DUE DATE

	201-6503		Printed in USA

shakespearean criticism

"Thou art a Monument without a tomb,
  And art alive still while thy Book doth
      live
  And we have wits to read and praise to
      give."

*Ben Jonson, from the preface
to the First Folio, 1623.*

MR. WILLIAM
SHAKESPEARES
COMEDIES,
HISTORIES, &
TRAGEDIES.

Published according to the True Originall Copies.

Martin Droeshout sculpsit London.

LONDON
Printed by Isaac Iaggard, and Ed. Blount. 1623.

Frontispiece to the First Folio (1623). By permission of the Folger Shakespeare Library.

Volume 1

shakespearean criticism

Excerpts from the Criticism of
William Shakespeare's Plays and Poetry,
from the First Published Appraisals
to Current Evaluations

Laurie Lanzen Harris
Editor

Mark W. Scott
Associate Editor

Gale Research Company
Book Tower
Detroit, Michigan 48226

STAFF

Laurie Lanzen Harris, *Senior Editor*

Mark W. Scott, *Associate Editor*

Hugh Grady, *Senior Assistant Editor*
Michael S. Corey, Melissa Reiff Hug, Jelena Obradovic Kronick,
Michele Roberge-Polizzi, and Robert Bruce Young, Jr., *Assistant Editors*

Sheila Fitzgerald and Phyllis Carmel Mendelson, *Contributing Editors*

Robert J. Elster, Jr., *Production Supervisor*
Lizbeth A. Purdy, *Production Coordinator*
Denise Michlewicz, *Assistant Production Coordinator*

Eric D. Berger, Laura L. Britton, Paula J. DiSante, Maureen Duffy,
Amy T. Marcaccio, Brenda Marshall, Marie M. Mazur, Janet S. Mullane,
Yvonne Huette Robinson, Gloria Anne Williams, *Editorial Assistants*

Linda Marcella Pugliese, *Manuscript Coordinator*
Donna D. Craft, *Assistant Manuscript Coordinator*
Colleen M. Crane, Maureen A. Puhl, Rosetta Irene Simms, *Manuscript Assistants*

Karen Rae Forsyth, *Research Coordinator*
Jeannine Schiffman Davidson, *Assistant Research Coordinator*
Victoria Cariappa, Ann Marie Dadah, Kathleen Gensley, Barbara Hammond, Robert J. Hill,
Harry Kronick, James A. MacEachern, Linda Mohler, Leslie Kyle Schell, Mary Spirito,
Margaret Stewart, Carol Angela Thomas, Valerie Webster, *Research Assistants*

L. Elizabeth Hardin, *Permissions Supervisor*
Filomena Sgambati, *Permissions Coordinator*
Janice M. Mach, *Assistant Permissions Coordinator*
Patricia A. Seefelt, *Assistant Permissions Coordinator, Illustrations*
Susan D. Nobles, *Senior Permissions Assistant*
Margaret Chamberlain, Anna Maria Pertner, Joan B. Weber, *Permissions Assistants*
Sandra C. Davis, Dorothy J. Fowler, Virgie T. Leavens, Diana M. Platzke, *Permissions Clerks*
Margaret Mary Missar, Audrey B. Wharton, *Photo Research*

Copyright © 1984 by Gale Research Company

Library of Congress Cataloging in Publication Data

Main entry under title:

Shakespearean criticism.

Includes bibliographies and index.
1. Shakespeare, William, 1564-1616--Criticism and
interpretation--History. 2. Shakespeare, William, 1564-
1616--Criticism and interpretation--Addresses, essays,
lectures. I. Harris, Laurie Lanzen. II. Scott, Mark.
III. Gale Research Company.
PR2965.S43   1984   822.3'3   84-4010
ISBN 0-8103-6125-6 (v. 1)

Contents

Preface

The works of William Shakespeare have delighted audiences and inspired scholars for nearly four hundred years. Shakespeare's appeal is universal, for in its depth and breadth his work evokes a timeless insight into the human condition.

The vast amount of Shakespearean criticism is a testament to his enduring popularity. Each epoch has contributed to this critical legacy, responding to the comments of their forebears, bringing the moral and intellectual atmosphere of their own era to the works, and suggesting interpretations which continue to inspire critics of today. Thus, to chart the history of criticism on Shakespeare is to note the changing aesthetic philosophies of the past four centuries.

The Scope of the Work

The success of Gale's four current literary series, *Contemporary Literary Criticism (CLC)*, *Twentieth-Century Literary Criticism (TCLC)*, *Nineteenth-Century Literature Criticism (NCLC)*, and *Children's Literature Review (CLR)*, suggests an equivalent need among students and teachers of Shakespeare. Moreover, since the criticism of Shakespeare's works spans four centuries and is larger in size and scope than that of any author, a prodigious amount of critical material confronts the student.

Shakespearean Criticism (SC) presents significant passages from published criticism on the works of Shakespeare. Five volumes of the series will be devoted to aesthetic criticism of the plays. Performance criticism will be treated in a separate special volume. Other special volumes will be devoted to such topics as Shakespeare's poetry, the authorship controversy and the apocrypha, and costume and set design. The first five volumes will each contain criticism on six or seven plays, with an equal balance of genres and an equal balance of plays based on their critical importance. Thus, Volume 1 contains criticism on one major tragedy *(Hamlet)*, one minor tragedy *(Timon of Athens)*, one major comedy *(Twelfth Night)*, one minor comedy *(Comedy of Errors)*, and two histories *(Henry IV, Part I* and *Henry IV, Part II)*, which because a great many critics have treated them together are handled as one entry.

The length of each entry is intended to represent the play's critical reception in English, including those works which have been translated into English. *SC* also includes several essays which have been translated specifically for this series and which will be appearing in English for the first time. We hope to expand this feature in future volumes. The editors have tried to identify only the major critics and lines of inquiry for each play. Each entry represents a historical overview of the critical response to the play: early criticism is presented to indicate initial responses and later selections represent significant trends in the history of criticism on the play. We have also attempted to identify and include excerpts from the seminal essays on each play by the most important Shakespearean critics. We have directed our series to students in late high school and early college who are beginning their study of Shakespeare. Thus, ours is not a work for the specialist, but is rather an introduction for the researcher newly acquainted with the works of Shakespeare.

The Organization of the Book

Each entry consists of the following elements: play heading, an introduction, excerpts of criticism (each followed by a citation), and an annotated bibliography of additional reading.

The *Introduction* begins with a discussion of the date, text, and sources of the play. This section is followed by a critical history which outlines the major critical trends and identifies the prominent commentators on the play.

Criticism is arranged chronologically within each play entry to provide a perspective on the changes in critical evaluation over the years. For purposes of easier identification, the critic's name and the date of the essay are given at the beginning of each piece. For an anonymous essay later attributed to a critic, the critic's name appears in brackets in the heading and in the citation. Within the text, all act, scene, and line designations have been changed to conform to *The Riverside Shakespeare,* published by Houghton Mifflin Company, which is a standard text used in many high school and college English classes. Many of the individual essays are prefaced with *explanatory notes* as an additional aid to students using *SC*. The explanatory notes provide several types of useful information, including: the importance of the critics in literary history, the critical schools with which they are identified, if any, and the importance of their comments on Shakespeare and the play discussed. The explanatory notes also identify the main issues in the commentary on each play and include a cross-reference to related criticism in the entry. The notes also provide previous publication information such as original title and date for foreign language publications.

A *bibliographical citation* designed to facilitate the location of the original essay or book follows each piece of criticism.

Within each play entry are facsimiles of title pages taken from the Quarto and First Folio editions of the plays as well as illustrations drawn from many sources, such as early editions of the collected works and artist's renderings of some of the famous scenes and characters of Shakespeare's plays. The captions following each illustration indicate act, scene, characters, and the artist and date, if known. The illustrations are arranged chronologically and, as a complement to the criticism, provide a historical perspective on Shakespeare throughout the centuries.

The *annotated bibliography* appearing at the end of each play entry suggests further reading on the play. This section includes references to the major discussions of the date, the text, and the sources of each play.

This volume includes an index to critics, which will cumulate with the second volume. Under each critic's name are listed the plays on which the critic has written and the volume and page where the criticism appears.

An appendix is included which lists the sources from which the material in the volume is reprinted. It does not, however, list every book or periodical consulted for the volume.

Acknowledgments

No work of this scope can be accomplished without the cooperation of many people. The editors wish to thank the copyright holders of the excerpts included in this Volume, the permissions managers of the book and magazine companies for assisting us in securing reprint rights, and the staffs of the Detroit Public Library, the University of Michigan libraries, and the Wayne State University library for making their resources available to us. We would especially like to thank the staff of the Rare Book Room of the University of Michigan for their research assistance and the Folger Shakespeare Library for their help in picture research. We would like to thank Michele L. Farrell and Almut McAuley for their assistance in translating, Jeri Yaryan for assistance with copyright research, and Norma J. Merry for her editorial assistance.

Suggestions Are Welcome

The editors welcome the comments and suggestions of readers to expand the coverage and enhance the usefulness of the series.

shakespearean criticism

The Comedy of Errors

DATE: Internal evidence suggests that *The Comedy of Errors* was written sometime between 1589 and 1594. Many critics have argued that because the play contains a reference to the war of succession in France, a probable date of composition is either 1591 or 1592, the fiercest years of the conflict. The latest possible date of composition is December, 1594, when the play was performed at Gray's Inn. Beyond these two pieces of evidence, the dating of *Comedy* is necessarily speculative, often involving a search for stylistic parallels with other dramas of the period. However, no consensus has been reached, save that *The Comedy of Errors* is one of Shakespeare's earliest plays, and quite possibly his first comedy.

TEXT: *The Comedy of Errors* was first printed in the First Folio of 1623. Critics generally believe that it was transcribed from Shakespeare's "foul papers," that is, an uncorrected manuscript written in the author's own hand. This speculation is based on the existence of contradictory character names and stage directions in the text. The textual scholar W. W. Greg suggested that the act divisions and certain stage directions indicate that a prompter added material to the text. R. A. Foakes argued that these interpolations merely show Shakespeare's inattention to detail while composing the play. Questions of authorship of the play were raised in the early twentieth century, prompted mainly by what was perceived as an uneven quality of the verse and the inclusion of doggerel, which some have suggested is the work of a different author. J. M. Robertson went so far as to propose that most of the play was written by Christopher Marlowe and that Shakespeare made only minor revisions. His theory has been dismissed by silence rather than rebuttal, and most critics now believe that Shakespeare wrote the entire play. Since no other text exists, the play as printed in the First Folio retains complete authority.

SOURCES: The chief source of *The Comedy of Errors* is considered to be a bawdy Roman play, the *Menaechmi* of Plautus. From this drama Shakespeare took his central plot, which revolves around "errors," or mistaken identity, involving identical twin brothers. In order to further complicate the plot, Shakespeare characterized the slaves of the two brothers also as identical twins and, in addition, borrowed an episode from another of Plautus's plays, *Amphitruo,* in which the foreign slave bars the native master from his own house. While keeping Plautus's tight plot structure, Shakespeare presented more fully developed characters and added the story of Aegeon. Critics have contended that this frame story was borrowed from the romance *Apollonius of Tyre,* a work which Shakespeare was to use again in *Pericles.* Peter G. Phialas suggested that this element of the play was borrowed from Plautus's *Captivi.*

CRITICAL HISTORY: The scarcity of commentary on *The Comedy of Errors* before the nineteenth century indicates that earlier critics did not consider the play to be of great importance. Samuel Taylor Coleridge's remarks on the play, however, inspired interest. Coleridge was the first to discuss the play as a unified work of art, asserting that it was a farce, and therefore should not be judged by the standards applied to comedy.

Efforts to categorize the play distinguish the history of *Comedy* criticism. Prominent among early commentators is Hermann

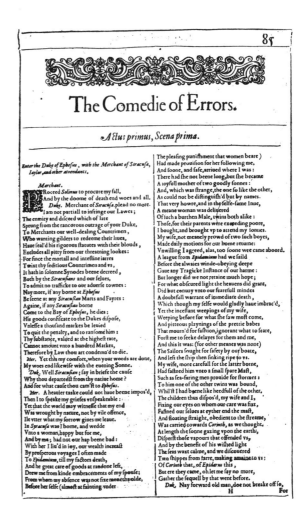

Ulrici, who created the category of "comedies of fancy" for those plays in which irrational elements are significant. Ulrici was also the first to take a serious philosophical view of a play that has generally been seen as a clever piece of apprentice work. Most other nineteenth-century commentary on the play, however, tends to focus on Shakespeare's sources. Only in the twentieth century did critics expand on the themes introduced by Ulrici.

Among the most important themes in the criticism of *The Comedy of Errors* are the generic classification of the play, the view of women the drama presents, particularly with regard to the contrasting perspectives of Adriana and Luciana, and the function of the potentially tragic frame story and its effect on the tone of the play. Critics also discuss Shakespeare's manipulation of his sources, his treatment of the problem of personal identity, and the success or failure of the play's characterization.

E. K. Chambers, like Coleridge, defended the play as a farce and distinguished between two different types of this sub-genre; one characterized by "the ruder vices and more robust virtues" and one in which interest in the plot completely dominates the play. *The Comedy of Errors,* according to Chambers, is a near perfect example of the latter. Arthur Quiller-Couch disputed Coleridge and his followers with the argument that any attempt to differentiate between farce and comedy is "a professional humbug of criticism." Hardin Craig described the play as a comedy because of Shakespeare's ability to expand the stock characters of farce into complex human beings. Gwyn Williams added a new dimension to the discussion by proposing that the constant threat of loss of personal identity constitutes an element of tragedy. Only Shakespeare's addition of the second pair of twins, contended Williams, distinguishes the play as a comedy.

Commentators are divided in their interpretation of the character of Adriana. Some, beginning with Frank Harris, saw her in a negative light, as a jealous shrew whose function is to convince the audience that, as Chambers put it, "the wiser course is not to rail." Later critics, however, tended to see Adriana's claims against her husband as justified, even if they found her invective too strong. H. B. Charlton noted that Adriana's views seem more reasonable to modern ears than do those of Luciana, while Derek Traversi claimed that the character of the passive sister acts as a foil to Adriana. In Traversi's view, by contrasting the attitudes of the two characters, Shakespeare was able to present "a truth greater than that which any single one of them can compass."

The frame provided by the story of Aegeon is first discussed by Quiller-Couch, who found it to be incongruous with the plot's farcical elements. But Alison Gaw asserted that the frame story advances the plot and lends dignity to the farcical atmosphere. The view that the Aegeon story enhances rather than detracts from the atmosphere of the play has become standard among modern commentators. G. Wilson Knight considered the shipwreck to be the central symbolic element of The Comedy of Errors, thus inaugurating a trend among critics to reconsider the romantic aspects of the drama. Mark Van Doren, speaking for a minority of critics, passed lightly over the frame story and dismissed the play as an "unfeeling farce."

Early and recent critics have devoted a good deal of commentary to Shakespeare's handling of his sources. Charles Gildon opened the discussion with his comment that Shakespeare had improved on Plautus's Menaechmi. William Hazlitt challenged this opinion, claiming that the classical mood is not congenial to Shakespeare's genius. Continuing the discussion, Ulrici proposed that the addition of the Dromios enabled Shakespeare to achieve a frenzied sequence of errors, thus heightening the question of personal identity raised in the play. In the early twentieth century, Chambers found The Comedy of Errors to be an improvement on its source, while Quiller-Couch dissented. Most critics writing later in the century, endorsed Chambers's view, including Thomas Marc Parrott, who asserted that the play was the best of the many interpretations of the Menaechmi.

Critics have often turned their attention to the question of personal identity suggested by Shakespeare's use of two sets of identical twins and the consequent errors of recognition in the play. First mentioned by Ulrici, who saw the play as "an amusing satire on man's power of observation and recognition," the problem of personal identity is one of the main focal points of twentieth-century criticism of The Comedy of Errors. G. R. Elliott contributed an evocative essay which noted the "weirdness" of the absolute resemblance between the twin characters. In Elliott's view, this eerie resemblance produces in the audience a feeling of "comic horror." Harold Brooks continued the discussion of this aspect, focusing on the themes of loss of identity, marriage, and community life evident in the play. Richard Henze associated the problem of identity with the confusion caused by the exchanges of the gold chain.

Shakespeare's handling of characterization in The Comedy of Errors has often been dismissed as weak. Writing in the eighteenth century, George Steevens claimed that the play features stock characters in a strong structure. In the twentieth century, Charlton proposed that The Comedy of Errors was written subsequent to Love's Labour's Lost and that Shakespeare was "recoiling" from a romantic viewpoint in writing Comedy. Thus, Charlton argued, Shakespeare chose a tight structure which excluded the possibility of deep and expanded character development. Other critics place the play among Shakespeare's earliest dramas, and see it as an "apprentice work," citing this as the reason for the weakness in characterization. The majority of critics, however, contend that interest in the play stems mainly from the strength of the plot rather than from characterization. And despite the attempts of such commentators as Knight, Bertrand Evans, and Blaze Odell Bonazza to link The Comedy of Errors to Shakespeare's later romantic comedies, many still consider the play to be something of an undistinguished early effort. Few critics view The Comedy of Errors as a play which expresses the full range of Shakespeare's genius.

GRAY'S INN RECORDS   (essay date 1594)

[The following excerpt is taken from the records of Gray's Inn, one of the four Inns of the Court which trained young men for the law. During the Christmas season of 1594, the Inn held revels to which the members invited an ambassador from the Inner Temple, another of the four Inns of Court. The revels were so unruly that the ambassador apparently left before the performance of the play mentioned, which is certainly Shakespeare's. This is a record of the first known performance of The Comedy of Errors, and the first known allusion to it.]

The next grand Night was intended to be upon Innocents-Day at Night. . . . The Ambassador [of the Inner Temple] came . . . about Nine of the Clock at Night . . . there arose such a disordered Tumult and Crowd upon the Stage, that there was no Opportunity to effect that which was intended. . . . The Lord Ambassador and his Train thought that they were not so kindly entertained as was before expected, and thereupon would not stay any longer at that time, but, in a sort, discontented and displeased. After their Departure the Throngs and Tumults did somewhat cease, although so much of them continued, as was able to disorder and confound any good Inventions whatsoever. In regard whereof, as also for that the Sports intended were especially for the gracing of the Templerians, it was thought good not to offer any thing of Account, saving Dancing and Revelling with Gentlewomen; and after such Sports, a Comedy of Errors (like to Plautus his Menechmus) was played by the Players. So that Night was begun, and continued to the end, in nothing but Confusion and Errors; whereupon, it was ever afterwards called, The Night of Errors. . . . We preferred Judgments . . . against a Sorcerer or Conjuror that was supposed to be the Cause of that confused Inconvenience. . . . And Lastly, that he had foisted a Company of base and common Fellows, to make up our Disorders with a Play of Errors and Confusions; and that that Night had gained to us Discredit, and itself a Nickname of Errors. (pp. 351)

An entry from "Gray's Inn Record" of December 28, 1594, in Shakespeare and His Critics *by F. E. Halliday, Gerald Duckworth & Co. Ltd., 1949, p. 351.*

CHARLES GILDON   (essay date 1710)

[*Gildon was the first critic to write an extended commentary on Shakespeare's plays. Like many other Neoclassicists, Gildon regarded Shakespeare as an imaginative playwright who nevertheless lacked knowledge of the dramatic "rules" necessary for correct writing. In the excerpt below, he makes two statements on* The Comedy of Errors *which are contested in later criticism of the play: that Shakespeare had knowledge of Latin—contradicted by William Hazlitt (1817), but supported by Hermann Ulrici (1839)—and that Shakespeare had improved on his Plautine source, a view that has been accepted by most modern critics but which was questioned by Hazlitt. The following excerpt is an extract from Gildon's "Remarks on the Plays of Shakespeare" in* The Works of Mr. William Shakespeare, Vol. 7, *first published in 1710.*]

[*The Comedy of Errors*] is exactly regular, as any one may see who will examine it by the Rules. The Place is part of one Town, the Time within the Artificial Day, and the Action the finding the lost Brother, &c. Allowing for the Puns, which were the Vice of the Age he liv'd in, it is extreamly diverting; the Incidents are wonderfully pleasant, and the *Catastrophe* very happy and strongly moving. . . .

This Comedy is an undeniable Proof that *Shakespeare* was not so ignorant of the *Latin* Tongue as some wou'd fain make him . . . for as it is beyond Contradiction plain that this Comedy is taken from that of *Plautus* so I think it as obvious to conclude from that that *Shakespeare* did understand *Latin* enough to read him, and knew so much of him as to be able to form a Design out of that of the *Roman* Poet; and which he has improv'd very much in my Opinion. He has made two Servants as like as their Masters, who are not in *Plautus*. (p. 240)

> *Charles Gildon, in an extract from his "Remarks on the Plays of Shakespeare," in* Shakespeare, the Critical Heritage: 1693-1733, Vol. 2, *edited by Brian Vickers, Routledge & Kegan Paul, 1974, pp. 226-62.*

[JOHN HOLT]   (essay date 1749)

[*The essay from which the excerpt below was taken first appeared in a 1749 edition of Holt's book.*]

[It] is surprising Mr. *Rowe* should so peremptorily assert, in his Account of *Shakespear*'s Life, &c. "That in his Works we scarce find any Traces of any Thing that looks like an Imitation of the Antients;" and yet mention his *Comedy of Errors*, the Plot of which is apparently taken from the *Menaechmi* of *Plautus;* and in which there are several Incidents borrowed also from the *Amphytrion* of the same Author: And in the fifth Act, a strong Imitation of *Plato's Dialogues,* in the *Socratic* Manner he makes the *Abbess* use, to draw from *Adriana,* the Cause of her Husband's supposed Madness. . . . (pp. x-xi)

> [*John Holt*], *in his preface to his* An Attempte to Rescue the Auciente, English Poet, and Play-Wrighte, Maister Williaume Shakespere, from the Maney Errours, Faulsely Charged on Him, by Certaine New-Fangled Wittes, *Manby and Cox, 1749 (and reprinted in* An Essay Upon English Tragedy *by William Guthrie together with* An Attempte to Rescue the Auciente, English Poet, and Play-Wrighte, Maister Williaume Shakespere, from the Maney Errours, Faulsely Charged on Him, by Certaine New-Fangled Wittes *by John Holt, Frank Cass & Co. Ltd., 1971, pp. iii-xii).*

GEORGE STEEVENS   (essay date 1773)

[*George Steevens was an English scholar who collaborated with Samuel Johnson on a ten-volume edition of Shakespeare's works in 1773. The subsequent revisions of this collection, along with Steevens's own edition of 1793, formed the textual basis for the first two Variorum editions of Shakespeare's plays. Many modern scholars also contend that Steevens was the sole theater critic for the* General Evening Post. *Steevens's argument that* Comedy *offers weak characterization within the frame of a strong plot has also been voiced by Alison Gaw (1926). This essay was first published in* The Plays of William Shakespeare, Vol. II, *edited by Steevens and Samuel Johnson and published in 1773.*]

In [*The Comedy of Errors*] we find more intricacy of plot than distinction of character; and our attention is less forcibly engaged because we can guess in great measure how it will conclude. Yet the poet seems unwilling to part with his subject, even in this last and unnecessary scene, where the same mistakes are continued till they have lost the power of affording any entertainment at all. (p. 521)

> *George Steevens, in his end-note to "The Comedy of Errors," in* Shakespeare, the Critical Heritage: 1765-1774, Vol. 5, *edited by Brian Vickers, Routledge & Kegan Paul, 1979, pp. 510-51.*

AUGUST WILHELM SCHLEGEL   (essay date 1808)

[*Schlegel holds a key place in the history of Shakespeare's reputation in European criticism. His translations of thirteen of the plays are still considered the best German translations of Shakespeare. Schlegel was also a leading spokesman for the Romantic movement which permanently overthrew the Neoclassical contention that Shakespeare was a child of nature whose plays lacked artistic form. In the following excerpt, he concludes that although* Comedy *is perhaps the worst of Shakespeare's plays, it is "the best of all written or possible Menaechmi." The excerpt is from a lecture written by Schlegel in 1808 and first published in 1811 in his* Über dramatische Kunst und Literatur.]

The Comedy of Errors is the subject of the *Menaechmi* of Plautus, entirely recast and enriched with new developments: of all the works of Shakspeare this is the only example of imitation of, or borrowing from, the ancients. To the two twin brothers of the same name are added two slaves, also twins, impossible to be distinguished from each other, and of the same name. The improbability becomes by this means doubled: but when once we have lent ourselves to the first, which certainly borders on the incredible, we shall not perhaps be disposed to cavil at the second; and if the spectator is to be entertained by mere perplexities they cannot be too much varied. In such pieces we must, to give to the sense at least an appearance of truth, always pre-suppose that the parts by which the misunderstandings are occasioned are played with masks, and this the poet no doubt observed. I cannot acquiesce in the censure that the discovery is too long deferred: so long as novelty and interest are possessed by the perplexing incidents, there is no need to be in dread of wearisomeness. And this is really the case here: matters are carried so far that one of the two brothers is first arrested for debt, then confined as a lunatic, and the other is forced to take refuge in a sanctuary to save his life. In a subject of this description it is impossible to steer clear of all sorts of low circumstances, abusive language, and blows; Shakspeare has however endeavoured to ennoble it in every possible way. A couple of scenes, dedicated to jealousy and love, interrupt the course of perplexities which are solely occasioned by the illusion of the external senses. A greater solemnity is given to the discovery, from the Prince presiding, and from the re-union of the long separated parents of the twins who are still alive. The exposition, by which the spectators are previously instructed while the characters themselves are still involved in ignorance, and which Plautus artlessly conveys in a prologue, is here masterly introduced in an affecting narrative by the father. In short, this is perhaps the best of all written or possible Menaechmi; and if the piece be inferior in worth to other pieces of Shakspeare, it is merely because nothing more could be made of the materials. (pp. 380-81)

> *August Wilhelm Schlegel, "Criticisms on Shakspeare's Comedies," in his* Lectures on Dramatic Art and Literature, *edited by Rev. A.J.W. Morrison, translated by John Black, second edition, George Bell & Sons, 1892, pp. 379-99.*

SAMUEL TAYLOR COLERIDGE (essay date 1808-18)

[*Coleridge's lectures and writings on Shakespeare form a major chapter in the history of English Shakespearean criticism. As the channel for the critical ideas of the German Romantics and as an original interpretor of Shakespeare in the new spirit of Romanticism, Coleridge played a strategic role in overthrowing the last remains of the Neoclassical approach to Shakespeare and in establishing the modern view of Shakespeare as a conscious artist and masterful portrayer of human character. Coleridge's remarks on Shakespeare come down to posterity largely as fragmentary notes, marginalia, and reports by auditors on the lectures, rather than in polished essays. The following remarks on* The Comedy of Errors *were taken from Coleridge's* Literary Remains, *which was published posthumously in 1836; however, his analysis of this play presumably dates from the years of Coleridge's public lectures on Shakespeare (1808-18). Coleridge asserts that* The Comedy of Errors *should be classed as a farce rather than as a comedy. The validity of this distinction, which Coleridge claims frees the play from criticisms of "improbability," is debated throughout the criticism of the play.*]

The myriad-minded man, our, and all men's, Shakspeare, has in [*The Comedy of Errors*] presented us with a legitimate farce in exactest consonance with the philosophical principles and character of farce, as distinguished from comedy and from entertainments. A proper farce is mainly distinguished from comedy by the license allowed, and even required, in the fable, in order to produce strange and laughable situations. The story need not be probable, it is enough that it is possible. A comedy would scarcely allow even the two Antipholuses; because, although there have been instances of almost indistinguishable likeness in two persons, yet these are mere individual accidents, *casus ludentis naturae,* and the *verum* will not excuse the *inverisimile.* But farce dares add the two Dromios, and is justifed in so doing by the laws of its end and constitution. In a word, farces commence in a postulate, which must be granted.

> *Samuel Taylor Coleridge, "Notes on 'Comedy of Errors'," in his* Shakespearean Criticism, Vol. I, *edited by Thomas Middleton Raysor, E. P. Dutton, 1960, p. 89.*

WILLIAM HAZLITT (essay date 1817)

[*Hazlitt is generally considered to be a leading Shakespearean critic of the English Romantic movement. A prolific essayist and critic on a wide range of subjects, Hazlitt remarked that he was inspired by the German critic August Wilhelm Schlegel and was determined to supplant what he considered the pernicious influence of Samuel Johnson's Shakespearean criticism. Hazlitt's criticism is typically Romantic in its emphasis on character studies. Unlike Samuel Taylor Coleridge, Hazlitt was a dramatic critic whose experience of Shakespeare in the theater influenced his interpretations. In the excerpt below, first published in his 1817 edition of* Characters of Shakespear's Plays, *Hazlitt disagrees with Charles Gildon's contention that Shakespeare had knowledge of Latin and that he had improved on his Plautine source (see excerpt above, 1710). He also suggests that Shakespeare's genius lay in his imagination rather than in his ability to imitate others' plays.*]

[*The Comedy of Errors*] is taken very much from the *Menaechmi* of Plautus, and is not an improvement on it. Shakespear appears to have bestowed no great pains on it, and there are but a few passages which bear the decided stamp of his genius. He seems to have relied on his author, and on the interest arising out of the intricacy of the plot. The curiosity excited is certainly very considerable, though not of the most pleasing kind. We are teazed as with a riddle, which notwithstanding we try to solve. In reading the play, from the sameness of the names of the two Antipholises and the two Dromios, as well from their being constantly taken for each other by those who see them, it is difficult, without a painful effort of attention, to keep the characters distinct in the mind. . . . We still, however, having a clue to the difficulty, can tell which is which, merely from the practical contradictions which arise, as soon as the different parties begin to speak; and we are indemnified for the perplexity and blunders into which we are thrown by seeing others thrown into greater and almost inextricable ones.— This play (among other considerations) leads us not to feel much regret that Shakespear was not what is called a classical scholar. We do not think his *forte* would ever have lain in imitating or improving on what others invented, so much as in inventing for himself, and perfecting what he invented,— not perhaps by the omission of faults, but by the addition of the highest excellencies. His own genius was strong enough to bear him up, and he soared longest and best on unborrowed plumes. (pp. 202-03)

> *William Hazlitt, "The Comedy of Errors," in his* Characters of Shakespear's Plays & Lectures on the English Poets, *Macmillan and Co. Limited, 1903, pp. 202-04.*

HERMANN ULRICI (essay date 1839)

[*A German scholar, Ulrici was a professor of philosophy and an author of works on Greek poetry and Shakespeare. The following excerpt is taken from an English translation of his* Über Shakspeares dramatische Kunst, und sein Verhältnis zu Calderon und Göthe, *first published in 1839. This work exemplifies the "philosophical criticism" developed in Germany during the nineteenth century. The immediate sources for Ulrici's critical approach appear to be August Wilhelm Schlegel's conception of the play as an organic, interconnected whole and Georg Wilhelm Friedrich Hegel's view of the drama Unlike his fellow German Shakespearean critic G. G. Gervinus, Ulrici sought to develop a specifically Christian aesthetics, but one which, as he carefully points out in the introduction to the work mentioned above, in no way intrudes on "that unity of idea, which preeminently constitutes a work of art a living creation in the world of beauty." His essay on* The Comedy of Errors *makes several important points: he dates the play at 1591 or 1592 based on stylistic considerations and its "peculiarly youthful air"; he treats the drama philosophically, considering it a satire on the ability to observe and recognize; and he views* The Comedy of*

Errors *as a "pendant" piece to* As You Like It, *categorizing them both as "comedies of fancy," in which irrational elements are seen as the dominant forces.*]

The ''Comedy of Errors'' may, in a certain sense, be regarded as the pendant to ''As You Like It.'' It is evidently one of Shakspeare's earlier works, and was probably written in 1591 or 1592. Many circumstances tend to corroborate this opinion; among others, the frequency of rhyme and the doggerel verses, which are quite in the style of Shakspeare's predecessors, and which he has here retained; and also the greater carefulness of the diction and versification, which betray all the anxiety of a youthful poet to deserve the approbation of the public, by the employment of all the external means at his command. For at a later period he entirely neglected such mere extrinsic embellishments. The correctness of the early date is further confirmed by the peculiarly youthful air which breathes over the wit and humour of the piece, and by a naïve, not to say puerile, delight in joke and fun, which, as yet unchecked by the cares and burden of life, moves lightly on the surface of things, and is without any of the force and elevation of thoughtful humour which distinguish the maturer works of our poet. In the ''Comedy of Errors'' life is depicted in its outward forms and more obvious appearances, and as it were only in its more general outline and colouring, the lights and shades, characterization and grouping, being touched with a light and unsteady hand. The irony too does, at most, but play with its object, or else passes hastily over it without probing its inmost depths. The gross improbability that it should never have occurred to Antipholus of Syracuse, after so many mistakes of his identity, that he had at last arrived at the residence of the lost brother whom he had left home purposely to seek, might of itself be adduced in proof of the early origin of the piece, if we did not know that Shakspeare, with his usual judgment, generally paid little attention to such trifles, which reflection alone discovers, and which do not disturb the poetical feeling.

This inconsistency overlooked, the ''Comedy of Errors'' must be pronounced a most amusing satire on man's boasted wisdom and discernment. The remarkable resemblance of two couples is sufficient to set a whole city in uproar and confusion. Life accordingly appears here as a continued but varying succession of delusion and mistake. Hence at the very outset, an accidental ignorance of the Ephesian laws is supposed to have brought the father of the twins into peril of his life,—a subordinate motive of the action, which otherwise might appear a superfluous appendage to it. In the same manner, the inconsistency which we have already noticed, and which at least implies great self-forgetfulness in the Syracusan Antipholus, appears, when viewed from its subjective side, perfectly consonant with the ground-idea of the entire piece. In the same way, the gradually increasing complication and perplexity, notwithstanding the obvious possibility of a mistake of identity, is not cleared up until the two pairs of twins are accidentally brought face to face. By all this the truth (not more comic than tragic) is most strikingly impressed upon us, that the knowledge and ignorance of man run so nicely into each other, that the boundary line almost disappears, and that the very convictions which we look upon as the most certain and best grounded may, perhaps, turn out to be nothing but error or deception. . . . All are in a moment disturbed by a mere freak of nature, in violating the seemingly most unimportant of her laws, and in neglecting those differences of the outward man by which the senses distinguish individuals. So artificial is the constitution of our world, that the derangement of the minutest of its members is sufficient to throw the whole into disorder.

It can scarcely be necessary to remind the reader, that such a state of things could have no existence except within the comic view of life, where caprice and chance, ignorance and error, mental stupidity and moral obliquity, are the immediate ruling principles. Within this view life is here contemplated exclusively in its dependence on the senses and the outward appearance. This dependence is most true; nevertheless the *exclusive consideration* of it exaggerates it into falsehood. It is a mistake to suppose, that human life depends *absolutely* and *entirely* on the sensuous appearance and perception; it is not true that knowledge is merely sensuous and empirical, and limited to the eye or ear. There is a knowledge, on the contrary, which is far above outward perception, and this, however, is left wholly untouched and disregarded in the present piece. This one-sidedness of view contains its own refutation; error ultimately destroys itself, and a scene of general recognition at last restores universal order. We are thus made to see that in itself error possesses no stability; that, although it may indeed prevail for a season, and as it were swallow up reality itself, it must invariably yield at last to the truth, and that a higher power guides us safely through the mistakes of life, and leads us from the darkness of error and delusion to the light, and to the good which we have long missed and sought for in vain.

We have called the ''Comedy of Errors'' a pendant to ''Twelfth Night'' or ''As You Like It,'' and place it in the class of comedies of fancy. Our meaning will be readily understood. In ''As You Like It,'' one aspect is presented of that contingency, which, according to the comic view of things, rules over human life; we there see nothing but caprice with its wayward and motiveless *resolves* and *deeds,* which are ultimately palsied by the comic dialectic of irony. In the ''Comedy of Errors'' we have the other aspect of subjective contingency; the ruling motive of this fable is error, as resulting from the groundless and vain conclusions of human *thought* and *cognition.* The capriciousness of conduct we there meet with is nothing but an error of judgment; its source is but the unwilling divorce of the world within us from the world without. Error and caprice appear equally groundless, since they have no objective and only a subjective foundation; and even on this account they both belong to the notion of contingency, in so far as the latter also consists in a seeming causelessness, in an apparent destruction of the necessary objective connexion between cause and effect. They differ, however, in this respect, that caprice appears to be voluntary and independent of external influences, whereas error is involuntary, relative, and dependent on outward circumstances. In ''As You Like It,'' accordingly, the influence of *objective* contingency is kept back, while in the ''Comedy of Errors'' it is brought prominently forward. This is apparent at once in the very groundwork of the piece, which is founded on the marvellous separation, by shipwreck, of the parents, as well as of the two pairs of twin brothers; all the subsequent perplexities, too, result from the mere play of chance, which again re-unites in Ephesus the divided family, and brings together husband and wife, servants, friends, and acquaintances; the happy re-union being brought about solely by means of the false Antipholus and Dromio. But now subjective as well as objective contingency belongs exclusively to the fantastic view of life; they are both essential elements of its fanciful colouring. Both alike undermine reality, as founded on the objective necessity of causal connexion, which disappears before a chequered and irregular play of whim and humour.

The circumstance, that in the "Comedy of Errors," as well as in the two pieces already noticed, the characters are but lightly sketched and inadequately developed, is perfectly consonant with our idea of fantastic comedy in general. The intrinsic license of fancy cannot become an object of description without investing with its own hues the mind and characters of all who enter its capricious maze. But a fantastic character is one in which the want of definiteness and consistency, as well as of steadiness of development, is predominant. (pp. 260-64)

> *Hermann Ulrici, " 'As You Like It'—'Comedy of Errors'—'Winter's Tale'," in his* Shakspeare's Dramatic Art: And His Relation to Calderon and Goethe, *translated by A.J.W. Morrison, Chapman, Brothers, 1846, pp. 253-69.*

ALGERNON CHARLES SWINBURNE (essay date 1880)

[*Swinburne was an English poet, dramatist, and critic who devoted much of his literary career to the study of Shakespeare and other Elizabethan writers. His three books on Shakespeare—*A Study of Shakespeare *(1880),* Shakespeare *(1909), and* Three Plays of Shakespeare *(1909)—all demonstrate his keen interest in Shakespeare's poetic talents and, especially, his major tragedies.*]

In the exquisite and delightful comedies of [Shakespeare's] earliest period we can hardly discern any sign, any promise of them at all. One only of these, the *Comedy of Errors*, has in it anything of dramatic composition and movement; and what it has of these, I need hardly remind the most cursory of students, is due by no means to Shakespeare. What is due to him, and to him alone, is the honour of having embroidered on the naked old canvas of comic action those flowers of elegiac beauty which vivify and diversify the scene of Plautus as reproduced by the art of Shakespeare. . . . But in this light and lovely work of the youth of Shakespeare we find for the first time that strange and sweet admixture of farce with fancy, of lyric charm with comic effect, which recurs so often in his later work, from the date of *As You Like It* to the date of *Winter's Tale*. . . . The sweetness and simplicity of lyric or elegiac loveliness which fill and inform the scenes where Adriana, her sister, and the Syracusan Antipholus exchange the expression of their errors and their loves, belong to Shakespeare alone; and may help us to understand how the young poet who at the outset of his divine career had struck into this fresh untrodden path of poetic comedy should have been, as we have seen that he was, loth to learn from another and an alien teacher the hard and necessary lesson that this flowery path would never lead him towards the loftier land of tragic poetry. For as yet, even in the nominally or intentionally tragic and historic work of the first period, we descry always and everywhere and still preponderant the lyric element, the fantastic element, or even the elegiac element. (pp. 44-6)

> *Algernon Charles Swinburne, "First Period: Lyric and Fantastic," in his* A Study of Shakespeare, *R. Worthington, 1880, pp. 1-65.*

EDWARD DOWDEN (essay date 1903)

[*Dowden was an Irish critic and biographer whose* Shakespeare: A Critical Study of His Mind and Art *was the leading example of the biographical criticism popular in the English-speaking world near the end of the nineteenth century. Biographical critics sought in the plays and poems a record of Shakespeare's personal development. As that approach gave way in the twentieth century*

to aesthetic theories with greater emphasis on the constructed, artificial nature of literary works, Dowden and other biographical critics came to be considered limited. The excerpt below is taken from his Representative English Comedies, *first published in 1903.*]

The Comedy of Errors is a comedy of incident. Here Shakespeare accepts his plot, his chief characters, and their adventures from Plautus. But the adventures are complicated by his addition of the two Dromios, which more than doubles the possibilities of ludicrous confusion. The fun cannot be too fast or furious; the unexpected always happens; the discovery is staved off to the fifth act with infinite skill; the nearer each brother approaches his fellow, the more impossible it becomes for them to meet. Nowhere has Shakespeare ravelled and unravelled the threads of an intrigue with such incomparable dexterity as in this early play. But Shakespeare's imagination could not rest satisfied with a farce, however laughable or however skilfully conducted. His vein of lyrical poetry breaks forth in the love-episode, for the sake of which he created Luciana. And he has set the entire comic business in a romantic and pathetic framework—the story of the afflicted old Aegeon and the Ephesian abbess, in whom he discovers his lost wife. The play opens with grief and the doom of death impending over an innocent life; it closes, after a cry of true pathos, with reconciling joy, and the interval is filled with laughter that peals to a climax. This is not the manner of Plautus; but laughter with Shakespeare would seem hard and barren—the crackling of thorns under a pot,—if it were wholly isolated from grief and love and joy. (p. 650)

> *Edward Dowden, "Shakespeare As a Comic Dramatist," in* Representative English Comedies: From the Beginnings to Shakespeare, Vol. I, *edited by Charles Mills Gayley, Macmillan Publishing Company, 1912, pp. 635-61.*

E. K. CHAMBERS (essay date 1906)

[*Chambers occupies a transitional position in Shakespearean criticism, one which connects the biographical sketches and character analyses of the nineteenth century with the historical, technical, and textual criticism of the twentieth century. While a member of the education department at Oxford University, Chambers earned his reputation as a scholar with his multivolume works,* The Medieval Stage *and* The Elizabethan Stage, *while he also edited* The Red Letter Shakespeare. *Chambers both investigated the purpose and limitations of each dramatic genre as Shakespeare presented it, and speculated on how the dramatist's work was influenced by contemporary historical issues and his own frame of mind. In the excerpt below, first published in Chamber's Red Letter edition of Shakespeare in 1906, he claims that the Elizabethans' interest in romance and the ethical issues of jealousy significantly influenced Shakespeare's writing of* The Comedy of Errors. *Chambers also maintains that Shakespeare's play is a "farce," a lower-class comedy "translated" for the bourgeoisie. For similar readings of* Comedy, *see the excerpts by Samuel Taylor Coleridge (1808-18), Algernon Charles Swinburne (1880), and Edward Dowden (1903).*]

Latin comedy, filtering down for the most part through Italian channels, has left its mark upon more than one of Shakespeare's plays. But it is in *The Comedy of Errors* alone, with its atmosphere of slaves and courtesans, its breathless dialogue, its strained domestic relations, its unity of action upon an open street between the convent and the house of Antipholus, that one may find any close reproduction of the manner of Plautus and of Terence. . . . It is a hazardous conjecture, and therefore has been made with much confidence, that a play performed at court by the choir-boys of St Paul's on the 1st of January, 1577, under the title of 'the historie of Error,' represents an earlier composition subsequently worked up by Shakespeare. That is, I think, too much to hang upon a similarity of name. 'Truth is one,' says Plato, 'but there are many kinds of error.' (pp. 21-2)

Shakespeare or another has of course introduced into the story certain elements which are quite alien to Plautus. There is the emotional interest, the note of romance, such as we find it in *The Merchant of Venice,* derived from the travels of Aegeon in search of wife and family, his condemnation, and the triple [recognition] which drenches the rather violent humours of the closing scene in sentiment. Such a situation is common form in Elizabethan comedy, just as it was common form in the tragedy of Euripides, but it will be admitted that the dramatic spirit had travelled long mediaeval roads before it could find its place among the situations of Plautus. Similarly it is a modern, rather than a Latin conception of the position of the wife in comedy, that determines the stress laid throughout the play upon the jealousy of Adriana, which again and again strikes a serious chord in the very midst of riot and horse-play, and finally leads up to the little sermon delivered by the Abbess to the foolish wife, for which the intrigue is stopped at a critical moment. . . . The commentators have been struck by the incongruity of this insistence upon the ethical issue with the general temper of the play, and have explained it after their fashion as due to the reaction of Shakespeare's own domestic circumstances upon his art. They regard him as preoccupied, both in *The Comedy of Errors* and in *The Taming of the Shrew,* with the relations of husband and wife and the interpretation of the marriage vow, because he too had married in haste and repented at leisure, and had suffered at bed and board from the tongue of Anne Hathaway, until he had been forced to solve his problem by a hasty flight upon the London road. . . . At any rate it is clear that, whether he had learnt the lesson by experience of his own fire-side, or by experience of the stormy fire-sides of his friends in comparison with that peaceful one which he so rarely visited in Stratford, Shakespeare was very much convinced, when he wrote *The Comedy of Errors,* of the sound practical truth that indiscretion in the expression of jealousy is by no means a way to remove the causes of jealousy; and that he was careful so to order his play as to give pointed utterance to this conviction. So much does the theme, in its serious aspect, turn upon jealousy, that when one finds the record of a play, new at a date about which *The Comedy of Errors* may very well have been written, acted by a company with which Shakespeare almost certainly had other relations, and bearing the title of *The Jealous Comedy,* one is tempted to ask whether this and *The Comedy of Errors* are not one and the same. . . . If the date which it indicates is correct, *The Comedy of Errors* is probably Shakespeare's first comedy, and so much, indeed, one might readily maintain on general grounds, and particularly upon the liberal use of verse, regular and doggerel, in clownish scenes, for which he had already learnt, by the time he came to write *The Two Gentlemen of Verona* and *Love's Labour's Lost,* that the proper medium is prose. (pp. 22-5)

In so far as it is concerned with jealousy and the ethical problems which hinge upon jealousy, *The Comedy of Errors* has an undeniable claim to the title which it bears. It is comedy in the true sense of a criticism of life, which is at heart profoundly serious, and employs all the machinery of wit or humour, with the deliberate intention of reaching through the laughter to the ultimate end of a purged outlook upon things.

Let an audience shake its sides at the plight into which a scold is brought by the railings of her tongue, and it is odds that they will go away with the conviction that the wiser course is not to rail. Whether they will actually cease to rail is perhaps hardly the concern of the dramatist, whose will to propagate his own vision of things is not necessarily identical with the pang with which the missionary aches for souls. From one point of view, then, *The Comedy of Errors* is to be classed as a comedy. But the label hardly applies to it as a whole, since, as I have already pointed out, the ethical element, no less than the element of romance, in the play has been imported into the original design under the promptings of the Elizabethan mood. Stripped of these ornaments, the interest declares itself as almost entirely one of plot, arising out of a succession of ingeniously interwoven situations brought about by the facial resemblances of the two pairs of twin brothers and the accident of their coming together, unknown to each other, in the same city. Too much praise cannot be given to the technical skill with which the idea is worked out; nor can it be denied that in this respect many improvements have been made in the original scheme of the *Menaechmi.* . . . If the rehandling of the Plautine structure is to be attributed to Shakespeare himself, he was already a master of stage-craft. To this particular type of drama it is possible to give the name of farce rather than of comedy, if certain distinctions are observed. Farce, indeed, is a term which has been used by literary historians in two rather different shades of meaning. In one acceptation, derived from its use as applied to *Maître Pathelin* and other examples of fifteenth-century French dramatic humour, it does not so much connote something other than comedy, as a variety of comedy itself. It is a matter of temper and *milieu.* Farce is comedy translated from the speech and manners of a cultivated society into the speech and manners of the *bourgeoisie;* or perhaps it would really be more historical to say that comedy represents a development out of farce, due to the sharpening of the wits and the refinement of the moral issues which accompany or form part of the growth of a cultivated society as distinct from a *bourgeoisie.* Such farce is a comedy of the ruder vices and the more robust virtues, a comedy in which fisticuffs, literal and verbal, take the place of rapier-play. In Shakespeare it is represented, magnificently enough, by *The Taming of the Shrew* and *The Merry Wives of Windsor.* And its primary dramatic interest is still, as in other forms of comedy, an interest of character, whatever other elements, of buffoonery or intrigue, may be added to this. . . . But the second application of the term farce is to a dramatic form which is sharply differentiated from comedy by the fact that in it the interest of character is wholly replaced by an interest of plot. The conception of farce in this sense may be defined as the deduction of a logical conclusion from absurd premises. The playwright starts with some impossible assumption, which you must take for granted; however unconvincing, however grotesque, it is beyond your criticism. From this he proceeds, without any further breach of the probabilities, to show what follows, and to work out a resulting tissue of absurdities, all inherent in the initial situation. . . . If, therefore, I call *The Comedy of Errors* a farce, it is not, as in the case of *The Merry Wives of Windsor* or *The Taming of the Shrew,* the temper of its ethics that I have in mind. There is nothing particularly farcical about the marital relations of Antipholus and Adriana or the sensible didactics of the Abbess. Farce has indeed generally a more brutal touch in such matters. There is horse-play, of course; but that is common to both types of farce. It is rather the plot of *The Comedy of Errors* that seems to me to answer very closely to the definition of a farcical plot. The initial assumption is of a personal similarity between two brothers so close as to extend to their raiment, and to deceive even those with whom they are most familiar. Given this, all the episodes of the play, however ridiculous the situations they involve, unwind themselves plausibly and naturally enough. One qualification must however be made. There is a weak point. Antipholus and Dromio of Ephesus did not know that they had twin brothers. . . . But Antipholus and Dromio of Syracuse did know. They had been brought up by Aegeon until they were eighteen years of age; and had only left him with the expressed intention of seeking out their brothers. One can hardly suppose that Aegeon had failed to tell them of the extraordinary likeness which had existed between the children. This being so, it is almost incredible that, when they found themselves being obviously and constantly mistaken at Ephesus for persons not themselves, the solution of the puzzle should have failed to suggest itself to them. The same criticism applies, in the last scene, to Aegeon, who, when he found himself repudiated by the son and slave whom he thought he knew, must surely, after his long narrative to the duke a few hours before, have guessed that these could only be the son and slave whom he did not know. There are therefore in reality two assumptions, not one, made in the play; an assumption of physical resemblance so close as to be mistaken for identity, and an assumption also of a very singular kind of oblivion in at least two of the personages. One such assumption is, as already explained, of the very essence of the game, but against a second we are entitled to protest. Had it not been for this lack of economy in hypothesis, *The Comedy of Errors* would have presented the very pink and perfection of a farcical plot. (pp. 25-30)

> E. K. Chambers, "The Comedy of Errors," in his
> Shakespeare: A Survey, *Sidgewick & Jackson, Ltd.,*
> *1925, pp. 21-30.*

FRANK HARRIS (essay date 1909)

[*Harris attempted to find a pattern in Shakespeare's work that would shed light on the nature of Shakespeare's life. His theories have been either ignored or ridiculed by most Shakespearean scholars. Nearly all modern commentators disagree with Harris's view of Adriana as a fully negative character, but his claim that* The Comedy of Errors *followed* Love's Labour's Lost *chronologically can also be found in the essays by H. B. Charlton (1931) and S. C. Sen Gupta (1950).*]

It is probable that "The Comedy of Errors" followed hard on the heels of "Love's Labour's Lost." It practically belongs to the same period: it has fewer lines of prose in it than "Love's Labour's Lost"; but, on the other hand, the intrigue-spinning is clever, and the whole play shows a riper knowledge of theatrical conditions. Perhaps because the intrigue is more interesting, the character-drawing is even feebler than that of the earlier comedy: indeed, so far as the men go there is hardly anything worth calling character-drawing at all. Shakespeare speaks through this or that mask as occasion tempts him: and if the women are sharply, crudely differentiated, it is because Shakespeare, as I shall show later, has sketched his wife for us in Adriana, and his view of her character is decided enough if not over kind. . . . When Aegeon, in the opening scenes, tells the Duke about the shipwreck in which he is separated from his wife and child, he declares that he himself "would gladly have embraced immediate death." No reason is given for this extraordinary contempt of living. It was the "incessant weepings" of his wife, the "piteous plainings of the pretty babes," that forced him, he says, to exert himself. But wives

don't weep incessantly in danger, nor are the "piteous plainings of the pretty babes" a feature of shipwreck; I find here a little picture of Shakespeare's early married life in Stratford—a snapshot of memory. . . . Aegeon is evidently a breath of Shakespeare himself, and not more than a breath, because he only appears again when the play is practically finished. Deep-brooding melancholy was the customary habit of Shakespeare even in youth. (pp. 169-71)

[Shakespeare] speaks through Aegeon and then at greater length through the protagonist Antipholus of Syracuse. Antipholus is introduced to us as new come to Ephesus, and Shakespeare is evidently thinking of his own first day in London when he puts in his mouth these words:

> Within this hour it will be dinner-time:
> Till that, I'll view the manners of the town,
> Peruse the traders, gaze upon the buildings,
> And then return and sleep within mine inn;
> For with long travel I am stiff and weary.
>
> [I. ii. 11-15]

Though "stiff and weary" he is too eager-young to rest; he will see everything—even "peruse the traders"—how the bookish metaphor always comes to Shakespeare's lips!—before he will eat or sleep. The utterly needless last line, with its emphatic description—"stiff and weary"—corroborates my belief that Shakespeare in this passage is telling us what he himself felt and did on his first arrival in London. . . . [When] the merchant leaves him, commending him to his own content, he talks to himself in this strain:

> He that commends me to mine own content,
> Commends me to the thing I cannot get, . . .
>
> So I, to find a mother and a brother,
> In quest of them, unhappy, lose myself.
>
> [I. ii. 32-4, 39-40]

A most curious way, it must be confessed, to seek for any one; but perfectly natural to the refined, melancholy, meditative, book-loving temperament which was already Shakespeare's. In this "unhappy" and "mother" I think I hear an echo of Shakespeare's sorrow at parting from his own mother. (pp. 171-73)

Now a word or two about Adriana. Shakespeare makes her a jealous, nagging, violent scold, who will have her husband arrested for debt, though she will give money to free him. But the comedy of the play would be better brought out if Adriana were pictured as loving and constant, inflicting her inconvenient affection upon the false husband as upon the true. Why did Shakespeare want to paint this unpleasant bitter-tongued wife?

When Adriana appears in the first scene of the second act she is at once sketched in her impatience and jealousy. . . . In the first five minutes of this act she is sketched to the life, and Shakespeare does nothing afterwards but repeat and deepen the same strokes: it seems as if he knew nothing about her or would depict nothing of her except her jealousy and nagging, her impatience and violence. We have had occasion to notice more than once that when Shakespeare repeats touches in this way, he is drawing from life, from memory, and not from imagination. Moreover, in this case, he shows us at once that he is telling of his wife, because she defends herself against the accusation of age, which no one brings against her, though every one knows that Shakespeare's wife was eight years older than himself. (pp. 175-76)

In the second scene of the third act there is a phrase from the hero, Antipholus of Syracuse, about Adriana which I find significant:

> She that doth call me husband, even my soul
> Doth for a wife abhor!
>
> [III. ii. 158-59]

There is no reason in the comedy for such strong words. Most men would be amused or pleased by a woman who makes up to them as Adriana makes up to Antipholus. I hear Shakespeare in this uncalled-for, over-emphatic "even my soul doth for a wife abhor."

In the fifth act Adriana is brought before the Abbess, and is proved to be a jealous scold. Shakespeare will not be satisfied till some impartial great person of Adriana's own sex has condemned her. . . . But Adriana will not accept the reproof: she will have her husband at all costs. The whole scene discovers personal feeling. Adriana is the portrait that Shakespeare wished to give us of his wife. (pp. 176-77)

> Frank Harris, "Shakespeare's Early Attempts to Portray Himself and His Wife: Biron, Adriana, Valentine," in his The Man Shakespeare and His Tragic Life Story, Frank Palmer, 1909, pp. 161-87.

Q [ARTHUR QUILLER-COUCH]   (essay date 1922)

[Quiller-Couch was editor with J. Dover Wilson of the New Cambridge edition of Shakespeare's works. In his study Shakespeare's Workmanship and in his Cambridge lectures on Shakespeare, Quiller-Couch based his interpretations on the assumption that Shakespeare was mainly a craftsman attempting, with the tools and materials at hand, to solve particular problems central to his plays. In the following excerpt, he challenges Samuel Taylor Coleridge's assertion that The Comedy of Errors is a farce (see excerpt above, 1808-18), claiming instead that it is an unsuccessful mixture of farce and romance. Quiller-Couch also attacks Coleridge's defense of the improbabilities in the play. For further commentary on the farcical nature of Comedy, see the excerpts by Algernon Charles Swinburne (1880) and Edward Dowden (1903).]

[In the Menaechmi] Plautus is content with one pair of twins: Shakespeare out-Plautusing Plautus, adds a second pair, the two Dromios. Now to double a pair of twins so alike that even a wife cannot tell one from the other is not merely to double that amount of the improbable which a play of 'mistaken identity' claims for credence, but to multiply it by more than a hundred—nay by more than a thousand. When all the changes have been rung on Aristotle's impossible probabilities and possible improbabilities, a fairy-tale is a fairy-tale, and we can concede a Fairy Prince incommoded by a nose a yard long. But a play supposed to be enacted by real persons exempt from magic must hold some claim of credence in its postulate, even though it call itself a farce. So when the condemned merchant Aegeon, telling his tale before the Duke, asserts that his wife arrived at an inn and became

> A joyful mother of two goodly sons:
> And, which was strange, the one so like the other,
> As could not be distinguished but by names. . . .
> That very hour, and in the self-same inn,
> A meaner woman was delivered
> Of such a burden male, twins both alike:
>
> [I. i. 50-5]

we must suspect that inn of more than dramatically-licensed victualling; or at least submit that here is behaviour beyond even the lax range of the Bonâ-fide Traveller. On the stage of Plautus the convention of two men being alike enough to deceive even a wife might pass. It was actually a convention of pasteboard since the actors wore masks; you had only to paint two masks alike, and the trick was done. But even on the stage of Plautus to present two pairs of doubles would have been to present an impossible improbability.

Shakespeare makes that improbability still more impossible by presenting it, on his stage, without masks. The critical excuse for The Comedy of Errors is usually borrowed from a passage in Coleridge's Literary Remains [see excerpt above]. . . . (pp. xix-xx)

With all respect to Coleridge we say that this has the air of special pleading; and we distrust it the more because of its categorising farce apart from comedy and giving it 'laws of its end and constitution.' As a matter of history, and even of nomenclature, farce and comedy never have been and never can be divided into compartments with separate literary laws. If Molière and Congreve be the norm of Comedy . . . , then Aristophanes is merely farcical, and—what does it matter? Who ever made these categories or gave them 'laws'? M. Maeterlinck's L'Oiseau Bleu or Sir James Barrie's Peter Pan are not farces as certainly as they are not tragedies. There is no line of demarcation—all such lines, or attempts at them, are a professional humbug of criticism. . . . We see no point at all in praising the Errors above the Menaechmi as 'the high water mark of elaborate farce in its highest signification.' It might (though we doubt it) have come near to deserve such praise had Shakespeare not set his artificial farce between the romantic-realism of the distressed merchant, with which he opens, and of the long-lost wife reclaimed, with which he concludes. . . . [In] this early play Shakespeare already discloses his propensity for infusing romance into each or every 'form' of drama; that unique propensity which in his later work makes him so magical and so hard to define. But, as yet, farce and romance were not one 'form' but two separate stools; and between them in The Comedy of Errors he fell to the ground. (pp. xxi-xxii)

Sundry passages, even in its farcical episodes, show us the born poet, the born romancer, itching to be at his trade. For an example:

> O, train me not, sweet mermaid, with thy note,
> To drown me in thy sister's flood of tears:
> Sing, siren, for thyself, and I will dote:
> Spread o'er the silver waves thy golden hairs;
> And as a bed I'll take them, and there lie:
> And, in that glorious supposition, think
> He gains by death that hath such means to die:
> Let Love, being light, be drownéd if she sink!
>
> [III. ii. 45-52]
>
> (p. xxii)

> Q [Arthur Quiller-Couch], in his introduction to The Comedy of Errors by William Shakespeare, Cambridge at the University Press, 1922, pp. vii-xxiii.

ALISON GAW   (essay date 1926)

[Gaw makes two new critical claims for The Comedy of Errors. First, she challenges the accepted view that Shakespeare borrowed only one scene from Plautus's Amphitruo and posits instead that Comedy contains a mixture of the plots of both the Menaechmi *and* Amphitruo. *Second, Gaw argues that the frame story of Aegeon is important to the structure of the play. Her emphasis on the necessity of the frame story opposes the earlier conclusion of Arthur Quiller-Couch (1922), who claimed that the frame story is simply imposed onto the farce and serves no dramatic purpose.]*

In general, editors of the *Comedy of Errors* give a somewhat misleading statement of the relationship of [the] two sources to the Shakespearean play. They say that the plot of the *Errors* is practically that of the *Menaechmi* with the addition of a scene borrowed from the *Amphitruo,* and some add that the idea of the Dromios also comes from the *Amphitruo.* A fairer statement would be that the two plots have been combined to the marked modification of both, and have also been very considerably amplified. The feature of the doubled principal characters (the two Menaechmi and Jupiter-Amphitryon) is central to both plays. But the conception of the servants as also doubles of each other (fundamental to the *Amphitruo,* where Mercury, Sosia's divine impersonator, is really the mischievous mainspring of the plot) is in the *Errors* borrowed from the *Amphitruo* and superimposed upon the *Menaechmi* plot. (p. 625)

In the *Comedy of Errors,* . . . both the preceding plots have been ethically cleansed and remotivated. The basic forces in the *Menaechmi* are three: Menaechmus' apparently habitual immorality, Sosicles' deliberate pilfering of the courtesan's mantle and bracelet, and the accidental confusion of the two brothers on account of their physical likeness. The motivation of the *Amphitruo* depends upon the licentiousness of Jupiter and the Puckish delight of Mercury in teasing Sosia and Amphitryon. In the *Comedy of Errors* the immoralities of the Roman plays largely disappear. Adriana's jealousy of her husband is baseless, and he visits the home of

> a wench of excellent discourse,
> Prettie and wittie; wilde, and yet too gentle;
> [III. i. 109-10]

only in exasperation at being shut out of his own home in the presence of his invited guests, taking them with him to dine at the other house and in the same exasperation ordering that there be delivered to her the gold chain he had previously intended as a gift to his wife. His brother, Antipholus of Syracuse, too, is no longer guilty of the clear-headed knavery of Sosicles' pilferings from the courtesan; he is dazed by the inexplicable familiar recognitions of him, and the play is filled with suggestions of conjuring and witchcraft that powerfully reflect his state of mind and explain his actions. . . . And as to the courtesan's bracelet (now a ring), the acquisition of which from that lady has been transferred from Sosicles (S. Antipholus) to Menaechmus (E. Antipholus), the misunderstanding is adjusted at the end of the play in two innocuous lines:

> *Cur[tesan].* Sir I must haue that Diamond from you.
> *E. Antiph[olus].* There take it, and much thanks for my
>   good cheere.   [V. i. 392-93]

In short, in the course of romanticizing the comedy, a fairly thorough moral disinfection has taken place. (pp. 626-27)

[About] this fundamental plot complex referring to the misadventures of the brothers Antipholus and the brothers Dromio has been woven a secondary plot-complex dealing with the experiences of . . . the father and . . . the mother of the brothers Antipholus. This material . . . is entirely new in the English version, the father in the *Menaechmi* having died long before the play opens and the mother being never mentioned. It is

contained wholly in the opening and closing scenes of the play. In I, i, Aegeon, the father, is brought before the Duke of Ephesus, under accusation of having, a Syracusan, visited the Ephesians despite the feud between the two towns. In peril of death, upon request of the Duke he tells his story. . . . The final scene of the play reunites father and mother at the same time that the perplexities of the main plot are solved by the bringing together of the two pairs of twins.

This frame-plot of the father and mother serves at least five dramaturgic functions:

1. For the extraneous Prologue of Plautus, detailing the events that precede the opening of the play and addressed as monologue directly to the audience, the frame of the *Comedy of Errors* substitutes an organic exposition in dramatic dialogue within the play proper. . . .

2. The frame is here an effective device for promoting plot unity. Without it the internal plot, even in the simpler form of the *Menaechmi,* impresses one as a rather loosely knit series of comic happenings. The frame gives a firm beginning and a firm, definite, and massive ending. That this is somewhat contrasted in tone with the misadventures that form the main plot merely, from this point of view, increases its effectiveness.

3. By its tone of romantic tragicomedy the frame also combines with other elements in the English play to lift the Plautan farce into an atmosphere of greater dignity.

4. The frame increases the general happiness of the ending. Among the many points which it adjusts we may note the reunion of the Antipholuses, the curing of Adriana's jealousy, the clearing up of the triangle situation between the two Dromios and Luce, the pairing off of Luciana with Antipholus of Syracuse, the release of the father from his imprisonment, and the reunion of the mother with her two sons and her husband.

5. The effectiveness of the conclusion is enhanced by surprise. The mother, Aemilia, is cleverly smuggled into the action . . . in the guise of an Abbess protecting a sane man from persecution as a lunatic. As she has not been mentioned since the opening scene of the play, the audience has wholly forgotten her; their attention has been skilfully diverted to another issue, and they have no reason for suspecting her identity until it is suddenly revealed. . . . (pp. 628-29)

It must be insisted on, therefore, that in the theatre the weakness of the *Comedy of Errors* does not lie in the plot. Neither, it may be added, does it consist in the improbability of the much criticized double twinship that is basic to the plot. Such a presupposition in a romantic drama the normal audience is always willing to accept. The weakness lies in the thinness and occasionally the falsity of the characterization, and in the wordiness and at times the triviality and irrelevance of the dialogue. Structurally the plot is . . . a skilful combination of materials drawn from two classic sources and amplified by five English additions—the Luce-E. Dromio-S. Dromio triangle, the Luciana-S. Antipholus situation, the Angelo-S. Antipholus episode, the Aegeon-Duke relation, and the Aemilia-Abbess identity—all of this material being knit into a compact structural whole.

Here, then, is our difficulty. How reconcile this adept plotcraftsmanship in the play with its weakness in characterization and dialogue, and with the patchwork structure of *Love's Labour's Lost,* the rambling of *The Two Gentlemen of Verona,* and the dramatic inadequacies of Shakespeare's amplification of *3 Henry VI*? (pp. 629-30)

Alison Gaw, "The Evolution of 'The Comedy of Errors'," in PMLA, 41, Vol. XLI, No. 3, September, 1926, pp. 620-66.

THOMAS WHITFIELD BALDWIN   (essay date 1928)

It is generally agreed that "a Comedy of Errors (like to *Plautus* his *Menechmus*)," which "was played by the Players" in the Gray's Inn Christmas Revels on December 28, 1594, was Shakespeare's play. This external evidence then indicates that *The Comedy* was written before December 28, 1594.

But the internal evidence still further limits and indicates the date. . . . [There] is an allusion in iii. 2 to the wars in France, which could have been written only between August, 1589, when they began, and July, 1593, when they ended. An allusion to the Great Armada of July, 1588, and to events directly following after it also shows that the writing of the play was done not earlier than 1589. Shakespeare borrows a character, Menaphon, and some geography from Marlowe's first part of *Tamburlaine,* in such a way as to show that he plotted *The Comedy* from the Latin sources later than *Tamburlaine,* so that he could not have written the play earlier than 1588. *The Comedy* also uses the anglicized form of the name Dromio, instead of Dromo, as the name appears in the Latin and in all known

Act V. Scene i. Egion, the Duke, Adriana, Dromio of Ephesus, Antipholus of Ephesus. Frontispiece to Rowe edition (1709). By permission of the Folger Shakespeare Library.

occurrences down to John Lyly's *Mother Bomby,* which is usually dated 1587-1590, this fact indicating a date probably not earlier than 1587. All these points together indicate, then, that *The Comedy* was not written before August, 1589. (pp. x-xi)

Several other pieces of evidence also show that the play was written not much later than August, 1589. As already pointed out, the allusion to French affairs shows that *The Comedy* was written before July, 1593. . . . *The Comedy* is earlier than *Romeo and Juliet,* which Shakespeare wrote in its first form for the summer season of 1591. Mr. J. J. Munro has shown that *The Two Gentlemen of Verona* is earlier than *Romeo and Juliet,* thus not later than the winter season 1590-1591. But *The Comedy* is in turn earlier than *The Two Gentlemen,* hence not later than the summer season of 1590. (pp. xi-xii)

The previous evidence, then, points to a date for *The Comedy* not earlier than August, 1589, nor later than the summer season of 1590. The play itself shows that it is for a winter season. Since a dramatist wrote his play for a particular season and since a play rarely lasted more than the one season, the seasonal allusions in the play are regularly to the time of intended performance. Dromio of Ephesus points out to his master "you stand here in the cold" (iii.1). The statement that "since Pentecost the sum is due," instead of "last Pentecost," or a year come next Pentecost, harmonizes with the preceding reference to indicate an autumn and winter play. A more curious indication is that in taking over the time scheme of *Menaechmi,* Shakespeare changes the sunset ending of that play to "Soon at five o'clock," which means "early in the evening about five o'clock." Thus the time of the year for the intended performance of *The Comedy* would be about November to February. Our indications of date thus agree that Shakespeare's version of *The Comedy* was written for the autumn and winter season of 1589-1590, probably for first performance between November, 1589, and February, 1590.

There is still another allusion in the play which further confirms our indications both that *The Comedy* was written for first performance around the Christmas of 1589-1590, and that the company performing it was Shakespeare's. In v. 1. . . . , which takes place before the Priory ruled over by an abbess, we hear:

> the duke himself in person
> Comes this way to the melancholy vale,
> The place of death and sorry execution,
> Behind the ditches of the abbey here.
> [V. i. 119-21]

Since "the melancholy vale" is a place of execution, Mr. Henry Cunningham identifies it as possibly Wapping, where maritime offenders, as Aegeon was, were executed. But Wapping was not a vale, so that the specific reference is not to that place, though in fact it ought to be. The vale would rather suggest Tyburn, so named for the bourne or brook it was on. But Tyburn was not behind a priory of nuns as was Shakespeare's vale, and hence the reference cannot be specifically to Tyburn. (pp. xii-xiii)

Mr. Cunningham again comes to our aid with the suggestion that the Priory of this passage is "beyond doubt the Priory of Holywell, near which Shakespeare lived and worked." The identification seems to be correct. For "The name of the Liberty was derived from an ancient holy well, which has now disappeared, and its status from the fact that it had been the property of a priory of Benedictine nuns." Here then is the priory governed by an abbess. This was the only such priory which in the period when *The Comedy* was written had any connection with acting, both the Curtain and the Theater being in this Liberty. The topography also accurately corresponds. . . . To reach [the] vale beyond the ditches behind the Priory, the Duke would have turned into Holywell Lane, where the Burbadges lived, to the south of which was the Curtain, to the north the Theater, though the entrance to the latter was not from Holywell Lane, but from the vale beyond the ditches, and presumably the same was true of the Curtain. The Duke may thus have been on his way to either theater to execute Aegeon.

It would appear then that the theater in which this play was to be performed was either the Curtain or the Theater. Since, on other evidence, it appears that the play dates around the Christmas of 1589, it is necessary to know what companies were performing at the Curtain and the Theater 1589-1590. The company which we call Shakespeare's was forced to stop performing at the Cross Keys on November 5, 1589, and is found at the Curtain before April, 1590, probably having gone there at once. It was seemingly coöperating with the Admiral's Men at the Theater in November of the same year, but in November the coöperating companies were both driven by dissensions from the Theater. Thus it would appear that this allusion was written for a performance at one of these buildings. If so, the whole conclusion of the play, centering as it does around the Priory, was written for this performance, and conversely the fact that the playhouse was in this Liberty is the source for the abbess disguise and the ending of the play in front of the Priory. We should thus on this evidence date the planning and completion of the fifth act as not earlier than November 5, 1589, nor later than November, 1590, which again confirms our date of the Christmas 1589-1590. (pp. xiii-xv)

[Some] dramatist wove two plays of Plautus together, and put the result into a new setting to form *The Comedy*. Since the geography of the new setting is based on the original Latin of one of these plays, it is apparent that all these main elements of the play were fitted together at the same time. But the geography and characters of the new setting were invented not earlier than November, 1589. . . . Since then, the new setting was manufactured pretty completely at the same time the other main structural elements of the play were fitted together, and since the Priory in Ephesus was put into this setting not earlier than November 5, 1589, it follows that the main structure of the play as we now have it was shaped from the sources not earlier than November, 1589. But the numerous references to contemporary events of 1588-1589, which occur in passages admitted by all critics to have been written by Shakespeare, show that Shakespeare wrote a version of *The Comedy* about the Christmas of 1589. It follows that Shakespeare shaped *The Comedy* from its original sources probably in November and December, 1589. It also follows that any later revisions, if such there were, could not have affected the fundamental structure of the play but only its minor details. (pp. xv-xvi)

Malone pointed out that Paul's Boys had performed "The Historie of Error" at court January 1, 1577. This play he suggested as the basis of Shakespeare's *Comedy of Errors*. Though many theories have been founded on this relationship, there has heretofore been nothing to indicate positively whether *The History of Error* was or was not the basis for Shakespeare's play. The fact that the one has "Error" and the other "Errors" in the title is the only definite connection that has been established. Indeed we cannot rely wholly even upon that connection. It is suggested that "A Historie of Ferrar," performed at court

January 6, 1583, by Sussex's Men is also really *The History of Error* with the *f* misplaced. But it is equally possible that our first entry is really a "History of Ferrar," changed to "Error" by dropping the *f*. . . . The truth of the matter is that we have no external evidence definitely to indicate that there was a preceding play on which Shakespeare founded his *Comedy*.

Modern proponents of the precedent play theory rely rather upon alleged internal evidence in *The Comedy* itself. Chief of these theories is that of Professor J. Dover Wilson, which has been further elaborated by Professor Allison Gaw [see excerpt above, 1926]. The general method is to discover inconsistencies in the play, then to group these together into more or less harmonious aggregations, and finally to assume that each of these groups represents a stage in the development of the play. But since minor inconsistency is characteristic of Shakespeare, as even his contemporaries knew, mere inconsistency in itself proves nothing as to divided authorship or precedent versions. There must be something peculiar about the inconsistencies if they are to be significant. The inconsistencies so far noted seem clearly explicable on other known principles, and consequently would not indicate a precedent version or versions. Thus there is no clear evidence either internal or external to prove that Shakespeare used an earlier English play on which to base his version. (pp. xviii-xix)

Shakespeare gets from Plautus general suggestions, situations, and materials; but . . . he has as completely and thoroughly replotted these as if his sources had not already been plays. Too, this has been so cleverly done that there is not a slow spot in the play, but once started all keeps moving in rapidly increasing cross-purposes up to the dénouement. It is so highly improbable as to be almost impossible that so smoothly and cleverly articulated a plot is the outcome of successive "rehashings" and repatchings of old material. Certainly this final version is a complete and harmonious reworking of the precedent material. And that precedent material for the essentials of all except the romance setting seems clearly to have been the *Menaechmi* and *Amphitruo* of Plautus, on which this final plot is directly based. But even the romance material pivots on, and furnishes the part for, Aegeon, one of the five chief rôles, who comes directly from *Menaechmi*. (pp. xxxi-xxxii)

[*The Comedy of Errors*] is a farce-comedy of situation. That it is intended to be a play of situation is indicated by the title itself; it is a comedy of errors, or mistaken identities. So Shakespeare has shaped his plot, from materials and on principles already shaped by one of the world's masters, in such a way as to obtain the maximum of mistakes. A great part of the interest in the play arises from the intellectual ingenuity Shakespeare has displayed in managing to continue getting the wrong persons together at exactly the right time to keep the confusions constantly increasing. (p. xxxii)

This elemental, and yet fundamental, part of the playwright's art he would early have had impressed upon him. . . . It was only in later days that he became careless, even contemptuous, of carefully articulated major plan, probably because of the realization that this was after all only machinery, a means and not an end. But now he is joyously exploring the possibilities of intricate plan to get every possible permutation and combination out of a given situation. If we enjoy such exercise, we can enter appreciatively into the game.

Too, we must have some ability to play make-believe. We must be able to believe "just for fun" in two sets of identical twins born in the same inn on the same night, or in the inability of the wandering pair to suspect what is wrong the minute the errors begin to occur. For its tone borders on that of farce, just as the story of Bully Bottom in *Midsummer Night's Dream* is farcical.

But in *Midsummer Night's Dream* Shakespeare had learned to base his fun on farcical character instead of farcical situations. That, he had not yet learned in *The Comedy.* He had learned how to make the machinery, but he had not learned the best motive power. His eventual motive power was character from which actions flow. But in *The Comedy* we must for the most part be content with the actions and assume the actuating character.

Not that Shakespeare does not appreciate differences in character. A reasonably careful reading will show that he differentiates the characters even of the Antipholi and of the Dromios. But those differentiations do not determine the action of the play. The situation is predominant over the characters, not the characters over the situation. What characterization we have is rather typical, assumed, or incidental; it is not indulged in for its own sake, or developed as having a main bearing on the outcome. Indeed, much characterization would have been in the way. (pp. xxxii-xxxiv)

If Shakespeare has not yet learned to make the characters dominate the situation, he has at least learned to make them support it. In the same way, while he has not yet learned to make each character say only or chiefly the things that would be peculiar to that character, yet he does not have the character saying things that are wholly inappropriate. A reasoned propriety of forms he has; instinctive propriety of thought and expression he has not yet attained. Thus he has but bare occasion even to attempt emotionally poetic expression, as when Antipholus of Syracuse makes love to Luciana; and poetic expression does not yet involuntarily flow from his pen. Instead, we have the characteristic, ingeniously artificial ornaments of puns and verbal quibbling of numerous varieties. Unless one enjoys the sheer nimbleness of mentality which these artificialities display, he will find little solace in the verbiage of this play.

But if one can induce the mood of rollicking, farcical hilarity of an Elizabethan Innocents' Night, and enter into the nimble spirit of the fun, *The Comedy of Errors* may prove to be his favorite farce-comedy. (pp. xxxiv-xxxv)

> *Thomas Whitfield Baldwin, in his introduction to* The Comedy of Errors *by William Shakespeare, edited by Thomas Whitfield Baldwin, D. C. Heath and Company, 1928, pp. v-xxxv.*

H. B. CHARLTON (essay date 1930)

[*An English scholar, Charlton is best known for his* Shakespearian Tragedy *and* Shakespearian Comedy—*two important studies in which he argues that the proponents of New Criticism, particularly T. S. Eliot and I. A. Richards, were reducing Shakespeare's drama to its poetic elements and in the process losing sight of his characters. In his introduction to* Shakespearian Tragedy, *Charlton described himself as a "devout" follower of A. C. Bradley, and like his mentor he adopted a psychological, character-oriented approach to Shakespeare's work. In the excerpt below, he suggests that Shakespeare turned to the highly structured, farcical plot of Plautus's* Menaechmi *because he was "recoiling" from the romantic method he used in* Love's Labour's Lost, *which Charlton believes was written earlier than* The Comedy of Errors. *This theory sets him apart from earlier critics, for although he agrees with such commentators as Samuel Taylor Coleridge (1808-*

18), *Algernon Charles Swinburne (1880), and Edward Dowden (1903) that* Comedy *is a farce, he does not follow the assumption that the play is a piece of apprentice work. For a later discussion of Charlton's ideas, see the excerpt by S. C. Sen Gupta (1950). The following excerpt is taken from a speech given in 1930; it was first published in* Bulletin of the John Rylands Library *in 1931.*]

[Though] *Love's Labour's Lost* is mere gay trifling, its peculiar gaiety almost frustrates itself by the formlessness and the spinelessness of the thing as a play. And Shakespeare's first recoil from the insouciant romantic formlessness of *Love's Labour's Lost* seems to have been a feeling that plays without backbone are hopelessly crippled. No plot, no play. And so apparently the recoil turned him to Classical comedy. Putting himself to school to Plautus for his *Comedy of Errors,* he submitted himself to a discipline which, however uncongenial to the spirit, was a salutary apprenticeship to the mechanics of play-building. But it was much more than that. When Shakespeare took the Roman comedians for his pattern, he was reverting to the practice on which his English predecessors, and French and Italian pioneers before them, had established the new comedy of modern Europe. Modern comedy begins with Plautus and Terence. . . . (p. 47)

It is easy to be unjust to classical comedy, and to Plautus and Terence. A modern, or even a sixteenth-century reader of Roman comedy, may find in it nothing but a string of ludicrous intrigues. It appears to be absorbed in mere incidents, to be farce at most, and rarely to attain to comedy in our modern sense. But events and situations which strike us as only isolated examples of the ludicrous, interesting or otherwise merely for themselves, may in the past have had a larger significance for contemporaries. When Shakespeare took the stories of Plautus for his *Comedy of Errors,* he could only take their material substance; their significance remained behind in the Roman civilisation of two thousand years ago. Even a colourable English imitation can impart little of the original but its external features. We roar hilariously at the ludicrous predicament and the crude discomfiture of bawd and pimp and procurer in play after play of Plautus and Terence. But the display is a farce for our entertainment, lacking almost all such repercussion in the circumstances of our social existence as would raise it to the level of comedy. Yet in our own day, if a dramatist calls any of Mrs. Warren's profession into his *dramatis personae,* without further thought he is taken to be a playwright obsessed with the notion of turning his plays to profound problems of our social life. (pp. 47-8)

The outstanding feature of the whole body of Roman comedy is that whilst it is full of sex, it is almost entirely devoid of love. There is nothing in it of love as modern literature makes love. (p. 52)

[Though Shakespeare] clung closely to Plautus, inevitably he lost much and changed still more of his originals. Transplanting stories to other societies in other and later periods of time is bound to sever them from that which gives them their essential significance. Moreover, these Roman stories are so closely built into the fabric of Roman society and its mind, that a transference of the mere story carries over with it elements, incidents, or scenes, which must remain alien in their new homes. In particular there are these all-important men-servants. The English bourgeoisie of the sixteenth-century had no exact counterpart of them in their households. Hence the Dromios are exotic on the English stage. In England, menial servants who are soundly kicked at frequent intervals are hardly likely to be taken into the confidential personal secrets of the masters; nor does one expect to find such pantry boys whiling away their leisure with sixth-form dissipations. There are, however, moments when their kitchen gossip brings the Dromios nearer home, and the fat cook's amorousness almost domesticates one of the Dromios permanently in England. . . . But though she haunted him, he escaped from her and ran back into the theatrical convention in which alone he has his existence. . . . Even as merely theatrical conventions, the Dromios are but shadows of their dramatic originals. In their new surroundings on an English stage, circumstance scarcely ever allows them to be the engineers of the story. Almost invariably, they are merely its clowns.

With less important persons of the Plautine plays, figures whose rôle is merely incidental, Shakespeare may effect a complete anglicisation. The man in buff, for instance, and Pinch the quack, are straight from the streets of London. But general naturalisation is impossible. Many of the favoured incidents, which make a Roman intrigue, lose all semblance of credibility when assembled in a modern play. Loss of children by shipwreck, drastic penal laws to safeguard petty economic systems, summary courts of justice at the street-corner—these are details harder to bring to life on a London stage than on one in ancient Rome.

But in taking his story from Plautus, Shakespeare frankly accepted all these limitations. The Dromios are mere stage clowns. Ephesus is a town where Lapland witches delight in playing spookish tricks on men and women. Farce expands to extravaganza. To give the farcical a larger scope, Shakespeare doubled the source of it in Plautus by providing twin Dromios for the twin Antipholi he took from his Roman original. The plot becomes a sort of mathematical exhibition of the maximum number of erroneous combinations of four people taken in pairs. The bustle leaves no room for characterisation, the persons in it enduring their lot as in a nightmare. Even the stock-types of the original are largely useless. The parasite, Peniculus, in Plautus was a genuine property of the Roman stage, and therefore Shakespeare dropped him overboard *en route,* as he would have been an utter foreigner in Elizabethan England. In one point only did the English dramatist find that he could import something of the social application of the Latin play.

In the *Menaechmi,* Plautus plays lightly with the folly of shrewish wives. It is a common theme in Roman comedy. It was an almost inevitable outcome of their marriage system: marriages were marriages of convenience, the wife bringing with her a dowry over which she retained control, and, though divorces were easily procurable, when a rejected wife returned to her parents, she took her dowry back with her. Such marriages must often have proved unhappy bargains; but release was an expensive luxury. Most of the husbands in Roman plays grumble at their hard lot. (pp. 64-6)

In the play to which Shakespeare turned for his *Comedy of Errors,* there is a wife and she is, of course, something of a shrew. But she is only half-heartedly so. She is, however, reprimanded for her behaviour; and, very significantly, the reprimand comes from the mouth of her own father. He has obviously more sympathy with the husband than with his daughter. He reminds her that it is her duty to be grateful for the material comforts her husband provides for her. . . . As a father, he reminds her, he has frequently had to urge her to be complacent, not to spy and pry into her husband's affairs. . . . He goes so far as explicitly to approve of the husband's resort to a courtesan in retaliation for his wife's nagging, adding that

to complain about the particular sort of pleasure he has chosen is to treat him as one would treat a slave! Only when the wife adds that the husband is stealing her property to provide presents for his mistress, does the old man find the husband clearly in the wrong. The attitude of mind is characteristic. He rebuked his daughter for her feminine inability to understand the material situation: by her blindness to the economic principles of house-keeping, she was causing an uneconomic distribution of the household's wealth between wife and courtesan. (p. 67)

But when a story embodying a situation like this of the *Menaechmi* is brought into sixteenth-century England, it has ceased to be a problem of domestic economy. The question of fidelity in wedlock is primary: and as the plot involves infidelity, Shakespeare is compelled to provide Antipholus with more immediate provocation for his lapse. So he draws on another play, the *Amphitruo,* and only allows Antipholus to resort to the courtesan when he has been locked out of his own house by his own wife who at the moment is entertaining a man whom she mistakenly assumes to be no other than her own husband. But even so, in the English play, the husband's drastic retaliation calls for a much greater emphasis on the shrewishness of his wife, Adriana, than appears in the Plautine counterpart.

Shakespeare's Adriana is doubtless shrew, virago and vixen to boot. She breaks the servants' pates across, though that hardly gives her characteristic distinction in a play in which fisticuffs are the regular means of intercourse. She rails at bed and board, and jealousy gives venom to her clamours, adding to them a virulence of which Plautus could scarcely avail himself, for it is only love in the modern sense "which is full of jealousy." An English shrew, moreover, much more than a Roman one, is hampered by memories of the affection she once had for the man of her choice. Adriana even fondles at times. But her single lapse into the broken-hearted bride who will weep and die in tears is a fall both from type and from character. A more credibly humanising trait appears in her excited enlargement of the tale of her husband's frenzied acts: the duke is treated to a display of rumour's growth, as facts swell with fancy when she recounts the incidents she thought she had seen. . . . Yet at the end of the play, the shrew is not so much out of countenance as she was meant to be. One cannot but remember that the person solemnly reproving Adriana for her shrewishness is not, as in Plautus, her own natural parent, but her mother-in-law. Nor does her husband appear to suffer much spiritual disquiet from her moods. A man who conducts a domestic tiff by calling his wife a dissembling harlot, and by threats to pluck out her eyes, is not too sensitive a fellow and has a sufficient protection in the thickness of his skin. Indeed, the general temper of the life depicted in *The Comedy of Errors* is so crude, coarse, and brutal, that Adriana's fault appears to be not so much her shrewishness as her undiplomatic use of it. Even the abbess accuses her of nothing more heinous than bad tactics. . . . (pp. 68-9)

But there is one person in the scene for whom this explanation is entirely inadequate. Luciana, sister of Adriana, breaks in on the abbess's reproaches:—

> She never reprehended him but mildly,
> When he demean'd himself rough, rude and wildly.
> Why bear you these rebukes and answer not?
>
> [V. i. 87-9]

The challenge is exactly what the woman of to-day would urge. Yet in the rest of the play, though it is our sentimental sympathy with Luciana which has reflected on Adriana a deeper condemnation than has any of the formal charges laid against her, our sympathy with Luciana is not in the least founded on a concurrence in her explicit propositions about the relationship of man and wife. It is indeed Adriana who speaks with the voice of to-day in these matters. "Why should man's liberty than our's be more?" she asks her sister, adding that none but asses will be bridled in such fashion by their husbands' will. But this is Luciana's creed:—

> There's nothing situate under heaven's eye
> But hath his bound, in earth, in sea, in sky:
> The beasts, the fishes and the winged fowls
> Are their males' subjects and at their controls:
> Men, more divine, the masters of all these,
> Lords of the wide world and wild watery seas
> Indued with intellectual sense and souls,
> Of more pre-eminence than fish and fowls,
> Are masters to their females, and their lords.
> Then let your will attend on their accords. . . .
>
> [II. i. 16-25]

No mortal in this world of ours now would venture to swear by such a creed: nor could a subject of Queen Elizabeth have easily dared to do so. And yet though Luciana's terms are mere relics of the past, she secures from the moderns more instinctive sympathy than does her sister, despite the almost Georgian modernity of Adriana's views on conjugal equality. For Luciana brings into the play a range of sentiment utterly incompatible with the atmosphere of this *Comedy of Errors*. When Antipholus of Syracuse woos her as

> mine own self's better part
> Mine eye's clear eye, my dear heart's dearest heart,
> My food, my fortune, and my sweet hope's arm,
> My sole earth's heaven, and my heaven's claim. . . .
>
> [III. ii. 61-4]

he is putting into words a way of looking on the relationship of man and woman different fundamentally from the point of view expressed in Roman comedy and in its English imitations. Between Plautus and Luciana are the centuries in which chivalry and its achievements in life and letters had evolved the love which, like God, makes earth and man anew. The world which is enshrined in mediaeval romance was embedded in the inherited experience of the sixteenth century. Even when he was recoiling from romanticism, Shakespeare could not divest himself of the romantic. And so these alien elements are stuffed within his imitation of a classical play. (pp. 69-70)

But Luciana is not the only romantic intruder into the gross Roman world of the *Comedy of Errors*. Old Aegeon and the abbess never lived in Rome. The father in the Plautine story died when he lost his sons, and not a word is heard of their mother. But Shakespeare's Aegeon brings into the story memories of tragic instances of harm reaching all but to the extremity of dire mishap. With echoes of mortal and intestine jars, he strikes a full note of pathos, the pity of age, and suffering, and frustrated hope. And these are plangent cries with which the heedless rollicking brutality of the comedy makes nothing but discord. Old men in Aegeon's sad situation are not unfamiliar to Roman comedy. But children were lost in Plautus, not to provide him with exhibitions of broken-hearted parents: they were lost simply that their finding might restore social status to such of the girls in a brothel as his young fellows might wish to marry. The old parent and his broken heart are useless to Plautus. (p. 71)

As there is neither the love of romanticism in Plautus, so neither is there its pity, except for the little of it which oddly creeps in to that abnormal play, the *Captivi*. But as love, so pity comes incongruously into the *Comedy of Errors*. Doubtless, much of the incongruity is hidden by Shakespeare's adroit use of Aegeon, who is not so much a figure in the play as a prologue and an epilogue to it. But at odd moments, the incongruity obtrudes itself. One is stupefied to learn that Antipholus of Ephesus, the thick-skinned man-about-town, has rendered knightly service in the field to his feudal overlord, bestriding him in battle, and taking in this deed of chivalric devotion, as deep a scar as ever hero won in mediaeval romance.

> Justice, most gracious duke, O, grant me justice!
> Even for the service that long since I did thee,
> When I bestrid thee in the wars, and took
> Deep scars to save thy life: even for the blood
> That then I lost for thee, now grant me justice. . . .
>
> [V. i. 190-94]

The *Comedy of Errors* is indeed a recoil, but a recoil which amply indicates that the recoiler will soon be turned again towards romance. It is in his blood and in the spirit of his times. The problem of reconciling romance and comedy was not to be avoided. It would have to be faced. (p. 72)

> *H. B. Charlton, "Shakespeare's Recoil from Romanticism," in his* Shakespearian Comedy, *Methuen & Co. Ltd., 1938, pp. 44-72.*

G. WILSON KNIGHT (essay date 1932)

[*One of the most influential of modern Shakespearean critics, Knight helped shape the twentieth-century reaction against the biographical and character studies of the nineteenth-century Shakespeareans. Knight's analytic practice stresses what he calls, in his study* The Wheel of Fire, *the "spatial" aspects of imagery, atmosphere, theme, and symbol in the plays. He thus parallels the New Critics with his emphasis on verbal texture; his discussions of symbolism are similar to Samuel Taylor Coleridge's notion of the symbolic as indefinite with multiple meanings. The excerpt below is from his* The Shakespearean Tempest, *first published in 1932, in which he develops his contention that Shakespeare's two most important symbols in* The Comedy of Errors *are the tempest and music.*]

In *The Comedy of Errors* a tempest is important. We are brought to a world of gold and fun where the tragic work of a tempest is finally remedied by reunions. The sea tempest is here an actual event, the tragic background to a romantic comedy. Aegeus describes, at length, the original tragedy, his words heavy with grief and the turbulence of his misfortunes. . . . Such a tempest is peculiarly Shakespearian. We meet it again and again. Tempests always, as here, tragic, tend to 'disperse', the resulting play to reunite, the people scattered in the tempest. Antipholus of Syracuse thus compares himself to a drop of water seeking for another drop, his mother and brother, in the world's ocean, and so he 'confounds' and loses himself in the 'quest': he is thus without 'content' [I. ii. 33-40]. These are typical thoughts. The ocean is the enemy to love's desire, seeking to engulf the searcher; and 'content', throughout Shakespeare, is an important word.

Now in this play a family is first dispersed by tempest. Next, the action shows a remarkable series of mistakes in a magic land of merchants and riches, with a final consummation in union and happiness. The play is full of riches imagery especially. There is the 'thousand marks in gold' [III. i. 8] that causes so much irritation; the 'two-hundred ducats' [IV. iv. 134] owed by Angelo; a 'bag of gold' [IV. iv. 96]. . . . There is the Syracusan Dromio's description of the kitchen wench in terms of geography including a fine riches-India association blended with 'caracks' [III. ii. 137]. . . . The central action turns on a 'chain of gold', made by the 'goldsmith', Angelo, for the Ephesian Antipholus. . . . Angelo owes money to a 'merchant' who is in direct need of it:

> . . . I am bound
> To Persia and want guilders for my voyage.
>
> [IV. i. 3-4]

He is in a hurry: 'both wind and tide' stays for him [IV. i. 46]. This chain of gold and all the violent troubles it gives rise to constitute much of the play's later action. 'Gold' is emphasized strongly throughout. Consider this speech:

> When I desired him to come home to dinner,
> He ask'd me for a thousand marks in gold:
> ''Tis dinner time', quoth I; 'My gold!' quoth he:
> 'Your meat doth burn', quoth I; 'My gold!' quoth he:
> 'Will you come home?' quoth I; 'My gold!' quoth he,
> 'Where is the thousand marks I gave thee, villain?'
> 'The pig', quoth I, 'is burn'd'; 'My gold!' quoth he.
>
> [II. i. 60-6]

Consider also the jealous Adriana's curious speech:

> I see the jewel best enamelled
> Will lose his beauty; yet the gold bides still,
> That others touch, and often touching will
> Wear gold: and no man that hath a name
> By falsehood and corruption doth it shame.
>
> [II. i. 109-13]

The play is full of gold and other riches, of merchants, and sea-voyages. There is continual suggestion both of the 'mart' and of the sea. (pp. 113-16)

[Here] love, as in the *Two Gentlemen*, may be expressed in luxuriantly coloured sea-imagery:

> O, train me not, sweet mermaid, with thy note,
>   To drown me in thy sister's flood of tears:
> Sing, siren, for thyself, and I will dote:
>   Spread o'er the silver waves thy golden hairs,
> And as a bed I'll take them and there lie,
>   And in that glorious supposition think
> He gains by death that hath such means to die:
> Let Love, being light, be drowned if she sink!
>
> [III. ii. 45-52]

Continually in Shakespeare such love sea-pictures are word-painted to suggest love immortal; continually they are juxtaposed with song or music. Of such, *The Tempest* itself is built: sirens, music, dances on the yellow sand, and still waters. This is the Shakespearian haven, and heaven, to storm-tossed mortality. But there are tragic essences in this play, too. And it is natural that in this atmosphere of riches, merchants, and tempests, human rage and unrest generally should be directly related to sea-loss:

> *Adriana.* This week he hath been heavy, sour, sad,
>   And much different from the man he was;
>   But till this afternoon his passion
>   Ne'er brake into extremity of rage.
> *Abbess.* Hath he not lost much wealth by wreck of sea?
>   Buried some dear friend?   [V. i. 45-50]

Notice how the 'wreck' is followed by thought of the death 'of some dear friend'. (pp. 116-17)

In *The Comedy of Errors* there is both tragedy and comedy interwoven. Our last quotation may lead us to consider the matter of Adriana's jealousy. She is a trying woman who troubles her husband, and in her much of the later thought of *The Taming of the Shrew* is personified. She, too, is 'shrewish' [III. i. 2]. Luciana tries to persuade her that women should be subject to their husbands' wills:

> Why, headstrong liberty is lash'd with woe.
> There's nothing situate under heaven's eye
> But hath his bound, in earth, in sea, in sky:
> The beasts, the fishes, and the winged fowls
> Are their males' subjects and at their controls:
> Men, more divine, the masters of all these,
> Lords of the wide world and wild watery seas,
> Indued with intellectual sense and souls,
> Of more pre-eminence than fish and fowls,
> Are masters to their females, and their lords:
> Then let your will attend on their accords.
>
> [II. i. 15-25]

Notice the comparison of human family order with vast symbols of order, natural and universal. (pp. 117-18)

Now, besides Adriana, there are the numerous other mistakes, dissensions, and difficulties that bring the action near to disaster. And we must remember the first grim scene where Aegeon is condemned to death:

> Merchant of Syracusa, plead no more.
>
> [I. i. 3]

'Merchant'. Every one here seems to be a merchant. The word occurs continually: 'merchant' and 'mart'. So Aegeon describes his tempest grief, the loss and dispersal of his family. And in this description, quoted at the start of my essay, we may observe that Aegeon's tragedy 'was wrought by nature, not by vile offence' [I. i. 34]. Such are our tempests often: they suggest the inscrutable enginry of fate that drives human barks on to their wreckage. Shakespeare does not only present tragedy in terms of weak 'character'. And we should here observe clearly how the tempest is closely associated with themes of birth—'a joyful mother of two goodly sons' [I. i. 50]. This happy family, this life-joy of father, mother, and their new-born children, is smashed, severed, 'dispersed' by 'tempest'. So the 'tempest' here is clearly opposed to life, a death force, 'tragic' [I. i. 64]. And throughout the action Aegeon's first organ dirge of sea sorrow lingers in our minds, together with the knowledge of his sentence to death. This play is dark with tragedy.

And yet, set against all this, is our gold-imagery, our passages of lyric beauty, our sense of rippling comedy. It is a glorious little play. And, at the close, all is united again, the end is peace, reunion, and pardon, outside the Abbey where Aemilia, Aegeon's wife, has long taken refuge. Aegeon is indeed a tragic figure. But all is quickly now resolved:

> *Aegeon.* If I dream not, thou art Aemilia:
>   If thou art she, tell me where is that son
>   That floated with thee on the fatal raft?
>
> [V. i. 347-49]

So this 'wreck at sea' . . . is at last remedied. This play concludes in joy, its reunions peculiarly forecasting *Pericles*. . . . Both plays show us a story starting with birth, with next the dispersal of a family in tempest, and then a final reunion. There is there a more intense religious and mythical suggestion. But here, too, it is more than once recognized that this Ephesus is a land of supernatural mystery:

> Sure, these are but imaginary wiles
> And Lapland sorcerers inhabit here.
>
> [IV. iii. 10-11]

In this land of gold, merchants, and mystery, all odds are made even, all sea sorrow finally dissolved in joy and love. This play, like *The Taming of the Shrew,* ends with a feast. (pp. 118-20)

> G. Wilson Knight, "The Romantic Comedies," in *his* The Shakespearian Tempest, *Oxford University Press, London, 1932, pp. 75-168.*

G. R. ELLIOTT   (essay date 1939)

[*Elliott's essay is considered one of the most important twentieth-century interpretations of* The Comedy of Errors. *Like the nineteenth-century critic Hermann Ulrici (1839), Elliott examines Shakespeare's philosophical concerns in* Comedy, *particularly the problem of personal identity central to the play. Elliott also claims that the highly developed structure of the play serves to mix the "fun" and the "horror" which arise from the loss of identity. This essay has been quite influential, and some of its ideas are developed in the essays by Harold Brooks (1961), Gwyn Williams (1964), and Richard Henze (1971).*]

The "The" in the title of [*The Comedy of Errors*] may be taken in a generic sense—that is, as the author's characteristically modest intimation that he has provided merely one more species of a well-recognized genus. "Here," says he, "are the Twins of Plautus again; here is the age-old comedy of resemblances." But time has made the "The" distinctive: here is indeed *the* comedy of errors. It is hard to see how the hoary sport of mistaken identities could be better worked up as the central theme of a drama.

I think the underlying reason for its success is the fact that Shakespeare was thoroughly penetrated by the comic horror, so to call it, implicit in the subject. Real horror attaches to the notion of the *complete* identity of two human beings; as in Poe's ghastly tale of a girl who turned out to be the re-embodiment of the mother who died in giving birth to her; and as in certain ancient legends of various lands, notably China. All normal persons (and especially Shakespeare) set so much store by human individuality that they shrink from the thought of its being submerged. And since the amusing, when intense, is nigh to the serious, there is something shuddery in the close resemblance of persons just when this appears to us intensely entertaining. . . . *The Comedy of Errors* has a note of real weirdness just when its mirth is keenest.

Another and related feature of this play that has also, I think, not been sufficiently appreciated is its structural excellence. Critics have regarded the piece as uninspired because of its comparatively conventional style. But whole form, no less than style, may be the vehicle of inspiration. And the intensity with which Shakespeare gave himself here to the limited but uncanny fun of twinship impelled him to weave his strands into a very close and telling pattern; which, moreover, is often subserved, as I shall point out in a striking instance below, by the very conventionality of the style. I think that in sheer composition this drama surpasses most of his early works and some of his mature ones. It testifies that this poet, who was later to achieve

the most expressive of styles, set his heart at the outset upon achieving wholeness of form. How much he was *directly* influenced in this matter by the Latin classics (not to speak of the Greek) cannot be known and is not very important. His friend to be, Ben Jonson, who was notoriously more intimate with those classics than he, was capable in maturity of producing such a work as *Bartholomew Fair,* rich in humour and humanity but hopelessly flimsy in architecture; no doubt it made Plautus turn in his grave. Compared with it *The Comedy of Errors,* by a young and "non-classical" writer, is a beautifully carved gem. (pp. 95-6)

[It] is clear that the budding dramatist, more or less influenced by the ancient classical sense of form, was reacting from the slipshod construction of contemporary romantic comedy. And indeed if he had not early been sharply critical of that mode at its lowest—that "most lamentable comedy," in Quince's phrase—he could not have learned how to carry it to its height, as in *Twelfth Night* and *As You Like It.* In this later period he vented through the mouth of Polonius a feeling which must have been at work in him all along, a kindly but critical sense of the amazing variety and confusion of forms in contemporary drama. He desired for his own work the variety without the confusion. From the first he aimed at the sort of drama so tellingly described by Hamlet soon after Polonius's outburst: "an excellent play, well digested in the scenes, set down with as much modesty as cunning." Accordingly in his first play (as I take the one under discussion to be) he preferred the "scene individable," the unity of place, to the "poem unlimited"; he followed the "law of writ" rather than "the liberty."

> Why, headstrong liberty is lashed with woe.
> There's nothing situate under heaven's eye
> But hath his bound, in earth, in sea, in sky. . . .
>
> [II. i. 15-17]

This thought, uttered by the gentle Luciana, is reiterated in Shakespeare's subsequent works. Of course it expresses the ancient doctrine of temperance which the writers of the Renaissance so much admired—often only verbally, but deeply at their best. . . . Often enough [Shakespeare's] work is poorly tempered, ill shaped. But one sees him continually striving for excellence of form even more than for variety of form. Thus it was natural for him in his earliest comedy to have recourse to the aid of unity of time and place.

Obviously he was free from the pedantic notion that this device is an essential principle of drama. But he saw that the outward sort of unity, observed strictly or approximately, could be an aid to inward form. And he saw that a strict observance of it was demanded by the material and mood of *The Comedy of Errors.* . . . No doubt a skipping series of scenes displaying . . . adventures on the stage would have pleased the average audience of the time. But that display would not have fitted the whole emotional pattern at which the author, consciously or not, was aiming and which may be described as follows. An initial mood of swift and strange, almost weird, romance is saturated, as the play proceeds, with fun that is swift, strange, weird. Thus the romance and the fun are congruent. And they are humanized by pathos at the first and last, and, in the central phase of the action, by touches of high comedy (comedy of character) involving pathos.

Such is the ideal mood-and-mode, so to speak, of this drama. It was fulfilled to a remarkable extent by the dramatist but, of course, not perfectly. The opening scene is too heavy—especially when its long speeches are not rendered by the actors "trippingly on the tongue." Aegeon's sorrowfulness is immense. The dramatist hints, unconvincingly, that it is not merely the fruit of circumstance: it is constitutional. The old man tells us that he "would gladly have embraced" death . . . on a certain occasion when he was still young, rich, and blessed with a happy household! We don't see why; but we see that this stroke is intended to intensify his air of sadness. . . . On the whole, his story takes hold of us. His emotion helps to float the strange episode of the mast that served as a "helpful ship" . . . to save the lives of six, and then to divide them nicely into the two triads required by the plot. But the author fails to bring out unmistakably the sole aspect of the tale that could render it fully plausible, namely its weirdness or uncanniness. Certainly this note is present, but not explicitly enough. In other words, the opening scene, from the standpoint of the play's whole mood, is not well tempered. Relatively too much stress is placed on the pathos of the romance, and too little on its weirdness. This error is not made in the final scene of the play. There the pathetic joy of the recognition and reunion of the members of Aegeon's household is skilfully intermixed with the characteristic comedy of this drama. But though the last scene of a play is important, the first scene is more so. And it is clear that in the present instance, as not in any later comedy, Shakespeare yielded to the temptation of capturing his audience at the outset by means of a heavy dose of heart-appeal.

The second scene, however, is finely turned: it provides exactly the right transition from the initial scene to the main body of the piece. The old despairing Aegeon is immediately succeeded by a young man who demeans himself very gravely. We are artfully informed at once that he too hails from Syracuse. . . . The fine point, however, is that his very air is felt to be *fathered* by Aegeon's, though quite different. The old man's voluble gloom gives place to the son's sober sadness. And this "humour" (mood) is susceptible of lightening. Antipholus, smiling slightly (not laughing, I think), at his Dromio's joke, remarks that the latter is

> A trusty villain, sir, that very oft,
> When I am dull with care and melancholy,
> Lightens my humour with his merry jests.
> [I. ii. 19-21]

Thus the mood of the play is modulated in the direction of mirth; and the way is actively opened by Antipholus's determination to relieve his lonely sorrow by wandering up and down in this foreign city, viewing its sights. Note the comic irony of his "I will go lose myself" [I. ii. 30], [repeated] just as Dromio of Ephesus enters to take him for his brother. Superb is the sudden but carefully prepared plunge, here, into the comedy of errors. The fact that Antipholus is "not in a sportive mood" is, of course, the soul of the sport. . . . The closing speech of the scene and act is notable. Antipholus soliloquizes:

> Upon my life, by some device or other
> The villain is o'er-raught of all my money.
> They say this town is full of cozenage;
> As, nimble jugglers that deceive the eye,
> Dark-working sorcerers that change the mind,
> Soul-killing witches that deform the body,
> Disguised cheaters, prating mountebanks,
> And many such-like liberties of sin.
> [I. ii. 95-102]

This sounds the note of weirdness; which, however, is not fully brought out till the close of the second act.

Meanwhile (II. i) high comedy, centred in Adriana, comes upon the scene. From now on, it gleams through the pattern of the play like a thin gold thread, appearing and disappearing. It is closely intertwined with the dominant comedy of action. . . . Her sister Luciana's rebuke of her—"Fie, how impatience loureth in your face!"—is histrionically revealing; such was the look that Shakespeare intended the boy-actor who "created" this part to employ continually. That look goes along with conduct, potentially at least, violent. And certainly the heroine of this drama has her full share in its mad doings. Yet louring impatience is merely on the surface of her; deep beneath is a devoted, yearning love for her husband. And the conflict of those two emotions in her is high-comic.

There is pathos, too, in her case, but the dramatist carefully subordinates it. . . . She is far from being a "wretched soul bruised with adversity." Her only real woe, here, is that her husband is very late for dinner. To be sure, she hints that he may be with another woman. . . . But this suspicion, entirely unfounded so far as the audience knows, is very faint and transient. All the more comical, therefore, is her great blaze of jealousy . . . when the strange demeanour of Antipholus of Syracuse, mistaken for her husband, has been reported to her. At this juncture the device of mistaken identity is superbly used for comedy of character. Antipholus of Syracuse, unlike his jaunty brother, is gravely moral. When finally he enters Adriana's presence and she regards him as Antipholus of Ephesus, he is exactly the man to "look strange and frown" [II. ii. 110]. No wonder his bearing turns Adriana's suspicion into a settled conviction. But now comes the finest stroke of all. Confronted with real trouble, with a real evil, as she believes, in her husband's life, her better nature comes to the fore. She drops her initial notion . . . that her own way of life should, by rights, be as free as her husband's. She maintains indeed that there should be (in modern parlance) a single standard for both sexes but she urges passionately that it should be pure and high. . . . Here the pathos, by itself, would be too keen for comedy. But it is checked for us, even as Adriana speaks, by the amazed looks of her two Syracusan listeners, wondering what it is all about; and it is submerged by the mirth, madder than ever, that ensues; to which I shall return presently.

In the next scene (III, i) the audience is kept outdoors with Antipholus of Ephesus to watch his obtrusive cheeriness give place to rage, which in turn yields to merry vengefulness; while his double dines with his wife inside. Thus the love and pathos of Adriana are literally kept *within door* at the crucial stage of the plot. Instead we are allowed to witness (III, ii) the slighter episode, couched in conventional rhymed verse, of the Syracusan Antipholus' love for Luciana. And just when that highly moral man has attempted to seize the hand of the gentle girl who believes him to be her sister's husband, Dromio of Syracuse dashes in, escaping the embraces of the spherical Nell. . . . This sudden explosion of fun from below stairs is a superb burlesque of the goings-on of the principal personages. Nell's mistaking the foreign Dromio for his brother at the end of the third act is the sequel of her mistress Adriana's similar error at the end of the second act. But the parallelism is not forced and obvious, as it so often is in Shakespeare's early work. The two episodes are at once vitally related and vitally different: they are at opposite poles in method and tone. Hence they beautifully complement each other.

More significantly, in each case the hyperbolical tone rises to eeriness. In the close of Act II, Dromio of Syracuse, dazed by the staid Luciana's seconding of her tense sister in taking him and his master for two other persons, cries out [II. ii. 188-92]:

> Oh for my beads! I cross me for a sinner.
> This is the fairy land; oh, spite of spites,
> We talk with goblins, owls, and elvish sprites!
> If we obey them not, this will ensue,
> They'll suck our breath or pinch us black and blue.

He and his Antipholus are overcome by a dreamlike sense of transformation, romantic in the master, grotesque ("'Tis so, I am an ass" . . .) in the man. This "complex" occurs again in the finale of Act III, but with overwhelming emphasis on the weird grotesquerie of the situation. Here the mounting hyperbole of Dromio's account of Nell renders dramatically plausible even the premiss that both he and his twin had a similar mark on the shoulder, a mole in the neck, and a great wart on the left arm! . . . Significantly Shakespeare refrains from bringing Nell onto the stage in person. The temptation to do so must have been great; the scene would have rejoiced the hearts of ninety per cent of his audience. But he sacrificed the physical fun of that scene to what we may call the metaphysical fun of Dromio's inspired narrative, culminating in his bizarre picture of the globular wench as a witch. Moreover, Nell's absence from the scene enables the audience to concentrate upon the all-important effect that the tale has on Dromio's master. (pp. 96-102)

Dromio's story of Nell is the last straw for Antipholus. The fun of the thing impresses this earnest gentleman far less than its weirdness. If the wench who claims his man for her betrothed is a sorceress, all the more so is "She that doth call me husband"; and he abhors Adriana "for a wife" as utterly as Dromio does Nell, though on higher grounds. These comparisons between his own and Dromio's case are not stated explicitly; Shakespeare's art is here too fine for that; but they are clearly implied in his speech. And the climactic implication is that even the sensible and normal Luciana is infected by the prevalent atmosphere of sorcery in which she lives. She,

> Possessed with such a sovereign gentle grace,
> Of such *enchanting* presence and discourse,
> Hath almost made me traitor to myself. . . .
> 　　　　　　　　　　　　　　[III. ii. 160-62]

The last line recalls the comic irony of his desire to lose himself, at the first, in this strange city. . . . And the word that I have italicized in the second line is deliciously ambiguous. By way of developing the equivoque we may say that the *bewitching* Luciana, as Antipholus now sees the matter in retrospect, put him almost *beside himself*. The more he made love to her, the more she insisted he was not himself; he was another man, well known to her, her brother-in-law unfortunately, making immoral advances to her. And he, so the implication runs, had been almost ready to lose his own identity if only thus he could win her interest. (p. 103)

He must speedily get away from this city, which he had felt at the first to be "full of cozenage" when it seemed that some "cheater" had made away with "all my money" [I. ii. 97ff]. But now an event of exactly opposite nature occurs as he is hastily moving off. A cheerful and trustful citizen enters, hands him a fine gold chain, refuses present payment, and terms him, what he least is, "a merry man, sir." It takes a good actor to represent Antipholus's state of mind in this masterly finale of the third act. He is so stunned that at first he can only ask weakly, "What is your will that I shall do with this?" In the upshot, despite his scrupulous nature, he retains the chain.

Why? Because one feature of this illusive city is, apparently, the giving of "such golden gifts" to strangers in the streets. Because, in short, Antipholus's mood, together with the mood of the play, has now become thoroughly fey. (pp. 103-04)

In Act IV the arrest of Antipholus of Ephesus, prominent and wealthy citizen, for the supposed theft of the gold chain brings this personage fully into the atmosphere of enchantment. Hitherto he had moved only in the outskirts of it; his healthy gaiety kept him aloof. . . . Soon he is wearing "pale and deadly looks" [IV. iv. 61], or at least something approximating thereto sufficiently for Pinch and others to imagine him insane. A similar look, we may assume, is on the face of Antipholus of Syracuse when he comes on at the close of this act with drawn sword, resolved finally to escape those whom he calls "these witches." Thus the two male principals co-operate, now, to intensify the note of bewitchment.

This note might easily have been overdone by Shakespeare. Of course he offsets the serious desperation of the two masters by the humorous desperation of the two servants, especially Dromio of Syracuse with his persistent nightmare of Nell. . . . A further offset to the two Antipholuses is needed, however, and it is provided by Pinch, the conjuring schoolmaster of "saffron face." . . . Later his complete appearance is given retrospectively by Antipholus of Ephesus [V. i. 238-42]:

> 　　a hungry lean-faced villain,
> A mere anatomy, a mountebank,
> A threadbare juggler, and a fortune-teller,
> A needy, hollow-eyed, sharp-looking wretch,
> A living dead man. . . .

In passing, notice that these words echo the tone-setting speech of Antipholus of Syracuse, at the end of the first act, upon jugglers, sorcerers, and so forth. Pinch is a tonal masterpiece. His pedantic gravity parodies and relieves the increasing angry seriousness of the two Antipholuses. But, above all, he bodies forth concretely the play's spirit of weird fun.

Adriana, again, contributes to that mood. Convinced that her husband has tried to make love to her sister, she vents her rage in a monstrous picturization of him [IV. ii. 19-22]:

> He is deformed, crooked, old and sere,
> Ill-faced, worse bodied, shapeless everywhere;
> Vicious, ungentle, foolish, blunt, unkind,
> Stigmatical in making, worse in mind.

Her wrathful, hyperbolic fancy is a better conjurer than Pinch. But the pathos and high comedy of her, though kept subordinate, come out in frequent touches. She closes the present episode with this simple cry: "My heart prays for him, though my tongue do curse." (The subjunctive "do" is nicely suggestive.) Thus we are prepared for the effective dialogue of Adriana and the Abbess early in the last act. Religiously beguiled by the older woman into confessing her fault, Adriana hugely exaggerates her scoldings of her husband . . . and is rebuked by the Abbess, with proportional severity, as the sole cause of his supposed madness. She makes no reply. . . . Her difficult silence is Adriana's self-imposed penance. Recalling her earlier line, quoted above, we may say that her heart is now praying so entirely for her husband that her tongue, so far from cursing, has no word even of proper self-defence.

That serious touch, together with the ensuing speech of the Second Merchant concerning "the melancholy vale" [V. i. 120], leads up to the re-entrance of the hapless and gloomy Aegeon. But, as remarked earlier, his pathos is not allowed anything like free rein here. He stands in the background during the long climax of the story of Antipholus of Ephesus. . . . Upon the close of this episode Aegeon is allowed the centre of the stage for fifty lines. The pathos of his appeal to him whom he takes to be "my only son" is very moving, but, of course, it is checked by his mistaking Antipholus of Ephesus for him of Syracuse. Thus Aegeon is drawn into the atmosphere of illusion; so is even the stiff-backed Duke a little later. . . . The tearful joys of the reunion of the old man's family are finely interwoven with enchanting mistakes . . . , and parodied at the close by the conference of the two Dromios. When Dromio of Syracuse declares to his new-found brother (italics mine),

> There is a fat *friend* at your master's house
> That kitchened me for you today at dinner:
> She now shall be my *sister, not* my wife . . .
> [V. i. 415-17]

the speaker's sense of relief is as vast as the girth of Nell. This speech brings us back towards everyday reality. Yet it reminds us, surely, of this Dromio's dread of Nell as a "diviner" and a "witch" [III. ii. 139ff]. Thus at the close there is a faint, last flicker of the ray of weird light, romantic and comic, that plays upon *The* Comedy of Errors. (pp. 104-06)

> G. R. Elliott, "Weirdness in 'The Comedy of Errors'," in University of Toronto Quarterly, Vol. IX, No. 1, October, 1939, pp. 95-106.

Act IV. Scene iv. Dromio of Ephesus, Antipholus of Ephesus, Adriana, Luciana, Pinch, Courtezan. By Francis Hayman (1744). From the Art Collection of the Folger Shakespeare Library.

MARK VAN DOREN   (essay date 1939)

[*Van Doren regards* The Comedy of Errors *as a simple farce and a work inferior to Shakespeare's later comedies. Interestingly, Van Doren sees the created world of the play as "matter-of-fact," whereas other critics, notably G. R. Elliot (1939), stress the play's "weirdness" and supernatural qualities.*]

"The Comedy of Errors" is not Shakespeare's only unfeeling farce. He wrote two others in "The Taming of the Shrew" and "The Merry Wives of Windsor," and a third if "Titus Andronicus" is one. In comedy, says Dr. Johnson, "he seems to repose, or to luxuriate, as in a mode of thinking congenial to his nature." If that is true, it is nevertheless not true of Shakespeare's comedies of situation: plays in which, obedient to the law governing such matters, he confines his interest, or almost confines it, to physical predicament—to things that happen to certain persons not because of who they are but because of what they are. In "The Comedy of Errors" they are not men but twins. The two Antipholuses and the two Dromios exist for no other purpose than to be mutually mistaken. They may groan and seem to go mad in their perplexity, but we only laugh the louder; for it is the figure that gestures, not the man, and our expectation indeed is that the playwright will strain his ingenuity still further in the invention of new tortures, provided new ones are possible. When no others are possible, or when the two hours are up, peace may be restored and the characters may cease to exercise that genius for misunderstanding the obvious which has distinguished them to date. If Shakespeare's spirit reposed in comedy it was not in this kind of comedy. He could write it very well and be hugely funny; but the heart of his interest was elsewhere, and the poet had abdicated.

The poet in "The Comedy of Errors" puffs with unnatural effort, as when for instance he asks us to believe that Aegeon said:

> Though now this grained face of mine be hid
> In sap-consuming winter's drizzled snow,
> And all the conduits of my blood froze up,
> Yet hath my night of life some memory,
> My wasting lamps some fading glimmer left. . . .
> [V. i. 312-16]

His rhymes, surviving from an old convention in comedy, rattle like bleached bones. . . . Even wit is unnecessary in a play which counts on beatings and beratings to amuse us, and indeed counts rightly. The mental fooling between Antipholus of Syracuse and his Dromio at the beginning of II, ii, is among the dullest things of its kind in Shakespeare. But it does not matter, for to Plautus's idea of twin masters Shakespeare has added the idea of twin servants, and there are riches in the fourfold result which he can mine by manipulation alone. Dromio of Syracuse, to be sure, makes excellent verbal use of his fat kitchen wench. . . . Yet there is no more need for such eloquence than there is for characters possessing qualities in excess of those required by the situation, or for verisimilitude in the plotted action. "What I should think of this, I cannot tell," says Antipholus of Syracuse [III. ii. 179]. What he should think of course is that his twin brother has turned up. He does not so think for the simple reason that he is in a conspiracy with Shakespeare to regale us with the spectacle of his talent for confusion.

The minds of these marionettes run regularly on the supernatural, on magic and witchcraft; but with the difference from "Henry VI" that there is no suggestion of vast state intrigues, and with the still more interesting difference from "A Midsummer Night's Dream" and "Othello" that no special atmosphere is created, whether charming or terrible. "This is the fairy land," whines Dromio of Syracuse [II. ii. 189]; "We talk with goblins, owls, and sprites." Dromio is consciously exaggerating; his world, like the world of the play, remains matter-of-fact, however frequent the angry references to jugglers, sorcerers, witches, cheaters, mountebanks, mermaids, wizards, conjurers, and the several fiends of folklore with their drugs and syrups, their nail-parings and pinpoint drops of blood. Cheaters is the word—pretenders to supernatural power, citizens in side streets who prey on the gullible. The play itself is never tinctured; farce must keep its head. (pp. 45-6)

Nor is the business of the shipwreck which has separated Aegeon from one of his sons more than a hint of the shipwrecks which in the last plays will be so beautiful and awful, and so important somehow to the life of Shakespeare's imagination. This catastrophe occurs only as a device to get twins separated, and to start the machinery of farce revolving. Yet it occurs. And Aegeon for all his bad poetry wrings a few drops of pathos from it. So Adriana for one moment, if only for one moment, outgrows her shrewish mold:

> Ah, but I think him better than I say. . . .
> Far from her nest the lapwing cries away.
> My heart prays for him, though my tongue do curse.
>   [IV. ii. 25-8]

There is a touch in her here of Beatrice, as well as of Shakespeare's silent heroines. And the lyric voice of her sister Luciana has perhaps no place at all in Ephesus, city of slapstick. Such elements, few and feeble though they are, point ahead to the time when Shakespeare will have found the kind of comedy in which his nature can repose, and to the year when he will have another try at twins but will make one of them a girl and give her the name Viola. (pp. 46-7)

> *Mark Van Doren, "'The Comedy of Errors'," in his*
> Shakespeare, *Henry Holt and Company, 1939, pp.*
> *44-7.*

HARDIN CRAIG   (essay date 1948)

[*Craig's* The Enchanted Glass, *which describes the intellectual background of the Elizabethan age, was an important contribution to the historical school of criticism, whose exponents attempted to analyze Shakespeare's works in the context of their age and audience. Craig also published two editions of Shakespeare and a volume of criticism,* An Interpretation of Shakespeare. *In the following essay, taken from the latter work, Craig points out significant differences between the characters of the two Antipholi, and, contrary to such critics as Samuel Taylor Coleridge (1808-18), Algernon Charles Swinburne (1880), Edward Dowden (1903), and H. B. Charlton (1930), defines the play as a comedy rather than a farce.*]

[*The Comedy of Errors*] is the most artificial of the comedies, as indicated by an abundance of doggerel verse, speeches balanced between speakers, characters set off formally against each other, alternate rhymes, puns and quibbles. It seems also to be a play designed, like *The Taming of the Shrew*, for the public stage. It lacks those typically Renaissance social features which appear in *Love's Labour's Lost* and *The Two Gentlemen of Verona*. For Shakespeare it must have functioned as an exercise in plot management. Not only does Shakespeare catch the resilient efficiency of Plautus, but he betters Plautus. The borrowing of a scene from the *Amphitruo*, the locking of An-

tipholus of Ephesus out of his own house, caused Shakespeare to make a most interesting change in comic method. Plautus in his realistic world begins with truth and then involves his characters in error; Shakespeare in the mad world of Ephesus begins his episodes with error and enlightens them with flashes of truth. In another respect, which is possibly an expression of Shakespeare's own nature, *The Comedy of Errors* is most significant in what it reveals about Shakespearean comedy. Shakespeare never writes comedy of the cool, objective kind that appears in Plautus, Ben Jonson, and Molière. Shakespeare loved to play with edged tools. Somebody's life or somebody's happiness is at stake even in his comedies. After the introduction of the good Aegeon, with his moving appeal to the duke to spare his life, we never get him out of our minds. In the midst of confusion worse confounded we continue to hope that he will be saved. Shakespeare is, moreover, unwilling for Adriana to remain a shrew, but characteristically provides for her reformation; nor is he willing for Antipholus of Syracuse to remain an eligible bachelor, but provides him with a Luciana. Such things as these indicate the popular intention of *The Comedy of Errors*.

Menaechmi is pure comedy, witty and clear, much simpler than *The Comedy of Errors*, of which it is the original form. There seem to have been many Greek and Latin comedies which depicted the confusion arising from identical twins, and in modern times such comedies are known as comedies of error. (pp. 20-1)

The genius of Plautus manifests itself splendidly in the fifth act [of *Menaechmi*], which is masterly. It contains a long and extremely amusing scene between Menaechmus the Traveler and his brother's wife, Mulier, which is heightened by an interview with Senex, her father, and further heightened by a side-splitting examination of the angry Citizen by Medicus in order to determine his sanity. It is much better than the encounter with Dr. Pinch (in *The Comedy of Errors*), for Shakespeare's play misses the humor of the situation. It is the Traveler who in Plautus was suspected of insanity, who actually counterfeited insanity, and it is the Citizen who undergoes the examination. Finally, Messenio is clever enough to see that he and his master, without knowing it, have actually found the twin brother of whom they had been in search, and he brings about a recognition. In cool cynicism Plautus has Menaechmus the Citizen, in order to accompany his brother to Syracuse, offer for sale his whole property, including Mulier, if any buyer appears—*si quis emptor venerit*.

When *Menaechmi* comes to us in Shakespearean form, it has been greatly amplified, first of all by such romantic additions as the story of Aegeon and Aemilia, which is but a variation of the theme of *Apollonius of Tyre*, later used in *Pericles;* secondly, by the adjustment which permits a love affair between Antipholus of Syracuse and Luciana, sister-in-law to Antipholus of Ephesus. There are also many minor ways in which human sentiment is added to the cool tale that Plautus tells.

In *The Comedy of Errors* Shakespeare shows already in operation his ability to discriminate among characters of all ranks, an ability which one would think of as fundamentally dramatic. This play discriminates lightly but surely between the identical brethren, masters, and slaves. A lesser genius might have contented himself with carrying external into internal likeness. The Antipholi are not alike in their characters and dispositions in spite of certain Plautine qualities which are carried over in both. Antipholus of Ephesus is a self-willed, rather dissolute man, not, however, to a point where his standing as a citizen of Ephesus is imperiled. His commercial credit is good, and he has been a valiant soldier in the service of the Duke. Plautus frankly depicts him as a lewd and dishonest man. The character in Shakespeare is far better than its prototype, but none the less has the markings of that prototype. Antipholus of Ephesus is in general a lively character. Plautus's discrimination between the masters is much less emphatic than that of Shakespeare. Menaechmus the Traveler, in Plautus, is quite as Greek as is his brother. He craftily accepts the cloak and the chain purloined by his brother, just, to be sure, as Antipholus of Syracuse accepts the chain; but the chain in Shakespeare is not stolen goods. Antipholus of Syracuse offers to pay the goldsmith for it, and later makes no attempt to conceal the facts. . . . Nowhere [in Plautus] is there any motive but simple selfishness, and both the Menaechmi are ordinary, rather shifty Greeks of the merchant class. Although Menaechmus the Traveler has journeyed widely he shows few marks of the man of the world except self-confidence and a disposition to take advantage. It is not so with Antipholus of Syracuse, who is an experienced traveler, curious about foreign lands, properly wary of the ways of strange peoples, a well-disposed man, capable of true love and honest sentiment.

It was a clever device on the part of the remaker of the plot to lay the scene in the famous city of witchcraft, Ephesus. The ancient city was noted for pagan worship, and St. Paul, who was aware of the reputation of the city, addressed to the Christians there perhaps the most magnificent of his epistles. The citizens of Ephesus seem to have utilized for profit their reputation for sorcery, and ancient Ephesus had a bad name. Antipholus of Syracuse knew well where he had landed, recognized his danger, and sought to escape. Just as Antipholus of Ephesus grows more and more indignant, so does his brother grow more and more frightened and bewildered. All in all, both characters have undergone in Shakespeare's hands changes in natural and appropriate ways.

The Dromios, possibly Shakespeare's own creations, have at least some marks of difference. Of course there is nothing important to be discovered in such light, clownish, and improbable characters; and yet the more staid and responsible traveler is given the more jocular and impudent Dromio, a sort of all-licensed fool, who apparently is flogged and expects to be flogged rather frequently. The more lively of the masters is given a rather more serious, protesting, bewildered slave.

Again, it is easy to say that Adriana is a shrew, one of the two types of women in earlier Elizabethan comedy, and that Luciana exemplifies the other type, the mild, ingenuous, sweet-tempered young woman who has no individuality. But these judgments are only relatively true. Adriana has some of the qualities of the wronged and neglected wife, as indeed had Mulier in the Plautine original, but Adriana's claims are recognized and respected; she is allowed to reform her conduct. Adriana is not unreasonable and has some individuality. Luciana is a responsible young woman and has more sense than does Bianca in *The Taming of the Shrew*. She deserves the good husband she gets in Antipholus of Syracuse. One might go so far as to say that *The Comedy of Errors* is a comedy rather than a farce, although it is usually played as a farce and although Coleridge in a famous passage describes it as a typical farce [see excerpt above]. (pp. 22-4)

It is not, however, in romantic materials only that the plot of *Menaechmi* has been expanded. There has also been added an increment in kind from another play by Plautus, *Amphitruo*.

In point of fact that comedy is a much bolder, more satirical, and more scandalous play than is *Menaechmi*. . . . One cannot see, however, that *The Comedy of Errors* was affected in any way by the tone of *Amphitruo* except perhaps in the vulgar description which Dromio of Syracuse gives his master of Nell (or Luce) in the second scene of the third act. (p. 25)

The Comedy of Errors is extremely deft in its handling. In spite of its many interests it is clear and easy to follow just as drama, without the aid of long explanatory speeches such as Plautus usually employs in order to make his action clear. (p. 26)

All the way through the play the characters react in perfect sincerity and with automatic faithfulness, which, it will be seen, is a necessary feature of a comedy of errors. The play is like Lucian or Swift in its adherence to a point of view. The characters speak and act what they believe to be truth while the audience, knowing the secret, chuckles in superiority. The recognition itself is held off until the latest possible time, an almost improbable time, since for either twin to see his fellow would have brought the comedy down like a house of cards. In dramatic manipulation *The Comedy of Errors* is not superior to *Menaechmi*, but it is far richer and of far greater general significance. It is worth pointing these things out because they show so well the difference between Elizabethan comedy and classical comedy. (pp. 28-9)

Hardin Craig, "The Beginnings," in his An Interpretation of Shakespeare, *The Citadel Press, 1948, pp. 19-46.*

NORTHROP FRYE (essay date 1949)

[*One of the most widely acclaimed critics of the recent past, Frye is best known for the theory and practice of "myth criticism" as elaborated especially in his* Anatomy of Criticism. *Although the following essay contains scant commentary on* The Comedy of Errors *itself, it is important in that it places the play in the history and theory of comedy as Frye interprets it. Alexander Leggatt (1974) argues against Frye's view of the "new social order" arising at the end of* The Comedy of Errors. *The essay was first published in* English Institute Essays *in 1949.*]

The Greeks produced two kinds of comedy, Old Comedy, represented by the eleven extant plays of Aristophanes, and New Comedy, of which the best known exponent is Menander. About two dozen New Comedies survive in the work of Plautus and Terence. . . . [Today] when we speak of comedy, we normally think of something that derives from the Menandrine tradition.

New Comedy unfolds from what may be described as a comic Oedipus situation. Its main theme is the successful effort of a young man to outwit an opponent and possess the girl of his choice. The opponent is usually the father (*senex*), and the psychological descent of the heroine from the mother is also sometimes hinted at. The father frequently wants the same girl, and is cheated out of her by the son, the mother thus becoming the son's ally. The girl is usually a slave or courtesan, and the plot turns on a *cognitio* or discovery of birth which makes her marriageable. . . . In Congreve's *Love for Love,* to take a modern instance well within the Menandrine tradition, there are two Oedipus themes in counterpoint: the hero cheats his father out of the heroine, and his best friend violates the wife of an impotent old man who is the heroine's guardian. Whether this analysis is sound or not, New Comedy is certainly concerned with the maneuvering of a young man toward a young woman, and marriage is the tonic chord on which it ends. The normal comic resolution is the surrender of the *senex* to the hero, never the reverse. Shakespeare tried to reverse the pattern in *All's Well That Ends Well,* where the king of France forces Bertram to marry Helena, and the critics have not yet stopped making faces over it.

New Comedy has the blessing of Aristotle, who greatly preferred it to its predecessor, and it exhibits the general pattern of Aristotelian causation. It has a material cause in the young man's sexual desire, and a formal cause in the social order represented by the *senex,* with which the hero comes to terms when he gratifies his desire. It has an efficient cause in the character who brings about the final situation. In classical times this character is a tricky slave; Renaissance dramatists often use some adaptation of the medieval ''vice''; modern writers generally like to pretend that nature or at least the natural course of events, is the efficient cause. The final cause is the audience, which is expected by its applause to take part in the comic resolution. All this takes place on a single order of existence. The action of New Comedy tends to become probable rather than fantastic, and it moves toward realism and away from myth and romance. The one romantic (originally mythical) feature in it, the fact that the hero or heroine turns out to be freeborn or someone's heir, is precisely the feature that trained New Comedy audiences tire of most quickly.

The conventions of New Comedy are the conventions of Jonson and Molière, and a fortiori of the English Restoration and the French rococo. When Ibsen started giving ironic twists to the same formulas, his startled hearers took them for portents of a social revolution. (pp. 79-80)

In all good New Comedy there is a social as well as an individual theme which must be sought in the general atmosphere of reconciliation that makes the final marriage possible. As the hero gets closer to the heroine and opposition is overcome, all the right-thinking people come over to his side. Thus a new social unit is formed on the stage, and the moment that this social unit crystallizes is the moment of the comic resolution. In the last scene, when the dramatist usually tries to get all his characters on the stage at once, the audience witnesses the birth of a renewed sense of social integration. . . .

This new social integration may be called, first, a kind of moral norm and, second, the pattern of a free society. We can see this more clearly if we look at the sort of characters who impede the progress of the comedy toward the hero's victory. These are always people who are in some kind of mental bondage, who are helplessly driven by ruling passions, neurotic compulsions, social rituals, and selfishness. . . . What we call the moral norm is, then, not morality but deliverance from moral bondage. Comedy is designed not to condemn evil, but to ridicule a lack of self-knowledge. It finds the virtues of Malvolio and Angelo as comic as the vices of Shylock.

The essential comic resolution, therefore, is an individual release which is also a social reconciliation. The normal individual is freed from the bonds of a humorous society, and a normal society is freed from the bonds imposed on it by humorous individuals. The Oedipus pattern we noted in New Comedy belongs to the individual side of this, and the sense of the ridiculousness of the humor to the social side. (p. 81)

The freer the society, the greater the variety of individuals it can tolerate, and the natural tendency of comedy is to include as many as possible in its final festival. The motto of comedy is Terence's ''Nothing human is alien to me.'' This may be one reason for the traditional comic importance of the parasite, who has no business to be at the festival but is nevertheless there. The spirit of reconciliation which pervades the comedies of Shakespeare is not to be ascribed to a personal attitude of his own, about which we know nothing whatever, but to his impersonal concentration on the laws of comic form.

Hence the moral quality of the society presented is not the point of the comic resolution. . . .

Aristophanes is the most personal of writers: his opinions on every subject are written all over his plays, and we have no doubt of his moral attitude. We know that he wanted peace with Sparta and that he hated Cleon, and when his comedy depicts the attaining of peace and the defeat of Cleon we know that he approved and wanted his audience to approve. But in *Ecclesiazusae* a band of women in disguise railroad a communistic scheme through the Assembly, which is a horrid parody of Plato's *Republic,* and proceed to inaugurate Plato's sexual communism with some astonishing improvements. Presumably Aristophanes did not applaud this, yet the comedy follows the same pattern and the same resolution. (p. 82)

Comedy, then, may show virtue her own feature and scorn her own image—for Hamlet's famous definition of drama was originally a definition of comedy. It may emphasize the birth of an ideal society as you like it, or the tawdriness of the sham society which is the way of the world. There is an important parallel here with tragedy. Tragedy, we are told, is expected to raise but not ultimately to accept the emotions of pity and terror. These I take to be the sense of moral good and evil, respectively, which we attach to the tragic hero. He may be as good as Caesar, and so appeal to our pity, or as bad as Macbeth, and so appeal to terror, but the particular thing called tragedy that happens to him does not depend on his moral status. The tragic catharsis passes beyond moral judgment, and while it is quite possible to construct a moral tragedy, what tragedy gains in morality it loses in cathartic power. The same is true of the comic catharsis, which raises sympathy and ridicule on a moral basis, but passes beyond both.

Many things are involved in the tragic catharsis, but one of them is a mental or imaginative form of the sacrificial ritual out of which tragedy arose. This is the ritual of the struggle, death, and rebirth of a God-Man, which is linked to the yearly triumph of spring over winter. The tragic hero is not really killed, and the audience no longer eats his body and drinks his blood, but the corresponding thing in art still takes place. The audience enters into communion with the body of the hero, becoming thereby a single body itself. Comedy grows out of the same ritual, for in the ritual the tragic story has a comic sequel. Divine men do not die: they die and rise again. The ritual pattern behind the catharsis of comedy is the resurrection that follows the death, the epiphany or manifestation of the risen hero. This is clear enough in Aristophanes, where the hero is treated as a risen God-Man, led in triumph with the divine honors of the Olympic victor, rejuvenated, or hailed as a new Zeus. In New Comedy the new human body is, as we have seen, both a hero and a social group. Aristophanes is not only closer to the ritual pattern, but contemporary with Plato; and his comedy, unlike Menander's, is Platonic and dialectic: it seeks not the entelechy of the soul but the Form of the Good, and finds it in the resurrection of the soul from the world of the cave to the sunlight. The audience gains a vision of that resurrection whether the conclusion is joyful or ironic, just as in tragedy it gains a vision of a heroic death whether the hero is morally innocent or guilty.

Two things follow from this: first, that tragedy is really implicit or uncompleted comedy; second, that comedy contains a potential tragedy within itself. With regard to the latter, Aristophanes is full of traces of the original death of the hero which preceded his resurrection in the ritual. Even in New Comedy the dramatist usually tries to bring his action as close to a tragic overthrow of the hero as he can get it, and reverses this movement as suddenly as possible. . . . Thus the resolution of New Comedy seems to be a realistic foreshortening of a death-and-resurrection pattern, in which the struggle and rebirth of a divine hero has shrunk into a marriage, the freeing of a slave, and the triumph of a young man over an older one.

As for the conception of tragedy as implicit comedy, we may notice how often tragedy closes on the major chord of comedy: the Aeschylean trilogy, for instance, proceeds to what is really a comic resolution, and so do many tragedies of Euripides. From the point of view of Christianity, too, tragedy is an episode in that larger scheme of redemption and resurrection to which Dante gave the name of *commedia*. . . . The sense of tragedy as a prelude to comedy is hardly separable from anything explicitly Christian. The serenity of the final double chorus in the St. Matthew Passion would hardly be attainable if composer and audience did not know that there was more to the story. (pp. 82-4)

New Comedy is thus contained, so to speak, within the symbolic structure of Old Comedy, which in its turn is contained within the Christian conception of *commedia*. This sounds like a logically exhaustive classification, but we have still not caught Shakespeare in it.

It is only in Jonson and the Restoration writers that English comedy can be called a form of New Comedy. The earlier tradition established by Peele and developed by Lyly, Greene, and the masque writers, which uses themes from romance and folklore and avoids the comedy of manners, is the one followed by Shakespeare. These themes are largely medieval in origin, and derive, not from the mysteries or the moralities or the interludes, but from a fourth dramatic tradition. This is the drama of folk ritual, of the St. George play and the mummers' play. . . . We may call this the drama of the green world, and its theme is once again the triumph of life over the waste land, the death and revival of the year impersonated by figures still human, and once divine as well.

When Shakespeare began to study Plautus and Terence, his dramatic instinct, stimulated by his predecessors, divined that there was a profounder pattern in the argument of comedy than appears in either of them. At once—for the process is beginning in *The Comedy of Errors*—he started groping toward that profounder pattern, the ritual of death and revival that also underlies Aristophanes, of which an exact equivalent lay ready to hand in the drama of the green world. (pp. 84-5)

Shakespeare's comedy is not Aristotelian and realistic like Menander's, nor Platonic and dialectic like Aristophanes', nor Thomist and sacramental like Dante's, but a fourth kind. It is an Elizabethan kind, and is not confined either to Shakespeare or to the drama. Spenser's epic is a wonderful contrapuntal intermingling of two orders of existence, one the red and white world of English history, the other the green world of the Faerie Queene. The latter is a world of crusading virtues proceeding from the Faerie Queene's court and designed to return to that court when the destiny of the other world is fulfilled. The fact that the Faerie Queene's knights are sent out during the twelve days of the Christmas festival suggests our next point.

Shakespeare too has his green world of comedy and his red and white world of history. The story of the latter is at one point interrupted by an invasion from the comic world, when Falstaff *senex et parasitus* throws his gigantic shadow over Prince Henry, assuming on one occasion the role of his father. Clearly, if the Prince is ever to conquer France he must reassert the moral norm. The moral norm is duly reasserted, but the rejection of Falstaff is not a comic resolution. In comedy the moral norm is not morality but deliverance, and we certainly do not feel delivered from Falstaff as we feel delivered from Shylock with his absurd and vicious bond. (p. 87)

We spend our lives partly in a waking world we call normal and partly in a dream world which we create out of our own desires. Shakespeare endows both worlds with equal imaginative power, brings them opposite one another, and makes each world seem unreal when seen by the light of the other. He uses freely both the heroic triumph of New Comedy and the ritual resurrection of its predecessor, but his distinctive comic resolution is different from either: it is a detachment of the spirit born of this reciprocal reflection of two illusory realities. We need not ask whether this brings us into a higher order of existence or not, for the question of existence is not relevant to poetry.

We have spoken of New Comedy as Aristotelian, Old Comedy as Platonic and Dante's *commedia* as Thomist, but it is difficult to suggest a philosophical spokesman for the form of Shakespeare's comedy. For Shakespeare, the subject matter of poetry is not life, or nature, or reality, or revelation, or anything else that the philosopher builds on, but poetry itself, a verbal universe. That is one reason why he is both the most elusive and the most substantial of poets. (pp. 88-9)

> *Northrop Frye, "The Argument of Comedy," in* Shakespeare: Modern Essays in Criticism, *edited by Leonard F. Dean, Oxford University Press, New York, 1957, pp. 79-89.*

S. C. SEN GUPTA (essay date 1950)

[Sen Gupta, India's leading Shakespearean scholar, discusses H. B. Charlton's commentary concerning Shakespeare's "recoil from romanticism" (see excerpt above, 1931). Sen Gupta also seconds Mark Van Doren's position that the play is weak in characterization, and challenges Hardin Craig's argument that the Antipholi are distinguishable (see excerpts above, 1939 and 1948).]

The Comedy of Errors is looked upon by Sir E. K. Chambers as Shakespeare's earliest comedy [see excerpt above, 1906], but other authorities regard *Love's Labour's Lost* (and possibly *The Two Gentlemen of Verona*) as anterior to it [see excerpt above by H. B. Charlton, 1931]. But this question of the exact place of the play in the Shakespearian canon is bound up with an interesting aspect of its plot and construction. Shakespeare's methods of workmanship are fundamentally different from those of the writers of classical comedies, and yet in this one play he derives his plot from two of Plautus's comedies and accepts not only the substance of the story as told in his originals but also something of the structure and technique. Did he, then, after writing *Love's Labour's Lost* and *The Two Gentlemen of Verona*, temporarily recoil from romanticism, or did he start his dramatic career with unromantic material and then discover that the really original things he could contribute were not the twin Dromios but the pathetic story of Aegeon and the romantic appeal of Luciana's beauty?

The question can never be satisfactorily answered. One thing, however, is definite and clear. *The Comedy of Errors,* although undoubtedly Shakespeare's work, deals with material not congenial to his genius. Shakespeare's greatness consists primarily in fathoming the depths of the human mind and only secondarily in enriching his plot with multiplicity of incidents. In this comedy he deals with a plot which does not allow of effective characterization and in which the main interest must be derived from the peculiarity of the situation. (pp. 104-05)

Shakespeare, accepting Plautus's story, improves upon it but not very much in his own way. Indeed, the addition of the twin Dromios involves so many new complications in the plot that there is but little room for the revelation of character. Professor Charlton argues that there was no room in Elizabethan society for any domestic corresponding to the Roman slave, for which reason it was not possible for Shakespeare to assign to the Dromios the part played by the intriguing servant in Latin comedy. But they are also very imperfect specimens of the Elizabethan clown. They are past masters in the art of punning and in twisting and mistaking the meanings of words, but there their affinity with the genuine Shakespearian clown ends. They have not that peculiar mixture of wisdom, sympathy, tolerance and humour which makes the Shakespearian fool such a remarkable specimen of humanity. . . . No one can know one Dromio from another in the same way in which one can know Launce from Speed in *The Two Gentlemen of Verona,* another early comedy. The twin Dromios are neither Roman slaves nor Elizabethan fools; they are marionettes, mechanically propelled, not living human beings with individual personalities.

The portraiture of the twin Antipholuses is open to the same objection. They are an improvement on the Menaechmus brothers in the sense that they are much more refined gentlemen. The Citizen has a concubine, but he does not steal his wife's mantle in order to enrich his mistress. The traveller-twin in Shakespeare's play is a much finer gentleman than his counterpart in Plautus. He beats his servant and prepares to leave Ephesus with a chain of gold he has not paid for, but he is not a thief like Menaechmus-Sosicles, who casts the festal garland in the wrong direction in order to throw possible pursuers off the scent. . . . On the whole both the brothers are more civilized than their prototypes in Plautus, but Shakespeare does not attempt to bring out their individual peculiarities in such a way as to make it possible for us to distinguish between the one twin and the other. . . . [The] difference is due not to any fundamental distinction in character but to the circumstances in which they are placed. Antipholus of Syracuse is a stranger in Ephesus. As he has no idea of the place or its inhabitants, he is naturally puzzled; he cannot be vindictive against any person, as his brother is, for the simple reason that he does not know anybody in the city. . . . All that can be said is that his situation is more romantic than his brother's. How strange it must be to him to be greeted familiarly in a place he is visiting for the first time!

Shakespeare must have realized that the theme of this play left little scope for the portraiture of character and, by adding the twin Dromios, he made the material more refractory than it was in the original play. The comic interest could be derived mainly from the artificial situations the collocation of the two pairs of twins brings about. . . . Coleridge, who ignores this fundamental defect in the plot, is lured into a hair-splitting discussion about the distinction between the probable and the merely possible [see excerpt above, 1808-18]. This distinction,

as Sir Arthur Quiller-Couch rightly points out [see excerpt above, 1922], is difficult to draw in practice. In fact, Shakespeare is anxious neither about the probable nor about the possible. Here he is writing a play—call it farce or comedy as you will—in which the interest must rest on situation rather than on character. The distinctive stamp of his genius is seen on the large diversity of incidents represented and on the variety of emotions aroused. The former quality is especially remarkable in this particular play in which he shows respect for the Unities and yet succeeds in introducing perplexing intricacies in the plot. . . . The denouement unravels a sore entanglement and brings with it an atmosphere of peace and harmony. In this way many strands of situation and emotion have been mingled to make a complex fabric, and farce is enriched with romance and pathos.

The introduction of Aegeon and Luciana is such an important thing that it calls for more than a passing notice. They import romance and sentiment into a comedy of confused identity. The romantic element which comes so unexpectedly into a classical comedy is Shakespeare's most daring innovation here and points the way in which he will discover his *métier.* Sir Arthur Quiller-Couch, however, thinks that the mixture of farce with romance and sentiment is far from happy. . . . It is hardly necessary to stress that *The Comedy of Errors* is one of Shakespeare's earliest plays in which we shall look in vain for evidence of his ripe magic. But what is lacking in this early work is deftness of characterization or profound insight into the deeper springs of life and not an ability to fuse different elements into a unified whole. The situation in the later acts of the comedy becomes so complicated that it is necessary for one of the Antipholuses to go to a place from which he cannot come out and be there confronted by his twin, and then only can the drama come to an end. Otherwise the confusions might have gone on multiplying till the spectator would be as much bewildered as the twins themselves. This is why the Abbess is introduced so that she may offer sanctuary to the ill-used citizen. Old Aegeon starts the story as a Prologue, arousing curiosity about his own fate and that of his son. When the comedy is afoot, he retires from the stage and re-enters only at the end to lend a mellow and tender touch to the conclusion. Far from disturbing the farce he only sets it off by supplying it with a suitable Prologue and also by adding sweetness to the denouement. The romance of Antipholus of Syracuse and Luciana is equally appropriate. As there is no attempt at probing psychological profundities, this romance has not the complex harmony which distinguishes that of Beatrice and Benedick or of Viola and Orsino. Indeed, it is inherent in the situation in which Antipholus meets Luciana. Antipholus is urged by a passionate longing to meet his long-lost brother; he has come to a strange land, which, he thinks, is infested by witches and from which he wants to flee. It is not surprising that in course of his sojourn he should be genuinely fascinated by the most attractive person in a land which he has reason to believe is enchanted. After the entanglement is over, the people of the comedy return to normal life, and he discovers in this enchantress the sister of his sister-in-law and his future wife who haunted and startled but would henceforth comfort and command. (pp. 106-11)

> *S. C. Sen Gupta, "Early Comedies," in his* Shakespearian Comedy, *Oxford University Press, Delhi, 1950, pp. 82-128.*

FRANCIS FERGUSSON (essay date 1954)

There is one strand running through the whole *Comedy of Errors* which might seem, on a first reading, to break the mood of farce: the troubled adventures of Antipholus of Ephesus' long-suffering wife. She is so disturbed when the other Antipholus treats her strangely that one might think Shakespeare wanted us to share her tears and frustrations. She and her sister and her maid, and eventually her real husband's mistress, form a dreary female procession through the quick twists of the plot. But I believe that Shakespeare expected us to laugh at them also, and that, in performance, would be largely a matter of tempo. The film of a funeral, even, may be made laughable if it is run off at twice the proper speed, and if we saw the bewildered women running and dripping at the same time we should understand how they fit into the whole farcical scheme.

When Shakespeare wrote *The Comedy of Errors* he was aiming, with great accuracy, at the perennial popular theatre. He demanded, therefore, very little of his audience. He does not expect us to be interested in the subtleties of character: the figures in this farce are labelled (as servant, man-about-town, wife or courtesan) just accurately enough to enable us to tell them apart. We are not called upon for much sympathy or imagination: in fact we must not try to see through these characters' eyes, or feel what they feel. It would ruin everything to take the wife's troubles, or Dromio's many beatings, at all seriously. All we have to do is grasp the broadly absurd situation, and follow the ingenious fugue of the plot. To get the point, nothing beyond mental alertness of an easy kind is required. The foolishness presented in this play is that of the incredible and arbitrary basic situation, not the ineluctable folly of mankind.

The play belongs in the stream of popular comedy, from Menander to Minsky; but it also shows an intelligence and control, on the part of the author, which is rare in any kind of play. It is much lighter and funnier than *The Two Menaechmuses*. This mastery is revealed, not so much in the language, though that is perfectly adequate to its modest purposes, as in the consistency with which its farcical limitations are accepted, and in the ingenuity of the plot. . . . Comedy of this type, or taste—rationalistic, built on a Latin base—was to be more fully explored in the succeeding age of the Enlightenment, in the innumerable comedies which lighted the theaters of Europe from Molière through Mozart. But Shakespeare was developing in a different direction, not toward the univocal perfection of the geometric diagram, but toward the harmonizing of complementary perspectives; not toward further ingenuity, but toward deeper insight.

The Comedy of Errors, like other comedies of that taste, is so clear that it *ought* to be reducible to a formula. Molière's comedies often strike us in the same way. Certainly one can find in them many standard and publicly available devices, whether of plotting, attitude, or conventional characterization. Without that heritage I do not suppose Shakespeare could, at so early an age, have written anything so easy and assured. Yet he uses it for his own purposes, like a good cook who first learns and then forgets the basic recipes, or a dress designer who assumes the clichés of fashion only to go beyond them to something not quite predictable. Only Shakespeare could derive *The Comedy of Errors* from Plautus, and only he could proceed from that simple fun to the enigmatic humor of his maturity. (pp. 28-9)

> *Francis Fergusson, "'The Comedy of Errors' and 'Much Ado about Nothing',"* in *The Sewanee Review, Vol. LXII, No. 1, Winter, 1954, pp. 24-37.*

JOHN RUSSELL BROWN   (essay date 1957)

[*The following essay was first published in 1957.*]

The Comedy of Errors is, in the main, an intrigue comedy which aims at making a certain number of characters look ridiculous; it deals therefore, not with the joys of giving in love, but with the follies and evils of possessiveness. Adriana's idea of love is to try to maintain a hold over her husband; the liberty of his actions galls her and she demands her rights. As part of this plan, she obtains the promise of a gold chain. Instead of the 'willing loan' of 'free' agents, Adriana sees love as a system of promises, duties and bonds. . . . Her sister, Luciana, proclaims herself ready to submit to the man she should marry, but, not being in love herself, she only uses the same kind of arguments on Adriana's behalf, urging rights and duties. . . . (p. 54)

This kind of love is further defined by contrasted loves, that of Antipholus of Syracuse who offers himself to Luciana unasked, and for whom giving is its own reward:

> Sing, siren, for thyself and I will dote:
>   Spread o'er the silver waves thy golden hairs,
> And as a bed I'll take them and there lie,
>   And in that glorious supposition think
> He *gains* by death that hath such means to die . . .
>
>   [III. ii. 47-52]

or that of Luce who deals only in claims and possessions:

> *Dromio of Syracuse.* . . . I am *due* to a woman; one that *claims* me, one that haunts me, one that will have me.
> *Antipholus of Syracuse.* What *claim lays* she to thee?
> *Dromio.* Marry, sir, such *claim* as you would lay to your horse; and she would have me as a beast: not that, I being a beast, she would have me; but that she, being a very beastly creature, *lays claim* to me. . . .
>
>   [III. ii. 81-8]

This is the level of merely possessive love; and the fact is driven home by bringing these three loves together in one brief scene.

There are further contrasts in the juxtaposition of misunderstandings about love and misunderstandings about the possession of servants, a gold chain, and a bag of ducats. For the like of Adriana there is little difference between them; so when the Goldsmith asks for his money on the strength of a bond, Antipholus of Ephesus in his refusal likens the confusion to Adriana's sort of marriage:

> Good Lord! you use this *dalliance* to excuse
> Your breach of promise to the Porpentine.
> I should have chid you for not bringing it,
> But, like a *shrew,* you first begin to brawl.
>
>   [IV. i. 48-51]

But there is one difference between the two kinds of misunderstandings: those between masters and men, and merchant and purchaser are occasioned solely by confused identities—even after he has lost his money, the Goldsmith acknowledges that Antipholus of Ephesus is of 'credit infinite, highly beloved' [V. i. 6]—but Adriana's misunderstandings, her claims of rights and wrongs, ante-date any mistaken identity. The merchants treat their possessions naturally as best they may, Adriana treats hers unnaturally—her merchandise requires the use of love's wealth in which giving is more important than taking or keeping. (pp. 55-6)

When the facts are made clear, the Goldsmith is readily satisfied, and so are masters and men. Adriana's reconciliation with her husband is not presented in dialogue; their misunderstanding involved more than mistaken identities, and cannot be cleared by such simple means. Yet the spirit of generosity is contagious and there is a hint that Adriana is now ready to give rather than demand: she has clamoured to the Abbess for possession of her husband, but to the Duke she uses a milder tone, basing her claim not on her rights but on the plea that Antipholus of Ephesus is the one 'Whom I made lord of me and all I had' [V. i. 137], instead of demanding, as of right, to be 'his nurse' [V. i. 98], she simply begs that he may be 'brought forth and borne hence for help' [V. i. 160]. (pp. 56-7)

No one would argue that *The Comedy of Errors* is a very profound play, but reference to Shakespeare's ideas about love's wealth and its difference from commercial wealth, does suggest that its action is not merely that of a merry-go-round. Its elements were not chosen at random, but serve to present, in lively dramatic form, some of Shakespeare's judgements on personal relationships. It is a play of greater promise than the mere dexterity of its plotting suggests; its contrasts of love, commerce, and justice are simple enough but they foreshadow the more complex treatment of *The Merchant of Venice*. Adriana's dilemma is perhaps the most subtle element in the play, but its resolution, the manner in which husband and wife can willingly agree, is not fully expressed; this theme was taken up in another early comedy, *The Taming of the Shrew*. (p. 57)

> *John Russell Brown, ''Love's Wealth and the Judgement of 'The Merchant of Venice','' in his* Shakespeare and His Comedies, *second edition, Methuen & Co. Ltd., 1962, pp. 45-81.*

BERTRAND EVANS   (essay date 1960)

[*Evans states that Shakespeare's dramatic method relied heavily on what he calls the ''arrangement of discrepant awarenesses,'' a method which gives an audience the advantage of seeing and knowing elements of the plot not known by the characters. He examines the way in which Shakespeare employs this method in* The Comedy of Errors.]

To describe the creation, maintenance, and exploitation of the gaps that separate the participants' awarenesses and ours in *The Comedy of Errors* is almost to describe the entire play, for in his first comedy Shakespeare came nearer than ever afterward to placing his whole reliance upon an arrangement of discrepant awarenesses. This comedy has no Falstaff, Toby Belch, Dogberry—not even an Armado. Comic effect emerges not once from character as such. If the Dromios prove laughable, it is not in themselves but in the incompleteness of their vision of situation that they prove so. Language, which regularly afterwards is squeezed for its comic potential, here serves chiefly to keep us advised of situation. Here are no malapropisms, dialectal oddities, few quirks and twists of phrase: the very pun, hereafter ubiquitous, is scanted. With neither character nor language making notable comic contribution, then, the great resource of laughter is the exploitable gulf spread between the participants' understanding and ours.

This gap is held open from beginning to end: it is available for exploitation and is exploited during ten of the eleven scenes. In the course of the action we hold an advantage in awareness

Act V. Scene i. Aemilia and the Duke. Engraving from Theobald edition by Hubert Gravelot (1762). From the Art Collection of the Folger Shakespeare Library.

over fifteen of the sixteen persons—Aemilia alone never being exhibited on a level beneath ours. Not until *The Tempest* (in the comedies) did Shakespeare again hold one gap open so long for exploitation; never again did he place so great a responsibility on a single gap.

As in most later plays, Shakespeare here opens the gap—that is to say, raises our vantage point above that of the participants—as soon as possible. After forty lines in Scene ii (at the entrance of Dromio of Ephesus) the facts of the enveloping situation are fixed in our minds. . . . [The] key fact that is quickly revealed to us is denied them: they are ignorant that all are in the same city. On our side, thus, is complete vision, and on theirs none at all. This condition, kept essentially unchanged, is made to yield virtually all of the comic effects during ten scenes.

In that the secret committed to our keeping is both simple and single, *The Comedy of Errors* is unique among the comedies. In later ones our awareness is packed, often even burdened, with multiple, complex, interrelated secrets, and the many circles of individual participants' visions, though they cross and recross one another, do not wholly coincide. . . . In *The Comedy of Errors* only a single great secret exists, which is ours alone; the participants, therefore, stand all on one footing of ignorance. Shakespeare never again used so simple an arrangement of the awarenesses.

The enveloping situation which makes both action and comic effects possible is itself static; it remains unchanged, until the last 100 lines, by the bustling incidents that fill up the scenes between beginning and end. Between the point midway in the second scene, at which all relevant facts have been put into our minds, and the ending, we neither need nor get additional information in order to hold our one great advantage over the participants. The many expository devices by which Shakespeare was later to sustain the advantage given us in the initial exposition—as soliloquies and asides strategically placed, scene-introductions which shed special light on following action, confidential dialogue of persons perpetrating some 'practice' on their unwitting fellows—are here absent because they would be superfluous. . . . The play has not one 'aside', and though there are brief soliloquies they exist not to advise us of what we had been ignorant but to exploit the speaker's ignorance of what we already know.

The Comedy of Errors is unique also in that its exploitable gap between awarenesses is created and sustained throughout the play without the use of a 'practiser'. No one here wilfully deceives another or even passively withholds a secret—for none here knows enough of the situation to deceive others about it, and none has a secret to withhold. (pp. 1-3)

The third distinguishing mark of *The Comedy of Errors,* seen from the point of view of its uses of awareness, is the universal depth of the participants' ignorance. In later plays persons ignorant of a situation occasionally glimpse the truth, even though dimly and obliquely, and the effect is an instant flash of irony. . . . But no person in *The Comedy of Errors* ever rises enough from the bottom of oblivion to glimpse the truth that we see steadily. In the first lines of Scene ii, the First Merchant mentions a fact which—if he but knew—would be enormously significant to Antipholus of Syracuse: 'This very day a Syracusian merchant / Is apprehended for arrival here.' And he goes on:

> And, not being able to buy out his life
> According to the statute of the town,
> Dies ere the weary sun set in the west.
> There is your money that I had to keep.
>
> [I. ii. 5-8]

Without a word about the plight of the 'Syracusian merchant', Antipholus takes the money—the very sum that would buy his father's life—and turns to instruct his servant. The intellectual remoteness of Antipholus from a truth that physically brushes against him at the outset of the action is matched constantly thereafter by the remoteness of other participants from truth that assaults their eyes and ears, and escapes detection. In his first use of the method, Shakespeare risks no dialogue that strikes the unsuspected truth. Nor, certainly, does he allow any participant to come close to guessing the truth. . . . Shakespeare keeps all persons safely oblivious. Though truth beats at them incessantly, it beats in vain.

The severest problem of the dramatist, accordingly, was to make it credible—at least sufficiently credible for farce—that such steady hammering, without which nothing would be comic, would never break in upon that obliviousness, without which action itself would cease. A partial solution was to emphasize the Ephesian reputation as a seat of the black arts. (pp. 4-5)

A second way of solving the problem of credibility was to emphasize the Syracusian brother's distrust of his own sanity.

At first the master had suspected that his servant was merely in a 'merry fit', and had beaten him. Next, he questioned his own wits, which seemed unable to distinguish dream from reality. . . . Finally, after other baffling encounters, he distrusts both his own and Dromio's sanity, and the witchery of the city, all in a breath. . . . In this condition, believing both himself and Dromio 'transformed', he grows hysterical when the Courtezan hails him as an old friend. 'Avaunt, thou witch!' he shouts, and runs off. When we see him again, it is with rapier drawn, ready, if necessary, to hack a path to the port. Though Dromio could 'find in my heart to stay here still and turn witch', Antipholus will bear no more: 'I will not stay tonight for all the town.'

It is, then, chiefly by concentrating on the mounting fears of Antipholus that he is losing his wits in a bewitched city that Shakespeare attacks the problem of making credible the continued unawareness of participants. It is clearly proper that the main effort should be spent on keeping the visiting Antipholus's ignorance plausible, since it is he who is searching for his brother and whom we might expect to be first to perceive that the search has ended when 'everyone knows us and we know none'. Little care is needed to make credible the obliviousness of Antipholus of Ephesus, since, separated from his family as an infant and lacking knowledge that any relative exists, he would be unlikely to guess the truth under any circumstances. As for Adriana—in whom, alone among these persons, Shakespeare designs character specifically appropriate to action— her special bent leads her to assume that her husband has tired of her; hence it is plausible that she should believe the report of his conduct toward Dromio of Ephesus and his refusal to come home to dinner. The tense relations of husband and wife, resulting from her shrewishness, thus help also to make it credible that error should become general and should prevail so long. The existing state of their affairs is enough to explain why Adriana is not simply astonished at the extraordinary conduct of her 'husband' when she meets the wrong Antipholus on the street and orders him home, and why the real husband readily accepts the situation when he comes home to find the door locked against him. . . . Further, as one inexplicable incident follows another, his fury itself comes to be blinding, and as his irrationality waxes it becomes less and less likely that he would guess the truth; in turn, because his fury comes to look more and more like lunacy, it also helps to prevent others from guessing the truth.

In these various ways, then, Shakespeare worked to make it credible that the participants should continue, throughout the bustling action, to be abused by error; that is to say, thus he kept open for his uses the exploitable gap from which rise the comic effects.

The participants' unawareness, however, is always but one side of the gap: the other is our awareness, which, with a few noteworthy exceptions in plays between *Henry VI* and *The Tempest,* Shakespeare always kept well informed. In this first try at comedy, he succeeded better in maintaining the participants' condition of plausible ignorance than in keeping our vantage point at the most effective height. Although our view of the incidents which are contained by the frame is perfect, our view of the frame itself is not.

His addition of the frame story of Aegeon and Aemilia greatly complicated for Shakespeare the system of awarenesses which prevails throughout the play. It also profoundly affects our view of the farcical scenes. In the opening scene, with Aegeon's speech and the dialogue that immediately follows it, the dramatist strikes a tragic note—indeed, strikes it very hard, as though he meant the tones to vibrate in our memories during the succession of explosions that make the hilarity of all the middle scenes. (pp. 6-7)

We are thus obliged to observe the comic action—which is the entire action except for the containing frame itself—while our minds hold a spot of anxiety for Aegeon. The method here first used, or its converse, Shakespeare would repeat in every comedy after this, and not only in the comedies, but also in the tragedies and the mature histories. It becomes a regular formula: we are required to look sometimes on hilarious scenes with a troubled awareness that shadows them, sometimes on dark and dangerous scenes with a secret and comforting assurance that lightens them. Because of the management of our awareness, scenes that would otherwise ask only a single, simple response demand instead conflicting responses simultaneously. In adding the frame story, then, fixing in our minds the tragic plight of Aegeon, Shakespeare was trying a dramatic method that at once became a principle of his dramaturgy.

At the same time, the handling of the frame story contrasts significantly with his later habitual method. Just this once, he withholds not only from the participants *but from us also* an all-important fact: he hides a key, that is to say, which exists all the while but of which we are denied knowledge. When we learn that there is an Abbess in Ephesus and that this Abbess is no other than old Aegeon's lost wife, the play is within eighty lines of the end. Had we been told of her existence at the outset, we would have been assured, even while recollection of Aegeon's desperate plight shadowed the hilarious scenes, that all would finally be well. As the play stands, with only half of the frame—Aegeon's plight—presented to us at the outset, it is plain that the dramatist has simply deceived us. He makes us believe our view complete when it is only partial. . . . There are a very great many 'Aemilias' in the comedies—keys, or key elements essential to the solution of problems—the identities or existences of which are hidden from participants until the denouement; but they are not hidden from us as audience. Shakespeare's regular practice after *The Comedy of Errors* is to expose to us at the outset the existence of the potential solvent. . . . By introducing Aemilia early in the action, Shakespeare could have added another level to the structure of awarenesses and thus have increased the complexity of our responses. Though we should then, as now, have observed the hilarity while our minds are troubled by recollection of Aegeon's plight, yet overlying our anxiety would have been the comforting assurance that, after all, all must be well. By denying us an early view of Aemilia, the dramatist did intensify the force of our anxiety; but the way of the mature comedies is to contain anxieties within a frame of warm reassurance. (pp. 8-9)

Bertrand Evans, "Here Sit I in the Sky: First Explorations," in his Shakespeare's Comedies, *Oxford at the Clarendon Press, Oxford, 1960, pp. 1-32.*

DEREK TRAVERSI (essay date 1960)

Whatever opinion we may form on the merits of Shakespeare's early plays, there can be no doubt that his artistic development was relatively slow. Had he died, like his contemporary Christopher Marlowe, at the early age of twenty-nine, it is far from certain that we should regard him to-day as the more forceful and striking figure of the two. This observation, however, though true, is only part of the truth. If the impact of Marlowe's

genius is at this stage more obviously powerful, emphatic in its effect, Shakespeare's earlier works already show a wider range, a closer adaptation to varied dramatic needs. The result is an instrument perhaps less obviously personal, but superior in theatrical possibilities: the instrument, in short, which the dramatist was already developing with considerable success in *The Comedy of Errors*. (pp. 8-9)

On the strictly formal side, and always within the prevailing convention, which is that of realistic Roman farce, we must be struck by Shakespeare's acceptance of the challenge implied in the added intricacy which he chose to confer upon [the plot derived from the *Menaechmi*]. . . . Since the working out of a complex pattern to its formal conclusion is an essential part of Shakespeare's mature comic conception, we should not underestimate the importance of this exercise in plot-making to his developing art.

Scarcely less important is the skilful use of different forms of verse, and where necessary of a contrasted prose, to point the contrasts which operate within the carefully contrived unity of the plot. The prose given to the servants, generally to convey a comic comment upon the way in which their masters are behaving, stands out effectively against the stiffness of much of the surrounding verse. It can rise on occasions to a notable vivacity. . . . Taken together with the lively use of the hitherto crude long verse line in a close chain of rhyming repartee . . . and the solid construction of the blank verse whenever the play's more serious moments require it, we must be struck with a facility, a fluent command of familiar modes of expression, that causes the play to stand out from its classical and contemporary models.

The true interest of the comedy, however, lies in the use to which the dramatist put these and similar effects. Beyond all its obvious crudities *The Comedy of Errors* aims at presenting a serious and humane view of human relationships. Most obviously of all, perhaps, the part played by the women in the entire series of farcical episodes is humanized in a way entirely foreign to the essential cynicism of the classical source. . . . [The] jealousy of Adriana is treated by Shakespeare with an effort at psychological plausibility which on occasion surpasses the hard-boiled attitude which we might have expected him to take over from his originals. (pp. 9-10)

More significantly still, Shakespeare has chosen to introduce another woman, Luciana, to act as a foil to his presentation of this jealous wife. It is here that we come into contact with the distinctive *seriousness* of his comic conception. Besides adding through contrast to the psychological depth of his portrayal, he gives himself the opportunity of presenting what is in effect a considered conception of marriage, completely foreign to Plautus and a main theme of his own comedies to come. The contrasted positions of the two women are developed with some insight. Luciana stresses the traditional view of marriage as resting upon the superiority of the male. . . . [Though] the argument is clearly intended to carry weight, there is substance in Adriana's retort that what is true in theory may not always be confirmed by practical experience:

> They can be meek that have no other cause.
> A wretched soul, bruised with adversity,
> We bid be quiet when we hear it cry;
> But were we burden'd with like weight of pain,
> As much, or more, we should ourselves complain.
> [II. i. 33-6]

We need not, indeed, exaggerate the force of this, though the attitude is hardly one that Plautus would have found conceivable; but the stress laid by Adriana, even in a situation composed of comic misunderstandings, upon mutual trust as an essential element in the marriage relationship, implies a seriousness which the intense vigour of the expression occasionally confirms:

> For if we two be one, and thou play false,
> I do digest the poison of thy flesh,
> Being strumpeted by thy contagion.
>
> [II. ii. 142-44]

The presentation of contrasted attitudes, leading to a truth greater than that which any single one of them can compass, is a dramatic device which will play a vital part in the development of Shakespeare's comic method. The introduction, through the twin Dromios, of a comic underplot, including a burlesque upon marriage itself in the pursuit of the Syracusan by the kitchen maid of Ephesus, presents yet another standpoint from which the central theme can be considered.

The Comedy of Errors, then, shows us a dramatist already intent upon giving a greater scope, more variety of human content, to the cynical realism of Roman farce. The play's emotional range is notably greater than any which Plautus could have contemplated. This is implied from the first in the deliberate seriousness of the story of Aegeon, which gives the entire action a new setting of gravity, a sense of tragic overtones which, elementary though it may be in its expression, is yet not without some intimation of later and finer effects. Such is especially the case with Aegeon's evocation of the storm which separated him from his wife and children and brought him face to face with his city's enemies at Ephesus. . . . [The] continuity of Shakespeare's development, as foreshadowed in these early and imperfect works, is even more impressive than might otherwise have been supposed.

At the end of the play, the serious framework to the main farce is confirmed by the introduction of that odd and entirely un-Roman figure, the Abbess. Here, at least, Plautus has nothing to contribute. When the Abbess with whom Adriana's supposed 'husband' has taken refuge speaks of the 'holy prayers' which will make him 'a formal man again', and claims this to be 'A charitable duty of my order', we can once more hear echoes which anticipate, uncertainly indeed, but none the less unmistakably, the 'symbolic' and spiritual order which haunts Shakespeare's last plays. It is through the actions of the Abbess that the opening discord is resolved, as Shakespearean comedy will always aim at resolving it, in marriage and the reconciliation of parents to their children. The Abbess, having disclosed that she is Aegeon's lost wife and mother of the twins, announces the dissolution of her sorrow in joy:

> Thirty-three years have I but gone in travail
> Of you, my sons; and till this present hour
> My heavy burthen ne'er delivered.
>
> [V. i. 401-03]

We may confess, indeed, that much in this conception is crude and perfunctory; but the situation is one to which Shakespeare will return with immeasurably greater conviction, and it is remarkable to find these intimations of the splendour of reconciliation in his first effort in this kind. For all the rough origins of his plot—origins which clearly survive in the story and the dramatist's treatment of it—we may reasonably find in *The Comedy of Errors* an attitude to his comic material which anticipates his mature presentation of human relationships. (pp. 11-14)

Derek Traversi, " 'The Comedy of Errors'," in his William Shakespeare: The Early Comedies, *British Council, 1960, pp. 8-14.*

HAROLD BROOKS (essay date 1961)

[*According to bibliographer Ronald Berman, Brooks's essay is the best critical treatment of* The Comedy of Errors. *Here Brooks continues the discussion of the problem of identity initiated by G. R. Elliott (see excerpt above, 1939), and gives a close analysis of Shakespeare's dramatic technique, which Brooks finds highly advanced. He also praises the "combinative power" of farce and the "averted-tragical" of the frame story, in contrast to Arthur Quiller-Couch (see excerpt above, 1922) and other commentators.*]

The Comedy of Errors has [a] large dramatic design, but is no less remarkable for its controlled detail, unparalleled at this date, except in *The Spanish Tragedy,* outside Shakespeare's other plays. His handling of the lesser units of structure, from the scene downwards, is already sure, and indeed within its conventions brilliant. These units include the scene, a new one beginning whenever the stage is clear; the sub-scene, or *scène* as understood in French drama, a new one beginning whenever the group on stage is altered by anyone leaving or joining it; the passage of dialogue or the set speech, more than one, sometimes, going to make up the *scène;* besides every physical action, whether procession, brawl, or bit of minor business. Fully to appreciate the close bonding of such units in the structure one has to ask what is contributed by every passage as it occurs, and how it is interrelated with others throughout the play. Some illustration is possible, however, by taking a single scene. Act I scene 2 will serve, the better as it is not exceptionally highly wrought. Yet even a scene so expository (being the first of the main action) is not allowed to lack the immediate interest that holds an audience. Shakespeare has already the art of fulfilling, and with the economy that secures dramatic compression, three principal requirements of dramatic structure: retrospect, preparation, and immediate interest. By retrospect and preparation the playwright keeps his action moving—the great virtue of dynamic or progressive structure—with the strongest continuity. Further, while he concerns himself with the matter of the present scene, he can add force and meaning to what has gone before, and pile them up for what is to come after, so that, in effect, he is building up several (perhaps widely separated) parts of his play at once. This can be of great value in what I will call the harmonic structure: the structure which by parallel, contrast, or cross-reference, independent perhaps of the cause-and-effect connections of the progressive action, makes us compare one passage or person of the play with another, and so find an enriched significance in both. (pp. 55-6)

With the first entry and speech of our illustrative scene, there is interest in the appearance of three fresh persons, and some tension: Antipholus the alien is warned that he is in danger of the fate which overtook Egeon in the scene before; a fate summarized in the natural course of the warning. This retrospect, and parallel of situation, link the opening of the main action and that of the Egeon action within which it is to be framed. The link is strengthened by reference to three themes already started in the Egeon episode: risk (and in particular the hazards of Ephesus), wealth and time. . . . Since these themes will now be developed throughout the main action, the references to them are preparatory no less than retrospective. The theme of moneyed wealth is emphasized by stage-'business': the merchant hands back to Antipholus

> . . . your money that I had to keep,
>
> [I. ii. 8]

and Antipholus passes it on to his Dromio. The bag of money is to furnish one of the two subjects of the first comic misunderstanding, due to occur later in the scene, and therefore is implanted visually on the audience's mind beforehand; moreover, it will form a parallel with the gold chain and the purse, other concrete visible properties which carry on the theme and become foci of similar cross-purposes in subsequent Acts. The second subject of the imminent misunderstanding, the summons to dinner by the Ephesian Dromio, is also prepared, and the time-theme touched, in Antipholus' observation:

> Within this hour it will be dinner-time.
>
> [I. ii. 11]

Another chief theme of the play is introduced when he is warned to conceal his Syracusan origin; for this concerns his identity. Again, when he bids Dromio depart with the money, Dromio's exit lines:

> Many a man would take you at your word,
> And go indeed, having so good a mean,
>
> [I. ii. 17-18]

foreshadow the suspicion that his master will shortly entertain, while preparing us to recognize it as groundless, a comic error. (pp. 56-7)

Dromio's jesting exit ends the first *scène*. It is Shakespeare's cue for underlining the promise of comedy: the note of tension at the start has now passed into the background. It is the cue also for Antipholus' direct comment upon Dromio's character, which adds to what has been gathered of his own and of the relations between the two of them. . . . Antipholus' experience of Dromio as a jester is needed to explain his coming assumption that the invitation to dinner is his servant's joke, and his slowly mounting surprise and anger when it is persisted in out of season. The rendezvous with the merchant, 'at five-o-clock', like that arranged in *scène* I with Dromio, helps to establish the theme of timing, and the motifs of timely or untimely meetings or failures to meet. It points forward, moreover, to the hour . . . so fateful for Egeon, the hour (though we do not yet know this) of the *dénouement*. . . . (pp. 57-8)

The *scènes* of three, then two persons, are succeeded by Antipholus' first soliloquy. Here and in the two remaining *scènes,* the immediate interest for the audience strengthens. From the point of view of comedy and the intrigue, *scène* 4, the encounter with the wrong Dromio, is the climax of the whole scene. It is flanked, in the ABA form so frequent in Shakespeare, by Antipholus' soliloquies, which are the imaginative climaxes and, together with the moment when he strikes the (Ephesian) Dromio, the emotional climaxes too, though there is contrast between his emotion as an exasperated and as a 'melancholy' imaginative man. From the imaginative, introspective man he is, soliloquies (his brother has none) come naturally; his allusion to his 'care and melancholy' has prepared the way for them.

The first of them explains both his special occasion of 'care', and his arrival, contributing by a single stroke to the logic at once of the character and of the plot. He has an aim, fruitlessly pursued: 'to find a mother and a brother'. It is a dull member of the audience who does not refer this back to Egeon's ret-

rospect (narrating much of the dramatist's 'fable', prior to the part enacted), and so conjecture who Antipholus must be. The audience is held, too, by the revelation of feeling. Antipholus' emotional reflections spring from the farewells just exchanged at the end of *scène* 2: 'I will go lose myself', he said, and was commended by the Merchant to his 'own content'. This is the phrase which prompts his soliloquy, where he laments that what would content him is precisely what he cannot get. . . . The theme of identity is here linked with those of relationship (dislocated or re-established), and of risk. To seek reunion with the lost members of the family, Antipholus is risking his identity; yet he must do so, for only if the full relationship is restored can he find content. And then, hints the image of one waterdrop seeking another, the present individual identity will be lost, or transformed, in another way. It is to claim a sinking of identity in the marriage-relation, with the emergence of a new identity, where each is also the other, that Adriana uses the closely similar image in II. ii. In the play's harmonic structure, while this soliloquy is thus recalled at that point, in its own place it recalls the situation of Egeon, who on virtually the same quest as Antipholus, has so risked his mortal identity that it is forfeit to the executioner. Antipholus' fear that he is losing himself is full of comic irony. No sooner has he expressed it, than, with the entry of his brother's Dromio, he begins to be the victim of the successive mistakes of identity to which his words are designed by Shakespeare as a prelude, and in the course of which he will come to wonder whether he is beside himself, and has lost himself indeed. . . . By Dromio's entrance are initiated the enigmas that beset the characters, and Antipholus is given an aptly enigmatic comment upon it:

> Here comes the almanack of my true date.
>
> [I. ii. 41]

The new arrival has the appearance of his Dromio, who constitutes a record of his span from the time of their simultaneous nativities; but by a comic irony, so does the Dromio who has really entered: the comment fits both the false inference from appearance, and the reality itself. Its enigmatic nature conceals, so one finds from the final speech of the Abbess after the *dénouement* . . . a further meaning: what approaches with this Dromio is the occasion which will secure Antipholus his true identity through a new date of birth—his true birth into the restored family relationship. That is the metaphor the Abbess employs.

It is by mistaking appearance for reality that Antipholus and his brother's Dromio misidentify one another. The threat to the very self involved in the confusion of appearance and reality is the thought most vividly conveyed in Antipholus' second soliloquy. The soliloquy rounds off the scene, not without certain resemblances to the beginning. Then, the theme of moneyed wealth was given prominence; and there was tension because the Ephesian law spelled danger to Antipholus' goods or life. Now, he is keenly anxious about his money; indeed, that is the motive for his final exit to seek Dromio at the Centaur. And tension rises again with his anxiety; but still more with the profoundly disturbing fears into which it merges, of worse perils than the law's in Ephesus, suggested by its repute as a place of illusions and shape-shifting, of jugglers that deceive the eye, of mountebanks and disguised cheaters, of

> Dark-working sorcerers that change the mind:
> Soul-killing witches that deform the body.
>
> [I. ii. 99-100]

The lines seize the imagination of the audience at the deep level where the ancient dread of losing the self or soul is very much alive. They are highly characteristic of the imaginative Antipholus, develop the idea in his first soliloquy that his self is at hazard, and set the pattern for his interpretations of the strange experiences that befall him henceforward. (pp. 58-60)

Every passage in our illustrative scene has thus its functions both in the scene itself, and in the wider dynamic, harmonic, thematic, comic structure of the play. Besides this close, economical texture, there are of course other proofs of Shakespeare's early command of construction in the dramatic medium. He constructs in terms of theatre: he knows, for instance, the value of business and of devices and episodes which belong peculiarly to the stage. . . . In *The Comedy of Errors*, the gold chain seen, the blows seen and heard, make double the effect they would in narrative. The asides or semi-asides of the alien Antipholus and Dromio in II. ii, by a sound use of dramatic convention, mark the dichotomy between their mental worlds and that of Adriana and Luciana with whom they are in converse. The hilarious and crucial episode of the rightful husband and his party shut out from dinner depends for its full impact upon the stage-arrangement: the parties in altercation are both plainly visible to the audience though not to each other. But the supreme power manifest in Shakespeare's art of dramatic construction is the combinative power well indicated by Hardin Craig, who writes of 'his unequalled [skill] in fitting parts together so that they [reinforce] one another', and notes that in working upon materials which often gave him much of his fable ready-made, his 'originality seems to have consisted in the selection of great significant patterns'. (pp. 60-1)

In *The Comedy of Errors*, the combinative power is exercised in drawing upon diverse sources to compose a play of diverse yet co-operating strands and tones, a play which ranges from the averted-tragical, in prologue and *dénouement*, to low comedy, as in the drubbings and the account of Luce; while the middle comedy of the Antipholi provides its central substance. The adventures of the alien Antipholus, particularly his falling in love with Luciana, have emotional chords that relate them to the tone of the Egeon story; the marital conflict of Antipholus the husband and his Adriana is bourgeois comedy, informed by intellectual and emotional discussion. Both Antipholi, through the association of master and man, take part with the Dromios in the lower comedy, which besides knockabout farce includes burlesque of academical logic and rhetoric, a comic parallel to the more serious concern with ideas at other levels of the action. (p. 61)

[When] through his neo-Plautine warp Shakespeare ran a weft dyed in colours of romance, he was making no extreme change from the Latin genre as then frequently understood. Rather, he was overgoing Plautus, and Terence, on their supposed romantic side, as well as on that of comic intrigue. For this purpose, and for 'copiousness', he drew on additional sources. The leading interests of romance—as one might exemplify from Arthurian romances, from *The Squire's Tale*, or, coming to the period of our play, from the romance aspects of *Arcadia* and *The Faerie Queene*—were adventure; marvel, especially enchantment; the high sentiment of love; and *sens*, the implications brought out in the *matière*, the meaning the reader takes away with him, as a result of the author's treatment. Shakespeare develops into an adventure-story, that of Egeon, the successful quest for the long-lost child which in *Menaechmi* is hardly more than a presupposition of the plot. For the initial peril demanded by a plot of this kind, he provides by translating

from hoax into fact the situation of the Sienese merchant in Gascoigne's *Supposes,* where it was already part of a drama of mistaken identities; and by heightening it from a potential threat to goods into a provisional sentence of death. The shipwreck and intervention of piratical fishermen, whereby, Egeon narrates, the family was first divided, have a probable source in Greene's *Menaphon*, and form a link with the source of the happy ending, the adventures of Apollonius of Tyre, related by Gower and Twine. . . . The interest of adventure is not confined to the *dénouement* and the opening scene; through the alien Antipholus it is carried into the main action. To him it seems that he has a series of adventures with the supernatural. His thoughts and feelings about them, like the providential coincidences that have brought all the members of the family to Ephesus, speak to our sense of marvel. His illusion of supernatural menace in these experiences is set against the real peril of Egeon, and against the truth of his love, even though his love-adventure, which brings the loftiest of love-sentiment into the comedy, seems to him supernatural and at least equivocally perilous too. In the idea of the town as a home of supernatural delusion, Shakespeare is again combining sources. The Epidamnum of *Menaechmi* . . . is notorious for cheats. The denizen's house there is associated by Shakespeare with Amphitruo's, a scene of supernatural shape-shifting. Epidamnum itself he has changed to Ephesus, no doubt as the site of Diana's Temple in the Apollonius story, which becomes his Abbey. Diana of the Ephesians inevitably recalls Acts XIX, whence Shakespeare would remember, besides the uproar on her account, the references to curious (that is, black) arts practised in Ephesus, and to the exorcists, with whom Dr. Pinch (founded on the Medicus in *Menaechmi*) has something in common. The Ephesians are warned against supernatural foes in St. Paul's Epistle, which also exhorts them . . . to domestic unity, dwelling on the right relationships of husbands and wives, parents and children, masters and servants. With the father's rebuke to the wife in *Menaechmi*, and the long tradition of marital debate in mediaeval and Tudor literature, it thus contributed, no doubt, to the *sens* of the play.

To consider the *sens* is to consider the themes. However they are deepened and interconnected by Shakespeare's treatment, they are not recondite: for the audience, they are the general ideas arising most naturally from the motives and development of the plot, and the response of the characters. The play begins and ends with relationship: a family torn asunder and reunited. . . . The chief entanglements spring from mistaken identity and mistiming:

> I see we still did meet each other's man,
> And I was ta'en for him, and he for me,
> And thereupon these ERRORS are arose.
> [V. i. 387-89]

The twins appear the same, but in reality are different; those who meet them are led by appearance into illusion. Repeatedly one of the persons assumes that he shared an experience with another, when in reality he shared it with a different one. In consequence, the persons cease to be able to follow each other's assumptions, and become isolated in more or less private worlds. Mistakes of identity all but destroy relationship, and loss of relationship calls true identity yet more in question; the chief persons suspect themselves or are suspected of insanity, or of being possessed, surrounded, or assailed by supernatural powers—madness or demoniac possession would be the eclipse of the true self, and sorcery might overwhelm it. . . . Yet the hazard of metamorphosis and of the loss of present identity is also the way to fresh or restored relationship. Antipholus the bachelor desires that Luciana will transform him and create him new; and Adriana's belief that in marriage the former identities coalesce and emerge identified with each other, is true if rightly interpreted. How the possessive interpretation, not relinquished by Adriana till almost the end, is at odds with the free giving and hazarding in which the wealth and debts of love differ from those of commerce, is another central theme, well traced by J. R. Brown [see excerpt above, 1957]. Adriana's envy of a husband's status contravenes principles of order that for Shakespeare and orthodox Elizabethans extended through the whole cosmos. (pp. 64-6)

Not only are the themes organically developed in the action; they are organically connected in themselves. At the centre is relationship: relationship between human beings, depending on their right relationship to truth and universal law: to the cosmic reality behind appearance, and the cosmic order. Trust in mere appearance results in illusion and mistakes of identity, thus dislocating relationship, and so disrupting order: blind conflict and disorder are inevitable when men misconceive true identity and become isolated in private worlds. Besides illusion, there are other factors of disorder: revolt against a wife's place in the cosmic hierarchy is the original source of discord in Adriana's marriage: order is broken, too, by everything untimely. . . . Here, and in the dread of Circean transformation into beasts, metamorphosis is seen in its hostile aspect; but, as we have observed, it can also transform for the better: time, too, when it is ripe, brings a new order. Till then, patience would mitigate disorder, which cannot be ended till the claims for justice, distorted by the claimants' assumption that their private worlds are real, are laid before those who in the hierarchy of order are founts of justice upon earth. More than justice is needed: without mercy, the godly prince is not himself; and amid the demonstrations of love's wealth, lacking which there would be little of the genial warmth that glows in the conclusion, Solinus is inspired to what he had declared impossible, and freely remits the debt Egeon owes the law. In this organic structure, of the two themes which next to relationship are the most inclusive, the first, cosmic order, presides in Shakespeare's early Histories; its importance in his drama is well recognized, and the importance of the second appearance and reality, is becoming so. The first is a familiar part of 'the Elizabethan world-picture'; the second, presumably, has affiliations with Renaissance neo-Platonism.

The themes are given prominence in several ways. They are voiced by the speakers, who often relate one theme to another: the examples in our analysis of I. ii are characteristic. The dominant imagery, of man as beast, reflects the ideas of illusory appearance and malign metamorphosis; above all, it mirrors the threats to identity and to status in the cosmic order. Appropriately, it stops on the brink of the *dénouement*, with the Duke's explicit formulation:

> I think you all have drunk of Circe's cup.
> [V. i. 271]

Thematic, likewise, are the two images of the water-drop, its identity lost for relationship's sake. The whole harmonic structure, of which the correspondence of images forms part, is a vehicle of the themes. . . . The supreme instance is the parallel between the 'gossips' feast' to which everyone is going at the end, and the dinner from which the husband and his guests were shut out. The gossips' or baptismal feast affirms relationship and identity: the kin are united, the Duke is patron, all are friends and godparents, witnesses to the identities now

truly established and christened into the family and the community; long travail is rewarded, and increase (the progressive aspect of cosmic order) which, despite the double birth of twins, was mocked by the intervention of mutable fortune, is now truly realized. It is not only as a sensational error of identity that the exclusion from dinner contrasts with this: balked or broken feasts (G. Wilson Knight has made us aware) are recurrent symbols in Shakespeare of the breakdown of human fellowship and its pieties. (pp. 67-8)

[The characters of *The Comedy of Errors*] are simple, but have just enough depth for the play, which Shakespeare, as we have seen, has deepened considerably beyond the expected limitations of neo-classical comedy.

Even so, in depth and scope he was, of course, far to surpass it. None the less, it is in its own kind an extraordinarily finished work. The kind being one that not even Shakespeare could extend beyond somewhat narrow limits, a less tight form, exemplified in *Two Gentlemen*, held more promise of *Twelfth Night*. Yet in recognizing this, one ought also to recognize how much, in the *Comedy*, he has in fact found room for. Like the other early plays, it will always be judged by two standards. One, quite properly, is the standard set later by Shakespeare himself. But the play should also be appreciated for what it is in its own right: still actable as a hilarious yet balanced comedy, more pregnant than has perhaps been supposed with Shakespearian ideas. (pp. 70-1)

> *Harold Brooks, "Themes and Structure in 'The Comedy of Errors'," in Early Shakespeare, Stratford-Upon-Avon Studies, No. 3, John Russell Brown and Bernard Harris, General Editors. Edward Arnold (Publishers) Ltd, 1961, pp. 55-72.*

ERNEST WILLIAM TALBERT (essay date 1963)

The Comedy of Errors] shows the vitality that the academic tradition had for a beginning playwright. In [*Titus Andronicus*], this vitality is apparent in the frequent use of classical myth and legend, in the closeness of incidents to Seneca's *Thyestes*, and in the intermittent echoes of the manner and the curriculum of Elizabethan schools; but in the first of Shakespeare's comedies, the academic discipline of the age provides the design for the entire play, both as *The Comedy of Errors* is derived from classical drama and as its development is controlled by precepts about five-act structure. Furthermore, to the well-educated spectator, this comedy might seem to effect a pleasing Terentian variation upon a multiple Plautine source; for Shakespeare matches each Antipholus with a woman.

In contrast with *Titus Andronicus*, however, there are no situations and no lines in *The Comedy of Errors* that specifically indicate for uneducated spectators that they are encountering in the vulgar theater matter that could be found in the schools. Yet such a difference should not be emphasized, for a classical note appears intermittently throughout the comedy from the time that the duke and hapless Aegeon set the milieu and Shakespeare writes a *narratio* about two converging ships "making amain," "Of Corinth that, of Epidaurus this" [I. i. 92-3].

In addition, the mystery and glamour of the world from "farthest Greece" "through the bounds of Asia" comes to rest with increasing emphasis upon Ephesus, a town of "nimble jugglers that deceive the eye," "Dark-working sorcerers," "Soul-killing witches" [I. i. 132-33, I. ii. 98-100]. With memories of the New Testament, and with the Elizabethans' belief in possession and witchcraft, this aura of mystery would heighten at first the dramatic irony in what will become a comic repetitive pattern that achieves multiplicity primarily by heaping up incidents of the same mistaken identities. (p. 143)

The preceding remarks obviously lead to a closer examination of Shakespeare's artistry, and a suitable beginning can be made by noticing how the structure of this play is derived from concepts about the parts of a comedy as they were elucidated by Renaissance scholars. Getting the Syracusans into the house of Antipholus of Ephesus is the narrative focal point of protasis (Acts I and II). The development of the complications then follows in the epitasis (Acts III and IV). Its narrative focal point is the binding of "mad" Antipholus of Ephesus. Out of this last incident develops the forward movement to the catastrophe. By a detailed use of the *Andria* formula, Shakespeare controls his nonclassical multiplicity.

The appearances of Aegeon at the beginning and the end of the play also give unity to the drama. In contrast with the political emphasis of *Titus,* the fate of Aegeon is not woven into the latter part of the main action; and thus Shakespeare's use of that brief narrative appears to be an even more obvious structural device than does his development of opening and closing emphases in his tragedy. This feature of the artistry of *The Comedy of Errors* gives added point to similar developments in other plays by Shakespeare and seems to confirm the unifying intent of the initial and final situations in *Titus.* (pp. 143-44)

In this respect, however, attention should be given to the change in tone between the farcical emphasis of *The Comedy of Errors* and its serious framing device that involves a perilous circumstance. Too great an emphasis upon the latter might well mitigate the comedy of mistaken identity. Thus it is pertinent to note that Aegeon is not called to an audience's attention after the opening lines of Act II [i. 1-8]. Although the clock ticks in this drama, it ticks explicitly toward dinner, five o'clock, supper, and night—not explicitly toward the fact and hour of Aegeon's possible death. . . . With crowded action building repetitiously upon an audience's expectation of another mistake, the return to seriousness when a "five o'clock" finally is joined to a "melancholy" "place of death" must have been largely unexpected [V. i. 120-21]. The "great thing forgot" in a welter of puns and compounded confusion must have been only faintly liminal at the best. The skill of a beginning playwright is obvious, however. Without mitigating the comic for an audience, he has delimited a play neatly; and his apparent desire to achieve an impression of unity through the use of Aegeon is certainly justifiable in the light of the multiplicity from Act I through Act V.

By Shakespeare's treatment of his mistakes, the comic intent of the drama would be realized during performance, and his skill in developing this aspect of the multiplicity in Elizabethan drama is especially worthy of attention. (pp. 144-45)

When the duke attempts to straighten out the situation, the basic confusions centered about the Antipholi have been eight. . . . While each incident tends to become more complicated, the first stretches through the protasis, two confusions appear within the third act, and three within the fourth act, plus another sequence begun as the fourth act closes and continued as the last act opens. Obviously Shakespeare wished to increase progressively the confusion that he also has compounded by twin servants until its greatest complication would be developed in the fourth act and lead into the catastrophe.

An audience's anticipation of comic confusion would be realized fully, even as an awareness of the probability of its resolution might increase.

Especially at the end of Act IV and in Act V, Shakespeare also elaborates the basic dramatic irony by developing situations wherein one character's account of events is confirmed at first by another character but then denied by the same figure. The technique is anticipated briefly at the end of the second act, becomes especially noticeable as the third confusion in the fourth act is dramatized, appears at the beginning of the fifth act, and is developed fully as the duke attempts to discover the truth. As a consequence, this aspect of mistaken identity also is elaborated progressively as the confrontation of twin with twin approaches.

During this comic process, word-play is emphasized, although it is, in general, subordinate to the increasing confusion. Probably Shakespeare derived this aspect of the comic from his classical sources, although Elizabethans delighted in verbal ingenuity and in the way a sentence could be "but a chev'ril glove to a good wit." . . . Although the punning in *The Comedy of Errors* may seem barren, the drama certainly would capitalize upon the fact that in equivocating word-play the "toe of the peasant" came "near the heels of our courtier."

Although punning may be emphasized, Shakespeare also reflects the popular merriment of his era. As the protasis is developed, a shrewish wife appears. . . . Both before and after Dromio of Ephesus is on the stage, the speeches of Luciana and Adriana are developed so that the scene might appear to carry on an argument between patience and jealousy in a "pleasant manner dialogue wise." Adriana's shrewishness, which is here most noticeable during the sequence with Dromio, is then mitigated. . . . Nevertheless, these scenes are closer than is anything in Plautus' *Menaechmi* to the noisy representation of that female attribute in one of the most widespread of comic motifs. In the later scene, Shakespeare also develops all other dialogue so that it approaches the wit-combat. . . . In it, the comedian maintains a statement with jests against an interrogator who would resolve the theme to naught. In both of the conversations with the Dromios, Luciana begins to take part in the merriment (II, i, 50). This tendency will be emphasized in the succeeding scene (III, i), and thereby the witty maid of Shakespeare's later plays is adumbrated faintly.

When viewed against current Elizabethan merriment, this last scene is especially interesting. The central situation is taken from Plautus' *Amphitruo* and dramatizes the exclusion of a husband and a servant because a "husband" and a "servant" are already at home. The incident is preceded by sententious dialogue between Balthazar and Antipholus of Ephesus and is followed by a similar dialogue that continues Luciana's theme of patience. . . . In this contrasting setting, the episode from *Amphitruo* is developed so that overtones of the jig must have been noticeable to any spectator. Witness the rhyming and the anapestic and dipodic meter that accords with a rollicking situation:

> But, soft! my door is lock'd. Go bid them let us in.
>   *Dro. E.* Maude, Bridget, Marian, Cicely, Gillian, Ginn!
>   *Dro. S.* [*Within*] Mome, malt-horse, capon, coxcomb, idiot, patch!
> Either get thee from the door or sit down at the hatch.
>   [III. i. 30-3]

Including word-play, especially on "ass,"—matter picked up from Luciana's last speech with a Dromio—the episode is complicated progressively. With the line given Antipholus of Ephesus . . . , dialogue between Dromio of Ephesus and his twin is enlarged for three participants. With that given Luciana . . . , it is enlarged for four. Then it is enlarged for six, with Luciana excluded but Adriana, Balthazar, and Angelo included. . . . Finally, in five instances, choric comments on the humor of the situation are given to the doubled role for the principal comic actor. . . . Here certainly, although the basic *inventio* is classical, the comic manner is compatible with constant features of Elizabethan merriment. (pp. 145-47)

This reflection of current mirth, which had been anticipated in the second act, continues through the rest of the third act and into the fourth. (pp. 147-48)

Except for humor at the expense of Doctor Pinch, . . . and except for the abbess' turn of the tables to condemn Adriana's shrewishness . . . , in the latter part of the drama beatings and word-play again make up the principal incidental comedy. It is revealing, indeed, that after the confusions have been resolved and even as the play closes, instead of utilizing matter akin to Elizabethan merriment, Shakespeare extends once more his Plautine mistakings by having Dromio of Syracuse and Antipholus of Ephesus momentarily mistaken all over again. . . . Although the device is well conceived as a brief echo of previous confusions now solvable and as a lingering, repetitive trick for laughter, it indicates what the total artistry of the play also indicates, namely, that Shakespeare here relies heavily upon his classical sources. Even when the epitasis was being developed in the third act, word-play, which accords with Plautus' practice, was rampant; and in spite of what has just been noted, Tudor merriment is not developed as fully in this comedy as it had been in the earlier, and much simpler, academic comedies by Udall and by "Mr. S."

Nevertheless, within its academic skill and within its emphasis upon mistaken identities, the comic intent and touch of *The Comedy of Errors* is [sure and knowledgeable]. . . . (p. 148)

By Shakespeare's use of the story of Aegeon and Aemilia, moreover, the scope of his play becomes wider than that of his classical sources. In this respect, *The Comedy of Errors* shows a slight kinship with Lyly's comedies, which constantly develop a thematic interest. After all identities have been established, the duke forgives the ransom necessary to save Aegeon's life. This contrasts with the fact that when the play began, even though the duke's "soul" would "sue as advocate" for Aegeon, this ruler was convinced that "passed sentence" could not be recalled but to his "honour's great disparagement" [I. i. 145, 147-48]. To the reunion of a family and the consequent readjustment of the society of the playworld, Shakespeare adds the ruler's readjustment to retaliation in kind upon all merchants from Syracuse—an action the duke had considered essential because of his "laws," "crown," "oath," and "dignity" [I. i. 142-43].

One should do no more than note this oblique comment on the conduct of rulers. Just as the occasional didacticism of the play is subordinate to its laughter, so the duke's remission of the ransom is but part of the alignment of the play-world as it ought to be. This act of mercy, moreover, is followed by Shakespeare's final extension of his comic confusions. The thematic lines in *The Comedy of Errors* are interesting, nevertheless—especially the final ones. (p. 149)

> Ernest William Talbert, " 'Titus' and the Earliest Comedies," in his Elizabethan Drama and Shakespeare's Early Plays: An Essay in Historical Criti-

cism, *University of North Carolina Press, 1963, pp. 132-60.*

GWYN WILLIAMS   (essay date 1964)

[*Williams, like G. R. Elliott and Harold Brooks (see excerpts above, 1939 and 1961) focuses on the problem of personal identity in* Comedy. *He concludes that the characters' confusion almost turns the play into a tragedy. This essay was originally published in* A Review of English Literature *in 1964.*]

There is no need to insist on or to exemplify the way in which *The Comedy of Errors* has until recently been considered a farce. . . . A careful analysis of this play, however, shows that it might easily have worked out as a tragedy.

Shakespeare criticism has from Meres to the present day been misled by the pedantic division of drama into comedy or tragedy. (p. 29)

A further analysis of the play seems called for, so that the reason may emerge for Shakespeare's addition of the two Dromios to the material he took from Plautus. This in turn may throw some light on the famous incongruities.

It will then appear that Shakespeare's purpose in making this duplication was not merely to increase the comic effect by repetition of a situation on a lower plane, a device he frequently used in comedy; it was not even to enhance the fun which could be elicited from the mistaking of identities. It was to save the play as comedy, to ensure, in fact, that there should be any fun at all.

As Shakespeare conceived the situation of Antipholus of Syracuse, the young man's bewilderment might well have made him desperate and against the solemn background of Egeon's predicament any act of violence could have carried Antipholus on to tragedy. On the other hand, this might have been precipitated by Antipholus of Ephesus, the more violent of the twins. The two Dromios, however, not only provide the low humour, the back-chat, the healthy indecencies; not only is their predicament kept firmly comic, but the occasional contact with Dromio of Syracuse, the only person in the play (before the final recognition by Egeon) who recognizes him for what he is, clearly saves the sanity of Antipholus of Syracuse. . . .

Without the two Dromios the play would hardly have had any farcical elements, except for the late introduction of Dr. Pinch, who is apt to be blown up into a music-hall act, not entirely without justification from the text. Much less a farce, the play might not even have ended as a comedy. After all, Antipholus of Ephesus had much more to go on than Othello was to have. (p. 30)

[Throughout the play, the] confusion of identity has been painful and potentially dangerous for the two Antipholuses. The denial of identity has been most complete for Antipholus of Syracuse, but he is in a foreign country, in a city renowned for witchcraft and sorcery, and he clings to his reason by reminding himself of this fact. He can always get away and this he is always on the point of doing. For Antipholus of Ephesus the case is very different. He is in a town where he has been a person of importance for twenty years. Quite suddenly to have his orders disregarded by his servant, to be refused admission to his own house and to be denied by his own wife in broad daylight in the presence of others, to be arrested for debt and to be treated as a madman, all this makes a galling, infuriating experience for the Ephesian twin. He is

Act I. Scene i. The Antipholus twins separated as infants. By Francis Wheatley (1796). From the Art Collection of the Folger Shakespeare Library.

a more violent character than his brother and he might quite easily have killed his wife. (p. 34)

The Comedy of Errors is an early study in the nature of personal identity. How soon does one's conception of oneself, the belief in one's own identity, break down before lack of recognition on the part of others? How far do we need others in order to have an identity at all? Is one's identity entirely dependent on the personal and social links and bonds, the ties of family, love, friendship and civic duty? In order that these questions might be tackled without in this case leading to madness and violent death, as they do in *King Lear,* Shakespeare added the twin servants. To condemn this on the grounds of improbability, as Quiller-Couch does [see excerpt above], . . . is to apply a standard which would not occur to one in the theatre, which is not relevant to drama or to great art of any kind. . . . It is curiously naïve to require more verisimilitude on the stage than is to be observed in life. Or perhaps absurdly sophisticated. The two Dromios of course provide a lot of fun, but this is not their main function. Whilst more often than not they unwittingly add to the confusion, they do sometimes recognize their true masters and the analysis made above shows this to be the only link that Antipholus of Syracuse has with his remembered identity, with reality. The fact that his servant is also taken for another person extends the predicament outside himself and makes it possible for him to hold the theory of witchcraft as a cause, thereby saving his reason. Antipholus

of Ephesus, whom Shakespeare makes less interesting and sympathetic, is not given this comfort, for there is little consolation for him in the fact that his servant is also refused admission to their house. This simply confirms the treachery of his wife to his mind.

There is an interesting ambivalence in the use made of Luciana. At a moment when Antipholus of Syracuse's identity seems to be disintegrating and he is in danger of losing all links with his past life, his new love for Luciana promises the building of a new bond, a new relationship to compensate for the loss of the old. But since a new identity is also involved, which is only viable in relation to her, this would be an act of treachery to his past and to the identity to which he is still clinging. Luciana is therefore a siren and a witch seducing him from his true self.

What seems to have happened in Shakespeare's handling of the story is this. He found the predicament of Antipholus of Syracuse far from farcical, but rather an opportunity to probe into the nature of personal identity. To provide another view of the problem he added to the story the ordeal of Egeon and his denial by Antipholus and Dromio of Ephesus, who of course do not know him but whom the old man takes to be those of Syracuse. The function of Luciana has already been discussed. The incongruities which have been seen in the play may be said to arise from Shakespeare's failure to accommodate the elements that really interested him in the play to a dramatic formula from which he could not yet quite escape. But since his additions to the story must indicate the nature and direction of his interest we should surely pay more attention to the serious elements in the play. . . . (pp. 35-6)

This is not to read something into the play which is not there but to find conspicuously laid out in it a concern which is central to the writing and thought of our mid-twentieth century, the whole matter of the nature of personal identity, the study of which in *The Comedy of Errors* was kept by Shakespeare on a comic level only by the introduction of the two Dromios. (p. 36)

> Gwyn Williams, " 'The Comedy of Errors' Rescued from Tragedy," in his Person and Persona: Studies in Shakespeare, *University of Wales Press, 1981, pp. 29-36.*

E.M.W. TILLYARD   (essay date 1965)

As the content of the *Comedy of Errors* is far more varied than is often allowed, so is the vehicle. In the main, blank verse prevails; but in the scenes where the low characters figure there can occur prose, after the fashion of Lyly, or four-stress doggerel after the fashion of *Ralph Roister Doister* and of much comic stuff in the primitive Elizabethan drama. The scene of Antipholus of Ephesus along with his Dromio bringing the Goldsmith and Balthazar back home to dine and being barred out of his own house begins with Antipholus talking in blank verse and goes on to Dromio's replying in doggerel, with doggerel continuing throughout this broadly comic episode, till Balthazar turns to stately blank verse in his efforts to dissuade Antipholus from the scandal of breaking in at this busy time of day when half Ephesus may see him. The next scene, showing the other Antipholus courting Luciana and her attempts to reprove him, is in rhymed quatrains which suggest partly a sonneteering context, apt to the courting, and partly a sententious one, apt to Luciana's moralizing. Its rhetoric is perfectly fitting. But, if Shakespeare varies his blank verse with prose or other metres, that verse is more varied than it is reputed to be. True, it is largely end-stopped but within such a norm he can be extremely expressive; though only to an ear that is both attentive and unprejudiced. Take this example, from the opening scene, where Aegeon in calm and unhurried despair begins his tale of misfortunes:

> In Syracusa was I born, and wed
> Unto a woman, happy but for me,
> And by me, had not our hap been bad.
>
> [I. i. 36-8]

Here not only does the verse depart from its end-stopped context, but the third line is unusual and most expressive in rhythm. It must be read: Ánd by me, had not our háp been bád, with *had* bearing a lighter stress than the other stressed words. Read thus, it suggests an afterthought following a long pause and serves to set up that feeling of the speaker's taking his time which is essential if we are to prepare ourselves for a long narrative. (pp. 49-50)

Then there are the passages that, by sheer poetic eminence, are exceptions to the usual norm of metrical competence and aptitude. Take these few lines of soliloquy [I. ii. 33-8] spoken by Antipholus of Syracuse after the merchant has 'commended him to his own content' and left him:

> He that commends me to mine own content
> Commends me to the thing I cannot get.
> I to the world am like a drop of water
> That in the ocean seeks another drop,
> Who, falling there to find his fellow forth,
> Unseen, inquisitive, confounds himself.

Here there is not only the slow melancholy cadence that confirms the sentiment but the surprising collocation of *unseen* and *inquisitive*. Normally the inquisitive person does not worry whether he is seen or not. But Antipholus feels all the loneliness of a stranger at large in an alien city in which he is about to 'lose himself and wander up and down to view' it. Yet it is his duty to be inquisitive, and the surprising collocation of the two adjectives expresses both that duty and his despair of ever fulfilling it. It is pleasant irony that as soon as he finishes his soliloquy he should cease to be unseen through being accosted by Dromio of Ephesus and prevented for good from taking his intended lonely walk round the town. (pp. 51-2)

In sum, Shakespeare's rhetoric in the *Comedy of Errors* is good for something more than simple farce. (p. 52)

In itself the romantic framework [of the *Comedy of Errors*] has no profound significance. It does not make us feel that either Aegeon or his younger son has surmounted an ordeal through the successful issue of his long wanderings; nor are we drawn anywhere near the feelings . . . apt to the natural human routine of setting out from home, coping successfully with a task, and returning to relax. No, the romantic framework in itself does not go beyond arousing our simple feelings of wonder. Aegeon tells his story of marine adventures well enough, though not as well as Prospero was destined to tell his, and keeps our mind happily busy, yet not seriously extended, by its strangenesses. But in conjunction with the rest of the play the romantic framework weighs more. It helped to satisfy Shakespeare's craving for a rich subject-matter and in particular for an extreme complication of plot needing skilful disentanglement in the last scene. For the latter the added presence of Aegeon and Aemilia was essential. . . . On the face of it, to graft remote romance on a crudely farcical plot was to court

disaster; but it is precisely over such difficulties that Shakespeare was able to triumph. As it is, the fantasy of the romance leads easily to the fantastic shape which he caused the old farcical material to take on. When it comes to degrees of fantasy, there is nothing to choose between Aegeon and Aemilia tying one twin son and one twin slave to this end of the mast and the other son and slave to that, and Antipholus and Dromio of Syracuse going about Ephesus with drawn swords convinced that they are surrounded by witches and devils.

Here, in the play that may be his first comedy, we find Shakespeare following what was to prove his permanent instinct: never to forsake the norm of social life. However distant he may get from that norm into inhuman horror, or wild romance, or lyrical fancy, or mystical heights, he always reverts, if only for a short spell, to the ordinary world of men and to its problems of how they are to live together. . . . You may say that he was forced to do this to please his public; but he was also following his instincts, which insisted on connecting, on demonstrating the unity of all experience. It is an instinct that has made Shakespeare so widely loved and the lack of which explains the comparative neglect of Spenser. The extent to which he indulged that instinct in the *Comedy of Errors* has not been fully recognized.

Take the setting. . . . Ephesus itself is a small ordinary town where everyone knows everyone else's business, where merchants predominate, and where dinner is a serious matter. The last item suggests an illustration of how Shakespeare added normal life to farce. . . . [Antipholus of Ephesus] has indeed been laying up trouble for himself, for not only is he shockingly late for dinner but he is bringing with him two guests, probably unnotified and certainly offensive to the housewife as eating a dinner that through over-cooking does an injustice to her domestic competence. No wonder Antipholus tries to excuse himself on the ground that it was his solicitude for his wife's chain that made him late and seeks further safety by getting Angelo to father the lie. So, in their way, his sins are great, but how ludicrously different from the sins Adriana imputes to him. (pp. 53-5)

Then there are the characters. For the farcical effect, Shakespeare did not need to diversify them. Situations he must of course diversify even to extravagance; but the characters of those who find themselves in the situations hardly count. It would not matter if the two Antipholi were identical not only in appearance but in character. The primary need is that they should be subjected to a variety of accidents. But Shakespeare could not be content simply to satisfy this primary need; his nature insisted on his giving the two brothers different characters. The elder brother, Antipholus of Ephesus, is the more energetic, the more practical, the more choleric; the younger Antipholus is in comparison melancholy, sensitive, and of a livelier imagination. . . . The contrast between the brothers is not thrust on us but it is there in all clarity. . . . By distinguishing between the Antipholi in this way Shakespeare adds the comic to the purely farcical.

The parents, Aegeon and Aemilia, on the other hand, are hardly characterized at all. Aegeon is little more than a humour of aged melancholy; rightly, because, if fully animated, he would have introduced an element of tragedy that the farcical core could not have sustained. Aemilia, a symbol of severe and stately authority, but again hardly characterized, serves the play substantially. Her unexpected appearance . . . is one of the great moments of the play; an abrupt check to the wild fantasy that has been accumulating through the previous acts and a sign that the resolution is at hand. She is also the agent of the final drawing out of Adriana's character, when she 'betrays her to her own reproof'. Yet, though thus an agent of normal human action, she is hardly humanized herself.

It is on the two sisters that Shakespeare expends his power of making ordinary, living people. Bradley noted how few lines Cordelia speaks in comparison with the impression she leaves behind. To a smaller extent this is true of Adriana and Luciana, to whose vivid characterization justice has hardly been done and whose natures, I venture to think, have not been properly understood. (pp. 56-8)

It is usual to describe Adriana as a jealous woman and to leave it at that. But this is too simple a description and indeed it heads us off the truth. It must be granted that she keeps on professing jealousy but her nature need not contain an excess of it. The root of her trouble is stupidity, and lack of reflection and restraint that makes her her own worst enemy. . . . She is also good-natured at bottom and quick to forgive. All these qualities save the last are evident in the scene (II, i) in which she first appears. Here she is shown in distraction because her husband is late for dinner and Dromio, sent to fetch him, has not returned. And Luciana's sensible advice—

> Perhaps some merchant hath invited him,
> And from the mart he's somewhere gone to dinner;
> Good sister, let us dine, and never fret.
>
> [II. i. 4-6]

makes no impression on her. Finally, when Dromio returns and reports his supposed master's strange behaviour, she loses all restraint and acts the greatly injured wife. Sense in the shape of Luciana now reproves Sensibility only to receive (as Jane Austen caused her Elinor to receive) the accusation of emotional coldness: 'Unfeeling fools can with such wrongs dispense' [II. i. 103]. The scene ends with Luciana's exclamation, 'How many fond fools serve mad jealousy!' She knows that stupidity is the root of the trouble. In the next scene, when the wrong Antipholus appears, Adriana lets him have the torrent of her complaint, once the supposed husband shows himself willing to enter the house for dinner, she cools rapidly:

> Come, come, no longer will I be a fool,
> To put the finger in the eye and weep,
> Whilst man and master laughs my woes to scorn.
> Come, sir, to dinner. Dromio, keep the gate.
> Husband, I'll dine above with you today,
> And shrive you of a thousand idle pranks.
>
> [II. ii. 203-08]

Alas, her resolution not to be a fool does not hold, and she has to pay the price. There is pathos in her relations with her husband; for when it comes to the point he trusts her, and we never doubt that in all practical matters she was an excellent wife. (pp. 58-9)

The critics have gone wrong over Luciana even more than over Adriana, and with less excuse. C. H. Herford in his introduction to the play in the Eversley edition writes, 'Luciana brings us altogether into the atmosphere of lyric love'; Charlton calls her 'a gentle-hearted girl'; and Pettet talks of her 'romantic love story'. *Good-natured,* yes, witness the forbearing and tactful way she deals with her maddening sister; but *gentle-hearted,* no: that swerves in the wrong direction, for Luciana is essentially resolute in character. And as for *lyrical* and *romantic,* these epithets are quite alien to this shrewd and practical young woman. Luciana is what D. H. Lawrence called a

'hen-sure' woman; and nothing could be less romantic than her advice to Antipholus of Syracuse, when, mistaken for her brother-in-law, he makes love to her. It is pure wordly wisdom, tempered by a loyal solicitude for her sister's happiness. . . . Unlike her blundering sister, Luciana is observant. In her loyalty she tells Adriana of Antipholus's advances (IV, ii). Though shocked at their impropriety, she takes note of their nature and admits that, addressed to the proper person, they would be in very good style. In another place her observant nature is conveyed with a subtlety that few readers would expect of Shakespeare in so early a play. In II, ii, Adriana and Luciana, mistaking one Antipholus for the other, try to persuade Antipholus of Syracuse to enter the house and eat the long-postponed dinner. Utterly bewildered, he allowed himself to be persuaded and tells us so in an aside. Whereupon Luciana cries out, 'Dromio, go bid the servants spread for dinner.' She has heard nothing, but she has been watching Antipholus's face and sees that he has changed his former mind. (pp. 61-2)

Not only did Shakespeare diversify farce by adding romance and comedy but he added delight and meaning to his farce by sharpening its elements and by taking farce beyond itself.

First, he subjects his brothers to different trials and adjusts their states of mind accordingly. Antipholus of Ephesus suffers a number of indignities and takes them seriously, at their face value. To an actor commanding a wide range of grim facial expressions he offers a superb part. And incongruity between the grim expression and the ultimately trivial nature of the things that cause it will be the main and most sufficient cause for laughter. The case of Antipholus of Syracuse is different and has not been fully understood. This Antipholus does not suffer indignities. On the contrary he is fortune's favourite; but he cannot relish her favours because he thinks they are illusory. The final states of mind of the brothers are alike in being strange, but in every other way they are sharply, and of course deliberately, contrasted. (pp. 62-3)

In remembering the intellectual charm of the *Comedy of Errors* we must not forget its sheer power of diverting a mixed audience and taking it out of itself. Granted that by some device the simplest among the spectators could know at once which Antipholus or Dromio was on the stage, the play progresses successfully from one hilarity to an ever wilder one, fulfilling superbly the basic function of a farce.

When an example of a lesser literary kind reaches a certain pitch of excellence it is apt to transcend the kind to which it belongs. And, if we are to perceive what the *Comedy of Errors* succeeds at last in doing, we should do well to consider high specimens of farce. Take first Chaucer's *Miller's Tale.* . . . I have pleaded in my *Poetry Direct and Oblique* that in the *Miller's Tale,* and especially at the supreme moment, Chaucer touches an area of the mind outside the area to which farce belongs. But Chaucer's tale is fairly simple, and I refer to it for the above general reason and not because it is much like the *Comedy of Errors.* Nearer to the *Comedy* are some of René Clair's films, particularly *Belles de Nuit* and the early films (*Les Deux Timides* for instance) founded on farces of Labiche. Like the usual run of farces, these begin in ordinary life; they then turn ordinary life into something fantastic and remote from life; and then somehow they seem to rejoin life, but at a different point, so that, instead of making us feel what an amusing holiday from life this is, they cause us to exclaim, 'Oh but life after all can be as strange as all this.' (pp. 69-70)

In transcending mere farce as I think it to do, the *Comedy of Errors* raises the question of what is the norm of reality. One need not suppose that, at any rate at this stage of his career, Shakespeare had consciously formulated any opinions on such matters; but it is certain that he was aware of many modes or standards of experience well before he came to write his play; and what literary kind more than farce, with its congenital bent to the fantastic, was likely to express that awareness? I have said what I think to be the culminating moment of the play: namely when Antipholus of Syracuse and his Dromio enter with drawn swords, and Adriana and the rest think them her husband and servant broken loose and fly in terror. Both parties suffer from an extremity of illusion, one as it were ratifying the illusion of the other. Moreover the states of mind have been arrived at by gradual and entirely logical processes. And we conclude that the state of violence presented has somehow acquired its own solidity and thus stands for a way of experiencing, alternative to the way common in the plain working world.

On the whole things go right in the *Comedy of Errors*. . . . Ignoring the blemishes, I find that the play is about as good as the verse allows. The verse has its limits and probably would not have reached to some subtle development of character, for instance. But it reaches to the things attempted; and the play has not been rated a major success only because it is Shakespeare's. (pp. 71-2)

> *E.M.W. Tillyard, "'The Comedy of Errors'," in his* Shakespeare's Early Comedies, *Chatto & Windus, 1965, pp. 46-72.*

MARION BODWELL SMITH   (essay date 1966)

The Comedy of Errors, generally regarded as an early play, is a farce, hilariously effective when produced with pace and verve. Yet its rhetorical style and careful observance of the unities of time and place are as "academic" as its source, the *Menaechmi* of Plautus. . . . [The] successive episodes of mistaken identity follow an almost mathematical pattern of permutations and combinations between the inner group of four, consisting of the twins, and an outer group of six, consisting of Balthazar, Angelo the goldsmith, the First Merchant, Adriana, Luciana, and the Courtesan, until, in the final scenes, the complications so proliferate as to include the minor characters of the main plot and those concerned primarily with the frame story. It is all as carefully worked out as the line-endings of a sestina, as is a somewhat less complicated pattern in *Love's Labour's Lost*. (p. 21)

In style, *The Comedy of Errors* is a microcosm of early Shakespeare: the frequent rhymes, the end-stopped lines, the quibbles, the rhetorical dialectic of question and answer in a single speech, the oxymoron and stichomythia, the echoes of Kyd and Marlowe, all are there. It is also a compendium of devices and situations Shakespeare used in other plays, early and late. The twins, the circumstances of the shipwreck, the kindly merchant, the comic exorcist, and the visitor who is convinced that the town is bewitched, appear in *Twelfth Night*, the turbulent wife lessoned in *The Taming of the Shrew*, the irrevocable law not enforced in *A Midsummer Night's Dream*. . . . The doubling of pairs occurs in *Love's Labour's Lost*, which has four pairs of lovers instead of the customary two and shapes its central action on the patterns of a dance. The same device is used in *As You Like It* to illustrate four varieties of love. It is not surprising, therefore, that we can find also in *The Comedy of Errors* many characteristic Shakespearean dualities other than the numerical.

Since his plot gives almost unlimited opportunity for the confusions, ironies of situation, and *double-entendres* which can be derived from mistaken identity, Shakespeare emphasizes here the comic aspects of appearance at variance with reality. It is a theme which he explores and re-explores in his Sonnets, Histories, Comedies, and Tragedies, as long as he can hold a pen. In *The Comedy of Errors* the two Antipholi resemble each other in personality as well as in appearance, but only outwardly are they identical. Both, in the tradition of Latin comedy, are choleric towards their servants, but in other respects Antipholus of Syracuse is the milder and less rash, the more courteous and considerate of the two. Where Antipholus of Ephesus meets obstacles head-on and is with difficulty persuaded by his friends to make the best of a bad situation, Antipholus of Syracuse is more inclined to go with the tide rather than fight against it.

To his two sets of twins Shakespeare adds a pair of sisters, and between them the differences are more marked. Indeed their two personalities are almost opposites, as is frequently the case with Shakespeare's siblings—honest Don Pedro and villainous Don John in *Much Ado About Nothing*, Edgar and Edmund, Isabella and Claudio, Antonio and Prospero, Katherine and Bianca, vacillating Clarence and single-purposed Richard, honourable Prince Hal and dishonourable Prince John, Cordelia and her sisters, Hamlet's father and Claudius, Oliver and Orlando in *As You Like It*, are some of them. "Good wombs have borne bad sons." But why? The paradoxical workings of nature by which the same elements of inheritance can be so variously compounded as to produce opposite characteristics in brothers and sisters are, for Shakespeare, one of the persistently fascinating anomalies of existence, and often a well-spring of tragedy.

But since this is a comedy, the characters of Adriana and Luciana complement rather than conflict with each other. Luciana's mildness balances Adriana's shrewishness, her submissiveness Adriana's jealous resentment of her husband's authority and liberty. Both, were they not mitigated by other qualities, might be seriously destructive, as such extreme characteristics are in other plays. But again as is appropriate to comedy, the attitudes of the sisters move closer together rather than farther apart, and the rapprochement is made easier by the fact that neither Adriana's curstness nor Luciana's mildness is as extreme as it professes to be. . . . The conflict between husband and wife ends in the triumph of order: Adriana has learned that "to obey is best" and has admitted her error. But it is not alone Luciana's scolding of the wrong Antipholus which suggests that Adriana is not solely at fault. That her husband is also culpable is indicated by the subtle and characteristically Shakespearean device of a buried biblical allusion in his complaint to the Duke:

> Justice, sweet Prince, against that woman there!
> She whom thou gav'st to me to be my wife,
> That hath abused and dishonoured me
> Even in the strength and height of injury.
> [V. i. 197-200]

In Shakespeare's plays the cry for "Justice!" is seldom heard without the accompaniment of some sort of irony.

Other characteristic dualities are the interweaving of the stories of two generations and the mingling of tones and genres. In setting his farce in a frame of romance Shakespeare departs from the New Comedy norm in which the conflict is between generations. His fathers are often enough, like Egeus in *A*

Midsummer Night's Dream, ''full of vexation'' against their children, and that vexation is usually unjustified, but he seldom bases the main action of a comedy on their opposition to the wishes of the young people. For Shakespeare the conflict of parents and children is the material of tragedy, and he reserves it as serious plot-motivation for tragic or tragi-comic action.

The declaration of Antipholus of Syracuse's love for Luciana adds a lyric note to the predominantly farcical main plot, and the romance frame is not entirely without touches of satire, or at least tongue-in-cheek burlesque. If the Duke's pompous exposition of the law which condemns Aegeon is not sufficient warning not to take too seriously the threat which surrounds the central comedy, what follows it makes the signposting unmistakable. Can Aegeon's reply,

> Yet this my comfort: when your words are done,
> My woes end likewise with the evening sun.
>
> [I. i. 26-7]

be taken otherwise than as indicating that the Duke's platitudes are among the woes? The gently ironic tone of the scene is underlined when, immediately afterwards, Aegeon takes no less than 105 lines (in three ''fits'') to speak his ''griefs unspeakable.'' In reply, the Duke demonstrates that in Ephesus as elsewhere the public scale of values sets legality above justice and official dignity above individual life by stating that though ''his soul would sue as advocate'' for Aegeon he cannot recall the sentence passed against him, ''but to our honour's great disparagement.'' . . . In his ''natural'' search for his lost son Aegeon has innocently violated an ''unnatural'' commercial blockade. The penalty is the forfeit of his life or a fine of a thousand marks. The satire is not stressed, but here we have another of Shakespeare's favourite themes of opposition, the disparity between law and justice, between the fertility of life and the sterility of ''barren metal.'' And what sort of ''honour'' is it that is founded on injustice?

The Duke is an ambiguous character, a well-meaning but not too effective representative of public order. He knows that there is no fault in the man, but considerations of legality and public policy tie his hands, as they did those of Pilate. (pp. 21-4)

> Marion Bodwell Smith, ''Two Distincts, Division None: The Nature of Shakespeare's Dualities,'' in her Dualities in Shakespeare, *University of Toronto Press,* 1966, pp. 19-52.

BLAZE ODELL BONAZZA (essay date 1966)

[*Bonazza analyses the dramatic structure of* The Comedy of Errors, *treating ''not only plot mechanics'' but also ''the incidents and their design, the use of characterization to further plot, the use of language to create character and tone, and the use of language and setting to create a motivating atmosphere.'' Bonazza posits that the play is an organic whole, and asserts that Shakespeare was working toward an ''A-B-C-D'' plot structure in which the A plot is the frame story or enveloping action; the B plot is the romantic love story which the A plot surrounds; the C plot incorporates the clowns, forming a parody and tonal contrast to the B plot; and the D plot provides atmosphere and makes possible the events of the B plot. Bonazza shows that by laying greater stress on characterization Shakespeare created a play with more humane qualities than are found in his Plautine source. This final point is also voiced by Derek Traversi (1960).*]

A structural analysis of [*The Comedy of Errors*] shows that the dramatist arranges his comic situations skillfully so that they lead up to a climactic effect. Allardyce Nicoll feels that at first

glance one might be tempted to pass the play with only an indulgent comment—that it is merely a farce with no direct bearing on the later comedies—but that a closer examination will show that it clearly outlines the greater comedies of the future.

Although this play uses only two elements of the A-B-C-D plot structure and, then, not in a multi-level fashion, it does exhibit a relation with the later, finished structure that first appears in *A Midsummer Night's Dream* in its use of tonal contrast. Shakespeare achieves this through the use of an enveloping action, or plot A, which contrasts a pathetic note with the farcical tone of the comedy of errors of the B plot. This may seem a trivial movement in the direction of the full tonally contrasting, multi-level formula, but it is an essential part of the pattern that develops later. Contrast in tones is as important an element as coterminous action in the fully evolved A-B-C-D pattern. In this early effort Shakespeare uses this important device of combining tones, thereby creating a harmonious blend instead of the single note he found in his sources. (p. 17)

[The characters of Plautus' *Menaechmi* are] coarse and repellent. They are interesting not in themselves but only as types. Mulier is the customary strident-voiced shrew; Peniculus is the conventional unscrupulous parasite motivated solely by greed and spite. The courtesan is the materialistic, grasping female representative of her profession; the father is the stereotyped comically ineffectual *senex iratus;* the doctor, the usual quack anxious to render the diagnosis necessary to earn a quick fee.

This facile, stock characterization is to be expected since Plautus' play makes no pretence of being anything other than pure farce, i.e., that type of comedy in which the action is unrelated to character or stems from characters so superficial or stereotyped that they are not engaged in any genuinely voluntary activity but are at the mercy of events, mostly coincidental. Since the heart of the action depends on the absence of dissimilarities between the Menaechmi, no attempt is made to delineate character differences by thought, word, or action. We have human identity reduced to the lowest possible level, that of physical appearance, and we must assume that human beings are somewhat less than human. . . . (pp. 19-20)

Since farce is situation-centered and the characters are primarily manipulatable puppets, there is no real focus of attention on the action of any one or two individuals. It is the state of confusion resulting from the improbable and extravagant action that attracts our attention and we find it difficult to identify with the weakly drawn characters. We do not care so much about what happens to a particular character as we do about the resolution of the absurd situation.

Along with the improbability and extravagance, the rapidity of the action affects our ability to identify with the characters. Many of Plautus' scenes are so short as to allow only an entrance, a few words, and then a hasty exit. . . . It is evident that this rapid shifting from one character to the other minimizes individuals and emphasizes situation.

But pure farce is not interested in delineating subtleties of character; its sole aim is to excite laughter, laughter of the raucous variety—''the non-reflective guffaw''. (p. 20)

Shakespeare attempts to shift the emphasis from situation to character by setting the mechanical elements of farce within a larger, more humane framework and by trying to create more subtle characters. (pp. 20-1)

Shakespeare has divided the dramatic emphasis between situation and story, with the latter receiving less emphasis. The classical play had revolved entirely about situation and incident and the tone was hard and cynical, the series of callous chicaneries of the various characters being capped by Sosicles' suggestion to Menaechmus that he abandon his wife, sell his possessions, and accompany him to Syracuse. By placing the events of the prologue within the play itself, as had already been done in Italian versions such as *I Simillimi* of Trissino and *La Moglie* of Cecchi, Shakespeare is following the tendency of medieval romance to tell a story from the very beginning to the end and, by so doing, he also changes the tone from the coarse to the pathetic. The playwright, even in a work derived primarily from classical sources, refuses to be cramped by the restraint imposed by the Greco-Roman stage conventions: instead of being confined into the one form of complicated situation resolving, he chooses to follow the involved story line of romance. . . . Thus in this early work we can already see the pattern of Shakespearean comedy evolving, i.e., the amalgamation of incident with romance or story tinged with the marvelous. Here the full story for its own sake is incorporated into the dramatic situation, made part of it, and made to bear on the central incidents within the play. It is easy to notice how the strong influence of romance, as seen in the element borrowed from Apollonius of Tyre, has swept aside all limitations of the classical dramatic form. Now there is no longer any obstacle to the intermingling of comic and tragic tones.

In Plautus all of the action in the play is contained within a single plot with the beginning of the story being relegated to a tongue-in-cheek prologue and the ending dismissed with a flippant proposal. In Shakespeare four separate but related plots, i.e., the arrest, scheduled execution, and salvation of Aegeon; the misunderstandings and resolution of the mistaken identities; the estrangement by jealousy and the reconciliation by love of the husband and wife; and the wooing and winning of Luciana, are interwoven into a single main plot. The peril and release of Aegeon is at the core of the serious action; it impinges on the comic action, resolves it, and is resolved in turn by it. The jealousy of Adriana leads to the estrangement from her husband and this in turn contributes to the complications of the comic action. The resolution of the comic action leads to a happy culmination of the embryonic love plot involving Antipholus of Syracuse and Luciana. The various elements of the plot are not all adequately developed and the pattern remains relatively simple, but the effort shows the future bent of the playwright's mind and offers promise of a later harmonious complexity of plot construction. (pp. 23-4)

In the first scene the playwright is concerned with laying the groundwork of the enveloping or serious action, i.e., the pathetic plight of Aegeon, and to indicate the basis of the internal or comic action, i.e., the mistaken identities. This two-fold objective is accomplished through a slender trial scene consisting mostly of exposition and stage setting for the final dual resolution. Aegeon is the first to speak and the audience is immediately informed that he is being sentenced to death. Since this is a comedy, the audience by convention realizes and expects that somehow this threatened execution will be averted no matter how inevitable it might seem on first acquaintance with the situation. The audience takes it for granted that the dramatist will sow the seeds of the eventual solution to the problem in the first scene. By doing so, the playwright provides his audience with the pleasure of anticipating how the happy resolution can be effected.

The Duke's first words inform us that Aegeon is a merchant of Syracuse hence subject to death for being apprehended in Ephesus. . . . The Duke is here represented as being reluctantly forced to carry out the stern mandate even though by nature he is a merciful man. In this way the mood appropriate to the breaking of the law is established. . . . The audience is secure in the belief that somehow the fine will be paid and the unfortunate old man rescued from death.

The next thing for the playwright to establish is when and how this will happen. With Aegeon's words, ''My woes end likewise with the evening sun,'' . . . the audience is made aware of the time limitations that will govern the ensuing action. . . . [The Duke's] gratuitous questioning provides the entré for a long expository section which has no legal bearing on the trial or the penalty but which is dramatically necessary to set the stage for the internal action and to prepare the audience for the comedy of errors arising from the improbable existence of two sets of identical twins whose destinies are closely woven together. . . . The main purpose of this portion of the exposition is, of course, to convince the audience that since not even the parents could tell the children apart, all kinds of confusion can be expected to result from this remarkable similarity.

Furthermore, the birth of another set of twins in the same inn on the same night that Aegeon's sons are born forewarns the audience to suspend the laws of probability for the sake of entertainment and to be willing to expect all sorts of coincidences based on the original one. (pp. 24-6)

The Duke is an exhaustive prober—all for the benefit of the audience. The dramatist uses him as a stalking-horse to elicit the full details of the enveloping action and to provide the material for the credibility of the forthcoming internal action.

Of the total 159 lines in the scene, 104 are spoken by Aegeon. The Duke's remarks are only to elicit background material of the doomed man's life, to provide further exposition of his own, and to prefigure the solution to the execution complication in the alternative which he offers. . . . [The] audience has been rendered receptive to coincidence and, knowing of the existence of the twin sons, is prepared for the old man's liberation and happy reunion with his family. When the Duke says,

> Therefore, merchant, I'll limit thee this day
> To seek thy life by beneficial help.
> Try all the friends thou hast in Ephesus;
> Beg thou, or borrow, to make up the sum
> And live; if no, then thou art doom'd to die.
>   [I. i. 150-54]

the audience is assured that justice will somehow be tempered with mercy. It realizes that as a stranger Aegeon has no friends in Ephesus and if he is to be saved, as surely he must be since this is a comedy, he must encounter his wandering son, the long-lost son, his wife, or most happily and most likely all of them. Since all of them escaped death in the shipwreck, reunion is demanded by convention. . . . The inevitable must be postponed until the internal action has been drained of its last comic possibility. When this occurs, the internal action will terminate in a juncture with the enveloping action centered about Aegeon's plight and impending execution at sunset.

Antipholus of Syracuse and his Dromio are the first to be introduced in the internal action of the play. Their presence affords an immediate opportunity to tie the enveloping action in with the internal action. Here the audience sees the twin the father had reared until he had left in search of his brother some seven years previously. To forestall the question of why he too is not apprehended as an enemy alien, the playwright uses the device of having the First Merchant warn him of Aegeon's fate and of the necessity for pretending to be from Epidamnum rather than from the hostile city of Syracuse. (pp. 26-8)

With Antipholus of Syracuse's first speech the internal action is set into motion. To provide the audience with its first view of one of the pairs of twins, Dromio of Syracuse must be sent from the stage on some pretext or other so that his double can appear and the audience thus see Aegeon's account of identical twins come to life before its eyes. To effect this necessary departure Dromio is given specific instructions, "and stay there, Dromio, till I come to thee" [I. ii. 10]. This serves as a signal to the audience: by this caution it knows that any Dromio reappearing shortly on the stage will be the twin from Ephesus. . . . The audience is required to accept the stipulation that the two masters never meet throughout the internal action. Coincidence is to operate only to bring master and slave together, never master and master or slave and slave. On Dromio's departure his master remarks on his trustworthiness and his tendency to practical joking. This rather unsubtle bit of characterization is introduced to prepare for the credibility of the later confusion of identities. At this point it is important that the First Merchant be provided with an excuse to leave the stage, otherwise he would be present to testify to the true identity of Antipholus of Syracuse and the comic conflict would not materialize. In a sense, the comic hero must be isolated to meet his fate.

In Antipholus' short soliloquy, "I to the world am like a drop of water / That in the ocean seeks another drop", the audience is informed through irony and metaphor that its expectations will be realized, that this one drop of water will meet its counterpart as unlikely as it may seem on the surface. In fact, this is the theme of the entire comedy: strange and comical events will transpire once unrestrained coincidence has its sway, but eventually all will turn out well. (pp. 28-9)

[The] characters in their attempts to act in accordance with commonsense will experience repeated reversals of intention and of fortune. Repetition will be the keynote of the comic action. Not just one or two but all of the characters will experience one or more reversals. The playwright will utilize his *donné*, the physical repetition of individuals, of master and slave, to produce repetition of incident. The audience has seen the first reversal of intention in the slave's invitation to the wrong master and the first reversal of fortune in the beating he receives. It can now anticipate a series of similar comic reversals, comic because of their repetitiveness and also because of their intrinsic variance from commonsense expectations. Although the basic element is the repetition of reversals, this principle of action must obviously be used with variations. These can be achieved by a shifting of scenes and characters so that the force of the original improbability draws all the characters into a widening circle of involvement. The audience as the arbiter of commonsense is moved to laughter by the thwarted anticipations and annoying frustrations of the characters as they undergo the various reversals. Laughter results from the fact that the violation of commonsense expectations leads not to disaster but only to temporary discomfiture and distress. (pp. 29-30)

Before the happy denouement, however, the comedy comes near pathos in Aegeon's fruitless appeal for aid to Antipholus of Ephesus. This is the one confusion of identities in the play that is not comic. Instead of being made the butt of the comedy

the old man is made a pathetic figure. The pathos is produced by Aegeon's acceptance of his son's denial as an understandable result of the changes that care and time have wrought in his visage. Since he does not protest, there is no comic conflict. The tension and tone are no longer comic and the playwright relieves it immediately. At this brush with pathos, the abbess appears with Antipholus of Syracuse and Dromio and all is instantly clear. With the resolution of the internal action with its series of mistaken identities, the enveloping action is also resolved. (pp. 40-1)

With this happy, sentimental outcome we can see that the playwright has turned the material of Plautine farce to a new use. In Plautus the *cognitio* had no significance beyond offering a resolution to the comic entanglement. In Shakespeare the *cognitio*, set as it is against a pathetic-romantic background, serves not only to bring clarity into the comic confusion but also to bring happiness into the somber situation. A whole series of reversals of intention on the comic level is contained within the framework of one serious reversal of fortune—the change from a death penalty to a last minute reprieve and happy family reunion. We can see that the playwright has added the tone of pathos to the ludicrous one of farce. It is an elementary harmony that he achieves here but this tentative mixture of antithetical tones represents a successful experiment. Comic and pathetic tones can be combined in one play to the enhancement of both. Shakespeare has learned that he does not have to be content with a pure specimen of either the comic or the serious. (p. 41)

The attempt to correlate the comic reversals with character is a further step away from Plautine farce in which the reversals are almost exclusively the result of coincidence. Shakespeare attempts to differentiate the characters of the two masters, the two slaves, the women, and even of some of the lesser characters so that the reversals will seem to emanate from character instead of from mere coincidence. (p. 42)

The most significant attempt to relate the reversals with character is made in the depiction of Adriana. From the totally unattractive Mulier of Plautus she is changed into a jealous, possessive woman genuinely in love with her husband, capable of reformation, and worthy of reconciliation. Luciana's reversal of fortune, i.e., from virginity to marriage is brought about by feminity, honesty, and loyalty. She confides all to her sister, and this frankness ironically leads to a happy resolution in which she finds a husband.

In this early effort Shakespeare is primarily concerned with the mechanics of plot, especially with the manipulation and multiplication of ironic reversals. As his main agencies of plot movement, he uses a motivating circumstance outside the main action—the shipwreck—and multiple accident and coincidence within the main plot, centering about two sets of identical twins whose destinies are intertwined. The central farcical tone is contrasted with a tone of pathos by wrapping the main incidents in an enveloping action involving the impending execution of Aegeon, the destitute old father of the twins in search for his long-lost wife and sons. This pathetic counter-tone lends significance to the denouement beyond that of simple comic *anagnorisis*. In this attempt to master the structuring and climactic arrangement of ironic reversals and to balance contrasting tones, beauty of language is neglected except for a few felicitous touches. Although characterization is elementary, he does experiment with the creation of the romantic heroine. His success here is very limited, but the attempt indicates that he is experimenting with character as a force to initiate and sustain the desired comic or serious action. (pp. 42-3)

*Blaze Odell Bonazza, "'The Comedy of Errors',"
in his* Shakespeare's Early Comedies: A Structural
Analysis, *Mouton & Co., Publishers, 1966, pp. 16-
43.*

PETER G. PHIALAS   (essay date 1966)

[*Contributing to the discussion of possible sources for* Comedy, *Phialas suggests that Shakespeare might have drawn the story of Egeon and Emilia from the* Captivi *of Plautus.*]

The Comedy of Errors, though not belonging to the [romantic] species of comedy . . . , nevertheless contains certain features of structure and theme, and even tone, which anticipate significant elements of Shakespeare's romantic comedies. As everyone knows, the play is an adaptation of Plautus' *Menaechmi,* but Shakespeare made changes and additions to the story which indicate clearly the way he was to follow in fashioning the special comic form which is the subject of this study. Perhaps the most significant over-all innovation is the presence of sentiment in Shakespeare's play, something utterly lacking in the Plautine source. Furthermore, *The Comedy of Errors* contains here and there a note of reflectiveness and serious purpose, a concern, however brief, with something deeper than accident and the surface show of things. (pp. 3-4)

Act V. Scene i. Antipholus of Syracuse, Aemilia, Luciana, Adriana, Egion, the Duke. By T. Stothard (1802). From the Art Collection of the Folger Shakespeare Library.

Though generally believed to be one of Shakespeare's early plays, *The Comedy of Errors* exhibits an astonishing command of his materials by the dramatist, a remarkable control of detail in adjusting the various themes to structure. (p. 5)

The Comedy of Errors, it is clear, stands apart from the comedies which followed it, differing from them in many significant ways. It is, the Arden editor writes, "a special kind of play, not easily compared with the other exploratory works." In particular, its plot, in part because of the story, lacks the complexity of the later plays. In his study of Shakespeare's comedies Bertrand Evans writes that "in his first comedy Shakespeare came nearer than ever afterward to placing his whole reliance upon an arrangement of discrepant awarenesses" [see excerpt above, 1960]. He finds the play unique in that it is built upon a single secret known only to the audience. (p. 6)

In thematic content, in structure, and in spirit, *The Comedy of Errors* is in the main a Roman, a Plautine comedy. And although there is another side of it created by the addition of two so-called romance themes, one of them may go back to a Roman original. Certainly the love-making of Antipholus of Syracuse is anything but Roman: it is in every detail a Shakespearean invention. But the other addition, the sentimental story of Egeon and Emilia which has been called romantic, may have been suggested by Plautus after all. (pp. 6-7)

[The] name Egeon and part of his story may have been suggested by yet another Plautine play, the *Captivi,* which in some important ways differs from Plautus' other comedies. In the *Captivi* the father's name is Hegio, which Shakespeare could easily have turned to Egeon, although of course the exact form of the name may have come from the legends of Theseus and his father Aegeus, King of Athens. Hegio, a wealthy Aetolian citizen, has lost two sons, one stolen while a child by a faithless servant, the other a war prisoner of the Eleans, with whom Aetolia is at present in conflict. In search of a way to recover the son held by the enemy, Hegio purchases a number of Eleans captured by his own country, hoping that among them he might find someone he can exchange for his own imprisoned son. Among the Elean prisoners is the aristocratic Philocrates attended by a devoted servant, who happens to be Tyndarus, Hegio's stolen son. After a near-tragic complication the play ends happily through the revelation of Tyndarus' identity. But the action creates a mood which sets the play apart from Plautus' other comedies. . . . [The *Captivi*] is a play of sentiment, of idealism, of powerful emotion. In order to enable his master Philocrates to escape slavery, Tyndarus exchanges identities with him, which in turn causes him to be put at hard labor in the stone quarries by his own father. In addition to sentiment generated by the devotion and friendship of the *captivi,* the play dramatizes extremes of passion, first in Hegio's violent indignation when he discovers that the two prisoners have duped him by exchanging identities, and second in the clash of emotions within Hegio when it is revealed that one of the prisoners is his own long-lost son. The passage describing Hegio's pain and joy at the moment of recognition is one that would have appealed strongly to Shakespeare. (pp. 7-8)

Another feature of the *Captivi* which would have impressed a young dramatist is the play's structure, which Lessing called the best in existence. Aristotle, had he had such a play at hand, would have given high praise to the unfolding of the action which leads, step by step, to the recognition and dénouement.

In the *Captivi* Shakespeare would have found much to interest him, especially the accommodation of sentiment as well as conflict and powerful emotion in a comic structure. It is often argued that by bringing to life the father of the twins, who in *Menaechmi* dies before the play opens, Shakespeare rounds off the action with an unclassical picture of family reunion and reconciliation. Although it is true that family reunion and reconciliation is very common in the prose romances and their derivatives, the theme is not altogether nonclassical. It is certainly a major element of the *Captivi*. And in the force of tearful happiness, of sheer emotion generated by such reunion, no comedy of Shakespeare's surpasses the closing scene of the *Captivi*. . . . What Shakespeare tried to do in *The Comedy of Errors* and in later comedies was to combine [farce and tragicomedy], to frame the farcical and boisterous action dealing with mistaken identity with a poignant story of sentiment and compassion. What is of interest is that Plautus' influence may have operated even in this so-called romantic addition to the story of *Menaechmi*.

Whether inspired by Plautus or not, the story of Egeon and Emilia initiates Shakespeare's habit of opening his romantic comedies with a secondary story or subplot of strife and pain which ends happily at the conclusion of each play. The other and more significant link with the romantic comedies is the invention of Luciana and the episode of her wooing by Antipholus of Syracuse. Although the love theme is here given the briefest treatment, both its presence and the expression it receives are of the greatest consequence in Shakespeare's development as a comic dramatist. In this respect, *The Comedy of Errors* bears a distinct relationship to the comedies which followed and should not, therefore, be seen in unbridgeable isolation from them.

Although successful in creating a farce which surpassed the Plautine original so early in his career, Shakespeare showed but slight interest in this sort of play, and he returned to the species only twice, in *The Taming of the Shrew* and *The Merry Wives of Windsor*. But here his main concern is no longer with incident, as it is in *The Comedy of Errors*. . . . [In] the later plays Shakespeare would attempt, in Francis Fergusson's phrase, "the harmonizing of complementary perspectives." In *The Comedy of Errors*, it is clear, he made no sustained attempt at such harmonizing. But it is equally clear that he at least essayed to express, however briefly and obliquely—by placing side by side conflicting points of view—an idea concerning love and wedded happiness. . . . Although the idea which the dramatist is trying to express never achieves explicitness, and although the relationship of Luciana and her Antipholus remains unresolved, what is of great significance is that here in a farce, in what may well have been his earliest comedy, Shakespeare introduces the chief structural principle of his romantic comedies: the juxtaposition of attitudes toward love and toward the ideal relationship of man and woman. (pp. 8-10)

Adriana thinks of love in terms of possession, ownership, mastery. And this is not strange, seeing that the concrete basis of her marriage had been financial, in terms of gold in the form of dowry. And even as she may still control and even repossess that dowry, that is, take back what she has given, she insists also on possession of her husband's liberty, a possession she calls her "right." Adriana's concept of love is the right to possess, to receive and own and be master of, whereas with her sister and Antipholus of Syracuse oppose to that concept their view of love as giving. It might be added here that the financial or commercial attitude towards human relationships is reinforced by the analogous misconception which underlies the Duke's judgment on Egeon. . . . (p. 12)

The folly of possessiveness as contrasted with love's giving forms a very small part of the action. But its dramatization here anticipates the much more extensive and meaningful treatment of it in *The Taming of the Shrew* and especially *The Merchant of Venice*. (p. 13)

There is no space in *The Comedy of Errors*, and perhaps neither inclination nor skill on Shakespeare's part, to pursue in detail the ideal basis for lovers' union and wedded happiness. This he was to do in the romantic comedies which followed. Nevertheless, he is able here to isolate, obliquely and in the briefest compass, one of the central conceptions of those later plays: that love does not possess, that it gives without needing to receive, for it gives to another self. "Call thyself sister, sweet, for I am thee," says Antipholus of Syracuse to Luciana.

Adriana's other misconception of the ideal union of lovers is the belief that such union is based on external beauty: that her husband has been driven away by her loss of physical attractiveness. That ideal love is not based on external beauty alone is much more directly and forcefully presented in the later comedies. (p. 14)

Adriana fears that she has lost her husband's love because her beauty is gone, and the bitterness of that loss turns into jealousy and vents itself in violent nagging. And that nagging, born of disappointment with the motion and change of things, sends our minds over a half dozen comedies to the tête-à-tête of Orlando and the disguised Rosalind in *As You Like It*. . . . The managing of the complex ironies here was quite beyond Shakespeare's abilities when he wrote *The Comedy of Errors*. Yet there is a palpable contact between the two plays and another instance of the unity of Shakespearean comedy. What puzzles Adriana, what in her own conduct remains beyond her awareness, is for Rosalind the most obvious fact in the nature of things. Both husbands and wives change, but their happiness need not be touched by such changes since that happiness should be based on something that remains constant: not outward beauty, not physical attraction, but inner beauty and worth.

The multiple attitudes toward love which are most skillfully woven into the fabric of *As You Like It* have no place in *The Comedy of Errors*. Here what we should note is the presence of the master-principle which controls the structure of Shakespeare's romantic comedies, namely the juxtaposition of attitudes toward love represented by different characters. This is a most significant aspect of *The Comedy of Errors*, a play dealing in the main with matters quite alien to romantic love. And it is certainly surprising to find that Shakespeare, in a severely limited space, could put in such a play so much of what was to be the chief matter of his romantic comedies. The treatment of love and the related motifs which we have noted above is elementary, lacking utterly the incisiveness as well as the ironic dramatization which we find in the later plays. But the fact remains that *The Comedy of Errors*, though in the main concerned with the farcical mistakings of identity, touches briefly a theme of far greater significance, the ideal relationship of man and woman. And it is here, rather than in the confusions of identity, that we find the element of reflectiveness and concern with something deeper than accident and the surface show of things to which we alluded at the beginning of this chapter. (pp. 15-16)

In these matters, then, *The Comedy of Errors* prefigures some of the significant features of Shakespeare's romantic comedies. It shows his general predilection for combining multiple actions into mutually qualifying relationships. More particularly, it initiates his custom of enclosing a comic action within a serious or near-tragic framing story or subplot. And most important of all it introduces into a farcical story of classical origin the theme of romantic love and attempts, in elementary fashion, to comment upon that theme by representing contrasted attitudes to it. In so doing, the play employs for the first time in Shakespeare's career the central thematic and structural characteristics of his romantic comedies. (p. 17)

> *Peter G. Phialas, "'The Comedy of Errors'," in his* Shakespeare's Romantic Comedies: The Development of Their Form and Meaning, *University of North Carolina Press, 1966, pp. 3-17.*

PAUL A. JORGENSEN (essay date 1969)

As the most elementally and transparently funny of Shakespeare's plays, *The Comedy of Errors* would seem to need slight introduction. . . . Indeed, this play is a good beginning one for the student of Shakespeare, for ability to enjoy the madness of total bewilderment is not a tutored one; every child has it. In the chaos created by two sets of twins (not to mention some four merchants), the expert is not of much help, as painstaking plot analyses of the play have shown. In telling who is who, or where, at any one time, the expert is about as helpful and impressive a guide as a professor leading a tour through a maze of mirrors in an amusement park. . . .

It is, for other reasons, a good play to begin on. Unlike Shakespeare's more mature comedies, its funniness is relatively uncomplicated by social criticism, by philosophy, or by characterization. Pure comedy of event can move more cleanly, more like a detective story, to its tidy solution. There are no lingering notes of greater problems unsolved. The value of life itself is not questioned (though the point of it all may be not too clear); all that matters is rearranging human puppets so that they can again go about their proper business. There are left over no Shylocks, no Malvolios. Indeed, there is left over nothing really to think about—except, if one wishes, the tremendously puzzling question of what so grips and amuses an audience during a play which has so little thought in it. . . .

One could speak more confidently of the elementary nature of this comedy, and of it as a significant beginning of Shakespeare's later development in the theatre, if one knew that it is indeed an extremely early play. It would be convenient to think of it as Shakespeare's first comedy. Unfortunately, the external evidence permits of a date anywhere from the beginning of Shakespeare's career to as late as 1594. . . .

Internal evidence suggests an earlier dating. There is the reference to Spain as having sent "whole armadoes of carracks," an allusion that would have lost some of its proud currency not long after 1588. There is also a tantalizingly specific topical allusion by Dromio of Syracuse to France as "armed and reverted, making war against her heir." This is clearly a reference to the French civil wars, which concerned England so much that Elizabeth sent over two expeditionary forces. . . . It is perhaps noteworthy that another very early play, *Love's Labor's Lost*, is paired with *The Comedy of Errors* in dealing with French affairs and specifically with Henry of Navarre.

The lack of compelling characterization also suggests an early date; but this quality may just as well be artistic design as immaturity, for it permits an economical exploitation of the speed and neatness of Latin comedy. *The Comedy of Errors* is precisely the sort of play that an artistically serious young dramatist, still without too much to say about love, politics, or human nature, might design as a reaction against contemporary (and perhaps his own) dabbling in romantic comedy. A date between 1589 and 1591 would accommodate most of the essential facts that we have about the play. (p. 55)

The Comedy of Errors, by having two sets of identical twins, strips all the dignity of individuality from its participants, and even in the joyful reunion there can be no identification with any one character.

With four mistakable persons wandering in a maze, plotting rather than other dramatic skills is most needed. And perhaps the symmetry and near flawlessness of this plot make it the best work of this not contemptible kind that Shakespeare was ever to do. However, though the characterization of the play is usually not praised, it is not negligible. Shakespeare merely succeeded, for one of the rare times in his career, in not allowing any one person to outgrow his function in the story. The characters, despite their comical external likenesses, are all distinct as personalities. (p. 56)

There are also other interesting persons (notably Luce, who with only a few slight lines is hugely comic), but the essence of this comedy is clearly not in character. If the critic examines closely the dialogue and stage business (remembering uneasily the singed beard and fool-cut hair of the scholarly Dr Pinch), he will find that the texture of the play is made up of incessant use of a small number of low comedy elements. There are endless quibbles (mainly by the Dromios), gross accounts of the structure of Luce, tireless jokes about the cuckold's horns and the "French disease." The dialogue is animated but not memorable; this is not a comedy of subtle or even realistic language. The stage business is equally innocent of subtlety. One is aware mainly of frantic running, angry expostulation, and a rapid shifting of confusable persons on the stage. . . . Each Dromio gets rewarded for his well-meaning efforts by the bloodying of the pate by both masters. Somehow the repeated act of having one's "sconce" broken is enormously satisfying to audiences. . . . It is not, of course, funny if the victim of a mighty blow stays down. Perhaps it is the resilience of the Dromios that reassures us, even as, on a much higher (and broader) level, Falstaff rebounds from blow after blow to his ego. (pp. 56-7)

But of course dialogue and stage business are secondary in this play to what it is classically famous for: mistaken identity. Mistaken identity is in itself an additional blow to the individual ego. One is seldom pleased to find that he is constantly being taken for someone else—usually, of course, someone much less impressive. There are, however, several kinds of mistaken identity. This play employs the lowest. The two higher forms of mistaken identity are mistaking the true nature of another person and mistaking one's own nature. Both lead to a reexamination of life and involve character growth. Exteriors are important only in so far as they lead to a realization of one's true nature. Of these two higher forms there are only hints in *The Comedy of Errors*. Antipholus of Syracuse asks a question that might have been all-important in a later comedy:

> Am I in earth, in heaven, or in hell?
> Sleeping or waking? mad or well advised?
> Known unto these, and to myself disguised!
> [II. ii. 212-14]

There is no probing of personality in *The Comedy of Errors*. No one learns more about himself or his neighbor as a result of the errors. Confusion leads to near-madness but does not bring about the breakdown of an ego prior to self-knowledge; it leads rather to drawn swords and headblows. The resolution of the play is not the serene elevation of vision which we find in the later comedies; it is simply a recognition of who, physically, is who.

There is still another peculiar limitation in this play of mistaken identity. No actor within the play pulls the strings of the human puppets. There is no Rosalind, no Prospero to make the confusion delightfully purposeful. In no other play is the ignorance of the participants more total, nor in any play is the purpose of the confusion less apparent. Perhaps Shakespeare felt that by widening the gap in awareness between audience and participants he was giving the audience a pleasant sense of superiority. This, however, does not seem to be the way it works out. The audience grows almost as baffled and impatient as the participants. But here there is no Iago upon whom to vent one's sense of outraged human dignity. The purposelessness of this confusion is perilously close to the purposelessness of uninstructed life. . . . Here is a basic comedy of human ineptitude without a comforting presiding spirit. Man laughing at the plight of the pointlessly outraged characters in this play is man laughing, not too comfortably, at his own most painful apprehension about life; but this apprehension, it must be stressed, is never brought brilliantly to the surface of consciousness by great poetry. It is an apprehension that might have seized Antipholus of Syracuse, but never one of the Dromios.

One must not, after all, forget that the play does not lead immediately to conclusions about human life. Theatrically it is superb farce—as so many of the so-called high comedies basically are. It is the farce of high-spirited, youthful characters, not like Egeon beyond the resilience of youth, who fight back at an intolerable situation. It is a farce set in a scene faintly anticipating the magic of *A Midsummer Night's Dream,* for Ephesus had acquired the reputation from Menander and from St Paul (Acts xix:19) of being a place of sorcerers and magic. The whole experience becomes, indeed, almost a dream. . . .

The play is all of these things, perhaps, for in it Shakespeare was feeling his way toward many possibilities of dramatic growth. He could not write simple farce without raising questions about the meaning of farce. But he does not ask such greater questions explicitly. In his last play, *The Tempest,* Shakespeare comments with great verbal beauty upon his craft and its strategies. *The Comedy of Errors* exhibits the legerdemain of Shakespeare's art without attempting to explain it. The basic techniques, still undisguised by weightier matters, are there. They are the more valuable in that they are not the commentary of Shakespeare the dramatic critic but of Shakespeare the dramatist. To understand the full range of Shakespeare's theatrical experiments, one should no more skip *The Comedy of Errors* than *The Tempest.* (p. 57)

Paul A. Jorgensen, in his introduction to "The Comedy of Errors," in William Shakespeare: The Complete Works, *Alfred Harbage, General Editor, revised edition, Penguin Books Inc., 1969, pp. 55-8.*

LARRY S. CHAMPION   (essay date 1970)

The one major consistency in Shakespeare's early comedies, which are quite literally plot-filled, is the superficial level of characterization. . . . The comic experience arises primarily from the situation itself, not from either a revelation of hypocrisy or a transformation in the characters who are manipulated in the scene.

More specifically, in *The Comedy of Errors* neither Antipholus of Ephesus nor Antipholus of Syracuse and neither of the Dromio servants undergoes a revelation of character or exposure of some comic flaw or hypocrisy, and none is in any way transformed in personality. The humor results from the improbable possibilities that occur when identical twin brothers with identical twin servants separated for twenty-three years are cast unwittingly into a single society. (p. 13)

The comic perspective in *The Comedy of Errors* is built upon two primary devices: stylized action—that is, action so flagrantly broad as to ensure the spectator's interest in *what* is happening (not to whom and how it emotionally affects them)—and a comic pointer—that is, a character or, in more primitive terms, a scene which exists partially (or primarily) as an explanation and a guide for the major complications of the plot.

The basic situation with its complex improbabilities is, of course, the dominant feature of exaggeration or stylization which prevents the spectator's interest in character from passing beyond the physical events themselves. . . . Even without the series of farcically disastrous events occasioned by mistaken identity, the plot invites interest in the action, not the character.

Certain features further emphasize the broad quality of the action. For one thing, the action is literally replete with the farcical action of physical slapstick. At least five scenes involve a Dromio beaten by his actual or his pretended master, the servant inevitably bearing the blame for the confusions of mistaken identity. Antipholus of Syracuse also contributes to the fantastic tone of the stage-world through the references to witchery and sorcery with which numerous scenes conclude. (pp. 17-18)

Two romantic features of the plot contribute especially to the stylization. Consider first the extreme comic shifts in Adriana, wife of Antipholus of Ephesus: One moment she is the stock shrew overwhelming anyone in earshot with an enumeration of her husband's flaws and allowing him liberty only to obey her mandates (II, i); the next moment she is the moralist attacking her husband as "an adulterate blot" [II. ii. 140]; on another occasion she is the clinging vine totally dependent upon her mate. (p. 19)

[In *The Comedy of Errors, The Taming of the Shrew,* and *Love's Labour's Lost*] Shakespeare does not dwell on or build his humor from character revelation. Even if Adriana has publicly confessed her shrewishness, the humor at the end of the scene arises from the shock that she has entertained the wrong man in the privacy of her home. (p. 20)

The second romantic feature of exaggeration involves the amatory interest of the Syracusan Antipholus and Dromio. That Antipholus of Ephesus should be married is not incredible, but that his twin, whom Adriana dines and woos as her own husband, should under such circumstances becomes enamored of the sister Luciana and pursue her hotly between moments with Adriana is convenient but fantastic. And what a price Dromio of Syracuse must pay for his twin's romantic taste: the "very beastly creature," "wondrous fat," a "kitchen wench and all grease" who "if she lives till doomsday" will "burn a week longer than the whole world" [III. ii. 88, 93, 95-6, 99-100]. (p. 21)

In short, such an exaggerated pattern of action forces characterization to the puppet level of farce: a broad doubletake or clever mugging can create humor from an otherwise somber situation; a ranting Herod or a shrewish uxor can turn a potentially serious moment to comedy. . . . Such broad action forces attention upon the physical events themselves and neither permits nor invites the spectator to consider the motivations of the characters or to become emotionally involved with them.

Regardless of the level of comic characterization, the reader must, of course, possess sufficient information to appreciate the comic confusion. . . . The characteristic method employed by Shakespeare to provide this information is a character or several characters who, consciously or unconsciously, develop a sufficiently objective rapport with the spectators to act as a guide or pointer. One aspect of Shakespeare's development as a comic playwright is the gradual integration of the pointer into the plot so that he performs the double function of comic guide and a character important to the plot in his own right.

Obviously, for the spectator to achieve the necessary comic perspective for *The Comedy of Errors*, he must understand the full situation. . . . In this respect, the comic structure of *The Comedy of Errors*—probably the clumsiest in all Shakespeare—belies its apprentice-creator. For to provide this information, Shakespeare has framed his plot (I, i; V, i) with the story of Aegeon and Aemilia, separated parents of the separated sons who likewise will be reunited. This material, appended to the Plautine sources, is not an integral part of the play; moreover, despite the duke's skillful mugging (even perhaps his falling asleep from ennui), Aegeon's lengthy opening speech is dramatically tedious and relatively ineffective. Indeed, of the one hundred fifty-nine lines in the scene, he speaks one hundred four. Even so, by establishing the problem of familial separation and emphasizing the desire for reunion, the scene does, albeit awkwardly, create a greater depth of dramatic interest than the farce of mistaken identity could provide. (pp. 21-2)

The connection between pointer and situation is admittedly clumsy in *The Comedy of Errors*. A situation comedy has been enveloped in an explanatory layer in a fashion at best peripheral. Yet, Shakespeare's method was clear. At a time when much of the contemporary comedy was still unfocused and disjointed, he approached his material with a concept of structural control not entirely dissimilar from that to be utilized a decade later by Ben Jonson for comic control of his satiric stage-worlds. And, as his comic vision grew, his method was refined. (p. 24)

> Larry S. Champion, *"The Comedies of Action," in his* The Evolution of Shakespeare's Comedy: A Study in Dramatic Perspective, *Cambridge, Mass.: Harvard University Press, 1970, pp. 12-59.*

RICHARD HENZE (essay date 1971)

[*Henze treats the gold chain as the chief symbol of* The Comedy of Errors, *claiming that as the chain passes from character to character it comes to represent the intricate social relationships so important to the play. Henze believes that Shakespeare meant to show that people could not function properly without this sense of relationship, and his thesis forms an interesting variation on the theme of identity discussed by such earlier critics as Hermann Ulrici (1839), G. R. Elliott (1939), and Harold Brooks (1961).*]

[In *The Comedy of Errors*, the gold chain begins] as a simple object—a gift purchased by Antipholus of Ephesus for his wife; but as the action develops, the chain becomes considerably more important than a simple property. As Plautus uses the mantle, it is just a gimmick that allows a few jokes about

perverse and bawdy topics. Shakespeare's chain, on the other hand, naturally symbolizes the cohesion of society as it asserts its orderly supremacy over prostitutes, wayward husbands, shrewish wives, and lost brothers. . . . [This] simple object becomes a complex symbol of the recommended norm in the play, the bridling of headstrong freedom and wandering individuality.

The major themes of the play are the finding of one's self by losing one's self and the freeing of one's self by binding one's self. Aegeon, in the first scene, is about to lose his life, a rather essential part of self. Then Antipholus of Syracuse decides that he will "go lose myself" [I. ii. 30]. Wandering around alone, looking at the city, he says that he cannot be content, and then:

> I to the world am like a drop of water
> That in the ocean seeks another drop,
> Who, falling there to find his fellow forth,
> (Unseen, inquisitive), confounds himself.
> So I, to find a mother and a brother,
> In quest of them (unhappy) lose myself.
>
> [I. ii. 35-40]

Alone, his attention on himself, Antipholus S. is unhappily lost from society on an unsatisfactory romantic quest. Only when he truly loses himself by losing part of this naked individuality by joining society, the rest of the ocean, does he find himself in any happy sense.

Then, when Adriana, jealous, meets Antipholus S., she rewords the metaphor:

> Ah, do not tear away thyself from me!
> For know, my love, as easy mayst thou fall
> A drop of water in the breaking gulf
> And take unmingled thence that drop again
> Without addition or diminishing,
> As take from me thyself, and not me too.
>
> [II. ii. 124-29]

Once enrolled in society, one cannot escape again. Society will hold Antipholus. To wander alone is to be unhappy. To intermingle is to join forever. But one cannot choose to refuse; mingling is mandatory. Antipholus S. at the end of Act IV decides that he "will not stay tonight for all the town" [IV. iv. 157]. But he does stay.

The major freeing-binding theme which accords the chain its significance begins with the first scene where Aegeon tells how the twins were bound to masts. (pp. 35-6)

The freeing-binding theme is continued by Antipholus E., who wants to be master of more liberty than social peace permits. He would like to be free to dine with a friendly prostitute (although, as he says, he actually has no mistress) without asking his wife's consent. Instead of freedom from all bonds, however, he gets freedom from no bonds at all and is finally symbolically tied in the bonds of marriage and society even as he is actually bound by ropes.

Adriana, too, would like unbridled liberty: "Why should their liberty than ours be more?" [II. i. 10]. But Luciana warns her that "headstrong liberty is lashed with woe." All things have their bounds, "in earth, in sea, in sky" [II. i. 15, 17]. (p. 36)

Adriana recommends mutual trust above any lord-servant relationship:

> For, if we two be one, and thou play false,
> I do digest the poison of thy flesh,
> Being strumpeted by thy contagion.
>
> [II. ii. 142-44]

The net result of the conflict of contrasting opinions, of Luciana's homily and Adriana's plea of experience, is to reinforce social, mutual responsibility of each married partner to the other and to the social pattern of marriage. Bridling is necessary, but the team needs to be bridled together lest they be asses alone, lashed with woe. (pp. 36-7)

Like Adriana and his brother, Antipholus of S. also seeks freedom. Thoroughly confused by his imagined "dark-working sorcerers" [I. ii. 99], he plans to leave Ephesus, to continue as a drop of water separate from the social ocean, but his departure is prevented; and he too is drawn from headstrong liberty to bridled security, from being a lost drop to joining the mingled waters.

The development of the themes parallels the development of the plot. At first we see Antipholus S. losing himself by remaining apart from society. This loss is prevented; immediately the social ocean engulfs the lost drop. Antipholus is invited to dinner the first time that he threatens to leave. The second time, after he wooes Luciana, he receives the chain, and, because of it, gets further embroiled in the confusion. Finally, after Dromio has arranged the departure, Antipholus S. is forced to flee into the abbey. At each point when the loss threatens, society prevents the loss. The finding is inevitable because society will have it so.

Not only Antipholus is found. Adriana, at first unaware that her nagging, and not Antipholus E., is destroying their marriage, is herself losing part of her social completeness. But Aemilia, with a bit of trickery and a short sermon, draws Adriana back in. Antipholus E. is too headstrong in his freedom. Again, society, through wife, merchant, and officer, intrudes and asserts its prerogative.

The finding of oneself is itself a losing, however, and this paradoxical relationship exists between the two parts of each major theme. Antipholus finds himself by rejoining the ocean from whence, once commingled with other drops, he cannot draw himself apart completely ever again, because his completeness, like Adriana's and Antipholus E.'s, requires the social submersion. Aegeon and Antipholus E. are both freed from the bonds of ropes only to enter the bonds of marriage and social limitation, bonds more restrictive than the bonds just lost. With freedom comes binding, but with the binding, paradoxically, comes freedom—freedom of trust, of fellowship, of love.

The use of the major devices in the play, chain and rope, reinforces the movement of plot and theme from unsocial or romantic to eminently social, and the chain quickly acquires its significance as a symbol of the social norm. (p. 37)

Antipholus E. has a chain made as a gift for his wife. When he finds himself locked out of his house, he decides to give the chain to a "wench of excellent discourse" [III. i. 109]. But the best laid plans need social mortar here. The chain goes instead to Antipholus S. and helps prevent his departure. The chain remains pretty obviously a social symbol, representing the bonds of society in spite of an attempt to make it work otherwise. . . .

The chain proceeds, after Antipholus E. orders it as a gift for his wife, through merchant to Antipholus S. and finally, we are sure, to Adriana, for whom it was intended in the first place. As a symbol of social bonds it consistently performs its symbolic function. It draws Antipholus S. into society and marriage, never gets into the prostitute's hands, and finally

helps rejuvenate Antipholus' and Adriana's marriage. . . . (p. 38)

Adriana firmly links the chain with truth to the marriage vow: "Sister, you know he promis'd me a chain" [II. i. 106].

> I see the Iewell best enamaled
> Will loose his beautie: yet the gold bides still
> That others touch, and often touching will,
> Where gold; and no man that hath a name,
> By falsehood and corruption doth it shame.
>
> [II. i. 109-13]

This oft-emended passage . . . is logical and clear if properly punctuated. Even the best enamelled jewel will lost its beauty eventually; gold, however, will bide even if often touched—where gold; "and no man that hath a name" will shame such gold. The gold, symbolized by the chain, is marriage and its sister bonds. The gold of marriage will abide much touching, in fact, requires much touching; and no man who deserves to be called a man, who has an awareness of the obligations of humanity, will shame marriages or the other bonds. But, the play indicates in addition, even if the man be willing to shame the gold, it will escape the shame and make the man a man in spite of himself.

The gold that bides often touching here is the social bond of marriage. By preventing this touching—being late to dinner, neglecting his wife—Antipholus E. is neglecting the gold for the sake of the jewel, self-centered freedom. The chain is already an emblem of the marriage bond, and as the chain gets misplaced, so the bond weakens. But as the chain, a symbol of other social bonds as well, fulfills its function even as it wanders, so the bonds, even as they apparently weaken, continue to do their job. (pp. 38-9)

Antipholus of Ephesus is incorporate with Adriana—to be himself whole he has to be loyal to her. Antipholus of S., on the other hand, is not yet linked to anyone; thus he is not complete. He attempts to get the completeness without the bond. He would have Luciana "create me new"; he seeks a sentimental stay at the shrine. Instead, however, he gets "transformed" by the chain from a wanderer into one of the social body. Only with proper incorporation can Luciana truly becomes Antipholus' "own self's better part", as he wishes [III. ii. 61].

Without proper incorporation, proper binding, Antipholus S. remains self-centered, afraid of involvement:

> But her fair sister,
> Possess'd with such a gentle sovereign grace,
> Of such enchanting presence and discourse,
> Hath almost made me traitor to myself.
> But, lest myself be guilty to self-wrong,
> I'll stop mine ears against the mermaid's song.
>
> [III. ii. 159-64]

At a very appropriate moment, however, Angelo enters with the chain and Antipholus S. is drawn back in. To reject love in favor of selfish melancholy and discontent is a fault that society does not allow. Antipholus is drawn back in by the whole network, chain, supper, time, merchant, and trust:

> *Ang.* And soon at supper time I'll visit you
> And then receive my money for the chain.
>
> [III. ii. 174-75]

Antipholus sensibly accepts the chain: "There's no man is so vain That would refuse so fair an offer'd chain" [III. ii. 180-81]; he echoes Adriana's words earlier: "No man that hath a name; By falsehood and corruption doth it shame'' [II. i. 112-13]. No man who is a man rejects or corrupts the binding chains. The gold chain, image of the golden bond that bides touching, is touching.

But the chain is now misplaced, and mistrust begins. The chain is an image of the golden bonds; the misplacement of the chain and weakening of the bonds bring distrust, confusion, loss of social stability. Antipholus E. sends Dromio E. for a rope's end to "bestow" on his wife just as he decided earlier to "bestow" the chain on the prostitute. In each case, Antipholus attempts to pervert the object's fundamental purpose—to bind. But just as the chain's purpose could not be perverted (it performs its social purpose in spite of Antipholus E.), so the rope is not perverted; Antipholus E., instead of his wife, is bound—his "headstrong liberty" is "lashed" with helpful woe.

With weakening of trust comes loosening of invisible bonds and need for material ones, for chains and ropes. When invisible bonds are again strong, on the other hand, rope and chain are loosened. Aemilia says of Aegeon, "Whoever bound him, I will loose his bonds, And gain a husband by his liberty" [V. i. 340-41].

From rope and chain the bridle is formed that guides men as they work mutually and inevitably toward harmony. . . . Such imagery also suggests, however, that throwing off of bonds of society—unbridling of asses—leads to a lower, animal level of existence. Humanity requires society; society requires social restraints. Each Antipholus attempts to reject the bonds, but each only succeeds in getting himself more securely bound. With both bridled, the teams are soon together. (pp. 40-1)

> *Richard Henze, " 'The Comedy of Errors': A Freely Binding Chain," in* Shakespeare *Quarterly, Vol. XXII, No. 1, Winter, 1971, pp. 35-41.*

THEODORE WEISS   (essay date 1971)

[Although *The Comedy of Errors*] proceeds in a brisk-paced, thoroughly self-possessed, old-style, farcical way, the settings, the occasions, and the personae, translated from Latin to contemporary Englishmen, must inevitably remind us of Shakespeare's England if not his middle-class home-town. It was apparently simple enough to transport a busy, Plautine, Mediterranean seaport town to the coast of England. Beyond references to the sea and the world at large, it is a small world, full of the bustle and business Shakespeare must have known; even with weather it is the trade winds that matter and that all bend to. But whether we credit Shakespeare with the play's leanness as a mark of his superb instinct for the rights and limitations of the form employed, or whether we attribute that leanness—and his wisdom therefore in starting with so popular and so handy a form—to talents not yet developed, the play normally hews to its original mark, winds up like a perfect top and equally perfectly unwinds again. Never, in a sense, will Shakespeare be in better shape. The play works so well by its honoring the interests and concerns of the middle-class world it treats, its people with a few exceptions alike in interests as in appearance as two guilders. Business, money, things, and pleasures out of things as they relate to money are an omnipresent consideration, the climate of the play, the motive power and shaper of the plot. Appropriately the lives of the characters turn on these. . . . Our chief pleasure consists of watching them being hauled and mauled about, and the variety of ways discovered to do so, that the maximum of profit be wrung out

of them. In this respect the characters are not much more than exploitable commodities.

In fact, a grimness out of such considerations so grips the play from the outset that in its materials and larger plot it is hard to believe it a comedy. The play is framed by the aged, long-parted, long-suffering parents of the twin Antipholi. Time, chance, adversity, money, and this play separate—as they will eventually unite—them all. . . . [In the] pathetic introduction, in the way in which fate or chance has steadily dogged him and his, poor Aegeon hardly looks like a comic character. Nor does his predicament seem the stuff of careless, carefree farce. Thus the play begins with a sentence of death and a desire to die. Law which should make society and men's living together possible and agreeable is here harsh, ruthless, even deadly, based on money, hostility, and war. . . . What intensifies the pathos is that love and its anguish, though necessarily muted here, are already at the center of Shakespeare's work; this family has long been seeking, however terrible the hazards and obstacles, to reunite.

Aegeon, looking for his sons, has landed on enemy territory. He begins:

> Proceed, Solinus, to procure my fall,
> And by the doom of death end woes and all.
>
>   [I. i. 1-2]

Who would think this, possibly his first couplet, Shakespeare! He seems to be at his oldest, flattest, because mainly derivative,

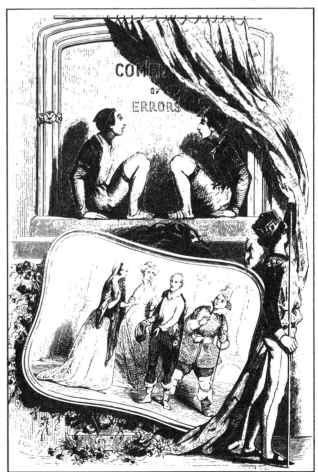

Engraving from Verplanck edition (1847). From the Art Collection of the Folger Shakespeare Library.

as a beginning young writer is likely to be. The laboriousness of this first scene's verse may be ascribable to Shakespeare's inexperience or, would we be more kind, to his sense of farce and especially to the framing of the play by romantic elements that, ultra-realistic in plot and action, must be fairly unreal in their verse, in this way distanced and subdued. Already, aside from the hardships and deprivations Aegeon has endured, he suggests a view of life that must be called melancholy. . . . When at the Duke's urging he tells his sad story, recounts the storm and the shipwreck that separated him and one son from his wife and the other, or the first 'error' as it means wandering, he says of the death which seemed imminent, '. . . myself would gladly have embraced. . . .' The background of the play then is the violence of nature in its wanton playfulness, expressed in storm as it sunders men. The opening of the play amounts to the violence of society expressed in war and an iron law that, as it separates men, also threatens to kill. The substance of the play will be the violence or at least the tumult of individual man immersed in his own storm of confusion. The havoc at large, the great winds, blow into the most domestic scenes and occasions. One might wonder how man, so embattled, survives at all—not to say thrives and realizes himself. Yet the same forces, we shall see, natural and/or human (we will not talk of supernatural ones), that scatter him somehow at the end gather him together again. (pp. 10-13)

The whole matter of the tempest and the shipwreck behind the play is a fascinating one, especially as we look ahead to later plays. The tempest here is a natural if not inevitable donée to an islander of a sea-going, mercantile nation; using it to get his play going, Shakespeare hardly seemed aware of its potential poetic reverberations. Nor, one must admit, for a self-respecting, well-behaved farce should he have sounded them had he been aware. Yet, though tempest and shipwreck may be part of the property of an island kingdom and though it is in the interest of farce to mute their effect on feeling, in Aegeon and his son some of the poignancy-to-be out of these images already stirs.

Similarly the grief, the sense of profound separation and loss, of Adriana, the wife of Antipholus of Ephesus, who thinks herself abandoned, amounts to an emotion far past farce. . . . One may dismiss her as a fairly conventional scold, a shrew expert as she should be in this play in complaint and tirade. But Shakespeare could not resist sympathy for her pain, could not resist at least the full expression of it. In such moments, as they strike against farce's customary grain, one might be tempted to see a breaking through, an almost involuntary criticism of, farce, its inadequacies for the human condition and for human expression. Certainly we know how common such criticism of the forms he used was with Shakespeare, how much the criticism became an intrinsic part of the form, an enlargement of it. Usually, however, it is the comic mocking the serious and the noble, especially when they become excessive, pretentious, hypocritical. Here in the first play the rare opposite occurs. But since the comic is this play's prevailing mode, such opposite is to be expected. (pp. 14-15)

Other grimness, or at least the potentiality of it, occurs in what is the major substance of the play, the confusions. A touch more and irreparable blows, maims, deaths must follow. One need simply notice her husband's violence against Adriana as he calls her 'dissembling harlot . . . false in all' and threatens 'with these nails I'll pluck out those false eyes. . . .' However, the one moment of real violence, the abuse by Antipholus of Ephesus and his Dromio of scrawny Pinch the conjurer, is not

shown but wittily, happily described (so were, of course, the hardships the Aegeon family endured before the play). As I suggested earlier, the family's 'natural' sufferings before the play would seem more than enough. Now they must go through more and at man's hands, mostly their own kin. This, however, is the last leg of their journey, the final purgatory or purging before reconciliation. Thrust out of a stormy sea by chance and its magic onto an island, an island that seems bewitched it is true, they are plunged into further turmoil, made to lose themselves—their names and so their persons—before they finally recover themselves, their identities, and each other. Through their confusion the law, moved by the same force which in the end reunites them, is also finally lightened and relaxed.

What is it then that, beyond its happy ending, wins this play the title of comedy and farce? Obviously the gags and slapstick that pervade it, particularly as they pertain to the two forever-put-upon Dromios, the choplogic that often serves for dialogue, especially among the Dromios and their masters, the absurdity of the confusions and, with the exception of Luciana, the Abbess, and those moments of Adriana we have commented on, the total submergence of the characters in the confusions. Fortunately the verbal exchanges tend to be brief and brisk, punctuated by well-administered blows. (pp. 18-19)

One other obvious main provision of amusement is the earthy low humor, the wit of the Dromios when it breaks loose from its laboriousness. . . . One of Shakespeare's first poetic wealths to come bubblingly alive was this exploitation of his day's colloquial world expressed in extravagant, yet realistically racy prose. (pp. 19-20)

Along with this low, delicious humor as well as its slapstick goes the constant insistence by the befuddled cast that they must be beset by goblins, witches, the supernatural. But clearly for such a play no magic is needed—nor may it be—beyond the cast's own prompt superstitiousness and confusion, and whatever power might waft over it from the framing romance, nature's mysterious, chance-ridden influence. Magic's very obvious absence intensifies the ludicrousness of the situations. The more so with magic insisted on. For characters immersed in materialism, money, business, time, and the commonplace pursuit of their own pleasures, the Duke's assertion that they have all 'drunk of Circe's cup' may not be too far from the mark. They have mixed most potent illusion with their daily sack. The senses alone relied on become their own mad seduction and confusion. (pp. 20-1)

The Comedy of Errors enjoys no magically releasing wood. Nor, for the kind of play it is, should it have one. On the contrary. The town itself, however, once the self-engendering errors begin, that is, the plot's masterly guarantee of chance and just right coincidence, is wood—not to say maze—enough. It may lack country elves and goblins, moonlit spells. But it possesses superabundantly, in the minds of its inhabitants for all their townish bustle and materialism, the necessary, fertile ground of superstition, enriched by sea tales and tales of other lands and times. A world that believes in magic and witchcraft, it is ready to find them everywhere.

One other source of witchcraft, and a potential embarrassment to the play as a farce even though it deepens it, a flickering instance of magic, the sovereign magic to be, is the brief amatory interlude between Luciana and Antipholus of Syracuse. Here begins one of the most persistent themes of the comedies, love as the great school, the enlightenment of a young man by a beautiful young woman. This is, since internal and natural, the true magic or witchery, the only source of transformation. It naturally produces the play's largest eruption into lyrical poetry, a positive one beside the plaintively lyrical outburst of Adriana: love as a promoter of feeling, of coming alive, or the great discoverer in all its confusingness of man's best nature and being. Antipholus says,

> Teach me, dear creature, how to think and speak;
> Lay open to my earthy-grass conceit,
> Smothered in errors, feeble, shallow, weak,
> The folded meaning of your words' deceit. . . .
> Are you a god? Would you create me new?
> Transform me, then, and to your power I'll yield.
> [III. ii. 33-40]

Though he is more thoroughly plunged into error than ever, he instinctively knows that she or love can alone free him to the truth. And like any good young Englishman, once touched by passion he is instantly ready and ready to give all; for recognizing good fortune come his way, he leaps ahead with all delighted might to seize it by its lovely golden forelock. Luciana, whatever siren-like confusion her words may throw him into, is the one and the only one to bring him with the speed of a word and a touch home to himself. (pp. 21-2)

[Since] this is farce and Shakespeare, he—as he will usually do hereafter in his multiple awareness of reality as well as for the fruitfulness of this awareness for drama—quickly comes down hard on this bit of extravagant poetry, ballasts it as he qualifies and rounds it out with his next scene, no less about men and women together and the transforming power of love, but love now at its earthiest, its seamiest, out of the English town and country life he knew so well and out of a realistic world of harbors, marketplaces, domestic business. Dromio of Syracuse, echoing Antipholus' very word, also admits that he is 'claimed'. But the claim for Antipholus was heavenly, a pure delight. Here it is being possessed in a most oozy, sticky way. At once we move from the open sea and heaven into the kitchen sink of love, from its spiritual to its most gross. The shimmering waves have turned to oil and grease! Accordingly, the human transformation, ennobling before, is now belittling. . . . In the comic mode, as well as comically, to live is to live up to whatever role we happen to be cast into. A lover leaps, a dog runs, an ass brays, and fulfilment and ripeness is all. Chance, the mother of comedy, if not of our lives, by our mettlesomeness, our ability to go with it, is made choice. (pp. 23-4)

Theodore Weiss, "In My Beginning Is My End," in his The Breath of Clowns and Kings: Shakespeare's Early Comedies and Histories, *Atheneum Publishers, 1971, pp. 9-43.*

ANNE BARTON (essay date 1974)

Although *The Comedy of Errors* is the only play by Shakespeare which includes the word *comedy* in its title, critics have persistently wanted to dismiss it as a farce, unworthy of serious consideration, however great its success as a theatrical frolic. It would be hard to deny that *The Comedy of Errors* has some of the characteristics of farce. As Coleridge observed [see excerpt above, 1808-18], the device of the identical Antipholuses which Shakespeare took from the *Menaechmi* of Plautus strains the verisimilitude usually thought appropriate to comedy. Shakespeare's insistence upon compounding this basic absurdity by inventing identical servants to wait upon the single pair

of twins provided in his Latin source pushes the story still further in the direction of that cloud-cuckoo-land of farce where, by special agreement between dramatist and audience, even the wildest and most coincidental plot structures become acceptable.

Twelfth Night, a play no one has ever wished to categorize as farce, also turns in part upon the confusions generated by twins identical in appearance. Viola and Sebastian, however, are both strangers in Illyria. They are mistaken for one another, pardonably, by new acquaintances; not, as in *The Comedy of Errors,* by those who know them well. Moreover, Viola recognizes at once what has happened. . . . Antipholus of Syracuse, by contrast, is journeying through the world in search of his lost twin. The extraordinary things that begin to happen to him as soon as he sets foot in Ephesus constitute a virtual proclamation that his seven-year quest is over, his missing brother found. Yet for almost five acts the Syracusan Antipholus fails to reach this glaringly obvious conclusion, preferring to invoke sorcery or hallucination to explain his situation. He is not meant to seem obtuse. His reactions are simply governed here, although not in other respects, by the rules of farce rather than comedy. Similarly, Shakespeare asks his audience to accept without question the fact that the Sicilian Antipholus and Dromio each manage to disembark at Ephesus in Asia Minor wearing clothes indistinguishable from those that the native Antipholus and Dromio happen to have put on that morning. In *Twelfth Night,* Viola goes out of her way to explain that her boy's disguise is a deliberate copy in its "fashion, color, ornament" of the garb habitually worn by her lost brother. No rationalization of this kind is even attempted in *The Comedy of Errors.* Again, the latitude of farce must be invoked, even as it must when considering that hail of blows and beatings which falls upon the perplexed and innocent Dromios without, as it seems, causing them any real physical or psychological harm.

Yet despite its emphasis on plot and situational absurdity, despite the merry violence in many of the scenes, it is not really possible to contain *The Comedy of Errors* within the bounds of farce as defined by the *Oxford English Dictionary:* "a dramatic work (usually short) which has as its sole object to excite laughter." A comparison here with Shakespeare's principal source is illuminating. . . . By Shakespearean standards, *The Comedy of Errors* is a short play, indeed the shortest in the canon, but the *Menaechmi* is very considerably shorter still. Plautus' play is also far less complex, concentrating almost entirely upon plot mistakings. Its characters are simple and rigidly type-cast. (pp. 79-80)

The Roman play is tightly constructed, lively and inventive, full of the atmosphere of a bustling harbor town. It would be difficult, however, to claim that it has any object or concern other than to turn the normal world upside down and to evoke laughter of a simple and unreflective kind.

Shakespeare retained the conventional city street of Roman comedy with its separate and stylized houses. . . . This setting, with its invisible but strongly contrasted off-stage localities—the mart with its world of business and, in the opposite direction, the more open and ambiguous sea-port—made it easy for Shakespeare to preserve the classical unity of place, while building up the image of a credible and populous town. . . .

Shakespeare may well have felt in the early 1590's that it would be a useful discipline to submit himself to the three unities, even if (as it turned out) he saw no subsequent need to employ them until he wrote *The Tempest* at the end of his career. He may also have turned to Plautus, as other Elizabethan dramatists had done before him, in order to learn something about the construction of a finely engineered dramatic plot after the more rambling organization typical of his own Henry VI plays or, possibly, of *The Two Gentlemen of Verona*. If so, he did not hesitate to create for himself technical problems far exceeding anything posed by his source. . . . [He] made *The Comedy of Errors* structurally as much a tour de force as one of the great Bach fugues. Even more important, he added three characters—Egeon, Luciana, and the Abbess—who have little or nothing to do with laughter.

Egeon derives not from classical comedy but from the story of Apollonius of Tyre as retold by the fourteenth-century poet John Gower in his *Confessio Amantis* (a story to which Shakespeare was to return years later for the plot of *Pericles*). The two appearances of old Egeon, at the beginning and end of *The Comedy of Errors*, not only define its time-span from morning until the sunset hour appointed for his execution: they greatly deepen the basic Plautine material in ways that often seem to anticipate *Pericles* and its successors. Parents in Roman comedy, like wives, were usually nothing but a nuisance, repressing and causing trouble for the young. Egeon cannot be fitted into such a scheme. It is true that his long opening account of the shipwreck which was the source of all his woes is faintly absurd. A family of six scattered by Fortune in a fashion at once so implausible and so ingeniously patterned announces itself fairly clearly as material for a comedy resolution. Yet it is wrong for actors to make Egeon's explanation to the Duke overtly comic. The anguish of the old man is real, even if the verse he speaks suggests delicately to a theatre audience that his loss will not prove irremediable. Later, in Act V, he addresses the son he believes to be guilty of forgetfulness and ingratitude in lines so bitter that they seem to prefigure the reproaches of Antonio in *Twelfth Night*, or even those of King Lear. Most important of all, Egeon allowed Shakespeare to open the play under the shadow of death and to keep this threat alive in the background, like a sword that has been drawn and not sheathed, until it flashes into prominence again in Act V only to dissolve before the discoveries and accords of the final scene. (p. 80)

Behind the *Menaechmi*, as behind all the plays of Plautus, lay a Greek original now lost. Mistaken identity and the recovery or reunion of lost children seem to have been almost obsessive preoccupations of the New Comedy written by Menander and his contemporaries towards the end of the 4th century B.C. A response, probably, to the political and economic chaos of a Hellenistic world that was filled with displaced persons, where children were often "lost" by parents too poor or too distracted to cope with them at the time of their birth, and where free citizens could become slaves overnight, the theme has an emotional resonance in the surviving Menandrian fragments which vanished in the later, Roman adaptations. For Plautus, living in a very different and more stable world, dealing with the Greek material at second hand, these plots became little more than an approved comic formula. *The Comedy of Errors* is remarkable on a number of counts, but not least because of the way it revitalizes and gives new meaning to a seemingly outworn dramatic convention. This meaning is not really Menandrian. Between Menander's *Epitrepontes* or *Periceiromene* and Shakespeare's play there stretches not only an immense gulf of space and time but also the fact of Christianity with its stress upon the inner life. Menander's characters were psychologically more complex than their Roman descendants but

it is still true that identity for them is principally a matter of establishing parentage and social class. Their quest is accomplished when they achieve the equivalent of a birth certificate. Antipholus of Syracuse, by contrast, has voluntarily left a father and a defined and satisfactory social role in order to find a missing mother and twin brother without whom he feels psychologically incomplete. . . .

Unlike Plautus, Shakespeare seems to have been less interested in the problems of the native twin angered by the perversity of a familiar world than he was in the more extreme situation of the traveller, especially vulnerable because far from home, who finds himself losing his own sense of self in an alien city of reputed sorcery and spells. . . . Where the equivalent character in the *Menaechmi* had thought Epidamnum bewildering but delightful, Antipholus of Syracuse comes to regard Ephesus as a nightmare country where "none but witches do inhabit." . . . Before long his self-confidence has been so badly shaken that he is asking Luciana to give him a new identity through the transforming power of romantic love. . . . (p. 81)

After the tension and accumulated mistakings of nearly five acts, [the] discovery generates an enormous sense of relief. The theatre audience, of course, unlike the characters in the play, has possessed the key to the situation all along: the knowledge that there are really two Dromios and two Antipholuses in Ephesus. The one surprise is Aemilia. When the Abbess recognizes Egeon as her long-lost husband and the two Antipholuses as her sons, Shakespeare deals a shrewd blow at the seeming omniscience of the spectators. Plautus had not restored this missing bit of the puzzle. There have been no hints in Shakespeare's play that Egeon's wife was alive and living in Ephesus. The discovery that she has been there all the time, that the virtuous and reverend lady who governs the abbey and has such decided views about a wife's duty to her husband is really the mother of the twins, is comical in the fullest sense of the word. As with Egeon's initial narrative of shipwreck and loss, there is something consciously absurd about this reunion which happens not only beyond hope but beyond any expectation explicitly generated by the play. Almost always, the theatre audience laughs when Aemilia identifies Egeon, but the laughter is not the laughter of farce.

At its ending *The Comedy of Errors* admits its own artificiality, its participation in that special realm of fairy-tale where the lost are always found, while reminding the theatre audience that it has not been in complete control of the situation after all. This last scene is consciously contrived but also moving in a way that seems to anticipate the marvellous discoveries of *Cymbeline* and *The Winter's Tale*. Certainly the emotions liberated look forward to the last plays. In the final moments of the comedy, the Syracusan Dromio makes another mistake. He addresses to the Ephesian Antipholus the question he ought to ask his own Syracusan master. . . . But, for the first time in the play, no altercation, no ferocious exchange of words and blows results. Instead, Antipholus of Syracuse points out gently,

> He speaks to me. I am your master, Dromio.
> Come go with us, we'll look to that anon.
> Embrace thy brother there, rejoice with him.
>
> [V. i. 412-14]

The basic situation of the play, the source of all the misunderstanding, remains but it has been robbed of its sting. There is no pain in this final confusion of identities and no violence, only delight: "After so long grief, such nativity!" (p. 82)

Anne Barton, in her introduction to "The Comedy of Errors," in The Riverside Shakespeare, *edited by G. Blakemore Evans, Houghton Mifflin Company, 1974, pp. 79-105.*

ALEXANDER LEGGATT (essay date 1974)

[*Leggatt's book* Shakespeare's Comedy of Love *stresses the variety rather than the unity of Shakespeare's love comedies. In his chapter on* The Comedy of Errors, *he delineates the "interweaving of the fantastic and the everyday" and explores the way in which Shakespeare developed the themes of his Plautine source to create a work of greater subtlety and complexity. For other discussions of the superiority of Shakespeare's play to its classical source, see the excerpts by Derek Traversi (1960) and Anne Barton (1974).*]

The Roman comedy of confusion [as, for example, the *Menaechmi*] takes place in a practical world, where nothing is inexplicable, and where the issues at stake are largely the material ones of who owns what and where the next meal is coming from. The play has a single vision and a uniform texture. But Shakespeare gives us a play in a more mixed dramatic idiom. The market-place atmosphere of Plautus is still present, but it no longer monopolizes the play; it is varied by suggestions of fantasy and mystery, and the result is a mixture of styles that goes much deeper than changes from prose to verse, or the varying of metres. It is a mixture of different ways of viewing the world, of which different dramatic styles are ultimately a reflection. Nor is the decision to mix idioms in this way artificially imposed; it springs from Shakespeare's own fresh and imaginative meditation on the central idea of Plautus, the idea of confusion. *The Comedy of Errors* is unusual in that mistaken identity is itself the primary motif, not (as in *As You Like It* or *Twelfth Night*) a technical device to aid the presentation of some other issue. Perhaps Shakespeare, before he could use mistaken identity as an instrument, had to give it a thorough examination. And in exploiting the situations arising from it, Shakespeare demonstrates that confusion, the gap of understanding between one mind and another, can exist at a deeper level than who's-got-the-chain or which-twin-is-it-*this*-time. These questions are important to the action, and much of the play's immediate comic life depends on them; but they are also signals of a deeper breakdown of understanding; the characters seem at times to inhabit different worlds, different orders of experience.

Some of this effect is created by the mingling—and, at times, the collision—of dramatic styles. In II. ii Adriana, meeting the man she thinks is her husband, attacks him passionately for straying from her, urging him to recognize that as husband and wife they are bound together in a single being, and that consequently she shares in his corruption. Taken out of context, the speech is passionate and earnest, idealistic in its view of marriage and urgent in its emotional response to the breaking of that ideal. But the context is all-important. Adriana's speech follows immediately—with no transition whatever—a racy comic turn between Dromio and Antipholus on time, falling hair and syphilis; she breaks in on two characters who are operating in quite a different dramatic world. . . . Or consider the following passage:

ANTIPHOLUS S: The fellow is distract, and so am I;
               And here we wander in illusions.
               Some blessed power deliver us from hence!
                                   [*Enter a* Courtezan.

COURTEZAN: Well met, well met, Master Antipholus.
               I see, sir, you have found the goldsmith now.
               Is that the chain you promis'd me to-day?
ANTIPHOLUS S: Satan, avoid! I charge thee, tempt me not.
DROMIO S: Master, is this Mistress Satan?
ANTIPHOLUS S: It is the devil.
                                 [IV. iii. 42-50]

Here, the attitude of each character is comically dislocated. The courtesan is simply living her casual, material life, while Antipholus is struggling between heaven and hell, in a metaphysical nightmare where even a call for 'some blessed power' is met by (for him) a fresh appearance of evil, and (for the audience) a comic anticlimax. The contrast is driven home, once again, by the different styles of speech—the casual chatter of the courtesan, the explosive horror of Antipholus and, on the side, Dromio's more familiar recognition of the powers of evil. This introduces us to a device we will see Shakespeare using throughout his comedies: a speech is comically dislocated by being placed in the wrong context, usually through being addressed to an unsympathetic or uncomprehending listener. The comic value of this device is obvious, and is exploited throughout the play. Yet, as with many such devices, it requires only a twist of emphasis, or a new situation, to make the effect pathetic or disturbing. The gaps of understanding between us are not always amusing. While we laugh easily enough when Adriana fires a long, emotional speech at the wrong Antipholus, it is not so funny when, later in the play, Aegeon pleads with his son to save his life, and his son refuses to acknowledge him.

The effect is to show how frail and vulnerable our attitudes and assumptions are, to bring into sharp focus the incompleteness of anything we may say or do, the fact that, however serious or important it may seem to us, there is always another viewpoint from which it is wrong, or trivial, or incomprehensible. . . . One of the most persistent comic points in Shakespeare is the disparity between theory and reality, the breakdown of philosophy in the face of experience—particularly when the experience is yours and the philosophy is someone else's. Throughout the play, Antipholus of Ephesus is (like his wife) the recipient of much good advice about the necessity of patience—from his friends . . . , from the officer who arrests him . . .—in short, from people who do not really share his problems. (pp. 3-6)

The gap between different understandings of the world is centred on the two Antipholus brothers. In *Menaechmi* the twin brothers inhabit the same prosaic, domestic world and undergo basically the same kind of experience; in *The Comedy of Errors* not only are their characters more sharply distinguished, but the difference between their experiences is more emphasized. In the words of A. C. Hamilton, Antipholus of Ephesus 'endures a nightmare' while his brother 'enjoys a delightful dream'. One is showered with gifts, money and women; the other is locked out of his house, arrested for debt and tied up as a lunatic. The difference in their experiences is signalled by a difference in style. The scene in which Antipholus of Ephesus is locked out of his house . . . is noisy, raucous and farcical, full of spluttering threats and bawdy insults; it is immediately followed . . . by his brother's courtship of Luciana, a quiet scene of romantic feeling shot through with more subtle comic irony, a scene in which the focus is on emotional rather than on physical problems. (pp. 6-7)

They seem to inhabit two different towns. For Antipholus of Ephesus, as for the rest of the native population (and initially for the audience) Ephesus is the familiar seaport town of Plautine comedy, a small world of commerce and domesticity, where, as E.M.W. Tillyard puts it [see excerpt above, 1965], 'everyone knows everyone else's business, where merchants predominate, and where dinner is a serious matter'. Shakespeare even sharpens the commercial interests of the town, giving them a distinctly unflattering emphasis. . . . This is the predicament in which Aegeon stands in the first scene. According to the Duke, he is condemned

> Unless a thousand marks be levied,
> To quit the penalty and to ransom him.
> Thy substance, valued at the highest rate,
> Cannot amount unto a hundred marks;
> Therefore by law thou art condemn'd to die.
>
> [I. i. 21-5]

Though the point is not much developed, this crude measuring of human life in financial terms anticipates the inhuman legalism of Shylock; and throughout the play there are several small touches conveying the Ephesians' narrow concern with money. (p. 7)

In the commercial and domestic spheres [Antipholus of Ephesus] inhabits, disruption may be fun for the audience, but it is unsettling and unpleasant for the victim. As we see throughout Shakespeare's comedies, love seems to thrive on irrationality and confusion, and emerges from it strengthened, renewed and satisfied: the experience of Antipholus of Syracuse is roughly parallel to that of Demetrius, Orlando and Sebastian. But the world of commerce simply goes crazy when an irrational factor is introduced, and the only satisfaction is for chains and ducats to be restored to their original owners, as though the confusion had never taken place. . . . What is enchantment and enrichment for one brother is simply confusion for the other, a confusion that must be put right. The only party to gain something is the audience: since commercial life has been depicted in such unflattering terms, we are bound to take a special, mischievous delight in seeing it disrupted.

One may even question whether the disruption of Antipholus's marriage leads to any good result for the characters. The disorder produced by mistaken identity is linked to a more familiar disorder, a longstanding unhappiness between husband and wife. Adriana tells the Abbess that her husband has not been himself all week, though his rage has only broken out that afternoon. . . . And when she confesses that her nagging has disrupted the normal rhythms of his life, the Abbess lectures her:

> In food, in sport, and life-preserving rest,
> To be disturb'd would mad or man or beast.
> The consequence is, then, thy jealous fits
> Hath scar'd thy husband from the use of wits.
>
> [V. i. 83-6]

We know, of course, that his 'madness' depends more on the mistaken-identity confusion than anything else (we have seen him cheated of a meal for reasons other than his wife's scolding tongue). But the Abbess's speech reminds us there are other, more familiar ways a man's life can be disrupted, and with similar results. It is clear enough that not all of Antipholus's problems stem from the fact that his brother is in town, and we may wonder if these problems can all be cured by the discovery of his brother. One curious feature of the ending is that, while the problems of the marriage have been thoroughly aired, there is no explicit reconciliation between husband and wife. . . . [The] final state of this marriage must remain an

open question. But we may suggest that in the domestic, commercial world of Ephesus there are no miracles.

No miracles, at least, for the native population. For the outsider, Antipholus of Syracuse, Ephesus is a different kind of town altogether, a place of magic and enchantment. His wonder and bewilderment remind us of the town's reputation as a centre of magic, a reputation to which none of the native population ever refers. And while—if we shake ourselves—we may remember that nothing supernatural actually takes place, we see the town to a great extent through the eyes of the outsiders, for they are given more dramatic prominence than the natives, and treated, on the whole, more sympathetically. Viewed from the special angle of the outsider, even the normal intercourse of life becomes bizarre and unsettling. . . . The prosaic, day-to-day business of a commercial town becomes something strange and dreamlike, because it is all happening to the wrong man.

Each brother's experience of the confusion of mistaken identity is matched by the more familiar experience of being unsettled by a woman. Antipholus of Ephesus has his domestic routine disrupted by an unseen brother and a nagging wife; Antipholus of Syracuse is enchanted by a strange town, and suddenly bewitched by love (the curious name given him in the Folio, 'Antipholus Erotes', suggests both wandering and love). Even when addressed by Adriana, he sees himself as in a dream, a dream to which he is willing to surrender. . . . [But his] surrender is still somewhat tentative; he offers himself to Luciana more recklessly: 'Are you a god? Would you create me new? / Transform me, then, and to your pow'r I'll yield' [III. ii. 39-40]. (pp. 8-11)

As the market-place and the tailor's shop acquire an aura of mystery for him, so too does Luciana. Here the special perspective of the outsider fuses with the special perspective of the lover, whose view of his lady is a transforming vision, comically at odds with reality. In their scene together, we note the practical, worldly manner of Luciana's advice:

> If you did wed my sister for her wealth,
> Then for her wealth's sake use her with more kindness;
> Or, if you like elsewhere, do it by stealth;
> Muffle your false love with some show of blindness.
>
> [III. ii. 5-8]

Her words appear cynical; but there is an undercurrent of sadness in them, as she tries to make the best of a difficult situation. Above all, she is realistic: there are no appeals to higher feelings, and she does not attempt to revive a dead love. But for Antipholus this rueful, worldly, but perfectly clear advice is transformed into a divine, oracular pronouncement, veiled in mystery. . . . But the comic disparity between Luciana as we see her and the lover's special vision, though clear enough, is less drastic than it might have been. The alternate rhyme they both use gives a heightened, formal quality to her speech. Despite its worldly content there *is* something oracular in its manner, and the result is a subtler comic effect than we might have expected. The double vision of Luciana is not just a matter of contrasting our reactions with the lover's; it is built into the presentation of Luciana herself—so that, while laughing at the lover, we can see his point of view. Though romantic love is a secondary motif in this play, the balance between mockery and sympathy, characteristic of later comedies, has already been struck.

This surrender to a special vision is placed ironically against Adriana's very different view of the transformations of love as they occur in marriage. Here the woman surrenders to the man (in courtship it is the other way round) and the surrender can be not life-enhancing but ruinous. . . . In the speeches of the lover, the idea of surrender is still innocent and uncomplicated, unbruised by reality. In the speeches of the wife, it has become tinged with self-pity and resentment, as we move from the idealism of courtship to the tensions of the sex war.

The idea of enchantment and transformation—including surrender in love—is seen from a third angle, that of Dromio of Syracuse, and there is a contrast between master and servant, as there is between brother and brother. What is normal life for the Ephesians and a dream for Antipholus of Syracuse is a folktale horror story come true for Dromio: 'This is the fairy land. O spite of spites! / We talk with goblins, owls, and sprites!' [II. ii. 189-90]. In place of his master's exotic 'Lapland sorcerers', Dromio imagines Ephesus as a town full of more familiar bugbears—fairies and devils. . . . And while Antipholus is eager to surrender himself to a woman and be transformed by her, Dromio's view of this surrender is (like the woman) radically different, and expressed in a comically contrasting style. (pp. 11-13)

One of the touching minor effects in the play is the way Antipholus and Dromio of Syracuse listen to each other, and sympathize with each other's point of view. When he hears what his servant has endured in the kitchen, Antipholus concludes, 'There's none but witches do inhabit here' [III. ii. 156] and decides, despite his love for Luciana, to 'stop mine ears against the mermaid's song' [III. ii. 164]. He yields to Dromio's pleas, and decides to leave town that night. But Dromio can also sink his own fears and recognize how his master is profiting from Ephesus:

> Faith, stay here this night; they will surely do
> us no harm; you saw they speak us fair, give
> us gold; methinks they are such a gentle nation
> that, but for the mountain of mad flesh that
> claims marriage of me, I could find in my heart
> to stay here still and turn witch.
>
> [IV. iv. 151-56]

To be cast adrift in a town of magic is both exhilarating and frightening; and the interplay between Dromio and Antipholus on this point conveys this dual quality subtly and even movingly. The interest of the play goes deeper than the farcical one of wondering what will happen next; we do wonder that, of course, but we also watch to see how the characters will *react* to what happens. (pp. 13-14)

[As] the knots are (figuratively and literally) untied, some of the wonder experienced by Antipholus of Syracuse begins to touch the more practical Ephesians. When the Duke sees the twins together he exclaims:

> One of these men is genius to the other;
> And so of these. Which is the natural man,
> And which the spirit? Who deciphers them?
>
> [V. i. 333-35]

To some extent the denouement is a practical, Plautine unravelling of the knots: the right people finally come together in the same place, and the various Ephesians who have lost money and property have it restored to them. But there are also strong suggestions that the denouement is an act of destiny (picking up Aegeon's concern with Fortune) and a miracle (recalling Antipholus of Syracuse's view that Ephesus is a town of magic). Certainly it cannot be brought about by institutional authority: the cry of 'justice' with which the Ephesians appeal to their

Duke is a confused babble that produces no result, since everyone's idea of 'justice' is different and the Duke has no idea what the problem is. In the last scene the Abbess, not the Duke, is the real figure of authority, remaining calm and clear-headed while he struggles to make sense of the matter. She alone registers no surprise, accepting the strange events as easily as if she had expected them to happen all along. And she presides over the final feast, suggesting in her invitation that what has taken place is a new birth—thus linking the miracle of the ending with the normal processes of life. . . . As the Abbess takes centre stage away from the Duke, so the fussy legalism he has represented is swept away by a deeper authority, the spontaneous force of life. (pp. 15-17)

The emphasis, at the end, is not on the creation of a 'new social unit' (as in Northrop Frye's theory of comedy [see excerpt above, 1949]) but on the renewal of an old family unit. Shakespeare is silent about the marriage of Adriana and Antipholus of Ephesus; and Antipholus of Syracuse's (presumably) approaching marriage is politely but firmly put to one side, as something to be discussed later. He says to Luciana:

> What I told you then,
> I hope I shall have leisure to make good;
> If this be not a dream I see and hear.
>
> [V. i. 375-77]

He is still caught up in the wonder of the family reunion. In Plautus, Menaechmus of Epidamnum sells all his household and returns to Syracuse with his brother; Shakespeare softens the emphasis considerably, but the point is the same: the final image of security is not a wedding dance but a christening feast, a *family* celebration. This may be because of the play's concern with identity: identity is surrendered in love and marriage, but when the original family is recreated, the characters join a comforting social group which asks only that they be their old selves. After the challenges to identity throughout the play the characters—and perhaps the audience—need this kind of comfort, a return to the old and familiar, rather than the start of something new which marriage symbolizes. Even at the end, the characters' disparate lives and experiences are not brought into a total harmony: security is achieved—and this is characteristic of Shakespeare's comedies—by selecting one experience, and fixing on that. Marriage is not brutally dismissed, as in Plautus; but it is quietly placed in the background, and no great hopes are pinned on it.

In the rejoining of the broken family, there is—as in most comic endings—a clear element of wish fulfilment. The play itself is a special, artificial ordering of experience, and, while we are not given the sort of distancing epilogue we find at the end of *A Midsummer Night's Dream* or *As You Like It*, the manner of the play throughout is sufficiently stylized to remind us that it is a work of literary and theatrical artifice. The play is, even for a Shakespearian comedy, unusually full of rhyme, of jingling verse and of comic turns and set pieces. . . . And the play presents a story starting from a fantastic premise and moving to an almost equally fantastic conclusion. But at the same time, for all its artificiality, it deals with the most normal and intimate relations of life—wives and husbands, parents and children. In comparing the different worlds the Antipholus brothers inhabit, we saw an intersection of the special and fantastic with the normal and everyday—Ephesus as a town of sorcerers, and as a town of merchants. The same intersection of the fantastic and the normal becomes part of the audience's own experience as it watches the play—a strange and stylized fable built out of the most familiar relationships of life. The result of this interweaving of the fantastic and the everyday is to make us see each kind of experience from the perspective of the other—just as Antipholus of Syracuse is brought to see ordinary tradesmen as 'Lapland sorcerers', or the Abbess sees the coincidental rejoining of a long-sundered family as an event as natural as childbirth. The comic strategy of the play is one of dislocation, forcing us to see experiences from a fresh perspective, reminding us that no one understanding of life is final. The mixed dramatic mode gives shading and variety to what could have been a one-note, mechanical farce; but it also embodies a comic vision of the instability of life itself. (pp. 17-19)

> Alexander Leggatt, '' 'The Comedy of Errors','' in his Shakespeare's Comedy of Love, *Methuen & Co Ltd, 1974, pp. 1-19.*

JAMES L. SANDERSON   (essay date 1975)

The Comedy of Errors is certainly not *Twelfth Night* (nor, perhaps, was meant to be, although they show parallels in plot structure and have several comic situations in common). *The Comedy of Errors* lacks the iridescent implication of *A Midsummer-Night's Dream* and the rich stylistic texture of *As You Like It*. But there is more substance to the play than the obvious

WHAT WILL YOU MURDER ME   ACT IV SCENE IV

Act IV. Scene iv. Antipholus of Ephesus and Officers. By John Byam Lister Shaw (1900?). From the Art Collection of the Folger Shakespeare Library.

noisy surface action, which seems too often to have absorbed critics' attention, to the exclusion of everything else. Event is better melded with ''character,'' and the two plots of the play achieve a closer unity than has usually been noted. More than an isolated, superficial apprentice exercise, *The Comedy of Errors* embodies an important theme that Shakespeare was to elaborate upon in a number of his later and greatest plays.

Perhaps profiting from the renewed critical interest in Shakespearean comedy in general, *The Comedy of Errors* has received more sensitive and imaginative readings in recent years. (p. 604)

Despite more careful critical attention, there remains a matter of thematic significance in *The Comedy of Errors*, and one of recurrent importance in Shakespeare's thought, which I believe has not been adequately appreciated and discussed. I refer to the theme of patience. Patience is a virtue whose absence among several main figures in the play promotes, perpetuates, and augments the ''errors'' bedeviling Ephesus and a virtue whose cultivation helps make possible the resolution of conflicts, the creation of a right understanding of oneself and others, and the eventual enjoyment of those ministrations of a benign Providence which despite man's frowardness, the play seems to suggest, eventually brings clarification out of bafflement, happiness out of adversity, indeed, life out of death. More than mechanical plot contrivances designed to pad out an evening of slapstick entertainment at Gray's Inn or the simple superimposition upon lifeless stick figures, the ''errors'' derive from the confrontation of impatient, impetuous human beings with unusual or distasteful circumstances, individuals whose impatience before complexities and whose restless intolerance of disappointment and frustration generate errors that deepen their confusion and beget additional errors. Furthermore, the theme of patience joins the drama's two plots and contributes to its unity.

The frequency with which *patience* occurs in *The Comedy of Errors* suggests that it is an idea of major thematic concern in the play. The word, sometimes with formal modification, appears twelve times and usually on an occasion of some moment or as part of some serious advice-giving, which would further support the view of its importance in the play.

Patience first appears in I.ii almost simultaneously with the first ''error'' of identity, an overturelike statement of the theme which receives more explicit development later. . . . To the emphatic question ''Where is the thousand marks thou hadst for me?'' Dromio replies:

> I have some marks of yours upon my pate,
> Some of mistress' marks upon my shoulders,
> But not a thousand marks between you both.
> If I should pay your worship those again,
> Perchance you will not bear them patiently.
> [I. ii. 82-6]
> (pp. 604-06)

Patience figures prominently in II.i, where Adriana peevishly fumes about her husband's tardiness and Luciana lectures her reprovingly on the customary ways and recognized rights of men, who, unlike women, are masters of their liberty. ''Time is their master, and when they see time / They'll go or come; if so, be patient sister'' [II. i. 8-9]. Adriana's discontent with her dependence upon the whims of her husband is hardly alleviated by Luciana's discourse on the Great Chain of Being in which examples of hierarchical ordering in the universe are cited to justify and sanction a master/servant relationship between man and wife. (p. 606)

Several significant reiterations of *patience* appear in III.i. Adriana has come upon the densely unsuspecting Antipholus S., and, thinking him to be her husband, invites him into her house to dine and orders the gates locked against all others. Unaware of this development, her husband, Antipholus E., approaches his house accompanied by his business associates Angelo and Balthasar, whom he expects to entertain. Denied entrance to his own house, frustrated and embarrassed, he explodes, demanding ''an iron crow'' with which he intends to force entry. In amazement, Balthasar pleads for restraint: ''Have patience, sir; O, let it not be so!'' [III. i. 85]. Insisting that there must surely be some satisfactory explanation for Adriana's unusual conduct, Balthasar urges his friend to ''depart in patience'' [III. i. 94]. (pp. 606-07)

A recommendation of patience recurs in IV.ii, when Luciana reports the flirtatious attention Antipholus S. has paid her during the entertainment at dinner. Suspicious that her husband is being unfaithful to her, Adriana threateningly questions whether her presumed rival had encouraged him with a pleasant response. Luciana responds pleadingly: ''Have patience, I beseech'' [IV. ii. 16]. Verbal violence gives way to physical in Scene iv of this Act. Dromio E. encounters his master, who expects him to have secured money from Adriana to pay the goldsmith. Under threat of arrest, perplexed and enraged by Dromio's incomprehensible unresponsiveness, Antipholus begins to beat his servant; at this point the arresting officer intervenes to urge, ''Good sir, be patient'' [IV. iv. 19]. Capable of a jest (and a biblical echo) even in such straits, Dromio replies: ''Nay, 'tis for me to be patient; I am in adversity'' [IV. iv. 20].

In Act V the unquiet principals in the play come with their various angers and partial understandings to the abbey, where Antipholus S. has taken refuge from the mad chaos whirling about him. The Abbess appears during the uproar and her first words are appropriately imperative: ''Be quiet, people'' [V. i. 38]. In the exchanges that follow she upbraids Adriana for her jealousy and unwifely conduct. When Adriana demands that she be permitted to minister to her husband, who she thinks is inside the abbey, the Abbess replies, ''Be patient'' [V. i. 102], and refuses to permit anyone to disturb Antipholus until he has regained his senses. (p. 607)

The theme of patience is not only given frequent verbal statement but is also reflected in the actions and thinking of the individuals involved. Both Antipholi and Adriana are prone to abuse their inferiors at moments of frustration and impatience. The pummeling of the brothers Dromio sometimes strikes modern audiences as a not-very-funny comic cliché from a socially primitive era, a cheap ploy to earn the guffaws of an unfeeling if not barbaric audience. In reality, however, Shakespeare has charged these attacks with meaning; they are the outward and visible signs of imperfections of character, of lapses from rational control and surrender to the passions—in short, manifestations of impatience. . . . Both Antipholi are subject to hasty generalization. To the embarrassed astonishment of his companions, Antipholus E. must be restrained from tearing down the door to his house, incapable of pausing to consider plausible explanations for the locked doors and the saucy statements issuing from within the house. Even more absurd in his impatience of doubt and inability to suspend his judgment is Antipholus S. For over five years he and his servant have been on a quest seeking their identical twin brothers. Antipholus'

mental opacity is remarkable as he is baffled by strangers who address him by his name, attractive ladies who familiarly invite him to dinner, and unfamiliar individuals who give him gifts and speak to him as if they have known him for many years. . . . The characterization that Shakespeare gives the principals here may be somewhat ''humorous,'' that is, limited to certain specific predispositions of character, and it is apparent that perspicacity in Antipholus would collapse the fragile plot. But it seems clear that Shakespeare also intends the audience to recognize certain traits of easy wrath, impetuosity in thought, and recklessness in conduct—in short, deficiencies in patience—and he dramatized the ''errors'' in the play as manifestations of such flaws of character. (pp. 608-09)

Patience may also be seen as an organizing idea that relates the two plots and promotes the overall unity of the play. The folly of impatience is clearly in evidence among the Antipholi and Adriana, but Solinus' decision concerning Aegeon's fate suggests that he too suffers from a proneness to facile and superficial generalization, a tendency to categorize a human being on imperfect knowledge and to determine his fate on superficial consideration. His judgment concerning Aegeon's punishment, which he says may not be set aside, is in fact easily rescinded later when he discovers his identity. . . . Aegeon and Aemelia both represent good examples of patience in adversity and suggest norms by which to measure the imprudent conduct of the twins and Adriana. Albeit with some understandable sadness, Aegeon approaches his execution without outcry or vehement display of emotion and bears his plight manfully. Living quietly in retreat from a world in which she has suffered great personal loss, Aemelia becomes an important spokesman for a charity that has suffered long, yet is kind to others, and that strives to work the peace of the present amid the clamors of a jealous wife, an angry husband, two pairs of very disoriented twins, clamoring servants, citizens, creditors, and one very confused duke. The composure and control of Aemelia contrast significantly with the vituperative and noisy petulance of the Antipholi and Adriana. In addition, Aemelia's calling for patience echoes earlier like pronouncements by Luciana, thereby drawing the two plots more closely together.

Many have noted that in adapting Plautus's comedy Shakespeare changed the setting from Epidamnum to Ephesus. . . . Shakespeare found Ephesus a particularly appropriate setting for a play elaborating the theme of patience. Through the letters of St. Paul, Ephesus was known as a place of social discord and unrest. The Apostle's admonitions to the Ephesians aptly spoke to the conditions of the figures in Shakespeare's play: ''Let not the Sunne goe downe upon your wrath, neither giue place to the backebiter. . . . Let all bitternes, and fiercenes, and wrath, and roaring, and cursed speaking be put away from you, with all maliciousnesse. Be ye courteous one to another, mercifull, forgiuing one another, euen as God for Christs sake hath forgiuen you.'' . . . Shakespeare may well have expected his audiences to place such domestic turmoil in a perspective of Christian history and teaching. (pp. 609-10)

Patience is a concept that occurs frequently throughout Shakespeare's plays. Although mechanical word-counts can be misleading, the importance of patience is at least suggested by its occurrence as a substantive, adverb, and adjective well over three hundred times. To this number should be added forty-two instances of the negative forms ''impatience,'' ''impatiently,'' and ''impatient.'' The wisdom and consolation of patience and the comic folly and tragic potential of impatience are themes commented upon by various Shakespearean characters and developed significantly in many of Shakespeare's plays. (p. 612)

If my contention that the theme of patience informs *The Comedy of Errors* is valid, the "unified field" of Shakespeare's thought and vision is considerably broadened, both in time and in the range of dramatic mode embodying the theme. Patience links Shakespeare's early work with his late, the young man from Stratford with the mature master looking homeward to retirement. No isolated "exercise in dramatic archeology," *The Comedy of Errors* adumbrates Shakespeare's more comprehensive art and reflects an important element of continuity in his vision which will help nurture the growth of diverse dramatic forms, myriad characters and episodes, and subtle emphases "to something of great constancy."

The Comedy of Errors also looks forward to Shakespeare's development of comedic form. It reflects his "sense of comedy as a moment in a larger cycle" in which the menaces of ignorance and death give way "to make the comic resolution a renewal of life, indeed explicitly a rebirth." The foolish, impatient mortals strut and fret their few hours about the streets of Ephesus, ignorantly struggling against their own best interests, committing errors of mind and heart which place in hazard, as much as Solinus' austere sentence, the fate of a family. But in this comedic vision of life their errors cannot forever triumph over enlightenment; some force for good refuses to permit them to hold back the emergence of a new, joyful, and restorative social order, which Northrop Frye has taught us to anticipate as the conclusion toward which Shakespearean comedy proceeds [see excerpt above, 1949].

It seems significant that a new and better society emerges at the portals of the abbey and is celebrated within its sanctuary. On his way to the execution of Aegeon, Solinus encounters the wrangling, recriminatory company outside the abbey. As the representative of an earthly law concerned with protecting rights and measuring out penalties, Solinus is urged by the loud claimants to give "justice," but the complexity of the issues confuses him and renders him ineffective. Another kind of mediation would seem necessary to disentangle the confusions at Ephesus, one devoted to a more kindly and loving code in the conduct of human relationships. From the cloistered tranquility of the abbey Aemelia again emerges to serve as such a peacemaker. Having earlier called for a patience that could make clarification of personal and social identity possible, the rewards of the faithful questers Aegeon, Antipholus, and Dromio available, and the restorative and loving ministrations of charity operative, she now brings forth Antipholus and Dromio of Syracuse at a moment truly propitious for the immediate resolution of the disputes. (pp. 617-18)

G. Wilson Knight's words are not excessive: *The Comedy of Errors* "is a glorious little play. And, at the close, all is united again, the end is peace, reunion, and pardon" [see excerpt above, 1932]. And our vision is refreshed and enhanced "in this land of gold, merchants, and mystery," where "all odds are made even, all sea sorrow finally dissolved in joy and love." (p. 618)

> *James L. Sanderson, "Patience in 'The Comedy of Errors'," in* Texas Studies in Literature and Language, *Vol. XVI, No. 4, Winter, 1975, pp. 603-18.*

ADDITIONAL BIBLIOGRAPHY

Arthos, John. "Shakespeare's Transformation of Plautus." *Comparative Drama* 1, No. 4 (Winter 1967-68): 239-53.*
> Discusses Shakespeare's substitution of a hierarchical social order for Plautus's disordered and confused collection of citizens, and asserts that such a change shows Shakespeare's predeliction for just and ordered societies. Arthos agrees with those critics who believe that *The Comedy of Errors* fits neatly into the canon. This essay also includes a brief discussion of the elaborate and varied verse schemes used by both Shakespeare and Plautus, and their relationship to music.

Baldwin, Thomas Whitfield. *William Shakespeare Adapts a Hanging.* Princeton: Princeton University Press, 1931, 201 p.
> An exposition of Baldwin's elaborate theory that Shakespeare attended the execution of William Hartley in 1588, and from that experience adapted the setting for the frame story of Aegeon in *The Comedy of Errors.* Baldwin uses his theory to date the play at 1589, earlier than the generally accepted date.

Baldwin, T[homas] W[hitfield]. "*The Comedy of Errors:* Main Sources" and "Genesis of *The Comedy of Errors.*" In his *Shakspeare's Five-Act Structure: Shakspeare's Early Plays on the Background of Renaissance Theories of Five-Act Structure from 1740,* pp. 665-90, pp. 691-718. Urbana: The University of Illinois Press, 1947.
> Describes how Shakespeare constructed his play around the Renaissance theory of five-act structure, which included a catastrophe at the end of each act. Baldwin contends that "the act structure of *The Comedy of Errors* is derived directly from that in *Menaechmi,* with some assistance from *Amphitruo* and a great deal from the five-act formula." The plays of Plautus were first divided into acts in the early sixteenth century, incorporating the formula used by the Roman playwright Terence.

Baldwin, T[homas] W[hitfield]. "Three Homilies in *The Comedy of Errors.*" In *Essays on Shakespeare and Elizabethan Drama in Honor of Hardin Craig,* edited by Richard Hosley, pp. 137-47. Columbia: University of Missouri Press, 1962.
> Explains the biblical sources for Luciana's homily, which recommends Adriana's "subjection" to her husband, and Adriana's two homilies concerning adultery.

Barber, C. L. "Shakespearian Comedy in *The Comedy of Errors.*" *College English* 25, No. 7 (April 1964): 493-97.
> Contrasts Shakespeare's use of fully developed characters, especially in portraying the marriage relationship, to Plautus's use of characters as "fractions of human nature in its aggressive, libidinal side."

Bradbrook, M. C. *The Growth and Structure of Elizabethan Comedy.* London: Chatto & Windus, 1955, 245 p.*
> In a brief passage, portrays *The Comedy of Errors* as a "Gray's Inn play," reflecting the taste of the age for wit of "quick, shallow dexterity." Bradbrook calls the doubling of the twins "a characteristically florid Elizabethan device."

Clubb, Louise George. "Italian Comedy and *The Comedy of Errors.*" *Comparative Literature* XIX, No. 3 (Summer 1967): 240-51.*
> Relates *The Comedy of Errors* to the *commedia grave* of the Italian counter-reformation. Though no direct link can be found in the compositional genetics of *The Comedy of Errors,* Clubb cites certain features that distinguish *Comedy* and the *commedia grave* from the medieval Italian comedies: the lesser role of the courtesan, the "addition of pathos," the theme of jealousy, the theme of madness and sorcery, and the reunification of the characters at the close of the play.

Feldman, A. Bronson. "Shakespeare's Early Errors." *The International Journal of Psycho-Analysis* XXXVI (1955): 114-33.
> A psychoanalytic interpretation of Shakespeare's motivation for writing *The Comedy of Errors* which bibliographer Ronald Berman claims "should either be avoided or approached only by the connoisseur of the intellectual grotesque." Feldman attributes the doubling of the hero to Shakespeare's "self-love" and claims that

the Syracusan Antipholus pursues Luciana because of Shakespeare's "irresistible urge to embrace strangers as lovers."

Foakes, R. A. Introduction to *The Comedy of Errors*, by William Shakespeare, pp. xi-lv. London: Methuen & Co., 1962.

A comprehensive overview of various commentators' opinions concerning the text, date, sources, and staging of the play. This essay also includes a critical introduction which considers many of the serious interpretations of the play, and offers a brief stage history.

French, Marilyn. "Marriage: *The Comedy of Errors*." In her *Shakespeare's Division of Experience*, pp. 77-81. New York: Summit Books, 1981.

A feminist interpretation designating Adriana and Luciana as embodiments of the "outlaw" and "inlaw" principles of the feminine nature as distinguished by Shakespeare.

Frye, Northrop. "Characterization in Shakespearian Comedy." *Shakespeare Quarterly* IV, No. 3 (July 1953): 271-77.

Argues against both the historical approach to Shakespeare's comedies as well as any method which focuses on character, claiming that "character depends on function." Thus, Frye concludes, we must examine the structure of a drama rather than its characters *per se* or the age in which the work was written. "The notion of an antithesis between the lifelike character and the stock type," he claims, "is a vulgar error."

Levin, Harry. "Two Comedies of Errors." In his *Refractions: Essays in Comparative Literature*, pp. 128-150. New York: Oxford University Press, 1966.*

Reviews the similarities and differences between *The Comedy of Errors* and the *Menaechmi*. Levin concentrates on the problem of identity and explains how Shakespeare deepened Plautus's two-dimensional play.

Petronella, Vincent F. "Structure and Theme through Separation and Union in Shakespeare's *The Comedy of Errors*." *Modern Language Review* 69, No. 3 (July 1974): 481-88.

Parallels Richard Henze's essay on the bonding themes in *The Comedy of Errors*. Petronella claims that the play works "not by means of senseless antics and heavy-handed sentimentality but by producing clear-sighted comedy that is not afraid to enhance its vision with an occasional sojourn into farce."

Pettet, E. C. "Shakespeare's 'Romantic' Comedies." In his *Shakespeare and the Romance Tradition*, pp. 67-100. London: Staples Press, 1949.

Sees *The Comedy of Errors* as an "oddity," at sharp variance with Shakespeare's romantic comedies. He does, however, note that the love story of Luciana and Antipholus of Syracuse and the frame story of Aegeon are two "minor elements" which reappear in Shakespeare's later plays.

Robertson, J. M. "The Authorship of *The Comedy of Errors*." In his *The Shakespeare Canon, Part II*, pp. 126-57. London: George Routledge & Sons, 1923.

An examination of the versification of *The Comedy of Errors*. Robertson, finding that *Comedy's* verse patterns differ from those of other Shakespearean plays of the same period, claims that the play was written by Christopher Marlowe, with only minor revisions by Shakespeare.

Stevenson, David Lloyd. "Shakespeare's Comedies of Courtship." In his *The Love-Game Comedy*, pp. 185-207. New York: Columbia University Press, 1946.

Claims that in *The Comedy of Errors* Shakespeare exaggerates "the basic unreality of romantic conventions" into farce. Stevenson focuses on the "antagonistic notions of love" presented in the play, claiming that Shakespeare makes no attempt to reconcile them.

Thomas, Sidney. "The Date of *The Comedy of Errors*." *Shakespeare Quarterly* VII, No. 4 (Autumn 1956): 377-84.

Disputes the standard dating of the play, claiming that it was not written until immediately before the 1594 performance at Gray's Inn. Thomas asserts that there is no reason to believe that the reference to the French civil war proves that the play was written at an earlier date. English interest in the war, he says, was evident as late as 1597.

Hamlet

DATE: The date of *Hamlet*'s composition has been designated as being after 1598 but prior to 1602. The earlier date is determined by its exclusion from the list of Shakespeare's works in Francis Meres's *Palladis Tamia*, published in September of 1598; the later is established by the 1602 entry of *Hamlet* in the Stationers' Register. Scholars have further narrowed the gap by noting that Polonius's statement that he "did enact Julius Caesar" is a reference to the play *Julius Caesar,* which was performed in 1599. The reference in *Hamlet* to the War of the Theatres, which was most intense in 1601, suggests that year as the date of composition. However, E.A.J. Honigmann has argued that the section that contains this reference, not included in either quarto text of the play, was added to the prompt-copy in 1601, which explains its inclusion in the Folio. This theory, if correct, could help to clear up the problems raised by another piece of external evidence. Gabriel Harvey's undated note in his copy of Speght's edition of the works of Chaucer, published in 1598, discusses *Hamlet,* and also describes Edmund Spenser, who died in 1599, as a "florishing metrician." Debate over this passage has centered on the meaning of "florishing." According to F. S. Boas and W. J. Lawrence, the word, in addition to the more common definition "thriving," can mean "popular" or "in demand." Thus, they argue, Spenser need not have been alive when Harvey's note was written. An additional piece of significant external evidence is Harvey's reference to the Earl of Essex in the present tense, which indicates that the play had been performed before Essex's execution in February, 1601. However, in the same passage that includes the reference to *Julius Caesar,* Rosencrantz speaks of an "innovation," a word usually used by Shakespeare to mean "uprising." If this refers, as some critics assume, to Essex's rebellion, the play would have to be dated after Essex's execution. No record of a court performance of *Hamlet* exists, a fact that gives weight to the theory that the play includes references to the Essex rebellion. In the face of a large body of conflicting evidence, most scholars have settled on a composition date of 1600 or 1601, with 1601 being the most often cited.

TEXT: There are three major texts for *Hamlet* and scholars hotly dispute their relationship. The earliest is the First Quarto, also called the Bad Quarto or Q1, published in 1603. The Second Quarto, Q2, published in 1604, is the longest version of the play. The third version is the Folio text, or F1, published in 1623. The highly corrupt nature of the text of Q1 has led most scholars to conclude that it was "pirated," that is, recollected by either actors or spectators and published without authorization. Though Q1 was originally assumed to be a first draft of the play, G. I. Duthie in his *The Bad Quarto of "Hamlet"* asserted that the text is actually a reconstruction of the play by the actor who played Marcellus, a theory that has been generally accepted by modern scholars. The Second Quarto and the Folio both contain passages not included in the other, and the two texts offer variant readings of many words and lines. In cases of contradictory readings, editors generally conferred authority on the Folio, but J. Dover Wilson, in *The Manuscript of Shakespeare's "Hamlet,"* reassessed this practice. In a detailed analysis of the three texts, Dover Wilson attempted to prove that the Second Quarto had been copied from Shakespeare's "foul papers," or uncorrected manuscript. The Folio text, Dover Wilson argued, was drawn from a play-

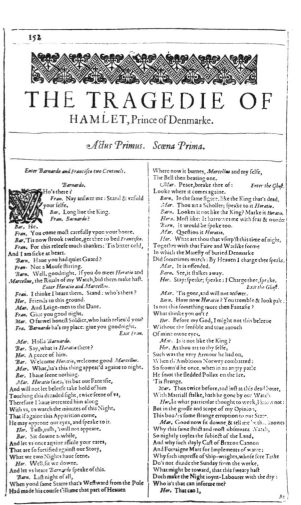

house copy, thus explaining the extensive differences between it and Q2. Dover Wilson explained many variant readings through his theory that various compositors and copiers misinterpreted Shakespeare's difficult handwriting. He proposed that a single, not necessarily reliable, compositor set the entire Second Quarto.

Alice Walker, in her *Textual Problems of the First Folio,* asserted that the Folio text of *Hamlet* is based not on a prompt-copy, but on a collation of the printed text of Q2 and a prompt-book. This weakens the authority of the Folio and undermines the theory that a correct reading can be based upon Q2 and the Folio. Walker's argument was challenged by Harold Jenkins, who suggested that the Folio copy was considerably altered by the actors.

Contrary to Dover Wilson, Fredson Bowers claimed that two compositors worked on the Q2 text, and furthermore, that they were the same two who had set the reliable 1600 quarto of *The Merchant of Venice.* Bowers therefore detected less evidence of misprinting in Q2 than Dover Wilson did, and argued that editors of the text should use less conjecture than Dover Wilson recommended in judging the reliability of passages in Q2.

Considering the disputed nature of the text, most editors of *Hamlet* have adopted an eclectic approach, choosing some variant readings from the Folio, and others from the Second Quarto. This leaves a number of "cruxes" in the text, where words or passages are uncertain. A well-known and much-discussed example is the reference in I.ii.129 to "solid," "sallied," or "sullied" flesh.

SOURCES: Shakespeare's immediate source for *Hamlet* is apparently a lost English play with a similar plot. Thomas Nashe's allusion to this play in his preface to Robert Greene's pamphlet *Menaphon* (1589) indicates that it was a Senecan tragedy, and Nashe makes a pun later in his commentary that suggests that Thomas Kyd was the author. This play is commonly referred to as the *Ur-Hamlet*. An earlier source is François de Belleforest's *Histoires Tragiques,* which scholars agree is the probable source for Kyd's, and possibly Shakespeare's, play. Belleforest derived his story from the Norse legend of *Amlothi* as rendered by Saxo Grammaticus in his *Historiae Danicae.* Although Grammaticus's version, written around 1200, contains a plot strikingly similar to that of *Hamlet,* there are important differences. The Hamlet character, Amleth, assumes madness in order to protect himself from his uncle, who is the acknowledged murderer of his father. Amleth revenges himself by slaying the king and courtiers at a banquet and assumes the throne. Belleforest retained this basic plot, but reduced the barbarism and made important additions, such as the adultery of the queen and uncle before the murder. Scholars dispute which further refinements and additions were made by Shakespeare and which by the author of the *Ur-Hamlet,* but some critics conjecture that an idea of the earlier play is evidenced in a seventeenth-century German drama, *Der bestrafte Brudermord.* This play is thought to be based on the *Ur-Hamlet,* though the relation between the two cannot be determined.

Some critics speculate that Shakespeare derived the melancholic aspects of Hamlet's character from Timothy Bright's *Treatise of Melancholy,* an Elizabethan medical text. In addition, several critics have noted a link between Hamlet and the Earl of Essex. Jacob Feis and J. M. Robertson have related Hamlet's skepticism to the philosophy of Michel de Montaigne, but most critics believe that Montaigne did not directly influence Shakespeare.

CRITICAL HISTORY: *Hamlet* has inspired more critical writing than any other work of Western literature. Clifford Leech wrote in 1956: "The criticism of *Hamlet* is marked by its extent, its variety, and its frequent aggressiveness." Scholars have disagreed on virtually every aspect of the play. In addition to the textual controversies, several key arguments predominate *Hamlet* criticism. In the eighteenth century, the Neoclassicists, who were the first notable commentators on *Hamlet,* praised the play for its emotional power and conceptual vigor, but found fault with its "irregularity" and "impropriety." As early as 1763, Thomas Sheridan foreshadowed the Romantic conception of Hamlet, which consists mainly of the analyses of the central figure, including what is known as the "sentimental" view of Hamlet, in addition to discussions of Hamlet's insanity and interpretations of the dilemma of his indecision. In the early twentieth century, proponents of the historical school pointed out that *Hamlet* should be evaluated in light of the values of the Elizabethan era, as a play which is derived from the tradition of the revenge tragedy and which reflects the moral, social, and theological attitudes of Shakespeare's times. The psychoanalytic movement influenced a group of critics who attempted to resolve the ambiguities of Hamlet's character by using the theories of Sigmund Freud. Writers influenced by the theories of New Criticism emphasized the

play's unity of imagery, symbolism, and language. A variety of approaches is evident in the commentary of critics of the present era, many of whom have applied modern theories of linguistics and semantics in their interpretation of *Hamlet.* While critical approaches to the play have varied through four centuries of interpretation, the same issues have predominated. Prominent among them are Hamlet's delay, his madness, the prayer scene, the nature of the ghost, Hamlet's attitude toward his mother and toward Ophelia, and the dumbshow. Various critics have selected one or another of these as the key to the play.

The first critical mention of *Hamlet* was made by Gabriel Harvey sometime after 1598. Noting that *Hamlet* and *The Rape of Lucrece* "have it in them to please the wiser sort," Harvey indicated that soon after its first performance the drama was known for its intellectual appeal. Throughout the seventeenth century, however, most allusions to the play are fragments, and it is not clear whether they refer to Shakespeare's play or to the *Ur-Hamlet.*

Jeremy Collier's attack on Ophelia's impropriety is typical of the arguments which dominated the Neoclassical period. Although some critics defended Shakespeare on this point, notably James Drake, who maintained that the play reflects an "admirable distribution of Poetick Justice," the madness and death of Ophelia distressed many commentators, including Charlotte Lennox and Samuel Johnson. Nicholas Rowe, drawing a comparison made by several critics of his time, asserted that *Hamlet* was superior to Sophocles's *Electra* in its handling of the theme of patricide and revenge. Such an interpretation, based on the exploration of mythic elements in the play, was developed in the twentieth century by such critics as Gilbert Murray and Francis Fergusson. Another fault commonly noted by the eighteenth-century critics concerned Hamlet's famous "To be or not to be" soliloquy. Charles Gildon pronounced the speech unnecessary in the drama, and Tobias Smollett added that it is out of character. Two questions which remain important today were first presented during this era in an anonymous essay, which scholars now attribute to either Thomas Hanmer or George Stubbes. In this, the first extended commentary on *Hamlet,* the critic replies simply to the problem of Hamlet's procrastination: "Had Hamlet gone naturally to work . . . there would have been the end of our play." Though often dismissed, this remark is cited by some twentieth-century historical critics, who place the play in the revenge-tragedy tradition and consider the delay a mere dramatic contrivance. The anonymous commentator also observed that in the prayerscene Hamlet's reasons for refusing to kill Claudius are offensive to Christian morals, an opinion that anticipates Johnson's charge that Hamlet's speech in this scene is "too horrible to read or be uttered." The exact nature of Hamlet's motives at this point in the drama have sparked one of the most important critical debates about the play.

The Romantic response to *Hamlet* was first expressed by Henry Mackenzie and William Richardson. Both asserted that Hamlet's irresolution is consistent with his character, thereby foreshadowing the so-called "sentimental" view of the character which Johann Wolfgang von Goethe was to expand upon and popularize over a decade later. Goethe described Hamlet as a "costly vase" in which "an oak tree is planted." According to Goethe, Hamlet is beautiful and sensitive, rather than heroic, even though his task requires heroic strength. The German Romantic critic August Wilhelm Schlegel modified this view, and defined the play as a "tragedy of thought." In Schlegel's opinion, Hamlet's inclination toward metaphysical thinking, most apparent in his soliloquies, makes action repugnant to him. Samuel Taylor Coleridge developed the same concept in a famous description of Hamlet's problem: "great, enormous, intellectual activity, and a consequent proportionate aversion to real action. . . ." The Schlegel-Coleridge interpretation of Hamlet's nature is one of the most influential in the play's critical history. The continued preoccupation with the main character is evident in a comment by the English Romantic critic William Hazlitt, who makes his identification with the hero clear: "It is *we* who are Hamlet."

Critics during the nineteenth century were also concerned with the question of Hamlet's madness. Some maintained that Hamlet is truly insane, while others believed that he merely feigns madness. Towards the end of the century this question receded, but psychoanalytic critics later revived it. The German scholars Hermann Ulrici and G. G. Gervinus concentrated on the play's ethical themes, recalling the critical preoccupation of eighteenth-century commentators, and anticipating twentieth-century critics who saw in the play a struggle with and gradual acceptance of Christian values. Both Ulrici and Gervinus cite the introspective side of Hamlet's nature as evidence of a superior morality, which is ruined when he is spurred to violent action. Søren Kierkegaard, a nineteenth-century philosopher, also discussed the religious aspects of *Hamlet*. Kierkegaard observed that the inner conflict implied by Hamlet's doubts could not be effectively conveyed through drama. Another nineteenth-century philosopher, Friedrich Nietzsche, contributed a new perspective to the play's criticism. Nietzsche proposed that Hamlet's procrastination is a product of his "Dionysian" awareness: because he has gained an understanding of the "true nature of things" Hamlet has lost the ability to act. The idea that Hamlet is prohibited from translating his metaphysical knowledge into action because of the materially corrupt nature of his society pervades twentieth-century criticism of the play.

Karl Werder offered yet another radical departure in the discussion of Hamlet's delay. Werder theorized that Hamlet's task was not to kill Claudius, but to expose him to public justice, a thesis that has been attacked by some of *Hamlet*'s most notable critics, including A. C. Bradley and J. Dover Wilson. Yet, with some modifications and refinements, this position has been generally accepted by other critics, among them Fredson Bowers, who posited that Hamlet must act as both "minister" and "scourge," and who discussed the relationship of these concepts to Elizabethan theology.

Two major developments occurred in *Hamlet* criticism at the beginning of the twentieth century. The first was the publication of Freud's *The Interpretation of Dreams,* in which Freud briefly outlined the way in which his theory of the Oedipus complex relates to the character of Hamlet. Ernest Jones elaborated on Freud's thesis in a series of essays which argued that Hamlet's Oedipal attachment to his mother caused both his reluctance to kill Claudius and his rejection of Ophelia. The second major event was the publication of A. C. Bradley's *Shakespearean Tragedy,* often regarded as the most important work on the tragedies since Coleridge's commentaries. Bradley rejected previous ideas concerning Hamlet's delay, stating that its cause is "a state of profound melancholy" brought about not by his father's death but by his mother's remarriage. These two approaches prompted some critics to respond that Hamlet is a character in an Elizabethan play, not an actual person with a psychological case history. This argument, posed by E. E.

Stoll and his colleagues in the historical school of criticism, led to a greater emphasis on studies of the sources of the play and of the society and culture of Shakespeare's time. More recently, Eleanor Prosser employed a historical approach, investigating Elizabethan attitudes toward revenge. Finding expressions of disapproval regarding private revenge in both political and theological writings, she contended that the ghost is "a devil," and that Hamlet's tragedy results from taking his advice.

Also in the early twentieth century, W. W. Greg brought forth the problem of the dumb-show. If Claudius does not react to the visual representation of his crime, Greg asked, what makes him respond to the spoken section of "The Mousetrap"? Greg's theory that the ghost's account of the murder was unreliable led him to doubt the ghost's objectivity. This argument was challenged by J. Dover Wilson, who proposed that Claudius does not witness the dumb-show because his attention is momentarily diverted. Dover Wilson expanded his analysis of the action of the play in his well-known book, *What Happens in "Hamlet."* Greg and Dover Wilson, along with Harley Granville-Barker, changed the focus of *Hamlet* criticism from character problems to questions of dramatic structure.

In the 1930s, G. Wilson Knight and other critics initiated an approach which concentrated on close explications of imagery and language and on the unity of a work of literature. This school of thought, which is characteristic of the approach known as New Criticism, made its mark on a generation of Shakespearean critics. Caroline F. E. Spurgeon, in her *Shakespeare's Imagery and What It Tells Us,* pioneered the technique of image pattern analysis. She found that the predominant images in *Hamlet* reflect the play's thematic preoccupation with disease, corruption, and death. Wolfgang Clemen also emphasized the play's images of disease and corruption, and related these to the prince's character and language. G. Wilson Knight also examined the play in terms of imagery and atmosphere and identified death as the unifying theme. Maynard Mack, in an explication of the play's verbal patterns, detected three major themes: mystery, the dichotomy of appearance and reality, and mortality. T. McAlindon explored the imagery in *Hamlet* that connotes abuse of speech. Other critics who focused on the language of *Hamlet* include Reuben A. Brower, Inga-Stina Ewbank, and Harry Levin, who in a rhetorical analysis focused on the play's uncertainty as it is manifested in its interrogative mood.

Two major critics have disputed the classification of *Hamlet* as a tragedy. E.M.W. Tillyard argued that the play was not principally tragic and that it should be considered a "problem play." Lionel Abel classified the play as "metatheatre," because each character has a radically different perception of events. Abel concludes that, rather than presenting a unified vision, Shakespeare permits each character to act as a separate "playwright."

A minor tradition of negative appraisals of the play began with F. M. de Voltaire, who, speaking from a French Neoclassical point of view, denounced the play as the work of a "drunken savage." T. S. Eliot later pronounced it "an artistic failure." Some critics, such as George Steevens, Ivan Turgenieff, and Salvador de Madariaga, have expressed a negative opinion of the main character. Rebecca West interpreted Hamlet as a Machiavellian figure who, tainted with original sin, is responsible for the evil which surrounds him. The majority of critics, however, like most readers and audiences, view the character sympathetically and consider the play a masterpiece.

No single critical approach dominates current *Hamlet* criticism. Commentators draw on diverse traditions in their writings on a work which continues to capture and sustain the interest of critics with radically varied approaches. As Paul Gottschalk wrote in his *The Meanings of Hamlet*, ''When a new book on *Hamlet* appears, and we have read it, our work has only begun. We still have to ask whether and how this book fits in with others of its school and of other schools . . . to discover how much it adds to what we already have and thus expands our horizons.''

JEREMY COLLIER   (essay date 1698)

[*Collier, a clergyman, is best remembered for his attack on the Restoration stage in a tract entitled* A Short View of the Immorality and Profaneness of the English Stage, *published in 1698 and excerpted here. Collier did not fully exempt Shakespeare from his condemnation of stage immorality, but he did find him a ''gentiler Enemy'' than the Restoration dramatists who were his chief targets. Here he faults Shakespeare's handling of Ophelia's madness, which, according to Collier, lacks ''Decorum.'' His thoughts on Ophelia are challenged by James Drake (1699). For additional commentary on Ophelia, see George Stubbes/Thomas Hanmer (1736), Charlotte Lennox (1753), and Thomas Campbell (1818).*]

Modesty, as Mr. *Rapin* observes, is the *Character* of Women. To represent them without this Quality is to make Monsters of them, and throw them out of their Kind. *Euripides*, who was no negligent Observer of Humane Nature, is always careful of this Decorum. Thus *Phaedra*, when possess'd with an infamous Passion, takes all imaginable Pains to conceal it. She is as regular and reserv'd in her Language as the most virtuous Matron. 'Tis true, the force of Shame and Desire, the Scandal of Satisfying, and the Difficulty of Parting with her Inclinations, disorder her to Distraction. However, her Frensy is not Lewd; She keeps her Modesty even after She has lost her Wits. Had *Shakespeare* secur'd this point for his young Virgin *Ophelia* the *Play* had been better contriv'd. Since he was resolv'd to drown the lady like a Kitten he should have set her a swimming a little sooner. To keep her alive only to sully her Reputation, and discover the Rankness of her Breath, was very cruel. But it may be said the Freedoms of Distraction go for nothing, a Fever has no Faults, and a Man *non Compos* may kill without Murther. It may be so: but then such People ought to be kept in dark Rooms and without Company. To shew them, or let them loose, is somewhat unreasonable. (p. 87)

Jeremy Collier, in his extract from ''The Immodesty of the Stage,'' in Shakespeare, the Critical Heritage: 1693-1733, Vol. 2, *edited by Brian Vickers, Routledge & Kegan Paul, 1974, p. 87.*

[JAMES DRAKE]   (essay date 1699)

[*In the essay below, first published in 1699 in his* The Antient and Modern Stages Survey'd, *Drake refutes the findings of Jeremy Collier (1698) on both Restoration drama and Shakespeare. He challenges Collier's opinion of Ophelia and also stresses the moral seriousness of* Hamlet, *citing its ''admirable distribution of Poetick Justice.'' For additional discussions of Ophelia, see George Stubbes/Thomas Hanmer (1736), Charlotte Lennox (1753), and Thomas Campbell (1818).*]

[Notwithstanding] the severity of Mr *Rymer* and the hard usage of Mr *Collier*, I must still think [Shakespeare] the *Proto-Dramatist* of *England*, tho he fell short of the Art of *Jonson* and

the Conversation of *Beaumont* and *Fletcher*. Upon that account he wants many of their Graces, yet his Beauties make large amends for his Defects, and Nature has richly provided him with the materials, tho his unkind Fortune denied him the Art of managing them to the best Advantage.

His *Hamlet*, a Play of the first rate, has the misfortune to fall under Mr *Collier*'s displeasure, and *Ophelia*, who has had the luck hitherto to keep her reputation, is at last censur'd for Lightness in her Frenzy. Nay, Mr *Collier* is so familiar with her as to make an unkind discovery of the unsavouriness of her Breath, which no Body suspected before. But it may be this is a groundless surmise, and Mr *Collier* is deceived by a bad Nose, or a rotten Tooth of his own; and then he is obliged to beg the Poet's and the Lady's pardon for the wrong he has done 'em. (p. 94)

Whatever defects the Criticks may find in this Fable [*Hamlet*], the Moral of it is excellent. Here was a Murther privately committed, strangely discover'd, and wonderfully punish'd. Nothing in Antiquity can rival this Plot for the admirable distribution of Poetick Justice. The Criminals are not only brought to execution, but they are taken in their own Toyls, their own Stratagems recoyl upon 'em, and they are involv'd themselves in that mischief and ruine which they had projected for *Hamlet*. *Polonius* by playing the Spy meets a Fate which was neither expected by nor intended for him. *Guildenstern* and *Rosencrantz*, the King's Decoys, are counterplotted and sent to meet that fate to which they were trepanning the Prince. The Tyrant himself falls by his own Plot, and by the hand of the Son of that Brother whom he had murther'd. *Laertes* suffers by his own Treachery, and dies by a Weapon of his own preparing. Thus every one's crime naturally produces his Punishment, and every one (the Tyrant excepted) commences a Wretch almost as soon as a Villain.

The Moral of all this is very obvious. It shews us *That the Greatness of the Offender does not qualifie the Offence, and that no Humane Power or Policy are a sufficient Guard against the Impartial Hand and Eye of Providence, which defeats their wicked purposes and turns their dangerous Machinations upon their own heads.* This Moral *Hamlet* himself insinuates to us when he tells *Horatio* that he ow'd the Discovery of the Design against his Life in *England* to a rash indiscreet curiosity, and thence makes this Inference:

Our Indiscretion sometimes serves as well,
When our dear Plots do fail, and this shou'd teach us,
There's a Divinity, that shapes our ends,
Rough hew 'em how we will.   [V.ii.8-11]
(p. 95)

Shakespeare's *Ophelia* comes first under [Collier's] Lash for not keeping her mouth clean under her distraction. He is so very nice that her breath, which for so many years has stood the test of the most critical Noses, smells rank to him. It may therefore be worth while to enquire whether the fault lies in her Mouth, or his Nose.

Ophelia was a modest young Virgin, beloved by *Hamlet*, and in Love with him. Her Passion was approv'd and directed by her Father, and her Pretensions to a match with *Hamlet*, the heir apparent to the Crown of *Denmark*, encouraged and supported by the Countenance and Assistance of the *King* and *Queen*. A warrantable Love, so naturally planted in so tender a Breast, so carefully nursed, so artfully manured, and so strongly forced up, must needs take very deep Root and bear a very great Head. Love, even in the most difficult Circumstances, is the Passion naturally most predominant in young Breasts, but when it is encouraged and cherish'd by those of whom they stand in awe it grows Masterly and Tyrannical, and will admit of no Check. This was poor *Ophelia*'s case. . . . Her hopes were full blown when they were miserably blasted. *Hamlet* by mistake kills her Father and runs mad; or, which is all one to her, counterfeits madness so well that she is cheated into a belief of the reality of it. Here Piety and Love concur to make her Affliction piercing and to impress her Sorrow more deep and lasting. . . . These Calamities distract her and she talks incoherently; at which Mr *Collier* is amaz'd, he is downright stupified; and thinks the Woman's mad to run out of her wits. But tho she talks a little light-headed, and seems to want sleep, I don't find she needed any *Cashew* in her Mouth to correct her Breath. That's a discovery of Mr *Collier*'s (like some other of his), who perhaps is of Opinion that the Breath and the Understanding have the same Lodging and must needs be vitiated together. However, *Shakespeare* has drown'd her at last, and Mr *Collier* is angry that he did it no sooner. He is for having Execution done upon her seriously, and in sober sadness, without the excuse of madness for Self-murther. To kill her is not sufficient with him unless she be damn'd into the bargain. . . . Mr *Collier* has not told us what he gounds his hard censure upon, but we may guess that if he be really so angry as he pretends 'tis at the mad Song which *Ophelia* sings to the Queen. . . . 'Tis strange stuff shou'd wamble so in Mr *Collier*'s Stomach and put him into such an Uproar. 'Tis silly, indeed, but very harmless and inoffensive; and 'tis no great Miracle that a Woman out of her Wits shou'd talk Nonsense, who at the soundest of her Intellects had no extraordinary Talent at Speech-making. Sure Mr *Collier*'s concoctive Faculty's extreamly deprav'd, that meer Water-Pap turns to such virulent Corruption with him. (pp. 99-101)

> [*James Drake*], *in his extract from* Shakespeare, the Critical Heritage: 1693-1733, Vol. 2, *edited by Brian Vickers, Routledge & Kegan Paul, 1974, pp. 93-101.*

RICHARD STEELE   (essay date 1709)

[*In 1709, Steele, an English poet, dramatist, critic, and essayist, founded the* Tatler, *which served as a platform for his strongly-held moral convictions. In the following essay, first published in the* Tatler *on December 12, 1709, he focuses on Hamlet's reaction to his mother's remarriage, an element of the play central to the argument of many later critics.*]

—That it should come to this!
But Two Months dead! Nay, not so much, not Two!
So excellent a King! That was to this
Hyperion to a Satyr! So loving to my Mother!
That he permitted not the Winds of Heav'n
To visit her Face too roughly! Heav'n and Earth!
Must I remember? Why she would hang on him!
As if Increase of Appetite had grown
By what it fed on! And yet, within a Month!
Let me not think on't—Frailty, thy Name is Woman!
A little Month! Or ere those Shoes were old,
With which she follow'd my poor Father's Body,
Like *Niobe* all Tears; Why she! ev'n she!
Oh Heav'n! a Brute, that wants Discourse of Reason,
Would have mourn'd longer!—Married with mine Uncle!
My Father's Brother! But no more like my Father,
Than I to *Hercules*! Within a Month!
Ere yet the Salt of most unrighteous Tears,

Had left the Flushing of her gauled Eyes,
She marry'd—O most wicked Speed! To post
With such Dexterity to incestuous Sheets!
It is not, nor it cannot come to Good!
But break, my Heart; for I must hold my Tongue!

[I.ii.137 ff]

The several Emotions of Mind and Breaks of Passion in this Speech are admirable. He has touched every Circumstance that aggravated the Fact and seemed capable of hurrying the Thoughts of a Son into Distraction. His Father's Tenderness for his Mother, expressed in so delicate a Particular; his Mother's Fondness for his Father no less exquisitely described; the great and amiable Figure of his dead Parent drawn by a true Filial Piety; his Disdain of so unworthy a Successor to his Bed; but above all the Shortness of the Time between his Father's Death and his Mother's Second Marriage, brought together with so much Disorder, make up as noble a Part as any in that celebrated Tragedy. The Circumstance of Time I never could enough admire. The Widowhood had lasted Two Months. This is his First Reflection. But as his Indignation rises, he sinks to 'scarce Two Months'; Afterwards into 'a Month'; and at last, into a 'Little Month'. But all this so naturally that the Reader accompanies him in the Violence of his Passion and finds the Time lessen insensibly, according to the different Workings of his Disdain. I have not mentioned the Incest of her Marriage, which is so obvious a Provocation, but can't forbear taking Notice that when his Fury is at it's Height he cries, *Frailty, thy Name is Woman!* As railing at the Sex in general, rather than giving himself Leave to think his Mother worse than others. (pp. 209-10)

> *Richard Steele, in his extract from* Shakespeare, the Critical Heritage: 1693-1733, Vol. 2, *edited by Brian Vickers, Routledge & Kegan Paul, 1974, pp. 209-10.*

NICHOLAS ROWE   (essay date 1709)

[*Rowe was the editor of the first critical edition of Shakespeare's plays (1709) and the author of the first authoritative Shakespeare biography. In the following excerpt from his edition of* The Works of William Shakespeare, *1709, Rowe compares* Hamlet *with Sophocles's* Electra, *an idea commented upon by Charles Gildon (1710) and Joseph Addison (1711), and expanded by Gilbert Murray (1914). Noting that both Hamlet and Orestes are avengers, Rowe contrasts the "terror" evoked by the death of Gertrude with the "horror" of the death of Clytemnestra, concluding that Shakespeare's play manifests the true passion of tragedy.*]

Hamlet is founded on much the same Tale with the *Electra* of *Sophocles*. In each of 'em a young Prince is engag'd to Revenge the Death of his Father; their Mothers are equally Guilty, are both concern'd in the Murder of their Husbands and are afterwards married to the Murderers. There is in the first Part of the *Greek* Tragedy something very moving in the Grief of *Electra*; but . . . there is something very unnatural and shocking in the Manners he has given that Princess and *Orestes* in the latter Part. *Orestes* embrues his Hands in the Blood of his own Mother; and that barbarous Action is perform'd, tho' not immediately upon the Stage, yet so near that the Audience hear *Clytemnestra* crying out to *Aegysthus* for Help, and to her Son for Mercy; while *Electra*, her Daughter, and a Princess—both of them Characters that ought to have appear'd with more Decency—stands upon the Stage and encourages her Brother in the Parricide. . . . [To] represent an Action of this Kind on the Stage is certainly an Offence against those Rules of Manners proper to the Persons that ought to be observ'd there. On the contrary, let us only look a little on the Conduct of *Shakespeare*. *Hamlet* is represented with the same Piety towards his Father, and Resolution to Revenge his Death, as *Orestes;* he has the same Abhorrence for his Mother's Guilt, which, to provoke him the more, is heighten'd by Incest. But 'tis with wonderful Art and Justness of Judgment that the Poet restrains him from doing Violence to his Mother. To prevent any thing of that Kind, he makes his Father's Ghost forbid that part of his Vengeance. . . . This is to distinguish rightly between *Horror* and *Terror*. The latter is a proper Passion of Tragedy, but the former ought always to be carefully avoided. And certainly no Dramatick Writer ever succeeded better in raising *Terror* in the Minds of an Audience than *Shakespeare* has done. (pp. 200-01)

> Nicholas Rowe, in his extract from Shakespeare, the Critical Heritage: 1693-1733, Vol. 2, edited by Brian Vickers, Routledge & Kegan Paul, 1974, pp. 190-202.

ANTHONY, EARL OF SHAFTESBURY   (essay date 1710)

[*In his brief account of* Hamlet, *first written in 1710 and published in 1732 in his* Characteristics of Men, Manners, Opinions, Times, *Shaftesbury makes several critical points that will be developed in later criticism. He echoes James Drake (1699) in acknowledging a moral purpose in the play and prefigures the work of many nineteenth- and twentieth-century critics in stressing the importance of the play's central figure. In noting the reflective nature of Hamlet, he anticipates the opinions of such Romantic critics as Johann Wolfgang von Goethe (1795), August Wilhelm Schlegel (1808), Charles Lamb (1811), Samuel Taylor Coleridge (1811 and 1813), William Hazlitt (1817), and A. C. Bradley (1905).*]

The Tragedy of *Hamlet*, which appears to have most affected *English* Hearts, and has perhaps been oftenest acted of any which have come upon our Stage, is almost one continu'd *Moral;* a Series of deep Reflections, drawn from *one* Mouth, upon the Subject of *one* single Accident and Calamity, naturally fitted to move Horror and Compassion. It may be properly said of this Play, if I mistake not, that it has only One *Character* or *principal Part*. It contains no Adoration or Flattery of *the Sex:* no ranting at *the Gods:* no blustring *Heroism:* nor any thing of that curious mixture of *the Fierce* and *Tender,* which makes the hinge of modern Tragedy, and nicely varies it between the Points of *Love* and *Honour*.

> Anthony, Earl of Shaftesbury, in his extract from A New Variorum Edition of Shakespeare: Hamlet, Vol. IV, edited by Horace Howard Furness, J. B. Lippincott Company, 1877, p. 143.

CHARLES GILDON   (essay date 1710)

[*Gildon was the first critic to write an extended commentary on Shakespeare's plays. Like many other Neoclassicists, Gildon regarded Shakespeare as an imaginative playwright who nevertheless lacked knowledge of the dramatic "rules" necessary for correct writing. In the following excerpt from his remarks on Shakespeare's works, first published in 1710 in* The Works of Mr. William Shakespeare, *Gildon contends that* Hamlet *is Shakespeare's masterpiece, but finds it inferior to Sophocles's* Electra, *thus challenging the position of Nicholas Rowe (1709). Joseph Addison (1711) also noted the parallel between* Electra *and* Hamlet.]

Tho' I look upon [*Hamlet*] as the Master-Piece of *Shakespeare* according to our Way of Writing yet there are abundance of Errors in the Conduct and Design which will not suffer us in Justice to prefer it to the *Electra* of *Sophocles,* with the Author of his Life who seems to mistake the Matter wide when he puts this on the same Foot with the *Electra. Hamlet*'s Mother has no Hand in the Death of her Husband, as far as we can discover in this Poem, but her fault was in yielding to the incestuous Amour with her Husband's Brother—that at least is all that the Ghost charges her with. Besides, *Shakespeare* was Master of this Story, but *Sophocles* was not. *Orestes*' father was commanded by the Oracle to kill his Mother, and therefore, all moral Duties yielding to the immediat Command of the Gods, his Action according to that System of Religion under which *Sophocles* wrote had nothing in it of Barbarity but was entirely pious, as *Agamemnon*'s Sacrificing his own Daughter *Iphigenia* on *Diana*'s Order.

This Play indeed is capable of being made more perfect than the *Electra* but then a great deal of it must be thrown away, and some of the darling Trifles of the Million, as all the comical Part entirely and many other things which relate not to the main Action, which seems here to be pretty entire, tho' not so artfully Conducted as it might be. But I wander from my Point. . . . *Hamlet* everywhere almost gives us Speeches that are full of the Nature of his Passion, his Grief, *&c.* The Advice of *Laertes* to his Sister is very moral and just and full of prudential Caution. And that of *Polonius* to his Son, and that of the same to his Daughter. . . . All the Scene betwixt *Hamlet* and the Ghost is admirable, as the Ghost's Description of his Residence in the other World. . . . (pp. 257-58)

The Discourse betwixt *Hamlet* and the Grave-Maker is full of moral Reflections, and worthy minding—tho' that Discourse itself has nothing to do there where it is, nor of any use to the Design, and may be as well left out; and whatever can be left out has no Business in a Play, but this being low Comedy has still less to do here. The Character *Hamlet* gives of *Osrick* is very satirical and wou'd be good anywhere else. (p. 258)

> Charles Gildon, in his extract from Shakespeare, the Critical Heritage: 1693-1733, Vol. 2, edited by Brian Vickers, Routledge & Kegan Paul, 1974, pp. 226-62.

JOSEPH ADDISON   (essay date 1711)

[*Addison was an English poet, dramatist, and essayist. In his essay below, first published in* The Spectator *on April 20, 1711, he praises Shakespeare's skill in drawing the character of the ghost, and, like Nicholas Rowe (1709) and Charles Gildon (1710), notes the parallel between* Hamlet *and Sophocles's* Electra. *For additional commentary on the ghost, see Gotthold Ephraim Lessing (1767), Elizabeth Montagu (1769), W. W. Greg (1917), J. Dover Wilson (1918), Sister Miriam Joseph (1962), and Eleanor Prosser (1971).*]

Among the several Artifices which are put in Practice by the Poets to fill the Minds of the Audience with Terrour, the first Place is due to Thunder and Lightning, which are often made use of at the Descending of a God or the Rising of a Ghost, at the Vanishing of a Devil or at the Death of a Tyrant. . . . [There] is nothing which delights and terrifies our *English* Theatre so much as a Ghost, especially when he appears in a bloody Shirt. A Spectre has very often saved a Play, though he has done nothing but stalked across the Stage, or rose through a Cleft of it, and sunk again without speaking one Word. . . .

The Appearance of the Ghost in *Hamlet* is a Masterpiece in its kind, and wrought up with all the Circumstances that can create either Attention or Horrour. The Mind of the Reader is wonderfully prepared for his Reception by the Discourses that precede it. His dumb Behaviour at his first Entrance strikes the Imagination very strongly; but every Time he enters he is still more terrifying. Who can read the Speech with which young *Hamlet* accosts him, without trembling? . . .

I do not therefore find Fault with the Artifices above-mentioned when they are introduced with Skill and accompanied by proportionable Sentiments and Expressions in the Writing. (pp. 275-76)

It may not be unaccepable to the Reader to see how *Sophocles* has conducted a Tragedy under the like delicate Circumstances. *Orestes* was in the same Condition with *Hamlet* in *Shakespeare*, his Mother having murder'd his Father and taken Possession of his Kingdom in Conspiracy with her Adulterer. (p. 277)

> *Joseph Addison, in his extract from* Shakespeare, the Critical Heritage: 1693-1733, Vol. 2, *edited by Brian Vickers, Routledge & Kegan Paul, 1974, pp. 275-77.*

CHARLES GILDON   (essay date 1721)

[*In this essay, first published in 1721 in* The Laws of Poetry Explain'd and Illustrated, *Gildon complains that Hamlet's famous "To be or not to be" soliloquy is unnecessary to the action and meaning of the drama. For further discussion of Hamlet's soliloquies, see William Guthrie (1747), Tobias Smollett (1756), Samuel Johnson (1765), A.J.A. Waldock (1931), Theodore Spencer (1942), and E.M.W. Tillyard (1949).*]

[The importance of Roscommon's precept that soliloquies should be few, short, and spoken in passion] is plain from the offences committed against it by all our poets. *Shakespeare* has frequently *soliloquies* of threescore lines, and those very often— if not always—calm, without any emotion of the passions, or indeed conducive to the business of the play; I mean, where there is any business in the play peculiar to it. That famous *soliloquy* which has been so much cry'd up in *Hamlet* has no more to do there than a description of the grove and altar of *Diana*, mention'd by *Horace*. *Hamlet* comes in talking to himself, and very sedately and exactly weighs the several reasons or considerations mention'd in that *soliloquy*,

> To be, or not to be, &c.   [III.i.55 ff]

As soon as he has done talking to himself he sees *Ophelia*, and passes to a conversation with her entirely different to the subject he had been mediating on with that earnestness, which as it was produc'd by nothing before, so has it no manner of influence on what follows after and is therefore a perfectly detach'd piece, and has nothing to do in the play. (p. 371)

> *Charles Gildon, in his extract from* Shakespeare, the Critical Heritage: 1693-1733, Vol. 2, *edited by Brian Vickers, Routledge & Kegan Paul, 1974, pp. 369-72.*

AARON HILL   (essay date 1735)

[*Hill's essay was first published in* The Prompter *on October 24, 1735.*]

[*Hamlet*] is the *Play* . . . which may be oftenest seen without *Satiety*. Here are *Touches of Nature* so numerous, and *mark'd* with so expressive a *Force* that Every *Heart* confesses their Energy: and in spite of Errors and Absurdities *Self-contradictory* and *indefensible* This Play has always pleas'd, still pleases, and will forever continue to please while *Apprehension* and *Humanity* have Power in *English* Audiences. . . .

The *Poet* has adorn'd [Hamlet] with a Succession of the most *opposite* Beauties, which are *varied*, like *Colours* on the Cameleon, according to the *different Lights* in which we behold him. (p. 35)

The characteristic Distinction that *marks* the Temper of *Hamlet* is a *pensive*, yet *genteel* Humanity.—He is by *Nature* of a *melancholy Cast*, but His polite Education has illuminated the *Sable*, and, like the Sun through a *wet* May *Morning*, mix'd a *Gleam* with his *Sadness*. When he *grieves*, he is never *Sullen;* When He *trifles*, he is never *light*. When *alone* He is *seriously solid;* When in Company, *designedly flexible*. He *assumes* what he pleases, but he *is* what He ought to be: the Lamenter of his murder'd *Father*, the Discerner of his *Mother's* Levity, and the Suspecter of his *Uncle's* Baseness. . . .

When he counterfeits Distraction with *Ophelia*, and perceives that she is *observing* him, All his Air is as light and as empty of Purpose as if *really as mad* as He designs She should *think* him. But no sooner has he delin'd himself from the Glances of Her Eye than His Own gives us Marks of his *Pity* and his *Prudence*. The Wildness He but *affects* quits his Air in a Moment, and a touching Sensation of Sorrow *paints* his *Soul* in his *Gesture:* which again the next Moment He transforms into *Wantonness*, in the very Instant of Time while He *returns* toward the Lady. (p. 36)

> *Aaron Hill, in his essay in* Shakespeare, the Critical Heritage: 1733-1752, Vol. 3, *edited by Brian Vickers, Routledge & Kegan Paul, 1975, pp. 29-39.*

[GEORGE STUBBES/THOMAS HANMER]   (essay date 1736)

[*This essay, the first full-length treatment of* Hamlet, *has been attributed by some scholars to George Stubbes and by others to Thomas Hanmer. The essay, published in* Some Remarks on the Tragedy of "Hamlet" *in 1736, not only offers a brief summary of eighteenth-century critical opinion on* Hamlet, *it also presents for the first time many ideas developed in subsequent criticism. The critic, who is the first to explore Hamlet's cruelty in the prayer scene, reflects the affinity of the Neoclassical Age for order and decorum in his discussion of the "shocking" nature of Ophelia's madness and the "improper" and "offensive" admixture of comedy and tragedy in* Hamlet. *This author's most important contribution to* Hamlet *criticism is his comment on Hamlet's delay: "Had Hamlet gone naturally to work . . . there would have been an end of our play." Thus, the anonymous critic attributes Hamlet's much-discussed procrastination to mere contrivance on Shakespeare's part. For other major essays on Hamlet's delay, see William Richardson (1774), Samuel Taylor Coleridge (1811), Hermann Ulrici (1839), Karl Werder (1859-60), Friedrich Nietzsche (1872), George Brandes (1895-96), and Sigmund Freud (1900).*]

Of all *Shakespeare*'s Tragedies none can surpass [Hamlet] as to the noble Passions which it naturally raises in us. (p. 42)

[In] my Examination of the whole Conduct of the Play the Reader must not be surprised if I censure any Part of it, although it be entirely in Conformity to the Plan the Author has chosen; because it is easy to conceive that a Poet's Judgment is particularly shewn in chusing the proper Circumstances, and rejecting the improper Ones of the Ground-work which he raises his Play upon. In general we are to take Notice that as History ran very low in his Days most of his Plays are founded upon some old wretched Chronicler, or some empty *Italian* Novelist; but the more base and mean were his Materials so much more ought we to admire His Skill, Who has been able to work up his Pieces to such Sublimity from such low Originals. . . . Nothing can be more conformable to Reason than that the Beginning of all Dramatick Performances (and indeed of every other kind of Poesie) should be with the greatest Simplicity, that so our Passions may be work'd upon by Degrees. This Rule is very happily observ'd in this Play, and it has this Advantage over many others that it has Majesty and Simplicity joined together. For [the] whole preparatory Discourse to the Ghost's coming in, at the same Time that it is necessary towards laying open the Scheme of the Play creates an Awe and Attention in the Spectators, such as very well fits them to receive the Appearance of a Messenger from the other World with all the Terror and Seriousness necessary on the Occasion. And surely the Poet has manag'd the Whole in such a Manner that it is all entirely Natural. And tho' most Men are well enough arm'd against all Belief of the Appearances of Ghosts yet they are forced during the Representation of this Piece entirely to suspend their most fixed Opinions, and believe that they do actually see a Phantom, and that the whole Plot of the Play is justly and naturally founded upon the Appearance of this Spectre. (pp. 42-4)

It is evident by the whole Tenour of *Polonius*'s Behaviour in this Play that he is intended to represent some Buffoonish Statesman, not too much fraught with Honesty. Whether any particular Person's Character was herein aim'd at I shall not determine, because it is not to the Purpose; for whoever reads our Author's Plays will find that in all of them (even the most serious ones) he has some regard for the meanest Part of his Audience and perhaps, too, for that Taste for low Jokes and Punns which prevailed in his Time among the better Sort. This, I think, was more pardonable in him when it was confined to Clowns and such like Persons in his Plays, but is by no Means excusable in a Man supposed to be in such a Station as *Polonius* is. Nay, granting that such Ministers of State were common (which surely they are not) it would even then be a Fault in our Author to introduce them in such Pieces as this, for every Thing that is natural is not to be made use of improperly: but when it is out of Nature this certainly much aggravates the Poet's Mistake. And to speak Truth, all Comick Circumstances, all Things tending to raise a Laugh are highly offensive in Tragedies, to good Judges. The Reason in my Opinion is evident, *viz.* that such Things degrade the Majesty and Dignity of Tragedy and destroy the Effect of the Intention which the Spectators had in being present at such Representations; that is, to acquire that pleasing Melancholy of Mind which is caus'd by them, and that Satisfaction which arises from the Consciousness that we are mov'd as we ought to be, and that we consequently have Sentiments suitable to the Dignity of our Nature. (pp. 49-50)

The Advice of *Laertes* to his Sister contains the soundest Reasoning express'd in the most nervous and poetical Manner, and is full of Beauties; particularly, I can never enough admire the Modesty inculcated in these Lines:

> The chariest Maid is prodigal enough,
> If She unmask her Beauty to the Moon.
> [I.iii.36-7]

Ophelia's modest Replies, the few Words she uses, and the virtuous Caution she gives her Brother after his Advice to her

are inimitably charming. This I have observed in general in our Author's Plays, that almost all his young Women (who are designed as good Characters) are made to behave with a Modesty and Decency peculiar to those Times, and which are of such pleasing Simplicity as seem too ignorant and unmeaning in our well taught knowing Age; so much do we despise the virtuous Plainness of our Fore-fathers! (p. 50)

[Hamlet's first encounter with the *Ghost* is] the sublimest Scene in this whole Piece, a Scene worthy of the greatest Attention: an Heroical Youth addressing the Shade of his departed Father, whom he tenderly loved, and who, we are told, was a Monarch of the greatest Worth. Surely there cannot be imagin'd any Scene more capable of stirring up our noblest Passions. . . . This Spectre has been once spoken to by the Friend of our young Hero, and it must be confessed that *Horatio*'s Speech to it is truly great and beautiful. But as the like Incident was again to happen—that is, as the Ghost was again to be addressed and with this Addition, by the Hero of the Play and Son to the King whose Spirit appears—it was necessary, I say, upon these Accounts that this Incident should be treated in a sublimer Manner than the Former. Accordingly we may take Notice that *Hamlet*'s Speech to his Father's Shade is as much superior to that of *Horatio* upon the same Occasion as his is to any Thing of that kind that I have ever met with in any other Dramatick Poet.

Hamlet's Invocation of the heavenly Ministers is extremely fine, and the begging their Protection upon the Appearance of a Sight so shocking to human Nature is entirely comfortable to the virtuous Character of this Prince, and gives an Air of Probability to the whole Scene. He accosts the Ghost with great Intrepidity, and his whole Speech is so full of the Marks of his Filial Piety that we may easily observe that his Tenderness for his Father gets the better of all Sentiments of Terror which we could suppose to arise. . . . (pp. 51-2)

The Ghost's Account of the base Murther committed on him is express'd in the strongest and most nervous Diction that Poetry can make use of; and he speaks with such Gravity and Weight of Language as well suits his Condition. The Ideas he raises in the Audience by his short Hint concerning the Secrets of his Prison-House are such as must cause that Terror which is the natural Effect of such Appearances, and must occasion such Images as should always accompany such Incidents in Tragedy.

The Ghost's bringing out the Account of his Murder by Degrees, and the Prince's Exclamations as he becomes farther acquainted with the Affair, are great Beauties in this Scene because it is all entirely conformable to Nature; that is, to those Ideas by which we naturally conceive how a Thing of this sort would be managed and treated were it really to happen.

We are to observe further that the King spurs on his Son to revenge his foul and unnatural Murder from these two Considerations chiefly, that he was sent into the other World without having had Time to repent of his Sins. . . . And, Secondly, That *Denmark* might not be the Scene of Usurpation and Incest, and the Throne thus polluted and profaned. For these Reasons he prompts the young Prince to Revenge; else it would have been more becoming the Character of such a Prince as *Hamlet*'s Father is represented to have been, and more suitable to his present Condition, to have left his Brother to the Divine Punishment, and to a Possibility of Repentance for his base Crime which, by cutting him off, he must be deprived of.

His Caution to his Son concerning his Mother is very fine and shews great Delicacy in our Author. . . . The Ghost's Interrupting himself *(but soft, methinks, I scent the Morning Air, &c.)* has much Beauty in it, particularly as it complys with the received Notions that Spirits shun the Light, and continues the Attention of the Audience by so particular a Circumstance.

The Sequel of this Scene by no Means answers the Dignity of what we have hitherto been treating of. *Hamlet*'s Soliloquy after the Ghost has disappeared is such as it should be. The Impatience of *Horatio, &c.* to know the Result of his Conference with the Phantom, and his putting them off from knowing it with his Caution concerning his future Conduct, and his intreating them to be silent in Relation to this whole Affair; all this, I say, is natural and right. But his light and even ludicrous Expressions to them, his making them swear by his Sword, and shift their Ground, with the Ghost's Crying under the Stage, and *Hamlet*'s Reflection thereupon, are all Circumstances certainly inferiour to the preceeding Part. (pp. 52-3)

I shall conclude what I have to say on this Scene with observing that I do not know any Tragedy, ancient or modern, in any Nation, where the Whole is made to turn so naturally and so justly upon such a supernatural Appearance as this is. Nor do I know of any Piece whatever where a Spectre is introduced with so much Majesty, such an Air of Probability, and where such an Apparition is manag'd with so much Dignity and Art; in short, which so little revolts the judgment and Belief of the Spectators. Nor have I ever met in all my Reading with a Scene in any Tragedy which creates so much Awe and serious Attention as this does, and which raises such a Multiplicity of the most exalted Sentiments. (p. 54)

Now I am come to mention *Hamlet*'s Madness I must speak my Opinion of our Poet's Conduct in this Particular. To conform to the Ground-work of his Plot *Shakespeare* makes the young Prince feign himself mad. I cannot but think this to be injudicious; for so far from Securing himself from any Violence which he fear'd from the Usurper, which was his Design in so doing, it seems to have been the most likely Way of getting himself confin'd, and, consequently, debarr'd from an Opportunity of Revenging his Father's Death, which now seem'd to be his only Aim; and accordingly it was the Occasion of his being sent away to *England*. Which Design, had it taken effect upon his Life, he never could have revenged his Father's Murder. To speak Truth, our Poet, by keeping too close to the Ground-work of his Plot, has fallen into an Absurdity; for there appears no Reason at all in Nature why the young Prince did not put the Usurper to Death as soon as possible, especially as *Hamlet* is represented as a Youth so brave, and so careless of his own Life.

The Case indeed is this: Had *Hamlet* gone naturally to work, as we could suppose such a Prince to do in parallel Circumstances, there would have been an End of our Play. The Poet therefore was obliged to delay his Hero's Revenge; but then he should have contrived some good Reason for it. (p. 55)

The whole Conduct of *Hamlet*'s Madness is, in my Opinion, too ludicrous for his Character, and for the situation his Mind was then really in. I must confess, nothing is more difficult than to draw a real Madness well, much more a feign'd one; for here the Poet in *Hamlet*'s Case was to paint such a Species of Madness as should not give cause of Suspicion of the real Grief which had taken Possession of the Prince's Mind. His Behaviour to those two Courtiers whom the Usurper had sent to dive into his Secret is very natural and just, because his chief Business was to baffle their Enquiries, as he does also in another Scene, where his falling into a sort of a Pun upon

bringing in the Pipe is a great Fault, for it is too low and mean for Tragedy. But our Author in this (as in all his Pieces) is glad of any Opportunity of falling in with the prevailing Humour of the Times, which ran into false Wit and a constant endeavour to produce affected Moral Sentences.

He was very capable of drawing *Hamlet* in Madness with much more Dignity, and without any Thing of the Comick; although it is difficult, as I said, to describe a feign'd Madness in a Tragedy, which is not to touch on the real Cause of Grief.

The Scene of the Players [II.ii.421ff.] is conducive to the whole Scheme of this Tragedy, and is managed with great Beauty. We are to observe that the Speeches spoken by the Prince and one of the Players are dismal Bombast, and intended, no doubt, to ridicule some Tragedy of those Days.

The Poet's stepping out of his Subject to lash the Custom of Plays being acted by the Children of the Chapel is not allowable in Tragedy, which is never to be a Satire upon any modern particular *Foible* or Vice that prevails, but is to be severe upon Crimes and Immoralities of all Ages and of all Countries. (p. 56)

The Prince's Design of confirming by the Play the Truth of what the Ghost told him is certainly well imagin'd, but as the coming of these Players is supposed to be accidental it could not be a Reason for his Delay.

> How smart a Lash, that Speech
> doth give my Conscience, &c.   [III.i.49ff.]

The Poet here is greatly to be commended for his Conduct. As consummate a Villain as this King of *Denmark* is represented to be yet we find him stung with the deepest Remorse, upon the least Sentence that can any ways be supposed to relate to his Crime. How instructive this is to the Audience, how much it answers the End of all publick Representations by inculcating a good Moral, I leave to the Consideration of every Reader.

Hamlet's Conversation with *Ophelia*, we may observe, is in the Stile of Madness; and it was proper that the Prince should conceal his Design from every one, which had he conversed with his Mistress in his natural Stile could not have been. (pp. 56-7)

Hamlet's whole Conduct during the Play which is acted before the King has, in my Opinion, too much Levity in it. His Madness is of too light a Kind, although I know he says he must be idle; but among other Things, his Pun to *Polonius* is not tolerable. I might also justly find Fault with the want of Decency in his Discourses to *Ophelia*, without being thought too severe. The Scene represented by the Players is in wretched Verse. This we may, without incurring the Denomination of an ill-natur'd Critick, venture to pronounce, that in almost every Place where *Shakespeare* has attempted Rhime, either in the Body of his Plays or at the Ends of Acts or Scenes, he falls far short of the Beauty and Force of his Blank Verse: one would think they were written by two different Persons. (p. 58)

Hamlet's Speech upon seeing the King at Prayers has always given me great Offence. There is something so very Bloody in it, so inhuman, so unworthy of a Hero that I wish our Poet had omitted it. To desire to destroy a Man's Soul, to make him eternally miserable by cutting him off from all hopes of Repentance; this surely, in a Christian Prince, is such a Piece of Revenge as no Tenderness for any Parent can justify. To put the Usurper to Death, to deprive him of the Fruits of his vile Crime, and to rescue the Throne of *Denmark* from Pollution, was highly requisite. But there our young Prince's Desires should have stop'd, nor should he have wished to pursue the Criminal in the other World, but rather have hoped for his Conversion before his putting him to Death; for even with his Repentance there was at least Purgatory for him to pass through, as we find even in a virtuous Prince, the Father of *Hamlet.* (p. 59)

Hamlet's killing *Polonius* was in Conformity to the Plan *Shakespeare* built his Play upon; and the Prince behaves himself on that Occasion as one who seems to have his Thoughts bent on Things of more Importance. I wish the Poet had omitted *Hamlet*'s last Reflection on the Occasion. . . . It has too much Levity in it; and his *tugging* him away into another Room is unbecoming the Gravity of the rest of the Scene and is a Circumstance too much calculated to raise a Laugh, which it always does. We must observe that *Polonius* is far from a good Character, and that his Death is absolutely necessary towards the *Denoüement* of the whole Piece. And our Hero had not put him to Death, had not he thought it to have been the Usurper hid behind the *Arras;* so that upon the Whole this is no Blemish to his Character. (p. 60)

Laertes's Character is a very odd one. It is not easy to say whether it is good or bad; but his consenting to the villainous Contrivance of the Usurper's to murder *Hamlet* makes him much more a bad Man than a good one. For surely Revenge for such an accidental Murder as was that of his Father's (which from the Queen, it is to be supposed, he was acquainted with all the Circumstances of) could never justify him in any treacherous Practices. . . .

The Scenes of *Ophelia*'s Madness are to me very shocking, in so noble a Piece as this. I am not against her having been represented mad; but surely it might have been done with less Levity and more Decency. Mistakes are less tolerable from such a Genius as *Shakespeare*'s, and especially in the very Pieces which give us such strong Proofs of his exalted Capacity. (p. 61)

The Scene of the Grave-Diggers I know is much applauded, but in my humble Opinion is very unbecoming such a Piece as this and is only pardonable as it gives Rise to *Hamlet*'s fine moral Reflections upon the Infirmity of human Nature.

Hamlet's Return to *Denmark* is not ill contriv'd; but I cannot think that his Stratagem is natural or easy by which he brings that Destruction upon the Heads of his Enemies which was to have fallen upon himself. It was possible, but not very probable; because methinks their Commission was kept in a very negligent Manner to be thus got from them without their knowing it. Their Punishment was just, because they had devoted themselves to the Service of the Usurper in whatever he should command, as appears in several Passages. (pp. 61-2)

Laertes's Death, and the Queen's, are truly poetical Justice, and very naturally brought about; although I do not conceive it to be so easy to change Rapiers in a Scuffle without knowing it at the Time.

The Death of the Queen is particularly according to the strictest Rules of Justice, for she loses her Life by the Villany of the very Person who had been the Cause of all her Crimes.

Since the Poet deferred so long the Usurper's Death, we must own that he has very naturally effected it, and still added fresh Crimes to those the Murderer had already committed. (p. 62)

It is not to be denied but that *Shakespeare*'s Dramatick Works are in general very much mix'd; his Gold is strangely mingled with Dross in most of his Pieces. He fell too much into the low Taste of the Age he liv'd in, which delighted in miserable Punns, low Wit, and affected sententious Maxims; and what is most unpardonable in him, he has interspersed his noblest Productions with this Poorness of Thought. This I have shewn in my Remarks on this Play. Yet, notwithstanding the Defects I have pointed out, it is, I think, beyond Dispute that there is much less of this in *Hamlet* than in any of his Plays; and that the Language in the Whole is much more pure, and much more free from Obscurity or Bombast, than any of our Author's Tragedies; for sometimes *Shakespeare* may be justly tax'd with that Fault. And we may moreover take Notice that the Conduct of this Piece is far from being bad; it is superior in that respect (in my Opinion) to many of those Performances in which the Rules are said to be exactly kept to. The Subject, which is of the nicest Kind, is managed with great Delicacy, much beyond that Piece wherein *Agamemnon*'s Death is revenged by his Son *Orestes,* so much admired by all the Lovers of Antiquity. . . . (pp. 63-4)

There is less Time employ'd in this Tragedy, as I observed else where, than in most of our Author's Pieces, and the Unity of Place is not much disturbed. But here give me leave to say that the Critick's Rules, in respect to those two Things, if they prove any Thing, prove too much; for if our Imagination will not bear a strong Imposition, surely no Play ought to be supposed to take more Time than is really employ'd in the Acting; nor should there be any Change of Place in the least. This shews the Absurdity of such Arbitrary Rules. (pp. 64-5)

Before I conclude I must point out another Beauty in the Tragedy of *Hamlet,* besides those already mentioned, which does indeed arise from our Author's conforming to a Rule which he followed (probably without knowing it) only because it is agreeable to Nature; and this is, that there is not one Scene in this Play but what some way or other conduces towards the *Denoüement* of the Whole; and thus the Unity of Action is indisputably kept up by every Thing tending to what we may call the main Design, and it all hangs by Consequence so close together that no Scene can be omitted without Prejudice to the Whole. Even *Laertes* going to *France,* and *Ophelia*'s Madness, however trivial they may seem (and how much soever I dislike the Method of that last mentioned) are Incidents absolutely necessary towards the concluding of all, as will appear to any one upon due Consideration. This all holds good, notwithstanding, it is my Opinion, that several of the Scenes might have been altered by our Author for the better; but as they all stand it is, as I said, quite impossible to separate them without a visible Prejudice to the Whole. (pp. 66-7)

> [*George Stubbes/Thomas Hanmer*], *in his extract from* Shakespeare, the Critical Heritage: 1733-1752, *Vol. 3, edited by Brian Vickers, Routledge & Kegan Paul, 1975, pp. 40-69.*

WILLIAM GUTHRIE (essay date 1747)

[*In this essay, from his* An Essay Upon English Tragedy, *published in 1747, Guthrie asserts that Hamlet lacks the "strong markings which commonly form the chief modern personage in a tragedy." According to Guthrie, Hamlet's doubts and perplexities only serve to indicate how much he is like his fellow man. Thus, Guthrie praises Hamlet's ordinariness, an opinion that runs counter to the ideas of most subsequent critics, who focus on Hamlet's unique qualities. Guthrie also compares the famous "To be or not to be'' soliloquy of Hamlet with that of Cato, from Joseph Addison's drama, concluding that Hamlet's is by far superior. For additional commentary on Hamlet's soliloquies, see Charles Gildon (1721), Tobias Smollett (1756), Samuel Johnson (1765), A.J.A. Waldock (1931), Theodore Spencer (1942), and E.M.W. Tillyard (1949).]*

[I] observe, though I have the prepossession of a whole age against me, that there is not the least necessity for the chief personage in a play to have either courage, wisdom, virtue, passion, or any other quality above what is to be found in his real history, or in common life. It is a sign of a poverty in genius when a poet invents a dress of good or bad qualities for a favourite character. The antients always brought the same men upon the stage which they saw in the world. But the French and the modern English in their tragedies have peopled the poetic world with a race of mortals unknown to life. This aiming at super-eminent qualities, were there no other, is a proof of the defect of genius; but the eternal practice of the French has, in modern times, given it a shameful sanction.

The field of imagination lyes higher than that of truth, and our modern poets generally take advantage of the ground to mount their Pegasus. But Shakespeare, like his own winged Mercury, vaults from the level soil into his seat.

He has supported the character of Hamlet entirely by the force of sentiment, without giving him any of those strong markings which commonly form the chief modern personage in a tragedy. He has not even made use of those advantages with which the great historian [Saxo Grammaticus] from whom he took his subject might have furnished him. He has omitted part of the marvellous to be met with in that writer, but has made excellent use of the following beautiful description of Hamlet's madness. . . . 'For Hamlet,' says Saxo, 'abhoring the imputation of a lye, so mingled cunning with truth that what he said was neither void of veracity, nor could the measure of his wit be betrayed by the discoveries of his sincerity.' Where is the poet but Shakespeare who could have worked so insipid a character into life by the justness of reflection and the strength of nature, without applying those colours which an inferior genius must have used to mark a principal figure? All that we see in Hamlet is a well-meaning, sensible young man, but full of doubts and perplexities even after his resolution is fixed. In this character there is nothing but what is common with the rest of mankind; he has no marking, no colouring, but its beautiful drawing, perhaps, cost Shakespeare more than any one figure he ever attempted. (pp. 198-99)

[Mr. Addison] has, to the immortal credit of his name and nation, exhibited upon the stage a Cato; but we must take the liberty to observe that he is not the Cato whom Rome produced, or Shakespeare would have drawn: he is so firm in virtue, so fortified in philosophy that he is above the reach of fate, and consequently he can be no object of compassion, one great end of tragedy. (p. 201)

All is indeed extremely well executed, and all bears the mark of a fine poet, but not of a great genius.

For a particular instance of the difference betwixt the poet and the genius, let us go to two speeches upon the very same subject by those two authors; I mean the two famous soliloquies of Cato and Hamlet. The speech of the first is that of a scholar, a philosopher, and a man of virtue: all the sentiments of such a speech are to be acquired by instruction, by reading, by conversation; Cato talks the language of the porch and academy. Hamlet, on the other hand, speaks that of the human heart, ready to enter upon a deep, a dreadful, a decisive act.

His is the real language of mankind, of its highest to its lowest order; from the king to the cottager; from the philosopher to the peasant. It is a language which a man may speak without learning; yet no learning can improve, nor philosophy mend it. This cannot be said of Cato's speech. It is dictated from the head rather than the heart; by courage rather than nature. . . . The words of Cato are not like those of Hamlet, the emanations of the soul; they are therefor improper for a soliloquy, where the discourse is supposed to be held with the heart, that fountain of truth. Cato seems instructed as to all he doubts: while irresolute, he appears determined; and bespeaks his quarters, while he questions whether there is lodging. How different from this is the conduct of Shakespeare on the same occasion! (pp. 201-02)

> *William Guthrie, in his extract from* Shakespeare, the Critical Heritage: 1733-1752, Vol. 3, *edited by Brian Vickers, Routledge & Kegan Paul, 1975, pp. 191-205.*

F. M. DE VOLTAIRE   (essay date 1752)

[Voltaire was a French novelist, satirist, philosopher, critic, dramatist, and poet. His vituperative attack on Hamlet *reflects his stringent adherence to the French Neoclassical ideals of restraint and rationalism, as well as his fear that Shakespeare's popularity would threaten that of the seventeenth-century French classical playwrights Corneille and Racine. Arthur Murphy (1753) defends Shakespeare against Voltaire's charges of "barbarity" and Voltaire's criticism of* Hamlet *is now generally considered an iconoclastic if interesting piece. Gotthold Ephraim Lessing (1767) contrasts the handling of the 'ghost' device in Voltaire's* Semiramis *with that in* Hamlet. *The essay first appeared as part of "Dissertation sur la tragédie" in 1752.]*

Englishmen believe in ghosts no more than the Romans did, yet they take pleasure in the tragedy of *Hamlet,* in which the ghost of a king appears on the stage. Far be it from me to justify everything in that tragedy; it is a vulgar and barbarous drama, which would not be tolerated by the vilest populace of France, or Italy. Hamlet becomes crazy in the second act, and his mistress becomes crazy in the third; the prince slays the father of his mistress under the pretence of killing a rat, and the heroine throws herself into the river; a grave is dug on the stage, and the grave-diggers talk quodlibets worthy of themselves, while holding skulls in their hands; Hamlet responds to their nasty vulgarities in silliness no less disgusting. In the meanwhile another of the actors conquers Poland. Hamlet, his mother, and his father-in-law, carouse on the stage; songs are sung at table; there is quarrelling, fighting, killing—one would imagine this piece to be the work of a drunken savage. But amidst all these vulgar irregularities, which to this day make the English drama so absurd and so barbarous, there are to be found in *Hamlet,* by a *bizarrerie* still greater, some sublime passages, worthy of the greatest genius. It seems as though nature had mingled in the brain of Shakespeare the greatest conceivable strength and grandeur with whatsoever witless vulgarity can devise that is lowest and most detestable.

It must be confessed that, amid the beauties which sparkle through this horrible extravagance, the ghost of Hamlet's father has a most striking theatrical effect. It always has a great effect upon the English—I mean upon those who are the most highly educated, and who see most clearly all the irregularity of their old drama. (pp. 18-19)

> *F. M. de Voltaire, in his extract from* Readings on the Character of Hamlet: 1661-1947, *edited by Claude*

C. H. Williamson, Gordian Press, Inc. 1972. pp. 18-19.

[CHARLOTTE LENNOX]   (essay date 1753)

[*Lennox was an American-born novelist and Shakespearean scholar who compiled a three-volume edition of translated texts of the sources used by Shakespeare in twenty-two of his plays, including some analyses of the ways in which he used these sources. In the following essay, first published in her* Shakespeare Illustrated *in 1753, she compares the plot of* Hamlet *with that of the story of Amleth from Saxo-Grammaticus. Her strict Neoclassical approach is evident: she finds Ophelia insufficiently modest in her frenzied madness, the catastrophe censorious, and Hamlet's death a violation of poetic justice. For additional discussions of Shakespeare's sources for* Hamlet, *see Thomas Kenny (1864), Charlton M. Lewis (1907), George Santayana (1908), Elmer Edgar Stoll (1933), and William Empson (1953).*]

All the principal Circumstances are the same in [*Hamlet* as in its source, the story of *Amleth* from Saxo-Grammaticus]. In both a Prince murders his Brother, usurps his Dignity, and marries his Widow; the Son of the murdered Prince resolves to revenge his Father; for that Purpose he feigns himself mad, and at last accomplishes his Design. Several of the lesser Circumstances are also as exactly copied, and others have afforded Hints for new ones. (pp. 126-27)

The Embassy to *England* is designed after the History. *Shakespeare* indeed makes *Hamlet* after two Days Absence be set on shore again at *Denmark;* and *Amleth* in the History arrives in *England,* has his Companions hanged, and marries the King's Daughter before he comes back. But *Shakespeare*'s Plan required the immediate Return of *Hamlet;* however, the Contrivance of changing the Letters are the same, and of punishing the treacherous Bearers of them. *Shakespeare* makes those Bearers the Schoolfellows and profest Friends of *Hamlet,* a Circumstance which heightens their Baseness, and justifies the Artifice he uses to procure their Punishment.

The Design of entrapping *Amleth* by means of a Girl has not been wholly neglected by *Shakespeare,* though he manages this Incident much more decently. *Ophelia,* with whom he is in Love, is ordered to throw herself in his way and the King and his Confident listen to their Conversation. . . . *Ophelia* is not a loose Wanton, as in the History, but a Woman of Honour with whom he is in love. The accidental killing of her Father, and her Distraction which was caused by it, is all his own Invention, and would have made a very affecting Episode if the Lady had been more modest in her Frenzy and the Lover more uniformly afflicted for her Death. For at his first hearing it he expresses only a slight Emotion; presently he jumps into her Grave, fiercely demands to be buried with her, fights with her Brother for professing to love her, then grows calm and never thinks of her any more.

The Ghost is wholly the Invention of *Shakespeare,* as is likewise the King's concerted Scheme with *Laertes* to kill *Hamlet* treacherously as they fenced, or if he failed, to poison the Wine. The King is killed by *Hamlet* both in the History and the Play, but in the Play he is stabb'd in the midst of his Friends, Guards, and Attendants; in the History as he is rising in Confusion from his Bed, and unable to draw his Sword to defend himself.

Here the Historian, romantic as his Relation seems, has the Advantage of the Poet in Probability. After *Amleth* has secured his Uncle's Attendants, taken away his Sword from him, and placed his own (which was fastened to the Scabbard) in its stead, it was not difficult for him to kill him disarmed, and without any Assistance.

But *Shakespeare* makes *Hamlet* execute his Vengeance on the King in a public Hall, crouded with his Attendants and Guards, and surrounded by his Friends. (pp. 127-28)

The Queen's Death, by drinking ignorantly of the poisoned Wine, is a beautiful Stroke of the Poet's. The History shews her unfortunate, but *Shakespeare* makes the same Man who seduced her to Wickedness be her involuntary Murderer, and at once the Cause and Punisher of her Guilt.

Shakespeare has with Reason been censored for the Catastrophe of this Tragedy. The brave, the injured *Hamlet* falls with the Murderers he punishes; one Fate overwhelms alike the innocent and the guilty. . . . *Shakespeare* would not so far deviate from the History as to leave him happy and in Peace, though he has hastened his Death as well as changed the Manner of it. He is killed by the treacherous Contrivance of the King, and *Laertes* is the Instrument of that Treachery, which is afterwards turned upon himself.

As *Laertes* is a subordinate Character in the Play, it seems to be a Fault in *Shakespeare* to shew him with a Similitude of Manners, under the same Circumstances, and acting upon the same Principles as *Hamlet,* his Hero. *Laertes* is brave and generous, his Father is murdered basely, as he is informed, Duty and Honour incite him to revenge his Death, and he does so.

This Sameness of Character and Parity of Circumstances with the Hero lessens his Importance, and almost divides our Attention and Concern between them; an Effect which *Shakespeare* certainly did not intend to produce. Nor can it be lessened by the Consideration of the treacherous Measures *Laertes* was prevailed upon to enter into against *Hamlet,* who had murdered his Father. In this he does not differ much from *Hamlet,* who did not attempt by open Force to revenge his Father's Murder on his Uncle, but designed to accomplish it by Subtilty and Craft.

The same Equality is preserved in their Deaths and in their Actions throughout the Play. *Laertes* wounds *Hamlet* with the poisoned Weapon, in the Scuffle they change Rapiers and *Hamlet* wounds *Laertes;* and they exchange Forgiveness with each other before they die.

Thus has *Shakespeare,* undesignedly no doubt, given us two Heroes instead of one in this Play; the only Difference between them is that one of them is a Prince, the other a Nobleman, and but for this slight Distinction the Play might have been as well called the *Tragedy of Laertes* as *Hamlet.* (pp. 128-29)

The Madness of *Hamlet* seems to be less essential to the Play than the History. In the latter it affords him the Means of executing a Contrivance which, absurd as it is, secures the Accomplishment of his Revenge, but in the Play it is of no other Use than to enliven the Dialogue, unless its Usefulness may be deduced from its bringing on such Accidents as it was assumed to prevent. For *Hamlet*'s Madness alarms the King's Suspicion, and that produces the treacherous Embassy to *England,* which failing, the Contrivance of the poisoned Rapier followed, and that does the Business.

But since the King's conscious Guilt and Terror might reasonably have created a Distrust of *Hamlet,* and that Distrust and a Desire of Security induced him to seek his Death, what need had *Shakespeare* to make his Heroe's Sense and Discretion appear doubtful by shewing him feigning a Madness destructive to his Safety, and which he himself knows to be so, and yet persists in?

Shakespeare has indeed followed the History in making *Hamlet* feign himself mad; but that Madness being of no Consequence to the principal Design of the Play (as it is in the History), or if of Consequence, it hurts the Reputation of his Heroe, 'tis certainly a Fault; for at least he only produces the same Events by a Blunder which might have happened without it.

The Violation of poetical Justice is not the only Fault that arises from the Death of *Hamlet*. The revenging his Father's Murder is the sole End of all his Designs and the great Business of the Play, and the noble and fixed Resolution of *Hamlet* to accomplish it makes up the most shining Part of his Character; yet this great End is delayed till after *Hamlet* is mortally wounded. He stabs the King immediately upon the Information of his Treachery to himself! Thus his Revenge becomes interested, and he seems to punish his Uncle rather for his own Death than the Murder of the King, his Father. (pp. 129-30)

> [*Charlotte Lennox*], in her extract from *Shakespeare, the Critical Heritage: 1753-1765, Vol. 4, edited by Brian Vickers, Routledge & Kegan Paul, 1976, pp. 126-30.*

ARTHUR MURPHY   (essay date 1753)

[*Murphy here responds to F. M. de Voltaire (1752), accusing him of unfairness and hyperbole in his criticism of* Hamlet. *The following is taken from a revision of a letter which originally appeared in the* Gray's Inn Journal *in 1753.*]

I have observed, Sir, that you are disposed upon all occasions to censure the *English* stage with some degree of acrimony whenever it comes in your way. Shakespeare stands at the head of our dramatic writers, perhaps at the head of all who have figured in that kind in every age and nation. With that great poet you have not hesitated to take unbounded liberty in a manner, if I am not mistaken, not consistent with that manly sense which seems to be your characteristic, and in a stile apparently destitute of your usual delicacy. Should I say that the boasted *bienséance* of your country has deserted you in some of these passages, I flatter myself that upon a review of them you will not totally disavow it. The most striking of the various judgments which you have vented against our immortal bard is found in the discourse prefixed to your tragedy of *Semiramis*. . . . (pp. 90-1)

I would ask yourself, Sir, is this criticism candid? Is it a fair analysis, a true account of the tragedy in question? We do not concern ourselves in this country with what is agreeable to the taste of the vulgar in *France* or *Italy;* we know that the *cliquant* of an opera, or a *comedie ballet*, is more acceptable to their refinement than the sterling bullion of an *English* performance; but we might expect from a writer of eminence a truer and more exact opinion. *Hamlet*, Sir, does not run mad; if he did, *King Lear* has proved what a beautiful distress might arise from it. *Hamlet* counterfeits madness, for his own private end. Nobody ever imagined that he thinks he is killing a rat when he says *Polonius*. If you will be pleased to recollect the passage you will find that he takes him for his better, meaning the King, and the rat is only mentioned to save appearances.

Ophelia does undoubtedly run mad. The desolation of her mind arises from filial piety: her virtue and her misfortunes make her respectable. Give me leave to add, her distress is perhaps the most pathetic upon any stage. It is true she sings in misery, and that is not usual in grave and serious tragedy; but it occurs in nature, and what *Shakespeare* saw in nature he transplanted into his drama. He knew of no rules to restrain him, and if he did he scorned the restraint. The beauty of *Ophelia*'s madness, Sir, consists in this: it gives the actings of the mind; it shews the course of the ideas in a disturbed imagination; and the poet who can thus turn the heart inside out does more than pompous declamation ever attained. That *Ophelia*'s grave is dug on the stage cannot be denied, but that very indecorum produces a string of beautiful reflections, and such a vein of morality as cannot be paralleled by the *Scene Francoise*. I cannot recollect that *Hamlet* ever shocked me with miserable jests upon this occasion; nor do I remember that any of the personages are such honest bottle companions as to carouse and sing merry catches on the stage. Pray consider, Sir, that our language, though no way inferior to the *French*, is not universally understood abroad. From your representation it may be inferred that our great poet is really the *drunken savage* you have thought proper to call him. This would be derogating from the greatest poet (*Milton* excepted) that the world has seen since the days of *Homer*, and, I believe you will grant, is dealing unfairly with a man whom you cannot but reverence.

When you confess that he has many flights of the highest elevation you make an approach towards justice, but I cannot help thinking that you are somewhat like a painter who lays on just and proper colouring and then instantly effaces it, when you add that you are astonished at his sublime excursions of fancy. I should have expected from your candour that you would rather have said, it is a pity that he who soared to such glorious heights should ever tire his eagle wing and fall beneath himself. You may remember that it is with this good temper *Longinus* talks of *Homer;* they are dreams, says he, but they are the dreams of *Homer*. He might have given the appellation of a *drunken savage;* he might have called *Homer* an *old dotard;* he might have said, in the fury of criticism, that some of his long stories are detestable; but a candid critic forgives the imbecilities of human nature, and passes sentence like a mild and good-natured judge. (pp. 91-2)

> *Arthur Murphy, in his extract from "Shakespeare Vindicated, in a Letter to Voltaire," in his* The Works of Arthur Murphy: Gray's Inn Journal, Vol. V, *T. Cadell, 1786 (and reprinted in* Shakespeare, the Critical Heritage: 1753-1765, Vol. 4, *edited by Brian Vickers, Routledge & Kegan Paul, 1976, pp. 90-3).*

[TOBIAS SMOLLETT]   (essay date 1756)

[*Smollett was a major eighteenth-century English novelist. Like Charles Gildon (1721), he considers the "To be" soliloquy in* Hamlet *to be a problem point, because, he suggests, the speech is "out of character" for Hamlet. For additional commentary on Hamlet's soliloquies, see Charles Gildon (1721), William Guthrie (1747), Samuel Johnson (1765), A.J.A. Waldock (1931), Theodore Spencer (1942), and E.M.W. Tillyard (1949). Smollett's essay first appeared in* The Critical Review *in 1756.*]

With respect to *Shakespeare*, though we revere the might of that creative genius we are not so dazzled with his excellencies but that we can perceive a number of imperfections scattered up and down his works. These his warmest admirers will not deny, and there an hundred characters in his plays that (if we may be allowed the expression) speak out of character. . . . The famous soliloquy of *Hamlet* is introduced by the head and shoulders. He had some reason to revenge his father's death upon his uncle, but he had none to take away his own life. Nor does it appear from any other part of the play that he had any such intention. On the contrary, when he had a fair opportunity of being put to death in *England* he very wisely retorted the villainy of his conductors on their own heads. (p. 266)

> [Tobias Smollett], *in his extract from* Shakespeare, the Critical Heritage: 1753-1765, *Vol. 4, edited by Brian Vickers, Routledge & Kegan Paul, 1976, pp. 266-67.*

THOMAS SHERIDAN [as reported by JAMES BOSWELL] (essay date 1763)

[*Sheridan, an Irish actor and author, distinguished himself in many of the leading roles of Shakespeare's plays, including Hamlet. Here he characterizes Hamlet as contemplative and lacking the "strength of mind" to carry out his task. As the first commentator to seek the cause of Hamlet's delay in the hero himself, Sheridan foreshadows the Romantic conception of Hamlet later developed by Johann Wolfgang von Goethe (1795), Samuel Taylor Coleridge (1811, 1813), and August Wilhelm Schlegel (1808), among others.*]

[Sheridan gave us] a most ingenious dissertation on the character of Hamlet. . . . He made it clear to us that Hamlet, notwithstanding of his seeming incongruities, is a perfectly consistent character. Shakespeare drew him as the portrait of a young man of a good heart and fine feelings who had led a studious contemplative life and so become delicate and irresolute. He shows him in very unfortunate circumstances, the author of which he knows he ought to punish, but wants strength of mind to exercise what he thinks right and wishes to do. In this dilemma he makes Hamlet feign himself mad, as in that way he might put his uncle to death with less fear of the consequences of such an attempt. We therefore see Hamlet sometimes like a man really mad and sometimes like a man reasonable enough, though much hurt in mind. His timidity being once admitted, all the strange fluctuations which we perceive in him may be easily traced to that source. We see when the Ghost appears (which his companions had beheld without extreme terror)—we see Hamlet in all the agony of consternation. Yet we hear him uttering extravagant sallies of rash intrepidity, by which he endeavours to stir up his languid mind to a manly boldness, but in vain. For he still continues backward to revenge, hesitates about believing the Ghost to be the real spirit of his father, so much that the Ghost chides him for being tardy. When he has a fair opportunity of killing his uncle, he neglects it and says he will not take him off while at his devotions, but will wait till he is in the midst of some atrocious crime, that he may put him to death with his guilt upon his head. Now this, if really from the heart, would make Hamlet the most black, revengeful man. But it coincides better with his character to suppose him here endeavouring to make an excuse to himself for his delay. We see too that after all he agrees to go to England and actually embarks. In short, Sheridan made out his character accurately, clearly, and justly. (pp. 234-35)

> *Thomas Sheridan [as reported by James Boswell], in his extract from a journal entry of April 6, 1763, in* Boswell's London Journal: 1762-1763 *by James Boswell, McGraw-Hill Book Co., 1950, pp. 233-35.*

SAMUEL JOHNSON (essay date 1765)

[*Johnson has long held an important place in the history of Shakespearean criticism. He is considered the foremost representative of moderate English Neoclassicism and is credited by some literary historians with freeing Shakespeare from the strictures of the three unities valued by strict Neoclassicists: that dramas should have a single setting, take place in less than twenty-four hours, and have a causally connected plot. More recent commentators portray him as a critic who was able to synthesize existing critical theory rather than as an innovative theoretician. Johnson was a master of the Augustan prose style and a personality who dominated the literary world of his day. The following excerpt from his 1765 edition of* The Plays of William Shakespeare *contains two of his more famous statements on* Hamlet: *the description of Polonius as "dotage encroaching upon wisdom" and the comment that Hamlet's soliloquy in the prayer-scene is "too horrible to be read or to be uttered." George Stubbes/Thomas Hanmer (1736) gives a similar interpretation of the prayer-scene. Other critics who commented on Hamlet's soliloquies include Charles Gildon (1721), William Guthrie (1747), Tobias Smollett (1756), A.J.A. Waldock (1931), Theodore Spencer (1942), and E.M.W. Tillyard (1949).*]

Polonius is a man bred in courts, exercised in business, stored with observation, confident of his knowledge, proud of his eloquence, and declining into dotage. His mode of oratory is truly represented as designed to ridicule the practice of those times, of prefaces that made no introduction, and of method that embarrassed rather than explained. This part of his character is accidental, the rest is natural. Such a man is positive and confident, because he knows that his mind was once strong, and knows not that it is become weak. Such a man excels in general principles, but fails in the particular application. He is knowing in retrospect, and ignorant in foresight. While he depends upon his memory and can draw from his repositories of knowledge he utters weighty sentences, and gives useful counsel; but as the mind in its enfeebled state cannot be kept long busy and intent, the old man is subject to sudden dereliction of his faculties, he loses the order of his ideas and entangles himself in his own thoughts, till he recovers the leading principle, and falls again into his former train. This idea of dotage encroaching upon wisdom will solve all the phaenomena of the character of *Polonius*. (pp. 156-57)

[Of the celebrated 'To be, or not to be'] soliloquy, which bursting from a man distracted with contrariety of desires and overwhelmed with the magnitude of his own purposes, is connected rather in the speaker's mind than on his tongue, I shall endeavour to discover the train, and to shew how one sentiment produces another.

Hamlet, knowing himself injured in the most enormous and atrocious degree, and seeing no means of redress but such as much expose him to the extremity of hazard, meditates on his situation in this manner: *Before I can form any rational scheme of action under this pressure of distress,* it is necessary to decide whether, *after our present state, we are* to be or not to be. That is the question which, as it shall be answered, will determine *whether 'tis nobler* and more suitable to the dignity of reason *to suffer the outrages of fortune* patiently, or to take arms against *them,* and by opposing end them, *though perhaps with the loss of life. If to die* were *to sleep, no more, and by a sleep to end* the miseries of our nature, such a sleep were *devoutly to be wished;* but if *to sleep* in death be *to dream,* to retain our powers of sensibility, we must *pause* to consider *in that sleep of death what dreams may come.* This consideration *makes calamity* so long endured; *for who would bear* the vexations of life, which might be ended *by a bare bodkin,* but that he is afraid of something in unknown futurity? This fear it is that gives efficacy to conscience, which by turning the mind upon *this regard* chills the ardour of *resolution,* checks the vigour of *enterprise,* and makes the *current* of desire stagnate in inactivity.

We may suppose that he would have applied these general observations to his own case, but that he discovered *Ophelia.* (pp. 157-58)

> *Hamlet.* Then trip him, that his heels may kick
> at heav'n;
> And that his soul may be as damn'd and black
> As hell, whereto it goes.   [III.iii.93-5]

This speech, in which *Hamlet,* represented as a virtuous character, is not content with taking blood for blood but contrives damnation for the man that he would punish, is too horrible to be read or to be uttered. (p. 159)

If the dramas of *Shakespeare* were to be characterised, each by the particular excellence which distinguishes it from the rest, we must allow to the tragedy of *Hamlet* the praise of variety. The incidents are so numerous that the argument of the play would make a long tale. The scenes are interchangeably diversified with merriment and solemnity; with merriment that includes judicious and instructive observations, and solemnity not strained by poetical violence above the natural sentiments of man. New characters appear from time to time in continual succession, exhibiting various forms of life and particular modes of conversation. The pretended madness of *Hamlet* causes much mirth, the mournful distraction of *Ophelia* fills the heart with tenderness, and every personage produces the effect intended, from the apparition that in the first act chills the blood with horror, to the fop in the last that exposes affectation to just contempt.

The conduct is perhaps not wholly secure against objections. The action is indeed for the most part in continual progression, but there are some scenes which neither forward nor retard it. Of the feigned madness of *Hamlet* there appears no adequate cause, for he does nothing which he might not have done with the reputation of sanity. He plays the madman most when he treats *Ophelia* with so much rudeness, which seems to be useless and wanton cruelty.

Hamlet is, through the whole play, rather an instrument than an agent. After he has, by the stratagem of the play, convicted the King he makes no attempt to punish him, and his death is at last effected by an incident which *Hamlet* has no part in producing.

The catastrophe is not very happily produced; the exchange of weapons is rather an expedient of necessity than a stroke of art. A scheme might easily have been formed to kill *Hamlet* with the dagger, and *Laertes* with the bowl.

The poet is accused of having shewn little regard to poetical justice, and may be charged with equal neglect of poetical probability. The apparition left the regions of the dead to little purpose; the revenge which he demands is not obtained but by the death of him that was required to take it; and the gratification which would arise from the destruction of an usurper and a murderer is abated by the untimely death of *Ophelia,* the young, the beautiful, the harmless, and the pious. (pp. 161-62)

> *Samuel Johnson, in his extracts from* Shakespeare,
> the Critical Heritage: 1765-1774, *Vol. 5, edited by*

Brian Vickers, Routledge & Kegan Paul, 1979, pp. 156-62.

GOTTHOLD EPHRAIM LESSING (essay date 1767)

[*Lessing, a German critic and playwright, rebelled against the influence of French classicism on German drama and praised the works of Shakespeare, which he promoted as the true model for German theater. In the excerpt below, Lessing contrasts the handling of the ghost device in Voltaire's* Semiramis *with that in Shakespeare's* Hamlet. *In the process, he ridicules Voltaire mercilessly and praises Shakespeare as the only dramatist who could truly make an audience believe in the reality of ghosts. Lessing believes that the comparison with Voltaire serves well to highlight Shakespeare's genius for realism on the stage. For additional commentary on the character of the ghost in* Hamlet, *see Joseph Addison (1711), Elizabeth Montagu (1769), W. W. Greg (1917), J. Dover Wilson (1918), Sister Miriam Joseph (1962), and Eleanor Prosser (1971).*]

The appearance of a ghost in a French tragedy was such a daring novelty, and the poet justified it with such curious reasons, that it might be well to pause here for a moment.

Everyone, claimed Monsieur Voltaire, was shouting that one didn't believe in ghosts anymore and that the re-appearance of the dead could only be viewed as ridiculous in the eyes of an enlightened nation. "What?" he countered; "all of antiquity believed in such miracles and we should deny ourselves the privilege? What? Our religion honored such extraordinary provisions, and now it should be ridiculous to renew them?"

It's true enough that antiquity believed in ghosts, but they also had perfectly good reasons to do so. We can't apply our present-day standards and judge them according to our views. When the poets of antiquity chose to resurrect a dead man in form of a ghost, they did so in accordance with their beliefs. Does this give the modern poet the same right? Surely not. What if he sets his tale in antiquity? Not then either. For the dramatist is not a historian; he doesn't write what happened in those days; rather, he lets it happen before our eyes one more time—not only because of its historical fact but with a completely new and different intent: the historical fact is not the end but only the means to his end. He wants to deceive us and, through his deception, move us. If we no longer believe in ghosts; if this disbelief should by necessity prevent this deception; if, without deception, it should be impossible for us to feel compassion—does this mean that the dramatist can no longer endow his stories with the stuff of fairytales? That it is no longer permissible to have ghosts and visions appear on the stage? That this source of the terrible and the sublime has dried up for us? No, this loss would be too great for the arts. Let's make another assumption: Who says we no longer believe in ghosts? And what is that supposed to mean? It cannot mean that we have become so enlightened that we can prove the impossibility of a ghost. It cannot mean that certain undeniable truths, which are in conflict with the belief in ghosts, have become so widely known that even the least sophisticated of men is so familiar with them that everything contradictory must needs strike him as ridiculous and cheap. That we don't believe in ghosts anymore can only mean that in this matter the current dominant way of thinking has given more weight to the reasons against it. Only a very few think this way, and these are the ones who raise their voices in protest and set the tone. The majority of the masses say nothing and remain indifferent; they believe now this, now that. When the sun shines they give their smiling approval to the ridicule of ghosts, and in the dark of night they shudder at the mere thought of one.

However, such a disbelief in ghosts cannot and must not deter the dramatist in any way from using this device. The seed for believing in it lies in us all, and everything depends on the artfulness with which the writer brings this seed to fruition and makes it believable and real with a few ingenious strokes. If he has these skills in his power, then we in our ordinary lives may believe whatever we wish: in the theater, we must believe whatever he wants us to believe.

Shakespeare is such a craftsman, and practically no one else but Shakespeare. The hair on our head stands up in terror before his ghost in *Hamlet*—regardless of whether it covers a believer's or non-believer's skull. Monsieur Voltaire made a grave mistake in citing this particular ghost [see excerpt above, 1752]; it makes him and his ghost Ninus ridiculous.

Shakespeare's ghost really does come from this world, or so it seems to us. For it comes in that solemn hour, in that shuddering stillness of the night, accompanied fully by all the ominous, mysterious connotations which we, from our wet-nurse on, have learned to expect and associate with ghosts. Voltaire's ghost, by contrast, wouldn't even make it as bogeyman to scare the children; it is nothing but a costumed buffoon who has nothing, says nothing, does nothing that would make him even half believable as that which it claims to be. Instead, all the circumstances under which it appears destroy the illusion and betray the creation of a cold poet who would dearly love to deceive and frighten us without knowing how to do it. Imagine, if you will, just this: in the middle of the day, in the middle of a gathering of all the ranks of the empire, announced by a thunder clap, the Voltairean ghost steps forth from its tomb. Wherever did Voltaire hear that ghosts are so brazen? What old woman couldn't have told him that ghosts shun the sunlight and dislike large gatherings? Voltaire must have known that too, but he was too timid, too fastidious to use these commonly known circumstances. He wanted to show us a ghost, but it had to be a ghost of a nobler sort, and this nobler sort spoiled everything. A ghost that violates everything that is considered tradition and consistent behavior among ghosts strikes me as no proper ghost at all; and whatever doesn't further the illusion destroys it.

If Voltaire had kept an eye on the capabilities of the actors, he would have realized another reason for the unsuitability of letting a ghost appear before a large mass of people: all of them must express fear and terror at the same time upon beholding the ghost, and all must express this in a different way if the scene is not to have the rigid symmetry of a ballet. Try teaching that to a herd of dull-witted extras, and once you have trained them as best you can, consider the degree to which this multiple group reaction to the ghost must distract from the attention focused on the principal actors. If the latter are to make the proper impression on us, we should not only see them alone, but nothing else but them. With Shakespeare, Hamlet is the only one with whom the ghost communicates; in the scene where the mother is also on the stage, it is neither seen nor heard by her. Thus, all our attention focuses on him, and the more signs of a soul shattered by awe and terror we perceive in him, the better prepared we are to consider the apparition which caused this condition in him to be exactly that for which he takes it. The ghost affects us more directly through Hamlet than through its own being. The impression it makes on him transfers itself to us, and the effect is too evident and too powerful for us to doubt its reality. How little Voltaire under-

stood of this artistic ruse! Many are frightened by his ghost, but many isn't much. At one point Semiramis exclaims: Heavens! I am dying! and the others don't fuss over him any more than they would over a friend, believed to be far away, who suddenly enters the room.

I note another difference between the ghosts of the French and the English poet. Voltaire's ghost is nothing but a poetic device to enhance plot; it is not in the least interesting for its own sake. Shakespeare's ghost, by contrast, is an actual character whom we see acting, in whose fate we actively participate; it arouses terror, but also pity.

No doubt this difference had its roots in the different concepts of ghosts held by the two playwrights. Voltaire saw the appearance of a dead person as a miracle, while Shakespeare saw it as a natural occurrence. Which of the two has the more philosophical bend should be obvious, but Shakespeare's thought was conceived in a more poetic way. At no time did Voltaire's ghost of Ninus strike us as a being which, even beyond the grave, could be capable of pleasant and unpleasant sensations; a being for whom we might feel pity. All he wanted to demonstrate was that even the highest authority, in order to uncover and punish hidden crimes, might make an exception to its eternal laws.

> *Gotthold Ephraim Lessing, in extracts from two of his essays dated June 5 and 9, 1767, in his* Hamburgische Dramaturgie, *Verlag Philipp Reclam jun., 1972* [translated for this publication].

Mrs. [ELIZABETH] MONTAGU   (essay date 1769)

[*Montagu compares Shakespeare favorably with classical Greek and French tragedians. In particular she is concerned with answering the attacks against Shakespeare by F. M. de Voltaire (1752) and other Neoclassical critics for their failure to observe the "rules" of Neoclassical dramatic composition. Montagu's response reflects the changing literary values evident in the work of European critics such as Gotthold Ephraim Lessing (1767), who regarded "modern" writers such as Shakespeare as equal or superior to the "ancients," and who preferred English to French drama. Montagu's essay was praised by her contemporary, the Shakespeare editor William Warburton, as "the most elegant and judicious piece of criticism this age has produced." In the following excerpt, first published in her* Essays on the Writings and Genius of Shakespeare *in 1769, she commends Shakespeare's handling of the ghost. For additional commentary on the ghost, see Joseph Addison (1711), W. W. Greg (1917), J. Dover Wilson (1918), Sister Miriam Joseph (1962), and Eleanor Prosser (1971).*]

The first propriety in dealing with preternatural beings seem to be that the ghost be intimately connected with the fable; that he increase the interest, add to the solemnity of it, and that his efficiency in bringing on the catastrophe be in some measure adequate to the violence done to the ordinary course of things in his visible interposition. To this end it is necessary that this being should be acknowledged and revered by the national superstition, and every operation that develops the attributes, which the vulgar opinion or nurse's legend taught us to ascribe to him, will augment our pleasure; whether we give the reins to imagination, and, as spectators, yield ourselves up to the pleasing delusion, or, as critics, examine the merit of the composition. In all these capital points Shakespeare has excelled. At the solemn midnight hour the scene opens, and Bernardo tells us that the ghost of the late monarch had appeared the night before 'When yon same star, that westward from the pole, Had made his course t'illume that part of heaven, Where now it burns, The bell then beating one ———.' Here enters the Ghost, after you are thus prepared. There is something solemn and sublime in thus regulating the walking of the spirit by the course of the star. It intimates a connection and correspondence between things beyond our ken, *and above the visible diurnal sphere.* Horatio is affected with that kind of fear which such an appearance would naturally excite. He trembles and turns pale. When the violence of the emotion subsides, he reflects that probably this supernatural event portends some danger lurking in the State. This suggestion gives importance to the phenomenon, and engages our attention. Such appearances, says he, preceded the fall of the mightiest Julius, and the ruin of the great commonwealth. There is great art in this conduct. The true cause of the royal Dane's discontent could not be guessed at; it was a secret which could be revealed only by himself. In the mean time it was necessary to captivate our attention by demonstrating that the poet was not going to exhibit such idle and frivolous gambols as ghosts are by the vulgar often represented to perform. Horatio's address to the Ghost is, in its whole purport, in accordance with the popular conception of such matters. The vanishing of the Ghost at the crowing of the cock is another circumstance of established superstition.

> *Mrs. [Elizabeth] Montagu, in her extract from* A New Variorum Edition of Shakespeare: Hamlet, Vol. IV, *edited by Horace Howard Furness, J. B. Lippincott Company, 1877, p. 146.*

LONGINUS [pseudonym of GEORGE STEEVENS] (essay date 1772)

[*Brian Vickers, editor of* Shakespeare: The Critical Heritage, *has attributed the following essay to George Steevens, an English scholar who collaborated with Samuel Johnson on a ten-volume edition of Shakespeare's works in 1773. The subsequent revisions of this collection, along with Steeven's own edition of 1793, formed the textual basis for the first two Variorum editions of Shakespeare's plays. Many modern scholars also contend that Steevens was the sole theater critic for the* General Evening Post, *in which the essay below was originally published. Steevens is convinced of the brutality of Hamlet's nature, an opinion challenged by the majority of Romantic critics; among the few commentators who have concurred with Steevens on this point are Ivan Turgenieff (1860), Salvador de Madariaga (1948) and Rebecca West (1957). In the following excerpt, first published in* General Evening Post *on January 1-2 and February 6-8, 1772, Steevens also discusses the scene in which Hamlet instructs the actor, which, according to Steevens, serves only to interrupt the action of the drama.*]

The character of Hamlet is evidently designed by its illustrious author as a picture of an amiable prince, an affectionate son, a fast friend, and a fine gentleman.—Yet in no one of these respects is it by any means intitled to our approbation. From the beginning of the play till his killing the King at the end of the fifth act we find him irresolute, unnatural, inconstant and brutal.—He assumes the appearance of madness to answer no purpose, and is perpetually talking of what he *ought* to do, without a single attempt of proceeding to action. His father has risen from the grave to call for vengeance upon a *kindless* murderer, and Hamlet promises solemnly to revenge his death, but never makes the smallest effort to effect it. . . . At the end of the fifth Act, indeed, when he finds himself mortally wounded and hears that he has not half an hour to live, then he proceeds to revenge his own death, and the inconsiderate are highly charmed with his heroism. Whereas in fact common sense

stands astonished at his cowardice, and wonders that a father bursting from the tomb cannot rouse him to a deed of manly resolution.

Characters assumed upon the stage should never be taken up but to answer some essential purposes. One half of the play in question is employed by Hamlet's madness; yet what individual consequence does this madness produce? The hero, to be sure, insults Ophelia (whom he tenderly loves) in the grossest manner, under the appearance of insanity; and he abuses her brother in the grossest manner, likewise under the same appearance, merely for the very conduct which should excite his esteem. In short, he does every thing wrong during his pretended madness, but never attempts any thing right; and after an outrageous violence on Laertes, in his sober senses, descends to the baseness of a serious lye to excuse himself by the plea of his *'sore distraction.'* (p. 488)

'Tis strange that he should have *spirit* enough to kill the innocent, and yet want resolution to punish the guilty; 'tis strange he should lament Ophelia's death, and yet insult her brother for lamenting it; and 'tis above all things strange that his rage is chiefly turned against *meritorious* objects, while the great object of his horror goes unpunished till he himself, by being in the agonies of death, has nothing farther to apprehend. *Hamlet* is generally stiled one of our dramatic *classics;* I could therefore wish to see it *somewhat* correct, and rendered really worthy of those tears which we usually conceive the due of superior virtue plunged into superior calamity. (p. 489)

- - - - -

However the various commentators on Shakespeare's tragedy of *Hamlet* may differ about particular parts of that celebrated piece, there is one scene which they all allow to be masterly, though certainly the very reason which they assign for calling it eminently excellent is the very reason why they should pronounce it peculiarly reprehensible.

The scene which I here allude to is that in which Hamlet instructs the player in the minutenesses of his profession, and exclaims against the absurdity of those actors who let the necessary business of the play stand still to introduce some impertinent witticism of their own. (p. 489)

That the lesson which Shakespeare thus gives to the players is admirable I shall readily acknowledge; and I shall also as readily acknowledge that the actors who fall into the error which he complains of deserve to be mentioned with the utmost severity of animadversion. Yet, with all possible deference to the genius of this great writer, I cannot help thinking that time and place are palpably wanting to render this scene in question a little more consonant to the laws of propriety. For if the reader considers but a moment he will find Shakespeare himself running into the very fault which incurs his own censure, and making the necessary business of the play stand still to dazzle the auditor's imagination with the lustre of his critical accuracy. (pp. 489-90)

A scene to be *proper* must advance the great business of the play; must serve to complicate the intrigue, or to develope the catastrophe. Unless it does this it is *impertinent,* however exquisite in itself, because we can only estimate its theatrical value by the relation which it bears to the piece, and are by no means to consider its merit as a separate composition, but its worth in a state of evident dependency. . . .

[Every] man who sees *Hamlet* is impatient during the performance of this scene, and burns with expectation of the vengeance which he hopes the young Prince will wreak on his father's murderer. What is Hecuba to Hamlet, or what is Hamlet to Hecuba? Yet, notwithstanding Shakespeare's own text manifestly rises against himself, the commentators *will* have the theatrical instruction a diamond of the finest water, though, *from the nature of its situation,* it is obviously a whiting's eye set in mud. (p. 490)

Longinus [pseudonym of George Steevens], in his essays in Shakespeare, the Critical Heritage: 1765-1774, Vol. 5, *edited by Brian Vickers, Routledge & Kegan Paul, 1979, pp. 487-89; 489-90.*

HIC ET UBIQUE [pseudonym of GEORGE STEEVENS] (essay date 1772)

[*Steevens's essay was originally published in the* St. James Chronicle *on February 18-20, 1772.*]

Hamlet is a curious Instance of the noblest Exertion of Dramatic Powers, and the greatest Abuse of them.—Considered as a Composition it is more, and less than Human. It rises to Inspiration, and sinks into Buffoonery. Greece, Rome, nor all the Kingdoms of the Earth, ancient and modern, can produce such Proofs of Genius as those Scenes where the Ghost appears, and those which are preparatory to them.—Perhaps the im-

Title page of the First Quarto of Hamlet *(1603). Reproduced by permission of The Huntington Library, San Marino, CA.*

mortal Author, in his more finished and consistent Dramas, has not any Parts superior, I may say equal to the Nature, Terror, Pathos, and Character, of those astonishing Exertions of his Powers! With this Consideration it is almost impious to mention his Errors, and yet they lie open to the Observation of every common Eye.

Now to his moral Part. *Hamlet,* a most exquisite Dramatic Character, young, warm, full of Grief for his Father's Death, and fuller of Resentment at his Mother's Marriage—before he sees the Ghost, and before he knows of his Father's Murder, expresses all the combined Passions of Rage, Sorrow, and Indignation, and yet when he is assured by his Father's Spirit that Murder has been added to Adultery and Incest, and he pledges himself—*with Wings as swift as Meditation, or the Thoughts of Love to sweep to his Revenge* [I.v.29ff.]—yet from that Moment—(notwithstanding all the Bitterness of Expression, his filial Tenderness and Horror at his Uncle's Crimes, with his Father's sacred Injunctions to spur him on—*'If thou hast Nature in thee bear it not'* [I.v.81])—Revenge, and all his former Passions are stagnated, and he goes on from Act to Act playing the Fool (inimitably I must confess), always *talking, threatening,* but never *executing.* He himself indeed, in one of the finest Soliloquies that can be imagined, produces a Kind of Excuse for his Cowardice, as he calls it, in *not fattening all the region Kites with the Slave's Offal!* [II.ii.579f.] which is, that that Devil might have appeared to him, *assumed his Father's Shape, and abused him to damn him* [II.ii.600ff.]; but when, by another Proof, he is convinced of his Uncle's Guilt, his Father again appears to him, *to whet his almost Blunted Purpose* [III.iv.111] (the best Critique upon the Play). Why does he not *then* bring about the Catastrophe? or why suffer himself to be tamely and unnaturally sent out of the Kingdom, to which he returns as unaccountably and as ineffectually as he left it. He does indeed make one Effort to kill the King before that divine Scene with his Mother in the 3d Act, but it is attended with such an abominable Reason for not doing it that it had better have been omitted. . . . (pp. 447-48)

All the remaining Part of the Play, from the 3d Act, seems as if his Genius, quite exhausted in the *Conception, Pregnancy,* and *Delivery* of such Wonders had wanted rest, fall'n asleep, and dreamt of going to England, coming back, Churchyards, Graves, Burials, Fencing Trials, Poison, Stabbing, and Death—all which are indeed

——Velut aegri somnia, vanae
Fingentur species

But they are Dreams of Genius! I shall speak of the Characters, in which Shakespeare seldom is wanting, when I speak of the Representation. In short, let it be said, more to the Honour of the Abilities of this astonishing Man, that notwithstanding all the Errors, Absurdities, and Extravagancies of this Play he alone could make it interesting without Progress in the Fable, and engage the Attention of an Audience by the Magic of his Imagery and Sentiments, by the wild irregular Sallies of an inspired Imagination, unassisted by Probability, or even Connection of Events.—This wonderful Secret no other Writer ever possessed, from the Beginning of the World to this Day! (pp. 448-49)

Hic et Ubique [pseudonym of George Steevens], in his extract from his "Dramatic Strictures on the Composition and Performance of 'Hamlet'," in Shakespeare, the Critical Heritage: 1765-1774, Vol.

5, *edited by Brian Vickers, Routledge & Kegan Paul, 1979, 446-49.*

WILLIAM RICHARDSON (essay date 1774)

[*Richardson was a Scottish author and educator whose philosophical leanings led him to focus on the psychological and moral aspects of Shakespeare's major characters, drawing from each a philosophical lesson, or what he termed a "ruling principle." For Richardson, such a guiding principle served to establish the psychological personalities of Shakespeare's characters—their motives, fears, delusions—and in the process defined the action of each play. Richardson was, with Henry Mackenzie (1780), one of the earliest critics to focus on the mind of the central figure, a practice which dominated the Romantic era and also influenced twentieth-century critics. In addition, he offered one of the first comprehensive examinations of the important question of Hamlet's delay. His Hamlet is a man of the highest morality and sensitivity who procrastinates because he is torn by the conflicting demands of his moral nature and his desire for vengeance. For additional commentary on Hamlet's delay, see Samuel Taylor Coleridge (1811), Hermann Ulrici (1839), Karl Werder (1859-60), Friedrich Nietzsche (1872), George Brandes (1895-96), and Sigmund Freud (1900). Richardson's essay was first published in 1774 in his* A Philosophical Analysis and Illustration of Some of Shakespeare's Remarkable Characters.]

Such is the condition of Hamlet. Exquisitely sensible of moral beauty and deformity, he discerns turpitude in a parent. Surprize, on a discovery so painful and unexpected, adds bitterness to his sorrow; and, led by the same moral principle to admire and glory in the high desert of his father, even this admiration contributes to his uneasiness. Aversion to his uncle, arising from the same origin, has a similar tendency and augments his anguish. All these feelings and emotions uniting together, are rendered still more violent, exasperated by his recent interview with the Queen, struggling for utterance, but restrained. (p. 121)

Hamlet's indignation [in the 'too too solid flesh' soliloquy] is not entirely effaced; and he expresses it by a general reflection: 'Frailty, thy name is woman!' This expression is too refined and artificial for a mind strongly agitated, yet it agrees entirely with just such a degree of emotion and pensiveness as disposes us to moralize. Considered as the language of a man violently affected, it is improper; considered in relation to what goes before and follows after, it appears perfectly natural. . . .

The condition of Hamlet's mind becomes still more curious and interesting. His suspicions are confirmed, and beget resentment. Conceiving designs of punishment, conscious of very violent perturbation, perceiving himself already suspected by the King, afraid lest his aspect, gesture, or demeanour should betray him, and knowing that his projects must be conducted with secrecy, he resolves to conceal himself under the disguise of madness. . . .

Accordingly, Hamlet, the more easily to deceive the King and his creatures, and to furnish them with an explication of his uncommon deportment, practises his artifice on Ophelia [when he comes to her with his doublet all unbrac'd]. (p. 122)

There is no change in his attachment, unless in so far as other passions of a violent and unpleasing character have assumed a temporary influence. His affection is permanent. Nor ought the pretended rudeness and seeming inconsistency of his behaviour to be at all attributed to inconstancy or an intention to insult. Engaged in a dangerous enterprise, agitated by impetuous emotions, desirous of concealing them, and for that reason feigning his understanding disordered; to confirm and publish

this report, seemingly so hurtful to his reputation, he would act in direct opposition to his former conduct and inconsistently with the genuine sentiments and affections of his soul. He would seem frivolous when the occasion required him to be sedate; and, celebrated for the wisdom and propriety of his conduct, he would assume appearances of impropriety. . . . To Ophelia he would shew dislike and indifference, because a change of this nature would be, of all others, the most remarkable, and because his affection for her was passionate and sincere. Of the sincerity and ardour of his regard he gives undoubted evidence.

> I lov'd Ophelia: forty thousand brothers
> Could not, with all their quantity of love,
> Make up my sum.   [V.i.269-71]
>   (pp. 122-23)

All the business of the tragedy, in regard to the display of character, is [concluded in the closet scene]. Hamlet, having detected the perfidy and inhumanity of his uncle, and having restored the Queen to a sense of her depravity, ought immediately to have triumphed in the utter ruin of his enemies, or to have fallen a victim to their deceit. The succeeding circumstances of the play are unnecessary; they are not essential to the catastrophe; and, excepting the madness of Ophelia and the scene of the grave-diggers, they exhibit nothing new in the characters. On the contrary, the delay cools our impatience; it diminishes our sollicitude for the fate of Hamlet, and almost lessens him in our esteem. Let him perish immediately, since the poet dooms him to perish; yet poetical justice would have decided otherwise.

On reviewing this analysis a sense of virtue—if I may use the language of an eminent philosopher without professing myself of his sect—seems to be the ruling principle. In other men it may appear with the ensigns of high authority; in Hamlet it possesses absolute power. United with amiable affections, with every graceful accomplishment, and every agreeable quality, it embellishes and exalts them. It rivets his attachment to his friends, when he finds them deserving; it is a source of sorrow, if they appear corrupted. It even sharpens his penetration; and if unexpectedly he discerns turpitude or impropriety in any character, it inclines him to think more deeply of their transgression than if his sentiments were less refined. . . . Men of other dispositions would think of gratifying their friends by contributing to their affluence, to their amusement, or external honour; but the acquisitions that Hamlet values, and the happiness he would confer, are a conscience void of offence, the peace and the honour of virtue. Yet with all this purity of moral sentiment, with eminent abilities, exceedingly cultivated and improved, with manners the most elegant and becoming, with the utmost rectitude of intention, and the most active zeal in the exercise of every duty, he is hated, persecuted, and destroyed. (pp. 123-24)

William Richardson, in his extract from "On the Character of Hamlet," in Shakespeare, the Critical Heritage: 1774-1801, *Vol. 6, edited by Brian Vickers, Routledge & Kegan Paul, 1981, pp. 121-24.*

HENRY MACKENZIE (essay date 1780)

[*Mackenzie, a Scottish novelist and essayist, wrote on Shakespeare for the journals* The Mirror *and* The Lounger. *In the following excerpt, published in* The Mirror *on April 17 and 22, 1780, he seconds William Richardson (1774) and anticipates such later Romantic critics as Johann Wolfgang von Goethe (1795),*

August Wilhelm Schlegel (1808), and Samuel Taylor Coleridge (1811, 1813), in judging Hamlet's irresolution consistent with his character. Thus, Mackenzie, like Richardson, by focusing on Hamlet's mind and personality, reconciled what previous critics perceived to be contradictory elements in Hamlet's character.]

Of all the characters of *Shakespeare* that of *Hamlet* has been generally thought the most difficult to be reduced to any fixed or settled principle. With the strongest purposes of revenge he is irresolute and inactive; amidst the gloom of the deepest melancholy he is gay and jocular; and while he is described as a passionate lover he seems indifferent about the object of his affections. It may be worth while to inquire whether any leading idea can be found upon which these apparent contradictions may be reconciled, and a character so pleasing in the closet, and so much applauded on the stage, rendered as unambiguous in the general as it is striking in detail. (p. 273)

The basis of *Hamlet's* character seems to be an extreme sensibility of mind, apt to be strongly impressed by its situation, and over-powered by the feelings which that situation excites. Naturally of the most virtuous and most amiable dispositions, the circumstances in which he was placed unhinged those principles of action which, in another situation, would have delighted mankind and made himself happy. . . . His misfortunes were not the misfortunes of accident, which, though they may overwhelm at first the mind will soon call up reflections to alleviate, and hopes to cheer; they were such as reflection only serves to irritate, such as rankle in the soul's tenderest part, his sense of virtue and feelings of natural affection; they arose from an uncle's villany, a mother's guilt, a father's murder!— Yet, amidst the gloom of melancholy and the agitation of passion in which his calamities involve him, there are occasional breakings-out of a mind richly endowed by nature and cultivated by education. We perceive gentleness in his demeanour, wit in his conversation, taste in his amusements, and wisdom in his reflections.

That *Hamlet's* character, thus formed by Nature, and thus modelled by situation, is often variable and uncertain I am not disposed to deny. I will content myself with the supposition that this is the very character which *Shakespeare* meant to allot him. (pp. 273-74)

Had *Shakespeare* made *Hamlet* pursue his vengeance with a steady determined purpose, had he led him through difficulties arising from accidental causes, and not from the doubts and hesitation of his own mind, the anxiety of the spectator might have been highly raised; but it would have been anxiety for the event, not for the person. As it is, we feel not only the virtues but the weaknesses of *Hamlet* as our own. . . . Our compassion for the first, and our anxiety for the latter, are excited in the strongest manner; and hence arises that indescribable charm in *Hamlet* which attracts every reader and every spectator, which the more perfect characters of other tragedies never dispose us to feel. (pp. 274-75)

Hamlet, from the very opening of the piece, is delineated as one under the dominion of melancholy, whose spirits were overborn by his feelings. Grief for his father's death, and displeasure at his mother's marriage prey on his mind, and he seems, with the weakness natural to such a disposition, to yield to their controul. He does not attempt to resist or combat these impressions, but is willing to fly from the contest, though it were into the grave:

Oh! that this too too solid flesh would melt, &c.

[I.ii.129ff.]

And indeed, he expressly delineates his own character as of the kind above mentioned when, hesitating on the evidence of his uncle's villainy, he says

The spirit that I have seen
May be the Devil, and the Devil hath power
T' assume a pleasing shape; yea, and perhaps,
Out of my weakness and my melancholy
Abuses me to damn me.

[II.ii.598ff.]

This doubt of the grounds on which our purpose is founded is as often the effect as the cause of irresolution, which first hesitates, and then seeks out an excuse for its hesitation. (pp. 275-76)

In the story of *Amleth,* the son of *Horwendil,* told by *Saxo-Grammaticus,* from which the tragedy of *Hamlet* is taken, the young prince who is to revenge the death of his father, murdered by his uncle *Fengo,* counterfeits madness that he may be allowed to remain about the court in safety and without suspicion. He never forgets his purposed vengeance, and acts with much more cunning towards its accomplishment than the *Hamlet* of *Shakespeare.* But *Shakespeare,* wishing to elevate the hero of his tragedy and at the same time to interest the audience in his behalf, throws around him from the beginning the majesty of melancholy, along with that sort of weakness and irresolution which frequently attend it. The incident of the *Ghost,* which is entirely the poet's own, and not to be found in the Danish legend, not only produces the happiest stage-effect but is also of the greatest advantage in unfolding that character which is stamped on the young prince at the opening of the play. In the communications of such a visionary being there is an uncertain kind of belief, and dark unlimited honour, which are aptly suited to display the wavering purpose and varied emotions of a mind endowed with a delicacy of feeling that often shakes its fortitude, with sensibility that overpowers its strength. (pp. 276-77)

•   •   •   •   •

[Some] have been induced to suppose the distraction of the Prince a strange unaccountable mixture, throughout, of real insanity and counterfeit disorder.

The distraction of *Hamlet,* however, is clearly affected through the whole play, always subject to the controul of his reason, and subservient to the accomplishment of his designs. At the grave of *Ophelia,* indeed, it exhibits some temporary marks of a real disorder. His mind, subject from Nature to all the weakness of sensibility, agitated by the incidental misfortune of *Ophelia's* death, amidst the dark and permanent impression of his revenge, is thrown for a while off its poise. . . . (p. 277)

Counterfeited madness, in a person of the character I have ascribed to *Hamlet,* could not be so uniformly kept up as not to allow the reigning impressions of his mind to shew themselves in the midst of his affected extravagance. It turned chiefly on his love to *Ophelia,* which he meant to hold forth as its greatest subject; but it frequently glanced on the wickedness of his uncle, his knowledge of which it was certainly his business to conceal.

In two of *Shakespeare's* tragedies are introduced at the same time instances of counterfeit madness and of real distraction. In both plays the same distinction is observed, and the false discriminated from the true by similar appearances. *Lear's* imagination constantly runs on the ingratitude of his daughters and the resignation of his crown; and *Ophelia,* after she has wasted the first ebullience of her distraction in some wild and incoherent sentences, fixes on the death of her father for the subject of her song. . . . But *Edgar* puts on a semblance as opposite as may be to his real situation and his ruling thoughts. He never ventures on any expression bordering on the subjects of a father's cruelty or a son's misfortune. *Hamlet*, in the same manner, were he as firm in mind as *Edgar*, would never have hinted any thing in his affected disorder that might lead to a suspicion of his having discovered the villany of his uncle; but his feeling, too powerful for his prudence, often breaks through that disguise which it seems to have been his original and ought to have continued his invariable purpose to maintain, till an opportunity should present itself of accomplishing the revenge which he meditated.

Of the reality of *Hamlet*'s love doubts also have been suggested. But if that delicacy of feeling, approaching to weakness, which I contend for be allowed him, the affected abuse, which he suffers at last to grow into scurrility of his mistress will, I think, be found not inconsistent with the truth of his affection for her. Feeling its real force, and designing to play the madman on that ground, he would naturally go as far from the reality as possible. . . . [Really] loving her, he would have been hurt by such a resemblance in the counterfeit. We can bear a downright caricature of our friend much easier than an unfavourable likeness.

It must be allowed, however, that the momentous scenes in which he is afterwards engaged seem to have smothered, if not extinguished the feelings of his love. His total forgetfulness of *Ophelia*, so soon after her death, cannot easily be justified. . . . Whether love is to be excited or resentment allayed, guilt to be made penitent or sorrow cheerful, the effect is frequently produced in a space hardly sufficient for words to express it. (pp. 277-79)

That gaiety and playfulness of deportment and of conversation which *Hamlet* sometimes not only assumes, but seems actually disposed to is, I apprehend, no contradiction to the general tone of melancholy in his character. That sort of melancholy which is the most genuine as well as the most amiable of any, neither arising from natural sourness of temper nor prompted by accidental chagrine, but the effect of delicate sensibility impressed with a sense of sorrow or a feeling of its own weakness, will, I believe, often be found indulging itself in a sportfulness of external behaviour amidst the pressure of a sad, or even the anguish of a broken heart. . . . The melancholy man feels in himself (if I may be allowed the expression) a sort of double person; one that, covered with the darkness of its imagination, looks not forth into the world nor takes any concern in vulgar objects or frivolous pursuits; another, which he lends, as it were, to ordinary men, which can accommodate itself to their tempers and manners, and indulge, without feeling any degradation from the indulgence, a smile with the chearful and a laugh with the giddy.

The conversation of *Hamlet* with the *Grave-digger* seems to me to be perfectly accounted for under this supposition; and instead of feeling it counteract the tragic effect of the story I never see him in that scene without receiving, from his transient jests with the clown before him, an idea of the deepest melancholy being rooted at his heart. The light point of view in which he places serious and important things marks the power of that great impression which swallows up every thing else in his mind, which makes *Caesar* and *Alexander* so indifferent to him that he can trace their remains in the plaster of a cottage or the stopper of a beer-barrel. (pp. 279-80)

Shakespeare's genius attended him in all his extravagancies. In the licence he took of departing from the regularity of the drama, or in his ignorance of those critical rules which might have restrained him within it, there is this advantage, that it gives him an opportunity of delineating the passions and affections of the human mind as they exist in reality, with all the various colourings which they receive in the mixed scenes of life; not as they are accommodated by the hands of more artificial poets to one great undivided impression, or an uninterrupted chain of congenial events. It seems, therefore, preposterous to endeavour to regularize his plays at the expence of depriving them of this peculiar excellence. . . . Within the bounds of a pleasure-garden we may be allowed to smooth our terrasses and trim our hedge-rows; but it were equally absurd and impracticable to apply the minute labours of the *roller* and the *pruning-knife* to the noble irregularity of trackless mountains and impenetrable forests. (p. 280)

> *Henry Mackenzie, in extracts from his essays in* Shakespeare, the Critical Heritage: 1774-1801, *Vol. 6, edited by Brian Vickers, Routledge & Kegan Paul, 1981, pp. 272-80.*

[JOSEPH] RITSON (essay date 1783)

[*Ritson's essay was first published in his* Remarks, Critical and Illustrative *in 1783.*]

Hamlet, the only child of the late king, upon whose death he became lawfully entitled to the crown, had, it seems, ever since that event been in a state of melancholy, owing to excessive grief for the suddenness with which it had taken place, and indignant horror at his mother's speedy and incestuous marriage. The spirit of the king, his father, appears, and makes him acquainted with the circumstances of his untimely fate, which he excites him to *revenge;* this Hamlet engages to do: an engagement it does not appear he ever forgot. It behoved him, however, to conduct hisself [*sic*] with the greatest prudence. The usurper was powerful, and had Hamlet carried his design into immediate execution, it could not but have been attended with the worst consequences to his own life and fame. No one knew what the Ghost had imparted to him, till he afterwards made Horatio acquainted with it; and though his interview with the spirit gave him certain proof and satisfactory reason to know and detest the usurper, it would scarcely, in the eye of the people, have justified his killing their king. To conceal, and, at a convenient time, to effect, his purpose, he counterfeits madness, and, for his greater assurance, puts the spirit's evidence and the usurper's guilt to the test of a play, by which the truth of each is manifested. . . .

Hamlet's conversation with Laertes immediately before the fencing scene was at the Queen's earnest entreaty; and though Dr Johnson [see excerpt above, 1765] be pleased to give it the harsh name of 'a dishonest fallacy,' there are better, because more natural, judges who consider it as a most gentle and pathetic address; certainly Hamlet did not intend the death of Polonius; of consequence, unwittingly and by mere accident, injured Laertes, who declared that he was 'satisfied in nature,' and that he only delayed his perfect reconcilement till his honor was satisfied by elder masters, whom at the same time (for he has the instrument of death in his hand) he never meant to consult. Let the conduct and sentiments of Laertes in this interview and in his conversation with the usurper, together with his villainous design against the life of Hamlet, be examined and tried by any rules of gentility, honor, or humanity, natural or artificial, he must be considered as a treacherous, cowardly, diabolical wretch. . . . (pp. 148-49)

> [*Joseph*] *Ritson, in his extract from* A New Variorum Edition of Shakespeare: Hamlet, *Vol. IV, edited by Horace Howard Furness, J. B. Lippincott Company, 1877, pp. 148-49.*

JOHANN WOLFGANG von GOETHE   (essay date 1795)

[*Goethe was an outstanding figure of German literature and a distinguished poet, dramatist, and novelist. His reverence for Shakespeare was inspired early in his career by his friendship with the German Romantic writer Johann Gottfried Herder. Many of Goethe's works bear Shakespeare's influence, particularly his first published drama,* Götz von Berlichingen mit der eisernen Hand (1773), *which is written in the manner of Shakespeare's history plays. His comments on* Hamlet *were incorporated into his autobiographical novel,* Wilhelm Meisters Lehrjahre, *first published in 1795. In his study of the character of Hamlet, Wilhelm, the novel's protagonist, is struck by the "inconsistencies" of the character. In order to understand them, he reviews the prince's history. Goethe's portrayal of Hamlet as a "lovely, pure, noble, and highly moral being" who lacks the hero's strength necessary to avenge his father's murder epitomizes the sentimental view of Hamlet that was initiated by William Richardson (1774) and Henry Mackenzie (1780), and further advanced by the Romantic critics. The image of Hamlet as an "oak-tree . . . planted in a costly vase" is one of the most often-repeated phrases in the history of criticism of the play, and his Romantic vision of the character is discussed throughout the criticism. For further examples of and commentary upon the Romantic conception of* Hamlet, *see August Wilhelm Schlegel (1808), Charles Lamb (1811), Samuel Taylor Coleridge (1811, 1813), William Hazlitt (1817), A. C. Bradley (1905), A.J.A. Waldock (1931), and H. B. Charlton (1942).*]

In accordance with his usual habit, [Wilhelm] was becoming talkative and instructive, and he wished to explain how he would have Hamlet performed. He stated in detail the result of his reflections upon the subject, and was at much pains to render his opinions acceptable, notwithstanding Serlo's doubts as to the correctness of his views. "But," exclaimed the latter at length, "supposing we admit all that you have said, what further explanation have you to add?"

"I have much to add," replied Wilhelm. "Picture to yourself a prince, such as I have described him, whose father has died suddenly. Ambition and the love of rule are not the passions which inspire him. He would have been satisfied with knowing that he was the offspring of a king. But now he is compelled for the first time to notice the difference between a monarch and a subject. His right to the throne was not hereditary, yet his father's longer life would have strengthened the claims of his only son, and secured his hopes of the crown. But he now sees himself excluded by his uncle perhaps for ever, in spite of all his specious promises. Destitute of all things and of favour, he is a stranger in the very place which from his youth he had considered as his own possession. At this point his disposition takes the first tinge of melancholy. He feels that now he is not more, but rather less, than a private nobleman. He becomes the servant of every one, and yet he is not courteous nor condescending, but degraded and needy.

"His past condition appears to him like a vanished dream. In vain does his uncle seek to console him, and to display his prospects in another light. The consciousness of his nothingness will not abandon him.

"The second blow that struck him, inflicted a deeper wound and bowed him to the earth. It was the marriage of his mother. After the death of his father, the true and tender son had yet a mother left, and he hoped that in the company of this noble parent, he might honour the heroic form of his deceased father, but he lost her also, and that by a more cruel fate than if he had been deprived of her by death. The hopeful picture which an affectionate child loves to form of his parents has for ever vanished. The dead can afford him no assistance and in the living he finds no constancy. She too is a woman and owns the frailty which belongs to all her sex.

"He feels for the first time that he is forsaken, that he is an orphan, and that no worldly happiness can restore to him what he has lost. Naturally, neither sorrowful nor reflective, sorrow and reflection now become to him a grievous burden. Thus it is that he appears before us. (pp. 225-26)

"Think of this youth," he exclaimed, "think of this prince vividly—reflect upon his condition and then observe him, when he learns that his father's spirit has appeared. Accompany him during that fearful night when the venerable ghost addresses him. A shuddering horror seizes him—he speaks to the mysterious form—it beckons to him, he follows and listens. The dreadful accusation of his uncle echoes in his ears, the injunction to revenge, and the imploring supplication again and again repeated, 'remember me!'

"And when the ghost has vanished, whom do we see standing before us? a young hero panting for revenge? a prince by birth who feels proud that he is enjoined to punish the usurper of his crown? No, astonishment and perplexity confound the solitary youth—he vents the bitterness of his soul against smiling villains—swears never to forget his father's departed spirit, and concludes with the expression of deep regret that

> The time is out of joint—O cursed spite,
> That ever I was born to set it right!
>   [I.v.188-89]

"It seems to me that in these words will be found the key to Hamlet's whole course of conduct, and it is evident that Shakspeare meant to describe a great duty imposed upon a soul unable to perform it. And in this sense I find that the whole play is conceived and worked out. An oak-tree is planted in a costly vase, which should only have borne beautiful flowers in its bosom,—the roots expand and the vase is shattered.

"A lovely, pure, noble and highly moral being, without the strength of mind which forms a hero, sinks beneath a load which it cannot bear and must not renounce. He views every duty as holy, but this one is too much for him. He is called upon to do what is impossible, not impossible in itself, but impossible to him. And as he turns and winds and torments himself, still advancing and retreating, ever reminded and remembering his purpose, he almost loses sight of it completely, without ever recovering his happiness." (p. 227)

"There is not much to be said about [Ophelia," said] Wilhelm, "for her character is drawn by a few master-strokes. Her whole existence flows in sweet and ripe sensation. Her attachment to the Prince, to whose hand she may aspire, flows so spontaneously, her affectionate heart yields so completely to its impulse, that both her father and brother are afraid, and both give her plain and direct warning of her danger. Decorum, like the thin crape upon her bosom, cannot conceal the motions of her heart, but on the contrary it betrays them. Her imagination is engaged, her silent modesty breathes a sweet desire, and if the convenient goddess Opportunity should shake the tree, the fruit would quickly fall.''

''And then,'' said Aurelia, ''when she sees herself forsaken, rejected and despised, when everything is overturned in the soul of her distracted lover, and he offers her the bitter goblet of sorrow in place of the sweet cup of affection—''

''Her heart breaks,''—cried Wilhelm, ''the entire edifice of her being is loosened from its hold, the death of her father knocks fearfully against it and the whole structure is over turned.'' (pp. 228-29)

Johann Wolfgang von Goethe, in his novel Wilhelm Meister's Apprenticeship, *translated by R. Dillon Boylan, Bell & Daldy, 1873, 570 p.*

AUGUST WILHELM SCHLEGEL (essay date 1808)

[*A prominent German Romantic critic, Schlegel holds a key place in the history of Shakespeare's reputation in European criticism. His translations of thirteen of the plays are still considered the best German translations of Shakespeare. Schlegel was also a leading spokesman for the Romantic movement, which permanently overthrew the Neoclassical contention that Shakespeare was a child of nature whose plays lacked artistic form. In the essay below, given as a lecture in 1808 and first published as* Über dramatische Kunst und Literatur *in 1811, Schlegel considers* Hamlet *to be a ''tragedy of thought'' and notes in the prince's nature weakness, hypocrisy, and a ''malicious joy'' in destroying his enemies. Thus, Schlegel, unlike Johann Wolfgang von Goethe (1795), perceives negative aspects in Hamlet's character. Schlegel's conception of Hamlet was significant in helping to shape the influential criticism of Samuel Taylor Coleridge (1811, 1813).*]

Hamlet is singular in its kind: a tragedy of thought inspired by continual and never-satisfied meditation on human destiny and the dark perplexity of the events of the world, and calculated to call forth the very same meditation in the minds of the spectators. This enigmatical work resembles those irrational equations on which a fraction of unknown magnitude always remains, that will in no way admit of solution. Much has been said, much written, on this piece, and yet no thinking head who anew expresses himself on it, will (in his view of the connexion and the signification of all the parts) entirely coincide with his predecessors. What naturally most astonishes us, is the fact that with such hidden purposes, with a foundation laid in such unfathomable depth, the whole should, at first view, exhibit an extremely popular appearance. The dread appearance of the Ghost takes possession of the mind and the imagination almost at the very commencement; then the play within the play, in which, as in a glass, we see reflected the crime, whose fruitlessly attempted punishment constitutes the subject-matter of the piece; the alarm with which it fills the King; Hamlet's pretended and Ophelia's real madness; her death and burial; the meeting of Hamlet and Laertes at her grave; their combat, and the grand determination; lastly, the appearance of the young hero Fortinbras, who, with warlike pomp, pays the last honours to an extinct family of kings; the interspersion of comic characteristic scenes with Polonius, the courtiers, and the grave-diggers, which have all of them their signification,—all this fills the stage with an animated and varied movement. The only circumstance from which this piece might be judged to be less theatrical than other tragedies of Shakspeare is that in the last scenes the main action either stands still or appears to retrograde. This, however, was inevitable, and lay in the nature of the subject. The whole is intended to show that a calculating consideration, which exhausts all the

relations and possible consequences of a deed, must cripple the power of acting; as Hamlet himself expresses it:—

> And thus the native hue of resolution
> Is sicklied o'er with the pale cast of thought;
> And enterprises of great pith and moment,
> With this regard, their currents turn awry,
> And lose the name of action.
>
> [III. i. 83-7]

With respect to Hamlet's character: I cannot, as I understand the poet's views, pronounce altogether so favourable a sentence upon it as Goethe does. . . . He is, it is true, of a highly cultivated mind, a prince of royal manners, endowed with the finest sense of propriety, susceptible of noble ambition, and open in the highest degree to an enthusiastic admiration of that excellence in others of which he himself is deficient. He acts the part of madness with unrivalled power, convincing the persons who are sent to examine into his supposed loss of reason, merely by telling them unwelcome truths, and rallying them with the most caustic wit. But in the resolutions which he so often embraces and always leaves unexecuted, his weakness is too apparent: he does himself only justice when he implies that there is no greater dissimilarity than between himself and Hercules. He is not solely impelled by necessity to artifice and dissimulation, he has a natural inclination for crooked ways; he is a hypocrite towards himself; his far-fetched scruples are often mere pretexts to cover his want of determination: thoughts, as he says on a different occasion, which have

> —but one part wisdom
> And ever three parts coward—
>
> [IV. iv. 42-3]

He has been chiefly condemned both for his harshness in repulsing the love of Ophelia, which he himself had cherished, and for his insensibility at her death. But he is too much overwhelmed with his own sorrow to have any compassion to spare for others. . . . On the other hand, we evidently perceive in him a malicious joy, when he has succeeded in getting rid of his enemies, more through necessity and accident, which alone are able to impel him to quick and decisive measures, than by the merit of his own courage, as he himself confesses after the murder of Polonius, and with respect to Rosencrantz and Guildenstern. Hamlet has no firm belief either in himself or in anything else; from expressions of religious confidence he passes over to sceptical doubts; he believes in the Ghost of his father as long as he sees it, but as soon as it has disappeared, it appears to him almost in the light of a deception. [Schlegel adds in a footnote: It has been censured as a contradiction, that Hamlet in the soliloquy on self-murder should say,

> The undiscover'd country, from whose bourn
> No traveller returns——   [III. i. 78-9]

For was not the Ghost a returned traveller? Shakspeare, however, purposely wished to show, that Hamlet could not fix himself in any conviction of any kind whatever].

He has even gone so far as to say, ''there is nothing either good or bad, but thinking makes it so''; with him the poet loses himself here in labyrinths of thought, in which neither end nor beginning is discoverable. The stars themselves, from the course of events, afford no answer to the question so urgently proposed to them. A voice from another world, commissioned it would appear, by heaven, demands vengeance for a monstrous enormity, and the demand remains without effect; the criminals are at last punished, but, as it were, by an accidental blow, and not in the solemn way requisite to convey to the world a warning example of justice; irresolute foresight, cunning treachery, and impetuous rage, hurry on to a common destruction; the less guilty and the innocent are equally involved in the general ruin. The destiny of humanity is there exhibited as a gigantic Sphinx, which threatens to precipitate into the abyss of scepticism all who are unable to solve her dreadful enigmas. (pp. 404-06)

> August Wilhelm Schlegel, "Criticisms on Shakespeare's Tragedies," in his Lectures on Dramatic Art and Literature, edited by Rev. A.J.W. Morrison, translated by John Black, second edition, George Bell & Sons, 1892, pp. 400-13.

CHARLES LAMB   (essay date 1811)

[Lamb is considered one of the leading figures of the Romantic movement and an authority on Elizabethan drama. A theatrical critic, Lamb argued that the stage was an improper medium for Shakespeare's plays, primarily because visual dramatizations marred their artistic and lyrical effects. Like Samuel Taylor Coleridge, Lamb reverenced Shakespeare as a poet rather than a playwright. Although many scholars consider his views sentimental and subjective and his interpretations of Shakespeare's characters extreme, Lamb remains an important contributor to the nineteenth-century's reevaluation of Shakespeare's genius. His criticism of Hamlet continues the Romantic tradition of focusing on Hamlet's powerful intellect and personality, but Lamb finds the character too complex to be understood through a performance of the play. According to Lamb, the ruminations of this "shy, negligent, retiring" character are so private and profound that his depth cannot be projected in a dramatic representation. For further examples of and commentary on the Romantic view of Hamlet, see Johann Wolfgang von Goethe (1795), August Wilhelm Schlegel (1808), Coleridge (1811, 1813), A. C. Bradley (1905), and A.J.A. Waldock (1931). Lamb's essay was originally published in The Reflector of October-December, 1811.]

It may seem a paradox, but I cannot help being of opinion that the plays of Shakspeare are less calculated for performance on a stage, than those of almost any other dramatist whatever. Their distinguished excellence is a reason that they should be so. There is so much in them, which comes not under the province of acting, with which eye, and tone, and gesture, have nothing to do. . . .

[In] all the best dramas, and in Shakspeare above all, how obvious it is, that the form of *speaking*, whether it be in soliloquy or dialogue, is only a medium, and often a highly artificial one, for putting the reader or spectator into possession of that knowledge of the inner structure and workings of mind in a character, which he could otherwise never have arrived at *in that form of composition* by any gift short of intuition. We do here as we do with novels written in the *epistolary form.* How many improprieties, solecisms in letter-writing, do we put up with in *Clarissa* and other books, for the sake of the delight which that form upon the whole gives us. (p. 127)

The character of Hamlet is perhaps that by which, since the days of Betterton, a succession of popular performers have had the greatest ambition to distinguish themselves. The length of the part may be one of their reasons. But for the character itself, we find it in a play, and therefore we judge it a fit subject of dramatic representation. The play itself abounds in maxims and reflexions beyond any other, and therefore we consider it as a proper vehicle for conveying moral instruction. But Hamlet himself—what does he suffer meanwhile by being dragged forth as a public schoolmaster, to give lectures to the crowd!

Why, nine parts in ten of what Hamlet does, are transactions between himself and his moral sense, they are the effusions of his solitary musings, which he retires to holes and corners and the most sequestered parts of the palace to pour forth; or rather, they are the silent meditations with which his bosom is bursting, reduced to *words* for the sake of the reader, who must else remain ignorant of what is passing there. These profound sorrows, these light-and-noise-abhorring ruminations, which the tongue scarce dares utter to deaf walls and chambers, how can they be represented by a gesticulating actor, who comes and mouths them out before an audience making four hundred people his confidants at once? I say not that it is the fault of the actor so to do; he must pronounce them *ore rotundo*, he must accompany them with his eye, he must insinuate them into his auditory by some trick of eye, tone, or gesture, or he fails. *He must be thinking all the while of his appearance, because he knows that all the while the spectators are judging of it.* And this is the way to represent the shy, negligent, retiring Hamlet.

It is true that there is no other mode of conveying a vast quantity of thought and feeling to a great portion of the audience, who otherwise would never earn it for themselves by reading, and the intellectual acquisition gained this way may, for aught I know, be inestimable; but I am not arguing that Hamlet should not be acted, but how much Hamlet is made another thing by being acted. I have heard much of the wonders which Garrick performed in this part; but as I never saw him, I must have leave to doubt whether the representation of such a character came within the province of his art. Those who tell me of him, speak of his eye, of the magic of his eye, and of his commanding voice: physical properties, vastly desirable in an actor, and without which he can never insinuate meaning into an auditory,—but what have they to do with Hamlet? what have they to do with intellect? . . . I see no reason to think that if the play of Hamlet were written over again by some such writer as Banks or Lillo, retaining the process of the story, but totally omitting all the poetry of it, all the divine features of Shakspeare, his stupendous intellect; and only taking care to give us enough of passionate dialogue, which Banks or Lillo were never at a loss to furnish; I see not how the effect could be much different upon an audience, nor how the actor has it in his power to represent Shakspeare to us differently from his representation of Banks or Lillo. Hamlet would still be a youthful accomplished prince, and must be gracefully personated; he might be puzzled in his mind, wavering in his conduct, seemingly-cruel to Ophelia, he might see a ghost, and start at it, and address it kindly when he found it to be his father; all this in the poorest and most homely language of the servilest creeper after nature that ever consulted the palate of an audience; without troubling Shakspeare for the matter: and I see not but there would be room for all the power which an actor has, to display itself. All the passions and changes of passion might remain: for those are much less difficult to write or act than is thought, it is a trick easy to be attained, it is but rising or falling a note or two in the voice, a whisper with a significant foreboding look to announce its approach, and so contagious the counterfeit appearance of any emotion is, that let the words be what they will, the look and tone shall carry it off and make it pass for deep skill in the passions. (pp. 128-30)

Among the distinguishing features of that wonderful character [Hamlet], one of the most interesting (yet painful) is that soreness of mind which makes him treat the intrusions of Polonius with harshness, and that asperity which he puts on in his interviews with Ophelia. These tokens of an unhinged mind (if they be not mixed in the latter case with a profound artifice of love, to alienate Ophelia by affected discourtesies, so to prepare her mind for the breaking off of that loving intercourse, which can no longer find a place amidst business so serious as that which he has to do) are parts of his character, which to reconcile with our admiration of Hamlet, the most patient consideration of his situation is no more than necessary; they are what we *forgive afterwards,* and explain by the whole of his character, but *at the time* they are harsh and unpleasant. Yet such is the actor's necessity of giving strong blows to the audience, that I have never seen a player in this character, who did not exaggerate and strain to the utmost these ambiguous features,— these temporary deformities in the character. They make him express a vulgar scorn at Polonius which utterly degrades his gentility, and which no explanation can render palateable; they make him shew contempt, and curl up the nose at Ophelia's father,—contempt in its very grossest and most hateful form; but they get applause by it: it is scornful, and the actor expresses scorn, and that they can judge of: but why so much scorn, and of that sort, they never think of asking.

So to Ophelia.—All the Hamlets that I have ever seen rant and rave at her as if she had committed some great crime, and the audience are highly pleased, because the words of the part are satirical, and they are enforced by the strongest expression of satirical indignation of which the face and voice are capable. But then, whether Hamlet is likely to have put on such brutal appearances to a lady whom he loved so dearly, is never thought on. The truth is, that in all such deep affections as had subsisted between Hamlet and Ophelia, there is a stock of *supererogatory love,* (if I venture to use the expression) which in any great grief of heart, especially where that which preys upon the mind cannot be communicated, confers a kind of indulgence upon the grieved party to express itself, even to its heart's dearest object, in the language of a temporary alienation; but it is not alienation, it is a distraction purely, and so it always makes itself to be felt by that object: it is not anger, but grief assuming the appearance of anger,—love awkwardly counterfeiting hate as sweet countenances when they try to frown: but such sternness and fierce disgust as Hamlet is made to shew is no counterfeit, but the real face of absolute aversion,—of irreconcileable alienation. It may be said he puts on the madman; but then he should only so far put on this counterfeit lunacy as his own real distraction will give him leave; that is, incompletely, imperfectly; not in that confirmed practised way, like a master of his art, or, as Dame Quickly would say, 'like one of those harlotry players.' (pp. 131-33)

When Hamlet compares the two pictures of Gertrude's first and second husband, who wants to see the pictures? But in the acting, a miniature must be lugged out; which we know not to be the picture, but only to shew how finely a miniature may be represented. This shewing of every thing, levels all things: it makes tricks, bows, and curtesies, of importance. Mrs. S. never got more fame by any thing than by the manner in which she dismisses the guests in the banquet-scene in Macbeth: it is as much remembered as any of her thrilling tones or impressive looks. But does such a trifle as this enter into the imaginations of the readers of that wild and wonderful scene? Does not the mind dismiss the feasters as rapidly as it can? Does it care about the gracefulness of the doing it? But by acting, and judging of acting, all these non-essentials are raised into an importance, injurious to the main interest of the play. (pp. 141-42)

Charles Lamb, "On the Tragedies of Shakspeare, Considered with Reference to Their Fitness for Stage Representation," in The Works in Prose and Verse *of Charles and Mary Lamb, Vol. I, edited by Thomas Hutchinson, Oxford University Press, Oxford, 1908, pp. 124-42.*

SAMUEL TAYLOR COLERIDGE [as reported by J. P. Collier] (essay date 1811)

[Coleridge's lectures and writings on Shakespeare form a major chapter in the history of English Shakespearean criticism. As the channel for the critical ideas of the German Romantics and as an original interpreter of Shakespeare in the new spirit of Romanticism, Coleridge played a strategic role in overthrowing the last remains of the Neoclassical approach to Shakespeare and in establishing the modern view of Shakespeare as a conscious artist and masterful portrayer of human character. Coleridge's remarks on Shakespeare come down to posterity largely as fragmentary notes, marginalia, and reports by auditors of the lectures, rather than in polished essays. The following remarks on Hamlet *were transcribed by J. P. Collier. Coleridge is one of the most important and influential commentators on* Hamlet. *Developing the concept described by August Wilhelm Schlegel (1808) that* Hamlet *is a tragedy of intellect rather than action, Coleridge identifies Hamlet as a man who is unable to act because his great intellectual activity makes him adverse to action. With his portrayal of Hamlet as a character who contains "a world within himself," Coleridge presents a highly Romantic view; he does not relate Hamlet's inner disposition to the action of the play, but effectively isolates him from the drama itself. Other critics who offer a Romantic conception of* Hamlet *include William Richardson (1774), Henry Mackenzie (1780), Johann Wolfgang von Goethe (1795), August Wilhelm Schlegel (1808), Charles Lamb (1811), William Hazlitt (1817), and A. C. Bradley (1905). Coleridge responds to the interpretation of the prayer-scene offered by Samuel Johnson (1765).]*

What then was the point to which Shakespeare directed himself in Hamlet? He intended to pourtray a person, in whose view the external world, and all its incidents and objects, were comparatively dim, and of no interest in themselves, and which began to interest only, when they were reflected in the mirror of his mind. Hamlet beheld external things in the same way that a man of vivid imagination, who shuts his eyes, sees what has previously made an impression on his organs.

The poet places him in the most stimulating circumstances that a human being can be placed in. He is the heir apparent of a throne; his father dies suspiciously; his mother excludes her son from his throne by marrying his uncle. This is not enough; but the Ghost of the murdered father is introduced, to assure the son that he was put to death by his own brother. What is the effect upon the son?—instant action and pursuit of revenge? No: endless reasoning and hesitating—constant urging and solicitation of the mind to act, and as constant an escape from action; ceaseless reproaches of himself for sloth and negligence, while the whole energy of his resolution evaporates in these reproaches. This, too, not from cowardice, for he is drawn as one of the bravest of his time—not from want of forethought or slowness of apprehension, for he sees through the very souls of all who surround him, but merely from that aversion to action, which prevails among such as have a world in themselves. (pp. 192-93)

There is no indecision about Hamlet, as far as his own sense of duty is concerned; he knows well what he ought to do, and over and over again he makes up his mind to do it. (p. 194)

Yet with all this strong conviction of duty, and with all this resolution arising out of strong conviction, nothing is done. This admirable and consistent character, deeply acquainted with his own feelings, painting them with such wonderful power and accuracy, and firmly persuaded that a moment ought not to be lost in executing the solemn charge committed to him, still yields to the same retiring from reality, which is the result of having, what we express by the terms, a world within himself. (p. 195)

[An] objection has been taken by Dr. Johnson, and Shakespeare has been taxed very severely. I refer to the scene where Hamlet enters and finds his uncle praying, and refuses to take his life, excepting when he is in the height of his iniquity. To assail him at such a moment of confession and repentance, Hamlet declares,

> Why, this is hire and salary, not revenge.
>
> [III. iii. 79]

He therefore forbears, and postpones his uncle's death, until he can catch him in some act

> That has no relish of salvation in't.
>
> [III. iii. 92]

This conduct, and this sentiment, Dr. Johnson has pronounced to be so atrocious and horrible, as to be unfit to put into the mouth of a human being. The fact, however, is that Dr. Johnson did not understand the character of Hamlet, and censured accordingly: the determination to allow the guilty King to escape at such a moment is only part of the indecision and irresoluteness of the hero. Hamlet seizes hold of a pretext for not acting, when he might have acted so instantly and effectually: therefore, he again defers the revenge he was bound to seek, and declares his determination to accomplish it at some time,

> When he is drunk, asleep, or in his rage,
> Or in th' incestuous pleasures of his bed.
>
> [III. iii. 89-90]

This, allow me to impress upon you most emphatically, was merely the excuse Hamlet made to himself for not taking advantage of this particular and favourable moment for doing justice upon his guilty uncle, at the urgent instance of the spirit of his father. (pp. 195-96)

Even after the scene with Osrick, we see Hamlet still indulging in reflection, and hardly thinking of the task he has just undertaken: he is all dispatch and resolution, as far as words and present intentions are concerned, but all hesitation and irresolution, when called upon to carry his words and intentions into effect; so that, resolving to do everything, he does nothing. He is full of purpose, but void of that quality of mind which accomplishes purpose.

Anything finer than this conception, and working out of a great character, is merely impossible. Shakespeare wished to impress upon us the truth, that action is the chief end of existence—that no faculties of intellect, however brilliant, can be considered valuable, or indeed otherwise than as misfortunes, if they withdraw us from, or render us repugnant to action, and lead us to think and think of doing, until the time has elapsed when we can do anything effectually. In enforcing this moral truth, Shakespeare has shown the fulness and force of his powers: all that is amiable and excellent in nature is combined in Hamlet, with the exception of one quality. He is a man living in meditation, called upon to act by every motive human and divine, but the great object of his life is defeated by continually resolving to do, yet doing nothing but resolve. (pp. 197-98)

Samuel Taylor Coleridge [as reported by J. P. Collier], in his lecture given before the London Philo-

sophical Society on December 28, 1811, in his Shakespearean Criticism, Vol. II, edited by Thomas Middleton Raysor, Harvard University Press, 1930, pp. 181-98.

SAMUEL TAYLOR COLERIDGE (essay date 1813)

[*This excerpt, taken from a transcript by E. H. Coleridge of one of Coleridge's notebooks, is believed to have been written for Coleridge's Bristol lectures of 1813. He offers a twelve-point analysis of the language of* Hamlet, *concluding that while the diction of the play is poetical rather than dramatic, it successfully reveals Hamlet's character. Coleridge, believing Hamlet to be near madness during his pretense of that state, remarks on Shakespeare's subtle treatment of the episode. For additional commentary on various aspects of the language of* Hamlet, *see Caroline F. E. Spurgeon, Wolfgang H. Clemen (1951), Harry Levin (1959), Reuben A. Brower (1971), and Inga-Stina Ewbank (1977).*]

Shakespeare's mode of conceiving characters out of his own intellectual and moral faculties, by conceiving any one intellectual or moral faculty in morbid excess and then placing himself, thus mutilated and diseased, under given circumstances. . . . In Hamlet I conceive him to have wished to exemplify the moral necessity of a due balance between our attention to outward objects and our meditation on inward thoughts—a due balance between the real and the imaginary world. In Hamlet this balance does not exist—his thoughts, images, and fancy [being] far more vivid than his perceptions, and his very perceptions instantly passing thro' the medium of his contemplations, and acquiring as they pass a form and color not naturally their own. Hence great, enormous, intellectual activity, and a consequent proportionate aversion to real action, with all its symptoms and accompanying qualities.

> Action is transitory, a step, a blow, etc.

Then as in the first instance proceed with a cursory survey thro' the play, with comments, etc.

(1) The easy language of ordinary life, contrasted with the direful music and wild rhythm of the opening of *Macbeth*. Yet the armour, the cold, the dead silence, all placing the mind in the state congruous with tragedy.

(2) The admirable judgement and yet confidence in his own marvellous powers in introducing the ghost twice, each rising in solemnity and awfulness before its third appearance to Hamlet himself.

(3) Shakespeare's tenderness with regard to all innocent superstition: no Tom Paine declamations and pompous philosophy.

(4) The first words that Hamlet speaks—

> A little more than kin, and less than kind.
>
> [I.ii.65]

He begins with that play of words, the complete absence of which characterizes *Macbeth*. . . . No one can have heard quarrels among the vulgar but must have noticed the close connection of punning with angry contempt. Add too what is highly characteristic of superfluous activity of mind, a sort of playing with a thread or watch chain or snuff box.

(5) And [note] how the character develops itself in the next speech—the aversion to externals, the betrayed habit of brooding over the world within him, and the prodigality of beautiful words, which are, as it were, the half embodyings of thoughts, that make them more than thoughts, give them an outness, a

reality *sui generis,* and yet retain their correspondence and shadowy approach to the images and movements within.

(6) The first soliloquy [I.ii.129ff]

O, that this too too solid flesh would melt.

[The] reasons why *taedium vitae* oppresses minds like Hamlet's: the exhaustion of bodily feeling from perpetual exertion of mind; that all mental form being indefinite and ideal, realities must needs become cold, and hence it is the indefinite that combines with passion.

(7) And in this mood the relation is made [by Horatio, who tells Hamlet of his father's ghost], of which no more than [that] it is a perfect model of dramatic narration and dramatic style, the purest poetry and yet the most natural language, equally distant from the inkhorn and the provincial plough.

(8) Hamlet's running into long reasonings [while waiting for the ghost], carrying off the impatience and uneasy feelings of expectation by running away from the *particular* in[to] the *general.* This aversion to personal, individual concerns, and escape to generalizations and general reasonings a most important characteristic. (pp. 37-9)

(9) The ghost [is] a superstition connected with the most [sacred?] truths of revealed religion and, therefore, O how contrasted from the withering and wild language of the [witches in] *Macbeth.*

(10) The instant and over violent resolve of Hamlet—how he wastes in the efforts of resolving the energies of action. (p. 39)

(11) Now comes the difficult task, [interpreting the jests of Hamlet when his companions overtake him].

The familiarity, comparative at least, of a brooding mind with shadows is something. Still more the necessary alternation when one muscle long strained is relaxed; the antagonist comes into action of itself. Terror [is] closely connected with the ludicrous; the latter [is] the common mode by which the mind tries to emancipate itself from terror. The laugh is rendered by nature itself the language of extremes, even as tears are. Add too, Hamlet's wildness is but *half-false.* O that subtle trick to pretend the *acting* only when we are very near *being* what we act. And this explanation of the same with Ophelia's vivid images [describing Hamlet's desperation when he visits her]; nigh akin to, and productive of, temporary mania. (pp. 39-40)

(12) Hamlet's character, as I have conceived [it, is] described by himself [in the soliloquy after the players leave him—

O, what a rogue and peasant slave am I, etc.]

[II.ii.550ff]

But previous to this, speak of the exquisite judgement in the diction of the introduced play. Absurd to suppose it extracted in order to be ridiculed from [an] old play. It is in thought and even in the separate parts of the diction highly poetical, so that this is its fault, that it is too poetical, the language of lyric vehemence and epic pomp, not of the drama. But what if Shakespeare had made the language truly dramatic? Where would have been the contrast between *Hamlet* and the play of *Hamlet*? (p. 40)

Samuel Taylor Coleridge, "Notes on the Tragedies of Shakespeare: The Character of Hamlet," in his Shakespearian Criticism, Vol. 1, *edited by Thomas Middleton Raysor, Cambridge, Mass.: Harvard University Press, 1930, pp. 37-40.*

WILLIAM HAZLITT   (essay date 1817)

[*Hazlitt is generally considered to be a leading Shakespearean critic of the English Romantic movement. A prolific essayist and critic on a wide range of subjects, Hazlitt remarked in the preface to his* Characters of Shakespeare's Plays, *first published in 1817, that he was inspired by the German critic August Wilhelm Schlegel and was determined to supplant what he considered the pernicious influence of Samuel Johnson's Shakespearean criticism. Hazlitt's criticism is typically Romantic in its emphasis on character studies. Unlike his fellow Romantic critic Samuel Taylor Coleridge, Hazlitt was a dramatic critic whose experience of Shakespeare in the theater influenced his interpretations. Hazlitt stresses the strong personal identification an audience feels toward Hamlet and focuses on both the intellectual and emotional depth of the character. For additional examples of the Romantic view of* Hamlet, *see Johann Wolfgang von Goethe (1795), August Wilhelm Schlegel (1808), Charles Lamb (1811), and Samuel Taylor Coleridge (1811, 1813).*]

Hamlet is a name; his speeches and sayings but the idle coinage of the poet's brain. What then, are they not real? They are as real as our own thoughts. Their reality is in the reader's mind. It is *we* who are Hamlet. This play has a prophetic truth, which is above that of history. Whoever has become thoughtful and melancholy through his own mishaps or those of others; whoever has borne about with him the clouded brow of reflection, and thought himself "too much i' the sun"; whoever has seen the golden lamp of day dimmed by envious mists rising in his own breast, and could find in the world before him only a dull blank with nothing left remarkable in it; whoever has known "the pangs of despised love, the insolence of office, or the spurns which patient merit of the unworthy takes"; he who has felt his mind sink within him, and sadness cling to his heart like a malady, who has had his hopes blighted and his youth staggered by the apparitions of strange things; who cannot be well at ease, while he sees evil hovering near him like a spectre; whose powers of action have been eaten up by thought, he to whom the universe seems infinite, and himself nothing; whose bitterness of soul makes him careless of consequences, and who goes to a play as his best resource to shove off, to a second remove, the evils of life by a mock representation of them— this is the true Hamlet.

We have been so used to this tragedy that we hardly know how to criticise it any more than we should know how to describe our own faces. But we must make such observations as we can. It is the one of Shakespear's plays that we think of the oftenest, because it abounds most in striking reflections on human life, and because the distresses of Hamlet are transferred, by the turn of his mind, to the general account of humanity. . . . He is a great moraliser; and what make him worth attending to is, that he moralises on his own feelings and experience. He is not a commonplace pedant. If *Lear* is distinguished by the greatest depth of passion, *Hamlet* is the most remarkable for the ingenuity, originality, and unstudied development of character. Shakespear had more magnanimity than any other poet, and he has shewn more of it in this play than in any other. There is no attempt to force an interest: everything is left for time and circumstances to unfold. The attention is excited without effort, the incidents succeed each other as matters of course, the characters think and speak and act just as they might do, if left entirely to themselves. There is no set purpose, no straining at a point. The observations are suggested by the passing scene—the gusts of passion come and go like sounds of music borne on the wind. . . . [Here] we are more than spectators. We have not only "the outward pageants and the signs of grief"; but "we have that within which passes shew.'' We read the thoughts of the heart, we catch the passions living as they rise. Other dramatic writers give us very fine versions and paraphrases of nature; but Shakespear, together with his own comments, gives us the original text, that we may judge for ourselves. This is a very great advantage.

The character of Hamlet stands quite by itself. It is not a character marked by strength of will or even of passion, but by refinement of thought and sentiment. Hamlet is as little of the hero as a man can well be: but he is a young and princely novice, full of high enthusiasm and quick sensibility—the sport of circumstances, questioning with fortune and refining on his own feelings, and forced from the natural bias of his disposition by the strangeness of his situation. He seems incapable of deliberate action, and is only hurried into extremities on the spur of the occasion, when he has no time to reflect. . . . At other times, when he is most bound to act, he remains puzzled, undecided, and sceptical, dallies with his purposes, till the occasion is lost, and finds out some pretence to relapse into indolence and thoughtfulness again. For this reason he refuses to kill the King when he is at his prayers, and by a refinement in malice, which is in truth only an excuse for his own want of resolution, defers his revenge to a more fatal opportunity, when he shall be engaged in some act "that has no relish of salvation in it." (pp. 79-82)

He is the prince of philosophical speculators; and because he cannot have his revenge perfect, according to the most refined idea his wish can form, he declines it altogether. So he scruples to trust the suggestions of the ghost, contrives the scene of the play to have surer proof of his uncle's guilt, and then rests satisfied with this confirmation of his suspicions, and the success of his experiment, instead of acting upon it. Yet he is sensible of his own weakness, taxes himself with it, and tries to reason himself out of it. . . . Still he does nothing; and this very speculation on his own infirmity only affords him another occasion for indulging it. It is not from any want of attachment to his father or of abhorrence of his murder that Hamlet is thus dilatory, but it is more to his taste to indulge his imagination in reflecting upon the enormity of the crime and refining on his schemes of vengeance, than to put them into immediate practice. His ruling passion is to think, not to act: and any vague pretext that flatters this propensity instantly diverts him from his previous purposes.

The moral perfection of this character has been called in question, we think, by those who did not understand it. It is more interesting than according to rules; amiable, though not faultless. . . . We confess we are a little shocked at the want of refinement in those who are shocked at the want of refinement in Hamlet. The neglect of punctilious exactness in his behaviour either partakes of the "licence of the time," or else belongs to the very excess of intellectual refinement in the character, which makes the common rules of life, as well as his own purposes, sit loose upon him. He may be said to be amenable only to the tribunal of his own thoughts, and is too much taken up with the airy world of contemplation to lay as much stress as he ought on the practical consequences of things. His habitual principles of action are unhinged and out of joint with the time. His conduct to Ophelia is quite natural in his circumstances. It is that of assumed severity only. It is the effect of disappointed hope, of bitter regrets, of affection suspended, not obliterated, by the distractions of the scene around him! Amidst the natural and preternatural horrors of his situation, he might be excused in delicacy from carrying on a regular

courtship. . . . His conduct does not contradict what he says when he sees her funeral,

> I loved Ophelia: forty thousand brothers
> Could not with all their quantity of love
> Make up my sum.   [V.i.269-71]

Nothing can be more affecting or beautiful than the Queen's apostrophe to Ophelia on throwing the flowers into the grave.

> ——Sweets to the sweet, farewell.
> I hop'd thou should'st have been my Hamlet's wife:
> I thought thy bride-bed to have deck'd, sweet maid,
> And not have strew'd thy grave.   [V.i.243-46]

Shakespear was thoroughly a master of the mixed motives of human character, and he here shews us the Queen, who was so criminal in some respects, not without sensibility and affection in other relations of life.—Ophelia is a character almost too exquisitely touching to be dwelt upon. Oh rose of May, oh flower too soon faded! Her love, her madness, her death, are described with the truest touches of tenderness and pathos. It is a character which nobody but Shakespear could have drawn in the way that he has done. . . . Her brother, Laertes, is a character we do not like so well: he is too hot and choleric, and somewhat rhodomontade. Polonius is a perfect character in its kind; nor is there any foundation for the objections which have been made to the consistency of this part. It is said that he acts very foolishly and talks very sensibly. There is no inconsistency in that. Again, that he talks wisely at one time and foolishly at another; that his advice to Laertes is very excellent, and his advice to the King and Queen on the subject of Hamlet's madness very ridiculous. But he gives the one as a father, and is sincere in it; he gives the other as a mere courtier, a busy-body, and is accordingly officious, garrulous, and impertinent. In short, Shakespear has been accused of inconsistency in this and other characters, only because he has kept up the distinction which there is in nature, between the understandings and the moral habits of men, between the absurdity of their ideas and the absurdity of their motives. Polonius is not a fool, but he makes himself so. (pp. 82-6)

William Hazlitt, "Hamlet," in his Characters of Shakespear's Plays, *J. M. Dent & Sons Ltd., 1906, pp. 79-87.*

T. C. [THOMAS CAMPBELL?]   (essay date 1818)

[*Campbell's proposal that a dramatic character should not be discussed as if he were among "our living brethren of mankind" runs counter to the Romantic critics' investigations into Hamlet's intellectual and emotional nature and anticipates the historical critics' attack on the Romantics' excessive concern with character. Campbell faults Shakespeare's portrayal of Hamlet's love for Ophelia, which he regards as unconvincing, although he praises the drawing of Ophelia's character and her part in the action of the play. For additional commentary on Ophelia, see Jeremy Collier (1698), James Drake (1699), George Stubbes/Thomas Hanmer (1736), and Charlotte Lennox (1753). Campbell's essay was first published in* Blackwood's Edinburgh Magazine *in February, 1818.*]

I have often thought that it is idle and absurd to try a poetical character on the stage, a creature existing in a Play, however like to real human nature it may be, precisely by the same rules which we apply to our living brethren of mankind in the substantial drama of life. No doubt a good Play is an imitation of life, as far as the actions, and events, and passions of a few hours can represent those of a whole lifetime. Yet, after all, it is but a segment of a circle that we can behold. . . . The pageants that move before us on the stage, however deeply they may interest us, are after all mere strangers. It is Shakespeare alone who can give to fleeting phantoms the definite interest of real personages. But we ought not to turn this glorious power against himself. We ought not to demand inexorably the same perfect, and universal, and embracing truth of character in an existence brought before us in a few hurried scenes (which is all a Play can be) that we sometimes may think we find in a real being, after long years of intimate knowledge, and which, did we know more, would perhaps seem to us to be truth no longer, but a chaos of the darkest and wildest inconsistencies. (p. 158)

If there is anything disproportionate in [Hamlet's] mind, it seems to be this only,—that intellect is in excess. It is even ungovernable, and too subtle. His own description of perfect man, ending with 'In apprehension how like a God!' appears to me consonant with this character, and spoken in the high and overwrought consciousness of intellect. Much that requires explanation in the Play may perhaps be explained by this predominance and consciousness of great intellectual power. Is it not possible that the instantaneous idea of feigning himself mad belongs to this? It is the power most present to his mind, and therefore in that, though in the denial of it, is his first thought to place his defence. . . .

Shakespeare never could have intended to represent [Hamlet's] love to Ophelia as very profound. If he did, how can we ever account for Hamlet's first exclamation, when in the churchyard he learns that he is standing by her grave, and beholds her coffin? 'What, the fair Ophelia!' Was this all that Hamlet would have uttered, when struck into sudden conviction by the ghastliest terrors of death, that all he loved in human life had perished? We can with difficulty reconcile such a tame ejaculation, even with extreme tenderness and sorrow. But had it been in the soul of Shakespeare to show Hamlet in the agony of hopeless despair,—and in hopeless despair he must at that moment have been, had Ophelia been all in all to him,—is there in all his writings so utter a failure in the attempt to give vent to overwhelming passion? When, afterwards, Hamlet leaps into the grave, do we see in that any power of love? I am sorry to confess that the whole of that scene is to me merely painful. It is anger with Laertes, not love for Ophelia, that makes Hamlet leap into the grave. (p. 159)

Hamlet is afterwards made acquainted with the sad history of Ophelia,—he knows that to the death of Polonius, and his own imagined madness, is to be attributed her miserable catastrophe. Yet, after the burial scene, he seems utterly to have forgotten that Ophelia ever existed; nor is there, as far as I recollect, a single allusion to her throughout the rest of the drama. The only way of accounting for this seems to be that Shakespeare had himself forgotten her,—that with her last rites she vanished from the world of his memory. But this of itself shows that it was not his intention to represent Ophelia as the dearest of all earthly things or thoughts to Hamlet, or surely there would have been some melancholy, some miserable hauntings of her image. But, even as it is, it seems not a little unaccountable that Hamlet should have been so slightly affected by her death.

Of the character of Ophelia, and the situation she holds in the action of the play, I need say little. Everything about her is young, beautiful, artless, innocent, and touching. She comes before us in striking contrast to the Queen, who, fallen as she is, feels the influence of her simple and happy virgin purity.

Amid the frivolity, flattery, fawning, and artifice of a corrupted court, she moves in all the unpolluted loveliness of nature. She is like an artless, gladsome, and spotless shepherdess, with the gracefulness of society hanging like a transparent veil over her natural beauty. . . . Perhaps the description of [her death] by the Queen is poetical rather than dramatic; but its exquisite beauty prevails, and Ophelia, dying and dead, is still the same Ophelia that first won our love. Perhaps the very forgetfulness of her, throughout the remainder of the play, leaves the soul at full liberty to dream of the departed. She has passed away from the earth like a beautiful air,—a delightful dream. There would have been no place for her in the agitation and tempest of the final catastrophe. (pp. 159-60)

T. C. [Thomas Campbell?], in his extract from A New Variorum Edition of Shakespeare: Hamlet, Vol. IV, *edited by Horace Howard Furness, J. B. Lippincott Company, 1877, pp. 157-60.*

HENRY HALLAM   (essay date 1837)

[*Hallam here anticipates the focus of the biographical critics of the later nineteenth century in his description of Shakespeare as "ill at ease" at the time he composed* Hamlet. *This excerpt is taken from the first edition of Hallam's* Introduction to the Literature of Europe in the Fifteenth, Sixteenth, and Seventeenth Centuries, *first published in 1837. For an additional example of biographical criticism, see Edward Dowden (1875).*]

There seems to have been a period of Shakespeare's life when his heart was ill at ease, and ill content with the world or his own conscience; the memory of hours misspent, the pang of affection misplaced or unrequited, the experience of man's worser nature which intercourse with ill-chosen associates, by choice or circumstance, peculiarly teaches; these, as they sank down into the depths of his great mind, seem not only to have inspired into it the conception of *Lear* and *Timon*, but that of one primary character, the censurer of mankind. This type is first seen in the philosophic melancholy of Jaques, gazing with an undiminished serenity, and with a gayety of fancy, though not of manners, on the follies of the world. It assumes a graver cast in the exiled Duke of the same play, and next one rather more severe in the Duke of *Measure for Measure*. In all these, however, it is merely contemplative philosophy. In Hamlet this is mingled with the impulses of a perturbed heart under the pressure of extraordinary circumstances; it shines no longer, as in the former characters, with a steady light, but plays in fitful coruscations amid feigned gayety and extravagance. In Lear it is the flash of sudden inspiration across the incongruous imagery of madness; in Timon it is obscured by the exaggerations of misanthropy. These plays all belong to nearly the same period: *As You Like It* being usually referred to 1600, *Hamlet*, in its altered form, to about 1602, *Timon* to the same year, *Measure for Measure* to 1603, and *Lear* to 1604. In the later plays of Shakespeare, especially in *Macbeth* and *The Tempest*, much of moral speculation will be found, but he has never returned to this type of character in the personages.

Henry Hallam, in his extract from A New Variorum Edition of Shakespeare: Hamlet, Vol. IV, *edited by Horace Howard Furness, J. B. Lippincott Company, 1877, p. 164.*

HERMANN ULRICI   (essay date 1839)

[*A German scholar, Ulrici was a professor of philosophy and an author of works on Greek poetry and Shakespeare. The following excerpt is taken from an English translation of his* Über Shak-speares dramatische Kunst, und sein Verhältnis zu Calderon und Göthe, *first published in 1839. This work exemplifies the "philosophical criticism" developed in Germany during the nineteenth century. The immediate sources for Ulrici's critical approach appear to be August Wilhelm Schlegel's conception of the play as an organic, interconnected whole and Georg Wilhelm Friedrich Hegel's view of the drama as an embodiment of the conflict of historical forces and ideas. Unlike his fellow German Shakespearean critic G. G. Gervinus, Ulrici sought to develop a specifically Christian aesthetics, but one which, as he carefully points out in the introduction to the work mentioned above, in no way intrudes on "that unity of idea, which preeminently constitutes a work of art a living creation in the world of beauty." Regarding Hamlet's delay and his personal character, Ulrici assumes a moderate position between Johann Wolfgang von Goethe (1795) and Schlegel (1808), both of whom he considers to be too extreme in their interpretations. Ulrici describes Hamlet as a character beset with moral doubts, and characterizes his dilemma as a struggle between the Christian and the natural man. For additional commentary on* Hamlet *as a religious drama, see Søren Kierkegaard (1845), H.D.F. Kitto (1956), Sister Miriam Joseph (1962), and Patrick Cruttwell (1963).]*

Every fresh commentator who studies and writes about "Hamlet," goes deeper and further than his predecessors, and thinks he has reached to the true foundation, which, nevertheless, lies all the while still deeper and far beyond his researches. This perhaps will be the fate also of my own speculations. However, I shall not be deterred by such a prospect, but comfort myself rather with the consoling certainty it affords of the surpassing fulness and the ever freshly-springing fertility of human genius.

Goethe, after quoting the complaint of Hamlet—"The times are awry: woe is me that I was born to set them straight again," observes—"These words, as it seems to me, contain the key to Hamlet's conduct, and it is quite clear to my mind, that Shakspeare designed to paint a great deed enjoined on an inferior mind". . . . [A. W. Schlegel, on the other hand] thinks that its purpose was to shew, that a deliberation which would exhaust to the farthest limits of human foresight all the possible contingencies and consequences of a particular act, must unnerve the resolution and cripple the powers of acting. . . . (pp. 213-14)

With respect also to the personal character of the Prince the two critics are no less at issue. Goethe calls him tender and noble; born a prince, and desirous of rule only to give free scope to goodness—of an agreeable person, moral by nature, amiable, not originally melancholy and reflective, but made so by circumstances alone. . . . But Schlegel, on the other hand, while he acknowledges his many excellent qualities, finds fault with his weakness of will, and charges him with a natural inclination for artifice and dissimulation, a want of resolution almost amounting to cowardice, a malicious joy in getting rid of his enemies through necessity and accident, rather than by his own decisive measures against them; and lastly, with scepticism, and with no firm belief either in himself or any thing else. . . . In the conflicting views of these two writers, we have, however, the reflection of the character of their own age. And yet with one or other of them, with greater or less modifications, Fr. Horn, and all the more distinguished critics both of England and Germany, agree.

For my part I cannot concur entirely with either. Hamlet, although of a highly noble disposition, is not the blameless ideal of Goethe, nor has he, though not impeccable, the faults which Schlegel imputes to him. In the first place, he is not wholly without courage and energy; this is shewn by the scene with

the Ghost, and his quarrel with Laertes in Ophelia's grave. It is no empty boast when he declares that "he does not set his life at a pin's fee." He wants, no doubt, the quick determination of a passionate and overflowing sensibility. This, however, is not infirmity of *will* or want of *resolution;* it is only to have the will guided by the *judgment,* that he is slow to act and backward to resolve. The charge of a natural inclination for crooked ways appears to me quite groundless, and I cannot conceive from what circumstance Schlegel has inferred it; for the wish to keep secret the fact of the Ghost's appearance, his pretended madness, and all his scruples and disinclination for a precipitate execution of his design, have their reason in the circumstance of his own position and the general posture of affairs. Hamlet has against him all the power and influence of apparently the legitimate King of Denmark. Because he cannot bring himself to flatter and play the hypocrite with his mother and his villainous uncle, and because he endeavours to arrive at a full certainty of the monstrous guilt of his nearest kinsfolk, he incurs the suspicions of the King, and then only, in order to elude the machinations against his own life, is he driven to have recourse to artifice and cunning. Still less does Hamlet's character exhibit, as Schlegel thinks, a malignant pleasure in inflicting pain. His own words, after killing Polonius—

> Thou wretched, rash, intruding fool, farewell;
> I took thee for thy betters; take thy fortune;
> Thou find'st to be too busy, is some danger.
>
> [III. iv. 31-3]

And again—

> . . . For this same lord
> I do repent; but heaven has pleased it so;—
> To punish this with me and me with this,
> That I must be their scourge and minister.
> I will bestow him, and will answer well
> The death I gave him. . . .   [III. iv. 172-77]

These words breathe rather compassion and sorrow for a rash deed than exultation, and if he does not express a very deep regret for the deaths of Rosencrantz and Guildenstern—those false and good-for-nothing tools of his worthless uncle—yet, in all this, there is nothing like malignity. Lastly, Hamlet has, no doubt, a profoundly thoughtful head, but he is far removed from scepticism and infidelity. (pp. 214-16)

Hamlet is, no doubt by nature, a subtle—or if the term be preferred, a philosophical spirit. This is the general basis of his character. He has the desire and the power to accomplish great things, but it must be in obedience to the dictates of his *own thoughts, and by his own independent, original, and creative energy.* On this account it goes against his disposition to perform a deed whose springs are external to himself, and which was *enjoined* upon him by outward circumstances, even though the execution of it be by no means beyond his powers. The praises of Ophelia, when she calls him—

> The courtier's, soldier's, scholar's eye, tongue, sword,
> The expectancy and rose of the fair state;
>
> [III. i. 151-52]

and ascribed to him both bravery and manly resolution, can scarcely be explained by the partiality of an admiring maiden. Equally far is Hamlet from self-deception, when he says of himself, that he has the will and strength, and means, to do what is to do; for the judgment which the wholly impartial Fortinbras passes on him is no less favourable. In short, he possesses all the good qualities which Goethe ascribes to him, with one virtue and one fault more; the wish, viz. to maintain in every case his self-possession and command over himself, but without sufficient strength to preserve this mastery and independence under all the trying circumstances of the difficult position in which he is placed. . . . With all his power does he strive to controul the adverse circumstances in which he is placed; with all his strength he labours to raise himself from the position assigned to him by fate, and by his own energy to mould the business which that position furnishes, or rather enjoins upon him, into a *spontaneous* and *independent* undertaking. By an internal impulse, he is continually aiming at his own idea of man, whom he calls ''a work of wonder, noble in reason, infinite in faculties, in *action* like to an *angel,* in apprehension like a god.'' And accordingly, because it is, on this account, repugnant to his nature to adopt any course of conduct upon external compulsion, there arises a conflict between the inward bias of his mind, and the pressure of *outward* circumstances He is unable to enter upon the enjoined work, not simply because it is too great and weighty for him, but because he cannot transmute it into an *inward spontaneous* impulse of his own. Hence comes his vacillation, his hesitating and procrastinating, and his fluctuating purpose, now advancing and now falling back: hence, too, the vehemence of his self-accusation, with which he would goad himself into prompt measures, without however being able to controul time and its flight; hence too the inconsistency and irresolution of his proceedings, and apparently also of his character. (pp. 216-17)

After the dreadful crime has been made known to him, the necessity of revenge does not at once press upon his mind; the vehemence of passion, and a constraining pressure to act, do not at once seize upon him. He is no doubt deeply horrified; but it is at most to him a lesson of experience; he will set it down,

> That one may smile and smile and be a villain,
> [I. v. 108]

and he comes immediately to a determination not to proceed further before he has assured himself of the certainty of the matter, and can see clearly what his own course ought to be. Accordingly, he entreats his friends to observe an unbroken silence as to the whole incident, even though his subsequent behaviour might appear to them strange and wonderful. The singular behaviour which he therefore adopted, his half madness, whose unreality it was not difficult to perceive, would have been most ill-timed and unaccountable, if from the first he had contemplated immediate action. But it is intelligible at once, if we suppose that this appearance was assumed with a view of awaking a suspicion in the mind of the king, that he possessed a hint or knowledge of the truth, and of drawing from his consequent behaviour a conclusion as to his guilt or innocence. The backwardness to give immediate credence to the word of the Ghost, which all this caution implies, would perhaps look like scepticism, were it not that the whole fable, as expressly intimated in the first scene, is based on the religious ideas and moral doctrines of *Christianity*. According to *these* ideas it cannot be a pure and heavenly spirit that wanders on earth in order to stimulate his son to avenge his murder. This, in fact, the Ghost admits of his own accord, and declares that he is

> Doomed for a certain time to walk the night,
> And for the day confined to fast in fires
> Till the foul crimes done in my days of nature
> Are purged and burnt away. . . .   [I. v. 10-13]

[Even] when, by the device of the play, Hamlet has assured himself of the King's guilt, he still hesitates, and forms no resolve; he is still beset with doubts and scruples; but preeminently *moral* doubts and *moral* scruples! Most justly. Even though the King were trebly a fratricide, in a *Christian* sense it would still be a sin to put him with one's own hand to death, without a trial and without justice; in a christian sense, the murder of an uncle and a second father is a deed from which every pure and thinking mind might well draw back and shudder, even though divine justice itself should seem to demand the punishment of the criminal, which in the present case none but Hamlet could accomplish. In Hamlet, therefore, we behold the christian struggling with the natural man, and its demand for revenge in a tone rendered still louder and deeper by the hereditary prejudices of the Teutonic nations. The natural man spurs him on to immediate action, and charges his doubts with cowardice and irresolution—the christian spirit—though indeed, as a feeling, rather than as a conviction—draws him back, though still resisting. . . . A regard for the eternal salvation of his soul, which he significantly alludes to at the first appearance of the Ghost, compels him to stand still and to consider, while the recollection of the solemn obligation to revenge, which his father's spirit has laid upon him, urges him onwards. . . . It is not, therefore, any sceptical and leisurely refining contemplation which seeks to exhaust all the possible consequences of a deed, but conscience, and a wish to act independently and in obedience to his own convictions, that, with propriety and justice, constrain his determination. Neither is it, as Goethe thinks, from any feeling of his own want of heroism or magnanimity, but from a sense of conscience, and of this his innate disposition, that he complains of being called upon to make straight the crooked times.

But, besides the moral question, whether he ought to attempt the deed, the how, also, tortures his soul. This is directly confessed in the soliloquy, Act III., Sc. 2. Granting that the deed must be done, still it must be accomplished in a way in accordance with the self-determining activity of the judgment, and in a form at once consistent with, and significant of, the end proposed. In this view, also, the affair appears both difficult and impracticable, and the whole posture of affairs is adverse to him. Again, therefore, he is plunged in doubt and procrastination. . . . It is only at the very last moment, and when he is himself at the point of death, that, incensed by the discovery of the fresh crimes of the King, and on the impulse of the moment, rather than acting freely and deliberately, he mortally wounds him, and then, with a sigh for human weakness, expires.

So far, no doubt, Hamlet is rightly styled a tragedy of *thought,* but in a sense far different from the one in which Schlegel employed the term. It is the highest and noblest attribute of man—thought in its freedom, and independent self-shaping energy, that the Poet seeks to illustrate in this play, as the fundamental principle of human conduct, and the leading motive in the history of the world. . . . The mind of Hamlet—not more noble and beautiful than it is strong and earnest, and as great as human greatness can reach to—is throughout struggling to retain the mastery which the judgment ought invariably to hold over the will, shaping and guiding the whole course of life. This aim he nevertheless misses. The weakness and irresolution of a finite being, aided by the force of the most unfavourable circumstances, are ever driving him from his true course; unforeseen events disappoint all his plans. *For in spite of all its grandeur and excellence, his mind is engrossed with this earthly existence; nay more—the ignorantly cherished and presumptuous wish, to be able, by the creative energy and perfection of thought, to rule and shape at pleasure the general course of things, bears on its very face the foul taint of sin,* for it is nothing less than the desire to reject the guiding hand of God, and to make of man's will an absolute law—to be a very god. Accordingly, whenever Hamlet does act, it is not upon the suggestion of his deliberate judgment, but hurried away rather by the heat of passion, or by a momentary impulse. (pp. 218-21)

With the character and fortunes of Hamlet—in whose story principally the grand tragic idea of the drama is embodied— the actions and sentiments of all the other personages correspond exactly. Laertes is the opposite and the pendant to Hamlet. The position of both is nearly the same: Laertes, too, has to avenge the death of a father and sister. His soul, however, kindles at once with passionate ardour. . . . The King himself is a mass of deception and hypocrisy; he is a practised actor, and the perfect master of his looks and movements, and of all his words and actions; his guilty designs are supported, in every case, by maturely weighed and well contrived plans; he too labours like Hamlet, though in an opposite sense, to direct his purpose by the power of thought and judgment, the course of events and the concurrence of circumstance. Nevertheless, we have here again the same result, the same fruitless trouble. . . . Polonius pays the penalty of his foolish *curiosity* and his empty cunning, with which he thinks he can see through and manage every thing: the sudden destruction of all her brilliant *dreams* of sensuous pleasure and earthly enjoyment, which with equal vanity and curiosity outran the present, upset the mind of Ophelia. By her side stands the Queen, whom a womanish weakness has made a sinner, talked over, cozened, and made the tool of designing man. She stands in the same class with Rosencrantz and Guildenstern, who, though directly they take no part in the action, are nevertheless willing, for the sake of their personal aggrandizement and influence, to become the guilty *instruments* of another's criminal design. . . . Opposed to all these stands *Horatio*, in direct and intrinsic contrast. He alone is *without* any ends of his own; he aims not at making any profit of life for himself, but devotes himself entirely and unreservedly to his friend. And by this disinterested conduct he gains that which all others lose. For it is clear that Fontinbras, young, and unacquainted with the circumstances of his new kingdom, will select Horatio—the friend of Hamlet, and named by the dying heir to the throne to be his exculpator and the defender of his fair fame—for the high but responsible office of restoring peace and order to the racked and disjointed kingdom. He is consequently anything but a superfluous character; not a part of the mere machinery of the plot, but an essential element of the fable. (pp. 222-23)

The several groups into which the characters fall during the complete development of the ground-work of the piece, move naturally and lightly forward; and by their hostile or friendly relations to each other, the march of the action is determined in Shakspeare's usual manner. Its principal movements are the behaviour of Hamlet after his discovery of the foul crime which forms the centre of interest, the play within the play, and the immediate consequences to which it gives rise—the deaths, viz. of Polonius and Ophelia—the return of Laertes, and his violent conduct, and the deaths of Rosencrantz and Guildenstern;—and lastly the particular form and evolution of the catastrophe. All these have been already noticed, and their significance respectively pointed out; or in other words we have ascertained their intrinsic necessity in the fundamental idea of the piece, and in the several characters and circumstances of

the story as limited and determined thereby. In this necessity, and in the purity and clearness with which the fundamental idea is kept before us in every turn of the plot, and in all the characters and details of the story, consist the beauty and perfection of its structure; and I have no hesitation in placing this grand and highly involved and complicated drama alongside of the best production of our poet, even though many have been found to find fault with its composition as highly defective.

A few points of detail may perhaps call for a closer examination. In the first place we will notice—which, after our previous disquisition scarcely called for further refutation—the objection which has been brought against Shakspeare, even by Goethe, that in the last act he has unnecessarily entangled and spun out the course of action by Hamlet's voyage to England, his adventures at sea, and his return, &c. These, however, appear indispensable, when we remember that the very purpose of the piece is to show that the poor plans and intentions of man do not miscarry merely through the weakness of their authors, but their baseless projects are also, by an intrinsic necessity, as frequently crossed and frustrated by the equally baseless empire of chance. The full establishment of this truth was requisite for the thorough working out of the ground idea. It was therefore necessary to interweave in the story a great variety of entangled incidents and relations, inasmuch as nothing less than such a thorough complication could fully exhibit the weakness of the unassisted human intellect. . . . For the same reason, and not for mere stage effect, does Shakspeare introduce the Ghost. This supernatural appearance is not only employed to bring suddenly to light the hidden crime, but to furnish the strongest motive that could influence such a character as Hamlet's, and so to heighten the conflict between his longing for free and deliberate action, and the constraining circumstances in which he was placed. With the same view has the poet brought folly and madness in such close juxtaposition with the shrewd understanding, the profound reflection, and the rare intellectual riches of Hamlet. (pp. 223-25)

Lastly, the concluding scene has been no less unjustly treated. The unexpected and sudden untying of the entangled knot by a series of accidents, and Hamlet's rash and passionate conduct, have, I think, been already shewn to be necessary. But another and a different fault has been found with it. It is objected, that the appearance of Fortinbras, even though preparation may have been made for it as early as in the first act, is irrelevant to the subject-matter, and is an insignificant piece of ornament capriciously stuck on to the story in order to close the scene with striking effect. . . .

It is enough for the reader to consult his own judgment, whether it would satisfy the essence of tragedy, to leave the spectator with the question unanswered, why so noble and powerful a race of kings is given up *so entirely* to destruction. This "murderous route" ought to have its reason, its intrinsic necessity, and its ideal significance; and so it has. Fortinbras, in whose favour Hamlet gives his dying voice, possesses an ancient claim and hereditary right to the throne of Denmark. Some deed of violence or injustice, by which his family were dispossessed of their just claims, hung in the dark back-ground over the head of that royal house which has now become extinct. Of this crime its last successors have now paid the penalty. And thus, in this closing scene, that idea of the overruling justice of God, which pervades all the other tragedies of Shakspeare, impresses on the whole play its seal of historical significance. (pp. 226-27)

Hermann Ulrici, "Criticisms of Shakspeare's Dramas: 'Hamlet'," in his Shakspeare's Dramatic Art: And His Relation to Calderon and Goethe, *translated by A.J.W. Morrison, Chapman, Brothers, 1846, pp. 213-33.*

FRATER TACITURNUS [pseudonym of SØREN KIERKEGAARD] (essay date 1845)

[*A Danish theologian and philosopher, Kierkegaard is a major figure in the development of modern existential thought. Hamlet fails, according to Kierkegaard, because it is impossible to convey the prince's essentially religious struggle in aesthetic, or dramatic, terms. Among other critics who analyze* Hamlet *as a religious drama are Hermann Ulrici (1839), H.D.F. Kitto (1956), Sister Miriam Joseph (1962), and Patrick Cruttwell (1963). Kierkegaard's essay was first published in 1845.*]

Börne says of "Hamlet," "It is a Christian drama." This to my thinking is a peculiarly good observation. I would alter it only by saying "a religious drama," and then would say that its fault is, not that it is a religious drama, but that it did not remain such to the end, or rather that it ought not to be drama at all. If Shakespeare will not give Hamlet religious postulates which conspire against him to produce religious doubt (wherewith the drama should properly end), then Hamlet is essentially a victim of morbid reserve, and the aesthetic demands a comic interpretation. His great plan of being the avenger ("to whom vengeance belongeth," says Hamlet) he has conceived. In case one does not see him at the same instant sink under the weight of this play (wherewith the scene becomes introspective and his unpoetic scruples, viewed psychologically, are a remarkable form of dialectic repentance, inasmuch as repentance comes as it were too early)—if this does not take place, one demands resolute action, for he has only to deal with outward circumstances where the poet puts no difficulties in his way. If the plan holds good, Hamlet is a dawdler who doesn't know how to act; if the plan does not hold good, he is a sort of self-tormentor who torments himself for and by wanting to be something great—and neither of these alternatives is tragic. (pp. 409-10)

If Hamlet is kept in purely aesthetic categories, one must see to it that he has demoniac strength to carry out such a resolution. His scruples are in this case of no interest at all; his procrastination and delay, his postponement and his self-deceitful pleasure in renewing his purpose when at the same time there is no outward hindrance, merely abase him, so that he does not become an aesthetic hero, and so becomes nothing at all. If he is conceived religiously, his scruples have great interest, they insure that he is a religious hero. (p. 410)

If Hamlet were to be interpreted religiously, one would either have to let him conceive the plan and then let the religious doubt take it from him, or else (the alternative which to my thinking illustrates better the religious, for in the first case there might possibly be mingled also doubt as to whether in reality he was capable of carrying out the plan) one must bestow upon him demoniac strength to carry out his plan resolutely and vigorously and then let him collapse within himself in the religious experience, until he should there find peace. A drama can of course never be made out of this, a poet cannot use this theme, which would have to begin with the last phase and let the first glimmer through it. (pp. 410-11)

Frater Taciturnus [pseudonym of Søren Kierkegaard], " 'Guilty?'/'Not Guilty?'," in his Stages on

Life's Way, *translated by Walter Lowrie, Princeton University Press, 1940, pp. 409-11.*

EDWARD STRACHEY (essay date 1848)

[*The following essay was originally published in Strachey's* Shakespeare's Hamlet *in 1848.*]

In all Shakespeare's varieties of characters there is none in which he has chosen to draw the *man of genius* so purely and adequately as in Hamlet; in Hamlet we see genius in itself, and not as it appears when its possessor is employing it in the accomplishment of some outward end; and this genius bursts forth with a sudden and prodigious expansion, into the regions of the pure intellect, as soon as its quiet course through its previous channel of the ordinary life of a brave, refined, and noble-minded prince-royal was violently stopped up by the circumstances with which we are familiar. Hamlet now shows himself in that character which is properly,—though not according to the popular appropriation of the word,—called *skeptical*. Partly because he is cut off from all legitimate practical outlet for his intellectual energies, partly from the instinctive desire to turn away from the harrowing contemplation of himself and his circumstances, he puts himself into the attitude of a bystander and *looker-on* . . . in the midst of the bustling world around him. And like other such skeptics he finds it more and more difficult to *act*, as his knowledge becomes more and more comprehensive and circular,—to take a *part* in the affairs of a world of which he seems to see the *whole;* and like them, too, he throws a satirical tone into his observation on men, who, however inferior to him in intellect, are always reminding him that he is dreaming while they are acting. (p. 172)

[We] can neither assert that Hamlet is mad, nor that his mind is perfectly healthy; much confusion and misapprehension about the character of Hamlet have arisen from thus attempting an impossible simplification of what is most complex. There are more things in heaven and earth than are dreamt of in the philosophy of the small critic who thinks he has only to rule two columns, with 'mad' at the top of one, and 'sane' at the top of the other, and then to put the name of Hamlet in one of the two. Hamlet, like all real men, and especially men such as he, has a character made up of many elements, ramifying themselves in many directions, some being healthy and some diseased, and intertwined now in harmony, now in contradiction with each other. And, accordingly, it presents different aspects to different observers, who look from opposite points of view, though each with considerable qualifications for judging rightly. We have just seen the view taken by Ophelia, whose deep love, and woman's tact and sentiment, can best appreciate the finer and more delicate features of Hamlet's character, though she, perhaps, exaggerates the extent of the untuning of his reason, from the influence of her own fears and of her father's declaration that he had gone mad. The shrewd, clear-headed King, with his wits sharpened by anxiety, considers the question from the side of its practical bearing on his own interests, and sees that as far as these are concerned Hamlet is not mad, but most dangerously sane. (pp. 172-73)

[We] must not only utterly reject the notion that Hamlet kills the King at last to revenge himself and not his father,—though we may allow that the treachery to himself helped to point the spur which was necessary to urge him on to instant action,— but we must also come to the conclusion which I proposed to prove by this inquiry into the whole plot and purpose of the Play,—that Hamlet does *not*, as Coleridge [see excerpts above,

THE
Tragicall Hiſtorie of
HAMLET,
Prince of Denmarke.

By William Shakeſpeare.

Newly imprinted and enlarged to almoſt as much
againe as it was, according to the true and perfect
Coppie.

AT LONDON,
Printed by I. R. for N. L. and are to be ſold at his
ſhoppe vnder Saint Dunſtons Church in

Title page of the Second Quarto of Hamlet *(1604). By permission of the Folger Shakespeare Library.*

1812 and 1813] and other great critics have asserted, 'delay action till action is of no use, and die the victim of mere circumstance and accident.' True it is that he delays action till it is of no use to himself, and has allowed his chains to hang on him till the time for *enjoying* liberty and life is past: and it is doubtless a part of the moral of the Play that we should recognize in this defect in Hamlet's character the origin of his tragic and untimely fate. He *ought* to have lived to enjoy his triumph, but surely he has triumphed, though only in death. If he had not triumphed, if he had not done his work before the night fell, but had been a mere idler and dreamer to the last, could we part from him with any feeling but that of the kind of pity which is half blame and contempt? . . . There is something so unpretending, and even homely (if I may apply the word to such a state of things) in the circumstances of Hamlet's death, that it does not strike us obviously that he dies for the cause to which he has been called to be the champion. Yet so it is. (p. 174)

> *Edward Strachey, in his extract from* A New Variorum Edition of Shakespeare: Hamlet, Vol. IV, *edited by Horace Howard Furness, J. B. Lippincott Company, 1877, pp. 172-74.*

G. G. GERVINUS (essay date 1849-50)

[*One of the most widely read Shakespearean critics of the latter half of the nineteenth century, the German critic Gervinus was praised by such eminent authors of his day as Edward Dowden, F.J. Furnivall, and James Russell Lowell; however, he is little known in the English-speaking world today. Like his predecessor*

Hermann Ulrici, Gervinus wrote in the tradition of the "philosophical criticism" developed in Germany in the mid-nineteenth century. Under the influence of August Wilhelm Schlegel's literary theory and Georg Wilhelm Friedrich Hegel's philosophy, German critics like Gervinus tended to focus their analyses around a search for the literary work's organic unity and ethical import. Gervinus perceived a rational ethical system independent of any religion in Shakespeare's works, in contrast to Ulrici, for whom Shakespeare's morality was basically Christian. In his discussion of Hamlet's delay, first published in his Shakespeare *in 1849-50, Gervinus describes how, when Hamlet is forced to action, "the beautiful qualities of his character become damaged and injured," and Rosencrantz and Guildenstern, as well as Ophelia, become his victims.*]

['Hamlet'] is a text from true life, and therefore a mine of the profoundest wisdom; a play which, next to 'Henry IV.', contains perhaps the most express information of Shakespeare's character and nature; a work of such a prophetic design, and of such anticipation of the growth of mind, that it has only been understood and appreciated after the lapse of nearly three centuries; a poem which has so influenced and entwined itself with our own later German life, as no other poem even of our own age and nation could boast of having done, with the exception of 'Faust' alone. (pp. 548-49)

All the want of design pointed out in Voltaire's censures [see excerpt above, 1752] suddenly . . . crumbled into dust, when Goethe demonstrated the strict logical consistency of the play; all that appeared to lie open to criticism in the reproaches of Johnson [see excerpt above, 1765] and Malone was changed at once into so many eulogiums, when it was shown that it was the very design of the poet to represent his hero as a man whose reason had been disturbed by the shock of too difficult a task; to lead him, according to that profound simile of Horatio's, to the dreadful summit of a steep whose height makes him giddy: as Goethe has expressed it, to delineate a mind oppressed by the weight of a deed which he fails to carry out [see excerpt above, 1795].

That this was really the design of the poet is evident from the facts themselves; but it is also made palpable by express and repeated reference to the meaning he intended to convey through them, and this even to a greater degree than in 'Romeo' or in any other play. (p. 551)

[In Hamlet's] first soliloquy it strikes us with surprise that the man so apparently resolute should immediately call on his heart to 'hold,' and to his sinews to 'grow not instant old, but to bear him stiffly up'; and that, in the deepest emotion, he should lament that time was 'out of joint,' and that he was born 'to set it right.' It is strange that he does not at once impart his secret to the friends to whom his father had appeared, and only subsequently to one of them, namely, to Horatio; that he chooses far-fetched means for a matter so simple, feigning himself mad like Brutus, when there was no mighty tyranny to overthrow. (pp. 552-53)

The play is acted. Before there ensues any appeal to the conscience of the king, the poet has made use of it to speak first to the conscience of Hamlet himself, and at once to convey to the spectator the meaning of his work. Scarcely has Hamlet interpreted the language of the acted queen into 'wormwood' for his mother, than he himself receives the same from Gonzago, who plays the part of his father, and the voice of the ghost speaks to him again. . . .

[Both Hamlet and Horatio] are now convinced of the guilt of the murderer. The poet now shows us the king alone, trying to pray and to repent (Act III. sc. 3). Almost every sentence of his soliloquy bears a comparison with the state of Hamlet's mind, in whom the duty of revenge exists in the same proportion as in Claudius the duty of repentance. The hypocritical murderer stands wavering between his deed and his revenge. The king has the will to pray, as Hamlet has to punish; but the impulse of their nature accords not with their task; 'the stronger guilt defeats the strong intent' of the praying man, the extreme of conscientiousness causes the backward ebb of the avenger's passion even when it has begun to flow. Thus it is with both, as Claudius says, that they 'like men to double business bound, stand in pause where they shall first begin, and both neglect.' . . . The king's soul, entangled in the meshes of crime, strives to free itself, and becomes more and more ensnared; Hamlet's excited feelings seem impatient of restraint, while all the more surely he is held captive by procrastination. (pp. 553-54)

[The] main action of the play and the conduct of the hero become still more evident from the unusually expressive contrast to Hamlet in which Shakespeare has placed Laertes, in whose history and behaviour Hamlet himself discovers the contrast to his own case. Perhaps nowhere else is the design of the poet so strikingly prominent in the touches of his characterisation as here. Hamlet has stabbed Polonius. His son Laertes—somewhat of a hero *à la mode*, a fencer, a knight of honour of the French school, of temperament as choleric as Hamlet's is melancholy, a man utterly unendowed with the splendid physical and mental gifts of Hamlet—flees from Paris to distant Denmark to avenge the death of his father. . . . The one thought of vengeance fills his mind, and every nerve in him is strained to action, even before he knows the murderer with any certainty. The king has had the body of Polonius secretly interred, and by this means draws suspicion upon himself. The position and power of the supposed murderer confuse not the avenger Laertes. . . . He has not the power nor the means which Hamlet has, but those which he has he will 'husband so well, that they shall go far with little.' He is not the lawful heir to the throne, he is not in the sight and favour of the people, not a prince of the house royal; but *he*, the subject, creates 'a rebellion which looks giant-like,' and shakes the king upon his throne. . . . He dooms his allegiance to hell, he sends conscience and grace to the profoundest pit, he dares damnation, whilst Hamlet speculates doubtfully in the sunlight. . . . Laertes goes so far as to poison his sword, that in single combat with Hamlet he may more surely obtain his end. He sullies by this his knightly honour, although he treats his revenge rather as a matter of honour, while for Hamlet it is a heavy matter of conscience. But in the midst of this passion, strained even to unscrupulousness, he is strictly confined to the one object of his revenge, whilst, owing to Hamlet's tardy steps, the guiltless Polonius falls, Ophelia becomes crazed, Rosencrantz and Guildenstern are made a sacrifice, and himself and his mother perish. . . . He desires alone to meet the murderer of his father, he has only this one object before him, and he expresses it in the first moment in which he appears before Claudius, in the short and sharp inquiry for his father; in this one endeavour not all the will of the world shall stay him.

And all this for what a father! Of Hamlet's father we hear those proud often-quoted words, the most splendid epithet of a great man—:

> He was a man, take him for all in all,
> I shall not look upon his like again.
>
> [I. ii. 187-88]

What a contrast to this is Polonius! The exact design of this contrast can never have been perceived by those who endeavoured to place this character in a favourable light, an endeavour which is not worth refutation. If Polonius' bad and ridiculous qualities had been even partially concealed by his good ones, why should Hamlet enjoin the players, when he commits them to *him*, the father of his beloved, to 'mock him not'? Why should he say, in the presence of his daughter, that her father is a fool? Why should he call him a tedious old fool? Why, moreover, should he say over his corpse, that he was 'in all his life a foolish prating knave'? We see him commit no especial acts of knavery, but we see him in a service and employ by no means over-honourable; he has an unwearied predilection for crooked ways, for aside-thrusts, and for eavesdropping, and at length he falls a sacrifice to them; he meddles with everything. (pp. 556-58)

Thus, then, the structure of the play stands in perfect unity and connection before us; the action throughout has one point in view, and the least conspicuous figures are in close and essential relation to the main subject. The truth-loving, moral hero stands in the midst of those wandering on crooked ways of hypocrisy, dissimulation, and untruth; his sensible, conscientious, and circumspect nature is opposed in strong contrast to the unprincipled conduct of all the others, and to the heartless or thoughtless heedlessness of their actions and their consequences. . . . [We] feel that with Shakespeare the action is ever secondary, that it ever holds a subordinate place, and that the true point of unity in his works ever leads to the source of the actions, to the actors themselves, and to the hidden grounds from which their actions spring. We could take but little interest for its own sake in the negative action of this play, in the evasion of the deed, in the lack of outward events, and in the absence of inward energy and vigor. Yet we take the deepest interest in this Hamlet—proof sufficient that the especial charm lies in the character. When we have thoroughly penetrated it, we may then feel that we have dived to the ground of the action. And not this alone; in our acquaintance with this source of the action we feel we have attained at once to an incomparably richer and more fertile perception; we can imagine this highly endowed man under other circumstances, different and yet ever the same; we learn to regard the action as a mere outlet, as merely one outlet of a deep original spring, from which can be traced the tide of similar or different actions; and we perceive the moral deduced from the story only as a lesson that may be traced to a higher, more comprehensive truth. It remains with us then to examine what form of character this is, what were the elements of its origin, and what pursuits and peculiarities affect this nature and render it so irresolute and incapable of action. (pp. 560-61)

Hamlet says himself that his uncle is no more like his father than he to Hercules. He lacked, therefore, says Goethe, the external strength of the hero, or we might say, more simply, the strength of a practical and active nature. His temperament is quiet, calm, phlegmatic, and free from choler. . . . In violent passion with Laertes, Hamlet says of himself that he is not 'splenetive and rash,' yet he has in him something dangerous, which the wisdom of his enemy may fear. This 'something dangerous' is his sensitive excitability, which originates in a heated imagination, and which supplies this passive nature with a goad for defence and a weapon for assault, but only at a moment of extreme necessity. For this very imagination is the source also of Hamlet's faintheartedness, and of his anxious uneasiness and weakness; it is a psychological circle, only too often verified by human nature. . . . His busy imagination suggests to him a condition with its fearful and remotest results; he sees himself surrounded by dangers and snares, and seeks to obviate them with elaborate preparation. He believes in ghosts and therefore sees them; differing in this from his more rational friend Horatio, who hardly believes, after he has seen it, that 'the thing' is the ghost of Hamlet; who in its very presence calls it an 'illusion,' and attempts to strike it with his partisan; who, according to his own confession, believes the traditions of Christian superstition only 'in part,' and according to his tone not at all. When the ghost appears to Hamlet, when his 'fate cries out,' in the excitement of the moment he fears not death, and 'each petty artery' in his body is 'as hardy as the Nemean lion's nerve'; but then too, according to Horatio's expression, he is 'desperate with imagination.' After the play, in the 'witching time of night,' when his imagination is heated, he could 'drink hot blood, and do such business as the bitter day would quake to look on'; then it seems to him as if the soul of Nero could enter his bosom; he sharpens the edge of his revenge, and when in this over-excited mood the occasion surprises him, and no time is left for consideration and doubt, he shows himself capable of the deed from which, in a calmer state, recollections and scruples restrain him. Nor is this excitement suddenly quieted by the disappointment of his mistaken vengeance; he torments his mother in the violence of his emotion more than his father permitted him; he speaks bitter words over the corpse of Polonius, and only subsequently weeps over it; the patience of the dove then comes sorrowfully back to him. So, too, when surprised by the tidings of Ophelia's death, he hears Laertes' ostentatious lament over her grave, a storm of passion rises within him, and finds vent in a burst of exaggerated language. By this excess of excitement Hamlet blunts the edge of purpose and action, which is rendered dull by the habitual tardiness of his nature; he alternately touches the chords of the two different moral themes of the drama, namely, that intentions conceived in passion vanish with the emotion, and the human will changes, and is influenced and enfeebled by delay. These waverings of his nature, this alternative inertness and passion, indolence and excitement, Hamlet perceives in himself, with all the torments, faults, and results which belong to them. (pp. 561-62)

This same elasticity in Hamlet's nature, which leads him from supineness to passion, and from vehemence to apathy, shows itself also in the contrast of good and bad temper, of spleen and humour, and in the balance of the sanguine with the melancholy side of his temperament. The poet has placed in close context with these witty satirical traits, which allow us to perceive in Hamlet a merry and happy nature, those of an elegiac sentimental character, which exhibit him a prey to deep melancholy; these affect his humour, scarcely alternately, but by being blended together, and the results are those bitter sarcasms which form his usual manner of expression. In prosperity the cheerful side of Hamlet's nature would have been developed; his predisposition to melancholy would then only have borne a contemplative character; he would perhaps have always visited churchyards and solitary places, and have given way to tender moods and emotions, but this inclination would never have degenerated into a melancholy that amounts to despair. The cause of this extremity of dejection lies in the events which befall him, events which suddenly impoverish him, which rob him, as Goethe says, of the true conception he had formed of his parents, which unhinge his mind and roll upon him a tide of affliction, sorrow, uneasiness, and dire forebodings, which in the course of their fulfilment produce unrestrained derangement. From the unfortified manner with which he bears misfortune, we should conclude that he was a man created rather

for happiness, whose distinguishing quality would then have been a witty cheerfulness and lightheartedness; this appears in him innate as well as acquired. He shows himself one of those ready and witty orators according to the taste of the age, more skilful in playing a part in comedy than in tragedy; the acuteness of mind which enables him to assume his tragic madness would under brighter circumstances have involuntarily taken a comic aspect. (p. 563)

In harmony with what we have seen of Hamlet's appearance, temperament, and natural disposition, are the rich endowments of mind and morals with which the poet has invested him. His uncle himself designates the kindly man as of a nature 'sweet and commendable'; all gentle virtues, all tender and delicate feelings, belong to him. His childlike piety is that which at once strikes us most forcibly. The reverence with which he reflects on his deceased father is unbounded; the sorrow which he endures for him testifies to the greatest warmth and sincerity of feeling; his grief at his mother's fickleness causes a shock to his whole moral nature; the certainty of his uncle's crime completely overwhelms him. The heaviness of this sorrow may indeed partly result from the innate susceptibility peculiar to Hamlet's nature; he has a kind of delight in dwelling upon gloomy ideas, and in revelling in thoughts of suicide and death. Yet the shock to his moral sensibilities adds essentially to the burden of his grief; and well may he call his indignation 'virtue,' when he gives it vent in the scene in which, with an ethical invective of the highest power, he urges his mother to confession and repentance. In great traits he is throughout placed before us, as a moral nature endowed with as much depth as delicacy. . . . [As Hamlet] appears opposed to the false culture of the age, he is equally vehement against its lack of refinement. He will know nothing of the brawls and revels of the generation; the intemperance of his uncle, the quarrels of Fortinbras, are far from his nature. Thus in the task assigned to him an inner conflict perplexes him; the strife of a higher law with the natural law of vengeance, the struggle of fine moral feelings with the instinct of nature. His irresolution results in nowise exclusively from weakness, but essentially also from conscientiousness and virtue; and it is just this subtle combination which renders Hamlet such an essentially tragic character. His doubts as to the certainty of the fact and the legitimacy of revenge, the gentleness of his soul which unconsciously struggles against the means of vengeance, the bent of his mind to reflect upon the nature and consequences of his deed and by this means to paralyse his active powers, all these scruples 'of thinking too precisely on the event,' he himself calls, in the warmth of self-blame,

> A thought, which quartered, hath but one part wisdom,
> And ever three parts coward;
>
> [IV. iv. 42-3]

but the poet has so well balanced the combination, that, in spite of Hamlet's witness against himself, we are inclined to impute the half at least to wisdom. (pp. 565-67)

[As soon as Hamlet rises] to his vocation for action, in the manner of one uncalled to the task, the beautiful qualities of his character become damaged and injured, and we see at last before us a man who has himself spoiled the best properties of his nature. He who bore the sufferings of humanity with such a feeling soul, becomes in his egotism cruel and severe towards those who stand nearest to his heart. He who is so irritable an enemy to all dissimulation, falsehood, and cunning, not venturing upon the straight path to action, himself takes the crooked way of cunning circumlocution and deceiving dissimulation. He who had weighed his task so conscientiously, veers round from conscientiousness itself, or from tardiness, into unconscientiousness, and converts his mildness into severity. When he finds his uncle kneeling in prayer, he will not kill him lest he should send the penitent to heaven; when, according to his propensity to neglect the near duty and to consider the remote one, and incapable of his own revenge, he wishes, as it were, to take upon himself the vengeance of God, does he not, in order to find excuse for his inaction, abandon himself to a refinement of wickedness and cruelty, such as before he would not have endured even in thought? He was still full of excitement and ardour, as at Polonius' death he was in the confusion of passion, but we see him presently sacrificing innocent men with cold premeditation—he, who was too over-thoughtful to strike the guilty. He is brought to England by Rosencrantz and Guildenstern. They carry with them a Urias-letter for his death, but they know it not. The open, upright Hamlet opens this letter, writes with feigned hand (an art he had practised in his youth) their names instead of his own, and thus these, the friends of the youth to whom, according to his mother's evidence, he adhered more than to any other, fell into the same pit which was dug for Hamlet, but not by them. They 'go to't?' asks his Horatio in reproachful surprise. But he lightly disregards this emotion of conscience; to dig a mine and prepare a trap suit his nature better than the direct open deed; his ever ingenious head had alone to act here; to plant a countermine is to him as easy as a clever idea; he rejoices inconsiderately and maliciously in these arts, praises himself for the quickness of his thought and the rapidity of its accomplishment, and sophistically sees God's help in the prosperous success—*he* who would not see the many distinct intimations which pointed out to him his duty of revenge! Thus then at last he himself reaches the same point of malice and cunning as his uncle, whose misdeeds he was called upon to revenge.

Still more reproachable does Hamlet appear to us in his relation to his beloved one. Goethe said of Hamlet's feeling for Ophelia, that it was without conspicuous passion. The poet has at any rate not exhibited him to us in a position in which this passion appears pre-eminent. When he casts his love in the scale with that of forty thousand brothers, the exaggeration of the tone affords no standard. Beyond this passage, Shakespeare has only once allowed him a direct opportunity, in a few aside-spoken words, to give us the key to his feeling for Ophelia, in those words which precede his conversation with her: 'Nymph, in thy orisons be all my sins remembered!' (pp. 578-79)

Of Polonius, Hamlet himself says expressly that the death of the innocent is his punishment who let the guilty live; a much greater punishment for him is the end of Ophelia, whose father *he*, the lover, had killed, and thus had rent in twain every bond which linked her to the world. To this death her songs incessantly relate; her real madness punishes the feigned insanity of Hamlet, which gave the first shock to her mind. In the same manner Rosencrantz and Guildenstern fall victims to Hamlet's ruined nature. If poetic justice appears too severe in these destinies, it is only that avenging justice may all the more severely recoil upon Hamlet himself. The poet has expressly placed in Hamlet's lips the fearful sentence of cold egotistical levity which exhibits these terrible bloody results of his dread of blood in the right light; a sentence which may be also applied to the end of Paris in 'Romeo and Juliet'. ' 'Tis dangerous,' he says at the death of his friends, 'when the *baser nature* comes between the pass and fell incensed points of mighty opposites.' In this manner does the man of great genius trifle

with the subordinate creature, whom he regards as appointed to play only inferior parts on this stage of life. Thus is it then that the conscientiousness, foresight, and consideration which restrain Hamlet from the murder and from the just punishment of a single man, bury at last the guilty and the guiltless in one common ruin; his own want of determination, the avenging rage of Laertes, the poisoned cup of his uncle, the careless weakness of his mother, the officiousness of his friends, the inoffensive folly of Polonius, the innocence of the devoted lover, each and all these—virtue, and pardonable faults, and inexpiable mortal crimes—suffer the same ruin, so that scarcely any of the living remain upon the stage. This has been declared to be a kind of barbarous, bloody tragedy, worthy of a rude age, all the characters at last being thus swept from the stage [see excerpt above by Voltaire, 1752]. But in so doing it was the aim of the poet to use this unnecessary bloodshed as part of the characterisation as well as punishment of his hero, who had not courage to shed necessary blood. Shakespeare himself has said this with distinct consciousness. The king asks Laertes whether it is 'writ in his revenge, that, sweepstake, he will draw both friend and foe, winner and loser?' The master of revenge, little conscientious as he is, is satisfied with the punishment of the one guilty one. But the conscientious Hamlet contrives that *he*, as the king designated it, should at one blow actually destroy all by his clumsy revenge. With one single significant word the poet evidently intimates his deep design at the end, and his reference to that question of the king to Laertes. Over the heaps of dead, Fortinbras exclaims, 'this quarry cries on havock!' a word which in sporting language signifies that game, useless from its amount and quality, which is killed by unpractised sportsmen; as here by the unskilful avenger. Thus then this bloody conclusion is not the consequence of an aesthetic fault on the part of the poet, but of a moral fault on that of his Hamlet, a consequence which the sense of the whole play and the design of this character aim at from the first. (pp. 581-82)

G. G. Gervinus, "Third Period of Shakespeare's Dramatic Poetry: 'Hamlet'," in his Shakespeare Commentaries, *translated by F. E. Bunnètt, revised edition, Smith, Elder, & Co., 1877, pp. 548-82.*

KARL WERDER   (essay date 1859-60)

[*Werder presents the radical thesis that Hamlet is not the procrastinator portrayed by earlier critics, but is a man of action whose task is to bring Claudius "to confession, to unmask and convict him" rather than to kill him. This interpretation runs counter to Johann Wolfgang von Goethe (1795), August Wilhelm Schlegel (1808), and the majority of early critics in its explication of Hamlet's delay. Werder's views were challenged by A. C. Bradley (1905), but have been adopted by such critics as Fredson Bowers (1955) and Sister Miriam Joseph (1962). This essay is taken from a series of lectures given from 1859 to 1860 by Werder at the University of Berlin. For additional commentary on Hamlet's delay, see William Richardson (1774), Samuel Taylor Coleridge (1811), Hermann Ulrici (1839), Friedrich Nietzsche (1872), George Brandes (1895-96), and Sigmund Freud (1900).*]

All the leading critics, with Goethe at the head, advance the idea that Hamlet is at fault on account of some subjective deficiency or weakness. If he had not been just the man he was, if he had been fitted by nature for the task imposed upon him, he would immediately have taken another and more direct course to accomplish it. He himself is the obstacle; he procrastinates from his own nature, and thus complicates the situation and drags everything out of place by giving it a direction wrong in itself and ruinous to himself and others.

For my own part, I must flatly dissent from this conclusion. Let me ask, first of all, would Hamlet have dared to act as these critics almost unanimously demand that he should have done? . . . I maintain that he could not have thus acted, and for purely objective reasons. The facts of the case, the force of all the circumstances, the very nature of his task, directly forbid it; so absolutely that Hamlet is compelled to respect the prohibition, even when his reason, his poetic and dramatic, yes, even his human judgment, would decide differently. The critics have been so absorbed in the study of his character that the task imposed upon him has been lost sight of. Here is the fundamental mistake.

What do the critics require of Hamlet? That he should attack the King immediately and make short work with him, indeed, the shortest possible. . . . He should go to the King at once and slay him. He can do this the first time he sees the King, if it be the very next hour. . . . Then, say the critics, he is to call the court and people together, justify his deed to them, and take possession of the throne.

And how is Hamlet to begin to justify his deed? By telling what his father's ghost had confided to him, say the critics. . . . Is it possible that they will believe him? Would they be convinced of the justice of his deed by evidence of this sort? The critics have assumed that he was by birth the supreme judge in the country and the legitimate heir to the throne, whom a usurper had deprived of his rights. Is there any proof of these assertions? Certainly none in Shakespeare. Hamlet himself breathes no word of complaint of having suffered any such wrong. And if such a wrong had existed, if there had been a usurpation, Hamlet would certainly have spoken of it, or if he had been silent Horatio and others would certainly have referred to it. Might not the courtiers have hinted that his madness proceeded from this cause? (pp. 41-3)

Hamlet understands his own position and cares for his own reputation very much better than the critics who have thus taken him to task. If he had killed the King immediately, what the critics call heroism would have served only to prove him a fool.

The Ghost himself has a better understanding of the case than the critics. He calls upon his son to avenge his murder, but he has by no means the passionate thirst for blood that the critics evince. He is in no such haste, and leaves time and place to his son. "*Howsoever* thou pursuest this act" are his words. He does not intimate that a thrust of the dagger will suffice, or that his demands would thereby be satisfied. (pp. 46-7)

What is Hamlet to do? What is his actual task? A sharply defined duty, but a very different one from that which the critics have imposed upon him. It is not to crush the King at once—he could commit no greater blunder—but to bring him to confession, to unmask and convict him. That is Hamlet's task, his first, nearest, inevitable duty. As things stand, truth and justice can come to light only from one mouth, that of the crowned criminal, and if he or some one connected with him does not speak, then the truth will be for ever hidden. That is the situation! Herein lie the terrors of this tragedy. This is the source of Hamlet's enigmatical horror and the bitterness of his misery. The secret of the encoffined and unprovable crime is the unfathomable source out of which flows its power to awaken fear and pity. (pp. 48-9)

Why did Hamlet delay if the task could be as easily accomplished as the critics insist? Alas! It is so difficult that it is almost impossible. Shakespeare himself lets us see that he understands it to be so. Claudius has no idea of confessing. Even if Hamlet should strike at him, there would be no disclosure of the truth. (pp. 49-50)

The main point of my declaration is by no means the doubtful results for Hamlet as an individual if he had been governed by the demands of the critics, but rather the effect such a course would have upon the fulfilment of his task. If Hamlet had struck down the King, without unmasking him, if he had obeyed the Ghost's prayer for revenge at the earliest opportunity by a bold dagger-thrust, the direct result would have surely been that no one would have believed in the apparition; its intentions would have been frustrated, and the true punishment, which should be memorable through the ages, would be rendered impossible. For no punishment can be real and effective unless the offender be condemned by the unanimous verdict of his world.

The apparition did not appear for the purpose of dethroning the King and having Hamlet succeed to the crown. The paternal spirit asked Hamlet, as any father might ask a son, to revenge his murder and not allow the kingly bed in which his own child was born to be stained with infamy, not to allow injustice to triumph and villany to remain unpunished. . . . (pp. 50-1)

If Hamlet had misunderstood the Ghost's meaning and had assassinated the King before he had unmasked him, he would really save rather than destroy him. He would make the King immortal, for the sympathy of the world would flow to him, and through all time the royal criminal would be regarded as the innocent victim of a wicked plot. Instead of being condemned he would be canonised. . . . What Hamlet has most at heart after he sees the Ghost is *not* the death, but, on the contrary, the *life* of the King, henceforth as precious to him as his own. These two lives are the only means by which he can fulfil his task. Now that he knows the crime and is enjoined to punish it, nothing worse could happen to him than that the King should suddenly die unexposed and thus escape his deserts. (pp. 52-3)

[The] resolution of Hamlet "to put an antic disposition on." As far back as the time of Johnson it had been a disputed problem. . . .

This decision is . . . supposed to favour the idea that Hamlet is really insane, which idea, according to the critics, his lack of resolution naturally confirms. But the question arises, can pretended lunacy and real distraction of mind exist in one and the same man? (p. 87)

As soon as Hamlet has heard what the Ghost tells him, his clear head instantly comprehends the whole dire pass to which *Truth* and *Right* have come, beyond all human power. The imminent agony, aye, the shudder of certainty that must seize him as to the impossibility, as things stand, of solving the problem; the horror and the crime coming so close to him; his murdered father's cry for revenge; the triumphant murderer, who, if the task can be achieved, is certainly not to be reached by force and hardly by cunning—with scarcely a glimmering hope of success, he is so sagacious and artful;—all this forms a condition of things so dark and dread, a dilemma of so terrible and monstrous a nature, that for a man involved in it to break through it alone, by his own unaided strength, is indeed a task which may well cost him the loss of his understanding.

In truth, if the situation is duly weighed, has there ever been another such task which was wholly placed within the power of a single person or any exertion or sacrifice that he personally can employ? Shakespeare has considered the task and therefore gives his hero this feeling and sense of the situation, although some may consider him a weakling and a shuffler, who tries to deceive himself and us in order to conceal his own want of energy. This, too, is thoroughly positive and not negative, not a blamable personal defect, but the monstrous, real objective trouble and dilemma; this natural immediate feeling is the *inmost* impulse to his purpose of "putting an antic disposition on." This instinctive motive is the first original motive. Hamlet's action is the direct outcome of his full sense of the situation.

Thus upon a sane mind is laid what is enough to destroy it, and in fact it does destroy *all* except the mind and the will and freedom of the mind. Because he knows that all in him of happiness and peace is already destroyed by the situation in which, with perfect innocence on his own part, he is placed—for even were he to fulfil his task, how shall he ever again be happy?—and because he knows, at the same time, that the demon of his task is ceaselessly menacing the last thing which is left to him unshattered—his mind; because this intense suffering has come upon him, and because it wholly possesses him, therefore he can do nothing else but give expression to this his condition; and this, too, out of the inmost core of his nature and out of the strength and fineness of his understanding. That from which he actually suffers, the truth of his position, he manifests; he moves in the element which his fate has made for him, and on *which alone* all that he may undertake henceforth hinges. All students see and feel Hamlet's blighted being and his clear head, but they do not understand it. The simple fact of his outward appearance alone strikes them; they do not grasp his inner being, the suffering of the shattered spirit, the agony and conflict of the free, strong mind.—And this is the second point to be noted: that instinctive impulse at once gives him some advantage and becomes effective as a purpose.

The behaviour for which, as something that may chance to be serviceable to him, he prepares his friends, and the connection of which with the appearance of the Ghost they were not to tattle about, is in fact of the greatest possible service to him. But they must never imagine that its true purpose concerns the downfall of the King, or they would understand the motive that prompts it; furthermore, this behaviour enables him at least to give vent to what is raging within him and what he would fain shriek out, while at the same time it diverts attention from the true cause of his trouble, from his secret, and thus assures its safety. . . . [By] the behaviour he adopts he has no longer any need to show respect for those whom he despises. Possibly also, if he is supposed to be crazy, he can, under this cover, should any favourable opportunity occur, make use of it for more active operations against the enemy than would be permitted to a sane man; play a more active game, be perhaps foolhardy, and, in case of failure, still have opportunity, under the protection of his supposed imbecility, for a new attack. (pp. 90-4)

He does what he must, takes the step which is directly before him, does what is actually at hand, does it without any other reflection, does what he in his situation must feel *is to be done*, and what he must recognise as most advantageous to his cause; and therefore, in thus acting, his thought must be that it will lead him the most surely through the darkness of his task. He cannot possibly have any other conception of the nature and the consequences of his course. (pp. 94-5)

How loosely does he wear his mask! how transparent it is! He is always showing his true face. The mask hides, not himself, but his secret; and, therefore, it so soon ceases to be useful to him. For as soon as the first opportunity for action comes—and how quickly it comes through the play within the play!—the King knows that the madness was no real madness. From the beginning his evil conscience scented under this madness a design against himself. . . . After the King listens his suspicion becomes certainty, and after the play he understands from what knowledge and to what end the madness was simulated.

Hamlet knows very well, at the point which he has then reached, that the old method is worn out. A new one must be found. But, first, his mother is to be enlightened and her conscience appealed to. This is *now*, after he has convinced himself of the guilt of the King, her husband,—this is the most important duty, which lies nearest to him, much nearer than killing the King. But this, in fact, seems to have escaped all observation—the inexorable necessity, according to the meaning of the play, of *just this action*.

That Shakespeare lets this action be introduced by the agency of others and not by Hamlet, by the interest of Polonius as a part of his machination against the Prince—this action not merely as an external agency but rather for the sake of it,—the impersonal power (the Ghost) intervening as the power instantaneously helping all forward, it is this that impresses this scene so powerfully with the stamp of that unparalleled art which characterises the play and makes it the central and turning point of the whole action.

Now comes a circumstance that changes all. *Hamlet kills Polonius*. He must now submit to be sent away to England. Thus, as the opportunity to adopt some new method of proceeding is cut off, the old one, although somewhat worn out, must be continued, because it suits both the King and the Prince; it suits the King to consider the Prince as really insane and so to get rid of him, and it suits the Prince to continue his eccentric behaviour, although more carelessly than before and without taking any pains to dissemble, because he himself has committed a murder.

It may be said, however, that Hamlet feigns only so far as it is necessary to make others reveal themselves. The real feigning is, in fact, always on their side. They all pretend to be honest, and play false parts. Hamlet speaks the truth to them and makes them tell their lies. The seriousness of Hamlet's fate is ever much more to him than the wish and care for his mask. Its use is only incidental, and it is soon cast aside. After the interview with his mother, he dissimulates no more. (pp. 96-9)

In act third Hamlet prepares his experiment,—he has neglected nothing up to this point,—the play will be presented and he will get the objective proof that he needed, and will also have confirmation by means of Horatio's testimony. He obtains the King's acknowledgment of guilt, but only as pantomime; he has not yet had any spoken confession. It suffices for his own moral conviction and that of his friend; but if nothing further is added to it, nothing has been gained so far as the belief of the world is concerned. . . . The traitor is almost beside himself from the possibility of betraying his secret, and the peril of trying to avoid justice. He can escape because he is King and the entire court is at his beck and call. They have all noticed, more or less, the design and meaning of the play and the impression and the effect on the King.

But the question is, how much of these impressions do they retain, and what use do they make of them? The relation of the fictitious marriage in the play to the real ceremony which they have seen is indubitable; but the people have taken no offence at the real one and therefore can take none at the ideal representation of the same. They perceive only Hamlet's anger and revolt, which are nothing new to them.

There is no mention of adultery in the play—the mother is to be spared. In the pantomime which precedes the representation, the poisoner first plots the murder to gain the woman, and later, after the action of the poisoning, Hamlet expressly tells the audience,

> You shall see anon how the murtherer gets the love of
> Gonzago's wife.   [III. ii. 263-64]

The murder, however, is discovered! Murder is cried aloud throughout the play. Hamlet insinuates that it is a "mouse-trap," that it is a cunningly contrived artifice. The murderer is a young relative of the aged duke; the crime happens in a garden by poisoning, only it is a man that does the deed instead of a snake; and—after this action the King starts up and runs away.

What ought the people to think? Can any one of the company ascribe the King's behaviour and his flight to any other cause than what he has seen and heard? Polonius cries in behalf of the company: "Give o'er the play." All that the public see in the play is the displeasure of the King and Hamlet's revolt. . . . They will *not* wish to see what may be more or less suspected. Suspicion against royalty would be a crime or an impropriety which should not be encouraged.

We can therefore perceive how little hold Hamlet has on this company which makes up his world. All the people would be concerned in the judicial procedure which he has to conduct, they are his jury. Not one takes part with him, no one save his Horatio. All have withdrawn from him after this demonstration as from a miscreant who has struck at the crown. They have all run after the King. Polonius has flown to the King's service, to overhear in the King's behalf the conversation between mother and son. Rosencranz and Guildenstern, acknowledging the sacred majesty of the King, are already at hand to conduct the Prince to England. (pp. 138-41)

For Hamlet and Horatio the King's action is a direct proof of guilt, but not for the other spectators. Let us suppose that the company did not prevent the thrust at the King and that it succeeded. What would then be attained? Nothing!

The critic's mistake originates in his impatience for the "duty-impelled stroke''; but if it fell as hastily and unwisely as he would like to have it, the single duty about which the Prince is concerned would be entirely thwarted instead of being fulfilled. (pp. 141-42)

Then he goes to his mother, and on his way Hamlet finds the King at prayer—the King who here, *for the first time,* makes a verbal confession before us that he is the murderer while confessing the crime to himself. So far have Hamlet and the poet brought him by means of the play. Here is progress in the rôle of the King, and from the negative side in the play. There is a depth or power of invention here which has not its parallel, the wisdom in the *rhythm of the development.* It is this which, if I may speak for myself, moves me most deeply. The *tempo* of the onward movement in the play, how measured is its step!—the course it takes, appearing to drag and yet

hurried onward by the storm of God, Heaven and Hell thundering together!

At this moment Hamlet finds the King alone, unarmed and unprotected. He draws his dagger, for after what he has learned from the play he dares to kill him; he wills to do it—and does not do it. And we know that this is well. He would defeat his purpose if he now made the King dumb before the world, when the first attack upon him by means of the play had succeeded in wresting from him at least the pantomime of a confession. Will it be replied, "No! for from this time the King will protect himself with good reason; now that he has learned the daring and the power of the avenger, there will be no further opportunity for Hamlet to attack him''? But Hamlet stands *inside* and *not* outside the action, and his own confidence in what he is capable of doing strengthens him. He knows, indeed, that his purpose is discovered. As he knows the enemy, so after this encounter the enemy knows him, and will do all in his power to destroy him and thus escape from the vengeance that threatens him. Hamlet knows this, and must be prepared for it and trust to his righteous cause. This is the one motive which restrains him. And even if nothing further should come out of it for the advancement of his purpose, if future developments should neutralise or destroy the present advantage, Hamlet dares not be the one through whose action it comes to naught. This would be the result if he struck at the King now. He can never by his own testimony alone accomplish his task if he makes the guilty one dumb for ever.

Hamlet himself, it is true, does not say this to us. No! But the facts say it for him. He himself says that for the King to die at this moment when he is praying would be so favourable to him that the stroke should be delayed until he can be made to fall past hope of salvation. Is it supposed to be a mere subterfuge of Hamlet's irresolution that he considers the moment when the King is praying is not the favourable moment for him to die? . . . Are the critics struck with blindness? How does the King fall at last? He so falls that we see that every other way would be more lenient, would be "hire and salary, not revenge," not the vengeance to which the criminal is condemned. He does not finally fall in a sudden fit, nor while drunk, asleep, or gaming—then his fate would have been all too easy,—but he falls in fact when in the very act of doing what puts him so utterly beyond all hope of salvation that even from the threatening words of Hamlet, terrible as they are, we neither can or should, when he utters them, anticipate the catastrophe. . . . Rather than be betrayed he suffers even his own wife to drink the poison which he had prepared for Hamlet; in this moment utterly hopeless of salvation he falls, so that his soul will be "as damned and black as hell whereto it goes." *Thus* the poet fulfils the words of Hamlet. *Thus* do they express to the letter Shakespeare's idea of vengeance, of punishment, of judgment, in such a case as this—*his* way of dealing justice to *this* transgressor. And it must not be forgotten that it is Hamlet who brings the King to this end. *He alone does it by his hits* and *by his misses,* by the play he uses and by the killing of Polonius. These things so work that "this physic but prolongs the sickly days" of the criminal.

Then he hastens to his mother, delaying the stroke, as he must, and putting it wholly out of mind, for his interest in the salvation of his mother is now infinitely the nearer and more pressing duty. As to striking the King down without bringing him to justice, he could do that the very next hour and more appropriately than now. (pp. 142-47)

Furious and frantic he rushes in wildly to his mother. He hears the cry behind the tapestry, and now supposing the King to be hidden there, he allows himself to be carried away by his hot impulsive rage, here in this place and in this still hour, close by the bed where he himself was begotten, where the worst personal dishonour had been inflicted upon him, here where the whole air is full of it—here the voice of the wretch (he is thinking only of the King and therefore believes that it is the King whom he has heard) calls up all his shame, and, forgetting the strict obligation of his task, he gives full course to his thirst for vengeance—for after the proof by means of the play, he is, of course, *morally* free to kill the King,—he is carried away into the grave error of plunging his sword through the tapestry. A grave error indeed! For there is no question here of his *moral* right and power. This is the turning-point of the play which includes in itself the second cardinal moment for the understanding of the whole. The first, that which I call the fundamental point, is the *conditio sine qua non* that guards the treasure, which can be exhumed only with the help and by the power of the second. Only with this second point do we get an insight into the *tragic depth* of the drama, into the plot. To understand this turning-point is to understand Hamlet.

Something new is here before us, something surprising for which we were not prepared. Hamlet commits an error! *and this error is Hamlet!*

But from now all hinges on this error, and of this error only shall we have to speak. That Hamlet stabs at the tapestry is no proof forsooth that he was a coward and would not have risked the act face to face with the enemy; it is wholly the expression and act of his blind passion.

Without stopping to consider whether he hit or miss, he stabs like lightning blindly into the dark; he looks neither to the right nor left; he listens only to his own thirst for vengeance and is deaf to his duty.

He has made the thrust at last. What has he accomplished? He has committed murder! And instead of being freed from the old burden, he has brought a new one upon his soul; instead of accomplishing what he was bound to do, he has become a criminal! Thus the error punishes itself! (pp. 148-50)

More pressingly and emphatically than ever must he feel himself obliged to proceed slowly and with redoubled caution; he must indeed feel himself driven to a standstill since he has suffered himself by a senseless burst of passion to stumble into the abyss to which he had come, driven to a full pause from the shock in his own mind, even though he perceives no circumstances forcing him thereto. And so the killing of Polonius is the turning-point of the drama. (p. 152)

Now follows the sea voyage. Hamlet,—as we learn from his communication to Horatio in the fifth act,—in the same frame of mind as when we left him, sleepless in his cabin, is tormented in regard to his all-too-correct suspicion of the royal document of which Rosencranz and Guildenstern are the bearers. He gets possession of the letter while they sleep. He sees therein, "black on white," his death-warrant. He writes another letter which resembles the first in outward appearance (he has his father's seal), with the earnest conjuration to the English King to put the bearers of the letter to death at sight, without respite even for confession. Hamlet puts this letter in place of the other, and the falsification is not detected.

We all know how the critics call that forgery a base crime, and we also know the tenderness and sympathy which is felt for the innocent victims of Hamlet's malice. I would like to know what the critics would have done in Hamlet's place. He

had endured intolerable suffering for his cause in order to accomplish it thoroughly and worthily. On his life hangs the possibility of its ultimate success, the revelation of heavenly justice on earth. And now he is about to be borne to death! . . . No, there is no possible way out of the difficulty, there can be no other course for Hamlet than this which he takes. No, *not here nor at any point in the whole destiny of Hamlet!* That is precisely the point again upon which hangs the correct understanding of the play. Rosencranz and Guildenstern—or himself! (pp. 162-65)

Rosencranz and Guildenstern perish justly because they serve the murderer against Hamlet, who is legally acting in the cause of justice, and also because they are not serving God.

That is the great tragical and rational point of view, and there is no higher reason than that of real tragedy. (p. 169)

[When] he made the thrust through the tapestry, Hamlet committed a grave error, causing the death of Polonius. The destruction of Rosencranz and Guidenstern was also the disastrous consequence of the same error. *Therefore,* on account of that error into which he allowed himself to fall, the original plot of the King is changed; *therefore,* instead of the commission to demand the arrears of tribute, the sentence of Hamlet's death is sent to England; *therefore,* Hamlet has to work against it; *therefore,* after an accident has rendered his counter-plotting useless and made it impossible for him to nullify it, these two fall; *therefore,* he himself also falls. For that one error, which has also for its consequence the madness of Ophelia, the poet lets his hero atone *with his own life.* (pp. 171-72)

The rapidity of pressing events in the fourth act, the detailed, minute preparation at the end of the act, and the apparent block in the fifth, are the foreshadowings of the catastrophe, the calm that often precedes the bursting of the tempest, the gathering clouds in which the thunderbolt of fated revenge is engendered.

This is the explanation of Hamlet's behaviour and of all his utterances in the last act. So far as he had the power *he has done his work, partly* for the task he has to perform, *partly against himself, not against the task,* for that is impossible, because it is just and because he was guided by the heavenly powers, and therefore what he did *against himself* becomes *active for good* in the hands of those powers. Hamlet is needed no more to lead, it is only for the execution of judgment that he is to be further used; his arm and his life are still necessary, no longer his mind, his wit, and his patience. Hamlet is *already at the goal,* although he does not know it.

Hence the mood of repose in which he appears in the churchyard, the tone of a man who has done all that he can and has nothing more to do, the disgust at the finite nature of things, the melancholy and sickening sense of mortality which fill him. It is this feeling which finds expression in his meditation upon the skull, in his horribly witty, bitter-sweet talk. (pp. 210-12)

He feels himself prepared, and therefore allows himself to become jocose and to ridicule the fop who invites him in the fatal fencing. More seriously he says:

> There's a special providence in the fall of a
> sparrow. If it be now, 't is not to come; if it
> be not to come, it will be now; if it be not now,
> yet it will come: the readiness is all. Since no
> man knows aught of what he leaves, what is 't
> to leave betimes? Let be.
>
> [V. ii. 219-24]

It is the influence of the Divine power by which every nerve in Hamlet is already stimulated and under whose spiritual control he stands. (p. 213)

Hamlet's *miss proves to be the hit*—because it is *his miss*, not *his hit*, but the *hit of Fate*. That is the most secret point in Hamlet's fate-guided course, the most hidden from himself. That is the most brilliant feature in the invention of Shakespeare, the turning-point of the play, the thing *inwardly accomplished* but outwardly apparent only in the catastrophe. This accidental death of Polonius is *the death of all*, but it also unmasks the criminal. Through that thrust by which Hamlet, in blind wrath, *tries to hit* the King and *does not hit* him, by this thrust the King *is really hit;* but only because Hamlet has *not* in reality hit him, therefore he is *in truth* hit, so hit that *the truth comes to light!* On this account Hamlet himself falls but his task is fulfilled, through the help which was secretly inherent and latent in his error in killing Polonius. By the death of Polonius, Hamlet stirs up against himself a vengeance similar to that which he has to inflict, but merely similar—it has no righteous claim to his life; and since, nevertheless, on account of it he suffers death, therefore it assists him *to do what he is bound to do.* And it assists him *because the criminal whom he is to punish avails himself of the error in order to secure himself and destroy Hamlet.* (pp. 215-16)

[Hamlet] allows himself to be led; in that he is ever intelligent and passive in the broadest sense, for he understands the difficulties of his task, understands in fear and agony; and thus he goes straight to the heart of the crime. And *by no means slowly.*

> [Werder adds in a footnote:] Consider how short is the space of time from the beginning of the second act—only a few days. This fact escapes notice because the text is so rich and deep, the subject so great, Hamlet's task so difficult, and his suffering so intense. It is this *inner* infinity that makes the process *seem* long.

The preposterous idea that he goes slowly has come to be generally accepted only from the silly desire that he should kill the King immediately.

The drama knows of no delay! The fulfilment, the judgment, even the death of the King, come quicker than Hamlet or we could have foreseen. All is accomplished *with one stroke*, in overwhelming surprise! *Now* Hamlet *may* strike the King down, *now* at last when he himself is dying, *now* he may *harken to his blood* when his blood is flowing! and *now* his thrust cannot injure the cause; it seals and fulfils it, but *never until this last moment* when Laertes and the Queen have also fallen.

The bloody havoc has been regarded by the critics as useless. Justice and her poet know better what blood is demanded in expiation and who is her debtor for the royal crime. Even now the King makes no confession. Death opens his mouth only for a lie, not for acknowledgment of the truth; but his own confession is no longer needed. Laertes confesses for him, and the corpse of the Queen and the blood of the Prince unite to proclaim the murderer to all the world. Now too Ophelia and Polonius, Rosencranz and Guildenstern, testify against him. All these victims of his crime now form the chorus to the solo of the Ghost, and when Horatio comes forward to tell Hamlet's story and to explain his cause to the unsatisfied, he will produce in all his hearers the conviction which he himself has and which we have, and the story which the grave told will be an unquestioned truth for the world—*now* when Hamlet lives no

more on earth and is no longer a party in the drama. (pp. 216-18)

Hamlet has reason as well as passion; full of the spirit of his task, as a noble and true hero he sets himself about the tragic atonement without making a false step at the start. He wins by the service he gives to the task, by the destiny arising from it, by his aim and action. Nothing but this service comes from Hamlet, nothing that can be explained as personal desire. He exists wholly for the task. He acts ever in its shadow, in the twilight of its inspiration, in its assurance and its torment. That is *Hamlet's attraction, his character, his originality.* It is this wonderful *clair-obscur* that gives the piece its tone. (pp. 221-22)

This play, in its depth, draws the soul to the abyss over which the mystery hovers which Shakespeare allows us to perceive but not to uncover. It represents essentially reality even in its gloom. Shakespeare extends his art to the unfathomable, and his limit is where our knowledge ends, but Shakespeare has made even this mysterious realm his own, *not* to explain the unfathomable, but to give us a human soul whom the riddle of destiny has carried beyond this world. (pp. 222-23)

> *Karl Werder, in his* The Heart of Hamlet's Mystery, *translated by Elizabeth Wilder, G. P. Putnam's Sons, 1907, 223 p.*

IVAN TURGENIEFF (essay date 1860)

[*Turgenieff, a Russian novelist, dramatist, poet, and essayist, was greatly influenced by the literature, culture, and politics of Western Europe, and promoted their acceptance in Russia. In the following essay, written in 1860, he offers a moral interpretation of* Hamlet *by contrasting Hamlet and Miguel de Cervantes's Don Quixote. According to Turgenieff, Quixote is a figure of faith and self-sacrifice who represents an ideal model for human behavior, whereas Hamlet, in his egotism and scepticism, conveys a negative moral lesson. Turgenieff's conception of Hamlet echoes that of George Steevens (1772), and anticipates the interpretations of such twentieth-century critics as Salvador de Madariaga (1948) and Rebecca West (1957).*]

The first edition of Shakespeare's tragedy, "Hamlet," and the first part of Cervantes' "Don Quixote" appeared in the same year at the very beginning of the seventeenth century.

This coincidence seems to me significant. . . . It seems to me that in these two types are embodied two opposite fundamental peculiarities of man's nature—the two ends of the axis about which it turns. I think that all people belong, more or less, to one of these two types; that nearly every one of us resembles either Don Quixote or Hamlet. In our day, it is true, the Hamlets have become far more numerous than the Don Quixotes, but the Don Quixotes have not become extinct. (p. 290)

What does Don Quixote represent?

Faith, in the first place; faith in something external, immutable; faith in the truth, in short, existing *outside* of the individual, which cannot easily be attained by him, but which is attainable only by constant devotion and the power of self-abnegation. . . . [His] life itself he values only in so far as it can become a means for the incarnation of the ideal, for the establishment of truth and justice on earth. I may be told that this ideal is borrowed by his disordered imagination from the fanciful world of knightly romance. Granted—and this makes up the comical side of Don Quixote; but the ideal itself remains in all its immaculate purity. To live for one's self, to care for one's self, Don Quixote would consider shameful. He lives—if I may so express myself—outside of himself, entirely for others, for his brethren, in order to abolish evil, to counteract the forces hostile to mankind—wizards, giants, in a word, the oppressors. There is no trace of egotism in him; he is not concerned with himself, he is wholly a self-sacrifice—appreciate this word; he believes, believes firmly, and without circumspection. . . . Don Quixote may seem to be either a perfect madman, since the most indubitable materialism vanishes before his eyes, melts like tallow before the fire of his enthusiasm (he really does see living Moors in the wooden puppets, and knights in the sheep); or shallow-minded, because he is unable lightly to sympathize or lightly to enjoy; but, like an ancient tree, he sends his roots deep into the soil, and can neither change his convictions nor pass from one subject to another. The stronghold of his moral constitution (note that this demented, wandering knight is everywhere and on all occasions the moral being) lends especial weight and dignity to all his judgments and speeches, to his whole figure, despite the ludicrous and humiliating situations into which he endlessly falls. (pp. 290-91)

Now what does Hamlet represent?

Analysis, first of all, and egotism, and therefore incredulity. He lives entirely for himself; he is an egotist. But even an egotist cannot believe in himself. We can only believe in that which is outside of and above ourselves. But this *I*, in which he does not believe, is dear to Hamlet. This is the point of departure, to which he constantly returns, because he finds nothing in the whole universe to which he can cling with all his heart. He is a skeptic, and always pothers about himself; he is ever busy, not with his duty, but with his condition. Doubting everything, Hamlet, of course, spares not himself; his mind is too much developed to be satisfied with what he finds within himself. He is conscious of his weakness; but even this self-consciousness is power: from it comes his irony, in contrast with the enthusiasm of Don Quixote. Hamlet delights in excessive self-depreciation. Constantly concerned with himself, always a creature of introspection, he knows minutely all his faults, scorns himself, and at the same time lives, so to speak, nourished by this scorn. He has no faith in himself, yet is vainglorious; he knows not what he wants nor why he lives, yet is attached to life. (pp. 291-92)

[He] will not sacrifice this flat and unprofitable life. He contemplates suicide even before he sees his father's ghost, and receives the awful commission which breaks down completely his already weakened will,—but he does not take his life. The love of life is expressed in the very thought of terminating it. Every youth of eighteen is familiar with such feelings as this: "When the blood boils, how prodigal the soul!"

I will not be too severe with Hamlet. He suffers, and his sufferings are more painful and galling than those of Don Quixote. The latter is pummeled by rough shepherds and convicts whom he has liberated; Hamlet inflicts his own wounds—teases himself. In his hands, too, is a lance—the two-edged lance of self-analysis.

Don Quixote, I must confess, is positively funny. His figure is perhaps the most comical that ever poet has drawn. His name has become a mocking nickname even on the lips of Russian peasants. . . .

Hamlet's appearance, on the contrary, is attractive. His melancholia; his pale tho not lean aspect (his mother remarks that he is stout, saying, "Our son is fat"); his black velvet clothes,

the feather crowning his hat; his elegant manners; the unmistakable poetry of his speeches; his steady feeling of complete superiority over others, alongside of the biting humor of his self-denunciation,—everything about him pleases, everything captivates. Everybody flatters himself on passing for a Hamlet. None would like to acquire the appellation of "Don Quixote." "Hamlet Baratynski," wrote Pushkin to his friend. No one ever thought of laughing at Hamlet, and herein lies his condemnation. To love him is almost impossible; only people like Horatio become attached to Hamlet. Of these I will speak later. Everyone sympathizes with Hamlet, and the reason is obvious: nearly everyone finds in Hamlet his own traits; but to love him is, I repeat, impossible, because he himself does not love anyone. . . .

Hamlet is the son of a king, murdered by his own brother, the usurper of the throne; his father comes forth from the grave—from "the jaws of Hades"—to charge Hamlet to avenge him; but the latter hesitates, keeps on quibbling with himself, finds consolation in self-depreciation, and finally kills his stepfather by chance. A deep psychological feature, for which many wise but short-sighted persons have ventured to censure Shakespeare! And Don Quixote, a poor man, almost destitute, without means or connections, old and lonely, undertakes the task of destroying evil and protecting the oppressed (total strangers to him) all over the world. It matters not that his first attempt to free innocence from the oppressor brings redoubled suffering upon the head of innocence. . . . It matters not that, in his crusades against harmful giants, Don Quixote attacks useful windmills. The comical setting of these pictures should not distract our eyes from their hidden meaning. The man who sets out to sacrifice himself with careful forethought and consideration of all the consequences—balancing all the probabilities of his acts proving beneficial—is hardly capable of self-sacrifice. Nothing of the kind can happen to Hamlet; it is not for him, with his penetrative, keen, and skeptical mind, to fall into so gross an error. No, he will not wage war on windmills; he does not believe in giants, and would not attack them if they did exist. We cannot imagine Hamlet exhibiting to each and all a barber's bowl, and maintaining, as Don Quixote does, that it is the real magic helmet of Mambrin. I suppose that, were truth itself to appear incarnate before his eyes, Hamlet would still have misgivings as to whether it really was the truth. (p. 292)

Remarkable are the attitudes of the mob, the so-called mass of the people, toward Hamlet and Don Quixote. In "Hamlet" Polonius, in "Don Quixote" Sancho Panza, symbolize the populace.

Polonius is an old man—active, practical, sensible, but at the same time narrow-minded and garrulous. He is an excellent chamberlain and an exemplary father. (Recollect his instructions to his son, Laertes, when going abroad—instructions which vie in wisdom with certain orders issued by Governor Sancho Panza on the Island of Barataria.) To Polonius Hamlet is not so much a madman as a child. Were he not a king's son, Polonius would despise him because of his utter uselessness and the impossibility of making a positive and practical application of his ideas. . . .

Polonius does not in the least believe Hamlet, and he is right. With all his natural, narrow presumptiveness, he ascribes Hamlet's capriciousness to his love for Ophelia, in which he is, of course, mistaken, but he makes no mistake in understanding Hamlet's character. The Hamlets are really useless to the people; they give it nothing, they cannot lead it anywhere, since they themselves are bound for nowhere. And, besides, how can one lead when he doubts the very ground he treads upon? Moreover, the Hamlets detest the masses. How can a man who does not respect himself respect any one or anything else? Besides, is it really worth while to bother about the masses? They are so rude and filthy! And much more than birth alone goes to make Hamlet an aristocrat.

An entirely different spectacle is presented by Sancho Panza. He laughs at Don Quixote, knows full well that he is demented; yet thrice forsakes the land of his birth, his home, wife and daughter, that he may follow this crazy man; follows him everywhere, undergoes all sorts of hardships, is devoted to him to his very death, believes him and is proud of him, then weeps, kneeling at the humble pallet where his master breathes his last. . . .

The masses of the people invariably end by following, in blind confidence, the very persons they themselves have mocked, or even cursed and persecuted. They give allegiance to those who fear neither curses nor persecution—nor even ridicule— but who go straight ahead, their spiritual gaze directed toward the goal which they alone see,—who seek, fall, and rise, and ultimately find. . . .

In their relations to woman, too, our two types present much that is noteworthy.

Don Quixote loves Dulcinea, a woman who exists only in his own imagination, and is ready to die for her. (p. 293)

Of sensuality there is not even a trace in Don Quixote. All his thoughts are chaste and innocent, and in the secret depths of his heart he hardly hopes for an ultimate union with Dulcinea,—indeed, he almost dreads such a union.

And does Hamlet really love? Has his ironic creator, a most profound judge of the human heart, really determined to give this egotist, this skeptic, saturated with every decomposing poison of self-analysis, a loving and devout heart? Shakespeare did not fall into this contradiction; and it does not cost the attentive reader much pains to convince himself that Hamlet is a sensual man, and even secretly voluptuous. (It is not for nothing that the courtier Rosencrantz smiles slily when Hamlet says in his hearing that he is tired of women.) Hamlet does not love, I say, but only pretends—and mawkishly—that he loves. On this we have the testimony of Shakespeare himself. In the first scene of the third act Hamlet says to Ophelia: ''I did love you once.'' Then ensues the colloquy:

> *Ophelia:* Indeed, my lord, you made me believe so.
> *Hamlet:* You should not have believed me . . . I loved you not.
>
> [III. i. 115-18]

And having uttered this last word, Hamlet is much nearer the truth than he supposed. His feelings for Ophelia—an innocent creature, pure as a saintess—are either cynical (recollect his words, his equivocal allusions, when, in the scene representing the theater, he asks her permission to lie . . . in her lap), or else hollow (direct your attention to the scene between him and Laertes, when Hamlet jumps into Ophelia's grave and says, in language worthy of Bramarbas or of Captain Pistol: ''Forty thousand brothers could not, with all their quantity of love, make up my sum. . . . Let them throw millions of acres on us,'' etc.).

All his relations with Ophelia are for Hamlet only the occasions for preoccupation with his own self, and in his exclamation, ''O, Nymph! in thy orisons be all my sins remembered!'' we see but the deep consciousness of his own sickly inanition, a lack of strength to love, on the part of the almost superstitious worshiper before ''the Saintess of Chastity.'' . . .

Hamlet embodies the doctrine of negation, that same doctrine which another great poet has divested of everything human and presented in the form of Mephistopheles. Hamlet is the self-same Mephistopheles, but a Mephistopheles embraced by the living circle of human nature: hence his negation is not an evil, but is itself directed against evil. Hamlet casts doubt upon goodness, but does not question the existence of evil; in fact, he wages relentless war upon it. He entertains suspicions concerning the genuineness and sincerity of good; yet his attacks are made not upon goodness, but upon a counterfeit goodness, beneath whose mask are secreted evil and falsehood, its immemorial enemies. He does not laugh the diabolic, impersonal laughter of Mephistopheles; in his bitterest smile there is pathos, which tells of his sufferings and therefore reconciles us to him. Hamlet's skepticism, moreover, is not indifferentism, and in this consists his significance and merit. In his makeup good and evil, truth and falsehood, beauty and ugliness, are not blurred into an accidental, dumb and vague something or other. The skepticism of Hamlet, which leads him to distrust things contemporaneous,—the realization of truth, so to speak,— is irreconcilably at war with falsehood, and through this very quality he becomes one of the foremost champions of a truth in which he himself cannot fully believe. But in negation, as in fire, there is a destructive force, and how can we keep it within bounds or show exactly where it is to stop, when that which it must destroy and that which it should spare are frequently blended and bound up together inseparably? (p. 349)

I know that, of all Shakespeare's works, ''Hamlet'' is perhaps the most popular. This tragedy belongs to the list of plays that never fail to crowd the theater. In view of the modern attitude of our public and its aspiration toward self-consciousness and reflection, its scruples about itself and its buoyancy of spirit, this phenomenon is clear. But, to say nothing of the beauties in which this most excellent expression of the modern spirit abounds, one cannot help marveling at the master-genius who, tho himself in many respects akin to his Hamlet, cleft him from himself by a free sweep of creative force, and set up his model for the lasting study of posterity. The spirit which created this model is that of a northern man, a spirit of meditation and analysis, a spirit heavy and gloomy, devoid of harmony and bright color, not rounded into exquisite, oftentimes shallow, forms; but deep, strong, varied, independent, and guiding. Out of his very bosom he has plucked the type of Hamlet; and in so doing has shown that, in the realm of poetry, as in other spheres of human life, he stands above his child, because he fully understands it. (p. 350)

Ivan Turgenieff, "Hamlet and Don Quixote—The Two Eternal Human Types," translated by David A. Modell, in Current Literature, *Vol. XLII, No. 3, March, 1907, pp. 290-93, 349-52.*

THOMAS KENNY (essay date 1864)

[*Kenny asserts that* Hamlet *is somewhat disharmonious because Shakespeare failed to integrate his original sources for the play with the creations of his imagination. He concludes that, even taking into account its inconsistencies,* Hamlet *will remain the "most enthralling of all the works of mortal hands." In his em-*

phasis on Shakespeare's assimilation of sources for Hamlet, *Kenny prefigures the critical arguments of Charlton M. Lewis (1907), George Santayana (1908), Elmer Edgar Stoll (1933), and William Empson (1953). Charlotte Lennox (1753) offered an early analysis of Shakespeare's sources for Hamlet. Kenny's essay was first published in his* The Life and Genius of Shakespeare *in 1864.*]

We cannot help thinking that the perplexity to which we are [exposed in *Hamlet*] is founded on conditions which, from their very nature, are more or less irremovable. It has its origin, as it seems to us, in two sources. It is owing, in the first place, to the essential character of the work itself; and in the second place it arises, in no small degree, from the large license which the poet has allowed himself in dealing with his intrinsically obscure and disordered materials.

All Nature has its impenetrable secrets, and there seems to be no reason why the poet should not restore to us any of the accidental forms of this universal mysteriousness. The world of art, like the world of real life, may have its obscure recesses, its vague instincts, its undeveloped passions, its unknown motives, its half-formed judgements, its wild aberrations, its momentary caprices. The mood of Hamlet is necessarily an extraordinary and an unaccountable mood. In him exceptional influences agitate an exceptional temperament. . . . Hamlet is not only in reality agitated and bewildered, but he is led to adopt the disguise of a feigned madness, and he is thus perpetually intensifying and distorting the peculiarities of an already over-excited imagination. It was, we think, inevitable that a composition which attempted to follow the workings of so unusual an individuality should itself seem abrupt and capricious; and this natural effect of the scene is still further deepened, not only by the exceptionally large genius, but by the exceptionally negligent workmanship, of the poet. . . .

We believe we can discover in the history of the drama a further reason why its details were not always perfectly harmonised. It was written under two different and somewhat conflicting influences. The poet throughout many portions of its composition had, no doubt, the old story which formed its groundwork directly present to his mind; but he did not apparently always clearly distinguish between the impressions in his memory and the creations of his imagination, and the result is, that some of his incidents now seem to his readers more or less inexplicable or discordant. (pp. 176-77)

Hamlet is, perhaps, of all the plays of Shakespeare the one which a great actor would find most difficult to embody in an ideally complete form. . . . Its whole action is devious, violent, spasmodic. Its distempered, inconstant irritability is its very essence. Its only order is the manifestation of a wholly disordered energy. It is a type of the endless perplexity with which man, stripped of the hopes and illusions of this life, harassed and oppressed by the immediate sense of his own helplessness and isolation, stands face to face with the silent and immovable world of destiny. In it the agony of an individual mind grows to the dimensions of the universe; and the genius of the poet himself, regardless of the passing and somewhat incongruous incidents with which it deals, rises before our astonished vision, apparently as illimitable and inexhaustible as the mystery which it unfolds.

It is manifest that *Hamlet* does not solve, or even attempt to solve, the riddle of life. It only serves to present the problem in its most vivid and most dramatic intensity. . . .

Wonder and mystery are the strongest and most abiding elements in all human interest; and, under this universal condition

of our nature, *Hamlet,* with its unexplained and inexplicable singularities, and even inconsistencies, will most probably for ever remain the most remarkable and the most enthralling of all the works of mortal hands. (p. 177)

Thomas Kenny, *in his extract from* A New Variorum Edition of Shakespeare: Hamlet, Vol. IV, *edited by Horace Howard Furness, J. B. Lippincott Company, 1877, pp. 176-77.*

FRIEDRICH NIETZSCHE (essay date 1872)

[*Nietzsche, a nineteenth-century German philosopher, essayist, poet, and autobiographer, exercised a great influence on modern philosophy, particularly in the area of existential thought. His first published work was a highly influential study of Greek art,* Die Geburt der Tragödie aus dem Geiste der Musik *in 1872, from which the following excerpt is taken. Nietzsche believed that before Socrates, Greek culture exhibited two tendencies: the Apollonian, marked by a concern with restraint, harmony, and measure, and the Dionysian, characterized by a primitive resistance to structure and reason. The first tendency found expression, according to Nietzsche, in Greek sculpture and architecture, while the second found its outlet in the drunken orgies of the Dionysian festivals and the music associated with them. In the following excerpt, he states that Hamlet is a Dionysian character because he has "looked truly into the essence of things" and "gained knowledge"; the result is "nausea" which prevents him from acting. Thus, Nietzsche rejects Samuel Taylor Coleridge's widely held Apollonian view of Hamlet as an intellectual paralyzed by his introspective nature (1811), and suggests that he is rather inhibited by a Dionysian awareness of the futility of action in a "world that is out of joint." Nietzsche thus expresses a view held by many modern critics, notably G. Wilson Knight (1930). For additional commentary on Hamlet's delay, see William Richardson (1774), Hermann Ulrici (1839), Karl Werder (1859-60), George Brandes (1895-96), and Sigmund Freud (1900).*]

[Tradition] tells us quite unequivocally *that tragedy arose from the tragic chorus,* and was originally only chorus and nothing but chorus. Hence we consider it our duty to look into the heart of this tragic chorus as the real proto-drama, without resting satisfied with such arty clichés as that the chorus is the "ideal spectator" or that it represents the people in contrast to the aristocratic region of the scene. (p. 56)

It is indeed an "ideal" domain, as Schiller correctly perceived, in which the Greek satyr chorus, the chorus of primitive tragedy, was wont to dwell. It is a domain raised high above the actual paths of mortals. . . . Yet it is no arbitrary world placed by whim between heaven and earth; rather it is a world with the same reality and credibility that Olympus with its inhabitants possessed for the believing Hellene. The satyr, as the Dionysian chorist, lives in a religiously acknowledged reality under the sanction of myth and cult. That tragedy should begin with him, that he should be the voice of the Dionysian wisdom of tragedy, is just as strange a phenomenon for us as the general derivation of tragedy from the chorus. (pp. 58-9)

[The] Greek man of culture felt himself nullified in the presence of the satyric chorus; and this is the most immediate effect of the Dionysian tragedy, that the state and society and, quite generally, the gulfs between man and man give way to an overwhelming feeling of unity leading back to the very heart of nature. The metaphysical comfort—with which, I am suggesting even now, every true tragedy leaves us—that life is at the bottom of things, despite all the changes of appearances, indestructibly powerful and pleasurable—this comfort appears in incarnate clarity in the chorus of satyrs, a chorus of natural beings who live ineradicably, as it were, behind all civilization and remain eternally the same, despite the changes of generations and of the history of nations.

With this chorus the profound Hellene, uniquely susceptible to the tenderest and deepest suffering, comforts himself, having looked boldly right into the terrible destructiveness of so-called world history as well as the cruelty of nature, and being in danger of longing for a Buddhistic negation of the will. Art saves him, and through art—life.

For the rapture of the Dionysian state with its annihilation of the ordinary bounds and limits of existence contains, while it lasts, a *lethargic* element in which all personal experiences of the past become immersed. This chasm of oblivion separates the worlds of everyday reality and of Dionysian reality. But as soon as this everyday reality re-enters consciousness, it is experienced as such, with nausea: an ascetic, will-negating mood is the fruit of these states.

In this sense the Dionysian man resembles Hamlet: both have once looked truly into the essence of things, they have *gained knowledge,* and nausea inhibits action; for their action could not change anything in the eternal nature of things; they feel it to be ridiculous or humiliating that they should be asked to set right a world that is out of joint. Knowledge kills action; action requires the veils of illusion: that is the doctrine of Hamlet, not that cheap wisdom of Jack the Dreamer who reflects too much and, as it were, from an excess of possibilities does not get around to action. Not reflection, no—true knowledge, an insight into the horrible truth, outweighs any motive for action, both in Hamlet and in the Dionysian man. (pp. 59-60)

> *Friedrich Nietzsche, "The Birth of Tragedy or: Hellenism and Pessimism," in his* The Birth of Tragedy and The Case of Wagner, *translated by Walter Kaufmann, Vintage Books, 1967, pp. 15-146.*

EDWARD DOWDEN   (essay date 1875)

[*Dowden was an Irish critic and biographer whose* Shakspere: A Critical Study of His Mind and Art, *first published in 1875, was the leading example of the biographical criticism popular in the English-speaking world near the end of the nineteenth century. Biographical critics sought in the plays and poems a record of Shakespeare's personal development. As this approach gave way in the twentieth century to aesthetic theories with greater emphasis on the constructed, artificial nature of literary works, Dowden and other biographical critics came to be considered limited. Dowden considers such tragic, though fascinating, characters as Hamlet to be creative embodiments of the dark side of Shakespeare's own personality. Drawing from the theories of August Wilhelm Schlegel (1808) and Samuel Taylor Coleridge (1811) regarding Hamlet's intellectualism, Dowden focuses in addition on the character's "sensitive heart" and emotional depth. Dowden influenced later critics with his perception of the play's essential mystery, its "baffling, vital obscurity," which, he believes, indicates the full range of Shakespeare's mature genius. For an earlier biographical view, see Henry Hallam (1837).*]

When *Hamlet* was written, Shakspere had passed through his years of apprenticeship and become a master-dramatist. In point of style the play stands midway between his early and his latest works. The studious superintendence of the poet over the development of his thought and imaginings, very apparent in Shakspere's early writings, now conceals itself; but the action of imagination and thought has not yet become embarrassing in its swiftness and multiplicity of direction. Rapid dialogue

in verse, admirable for its combination of verisimilitude with artistic metrical effects, occurs in the scene in which Hamlet questions his friends respecting the appearance of the ghost (act i., sc. 2); the soliloquies of Hamlet are excellent examples of the slow, dwelling verse which Shakspere appropriates to the utterance of thought in solitude; and nowhere did Shakspere write a nobler piece of prose than the speech in which Hamlet describes to Rosencrantz and Guildenstern his melancholy. But such particulars as these do not constitute the chief evidence which proves that the poet had now attained maturity. The mystery, the baffling, vital obscurity of the play, and, in particular, of the character of its chief person, make it evident that Shakspere had left far behind him that early stage of development when an artist obtrudes his intentions, or, distrusting his own ability to keep sight of one uniform design, deliberately and with effort holds that design persistently before him. . . . Hamlet might so easily have been manufactured into an enigma or a puzzle; and then the puzzle, if sufficient pains were bestowed, could be completely taken to pieces and explained. But Shakspere created it a mystery, and therefore it is forever suggestive; forever suggestive, and never wholly explicable.

It must not be supposed, then, that any *idea,* any magic phrase, will solve the difficulties presented by the play, or suddenly illuminate everything in it which is obscure. The obscurity itself is a vital part of the work of art which deals not with a problem, but with a life; and in that life, the history of a soul which moved through shadowy borderlands between the night and day, there is much (as in many a life that is real) to elude and baffle inquiry. (pp. 111-12)

We may at once set aside as misdirected a certain class of *Hamlet* interpretations—those which would transform this tragedy of an individual life into a dramatic study of some general social phenomenon, or of some period in the history of civilization. . . . We must not allow any theory, however ingenious, to divert our attention from fixing itself on this fact, that Hamlet is the central point of the play of *Hamlet.* It is not the general cataclysm in which a decayed order of things is swept away to give place to new rough material; it is not the downfall of the Danish monarchy and of a corrupt society, together with the accession of a new dynasty and of a hardier civilization, that chiefly interested Shakspere. The vital heart of the tragedy of *Hamlet* cannot be an idea; neither can it be a fragment of political philosophy. Out of Shakspere's profound sympathy with an individual soul and a personal life, the wonderful creation came into being. (p. 113)

Shakspere, who felt so truly the significance of external nature as the environing medium of human passion, understood also that no man is independent of the social and moral conditions under which he lives and acts. Goethe, in the celebrated criticism upon this play contained in his "Wilhelm Meister" [see excerpt above, 1795], has only offered a half-interpretation of its difficulties; and subsequent criticism, under the influence of Goethe, has exhibited a tendency too exclusively subjective. "To me," wrote Goethe, "it is clear that Shakspere meant . . . to represent the effects of a great action laid upon a soul unfit for the performance of it. In this view the whole piece seems to be composed. . . ." (pp. 113-14)

This is one half of the truth; but only one half. In several of the tragedies of Shakspere, the tragic disturbance of character and life is caused by the subjection of the chief person of the drama to some dominant passion, essentially antipathetic to his nature, though proceeding from some inherent weakness or imperfection—a passion from which the victim cannot deliver himself, and which finally works out his destruction. . . . We may reasonably conjecture that the Hamlet of the old play— a play at least as old as that group of bloody tragedies inspired by the earlier works of Marlowe—was actually what Shakspere's Hamlet, with a bitter pleasure in misrepresenting his own nature, describes himself as being, "very proud, revengeful, ambitious." . . . But Shakespere, in accordance with his dramatic method, and his interest as artist in complex rather than simple phenomena of human passion and experience, when recreating the character of the Danish Prince, fashions him as a man to whom persistent action, and in an especial degree the duty of deliberate revenge, is peculiarly antipathetic. Under the pitiless burden imposed upon him, Hamlet trembles, totters, falls. Thus far Goethe is right.

But the tragic *nodus* in Shakspere's first tragedy—*Romeo and Juliet*—was not wholly of a subjective character. The two lovers are in harmony with one another, and with the purest and highest impulses of their own hearts. . . . The world fought against Romeo and Juliet, and they fell in the unequal strife. Now, Goethe failed to observe, or did not observe sufficiently, that this is also the case with Hamlet:

> The time is out of joint: O cursed spite,
> That ever I was born to set it right!
>
> [I. v. 188-89]

Hamlet is called upon to assert moral order in a world of moral confusion and obscurity. He has not an open plain or a hillside on which to fight his battle, but a place dangerous and misleading, with dim and winding ways. He is made for honesty, and he is compelled to use the weapons of his adversaries, compelled to practise a shifting and subtle stratagem; thus he comes to waste himself in ingenuity and crafty device. . . . His idealism, at thirty years of age, almost takes the form of pessimism; his life and his heart become sterile; he loses the energy which sound and joyous feeling supplies; and in the wide-spreading waste of corruption which lies around him, he is tempted to understand and detest things rather than accomplish some limited practical service. (pp. 114-16)

If Goethe's study of the play, admirable as it was, misled criticism in one way by directing attention too exclusively upon the inner nature of Hamlet, the studies by Schlegel and by Coleridge tended to mislead criticism in another by attaching an exaggerated importance to one element of Hamlet's character. "The whole," wrote Schlegel, "is intended to show that a calculating consideration, which exhausts all the relations and possible consequences of a deed, must cripple the power of acting." It is true that Hamlet's power of acting was crippled by his habit of "thinking too precisely on the event"; and it is true, as Coleridge said, that in Hamlet we see "a great, an almost enormous intellectual activity, and a proportionate aversion to real action consequent upon it." But Hamlet is not merely or chiefly intellectual; the emotional side of his character is quite as important as the intellectual; his malady is as deep-seated in his sensibilities and in his heart as it is in the brain. If all his feelings translate themselves into thoughts, it is no less true that all his thoughts are impregnated with feeling. To represent Hamlet as a man of preponderating power of reflection, and to disregard his craving, sensitive heart is to make the whole play incoherent and unintelligible.

It is Hamlet's intellect, however, together with his deep and abiding sense of the moral qualities of things, which distinguishes him, upon the glance of a moment, from the hero of Shakspere's first tragedy, Romeo. If Romeo fail[s] to retain a

sense of fact and of the real world because the fact, as it were, melts away and disappears in a solvent of delicious emotion, Hamlet equally loses a sense of fact because with him each object and event transforms and expands itself into an idea. (pp. 116-17)

This long course of thinking, apart from action, has destroyed Hamlet's very capacity for belief, since in belief there exists a certain element contributed by the will. Hamlet cannot adjust the infinite part of him to the finite; the one invades the other and infects it; or, rather, the finite dislimns and dissolves, and leaves him only in presence of the idea. He cannot make real to himself the actual world, even while he supposes himself a materialist; he cannot steadily keep alive within himself a sense of the importance of any positive, limited thing—a deed, for example. Things in their actual, phenomenal aspect flit before him as transitory, accidental, and unreal. And the absolute truth of things is so hard to attain, and only, if at all, is to be attained in the *mind*. Accordingly, Hamlet can lay hold of nothing with calm, resolved energy; he cannot even retain a thought in indefeasible possession. Thus all through the play he wavers between materialism and spiritualism, between belief in immortality and disbelief, between reliance upon providence and a bowing under fate. (pp. 117-18)

Does Hamlet finally attain deliverance from his disease of will? Shakspere has left the answer to that question doubtful. Probably if anything could supply the link which was wanting between the purpose and the deed, it was the achievement of some supreme action. The last moments of Hamlet's life are well spent, and, for energy and foresight, are the noblest moments of his existence. He snatches the poisoned bowl from Horatio, and saves his friend; he gives his dying voice for Fortinbras, and saves his country. The rest is silence:

> Had I but time (as this fell sergeant, death,
> Is strict in his arrest), O, I could tell you.
>
> [V. ii. 336-37]

But he has not told. Let us not too readily assume that we "know the stops" of Hamlet, that we can "pluck out the heart of his mystery."

One thing, however, we *do* know—that the man who wrote the play of *Hamlet* had obtained a thorough comprehension of Hamlet's malady. And, assured, as we are by abundant evidence, that Shakspere transformed with energetic will his knowledge into fact, we may be confident that when *Hamlet* was written Shakspere had gained a further stage in his culture of self-control, and that he had become not only adult as an author, but had entered upon the full maturity of his manhood. (pp. 141-42)

> *Edward Dowden, "The First and the Second Tragedy: 'Romeo and Juliet'; 'Hamlet',"* in his Shakspere: A Critical Study of His Mind and Art, *third edition, Harper & Brothers Publishers, 1881, pp. 84-143.*

GEORGE BRANDES (essay date 1895-96)

[*Brandes was a scholar and the most influential literary critic of late nineteenth-century Denmark whose work on Shakespeare, originally published in 1895-96, was translated and widely read in his day. A writer with a broad knowledge of literature, Brandes placed Shakespeare in a European context, comparing him with other important dramatists. For Brandes, Hamlet is "the first typical modern character," an emotionally and intellectually complex figure who suffers the conflict between the ideal and actual worlds. Brandes asserts that Shakespeare is misunderstood if Hamlet is interpreted merely as a character who reflects the fin-de-siècle malady of "a mind diseased by morbid reflection," and stresses that although Hamlet hesitates before his final, decisive act, he "is not, in the main, incapable of action." For additional commentary on Hamlet's delay, see William Richardson (1774), Samuel Taylor Coleridge (1811), Hermann Ulrici (1839), Friedrich Nietzsche (1872), and Sigmund Freud (1900).]*

Though there are in *Hamlet* more direct utterances of the poet's inmost spiritual life than in any of his earlier works, he has none the less succeeded in thoroughly disengaging his hero's figure, and making it an independent entity. What he gave him of his own nature was its unfathomable depth; for the rest, he retained the situation and the circumstances much as he found them in his authorities. It cannot be denied that he thus involved himself in difficulties which he by no means entirely overcame. The old legend, with its harsh outlines, its mediaeval order of ideas, its heathen groundwork under a varnish of dogmatic Catholicism, its assumption of vengeance as the unquestionable right, or rather duty, of the individual, did not very readily harmonise with the rich life of thoughts, dreams, and feelings which Shakespeare imparted to his hero. . . . Now and then, in the course of the drama, a rift seems to open between the shell of the action and its kernel.

But Shakespeare, with his consummate instinct, managed to find an advantage precisely in this discrepancy, and to turn it to account. His Hamlet believes in the ghost and—doubts. He accepts the summons to the deed of vengeance and—delays. Much of the originality of the figure, and of the drama as a whole, springs almost inevitably from this discrepancy between the mediaeval character of the fable and its Renaissance hero, who is so deep and many-sided that he has almost a modern air. (p. 366)

[Goethe's] interpretation is brilliant and thoughtful, but not entirely just [see excerpt above, 1795]. One can trace in it the spirit of the period of humanity, transforming in its own image a figure belonging to the Renaissance. Hamlet cannot really be called, without qualification, "lovely, pure, noble and most moral"—he who says to Ophelia the penetratingly true, unforgettable words, "I am myself indifferent honest; but yet I could accuse me of such things, that it were better my mother had not borne me." The light of such a saying as this takes the colour out of Goethe's adjectives. It is true that Hamlet goes on to ascribe to himself evil qualities of which he is quite innocent; but he was doubtless sincere in the general tenor of his speech, to which all men of the better sort will subscribe. Hamlet is no model of virtue. He is not simply pure, noble, moral, &c., but is, or becomes, other things as well—wild, bitter, harsh, now tender, now coarse, wrought up to the verge of madness, callous, cruel. No doubt he is too weak for his task, or rather wholly unsuited to it; but he is by no means devoid of physical strength or power of action. He is no child of the period of humanity, moral and pure, but a child of the Renaissance, with its impulsive energy, its irrepressible fulness of life and its undaunted habit of looking death in the eyes.

Shakespeare at first conceived Hamlet as a youth. In the First Quarto he is quite young, probably nineteen. It accords with this age that he should be a student at Wittenberg; young men at that time began and ended their university course much earlier than in our days. It accords with this age that his mother should address him as "boy" ("How now, boy!" iii. 4—a phrase which is deleted in the next edition), and that the word "young" should be continually prefixed to his name, not merely to distinguish him from his father. The King, too, in the early

edition (not in that of 1604) currently addresses him as "son Hamlet"; and finally his mother is still young enough to arouse—or at least to enable Claudius plausibly to pretend—the passion which has such terrible results. Hamlet's speech to his mother—

> At your age
> The hey-day of the blood is tame, it's humble,
> And waits upon the judgment,   [III. iv. 68-70]

does not occur in the 1603 edition. The decisive proof, however, of the fact that Hamlet at first appeared in Shakespeare's eyes much younger (eleven years, to be precise) than he afterwards made him, is to be found in the graveyard scene (V. I). In the older edition, the First Gravedigger says that the skull of the jester Yorick has lain a dozen years in the earth; in the edition of 1604 this is changed to twenty-three years. (pp. 367-68)

The process of thought in Shakespeare's mind is evident. At first it seemed to him as if the circumstances of the case demanded that Hamlet should be a youth; for thus the overwhelming effect produced upon him by his mother's prompt forgetfulness of his father and hasty marriage seemed most intelligible. He had been living far from the great world, in quiet Wittenberg, never doubting that life was in fact as harmonious as it is apt to appear in the eyes of a young prince. . . . From the moment he loses his father, and is forced to change his opinion of his mother, this serene view of life is darkened. If his mother has been able to forget his father and marry this man, what is woman worth? and what is life worth? At the very outset, then, when he has not even heard of his father's ghost, much less seen or held converse with it, sheer despair speaks in his monologue:

> O that this too too solid flesh would melt,
> Thaw, and resolve itself into a dew;
> Or that the Everlasting had not fix'd
> His canon 'gainst self-slaughter!   [I. ii. 129-32]

Hence, also, his naïve surprise that one may smile and smile and yet be a villain. He regards what has happened as a typical occurrence, a specimen of what the world really is. (pp. 368-69)

Hence arise his thoughts of suicide. The finer a young man's character, the stronger is his desire, on entering life, to see his ideals consummated in persons and circumstances. Hamlet suddenly realises that everything is entirely different from what he had imagined, and feels as if he must die because he cannot set it right.

He finds it very difficult to believe that the world is so bad; therefore he is always seeking for new proofs of it; therefore, for instance, he plans the performance of the play. His joy whenever he tears the mask from baseness is simply the joy of realisation, with deep sorrow in the background—abstract satisfaction produced by the feeling that at last he understands the worthlessness of the world. His divination was just—events confirm it. There is no cold-hearted pessimism here. Hamlet's fire is never quenched; his wound never heals. Laertes' poisoned blade gives the quietus to a still tortured soul.

All this, though we can quite well imagine it of a man of thirty, is more natural, more what we should expect, in one of nineteen. But as Shakespeare worked on at his drama, and came to deposit in Hamlet's mind, as in a treasury, more and more of his own life-wisdom, of his own experience, and of his own keen and virile wit, he saw that early youth was too slight a framework to support this intellectual weight, and gave Hamlet the age of ripening manhood.

Hamlet's faith and trust in humankind are shattered before the Ghost appears to him. From the moment when his father's spirit communicates to him a far more appalling insight into the facts of the situation, his whole inner man is in wild revolt.

This is the cause of the leave-taking, the silent leave-taking, from Ophelia, whom in letters he had called his soul's idol. His ideal of womanhood no longer exists. Ophelia now belongs to those "trivial fond records" which the sense of his great mission impels him to efface from the tablets of his memory. There is no room in his soul for his task and for her, passive and obedient to her father as she is. (pp. 369-70)

He intends to proceed at once to action, but too many thoughts crowd in upon him. He broods over that horror which the Ghost has revealed to him, and over the world in which such a thing could happen; he doubts whether the apparition was really his father, or perhaps a deceptive, malignant spirit; and, lastly, he has doubts of himself, of his ability to upraise and restore what has been overthrown, of his fitness for the vocation of avenger and judge. . . .

During the course of the play it is sufficiently proved that he is not, in the main, incapable of action. He does not hesitate to stab the eavesdropper behind the arras; without wavering and without pity he sends Rosencrantz and Guildenstern to certain death; he boards a hostile ship; and, never having lost sight of his purpose, he takes vengeance before he dies. But it is clear, none the less, that he has a great inward obstacle to overcome before he proceeds to the decisive act. Reflection hinders him; his "resolution is sicklied o'er with the pale cast of thought," as he says in his soliloquy.

He has become to the popular mind the great type of the procrastinator and dreamer; and far on into this century, hundreds of individuals, and even whole races, have seen themselves reflected in him as in a mirror. (p. 370)

Shakespeare is misunderstood when Hamlet is taken for that entirely modern product—a mind diseased by morbid reflection, without capacity for action. It is nothing less than a freak of ironic fate that *he* should have become a sort of symbol of reflective sloth, this man who has gunpowder in every nerve, and all the dynamite of genius in his nature. (p. 371)

It is natural that he should feel ashamed at the sight of Fortinbras marching off to the sound of drum and trumpet at the head of his forces—he, who has not carried out, or even laid, any plan; who, after having by means of the play satisfied himself of the King's guilt, and at the same time betrayed his own state of mind, is now writhing under the consciousness of impotence. But the sole cause of this impotence is the paralysing grasp laid on all his faculties by his new realisation of what life is, and the broodings born of this realisation. Even his mission of vengeance sinks into the background of his mind. Everything is at strife within him—his duty to his father, his duty to his mother, reverence, horror of crime, hatred, pity, fear of action, and fear of inaction. He feels, even if he does not expressly say so, how little is gained by getting rid of a single noxious animal. He himself is already so much more than what he was at first—the youth chosen to execute a vendetta. He has become the great sufferer, who jeers and mocks, and rebukes the world that racks him. He is the cry of humanity horror-struck at its own visage.

There is no "general meaning" on the surface of *Hamlet*. Lucidity was not the ideal Shakespeare had before him while he was producing this tragedy, as it had been when he was composing *Richard III*. Here there are plenty of riddles and self-contradictions; but not a little of the attraction of the play depends on this very obscurity.

We all know that kind of well-written book which is blameless in form, obvious in intention, and in which the characters stand out sharply defined. We read it with pleasure; but when we have read it, we are done with it. . . . [There are other books whose fundamental idea is capable of many interpretations, and affords matter for much dispute, but whose significance lies less in what they say to us than in what they lead us to imagine, to divine. They have the peculiar faculty of setting thoughts and feelings in motion; more thoughts than they themselves contain, and perhaps of a quite different character. *Hamlet* is such a book. As a piece of psychological development, it lacks the lucidity of classical art; the hero's soul has all the untranspicuousness and complexity of a real soul; but one generation after another has thrown its imagination into the problem, and has deposited in Hamlet's soul the sum of its experience.

To Hamlet life is half reality, half a dream. He sometimes resembles a somnambulist, though he is often as wakeful as a spy. He has so much presence of mind that he is never at a loss for the aptest retort, and, along with it, such absence of mind that he lets go his fixed determination in order to follow up some train of thought or thread some dream-labyrinth. He appals, amuses, captivates, perplexes, disquiets us. Few characters in fiction have so disquieted the world. Although he is incessantly talking, he is solitary by nature. He typifies, indeed, that solitude of soul which cannot impart itself. (pp. 371-72)

There is in him no less indignation than melancholy; in fact, his melancholy is a result of his indignation. Sufferers and thinkers have found in him a brother. Hence the extraordinary popularity of the character, in spite of its being the reverse of obvious.

Audiences and readers feel with Hamlet and understand him; for all the better-disposed among us make the discovery, when we go forth into life as grown-up men and women, that it is not what we had imagined it to be, but a thousandfold more terrible. Something is rotten in the state of Denmark. Denmark is a prison, and the world is full of such dungeons. A spectral voice says to us: "Horrible things have happened; horrible things are happening every day. Be it your task to repair the evil, to rearrange the course of things. The world is out of joint; it is for you to set it right." But our arms fall powerless by our sides. Evil is too strong, too cunning for us.

In *Hamlet*, the first philosophical drama of the modern era, we meet for the first time the typical modern character, with its intense feeling of the strife between the ideal and the actual world, with its keen sense of the chasm between power and aspiration, and with that complexity of nature which shows itself in wit without mirth, cruelty combined with sensitiveness, frenzied impatience at war with inveterate procrastination. (pp. 372-73)

George Brandes, "The Psychology of Hamlet," *translated by William Archer with Mary Morison, in* *his* William Shakespeare, *Heinemann, 1920, pp. 366-73.*

Act III. Scene iv. Hamlet, Gertrude, the ghost. Frontispiece to Rowe edition (1709). By permission of the Folger Shakespeare Library.

SIGMUND FREUD (essay date 1900)

[The influence of Freud's theory of psychoanalysis profoundly affected modern life and art, inspiring psychoanalytical studies in diverse fields. Freud analyzed Hamlet *and other Shakespeare plays for evidence supporting his theories about the personality. In the following excerpt, first published as* Die traumdeutung *in 1900, he identifies the Oedipus complex revealed in Hamlet. Freud theorizes that Hamlet is unable to act because he unconsciously identifies with Claudius, who, by eliminating Hamlet's father and taking his father's place with his mother, has realized Hamlet's repressed childhood wishes. Subsequently, according to Freud, Hamlet's desire for revenge is replaced "by scruples of conscience, which remind him that he himself is literally no better than the sinner whom he is to punish." Ernest Jones expands upon this theme (1949). For additional remarks on Hamlet's delay, see William Richardson (1774), Samuel Taylor Coleridge (1811), Hermann Ulrici (1839), Karl Werder (1859-60), Friedrich Nietzsche (1872), A.J.A. Waldock (1931), H. B. Charlton (1942), and D. G. James (1951).]*

Another of the great creations of tragic poetry, Shakespeare's *Hamlet,* has its roots in the same soil as *Oedipus Rex.* But the changed treatment of the same material reveals the whole difference in the mental life of these two widely separated epochs of civilization: the secular advance of repression in the emotional life of mankind. In the *Oedipus* the child's wishful phan-

tasy that underlies it is brought into the open and realized as it would be in a dream. In *Hamlet* it remains repressed; and—just as in the case of a neurosis—we only learn of its existence from its inhibiting consequences. Strangely enough, the overwhelming effect produced by the more modern tragedy has turned out to be compatible with the fact that people have remained completely in the dark as to the hero's character. The play is built up on Hamlet's hesitations over fulfilling the task of revenge that is assigned to him; but its text offers no reasons or motives for these hesitations and an immense variety of attempts at interpreting them have failed to produce a result. According to the view which was originated by Goethe [see excerpt above, 1795] and is still the prevailing one to-day, Hamlet represents the type of man whose power of direct action is paralysed by an excessive development of his intellect. (He is 'sicklied o'er with the pale cast of thought'.) According to another view, the dramatist has tried to portray a pathologically irresolute character which might be classed as neurasthenic. The plot of the drama shows us, however, that Hamlet is far from being represented as a person incapable of taking any action. We see him doing so on two occasions: first in a sudden outburst of temper, when he runs his sword through the eavesdropper behind the arras, and secondly in a premeditated and even crafty fashion, when, with all the callousness of a Renaissance prince, he sends the two courtiers to the death that had been planned for himself. What is it, then, that inhibits him in fulfilling the task set him by his father's ghost? The answer, once again, is that it is the peculiar nature of the task. Hamlet is able to do anything—except take vengeance on the man who did away with his father and took that father's place with his mother, the man who shows him the repressed wishes of his own childhood realized. Thus the loathing which should drive him on to revenge is replaced in him by self-reproaches, by scruples of conscience, which remind him that he himself is literally no better than the sinner whom he is to punish. Here I have translated into conscious terms what was bound to remain unconscious in Hamlet's mind; and if anyone is inclined to call him a hysteric, I can only accept the fact as one that is implied by my interpretation. The distaste for sexuality expressed by Hamlet in his conversation with Ophelia fits in very well with this: the same distaste which was destined to take possession of the poet's mind more and more during the years that followed, and which reached its extreme expression in *Timon of Athens.* For it can of course only be the poet's own mind which confronts us in Hamlet. I observe in a book on Shakespeare by George Brandes [see excerpt above, 1895-96] a statement that *Hamlet* was written immediately after the death of Shakespeare's father (in 1601), that is, under the immediate impact of his bereavement and, as we may well assume, while his childhood feelings about his father had been freshly revived. It is known, too, that Shakespeare's own son who died at an early age bore the name of 'Hamnet', which is identical with 'Hamlet'. Just as *Hamlet* deals with the relation of a son to his parents, so *Macbeth* (written at approximately the same period) is concerned with the subject of childlessness. But just as all neurotic symptoms, and, for that matter, dreams, are capable of being 'over-interpreted' and indeed need to be, if they are to be fully understood, so all genuinely creative writings are the product of more than a single motive and more than a single impulse in the poet's mind, and are open to more than a single interpretation. In what I have written I have only attempted to interpret the deepest layer of impulses in the mind of the creative writer. (pp. 264-66)

Sigmund Freud, "The Material and Sources of Dreams," in his The Interpretation of Dreams, *edited* *and translated by James Strachey, Basic Books, Inc., Publishers, 1955, pp. 163-276.**

A. C. BRADLEY (essay date 1905)

[*Bradley is a major Shakespearean critic whose work culminated the nineteenth-century method of character analysis initiated in the Romantic era. He is best known for his* Shakespearean Tragedy, *a close analysis of* Hamlet, Othello, King Lear, *and* Macbeth. *Bradley concentrated on Shakespeare as a dramatist, and particularly on his characters, excluding not only the biographical concerns so prominent in the works of his immediate predecessors but also questions of poetic structure, symbolism, and thematics, which became prominent in later criticism. He thus may be seen as a pivotal figure in the transition in Shakespearean studies from the nineteenth to the twentieth century. He has been a major target for critics reacting against Romantic criticism, but he has continued to be widely read to the present day. The influence of nineteenth-century criticism is clear in Bradley's emphasis on the character of Hamlet. He disputes several of the Romantic commentators, including Johann Wolfgang von Goethe (1795), August Wilhelm Schlegel (1808), and Samuel Taylor Coleridge (1811), on the theory of Hamlet's delay. Bradley asserts that it is the melancholy brought about by his mother's remarriage that renders Hamlet unable to act.*]

Suppose you were to describe the plot of *Hamlet* to a person quite ignorant of the play, and suppose you were careful to tell your hearer nothing about Hamlet's character, what impression would your sketch make on him? Would he not exclaim: 'What a sensational story! Why, here are some eight violent deaths, not to speak of adultery, a ghost, a mad woman, and a fight in a grave! If I did not know that the play was Shakespeare's, I should have thought it must have been one of those early tragedies of blood and horror from which he is said to have redeemed the stage'? (p. 89)

[The] whole story turns upon the peculiar character of the hero. For without this character the story would appear sensational and horrible; and yet the actual *Hamlet* is very far from being so, and even has a less terrible effect than *Othello, King Lear* or *Macbeth*. And again, if we had no knowledge of this character, the story would hardly be intelligible; it would at any rate at once suggest that wondering question about the conduct of the hero; while the story of any of the other three tragedies would sound plain enough and would raise no such question. . . . [The] tragedy of *Hamlet* with Hamlet left out has become the symbol of extreme absurdity; while the character itself has probably exerted a greater fascination, and certainly has been the subject of more discussion, than any other in the whole literature of the world. (pp. 89-90)

Hamlet seems from the first to have been a favourite play; but until late in the eighteenth century, I believe, scarcely a critic showed that he perceived anything specially interesting in the character. Hanmer, in 1736, to be sure, remarks that 'there appears no reason at all in nature why this young prince did not put the usurper to death as soon as possible' [see excerpt above]; but it does not even cross his mind that this apparent 'absurdity' is odd and might possibly be due to some design on the part of the poet. . . . How significant is the fact (if it be the fact) that it was only when the slowly rising sun of Romance began to flush the sky that the wonder, beauty and pathos of this most marvellous of Shakespeare's creations began to be visible! We do not know that they were perceived even in his own day, and perhaps those are not wholly wrong

who declare that this creation, so far from being a characteristic product of the time, was a vision of

the prophetic soul
Of the wide world dreaming on things to come.
[Sonnet 107]

But the dramatic splendour of the whole tragedy is another matter, and must have been manifest not only in Shakespeare's day but even in Hanmer's.

It is indeed so obvious that I pass it by, and proceed at once to the central question of Hamlet's character. And I believe time will be saved, and a good deal of positive interpretation may be introduced, if, without examining in detail any one theory, we first distinguish classes or types of theory which appear to be in various ways and degrees insufficient or mistaken. (pp. 91-2)

But, before we come to our types of theory, it is necessary to touch on an idea, not unfrequently met with, which would make it vain labour to discuss or propose any theory at all. It is sometimes said that Hamlet's character is not only intricate but unintelligible. . . . What is meant is that Shakespeare *intended* him to be so, because he himself was feeling strongly, and wished his audience to feel strongly, what a mystery life is, and how impossible it is for us to understand it. Now here, surely, we have mere confusion of mind. The mysteriousness of life is one thing, the psychological unintelligibility of a dramatic character is quite another; and the second does not show the first, it shows only the incapacity or folly of the dramatist. (p. 93)

(1) To come, then, to our typical views, we may lay it down, first, that no theory will hold water which finds the cause of Hamlet's delay merely, or mainly, or even to any considerable extent, in external difficulties. Nothing is easier than to spin a plausible theory of this kind. What, it may be asked, was Hamlet to do when the Ghost had left him with its commission of vengeance? The King was surrounded not merely by courtiers but by a Swiss body-guard: how was Hamlet to get at him? (p. 94)

A theory like this sounds very plausible—so long as you do not remember the text. But no unsophisticated mind, fresh from the reading of *Hamlet*, will accept it; and, as soon as we begin to probe it, fatal objections arise in such numbers that I choose but a few, and indeed I think the first of them is enough.

(a) From beginning to end of the play, Hamlet never makes the slightest reference to any external difficulty. How is it possible to explain this fact in conformity with the theory? For what conceivable reason should Shakespeare conceal from us so carefully the key to the problem?

(b) Not only does Hamlet fail to allude to such difficulties, but he always assumes that he *can* obey the Ghost, and he once asserts this in so many words ('Sith I have cause and will and strength and means To do't,' [IV. iv. 45]).

(c) Again, why does Shakespeare exhibit Laertes quite easily raising the people against the King? Why but to show how much more easily Hamlet, whom the people loved, could have done the same thing, if that was the plan he preferred?

(d) Again, Hamlet did *not* plan the play-scene in the hope that the King would betray his guilt to the court. He planned it, according to his own account, in order to convince *himself* by the King's agitation that the Ghost had spoken the truth. (pp. 95-6) *(e)* Again, Hamlet never once talks, or shows a sign of thinking, of the plan of bringing the King to public justice; he always talks of using his 'sword' or his 'arm.' And this is so just as much after he has returned to Denmark with the commission in his pocket as it was before this event. When he has told Horatio the story of the voyage, he does not say, 'Now I can convict him': he says, 'Now am I not justified in using this arm?' (p. 96)

(2) Assuming, now, that Hamlet's main difficulty—almost the whole of his difficulty—was internal, I pass to views which, acknowledging this, are still unsatisfactory because they isolate one element in his character and situation and treat it as the whole.

According to the first of these typical views, Hamlet was restrained by conscience or a moral scruple; he could not satisfy himself that it was right to avenge his father.

This idea, like the first, can easily be made to look very plausible if we vaguely imagine the circumstances without attending to the text. But attention to the text is fatal to it. For, on the one hand, scarcely anything can be produced in support of it, and, on the other hand, a great deal can be produced in its disproof. To take the latter point first, Hamlet, it is impossible to deny, habitually assumes, without any questioning, that he *ought* to avenge his father. Even when he doubts, or thinks that he doubts, the honesty of the Ghost, he expresses no doubt as to what his duty will be if the Ghost turns out honest: 'If he but blench I know my course.' (p. 97)

Perhaps, however, it may be answered: 'Your explanation of this passage may be correct, and the facts you have mentioned do seem to be fatal to the theory of conscience in its usual form. But there is another and subtler theory of conscience. According to it, Hamlet, so far as his explicit consciousness went, was sure that he ought to obey the Ghost; but in the depths of his nature, and unknown to himself, there was a moral repulsion to the deed. The conventional moral ideas of his time, which he shared with the Ghost, told him plainly that he ought to avenge his father; but a deeper conscience in him, which was in advance of his time, contended with these explicit conventional ideas.' (p. 99)

Now I at once admit not only that this view is much more attractive and more truly tragic than the ordinary conscience theory, but that it has more verisimilitude. But I feel no doubt that it does not answer to Shakespeare's meaning, and I will simply mention, out of many objections to it, three which seem to be fatal. *(a)* If it answers to Shakespeare's meaning, why in the world did he conceal that meaning until the last Act? The facts adduced above seem to show beyond question that, on the hypothesis, he did so. That he did so is surely next door to incredible. In any case, it certainly requires an explanation, and certainly has not received one. *(b)* Let us test the theory by reference to a single important passage, that where Hamlet finds the King at prayer and spares him. The reason Hamlet gives himself for sparing the King is that, if he kills now, he will send him to heaven, whereas he desires to send him to hell. Now, this reason may be an unconscious excuse, but is it believable that, if the real reason had been the stirrings of his deeper conscience, *that* could have masked itself in the form of a desire to send his enemy's soul to hell? Is not the idea quite ludicrous? *(c)* The theory requires us to suppose that, when the Ghost enjoins Hamlet to avenge the murder of his father, it is laying on him a duty which *we* are to understand to be no duty but the very reverse. And is not that supposition

wholly contrary to the natural impression which we all receive in reading the play? (p. 100)

(3) We come next to what may be called the sentimental view of Hamlet, a view common both among his worshippers and among his defamers. Its germ may perhaps be found in an unfortunate phrase of Goethe's (who of course is not responsible for the whole view): 'a lovely, pure and most moral nature, *without the strength of nerve which forms a hero,* sinks beneath a burden which it cannot bear and must not cast away'. When this idea is isolated, developed and popularised, we get the picture of a graceful youth, sweet and sensitive, full of delicate sympathies and yearning aspirations, shrinking from the touch of everything gross and earthly; but frail and weak, a kind of Werther, with a face like Shelley's and a voice like Mr. Tree's. And then we ask in tender pity, how could such a man perform the terrible duty laid on him?

How, indeed! And what a foolish Ghost even to suggest such a duty! But this conception, though not without its basis in certain beautiful traits of Hamlet's nature, is utterly untrue. It is too kind to Hamlet on one side, and it is quite unjust to him on another. The 'conscience' theory at any rate leaves Hamlet a great nature which you can admire and even revere. But for the 'sentimental' Hamlet you can feel only pity not unmingled with contempt. Whatever else he is, he is no *hero*.

But consider the text. This shrinking, flower-like youth—how could he possibly have done what we *see* Hamlet do? What likeness to him is there in the Hamlet who, summoned by the Ghost, bursts from his terrified friends with the cry:

> Unhand me, gentlemen!
> By heaven, I'll make a ghost of him that lets me;
>
> [I. iv. 84-5]

the Hamlet who scarcely once speaks to the King without an insult, or to Polonius without a gibe; the Hamlet who storms at Ophelia and speaks daggers to his mother; the Hamlet who, hearing a cry behind the arras, whips out his sword in an instant and runs the eavesdropper through; the Hamlet who sends his 'school-fellows' to their death and never troubles his head about them more; the Hamlet who is the first man to board a pirate ship, and who fights with Laertes in the grave; the Hamlet of the catastrophe, an omnipotent fate, before whom all the court stands helpless, who, as the truth breaks upon him, rushes on the King, drives his foil right through his body, then seizes the poisoned cup and forces it violently between the wretched man's lips, and in the throes of death has force and fire enough to wrest the cup from Horatio's hand ('By heaven, I'll have it!') lest he should drink and die? This man, the Hamlet of the play, is a heroic, terrible figure. He would have been formidable to Othello or Macbeth. If the sentimental Hamlet had crossed him, he would have hurled him from his path with one sweep of his arm. (pp. 101-03)

(4) There remains, finally, that class of view which may be named after Schlegel and Coleridge. According to this, *Hamlet* is the tragedy of reflection. The cause of the hero's delay is irresolution; and the cause of this irresolution is excess of the reflective or speculative habit of mind. He has a general intention to obey the Ghost, but 'the native hue of resolution is sicklied o'er with the pale cast of thought.' He is 'thought-sick.' . . . Professor Dowden objects to this view, very justly, that it neglects the emotional side of Hamlet's character, 'which is quite as important as the intellectual'; but, with this supplement, he appears on the whole to adopt it [see excerpt above, 1875]. (pp. 104-05)

On the whole, the Schlegel-Coleridge theory (with or without Professor Dowden's modification and amplification) is the most widely received view of Hamlet's character. And with it we come at last into close contact with the text of the play. It not only answers, in some fundamental respects, to the general impression produced by the drama, but it can be supported by Hamlet's own words in his soliloquies—such words, for example, as those about the native hue of resolution, or those about the craven scruple of thinking too precisely on the event. It is confirmed, also, by the contrast between Hamlet on the one side and Laertes and Fortinbras on the other. . . . And, lastly, even if the view itself does not suffice, the *description* given by its adherents of Hamlet's state of mind, as we see him in the last four Acts, is, on the whole and so far as it goes, a true description. The energy of resolve is dissipated in an endless brooding on the deed required. (pp. 105-06)

Nevertheless this theory fails to satisfy. And it fails not merely in this or that detail, but as a whole. We feel that its Hamlet does not fully answer to our imaginative impression. He is not nearly so inadequate to this impression as the sentimental Hamlet, but still we feel he is inferior to Shakespeare's man and does him wrong. And when we come to examine the theory we find that it is partial and leaves much unexplained. I pass that by for the present, for we shall find, I believe, that the theory is also positively misleading, and that in a most important way. (pp. 106-07)

Hamlet's irresolution, or his aversion to real action, is, according to the theory, the *direct* result of 'an almost enormous intellectual activity' in the way of 'a calculating consideration which attempts to exhaust all the relations and possible consequences of a deed.' And this again proceeds from an original one-sidedness of nature, strengthened by habit, and, perhaps, by years of speculative inaction. The theory describes, therefore, a man in certain respects like Coleridge himself, on one side a man of genius, on the other side, the side of will, deplorably weak, always procrastinating and avoiding unpleasant duties, and often reproaching himself in vain; a man, observe, who at *any* time and in *any* circumstances would be unequal to the task assigned to Hamlet. And thus, I must maintain, it degrades Hamlet and travesties the play. For Hamlet, according to all the indications in the text, was not naturally or normally such a man, but rather, I venture to affirm, a man who at any *other* time and in any *other* circumstances than those presented would have been perfectly equal to his task; and it is, in fact, the very cruelty of his fate that the crisis of his life comes on him at the one moment when he cannot meet it, and when his highest gifts, instead of helping him, conspire to paralyse him. This aspect of the tragedy the theory quite misses; and it does so because it misconceives the cause of that irresolution which, on the whole, it truly describes. For the cause was not directly or mainly an habitual excess of reflectiveness. The direct cause was a state of mind quite abnormal and induced by special circumstances,—a state of profound melancholy. (pp. 107-08)

Let us first ask ourselves what we can gather from the play, immediately or by inference, concerning Hamlet as he was just before his father's death. And I begin by observing that the text does not bear out the idea that he was one-sidedly reflective and indisposed to action. Nobody who knew him seems to have noticed this weakness. Nobody regards him as a mere scholar who has 'never formed a resolution or executed a deed.' . . . So far as we can conjecture from what we see of him in those bad days, he must normally have been charmingly frank, cour-

teous and kindly to everyone, of whatever rank, whom he liked or respected, but by no means timid or deferential to others; indeed, one would gather that he was rather the reverse, and also that he was apt to be decided and even imperious if thwarted or interfered with. He must always have been fearless,—in the play he appears insensible to fear of any ordinary kind. And, finally, he must have been quick and impetuous in action; for it is downright impossible that the man we see rushing after the Ghost, killing Polonius, dealing with the King's commission on the ship, boarding the pirate, leaping into the grave, executing his final vengeance, could *ever* have been shrinking or slow in an emergency. Imagine Coleridge doing any of these things! (pp. 108-09)

Where then are we to look for the seeds of danger?

(1) Trying to reconstruct from the Hamlet of the play, one would not judge that his temperament was melancholy in the present sense of the word; there seems nothing to show that; but one would judge that by temperament he was inclined to nervous instability, to rapid and perhaps extreme changes of feeling and mood, and that he was disposed to be, for the time, absorbed in the feeling or mood that possessed him, whether it were joyous or depressed. This temperament the Elizabethans would have called melancholic; and Hamlet seems to be an example of it, as Lear is of a temperament mixedly choleric and sanguine. . . . [Shakespeare] gives to Hamlet a temperament which would not develop into melancholy unless under some exceptional strain, but which still involved a danger. In the play we see the danger realised, and find a melancholy quite unlike any that Shakespeare had as yet depicted, because the temperament of Hamlet is quite different.

(2) Next, we cannot be mistaken in attributing to the Hamlet of earlier days an exquisite sensibility, to which we may give the name 'moral,' if that word is taken in the wide meaning it ought to bear. This, though it suffers cruelly in later days, as we saw in criticising the sentimental view of Hamlet, never deserts him; it makes all his cynicism, grossness and hardness appear to us morbidities, and has an inexpressibly attractive and pathetic effect. He had the soul of the youthful poet as Shelley and Tennyson have described it, an unbounded delight and faith in everything good and beautiful. (pp. 109-11)

Where else in Shakespeare is there anything like Hamlet's adoration of his father? The words melt into music whenever he speaks of him. And, if there are no signs of any such feeling towards his mother, though many signs of love, it is characteristic that he evidently never entertained a suspicion of anything unworthy in her,—characteristic, and significant of his tendency to see only what is good unless he is forced to see the reverse. (p. 111)

And the negative side of his idealism, the aversion to evil, is perhaps even more developed in the hero of the tragedy than in the Hamlet of earlier days. It is intensely characteristic. Nothing, I believe, is to be found elsewhere in Shakespeare (unless in the rage of the disillusioned idealist Timon) of quite the same kind as Hamlet's disgust at his uncle's drunkenness, his loathing of his mother's sensuality, his astonishment and horror at her shallowness, his contempt for everything pretentious or false, his indifference to everything merely external. (p. 112)

Now, in Hamlet's moral sensibility there undoubtedly lay a danger. Any great shock that life might inflict on it would be felt with extreme intensity. Such a shock might even produce tragic results. And, in fact, *Hamlet* deserves the title 'tragedy of moral idealism' quite as much as the title 'tragedy of reflection.'

(3) With this temperament and this sensibility we find, lastly, in the Hamlet of earlier days, as of later, intellectual genius. It is chiefly this that makes him so different from all those about him, good and bad alike, and hardly less different from most of Shakespeare's other heroes. And this, though on the whole the most important trait in his nature, is also so obvious and so famous that I need not dwell on it at length. But against one prevalent misconception I must say a word of warning. Hamlet's intellectual power is not a specific gift, like a genius for music or mathematics or philosophy. It shows itself, fitfully, in the affairs of life as unusual quickness of perception, great agility in shifting the mental attitude, a striking rapidity and fertility in resource; so that, when his natural belief in others does not make him unwary, Hamlet easily sees through them and masters them, and no one can be much less like the typical helpless dreamer. (p. 113)

[The] Schlegel-Coleridge view (apart from its descriptive value) seems to me fatally untrue, for it implies that Hamlet's procrastination was the normal response of an over-speculative nature confronted with a difficult practical problem.

On the other hand, under conditions of a peculiar kind, Hamlet's reflectiveness certainly might prove dangerous to him, and his genius might even (to exaggerate a little) become his doom. Suppose that violent shock to his moral being of which I spoke; and suppose that under this shock, any possible action being denied to him, he began to sink into melancholy; then, no doubt, his imaginative and generalising habit of mind might extend the effects of this shock through his whole being and mental world. And if, the state of melancholy being thus deepened and fixed, a sudden demand for difficult and decisive action in a matter connected with the melancholy arose, this state might well have for one of its symptoms an endless and futile mental dissection of the required deed. And, finally, the futility of this process, and the shame of his delay, would further weaken him and enslave him to his melancholy still more. Thus the speculative habit would be *one* indirect cause of the morbid state which hindered action; and it would also reappear in a degenerate form as one of the *symptoms* of this morbid state.

Now this is what actually happens in the play. Turn to the first words Hamlet utters when he is alone; turn, that is to say, to the place where the author is likely to indicate his meaning most plainly. What do you hear?

O, that this too too solid flesh would melt,
Thaw and resolve itself into a dew!
Or that the Everlasting had not fix'd
His canon 'gainst self-slaughter! O God! God!
How weary, stale, flat and unprofitable,
Seem to me all the uses of this world!
Fie on't! ah fie! 'tis an unweeded garden,
That grows to seed; things rank and gross in nature
Possess it merely.   [I. ii. 129-37]

Here are a sickness of life, and even a longing for death, so intense that nothing stands between Hamlet and suicide except religious awe. And what has caused them? The rest of the soliloquy so thrusts the answer upon us that it might seem impossible to miss it. It was not his father's death; that doubtless brought deep grief, but mere grief for some one loved and lost does not make a noble spirit loathe the world as a place full only of things rank and gross. It was not the vague suspicion

that we know Hamlet felt. Still less was it the loss of the crown; for though the subserviency of the electors might well disgust him, there is not a reference to the subject in the soliloquy, nor any sign elsewhere that it greatly occupied his mind. It was the moral shock of the sudden ghastly disclosure of his mother's true nature, falling on him when his heart was aching with love, and his body doubtless was weakened by sorrow. And it is essential, however disagreeable, to realise the nature of this shock. It matters little here whether Hamlet's age was twenty or thirty: in either case his mother was a matron of mature years. All his life he had believed in her, we may be sure, as such a son would. He had seen her not merely devoted to his father, but hanging on him like a newly-wedded bride, hanging on him

As if increase of appetite had grown
By what it fed on.   [I. ii. 144-45]

He had seen her following his body 'like Niobe, all tears.' And then within a month—'O God! a beast would have mourned longer'—she married again, and married Hamlet's uncle, a man utterly contemptible and loathsome in his eyes; married him in what to Hamlet was incestuous wedlock; married him not for any reason of state, nor even out of old family affection, but in such a way that her son was forced to see in her action not only an astounding shallowness of feeling but an eruption of coarse sensuality, 'rank and gross,' speeding post-haste to its horrible delight. Is it possible to conceive an experience more desolating to a man such as we have seen Hamlet to be; and is its result anything but perfectly natural? It brings bewildered horror, then loathing, then despair of human nature. (pp. 116-19)

[In Hamlet's] hour of uttermost weakness, this sinking of his whole being towards annihilation, there comes on him, bursting the bounds of the natural world with a shock of astonishment and terror, the revelation of his mother's adultery and his father's murder, and, with this, the demand on him, in the name of everything dearest and most sacred, to arise and act. And for a moment, though his brain reels and totters, his soul leaps up in passion to answer this demand. But it comes too late. It does but strike home the last rivet in the melancholy which holds him bound.

The time is out of joint! O cursed spite
That ever I was born to set it right,—
                            [I. v. 188-89]

so he mutters within an hour of the moment when he vowed to give his life to the duty of revenge; and the rest of the story exhibits his vain efforts to fulfil this duty, his unconscious self-excuses and unavailing self-reproaches, and the tragic results of his delay. (p. 120)

[Hamlet's] melancholy is something very different from insanity, in anything like the usual meaning of that word. No doubt it might develop into insanity. The longing for death might become an irresistible impulse to self-destruction; the disorder of feeling and will might extend to sense and intellect; delusions might arise; and the man might become, as we say, incapable and irresponsible. But Hamlet's melancholy is some way from this condition. It is a totally different thing from the madness which he feigns; and he never, when alone or in company with Horatio alone, exhibits the signs of that madness. Nor is the dramatic use of this melancholy, again, open to the objections which would justly be made to the portrayal of an insanity which brought the hero to a tragic end. (p. 121)

Let me try to show now, briefly, how much this melancholy accounts for.

It accounts for the main fact, Hamlet's inaction. For the *immediate* cause of that is simply that his habitual feeling is one of disgust at life and everything in it, himself included,—a disgust which varies in intensity, rising at times into a longing for death, sinking often into weary apathy, but is never dispelled for more than brief intervals. Such a state of feeling is inevitably adverse to *any* kind of decided action; the body is inert, the mind indifferent or worse; its response is, 'it does not matter,' 'it is not worth while,' 'it is no good.' And the action required of Hamlet is very exceptional. . . . [This] melancholy is perfectly consistent also with that incessant dissection of the task assigned, of which the Schlegel-Coleridge theory makes so much. For those endless questions (as we may imagine them), 'Was I deceived by the Ghost? How am I to do the deed? When? Where? What will be the consequence of attempting it—success, my death, utter misunderstanding, mere mischief to the State? Can it be right to do it, or noble to kill a defenceless man? What is the good of doing it in such a world as this?'—all this, and whatever else passed in a sickening round through Hamlet's mind, was not the healthy and right deliberation of a man with such a task, but otiose thinking hardly deserving the name of thought, an unconscious weaving of pretexts for inaction, aimless tossings on a sick bed, symptoms of melancholy which only increased it by deepening self-contempt.

Again, *(a)* this state accounts for Hamlet's energy as well as for his lassitude, those quick decided actions of his being the outcome of a nature normally far from passive, now suddenly stimulated, and producing healthy impulses which work themselves out before they have time to subside. *(b)* It accounts for the evidently keen satisfaction which some of these actions give to him. He arranges the play-scene with lively interest, and exults in its success, not really because it brings him nearer to his goal, but partly because it has hurt his enemy and partly because it has demonstrated his own skill (III. ii. 286-304). . . . *(c)* It accounts for the pleasure with which he meets old acquaintances, like his 'school-fellows' or the actors. The former observed (and we can observe) in him a 'kind of joy' at first, though it is followed by 'much forcing of his disposition' as he attempts to keep this joy and his courtesy alive in spite of the misery which so soon returns upon him and the suspicion he is forced to feel. *(d)* It accounts no less for the painful features of his character as seen in the play, his almost savage irritability on the one hand, and on the other his self-absorption, his callousness, his insensibility to the fates of those whom he despises, and to the feelings even of those whom he loves. These are frequent symptoms of such melancholy, and *(e)* they sometimes alternate, as they do in Hamlet, with bursts of transitory, almost hysterical, and quite fruitless emotion. (pp. 122-24)

Finally, Hamlet's melancholy accounts for two things which seem to be explained by nothing else. The first of these is his apathy or 'lethargy.' We are bound to consider the evidence which the text supplies of this, though it is usual to ignore it. When Hamlet mentions, as one possible cause of his inaction, his 'thinking too precisely on the event,' he mentions another, 'bestial oblivion'; and the thing against which he inveighs in the greater part of that soliloquy (IV. iv.) is not the excess or the misuse of reason (which for him here and always is god-like), but this *bestial* oblivion or '*dullness*,' this 'letting all *sleep*,' this allowing of heaven-sent reason to 'fust unused'. . . . (p. 125)

The second trait which is fully explained only by Hamlet's melancholy is his own inability to understand why he delays. This emerges in a marked degree when an occasion like the player's emotion or the sight of Fortinbras's army stings Hamlet into shame at his inaction. . . . A man irresolute merely because he was considering a proposed action too minutely would not feel this bewilderment. A man might feel it whose conscience secretly condemned the act which his explicit consciousness approved; but we have seen that there is no sufficient evidence to justify us in conceiving Hamlet thus. These are the questions of a man stimulated for the moment to shake off the weight of his melancholy, and, because for the moment he is free from it, unable to understand the paralysing pressure which it exerts at other times. (pp. 126-27)

[Having] once given its due weight to the fact of Hamlet's melancholy, we may freely admit, or rather may be anxious to insist, that this pathological condition would excite but little, if any, tragic interest if it were not the condition of a nature distinguished by that speculative genius on which the Schlegel-Coleridge type of theory lays stress. Such theories misinterpret the connection between that genius and Hamlet's failure, but still it is this connection which gives to his story its peculiar fascination and makes it appear (if the phrase may be allowed) as the symbol of a tragic mystery inherent in human nature. Wherever this mystery touches us, wherever we are forced to feel the wonder and awe of man's godlike 'apprehension' and his 'thoughts that wander through eternity,' and at the same time are forced to see him powerless in his petty sphere of action, and powerless (it would appear) from the very divinity of his thought, we remember Hamlet. And this is the reason why, in the great ideal movement which began towards the close of the eighteenth century, this tragedy acquired a position unique among Shakespeare's dramas, and shared only by Goethe's *Faust*. It was not that *Hamlet* is Shakespeare's greatest tragedy or most perfect work of art; it was that *Hamlet* most brings home to us at once the sense of the soul's infinity, and the sense of the doom which not only circumscribes that infinity but appears to be its offspring. (pp. 127-28)

The emotion shown by the player in reciting the speech which tells of Hecuba's grief for her slaughtered husband awakes into burning life the slumbering sense of duty and shame. He must act. With the extreme rapidity which always distinguishes him in his healthier moments, he conceives and arranges the plan of having the 'Murder of Gonzago' played before the King and Queen, with the addition of a speech written by himself for the occasion. Then, longing to be alone, he abruptly dismisses his guests, and pours out a passion of self-reproach for his delay, asks himself in bewilderment what can be its cause, lashes himself into a fury of hatred against his foe, checks himself in disgust at his futile emotion, and quiets his conscience for the moment by trying to convince himself that he has doubts about the Ghost, and by assuring himself that, if the King's behaviour at the play-scene shows but a sign of guilt, he 'knows his course.'

Nothing, surely, can be clearer than the meaning of this famous soliloquy. The doubt which appears at its close, instead of being the natural conclusion of the preceding thoughts, is totally inconsistent with them. For Hamlet's self-reproaches, his curses on his enemy, and his perplexity about his own inaction, one and all imply his faith in the identity and truthfulness of the Ghost. Evidently this sudden doubt, of which there has not been the slightest trace before, is no genuine doubt; it is an unconscious fiction, an excuse for his delay—and for its continuance. (p. 131)

[On] his way to his mother's chamber, [Hamlet] comes upon the King, alone, kneeling, conscience-stricken and attempting to pray. His enemy is delivered into his hands.

> Now might I do it pat, now he is praying:
> And now I'll do it: and so he goes to heaven:
> And so am I revenged. That would be scanned.
> [III. iii. 73-5]

He scans it; and the sword that he drew at the words, 'And now I'll do it,' is thrust back into its sheath. If he killed the villain now he would send his soul to heaven; and he would fain kill soul as well as body.

That this again is an unconscious excuse for delay is now pretty generally agreed. . . . The first five words he utters, 'Now might I do it,' show that he has no effective *desire* to 'do it'; and in the little sentences that follow, and the long pauses between them, the endeavour at a resolution, and the sickening return of melancholic paralysis, however difficult a task they set to the actor, are plain enough to a reader. And any reader who may retain a doubt should observe the fact that, when the Ghost reappears, Hamlet does not think of justifying his delay by the plea that he was waiting for a more perfect vengeance. But in one point the great majority of critics, I think, go astray. . . . The reason for refusing to accept his own version of his motive in sparing Claudius is not that his sentiments are horrible, but that elsewhere, and also in the opening of his speech here, we can see that his reluctance to act is due to other causes. (pp. 134-35)

In *Macbeth* and *Hamlet* not only is the feeling of a supreme power or destiny peculiarly marked, but it has also at times a peculiar tone, which may be called, in a sense, religious. I cannot make my meaning clear without using language too definite to describe truly the imaginative impression produced; but it is roughly true that, while we do not imagine the supreme power as a divine being who avenges crime, or as a providence which supernaturally interferes, our sense of it is influenced by the fact that Shakespeare uses current religious ideas here much more decidedly than in *Othello* or *King Lear*. The horror in Macbeth's soul is more than once represented as desperation at the thought that he is eternally 'lost'; the same idea appears in the attempt of Claudius at repentance; and as *Hamlet* nears its close the 'religious' tone of the tragedy is deepened in two ways. In the first place, 'accident' is introduced into the plot in its barest and least dramatic form, when Hamlet is brought back to Denmark by the chance of the meeting with the pirate ship. This incident has been therefore severely criticised as a lame expedient, but it appears probable that the 'accident' is meant to impress the imagination as the very reverse of accidental, and with many readers it certainly does so. And that this was the intention is made the more likely by a second fact, the fact that in connection with the events of the voyage Shakespeare introduces that feeling, on Hamlet's part, of his being in the hands of Providence. (pp. 172-73)

Observing this, we may remember another significant point of resemblance between *Hamlet* and *Macbeth*, the appearance in each play of a Ghost,—a figure which seems quite in place in either, whereas it would seem utterly out of place in *Othello* or *King Lear*. Much might be said of the Ghost in *Hamlet*, but I confine myself to the matter which we are now considering. What is the effect of the appearance of the Ghost? And, in particular, why does Shakespeare make this Ghost so *majestical* a phantom, giving it that measured and solemn utterance, and that air of impersonal abstraction which forbids, for example,

all expression of affection for Hamlet and checks in Hamlet the outburst of pity for his father? Whatever the intention may have been, the result is that the Ghost affects imagination not simply as the apparition of a dead king who desires the accomplishment of *his* purposes, but also as the representative of that hidden ultimate power, the messenger of divine justice set upon the expiation of offences which it appeared impossible for man to discover and avenge, a reminder or a symbol of the connexion of the limited world of ordinary experience with the vaster life of which it is but a partial appearance. (pp. 173-74)

If these various peculiarities of the tragedy are considered, it will be agreed that, while *Hamlet* certainly cannot be called in the specific sense a 'religious drama,' there is in it nevertheless both a freer use of popular religious ideas, and a more decided, though always imaginative, intimation of a supreme power concerned in human evil and good, than can be found in any other of Shakespeare's tragedies. And this is probably one of the causes of the special popularity of this play, just as *Macbeth*, the tragedy which in these respects most nearly approaches it, has also the place next to it in general esteem. (p. 174)

> A. C. Bradley, "Shakespeare's Tragic Period— 'Hamlet'" and "'Hamlet'," in his Shakespearean Tragedy: Lectures on "Hamlet", "Othello", "King Lear", "Macbeth", *second edition, Macmillan, 1905, pp. 79-128, 129-74.*

CHARLTON M. LEWIS (essay date 1907)

[*In his* The Genesis of "Hamlet," *from which the following is drawn, Lewis evaluates the sources for the play. He concludes that* Hamlet *is essentially an inharmonious melding of Shakespeare's thought onto the plot of the lost* Ur-Hamlet, *which Lewis believes was written by Thomas Kyd. Lewis disputes the Coleridgeans with his assertion that* Hamlet *is a "composite" of the work of Shakespeare and Kyd, "not an entity at all, and therefore not a subject for psychological analysis." Lewis's assertion that* Hamlet *lacks unity is echoed in part by George Santayana (1908) as well as A.J.A. Waldock (1931). Such critics as Francis Fergusson (1949), Wolfgang H. Clemen (1951), Maynard Mack (1952), and Harry Levin (1959) argue that the play has, indeed, a unified structure. For additional studies of the sources of* Hamlet, *see Charlotte Lennox (1753), Thomas Kenny (1864), Elmer Edgar Stoll (1933), and William Empson (1953).*]

Shakespeare was not a ready inventor of incident. He took full advantage of the Elizabethan license of borrowing, and adopted ready-made plots wherever he found them. He made alterations, of course; but they were usually slight. . . . The making of plot-material was not his business.

What he did feel to be his business was the realization of character. His original provided him with a good story, but the characters were often no more than puppets. Stirring deeds were done, but as to what manner of men did them the older writers were apt to be noncommittal. (p. 70)

In *Hamlet*, therefore, it does not surprise us to discover that almost all the plot was old. Shakespeare would be especially sparing of invention when he was not newly dramatizing fiction or history, but only remodeling material already dramatized. In such cases he always retained the main outlines of his original, sometimes even minute details of the scenario. He was content to put new wine in the old bottles.

Of course Shakespeare reproduced those inconsistencies which Kyd had already imported into the Hamlet story. By making the murder secret, Kyd had made the pretence of madness absurd; yet he had retained it, and Shakespeare retained it too. Kyd's Hamlet had had a very difficult task to accomplish, and had foreseen that it would take a long time; and Shakespeare followed Kyd step by step through the scenes in which this foresight was shown. His Hamlet, like Kyd's, resolves at once upon the pretence of madness, and prepares for an indefinite period of suspense by swearing everybody to secrecy.

Here, however, Shakespeare is not content with merely taking over the existing difficulties of his plot; he actually creates new difficulties. Kyd . . . had narrowed the scope of Hamlet's task, limiting it to mere savage vengeance; but he had retained from Belleforest the notion that Claudius was hard to get at. Hence it was proper for Hamlet to foresee long delay and at once plan to face it. But Shakespeare, though he keeps the passage in which the difficulty of the task is foreseen, eliminates the difficulty itself. In Shakespeare's play Claudius is not hard to get at. There is no evidence that Hamlet could not have run upon him and given him his death at any time, had he so chosen.

Shakespeare's reasons for retaining those passages which his own exposition thus made absurd were doubtless very simple. The passages were good in themselves, and they were already in the play. I believe that he could not have written any such passages if the whole play had been a new invention of his own. . . . But the nature of Shakespeare's genius was creative, not critical. The unity and consistency which in a wholly original creation would come unsought, could hardly come in a revision of Kyd's curious play unless by processes of rigid critical analysis. For such processes Shakespeare had neither time nor inclination. (pp. 71-3)

It is easy, therefore, to understand why Shakespeare retained the embarrassments created by Kyd; but why did he create new ones by eliminating the difficulty of Hamlet's task? Why is it only in the German Hamlet that we hear of the King's bodyguard, of Hamlet's vigilant watch for an opportunity to kill, and of the possibility that his dead body may be found somewhere by Horatio?

The obvious answer is that Shakespeare suppressed all this evidence of the difficulty of the task chiefly because that difficulty did not interest him. He cared little for adventure. . . . He saw men's acts not as exertions made upon external objects but as results of internal struggles; he was interested in effects of character and will, not of muscle and agility.

Accordingly Shakespeare instinctively slighted things that to Kyd were essentials. In Kyd, as in Belleforest, Hamlet *could* not kill Claudius, while to Shakespeare the only question of any interest was whether Hamlet *would*. The evidence that he could not, therefore, has been quietly dropped out as immaterial and irrelevant. Yet Shakespeare has confused his own design by retaining passages appropriate only to the design of his predecessors; he allows his Hamlet to act on occasion as if he *could* not, although it seems clear all the time that he could if he would. (pp. 73-4)

As was his wont, he addressed himself to the creation of the necessary characters, and the first question that suggested itself may well have been this: "What kind of man must this Hamlet have been, the impossible hero of this impossible plot? What kind of man, with such a task thrust upon him, would go off on so impracticable a side-track? What is the meaning of this absurd pretence of madness? How can I possibly make it go?"

In some such way as this, I think, the pretence of madness was the starting-point from which Hamlet's character was evolved, and it may well have determined the whole course of its development. The sensitive, passionate nature of the Hamlet whom we know, the hysterical intensity of his agony when his cherished ideals are shattered, even his histrionic fancy for playing with his own instinctive loathings—all these traits seem to have sprung up in Shakespeare's imagination as he worked backwards from the feigned madness. He could account for that strange device only as a safety-valve for the ebullitions of Hamlet's own passion. He could see no exterior motive for it at all; and as the motives assigned by Kyd were uninteresting as well as insufficient, he suppressed all reference to them. I do not believe, however, that this suppression was conscious and deliberate.

The idea of the safety-valve was, I think, wholly original with Shakespeare; but even if we suppose some germ to have been latent in Kyd's play, we must recognize in Shakespeare's development of it a brilliant feat of genius. Yet in working it out he has had to bring Hamlet so near the verge of chronic hysteria that some critics have denied his sanity, while most have thought him an incapable weakling: and even by going to this extreme Shakespeare has not achieved the impossible task of making the plot plausible. (pp. 74-6)

[We] must remind ourselves that the play is not fact, but imperfectly digested fiction. If it were fact, we might argue from Hamlet's dilatory pretence of madness, from his willing departure for England, indeed from all his conduct that is known to us, that he was just such a palterer as the Coleridgeans think him. But as it is, we know that we have no right to reason so. We may not call the pretence of madness dilatory. It was clever and practical strategy in the original; and Kyd and Shakespeare, by obscuring its practical value, have not necessarily converted it into imbecility. The journey to England was not a willing abandonment of Hamlet's design. In the original it was a plan imposed upon him by irresistible authority, and no other course was open to him under the circumstances. Shakespeare has projected some of these circumstances into the fourth dimension, but by what right may we treat them as non-existent?

It would be very strange if Shakespeare adopted for his Hamlet the whole Coleridgean conception. He was merely repolishing a play with a typical romantic hero, a man ready and quick in action and whole-souled in devotion to his task. There is no hint that his conduct deserves anything but praise. Both Kyd and Belleforest clearly meant to represent Hamlet as doing just what they imagined he ought to do; or at any rate he did more than this, rather than less. Now Shakespeare read character more profoundly than his predecessors, and sometimes took new views of his heroes' difficulties and duties; but I recall no instance of his turning a model of virtue into a dreadful example of vice. When he follows an old plot as closely as he does in Hamlet, retaining the whole story practically intact, together with most of the stage business, is it conceivable that he would transfigure its entire meaning? It would be as if in Othello he had made Desdemona really guilty, and Iago an honest counselor! (pp. 77-9)

Kyd was a shallow philosopher. He studied passions, not men. He meant to represent Hamlet as doing just what he ought to do; but his Hamlet was primarily a personified craving for revenge. Like Hieronimo, he belonged not to real life but to the conventional world of the old revenge tragedy. . . . (p. 81)

This view could not interest Shakespeare; but much else in the play interested him deeply. He found there a noble, capable, and strong man, a man in every way admirable, suddenly called upon to dedicate himself to a savage passion. The call is the most urgent one conceivable, proceeding from his father's grave; and the hero obeys it and gives his life in the pursuit of his revenge. This was the story Shakespeare had to tell, and our question is: how would he be likely to tell it?

He would be likely to repeat substantially as he found them all facts that interested him; he would make no change, even in characterization, except such as the situation itself suggested, or such as were necessitated by his own larger views of life; but he certainly could not take over the shallow psychology of Kyd. He would follow Kyd in presenting an admirably heroic youth driven to vengeance by an irresistible impulse; but he would emancipate himself wholly from Kyd when he came to consider how the youth would feel about it. Shakespeare's hero would *not* be an incarnate demon of revenge, and the conventional standards of the revenge tragedy would be thrown overboard. Hamlet himself says, "Give me that man that is not passion's slave, and I will wear him in my heart's core." Those words, as everybody perceives, seem to express Shakespeare's own mature ideal of manhood; and it is that ideal that we should expect to see put to the test in Hamlet. (pp. 81-2)

The interesting problem was how it would feel to be in Hamlet's place. The sensitive, affectionate, impulsive character of Hamlet has already sprung to light in Shakespeare's imagination, out of the pretence of madness; and the answer to the present problem is that such a man in such a situation would be in an almost hopeless quandary. At times he would be all for blood, for in the best of us the brutish passions are still strong; but in the best of us such moods are not enduring, and there would be times when Hamlet could hardly persuade himself back into his fury if he tried. He achieves his revenge; he achieves it, indeed, as soon as circumstances permit; but that is not the point. The point is that, looking down deep into his soul, we see him achieving it in spite of almost infinite reluctance.

Such, I think, was Shakespeare's conception of his hero. I cannot believe that his Hamlet is to blame for any irresoluteness. If we judge him by the standards that prevail in *The Spanish Tragedy,* and especially if we accept the data of the play as a complete account of the situation, we must condemn Hamlet for not taking the life of Claudius at once. But our judgments are not regulated by those standards, and we know that the play tells the story but imperfectly.

The Coleridgeans, I think, read Hamlet's character just as Shakespeare read it, except for their imputation of a feeble will. They have superposed this defect upon the character because they have made both the mistakes mentioned in the last paragraph. In the first place, they have taken such things as the pretence of madness and the journey to England for facts by which Hamlet was to be interpreted; and, in the second place, they have judged that he falls short of perfection just in so far as he falls short of the pre-Shakespearean ideal of the avenger.

So far as we know, it never occurred to Shakespeare that Hamlet was incapable of achieving any task, however great, if he wanted to; or that, in the present instance, he ought to have been more eager than he was. In a sense, Shakespeare did with the character exactly what Kyd had done; that is, he let Hamlet behave exactly as he imagined a noble-minded prince would behave under the circumstances. Kyd, however, saw the story in the lime-light of a conventional stage, while Shakespeare saw it in the light of a profound knowledge of human nature. (pp. 83-5)

In the existing tragedy we find two distinct heroes imperfectly melted into one. Kyd's Hamlet and Shakespeare's Hamlet, taken separately, are comparatively simple and intelligible persons; but the Kyd-Shakespeare compound is a "monstr'-horrend'-inform'-ingendous" mystery, *cui lumen ademptum*. Kyd's Hamlet does most of the deeds of the play, and Shakespeare's Hamlet thinks most of the thoughts. Kyd is responsible for most of the plot, and Shakespeare for most of the characterization; Kyd for the hero's actual environment, Shakespeare for the imperfect description of his environment that has come down to us. Thus the Kyd-Shakespeare composite hero follows up one man's thoughts with another man's deeds, and confronts with Shakespeare's soul a situation of Kyd's devising.

The complexity of this compound is further confused by the complexity of one of the components; for Kyd's Hamlet himself was an ill-assorted blend of Kyd and Belleforest. This fact, indeed, is the first cause of the greatness of the existing tragedy, as well as of its defects; for it was the irrational behavior of Kyd's hero that piqued Shakespeare's curiosity and drove him to depart as far from Kyd as Kyd had departed from Belleforest. But if we want a clear conception of Shakespeare's own Hamlet, we must put out of our minds those parts of the play which belong to the Hamlets of Belleforest and Kyd. Those parts are important as clues to guide us in running down Shakespeare's meaning, but we must not treat them as direct evidence by which his meaning may be proved. They are direct evidence only of the meaning of the Belleforest-Kyd-Shakespeare compound; and that compound is meaningless. It is because this condition has been so long overlooked that the Hamlet mystery has remained unsolved.

Shakespeare's purpose was to tell the story of Hamlet, and to explain it as he went along; and the reason why he failed in the latter part of his purpose was that the story was inexplicable. Like many other inexplicable stories, however, it was an exceedingly good one; and Shakespeare has told a considerable part of it supremely well.

The story included the revelation by the Ghost, the feigned madness (with an elaborate scene ready-made in which it was planned), the doubt of the Ghost's veracity, and the stirring demonstration thereof by The Mouse-Trap. It included also the dramatic scene with the hero's mother, the killing of Polonius, the thwarting of the embassy to England, and the final riot at the fencing-bout. Into the thick of these adventures Shakespeare projected his own hero, a young man of ideal excellence in general, but with such specific refinements of temper as might most nearly explain his pretence of madness. The very intensity of Shakespeare's interest in this hero's inner experiences made some essential features of the plot seem irrelevant; and other features were not merely irrelevant but actually incongruous. (pp. 116-19)

[Hamlet] would never willingly prefer his injuries to his heart, nor bring his heart into danger by cherishing an alien passion; but the injuries are preferred for him by his father's spirit, and the passion is commended to him by filial love. He therefore accepts his mission, and achieves it, in spite of its repugnancy. It is this that makes him a tragic hero.

The theories of Coleridge and Werder [see excerpts above, 1811 and 1859-60] are attempts to explain the Hamlet of Belleforest, Kyd, and Shakespeare. Coleridge finds that this Hamlet's delays are due to internal difficulties, for which he is to blame. Werder finds that they are due to external difficulties, for which he is not to blame. If we are asked to decide between these theories we must first demur on the ground that the composite Hamlet is not an entity at all, and therefore not a subject for psychological analysis. But if this ground of demurrer be waived, we may suggest a compromise between the opposing theories. We will say with Coleridge that Hamlet's difficulties are internal, and with Werder that he is not to blame for them; but we must add, in disagreement with both disputants, that these difficulties are not the causes of the delay. The causes of the delay are those external difficulties which have vanished into the fourth dimension. (pp. 120-21)

Charlton M. Lewis, in his The Genesis of ''Hamlet,''
Henry Holt and Company, 1907, 121 p.

GEORGE SANTAYANA   (essay date 1908)

[*Santayana was a Spanish-born American philosopher. Noting, like Charlton M. Lewis (1907), inconsistencies in* Hamlet *that result from Shakespeare's handling of his sources, Santayana finds, unlike Lewis, that it is exactly these incongruous elements which give depth and range to Hamlet's character. For additional commentary on the sources of* Hamlet, *see Charlotte Lennox (1753), Thomas Kenny (1864), Elmer Edgar Stoll (1933), and William Empson (1953). The following essay was first published in* The Works of William Shakespeare: Hamlet *in 1908.*]

[Readers] of *Hamlet* should not be surprised if this most psychological of tragedies should turn out to be a product of gradual accretions, or if its hero, most spontaneous and individual of characters, should be an afterthought and a discovery. Shakespeare followed a classic precept in this romantic drama: he allowed the plot to suggest the characters, and conceived their motives and psychological movement only as an underpinning and satiric deepening for their known actions. The play is an ordinary story with an extraordinary elaboration. . . . Some of Hamlet's actions and speeches seem anterior to his true character. They apparently remain over from the old melodrama and mark the points neglected by the poet and left untransmuted by his intuition.

These survivals of cruder methods, if survivals they be, give a touch of positive incoherence to Hamlet's character, otherwise sufficiently complex. His behaviour, for instance, before the praying King, and the reasons he gives there for sparing the villain, are apparently a remnant of bombast belonging to the old story, far more Christian and conventional in its motives than Shakespeare's is. So the grotesque bout with Laertes in Ophelia's grave is perhaps a bit of old rodomontade left unexpunged. . . . These passages may contain remnants of that conventional farce which, as some think, was inherited by Elizabethan drama from the Middle Ages, when piety and obscenity, quaint simplicity and rant, could be jumbled together without offence. Yet this barbaric medley, surviving by chance or by inertia, is the occasion for the creation of a spirit that shall justify it, and shall express therein its own profound discord. The historical accidents that make these patches in the play are embodied and personified in a mind that can cover them all by its own complexity and dislocation. Each of these blots thus becomes a beauty, each of these accidents a piece of profound characterization. In Hamlet's personality incoherent sentiments, due, in a genetic sense, to the imperfect recasting of a grotesque old story, are made attributable ideally to his habit of acting out a mood irresponsibly and of giving a mock expression to every successive intuition. Thus his false rhetoric before the praying King becomes characteristic, and may be taken to betray an inveterate vacillation which seizes on verbal excuses and plays with unreal sentiments in order to

put off the moment of action. . . . So, too, his sardonic humour and nonsensical verbiage at the most tragic junctures may justify themselves ideally and seem to be deeply inspired. These wild starts suggest a mind inwardly rent asunder, a delicate genius disordered, such as we now learn that Hamlet's was, a mind that with infinite sensibility possessed no mastery over itself nor over things. Thus the least digested elements in the fable come, by a happy turn, to constitute its profoundest suggestion.

Evidently the same thing happened to Shakespeare with his histrionic Prince that happened to Cervantes with his mad Knight: he fell in love with his hero. He caught in that figure, at first only grotesque and melodramatic, the suggestion of something noble, spiritual, and pathetic, and he devoted all his imaginative powers to developing that suggestion. He enriched the lines with all that reflection could furnish that was most pungent and poetical; he added the philosophic play of mind, gave free rein to soliloquy, insisted everywhere on what might seem keen and significant. At the same time he found pleasure in elaborating the story. He constructed, for instance, a young Hamlet, to stand behind the tragic hero, a witty, tender, and accomplished prince, to be overtaken by that cursed spite which he should prove incapable of turning aside. Here we have a piece of deliberate art. By numerous and well-chosen phrases scattered throughout the play, Shakespeare takes pains to evoke the image of a consummate and admirable nature, so that the charm and pathos of the tragedy which ruins it may be enhanced.

Yet he is not without a soberer and more settled affection than that expressed in his fancy for the fair Ophelia; his deepest sentiment is a great love and admiration for the King, his father. On this natural piety in the young Hamlet, his new tragic life is to be grafted. By striking rudely in this quarter fate strikes not merely at his filial affection, but at his intellectual peace and at his confidence in justice. The wound is mortal and saps his moral being.

We might say that to see—or if the spiritualistic reader prefers, to call up—a ghost is a first sign of Hamlet's moral dissolution. It would be easy to rationalize this part of the story, and explain the Ghost as a sort of symbol or allegory. Hamlet's character and situation were well conceived to base such a hallucination upon. His prophetic soul might easily have cheated him with such a counterfeit presentment of its own suspicions. But Shakespeare was evidently content to take the Ghost literally, and expected his audience naturally to do the same. Although not visible to the Queen on its final appearance, the Ghost is seen by Horatio and others on several occasions. The report it gives of its torments corresponds to the popular and orthodox conception of Purgatory, so that a Christian public might accept this ghost as a possible wanderer from the other world. Had Shakespeare cared much about ghosts, or wished to give, as in *Macbeth,* a realistic picture of the shabby supernatural, Hamlet's Ghost might well have been a much less theological and conventional being. . . . It is a Christian soul in Purgatory, which ought, in theological strictness, to be a holy and redeemed soul, a phase of penitential and spiritual experience; yet this soul fears to scent the morning air, trembles at the cock-crow, and instigates the revenging of crime by crime. That is, it is no Christian soul, but a heathen and pathological spectre. It speaks, as Hamlet justly feels, by the ambiguous authority of hell and heaven at once. This hybrid personage, however, like the other anomalies in the play, comes to have its expressive value. It unites in a single image various threads of superstition actually tangled in the public mind.

The first effect of the Ghost's revelation is characteristic of Hamlet's nature. He and the Ghost both insist on secrecy, as if too much had already been done. Hamlet induces his fellow-witnesses to swear to keep silence about the marvel they have seen; he checks a natural impulse to repeat the Ghost's story; and the Ghost himself, on its way to its subterranean torture-chamber, echoes Hamlet's demand—"Swear, Swear"—in hollow and melodramatic accents. Why this fear to divulge the truth? Why this unnecessary precaution and delay? Why this fantastic notion, at once imposing itself on the hero's mind, that there would be occasion for him to feign madness and put an antic disposition on? The simple truth is, that the play pre-exists and imposes itself here on the poet, who is reduced to paving the way as best he can for the foregone complications.

Those who have maintained that Hamlet is really mad had this partial justification for their paradox, that Hamlet is irrational. He acts without reflection, as he reflects without acting. At the basis of all his ingenuity and reasoning, of his nimble wit and varied fooling, lies this act of inexplicable folly: that he conceals his discovery, postpones his vengeance before questioning its propriety, and descends with no motive to a grotesque and pitiful piece of dissimulation. This unreason is not madness, because his intellect remains clear, his discourse sound and comprehensive; but it is a sort of passionate weakness and indirection in his will, which mocks its own ends, strikes fantastic attitudes, and invents elaborate schemes of action useless for his declared purposes. The psychology of Hamlet is like that which some German metaphysicians have attributed to their Spirit of the World, which is the prey to its own perversity and to what is called romantic irony, so that it eternally pursues the good in a way especially designed never to attain it. In Hamlet, as in them, beneath this histrionic duplicity and earnestness about the unreal, there is a very genuine pathos. . . . It is the tragedy of a soul buzzing in the glass prison of a world which it can neither escape nor understand, in which it flutters about without direction, without clear hope, and yet with many a keen pang, many a dire imaginary problem, and much exquisite music.

This morbid indirection of Hamlet's, in the given situation, yields the rest of the play. Its theme is a hidden crime met by a fantastic and incapable virtue. The hero's reaction takes various forms: his soliloquies and reflections, his moody and artful treatment of other persons, his plans and spurts of action. In soliloquy Hamlet is much the same from the beginning to the end of the piece. His philosophy learns little from events and consequently makes little progress.

Hamlet's attitude towards the minor characters in the play is a source of perennial joy to spectators and readers. His words and manner to Polonius, Horatio, Rosencrantz, and Guildenstern, the players, the grave-diggers, the court messengers, are alike keen, kindly, witty, and noble. Since he is playing at madness he can allow his humour to be broader, his scorn franker, his fancy more wayward than they could well have been otherwise; yet in all mock disguises appears the same exquisite courtesy, even in that clever and cruel parrying of the King's treachery during the expedition to England. It is when we come to Hamlet's attitude towards the other chief figures—the Ghost, Ophelia, the Queen—that we observe a certain indistinctness and dispersion of mind, so that both the hero's character and the poet's intentions are, to say the least, less obvious. In the Ghost's presence Hamlet is overcome with feeling, in its absence with doubts. What he ostensibly wishes to have confirmed is the veracity of that witness, and the play-

scene is arranged to obtain corroboration of this. Yet when that ostensible doubt is solved and the facts are beyond question, he is no more ready for action than before. . . . Hamlet feels that he is leaving a duty unperformed and at the same time that he is being driven on by the devil. If his instinctive hesitation could have expressed itself theoretically he might perhaps have asked whether the treacherous murder of one innocent man could well be righted by more treachery and more murder, involving disaster to many innocent persons. . . . So Hamlet's whole entanglement with the Ghost, and with the crude morality of vengeance which the plot imposes upon him, fails to bring his own soul to a right utterance, and this stifling of his better potential mind is no small part of his tragedy. Or is it only a fond critic's illusion that makes us read that better idea into what is a purely unconscious barbarism and a vacillation useful for theatrical purposes?

Towards his mother Hamlet maintains throughout the greater part of the play a wounded reserve appropriate to the situation. He speaks of her with sarcasm, but addresses her with curt respect. Only in the closet scene does he unbosom himself with a somewhat emphatic eloquence which shows touches of dignity and pathos; yet this scene, central as it is in the plot, hardly rises in power above the level of its neighbours. In comparison, for instance, the scenes with Ophelia are full of wonder and charm. There the poet's imagination flowers out, and Hamlet appears in all his originality and wild inspiration. Yet Ophelia and Hamlet's relation to her are incidental to the drama, while the Queen and her fate are essential to it. We may observe in general that Shakespeare's genius shines in the texture of his poems rather than in their structure, in imagery and happy strokes rather than in integrating ideas. His poetry plays about life like ivy about a house, and is more akin to landscape than to architecture.

Hamlet's positive and deliberate action is limited to two stratagems, one with the players, to catch the King's conscience, and one by which he makes Rosencrantz and Guildenstern suffer the fate prepared for himself in England. In both cases Hamlet betrays a sort of exuberance and wild delight. He feels the luxury of hitting home, the absolute joy of playing the game, without particular reference to the end in view. . . . If he acts seldom and with difficulty, it is not because he does not hugely enjoy action. Yet his delight is in the shimmer and movement of action rather than in its use; so that the weakness of his character appears just as much in his bursts of activity as in his long hesitations. He kills Polonius by accident, hoping that in a blind thrust through the arras he might turn out at last to have dispatched the King; and when, himself mortally wounded, he finally executes that long-meditated sentence, he can do so only by yielding to a sudden hysterical impulse. So consistently does unreason pursue him: an inexplicable crime is followed by a miraculous vision; that portent he meets by a senseless and too congenial pretence of madness; a successful stratagem confirms the King's guilt, but does not lead to exposure or punishment, rather to a passive reconciliation with him on Hamlet's part. Innocent persons meantime perish, and the end is a general but casual slaughter, amid treachery, misunderstandings, and ghastly confusions.

This picture of universal madness is relieved by the very finest and purest glints of wit, intelligence, and feeling. It is crammed with exquisite lines, and vivified by most interesting and moving characters in great variety, all drawn with masterly breadth, depth, and precision. Hamlet, in particular, as our analysis testifies, is more than a vivid dramatic figure, more than an unparalleled poetic vision. He lays bare the heart of a whole race, or, perhaps we should rather say, expresses a conflict to which every soul is more or less liable.

The impression of utter gloom which the plot leaves when taken, so to speak, realistically, as if it were a picture of actual existences, is not the impression which it leaves when we take it as lyric poetry, as music, as an abstract representation of sundry moods and loyalties traversing a noble mind. The world which is here set before us may be grotesque and distracted; but we are not asked to be interested in that world. Had Hamlet himself been interested in it, he would have acted more rationally. It was not intelligence or courage that he lacked; it was practical conviction or sense for reality. . . . At any rate, express it how we will, the sympathetic reader will instinctively feel that he should pass over lightly the experience which the play depicts and carry away from it only the moral feeling, the spiritual sentiment, which it calls forth in the characters. As the poet himself thought a violent and somewhat absurd fable not unworthy to support his richest verse and subtlest characterizations, so we must take the fabric of destiny, in this tragedy and in that, too, which we enact in the world, as it happens to be, and think the moral lights that flicker through it bright enough to redeem it.

So absolute a feat of imagination cannot be ranked in comparison with other works, nor estimated by any standard of which it does not itself furnish the suggestion and type. It is rather to be studied and absorbed, to be made a part of our habitual landscape and mental furniture, lest we should miss much of what is deepest and rarest in human feeling. If we care to pass, however, from admiration of the masterpiece to reflection on the experience which it expresses, we see that here is no necessary human tragedy, no universal destiny or divine law. It is a picture of incidental unfitness, of a genius wasted for being plucked quite unripe from the sunny places of the world. In Hamlet our incoherent souls see their own image; in him romantic potentiality and romantic failure wears each its own feature. In him we see the gifts most congenial and appealing to us reduced to a pathetic impotence because of the disarray in which we are content to leave them.

> *George Santayana, in his* Definitive Edition of the Works of George Santayana: Persons and Places, Vol. I, *edited by Herman J. Saatkamp, Jr. and William J. Holzberger, The MIT Press, to be published in 1984.*

GILBERT MURRAY   (essay date 1914)

[*Developing a parallel first noted by seventeenth-century critics, Murray compares the characters of Hamlet and Orestes. He discusses Orestes as he appears in seven Greek tragedies, and Hamlet as he is rendered in the Norse sagas and in Shakespeare's play. For Murray, both* Hamlet *and the various dramatic interpretations of the Orestes story have their roots in primitive myth and ritual, and specifically in the stories of the Golden-Bough Kings, ritual explanations of the seasonal changes in which "a Summer-king or Vegetation-spirit is slain by Winter and rises from the dead in the spring." Murray's approach to the text through the analysis of its mythic aspects prefigures a major movement in the criticism of Shakespeare's work. Francis Fergusson (1949) expands upon Murry's analysis in his investigation of the mythical roots of* Hamlet; *H.D.F. Kitto (1956) also examines* Hamlet's *mythic sources. Murray's essay is a revision of a lecture given in 1914.*]

My subject is the study of two great tragic characters, Hamlet and Orestes, regarded as traditional types. I do not compare play with play, but simply character with character, though in the course of the comparison I shall naturally consider the situations in which my heroes are placed and the other persons with whom they are associated.

Orestes in Greek is very clearly a traditional character. He occurs in poem after poem, in tragedy after tragedy, varying slightly in each one but always true to type. He is, I think, the most central and typical tragic hero on the Greek stage; and he occurs in no less than seven of our extant tragedies. . . . I shall use all these seven plays as material: namely, Aeschylus, *Choephoroe* and *Eumenides; * Sophocles, *Electra; * and Euripides, *Electra, Orestes, Iphigenia in Tauris* and *Andromache.* And we must realize that before any of these plays was written Orestes was a well-established character both in religious worship and in epic and lyric tradition.

As for *Hamlet,* I note, in passing, the well-known fragments of evidence which indicate the existence of a Hamlet tragedy before the publication of Shakespeare's Second Quarto in 1604. (pp. 205-06)

Hamlet, like most of the great Elizabethan plays, presents itself to us as a whole that has been gradually built up, not as a single definitive creation made by one man in one effort. There was an old play called *Hamlet* extant about 1587, perhaps written by Kyd. It was worked over and improved by Shakespeare; improved doubtless again and again in the course of its different productions. We can trace additions; we can even trace changes of mind or repentances, as when the Folio of 1623 goes back to a discarded passage in the First Quarto. It is a live and growing play, apt no doubt to be slightly different at each performance, and growing steadily more profound, more rich, and more varied in its appeal.

And before it was an English play, it was a Scandinavian story: a very ancient Northern tale, not invented by any person, but just living, and doubtless from time to time growing and decaying, in oral tradition. (p. 208)

Besides Saxo we have a later form of the same legend in the Icelandic *Ambales Saga.* The earliest extant manuscripts of this belong to the seventeenth century. (p. 209)

Now to our comparison.

1. The general situation. In all the versions, both Northern and Greek, the hero is the son of a king who has been murdered and succeeded on the throne by a younger kinsman—a cousin, Aegisthus, in the Greek; a younger brother, Feng or Claudius, in the Northern. The dead king's wife has married his murderer. The hero, driven by supernatural commands, undertakes and carries through the duty of vengeance.

In Shakespeare the hero dies as his vengeance is accomplished; but this seems to be an innovation. In Saxo, *Ambales,* and the Greek he duly succeeds to the kingdom. In Saxo there is no mention of a ghost; the duty of vengeance is perhaps accepted as natural. In *Ambales,* however, there are angels; in the English, a ghost; in the Greek, dreams and visions of the dead father, and an oracle.

2. In all versions of the story there is some shyness about the mother-murder. In Saxo the mother is not slain; in Shakespeare she is slain by accident, not deliberately murdered; in *Ambales* she is warned and leaves the burning hall just in time. . . . In the Greek versions she is deliberately slain, but the horror of

the deed unseats the hero's reason. We shall consider this mother more at length later on.

3. In all the versions the hero is in some way under the shadow of madness. This is immensely important, indeed essential, in his whole dramatic character. It is present in all the versions, but is somewhat different in each.

In *Hamlet* the madness is assumed, but I trust I am safe in saying that there is something in the hero's character which at least makes one wonder if it is entirely assumed. I think the same may be said of Amlodi and Ambales.

In the Greek the complete madness comes only as a result of the mother-murder; yet here too there is that in the hero's character which makes it easy for him to go mad. In the *Choephoroe,* where we see him before the deed, he is not normal. His language is strange and broken amid its amazing eloquence; he is a haunted man. In other plays, after the deed, he is seldom actually raving. But, like Hamlet in his mother's chamber, he sees visions which others cannot. . . . He indulges freely in soliloquies; especially, like Hamlet, he is subject to paralyzing doubts and hesitations, alternating with hot fits. (pp. 209-11)

Both in Saxo and in *Ambales* the madness is assumed, entirely or mainly, but in its quality also it is utterly different from that of Shakespeare's hero. The saga Hamlet is not a highly wrought and sensitive man with his mind shaken by a terrible experience, he is a Fool, a gross Jester, covered with dirt and ashes, grinning and mowing and eating like a hog, spared by the murderer simply because he is considered too witless to be dangerous. The name "Amlodi" itself means a fool. This side is emphasised most in *Ambales,* but it is clear enough in Saxo also and explains why he has combined his hero with the Fool, Brutus. Hamlet is a Fool, though his folly is partly assumed and hides unsuspected cunning.

4. The Fool.—It is very remarkable that Shakespeare, who did such wonders in his idealized and half-mystic treatment of the real Fool, should also have made his greatest tragic hero out of a Fool transfigured. Let us spend a few moments on noticing the remnants of the old Fool that subsist in the transfigured hero of the tragedies. For one thing . . . Hamlet's actual language is at times exactly that of the regular Shakespearean Fool: for example, with Polonius in Act II, scene 2; just before the play in Act III, scene 2, and after. But apart from that, there are other significant elements.

(a) The Fool's disguise.—Amlodi and Brutus and Shakespeare's Hamlet feign madness; Orestes does not. Yet the element of disguise is very strong in Orestes. He is always disguising his feelings: he does so in the *Choephoroe,* Sophocles' *Electra,* Euripides' *Electra* and *Iphigenia in Tauris.* (pp. 212-13)

Again, it is a marked feature of Orestes to be present in disguise, especially when he is supposed to be dead, and then at some crisis to reveal himself with startling effect. He is apt to be greeted by such words as "Undreamed-of phantom!" or "Who is this risen from the dead?" He is present disguised and unknown in the *Choephoroe,* Sophocles' *Electra,* Euripides' *Electra* and *Iphigenia in Tauris;* he is in nearly every case supposed to be dead. (pp. 213-14)

No other character in Greek tragedy behaves in this extraordinary way. But Saxo's Amlodi does. When Amlodi goes to England, he is supposed to be dead, and his funeral feast is in progress, when he walks in, "striking all men utterly aghast."

In *Hamlet* there is surely a remnant of this motive, considerably softened. In Act V, 2, the Gravedigger scene, Hamlet has been present in disguise while the Gravedigger and the public thought he was in England, and the King and his confidants must have believed him dead, as they do in Saxo. Then comes the funeral—not his own, but Ophelia's; he stays hidden for a time, and then springs out, revealing himself: "This is I, Hamlet the Dane!" The words seem like an echo of that cry that is so typical in the Greek tragedies: "'Tis I, Orestes, Agamemnon's son!" (p. 214)

(b) The disorder of the Fool.—This disguise motive has led us away from the Fool, though it is closely connected with him. Another curious element of the Fool that lingers on is his dirtiness and disorder in dress. . . . We remember Ophelia's description of Hamlet's coming to her chamber:

> his doublet all unbraced;
> No hat upon his head; his stockings fouled,
> Ungartered and down-gyvèd to the ankle,
> Pale as his shirt. . . .   [II. i. 75-8]

Similarly, Orestes, at the beginning of the play that bears his name, is found with his sister, ghastly pale, with foam on his mouth, gouts of rheum in his eyes, his long hair matted with dirt and "made wild with long unwashenness." "Poor curls, poor filthy face," his sister says to him. (p. 215)

(c) The Fool's rudeness of speech.—Besides being dirty and talking in riddles, the Fool was abusive and gross in his language. This is the case to some degree in Saxo, though no doubt the monk has softened Amlodi's words. It is much emphasized in Ambales. That hero's language is habitually outrageous, especially to women. This outrageousness of speech has clearly descended to Hamlet, in whom it seems to be definitely intended as a morbid trait. He is obsessed by revolting images. He does

> like a whore unpack his heart in words
> And fall a-cursing like a very drab,
>   [II. ii. 585-86]

and he rages at himself because of it.

(d) The Fool on women.—Now the general style of Greek tragedy will not admit any gross language. So Orestes has lost this trait. But a trace of it perhaps remains. Both Orestes and Hamlet are given to expressing violently cynical opinions about women. The *Orestes* bristles with parallels to the ravings of Hamlet's "Get-thee-to-a-nunnery" scene. The hero is haunted by his "most pernicious woman." All women want to murder their husbands; it is only a question of time. Then they will fly in tears to their children, show their breasts, and cry for sympathy. We may, perhaps, couple with these passages the famous speech where [Orestes] denies any blood relationship with his mother, and the horrible mad line where he says he could never weary of killing evil women. (pp. 215-16)

The above, I think, are, all of them, elements that go deep into the character of the hero as a stage figure. I will now add some slighter and more external points of resemblance.

1. In both traditions the hero has been away from home when the main drama begins, Orestes in Phocis, Hamlet in Wittenberg. This point, as we shall see later, has some significance.

2. The hero in both traditions—and in both rather strangely—goes on a ship, is captured by enemies who want to kill him, but escapes. And as Hamlet has a sort of double escape, first from the King's treacherous letter, and next from the pirates,

so Orestes, in the *Iphigenia,* escapes once from the Taurians who catch him on the shore, and again from the pursuers in the ship. (p. 217)

[One] of the greatest horrors about the father's death in both traditions is that he died without the due religious observances. In the Greek tragedies, this lack of religious burial is almost the central horror of the whole story. Wherever it is mentioned it comes as something intolerable, maddening; it breaks Orestes down. (p. 220)

The atmosphere is quite different in the English. But the lack of dying rites remains, and retains a strange dreadfulness:

> Cut off even in the blossom of my sin,
> Unhousel'd, disappointed, unanel'd.   [I. v. 76-7]

To turn to the other characters: in both the dramatic traditions the hero has a faithful friend and confidant, who also arrives from Phocis-Wittenberg, and advises him about his revenge. This friend, when the hero is threatened with death, wishes to die too, but is prevented by the hero and told to "absent him from felicity awhile." This motive is worked out more at length in the Greek than in the English. (p. 221)

Next comes a curious point. At first sight it seems as if all the Electra motive were lacking in the modern play, all the Ophelia-Polonius motive in the ancient. Yet I am not sure.

In all the ancient plays Orestes is closely connected with a strange couple—a young woman and a very old man. They are his sister Electra and her only true friend, an old and trusted servant of the dead King, who saved Orestes' life in childhood. (pp. 221-22)

In the Elizabethan play this couple—if we may so beg the question—has been transformed. The sister is now the mistress, Ophelia; the old servant of the King—for so we must surely describe Polonius or Corambis—remains, but has become Ophelia's real father. And the relations of both to the hero are quite different.

The change is made more intelligible when we look at the sagas. There the young woman is not a sister but a foster-sister; like Electra she helps Amlodi, like Ophelia she is his beloved. The old servant of the King is not her father—so far like the Greek; but there the likeness stops. He spies on Amlodi in his mother's chamber and is killed for his pains, as in the English.

We may notice, further, that in all the Electra plays alike a peculiar effect is got from Orestes' first sight of his sister, either walking in a funeral procession or alone in mourning garb. He takes her for a slave, and cries, "Can that be the unhappy Electra?" A similar but stronger effect is reached in *Hamlet,* when Hamlet, seeing an unknown funeral procession approach, gradually discovers whose it is and cries in horror: "What, the fair Ophelia?"

Lastly, there is something peculiar, at any rate in the Northern tradition,—I will take the Greek later,—about the hero's mother. Essentially it is this: she has married the murderer of her first husband and is in part implicated in the murder, and yet the tradition instinctively keeps her sympathetic. In our *Hamlet* she is startled to hear that her first husband was murdered, yet one does not feel clear that she is perfectly honest with herself. She did not know Claudius had poisoned him, but probably that was because she obstinately refused to put together things which she did know and which pointed towards that conclusion. At any rate, though she does not betray Hamlet, she sticks to Claudius and shares his doom. (pp. 222-23)

A wife who loves her husband and bears him children, and then is wedded to his slayer and equally loves him, and does it all in a natural and unemotional manner: it seems somewhat unusual. (p. 223)

Now I hope I have not tried artificially to make a case or to press my facts too hard. I think it will be conceded that the points of similarity, some fundamental and some perhaps superficial, between these two tragic heroes are rather extraordinary, and are made the more striking by the fact that Hamlet and Orestes are respectively the very greatest or most famous heroes of the world's two great ages of tragedy.

The points of similarity, we must notice, fall into two parts. There are, first, the broad similarities of situation between what we may call the original sagas on both sides; that is, the general story of Orestes and of Hamlet respectively. But, secondly, there is something much more remarkable: when these sagas were worked up into tragedies, quite independently and on very different lines, by the great dramatists of Greece and England, not only do most of the old similarities remain, but a number of new similarities are developed. That is, Aeschylus, Euripides, and Shakespeare are strikingly similar in certain points which do not occur at all in Saxo or *Ambales* or the Greek epic. For instance, the hero's madness is the same in Shakespeare and Euripides, but is totally different from the madness in Saxo or *Ambales.*

What is the connexion? All critics seem to be agreed that Shakespeare did not study these Greek tragedians directly. And, if any one should suggest that he did, there are many considerations which would, I think, make that hypothesis unserviceable. (pp. 224-25)

There seems to have been, so far as our recorded history goes, no chance of imitation, either direct or indirect. Are we thrown back, then, on a much broader and simpler though rather terrifying hypothesis, that the field of tragedy is by nature so limited that these similarities are inevitable? Certain situations and stories and characters—certain subjects, we may say, for shortness—are naturally tragic; these subjects are quite few in number, and, consequently, two poets or sets of poets trying to find or invent tragic subjects are pretty sure to fall into the same paths. . . . But I do not think that in itself it is enough, or nearly enough, to explain such close similarities, both detailed and fundamental, as those we are considering. I feel as I look at these two traditions that there must be a connexion somewhere.

There is none within the limits of our historical record; but can there be any outside? There is none between the dramas, nor even directly between the sagas; but can there be some original connexion between the myths, or the primitive religious rituals, on which the dramas are ultimately based? And can it be that in the last analysis the similarities between Euripides and Shakespeare are simply due to the natural working out, by playwrights of special genius, of the dramatic possibilities latent in that original seed? If this is so, it will lead us to some interesting conclusions.

To begin with, then, can we discover the original myth out of which the Greek Orestes-saga has grown? (pp. 226-27)

The story falls into its place in a clearly marked group of Greek or pre-Greek legends. Let us recall the primeval kings of the world in Hesiod.

First there was Ouranos and his wife Gaia. Ouranos lived in dread of his children, and "hid them away" till his son Kronos rose and cast him out, helped by the Queen-Mother Gaia.

Then came King Kronos with his wife Rhea. He, too, feared his children and ''swallowed them,'' till his son Zeus rose and cast him out, helped by the Queen-Mother Rhea.

Then, thirdly—but the story cannot continue. For Zeus is still ruling and cannot have been cast out. But he was saved by a narrow margin. He was about to marry the sea-maiden Thetis, when Prometheus warned him that, if he did so, the son of Thetis would be greater than he and cast him out from heaven. And, great as is my love for Thetis, I have little doubt that she would have been found helping her son in his criminal behaviour.

In the above cases the new usurper is represented as the son of the old King and Queen. Consequently the Queen-Mother, though she helps him, does not marry him, as she does when he is merely a younger kinsman. But there is one great saga in which the marriage of mother and son has remained, quite unsoftened and unexpurgated. In Thebes King Laïus and his wife Jocasta knew that their son would slay and dethrone his father. Laïus orders the son's death, but he is saved by the Queen-Mother, and, after slaying and dethroning his father, marries her. She is afterwards slain or dethroned with him, as Clytemnestra is with Aegisthus, and Gertrude with Claudius.

There is clearly a common element in all these stories, and the reader will doubtless have recognised it. It is the world-wide ritual story of what we may call the Golden-Bough Kings. That ritual story is . . . the fundamental conception that forms the basis of Greek tragedy, and not Greek tragedy only. It forms the basis of the traditional Mummers' Play, which, though deeply degraded and vulgarized, is not quite dead yet in the countries of Northern Europe and lies at the root of so large a part of all the religions of mankind.

It is unnecessary, I hope, to make any long explanation of the Vegetation-kings or Year-daemons. But there are perhaps two points that we should remember, to save us from confusion later on. First, there are two early modes of reckoning: you can reckon by seasons or half-years, by summers and winters; or you can reckon with the whole year as your unit. On the first system a Summer-king or Vegetation-spirit is slain by Winter and rises from the dead in the spring. On the second each Year-king comes first as a wintry slayer, weds the queen, grows proud and royal, and then is slain by the Avenger of his predecessor. These two conceptions cause some confusion in the myths, as they do in most forms of the Mummers' Play.

The second point to remember is that this death and vengeance was really enacted among our remote ancestors in terms of human bloodshed. The sacred king really had ''slain the slayer'' and was doomed himself to be slain. The queen might either be taken on by her husband's slayer, or else slain with her husband. It is no pale myth or allegory that has so deeply dyed the first pages of human history. It is man's passionate desire for the food that will save him from starvation, his passionate memory of the streams of blood, willing and unwilling, that have been shed to keep him alive. (pp. 227-29)

Thus Orestes, the madman and king-slayer, takes his place beside Brutus the Fool, who expelled the Tarquins, and Amlodi the Fool, who burnt King Feng at his winter feast. (p. 229)

[It] seems beyond doubt, even to my most imperfect scrutiny of the material, that the same forms of myth and the same range of primitive religious conceptions are to be found in Scandinavia as in other Arian countries.

There are several wives in the Ynglinga saga who seem to belong to the Gaia-Rhea-Clytemnestra-Jocasta type. For instance, King Vanlandi was married to Drifa of Finland, and was killed by her in conjunction with their son Visburr, who succeeded to the kingdom. (p. 230)

Visburr in turn married the daughter of Aude the Wealthy. Like Agamemnon, he was unfaithful to his wife, so she left him and sent her two sons to talk to him, and duly, in the proper ritual manner, to burn him in his house—just as the Hamlet of saga burned King Feng, just as the actual Northern villagers at their festival burned the Old Year.

Again, there are clear traces of kings who are sacrificed and are succeeded by their slayers. Most of the Yngling kings die in sacrificial ways. One is confessedly sacrificed to avert famine, one killed by a sacrificial bull, one falls off his horse in a temple and dies, one burns himself on a pyre at a festival. (pp. 230-31)

[When] we find that the Hamlet of saga resembles Orestes so closely; when we find that he is the Bitter Fool and king-slayer; when especially we find that this strange part of wedding—if not helping—their husband's slayer and successor is played alike by Hamlet's mother, whatever her name, Gerutha, Gertrude, or Amba; and by Amlodi's mother and by Ambales' mother, and by the mother of divers variants of Hamlet, like Helgi and Hroar; and by Hamlet's wife, and by the wife of Anlaf Curan, who is partly identified with Hamlet, we can hardly hesitate to draw the same sort of conclusion as would naturally follow in a Greek story. Hamlet is more deeply involved in this Clytemnestra-like atmosphere than any person I know of outside Hesiod. And one cannot fail to be reminded of Oedipus and Jocasta by the fact, which is itself of no value in the story but is preserved both in Saxo and the *Ambales Saga,* that Amlodi slept in his mother's chamber.

There is something strangely characteristic in the saga treatment of this ancient Queen-Mother, a woman under the shadow of adultery, the shadow of incest, the shadow of murder, who is yet left in most of the stories a motherly and sympathetic character. . . . The trait remains even in Shakespeare. ''Gertrude,'' says Professor Bradley, ''had a soft animal nature. . . . She loved to be happy like a sheep in the sun, and to do her justice she loved to see others happy, like more sheep in the sun.'' Just the right character for our Mother Earth! For, of course, that is who she is. . . . One cannot apply moral disapproval to the annual re-marriages of Mother Earth with the new Spring-god; nor yet possibly to the impersonal and compulsory marriages of the human queen in certain very primitive stages of society. But later on, when life has become more self-conscious and sensitive, if once a poet or dramatist gets to thinking of the story, and tries to realise the position and feelings of this eternally traitorous wife, this eternally fostering and protecting mother, he cannot but feel in her that element of inward conflict which is the seed of great drama. She is torn between husband, lover, and son; and the avenging son, the mother-murderer, how is he torn?

English tragedy has followed the son. Yet Gerutha, Amba, Gertrude, Hermutrude, Gormflaith, Gaia, Rhea, Jocasta—there is tragedy in all of them, and it is in the main the same tragedy. (pp. 231-33)

And what of Hamlet himself as a mythical character? I find, almost to my surprise, exactly the evidence I should have liked to find. Hamlet in Saxo is the son of Horvendillus or Ørvandil, an ancient Teutonic god connected with dawn and the spring.

His great toe, for instance, is now the morning star. (It was frozen off; that is why it shines like ice.) His wife was Groa, who is said to be the Green Earth; he slew his enemy Collerus—Kollr the Hooded, or perhaps the Cold—in what Saxo calls "a sweet and spring-green spot" in a budding wood. He was slain by his brother and avenged by his son. (pp. 233-34)

Thus, if these arguments are trustworthy, we finally run the Hamlet-saga to earth in the same ground as the Orestes-saga: in that prehistoric and world-wide ritual battle of Summer and Winter, of Life and Death, which has played so vast a part in the mental development of the human race and especially, as Mr. E. K. Chambers has shown us, in the history of mediaeval drama. Both heroes have the notes of the winter about them rather than summer, though both are on the side of right against wrong. Hamlet is no joyous and triumphant slayer. He is clad in black, he rages alone, he is the Bitter Fool who must slay the King.

It seems a strange thing, this gradual shaping and reshaping of a primitive folk-tale, in itself rather empty and devoid of character, until it issues in a great tragedy which shakes the world. Yet in Greek literature, I am sure, the process is a common, almost a normal, one. Myth is defined by a Greek writer as . . . "the things said over a ritual act." For a certain agricultural rite, let us suppose, you tore a cornsheaf in pieces and scattered the grain; and to explain why you did so, you told a myth. . . . The things that thrill and amaze us in *Hamlet* or the *Agamemnon* are not any historical particulars about mediaeval Elsinore or prehistoric Mycenae, but things belonging to the old stories and the old magic rites, which stirred and thrilled our forefathers five and six thousand years ago; set them dancing all night on the hills, tearing beasts and men in pieces, and giving up their own bodies to a ghastly death, in hope thereby to keep the green world from dying and to be the saviours of their own people.

I am not trying to utter a paradox, or even to formulate a theory. I am not for a moment questioning or belittling the existence, or the overwhelming artistic value, of individual genius. I trust no one will suspect me of so doing. I am simply trying to understand a phenomenon which seems, before the days of the printed book and the widespread reading public, to have occurred quite normally and constantly in works of imaginative literature, and doubtless in some degree is occurring still.

What does our hypothesis imply? It seems to imply, first, a great unconscious solidarity and continuity, lasting from age to age, among all the children of the poets, both the makers and the callers-forth, both the artists and the audiences. In artistic creation, as in all the rest of life, the traditional element is far larger, the purely inventive element far smaller, than the unsophisticated man supposes.

Further, it implies that in the process of *traditio*—that is, of being handed on from generation to generation, constantly modified and expurgated, re-felt and re-thought—a subject sometimes shows a curious power of almost eternal durability. It can be vastly altered; it may seem utterly transformed. Yet some inherent quality still remains, and significant details are repeated quite unconsciously by generation after generation of poets. Nay, more. It seems to show that often there is latent in some primitive myth a wealth of detailed drama, waiting only for the dramatist of genius to discover it and draw it forth. Of course, we must not exaggerate this point. We must not say that *Hamlet* or the *Electra* is latent in the original ritual as

a flower is latent in the seed. The seed, if it just gets its food, is bound to develop along a certain fixed line; the myth or ritual is not. It depends for its development on too many live people and too many changing and complex conditions. We can only say that some natural line of growth is there, and in the case before us it seems to have asserted itself both in large features and in fine details, in a rather extraordinary way. The two societies in which the Hamlet and Orestes tragedies arose were very dissimilar; the poets were quite different in character, and quite independent; even the particular plays themselves differed greatly in plot and setting and technique and most other qualities; the only point of contact lies at their common origin many thousand years ago, and yet the fundamental identity still shows itself, almost unmistakable.

This conception may seem strange; but after all, in the history of religion it is already a proved and accepted fact, this "almost eternal durability" of primitive conceptions and even primitive rites. Our hypothesis will imply that what is already known to happen in religion may also occur in imaginative drama.

If this is so, it seems only natural that those subjects, or some of those subjects, which particularly stirred the interest of primitive men, should still have an appeal to certain very deep-rooted human instincts. I do not say that they will always move us now; but, when they do, they will tend to do so in ways which we recognize as particularly profound and poetical. This comes in part from their original quality; in part, I suspect, it depends on mere repetition. We all know the emotional charm possessed by famous and familiar words and names, even to hearers who do not understand the words and know little of the bearers of the names. I suspect that a charm of that sort lies in these stories and situations, which are—I cannot quite keep clear of metaphor—deeply implanted in the memory of the race, stamped, as it were, upon our physical organism. We have forgotten their faces and their voices; we say that they are strange to us. Yet there is that within us which leaps at the sight of them, a cry of the blood which tells us we have known them always. (pp. 234-39)

> *Gilbert Murray, "Hamlet and Orestes," in his* The Classical Tradition in Poetry: The Charles Eliot Norton Lectures, *Cambridge, Mass.: Harvard University Press, 1927, pp. 205-40.*

W. W. GREG (essay date 1917)

[*Greg was an English scholar and a major figure in the development of the principles of textual scholarship in Shakespeare studies. In the excerpt here, Greg contends that the ghost in* Hamlet *is not genuine or objective; rather, that it is suggested by Hamlet's hallucination. Thus Greg challenges the accepted view of that figure's nature and purpose. As proof, he points out that while both the dumb-show and the* Murder of Gonzago *purport to reenact King Hamlet's murder and Gertrude's remarriage, they have no effect on Claudius. Greg's argument is challenged by J. Dover Wilson (1918). For additional commentary on the ghost, see Joseph Addison (1711), Gotthold Ephraim Lessing (1767), Elizabeth Montagu (1769), Sister Miriam Joseph (1962), and Eleanor Prosser (1971).*]

Belief in the genuineness and objectivity of the Ghost in *Hamlet* has been almost universal. It is the natural view, based on the obvious and naïve interpretation of the text. Any other view supposes a considerable amount of subtlety on the part of the author in hinting that statements, and even apparent action, are not to be taken at their face value; a kind of subtlety which may, indeed, possess high dramatic value, but is not of a kind

Act III. Scene ii. Claudius, the Players, Hamlet, Ophelia. Frontispiece to Hanmer edition by F. Hayman (1744). By permission of the Folger Shakespeare Library.

commonly credited to Shakespeare, and certainly not to be presumed without cogent reasons.

Now the claim of the naïve view to be obviously correct is based, it seems to me, upon two considerations: the elaborate external evidence for the reality of the Ghost, and the fact that the Ghost reveals to Hamlet true information which he could not otherwise have acquired. But observe that these two arguments are not of equal importance. For should the second, upon examination, break down (through the information proving false), its collapse would leave the orthodox view a chaotic mass of ruins; whereas, so long as it holds, it is of itself ample to support the conclusion, no matter how weak the other may prove to be. We may as well, therefore, consider the more important point first. (pp. 395-96)

There is a curious feature of the action which exponents of *Hamlet* commonly ignore, and the purpose of which has never been discovered. If we turn to the text we shall find that the regular performance of the *Murder of Gonzago,* the piece acted by the players, is preceded by a dumb-show. (p. 397)

The full significance of this dumb-show has never been appreciated. Here and there a critic has dimly apprehended what it involved, but the vast majority have passed by with obstinate blindness. Yet the difficulty it raises is obvious enough. The King, we have seen, when he beholds his secret crime repro-

duced before the assembled court, loses his nerve, and retires in evident agitation. How comes it then that he sat unmoved through the representation of the same action in equal detail in the dumb-show? It is impossible that, seeing that show, he could fail to understand that his secret was betrayed. Crown, poison, queen, these might conceivably be coincidences; not so the almost unique method by which the poison is administered. That is conclusive. If the king could sit unmoved through the representation in pantomime of these events there is no imaginable reason why they should move him when acted with words. (pp. 397-98)

There are several things to be observed about this dumb-show. To begin with, there is no getting rid of it. Not only is the textual tradition unassailable, but the show is actually the subject of comment by Ophelia and Hamlet, a fact that proves it to be no mere oversight, no intrusion accidentally foisted into the text, but an integral, and presumably rational, part of the scene in which it occurs. And there is a further and exceedingly important point to be noticed. The dumb-show is not, as one might be tempted to suppose, a fossilized relic of the original *Hamlet.* . . . [Of] one thing we can be absolutely certain: if the play was shown in pantomime only it broke off with the poisoning. The fact that in both versions of the play, as we have it, the action is carried beyond this point, proves conclusively that the extant dumb-show is not the survival of an original pantomime play. It follows that the dumb-show was actually designed for its present position, and was intentionally made to anticipate the representation of the spoken play. And no theory of *Hamlet* is tolerable that does not face this fact and offer a rational explanation of it. (pp. 398-99)

One or two commentators have wondered why Hamlet should have risked the success of his play by anticipating the action in the dumb-show. It has been suggested that, in order to avoid the possibility of failure through an accidental wandering of the King's attention, Hamlet presented the situation twice over, and that there should be a direction to the effect that during the dumb-show the King and Queen are absorbed in close conversation and pay no attention to the stage. The explanation is, indeed, a lame one, but such as it is it has had to serve, for no other has been forthcoming.

We are now in a position to appreciate the extraordinary nature of this intrusive dumb-show. It is an integral and intentional factor of the scene, deliberately designed for the position it now occupies. It is unique in type, unparalleled by anything to be found elsewhere in the Elizabethan drama. It serves no discovered purpose of the plot. And, on the accepted interpretation of the action, it not merely threatens the logical structure of one of the most crucial scenes of the play, but reduces it to meaningless confusion. How are we to account for its presence? . . . We have to choose between giving up Shakespeare as a rational playwright, and giving up our inherited beliefs regarding the story of *Hamlet.*

And, if only we will look at the matter with our minds freed from certain prepossessions, we shall soon, I think, perceive a possible line of advance. Since there appears to be a contradiction between the dumb-show and the subsequent conduct of the King, and since the former is a hard fact which cannot be explained away, it is worth while to consider whether our view of the latter may not be at fault.

Let us for the moment suppose (what I hope later to show is the case) that the King's action in breaking up the court has nothing directly to do with either the plot or the words of the play. The gross contradiction we have been considering will then be removed, and, although we shall be no nearer explaining the motive for the dumb-show, the scene should be at least logically coherent. On examination, however, we shall find that we have only removed a glaring absurdity to be faced with a more subtle obstacle. We are bound to believe that, as soon as the dumb-show has been performed, the King is aware that the story of his crime down to its minutest details is known, and known to Hamlet. There can be no possible doubt on that head. But how does his subsequent behaviour (even upon our revised hypothesis, and basing ourselves solely upon the actual text of the play) square with this fundamental assumption? The answer is that it does not square at all. The King, it will be observed, gives not the smallest sign of disturbance during or after the all-important dumb-show, and yet when the play comes to be acted his uneasiness quickly makes itself apparent. . . . [The] only hypothesis consistent with the King's behaviour is that in the dumb-show he actually fails to recognize the representation of his own crime. This, however, on the ordinary assumptions, is impossible. The manner in which the poison is administered makes even the shadow of a doubt absurd. There is but one rational conclusion: *Claudius did not murder his brother by pouring poison into his ears.*

This inference appears to be as certain as anything in criticism can be. But a far more important inference follows immediately, and as certainly, from it. If the facts of King Hamlet's death were not as represented in the players' play, then the Ghost was no honest ghost, but a liar. In other words, *the Ghost's story was not a revelation, but a mere figment of Hamlet's brain.* (pp. 399-401)

Objections must at once occur to the reader, the weight of which I do not seek to deny. They are, I think, in the main two: (1) that we know from the earlier scenes that the Ghost is an objective reality and no mere hallucination; and (2) that, as a fact, the King, whatever his behaviour during the dumb-show, does break down 'upon the talk of the poisoning.' The first of these is our old friend, the external evidence for the reality of the Ghost, the consideration of which still awaits us. Meanwhile we will complete our investigation of the 'Mouse-Trap' by attending to the second objection. For if we are to re-establish the play-scene upon a new and logical basis, it behoves us to show that it can be rationally interpreted throughout on the assumptions which consideration of one point in it have forced upon us, and in particular it will be necessary for us to offer a satisfactory explanation of the King's behaviour. (pp. 401-02)

To begin with, let us consider the inserted play, chosen by Hamlet as being 'something like the murder of my father.' We have already observed that this is hardly an adequate description of the *Murder of Gonzago* as actually performed: it is, indeed, a minutely applicable representation of the affairs of the Danish court, and of the alleged murder of the late King. The strangeness of this coincidence has been hidden from critics by a vague idea that Hamlet had considerably altered the play in order to make it serve his purpose. But for this belief there is no warrant. We know that, to bring home the situation, Hamlet proposed to insert in the play an original 'speech of some dozen or sixteen lines': he says nothing to justify our supposing that he intended to, or in fact did, in any way interfere with the action. . . . Now commentators have never been able to agree as to where this speech of Hamlet's is to be found, and it seems probable that all Shakespeare wished to do was to prepare his audience for the striking relevance of the *language* of the play to the

known circumstances of the Danish court, noticeably to the marriage of the Queen. There is no allusion to the hidden matter of the King's guilt. The only relevance here is in the *action*, and of this, startling as it is, Shakespeare gives us no hint beforehand. Indeed, he has rather gone out of his way to imply, by laying stress on the language, that the action has been left undisturbed. We are bound, on the evidence to assume that the plot of the play is untouched, and that the words alone have been altered.

But, this being so, it must strike the reader that, if Claudius really poisoned his brother in the manner described by the Ghost, it is unbelievable that the players should chance to have in stock a play, which not only reproduced so closely the general situation, but in which the murderer adopted just this exceptional method by which to dispatch his victim. A dramatist is, no doubt, entitled to draw in some measure upon coincidence, but to draw to this extent for a mere piece of theatrical machinery, which could quite easily have been otherwise supplied, is to make impossible demands upon the credulity of his audience. (pp. 402-03)

[If] the dumb-show was unexpected on Hamlet's part, it must have been singularly unwelcome. The plot has been prematurely divulged, and the King has shown no symptom of alarm. Is the trap going to prove a failure after all? Of course, Hamlet ought to begin to suspect that the Ghost was, indeed, no messenger of truth; but his growing excitement and the shock of the unexpected turn of events have put his critical purpose from his mind; his attention is bent on tripping the King, he forgets the object with which he desires to trip him. At first Hamlet hardly counted on any public outbreak—such as actually occurs—'if he but blench, I know my course.' But will he even achieve this much? If the King is really endowed with such iron nerves as to watch unmoved the dumb-show, will he not be equally able to sit and smile on the play, and betray no sign of guilt? Or, if Hamlet still counts on the efficacy of his 'speech,' there is another danger. Will that speech ever be spoken? Warned by the unfortunate dumb-show, will not the King make some excuse for stopping the performance? He knows not what public exposure may be in store. However firm his nerves, can he afford to run the risk? To Hamlet the doubt and suspense must be torture. He now assumes the King's guilt, and sets himself to ensure that the play itself shall not fail as the dumb-show failed. Moreover, it is no longer some slight tremor that Hamlet looks for—he is now playing for a full and open betrayal. If only he can break down the King's defences, if only he can frighten him sufficiently, he *must* give himself away by some manifest and public act. (p. 404)

The play begins. It is strange stuff, with its childish crudity and directness, strange in its passionate rhetoric, strangest of all in its harping on the idea of remarriage. It is such a play as Hamlet might have dreamed. The protests of the lady are certainly too much: they are extravagant, irrational. The effect on the audience may be imagined. Whatever else the performance may be, it is a coarse insult to the Queen—gross, open, palpable. And Hamlet's question: 'Madam, how like you the play?' is a slap in the face before the whole court. The King is naturally disturbed. It is impossible to feign blindness. Can it be mere coincidence? For assurance he turns to Hamlet. To Hamlet! whom, on the usual assumptions, he must by this time know for his deadly enemy. How far is this unseemly matter to be pursued? 'Have you heard the argument? *Is there no offence in't?*' No offence in the public representation of his own crime! Were there still room for doubt in Hamlet's mind, this remark of the King's ought surely to shake his confidence in the Ghost. But he is now too excited to notice anything. . . . His original purpose is long forgotten. In his excitement he lashes out all round: he insults Ophelia, outrages the Queen, jibes at the King and taunts him before the assembled court. In fine, he behaves like a madman; there is no telling what he may say or do next. When the poisoner appears he can hardly contain himself. Delay is torture. 'Begin, murderer; pox, leave thy damnable faces, and begin. Come: the croaking raven doth bellow for revenge.' He shouts the words across the hall at the actor on the stage. Revenge! There is no question of revenge in the play; as yet there is nothing to revenge. But it is not of the play that Hamlet is thinking. The word must fall ominously on the ears of the assembled courtiers, who behold the dispossessed heir first insult the Queen, and now covertly threaten the usurper. We can see them exchange looks. But Hamlet heeds them not. His excitement rises to an agony of suspense as the critical moment—to his thinking—approaches. The poisoner speaks:

Thoughts black, hands apt, drugs fit, and time agreeing;
Confederate season, else no creature seeing;
Thou mixture rank, of midnight weeds collected,
With Hecate's ban thrice blasted, thrice infected,
Thy natural magic and dire property,
On wholesome life usurp immediately.

[III. iv. 254-60]

It would be difficult to imagine more stilted commonplace, a speech less calculated to unnerve a guilty spectator. But for Hamlet the supreme moment, so long anxiously expected, has arrived. The murderer empties his poison into the sleeper's ears, and—the King rises? Not a bit of it. Hamlet is unable to restrain himself any longer; he breaks out, hurling the crude facts of the story in the King's face, shouting, gesticulating, past reason and control. It seems as though the next moment he must spring at his throat. Naturally the court breaks up, the King rises, calls for lights, and retires to his private apartments, convinced—not that his guilt has been discovered, but that Hamlet is a dangerous madman, who has designs on his life, and must, at all costs, be got quietly out of the country, and, if possible, out of the world. (pp. 405-06)

We have (1) found evidence that the circumstances of King Hamlet's death were not as represented by the Ghost, and (2) we have further discovered that the action of the scene is perfectly consistent with this hypothesis, and in particular that the behaviour of Claudius, which seemed at first sight to confirm the Ghost's story, is readily explained in another manner. It remains, therefore, to consider what I have called the external evidence for the genuineness of the Ghost. . . .

If the theory advanced above is to be made good, it will be necessary to maintain that the Ghost's communications to Hamlet are no more than hallucinations of Hamlet's own mind, and we shall expect to find internal evidence of this in the text. But we are not bound to maintain that the appearances of the Ghost to Horatio and the rest are mere illusion. (p. 407)

At the opening of the play Marcellus and Bernardo have twice already seen the apparition, and have invited Horatio, the scholar and friend of the Prince, to come and share their watch, in the belief that it will manifest itself again. He does so, sees the Ghost, and speaks to it. The account he subsequently gives to Hamlet is very circumstantial. 'A figure like your father. Armed at point exactly, cap-a-pie.—I knew your father; These hands are not more like.—He wore his beaver up.—A countenance

more in sorrow than in anger . . . very pale.—His beard . . . was, as I have seen it in his life, A sable silver'd.' All this is very satisfactory, and these details, if they can be accepted as the direct result of observation, are conclusive of an apparition so clear and definite that we shall probably be content to accept it as genuine. But they are given some hours after the occurrence; there is time for imagination to have been at work. How much of the description is due to observation, how much, possibly, to suggestion? It will be noticed that from the first the two soldiers have made up their minds that the Ghost is none other than the late King. . . . Horatio is a simple, honest, and healthy, but not a critical soul. He is overwhelmed by the unexpectedness of his experience, and his abnormal agitation may be traced in the words he utters at the time. We do not here find the lucid and orderly evidence he gives later on. 'Is it not like the king?' asks Marcellus, seeking confirmation of his own belief. 'As thou art to thyself,' replies Horatio, now but a mirror of the others' thoughts; and he proceeds:

Such was the very armour he had on
When he the ambitious Norway combated;
So frown'd he once, when, in an angry parle,
He smote the sledded Polacks on the ice.

[I. i. 60-3]

Now, we have very good reason to believe that Horatio, the fellow student of Hamlet, can have been at most a baby in arms at the time of the Norwegian contest, and although we know nothing as to the date of the 'angry parle,' it seems unlikely that the Wittenberg scholar should have witnessed it. In short, Horatio here is not giving personal evidence of value, but indulging in mere imaginative rhetoric, and incidentally sowing the seed of the suggestion that bears fruit in his subsequent interview with the Prince. . . . It is also to be noticed that, in spite of all this pretended certainty, Horatio does not in the least persuade himself that the apparition really is the spirit of the dead King, for on its re-appearance he hails it with the exclamation: 'Stay, illusion!' (pp. 407-09)

How, then, does the question stand as regards the reality of the Ghost? The assumption that it is genuine certainly leads to no contradiction; we are perfectly at liberty to make it. But are we compelled to do so? No one will suggest that the apparition is pure fancy, but it is a long cry from that to the belief that it is supernatural. Further, it seems evident that there is about the appearance something to confirm the belief that it is the dead King in a mind in which the suggestion is already present. But we do not know how the belief originally arose; whether from an actually convincing resemblance, or whether through the opportune congress of some chance phenomenon with a preoccupation in the minds of the officers, Marcellus and Bernardo. From the freedom of Hamlet's discourse in their presence, we may suppose them to have been loyal followers of his father; and the events of the last few weeks must have given rise to speculation and suspicion in the minds of others than the Prince. They may or may not have been personally familiar with the late King's appearance. From them the suggestion passes to Horatio, who we know was not. To many people Horatio's evidence is conclusive regarding the genuineness of the Ghost. But on close examination we have found that, for all his honesty, he is a very bad witness indeed. From him the suggestion passes to Hamlet. And we may fancy we trace how the idea, once formed, works in diverse ways upon the belief of each. There is the appearance of mutual suggestion; the characters encourage one another to trace the likeness of the King. And yet, previous to the pretended revelation, not one of them is really persuaded that the Ghost is genuine. It is an 'illusion,' an 'imagination,' a 'horrible shape,' a 'spirit of health or goblin damn'd'; while, on a later occasion, Hamlet admits bluntly that it may be the devil. There is, it seems to me, a good deal here to shake our confidence in the supernatural character of the apparition. But it falls far short of disproof. If we please to accept the Ghost as genuine we may; at the same time Shakespeare seems clearly to leave the way open for an alternative, to hint that we may, if we will, regard it as a freak of collective suggestion, and explain it away as we should any other spook. (p. 410)

Let me try to make clear what I conceive to be the position. Shakespeare, it must be supposed, expected his ghost and its story to be generally taken on the stage at their face value. To the bulk of his audience *Hamlet* would just be another—and the greatest—of the Senecan revenge dramas. But may we not believe that for himself, as for other humaner minds among his contemporaries, such crude machinery would appear as a blot upon a noble piece of work? For such minds he would appear to have designed an alternative explanation, and as a warning of his real intention to have introduced the dumb-show. This piece of business does not obtrude itself on the attention when the play is acted, but in reading and upon consideration its absolute redundancy and its extraordinary results *should* immediately become apparent. It is then seen that the obvious interpretation of the action, which satisfies the generality, makes Shakespeare an astonishingly perverse bungler; while the alternative shows him not only a skilful craftsman, but likewise a considerable master of innuendo. That we are not in the habit of regarding Shakespeare in this light is true, and in the case of most of his work it might hardly be legitimate to do so. But are we not perhaps justified, in the case of *Hamlet*, in looking for subtleties we do not meet elsewhere? or need we be surprised at finding literary devices employed in that play that would miss their effect under the conditions of the Elizabethan stage? *Hamlet* stands more or less alone among its author's works. In writing it Shakespeare built upon the foundation of an earlier piece by Kyd or somebody, rewriting and revising probably more than once, and it is clear that in doing so he got carried away by his interest in the story, and allowed his work to burst the bounds of its theatrical limitations. The length of the play is excessive; it would almost make two pieces of ordinary dimensions. As a practical dramatist Shakespeare must have known that it could never be performed in its entirety, even under the most favourable conditions of the great London theatres. We know that, in fact, it was mercilessly cut by the company for which it was written. In composition Shakespeare *must* have had in mind readers as well as spectators; he must have written for the closet as well as for the stage. Is it reasonable to suppose that this knowledge had no influence on his treatment of his theme? It would be a rash assumption in the case of any professional writer: we certainly have no right to make it in the case of Shakespeare. (pp. 419-21)

W. W. Greg, ''Hamlet's Hallucination,'' in The Modern Language Review, *Vol. XII, No. 4, October, 1917, pp. 393-421.*

J. DOVER WILSON (essay date 1918)

[*Dover Wilson was a highly regarded Shakespearean scholar who was involved in several aspects of Shakespeare studies. As an editor of the* New Cambridge Shakespeare, *he made numerous contributions to twentieth-century textual criticism of Shake-speare, making use of the scientific bibliography developed by W. W. Greg and Charlton Hinman. As a critic, Dover Wilson combines several contemporary approaches and does not fit easily into any one critical ''school.'' He is concerned with character analysis in the tradition of A. C. Bradley; he delves into Elizabethan culture like the historical critics, but without their usual emphasis on hierarchy and the Great Chain of Being; and his interest in visualizing possible dramatic performances of the plays links him with his contemporary, Harley Granville-Barker. In the following reply to Greg (1917), Dover Wilson points out many flaws in Greg's argument regarding the ghost, the play-scene, and the dumb-show in* Hamlet, *and contends that the ghost is objective. Stressing that the ghost reveals the news of his mother's adultery to Hamlet, Wilson disputes Greg's claim that the ghost gives Hamlet only one piece of new information. Wilson also identifies and refutes six assumptions on which Greg's theory of the play-scene is based. Finally, he offers his own theory regarding the dumb-show, asserting that Claudius does not watch it. Granville-Barker (1937) contradicts Dover Wilson's theory. Wilson included his analysis of the ghost in his* What Happens in Hamlet *(see excerpt below, 1935). For additional commentary on the ghost, see Joseph Addison (1711), Gotthold Ephraim Lessing (1767), Elizabeth Montagu (1769), Sister Miriam Joseph (1962), and Eleanor Prosser (1971).*]

Dr Greg's article, 'Hamlet's Hallucination,' . . . is a fascinating, far-reaching and extraordinarily ingenious piece of work. Arguing from an apparently weak spot in the dramatic structure of the play, he has produced a theory which, if true, forces us to recast completely our traditional conception of Shakespeare's intention, our time-honoured beliefs as to what actually took place in the palace of Elsinore, and—a point which has seemingly escaped his notice—our general ideas on the character of the prince of Denmark. (p. 129)

Clearly what started him off on his enquiry was a remarkable point in connexion with the dumb-show in the play-scene. . . . The conclusions which Dr Greg draws from [the anomalies in the play-scene] are startling and at first reading overwhelming. They may be briefly summed up as follows:

(1) The King did not blench at the dumb-show for the simple reason that he did not recognise his own crime either in that or in the Gonzago play itself, which is mere verbal repetition of it.

(2) The information which the Ghost gives to Hamlet is, therefore, an incorrect version of what took place.

(3) Consequently the Ghost's speech must be interpreted as nothing but a figment of Hamlet's overwrought brain.

(4) And finally, the essential feature of the story (the poisoning through the ears) could only have taken root in Hamlet's mind through a sub-conscious memory of the very play which he afterwards employed 'to catch the conscience of the king.' (pp. 129-30)

[The] whole hypothesis, the construction of which occupies nearly thirty tightly packed pages of print, stands on a foundation which is strikingly slender. The stone which, ignored by all previous critics, Dr Greg makes the head-stone of his corner, is, dramatically considered, scarcely larger than a pebble. Once prove that the dumb-show business can be reconciled with the traditional interpretation of *Hamlet*, and the beautiful edifice reared so patiently and ingeniously, falls toppling to the ground. (p. 131)

The dumb-show, which occurs about a third of the way through Act III, is almost exactly the middle point of the play. Dr Greg's argument touches very slightly upon what happens in

Acts IV and V, and in effect he is asking us, on the evidence of the dumb-show, in itself a brief incident enough, to revise all our impressions of what has taken place previously. Now Shakespeare undoubtedly aimed at coherence and continuity of general impression rather than at historical consistency. The play moves forward from scene to scene and from act to act, the spectator all the while absorbing new details which he builds up into the memory of all that has already happened. Surely if Shakespeare wished to give the 'judicious' section of his audience a clue, warning them not to accept the Ghost's word for a thousand pound, it is strange that he should have inserted it so late in the play. Let us imagine one of these judicious folk at a performance of *Hamlet*. The first act is almost exclusively concerned with the doings of the Ghost; it appears on three separate occasions, and more than 550 lines are devoted to it. At the end of all this our judicious gentleman, however much he may disbelieve in ghosts in the world of phenomena, can hardly avoid the conviction that, as far as the play is concerned, he must take this particular spook as an objective reality. This general impression he carries with him right through the second and part way through the third act. The hautboys play; the dumb-show enters, performs its pantomime and goes off; Claudius makes no sign of guilt. Does the spectator at once surrender his carefully built up impression of the Ghost's reality, recognise that the speech was an hallucination of Hamlet's brain, and conclude that the Gonzago story is the true origin of the whole business? It would be ridiculous to suppose it. . . . He cannot turn back the pages or bid the actors stop while he thinks the matter out. He is forced to go on receiving new impressions, one of which, the King's consternation on the talk of poisoning, lays to rest any possible suspicions that may have arisen. Dr Greg complains, justly enough, that the commentators habitually fall into the 'mistake of criticizing drama as history.' Has he not also fallen into the same error? Not so, he replies, for *Hamlet* differs from Shakespeare's other plays, inasmuch as it was written for the closet not the stage, for the reader not the spectator. This is to beg the whole question of the relation between the First Quarto and the subsequent texts. But grant the point, admit that the play was written *first of all* by Shakespeare to be read, a large and generous admission, and we still have two questions to ask. The First Quarto was, in Dr Greg's words, 'undoubtedly based on an acting version,' why then does the dumb-show appear in it? Why did the players, who cut out so much else, retain this 'superfluous piece of business,' which on the orthodox interpretation, the only one possible for a spectator, 'not merely threatens the logical structure of one of the crucial scenes of the play, but reduces it to meaningless confusion'? And again, if 'in reading and upon consideration' the dumb-show's 'absolute redundancy and its extraordinary results should immediately become apparent,' why has not a single one of Shakespeare's many thousand readers through the centuries ever drawn attention to the fact until October 1917? (pp. 131-33)

Whatever Shakespeare's own beliefs may have been, and whatever secret understanding he may have wished to establish with the 'judicious' among his audience, he took very great care indeed to make this ghost as real and as convincing as possible to the 'generality.' *Hamlet* opens as a ghost-story. The whole setting of the first scene, the midnight hour, the starlight, the ancient castle in the background, the handful of soldiers in the foreground who can barely see each other's faces, so dark is it, all this is deliberately calculated to throw the audience into that 'willing suspension of disbelief' which Shakespeare needed for his play. Marcellus and Bernardo have already seen the

Ghost twice before, and have hardly begun to tell the tale once again to Horatio when the apparition glides on to the stage, only forty brief lines from the beginning of the play. Beforehand Horatio is represented as sceptical. Why? In order that he may be convinced against his daylight judgment and so help to convince the audience. The Ghost appears twice in the first scene. Why? In order that the impression may take firmer grip upon the audience. (p. 133)

[Dr Greg's] hallucination-theory demands a 'dumb ghost.' Believe or disbelieve in the Ghost, as you will, you cannot believe in the Ghost's revelation to Hamlet, since the events of the play-scene give it the lie direct. Leaving the play-scene for later consideration, in order to preserve Shakespeare's sequence of events, let us consider this revelation. In so doing we shall discover at least two curious points which Dr Greg has strangely overlooked, and which make things very awkward for his argument. Personally, I feel that the impression of the Ghost's objective reality has been so firmly built up in the minds of the audience before it opens its mouth, that the average spectator is prepared to take on trust almost anything it chooses to say. Possibly, however, the critical faculty of the 'judicious' may still be awake. If so, what is there in the revelation-scene to create suspicion? First, Dr Greg tells us, there is the style of the Ghost's speech. 'Did the dubious influence of Seneca ever produce a more frigid piece of academic declamation? Is this the way Shakespeare writes when he is in earnest?' To this we reply that it is exceedingly dangerous to assume that Shakespeare shared the views of the modern literary man on questions of style. Is the speech of the Ghost more academic, rhetorical or Senecan than the Pyrrhus-cum-Priam speech, which so moved Hamlet in Act II, scene 2? Yet it is almost certain that Shakespeare agreed with Hamlet in admiring the latter. (p. 138)

Let us pass to the more profitable matter of the actual information which the Ghost conveys. 'The Ghost gives Hamlet one, and only one, piece of information he did not already possess'—the fact that the poison was administered through the ears of the victim. Thus Dr Greg. But is it so? Did Hamlet know, until the Ghost told him, that his father had been murdered? He began to suspect it when he heard that his 'father's spirit in arms' was walking the castle battlements; and the exclamation 'O my prophetic soul' shows that the suspicion had grown in the waiting interval. But he could not and did not *know* before he had speech with the Ghost itself. Dr Greg, however, will no doubt explain this as surmise ripening by hallucination into certainty. Be it so. But what of another piece of information imparted by the Ghost, which Dr Greg passes over entirely? The passage is not a pleasant one, but it has never been properly faced by critics, and must therefore be quoted in full.

> Ay, that incestuous, that *adulterate* beast,
> With witchcraft of his wit, with traitorous gifts,
> O wicked wit and gifts, that have the power
> So to *seduce!—won to his shameful lust*
> *The will of my most seeming-virtuous queen;*
> O Hamlet, what a falling off was there!
> From me, whose love was of that dignity
> That it went hand in hand *even with the vow*
> *I made to her in marriage;* and to decline
> Upon a wretch, whose natural gifts were poor
> To those of mine!
> But virtue, as it never will be moved,
> Though lewdness court it in the shape of heaven,

So lust, though to a radiant angel link'd,
Will sate itself in a celestial bed,
And prey on garbage.   [I. v. 42-57]

Is the Ghost speaking here of the o'er hasty marriage of Claudius and Gertrude? Assuredly not. His 'certain term' was drawing rapidly to an end, and he was already beginning to 'scent the morning air.' Hamlet knew of the marriage, and his whole soul was filled with nausea at the thought of the speedy hasting to 'incestuous sheets.' Why then should the Ghost waste his precious moments in telling Hamlet what he was fully cognisant of before? He had come from his 'prison house' to incite Hamlet to revenge by bringing him *news*, news which only he could communicate to his son. Again, the passage occurs before the account of the murder, and therefore presumably deals with events preceding the crime in the orchard. Moreover, though the word 'incestuous' was applicable to the marriage, and had already been used by Hamlet in speaking of it before he heard of the Ghost, the rest of the passage is entirely inapplicable to it. Marriage, even if, like that of Claudius, contrary to the Church's law, cannot be described as 'adulterate.' Nor do the words 'witchcraft,' 'traitorous gifts,' 'seduce,' 'shameful lust,' and 'seeming-virtuous' seem at all suitable to Gertrude's second marriage, which, though may-be uncanonical, indecently swift, and to Hamlet, with his devotion for his father, shocking in the extreme, was not an uncommon act in royal households, or considered reprehensible by the worldly-minded. But the rest of the quotation (the first six lines of which are cited by Dr Greg as an illustration of the Ghost's comicality!) leave no doubt upon the matter. The comparison of the 'natural gifts' of King Hamlet with those of his brother, taken in conjunction with the reference to the 'marriage-vow,' 'celestial bed,' and 'preying on garbage,' can have but one meaning. *The Ghost is speaking of Gertrude's infidelity before his death,* an infidelity for which she had not the shadow of an excuse. (pp. 139-41)

What then is Dr Greg to make of all this? The information which the Ghost gives as to the method of the poisoning may be false, but the speech as a whole cannot possibly be 'a mere figment of Hamlet's brain,' since it communicates to Hamlet a fact, of which he shows previously not the least suspicion, and which is at the same time undoubtedly true.

And there is another point. The Ghost tells the spectators only one fact about the murder the truth of which they cannot test. Dr Greg makes much of this without seeing that it recoils upon his own interpretation of the play. We know that Claudius murdered his brother because he confesses it in the prayer-scene; we know that the deed was done by means of poison because it was given out that a serpent had stung the victim: we know that the old king was murdered in his orchard or garden, during his after-dinner nap; we know finally that Claudius seized the crown and married the Queen. Now all these facts are mentioned not only in the speech of the Ghost, but also in the story of Gonzago. One of Dr Greg's principal arguments is the strange coincidence that the players should have in stock a play which was 'a minutely applicable representation of the affairs of the Danish Court, and of the alleged murder of the late king.' Once Dr Greg points the matter out to us, it certainly does seem remarkable. But let us suppose that the Ghost lies in the one particular in which we cannot bring his testimony to the proof; let us suppose that Claudius administered the poison, not through the ears, but through the mouth, or by injection of some kind. Is not the coincidence between the Gonzago-play and the verified facts still sufficiently close

to merit Dr Greg's criticism that 'it makes impossible demands upon the credulity of the audience'? And yet how many spectators or even readers have noticed the coincidence? (p. 142)

[There are six distinct assumptions in Dr Greg's] reading of the play-scene. (i) Hamlet is in a state of excitement when the scene opens. (ii) This excitement grows more and more violent as the scene proceeds. (iii) The unlooked-for dumb-show, and its failure to stir the King's conscience, cause Hamlet to change his intention, and to force Claudius to self-exposure by frightening him, instead of leaving the play to do the work. (iv) The King does *not* rise at the poisoning. (v) Hamlet, thereupon, becomes unbearably violent, and the court disperses in confusion. (vi) In the prayer-scene the King gives no hint of recent exposure. He does not know that Hamlet knows.

It is an exceedingly pretty piece of critical exposition. The only flaw in it is that not a single one of the six pillars which support it has any real basis in the text of Shakespeare. Let us take them one by one and see.

(i) On Dr Greg's own showing, Hamlet during his talks with the First Player, and with Horatio earlier in the scene, 'has been his own self, calm and collected.' Does his mood change as the play-scene opens? Shakespeare, whom we have seen to be sometimes a careless historian, is in general as a dramatist a painstaking fellow enough; he has a habit, for example, of giving clues to the moods of his principal characters just before or just after an important scene begins. In the present instance the clue is a very obvious one. Hamlet, seeing the court procession about to enter, breaks off his talk with Horatio, with these words: 'They are coming to the play; *I must be idle*: Get you a place.' The meaning is unmistakable. The two have just been plotting to watch the King together; he must not see them in collusion; 'get you a place' says Hamlet in a hurried whisper. Hamlet, too, has a part to play in this drama. 'I must be idle,' that is to say 'crazy.' . . . And the conversation before the entrance of the dumb-show is exactly what one would expect from his words to Horatio; it is all 'idle,' and, though it is full of double meaning, there is not a trace of excitement in it.

(ii) We may agree that Hamlet was upset at the appearance of the dumb-show, and that 'miching mallecho; it means mischief' is an indication that it was unexpected. But what evidence is there for the growing mental excitement which Dr Greg posits? There is a brief conversation with Ophelia about the Prologue, intermingled with a little ribaldry, at one point perhaps unnecessarily strong—a conversation, which as the *real* audience knows, partly reflects upon the Queen. Then follow seventy lines of the Gonzago-play, during which Hamlet makes two remarks, which are sardonic but certainly not excited. . . . Hamlet's whole behaviour except for one brief lapse is masterly in its self-control up to the entrance of the Poisoner.

(iii) As there is no evidence for Hamlet's 'excitement' so there is none for that 'change of intention' of which Dr Greg makes so much. Such a change in the mind of Hamlet, if it actually took place, would be one of the turning-points of the play, and it is inconceivable that Shakespeare should not have inserted some clue to it, obvious to the 'judicious' but perhaps passing unnoticed by the attention of the 'generality' as part of Hamlet's 'antic disposition.' And without Shakespeare's help, the actor can do nothing. . . . In short, Dr Greg has torn out Shakespeare's pages and inserted a chapter from a psychological novel of his own invention.

(iv) We now reach the crucial point of Dr Greg's interpretation of the scene. He has to show that it is Hamlet's conduct and not the poisoning which causes Claudius to rise, and he bends all his ingenuity to the task. 'The murderer empties his poison into the sleeper's ears, and—the King rises? Not a bit of it.' And the statement is expanded in a footnote: 'This is really the only legitimate interpretation of the text. Hamlet has time for a speech of four lines before Ophelia says: "The King rises." Note too that Hamlet's words, "you shall see anon," assume that the play is going forward.' Alas, we are down to the bone here. Four lines! Four little lines; it is a thin covering for Dr Greg's theory against the searching winds of common-sense. Four lines! Think of those 'judicious' spectators; what lightning intelligences they must possess to catch the point! . . . Had Dr Greg but looked twenty-five lines farther on, as he wrote, he would have seen that this, and not *his* reading, is 'the only legitimate interpretation of the text.'

> *Hamlet.* O good Horatio, I'll take the Ghost's
> word for a thousand pound. Didst perceive?
> *Horatio.* Very well, my lord.
> *Hamlet. Upon the talk of the poisoning?*
> *Horatio.* I did very well note him.
>   [III. ii. 286-90]

Hamlet and Horatio had agreed before the play-scene to 'rivet' their eyes upon the face of Claudius, and they are comparing notes. When had 'his occulted guilt' first unkennelled itself? When the murderer poured the poison into the sleeper's ears? Not a bit of it! It was upon the *talk* of the poisoning. In other words, the King betrayed himself in the eyes of both Hamlet and Horatio (I trust Dr Greg will allow Horatio to be considered a credible witness on this point) *before he had actually seen the manner in which the poison was to be administered.* Even had the Ghost been wrong in the one statement which we cannot bring to the test of external evidence, it would have made no difference. (pp. 145-48)

(v) And if Hamlet, with his eyes upon Claudius, has seen him blench at the talk of the poisoning, why should he break out, 'hurling the crude facts of the story in the King's face, shouting, gesticulating, past reason and control'? Will not his mood be one of exultancy and elation, the mood which 'breaks out' in ballad-snatches and doggerel, directly he has Horatio to himself? There is not the smallest symptom of anger, hatred or madness in this later conversation. He is triumphant, jocular— a jocularity which Horatio shares; it is the happiest moment in his career, for he has succeeded! But those 'four lines.' Well, look at them!

> He poisons him i' the garden for 's estate, his
> name 's Gonzago, the story is extant, and writ-
> ten in very choice Italian, you shall see anon
> how the murderer gets the love of Gonzago's
> wife.   [III. ii. 261-64]

Hamlet sees the hunted look of Claudius, sees that the speech-poison has penetrated his ears, and that the King can stand no more. But he will keep up his own part to the last, the part of 'chorus,' and his final words on the play are in strict accordance with all that he has said to the King hitherto. (pp. 148-49)

(vi) In the concluding sentence of his interpretation of the play-scene Dr Greg makes an important admission in regard to Claudius. 'It is true,' he writes, 'that his conscience is touched, and that in the next scene we see its final wriggles.' So, after all these pages of exposition and all this clever juggling with the plain meaning of the text, we have the concession that the play has caught the conscience of the King and that there *is* something in the orthodox theory. . . . The prayer-scene is the direct consequence of the talk of poisoning and its representation before his eyes. It is an awkward point for Dr Greg, and he wisely glides quickly over it. Yet he makes a valiant attempt to pluck victory out of the jaws of defeat, by insisting that Claudius gives no hint throughout his soliloquy that his secret has been discovered. That he should not do so, would be no point against the orthodox theory. Even Claudius, we might suppose, would hesitate to admit to his Maker that repentance had been forced upon him by discovery. (pp. 149-50)

We have seen that Dr Greg's reading of the play-scene is entirely unsupported by the evidence of the text, that Claudius does recognise his crime in the speech of the murderer and that, therefore, the veracity of the Ghost has received its crowning proof. What then remains of the beautiful hallucination-edifice so cunningly reared by Dr Greg? Nothing at all, except these two strange features of *Hamlet* upon which he rears his whole hypothesis: the parallel plots and the puzzle of the dumb-show. In order to round off the subject it is necessary to provide an explanation of these anomalies which is dramatically a satisfactory one. (p. 150)

Surely what we are here confronted with is an extraordinarily ingenious piece of stage-craft! For consider Shakespeare's problem. The idea of having a play within the play is a famous one, we can imagine him saying to himself, but it is attended with certain difficulties. To serve its dramatic purpose, the actors' play must come as close as possible to the situation at the Danish court; for not only has Hamlet to catch the King's conscience but I have to catch and rivet the attention of my audience. 'Something like' will not do at all; it must be identical, or, at least differing only in such a way as will indicate that it is another story, without impairing the overwhelming dramatic effect of its similarity upon the mind of Claudius and of the spectators in the theatre. . . . But if these differences are small, as they must be, if the scene is to be really effective, will not the audience be asking themselves how it comes about that the actors should have a play, the plot of which is to all intents identical with what had taken place at Elsinore? To avoid such questions it will be necessary to throw them off the scent. They shall be told that the Gonzago-story is 'something like the murder' of the late King, that 'one scene of it comes near the circumstance' of the actual poisoning, that Hamlet has to adapt it for his purposes; but they shall know nothing more about the matter until they see the play itself. (pp. 151-52)

Further, if for the reasons just given it was impossible for Shakespeare to divulge the plot of the Gonzago-story before the play-scene was reached, it was equally impossible for him to set out the plot in full in the Gonzago-play itself. The play is a Mouse-trap, the jaws of which must snap upon the imprisoned Claudius, suddenly, unexpectedly, overwhelmingly. The King must be taken by complete surprise or Hamlet's purpose will be frustrated. Accordingly we have seventy lines of dialogue, between a king and queen, on the subject of widowhood and second marriage, then a sudden murder by a person of whose name and motive we should know nothing did not Hamlet enlighten us,—and that is all! It is not a play; it is not even a scene; it is a piece of a scene, terminated by Claudius at the very moment when the only action which occurs in it is taking place. Thus neither before nor during the play can Shakespeare tell his audience what the plot of the whole business is. And yet somehow he must take them into his confidence, or they will not realise what is going to happen and so will miss the pleasure of watching, with Hamlet, the unconscious criminal drawing nearer and nearer to the trap. Their memories too need refreshing, for by this time the details of the crime will have been partly forgotten. Moreover, if the parallelism between the Gonzago-story and the speech of the Ghost is not made absolutely clear, the whole dramatic effect of the play-scene will be ruined. It was a pretty dilemma; how was Shakespeare to get out of it? Stage-craft afforded him the only possible means of escape. (pp. 152-53)

But what about Claudius? If he is to be lured unsuspectingly into the trap, how can he face the detailed parallelism of the dumb-show? Here we stumble upon the dramatic pebble which Dr Greg has made the head-stone of his corner. But Shakespeare saw it three hundred years and more before Dr Greg, and he avoided it by yet another simple stage-trick. *He had to make it quite apparent to his audience that Claudius was not looking at the dumb-show*. There is nothing new in this explanation. It was first suggested by Halliwell, and has since found its way into all the text-books. Dr Greg calls it 'tame,' but it is only tame, in so far as the critics have put it forward timidly, have not seen that it can be proved from the text, and have failed to observe how cleverly Shakespeare managed the business. It should be as apparent to the modern reader as it undoubtedly was to the Elizabethan spectator that Claudius did not see the dumb-show, because he himself tells us so in unmistakable terms. The Player King and Queen speak their seventy lines, and during the pause before the murderer appears, Claudius turns to Hamlet with these words: 'Have you heard the *argument*? Is there no offence in't?' It is a question which would have been quite impossible if Claudius had seen the dumb-show, the dumb-show which *is* the 'argument of the play' as Shakespeare has carefully informed us through the mouth of Ophelia. (pp. 153-54)

When Claudius and Polonius come to the play their minds are full of what they have recently overheard Hamlet say to Ophelia in the Nunnery scene which immediately precedes the play. Hamlet's references to his 'proud, revengeful, ambitious' nature and the threat in his assertion that 'those that are married already, *all but one*, shall live' have convinced Claudius, not that his nephew knows his secret (of that he has no suspicion until the play-scene draws to an end), but that Hamlet, the dispossessed heir, has designs upon the crown. Polonius, on the other hand, is equally convinced by the general tenor of Hamlet's remarks to Ophelia that 'the origin and commencement of his grief sprung from neglected love.' Before the dumb-show comes on Hamlet plays up to both these explanations of his antic disposition. He supports the King's theory by his 'promise-crammed' reference, which is clearly a hint at his starved ambition and the King's promise of the succession in Act I, scene 2, and by his reminding Polonius of the scene upon the Capitol. On the other hand, he supports the theory of Polonius himself by ostentatiously refusing to sit by his mother and by taking a place at Ophelia's feet. 'O ho! do you mark that?' exclaims the old man exultantly to the King, thereby revealing what the two had been discussing in the interval between their eavesdropping and their appearance at the play. It is a discussion which Hamlet's action now revives in full force, and his ribaldry with Ophelia, clear indication of love-madness, supplies Polonius with still further argument. But there is yet a third explanation of the Prince's madness, the theory of Gertrude,—'his father's death and our o'er-hasty marriage'; and it amuses Hamlet to give this an innings also. 'Look you,' he says, 'how cheerfully my mother looks, and my father died within these two hours,' and he continues fiddling on the same string until the dumb-show appears. This sally complicates the matter between Claudius and Polonius

and drags the Queen in also. It arrests too the attention of Shakespeare's audience, who at Hamlet's 'Look you' turn their full gaze upon the royal group to see how they take this attack. Thus they are fully aware of Claudius's preoccupation at this critical point; they observe the three figures with their heads together, closely engaged in whispered and exciting controversy, controversy which becomes half-audible directly Hamlet ceases speaking. The dumb-show enters and performs its pantomime, quite unnoticed by the three disputants, and the audience *know* that it is so. Doubtless, the dumb-show over, they turn to make sure that Claudius has not seen this striking representation of his crime. If so their anxiety is set at rest by finding him still at it, gesticulating angrily in his efforts to enlighten the darkness of his obstinate interlocutors. (pp. 154-55)

The hallucination-theory would make Shakespeare out to be a far more sophisticated person than we had taken him for; its disproof has shown him to be a subtler dramatist and stage-craftsman than we knew. And the distinction between the two audiences, which Dr Greg makes, still holds good; the only difference being that, whereas he would draw the line between the credulous and the sceptical, we draw it where Hamlet did himself, i.e. between the 'generality' who flocked to the theatre to see a tragedy of revenge and cared for nothing but the story, and the 'judicious' who were interested in the niceties of drama, Shakespeare's fellow-dramatists and cultured patrons, who would catch points in the play which the ordinary spectator would miss, and which indeed have also been missed by the generality of modern critics. In particular the marvellous ingenuity of the play-scene as a whole has been totally obscured since the day when the dramatist himself stage-managed his own performances, an obscurity which we can see beginning as far back as the First Folio. But that is another story. (pp. 155-56)

> *J. Dover Wilson, "The Parallel Plots in 'Hamlet':* *A Reply to Dr. W. W. Greg," in* The Modern Language Review, *Vol. XIII, No. 2, April, 1918, pp. 129-56.*

T. S. ELIOT   (essay date 1919)

[*Eliot, a celebrated American-born English poet, essayist, and critic, stressed in his criticism the importance of tradition, religion, and morality in literature. His emphasis on imagery, symbolism, and meaning helped to establish the theories of New Criticism. Eliot's concept of the "objective correlative" is considered a major contribution to literary analysis. In his* Selected Essays, *Eliot defines the objective correlative as "a set of objects, a situation, a chain of events which shall be the formula of [a] particular emotion" and which have the ability to evoke that emotion in the reader. Eliot cites the scholar, J. M. Robertson (see Additional Bibliography), whose theories regarding the authorship of Shakespeare's plays were popular in Eliot's time, but are now considered extreme. Eliot concurs with Robertson's theory that the play's central emotion is "the feeling of a son toward a guilty mother," but he notes Shakespeare's failure to create for Hamlet's passion an objective correlative that provides a means to express "emotion in the form of art." Francis Fergusson (1949) challenges Eliot's perception of the play's central emotion. Eliot's essay was first published in 1919.*]

Few critics have ever admitted that *Hamlet* the play is the primary problem, and Hamlet the character only secondary. And Hamlet the character has had an especial temptation for that most dangerous type of critic: the critic with a mind which is naturally of the creative order, but which through some weakness in creative power exercises itself in criticism instead.

These minds often find in Hamlet a vicarious existence for their own artistic realization. Such a mind had Goethe, who made of Hamlet a Werther; and such had Coleridge, who made of Hamlet a Coleridge [see excerpts above, 1795 and 1811, 1813]; and probably neither of these men in writing about Hamlet remembered that his first business was to study a work of art (p. 121)

Qua work of art, the work of art cannot be interpreted; there is nothing to interpret; we can only criticize it according to standards, in comparison to other works of art; and for 'interpretation' the chief task is the presentation of relevant historical facts which the reader is not assumed to know. Mr. Robertson points out, very pertinently, how critics have failed in their 'interpretation' of *Hamlet* by ignoring what ought to be very obvious: that *Hamlet* is a stratification, that it represents the efforts of a series of men, each making what he could out of the work of his predecessors. The *Hamlet* of Shakespeare will appear to us very differently if, instead of treating the whole action of the play as due to Shakespeare's design, we perceive his *Hamlet* to be superposed upon much cruder material which persists even in the final form. (p. 122)

The upshot of Mr. Robertson's examination is, we believe, irrefragable: that Shakespeare's *Hamlet,* so far as it is Shakespeare's, is a play dealing with the effect of a mother's guilt upon her son, and that Shakespeare was unable to impose this motive successfully upon the 'intractable' material of the old play.

Of the intractability there can be no doubt. So far from being Shakespeare's masterpiece, the play is most certainly an artistic failure. In several ways the play is puzzling, and disquieting as is none of the others. Of all the plays it is the longest and is possibly the one on which Shakespeare spent most pains; and yet he has left in it superfluous and inconsistent scenes which even hasty revision should have noticed. The versification is variable. Lines like

> Look, the morn, in russet mantle clad,
> Walks o'er the dew of yon high eastern hill,
> [I. i. 166-67]

are of the Shakespeare of *Romeo and Juliet.* The lines in Act V. Sc. ii,

> Sir, in my heart there was a kind of fighting
> That would not let me sleep . . .
> Up from my cabin,
> My sea-gown scarf'd about me, in the dark
> Grop'd I to find out them: had my desire;
> Finger'd their packet; [V. ii. 4-15]

are of his quite mature. Both workmanship and thought are in an unstable position. We are surely justified in attributing the play, with that other profoundly interesting play of 'intractable' material and astonishing versification, *Measure for Measure,* to a period of crisis, after which follow the tragic successes which culminate in *Coriolanus. Coriolanus* may be not as 'interesting' as *Hamlet,* but it is, with *Antony and Cleopatra,* Shakespeare's most assured artistic success. And probably more people have thought *Hamlet* a work of art because they found it interesting, than have found it interesting because it is a work of art. It is the 'Mona Lisa' of literature.

The grounds of *Hamlet*'s failure are not immediately obvious. Mr. Robertson is undoubtedly correct in concluding that the essential emotion of the play is the feeling of a son towards a guilty mother. . . . (pp. 123-24)

This, however, is by no means the whole story. It is not merely the 'guilt of a mother' that cannot be handled as Shakespeare handled the suspicion of Othello, the infatuation of Antony, or the pride of Coriolanus. The subject might conceivably have expanded into a tragedy like these, intelligible, self-complete, in the sunlight. *Hamlet,* like the sonnets, is full of some stuff that the writer could not drag to light, contemplate, or manipulate into art. And when we search for this feeling, we find it, as in the sonnets, very difficult to localize. . . . We find Shakespeare's *Hamlet* not in the action, not in any quotations that we might select, so much as in an unmistakable tone which is unmistakably not in the earlier play.

The only way of expressing emotion in the form of art is by finding an 'objective correlative'; in other words, a set of objects, a situation, a chain of events which shall be the formula of that *particular* emotion; such that when the external facts, which must terminate in sensory experience, are given, the emotion is immediately evoked. If you examine any of Shakespeare's more successful tragedies, you will find this exact equivalence. . . .

[The] words of Macbeth on hearing of his wife's death strike us as if, given the sequence of events, these words were automatically released by the last event in the series. The artistic 'inevitability' lies in this complete adequacy of the external to the emotion; and this is precisely what is deficient in *Hamlet.* Hamlet (the man) is dominated by an emotion which is inexpressible, because it is in *excess* of the facts as they appear. And the supposed identity of Hamlet with his author is genuine to this point: that Hamlet's bafflement at the absence of objective equivalent to his feelings is a prolongation of the bafflement of his creator in the face of his artistic problem. Hamlet is up against the difficulty that his disgust is occasioned by his mother, but that his mother is not an adequate equivalent for it; his disgust envelops and exceeds her. It is thus a feeling which he cannot understand; he cannot objectify it, and it therefore remains to poison life and obstruct action. None of the possible actions can satisfy it; and nothing that Shakespeare can do with the plot can express Hamlet for him. And it must be noticed that the very nature of the *données* of the problem precludes objective equivalence. To have heightened the criminality of Gertrude would have been to provide the formula for a totally different emotion in Hamlet; it is just *because* her character is so negative and insignificant that she arouses in Hamlet the feeling which she is incapable of representing.

The 'madness' of Hamlet lay to Shakespeare's hand; in the earlier play a simple ruse, and to the end, we may presume, understood as a ruse by the audience. For Shakespeare it is less than madness and more than feigned. The levity of Hamlet, his repetition of phrase, his puns, are not part of a deliberate plan of dissimulation, but a form of emotional relief. In the character Hamlet it is the buffoonery of an emotion which can find no outlet in action; in the dramatist it is the buffoonery of an emotion which he cannot express in art. The intense feeling, ecstatic or terrible, without an object or exceeding its object, is something which every person of sensibility has known; it is doubtless a subject of study for pathologists. . . .

We must simply admit that here Shakespeare tackled a problem which proved too much for him. Why he attempted it at all is an insoluble puzzle; under compulsion of what experience he attempted to express the inexpressibly horrible, we cannot ever know. We need a great many facts in his biography; and we should like to know whether, and when, and after or at the same time as what personal experience, he read [Michel de

Montaigne's] *Apologie de Raimand Sebond*. We should have, finally, to know something which is by hypothesis unknowable, for we assume it to be an experience which, in the manner indicated, exceeded the facts. We should have to understand things which Shakespeare did not understand himself. (pp. 124-26)

> T. S. Eliot, ''Hamlet and His Problems,'' in his Selected Essays, *Harcourt Brace Jovanovich, 1932, pp. 121-26.*

G. WILSON KNIGHT (essay date 1930)

[*One of the most influential of modern Shakespearean critics, Knight helped shape the twentieth-century reaction against the biographical and character studies of the nineteenth-century Shakespeareans. Knight's analytic practice stresses what he calls, in* The Wheel of Fire, *the ''spatial'' aspects of imagery, atmosphere, theme, and symbol in the plays. He thus parallels the New Critics with his emphasis on verbal texture; his discussions of symbolism are similar to Samuel Taylor Coleridge's notions of the symbolic as indefinite with multiple meanings. Like Friedrich Nietzsche (1872), Knight defines Hamlet as a character who truly comprehends the futility of his situation and who is paralyzed by that knowledge. His is not Johann Wolfgang von Goethe's gentle, sensitive Hamlet (1795), but is a ''sick soul, commanded to heal, to cleanse, to create harmony.'' For Knight, Hamlet is an agent of death who poisons the life around him. Caroline F. E. Spurgeon (1935) and Wolfgang H. Clemen (1951) also discuss the imagery of disease in the play. For additional commentary on theme and imagery in* Hamlet, *see Francis Fergusson (1949), Maynard Mack (1952), and T. McAlindon (1970). Additional studies focusing on language in* Hamlet *include those of Harry Levin (1959), Reuben A. Brower (1971), and Inga-Stina Ewbank (1977). Knight's essay was first published in 1930.*]

Our attention is early drawn to the figure of Hamlet. Alone in the gay glitter of the court, silhouetted against brilliance, robustness, health, and happiness, is the pale, black-robed Hamlet, mourning. When first we meet him, his words point the essential inwardness of his suffering:

> But I have that within which passeth show;
> These but the trappings and the suits of woe. . . .
>> [I. ii. 85-6]

The mood expressed by these lines is patent. To Hamlet the light has been extinguished from the things of earth. He has lost all sense of purpose. We already know one reason for Hamlet's state: his father's death. . . . Now, during Hamlet's soliloquy, we see another reason: disgust at his mother's second marriage:

> . . . within a month:
> Ere yet the salt of most unrighteous tears
> Had left the flushing in her galled eyes,
> She married. O, most wicked speed, to post
> With such dexterity to incestuous sheets!
>> [I. ii. 153-57]

These two concrete embodiments of Hamlet's misery are closely related. He suffers from misery at his father's death and agony at his mother's quick forgetfulness: such callousness is infidelity, and so impurity, and, since Claudius is the brother of the King, incest. It is reasonable to suppose that Hamlet's state of mind, if not wholly caused by these events, is at least definitely related to them. Of his two loved parents, one has been taken for ever by death, the other dishonoured for ever by her act of marriage. To Hamlet the world is now an 'unweeded garden'.

Hamlet hears of his father's Ghost, sees it, and speaks to it. His original pain is intensified by knowledge of the unrestful spirit, by the terrible secrets of death hinted by the Ghost's words:

> I could a tale unfold whose lightest word
> Would harrow up thy soul, freeze thy young blood . . .
>> [I. v. 15-16]

This is added to Hamlet's sense of loss: this knowledge of the father he loved suffering in death:

> Doom'd for a certain time to walk the night,
> And for the day confin'd to fast in fires . . .
>> [I. v. 10-11]

Nor is this all. He next learns that his father's murderer now wears the crown, is married to his faithless mother. Both elements in his original pain are thus horribly intensified. His hope of recovery to the normal state of healthy mental life depended largely on his ability to forget his father, to forgive his mother. Claudius advised him well. Now his mother's honour is more foully smirched than ever; and the living cause and symbol of his father's death is firmly placed on Denmark's throne. Forgetfulness is impossible, forgetfulness that might have brought peace. The irony of the Ghost's parting word is terrible:

> Adieu, adieu! Hamlet, remember me.
>> [I. v. 91]

If the spirit had been kind, it would have prayed that Hamlet might forget. (pp. 17-19)

Hamlet, when we first meet him, has lost all sense of life's significance. To a man bereft of the sense of purpose there is no possibility of creative action, it has no meaning. No act but suicide is rational. Yet to Hamlet comes the command of a great act—revenge: therein lies the unique quality of the play—a sick soul is commanded to heal, to cleanse, to create harmony. But good cannot come of evil: it is seen that the sickness of his soul only further infects the state—his disintegration spreads out, disintegrating.

Hamlet's soul is sick to death—and yet there was one thing left that might have saved him. In the deserts of his mind, void with the utter vacuity of the knowledge of death—death of his father, death of his mother's faith—was yet one flower, his love of Ophelia. . . . Now there is one supreme enemy to the demon of neurotic despair, its antithesis and bright antagonist: romantic love. . . . The love of Ophelia is thus Hamlet's last hope. This, too, is taken from him. Her repelling of his letters and refusing to see him, in obedience to Polonius' command, synchronizes unmercifully with the terrible burden of knowledge laid on Hamlet by the revelation of the Ghost. The result is given to us indirectly—but with excruciating vividness:

> *Ophelia*. My lord, as I was sewing in my closet,
> Lord Hamlet, with his doublet all unbraced;
> No hat upon his head; his stockings foul'd,
> Ungarter'd, and down-gyved to his ankle;
> Pale as his shirt; his knees knocking each other;
> And with a look so piteous in purport
> As if he had been loosed out of hell
> To speak of horrors—he comes before me.
>> [II. i. 74-81]

This is no mock-madness. To see it as such is to miss the power of the central theme of the play. Hamlet would not first try the practical joke of pretended madness on Ophelia whom he loved. That pallor was clearly no cosmetic. Hamlet was in truth 'loosed out of hell to speak of horrors': on top of the Ghost's revelation has come Ophelia's unreasonable repulsion of that his last contact with life, his love for her. Therefore

> He took me by the wrist and held me hard;
> Then goes he to the length of all his arm;
> And, with his other hand thus o'er his brow,
> He falls to such perusal of my face
> As he would draw it. Long stay'd he so;
> At last, a little shaking of mine arm,
> And thrice his head thus waving up and down,
> He raised a sigh so piteous and profound
> As it did seem to shatter all his bulk
> And end his being . . .   [II. i. 84-93]

From henceforth he must walk alone within the prison of mental death. There is surely no more pitiful thing in literature than this description. . . . The suggestion that in these circumstances, at this moment in his history, he has the presence of mind to pretend madness to Ophelia is a perversion of commentary.

It is, however, certain that Hamlet does simulate madness before the Court, and the King and Queen are both rightly unwilling to relate this madness to Hamlet's love of Ophelia. . . . Hamlet's pain is a complex of different themes of grief. But absolute loss of control is apparent only in his dealings with Ophelia. Three times after the Ghost scene he utterly loses mental control: first, in the incident narrated by Ophelia; second, in his meeting with her in III. i.; and third, in the Graveyard scene, with Laertes over Ophelia's body. On all other occasions his abnormal behaviour, though it certainly tends towards, and might even be called, madness in relation to his environment, is yet rather the abnormality of extreme melancholia and cynicism.

Throughout the middle scenes of the play we become more closely acquainted with Hamlet's peculiar disease. He is bitterly cynical:

> . . . to be honest, as this world goes, is to be
> one man picked out of ten thousand.
>   [II. ii. 178-79]

and

> Use every man after his desert, and who should
> 'scape whipping?   [II. ii. 529-30]

To Hamlet the world is a 'goodly' prison

> in which there are many confines, wards, and
> dungeons, Denmark being one o' the worst.
>   [II. ii. 245-47]

His mind is drawn to images in themselves repellent, and he dwells on the thought of foulness as the basis of life:

> For if the sun breed maggots in a dead dog . . .
>   [II. ii. 181]

Hamlet's soul is sick. The symptoms are, horror at the fact of death and an equal detestation of life, a sense of uncleanliness and evil in the things of nature; a disgust at the physical body of man; bitterness, cynicism, hate. It tends towards insanity. All these elements are insistent in Hamlet. He can describe the glories of heaven and earth—but for him those glories are gone. And he knows not why. The disease is deeper than his loss of Ophelia, deeper than his mother's sexual impurity and his father's death. These are, like his mourning dress, the 'trappings

and the suits of woe'. They are the outward symbols of it, the 'causes' of it: but the thing itself is ultimate, beyond causality. (pp. 19-23)

It will be clear that Hamlet's outstanding peculiarity in the action of this play may be regarded as a symptom of this sickness in his soul. He does not avenge his father's death, not because he dare not, not because he hates the thought of bloodshed, but because his 'wit's diseased' [III. ii. 321-22]; his will is snapped and useless, like a broken leg. Nothing is worth while. After the player has worked himself into a tragic passion in the recitation of 'Aeneas' Tale to Dido', Hamlet looks inward and curses and hates himself for his lack of passion, and then again he hates himself the more for his futile self-hatred. He cannot understand himself:

> . . . it cannot be
> But I am pigeon-liver'd and lack gall
> To make oppression bitter.
>   [III. i. 576-78]
>   (pp. 23-4)

There are often moments when reincarnations of what must have been his former courteous and kindly nature—of which we hear, but which we only see by fits and starts—break through the bitterness of Hamlet as he appears in the play, but they do not last: cynicism and consequent cruelty, born of the burden of pain within him, blight the spontaneous gentleness that occasionally shows itself, strangle it. There is a continual process of self-murder at work in Hamlet's mind. He is cruel to Ophelia and his mother. He exults in tormenting the King by the murder of Gonzago, and when he finds him conscience-stricken, at prayer, takes a demoniac pleasure in the thought of preserving his life for a more damning death. . . . With a callousness and a most evident delight that shocks Horatio he sends his former school-friends to an undeserved death, 'not shriving time allowed', again hoping to compass the eternal damnation of his enemy. . . . Hamlet thus takes a devilish joy in cruelty towards the end of the play: he is like Iago. It is difficult to see the conventional courtly Prince of Denmark in these incidents. We have done ill to sentimentalize his personality. We have paid for it—by failing to understand him; and, failing to understand, we have been unable to sympathize with the demon of cynicism, and its logical result of callous cruelty, that has Hamlet's soul in its remorseless grip. Sentiment is an easy road to an unprofitable and unreal sympathy. Hamlet is cruel. . . . At the end of his scene with his mother there is one beautiful moment when Hamlet gains possession of his soul:

> For this same lord,
> I do repent: but heaven hath pleased it so,
> To punish me with this, and this with me.
>   [III. iv. 172-74]

And his filial love wells up in:

> So, again, good-night.
> I must be cruel only to be kind:
> Thus bad begins and worse remains behind.
>   [III. iv. 177-79]

But it is short-lived. Next comes a long speech of the most withering, brutal, and unnecessary sarcasm:

> Let the bloat king tempt you again to bed;
> Pinch wanton on your cheek; call you his mouse . . .
>   [III. iv. 182-83]

Even more horrible are his disgusting words about Polonius, whom he has unjustly killed, to the King.

> *King.* Now, Hamlet, where's Polonius?
> *Hamlet.* At supper.
> *King.* At supper! where?
> *Hamlet.* Not where he eats, but where he is eaten: a certain convocation of politic worms are e'en at him. Your worm is your only emperor for diet: we fat all creatures else to fat us, and we fat ourselves for maggots: your fat king and your lean beggar is but variable service, two dishes, but to one table: that's the end.
> *King.* Alas, alas!
> *Hamlet.* A man may fish with the worm that hath eat of a king, and eat of the fish that hath fed of that worm.
> *King.* What dost thou mean by this?
> *Hamlet.* Nothing but to show you how a king may go a progress through the guts of a beggar.
> *King.* Where is Polonius?
> *Hamlet.* In heaven; send thither to see: if your messenger find him not there, seek him i' the other place yourself. But indeed, if you find him not within this month, you shall nose him as you go up the stairs into the lobby.
>
> [IV. iii. 17-37]

A long and unpleasant quotation, I know. But it is necessary. The horror of humanity doomed to death and decay has disintegrated Hamlet's mind. From the first scene to the last the shadow of death broods over this play. In the exquisite prose threnody of the Graveyard scene the thought of physical death is again given utterance. There its pathos, its inevitability, its moral, are emphasized: but also its hideousness. Death is the theme of this play, for Hamlet's disease is mental and spiritual death. So Hamlet, in his most famous soliloquy, concentrates on the terrors of an after life. The uninspired, devitalized intellect of Hamlet thinks pre-eminently in terms of time. To him, the body disintegrates in time; the soul persists in time too; and both are horrible. His consciousness, functioning in terms of evil and negation, sees Hell but not Heaven. . . . Therefore he dwells on the foul appearances of sex, the hideous decay of flesh, the deceit of beauty either of the spirit or the body, the torments of eternity if eternity exist. The universe is an 'unweeded garden', or a 'prison', the canopy of the sky but a 'pestilent congregation of vapours', and man but a 'quintessence of dust', waiting for the worms of death.

It might be objected that I have concentrated unduly on the unpleasant parts of the play. It has been my intention to concentrate. They are the most significant parts. I have tried by various quotations and by suggestive phrases to indicate this sickness which eats into Hamlet's soul. . . . Now by emphasizing these elements in the figure of Hamlet I have essayed to pluck out the heart of his mystery. And it will be clear that the elements which I have emphasized, the matter of Hamlet's madness, his patent cruelty, his coarse humour, his strange dialogue with Ophelia, his inability to avenge his father's death, are all equally related to the same sickness within. The coherence of these elements in the play must be evident. Creative action; love; passion—all these can find none but a momentary home in Hamlet's paralysed mind. (pp. 26-9)

The impression of the play, as a whole, is not so gloomy as the main theme: if it were, it would not have been so popular. There are many individual scenes of action, passion, humour, and beauty, that take our thoughts from the essentially morbid

impact of Hamlet's melancholia. Hamlet himself at times recovers his old instinctive friendliness, humour, and gentleness. We can guess what he was like before. That side of his nature which never quite dies, appearing intermittently until the end, is important: it lends point and pathos to the inroads of his cynicism and disgust. His mind wavers between the principle of good, which is love, and that of evil, which is loathing and cruelty. But too much emphasis has been laid on this element of Hamlet. The popularity of the play is not innocent of misunderstanding. To ignore the unpleasant aspects of Hamlet blurs our vision of the protagonist, the play as a whole, and its place in Shakespeare's work. The matter of the disease-theme in relation to the rest of the play is difficult. The total impression, the imaginative impact of the whole, leaves us with a sense of gaiety, health, superficiality, and colour, against which is silhouetted the pale black-robed figure of Hamlet who has seen what lies behind the smiles of benevolence, who has broken free of the folly of love because he has found its inward tawdriness and deceit, who knows that king and beggar alike are bound for the same disgusting 'convocation of worms', and that even an 'indifferent honest' man is too vile to be 'crawling between heaven and earth'.

There is no fallacy in Hamlet's reasoning. We cannot pick on this or that of his most bitter words, and prove them false. The solitary and inactive figure of Hamlet is contrasted with the bustle and the glitter of the court, the cancer of cynicism in his mind, himself a discordant and destructive thing whose very presence is a poison and a menace to the happiness and health of Denmark, fulfilling to the letter the devilish command of the Ghost:

> Adieu, Adieu, Hamlet, remember me.
>
> [I. v. 91]

Hamlet does not neglect his father's final behest—he obeys it, not wisely but only too well. Hamlet remembers—not alone his father's ghost, but all the death of which it is a symbol. What would have been the use of killing Claudius? Would that have saved his mother's honour, have brought life to his father's mouldering body, have enabled Hamlet himself, who had so long lived in death, to have found again childish joy in the kisses of Ophelia? Would that have altered the universal scheme? To Hamlet, the universe smells of mortality; and his soul is sick to death. (pp. 29-30)

The general thought of death, intimately related to the predominating human theme, the pain in Hamlet's mind, is thus suffused through the whole play. And yet the play, as a whole, scarcely gives us that sense of blackness and the abysms of spiritual evil which we find in *Macbeth;* nor is there the universal gloom of *King Lear*. This is due partly to the difference in the technique of *Hamlet* from that of *Macbeth* or *King Lear*. Macbeth, the protagonist and heroic victim of evil, rises gigantic from the murk of an evil universe; Lear, the king of suffering, towers over a universe that itself toils in pain. Thus in *Macbeth* and *King Lear* the predominating imaginative atmospheres are used not to contrast with the mental universe of the hero, but to aid and support it, as it were, with similarity, to render realistic the extravagant and daring effects of volcanic passion to which the poet allows his protagonist to give voice. We are forced by the attendant personification, the verbal colour, the symbolism and events of the play as a whole, to feel the hero's suffering, to see with his eyes. Now in *Hamlet* this is not so. We need not see through Hamlet's eyes. Though the idea of death is recurrent through the play, it is not implanted in the minds of other persons as is the consciousness of evil throughout *Macbeth* and the consciousness of suffering throughout *King Lear*. Except for the original murder of Hamlet's father, the Hamlet universe is one of healthy and robust life, good-nature, humour, romantic strength, and welfare: against this background is the figure of Hamlet pale with the consciousness of death. He is the ambassador of death, walking amid life. The effect is at first one of separation. Nevertheless it is to be noted that the consciousness of death, and consequent bitterness, cruelty, and inaction, in Hamlet not only grows in his own mind disintegrating it as we watch, but also spreads its effects outward among the other persons like a blighting disease, and, as the play progresses, by its very passivity and negation of purpose, insidiously undermines the health of the state, and adds victim to victim until at the end the stage is filled with corpses. It is, as it were, a nihilistic birth in the consciousness of Hamlet that spreads its deadly venom around. That Hamlet is originally blameless, that the King is originally guilty, may well be granted. But, if we refuse to be diverted from a clear vision by questions of praise and blame, responsibility and causality, and watch only the actions and reactions of the persons as they appear, we shall observe a striking reversal of the usual commentary. (pp. 32-3)

Now Claudius is not drawn as wholly evil—far from it. We see the government of Denmark working smoothly. Claudius shows every sign of being an excellent diplomatist and king. . . . The impression given by [his early] speeches is one of quick efficiency—the efficiency of the man who can dispose of business without unnecessary circumstance, and so leaves himself time for enjoying the good things of life: a man kindly, confident, and fond of pleasure.

Throughout the first half of the play Claudius is the typical kindly uncle, besides being a good king. His advice to Hamlet about his exaggerated mourning for his father's death is admirable common sense. . . . It is the advice of worldly common sense opposed to the extreme misery of a sensitive nature paralysed by the facts of death and unfaithfulness. This contrast points the relative significance of the King and his court to Hamlet. They are of the world—with their crimes, their follies, their shallownesses, their pomp and glitter; they are of humanity, with all its failings, it is true, but yet of humanity. They assert the importance of human life, they believe in it, in themselves. Whereas Hamlet is inhuman, since he has seen through the tinsel of life and love, he believes in nothing, not even himself, except the memory of a ghost, and his black-robed presence is a reminder to every one of the fact of death. There is no question but that Hamlet is right. The King's smiles hide murder, his mother's love for her new consort is unfaithfulness to Hamlet's father, Ophelia has deserted Hamlet at the hour of his need. Hamlet's philosophy may be inevitable, blameless, and irrefutable. But it is the negation of life. It is death. Hence Hamlet is a continual fear to Claudius, a reminder of his crime. It is a mistake to consider Claudius as a hardened criminal. When Polonius remarks on the hypocrisy of mankind, he murmurs to himself:

> O, 'tis too true!
> How smart a lash that speech doth give my conscience!
> The harlot's cheek, beautied with plastering art,
> Is not more ugly to the thing that helps it
> Than is my deed to my most painted word:
> O heavy burthen! [III. i. 48-53]

Again, Hamlet's play wrenches his soul with remorse—primarily not fear of Hamlet, as one might expect, but a genuine remorse—and gives us that most beautiful prayer of a stricken soul beginning, 'O, my offence is rank, it smells to Heaven' [III. iii. 36]. . . . He fears that his prayer is worthless. He is still trammelled by the enjoyment of the fruits of his crime. 'My fault is past', he cries. But what does that avail, since he has his crown and his queen still, the prizes of murder? His dilemma is profound and raises the problem I am pointing in this essay. Claudius, as he appears in the play, is not a criminal. He is—strange as it may seem—a good and gentle king, enmeshed by the chain of causality linking him with his crime. And this chain he might, perhaps, have broken except for Hamlet, and all would have been well. Now, granted the presence of Hamlet—which Claudius at first genuinely desired, persuading him not to return to Wittenberg as he wished—and granted the fact of his original crime which cannot now be altered, Claudius can hardly be blamed for his later actions. They are forced on him. As King, he could scarcely be expected to do otherwise. Hamlet is a danger to the state, even apart from his knowledge of Claudius' guilt. He is an inhuman—or superhuman—presence, whose consciousness—somewhat like Dostoievsky's Stavrogin—is centred on death. Like Stavrogin, he is feared by those around him. They are always trying in vain to find out what is wrong with him. They cannot understand him. He is a creature of another world. As King of Denmark he would have been a thousand times more dangerous than Claudius. (pp. 33-5)

[I have concentrated on Claudius' virtues. They are manifest. So are his faults, his original crime, his skill in the less admirable kind of policy, treachery, and intrigue. But I would point clearly that, in the movement of the play, his faults are forced on him, and he is distinguished by creative and wise action, a sense of purpose, benevolence, a faith in himself and those around him, by love of his Queen. . . . Instinctively the creatures of earth—Laertes, Polonius, Ophelia, Rosencrantz and Guildenstern, league themselves with Claudius: they are of his kind. They sever themselves from Hamlet. Laertes sternly warns Ophelia against her intimacy with Hamlet, so does Polonius. They are, in fact, all leagued against him, they are puzzled by him or fear him: he has no friend except Horatio, and Horatio, after the Ghost scenes, becomes a queer shadowy character who rarely gets beyond 'E'en so, my lord', 'My lord—', and such-like phrases. The other persons are firmly drawn, in the round, creatures of flesh and blood. But Hamlet is not of flesh and blood, he is a spirit of penetrating intellect and cynicism and misery, without faith in himself or any one-else, murdering his love of Ophelia, on the brink of insanity, taking delight in cruelty, torturing Claudius, wringing his mother's heart, a poison in the midst of the healthy bustle of the court. He is a superman among men. And he is a superman because he has walked and held converse with death, and his consciousness works in terms of death and the negation of cynicism. He has seen the truth, not alone of Denmark, but of humanity, of the universe: and the truth is evil. Thus Hamlet is an element of evil in the state of Denmark. The poison of his mental existence spreads outwards among things of flesh and blood, like acid eating into metal. They are helpless before his very inactivity and fall one after the other, like victims of an infectious disease. They are strong with the strength of health—but the demon of Hamlet's mind is a stronger thing than they. Futilely they try to get him out of their country; anything to get rid of him, he is not safe. But he goes with a cynical smile, and is no sooner gone than he is back again in their midst, meditating in graveyards, at home with death. Not till it has slain all, is the demon that grips Hamlet satisfied. And last it slays Hamlet himself:

The spirit that I have seen

May be the devil . . .   [II. ii. 598-99]

It was.   (pp. 37-9)

> *G. Wilson Knight, "The Embassy of Death: An Essay on Hamlet," in his* The Wheel of Fire: Interpretations of Shakespearian Tragedy, *revised edition, Methuen & Co Ltd, 1949, pp. 17-46.*

A.J.A. WALDOCK (essay date 1931)

[*Waldock, contending that "a play is not a mine of secret motives," challenges several generally accepted critical approaches to* Hamlet. *First, he posits that critics have overemphasized the problem of the delay, which he believes is a matter of minor significance. He charges that Hamlet's personality and motives have been overanalyzed and that such critics as William Richardson (1774) and A. C. Bradley (1905) reinvent the character for themselves, rather than accept Shakespeare's creation as he appears in the play. Waldock also denies the importance of Ernest Jones's psychoanalytic argument (1949). One need not resolve all the inconsistencies in the play, the critic concludes, for "what would* Hamlet *be without its puzzles?" For additional commentary on Hamlet's delay, see Samuel Taylor Coleridge (1811), Hermann Ulrici (1839), Karl Werder (1859-60), Friedrich Nietzsche (1872), Sigmund Freud (1900), H. B. Charlton (1942), Ernest Jones (1949), and D. G. James (1951).*]

We do not know whether *Hamlet* perplexed the first audiences or not. We do know that we are unable to find any records of perplexity until more than a century after the performance of the play. We need not, perhaps, attach great significance to such a failure. But it is interesting to observe that the first commentators were not unduly worried by what puzzled them. Sir Thomas Hanmer, writing in 1736, noticed some difficulties [see excerpt above]. It is worth while noting what his difficulties were. They were the big problems, or what were to become the big problems. . . . [Hanmer] was struck by what was to become the problem of problems. "There appears no reason at all in nature", he observed, "why this young Prince did not put the usurper to death as soon as possible", for the young man was represented as very brave and careless of his own life. "The case, indeed, is this," he goes on, "had Hamlet gone naturally to work, there would have been an end of the play. The poet, therefore, was obliged to delay his hero's revenge; but then he should have contrived some good reason for it." Such are the modest observations of one of our early critics of *Hamlet*. Naïve perhaps they are; but it is by no means certain, for all the wealth of later speculation, that we have got very far beyond them. (pp. 3-4)

It was towards the end of the eighteenth century that the *Hamlet* problem, as a problem, began to emerge. . . . Richardson, finally, is the discoverer of excessive sensibility as the cause of Hamlet's indecision. His account of the sparing by Hamlet of the King at prayer might have set the traditional treatment. "The sentiments that Hamlet expresses when he finds Claudius at prayer are not, I will venture to affirm, his real ones. There is nothing in his whole character to justify such savage enormity." How, then, is the episode to be explained? Ingeniously, on the lines which were to become orthodox, Richardson reconstructs the event. Do we not ourselves, he very plausibly asks, often allege false motives for our behaviour? Do we not sometimes do so almost without our knowledge? Apply all this to Hamlet. Really, he is withheld "by the ascendant of a gentle disposition, by the scruples, and perhaps weakness, of extreme

sensibility". But his sense of duty will not allow him to acknowledge the truth even to himself. (pp. 4, 6)

It is, of course, strange that a play should ever have become a problem. Musical compositions, paintings, poems, even novels might well be or contain problems. But a play depends so much for its effect on ready comprehensibility. That a play which had been so successful should have had to wait so long until its true import began to be discovered, surely literary or dramatic history can contain few queerer phenomena than this. Of course, the strangeness has often been noted—then, generally, ignored or explained away. It seems to me difficult to explain it quite away. It is rather far-fetched, in this instance, to speak of artists who in the joy of creation work more subtly than they know, or of evasive meanings secreted within a disguise of melodrama. Nor is it a question of intricacies of detail, that might naturally require a more leisurely appreciation than the theatre affords. We cannot too often remind ourselves that the problem of *Hamlet* is the problem of the very central action of the piece. The difficulty, in ultimate terms, is to know what the play is really about. This is what is so very strange, that it should be difficult, or should have become difficult, to grasp the central drift of a play that has always been popular and successful.

In the second place, it is interesting to observe the methods of attacking this problem already adopted by Mackenzie [see excerpt above, 1780] and Richardson. Richardson, in particular, it will be noticed, yielded a very free rein to his imagination. In his discussion, for example, of the prayer-scene, where Hamlet spares Claudius, that was his deliberate method, to use his imagination to reconstruct a mysterious incident in the play. As we have seen, he reconstructs the incident very cleverly and no later commentator who has used the same method has been able to add much of importance to Richardson's interpretation of this scene. Only, let us note the word *reconstruct*, which his procedure inevitably suggests. . . . There are scenes in Shakespeare, we know, which are, by his own or another's fault, imperfect. There is nothing to be done with the last scene of *The Two Gentlemen of Verona*, if we do anything with it, but to try to reconstruct it. Parts of *Antony and Cleopatra* require some piecing together. But we are not, here, obviously dealing with such a scene. The prayer-scene in *Hamlet* is not garbled or incomplete; nor is it in Shakespeare's "shorthand" style. It bears every mark of being exactly what Shakespeare wished it to be: it is eminently finished and entire. Why, then, should we be obliged to reconstruct it? Why should any event, in any well-written play, require to be reconstructed? It is already constructed. It carries (or should carry) its own meaning with it: for is not that precisely how drama differs from life? If dramas need to be put together as fragments of real life are put together in the law courts, why, it must occur to one, write dramas? Where is their advantage? It is fairly clear that this contradiction pervades a good deal of *Hamlet* commentary: it is produced by a radical fallacy in method. (pp. 7-9)

[What] is to be made of [the prayer scene]? It is instructive to remember how Richardson set about explaining the passage. He assumed, to begin with, that it stood in need of interpretation. Hamlet's expressed sentiments are not his real ones: "there is nothing in Hamlet's whole character that justifies such savage enormity". The speech, in short, is too horrible ever to have been genuinely representative of Hamlet. It is some sort of a disguise thrown up by his unconscious self. . . . Hamlet excuses to himself his natural mercy by covering it in this hideous garb. Professor Bradley, of course, does not follow

Richardson in all these details. When Richardson affirms that "there is nothing in Hamlet's whole character that justifies such savage enormity" he is simply not remembering the play clearly. We think once more of the Hamlet who was to take vengeance on his treacherous friends; the Hamlet who "lugs the guts" of the slain Polonius into the neighbour room. There *is* in the Hamlet we see a strain of savagery: the terms of the speech are not in themselves at all inconsistent with a side of his (present, jangled) nature that is exhibited more than once. And, again, as Bradley objects, nothing could be more unfaithful to the play than to minimize the intensity of Hamlet's hatred of the King. . . . No, there is assuredly no reason for believing that the horrible sentiments of this speech are not authentically and profoundly Hamlet's. Bradley, however, finds still a reason for rejecting the surface value of the words. The reason is, not that Hamlet's sentiments are horrible, "but that elsewhere, and also in the opening of his speech here, we can see that his reluctance to act is due to other causes". Take the opening of the speech again:

> Now might I do it pat, now he is praying;
> And now I'll do't: and so he goes to heaven:
> And so am I revenged. That would be scann'd.
>   [III. iii. 73-5]

"The first five words he utters 'Now might I do it' show that he has no effective desire to 'do it'." Thus Bradley. But surely this is the very ecstasy of sophistication. "Now *might* I do it": that little *might*! But whoever in an audience could have taken such a hint as that; whoever, reading the play with unbiased mind, could possibly check at such a subtlety! . . . It will be remembered that Hamlet is thinking quickly: he has come accidentally upon the King: he is to decide in a matter of seconds if he will choose this or another occasion (and there is no suggestion that occasions were scarce). Then, as he is on the brink of action, a counter-thought suddenly strikes him: "and so he goes to heaven": the irony of such a revenge! And in the rest of the speech this second thought slowly prevails. . . . I feel that the sequence of the speech is in every detail simple and clear: it is a speech with a plain and obvious meaning; and it is something of a responsibility to refuse obvious meanings in a Shakespearean play.

This is really a test-passage of great importance, and I follow the matter a little farther. Bradley himself admits that the actability of the incident, in the sense in which he interprets it, is at least questionable: "in the little sentences that follow [the first five words], and the long pauses between them, the endeavour at a resolution, and the sickening return of melancholic paralysis, *however difficult a task they set to the actor* . . .": difficult task indeed, and one wonders when performed. But not so difficult, Bradley thinks, for the reader: such meanings are plain enough to him. But surely this is begging the question. The plain meaning is the meaning which the passage bears on its face. The Bradleian meaning, even if it were the true meaning, is certainly not the plain meaning. And it cannot be too emphatically urged that the onus is on the critic, in such a case, to demonstrate beyond doubt the subtler significance he finds. Is it really possible, in the present instance, to demonstrate such a significance? (pp. 38-41)

The chance offered to Hamlet is, as Bradley rightly observes, a repulsive chance—to us. We shrink from his accepting it. We could not help thinking less of him if he did accept it (although contradictorily, we are asked also to think less of him because he did not). The whole incident, to our present feelings, is strange, and Hamlet's scruples, as he expresses

them, strike no very sympathetic chord. To put it in a word, the theology of the speech impresses us as incredibly primitive. That it is primitive is readily granted. But it can make no difference, Hamlet is by no means the only Elizabethan character who is made to utter sentiments of this kind. Their primitiveness is merely to be accepted. We are all tempted to over-modernise Hamlet. Near as we feel him to be to ourselves, he still remains a literary creation of some years in the past. It is a passage like the present that should remind us, even if somewhat to our disturbance, of this truth. (pp. 41-2)

He *is* ready for bitter business. The occasion offers, and he is about to accept it. Then the qualm comes, itself evidence of the intensity of his feeling, and he postpones this chance of a vengeance too mild: meaning every word he says. If such a literal acceptation, after the elaborate reconstructions which have become familiar to us, now seems almost crude, it cannot be helped. (p. 43)

[Another passage of great importance is] the speech in which Hamlet announces his plans for [the] play [II. ii. 575 ff.]. . . . (pp. 43-4)

This is Bradley's comment: "Nothing, surely, can be clearer than the meaning of this famous soliloquy. The doubt which appears at its close, instead of being the natural conclusion of the preceding thoughts, is totally inconsistent with them. For Hamlet's self-reproaches, his curses on his enemy, and his perplexity about his own inaction, one and all imply his faith in the identity and truthfulness of the Ghost. Evidently this sudden doubt, of which there has not been the slightest trace before, is no genuine doubt; it is an unconscious fiction, an excuse for his delay—and for its continuance".

Now, in the first place, it is very important to recognise that Hamlet's doubt, whether it is genuine or not, is at least based on legitimate grounds. Here, again, our modern view requires some readjustment. There is no difficulty in obtaining information about the Elizabethan attitude to the supernatural. All the suspicions that Hamlet expresses here had their root in popular belief. He is perfectly orthodox in his demonology. When Hamlet alleges, as his reason for obtaining confirmation, that the spirit that he has seen may be the devil, he is alleging something that, in itself, is extremely likely. It is also quite true, as he says, that the devil has power to assume a pleasing shape. It is, finally, only too probable that, supposing this Ghost were diabolic, he would have selected this time of lowered resistance in Hamlet, of weakness and melancholy, for attacking him. All these considerations, to us, seem far-fetched. We do not sympathise with such reasons, as we do not sympathise with the sentiments of the prayer-scene. It is easy for us to see in such arguments thin excuses. Would it have been as easy for an Elizabethan audience to see in them thin excuses: arguments so clear, so logical, so well-founded in doctrine and experience? (pp. 45-6)

As Professor Bradley says, those curses, those reproaches, those perplexities that make up the bulk of the soliloquy, one and all imply complete confidence in the genuineness and veracity of the apparition. Nor have we had any previous warnings (at least on Hamlet's part) of these doubts: they appear suddenly out of a clear sky. All this is true enough. Yet it is impossible to believe that if Shakespeare had really desired to convey such a meaning as Bradley finds he would not have made it more unmistakable. As it stands, it is extremely mistakable. The explanation, surely, is much simpler; and it is an explanation that covers, quite adequately, certain other passages from which intricate deductions have been drawn. It is merely that the workmanship is rather transparent. Is it not fairly clear? The next major event due in the plot is the play-scene. The concluding parts of this soliloquy provide the bridge to that scene. It is not, perhaps, a thoroughly sound bridge; if we step heavily on it, it gives alarmingly. If we slip by more lightly, it serves well enough. (p. 47)

There is one other thing. We suspect Hamlet's motives. Why is not Horatio made to suspect them? He agrees quite simply to the plan [III. ii. 87-9]. Then, after the play is over, and as the company breaks up in confusion, Hamlet turns excitedly to his friend [III. ii. 286-90]:

> HAMLET. O good Horatio, I'll take the ghost's word for
>   a thousand pound. Didst perceive?
> HORATIO. Very well, my lord.
> HAMLET. Upon the talk of the poisoning?
> HORATIO. I did very well note him.
>
> [III. ii. 286-90]

I will not stop to discuss the suggestion that Horatio is here speaking "dryly"!

It seems clear, in short, that the Bradleian interpretation of this speech rests on a balancing of afterthoughts. It is not the meaning which the passage naturally and immediately carries. When we scrutinise this passage closely, we are struck by the inconsistency between beginning and end. If we have already in our mind ideas about the cause of Hamlet's irresolution, we can find in this inconsistency ingenious support for them. But I doubt if any reader, perusing the passage for the first time, in its natural order, and without prejudice, is really checked by the inconsistency: and still more that he would immediately infer from it that Hamlet was inventing unconscious fictions. As for the playgoer, and above all for the Elizabethan playgoer, it is absurd, surely, to imagine that he could ever catch such a drift. (pp. 48-9)

It was inevitable that Hamlet, sooner or later, should be psychoanalysed, for he is a perfect subject. It is, indeed, very interesting to note what the new psychology has to say about him.

We owe the major elucidation of him from this point of view to Dr Ernest Jones. (p. 50)

In the first place one wonders where [Jones's] principle, of an author's unconsciousness of his own purposes, might eventually lead us. . . . We can easily think of writers to whom such phrases might seem to apply with greater aptness. But it is surely not going too far to feel with Jones that much of the stuff of *Hamlet* came from inspirations that took their origin in the "deepest and darkest regions" of Shakespeare's mind. No one would suggest at least that a writer needs to be able to supply a coherent psychological analysis, with terms complete, of the characters he creates: his business is rather to feel his characters very intensely. We can have no doubt, for all the perplexities of the play, that if ever Shakespeare did feel a character intensely, it was Hamlet. Nor does there seem a reason to refuse the suggestion, which Jones (after Bradley) makes, that the behaviour of Hamlet might well represent Shakespeare's sense of what his own behaviour in such circumstances could have been. . . . It is still a good deal to ask us to believe that not this or that touch, not an intimation here, a suggestion there, but the central plot of this play, depends on, *is*, a complex of the author's, the nature of which, the existence of which, were of course quite hidden from his conscious mind. One wonders what Shakespeare himself thought

of Hamlet's symptoms; and seeing that, when he had produced them, he could gain no glimmer of an idea of what they meant (as of course by hypothesis he could not), why he did not become anxious about them. . . . Why, in *Hamlet,* he should have departed from what seems to have been his usual practice (namely, of working as a more or less conscious artist) and have suddenly decided to abandon himself to the whims of his subconscious nature, is hard to see. (pp. 53-4)

If Hamlet has a complex, what business is it of ours? When a complex is made into dramatic material it becomes our business, not before. And even to speak of Hamlet's complex is to speak of something in another dimension: it is a thing that has no being in the world of our play. With as much reason might we set about explaining Macbeth's crime by an investigation of the medical history of his grandfather. The reply, in short, to all such attempts is that, whatever illumination they may shed by the way, they are in bulk devoid of all dramatic relevance.

Dr Jones *does* shed illumination by the way. It seems to me that few investigators have laid emphasis so valuably on an aspect of the play strangely ignored or underestimated in *Hamlet* criticism: I mean, using the term in a rather special sense, its sexual quality. . . . Let us return to that first soliloquy. Really, "moral shock" hardly seems adequate to the impression this soliloquy conveys. There is in some of the lines almost a physical nausea. Hamlet is sick with disgust. He could retch with the thought of the things his mother has been doing. Now this impression seems of very great importance indeed. There is, if we like, something abnormal in the quality of Hamlet's feeling. But, above all, it is no *abstract* feeling (although, as we know, the despair does universalise itself). The feeling is in its essential nature exceedingly intimate. And it does, surely, put us in mind strongly of the things on which Jones fixes his attention. There is a suggestion that Hamlet has received damage of a kind analogous to the damage sometimes revealed by the procedures of psycho-analysis. I see no possibility, in a dramatic appreciation of the play, of going much farther than this. (pp. 55-6)

I would suggest . . . that the question "Why did Hamlet delay?", instead of being *the* question about Hamlet, is a question that in our immediate experience of the play (which is our all-important experience) does not, after all, very seriously arise. No one can deny the positive indications of delay; they are not, however, quite so numerous or quite so urgent as one might be led to think from some of the critical accounts; and their cumulative effect is not, perhaps, so powerful as has been assumed. The play is not dyed in delay. Now that means, simply, that the problem of the inaction recedes. It does not vanish. But it becomes less obtrusive.

Nor does it seem necessary, even if we suppose that the inaction is accounted for, by Shakespeare, rather less certainly, with rather less logic, than it is accounted for by Coleridge [see excerpts above, 1811 and 1813] and Bradley, that we should rush into a kind of critical atheism, proclaiming the shattering of our belief in the dramatist. Dramas are of many kinds. We have no reason to require of Shakespeare that every play should match a set technique. The inaction (as much of it as is dramatically urgent, as much of it as Shakespeare permits to become stuff of the drama) is accounted for, when all is said, with fair sufficiency. It does not worry us, unless we let it worry us. We take it in our stride. And it was surely open to Shakespeare, when he wished, to keep motives subdued, as it was open to him, when he wished, to enforce them.

We still, of course, have our difficulties: plenty of them. Some of these, as we have seen, seem inherent in the design. The play, from one point of view, is a tremendous *tour de force*. An old plot is wrenched to new significances, significances, in places, that to the end it refuses to take. It was, perhaps, inevitable that the play should show signs, in fissures and strain, of all this forceful bending. There are other difficulties that we can hardly venture to account for. Motives vaguely indicated ("blunted purpose", "lapsed in time") fade, seem somehow thwarted in their working out. We are left to surmises. Chords are sounded, dimly, suggestively, then become blurred. We seem to gain partial visions of intentions not clearly formulated. . . . But what would *Hamlet* be without its puzzles: the eternal piquancy of its imperfection?

Imperfection. For the play, after all, is just a play: a work of art with a design that is deceptive and intricate and somewhat misleading. We are discouraged if we cannot trace the design as evenly as we could wish, we are disappointed if we find the pattern a little mixed and bewildering. But at least we must keep to the design as it appears, abide by the patterns as we find them. Nothing is to be gained by compelling system from what is not system. If the filaments are not everywhere tight, it is not for us to tighten them; if the design relaxes, we cannot put it right.

But there is an inveterate temptation to try. We are for ever discovering new causes for Hamlet's inaction. . . . A play is not a mine of secret motives. We persist in digging for them; what happens usually is that our spade goes through the other side of the drama.

Is it, finally, of very great moment that we must admit these difficulties? The play, in spite of its discrepancies, has a fine harmony. Can we look usually in Shakespeare for the precise and narrow consistency that distinguishes the work of some other great literary craftsmen? Invincible logic of plot was scarcely his special glory. How different is, say, a novel by Henry James, the technique so deliberate, the fashioning so conscious; the work *sound* through and through! Shakespeare is rarely *sound* in that sense: how majestically careless, in comparison, he can be! He gives us things that were beyond James's range: he does not give us just that. To look for it is rather to wrong him. We know what, among other things, he has given us in *Hamlet*: the portrait of a man who seems to express (and the more in his sufferings and his disasters) all that Shakespeare found of greatest beauty and worth in the human spirit. There is no one, in history or in literature, like Hamlet. All that humanity is, all that humanity might be, seem figured in him. It is no wonder if we find it a task of some difficulty to pluck out all the mysteries of his soul. (pp. 96-9)

> A.J.A. Waldock, in his "Hamlet": A Study in Critical Method, *Cambridge at the University Press, 1931, 99 p.*

ELMER EDGAR STOLL   (essay date 1933)

[*Stoll was one of the earliest critics to attack the method of character analysis that had dominated nineteenth-century Shakespearean criticism. Instead, he maintained that Shakespeare was primarily a man of the professional theater and that his works had to be interpreted in the light of Elizabethan stage conventions and understood for their theatrical effects rather than their psychological insight. Stoll has in turn been criticized for seeing only one dimension of Shakespeare's art. Stoll argues that* Hamlet *falls within the tradition of the Elizabethan revenge tragedy. In that context, the delay is not a critical problem, but a theatrical device*

Act III. Scene iv. Gertrude and Hamlet. By W. Hamilton (1802). From the Art Collection of the Folger Shakespeare Library.

which was acceptable to the Elizabethans and, despite the opposing opinions of the Romantic critics, is still valid. Stoll's approach was anticipated in the criticism of Thomas Campbell (1818). Later critics who adopted a historical approach similar to Stoll's include A.J.A. Waldock (1931), J. Dover Wilson (1935), E.M.W. Tillyard (1949), William Empson (1953), Fredson Bowers (1955), and Eleanor Prosser (1971).]

[In *Hamlet*] the hero is put in a plight—made superior to his conduct and somewhat averse to it. . . . [The] highly effective situation is brought about by external means—by the ghost, which is, of course, no figment of the hero's imagination, and no more an allegory or symbol than is the goddess Athena in the epic or the Weird Sisters in the tragedy, who perform much the same dramatic function. . . . [The] improbabilities are allayed by the reality of the characterization, the interest of a quickly moving story, a veiled confusion of motive, and the all-reconciling power of poetry.

Of the dramatist's particular purpose, however, and his success in achieving it, we are here less able rightly to judge because the original *Hamlet* is lost; though of this we indirectly know enough (that is, through the sister play *The Spanish Tragedy*, by the same author; the German *Hamlet*; and Quarto I, which is Shakespeare's first revision, piratically printed and inadequately reported) to be sure that for the resulting obscurity it was much to blame. This rudely written but cunningly constructed Senecan melodrama of Kyd's was popular—hence the two revisions of it by the most popular dramatist of the London stage; and yielding to the demand of his company and their public, the poet was not free, if indeed, in view of the practical necessities and advantages, he was much disposed, to make sweeping changes. Until his life-giving hand retouched it the play had not been so popular as *The Spanish Tragedy,* which had, in the last months, taken a new lease of life from the mad-scenes added by Jonson; it was this success that the Chamberlain's company was now emulating; and since the most unreasonable features of the Danish tragedy, shared by the Spanish, were its most unmistakable attractions, they must be not only retained but, in Jonson's fashion, heightened and set off. The story must in general be the same story, though better told, or both company and public would be disappointed; and the principal improvement expected was no doubt in style and metre.

With merely that Shakespeare could not have contented himself, but just how far was he to go? Because not only of the popular demand but of dramatic requirements, the ghost must still appear at the beginning, and the tragic deed be accomplished, as in all good revenge plays, ancient or modern, at the end. How, then, was the revenger to be occupied in the meantime? As in the old *Hamlet,* of course—secretly, with intrigue and melancholy meditation, which to us seem not greatly to advance the business in hand (but must needs not too greatly advance it); and publicly, with a pretence of madness, which to us seems only to thwart it. But there these matters were, superficially at least, less unplausible. There the delay, though like Hieronimo, in *The Spanish Tragedy,* the hero reproached himself for it, was attributed to the King's being difficult of access; and the feigned madness was represented as a means to reach him. . . . The dramatist taking it as a matter of course, the audience would so take it; and not, like the critics, scratch their heads, and cunningly conclude (as a generation ago) that it is a "safety-valve" [see excerpt above by Charlton M. Lewis, 1907], or (as nowadays) a case of "double consciousness", or any of the numerous other things it has been thought to be, and still less, that the man is crazy in reality. Thus, and by his subtler treatment and phrasing, he intensified an effect of contrast provided in the melodrama, similar (as we shall see) to that later invented for Othello, and, however improbable, too precious to be surrendered. And profiting by the familiarity of the rest of the intrigue—the baffling of the spies, the doubt of the ghost and the theatrical performance to satisfy it, the sparing of the King at his devotions, the killing of him (as is intended) behind the arras and the reproachful conference with his mother, the trip to England—the dramatist (to judge by the changes from Quarto I to Quarto II and the Folio) subdued, instead of emphasizing, its irrelevance, but accentuated and complicated its dangers; letting Hamlet perilously play the King's game (but beat him at it) as if it were his own, and, unlike Kyd's Hamlet, keep the secret of his revengeful purpose from his friends, his mother, and even from Horatio until near the end of the tragedy, and his plan to the very end. Thus he heightened the suspense and mystery, imparted to the hero dignity, delicacy, and pathos, and threw the whole burden of motivation, or explanation, upon his self-reproaches. (pp. 90-4)

In effect the reproaches are, as often in ancient and Renaissance soliloquy, exhortations, addressed by the character to himself. They motive the delay, not in the sense of grounding it in character, but of explaining it and bridging it over; they motive it by reminding the audience that the main business in hand, though retarded, is not lost to view. They provide an epical motive, if I may so call it . . . rather than a dramatic one. . . . [In] the Renaissance drama, reproaches beforehand for failure to act do not discredit the hero or reveal an inner flaw. And,

indeed, is not this simpler technique more in keeping with the surface and common course of life? "Yea, a man will pause", replies the Chorus to the complaint of Sophocles' Electra against Hamlet's prototype, Orestes, "on the verge of a great work". Who does not?

This is a case where what the character says of himself in soliloquy, even though (as with both Sophocles and Kyd) his confidants say it too, is not, according to the usual expectation of the dramatist, to be taken at its face value; or, we might better say, it is to be taken at that and no more, being the sort of charge that Elizabethan and ancient tragedy, concerned with ethical rather than psychical defects, made no further account of. In those days not everything in conduct was reduced to a psychological or sociological phenomenon, or was given an inner meaning, even as it is not by ordinary people in ours; and, in particular, not such a matter as the pausing or hesitating which holds the situation, which prolongs the story. . . . [What] counts in drama is the positive; and Hamlet not only is never blamed or criticized but is esteemed and openly praised on every hand. If at any other time he had shown himself a procrastinator or a weakling, Horatio or Laertes, the King or the Queen could have said or hinted as much; and by the laws of dramatic technique, both in that day and in this, they were under a heavy necessity of saying it, and not the contrary, now. A villain who reveals his inner nature in soliloquy may conceal it from the world until the end; but Hamlet, if he has anything worth concealing, does so even beyond the end, while Fortinbras is declaring he would have made a kingly king. . . . Where else in Shakespeare is any secret, needful for the comprehension of the action, kept from the other characters—and really from the audience too!—for good and all? (pp. 94-7)

As psychology, certainly, the trouble is not made clear; yet, depending upon the success with which the character has already been enforced upon the audience, the dramatist avails himself of the familiar fact that the most practical person in the world may, sometime or other, say "I don't know why I haven't done that", only telling the truth. His friends press him no further, and Hamlet's friends in the theatre should not either. It is action, indeed, and little more, that he now engages in—checkmating the King, not killing him; but Shakespeare is again manoeuvring, and making the best of a picturesque and exciting but irrational old plot. Here, as at the end of "O what a rogue", he is counting on the audience being, in their familiarity with the circuitous movement of revenge plays, satisfied with any action against the murderer. And only this defensive movement it must as yet be, for to resolve upon immediately killing him, and not kill him (as indeed by the requirements of the story, until the last act, he cannot) would make the Prince look more futile than ever. (pp. 100-01)

Hamlet's case is much the same as Othello's and Macbeth's; only, the material being different, and the old play intervening, the treatment must be a little different too. The Weird Sisters and the villain alike touch responsive chords; but in Hamlet the chord struck by the Ghost is the noblest within him, his love for his father. His vengeance, unlike the Moor's and unlike the regicide at Glamis, is a duty; and his aversion, unlike theirs, is not a virtue, although no flagrant fault. It serves to motive the circuitousness of the plot, and, when there is no more need of it, disappears. Not far from the end it vanishes, like Lear's irascibility and Macbeth's ambition shortly after the beginning. (p. 106)

How strange that [Horatio], neither through confession, on the one hand, nor observation, on the other, has any inkling of the

Prince's mental malady; and it is not to deal with him alone, and not at all with his dilatoriness, *his* story "of carnal, bloody, and unnatural acts", "of deaths put on by cunning and forc'd cause",

> And, in this upshot, purposes mistook
> Fallen on the inventors' heads!
>
> [V. ii. 384-85]

How strange that Horatio, like Fortinbras, misses the point of the tragedy! Indeed, so strange a drama (if such there be) would be inconceivable on the stage. But from . . . the other frequent discussions, down to the time of the Scottish—untheatrical— Richardson and Mackenzie [see excerpts above, 1774 and 1780], as well as from the play's continual popularity, it is apparent that Shakespeare had not misjudged his theatrical public, contemporary or posthumous. These only delighted in the intrigue, circuitous but cunning, bloody but poetically "just", and took it for what he intended it to be, a story, not of Hamlet's procrastination—that they would not have taken for a story!—but of a prolonged and artful struggle between him and the King. (pp. 107-08)

The author of *Some Remarks* [see excerpt above by George Stubbes/Thomas Hanmer, 1736] thinks Shakespeare "should have contrived some good reason" for his delay, but—"so brave and careless of his own life"—discovers none. In all that period the play was, as the Earl of Shaftesbury, in 1710, justly recognized, "that piece of his which appears to have most affected English hearts, and has been oftenest acted of any which have come upon our stage" [see excerpt above],— something it could not have been if the leading character had been represented as a hesitant weakling, a psychopathic case. Once he was so represented, he gradually retreated from the theatre, now a stranger to it. . . . But others may hesitate so lightly to reverse the verdict of two centuries of popular opinion and applause in the theatre, concerning a play written for the theatre, not published with the author's consent, and in both Quartos garbled, in favour of the judgment of Scotch professors and sentimentalists, Romantic poets and German philosophers, and present-day psychologists and psycho-analysts, exploring their own consciousness, in the study. Others still may have misgivings in acknowledging in a popular hero a tragic fault not discovered by a moral philosopher like Shaftesbury, or by neo-classical dramatists and critics, professionally on the alert for it, such as Nicholas Rowe, Fielding, Dennis, Tom Davies, Malone, Aaron Hill, Voltaire, and above all Johnson (who sought for it and was troubled by the lack of it), and first revealed to those who knew not and loved not the stage or its ways. The dramatic idiom is not one of words and phrases merely, but of traditions and conventions; and why should not these successive generations of dramatists, actors, and spectators have far better understood it? A novel or a poem may, in its own time and after, be neglected because misunderstood; but criticism should be wary of finding this to be the case with an extraordinarily popular play by an expert playwright; and of stepping into the breach itself, when the idiom has grown unfamiliar, with an interpretation diametrically opposed. (pp. 108-09)

> Elmer Edgar Stoll, "'Hamlet'," in his Art and Artifice in Shakespeare: A Study in Dramatic Contrast and Illusion, *Cambridge at the University Press, 1933, pp. 90-137.*

CAROLINE F. E. SPURGEON (essay date 1935)

[*Spurgeon's* Shakespeare's Imagery, *first published in 1935, inaugurated the "image-pattern analysis" method of studying*

Shakespeare's plays. In this work, she interprets the thematic structure of the plays through an examination of patterns in the imagery. This critical approach was one of the most widely used methods of the mid-twentieth century. Spurgeon also sought to learn about Shakespeare's personality from a study of his images, a direction which few of her disciples followed. Since publication of her book, earlier works on image patterns in Shakespeare have been discovered, but none was as important in the history of Shakespearean criticism as Spurgeon's. Concentrating on imagery and the unity it gives the play, Spurgeon, like G. Wilson Knight (1930), finds Hamlet *permeated with images of sickness and death. For additional commentary on images of sickness in* Hamlet, *see the excerpt by Wolfgang H. Clemen (1951), who, like Spurgeon, presents an image analysis of the play. For further discussion of imagery and language, see Samuel Taylor Coleridge (1813), Maynard Mack (1952), Harry Levin (1957), T. McAlindon (1970), Reuben A. Brower (1971), and Inga-Stina Ewbank (1977).*]

[In] *Hamlet*, we find in the 'sickness' images a feeling of horror, disgust and even helplessness not met before (save for a touch of the first two in Jacques' bitter moralising and the duke's answer, [*A.Y.L.I.* II. vii. 58-61 and 64-9]; and the general sense of inward and unseen corruption, of the man helplessly succumbing to a deadly and 'foul disease', which feeds 'even on the pith of life' [IV. i. 23], is very strong. This is accompanied by the impression that for such a terrible ill the remedy must be drastic, for

> diseases desperate grown
> By desperate appliance are relieved,
> Or not at all,   [IV. iii. 9]

and that anything short of this is but to

> skin and film the ulcerous place,
> Whiles rank corruption, mining all within,
> Infects unseen.   [III. iv. 147-49]

This is, as we shall see later, the general symbolic trend of these images in the play, and Hamlet and the others pay the price demanded for the necessary cleansing of the 'foul body of the infected world'. (pp. 133-34)

Hamlet speaks of his mother's sin as a blister on the 'fair forehead of an innocent love', she speaks of her sick soul', and as in *King Lear* the emotion is so strong and the picture so vivid, that the metaphor overflows into the verbs and adjectives: heaven's face, he tells her, is *thought-sick* at the act; her husband is a *mildew'd ear*, blasting his *wholesome* brother; to have married him, her sense must be not only *sickly*, but *apoplex'd*. Finally, at the end of that terrific scene [III. iv], he implores her not to soothe herself with the belief that his father's apparition is due to her son's madness, and not to her own guilt, for that

> will but skin and film the ulcerous place,
> Whiles rank corruption, mining all within,
> Infects unseen.   [III. iv. 147-49]

So also, later, he compares the unnecessary fighting between Norway and Poland to a kind of tumour which grows out of too much prosperity. He sees the country and the people in it alike in terms of a sick body needing medicine or the surgeon's knife. When he surprises Claudius at his prayers, he exclaims,

> This physic but prolongs thy sickly days;
>
> [III. iii. 96]

and he describes the action of conscience in the unforgettable picture of the healthy, ruddy countenance turning pale with sickness. A mote in the eye, a 'vicious mole', a galled chilblain, a probed wound and purgation, are also among Hamlet's images; and the mind of Claudius runs equally on the same theme.

When he hears of the murder of Polonius, he declares that his weakness in not sooner having had Hamlet shut up was comparable to the cowardly action of a man with a 'foul disease' who

> To keep it from divulging, let it feed
> Even on the pith of life;   [IV. i. 22-3]

and later, when arranging to send Hamlet to England and to his death, he justifies it by the proverbial tag:

> diseases desperate grown
> By desperate appliance are relieved,
> Or not at all;   [IV. iii. 9-11]

and adjures the English king to carry out his behest, in the words of a fever patient seeking a sedative;

> For like the hectic in my blood he rages,
> And thou must cure me.   [IV. iii. 66-7]

When working on Laertes, so that he will easily fall in with the design for the fencing match, his speech is full of the same underlying thought of a body sick, or ill at ease:

> goodness, growing to a plurisy,
> Dies in his own too much;   [IV. vii. 117-18]

and finally, he sums up the essence of the position and its urgency with lightning vividness in a short medical phrase:

> But, to the quick o' the ulcer:
> Hamlet comes back.   [IV. vii. 123-24]

In marked contrast to *King Lear,* though bodily disease is emphasised, bodily action and strain are little drawn upon; indeed, only in Hamlet's great speech are they brought before us at all (*to be shot at* with slings and arrows, *to take arms against* troubles and *oppose* them, *to suffer* shocks, *to bear* the lash of whips, and *endure* pangs, *to grunt* and *sweat* under burdens, and so on), and here, as in *King Lear,* they serve to intensify the feeling of mental anguish. In *Hamlet,* however, anguish is not the dominating thought, but *rottenness,* disease, corruption, the result of *dirt;* the people are 'muddied',

> Thick and unwholesome in their thoughts and
>   whispers;   [IV. v. 82]

and this corruption is, in the words of Claudius, 'rank' and 'smells to heaven', so that the state of things in Denmark which shocks, paralyses and finally overwhelms Hamlet, is as the foul tumour breaking inwardly and poisoning the whole body, while showing

> no cause without
> Why the man dies.   [IV. iv. 28-9]

This image pictures and reflects not only the outward condition which causes Hamlet's spiritual illness, but also his own state. Indeed, the shock of the discovery of his father's murder and the sight of his mother's conduct have been such that when the play opens Hamlet has already begun to die, to die internally; because all the springs of life—love, laughter, joy, hope, belief in others—are becoming frozen at their source, are being gradually infected by the disease of the spirit which is—unknown to him—killing him.

To Shakespeare's pictorial imagination, therefore, the problem in *Hamlet* is not predominantly that of will and reason, of a

mind too philosophic or a nature temperamentally unfitted to act quickly; he sees it pictorially *not as the problem of an individual at all,* but as something greater and even more mysterious, as a *condition* for which the individual himself is apparently not responsible, any more than the sick man is to blame for the infection which strikes and devours him, but which, nevertheless, in its course and development, impartially and relentlessly, annihilates him and others, innocent and guilty alike. That is the tragedy of *Hamlet,* as it is perhaps the chief tragic mystery of life.

It is hardly necessary to point out, in a play so well known, and of such rich imaginative quality, how the ugliness of the dominating image (disease, ulcer) is counteracted, and the whole lighted up by flashes of sheer beauty in the imagery; beauty of picture, of sound and association, more particularly in the classical group and in the personifications. Thus, the tragic, murky atmosphere of Hamlet's interview with his mother, with its ever-repeated insistence on physical sickness and revolting disease, is illumined by the glow of his description of his father's portrait, the associations of beauty called up by Hyperion, Jove and Mars, or the exquisite picture evoked by the contemplation of the grace of his father's poise:

> like the herald Mercury
> New-lighted on a heaven-kissing hill.
>
>   [III. iv. 58-9]

These beauties are specially noticeable in the many personifications, as when, with Horatio, we see 'the morn, in russet mantle clad', as she 'walks o'er the dew of yon high eastward hill', or, with Hamlet, watch Laertes leaping into Ophelia's grave, and ask,

> Whose phrase of sorrow
> Conjures the wandering stars and makes them stand
> Like wonder-wounded hearers?   [V. i. 255-57]

Peace, with her wheaten garland, Niobe all tears, Ophelia's garments 'heavy with their drink', which pull her from her 'melodious lay' to muddy death, or the magnificent picture of the two sides of the queen's nature at war, as seen by the elder Hamlet:

> But look, amazement on thy mother sits:
> O, step between her and her fighting soul;
>
>   [III. iv. 112-13]

these, and many more, are the unforgettable and radiant touches of beauty in a play which has, as images, much that is sombre and unpleasant. (pp. 316-20)

> *Caroline F. E. Spurgeon, "Shakespeare's Tastes and Interests: Indoor and Other Interests" and "Leading Motives in the Tragedies," in her* Shakespeare's Imagery and What It Tells Us, *Cambridge at the University Press, 1968, pp. 112-45, 309-56.*

J. DOVER WILSON   (essay date 1935)

[*Wilson's* What Happens in Hamlet *is one of the most important works on the play. Wilson urges readers to maintain the ability to see the play with Elizabethan eyes; in this he agrees with A.J.A. Waldock (1931) and Elmer Edgar Stoll (1933). Wilson examines specific words and phrases for connotations understood by Elizabethans that are lost on modern audiences. Analyzing the plot in terms of an Elizabethan's vocabulary and attitudes, Wilson asserts that three points would have been evident to an Elizabethan audience: (1) Claudius usurped Hamlet, the rightful heir; (2) Gertrude's incest is abhorent; (3) the ghost is an important, ob-*

jective character in the play. This last point is developed in Wilson's earlier essay (1918), which refutes the theory of W. W. Greg (1917) regarding the nature of the ghost. E.M.W. Tillyard (1949), William Empson (1953), Fredson Bowers (1955), and Eleanor Prosser (1971) adopted in their criticism a historical approach similar to Wilson's.]

The first act of *Hamlet* unfolds the situation in which the Prince of Denmark finds himself at the beginning of his tragedy, and the nature of the task which that situation lays upon him. But the drama of which he is the hero was written by an Elizabethan for Elizabethans. If therefore we of the twentieth century desire to enter fully into that situation we must ask ourselves how it would present itself to English minds at the end of the sixteenth. Further, in our endeavour to see the play in its contemporary perspective, we must be careful not to overlook those tacit understandings between Shakespeare and his audience which, just because they were tacit, because that is to say they were part of the atmosphere of the time, are most likely to escape us. (p. 26)

What kind of constitution and state, for example, would a sixteenth-century dramatist and his public imagine as an appropriate setting for this Danish tragedy? The events of the story take place at a court; the principal characters are members of a royal house; we are told of Norwegian and Polack wars; the presence of young Fortinbras is felt long before he actually makes his appearance; there is a going and coming of ambassadors; at one point a popular insurrection threatens to break out; and the last problem that agitates the mind of the dying Hamlet is the question of the succession to the throne. Shakespeare has etched this background in strokes masterly but few, for he would not detract from the main human interest. What was his model? With what thoughts did the spectators for whom he wrote piece out the hints he gave them? (p. 27)

Nothing is more certain than that Shakespeare has England chiefly in mind in other plays. The scene may be Rome, Venice, Messina, Vienna, Athens, Verona, or what not, and the game of make-believe may be kept alive by a splash of local colour here and there, but the characters, their habits, their outlook, and even generally their costumes are "mere English". . . . (pp. 27-8)

Why should *Hamlet* be an exception to all this? The references to "ambitious Norway" or "the sledded Polacks on the ice" do not deceive us. Shakespeare no doubt took what he fancied from the old play over which he worked, and glanced now and again into Saxo or Belleforest; but to make him out a deep student of Danish history and customs is absurd. Hamlet is an English prince, the court of Elsinore is modelled upon the English court, and the Danish constitution that of England under the Virgin Queen.

Take the second scene. By following the stage-directions of the First Folio text editors have overlooked the fact that it is intended to represent a meeting of the Privy Council. *Enter Claudius, King of Denmarke, Gertrud the Queene, Councillors, Polonius, and his Sonne Laertes, Hamlet, Cum Alijs* is the opening direction according to the Second Quarto, which is almost certainly printed direct from Shakespeare's autograph manuscript. Here the presence of councillors is unquestionable. Moreover, the business which is transacted stamps the character of the assembly. Questions of foreign policy are discussed; ambassadors are given their commission; Hamlet is solemnly announced as next in order of succession: all this could only be done by "The King in Council". The tone, too, of Clau-

dius's speech is that of a monarch addressing his advisers, not of one at a court gala. (pp. 28-9)

A trivial point, it may be said; yet it is one that raises considerations of far-reaching importance. For if Shakespeare and his audience thought of the constitution of Denmark in English terms, then *Hamlet was the rightful heir to the throne and Claudius a usurper*. . . . Hamlet describes his uncle as a usurper and refers to his own blighted hopes of the succession on two occasions:

> A murderer and a villain,
> A slave that is not twentieth part the tithe
> Of your precedent lord, a vice of kings,
> A cutpurse of the empire and the rule,
> That from a shelf the precious diadem stole
> And put it in his pocket.   [III. iv. 96-101]

These words, spoken to the Queen just before the apparition in the bedroom, are surely sufficiently plain. Equally so—apart from the word "election", to which I shall return—is another outburst, in the ear of Horatio this time, against the triple criminal who

> hath killed my king, and whored my mother,
> Popped in between th'election and my hopes.
>   [V. ii. 64-5]

It will be objected that these references occur very late in the play, and that had Shakespeare attached importance to the fact of usurpation he would have made it obvious at the beginning. The argument really cuts the other way. That Hamlet regarded the accession of Claudius as a grievance is proved by his words; and his expression of them so late in the play proves that Shakespeare did not think it necessary to make it plainer, that he knew his audience would assume the situation from the outset. The point was, indeed, so clear that it needed no stressing. (pp. 30-1)

[Hamlet's] sardonic air and his brief but bitter replies to his mother and uncle signify a consciousness of grievous wrong.

> But now my cousin Hamlet, and my son,
>   [I. ii. 64]

begins Claudius; and Hamlet comments in an audible aside:

> A little more than kin, and less than kind.
>   [I. ii. 65]

The alliteration will fix the words in the memory of those who hear them, and later they will perceive in the quibble "less than kind" a sinister point not immediately apparent. But the surface meaning is clear enough. It refers to Hamlet's disappointed hopes of the succession, as is proved by what follows; for when the King continues:

> How is it that the clouds still hang on you?
>   [I. ii. 66]

he gets the only reply that Hamlet vouchsafes him throughout the scene:

> Not so, my lord, I am too much in the "son".
>   [I. ii. 67]

It is another quibble, but this time direct, defiant and (to Elizabethan ears) unambiguous. I say to Elizabethan ears, because unfortunately until recently the point has been missed by modern readers. Hamlet was known, by comparison with similar quibbles in *King Lear* and other books of the period, to be alluding to the now obsolete proverbial expression "Out of heaven's blessing to the warm sun''; but it was only discovered four years ago that the true interpretation of this expression was ''From an exalted, or honourable, state or occupation to a low or ignoble one'', an interpretation, to quote the words of the discoverer himself, which ''seems to favour the belief that one cause, among others, of Hamlet's bitterness was his exclusion from the throne''. (pp. 32-3)

The usurpation is one of the main factors in the plot of *Hamlet,* and it is vital that we moderns should not lose sight of it. Hamlet, as we have seen, is not unmindful of it; still more important, Claudius is not unmindful either. In short, Hamlet's ambitious designs, or what his uncle takes so to be, form, not of course the most important, but a leading element in the relations between the two men throughout the play. During the first half Claudius is constantly trying to probe them; they explain much in the conversations between Hamlet and the two spies Rosencrantz and Guildenstern; they clarify the whole puzzling situation after the play scene; and they add surprising force and meaning to one of the most dramatic moments of the play scene itself. In a word, suppress the usurpation-motive and we miss half the meaning of what happens in acts 2 and 3. As an aid to the operation of the plot it is second only in importance to a true understanding of the Ghost. And this in itself is strong evidence in its favour. (p. 34)

We can rest assured that few if any spectators and readers of *Hamlet* at the beginning of the seventeenth century gave even a passing thought to the constitutional practices of Denmark. And, if after the accession of James and his Danish consort, the audience came to include a sprinkling of courtiers more knowing than the rest, what then? The election in Denmark, as even Blackstone admitted, was in practice limited to members of the blood royal; in other words, on the death of King Hamlet the choice lay between his son and his brother. In the eyes of such spectators, therefore, Hamlet's disappointment would seem just as keen and his ambitious designs just as natural, as if the succession was legally according to the principle of primogeniture. However it be looked at, the elective throne in Shakespeare's Denmark is a mirage.

Hamlet is a tragedy, the tragedy of a genius caught fast in the toils of circumstance and unable to fling free. Shakespeare unfolds to us the full horror of Hamlet's situation gradually, adding one load after another to the burden he has to bear until we feel that he must sink beneath it. The apparition in the first scene forewarns us of ''some strange eruption'' that threatens the state of Denmark. The opening of the second scene shows us the Prince robbed of his inheritance by his uncle and mourning a beloved father whom his mother has already forgotten. Here is matter for pathos, though scarcely for tragic issues. But Hamlet now steps forward and tells us what is in his heart, what overshadows his disinheritance so completely that he does not mention it. His mother is a criminal, has been guilty of a sin which blots out the stars for him, makes life a bestial thing, and even infects his very blood. She has committed incest. Modern readers, living in an age when marriage laws are the subject of free discussion and with a deceased wife's sister act upon the statute-book, can hardly be expected to enter fully into Hamlet's feelings on this matter. Yet no one who reads the first soliloquy in the Second Quarto text, with its illuminating dramatic punctuation, can doubt for one moment that Shakespeare wished here to make full dramatic capital out of Gertrude's infringement of ecclesiastical law, and expected his audience to look upon it with as much abhorrence as the Athenians felt for what we should consider the more venial, be-

cause unwitting, crime of the Oedipus of Sophocles. (pp. 38-9)

This incest-business is so important that it is scarcely possible to make too much of it. Shakespeare places it in the very forefront of the play, he devotes a whole soliloquy to it, he shows us Hamlet's mind filled with the fumes of its poison, writhing in anguish, longing for death as an escape. I am anxious at this stage not to prejudge the question of Hamlet's ''character''; but in dealing with it the critics have certainly neglected to give full weight to the opening soliloquy. It is the first occasion on which Hamlet takes us into his confidence, and its position makes it, as it were, a window through which we view the rest of the drama. . . . Goethe's condescending sentimentalism in particular moves one almost to anger [see excerpt above, 1795]. The datum of the tragedy is not ''a great deed imposed upon a soul unequal to the performance of it'', but a great and noble spirit subjected to a moral shock so overwhelming that it shatters all zest for life and all belief in it. And as yet he has not begun to feel the full weight of the ''yoke of inauspicious stars''; for the Ghost still awaits him on the battlements.

The interview with his father's spirit doubles the load upon Hamlet's shoulders. He learns two new facts about his father, his mother and his uncle, both more terrible than anything he has known hitherto—and he is given a commission of extraordinary difficulty and delicacy. He learns that Claudius has murdered his father, done him to death in a fashion horrible to think of, sent him suddenly into the next world ''in the blossoms of his sin'' with no time even to make his peace with Heaven. Claudius had seemed to Hamlet a satyr before this, now he knows him as something more deadly, a smiling, creeping, serpent—very venomous. He learns too that his mother, who would hang upon her first husband, ''as if increase of appetite had grown by what it fed on'', was even then, in his life-time, unfaithful to him, would steal from her ''celestial bed'' to ''prey on garbage''. He had known she was a criminal, guilty of the filthy sin of incest; but this new revelation shows her as rotten through and through. (pp. 43-4)

Hamlet is Shakespeare's most realistic, most modern, tragedy; the play of all others in which we seem to come closest to the spirit and life of his time, and he closest to the spirit and life of ours. It is therefore remarkable, and perhaps not without a personal significance, that he should have made the supernatural element more prominent here than in any other of his dramas. The first act is a little play in itself, and the Ghost is the hero of it; 550 out of 850 lines are concerned with him. Moreover, he is a very real spirit. Caesar at Philippi may be a student's dream; Banquo at the feast may be a false creation proceeding from Macbeth's crime-oppressed brain; but there can be no doubt, if Dr Greg will forgive me, about the objectivity of the spectre of King Hamlet. He is a character in the play in the fullest sense of the term. He retains a human heart, for all his stateliness, and there is more than a touch of pathos about his majestical figure. I do not claim that Shakespeare ''believed in ghosts''; we do not know what Shakespeare believed, though it seems by no means improbable that he regarded ghosts as at least a sublunary possibility. Certainly as a poet he believed in *this* ghost, and determined that his audience should believe in it likewise. The Ghost is the linchpin of *Hamlet;* remove it and the play falls to pieces. (p. 52)

The majesty of buried Denmark is an English spirit, English of the late sixteenth and early seventeenth centuries, and the story of *Hamlet* turns upon this fact. Thus, unless we can see it as the Elizabethans did, we shall inevitably miss, not only many beautiful touches, but, more important still, matters which concern the plot of the play, to which the Ghost is intimately related, seeing that he is the instrument which sets it in motion. (p. 53)

The attitude of Hamlet towards Ophelia is without doubt the greatest of all the puzzles in the play, greater even than that of the delay itself, a fact which should long ago have created suspicion that in the course of three centuries Shakespeare's original intentions have somehow been obscured. The difficulty is not that, having once loved Ophelia, Hamlet ceases to do so. This is explained, as most critics have agreed, by his mother's conduct which has put him quite out of love with Love and has poisoned his whole imagination. The exclamation "Frailty thy name is woman!" in the first soliloquy, we come to feel later, embraces Ophelia as well as Gertrude, while in the bedroom scene he as good as taxes his mother with destroying his capacity for affection, when he accuses her of

> such an act
> That blurs the grace and blush of modesty,
> Calls virtue hypocrite, *takes off the rose*
> *From the fair forehead of an innocent love*
> And sets a blister there.   [III. iv. 40-4]

Moreover, it is clear that in the tirades of the nunnery scene he is thinking almost as much of his mother as of Ophelia.

The word "blister" in the passage just quoted introduces us to the real problem; for it refers to the branding of a harlot. Why brand "an *innocent* love" thus? Gertrude had played the harlot with Claudius; why pour abuse which might be appropriate to her upon the unoffending head of Ophelia? . . . [That] Shakespeare intended us to interpret Hamlet's speeches here, together with some of those in the nunnery scene, as, like Othello's, belonging to the brothel is, I think, incontestable. We may try and palliate this conduct by dwelling upon Hamlet's morbid state of mind, by recalling that manners were ruder and speech more direct with the Elizabethans than with ourselves, by noting that since Ophelia and the rest thought he was mad they would be ready to extenuate his behaviour on that ground (as for instance Ophelia's outspoken song in 4.5 is generally regarded as a pathetic symptom of her condition), and by emphasising the fact that she had jilted him and that he had therefore a grievance against her. Yet all will not do; Hamlet's treatment of her remains inexcusable on the ordinary reading of the story, and as such it endangers the very life of the play. (pp. 101-02)

There is a savage side to Hamlet, which comes out in his ruthlessness towards Rosencrantz and Guildenstern, and in the speech as the King kneels in prayer, a speech that Dr Johnson found "too horrible to be read or to be uttered" [see excerpt above, 1765]. Yet this savagery, discordant as it is with our scale of values, does not detract from our general sense of the nobility and greatness of the man. But savagery towards a gentle and inoffensive child, one whom he had loved and whose worst crime towards him is lack of understanding and inability to disobey her father's commands, is a very different matter. It is, in fact, irreconcilable with everything else we are told about him.

Hamlet treats Ophelia like a prostitute; and the only possible defence for him is to show that he had grounds for so doing. What can they have been? . . . [Early] in 2.2, at which Polonius and Claudius devise the plot of listening to Hamlet and Ophelia

behind the arras, . . . my attention was arrested by this line in the speech of Polonius:

> At such a time I'll loose my daughter to him.
>
>   [II. ii. 162]

The expression was not new to me. I had met it before in *The Tempest* at II. i. 126, where the cynical Sebastian sneers at Alonso because he would not marry his daughter to a European prince,

> But rather loose her to an African;

and in *The Merry Wives* at II. i. 181-84, where the confident Master Page declares of Falstaff that "if he should intend this voyage towards my wife, I would turn her loose to him; and what he gets more of her than sharp words, let it lie on my head". I had met it also, listening to present-day farmers in the north of England discussing the breeding of horses and cattle; and that this was the meaning intended, a meaning that would assuredly not escape an Elizabethan audience, was confirmed to my mind by Polonius speaking of "a farm and carters" five lines later, in accordance with Shakespeare's habit of sustained imagery.

But to understand the point of it and its connection with what follows, we must have the whole context before us. I quote from the Second Quarto text:

> *King.* How may we try it further?
> *Pol.* You know sometimes he walkes foure houres
> together heere in the Lobby.
> *Quee.* So he dooes indeede.
> *Pol.* At such a time, Ile loose my daughter to him,
> Be you and I behind an Arras then,
> Marke the encounter, if he loue her not,
> And be not from his reason falne thereon
> Let me be no assistant for a state
> But keepe a farme and carters.
> *King.* We will try it.
>   *Enter Hamlet.*
> *Quee.* But looke where sadly the poore wretch
> comes reading.
> *Pol.* Away, I doe beseech you both away, *Exit*
> *King and Queene.*
> Ile bord him presently, oh giue me leaue,
> How dooes my good Lord Hamlet?
> *Ham.* Well, God a mercy.
> *Pol.* Doe you knowe me my Lord?
> *Ham.* Excellent well, you are a Fishmonger.
> *Pol.* Not I my Lord.
> *Ham.* Then I would you were so honest a man.
> *Pol.* Honest my Lord.
> *Ham.* I sir to be honest as this world goes,
> Is to be one man pickt out of tenne thousand.
> *Pol.* That's very true my Lord.
> *Ham.* For if the sunne breede maggots in a dead
> dogge, being a good kissing carrion. Haue you a
> daughter?
> *Pol.* I haue my Lord.
> *Ham.* Let her not walke i'th Sunne, conception is
> a blessing, but as your daughter may conceaue,
> friend looke to't.   [II. ii. 158-86]

Everything that Hamlet here says is capable of an equivocal interpretation reflecting upon Polonius and Ophelia. "Fishmonger", as many commentators have noted, means a pandar or procurer; "carrion" was a common expression at that time for "flesh" in the carnal sense; while the quibble in "conception" needs no explaining. And when I asked myself why Hamlet should suddenly call Polonius a bawd and his daughter a prostitute—for that is what it all amounts to—I could discover but one possible answer to my question, namely that "Fishmonger" and the rest follows immediately upon "loose my daughter to him". Nor was this the end of the matter. For what might Hamlet mean by his sarcastic advice to the father not to let the daughter "walke i'th Sunne", or by the reference to the sun breeding in the "carrion" exposed to it? Bearing in mind Hamlet's punning retort "I am too much in the 'son'", in answer to Claudius's unctuous question at I. ii. 64, 66,

> And now my cousin Hamlet, and my son,
> How is it that the clouds still hang on you?—
>
> [I. ii. 64, 66]

and recalling Falstaff's apostrophe to Prince Hal: "Shall the blessed sun of heaven prove a micher and eat blackberries? a question not to be asked. Shall the son of England prove a thief and take purses? a question to be asked", is it not obvious that Hamlet here means by "Sunne" the sun or son of Denmark, the heir apparent, in other words himself? And if so, "let her not walke i'th Sunne" is to be paraphrased "take care that you do not loose your daughter to me!"

What then? *Hamlet must have overheard what Polonius said to the King.* The context allows no escape from this conclusion, inasmuch as what Hamlet says to Polonius is only intelligible if the conclusion is allowed. (pp. 102-06)

Hamlet walks into the trap in complete unconsciousness. As he enters, his mind is not on the plot, his uncle or Ophelia. If he remembers the Ghost at all, it is to write it off as a snare of the evil one. He is back again where he was when he first had sight of his inner self; back in the mood of the soliloquy which begins

> O that this too too sullied flesh would melt,
> Thaw and resolve itself into a dew,
> Or that the Everlasting had not fixed
> His canon 'gainst self-slaughter.
>
> [I. ii. 129-32]

But he is no longer thinking of his own "sullied flesh", still less of the divine command. By constantly turning it over he has worn the problem to the bone:

> To be, or not to be, that is the question.
>
> [III. i. 55]

A like expression of utter weariness is not to be found in the rest of human literature. Sleep, death, annihilation, his whole mind is concentrated upon these; and the only thing that holds his arm from striking home with "the bare bodkin" is the thought of "what dreams may come", "the dread of something after death". (p. 127)

As the meditation finishes, Hamlet sees Ophelia behind him upon her knees. The sight reminds him of nothing except "the pangs of disprized love", and those have long been drowned in "a sea of troubles". "The fair Ophelia!" he exclaims; the words have no warmth in them. And, when he addresses her, he speaks in irony:

> Nymph, in thy orisons
> Be all my sins remembered. . . .
>
> [III. i. 88-9]

She had refused to see him and had returned his letters; she could not even speak a word of comfort when in deep trouble he forced his way into her room with mute pitiable appeal. After that he had done with her; and the Ophelia he now meets is a stranger. Stranger indeed! For listen:

> Good my lord,
> How does your honour for this many a day?
>
> [III. i. 89-90]

Is she implying that *he* has neglected *her*? It was only yesterday he had been with her despite her denial of his access. But at first he takes small note of her words and answers with polite aloofness:

> I humbly thank you, well, well, well.
>
> [III. i. 91]

It is a form of address he employs later with people like the Norwegian Captain and Osric, while the repeated "well" sounds bored. Nevertheless, she continues:

> My lord, I have remembrances of yours,
> That I have longed long to re-deliver.
> I pray you now receive them.   [III. i. 92-4]

What should that mean? Once again, however, he brushes it aside: "I never gave *you* aught,"—the woman to whom I once gave gifts is dead. Yet still she persists:

> My honoured lord, you know right well you did,
> And with them words of so sweet breath composed
> As made the things more rich. Their perfume lost,
> Take these again, for to the noble mind
> Rich gifts wax poor when givers prove unkind.
> There, my lord.   [III. i. 96-101]

And here she draws the trinkets from her bosom and places them on the table before him.

The unhappy girl has sadly overplayed her part. Her little speech, ending with a sententious couplet, as Dowden notes, "has an air of being prepared". Worse than that, she, the jilt, is accusing him of coldness towards her. Worst of all, Hamlet who has been "sent for", who meets her in the lobby "by accident", finds her prepared not only with a speech but with the gifts also. She means no harm; she has romantically arranged a little play scene, in the hope no doubt of provoking a passionate declaration of affection, which perhaps

> Will bring him to his wonted way again,
>
> [III. i. 40]

as the Queen had remarked just before Hamlet's entrance, and will at any rate prove to the King that she and her father are right in their diagnosis of the distemper. But the effect upon Hamlet is disastrous. Until that moment he had forgotten the plot; it is a far cry from thoughts of "the undiscovered country" to this discovery. But he is now thoroughly awake, and sees it all. Here is the lobby and the decoy, playing a part, only too unblushingly; and there at the back is the arras, behind which lurk the Fishmonger and Uncle Claudius. His wild "Ha, ha!" the fierce question "are you honest?" that is to say "are you not a whore?" together with a significant glance round the room, are enough to show the audience that he realises at last, and warn them to expect "antic disposition". Everything he says for the rest of the scene is intended for the ears of the eavesdroppers. As for the daughter who has been "loosed" to him, she will only get what she deserves. . . . He puts her to one final test before the scene is over; but the dice are loaded against her. Thus, through a chain of misconceptions, due to nothing worse than narrowness of vision and over-readiness to comply with her father's commands, Ophelia blackens her own character in her lover's eyes. The process has been obscured hitherto owing to the absence of one important link in the chain; but the link now in place makes all clear, explains Hamlet's attitude, and shows her fate as even more pathetic than we had supposed.

Everything he says, I repeat, for the rest of the scene is intended for the ears of Claudius and Polonius, whom he knows to be behind the arras. . . . He speaks at both; but he speaks, of course, to Ophelia, while as he speaks he has yet a fourth person constantly in mind, his mother. If this be remembered, and if we also keep in view Hamlet's habitual lack of self-control once he becomes excited, the dialogue is easy to follow.

I return to it:

> *Hamlet.* Ha, ha! are you honest?
> *Ophelia.* My lord?
> *Hamlet.* Are you fair?
> *Ophelia.* What means your lordship?
> *Hamlet.* That if you be honest and fair, your honesty
>   should admit no discourse to your beauty.
>
> [III. i. 102-07]

If, that is, you were the chaste maiden you pretend to be, you would not allow your beauty to be used as a bait in this fashion. (pp. 128-32)

So far Hamlet's talk has been in fishmonger-vein, and is meant for the Jephthah behind the arras. But now is the turn for Uncle Claudius. The mention of corrupt stock leads by natural transition to an elaborate confession of criminal propensities on Hamlet's part which *we* know to be ridiculous, but which is intended to make the King's blood run cold. "I am very proud, revengeful, ambitious" is the gist of it. Could any other three epithets be found less appropriate to Hamlet? But Claudius says he is ambitious; and Claudius is a reasonable man. The following, too, sounds terrible:

> with more offences at my beck, than I have
> thoughts to put them in, imagination to give
> them shape, or time to act them in:
>
> [III. i. 124-26]

—until we scan it and find that it amounts to nothing at all, since the same might be said of any mortal.

At this point Hamlet gives Ophelia her last chance with his sudden "Where's your father?" She answers with a lie, as it would seem to him, though of course she is observing the most ordinary precautions and, as she thinks, humouring a madman. But it is this crowning proof of her treachery, I suggest, that provokes the frenzy with which the episode closes. He goes out, perhaps in the hope that the rats may emerge from their hole and that he may catch them in the act of so doing. Twice he rushes from the room and with each return his manner grows more excited. His two final speeches are mainly food for fish-mongers, and he concludes by coming very near to calling Ophelia a prostitute to her face. The repeated injunction "to a nunnery go" is significant in this connection, since "nun-nery" was in common Elizabethan use a cant term for a house of ill-fame. (pp. 133-34)

As he leaves for the last time he throws his uncle one more morsel to chew: "I say we will have no mo marriage—those that are married already, *all but one,* shall live, the rest shall

keep as they are." . . . [These] threats show that the Prince has thoroughly grasped the hints about ambition dropped by Rosencrantz and Guildenstern; and is now posing as the discontented heir thirsting for revenge. . . . (pp. 134-35)

After his disillusionment with Rosencrantz and Guildenstern, Hamlet is delighted to welcome the players to Elsinore. He selects immediately a rather bombastic passionate speech from a *Dido and Aeneas* play, and bids the First Player recite it. . . . [When] the First Player next appears, Hamlet is giving him careful instructions how the all-important "dozen or sixteen lines", inserted by his own hand, are to be delivered. Commentators have dwelt much upon this conversation, since it seems to let us into Shakespeare's own views about the methods of his craft; but in so doing they have overlooked its connection with the Hamlet story. . . . [Despite] his general approval of the rendering of the Pyrrhus speech, Hamlet is nervous, very nervous, about the First Player's capacity to recite his lines properly. This is natural, of course, seeing that the speech is to be the chief instrument in his unmasking of the King. Yet Hamlet, it is quite obvious, is not thinking primarily about Claudius at all; he is thinking of his lines. He wants full justice done to his essay in the art of drama. Note, too, what it is particularly that he fears:

> If you *mouth* it as many of your players do, I
> had as lief the town-crier spoke my lines. Nor
> *do not saw the air* too much with your hand
> thus, but use all gently. . . . O, it offends me
> to the soul, to hear a robustious periwig-pated
> fellow *tear a passion to tatters,* to very rags,
> to split the ears of the groundlings, who for the
> most part are capable of nothing but *inexpli-*
> *cable dumb-shows and noise:* I would have such
> a fellow whipped for o'erdoing Termagant, it
> out-herods Herod, pray you avoid it. . . . O
> there be players that I have seen play—and
> heard others praise, and that highly—not to
> speak it profanely, that neither having th'accent
> of Christians, nor the gait of Christian, pagan,
> nor man, have so *strutted and bellowed,* that I
> have thought some of nature's journeymen had
> made men, and not made them well, they im-
> itated humanity so abominably.
>
> [III. ii. 2-14, 28-35]

Surely all this sheds a very curious light upon what happens immediately after in the play scene? First of all we have one of those dumb-shows that Hamlet thinks fit for groundlings alone—here, alas! only too explicable. Next we have a ridiculous prologue-jingle which Hamlet treats with undisguised contempt. Is it possible to hold him responsible for either of these effects?

Critics have seen that the dumb-show creates difficulties in regard to Claudius; they have not seen that it creates difficulties quite as great in regard to Hamlet himself. For what is he to make of this premature exhibition of his mouse-trap in all its naked outline? If he has not ordered it, will he not be vexed at its appearance? The dialogue that follows it between Ophelia and himself makes it quite clear, or at least should make it quite clear if only people would read *Hamlet* with their eyes open, that he is very angry indeed; and his comment, "Marry, this is miching mallecho, it means mischief", shows upon whom he fastens the blame. (pp. 154-56)

Hamlet sees that his speech is about to be rendered superfluous, and the spring of the mouse-trap released before the moment has arrived. His anxiety is evident in the sentence that follows the one just quoted: ''The players *cannot* keep counsel, they'll tell all!'' It is evident too, surely, in the dialogue that takes place immediately after the dumb-show, which exhibits Ophelia's attention concentrated upon the meaning of the pantomime and Hamlet's upon something quite different, viz. the conduct of the players, conduct which ''means mischief''. For the words ''miching mallecho'' I take to refer, not to the crime of Claudius, as most commentators seem vaguely to imagine, but to the *skulking iniquity* of the players, who have introduced this unauthorised and ridiculous dumb-show, and so have almost ruined the whole plot. (p. 157)

Shakespeare meant us to imagine Hamlet suffering from some kind of mental disorder throughout the play. Directly, however, such critics begin trying to define the exact nature of the disorder, they go astray. Its immediate origin cannot be questioned; it is caused, as we have seen, by the burden which fate lays upon his shoulders. We are not, however, at liberty to go outside the frame of the play and seek remoter origins in his past history. It is now well known, for instance, that a breakdown like Hamlet's is often due to seeds of disturbance planted in infancy and brought to evil fruition under the influence of mental strain of some kind in later life. Had Shakespeare been composing *Hamlet* to-day, he might conceivably have given us a hint of such an infantile complex. But he knew nothing of these matters and to write as if he did is to beat the air. We may go further. It is entirely misleading to attempt to describe Hamlet's state of mind in terms of modern psychology at all, not merely because Shakespeare did not think in these terms, but because—once again—Hamlet is a character in a play, not in history. He is part only, if the most important part, of an artistic masterpiece, of what is perhaps the most successful piece of dramatic illusion the world has ever known. And at no point of the composition is the illusion more masterly contrived than in this matter of his distraction.

In *Hamlet* Shakespeare set out to create a hero labouring under mental infirmity, just as later in *Macbeth* he depicted a hero afflicted by moral infirmity, or in *Othello* a hero tortured by an excessive and morbid jealousy. Hamlet struggles against his weakness, and the struggle is in great measure the ground-work of his tragedy. But though he struggles in vain, and is in the end brought to disaster, a disaster largely of his own making and involving his own house and that of Polonius, we are never allowed to feel that his spirit is vanquished until ''the potent poison quite o'er-crows'' it. Had he been represented as a mere madman, we should of course have felt this; he would have ceased to be a hero and, while retaining our pity, would have forfeited our sympathy, our admiration—and our censure. Ophelia exclaims,

> O, what a noble mind is here o'erthrown!
>
> [III. i. 150]

We know better: we realise that the mind is impaired, but we do not doubt for a moment that its nobility remains untouched; we see his sovereign reason often

> Like sweet bells jangled, out of tune and harsh,
>
> [III. i. 158]

yet all the while it retains its sovereignty and can recall its sweetness. There may be contradiction here; but we are not moving in the realm of logic. From the point of view of analytic psychology such a character may even seem a monster of inconsistency. This does not matter, if as here it also seems to spectators in the theatre to be more convincingly life-like than

any other character in literature. For most critics have agreed that Hamlet is one of the greatest and most fascinating of Shakespeare's creations; that he is a study in genius. Shakespeare, in short, accomplished that which he intended; he wrote a supreme tragedy. In poetic tragedy we contemplate beings greater than ourselves, greater than it is possible for man to be, enduring and brought to a calamitous end by sorrow or affliction or weakness of character which we should find unendurable; and we contemplate all this with unquestioning assent and with astonishment that deepens to awe. In the making of Hamlet, therefore, Shakespeare's task was not to produce a being psychologically explicable or consistent, but one who would evoke the affection, the wonder and the tears of his audience, and would yet be accepted as entirely human. (pp. 217-20)

> *J. Dover Wilson, in his* What Happens in ''Hamlet,'' *Cambridge at the University Press, 1935, 334 p.*

HARLEY GRANVILLE-BARKER (essay date 1937)

[*Granville-Barker was a noted actor, playwright, director, and critic. His work as a Shakespearean critic is at all times informed by his experience as a director, for he treats Shakespeare's plays not as works of literature better understood divorced from the theater, as did such Romantic critics as Charles Lamb, but as pieces meant for the stage. As a director, he emphasized simplicity in staging, set design, and costuming. He believed that elaborate scenery obscured the poetry which was of central importance to Shakespeare's plays. Granville-Barker also eschewed the approach of directors who scrupulously reconstruct a production based upon Elizabethan stage techniques; he felt that this, too, detracted from the play's meaning. Granville-Barker contests the accepted five-act division of* Hamlet *and proposes instead a three-act division based upon the flow of the action. Commenting on the dumb-show, he disagrees with J. Dover Wilson (1918), stating that Claudius does indeed see the dumb-show. Both the dumb-show and the ''Murder of Gonzago,'' according to Granville-Barker, represent ''the culmination of a long, tense, deliberate struggle to break down the king's composure.'' He urges an understanding of the piece as a ''play not a pamphlet,'' and also stresses that Shakespeare did not intend a clinical definition of madness in his depiction of Hamlet. Granville-Barker's essay was written in 1937, and first published in 1946 in his* Prefaces to Shakespeare.]

The long-accepted division of [*Hamlet*] into five acts is not, of course, authentic. Here, as with other plays, the editors of the Folio were bent upon giving their author this classic dignity; and it may be, besides, that by 1623 theatrical practice had itself imposed this division upon such of his plays as were still being acted. . . . [Shakespeare] certainly did not (except for one instance) think out his plays in five-act form; whatever the exigencies of its performance are to be, the play itself is an indivisible whole. It was the telling of a story; its shape would be dictated by the nature of the story and the need to make this dramatically effective. And that meant, among other things, that if there were to be breaks in its progress, one generally did better to minimize than to accentuate them; for the attention of an audience, once captured, must be held. (pp. 34-5)

There is both a place-structure and a time-structure in *Hamlet*. The place-structure depends upon no exact localization of scenes. The time-structure answers to no scheme of act-division. But each has its dramatic import.

The action of *Hamlet* is concentrated at Elsinore; and this though there is much external interest, and the story abounds in journeys. As a rule in such a case, unless they are mere messengers, we travel with the travelers. But we do not see Laertes in Paris, nor, more surprisingly, Hamlet among the pirates; and the Norwegian affair is dealt with by hearsay till the play is two-thirds over. This is not done to economize time, or to leave space for more capital events. Scenes in Norway or Paris or aboard ship need be no longer than the talk of them, and Hamlet's discovery of the King's plot against him is a capital event. Shakespeare is deliberately concentrating his action at Elsinore. When he does at last introduce Fortinbras he stretches probability to bring him and his army seemingly to its very suburbs; and, sooner than that Hamlet should carry the action abroad with him, Horatio is left behind there to keep him in our minds. On the other hand he still, by allusion, makes the most of this movement abroad which he does not represent; he even adds to our sense of it by such seemingly superfluous touches as tell us that Horatio has journeyed from Wittenberg, that Rosencrantz and Guildenstern have been "sent for"—and even the Players are traveling.

The double dramatic purpose is plain. Here is a tragedy of inaction; the center of it is Hamlet, who is physically inactive too, has "foregone all custom of exercises," will not "walk out of the air," but only, book in hand, for "four hours together, here in the lobby." The concentration at Elsinore of all that happens enhances the impression of this inactivity, which is enhanced again by the sense also given us of the constant coming and going around Hamlet of the busier world without. The place itself, moreover, thus acquires a personality, and even develops a sort of sinister power; so that when at last Hamlet does depart from it (his duty still unfulfilled) and we are left with the conscience-sick Gertrude and the guilty King, the mad Ophelia, a Laertes set on his own revenge, among a

> people muddied.
> Thick and unwholesome in their thoughts and whispers . . .
> [IV. v. 81-2]

we almost seem to feel it, and the unpurged sin of it, summoning him back to his duty and his doom. Shakespeare has, in fact, here adopted something very like unity of place; upon no principle, but to gain a specific dramatic end. (pp. 40-1)

Throughout the play Shakespeare makes much use of suspense. The story is, it might be said, one long essay in it; the single deed to be done, and to the last minute the doubt that it ever will be. And its incidental use is continual and various. We have had the suspense between the Ghost's first two appearances, the delay between the telling of the tale of them and this midnight; and now that the moment has come, we have this still obstinate silence. And when it is not suspense incidental to the action and imposed on him, there will be the checks, the delays, the zigzags of thought and intention in Hamlet himself to hold us in suspense.

[How "mad" is Hamlet? Or,] whether by a modern alienist's standard certifiably so—Shakespeare does not think in those terms. He uses the word as unprecisely as we still commonly do. Says Polonius,

> to define true madness,
> What is't but to be nothing else but mad?
> [II. ii. 93-4]

Hamlet speaks of himself as mad; half ironically, while he is under the spell; when he is free of it, as having been

> punished
> With sore distraction.   [V. ii. 229-30]

He is not ironical there. But he speaks in riddles. And this we may fairly accept as Shakespeare's conclusion too; that the thing in itself is a riddle. He attempts no answer. Nor need he, since he is writing a play, not a pamphlet. All he has to do is to show us what madness amounts to in this particular case. Hamlet will also pretend to be mad, and the pretense and the reality will not easily be distinguished. That there is reality mixed with the pretense—so much is plain. The reality, and the riddle of it, is Shakespeare's addition to the old story and its pretense, and is the leaven which, lifting the character above the story's needs, gives the play its enduring significance. For while few of us have murdered fathers to avenge, and not so many adulterous mothers to shame us, there will be hardly a man in any audience to whom that word "madness," in some one of its meanings, has not at one time or another come dreadfully home. (p. 66)

Does not [the Dumb Show] fatally anticipate the promised critical scene? Will Claudius not "blench" at so close a picturing—though a picturing only—of his crime? Let him do so, and is not Hamlet's purpose at once served, but Shakespeare's (so to say) aborted, the rest of the scene being then superfluous? Or, if Claudius manages to control himself, will he not, since "this show imports the argument of the play," stop the proceedings then and there? These questions have fomented controversy enough about the Dumb Show. Editors have answered them variously, producers in the main by omitting it. One editorial answer is that the King is at the moment talking to the Queen or Polonius, and does not see it [see excerpt above by J. Dover Wilson, 1935]. That can hardly be. Shakespeare does not leave such crucial matters in the air. Failing plain indication to the contrary, we must assume, I think, that whatever there is to be seen the King sees. Another answer is that while he sees the Show he does not suppose it to "import the argument," and is content to let it pass for an unlucky coincidence which no one can remark but he; for dumb shows are apt to be, as Hamlet says, "inexplicable," and the likeness may not be striking. This is more tenable; the Folio's labeling of the murderer as *a Fellow* does, in fact, suggest no such figure as the King's. And it is likely, I think, that the method of acting a dumb show differed greatly from that developed by this time for the acting of a play. It must inevitably have had more of the formal mime in it, which we commonly associate with ballet and the *Commedia dell' Arte*. But the right answer will emerge from the text and the situation involved in it; we have only straightforwardly to work this out, instead of dodging or shirking the issue.

When the King sees the Dumb Show he is at once alert. Though here may be a coincidence and no more, whatever Hamlet has a hand in will now be matter for suspicion. But what should he do? If the thing is mere coincidence, nothing. If it is a trap laid, he is not the man to walk straight into it—as he would by stopping the play for no reason he could give before it had well begun. He must wait and be wary. Ophelia (the acting of the Dumb Show has let her recover herself a little) voices the question for him:

> What means this, my lord? . . . Belike this
> show imports the argument of the play?
> [III. ii. 136, 139-40]

And Hamlet's answer:

> Marry, this is miching mallecho; it means mischief.
> [III. ii. 137-38]

and his comment on the Prologue:

the players cannot keep counsel: they'll tell all.

[III. ii. 141-42]

point disquietingly away from coincidence. "Miching malle-cho . . . mischief . . . tell all''; Claudius must be wary indeed.

Here, then, is the battle joined at once, between the watcher and the watched. On the defensive is the King, whose best tactics, without doubt, are to brave the business out, calmly, smilingly, giving no slightest sign that he sees anything ex-traordinary in it; for the attack, Horatio, whose steady eye—he has assured us—nothing will escape, and Hamlet, a-quiver with suppressed excitement, who after a while will try—still vainly—by mocking look and word, to pierce that admirable composure. But for a long first round, from the entry of the player King and Queen, it is a still and silent battle. Its back-ground is the line after line of their smoothly flowing verse, which we hear but need not greatly heed. Our attention is for the three: for Claudius, conscious that he is being watched, and Hamlet and Horatio, their eyes riveted to his face.

The Dumb Show falls quite pertinently into Hamlet's—and Shakespeare's—scheme. The mimic play as a whole is a cal-culated insult both to King and Queen. The "one scene" which "comes near the circumstance" of the old King's death, and into which Hamlet has inserted his "dozen or sixteen lines," is to be the finishing stroke merely. Were it a single one, Claudius might outface it. It is the prolonged preliminary ordeal which is to wear him down. Upon the point of dramatic tech-nique, too, if the test of his guilt is to be limited to the one scrambled and excited moment of the

Thoughts black, hands apt, drugs fit . . .

[III. ii. 255]

—when our eyes and ears are everywhere at once, upon Ham-let, Lucianus and the King, upon the Queen and the courtiers, too—the play's most vital crisis must be half lost in confusion. What Shakespeare means, surely, is to make this simply the culmination of a long, tense, deliberate struggle to break down the King's composure, on his part to maintain it. Treat it thus and the confusion, when at last it comes, makes its true effect. And the eighty lines of the spineless verse of *The Murder of Gonzago* are all they should be as a placid accompaniment to a silent and enthralling struggle. If the struggle is not the salient thing, if the ambling of the verse is made so instead, it must lower the tension of the scene disastrously. And we may, I think, acquit Shakespeare of meaning to do that. (pp. 93-5)

Rosencrantz and Guildenstern departed to arm them for their "speedy voyage," Polonius to warn the Queen of Hamlet's coming and "convey" himself behind the arras before he can arrive, Claudius is left alone. It is the first time that we see him so. And the adulterer, the murderer and usurper, so cool and collected till now—but for that one moment during the mimic play—now incontinently bends and writhes under the dreadful burden of his remorse. We have been prepared for some such revulsion by the earlier lines, spoken aside, about the harlot's cheek beautied with plastering art being not more ugly than is his deed to his painted word, and by the "O heavy burden!" with which they end. But I strongly suspect that these were inserted as an afterthought (lest the turn here should prove *too* unexpected to be convincing, or seem a mere superficial consequence of the shock of the play-scene), and that the orig-inal effect was meant to be one of arresting surprise. For here, not in the revelation during the play-scene, is the action's true turning point. That was a flash in the pan. But upon what happens now—or, rather does *not* happen—the rest of the play

depends; from this moment the tragedy and its holocaust are precipitated. Incidentally, it is always referred to as "the prayer-scene." But this is a misnomer more than usually misleading; since the whole point is that though Claudius strives to pray he cannot, that Hamlet spares him because he thinks he is praying, while, if he knew what was in his mind, he would presumably dispatch him then and there, and all, but for Ger-trude's grief and the scandal, would be well over. It is upon this master stroke of irony that everything turns; upon a Clau-dius battling within himself for his salvation and losing, and a Hamlet refusing to kill him lest he should *not* be damned.

The technical make-up of the scene, Claudius' soliloquy laps-ing into the silence of the attempted prayer, the surprise of Hamlet's appearance (we imagine him, as Claudius must, al-ready with his mother, Polonius having outsped him there), *his* surprise at the chance offered him, his soliloquy imposed, so to speak, upon the other—all that is unique in the play. Nor are we anywhere given harder or closer-knit argument. Each competes with the other in this; and we have a solid intellectual knot tied, a steadying interlude between the excitements of the play-scene and the emotions of the coming encounter with the Queen. Each antagonist is unaware of the other, Claudius of Hamlet's presence, Hamlet of what is in Claudius' mind. Each reaches a characteristic conclusion; Hamlet, with his revenge to his hand, is dissatisfied with its quality and refuses it; Clau-dius faces the truth about himself as he rises from his knees—

My words fly up, my thoughts remain below;
Words without thoughts never to heaven go.

[III. iii. 97-8]

—and, his own life spared, goes, single-minded again, to write the letter which is to compass Hamlet's death. And all Hamlet has gained is a fresh reminder of him

in the incestuous pleasure of his bed . . .

[III. iii. 90]

—more fuel, that is to say, for the already dangerous mood in which he now takes his interrupted way to his mother. (pp. 107-08)

The encounter with the Queen, as acted, too often becomes a moral lecture delivered by a grieved young man to a con-science-stricken matron. It is not meant, of course, to be any-thing of the sort. For one thing, Shakespeare would never bring this most passionate theme to a sententious crisis. For another, he habitually treats age in his characters as freely as he treats time in a play's action, conventionally, or (within the bounds of likelihood) for dramatic effect alone—and so he does here. Hamlet is "young." It looks as if Shakespeare first thought of him as about twenty, as the student returning to Wittenberg; late in the play he takes the trouble to make him a definite thirty, evidently to justify the developed maturity of his mind. But he remains conventionally "young." Gertrude—if we ar-gue the matter out, but we do not—might then be approaching fifty by the calendar, and in real life have come to look matronly and middle-aged enough. But, played by a boy upon Shake-speare's stage, this is just what she could not plausibly be made to look. There she must be either conventionally "old" or conventionally "young." And since she must be shown sen-sually in love with Claudius, and seductive enough to make him commit murder for her sake, she clearly—the sole choice lying between the two—must be "young." And the force of Hamlet's reproach that at her age

The heyday in the blood is tame, it's humble,
And waits upon the judgment. . . .

[III. iv. 69-70]

is that, while to intolerant youth (never so intolerant as upon this issue) this should be so with her, it all too patently is not. From this, in fact, springs the tragedy; poor Gertrude's blood was not tame. In this the story of the play is rooted, and much of its meaning will be missed if the point is not from first to last kept clear. (p. 109)

[After killing Polonius] Hamlet turns to the slain:

> Thou wretched, rash, intruding fool, farewell!
> I took thee for thy better; take thy fortune;
> Thou find'st to be too busy is some danger.
> [III. iv. 31-3]

But this, in cold blood, from the sensitive and chivalrous Hamlet for elegy upon an old man—Ophelia's father too—whom he has recklessly killed! It is proof of the dire change worked in him; and for Gertrude, as he turns back to her, some warning of what—be he mad or sane—she may now expect. The deed itself, too, futile as it proves to be, its mere doing (for him, the *doing* of anything after the long thwarting and inaction), gives him, for the moment, a terrible authority, under which she shrinks cowed. . . .

[We] may call Polonius' fate the catastrophe of his busybodying through the two preceding scenes, and the uninterrupted action makes this view of it effective—the encounter [with Gertrude], as Hamlet has meant it to be, begins; with his

> Peace! sit you down,
> And let me wring your heart. . . .
> [III. iv. 34-5]

But he talks a language she does not understand, less of ill deeds themselves than the hidden springs of them, and of the infection their evil may spread till the whole world be "thought-sick" with it. (pp. 111-12)

Such sparks of the dreaded "soul of Nero" as there were in him flamed and died with the killing of Polonius. But here is cruelty enough, in the loosing upon the wretched woman of this long-pent store of resentful rage. And so transported is he as to come again to the very point of dealing her the deadlier blow, which will turn these mad hints of murder to plain fact—when, providentially, the Ghost appears.

A very different "visitation" this from the imposing vision of the battlements; no armed imperious figure, but

> My father, in his habit as he liv'd!
> [III. iv. 135]

—lived even here in unsuspicious happiness with wife and son; no sternly renewed mandate, nor the condemnation Hamlet looks for of his lapse in time and passion. But a gently reproachful

> Do not forget. . . .   [III. iv. 109]

—a pale, inverted, echo of that parting, commanding "Remember me," and the pitiful

> But look! amazement on thy mother sits;
> O, step between her and her fighting soul. . . .
> [III. iv. 111-12]

—for he divines a grace in her, as Hamlet does not, as she herself, it may be, does not yet. Then, after a little, a silent stealing-away. It is as if, with the passing of time, the spirit had lost material power, was nearer to its rest, and to oblivion.

These thirty-five lines make a center of calm in storm. It is a strange reunion for the three; and its pathos is epitomized in the question and answer between mother and son:

> To whom do you speak this?
>   Do you see nothing there?
> Nothing at all; yet all that is I see.
> Nor did you nothing hear?
>   No, nothing but ourselves.
> [III. iv. 131-33]

"Nothing at all; *yet all that is I see*." So speak the spiritually blind.

Hamlet rages at her no more. But the compassion stirred in him soon hardens to irony. He has, she tells him, cleft her heart in twain. His

> O, throw away the worser part of it,
> And live the purer with the other half. . . .
> [III. iv. 157-58]

only preludes the

> Good-night; but go not to mine uncle's bed;
> Assume a virtue if you have it not. . . .
> [III. iv. 159-60]

and praise of "that monster custom." Trust not to change of heart. Put on the "frock and livery" of repentance, and you may come to be what you pretend to be. The unheroic way is best. For him, he must be Heaven's "scourge and minister" and "cruel to be kind." Yet these so "stern effects" in him are, it would seem, something of a frock and livery too. For, his passion spent, his cruelty sated, he now himself melts into repentant tears over old Polonius' body. But worse than this ill deed "remains behind"; the work prescribed him is still to do. (pp. 113-14)

[There] falls about Hamlet [upon accepting the fencing match] the shadow of death. He is aware of it without knowing it. Through his answer:

> I am constant to my purposes. They follow the
> King's pleasure. If his fitness speaks, mine is
> ready, now or whensoever, provided I be so
> able as now.
> [V. ii. 200-02]

sounds a constancy, a fitness, a readiness to meet a weightier challenge than this. And his quiet

>   In happy time.   [V. ii. 205]

accepts more than the mere fact that

> The King, and Queen, and all are coming down.
> [V. ii. 203-04]

It is as if the vanished "madness" had left something like clairvoyance behind. (p. 157)

Horatio is . . . troubled for him:

> If your mind dislike anything, obey it; I will
> forestall their repair hither, and say you are not
> fit.
> [V. ii. 217-18]

and the intimate simplicity of it all sets off the simple nobility of the valediction:

> Not a whit; we defy augury; there's a special
> providence in the fall of a sparrow. If it be

now, 'tis not to come; if it be not to come, it
will be now; if it be not now, yet it will come:
the readiness is all. Since no man has aught of
what he leaves, what is't to leave betimes? Let
be.

[V. ii. 219-24]

It is no more than this, at the last, that the subtly questing mind
has come.

As the curtains of the inner stage part, the disquieted Horatio
is silenced by a gesture; and there once more—it is much the
same picture as at the play's beginning—is the sinister brilliance of Claudius and his Court, Hamlet's somber figure outlined against it as before.

The scene of catastrophe which follows is full of complicated
matter, close-packed. Shakespeare will have inherited its holocaust—which may suit him well enough, but he has to harmonize it with his own enrichment of the play's theme. The
sudden huddle of violent events is in itself effective after the
long delays of plot and counterplot, but character must be
eloquent in them still. And this network of action is lucid with
character. (pp. 158-59)

Shakespeare has to reconcile the creature of his imagination
with the figure of the borrowed story; the Hamlet we have is
the tragic product of his very failure to do so.

The unfitness of the man for his task is at once plain. But
Hamlet's continuing effort to be at the same time—so to put
it—Kyd's hero and Shakespeare's reveals deeper incongruities.
It involves him in a rupture of the entire spiritual treaty between
himself and the world in which he must live, and in a conflict
between two selves within him, the one that could agree with
this world, the other that cannot. There is the fundamental
tragedy, exhibited by setting him in contact with a variety of
his world's inhabitants; his mother, the girl he has loved, a
true friend and two false ones, his secret enemy, the man he
unwittingly wrongs, an old Court wiseacre, a shrewd old peasant, those shadows of reality, the Players, and that other shadow,
his father's ghost. Each contact has its discord, and sets him
playing false to what common sense would expect of him, and
to what he once might have expected of himself. (pp. 252-53)

[Hamlet's] heresies, worn by three centuries currency, no longer
shock us. But they are grave enough—and gravest when he
faces suicide—for him to have good cause to wish that his sins
may be remembered in Ophelia's prayers. Shakespeare (with
his play's licensing to consider) cannot, if he would, meddle
with theology. But he has managed before now to deal with
much belonging to it; and, in this case, the problem of the
Ghost brings him as near to the kernel of the matter as he needs
to go.

Hamlet's heart tells him that it is his father's ghost, but his
mind as promptly questions whether it be

a spirit of health or goblin damned . . .

[I. iv. 40]

While he listens he believes; but when, on its vanishing, he
invokes the host of heaven, he adds

And shall I couple hell?　　　[I. v. 93]

And later, at his calmest, he thinks it well may be

a damned ghost that we have seen . . .

[III. ii. 82]

In this again, then, his native faith is flawed; and the rift but
opens deeper doubts. Insoluble doubts; for if man's mind cannot master the mortal world, what chance has it against mysteries beyond? Yet if they can touch him so nearly as this, and
since death is the common door to them, bring himself to
braving them he must. Hamlet, the intellectual hero, very certainly must be allowed to face them. It is the crown to his
dignity that he should. Subtract these reckonings from his account, indeterminate though they are, and by how much would
not his dramatic stature be diminished?

Little explicit argument emerges; in this, as in the struggle for
self-understanding, no more than the play's action can be brought
to engender. But that central soliloquy questions eternity itself:

To be, or not to be . . .　　　[III. i. 55]

not simply here—a dagger thrust will settle that—but hereafter.
And the

consummation
Devoutly to be wished . . .

[III. i. 62-3]

is not merely the body's death, but the soul's. The proud faith
that could still brave the Ghost with

And for my soul, what can it do to that,
Being a thing immortal as itself?

[I. iv. 66-7]

is gone, and doubt and dread replace it. The infection, which
his mother's treachery to his faith in her sowed in his heart,
has spread and deepened. The disillusioned mind now asks:
may not this seeming spirit of my father be even as treacherous,
be abusing me to damn me? And out of such doubt he builds
a dreadfully imagined limbo around him, where evil is still
potent and the departed soul as helpless as in a dream.

The Ghost is proved to be an honest ghost, but this does not
give Hamlet back the old confident possession of his soul. He
has let himself be made an instrument of these supernatural
powers. No blind instrument; the enfranchised mind rebels
against the indignity of that, against working for mere "bait
and salary." He is lending his mind to their work to better the
occasion offered him when he spares for a worse fate the
kneeling, guilty King. A minute later he has involuntarily killed
Polonius. These powers he serves—who have tricked him into
that—are truly not nice in their dealings:

but heaven hath pleased it so,
To punish me with this and this with me,
That I must be their scourge and minister. . . .

[III. iv. 173-75]

To punish him with this indeed; a lonely soul seeking its right
and wrong amidst such anarchy!

The strange little scene of the Ghost's return opens sadder
uncertainties. The armored figure of the battlements is now:

My father, in his habit as he liv'd!

[III. iv. 135]

—here in a fleeting happiness with wife and son. Commands
to vengeance have become "this piteous action"; the majestic,
memorable farewell turns to a stealing-away out at the portal;
and his mother is blind and deaf to what he must still believe
he sees. Evil which no vengeance can expiate; the helpless
suffering of the dead, the irremediable estrangement of these

three that once were one. Matter, indeed, far more for tears than blood.

Hamlet, after this, talks no more of the Ghost, nor of the soul. As to the hereafter:

> To what base uses we may return, Horatio! . . .
> Alexander died, Alexander was buried, Alex-
> ander returneth into dust; the dust is earth, of
> earth we make loam; and why of that loam,
> whereto he was converted, might they not stop
> a beer barrel?
>
> [V. i. 202, 208-12]

And when he comes to die, his hope is simply that the rest will be silence.

To the more perceptive of Shakespeare's audience the most interesting thing about *Hamlet* must have been that in the old story retold an old issue was dealt with afresh. There must always be interest in this. To every age the same problems recur, differently decked out; and men have to decide whether to attack them as their fathers did, obey habit and authority, or seek and take their own conscientious way. And in that age of the breaking-up of creeds which was Shakespeare's, this, under one guise or another, was a dilemma with which many men were faced.

Hamlet is a man adrift from old faiths and not yet anchored in new; a man of his time in that, more particularly. The theologians had been busy, patching and repatching. But formulas, which the mind may accept, are one thing; and the lively faith, by which we live in unconscious harmony with our surroundings, is very much another. This faith extends to secular everyday things. Let it be flawed here and there, it will be weakened everywhere. Put it then to some extraordinary test, and we at once find that its integrity is broken. Reason, brought to the rescue, cannot help, for it works by other means; it cannot even tell us what is wrong. Act we must, if action is what is asked of us, for the world will not stand still. But with crippled faith and enfranchised reason at odds in us we do self-defeating things, and may lapse into impotence and despair. That is Hamlet's case. And while none of those first spectators may have stood, as he did, with

> a father killed, a mother stained . . .
>
> [IV. iv. 57]

and under ghostly command to avenge the crime, not a few of them must have seen in his spiritual troubles only a more vivid shadowing-forth of their own.

He is of an intellectual generation to whom the word has been let penetrate: Prove all things; for only so can one learn to hold fast that which is good. Could he simply have been set to prove the theory of a carefully selected few—he and his fellow-student Horatio—in the shelter of that Protestant Wittenberg to which he so longed to return, all might have been well. But he has to face an urgent, practical problem, which is colored for him, moreover, by his own most intimate concern with it. How can a man treat such a matter dispassionately and trust to his own isolated judgment of the right and the wrong of it? And if it is a question, as this is, of life and death, and even worse, of salvation or damnation—let him go arguing such issues as these forth and back and back and forth again in terms of his own doubts and griefs and fears, into what dark and vertiginous places may not the lonely mind be lured? (pp. 278-82)

Many a man, then, can find touches of himself in the later Hamlet at least, who returns weary of questioning, hardened (by a sea-fight and some ruthless practice upon his jailers) to his deadly task, and looking back to the old self-torture as "madness."

Yet his soul's adventure, which seemed but to lead him to defeat, was heroic too. For if men shirk such perils, how are these high matters to be brought home to spiritual freedmen? Nor will mere intellectual venturing suffice, if lively faith, in its health and strength, is to be found and enjoyed again. Hamlet, being called upon, flings his whole being—mind and affections both, the best and the worst of him, weakness no less than strength—into the trial. And he widens the issue till he sees eternal life and death, his own and his enemy's, at stake. He will reconcile himself, as he is and in all he is, with these now unveiled verities of this world and the next, if that may be. In which Promethean struggle towards the light he is beaten—as who has not been?—with havoc wrought, not in him only, but by him, even to his own despite. It is none the less a heroic struggle.

Here, for me, is the master-clue to Hamlet's "mystery." The "sane" world around him has naturally no sense of it, nor the too sane spectator of the play. He does not pluck out the heart of it himself. Neither are we meant to. For his trouble is rooted in the fact that it is a mystery. Shakespeare, for his part, must order his play in terms of action (even as Hamlet is called on to act); the tragedy of thwarted thought and tortured spirit is the rich soil in which he replants his borrowings. Yet while the action keeps us interested, it is this tragedy and the mystery of it, which is enthralling. (pp. 282-83)

The play is attractively alive on the surface; the riches of its underworkings of emotion and thought fall to those whose own are a touchstone for them. And it fulfills, in this, the double demand of drama, which is not for action alone nor the revelation of character only, but for character in action. Pertinently so; since the character-revealing problems of life present themselves as problems of action, which men attack even as Hamlet does, imaginatively, thoughtfully, passionately too. And the play's progress, like a stream in flood, here flowing deeply and evenly, here eddying and spreading, there rushing down some steep channel—it is thus, and not to any clocklike measure, that human affairs do move.

In England, for the best part of a century before *Hamlet* was written, and for sixty years after, the finer issues of the spiritual revolution which the Renaissance had begun were obscured by secular discord, persecution and civil war; and the ensuing peace left them hardened into formula. To the popular mind thus distressed and coarsened the finer issues implicit either in play or character might well make small appeal. Nor would they be likelier to touch the conscience of the positive eighteenth century. Not till it was waning, and many men had come to find their set creeds unsatisfying, till they began to ask the old essential questions once again, to have a better answer if they might, did the Hamlet of spiritual tragedy come by his own; then to become, indeed, the typical hero of a new "age of doubt." It was as if Shakespeare, so alive to the spirit of his own time, had been in this mysteriously attuned besides to some

> prophetic soul
> Of the wide world dreaming on things to come.
>
> [Sonnet 107]

While our age of doubt endures, and men still cry despairingly, "I do not know . . . ," and must go on uncomforted, the play will keep, I should suppose, its hold on us. If a new age of faith or reason should succeed, or one for a while too crushed by brute reality to value either, Hamlet may then be seen again simply as the good Polonius saw him. (pp. 283-84)

Harley Granville-Barker, in his Preface to "Hamlet," *Hill and Wang, 1957, 284 p.*

H. B. CHARLTON (essay date 1942)

[*An English scholar, Charlton is best known for his* Shakespearian Tragedy *and* Shakespearian Comedy—*two important studies in which he argues that the proponents of New Criticism, particularly T. S. Eliot and I. A. Richards, were reducing Shakespeare's drama to its poetic elements and in the process losing sight of his characters. In his introduction to* Shakespearian Tragedy, *Charlton described himself as a "devout" follower of A. C. Bradley, and like his mentor he adopted a psychological, character-oriented approach to Shakespeare's work. In his discussion of* Hamlet, *originally published in* Bulletin of the John Rylands Library, *April-May, 1942, Charlton concentrates on the prince's manner of thought as the key to his irresolution. According to Charlton, Hamlet is called upon to act in the physical world, yet his "supreme gift for philosophic thought" does not equip him to dwell in the world of action. Thus Charlton follows in the tradition of Romantic critics such as Johann Wolfgang von Goethe (1795), August Wilhelm Schlegel (1808), Charles Lamb (1811), Samuel Taylor Coleridge (1811, 1813), William Hazlitt (1817), and, fi-* *nally, Bradley, whose work culminated the Romantic perception of Hamlet.*]

[If] the play within the play was devised by Hamlet to give him a really necessary confirmation of the ghost's evidence, why is this the moment he chooses to utter his profoundest expression of despair, 'To be, or not to be, that is the question'? For, if his difficulty is what he says it is, this surely is the moment when the strings are all in his own hands. He has by chance found an occasion for an appropriate play, and, as the king's ready acceptance of the invitation to attend shows, he can be morally certain that the test will take place; and so, if one supposes him to need confirmation, within a trice he will really know. Yet this very situation finds him in the depths of despair. Can he really have needed the play within the play? The point is of some importance, because in the 1603 Quarto of *Hamlet*, this 'To be, or not to be' speech occurs before Hamlet has devised the incriminating play. In the 1604 and later versions, the speech comes where we now read it. I know no more convincing argument that the 1604 Quarto is a master-dramatist's revision of his own first draft of a play. (pp. 89-90)

More difficult to set aside is the Freudian or the semi- or pseudo-Freudian explanation that a mother- or a sex-complex is the primary cause of Hamlet's delay. But the difficulty is one of terminology, not one of substance. The Elizabethans believed that a man could love his mother without being in

Act I. Scene iv. Marcellus, Horatio, Hamlet, the ghost. By Henry Fuseli (1803).

love with her or without unconsciously lusting for her. Hamlet's filial love for his mother is certainly a main cause of his estrangement from the people who inhabit the world in which he lives, the world in which he must build his own soul. Certainly, too, her 'o'er' hasty re-marriage shatters the pillars of his moral universe. He has lived in an ideal world, that is, a world fashioned in his own idea, a world in which chastity is a main prop: and when he finds that, of all the women in his world, it is his own mother who seems unaware of this mainstay of the moral order, the structure topples over him. The only way to preserve purity is for womankind to seclude themselves from men: 'get thee to a nunnery'; and Ophelia becomes a potential source of contagion. (pp. 90-1)

[Consider] the difference in depth between his first soliloquy, 'O, that this too solid flesh' and the later one, 'To be, or not to be'. Both are contemplations of suicide. But what immeasurable difference between the constraining sanctions! When Hamlet speaks the first soliloquy, all that he knows to his own grief is that his father has died and that his mother has married again o'er-hastily. . . . But this death and, still more, his mother's remarriage, have reduced Hamlet's ideal universe to chaos. His rich and exquisitely sensitive nature, the observed of all observers, has suffered a shock which starts it reeling. A father dead, and untimely dead, though in itself a common experience, may prompt some sceptical scrutiny of divine providence; but worse still, a mother so soon married again seems to reveal an even more immediate despair; for here, not the divine but the human will seems to be working without moral sensibility. Yet the seat of the sorrow is nothing near so deep in human experience as is that which Hamlet utters when later he knows that his father has been murdered by his uncle.

In the first soliloquy, 'O, that this too too solid flesh', Hamlet is not so much actively contemplating suicide as passively longing to be dead. And the respect which makes it unthinkable to resort to self-slaughter is that the Everlasting has set his canon against it. In a way there is something of a pose in Hamlet's gesture: as if a young poet peering into the waters of a pool should long for the eternal quiet of its depths, but should be kept to the bank for fear that the water might be too cold. How much deeper in human nature are the constraints which withhold the Hamlet of the 'To be, or not to be' soliloquy! No merely intellectual recognition of a theological injunction, but a primitive fear of the unknown after-world. 'What dreams may come when we have shuffled off this mortal coil.' The first speech is that of a sensitive soul in spiritual discomfort, the second is that of a man in profound despair. The discovery of the murder of his father by his uncle, of an act of uttermost human sacrilege, drives him to abysses of grief deeper than those occasioned by his mother's frailty. Something more human, more overt and intelligible than the Freudian hypothesis is the main stress of Hamlet's tragic incapacitation. (pp. 91-2)

Nor will it do to say that Hamlet fails, not because he thinks, but because he thinks too much. In one sense, if thought is what will save the world, there cannot be too much of it. In another, if all that is meant is that Hamlet thinks too often, then clearly this is no matter for tragedy: it is merely a question of a revised time-table, more time to be allocated for field sports and other non-intellectual forms of activity.

What is wrong is not that Hamlet thinks or thinks too much or too often, but that his way of thinking frustrates the object of thought. It is the kind of distortion to which cerebration is liable when it is fired by a temperamental emotionalism and guided by an easily excited imagination. The emotion thrusts one factor of the thinker's experience into especial prominence, and the imagination freely builds a speculative universe in which this prominence is a fundamental pillar. Hence, the business of thinking overreaches itself. The mind's function to construct an intellectual pattern of reality becomes merely a capacity to build abstract patterns, and the relation of these patterns to reality is misapprehended, if not discounted entirely. In the main, this way of thinking constructs a cosmic picture which only serves to give apparent validity to what the feeling of the person and of the moment makes most immediately significant. But examples will help to make the effect of it apparent. They will be better, because more certainly characteristic of the more normal working of Hamlet's mind, if they are taken from scenes before Hamlet is given the additional shock of discovery that his uncle is a murderer and has murdered his father. There are sufficient of them in his first soliloquy.

The scene of it is worth recalling to establish other qualities of Hamlet which are easily overlooked. He is the hero: and in our backward rumination when we have come to know him, unconsciously we idealise his earlier appearances. But in this first episode, he is not an altogether attractive person. The Court is in session: he is in the royal train, but not a part of it. In manner, in dress and in place, he is staging his contemptuous aloofness from it. He stands apart, taking no share in the social formalities of the occasion, and he draws attention to his aloofness by an extravagant garb of mourning and by excessive display of the conventional gestures of grief. . . . Nor is this possibility of a Pharisaic isolation weakened by memory of his only other words, his earlier sardonic interjections and his affectedly humorous comments on the king's greeting. . . .

Hence, when he soliloquises, our willingness to sympathise with a son whose father has died and whose mother has hastily married again is suspended by our suspicion of the son's leaning to morbidity. His words appear to justify suspicion to the full:

> O, that this too too solid flesh would melt,
> Thaw and resolve itself into a dew!
> Or that the Everlasting had not fix'd
> His canon 'gainst self-slaughter!
>
> [I. ii. 129-32]

We have seen that the utterance of a wish for death in such phrase lacks the convincing urgency of the constraints expressed in the incalculable fears of the 'To be, or not to be' speech. His imagination goes on to explore illimitable stretches of despair; 'weary' and 'stale' and 'flat' and 'unprofitable' are the suggestions by which it deprives the uses of the world of all their value. 'Things rank and gross in nature possess it merely.' Yet the absoluteness of this denunciation prompts our question. Hamlet has hitherto enjoyed a privileged life, and the good things of the world, material and spiritual, have been fully and freely at his disposal: but the passionate sorrow of the moment blots these out of his intellectual picture of the universe. (pp. 93-5)

This very soliloquy includes another striking instance of similar intellectual transformation. As he remembers his mother's lapse, his passion prompts the general condemnation, 'Frailty, thy name is woman'. As far as one knows, Hamlet, of all the women in the world, has known but two, his mother and Ophelia. His mother has unexpectedly proved 'frail', but, in the Elizabethan sense of the word, Ophelia is entirely free of such charge. Yet the generalisation: all women are frail. (pp. 96-7)

This does not mean, of course, that Hamlet's thinking is generally or regularly so prone to fallacious conclusions. His philosophic grasp of much of life's riddle is sure and permanent: and imagination has prompted his discoveries. But when the thought springs from a particular incident which moves his own feelings to new depths, imagination leads his speculations awry. Into the fate of man at large he has a deep and broad view: he holds the macrocosm more securely than the microcosm of his own personal experiences. Hence the magnificent appeal of the most famous of all the speeches in the play, 'To be, or not to be'. Here is a purely philosophical or speculative statement of the general tragedy of man. The problem is a universal, not a particular, one. . . . That is, it is not really a question of whether Hamlet shall commit suicide, but whether all men ought not to do so. For Hamlet is a metaphysician, not a psychologist; he is speculative, but not essentially introspective. (p. 97)

This flair of Hamlet's for abstract thinking is perpetually liable to make him momentarily indifferent to the concrete world about him. Another speech spoken before his mind is doubly strained by knowledge of the murder will show us how the natural functioning of his brain works. The situation is exciting. A ghost has been seen by Hamlet's friends. They have informed Hamlet that his father's spirit in arms has twice appeared at midnight. Hamlet is agog with excitement. The three of them plan to be in wait for the ghost: they are here on the battlements at midnight. 'The air bites shrewdly', 'very cold', 'a nipping and an eager air', 'it has struck twelve'—the whole atmosphere is one of strained excited nerves: suddenly, as they peer in hushed expectation, the silence is broken by the blast of cannon. It is a situation not likely, one would think, to soothe nerves on edge. Horatio, normally calmest of men, is rattled: 'What does this mean, my lord?' asking questions more from discomposure than from desire to have repeated what he surely knows. Yet at this very moment, of all moments the most inopportune, unexpected and inappropriate, Hamlet solemnly embarks on a regular professorial disquisition about the nature of habit and its influence on moral character. . . . The very syntax of this speech, with its interrupted and broken structure, is Hamlet's brain in action under our eyes. And again he is so enthralled in its operations that when the ghost does appear, his attention to it has to be called, 'Look, my lord, it comes'. (p. 99)

Hamlet's habit of mind will in some way or another complicate his procedure. His tendency to abstraction, his proneness to let imagination stimulate and direct his intellectual voyagings beyond the reaches of the soul, his liability to set the mind awork before the body takes its appropriate complementary posture: these may recurrently obstruct a ready response in action. But in themselves they will not induce a general paralysis: and, in fact, Hamlet is normally very ready to act. . . . When, towards the end, he comes on Ophelia's funeral, he acts with almost a madman's precipitancy, and jumps into the grave; and though it is a frenzied display, it is not one of a man whose sinews have atrophied in general paralysis. It is, indeed, a very significant action. It has energy, deliberateness, and the application of force on circumstances in the world about him: and these qualities are what distinguish action from mere reflex activities. But its significance for the tragedy is this: it is the wrong action for the actual world in which Hamlet must live; it is proper only to the ideal world (that is, the picture of the world which he has built in his own mind) in which he now lives without knowing that it is a distorted image of reality. If his ideal world were a valid intellectual projection of the real world, his action would be apt and effective. A crucial illustration of this is provided by his treatment of Ophelia.

Nothing is more difficult to reconcile with our impulse to sympathise with Hamlet than are his dealings with Ophelia. However docile she may be to her father (and that has not always been regarded as a sign of weakness; moreover, she stands up triumphantly to her preachifying brother), she cannot hide her love for Hamlet from us. She is not forthcoming in the way of the modern girl, nor even as naturally wise as Shakespeare's comic heroines. But is this a moral defect? And can anybody suppose for a moment that it justifies Hamlet's abominable treatment of her? It is not so much that he determines to break with her. It is the manner of the breaking. He talks to her, at best, as a salvationist preacher would reprove a woman of the street, and then as a roué who is being cynical with an associate in looseness. His remarks are disgusting and even revolting; they offend because they are preposterously out of place, for Ophelia is in no wise deserving of such ineptitudes. But if frailty (that is, immorality) is woman's name, if Ophelia, because a woman, is therefore necessarily frail, then of course everything fits. The serious advice, 'get thee to a nunnery', is the only way to save the world; and the smut of the wise-cracks in the play-within-the-play scene is a proper garb. But, of course, these hypotheses are pure fiction. They are real only in Hamlet's 'ideal' world, and it is only in that world that his actions would be appropriate. The other and the real world, the one in which he must live and act and succeed or fail, is a different one; and we have seen how Hamlet came to create his ideal world and then to mistake it for a true intellectual projection of the real one.

This, it would appear, is the way of Hamlet's tragedy. His supreme gift for philosophic thought allows him to know the universe better than the little world of which he is bodily a part. But his acts must be in this physical world: and his mind has distorted for him the particular objects of his actual environment. So he cannot act properly within it: or rather, towards those parts of it which the stress of his feeling and the heat of his imagination have made especially liable to intellectual distortion, he cannot oppose the right response. He can kill a Rosencrantz, but not his villainous uncle. Yet though the paralysis is localised at first, it tends to be progressive. The world of action, or the world in which outward act is alone possible, becomes increasingly different from the world as his mind conceives it. Yet the mind increasingly imposes its own picture on him as absolute. The end is despair. The will to act in the one necessary direction is first frustrated and then gradually atrophied. Worst of all, the recognition of the will's impotence is accepted as spiritual resignation; and the resignation is not seen as the moral abnegation, the *gran rifiuto*, which it certainly is; on the contrary, it is phrased as if it were the calm attainment of a higher benignity, whereas it is nothing more than a fatalist's surrender of his personal responsibility. That is the nadir of Hamlet's fall. The temper of Hamlet's converse with Horatio in the graveyard, the placidity of his comments on disinterred bones, his reminiscent ruminations on Yorick's skull, and his assumed hilarity in tracking Alexander's progress till the loam whereto he is converted serves to stop a beer-barrel—these are traits of his final frame of mind and they indicate no ascent to the serenity of philosophic calm. They are only processes which reconcile him to his last stage of failure. (pp. 101-03)

H. B. Charlton, "'Hamlet'," in his Shakespearian Tragedy, *Cambridge at the University Press, 1948, pp. 83-112.*

THEODORE SPENCER (essay date 1942)

[*Spencer demonstrates that in Hamlet's character Shakespeare presents a central conflict in Renaissance thought: the disparity between the ideal and the real. Spencer asserts that Hamlet's awareness of the conflict between the apparent good of the universe and the evil which underlies it causes his preoccupation with appearance and reality. Like George Brandes (1895-96), Spencer notes that Hamlet matures more during the course of the play than the passage of time justifies. Maynard Mack (1952) further explores the relationship between appearance and reality in* Hamlet. *In the following excerpt, Spencer focuses on Hamlet's soliloquies. For additional commentary on these soliloquies, see Charles Gildon (1721), William Guthrie (1747), Tobias Smollett (1756), Samuel Johnson (1765), A.J.A. Waldock (1931), and E.M.W. Tillyard (1949).*]

[With] *Hamlet* we feel as if Shakespeare had had a new vision of what a play could contain, and in this play, as in the other tragedies that follow it, the characters and events become larger than the characters of the 1590's; they make more reverberations in our minds; they take on a symbolic and universal meaning.

To describe how this is accomplished is one of the central problems in Shakespearean criticism: I suggest that we can understand it best by realizing that in *Hamlet* Shakespeare for the first time used to the full the conflict between the two views of man's nature which was so deeply felt in his age. On one side was the picture of man as he should be—it was bright, orderly and optimistic. On the other was the picture of man as he is—it was full of darkness and chaos. Shakespeare puts an awareness of this contrast into the character of Hamlet, and his having done so is one of the main reasons for *Hamlet*'s greatness. Previously Shakespeare had used the traditional beliefs *descriptively* as part of the background—the sun is compared to the king, the human body is compared to the state—and there is no question as to whether the beliefs are true. But in *Hamlet* they are not in the background, they are an essential part of the hero's consciousness, and his discovery that they are not true, his awareness of the conflict between what theory taught and what experience proves, wrecks him. Shakespeare had used the difference between appearance and reality as a dramatic device many times before, but never like this, and never in such close relation to the thought and feeling of his time.

For Hamlet, before his mother's second marriage, had been, as Shakespeare is careful to point out, the ideal Renaissance nobleman; according to Ophelia, he had a "noble mind," "the courtier's, soldier's, scholar's, eye, tongue, sword." He was

> The expectancy and rose of the fair state,
> The glass of fashion and the mould of form;
> [III. i. 152-53]

he had, to use Bradley's somewhat romantic expression, "an unbounded delight and faith in everything good and beautiful" [see excerpt above, 1905]. He was conceived by Shakespeare, in other words, as a young man who had been trained to believe, and by temperament was inclined to believe, in the traditional optimistic view of the nature of man. But the discovery of his mother's lust and the fact that the kingdom is in the hands of a man he considers unworthy—these shatter his belief into ruins, and the world, the state and the individual are to him suddenly corrupt. (pp. 94-5)

There are two related aspects of Hamlet's thought which Shakespeare deliberately emphasizes in first presenting him to the audience. Hamlet is preoccupied with the difference between appearance and reality, and he extends his feelings about his particular situation to cover his feelings about the world as a whole.

> *King:* But now, my cousin Hamlet, and my son,—
> *Hamlet: (Aside.)* A little more than kin, and less than kind.
> *King:* How is it that the clouds still hang on you?
> *Hamlet:* Not so, my lord; I am too much i' the sun.
> [I. ii. 64-7]

Again, when the queen asks him why the death of his father seems so particular with him, he answers,

> Seems, madam! Nay, it is; I know not 'seems,'
> [I. ii. 76]

and he discourses, roused for the first time, on the contrast between the outer trappings of grief, and the feeling within "which passeth show."

So much he can say in public, but when he is left alone, we see that his whole view of life is turned upside down. It is characteristic of Shakespeare's conception of Hamlet's universalizing mind that he should make Hamlet think first of the general rottenness; to him *all* the uses of the world are weary, stale, flat and unprofitable; things rank and gross in nature possess it completely. From this he passes to the king, the head of the state, bitterly comparing his god-like father to his satyr-like uncle, and he finally dwells at length on individual perversion, the lustfulness of his mother, who has violated natural law by the brevity of her grief and the haste of her marriage. (pp. 95-6)

Hamlet's generalizing mind is everywhere emphasized; his thought invariably leaps out to embrace the world as a whole, he talks of infinite space, his rhetoric includes the stars. (p. 96)

[The] occasion on which Hamlet speaks at greatest length of the heavens is, of course, when he describes his state of mind to Rosencrantz and Guildenstern in the second act. The situation is a critical one for Hamlet. He knows that his former fellow-students are spies of the king, and he obviously cannot tell them the real cause of his distemper. What explanation can he give them? He gives them just the kind of explanation that would be most clearly understood by young intellectuals, particularly young intellectuals who were familiar with his own generalizing type of mind and who might be expected to have shared his previous acceptance of the optimistic view of the world. All three young men had been taught that the surest way to comprehend man's place in the universe and to realize the magnificence of God's creation, was to contemplate the glory of the superior heavens which surrounded the earth. . . . La Primaudaye and countless other Renaissance writers had written in the same way, and had inevitably turned, as Hamlet turns, from the contemplation of the stars to the contemplation of man, for whom all this splendor had been made. But Hamlet reverses the application, and the clearest way he can explain his melancholy to his fellow-students is to tell them that he sees in the heavens, as well as in the world around him, the reality of evil underneath the appearance of good. (pp. 97-8)

Shakespeare uses the traditional views of kingship in the same way that he uses cosmology and psychology. Throughout *Hamlet* there is an emphasis on the importance of the king as the center of the state. . . . Much state business is transacted before the king, in the second scene of the first act, finally turns to the particular problem of Hamlet's melancholy; Shakespeare deliberately puts Hamlet's situation in a political environment.

This not only increases the scope of the play, it also emphasizes the dramatic conflict. For from whatever side we regard the action there is something politically wrong. From Claudius' point of view it is bad for the state to have a disaffected heir, particularly since he is so much loved by the multitude. From Hamlet's point of view it is abominable to have an unworthy and lustful king. And the appearance of the ghost emphasizes in more general terms our sense of uneasiness about the condition of the state. It bodes, says Horatio, ''some strange eruption to our state,'' Hamlet dwells on the fact that the ghost is armed, and the armor implies that the ghost has more than a private purpose in showing himself. No wonder Marcellus says that there is something rotten in the *state* of Denmark. He, and the king, and the ghost, reinforce Hamlet's feelings about the situation, and the speeches of Rosencrantz and Laertes on kingship apply not only to an immediate necessity but also to the importance of kingship itself, and hence they emphasize the enormity of Claudius' previous action in murdering his kingly brother. Again it is worth remembering the strength of Hamlet's feeling about his uncle's unworthiness as a king—a feeling that shocks, as Hamlet means it to do, the conventional Guildenstern [IV. ii. 28-9]:

> *Hamlet:* The king is a thing—
> *Guildenstern:* A thing, my lord!
>
> (pp. 102-03)

[The] way Hamlet treats Ophelia, like the way he treats love in general, is a further striking example of Shakespeare's handling of the contrast between appearance and truth. For here too there is an ideal in the background against which the present reality seems coarse and vile. The relation between Hamlet's mother and father had been perfect; he was as fine a husband as he had been a king, his

> love was of that dignity
> That it went hand in hand even with that vow
> (He) made to her in marriage;
>
> [I. v. 48-50]

he was, says Hamlet,

> so loving to my mother
> That he might not beteem the winds of heaven
> Visit her face too roughly.
>
> [I. ii. 140-42]

But this ideal, an ideal as deeply embedded in the sixteenth-century mind as the ideal of kingship and of human reason, is violated by Gertrude's marriage to Claudius, which he calls ''incestuous,'' as according to the law of Nature, it actually was. Hamlet throughout the play can think of the relations between the sexes only in the coarsest terms; he tortures both Ophelia and himself by doing so, attributing to her in his usual generalizing way the faults of her sex as a whole which his mother's behavior had revealed. And the innocent Ophelia herself, in delirium, sings songs at which her maidenly sanity would have blushed.

This sense of the reality of evil—in the cosmos, in the state, and in man—this enlargement of dramatic dimension by significant generalization, this dramatic use of one of the essential conflicts of the age, is what helps to make *Hamlet* so large an organism, and to give it, as the expression of a universal situation, so profound a meaning. Hamlet's disillusionment is a partial expression of a general predicament; the emotions he gives voice to were shared in his own time and have been shared ever since by many people less miraculously articulate

than himself. His discovery of the difference between appearance and reality, which produced in his mind an effect so disillusioning that it paralysed the sources of deliberate action, was a symptom that the Renaissance in general had brought with it a new set of problems, had opened new psychological vistas, which the earlier views of man had not so completely explored. (pp. 104-06)

But we can find, if we return to the play itself, more in Shakespeare's conception of Hamlet's character than an embodiment, however profound, of the difference between appearance and reality. Shakespeare had made several earlier experiments with the development of character; in portraying Romeo and Prince Hal, among others, he had shown his ability to make a hero change as the result of the play's action. But just as *Hamlet* illustrates both a more expanded and a more fused control of dramatic convention and traditional belief than the earlier plays, so it shows a greater mastery of how to describe the growth, inside dramatic limits, of a hero. This can be clearly seen if we examine, in order, Hamlet's great soliloquies. When we first see Hamlet alone, he is emotionally in pieces, and the chaos of his thought and feeling is reflected in the grammatical chaos of his utterances; before he can finish a sentence some new agonizing disruptive thought explodes to distract his mind. The order of the world, of the state, and of the individual are all in pieces, and the chaotic grammar reflects the universal chaos of his thought. The same is true of his second great soliloquy, the one beginning,

> O, what a rogue and peasant slave am I!
>
> [III. i. 550]

in which he bursts into violent self-deprecation as he thinks of the difference between stage-playing and real action. But even in this speech, at the end, he pulls himself together and orders his thought to plan the testing of the king. Planned action takes the place, as it had not before, of emotional desperation.

In the soliloquy that follows (as far as the audience is concerned, about three minutes later), the ''To be or not to be'' soliloquy, we see a Hamlet who is able to generalize on a new level. No longer is there a grammatical torrent, and no longer is Hamlet thinking about existence as opposed to non-existence only in relation to himself; he has grown, psychologically and philosophically, so that he can think of the problem more universally. In the first soliloquy it was ''*This* too too solid flesh''— Hamlet's own—about which he was concerned. Now, as the play reaches its center, it is no longer ''I,'' but ''we''—all humanity—that he reflects upon: ''When *we* have shuffled off this mortal coil'' . . .

> And makes *us* rather bear those ills *we* have
> Than fly to others that *we* know not of.
> Thus conscience doth make cowards of *us all*. . . .
>
> [III. i. 80-2]

Even the soliloquy in the fourth act—''How all occasions do inform against me''—when Hamlet compares his behavior to that of Fortinbras, combining, as usual personal and general reflection—even this agonized soliloquy has much more order, both logically and grammatically, than the first two violent outbursts. In fact there can be little doubt that Shakespeare thought of Hamlet as growing much older, emotionally, intellectually and even physically, during the course of the play, than the literal time covered by the action could possibly justify. At the beginning Hamlet is fresh from the university; he is about twenty. In the graveyard scene he is unmistakably described as thirty. Shakespeare was in the habit of using concrete numerical details to make a particular scene vivid, regardless of previous data, and this is an obvious example of how his view of his hero had changed, perhaps unconsciously, at the end of the play. Throughout the fifth act, Hamlet is a very different man from the distracted undergraduate he was at the beginning. At the beginning there was a horrible split between his view of the world as it should be and the world as it is. At the end he is reconciled; and his reconciliation has both matured and ennobled him. . . .

> If it be now, 'tis not to come; if it be not to
> come, it will be now; if it be not now, yet it
> will come: the readiness is all.
>
> [V. ii. 220-22]

The thought may be a neo-stoic Renaissance commonplace, but Hamlet's expression of it, through his incomparable control of rhythm, enlarges our feeling about Hamlet's character. To be resigned, as Hamlet is resigned, is to be made, by experience instead of by theory, once more aware of the world's order. The last time we know Hamlet emotionally, he has transcended his own situation; he is no longer a victim of it. That is why we feel so moved, so in a way glorified, by the inevitability of his death. We have seen the purgation of a soul, and when Fortinbras enters at the end to be the king that Hamlet might have been, we know in another way and on another level—a more practical level that brings us back to the world in which we live—that we have also seen, with the accomplishment of Hamlet's revenge, the purgation of a state. (pp. 106-09)

> *Theodore Spencer, " 'Hamlet' and 'Troilus and Cressida'," in his* Shakespeare and the Nature of Man, *Macmillan Publishing Company, 1942, pp. 93-121.*

SALVADOR DE MADARIAGA (essay date 1948)

[*According to Madariaga, Hamlet's character has been deformed and adapted by succeeding generations of critics, such as A. C. Bradley (1905) and J. Dover Wilson (1935), who have obscured his true nature, that of an egocentric, Renaissance aristocrat. Rebecca West (1957) concurs with Madariaga, in highlighting Hamlet's brutal aspects. George Steevens (1772) and Ivan Turgenieff (1860) also stressed Hamlet's negative characteristics.*]

Most of the difficulties we encounter in understanding *Hamlet* come from a disharmony between the taste of present day Britain and that of Shakespearean England. In Shakespeare's days, England was still uninhibited; and puritanism—the making of her greatness-in-action—had not yet blasted her greatness-in-art. . . . The Britain of Wordsworth, prim and respectable, had to adapt Shakespeare to her tastes and ways. Hamlet the Elizabethan had to be modernised. And to begin with he had to shave. For Hamlet was bearded like Drake and not clean shaven like Mr. Winston Churchill.

> Who calls me villain, breaks my pate across,
> Plucks off my beard and blows it in my face,
>
> [II. ii. 572-73.]

Then, he had to take off his hat indoors; for Hamlet, indoors, like all Elizabethans, kept his hat on his head; a custom so well established that Ophelia was ever "so affrighted" on seeing him come before her into her closet "No hat upon his head". (pp. 1-2)

These, it may be argued, are but trifling infidelities. And so, up to a point, they are. But they surely must conceal some substantial import or else we should not insist so much on inflicting them on *Hamlet*. At any rate, they suggest the process of deformation and adaptation which the character has undergone. The beard, the hat and feathers, are all outward signs of a barbarous (if brilliant) age; they have to be sacrificed, not in themselves, but because we must first get rid of these outward signs before we come to alter the inner man. It is Hamlet himself, his person and spirit, we want to assimilate to our century. He, the Elizabethan, the volcano of manly energies, ever in spontaneous eruption, must be turned into a grassy hill and become genteel. Hamlet, the man born in an era of no gentleness whatever, must become a gentleman. (p. 2)

Much of what has been written on Hamlet, is biased in his favour. The critic, we feel, does not face the full impact of the facts, drawing then the conclusions which inevitably follow as to the character; he starts determined to "explain", and, if need be, to "explain away" all the facts more or less awkward for Hamlet the hero, Hamlet the gentleman, Hamlet the sweet, for that "peculiar beauty and nobility of his nature" [see excerpt above by A. C. Bradley, 1905] which goes without saying. Owing to this defective 'stance' of their affections, even acute observers are apt to describe the events in *Hamlet* in a manner which bears little relation to the actual facts of the play. (pp. 3-4)

[We] must endeavour to find the *key to unity* in Hamlet's character. We must be certain that Shakespeare could not have felt so free to present his protagonist under so many lights, had he not possessed a guide, a principle to endow his character with the inner unity his outward pranks and adventures were bound to lack. (p. 7)

At the outset we must get rid of a popular though, of course, by no means scholarly misconception about Hamlet. He is not irresolute. Nothing more unlike Hamlet than the effeminate fastidiousness with which he is at times represented. He is resolute to a fault, indeed to two faults: impulsiveness and brutality. The man who could hoist Rosencrantz and Guildenstern with their own petard, or coldly drag Polonius' body out of the room in which he had killed him, was not squeamish, fastidious or irresolute. But, of course, misconceptions do not arise out of nothing. Hamlet is at times believed to be irresolute because the whole play is woven of his hesitations on the threshold of the task the Ghost has set before him. It is, however, evident that Hamlet, to borrow his own image, is only irresolute north-north-west. When the Ghost beckons him away from his companions, he is resolute; when the Ghost points to King Claudius as a man to be slain, he hesitates.

He hesitates, but he does not refuse. He is, as the pregnant English saying goes, in two minds about it. And the question arises: whence the two minds? It is the crucial question to the interpretation of Hamlet. The answer to this question will reveal the essentially European and ever modern character of this Englishman who stalks the European Olympus clad in the garb of a Prince of Denmark.

Let us see him first in his setting, as Ophelia, in her lamentations, describes him for us.

> O, what a noble mind is here o'erthrown!
> The courtier's, soldier's, scholar's, eye, tongue, sword:
> The expectancy and rose of the fair State,
> The glass of fashion and the mould of form,
> The observed of all observers,
>
> [III. ii. 150-54]

In these words, Ophelia reveals one of the most important factors about Hamlet. He occupies the centre of his world, the apex of his society. (pp. 7-8)

This then is the initial position. A young, vigorous, brave, intelligent, active man (he tells his friend he has of late "forgone all custom of exercises"), a man, therefore, bound to have a mind of his own, finds himself confined within a society of closely knit traditions, ways and ideas. (p. 8)

We see thus from the outset the nature of the conflict: the society known as the State of Denmark is bent on moulding Hamlet to its image and expectations, setting all its observers on him; and the individual Hamlet asserts his right to judge for himself when and why he will follow the dictates of the society in the midst of which he was born.

At this stage, the Ghost appears. Why a Ghost? Because he represents tradition, the voice of the dead who still live and beyond death still order us about. We need not assume that Shakespeare deliberately brings the Ghost on to the stage because of this symbolic value; he probably did not, and in any case, the Ghost was traditional in the plot—but the facts of nature, not the poet, grant him this power to represent the voice of the dead—i.e. tradition. The Ghost orders Hamlet to avenge a crime with another crime. All that is social in Hamlet pushes Hamlet to his deed: he must obey his father, tradition, the Ghost, the vindictiveness of society whereby it protects itself against deeds which would destroy it; in other words, against all that is rotten in the Kingdom of Denmark. But the individual Hamlet cannot bring himself to commit that individual crime which is a social execution. The conflict is absolute; and the whole play moves inexorably towards Hamlet's death. (pp. 9-10)

[The] distance which Hamlet manages to establish between himself and the world is a great dramatic asset. It contributes not a little to that feeling that in this tragedy he and he alone matters. Not even Ophelia can retain our attention for long; and her sad fate, her mad scene, her death, her burial, soon become a mere part of Hamlet's dream, mere clouds in Hamlet's sky. As soon as Hamlet is on the stage, everything and everybody becomes background. *Hamlet* is a Hamlet-centric play.

It follows that Hamlet is egocentric. And this is the key we were looking for. The only principle capable of giving an order and a coherence to the character, the only explanation for all he says and does, is that Hamlet is egocentric. This is the meaning to be attached to the famous line "for there is nothing either good or bad, but thinking (i.e. *my* thinking) makes it so". There is—he means—no objective standard. He has just said Denmark is a prison. Rosencrantz retorts: "We think not so, my Lord"; and he, at once, concedes: "Why, then 'tis none to you, for there is nothing either good or bad, but thinking makes it so: to me it is a prison".

This is the triumph of subjectivity. In these words, Hamlet defines what throughout the play he performs: good or bad are to be understood in relation to him. Hamlet is as egocentric in his standards of action as in his standards of thought. It is in so far as, and in the way in which, situations affect him that he reacts. Once this principle is recognised, the play, so much involved and so difficult, becomes crystal clear. The only reason why so many of Hamlet's actions give rise to interminable discussions and to complicated explanations is that the bias which will make of him a refined, noble, sweet, generous gentleman—no doubt with his 'weaknesses' and even his 'sav-

agery' but a gentleman at heart—provides no definite set of co-ordinates for them. But when we realise that the centre of Hamlet's interest, thought, motive and emotion is his own self, the play becomes as clear as the solar system after Copernicus, when astronomers were able at last to drop their cycles and epicycles and refer everything in simple ellipses to the sun. (pp. 12-13)

We have put forward the view that Hamlet is an egocentric man, and that his actions must remain obscure until we realise that he only acts when his own interests are directly concerned. He is going to prove us right. Even nowadays, the best authorities can write that Hamlet's procrastination "is considered his most mysterious feature" [see excerpt above by J. Dover Wilson, 1935]. But why? Because its motives are sought where they cannot be found. This procrastination cannot be due to an instinctive and fastidious repugnance to killing, for Hamlet kills Polonius, and Laertes, and in the end the King himself; and he dispatches Rosencrantz and Guildenstern to their doom with true alacrity. Whence then does it come?

The answer will be found by examining all these cases. And before them all, let us look at those two lines in I. iv. 84-5

> unhand me gentlemen,
> By heaven I'll make a ghost of him that lets me!

It is one of the key points in the drawing of his character. When it comes to doing what he is determined to do, he will not hesitate to kill even his closest friend, for Horatio is one of the gentlemen whom he threatens sword in hand. Hamlet's spontaneous tendencies are therefore essentially individualistic; and, the point must be emphasised, not even death of others, if need be, will stand in his way. (pp. 13-14)

[Hamlet] himself imparts to Horatio how, having broken the seals, and read what his uncle had in store for him, he wrote another commission requiring the King of England to put his two school fellows to death. Why? What had they done to him? They would have been horrified had they known either about the contents of the sealed letter or about the murder of Hamlet's father. What is Hamlet's reason for committing so dastardly an action? Here it is:

> Why, man, they did make love to this employment,
> They are not near my conscience, their defeat
> Does by their own insinuation grow.
> 'Tis dangerous when the baser nature comes
> Between the pass and fell incensèd points
> Of mighty opposites
>
> [V. ii. 57-62.]

And that is all. Unless one adds these revealing words to his mother on the same theme:

> O, 'tis most sweet
> When in one line two crafts directly meet.

These words describe the man. Hamlet was a Renaissance European who thought that all was permissible to the powerful for the sake of power, and that those who were not of 'the baser nature' need not follow the rules of the game. Shakespeare, as was his wont, has rendered this feature of his character not merely by deeds, not merely by words, but by moods. Clearer even than the cool explanation of what amounts to his murder of Rosencrantz and Guildenstern, is the flippant, frivolous way in which he relates it:

> Wilt thou know
> Th' effect of what I wrote?

he asks Horatio; and then, relishing every word of it with the gusto of a true *dilettante*, he speaks on:

An earnest conjuration from the king,
As England was his faithful tributary,
As love between them like the palm might flourish,
As peace should still her wheaten garland wear
And stand a comma 'tween their amities,
And many such like 'as'es' of great charge,
That on the view and knowing of these contents,
Without debatement further, more or less,
He should those bearers put to sudden death,
Not shriving-time allowed.

[V. ii. 38-46.]

Genius could go no higher to represent the utter human callousness of a brilliant wit, for whom the very detail of not allowing time for confession, a truly terrible cruelty in those days, is reserved for an effect in the story. Hamlet in this scene is happy, thoroughly happy. He has won; he has played his uncle a mighty trick; he pokes witty fun at diplomatic papers; he tells a story as no one else can; that he kills two men so to enjoy himself, is a mere detail—moreover, they were of 'the baser nature'.

In his attitude towards his two schoolfellows, Hamlet, therefore, confirms our view of him as a man predominantly interested in himself; a man, therefore, for whom the other persons, without exception, are but pawns in his game. For such a character the worst crime that can be committed by an outsider is an aggression against his own self. The savagery with which Hamlet sends Rosencrantz and Guildenstern to their doom is due to his sudden discovery that the King meant to have him put to death. This personal aggression is for Hamlet the very apex of crime. His emotion at seeing himself thus attacked seals the fate of his two schoolfellows, even though he knew them to be innocent. He would not tell them his secret—the Ghost's secret—which would almost certainly have brought them over to his party; and he made them responsible for a loyalty to the King which in the circumstances was imperative. This had been enough to create in his Machiavellian or Borgian mind the desire to blow them to the moon. The energy for the explosion came from the thrust at his body which the commission revealed when he broke the seals. At no time did he think of his two school fellows as human beings in their own right. And when, even in imagination, his skin was threatened, he took their lives. (pp. 17-19)

Hamlet does not react so quickly to threats to his skin because he fears death or pain. He is brave. His threat to make a ghost of him who 'lets', i.e. who prevents, him from following the Ghost is virile; he is the first to board that pirate ship, and though we have no word but his for it, we do not hesitate to believe him; for despite his subtleties and his "pranks" he strikes that note of frankness which always goes with courage. No. The swiftness of his reactions when attacked is not cowardice; it is egotism. It means: "you are welcome to do anything you like in the world, but you must not touch ME." (pp. 19-20)

[Essential] as it is, this egotism of Hamlet is but his psychological backbone; and to make up the whole there remain many other features, over which there is hardly a difference of opinion nowadays. They are the powers and graces of the most fascinating character of the European stage.

This fascination which Hamlet exerts on all has powerfully contributed to the misunderstanding which prevails over his relations with Ophelia. The critic starts with the prepossession that these relations must satisfy the standards of a cultivated, refined, honest, 'decent' gentleman of his contemporary Britain; and when he comes across facts and words which do not tally in the least with his prepossession, he just stalls. It is crucial to begin by emphasising this fact: orthodox criticism of Hamlet has failed to provide a coherent explanation of the Hamlet-Ophelia problem. (p. 31)

The chief cause of the trouble may well be the height of poetical power and pathos to which Shakespeare raises the play in the scene of Ophelia's madness; the songs, the flowers, "the pity of it", work our emotions to such a pitch and tension that Ophelia is thereby transfigured and her whole life is retrospectively coloured by this hectic sunset of her mind. By a curious effect of this alchemy, not only Ophelia but Hamlet as well becomes transfigured and sentimentalised. And so, Ophelia has been established as the paragon of innocence, love and undeserved tragedy, not very clever perhaps, but so sweet! As for Hamlet, it soon became a habit to convey to the audience, by some tender gesture when Ophelia was not looking, that though he might speak harsh and insulting words to her, he still at heart loved her. (p. 32)

"That Hamlet was at one time genuinely in love with Ophelia"—writes an eminent authority—"no serious critic has, I think, ever questioned" [see excerpt above by J. Dover Wilson, 1935]. Then I am no serious critic, for I hold that Hamlet never was meant by Shakespeare to have been in love with Ophelia. Indeed the idea that Hamlet could be in love at all with anybody but himself is incompatible with Hamlet's character. . . . [Whatever] the circumstances, whatever the excuses, is it possible that a man who had loved a woman should treat her as Hamlet treats Ophelia repeatedly? Are the 'nunnery' scene and the conversation at the play reconcilable even with a love that is past? "Hamlet"—writes the same authority—"treats Ophelia like a prostitute"; and while in this, the eminent critic may go too far, his award is surely proof enough that Hamlet had never loved Ophelia! For, no matter her crimes, and we have seen her commit none so far to justify Hamlet's behaviour, a man of Hamlet's stamp would demean himself by "treating like a prostitute" a woman he had once loved.

But that is not all. For surely a true love, even if extinct, would leave behind enough embers of respect towards the once beloved and towards her family. Now, Polonius might be garrulous and meddlesome, but he was the father of Ophelia. He might conspire to test Hamlet by eavesdropping; but that was not such a crime as to justify the gibes, the mockery, the actual insults to an old man who was the father of the once beloved. And the callous words he addresses the body after slaying him behind the arras—not a thought for Ophelia then!—and that gruesome line:

I'll lug the guts into the neighbour room

[III. iv. 212]

and that stark stage direction *"he drags the body from the room"*, are any of these things compatible even with extinct love?

Shakespeare did everything he could to convey to his audience the fact that Hamlet had never loved Ophelia. True he makes Ophelia speak of the "words of so sweet breath composed"; note she speaks of *words;* true he says: *I did love you once,* but this whole dialogue to which we must return, ends with a remarkable exchange of hard truths: *"I loved you not,"* says Hamlet, and Ophelia retorts: *"I was the more deceived."* The only other pronouncement on the subject we hear from Hamlet's own lips in his frantic:

> I loved Ophelia, forty thousand brothers
> Could not with all their quality of love
> Make up my sum—   [V. i. 269-71]

words which were certainly not meant to convey to anyone in his senses that Hamlet loved Ophelia; but merely that he was ready to outdo Laertes in anything, from loving Ophelia to drinking vinegar or ranting as well as any man. (pp. 36-8)

It might be argued—if with but little force—that all this happens when Hamlet has already lost his love for Ophelia. But lest we were thus led astray, Shakespeare took care to provide us with a first-hand document of the period before, on any hypothesis, his love had "ceased". Hamlet's love letter which Polonius reads to the King and Queen in II.2 raises one of the many problems in Shakespeare. Polonius brings it in triumph to the King after the scene in which Ophelia "affrighted" reports Hamlet's sudden visit to her. When was this letter written? Recently? But how could Hamlet play with such "numbers" when he was so sorely tried by the revelations of the Ghost? And how could Ophelia possess it since in the previous scene she tells her father "I did repel his letters"? Was then the letter old, previous to the King's murder? But then how is it Polonius makes news of it? Shakespeare is precise in essence, vague in detail. The solution is this: the letter is old. Polonius lies when he says it was given him by his daughter "in her duty and obedience". We know he lies because the vain old man goes on to say:

> This in obedience hath my daughter shown me,
> And more above hath his solicitings,
> As they fell out by time, by means and place,
> All given to mine ear   [II. ii. 125-28]

which we know is not true, since we have heard father and daughter talk the matter *over* but—so far as Ophelia is concerned—by no means *out*. (pp. 38-9)

[This] goes to show that this letter comes from the period before the play, when, if ever Hamlet was in love with Ophelia, no cloud had come to disturb his feelings. Now, is this a love letter at all? . . . No girl of average feminine acumen would take such stuff for the style of love. "To the celestial, and my soul's idol, the most beautified Ophelia" might do for Osric; but from Hamlet's pen it can only mean *fun*. He is having fun out of her as he does out of everybody; playing *on* her as if she were an instrument. . . . "Most beautiful Ophelia" does mean "most made-up Ophelia"; not merely because it tallies with "I have heard of your paintings" at III.1, but (which is even more to the point) because Hamlet was not a man who could write *beautified* when he meant *beautiful;* so that the argument that "Polonius' condemnation of 'beautified' is sufficient to show that it is an innocent word" should be inverted: it shows that Hamlet did not mean it in the sense in which Polonius rightly criticised it. Then come four lines of doggerel which Hamlet must have known had nothing to do with either genuine love or genuine poetry:

> Doubt thou the stars are fire
>   Doubt that the sun doth move,
> Doubt truth to be a liar
>   But never doubt I love.
>   [II. ii. 116-19]

and then the "Oh bother" perfunctory paragraph: "O dear Ophelia, I am ill at these numbers, I have not art to reckon

my groans, but that I love thee best, O most best, believe it. Adieu. Thine evermore, most dear lady, whilst this machine is to him, Hamlet."

If that is the way Shakespeare made Hamlet express his love for Ophelia, he who has endowed the English language with one of the richest anthologies of love the world possesses, from the adolescent love of Romeo to the autumnal and hectic love of Anthony, we are right in concluding that Hamlet was at no time in love with Ophelia. (pp. 39-40)

[That Ophelia was not in love with Hamlet] is proved by her very acquiescence in her father's designs. Any young woman with a genuine love for a man would have resisted the part assigned to her in that comedy, and instinctively sided with her lover against the two "lawful espials". She makes no opposition whatever and she enters fully into the plot. (pp. 40-1)

We are advised by an authority on Hamlet to bear in mind that, in order not to misunderstand the 'nunnery' scene we must remember that it is not Hamlet who has repelled Ophelia but Ophelia Hamlet [see excerpt above by J. Dover Wilson, 1935]. What evidence is there for such a conclusion? Let us listen to the play: We first hear of Hamlet's interest in Ophelia when Laertes gives her advice about it, prolix enough to augur for the young man as garrulous an old age as his father's. What is her reaction? Does she raise the slightest objection to all the indirect accusations against Hamlet implicit in her brother's sermon? None. . . . And, most revealing of all, these lines:

> But good my brother
> Do not, as some ungracious pastors do,
> Show me the steep and thorny way to heaven,
> Whiles like a puffed and reckless libertine
> Himself the primrose path of dalliance treads
> And recks not his own rede.   [I. ii. 46-51]

Could Shakespeare give us a broader hint on what was in Ophelia's mind and on the way she conceived her own relations with Hamlet?

Then, Laertes gone, Polonius takes on the subject again, in a scene in which, again, Ophelia gives not a shadow of a sign, direct or indirect, that she is in love with Hamlet. (p. 41)

[When] ordered no longer "to give words or talk with the Lord Hamlet", she promptly bows: "I shall obey, my lord."

The next thing that happens is Hamlet's dramatic, silent visit to her which she comes, still 'affrighted', to report to her father (II.1). "Mad for thy love?"—he asks; and she, who knows better, answers ambiguously: "My Lord, I do not know but truly I do fear it." Then Polonius asks an extraordinary question:

> What, have you given him any hard words of late?
>   [II. i. 104]

This shows how little faith the old man laid in his daughter's obedience. But she dutifully answers:

> No, my good Lord, but as you did command,
> I did repel his letters, and denied
> His access to me.   [II. i. 105-07]

That is what she says to her father. But can it be true? Evidently not. For were it true, she would not return the trinkets alleging that:

Rich gifts wax poor when givers prove unkind!

[III. i. 100]

This little scene proves that Ophelia had paid no notice either to her brother's or to her father's sermons; that she promised Laertes with her lips what she was determined not to carry out; and that she bowed at once with a 'I shall obey' to her father's orders not to receive Hamlet, because she had not the slightest intention of obeying them. If this interpretation is not accepted, the trinkets scene has no sense.

Ophelia is in fact a flirt; a fast girl such as at Elizabeth's court was the rule rather than the exception; a girl whose model was Ann Boleyn, the young beauty who ascended the throne by way of the King's bedroom. This much can be concluded from all that precedes. An examination of the play scene will confirm it. The very first words and action of Hamlet with regard to Ophelia in this scene confirm our view of their relationship. "Come hither, my dear Hamlet, sit by me," says the Queen; and he, sitting at Ophelia's feet, retorts: "No, good mother, here is metal more attractive." This disposes of all explanations which would account for Hamlet's brutality towards Ophelia by dividing their relationship into two phases: a love-phase and a no-love or even hate-phase. No. After their 'nunnery' scene and a few seconds before that obscene dialogue during the play scene, Ophelia is attractive metal to Hamlet. Their relationship was ever the same: one which enabled Hamlet to write a mock-and-bother letter during the "love" period, and to seek her company during the "no-love" period; in fact, one of neither love nor no-love, hereafter to be analysed.

Then comes the obscene dialogue; for it is a dialogue. Now if Ophelia was the innocent, candid maid she is supposed to be, this dialogue could not have gone beyond the "I think nothing, my Lord"; the only decent answer Ophelia gives Hamlet in the scene. But what sort of maiden's innocence is it which, to:

That's a fair thought to lie between maid's legs,

asks:

What is, my Lord?

[III. ii. 118-20]

These four words should have been enough to reveal Ophelia's true character to all but hopeless romantics and sentimentalists. And to Hamlet's "Nothing", Ophelia comments: "You are merry, my Lord." Let critics think that he is "disgusting", "insulting" and "gross" [see excerpt above by A. C. Bradley, 1905]; but Ophelia just thinks he is "merry". And this difference in words measures the difference in values between the XIXth century critic and the XVIth century author: Hamlet does not treat Ophelia like a prostitute; he treats her as a young Elizabethan courtier would a young Elizabethan flirt with no particular inhibition about anything.

A girl of the stamp orthodox critics still see in Ophelia would either have left the room, or moved away from Hamlet or never addressed a word to him after his obscene opening gambit. Ophelia talks and even engages him in conversation when he is silent, as if wanting more "insults". She asks "What means this, my Lord?" and "Will a'tell us what this show meant?" To which Hamlet answers, not in the least "savagely", but in the same jesting-indecent-sardonic mood: "Ay, or any show that you'll show him; be not you ashamed to show, he'll not shame to tell you what it means."

To this, she comments: "You are naught, you are naught, I'll mark the play"—which in the circumstances is downright encouragement. But he has of course other things to attend to; so she has to wait till a later phase, when Hamlet having explained

This is one Lucianus, nephew to the King,

[III. ii. 244]

the much insulted but never enough insulted young lady, puts in: "You are as good as a chorus, my Lord". This brings him out in his best form: "I could interpret between you and your love, if I could see the puppets dallying".

Could any one in his senses believe that this man had ever been in love with the woman to whom he spoke thus? And how revealing her answer: "You are keen, my Lord, you are keen". This answer shatters the accepted view that she is undeservedly repelled. He treats her "love" as a puppet show and she—well, does she not acknowledge that he is not altogether mistaken? Then, Hamlet goes on worse: "It would cost you a groaning to take off my edge"—a remark she ought not to understand, were she "sweet, innocent Ophelia"; but which simply delights her, for she answers: "Still better and worse". That is: "You are naught, but I like it." (pp. 42-4)

[Hamlet] talks much more than anyone else in the play, nearly three times as much as the King, who comes next on the list of lines spoken. Here lies the tragedy. The self-centred man gives nothing to the human beings that surround him; he wipes them out of existence so far as he is concerned—but he needs them. He needs them more anxiously perhaps than more open and generous souls would. For, by nature, the self-centred man is lonely,—inwardly lonely, and, unless he can drown this inner loneliness in outer company, he is bound to fall into misanthropy, melancholy and even madness. Hamlet was apt to feel misanthropic: "man delights not me; no, nor woman either." And his melancholy lends a sombre background to the whole play. He is ever wandering in that zone of disenchanted boredom, yet of attraction and tension towards others, to be expected of his inner contradiction—refusal to give himself to the world of men—need of the world of men.

Shakespeare has managed to convey this struggle of the two antagonistic forces right to the end. Hamlet dies in the midst of dead bodies. His mother, the King, Laertes are no more. He himself is dying. And in this solemn hour, when he might have thought of Ophelia, or of Polonius, both his victims, or of his father, at last avenged, or of his mother, poisoned, of whom, of what does he think? Of himself and of his cause. In the strongest and most moving words, he entreats Horatio to absent himself from felicity awhile "to tell my story", to "report me and my cause aright to the unsatisfied". To his dying hour, Hamlet can think of nothing but Hamlet. Both in its utter neglect of all his partners in his life and in his pathetic dependence on "the unsatisfied", this last utterance of the unhappy Prince is typical of the self-centred man.

Shakespeare could not have remained more faithful to the type which he began to draw with a firm hand from the very first scene in which he comes on the stage. There is no mystery about Hamlet. Once the film of prejudice and misinterpretation is removed, the play stands perfectly clear; and its chief character, solidly built on sound psychological premises, is treated with all the freedom and subtle mastery of true creative genius. (pp. 106-07)

Salvador de Madariaga, in his On Hamlet, *Hollis & Carter, 1948, 130 p.*

E.M.W. TILLYARD   (essay date 1949)

[*Tillyard's* Shakespeare's History Plays *(1944), one of the most influential twentieth-century works in Shakespearean studies, is considered a leading example of historical criticism. Tillyard's thesis, which is shared, with variations, by other historical critics, discerns a systematic world view in Shakespeare's plays—and one common to educated Elizabethans—in which reality is understood to be structured in a hierarchal Great Chain of Being. On a social level such a philosophy valued order, hierarchy, and civil peace as the chief political goals. For Tillyard,* Hamlet *is, like* Measure for Measure, All's Well That Ends Well, *and* Troilus and Cressida, *a problem play. He posits that in tragedy, motives are unambiguous and life is depicted with clarity and force. In* Hamlet, *the emphasis is on the variety and complexity of human thought and experience, and so the play is removed from the realm of tragedy. According to Tillyard's theory, tragedy requires three ''types of feeling or situation'': suffering, sacrificial purgation, and spiritual renewal. While acknowledging that the first two criteria are found in* Hamlet, *he maintains that Hamlet himself does not experience any kind of spiritual renewal or enlightenment. Tillyard disagrees with Theodore Spencer (1942) regarding Hamlet's soliloquies. For additional commentary on Hamlet's soliloquies, see Charles Gildon (1721), William Guthrie (1747), Tobias Smollett (1756), Samuel Johnson (1765), and A.J.A. Waldock (1931).*]

Since *Hamlet* is usually classed as a tragedy, I recognize my obligation to explain why I go against habit and class it as a problem play. Where you class it will depend on your notion of tragedy; so I must begin by stating my own.

No single formula will cover all those works we agree to call tragic: at least three types of feeling or situation are included in the word. The first and simplest is that of mere suffering; and it has been very well set forth by J. S. Smart. Suffering becomes tragic when it befalls a strong (even a momentarily strong) nature who is not merely passive but reacts against calamity. Then "there is a sense of wonder," and the tragic victim

> contrasts the present, weighed as it is with unforeseen disaster and sorrow, with the past which has been torn from him: it seems as if the past alone had a right to exist, and the present were in some way unreal. . . . The stricken individual marvels why his lot should be so different from that of others; what is his position among men; and what is the position of man in the universe.

This simple conception is needed because it includes certain things which we recognize as tragic but which elude any conception more rigid or more complicated. *The Trojan Women* and *The Duchess of Malfi* are tragedies of simple suffering, where the sufferers are not greatly to blame. . . . *Hamlet* is certainly, among other things, a tragedy of this kind. Terrible things do befall its protagonist; while as a tragic hero Hamlet lacks a complication and an enrichment common in much tragedy: that of being to some extent, even a tiny extent, responsible for his misfortunes. Othello and Samson were in part responsible for theirs. . . . No one could accuse Hamlet of being the kind of person whose mother was bound to enter into a hasty and incestuous remarriage, of being such a prig that his mother *must* give him a shock at any cost. If you read the play with a main eye to the soliloquies, you can easily persuade yourself that *Hamlet* is principally a tragedy of this first simple kind.

The second type of tragic feeling has to do with sacrificial purgation and it is rooted in religion. The necessary parties in

a sacrifice are a god, a victim, a killer, and an audience; and the aim is to rid the social organism of a taint. The audience will be the more moved as the victim is or represents one of themselves. . . . Once again, *Hamlet* is tragic, and in this second way. There is something rotten in the state of Denmark, and one of its citizens, blameless hitherto and a distinguished member of society, is mysteriously called upon to be the victim by whose agency the rottenness is cut away. . . . Like the first, we can make this second tragic feeling the principal thing, if we narrow our vision sufficiently. But we should be wrong, for in actual fact our sense of Denmark's rottenness is much weaker than our sense of what a lot happens there. There is simply no comparison with Macbeth's Scotland, for instance. (pp. 14-16)

A third kind of tragic feeling has to do with renewal consequent on destruction. It occurs when there is an enlightenment and through this the assurance of a new state of being. This kind penetrates deep into our nature because it expresses not merely the tragedy of abnormal suffering but a fundamental tragic fact of all human life: namely, that a good state cannot stay such but must be changed, even partially destroyed, if a succeeding good is to be engendered. . . . The usual dramatic means of fulfilling this tragic function is through a change in the mind of the hero. His normal world has been upset, but some enlightenment has dawned, and through it, however faintly, a new order of things. Milton's Samson is for a second time reconciled to God, and this second reconciliation is other than the earlier state of friendship with God, which was destroyed. Othello is more than the stoical victim of great misfortune. He has been enlightened and, though he cannot live, it is a different man who dies. Those tragedies which we feel most centrally tragic contain, with other tragic conceptions, this third one. It is partly through failing to contain this conception that *Hamlet* is separated from the three great tragedies with which it is popularly joined. But this is a contentious statement which must be substantiated.

The main point at issue is whether Hamlet's mind undergoes during the course of the play a revolution comparable to that which takes place in the minds of Oedipus, or Lear, or Samson. If it does not, there can be no question of tragedy in the third sense. . . . [Recently] a fundamental change in Hamlet's mind has been very confidently asserted. . . . C. S. Lewis speaks of *Hamlet* largely in terms of a state of mind, the state of thinking about being dead, but he . . . [finds] progress in the mind of the hero [see Additional Bibliography]. [Such critics] rely for their opinions mainly on a single passage, the prose conversation between Hamlet and Horatio in V. 2 after Osric has gone out bearing with him Hamlet's acceptance of an immediate fencing-match with Laertes. They think this passage (containing Hamlet's ''defiance of augury'') marks the revolution in Hamlet's mind. If they are wrong here, their argument cannot hold. (pp. 16-18)

As I read it the passage shows no fundamental change in Hamlet's mind; and for two main reasons.

First, any piety shown here by him was anticipated earlier in the play. He has been from the first remote from natural, unregenerate man. He is deeply religious, as the complete man of the Renaissance ought to be. And the signs of his piety and his belief that "the readiness is all" in other and earlier parts of the play argue that in the present passage he exhibits no spiritual development. . . . [He] had already protested that the Ghost could do nothing to his soul, "being a thing immortal as itself." His sense of the glory of man as created in God's image (''What a piece of work is a man!'') and of his ignominy as a fallen creature (''Virtue cannot so inoculate our old stock but we shall relish of it'') is theologically impeccable. And his words on Polonius's dead body are equally so:

> For this same lord
> I do repent: but heaven hath pleased it so,
> To punish me with this and this with me,
> That I must be their scourge and minister.
> I will bestow him and will answer well
> The death I gave him.   [III. iv. 172-77]

Nothing in the ''defiance of augury'' speech is more pious and regenerate than this. Hamlet did not change.

But a more important reason is the tone of the passage. And this is not new and profound and significant, but elegantly conventional. Quietism not religious enlightenment is the dominant note. Hamlet is ready for anything that will come along; he has not acquired a new and liberating mastery of his own fate.

If therefore this crucial passage shows nothing new, the notions of a regenerate Hamlet, and hence of a play tragic in the fullest sense, are ruled out. Further, even though *Hamlet* is tragic in certain senses, that tragic quality is not the principal quality. (pp. 18-19)

In denying to Hamlet any powerful spiritual growth, any definitive spiritual revolution, I may have given the impression that his mind was quite static. This I did not intend; for the religious is not the only type of mental growth, and it is possible that Hamlet without undergoing a religious regeneration does change in some sort. Indeed it would be strange if all the things Hamlet had to suffer made no impression on his mind. Thus Theodore Spencer argues that Hamlet's soliloquies show a progress in his power to convert the personal into the general, and that in the end he is above rather than in the tumult. This, I believe, is to argue from single passages in abstraction from the play. And even if Hamlet's soliloquies do show a progression from the personal, his behaviour at Ophelia's funeral, which comes after all the soliloquies, shows a very thorough relapse. On the other hand, the notion that Hamlet grows older during the play is surely true. (pp. 19-20)

[Though] the things Hamlet endures may not work a spiritual revolution in him they do have their effect on the given ingredients of his mind. And that effect has its own order. Again, this order is not the principal thing in *Hamlet*, but it has high importance. To speak of this importance is useless till I have made out a case for the order itself. In so doing I shall have to be highly subjective, for the order will depend less on what is stated than on the ways in which the poetic stress appears to the reader to fall. Further, to be at all brief, I shall have to be dogmatic on just those matters which have been the subject of doubt and controversy, namely, on what passes in Hamlet's mind; for what creates the order I seek to elucidate is the degree of prominence different events assume in Hamlet's mind and any action he takes to meet them.

First, I must recall Granville-Barker's timely and emphatic reminder that the accepted act divisions are misleading and that the play falls naturally into three parts [see excerpt above, 1937]. The first corresponds with the first act and ends with Hamlet's acceptance of the task given him by the Ghost. The second begins with Polonius sending Reynaldo to Paris (II. 1) and ends with Hamlet's departure to England (IV. 4). The last begins with Ophelia's madness (IV. 5) and comprises the rest

of the play. Between the parts there are long lapses of time. The first part presents Hamlet's state of mind, the position he is in, and the problems of action involved; the second presents the action and counter-action of Hamlet and Claudius; the third presents the consequences of what happened in the second.

Next, I must record my agreement with Waldock [see excerpt above, 1931] in the great prominence he gives to Hamlet's first soliloquy ''O that this too too solid flesh would melt'' and in his surprise that from Goethe and Coleridge (and one might now add from . . . C. S. Lewis) one would not gather that before the coming of the Ghost anything had happened to trouble Hamlet. . . . It was a fact that his mother would hang on his father as if increase of appetite had grown by what it fed on; and it was another fact that within a month she had married his uncle. And the two facts, of which he had utter personal evidence, could not be reconciled. When such a shock is recounted in the earliest place in the play where Hamlet is able to reveal himself, that is, his soliloquy in the second scene, we may surely expect that the rest of the play will deal largely with the working out of this shock. It should also be observed that in his soliloquy Hamlet says nothing about his uncle having cheated him of the succession. . . . (pp. 20-3)

In the next scene—that is, before Hamlet meets his father's ghost—we hear of his courtship of Ophelia; and I think the critics have been backward in seeing the great prominence of this motive, which occurs so early in the play and at the very time when the themes that are to prevail are being set forth. . . . [The] way Act One is organized suggests that Hamlet's very first advances to Ophelia had to do with his mother's second marriage. He hoped to find in Ophelia evidence to contradict what his mother's action appeared to prove. Not that we are justified in working out a time-table for Hamlet . . . ; but the order of dramatic presentation bids us connect Gertrude and Ophelia closely and expect that Polonius's orders to Ophelia to deny her presence to Hamlet will have a powerful bearing on the course of the play. By the end of the third scene, therefore, the overwhelmingly important theme is Gertrude's remarriage, its effect on Hamlet reinforced by Ophelia's behaviour, and the probability of further consequences. . . . [The] Ghost commands Hamlet to avenge his murder and, though putting an end to the incestuous connection of Claudius and Gertrude, not to contrive anything against his mother:

> Let not the royal bed of Denmark be
> A couch for luxury and damned incest.
> But, howsoever thou pursuest this act,
> Taint not thy mind; nor let thy soul contrive
> Against thy mother aught. Leave her to heaven
> And to those thorns that in her bosom lodge
> To prick and sting her.   [I. v. 82-8]

The words are ambiguous. It is not clear whether in upbraiding his mother as Hamlet later did he was transgressing his father's command. But at least the Ghost couples what are by now evidently the master-themes, the vengeance on Claudius and the lascivious and incestuous guilt of Gertrude. And it is the coexistence of the two themes and the contrasted ways in which Hamlet responds to them that give the play what regularity of structure it possesses. (pp. 20-5)

The second act, which begins the true second part, develops both themes without bringing them to a crisis. Hamlet's disgust at his mother had promoted his dealing with Ophelia; and her actions in their turn exacerbate his feelings against her, his mother, and all women. Hamlet's experience with his father's ghost had dealt a second shock to his mind, bringing with it the danger of derangement and prompting him to assume a fictitious derangement in addition and to express the conflict in his feelings through long soliloquies. This derangement alarms Claudius and causes him to take precautions. The next act contains Hamlet's answers to the two shocks he has suffered in the first act; and they consist of his testing the Ghost's veracity through the play, followed by his sparing Claudius immediately after, and of his upbraiding his mother. There is no interval between his dealing with Claudius and his dealing with his mother, and these should be considered jointly yet in contrast; so considered, they match the manner in which the two themes had been set forth in the first act. . . . My impression is that Hamlet forces himself in his dealings with Claudius, lashing himself to hysteria but not acting with his whole heart, while he puts his whole self into his words to his mother. In the deepest sense, therefore, he disobeys the Ghost's commands. Hamlet's brutal words to Ophelia in the play scene tell the same tale, for they show him thinking of his mother's action and of his disgust at womankind during the very crisis of his dealings with Claudius. While, then, in the two scenes that mainly concern Claudius Hamlet shows himself histrionic, artificially self-excited, and even hysterical, in talking to his mother he shows the full range of his character and relieves his long-suppressed feelings by speaking from his heart. Moreover in his positive advice to her he finds an outlet for the active side of his nature. This is the supreme scene of the play. Psychologically, what resolution there is in the play is mainly here. Once Hamlet can face his mother and share with her the burden of what he thinks of her, he can at least begin to see the world as something other than a prison. . . . It is in this scene too that Hamlet, although terrified by the Ghost, overwhelmingly vehement in denouncing the loathesomeness of his mother's sexual sin, and callous over the body of Polonius (''I'll lug the guts into the neighbour room''), shows his most winning sanity and the utmost delicacy of his sensibilities. When, on the Ghost's exit, he protests that his pulse keeps time as temperately as his mother's, the words that follow bear his protest out. What better could illustrate his sane and delicate and critical temper than the sudden interpolation into his preaching to his mother of

> forgive me this my virtue,
> For in the fatness of these pursy times
> Virtue itself of vice must pardon beg,
> Yea, curb and woo for leave to do him good.
> [III. iv. 152-55]

His final callousness over Polonius's body does not exclude his pious words quoted earlier about his deed, while his final disposition towards his mother is tender. All these exhibitions, even if they are fragmentary, of sanity and clean feeling, come after Hamlet has relieved his mind of his horror at his mother's act; and, coming also after and in spite of the Ghost's interposition urging revenge, are surely meant to show us that his mother's act rather than the obligation to his dead father usurps the main part of his mind. What we learn from this most revealing scene is that Hamlet (unlike the world at large) does not really believe that it is relevant to kill Claudius: that will not bring his father back to life. To awaken Gertrude's sense of guilt is his fundamental need.

Hamlet's conversation with his mother does not cure him, does not altogether rescue him from his prison, but it does either initiate a slow healing process or render him less impatient of his burdens. His bad conscience about the revenge stirs again,

on his way to take ship to England, in his last soliloquy (''How all occasions . . .''). Later, on his return, he exhibits violent passions at Ophelia's funeral. Yet these relapses do not efface the sense of Hamlet's having obtained a real relief and being more resigned. And this more resigned temper persists till the end of the play. In the third part (after Hamlet's return from England) the psychological interest, through the preponderant motives of Hamlet's mind having been revealed, shifts partly to the other characters; and now counts for less compared with the interest of the plot, the details of which evolve with perfect propriety from the events recounted in the second part.

Hamlet, then, does possess a shape. The states of mind presented in the first act lead to certain actions in the second act and are tested and clarified in the third. Thus clarified they persist to the end of the play. This shape contributes substantially to the poetic quality; and mainly on the intellectual side, giving the sense of a masterly controlling brain. But psychological explication showing intellectual mastery and spiritual action are not the same. At most Hamlet regains some of the dignity and composure that we know to have been part of his original endowment. . . . But, with no great revelation or reversal of direction or regeneration, the play cannot answer to one of our expectations from the highest tragedy.

This failure does not mean that *Hamlet* is not one of the greatest plays. On the contrary, the subtlety and the fascination of its psychological appeal (within the limits indicated) joined with the simple but firm lines of its general shaping exalt it to eminence.

Even so I do not make these matters, however important, quite the principal matters, and it remains to say which I consider these to be.

The first is the sheer wealth and vigour and brilliance of all the things that happen. . . . One is tempted to call *Hamlet* the greatest display of sheer imaginative vitality in literary form that a man has so far achieved. It is here we feel that Shakespeare first reached the full extent of his powers; and he gives us the sense of glorying in them. And no other play of Shakespeare gives us just that touch of sheer exultation.

The second principal matter has to do as much with the setting as with the business of the play. . . . Thoughtful people are puzzled by the appearance life presents to them. Their hour-to-hour experiences do not satisfy them and are felt to convey a false impression. The impression is both impoverished and unordered, and they wish to have it enlarged and interpreted. In fulfilling this wish people will do the work for themselves or obtain help from others in proportions that accord with their capacities. The great artists do a great deal of the work for themselves and offer a great deal of help to others. . . . The artists by the richness of their presentation enlarge the range of experience comprehensible by the unaided efforts of the ordinary person, and by the form of their presentation suggest some order in this range of experience. A great artist will excel in both functions. But, however great he is, he has to compromise and to adjust the scope of one function to that of the other. If he is very great, he will wish to present a variety of such compromises, for each type of compromise will express something that none of the others can. (pp. 25-31)

Hamlet is best understood as a play less of ordering than of sheer explication or presentation, as a play presenting the utmost variety of human experience in the largest possible cosmic setting. (p. 31)

Shakespeare's picture of the varieties of human experience was of course conditioned by the contemporary world picture. And I doubt if in any other play of Shakespeare there is so strong an impression of the total range of creation from the angels to the beasts. Maybe in *The Tempest* the lower stretches of the chain of being and the doubtful stretches between man and angel are more fully presented, but the angels and man's variety in his own great stretch of the chain are presented there with less emphasis. This way of looking at creation is powerfully traditional and Christian; and in *Hamlet* if anywhere in Shakespeare we notice the genealogy from the Miracle Plays with their setting of Heaven, Purgatory, and Hell, as for instance in the hero's description of himself as a fellow "crawling between heaven and earth." . . . *Hamlet* is one of the most medieval as well as one of the most acutely modern of Shakespeare's plays. And though the theme of spiritual regeneration may be absent from the plot, the setting includes the religious consciousness most eminently. (pp. 32-3)

The tragic mode is ideally very definite and formal. Motives are clear in the characters, and the spectator has no doubt where his sympathies should lie. We know that Medea had been hardly treated and also that she acted with deplorable violence. We know that Macbeth was a villain in having Banquo murdered. Further, in ideal tragedy life is presented in a startlingly clear and unmistakable shape: we are meant to see it indubitably so and not otherwise. When sheer explication, or abundance of things presented, takes first place, then we leave the realm of tragedy for that of the problem play. Here it is the problems themselves, their richness, their interest, and their diversity, and not their solution or significant arrangement that come first. I have argued that *Hamlet*, though containing tragedy of sorts, and though reinforced intellectually by a noble general shape, belongs principally to this type. (pp. 33-4)

> *E.M.W. Tillyard, "'Hamlet'," in his* Shakespeare's Problem Plays, *University of Toronto Press, 1949, pp. 14-35.*

ERNEST JONES (essay date 1949)

[*A disciple of Sigmund Freud, Jones here develops Freud's thesis that Hamlet's procrastination is the result of an Oedipus complex (see excerpt above, 1900). Jones's essay was originally published in 1910. It was expanded in 1923 and published in final form in 1949. A.J.A. Waldock (1931) challenges the validity of Jones's approach.*]

The first writer clearly to recognize that Hamlet was a man not baffled in his endeavours but struggling in an internal conflict was Ulrici, in 1839 [see excerpt above]. The details of Ulrici's hypothesis, which . . . originated in the Hegelian views of morality, are not easy to follow, but the essence of it is the contention that Hamlet gravely doubted the moral legitimacy of revenge. He was thus plunged into a struggle between his natural tendency to avenge his father and his highly developed ethical and Christian views, which forbade the indulging of this instinctive desire. . . . [Some critics] have suggested that the conflict was a purely intellectual one, Hamlet being unable to satisfy himself of the adequacy or reliability of the Ghost's evidence. (pp. 45-7)

The obvious question that one puts to the upholders of . . . the [hypothesis] just mentioned is: why did Hamlet in his monologues give us no indication whatsoever of the nature of the conflict in his mind? As we shall presently note, he gave several pretended excuses for his hesitancy, but never once did he hint at any doubt about what his duty was in the matter. He was always clear enough about what he *ought* to do; the conflict in his mind ranged about the question why he couldn't bring himself to do it. . . . [Ulrici meets] this difficulty by assuming that the ethical objection to personal revenge was never clearly present to Hamlet's mind; it was a deep and undeveloped feeling which had not fully dawned. I would agree that only in some such way as this can the difficulty be logically met, and further that in recognizing Hamlet's non-consciousness of the cause of his repugnance to his task we are nearing the core of the mystery. In fact Hamlet tells us so himself in so many words (in his bitter cry—Act IV, Sc. 3—*I do not know why,* etc.). But an insurmountable obstacle in the way of accepting any of the causes of repugnance suggested above is that the nature of them is such that a keen and introspective thinker, as Hamlet was, would infallibly have recognized some indication of their presence, and would have openly debated them instead of deceiving himself with a number of false pretexts in the way we shall presently recall. (pp. 47-8)

That Hamlet is suffering from an internal conflict the essential nature of which is inaccessible to his introspection is evidenced by the following considerations. Throughout the play we have the clearest picture of a man who sees his duty plain before him, but who shirks it at every opportunity and suffers in consequence the most intense remorse. To paraphrase Sir James Paget's well-known description of hysterical paralysis: Hamlet's advocates say he cannot do his duty, his detractors say he will not, whereas the truth is that he cannot will. Further than this, the deficient will-power is localized to the one question of killing his uncle; it is what may be termed a *specific aboulia*. Now instances of such specific aboulias in real life invariably prove, when analysed, to be due to an unconscious repulsion against the act that cannot be performed (or else against something closely associated with the act, so that the idea of the act becomes also involved in the repulsion). In other words, whenever a person cannot bring himself to do something that every conscious consideration tells him he should do— and which he may have the strongest conscious desire to do— it is always because there is some hidden reason why a part of him doesn't want to do it; this reason he will not own to himself and is only dimly if at all aware of. That is exactly the case with Hamlet. Time and again he works himself up, points out to himself his obvious duty, with the cruellest self-reproaches lashes himself to agonies of remorse—and once more falls away into inaction. (pp. 52-3)

Highly significant is the fact that the grounds Hamlet gives for his hesitancy are grounds none of which will stand any serious consideration, and which continually change from one time to another. One moment he pretends he is too cowardly to perform the deed, at another he questions the truthfulness of the ghost, at another—when the opportunity presents itself in its naked form—he thinks the time is unsuited, it would be better to wait till the King was at some evil act and then to kill him, and so on. They have each of them, it is true, a certain plausibility— so much so that some writers have accepted them at face value; but surely no pretext would be of any use if it were not plausible. (pp. 53-4)

When a man gives at different times a different reason for his conduct it is safe to infer that, whether consciously or not, he is concealing the true reason. . . . We can therefore safely dismiss all the alleged motives that Hamlet propounds, as being more or less successful attempts on his part to blind himself with self-deception. (pp. 54-5)

In short, the whole picture presented by Hamlet, his deep depression, the hopeless note in his attitude towards the world and towards the value of life, his dread of death, his repeated reference to bad dreams, his self-accusations, his desperate efforts to get away from the thoughts of his duty, and his vain attempts to find an excuse for his procrastination: all this unequivocally points to a *tortured conscience,* to some hidden ground for shirking his task, a ground which he dare not or cannot avow to himself. We have, therefore, to take up the argument again at this point, and to seek for some evidence that may serve to bring to light the hidden counter-motive.

The extensive experience of the psycho-analytic researches carried out by Freud and his school during the past half-century has amply demonstrated that certain kinds of mental process show a greater tendency to be inaccessible to consciousness (put technically, to be "repressed") than others. . . . [Those] processes are most likely to be "repressed" by the individual which are most disapproved of by the particular circle of society to whose influence he has chiefly been subjected during the period when his character was being formed. (pp. 57-8)

The language used in the previous paragraph will have indicated that by the term "repression" we denote an active dynamic process. Thoughts that are "repressed" are actively kept from consciousness by a definite force and with the expenditure of more or less mental effort, though the person concerned is rarely aware of this. . . . It only remains to add the obvious corollary that, as the herd unquestionably selects from the "natural" instincts the sexual one on which to lay its heaviest ban, so it is the various psycho-sexual trends that are most often "repressed" by the individual. We have here the explanation of the clinical experience that the more intense and the more obscure is a given case of deep mental conflict the more certainly will it be found on adequate analysis to centre about a sexual problem. On the surface, of course, this does not appear so, for, by means of various psychological defensive mechanisms, the depression, doubt, despair, and other manifestations of the conflict are transferred on to more tolerable and permissible topics, such as anxiety about worldly success or failure, about immortality and the salvation of the soul, philosophical considerations about the value of life, the future of the world, and so on.

Bearing these considerations in mind, let us return to Hamlet. It should now be evident that the conflict hypotheses discussed above, which see Hamlet's conscious impulse towards revenge inhibited by an unconscious misgiving of a highly ethical kind, are based on ignorance of what actually happens in real life, since misgivings of this order belong in fact to the more conscious layers of the mind rather than to the deeper, unconscious ones. Hamlet's intense self-study would speedily have made him aware of any such misgivings and, although he might subsequently have ignored them, it would almost certainly have been by the aid of some process of rationalization which would have enabled him to deceive himself into believing that they were ill-founded; he would in any case have remained conscious of the nature of them. We have therefore to invert these hypotheses and realize—as his words so often indicate—that the positive striving for vengeance, the pious task laid on him by his father, was to him the moral and social one, the one approved of by his consciousness, and that the "repressed" inhibiting striving against the act of vengeance arose in some hidden source connected with his more personal, natural instincts. The former striving has already been considered, and indeed is manifest in every speech in which Hamlet debates

the matter: the second is, from its nature, more obscure and has next to be investigated.

This is perhaps most easily done by inquiring more intently into Hamlet's precise attitude towards the object of his vengeance, Claudius, and towards the crimes that have to be avenged. These are two: Claudius' incest with the Queen, and his murder of his brother. Now it is of great importance to note the profound difference in Hamlet's attitude towards these two crimes. Intellectually of course he abhors both, but there can be no question as to which arouses in him the deeper loathing. Whereas the murder of his father evokes in him indignation and a plain recognition of his obvious duty to avenge it, his mother's guilty conduct awakes in him the intensest horror. (pp. 58-61)

The uncle has not merely committed *each* crime, he has committed *both* crimes, a distinction of considerable importance, since the *combination* of crimes allows the admittance of a new factor, produced by the possible inter-relation of the two, which may prevent the result from being simply one of summation. In addition, it has to be borne in mind that the perpetrator of the crimes is a relative, and an exceedingly near relative. The possible inter-relationship of the crimes, and the fact that the author of them is an actual member of the family, give scope for a confusion in their influence on Hamlet's mind which may be the cause of the very obscurity we are seeking to clarify.

Let us first pursue further the effect on Hamlet of his mother's misconduct. Before he even knows with any certitude, however much he may suspect it, that his father has been murdered he is in the deepest depression, and evidently on account of this misconduct. (pp. 61-2)

If we ask, not what ought to produce such soul-paralysing grief and distaste for life, but what in actual fact does produce it, we are compelled to go beyond this explanation and seek for some deeper cause. In real life speedy second marriages occur commonly enough without leading to any such result as is here depicted, and when we see them followed by this result we invariably find, if the opportunity for an analysis of the subject's mind presents itself, that there is some other and more hidden reason why the event is followed by this inordinately great effect. The reason always is that the event has awakened to increased activity mental processes that have been "repressed" from the subject's consciousness. (pp. 64-5)

We come at this point to the vexed question of Hamlet's sanity, about which so many controversies have raged. Dover Wilson authoritatively writes: "I agree with Loening, Bradley and others that Shakespeare meant us to imagine Hamlet as suffering from some kind of mental disorder throughout the play" [see excerpt above, 1935]. The question is what kind of mental disorder and what is its significance dramatically and psychologically. The matter is complicated by Hamlet's frequently displaying simulation (the Antic Disposition), and it has been asked whether this is to conceal his real mental disturbance or cunningly to conceal his purposes in coping with the practical problems of this task? (p. 65)

More to the point is the actual account given in the play by the King, the Queen, Ophelia, and above all, Polonius. In his description, for example, we note—if the Elizabethan language is translated into modern English—the symptoms of dejection, refusal of food, insomnia, crazy behaviour, fits of delirium, and finally of raving madness; Hamlet's poignant parting words to Polonius ("except my life", etc.) cannot mean other than a craving for death. These are undoubtedly suggestive of certain forms of melancholia, and the likeness to manic-depressive insanity, of which melancholia is now known to be but a part, is completed by the occurrence of attacks of great excitement that would nowadays be called "hypomanic", of which Dover Wilson counts no fewer than eight. . . . Nevertheless, the rapid and startling oscillations between intense excitement and profound depression do not accord with the accepted picture of this disorder, and if I had to describe such a condition as Hamlet's in clinical terms—which I am not particularly inclined to—it would have to be as a severe case of hysteria on a cyclothymic basis.

All this, however, is of academic interest only. What we are essentially concerned with is the psychological understanding of the dramatic effect produced by Hamlet's personality and behaviour. That effect would be quite other were the central figure in the play to represent merely a "case of insanity". When that happens, as with Ophelia, such a person passes beyond our ken, is in a sense no more human, whereas Hamlet successfully claims our interest and sympathy to the very end. Shakespeare certainly never intended us to regard Hamlet as insane, so that the "mind o'erthrown" must have some other meaning than its literal one. . . . I would suggest that in this Shakespeare's extraordinary powers of observation and penetration granted him a degree of insight that it has taken the world three subsequent centuries to reach. Until our generation (and even now in the juristic sphere) a dividing line separated the sane and responsible from the irresponsible insane. It is now becoming more and more widely recognized that much of mankind lives in an intermediate and unhappy state charged with what Dover Wilson well calls "that sense of frustration, futility and human inadequacy which is the burden of the whole symphony" and of which Hamlet is the supreme example in literature. This intermediate plight, in the toils of which perhaps the greater part of mankind struggles and suffers, is given the name of psychoneurosis, and long ago the genius of Shakespeare depicted it for us with faultless insight.

Extensive studies of the past half century, inspired by Freud, have taught us that a psychoneurosis means a state of mind where the person is unduly, and often painfully, driven or thwarted by the "unconscious" part of his mind, that buried part that was once the infant's mind and still lives on side by side with the adult mentality that has developed out of it and should have taken its place. It signifies *internal* mental conflict. We have here the reason why it is impossible to discuss intelligently the state of mind of anyone suffering from a psychoneurosis, whether the description is of a living person or an imagined one, without correlating the manifestations with what must have operated in his infancy and is *still operating*. That is what I propose to attempt here.

For some deep-seated reason, which is to him unacceptable, Hamlet is plunged into anguish at the thought of his father being replaced in his mother's affections by someone else. It is as if his devotion to his mother had made him so jealous for her affection that he had found it hard enough to share this even with his father and could not endure to share it with still another man. Against this thought, however, suggestive as it is, may be urged three objections. First, if it were in itself a full statement of the matter, Hamlet would have been aware of the jealousy, whereas we have concluded that the mental process we are seeking is hidden from him. Secondly, we see in it no evidence of the arousing of an old and forgotten memory. And, thirdly, Hamlet is being deprived by Claudius of no greater share in the Queen's affection than he had been by his own father, for the two brothers made exactly similar claims in this respect—namely, those of a loved husband. The last-named objection, however, leads us to the heart of the situation. How if, in fact, Hamlet had in years gone by, as a child, bitterly resented having had to share his mother's affection even with his own father, had regarded him as a rival, and had secretly wished him out of the way so that he might enjoy undisputed and undisturbed the monopoly of that affection? If such thoughts had been present in his mind in childhood days they evidently would have been "repressed", and all traces of them obliterated, by filial piety and other educative influences. The actual realization of his early wish in the death of his father at the hands of a jealous rival would then have stimulated into activity these "repressed" memories, which would have produced, in the form of depression and other suffering, an obscure aftermath of his childhood's conflict. This is at all events the mechanism that is actually found in the real Hamlets who are investigated psychologically.

The explanation, therefore, of the delay and self-frustration exhibited in the endeavour to fulfil his father's demand for vengeance is that to Hamlet the thought of incest and parricide combined is too intolerable to be borne. One part of him tries to carry out the task, the other flinches inexorably from the thought of it. How fain would he blot it out in that "bestial oblivion" which unfortunately for him his conscience contemns. He is torn and tortured in an insoluble inner conflict. (pp. 67-70)

[It] is often overlooked that childhood (roughly speaking, between the ages of three and twelve) is preceded by another period, that of infancy, which is vastly more fateful for the future than anything that happens in childhood. The congeries of emotions, phantasies, and impulses, forgotten or never even conscious, that occupy the dawning mind was only made accessible to our knowledge when Freud devised his psychoanalytic method for penetrating to the unconscious mental layers. . . . The main discoveries here may be summed up in the statement that, side by side with loving attitudes and peaceful contentment, there are always to be found mental processes reminiscent of the most primitive aspects of savage life of an intensity that is only faintly mirrored later on by the distressing aspects of our international relations, including even the tortures and other atrocities. Violent and ruthless impulses of destruction (i.e. murder in adult language) follow on the inevitable minor privations of this period. The jealousies, hatreds, and murderous impulses of which signs may be detected in childhood are, in fact, the weakened derivatives of a very sinister inheritance we bring to the world and which somehow has to be worked through and chastened in the painful conflicts and emotions of infancy. (pp. 74-5)

Of the infantile jealousies the most important, and the one with which we are here occupied, is that experienced by a boy towards his father. The precise form of early relationship between child and father is in general a matter of vast importance in both sexes and plays a predominating part in the future development of the child's character. . . . The only aspect that at present concerns us is the resentment felt by a boy towards his father when the latter disturbs, as he necessarily must, his enjoyment of his mother's exclusive affection. This feeling is the deepest source of the world-old conflict between father and son, between the younger and the older generation, the favourite theme of so many poets and writers, the central *motif* of most mythologies and religions. (pp. 75-6)

It was Freud who first demonstrated, when dealing with the subject of the earliest manifestations of the sexual instinct in children, that the conflict in question rests in the last resort on sexual grounds. (p. 76)

The complete expression of the "repressed" wish is not only that the father should die, but that the son should then espouse the mother. . . . The attitude of son to parents is so transpicuously illustrated in the Oedipus legend, as developed for instance in Sophocles' tragedy, that the group of mental processes in question is generally known under the name of the "Oedipus-complex".

We are now in a position to expand and complete the suggestions offered above in connection with the Hamlet problem. The story thus interpreted would run somewhat as follows.

As a child Hamlet had experienced the warmest affection for his mother, and this, as is always so, had contained elements of a disguised erotic quality, still more so in infancy. The presence of two traits in the Queen's character accord with this assumption, namely her markedly sensual nature and her passionate fondness for her son. . . . Nevertheless Hamlet appears to have with more or less success weaned himself from her and to have fallen in love with Ophelia. The precise nature of his original feeling for Ophelia is a little obscure. We may assume that at least in part it was composed of a normal love for a prospective bride, though the extravagance of the language used (the passionate need for absolute certainty, etc.) suggests a somewhat morbid frame of mind. There are indications that even here the influence of the old attraction for the mother is still exerting itself. Although some writers, following Goethe [see excerpt above, 1795], see in Ophelia many traits of resemblance to the Queen, perhaps just as striking are the traits contrasting with those of the Queen. . . . Her naïve piety, her obedient resignation, and her unreflecting simplicity sharply contrast with the Queen's character, and seem to indicate that

Hamlet by a characteristic reaction towards the opposite extreme had unknowingly been impelled to choose a woman who should least remind him of his mother. A case might even be made out for the view that part of his courtship originated not so much in direct attraction for Ophelia as in an unconscious desire to play her off against his mother, just as a disappointed and piqued lover so often has resort to the arms of a more willing rival. It would not be easy otherwise to understand the readiness with which he later throws himself into this part. When, for instance, in the play scene he replies to his mother's request to sit by her with the words "No, good mother, here's metal more attractive" and proceeds to lie at Ophelia's feet, we seem to have a direct indication of this attitude; and his coarse familiarity and bandying of ambiguous jests with the woman he has recently so ruthlessly jilted are hardly intelligible unless we bear in mind that they were carried out under the heedful gaze of the Queen. It is as if his unconscious were trying to convey to her the following thought: "You give yourself to other men whom you prefer to me. Let me assure you that I can dispense with your favours and even prefer those of a woman whom I no longer love." His extraordinary outburst of bawdiness on this occasion, so unexpected in a man of obviously fine feeling, points unequivocally to the sexual nature of the underlying turmoil.

Now comes the father's death and the mother's second marriage. The association of the idea of sexuality with his mother, buried since infancy, can no longer be concealed from his consciousness. . . . Feelings which once, in the infancy of long ago, were pleasurable desires can now, because of his repressions, only fill him with repulsion. The long "repressed" desire to take his father's place in his mother's affection is stimulated to unconscious activity by the sight of someone usurping this place exactly as he himself had once longed to do. More,

Act III. Scene ii. Horatio, Ophelia, Hamlet, the Players, Polonius, Gertrude, Claudius, members of the court. By D. Maclise (n.d.). From the Art Collection of the Folger Shakespeare Library.

this someone was a member of the same family, so that the actual usurpation further resembled the imaginary one in being incestuous. Without his being in the least aware of it these ancient desires are ringing in his mind, are once more struggling to find conscious expression, and need such an expenditure of energy again to ''repress'' them that he is reduced to the deplorable mental state he himself so vividly depicts.

There follows the Ghost's announcement that the father's death was a willed one, was due to murder. Hamlet, having at the moment his mind filled with natural indignation at the news, answers normally enough with the cry (Act I, Sc. 5):

> Haste me to know 't, that I with wings as swift
> As meditation or the thoughts of love,
> May sweep to my revenge.   [I. v. 29-31]

The momentous words follow revealing who was the guilty person, namely a relative who had committed the deed at the bidding of lust. Hamlet's second guilty wish had thus also been realized by his uncle, namely to procure the fulfilment of the first—the possession of the mother—by a personal deed, in fact by murder of the father. The two recent events, the father's death and the mother's second marriage, seemed to the world to have no inner causal relation to each other, but they represented ideas which in Hamlet's unconscious fantasy had always been closely associated. These ideas now in a moment forced their way to conscious recognition in spite of all ''repressing forces'', and found immediate expression in his almost reflex cry: ''O my prophetic soul! My uncle?''. The frightful truth his unconscious had already intuitively divined, his consciousness had now to assimilate as best it could. For the rest of the interview Hamlet is stunned by the effect of the internal conflict thus re-awakened, which from now on never ceases, and into the essential nature of which he never penetrates. (pp. 79-83)

In the first place, there is a complex reaction in regard to his mother. As was explained above, the being forced to connect the thought of his mother with sensuality leads to an intense sexual revulsion, one that is only temporarily broken down by the coarse outburst discussed above. Combined with this is a fierce jealousy, unconscious because of its forbidden origin, at the sight of her giving herself to another man, a man whom he had no reason whatever either to love or to respect. Consciously this is allowed to express itself, for instance after the prayer scene, only in the form of extreme resentment and bitter reproaches against her. His resentment against women is still further inflamed by the hypocritical prudishness with which .Ophelia follows her father and brother in seeing evil in his natural affection, an attitude which poisons his love in exactly the same way that the love of his childhood, like that of all children, must have been poisoned. He can forgive a woman neither her rejection of his sexual advances nor, still less, her alliance with another man. Most intolerable of all to him, as Bradley well remarks, is the sight of sensuality in a quarter from which he had trained himself ever since infancy rigorously to exclude it [see excerpt above, 1904]. The total reaction culminates in the bitter misogyny of his outburst against Ophelia, who is devastated at having to bear a reaction so wholly out of proportion to her own offence and has no idea that in reviling her Hamlet is really expressing his bitter resentment against his mother. (p. 84)

The underlying theme relates ultimately to the splitting of the mother image which the infantile unconscious effects into two opposite pictures: one of a virginal Madonna, an inaccessible saint towards whom all sensual approaches are unthinkable, and the other of a sensual creature accessible to everyone. Indications of this dichotomy between love and lust (Titian's Sacred and Profane Love) are to be found later in most men's sexual experiences. When sexual repression is highly pronounced, as with Hamlet, then both types of women are felt to be hostile: the pure one out of resentment at her repulses, the sensual one out of the temptation she offers to plunge into guiltiness. Misogyny, as in the play, is the inevitable result. (p. 86)

Hamlet's attitude towards his uncle-father is far more complex than is generally supposed. He of course detests him, but it is the jealous detestation of one evil-doer towards his successful fellow. Much as he hates him, he can never denounce him with the ardent indignation that boils straight from his blood when he reproaches his mother, for the more vigorously he denounces his uncle the more powerfully does he stimulate to activity his own unconscious and ''repressed'' complexes. He is therefore in a dilemma between on the one hand allowing his natural detestation of his uncle to have free play, a consummation which would stir still further his own horrible wishes, and on the other hand ignoring the imperative call for the vengeance that his obvious duty demands. His own ''evil'' prevents him from completely denouncing his uncle's, and in continuing to ''repress'' the former he must strive to ignore, to condone, and if possible even to forget the latter; *his moral fate is bound up with his uncle's for good or ill.* In reality his uncle incorporates the deepest and most buried part of his own personality, so that he cannot kill him without also killing himself. This solution, one closely akin to what Freud has shown to be the motive of suicide in melancholia, is actually the one that Hamlet finally adopts. The course of alternate action and inaction that he embarks on, and the provocations he gives to his suspicious uncle, can lead to no other end than to his own ruin and, incidentally, to that of his uncle. Only when he has made the final sacrifice and brought himself to the door of death is he free to fulfil his duty, to avenge his father, and to slay his other self—his uncle. (p. 88)

The call of duty to kill his stepfather cannot be obeyed because it links itself with the unconscious call of his nature to kill his mother's husband, whether this is the first or the second; the absolute ''repression'' of the former impulse involves the inner prohibition of the latter also. It is no chance that Hamlet says of himself that he is prompted to his revenge ''by heaven and hell''.

In this discussion of the motives that move or restrain Hamlet we have purposely depreciated the subsidiary ones—such as his exclusion from the throne where Claudius has blocked the normal solution of the Oedipus complex (to succeed the father in due course)—which also play a part, so as to bring out in greater relief the deeper and effective ones that are of preponderating importance. These, as we have seen, spring from sources of which he is quite unaware, and we might summarize the internal conflict of which he is the victim as consisting in a struggle of the ''repressed'' mental processes to become conscious. The call of duty, which automatically arouses to activity these unconscious processes, conflicts with the necessity of ''repressing'' them still more strongly; for the more urgent is the need for external action the greater is the effort demanded of the ''repressing'' forces. It is his moral duty, to which his father exhorts him, to put an end to the incestuous activities of his mother (by killing Claudius), but his unconscious does not want to put an end to them (he being identified with Claudius in the situation), and so he cannot. His lashings of self-reproach and remorse are ultimately because of this very failure, i.e. the refusal of his guilty wishes to undo the sin. By refusing to abandon his own incestuous wishes he perpetuates the sin and so must endure the stings of torturing conscience. And yet killing his mother's husband would be equivalent to committing the original sin himself, which would if anything be even more guilty. So of the two impossible alternatives he adopts the passive solution of letting the incest continue vicariously, but at the same time provoking destruction at the King's hand. Was ever a tragic figure so torn and tortured!

Action is paralysed at its very inception, and there is thus produced the picture of apparently causeless inhibition which is so inexplicable both to Hamlet and to readers of the play. This paralysis arises, however, not from physical or moral cowardice, but from that intellectual cowardice, that reluctance to dare the exploration of his inmost soul, which Hamlet shares with the rest of the human race. "Thus conscience does make cowards of us all." (pp. 90-1)

Ernest Jones, "The Psycho-Analytical Solution" and "Tragedy and the Mind of the Infant," in his Hamlet and Oedipus, *W. W. Norton & Company, Inc., 1949, Victor Gollancz, Ltd, 1949, pp. 45-70, 71-91.*

FRANCIS FERGUSSON (essay date 1949)

[*Fergusson traces* Hamlet *to its dramatic sources in the ritual drama of Greece, the Middle Ages, and early rituals. In discussing Greek drama, he makes use of Aristotle's "notion of analogous action," pointing out that in* Hamlet *the prince's story is interwoven with the story of Denmark. T. S. Eliot (1919), contends Fergusson, fails to discern unity in the play because he deals with the character without reference to his society or to the action around him. Fergusson's approach is similar to that of Gilbert Murray (1914) and H.D.F. Kitto (1956) in its focus on the mythic origins of the play, and to that of G. Wilson Knight (1930) in its thematic concerns.*]

Through *Hamlet* was written long before *Bérénice*, or *Tristan*, modern readers are more at ease with it than with either of the others. We may admire the masterpiece of Racine, or be genuinely "sunk" by *Tristan*, but compared with *Hamlet* they are artificial, limited, and arbitrary. Shakespeare's mysterious play has, even in our day, a directness and an intimacy which the others lack.

That is because *Hamlet* was formed in a Theater which was close to the root of drama itself—that art which is both more primitive and more subtle than Philosophy. Since the destruction of the great "mirror" of the Elizabethan theater, it has been necessary to restore or invent the theater; and modern drama has been a succession of more limited *genres*, based upon more limited postulates about human life, like Racine's "action as rational," or Wagner's "action as passion." These sharp perspectives may seem to their own times to reveal the essence of life but to the next generation they may appear partial or even depraved. But *Hamlet*, like *Oedipus* and the *Purgatorio*, can take myth and ritual as still alive. Its imitation of human action "undercuts" or precedes all theory. If it is "the" modern play, it is also very ancient, the heir of the great tradition in its completeness. Thus it is necessary to examine *Hamlet* (mysterious though it is) in order to complete the study of the idea of a theater in our tradition.

This view of *Hamlet* has been emerging slowly since the end of the eighteenth century. Every generation has regarded it in the light of its own taste which was formed by the then regnant form of drama. The critics have been fascinated with it, but they have made it over in their own image: as Hamlet himself tells Ophelia, "the power of beauty will sooner transform honesty from what it is to a bawd than the force of honesty can translate beauty into his likeness: this was sometime a paradox, but now the time gives it proof." The beauty of *Hamlet*, its endless suggestiveness, the iridescent play of the analogical relationships within it, will no doubt continue to seduce, and then show up its well-intentioned lovers. (pp. 98-9)

Robertson's essay on *Hamlet* [see Additional Bibliography] together with Mr. Eliot's essay, which was apparently inspired by a reading of Robertson, may be taken as typical of the objections which many critics make to the play: they cannot find that it has any unity, or intellectual consistency, as a whole. Thus Robertson, while he admits that it makes superb entertainment and that it is full of brilliant characterization and passages of wonderful poetry, reports that it leaves the critical intellect unsatisfied. He suggests that Shakespeare may have intended nothing more than an entertainment and never bothered about the deeper unity or wider meaning of the whole. . . . (p. 99)

Robertson, and after him Mr. Eliot, seek in *Hamlet* conceptual truth, and do not find it. They wish to be able to reduce *Hamlet* to terms which the reason can accept; and, in the attempt to satisfy this demand, they make an interpretation of the play which certainly makes it appear confused, formless, and, in short, a failure. "Mr. Robertson is undoubtedly correct." Mr. Eliot writes, "in concluding that the essential emotion of the play is the feeling of a son toward a guilty mother." He then shows that there are many elements and several entire scenes in the play which have nothing to do with the feeling of a son toward a guilty mother. He shows that on this interpretation, Hamlet himself is incomprehensible. . . . (p. 100)

The view that "the essential emotion of the play is the feeling of a son toward a guilty mother" is a drastic reduction of the play as Shakespeare wrote it. Hamlet's feeling toward his guilty mother is certainly essential, but not more essential than his dismay at the loss of a father. . . . Mr. Dover Wilson offers an explanation of Hamlet's feeling which is perhaps . . . more fruitful: Hamlet has lost a throne, and he has lost thereby a social, publicly acceptable *persona*: a local habitation and a name [see excerpt above, 1935]. It is for this reason that he haunts the stage like the dispossessed of classical drama: like an Electra, who has lost the traditional life which was her due as daughter, wife, and mother—or even like the ghost of Polyneikes, who cannot rest because the ritual order of society which might have provided such a place has been destroyed. And Mr. Wilson assures us that an Elizabethan audience (more or less aware of such implications as these) would have accepted the loss of the throne as sufficient explanation for Hamlet's dismay. (pp. 100-01)

[One] of the chief objections to the type of criticism which Mr. Eliot brings to bear, is that it does not distinguish clearly between the story of Hamlet the individual and the story of the play as a whole. He objects to the criticism of Hamlet abstracted from the work in which he appears; but his own essay deals with "Hamlet without the Prince of Denmark"—i.e., the character without reference to the society in which he endeavors to realize himself. Hence he cannot understand the relevance of the minor characters, nor the significance of certain scenes which do not bear directly upon Hamlet's individual fate.

"There are unexplained scenes," he writes, "the Polonius-Laertes and the Polonius-Reynaldo scene—for which there is little excuse." There is no explanation and no excuse for them if Shakespeare was merely trying to convey the feeling of a son toward a guilty mother. If he was also picturing the relation of a son to his father, then the whole Polonius-Laertes-Reynaldo sequence makes sense as a comic-pathetic sub-plot, with many ironic parallels to the story of Hamlet and his father's Ghost. If to this we add Mr. Dover Wilson's suggestions, we see that the welfare of Denmark—the traditional order of society, with its father-king upon whom depend "the lives of many"—is the matter of the play as a whole, rather than Hamlet's individual plight. In the welfare of Denmark, Polonius, Laertes and Reynaldo have a stake also. The postulate upon which the entire action is based (from the first scene on the parapet, with the soldiers peering through the darkness to discern what danger may threaten the body politic) is that "the times are out of joint." It is Hamlet's misfortune that, as Prince, and as a man of profound insight, he especially should have been "born to set them right." (pp. 101-02)

It has been well established by now that the Elizabethan "double plot," at its best, is more than a device for resting the audience. The comic sequences which are woven through the tragedies are not to be dismissed as mere "comic relief," or as punctuation for the main story, like the music that Corneille used between the acts. In Shakespeare, and in the best of his contemporaries, the minor plots are essential parts of the whole composition. This much is, I think, generally recognized. But there is little agreement about the nature of these relationships: we lack a generally accepted critical vocabulary for describing them.

Thus Moulton, in his *Shakespeare the Dramatic Artist,* studied the plots themselves as intelligible chains of events, and showed (for *Lear* and *The Merchant of Venice,* for example) that the various narrative strands depend causally upon each other; that their climaxes, coming together, reinforce each other; and that their denouements are interdependent. . . . Mr. William Empson, in his extremely illuminating study, *Some Versions of Pastoral,* is interested, not in the logical concatenation of the stories, but in the ironic parallels between them: the tragi-comic parallel between the motivations of love and war, as in *Troilus and Cressida;* between the lives of "clowns" and the lives of "heroes" in the whole tradition of British drama to the middle of the eighteenth century.

Henry James's technical concept of the "reflector" is akin to the notion of the double plot as Mr. Empson explains it. The "occasions," or the more or less peripheral intelligences which James used to mirror his action, serve to reveal it from various (ironically different) angles. Neither the author nor the protagonist is to be allowed to break down and "tell all": that would not be truly dramatic; it would not be "objective" in the realist scene. The situation, the moral and metaphysical "scene" of the drama, is presented only as one character after another sees and reflects it; and the action of the drama as a whole is presented only as each character in turn actualizes it in his story and according to his lights. This is as much as to say that the various stories with their diverse casts of characters are analogous, and that the drama as a whole is therefore "one by analogy" only. It does not have the literal and rational unity of the single logically and causally connected chain of events or story. And if we are to grasp a novel of Henry James or a

play by Shakespeare, we must be prepared to follow these shifting perspectives, as we move from character to character and from story to story, trying, as we go, to divine the supreme analogue, the underlying theme, to which they all point in their various ways.

This "supreme analogue" or "underlying theme" is the main action of the play, as Aristotle explains in a neglected passage of the *Poetics.* Aristotle knew plays with a double plot-thread, one of which issues "happily," the other tragically; and he did not like them—they are "less perfect," he says, than pure tragedy; a concession to popular taste. But in his few remarks on the *Odyssey* he comes closer to describing a multiple plot as Shakespeare employed it. The *Odyssey* has neither the literal unity of the one cast of characters, nor the rational unity of the single plot-line. (pp. 103-04)

In considering the structure of *Hamlet,* all of these studies of the properties of the double plot are useful. The stories of the play—the struggle between Hamlet and Claudius; between Hamlet, Polonius and Laertes; between Fortinbras and Claudius' regime—are tightly woven together, causally and logically interdependent, in the manner Moulton demonstrates for *The Merchant of Venice.* At the same time the various stories are presented as ironically parallel in the ways Mr. Empson describes. Polonius, for instance, plays the "clown" to Hamlet's "hero," to use Mr. Empson's words; at the same time Hamlet frequently feels himself in the role of clown in relation to Fortinbras and even Laertes. Or, taking Henry James's phrase, you may put it that we are continually shifting from reflector to reflector throughout the play. . . . The action is illumined from so many angles that we have an embarrassment of riches; the problem is not to demonstrate that the play moves in ironic parallels but rather to show that they add up to something— are intended to convey (with however rich a profusion) an underlying unity of theme. For this purpose Aristotle's notion of analogous actions is the most useful.

The main action of Hamlet may be described as the attempt to find and destroy the hidden "imposthume" which is poisoning the life of Claudius' Denmark. All of the characters— from Polonius with his "windlasses" and "assays of bias," to Hamlet with his parables and symbolic shows—realize this action, in comic, or evil, or inspired ways. (p. 105)

If one could see a performance of *Hamlet,* uncut, unbroken by intermissions, and employing the kind of simple make-believe which Shakespeare, with his bare stage, must have intended, we should find much to enthrall us besides the stories themselves. The stories, of course, start at once, and are felt continuously as working themselves out: fate, behind the scenes, makes, from time to time, its sudden pronouncements. But onstage, the music and the drums and the marching of royal and military pageantry, are directly absorbing, and they assure us that something of great and general significance is going on. From time to time the stage is emptied; the pageantry is gone; the stories seem to be marking time—and Hamlet emerges, alone, or with one or two interlocutors. Sometimes he suffers his visions before us; sometimes he makes jokes and topical allusions; sometimes he spars with his interlocutors like the gag-man in a minstrel show, or the master of ceremonies in a modern musical. (pp. 112-13)

Both the ritual and the improvisational elements in *Hamlet* are essential—as essential as the stories—in the structure of the whole. The Elizabethan theater, at once as frankly "theatrical" as vaudeville, and as central to the life of its time as an ancient rite, offered Shakespeare two resources, two theatrical "dimensions" which the modern naturalistic tradition of serious drama must try, or pretend, to do without. (pp. 113-14)

If one thinks over the succession of ritual scenes as they appear in the play, it is clear that they serve to focus attention on the Danish body politic and its hidden malady: they are ceremonious invocations of the well-being of society, and secular or religious devices for securing it. As the play progresses, the rituals change in character, from the dim but honest changing of the guard, through Ophelia's mock rites, to the black mass of Claudius' last court. And it appears that the improvisational scenes bear a significant and developing relationship to the rituals. In general, they throw doubt upon the efficacy of the official magic, as when Hamlet refuses to take Claudius' first court at its face value; yet even the most cutting ironies of Hamlet do not disavow the mystery which the rituals celebrate, or reject the purposes that inform them.

The rituals, the stories, and the improvisations together make the peculiar rhythm of *Hamlet* as a performance. Denmark is shown as waiting, as it were, in the darkness of its ineffective ceremonies and hollow communal prayers while the infection, "mining all within," divides every man in secret from every other and bursts forth, from time to time, in savage but brief and ineffective fights. (p. 114)

The main evidence (apart from the play itself) for taking *Hamlet* as a species of ritual drama, is provided by recent studies which show that a great deal of the religious culture of the Middle Ages was still alive in Shakespeare's time. Tilyard's *The Elizabethan World Picture,* for example, makes this clear. Mr. Tilyard quotes Hamlet's famous speech on man: "What a piece of work is a man". . . . "This has been taken," Mr. Tilyard explains, "as one of the great English versions of Renaissance humanism, an assertion of the dignity of man against the asceticism of medieval misanthropy. Actually it is in the purest medieval tradition: Shakespeare's version of the orthodox encomia of what man, created in God's image, was like in his prelapsarian state and of what ideally he is still capable of being. It also shows Shakespeare placing man in the traditional cosmic setting between the angels and the beasts. It is what the theologians had been saying for centuries." (pp. 114, 116)

The Elizabethan stage itself, that central mirror of life of its times, was a symbolic representation of this traditional cosmos: it was thus taken both as the physical and as the metaphysical "scene" of man's life. Mr. Kernodle has shown this in detail in his illuminating study, *From Art to Theater.* He traces the genealogy of the symbolic façade of the Elizabethan stage house back through street pageantry to painting and to the architecture of tombs and altars; and thence to the arcade screen of the Greek tragic theater itself. (p. 116)

The symbolic character of this stage seems to imply a conception of the theater akin to that of ritual: the celebration of the mystery of human life. This stage and its drama did not, it is true, develop directly from the Mass; it developed from the secular theater of the Middle Ages and, as Mr. Kernodle shows, from royal and civic pageantry. But in the Renaissance the monarchy and its rites was taking over some of the religious significance of the church and its rites. The pope tended to be superseded by the prince as vicar, or "type" of Christ, the pageantry and ceremony of the church by the pageantry and ceremony of the national state. . . . The role of the monarch in Shakespeare's time (and in his plays) was thus very close to that of Sophocles' Oedipus or Creon: he was at once ruler,

high priest, and father of the community. And the ceremonies which Shakespeare and Hamlet's Danes engaged in—whether obviously religious, like the funeral, or more secular, like the Court—were taken as celebrating and securing the welfare of the whole, of the monarchy, and of the "lives of many" that depended on it.

The Elizabethan theater may thus be regarded as the heir of the Greek tragic theater with its ritual basis. The Elizabethan cosmos is still that of the great tradition, which the Middle Ages inherited from the city state. (pp. 116-17)

If Shakespeare's theater is thus akin to the theater of Sophocles, their drama should be composed on similar principles: appealing in both cases to ancient and publicly accepted values and modes of understanding, rather than preaching, inventing, and arguing in the manner of modern drama. And the comparison should throw some light on both.

The themes of *Oedipus* are, from many points of view, strikingly similar to those of *Hamlet.* Oedipus gave his name to that "complex" to which . . . Ernest Jones reduces *Hamlet* [see excerpt above, 1949]. Whatever one may think of this reduction, it is clear that in both plays a royal sufferer is associated with pollution, in its very sources, of an entire social order. Both plays open with an invocation of the well-being of the endangered body politic. In both, the destiny of the individual and of society are closely intertwined; and in both the suffering of the royal victim seems to be necessary before purgation and renewal can be achieved.

But my purpose here is not to attempt an extended comparison of the two plays; it is, rather, to contrast the structural principles of these two ritual dramas, one from the beginnings of the tradition, the other from the end, at the very brink of the modern world.

The extraordinary unity and clarity of *Oedipus,* in comparison with *Hamlet,* is perhaps due to the fact that it is closer to the form, purpose, and occasion (the Festival of Dionysos) of its ritual source than *Hamlet,* in the Globe Theater, is to its ritual sources. Oedipus is the one and obvious protagonist, his story the literal subject of the play. He is the diagrammatic royal scapegoat, a marked man, from the first. And the parts of the play, which show the stages of his destruction, correspond very closely to the stages of the ancient ritual sacrifice.

In *Hamlet* it is as though every one of these elements had been elaborated by a process of critical analysis. Hamlet himself, though a prince, is without a throne; though a sufferer for the truth, he can appear in public as a mere infatuated or whimsical youth. We have seen how many ironic parallels Shakespeare provides to his story—and to this I may add that it takes both Hamlet and Claudius to represent the royal victim of the tradition. Though the play has the general shape of the tragic rhythm, and the traditional parts of the plot, each part is presented in several ironically analogous versions. (pp. 117-19)

Even the ritual process itself is, in *Hamlet,* directly dramatized: i.e., presented in a tragic, ironic light. There are no rituals in *Oedipus:* Oedipus is a ritual. But Hamlet has an extremely modern and skeptical, a Pirandellesque, theatricality as well; Shakespeare plays with the basis of his own make-believe. Sophocles uses the tragic theater with its ritual basis to mirror human life directly. Shakespeare uses the Elizabethan theater in the same way; but at the same time he has another mirror—his own and Hamlet's supermodern awareness—in which the making of the ritual is itself ironically reflected. (p. 119)

Shakespeare's theater, because of its ancient roots and its central place in society, permitted the development of ritual drama—or at least a drama which had this dimension as well as others. In the structure of *Hamlet* the rituals, as distinguished from the plots, serve to present the main action at various points in its development. . . .

[The] social rite or occasion is taken as a thing by itself; it enables the author to assemble his dramatis personae in a wider light than any of their individual intelligences could provide. . . .

[The players' scene] has a ritual aspect, it is Hamlet's most ambitious improvisation, and it is the climax and peripety of the whole complex plot-scheme. If one can understand this scene, one will be close to grasping Shakespeare's sense of the theater, and his direct, profoundly histrionic dramaturgy. (p. 120)

First of all the play presents the hidden crime (the murder of a king and the more or less incestuous theft of his queen and his throne) upon which, as in *Oedipus,* all the threads of the interwoven plots depend. It is the presentation of this literal fact which has the immediate effect upon the innocent bystanders of the court and upon the innocent groundlings in the audience, though in Hamlet's violent view none are innocent. Because the security of the regime and the purposes of its supporters depend either upon ignorance or concealment, the public representation of the crime is itself an act of aggression, Hamlet's attack, the turning point in the story. This attack reaches the guilty Claudius first, Gertrude second, Polonius third; then Laertes and Ophelia. And at length it clears the way for Fortinbras, the new faith and the new regime.

But though the fact of murder, incest, and usurpation is clearly presented, the time of the murder—is it still to come?—is vague; and the dramatis personae in the playlet are shifted about in such a way as to leave the identity of the criminal in question, and so to spread the guilt. The actual crime was that of Claudius; but in the play the guilty one is nephew to the King. This could mean (as Polonius and Gertrude seem to think) a direct threat by Hamlet to Claudius. . . . Neither Hamlet nor Shakespeare seem to rule out a Freudian interpretation of the tangle; Hamlet comes close to representing himself as the diagrammatic son of the Oedipus complex, killing the father and possessing the mother. Yet his awareness of such motivations lifts the problems from the level of pathology to that of drama; he sees himself, Claudius, Denmark, the race itself, as subject to greeds and lusts which the hypocritical façade of the regime guiltily conceals.

Thus the literal meaning of the playlet is the fact of the crime; but the trope and the anagoge convey a picture of the human in general as weak, guilty, and foolish: the deepest and most sinister version of the malady of Claudius' regime in Denmark. This picture should emerge directly from the staging of the playlet before the corrupt and hypocritical court, under the inspired and triumphant irony of the regisseur-prince. The whining of pipes, the parade of mummers, the wooden gestures of the dumb-show, the tinkle of the rhymes, should have the magical solemnity of a play-party or children's singing-game ("London bridge is falling down"). Yet because of the crimes represented, this atmosphere is felt as unbearably weak and frivolous, a parody of all solemn rites. (pp. 122-23)

Hamlet's audience on-stage (and perhaps off-stage as well) misses the deeper meanings of his play. Yet he and his author have put it as simply as possible in the weary couplets of the Player-King. The Player-King seems to stand for Hamlet's father, and thus for the Ghost; and he speaks in fact with the clarity but helplessness (in this world) of the dead—addressing the frivolous Player-Queen without much hope of understanding. Since he is Hamlet's puppet, he speaks also for Hamlet, and since he is the King, he stands also for Claudius. Claudius, in the course of the play, will gradually acquire a helplessness like that of the Ghost; a faithlessness and an indecision like that of Hamlet. It is the function of the Player-King to state as directly as possible that gloomy and fatalistic sense of human action which is the subject of the play, and which all the various characters have by analogy. (p. 124)

[The] Player-King presents very pithily the basic vision of human action in the play, at a level so deep that it applies to all the characters: the guilty, the free, the principals, the bystanders, those in power and the dispossessed. This vision of course comes directly from the crime of Claudius and the other "accidental judgements, casual slaughters, purposes mistook" (as Horatio describes them when summing up for Fortinbras) upon which the complicated plot depends; yet this generalized vision is more terrible than any of the particular crimes, and much more important for understanding Hamlet's motivation. (p. 126)

Though Hamlet accepts [the traditional ordered universe], he does not know where he belongs in it; he is not even sure which way is up. He would have felt the force of that remark of Heracleitus which Eliot uses as epigraph to *Burnt Norton:* "The way up and the way down are one and the same." His intellect plays over the world of the religious tradition with an all-dissolving irony like that of Montaigne in the *Apologie de Raimond Sebonde:* a truly double-edged irony, for he can neither do with nor do without the ancient moral and cosmic order. (p. 129)

[By Act V, Hamlet] feels the poetic rightness of his own death. One could say, with Ernest Jones, that because of his Oedipus complex he had a death-wish all along. Or one could say that his death was the only adequate expiation for the evil of Denmark, according to the ancient emotional logic of the scapegoat; or one could say that only by accepting death to prove it could the truth of his vision be properly affirmed.

However one may interpret it, when his death comes it "feels right," the only possible end for the play. Horatio makes music for his going-off like that which accompanies Oedipus' death at Colonnus: "Good night, sweet prince, and flights of angels sing thee to thy rest." And Fortinbras treats him like one of those honor-seekers that had puzzled him all along, as though in his career the hero had somehow been subsumed in the martyr: "Let four captains bear Hamlet, like a soldier, to the stage." We are certainly intended to feel that Hamlet, however darkly and uncertainly he worked, had discerned the way to be obedient to his deepest values, and accomplished some sort of purgatorial progress for himself and Denmark. (pp. 131-33)

[The] role of Fortinbras, in *Hamlet,* corresponds to those of Malcolm, Macduff, and King [Duncan] in *Macbeth.* Like them, he is felt as a constant, though off-stage, threat to the corrupt regime. Like them, he does not appear in the flesh until after the peripety and, though we feel his approach, does not enter Denmark until Claudius is gone. Like Malcolm and Macduff, he has his own version of the main action of the play. He moves and fights in the dark as much as his contemporaries, Hamlet and Laertes; but his darkness is not the artificial shadow of Claudius but the natural darkness of inexperience. He confronts it with a kind of sanguine natural faith, "exposing all that's mortal and unsure even for an eggshell"—as he could not (Laertes' example is there to prove it) in Denmark. That is why he cannot enter Denmark until the end. . . . [When] Fortinbras comes in at the end, he places the action we have seen in Denmark, both with reference to the wider world from which he comes, and with reference to his healthier version of "the fight in the dark," the "quest for the unseen danger." Fortinbras' darkness of natural faith is the last variation, this time in a major key, which Shakespeare plays upon his great theme.

This does not mean that Fortinbras, either in his character or in his vision, provides an answer to Hamlet's "problem"— nor does it mean that his example is intended to show that the experience of the play was simply illusory. This experience was "real," just as Dante's experience of Hell was real. . . . Hamlet sees a great deal that Fortinbras will never see; but Hamlet, who has his own limited being, is defined by it, and by the spiritual realm in which he moves; and this is not all of life. Fortinbras does not destroy, he "places" the action of the play by suddenly revealing a new analogue of this action. The effect, once more, is not to provide us with an intellectual key, an explicit philosophy, but to release us from the contemplation of the limited mystery of Denmark by returning us to the wider mystery of life in the world at large.

Thus it seems to me that the elements of Shakespeare's composition (like those of Sophocles and Dante before him) are not qualities, like those of the romantics with their logic of feeling, not abstract concepts, like those of the dramatists of the Age of Reason, with their clear and distinct moral ideas, but beings, real people in a real world, related to each other in a vast and intricate web of analogies. (pp. 139-40)

[The] anagoge, or ultimate meaning of the play, can only be sought through a study of the analogical relationships within the play and between the world of Denmark and the traditional cosmos. There are the analogous actions of all the characters, pointing to the action which is the underlying substance of the play. There are the analogous father-son relationships, and the analogous man-woman relationships. There are the analogous stories, or chains of events, the fated results of the characters' actions. And stretching beyond the play in all directions are the analogies between Denmark and England; Denmark and Rome under "the mightiest Julius"; Hamlet's stage and Shakespeare's stage; the theater and life. Because Shakespeare takes all these elements as "real," he can respect their essential mystery, not replacing them with abstractions, nor merely exploiting their qualities as mood-makers, nor confining us in an artificial world with no exit. He asks us to sense the unity of his play through the direct perception of these analogies; he does not ask us to replace our sense of a real and mysterious world with a consistent artifact, "the world of the play."

If Shakespeare's Hamlet is realist in the tradition represented by Sophocles and Dante, if he composes by analogy rather than by "qualitative progress" or "syllogistic progression," then the question of *Hamlet* as an artistic success appears in a different light. Because it is rooted in an ancient tradition, and in a theater central to its culture, it is not only a work of art, but a kind of more-than-individual natural growth, like the culture itself, and Shakespeare is not so much its inventor as its god-like recorder. . . . (pp. 140-41)

The age of Shakespeare "moved toward chaos," and the great mirror of his theater was broken into fragments. But it lasted

long enough to give us the last image of western man in the light of his great tradition. (p. 142)

> *Francis Fergusson, "'Hamlet, Prince of Denmark':*
> *The Analogy of Action," in his* The Idea of a Theater:
> A Study of Ten Plays; The Art of Drama in Changing
> Perspective, *Princeton University Press, 1949, pp.*
> *98-142.*

WOLFGANG H. CLEMEN (essay date 1951)

[*Clemen's analysis of* Hamlet *deals with the patterns of imagery which unify the play and thus recalls the comments of G. Wilson Knight (1930) and Caroline F. E. Spurgeon (1935). Like Knight and Spurgeon, Clemen notes the preponderance of disease imagery in the play, particularly in the language of the prince. He finds the source of this imagery in the ghost's description of his death by poisoning in Act I. For Clemen, this image becomes a leitmotif as the "corruption of land and people throughout Denmark is understood as an imperceptible and irresistible process of poisoning." For further commentary on imagery and language in Hamlet, see Samuel Taylor Coleridge (1813), Maynard Mack (1952), Harry Levin (1959), T. McAlindon (1970), Reuben A. Brower (1971), and Inga-Stina Ewbank (1977).*]

Hamlet's way of employing images is unique in Shakespeare's drama. When he begins to speak, the images fairly stream to him without the slightest effort—not as similes or conscious paraphrases, but as immediate and spontaneous visions. Hamlet's imagery shows us that whenever he thinks and speaks, he is at the same time a visionary, a seer, for whom the living things of the world about him embody and symbolize thought. His first monologue may show this; the short space of time which lies between his father's death and his mother's remarriage is to him a series of pictures taken from real life:

> A little month, or ere those shoes were old
> With which she follow'd my poor father's body,Like
> Niobe, all tears: [I. ii. 147-49]
>
> Ere yet the salt of most unrighteous tears
> Had left the flushing in her galled eyes,
>   [I. ii. 154-55]

or a little later, addressed to Horatio:

> the funeral baked meats
> Did coldly furnish forth the marriage tables.
>   [I. ii. 180-81]

These are no poetic similes, but keen observations of reality. Hamlet does not translate the general thought into an image paraphrasing it; on the contrary, he uses the opposite method; he refers the generalization to the events and objects of the reality underlying the thought. This sense of reality finds expression in all the images Hamlet employs. Peculiar to them all is that closeness to reality which is often carried to the point of an unsparing poignancy. They are mostly very concrete and precise, simple and, as to their subject matter, easy to understand; common and ordinary things, things familiar to the man in the street dominate, rather than lofty, strange or rare objects. . . . In contrast to Othello or Lear, for example, who awaken heaven and the elements in their imagery and who lend expression to their mighty passions in images of soaring magnificence, Hamlet prefers to keep his language within the scope of reality, indeed, within the everyday world. It is not spacious scenery and nature which dominate in Hamlet's imagery, but rather trades and callings, objects of daily use, popular games and technical terms; his images are not beautiful, poetic, magnificent, but they always hit their mark, the matter in question, with surprisingly unerring sureness. . . . As his imagery betrays to us, he is rather a man gifted with greater powers of observation than the others. He is capable of scanning reality with a keener eye and of penetrating the veil of semblance even to the very core of things. "I know not seems."

At the same time, Hamlet's imagery reveals the hero's wide educational background, his many-sidedness and the extraordinary range of his experience. That metaphors taken from natural sciences are specially frequent in Hamlet's language again emphasizes his power of observation, his critical objective way of looking at things. But Hamlet is also at home in classical antiquity or Greek mythology, in the terminology of law, he is not only familiar with the theatre and with acting—as everyone knows—but also with the fine arts, with falconry and hunting, with the soldier's trade and strategy, with the courtier's way of life. . . . Hamlet commands so many levels of expression that he can attune his diction as well as his imagery to the situation and to the person to whom he is speaking. (pp. 106-09)

At the same time, this wide range of imagery can, in certain passages, serve to give relief to his conflicting moods, to his being torn between extremes and to the abruptness of his changes of mood. This characteristic which has been particularly emphasized and partly attributed to "melancholy" by L. L. Schücking and John Dover Wilson [see excerpts above, 1937 and 1935], also expresses itself in the sudden change of language and in the juxtaposition of passages which are sharply contrasted in their diction. With no other character in Shakespeare do we find this sharp contrast between images marked by a pensive mood and those which unsparingly use vulgar words and display a frivolous and sarcastic disgust for the world.

Let us consider further how Hamlet's use of imagery reflects his ability to penetrate to the real nature of men and things and his relentless breaking down of the barriers raised by hypocrisy. Many of his images seem in fact designed to unmask men; they are meant to strip them of their fine appearances and to show them up in their true nature. Thus, by means of the simile of fortune's pipe, Hamlet shows Rosencrantz and Guildenstern that he has seen through their intent, and thus he unmasks Rosencrantz when he calls him a "sponge", "that soaks up the king's countenance" [IV. ii. 14-16]. He splits his mother's heart "in twain", because he tells her the truth from which she shrinks and which she conceals from herself. (p. 109)

Hamlet's imagery, which thus calls things by their right names, acquires a peculiar freedom from his feigned madness. Hamlet needs images for his "antic disposition". He would betray himself if he used open, direct language. Hence he must speak ambiguously and cloak his real meaning with quibbles and puns, images and parables. The other characters do not understand him and continue to think he is mad, but the audience can gain an insight into the true situation. Under the protection of that mask of "antic disposition", Hamlet says more shrewd things than all the rest of the courtiers together. So we find the images here in an entirely new rôle, unique in Shakespeare's drama. Only the images of the fool in *King Lear* have a similar function.

Hamlet suffers an injustice when he is accused of merely theoretical and abstract speculation which would lead him away from reality. His thoughts carry further than those of others, because he sees more and deeper than they, not because he

would leave reality unheeded. It is true that his is a nature more prone to thought than to action; but that signifies by no means, as the Hamlet critics would often have us believe, that he is a philosopher and dreamer and no man of the world. When, in the graveyard scene, he holds Yorick's skull in his hand, he sees *more* in it than the others, for whom the skull is merely a lifeless object. . . . The comparisons which spring from [his] faculty of thinking a thing to the end, as it were, derive in fact from a more intense experience of reality.

It is a fundamental tenet of Hamlet criticism that Hamlet's over-developed intellect makes it impossible for him to act. In this connection the following famous passage is generally quoted:

> And thus the native hue of resolution
> Is sicklied o'er with the pale cast of thought,
> And enterprises of great pith and moment
> With this regard their currents turn awry,
> And lose the name of action.—   [III. i. 83-7]

The customary interpretation of this passage, "reflection hinders action", does it an injustice. For Hamlet does not say "reflection hinders action", he simply utters this image. The fact that he does not utter that general maxim, but this image, makes all the difference. For this image is the unique and specific form of expression of the thought underlying it, it cannot be separated from it. . . . Here the image does not serve the purpose of merely casting a decorative cloak about the thought; it is much rather an intrinsic part of the thought.

"Reflection hinders action"—this phrase carries in it something absolute, something damning. We sense a moralizing undertone. Action and reflection are thus conceived of as two mutually inimical abstract principles. But not so in Shakespeare's metaphorical language. "Native hue of resolution" suggests that Shakespeare viewed resolution as an innate human quality, not as a moral virtue to be consciously striven after. (pp. 110-12)

"Reflection hinders action." Polonius, the sententious lover of maxims, could have said this, for a general saying carries no sense of personal obligation; it places a distance between the speaker and what he would say. But just as it is characteristic of Polonius to utter banalities and sententious effusions, so, too, it is characteristic of Hamlet, to express even those things which would have permitted of a generalizing formulation, in a language which bears the stamp of a unique and personal experience.

Hamlet sees this problem under the aspect of a process of the human organism. The original bright colouring of the skin is concealed by an ailment. Thus the relation between thought and action appears not as an opposition between two abstract principles between which a free choice is possible, but as an unavoidable condition of human nature. The image of the leprous ailment emphasizes the malignant, disabling, slowly disintegrating nature of the process. It is by no mere chance that Hamlet employs just this image. Perusing the description which the ghost of Hamlet's father gives of his poisoning by Claudius [I. v. 63-73] one cannot help being struck by the vividness with which the process of poisoning, the malicious spreading of the disease, is portrayed:

> And in the porches of my ears did pour
> The leperous distilment; whose effect
> Holds such an enmity with blood of man
> That swift as quicksilver it courses through
> The natural gates and alleys of the body,

> And with a sudden vigour it doth posset
> And curd, like eager droppings into milk,
> The thin and wholesome blood: so did it mine;
> And a most instant tetter bark'd about,
> Most lazar-like, with vile and loathsome crust,
> All my smooth body.
>
>   (pp. 112-13)

What is later metaphor, is here still reality. The picture of the leprous skin disease, which is here—in the first act—described by Hamlet's father, has buried itself deep in Hamlet's imagination and continues to lead its subterranean existence, as it were, until it reappears in metaphorical form.

As Miss Spurgeon has shown, the idea of an ulcer dominates the imagery, infecting and fatally eating away the whole body; on every occasion repulsive images of sickness make their appearance. It is certain that this imagery is derived from that one real event. Hamlet's father describes in that passage how the poison invades the body during sleep and how the healthy organism is destroyed from within, not having a chance to defend itself against attack. But this now becomes the *leitmotif* of the imagery: the individual occurrence is expanded into a symbol for the central problem of the play. The corruption of land and people throughout Denmark is understood as an imperceptible and irresistible process of poisoning. And, furthermore, this poisoning reappears as a *leitmotif* in the action as well—as a poisoning in the "dumb-show", and finally, as the poisoning of all the major characters in the last act. Thus imagery and action continually play into each other's hands and we see how the term "dramatic imagery" gains a new significance.

The imagery appears to be influenced by yet another event in the action underlying the play: Hamlet feels himself to be sullied by his mother's incest which, according to the conception of the time, she committed in marrying Claudius. For him this is a poisoning idea which finds expression in his language. (pp. 113-14)

The *leitmotif* occasionally appears in a disguised form at a point where it seems to have no real connection with the main issue of the play, for instance, in the following passage:

> So, oft it chances in particular men,
> That for some vicious mole of nature in them,
> As, in their birth—wherein they are not guilty
> Since nature cannot choose his origin—
> By the o'ergrowth of some complexion,
> Oft breaking down the pales and forts of reason,
> Or by some habit, that too much o'er-leavens
> The form of plausive manners, that these men,
> Carrying, I say, the stamp of one defect,
> Being nature's livery, or fortune's star,
> Their virtues else—be they as pure as grace,
> As infinite as man may undergo—
> Shall in the general censure take corruption
> From that particular fault: the dram of eale
> Doth all the noble substance of a doubt
> To his own scandal.
>
>   [I. iv. 23-38]

Hamlet has spoken of the excessive revels and drinking-bouts among his people and has said that this was disparaging to the Danes in the eyes of the other peoples. Then follows this general reflection. The question arises: why does Hamlet speak in such detail of these matters here? For at this point in the play he has as yet heard nothing of his uncle's murderous deed. And still he touches in this speech upon that *leitmotif* of the

whole play; he describes how human nature may be brought to decay through a tiny birth-mark, just as from one "dram of evil" a destructive effect may spread over the whole organism. *O'er-leavens* already points to *sicklied o'er*, and, as in the passage discussed, the notion of the human body is in the background. As in later passages, the balance of the powers in man is the theme here, and "corruption", a basic motif in the whole play, already makes its appearance. This general reflection on gradual and irresistible infection is made in passing, as it were. Thus Shakespeare makes use of every opportunity to suggest the fundamental theme of the play. (pp. 114-15)

The imagery in Shakespeare's tragedies often shows how a number of other images are grouped around the central symbol which express the same idea, but in quite other terms. Several degrees, as it were, of the metaphorical expression of a fundamental idea may be distinguished. Besides images which express a motif with the greatest clarity and emphasis, we find others which utter the thought in a veiled and indirect manner. An examination of the way in which the images are spread over the play, can reveal how subtly Shakespeare modifies and varies according to character and situation.

The most striking images of sickness, which Miss Spurgeon has already listed, make their first appearance, significantly enough, in the second half of the play, and most notably in the scene in which Hamlet seeks to bring his mother to a change of heart. Here the plainness and clarity of the images is meant to awaken the conscience of the Queen; they can scarcely be forceful enough; "let me wring your heart", Hamlet has said at the beginning of the meeting. In the first part of the play the atmosphere of corruption and decay is spread in a more indirect and general way. Hamlet declares in the first and second acts how the world appears to him:

> . . . Ah fie! 'tis an unweeded garden,
> That grows to seed; things rank and gross in nature
> Possess it merely.   [I. ii. 135-39]

The image of weeds, touched upon in the word "unweeded", is related to the imagery of sickness in Shakespeare's work. It appears three times in *Hamlet*. The ghost says to Hamlet:

> And duller shouldst thou be than the fat weed
> That roots itself in ease on Lethe wharf,
>
>   [I. v. 32-3]

In the dialogue with his mother, this image immediately follows upon the image of the ulcer:

> And do not spread the compost on the weeds,
> To make them ranker,   [III. iv. 151-52]

Images of rot, decay and corruption are especially numerous in the long second scene of the second act. There are, for example, Hamlet's remarks on the maggots which the sun breeds in a dead dog [II. ii. 181], on the deep dungeons in the prison Denmark [II. ii. 246], on the strumpet Fortune [II. ii. 236], who reappears in the speech of the first Player [II. ii. 493], his comparison of himself with a whore, a drab and a scullion [II. ii. 585-87].

Seen individually, such images do not seem to be very important. But in their totality they contribute considerably to the tone of the play. (pp. 116-18)

    Wolfgang H. Clemen, "'Hamlet'," in his The Development of Shakespeare's Imagery, *Methuen & Co Ltd, 1951, pp. 106-18.*

D. G. JAMES (essay date 1951)

[*James proposes that Hamlet's is the uncertainty of an intellectual faced with metaphysical and religious as well as ethical decisions. Hamlet's tragedy is not that he thinks too much, but that thinking provides no resolution. He may suffer eternal punishment "for a wrong choice," yet he "does not know; and he knows of no way of knowing" whether this is true. Thus, "Hamlet has for its soul and centre a passionate and deeply reflective concern with the problem of conduct." James proposes that Michel de Montaigne's discussion of Socrates's* Apology, *was a source of Shakespeare's themes in* Hamlet. *For additional commentary on Hamlet's delay, see William Richardson (1774), Samuel Taylor Coleridge (1811, 1813), Hermann Ulrici (1839), Karl Werder (1859-60), Friedrich Nietzsche (1872), George Brandes (1895-96), Sigmund Freud (1900), A. C. Bradley (1905), and H. B. Charlton (1942).*]

Some have seen Hamlet as congenitally indisposed to action: Goethe and Coleridge saw him largely in this way [see excerpts above, 1795 and 1811, 1813]. But in fact, the play forbids this; and Ophelia's description of Hamlet is no doubt intended to suggest to us a difference between the Hamlet we see now and the Hamlet of earlier days. He had been the courtier, the soldier, and the scholar,

> The expectancy and rose of the fair state,
> The glass of fashion, and the mould of form,
> The observed of all observers . . .
>
> [III. i. 152-54]

But now he is quite, quite down. New circumstances have arisen, and in them he is distracted, uncertain of his way, unable to resolve an intolerable state of things; and the play presents this man in this condition, what he does and what happens to him. This indeed is not all it does; but this it does chiefly.

To see Hamlet as merely a perplexed mind, an uncertain intellect, would be grossly to simplify; no play could be enacted out of such abstracted matter. Hamlet is a man of strong passion, if he is also one of weak will; but the weakness of his will and the strength of his feelings, whether of contempt and disgust for Claudius or of admiration for Horatio, are of a piece with his intellectual condition; and if I appear to speak of Hamlet as of some ghostly and bloodless intellectual, it will not be in entire forgetfulness of the rest of him. (p. 37)

Now we have, in the first place, to see Hamlet as a man uncertain of his duty in the circumstances in which he finds himself. Ought he to murder the murderer of his father and the seducer of his mother? That is the question:

> To be, or not to be: that is the question:
> Whether 'tis nobler in the mind to suffer
> The slings and arrows of outrageous fortune,
> Or to take arms against a sea of troubles,
> And by opposing end them? To die,—to sleep . . .
>
> [III. i. 55-9]

I am not unaware that I am plunging into, to say the least, debated territory. But it is better, I think, for me to declare myself at once and make clear where, on this battlefield, I stand and fight. . . . [Dr. Johnson's] interpretation of this soliloquy seems to me incomparably the best yet offered [see excerpt above, 1765]. The thought of the soliloquy is not, at the outset, of suicide at all, but of personal immortality: whether we are to be or not to be, to live or in truth to die; and in the context of this thought, which recurs at the conclusion of the lines I quoted (. . . *and by opposing end them? To die,—to sleep . . .*), Hamlet asks whether it be nobler to suffer the slings of fortune or to take arms against troubles and end them.

Hamlet's mind is moving fast: we may read the 'that is the question' as referring both backwards and forwards; and the two questions, Whether we shall live or die? and, Whether it is nobler to suffer or to take arms against our troubles? are tied up with each other and are in Hamlet's mind quite inseparable. Certainly, the thought of suicide occurs later with the talk of a bare bodkin making a quietus for us; this is one way of taking arms against a sea of troubles; and then Hamlet's thought turns at once, again, to death and a life to come. He had spoken first of taking arms against others with the chance that he be killed; and his mind had passed at once to the thought of what might come in another world than this. Now he speaks of killing himself; and now, again, his mind turns to what would come in another world. . . . We do offence to the speech, or so it seems to me, unless we see Hamlet contemplating first, the killing of others with perhaps, then, his own death, and second, a suicide; both are ways of taking arms against a sea of troubles; and the taking arms in either form is seen against the fearful background of a world to come in which condign punishment may be inflicted by a righteous God. What kind of an eternity will the taking up of arms, whether against others or oneself, bring one? Therefore the overriding question is, Whether 'tis nobler . . .? This we must know; for God, if there be a God, may punish us through eternity for a wrong choice. There is the intrinsic ethical question,—Which is in itself nobler? But Hamlet ties up this question along with the thought of eternal sanctions imposed by God. If there were no after-life it would not matter, or matter less, which line he took; but he cannot here, upon this bank and shoal of time, jump the thought of a life to come. There is, then, an ethical question; there is also a metaphysical and religious question; and to neither does he know the answer. (pp. 38-40)

My own wish is frankly to elevate Hamlet's intellectual distresses to an equality in importance with his emotional state; the strength of the emotional shock he has suffered is equalled by the weakness of his mind in the face of difficult moral and metaphysical issues. Hamlet was, after all, an intellectual. We must bear in mind that Shakespeare was the first to make him a member of a university; and *Hamlet* was acted before the universities of Oxford and Cambridge. . . . But my point is that *Hamlet* is not a tragedy of excessive thought; so far as we are to see the cause of Hamlet's destiny in intellectual terms, it is a tragedy not of excessive thought but of defeated thought. Hamlet does not know; and he knows of no way of knowing. And then comes the line,

> Thus conscience does make cowards of us all;
>
> [III. i. 82]

resolution is sicklied o'er, and enterprise loses the name of action. It is hard to know what it is right to do; and we do not know whether in fact we live after we die, and in a universe in which a moral order asserts itself. No doubt Shakespeare had to be careful how he expressed the issues which confronted Hamlet. But the plain issue was, Does God exist or not? What was at stake in Hamlet's mind was nothing less than the greatest which confronts our mortal minds. (pp. 41-2)

It is precisely his duty Hamlet thinks of, and of his duty, which he finds it hard to decide, in relation to a possible world to come; and the difficulty of knowing what is right, and the uncertainty of our last destiny, together puzzle and arrest the will. Conscience requires that we do what is right; but then, what *is* right or wrong in these circumstances? Anxious reflection discloses no clear conviction; nor does it provide knowledge of a world to come. This is the moral and metaphysical uncertainty in which Hamlet finds himself. He does not know and cannot find out. Conscience makes demands; but it also provides no clear moral or metaphysical sense. Until he finds himself in this climacteric condition, life has gone on smoothly enough; but now, and suddenly, he knows that he lacks the insight, or the knowledge, or the faith, which will steady him, and carry him forward in a single and continuous course of action. In this, Hamlet knows he is different from Horatio, whose calm and steadily appointed way of life we are expected to admire. Horatio is precisely one who in suffering all, suffers nothing; he has accepted the first alternative Hamlet had proposed to himself: 'whether 'tis nobler in the mind to suffer the slings and arrows . . .'. Horatio has, we are expected to understand, decided that it is nobler so to suffer, and he has taken the buffets and the rewards of fortune with equal thanks; he knows his line and he is steady in it. Hamlet has not decided; and hence his peculiar distress.

It is very important to observe the play here on the word 'suffer'. Horatio is one who suffers everything and suffers nothing. What does this mean? I take it to mean, in the first sense, that Horatio accepts equally the fortunes and misfortunes of life; he embraces his good fortune with restraint and he endures his misfortunes. Therefore, in the second sense, he suffers nothing; he is not put out or mastered by circumstance; he is master of himself and of circumstance; he sustains a steady and imperturbable calm. In the one sense of the word, he takes what comes, without rebellion against it; he does not oppose it to end it; he is thus passive. But in the other sense, he is precisely not passive, but pre-eminently active and creative in his life. Such a steadiness and even tenour, in a philosophy of 'suffering', Hamlet does not possess. Horatio is one who, in suffering all, suffers nothing; Hamlet is one who, in suffering nothing, suffers everything. He is active where Horatio is passive, and passive where Horatio is active. His passivity is of the wrong sort; he is blown about by every gust of passion. But it is the same when he is active: his activity, like his passivity, is an affair of passion merely. Judgement is not in it. He is passion's slave, played on like a pipe, lapsed in time and circumstance, unaccountable, now listless, now violent.

But we must remark how Hamlet speaks of Horatio; he does so in words of passionate admiration. His election had sealed Horatio for himself because in suffering all, Horatio suffered nothing; and it is the man who is not passion's slave whom he would wear in his heart's core. How clearly he would be like Horatio! And yet, in the face of what has happened, ought he to be like Horatio? or ought he not to take up arms against his troubles, and violently end them and perhaps thereby himself? He did not know. The ghost had given Hamlet specific instructions to contrive nothing against his mother:

> . . . leave her to heaven,
> And to those thorns that in her bosom lodge,
> To prick and sting her.   [I. v. 86-8]

But ought he perhaps to leave Claudius to heaven also? When his guilt was proved beyond any doubt, Hamlet still did not kill him; he left him alone, giving a reason, plausible enough in Hamlet's eyes, in the eyes of his audience, and in our eyes, and yet inhabiting a middle region between sincerity and insincerity. We are told that in explaining why he does not there kill the King, Hamlet was sincere; it was a belief of the time. But it was certainly not universal. Claudius at least could have told him it was nonsense; Claudius has made just clear to us what was necessary if he, Claudius, was to win heaven. And could a Hamlet who half his time believed neither in heaven

nor hell, sincerely and with a whole mind say these things? (pp. 43-6)

[If] his precise thinking issues in no results, no assured decision, no clear path of duty, how can he be other than afraid of doing one thing rather than the other? He has cause and will and strength and means to do it; yes, all these he has; but has he the conscience to do it? That is the question; and conscience makes cowards of us. But where is a resolution of this distress to come from? From thinking precisely on the event? Apparently not; Hamlet is a thinker and has thought enough. Then let him plunge, and do what no doubt most people would expect of him; he talks fustian at himself about greatly finding quarrel in a straw when honour's at the stake; and this in future will be his line. But will it? Of course not. It is better to have three-quarters cowardice and one quarter wisdom than four quarters of bravado and tomfoolery; and Hamlet knows this well enough. But where and how will he find escape from this proper and rightminded cowardice? This is his problem; and it is, I suppose, everybody's problem. (pp. 46-7)

I confess to some impatience with what seems to me the present-day willingness to give up Hamlet for a mystery. Now it is true, no doubt, that we must not see the play as merely an affair of the character of its hero. But few of us will deny that Hamlet's procrastination is the major fact in the play and that it was intended by Shakespeare to be so. But are we really to find his procrastination a mystery and to leave it a mystery? Is there really anything mysterious about a man who has come to no clear and practised sense of life, and who in the face of a shocking situation which quite peculiarly involves him, shuffles, deceives himself, procrastinates, and in his exasperation cruelly persecutes the person he loves best in the world? Is this beyond our understanding? If we fail to understand it, is it not only because it is all so near to us and not because it is far off in Elizabethan times? Conscience, Hamlet said, makes cowards *of us all.* He was thinking of himself not as the exception, but as the rule. (pp. 47-8)

Everywhere in this play there is uncertainty and doubt; everywhere also there is incalculable and almost incredible conduct. In belief as in conduct nothing is firm and clear. If we look to belief: the ghost may be an honest ghost; he may be the devil; he may be an illusion. Man has an immortal soul; he is also the quintessence of dust. Death may be a nothing, or a sleep, or its world may contain a heaven and a hell. It may be right to leave criminals to the action of heaven; it may also be right to find quarrel in a straw when honour (whatever that may be) is at the stake. There may be a God to point his canon at self-slaughter; but also there may not be, and only, in his place, a congregation of vapours. And if we look to the conduct of others: a brother can murder his brother whose wife he has seduced, and he can smile and be a villain. A loving wife will betray her husband and promptly marry again with no obvious compunction; and before these two a Court will cringe and crawl. Ophelia will apparently play in with the others. Of clarity of belief and clarity of conduct there is nothing. The world has crumbled to shifting sand; there is nothing which is firm and no one on whom to rely. Except indeed Horatio, who in suffering all suffers nothing; who has made a choice; and him Hamlet wears in his heart's core, ay, in his heart of heart.

But can we, before we go further, say anything which is at all clear about the fundamental ethical issue which confronted Hamlet? I think it is possible to do so; and to do so in the first place in terms of an opposition, with which Hamlet plays a good deal, between 'blood' and 'judgment'. Hamlet has said to Horatio that he suffers nothing in suffering all; and he goes on to say that they are blessed

> Whose blood and judgment are so well commingled
> That they are not a pipe for fortune's finger
> To sound what stop she please. Give me that man
> That is not passion's slave . . .
>
> [III. ii. 69-72]

'Blood', here, is the same as 'passion', and together are opposed to 'judgment', a word which is frequent in Shakespeare's plays of this time. . . . The opposition of these two is frequent and clear. Besides, the King speaks of Ophelia in her madness as

> Divided from herself and her fair judgment,
> Without the which we are pictures, or mere beasts;
>
> [IV. v. 85-6]

and this chimes in with Hamlet's

> What is a man,
> If the chief good and market of his time
> Be but to sleep and feed? a beast, no more.
> Sure he that made us with such large discourse,
> Looking before and after, gave us not
> That capability and god-like reason
> To fust in us unused.   [IV. iv. 33-9]

It is clear that what is of the blood is animal and is opposed to judgement, which is reason; and Hamlet in one place declares that reason is from God and god-like.

Now we observe that Hamlet, in the soliloquy in the fourth Act, speaks of 'excitements of my reason and my blood': both his reason and his blood are roused, he says; and in the mood in which he finds himself after hearing of Fortinbras, he implies that both his reason and his blood require that he takes arms. But in the speech to Horatio he speaks of blood and judgement, which are also passion and reason, being so well commingled in Horatio that he is neither a pipe for fortune to play upon nor a slave of passion; this is part and parcel, apparently, of Horatio's power to suffer all and to suffer nothing. . . . (pp. 52-4)

[It] seems certain to me that Shakespeare . . . had read Montaigne before writing *Hamlet* and *Troilus*. I cannot now attempt to give chapter and verse; but the evidence that can be compiled is, it seems to me, decisive. It is not, however, necessary for my purpose to prove that this is so: I wish only to mention briefly those things in which Shakespeare in these plays manifests a mind deeply concerned with matters discursively treated by Montaigne.

There is of course Montaigne's scepticism. But it is not of this only that . . . I think now. Everybody knows that it has frequently been thought, and reasonably enough, that some lines in the soliloquy in Act III derive from an essay in the Third Book; in that essay Montaigne gives a loose version of some passages which occur in the Apology of Socrates; and, if we are at all right in thinking that Shakespeare read these pages, it is striking to reflect that here at least he encountered a version of a part of the *Apology*. I shall quote soon a few sentences from the *Apology* . . . in order further to emphasize, what is my main thesis, that the play of *Hamlet* has for its soul and centre a passionate and deeply reflective concern with the problem of conduct; and if this is so, it is natural to bring together in our minds Shakespeare and Socrates. Socrates, we know, declared that he turned away from natural philosophy to concern himself with conduct; . . . in *Hamlet* we see Shakespeare writing one of his greatest plays, after reading an essay by Montaigne in which Socrates is exhibited as the model and pattern of human wisdom.

> You do not speak wisely . . . if you think a man of any worth should weigh the risks of life against the risks of death. What he should consider is only whether what he does is right or wrong, and is the action of a good or a bad man. . . . For, my friends, to fear Death is only to think yourself wise when you are not; it is to think you know when in fact you do not know. For no one can be sure that Death is not the greatest of all benefits; but men fear it in the firm belief that it is the greatest of all evils. But is it not the most contemptible kind of ignorance to think you know when you do not? . . . For to be dead is one of two things: either it is as good as being nothing, so that a dead man has no consciousness of anything; or it is, as people say, a transition and a moving of the soul's abode from here to another place.
>
> Now if to be dead is to be unconscious and, as it were, a sleep in which dreams do not appear, how wonderful a benefit Death becomes! Let a man compare a night in which he sleeps without dreaming with other nights and days of his life. Then let him reflect carefully and declare how many of those days and nights he has passed to more advantage and more pleasantly than his night of dreamless sleep. I think that, whether he is a private citizen or the great Persian King himself, he would find that he could count them on one hand. Now if Death were a dreamless sleep, I certainly would count it a great gain: the whole of time would then be no longer than a night. But if, instead, Death is a change of abode from here to another place, and if it is true, as we are told, that all the dead are there, what greater boon can there be . . .? For if a man on coming to the other world escapes from so-called judges and finds real judges . . . is his change of abode of no account? . . . But you, my judges, must be of good hope when you think of Death. Have in mind this one truth: that nothing evil can befall a good man in life or in death; and the Gods are never unmindful of him.

I have quoted these passages from the *Apology*, not as they are given in Montaigne, but in a close translation, because I venture to think we shall better understand Shakespeare's play by a reading of Plato than by indulging the naturalistic temper of our time and seeking therefore to see Shakespeare only as a professional playwright, who dealt cleverly with intractable material or contrived merely to stretch out a play for the appointed time. Socrates spoke these words near to his death; Hamlet spoke his words with death, as he might well think, not far off. Socrates knew his line; he knew where he stood; and he was ready. Shakespeare exhibits Hamlet as a man seeing indeed the issues, and with his imagination complicated by centuries of Christian eschatology, but not knowing his line or where he stood; he was not ready. He could not keep his mind in a pious and cheerful agnosticism of what came after; and he could not do so because he swayed between the clamour of a traditional moral code which might be only the clamour of blood, passion, and revenge, and the calm demands of what might be true judgement and reason. What he should do was not clear to him, in the face of his dreadful situation; and not knowing this, he could not calmly face the prospect of a world to come. By Socratic standards he fell short and was lost; he was not enough of a philosopher, after all.

He falls short by the standards of Socrates; and he falls short by the standards of Montaigne, who holds up Socrates for a paragon of virtue and wisdom. The burden of much of Montaigne's writing is the folly of passion which masters conduct. (pp. 57-60)

Hamlet is a man having a sense of the high stoical impassibility; he beholds it lived by Horatio; and Horatio he wears in his heart's core. But he is also moved, and naturally, by the passions of disgust and revenge; what they say may be right; 'is't not perfect conscience to kill him with this arm?' He does not rise to the demands of philosophy; he cannot sink into passion; he inhabits a middle region where philosophy and passion, judgement and honour, reason and blood, annul each other and leave him, for all essential purposes, helpless and angry, passive and violent.

This I take to be Hamlet; and we see him in a world of distress which does not appear in the philosophy of his contemporary Bacon. Bacon enjoined natural philosophy and complete religious faith. It is hard to see how natural philosophy could have helped Hamlet; and he had failed to come by that other kind of philosophy which might rule his conduct. But are there signs that, in his troubles, he turned to faith?

The name of God is indeed sometimes on his lips; and once, in the closet scene with his mother, he tells her that what she had done

> As from the body of contraction plucks
> The very soul, and sweet religion makes
> A rhapsody of words. . . .
>
> [III. iv. 46-8]

Now I do not think there are any grounds whatever for seeing Horatio as a Christian; he seems nearer to Stoicism; and it is natural to think that just commingling of blood and judgement, the philosophy of right suffering, which animates Horatio and is so admired by Hamlet in him, is vaguely a Stoicism. Certainly, also, Hamlet exhibits no touch of piety or devotion; he does not turn, or show signs of turning, to supernatural power for light or strength. Once indeed, in the conversation with Horatio which immediately precedes the fencing, he quotes, or almost quotes, the Gospels: 'there's a special providence in the fall of a sparrow'; he seems here to suggest that his fate is in the hand of a God who knows and loves him. But this comes late in the play; there is not a hint of this earlier; and besides, and even more important, the Hamlet who speaks in these lines is a defeated Hamlet who has given up the struggle. All's ill indeed about his heart; but we are clearly given to understand that he is resigned to death and foresees it coming soon. This is not the Hamlet who had earlier struggled with his conscience and urged himself, now with shame, now with exasperation, into some line of action. Then, as he was then, we must see him as fundamentally secular, and not inclined to faith and to belief that he might find succour in religion. The struggles of Hamlet within himself and with his conscience were the struggles of the secular soul, reared indeed in 'sweet

religion' but looking to it now not at all for help and deliverance. (pp. 62-4)

Still, we also observe that Christianity is not excluded from the play. Claudius turns, in desperation, to the hope of divine pardon and absolution. I believe that not enough attention— or indeed, weight—is given to this remarkable soliloquy of Claudius. Claudius is a murderer of his brother and a seducer of his brother's wife. His guilt is finally disclosed. Then, in his desperation and alone, not now maintaining a restrained and clever imposture, but alone, he speaks the lines:

> Oh, my offence is rank, it smells to heaven . . .
>
> [III. iii. 36]

Claudius's enormous wickedness is the source and beginning of all the trouble which the play sets forth. But he, too, has a conscience; and conscience makes cowards of us all. Claudius has no illusions about the issue that confronts him. He must either go on in crime or, for expiation and forgiveness, give up his crown, his own ambition, and his queen. Which shall it be? . . . Soon Hamlet will come by. Both of them are at the turning-point; both of them will either cease from their divided wills or be carried helplessly by time and circumstance to their disastrous ends. Hamlet has declared that conscience makes a coward of him; and he will soon prove it to the uttermost when he excuses himself from killing Claudius then. But Claudius, too, in his way, is conscience's coward. He at least knows what is required of him. Here he is different from Hamlet. If they are both conscience's cowards, there is also a difference: Hamlet does not know what is required of him; but Claudius cannot rise to what his conscience clearly requires. Out of these, their respective situations, both will shuffle. 'There is no shuffling', says Claudius; but he kneels to his prayers with a weak 'All may be well': it is a faint hope and not a resolve. Then Hamlet, as Claudius prays, does *his* shuffling; he utters a resolve indeed, to kill him when he is drunk, asleep, or in his rage; but we know there is nothing in it. And Claudius, rising, says only what we expected: 'words without thoughts never to Heaven go'. Could there be a clearer comment on Hamlet's talk of sending the soul of Claudius to Heaven as he prays?

My point now is chiefly that here, in this speech of Claudius, we see the promptings of religion. Shakespeare does not exclude Christianity from the play and from the soul of Claudius; nowhere do we see it touching or inclining the soul of Hamlet. Hamlet seems to be entirely without the faith which Bacon enjoined. (pp. 64-6)

> *D. G. James, "The New Doubt," in his* The Dream of Learning *(reprinted by permission of Oxford University Press), Oxford at the Clarendon Press, 1951, pp. 33-68.*

HAROLD C. GODDARD   (essay date 1951)

[*Goddard interprets Hamlet as the combination of Shakespeare's greatest characters, and as an embodiment of Shakespeare's continuing exploration into the philosophical issue of vengeance which he began with Romeo and Richard II and culminated with Othello, Macbeth, and Lear. For additional commentary on revenge in* Hamlet *see Fredson Bowers (1955), Helen Gardner (1959), and Eleanor Prosser (1971). Goddard's essay was first published in 1951.*]

[There] is no doubt that Shakespeare endowed Hamlet with the best he had acquired up to the time he conceived him. He

Act V. Scene i. Hamlet and Horatio. By Eugene Delacroix (1836). From the Art Collection of the Folger Shakespeare Library.

inherits the virtues of a score of his predecessors—and some of their weaknesses. Yet he is no mere recapitulation of them. In him, rather, they recombine to make a man as individual as he is universal. He has the passion of Romeo ("Romeo is Hamlet in love," says Hazlitt), the dash and audacity of Hotspur, the tenderness and genius for friendship of Antonio, the wit, wisdom, resourcefulness, and histrionic gift of Falstaff, the bravery of Faulconbridge, the boyish charm of the earlier Hal at his best, the poetic fancy of Richard II, the analogic power and meditative melancholy of Jaques, the idealism of Brutus, the simplicity and human sympathy of Henry VI, and, after the assumption of his antic disposition, the wiliness and talent for disguise of Henry IV and the cynicism and irony of Richard III—not to mention gifts and graces that stem more from certain of Shakespeare's heroines than from his heroes— for, like Rosalind, that inimitable boy-girl, Hamlet is an early draft of a new creature on the Platonic order, conceived in the *Upanishads,* who begins to synthesize the sexes. "He who understands the masculine and keeps to the feminine shall become the whole world's channel. Eternal virtue shall not depart from him and he shall return to the state of an infant." If Hamlet does not attain the consummation that Laotse thus describes, he at least gives promise of it. (pp. 332-33)

For what was such a man made? Plainly for the ultimate things: for wonder, for curiosity and the pursuit of truth, for love, for creation—but first of all for freedom, the condition of the other four. He was made, that is, for religion and philosophy, for love and art, for liberty to "grow unto himself"—five forces that are the elemental enemies of Force.

And this man is called upon to kill. It is almost as if Jesus had been asked to play the role of Napoleon (as the temptation in the wilderness suggests that in some sense he was). If Jesus had been, ought he to have accepted it? The absurdity of the question prompts the recording of the strangest of all the strange facts in the history of *Hamlet:* the fact, namely, that nearly all readers, commentators, and critics are agreed in thinking that it was Hamlet's duty to kill, that he ought indeed to have killed much sooner than he did. His delay, they say, was a weakness and disaster, entailing, as it did, many unintended deaths, including his own. He should have obeyed much earlier the Ghost's injunction to avenge his father's murder. (p. 333)

Now whatever we are "meant" to assume, there is no doubt that nearly every spectator and reader the first time he encounters the play does assume that Hamlet ought to kill the King—and nearly all continue in that opinion on further acquaintance in the face of the paradox just stated.

How can that be?

It can be for the same reason that we exult when Gratiano cries, "Now, infidel, I have thee on the hip," and we see Shylock get what he was about to give, for the same reason that we applaud when Romeo sends Tybalt to death, and are enthralled by Henry V's rant before Harfleur or his injunction to his soldiers to imitate the action of the tiger. It can be because we all have stored up within ourselves so many unrequited wrongs and injuries, forgotten and unforgotten, and beneath these such an inheritance of racial revenge, that we like nothing better than to rid ourselves of a little of the accumulation by projecting it, in a crowd of persons similarly disposed, on the defenseless puppets of the dramatic imagination. There is no mystery about it. Anyone can follow the effect along his own backbone.

But if we are all repositories of racial revenge, we are also repositories of the rarer tendencies that over the centuries have resisted revenge. Against the contagion of a theater audience these ethereal forces have practically no chance, for in the crowd we are bound to take the play as drama rather than as poetry. But in solitude and in silence these forces are sure to lead a certain number of sensitive readers to shudder at the thought of Hamlet shedding blood. Let them express their revulsion, however, and instantly there will be someone to remind them that, whatever may be true now, "in those days" blood revenge was an accepted part of the moral code. As if Shakespeare were a historian and not a poet!

"Those days" never existed. They never existed poetically, I mean. No doubt the code of the vendetta has prevailed in many ages in many lands and revenge has been a favorite theme of the poets from Homer down. History itself, as William James remarked, has been a bath of blood. Yet there is a sense in which the dictum "Thou shalt not kill" has remained just as absolute in the kingdom of the imagination as in the Mosaic law. Moralize bloodshed by custom, legalize it by the state, camouflage it by romance, and still to the finer side of human nature it is just bloodshed; and always where poetry has become purest and risen highest there has been some parting of Hector and Andromache, some lament of the Trojan women, to show that those very deeds of vengeance and martial glory that the poet himself is ostensibly glorifying have somehow failed to utter the last word. To utter that last word—or try to—is poetry's ultimate function, to defend man against his own brutality, against

> That monster, custom, who all sense doth eat,
> Of habits devil,   [III. iv. 161-62]

a much emended line-and-a-half of Hamlet that makes excellent sense exactly as it stands.

If Shakespeare was bent in this play on presenting the morality of a primitive time, why did he make the mistake of centering it around a man who in endowment is as far ahead of either the Elizabethan age or our own as the code of blood revenge is behind both? . . . The greatest poetry has always depicted the world as a little citadel of nobility threatened by an immense barbarism, a flickering candle surrounded by infinite night. The "historical" impossibility of *Hamlet* is its poetical truth, and the paradox of its central figure is the universal psychology of man.

Yet, in the face of the correspondingly universal fascination that both the play and its hero have exercised, T. S. Eliot can write: "*Hamlet,* like the sonnets, is full of some stuff that the writer could not drag to light, contemplate, or manipulate into art. We must simply admit that here Shakespeare tackled a problem which proved too much for him. Why he attempted it at all is an insoluble enigma" [see excerpt above, 1919]. In which case, why all this fuss over a play that failed? To reason as Eliot does is to indict the taste and intelligence of three centuries. If Hamlet is just a puzzle, why has the world not long since transferred its adulation to Fortinbras and Laertes? They, at any rate, are clear. If action and revenge were what was wanted, they understood them. The trouble is that by no stretch of the imagination can we think of Shakespeare preferring their morality to that of his hero. They are living answers to the contention that Hamlet ought to have done what either of them, in his situation, would have done instantly. For what other purpose indeed did Shakespeare put them in than to make that plain?

But Hamlet himself, it will be said, accepts the code of blood revenge. Why should we question what one we so admire embraces with such unquestioning eagerness? With such *suspicious* eagerness might be closer to the mark. But waiving that for the moment, let us see what is involved in the assumption that Shakespeare thought it was Hamlet's duty to kill the King.

It involves nothing less than the retraction of all the Histories, of *Romeo and Juliet* and *Julius Caesar*. Private injury, domestic feud, civil revolution, imperialistic conquest: one by one in these plays Shakespeare had demonstrated how bloodshed invoked in their name brings on the very thing it was intended to avert, how, like seeds that propagate their own kind, force begets force and vengeance vengeance. And now in *Hamlet* Shakespeare is supposed to say: "I was wrong. I take it all back. Blood should be shed to avenge blood." And more incredible yet, we must picture him a year or two later taking his new opinion back and being reconverted in turn to his original conviction in *Othello, Macbeth, King Lear,* and the rest. If you find a term in a mathematical series fitting perfectly between what has gone before and what follows, you naturally assume it is in its right place, as you do a piece that fits into the surrounding pieces in a jigsaw puzzle. Only on the assumption that Hamlet ought not to have killed the King can the play be fitted into what then becomes the unbroken progression of Shakespeare's spiritual development. The only other way out of the difficulty for those who do not themselves

believe in blood revenge is to hold that Shakespeare in *Hamlet* is an archeologist or anthropologist interested in the customs of primitive society rather than a poet concerned with the eternal problems of man. (pp. 334-36)

Of course Shakespeare expected his audience to assume that Hamlet should kill the King, exactly as he expected them to assume that Katharine was a shrew, and that Henry V was a glorious hero for attempting to steal the kingdom of France. He was not so ignorant of human nature as not to know how it reacts under the stimulus of primitive emotion. He understood too that what ought to be can be seen only against a background of what is. (pp. 336-37)

Shakespeare, I am convinced, wanted us at first to believe that Hamlet ought to kill the King in order that we might undergo his agony with him. But he did not want us, I am equally convinced, to persist in that belief. We must view Hamlet first under the aspect of time so that later we may view him under the aspect of eternity. We must be him before we can understand him.

And here, oddly, we have an advantage over Shakespeare. The author of *Hamlet,* when he wrote it, had not had the privilege of reading *King Lear* and other post-Hamletian masterpieces. But we have had it, and can read *Hamlet* in their light. This does not mean that we import into *Hamlet* from later plays anything that is not already there. A work of art must stand or fall by itself. It merely means that, with vision sharpened by later plays, we are enabled to see in *Hamlet* what was already there but hidden from us—as a later dream does not alter an earlier one but may render it intelligible because of a mutual relation. . . .

And even if we do not look beyond *Hamlet,* our vantage point enables us to see from the past the direction that road was taking. Roads, to be sure, may make unexpected turns, and even a long-maintained general course is no guarantee against its interruption. But highways of Shakespearean breadth seldom go off abruptly at right angles. And so it is permissible to ask as we come to *Hamlet:* What, judging from what he had been doing, might Shakespeare be expected to do next?

The answer is plain. Having given us in Hal-Henry (not to mention Romeo and Richard II) a divided man easily won by circumstances to the side of violence, and in Brutus a man so won only after a brief but terrible inner struggle, what then? Why, naturally, the next step in the progression: a divided man won to the side of violence only after a protracted struggle. And this is precisely what we have in Hamlet. Moreover, there is a passage in the play that confirms just this development. (p. 338)

The passage is brief and apparently parenthetical. Shortly before the performance of *The Murder of Gonzago,* Hamlet suddenly addresses Polonius:

> HAM.: My lord, you played once i' the university, you
>   say?
> POL.: That did I, my lord, and was accounted a good
>   actor.
> HAM.: What did you enact?
> POL.: I did enact Julius Caesar: I was killed i' the
>   Capitol; Brutus killed me.
> HAM.: It was a brute part of him to kill so capital a calf
>   there.   [III. ii. 98-106]

It is interesting, to begin with, that Polonius was accounted a good actor in his youth. He has been playing a part ever since, until his mask has become a part of his face. The roles that men cast themselves for often reveal what they are and may prophesy what they will become. That Polonius acted Julius Caesar characterizes both men: Caesar, the synonym of imperialism, Polonius, the petty domestic despot—the very disparity of their kingdoms makes the comparison all the more illuminating.

But it is not just Caesar and Polonius. Brutus is mentioned too. And Brutus killed Caesar. In an hour or so Hamlet is to kill Polonius. If Polonius is Caesar, Hamlet is Brutus. This is the rehearsal of the deed. For to hate or scorn is to kill a little. "It was a brute part . . . to kill so capital a calf there." The unconscious is an inveterate punster and in that "brute part" Hamlet passes judgment in advance on his own deed in his mother's chamber. Prophecy, rehearsal, judgment: was ever more packed into fewer words? *Et tu*, Hamlet?

And it is not Brutus only who stands behind Hamlet. There is another behind him. And another behind *him*. . . . [As] Hamlet listens to the spirit of his father, behind him are the ghosts of Brutus, Hal, and Romeo. "Beware, Hamlet," says Romeo, "my soul told me to embrace Juliet and with her all the Capulets. But my 'father' bade me kill Tybalt and carry on the hereditary quarrel. And I obeyed him." "Beware, Hamlet," says Hal, "my soul told me to hold fast to Falstaff's love of life. But, instead, I did what is expected of a king, rejected Falstaff, and following my dying father's advice, made war on France." "Beware, Hamlet," says Brutus, "Portia and my soul gave ample warning. But Cassius reminded me that there was once a Brutus who expelled a tyrant from Rome, and, in the name of 'our fathers,' tempted me to exceed him in virtue by killing one. And I did. Beware, Hamlet." Each of these men wanted to dedicate himself to life. Romeo wanted to love. Hal wanted to play. Brutus wanted to read philosophy. But in each case a commanding hand was placed on the man's shoulder that disputed the claim of life in the name of death. Romeo defied that command for a few hours, and then circumstances proved too strong for him. Hal evaded it for a while, and then capitulated utterly. Brutus tried to face the issue, with the result of civil war within himself. But death won. Brutus' suppressed compunctions, however, ejected themselves in the form of a ghost that, Delphically, was both Caesar and Brutus' own evil spirit, his reliance on force.

Hamlet is the next step. He is a man as much more spiritually gifted than Brutus as Brutus is than Hal. The story of Hamlet is the story of Hal over again, subtilized, amplified, with a different ending. The men themselves seem so unlike that the similarities of their situations and acts are obscured. Like Hal, Hamlet is a prince of charming quality who cares nothing at the outset for his royal prospects but is absorbed in playing and savoring life. Only with him it is playing in a higher sense: dramatic art, acting, and playwriting rather than roistering in taverns and perpetrating practical jokes. And, like all men genuinely devoted to art, he is deeply interested in philosophy and religion, drawing no sharp lines indeed between or among the three. Because he is himself an imaginative genius, he needs no Falstaff to spur him on. Hamlet is his own Falstaff.

Hamlet's father, like Hal's, was primarily concerned with war, and after death calls his son to a deed of violence, not to imperial conquest, as the elder Henry did, but to revenge. Like Hal, Hamlet accepts the injunction. But instead of initiating a change that gradually alters him into his father's likeness, the decision immediately shakes his being to its foundations. (pp. 339-41)

The far more shattering effect on Hamlet than on Hal or even on Brutus of the task he assumes shows how much more nearly balanced are the opposing forces in his case. Loyalty to his father and the desire to grow unto himself—thirst for revenge and thirst for creation—are in Hamlet almost in equilibrium, though of course he does not know it. Henry V was vaguely troubled by nocturnal stirrings of the spirit. He saw no ghost. Brutus became the victim of insomnia. He stifled his conscience by action and saw no ghost until after the deed. Hamlet saw his before the deed—as Brutus would have if his soul had been stronger—and it made night hideous for him. No spirit but one from below would have produced that effect, and the fact that "this fellow in the cellarage" speaks from under the platform when he echoes Hamlet's "swear" is in keeping with Shakespeare's frequent use of the symbolism that associates what is physically low with what is morally wrong. Hamlet's delay, then, instead of giving ground for condemnation, does him credit. It shows his soul is still alive and will not submit to the demands of the father without a struggle. . . . In a tug of war between evenly matched teams the rope at first is almost motionless, but ultimately the strength of one side ebbs and then the rope moves suddenly and violently. So mysterious, and no more, is Hamlet's hesitation, followed, as it finally was, by lightning-like action. . . . Shakespeare puts in the mouth of Claudius words that seem expressly inserted to explain the riddle. The King, caught in the same way between opposing forces—desire to keep the fruits of his sin and desire to pray—declares:

> And, like a man to double business bound,
> I stand in pause where I shall first begin,
> And both neglect.   [III. iii. 41-3]

That seems plain enough. But what is true of Claudius in this one scene is true of Hamlet during all the earlier part of the play. It is as if his soul were a body in space so delicately poised between the gravitation of the earth and the gravitation, or we might say the levitation, of the sun that it "hesitates" whether to drop into the one or fly up to the other. It sometimes seems as if *Homo sapiens* were in just that situation.

People who think Shakespeare was just a playwright say Hamlet delayed that there might be a five-act play! Others, who calmly neglect much of the text, say he delayed because of external obstacles. Coleridge thinks it was because he thought too much. Bradley, because he was so melancholy [see excerpts above, 1813 and 1905]. It would be nearer the truth to say he thought too much and was melancholy because he delayed. The more powerful an unconscious urge, the stronger and the more numerous the compensations and rationalizations with which consciousness attempts to fight it. Hence the excess of thought and feeling. Goethe, I would say, is far closer to the mark than Coleridge and Bradley in attributing Hamlet's hesitation to a feminine element in the man [see excerpt above, 1795]. But then he proceeds to spoil it all by implying that Hamlet is weak and effeminate: "a lovely, pure and most moral nature, without the strength of nerve that makes a hero, sinks beneath a burden which it cannot bear and must not cast away." The implication is that Hamlet ought to have killed the King at once; also that loveliness, purity, and moral insight are not sources of strengh and heroism!

On the contrary, they are the very higher heroism that challenges a more primitive one in this play. Hamlet is the battlefield where the two meet. It is war in that psychological realm where all war begins. Hamlet is like Thermopylae, the battle that stands first among all battles in the human imagination because of its symbolic quality—a contest between the Persian hordes of the lower appetites and the little Greek band of heroic instincts.

> They have the numbers, we, the heights.

At Thermopylae the Persians won. Yet we think of it as a Greek victory because it was the promise of Salamis and Plataea. So with Hamlet. Hamlet lost. But *Hamlet* is the promise of *Othello* and *King Lear*. (pp. 341-43)

> Harold C. Goddard, "'Hamlet'," in his The Meaning of Shakespeare, *University of Chicago Press, 1960, pp. 331-86.*

MAYNARD MACK   (essay date 1952)

[*Mack describes the world of* Hamlet *in terms of three pervasive characteristics: mysteriousness, the problematic nature of reality, and mortality. Mack discovers evidence of these attributes in the language and imagery patterns of the play, an approach employed by G. Wilson Knight (1930), Caroline F. E. Spurgeon (1935), and Wolfgang H. Clemen (1951). For additional commentary on the language of the play, see Samuel Taylor Coleridge (1813), Harry Levin (1959), T. McAlindon (1970), Reuben A. Brower (1971), and Inga-Stina Ewbank (1977).*]

My subject is the world of "Hamlet." I do not of course mean Denmark, except as Denmark is given a body by the play; and I do not mean Elizabethan England, though this is necessarily close behind the scenes. I mean simply the imaginative environment that the play asks us to enter when we read it or go to see it.

Great plays, as we know, do present us with something that can be called a world, a microcosm—a world like our own in being made of people, actions, situations, thoughts, feelings, and much more, but unlike our own in being perfectly, or almost perfectly, significant and coherent. In a play's world, each part implies the other parts, and each lives, each means, with the life and meaning of the rest.

This is the reason, as we also know, that the worlds of great plays greatly differ. Othello in Hamlet's position, we sometimes say, would have no problem; but what we are really saying is that Othello in Hamlet's position would not exist. (p. 502)

Without his particular world of voices, persons, events, the world that both expresses and contains him, Othello is unimaginable. And so, I think, are Antony, King Lear, Macbeth—and Hamlet. We come back then to Hamlet's world, of all the tragic worlds that Shakespeare made, easily the most various and brilliant, the most elusive. It is with no thought of doing justice to it that I have singled out three of its attributes for comment. . . . All I would say in defense of the materials I have chosen is that they seem to me interesting, close to the root of the matter even if we continue to differ about what the root of the matter is, and explanatory, in a modest way, of this play's peculiar hold on everyone's imagination, its almost mythic status, one might say, as a paradigm of the life of man.

The first attribute that impresses us, I think, is mysteriousness. We often hear it said, perhaps with truth, that every great work of art has a mystery at the heart; but the mystery of "Hamlet" is something else. We feel its presence in the numberless explanations that have been brought forward for Hamlet's delay, his madness, his ghost, his treatment of Polonius, or Ophelia, or his mother. . . . (pp. 503-04)

[In] Hamlet, to paraphrase a remark of Falstaff's, we have a character who is not only mad in himself but a cause that madness is in the rest of us. Still, the very existence of so many theories and counter-theories, many of them formulated by sober heads, gives food for thought. "Hamlet" seems to lie closer to the illogical logic of life than Shakespeare's other tragedies. And while the causes of this situation may be sought by saying that Shakespeare revised the play so often that eventually the motivations were smudged over, or that the original old play has been here or there imperfectly digested, or that the problems of Hamlet lay so close to Shakespeare's heart that he could not quite distance them in the formal terms of art, we have still as critics to deal with effects, not causes. (p. 504)

Moreover, the matter goes deeper than this. Hamlet's world is preëminently in the interrogative mood. It reverberates with questions, anguished, meditative, alarmed. There are questions that in this play, to an extent I think unparalleled in any other, mark the phases and even the nuances of the action, helping to establish its peculiar baffled tone. There are other questions whose interrogations, innocent at first glance, are subsequently seen to have reached beyond their contexts and to point towards some pervasive inscrutability in Hamlet's world as a whole. Such is that tense series of challenges with which the tragedy begins: Bernardo's of Francisco, "Who's there?" Francisco's of Horatio and Marcellus, "Who is there?" Horatio's of the ghost, "What art thou . . .?" And then there are the famous questions. In them the interrogations seem to point not only beyond the context but beyond the play, out of Hamlet's predicaments into everyone's: "What a piece of work is a man! . . . And yet to me what is this quintessence of dust?" "To be, or not to be, that is the question." "Get thee to a nunnery. Why wouldst thou be a breeder of sinners?" (pp. 504-05)

Further, Hamlet's world is a world of riddles. The hero's own language is often riddling, as the critics have pointed out. When he puns, his puns have receding depths in them, like the one which constitutes his first speech: "A little more than kin, and less than kind." His utterances in madness, even if wild and whirling, are simultaneously, as Polonius discovers, pregnant: "Do you know me, my lord?" "Excellent well. You are a fishmonger." Even the madness itself is riddling: How much is real? How much is feigned? What does it mean? Sane or mad, Hamlet's mind plays restlessly about his world, turning up one riddle upon another. The riddle of character, for example, and how it is that in a man whose virtues else are "pure as grace," some vicious mole of nature, some "dram of eale," can "all the noble substance oft adulter." Or the riddle of the player's art, and how a man can so project himself into a fiction, a dream of passion, that he can weep for Hecuba. (p. 505)

There are also more immediate riddles. His mother—how could she "on this fair mountain leave to feed, And batten on this moor?" The ghost—which may be a devil, for "the de'il hath power T' assume a pleasing shape." Ophelia—what does her behavior to him mean? Surprising her in her closet, he falls to such perusal of her face as he would draw it. Even the king at his prayers is a riddle. Will a revenge that takes him in the purging of his soul be vengeance, or hire and salary? As for himself, Hamlet realizes, he is the greatest riddle of all—a mystery, he warns Rosencrantz and Guildenstern, from which he will not have the heart plucked out. . . .

Thus the mysteriousness of Hamlet's world is of a piece. It is not simply a matter of missing motivations, to be expunged if only we could find the perfect clue. It is built in. It is evidently an important part of what the play wishes to say to us. And it is certainly an element that the play thrusts upon us from the opening word. Everyone, I think, recalls the mysteriousness of that first scene. The cold middle of the night on the castle platform, the muffled sentries, the uneasy atmosphere of apprehension, the challenges leaping out of the dark, the questions that follow the challenges, feeling out the darkness, searching for identities, for relations, for assurance. (p. 506)

We need not be surprised that critics and playgoers alike have been tempted to see in this an evocation not simply of Hamlet's world but of their own. Man in his aspect of bafflement, moving in darkness on a rampart between two worlds, unable to reject, or quite accept, the one that, when he faces it, ''to-shakes'' his disposition with thoughts beyond the reaches of his soul—comforting himself with hints and guesses. We hear these hints and guesses whispering through the darkness as the several watchers speak. . . . However we choose to take the scene, it is clear that it creates a world where uncertainties are of the essence.

Meantime, such is Shakespeare's economy, a second attribute of Hamlet's world has been put before us. This is the problematic nature of reality and the relation of reality to appearance. The play begins with an appearance, an ''apparition,'' to use Marcellus's term—the ghost. And the ghost is somehow real, indeed the vehicle of realities. Through its revelation, the glittering surface of Claudius's court is pierced, and Hamlet comes to know, and we do, that the king is not only hateful to him but the murderer of his father, that his mother is guilty of adultery as well as incest. Yet there is a dilemma in the revelation. For possibly the apparition *is* an apparition, a devil who has assumed his father's shape.

This dilemma, once established, recurs on every hand. From the court's point of view, there is Hamlet's madness. (p. 507)

On the other hand, from Hamlet's point of view, there is Ophelia. Kneeling here at her prayers, she seems the image of innocence and devotion. Yet she is of the sex for whom he has already found the name Frailty, and she is also, as he seems either madly or sanely to divine, a decoy in a trick. The famous cry—''Get thee to a nunnery''—shows the anguish of his uncertainty. If Ophelia is what she seems, this dirty-minded world of murder, incest, lust, adultery, is no place for her. Were she ''as chaste as ice, as pure as snow,'' she could not escape its calumny. And if she is not what she seems, then a nunnery in its other sense of brothel is relevant to her. In the scene that follows he treats her as if she were indeed an inmate of a brothel.

Likewise, from Hamlet's point of view, there is the enigma of the king. If the ghost is *only* an appearance, then possibly the king's appearance is reality. He must try it further. By means of a second and different kind of ''apparition,'' the play within the play, he does so. But then, immediately after, he stumbles on the king at prayer. This appearance has a relish of salvation in it. If the king dies now, his soul may yet be saved. Yet actually, as we know, the king's efforts to come to terms with heaven have been unavailing; his words fly up, his thoughts remain below. If Hamlet means the conventional revenger's reasons that he gives for sparing Claudius, it was the perfect moment not to spare him—when the sinner was acknowledging his guilt, yet unrepentant. The perfect moment, but it was hidden, like so much else in the play, behind an arras.

There are two arrases in his mother's room. Hamlet thrusts his sword through one of them. Now at last he has got to the heart of the evil, or so he thinks. But now it is the wrong man; now he himself is a murderer. The other arras he stabs through with his words—like daggers, says the queen. He makes her shrink under the contrast he points between her present husband and his father. But as the play now stands (matters are somewhat clearer in the bad Quarto), it is hard to be sure how far the queen grasps the fact that her second husband is the murderer of her first. And it is hard to say what may be signified by her inability to see the ghost, who now for the last time appears. In one sense at least, the ghost is the supreme reality, representative of the hidden ultimate power, in Bradley's terms—witnessing from beyond the grave against this hollow world. Yet the man who is capable of seeing through to this reality, the queen thinks is mad. . . . Here certainly we have the imperturbable self-confidence of the worldly world, its layers on layers of habituation, so that when the reality is before its very eyes it cannot detect its presence.

Like mystery, this problem of reality is central to the play and written deep into its idiom. Shakespeare's favorite terms in ''Hamlet'' are words of ordinary usage that pose the question of appearances in a fundamental form. ''Apparition'' I have already mentioned. Another term is ''seems.'' When we say, as Ophelia says of Hamlet leaving her closet, ''He seem'd to find his way without his eyes,'' we mean one thing. When we say, as Hamlet says to his mother in the first court-scene, ''Seems, Madam! . . . I know not 'seems,''' we mean another. And when we say, as Hamlet says to Horatio before the play within the play, ''And after, we will both our judgments join in censure of his seeming,'' we mean both at once. The ambiguities of ''seem'' coil and uncoil throughout this play, and over agaisnt them is set the idea of ''seeing.'' So Hamlet challenges the king in his triumphant letter announcing his return to Denmark: ''Tomorrow shall I beg leave to see your kingly eyes.'' Yet ''seeing'' itself can be ambiguous, as we recognize from Hamlet's uncertainty about the ghost; or from that statement of his mother's already quoted: ''Nothing at all; yet all that is I see.''

Another term of like importance is ''assume.'' What we assume may be what we are not: ''The de'il hath power T' assume a pleasing shape.'' But it may be what we are: ''If it assume my noble father's person, I'll speak to it.'' And it may be what we are not yet, but would become; thus Hamlet advises his mother, ''Assume a virtue, if you have it not.'' The perplexity in the word points to a real perplexity in Hamlet's and our own experience. (pp. 508-10)

Two other terms I wish to instance are ''put on'' and ''shape.'' The shape of something is the form under which we are accustomed to apprehend it: ''Do you see yonder cloud that's almost in shape of a camel?'' But a shape may also be a disguise—even, in Shakespeare's time, an actor's costume or an actor's role. . . . ''Put on'' supplies an analogous ambiguity. Shakespeare's mind seems to worry this phrase in the play much as Hamlet's mind worries the problem of acting in a world of surfaces, or the king's mind worries the meaning of Hamlet's transformation. Hamlet has put an antic disposition on, that the king knows. But what does ''put on'' mean? A mask, or a frock or livery—our ''habit''? The king is left guessing, and so are we.

What is found in the play's key terms is also found in its imagery. Miss Spurgeon has called attention to a pattern of disease images in ''Hamlet'', to which I shall return. But the play has other patterns equally striking. One of these, as my earlier quotations hint, is based on clothes. In the world of surfaces to which Shakespeare exposes us in "Hamlet" clothes are naturally a factor of importance. "The apparel oft proclaims the man," Polonius assures Laertes, cataloguing maxims in the young man's ear as he is about to leave for Paris. Oft, but not always. And so he sends his man Reynaldo to look into Laertes' life there—even, if need be, to put a false dress of accusation upon his son ("What forgeries you please"), the better by indirections to find directions out. On the same grounds, he takes Hamlet's vows to Ophelia as false apparel. (pp. 510-11)

This breach between the outer and the inner stirs no special emotion in Polonius, because he is always either behind an arras or prying into one, but it shakes Hamlet to the core. Here so recently was his mother in her widow's weeds, the tears still flushing in her gallèd eyes; yet now within a month, a little month, before even her funeral shoes are old, she has married with his uncle. Her mourning was all clothes. Not so his own, he bitterly replies, when she asks him to cast his "nighted color off." . . .

What we must not overlook here is Hamlet's visible attire, giving the verbal imagery a theatrical extension. Hamlet's apparel now is his inky cloak, mark of his grief for his father, mark also of his character as a man of melancholy, mark possibly too of his being one in whom appearance and reality are attuned. Later, in his madness, with his mind disordered, he will wear his costume in a corresponding disarray, the disarray that Ophelia describes so vividly to Polonius. . . . (p. 511)

A second pattern of imagery springs from terms of painting: the paints, the colorings, the varnishes that may either conceal, or, as in the painter's art, reveal. Art in Claudius conceals. "The harlot's cheek," he tells us in his one aside, "beautied with plastering art, Is not more ugly to the thing that helps it Than is my deed to my most painted word." Art in Ophelia, loosed to Hamlet in the episode . . . to which this speech of the king's is prelude, is more complex. She looks so beautiful— "the celestial, and my soul's idol, the most beautified Ophelia," Hamlet has called her in his love letter. But now, what does beautified mean? Perfected with all the innocent beauties of a lovely woman? Or "beautied" like the harlot's cheek? "I have heard of your paintings too, well enough. God hath given you one face, and you make yourselves another."

Yet art, differently used, may serve the truth. By using an "image" (his own word) of a murder done in Vienna, Hamlet cuts through to the king's guilt; holds "as 'twere, the mirror up to nature," shows "virtue her own feature, scorn her own image, and the very age and body of the time"—which is out of joint—"his form and pressure." (p. 512)

The most pervasive of Shakespeare's image patterns in this play, however, is the pattern evolved around the three words, show, act, play. "Show" seems to be Shakespeare's unifying image in "Hamlet." Through it he pulls together and exhibits in a single focus much of the diverse material in his play. The ideas of seeming, assuming, and putting on; the images of clothing, painting, mirroring; the episode of the dumb show and the play within the play; the characters of Polonius, Laertes, Ophelia, Claudius, Gertrude, Rosencrantz and Guildenstern, Hamlet himself—all these at one time or another, and usually more than once, are drawn into the range of implications flung round the play by "show."

"Act," on the other hand, I take to be the play's radical metaphor. It distills the various perplexities about the character of reality into a residual perplexity about the character of an

act. What, this play asks again and again, is an act? What is its relation to the inner act, the intent? "If I drown myself wittingly," says the clown in the graveyard, "it argues an act, and an act hath three branches; it is to act, to do, to perform." Or again, the play asks, how does action relate to passion, that "laps'd in time and passion" I can let "go by Th' important acting of your dread command"; and to thought, which can so sickly o'er the native hue of resolution that "enterprises of great pitch and moment With this regard their currents turn awry, And lose the name of action"; and to words, which are not acts, and so we dare not be content to unpack our hearts with them, and yet are acts of a sort, for we may speak daggers though we use none. Or still again, how does an act (a deed) relate to an act (a pretense)? For an action may be nothing but pretense. . . . Or it may be a pretense that is also the first foothold of a new reality, as when we assume a virtue though we have it not. Or it may be a pretense that is actually a mirroring of reality, like the play within the play, or the tragedy of "Hamlet."

To this network of implications, the third term, play, adds an additional dimension. "Play" is a more precise word, in Elizabethan parlance at least, for all the elements in "Hamlet" that pertain to the art of the theatre; and it extends their field of reference till we see that every major personage in the tragedy is a player in some sense, and every major episode a play. The court plays, Hamlet plays, the players play, Rosencrantz and Guildenstern try to play on Hamlet, though they cannot play on his recorders—here we have an extension to a musical sense. And the final duel, by a further extension, becomes itself a play, in which everyone but Claudius and Laertes plays his role in ignorance: "The queen desires you to show some gentle entertainment to Laertes before you fall to play." "I . . . will this brother's wager frankly play." "Give him the cup."—"I'll play this bout first."

The full extension of this theme is best evidenced in the play within the play itself. Here, in the bodily presence of these traveling players, bringing with them the latest playhouse gossip out of London, we have suddenly a situation that tends to dissolve the normal barriers between the fictive and the real. For here on the stage before us is a play of false appearances in which an actor called the player-king is playing. But there is also on the stage, Claudius, another player-king, who is a spectator of this player. And there is on the stage, besides, a prince who is a spectator of both these player-kings and who plays with great intensity a player's role himself. And around these kings and that prince is a group of courtly spectators— Gertrude, Rosencrantz, Guildenstern, Polonius, and the rest— and they, as we have come to know, are players too. And lastly there are ourselves, an audience watching all these audiences who are also players. Where, it may suddenly occur to us to ask, does the playing end? (pp. 512-14)

The mysteriousness of Hamlet's world, while it pervades the tragedy, finds its point of greatest dramatic concentration in the first act, and its symbol in the first scene. The problems of appearance and reality also pervade the play as a whole, but come to a climax in Acts II and III, and possibly their best symbol is the play within the play. Our third attribute, though again it is one that crops out everywhere, reaches its full development in Acts IV and V. It is not easy to find an appropriate name for this attribute, but perhaps "mortality" will serve, if we remember to mean by mortality the heartache and the thousand natural shocks that flesh is heir to, not simply death.

The powerful sense of mortality in "Hamlet" is conveyed to us, I think, in three ways. First, there is the play's emphasis on human weakness, the instability of human purpose, the subjection of humanity to fortune—all that we might call the aspect of failure in man. Hamlet opens this theme in Act I, when he describes how from that single blemish, perhaps not even the victim's fault, a man's whole character may take corruption. Claudius dwells on it again, to an extent that goes far beyond the needs of the occasion, while engaged in seducing Laertes to step behind the arras of a seemer's world and dispose of Hamlet by a trick. Time qualifies everything, Claudius says, including love, including purpose. As for love—it has a "plurisy" in it and dies of its own too much. As for purpose—"That we would do, We should do when we would, for this 'would' changes, And hath abatements and delays as many As there are tongues, are hands, are accidents; And then this 'should' is like a spendthrift's sigh, That hurts by easing." The player-king, in his long speeches to his queen in the play within the play, sets the matter in a still darker light. She means these protestations of undying love, he knows, but our purposes depend on our memory, and our memory fades fast. . . . The subjection of human aims to fortune is a reiterated theme in "Hamlet," as subsequently in "Lear." Fortune is the harlot goddess in whose secret parts men like Rosencrantz and Guildenstern live and thrive; the strumpet who threw down Troy and Hecuba and Priam; the outrageous foe whose slings and arrows a man of principle must suffer or seek release in suicide. Horatio suffers them with composure: he is one of the blessed few "Whose blood and judgment are so well co-mingled That they are not a pipe for fortune's finger To sound what stop she please." For Hamlet the task is of a greater difficulty.

Next, and intimately related to this matter of infirmity, is the emphasis on infection—the ulcer, the hidden abscess, "th' imposthume of much wealth and peace That inward breaks and shows no cause without Why the man dies." Miss Spurgeon, who was the first to call attention to this aspect of the play, has well remarked that so far as Shakespeare's pictorial imagination is concerned, the problem in "Hamlet" is not a problem of the will and reason, "of a mind too philosophical or a nature temperamentally unfitted to act quickly," nor even a problem of an individual at all. Rather, it is a condition—"a condition for which the individual himself is apparently not responsible, any more than the sick man is to blame for the infection which strikes and devours him. . .". "That," she adds, "is the tragedy of 'Hamlet,' as it is perhaps the chief tragic mystery of life." This is a perceptive comment, for it reminds us that Hamlet's situation is mainly not of his own manufacture, as are the situations of Shakespeare's other tragic heroes. He has inherited it; he is "born to set it right."

We must not, however, neglect to add to this what another student of Shakespeare's imagery has noticed—that the infection in Denmark is presented alternatively as poison. Here, of course, responsibility is implied, for the poisoner of the play is Claudius. The juice he pours into the ear of the elder Hamlet is a combined poison and disease, a "leperous distilment" that curds "the thin and wholesome blood." From this fatal center, unwholesomeness spreads out till there is something rotten in all Denmark. Hamlet tells us that his "wit's diseased," the queen speaks of her "sick soul," the king is troubled by "the hectic" in his blood. . . . In the end, all save Ophelia die of that poison in a literal as well as figurative sense.

But the chief form in which the theme of mortality reaches us, it seems to me, is as a profound consciousness of loss. Hamlet's father expresses something of the kind when he tells Hamlet how his "most seeming-virtuous queen," betraying a love

which "was of that dignity That it went hand in hand even with the vow I made to her in marriage," had chosen to "decline Upon a wretch whose natural gifts were poor To those of mind." "O Hamlet, what a falling off was there!" Ophelia expresses it again, on hearing Hamlet's denunciation of love and woman in the nunnery scene, which she takes to be the product of a disordered brain. . . . And then there is that further falling off, if I may call it so, when Ophelia too goes mad—"Divided from herself and her fair judgment, Without the which we are pictures, or mere beasts."

Time was, the play keeps reminding us, when Denmark was a different place. That was before Hamlet's mother took off "the rose From the fair forehead of an innocent love" and set a blister there. Hamlet then was still "th' expectancy and rose of the fair state"; Ophelia, the "rose of May." For Denmark was a garden then, when his father ruled. There had been something heroic about his father—a king who met the threats to Denmark in open battle. . . . But, the ghost reveals, a serpent was in the garden, and "the serpent that did sting thy father's life Now wears his crown." The martial virtues are put by now. The threats to Denmark are attended to by policy, by agents working deviously for and through an uncle. The moral virtues are put by too. Hyperion's throne is occupied by "a vice of king," "a king of shreds and patches"; Hyperion's bed, by a satyr, a paddock, a bat, a gib, a bloat king with reechy kisses. The garden is unweeded now, and "grows to seed; things rank and gross in nature Possess it merely." Even in himself he feels the taint, the taint of being his mother's son; and that other taint, from an earlier garden, of which he admonishes Ophelia: "Our virtue cannot so inoculate our old stock but we shall relish of it." (pp. 514-18)

Hamlet's problem, in its crudest form, is simply the problem of the avenger: he must carry out the injunction of the ghost and kill the king. But this problem, as I ventured to suggest at the outset, is presented in terms of a certain kind of world. The ghost's injunction to act becomes so inextricably bound up for Hamlet with the character of the world in which the action must be taken—its mysteriousness, its baffling appearances, its deep consciousness of infection, frailty, and loss—that he cannot come to terms with either without coming to terms with both. (p. 518)

The ghost's injunction to revenge unfolds a different facet of his problem. The young man growing up is not to be allowed simply to endure a rotten world, he must also act in it. Yet how to begin, among so many enigmatic surfaces? Even Claudius, whom he now knows to be the core of the ulcer, has a plausible exterior. And around Claudius, swathing the evil out of sight, he encounters all those other exteriors, as we have seen. Some of them already deeply infected beneath, like his mother. Some noble, but marked for infection, like Laertes. Some not particularly corrupt but infinitely corruptible, like Rosencrantz and Guildenstern; some mostly weak and foolish like Polonius and Osric. Some, like Ophelia, innocent, yet in their innocence still serving to "skin and film the ulcerous place."

And this is not all. The act required of him, though retributive justice, is one that necessarily involves the doer in the general guilt. Not only because it involves a killing; but because to get at the world of seeming one sometimes has to use its weapons. He himself, before he finishes, has become a player, has put an antic disposition on, has killed a man—the wrong man—has helped drive Ophelia mad, and has sent two friends of his youth to death, mining below their mines, and hoisting the engineer with his own petard. He had never meant to dirty himself with these things, but from the moment of the ghost's challenge to act, this dirtying was inevitable. It is the condition of living at all in such a world. To quote Polonius, who knew that world so well, men become "a little soil'd i' th' working." Here is another matter with which Hamlet has to come to terms. (pp. 519-20)

In the last act of the play (or so it seems to me, for I know there can be differences on this point), Hamlet accepts his world and we discover a different man. Shakespeare does not outline for us the process of acceptance any more than he had done with Romeo or was to do with Othello. But he leads us strongly to expect an altered Hamlet, and then, in my opinion, provides him. We must recall that at this point Hamlet has been absent from the stage during several scenes, and that such absences in Shakespearean tragedy usually warn us to be on the watch for a new phase in the development of the character. It is so when we leave King Lear in Gloucester's farmhouse and find him again in Dover fields. It is so when we leave Macbeth at the witches' cave and rejoin him at Dunsinane, hearing of the armies that beset it. Furthermore, and this is an important matter in the theatre—especially important in a play in which the symbolism of clothing has figured largely—Hamlet now looks different. He is wearing a different dress—probably, as Granville-Barker thinks, his "sea-gown scarf'd" about him [see excerpt above, 1937], but in any case no longer the disordered costume of his antic disposition. The effect is not entirely dissimilar to that in "Lear," when the old king wakes out of his madness to find fresh garments on him.

Still more important, Hamlet displays a considerable change of mood. This is not a matter of the way we take the passage about defying augury, as Mr. Tillyard among others seems to think [see excerpt above, 1949]. It is a matter of Hamlet's whole deportment, in which I feel we may legitimately see the deportment of a man who has been "illuminated" in the tragic sense. Bradley's term for it is fatalism [see excerpt above, 1904], but if this is what we wish to call it, we must at least acknowledge that it is fatalism of a very distinctive kind—a kind that Shakespeare has been willing to touch with the associations of the saying in St. Matthew about the fall of a sparrow, and with Hamlet's recognition that a divinity shapes our ends. The point is not that Hamlet has suddenly become religious; he has been religious all through the play. The point is that he has now learned, and accepted, the boundaries in which human action, human judgment, are enclosed.

Till his return from the voyage he had been trying to act beyond these, had been encroaching on the role of providence, if I may exaggerate to make a vital point. He had been too quick to take the burden of the whole world and its condition upon his limited and finite self. Faced with a task of sufficient difficulty in its own right, he had dilated it into a cosmic problem—as indeed every task is, but if we think about this too precisely we cannot act at all. The whole time is out of joint, he feels, and in his young man's egocentricity, he will set it right. . . . Even with the king, Hamlet has sought to play at God. *He* it must be who decides the issue of Claudius's salvation, saving him for a more damnable occasion. Now, he has learned that there are limits to the before and after that human reason can comprehend. Rashness, even, is sometimes good. Through rashness he has saved his life from the commission for his death, "and prais'd be rashness for it." This happy circumstance and the unexpected arrival of the pirate ship make it plain that the roles of life are not entirely self-assigned. (pp. 520-22)

The crucial evidence of Hamlet's new frame of mind, as I understand it, is the graveyard scene. Here, in its ultimate symbol, he confronts, recognizes, and accepts the condition of being man. It is not simply that he now accepts death, though Shakespeare shows him accepting it in ever more poignant forms: first, in the imagined persons of the politician, the courtier, and the lawyer, who laid their little schemes "to circumvent God," as Hamlet puts it, but now lie here; then in Yorick, whom he knew and played with as a child; and then in Ophelia. This last death tears from him a final cry of passion, but the striking contrast between his behavior and Laertes's reveals how deeply he has changed.

Still, it is not the fact of death that invests this scene with its peculiar power. It is instead the haunting mystery of life itself that Hamlet's speeches point to, holding in its inscrutable folds those other mysteries that he has wrestled with so long. These he now knows for what they are, and lays them by. The mystery of evil is present here—for this is after all the universal graveyard, where, as the clown says humorously, he holds up Adam's profession; where the scheming politician, the hollow courtier, the tricky lawyer, the emperor and the clown and the beautiful young maiden, all come together in an emblem of the world; where even, Hamlet murmurs, one might expect to stumble on "Cain's jawbone, that did the first murther." (pp. 522-23)

After the graveyard and what it indicates has come to pass in him, we know that Hamlet is ready for the final contest of mighty opposites. He accepts the world as it is, the world as a duel, in which, whether we know it or not, evil holds the poisoned rapier and the poisoned chalice waits; and in which, if we win at all, it costs not less than everything. I think we understand by the close of Shakespeare's "Hamlet" why it is that unlike the other tragic heroes he is given a soldier's rites upon the stage. For as William Butler Yeats once said, "Why should we honor those who die on the field of battle? A man may show as reckless a courage in entering into the abyss of himself." (p. 523)

Maynard Mack, "The World of Hamlet," in The Yale Review *(© 1952 by Yale University; reprinted by permission of the editors), Vol. XLI, No. 4, June, 1952, pp. 502-23.*

WILLIAM EMPSON   (essay date 1953)

[Empson is an English poet, critic, and scholar. His Seven Types of Ambiguity *(1930), with its emphasis on interpreting a literary work as a complex combination of multiple meanings, was a major influence in the development of New Criticism. Empson here argues that the Elizabethan audience had grown tired of the revenge tragedy that was at the base of* Hamlet's *plot, and that Shakespeare revised his sources in an attempt to modernize the story and to make it more appealing. Thus, Shakespeare developed the delay into a theatrical device which would heighten the mysterious nature of the play. Empson concludes his essay with a discussion of the Freudian interpretation of Hamlet. Other critics who adopted a historical approach to* Hamlet *include A.J.A. Waldock (1931), E. E. Stoll (1933), J. Dover Wilson (1935), E.M.W. Tillyard (1949), Fredson Bowers (1955), and Eleanor Prosser (1971).]*

The real "Hamlet problem," it seems clear, is a problem about his first audiences. This is not to deny (as Professor Stoll has sometimes done) that Hamlet himself is a problem [see excerpt above, 1933]; he must be one, because he says he is; and he is a magnificent one, which has been exhaustively examined in the last hundred and fifty years. What is peculiar is that he does not seem to have become one till towards the end of the eighteenth century. . . . [As] the Hamlet Problem has developed, yielding increasingly subtle and profound reasons for his delay, there has naturally developed in its wake a considerable backwash from critics who say ''But how can such a drama as you describe conceivably have been written by an Elizabethan, for an Elizabethan audience?'' Some kind of mediating process is really required here; one needs to explain how the first audiences could take a more interesting view than Dr. Johnson's [see excerpt above, 1765], without taking an improbably profound one.

The political atmosphere may be dealt with first. Professor Stoll has successfully argued that even the theme of delay need not be grasped at all by an audience, except as a convention; however, Mr. Dover Wilson has pointed out that the first audiences had a striking example before them in Essex, who was, or had just been, refusing to make up his mind in a public and alarming manner; his attempt at revolt might have caused civil war. Surely one need not limit it to Essex; the Queen herself had long used vacillation as a major instrument of policy, but the habit was becoming unnerving because though presumably dying she still refused to name a successor, which in itself might cause civil war. Her various foreign wars were also dragging on indecisively. A play about a prince who brought disaster by failing to make up his mind was bound to ring straight on the nerves of the audience when Shakespeare rewrote *Hamlet;* it is not a question of intellectual subtlety but of what they were being forced to think about already. (pp. 16-18)

[The] political angle was not the first problem of the assignment, the thing [Shakespeare] had to solve before he could face an audience; it was more like an extra gift which the correct solution tossed into his hand. The current objection to the old play *Hamlet,* which must have seemed very hard to surmount, can be glimpsed in the surviving references to it. It was thought absurdly theatrical. (p. 19)

The difficulty was particularly sharp for Shakespeare's company, which set out to be less ham than its rivals, and the Globe Theatre itself, only just built, asked for something impressively new. And yet there was a revival of the taste for Revenge Plays in spite of a half-resentful feeling that they had become absurd. (pp. 19-20)

What Shakespeare was famous for, just before writing *Hamlet,* was Falstaff and patriotic stuff about Henry V. *Julius Caesar,* the play immediately previous to *Hamlet,* is the most plausible candidate for a previous tragedy or indeed Revenge Play, not surprisingly, but the style is dry and the interest mainly in the politics of the thing. One can easily imagine that the external cause, the question of what the audience would like, was prominent when the theme was chosen. . . . [He] must have seemed an unlikely person just then to start on a great Tragic Period, and he never wrote a Revenge Play afterwards; we can reasonably suppose that he first thought of *Hamlet* as a pretty specialized assignment, a matter, indeed, of trying to satisfy audiences who demanded a Revenge Play and then laughed when it was provided. . . . It was a bold decision, and probably decided his subsequent career, but it was a purely technical one. He thought: ''The only way to shut this hole is to make it big. I shall make Hamlet walk up to the audience and tell them, again and again, 'I don't know why I'm delaying any more than you do; the motivation of this play is just as blank to me as it is to you; but I can't help it.' What is more, I shall make it impossible for them to blame him. And *then* they

daren't laugh.'' It turned out, of course, that this method, instead of reducing the old play to farce, made it thrillingly life-like and profound. A great deal more was required; one had to get a character who could do it convincingly, and bring in large enough issues for the puzzle not to appear gratuitous. I do not want to commit the Fallacy of Reduction, only to remove the suspicion that the first audiences could not tell what was going on. (pp. 20-1)

To be sure, we cannot suppose them really very ''sophisticated,'' considering the plays by other authors they admired. . . . But that they *imagined* that they were too sophisticated for the old *Hamlet* does seem to emerge from the surviving jokes about it, and that is all that was required. We need not suppose, therefore, that they missed the purpose of the changes; ''he is cunning past man's thought'' they are more likely to have muttered unwillingly into their beards, as they abandoned the intention to jeer.

As was necessary for this purpose, the play uses the device of throwing away dramatic illusion much more boldly than Shakespeare does anywhere else. . . . A particularly startling case is planted early in the play, when the Ghost pursues Hamlet and his fellows underground and says ''Swear'' (to be secret) wherever they go, and Hamlet says

> Come on, you hear this fellow in the cellarage,
> Consent to swear.   [I. v. 151-52]

It seems that the area under the stage was *technically* called the cellarage, but the point is clear enough without this extra sharpening; it is a recklessly comic throw-away of illusion, especially for a repertory audience, who know who is crawling about among the trestles at this point (Shakespeare himself, we are told), and have their own views on his style of acting. But the effect is still meant to be frightening; it is like Zoo in *Back to Methusaleh,* who says ''This kind of thing is got up to impress you, not to impress me''; and it is very outfacing for persons in the audience who come expecting to make that kind of joke themselves. (pp. 22-3)

Critics have wondered how it could be endurable for Shakespeare to make the actor of Hamlet upbraid for their cravings for theatricality not merely his fellow actors but part of his audience (the term ''groundlings'' must have appeared an insult and comes nowhere else); but surely this carries on the central joke, and wouldn't make the author prominent. . . . What is technically so clever is to turn this calculated collapse of dramatic illusion into an illustration of the central theme. The first problem was how to get the audience to attend to the story again, solved completely by ''O what a rogue'' and so forth, which moves from the shame of theatrical behavior and the paradoxes of sincerity into an immediate scheme to expose the King. . . . We next see Hamlet in the ''To be or not to be'' soliloquy, and he has completely forgotten his passionate and apparently decisive self-criticism—but this time the collapse of interest in the story comes from the Prince, not merely from the audience; then when Ophelia enters he swings away from being completely disinterested into being more disgracefully theatrical than anywhere else. . . . The metaphor of the pipe which Fortune can blow upon as she pleases, which [Hamlet] used to Horatio, is made a symbol by bringing a recorder into bodily prominence during his moment of triumph after the Play scene, and he now boasts to the courtiers that he is a mystery, therefore they cannot play on him—we are meant to feel that there are real merits in the condition, but he has already told us he despises himself for it. Incidentally he has just told

Horatio that he deserves a fellowship in a "cry" of players (another searching joke phrase not used elsewhere) but Horatio only thinks "half of one." The recovery from the point where the story seemed most completely thrown away has been turned into an exposition of the character of the hero and the central dramatic theme. No doubt this has been fully recognized, but I do not think it has been viewed as a frank treatment of the central task, that of making the old play seem real by making the hero life-like. (pp. 23-5)

However, the theme of a major play by Shakespeare is usually repeated by several characters in different forms, and Hamlet is not the only theatrical one here. Everybody is "acting a part" except Horatio, as far as that goes; and Laertes is very theatrical, as Hamlet rightly insists over the body of Ophelia ("I'll rant as well as thou"). One might reflect that both of them trample on her, both literally and figuratively, just because of their common trait. And yet Laertes is presented as opposite to Hamlet in not being subject to delay about avenging his father or to scruples about his methods; the tragic flaw in Hamlet must be something deeper or more specific. We need therefore to consider what his "theatricality" may be. . . . The *plot* of a Revenge Play seemed theatrical because it kept the audience waiting without obvious reason in the characters; then a theatrical *character* (in such a play) appears as one who gets undeserved effects, "cheap" because not justified by the plot as a whole. However, theatrical behavior is never only "mean" in the sense of losing the ultimate aim for a petty advantage, because it must also "give itself away"—the idea "greedy to impress an audience" is required. Now the basic legend about Hamlet was that he did exactly this and yet was somehow right for it; he successfully kept a secret by displaying he had got one. The idea is already prominent in Saxo Grammaticus. . . . (pp. 26-7)

Kyd would probably keep [Hamlet] sane and rather tedious in soliloquy but give him powerful single-line jokes when answering other characters; the extreme and sordid pretence of madness implied by Saxo would not fit Kyd's idea of tragic decorum. I think that Shakespeare's opening words for Hamlet, "A little more than kin and less than kind," are simply repeated from Kyd; a dramatic moment for the first-night audience, because they wanted to know whether the new Hamlet would be different. His next words are a passionate assertion that he is *not* the theatrical Hamlet—"I know not seems." Now this technique from Kyd, though trivial beside the final Hamlet, would present the inherent paradox of the legend very firmly: why are these jokes supposed to give a kind of magical success to a character who had obviously better keep his mouth shut? All Elizabethans, including Elizabeth, had met the need to keep one's mouth shut at times; the paradox might well seem sharper to them than it does to us. Shakespeare took care to laugh at this as early as possible in his version of the play. The idea that it is silly to drop hints as Hamlet does is expressed by Hamlet himself, not only with force but with winning intimacy, when he tells the other observers of the Ghost that they must keep silence completely, and not say "I could an I would, there be an if they might" and so on, which is precisely what he does himself for the rest of the play. No doubt he needs a monopoly of this technique. But the first effect in the theatre was another case of "closing the hole by making it big"; if you can make the audience laugh *with* Hamlet about his method early, they aren't going to laugh *at* him for it afterwards. . . . I fancy Shakespeare could rely on some of his audience to add the apparently modern theory that the relief of self-expression saved Hamlet from going finally mad, because it fits well enough onto their beliefs about the disease "melancholy." But in any case the basic legend is a dream glorification of both having your cake and eating it, keeping your secret for years, till you kill, and yet perpetually enjoying boasts about it. Here we are among the roots of the race of man; rather a smelly bit perhaps, but a bit that appeals at once to any child. It is ridiculous for critics to *blame* Shakespeare for accentuating this traditional theme till it became enormous.

The view that Hamlet "is Shakespeare," or at least more like him than his other characters, I hope falls into shape now. It has a basic truth, because he was drawing on his experience as actor and playwright; these professions often do puzzle their practitioners about what is theatrical and what is not, as their friends and audiences can easily recognize; but he was only using what the theme required. To have to give posterity, let alone the immediate audiences, a picture of himself would have struck him as laying a farcical extra burden on an already difficult assignment. (pp. 28-9)

We should now be able to reconsider the view which Professor Stoll has done real service by following up: Hamlet's reasons are so good that he not only never delays at all but was never supposed to; the self-accusations of the Revenger are always prominent in Revenge Plays, even classical Greek ones, being merely a necessary part of the machine—to make the audience continue waiting with attention. . . . In making the old play "life-like" Shakespeare merely altered the style, not the story; except that it was probably he who (by way of adding "body") gave Hamlet very much better reasons for delay than any previous Revenger, so that it is peculiarly absurd of us to pick him out and puzzle over *his* delay. I do not at all want to weaken this line of argument; I think Shakespeare did, intentionally, pile up all the excuses for delay he could imagine, while at the same time making Hamlet bewail and denounce his delay far more strongly than ever Revenger had done before. It is the force and intimacy of the self-reproaches of Hamlet, of course, which ordinary opinion has rightly given first place; that is why these legal arguments that he didn't delay appear farcical. But the two lines of argument are only two halves of the same thing. Those members of the audience who simply wanted to see a Revenge Play again, without any hooting at it from smarter persons, deserved to be satisfied; and anyhow, for all parties, the suspicion that Hamlet was a coward or merely fatuous had to be avoided. The ambiguity was an essential part of the intention, because the more you tried to translate the balance of impulses in the old drama into a realistic story the more peculiar this story had to be made. The old structure was still kept firm, but its foundations had to be strengthened to carry so much extra weight. At the same time, a simpler view could be taken; whatever the stage characters may say, the real situation in the theatre is still that the audience knows the revenge won't come till the end. Their own foreknowledge is what they had laughed at, rather than any lack of motive in the puppets, and however much the motives of the Revenger for delay were increased he could still very properly blame himself for keeping the audience waiting. One could therefore sit through the new *Hamlet* (as for that matter the eighteenth century did) without feeling too startled by his self-reproaches. But of course the idea that "bringing the style up to date" did not involve any change of content seems to me absurd, whether held by Shakespeare's committee or by Professor Stoll; for one thing, it made the old theatrical convention appear bafflingly indistinguishable from a current political danger. The whole story was brought into a new air, so that one felt there was much more "in it." (pp. 30-1)

[It] is reasonable to revive the idea that [Shakespeare] wrote two versions of *Hamlet,* and . . . the mangled First Quarto gives indirect evidence about the first one. . . . The first version, for 1600, solved the technical problem so well that it established Hamlet as a ''mystery'' among the first audiences; then a minor revision for 1601 gratified this line of interest by making him a baffling one and spreading mystery all round. (p. 185)

I assume, then, that the First Quarto gives evidence about the first draft, so that the main changes for the second concern Ophelia and the Queen; whom I will consider in turn. The scolding of Ophelia by Hamlet, and the soliloquy ''To be or not to be'' before it, were put later in the play. The main purpose in this, I think, was to screw up the paradoxes in the character of Hamlet rather than to affect Ophelia herself. (pp. 185-86)

[The] worst behavior of Hamlet is towards Ophelia, whether you call it theatrical or not; the critics who have turned against him usually seem to do so on her behalf, and his relations with the two women raise more obvious questions about whether he is neurotic than the delay. The first question here is how Shakespeare *expected* the audience to take the scolding of Ophelia, admitting that an audience has different parts. We can all see Hamlet has excuses for treating her badly, but if we are to think him a hero for yielding to them the thing becomes barbaric; he punishes her savagely for a plot against him when he has practically forced her to behave like a hospital nurse. I feel sure that Mr. Dover Wilson is getting at something important, though as so often from a wrong angle, when he makes a fuss about adding a stage direction at II, ii, 158, and insists that Hamlet must visibly overhear the King and Polonius plotting to use Ophelia against him [see excerpt above, 1935]. No doubt this is better for a modern audience, but we need to consider the sequence of changes in the traditional play. In our present text, even granting Mr. Dover Wilson his tiny stage direction, what Hamlet overhears is very harmless and indeed what he himself has planned for; it was he who started using Ophelia as a pawn, however much excused by passion or despair. (pp. 186-87)

I think the Shakespeare Hamlet was meant to be regarded by most of the audience as behaving shockingly towards Ophelia, almost too much so to remain a tragic hero; to swing round the whole audience into reverence for Hamlet before he died was something of a lion-taming act. This was part of the rule that all his behavior must be startling, and was only slightly heightened in revision. But to see it in its right proportion we must remember another factor; the theatre, as various critics have pointed out, clung to an apparently muddled but no doubt tactical position of both grumbling against Puritans and accepting their main claims. The Victorians still felt that Hamlet was simply high-minded here. (p. 188)

Here I think we have the right approach to another Victorian view of Hamlet, of which Bernard Shaw is perhaps the only representative still commonly read: that he was morally too advanced to accept feudal ideas about revenge, and felt, but could not say, that his father had given him an out-of-date duty; that was why he gave such an absurd excuse for not killing the King at prayer. . . . The word ''feudal'' needs to be removed (as so often); it is royal persons who cannot escape the duty of revenge by an appeal to public justice; this is one of the reasons why they have long been felt to make interesting subjects for plays. But I think Shakespeare's audiences did regard his Hamlet as taking a ''modern'' attitude to his situation, just as Bernard Shaw did. This indeed was one of the major dramatic effects of the new treatment. He walks out to the audience and says ''You think this an absurd old play, and so it is, *but I'm in it,* and what can I do?'' The theatrical device in itself expresses no theory about the duty of revenge, but it does ask the crowd to share in the question. (pp. 188-89)

Turning now to the Queen: Mr. Dover Wilson argued that the First Quarto was merely a perversion of the single play by Shakespeare, with a less ''subtle'' treatment of the Queen. I do not think we need at once call it subtle of Shakespeare to make her into an extra mystery by simply cutting out all her explanations of her behavior. The idea of a great lady who speaks nobly but is treacherous to an uncertain degree was familiar on the stage, as in Marlowe's *Edward II,* not a new idea deserving praise. No doubt the treatment is subtle; several of her replies seem unconscious proofs of complete innocence, whereas when she says her guilt ''spills itself in fearing to be spilt'' she must imply a guilty secret. But we must ask why the subtlety is wanted. An important factor here is the instruction of the Ghost to Hamlet, in the first Act, that he must contrive nothing against his mother. I think this was supplied by Kyd; he would see its usefulness as an excuse for the necessary delay, and would want his characters to be high-minded. Also he had to give his Ghost a reason for returning later, because the audience would not want this interesting character to be dropped. In Kyd's first act, therefore, the Ghost said Claudius must be killed and the Queen protected; then in the third Act, when Hamlet was questioning her suspiciously, the Ghost came back and said she hadn't known about his murder, supporting her own statement to that effect; meanwhile he told Hamlet that it would be dangerous to wait any longer about killing Claudius, because the Play Scene has warned him. Hamlet had felt he still ought to wait till he knew how much his mother was involved. The Ghost had already forgiven her for what she had done—perhaps adultery, probably only the hasty re-marriage to his brother—but had not cared to discuss it much; the tragic effect in the third act is that he clears up too late an unfortunate bit of vagueness in his first instructions. This makes him a bit absurd, but the motives of Ghosts seldom do bear much scrutiny, and he is better than most of them. (On this account, Hamlet is still liable to have different motives in different scenes for sparing the King at prayer, but that seems a normal bit of Elizabethan confusion.) Thus there is no reason why Kyd's Queen should not have satisfied the curiosity of the audience fully; she would admit to Hamlet that her second marriage was wrong, clear herself of anything else, offer to help him, and be shown doing it. Shakespeare, in his first treatment of the play, had no reason not to keep all this, as the First Quarto implies; his problem was to make the audience accept the delay as life-like, and once Hamlet is surrounded by guards that problem is solved. But if we next suppose him making a minor revision, for audiences who have become interested in the mystery of Hamlet, then it is clearly better to surround him with mystery and make him drive into a situation which the audience too feels to be unplumbable. (pp. 193-95)

I think the fundamental reason why the change was ''subtle,'' to recall the term of Mr. Dover Wilson, was something very close to the Freudian one which he is so quick at jumping away from; to make both parents a mystery at least pushes the audience towards fundamental childhood situations. But it would have a sufficient immediate effect from thickening the atmosphere and broadening the field. (p. 196)

I ought finally to say something about the Freudian view of *Hamlet,* the most extraordinary of the claims that it means something very profound which the first audiences could not know about. I think that literary critics, when this theory appeared, were thrown into excessive anxiety. A. C. Bradley had made the essential points before [see excerpt above, 1905], that Hamlet's first soliloquy drives home (rather as a surprise to the first audiences, who expected something about losing the throne) that some kind of sex nausea about his mother is what is really poisoning him; also that in the sequence around the Prayer scene his failure to kill Claudius is firmly and intentionally tied up with a preference for scolding his mother instead. I have been trying to argue that his relations with the two women were made increasingly oppressive as the play was altered, but in any case the Freudian atmosphere of the final version is obvious even if distasteful. Surely the first point here is that the original legend is a kind of gift for the Freudian approach (even if Freud is wrong); it need not be painful to suppose that Shakespeare expressed this legend with a unique power. There is a fairy-story or childish fascination because Hamlet can boast of his secret and yet keep it, and because this crazy magical behaviour kills plenty of grown-ups; to base it on a conflict about killing Mother's husband is more specifically Freudian but still not secret. The Freudian theory makes a literary problem when its conclusions oppose what the author thought he intended; but it seems clear that Shakespeare wouldn't have wanted to alter anything if he had been told about Freud, whether he laughed at the theory or not. Then again, what is tiresome for the reader about the Freudian approach is that it seems to tell us we are merely deluded in the reasons we give for our preferences, because the real grounds for them are deep in the Unconscious, but here the passage to the underground is fairly open. A feeling that this hero is allowed to act in a peculiar way which is yet somehow familiar, because one has been tempted to do it oneself, is surely part of the essence of the story. There is a clear contrast with Oedipus, who had no Oedipus Complex. He had not wanted to kill his father and marry his mother, even "unconsciously"; if he came to recognize that he had wanted it, that would weaken his bleak surprise at learning he has done it. The claim is that his audiences wanted to do it unconsciously—that is why they were so deeply stirred by the play, and why Aristotle could treat it as the supreme tragedy though in logic it doesn't fit his case at all, being only a bad luck story. This position is an uneasy one, I think; one feels there ought to be some mediation between the surface and the depths, and probably the play did mean more to its first audiences than we realize. But Hamlet is himself suffering from the Complex, in the grand treatment by Ernest Jones [see excerpt above, 1949], though the reactions of the audience are also considered when he makes the other characters "fit in." And this is not unreasonable, because Hamlet is at least peculiar in Saxo, and Shakespeare overtly treats him as a "case" of Melancholy, a specific though baffling mental disease which medical textbooks were being written about.

What does seem doubtful is whether his mental disease was supposed to be what made him spare the King at prayer. We may take it that Kyd already had the scene, and gave the reason (that this might not send him to Hell), and meant it to be taken seriously; and also meant its effect to be seen as fatal, a tragic failure of state-craft. A moral to this, that a desire for excessive revenge may sometimes spoil a whole design, would seem quite in order. But, by the time Shakespeare had finished raising puzzles about the motives, even the motive for this part, though apparently taken over directly, might well come into doubt; for one thing, the failure of Hamlet even to consider his own danger, now that the King knows his secret, is so very glaring.

Even the wildly opposite reason suggested by Mr. Dover Wilson, that he feels it wouldn't be sporting though he can't tell himself so, might crop up among contemporary audiences; in any case, the idea that there was some puzzle about it could easily occur to them. And the idea of a man grown-up in everything else who still acts like a child towards his elder relations is familiar; it could occur to a reflective mind, not only be sensed by the Unconscious, as soon as behavior like Hamlet's was presented as a puzzle. The trouble with it if made prominent would be from making the hero contemptible, but Hamlet has many escapes from that besides his claim to mental disease. That his mother's marriage was considered incest made his initial disturbance seem more rational then than it does now; but his horror and jealousy are made to feel, as Mr. Eliot pointed out for purposes of complaint, a spreading miasma and in excess of this cause [see excerpt above, 1919]. . . . Unconscious resistance to killing a *King* is what the audience would be likely to invent, if any; for Claudius to talk about the divinity that doth hedge a king is irony, because he has killed one, but we are still meant to feel its truth. . . . But none of this is a rebuttal of the Freudian view; the feeling about a King is derived very directly from childhood feelings about Father.

We have to consider, not merely how a play came to be written which allows of being searched so deeply so long after, but why it has steadily continued to hold audiences who on any view do not see all round it. The Freudian view is that it satisfies the universal Unconscious, but one feels more practical in saying, as Hugh Kingsmill did, that they enjoy the imaginative release of indulging in very "theatrical" behavior, which in this case is hard to distinguish from "neurotic" behavior. The business of the plot is to prevent them from feeling it as an indulgence, because the assumption that Hamlet has plenty of reasons for it somehow is always kept up. If we leave the matter there, I think, the play appears a rather offensive trick and even likely to be harmful. Indeed common sense has decided that people who feel encouraged to imitate Hamlet, or to follow what appear to be the instructions of Freud, actually are liable to behave badly. But the first audiences were being asked to consider this hero of legend as admittedly theatrical (already laughed at for it) and yet unbreakably true about life; in one way because he illustrated a recognized neurosis, in another because he extracted from it virtues which could not but be called great however much the story proved them to be fatal. So far as the spectator was tempted forward to examine the "reasons" behind Hamlet he was no longer indulging a delusion but considering a frequent and important, even if delusory, mental state, and trying to handle it. If one conceives the play as finally rewritten with that kind of purpose and that kind of audience, there is no need to be astonished that it happened to illustrate the Freudian theory. Indeed it would seem rather trivial, I think, to go on now and examine whether the successive versions were getting more Freudian. The eventual question is whether you can put up with the final Hamlet, a person who frequently appears in the modern world under various disguises, whether by Shakespeare's fault or not. I would always sympathize with anyone who says, like Hugh Kingsmill, that he can't put up with Hamlet at all. But I am afraid it is within hail of the more painful question whether you can put up with yourself and the race of man. (pp. 201-05)

William Empson, "'Hamlet' When New" and "'Hamlet' When New (Part II)," in The Sewanee Review, *Vol. LXI, Nos. 1 and 2, January-March and April-June, 1953, pp. 15-42; 185-205.*

ANDREW J. GREEN (essay date 1953)

[*Green debates the relation of the Mousetrap to Hamlet's essential nature. He refutes the contention of J. Dover Wilson (1935) that the dumb-show "took Hamlet by surprise."*]

In Hamlet's advice to the players Shakespeare goes further than merely to voice his own sentiments on the art of acting. There are clues in this speech, in the Pyrrhus passage, and in The Mousetrap to Shakespeare's own full-bodied concept of the power of drama. The evidence for the presence in *Hamlet* of this developed concept does not necessarily prove or refute either the theory of an indecisive or of a decisive protagonist. It is here presented, however, from the point of view that Hamlet, though amazingly and even mystifyingly complex, is essentially a man of action.

That after a dozen years of work in and for the theater Shakespeare had become intensely conscious of the power of drama upon the human soul, and that in *Hamlet* he found a perfect means of dramatic representation of this concept, is the thesis of this article. The crux of the evidence lies in an affirmation of the structural necessity in the play of the Pyrrhus passage. No Hamlet criticism or scholarship familiar to this author has ever explicitly—let alone heartily—made this affirmation, although mere dramatic probability and, at least at the height of his maturity, Shakespeare's much-praised dramatic economy, present two compelling arguments in its favor. But once the Pyrrhus material is seen as a structural necessity, much follows. . . .

The exponents of delay see the Pyrrhus passage merely as a cue for the John-a-dreams soliloquy which follows. But for the performance of a function so simple Shakespeare, who can effectively motivate Edmund, Richard II, or Reynaldo in a single line or two, has given it much too much space. (p. 395)

The passage is also too long to account for as an intrusion. The young Shakespeare was capable of dragging out the murder of Clarence for its theatrical appeal, and of employing Queen Elizabeth as a necessary cog in the machinery of *A Midsummer Night's Dream;* the mature Shakespeare can expand ad libitum Malcolm's not very dramatic testing of Macduff because what could be forgiven and what could not be forgiven in a king was of profound interest to Englishmen, and, because of its timely appeal, he could also insert into *Hamlet* a dialogue on children's companies. But the Pyrrhus passage is not intrinsically worth while as melodrama, or as praise of Elizabeth or James, or as timely commentary, or as an appeal to patriotic fervor or insular pride. Its *raison d'etre* cannot be found outside of the play. It must therefore be looked for where it has never been looked for—in the dramatic economy of *Hamlet* itself.

Once mentioned, the fact that the Pyrrhus passage provides solid motivation for the Mousetrap may seem obvious. But it has not been obvious in the past. . . . The absence in criticism and scholarship of significant comment on the necessity of the material indicates that its function has been understood by few or none. (p. 396)

Probably one reason that its relation to the Mousetrap has not been seen is that readers and critics conditioned by the indecisive Hamlet of Goethe and Coleridge [see excerpts above, 1795 and 1811] would be unlikely to see it, or to give it any emphasis or reflection if they did. Hamlet, paralyzed in will, snatches at any excuse for delay. The Mousetrap therefore appears as an easy stratagem to conceive of, the kind of idea that would occur to any procrastinator. A second reason is that

Hamlet is so familiar to us all that we take the events of the plot for granted. We have read it many times, and always under the mesmerism of its traditional greatness. The Mousetrap is merely something to be expected, something that happens next. At best it is admired as a thought that came to Hamlet by lucky chance, or was momentarily suggested by the casual advent of the players—the most natural idea in the world.

It could not have been taken in this way by the Elizabethans who enjoyed its first run at the Globe. . . . Attending either the *Ur-Hamlet* or Shakespeare's *Hamlet,* [this audience] did not know for sure what was coming next. It felt a sense of curiosity and expectancy impossible for us moderns to recapture, no matter how much we try to approach the play in the mood of a first-nighter. Not that modern criticism has not glorified the Mousetrap, but it has always been for its effect on Claudius and for Hamlet's histrionics rather than for its inception. A clever stratagem: yes, but *how* clever is it, and *why* is it so clever? (pp. 396-97)

Hamlet's dramatic task is to possess himself of unquestionable evidence of the King's innocence or guilt, avenge the crime, and expose the guilt to the world; his task is to execute justice, not to commit murder.

But the crime of Claudius is dark, occult, undivulged; the bloody hand is hidden. . . . All knowledge of it is locked in the soul of Claudius. There are no wisps of hair, no telltale finger-prints, no bits of torn clothing, no blood-stains, no buttons. Hamlet is cast in the role of a detective to whom the discovery of any convincing evidence seems utterly impossible. (p. 397)

A playwright could scarcely devise for his protagonist a problem more baffling and maddening than Hamlet's. Small wonder that the close of Act II his frustration bursts forth with such vehemence.

No rogue, peasant slave, or John-a-dreams, however, could escape from this labyrinthine maze as does Hamlet.

The thought that Claudius may be made to reveal his secret if his crime is dramatically enacted before his eyes does not occur to Hamlet in a vacuum. It does not come with the arrival of the players, though that is certainly opportune. Instead, Shakespeare carefully motivates it and prepares for it. . . . Admiration for Hamlet's stratagem is, in fact, a necessary assumption of the play.

In *Der Bestrafte Brudermord* the motif is employed as a stratagem; it therefore probably occurred in the *Ur-Hamlet,* the author of which undoubtedly derived it from three or four contemporary stories. What Shakespeare did was to motivate the device far beyond the motivation of his sources: that is, he has made it artistically convincing.

In Shakespeare, the man to whom such a stratagem could occur must not merely possess a profound and penetrating mind and a knowledge of the souls of men, but must also be a lover of drama and thoroughly versed in the field. Such is Hamlet: he banters with the players on terms of intimacy. The First Player is an "old friend." Hamlet knows two plays thoroughly; he must know many well. Of one he has at least seventeen consecutive lines by heart. Another he knows well enough to insert some dozen or sixteen lines at the most critical point. (pp. 397-98)

Hamlet is also an actor: in this speech we have an excellent sample of his quality. In the Mousetrap, too, he is superb: he plays one part to the court, another to Ophelia, another to the Queen, another—the finest and best—to the King. . . .

His dramatic sensitivity is prompter to his expectant spiritual intuition. As Hamlet begins to quote the speech he chiefly loved—

> 'twas Aeneas' tale to Dido, and thereabout of
> it especially where he speaks of Priam's slaugh-
> ter
>
> [II. ii. 446-48]

—a sense of empathy with Aeneas and the poetic material captures him. He becomes an eye-witness of the bloody figure of Pyrrhus. Instinctively, as he recites, he begins to act the part, and at the same time his feeling for the dramatic art becomes so keen that he wants a professional to continue— that is, to heighten the empathy still further. (p. 398)

With the passion of Hecuba the First Player is at his best, for he has forced his soul

> so to his own conceit
> That from her working all his visage wann'd,
> Tears in his eyes, distraction in 's aspect,
> A broken voice, and his whole function suiting
> With forms to his conceit.
>
> [II. ii. 553-57]

The empathetic emotion is at its height. Even old Polonius, forgetting for a moment his own self-importance, is on the verge of weeping:

> Look, whe'er he has not turned his colour and
> has tears in 's eyes. Prithee, no more.
>
> [II. ii. 519-20]

Hamlet, startled, notes the power of drama on Polonius and feels it on himself. The idea falls from heaven: here is a means to pierce the deepest recesses of a guilty soul. (p. 399)

The Pyrrhus material was not included in *Der Bestrafte Brudermord* and therefore probably did not appear in the *Ur-Hamlet.* It is in all likelihood an addition by Shakespeare to his sources to provide convincing motivation for the Mousetrap.

If it is through the power of drama that Claudius is to be trapped, the drama which traps him must be powerful. Hamlet is much concerned with this: it can be no other than his speech of a dozen or sixteen lines which is the subject, probably just after the conclusion of a rehearsal, of his advice to the First Player:

> Speak the speech, I pray you trippingly on the
> tongue, but if you mouth it, as some of your
> players do, I had as lief the town-crier had
> spoke my lines.
>
> [III. ii. 1-4]
> (pp. 399-400)

Both Hamlet's concern about the Mousetrap and an emphasis upon the ingenuity of his stratagem tell against Dover Wilson's ingenious theory that the dumb-show took Hamlet by surprise [see excerpt above, 1935]. He further supposes the King and Queen so engaged in merry talk that they happen not to look at the dumb-show. But Hamlet knew "The Murder of Gonzago" thoroughly enough to set down a dozen or sixteen lines in it; therefore he knew of the dumb-show. . . . Dover Wilson's theory, moreover, is almost certainly beyond the possibilities of lucid representation to any audience. (p. 400)

It is a commonplace of criticism that Shakespeare distinguishes the verse of the Pyrrhus passage and of the Mousetrap from the style of *Hamlet* itself in order to set off the interpolated recitation and play from the main drama. The verse of both is excellent in one sense at least: it effectively achieves this purpose. And Hamlet and Shakespeare both require us to assume its excellence as dramatic verse. We have no independent judgment in this matter: it is excellent because they say it is. And the play within the play cannot be like the play. But most direction has stopped with the unlikeness, and we behold the spectacle of Claudius being bowled over by mere puppetry. (p. 401)

The principle of dramatic empathy forbids [a static] presentation. When the trap is sprung, Claudius must be in a state of hypnotic attention to the play. What must influence him so powerfully ought at least to possess, at that moment, a convincing degree of probability and verisimilitude for the audience. There must be, in short, a doubly empathetic development in the Mousetrap itself—the empathetic spell of Claudius must be seen (this is worth repeating) and the tension of the Mousetrap and the horror of the murder must be felt, by the audience of *Hamlet.* (pp. 401-02)

The dialogue of the Player King and the Player Queen is just sufficiently extended to provide time for a progression from a sense of quaintness and unreality to one of reasonable familiarity. The passage is directed to test Gertrude, not Claudius. This is good incidental theater, but, being tangential to Hamlet's central purpose, it is not good enough to account for the prolixity of the dialogue. Three better reasons for the dramatic interval are that Claudius cannot miss the developing parallelism between the dumb-show and the play, that it permits his growing dread to increase to a gripping fear, and that it permits the audience time enough to adjust to the new illusion. (p. 402)

The climax of the Mousetrap is at once high theater and high drama. When Claudius saw his crime in the puppetlike action of the dumb-show, he felt more surprise than empathy. But Hamlet fixes in his mind the conviction that the pantomime was no accident—

> Marry, this is miching mallecho; it means MISCHIEF
>
> [III. ii. 137-38]

—and also fixes the apprehension of what may follow. Thus warned, Claudius knows for certain that the developing parallelism between the dumb-show and "The Murder of Gonzago" now being acted will be carried further, will be carried out; during the dialogue of the Player King and Queen his guilt and fear must steadily mount as he waits to participate vicariously in the murder he had himself performed.
The Player King sleeps. The victim of Hamlet's psychological rack endures his anguish heroically:

> Have you heard the argument? Is there no of-
> fense in it?
>
> [III. ii. 232-33]

Hamlet's reply insistently increases the illusion. He hurls the King's guilt in his face:

> No, no, they do but jest, POISON in jest; no
> offense i' th' world.
>
> [III. ii. 234-35]

Lucianus enters. Action and illusion are now swiftly, vividly stepped up. This is the finest actor of the troupe, the Aeneas who so moved Polonius. There is a moment of tableau before

Lucianus-Claudius speaks. His black thoughts are to be read in his looks, in his "damnable faces." Hamlet ("Begin, MURDERER") turns the screw still harder. Can Claudius sit through this when it will be accentuated by voice and gesture? Lucianus speaks. Claudius has heard that voice before; it is the voice of his own soul. Swiftly the illusion intensifies. Claudius sees himself and the audience sees Claudius pour the poison into the sleeper's ears. The realities of play and play within play have coalesced; and Hamlet gives one last fierce, triumphant wrench to the screw. And Claudius gives way.

The argument upon the subject of Hamlet's decisiveness is too complex to be settled by this interpretation. If the interpretation itself is acceptable, it can be fitted into the picture of either a decisive or an indecisive Hamlet. But it strengthens the argument for his decisiveness. The Mousetrap of a mere procrastinator would hardly require the ingenious structural motivation which Shakespeare has so skillfully provided. Nor would it require the exercise by Hamlet of high genius in its inception, or of such remarkable spiritual and intellectual subtlety. If Hamlet is still a delayer, these qualities appear as symptoms of frenetic self-delusion, genius gone crazy; the play itself becomes a document in psychic disorder, and the hero a psychopathic case well outside of humanity.

The Hamlet of the Great Stratagem appears in his main outlines as a man of action, a hero who solves the first half of his terrible problem by an amazing tour de force, and then hews his way through almost insuperable difficulties to the magnificence of his final success and failure. He is a subtler, more complex, more mystifying, more brilliant protagonist than before. He is not, like the delaying Hamlet, a paradoxical inversion of pre-Shakespearian tradition. The shrewdness of his ancestral archetype in Saxo, Belleforest, and Kyd is raised through Shakespeare's transforming power to qualities of subtle intuitive perception and intellectual brilliance. The Hamlet who has delved deeply into criminal psychology, who has employed the power of drama to rive a guilty heart, is much more admirable than the delayer of the Romantics and the less complex driving avenger of Professor Stoll.

If this interpretation is convincing, how congenial to Shakespeare the motif must have been! If it is true that in Hamlet he put more of himself than into any other character, then into Hamlet the protagonist and *Hamlet* the play he must have put more of himself as a dramatist. This propriety of relationship of play and protagonist to the dramatist, to his temperament and imagination, to the seriousness and depth of his sense of his art, to the daily stuff of his thoughts, is a contributing argument in support of the interpretation. In the Pyrrhus speech, in Hamlet's advice to the players, and in the Mousetrap, in short, Shakespeare has made his greatest play an eloquent tribute to his own love of the dramatic art and his respect for its power to influence the souls of men. (pp. 403-04)

> *Andrew J. Green, "The Cunning of the Scene," in* Shakespeare Quarterly, *Vol. IV, No. 4, October, 1953, pp. 395-404.*

FREDSON BOWERS   (essay date 1955)

[*Bowers identifies the central focus of the play as Hamlet's speech following the murder of Polonius, in which Hamlet defines himself as "scourge and minister." Bowers examines Hamlet in both of these roles in terms of their religious significance during the Elizabethan era. While a scourge is an agent for God's vengeance, and is damned even before he acts, a minister carries out divine*

vengeance in order to overthrow evil and promote justice, and is therefore an agent of good. Bowers contends that Hamlet delays while he waits for heaven to define his role. For additional commentary on the theme of revenge in the play, see the excerpts by Harold C. Goddard (1955), Helen Gardner (1959), and Eleanor Prosser (1971).]

When Hamlet is first preparing to leave his mother's chamber after harrowing her to repentance, he turns to the dead body of Polonius:

> For this same lord,
> I do repent; but heaven hath pleas'd it so,
> To punish me with this, and this with me,
> That I must be their scourge and minister.
> I will bestow him, and will answer well
> The death I gave him.   [III. iv. 172-77]

These provocative, if not enigmatic, lines have received comparatively small attention. In my opinion they contain perhaps the clearest analysis Hamlet makes of his predicament, and are therefore worth a scrupulous enquiry.

The Variorum quotes Malone's paraphrase, "To punish me by making me the instrument of this man's death, and to punish this man by my hand." This is surely the literal meaning of the first lines. Going beyond Malone by seeking the nature of Hamlet's punishment, [Dover Wilson finds] that "To punish me with this" means, substantially, that Hamlet perceives his secret will be revealed to Claudius, with serious consequences to himself [see excerpt above, 1935]. . . .

This view is only superficially plausible, and it should not satisfy as offering the complete, or even the true, interpretation. The reason for Heaven's punishment is left unexamined, and no account is taken of the close syntactical relationship between the first statement about the double punishment, and the second, "That I must be their [i.e. Heaven's] scourge and minister." (p. 740)

"For this same lord, I do repent." In spite of whatever callousness Hamlet exhibits in "Thou wretched, rash, intruding fool, farewell!" and in "I'll lug the guts into the neighbour room," or in "Safely stow'd," his stated repentance must be based on more than merely practical considerations that now the hunt will be up. Although Polonius' folly has been punished by Hamlet, yet an innocent man has been killed, and Hamlet has stained his hands with blood without attaining his main objective. His attempt at revenge has led him to commit a murder which he had never contemplated. A modern audience is less likely to feel the horror of Polonius' death than an Elizabethan, which would have known from the moment the rapier flashed through the arras that Hamlet was thereafter a doomed man. On the Elizabethan stage, blood demanded blood; and at the most only two or three tragic characters who draw blood for private motives survive the denouement, and then only at the expense of a retirement to the cloister for the rest of their lives. (pp. 740-41)

Hamlet repents at the personal level, yet adds, "but heaven hath pleas'd it so, / To punish me with this." There are two implications here. First, Hamlet recognizes that his repentance cannot wash the blood from his hands, and that he must accept whatever penalty is in store for him. Second, the "this" with which he is punished is certainly the body of Polonius, and thus the fact of murder, carrying with it the inevitable penalty for blood. (p. 741)

If Heaven's punishment is taken merely as the revelation of Hamlet's secret to Claudius, with all the consequences that are

"Ophelia," by Arthur Hughes (1852). From the Art Collection of the Folger Shakespeare Library.

sure to follow, the punishment would have been comparatively mild, for the play-within-a-play had already effectively revealed Hamlet to Claudius, as well as Claudius to Hamlet. If we carefully follow the implications of the action within the setting of the time-scheme, it is clear that immediately following the mousetrap, and before the killing of Polonius, Claudius has seen Hamlet's murderous intents and has set on foot a plot to kill him. When first conceived after the eavesdropping on Hamlet and Ophelia in the nunnery scene, the English voyage was an innocent expedient to get a peculiarly behaving Hamlet out of the country, perhaps to his cure. However, it becomes a murderous scheme immediately after the play-within-a-play when Claudius changes the ceremonious details and plans to send Hamlet away in the same ship with Rosencrantz and Guildenstern, a necessary factor for the altered commission ordering Hamlet's execution in England. No hint is given that Claudius has altered the original commission in the short interval between the Queen's announcement of Polonius' death and the appearance of Hamlet before him for questioning, nor would there have been time. We learn only that Polonius' death must expedite Hamlet's departure; and hence we are required to assume that the discussion of the commission immediately following the mousetrap play involved what we later learn to have been the important change commanding Hamlet's death. Viewed in this light, the dead body of Polonius cannot punish Hamlet by revealing his secret to Claudius, for that has previously been revealed, and Claudius has already set on foot a lethal plot to dispose of his stepson.

Of course, Hamlet does not know of the change in the purport of the commission, it might be argued. But it would be most difficult to argue that Hamlet was not quite aware that in stripping the truth from Claudius by the doctored-up *Murder of Gonzago,* he had simultaneously revealed himself. . . . Hence I take it that the conventional interpretation of Hamlet's words

ignores their deeper religious significance, and offers only a meaningless redundancy as a substitute.

> but heaven hath pleas'd it so,
> To punish me with this, and this with me,
> That I must be their scourge and minister.
> [III. iv. 173-75]

We may paraphrase thus: Heaven has contrived this killing as a means of punishing us both and as a means of indicating to me that I must be its scourge and minister.

One need only dig down to this bare meaning to reveal how little the basic ideas have really been explained. Three difficult questions immediately assert themselves. Why was Heaven punishing Hamlet by making him the instrument of Polonius' death? Why does this punishment place him in the position of scourge and minister? What is the difference, if any, between scourge and minister? These are best answered, perhaps, in inverse order. The standard religious concept of the time was that God intervened in human affairs in two ways, internally and externally. Internally, God could punish sin by arousing the conscience of an individual to a sense of grief and remorse, which might in extraordinary cases grow so acute as to lead to madness. Externally, God worked through inanimate, or at least sub-human objects, through the forces of Nature, and through the agency of human beings. God's vengeance might strike a criminal by causing a sudden and abnormal mortal sickness, by sinking him in a squall at sea, by hitting him over the head with a falling timber, by leading him accidentally into a deep quicksand or unseen pool. The Elizabethans, if there was any suspected reason, were inclined to see God's hand in most such accidents. But sometimes Heaven punished crime by human agents, and it was standard belief that for this purpose God chose for His instruments those who were already so steeped in crime as to be past salvation. . . . When a human agent was selected to be the instrument of God's vengeance, and the act of vengeance on the guilty necessitated the performance by the agent of a crime, like murder, only a man already damned for his sins was selected, and he was called a scourge.

Any man who knew himself to be such a scourge knew both his function and his fate: his powers were not his own. Taking the long view, no matter how much he could glory in the triumphs of the present, his position was not an enviable one. Any human agent used by God to visit wrath and to scourge evil by evil was already condemned. . . . When Hamlet called himself a scourge of Heaven, it is inconceivable that the Elizabethan audience did not know what he meant, and that Hamlet did not realize to the full what he was saying.

Although some writers, as in Fortescue's translation *The Forest,* used scourge and minister interchangeably, there was a general tendency to distinguish them. The references in the concordance show, for our purposes, that Shakespeare always means minister in a good sense unless he specifies that the minister is of hell. A minister of God, in contrast to a scourge, is an agent who directly performs some good. In this sense, heavenly spirits are ministers of grace, as Hamlet calls them. The good performed by a human minister, however, may be some positive good in neutral or in good circumstances, or it may be some good which acts as a direct retribution for evil by overthrowing it and setting up a positive good in its place. The distinction between minister and scourge, thus, lies in two respects. First, a retributive minister may visit God's wrath on sin but only as the necessary final act to the overthrow of evil, whereas a scourge visits wrath alone, the delayed good to rest in another's hands. To take a rough and ready example, Richard III was thought of as a scourge for England, the final agent of God's vengeance for the deposition and murder of the anointed Richard II; but the good wishes of the ghosts make young Henry Richmond, in Raleigh's description, "the immediate instrument of God's justice," that is, a minister who will bring to a close God's wrath by exacting public justice in battle on the tyrant Richard, this triumph to be followed by a reign of peace and glory under the Tudor dynasty. In the second respect, as a contrast to the evil and damned scourge, if a minister's duty is to exact God's punishment or retribution as an act of good, his hands will not be stained with crime. If in some sense he is the cause of the criminal's death, the means provided him by Heaven will lie in some act of public justice, or of vengeance, rather than in criminal private revenge.

We are now in a position to examine Hamlet's "scourge and minister." We must recognize that the Ghost's command, though not explicit, was at first interpreted by Hamlet as a call to an act of private blood-revenge. Yet there is no getting around the fact that to an Elizabethan audience this was a criminal act of blood, not to be condoned by God, and therefore represented a particularly agonizing position for a tragic hero to be placed in. If Hamlet hopes to right the wrong done him and his father, and to ascend the throne of Denmark with honor, he must contrive a public vengeance which will demonstrate him to be a minister of Heaven's justice. Yet the secret murder of his father, so far as he can see, prevents all hope of public justice; and therefore the circumstances appear to him to enforce a criminal private revenge even after he realizes that he has been supernaturally appointed as a minister. The enormous contrast between Hamlet's first promise to sweep to his revenge and his concluding, "The time is out of joint. O cursed spite, / That ever I was born to set it right," has often been remarked,

but not sufficiently against this background. Moreover, it has not been well considered that if the Ghost is a spirit of health, it could not escape from purgatory under its own volition in order to influence affairs on earth. Since divine permission alone could free the Ghost to revisit the earth, the Ghost's demand for the external punishment of Claudius, and its prophecy of the internal punishment of Gertrude, is not alone a personal call but in effect the transmission of a divine command, appointing Hamlet as God's agent to punish the specific criminal, Claudius.

With the final line of [John Fletcher's] *The Maid's Tragedy* in our ears—"But curs'd is he that is their instrument"—we may see with full force the anomalous position Hamlet conceives for himself: is he to be the private-revenger scourge *or* the public-revenger minister? If scourge, he will make his own opportunities, will revenge murder with murder, and by this means visit God's wrath on corruption. If minister, God will see to it that a proper opportunity is offered in some way that will keep him clear from crime, one which will preserve him to initiate a good rule over Denmark. (pp. 741-45)

As a consequence, Hamlet at the start finds himself in this peculiarly depressing position. He has been set aside from other human beings as an agent of God to set right the disjointed times, and he may reasonably assume from the circumstances of the ghostly visitation that he is a minister. Every private emotion urges him to a personal revenge of blood as the only means of solving his problem, and this revenge seems enforced by the secrecy of the original crime. But if he acts thus, he will be anticipating God's will, which in its good time will provide the just opportunity. If he anticipates and revenges, he risks damnation. If he does not revenge, he must torture himself with his seeming incompetence. In moments of the deepest depression, it could be natural for doubts to arise as to his role, and whether because of his "too too sullied flesh" he may not in fact have been appointed as a scourge, in which case his delay is indeed cowardly. Finally, there arises the important doubt whether the Ghost has been a demon to delude him into damning his soul by the murder of an innocent man, or indeed an agent of Heaven appointing him to an act of justice.

With these considerations in mind, the two months' delay between the Ghost's visitation and the next appearance of Hamlet in Act II may seem to have more validity than certain rather bloodthirsty critics will allow. I suggest that this delay, which Shakespeare never explicitly motivates, was caused not alone by rising doubts of the Ghost, or by the physical difficulties of getting at Claudius, or by the repugnance of a sensitive young man to commit an act of murder, or by his examining the circumstances so over-scrupulously as to become lost in the mazes of thought, motive, and doubt; but instead as much as anything by Hamlet as minister waiting on the expected opportunity which should be provided him, and not finding it. . . . The corruption of the world, of men and women, and of Denmark with its interfering Polonius, its complaisant Ophelia, its traitorous Rosencrantz and Guildenstern whose love has been bought away from their schoolfellow—but especially of Denmark's source of corruption, its murderer-King and lustful, incestuous Queen—seem to cry out for scourging. To satisfy at least one question, he contrives the mousetrap and secures his answer, in the process revealing himself. And immediately an opportunity is given him for private revenge in the prayer scene, but one so far different from divinely appointed public vengeance that Heaven would never have provided it for its minister, a sign that the time is not yet. He passes on, racking himself with blood-thirsty promises, and—no longer trusting to Heaven's delays—impulsively takes the next action upon himself. He kills Polonius, thinking him the King. He repents, but does not expect his repentance to alter the scales of justice. Heaven, it is clear, has punished him for anticipating by his own deed the opportunity that was designed for the future. The precise form of the punishment consists in the fact that in killing, he has slain the wrong man; and the fact that it was Polonius and not the King behind the arras is the evidence for Heaven's punishment. He has irretrievably stained his hands with innocent blood by his usurping action, and foreseeing Heaven withheld his proper victim as its punishment.

As I interpret it, therefore, Hamlet is not only punished *for* the murder of Polonius but *with* his murder, since Polonius was not his assigned victim; hence this fact is the evidence for Heaven's displeasure at his private revenge. The punishment *for* the murder will come, as indeed it does: it is this incident which for the Elizabethan audience motivated the justice of the tragic catastrophe and makes the closet scene the climax of the play. Hamlet's words show his own recognition that he has in part made himself a scourge by the mistaken murder; and I suggest that it is his acceptance of this part of his total role that leads him to send Rosencrantz and Guildenstern so cheerfully, at least on the surface, to their doom. In his mind they are of the essence of the court's corruption under Claudius. They are adders fanged.

When next we see Hamlet, after the interlude of the graveyard scene, a manifest change has taken place. When he left for England, as shown by his "How all occasions do inform against me" soliloquy, he was still torn by his earlier dilemma of somehow reconciling the combat of his private emotions for revengeful action against the restraint of waiting on divine will. But it appears to him that very shortly Heaven reversed its course and actively demonstrated its guidance by preserving his life from the King's plot and returning him to Denmark, short-circuiting the delay of an English adventure. The conflict has certainly been resolved, and it is a different Hamlet indeed who tells Horatio that "There's a divinity that shapes our ends, / Rough-hew them how we will." (pp. 745-48)

When he recapitulates his wrongs, a new and quite different item is appended. It is true that Claudius, as he says, has killed his father, whored his mother, popped in between the election and his hopes, and has even attempted Hamlet's life by treacherous device. He demands for these, "Is't not perfect conscience / To quit him with this arm?" And then, significantly, he adds, "And is't not to be damn'd / To let this canker of our nature come / To further evil?" This is a note not heard before, an argument which would be used not by a private revenger but by one seeking public vengeance and justice. It says in effect: knowing what I know now, especially in this attempt on my life, I should be an accessory before the fact, and thus equally guilty with Claudius, if by further delay I permit him to enact more crimes. (p. 748)

Shakespeare here, as elsewhere, gives Hamlet no precise plan. But the note of confidence, not hitherto heard, is of the utmost importance. Before, when the ways of God were not at all apparent to his mind, we had "O what a rogue and peasant slave," or "How all occasions do inform against me." Now he says to Horatio, "The interim is mine," serene in trust that divine providence will guide him. Critics have noted this end to self-recrimination and conflict but have thought it odd that his confidence was based on no definite plan of action. Properly

viewed, that is the precise point and it is one of great importance. His lack of plan and thus his insistence on providence arises from his confidence in Heaven. This is not lip-service or religious commonplace, but the very heart of the matter.

Immediately, Claudius' counterplot begins and the fencing match is arranged. Hamlet's assured feeling that he is only an instrument in the hands of God sustains him against the ominous portent of disaster that seizes on his heart. For he has learned his lesson from the results of killing Polonius. "There's a special providence in the fall of a sparrow," he says to Horatio; "if it be not now, yet it will come"; and, finally, the summation, "The readiness is all."

From the Elizabethan point of view, divine providence works out the catastrophe with justice. The plotters are hoist by their own villainous schemes; and then, triumphantly, the opportunity is given Hamlet to kill Claudius in circumstances which relieve him from immortal penalty for blood. By stage doctrine he must die for the slaying of Polonius, and, more doubtfully, for that of Rosencrantz and Guildenstern perhaps, the first in which he was inadvertently and the second consciously a scourge; and that penalty is being exacted. Since he cannot now ascend the throne over Claudius' body, all possible self-interest is removed. He has not plotted Claudius' death in cold blood, but seized an opportunity which under no circumstances he could have contrived by blood-revenge, to kill as a dying act of public justice a manifest and open murderer, exposed by the death of Gertrude, while himself suffering the pangs of death as his victim. . . . Hamlet's death is sufficient to expiate that of Polonius in the past and of Laertes in the present. With Christian charity Hamlet accepts Laertes' repentance and forgiveness accompanied by the prayer that "Mine and my father's death come not upon thee" in the future life; and in turn he prays that Heaven will make Laertes free from the guilt of his own. Finally, Horatio's blessing, "Flights of angels sing thee to thy rest," are words of benediction for a minister of providence who died through anticipating heavenly justice but, like Samson, was never wholly cast off for his tragic fault and in the end was honored by fulfilling divine plan in expiatory death. In more ways than one, but not necessarily more than he meant by his prophecy, Hamlet kept his promise for Polonius, "I will answer well the death I gave him." (pp. 748-49)

Fredson Bowers, "Hamlet As Minister and Scourge," in PMLA, Vol. LXX, No. 4, September, 1955, pp. 740-49.

H.D.F. KITTO (essay date 1956)

[*Arguing that* Hamlet *is a religious drama, Kitto explores the way in which Divine Providence structurally and thematically informs the play. He claims that we disregard Shakespeare's intent if we focus solely on the character of Hamlet. Although he concentrates on religious, rather than mythical or ritualistic matters, Kitto follows Gilbert Murray (1914) and Francis Fergusson (1949) in comparing* Hamlet *with classical Greek dramas. Kitto's thesis is supported by Sister Miriam Joseph (1962), but challenged by Eleanor Prosser (1971). For additional commentary on* Hamlet *as a religious drama, see Hermann Ulrici (1839), Søren Kierkegaard (1845), and Patrick Cruttwell (1963). Kitto's essay was first published in 1956.*]

In *Hamlet*, eight people are killed, not counting Hamlet's father; of the two families concerned in the play, those of King Hamlet and Polonius, both are wiped out. Eight deaths are enough to attract attention, and to make us wonder if the essential thing has been said when the play is called 'the tragedy of a man who could not make up his mind'. And the manner of these deaths is no less significant than their number. Claudius murders King Hamlet by poison; thereafter, a metaphorical poison seeps through the play: rottenness, cankers, 'things rank and gross in nature' meet us at every turn. Then at the end it once more becomes literal poison: Gertrude, Claudius, Laertes, Hamlet are all poisoned; and on Claudius, already dead or dying from the poisoned rapier, Hamlet forces the poisoned cup. The Ghost had said:

> Nor let thy soul contrive
> Against thy mother aught; leave her to Heaven.
>
> [I. v. 85-6]

So too Horatio observed:

> Heaven will direct it.
>
> [I. iv. 91]

And what does Heaven do with Gertrude? Of her own accord, and in spite of a warning, she drinks poison. These are plain and striking dramatic facts; how far does 'Hamlet's fatal indecision' explain them? Are they an organic part of a tragedy of character? Or did Shakespeare kill so many people merely from force of habit? (pp. 249-50)

In Act III Scene 1—a magnificent scene, provided we do not try to be clever with it—Claudius and Polonius arrange to spy on Ophelia and Hamlet. There will be occasion later to consider the scene in detail; for the moment we will consider only this, that Shakespeare is concerned to emphasise the indecency of it. Hamlet is—or was—in love with Ophelia and she with him. (The other view, that she is a hussy and he a trifler, brings to mind an unamiable phrase of Housman's: 'This suggestion does dishonour to the human intellect.') It will do us no harm to remember what Love so often is in Shakespeare: not merely a romantic emotion, but a symbol of goodness, even a redemptive power. We have been told often enough in the play what Claudius and Gertrude have made of Love; we ought to have noticed how Polonius thinks of it. In this scene the pure love of Ophelia is being used by two evil men who besmirch everything they touch. This would need argument—and plenty is available—except that in this very scene Shakespeare makes further argument unnecessary: Polonius gives Ophelia a book, evidently a holy book. Lying, spying, double-dealing, are second nature to this wise old counsellor; even so, the formal indecency of what he is doing now makes him uneasy:

> Read on this book,
> That show of such an exercise may colour
> Your loneliness.—We are oft to blame in this,
> 'Tis too much proved, that with devotion's visage
> And pious action we do sugar o'er
> The Devil himself.   [III. i. 43-8]

So, Polonius, there you are—and there too is Claudius, who also confesses at this moment the rottenness of his soul. (pp. 250-51)

Evidently, the character of Hamlet and the death of Polonius are not unconnected, but it is not the case that Shakespeare contrived the latter merely to illustrate the former. The perspective is wider than this. If we will not see the 'divine background', whatever that may prove to be in this play, what shall we make of what Hamlet now says?—

> For this same lord
> I do repent: but Heaven hath pleased it so,
> To punish me with this, and this with me,
> That I must be their scourge and minister.
>
> [III. iv. 172-75]

A shuffling-off of responsibility? No; this has the authentic ring of Greek, that is to say of 'religious', tragedy. The deed is Hamlet's, and Hamlet must answer for it. But at the same time it is the work of Heaven; it is, so to speak, what *would* happen, what ought to happen, to a man who has been sugaring o'er the Devil himself. Denmark is rotten, Polonius is rotten; his death, and the death of seven others, are the natural outcome.

The case is similar with Rosencrantz and Guildenstern. What kind of a man, we may ask, was this Hamlet, that without turning a hair he should so alter the commission that

> He should the bearers put to sudden death,
> No shriving-time allowed?
>
> [V. ii. 46-7]

It is a legitimate question, but not the first one to ask. The first question is: what is the significance of the whole incident in the total design of the play? Where does Shakespeare himself lay the emphasis? For after all, it is his play. When Hamlet tells the story to Horatio, Shakespeare might have made Horatio say:

> Why, man, this was a rash and bloody deed!

What Horatio does say is very different:

> So Guildenstern and Rosencrantz go to 't.
>
> [V. ii. 56]

Before we tell Shakespeare what we think of Hamlet's behaviour we should listen to what Shakespeare tells us. (pp. 251-52)

[Something] has just happened to these two young men: they have been suborned by Claudius and Gertrude:

> GUILDENSTERN: But we both obey.
> And here give up ourselves in the full bent
> To lay our service freely at your feet
> To be commanded.   [II. ii. 29-32]

'We here give up ourselves'—to a murderer and to his guilty wife. Nor is this all that Shakespeare has to tell us about them:

> The cease of majesty
> Dies not alone, but like a gulf doth draw
> What's near it with it; it's a massy wheel
> Fixed on the summit of the highest mount,
> To whose huge spokes ten thousand lesser things
> Are mortis'd and adjoined; which when it falls,
> Each small annexment, petty consequence,
> Attends the boisterous ruin. Never alone
> Did the king sigh, but with a general groan.
>
> [III. iii. 15-23]

Sophocles was not the only tragic poet to understand tragic irony. For these words, spoken of King Claudius, have a much more vigorous reference to the death of King Hamlet; he is the 'massy wheel' which in its fall brings down sundry small annexments—one of whom is the wise speaker of these verses; for they are spoken by Rosencrantz. If then our first question is, What kind of man is Hamlet, that he sends these two to their death? the fault is not Shakespeare's but our own, for lowering our sights contrary to his instructions.

Much of what has just been said needs further justification. We have also many other dramatic facts to note and to use. Perhaps we can kill two birds with one stone by surveying the first six scenes of the play, in which are laid down the foundations of the whole structure, and by prefixing to this a consideration of a matter which has not indeed escaped notice, that there is a resemblance between *Hamlet* and the *Oedipus*.

The *Oedipus Tyrannus* begins by describing twice, once in dialogue and once in lyrics, the plague which is afflicting Thebes. The cause of the plague is the presence in the city of a man who has done two things foul and unnatural above all others: he has killed his own father, and he is living incestuously with his own mother. The details of the plague are so described that we can see how its nature is strictly proportioned to its cause: to death is added sterility; the soil of Thebes, the animals, and the human kind are all barren. The meaning is obvious—unless we make it invisible by reducing the play to the stature of Tragedy of Character: what Oedipus has done is an affront to what we should call Nature, to what Sophocles calls Diké; and since it is the first law of Nature, or Diké, that she cannot indefinitely tolerate what is . . . contrary to Nature, she rises at last against these unpurged affronts. The plague of sterility is the outcome of the unnatural things which Oedipus has done to his parents.

Hamlet begins in the same way. The two soldiers Marcellus and Bernardo, and Horatio, who is both a soldier and a scholar, are almost terrified out of their wits by something so clean contrary to the natural order that

> I might not this believe
> Without the sensible and true avouch
> Of mine own eyes.   [I. i. 56-8]

Professor Dover Wilson, learned in sixteenth-century demonology, has explained that the eschatology of Horatio and Hamlet is Protestant, that the Ghost is a Catholic ghost, and that Bernardo and Marcellus are plain untheological Elizabethans. On this it would be impertinent for an ignoramus to express an opinion, but it does seem that if the 'statists' in Shakespeare's audience, and scholars from the Inns of Court, saw and savoured theological *expertise* in this scene, they would be in danger of missing the main point: that the repeated appearances of the Ghost are something quite outside ordinary experience. Horatio the scholar has heard of something similar, in ancient history, 'a little ere the mightiest Julius fell'. (pp. 252-54)

[At] this point Shakespeare decides to write some poetry—and he is never so dangerous as when he is writing poetry:

> It faded on the crowing of the cock.
> Some say that ever 'gainst that season comes
> Wherein our Savour's birth is celebrated,
> The bird of dawning singeth all night long:
> And then, they say, no spirit dare stir abroad,
> The nights are wholesome; then no planets strike,
> No fairy takes, nor witch hath power to charm,
> So hallowed and so gracious is the time.
>   [I. i. 157-64]

Pretty good, for a simple soldier. The intense and solemn beauty of these verses lifts us, and was designed to lift us, high above the level of Horatio's conjectures. The night 'wherein our Saviour's birth is celebrated' is holy and pure beyond all others; therefore these nights which the Ghost makes hideous by rising so incredibly from the grave, are impure beyond most. Unless Greek Tragedy has bemused me, this passage does more than 'give a religious background to the supernatural happenings' of the scene; they give the 'background', that is, the

logical and dynamic centre, of the whole play. We are in the presence of evil. [Enquiring with Hamlet:]

> Why thy canonized bones, hearsed in death,
> Have burst their cerements; why the sepulchre
> Wherein we saw thee quietly inurned
> Hath o'ped his ponderous and marble jaws
> To cast thee up again—   [I. iv. 47-51]

we learn the cause: fratricide, incest, 'Murder most foul, strange and unnatural'.

Here, most emphatically stated, are the very foundations and framework of the tragedy. We can, of course, neglect these, and erect a framework of our own which we find more interesting or more congenial to us. We can say, with Dr Gregg, that the Ghost is all my eye; or, with Professor Dover Wilson, that the first act, 'a little play of itself', is 'an epitome of the ghost-lore of the age'—in which case it becomes something of a learned Prologue to the real play; or, like Dr de Madariaga, we can neglect this encircling presence of evil, and substitute what we know of sixteenth-century Court manners [see excerpts above, 1917, 1935, and 1948], or, again without constant reference to the background which Shakespeare himself erected, we can subtly anatomise the soul and mind of Hamlet, on the assumption that Hamlet is the whole play. But if we do these things, let us not then complain that Shakespeare attempted a task too difficult for him, or conclude that the play is an ineffable mystery. Turning it into 'secular' tragedy we shall be using the wrong focus. The correct focus is one which will set the whole action against a background of Nature and Heaven; for this is the background which the dramatist himself has provided. (pp. 254-56)

Laertes, paired with Hamlet in the second scene, is removed before we gain a clear impression of him, except that he seems to be a dutiful son, an affectionate brother, and not without sense. His part in the tragedy does not properly begin before Act IV. But if we look at it now, it may help us to understand Hamlet, since in several ways Shakespeare clearly treats him as Hamlet's counterpart. Laertes, with a father to avenge, is placed in exactly the same position as Hamlet; his behaviour in this position is utterly different; but they share a common destruction.

Unlike Hamlet, Laertes acts with vigour. He is a headstrong youth; he is grievously hurt. On bare suspicion he forces his way into the King's presence, ready to kill him at once. Where Hamlet had said 'Look you, I'll go pray', Laertes is ready to 'cut his throat i' the church'. Hamlet shrank from 'the dread of something after death', remembered 'God's canon 'gainst self-slaughter', contemplated even the possibility that 'It is a damned ghost that we have seen'. To kill Claudius is 'such bitter business as the day would quake to look on'. He sees everything in the light of conscience:

> Is't not perfect conscience
> To quit him with this arm?
>   [V. ii. 67-8]

Laertes on the other hand has no scruples:

> To Hell, allegiance! vows, to the blackest devil!
> Conscience and grace, to the profoundest pit!
> I dare damnation: to this point I stand,
> That both the worlds I give to negligence,
> Let come what comes; only I'll be revenged
> Most throughly for my father.
>   [IV. v. 132-37]

Nothing could be sharper than this contrast; yet the two men come to the same end. How? Why? With Laertes the case is plain. Since it is so plain, it may help us to understand the case of Hamlet, because we may certainly assume, as a reasonable working hypothesis, that these two personal tragedies are designed to be coherent parts of the complete tragedy. Laertes is drawn into the spreading circle of evil, is corrupted by it, and is destroyed. . . . [As] Polonius first gave unctuous advice about Honour to Laertes, and then sent Reynaldo so disgustingly to spy on him, so now Laertes talks pedantically of his honour in the midst of the blackest treachery:

> . . . But in my terms of honour
> I stand aloof, and will no reconcilement
> Till by some elder masters of known honour
> I have a voice and precedent of peace
> To keep my name ungored.   [V. ii. 246-50]

We can note these faults without in the least failing in sympathy towards him; uncritical sympathy may be agreeable in life, but it will not help us to understand plays. We can sympathise with him—and, what is more, we can understand Shakespeare—when we remember what he has suffered, what he is by training, and how plausibly—how truly indeed—Claudius accuses Hamlet. Most of all do we sympathise with him and pity him when he sees the truth, too late:

> The foul practice
> Hath turned itself on me: lo, here I lie,
> Never to rise again . . .
> Exchange forgiveness with me, noble Hamlet.
>   [V. ii. 317-19, 329]

We can certainly interpret Laertes as an Aristotelian tragic hero; but Shakespeare's tragedy here is wider than anything that Aristotle describes; it is Aeschylean in its amplitude: the original crime, and the rottenness that prompted it, surrounds it, and flows from it, corrupts this essentially decent youth and leads him to dishonour and death. The point is made explicitly when Laertes cries:

> The King, the King's to blame.
>   [V. ii. 320]

He and Hamlet may fittingly 'exchange forgiveness'; they are colleagues in tragedy, just as are Hamlet and Ophelia. (pp. 267-69)

Since the arrival of the players Hamlet has recovered the will to act. Although he has not swept to his revenge, he has swept to the brink of it. That the Gonzago-play has completely changed the situation, for Hamlet, is plain; he has made open declaration of war on Claudius. But we should take a wider view than this; and the play, if we attend to its design, will see to it that we do. . . . The first critical scene here is of course the very remarkable one that passes between Hamlet and Claudius. (p. 312)

From now on we see much more of Claudius than we have done yet. We know of his two great crimes; we know from his own lips that he is oppressed by the evil that he has done. Now, by Hamlet's declaration of war, he is driven further and further into villainy. First, he will, for his own safety, send Hamlet into exile—for exile is all that is mentioned yet. Rosencrantz receives his commission, and in his ignorance answers with the unconscious irony that we have already noted:

> The cease of majesty
> Dies not alone, but like a gulf doth draw
> What's near it with it.   [III. iii. 15-17]

The death of King Hamlet is indeed a 'gulf', a whirlpool; already we have passed its perimeter and are approaching its centre. Polonius indeed is very close to it:

> Fare you well, my liege;
> I'll call upon you ere I go to bed.
>   [III. ii. 33-4]

Now it is the turn of Claudius to bare his soul in a soliloquy—his 'limed soul', as he truly says. A frightening speech, if we can remember that once upon a time men believed in the possibility of eternal damnation.

> Is there not rain enough in the sweet Heavens
> To wash it white as snow?   [III. iv. 45-6]

Doubtless there is, if Claudius will fulfil Heaven's conditions. What they are, he knows; fulfil them, he cannot; he cannot give up his crown, his own ambition, and his Queen. But at least he can bow his stubborn knees, and, like more than one person in the *Agamemnon*, he says: All may be well. But that is not the way of the gods, either there or here.

The imaginative energy of Shakespeare is a thing to wonder at. On top of this profoundly tragic soliloquy comes Hamlet, and a stroke of tragic irony as great as any in Sophocles—and very like some of them. It is the only moment in the play when Hamlet is alone with Claudius; it is a moment in which he is in a black enough mood to kill him. Yet he fails to do it, and thereby, as it happens, he leads to his own death. Clearly it is a moment of great significance, but the real significance has not always been seen.

'Now might I do it pat, now he is praying'; which meant, to Bradley, 'Now I *might* do it—if only I were not irresolute' [see excerpt above, 1905]. But this is ruinous to the play; for if this were the reason, there would be a most inartistic disparity between the amplitude of the play and the individual, personal nature of its theme; tragedy of character, however great the character, ought not to be so indiscriminate as to involve the death of seven others. But Hamlet makes it clear in the rest of his speech what the reason is—and it is one which has given great offence to some of his admirers. It is not religious scruple, as if he were obeying a maxim: never kill a man while he is praying. On the contrary, it is the thought that if he strikes now, Claudius will go to Heaven. About this, let us by all means say that it shows Hamlet to be disconcertingly ruthless and unchristian in his lack of charity. But having said this let us not suppose that we have said the significant thing. The tragic point here is something much more wide-reaching than this. Hamlet is conspicuously a man of intellect, 'in apprehension how like a god'; at this, his one opportunity (as it proves), he brings his intellect to bear, and—like Oedipus—he is betrayed by it. His reason is almost god-like, but not quite; it does not show him that the whole basis of his present calculation is false. He reasons, being ignorant of the material fact; and the material fact is:

> My words fly up, my thoughts remain below;
> Words without thoughts never to Heaven go.
>   [III. iii. 97-8]

A Laertes in Hamlet's position would have killed his man and been safe. He would have felt no more religious scruple than Hamlet; on the other hand, he would not have 'scanned' the question. He would have acted on the instant, just as Hamlet himself does ten minutes later, with Polonius. (pp. 313-15)

So, immediately after the Gonzago-play, we see how two of the chief actors in the tragedy move perceptibly nearer the centre of the 'gulf'. In the scene that follows a third is sucked down. Hamlet 'took him for his better', but things are not allowed to fall out so simply for Hamlet, and it was only Polonius. It was a 'rash and bloody deed'; but Shakespeare bespeaks no pity either for Polonius or, later, for Rosencrantz and Guildenstern, who did make love to the same employment. What he does say—or rather, what he makes Hamlet say, though without any hint of correction or dissent—is:

> For this same lord
> I do repent; but Heaven hath pleased it so,
> To punish me with this, and this with me,
> That I must be their scourge and minister.
>   [III. iv. 172-75]

This is the first of a series of events in which we are given to understand—again without any contradiction—that 'Heaven is ordinant'. What does Shakespeare mean by this? For we shall not easily suppose that on each occasion he is using only an empty formula, or simply 'characterising' Hamlet as a religious man. Shakespeare, it may be, means what Sophocles meant when his chorus-leader said:

> Do we not see in this the hand of God?

or when he indicates that Apollo presides over the vengeance which Electra and Orestes took on their father's murderers. It is not that the god, or Heaven, *makes* these things happen; rather that there is an overruling Order, a Divine Justice, which makes itself perceptible in affairs like these; and sometimes the dramatist will make use of an apparent miracle, or a strange coincidence, to emphasise the idea that a universal law is operating.

Certainly we are left to suppose that Justice is operating here, and that it operates, on this occasion at least, when Hamlet acts on the spur of the moment. He kills an intruder, imagining, hoping, that it is Claudius. 'As kill a king!' Gertrude, horror-stricken, repeats Hamlet's dreadful accusation. 'Ay, lady, 'twas my word'—and he raises the arras; but he has not killed the king who killed a king. Yet he has hardly killed the wrong man, for the dead man was at least the king's counsellor and supporter, the treacherous father, the spy who was ready to sugar o'er the Devil himself.

In the scene with Gertrude, Shakespeare makes Hamlet cover ground which we have trodden already. There is very good reason why he should; our attention is kept fixed on what is the basis of the whole tragedy. The wickedness of Gertrude's 'incest', the sheer unreason of her preferring a man like Claudius to a paragon like her true husband—these are instances of that evil which 'takes off the rose from the fair forehead of an innocent love', and 'sweet religion makes a rhapsody of words'. Scholars speak of Shakespeare's 'obsession with sex'. In this play at least, when we listen to Hamlet's horrifying language about

> honeying and making love
> Over the nasty sty,   [III. iv. 93-4]

let us be clear what the poet is really obsessed with: it is with sin and corruption. (pp. 315-16)

The struggle for Gertrude's soul ends with a return to the struggle against Claudius:

> I must to England; you know that?
>   [III. iv. 200]

At once Hamlet returns to the mood of the last soliloquy, in which Hell itself was breathing out contagion to the world. The knavery of Claudius he will meet by knavery of his own: 'Let it work!' (p. 317)

What we are to be concerned with is the madness and then the death of Ophelia, the return of Laertes, the willingness of 'the false Danish dogs' to rebel against Claudius, the failure of his present plot against Hamlet, and the hatching of the new double plot by Claudius and Laertes together. If we try to take, as the essence of the play, the duel between Hamlet and Claudius, or the indecision of Hamlet, or any other theme which is only a part, not the whole, of the play, then much of this act is only peripheral; but everything coheres closely and organically when we see that the central theme is the disastrous growth of evil. (p. 321)

At the end of the Churchyard-scene we are told what happened on the North Sea. We last saw Hamlet being sent away, under guard, for 'instant death'. It looked as if Claudius might triumph. But Hamlet is home again. All we know of the manner of his escape is what we have learned from his letter to Horatio; everything turned on the veriest accident—seconded by Hamlet's own impetuous valour. Shakespeare now chooses to amplify the story; and the colour he gives it is surely a definite and significant one, and entirely harmonious with the colours of the whole play.

> Sir, in my heart there was a kind of fighting
> That would not let me sleep.   [V. ii. 4-5]

This time, as when he killed Polonius, and as always henceforth, Hamlet yields to the prompting of the occasion:

> HAMLET: Rashly—
> And praised be rashness for it: let us know
> Our indiscretion sometimes serves us well
> When our deep plots do pall; and that should teach us
> There's a divinity that shapes our ends
> Rough-hew them how we will,—
> HORATIO: That is most certain.
> HAMLET: Up from my cabin . . .
>   [V. ii. 6-12]

This is a very different Hamlet from the one who sought confirmation—or disproof—of what the Ghost had told him, and who sought more than mere death for Claudius. It is the Hamlet who did the 'rash and bloody deed' on Polonius, where also 'rashness' serves the ends of Providence.

As for what Hamlet did to Rosencrantz and Guildenstern, we must be on our guard against seeing the obvious and missing what is significant. There is no irrelevant reproof in Horatio's brief comment:

> So Rosencrantz and Guildenstern go to 't.
>   [V. ii. 56]

Hamlet continues:

> Why, man, they did make love to this employment;
> They are not on my conscience; their defeat
> Doth by their own insinuation grow.
> 'Tis dangerous when the baser nature comes
> Between the pass and fell incensèd points
> Of might opposites.   [V. ii. 57-62]

This is not Hamlet trying to exculpate himself. Shakespeare is not interested in that kind of thing here. He is saying: 'This is what happens in life, when foolish men allow themselves to be used by such as Claudius, and to get themselves involved in desperate affairs like these.' To prove that this is what he meant, we may once more reflect what Horatio might have said, and then listen to what he does say:

> Why, what a King is this!
>
> [V. ii. 62]

How could Shakespeare more decisively draw our attention away from a nice and private appraisal of Hamlet's character, as expressed in this affair, and direct it to the philosophic or 'religious' framework in which it is set? Horatio says just what Laertes says later: 'The King! the King's to blame.' (pp. 324-25)

[The] first thing that strikes us, or should strike us, when we contemplate the play is that it ends in the complete destruction of the two houses that are concerned. The character of Hamlet and the inner experience that he undergoes are indeed drawn at length and with great subtlety, and we must not overlook the fact; nevertheless, the architectonic pattern just indicated is so vast as to suggest at once that what we are dealing with is no individual tragedy of character, however profound, but something more like religious drama; and this means that unless we are ready, at every step, to relate the dramatic situation to its religious or philosophical background—in other words, to look at the play from a point of view to which more recent drama has not accustomed us—then we may not see either the structure or the meaning of the play as Shakespeare thought them.

Why do Rosencrantz and Guildenstern die, and Ophelia, and Laertes? Are these disasters casual by-products of 'the tragedy of a man who could not make up his mind'? Or are they necessary parts of a firm structure? Each of these disasters we can refer to something that Hamlet has done or failed to do, and we can say that each reveals something more of Hamlet's character; but if we see no more than this we are short-sighted, and are neglecting Shakespeare's plain directions in favour of our own. We are told much more than this when we hear Horatio, and then Laertes, cry 'Why, what a King is this!', 'The King, the King's to blame'; also when Guildenstern says, with a deep and unconscious irony 'We here give up ourselves . . .', and when Laertes talks of 'contagious blastments'. Shakespeare puts before us a group of young people, friends or lovers, none of them wicked, one of them at least entirely virtuous, all surrounded by the poisonous air of Denmark (which also Shakespeare brings frequently and vividly before our minds), all of them brought to death because of its evil influences. Time after time, either in some significant patterning or with some phrase pregnant with irony, he makes us see that these people are partners in disaster, all of them borne down on the 'massy wheel' to 'boisterous ruin'.

In this, the natural working-out of sin, there is nothing mechanical. That is the philosophic reason why character and situation must be drawn vividly. Neither here nor in Greek drama have we anything to do with characters who are puppets in the hands of Fate. In both, we see something of the power of the gods, or the designs of Providence; but these no more override or reduce to unimportance the natural working of individual character than the existence, in the physical world, of universal laws overrides the natural behaviour of natural bodies. It is indeed precisely in the natural behaviour of men, and its natural results, in given circumstances, that the operation of the divine laws can be discerned. In *Hamlet,* Shakespeare draws a complete character, not for the comparatively

barren purpose of 'creating' a Hamlet for our admiration, but in order to show how he, like the others, is inevitably engulfed by the evil that has been set in motion, and how he himself becomes the cause of further ruin. The conception which unites these eight persons in one coherent catastrophe may be said to be this: evil, once started on its course, will so work as to attack and overthrow impartially the good and the bad; and if the dramatist makes us feel, as he does, that a Providence is ordinant in all this, that, as with the Greeks, is his way of universalising the particular event. (pp. 329-30)

The structure of *Hamlet,* then, suggests that we should treat it as religious drama, and when we do, it certainly does not lose either in significance or in artistic integrity. As we have seen more than once, it has fundamental things in common with Greek religious drama—yet in other respects it is very different, being so complex in form and texture. It may be worth while to enquire, briefly, why this should be so.

One naturally compares it with the two Greek revenge-tragedies, the *Choephori* and Sophocles' *Electra,* but whether we do this, or extend the comparison to other Greek religious tragedies like the *Agamemnon* or *Oedipus Tyrannus* or *Antigone,* we find one difference which is obviously pertinent to our enquiry: in the Greek plays the sin, crime or error which is the mainspring of the action is specific, while in Hamlet it is something more general, a quality rather than a single act. (p. 334)

Hamlet resmebles the *Choephori* in this, that the murder of a King, and adultery, or something like it, are the crimes which have to be avenged; also that these can be avenged only through another crime, though perhaps a sinless one; but the differences are deep and far-reaching. They are not merely that Orestes kills, and Hamlet shrinks from killing. We may say that both in the Greek trilogy and in Shakespeare's play the Tragic Hero, ultimately, is humanity itself; and what humanity is suffering from, in *Hamlet* is not a specific evil, but Evil itself. The murder is only the chief of many manifestations of it, the particular case which is the mainspring of the tragic action.

This seems to be typical. In the *Antigone* a whole house is brought down in ruin, and, again, the cause is quite a specific one. It is nothing like the comprehensive wickedness of Iago, or the devouring ambition of Macbeth, or the consuming and all-excluding love of Antony and Cleopatra. It is, quite precisely, that Creon makes, and repeats, a certain error of judgment . . . ; and I use the phrase 'error of judgment' meaning not that it is venial, nor that it is purely intellectual, but that it is specific. It is not a trivial nor a purely intellectual mistake if a man, in certain circumstances, rejects the promptings of humanity, and thinks that the gods will approve; but this is what Creon does, and the tragedy springs from this and from nothing else. He is not a wicked man—not lecherous or envious or ambitious or vindictive. All this is irrelevant. He is simply the man to make and maintain this one specific and disastrous error.

This contrast between the specific and the general obviously has a close connexion with the contrast between the singleness of the normal Greek tragic structure and the complexity of *Hamlet.* In the first place, since Shakespeare's real theme is not the moral or theological or social problem of crime and vengeance, still less its effect on a single mind and soul, but the corroding power of sin, he will present it not as a single 'error of judgment' but as a hydra with many heads. We have shown, let us hope, how this explains, or helps to explain, such features of the play as, so to speak, the simultaneous presentation of three Creons: Claudius, Gertrude and Polonius, each of them, in his own degree, an embodiment of the general evil. Hence too the richer character-drawing. Claudius is a drunkard, and the fact makes its own contribution to the complete structure; if Sophocles had made Creon a drunkard, it would have been an excrescence on the play. Hence too the frequent changes of scene in the first part of the play; also the style of speech invented for Polonius and Osric. The general enemy is the rottenness that pervades Denmark; therefore it is shown in many persons and many guises. (pp. 335-36)

It is, in short, a general statement which I think will bear examination, that Greek tragedy presents sudden and complete disaster, or one disaster linked to another in linear fashion, while Shakespearean tragedy presents the complexive, menacing spread of ruin; and that at least one explanation of this is that the Greek poets thought of the tragic error as the breaking of a divine law (or sometimes, in Aeschylus, as the breaking down of a temporary divine law), while Shakespeare saw it as an evil quality which, once it has broken loose, will feed on itself and on anything else that it can find until it reaches its natural end. So, for example in *Macbeth:* in 'noble Macbeth', ambition is stimulated, and is not controlled by reason or religion; it meets with a stronger response from Lady Macbeth, and grows insanely into a monstrous passion that threatens a whole kingdom. It is a tragic conception which is essentially dynamic, and demands the very unhellenic fluidity and expansiveness of expression which the Elizabethan theatre afforded. (p. 337)

> H.D.F. Kitto, "'Hamlet'," in his Form and Meaning in Drama: A Study of Six Greek Plays and of "Hamlet," *Methuen & Co Ltd, 1964, pp. 246-337.*

REBECCA WEST (essay date 1957)

[*West's concept of Hamlet runs counter to the mainstream of nearly four centuries of interpretation. She contends that the character has been consistently misread; he is actually "a bad man," in a thoroughly corrupt society. West maintains that in Hamlet Shakespeare "makes the Renaissance man his own Mephistopheles." Her concept of Hamlet as a negative character echoes George Steevens (1772) and Ivan Turgenieff (1860), and her interpretation of Hamlet as an egocentric, often brutal Renaissance figure supports the reading of Salvador de Madariaga (1948).*]

If a work of art should make a revelation which discredits what most human beings wish to believe, they will try to expose it as unsound. If they cannot do that, if the point the artist makes is incontrovertible, they may undertake the defense of their shattered universe in another way. They may pretend that he wrote something quite other than what he did. Then it is that the long life-span of literature is a source of danger, for though it gives the writer a many-branched and deep-rooted tradition to uphold him, it also gives time for his readers to repeat these defense tactics to the point of success. The repetition may be carried on so extensively through the centuries that in time a very large number of persons among those who have relations with literature, who move within the sphere of culture, may be under the impression that the content of a famous work of art is not that which the artist has carefully set down on his page.

This is surely what has happened to the play of *Hamlet,* and it is unfortunate that it should be so, for there has thus been obscured Shakespeare's development of a theme which runs

through Western literature and has often provided genius with its material. . . . [The] practice of misreading the character of Hamlet, and hence the significance of the play, had been carried on by generation after generation of persons interested in the play on widely different levels, all over the world; by many scholars, by people who are true readers—that is, who read all their lives—as well as by people who read only when they are at school or the university, by people who do not read at all but who have seen a version of the play acted in a theater or as a film or on television, or heard it on the radio. . . . A host of such people, vastly as they differ from one another intellectually and socially, misread the character of Hamlet in exactly the same way. They see him as a symbol of irresolution; and their unanimity is remarkable if it be considered that there is no justification for this view in the text. (pp. 6-7)

There is no sign in the text that he was averse from any action, even of the most violent kind. It is true that he was sensitive and thoughtful and melancholy; but he was cruel as well as sensitive, impulsive as well as thoughtful, and though melancholy he was coarse as any barroom drunk. These less attractive attributes have been traced through the play by Salvador de Madariaga in an attempt to disprove the myth of Hamlet's irresolution, in a volume which has plainly been inspired by Turgenev's essay though it does not name it. This volume is not entirely satisfactory, for it is marred by a punitive manner suggesting that it is based on the private papers of a District Attorney of Elsinore who had hoped to make an arrest, and would have made one had it not been for the holocaust in the last scene. But there is no use in quarreling with Madariaga's findings, which are not really much less favorable than the reluctant admissions of that wise and loving Shakespearean scholar, Wilson Knight [see excerpt above, 1935]. From the admissions of Hamlet's faults which these two very different critics are forced to make in common, we get some indication of the reason why the vast audience of Western readers has been shy about accepting Hamlet as Shakespeare drew him. Hamlet is universal.

"We all," Turgenev says, "sympathize with Hamlet because there is not one of us but recognizes in the prince one or more of our own characteristics." That is in part, perhaps, a matter of technique. The verse which Hamlet speaks runs with the quick, ranging gait of thought, of the interior monologue, and as we listen to it we recognize that that is how we think. And thus identifying ourselves with Hamlet, we come to the conclusion that we, too, think well. "We have," Turgenev goes on, "a constant persuasion of his high value. No man but is flattered to learn he is Hamlet." So Hamlet is ourselves at our most attractive. Therefore we do not want to learn that he, who is us at our best, has some of the worst of human attributes.

Hamlet was so far from being incapable of action that he committed without remorse that extreme action, murder, and he committed it four times and killed one man in self-defense. It is sometimes said that the violence of the times in which Shakespeare lived accounts for the many crimes in his plays. But there is surely a constant way of regarding murder, as we ourselves should know. . . . [At] no time during the recent degeneration of history would an artist engaged on a pure work of art not involved in propaganda, or a person engaged in the disinterested study of a pure work of art, have considered murder as other than a horrible deed. There is built into our flesh a strong prejudice in favor of natural death. Moreover, Shakespeare was writing at the court of Elizabeth, which, despite certain outrageous deeds of royal vengeance, was a shrine of mercy compared to the slaughter-houses presided over by Henry the Eighth and Mary Tudor, and to him murder must have had all the horror of a recently escaped danger. (pp. 11-13)

Hamlet committed both kinds of murder, premeditated and unpremeditated. On hot impulse he stabbed Polonius as he hid behind the arras; and he sent Rosenkrantz and Guildenstern off to England bearing their own death warrant in the forged letter to the King of England, requesting him to kill them.

Hamlet was, indeed, an exceptionally callous murderer. Not in the first heat of crime, but after he has had his long scene with his mother with Polonius' corpse lying on the floor, he says, ''I'll lug the guts into the neighbor room'' [III. iv. 212]. . . . His insensibility toward Rosenkrantz and Guildenstern is worse. When, after his return from the sea voyage to Denmark, he tells Horatio how he sent the pair to their deaths by forging the letter to the King of England requesting that ''He should the bearers put to sudden death, Not shriving-time allow'd'' [V. ii. 46-7], he is quite jaunty about it. The excuse he gives is, ''Why, man, they did make love to this employment'' [V. ii. 57]—that is, to their employment by Claudius to take him to his execution in England. But there is no indication that they were aware of the fate which Claudius had contrived for Hamlet on his arrival. . . . Yet of Rosenkrantz and Guildenstern Hamlet says, ''They are not near my conscience'' [V. ii. 58], so easy does he find it to commit murder.

He can kill only on his own behalf. When his father returns from the grave and bids his son avenge his death by killing Claudius, he cannot obey. It is true that he kills Polonius in the belief that he is Claudius, but this is so confused an action that it is almost a repudiation of the one desired. He could have sought out his stepfather at any hour he pleased and murdered him as they talked, but he chose to run a sword through an unidentified body on the off chance that it was his stepfather. It is true that he ultimately kills Claudius, but it is because Claudius, by inducing Laertes to fight with an envenomed sword, has committed the only offense which Hamlet recognizes an offense, that is, an offense against himself. He meets the ghost's command with an abstracted disobedience, and it is part of the oddity of *Hamlet* which so greatly distressed Thomas Rymer and in our own day T. S. Eliot [see excerpt above, 1919], that the reader knows this to be a sin, though the ghost is to us one of the most ridiculous preternatural beings ever invented. He talks fustian and he cannot establish his authority, even with the advantage of his supernatural state behind him; he is addressed by his son, whose blood he has sought to freeze, as old mole and truepenny. His requests are disregarded even when he pays a special daylight visit to repeat them; and on this occasion he is seen in circumstances peculiarly unfavorable to the suspension of disbelief, for he is on the stage at the same time as the corpse of Polonius, who should, if the universe be consistent, also have a ghost. Yet Hamlet's father's ghost has authority over the reader, and over any audience, because he is the symbol of a reality. He represents tradition. His insistence that Hamlet should avenge his murder is an invocation of the Rule of Law, a warning that the existence of our kind depends on observance of the Commandments. When Hamlet fails to obey, he rejects the accumulated experience of his race; he has refused to aid society by transmitting a message; and he has taken as his government his individual impulses. (pp. 14-16)

[Tradition] is the distillation of human experience, and it must be condemned if humanity is condemned; and Hamlet was disgusted by his own kind.

There are other crimes afoot in Elsinore, in the world, as well as murder. The ghost wishes Hamlet to avenge his murder and also to put an end to the unholy offense of the marriage between his widow and his murderer. But when Hamlet talks of these matters with his mother he loses all interest in that part of the command which relates to his father's murder, and in the course of over eighty lines addressed to her he devotes only three to a perfunctory mention of the fact that her present husband murdered her previous husband, and when she shows that she did not know that any such crime had been committed he does not take the opportunity of enlightening her. He simply tells her that she is behaving reprehensibly in living with her present husband, not because he had murdered her dead husband and his own brother, but because he was not so good looking as her dead husband. . . . Claudius is guilty, the Queen is guilty, and so as this scene makes quite plain, is Hamlet. All that he says is smeared with a slime which is the mark of sexual corruption. His curious emphasis on the physical difference between the dead King and the living Claudius hints at a homosexual element in his nature, but that is irrelevant. Hamlet could be neither a heterosexual nor a homosexual lover. Such an egotist would be restricted to lust, for he could not afford the outgoings of love.

That has been indicated earlier in the play by his scenes with Ophelia. There is no more bizarre aspect of the misreading of Hamlet's character than the assumption that his relations with Ophelia were innocent and that Ophelia was a correct and timid virgin of exquisite sensibilities. . . . We have certainly put Ophelia into the wrong category and into the wrong century. She was not a chaste young woman. That is shown by her tolerance of Hamlet's obscene conversations, which cannot be explained as consistent with the custom of the time. If that were the reason for it, all the men and women in Shakespeare's plays, Romeo and Juliet, Beatrice and Benedict, Miranda and Ferdinand, Antony and Cleopatra, would have talked obscenely together, which is not the case. . . . The truth is that Ophelia was a disreputable young woman: not scandalously so, but still disreputable. She was foredoomed to it by her father, whom it is a mistake to regard as a simple platitudinarian. . . . Polonius is interesting because he was a cunning old intriguer who, like an iceberg, only showed one-eighth of himself above the surface. The innocuous sort of worldly wisdom that rolled off his tongue in butter balls was a very small part of what he knew. It has been insufficiently noted that Shakespeare would never have held up the action in order that Polonius should give his son advice as to how to conduct himself abroad, unless the scene helped him to develop his theme. But ''This above all—to thine own self be true; And it must follow, as the night the day, Thou canst not then be false to any man'' [I. iii. 78-80], has considerable contrapuntal value when it is spoken by an old gentleman who is presently going to instruct a servant to spy on his son, and to profess great anxiety about his daughter's morals, when plainly he needed to send her away into the country if he really wanted her to retain any. (pp. 17-20)

The girl is not to be kept out of harm's way. She is a card that can be played to take several sorts of tricks. She might be Hamlet's mistress; but she might be more honored for resistance. And if Hamlet was himself an enemy of the King, and an entanglement with him had ceased to be a means of winning favor, then she can give a spy's report on him to Claudius. Surely Ophelia is one of the few authentic portraits of that army of not virgin martyrs, the poor little girls who were sacrificed to family ambition in the days when a court was a cat's cradle of conspiracies. Man's persuasion that his honor depends on the chastity of his womenfolk has always been liable to waste away and perish within sight of a throne. Particularly where monarchy had grown from a yeasty mass of feudalism, few families found themselves able to resist the temptation to hawk any young beauty in their brood, if it seemed likely that she might catch the eye of the king or any man close to the king. Unfortunately the king's true favorite was usually not a woman but an ideology. If royal approval was withdrawn from the religious or political faith held by the family which had hawked the girl, she was as apt to suffer fatality as any of her kinsmen. The axe has never known chivalry. Shakespeare, writing this play only three reigns from Henry the Eighth, had heard of such outrages on half-grown girls from the lips of those who had seen the final blood-letting. (pp. 20-1)

Like Anne Boleyn, Ophelia has lost her integrity. She fiddles with the truth when she speaks of Hamlet to her father, and she fiddles with the truth when she talks to Hamlet as her father and Claudius eavesdrop; and she contemplates without surprise or distaste Hamlet's obscenity, the scab on his spiritual sore.

Surely the picture of Ophelia shows that Shakespeare, who wrote more often of cruelty than any other great writer, was not a cruel man, and was great in pity, that rare emotion. He shows the poor little creature, whom the court had robbed of her honesty, receiving no compensation for the loss, but being driven to madness and done to death. For the myth which has been built round Hamlet is never more perverse than when it pretends that Ophelia went mad for love and killed herself. No line in the play suggests that she felt either passion or affection for Hamlet. She never mentions him in the mad scene, and Horatio says of her, "She speaks much of her father." Indeed she was in a situation which requires no sexual gloss. Her father had been murdered by a member of the royal house, and she found herself without protection, since her brother Laertes was in France, in the midst of a crisis such as might well send her out of her wits with fear. For the Danes hostile to the royal house made of her wrong a new pretext for their hostility, and the royal house, noting this, turned against her, helpless though she was. (pp. 22-3)

But neither from fear nor from love did Ophelia kill herself. She did not kill herself at all. The Queen describes her drowning as an accident. "An envious sliver broke," she says, and there is no indication that she was lying. Many things are packed into the passage which begins "There is a willow grows aslant a brook," but insincerity is not among them. These lines achieve a dramatic value often not exploited in the theater. They are beautiful and expressive verse: their sound suggests heaviness submerging lightness, the soaked clothes dragging down the fragile body they encase, the inanimate flesh grown leaden round the spirit. But the lines are also in character. The Queen is one of the most poorly endowed human beings which Shakespeare ever drew. Very often he created fools, but there is a richness in their folly, whereas Gertrude is simply a stately defective. The whole play depends on her not noticing, and not understanding; and in this passage there are samples of her stupidity. The botanical digression about the long purples is ill-timed, and the epithet "mermaid-like" is not applicable to someone saved from drowning by an amplitude of skirts or to the skirts themselves. But the fusion of perception and obtuseness in these lines, and the contrast between their distinction and the empty rotundity of all the Queen's other speeches, convince us that just once this dull woman was so moved that her tongue became alive. It is not credible that at that moment

she would have taken thought to deceive Laertes about the object of her emotion; nor indeed does Shakespeare suggest that she practiced any such deception.

For that Ophelia drowned herself is stated definitely only by two people: the clowns in the graveyard, typical examples of the idiot groundlings gorged on false rumor who appear so often in Shakespeare's plays. Whether we like it or not, we must admit that there is very little in the works of Shakespeare which could be used as propaganda for adult suffrage. For the rest, the priest declares that "her death was doubtful" [V. i. 227], and that the doubt was enough to make it necessary that she should be buried with "maimed rites" [V. i. 219]. But surely we are not intended to believe him, for he is drawn as a bigot, who finds it possible to answer her brother coldly when he asks, "What ceremony else?" [V. i. 223], and it is to be presumed that such lack of charity would invent a doubt. Shakespeare will not allow anyone in the graveyard scene, even to the priest, to be without sin. Each of them has helped to dig the girl's grave. Hamlet was the most guilty, for he had been her spurious lover and a tyrant prince, giving her no protection as a mistress or as one of his people; but it was the whole court that had destroyed her. She was a victim of society, which abandons principle for statecraft, for politics, for intrigue, because of its too urgent sense that it must survive at all costs, and in its panic loses cognizance of all the essentials by which it lives. Even her brother Laertes was not fully aware of his sister's tragedy, for he was tainted with the vice which Shakespeare feared most as a distraction: he was subject to lust. (pp. 24-5)

It is Shakespeare's contention that the whole of the court is corrupt: society is corrupt. There is a flaw running horizontally through humanity wherever it is gathered together in space. It would seem natural therefore that Hamlet should obey the ghost and punish Claudius, who controls the court, who is an emblem of society. But the flaw runs vertically also; it runs through time, into the past. For Hamlet's father, the ghost, is in purgatory, doing penance for his sins, which were of the same gross kind as those he desires his son to punish. . . . The ghost was indeed a sinner; the voice of tradition speaks from a tainted source. The evil in the world is not the product of the specially corrupt present generation, it has its roots in the generations that went before and also were corrupt; it has its roots in the race. There is no use pretending that we can frustrate our sinful dispositions by calling on tradition, because that also is the work of sinful man. This is the situation of our kind as it is shown to us in *Hamlet*, which is as pessimistic as any great work of literature ever written. The theme of the play could never appear to any reader who kept his eye on the text as the irresolution of Hamlet, his lack of the nerve which forms a hero (as Goethe put it) [see excerpt above, 1796], his failure to achieve a virtue which would consist simply of capacity for action. For what excites Shakespeare in this play is the impossibility of conceiving an action which could justly be termed virtuous, in view of the bias of original sin. (pp. 27-8)

[Shakespeare] in Hamlet makes the Renaissance man his own Mephistopheles, and depicts a being so gifted that he needs no supernatural being to raise him above the common lot. But Shakespeare, the supreme artist observing this supreme man, immediately adds, "And yet to me what is the quintessence of dust?" And his genius has been asking that question throughout the play. Scene after scene has demonstrated the paragon of animals to be an animal, the world to be so diseased that even its beauty is infected. This speech of homage to man is indeed an example of teasing ambiguity; it can be read without irony or with irony; each reading is equally faithful to the text.

Shakespeare hopes for little from the dust. It is quite certain that he wished to present Hamlet as a bad man, because he twice makes him rejoice at the thought of murdering men who had not made their peace with God. He might have killed Claudius when he came on him at prayer. But he decided this might mean that Claudius would go straight to heaven. . . . Later on, when he tells Horatio of his peculiarly cold-blooded murder of Rosenkrantz and Guildenstern, his description of the letter he forged to the King of England shows traces of a like perverse determination to kill the soul as well as the body. . . . There would be no question at all in the minds of an Elizabethan audience that a murderer who could cheat his victims of their chance of salvation was a very bad man indeed; and indeed most of us would think with repulsion of such an action, if, through the hazards of war or dictatorship, it came within our experience.

But to this bad man Shakespeare ascribes one virtuous action; and the nature of that action is determined by his most lasting preoccupation. It is a political action. Hamlet gives his dying breath to thought for the future of his people; his last words choose a ruler for them [V. ii. 352-58]:

> O, I die, Horatio;
> The potent poison quite o'ercrows my spirit;
> I cannot live to hear the news from England;
> But I do prophesy th' election lights
> On Fortinbras: he has my dying voice.
> So tell him, with the occurents, more and less,
> Which have solicited—the rest is silence.
>
> [V. ii. 352-58]

Hamlet was never more the Renaissance man—who was a statesman, a true Macchiavellian, a prince careful for the safety of his subjects. Even if one be disillusioned with the race, and suspect paragons and the beauty of the world, this is still admirable. These fragile creatures, so little changed from dust that they constantly revert to it, show bravery in their intention that their species shall survive as if it were marble. Yet, all the same, how horrid is the sphere in which they show their excellence. The court was saved by its political conscience; yet it was damned by it too. (pp. 29-32)

> Rebecca West, "Was Hamlet without Will?" and "The Nature of Will," in her The Court and the Castle: Some Treatments of a Recurrent Theme, Yale University Press, 1957, pp. 3-16, 17-32.

L. C. KNIGHTS (essay date 1959)

[A renowned English Shakespearean scholar, Knights is best known for his How Many Children Had Lady Macbeth? (1933)—a milestone study in the twentieth-century reaction to the Shakespearean criticism of the previous century in which he criticizes the traditional emphasis on character as an approach which inhibits the reader's total response to Shakespeare's plays. Knights, like E.M.W. Tillyard (1949), claims that Hamlet achieves no breakthrough to self-awareness; rather, he is a symbol of "corruption of consciousness." Knights disagrees with the contention of H.D.F. Kitto (1956) that "in Denmark, Hamlet's fineness must necessarily suffer corruption." Knights's essay is drawn from a series of lectures given at Stratford-Upon-Avon in 1959.]

I wish to start this lecture by drawing your attention to Professor H.D.F. Kitto's Form and Meaning in Drama. It would be almost an impertinence for me to praise it, but I may say that even for a Greekless reader it is a fascinating experience to see how a scholar who is also a critic sets about his task of eliciting the moral centre and the unifying pattern of plays by Aeschylus and Sophocles. Now in this book Professor Kitto has a long chapter on Hamlet that can be read with profit by any student of Shakespeare, and I want to use that chapter—both by way of agreement and of disagreement—as a means of introducing my own reflections on the play. (p. 31)

I feel sure that Professor Kitto is right about the nature of Hamlet's paralysis; but I also think that his development of the idea of the 'contagion' . . . suffered by Hamlet is not a full or adequate answer to the questions raised by the play. Is it enough to say that Hamlet 'feels himself being inexorably dragged down . . . to actions which, being free, he would condemn'— such as the murder of Rosencrantz and Guildenstern? . . . Is it enough to say that 'Hamlet's "madness" was but the reflection of the evil with which he found himself surrounded, of which Claudius was the most prolific source'? . . . I think this is, at best, a partial summing-up; and I also think that there is some confusion that we should try to dissipate. Evil of course can 'overthrow' the good as well as the bad, in the sense that it can torture and kill them. But to the extent that they are 'engulfed' by it, as Hamlet is said to be engulfed— and this, in context, refers not to his happiness but to his nature—to that extent they deviate from goodness. Kitto tells us that 'in Denmark, Hamlet's fineness must necessarily suffer corruption'. . . . But why? I cannot feel that 'contagion' is an adequate answer. What I do feel is that the play prompts us to look much more closely at the attitudes with which Hamlet confronts his world and the gross evil in that world. (pp. 32-4)

Kitto writes, 'we may say that both in the Greek trilogy (the Oresteia) and in Shakespeare's play the Tragic Hero, ultimately, is humanity itself; and what humanity is suffering from, in Hamlet, is not a specific evil, but Evil itself'. . . . Yes, in Hamlet the preoccupation is with Evil itself, but this is presented with a greater immediacy than Kitto's account, taken as a whole, suggests. And when we attend to this—the full imaginative effect—there is a timbre or quality that perplexes us. Our perplexities centre on Hamlet, and when we attend to them we find that Shakespeare is not simply presenting the working out of Law, Dikê, he is also—I think—questioning the perceiver. (p. 35)

It is well known how, right at the start of each of his tragedies, Shakespeare establishes the 'atmosphere'—something that is not just a vaguely effective background but an integral part of the play's structure of meanings. In Hamlet, with the usual effective economy of means, we are made aware of a cold darkness that makes men 'sick at heart'. In the surrounding stillness ('not a mouse stirring') men's voices ring out sharply and with subdued apprehension. In this 'dead vast'—vacancy, void, emptiness—'and middle of the night', when Bernardo points to the 'star that's westward from the pole', and speaks of 'the bell then beating one', there is something of that sense of a surrounding non-human that reverberates from the steeples in Robert Frost's 'I will sing you One-O':

> In that grave One
> They spoke of the sun
> And moon and stars,
> Saturn and Mars . . .

In that setting—which will shortly contrast so strongly with the light and pomp and self-important complacency of King

Claudius's court—we first hear of, then see, a dead man's ghost. It is of course important not to rewrite Shakespeare's plays for him but to follow his lead as closely as we may. But the emphasis here is indeed Shakespeare's. . . . The dead man's ghost is the mainspring of the action, which involves, finally, eight other deaths. Of that original death the memory is indeed 'green', from the first scene, through the re-enactment of the murder by the Players, to the rhetorical question of Fortinbras at the end,

> O proud Death!
> What feast is toward in thine eternal cell . . . ?
> [V. ii. 364-65]

And it is quite early offered as an example of obvious and inescapable mortality: 'your father lost a father, That father lost, lost his'; it is 'as common As any the most vulgar thing to sense'; the 'common theme' 'is death of fathers', and reason

>   still hath cried,
> From the first corse [ironically Abel's] till he that
>   died to-day,
> 'This must be so'.   [I. ii. 104-06]

From this until the Play scene the theme is mainly expressed by Hamlet, but from the killing of Polonius the presence of death is very close indeed. Polonius, interred 'in hugger-mugger', is 'compounded with dust'; death shares with sex the burden of Ophelia's mad songs; there is the long elegiac description of her drowning. Above all, there is Act V, scene i—the scene with the grave-diggers. Here, as so often in Shakespeare, a dominant theme entwined in a complex action is for a short space given full and exclusive prominence.

> What is he that builds stronger than either the
>   mason, the shipwright, or the carpenter? . . .
> a gravemaker; the houses that he makes last till
>   doomsday.   [V. i. 41-2, 58-9]

To the accompaniment of snatches of song, in which love gives way to death, the Clown throws up the skulls that Hamlet comments on: politician, courtier, lawyer, tanner, fine lady, jester, Caesar, Alexander—not one can escape this fate. The moral is enforced with the simplification of a *danse macabre:*

> Now get you to my lady's chamber, and tell
>   her, let her paint an inch thick, to this favour
> she must come; make her laugh at that.
> [V. i. 192-95]

On the one hand, then, is death, on the other is life lived with a peculiarly crude vigour of self-assertion. In the world that Hamlet confronts, men mostly, as the phrase goes, know what they want—plenty to eat and drink, sexual satisfaction, and power—and they see that they get it, pursuing their limited aims with a gross complacence, fat weeds that rot themselves in ease on the wharf of oblivion. (pp. 38-41)

Now it is well known that some other plays of this period exhibit, with an almost obsessive insistence, death and corruption—Webster's tragedies, for example. But when we have finished *The White Devil* or *The Duchess of Malfi,* we are likely to find ourselves in some perplexity concerning what it is all about. What is the point of it? When we have finished reading *Hamlet,* we have at least a fair idea of what it is about. The point is not a display of accumulated horrors; it is the effect of these on a particular kind of consciousness. . . . Hamlet, in his confrontation of this world, feels himself paralysed because an exclusive concentration on evil, or—say—some-

thing in the manner of the concentration, is itself corrupting. (p. 43)

The climax of the first movement of the play—that is, of Act I—is Hamlet's encounter with the Ghost. It is important that we should get clear with ourselves how we are intended to take it. At first it seems that Shakespeare is careful to keep the status of the Ghost more or less neutral. The first we hear of it is Marcellus's 'What, has this thing appear'd again to-night?' As a ghost, it is of course a 'dreaded sight', a 'portentous figure', but it is also, simply, 'this apparition', 'illusion', 'this present object'. When Horatio tells Hamlet what has happened, it is 'a figure like your father' and 'the apparition'. None of this provides any very clear answer to the question that an audience is likely to ask—What sort of a ghost is this? Is it good or bad? There are however some suggestive tonings. The Ghost, though 'majestical', starts 'like a guilty thing' when the cock crows, and we are told that this is because the bird's 'lofty and shrill-sounding throat' awakes 'the god of day', but dismisses 'to his confine' 'the extravagant and erring spirit'. Both these adjectives may mean no more than wandering out of bounds or straying, but the immediately following lines suggest rather more than this.

> It faded on the crowing of the cock.
> Some say that ever 'gainst that season comes
> Wherein our Saviour's birth is celebrated,
> The bird of dawning singeth all night long;
> And then, they say, no spirit dare stir abroad;
> The nights are wholesome; then no planets strike,
> No fairy takes, nor witch hath power to charm,
> So hallow'd and so gracious is that time.
> [I. i. 157-64]

Now I cannot believe that these lines were put in for the sake of an incidental bit of 'poetry'—no more than I could believe it of the temple-haunting martlets passage in *Macbeth,* which similarly contrasts so markedly with the thick and oppressive atmosphere that permeates most of the play. Here, in the passage before us, not only is Christmas night wholesome, hallowed and gracious, because various malign influences are as powerless to act as spirits such as this are to stir abroad, the limpid freshness of the verse emphasizes an accepted Christianity ('our Saviour's birth') which, it seems in place to remark, is directly opposed to the code of revenge. Ah but, we may be told, in *Hamlet* Shakespeare is using the conventions of the revenge play, in which quite different assumptions about the duty of revenge prevail. This has always seemed to me a very rum argument indeed. Shakespeare may use various dramatic conventions—such as the foreshortening of time or the impenetrability of disguise—when they suit his purpose; but he never—what great poet could?—allows convention to shape his essential matter. I cannot believe that the poet who was going on to write *Measure for Measure* (perhaps his next play), which is about forgiveness, who was going on to create the figure of Cordelia, and to write those plays of which a main part of the burden is that 'the rarer action is in virtue than in vengeance'—I cannot believe that such a poet could temporarily waive his deepest ethical convictions for the sake of an exciting dramatic effect. It is almost like believing that Dante, for a canto or two, could change his ground and write approvingly, say, of the enemies of the Empire. (pp. 44-6)

The point of view that I am putting forward is that what we have in *Hamlet*—as in *Othello* and, less successfully, in *Timon*—is the exploration and implicit criticism of a particular state of mind or consciousness. It is an extremely complex state of mind, in which reason and emotion, attitudes towards the self and towards other persons and the world at large, are revealed both directly and through a series of encounters; and our business is to see how the different ingredients (so to speak) are related in such a way that a particular judgment or assessment of experience is precipitated. (p. 49)

Hamlet's state of mind, the Hamlet consciousness, is revealed not only at the level of formulable motive, but in its obscure depths; and it is revealed through the poetry. . . . [The] judgment of which I spoke is not a matter of formal approval or condemnation of a dramatic figure conceived as a real person. No doubt it is partly that; but essentially it is part of an imaginative apprehension of life in which, with the whole force of our personality ('judgment ever awake and steady self-possession combined with enthusiasm and feeling profound or vehement'), we try to see fundamental aspects of human life in their true status and relationships. And what we judge, in this sense, is not someone 'out there', but potentialities of our own being.

In the particular complex of feelings and attitudes that constitute the Hamlet consciousness it is not easy to separate causes and effects, but I think that most people would agree that what is emphasized from the opening scenes is a movement of recoil and disgust of a peculiar intensity. . . . [The] determining moment, when this imbalance is accepted as a kind of compulsion is . . . the encounter with the Ghost. When Hamlet swears to 'remember'—with such ominous repetition of the word—he commits himself to a passion that has all the exclusiveness of an infatuation. . . . [For Hamlet] death is mere negation; but at the same time he is fascinated by it, fascinated not merely by 'the dread of something after death', but by the whole process of earthly corruption, as in the long brooding on the skulls in the churchyard, culminating in the gratuitous fantasy of the progress of Alexander:

> To what base uses we may return, Horatio!
> Why may not imagination trace the noble dust
> of Alexander, till he find it stopping a bung-
> hole?   [V. i. 202-04]

To which, you remember, Horatio replies, ' 'Twere to consider too curiously, to consider so'; but Hamlet does not heed him. Certainly the facts that Hamlet dwells on here, as he had dwelt on them in connexion with the death of Polonius, are facts that have to be assimilated somehow, but it is the tone and manner that are betraying:

> —Now, Hamlet, where's Polonius?
> —At supper . . . Not where he eats, but where he is
>   eaten; a certain convocation of politic
>   worms are e'en at him. Your worm is your
>   only emperor for diet; we fat all creatures
>   else to fat us, and we fat ourselves for
>   maggots . . .   [IV. iii. 16-23]

and again:

> —Dost thou think Alexander looked o' this fashion
> —i' the earth?
> —E'en so.
> —And smelt so? pah!   [V. i. 197-200]

It need cause no surprise that these attitudes of fascinated revulsion combine with a regressive longing for the death that, from another point of view, appears so repulsive. (pp. 50-4)

Hamlet is a man who in the face of life and of death can make no affirmation, and it may well be that this irresolution—which goes far deeper than irresolution about the performance of a specific act—this fundamental doubt, explains the great appeal of the play in modern times. The point has been made by D. G. James in *The Dream of Learning* [see excerpt above, 1951]. Shakespeare's play, he says, 'is an image of modernity, of the soul without clear belief losing its way, and bringing itself and others to great distress and finally to disaster'; it is 'a tragedy not of excessive thought but of defeated thought', and Hamlet himself is 'a man caught in ethical and metaphysical uncertainties'. Now I am sure that Mr. James is right in emphasizing the element of scepticism in Hamlet's make-up—the weighing of alternative possibilities in such a way as to make choice between them virtually impossible; and I sympathize with his wish 'to elevate Hamlet's intellectual distresses to an equality in importance with his emotional state', for 'the strength of the emotional shock he has suffered is equalled by the weakness of his mind in the face of difficult moral and metaphysical issues. Hamlet was, after all, an intellectual.' But at the same time I feel that the play incites us to a closer examination of the intimate and complex relationship of thought and feeling, of intellectual bafflement and certain aspects of the emotional life; in the play before us the dominant emotions are activated by certain specific shocks but they cannot be attributed solely to these. (p. 55)

I think we shall not be far wrong if, in seeking to account for Hamlet's paralysis, his inability to affirm, we give special prominence to his isolation and self-consciousness. Now consciousness, as distinguished from Hamlet's self-consciousness, is dependent upon love and relationship, and the name that Blake gave to consciousness, . . .is the Imagination. Hamlet, for all his ranging mind and his nervous susceptibility, is not in this sense imaginative; in Blakean terms he is in the power of his Spectre.

> Each Man is in his Spectre's power
> Untill the arrival of that hour,
> When his Humanity awake
> And cast his own Spectre into the Lake. . . .

Looking up other instances of 'Spectre' in the Index to the edition of the Prophetic Writings by Sloss and Wallis, I found (what I had not noticed before) that Blake also used them in *Jerusalem:* in the drawing showing Albion in despair (Plate 41) they are engraved in reverse on the stone at the feet of the seated bowed figure, his face covered by his hands; and it is not irrelevant to our present concerns to notice that the passage immediately following this illustration begins,

> Thus Albion sat, studious of others in his pale disease,
> Brooding on evil . . .

I hope you will not misunderstand me. I do not think that Shakespeare wrote *Hamlet* as an esoteric commentary on Blake's Prophetic Books, or that Hamlet's Ghost is to be identified with Blake's Spectre. It is simply that both poets had some comparable insights, and the one may be used to bring out the meaning of the other. Blake's Spectre is the rationalizing faculty, self-centred and moralistic, working in isolation from the other powers and potentialities of the mind. Unless redeemed by Los, the Imagination, in dealing with the self and with others it can only criticize and accuse, creating around itself what Wordsworth was to call 'a universe of death.'

Hamlet, 'studious of others in his pale disease, Brooding on evil,' is, in this sense, in the power of his Spectre. He is indeed, as Mr James and many others have insisted, an intellectual, a man given to reason and reflection. But what Shakespeare is bringing in question in this play is what it means to be an intellectual in any but a sterile sense, the conditions on which this capability can be indeed 'god-like'. Hamlet's intellectuality, the working of his mind, is largely at the service of attitudes of rejection and disgust that are indiscriminate in their working. Let me repeat what I have said before: the Denmark of this play is indeed an unweeded garden; there are facts enough to justify almost everything Hamlet says about this world; but what we have to take note of is not only what he says but a particular vibration in the saying. We can define this in relation to his self-disgust, his spreading sexual nausea, and his condemnation of others. (pp. 57-9)

Now to say that Hamlet adopts histrionic, even at times melodramatic, postures is to bring into view another matter of central importance—that is, the static quality of Hamlet's consciousness. It is not for nothing that the popular conception is that this is a play about delay. Delay in the action, that is in the carrying out of Hamlet's strategy against the King, can of course be explained: he had to find out if the Ghost was telling the truth about the murder, and so on. But the fact remains that one of the most powerful imaginative effects is of a sense of paralysis. Hamlet feels, and we are made to feel, that he is 'stuck', as we say on more homely occasions.

> Sure he that made us with such large discourse,
> Looking before and after, gave us not
> That capability and god-like reason
> To fust in us unused. Now, whether it be
> Bestial oblivion, or some craven scruple
> Of thinking too precisely on the event,—
> A thought which, quarter'd, hath but one part
> —wisdom
> And ever three parts coward,—I do not know
> Why yet I live to say 'This thing's to do,'
> Sith I have cause, and will, and strength, and means
> To do't.   [IV. iv. 36-46]

Hamlet is here of course referring to the specific action of revenge, and commentators have been quick to point out that in regard to outward action he is neither slow nor a coward. But there is another and more important sense in which his self-accusation here is entirely justified, in which he is indeed 'lapsed in time and passion'—that is, as Dover Wilson explains, arrested or taken prisoner ('lapsed') by circumstances and passion [see excerpt above, 1935]. Hamlet, as every one says, is an intellectual, but he does little enough effective thinking on the moral and metaphysical problems that beset him: his god-like reason is clogged and impeded by the emotions of disgust, revulsion and self-contempt that bring him back, again and again, to the isolation of his obsession. Effective thinking, in the regions that most concern Hamlet, implies a capacity for self-forgetfulness and a capacity for true relationship.

With this, I think, we reach the heart of the play. If .. in the world of the play there is, on the one hand death, on the other, life lived with a peculiarly crude vigour of self-assertion, in such a world where are values to be found? If we are true to our direct impressions we must admit that *that* is Hamlet's problem, and questions concerning the authenticity of the Ghost or the means whereby Claudius may be trapped are subordinate to it. Hamlet's question, the question that he is continually asking himself is, How can I live? What shall I do to rid myself of this numbing sense of meaninglessness brought by the

knowledge of corruption? But behind this, and implicit in the play as a whole, is the question of being, of the activated consciousness. Hamlet comes close to putting this question directly in the great central soliloquy, but he glides away from it. And no wonder, for the problem is insoluble in the state of unresolved emotion in which he delivers himself of his thoughts; as Coleridge was never tired of insisting, thinking at the higher levels is an activity of the personality as a whole. (pp. 67-9)

What I have tried to do is to suggest that we are likely to see *Hamlet* more clearly if we see it as one of a series of studies of the mind's engagement with the world, of the intimate and intricate relations of self and world. In each of these plays— I have named *Othello, Timon,* and some others—there is an exploration of the ways in which 'being' and 'knowing' are related, so that failure in being, the corruption of consciousness, results either in a false affirmation, as with Othello, or in an inability to affirm at all, as with Hamlet. In *King Lear,* where so many lines of Shakespeare's thought converge, Lear only comes to 'see better' through a purgatorial progress of self-knowledge which enables him finally to respond to love. Perhaps we may say that Hamlet's consciousness is not unlike the consciousness of the unregenerate Lear, full of the knowledge of bitter wrong, of evil seemingly inherent in human nature. But Hamlet, unlike Lear—even if, initially, he is less greatly sinning—cannot break out of the closed circle of loathing and self-contempt, so that his nature is 'subdued to what it works in, like the dyer's hand'. The awareness that he embodies is at best an intermediate stage of the spirit, at worst a blind alley. Most certainly Hamlet's way of knowing the world is not Shakespeare's own. (pp. 90-1)

L. C. Knights, in his An Approach to "Hamlet," *Stanford University Press, 1961, 91 p.*

HELEN GARDNER   (essay date 1959)

[*Gardner compares* Hamlet *with other revenge tragedies of the period in an attempt to understand the complexities of Shakespeare's work. Gardner agrees with Samuel Johnson (1765) that Hamlet is "an instrument rather than an agent." For additional commentary on revenge in* Hamlet, *see Harold C. Goddard (1951), Fredson Bowers (1955), and Eleanor Prosser (1971).*]

[A] complex and delicate question, which takes us near to the heart of the play, is raised by the complaint which Johnson makes about the plot of *Hamlet.* 'Hamlet is, through the whole play, rather an instrument than an agent. After he has, by the stratagem of the play, convicted the King, he makes no attempt to punish him, and his death is at last effected by an incident which Hamlet has no part in producing.' Bradley's celebrated question, which he thinks anyone would ask on hearing the plot of *Hamlet,* converts Johnson's objection to the conduct of the plot into censure of the conduct of the hero: 'But why in the world did not Hamlet obey the ghost at once, and so save seven of those eight lives?' [See excerpt above, 1904.] And a highly unsympathetic aside of Mr. Eliot's converts Bradley's complaint at Hamlet's incompetence into a reproach to him for not being aware, as we are, that he 'has made a pretty considerable mess of things'. Mr. Eliot's rebuke to Hamlet for 'dying fairly well pleased with himself' is only logical from a severe moralist if we accept that what the play has shown us is the mess which Hamlet has made of things. Mr. Eliot might, however, have noticed that it is not merely Hamlet who appears to feel at the close that if only the whole truth were known— as we, the audience, know it—the name which he leaves behind

"Ophelia," by John Everett Millais (1852). From the Art Collection of the Folger Shakespeare Library.

him would not be 'a wounded name'. Horatio's farewell to him and Fortinbras's comment make no suggestion that what we have witnessed is a story of personal failure and inadequacy. . . . No need of extenuation appears to be felt. On the contrary, the play ends with 'the soldiers' music and the rites of war' and a final volley in salute of a dead hero.

The question here, which arises out of the play itself, is how we are to find consistency between the fact of Hamlet's delay, with which he bitterly reproaches himself, the fact, which Johnson pointed out, that the final denouement is not of his making, and the tone of the close of the play, which suggests so strongly that Hamlet has 'parted well and paid his score'. . . . When faced with a contradiction of this kind, the critic is bound to ask himself whether he has got the play out of focus. Is there some element in it which he is unaware of, which will, when perceived, make the close seem a full and fitting close? He needs to discover whether there is any means by which he can decide whether Shakespeare intended his audience to regard Hamlet as having 'made a mess of things'. And he must ask himself whether what Johnson thought an objection to the conduct of the plot, that the hero does so little to forward it, is a real objection: whether it does actually affect the 'satisfaction' which Johnson thought we should feel at the close of the play. The historical fact to which we can turn is that Shakespeare did not invent the plot of *Hamlet*. He chose, presumably because it in some way appealed to his imagination, to remake an older play. And, although this older play no longer exists,

there exist other plays on the same kind of subject. A study of these, to see what they have in common with *Hamlet*, may, at the least, suggest to us things which we should take into account in trying to understand the masterpiece which Shakespeare created in this genre. Such a study shows that the answer which Bradley gave to his question 'Why in the world did not Hamlet obey the ghost at once?' is only a partial answer. To Bradley's assertion, 'The whole story turns upon the peculiar character of the hero', we can object that heroes of very different character also fail to act promptly and also involve themselves and others in the final catastrophe. As for Johnson's comment on the conduct of the plot, we can say that the same complaint can be made to some degree against the plots of other revenge tragedies in the period. What Johnson thought to be a weakness in the plot of *Hamlet* appears to be a feature of the plots of other plays of the same kind and may point us towards a reason for their popularity and even towards what attracted Shakespeare in the old play which he re-made.

The essence of any tragedy of revenge is that its hero has not created the situation in which he finds himself and out of which the tragedy arises. . . . When the action opens the hero is seen in a situation which is horrible, and felt by him and the audience to be intolerable, but for which he has no responsibility. . . . [In] Elizabethan revenge plays it is not merely the initial situation which is created by the villain. The denouement also comes about through his initiative. It is not the result of a successfully carried out scheme of the revenger. The revenger takes an opportunity unconsciously provided for him by the villain. Given this opportunity, which he seems unable to create for himself, he forms his scheme on the spur of the moment. Thus, in *The Spanish Tragedy*, Lorenzo, believing himself safe and that the secret of Horatio's murder lies buried with Serberine and Pedringano, feigns reconcilement with Hieronymo and invites him to provide a play for the entertainment of the court. By means of this play Hieronymo achieves his vengeance and brings to light the secret crime of Lorenzo. . . . It seems as if in plays of this kind it was a necessary part of the total effect that the villain should be to some extent the agent of his own destruction. As initiator of the action he must be the initiator of its resolution. The satisfaction of the close included to a less or greater degree the sombre satisfaction which the Psalmist felt at the spectacle of the wicked falling into pits which they had digged for others. (pp. 38-42)

Shakespeare has very greatly developed this basic element in the revenge play of his day. He has developed it to make clear what in them is confused by sensationalism, and by that moral indignation which so easily converts itself to immorality. Great writers perceive what is only half perceived by their lesser contemporaries and express what in them finds only partial or imperfect expression. In other revenge plays, once the signal is given, the revenger produces a scheme of horror by which he destroys his opponent. He becomes an agent, bent on fulfilling the hateful Senecan maxim that crimes are only to be avenged by greater crimes. The irony is only mild. It is ironic that the villain, acting as if all were well, invites his destroyer to destroy him. Once invited, the hero descends with alacrity to the moral level of his opponent. The vengeance when it comes is as hideous as the original crime, or even more hideous, and the moral feelings of the audience are confused between satisfaction and outrage. In the denouement of *Hamlet* the irony is profound. Claudius, who has arranged the whole performance in order to destroy Hamlet, is himself destroyed and destroys his Queen. He is 'hoist with his own petard'. His tool Laertes acknowledges the justice of his fate as he reveals the plot to which he had consented: 'I am justly killed with mine own treachery.' Claudius himself makes no such acknowledgement. He dies impenitent; there is 'no relish of salvation' in his death. . . . Hamlet dies as a victim to that constancy to his purposes which has made him 'follow the king's pleasure' throughout. The end comes because he has accepted every challenge: 'If his fitness speaks, mine is ready.' . . . [There] is another point in which an Elizabethan tragedy of revenge differs from the legend of Orestes and from the original Hamlet legend. Everyone in Argos is perfectly well aware that Clytemnestra, with the help of her paramour, Aegisthus, murdered her husband, Agamemnon, just as in the old story of Hamlet everyone knows that his uncle Feng is the murderer of his father. In these ancient stories of revenge for blood the criminals are known to be criminals by all their world. They are not 'secret men of blood'. The secrecy with which Kyd invests the murder of Horatio is carried to such fantastic lengths that at one point in the play it appears that the world in general does not even realize that he is dead. In *Hamlet,* as we know it, whether it was so in the old play or not, only his murderer among living men knows at the beginning of the action that Hamlet the elder was murdered. *The Spanish Tragedy* is built on a powerful moral contrast between the treacherous, subtle, politic Lorenzo and the honest man, Hieronymo, who lives by conscience and the law. At the crisis of the play this contrast is blurred and Hieronymo becomes as crafty as his enemy. In *Hamlet* it is preserved to the end, and Hamlet himself is far

more of an instrument and far less of an agent than are his fellow revengers.

The view that the revenger's role was essentially a waiting role, that he was committed by the situation in which he found himself to counter-action, and differentiated from his opponent by lack of guile, does not answer the question 'Why does Hamlet delay?' It sets it in a different light. We must still find consistency between his character and his actions, and Bradley's statement that 'the whole story turns on the peculiar character of the hero' retains its truth. But to set *Hamlet* against other plays of its time which handle the same kind of subject is to suggest that however much he may reproach himself with his delay, that delay is part of a pattern which is made clear at the close. To ask 'Why in the world did not Hamlet act at once?' is to fail to grasp the nature of the dilemma which Kyd crudely adumbrated when he set the man of conscience and duty against the conscienceless and treacherous villain. Hamlet's agony of mind and indecision are precisely the things which differentiate him from that smooth, swift plotter Claudius, and from the coarse, unthinking Laertes, ready to 'dare damnation' and cut his enemy's throat in a churchyard. He quickly learns from Claudius how to entrap the unwary and the generous, and betters the instruction. 'He will never have a better opportunity', say many critics, when Hamlet, convinced of his uncle's guilt and hot for vengeance, comes on Claudius on his knees. . . . Do we really want to see Hamlet stab a defenceless, kneeling man? This 'opportunity' is no opportunity at all; the enemy is within touching distance, but out of reach. Hamlet's baffled rage finds an outlet in the speech which shocked Johnson by its depth of hatred. The speech reveals more than its speaker's character. Like many soliloquies, it is proleptic. The moment which Hamlet here declares that he will wait for, the real opportunity, will come. When Hamlet has gone and Claudius has risen from his knees, and not before, we know that Claudius has not found grace. The opportunity which Hamlet awaits Claudius will now provide. The play has made Hamlet certain of his uncle's guilt; it has also shown Claudius that his guilt is no longer his own secret. If he cannot repent, he must, for his own safety, destroy Hamlet. He will do it in his own characteristic way, by the hand of an accomplice and by the treacherous man's characteristic weapon, poison. And Hamlet will destroy Claudius in his own characteristic way also: by 'rashness' and 'indiscretion', and not by 'deep plots'. He will catch him at the moment when his guilt has been made clear to all the bystanders, so that as he runs the sword through him he will do so not as an assassin but as an executioner. The dark and devious world in which Hamlet finds himself, when he accepts the necessity of obeying the command of the Ghost, involves all who enter it in guilt. But Hamlet's most terrible deed, when he allows himself to be 'marshalled to knavery' and is most contaminated by his world, the sending of the traitors Rosencrantz and Guildenstern to their deaths, is a spontaneous, savage response to the discovery of their treachery; and his other crime, the killing of Polonius, with its consequence in the madness and death of Ophelia, is also unpremeditated. (pp. 43-7)

Hamlet is fittingly borne 'like a soldier, to the stage', because in the secret war which he has waged he has shown a soldier's virtues. Pre-eminently he has shown the virtue of constancy. He has not laid down his arms and quitted the field. For Bradley's comment, 'Two months have passed and he has done nothing', we might better say, 'Two months have passed and he is still there, at his post, on guard.' The play ends with a soldier's funeral. It opens with sentries at their watch, being relieved. . . . The play of *Hamlet* continually recurs to the thought of suicide, and the temptation to give up the battle of life. Hamlet's first soliloquy opens with the lament that the Almighty has 'fixed his canon 'gainst self-slaughter', and his last action is to snatch the poisoned cup from the lips of Horatio. Within this frame of soldiers on the watch, being relieved, and of a soldier's laying to rest, I do not believe that the Elizabethans thought that they were witnessing a story of personal failure. Nor do I think that we should do so either, unless we are certain of what, in this situation, would be success.

The tragedy of *Hamlet,* and of plays of its kind, of which it is the supreme example, does not lie in 'the unfitness of the hero for his task', or in some 'fatal flaw'. It is not true that a coarser nature could have cleansed the state of Denmark. . . . The tragedy lies in the nature of the task, which only the noble will feel called on to undertake, or rather, in the nature of the world which is exposed to the hero's contemplation and in his sense of responsibility to the world in which he finds himself. *Hamlet* towers above other plays of its kind through the heroism and nobility of its hero, his superior power of insight into, and reflection upon, his situation, and his capacity to suffer the moral anguish which moral responsibility brings. Hamlet is the quintessence of European man, who holds that man is 'ordained to govern the world according to equity and righteousness with an upright heart', and not to renounce the world and leave it to its corruption. By that conception of man's duty and destiny he is involved in those tragic dilemmas with which our own age is so terribly familiar. For how can man secure justice except by committing injustice, and how can he act without outraging the very conscience which demands that he should act? (pp. 48-50)

Hamlet is not a problem to which a final solution exists. It is a work of art about which questions can always be asked. Each generation asks its own questions and finds its own answers, and the final test of the validity of those answers can only be time. Johnson, Coleridge, Bradley, all tell us things about *Hamlet* which are consistent with the play as we read it. A critic today cannot hope for more than that his questions and answers will seem relevant, and will continue to seem relevant, to others who read and ponder the play. The reward of the historical approach is not that it leads us to a final and infallible interpretation. (p. 51)

> Helen Gardner, ''The Historical Approach,'' in her The Business of Criticism, *Oxford University Press, Oxford, 1959, pp. 25-51.*

HARRY LEVIN (essay date 1959)

[*Levin's study of* Hamlet *is a rhetorical analysis in which he identifies interrogation, doubt, and irony as three "figures of speech and thought" which recur in the play. Levin asserts that these three elements are manifested in a dialectical fashion: interrogation is the thesis, doubt the antithesis, and irony the synthesis. Levin examines the language of* Hamlet *for expression of these qualities throughout the play. For additional commentary on language and imagery in* Hamlet, *see Samuel Taylor Coleridge (1813), G. Wilson Knight (1930), Caroline F. E. Spurgeon (1935), Wolfgang H. Clemen (1951), Maynard Mack (1952), T. McAlindon (1970), Reuben A. Brower (1971), and Inga-Stina Ewbank (1977).*]

Maynard Mack has lately noted, 'is pre-eminently in the interrogative mood,' Precisely; and this questioning spirit takes a structural form which invites a technical analysis. The interchange of question and answer, as a basis of dialogue, is

fundamental to dramatic technique; and dialogue, whenever it serves a purpose, becomes dialectic. In the stichomythy of Greek tragedy, it serves not only to forward the exposition but to precipitate the discovery. Shakespeare is adroit in his handling of it throughout his work: note how he opens the first four scenes of *Macbeth,* or brings out the inquisitorial predisposition of King Lear. Comparative statistics would prove little, given the variances of Elizabethan punctuation; but Hamlet's Graveyard Scene provides a cogent sampling, with seventy question-marks in 322 lines.

What is more revealing, the word 'question' occurs in *Hamlet* no less than seventeen times, much more frequently than in any of Shakespeare's other plays. Recalling that it comes as the final word in Hamlet's most famous line, we may well regard it as the key-word of the play. Many other words contribute to the general atmosphere of uncertainty, as we shall soon have occasion to recall. Furthermore, besides direct inquiry, there are other modes of questioning, notably doubt and irony, which we shall be considering in due sequence. Each of these three devices is a figure of speech and simultaneously a figure of thought, to take them as they are categorized by Quintilian. This overlapping classification is useful, if it helps us to understand how words adapt their structure to ideas, how the very process of cogitation can be dramatized. *Interrogatio* is the simplest mode, with the rhetorical question indicating its own response, or with the catechism preordaining its set replies. But when the answer is unforeseen, or when there is no answer—that is the kind of open question which *Hamlet* is more particularly concerned to pose. The play begins with such a question: 'Who's there?' This, at first glance, would seem to be no more than a sentry's perfunctory challenge. With the second line and its counter-question, we become aware that the original speaker was not the sentry on duty but the nervous officer who has just arrived to relieve him. As the exposition develops, we come to realize that the change of guard constitutes a symbolic prologue, a re-enactment of those dynastic changes which frame the play. *Qui vive? Vive le roi!* The watchword, in ghostly reverberation, gathers ironic overtones. 'Long live the King!' Which king? *Le roi est mort. Vive le roi!*

Now Bernardo, the arriving sentry, presumably knew that Francisco, the watchman, was there. Whom else then, we may wonder, could he have been expecting to encounter? 'Who's there?' might be the cry of a frightened child in the dark; it might also be the query of a metaphysician scanning the void for evidence of God. The nocturnal setting from which it is launched, a fortified elevation by the edge of a northern sea, an outpost of reason on the frontier of unconsciousness, starkly accords with the interrogative theme. Francisco's departure strikes the note of foreboding: the night is very cold and he is heartsick. The entrance of Horatio and Marcellus, with their expository conversation, raises further questions: why are these feverish preparations for war going on in the background, nightly as well as daily? and can this be some civic portent, which we are here to watch, like the baneful omens that portended the fall of Caesar at Rome? Speculations are rife during the interim of suspense between the appearance and the reappearance of the Ghost, which is nothing if not a personified question. (pp. 18-21)

In the following scene, the brilliantly lighted Council Scene, it is Hamlet who is questioned in turn by Claudius and Gertrude. His answers are reluctant and elusive, preceded by an enigmatic aside and followed by his First Soliloquy, which voices his melancholy state of mind and especially his distaste for his mother's remarriage. After this self-questioning, Horatio and Marcellus arrive to tell him about the Ghost, and he responds with a volley of questions to them: 'Saw? who? . . . But where was this? . . . Did you not speak to it? . . . Arm'd, say you? . . . Stay'd it long? . . . His beard was grizzled—no?' [I. ii. 190-239]. Subsequently he has his turn as investigator; and he too is overwhelmingly conscious of the conflicting possibilities that might account for this 'questionable shape.' Why has the tomb cast up a corpse, if indeed it has? What can it mean, and what can it lead to? 'Say, why is this? wherefore? what should we do?' [I. iv. 57]. The spectre will not speak until Hamlet faces it alone, ignoring the terrors envisioned by Horatio. Horatio, as befits a student from Wittenberg University, has been skeptical; he has begun by saying 'tush' and attributing the manifestation to fantasy; but he has come around to believing, at least 'in part.' The Ghost's narration, with its pointed refusal to reveal the purgatorial secrets of its prison house, ends by deepening the mystery. Hamlet's reaction to the disclosure of his father's murder and his uncle's hypocrisy is registered in his Second Soliloquy. His new awareness, that Claudius could smile and be a villain, makes him distrustful of everyone about him. Hesitant to impart what the Ghost has confided, he swears his companions to a conspiratorial secrecy, while the Ghost's voice echoes from the cellarage, the cavernous area under the Elizabethan stage that was commonly designated as hell.

Hamlet is understandably anxious to identify this ambiguous figure with the late King, his father, and consequently to trust it. But Horatio's doubt cannot be dismissed so easily. It is already present as an alternative at the moment of recognition:

Be thou a spirit of health or goblin damn'd,
Bring with thee airs from heaven or blasts from hell . . .

[I. iv. 40-1]

And from that moment Hamlet is constantly glancing upward and downward, balancing every decision and making every move in full view of a perspective which now extends, as in the medieval mysteries, from the celestial to the infernal sphere. 'Heaven and earth!' was his exclamation in the First Soliloquy [I. ii. 42]. The Second widens his frame of reference:

O all you host of heaven! O earth! What else?
And shall I couple hell?   [I. v. 92-3]

Whether heaven or hell is ordinant, whether good or evil prevails in this world, seems to hinge on Hamlet's identification of the Ghost. Yet that would not resolve the ambiguity; for if he takes the Ghost's word, the world is far more corrupt than he has previously imagined; but if the Ghost is false, then that corruption undermines the very foundations of the universe. Taking our ghostly witness at face value, we might recognize it as the soul of Hamlet the Elder, returning to earth on a special mission from purgatory, in accordance with the orthodox tenets of the Catholic faith. The Reformation, however, rejected the dogma of purgatory; and we associate Wittenberg with Protestantism. The ardent Protestant soon to be King of England had recently published a treatise arguing that ghosts were not souls of the dead but demons who tempted the living. Whether Hamlet was being led astray to eternal damnation or being enjoined to perform a sacred duty would thus be contingent on theological questions which were moot. Even more perplexing are the moral implications of the Ghost's command. It is based upon the *lex talionis*, the primitive law of the blood-feud, whereby the nearest of kin to a murdered person is bound

to avenge him by slaying his murderer. This barbarous principle, which Hamlet seems ready to act on, runs counter to both the Catholic and Protestant religions. It is altogether incompatible with the teaching of Christianity. 'Vengeance is mine,' says the Lord, in both the Old and New Testaments, 'I will repay.'

Hamlet's outlook is clouded by two problematic assumptions, closely related yet somewhat contradictory, each of them deeply rooted in tradition yet increasingly subject to questioning: the belief in ghosts and the code of revenge. Happily, it is not for us to solve his problems; it is enough if we appreciate their immediacy to him and their complexity for him. (pp. 21-4)

Hamlet takes place in an open universe; its signs and omens, though evident, are equivocal; and it is not merely Claudius, it is Hamlet and nearly everyone else, who dies cut off from confession and absolution, 'Not shriving time allow'd' [V. ii. 47]. Death is sudden and birth unsought for; the conditions of existence are questionable from first to last; nothing is certain except that churchyards yawn and gravedigging is a useful employment. Yorick's grin is the sole retort to Hamlet's *ubi sunt*. Where indeed are they now, those travelers to the undiscovered country? Only the Ghost can say, and it will not. But it will haunt us all the more, because it materializes 'the dread of something after death,' because it prefigures our vague apprehension of godhead [III. i. 77]. And we must acknowledge its effect, with the skeptic Horatio, 'It harrows me with fear and wonder'' [I. i. 44], or with Hamlet himself, 'O wonderful' [I. v. 118]. Pity and fear are the usual tragic components; but here, while Fortinbras surveys the damage, Horatio bespeaks the emotions of 'woe or wonder' [V. ii. 363]. The play has kept us guessing; it leaves us wondering.

With *Hamlet*, 'why' and 'wherefore' are brushed aside, as the interrogative gives way to the imperative, 'what should we do?' The first-person plural supports the suggestions, put forward by Hazlitt [1817] and endorsed by other perceptive critics, that our interest in the protagonist is a self-involvement; that we are Hamlet. His circumstances are ours, to the extent that every man, in some measure, is born to privilege and anxiety, committed where he has never been consulted, hemmed in on all sides by an overbearing situation, and called upon to perform what must seem an ungrateful task. No wonder he undertakes it with many misgivings, tests it with much groping and some backsliding, pursues it with revisions and indecisions, and parses every affirmation by the grammar of doubt. (pp. 41-3)

* * * * *

In reconsidering *Hamlet*, we cannot pretend that we are unaware of what happens next or how it all comes out. Knowing what will finally be decided, critics have grown impatient over its agonies of decision, and have blamed Hamlet for undue procrastination. But what may be a foregone conclusion to them must be an open question to him, as we have reminded ourselves by watching the process unfold, and observing how the tone is set through the interaction of questions, answers, and unanswered speculations. Having rehearsed the play once with an emphasis on the interrogative mood, let us push the interrogation further by returning to certain indicative passages, tracing now an inner train of thought, and later placing it in a broader perpsective. *Interrogatio* is classified—by the rhetorician, Henry Peacham—as a form of *pathopoeia*, which in turn is neither more nor less than a device for arousing emotions: 'Examples hereof are common in Tragedies.' *Dubitatio*, our next figure of speech and thought, is less emotional and more deliberative. As it is defined by Abraham Fraunce, in *The Arcadian Rhetorike*, 'Addubitation or doubting is a kinde of deliberation with our selues.' The orator deliberates between rival options: either to revenge or not to revenge, whether a visitant comes from heaven or hell. For doubt is that state of mind where the questioner faces no single answer nor the lack of one, but rather a choice between a pair of alternatives. Etymologically, the word stems from *dubitare*, which means precisely to hesitate in the face of two possibilities. The structure of *Hamlet* seems, at every level, to have been determined by this duality. 'A double blessing is a double grace' [I. iii. 53].

Similarly, the texture is characterized by a tendency to double and redouble words and phrases. From the very first scene, the speeches abound in hendiadys; 'gross and scope,' 'law and heraldry.' Sometimes the paired nouns are redundant synonyms: 'food and diet,' 'pith and moment'—Saxon balancing Latin as in the doublets of Sir Thomas Browne. Adjectives or verbs are coupled at other times: 'impotent and bedrid,' 'countenance and excuse.' This reduplication seems to be a habit of courtly diction into which Hamlet himself falls now and then: 'the purpose of playing . . . is . . . to show . . . the very age and body of the time his form and pressure' [III. ii. 20-4]. By the count of R. A. Foakes, no less than 247 such pairings are scattered through the play. They are doubtless more ornamental than functional; yet they charge the air with overtones of wavering and indecision. The Clown goes farther with his equivocations, putting his finger on serious ambiguities. And Hamlet goes too far with his *double-entendres*, besmirching the maidenly innocence of Ophelia. Claudius, in his opening address to the Council, establishes himself as a practiced exponent of stately double-talk. With unctuous skill, he manages a transition from the old King's death to himself and his inherited queen. Antithesis is condensed into oxymoron: 'delight and dole,' 'defeated joy.' (pp. 48-9)

The incrimination of Claudius by the Ghost, duly recorded in the book of Hamlet's brain, is an object-lesson in duplicity. Claudius himself is unremittingly conscious of the distinction between the 'exterior' and 'the inward man' [II. ii. 6]. Both in communing with himself and in dealing with others, he seldom fails to distinguish between words and deeds, or face and heart. He introduces Gertrude by publicly casting her in a dual role, 'our sometime sister, now our queen,' as he does his nephew shortly afterward, 'my cousin Hamlet, and my son' [I. ii. 8, 64]. Hamlet resentfully picks up the implications, and caustically refers to his 'uncle-father and aunt-mother' [II. ii. 376]. On the premise that 'man and wife is one flesh,' he perversely carries the logic of incest to its conclusion by bidding farewell to Claudius as his 'dear mother' [IV. iii. 49]. . . . [Hamlet,] learns to live at court, in an arena where men and women must be actors and actresses. He must learn an etymology which may not have struck him during his humanistic studies at Wittenberg—that the word 'hypocrite,' in the original Greek, designated an actor.

Claudius, invoking the 'twofold force' of prayer, acknowledges his own hypocrisy, caught as he is between guilt and repentance:

> . . . like a man to double business bound,
> I stand in pause where I should first begin.
> [III. iii. 41-2]

A moment later, Hamlet will stand in pause before the double business of whether Claudius should be saved or damned, and will give him the benefit of an unforeseen doubt. The smiling villain is a double-dealer; but so is Hamlet, in another sense. At the beginning he is single-minded, all of a piece, all melancholia; then he puts on his mask and plays the antic, carrying his buffoonery to the verge of hysteria; his disposition is manic in the presence of others and depressive when he is by himself. Where the vicious Claudius assumes an air of respectability, the virtuous Hamlet must assimilate the atmosphere of licentiousness.(pp. 49-51)

This world, in Hamlet's opening description, is 'an unweeded garden' [I. ii. 135]. Well-tended gardens always stand for the norms of nature in Shakespeare's imagery; here the blight is traceable not merely to neglect, but to a kind of perverse cultivation; and Gertrude will be cautioned by Hamlet against spreading compost on the weeds [III. iv. 151]. The Ghost is manifestly a sign that something is rotten; more problematically, it points a course of action for setting things right. By obeying its supernatural behest, Hamlet might solve the political and personal problems at one fell swoop, removing his uncle from his father's throne and from his mother's bed. But, having been led to question all that seems most familiar, how can he be expected to trust the unknown? (pp. 52-4)

As a poet who mixes cosmology with intimacy, Hamlet obviously belongs to the Metaphysical School. The purport of his stanza does not differ much from the conclusion of Arnold's 'Dover Beach,' the affirmation that, in a universe of illusion and pain, the only true relationship is love. But Hamlet recants his love soon afterward, while Ophelia herself is enveloped from first to last in an astral nimbus of uncertainty. Her first speech, in response to her brother's parting request, is the question, 'Do you doubt that?' [I. iii. 4]. Her last rites are curtailed by the Priest because 'Her death was doubtful' [V. i. 227]. The tenderness of lovers can be no more than a trivial fond record which Hamlet must erase from his tablets of memory. Only the filial relationship can retain its meaning for him; and it is, to put it mildly, a peculiar one; for he is not the son and heir of his father so much as the son and revenger of a ghost; he is, we might deduce, the incarnate member of an unhallowed trinity. (pp. 54-5)

'There is nothing either good or bad but thinking makes it so,' Hamlet explains to Rosencrántz and Guildenstern [II. ii. 249-50]. The identical situation, the state of Denmark, may seem good to them and bad to him. Similarly, an intellectual might have disagreed with a pair of courtiers about the state of England in 1601, though he could hardly have publicized his plaint. In the year of *Hamlet*, John Donne poured his disillusionment into an elaborate poetic fragment, 'The Progress of the Soul,' which breaks off with this triplet:

> Ther's nothing simply good, nor ill alone,
> Of every quality comparison,
>   The only measure is, and judge, opinion.

Montaigne, under more tranquil circumstances two decades before, had reached an analogous position in an essay demonstrating 'That the taste of goods or evils doth greatly depend on the opinion we have of them.' Of these three formulations, Hamlet's is the boldest, though his boldness must be qualified by the realization that he is a fictitious character, speaking not for Shakespeare but for himself, and for himself in a particularly saturnine humor. Yet he is willing, at all events, to declare that there are no ethical absolutes, that good and evil are value-judgements determined by relative standards. Troilus, starting from the same relativism, strives to imbue it with all the enthusiasm that Hamlet so consciously lacks. 'What is aught save as 'tis valu'd?' asks Troilus. The upshot, for him, is a relentless devaluation of both the heroic and the romantic ideals. *Troilus and Cressida* has close affinities with *Hamlet* in composition and in temper; but it terminates with its difficulties unresolved. As for *Hamlet*, it never regains its lost certitudes; nor does it ever relax its movement of vacillation; but it derives new meaning out of its clash of values; and its overclouded patterns merge into a grander design. 'What doubt is to knowledge, irony is to the personal life,' wrote another melancholy Dane, Sören Kierkegaard, who was to strike his balance under the heading of *Either/Or*. That pronouncement asks for application, when Kierkegaard singles out Shakespeare as 'the grand master of irony.' (pp. 74-5)

With *Hamlet*, as we have seen, we are involved in two sets of complementary problems. One set is speculative: why? wherefore? who is the Ghost? and what is the ultimate mystery that it prefigures? The other is practical: what shall we do? how should Hamlet bear himself amid these unexampled difficulties? and how should he accomplish his unsought vocation, revenge? Shakespearean tragedy is deeply concerned with the individual as he faces opportunity, responsibility, and moral choice. It is equally preoccupied with the pattern of events, and whether this is determined by casual accident, fatal necessity, or divine intervention. Given the motive, one must await one's cue. The interplay between these preoccupations is the source of innumerable ironies, both conscious and unconscious, some of them attached to the hero's viewpoint, others detached in a reminiscent overview. 'Hamlet has no plan, but *Hamlet* has,' as Goethe observed, with a fellow-dramatist's understanding [see excerpt above, 1795]. The play has a plot; and, so, in another sense, has the Prince; but he cannot foresee the fulfilment of his intentions; he can only test them against hugger-mugger conditions. Yet, as producer of 'The Murder of Gonzago,' he can take charge of a miniature drama which exerts an effect on the drama at large; he can play god and look down on his creation, in the self-conscious mood of romantic irony. Whereas in *Hamlet* itself, he is no more than a leading actor, whose body will be placed 'on a stage'—on a funeral bier which may likewise be viewed as a theatrical platform—among the other corpses at the end. (pp. 83-4)

With Shakespeare the dramatic resolution conveys us, beyond the man-made sphere of poetic justice, toward the ever-receding horizons of cosmic irony.

This is peculiarly the case with *Hamlet*, for the same reasons that it excites such intensive empathy from actors and readers, critics and writers alike. There may be other Shakespearean characters who are just as memorable, and other plots which are no less impressive; but nowhere else has the outlook of the individual in a dilemma been so profoundly realized; and a dilemma, by definition, is an all but unresolvable choice between evils. Rather than with calculation or casuistry, it should be met with the virtue of readiness; sooner or later it will have to be grasped by one or the other of its horns. These, in their broadest terms, have been—for Hamlet, as we interpret him—the problem of what to believe and the problem of how to act. Hamlet is unwittingly compelled to act as if life were a duel, with unbated swords and against a series of furtive assailants. He is unwillingly led to believe that death comes as a cup, filled with poisonous wine and containing a flawless pearl. His doom is generalized in Fulke Greville's chorus:

> Oh, wearisome condition of humanity,
> Born under one law, to another bound . . .

Irony cannot solve the incalculable contradictions between the personal life and the nature of things. Yet it can teach us to live with them; and that is no mean achievement; for Hamlet's knowledge was not idle reflection, according to Nietzsche [see excerpt above, 1872]. It was an insight which hindered action by stripping the veil of illusion from the terrible truth, the terror or the absurdity of existence. This would be intolerable, were it not for the transformations of art, which asserts man's conquest over his fears, and which thereby allays his vexation of spirit. Thus Hamlet's limited victory commences with the play-within-the-play, a working-model of the play itself, which repeats the lesson in mastery on a larger scale within our minds. From its very commencement, after the stroke of midnight, we are brought face to face with the supernatural. Volleys of gunfire augment and accelerate the sound effects until, at the conclusion of the dead-march, '*a peal of ordinance*' signalizes a battle lost and won. (pp. 104-06)

Up to a certain point, the modern mind has taken the course of Faust; it has felt free to experiment, to cultivate the widest experience, to develop and enrich personality. Past that point, it has been taking the way of Hamlet; it has been curbed and sidetracked, commandeered by unexpected emergencies and forced to expend itself on objects unworthy of its talents. But, happily, the parable does not end with our ephemeral efforts to apply it. It persists while thinking man is interested in viewing his finest self-portrait, in asking himself the reason for his existence, or in responding to those demands which may prove, in the long run, to be its justification. (pp. 106-07)

> *Harry Levin, "Interrogation," "Doubt," and "Irony," in his* The Question of "Hamlet," *Oxford University Press, New York, 1959, pp. 17-43, 47-75, 79-107.*

ROBERT ORNSTEIN (essay date 1960)

[*Ornstein explores the moral atmosphere of* Hamlet.]

The impression of vastness in *Macbeth* is created almost entirely by poetic suggestion. The play lacks the intellectual dimension and richness of thought which make *Hamlet* seem to the critics the most philosophical of Shakespeare's plays. Honor, revenge, justice, political order, Stoicism, friendship, familial piety—how many Renaissance ideas and ideals come under scrutiny in the halls of Elsinore. And yet how little is there in the lines of *Hamlet* which testifies to Shakespeare's intellectual or philosophical powers. Subjected to philosophical analysis the great speeches in *Hamlet* yield commonplaces. We treasure them for their incomparable poetry, not for their depth and originality of thought—for their revelation of Hamlet's soul, not for their discovery of the human condition. Many questions are raised in the play but few are answered. The question of action in an evil society, one might say, is resolved by an expedient dear to Victorian novelists: a change of air, a sea voyage from which the hero returns calm if not resolute, buoyed by a vaguely optimistic fatalism that is half-Christian, half-Stoic.

My point is not that Shakespeare tricks us into accepting a sham or meretricious resolution in *Hamlet*, but that we do not find in Shakespearean drama the intellectual schemes of Chapman's tragedies. Even when Shakespeare seems to dramatize a thesis, he does not debate philosophical positions. He is not interested in abstract thought but in characters who think, who have intellectual as well as emotional needs, and who, like Pirandello's characters, cry aloud the reason of their suffering.

The "problem" of *Hamlet* is not an intellectual puzzle. It arises because the play creates so marvelous a sense of the actual improvisation of life that we can find no simple logic in its sprawling action. Unable to comprehend or accept the totality of Shakespeare's many-sided hero, we search for a more logical, more consistent, or more pleasant Hamlet than the play affords. We try to arrive at Shakespeare's moral ideas by reading Elizabethan treatises of psychology and moral philosophy, when it is only by studying the total artifice of *Hamlet* that we can understand why its hero seems to us the most noble, pureminded, and blameless of Shakespeare's tragic protagonists. What is not near Hamlet's conscience is not near our own because he is our moral interpreter. He is the voice of ethical sensibility in a sophisticated, courtly milieu; his bitter asides, which penetrate Claudius' facade of kingly virtue and propriety, initiate, so to speak, the moral action of the play. And throughout the play our identification with Hamlet's moral vision is such that we hate what he hates, admire what he admires. As centuries of Shakespeare criticism reveal, we accuse Hamlet primarily of what he accuses himself: namely, his slowness to revenge.

Our moral impression of Hamlet's character derives primarily from what he says rather than what he does. It is an almost intuitive awareness of the beauty, depth, and refinement of his moral nature, upon which is thrust a savage burden of revenge and of disillusion. If Shakespeare's characters are illusions created by dramatic artifice, then what we love in Hamlet is an illusion within an illusion: i.e., the suggestion of Hamlet's former self, the Hamlet whom Ophelia remembers and who poignantly reappears in the conversations with Horatio, particularly before the catastrophe. Through his consummate artistry Shakespeare creates within us a sympathy with Hamlet which becomes almost an act of faith—a confidence in the untouched and untouchable core of his spiritual nature. This act of faith, renewed by the great speeches throughout the play, allows us to accept Hamlet's brutality towards Ophelia, his reaction to Polonius' death, his savage refusal to kill Claudius at prayer, and his Machiavellian delight in disposing of Rosencrantz and Guildenstern. Without the memory of the great soliloquies which preceded it, our impression of the closet scene would be vastly different. And, in fact, to attempt to define Hamlet's character by weighing his motives and actions against any system of Renaissance thought is to stage *Hamlet* morally without the Prince of Denmark, i.e., without the felt impression of Hamlet's moral nature which is created by poetic nuance. (pp. 234-35)

If the ambiguities and the mysteries of *Hamlet* irritate us, it is because we expect an omniscient view of character in drama; we are not used to seeing a play almost entirely from the point of view of a single character. We do not realize that our identification with Hamlet is as complete as with a first-person narrator of a novel. We see little more than he sees; we know little more about the other characters—about Gertrude's crimes or Rosencrantz and Guildenstern's treachery—than he finally knows. If we had to examine objectively the facts of the play to decide whether Hamlet should have had Rosencrantz and Guildenstern executed, then their innocence or guilt would be a crucial matter; but since like Hamlet we identify Rosencrantz and Guildenstern with Claudius' cause, what they knew or did not know of Claudius' plans "does not matter."

It is Hamlet (not the Romantic critics) who creates the problem of his delay in revenge. Were it not for the self-lacerating soliloquies in which he accuses himself of the grossness and

insensitivity which he despises in his mother, the thought that he delays would not occur to us. . . . In the study a critic can be quite bloodthirsty about Hamlet's failure to dispatch Claudius. In the theater, however, one does not feel that Hamlet should have skewered Claudius at prayer or should have been more interested in Claudius' damnation than his mother's salvation. Nor does one feel that the Hamlet who says, "The interim is mine" is "delaying."

This is not to say that Shakespeare posed an artificial problem in Hamlet's soliloquies in order to make mad the critics and appall the scholars. The problem of action in an evil world is as real in *Hamlet* as in many of the revenge plays of the period. True to his father's command, Hamlet engages in fierce struggle against the world without tainting his mind. False to himself and to his father's advice, Laertes is corrupted and debased by the hunger for vengeance. Although Hamlet commits rash and bloody deeds and comes to take a sardonic delight in flanking policy with policy, he does not, like Vindice, become unfit for life. . . . The inevitability of his death is an aesthetic, not moral, expectation created by the insistent imagery of death, by the mood of the graveyard scene, by Hamlet's premonitions, and by the finality of Claudius' triple-stopped treachery. The calm of the graveyard scene, coming after the feverish action that preceded Hamlet's departure for England, seems a false recovery before death, that brief moment of detachment and lucidity which is often granted dying men. Enhancing this poignant impression are the very simple, quiet responses of Horatio, who attends the final hours of his Prince.

The problem of action in *Hamlet* is posed immediately and ultimately by Death, the philosophical tutor who forces man to consider the value of existence. Because the death of his father has made life meaningless, Hamlet wishes for the release of suicide, which is by traditional standards a cowardly evasion and negation of life. Yet, paradoxically, the willingness and eagerness of Fortinbras' army to die seems to give meaning to a cause that would be otherwise contemptible and valueless. And whether one takes arms against a sea of troubles (an apparently hopeless undertaking) or suffers the arrows and slings of outrageous fortune, there is only one possible conclusion to the action of life, the stillness of the grave. *Hamlet* begins with terrified sentries awaiting the return of the dead. It closes with the solemn march of soldiers bearing Hamlet's body "to the stage." Throughout the play Hamlet faces the most ancient and abiding philosophical problem: he must "learn how to die," i.e., how to live with the fact and thought of death. (pp. 236-37)

More clearly in *Hamlet* than in *The Spanish Tragedy* or *Tamburlaine* one can see the inner direction which great tragedy takes at the close of the Elizabethan age. For Shakespeare as for Kyd and Marlowe the fact of man's mortality is not the essential pathos of tragedy. That pathos lies in their heroes' anguished discovery of a universe more vast, more terrible, and more inscrutable than is dreamt of in philosophy. In *Hamlet* and Jacobean tragedy man suffers to be wise, and, indeed, his knowledge of reality is a more intense form of suffering than the illustrators of *De casibus* tales could imagine. (p. 240)

Robert Ornstein, "Shakespeare," in his The Moral Vision of Jacobean Tragedy, *University of Wisconsin Press, 1960, pp. 222-76.*

SISTER MIRIAM JOSEPH, C.S.C.   (essay date 1962)

[*Sister Miriam Joseph considers* Hamlet *to be a specifically Christian tragedy, "with a Christian atmosphere and Christian char-*

acters." She proposes that Hamlet has good reason to believe that, through the ghost's message, he has been granted divine authority to kill Claudius. Yet he ignores the ghost's warning, "taint not thy mind," and his hatred for Claudius overcomes his Christian nature. This, according to Sister Miriam Joseph, is his tragic flaw. In contrast to this view, Eleanor Prosser (1967) defines the ghost as evil in origin rather than good. For additional commentary on Hamlet from a religious perspective, see the excerpts by Hermann Ulrici (1839), Søren Kierkegaard (1845), H.D.F. Kitto (1956), and Patrick Cruttwell (1963). For further discussion of the ghost, see Joseph Addison (1811), Gotthold Ephraim Lessing (1767), Elizabeth Montagu (1769), W. W. Greg (1917), and J. Dover Wilson (1918).]

If we agree with Aristotle that a tragedy is the imitation of a serious action in dramatic form having as its specific function to arouse pity and fear in the audience through its incidents and thereby to purify their emotions, then a Christian tragedy must accomplish this purification through incidents that have Christian significance. And if a tragic hero must be a man, not perfect, but on the whole good and likable, who brings upon himself through a flaw in his character or an error of judgment the misfortune he suffers (and the audience with him), then a Christian tragic hero must bring upon himself misfortune and suffering through a flaw in his character as a Christian.

I hope to demonstrate that the play *Hamlet* is in the strict sense a Christian tragedy and that Hamlet is a Christian hero whose tragic flaw is his failure at the moment of crisis to measure up to the heroic Christian virtue demanded of him by the moral situation and by the ghost. I believe that the centuries-old Christian doctrine of the discernment of spirits is a key to the understanding of the ghost.

The ghost reveals the moral situation in Denmark and prescribes the remedy to rectify it. King Claudius occupies and stains the throne which he won by murdering the king, his brother. The ghost commands his son Hamlet to revenge the murder and thereby cleanse the state. (p. 119)

I maintain that a careful study of the text of *Hamlet* shows the four witnesses testing the apparition in accordance with the ancient, traditional doctrine for the discernment of spirits, current in Shakespeare's time. It prescribes an investigation of the three basic possibilities by successive steps to determine the nature of the spirit: Can a natural explanation, such as 1) *delusion or hallucination* caused by faulty apprehension of the senses or illness or a too lively or disordered imagination account for the appearance or the occurrence under consideration? If natural causes must be ruled out and yet the objective reality of the phenomenon cannot be denied, it is preternatural and must be produced by either 2) *an evil spirit* or 3) *a good spirit*, God acting either directly or else indirectly through a holy angel or through a sanctified human spirit.

These three steps are stages in elimination in the process of reaching the truth in a given instance. This rationale inherently generates the most intense dramatic suspense because it holds together in one unified theory the alternatives of hallucination, an evil spirit, and a good spirit as possibilities to be tested rigorously and successively, the second to be considered only after the first has been rejected, the third only after the second has had to be eliminated. It does not regard them as views of separate and opposing schools of thought concerning spirits. It poses a problem in the play, as it did in life itself, but it furnishes a key to the solution. Not only the belief in the ghost engendered in the four witnesses by their experiences of seeing it [I. i. 23-5, 56-8, I. iv. 38] but even Hamlet's subsequent doubts [II. ii. 598-603] accord with this traditional doctrine.

Through the play-test Hamlet becomes convinced on grounds of reason that the third alternative is the true one, that the ghost is a good spirit, his revelation true [III. ii. 286], his command just. (pp. 120-21)

I maintain that the words of the ghost are not inconsistent with the character of a Christian soul temporarily suffering the fire of purgatory until he be cleansed and admitted to heaven. The ghost devotes one line to the three-fold but minor loss he suffered from death itself [I. v. 75], but he laments in a five-line crescendo his major spiritual loss in being deprived of the sacraments [I. v. 76-80]. I believe that those who charge the ghost with self-praise and personal vindictiveness overlook profound differences between a living man and the soul of a dead man, between a man in time seeking the truth and a soul in eternity knowing the truth. In my opinion, the ghost, who impersonally silences his son's pity for his sufferings [I. v. 5] and is now enlightened as to truth and holiness, can without vanity but with frank objectivity and balance speak of his own virtue [I. v. 47-50] as well as his own sins [I. v. 12, 76, 79]. . . . (p. 121)

I have considered the morality of the ghost's command from three points of view: the moral situation as grounded on custom and reason, the legal aspect, and the special command.

The authority that St. Paul says is God's minister to punish evildoers (Rom. xiii. 1, 3, 4) cannot reside in Claudius, who won the throne by murder. One cannot win a right with wrong. Claudius has disqualified himself, for he lacks a condition necessary to make him God's deputy. . . . If reason demands that the state protect the common good by punishing a murderer much more does it demand that the murderer be punished when he corrupts the very seat of government itself. Although the king of Denmark is elected by the nobles from among members of the royal family, we gather that he (and the king of England also) is an absolute monarch whose will is law and who directly exercises power over life and death [V. ii. 18-25]. He *is* the state. How then can he be punished? In whom does the authority from God really exist? Surely in Hamlet. Had his life not been cut off by violence, his father would undoubtedly have named Hamlet his successor, as Hamlet later named Fortinbras. . . . Because of the situation itself the throne is morally vacant and we may conclude that Hamlet is the rightful ruler, the one in whom according to custom and reason the authority from God really resides and that Claudius is the arch-criminal whom the true ruler should cut away for the health of the whole body politic. (pp. 122-23)

Since the throne is morally vacant, although this fact is not publicly known, Hamlet is in truth the legal ruler in whom the authority from God resides and through whom as God's *minister* the divine prerogative may be verified: "'Vengeance is mine, I will repay, says the Lord'" (Rom., xii. 19; Deut. xxxii. 35).

Hamlet has a third reason, a special and explicit one, to regard himself as having authority from God to punish the murderer and cleanse Denmark. If the ghost is a good spirit, as Hamlet is satisfied he is after the play-test, the command he brings can come only from God, the sole master of life and death. (p. 123)

Hamlet is a play with a Christian atmosphere and Christian characters who are confronted with moral problems of deep import; recognition of this fact is essential to an understanding of the tragedy.

Almost every character in the play, whether good or evil, has a Christian mentality and uses Christian terms. The accumulation of Christian details is assuredly both deliberate and significant. (p. 125)

It is significant that the word "conscience" is used eight times in *Hamlet,* four times by Hamlet, twice by Claudius, and twice by Laertes, all in the Christian sense of an act whereby the practical reason consciously reflects on and judges a personal particular act as morally good or evil. In addition, the idea of conscience, but not the word, is present in the remark about the sinner's salutary pricks and stings [I. v. 86-8], in the king's prayer [III. iii. 36-69, 97-8], and in the talk between Hamlet and his mother [III. iv.19-20, 35, 89, 113, 156].

Hamlet is a Christian prince whose basic moral sensitivity and rectitude fit him to be the hero in a Christian tragedy. We learn from his first soliloquy that his moral and emotional revulsion against his mother's remarriage to his uncle causes him such anguish of heart that he would seek respite in suicide, if God did not forbid self-slaughter. It is obvious that he dislikes his uncle, but the unseemly haste and the sin of incest (as ecclesiastical law defined it) are the two offenses that revolt his soul. Again tempted to suicide, he asks himself who would bear the sufferings of life

> But that the dread of something after death
> . . . makes us rather bear those ills we have
> Then fly to others that we know not of?
> Thus conscience does make cowards of us all.
>   [III. i. 78, 80-2]

Hamlet notes the conflict between conscience and false codes of honor. By conscience he means that "regard" for the moral consequences of our acts which here prescribes 1) bearing even "the oppressor's wrong" rather than violate conscience by suicide and 2) a turning from "enterprises of great pith and moment," although such conduct be termed cowardly by fiery young men, such as Fortinbras and Laertes, who do not let "the pale cast of thought" affect "the native hue of resolution" [III. i. 83-7] "When honour's at the stake" [IV. iv. 56]. This "honor" is clearly not a moral but a social concept that does not scruple to lead two thousand men to death for a straw [IV. iv. 25; cf. Laertes' words, V. ii. 244-52]. Hamlet could not and should not act upon the dictates of such "honor." (pp. 126-27)

Conscience is, I believe, the primary cause of Hamlet's delay in fulfilling the ghost's command. He had conscientious doubts about the ghost which he found no means to settle until the players came to Elsinore and provided him an opportunity to gain human evidence to test and corroborate the ghost's message. Why then did he blame himself for the delay? In my opinion, not because he was incapable of action . . . but for emotional reasons natural to a normal human being in such circumstances. When a man berates himself, we do not always take him at his own devaluation. Thus, Hamlet replies to Horatio, who has spoken slightingly of himself:

> Nor shall you do my ear that violence
> To make it truster of your own report
> Against yourself.   [I. ii. 171-73]

I think it likely that Shakespeare wishes to alert the audience to keep this point in mind later in judging Hamlet himself. (pp. 127-28)

Hamlet is free in conscience to fulfill the command to punish the regicide and cleanse Denmark, but he must observe the two conditions which the ghost prescribed:

> *howsoever* thou pursuest this act,
> [1] Taint not thy mind, [2] nor let thy soul contrive
> Against thy mother aught; leave her to heaven,
> And to those thorns that in her bosom lodge
> To prick and sting her.   [I. v. 84-8]

At this point Shakespeare illustrates dramatic genius at a peak. In rapid sequence he shows this likable prince, his sensitive conscience concerning the command now settled, act swiftly and energetically; but he violates the first and then the second of the prescribed conditions and thereby brings upon himself an avalanche of sorrow. Thus the play becomes a tense and essentially Christian tragedy.

How might Hamlet taint his mind and thereby vitiate an act in itself justifiable? There is an essential difference between acting as a privately commissioned executioner and seeking private revenge. The ghost commissioned Hamlet to execute justice, for which there is Scriptural warrant . . . , but he expressly forbade him to violate supernatural charity. (pp. 128-29)

The hatred that Hamlet expresses [in the prayer scene] is, I submit, his tragic flaw. By thus yielding to his personal hatred for Claudius 1) he radically disregards the ghost's warning, "Taint not thy mind"; 2) ironically, he misjudges from the outward posture of prayer that Claudius is repentant, forgiven, restored to God's friendship, no longer in a state of sin; 3) this Christian prince who has justly delayed to kill Claudius until his reason and his conscience were satisfied that the king is guilty and the ghost true, now through hatred disqualifies himself morally as the agent of retributive justice which the ghost's command made him. (p. 131)

Hamlet is a Christian tragedy because the hero, who was called upon to exercise heroic Christian charity, not to taint his mind and soul with personal hatred in spite of the strongest impulses of nature to do so, failed signally to practise such virtue, and, on the contrary, indulged in such intense hate as to will explicitly the eternal damnation of the criminal. Furthermore, through this flaw in his character and his double error of judgment in assuming the king to be repentant and in killing Polonius whom he mistook to be Claudius, Hamlet brought upon himself great sufferings: the dispatch to England, the madness and death of Ophelia, the plot of Laertes and Claudius, the death of his mother, and his own death. Dramatically, however, these errors are the very virtues of the play, for they increase the conflict of "mighty opposites," the tempo, the suspense, the tragic quality. For full dramatic effect, the moral aberration and its powerful dramatic function need to be kept simultaneously in mind. Thus the hero's flaw, which makes him a tragic hero, is precisely and concomitantly a failure in his character as a Christian; and the decision which is the crucial instance of his failure to exercise charity, the most necessary and the most Christian of virtues (cf. Jn. xiii. 35), constitutes the interior peripety of his character which leads almost immediately to killing Polonius, the act which constitutes the exterior or structural peripety of the tragedy. (pp. 131-32)

Hamlet violated the ghost's second prohibition by speaking harshly to his mother. Then, significantly in domestic dress, the ghost appeared again to Hamlet and bade him adopt a more kindly attitude toward her: "O step between her and her fighting soul" [III. iv. 113]. Immediately Hamlet changes his attitude, speaks gently to his mother, and thereafter concerns himself not with angry reproof as before, but with sound spiritual advice, urging her to remedy the sinful state of her soul by taking three necessary steps to reconciliation with God—confession, contrition, and a firm purpose of amendment.

> Mother, for love of grace, . . .
> [1] Confess yourself to heaven,
> [2] Repent what's past, [3] avoid what is to come . . .
> . . . go not to my uncle's bed . . . Refrain tonight,
> And that shall lend a kind of easiness
> To the next abstinence, the next more easy;
> For use almost can change the stamp of nature.
> [III. iv. 144-68)

Thus we see that Hamlet, prompted by the ghost, in this crisis in his mother's life, urges her to use Christian means to cleanse her soul. (pp. 134-35)

Laertes admits having wounded Hamlet with an unbated, poisoned foil, but for the poisoned drink which killed the queen, he says, "The King, the King's to blame" [V. ii. 320]. Thereupon Hamlet kills Claudius. The attendants cry, "Treason!" [V. ii. 323], but the testimony of the dying Laertes has its effect. (p. 136)

Thus publicly before the lords and attendants made vividly aware of the king's crimes, Hamlet fulfills the ghost's command to punish this murderer. The brief outcry of the attendants indicates the difficulty Hamlet would have faced had he killed Claudius under circumstances that did not thus publicly expose the royal criminal. Although the ghost's command did not impose this public cleansing of the desecrated throne, it has psychological and dramatic fitness. The audience is now emotionally ready to see Claudius punished with retributive justice, because his multiplied crimes have alienated the sympathy they naturally had for him in the prayer scene. The play gains as tragedy from so many deaths, especially that of Hamlet. The prince's final act of killing the regicide has two new motives added—the king's part in both Hamlet's own mortal wound [V. ii. 333] and in his mother's death—two additional murders, the first intended, the second unintentional, although Claudius is too cowardly to risk exposure by effectually trying to prevent the queen from drinking the poison [V. ii. 290] and he vainly tries to divert attention from her fall by a lie, "She swounds to see them bleed" [V. ii. 308]. (pp. 136-37)

An act of Hamlet particularly difficult for us to judge morally is his changing of the "grand commission" whereby Rosencrantz and Guildenstern suffer the immediate death, "not shriving time allowed" [V. ii. 47], which Claudius had ordered for Hamlet through their agency. These two schoolfellows, we must remember, are the king's spies, one of the reasons why, "at each ear a hearer" [II. ii. 382], Hamlet "can say nothing" [II. ii. 569]. He protests, "You would pluck out the heart of my mystery . . . do you think I am easier to be played on than a pipe? . . . You cannot play upon me" [III. ii. 365-72]. . . . To Prince Hamlet these friends turned spies and willing agents of the malevolent murderer-king may have seemed traitors not only to friendship but to the public weal. Although his schoolfellows did not know the contents of the sealed documents they carried [IV. iii. 56, 63-5], Hamlet apparently believes they did and that they were willing accomplices. It is worth noting that he judges this act just. He explicitly asserts to Horatio:

> Why man, they did make love to this employment.
> They are not near my conscience, their defeat
> Does by their own insinuation grow.   [V. ii. 57-9]

Furthermore, Hamlet cites the incident as clear, instructive evidence that Providence works pervasively in the affairs of men, whether they realize it or not.

> . . . and that should learn us
> There's a divinity that shapes our ends,
> Rough-hew them how we will.   [V. ii. 9-11]

Horatio agrees: "That is most certain" [V. ii. 11]. Asked how he sealed the altered document, Hamlet answers:

> Why even in that was heaven ordinant.
> I had my father's signet in my purse. [V. ii. 48-9]

Hence, it is simply "given" that this act is explicitly justified in the subjective forum of Hamlet's conscience, whether or not it is objectively justified. (pp. 137-38)

We conclude, accordingly, that *Hamlet* is a Christian tragedy in the strict sense. Christian issues impregnate its essential structure: the revelation and command of the Christian ghost initiate the action; Hamlet's decision through hate not to kill Claudius until he is fit for damnation is the turning point; and his final fulfillment of the ghost's command is the denouement. Christian problems, especially that of discerning the character of the ghost, determine the moral situation. In their response to the moral and dramatic situation the characters consciously accept or reject Christian principles. And finally the flaw in the tragic hero is his failure in the moment of crisis to measure up to the requirements of Christian charity which the ghost demanded. (pp. 139-40)

> *Sister Miriam Joseph, C.S.C., "'Hamlet,' a Christian Tragedy," in* Studies in Philology, *Vol. LIX, No. 2, Pt. 1, April, 1962, pp. 119-40.*

PATRICK CRUTTWELL   (essay date 1963)

[*For Cruttwell, the central question of the play is whether Hamlet is a good or bad man. In the following essay, he considers Hamlet's madness and the nature of his revenge, and discusses the various critical responses to Shakespeare's handling of Hamlet's revenge, citing G. Wilson Knight (1930), A.J.A. Waldock (1931), and L. C. Knights (1959), as well as Bertram Joseph (see Additional Bibliography). Cruttwell concludes that the confusion of both Hamlet and the critics who attempt to interpret him arises from the "muddle of two moralities": the Christian ethic and the pagan "ethic of revenge." For additional commentary on religious aspects of* Hamlet, *see Hermann Ulrici (1839), Søren Kierkegaard (1845), H.D.F. Kitto (1956), and Sister Miriam Joseph (1962).*]

Was Hamlet a good man or was he a bad one?

I cannot think it illegitimate to ask that simple question (though, of course, the answer need not be simple); it is, I believe, a question which every reader or playgoer 'uncorrupted by literary prejudices' asks himself, and which the play as a whole insists that we should ask. But the answers it has received range no less widely than those given to the other questions which play and characters provoke. . . . (p. 110)

Hamlet is one of the handful of literary creations which have turned into something more than simply characters in a novel or poem or play. He has become a figure of myth; and just as Odysseus is the myth-character of the Traveller, Faust of the Seeker, Quixote of the Knight, and Juan of the Lover, so Hamlet has been made the myth-character of the doubting, self-contemplating Intellectual. It is only appropriate, then, that his outlines should be so much hazier than those of the other myth-characters. The haziness is inherent in the myth and in the manner by which the myth has been made, for Hamlet, the puzzled self-contemplator, has been created through the self-projections of a long line of puzzled self-contemplators. Everything about him has for long been hazy; and why should we expect an exemption from haziness in the moral judgements which men have passed on him? (p. 111)

The question to be asked, I repeat, is the question: Was Hamlet a good man or was he a bad one? I shall look at this as it appears in most of the play's major episodes; but underlying it throughout, and decisive for our answer, are two other questions. How do we take his madness—feigned or real, or, if mixed, mixed in what proportions? And how do we take the obligation of revenge laid on him by the ghost—as a true moral duty, recognised as such by the prince himself and to be accepted as such by us, or as a temptation to wrongdoing?

The former is clearly paramount in deciding Hamlet's moral responsibility. When, for example, he says to Ophelia: 'I loved you not', but to Laertes, over her dead body: 'I loved Ophelia'—when he behaves to her as we see him doing in the nunnery-scene but also as she reports him to have done before—then surely the natural and immediate response of most of us is that unless we can allow him a degree of genuine mental disturbance, the only possible verdict is Johnson's 'useless and wanton cruelty' [see excerpt above, 1765]. (But the 'natural and immediate response' is not always the right one.) And a survey of *Hamlet* commentators would show, I believe, a certain correlation. Those who like the prince and admire him as a good man will tend to see a part at least of his madness as genuine; those who do not will see it all as feigned. We assume, of course, that in the lost 'Kydian' *Hamlet,* the hero simply put it on as a trick. But Kyd's own example, *The Spanish Tragedy,* is enough to show how easily that can slide into something more than a trick: for the 'mad Hieronymo' of the later additions makes an effect dramatically indistinguishable from the effect of the real thing. . . . Whether an audience thought his madness feigned or real—and remember we are criticising a play, not a treatise of psychiatry—the effect was bound to be: 'This isn't the *real* Hamlet!' And for such a way of playing, for such violent alternations of behaviour, the text gives ample warrant, indeed specific instructions. From Hamlet's own 'put an antick disposition on' through Ophelia's description of neglected clothes, physical collapse ('pale as his shirt, his knees knocking together'), hysterical gestures and deep sighs, and the king's 'transformation, sith nor the exterior nor the inward man Resembles that it was', to the Queen's 'mad as the sea and wind when they contend', and in many other places, the text is insisting on an extravagance of behaviour which could scarcely be overacted. . . . The modern tendency is to present not a Hamlet who is at times perfectly sane and at other times perfectly lunatic, or behaving as if perfectly lunatic, but a Hamlet who is all the time just a trifle and part of the time more than a trifle—neurotic. This, I suppose, in the age of Freud, may be expected. (pp. 113-15)

Right or wrong, it has had a curious effect on the moral issue. If one imagined Hamlet as a real person, outside the theatre and the play, then clearly his moral responsibility would be greatly lessened if he could be thought of as all the time mentally and emotionally disturbed. But the effect of this *in the play* is to keep him all the time before us as a person behaving, if not quite normally, then at least within sight of normality and therefore within reach of moral judgement; whereas if he is allowed now and then to rant and caper, heave profound

sighs and wear his stockings down-gyved to the ankles, we forget, in practice, that this is 'feigning' and simply discount it. If—to take a concrete instance—the scene with Ophelia can be played as Aaron Hill in the early eighteenth century suggested—that is, Hamlet must quite unmistakably 'act mad' when she is watching but look sanely miserable when she doesn't see him—then his behaviour to her becomes perfectly plausible. But no modern actor does play the scene in that way. The reasons are clear. Partly it is that our greater reluctance to accept on the stage a 'make-believe' we would not credit offstage renders an acted madness unacceptable; partly that our greater sensitiveness to mental illness makes the mere idea of pretending to be mad more than a little distasteful. So in the names of realism and sensitiveness, Hamlet is never allowed to behave as practically everyone in the play (including himself) assures us he does frequently behave. And this implies a very different Hamlet. Instead of a man sufficiently in command of himself to sustain for long periods an exceedingly difficult masquerade, and sustain it well enough to deceive everybody, we have someone always on the edge of breakdown and sometimes over it. The former, I believe, is a great deal nearer than the latter to Shakespeare's conception: though I must agree with Waldock that here Shakespeare himself is partly to blame. He has not completely 'assimilated, re-explained' the inherited theme of feigned madness into his own creation. (pp. 115-16)

Shakespeare does show characters who are what we would call neurotic—Don Juan of *Much Ado,* Jaques, Angelo, Leontes, Apemantus—and these are truly unbalanced in ways that Hamlet is not. They show it by an alienation from reality which breeds irremovable delusions, violently anti-social behaviour, and above all a tendency to shun and hate their fellow-creatures. In none of them are the easy sociability, the unforced authority, the capacity to love and be loved, which Hamlet shows. And as for the disgust for life which Hamlet expresses, isn't this very adequately accounted for by what happens to him? Eliot's famous remark, that 'Hamlet . . . is dominated by an emotion which . . . is in *excess* of the facts as they appear' [see excerpt above, 1919], has always, I must confess, filled me with stupefaction; for when I consider the 'facts' as they did 'appear' to Hamlet—the sudden death of a much-loved father, followed immediately by the indecently hasty and incestuous remarriage of his mother to a man whom Hamlet hated and despised and who then proceeded to cheat him out of the throne, this followed in turn by the supernatural reappearance of his late father with the information that Hamlet's stepfather was his father's murderer and the peremptory command that he, Hamlet, should set to work at once on vengeance—when I consider all this, I find it hard to imagine any degree of emotion which ought to be censured as 'excessive' and I am deep in admiration for the high behaviour-standards of those critics who find in Hamlet's occasional outbursts of hysteria evidence that he must be neurotic. (pp. 116-17)

If, then, we conclude that Hamlet is not a neurotic, he is a normal man in a situation of intense strain, what effect will this have on the moral question? It must clearly make Hamlet a good deal more culpable when he misbehaves, at least when we reflect about him afterwards, if not when we are actually seeing him on the stage. We can rescue him only on one assumption—that he has had laid on him a moral duty so stern and undeniable as to excuse any behaviour which is directed to its performance. And this brings us to the question of revenge.

The original Hamlet, there is no doubt, was almost nothing but an embodiment of Revenge. . . . We cannot tell for how long this Ur-Hamlet held the stage instead of—or together with—his more complex descendant; it looks as if for a time there must have been one Hamlet for the groundlings and another for the highbrows. Waldock seems to me in the right when he suggests . . . that in Shakespeare's handling of his inherited story 'the revenge theme has been considerably damaged'; but, damaged or not, it is still very much there. We cannot ignore it, we must not play down its sometimes unpleasing effects—or play them up, given them a quality of moral repulsiveness which may not have been meant—for it is this, more than anything else, which has divided the prince's interpreters. Was he right to take the command 'Revenge!' as a true moral duty? Does the play as a whole insist that we should agree with this—as powerfully as the *Choephori*, for instance, insists that Orestes must take vengeance for his father's murder? There is a whole spectrum of answers to these questions—of which we may take [Bertram] Joseph as representative of the one end, Knights and Wilson Knight of the other. Joseph, accepting the revenge-ethic as the ethic which governs the play, argues that 'in a revenge play a nobleman was bound to kill Claudius, and many of Shakespeare's first audiences would have expected this in real life as well'. . . . Knights replies that a ghost who 'clamours for revenge' must be a ghost concerning whom Shakespeare entertains 'grave doubts' and that Hamlet's acceptance of his command is simply a yielding to temptation. . . . Wilson Knight agrees; the ghost's command was 'devilish', he was 'a portent not kind but sinister'.

Disagreement could hardly be more absolute. It is part, of course, of a wider disagreement. Joseph sees the character relatively, in terms partly historical, Knights and Wilson Knight absolutely, in terms entirely moral. My own verdict inclines to agree with Joseph, mainly, I think, because this reading seems to stay more scrupulously within the play itself and within the framework of time and form in which the play was made. Knights's reply to this is that he *is* seeing the play within a 'framework'—and the framework is that of Shakespeare's other plays written in the same period as *Hamlet*. These, he thinks, enforce a morality which exposes the inadequacy, the wrongness of the revenge-ethic; and would Shakespeare, at about the same time, write a play to the opposite effect? But this, I believe, falls into two errors. It minimises the difference between an imaginative artist and a moralising arguer; and it is based on selective reading. We may be entitled to draw from Isabella's pardoning of Angelo and Cordelia's of Lear the message that forgiveness is better than vengeance; but surely it is equally true that the whole moral weight of *Macbeth* is behind the personal and bloody vengeance which Macduff vows and takes on the man who has killed his wife and children, and the whole moral weight of *Lear* is no less behind Edgar's challenging and killing of Edmund. . . . This reluctance to believe that Shakespeare could possibly have conceived a character who was 'represented as virtuous', in Johnson's words, but who also pursued revenge as a moral duty—and even greater reluctance to believe that Shakespeare could have thought such a character right to do so—springs, to my mind, from the very powerful quasi-pacifist emotions of many twentieth-century liberal intellectuals and especially of those literary critics whose preoccupations are more with morality than with history. They hate the use of physical force; they are enormously suspicious of what were once called the 'military virtues'; they do not like the idea that a poet whom they admire could have admired a fighting-man. . . . [It] is this which I detect in Knights's phrase 'the *murder* of Rosencrantz and Guildenstern'. . . . Murder? Well, yes, in a sense I suppose it was; but I fancy

that most readers, when they come to that word, are brought up with a shock—a shock of spontaneous disagreement—which, if they reflect on it, they will explain in words like these: 'Knights has forgotten something. He has forgotten that *Hamlet is at war*.' Shakespeare did his best to remind him, with pointed use of military imagery—'the enginer / Hoist with his own petar' and 'the pass and fell incensed points / Of mighty opposites', both of which refer directly to Rosencrantz and Guildenstern—but I suspect that these signposts failed to show the right way because, for this critic, 'war' and 'murder' are emotionally synonymous. They were not so for Shakespeare; nor for Hamlet. And revenge, in effect, was a private war. (pp. 117-19)

But could it not still be argued that even if Hamlet, and even if the play of *Hamlet,* accept revenge as a moral duty, nevertheless its execution, and the nasty things that must be done on the way to it, do in fact degrade and contaminate the prince? This is Kitto's argument [see excerpt above, 1956]. Hamlet, he thinks, is paralysed and 'left prostrate' by 'his comprehensive awareness of evil' and 'the destructive power of evil'. Knights finds this inadequate. Part of the corruption is in Hamlet himself, not all in the world around him, and the play 'urges' us to question and criticise 'the attitudes with which Hamlet confronts his world'. . . . Does it? I wish I could see just where the play is 'urging' this. . . . [The] overall tone of the play is urging us very strongly to admire this prince, and to sympathise with him, at least, all through. Denial of this implies, of course, that the ending of the play must be totally ironic: not merely Horatio's elegy—which I suppose may be discounted (though against the emotional grain) as the words of a deeply moved friend—but also the verdict of the uninvolved Fortinbras:

> For he was likely, had he been put on,
> To have proved most royal . . .   [V. ii. 397-98]

He could never have said that of Knights's Hamlet.

Nor can I believe, in any case, that Elizabethan minds would accept the proposition that a man who pursues a cause just in itself can be corrupted by the pursuit of it. Their minds were more theological than ours, more closely keyed to an ultimate destiny of total black or white, damned or saved. . . . If then we accept, as I have argued we must, Shakespeare's acceptance in *Hamlet* of the ethic of revenge, we must accept also that the man who follows this ethic with courage and responsibility cannot be doing wrong, whatever mistakes or inevitable damage to others may befall him on the way. And Hamlet does show responsibility, when he doubts the *bona fides* of the ghost and arranges that its story shall be tested. (If only Othello had tested Iago's story with as much responsibility—!)

Nevertheless, it would be absurd to argue that Shakespeare's Hamlet—prince *and* poem—can yield a moral effect as simple as that of *The Spanish Tragedy* or, we may presume, of the original Kydian *Hamlet*. Waldock and Joseph are right, I believe, when they point out . . . that there are no signs from Hamlet of conscientious scruples about undertaking the task of revenge, and no other expressions of such feelings in the play: but is it not strange that there should be none? For both play and character are notably Christian. The ghost's speech about Purgatory; the wonderful lines of Marcellus describing the miracles at Christmas; the King at prayer; the burial of Ophelia; Hamlet's references to Christian doctrine on suicide: these give the play terms of reference much more specifically Christian than those of the other tragedies. And yet the completely anti-Christian ethic of revenge is never, as it were, tested by, never even brought up against, this Christian world in which it lives. It is this which makes the moral effect so much more ambiguous than that of a play which is revenge-play and nothing else, such as *The Spanish Tragedy;* for in that the moral universe is completely pagan, and the fact that the story is supposed to be set in Christian Spain is simply forgotten. This, too, invalidates Kitto's reading of *Hamlet* as a 'religious drama', one which shows 'the natural working-out of sin' and the 'operation of the divine laws'. . . . Such words would apply only to dramas where the religious basis was clear-cut and single; but what we have in *Hamlet* is an extraordinary muddle of *two* moralities, one avowed, the other not avowed, but both playing heavily and continuously on the central character. This, I believe, is very largely responsible both for Hamlet's own confusions and for the confusions of his critics; it is certainly responsible for one or two crucially ambiguous episodes—and above all for that in which Hamlet spares the King at prayer because he thinks that if he kills him then, his victim will go straight to heaven. . . . [The] irony is that Hamlet is here behaving as he does because he is a Christian, convinced, as most believers were, of the vital importance of 'dying well'. The pagan revenger could have taken his vengeance then and there—the only vengeance available to a pagan, the bringing to an end of bodily life—if he were not also a Christian believer.

How aware was Shakespeare of this moral muddle at the core of his play? And how aware was Hamlet that his behaviour as revenger and his beliefs as Christian were scarcely compatible? We shall never be able to answer these questions; but it is a fact that in the Renaissance the Christian ethic which says: 'Vengeance is mine, saith the Lord; I will repay' and the ethic of personal revenge co-existed side by side not merely as ways in which men actually behaved but as accepted, one might almost say respectable, moralities. (They continued to do so, of course, till much later: revenge became duelling, a narrower code but recognisably the same.) Whether the play intends this or not, the curious spectacle it presents of two rival moralities going their ways apparently without noticing each other is no bad representation of the actual contemporary state of affairs outside the theatre; and Hamlet himself, morally divided so perfectly that he does not seem aware of the division, may have seemed to many young men of the early 1600s a remarkably penetrating analysis of a young man like themselves. (pp. 120-22)

Hamlet, then, was a very 'contemporary' character. But this character Shakespeare put in a setting almost as incongruous as he could have found. Whether he did this knowingly or not, no one can say. I should say not; it was rather the inherent effect of taking over an old story for new times. But I am sure that it is here, in this continuous incongruity between central character and setting, that the clue lies to the moral problems which play and character present. For, first of all, he is made a prince, heir presumptive to the throne; the would-be scholar, the quick-witted affable talker, is put in a position where tradition required of him gravity, haughtiness, aloofness. (Of which expected distance Polonius's warning-off of Ophelia is a symptom: 'Lord Hamlet is a Prince, out of thy star' [II. ii. 141].) And then he is placed, this fastidious hater of debauchery and lover of the theatre, in a court peculiarly sombre, sordid and tasteless; and there, against his expressed desire, he is forced to remain. There comes to him next a direct supernatural intervention—one which he must and does believe in (for under his flippant wit he is a believing Christian) but which shocks him with doubts and questions as it would not have shocked

the credulity of earlier ages or simpler types. And finally, there is imposed on him the demand of Revenge. This he accepts as a moral duty, for he has enough in him of the inherited concept of a prince's and a gentleman's honour; but though his reason and his conscience tell him Yes, his nerves tell him No. It is not that he cannot do it; he can, and knows he can. Nor is it that he does not want to through some delicate reluctance to kill in general or some Freudian reluctance to kill his 'father-uncle' in particular. It is the whole life of action, violence, intrigue and public duty that he is reluctant to enter; he would rather be in Wittenberg, with his books. What he really is, is a conscript in a war. He has done things, as we all do in wars, he would rather not have done; but he believes it to be a just war, and all in all, he has borne himself well. That this was how Shakespeare saw it, the ending of the play convinces me; for why else should

> The soldier's music and the rite of war
> Speak loudly for him?   [V. ii. 399-400]
>   (pp. 127-28)

Patrick Cruttwell, "The Morality of Hamlet—'Sweet Prince' or 'Arrant Knave'?" in Hamlet, *John Russell Brown and Bernard Harris, Stratford-Upon-Avon Studies, No. 5, General Editors, Edward Arnold (Publishers) Ltd., 1963, pp. 110-28.*

LIONEL ABEL   (essay date 1963)

[*Abel defines* Hamlet *as the first in a new form of drama which he terms "metatheatre." Characters in such plays "are aware of their own theatricality," and the dramatist presents a vision which stresses the inherent artificiality of life. In* Hamlet, *Abel notes, "almost every important character acts at some moment like a playwright, employing a playwright's consciousness of drama to impose a certain posture or attitude on another."*]

[Eliot's view] marks a turning point in the history of *Hamlet* criticism [see excerpt above, 1919]. If Eliot was right, then a purely literary or dramatic analysis of *Hamlet* would have to be barren; the real explanation of the play's difficulties must be left to psychologists.

Since Eliot's essay, of course, other critics have defended the form of the play; they defended the play as tragedy. In so doing, I think, they have ignored or glossed over *Hamlet*'s very real difficulties. So that of the two views, (1) that *Hamlet* is defective as tragedy and (2) that *Hamlet* is a tragedy and great, the first must be preferred.

But a third view is possible. What if our own misunderstanding of the form of *Hamlet* has made its content seem so complicated? What if *Hamlet* is not essentially a tragedy? Then the play might be explained without our having to psychoanalyze either Shakespeare or Hamlet—as if this were even possible, when we have no biography of Shakespeare to guide us! (pp. 40-1)

Would *Hamlet* have been a tragedy if the Ghost had told Hamlet to kill his mother, along with Claudius? Instead of this, as we know, the Ghost expressly forbids Hamlet to harm his mother in any way, urging him to "leave her to heaven," and devote his energies to killing his uncle. But it is not tragic to kill one's uncle nor to have been told to do so, even by one's father's ghost. Hamlet, so ready for tragedy in his attitude and character, with such a perfect disposition for the part, is asked by his father's ghost to do something of little tragic consequence. . . . What if Gertrude had committed suicide? Then

Hamlet would have killed his mother, though indirectly, and would have had to sustain the inevitable remorse. Still, even if done in that way, the story of Hamlet would have been a weak one, far weaker than that of Orestes in the *Oresteia* of Aeschylus or of Orestes and Electra in the *Electra* of Sophocles. (p. 41)

Why did the Ghost not tell Hamlet to kill his mother, as Apollo in the *Oresteia* told Orestes to kill Clytemnestra? It will be said that in *Hamlet* the role of Gertrude in the murder of Hamlet's father was left ambiguous. But Shakespeare could have made Gertrude a participant in the murder, had he wanted to. (p. 42)

Let us assume that Shakespeare has resolved to write his *Hamlet* and does not know how to make the story tragic. If the Prince obeys the injunction of the Ghost and kills his uncle, there is no tragedy; if the Prince kills his mother without a divine order, there is no tragedy either; then how could the play be a tragedy at all? With these questions, which Shakespeare may never have put, we come closer to his intention and to his peculiar resolution of the drama he set himself to write. Since there could be no tragedy in prompt action on Hamlet's part, Shakespeare dignifies Hamlet's inactivity, making it philosophic.

So we have the wonderful soliloquy on being and non-being, which quickly becomes a question put by Hamlet as to whether or not he should take his own life. But if it is better to be dead than to live, then how could killing Claudius avenge the murder of Hamlet's father? If there is a question as to whether one should be or not be, then there is surely no answer as to why Hamlet should kill Claudius. The great soliloquy is a complete contradiction of the assignment given Hamlet; it is much more than that; it is a contradiction of any assignment, of any action. But since we are speaking of a character in a play we are also speaking of that character's author. Shakespeare, too, had no reason to make Hamlet act, and a very strong reason for making him philosophize at the moment of the famous soliloquy.

Thus it is that Shakespeare, with his unfailing feeling for the common, appealed to a very gross opinion, that thought and action contradict each other. This opinion has helped make Hamlet loved by audiences, who feel him to be a victim, not of his situation, but of his thought. (p. 44)

Shakespeare, to dignify Hamlet's inactivity, gave it, as I have said, a philosophic quality. Those critics who have considered Hamlet the victim of his own irresolution, beguiled by this notion, have lost sight of the dramatic movement of the play as a whole. What is that movement? When this movement is grasped, the new form Shakespeare would turn to, later in his career, may be glimpsed.

Everyone has noticed that there is a play within a play, for Hamlet puts on a· show in order to catch, as he says, the "conscience of the King." What has not been noticed, though, but becomes evident once one abandons the notion that the play is a tragedy, or that Shakespeare could make it one, is that there is hardly a scene in the whole work in which some character is not trying to dramatize another. Almost every important character acts at some moment like a playwright, employing a playwright's consciousness of drama to impose a certain posture or attitude on another. Here is Gertrude urging Hamlet to look less melancholy:

> Good Hamlet, cast thy nighted color off,
> And let thine eye look like a friend on Denmark.
> [I. ii. 68-9]

The sense of Hamlet's reply is that there is that within him which cannot be dramatized:

> 'Tis not alone my inky cloak, good mother,
> Nor customary suits of solemn black,
> Nor windy suspiration of forc'd breath,
> No, nor the fruitful river in the eye,
> Nor the dejected havior of the visage,
> Together with all forms, moods, shows of grief,
> That can denote me truly. These indeed seem,
> For they are actions that a man might play;
> But I have that within which passeth show,
> These but the trappings and the suits of woe.
> [I. ii. 77-86]

The next attempt to dramatize Hamlet and impose on him a particular posture comes from the Ghost, whose revelation is couched in the most theatrical and stagey terms. In fact the Ghost tells Hamlet that he could easily, by revealing the secrets of his prison house, produce an immediate effect upon the Prince:

> I could a tale unfold whose lightest word
> Would harrow up thy soul, freeze thy young blood,
> Make thy two eyes, like stars, start from their spheres,
> Thy knotty and combined locks to part
> And each particular hair to stand on end,
> Like quills upon the fretful porpentine.
> [I. v. 15-20]

This is what the Ghost could do to Hamlet. However, he will not, having been forbidden to tell of his supernatural sufferings. All the same, the Ghost is determined to impose on Hamlet a definite posture. . . . But immediately afterward Hamlet retaliates against the Ghost by trying to dramatize him in turn, in the wonderful and otherwise inexplicable scene when the Ghost has disappeared under the boards and Hamlet asks the guards and Horatio to swear that they have seen nothing. The remarkable thing about this scene is the fond contempt with which Hamlet addresses the Ghost, who has just sworn him to devote his whole life to revenge. Hamlet calls the Ghost "boy," "truepenny," "old mole," and "worthy pioneer." How are we to understand these contemptuous epithets addressed by Hamlet to the Ghost of his father? . . . [I suggest] that the reaction of Hamlet is that of a man with a playwright's consciousness who has just been told to be an actor, and is now determined to make an actor of the very playwright who had cast him for an undesired role. What makes the Ghost a serious playwright is what has happened to him. He has the force of death and hell behind his stage instructions. Hamlet, however, has the force of his—that is, Shakespeare's—dramatic imagination. The scene is one of the most wonderful in all drama. This is not a struggle between two characters, but between two playwrights. And the better playwright, Hamlet—in terms of consciousness—happens to be the lesser playwright in terms of zeal. Hence his dramatic retaliation has to be humorous.

Is not any son forced to be an actor in his parents' script? They chide him, spank him, dress him, coddle him, order him around: to be a child means to take direction. (Actors in general are childish.) Certainly Hamlet, as a child, must have been through all that. But having been in the play of his parents, almost any individual will want to be in another play, when grown up. Besides, it was not Hamlet's father who authored the situation he asks Hamlet to play a part in. The author of this situation was Hamlet's uncle. Who could want to become an actor in a bloody show put on by a villainous uncle? Certainly not Hamlet.

Polonius, who dramatizes himself as wise, treats his son Laertes and his daughter Ophelia as if they were actors in a play whose meaning he, Polonius, alone understands. In the famous speech Polonius makes to Laertes, he even tells the young man the kind of clothes he should wear, the kind of figure he should cut. With more at stake, Polonius instructs Ophelia on how to test Hamlet's real intentions toward herself and toward the King. Ophelia obeys her father's directions, but Hamlet, with his sensitivity to stage technique, sees through her guise of innocence at once. Polonius, who is able to dramatize both his son and his daughter, does not try to dramatize Hamlet; this is because Polonius, amateur playwright that he is, thinks Hamlet is already dramatized, and that he, Polonius, knows exactly the plot of the drama Hamlet is in. . . . Finally Polonius goes too far, spies on Hamlet's violent scene with his mother, and is killed by Hamlet, who mistakes him for the King. (pp. 45-8)

What is most interesting in the scene . . . is that two playwrights are present in it, Polonius behind the arras, and Hamlet, who gives his mother a playwright's instructions about her future behavior: she is to avoid her husband's bed, and, as Hamlet indicates, by making such avoidance habitual, she may be able to arrive at a truer consciousness of her responsibilities. In this scene Hamlet urges his mother to act without sincerity until that moment when her motives, by force of repeated acting, become sincere. At this point it is necessary for a third playwright to put in an appearance. The Ghost does just that, appearing to Hamlet and reminding him that he, so eloquent in instructing his mother how to act, has forgotten his own role, which is to kill Claudius.

Two vain and very minor playwrights are quickly called upon by Claudius. These are Rosencrantz and Guildenstern, who first try to find out what is in Hamlet's mind and are told by him that they cannot play on him. Nor can they. Their final instructions are to dramatize Hamlet as a corpse when he sails with them for England. They have sealed orders requesting his execution on arrival. Hamlet, of course, rewrites the orders, and when the three arrive in England, Rosencrantz and Guildenstern are executed instead of him.

All of the characters in the play can be distinguished as follows: some are fundamentally dramatists or would-be dramatists, the others are fundamentally actors.

> [Abel adds in a footnote: In calling the important characters of *Hamlet* "playwrights," am I relying on a metaphor? To an extent, yes. On the other hand, I claim that no other metaphor could throw an equal light on the play's movement. Suppose that we called Hamlet, the Ghost, Claudius, and Polonius "poets" and compared their rhetoric. This could be done, and might lead to some discovery. But not, I think, to any important discovery about the play as a whole. When I say that the important characters are "playwrights" what I want to underscore is that each of them has the consciousness of a dramatist as well as that of a character.]

Thus Gertrude and Ophelia are actors; so is Laertes; but Hamlet, Claudius, Polonius, and the Ghost are dramatists. There is still another dramatist, whose dramaturgy in the end Hamlet will consent to.

This dramatist is death. When Hamlet has returned from England, after having defeated the crude intrigue of Claudius,

Rosencrantz, and Guildenstern, he is ready for death. As he says, "the readiness is all." He passes with Horatio by the cemetery, sees the gravedigger at work, and finds the skull of Yorick, the court clown he had loved. At this moment Hamlet recognizes the truth of that dramatic script in which no one can refuse to act: death will make us all theatrical, no matter what we have done in life. The skull is pure theatre. It is a perfect mask. I think it is at this moment that Hamlet accepts death's dramaturgy, not his father's, not his own. He is ready to die now, no matter what the occasion. (pp. 48-9)

Hamlet had found the terrible dramatist who could dramatize even him. And this is why he falls in with the crude, melodramatic scheming of Claudius; the latter promotes a duel between Hamlet and Laertes. There could be no cruder plotting. The foil of Laertes is poisoned, and there is a poisoned wine for Hamlet to drink if, after exertion, he needs refreshment. Hamlet gives not the slightest thought to the details of the duel, and acts as if he suspects nothing. He is ready now to be in the worst play possible, to act in it, play his part, pretend to believe in it; he has not accepted the role the Ghost has tried to force on him, but the role from which he cannot escape anyway, the role death will inevitably make him play. (pp. 49-50)

I have said that there are four playwrights among the characters of *Hamlet:* Claudius, the Ghost, Polonius, and Hamlet. What kinds of playwrights are they; in other words, what kinds of plays are they capable of?

Claudius is a writer of melodrama from start to finish. He kills his brother horribly, pouring into "the porches of his ear a leprous distillment"; the peculiar detail that the poison was poured into the victim's ear and not given him to drink, as would be more natural, suggests the creator of a sensational story, as well as an assassin.

The Ghost is a typically Elizabethan writer of melodrama; though himself tragically victimized, killed by his brother, and subject to eternal punishment in hell, all he requires of Hamlet is the murder of Claudius. He expressly forbids Hamlet to harm Gertrude in any way. His conception of life, even after death, is extremely gross: he wants what began as tragedy to end as melodrama.

Polonius is the amateur playwright par excellence. Though caught in the bloody intrigue of Denmark's royal family, he looks forward to a happy and practical consummation of events fraught with terror. He thinks that his plotting will resolve the problems of Denmark and of his daughter's relationship with Hamlet. . . . No playwright could have been more mistaken in his understanding of events than Polonius, striving to control all the other characters by intrigue.

What kind of playwright is Hamlet? This question is more difficult to answer. Like his creator, he has the most excellent sense of theatre, as is shown in his advice to the actors. Certainly Hamlet's melancholy has endowed him greatly for tragic poetry; but he is in a situation which the Ghost of his own father has forbidden him to define tragically. Now we can assume Hamlet's taste to be quite different from the Ghost's, Hamlet, then, with his gifted playwright's consciousness has the problem of rewriting the melodrama he has been placed in, but with no alternative form in view. For he has been expressly forbidden to convert this melodrama into tragedy. Finally, he yields to the appeal of the one dramatist whose script, like tragedy, involves necessity and places one beyond chance. This dramatist is death. . . . Death, which I have called somewhat metaphorically the dramatist in whose script all must act, Hamlet appeals to as an ultimate form. To a modern consciousness is not death equal to the immortal gods?

Let us now see if the questions to which the play has given rise cannot be settled once and for all. If it is borne in mind that Hamlet does not know the form of the play he is in, in other words, that Shakespeare was unable to make a tragedy of *Hamlet,* the major questions about the play can be answered definitively.

(1) Is Hamlet irresolute? Coleridge and Goethe [see excerpts above, 1811 and 1795] held this view, though they nuanced their judgments differently. Is Hamlet, on the contrary, resolute? That was A. C. Bradley's contention [see excerpt above, 1904]. These questions become nonsensical when we keep clearly in mind that for a character in a play to be judged either resolute or irresolute, the type or form of play he is in has to be clearly defined. But there is no clear definition for the kind of play Hamlet was placed in by Shakespeare.

(2) Is Hamlet mad? He warns his friends that he may put on an "antic disposition," but we may well wonder whether he does so with any other purpose than to avoid the purposelessness of the plot. No doubt Hamlet enjoys acting as if he were mad. He likes the role no one gave him. In pretended madness there is, of course, a refuge from the seriousness of his task. . . . Since the structure of the play he is in is so indefinite, and not to his taste, he can only get outside of it by acting as if he were mad.

(3) Is Hamlet in love with Ophelia? He is not. Replying to Laertes' expression of love for Ophelia by her grave, Hamlet does declare:

> . . . Forty thousand brothers
> Could not, with all their quantity of love,
> Make up my sum. . . .   [V. i. 269-71]

but adds immediately afterward:

> Nay, an thou'lt mouth. I'll rant as well as thou
>   [V. i. 283-84]

thus negating his declaration. (pp. 50-2)

Hamlet, in the play he is in, cannot love Ophelia. He would, of course, have preferred to be in another play.

(4) Is Hamlet in love with his mother? There is no evidence for any such assumption, except Hamlet's greater interest in his mother's guilt than in his uncle's, which seems to me perfectly normal.

(5) Does Hamlet believe or not believe in the Ghost? Certainly he believes in the Ghost. The entire action of the play comes from the Ghost's appearing to Hamlet and setting him the most unambiguous of tasks; Hamlet shirks the task, finding excuses for inaction. But the concern and guilt for nondoing which Hamlet expresses throughout imply that he believes in the Ghost's honesty, and ought to obey his command. But what the Ghost has commanded him to do holds no interest for Hamlet.

(6) How is it that the sentinels of Elsinore, as well as Marcellus and Horatio, all see the Ghost, while Gertrude, during the scene in which the Ghost appears to Hamlet in her presence, does not see him? Why should not Gertrude have seen the Ghost too? . . . [This] question, raised so many times, suggests a much more interesting one: why did not the Ghost deliberately reveal himself to Gertrude? Why was he not interested in touching *her* conscience? Why was he so exclusively interested in

getting Hamlet to kill his murderer? This is in Hamlet's own phrase "a poor ghost." That is to say, one uninterested in tragedy.

(7) When Hamlet in the third act sees Claudius kneeling in prayer and has a chance to kill him, why doesn't he kill him? (p. 53)

[Is his] explanation a rationalization by Hamlet of his inability to act? After all, what likelihood is there that Hamlet will have the opportunity to find Claudius physically defenseless at some moment when he is also morally and metaphysically helpless? Certainly Hamlet is expecting too much of chance for us to consider his explanation reasonable. The explanation is illogical in another sense, too. The Ghost has demanded of Hamlet only that he kill Claudius, not that he decide on the supernatural destiny of Claudius' soul. And if Hamlet believed in the reality of a final destiny for the soul, would he not also have had the piety—unless he were willing to incur damnation—to leave that supernatural destiny to the judgment of God? Certainly he was rationalizing his inaction. But I think there is sincerity in what he says. He can find no satisfaction in a mere physical dispatch of his villainous uncle; Hamlet, once again, has little taste for melodrama. What he wants is something more—a deeper, a more ultimate meaning for his act. The only moral significance killing Claudius could have had for Hamlet would have been to kill him in front of Gertrude and thus quicken her conscience.

(8) When Hamlet killed Polonius, did he know Claudius was not behind the arras? The psychoanalytic critics who maintain that Hamlet must have known since he had just left the King praying, have to assume two things:

(a) Hamlet went straight from seeing the King to his mother and did not delay, which he might have done, for all we know. If he did delay, then the King would have had time to get to Gertrude's chamber before Hamlet.

(b) Shakespeare did not know what he was doing in writing the two successive scenes, any more than Hamlet knew what he was doing in either of them. For if Shakespeare had wanted us to think that Hamlet was only pretending to kill the King, knowing all the time the King could not be behind the arras, would Shakespeare have made Hamlet say, looking at Polonius' corpse. "I took you for your better"? (pp. 54-5)

It seems far more plausible to me that what Shakespeare intended in the two successive scenes was to contrast Hamlet's lack of interest in killing Claudius and his very great interest in touching his mother's conscience. Hamlet leaves the King whom he has been sworn to kill and goes to his mother to tell her what she must do. In the first scene, the scene with the King praying, Hamlet is supposed to act and does not. In the second scene, with the queen, he does what we know he likes to do—he directs.

(9) What is the dramatic function of the "To be or not to be" soliloquy? I have remarked already that the soliloquy denies the value of action as such; in speaking as he does, Hamlet takes refuge in philosophy, just as he has already taken refuge in pretended madness. So understood, the soliloquy has only psychological meaning. But I think it also has a function in the play's progress. Hamlet's resort to pretended madness takes him out of the plot; so does philosophizing; but, on the other hand, it is through philosophizing that he finally submits willingly to the crudest plotting of all: Claudius' plot with Laertes to kill him. Hamlet's philosophizing is a meditation on death. . . .

Hamlet's meditation takes him from the plot into metaphysics, and then, turning him toward death, enables him to feel something metaphysical in the plot. (pp. 55-6)

T. S. Eliot judged *Hamlet* a defective tragedy [see excerpt above, 1919]. He was right; as tragedy it is defective. He was wrong, though, in judging the play as tragedy. . . . According to Eliot, Hamlet's feelings are excessive with respect to his situation: he lacks an objective reason for feeling such melancholy and cuts the figure of an adolescent, exaggerating his own anguish and trying to impose on others the norms of an idealism doomed to remain vague.

To be sure, Hamlet is an objective expression of Shakespeare's inability to make of his play a tragedy. But Shakespeare made something else of his play, something quite as extraordinary as tragedy. It is to be noted that Eliot ignores the originality of the character and of the play, too, in which, for the first time in the history of drama, the problem of the protagonist is that he has a playwright's consciousness. Hamlet is not an adolescent; he is the first stage figure with an acute awareness of what it means to be staged. How be dramatized when one has the imagination to be a dramatist? After *Hamlet* it would be difficult for any playwright to make us respect any character lacking dramatic consciousness. . . . The problem of author versus character was I think first envisaged in *Hamlet*. From now on—unless there is to be a new culture whose values we can scarcely foresee—no dramatist has the right to set any supposedly self-conscious character on the stage who does not collaborate in his dramatization. In this sense Jean-Paul Sartre was profoundly correct. No one with self-consciousness can ever do anything drastic in life or on the stage, with our respect, that is, unless he has agreed to his commitment.

What Eliot did not take into account is that none of us, no matter what our situation, really knows the form of the plot he is in, and Hamlet was the first theatrical figure who expressed this fact fully. (pp. 57-8)

Only certain plays tell us at once that the happenings and characters in them are of the playwright's invention, and that insofar as they were discovered—where there is invention there also has to be discovery—they were found by the playwright's imagining rather than by his observing the world. Such plays have truth in them, not because they convince us of real occurrences or existing persons, but because they show the reality of the dramatic imagination, instanced by the playwright's and also by that of his characters. Of such plays, it may indeed be said: "The play's the thing." Plays of this type, it seems to me, belong to a special genre and deserve a distinctive name.

But is there not already an adequate name for such plays, one which has the advantage of being well known? Are not plays of the kind I mean essentially comedies? We do not believe that what takes place in comedy has really occurred: events in comedy are reduced by humor to examples for reflection and are not irrevocable, as in tragedy. Nor do characters in comedy have to convince us they exist; all they have to do is to make us laugh. Humor, I suppose, consecrates nonexistence. But that which does not exist can scarcely make us sad. So comedies have to end happily.

It is true that the plays I have in mind end happily in the main, but many of them are able to do what comedy never can do, that is, to instill a grave silence—a speculative sadness—at their close. They can do this without being tragedies, which means, without making us believe that the events presented, responsible for our sadness, happened once and for all. More-

over, such plays make us feel concerned for characters who tell us frankly they were invented to make us feel concerned for them.

Should the plays I am speaking of—if there is any humor in them—be called tragi-comedies? I object to this self-contradictory term, which tells us only that humor and pathos may alternate in a play, but does not define that kind of play in which humor and pathos may alternate. Besides, if the events on the stage are not irrevocable, then wherein lies their tragic content? If the events are irrevocable, wherein lies their comedy? The term tragicomedy implies, it seems to me, two different kinds of plays, amalgamated no one knows just how. If it is said: by the "genius" of the playwright—is that not asking the playwright's genius to do the critic's task? (pp. 59-60)

[Some of the plays I am referring to] can, of course, be classified as instances of the play-within-a-play, but this term, also well known, suggests only a device, and not a definite form. Moreover, I wish to designate a whole range of plays, some of which do not employ the play-within-a-play, even as a device. Yet the plays I am pointing at do have a common character: all of them are theatre pieces about life seen as already theatricalized. By this I mean that the persons appearing on the stage in these plays are there not simply because they were caught by the playwright in dramatic postures as a camera might catch them, but because they themselves knew they were dramatic before the playwright took note of them. What dramatized them originally? Myth, legend, past literature, themselves. They represent to the playwright the effect of dramatic imagination before he has begun to exercise his own; on the other hand, unlike figures in tragedy, they are aware of their own theatricality. Now, from a certain modern point of view, only that life which has acknowledged its inherent theatricality can be made interesting on the stage. From the same modern view, events, when interesting, will have the quality of having been thought, rather than of having simply occurred. But then the playwright has the obligation to acknowledge in the very structure of his play that it was his imagination which controlled the event from beginning to end.

Plays of the kind I have in mind exist. I did not invent them. However, I shall presume to designate them. I call them metaplays, works of metatheatre.

Consider a great seventeenth-century play, Molière's *Tartuffe*. Molière called it a comedy, and it is generally played as such. Stendhal, however, noticed that he laughed only twice during a performance of *Tartuffe*, and that the audience around him laughed hardly more. The difficulty in laughing when *Tartuffe* is performed is not because the characterization or the plot lacks humor, but because Tartuffe, the villain, bulks so much larger than his victims, and is so much more interesting. (pp. 60-1)

Tartuffe happens to be much bigger than the conventional comedy in which Molière put him. So, if Molière wrote *Tartuffe* in order to criticize religious bigotry and moral hypocrisy, his play is self-defeating: Molière's hypocrite and bigot is not odious, but interesting to us. No doubt Molière intended a much different effect. We know from his other plays how he valued sincerity. Should we think of *Tartuffe*, then, as designed to attack something going on in society, outside the action it presents? But the villain of that action is not a statement about the world, but a statement about himself. If we refer Tartuffe to the world, he will give it more meaning, I think, than it could have without him. I think, too, he was addressed to the imagination of Molière's audience, while the play he is in was addressed to their social reason. In any case, Tartuffe looms up out of Molière's comedy, greater than it, and destroys it.

But in what kind of play should a character of this imaginative size have been placed? In what kind of play should Hamlet have been put? In *Six Characters in Search of an Author*, perhaps the most original play-within-a-play written in this century, the remark is made that certain dramatic characters— Hamlet is one mentioned—cannot be contained in the works they first appeared in and have had to venture far from their creators into other works by other authors. Now I would say that if Tartuffe and Hamlet seem to break out of the plays and situations they were first placed in, this is not merely because the right dramatic form had not been found for them, but perhaps more importantly, because these characters are themselves dramatists, capable of making other situations dramatic besides the ones they originally appeared in.

Any play written at a certain depth should have some other aim than to suggest social change or moral reform. The contemplative imagination can and does delight in what moral and practical wisdom urges us to reject. We are all more profound than our purposes seem to indicate. And the playwright who ventures to touch us very deeply ought to know that he is touching a part of us which is irrelevant to the achievement of our most rational goals. Molière was, I think, too profound for the form he relied on in *Tartuffe*.

Take another play, an Elizabethan play—a great play, too, but one in which the events are made unreal by the playwright's inability to decide whether they actually happened or not. When he wrote *Doctor Faustus,* Marlowe lacked, I think, a definite dramatic horizon. What kind of play is *Doctor Faustus*? Marlowe thought he had written a tragedy, as Molière thought he had written a comedy in *Tartuffe*. But is Marlowe's Doctor Faustus truly tragic? Do we feel that Faustus actually sold his soul to the Devil, signed his transaction with Hell in his own blood, and thus was enabled to regain youthfulness, pride, power, and lust at the price of eternal damnation? Do we believe when we watch *Doctor Faustus* that anything of this sort ever happened in the same way we believe when we watch *Macbeth* that Macbeth really talked to the witches, murdered Duncan and Banquo, conversed with Banquo's ghost, massacred Macduff's family, and was finally killed by Macduff?

I am convinced that no one genuinely believes the events in *Doctor Faustus* in any such way. Nor are the events adequately understood by Marlowe. For instance, Marlowe should have made it clear that the transaction between Faustus and the Devil was essentially a theatrical one. Faustus, an old man, is asking the Devil to dramatize him as a youth; here we are on the verge of a new theatrical form. But Marlowe thought of the transaction as one in which Faustus became the tragic protagonist in a play written by the Devil. Therefore Faustus had to be damned. But when we think about the story with a little more sophistication, does it not appear that the Devil was the actor and Faust the dramatist, since it was he, Faust, who called upon the Devil to dramatize him? Such was the interpretation Goethe made when he took up the story, and he was able to give it such clarity and lightness—not simply because he was more philosophical than Marlowe, but because the form for a play like his *Faust* had already been invented. Goethe found that form in Shakespeare and in Calderón.

Why is it that neither Marlowe nor Molière was able to invent the dramatic form both needed, Molière for a proper presen-

tation of his character Tartuffe, Marlowe for phantasizing adequately the dealings of Doctor Faustus with the Devil? But then how is it that neither Lope de Vega, Calderón's predecessor, nor Corneille, with whom the great period of French theatre began, nor any of the English dramatists before Shakespeare had been able to lift the play-within-a-play—which many of them used as a device—to a truly philosophic height?

Of all the European dramatists, Shakespeare was the only one possessed by a complete confidence in the power of imagination, not simply in its power to make speech splendid— Marlowe had that, too—but in its power to arrange, order, and judge all manners of persons and every single type of action; in other words, to put the whole world on stage. Generalizing that power of imagination which guided his best inventions, Shakespeare could make his philosopher, Jaques, say, "the world's a stage." (pp. 61-4)

Lionel Abel, "'Hamlet' 'Q.E.D.' and Metatheatre: Shakespeare and Calderón," in his Metatheatre: A New View of Dramatic Form, *Hill and Wang, 1963, pp. 41-58, 59-72.*

B. L. REID (essay date 1964)

[*Reid examines Act V scene 1 of the play, which he terms "the Passion of Hamlet." In this scene, death becomes generalized; it is shown as the "universal human essence," and Hamlet accepts his own death as the "grandest, the ultimate, human limitation."*]

The opening of Act V of *Hamlet* brings a shock, even to students of the plays who have grown to admire the liberties the master takes with dramatic structures, the ordinary logic of sequence. The shock is the greater for being received from the common modern forms of the play, printed or staged, which stiffen the sequence, as it were, canonize the new act *as* new, insist on both its reality and its artifice. (p. 59)

The shock really is two shocks, one being the terrible, doubly "untimely" comedy of the graveyard, the other the astonishing change in the mood, almost in the nature, of Hamlet himself since last we saw him. His new presence, quiet, ruminative, fatalistic, strongly but easily reined in, is unexplained, unmotivated by anything we know. And these two strange sensations are offered us as matter transitional between two dramatic units which do stand in clear relationship: the close of Act IV on the plot of Claudius and Laertes to kill Hamlet in the rigged fencing match and the bare lyric notice of the death of Ophelia; and the fencing scene itself with its general carnage, "so many princes at a shot." How is the matter of Act V, scene i related to these matters, and to the matter of the play as a whole? (pp. 59-60)

[The] problem is not only one of the scene's "local" relevance, its work in the immediate context; the question it raises cannot be understood except in the light of the whole play, "the action" of Aristotle—that which being "imitated" forms the work of art. (p. 60)

Our psychological difficulty arises from Aristotle's insistence on the primacy of action, the subordination of character. When he says, "They do not act in order to portray the characters; they include the characters for the sake of the action"; or, "We maintain that tragedy is primarily an imitation of action, and that it is mainly for the sake of the action that it imitates the personal agents," we feel rudely and intimately attacked. Our modern cult of personality, our faith in the importance of self-expression, finds the whole idea insulting—but peculiarly so

Act I. Scene iv. The ghost, Hamlet, Horatio, Marcellus (1887). From the Art Collection of the Folger Shakespeare Library.

as applied to Hamlet. For Hamlet is at once the culture-hero and the dramatic personality with whom everyone identifies with haunting intimacy—as lover, son, or second self—such is the closeness and the variety of his humanity. (pp. 60-1)

Of course the play is "about" Hamlet, there would be no play without him. But Aristotle would insist that the play is primarily an action of which Hamlet is the chief agent; what is "imitated," the objective thing that is offered us to see, is events in a significant sequence. The center of our experience is not the personality of Hamlet, Coleridgean or otherwise, but the tragic order of things that happen to him and through him. Hamlet does not summon the tragic action, Shakespeare summons him to serve it. But this is not to say that any hero would work equally well; the particular action summons the particular hero. . . . In understanding the ado about Hamlet, in "The Tragedy of Hamlet, Prince of Denmarke" or "The Revenge of Hamlett Prince Denmarke," there is good advice in the full title. It suggests that the action of which Hamlet is agent is an affair of public moment; it is stately, courtly, civic. The full title imposes the same sort of qualification as that of *Oedipus Rex*—there the agent is "the King," "Tyrannos." The ado in *Hamlet* is about a prince on princely errands; the play is not a character sketch of a brilliant but unsatisfactory young man.

If we try to borrow from *Hamlet* a Stanislavskian text or motto, an infinitive or imperative phrase to stand for the whole, as

Francis Fergusson has done in defining the action of *Macbeth* ("'To outrun the pauser, Reason'"), the case proves difficult or impossible. This play's fusion of positives, negatives, and ambiguities is too complex to accommodate in a single formula—though there are phrases, "By indirections find directions out," for example, or "I must be their scourge and minister," which carry one far. And the chronicle of sheer disaster which Horatio draws up at the end is in one sense the play:

> So shall you hear
> Of carnal, bloody, and unnatural acts,
> Of accidental judgements, casual slaughters,
> Of deaths put on by cunning and forc'd cause,
> And, in this upshot, purposes mistook
> Fall'n on the inventors' heads. . . .
>
> [V. ii. 380-85]

Mr. Fergusson's formula for the action of *Hamlet* goes as follows: "to identify and destroy the hidden imposthume which is endangering the life of Denmark" [see excerpt above, 1949]. It is fairly satisfactory, but it does not convey much of the flavor of the play, and I must say, at some risk of paradox, that I wish to hear something of the hero: a particular action summons a particular hero. My suggestion would run as follows: "A brilliant and idealistic young prince cleanses his country and avenges his father's murder at the expense of many lives, among them his own." Let us try to trace the design of the action pointing to and beyond the problematical scene, the opening scene of the final act.

If the action is stately, having to do with the "state" of Denmark, then clearly the first scene is not a prologue but an organic member of the action, in fact a singularly forceful Aristotelian "beginning." The guards on the parapet, soon joined by Horatio, peering into the murk, putting edgy questions, speaking nervously of wars and mysteries and spirits, are types of the citizenry of the state, enacting the common condition. The melodrama of the ghost's silent first appearance dominates the movement of the scene. But that too is symptomatic, and a type of the general dis-ease and upending of things—"post-haste and romage in the land," "the night joint-labourer with the day," stars that are "sick"—such forms the climate enclosing the whole action. . . . The watch breaks up on the resolution to tell Hamlet of the ghost. Thus the first mention of the hero comes on the energetic rising tone of the Savior, the wholesome time, the morn, the dew on high eastern hills. The language, the words of the action, has told us what Hamlet's function is to be: he must restore the land's lost order, must "redeem the time."

Yet it is significant that we hear next not from Hamlet but from Claudius, in the first of the play's three grand court scenes. As the usurper speaks we feel at once the size of Hamlet's adversary and of his problem. The speech is a brilliant piece of public rhetoric, full of jaunty-stately turns and glides. What is most interesting in all Claudius's first speeches is the thickness of equivocation in them, the texture of paradox, ambiguity, multiplication of terms. . . . [Hamlet's] first speech of any length, in response to his mother's unfeeling question as to why his father's death "seems . . . so particular," is a bitter insistence on candor and right feeling, on open truth: "Seems, madam! Nay, it is; I know not seems," the speech begins. And that too is one of the things the play is about, a part of its "significant design"; Hamlet must restore the world's honesty of face, make it again a place where things seem what they are. If the play itself refuses us a handy motto, perhaps we may find one in a line from Wallace Stevens, "Let be be finale of seem."

The promising morn at the end of the soldiers' scene, as inductive of Hamlet, has proved a false dawn. His "nighted colour" of costume and of mind is crow-black against the peacock glitter of the court. Claudius, having royally identified himself with the state, as "the Dane" and "Denmark," leads the court off to drink "jocund health"; and the first soliloquy shows Hamlet in a mood perfectly reverse, in a condition of confused and suicidal moral nausea. The image of the sick and ambiguous world is now carried by the great trope of the "unweeded garden." The real world is not merely worse than he had grown up believing, it is foully inhuman. . . . We see a high-minded young man suffering the shock of a corrected vision of the real world. Among other things, *Hamlet* is one of the greatest of all stories on the theme of initiation, a moral and intellectual ceremony in which the idealizing veil of youth is drawn aside. The shock of this corrected vision accounts in part for the savagery of the wit, a kind of murderousness, that marks Hamlet's speech at crucial points of the play, as now in the quickly ensuing passage with his friends, "Thrift, thrift, Horatio! The funeral bak'd-meats / Did coldly furnish forth the marriage tables." (pp. 61-5)

The marvelous business of the players' arrival is turned into the most complex and brilliant assay of all, the mousetrap, "to catch the conscience of the king," observed by Horatio "Even

with the very comment of [his] soul." This second of the three great court scenes is a triumph of Shakespeare's dramatic intelligence, a set piece made of planes or stages of fabrication ranging away from the viewer's eye, in complex grades of stylization and verisimilitude. We as spectators spy upon actors playing Hamlet and the court, observing actors playing actors playing a play, which includes both a false play and a pantomime. The dumb-show is at once the most stylized and the most primitively real, brutally "true," element of the scene; it mimes an elementary horror beyond language, which the outer frame-play, our play, is in the midst of proving possible for art after all. We can call it either the farthest or the nearest stage of reality. We are farthest from the whole, of course, just beyond Horatio who overlooks the action with a special eye to Claudius. Hamlet himself at this point is playing a nonce-part of great intricacy, stage-managing both the outer play and the inner play, and punishing Ophelia with savage lewdness even while spying upon Claudius.

The scene is a hall of mirrors, and that in a double sense. For in fact this whole long portion of the play is marked by imagery of imagery, so to speak—mirrors, pictures, true and false faces. When Hamlet says to the player in the mousetrap, "Begin, murderer; pox, leave thy damnable faces and begin," he fairly spits his impatience for the thing to come to the point. "Let be be finale of seem." Hamlet's obsessive need to distinguish, and to publish, the difference between appearance and reality, the drive to come at the truth, is working everywhere now. (pp. 68-9)

The "purpose of playing" is the revelation of truth, and Hamlet, who is "playing" throughout these three acts, has that moral end in view. His policy is necessary, wise, and in part pleasant to him. One side of his nature takes both physical and intellectual pleasure in the dangerous ingenuity of his strategy. As he says at the end of Act III, "O, 'tis most sweet, / When in one line two crafts directly meet." Hamlet knows that craft is necessary, as is occasional cruelty: "I must be cruel, only to be kind." His cruelty, to Ophelia, to Gertrude, later to Rosencrantz and Guildenstern, is zestful and brilliant, like everything he does. But accompanying the zest is a profound disgust; he knows he is being forced to proceed through, and thus to share in, corrupt practices which are his object of attack. His general revulsion against his destroyed image of an ideal humanity—"And yet, to me, what is this quintessence of dust?"—is given in his early speech to Rosencrantz and Guildenstern. "Use every man after his desert, and who should scape whipping?" he says to Polonius before that scene is over, not excepting himself. (pp. 69-70)

The meeting of two crafts in one line is sweet to one kind of psychology; it is dangerous to all hands, and the fatal consequences of all the spying and dissembling begin to arrive. Polonius hides behind one arras too many, and finds "to be too busy is some danger." Ophelia, broken by brutal and tricky usage, dies a suicide. Brutality as well as deviousness grows toward murder in these three acts. They are very wrong who read the action of this play as fretfully passive waiting upon events which have the quality of hysteria when they finally arrive. Deviousness, "practice," reaches a kind of crude perfection at the end of Act IV, in the scheme of Claudius and Laertes to put an end to Hamlet: they prepare not one but three potentially fatal devices, the "sword unbated," the poisoned tip, and the poisoned chalice. The preoccupation with death and the corruption of the body, so central in the last act, is prefigured in Act IV by Hamlet's gross treatment, in word and deed, of the body of Polonius. By the "end of the middle," we feel that the rottenness of the body politic is swollen to bursting. We may leave it in that state for a moment in order to think about the function of a healthy member, Horatio, in the general design of the action.

Until Hamlet's death, Horatio inhabits the play with a grave and laconic placidness that one calls stoicism after deciding it is not stupidity. He seems to be a man of perfect emotional balance, his "blood and judgement / . . . so well commingled" that he is "not passion's slave." He is a complete integrity, absolutely sane and true. That his nature is extraordinary is the point of his function; his abnormal soundness defines the unsound norm of this world, as he stands firm amid its melodrama and moral inversion. If the play is in part a drama of initiation, it is so not only for Hamlet but for his whole visible generation—for Horatio, Ophelia, Laertes, Fortinbras, even Rosencrantz and Guildenstern. . . . The conflict of generations within the play is one of the ways in which it expresses the theme of initiation. The conflict is a norm of human experience, a thing that happens to everybody; but Shakespeare here makes it into a structural member, and thereby incorporates it into the vision of life he is imitating. Hamlet and Claudius captain the opposed generations and the moral destiny of the young seems to be determined by the direction of their allegiance. Thus Horatio is important (as is Fortinbras fleetingly at the end) in forming with Hamlet a moral unit, an oasis of probity in the moral desert of Claudius's Denmark. One feels that they carry about with them a little country inside Claudius's country; they move in the loneliness of honor. By refusing to offer a single uncorrupted person of the older generation, the play makes the dreadful suggestion that moral decay is an automatic concomitant of growing older. And watching him grow wise and weary in his terrible sudden aging, we know that Hamlet himself is not wholly innocent. (pp. 70-2)

It may matter in the Christian way, among others, that the last act opens in a Place of Skulls. One way to see the last unit in the action is to see it as the Passion of Hamlet. Yet the act opens as if the play had all the time in the world, and its long first movement especially is slow and ruminative. We are returned to our original problem of the seeming disjunction and that mysterious calm that dominates the opening and indeed all but two passages in the act. If Act V does present the Passion of Hamlet, as I think it does, it does so in complex (not paradoxical) forms. But before entering the calm of this act, we need to notice that Shakespeare has already given it a subtle preparation in his treatment of the death of Ophelia. For we enter the fifth act with the excitement of the melodrama of the fourth—Hamlet's defiant response to Claudius over the death of Polonius, Ophelia's mad scenes, the enraged return of Laertes, the news of Hamlet's offstage sea fight, the new scheme for his murder—slowed and softened by Gertrude's elegiac description of Ophelia's dying and Laertes's reticent manner of accepting that news. From this point of view the approach to Ophelia's grave and the "maimed rites" of her burial in Act V form a natural and logical elision in the action.

But Shakespeare complicates that elision, and makes at once so much and so little of the grave and the burial, and this creates the problem in the unity. The body of the sweet girl is treated to more than three hundred lines—in prose—of coarse jest, travesty, forgetfulness, and ugly quarreling. The effect is both to lower and to generalize, though never to vulgarize, the total action of which this is a part. The process begins at once with the anonymity and ignorance of the gravediggers, who

are nobodies from nowhere, mere men, of no provenance—the people; they give us, more loosely and less intensively than the soldiers at the beginning, the state, the mass of the body politic, the now ironic extension of the microcosm, in which for four acts we have been held tense and airless, out into the flaccid and insensitive macrocosm. In this scene we have for the first time the sense of a really "public" action, where there is space and time and people talk prose. In the second scene the play reverts to its normal constriction, its dreadful "stately" atmosphere, and the heroic and tragic quality of the action is not relieved but intensified by the interval which has come between. But the central action is going forward, in its beautifully complex way, from the first word of the act. (pp. 72-3)

The gravediggers help to create a theatre for the special shapes the "passion" of Hamlet is about to take. They "hold up Adam's profession"; they are mere men, men of clay, and they pull the scene to the literal earth on which Hamlet walks for this time. The movement of the whole first scene, until it explodes in the quarrel at the grave, is ambulatory, processional. . . . The scene is a sort of triptych, three interlinked panels. The gravediggers talk alone in the landscape, one leaves, and Hamlet and Horatio enter through the landscape to join the one who remains; the three talk, and the funeral procession enters through the landscape; Hamlet and Horatio retire to observe the ceremony, the identity of the corpse is revealed, and the quarrel ensues. We have moved from the general to the special, the imminent, tragic atmosphere.

The "subject" of all this is of course death. But death is not merely the current form of the action. It is also the philosophical object of the talk, and the gravediggers, who act and speak as members of the action, help Hamlet to speak in a new philosophical way. Hamlet's mission has been to redeem the time, to "set it right," to be "scourge and minister" of the whole state. What has happened to him since we saw him off for England, I think, is that he has come to see his reading of his mission as grandiose and unreal. He sees that he himself, by reasonable standards, has been "out of joint." He is still a good man in a bad world, and he will act as heroically as a man can, but he claims no more than that. Earlier in the action Hamlet has asked, in effect, "This cup pass from me"; now he rests a mere man in the hands of God: "Not my will but thine be done."

Thus death in Act V is not primarily important in itself, or as the subject of the action, or as the object of talk; it is more important as the universal human essence, the generic shape that destiny takes, the omnipresent real. "Ay, madam, it is common," Hamlet had said to his mother long ago. In Act V, with no essential retreat from its courtliness and high heroism, the play turns into the tragedy of common life; that is, it enacts the tragic drama of human limits. . . . The scene shows the pitiful inadequacy of the old notion of "comic relief"; the scene is not relief, not an eddy, not extraneous or superimposed in any way. It is an intensified expression of the unbroken action, an imitation in a mode almost unbearably poignant. "Death is the mother of beauty"—to borrow another motto from Wallace Stevens. The play has been throughout a gorgeous exercise of intellect and emotion, the mind and the heart; now the action, moving to complete itself, insists on its tie to the earth, and takes up the subject of the elemental body and its end, man as corpus, corpse. The ineluctable modality of the fatal, we might call it in Joycean terms. (pp. 73-5)

I have spoken of the scene as a generalizing one because of its extensiveness in space and time, its crosscutting of social strata, its ambulatory, horizontal movement; for the same reasons, and for its closeness to the plane of the earth, we might equally well speak of it as leveling. The earth is both fact and trope in the action now, and Hamlet and the clowns inhabit it equally. The typicality of the modes of death is traced out in Hamlet's ruminative reflection on the skull, finally revealed as Yorick's, which the sexton tosses up like any other troublesome stone. The grave the sexton digs is every man's and no man's; it was Yorick's and is now Ophelia's—"One that was a woman, sir; but, rest her soul, she's dead"; it could as well be Alexander's. It is in fact the destination of human vanity: "To what base uses we may return, Horatio! Why may not imagination trace the noble dust of Alexander, till he find it stopping a bung-hole?" Shakespeare's point now is not merely that all men die, but that no man is great in the eye of time.

What Maynard Mack says about the "new" Hamlet of Act V seems to me just right: "It is a matter of Hamlet's whole deportment, . . . the deportment of a man who has been 'illuminated' in the tragic sense" [see excerpt above, 1952]. Mr. Mack seems to me right again in his account of the psychology of Hamlet's change: "The point is not that Hamlet has suddenly become religious; he has been religious all through the play. The point is that he has now learned, and accepted, the boundaries in which human action, human judgment, are enclosed." Hamlet has rediscovered his humanity, all of it, and that is to confess the limits of the creature. Act V insists upon death because that is the grandest, the ultimate, human limitation. But the change in the hero and the insistence upon death occur because the tragic action calls for them. Tragedy is an imitation, and what it imitates is action and life, as Aristotle says. Critics have said that in the final act Hamlet lashes out, "the serpent unwinds," at last. Certainly it is true that he performs with great efficiency, a careless, almost insolent, ease, the tasks required of him in "The Revenge of Hamlett Prince Denmarke." But this is the less significant change in the hero. The greater change is in fact an intensification of the intellectualizing Hamlet we have known all along. For Hamlet's mood throughout Act V is marked by a strange and beautiful detachment from the very acts he performs and witnesses, a sort of spectatorship or connoisseurship of life as panorama. It is essentially in that spirit that he and the play look at death in the long first scene. In this tragic vision, tragedy and comedy fuse into irony—but that is still tragedy. (pp. 75-6)

[It] is wonderful to see how the encompassing design of the action accommodates these extremes of modulation. We should not miss, for example, how the prince's "This is I, / Hamlet the Dane" echoes and displaces Claudius's similar nomination of himself in the first act. The revenge and the cleansing are going forward. But the new calmer Hamlet returns to himself in his following speech:

> Hear you, sir,
> What is the reason that you use me thus?
> I lov'd you ever. But it is no matter.
> Let Hercules himself do what he may,
> The cat will mew, and dog will have his day.
> [V. i. 288-92]

That dignity, softened by knowledge, acidified by irony, saddened by despair, lasts out the play.

That dignity, and what I have called Hamlet's connoisseurship of the spectacle of life, the irony deepening in seriousness as the action moves toward fatality, commands the tone and the tempo now to the end. The sorting of the language to the action

and its meaning, its expression of those essences, is almost incredibly fine. In a few lines of compact plain narrative, Hamlet tells Horatio of discovering Claudius's commission to England for his death, his substitution of his own counterfeit message and of Rosencrantz and Guildenstern as victims, and the sea-fight that freed him to return to Denmark. Hamlet's keen intellectual pleasure in precise and vivid speech, in words as instruments to true or false ends, shows again here in his mocking description of Claudius's "state" message and his own. The confident heart-wholeness of the new Hamlet shows in the brusque terms with which he dismisses Rosencrantz and Guildenstern to death:

> Why, man, they did make love to this employment;
> They are not near my conscience. Their defeat
> Doth by their own insinuation grow.
> 'Tis dangerous when the baser nature comes
> Between the pass and fell incensed points
> Of mighty opposites.   [V. ii. 57-62]

It is instructive to compare the end of this speech with the language of a related statement at the end of Act III: "O, 'tis most sweet, / When in one line two crafts directly meet." The juvenility, the petulance, the cant are all gone, and what remains is the blunt pragmatic confrontation. (pp. 77-8)

Everyone has remarked Hamlet's "fatalism" . . . in the late action, and the text is rich in support of such a reading: heaven is "ordinant"; "There's a divinity that shapes our ends"; "a man's life's no more than to say 'One'"; "the readiness is all." These are great, moving, and appropriate statements; but I agree with Mr. Mack that it is Hamlet's acceptance they are appropriate to, not his fatalism. Hamlet has been demanding all through the play, "Let be be finale of seem," demanding the identification, the making-one, of appearance and reality, the bringing of things into moral focus or register. But the terms of the proposition have changed, shrunk and cooled to the scale of the real world of men. Hamlet acts out now nothing so grandiloquent as destiny, only the limits of his powers. They are heroic powers, but human ones, and they perform in the eye of God. Hamlet himself has fallen into register with the human condition.

The violent and beautiful melodrama of the sword fight, the deadly "brother's wager," the triumphant saturnalia of the occulted evil of the play's action—an event which Aristotle might have called a "probable impossibility"—precedes the elegiac close, the epiphany or showing forth of the bodies and their meaning. The "fell sergeant, Death" arrests Hamlet, Claudius, Gertrude, Laertes. Horatio is left to draw his breath in pain. We breathe with him. The best and the worst in the state have died, and the state has nearly died with them. Hamlet has brought the state out of terrible sickness at the cost of his own life. Now it is weakly convalescent. But that is not how the spectators, "You that look pale and tremble at this chance, / That are but mutes or audience to this act," feel. Our response is better rendered by the paired terms, "woe" and "wonder," of Horatio's heartbroken address to Fortinbras: "What is it ye would see? / If aught of woe or wonder, cease your search." The action has been an inextricable union of woe and wonder from the first lines: the events of the action make the woe; the tone and spirit of the action, shaping events into meaning to compose the significant design of the action, provide the beauty and truth to create the wonder that lets us bear the woe. The play "ends in speculation," as Keats says deep enterprises always end, the long wide look into the woe and wonder of the human condition in its grand generic forms.

We have seen the best of our time. Hamlet is not other than fatally dead. Horatio's farewell, ''Good-night, sweet prince, / And flights of angels sing thee to thy rest!'' points to a cloudy region outside the competence of the dramatic action, and comforts us only with the beauty of its language. But the air is clear, and we can breathe it with pride and some confidence as well as with Horatio's pain. The action has cleared its own corrupted air through the agency of Hamlet's sacrifice, his lustration. The bad old ones at least are gone, and the visible state is left in the hands of the instructed young. We are free at last to recollect the soldier's words from the play's first scene:

> Some say that ever 'gainst that season comes
> Wherein our Saviour's birth is celebrated
> The bird of dawning singeth all night long;
> And then, they say, no spirit can walk abroad;
> The nights are wholesome; then no planets strike,
> No fairy takes, nor witch hath power to charm,
> So hallow'd and so gracious is the time.
>
> 　　　　　　　　　　　　　　　　[I. i. 158-64]

But of course the only miracle that has been passed is the miracle of art. The action leaves us in the real, fallen, endlessly corruptible world, the current embodiment of the great enemy vanquished for the time by heroic courage and sacrifice. Tragedy cannot put an end to pity and fear, it can only make the terrible beautiful. (pp. 78-80)

> *B. L. Reid, ''The Last Act and the Action of 'Hamlet','' in* The Yale Review, *Vol. LIV, No. 1, Autumn, 1964, pp. 59-80.*

JAN KOTT (essay date 1964)

[*Kott is a Polish-born critic now residing in the United States. Here he focuses on the innumerable possibilities, all valid, for interpreting the play and its characters, particularly in the modern theater. According to Kott, the genius of* Hamlet *lies in that versatility, for ''like a sponge,'' the play ''absorbs all the problems of our time.'' In his conception of* Hamlet *as a modern character, Kott expands upon an observation made by George Brandes (1895-96). Kott's essay was originally published in his* Skice o Szekspirze, 1964.]

Innumerable glossaries and commentaries have grown round Hamlet, and he is one of the few literary heroes who live apart from the text, apart from the theatre. His name means something even to those who have never seen or read Shakespeare's play. In this respect he is rather like Leonardo's Mona Lisa. We know she is smiling even before we have seen the picture. Mona Lisa's smile has been separated from the picture, as it were. . . . It is not just Mona Lisa that is smiling at us now, but all those who have tried to analyze, or imitate, that smile.

This is also the case with *Hamlet*, or rather—with *Hamlet* in the theatre. For we have been separated from the text not only by Hamlet's ''independent life'' in our culture, but simply by the size of the play. *Hamlet* cannot be performed in its entirety, because the performance would last nearly six hours. One has to select, curtail and cut. One can perform only one of several *Hamlets* potentially existing in this arch-play. It will always be a poorer *Hamlet* than Shakespeare's *Hamlet* is; but it may also be a *Hamlet* enriched by being of our time. (p. 52)

The genius of *Hamlet* consists, perhaps, in the fact that the play can serve as a mirror. An ideal *Hamlet* would be one most true to Shakespeare and most modern at the same time. Is this

possible? I do not know. But we can only appraise any Shakespearean production by asking how much there is of Shakespeare in it, and how much of us.

Costumes do not matter. What matters is that through Shakespeare's text we ought to get at our modern experience, anxiety and sensibility.

There are many subjects in *Hamlet*. There is politics, force opposed to morality; there is discussion of the divergence between theory and practice, of the ultimate purpose of life; there is tragedy of love, as well as family drama; political, eschatological and metaphysical problems are considered. There is everything you want, including deep psychological analysis, a bloody story, a duel, and general slaughter. One can select at will. But one must know what one selects, and why.

The *Hamlet* produced in Cracow a few weeks after the XXth Congress of the Soviet Communist Party lasted exactly three hours. It was light and clear, tense and sharp, modern and consistent, limited to one issue only. It was a political drama par excellence. ''Something is rotten in the state of Denmark'' was the first chord of *Hamlet*'s new meaning. And then the dead sound of the words ''Denmark's a prison'', three times repeated. Finally the magnificent churchyard scene, with the gravediggers' dialogue rid of metaphysics, brutal and unequivocal. Gravediggers know for whom they dig graves. ''The gallows is built stronger than the church,'' they say.

''Watch'' and ''enquire'' were the words most commonly heard from the stage. In this performance everybody, without exception, was being constantly watched. (pp. 52-3)

Everything at Elsinore has been corroded by fear: marriage, love and friendship. Shakespeare, indeed, must have experienced terrible things at the time of Essex's plot and execution, since he came to learn so well the working of the Grand Mechanism. (p. 54)

The murderous uncle keeps a constant watchful eye on Hamlet. Why does he not want him to leave Denmark? His presence at court is inconvenient, reminding everybody of what they would like to forget. Perhaps he suspects something? Would it not be better not to issue him a passport and keep him at hand? Or does the King wish to get rid of Hamlet as soon as possible, but give way to the Queen, who wants to have her son near her? And the Queen? What does she think about it all? Does she feel guilty? What does the Queen know? She has been through passion, murder and silence. She had to suppress everything inside her. One can sense a volcano under her superficial poise.

Ophelia, too, has been drawn into the big game. They listen in to her conversations, ask questions, read her letters. It is true that she gives them up herself. She is at the same time part of the Mechanism, and its victim. Politics hangs here over every feeling, and there is no getting away from it. All the characters are poisoned by it. The only subject of their conversations is politics. It is a kind of madness.

Hamlet loves Ophelia. But he knows he is being watched; moreover—he has more important matters to attend to. Love is gradually fading away. There is no room for it in this world. Hamlet's dramatic cry: ''Get thee to a nunnery!'' is addressed not to Ophelia alone, but also to those who are overhearing the two lovers. It is to confirm their impression of his alleged madness. But for Hamlet and Ophelia it means that in the world where murder holds sway, there is no room for love. (pp. 54-5)

I have nothing against such an interpretation. And I do not regret all the other Hamlets: the moralist, unable to draw a clear-cut line between good and evil; the intellectual, unable to find a sufficient reason for action; the philosopher, to whom the world's existence is a matter of doubt.

I prefer the youth, deeply involved in politics, rid of illusions, sarcastic, passionate and brutal. A young rebel who has about him something of the charm of James Dean. His passion sometimes seems childish. No doubt he is more primitive than all previous Hamlets. Action, not reflection, is his forte. He is wild and drunk with indignation. The Polish Hamlet after the XXth Party Congress. One of many. He does not yet experience deep moral doubts, but he is not a simpleton. He wants to know if his father has really been murdered. He cannot fully trust the Ghost, or any ghosts for that matter. He looks for more convincing evidence, and that is why he arranges a psychological test by staging the crime that has been committed. He loathes the world, and that is why he sacrifices Ophelia. But he does not flinch from a coup d'état. He knows, however, that a coup is a difficult affair. He considers all pros and cons. He is a born conspirator. "To be" means for him to revenge his father and to assassinate the King; while "not to be" means— to give up the fight. (pp. 55-6)

Hamlet is like a sponge. Unless it is produced in a stylized or antiquarian fashion, it immediately absorbs all the problems of our time. It is the strangest play ever written, by its very imperfections. *Hamlet* is a great scenario, in which every character has a more or less tragic and cruel part to play, and has magnificent things to say. Every character has an irrevocable task to fulfil, a task imposed by the author. This scenario is independent of the characters; it has been devised earlier. It defines the situations, as well as the mutual relations of the characters; it dictates their words and gestures. But it does not say who the characters are. It is something external in relation to them. And that is why the scenario of *Hamlet* can be played by different sorts of characters. (pp. 57-8)

Hamlet can be summarised in a number of ways: as an historical chronicle, as a thriller, or as a philosophical drama. They will probably be three different plays, though all three have been written by Shakespeare. But if the summary is fair, scenarios of the three plays will be the same. Except that every time there will be a different Ophelia, or Hamlet, or Laertes. The parts are the same, but performed by different actors.

Let us have a look at the scenario. For, after all, Shakespeare had written, or rather re-written, an old scenario, and the parts in it. But he did not distribute the parts. This has been done anew in every age. Every age has its own Poloniuses, Fortinbrases, Hamlets and Ophelias. (pp. 58-9)

Let us have a look at the scenario in order to find out what parts it contains, knowing that they will be played by modern characters. *Hamlet,* envisaged as a scenario, is the story of three young boys and one girl. The boys are of the same age. They are called Hamlet, Laertes, Fortinbras. The girl is younger, and her name is Ophelia. They are all involved in a bloody political and family drama. As a result, three of them will die; the fourth will, more or less by chance, become the King of Denmark.

I have deliberately written that they are involved in a drama. For none of them has chosen his part; it is imposed on them from outside, having been conceived in the scenario. The scenario has to be played to the end, no matter who Hamlet, Ophelia, and other characters are. I am not concerned at the moment with the question of what the scenario itself is supposed to be. It may be the mechanism of history, fate, human condition, depending on how we want to envisage *Hamlet. Hamlet* is a drama of imposed situations, and here lies the key to modern interpretations of the play.

The King, the Queen, Polonius, Rosenkrantz and Guildenstern have been clearly defined by their situations. It may be a tragic situation, as in the case of the Queen; or grotesque, as in the case of Polonius. But character and situation are closely connected. Claudius does not play the part of a murderer and a king. He *is* the murderer and the King. Polonius does not play the part of a despotic father and a king's councillor. He *is* the despotic father and the King's councillor.

It is different with Hamlet. He is more than the heir to the throne who tries to revenge himself for the murder of his father. The situation does not define Hamlet, or at any rate does not define him beyond doubt. The situation has been imposed on him. Hamlet accepts it, but at the same time revolts against it. He accepts the part, but is beyond and above it. (pp. 60-1)

Every Hamlet has a book in his hand. What book does the modern Hamlet read? Hamlet in the Cracow production of late autumn, 1956, read only newspapers. He shouted that "Denmark's a prison", and wanted to improve the world. He was a rebellious ideologist, and lived only for action. Hamlet in the Warsaw production of 1959 was full of doubts again; and again was the "sad boy with a book in his hand . . ." We can easily visualize him in black sweater and blue jeans. The book he is holding is not by Montaigne, but by Sartre, Camus or Kafka. He studied in Paris, or Brussels, or even—like the real Hamlet—in Wittenberg. He returned to Poland three or four years ago. He very much doubts that the world can be reduced to a few simple statements. Occasionally he is tormented by thoughts of the fundamental absurdity of existence.

This latest, the most modern of Hamlets, returned to the country at a moment of tension. Father's ghost demands revenge. Friends expect him to fight for succession to the throne. He wants to go away again. He cannot. Everybody involves him in politics. He has been trapped into finding himself in a compulsory situation, a situation he does not want but which has been thrust upon him. He is looking for inner freedom, and does not want to commit himself. At last he accepts the choice imposed on him; but only in the sphere of action. He is committed but only in what he does, not in what he thinks. He knows that all action is clear-cut, but he refuses to let his thought be thus limited. He does not want practice to be equated with theory.

He is inwardly starved. He considers life to be a lost cause from the outset. He would rather be excused from this big game, but remains loyal to its rules. He knows that "though man does not do what he wants, he is responsible for his life". And that "it does not matter what has been made of us; what matters is what we ourselves make of what has been made of us". Sometimes he thinks himself an existentialist; at other times—just a Marxist who has revolted. But he knows that "death transforms life into destiny". He has read Malraux's *Condition humaine.*

This attitude of the modern Hamlet is a defence of his inner freedom. This Hamlet fears, most of all, a clear-cut definition. But act he must. Ophelia may have a hair-do like Leonardo's *Lady with a weasel,* or her hair may be let down loose; she may wear a pigtail, or a pony-tail. But she, too, knows that life is a hopeless business from the start. So she does not want to play her game with life at too high a stake. It is the events that compel her to over-play. Her boy friend has been involved in high politics. She has slept with him. But she is a daughter of a minister of the crown; an obedient daughter. She agrees to her conversation with Hamlet being overheard by her father. Maybe she wants to save Hamlet. But she falls into the trap herself. The events have driven her into a blind alley from which there is no way out. An ordinary girl, who loved her boy, has been given by the scenario of history a tragic part.

Traditional nineteenth-century Hamletology devoted itself almost exclusively to the study of the problem who Hamlet really was. Those traditional scholars charged Shakespeare with having written an untidy, inconsistent and badly constructed masterpiece. Whereas modern essays consider *Hamlet* from a theatrical standpoint. *Hamlet* is not a philosophical, moral or psychological treatise; it is a piece for the theatre, that is to say, a scenario with parts. If this is so, then one must begin with Fortinbras, who plays a decisive role, as far as the scenario of *Hamlet* is concerned. (pp. 61-3)

In all modern analyses of *Hamlet* (H. Granville-Barker, F. Fergusson, J. Paris) the character of Fortinbras has been brought to the foreground. In structural interpretations *Hamlet* is a drama of analogical situations, a system of mirrors, in which the same problem is in turn reflected tragically, pathetically, ironically and grotesquely: three sons who have lost their fathers, one after the other, or Hamlet's and Ophelia's madness. In predominantly historical interpretations *Hamlet* is a drama of power and heredity. In the first instance, Fortinbras is one of Hamlet's "doubles", "alter egos", "mediums". In the other he is the heir to the throne of Denmark; the man who has broken the chain of crime and revenge, who has restored order to the Danish kingdom. This order may be understood as restoration of moral law, or as *neue Ordnung in Europa*. The ending of the tragedy has been interpreted in both ways. For if one wishes to place *Hamlet*'s moral conflicts in an historical context, no matter whether Renaissance or modern, one cannot ignore the part played by Fortinbras.

The difficulty is that in the text of the play Fortinbras is only broadly sketched. On the stage he appears only twice: for the first time in Act IV, when he and his troops are on the way to Poland; for the second time when he comes to claim the throne after the general slaughter. But young Fortinbras is mentioned many times. His father has been killed in a duel by Hamlet's father. Fathers of all the young people in this play—Hamlet, Laertes and Ophelia—have been murdered. Spectators get confused when tracing the history of young Fortinbras. From the prologue we learn that he wants to wage war against Denmark; then he fights with the Poles for a piece of sand hardly worth having; at the end he appears in Elsinore. It is he who speaks the final words of this cruel drama.

Who is this young Norwegian prince? We do not know. Shakespeare does not tell us. What does he represent? Blind fate, absurdity of the world, or victory of justice? Shakespearean scholars have made a case for all these interpretations in turn. The producer has to decide. Fortinbras is a young, strong and cheerful fellow. On his arrival he delivers a speech to this effect: "Take away these corpses. Hamlet was a good boy, but he is dead. Now I shall be your king. I have just remembered that I happen to have certain rights to this crown." Then he smiles and is very pleased with himself.

A great drama has been concluded. People fought, plotted, killed one another, committed crimes for love, and went mad

for love. They told amazing things about life, death and human fate. They set traps for each other, and fell into them. They defended their power, or revolted against power. They wanted to build a better world, or just save themselves. They all stood for something. Even their crimes had a certain greatness. And then a vigorous young lad comes, and says with a charming smile: "Take away these corpses. Now I shall be your king." (pp. 64-5)

Jan Kott, "Hamlet of the Mid-Century," in his Shakespeare, Our Contemporary, *translated by Boleslaw Taborski, Doubleday & Company, Inc., 1964, pp. 51-65.*

T. McALINDON (essay date 1970)

[*McAlindon discusses aspects of form and duty, or "the proper and fitting," and their relationship in* Hamlet, *discerning a pattern which illustrates "Shakespeare's magnificent conception of his art as one which mirrors disorder in the drama of life and so achieves decorous indecorum". The critic also focuses on the language of the play, noting recurrent imagery which connotes abuse of speech. For additional discussions of Shakespeare's use of imagery in the play, see the excerpts by G. Wilson Knight (1930), Caroline F. E. Spurgeon (1935), Wolfgang H. Clemen (1951), Maynard Mack (1952), and Inga-Stina Ewbank (1977). McAlindon's essay was originally published in* Shakespeare Studies *in 1970.*]

In Shakespeare's great tragedies, as in his histories, the individual's loss of identity (or assumption of a false role) is the most emphatic sign of disorder and indecorum. But this phenomenon is much more intensively explored in the tragedies than in the histories since, in them, the fate of the individual rather than that of society or the nation is the chief source of interest. In *Hamlet*, the problem of lost and false identity is virtually identified with the loss or abuse of 'form'. Thus, in her moving but noticeably formalized lament for the man who was once his country's 'chiefest courtier' [I. ii. 117], Ophelia equates the true Hamlet with form itself: he was 'the glass of fashion and the mould of form', the 'unmatch'd form and feature of blown youth' [III. i. 153, 159]. Hamlet's grievous 'transformation' [II. ii. 5], too, has been caused to a great extent by his horror at what can be called the violation of form around him: within two months of his father's death, his mother has married his uncle, and so a bed and a throne once occupied by a king of consummate grace and dignity—'A combination and a form . . . Where every god did seem to set his seal / To give the world assurance of a man' [III. iv. 60-2]—have been usurped by a satyr, a Vice, a king of shreds and patches.

Hamlet, moreover, is called upon to correct the disorders which disgust him; and for the most part he is eager to do so—just as he is eager to reform the disorders in that art which he sees as the mirror of nature: 'O, reform it altogether' [III. ii. 37]. But he is haunted by a spirit which assumes his father's 'fair and warlike form' [I. i. 47], has to contend with an opponent endowed with devilish skill 'in forgery of shapes and tricks' [IV. vii. 89], moves in a world where 'forms, moods, shapes' no longer 'denote' [I. ii. 82] what they should, and is unhealthily attracted by Death itself and its strange transformations. So the task proves too much for him. Not the first who, with best meaning, have incurred the worst, the prince reduces himself to an antic—half real, half false—and his world to a shambles before reformation can even begin. Not surprisingly, then, this tragedy exhibits a greater range and concentration of formal disorder than any other of Shakespeare's plays. Manners, dress, speech, 'action' (delivery), acting, drama, game and rite are all abused in it either by excess or deficiency, fradulence or disarray.

Almost as important in *Hamlet* as the notion of form is that of duty. The relationship between the two notions in the philosophical structure of the play is partly determined by the fact that Hamlet has a duty which involves the restoration of true form in a world which is out of joint: the works of the crowned Vice must be exposed. But the connection between form and duty is not limited to the conditions of Hamlet's predicament: they have a kinship which is essential, each being indissolubly bound up with the idea of the proper and fitting. Whereas form is the proper combination or fitting together of parts, the apt relationship of substance and shape, of thought and expression, duty (as Cicero taught) arises from that which is proper in a given set of circumstances and so is indistinguishable from decorum. (pp. 44-5)

In *Hamlet* duty is first invoked in relation to fitness; both words are prominent in the play's vocabulary and are obviously deemed to be intimately related if not synonymous. Almost every character in the play professes or shows an eagerness to do his duty; and some, too—including the ghost, Claudius, Gertrude, Laertes, Polonius and Hamlet—are quick to give others 'lecture and advice' [II. i. 64] on *their* duty. All of which should augur well for the moral health of Denmark. But apart from the fact that what passes for dutifulness may be only an adherence to outward forms [cf. *Othello*, I. i. 50-2], a willingness to do one's duty and to see that others do theirs is no guarantee that good deeds will be done and bad avoided. Since fitness depends on variable factors, there will always be occasions when only a man of exceptional judgement can determine what words and deeds are appropriate. 'Judgement', 'discretion', 'reason' and 'understanding' are words which keep recurring in the dialogue and monologues of *Hamlet;* but they serve principally to emphasise that no one of any importance in Elsinore knows what is fitting or can distinguish the true from the false in matters of form and duty. The most significant use of the word 'fit' occurs then in a speech where Claudius offers Gertrude a hypocritical explanation of his indulgent treatment of Hamlet: 'But so much was our love, / We would not understand what was most fit' [IV. i. 19-20]. In the court of the fratricidal and incestuous usurper, men spy on their friends, come between lovers, 'loose' their daughters, eavesdrop, pretend lunacy, calumniate, murder well-meaning blunderers, bury the innocent with 'maimed rites', and tip unbated foils with poison in the execution of what they believe to be 'fitting our duty'. (pp. 45-6)

Although Hamlet detests noisy acting and the intemperateness it denotes, he is nevertheless the First Player in a piece which—if properly acted and staged—does considerable violence to the ear. The original assault upon the ear, that from which all the others follow, occurs in the murder of the old king, poisoned in a manner which Shakespeare chose purely for its emblematic potential. Powerfully impressed on the mind by the ghost's speech and later by the dumb show (there is emblematic intention here, too), the act of killing through the ear lies at the centre of a whole network of images whose function is to suggest that the excesses and disorders which afflict Denmark are closely related to the abuse of speech, to what we hear. Speech is violent, frightening, poisonous—not calculated to enlighten and to elicit an intelligible and civilized response but to drive 'wonder-wounded hearers' [V. i. 257] into strange silence or passionate execration: 'I have words to speak in thine ear will make thee dumb' [IV. vi. 24-5].

The first instance of violence to the ear occurs when Hamlet and his friends are waiting for the ghost at midnight and the silence is suddenly shattered by the sound of trumpets, kettle-drums and cannon. In reply to Horatio's astonished question, 'What does this mean, my lord?' [I. iv. 7], Hamlet explains that such noise is the language of swaggering drunkenness and revelry whereby the king 'brays out' his bombastic drinking pledges [I. iv. 11-12]. His claim that this has become the norm is confirmed in the last scene of the play [V. ii. 267-71] and, in fact, evidence for it has already been provided in the king's jovial assurance that he would 'grace' Hamlet's 'unforced' show of filial duty with resounding toasts [I. ii. 123-28]:

> No jocund health that Denmark drinks today
> But the great cannon to the clouds shall tell,
> And the King's rouse the heaven shall bruit again,
> Re-speaking earthly thunder. Come away.
>   *(Flourish. Exeunt all but Hamlet.)*

This association of Claudius with noisy self-expression may seem inconsistent, since as a speaker he is glib and oily rather than loud; a true 'politician', he never gives way to ranting passion. But the guns, drums and trumpets are carefully used by Shakespeare to suggest that the vulgar and bombastic mode of utterance, which ultimately disgraces the two most promising young men in Denmark, begins with him, the complacent cutpurse of the empire. (pp. 48-9)

[The] most eloquent and persuasive character is the ghost, whose power to bewitch both eye and ear is irresistible. The chief secret of his art is that he is so slow to speak. Rather like Antony in his refusal to read Caesar's will to the mob ('I must not read it . . . It will inflame you, it will make you mad'), he excites an overpowering desire to hear him utter what he alone knows. Being 'distill'd / Almost to jelly with the act of fear', Marcellus and Barnardo 'stand dumb and speak not to him' [I. ii. 204-06]; nor does he speak to them. But the mere 'sight' of him is such that they 'assail' the 'ears' of Horatio [I. i. 25, 31] until he, too, becomes involved. . . . Later, Hamlet gives 'an attent ear' to Horatio's description of this 'dumb' ghost [I. i. 171; I. ii. 193] and shows a desire to hear it speak which will not be mastered by any consideration: 'I'll speak to it, though hell itself should gape / And bid me hold my peace' [I. ii. 244-45]. And when he is confronted by the ghost, he presents the picture of a man so obsessed with a desire to know and listen that he has become a tool in the hands of the speaker even before a single word is uttered: 'I will speak to thee . . . O, answer me! / Let me not burst in ignorance . . . why . . . why . . . what . . . Say, why is this? Wherefore? What should we do?' [I. iv. 44-57].

What should he do? First, he must open his ears wide to an astounding tale of poisoning through the ear. . . . From start to finish, the ghost's speech is calculated to excite the kind of horrified pity which leads to rage and vengeance. And his advice to Hamlet that 'howsomever' he pursues 'this act' (that is, of vengeance) he must not taint his mind [I. iv. 84-5], seems rather similar in its context to the appeals for moderation made by Antony and Iago to the men whom they have just worked up into a frenzy of uncontrollable hatred [*Julius Caesar* III. ii. 210; *Othello*, III. iii. 452]. (pp. 51-2)

[In] *Hamlet*, the destruction of the innocent together with the guilty is dependent upon the shrouding of truth in secrecy and the use of words as a disguise. One must admit, of course, that some of Hamlet's riddling manifests his fine sense of humour and his ready command of those 'privy nips' and 'merry conceits' which help to make the courtier a socially attractive person. Most of it, however, is a private language begotten by disgust and hatred; and it is intimately related to the secret justice (and therefore non-justice) of revenge. It must be considered, then, not only as a superb revelation of a penetrating, restless and unhappy mind, but as a sign of the isolation of the individual and the collapse of society. (p. 59)

Hamlet's rejection of normal verbal intercourse, his retreat from dialogue to monologue, is not idiosyncratic: it is part of a prevailing disease whereby words and thoughts, questions and answers are deprived of their pre-ordained natural relationships. . . . The transformation of Hamlet's honey vows into bitter riddles begins with Polonius' claim that those vows are treacherous lies rather than sanctified bonds [I. iii. 115-31] and with his command that Ophelia should cease 'to give words or talk with the Lord Hamlet' [I. iii. 134], should 'repel his letters' [II. i. 106], 'admit no messengers, receive no tokens' [II. ii. 144]. Polonius thus coins words which are socially destructive (slanders) and destroys those which are socially binding. But he also twists ordinary words to fit his own devious mind and so deprives them of their accepted meanings. (p. 60)

From the beginning of his career, Shakespeare frequently made good use of sophistry and unconsciously fallacious reasoning as vehicles of deception and self-deception and as pointers to moral and psychological confusion. Of particular interest in relation to *Hamlet* are those noblemen whose judgement is clouded by passion, an over-active imagination, a thirst for revenge, and a muddled devotion to honour. (pp. 61-2)

Distinguished as it is by continual reference to reason, judgement and understanding, the play itself invites this approach. Moreover, although Claudius argues that Hamlet's attitude to his dead father shows 'an understanding simple and unschool'd' and is 'to reason most absurd' [I. ii. 97, 103], it is perfectly clear that the prince has an excellent understanding of the rules of formal logic: a fact which makes the overthrow of his 'noble and most sovereign reason' [III. i. 157] all the more noticeable and tragic. When Hamlet says to himself, 'I'll have grounds / More *relative* than this' [II. ii. 603-04] [my italics], he uses a technical term from formal logic with complete precision and thereby emphasises his determination to proceed in a thoroughly rational manner to decide on the nature of the ghost and the guilt or innocence of Claudius. (p. 62)

In Hamlet's handling of the questions which vex his mind so profoundly the chief source of error is the hidden, false assumption—he can 'sweep' to conclusions in much the same way as he can stab a man to death from the wrong side of an arras. It is noticeably in relation to the ghost that this fault first shows itself. When Horatio warns him not to follow the ghost, Hamlet replies:

Why, what should be the fear?
I do not set my life at a pin's fee;
And for my soul, what can it do to that
Being a thing immortal as itself?   [I. iv. 64-7]

The most effective way of objecting to this would be to point out that murderers can send the souls of men to the 'sulphurous flames' of purgatory ('not shriving time allow'd') and that revengers often do their best to ensure that their victims are damned forever in hell. Hamlet has here implied that what endures forever cannot be harmed—an error which finds support in an equivocal use of the word 'immortal'. (pp. 63-4)

But an even more palpable—indeed an astonishing—error of this kind lies in the argument that if the king blenches at the play he must be guilty of murdering his brother. Since the Player King is killed by his nephew and not his brother, those who do not know that Claudius is guilty (that is, everyone on and off stage) must recognise that two antithetical and therefore useless inferences can be made from his fright at false fire: (1) he did kill his brother and is terrified by Hamlet's knowledge of the fact; (2) he did not kill his brother and is filled with rage or fear at what he takes to be a crudely disguised threat of murder from his insulting and deranged nephew. Hamlet automatically makes the first inference and the court (no less automatically) makes the second. The judicious spectator will at least suspend his judgement until he overhears Claudius confessing his guilt in the prayer scene (a confession which Hamlet does not hear)—though the fact that Hamlet has been making hints about his own dissatisfied ambition, and that Claudius is not in the least perturbed by the dumb-show's image of ear-poisoning, might well incline such a spectator to feel that the court's interpretation has more probability. At any rate, no reliable conclusion whatever about Claudius' innocence or guilt can be drawn from the fact that he blenches.

Virtually inseparable from these errors is Hamlet's failure to specify and test the assumption that private revenge is right and proper: if Claudius killed his brother then he undoubtedly deserves to be punished; but 'if 'a do blench I know my course'— 'Nay, that follows not'. . . . It can, of course, be argued that since there is no allusion whatever to the moral problem of revenge, we must simply ignore it; and that for a similar reason we must ignore Hamlet's obliviousness to the teaching that evil spirits can tell the truth. This would be a valid argument if Hamlet were presented as an unsophisticated hero in a barbarous or pagan setting; if Shakespeare and his contemporaries were indifferent to the serious implications of revenge; and if the truth-telling of treacherous spirits was an unfamiliar notion. The facts being otherwise, the argument seems to me to be unacceptable. Hamlet's failure to question his assumptions about ghosts and revenge must have been intended as an indication of the extent to which 'the poison of deep grief' [IV. v. 75]— and the poison of hatred—can break down 'the pales and forts of reason' [I. iv. 28]. In the Shakespearian canon, it is a new and subtle way of showing that 'revenge' has 'ears more deaf than adders to the voice of / Any true decision' [*Troilus*, II. ii. 172-73].

Polonius, Rosencrantz and Guildenstern are the most obvious victims of Hamlet's passion and of his commitment to quick revenge. Panic and impetuosity help to palliate the impression of these killings; but the self-righteous and specious arguments with which Hamlet justifies them do not. His contention that the death of Polonius fits into the scheme of divine providence is true in a strict theological sense, but is a point of which every murderer could avail himself. And Hamlet's promise (to his mother) that he 'will answer well' the death he has given Polonius [III. iv. 176-77] is eventually kept thus:

What I have done
That might your nature, honour, and exception
Roughly awake, I here proclaim was madness.
Was't Hamlet wrong'd Laertes? Never Hamlet.
If Hamlet from himself be ta'en away,
And when he's not himself does wrong Laertes,
Then Hamlet does it not, Hamlet denies it.
Who does it, then? His madness. If't be so,
Hamlet is of the faction that is wrong'd;

His madness is poor Hamlet's enemy.

[V. ii. 230-39]

'If't be so' indeed. Is it unfair to recall that when Hamlet promised Gertrude to 'answer well' for Polonius' death he also urged her most vehemently to confess herself to heaven and not to cover up her sins with the flattering and entirely erroneous belief that her moralising son was mad? (pp. 64-6)

What Hamlet says to his mother and to Laertes concerning his madness is one of several indications that his 'discourse'—his speaking and reasoning—on fundamental issues has a strong element of self-contradiction, ambivalence, and ambiguity which, in turn, emphasises the presence of unquestioned assumptions and dubious conclusions. In his first soliloquy he rejects suicide because it is condemned by divine law, but in his second he accepts revenge although it, too, is condemned by divine law. In his third soliloquy he assures himself that he is prompted to revenge 'by heaven and hell' [II. ii. 584]: a most improbable liaison. And his final soliloquy (prompted by Fortinbras) is one long tangle of contradictory argument, in which most of the errors of reasoning that have dogged him since the appearance of his father's form coalesce and demand scrutiny [IV. iv. 24-66]. (p. 67)

In listening to Hamlet's soliloquies, we, the theatre audience, cannot but be as puzzled as the stage audience which eavesdrops on his fourth soliloquy [III. i. 55] and attends to his every word and gesture in an effort to 'frankly judge' [III. i. 33] his mind. This phenomenon of puzzling speaker and puzzled audience is discussed, and its full implications explained, in a dialogue which follows immediately upon Hamlet's last and most confusing soliloquy. It introduces a scene in which dark speech combines with other abuses of the word to make manifest the coming disintegration of society: with the blank refusal of the frightened to speak and to listen ('dumbness'), the noise of the rabble, the rant of the avenger, and the ear-poisoning of the Machiavel. In terms of plot, this dialogue could easily be dispensed with; but it greatly illuminates the form and meaning (and non-meaning) of the play, and it serves as an oblique but lucid and dispassionate comment on the words of the man who has just left the stage:

> Queen.   I will not speak with her.
> Gent.   She is importunate, indeed distract.
>   Her moods will needs be pitied.
> Queen.   What would she have?
> Gent.   She speaks much of her father; says she hears
>   There's tricks i' th' world, and hems, and beats her
>   heart;
>   Spurns enviously at straws; speaks things in doubt,
>   That carry but half sense. Her speech is nothing,
>   Yet the unshaped use of it doth move
>   The hearers to collection; they yawn at it,
>   And botch the words up fit to their own thoughts;
>   Which, as her winks and nods and gestures yield
>   them,
>   Indeed would make one think there might be thought,
>   Though nothing sure, yet much unhappily.
> Hor.   'twere good she were spoken with; for she may
>   strew
>   Dangerous conjectures in ill-breeding minds.

[IV. v. 1-15]

A dialogue on the relationship between speaker and audience such as this fits easily into a play profoundly affected by the use of drama-within-drama. Although 'The Murder of Gon-

zago' and its preliminaries constitute the most striking feature of the play's dramatic content, this nevertheless is made up of ritual and theatrical ingredients in fairly even proportion. And the relationship between these two forms of the dramatic is finely established, too: the first allusion to acting occurs in Hamlet's comments on mourning and funeral, while in the fencing 'play' [IV. vii. 105; V. ii. 190, 198 etc.]—as in many formalised games—there is a distinct fusion of the theatrical and the ritual.

Ceremonies are abused in *Hamlet* from (literally) the first line to the last. The action commences with a breach in military rite, the nervous, oncoming guard challenging the man he is about to replace [I. i. 1-2]; and it closes with the rite of a soldier killed on the field being given to a prince who has been poisoned at court in a game of foils: 'such a sight as this / Becomes the field, but here shows much amiss' [V. ii. 401-02]. This blending at the close of two ceremonial disorders (the military and the funeral) is wonderfully artful, for it allows Shakespeare not only to echo the first words of the play but to sustain to the last the basic ritual disorder of the action: the individual violation, and the confusion, of funeral and marriage. The funeral rite at the close is improper not merely because it is unfitted to person and place; it should not have occurred at all: it is a mistake for a marriage.

The clash of funeral and marriage is visually defined at the beginning of the play by the melancholy figure of the hero dressed in a suit of solemn black amid a gay assembly of courtiers robed for marriage and coronation. Subsequently, Hamlet's mourning garb will be in complete disarray and it will be impossible to determine from it whether he is a grief-stricken son or a distracted lover. But here—contrary to appearances—his dress is what it should be and shows that he is the only one at court with a true sense of what is fitting. . . . Insisting in deceptively smooth phrases that 'discretion fought with nature' [I. ii. 5] to demand that sorrow give way to joy, mourning to marriage, Claudius involves himself in a form of contradictory thought which leads inevitably to his glib approval of something so unnatural as 'mirth in funeral and . . . dirge in marriage' [I. ii. 12].

Claudius' allusion in these opening speeches to 'our sometime sister, now our queen' [I. ii. 8], and to 'my cousin Hamlet, and my son' [I. ii. 64], further emphasises that the marriage now being celebrated is one in which categories that are totally distinct in nature have become indistinguishable. But the untimeliness of the marriage is of greater importance in the total design of the play than its incestuous nature; for the haste with which Claudius and Gertrude unite necessarily involves an abuse of two ceremonies. The last line of Claudius' opening speech is, then, an omen of what is going wrong: 'Farewell; and let your haste commend your duty'; Claudius rules over a nation where haste is intimately related to a failure in the performance of duty. We have had hints of this even in the opening scene of the play, hints too which show that serious violations of time lead naturally to a confusion in ritual order: the impetuous Fortinbras' contempt for law and heraldry and his military threats have caused 'poste-haste and romage in the land', 'sweaty haste' which 'doth make the night joint-labourer with the day', and which, moreover, makes it impossible to 'divide the Sunday from the week' [I. i. 76-8, 107]. Such remarks fall into a significant pattern when we hear Hamlet's most bitter comments on the marriage now being loudly celebrated:

> But two months dead! Nay, not so much, not two . . .
> O, most wicked speed to post

With such dexterity to incestuous sheets!
It is not, nor it cannot come to good.   [I. ii. 138-58]

From Gertrude's 'original sin' other ceremonial disorders follow and, as a result, a history which begins with a marriage that has displaced a funeral concludes with funerals that have displaced marriage: such is the symmetry of tragic justice. . . . Echoing Hamlet, Laertes rages against the impropriety of his father's funeral rites:

His means of death, his obscure funeral—
No trophy, sword, nor hatchment o'er his bones,
No noble rite nor formal ostentation—
Cry to be heard, as 'twere from heaven to earth,
That I must call't in question.   [IV. v. 214-18]

But the ritual impropriety here is almost inoffensive in comparison to that which prevails at the funeral of the bride-to-be. Not only does the church curtail that ceremony on the debatable assumption that Ophelia committed suicide; the conduct of her lover and her brother ensures that it suffers from monstrous excess as well as deficiency. (pp. 70-3)

Hamlet (as audience) introduces the funeral as one performed with 'maimed rites'—dubiously inferring that this really 'doth betoken' suicide [V. i. 219-21]. What focuses all our attention on the ritual defects of the funeral, however, is the outraged questioning of Laertes: 'What ceremony else?' [V. i. 223]; 'What ceremony else?' [V. i. 225]; 'Must there no more be done?' [V. i. 235]. An impression of even greater impropriety than actually occurs is induced by means of the 'churlish priest', who insists that in addition to being denied requiem music [V. i. 242], Ophelia should also have been buried in unsanctified ground and denied a final prayer: indeed, 'for charitable prayers, / Shards, flints, and pebbles, should be thrown on her' [V. i. 230-31]. The discordant character of these words brings to mind the noise of kettle-drums, cannon and upspring reels which grated on the ear of Hamlet as he mourned for his father; and it anticipates further discord in requiem harmony at the close of the play.

The ranting and wrestling match on the coffin between the two chief mourners is the very nadir of ritual indecorum. At such a time, noise and violence would appal even the most uncultivated sensibility. But the offensiveness of Laertes and Hamlet here is intensified for more sensitive minds by the touch of insincerity and egotism in their conduct and by the confusion in roles and relationships: who is the distracted lover? Moreover, just as lover and brother are confused, so are marriage and funeral. Both forms of confusion, it should be noted, have been finely foreshadowed in the mad speech of Ophelia herself. When she sang: 'Larded with sweet flowers; / Which bewept to the grave did not go / With true-love showers' [IV. v. 38-40], it was apparent that her mind would always be haunted by, but would never distinguish between, sorrow for a lost lover and a dead father. (pp. 73-4)

Claudius, Gertrude and Laertes being dead, the last moments of Hamlet are necessarily less discordant than Ophelia's; but the tragic cycle of ritual confusion is not yet complete—and besides, the first rash youth is still alive. As Hamlet lies dying in the arms of Horatio, speaking now some of the quietest and most beautiful verse he has ever spoken, his words are suddenly drowned in the tread of soldiers' feet and the crash of cannon: 'What warlike noise is this?', he asks—and then dies, with words of marvellous aptness: 'The rest is silence' [V. ii. 349, 358]. However, although he has escaped from noise at last, the mourners and 'mutes or audience to this act' [V. ii. 335]

[my italics] have not. Horatio prays that angels will sing the prince's requiem, and in effect proceeds to do so himself. But what might have become a noble panegyric is lost in the clatter of kettle-drums, reduced to a dozen words, 'maimed':

Now cracks a noble heart. Good night, sweet prince,
And flights of angels sing thee to thy rest! [March
within.]
Why does the drum come hither?   [V. ii. 359-61]

It is, of course, the drum of the delicate and tender prince who, for the sake of an eggshell, will send twenty thousand men to their graves as if to their beds. Being so happily a soldier, he confidently orders a soldier's funeral for Hamlet, thinking it would be appropriate. But is it? Even he has enough wit to almost suspect that it is not—but no more:

. . . and for his passage
The soldier's music and the rite of war
Speak loudly for him.
Take up the bodies. Such a sight as this
Becomes the field, but here shows much amiss.
Go, bid the soldiers shoot. [Exeunt marching; after the
which a peal of ordnance are shot off.]
          [V. ii. 398-404]

After which—possibly—the rest is silence.

Moving from rite to play, from form as social morality to form as entertainment, we begin to see in perspective Shakespeare's magnificent conception of his art as one which mirrors disorder in the drama of life and so achieves decorous indecorum. The crisis of the tragedy is caused by one kind of play, the catastrophe by another. Both plays are prepared for and staged with great deliberation. But the purpose for which they are presented is utterly at variance with the customary and natural end of all organised 'pastime' [III. i. 15; IV. vii. 33]. On the sacrilegious principle that 'no place . . . should murder sanctuarize' [IV. vii. 127], they are designed not as joyous social events but as death traps. Their words and actions, therefore (like those in the burial of Ophelia), do not 'betoken' their true meaning; in fact, as each producer realises, only a bad performance can reveal the truth [III. ii. 137; IV. vii. 151]. Moreover, both of these plays collapse before their natural conclusion, leaving the audience bewildered, horrified, 'mute': in each of them 'the mould of form' is 'blasted'. (pp. 75-6)

My primary concern so far has been with form. As I have suggested, however, at the beginning of this chapter, and as becomes apparent whenever we examine speech which (in Claudius' phrase) 'lacks form a little', form itself is the revelation of meaning. It is to be hoped, therefore, that my analysis of (significant) formal disorder in Hamlet has helped to clarify not only the dramatic techniques of the play but also the ideas which it was intended to express. Indeed, the nature of my approach is such that an attempt to answer the evergreen question—What is the secret meaning of Hamlet? Why does it baffle?—is the next logical step. The attempt may, of course, seem as pretentious as it is logical, but it will at least have the virtue of brevity; for the answer I propose to give has been implied in almost everything I have already said.

In trying to answer this question, it is first of all necessary to bear in mind that similar questions are asked throughout the play itself: 'What may this mean . . .? [I. iv. 51]; 'What means your lordship?' [III. i. 105]; 'What means this my lord? . . . Belike this show imports the argument of the play . . . Will 'a tell us what this show meant?' [III. ii. 136, 140, 143];

'There's matter in these sighs, these profound heaves, / You must translate; 'tis fit we understand them' [IV. i. 1-2]; 'What dost thou mean by this?' [IV. iii. 29]; 'Alas, sweet lady, what imports this song?' [IV. v. 27]; 'Pray you, let's have no words of this; but when they ask you what it means, say you this' [IV. v. 46-7]; 'This nothing's more than matter' [IV. v. 174]; 'What should this mean? . . . Or is it some abuse and no such thing?' [IV. vii. 49-50]. But to all such queries in Elsinore there are no really satisfactory answers. The subjects of Claudius live in 'a strange-disposed time' when (to quote Shakespeare's Cicero) 'men may construe things after their fashion, / Clean from the purpose of the things themselves' [*Julius Caesar*, I. iii. 33-5]; judgement being impaired or perverted, the signs are improper and meaning is necessarily elusive. And so with *Hamlet* and us. It has an enigmatic quality, not because its author or protagonist discovered that life is meaningless or absurd or that certain moral questions are inherently unanswerable; it is enigmatic, rather, because it is the sum total of all the imperfect signs, rites and plays which it contains and so—with daring logic—has been made to share in their indirect and reluctant surrender of meaning. Given a protagonist who swears his friends to silence, who talks mostly to himself and renounces dialogue on major issues, whose 'discourse of reason' is seriously flawed, and who cannot so much as formulate (though he *may* sense) what every rational Elizabethan would have considered to be his chief moral problem—given all this, the audience is compelled to rely on far more conjecture than would normally be required of it, and to be on its guard against grave misinterpretations: 'And you, the judges, bear a wary eye' [V. ii. 279]. *Hamlet*, then, has been so written that the experience of the audience on the stage (which includes *all* the *dramatis personae*) is shared by that in the theatre. An exceptionally mimetic play, it enacts its own meaning, exemplifies its own moral. It is what it is about. (pp. 78-9)

> T. McAlindon, "'Hamlet, Prince of Denmark'," in Shakespeare and Decorum by T. McAlindon, Macmillan, 1973, pp. 44-79.

ELEANOR PROSSER (essay date 1971)

[*Like Harold C. Goddard (1951), Fredson Bowers (1955), and Helen Gardner (1959), Prosser explores Shakespeare's handling of revenge in* Hamlet. *After investigating the Elizabethan attitude toward revenge, she concludes that Shakespeare, in accordance with the strictures of Church and State, denounces revenge in the play. Prosser's theory differs from earlier explanations of the ghost, particularly that of Sister Miriam Joseph (1962), in seeing it as an evil force who, by insisting on vengeance, sets Hamlet on a path that leads to "barbarism, destruction, and Hell." For additional views of the ghost, see Joseph Addison (1711), Gotthold Ephraim Lessing (1767), W. W. Greg (1917), and J. Dover Wilson (1918).*]

Any critical study of *Hamlet* must at some time face a fundamental question: is the Ghost's command morally binding? Since the ethical question underlies the basic dramatic question it cannot be avoided. Is the play predicated on the assumption that Hamlet is morally obligated to revenge his father's death? With few exceptions, critics have long agreed that in Shakespeare's time the answer was an unqualified "yes," and that the modern reader must adjust to this Elizabethan premise even if it runs counter to his own ethical intuitions. (p. 3)

[Most] critics still hold that the average Elizabethan believed a son morally bound to revenge his father's death. The most thoughtful of these critics have not ignored the orthodox code;

they have insisted, rather, that a popular code approving revenge had far more influence than the code of the Elizabethan Establishment.

A synthesis of their views might read as follows: "To be sure, the Establishment condemned private revenge, but history denies that its campaign had widespread influence. The tumultuous temper of the Elizabethan age stood in direct opposition to official platitudes about obedience, humility, resignation, patience. Far more influential than the orthodox code of the Establishment were two popular codes that placed the demands of revenge above the strictures of religion and law: an aristocratic counter-code of honor and a long-established folk code rooted deep in racial hungers. The popular Elizabethan revenge play arose in a theatrical tradition that appealed to popular, not official, attitudes. The Establishment's condemnation of those popular attitudes is surely no guide in determining either the playwright's intention or the audience's response."

The argument is persuasive and has found many able proponents. The present investigation suggests, however, that the "popular" attitude toward revenge was far more complex than has been generally assumed. Popular literature and dramatic conventions indicate that the orthodox code did in fact have widespread influence. At the same time, they indicate that the average spectator at a revenge play was probably trapped in an ethical dilemma—a dilemma, to put it most simply, between what he believed and what he felt. (p. 4)

Our average Elizabethan could not have failed to hear the voice of the Establishment. Throughout the last half of the sixteenth century, Church, State, and conventional morality fulminated against private revenge in any form and under any circumstances. The vigorous campaign may perhaps best be seen as a response to the natural energies and contentiousness of the age, an age of new and unsettled political loyalties, new economic and class struggles, new fears, new hungers, new hopes. Conflicts were inevitable. More specifically, the Establishment's denunciation of revenge was related to its recurrent fears of civil disorder. As Bacon was later to argue in prosecuting a dueling case, private revenge could lead to quarrels, thence to public tumult, thence to dissension between families, and thence to national quarrels. Since punishment was the prerogative of the State, every possible argument was induced to convince the private citizen that he must leave revenge to God, and thus to the magistrates, His appointed agents. (p. 5)

Revenge was a reprehensible blasphemy, as the most frequently cited Scriptural text made clear: "Dearly beloved, avenge not yourselves, but rather give place unto wrath: for it is written, Vengeance is mine; I will repay, saith the Lord." Echoes of this divine command and promise reverberate throughout Elizabethan literature, and not merely in didactic works. It is heard as a direct quotation in Hieronimo's "*Vindicta mihi*," and is paraphrased in John of Gaunt's "God's is the quarrel." For private men to take revenge is not merely, like Lucifer, to seek to rival God; it is actually "to usurp Christ's office," "as if God had resigned his own right into their hands." Such rebellion against Divine Providence shows that man but little knows himself or his relation to his Maker. (pp. 6-7)

The primary argument against revenge, therefore, was that the revenger endangered his own soul. No matter how righteous a man might think his motives, the act of revenge would inevitably make him as evil as his injurer in the eyes of God. "In so going about to revenge evil, we shew our selves to be evil, and, while we will punnish, and revenge another mans folly, we double, and augment our owne folly.'' A revenger may honestly think he seeks justice, but the nature of revenge makes justice impossible. (p. 7)

Critics have generally agreed that . . . a counter-code led the Elizabethan audience to regard private revenge as an obligation of honor rather than an offense against God, as a virtue rather than a sin. There are several important objections to this view. On the simplest level, even if we grant that many members of the nobility adhered to a highly sophisticated counter-code of honor, can we assume that it was accepted or even recognized by the majority of the theatergoing public? It may be argued that Shakespeare and his contemporaries appealed primarily to the ''judicious,'' not to the groundling. Undoubtedly there is some truth in this argument; any serious playwright knows that his audiences represent many degrees of comprehension. But is it conceivable that Elizabethan playwrights expected different members of their audiences to apply diametrically opposed moral judgments? (p. 13)

Undoubtedly, the average Elizabethan sympathized strongly with a revenger, but we cannot assume that he therefore ignored all the ethical and religious precepts he heard daily and which, according to the available evidence, he generally accepted. The ''willing suspension of disbelief'' does not imply that an audience leaves all of its knowledge, its ethics, its religious faith, at the box office. Is it not at least possible that the Elizabethan audience could instinctively identify with the revenger and yet—either at the same time or later, when released from emotional involvement—judge him, too? (p. 34)

[We] find no suggestion that Shakespeare expected his audience to accept without question the validity of private blood revenge. The evidence suggests, rather, that his plays rely on the orthodox ethical and religious injunctions against it. Despite a maturing of both dramatic skill and thought between *Titus Andronicus* and *The Tempest*, the portrayal of the revenger seems to remain constant. Titus and Prospero are two sides of the same coin: Titus in his madness embracing revenge and thus descending to the hell of barbarism and destruction; Prospero in his sanity exercising his nobler reason and thus rising to forgiveness and reconciliation.

Revenge motifs recur throughout the plays. Again and again the surrender to revenge is seen as the surrender of reason, the surrender at least to rashness and at most to madness. Similarly, a decision to take revenge is often accompanied by an explicit rejection of some clear virtue or good. Just as Lear denies his daughters, Coriolanus predicates his revenge on the total rejection of the natural bonds of family (''Wife, mother, child I know not''). The rejection may take the form of symbolically flinging virtue back to heaven before vowing vengeance: Othello blows ''all [his] fond love . . . to heaven'' and Romeo cries, ''Away to heaven respective lenity.''

Of special pertinence is the frequency with which revengers associate their motives and actions with Hell and the demonic. In *Titus Andronicus* we hear that the man who seeks private revenge must dive to the bowels of hell. In his madness, Titus takes that plunge. Antony envisions Caesar's spirit, an epitome of revenge, rising ''with Ate by his side come hot from hell.'' Othello calls up ''black vengeance, from the hollow hell.'' Coriolanus resolves to pursue his revenge ''with the spleen / Of all the under fiends.'' None of these characters is originally demonic in purpose, as are Iago and Aaron. The language is not the mere rhetoric of villainy.

In none of the foregoing do I intend to suggest that Shakespeare was a dour, inflexible moralist, consigning his revengers to

Hell with grim satisfaction. At a given moment in a play—the moment when Romeo stabs Tybalt, when Coriolanus defies the screaming mob, when Hotspur rages at personal insult— we often instinctively identify with the very action that later, when we are released from emotional involvement, we see in ethical perspective. Shakespeare's plays show a deeper penetration into the nature of the ethical dilemma involved in revenge and a greater compassion for the revenger than do the plays of his contemporaries. Even so, they bear out Cutwolfe's view that revenge in Elizabethan drama was ''continually raised from hell.''

With—let us note—the possible exception of *Hamlet*. In his treatment of the Ghost, Shakespeare breaks new ground, demanding a fresh response by transforming a theatrical convention. If we approach the play with certain preconceptions, we may be blind to a radical change in ethical perspective. This chapter has not attempted to use Shakespeare's other plays to interpret *Hamlet* It has merely questioned one particular preconception: that Shakespeare's plays in general reflect an approved code of private blood revenge.

On the contrary, on the subject of revenge, his plays reflect agreement with sermons, moralist tracts, poetry, and other plays of his day. No matter how base the injury, no matter how evil your enemy, no matter how dim all hope of legal redress, leave the issue to Heaven; ''God's is the quarrel.'' In *Richard III*, Clarence's words to his murderers succinctly state a plea implicit in play after play:

> If God will be revenged for this deed,
> O, know you yet, he doth it publicly:
> Take not the quarrel from his powerful arm;
> He needs no indirect nor lawless course
> To cut off those that have offended him.
>   [I. iv. 215-19]
>   (pp. 93-4)

No one in the first scene [of *Hamlet*] gives any indication of believing the Ghost to be the true soul of the dead King. The point of view is Protestant. Horatio, Marcellus, and Bernardo all consistently refer to the apparition as ''it'': not as the soul of the King himself, but as a spirit whose identity is in doubt. When Marcellus asks if this ''thing'' has appeared, his diction suggests not contemptuous levity but the cautious Protestant's awareness that the Ghost cannot be the actual King. It is an unknown, the nature of which is still to be determined. Similarly, Horatio's ''Stay, illusion'' is not an echo of his earlier skepticism but the correct response of a wary Protestant. The Ghost is, indeed, an ''illusion.'' The point at issue is what kind of illusion.

In its first minute on stage, the Ghost reveals that something is seriously wrong. What is the purpose of its first appearance? It merely enters and leaves. Little is established that could not be included in the second appearance. The usual explanation is that its first entrance is a shrewd bit of theatrical trickery intended to catch the audience's attention. The episode does much more than that. It firmly establishes one point: this Ghost is forced to leave when Heaven is invoked. Horatio follows the warnings of religion. He charges the Ghost in the name of Heaven to identify itself, and it took no pious scholar to know that only demons would be ''chased'' by the invocation of God. The first episode reaches its climax as the Ghost is ''offended'' and stalks away, leaving Horatio pale and trembling. (pp. 118-19)

The physical appearance of the Ghost may also suggest that it is suspect. As Catholics believed and Protestants had heard,

Purgatory souls and good spirits both were "of sweet and amiable aspect," moved only by grace and charity. This ghost frowns as did the dead King once when he was angry with the Polacks. Moreover, Purgatory souls and good spirits are both spirits of peace. Many have noted the curious fact that the Ghost is in arms, bearing a truncheon as it moves with martial stalk. (p. 121)

A wise scholar, Horatio addresses the Ghost as both Protestants and Catholics advised. He does not question it. He charges it to speak, but only if it is a good spirit come upon some mission of grace. This time, it will be recalled, Horatio has not invoked Heaven, and the Ghost is about to speak when it is suddenly arrested by the crow of the cock. Modern editors who place the notation "Cock crows" in the middle of Horatio's speech create a misleading impression. In Q_2, the only version to indicate the sound effect, it appears opposite Horatio's last line. The Ghost is meant to react as suddenly to the voice of the cock as it did to Horatio's invocation of Heaven.

There can be little doubt that Shakespeare's audience was acquainted with the symbolic meaning of the cock. An ancient belief—found in traditional Jewish writings and later made specifically Christian by such writers as Prudentius and St. Ambrose—held that roving demons scattered in fear at cock-crow, and Le Loyer specially related the belief to his discussion of demons appearing as dead souls. The Witches' Sabbath customarily began at midnight and lasted until cockcrow, at which time Satan fled terrified. As the herald of the day, the cock is the voice of light and thus of grace; in banishing night, he banishes darkness and sin. (pp. 121-22)

The first scene thus serves several important functions. It establishes that the Ghost is not a hallucination. It establishes that something is rotten in the state of Denmark. It establishes suspense. It establishes the Christian framework. But, above all, it establishes that the Ghost is probably malignant. The first four purposes could have been served by one appearance of the Ghost in a scene half the length, but the fifth required that the audience recognize a suspicious pattern. Many members of the audience would probably have been alerted when the Ghost vanished at the invocation of Heaven, but some might have missed the full significance of such a swift action. When the Ghost vanishes a second time for an equally suspicious reason, the inference is unavoidable.

I do not mean to suggest that the Ghost is established as unquestionably demonic by the end of the first scene. It is an awe-inspiring figure of regal majesty whom a loving son will, understandably, be inclined to credit. When the Ghost and Hamlet meet, we will be seeing through Hamlet's eyes and might easily overlook hints of danger. In the first scene, however, we are not yet emotionally involved. While we are still fairly objective, Shakespeare plants several clear warnings that this "guilty thing" is a creature that must be tested with extreme caution, and tested by the teachings of the Church. (pp. 122-23)

What is the mission of the Ghost? Even before it announces its identity, we are warned: it comes to command revenge. Its first long speech is skillfully adapted to its mission. It appeals to Hamlet's love and grief, relentlessly aggravating the son's anguish by describing the pains of Purgatory. Note that it does not state one specific fact, though literature abounded with useful details. It announces that it is forbidden to tell such secrets to mortal men, and then proceeds to create an even more horrifying impression than any description would. Of

course Purgatory ghosts were under no such proscription. One of their purposes in returning was to make man understand the specific pains they were suffering, and thus their mission required them to give as much graphic detail as possible. Why does this Ghost rely on the ghastly inference, the harrowing hint? It is skillfully arousing Hamlet's imagination, working entirely on his emotions. The speech builds to a compelling climax in "If thou didst ever thy dear father love—" What loving son could possibly remain calm? (pp. 133-34)

If we read the Ghost's long speech without preconceptions, we should be struck by its almost exclusive reliance on sensual imagery. Like Iago, it paints a series of obscene pictures and then insistently highlights the very images that Hamlet had tried to blot out in his early soliloquy: "that incestuous, that adulterate beast . . . shameful lust . . . lewdness . . . sate itself in a celestial bed . . . prey on garbage." Hamlet had known that for his own sanity he must not visualize that bed, but the Ghost rivets his eyes upon it. The culminating exhortation is not to purge the "royal throne of Denmark." It forces Hamlet again to peer into the horror that sickens him:

> Let not the royal bed of Denmark be
> A couch for luxury and damned incest.
>
> [I. v. 82-3]

Can this be a divine agent on a mission of health and consolation?

Moreover, if a pious son should immediately recognize that swift revenge was a "sacred duty," why does the Ghost find it necessary to present an extended, revolting description of the poisoning? Again its appeal is entirely to the senses. This Ghost is not appealing to Hamlet's love of virtue; it is not arousing his determination to serve the justice of God. It is doing everything possible to arouse nausea and loathing.

This Ghost cannot be a penitent soul from Purgatory. It says it is, but are we intended to believe it? It does, to be sure, speak of its agony at dying without the sacraments, but the reference serves as one more detail to intensify Hamlet's pain. Moreover, a subtle hint has been planted that is to bear terrible fruit in the Prayer Scene. The Ghost's attitude toward its suffering is also telling. Does it humbly confess its sins, acknowledging the justice of its punishment? On the contrary, it "groans" and "complains" of the agony resulting from its being unfairly deprived of final sacraments. For centuries editors have tried to give "O, horrible! O, horrible! most horrible!" to Hamlet on the grounds that the reaction ill befits a spirit of grace. So it does. A Purgatorial penitent would be a loving figure of consolation, but the Ghost that Shakespeare created dwells on the horror of its pains. The exclamation is a logical climax to the extended assault on Hamlet's emotions. (pp. 134-35)

In my judgment, a production following Shakespeare's every clue would create the same response in us today as I have suggested it did in the original audience. If we heard the terrible human passions in the Ghost's voice and saw them in its face, if we were startled by its sudden recoil at Horatio's invocation of Heaven, if we were made aware of the significance of the cock—if, in short, we could once see the Ghost that Shakespeare created, would we not instinctively sense that we were in the presence of evil?

Throughout the preceding analysis, I have, of course, often viewed the action from a dispassionate perspective no audience can reach so long as it remains an audience. Although I have tried to maintain awareness of this fact, in emphasizing the

Ghost's malignity I may have created a misconception. I am not suggesting that we are consciously aware of the Ghost's true nature or that we want Hamlet to ignore its terrible revelations. During a good production, we rarely make objective judgments. When Hamlet is onstage, we enter his world, seeing much as he sees, feeling much as he feels. But not completely. I have stressed the many warnings of evil to suggest that our response to the Ghost is too complicated to be accounted for solely by the fact that we identify with Hamlet.

The audience cannot meet the Ghost for the first time with Hamlet in the fourth scene. We have seen things that Hamlet does not see. The first Ghost Scene created a series of impressions that will necessarily color, if only slightly, our response to the second. And throughout the opening scene, the Ghost is consistently suspect. Later, however, ambiguities begin to appear. In the first scene, Horatio had said that the Ghost was frowning as ''in an angry parle''; now, in the third, he tells Hamlet that it had ''a countenance more in sorrow than in anger.'' In the fourth scene, the Ghost is addressed as a mouldering corpse from the grave, but it speaks as a suffering soul from Purgatory. It cries for revenge against Claudius, but pleads for forbearance with Gertrude. Each of these details can be harmonized into a consistent interpretation, but only by hindsight. In the theater, Shakespeare keeps shifting our point of view. Our response is further complicated by Hamlet's own shifting perspective. He defies damnation; he weeps for his dead father; he plays games with a devil; he affirms that the Ghost is ''honest.'' We have been asked to test the Ghost, but we have not been allowed an easy answer.

Given the perspective of the entire play, we can discern a probability; but in the fleeting perspective of the dramatic moment, we find only questions. If we could unequivocally pronounce the Ghost a demon and its command a damnable temptation, the tragedy would be destroyed. We cannot, and as a result are caught up in Hamlet's dilemma. The warnings have not made us pull back and condemn his vow to take revenge; they have made us aware of the intolerable alternatives he faces. He says he will go pray, but he will not be the man we want him to be if prayer is his only recourse. Somehow, in some way, we surely want him to act. To retreat into patience would be to acquiesce in the evil. But, as both Hamlet and the audience now know, to act may be to couple Hell. (pp. 142-43)

The theory that Hamlet instinctively shrinks from a dread command for which he is ill-fitted is belied by his obvious jubilation at having proof of Claudius's guilt, and by the ferocious eagerness with which he now allies himself with the powers of Hell:

> 'Tis now the very witching time of night,
> When churchyards yawn and hell itself breathes out
> Contagion to this world: now could I drink hot blood,
> And do such bitter business as the day
> Would quake to look on.   [III. ii. 387-92]

The speech is appalling in its implications. . . . The night that Hamlet welcomes is even more ghastly than most in its explicit association with Hell, the demonic practices of witchcraft, and the blasts of contagion.

We cannot lightly dismiss Hamlet's grisly avowal that now he could ''drink hot blood.'' To the Elizabethan audience, the statement would inevitably have suggested one of the most degenerate practices of the Black Mass. . . . If we accept the speech on its own terms, we find Hamlet's thirst for blood a terrifying indication of his state of mind. The thought of murder does not appall him. It excites him to a state of inhuman frenzy. (pp. 183-84)

The Prayer Scene provides one of the most profoundly moving movements of the play. Claudius is himself a tragic figure, not the greasy, vulture-eyed villain pictured by those who bolster Hamlet's virtue by blackening his opponents. He is a strong and self-willed but sensitive man, whose passions have led him to choose evil but who has never deluded himself into calling that evil good. He has an active conscience that cannot be silenced. He is far closer to Macbeth than to Iago or Richard III.

Perhaps no character is more compelling on stage than the contrite sinner struggling to repent, a fact that medieval dramatists put to good use in their treatments of Mary Magdalene. No situation so clearly unites a dramatic character with his audience by a bond of shared humanity. No matter what his religious or cultural heritage, every man but the amoral freak tries and fails, feels the pangs of guilt and regret, and struggles to shape himself anew to that image of good toward which he strives.

Shakespeare dramatizes this struggle in Christian terms, using specific points of doctrine his audience would recognize. One by one, Claudius mounts three of the four steps comprising what was known as the ''ladder of repentance'': contrition, confession, faith, and amendment. His prayer is not motivated by fear of detection. His conscience has led him to true contrition: loathing of his sin because it is an offense to God, because ''it smells to heaven.'' Moreover, it has led him to confession: acknowledgment before God that he knows the full horror of his sin. Compelled by the inexorable witness of conscience to see his past action in its true nature and be revolted by it, he nonetheless cannot bring himself to surrender the motives which led him to that action and which still dominate him. He is trapped. Claudius is in a state of human torment, not of theological despair. He has absolute faith: even if his sin were greater than the crime first cursed of God, the gracious rain of divine mercy could wash the blood from his hand. The fault of the murder itself is past and easily repented. If his ''strong intent,'' his genuine longing to find peace, can but defeat his ''stronger guilt''—the sins of ambition and lust that still corrupt him—forgiveness, he knows, awaits. He has but to choose by an act of will.

But can he make that choice? The tortured outcries reveal the intense agony of a man paralyzed between the longing of soul and the solicitation of appetite: ''O limed soul, that, struggling to be free, / Art more engaged!'' Ironically, Claudius knows that this movement to repent has necessarily enslaved him even more to his sin. He has honestly diagnosed the cancer that is destroying him, but has consciously refused the only medicine that could heal him. Because he has brought all the evil out into the open but has deliberately rejected grace, he is doubly damned. Even at this moment, however, he decides to make one final attempt and retires to pray. ''All may be well.'' The line is a masterly stroke. The impotence of his will, his half-hope, half-rejection—all are pointed in this indefinite half-promise. It is the final summation of his ''limed soul,'' and at the same time it serves a brilliant dramatic function. It leaves the audience in a state of suspense throughout Hamlet's hesitation. Will Claudius be able to take that final step? There is little doubt, but there is still some. Irony and suspense are both maintained until his final lines before retiring:

> My words fly up, my thoughts remain below:
> Words without thoughts never to heaven go.
>   [III. iii. 97-8]

With a rush of irony, the audience now realizes that Hamlet's moment was ideal for the total revenge he intended: death at the very moment Claudius was rejecting the call of grace and thus willfully choosing damnation. (pp. 185-87)

I have dealt rather extensively with the religious issues in Claudius's speech in order to justify two important premises that will be crucial in interpreting Hamlet's ensuing soliloquy. First, no matter how we have seen Claudius previously, we sympathize with him in the Prayer Scene. He is a human being in torment, facing his own question of "being." Only a bigoted Pharisee swelling with more spiritual sins than Claudius would sit back smugly and crow, "It serves him right." Second, the profound and moving presentation of Christian doctrine in the speech makes it inconceivable that Shakespeare intended his audience simply to forget its religious values when Hamlet enters. He has pointedly insisted that the world of *Hamlet* is a Christian world in which the redeeming values are self-knowledge, forgiveness, and mercy, a world in which eternal salvation is man's ultimate goal. Would Shakespeare have devoted such attention to Claudius's moral struggle if he wanted us to approve without question of Hamlet's ensuing actions?

Picture the scene. His stubborn knees at last bent, Claudius is kneeling in prayer. Hamlet runs in, on his way to Gertrude's chamber. He stops short, pulls his sword, sneaks up behind the bent figure, raises his arm—Is it possible that any normally sensitive, decent man could genuinely want him to strike? Stab a defenseless man? In the back? While he is praying? If we forget all we have heard about pagan ethics and Elizabethan revenge codes and dramatic conventions, does not the voice of instinct cry "No"?

Unexpectedly, Hamlet stays his hand, but his reason is frightful. A terrible hint had been planted by the Ghost: Hamlet's father had been cut off in a state of sin. Would it then be "revenge" to kill Claudius while he is praying? If, perchance, he is repenting, his soul would go to Heaven. (pp. 187-88)

For over two centuries critics have been personally appalled by Hamlet's expressed reason for refusing to kill Claudius at prayer. The speech is "too horrible to be read or to be uttered" [see excerpt above by Samuel Johnson, 1765]; it expresses "one of the most revolting sentiments in all Shakespeare . . . in language hardly equalled for repulsiveness"; the words are "frightful," the idea "fiendish." Almost to a man, however, critics believe that the speech could not possibly reflect Hamlet's real sentiments and that their personal revulsion is therefore invalid. Seeking for some logical explanation, they have generally divided into two camps. Many have argued that Hamlet's vicious reason is so inconsistent with his character that it cannot be his real reason. Actually he finds undercover tactics abhorrent, or he realizes a public occasion would be more fitting, or he shrinks from killing a defenseless man, or he really does not want to act at all. There is, however, an obvious objection to any theory that Hamlet is rationalizing. Rationalization is a process of attributing morally acceptable motives to unacceptable desires or actions. If Hamlet's real motive were as commendable as the desire for public justice or the refusal to stab a defenseless man in the back, why would he need to conceal the motive from himself? More important, why would Shakespeare conceal it from the audience? If Hamlet's motive is not commendable, if he is temporizing out of weakness, why did not Shakespeare offer a rationalization that sounds virtuous? Hamlet could easily hesitate on the grounds that Claudius may be repenting and hence may confess publicly. The audience might then sense the contradiction between his stated thirst for

blood and his hesitation and realize that he is rationalizing. In the play as Shakespeare wrote it, however, there is no contradiction between Hamlet's expressed motives and his actions.

A second group of critics accept Hamlet's reason, although they agree it is abhorrent to the modern mind. They assert, however, that he is merely voicing a conventional sentiment of the Elizabethan stage and that we should therefore suspend moral judgment. The speech, it is argued, does not reflect a vicious state of mind but a dutiful attempt to heed an ethic of revenge that Shakespeare's audience never questioned, a code that made the damnation of one's victim a moral requisite to a perfect revenge. Thus Hamlet is not to blame. In spite of his own moral sensibilities, he is courageously trying to effect equal justice by a device long approved in the theater.

Outside the theater, the voices of Elizabethan morality were, of course, unanimous. Their attitude is implicit in recurrent assertions that we must pray for the salvation of our enemies, that private revenge is a blasphemous usurpation of God's prerogative. . . . Despite this evidence, many believe that audiences were trained to accept a pagan revenge code in the theater and thus to accord the dramatic convention of "immortal vengeance" full moral approval.

But does the drama of the period support this assumption? To my knowledge, no one has ever studied the convention in its dramatic context. Plays have been named, characters listed, and lines quoted, but no attempt has been made to determine audience response. What kinds of characters either desire or plan to kill their victims in a way that will ensure their damnation? What was the audience's moral attitude? Where did its sympathies lie? The answers to these questions constitute an astounding contradiction of the widespread belief that the revenger who sets out to damn his victim is merely fulfilling an ethical obligation.

In twenty-six works of both dramatic and non-dramatic literature written between 1585 and 1642, we find the convention reflected in twenty-three characters who either desire or act upon the desire to damn their victims, and in three characters who reject any such motive. In only three instances is there any possibility that the convention received either the moral approval or the sympathy of the audience. Of these three, one occurs in *Antonio's Revenge*, a play so contradictory in its appeals that the modern reader cannot know where the audience's sympathies lay; one is found in the wish, but not the actions, of the virtuous Iden of *2 Henry VI*, who regrets that his sword could not have killed the soul as well as the body of a traitor. We have, then, only one clear example of an ostensibly virtuous hero who acts upon the desire to damn his enemy—Perolet in *Four Plays* (1608)—and even this example is doubtful because of the confused ethics so typical of Beaumont and Fletcher.

Of the remaining twenty-three examples, not one could be offered in support of the traditional view. In all twenty-three cases, even the mere desire to damn another soul for eternity was unquestionably viewed by the audience as morally reprehensible and emotionally horrifying. In some cases, a basically good man refuses to send an unprepared soul to Hell, a sentiment arousing obvious sympathy. In some cases, a virtuous man momentarily wishes that he could damn a sinner but is immediately castigated for even entertaining such a thought. In most cases—eighteen in all—the character who merely considers the idea is unmistakably evil. (pp. 189-91)

Let us, then, return to our intuitive response. Hamlet states his reason for hesitating to kill Claudius, and nothing suggests that we should doubt him. The sentiment is wholly consistent with what has preceded and what will follow. At the end of the Play Scene, he had been violent and bloodthirsty, eagerly allying himself with the forces of Hell; now he viciously determines to be the agent of Claudius's damnation; shortly, in the Closet Scene, he will still be violent and murderous. Moreover, he will do exactly what he said he would do: strike out the minute he believes Claudius to be trapped in an act "that has no relish of salvation in 't." His stated motive is confirmed by his actions. Once we accept the soliloquy as a true expression of Hamlet's state of mind, we see the Prayer Scene as the inevitable culmination of all that has preceded, the terrible fulfillment of the many warnings so carefully planted. It matters little whether we recall the Ghost at this point. No reminders are necessary to make us realize that Hamlet at this moment is the servant of malign forces.

Once we accept the soliloquy at face value, we also see that Hamlet, at least at this point in the play, is closely allied to many of the villain-revengers in Elizabethan and Jacobean drama. Echoing many familiar conventions, he has defied patience, hailed the black night as congenial to his purpose, aligned himself with Hell, expressed a thirst for blood, and descended into savagery. Even more significant, he is following the pattern that we have found in several of Shakespeare's plays. The surrender to revenge is accompanied by a rejection of "all forms, all pressures past," and of all natural ties; it is followed by a surrender to instinct with a resulting loss of rational control. Any interpretation of *Hamlet* must stand or fall on the play itself, but other plays by both Shakespeare and his contemporaries would seem to confirm the view that Hamlet has set his foot on a path that can lead only to barbarism, destruction, and Hell. (pp. 192-93)

Only when we grant that the world of *Hamlet* is not an ethical never-never land, governed by some artificial theatrical code at variance with the code of daily life, can we grant that Shakespeare probably intended his audience to respond naturally.

Is it not likely, then, that the best way to approach *Hamlet* today is to forget all one has ever heard about Elizabethan codes and counter-codes, about dramatic sources and theatrical conventions—to respond as naturally as one would to a modern play? Our attitude toward revenge is almost the same as the Elizabethan attitude, and it is doubtful that human nature has changed. If we recognize that our intuitions have always been valid, that, despite our sympathy for Hamlet's agony, the savage course on which he embarks is designed to appall us, we find the tragic issue to be rooted in an ethical dilemma that is universal. (p. 256)

> *Eleanor Prosser, in her* Hamlet & Revenge, *second edition, Stanford University Press, 1971, 304 p.*

REUBEN A. BROWER   (essay date 1971)

[*Through an analysis of the language of the play, Brower traces the influence of the ancient heroic tradition on the character of Hamlet. Additional commentary on Shakespeare's handling of language in the play is provided in the excerpts by Samuel Taylor Coleridge (1813), Wolfgang H. Clemen (1951), Harry Levin (1959), and Inga-Stina Ewbank (1977).*]

The ghost that haunts Hamlet is the ghost of the ancient hero in its more primitive forms, Homeric and Germanic. How to be both the hero-avenger and the just hero of the Renaissance— that is the question. The formula, though reasonably true, is

"The Rest is Silence," by John Austen (1922?). From the Art Collection of the Folger Shakespeare Library.

both partial and misleading, since a Hamlet so described sounds like a Corneillian hero clearly aware of conflicting moral claims, whereas the essence of Shakespeare's hero lies in his 'trouble', in his confusion as he faces the conflict. (p. 277)

Marcellus asks why all this preparation for war in the present Denmark, and Horatio tells him that it is connected with the cause in which old Hamlet had fought. His story, a typical heroic exploit of challenge and single combat, is told in answering style:

> Our last king,
> Whose image even but now appear'd to us,
> Was, as you know, by Fortinbras of Norway,
> Thereto prick'd on by a most emulate pride,
> Dar'd to the combat; in which our valiant Hamlet
> (For so this side of our known world esteem'd him)
> Did slay this Fortinbras. . . .   [I. i. 80-6]

'Young Fortinbras' ('Strong-in-arm'), who is now taking up his father's quarrel, is like his father and old Hamlet a man of 'mettle hot and full', eager to undertake an 'enterprise / That hath a stomach in 't'. The new wars are only the old wars again:

> *Bernardo*. Well may it sort that this portentous figure
> Comes armed through our watch, so like the King
> That was and is the question of these wars.
>   [I. i. 109-11]

Bernardo's and Horatio's speeches foreshadow later contrasts of theme and character: old Fortinbras and 'young Fortinbras', old Hamlet and 'young Hamlet'. What will 'young Denmark' be when measured against his contemporary and against the 'warlike form' of 'the King his father'? Parallels introduced here set the frame for the action, anticipating its destination when Fortinbras, now ruler of both kingdoms, will give his order to

> Bear Hamlet like a soldier to the stage . . .
>
> [V. ii. 396]

As this line unfolds in our later recollection of the play, it embraces much of the meaning and the mystery of Hamlet's career. How 'like a soldier' has he been? To what 'stage' will he be borne? A mere platform raised for viewers to see, or the stage of an imaginary theatre? Or does the image suggest a more heroic resting-place, like the monument of Sir Francis Vere, in which the hero's body is borne by four fellow soldiers? The heroic image of the warrior young and old, and the Virgilian contrast of father and son, are always present in the imaginative background of *Hamlet,* the night-time of past and present in one. (The romantic sense of the past within the present, and night and darkness as a setting for important actions, are also Virgilian.)

'This portentous figure' moves Horatio to draw the first of many parallels between the Northern and the Roman heroic worlds. His style, recalling Plutarch and *Julius Caesar,* is learned and splendidly Roman:

> In the most high and palmy state of Rome,
> A little ere the mightiest Julius fell,
> The graves stood tenantless, and the sheeted dead
> Did squeak and gibber in the Roman streets. . . .
> As stars with trains of fire, and dews of blood,
> Disasters in the sun; and the moist star
> Upon whose influence Neptune's empire stands
> Was sick almost to doomsday with eclipse.
> And even the like precurse of fierce events,
> As harbingers preceding still the fates
> And prologue to the omen coming on,
> Have heaven and earth together demonstrated
> Unto our climature and countrymen.   [I. i. 113-25]

The epithets, the Latin use of the superlative ('mightiest'), the etymological pun on 'dis-asters', the out-of-the-way 'precurse' (which occurs only here in Shakespeare), the allusion to Virgil's *imperium pelagi* in 'Neptune's empire', the curious use of 'omen' for 'the event'—these features and the grandeur of rhythm are typical of the contemporary Virgilian manner. The impression of disease in Nature and in the state, and of ambiguously evil fantasies, stands out in sharp contrast with the rare purity of the Nativity season, when

> The nights are wholesome, then no planets strike,
> No fairy tales, nor witch hath power to charm,
> So hallow'd and so gracious is the time.
>
> [I. i. 162-64]

For the first time in the play, Christian and pagan are opposed to one another.

The description of the Ghost as '*like* the King' and the stress on its 'form', walk, and costume, anticipate a central theme in *Hamlet,* one of the most important for understanding the temperament of the man who is to face the claims of ancient and Renaissance heroic ideals. The theme is also implied in Claudius' picture of himself in his opening speech,

> With an auspicious, and a dropping eye,
> With mirth in funeral, and with dirge in marriage,
> In equal scale weighing delight and dole. . . .
>
> [I. ii. 11-13]

With unconscious irony Claudius explains how 'discretion' has 'fought with nature', how his judgement has resisted the natural and normal response to a brother's death. The number of opposites in this address of studied majesty seems strange coming from a man who will shortly reject any motion that his 'state' is 'disjoint and out of frame'. Although the style may have been what Elizabethans expected from royalty, it is fairly obvious that Claudius, like the player queen, is overplaying his part. (pp. 279-82)

In Hamlet's first soliloquy ('O that this too too sullied flesh . . .') there are further traces of this consciousness of roles and of the contrast between outer appearance and inner reality. There are also many allusions, more or less direct, to Hamlet's state of mind as the play begins: the feeling of corruption and foulness, the fixing on the sensuality of his mother's love, the horror of incest, the *taedium vitae* and longing for death. By any definition, modern or Elizabethan, Hamlet is melancholy-sick, though his language is not ours, whether by 'ours' we mean Romantic or Freudian. Hamlet sees, feels, and speaks in an idiom that fuses the Christian,

> that the Everlasting had not fix'd
> His canon 'gainst self-slaughter!
>
> [I. ii. 131-32]

with the heroic: his father, 'So excellent a king', was 'Hyperion' to this 'satyr'; his mother had seemed 'Like Niobe, all tears' (an example Achilles recommended to Priam); and he himself is *not* like Hercules. The last comparison does not imply that Hamlet is weak, but that he feels unequal to the 'saviour and purger' role of the favourite Stoic hero. His asides show that like Brutus he tends to fall into abstractions and personifications,

> Frailty, thy name is woman!   [I. ii. 146]

and that he is familiar with the moral psychology of the Stoics and contemporary intellectuals,

> (O God! a beast that wants discourse of reason . . .)
>
> [I. ii. 150]

These classical and philosophical turns of speech point to another Hamlet, the university man who speaks to Horatio with affection and bright wit. But this is no more the 'real' Hamlet than the grieving son who bursts into violent exclamations, breaking the rhythm of his speech with asides and incomplete sentences. There is also the Hamlet who is lightly—or seriously—in love with Ophelia, and the man of 'noble mind' (another Stoic idiom),

> The courtier's, scholar's, soldier's, eye, tongue, sword . . .

—the complete prince. It is to all these Hamlets in one, the total image of eloquent courtier, soldier-hero, philosopher, actor, and son sick with grief and loathing for his mother's marriage, that the puzzling 'thing' comes. What part will the player play in that terrifying scene?

The progress of Hamlet's response to his heroic mission may be suggested by focusing on two expressions, each connected with one of the major themes: 'taint not thy mind', the warning of the Ghost, and Hamlet's hint to his friends that he may 'put an antic disposition on'.

The first of these phrases occurs in the Ghost's speech following his monstrous revelations of the father's murder and the mother's 'lewdness':

> Let not the royal bed of Denmark be
> A couch for luxury and damned incest.

But, howsoever thou pursuest this act,
Taint not thy mind, nor let thy soul contrive
Against thy mother aught.

[I. v. 82-6]

The meaning of 'taint' is well illustrated by Maria's libel on Malvolio, 'for sure, the man is tainted in 's wits'. Hamlet is warned to beware of disease of mind, the thought-sickness known to the Elizabethans as 'melancholy'. As he says to Rosencrantz and Guildenstern, 'my wit's diseased'. Recent critics have been fond of noting symptoms of a neurosis, of Hamlet's compulsive fixing on his mother's lust and of his extreme revulsion from it. But the terms Hamlet uses indicate that the feeling is more normal and more conventional than a Freudian diagnosis alone would suggest. When Hamlet talks of this 'sterile promontory' and of sexual disgust, he is speaking the language of medieval pessimism, *contemptu mundi*, of which we saw a trace in Chapman's Hector, an attitude that fits in easily with the Stoicism of the Renaissance hero. To the Elizabethans Hamlet might have sounded no more and no less 'sick' than St. Paul or St. Augustine, prime authors of the medieval attitude. (pp. 283-85)

Hamlet gives no sign that he may on occasion deliberately assume madness until near the end of [the cellerage] scene:

How strange or odd soe'er I bear myself
(As I perchance herafter shall think meet
To put an antic disposition on). . . .

[I. v. 170-72]

'Put on', like the Queen's 'cast off' and the King's 'throw to earth', implies 'putting on' garb of some sort. 'Putting on a costume' is a fair translation, since 'antic' (here in the sense of 'fantastic') is closely connected with the 'antic', the motley-clad buffoon or clown, and with 'antics' of the kind Hamlet himself has just been indulging in. The metaphor enters in a parenthesis, as an afterthought: he may 'perchance' at some later time—good evidence that he has not done so yet—'think meet' to assume a role that will conceal his real self. We cannot press a casual aside to mean that Hamlet is working up an elaborate counterplot, or that in the future every 'antic' gesture will be a piece of deliberate trickery. Hamlet has said that he *may* sometimes act queerly,

How strange or odd soe'er I bear myself . . .

[I. v. 70]

—which suggests not a plot but the way he had been behaving a few moments before. This tentative speech expresses Hamlet's growing recognition of how odd his behaviour must have seemed, and a vague realization of its usefulness. Like a good many actors Hamlet has had the experience of discovering that a piece of business he stumbled into went over surprisingly well.

Two examples from many will illustrate the subtle interrelation in later scenes between playing and melancholy, between 'antic' behaviour and 'tainting' of mind. In the first, Ophelia, 'affrighted', gives Polonius and the audience a preview of what Hamlet's 'antic disposition' may be like. The Hamlet who rushes in 'with his doublet all unbrac'd' has costumed himself for some role, though exactly what, it is hard to see. One thing is certain, Hamlet's appearance and gestures cannot be dismissed as 'fooling'. That 'look so piteous in purport / As if he had been loosed out of hell' is a look Hamlet must have had in all seriousness. In listening to the Ghost he had in effect been 'loosed from hell', and he had heard 'horrors' enough.

If he is acting, he is dramatizing his own terror, the state of a man shaken by thoughts beyond the mind's reach. Polonius as usual is wrong: this is not simply the 'ecstasy of love'. Hamlet's 'look' and 'sigh so piteous and profound' bring to mind many things—the Ghost and his response to it, the earlier 'tainting' of his imagination by his mother's unfaithfulness, Ophelia's coolness, the rottenness of Denmark and the 'perniciousness' of the King's action, and the half-formed notion of exploiting antic behaviour as a ruse. To see in Hamlet's appearance and gestures here or hereafter, where playing ends and melancholy begins, will require considerable discretion if we too are not

To cast beyond ourselves in our opinions. . . .

[II. i. 112]

The second example of the close bond between the two states (and metaphors) is Hamlet's first meeting with Rosencrantz and Guildenstern, where he displays much wit, the wit of one who plays the courtier, but not of one who is playing madness. 'Bad dreams', a symptom of melancholy, intrude when the conversation touches obliquely on Hamlet's concern that he may have to act the part of king and hero. He finishes off the silly argument about 'ambition' and 'shadows' neatly enough—

Then are our beggars bodies, and our monarchs
and outstretch'd heroes the beggars' shadows.

[II. ii. 263-64]

—but the joking conclusion is belied by his earlier horrified and reverent reaction to his father's 'warlike form'. Once Hamlet has pierced the pretences, the play-acting, of his 'excellent good friends', he launches into his second great speech of world weariness, in which the depth of his depression is measured by the splendour of his vision of the Dignity of Man: 'How noble in reason! how infinite in faculties!' As Hamlet progressively senses the gap between this ideal and the cruel necessity of the role imposed by 'King, father, royal Dane', the interplay in consciousness between the histrionic and the melancholy will continue. (pp. 288-90)

Hamlet's performance in the [scenes following the play] can be judged best in connection with another of the Ghost's warnings and the question it raises,

nor let thy soul contrive
Against thy mother aught. . . .

[I. v. 85-6]

How to play the avenger without the taint of cruelty, without loss of heroic balance? The boundary between acting and madness will prove to be even harder to maintain than before. The language of Hamlet's fresh resolves is worth attending to:

'Tis now the very witching time of night,
When churchyards yawn, and hell itself breathes out
Contagion to this world. Now could I drink hot blood,
And do such bitter business as the day
Would quake to look on. Soft! now to my mother!
O heart, lose not thy nature; let not ever
The soul of Nero enter this firm bosom.
Let me be cruel, not unnatural;
I will speak daggers to her, but use none.
My tongue and soul in this be hypocrites—
How in my words somever she be shent,
To give them seals never, my soul, consent!

[III. ii. 388-99]

The imagery goes back to the night-time fantasy and foulness, the 'contagion' associated with the late King's murder and the state of Denmark, and with Hamlet's first symptoms of melancholy. Ophelia's view seems momentarily justified: this might be the speech of someone 'blasted with ecstasy'. But it also is in key with Hamlet's melodramatic summons to the actor-murderer: 'Come, the croaking raven doth bellow for revenge' [III. ii. 253-54]. 'Now could I drink hot blood' is in the true 'raven-bellowing' vein of a revenger's tragedy.

The infection Hamlet suffers is more than rhetorical and histrionic, and with 'Soft! now to my mother!' the tragic tensions of his role become acute: 'O heart, lose not thy nature . . .' He is struggling to retain humanity with firmness of heart, to be a son, natural, just, and not cruel. The Roman analogy, which accentuates the irony of the part Hamlet is attempting to play, is to the point: he prays that he may not be a Nero, but as constant as the emperor's tutor, Seneca. Like Brutus and Othello, Hamlet would be the instrument of justice while committing murder or the emotional equivalent of murder. His solution is in character; he will make an 'act' of it, 'Speak daggers . . . but use none'. (pp. 297-98)

> Now might I do it pat, now he is praying;
> And now I'll do't.
>
> [III. iii. 73-4]

How easy this sounds, as if Hamlet were playing 'villainous' Edmund's part ('pat! he comes, like the catastrophe of the old comedy'). But the dramatic effect of the rest of Hamlet's speech is very different: this is not the talk of the active revenger he supposes himself to be. It *is* the talk of a man suffering an obscure 'taint' from the 'bitter business' he is forcing himself to do. As before, Hamlet is caught, not by any one defect or condition of his nature, not alone by thinking too 'precisely', nor by play-acting too much, nor by being melancholy sick—but by being Hamlet, the man who is trying to harmonize his many selves.

In the scene with his mother, Hamlet returns to the resolve of his soliloquy, to 'speak daggers . . . but use none'. The intention is half-betrayed by the thrust of his speeches:

> *Hamlet.* Now, mother, what's the matter?
> *Queen.* Hamlet, thou hast thy father much offended.
> *Hamlet.* Mother, you have my father much offended.
> *Queen.* Come, come, you answer with an idle tongue.
> *Hamlet.* Go, go, you question with a wicked tongue.
>
> [III. iv. 8-12]

> *Queen.*   Ay me, what act,
> That roars so loud and thunders in the index?
>
> [III. iv. 51-2]

> *Queen.*   O, speak to me no more!
> These words like daggers enter in mine ears.
> No more, sweet Hamlet!   [III. iv. 94-6]

We see, though with sympathy, that 'Hamlet from himself' is 'ta'en away', as he will explain his violence in the graveyard. Two great themes of the heroic tradition which are also two leading Shakespearian themes, are present in the dialogue of the scene—the hero's struggle to be 'like himself' and the closeness of the heroic to the monstrous. The struggle is more complicated for Hamlet than for Achilles or Aeneas, because like later heroes in fiction he finds it infinitely harder to decide which is his true self and to know when justice becomes sadism. (pp. 298-99)

With the entrance of Fortinbras comes the voice of action uncoloured by antic high spirits, the voice of the normal hero in Northern and Homeric epic:

> *Fortinbras.* Go, Captain, from me greet the Danish king . . .
> If that his Majesty would aught with us,
> We shall express our duty in his eye;
> And let him know so.
>
> [IV. iv. 1, 5-7]
> (p. 301)

Hamlet interprets Fortinbras' challenge in his own way, seeing in young Norway, as in Horatio, an alter ego, a true Prince, tender, not 'robust', but of a fine ('delicate') nature, inspired by 'divine' (glorious, heroic) 'ambition', a motive to which Hamlet is not a complete stranger. Like the ancient hero, Fortinbras goes to meet fate, danger, and death, 'Even for an eggshell'. Such is heroic greatness—or nobility—which Hamlet defines in terms fully understandable to his contemporaries:

> Rightly to be great
> Is not to stir without great argument,
> But greatly to find quarrel in a straw
> When honour's at the stake.
>
> [IV. iv. 53-6]

'But', instead of setting up the expected pair of opposites, introduces a further and more striking test of nobility: it is even greater to find the 'great argument' in the slightest loss of honour. Although, as Dr. Johnson says, this is 'the idea of a modern hero', the chivalric term 'honour' in this context is a fair translation for *timé*, the share of respect and material rewards due to the Homeric hero. Achilles would have had little difficulty in grasping what Hamlet means. The loss of Briseis was 'a straw' of the kind that a hero cannot ignore, because it symbolized a loss of heroic prestige. It is often said that the irony of 'straw' and 'eggshell' proves that the attitude of Hamlet and Shakespeare is mock heroic. But as Achilles proves, 'divine' heroism can include the high irony of acknowledging how slight and unsatisfying are the usual rewards of action. (p. 303)

Hamlet has had his vision of the heroic in its purer Achillean and Renaissance forms; but Shakespeare's grasp of character remains complexly true. As there had been no outright 'transformation' of the kind imagined by Polonius and Ophelia, or by the King and Queen, no 'bemonstering' such as seemed imminent in the scene between Hamlet and his mother, so there is no complete about-face from meditation to revenge. But there is increased clarity of vision, which makes Hamlet more rather than less tragic as he continues to feel the gap between his motive for action and the lethargy that 'lets all sleep'. Histrionics and 'thinking too precisely', symptoms of the disease he cannot shake, have betrayed him when he would be heroic 'scourge and minister'. (p. 304)

The transition to the final episode is made by a kind of theatrical pun, as Hamlet goes from his play-acting with Osric to 'playing with Laertes' in the fencing match. His cheerfulness is of the surface: 'But thou wouldst not think', he tells Horatio, 'how ill all's here about my heart' [V. ii. 212-13]. There is again the feeling of being borne along by fate:

> we defy augury; there's a special providence in
> the fall of a sparrow. If it be now, 'tis not to
> come; if it be not to come, it will be now; if
> it be not now, yet it will come: the readiness
> is all. Since no man knows aught of what he
> leaves, what is't to leave betimes? Let be.
>
> [V. ii. 219-24]

Here Hamlet approaches the style and pose of Brutus and Caesar in their Stoic meditations on fate and death.

His apology to Laertes before they start to fence, adds one more piece of evidence that Hamlet has not been wholly sane 'underneath' his odd behaviour. If in all his strange actions he had been deliberately deceiving others, his present excuse of 'madness' would be despicable. It is hard to think that Shakespeare would at this point in the play sacrifice a character for whom he has aroused so much sympathy, and whose death will be presented with dignity and tenderness. Hamlet is not always mad, he explains, but 'punish'd / With sore distraction'; and at times 'he's not himself', not Hamlet. The considerateness of tone and the noble generosity of the words, reminding us of Plutarch's 'gentle' and 'courteous' heroes, go naturally with the heart-sickness and the Stoic resignation of his conversation with Horatio. These are heroic attitudes—Plutarchan, Stoic, and Renaissance-Virgilian—that Hamlet can embrace, however hard he finds it to attain to the martial virtue of Graeco-Roman or Northern warrior-heroes.

Such is the hero who kills the King: a man with the imaginative understanding of the heroic role in its simpler and in its most sophisticated forms, a man given to moments of melancholy madness, but capable of dramatizing and foreseeing and occasionally effecting the necessary action, a man who will take with the resignation of a Stoic what the impulse of the moment brings: 'Prais'd be rashness!' With this passively active figure in mind, we can justify more easily Shakespeare's use of Elizabethan revenge-play clap-trap to end his tragedy: duels, poisoned swords, mistakes, hit-and-miss killings, and desperate acts of suicide. However little we may like this business—this is the way *Hamlet* ends. If we think of the outright vengeful heroes of Elizabethan drama, or of the decisive heroes of ancient epic and tragedy—an Achilles or a Turnus, an Orestes or an Electra—or of Chapman's morally 'composed' heroes, then Shakespeare's ending will not be at all what we want.

But Hamlet's inheritance is too inclusive and too complex for him to fit any single one of these well-defined roles. He is cursed with 'indirection' of many kinds, from a weakness for play-acting and over-nice speculation, to religious fears and inexplicable procrastination (caused in part by sexual revulsion), to troubling visions of the Renaissance moral hero and his ancient originals, Graeco-Roman and German. He is given to sudden melancholy impulses and over-dramatic gestures, but he is also capable of momentary perceptions of what it would be to act with full 'unity of being'. Hamlet's tragic complexity and pathos arise from this terrible openness to so many possible modes of thought, feeling, and action. In the gestures and words of the final scene, his various selves, concerns, and loyalties come to expression in flashes of poetic and theatrical power. (pp. 309-10)

In the early stages of the fencing match, Hamlet is very agile in speech and movement. When the Queen dies, he is still the alert if slightly stagey avenger:

> O villany! Ho! let the door be lock'd.
> Treachery! Seek it out.
>
> [V. ii. 311-12]

But when he discovers the foul practice of the King and Laertes, the actor comes again to the fore. The moment is one of high melodrama, and Hamlet plays up to it:

> Here, thou incestuous, murd'rous, damned Dane,
> Drink off this potion! Is thy union here?
> Follow my mother.
>
> [V. ii. 324-27]

The first line is in the style of 'Bloody, bawdy villain! / Remorseless, treacherous, lecherous, kindless villain!' But this time the act is as violent as the language: Hamlet has at last attained some kind of harmony between act and word. That the harmony is not very inclusive, and hardly satisfying to the total man, makes the moment more poignant. These are very much 'actions that a man might play' in a fit of passion, not the controlled deeds of one executing divine justice. Through rashness, not through deliberate action, Hamlet has reached his end.

His theatrical sense remains as strong as ever:

> You that look pale and tremble at this chance,
> That are but mutes or audience to this act . . .
>
> [V. ii. 334-35]

But Hamlet's concern is more than a desire to stage a handsome death-scene:

> Horatio, I am dead;
> Thou Liv'st; report me and my cause aright
> To the unsatisfied . . .
>
> O good Horatio, what a wounded name
> (Things standing thus unknown) shall live behind me!
>
> [V.ii. 338-40, 344-45]

Hamlet fears that his 'name' may be known only by the casual and ruthless impulses of the present scene, that he himself, his true 'cause' and 'story' will be 'unknown'. In these last speeches, which convey so well Hamlet's sense of the distance between the ideal and the actual, between what 'seems' and what 'is', he attains tragic and even heroic stature. (pp. 310-11)

The reply to Hamlet's request made by Horatio is consistent with his Brutus-like character of composed Roman hero: 'I am more an antique Roman than a Dane.' The line compactly symbolizes the conflict within the heroic tradition, between the plain soldier-hero ('Old Hamlet') and the consciously controlled moral hero, which has been a major source of Hamlet's suffering and failure. Hamlet too is more 'antique Roman' than 'Hamlet, the Dane'. But in his strangely 'mixed' nature primitive concern for personal glory and self-conscious Roman nobility are further modified by Christian attitudes:

> If thou didst ever hold me in thy heart,
> Absent thee from felicity awhile,
> And in this harsh world draw thy breath in pain,
> To tell my story.   [V. ii. 346-49]

'Felicity' lies not here but in death, which is not at all the view of the Homeric hero, for whom the after world is a grey unsatisfying substitute for the 'harsh world' of action. Hamlet's language is more like that of Chapman's Athena, or North's Brutus, who speaks of being rid 'of this miserable world' and living 'in another more glorious worlde'. 'The rest is silence'— which might mean for the heroes of Seneca a mere end—takes on another meaning when followed by Horatio's

> And flights of angels sing thee to thy rest!
>
> [V. ii. 360]

So saints ascend to their reward. The prayer and the hope it expresses introduce two more Christian notes into this final scene. Hamlet, like his author, is poised between ancient and modern worlds. (pp. 311-12)

Shakespeare was not writing an essay on the Renaissance man, but pursuing a question, which he explored dramatically through a particular temperament, one he knew very well, the player-poet. It is the actor's self that lends a special quality to the princely 'composition' of

> The courtier's, scholar's, soldier's, eye, tongue, sword . . .
>   [III. i. 151]

The distinguishing mark of the actor is to assume all men's parts and be nobody, to be carried outside himself in an 'ecstasy' of identification with someone else. Hence the actor's peculiar liability to the fear of not 'being himself'. For a man of this temperament to be burdened with the heroic aim of 'being like one's self', of maintaining firm consistency according to an ideal of noble action—whether old simple heroic or new complex moral-heroic—is past enduring. The praise of Fortinbras is restrained,

> Bear Hamlet like a soldier to the stage;
> For he was likely, had he been put on,
> To have prov'd most royally. . . .
>   [V. ii. 396-98]

He was potentially soldier and 'royal Dane', potentially capable of being the hero he dreamed of being, the soldier who would embrace the old martial and the new princely ideal of the courtier. There is an irony in Fortinbras' 'like', and in the suggestion that Hamlet's ultimate role will be played 'high' on the 'stage', when Horatio will tell his half-heroic story. The tragedy of Hamlet's life and death lies in the painfully experienced gap between seeming and being, a gap that the actor-playwright-poet would well understand.

Looking back to the heroic tragedy of Achilles and to its Renaissance reinterpretation in Chapman, North, and other translators, we may be able to define a little more exactly the kind of tragedy *Hamlet* is and is not. We have said that a character who faced clearly the conflicts implicit in the Renaissance version of the Homeric hero, would be tragic 'in the fullest sense'. 'The fullest sense' for European literature is defined, not by Aristotle, but by Sophocles in the unflinching but exhilarating recognitions of Oedipus and Antigone, of Ajax and Philoctetes. But there were conflicts within the heroic ideal before the age of Pericles or the age of Augustus, and before the Renaissance. Achilles in darker moments questions the simple heroic aims of his society, and he goes to revenge Patroclus with less satisfaction than we might expect. The usual heroic rewards seem increasingly petty as he lives out his *pathos,* and though the demand of absolute honour would seem to have been satisfied by the death of Hector, and though the will of Zeus has been fulfilled, Achilles' godlike self remains unsatisfied. In the vision he shares with Priam, heroic violence seems as unrewarding and destructive as it is inevitable. Greatness comes not from the deed, but from daring to face the terribleness of achievement. In Robert Frost's noble line, he finds

> that the utmost reward
> Of daring should be still to dare.

Beside the tragedy of Achilles,

> Tragedy wrought to the uttermost,

Hamlet's drama is incomplete, although his tragic disturbance of mind is much more extensive and vastly more complex. He is the most extreme example of Chapman's finely meditating Homeric hero, responsive to the claims of ancient and modern nobility, pagan and Christian. To be at once Achilles and the moral hero of the Virgilian and Christian traditions is beyond action and almost beyond expression. The hero faced with such

an aim, if he is a 'Hamlet', a player who enacts too vividly every demand of his imagined roles, cannot move through the cycle of passion and action to a clarifying vision. His last word—and Shakespeare's—is 'silence'. (pp. 314-16)

> *Reuben A. Brower, "Hamlet Hero," in his* Hero & Saint: Shakespeare and the Graeco-Roman Heroic Tradition, *Oxford University Press, New York, 1971, pp. 277-316.*

MAYNARD MACK, JR.   (essay date 1973)

[*Positing that* Hamlet *is more complex than* Richard II, *Mack compares Shakespeare's handling of the theme of regicide in the two plays.*]

Richard II and *Hamlet* are both plays about king killing. While the history play, however, leads steadily toward the death of the king, the tragedy moves steadily away from the death of one king and haltingly toward the death of another. *Richard II* reveals the conflict that leads to regicide; *Hamlet* uncovers layer by layer the effects of having killed the king and simultaneously shows the uneven path toward a new, different act of regicide under the label of revenge.

Hamlet, as we might expect, is uniformly more complex than *Richard II*. In place of one dead king, *Hamlet* shows two—old Hamlet and eventually Claudius—besides a dead prince. The opening confusion of conflicting, fiercely held, clearly articulated political claims in *Richard II* gives way in *Hamlet* to the more mysterious uneasiness of frightened guards confronted with a Ghost. (p. 75)

In the second scene of *Richard II* we are informed plainly of certain political facts; in the same scene of *Hamlet* we watch Claudius's virtuoso solo performance which accomplishes much business but as a whole only enhances our uncertainties concerning the Ghost. Instead of an emblematic garden scene summarizing the ideals underlying the confused race of historical events, *Hamlet* presents a troupe of players from England—actors acting—who for the most part only add to the pervading ambiguity despite Hamlet's confidence that a "play" is "the thing" to cut through this problem. The single prison soliloquy at Pomfret becomes in *Hamlet* four soliloquies and a long encounter in the graveyard. Richard's prison seems to symbolize the closing in on him of the forces of history, and perhaps also his solipsism, the imprisonment in his own image-making theatrical ego that has characterized him from the start. The graveyard in *Hamlet,* with its references to Caesar and Alexander and all sorts of ages and professions, may also intend this, but it makes us more conscious as well of the broader forces of mortality closing in, and at the same time of the omnipresence of Claudius as he and his court literally invade Denmark's boneyard.

Even to the extent that it shares elements of structure with *Richard II*—as in the close, where in both cases we have movement from meditation to violent death to continuing activities of state—*Hamlet* is more complicated, confused, and subtle. *Richard II* is a play enacted in the main against a background of clear political standards and ideals which cast a certain glow of irony on both the usurper and the king. *Hamlet* is a play of intricate tragic ironies where the background is never clear but where prince and king, especially the former, are granted moments of clairvoyance. Here, too, however, there is a middle ground of resemblance. In both plays, what clarity there is has to do with two opposing sorts of life-style:

one that is simpler, infinitely appealing, but no longer viable, especially in the area of kingship; the other complicated, shrewd, and ambiguous. In both plays, the hero manages a peculiar and limited reconciliation of the two—untidy, contingent, but splendid—through a painful growth of insight. But whereas much of the imaginative energy in the history play stems from what I have called a nostalgic vision of an English monarchy supported by the whole host of heaven and responding with Christian service and true chivalry, in *Hamlet,* although the Ghost's command ostensibly moves the plot, the imaginative center lies in the realm that in the preceding play is given to Bolingbroke, the mixed realm of "the indifferent children of the earth" [II. ii. 227]. The immense variety of an "unweeded garden" now replaces, as the focus of attention, the order of "this other Eden, demi-paradise." (pp. 75-6)

[The] Ghost's addresses to Hamlet have a drive and confidence that has been lacking in the language of the play before. He quickly reveals his demand—"Revenge his foul and most unnatural murder" [I. v. 25]—tells the story of his death, and vanishes with the instruction: "remember me" [I. v. 91]. Within the space of ninety lines, he has not only supplied the facts that have been so confusingly missing to this point, but has revealed his personality and values, besides adding (simply by his status as one returned from the dead) a mythic dimension to the meaning of the old king's death. Predictably, from Horatio's description in the first scene of the kind of man he was in life, the Ghost's views are extremely clear and firm. . . . [He] has a mind evidently used to making direct and rather unqualified projections from interior self to exterior reality. Thus he easily takes for granted in talking to his son that he is "thy dear father" (in this assessment he is right), and satisfies himself with a generalization, as we have just seen, that shrinks everyone involved in his story to a morality figure: Gertrude is equated with lust, Claudius with garbage, and the injured husband with "a radiant angel" (in at least the first of these simplifications he is wrong, as his own concern for Gertrude indicates). (pp. 80-2)

Since the elder Hamlet represents a world in which the boundaries of things—moral, psychological, and philosophical—are settled and rather clearly drawn, its similarities to Gaunt's world are obvious. Its major difference from his is, however, more important for our present purposes. In *Richard II* the stress falls on the idea of a king who is active in Christ's service and, as corollary to that, in the service of the nation; in *Hamlet* it falls on the philosophical or even psychological integration that causes and inspires wholesome action, rather than on the political acts and disciplines in themselves. Though it is a mistake, I think, to see *Hamlet* as merely a personal tragedy, the many critics who do so are right in arguing that the play focuses on peculiarly personal and psychic aspects of problems that Shakespeare elsewhere considers in other terms. (p. 83)

Nevertheless, in *Hamlet* an image of direct action, embodied primarily in the dead king and his dead and dying colleagues, does inform the play with a happy contrast to the muddled present. The overtones from medieval chivalry and from the classical Pantheon contrast with the "weary, stale, flat, and unprofitable" [I. ii. 133] quality of the present times under a "satyr" king; and the Edenic overtones of a period before time, or of a period when at least one could count on his "secure hour" [I. v. 61], contrast with the unweeded Elsinore of the play, where "Time qualifies" not only the spark and fire of love [IV. vii. 113] but everything.

To these contrasts Shakespeare has added one more that deeply humanizes the whole question of direct action—the contrast of father and son. The impact of this special emphasis is obvious from the proliferation in this century of psychoanalytic criticism. Though one suspects this new trend in criticism does not so much explain the special fascination of *Hamlet* as pay it tribute, the psychoanalysts do at least point to a profound reservoir of meanings and implications in the play's images of action as they involve the personal relationship between father and son. (p. 84)

I have mentioned that in every respect *Hamlet* is immensely more complex than *Richard II*. Nowhere is this clearer than in its vast array of "indifferent children of the earth" who fill the role that was assigned in *Richard II* primarily to Bolingbroke and Northumberland. In *Hamlet* the attitudes of Bolingbroke and Northumberland, treated in the earlier play within the limited frame of politics and especially kingship, leaf out to become a whole world of people, relationships, and actions that are as old as Adam and as new as Osric's fashionable modernisms, as socially exalted as the king and as lowly as the Gravedigger, as active as Hamlet (for by the lights of this world, Hamlet *is* active; it would never have occurred to Claudius to reproach Hamlet with delay!) and as passive as Ophelia. (p. 93)

Not only does the portrayal of multiplicity and variety replace what in *Richard II* was essentially a confrontation of an old and a new kind of power, but the killing of the king and his murderer's succession to his power is used as a means of exploring in detail aspects of life that have nothing to do with kingship. . . . [The] motto of everyone in this new world is that time modifies all intentions and changes all values and realities. Only Fortinbras and Horatio manage to escape it, and even the Ghost registers its reality—"O Hamlet, what a falling-off was there!" [I. v. 47]—though he, of course, opposes his own binding command "remember me" [I. v. 91] to this tendency toward degeneration and change.

Prominent among those for whom time qualifies all things are Rosencrantz and Guildenstern, contrasted with Horatio as Hamlet's schoolmates. His joy at first seeing them is obviously genuine—"My excellent good friends!" [II. ii. 224]—but he quickly senses that they, unlike Horatio, have changed with time. After this, he treats them as the tools they have become. Shakespeare's touch was sure in the creation of this pair. Their names (which vary a good deal in the early editions, as if no one could keep them straight, or cared to) perfectly suit the idea of busy little agents going cheerfully and ineffectively about the business of betrayal. Their lack of differentiation, to which Gertrude draws attention [II. ii. 34], renders their shallow frivolity unforgettable. It would be wrong to see them as villains. They are merely (in their own Broadway idiom) Fortune's "privates" [II. ii. 234]—witty, shallow, corrupt, and irrelevant. Having betrayed a friend, in time they are in turn betrayed—the pattern is a little demonstration of the complex ways in which time qualifies all in Denmark.

The creation of the Polonius family was another stroke of genius. Here the family relationship expresses ideally the similarity that exists underneath all variety among the indifferent children of the earth; their total annihilation exemplifies the fierceness of the struggle begun by old Hamlet's murder; and the father-child relationships within the family reverberate, as we have seen, throughout the play against other parent-child relations. Through the three members of the Polonius family, Shakespeare develops with care and variety the theme of Claudius's world, showing in several new ways how time qualifies all. At the same time, especially in the two men, another theme is introduced and developed: the question of what an action is in a world whose layers of deception and self-delusion make it unresponsive to actions either resolute or reckless. (pp. 93-5)

Claudius, while clearly not the cause or creator of all the indifferent children of the earth, is appropriately their king—their best and worst. Murderer of the old king, he is the epitome and the dynamic center of all the ambiguities, changes, and masks that now fill Elsinore. With him, the medieval dream of the prince who is a mirror of all knighthood has darkened into Machiavelli's prince who is a master of treasons, stratagems, and spoils: he has become the manipulator, the mask wearer, the stage manager. Polonius displays traces of this function but is too old, awkward, bumbling, and too much pleased with his own sagacity to be effective at it. Neither of his little plays managed from behind curtains (III. i and III. iv) turns out successfully. (p. 108)

In fact, Claudius himself is not so much an indifferent child of the earth like the others as he is (drawing on the same nonbiblical tradition Milton was to popularize) a fallen angel, who, though darkened, yet shines. His main characteristic is ambiguity. It is an ambiguity of which he is fully conscious, and in this respect he is unlike Bolingbroke. It is also an active ambiguity, and in this he differs from his victims. Ophelia and Laertes collaborate in ambiguous situations, but they do not make them. Claudius does. He is "creatively" ambiguous. Before the final duel at one moment—and only one—he sounds like a traditional uncomplicated villain.

> And, England, if my love thou hold'st at aught,—
> . . . .
> thou may'st not coldly set
> Our sovereign process; which imports at full,
> By letters conjuring to that effect,
> The present death of Hamlet. Do it, England;
> For like the hectic in my blood he rages,
> And thou must cure me.
>
> [IV. iii. 58-67]

But only when under extreme pressure from Hamlet, as here, does Claudius appear like the kind of man we would expect to have murdered old Hamlet. At other times, he sounds precisely like a proper king, in the vein of Gaunt, Richard, or his own older brother:

> do not fear our person;
> There's such divinity doth hedge a king,
> That treason can but peep to what it would,
> Acts little of his will.
>
> [IV. v. 123-26]

This is undercut, of course, by irony. No one knows better than Claudius just how inadequate "divinity" was to "hedge" the previous king. The same irony (in Claudius's mind and ours) pervades the comment of Rosencrantz and Guildenstern when they take up the king's view that Hamlet has become a personal danger to him.

> The cease of majesty
> Dies not alone, but like a gulf doth draw
> What's near it with it; it is a massy wheel,
> Fix'd on the summit of the highest mount,
> To whose huge spokes ten thousand lesser things
> Are mortised and adjoin'd; which, when it falls,
> Each small annexment, petty consequence,
> Attends the boisterous ruin. Never alone
> Did the king sigh, but with a general groan.
>
> [III. iii. 15-23]

And here the irony is sharpened by our suspicion that they speak only what they know Claudius wants to hear. Nevertheless, these traditional reverberations have the effect of adding to Claudius's dignity because he is in fact a king, and, in the course of the play, all the characters except Hamlet (and Horatio and Fortinbras, of course) do in some way come to "serve" him. (pp. 108-10)

If at one moment Claudius sounds like a villain, at another like a king, at still other moments he sounds like a wise observer with a broad awareness of the human condition.

> Not that I think you did not love your father,
> But that I know love is begun by time,
> And that I see, in passages of proof,
> Time qualifies the spark and fire of it.
> There lives within the very flame of love
> A kind of wick or snuff that will abate it;
> And nothing is at a like goodness still,
> For goodness, growing to a plurisy,
> Dies in his own too-much; that we would do
> We should do when we would; for this "would" changes,
> And hath abatements and delays as many
> As there are tongues, are hands, are accidents;
> And then this "should" is like a spendthrift sigh,
> That hurts by easing.
>
> [IV. vii. 110-23]

This is a remarkable passage. It offers an approach to life that could conceivably explain Claudius's earlier act of murder ("that we would do / We should do when we would") and it is also part of Claudius's seduction of Laertes. But there is more here. The idea that the "wick" or "snuff" in the very flame of love must kill it is an even bleaker image of human limitation than the Gravedigger's view of the "many pocky corpses" rotten before they die. For Claudius's image claims that time qualifies not from without but from within, from some internal dynamic or divisiveness inside love itself. These are hardly the typical views of a king-killing "over-reacher." The notion that goodness "Dies in his own too-much" might even be used to raise questions about Hamlet and old Hamlet, if, as appears, it may be stretched to imply that murder is not a moral outrage, since goodness destroys itself if it is not destroyed by something else.

This speech alone establishes Claudius's view of the world as fascinating and frightening. What he says about love has certainly been shown to be true in a play of hasty remarriage, betrayal of friends and loved ones, deceit, confusion, madness, death. Yet at the same time there is considerable evidence of his continuing affection for Gertrude even in this very scene.

> She's so conjunctive to my life and soul,
> That, as the star moves not but in his sphere,
> I could not but by her.
>
> [IV. vii. 14-16]

His star-imagery evokes the full weight of the traditional correspondences between man and the hierarchical universe to emphasize the quality and permanence of his love. Are we to suppose that there are more things in heaven and earth than are dreamt of in Claudius's conscious philosophy? or are we to assume that all this is put on for the benefit of Laertes? (pp. 110-12)

In the prayer scene, we . . . see Claudius torn by his double awareness of the nature of his deed and the standards he has ignored. . . . The constant problem of action and its ambiguous relationship to will reappears.

> Pray can I not,
> Though inclination be as sharp as will:
> My stronger guilt defeats my strong intent,
> And, like a man to double business bound,
> I stand in pause where I shall first begin,
> And both neglect.
>
> [III. iii. 38-43]

The mention of "double business" may just possibly recall the biblical warning that no man can serve two masters, but the main emphasis still is on the theme of action ending in inaction, which is also to prove to be the experience of the hero. Claudius's comments on the same problem link the two opposite characters in a common experience.

In this condition of confusion, Claudius longs for a simplicity that the other indifferent children of Elsinore (excepting Ophelia) never seem to miss:

> Is not there rain enough in the sweet heavens
> To wash [this cursed hand] white as snow?
>
> [III. iii. 45-6]
> (pp. 115-16)

Claudius also discovers that being a king involves more than merely killing a king and imitating a royal style. This may suffice for a while in Elsinore, but there is a bigger world:

> In the corrupted currents of this world
> Offence's gilded hand may shove by justice,
> And oft 'tis seen the wicked prize itself
> Buys out the law; but 'tis not so above;
> There, is no shuffling; there, the action lies
> In his true nature. . . .
>
> [III. iii. 57-62]

Pervasively a religious play, though in nontheological terms, *Hamlet* constantly expands, as here, the private story of Denmark's royal family to include all Denmark, all Europe, all this world, and adumbrations of another. The particular terms, however, in which Claudius puts his conception of a realm of clarity and directness opposed to the "gilded" ambiguity of this world are revealing, for once again the difference is seen in terms of action: "there, the action lies / In his true nature." Throughout the play, this intuition of direct action beckons elusively in the middle of all the acting, lies, masks, confusion, and change.

As usual, however, time qualifies. Claudius is soon back to playing the efficient king and loving uncle, grieved by Hamlet's rashness in killing Polonius. Indeed, after this scene in act III, he never again evinces this kind of dramatic internal awareness, but becomes increasingly villainous and crafty—if also increasingly weary—until the very end. His only moment of dramatic complexity in the last acts comes at the close when he warns his wife, "Gertrude, do not drink!" [V. ii. 290]. This moment will depend largely on staging for its effect. In the text, it is not clear whether Claudius could have done more to stop Gertrude or whether, as he says, "it is too late!" [V. ii. 292]. Having lost, or sacrificed, Gertrude, Claudius dies the villain, thinking only of his own defense ("Oh, yet defend me, friends; I am but hurt" [V. ii. 323], still trying to hide fatal realities under a mask of calming words.

It is in such a world—corrupt, wordy, changing, ambiguous— that Hamlet is ordered by the Ghost to "revenge his foul and most unnatural murder" [I. v. 25] by killing the king. Though Elsinore is still informed with faint recollections of direct action in the reported talk of a character like Fortinbras, and in brief glimpses of a simpler, clearer world like Norway's [I. i. 60-3] and Lamord's—nonetheless, the Ghost's command stands apart as if it were some timeless norm in an essentially time-bound atmosphere.

Hamlet, like Richard II, is caught between two opposed value systems, but his problem from the start is much more an internal, even psychic, one than Richard's. The emphasis has shifted inward, and now the problems are not armies, allies, finances, crusades, and castles so much as will, insight, guilt, self-control, and intention.

Hamlet's development through the play is characterized by fluctuations between brief glimpses of clarity and long periods of confusion. When he confronts Claudius in the council scene, he is keenly aware but resigned. He sees all the disparity between word and deed, intention and action, appearance and reality that life in Elsinore reveals, but he is unable to do anything about it. He is reduced to defending himself with the double meanings of words ("kin," "kind," "common," "seems"), which Claudius seems rightly to see as a threat: anyone who can play with words clearly threatens the king's house of words.

In the midst of such frustration and confusion, the Ghost shows Hamlet a way to clear action. Told of his father's murder, he enthusiastically embraces revenge. He vows, in effect, to give over his torturing awareness of the disparity between ideal and real in favor of a simpler view.

> And thy commandment all alone shall live
> Within the book and volume of my brain,
> Unmix'd with baser matter.
>
> [I. v. 102-04]

The last line seems to reflect the same desire for clarity and simplicity that Claudius shows in act III. (pp. 116-18)

In act IV, Shakespeare shows us for the last time the two extremes of Hamlet's temperament and in these two extremes the competing views of action and thought on which the play turns. Questioned by Claudius about the location of Polonius's body, Hamlet's words [IV. iii. 19-37] echo his earlier conversation with Rosencrantz and Guildenstern about kings and beggars [II. ii. 263-70], this time taking a literal approach that foreshadows the Gravedigger's and leads him to the same conclusion: "your fat king and your lean beggar is but variable service, two dishes, but to one table" [IV. iii. 22-4]. Here, Hamlet's wit is at its most strained and brittle, his antic disposition—though more necessary than ever before—at its most abrasive. Later, the stirring passage of Fortinbras's army, though not free of ambiguities . . . , effects a certain clearing of the air and tightening of nerves. Action remains possible if one is either resolute enough or insensitive enough (characteristically, the two conditions are as impossible to distinguish clearly in Hamlet's world as in our own) to pay its price: "My thoughts be bloody, or be nothing worth" [IV. iv. 66]. This is followed, in turn, by the letter that Horatio receives, with its account of an action undertaken *without* thinking too deeply on the event: "and in the grapple I boarded them" [IV. vi. 18-9]. We become anxious for the hero's return.

When we see Hamlet next, in the graveyard, all of the old terms reappear, but with a difference. For the first time, he is primarily the connoisseur of puns, not the punster. His meditation on Yorick's skull is quiet and controlled, a balanced mixture of affection ["a fellow of infinite jest, of most excellent fancy" V. i. 185] and disgust ["my gorge rises at it" V. i. 187] that we have not seen before. His tracing of Alexander to the stopper for a bunghole recalls all the previous references to the ways in which time qualifies, but shows a detachment that is new. (pp. 132-33)

In the last scene, Hamlet indirectly reveals the basis of his new confidence and command: "The interim is mine" [V. ii. 73]. There is occasion for action, but that occasion and action will be necessarily limited. Giving up his extreme desire for a total cure of Denmark's woes, Hamlet can discover the limited possibilities that are actually his. It is only by abandoning the letter of old Hamlet's command that he is able to accomplish the spirit. The point is not, of course, that he now has a simple solution to the ambiguities and corruption in Elsinore, but that he displays an attitude ready to accept what partial solutions become possible. (p. 133)

The unknown and the unanticipated lead to Hamlet's success and to his death. There is a splendid poetic aptness in his spontaneous double murder of Claudius. The thrust of the sword with which Hamlet cuts down the king brings to mind the heroic individualism of old Hamlet's defeat of the elder Fortinbras (though, appropriately, flexible foils have replaced the heavier weapons of the past). The poisoned cup, on the other hand, which Hamlet now forces on Claudius—death disguised as celebration—is thoroughly a product of Claudius's deceitful rule, a final dramatization of the way indirections can, and must, find directions out in the murky atmosphere of Elsinore. The Ghost's command has been done, though not as directly as he desired, and the villain has been "Hoist with his own petar" [III. iv. 207]. Both the world's call for revenge and evil's own tendency toward self-destruction are balanced in the symbolism of this double killing with sword and drink. (pp. 133-34)

Structurally, the whole of *Hamlet* can be seen as an expansion of the last scene of *Richard II:* the effects on a new king and his court of the death of the old king. But there the likeness ends. Certain questions are posed by *Richard II* that seem to cry out to be resolved in the following plays—most obviously, the question whether Bolingbroke is essentially protean or merely expedient, and the question whether his vigor and energy have any real relationship to Gaunt's conception of Christian service. To *Hamlet,* however, future events would add nothing. The story is complete and most of the characters are dead.

More important, the play is imaginatively complete. It has taken an action—the murder of a king—and has worked out the meanings and consequences of this action in complete detail. Furthermore, it has added to the study of regicide a different kind of king killing, a consequential revenge. Obviously, the "facts" of received Renaissance history would not have allowed Shakespeare to show vengeance being taken on Bolingbroke, had he wanted to. And though such speculation is always uncertain, it would appear that when Shakespeare wrote his second historical tetralogy, he was interested in a different kind of revenge for regicide, not personal and local, but political and historical. . . . In the Danish court, the religious, philosophic, political, familial, personal, and psychic dimensions of the initial murder and the immensely more complex reaction are all explored. What the story fails to show about one aspect, the poetry does show. The central questions of action, responsibility, motive, intention, will, consequences, roles, identities have all been raised, and with respect to gods,

kings, soldiers, courtiers, fathers, children, lovers, friends. *Hamlet* is almost bewilderingly complete. (pp. 135-36)

But no, or very few, answers are given. The overriding question, whether anything is "either good or bad, but thinking makes it so" or whether "foul deeds will rise, / Though all the earth o'erwhelm them, to men's eyes" [I. ii. 256-57] is left hanging. No very clear resolution is offered to the enigma of action, and indeed the end, with death in game and victory in defeat, merely complicates the matter. The question of human responsibility is raised but not settled. Above all, the most personal of questions, the one which underlies all religious, metaphysical, and moral problems, the question of conscience, is unresolved. Does conscience make cowards of us all or is it man's "chief good and market of his time"? [IV. iv. 34] Can it transform regicide into revenge? Who best understood the meaning of regicide, the Ghost with his call for revenge or the prince with his complicated response?

In the figure of its hero the play commends an imaginative flexibility that casts light on all the issues it encounters. Hamlet does very little, accomplishes successfully even less, but encounters imaginatively practically the whole range of possible experience. Unlike Richard II, who develops deep, internal awareness only under the pressure of suffering and external events, Hamlet displays this complex awareness from his opening pun on "kin" and "kind." His final development is not increased insight so much as a new sense of stability among old insights. He achieves a balance which, acknowledging that the readiness is all, can kill a king without committing the same overreaching crime that Claudius originally committed. In *Richard II*, killing the king meant the replacement of one conception of kingship with another, but, in *Hamlet,* killing the king exfoliates into action—action in all its meanings, public and private, physical and psychic, ranging from a secret murder to a mistaken stab through an arras, from a doubtful suicide to a public revenge. The dramatic growth of awareness that became a major aspect only in the last acts of *Richard II* occupies in *Hamlet* the whole play. (pp. 136-37)

    Maynard Mack, Jr., "The Name of Action," in his Killing the King: Three Studies in Shakespeare's Tragic Structure, *Yale University Press, 1973, pp. 75-137.*

BARBARA EVERETT   (essay date 1976)

[*Everett discusses* Hamlet *as a Time Play, or Time Tragedy. Her essay was originally presented as a speech at Stratford-upon-Avon in 1976.*]

'Why does Hamlet delay?' The question has been asked for over two hundred years now. And whether or not it is the best way to interrogate the play, it seems now a natural one. For after every new reading or performance, it's difficult to avoid that prickling, sympathetic and exasperated sensation which formulates itself as: '*Why* does Hamlet delay?' Whatever more correct form the enquiry takes, something to do with time does seem to be at the centre of *Hamlet:* which—to the extent that the play tells this kind of truth at all—makes the whole of life a great waiting game. (p. 117)

Why does Hamlet delay in revenging his father? Beyond a certain point, Hamlet didn't delay in revenging his father; because he didn't revenge his father. In the end he revenged only himself. The ghost is a presence that fades. And this fading of the Ghost is a part of the narrative of *Hamlet,* a play which offers such temporal changes and transformations as simply an aspect of the real that we know. The Ghost is first a royal presence coming to the waiting sentries; and then he is the great shadow of a loved father burdening the son with dread; and then a devil in the cellarage, friendly and bad; and finally a man in a dressing-gown whose wife cannot even see him. In the closet scene the Ghost stays just long enough to make us realise that we had almost forgotten him. After it, Hamlet Senior is neither present nor missed, and there is no word of him at the end of the play. The Ghost fades; and Hamlet comes into being, already a dead man. In the graveyard he says suddenly

> This is I,
> Hamlet the Dane   [V. i. 257-58]

taking on, *faute de mieux*, the royal title. Those who survive loss become the dead person; Hamlet ages onstage before us, slowing down into the tiredness of 'Let be'. The prince never does revenge his father; he does something more natural and perhaps more terrible, he becomes his father. He kills Claudius when he recognizes the similarity: 'I am dead, Horatio'. (p. 118)

The fading of the Ghost, the slow and yet sudden approach of Fortinbras—diminishing Hamlet, overtaking him—are equally the play's rendering of certain great natural and impersonal laws which the individual apprehends but hardly governs. They constitute the real form of the tragedy, that quality of elastic and problematic life which makes the work seem to shift in our hands, but to shift around a centre: the curve of its own plot. The process can be given many true names, but the play leads us unusually often to think of it in terms of the laws of time, and to call *Hamlet*, if we wish, a Time Play. A human experience of living impossibility, Hamlet's crux, can be paraphrased into a very old and frequently recurring philosophical conundrum. . . . Its earliest spokesman seems to have been the Heracleitus who said

> You cannot step twice into the same river; for
> other waters are ever flowing on to you. . . .

It is [this saying] of Heracleitus that is the best-known of his utterances: and what has made it, I think, so permanently available is the absoluteness of that 'You cannot' with which the phrase begins in English. The sentence makes a natural epigram for an experience of negation radical to human life, and does so the more believably for the lack of any doctrine. An outdated physics may do very well for wisdom. Shakespeare's tragedies are founded on this acquaintance with impossibilities, and *Hamlet* more than any. At every turning in it, in phrase and image and situation, we meet an inbuilt 'You cannot', a kind of wholly intrinsic 'No Road' sign. And these negations can't in the end be resolved into inhibition, some private trouble of Hamlet's: they are, like the sayings of Heracleitus, laws of nature, statements of human physics. (p. 119)

When we say *Time*, time stops. Dürer's remarkable engraving of that beautiful, wild-eyed Melancholia who is Hamlet's patron saint—a melancholia that is almost the Renaissance word for consciousness—has, up in the right-hand corner, an hourglass, and the sand is running, and yet also (because we look at it) is completely still. Shakespeare made of his revenge-plot something like the pictured hour-glass. He changed his resources to give father and son the same name, Hamlet old and young: or perhaps he took this brilliant device from the imputed early *Hamlet* of Kyd. . . . In Shakespeare's *Hamlet*, whether or not elsewhere, the revenge-plot becomes a mirror-image reversal from generation to generation: Hamlet is killed, Hamlet kills; the king is dead, long live the king. Behind *Hamlet*

lie the two interlocking cycles of the Histories, from weak Harry to strong Harry, from the son to the father, from the loser to the winner and so *da capo*. The plot of *Hamlet* is a résumé of the Histories, or of history, just as the play-within-the-play is a résumé of *Hamlet:* an inset which, by the mirror-image logic that governs the entire play, opens out at the heart of its curious individual fable into a grey vista of commonplace history:

> The great man down, you mark his favourite flies;
> The poor advanced makes friends of enemies.
>   [III. ii. 204-05]

The plot of *Hamlet* maintains this strange static fixity, as of an object balancing its mirrored image. From the opening to the play-scene Hamlet is Revenger, a mere function or shadow of that ghost-father whose appearances frame this half of the play. The dynamic centre of the tragedy lies at that point where Hamlet, with a gesture like that Milton was to give to the tempted Eve in *Paradise Lost* ('she plucked, she ate') waves his arm and impales on his sword—as a pig on a spit—the hapless Polonius. From that vital and ludicrous moment to the end of the play Hamlet is Revengee, an introverted virtual image, a shadow of a shadow. And by this passive and humiliating function he achieves his end, or what seemed the end when he began. . . . [To] any steady consciousness of the situation, the play stands still. 'Denmark is a prison'; the hourglass does not move. Everything in the court is a frozen shifting, an endless descent of sand: like the movement of that wonderfully distinguished speech in which Claudius sees the laws of his own and his kingdom's dissolution. In the kingdom of power and will,

> That we would do
> We should do when we would; for this *would* changes
> And hath abatements and delays as many
> As there are tongues, are hands, are accidents;
> And then this *should* is like a spendthrift's sigh
> That hurts by easing. But to the quick of the ulcer:
> Hamlet comes back; what would you undertake
> To show yourself indeed your father's son
> More than in words?   [IV. vii. 118-26]

In Claudius's dreamy transition, the only paternal bequest is the will to kill. 'Hamlet comes back' in time to this.

Hamlet comes back *in time*. Similarly, Claudius lives 'when we would'. He inhabits a moment of existence conceived by Shakespeare as the time of the politicians. (pp. 119-20)

It's easier than it once was—perhaps almost too easy—to turn that hour-glass, sixty years after the advent of Modernism, which showed that the convention of space in a painting comes to little more than the relation of one brush-stroke to another, and that time is after all only a dimension. . . . Drama, particularly when staged, has a peculiar *vraisemblance* that can make it seem sensible to talk, as several generations once did, of time-schemes, of calendars of days and weeks and months: so that one ought for instance to be able to prove that Hamlet's time is or is not 'enough', that he does or does not *delay*. But even drama, insofar as it is art, is a mental act, and therefore almost timeless, its running-time a metaphor for as long as we like. In Peele's *Old Wives' Tale* an old woman tells a story and its characters walk onstage and are the play. To ask 'When?' would be as misplaced as Laertes's characteristic 'Oh, where?' when he hears his sister's drowned. . . . Peele's work balances on a point somewhere between the aesthetic sophistication rediscovered in Modernism, and the simple crude fact that in England in 1590 no clock told the right time. (p. 121)

Shakespeare's plays time themselves, as country people did for many centuries, by the sun, and he starts up indoor clocks only as and when he pleases. . . . [In] the middle of *Twelfth Night* Olivia is with finality turned down by Viola. There is— one presumes—a sudden offstage bell-note and Olivia says 'The clock upbraids me with the waste of time'. The death of a fantasy, the pang of a real despised love, are a simple and hard slap in the face strong enough to start up a clock in Olivia's mind. The ghost of Hamlet's father enters at just such another stroke, 'The bell then beating *One!*'. And Hamlet himself says '*One!*' like an echo of the clock, as he gives his first blow to Laertes, to whom he has said 'I loved you ever' and who in response kills him.

The word *One,* used in this way, in fact occurs with weight a third time in *Hamlet.* At the beginning of the last scene, whose packed action so crystallizes into the ritual of the duel as to seem to stand still, to be timeless one might say, Hamlet absently reassures the anxious Horatio:

> It will be short: the interim is mine,
> And a man's life's no more than to say *One.*
>
> [V. ii. 73-4]

The phrase is definitive though enigmatic. Its resonance has something to do with those two other bell-notes to which it looks forward and back, the clock that strikes at the Ghost's entry and the call of the first blow struck in the duel. The three *One*'s hold together like a linked irregular chain, or like the echoes of a stone going down a deep place. The *One*'s can seem echoic in this way because the first of the sequence, the bell-note that brings in the Ghost, encourages the image, and is, moreover, itself an echo. The entry of the Ghost is an extraordinary dramatic event that helps to define something of what one might mean by calling *Hamlet* a Time Tragedy. . . . This first appearance of the Ghost is perhaps the most quietly startling moment in all Elizabethan drama. The Ghost brings to their feet the intent seated group of listening soldiers, shattering their circle as it interposes itself within Barnardo's very sentences. It brings its own ending to his unfinished story, a subject relegating his own unspoken object to nothingness: it leaves 'Marcellus and myself' suspended forever in the air, just as it will the next night dislocate Hamlet's life, leaving thirty years unfinished for always. The Ghost's effect is even more radical than this, more transforming and more philosophical: it alters the temporal dimension of the moment. The story that was begun has created on stage that rapt enclosure of the historic where all narratives take place, a security reflected in the lamplit circle of listeners. When the Ghost comes on, when the Ghost—unnoticed through the familiar conjurors' distraction of spell-binding anecdote—suddenly *is* on, that security is broken; narrative is drama and the past is present. Theatre and metaphysics come together: the *shadow* behind the soldiers is a true *ghost* because a real *actor,* just as later in the play the Players crowd onstage as 'the brief chronicles of the time', to deny that the past was ever anything but living. In this first scene of the play, time is a great continuum like an open stage. As Barnardo remembers, and the bell beats, and the Ghost comes and stands in the darkness, the present moment dissolves into a receding sequence of shadows, of haunted imagined nights all reaching back for their meaning to a time when 'the king that's dead' really lived. (pp. 122-23)

The first appearance of the Ghost is a brilliant stage moment, like a flash of lightning. It is, that is to say, only a moment, but it extends in the mind into concepts and reactions much wider-reaching, their outer limits being the boundaries of the play, which are perhaps the boundaries of human society itself. The moment is a definition, as of law. Barnardo has 'called back yesterday'; from now on, every hour struck in *Hamlet* is a passing-bell. History begins when the bell strikes *One,* and the prince's vocation is to give meaning to the clock, saying *One* until the Ghost is laid at last. For the play's hero is introduced to us as *Young Hamlet,* the child of the Ghost, and the first important thing that we learn about him is that he is, in his black garments, true to the darkness, and incapable of forgetting:

> Heaven and earth,
> Must I remember?
>
> [I. ii. 142-43]

The court of Denmark lives by daylight and survives by forgetting, its time-servers drifting on the present moment as Ophelia will on the brook that finally drags her down. In such a world, Hamlet's only freedom is to follow the Ghost; to be caught into that huge individual act of confronting Time which the play summarizes as memory, or delay: a death in life, but the life, also, of all human civility, and the source from which the prince derives his royalty. While he thus follows the Ghost, life becomes for him 'a time to die'. This is the impasse or crux on which Hamlet rests, and it makes of him a figure not unlike that image of Melancholy which I mentioned earlier, one created at a time when the mechanical clock and the sense of History were together beginning to master Europe. Benighted and moonlit, Dürer's powerful, winged but seated Melancholy lifts a heavy frowning head: and behind her head, next to the hour-glass, there hangs a bell, its rope drawn sideways and out of the picture, about to ring and never ringing. In just such a condition of pause, Hamlet is held: always potential and always too late. (p. 123)

> Barbara Everett, "'Hamlet': A Time To Die," in Shakespeare Survey: An Annual Survey of Shakespearian Study and Production, Vol. 30, *edited by Kenneth Muir, Cambridge University Press, 1977, pp. 117-23.*

INGA-STINA EWBANK (essay date 1977)

[*Ewbank focuses on the language of* Hamlet. *She reviews the way in which the characters of the play are "self-conscious speakers," able subtly to adapt, or "translate," their style of speech for a particular listener or effect. For additional commentary on Shakespeare's handling of language in* Hamlet, *see the excerpts by Samuel Taylor Coleridge (1813), Wolfgang H. Clemen (1951), Harry Levin (1959), and Reuben A. Brower (1971). Ewbank's essay was first published in* Shakespeare Survey *in 1977.*]

If the first law of literary and dramatic criticism is that the approach to a work should be determined by the nature of that work, then I take courage from the fact that *Hamlet* is a play in which, in scene after scene, fools tend to rush in where angels fear to tread. . . .

The area into which I propose to rush is the language of *Hamlet.* The method of entry is eclectic. . . . A recent book on Shakespeare's *Tragic Alphabet* speaks of the play being about 'a world where words and gestures have become largely meaningless', and even as long as twenty-five years ago an article on 'The Word in *Hamlet*' began by drawing attention to the

intensely critical, almost disillusionist, attitude of the play towards language itself'. Against these, I must confess a firm
(and perhaps old-fashioned) belief that *Hamlet*, the play, belongs not so much in No Man's as in Everyman's Land: that
it is a vision of the human condition realized in the whole
visual and verbal language of the theatre with such intensity
and gusto that from any point of view it becomes meaningless
to call that language meaningless; and that in the play as a
whole speech is something far more complex, with powers for
good and ill, than the 'words, words, words' of Hamlet's disillusionment. . . .

At the opening of act IV—or, as some would prefer to describe
it, at the close of the closet scene—Claudius pleads with Gertrude, whom he has found in considerable distress:

> There's matter in these sighs, these profound heaves,
> You must translate; 'tis fit we understand them.
>
> [IV. i. 1-2]

Of course he thinks he knows what the 'matter' is, for he also
immediately adds 'Where is your son?'. Gertrude has just been
through the most harrowing experience: Hamlet's words to her
have 'like daggers' entered into her 'ears' and turned her 'eyes
into [her] very soul' where she has gained such unspeakable
knowledge of her 'black and grained spots' as might well have
made her feel unable to comply with Claudius's request for a
'translation'. Indeed, in a modern play, where husbands and
wives tend to find that on the whole they don't speak the same
language, the shock of insight might well have led her to make
some statement of noncommunication. . . . In fact, of course,
Gertrude does the opposite. She provides a translation of the
preceding scene which manages to avoid saying anything about
herself but to describe Hamlet's madness, his killing of Polonius, and his treatment of the body. As so often in this play,
we have a retelling of an episode which we have already witnessed. And so we can see at once that Gertrude's translation
is a mixture of three kinds of components: first, of what really
happened and was said (including a direct quotation of Hamlet's cry 'a rat', though she doubles it and changes it from a
question to an exclamation); secondly, of what she thinks, or
would like to think, happened and was said. She is prepared
to read into Hamlet's behaviour such motivations, and to add
such details, as she would have liked to find. . . . Thirdly, but
most importantly, as it most controls both what she says and
how she says it, her translation consists of what she wants the
king to think did happen: that the scene demonstrated what
Hamlet in a doubly ironic figure of speech had told her not to
say, i.e. that he is 'essentially' mad and not 'mad in craft'.
Her emotion is released, and her verbal energy spends itself,
not on the part of the recent experience which concerns herself
most radically, but on convincing her husband that her son is

> Mad as the sea and wind, when both contend
> Which is the mightier.   [IV. i. 7-8]

Claudius may end the scene 'full of discord and dismay', but—
and this seems usually to be the most Gertrude can hope for—
things are not as bad as they might have been. (pp. 84-5)

In so far as anything in this play, so full of surprises at every
corner, is typical of the whole, the scene seems to me a model
for how language functions within much of the play: communicating by adapting words to thought and feeling, in a
process which involves strong awareness in the speaker of who
is being spoken to. Of course there has not been much truth
spoken and on that score, no doubt, the scene is a thematic
illustration of that dreaded pair of abstracts, Appearance and

Reality; and the author's attitude is 'disillusionist' enough. And
of course the scene in one sense speaks of non-communication
between husband and wife. . . . But, in its dramatic context,
the language does a great deal more than that. There is, as
Polonius has said, 'some more audience' in the theatre, and to
them—to us—the language speaks eloquently of the strange
complexities of human life, of motives and responses and the
re-alignment of relationships under stress. It speaks of Gertrude's desperate attempt to remain loyal to her son but also
(however misguidedly) to her husband and to his chief councillor. Ultimately the power of the words is Shakespeare's, not
Gertrude's, and it operates even through the total muteness of
Rosencrantz and Guildenstern who, like parcels, are, most
Stoppardlike, sent out and in and out again in the course of
the scene.

Claudius's verb for what he asks Gertrude to do is apter than
he knew himself: 'You must translate'. Presumably . . . he
simply wants her to interpret her signs of emotion in words,
to change a visual language into a verbal. But, as anyone knows
who has attempted translation in its now most commonly accepted sense, the processes involved in finding equivalents in
one language for the signs of another are far from simple.
There is a troublesome tension—indeed often an insoluble contradiction—between the demands of 'interpretation' and those
of 'change', between original meaning and meaningfulness in
another language. That Shakespeare was aware of this—although, unlike many of his fellow poets and dramatists, he
was apparently not an inter-lingual translator—is suggested, in
the first place, by the various ways in which he uses the word
'translate' in his plays. Alexander Schmidt's *Shakespeare-Lex-
icon* separates three clearly defined meanings: 1. to transform
or to change, as Bottom is 'translated', or as beauty is *not*
translated into honesty in the nunnery scene; 2. 'to render into
another language (or rather to change by rendering into another
language)', as Falstaff translates Mistress Ford's inclinations
'out of honesty into English' . . . ; and 3. to interpret or explain, as in the Claudius line I have been discussing, or as
Aeneas has translated Troilus to Ulysses. . . . [As] the examples I have given indicate, meanings seem to overlap within
Shakespeare's uses of the word—so that all three hover around
the following lines from Sonnet 96:

> So are those errors that in thee are seen
> To truths translated and for true things deem'd.

That sonnet is in a sense about the problem of finding a language for the 'grace and faults' of the beloved—a problem
which haunts many of the Sonnets and can be solved, the poems
show, only by fusing change and interpretation into a single
poetic act. In much the same way, *Hamlet* is dominated by the
hero's search for a way to translate (though Shakespeare does
not use the word here) the contradictory demands of the Ghost:

> If thou hast nature in thee, bear it not;
>
> . . . .
>
> But, howsomever thou pursuest this act,
> Taint not thy mind. . . .   [I. v. 81, 84-5]
>
>   (pp. 85-7)

George Steiner, in *After Babel*, maintains that '*inside or between languages, human communication equals translation*'.
Hamlet, I think, bears out the truth of this. Hamlet himself is
throughout the play trying to find a language to express himself
through, as well as languages to speak to others in; and round
him—against him and for him—the members of the court of
Elsinore are engaging in acts of translation. The first meeting

with Rosencrantz and Guildenstern, in II, ii, would be a specific example of this general statement. . . . [The] verbal hide-and-seek of the whole episode turns what might have been a simple spy/counterspy scene into a complex study of people trying to control each other by words. Here, and elsewhere in the play, the mystery of human intercourse is enacted and the power of words demonstrated: what we say, and by saying do, to each other, creating and destroying as we go along. (p. 87)

Words govern the action of the play, from the ironical watch-word—'Long live the King!'—which allays Francisco's fears at the opening, to Hamlet's 'dying voice' which gives the throne of Denmark to Fortinbras at the end; and, beyond, to the speech which will be given by Horatio when it is all over, explaining 'to th'yet unknowing world / How these things came about'. Words control the fates and the development of the characters, and not only when they are spoken by the Ghost to Hamlet and turned by him into a principle of action ['Now to my word', I. v. 110]. Words can open Gertrude's eyes, help to drive Ophelia mad, unpack Hamlet's heart (however much he regrets it); and if Claudius finds that 'words without thoughts never to heaven go' [III. iii. 98], this merely validates those words which have thoughts. Sometimes the words deceive, sometimes they say what is felt and meant, sometimes they are inadequate—but the inadequacy reflects on the speaker rather than the language. (pp. 87-8)

Language is being stretched and re-shaped to show the form and pressure of the *Hamlet* world. The extraordinary variety of language modes is important, too: we move, between scenes or within a scene or even with a speech, from moments of high elaboration and formality to moments of what Yeats would have called 'walking naked', where speech is what the Sonnets call 'true and plain' and we call 'naturalistic'. (pp. 88-9)

In *Hamlet*, unlike *King Lear*, seeing is rarely enough. Ophelia's lament at the end of the nunnery scene—

O, woe is me
T' have seen what I have seen, see what I see!—
[III. i. 160-61]

follows upon an unusually (for her) eloquent analysis of both what she has seen and what she is seeing ('O, what a noble mind is here o'er-thrown!'); and Gertrude, we know, soon finds words to translate into words her exclamation, 'Ah, mine own lord, what have I seen tonight!' Often seeing has to be achieved through hearing. 'You go not till I set you up a glass', Hamlet tells his mother, but that 'glass' is not so much 'the counterfeit presentment of two brothers' as Hamlet's speech on Gertrude's lack of 'eyes'. . . . One begins to feel that the ear is the main sense organ in *Hamlet*, and concordances confirm that the word 'ear' occurs in this play more times than in any other of Shakespeare's. Through the ear—'attent', or 'knowing'—comes the understanding which Claudius asks Gertrude for in IV, i; but through the 'too credent' or 'foolish' ear come deception and corruption. Claudius seems obsessed with a sense of Laertes's ear being infected 'with pestilent speeches' while he himself is being arraigned 'in ear and ear' [IV. v. 91-4]. Well he might be, for in the Ghost's speech all of Denmark had, as in a Bosch vision, been contracted into a single ear:

so the whole ear of Denmark
Is by a forged process of my death
Rankly abus'd;
[I. v. 36-8]

and the ironic source and sounding-board of all these images is of course the literal poisoning by ear on which the plot of the play rests. (p. 89)

[The characters] take a conscious and delighted interest in the idiosyncrasies of individual and national idioms, in how people speak, as Polonius says, 'according to the phrase and the addition / Of man and country' [II. i. 47-8]. Hamlet's parodies of spoken and written styles are outstanding, but Polonius—in instructing Reynaldo—is just as good at imitating potential conversations. Seen from our point of view or the characters', the play is alive with interest in how people react to each other and to each other's language.

Like Claudius, in the scene from which I began, the characters, when they urge each other to speak, expect to understand the 'matter', or meaning, of what is said. Hence they are particularly disturbed by the apparent meaninglessness of 'antic' speech—'I have nothing with this answer, Hamlet; these words are not mine', is Claudius's sharpest and most direct rebuke to his nephew/son [III. ii. 96-7]—and by the dim apprehension, again expressed by Claudius, after overhearing the nunnery scene, that the lack of 'form' in such speech may conceal 'something' [III. i. 164ff]. (pp. 89-90)

We have returned to the idea of translation, for in their intercourse the characters seem unusually aware of their interlocutors' tendency to 'botch the words up fit to their own thoughts'. One main aspect of this is the belief, demonstrated throughout the play, in the importance of finding the right language for the right person. The opening scene is a model of this. Horatio had been brought in as a translator ('Thou art a scholar; speak to it, Horatio') but, though the Ghost's first appearance turns him from scepticism to 'fear and wonder', he is unsure of his language. His vocabulary is wrong: 'What art thou that usurp'st [a particularly unfortunate verb in the circumstances] this time of night . . .?' and so is his tone: 'By heaven I charge thee, speak!'. On the Ghost's second appearance, Horatio's litany of appeals—'If . . . Speak to me'—more nearly approaches the ceremony which befits a king. . . . Time in the form of a cock's crow interrupts any possible interchange. A 'show of violence' signals the hopeless defeat of verbal communication. Horatio now knows that none but Hamlet can find the language needed, and so the scene ends with the decision to 'impart what we have seen tonight / Unto young Hamlet', for:

This spirit, dumb to us, will speak to him.
[I. i. 171]

But the gap between speakers which—they are aware—must be bridged by translation is not always as wide as the grave. The king appeals to Rosencrantz and Guildenstern as being on the same side of the generation gap as Hamlet—

being of so young days brought up with him,
And sith so neighboured to his youth and haviour—
[II. ii. 11-2]

which should give them a language 'to gather, / So much as from occasion you may glean'; and Hamlet conjures them to tell the truth 'by the consonancy of our youth' [II. ii. 284-85]. When the opening of the closet scene has demonstrated that Gertrude's language and her son's are in diametrical opposition—

Hamlet, thou hast thy father much offended.
Mother, you have my father much offended.—
[III. iv. 9-10]

and that he will not adopt the language of a son to a mother ('Have you forgot me?') but insists on a vocabulary and syntax which ram home the confusion in the state of Denmark—

No, by the rood, not so:
You are the Queen, your husband's brother's wife.

And—would it were not so!—you are my mother—

[III. iv. 14-16]

then Getrude can see no other way out of the deadlock but to call for translators:

Nay then, I'll set those to you that can speak.

[III. iv. 17]

Hamlet's refusal to be thus translated is what leads to Polonius's death. Polonius spends much energy, in his last few days of life, on finding a language for a madman, trying—as in II, ii—at the same time to humour and to analyse Hamlet. But Rosencrantz and Guildenstern are perhaps even more supremely aware of the necessity of different languages for different persons. They take their colour, their style, tone and imagery, from their interlocutors, whether it is a question of speaking the snappy, quibbling dialogue of clever young students with Hamlet on first meeting him, or enlarging before Claudius on the idea of 'the cease of majesty' so that it becomes an extended image of 'a massy wheel, / Fixed on the summit of the highest mount' [III. iii. 17 ff]. (pp. 90-1)

The characters of the play, then, are on the whole very self-conscious speakers, in a way which involves consciousness of others: they believe in the word and its powers, but they are also aware of the necessity so to translate intentions and experiences into words as to make them meaningful to the interlocutor. And not only vaguely meaningful: they know the effect they want to produce and take careful steps to achieve it. (p. 91)

[Claudius's speech in Act I, scene 2] establishes him as a very clever chairman of the board. First he gets the minutes of past proceedings accepted without query, by a carefully arranged structure of oxymorons:

Therefore our sometime sister, now our queen,
Th'imperial jointress to this warlike state,
Have we, as 'twere with a defeated joy,
With an auspicious and a dropping eye,
With mirth in funeral, and with dirge in marriage,
In equal scale weighing delight and dole,
Taken to wife.   [I. ii. 8-14]

The oxymorons, in a relentless series of pairings, operate to cancel each other out, smoothing over the embarrassment (or worse) involved in 'our sometime sister, now our queen', stilling criticism and enforcing acceptance of the apparent logic of the argument, so that by the time we finally get to the verb ('Taken to wife') the 'Therefore' seems legitimate. . . . He intends to deal with Hamlet, too, through the technique of dissolving contradictions—

But now, my cousin Hamlet, and my son—

[I. ii. 64]

but his briskness here comes to grief, as Hamlet becomes the first to raise a voice, albeit in an aside, which punctures such use of language:

A little more than kin, and less than kind.

[I. ii. 65]

Intrepidly, Claudius continues in an image suggesting the tone of decorous grief which ought to be adopted—'How is it that the clouds still hang on you?'—but this again founders on Hamlet's pun on sun/son. The pun, according to Sigurd Burckhardt in *Shakespearean Meanings*, 'gives the lie direct to the social convention which is language. . . . It denies the mean-

ingfulness of words.' But in their dramatic context here, Hamlet's puns do no such thing: they deny the logic and sincerity and meaningfulness of Claudius's words but suggest that there is a language elsewhere.

The rest of the scene, until it closes on Hamlet's decision to 'hold my tongue', is a series of contrasts and clashes between different languages. Hamlet's 'common' is not the queen's and implies a far-reaching criticism of hers. Gertrude's reply suggests that she is not aware of the difference, Claudius's that he is trying to pretend that he is not, as he follows Hamlet's terrible outburst against seeming with an, in its way, equally terrible refusal to acknowledge any jar:

'Tis sweet and commendable in your nature, Hamlet,
To give these mourning duties to your father.

[I. ii. 87-8]

Hamlet has no reply to Claudius's appeal to the 'common theme' of death of fathers, nor to the request that he give up Wittenberg for 'the cheer and comfort of our eye'; his reply, promising to 'obey', is made to his mother. But it is Claudius who comments on it as 'loving' and 'fair', and it is he who sums up the conversation, translating the tense scene just past into an image of domestic and national harmony—

This gentle and unforc'd account of Hamlet
Sits smiling to my heart—   [I. ii. 123-24]

and an excuse for a 'wassail'. The incongruity is as if a satire and a masque by Jonson were being simultaneously performed on the same stage. (pp. 92-3)

The different languages spoken in a scene like this clearly add up to a kind of moral map. That is, the adding up is clear, the map itself not necessarily so. It is not just a matter of Hamlet's words being sincere and Claudius's not. In the dialogue Hamlet is striving for effect in his way just as much as Claudius in his. And Claudius is soon going to be sincere enough, when we learn from his own mouth, in an image that could well have been used by Hamlet, that he is aware of the ugliness of his deed as against his 'most painted word' [III. i. 48-52] and that his words are unable to rise in prayer [III. iii. 36 ff.]. Morality and sensitivity to language are peculiarly tied up with each other in this play; and in trying to think how they are related I, at least, am driven back to James and 'The Question of Our Speech': to the importance of 'The way we say a thing, or fail to say it, fail to learn to say it'. In a play peopled by translators, it is in the end the range of languages available to each character—those they 'fail to learn' as well as those they speak—which measures their moral stature. Both Claudius and Gertrude at various times have their consciences stung, but neither seems able to find a language for his or her own inner self. (p. 93)

Hamlet's own language is in many ways that of Elsinore. As others, notably R. A. Foakes, have pointed out, his speech modes and habits are largely those of the court: wordiness, formality, sententiousness, fondness of puns and other forms of word-play, etc. He too uses language in all the ways practised by Claudius and his entourage: for persuasion, diplomacy, deception, and so on. His sheer range, which is as large almost as that of the play itself, has made it difficult for critics to define his own linguistic and stylistic attributes. . . . [We] still need a way of talking about Hamlet's language which includes his uncontrolled and (surely) revealing moments, such as the nunnery scene or the leaping into Ophelia's grave, as well as his moments of deliberately antic disposition; and the simple statements in the dialogues with Horatio as well as the tortuous questioning in the monologues. It might be helpful, then, to think of Hamlet as the most sensitive translator in the play: as the one who has the keenest sense both of the expressive and the persuasive powers of words, and also and more radically the keenest sense both of the limitations and the possibilities of words. (p. 94)

No other Shakespearian hero, tragic or comic, has to face so many situations in which different speakers have different palpable designs on him, and where he so has to get hold of the verbal initiative. No other hero, not even Falstaff or Benedick, is so good at grasping the initiative, leading his interlocutor by the nose while—as with Polonius and Osric—playing with the very shape and temperature of reality. Many of the play's comic effects stem from this activity, and the strange tonal mixture of the graveyard scene has much to do with Hamlet, for once, almost playing the stooge to the indomitable wit of the First Gravedigger. No other Shakespearian hero is so good at running his antagonists right down to their basic premises and striking them dumb, as with Rosencrantz and Guildenstern in the recorder scene. . . .

But, unlike many other Shakespearian tragic heroes, Hamlet also listens in a more reflective way—listens and evaluates, as Othello does not (but Hamlet surely would have done) with Iago. In some situations we begin to feel that his linguistic flexibility is founded on a sympathetic imagination. In him, alone in the play, the ability to speak different languages to different people seems to stem from an awareness that, in George Eliot's words, another being may have 'an equivalent centre of self, whence the lights and shadows must always fall with a certain difference'. Other characters meet to plot or to remonstrate, or they step aside for an odd twitch of conscience. To Hamlet, conversations may become extensions of moral sympathy. (p. 95)

Yet by the same measurement there is only a hair's breadth between moral sympathy and callousness, and *Hamlet* shows this too. Hamlet's awareness of others as autonomous beings with 'causes', and accordingly with languages, of their own also helps to explain why he despises Rosencrantz and Guildenstern so, and can so unflinchingly let them 'go to't', re-counting his dealings with them as 'not near my conscience' only a few lines before he speaks to Horatio of his regret for what he did and said to Laertes. To him they lack any 'centre of self'; they are instruments used to turn others into 'unworthy' things [III. ii. 363]; they are sponges whose only function is to be 'at each ear a hearer' [II. ii. 382]. Hamlet's sympathetic imagination falls far short of Stoppard's, and of Christian charity. The killing of Polonius, whom he sees only as an over-hearer and a mouthpiece, affects him no more than a putting-down in verbal repartee:

> Take thy fortune;
> Thou find'st that to be busy is some danger.
>   [III. iv. 32-3]
>   (p. 96)

[It] is in his dealings with Ophelia—which is as much as to say his language to Ophelia—that Hamlet most shows the destructive powers of speech. His vision of the world as 'an unweeded garden' ultimately drives Ophelia to her death, wearing the 'coronet weeds' of her madness. . . . [The] Hamlet-Ophelia relationship reveals something essential to Hamlet's and his creator's vision of the power of words; and also that it illuminates the way in which Hamlet contracts what Kenneth

Muir has called 'the occupational disease of avengers'—how he is tainted by the world in which he is trying to take revenge. (pp. 97-8)

Hamlet's vision of Ophelia has changed with his vision of the world. The language to be spoken to her is that current in a world where frailty is the name of woman, love equals appetite, vows are 'as false as dicers' oaths' [III. iv. 45], and nothing is constant. It is a terrible coincidence, and a masterly dramatic stroke, that before Hamlet and Ophelia meet within this vision, Laertes and Polonius have been speaking the same language to her, articulating out of their worldly wisdom much the same view of their love as the one Hamlet has arrived at through his shock of revulsion from the world. In I, iii, while Hamlet offstage goes to meet the Ghost, Ophelia meets with equally shattering (to her world) commands from her father, attacking her past, present and future relations with Hamlet. (p. 98)

Polonius's method is particularly undermining in that he lets Ophelia provide the keywords which he then picks up and translates by devaluing them—painfully literally so when Ophelia's 'many tenders / Of his affection' provokes:

> . . . think yourself a baby
> That you have ta'en these tenders for true pay
> Which are not sterling.   [I. iii. 105-07]

His translation is partly a matter of devaluation by direct sneer ('think' and 'fashion' are thus dealt with), partly a matter of using the ambiguities of the English language to shift the meanings of words (thus 'tender' is translated into the language of finance and 'entreatment' into that of diplomacy); and partly a dizzying matter of making one meaning slide into another by a pun. In this last way Hamlet's vows are translated, first into finance, then into religion—

> Do not believe his vows; for they are brokers,
> Not of that dye which their investments show,
> But mere implorators of unholy suits,
> Breathing like sanctified and pious bonds—
>   [I. iii. 127-30]

but always in proof of their falsehood: 'The better to beguile'. What supplies the power of Polonius's words is also a logic which, like Iago's, strikes at the root of the victim's hold on reality:

> You do not understand yourself so clearly
> As it behoves my daughter and your honour;
>   [I. iii. 96-7]

and which has a kind of general empirical truth—such as in the comedies might have been spoken by a sensible and normative heroine:

>   I do know,
> When the blood burns, how prodigal the soul
> Lends the tongue vows.   [I. iii. 115-17]

By the end of the scene, Polonius's words have left Ophelia with no hold on her love and with nothing to say but 'I shall obey, my lord'. When there is no one left even to obey, she will go to pieces. But before then she has to be pushed to the limit by Hamlet's verbal brutality which doubly frightens and hurts her because it seems to prove both that Hamlet is mad and that Polonius was right. . . . The two of them are speaking *about* each other, Hamlet's stream-of-consciousness circling around nuns and painted harlots and Ophelia appealing, twice, to an invisible and silent audience: 'O, help him, you sweet heavens!' and 'O heavenly powers, restore him!' (pp. 99-100)

Hamlet and Ophelia no longer speak the same language. I dwelt at some length on the Polonius-Ophelia scene because it brings out, ironically and indirectly, an important aspect of the 'tainting' of Hamlet. Though he does not know it, and would hate to be told so, his language has moved away from Ophelia's and towards Polonius's. It is a language based on the general idea of 'woman' rather than a specific awareness of Ophelia (to whom he now listens only to score verbal points off her, usually bawdy ones, too). Even his technique is like Polonius's as he picks up words only to demolish them, and her. Thus, in perhaps the cruellest stretch of dialogue in the whole play, Ophelia is allowed, briefly, to think that she knows what Hamlet means, only to have this understanding taken from her:

> *Hamlet*. . . . I did love you once.
> *Ophelia*. Indeed, my lord, you made me believe so.
> *Hamlet*. You should not have believ'd me; for virtue cannot so inoculate our old stock but we shall relish of it. I loved you not.
> *Ophelia*. I was the more deceived.
>
>   [III. i. 114-19]

Polonius turned her into an object, an instrument, by 'loosing' her to Hamlet in the nunnery scene; Hamlet turns her into a thing—as 'unworthy a thing' as he ever may accuse Rosencrantz and Guildenstern of attempting to make out of him—in the play scene where, in public and listening to a play which from her point of view must seem to be mainly about women's inconstancy and sexual promiscuity, she is all but sexually assaulted by Hamlet's language. (p. 100)

So we seem in the end to be left with a long row of contradictions: Hamlet's use of language is sensitive and brutal; he listens and he does not listen; his speech is built on sympathy and on total disregard of other selves; his relationship with words is his greatest strength and his greatest weakness. Only a Claudius could pretend that these are not contradictions and only he could translate them into a simple unity. Hamlet's soliloquies are not much help to this end. Even they speak different languages and add up, if anything, to a representation of a man searching for a language for the experiences which are forcing themselves upon him, finding it now in the free flow of I-centered exclamations of 'O, that this too too solid flesh would melt', now in the formally structured and altogether generalized questions and statements of 'To be, or not to be'. It is tempting to hear in Hamlet's self-analytical speeches a progression towards clarity, reaching its goal in the fusion of the individual and the general, of simple form and complex thought, in the speech about defying augury—

> If it be now, 'tis not to come; if it be not to come, it will be now; if it be not now, yet it will come—the readiness is all—
>
>   [V. ii. 220-22]

and coming to rest on 'Let be'. It is tempting because many Jacobean tragic heroes and heroines were to go through such a progression, through tortured and verbally elaborate attempts at definition of their vision of life to simple statements of—as in Herbert's poem 'Prayer'—'something understood'. But to me this seems too smooth a curve, too cathartic a movement, more indicative of critics' need to experience the peace which Hamlet himself happily appears to gain at the end than of the true impact of the language of the play as a whole. That impact is surely much closer to the sense that for a complex personality in an impossible situation—and in 'situation' I include a number of difficult human relationships—there is no single language. This does not mean that the play ultimately sees speech as meaningless, or that Shakespeare (or even Hamlet) is finally trapped in a disillusionist attitude to language. It means that we are given a very wide demonstration of the power of words to express and communicate—it is, after all, words which tell Horatio and us even that 'the rest is silence'—but also, and at the same time, an intimation that there is something inexpressible and incommunicable at the heart of the play. (pp. 100-01)

To me the final greatness of the play lies just there: in its power to express so much and yet also to call a halt on the edge of the inexpressible where, to misquote Claudius, we must learn to say ''Tis fit we do not understand'. This, I think, is the hallmark of Shakespeare as a translator, into tragedy, of the human condition. (p. 101)

Inga-Stina Ewbank, "'Hamlet' and the Power of Words, in Aspects of Hamlet: Articles Reprinted from "Shakespeare Survey," *edited by Kenneth Muir and Stanley Wells, Cambridge University Press, 1979, pp. 84-101.*

ADDITIONAL BIBLIOGRAPHY

Adams, Joseph Quincy. "Joyous Comedies; *Hamlet*." In his *A Life of William Shakespeare*, pp. 289-314. Boston: Houghton Mifflin Co., 1923.
  Traces the history of the quarto and folio editions of *Hamlet* and offers explanations for the differences between them.

Aldus, P. J. *Mousetrap: Structure and Meaning in "Hamlet"*. Toronto: University of Toronto Press, 1977, 235 p.
  An interpretation of *Hamlet* as a literary myth, with a meticulous examination of the verbal and structural detail. Aldus interprets Hamlet as a mythic representative of humankind, and he identifies the supporting characters as different aspects of Hamlet's psyche. Aldus finds that Hamlet is driven by sexual obsession that causes him to direct the Mousetrap at Gertrude rather than Claudius. Aldus concludes that Hamlet "is beyond ordinary conception, one figure whose 'hallucinations', never cancelling each other, create the obsessed, mad Hamlet who bears all of the desolations that destroy man."

Alexander, Nigel. *Poison, Play, and Duel*. Lincoln, Neb.: University of Nebraska Press, 1971, 212 p.
  Contends that Hamlet's dilemma is caused by a dual problem: he must combat the evil that surrounds him and control the violence within himself. Alexander also examines the dramatic purpose of the ghost and explains that it accentuates "the division within Hamlet's mind and will."

Alexander, Peter. *Hamlet: Father and Son*. London: Oxford at the Clarendon Press, 1955, 189 p.
  Describes Hamlet as a blend of opposites whose ability to reconcile "heroic passion" and "meditative wisdom" reveals his tragic greatness. Alexander's theories present important interpretations concerning criticism of both *Hamlet* and the nature of tragedy in general.

Altick, Richard D. "*Hamlet* and the Odor of Mortality." *Shakespeare Quarterly* V (1954): 167-76.
  Describes the imagery of physical corruption in the play and concludes that "the sense of evil which permeates" *Hamlet* "is deepened and made more repulsive by being constantly associated with one of the most unpleasant of man's sensory experiences."

Andrews, Michael Cameron. "*Hamlet*: Revenge and the Critical Mirror." *English Literary Renaissance* 8, No. 1 (Winter 1978): 9-23.

Disagrees with Eleanor Prosser's interpretation of the Elizabethan attitude toward revenge. He endeavors to demonstrate that "an Elizabethan audience did not necessarily respond to revenge in moral terms; that Shakespeare does not impose moral judgment on all his revengers; and that *Hamlet* would not be a startling play if it presented blood revenge in a way that aroused approval as well as sympathy."

Babb, Lawrence. "Pathological Grief and Other Forms of Grief in the Drama." In his *The Elizabethan Malady: A Study of Melancholia in English Literature from 1580 to 1642*, pp. 102-27. East Lansing, Mich.: Michigan State University Press, 1951.
Defines melancholia as "a purely intellectual phenomenon" caused by "grief and frustration." Babb remarks that Elizabethans would have recognized this malady in Hamlet and would have accepted his procrastination as a symptom of the ailment in a man who "reflects rather than acts."

Babcock, Weston. *"Hamlet": A Tragedy of Errors*. West Lafayette, Ind.: Purdue University Press, 1961, 134 p.
An analysis of the play which concentrates on the characters' misconceptions. Babcock sees these misconceptions as errors that lead to the catastrophe, chief among them being Hamlet's belief that Gertrude is guilty of complicity in Claudius's crime.

Battenhouse, Roy. "The Ghost in *Hamlet*: A Catholic 'Lynchpin'?" *Studies in Philology* XLVIII, No. 2 (April 1951): 161-92.
Challenges J. Dover Wilson's statement that the ghost is Catholic, that he "comes from Purgatory," and that he has a Catholic concern for the sacraments. Instead, Battenhouse demonstrates his contention that the ghost is a "post-Christian" pagan.

Battenhouse, Roy. "Hamlet's Apostrophe on Man: Clue to the Tragedy." *PMLA* LXVI, No. 6 (December 1951): 1073-1113.
Asserts that Shakespeare selected a "recognizable complex of character-motivation" that falls short of Christian spirituality. Battenhouse illustrates how Hamlet is intellectually lost "within the self-made toils of a noble reason turned in upon itself."

Battenhouse, Roy W. "Hamartia in Aristotle, Christian Doctrine, and *Hamlet*." In his *Shakespearean Tragedy: Its Art and Its Christian Premises*, pp. 204-66. Bloomington, Ind.: Indiana University Press, 1969.
A religious interpretation of *Hamlet*, describing a combination of the philosophies of Aristotle, Augustine, and Aquinas in Shakespeare's tragedies. Battenhouse notes that Hamlet's "tragic flaw" is narcissism and that his actions fulfill one of St. Augustine's precepts about man: he perversely imitates the role of Christ.

Berry, Francis. "Young Fortinbras." *Life and Letters and the London Mercury* LII, No. 114 (February 1947): 94-103.
Bases theories about Fortinbras on the commentary of Goethe and concludes that the Norwegian prince can legitimately claim the throne of Denmark "because he is spiritually the heir of his father's foe."

Bevington, David, ed. *Twentieth-Century Interpretations of "Hamlet": A Collection of Critical Essays*. Englewood Cliffs, N.J.: Prentice-Hall, 1968, 120 p.
Presents seventeen essays on *Hamlet* by prominent twentieth-century critics.

Bowers, Fredson. "The Death of Hamlet: A Study in Plot and Character." In *Studies in the English Renaissance Drama in Memory of Karl Holzknecht*, edited by J. W. Bennett and Oscar Cargill, pp. 28-42. New York: New York University Press, 1959.
Claims that Shakespeare's handling of plot and character clearly directs the audience's response to Hamlet's revenge. Bowers suggests that "this unusual interposition" assures our acceptance of Hamlet as a tragic hero.

Braddy, Haldeen. *Hamlet's Wounded Name*. El Paso, Tex.: Texas Western College Press, 1964, 82 p.
Compares the plot of the play "with folklore motifs and medieval conventions that justify Hamlet's course of action." Braddy claims that Hamlet rejects Ophelia because she allows herself to be used

as a pawn by Claudius. Braddy also asserts that Gertrude redeems herself by lying to Claudius.

Brockbank, J. Philip. "Hamlet the Bonesetter." *Shakespeare Survey* 30 (1977): 103-15.*
Traces the "lines of continuity" between *Hamlet* and ancient sacrificial rituals. Brockbank maintains that the discovery of communal guilt is the central theme of the play, because "the tragic effects of both *Hamlet* and *Oedipus Rex* may be set down . . . to a sacrificial law, working through 'accidents' as well as through human choice and disposition, towards the discovery and purgation of guilt."

Brooke, Stopford A. *"Hamlet."* In his *Ten More Plays of Shakespeare*, pp. 91-138. London: Constable and Co., 1913.
Reviews the play through the eyes of Hamlet in an attempt to ascertain how all of the characters are developed in relation to the central figure. Brooke contends that it is the inability of "active, practical" types to understand the "sensitive, imaginative" idealist that leads some to conclude that Hamlet actually is mad. Brooke states that Hamlet's dilemma is answered by accident and not design, for Hamlet's dying thought reveals that he fears to "be mistaken by the world."

Brophy, Brigid; Levey, Michael; and Osborne, Charles. "William Shakespeare: *Hamlet, Prince of Denmark*." In their *Fifty Works of English and American Literature We Could Do Without*, pp. 11-12. New York: Stein and Day, 1968.
Judges *Hamlet* one of the weakest of Shakespeare's plays, and attributes its popularity to the poor taste of the reading public. According to these critics, the hero is "the posturing, self-pitying, egotistical baby-cum-adolescent in us all, and the play is the prototype of western literature's most deplorable and most formless form, autobiographical fiction."

Brown, John R., and Harris, Bernard, eds. *"Hamlet": Stratford-upon-Avon Studies 5*. London: Arnold, 1963, 212 p.
Includes recent essays that deal with "the relationship of prince and play, human character and dramatic role, role and structure, character and speech."

Calderwood, James L. "Hamlet: The Name of Action." *Modern Language Quarterly* XXXIX, No. 4 (December 1978): 331-62.
Defines Hamlet's "problem" as an identity crisis. Calderwood contends that, in swearing to avenge his father, Hamlet must temporarily relinquish his personal identity and unite with his father "in actional fact" as well as in name. According to Calderwood, Hamlet's search for self-definition parallels Shakespeare's form-exploration in the play itself; in the play's conclusion, Hamlet earns his name, "investing it with his own meaning," while the play, "having gone its own self-defining route," fulfills the requirements of the revenge tragedy form.

Camden, Carroll. "On Ophelia's Madness." *Shakespeare Quarterly* XV, No. 2 (Spring 1964): 247-55.
Suggests that Ophelia's madness chiefly stems not from the death of her father, but rather from her rejection by Hamlet. Camden further argues that an Elizabethan audience would have clearly recognized Ophelia's symptoms as erotomania.

Campbell, Lily B. *"Hamlet: A Tragedy of Grief."* In her *Shakespeare's Tragic Heroes: Slaves of Passion*, pp. 109-47. New York: Barnes & Noble, 1930.
Disputes the traditional view that Hamlet is under the influence of the melancholy humor. According to Campbell, Hamlet is sanguine and becomes melancholy when moved to passion. Thus his melancholy is sanguine "adust," an unnatural and destructive humor.

Campbell, Oscar James. "What Is the Matter with Hamlet?" *The Yale Review* XXXII, No. 2 (Winter 1943): 309-22.
Proposes that Hamlet's melancholy makes him incapable of action until his "emotional equilibrium" is restored by the fatal wound he receives from Laertes.

Capell, Edward. "Notes on Shakespeare." In *Shakespeare: The Critical Heritage, Vol. 5, 1765-1774,* edited by Brian Vickers, pp. 555-58. London: Routledge & Kegan Paul, 1979.

Several notes on Hamlet by the seventeenth-century scholar, including an analysis of Ophelia's flower imagery.

Chambers, E. K. *"Hamlet."* In his *William Shakespeare: A Study of Facts and Problems,* pp. 408-25. London: Oxford at the Clarendon Press, 1930.

An examination of the textual genesis of *Hamlet* in which Chambers claims, in agreement with John Dover Wilson, that the second quarto represents the original text of the play.

Chambers, E. K. "The Date of *Hamlet.*" In his *Shakespearean Gleanings,* pp. 68-75. London: Oxford University Press, 1944.

Sets the date of the play, on evidence of the reference to the Essex rebellion, at 1601. In this essay Chambers revises his earlier proposed date of 1600, based on an interpretation which attaches less importance to the note in Gabriel Harvey's copy of Speght's Chaucer.

Charney, Maurice. *Style in "Hamlet."* Princeton: Princeton University Press, 1969, 333 p.

A three-part examination of *Hamlet* that analyzes theatrical images and style in the development of characterization. Charney devotes the first part to the play's important images, the second section to the theatrical effects, and the third part to a stylistic study of Polonius, Claudius, and Hamlet. He suggests that Hamlet "thinks of experience as a work of art that can only be mastered by aesthetic means."

Conklin, Paul S. *A History of Hamlet Criticism: 1601-1821.* New York: King's Crown Press, 1947, 176 p.

A detailed account of the earliest criticism of *Hamlet.* Conklin provides valuable insight on the ideas of the commentators of the period.

Cooperman, Stanley. "Shakespeare's Anti-Hero: Hamlet and the Underground Man." *Shakespeare Studies* I (1965): 37-63.

A comparison of Hamlet with the protagonist of Dostoevski's *Notes from Underground.* Cooperman claims that both characters suffer from the same existential dilemma—neither can accommodate himself to the world's pervasive evil.

Corbin, John. *The Elizabethan Hamlet.* 1895. Reprint. New York: AMS Press, 1970, 89 p.

Ascertains, through a study of the sources, Elizabethan customs, and earlier plays, that madness was often treated as a source of comedy in Shakespeare's era. Corbin concludes that "there are distinct traces" of humor in scenes that modern readers consider the most tragic, and this accounts for "the divergent views of the critics."

Cox, Roger L. "Hamlet's Hamartia: Aristotle or St. Paul?" *The Yale Review* LV, No. 3 (Spring 1966): 347-64.

Argues that critics' attempts to illuminate Hamlet's "tragic flaw" by means of Aristotle's *Poetics* are misguided, mainly because Aristotle's aesthetics fail to explain Hamlet's "madness" and his inability to act. Instead, Cox maintains that the Christian doctrine of sin, as stated by St. Paul in the seventh chapter of his letter to the Romans, serves as a more satisfactory basis for Hamlet's dilemma. Cox concludes that Hamlet's actions show that he is dominated by sin, and that the delay "comes about not because he consistently fails to act, but because his actions utterly miss the mark."

Craig, Hardin. "The Great Trio: Hamlet, Othello, King Lear." In his *An Interpretation of Shakespeare,* pp. 178-219. New York: The Citadel Press, 1948.

Describes Hamlet as an Everyman figure, prone to two human weaknesses: a propensity to hesitation and a difficulty in mustering enough courage to act. Hamlet thus becomes "a hero in whom we recognize our common humanity."

Craig, Hardin. "A Cutpurse of the Empire: On Shakespeare Cosmology." In *A Tribute to George Coffin Taylor,* edited by Arnold

Williams, pp. 3-16. Chapel Hill, N.C.: University of North Carolina Press, 1952.

Interprets *Hamlet* according to the "Great Chain of Being" concept. Craig compares the play with Shakespeare's other tragedies, as well as the revenge dramas of the era, and concludes that Hamlet's duty to rectify the wrongs committed against his family and country and to reestablish God's order relieves him of any guilt.

Croce, Benedetto. *Aristo, Shakespeare and Corneille.* Translated by Douglas Ainslee. London: George Allen & Unwin, 440 p.

Claims that there is no real obstacle which thwarts Hamlet's will, but that his inability to act is ultimately the result of "painful impressions" which have paralyzed his psyche. Croce views the play as "the expression of disaffection and distaste for life."

Dennis, John. *An Essay upon the Genius and Writings of Shakespeare: With Some Letters of Criticism to the "Spectator."* London: Bernard Linlott, 1712, 66 p.

Contains a letter of February 1, 1711 in which Dennis stresses the lack of poetic justice in Shakespeare's tragedies. Even though Hamlet is justified in taking his revenge by "no less than a Call from Heaven," both the innocent and the guilty die in the conclusion. Therefore, "there can be either none or very weak instruction" in this tragedy.

Dent, R. W. "Hamlet: Scourge and Minister." *Shakespeare Quarterly* 29, No. 1 (Winter 1978): 82-4.

Disputes the claim of Fredson Bowers that the terms "scourge" and "minister" contained a contrast in Elizabethan usage. Dent find's no evidence that "scourge" bore a necessary implication of evil, and considers the use of the two words as "another of the play's innumerable pairings of synonyms or near synonyms."

Doran, Madeleine. "The Language of *Hamlet.*" *Huntington Library Quarterly* XXVII, No. 3 (May 1964): 259-78.

Detailed analysis of the language of the play. Doran regards Hamlet's final feeling as one of failure, and maintains that ultimately, he remains a misunderstood figure, or worse, a "common assassin," after his tragic act.

Draper, John W. *The "Hamlet" of Shakespeare's Audience.* Durham, N.C.: Duke University Press, 1938, 254 p.

Discusses *Hamlet* in terms of the social background of the play's Elizabethan audience. Draper posits that the audience's understanding of the characters in *Hamlet* was influenced by each one's social status. For such an audience, Hamlet thus represented a combination of character types, including "an ideal courtier," a "feigning madman," and an "all-too-human human being."

Duthie, G. I. *The Bad Quarto of "Hamlet."* Cambridge: Cambridge University Press, 1941, 279 p.

Study of the 1603 Quarto which presents evidence suggesting that that edition was a pirated text, probably reconstructed from the memory of the actor who played Marcellus. Duthie's study has had an enormous impact on scholars, virtually putting to rest speculation that Q1 was an earlier version by Shakespeare.

Elliott, G. R. *Scourge and Minister: A Study of "Hamlet" as Tragedy of Revengefulness and Justice.* Durham, N.C.: Duke University Press, 1951, 208 p.

Attributes Hamlet's delay to his awareness of the sinfulness and futility of personal revenge. Elliott classifies *Hamlet* not as a character study, but instead as a dramatization of emerging Renaissance Christian humanism.

Erlich, Avi. *Hamlet's Absent Father.* Princeton: Princeton University Press, 1977, 308 p.

Disputes the Freudian interpretation of Hamlet's character, stressing that Oedipal conflicts manifest themselves differently in different people. Erlich claims that had Hamlet subconsciously desired to kill his father, the punishment of Claudius for that act would be an ideal displacement of guilt. Hamlet's conflict, according to Erlich, stems from the fact that his father's victimization contradicts Hamlet's image of him as a strong, ideal figure.

Evans, Ifor. *"Hamlet."* In his *The Language of Shakespeare's Plays,* pp. 116-31. London: Methuen & Co., 1952.
Notes the "exceptional importance in *Hamlet* of the linguistic interest." Evans claims that Hamlet is such a unique character because no other personage in Shakespeare possesses his pronounced ability to alternate between modes of discourse.

Farnham, Willard. Introduction to *Hamlet Prince of Denmark,* by William Shakespeare. In *William Shakespeare: The Complete Works,* edited by Alfred Harbage, pp. 930-32. Baltimore: Penguin Books, 1969.
Brief introduction that contrasts the search for truth and the search for revenge in the play.

Feis, Jacob. *Shakespeare and Montaigne: An Endeavour to Explain the Tendency of "Hamlet" from Allusions in Contemporary Works.* London: Kegan Paul, Trench, & Co., 1884, 210 p.
Textual study that advances the argument that Shakespeare wrote *Hamlet* to counter the influence of Montaigne. This thesis is hotly disputed by J. M. Robertson.

Flatter, Richard. *Hamlet's Father.* New Haven: Yale University Press, 1949, 207 p.
Contains many observations that derive from Flatter's experience in producing *Hamlet.* Flatter presents the Ghost as the controlling force in the play and the source of Hamlet's dilemma in choosing between justice and all-forgiving love.

Foreman, Walter C., Jr. *"Hamlet."* In his *The Music of the Close: The Final Scenes of Shakespeare's Tragedies,* pp. 73-112. Lexington: The University Press of Kentucky, 1978.
Concentrates on the antagonism of Claudius and Hamlet. The play, according to Foreman, consists of a series of deferrals of the main conflict until the fencing scene at the close of the drama. Foreman regards Fortinbras not as a restorer of health, but as a cynical opportunist who takes advantage of a tragic situation.

Gottschalk, Paul. *The Meanings of "Hamlet": Modes of Literary Interpretation Since Bradley.* Albuquerque: The University of New Mexico Press, 1972, 197 p.
Survey of critical approaches to *Hamlet* in the twentieth century. In his conclusion, Gottschalk argues for a "critical pluralism," claiming that "although no interpretation can explain *Hamlet* utterly, many may be coordinate" and that "interpretative difference need not be interpretative conflict."

Gray, Henry David. "Reconstruction of a Lost Play." *Philological Quarterly* VII, No. 3 (July 1928): 254-74.
Attempts to construct an outline of the *Ur-Hamlet* using the Belleforest version and *Der Bestrafte Brudermord.* Gray claims that this early version of the play was written by Thomas Kyd, and that the plot follows the line of his *The Spanish Tragedy.*

Gray, Henry David. "The Date of *Hamlet.*" *Journal of English and Germanic Philology* 31, No. 1 (January 1932): 51-61.
Dates the play at 1601, relying on the evidence of the internal reference to the War of the Theatres.

Grebanier, Bernard. *The Heart of Hamlet.* New York: Thomas Y. Crowell, 1960, 311 p.
Argues that Hamlet is neither mad nor pretending to be mad, and that his tragic flaw comes not from his delay but from his rashness. Grebanier considers the climax of the play to be Hamlet's killing of Polonius—"the rash and bloody deed" which insures his downfall.

Greg, W. W. "What Happens in *Hamlet.*" *The Modern Language Review* XXXI, No. 2 (April 1936): 145-54.
Rejects J. Dover Wilson's interpretation of *Hamlet* and presents opposing readings on such contested points as the nature of the ghost, Hamlet's feelings for Ophelia, and the amount of protection afforded Claudius.

Hardison, O. B., Jr. "The Dramatic Triad in *Hamlet.*" *Studies in Philology* LXII, No. 1 (January 1960): 144-64.
Presents Fortinbras, Laertes, and Ophelia as a dramatic triad and describes their function as dramatic foils to Hamlet. Hardison

identifies the way in which these characters respond to a father's violent death as forbearance (Fortinbras), revenge (Laertes), and suicide (Ophelia), and examines how their reactions represent a dramatization of Hamlet's dilemma.

Hawkes, Terence. *"Hamlet"* and *"Conclusion."* In his *Shakespeare and the Reason: A Study of the Tragedies and the Problem Plays,* pp. 39-71, pp. 194-201. London: Routledge & Kegan Paul, 1964.
Examines the play to determine Hamlet's role in his society. Hawkes finds that the contemplative values of Wittenberg are opposed to the masculine, aggressive world of action and reason that characterizes Elsinore.

Haydn, Hiram. "Shakespeare and the Counter-Renaissance: Hamlet, Honor vs. Stoicism." In his *The Counter-Renaissance,* pp. 619-35. New York: Harcourt, Brace & World, 1950.
Discusses the acceptance of private revenge in Shakespeare's society. Haydn maintains that this approach should be given more consideration than the interpretations of the play that stress the Church's attitude toward revenge.

Heilbrun, Carolyn. "The Character of Hamlet's Mother." *Shakespeare Quarterly* VIII, No. 2 (Spring 1957): 201-06.
Perceives Gertrude not solely as a creature of lust, but also as "intelligent, penetrating, and gifted with a remarkable talent for concise and pithy speech."

Holland, Norman N. "Hamlet: My Greatest Creation." *The Journal of the American Academy of Psychoanalysis* 3, No. 4 (October 1975): 419-27.
Claims that the language of the play creates a "potential space" which gives the reader or auditor a chance to create his or her own alternate meanings and dramatic possibilities. Thus, according to Holland, each creates his own "play."

Holloway, John. *"Hamlet."* In his *The Story of the Night: Studies in Shakespeare's Major Tragedies,* pp. 21-36. Lincoln: University of Nebraska Press, 1961.
Characterizes Shakespeare's presentation of the protagonist in his tragedies, especially in *Hamlet,* as "the assumption, and then the enactment, of a determinate *role* instead of the deployment of a determinate character." Holloway also analyzes two themes in the play: the disintegration of a society and the idea that random chance is actually an operation of "Divine Justice."

Holmes, Martin. *The Guns of Elsinore.* New York: Barnes & Noble, 1964, 188 p.
Historical study which attempts to recreate the original production of *Hamlet.* Holmes adds a detailed commentary on the play, stressing its military and political aspects.

Honigmann, E.A.J. "The Date of *Hamlet.*" *Shakespeare Survey* 9 (1956): 24-34.
Presents evidence that points to late 1599 or early 1600 as the date of the play's composition.

Hoy, Cyrus, ed. *William Shakespeare: "Hamlet".* New York: W. W. Norton, 1963, 270 p.
Presents a collection of some of the most important critical essays in the history of *Hamlet* commentary.

Hugo, Victor. "Shakespeare: His Work, the Culminating Points." In his *The Works of Victor Hugo,* Vol. X, pp. 156-78. Boston, New York: The Jefferson Press, 1864.
Romantic panegyric to the play and its hero. Hugo calls *Hamlet* an "overwhelming and vertiginous work, in which is seen the depth of everything."

Hunter, Joseph. *New Illustrations of the Life, Studies, and Writings of Shakespeare,* Vol. II. London: J. B. Nichols and Son, 1845, 205 p.
Considers *Hamlet* a "spotty" play and one which only gives evidence "of a noble promise . . . left unfulfilled." Hunter greatly admires the first act, but objects to the introduction of Osric and Fortinbras near the end of the play, to Ophelia's madness, and to the lack of poetic justice.

Jameson, Anna Brownell. *Characteristics of Women: Moral, Political, and Historical,* Vol. I. London: 1832, 254 p.

Contains a passage on Ophelia, stressing her beauty and innocence. This is an example of one of the more extreme nineteenth-century hommages to Ophelia.

Jenkins, Harold. "The Relation Between the Second Quarto and the Folio Text of *Hamlet.*" *Studies in Bibliography* 7 (1955): 69-83.

Claims, contrary to John Dover Wilson, that the Second Quarto was used in the preparation of the Folio text. Thus, though editors must still use Q2 as a primary text, a greater amount of authority may be given to the Folio than Wilson suggested.

Jenkins, Harold. Introduction to *Hamlet,* by William Shakespeare, edited by Harold Jenkins, pp. 1-159. London and New York: Methuen, 1982.

Considered by some scholars to be the most authoritative, scholarly edition of *Hamlet* yet published. As the editor of the New Arden edition, Jenkins surveys the history of criticism on the play and presents a comprehensive overview of the date, publication history, texts, editorial problems, and sources of *Hamlet.* In the conclusion to his critical introduction, Jenkins maintains that Hamlet's refusal to act is a result of his unusual situation: he is asked to perform the kind of evil he wishes to punish.

Johnson, S. F. "The Regeneration of Hamlet: A Reply to E.M.W. Tillyard with a Counter-proposal." *Shakespeare Quarterly* III, No. 3 (July 1952): 187-207.

Attacks E.M.W. Tillyard's thesis that *Hamlet* is a "problem play." Johnson asserts that Hamlet does in fact gain a tragic awareness at the end of the play, as evidenced by his final acceptance of providence.

Joseph, Bertram. *Conscience and the King: A Study of "Hamlet."* London: Chatto & Windus, 1953, 175 p.

Historical approach to the play which stresses the importance of an interpretation based on an Elizabethan perspective.

Joyce, James. In his *Ulysses,* pp. 182-215. New York: Random House, 1934.

Discussion of *Hamlet* by several characters in Joyce's novel. Stephen Dedalus theorizes that Shakespeare wrote *Hamlet* after discovering that he had been cuckolded by one of his brothers. Stephen believes that King Hamlet and Prince Hamlet represent the two sides of Shakespeare's personality. Joyce draws parallels between the fatherless Stephen and Hamlet throughout his novel.

Kermode, Frank. Introduction to *The Tragedy of Hamlet. Prince of Denmark,* by William Shakespeare. In *The Riverside Shakespeare,* edited by G. Blakemore Evans, pp. 1135-40. Boston: Houghton Mifflin Co., 1974.

Introduction containing an overview of the sources of the play in some detail. Kermode describes one of the chief pleasures in reading *Hamlet* to be "the great rhythmical pulse of the play, in its invention of a new mirror to hold up to a changed nature."

Kirsch, Arthur. "Hamlet's Grief." *ELH: A Journal of English Literary History* 48, No. 1 (Spring 1981): 17-36.

Suggests that Hamlet's grief over the loss of his father informs his actions throughout the play. Kirsch defines mourning as a component of anger and protest—"anger at being wounded and abandoned" and a protest "against the inescapably mortal condition of mortal life." And, Kirsch states, the ghost intensifies Hamlet's mourning by forbidding "the internal process by which the ego heals its wounds."

Kirschbaum, Leo. "The Date of Shakespeare's *Hamlet.*" *Studies in Philology* XXXIV, No. 2 (April 1937): 168-79.

Rejects the assumption that *Hamlet* was written in 1598, finding no credibility in Gabriel Harvey's note referring to the play. Kirschbaum instead uses the reference in the play to the War of the Theatres to date it no earlier than 1601.

Kirschbaum, Leo. "Hamlet and Ophelia." *Philological Quarterly* XXXV, No. 4 (October 1956): 376-93.

Discusses the relationship between Hamlet and Ophelia. Kirschbaum argues that Ophelia is indeed morally responsible for the consequences of obeying Polonius: "What else should she do as a good daughter? Well, there is a long list: Desdemona, Jessica, Cordelia, Sylvia, etc."

Kittredge, George Lyman. Introduction to *The Tragedy of Hamlet, Prince of Denmark,* by William Shakespeare, edited by George Lyman Kittredge, pp. vii-xx. Boston: Ginn and Co., 1939.

Brief introduction in which Kittredge gives his opinion on several disputed matters of interpretation. Kittredge believes that Hamlet's professed reason for not killing Claudius in the prayer scene is a mere pretext for delay, that Denmark's throne is elective, that Hamlet is a very young man, and that Claudius feels genuine remorse over his crime.

Knight, G. Wilson. "Rose of May: An Essay on Life-themes in *Hamlet.*" In his *The Imperial Throne: Further Interpretations of Shakespeare's Tragedies Including the Roman Plays,* pp. 96-124. London: Oxford University Press, 1931.

Further elaborates on his interpretation from *The Wheel of Fire,* in which he considers Hamlet the instrument of the forces of death. Knight explains that Hamlet's rejection of existence has been caused by "Death, in the form of the ghost." According to Knight, Hamlet developed his philosophy of death because "the life-forces are shown to have a hideous evil at their source."

Kott, Jan. "Letters on *Hamlet.*" *Theater* 10, No. 3 (Summer 1979): 92-4.

Suggests that a director must emphasize the resemblance of the gravediggers' scene to the medieval "dance of death" in order to link the scene with the appearances of the Ghost.

Lawrence, W. J. "The Date of Shakespeare's *Hamlet*" and "The Ghost in *Hamlet.*" In his *Shakespeare's Workshop,* pp. 98-109, 124-36. Boston and New York: Houghton Mifflin, 1928.

Regards the Second Quarto as the original Shakespearean text of *Hamlet,* and claims that the play was first performed around Easter of 1600. Lawrence provides external, internal, and speculative evidence to support his theory. In the second essay, he uses an historical approach to comment upon the ghost, describing it as vitally important to the plot.

Lawrence, W. W. "The Play Scene in *Hamlet.*" *Journal of English and Germanic Philology* XVIII (1919): 1-22.

Explication of the Mousetrap. Lawrence claims that both Claudius and Gertrude witness the dumb-show and that Claudius "does not stop the play, because to do so would be a tacit confession of guilt."

LeComte, Edward S. "The Ending of *Hamlet* as a Farewell to Essex." *ELH: A Journal of English Literary History* 17, No. 2 (June 1950): 87-114.

Review of the different studies that have posited the theory that Hamlet is based on the Earl of Essex. LeComte presents four possible refutations of the theory.

Leech, Clifford. "Studies in *Hamlet,* 1901-1955." *Shakespeare Survey* 9 (1956): 1-15.

Outlines the theories and influence of the major twentieth-century critics of *Hamlet.*

Levenson, J. C., ed. *Discussions of "Hamlet".* Boston: D. C. Heath, 1960, 113 p.

Includes the commentaries of twelve major Shakespearean critics.

Lidz, Theodore. *Hamlet's Enemy: Madness and Myth in "Hamlet".* New York: Basic Books, 1975, 258 p.

Psychoanalytic approach which claims that *Hamlet* focuses specifically on "the importance of the family as a unit." Lidz stresses the importance of "intrafamilial relationships" in the growth of a person's emotional stability and notes that the questions about the value of life in the play are intimately related to these interpersonal and family themes.

Maginn, William. *The Shakespeare Papers of the Late William Maginn.* London: Refield, 1856, 275 p.

Describes *Hamlet* as the Shakespeare play in which "the Spirit of Love is weakest," and as a "psychological exercise and study." Magin contends that Hamlet is insane, but that his "malady . . . is of the subtlest character."

Mahood, M. M. *"Hamlet."* In his *Shakespeare's Wordplay*, pp. 111-29. London: Methuen & Co., 1957.
    Focuses on the language of the play. Mahood demonstrates the way in which Shakespeare's wordplay provides the dramatic realization of "the conflict between the demands of an accepted ethical code and Hamlet's particular vision of evil."

Maxwell, Baldwin. "Hamlet's Mother." *Shakespeare Quarterly* XV, No. 2 (Spring 1964): 235-46.
    Examines the role of Gertrude and concludes that she is weak and indecisive. Maxwell asserts that "her one act of independence"—accusing Claudius of preparing the poisoned drink—leads to her death.

McDonald, David J. "*Hamlet* and the Mimesis of Absence: A Post-Structuralist Analysis." *Educational Theatre Journal* 30, No. 1 (March 1978): 36-53.
    Discussion of *Hamlet* which employs Jacques Derrida's deconstructionist method. McDonald concentrates on the "presence of absence"—the continual substitutions and discontinuities that occur in the play.

Morris, Harry. "*Hamlet* as a Memento Mori Poem." *PMLA* 85, No. 5 (October 1970): 1035-40.
    Maintains that Shakespeare's "close and detailed concern with the plight of the soul of each character who is to die" argues for an eschatological reading of the play, and that such a reading is enhanced "by the structure of the five acts insofar as it is modeled on the *memento mori-timor mortis* lyric."

Muir, Kenneth. "Some Freudian Interpretations of Shakespeare." *Proceedings of the Leeds Philosophical and Literary Society: Literary and Historical Section* VII (July 1952): 43-52.*
    Summarizes the psychoanalytic approach of Freudian criticism and upholds the value of this method in studying *Hamlet*.

Muir, Kenneth. "Imagery and Symbolism in *Hamlet*." *Études Anglaises* XVII, No. 4 (October-December 1964): 352-63.
    Studies the image patterns of war and violence, corruption, the contrast between appearance and reality, and disease in the play.

Murray, John Middleton. "Whether 'Tis Nobler?" In his *Shakespeare*, pp. 235-70. London: Jonathan Cape, 1936.
    Claims that Hamlet goes to the fencing match in a spirit of Christian forgiveness, with no intention of killing the king. Only when he becomes aware of Claudius's final treachery does Hamlet become inspired to kill him.

Nevo, Ruth. *"Hamlet."* In her *Tragic Form in Shakespeare*, pp. 128-77. Princeton: Princeton Univeristy Press, 1972.
    Analyzes the dramatic structure of *Hamlet* and identifies a mode of action characterized by "speculation, interrogation, spying into, finding out, testing, probing, observing, and discovering."

Newell, Alex. "The Dramatic Context and Meaning of Hamlet's 'To Be or Not To Be' Soliloquy." *PMLA* LXXX, No. 1 (March 1965): 38-50.
    Suggests that Hamlet's famous soliloquy dramatically reveals "that he is grappling with a particular problem that is an outgrowth of the developing event, the presentation of the mousetrap play."

Nosworthy, J. M. "The Structural Experiment in *Hamlet*." *The Review of English Studies* XXII, No. 88 (October 1946): 382-88.
    Theorizes that the scenes with the players serve as an experiment in which Shakespeare could air his views on the War of the Theaters.

Paterson, John. "The Word in *Hamlet*." *Shakespeare Quarterly* II, No. 1 (January 1951): 47-55.
    Asserts that the central theme of *Hamlet*—the "confusion of appearance with reality," in which the human mind "cries forever after certitude and truth"—is underscored by the "rhetorical full-

ness and the linguistic criticism" inherent in the speech of every character.

Pearn, B. R. "Dumb-Show in Elizabethan Drama." *The Review of English Studies* XI, No. 44 (October 1935): 385-405.
    Review of the use of the dumb-show by Elizabethan dramatists, with a complete listing of plays in which the device occurs. Pearn demonstrates that, contrary to earlier opinion, this device had not in fact become rare by the time that Shakespeare wrote *Hamlet*. He notes that the use of the dumb-show in Shakespeare's play is unique in that it functions as a significant part of the main action.

Prior, Moody E. "The Thought of *Hamlet* and the Modern Temper." *ELH: A Journal of English Literary History* 15, No. 4 (December 1948): 261-87.
    Argues for an interpretation of the play which integrates the dramatic element with the philosophical aspects and gives "attention to the continuous and developing relationship of character and action which is one of the distinguishing features of Shakespeare's tragedies." Prior proposes that the play's continuing popularity stems from the ability of modern readers and viewers to understand and sympathize with Hamlet's dilemma.

Quinn, Edward. *"Hamlet."* In *The Major Shakespearean Tragedies*, by Edward Quinn, James Ruoff, and Joseph Grennen, pp. 1-75. New York: The Free Press, 1973.
    Annotated bibliography of important criticism on *Hamlet*, covering essays from 1736 to 1971.

Ribner, Irving. "The Pattern of Growth: *Hamlet*." In his *Patterns in Shakespearian Tragedy*, pp. 65-90. London: Methuen & Co., 1960.
    Christian interpretation of the play. Ribner contends that Hamlet is unable to destroy the evil which surrounds him without first accepting his own human weakness and becoming, like Horatio, a stoic Christian. When he does so, in the fifth act, his task is soon accomplished and he dies a heroic death.

Richardson, William. "Additional Observations on Shakespeare's Dramatic Character of Hamlet." In his *Essays on Shakespeare's Dramatic Characters of Richard the Third, King Lear, and Timon of Athens: To Which Are Added, an Essay on the Faults of Shakespeare; and, Additional Observations of the Character of Hamlet*. London: J. Murray, 1784.
    Early essay in the romantic tradition of *Hamlet* criticism. Richardson defends the consistency of Hamlet's character, asserting that Hamlet fails in his task because he is unable to perform tasks too great for his extreme sensitivity. Thus, for the audience, Hamlet "becomes an object not of blame, but of genuine and tender regret."

Righter, Anne. "The Power of Illusion: *Hamlet* and the Contemporary Stage." In her *Shakespeare and the Idea of the Play*, pp. 154-64. London: Chatto & Windus, 1962.
    Discusses the allusions to the Elizabethan theater in *Hamlet*. Righter covers both the topical allusions to Shakespeare's contemporary stage and the philosophical issues, such as the nature of reality and illusion, which Shakespeare confronted in his drama.

Robertson, J. M. "Montaigne and Shakespeare." In his *Montaigne and Shakespeare, and Other Essays on Cognate Questions*, pp. 3-232. London: Adam and Charles Black, 1909.
    Disputes Jacob Feis's contention that Shakespeare intended *Hamlet* to be a criticism of Montaigne's philosophy. Robertson claims that *Hamlet* is a far more skeptical play than its sources and that it is permeated with an apparent disbelief in immortality. He concludes that Feis's thesis is "a shallow interpretation of the play" and "merely ridiculous."

Robertson, J. M. *The Problem of "Hamlet."* New York: Harcourt, Brace & Howe, 1920, 90 p.
    Maintains that inconsistencies in the play can be attributed to Shakespeare's failure to fully integrate his sources with his theme. This essay had a considerable influence on T. S. Eliot's ideas about *Hamlet*.

Robson, W. W. "Did the King See the Dumb-Show?" *Cambridge Quarterly* VI, No. 4 (1975): 303-26.

Presents a "cubist" interpretation of the action in the dumb-show. Robson finds all the theories inconsistent with the text, and suggests that "the various points of view in the play are not subordinated to a single synoptic vision." This, Robson believes, was Shakespeare's intention.

Sacks, Claire, and Whan, Edgar, eds. *"Hamlet": Enter Critic.* New York: Appleton-Century-Crofts, 1960, 298 p.

Contains critical essays that offer divergent, contradictory, and unusual answers to interpretive problems in *Hamlet.*

Skulsky, Harold. "Revenge, Honor, and Conscience in *Hamlet.*" *PMLA* 85, No. 1 (January 1970): 78-87.

Perceives Hamlet as torn between the ancient honor code of Pyhrrus and the more "courtly" revenge codes represented by Laertes and Fortinbras. Hamlet's inability to integrate these two codes constitutes his tragedy, which Skulsky sees as "a tragedy of spiritual decline."

Smith, Rebecca. "A Heart Cleft in Twain: The Dilemma of Shakespeare's Gertrude." In *The Woman's Part: Feminist Criticism of Shakespeare,* edited by Carolyn Ruth Swift Lenz, Gayle Greene, and Carol Thomas Neely, pp. 194-210. Urbana: University of Illinois Press, 1980.

Disputes the interpretation of Gertrude as a duplicitous and lustful woman. Smith argues that such an interpretation is based on the statements of the male characters of the play, whereas an examination of Gertrude's own words and actions shows her to be a "soft, obedient, dependent, unimaginative woman who is caught miserably at the center of a desperate struggle between two 'mighty opposites'. . . ." Smith also traces the evolution of the character of Gertrude through Shakespeare's sources, claiming that Shakespeare purposely modified her nature and her role in the play.

Stoll, Elmer Edgar. *"Hamlet": An Historical and Comparative Study.* Minneapolis: University of Minnesota, 1919, 75 p.

Argues that inconsistencies in Hamlet's character are due to the fact that Shakespeare was drawing from Elizabethan tradition and did not fully integrate his conception of Hamlet's nature.

Swinburne, Algernon Charles. "Second Period: Comic and Historic." In his *A Study of Shakespeare,* pp. 66-169. London: William Heinemann, 1920.

Classifies the play as a bridge between Shakespeare's middle and final periods, "the deeper complexities of the subject . . . merely indicated." Swinburne's interpretation of Hamlet's character follows the romantic tradition of Goethe and Coleridge.

Tolstoy, Leo. "Tolstoy on Shakespeare." In his *Tolstoy on Shakespeare: A Critical Essay on Shakespeare,* translated by V. Tchertkoff and I.F.M., pp. 1-124. New York, London: Funk & Wagnalls, 1907.

States that Shakespeare makes Hamlet's character incomprehensible by "introducing quite inappropriately (as indeed he always does) into the mouth of the principal person all those thoughts of his own which appeared to him worthy of attention." Only idolatry of Shakespeare, in Tolstoy's view, inspires critics to make any sense of the drama.

Trench, Wilbraham Fitzjohn. *Shakespeare's "Hamlet": A New Commentary, with a Chapter on First Principles.* London: Smith, Elder & Co., 1913, 274 p.

Scene-by-scene analysis of the play. Trench concludes by stating that no absolute interpretation of the drama is possible, but that the text is a rich ground of subtleties and profundities.

Very, Jones. *Essays and Poems: "Hamlet".* Boston: C. C. Little and J. Brown, 1839, 82 p.

Attributes Hamlet's indecision to the one thing he fears: death. Very argues that his fear of death is "the hinge on which [Hamlet's] every endeavor turns."

Vickers, Brian. "Two Tragic Heroes." In his *The Artistry of Shakespeare's Prose,* pp. 240-71. London: Methuen & Co., 1968.

Examination of the prose speeches of Brutus and Hamlet. Vickers concentrates on the "expansiveness" of Hamlet's prose and its relation to the poetic speeches. He also includes a lengthy section on the gravedigger scene, which he says shows "the first signs of that application of comic prose to tragedy which is shortly to come to fruition" in Shakespeare's work.

Walker, Roy. *The Time Is Out of Joint: A Study of "Hamlet."* London: Andrew Darkers Limited, 1948, 157 p.

Examines the ways in which Hamlet is portrayed as a figure of sacrifice whose purpose is to cleanse Elsinore of its sickness.

Weitz, Morris. *"Hamlet" and the Philosophy of Literary Criticism.* Chicago, London: The University of Chicago Press, 1964, 335 p.

Linguistic analysis which focuses on the various approaches used by the critics of *Hamlet.* Weitz determines that each commentator has followed one of four procedures in interpreting *Hamlet:* description, explanation, evaluation, or poetics.

West, Robert H. "King Hamlet's Ambiguous Ghost." *PMLA* LXX, No. 5 (December 1955): 1107-17.*

Rejects Roy Battenhouse's theory that the ghost is not Christian and surveys Renaissance drama in an attempt to understand Shakespeare's handling of the supernatural. West concludes that the ghost is Christian, but that "we do not need to know the ghost's denomination, and to insist upon it is gratuitous."

Williamson, Claude C.H., ed. *Readings on the Character of Hamlet: 1661-1947.* London: George Allen & Unwin, 1950, 783 p.

Presents a compilation of almost three hundred years of *Hamlet* criticism.

Winstanley, Lilian. *"Hamlet" and the Scottish Succession: Being an Examination of the Relations of the Play of "Hamlet" to the Scottish Succession and the Essex Conspiracy.* London: Cambridge at the University Press, 1921, 188 p.

Regards *Hamlet* as a political allegory that deals with the revolt of the Earl of Essex and the succession of Scotland's James VI to the English throne. Winstanley sees Hamlet as a combination of James and Essex.

Zitner, S. P. "Hamlet, Duellist." *University of Toronto Quarterly* XXXIX, No. 1 (October 1969): 1-18.

Studies the use of weapons in the play. Zitner focuses on Shakespeare's opposition to the aristocratic code of duelling to which Hamlet feels bound—an opposition which expresses itself in the play's depiction of the inadequacy of that code and its cost to human life.

Henry IV, Part I and Henry IV, Part II

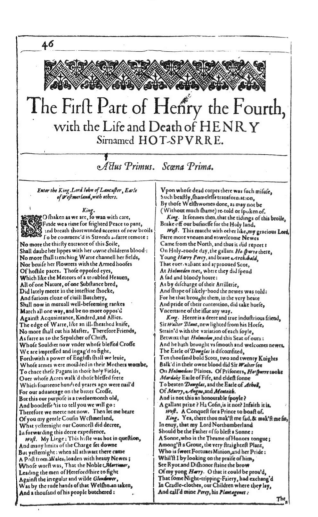

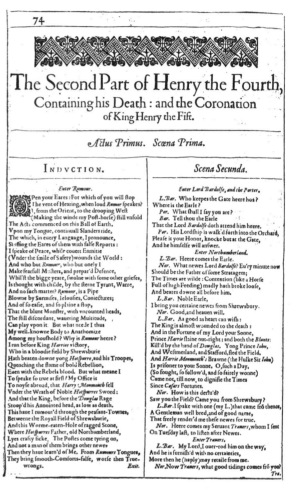

DATE: *Henry IV, Part 1* appears to have been written by Shakespeare in late 1596 or early 1597, and scholars generally agree that it was first performed shortly after its composition. It was entered in the Stationers' Register on February 25, 1598 (without the designation "Part One"), and a quarto text of the play appeared in 1598. Francis Meres mentions "Henry the 4" in his list of Shakespeare's works in his *Palladis Tamia* (1598) as among Shakespeare's tragedies, presumably referring to Part One.

There is widespread agreement that *Henry IV, Part 2* was written shortly after Part One, with late 1597 or early 1598 frequently given as its date of composition. It is also generally agreed that it was first staged immediately after the production of *Henry IV, Part 1*. It was entered in the Stationers' Register on August 23, 1600, and a quarto text appeared in that same year.

TEXT: Six quarto editions of *Henry IV, Part 1* are known, which is an unusually large number for an Elizabethan play. The earliest known text survives only as a four-leaf fragment, and five later editions—dated 1598, 1604, 1608, 1613, and 1622—have survived intact to the present. The Folio version appears to have been based on the 1613 quarto; hence, the earliest complete quarto (1598), supplemented by the still earlier fragment, remains the most authoritative text for *Henry IV, Part 1*. Only one quarto edition of *Henry IV, Part 2*, dated 1600, is known. In some copies of this edition, however, a scene was omitted, apparently as a result of a printing error. The Folio text of *Henry IV, Part 2* adds eight passages not found in the earlier text. Many scholars believe these were struck from the quarto by censors for political reasons connected with developing tensions between the Earl of Essex and Queen Elizabeth—tensions which eventually led to an unsuccessful rebellion by Essex in February, 1601. The Folio text of Part Two is otherwise very similar to the quarto, which, except for the omitted passages, is considered more authoritative.

SOURCES: For the historical plots of both plays, Shakespeare drew from several accounts of English history written during the Elizabethan period, selecting, pruning, and condensing the considerable detail available. His chief source for the historical plot was Raphael Holinshed's *Chronicles of England, Scotland, and Ireland* (2d edition, 1586-87), a work Shakespeare used on several other occasions. He also consulted Samuel Daniel's narrative poem, *The Civile Wars between the two houses of Lancaster and York* (1595) and Edward Hall's *Chron-*

icle of the Union of the Two Noble and Illustre Famelies of Lancastre and Yorke (1540).

For the Hal-Falstaff plot, Shakespeare was apparently indebted to a crude, anonymous chronicle-play entitled *The Famous Victories of Henry V* (1594?). This play survives in manuscript, although the surviving copy was probably changed or condensed. However, some scholars have speculated that both *The Famous Victories* and *Henry IV* were derived from an earlier source now lost.

A major preoccupation of twentieth-century scholarship has been to trace the dramatic forebears of the character of Falstaff, and sources for him have been proposed from a wide range of previous literature. The most prominent of these supposed dramatic ancestors are the stock characters of the Vice and the Devil from medieval morality plays and the *miles gloriosus* from ancient Latin comedy. It is possible that Shakespeare derived Falstaff from the character Sir John Oldcastle in *The Famous Victories,* and there is substantial evidence that Shakespeare's character was in fact originally called Oldcastle. It is thought that Shakespeare changed the name after the descendants of the real Sir John protested that their ancestor's good name had been slandered. Hal's address to Falstaff as "my old lad of the castle" (*1H4,* I. ii. 47) and the assertion in the Epilogue of Part Two that "Oldcastle died a martyr, and this [Falstaff] is not the man" are among the chief bits of textual evidence that Shakespeare did indeed change the name.

CRITICAL HISTORY: Henry IV, Part 1 and *Part 2* have received a substantial amount of diverse criticism over the past four centuries, making them undoubtedly the most discussed of Shakespeare's historical dramas. However, over the past four hundred years of commentary a core of major issues has dominated critics' interests. Perhaps the most significant, and the most essential to an understanding of *Henry IV,* is the nature of Falstaff's character and his relation to both the other characters and the main action of the two plays. Critics have also focused on the question of the unity of the plays, the relation of *Henry IV* to Shakespeare's other histories, its mixture of history and comedy, and the meaning of Hal's rejection of Falstaff.

During the seventeenth century, nearly all commentators on *Henry IV* focused on the issue of morality in the plays. Falstaff was generally seen as the embodiment of humanity's baser qualities, and his rejection by Prince Hal was considered both proper and necessary in establishing the moral intention of the plays. This view is best exemplified in the essays by John Dryden and Jeremy Collier, both of whom regarded Sir John as a "coward" and a "drunk" who hardly demanded the sympathy of a civilized society. However, their interpretation of Falstaff's character left much unexamined and unexplained in Shakespeare's plays. It wasn't until the beginning of the following century that critics began to see the rejection of Falstaff and Hal's reformation as more complex. Similarly, other concerns came to the forefront, such as the validity of Shakespeare's mixture of tragic and comic forms, his supposed ignorance of the Neoclassical rules for successful drama, and the relation between the two *Henry IV* plays. Nicholas Rowe was one of the earliest critics to disapprove of Shakespeare's hybrid genre on the grounds of dramatic purity and the first to question Hal's rejection of Falstaff as both inhumane and at odds with the author's sympathetic portrait of the fat knight. Rowe claimed that Falstaff was "almost too agreeable" and wondered whether "some People have not, in remembrance of the Diversion he had formerly afforded 'em, been sorry to see his Friend *Hal*

use him so scurvily, when he comes to the Crown." Rowe's comments on the nature of Falstaff's character foreshadowed a century of debate over the issue; indeed, the great topic of *Henry IV* criticism in the eighteenth-century can be termed the paradox of Falstaff. Other eighteenth century critics who addressed the issue include Corbyn Morris, Samuel Johnson, Richard Cumberland, and Henry Mackenzie. Morris, one of the earliest of Falstaff's unabashed champions, denied the presence of a moral dilemma in *Henry IV* and considered the rejection of Sir John as merely Shakespeare's accomodation to the "Austerity of the Times." Johnson, on the other hand, concluded that Hal's rejection of Falstaff, despite the delight the "unimitable" Sir John provides his audience, was both proper and necessary to the reestablishment of a moral order in the plays. Cumberland appealed to the exigencies of the plot, claiming that Falstaff had to be evil enough to threaten to corrupt the prince, but amiable enough to appeal to him. The novelist Mackenzie admired Falstaff's combination of wit, physical obsession, and high imagination, and became the first to compare the fat knight to another Renaissance comic hero, Don Quixote.

However, the most celebrated of all eighteenth-century writings on Falstaff was Maurice Morgann's "An Essay on the Dramatic Character of Sir John Falstaff." In this study, Morgann argued that the "apparent" Falstaff—the drunk and intemperate coward—is in reality a misconception of the "real" Falstaff, who is an individual of "much Natural courage and resolution." Morgann's essay overturned a number of previously held assumptions and established, in the following centuries, the lines of argument opposing critics employed to defend their interpretations of *Henry IV.*

Critics in the nineteenth century continued the debate over many of the questions raised in the preceding two hundred years and identified additional areas of discussion. Perhaps the most influential of theories prevalent during this time was the idea, first suggested by August Wilhelm Schlegel and continued by Hermann Ulrici and Beverley Warner, that *Henry IV* was part of Shakespeare's ten-play "epic" dramatization of English history, from *King John* to *Henry VIII.* Although the question of the relation of the *Henry IV* plays to Shakespeare's other historical dramas seems largely confined to the nineteenth century, E.M.W. Tillyard revived the issue in the twentieth century with his interpretation of Shakespeare's histories as thematically unified in their presentation of an orthodox Elizabethan world view. Other twentieth-century critics such as Una Ellis-Fermor and Alvin Kernan considered *Henry IV* as part of a Shakespearean tetralogy, often referred to as The Henriad, consisting of *Richard II, Henry IV, Part 1* and *Part 2,* and *Henry V.* Another important contribution during the nineteenth century was Ulrici's essay on the historical and comic plots in *Henry IV.* In this study, the German critic maintained that Prince Hal is indeed the hero of the plays—and, most significantly, that the Falstaff story serves as a kind of parody of the main action, suggesting both the hollowness and licentiousness of the Lancastrian monarchy. This assessment of the dramatic structure of *Henry IV* was developed in the twentieth century by L. C. Knights and William Empson.

Other important nineteenth-century critics who discussed *Henry IV* include Samuel Taylor Coleridge, William Hazlitt, and G. G. Gervinus. Coleridge never lectured at length on *Henry IV,* but his scattered remarks reveal his admiration for both plays, particularly the character of Falstaff, whom he compared to Richard III and Iago. He saw all three as characters dominated by their intellectual faculties, a view expressed in the eighteenth century by Mackenzie and in the twentieth century by Wyndham Lewis. Hazlitt devoted a considerable amount of attention to the plays. He continued Morgann's sympathetic interpretation of Falstaff's character and argued that Hal's rejection of the knight was both emotionally disconcerting and intellectually unjustified. Unlike Hazlitt, Gervinus belittled Falstaff and called him ''the personification of the inferior side of man,'' while at the same time he voiced perhaps the highest praise of Hal in calling him an ''ideal prince'' and the central figure in the plays. Gervinus also joined in the controversy surrounding the relation of *Henry IV, Part 1* and *Part 2,* claiming that the two plays represent a unified work, each based on a system of parallels and interconnections formed by the major characters.

Both Morgann's and Hazlitt's pro-Falstaff reading of *Henry IV* was continued in the twentieth century by A. C. Bradley, who regarded Sir John as ''the bliss of freedom gained in humour,'' and who saw Hal's rejection of the knight as a grevious error on Shakespeare's part. This error consisted of Shakespeare's attempt to divorce the audience's sympathies from Falstaff in order to prepare for his eventual repudiation—an attempt, Bradley claimed, doomed to failure because of the attractiveness of Falstaff's character. Although Bradley acknowledged the same vices in Falstaff noted by previous critics, he concluded that the experience of comedy itself demanded that their moral implications be set aside.

The reaction to Bradley's essay on this and many other points was generally quite negative. Over a decade after its appearance, E. E. Stoll denounced both Bradley and Morgann as hopeless romantics, and he dismissed all previous Anglo-American criticism of Shakespeare as amateurish and ignorant of the history of drama. Stoll posited that Falstaff was not the sympathetic and transcendent figure imagined by Bradley and the Romantic critics, but a conventional stage character derived from the *miles gloriosus,* or ''braggart soldier,'' of Latin comedy. This approach, which sought in *Henry IV* evidence of the literary traditions and beliefs popular during the Elizabethan age, was also adopted by such later critics as John Webster Spargo, T. A. Jackson, J. Dover Wilson, and Tillyard. Other critics, such as L. C. Knights and William Empson, interpreted *Henry IV* according to the strictures of New Criticism, while J.I.M. Stewart and C. L. Barber followed the methods of the ''myth'' critics—a school which sought to identify universal archetypes present in all literature. What all these commentators held in common, however, was the view that Shakespeare created not sympathetic human figures in *Henry IV,* but dramatic ''types'' designed to carry out specific functions in the plays. Perhaps the most controversial of the different conclusions was that reached by Spargo, Jackson, Dover Wilson, and Tillyard—all of whom regarded *Henry IV* as Shakespeare's adaptation of medieval morality drama, and who saw such characters as Prince Hal and Falstaff, Hotspur and the Lord Chief Justice, as representations of distinct moral or ethical attitudes. With some minor variations in their thinking, these critics conceived the action of *Henry IV, Part 1* and *Part 2* as moving towards the eventual repudiation of Vice by the Prodigal Prince and Hal's acceptance of the divine responsibilities of kingship.

Dover Wilson was perhaps the most influential critic on *Henry IV* in the first half of the twentieth century. He argued that only through a historical reading of the plays is the scholar able to uncover Shakespeare's basic allegorical structure—a

structure, he claimed, which was immediately recognizable to Shakespeare's Elizabethan audience. Importantly, Dover Wilson also maintained that the modern dilemma over the rejection of Falstaff would not have existed for Shakespeare's contemporaries, since they would have seen Sir John only in this moral context and, therefore, demanded his expulsion and repudiation as a matter of principle. Later critics adopted Dover Wilson's thesis and added insights of their own. Tillyard, for example, claimed that *Henry IV* reflects an ''Elizabethan world picture'' and demonstrates Shakespeare's acceptance of the Tudor myth popular during his lifetime. Stewart and Barber applied a more anthropological approach to the *Henry IV* plays. Stewart interpreted Hal's rejection of Falstaff as Shakespeare's dramatization of the ''scapegoat ritual'' practiced in primitive cultures; similarly, Barber regarded the repudiation of Falstaff not as a moral event, as did Dover Wilson, but as Shakespeare's adaptation of the traditional banishment of the Lord of Misrule enacted in numerous cultures during holiday festivities. A final mention should be given here to both Knights and Empson. Also anti-Romantic in their approach to *Henry IV,* these two critics asserted that the single-minded attention given the character of Falstaff obscures the recognition of his true dramatic role—that of the ironic foil who parodies and deflates the dubious heroics present in the main plot. Thus, similar to Spargo, Jackson, Dover Wilson, Tillyard, Stewart, and Barber, Knights and Empson considered Falstaff not the human figure of Morgann and Bradley, but a dramatic type who serves a specific function in Shakespeare's plays.

The debate over the exact relationship of *Henry IV, Part 1* and *Part 2* also intensified during the twentieth century. Such recent critics as Harry T. Baker, Robert Adger Law, M. A. Shaaber, and Clifford Leech all contested the nineteenth-century assumption that the two parts constitute a unified ten-act play. Some critics, especially Law, Leech, Knights, and A. R. Humphreys, suggested that the second part was superior to the first, an opinion which received little support before the twentieth century. Other commentators, most notably G. K. Hunter and Harold Jenkins, suggested new approaches to the question of unity between the plays. Hunter analyzed the parallels in dramatic structure of the two dramas and found the entire work similar in design to other Renaissance two-part plays. On the other hand, Jenkins argued that the two plays are both unified and separate, complimentary and incompatible, basing his theory on the idea that Shakespeare changed his mind during the composition of *Henry IV, Part 1* and decided that a single play would be insufficient to portray the action or characters he intended.

Critics influenced by the theories of New Criticism, such as Cleanth Brooks and Robert Heilman, Ellis-Fermor, and D. A. Traversi, as well as other Shakespearean scholars, began to question the validity of the historical critics' approach to *Henry IV.* Most often disputed was the idea that Shakespeare's play could be reduced to any type of historical, moral, or social evaluation. Stressing the ambiguity, linguistic complexity, and irony inherent in the *Henry IV* plays, Ellis-Fermor, Brooks and Heilman, and Traversi all argued that the central conflict in *Henry IV* has nothing to do with such concepts as Virtue or Vice, Vanity or Political Authority, but consists of Hal's choice to reform and become an ''ideal'' king and the effect such a decision has on the development of the characters and the play itself. Two other important critics who disapproved of the methods of the historical critics were Harold C. Goddard and Samuel B. Hemingway. The first of these combined both the Romantic and anti-Romantic interpretations of Hal and Falstaff and posited the idea that Shakespeare intended to create two Hals, as well as two Falstaffs, in the *Henry IV* plays. Hemingway, in a similar fashion, united the approaches of Morgann and Bradley with those of Stoll and Dover Wilson in an attempt to achieve a "two-leveled" critical assessment of Falstaff's character, claiming that neither approach by itself can accomplish a reliable evaluation of Shakespeare's comic hero.

In recent years, *Henry IV* criticism has continued to move away from the historical methods of Tillyard and Dover Wilson and focus instead on the structural and linguistic elements in the plays. Such critics as Joseph Porter and Edward Pechter have begun to examine internal evidence in *Henry IV* as a means of solving certain problems which have continued to plague scholars. For Porter, this examination consisted of a reinterpretation of Hal's first soliloquy using the "speech-act" theory of the British philosopher J. L. Austin. Pechter, on the other hand, disputed the theories of Tillyard and maintained that *Henry IV, Part 1* has no relation to the Tudor myth popular during Shakespeare's lifetime. Instead, he regarded the drama as an open-ended play lacking a clear center of authority and resistent to any external scheme as a model of interpretation.

Despite the critical shift towards studies focusing on the plays' language and structure, there are still some critics, such as Herbert B. Rothschild, Jr. and Roy Battenhouse, whose work reflects the influence of Tillyard and Dover Wilson. Still others have tried to synthesize the various approaches, combining the Romantic and the modern, the historical and the linguistic, in order to achieve a fuller understanding of the *Henry IV* plays. What most critics have found is that Shakespeare's drama is a complex creation, unyielding to any single formula or to the critical methods of the past. Perhaps for this reason, *Henry IV, Part 1* and *Part 2* remain the most controversial of Shakespeare's histories and, for many readers, the most satisfying.

THOMAS FULLER (essay date 1662)

[*The following passage from the English biographer Thomas Fuller is one of the most unequivocal items of external evidence that Shakespeare's Falstaff had originally been named Oldcastle. The passage also has critical interest as an early interpretation of Falstaff as a coward, a designation challenged by such later critics as Corbyn Morris (1744), Maurice Morgann (1777), William Hazlitt (1817), and A. C. Bradley (1902). Fuller's reference to Oldcastle as a character in "all Plays" could refer not only to Shakespeare's 1 and 2 Henry IV but also to* The Famous Victories of Henry V, *an anonymous chronicle-play in which Oldcastle appears as a dissolute companion to Prince Henry, and which was apparently one of Shakespeare's sources; "our Comedian" clearly refers to Shakespeare. The essay was first published in 1662.*]

John Fastolfe, Knight, was a native of this County [Norfolk]. . . . To avouch him by many arguments valiant, is to maintain that the Sun is bright, though since the *Stage* hath been overbold with his memory, making him a *Thrasonical Puff*, and emblem of *Mock-valour*.

True it is, Sir *John Oldcastle* did first bear the brunt of the one, being made the *make-sport* in all Plays for a *Coward*. It is easily known out of what *purse* this black *peny* came; the Papists railing on him for a *Heretick*, and therefore he must also be a *Coward*, though indeed he was a *man* of *arms, every inch of him,* and as valiant as any in his age.

Now as I am glad that Sir John Oldcastle is *put out,* so I am sorry that Sir John Fastolfe is *put in,* to relieve his memory in this base service, to be the *anvil* for every *dull wit* to strike upon. Nor is our Comedian excusable, by some alteration of his name, writing him Sir *John Falstafe* (and making him the *property* of *pleasure* for King Henry the Fifth, to abuse), seeing the *vicinity* of sounds intrench on the memory of *that worthy Knight,* and few do heed the *inconsiderable difference* in spelling of their name. (pp. 131-32)

> Thomas Fuller, "Norfolk," in his The History of the Worthies of England, *edited by Thomas Fuller, F. C. and J. Rivington, in 1811, pp. 124-53.*

JOHN DRYDEN (essay date 1668)

[*Dryden, the leading poet and playwright of Restoration England, helped formulate the Neoclassical view of Shakespeare as an irregular genius whose native talent overcame his ignorance of the proper "rules" and language for serious drama. He was also instrumental in establishing Shakespeare's reputation as the foremost English dramatist, and his assessment of Shakespeare influenced critics well into the following century. Dryden's best-known remarks on Falstaff—in which he characterizes Sir John as "Cowardly," "Drunken," and "Vain"—occur as a digression in a discussion of Ben Jonson's play,* The Silent Woman; or Epicoene. *The following essay was first published in Dryden's* Of Dramatic Poesie: An Essay *in 1668.*]

I am assur'd from diverse persons, that *Ben. Johnson* was actually acquainted with such a man [as Morose], one altogether as ridiculous as he is [represented in *The Silent Woman; or, Epicoene*]. Others say it is not enough to find one man of such an humour; it must be common to more, and the more common the more natural. To prove this they instance in the best of Comical Characters, Falstaff: There are many men resembling him; Old, Fat, Merry, Cowardly, Drunken, Amorous, Vain, and Lying: But to convince these people I need but tell them, that humour is the ridiculous extravagance of conversation, wherein one man differs from all others. If then it be common or communicated to many, how differs it from other mens? or what indeed causes it to be ridiculous so much as the singularity of it? As for Falstaffe, he is not properly one humour, but a Miscellany of Humours or Images, drawn from so many several men; that wherein he is singular in his wit, or those things he sayes, *praeter expectatum,* unexpected by the Audience; his quick evasions when you imagine him surpriz'd, which as they are extreamly diverting of themselves, so receive a great addition from his person; for the very sight of such an unwieldy old debauch'd fellow is a Comedy alone. . . . (p. 146)

> John Dryden, in an extract from The Shakespere Allusion Book: A Collection of Allusions to Shakespere from 1591-1700, Vol. II, *edited by John Munro, Oxford University Press, London, 1932, pp. 143-48.*

JOHN DRYDEN (essay date 1679)

[*Dryden's views on the proper meaning of the term "humour" appear to have shifted somewhat in the years between* Of Dramatick Poesy *(see excerpt above, 1668) and the following passage, but Shakespeare's Falstaff appears to be a constant in his thinking on the subject. The following extract was first published in Dryden's* Troilus and Cressida; or, Truth Found Too Late, *in 1679.*]

A character, or that which distinguishes one man from all others, cannot be suppos'd to consist of one particular Virtue, or Vice, or passion only; but 't is a composition of qualities which are not contrary to one another in the same person: thus the same man may be liberal and valiant, but not liberal and covetous; so in a Comical character, or humour, (which is an inclination to this, or that particular folly) *Falstaff* is a lyar, and a coward, a Glutton, and a Buffon, because all these qualities may agree in the same man. . . . Our *Shakespear*, having ascrib'd to *Henry the Fourth* the character of a King, and of a Father, gives him the perfect manners of each Relation, when either he transacts with his Son, or with his Subjects. (pp. 246-47)

> *John Dryden, in an extract from his "The Grounds of Criticism in Tragedy," in* The Shakespere Allusion-Book: A Collection of Allusions to Shakespere from 1591-1700, *Vol. II, edited by John Munro, Oxford University Press, London, 1932, pp. 244-50.*

JEREMY COLLIER   (essay date 1698)

[Collier, an English clergyman, is best remembered for his attack on the Restoration stage in a tract entitled A Short View of the Immorality and Profaneness of the English Stage. *Collier did not fully exempt Shakespeare from his condemnation of stage immorality, but he did find him a "gentiler Enemy" than the Restoration dramatists who were his chief targets. In the excerpt below, taken from that work, first published in 1698, he uses the rejection of Falstaff as a positive example of stage morality, in sharp contrast to such later critics as Nicholas Rowe (1709), William Hazlitt (1817), and A. C. Bradley (1902), all of whom have found the rejection callous and hypocritical.]*

I shall take a Testimony or two from *Shakespear*. And here we may observe the admir'd *Falstaffe* goes off in Disappointment. He is thrown out of Favour as being a *Rake*, and dies like a Rat behind the Hangings. The Pleasure he has given, would not excuse him. The *Poet* was not so partial, as to let his Humour compound for his Lewdness. If 'tis objected that this remark is wide of the Point, because *Falstaffe* is represented in Tragedy, where the Laws of Justice are more strickly observ'd. To this I answer, that you may call *Henry the Fourth* and *Fifth*, Tragedies if you please. But for all that, *Falstaffe* wears no *Buskins*, his Character is perfectly Comical from end to end. (pp. 408-09)

> *Jeremy Collier, in his extract from* The Shakespere Allusion Book: A Collection of Allusions to Shakespere from 1591-1700, *Vol. II, edited by John Munro, Oxford University Press, London, 1932, pp. 407-09.*

NICHOLAS ROWE   (essay date 1709)

[Rowe was the editor of the first critical edition of Shakespeare's plays (1709) and the author of the first authoritative Shakespeare biography. In the following excerpt, taken from Rowe's The Works of William Shakespeare, *Vol. 1, published in 1709, Rowe reveals a typical Neoclassical disapproval for the mixed genre of "Trage-Comedy." His essay also suggests that the disapproval of Hal's rejection of Falstaff, prominent in the nineteenth and twentieth centuries, was voiced as early as the first years of the eighteenth century.]*

[Shakespeare's] plays are properly to be distinguish'd only into Comedies and Tragedies. Those which are called Histories, and even some of his Comedies, are really Tragedies, with a run or mixture of Comedy amongst 'em. That way of Trage-Comedy was the common Mistake of that Age, and is indeed become so agreeable to the *English* Tast, that tho' the severer Critiques among us cannot bear it, yet the generality of our

Audiences seem to be better pleas'd with it than with an exact Tragedy. *The Merry Wives of Windsor, The Comedy of Errors,* and *The Taming of the Shrew,* are all pure Comedy; the rest, however they are call'd, have something of both Kinds. 'Tis not very easie to determine which way of Writing he was most Excellent in. There is certainly a great deal of Entertainment in his Comical Humours; and tho' they did not then strike at all Ranks of People, as the Satyr of the present Age has taken the Liberty to do, yet there is a pleasing and a well-distinguish'd Variety in those Characters which he thought fit to meddle with. *Falstaff* is allow'd by every body to be a Master-piece; the Character is always well-sustain'd, tho' drawn out into the length of three Plays; and even the Account of his Death, given by his Old Landlady Mrs. *Quickly,* in the first act of *Henry V.* tho' it be extremely Natural, is yet as diverting as any Part of his Life. If there be any Fault in the Draught he has made of this lewd old Fellow, it is, that tho' he has made him a Thief, Lying, Cowardly, Vain-glorious, and in short every way Vicious, yet he has given him so much Wit as to make him almost too agreeable; and I don't know whether some People have not, in remembrance of the Diversion he had formerly afforded 'em, been sorry to see his Friend *Hal* use him so scurvily, when he comes to the Crown in the End of the Second Part of *Henry* the Fourth. (pp. 9-10)

> *Nicholas Rowe, "Some Account of the Life, etc., of Mr. William Shakespear," in* Eighteenth Century Essays on Shakespeare, *edited by D. Nichol Smith, second edition, Oxford at the Clarendon Press, 1963, pp. 1-22.*

CHARLES GILDON   (essay date 1710)

[Gildon was the first critic to write an extended commentary on Shakespeare's plays. Like many other Neoclassicists, Gildon regarded Shakespeare as an imaginative playwright who nevertheless lacked knowledge of the dramatic "rules" necessary for correct writing. In the following excerpt, Gildon takes exception to Nicholas Rowe's classification of Shakespeare's histories as tragedies with a comic admixture (see excerpt above, 1709); instead, he considers them not tragedies at all, but works similar to early Greek poetry in their mixture of serious and comic characters. The following extract first appeared in The Works of Mr. William Shakespeare *in 1710.]*

I come now to the Historical Plays of *Shakespeare,* which . . . cannot be placed under *Tragedy* because they contain no Tragic Imitation. They are Draughts of the Lives of Princes brought into *Dialogue,* and in Regard of their Mixture of serious and comical Characters may be compared to the Greek Pieces that were wrote before *Æschylus* and *Sophocles* had reformed the Stage of *Athens,* or the rambling unartful Pieces first represented in *Rome* after the calling in of the *Etrurian* Players, nay after the Time of *Livius Andronicus.* In their Extent they may be compar'd to the *Theseids,* the *Heracleids,* written by some Greek Poets and reflected on by *Aristotle* in his Art of Poetry for imagining that the Unity of the Hero made the Unity of the Action.

These Instances from this polite Nation will be a very good Plea for this Error of *Shakespeare,* who liv'd when the Stage was not regarded by the State as it was in *Athens.* For had a Reformation then begun he wou'd doubtless have done as Mr. *Corneille* did upon the studying the Art of the Stage, by which the Plays which he wrote afterwards excell'd those he wrote without any Knowledge of that Art.

I shall only add here that since these Plays are Histories there can be no Manner of Fable or Design in them. I shall not therefore give the Plot but refer the Reader to those Historians where he may find the Stories at large, and by them judge how near *Shakespeare* has kept to the Character History has given us of them. (p. 245)

Tho' the Humour of *Falstaff* be what is most valuable in both these Parts [*1* and *2 Henry IV*] yet that is far more excellent in the first, for Sir *John* is not near so Diverting in the second Part. *Hotspur* is the next in Goodness, but that wou'd have shew'd much more had it been in a regular Tragedy, where the Manners had not only been necessary but productive of Incidents Noble, and Charming. *Glendower* is fine for Comedy. (p. 248)

> *Charles Gildon, in an extract from his "Remarks on the Plays of Shakespeare," in* Shakespeare, the Critical Heritage: 1693-1733, Vol. 2, *edited by Brian Vickers, Routledge & Kegan Paul, 1974, pp. 226-62.*

[JOSEPH ADDISON]   (essay date 1711)

[*The following piece was originally an unsigned essay published in* The Spectator, *No. 47, April 24, 1711.*]

Mr. Hobbs, in his Discourse of Human Nature, which, in my humble Opinion, is much the best of all his Works, after some very curious Observations upon Laughter, concludes thus: 'The Passion of Laughter is nothing else but sudden Glory arising from some sudden Conception of some Eminency in our selves, by Comparison with the Infirmity of others, or with our own formerly: For Men laugh at the Follies of themselves past, when they come suddenly to Remembrance, except they bring with them any present Dishonour.'

According to this Author therefore, when we hear a Man laugh excessively, instead of saying he is very Merry, we ought to tell him he is very Proud. And indeed, if we look into the bottom of this Matter, we shall meet with many Observations to confirm us in his Opinion. Every one laughs at some Body that is in an inferior State of Folly to himself. (p. 200)

I shall pass by the Consideration of those Stage Coxcombs that are able to shake a whole Audience, and take Notice of a particular sort of Men who are such Provokers of Mirth in Conversation, that it is impossible for a Club or Merry-meeting to subsist without them; I mean, those honest Gentlemen that are always exposed to the Wit and Raillery of their Well-wishers and Companions; that are pelted by Men, Women and Children, Friends and Foes, and, in a word, stand as *Butts* in Conversation, for every one to shoot at that pleases. . . . A stupid *Butt* is only fit for the Conversation of ordinary People: Men of Wit require one that will give them Play, and bestir himself in the absurd part of his Behaviour. A *Butt* with these Accomplishments, frequently gets the Laugh of his side, and turns the Ridicule upon him that attacks him. Sir *John Falstaff* was an Hero of this Species, and gives a good Description of himself in his Capacity of a *Butt*, after the following manner; *Men of all Sorts* (says that merry Knight) *take a pride to gird at me. The Brain of Man is not able to invent any thing that tends to Laughter more than I invent, or is invented on me. I am not only Witty in my self, but the Cause that Wit is in other Men.* (pp. 203-04)

[*Joseph Addison*], *in his essay in* The Spectator, Vol. I, *edited by Donald F. Bond, Oxford at the Clarendon Press, Oxford, 1965, pp. 200-04.*

[WILLIAM WARBURTON]   (essay date 1733)

[*Correspondence first published in 1817 proved that the Shakespearean editor Lewis Theobald incorporated notes and letters by Warburton in his 1733 edition of* The Works of Shakespeare, *from which the following extract is taken. Brian Vickers, editor of* Shakespeare, the Critical Heritage, *assigns the following passage to Warburton. The "Rule" mentioned in the first sentence of the following passage refers to Horace's admonition that the playwright must make characters self-consistent throughout a play. Warburton claims that Shakespeare did not transgress this rule in his portrait of Prince Hal.*]

It may be objected, perhaps, by some who do not go to the Bottom of [Shakespeare's] Conduct, that he has . . . transgress'd against the Rule himself by making Prince *Harry* at once, upon coming to the Crown, throw off his former Dissoluteness and take up the Practice of a sober Morality and all the kingly Virtues. But this would be a mistaken Objection. The Prince's Reformation is not so sudden as not to be prepar'd and expected by the Audience. He gives, indeed, a Loose to Vanity and a light unweigh'd Behaviour when he is trifling among his dissolute Companions, but the Sparks of innate Honour and true Nobleness break from him upon every proper Occasion where we would hope to see him awake to Sentiments suiting his Birth and Dignity. And our Poet has so well and artfully guarded his Character from the Suspicions of habitual and unreformable Profligateness that even from the first shewing him upon the Stage, in the first Part of *Henry IV*, when he made him consent to join with *Falstaff* in a Robbery on the Highway, he has taken care not to carry him off the Scene without an Intimation that he knows them all, and their unyok'd Humour; and that, like the Sun, he will permit them only for a while to obscure and cloud his Brightness, then break thro' the Mist when he pleases to be himself again, that his Lustre, when wanted, may be the more wonder'd at.

> [*William Warburton*], *in his extract from* Shakespeare, the Critical Heritage: 1693-1733, Vol. 2, *edited by Brian Vickers, Routledge & Kegan Paul, 1974, p. 479.*

CORBYN MORRIS   (essay date 1744)

[*Morris, an Englishman who became commissioner of customs in 1763, wrote mainly on economic and statistical subjects. But he is also the author of perhaps the earliest extended celebration of Falstaff as an entirely positive character and the perfect combination of wit and humor, a position in sharp contrast to John Dryden (1668 and 1679) and to such later critics as Samuel Johnson (1765), Richard Stark (1788), William Richardson (1788), A. S. Pushkin (1836), Victor Hugo (1864), E. E. Stoll (1914), L. C. Knights (1934), and H. B. Charlton (1935). Morris's position anticipated in some ways the Romantic and post-Romantic celebration of Falstaff by Maurice Morgann (1777), Samuel Taylor Coleridge (1810 and 1813), William Hazlitt (1817), and A. C. Bradley (1902). The following excerpt is from Morris's* An Essay Towards Fixing the True Standards of Wit, Humour, Raillery, Satire, and Ridicule, *first published in 1744.*]

As to the the Character of Sir *John Falstaff*, it is chiefly extracted from *Shakespeare*, in his *1st Part of King Henry the IVth*. But so far as *Sir John* in *Shakespeare*'s Description sinks into a *Cheat* or a *Scoundrel* upon any Occasion, he is different from that *Falstaff* who is designed in the following *Essay,* and is entirely an amiable Character. . . . His Imprisonment and Death in the latter Part of *King Henry the IVth,* seem also to have been written by *Shakespeare* in Compliance with the *Austerity* of the Times, and in order to avoid the Imputation of encouraging *Idleness* and mirthful *Riot* by too amiable and happy an Example. (p. 122)

For HUMOUR, extensively and fully understood, is *any remarkable* Oddity *or* Foible *belonging to a* Person *in* real Life; *whether this* Foible *be constitutional, habitual,* or *only affected; whether partial in one or two Circumstances or tinging the whole Temper and Conduct of the* Person.

It has from hence been observ'd that there is more HUMOUR in the *English* Comedies than in others; as we have more various odd *Characters* in real Life than any other Nation, or perhaps than all other Nations together.

That HUMOUR gives more Delight and leaves a more pleasurable Impression behind it than WIT, is universally felt and established, though the Reasons for this have not yet been assign'd. I shall therefore beg Leave to submit the following.

1. HUMOUR is more *interesting* than WIT in general, as the *Oddities* and *Foibles* of *Persons* in *real Life* are more apt to affect our Passions than any Oppositions or Relations between *inanimate* Objects.

2. HUMOUR is *Nature,* or what really appears in the Subject, without any Embellishments; WIT only a Stroke of *Art* where the original Subject, being insufficient of itself, is garnished and deck'd with auxiliary Objects.

3. HUMOUR, or the Foible of a *Character* in real Life, is usually insisted upon for some Length of Time. From whence, and from the common Knowledge of the Character, it is universally felt and understood. Whereas the Strokes of WIT are like sudden *Flashes,* vanishing in an Instant, and usually flying too fast to be sufficiently marked and pursued by the Audience.

4. HUMOUR, if the Representation of it be just, is compleat and perfect in its Kind, and entirely fair and unstrain'd. Whereas in the Allusions of WIT the Affinity is generally imperfect and defective in one Part or other; and even in those Points where the Affinity may be allow'd to subsist some Nicety and Strain is usually requir'd to make it appear.

5. HUMOUR generally appears in such Foibles as each of the Company thinks himself superior to. Whereas WIT shews the Quickness and Abilities of the Person who discovers it, and places him superior to the rest of the Company.

6. HUMOUR, in the Representation of the *Foibles* of *Persons* in *real Life,* frequently exhibits very *generous benevolent* Sentiments of Heart, and these, tho' exerted in a particular odd Manner, justly command our Fondness and Love. Whereas in all Allusions of WIT, *Severity, Bitterness,* and *Satire* are frequently exhibited. And where these are avoided, not worthy amiable Sentiments of the *Heart* but quick unexpected Efforts of the *Fancy* are presented.

7. The odd Adventures and Embarrassments which *Persons* in *real Life* are drawn into by their *Foibles* are fit Subjects of *Mirth.* Whereas in pure WIT the Allusions are rather *surprizing* than *mirthful;* and the *Agreements* or *Contrasts* which are started between Objects without any relation to the *Foibles* of *Persons* in real Life, are more fit to be *admired* for their *Happiness* and *Propriety* than to excite our *Laughter.* Besides, WIT, in the frequent Repetition of it, tires the Imagination with its

precipitate Sallies and Flights, and teizes the Judgment. Whereas HUMOUR, in the Representation of it, puts no Fatigue upon the *Imagination* and gives exquisite Pleasure to the *Judgment.*

These seem to me to be the different Powers and Effects of HUMOUR and WIT. However, the most agreeable Representations or Compositions of all others appear not where they *separately* exist but where they are *united* together in the same Fabric; where HUMOUR is the *Groundwork* and chief Substance and WIT, happily spread, *quickens* the whole with Embellishments.

This is the Excellency of the *Character* of Sir *John Falstaff.* The *Ground-work* is *Humour,* or the Representation and Detection of a bragging and vaunting *Coward* in *real Life.* However, this alone would only have expos'd the *Knight* as a meer *Noll Bluff,* to the Derision of the Company, and after they had once been gratify'd with his Chastisement he would have sunk into Infamy, and become quite odious and intolerable. But here the inimitable *Wit* of Sir *John* comes in to his Support, and gives a new *Rise* and *Lustre* to his Character: for the sake of his *Wit* you forgive his *Cowardice;* or rather, are fond of his *Cowardice* for the Occasions it gives to his *Wit.* In short, the *Humour* furnishes a Subject and Spur to the *Wit,* and the *Wit* again supports and embellishes the *Humour.*

At the *first* Entrance of the *Knight* your good Humour and Tendency to *Mirth* are irresistibly excited by his jolly Appearance and Corpulency; you feel and acknowledge him to be the fittest Subject imaginable for yielding *Diversion* and *Merriment.* But when you see him immediately set up for *Enterprize* and *Activity* with his evident *Weight* and *Unweildiness* your Attention is all call'd forth, and you are eager to watch him to the End of his Adventures, your Imagination pointing out with a full Scope his future Embarrassments. All the while, as you accompany him forwards, he *heightens* your Relish for his future Disasters by his happy Opinion of his own Sufficiency, and the gay Vaunts which he makes of his Talents and Accomplishments; so that at last when he falls into a Scrape your Expectation is exquisitely gratify'd, and you have the full Pleasure of seeing all his trumpeted Honour laid in the Dust. When, in the midst of his Misfortunes, instead of being utterly demolish'd and sunk he rises again by the superior Force of his *Wit,* and begins a *new* Course with fresh Spirit and Alacrity, this excites you the more to *renew* the Chace, in full View of his *second* Defeat; out of which he recovers again, and triumphs with new Pretensions and Boastings. After this he immediately starts upon a *third* Race, and so on, continually detected and caught, and yet constantly extricating himself by his inimitable *Wit* and *Invention;* thus yielding a perpetual *Round* of Sport and Diversion.

Again, the genteel *Quality* of Sir *John* is of great Use in supporting his Character: it prevents his *sinking* too low after several of his Misfortunes. Besides, you allow him, in consequence of his *Rank* and *Seniority,* the Privilege to dictate and take the Lead, and to rebuke others upon many Occasions; by this he is sav'd from appearing too *nauseous* and *impudent.* The good *Sense* which he possesses comes also to his Aid, and saves him from being *despicable* by forcing your Esteem for his real Abilities. Again, the *Privilege* you allow him of rebuking and checking others, when he assumes it with proper Firmness and Superiority, helps to *settle* anew, and *compose* his Character after an Embarrassment; and reduces in some measure the *Spirit* of the Company to a proper *Level* before he sets out again upon a fresh Adventure—without this, they would be kept continually *strain'd* and *wound up* to the highest Pitch without sufficient Relief and Diversity.

It may also deserve to be remark'd of *Falstaff* that the *Figure* of his *Person* is admirably suited to the *Turn* of his *Mind;* so that there arises before you a perpetual *Allusion* from one to the other, which forms an incessant Series of *Wit* whether they are in *Contrast* or *Agreement* together. When he pretends to *Activity* there is *Wit* in the *Contrast* between his *Mind* and his *Person,* and *Wit* in their *Agreement,* when he triumphs in *Jollity*.

To compleat the whole, you have in this Character of *Falstaff* not only a free Course of *Humour,* supported and embellish'd with admirable *Wit,* but this *Humour* is of a Species the most *jovial* and *gay* in all Nature. Sir *John Falstaff* possesses Generosity, Chearfulness, Alacrity, Invention, Frolic and Fancy superior to all other Men. The *Figure* of his *Person* is the Picture of Jollity, Mirth, and Good-nature, and banishes at once all other Ideas from your Breast; he is happy himself, and makes you happy. If you examine him further, he has no Fierceness, Reserve, Malice or Peevishness lurking in his Heart; his Intentions are all pointed at innocent Riot and Merriment; nor has the Knight any inveterate Design, except against *Sack,* and that too he *loves.* If, besides this, he desires to pass for a Man of *Activity* and *Valour* you can easily excuse so harmless a *Foible* which yields you the highest Pleasure in its constant *Detection.*

If you put all these together, it is impossible to *hate* honest *Jack Falstaff.* If you observe them again, it is impossible to avoid *loving* him. He is the gay, the witty, the frolicksome, happy, and fat *Jack Falstaff,* the most delightful *Swaggerer* in all Nature. You must *love* him for your *own* sake, at the same time you cannot but *love* him for *his own* Talents. And when you have *enjoy'd* them you cannot but *love* him in *Gratitude;* he has nothing to disgust you, and every thing to give you Joy. His *Sense* and his *Foibles* are equally directed to advance your Pleasure, and it is impossible to be tired or unhappy in his Company.

This *jovial* and *gay* Humour, without any thing *envious, malicious, mischievous,* or *despicable,* and continually *quicken'd* and adorn'd with *Wit,* yields that peculiar Delight, without any *Alloy,* which we all feel and acknowledge in *Falstaff's* Company. *Ben Jonson* has *Humour* in his *Characters,* drawn with the most masterly Skill and Judgment. In Accuracy, Depth, Propriety, and Truth he has no *Superior* or *Equal* amongst *Ancients* or *Moderns.* But the *Characters* he exhibits are of a *satirical* and *deceitful,* or of a *peevish* or *despicable* Species: as *Volpone, Subtle, Morose,* and *Abel Drugger,* in all of which there is something very justly to be *hated* or *despised.* And you feel the same Sentiments of *Dislike* for every other *Character* of *Jonson's,* so that after you have been *gratify'd* with their *Detection* and *Punishment* you are quite tired and disgusted with their Company. Whereas *Shakespeare,* besides the peculiar *Gaiety* in the *Humour* of *Falstaff,* has guarded him from disgusting you with his *forward Advances* by giving him *Rank* and *Quality;* from being *despicable,* by his real good *Sense* and excellent *Abilities;* from being *odious,* by his *harmless Plots* and *Designs;* and from being *tiresome,* by his inimitable *Wit* and his new and incessant *Sallies* of highest *Fancy* and Frolick. (pp. 122-26)

It may be further remark'd that *Jonson,* by pursuing the most useful Intention of *Comedy,* is in Justice oblig'd to *hunt down* and *demolish* his own Characters. Upon this Plan he must

necessarily expose them to your *Hatred,* and of course can never bring out an amiable Person. His *Subtle* and *Face* are detected at last, and become mean and despicable. Sir *Epicure Mammon* is properly trick'd, and goes off ridiculous and detestable. The *Puritan Elders* suffer for their Lust of Money and are quite nauseous and abominable, and his *Morose* meets with a severe Punishment after having sufficiently tir'd you with his Peevishness. But *Shakespeare,* with happier Insight, always supports his Characters in your *Favour.* His Justice *Shallow* withdraws before he is tedious; the *French* Doctor and *Welch* Parson go off in full Vigour and Spirit. Ancient *Pistol,* indeed, is scurvily treated: however, he keeps up his Spirits, and continues to threaten so well that you are still desirous of his Company; and it is impossible to be tir'd or dull with the gay unfading Evergreen *Falstaff.* (p. 128)

Upon the whole, *Jonson's* Compositions are like finished Cabinets, where every Part is wrought up with the most excellent Skill and Exactness; *Shakespeare's* like magnificent Castles, not perfectly finished or regular, but adorn'd with such bold and magnificent Designs as at once delight and astonish you with their Beauty and Grandeur. (p. 129)

> *Corbyn Morris, in an extract from* Shakespeare, the Critical Heritage: 1733-1752, Vol. 3, *edited by Brian Vickers, Routledge & Kegan Paul, 1975, pp. 122-29.*

JOHN UPTON   (essay date 1748)

[*A clergyman and Spenserean scholar, Upton was apparently the first to give an opinion on a question still discussed by critics: whether* 1 Henry IV *and* 2 Henry IV *are separate, autonomous plays or the parts of a single, unified work. Upton's view that they are separate plays was contested by Samuel Johnson (1765),who considered both parts a single, unified work, but has been supported by such twentieth-century critics as E. E. Stoll (1914), Harry T. Baker (1926), Robert Adger Law (1927), M. A. Shaaber (1948), and Muriel C. Bradbrook (1965). This essay first appeared in Upton's* Critical Observations on Shakespeare, *1748.*]

Other plays of our poet are called *First and second parts,* as *The first and second parts of King Henry IV.* But these plays are independent each of the other. *The first part,* as 'tis named, ends with the settlement in the throne of King Henry IV when he had gained a compleat victory over his rebellious subjects. *The second part* contains King Henry's death; shewing his son, afterwards Henry V, in the various lights of a good-natured rake, 'till he comes to the crown; when 'twas necessary for him to assume a more manlike character and princely dignity. To call these two plays *first and second parts* is as injurious to the author-character of Shakespeare as it would be to Sophocles to call his two plays on Oedipus, *first and second parts of King Oedipus.* Whereas the one is *Oedipus King of Thebes,* the other, *Oedipus at Athens.* (pp. 294-95)

> *John Upton, in an extract from* Shakespeare, the Critical Heritage: 1733-1752, Vol. 3, *edited by Brian Vickers, Routledge & Kegan Paul, 1975, pp. 290-323.*

[CHARLOTTE LENNOX]   (essay date 1754)

[*Lennox was an American-born novelist and Shakespearean scholar who compiled a three-volume edition of translated texts of the sources used by Shakespeare in twenty-two of his works, including some analyses of the manner in which he used these sources. In the following excerpt, first published in 1754 in her* Shakespear

Illustrated, *she praises Shakespeare for his portrait of Prince Hal. For other early assessments of the character of Prince Hal see the excerpts by William Warburton (1733) and Samuel Johnson (1765).*]

[In *1 Henry IV*] *Shakespeare* has copied *Holinshed* very closely, as well in the Historical Facts as the Characters of his Persons; *Percy*'s and *Glendower*'s are indeed greatly heightened, but both with wonderful Propriety and Beauty. The Episodical Part of the Drama, which is made up of the extravagant Sallies of the Prince of *Wales* and the inimitable Humour of *Falstaff*, is entirely of his own Invention. The Character of Prince *Henry*, tho' drawn after the Historians, is considerably improved by *Shakespeare*, and through the Veil of his Vices and Irregularities we see a Dawn of Greatness and Virtue that promises the future Splendor of his Life and Reign.

The Poet has indeed deviated from History in making this young Prince kill the gallant *Percy* at the Battle of *Shrewsbury*. According to them it is uncertain by whom he fell; however, this Circumstance is beautifully imagined by *Shakespeare* in order to exalt the Character of Prince *Henry*, which had before been obscured by the Glory of that Heroe. (pp. 136-37)

> [*Charlotte Lennox*], in an extract from her notes on *"1 Henry IV,"* in Shakespeare, the Critical Heritage: 1753-1765, Vol. 4, edited by Brian Vickers, Routledge & Kegan Paul, 1976, pp. 136-37.

ARTHUR MURPHY (essay date 1757)

[*In the following excerpt, first published in the* London Chronicle *in 1757, Murphy voices two critical assessments common to the Neoclassical age: that Shakespeare was a genius ignorant of the necessary rules of art and that Falstaff was one of his great creations. The first of these assessments was also put forth by Nicholas Rowe (1709) and Charles Gildon (1710).*]

The Plays of [Shakespeare] must never be judged by the strict Rules of Dramatic Poetry, with which it is to be imagined he was not acquainted; and therefore to try him by what he did not know would be trying him by a Kind of *ex post facto* Law, Regularity of Design being introduced in this Country since the Decease of that great Genius. Mr. *Hume*, in his *History of Great Britain*, has given a pretty just Character of him when he says 'A striking Peculiarity of Sentiment, adapted to a singular Character, he frequently hits as it were by Inspiration; but a reasonable Propriety of Thought he cannot for any Time uphold;' unless the Character of *Falstaff* be an Exception to this very sensible Writer's Opinion. For indeed the Character of Sir *John* no where flags, and he generally upholds a Propriety of Thought if it be considered in regard to the Manners of the Speaker. Bullying, Cowardice, Vaunting, Detection, boasted Activity and bodily Indolence, Profligacy and Pretensions to Decorum, form such a party-coloured Groupe as moves our Laughter irresistibly. His Wit and, on all Occasions, the Pleasantry of his Ideas provoke us to laugh with him, and hinder the Knight's Character from sinking into Contempt; and we love him, in Spight of his degrading Foibles, for his enlivened Humour and his companionable Qualities. (pp. 274-75)

> *Arthur Murphy, in his review of "1 Henry the Fourth,"* in Shakespeare, the Critical Heritage: 1753-1765,

Vol. 4, *edited by Brian Vickers, Routledge & Kegan Paul, 1976, pp. 274-75.*

SAMUEL JOHNSON (essay date 1765)

[*Johnson has long held an important place in the history of Shakespearean criticism. He is considered the foremost representative of moderate English Neoclassicism and is credited by some literary historians as having freed Shakespeare from the strictures of the three unities—the belief of strict Neoclassicists that dramas should have a single setting, take place in less than twenty-four hours, and have a causally connected plot. He is seen by more recent commentators as a synthesizer of existing critical theory rather than as an innovative theoretician. Johnson was a master of Augustan prose style and a personality who dominated the literary world of his day. The following excerpt is from Johnson's editorial notes in his 1765 edition of* The Plays of William Shakespeare. *In accordance with the practice of Arthur Sherbo, editor of* Johnson on Shakespeare *(the volume excerpted here), the act, scene, and life references given in the excerpt are from W. Aldis Wright's Cambridge edition of Shakespeare, but the Shakespearean text to which Johnson's notes refer is taken from Johnson's first edition. He makes a number of assertions that are both influential and controversial in subsequent* Henry IV *criticism. In response to John Upton (1748), Johnson argues for the unity of Parts One and Two, calling Prince Hal the hero of both plays and of both the comic and tragic parts. He defends Hal's first soliloquy and the rejection of Falstaff, criticizes the ending of Part Two as "lame", and gives in a few lines a memorable reference to Falstaff as a complex mixture of the admirable and the objectionable. Johnson's views were reconsidered in the twentieth century by J. Dover Wilson (1943), who praised the eighteenth-century critic for his understanding of the character of Prince Hal. For similar views on the essential unity of* Henry IV, Part 1 *and* Part 2, *see the excerpts by Hermann Ulrici (1839), G. G. Gervinus (1849-50), E.M.W. Tillyard (1944), and A. R. Humphreys (1966).*]

I.i.1   KING HENRY. So shaken as we are, so wan with care,
         Find we a time for frighted peace to pant,
         And breathe short-winded accents of new broils
         To be commenc'd in stronds a-far remote.

Shakespeare has apparently designed a regular connection of these dramatick histories from Richard the Second to Henry the Fifth. King Henry, at the end of *Richard the Second*, declares his purpose to visit the Holy Land, which he resumes in this speech. The complaint made by King Henry in the last act of *Richard the Second*, of the wildness of his son, prepares the reader for the frolicks which are here to be recounted, and the characters which are now to be exhibited. (p. 453)

I.ii.201 PRINCE HENRY. So, when this loose behaviour I throw off,
          And pay the debt I never promised;
          By how much better than my word I am,
          By so much shall I falsifie men's hopes. . . .

To "falsify hope" is to "exceed hope," to give much where men "hoped" for little.

This speech is very artfully introduced to keep the Prince from appearing vile in the opinion of the audience; it prepares them for his future reformation, and, what is yet more valuable, exhibits a natural picture of a great mind offering excuses to itself, and palliating those follies which it can neither justify nor forsake. (p. 458)

I.iii.286   WORCESTER. The King will always think him
             in our debt;
             And think, we deem ourselves unsatisfy'd,
             Till he hath found a time to pay us home.
             And see already, how he doth begin
             To make us strangers to his looks of love.

This is a natural description of the state of mind between those
that have conferred, and those that have received, obligations
too great to be satisfied. (p. 463)

II.iv.34   [Stage direction] Enter Francis the Drawer.

This scene, helped by the distraction of the drawer, and gri-
maces of the prince, may entertain upon the stage, but affords
not much delight to the reader. The authour has judiciously
made it short. (p. 468)

II.iv.335   PRINCE HENRY. He that rides at high speed,
             and with a pistol kills a sparrow flying.

Shakespeare never has any care to preserve the manners of the
time. "Pistols" were not known in the age of Henry. Pistols
were, I believe, about our authour's time, eminently used by
the Scots. (p. 471)

II.iv.387   FALSTAFF. Harry, I do not only marvel, where
             thou spendest thy time, but also, how thou art
             accompany'd; for though the camomile, the more
             it is trodden on, the faster it grows, yet youth,
             the more it is wasted, the sooner it wears.

This whole speech is supremely comick. The simile of ca-
momile used to illustrate a contrary effect, brings to my remembrance an observation of a later writer of some merit,
whom the desire of being witty has betrayed into a like thought.
Meaning to enforce with great vehemence the mad temerity of
young soldiers, he remarks, that "though Bedlam be in the
road to Hogsden, it is out of the way to promotion." (pp. 472-
73)

II.iv.482   PRINCE HENRY. Go, hide thee behind the
             arras

The bulk of Falstaff made him not the fittest to be concealed
behind the hangings, but every poet sacrifices something to
the scenery; if Falstaff had not been hidden he could not have
been found asleep, nor had his pockets searched. (p. 474)

III.i.25   HOTSPUR. O, then the earth shook to see the
             heav'ns on fire,
             And not in fear of your nativity.
             Diseased Nature oftentimes breaks forth
             In strange eruptions; and the teeming earth
             Is with a kind of colick pinch'd and vext,
             By the imprisoning of unruly wind
             Within her womb

The poet has here taken, from the perverseness and contra-
riousness of Hotspur's temper, an opportunity of raising his
character, by a very rational and philosophical confutation of
superstitious errour. (p. 475)

IV.i.97   VERNON. All furnish't, all in arms,
             All plum'd like estridges, that with the wind
             Baited like eagles, having lately bath'd

"To bait with the wind" appears to me an improper expression.
To "bait" is in the style of falconry, to "beat the wing," from
the French *battre*, that is, to flutter in preparation for flight.

Besides, what is the meaning of "estridges, that baited with
the wind like eagles"; for the relative "that," in the usual
construction, must relate to "estridges." (pp. 481-82)

             All furnish'd, all in arms,
             All plum'd like estridges that *wing* the wind
             Baited like eagles.

This gives a strong image. They were not only plum'd like
estridges, but their plumes fluttered like those of an estridge
on the wing mounting against the wind. A more lively representation of young men ardent for enterprize perhaps no writer
has ever given. (p. 482)

Mr. Upton thinks these two plays improperly called *The First*
and *Second Parts of Henry the Fourth* [see excerpt above,
1748]. The first play ends, he says, with the peaceful settlement
of Henry in the kingdom by the defeat of the rebels. This is
hardly true, for the rebels are not yet finally suppressed. The
second, he tells us, shews Henry the Fifth in the various lights
of a good-natured rake, till, on his father's death, he assumes
a more manly character. This is true; but this representation
gives us no idea of a dramatick action. These two plays will
appear to every reader, who shall peruse them without ambition
of critical discoveries, to be so connected that the second is
merely a sequel to the first; to be two only because they are
too long to be one.

Induction.1   RUMOUR. Open your ears; for which of
               you will stop
               The vent of hearing, when loud Rumour
               speaks?

This speech of Rumour is not inelegant or unpoetical, but is
wholly useless, since we are told nothing which the first scene
does not clearly and naturally discover. The only end of such
prologues is to inform the audience of some facts previous to
the action, of which they can have no knowledge from the
persons of the drama.

Induction.15   RUMOUR. Rumour is a pipe
               Blown by surmises, jealousies, conjec-
               tures

Here the poet imagines himself describing Rumour, and forgets
that Rumour is the speaker. (p. 490)

I.i.157   NORTHUMBERLAND. But let one spirit of the
             first-born Cain
             Reign in all bosoms, that each heart being
             set
             On bloody courses, the rude scene may end,
             And darkness be the burier of the dead!

The conclusion of this noble speech is extremely striking. There
is no need to suppose it exactly philosophical, "darkness" in
poetry may be absence of eyes as well as privation of light.
Yet we may remark, that by an ancient opinion it has been
held, that if the human race, for whom the world was made,
were extirpated, the whole system of sublunary nature would
cease. (p. 493)

II.ii.163   PRINCE HENRY. How might we see Falstaff
             bestow himself to night in his true colours,
             and not ourselves be seen?

             POINS. Put on two leather jerkins and aprons,
             and wait upon him at his table, as drawers.

This was a plot very unlikely to succeed where the Prince and the drawers were all known, but it produces merriment, which our authour found more useful than probability. (p. 499)

III.i.106   KING HENRY. I will take your counsel;
             And were these inward wars once out of
             hand,
             We would, dear lords, unto the Holy Land.

This play, like the former, proceeds in one unbroken tenour through the first edition, and there is therefore no evidence that the division of the acts was made by the authour. Since then every editor has the same right to mark the intervals of action as the players, who made the present distribution, I should propose that this scene may be added to the foregoing act, and the remove from London to Gloucestershire be made in the intermediate time, but that it would shorten the next act too much, which has not even now its due proportion to the rest. (p. 505)

IV.ii.122   LANCASTER. Some guard these traitors to the
             block of death,
             Treason's true bed and yielder up of breath.

It cannot but raise some indignation to find this horrible violation of faith passed over thus slightly by the poet, without any note of censure or detestation. (p. 512)

IV.iii.86   FALSTAFF. Good faith, this same young so-
             ber-blooded boy doth not love me; nor a man
             cannot make him laugh.

Falstaff speaks here like a veteran in life. The young prince did not love him, and he despaired to gain his affection, for he could not make him laugh. Men only become friends by community of pleasures. He who cannot be softened into gayety cannot easily be melted into kindness. (p. 513)

IV.v.210   KING HENRY. I cut them off, and had a
             purpose now
             To lead out many to the Holy Land. . . .

This journey to the Holy Land, of which the King very frequently revives the mention, had two motives, religion and policy. He durst not wear the ill-gotten crown without expiation, but in the act of expiation he contrives to make his wickedness successful. (pp. 516-17)

IV.v.219   KING HENRY. How I came by the crown,
             O God, forgive!
             And grant it may with thee in true peace
             live.

This is a true picture of a mind divided between heaven and earth. He prays for the prosperity of guilt while he deprecates its punishment. (p. 517)

V.v.64   KING HENRY V. Till then I banish thee, on
             pain of death,
             As I have done the rest of my mis-leaders,
             Not to come near our person by ten miles.

Mr. Rowe observes, that many readers lament to see Falstaff so hardly used by his old friend [see excerpt above, 1709]. But if it be considered that the fat knight has never uttered one sentiment of generosity, and with all his power of exciting mirth, has nothing in him that can be esteemed, no great pain will be suffered from the reflection that he is compelled to live honestly, and maintained by the king, with a promise of advancement when he shall deserve it. (p. 521)

I think the poet more blameable for Poins, who is always represented as joining some virtues with his vices, and is there-

fore treated by the Prince with apparent distinction, yet he does nothing in the time of action, and though after the bustle is over he is again a favourite, at last vanishes without notice. Shakespeare certainly lost him by heedlessness, in the multiplicity of his characters, the variety of his action, and his eagerness to end the play. . . .

V.v.92   CHIEF JUSTICE. Go, carry Sir John Falstaff
             to the Fleet.

I do not see why Falstaff is carried to the Fleet. We have never lost sight of him since his dismission from the king; he has committed no new fault, and therefore incurred no punishment; but the different agitations of fear, anger, and surprise in him and his company, made a good scene to the eye; and our authour, who wanted them no longer on the stage, was glad to find this method of sweeping them away. (p. 522)

I fancy every reader, when he ends this play, cries out with Desdemona, ''O most lame and impotent conclusion!'' As this play was not, to our knowledge, divided into acts by the authour, I could be content to conclude it with the death of Henry the Fourth.

In that Jerusalem shall Harry dye.

These scenes which now make the fifth act of *Henry the Fourth*, might then be the first of *Henry the Fifth;* but the truth is, that they do unite very commodiously to either play. When these plays were represented, I believe they ended as they are now ended in the books; but Shakespeare seems to have designed that the whole series of action from the beginning of *Richard the Second*, to the end of *Henry the Fifth*, should be considered by the reader as one work, upon one plan, only broken into parts by the necessity of exhibition.

None of Shakespeare's plays are more read than the *First and Second Parts of Henry the Fourth*. Perhaps no authour has ever in two plays afforded so much delight. The great events are interesting, for the fate of kingdoms depends upon them; the slighter occurrences are diverting, and, except one or two, sufficiently probable; the incidents are multiplied with wonderful fertility of invention, and the characters diversified with the utmost nicety of discernment, and the profoundest skill in the nature of man.

The Prince, who is the hero both of the comick and tragick part, is a young man of great abilities and violent passions, whose sentiments are right, though his actions are wrong; whose virtues are obscured by negligence, and whose understanding is dissipated by levity. In his idle hours he is rather loose than wicked, and when the occasion forces out his latent qualities, he is great without effort, and brave without tumult. The trifler is roused into a hero, and the hero again reposes in the trifler. This character is great, original, and just.

Percy is a rugged soldier, cholerick, and quarrelsome, and has only the soldier's virtues, generosity and courage.

But Falstaff unimitated, unimitable Falstaff, how shall I describe thee? Thou compound of sense and vice; of sense which may be admired but not esteemed, of vice which may be despised, but hardly detested. Falstaff is a character loaded with faults, and with those faults which naturally produce contempt. He is a thief, and a glutton, a coward, and a boaster, always ready to cheat the weak, and prey upon the poor; to terrify the timorous and insult the defenceless. At once obsequious and malignant, he satirises in their absence those whom he lives by flattering. He is familiar with the Prince only as an agent of vice, but of this familiarity he is so proud as not only to be supercilious and haughty with common men, but to think his interest of importance to the Duke of Lancaster. Yet the man thus corrupt, thus despicable, makes himself necessary to the prince that despises him, by the most pleasing of all qualities, perpetual gaiety, by an unfailing power of exciting laughter, which is the more freely indulged, as his wit is not of the splendid or ambitious kind, but consists in easy escapes and sallies of levity, which make sport but raise no envy. It must be observed that he is stained with no enormous or sanguinary crimes, so that his licentiousness is not so offensive but that it may be borne for his mirth.

The moral to be drawn from this representation is, that no man is more dangerous than he that with a will to corrupt, hath the power to please; and that neither wit nor honesty ought to think themselves safe with such a companion when they see Henry seduced by Falstaff. (pp. 522-24)

> Samuel Johnson, "Notes on Shakespeare's Plays: '1 Henry IV'" and "Notes on Shakespeare's Plays: '2 Henry IV'," in The Yale Edition of the Works of Samuel Johnson: Johnson on Shakespeare, Vol. VII, edited by Arthur Sherbo, Yale University Press, 1968, pp. 453-89, 490-524.

[ELIZABETH] MONTAGU (essay date 1769)

[In the essay below, first published in 1769, Montagu favorably compares Shakespeare to classical Greek and modern French tragedians. In particular, she addresses Voltaire and the Neoclassical critics regarding their comments on Shakespeare's failure to observe the "rules" of Neoclassical dramatic composition. The Neoclassicists favored "pure" comedy and tragedy over tragi-comedy and other mixed genres, such as Shakespeare's history plays. Montagu's response was consistent with a growing body of European opinion that began to see "modern" writers like Shakespeare as equal or superior to the "ancients," and with an English tradition begun by John Dryden of preferring English to French drama. Montagu's essay was praised by her contemporary, the Shakespearean editor William Warburton, as "the most elegant and judicious piece of criticism this age has produced." For examples of the Neoclassical reaction to Shakespeare's work, see the excerpts by Nicholas Rowe (1709), Charles Gildon (1710), and Arthur Murphy (1757).]

Those Dramas of Shakspeare, which he distinguishes by the name of his Histories, being of an original kind and peculiar construction, cannot come within any rules, prior to their existence. The office of the Critic, in regard to Poetry, is like that of the Grammarian and Rhetorician in respect to Language: it is the business of both to shew why such and such modes of speech, are proper and graceful, others improper and ungraceful: but they pronounce on such words and expressions only, as are actually extant.

The rules of Aristotle were drawn from the tragedies of Æschylus, Sophocles, &c. Had that great critic seen a play as fashioned on the chronicles of his country, thus representative of the manners of the times, and of the characters of the most illustrious persons concerned in a series of important events, perhaps he would have esteemed such a sort of drama well worth his attention, as very peculiarly adapted to those ends, which the Grecian philosophers proposed in popular entertainments. If it be the chief use of history, to teach philosophy by example, this species of history must be allowed to be the best preceptor. The catastrophe of these plays is not built on a vain and idle fable of the wrath of Juno, or of the revenge of [slighted]

Bacchus; nor is a man represented entangled in the web of Fate, from which his Virtues and his Deities cannot extricate him: but here we are admonished to observe the effects of pride and ambition, the tyrant's dangers and the traitor's fate. The sentiments and the manners, the passions and their consequences, are fully set before you; the force and lustre of poetical language join with the weight and authority of history, to impress the moral lesson on the heart. The poet collects, as it were, into a focus, those truths, which lie scattered in the diffuse volume of the historian, and kindles the flame of virtue, while he shews the miseries and calamities of vice.

The common interests of humanity make us attentive to every story that has an air of reality, but we are more affected if we know it to be true; and the interest is still heightened if we have any relation to the persons concerned. Our noble countryman, Percy, engages us much more than Achilles, or any Grecian hero. The people, for whose use these public entertainments should be chiefly intended, know the battle of Shrewsbury to be a fact; they are informed of what passed on the banks of the Severn: all that happened on the shore of the Scamander has, to them, the appearance of a fiction. (pp. 33-5)

The nature of the Historical Play gave scope to the extensive talents of Shakspeare. He had an uncommon felicity in painting manners, and developing characters, which he could employ with peculiar grace and propriety, when he exhibited the chiefs in our civil wars. The great earl of Warwick, Cardinal Beaufort, Humphrey duke of Gloucester, the renowned Hotspur, were very interesting objects to their countrymen. Whatever shewed them in a strong light, and represented them with sentiments and manners agreeable to their historical characters, and to those things which common fame had divulged of them, must have engaged the attention of the spectator, and assisted in that delusion of his imagination, whence his sympathy with the story must arise. (pp. 36-7)

Nothing great is to be expected from any set of artists, who are to give only copies of copies. The treasures of nature are inexhaustible, as well in moral as in physical subjects. The talents of Shakspeare were universal, his penetrating mind saw through all characters; and, as Mr. Pope says of him, he was not more a master of our strongest emotions, than of our idlest sensations.

One cannot wonder, that, endued with so great and various powers, he broke down the barriers that had before confined the dramatic writers to the regions of Comedy, or Tragedy. He perceived the fertility of the subjects that lay between the two extremes; he saw, that in the historical play he could represent the manners of the whole people, give the general temper of the times, and bring in view the incidents that affected the common fate of his country. The Gothic muse had a rude spirit of liberty, and delighted in painting popular tumults, the progress of civil wars, and the revolutions of government, rather than a catastrophe within the walls of a palace. (pp. 43-4)

The tragedians who took their subjects from Homer, had all the advantage a painter would have, who was to draw a picture from a statue of Phidias or Praxiteles. Poor Shakspeare from the wooden images in our mean chronicles was to form his portraits. What judgment was there in discovering, that by moulding them to an exact resemblance he should engage and please! And what discernment and penetration into characters, and what amazing skill in moral painting, to be able, from such uncouth models, to bring forth not only a perfect, but, when occasion required, a graceful likeness!

The patterns from which he drew, were not only void of poetical spirit and ornament, but also of all historical dignity. The histories of those times were a mere heap of rude undigested annals, coarse in their style, and crowded with trivial anecdotes. No Tacitus had investigated the obliquities of our statesmen, or, by diving into the profound secrets of policy, had dragged into light the latent motives, the secret machinations of our politicians: yet how does he enter into the deepest mysteries of state! (pp. 45-7)

[Hotspur] is hurried by an impetuosity of soul out of the sphere of obedience, and, like a comet, though dangerous to the general system, is still an object of admiration and wonder to every beholder. It is marvellous, that Shakspeare, from bare chronicles, coarse history, and traditional tales, could thus extract the wisdom and caution of the politician Henry, and catch the fire of the martial spirit of Hotspur. The wrath of Achilles in Homer is not sustained with more dignity. Each hero is offended that the prize of valour,

> Due to many a well-fought day,

is rudely snatched from him by the hand of power.—One should suspect an author of more learning to have had the character of Achilles in his eye. . . . (pp. 72-3)

[Hotspur] has also the frankness of Achilles, and the same abhorrence of falsehood; he is as impatient of Glendower's pretensions to supernatural powers, as to the king's assuming a right over his prisoners. In dividing the kingdom, he will not yield a foot of ground to those who dispute with him; but would give any thing to a well-deserving friend. It is a pardonable violation of historical truth, to give the Prince of Wales, who behaved very gallantly at the battle of Shrewsbury, the honour of conquering him; and it is more agreeable to the spectator, as the event was, to beat down

> The never-daunted Percy to the earth,
>
> [*2 Henry IV*, I. i. 110]

to suppose it did not happen from the arrow of a peasant, but from the sword of Henry Monmouth, whose spirit came with a higher commission from the same fiery sphere.

In Worcester, the rebel appears in all his odious colours; proud, envious, malignant, artful, he is finely contrasted by the noble Percy. Shakspeare, with the sagacity of a Tacitus, observes the jealousies which must naturally arise between a family, who have conferred a crown, and the king who has received it, who will always think the presence of such benefactors *too bold and peremptory.*

The character of Henry IV. is perfectly agreeable to that given him by historians. The play opens by his declaring his intention to war against the infidels, which he does not undertake, as was usual in those times, from a religious enthusiasm, but is induced to it by political motives: that the martial spirit may not break out at home in civil wars; nor peace and idleness give men opportunity to enquire into his title to the crown, and too much discuss a point which would not bear a cool and close examination. (pp. 74-6)

Our author is so little under the discipline of art, that we are apt to ascribe his happiest successes, as well as his most unfortunate failings, to chance. But I cannot help thinking, there is more of contrivance and care in his execution of this play, than in almost any he has written. It is a more regular drama than his other historical plays, less charged with absurdities,

and less involved in confusion. It is indeed liable to those objections, which are made to Tragi-comedy. But if the pedantry of learning could ever recede from its dogmatical rules, I think that this play, instead of being condemned for being of that species, would obtain favour for the species itself, though perhaps correct taste may be offended with the transitions from grave and important to light and ludicrous subjects: and more still with those from great and illustrious, to low and mean persons. Foreigners, unused to these compositions, will be much disgusted at them. The vulgar call all animals that are not natives of their own country, monsters, however beautiful they may be in their form, or wisely adapted to their climate, and natural destination. (pp. 81-2)

How skilfully does our author follow the tradition of the Prince's having been engaged in a robbery, yet make his part in it a mere frolic to play on the cowardly and braggart temper of Falstaffe! The whole conduct of that incident is very artful: he rejects the proposal of the robbery, and only complies with the playing a trick on the robbers; and care is taken to inform you, that the money is returned to its owners.—There is great propriety likewise in the behaviour of Prince Henry, when he supposes Falstaffe to lie dead before him: to have expressed no concern, would have appeared unfeeling; to have lamented such a companion too seriously, ungraceful: with a suitable mixture of tenderness and contempt he thus addresses the body:

> What! old acquaintance! could not all this flesh
> Keep in a little life? Poor Jack! farewell!
> I could have better spar'd a better man.
>
> [*1 Henry IV*, V. iv. 102-04]

The Prince seems always diverted, rather than seduced by Falstaffe; he despises his vices while he is entertained by his humour; and though Falstaffe is for a while a stain upon his character, yet it is of a kind with those colours, which are used for a disguise in sport, being of such a nature as are easily washed out, without leaving any bad tincture. And we see Henry, as soon as he is called to the high and serious duties of a king, come forth at once with unblemished majesty. The disposition of the hero is made to pierce through the idle frolics of the boy, throughout the whole piece; for his reformation is not effected in the last scene of the last act, as is usual in our comedies, but is prepared from the very beginning of the play. The scene between the Prince and Francis, is low and ridiculous, and seems one of the greatest indecorums of the piece; at the same time the attentive spectator will find the purpose of it is to shew him, that Henry was studying human nature, in all her variety of tempers and faculties. I am now, says he, acquainted with all humours, (meaning dispositions) since the days of good man Adam to the present hour. (pp. 83-5)

Whether Henry, in the early part of his life, was indulging a humour that inclined him to low and wild company, or endeavouring to acquire a deeper and more extensive knowledge of human nature, by a general acquaintance with mankind, is the business of his historians to determine. But a critic must surely applaud the dexterity of Shakspeare for throwing this colour over that part of his conduct. . . . (p. 86)

Whether we consider the character of Falstaffe as adapted to encourage and excuse the extravagances of the Prince, or by itself, we must certainly admire it, and own it to be perfectly original.

The professed wit, either in life or on the stage, is usually severe and satirical. But mirth is the source of Falstaffe's wit. He seems rather to invite you to partake of his merriment, than to attend to his jest: a man must be ill-natured, as well as dull, who does not join in the mirth of this jovial companion, the best calculated, in all respects, to raise laughter of any that ever appeared on a stage. (p. 87)

As Falstaffe, whom the author certainly intended to be perfectly witty, is less addicted to quibble and play on words, than any of his comic characters, I think we may fairly conclude, our author was sensible that it was but a false kind of wit, which he practised from the hard necessity of the times: for in that age, the professor quibbled in his chair, the judge quibbled on the bench, the prelate quibbled in the pulpit, the statesman quibbled at the council-board; nay, even majesty quibbled on the throne. (p. 89)

It is uncommon to find the same spirit and interest diffused through the sequel, as in the first part of a play: but the fertile and happy mind of Shakspeare could create or diversify at pleasure; could produce new characters, or vary the attitudes of those before exhibited, according to the occasion. He leaves us in doubt, whether most to admire the fecundity of his imagination in the variety of its productions; or the strength and steadiness of his genius in sustaining the spirit, and preserving unimpaired, through various circumstances and situations, what his invention had originally produced. (p. 93)

We shall hardly find any man to-day more like to what he was yesterday, than the persons here are like to what they were in the First Part of Henry IV. (p. 94)

I cannot help taking notice of the remarkable attention of the poet, to the cautious and politic temper of Henry, when he makes him, even in speaking to his friends and partisans, dissemble so far, in relating Richard's prophecy, that Northumberland, who helped him to the throne, would one day revolt from him, as to add,

> Though then, Heaven knows, I had no such intent;
> But that necessity so bow'd the state,
> That I and Greatness were compell'd to kiss.
> > [*2 Henry IV*, III. i. 72-4]

To his successor he expresses himself very differently, when he says,

> Heaven knows, my son,
> By what by-paths and indirect crook'd ways
> I met this crown.
> > [*2 Henry IV*, IV. v. 183-85]

These delicacies of conduct lie hardly within the poet's province, but have their source in that great and universal capacity, which the attentive reader will find to belong to our author, beyond any other writer. (pp. 95-6)

Justice Shallow is an admirably well-drawn comic character, but he never appears better, than by reflection in the mirror of Falstaffe's wit, in whose descriptions he is most strongly exhibited.—It is said by some, that the Justice was meant for a particular gentleman, who had prosecuted the author for deer-stealing. I know not whether that story be well grounded. The Shallows are to be found every where, in every age; but they who have least character of their own, are most formed and modified by the fashion of the times, and by their peculiar profession or calling. So, though we often meet with a resemblance to this Justice, we shall never find an exact parallel to him, now when manners are so much changed. (p. 99)

The Archbishop of York, even when he appears an iron man, keeps up the gravity and seeming sanctity of his character, and

wears the mitre over his helmet. He is not, like Hotspur, a valiant rebel, full of noble anger and fierce defiance: he speaks like a cool politician to his friends, and like a deep designing hypocrite to his enemies, and pretends he is only acting as physician to the state. (p. 103)

Pistol is an odd kind of personage, intended probably to ridicule some fashionable affectation of bombast language. When such characters exist no longer but in the writings, where they have been ridiculed, they seem to have been monsters of the poet's brain. The originals lost and the mode forgotten, one can neither praise the imitation, nor laugh at the ridicule. (p. 104)

Mine hostess Quickly is of a species not extinct. It may be said, the author there sinks from comedy to farce; but she helps to complete the character of Falstaffe, and some of the dialogues in which she is engaged are diverting. Every scene in which Doll Tearsheet appears, is indecent, and therefore not only indefensible but inexcusable. There are delicacies of decorum in one age unknown to another age; but whatever is immoral, is equally blameable in all ages, and every approach to obscenity is an offence for which wit cannot atone, nor the barbarity or the corruption of the times excuse. (p. 105)

Having considered the characters of this piece, I cannot pass over the conduct of it without taking notice of the peculiar felicity, with which the fable unfolds itself from the very beginning.

The first scenes give the outlines of the characters, and the argument of the drama. Where is there an instance of any opening of a play equal to this? And I think I did not rashly assert, that it is one of the most difficult parts of the dramatic art: for that surely may be allowed so, in which the greatest masters have very seldom succeeded. (p. 106)

> [*Elizabeth*] *Montagu, in her* An Essay on the Writings and Genius of Shakspeare, *R. Priestley, 1810, pp. 33-111.*

FRANCIS GENTLEMAN   (essay date 1774)

> [*The often-repeated view that Part Two is a dramatically inferior sequel to Part One finds one of its earliest exponents in Gentleman. Other commentators who agree with this assessment include Samuel Johnson (1765), George Brandes (1895-96), and Caroline F.E. Spurgeon (1935); such twentieth-century critics as Robert Adger Law (1927), Clifford Leech (1951), and L. C. Knights (1959) have all stressed the integrity of* Henry IV, Part 2. *Gentleman's comments were originally published in* Bell's Edition of Shakespeare's Plays *in 1744.*]

[On *1 Henry IV*, 5.4: Hal's defeat of Hotspur]
Though *Henry's* gallant behaviour must give pleasure, yet we think every generous mind must feel for *Percy's* fall; as, though a rebel, he seems to act upon just principles and very aggravated provocation. It is a very nice, and almost unparalleled point, to bring two characters in mortal conflict on the stage where, as in the present case, we must rejoice at the success of one and grieve for the fate of the other. (pp. 93-4)

[On *1 Henry IV*, 5.4: 'Embowelled?']
The supposed dead man's rising is a most risible incident, and his soliloquy keeps pace with it; however, we conceive the son of sack's rolling and tumbling about the stage to get *Hotspur* on his back, is too much in the stile of pantomime mummery; it may, and certainly does, create laughter for the time; but such ludicrous attacks upon reason are beneath *Shakespeare* and the stage. . . .

[On *2 Henry IV*, 5.5.47ff.: Hal's rejection of Falstaff]
A truly majestic rebuff to the licentious companion of his dissipated hours; mingled with a humane attention for one whom, though he can no longer sport with, he may justly pity. (p. 94)

[End-note to *2 Henry IV*]
This dramatic Olio, for such *Henry* the Fourth's second part is, contains some very insipid ingredients, with several richly seasoned for critical taste. The author has been complimented for his support of *Falstaff*'s character; but though it may be a better second part than any other author could have drawn, yet we are bold to pronounce all the comedy of this piece, out of comparison, inferior to that of the first part: more low, much more indecent, consequently less deserving of approbation. Several passages in the tragic scenes are inimitably fine; but, on the whole, we cannot think it either a good acting or reading composition. . . . (pp. 94-5)

> *Francis Gentleman, in his notes to "1 Henry IV" and "2 Henry IV," in* Shakespeare, the Critical Heritage: 1774-1801, Vol. 6, *edited by Brian Vickers, Routledge & Kegan Paul, 1981, pp. 93-5.*

SHAKESPEARE: CONTAINING THE TRAITS OF HIS CHARACTERS (essay date 1774?)

[*The following piece is an unsigned essay from* Shakespeare: Containing the Traits of His Characters, *believed to have been published in 1774.*]

In Falstaff are to be found the traits of an artful, ambitious, vain, voluptuous, avaricious, cowardly, satirical, pleasant-witted knave.

It may be matter for astonishment that so conspicuous a knave could render himself so agreeable to an audience as to afford more general entertainment than, I believe, any character has done that was ever exhibited on the stage. Consider the above motto ['That reverend vice, that grey iniquity, that father ruffian that vanity in years!' (2.4.453ff.)], which perfectly agrees with his character, and if possible with-hold your astonishment that, instead of his being an object of entertainment, he is not an object of disgust and detestation. . . .

Falstaff made the pleasantness of his wit the ladder to his knavish designs, and dependence on Prince Henry. . . . His intimacy with the Prince he cherished for these reasons: it gratified his vanity, fed his expectations, was his shield from justice, and gained him credit and authority over his myrmidons.

He displays his knowledge how to win the heart by considering, that when a man herds with his inferiors it is most commonly for the purpose merely of enjoying that authority and complimentary homage which he could not among his equals. . . .

The reason of his affording so much entertainment is the same that excuses Prince Henry's being so fond of his company. He flatters while he reproves, is always in a good temper, tho' apparently against his inclination. His knavery, vices, and follies he frankly confesses, which lessens that abhorrence we should otherwise have for him, and prepares us to be the more pleased with the pleasantry of his humour; this being much greater than his wit, which is in general but paltry puns, 'quips and quidities,' to use his own expression. I quote the following as an example of his admirable mixture of flattery with reproof, and frankness in confessing his viciousness: '—Before I knew

thee, Hal, I knew nothing; and now am I, if a man should speak truly, little better than one of the wicked.' [1.2.92ff.]

Falstaff, like other villains, can excuse himself to himself at the same time he does to others. He says, 'Why, Hal, 'tis my vocation, Hal, 'tis no sin for a man to labour in his vocation.' (pp. 134-35)

His observations on honour, although they be natural to his character, I think should be suppressed in the representation; by reason as honour is the soul of society nothing should be so publicly expressed as to lessen our esteem for it.

Among all the villainous acts of Falstaff there is not one which disgusts us, except his wounding the vanquished Percy. In this he appears more than the coward—the cruel assassin. I should suppose Shakespeare made him guilty of it to prevent our being too fond of such a villain. . . . (p. 136)

> *An extract from "Falstaff," in* Shakespeare, the Critical Heritage: 1774-1801, Vol. 6, *edited by Brian Vickers, Routledge & Kegan Paul, 1981, pp. 134-36.*

[ELIZABETH] GRIFFITH (essay date 1775)

[*Griffith exemplifies the seventeenth- and eighteenth-century preoccupation with searching through Shakespeare's plays for set speeches and passages that could be read out of dramatic context for their own sake. Griffith, however, avoided the more usual practice of collecting and commenting on poetic "beauties" and concentrated instead on the "moral" subjects treated in the text. The result will strike most readers as painfully didactic—her most recent editor, Arthur Freeman, wrote of her: "Elizabeth Griffith's Shakespearean criticism has in general been lightly dismissed, and with good reason." But her views on* Henry IV *are of interest as a reflection of eighteenth-century enthusiasm for the play and its characters. The essay was first published in 1775.*]

The method that men take to disguise the nature of their vices, by palliating epithets, is of dangerous consequences in life. It not only serves to blunt the edge of remorse in ourselves, but often helps to induce a milder censure in others, upon the most flagrant enormities.

Thus a profligate fellow, who debauches every woman in his power, is stiled *a man of galantry;* a pennyless adventurer, who carries off a rich heiress, is called *a soldier of fortune;* a duellist, dubbed with the title of *a man of honour;* a sharper, *un chevalier d'industrie;* an atheist, *a free-thinker;* and so forth.

A good specimen of this sort of deceitful phraseology is presented to us in part of this Scene.

> Falstaff *to the Prince.*
>
> Marry, then, sweet wag, when thou art king,
> let not us that are *squires* of the night's body,
> be called thieves of the day's booty. Let us be
> *Diana's foresters, gentlemen of the shade, minions of the moon;* and let them say we be *men of good government,* being governed as the sea is, by *our noble and chaste mistress the moon;* under whose countenance we—steal.
>
> [*1 Henry IV*, I. ii. 23-9]
> (pp. 207-08)

The following speech affords us a beautiful instance of this method of amusing our too flexible and indolent tempers of mind; which I copy here with the greater pleasure, as the speaker of it did effectually reform his life and manners, and has enriched the annals of England with a memoir of true glory.

The Prince of Wales, speaking of his loose companions, who had just quitted the scene, says,

> I know ye all, and will a-while uphold
> The unyoked humour of your idleness;
> Yet herein will I imitate the fun,
> Who doth permit the base contagious clouds
> To smother up his beauty from the world;
> That when he please again to be himself,
> Being wanted, he may be more wondered at,
> By breaking through the foul and ugly mists
> Of vapours, that did seem to strangle him.
>
> [*1 Henry IV*, I. ii. 195-203]
> (p. 209)

There is hardly a line in the above speech of the King [in *1 Hen. IV*, Act III, Scene II] that is not worth the whole of what Sophocles makes Oedipus say to his son in the same circumstances. But I don't expect that *the learned* will ever give up this point to me, *while one passage remains in Greek, and the other only in English.* (p. 222)

The arguments of cowardice are whimsically discussed and exposed, in the following passage. The Prince, just as he goes out, says to Falstaff,

> Why, thou owest Heaven a death.
>
> [*1 Henry IV*, V. i. 126]

Upon which the fat Knight takes occasion to hold this humorous soliloquy with himself:

> *Falstaff.* 'Tis not due, yet—I would be loath
> to pay him before his day. What need I be so
> forward with him, that calls not on me? Well,
> 'tis no matter; honour pricks me on; but how
> if honour pricks me off again, when I come
> on? Can honour set to a leg? No—Or an arm?
> No—Or take away the grief of a wound? No.
> Honour hath no skill in surgery, then? No—
> What is honour? A word—What is that word
> Honour? Air?—A trim reckoning—Who hath it?
> He that died on Wednesday.
>
> [*1 Henry IV*, V. i. 127-36]
> (pp. 224-25)

I thought that my task was done with this Play, when I had got to the end of it; but there is something so very great, singular, and attractive, in the two principal characters of this historic piece, that I find a pleasure in keeping them still in view, and contemplating them both in my mind.

Whenever Hotspur or the Prince *filled the Scene,* which they are either of them, singly, sufficient to do, I confess that my heart was sensible of such an emotion, as Sir Philip Sidney said he used to be affected with, on a perusal of the old Ballad of Chevy-Chase; *as if he had heard the sound of a trumpet.* (p. 226)

They are both equally brave; but the courage of Hotspur has a greater portion of fierceness in it—The Prince's magnanimity is more heroic. The first resembles Achilles; the latter is more like Hector. The different principles, too, of their actions help to form and justify this distinction; as the one *invades,* and the other *defends,* a right. Hotspur speaks nobly of his rival Dowglas, to his face, but after he is become his friend; the Prince does

the same of Hotspur, behind his back, and while he is still his enemy.

They both of them possess a sportive vein of humour in their scenes of common life; but Hotspur still preserves the surly and refractory haughtiness of his character, throughout, even in the relaxations he indulges himself in. The Prince has more of ease and nature in his; delivering himself over to mirth and dissipation, without reserve. Hotspur's festivity seems to resemble that of Hamlet; as assumed merely to relieve anxiety of mind, and cover sanguinary purposes; the Prince's gaiety, like that of Faulconbridge, appears to be more genuine, arising from natural temper, and an healthful flow of spirits. The Prince is Alcibiades—Percy is—himself.

There is likewise another character in this rich Play, of a most peculiar distinction; as being not only *original,* but *inimitable,* also—No copy of it has ever since appeared, either in life or description. Any one of the Dramatis Personae in Congreve's Comedies, or, indeed, in most of the modern ones, might repeat the wit or humour of the separate parts, with equal effect on the audience, as the person to whose rôle they are appropriated; but there is a certain characteristic peculiarity in all the humour of Falstaff, that would sound flatly in the mouths of Bardolph, Poins, or Peto. In fine, the portrait of this extraordinary personage is delineated by so masterly a hand, that we may venture to pronounce it to be the only one that ever afforded so high a degree of pleasure, without the least pretence to merit or virtue to support it.

I was obliged to pass by many of his strokes of humour, character, and description, because they did not fall within the rule I had prescribed to myself in these notes; but I honestly confess that it was with regret, whenever I did so; for, were there as much moral, as there certainly is physical, good in laughing, I might have transcribed every Scene of his, throughout this, the following Play, and the *Merry Wives of Windsor,* for the advantage of the health, as well as the entertainment, of my readers. (pp. 227-28)

The delicacy of the Prince's difficulty upon this occasion [in his dialogue with Poins in 2 Henry IV, Act II, Scene II], in not being able to manifest the concern he was really sensible of for his father's illness, lest, from the former complexion of his life and manners, he might be suspected of insincerity in such professions, must have a fine effect on the sentiment of a reader who is possessed of the least refinement of principle or virtue.

A most useful lesson might be framed, upon the very singular character of this amiable person. The pattern is not perfect; and therefore—shall I venture to say it? the example is the better, for that reason. His manners are idle, but his morals uncorrupt. He suffers Falstaff to make as free with him as he pleases, but breaks his head, as Mrs. Quickly tells us in a former Scene, for his having thrown out a jest upon his father. Young men may learn from him never to be guilty of more vice, than the temptation to it might precipitate them into. He connives at the robbery of his companions, for the diversion of playing the same game upon them, again; but resolves to make ample restitution for the wrong. He offends his father by the dissoluteness of his conduct; but his filial affection and respect are still unremitted towards him. He shews a spirit of justice in injustice, and of duty, even in disobedience.

I here offer this comment as a supplement to the character I have already drawn of this Prince, at the end of the former Play. I could not have fairly added it there, as any thing that did not immediately relate to the comparison between him and Hotspur, would have been improperly introduced in the Parallel. (p. 236)

[Elizabeth] Griffith, "'Henry the Fourth: First Part'" and "'Henry the Fourth: Second Part'," in her The Morality of Shakespeare's Drama Illustrated, Frank Cass & Co. Ltd., 1971, pp. 207-28, 229-52.

MAURICE MORGANN   (essay date 1777)

[Morgann holds an assured place in the history of Shakespearean criticism on the basis of the following essay, first published in 1777 in his An Essay on the Dramatic Character of Sir John Falstaff. It is the longest and most detailed study of a single Shakespearean character to its date—and still controversial in the twentieth century. Of all the eighteenth-century character analyses, Morgann's most closely approaches the Romantic view that Shakespeare's characters are organic creations not to be reduced to psychological models. In the excerpt below, he maintains that Shakespeare did not intend Falstaff to be merely a "coward," but that, like all Shakespeare's characters, he was meant to possess a combination of real and apparent qualities, all in themselves irreducible to a simple psychological behavior, such as cowardice or vanity. In fact, Morgann suggests that the "apparent" Falstaff—the drunk and intemperate coward—is in

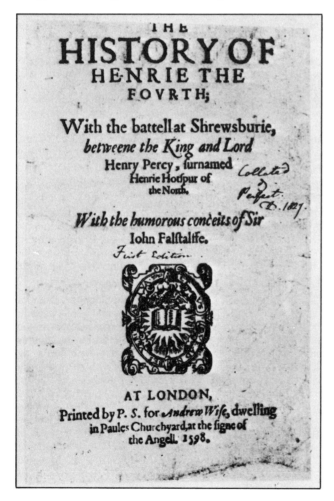

Title page of the Quarto of Henry IV, Part I (1598). Reproduced by permission of The Huntington Library, San Marino, CA.

reality a misconception of the "real" Falstaff, who is a character of "much Natural courage and resolution." Morgann's interpretation of Sir John was virtually ignored until the beginning of the twentieth century, when it was enthusiastically praised by A. C. Bradley (1902). Other critics who are often considered "pro-Morgann" in their views of Falstaff and Prince Hal include William Hazlitt (1817), Charles Cowden Clarke (1863), Charles Algernon Swinburne (1880), J. B. Priestley (1925), J. I. M. Stewart (1948), and Roy Battenhouse (1975). For opposing interpretations of Falstaff's character, see the excerpts by Samuel Johnson (1765), A. S. Pushkin (1836), G. G. Gervinus (1849-50), Leo Tolstoy (1906), E. E. Stoll (1914), L. C. Knights (1934), J. Dover Wilson (1943), E.M.W. Tillyard (1944), and Arthur Sewell (1951).]

The following sheets were written in consequence of a friendly conversation, turning by some chance upon the Character of FALSTAFF, wherein the Writer, maintaining, contrary to the general Opinion, that this Character was not intended to be shewn as a Coward, he was challenged to deliver and support that Opinion from the Press, with an engagement, now he fears forgotten, for it was three years ago, that he should be answered thro' the same channel. . . . (p. 203)

The vindication of FALSTAFF's Courage is truly no otherwise the object than some old fantastic Oak, or grotesque Rock, may be the object of a morning's ride; yet being proposed as such, may serve to limit the distance, and shape the course: The real object is Exercise, and the Delight which a rich, beautiful, picturesque, and perhaps unknown Country, may excite from every side. Such an Exercise may admit of some little excursion, keeping however the Road in view; but seems to exclude every appearance of labour and of toil.—Under the impression of such Feelings, the Writer has endeavoured to preserve to his Text a certain lightness of air, and chearfulness of tone; but is sensible, however, that the manner of discussion does not *every where*, particularly near the commencement, sufficiently correspond with his design.—If the Book shall be fortunate enough to obtain another Impression, a separation may be made; and such of the heavier parts as cannot be wholly dispensed with, sink to their more proper station,—a Note.

He is fearful likewise that he may have erred in the other extreme; and that having thought himself intitled, even in argument, to a certain degree of playful discussion, may have pushed it, in a few places, even to levity. (p. 204)

I presume to declare it as my opinion, that Cowardice *is not* the *Impression* which the *whole* character of *Falstaff* is calculated to make on the minds of an unprejudiced audience; tho' there be, I confess, a great deal of something in the *composition* likely enough to puzzle, and consequently to mislead the Understanding.—The reader will perceive that I distinguish between *mental Impressions* and the *Understanding*.—I wish to avoid every thing that looks like subtlety and refinement; but this is a distinction which we all comprehend.—There are none of us unconscious of certain feelings or sensations of mind which do not seem to have passed thro' the Understanding; the effects, I suppose, of some secret influences from without, acting upon a certain mental sense, and producing feelings and passions in just correspondence to the force and variety of those influences on the one hand, and to the quickness of our sensibility on the other. Be the cause, however, what it may, the fact is undoubtedly so; which is all I am concerned in. And it is equally a fact, which every man's experience may avouch, that the Understanding and those feelings are frequently at variance. The latter often arise from the most minute circumstances, and frequently from such as the Understanding cannot estimate, or even recognize; whereas the Understanding delights in abstraction, and in general propositions; which, however true considered as such, are very seldom, I had like to have said *never*, perfectly applicable to any particular case. And hence, among other causes, it is, that we often condemn or applaud characters and actions on the credit of some logical process, while our hearts revolt, and would fain lead us to a very different conclusion. (pp. 206-07)

It is not to the *Courage* only of *Falstaff* that we think these observations will apply: No part whatever of his character seems to be fully settled in our minds; at least there is something strangely incongruous in our discourse and affections concerning him. We all like *Old Jack;* yet, by some strange perverse fate, we all abuse him, and deny him the possession of any one single good or respectable quality. There is something extraordinary in this: It must be a strange art in *Shakespeare* which can draw our liking and good will towards so offensive an object. He has wit, it will be said; chearfulness and humour of the most characteristic and captivating sort. And is this enough? Is the humour and gaiety of vice so very captivating? Is the wit, characteristic of baseness and every ill quality, capable of attaching the heart and winning the affections? Or does not the apparency of such humour, and the flashes of such wit, by more strongly disclosing the deformity of character, but the more effectually excite our hatred and contempt of the man? And yet this is not our *feeling* of *Falstaff*'s character. When he has ceased to amuse us, we find no emotions of disgust; we can scarcely forgive the ingratitude of the Prince in the new-born virtue of the King, and we curse the severity of that poetic justice which consigns our old good-natured delightful companion to the custody of the *warden*, and the dishonours of the *Fleet*. (p. 209)

[What] can be the cause that we are not at all surprized at the gaiety and ease of *Falstaff* under the most trying circumstances; and that we never think of charging *Shakespeare* with departing, on this account, from the truth and coherence of character? Perhaps, after all, the *real* character of *Falstaff* may be different from his *apparent* one; and possibly this difference between reality and appearance, whilst it accounts at once for our liking and our censure, may be the true point of humour in the character, and the source of all our laughter and delight. We may chance to find, if we will but examine a little into the nature of those circumstances which have accidentally involved him, that he was intended to be drawn as a character of much Natural courage and resolution; and be obliged thereupon to repeal those decisions which may have been made upon the credit of some general tho' unapplicable propositions; the common source of error in other and higher matters. A little reflection may perhaps bring us round again to the point of our departure, and unite our Understandings to our instinct.—Let us then for a moment *suspend* at least our decisions, and candidly and coolly inquire if Sir *John Falstaff* be, indeed, what he has so often been called by critic and commentator, male and female,—a *Constitutional Coward*. (pp. 210-11)

To me . . . it appears that the leading quality in *Falstaff*'s character, and that from which all the rest take their colour, is a high degree of wit and humour, accompanied with great natural vigour and alacrity of mind. This quality, so accompanied, led him probably very early into life, and made him highly acceptable to society; so acceptable, as to make it seem unnecessary for him to acquire any other virtue. Hence, perhaps, his continued debaucheries and dissipations of every kind.—He seems, by nature, to have had a mind free of malice or any evil principle; but he never took the trouble of acquiring

any good one. He found himself esteemed and beloved with all his faults; nay *for* his faults, which were all connected with humour, and for the most part grew out of it. As he had, possibly, no vices but such as he thought might be openly professed, so he appeared more dissolute thro' ostentation. To the character of wit and humour, to which all his other qualities seem to have conformed themselves, he appears to have added a very necessary support, *that* of the profession of a *Soldier*. He had from nature, as I presume to say, a spirit of boldness and enterprise; which in a Military age, tho' employment was only occasional, kept him always above contempt, secured him an honourable reception among the Great, and suited best both his particular mode of humour and of vice. Thus living continually in society, nay even in Taverns, and indulging himself, and being indulged by others, in every debauchery; drinking, whoring, gluttony, and ease, assuming a liberty of fiction, necessary perhaps to his wit, and often falling into falsity and lies, he seems to have set, by degrees, all sober reputation at defiance; and finding eternal resources in his wit, he borrows, shifts, defrauds, and even robs, without dishonour. (pp. 212-13)

Let us then examine, as a source of very authentic information, what Impressions *Sir John Falstaff* had made on the characters of the Drama; and in what estimation he is supposed to stand with mankind in general as to the point of Personal Courage. . . .

The *Hostess Quickly* employs two officers to arrest *Falstaff*: On the mention of his name, one of them immediately observes, '*that it may chance to cost some of them their lives, for that he will stab.*'—'*Alas a day,*' says the hostess, '*take heed of him, he cares not what 'mischief he doth; if his weapon be out, he will 'foin like any devil; He will 'spare neither man, woman, or child.*' (p. 217)

But to go a little higher, if, indeed, to consider *Shallow*'s opinion be to go *higher:* It is from him, however, that we get the earliest account of *Falstaff*. He *remembers him a Page to Thomas Mowbray, Duke of Norfolk: 'He broke,*' says he, '*Schoggan's head at the 'Court-Gate when he was but a crack thus high.*' *Shallow*, throughout, considers him as a great Leader and Soldier, and relates this fact as an early indication only of his future Prowess. *Shallow*, it is true, is a very ridiculous character; but he picked up these Impressions somewhere; and he picked up none of a contrary tendency.—I want at present only to prove that *Falstaff* stood well in the report of common fame as to this point; and he was now near seventy years of age, and had passed in a Military line thro' the active part of his life. At this period common fame may be well considered as the *seal* of his character; a seal which ought not perhaps to be broke open on the evidence of any future transaction. (p. 218)

It has been remarked, and very truly I believe, that no man is a hero in the eye of his valet-de-chambre; and *thus* it is, we are witnesses only of *Falstaff*'s weakness and buffoonery; our acquaintance is with *Jack Falstaff, Plump Jack,* and *Sir John Paunch;* but if we would look for *Sir John Falstaff*, we must put on, as *Bunyan* would have expressed it, the spectacles of observation. With respect, for instance, to his Military command at Shrewsbury, nothing appears on the surface but the Prince's familiarly saying, in the tone usually assumed when speaking of *Falstaff*, '*I will procure this fat rogue a Charge of foot*'; and in another place, '*I will procure thee Jack a Charge of foot; meet 'me to-morrow in the Temple Hall.*' Indeed we might venture to infer from this, that a Prince of so great ability, whose wildness was only external and assumed, would not have procured, in so nice and critical a conjuncture, a Charge of foot for a known Coward. (p. 219)

Even at the age at which [Falstaff] is exhibited to us, we find him *foundering, as he calls it, nine score and odd miles,* with wonderful expedition, to join the army of Prince *John* of *Lancaster;* and declaring, after the surrender of *Coleville,* that *'had he but a belly of any indifferency, he 'were simply the most active fellow in Europe'.* Nor ought we here to pass over his Knighthood without notice. It was, I grant, intended by the author as a dignity which, like his Courage and his wit, was to be debased; his knighthood by low situations, his Courage by circumstances and imputations of cowardice, and his wit by buffoonery. But how are we to suppose this honour was acquired? By that very Courage, it should seem, which we so obstinately deny him. It was not certainly given him, like a modern City Knighthood, for his wealth or gravity: It was in these days a Military honour, and an authentic badge of Military merit. (pp. 228-29)

I cannot foresee the temper of the reader, nor whether he be content to go along with me in these kind of observations. Some of the incidents which I have drawn out of the Play may appear too minute, whilst yet they refer to principles which may seem too general. Many points require explanation; something should be said of the nature of *Shakespeare*'s Dramatic characters. . . . (p. 230)

> [Morgan adds in a footnote:] The reader must be sensible of something in the composition of *Shakespeare*'s characters, which renders them essentially different from those drawn by other writers. The characters of every Drama must indeed be grouped; but in the groupes of other poets the parts which are not seen do not in fact exist. But there is a certain roundness and integrity in the forms of *Shakespeare,* which give them an independence as well as a relation, insomuch that we often meet with passages which, tho' perfectly felt, cannot be sufficiently explained in words, without unfolding the whole character of the speaker. . . .
>
> Bodies of all kinds, whether of metals, plants, or animals, are supposed to possess certain first principles of *being,* and to have an existence independent of the accidents which form their magnitude or growth: Those accidents are supposed to be drawn in from the surrounding elements, but not indiscriminately; each plant and each animal imbibes those things only which are proper to its own distinct nature, and which have besides such a secret relation to each other as to be capable of forming a perfect union and coalescence: But so variously are the surrounding elements mingled and disposed, that each particular body, even of those under the same species, has yet some *peculiar* of its own. *Shakespeare* appears to have considered the being and growth of the human mind as analogous to this system: There are certain qualities and capacities which he seems to have considered as first principles; the chief of which are certain energies of courage and activity, according to their degrees; together with different degrees and sorts of sensibilities, and a capacity, varying likewise in *degree,* of discernment and in-

telligence. The rest of the composition is drawn in from an atmosphere of surrounding things; that is, from the various influences of the different laws, religions and governments in the world; and from those of the different ranks and inequalities in society; and from the different professions of men, encouraging or repressing passions of particular sorts, and inducing different modes of thinking and habits of life; and he seems to have known intuitively what those influences in particular were which this or that original constitution would most freely imbibe and which would most easily associate and coalesce.

> (n., p. 230)

But it was not enough for *Shakespeare* to have formed his characters with the most perfect truth and coherence; it was further necessary that he should possess a wonderful facility of compressing, as it were, his own spirit into these images, and of giving alternate animation to the forms. This was not to be done *from without;* he must have *felt* every varied situation, and have spoken thro' the organ he had formed. Such an intuitive comprehension of things and such a facility must unite to produce a *Shakespeare.* The reader will not now be surprised if I affirm that those characters in *Shakespeare,* which are seen only in part, are yet capable of being unfolded and understood in the whole; every part being in fact relative, and inferring all the rest.

> (n., p. 231)

Shakespeare is, in truth, an author whose mimic creation agrees in general so perfectly with that of nature, that it is not only wonderful in the great, but opens another scene of amazement to the discoveries of the microscope. (p. 231)

When the hand of time shall have brushed off his present Editors and Commentators, and when the very name of *Voltaire,* and even the memory of the language in which he has written, shall be no more, the *Apalachian* mountains, the banks of the *Ohio,* and the plains of *Sciota* shall resound with the accents of this Barbarian: In his native tongue he shall roll the genuine passions of nature; nor shall the griefs of *Lear* be alleviated, or the charms and wit of *Rosalind* be abated by time. (p. 233)

True Poesy is *magic,* not *nature;* an effect from causes hidden or unknown. To the Magician I prescribed no laws; his law and his power are one; his power is his law. Him, who neither imitates, nor is within the reach of imitation, no precedent can or ought to bind, no limits to contain. If his end is obtained, who shall question his course? Means, whether apparent or hidden, are justified in Poesy by success; but then most perfect and most admirable when most concealed. (p. 235)

If *Falstaff* had been intended for the character of a *Miles Gloriosus,* his behaviour ought and therefore would have been commented upon by others. *Shakespeare* seldom trusts to the apprehensions of his audience; his characters interpret for one another continually, and when we least suspect such artful and secret management: The conduct of *Shakespeare* in this respect is admirable, and I could point out a thousand passages which might put to shame the advocates of a formal Chorus, and prove that there is as little of necessity as grace in so mechanic a contrivance. But I confine my censure of the Chorus to its supposed use of comment and interpretation only.

Falstaff is, indeed, so far from appearing to my eye in the light of a *Miles Gloriosus,* that, in the best of my taste and judgment, he does not discover, except in consequence of the robbery, the least *trait* of such a character. All his boasting speeches are humour, mere humour, and carefully spoken to persons who cannot misapprehend them, who cannot be imposed on: They contain indeed, for the most part, an unreasonable and imprudent ridicule of himself, the usual subject of his good humoured merriment. . . . (pp. 237-38)

But to come to the very serious reproach thrown upon him by that *cold blooded* boy, as he calls him, *Lancaster.—Lancaster* makes a solemn treaty of peace with the *Archbishop of York, Mowbray,* &c. upon the faith of which they disperse their troops; which is no sooner done than *Lancaster* arrests the Principals, and pursues the *scattered stray:* A transaction, by the bye, so singularly perfidious, that I wish *Shakespeare,* for his own credit, had not suffered it to pass under his pen without marking it with the blackest strokes of Infamy.—During this transaction, *Falstaff* arrives, joins in the pursuit, and takes Sir *John Coleville* prisoner. Upon being seen by *Lancaster* he is thus addressed:—

> Now, Falstaff, where have you been all this while?
> When every thing is over, then you come:
> These tardy tricks of yours will, on my life,
> One time or other break some gallows' back.
> [*2 Henry IV,* IV. iii. 26-9]

This may appear to many a very formidable passage. It is spoken, as we may say, in the hearing of the army, and by one intitled as it were by his station to decide on military conduct; and if no punishment immediately follows, the forbearance may be imputed to a regard for the Prince of Wales, whose favour the delinquent was known so unworthily to possess. But this reasoning will by no means apply to the real circumstances of the case. The effect of this passage will depend on the credit we shall be inclined to give to *Lancaster* for integrity and candour. . . . (pp. 238-39)

We are already well prepared what to think of this young man:—We have just seen a very pretty manoeuvre of his in a matter of the highest moment, and have therefore the less reason to be surprized if we find him practising a more petty fraud with suitable skill and address. He appears in truth to have been what *Falstaff* calls him, *a cold, reserved, soberblooded boy;* a politician, as it should seem, by nature; bred up moreover in the school of *Bolingbroke* his father, and tutored to betray: With sufficient courage and ability perhaps, but with too much of the knave in his composition, and too little of enthusiasm, ever to be a great and superior character. That such a youth as this should, even from the propensities of character alone, take any plausible occasion to injure a frank unguarded man of wit and pleasure, will not appear unnatural. But he had other inducements. *Falstaff* had given very general scandal by his distinguished wit and noted poverty, insomuch that a little cruelty and injustice towards him was likely to pass, in the eye of the grave and prudent part of mankind, as a very creditable piece of fraud, and to be accounted to *Lancaster* for virtue and good service. But *Lancaster* had motives yet more prevailing; *Falstaff* was a Favourite, without the power which belongs to that character; and the tone of the Court was strongly against him, as the misleader and corrupter of the Prince; who

was now at too great a distance to afford him immediate countenance and protection. (pp. 239-40)

But as yet we have dealt principally in parole and circumstantial evidence, and have referred to *Fact* only incidentally. But *Facts* have a much more operative influence: They may be produced, not as arguments only, but Records; not to dispute alone, but to decide.—It is time then to behold *Falstaff* in actual service as a soldier, in danger, and in battle. . . . In the midst and in the heat of battle [at Shrewsbury], we see him come forwards;—what are his words? '*I have led my Rag-o-muffians where* 'they are peppered; there's not three of my hundred and fifty left alive.' But to *whom* does he say this? To himself only; he speaks *in soliloquy.* There is no questioning the fact, *he had* led *them; they were peppered; there were not* three *left alive.* He was in luck, being in bulk equal to any two of them, to escape unhurt. Let the author answer for that, I have nothing to do with it: He was the Poetic maker of the whole *Corps,* and he might dispose of them as he pleased. Well might the Chief justice, as we now find, acknowledge *Falstaff'*s services in this day's battle; an acknowledgment which amply confirms the fact. A Modern officer, who had performed a feat of this kind, would expect, not only the praise of having done his duty, but the appellation of a hero. (pp. 244-45)

In the following passages the true character of *Falstaff* as to Courage and Principle is finely touched, and the different colours at once nicely blended and distinguished. '*If Percy be alive, I'll* 'pierce *him. If he do come in my way, so:—If he do not, if I come in* his 'willingly, let him make a Carbonado of me. I like not such grinning 'honour as Sir Walter hath; give me life; which if I can save, so; if not, 'honour comes unlook'd for, and there's an end.' One cannot say which prevails most here, profligacy or courage; they are both tinged alike by the same humour, and mingled in one common mass; yet when we consider the superior force of *Percy,* as we must presently also that of *Douglas,* we shall be apt, I believe, in our secret heart, to forgive him. These passages are spoken in soliloquy and in battle: If every soliloquy made under similar circumstances were as audible as *Falstaff'*s, the imputation might perhaps be found too general for censure. These are among the passages that have impressed on the world an idea of Cowardice in *Falstaff;*—yet why? He is resolute to take his fate: If *Percy* do come in his way, *so;*—if not, he will not seek inevitable destruction; he is willing to save his life, but if that cannot be, why,—'honour comes unlook'd for, and there's an end.' This surely is not the language of Cowardice: It contains neither the Bounce or Whine of the character; he derides, it is true, and seems to renounce that grinning idol of Military zealots, Honour. But *Falstaff* was a kind of Military free-thinker, and has accordingly incurred the obloquy of his condition. He stands upon the ground of natural Courage only and common sense, and has, it seems, too much wit for a hero.—But let me be well understood;—I do not justify *Falstaff* for renouncing the point of honour; it proceeded doubtless from a general relaxation of mind, and profligacy of temper. Honour is calculated to aid and strengthen natural courage, and lift it up to heroism; but natural courage, which can act as such without honour, is natural courage still; the very quality I wish to maintain to *Falstaff.* And if, without the aid of honour, he can act with firmness, his portion is only the more eminent and distinguished. In such a character, it is to his actions, not his sentiments, that we are to look for conviction. But it may be still further urged in behalf of *Falstaff,* that there may be false honour as well as false religion. It is true; yet even in that case candour obliges me to confess that the best men are most disposed to conform, and most likely to become the dupes of their own virtue. But it may however be more reasonably urged that there are particular tenets both in honour and religion, which it is the grossness of folly not to question. To seek out, to court assured destruction, without leaving a single benefit behind, may be well reckoned in the number: And this is precisely the very folly which *Falstaff* seems to abjure;—nor are we, perhaps, intitled to say more, in the way of censure, than that he had not virtue enough to become the dupe of honour, nor prudence enough to hold his tongue. (pp. 246-47)

But there is a formidable objection behind. *Falstaff* counterfeits beasely on being attacked by *Douglas;* he assumes, in a cowardly spirit, the appearance of death to avoid the reality. But there was no equality of force; not the least chance for victory, or life. And is it the duty then, *think we still,* of true Courage, to meet, without benefit to society, *certain death*? Or is it only the phantasy of honour?—But such a fiction is highly disgraceful;—true, and a man of nice honour might perhaps have *grinned* for it. But we must remember that *Falstaff* had a double character; he was a *wit* as well as a *soldier;* and his Courage, however eminent, was but the *accessary;* his wit was the *principal;* and the part, which, if they should come in competition, he had the greatest interest in maintaining. Vain indeed were the licentiousness of his principles, if he should seek death like a bigot, yet without the meed of honour; when he might live by wit, and encrease the reputation of that wit by living. But why do I labour this point? It has been already anticipated, and our improved acquaintance with *Falstaff* will now require no more than a short narrative of the fact.

Whilst in the battle of *Shrewsbury* he is exhorting and encouraging the Prince who is engaged with the *Spirit Percy*— *'Well said Hal, to him Hal,'*—he is himself attacked by the *Fiend Douglas.* There was no match; nothing remained but death or stratagem; grinning honour, or laughing life. But an expedient offers, a mirthful one,—Take your choice *Falstaff,* a point of honour, or a point of drollery.—It could not be a question;—*Falstaff* falls, *Douglas* is cheated, and the world laughs. But does he fall like a Coward? No, like a buffoon only; the superior principle prevails, and *Falstaff* lives by a stratagem growing out of his character, to prove himself *no counterfeit,* to jest, to be employed, and to fight again. . . . The circumstance of his wounding *Percy* in the thigh, and carrying the dead body on his back like luggage, is *indecent* but not cowardly. The declaring, though in jest, that he killed *Percy,* seems to me *idle,* but it is not meant or calculated for *imposition;* it is spoken to the *Prince himself,* the man in the world who could not be, or be supposed to be, imposed on. (pp. 247-49)

I know not what Impression has been made on the reader; a good deal of evidence has been produced, and much more remains to be offered. But how many sorts of men are there whom no evidence can persuade! How many, who, ignorant of *Shakespeare,* or forgetful of the text, may as well read heathen Greek, or the laws of the land, as this unfortunate Commentary? How many, who, proud and pedantic, hate all novelty, and damn it without mercy under one compendious word, Paradox? (pp. 250-51)

As for you, *Mrs.* MONTAGUE, I am grieved to find that *you* have been involved in a popular error [see excerpt above, 1769]; so much you must allow me to say;—for the rest, I bow to your genius and your virtues: You have given to the world a very elegant composition; and I am told your manners and your mind are yet more pure, more elegant than your book.

Falstaff was too gross, too infirm, for your inspection; but if you durst have looked nearer, you would not have found Cowardice in the number of his infirmities.—We will try if we cannot redeem him from this universal censure.—Let the venal corporation of authors duck *to the golden fool,* let them shape their sordid quills to the mercenary ends of unmerited praise, or of baser detraction;—*old Jack,* though deserted by princes, though censured by an ungrateful world, and persecuted from age to age by Critic and Commentator, and though never rich enough to hire one literary prostitute, shall find a Voluntary defender. . . . (p. 252)

[We] behold all the parties at *Gads-Hill* in preparation for the robbery. Let us carefully examine if it contains any intimation of Cowardice in *Falstaff.* He is shewn under a very ridiculous vexation about his horse, which is hid from him; but this is nothing to the purpose, or only proves that *Falstaff* knew no terror equal to that of walking *eight yards of uneven ground.* But on occasion of *Gadshil's* being asked concerning the number of the travellers, and having reported that they were eight or ten, *Falstaff* exclaims, *'Zounds! will they not rob us!'* If he had said more seriously, 'I doubt they will be too hard for us,'—he would then have only used the Prince's own words upon a less alarming occasion. This cannot need defence. But the Prince, in his usual stile of mirth, replies, *'What a Coward, Sir 'John Paunch!'* To this one would naturally expect from *Falstaff* some light answer; but we are surprized with a very serious one;—'*I am not indeed* John of Gaunt *your grandfather, but yet no 'Coward, Hal.'* This is singular: It contains, I think, the true character of *Falstaff;* and it seems to be thrown out *here,* at a very critical conjuncture, as a caution to the audience not to take too sadly what was intended only (to use the Prince's words) *'as 'argument for a week, laughter for a month, and a good jest for ever 'after.'* (pp. 256-57)

But now comes on the concerted transaction, which has been the source of so much dishonour. *As they are sharing the booty* (says the stage direction) *the Prince and* Poins *set upon them, they all run away; and* Falstaff *after a blow or two runs away too, leaving the booty behind them.*—'Got with much 'ease,' says the Prince, as an event beyond expectation, 'Now 'merrily to horse.'—Poins adds, as they are going off, 'How the 'rogue roared!' This observation is afterwards remembered by the Prince, who, urging the jest to *Falstaff,* says, doubtless with all the licence of exaggeration,—'*And you,* Falstaff, *carried your guts 'away as nimbly, with as quick dexterity, and roared for mercy, and still 'ran and roared, as I ever heard bull-calf.'* If he did roar for mercy, it must have been a very inarticulate sort of roaring; for there is not a single word set down for *Falstaff* from which this roaring may be inferred, or any stage direction to the actor for that purpose: But, in the spirit of mirth and derision, the lightest exclamation might be easily converted into the roar of a bull-calf. (pp. 257-58)

That the whole transaction was considered as a mere jest, and as carrying with it no serious imputation of the Courage of *Falstaff,* is manifest, not only from his being allowed, when the laugh was past, to call himself, without contradiction in the personated character of *Hal* himself, 'valiant *Jack Falstaff, and the 'more* valiant *being, as he is,* old Jack Falstaff,' but from various other particulars, and, above all, from the declaration, which the Prince makes on that very night, of his intention of procuring this *fat rogue a Charge of foot;*—a circumstance, doubtless, contrived by *Shakespeare* to wipe off the seeming dishonour of the day: And from this time forward we hear of no imputation arising from this transaction; it is born and dies in a convivial hour; it leaves no trace behind, nor do we see any longer in the character of *Falstaff* the boasting or braggadocio of a Coward. (p. 266)

What then upon the whole shall be said but that *Shakespeare* has made certain Impressions, or produced certain effects, of which he has thought fit to conceal or obscure the cause? How he has done this, and for what special ends, we shall now presume to guess.—Before the period in which *Shakespeare* wrote, the fools and Zanys of the stage were drawn out of the coarsest and cheapest materials: Some essential folly, with a dash of knave and coxcomb, did the feat. But *Shakespeare*, who delighted in difficulties, was resolved to furnish a richer repast, and to give to one eminent buffoon the high relish of wit, humour, birth, dignity, and Courage. But this was a process which required the nicest hand, and the utmost management and address: These enumerated qualities are, in their own nature, productive of *respect;* an Impression the most opposite to laughter that can be. This Impression then, it was, at all adventures, necessary to withhold; which could not perhaps well be without dressing up these qualities in fantastic forms, and colours not their own; and thereby cheating the eye with shews of baseness and of folly, whilst he stole as it were upon the palate a richer and a fuller *goût*. To this end, what arts, what contrivances, has he not practised! How has he steeped this singular character in bad habits for fifty years together, and brought him forth saturated with every folly and with every vice not destructive of his essential character, or incompatible with his own primary design! For this end, he has deprived *Falstaff* of every good principle; and . . . he has concealed every bad one. He has given him also every infirmity of body that is not likely to awaken our compassion, and which is most proper to render both his better qualities and his vices ridiculous: he has associated levity and debauch with *age*, corpulence and inactivity with *courage*, and has roguishly coupled the gout with *Military honours*, and a *pension* with the *pox*. He has likewise involved this character in situations, out of which neither wit nor Courage can extricate him with honour. The surprize at *Gads-Hill* might have betrayed a hero into flight, and the encounter with *Douglas* left him no choice but death or stratagem. If he plays an after-game, and endeavours to redeem his ill fortune by lyes and braggadocio, his ground fails him; no wit, no evasion will avail: Or is he likely to appear respectable in his person, rank, and demeanor, how is that respect abated or discharged! *Shakespeare* has given him a kind of state indeed; but of what is it composed? Of that fustian cowardly rascal *Pistol*, and his yoke-fellow of few words, the equally deedless *Nym;* of his cup-bearer the fiery *Trigon*, whose zeal burns in his nose, *Bardolph;* and of the boy, who bears the purse with *seven groats and two-pence;*—a boy who was given him on purpose to set him off, and whom he walks *before*, according to his own description, *'like a sow that had overwhelmed all her litter but one.'*

But it was not enough to render *Falstaff* ridiculous in his figure, situations, and equipage; *still* his respectable qualities would have come forth, at least occasionally, to spoil our mirth; or they might have burst the intervention of such slight impediments, and have every where shone through: It was necessary then to go farther, and throw on him that substantial ridicule, which only the incongruities of real vice can furnish; of vice, which was to be so mixed and blended with his frame as to give a durable character and colour to the whole. (pp. 267-69)

I have 'till now looked only to the Courage of *Falstaff*, a quality which, having been denied, in terms, to belong to his consti-

tution, I have endeavoured to vindicate to the Understandings of my readers; the Impression on their Feelings (in which all Dramatic truth consists) being already, as I have supposed, in favour of the character. In the pursuit of this subject I have taken the general Impression of the whole character pretty much, I suppose, like other men. . . . But if we would account for our Impressions, or for certain sentiments or actions in a character, not derived from its apparent principles, yet appearing, we know not why, natural, we are then compelled to look farther, and examine if there be not something more in the character than is *shewn;* something inferred, which is not brought under our special notice: In short, we must look to the art of the writer, and to the principles of human nature, to discover the hidden causes of such effects.—Now this is a very different matter.—The former considerations respected the Impression only, without regard to the Understanding; but this question relates to the Understanding alone. . . . If therefore, for further proofs of *Falstaff*'s Courage, or for the sake of curious speculation, or for both, I change my position, and look to causes instead of effects, the reader must not be surprized if he finds the former *Falstaff* vanish like a dream, and another, of more disgustful form, presented to his view; one whose final punishment we shall be so far from regretting, that we ourselves shall be ready to consign him to a severer doom. (pp. 269-70)

We have frequently referred to [Falstaff's vices] under the name of ill habits;—but perhaps the reader is not fully aware how very vicious he indeed is;—he is a robber, a glutton, a cheat, a drunkard, and a lyar; lascivious, vain, insolent, profligate, and profane:—A fine infusion this, and such as without very excellent cookery must have thrown into the dish a great deal too much of the *fumet*. (pp. 270-71)

It ought not . . . to be forgotten, that if *Shakespeare* has used arts to abate our respect of *Falstaff*, it should follow by just inference, that, without such arts, his character would have grown into a *respect* inconsistent with laughter; and that yet, without Courage, he could not have been respectable at all;—that it required nothing less than the union of ability and Courage to support his other more accidental qualities with any tolerable coherence. (p. 274)

[It] may be well worth our curiosity to inquire into the composition of *Falstaff*'s character.—Every man we may observe has two characters; that is, every man may be seen externally, and from without;—or a section may be made of him, and he may be illuminated from within.

Of the external character of *Falstaff*, we can scarcely be said to have any steady view. *Jack Falstaff* we are familiar with, but *Sir John* was better known, it seems, *to the rest of Europe*, than to his intimate companions; yet we have so many glimpses of him, and he is opened to us occasionally in such various points of view, that we cannot be mistaken in describing him as a man of birth and fashion, bred up in all the learning and accomplishments of the times;—of ability and Courage equal to any situation, and capable by nature of the highest affairs; trained to arms, and possessing the tone, the deportment, and the manners of a gentleman;—but yet these accomplishments and advantages seem to hang loose on him, and to be worn with a slovenly carelessness and inattention: A too great indulgence of the qualities of humour and wit seems to draw him too much one way, and to destroy the grace and orderly arrangement of his other accomplishments;—and hence he becomes strongly marked for one advantage, to the injury, and almost forgetfulness in the beholder, of all the rest. Some of his vices likewise strike through, and stain his Exterior;—his modes of speech betray a certain licentiousness of mind; and that high Aristocratic tone which belonged to his situation was pushed on, and aggravated into unfeeling insolence and oppression. (pp. 275-76)

We are next to see him *from within:* And here we shall behold him most villainously unprincipled and debauched; possessing indeed the same Courage and ability, yet stained with numerous vices, unsuited not only to his primary qualities, but to his age, corpulency, rank, and profession;—reduced by these vices to a state of dependence, yet resolutely bent to indulge them at any price. These vices have been already enumerated; they are many, and become still more intolerable by an excess of unfeeling insolence on one hand, and of base accommodation on the other.

But what then, after all, is become of *old Jack?* Is this the jovial delightful companion—*Falstaff,* the favourite and the boast of the Stage?—by no means. But it is, I think however, the *Falstaff* of Nature; the very stuff out of which the *Stage Falstaff* is composed; nor was it possible, I believe, out of any other materials he could have been formed. From this disagreeable draught we shall be able, I trust, by a proper disposition of light and shade, and from the influence of compression of external things, to produce *plump Jack,* the life of humour, the spirit of pleasantry, and the soul of mirth.

To this end, *Falstaff* must no longer be considered as a single independent character, but grouped, as we find him shewn to us in the Play;—his ability must be disgraced by buffoonery, and his Courage by circumstances of imputation; and those qualities be thereupon reduced into subjects of mirth and laughter:—His vices must be concealed at each end from vicious design and evil effect, and must thereupon be turned into incongruities, and assume the name of humour only;—his insolence must be repressed by the superior tone of *Hal* and *Poins,* and take the softer name of spirit only, or alacrity of mind;—his state of dependence, his temper of accommodation, and his activity, must fall in precisely with the indulgence of his humours; that is, he must thrive best and flatter most, by being extravagantly incongruous; and his own tendency, impelled by so much activity, will carry him with perfect ease and freedom to all the necessary excesses. But why, it may be asked, should incongruities recommend *Falstaff* to the favour of the Prince?—Because the Prince is supposed to possess a high relish of humour and to have a temper and a force about him, which, whatever was his pursuit, delighted in excess. This, *Falstaff* is supposed perfectly to comprehend; and thereupon not only to indulge himself in all kinds of incongruity, but to lend out his own superior wit and humour against himself, and to heighten the ridicule by all the tricks and arts of buffoonery for which his corpulence, his age, and situation, furnish such excellent materials. This compleats the Dramatic character of *Falstaff,* and gives him that appearance of perfect good-nature, pleasantry, mellowness, and hilarity of mind, for which we admire and almost love him, tho' we feel certain reserves which forbid our going that length; the true reason of which is, that there will be always found a difference between mere appearances and reality: Nor are we, nor can we be, insensible that whenever the action of external influence upon him is in whole or in part relaxed, the character restores itself proportionably to its more unpleasing condition. (pp. 277-78)

[At the Play's end,] the curtain must not only be dropt before the eyes, but over the minds of the spectators, and nothing left for further examination and curiosity.—But how was this to be done in regard to *Falstaff?* He was not involved in the fortune of the Play; he was engaged in no action which, as to him, was to be compleated; he had reference to no system, he was attracted to no center; he passes thro' the Play as a lawless meteor, and we wish to know what course he is afterwards likely to take: He is detected and disgraced, it is true; but he lives by detection, and thrives on disgrace; and as we are desirous to see him detected and disgraced again. The *Fleet* might be no bad scene of further amusement;—he carries *all* within him, *and what matter* where, *if he be still the same,* possessing the same force of mind, the same wit, and the same incongruity. This, *Shakespeare* was fully sensible of, and knew that this character could not be compleatly dismissed but by death.— 'Our author,' says the Epilogue to the Second Part of Henry IV., 'will continue the story with Sir *John* in it, and make 'you merry with fair *Catherine* of *France; where,* for any thing I know, *Falstaff* shall dye of a sweat, unless already he be killed with your hard opinions.' If it had been prudent in *Shakespeare* to have killed *Falstaff* with *hard opinion,* he had the means in his hand to effect it;—but dye, it seems, he must, in one form or another, and a *sweat* would have been no unsuitable catastrophe. However we have reason to be satisfied as it is;—his death was worthy of his birth and of his life: '*He was born,*' he says, '*about 'three o'clock in the afternoon, with a white head, and something a round belly.*' But if he came into the world in the evening with these marks of age, he departs out of it in the morning in all the follies and vanities of youth;— '*He was shaked*' (we are told) '*of a burning quotidian tertian;— the young King had run bad humours on the knight;—his heart was fracted and corroborate; and a' parted just between twelve and one, even at the turning of the tide, yielding the crow a pudding, and passing directly into* Arthur's bosom, *if ever man went into the bosom of* Arthur.'—So ended this singular buffoon; and with him ends an Essay, on which the reader is left to bestow what character he pleases: An Essay professing to treat of the Courage of *Falstaff,* but extending itself to his Whole character; to the arts and genius of his Poetic-Maker, SHAKESPEARE; and thro' him sometimes, with ambitious aim, even to the principles of human nature itself. (pp. 282-83)

> Maurice Morgann, "An Essay on the Dramatic Character of Sir John Falstaff," in Eighteenth Century Essays on Shakespeare, *edited by D. Nichol Smith, second edition, Oxford University Press, Oxford, 1963, pp. 203-83.*

HENRY MACKENZIE   (essay date 1786)

[*A Scottish novelist and essayist, Mackenzie wrote four essays in Shakespearean criticism, including the following sketch of Falstaff, first published in* Lounger *in 1786. He was apparently the first of a long line of critics to compare Falstaff with Don Quixote, and his conception of Falstaff as having affinities with Richard III anticipates Samuel Taylor Coleridge's discussion of Falstaff, Iago, and Richard III as Shakespeare's men of intellect (see excerpt below, 1813).*]

By a very singular felicity of invention [Shakespeare] has produced in the beaten field of ordinary life characters of such perfect originality that we look on them with no less wonder at his invention than on those preternatural beings [as in *Macbeth* and *The Tempest*], which 'are not of this earth;' and yet they speak a language so purely that of common society that we have but to step abroad into the world to hear every expression of which it is composed. Of this sort is the character of *Falstaff.* (p. 441)

Falstaff is truly and literally 'ex Epicuri grege porcus' [Horace, *Epistles*, 1.4.6: 'fat and sleek, a hog from Epicurus' herd'], placed here within the pale of this world to fatten at his leisure, neither disturbed by feeling nor restrained by virtue. He is not, however, positively much a villain, though he never starts aside in the pursuit of interest or of pleasure when knavery comes in his way. We feel contempt, therefore, and not indignation at his crimes, which rather promotes than hinders our enjoying the ridicule of the situation, and the admirable wit with which he expresses himself in it. As a man of this world he is endowed with the most superior degree of good sense and discernment of character; his conceptions, equally acute and just, he delivers with the expression of a clear and vigorous understanding; and we see that he thinks like a wise man, even when he is not at the pains to talk wisely. (pp. 441-42)

With [a] sagacity and penetration into the characters and motives of mankind Shakespeare has invested Falstaff in a remarkable degree: he never utters it, however, out of character, or at a season where it might better be spared. Indeed, his good sense is rather in his thoughts than in his speech; for so we may call those soliloquies in which he generally utters it. He knew what coin was most current with those he dealt withal, and fashioned his discourse according to the disposition of his hearers; and he sometimes lends himself to the ridicule of his companions when he has a chance of getting any interest on the loan. (pp. 442-43)

The greatest refinement of morals, as well as of mind, is produced by the culture and exercise of the imagination, which derives, or is taught to derive its objects of pursuit, and its motives of action, not from the senses merely but from future considerations which fancy anticipates and realizes. Of this, either as the prompter or the restraint of conduct, Falstaff is utterly devoid; yet his imagination is wonderfully quick and creative in the pictures of humour and the associations of wit. But the 'pregnancy of his wit,' according to his own phrase, 'is made a tapster;' [*2 Henry IV*, 1.2.170-71] and his fancy, how vivid soever, still subjects itself to the grossness of those sensual conceptions which are familiar to his mind. We are astonished at that art by which Shakespeare leads the powers of genius, imagination, and wisdom in captivity to this son of earth; 'tis as if transported into the enchanted island in the *Tempest,* we saw the rebellion of *Caliban* successful, and the airy spirits of *Prospero* ministering to the brutality of his slave. (p. 444)

In the immortal work of *Cervantes* we find a character with a remarkable mixture of wisdom and absurdity, which in one page excites our highest ridicule and in the next is entitled to our highest respect. *Don Quixote,* like Falstaff, is endowed with excellent discernment, sagacity, and genius; but his good sense holds fief of his diseased imagination, of his over-ruling madness for the atchievements of knight-errantry, for heroic valour and heroic love. The ridicule in the character of Don Quixote consists in raising low and vulgar incidents, through the medium of his disordered fancy, to a rank of importance, dignity, and solemnity to which in their nature they are the most opposite that can be imagined. With Falstaff it is nearly the reverse; the ridicule is produced by subjecting wisdom, honour, and other the most grave and dignified principles to the controul of grossness, buffoonery, and folly. 'Tis like the pastime of a family-masquerade, where laughter is equally excited by dressing clowns as gentlemen or gentlemen as clowns. In Falstaff the heroic attributes of our nature are made to wear the garb of meanness and absurdity. In Don Quixote the com-mon and the servile are clothed in the dresses of the dignified and the majestic; while to heighten the ridicule *Sancho,* in the half deceived simplicity and half discerning shrewdness of his character, is every now and then employed to pull off the mask. (pp. 444-45)

Shakespeare has drawn, in one of his immediately subsequent plays, a tragic character very much resembling the comic one of Falstaff, I mean that of *Richard III.* Both are men of the world, both possess the sagacity and understanding which is fitted for its purposes, both despise those refined feelings, those motives of delicacy, those restraints of virtue which might obstruct the course they have marked out for themselves. The hypocrisy of both costs them nothing, and they never feel that detection of it to themselves which rankles in the conscience of less determined hypocrites. Both use the weaknesses of others as skilful players at a game do the ignorance of their opponents; they enjoy the advantage not only without self-reproach but with the pride of superiority. Richard indeed aspires to the Crown of England, because Richard is wicked and ambitious: Falstaff is contented with a thousand pounds of Justice Shallow's, because he is only luxurious and dissipated. Richard courts Lady Anne and the Princess Elisabeth for his purposes: Falstaff makes love to Mrs. Ford and Mrs. Page for his. Richard is witty like Falstaff, and talks of his own figure with the same sarcastic indifference. Indeed, so much does Richard, in the higher walk of villany, resemble Falstaff in the lower region of roguery and dissipation, that it were not difficult to shew in the dialogue of the two characters, however dissimilar in situation, many passages and expressions in a style of remarkable resemblance. (p. 445)

Falstaff is the work of *Circe* and her swinish associates, who, in some favoured hour of revelry and riot, moulded this compound of gross debauchery, acute discernment, admirable invention, and nimble wit, and sent him for a consort to England's madcap Prince; to stamp currency on idleness and vice, and to wave the flag of folly and dissipation over the seats of gravity, of wisdom, and virtue. (p. 446)

> *Henry Mackenzie, in an extract from* Shakespeare, the Critical Heritage: 1774-1801, Vol. 6, *edited by Brian Vickers, Routledge & Kegan Paul, 1981, pp. 440-46.*

RICHARD CUMBERLAND (essay date 1786)

> [*Cumberland relates the dramatic structure of* Henry IV *to Falstaff's character, finding him less witty and amusing in Part Two than in Part One. This conclusion was also reached by George Brandes (1895-96) and Caroline F.E. Spurgeon (1935). The following extract originally appeared in* The Observer *in 1786.*]

When it had entered into the mind of Shakespeare to form an historical play upon certain events in the reign of Henry the fourth of England, the character of the Prince of Wales recommended itself to his fancy as likely to supply him with a fund of dramatic incidents. For what could invention have more happily suggested than this character, which history presented ready to his hands? a riotous disorderly young libertine, in whose nature lay hidden those seeds of heroism and ambition which were to burst forth at once to the astonishment of the world and to atchieve the conquest of France. . . .

With these materials ready for creation the great artist sate down to his work. . . . His first concern was to give a chief or captain to this gang of rioters; this would naturally be the first outline he drew. To fill up the drawing of this personage he conceived a voluptuary, in whose figure and character there should be an assemblage of comic qualities. In his person he should be bloated and blown up to the size of a *Silenus,* lazy, luxurious, in sensuality a satyr, in intemperance a bacchanalian. As he was to stand in the post of a ringleader amongst thieves and cutpurses he made him a notorious liar, a swaggering coward, vain-glorious, arbitrary, knavish, crafty, voracious of plunder, lavish of his gains, without credit, honour or honesty, and in debt to every body about him. As he was to be the chief seducer and misleader of the heir apparent of the crown, it was incumbent on the poet to qualify him for that part in such a manner as should give probability and even a plea to the temptation. This was only to be done by the strongest touches and the highest colourings of a master; by hitting off a humour of so happy, so facetious and so alluring a cast as should tempt even royalty to forget itself, and virtue to turn reveller in his company. His lies, his vanity and his cowardice, too gross to deceive, were to be so ingenious as to give delight; his cunning evasions, his witty resources, his mock solemnity, his vapouring self-consequence, were to furnish a continual feast of laughter to his royal companion. He was not only to be witty himself, but the cause of wit in other people; a whetstone for raillery; a buffoon, whose very person was a jest. Compounded of these humours, Shakespeare produced the character of *Sir John Falstaff;* a character which neither ancient nor modern comedy has ever equalled, which was so much the favourite of its author as to be introduced in three several plays, and which is likely to be the idol of the English stage as long as it shall speak the language of Shakespeare. (pp. 456-57)

The humour of Falstaff opens into full display upon his very first introduction with the prince. The incident of the robbery on the highway, the scene in Eastcheap in consequence of that ridiculous encounter, and the whole of his conduct during the action with Percy, are so exquisitely pleasant that upon the renovation of his dramatic life in the second part of *Henry the fourth* I question if the humour does not in part evaporate by continuation. At least I am persuaded that it flattens a little in the outset, and though his wit may not flow less copiously yet it comes with more labour and is farther fetcht. The poet seems to have been sensible how difficult it was to preserve the vein as rich as at first, and has therefore strengthened his comic plot in the second play with several new recruits who may take a share with Falstaff, to whom he no longer entrusts the whole burthen of the humour. In the front of these auxiliaries stands Pistol, a character so new, whimsical and extravagant that if it were not for a commentator now living, whose very extraordinary researches amongst our old authors have supplied us with passages to illuminate the strange rhapsodies which Shakespeare has put into his mouth, I should for one have thought Antient Pistol as wild and imaginary a being as Caliban. But I now perceive, by the help of these discoveries, that the character is *made up in great part of absurd and fustian passages from many plays, in which Shakespeare* was versed and perhaps *had been a performer.* Pistol's dialogue is a tissue of old tags of bombast, like the middle comedy of the Greeks, which dealt in parody. I abate of my astonishment at the invention and originality of the poet, but it does not lessen my respect for his ingenuity. Shakespeare founded his bully in parody, Jonson copied his from nature, and the palm seems due to Bobadil upon a comparison with Pistol. . . . (pp. 457-58)

Shallow and Silence are two very strong auxiliaries to this second part of Falstaff's humours, and though they do not absolutely belong to his family they are nevertheless near of

kin, and derivatives from his stock. Surely two pleasanter fellows never trode the stage; they not only contrast and play upon each other, but Silence sober and Silence tipsy make the most comical reverse in nature; never was drunkenness so well introduced or so happily employed in any drama.

Dame Quickly also in this second part resumes her rôle with great comic spirit but with some variation of character, for the purpose of introducing a new member into the troop in the person of Doll Tearsheet, the common trull of the times. Though this part is very strongly coloured, and though the scene with her and Falstaff is of a loose as well as ludicrous nature, yet if we compare Shakespeare's conduct of this incident with that of the dramatic writers of his time, and even since his time, we must confess he has managed it with more than common care, and exhibited his comic hero in a very ridiculous light without any of those gross indecencies which the poets of his age indulged themselves in without restraint.

The humour of the Prince of Wales is not so free and unconstrained as in the first part. Though he still demeans himself in the course of his revels yet it is with frequent marks of repugnance and self-consideration, as becomes the conqueror of Percy, and we see his character approaching fast towards a thorough reformation. But though we are thus prepared for the change that is to happen when this young hero throws off the reveller and assumes the king, yet we are not fortified against the weakness of pity when the disappointment and banishment of Falstaff takes place, and the poet executes justice upon his inimitable delinquent with all the rigour of an unrelenting moralist. The reader or spectator who has accompanied Falstaff through his dramatic story is in debt to him for so many pleasant moments that all his failings, which should have raised contempt, have only provoked laughter, and he begins to think they are not natural to his character but assumed for his amusement. With these impressions we see him delivered over to mortification and disgrace, and bewail his punishment with a sensibility that is only due to the sufferings of the virtuous. (pp. 458-59)

> *Richard Cumberland, in an extract from his "Remarks Upon the Characters of Falstaff and His Group," in* Shakespeare, the Critical Heritage: 1774-1801, Vol. 6, *edited by Brian Vickers, Routledge & Kegan Paul, 1981, pp. 456-60.*

REV. RICHARD STACK (essay date 1788)

[*Stack was one of the first critics to refute Maurice Morgann's interpretation of Falstaff as a courageous character, rather than a coward (see excerpt above, 1777). His essay was originally given as a paper in 1788.*]

[Morgann] introduces his essay with a distinction between the conclusions of the understanding formed upon actions, and the impressions upon a certain sense somewhat like instinct, which immediately acquaints us with the principles of character without any consideration of actions, and sometimes determines our heart even against the conclusions of our reason. (p. 470)

I am willing . . . for the present to admit that all men are conscious to themselves of certain feelings about character, independent of and even in opposition to the conclusions of the understanding. And upon the ground of this very distinction I think it might be shewn that Shakespeare has designed cowardice, rather than constitutional courage, to be a part of Falstaff's real character. (p. 471)

That Falstaff is vicious, a rogue, a liar, and a profligate, is allowed on all hands; yet covered with all this infamy, he entertains, surprises and charms, nay he engages our hearts. What then? Shall an infusion of cowardice reduce the character to a caput mortuum, and no spirit, no salt remain? For my part, I can see no reason for this. A man may, in my opinion, be very witty and pleasant upon his own defects, and even upon such qualities as, though acknowledged vices, cannot be deemed flagitious. Now cowardice, if it can be called by a harsher name than defect, will at least be allowed to have in it nothing flagitious. It certainly gives a mean and contemptible idea of its possessor; but so do fraud and lying. But neither these, nor any other qualities bestowed upon Falstaff, are in their nature so far detestable, but that great endowments of mind, especially if they be such as universally charm, shall be able completely to discharge the disgust arising from them. Genius and wit never fail to recommend themselves to the notice and admiration of mankind; and always throw a dignity round a character even above its true merit. These principles are sufficient to explain the superior pleasure and peculiar interest we feel in Falstaff above all other characters which have not half his vices. His creative fancy, playful wit, characteristic humour, admirable judgment and nice discernment of character, are so rare and excellent endowments that we lose the exceptionable matter in contemplating them. Nor is it owing to these alone that we admire and almost love Falstaff, but to another exquisite contrivance of the poet in catching occasions of mirth from his very vices. Thus, by making them the ground into which he has wrought the most entertaining fancies and delightful humour, he has made it almost impossible to separate matters thus closely interwoven, and has seduced judgment to the side of wit. These are the strange arts by which Shakespeare has drawn our liking toward so offensive an object; or to speak with more precision, has contrived to veil the offensive parts of his character. Defence is a thing of too serious a nature for Falstaff, he laughs at all vindication; *crescit sub pondere virtus* ["virtue grows under a burden"]. His elastic vigour of mind repels all difficulties; his alacrity bears him above all disgust; and in the gay wit we forget the contemptible coward. (pp. 478-79)

Rev. Richard Stack, in an extract from his "An Examination of an Essay on the Dramatic Character of Sir John Falstaff" in Shakespeare, the Critical Heritage: 1774-1801, Vol. 6, *edited by Brian Vickers, Routledge & Kegan Paul, 1981, pp. 469-79.*

WILLIAM RICHARDSON   (essay date 1788)

[*Richardson was a Scottish author and educator whose philosophical leanings led him to focus on the psychological and moral aspects of Shakespeare's major characters, drawing from each a philosophical lesson, or what he termed a "ruling principle." For Richardson, such a guiding principle served to establish the psychological personalities of Shakespeare's characters—their motives, fears, delusions—and in the process defined the action of each play. In the following excerpt, first published in his* Essays on Shakespeare's Dramatic Character of Sir John Falstaff, and On His Imitation of Female Characters *in 1788, he maintains that the "gratification of bodily pleasure" is the principle which guides all of Falstaff's actions and determines his personality. For other major essays on Falstaff, see the excerpts by Corbyn Morris (1744), Maurice Morgann (1777), William Hazlitt (1817), A. C. Bradley (1902), E. E. Stoll (1914), J. Dover Wilson (1943), and Roy Battenhouse (1975).*]

'The desire of gratifying the grosser and lower appetites, is the ruling and strongest principle in the mind of Falstaff.' Such indulgence is the aim of his projects; upon this his conduct very uniformly hinges; and to this his other passions are not only subordinate but subservient. His gluttony and love of dainty fare are admirably delineated in many passages: but with peculiar felicity in the following, where the poet displaying Falstaff's sensuality in a method that is humorous and indirect, and placing him in a ludicrous situation reconciles us by his exquisite pleasantry to a mean object [i.e., the scene in which the bill of fare is found in Falstaff's pocket in *1 Henry IV*, 204]. Who but Shakespeare could have made a tavern-bill the subject of so much mirth; and so happily instrumental in the display of character? The sensuality of the character is also held forth in the humorous and ludicrous views that are given of his person [in *1 Henry IV*, 2.2.10ff].

Pursuing no other object than the gratification of bodily pleasure, it is not wonderful that in situations of danger the care of the body should be his chief concern. He avoids situations of danger: he does not wish to be valiant; and without struggle or reluctance adheres to his resolution. Thus his cowardice seems to be the result of deliberation rather than the effect of constitution: and is a determined purpose of not exposing to injury or destruction that corporeal structure, foul and unwieldy tho' it be, on which his supreme enjoyment so completely depends. His well-known soliloquy on honor displays a mind that, having neither enthusiasm for fame, nor sense of reputation, is influenced in the hour of danger by no principle but the fear of bodily pain; and if man were a mere sentient and mortal animal, governed by no higher principle than sensual appetite, we might accede to his reasoning.

Thus while the speaker, in expressing his real sentiments, affects a playful manner he affords a curious example of self-imposition, of an attempt to disguise conscious demerit and escape from conscious disapprobation. . . .

Falstaff is also deceitful: for the connection between vainglorious affectation and unembarrassed, unreluctant deceit is natural and intimate. He is deceitful in every form of falsehood. He is a flatterer: he is even hypocritical; and tells the chief justice that he has 'lost his voice singing anthems.' (p. 491)

From the foregoing enumeration it appears abundantly manifest that our poet intended to represent Falstaff as very mean and worthless. . . . How then comes Falstaff to be a favorite? a favorite with Prince Henry? and a favorite on the English stage? For he not only makes us laugh but, it must be acknowledged, is regarded with some affection. (p. 492)

Those qualities in the character of Sir John Falstaff which may be accounted estimable are of two different kinds, the social and intellectual.

His social qualities are joviality and good-humour. These dispositions, though they are generally agreeable, and may in one sense of the word be termed moral, as influencing the manners and deportment of mankind, are not on all occasions, as we shall see exemplified in the present instance, to be accounted virtuous. They may be agreeable without being objects of approbation. . . .

Falstaff's love of society needs no illustration; and that it is unconnected with friendship or affection is no less apparent. Yet the quality renders him acceptable.—It receives great additional recommendation from his good-humour. . . . Such seems to be the good-humour of Falstaff; for our poet discriminates with exquisite judgment, and delineates his conception with power. He does not attribute to Falstaff the good temper flowing from inherent goodness and genuine mildness of disposition; for in company with those about whose good opinion he has little concern, though his vacuity of mind obliges him to have recourse to their company he is often insolent and overbearing. It is chiefly with Prince Henry and those whom he wishes, from vanity or some selfish purpose, to think well of him, that he is most facetious. (pp. 492-93)

His wit is of various kinds. It is sometimes a play upon words [as in *1 Henry IV*, 2.4.146ff]. One of the most agreeable species of wit, and which Falstaff uses with great success, is the ridiculous comparison. It consists in classing or uniting together by similitude objects that excite feelings so opposite as that some may be accounted great, and others little, some noble, and others mean: and this is done when in their structure, appearance, or effects they have circumstances of resemblance abundantly obvious when pointed out, though on account of the great difference in their general impression not usually attended to; but which being selected by the man of witty invention, as bonds of intimate union, enable him by an unexpected connection to produce surprise.

> *Falstaff. (speaking of Shallow).* I do remember him at Clement's-inn, like a man made after supper with a cheese-paring. When he was naked, he was for all the world like a forked radish, with a head fantastically carved upon it with a knife.
>
> [*2 Henry IV*, 3.2.308ff]

Another very exquisite species of wit consists in explaining great, serious, or important appearances by inadequate and trifling causes. This, if one may say so, is a grave and solemn species; and produces its effect by the affectation of formal and deep research. (p. 493)

Falstaff is not unacquainted with the nature and value of his talents. He employs them not merely for the sake of merriment but to promote some design. He wishes, by his drollery in [4.3.96ff], to cajole the Chief Justice. In one of the following acts he practises the same artifice with the Prince of Lancaster. He fails, however, in his attempt: and that it was a studied attempt appears from his subsequent reflections: 'Good faith, this same young sober-blooded boy doth not love me; nor a man cannot make him laugh.' (pp. 493-94)

It may also be remarked that the guise or raiment with which Falstaff invests those different species of wit and humour is universally the same. It is grave, and even solemn. He would always appear in earnest. He does not laugh himself, unless compelled by a sympathetic emotion with the laughter of others. He may sometimes indeed indulge a smile of seeming contempt or indignation: but it is perhaps on no occasion when he would be witty or humorous. Shakespeare seems to have thought this particular of importance, and has therefore put it out of all doubt by making Falstaff himself inform us: 'O it is much that a lie with a slight oath, and a jest with a *sad brow*, will do with a fellow that never had the ache in his shoulders.' (p. 494)

We may remark his discernment of mankind, and his dexterity in employing them, in his conduct towards the Prince, to Shallow, and his inferior associates.—He flatters the Prince, but he uses such flattery as is intended to impose on a person of understanding. He flatters him indirectly. He seems to treat him with familiarity: he affects to be displeased with him: he rallies him; and contends with him in the field of wit. When he gives praise it is insinuated; or it seems reluctant, accidental,

and extorted by the power of truth. In like manner, when he would impress him with a belief of his affectionate and firm attachment he proceeds by insinuation; he would have it appear involuntary, the effect of strong irresistible impulse; so strong as to appear preternatural. 'If the rascal hath not given me medicines to make me love him, I'll be hang'd.' [*1 Henry IV*, 2.2.18f.] Yet his aim is not merely to please the Prince: it is to corrupt and govern him; and to make him bend to his purposes, and become the instrument of his pleasures. (p. 495)

Falstaff, who was studious of imposing on others, imposes upon himself. He becomes the dupe of his own artifice. Confident in his versatility, command of temper, presence of mind, and unabashed invention; encouraged too by the notice of the Prince, and thus flattering himself that he shall have some sway in his counsels, he lays the foundation of his own disappointment. Though the flatterer and parasite of Prince Henry he does not deceive him. The Prince is thoroughly acquainted with his character, and is aware of his views. Yet in his wit, humour, and invention, he finds Amusement.—Parasites, in the works of other poets, are the flatterers of weak men, and impress them with a belief of their merit or attachment. But Falstaff is the parasite of a person distinguished for ability or understanding. The Prince sees him in his real colours; yet, for the sake of present pastime, he suffers himself to seem deceived; and allows the parasite to flatter himself that his arts are not unsuccessful. The real state of his sentiments and feelings is finely described when, at the battle of Shrewsbury, seeing Falstaff lying among some dead bodies, he supposes him dead.

> What! old acquaintance! could not all this flesh keep in a little life? Poor Jack, farewell, I could have better spared a better man: O I should have a heavy miss of thee, if I were much in love with vanity.
>
> [*1 Henry IV*, 5.4.102ff.]

But Prince Henry is not much in love with vanity. (p. 497)

[In] the self-deceit of Falstaff, and in the discernment of Henry, held out to us on all occasions, we have a natural foundation for the catastrophe. The incidents too, by which it is accomplished, are judiciously managed. None of them are foreign or external, but grow, as it were, out of the characters. (p. 498)

Shakespeare, whose morality is no less sublime than his skill in the display of character is masterly and unrivalled, represents Falstaff not only as a voluptuous and base sycophant but totally incorrigible. He displays no quality or disposition which can serve as a basis for reformation. Even his abilities and agreeable qualities contribute to his depravity. Had he been less facetious, less witty, less dexterous, and less inventive he might have been urged to self-condemnation, and so inclined to amendment. But mortification leads him to no conviction of folly, nor determines him to any change of life. (pp. 498-99)

I may be thought perhaps to have treated Falstaff with too much severity. I am aware of his being a favourite. Persons of eminent worth feel for him some attachment, and think him hardly used by the King. But if they will allow themselves to examine the character in all its parts they will perhaps agree with me that such feeling is delusive, and arises from partial views. They will not take it amiss, if I say that they are deluded in the same manner with Prince Henry. They are amused, and conceive an improper attachment to the means of their pleasure and amusement. (p. 499)

William Richardson, in an extract from Shakespeare, the Critical Heritage: 1774-1801, Vol. 6, *edited by*

Brian Vickers, Routledge & Kegan Paul, 1981, pp. 490-99.

[ELIZABETH] INCHBALD   (essay date 1808)

[*1 Henry IV*] is a play which all men admire, and which most women dislike. Many revolting expressions in the comic parts, much boisterous courage in some of the graver scenes, together with Falstaff's unwieldy person, offend every female auditor; and whilst a facetious Prince of Wales is employed in taking purses on the highway, a lady would rather see him stealing hearts at a ball, though the event might produce more fatal consequences.

The great Percy, they confess, pays some attention to his wife, but still more to his horse: and, as the king was a rebel before he mounted the throne, and all women are naturally loyal, they shudder at a crowned head leagued with a traitor's heart.

With all these plausible objections, infinite entertainment and instruction, may be received from this drama, even by the most delicate readers. They will observe the pen of a faithful historian, as well as of a great poet; and they ought, surely, to be charmed with every character, as a complete copy of nature; admiring even the delinquency of them all, far beyond that false display of unsullied virtue, so easy for a bard to bestow upon the creatures of his fancy, when truth of description is sacrificed to brilliant impossibilities.

The reader, who is too refined to laugh at the wit of Sir John, must yet enjoy Hotspur's picture of a coxcomb; and receive high delight from those sentences of self-reproach, and purpose of amendment, which occasionally drop from the lips of the youthful and royal profligate.

If the licentious faults of old fashioned dialogue should here too frequently offend the strictly nice, they must, at least, confer the tribute of their praises upon every soliloquy. It is impossible for puritanism not to be merry, when Falstaff is ever found talking to himself; or holding discourse over the honoured dead. It is nearly as impossible for stupidity to be insensible of the merit of those sentiments, delivered by the prince, over the same extended corse; or, to be unmoved by various other beauties, with which this work abounds.

In order to form a proper judgment of the manners and conversations of the characters in this play, and, to partake of their genuine spirit, the reader must keep in mind that the era, in which all those remarkable personages lived, thought, spoke, and acted, has now been passed more than four hundred years. (pp. 3-4)

It will be vain to endeavour to prevent many tender-hearted readers, who sign over the horrors of a battle, from wishing, that the prince's challenge to Hotspur had produced the single combat he desired; and that the victory of the day had been so decided.

Such tender and compassionate persons should not suffer their estimation of honour thus to sink into an equality with the cowardly Falstaff's; but they should call to mind—that, though it was, in ancient times, considered as a token of valour, for a prince at the head of an army, to challenge to single contest the chief warrior on the opposite side; yet, in modern days, when a powerful monarch threw his gauntlet down, to save the effusion of blood, this act of self-sacrifice was considered as a token of mere madness. . . .

The discarding of his vile companions, by the newly crowned king, as [*2 Henry IV*, Act V] describes, is . . . authenticated by history—and although such an incident is, perhaps, the best moral which can be drawn from any part of the whole play, it is, nevertheless, such a one, as does not come with entire welcome to the breast of every spectator. (p. 5)

[*Elizabeth*] Inchbald, ''Remarks: 'King Henry IV, First Part''' and ''Remarks: 'King Henry IV, Second Part','' in The British Theatre; or, A Collection of Plays, Vol. II, *1808, pp. 3-5.*

AUGUST WILHELM SCHLEGEL   (essay date 1808)

[*Schlegel holds a key place in the history of Shakespeare's reputation in European criticism. His translations of thirteen of the plays are still considered the best German translations of Shakespeare. Schlegel was also a leading spokesman for the Romantic movement which permanently overthrew the Neoclassical contention that Shakespeare was a child of nature whose plays lacked artistic form. Schlegel treated the* Henry IV *plays as part of a larger Shakespearean epic comprising the ten English history plays. The theory that the* Henry IV *plays are part of a larger historical series has also been suggested by Hermann Ulrici (1839), Beverley Warner (1894), Una Ellis-Fermor (1945), and E.M.W. Tillyard (1944). Schlegel's essay was written in 1808 and first published in 1811 in his* Über dramatische Kunst und Literatur.]

The dramas derived from the English history, ten in number, form one of the most valuable of Shakspeare's works, and partly the fruit of his maturest age. I say advisedly *one* of his works, for the poet evidently intended them to form one great whole. It is, as it were, an historical heroic poem in the dramatic form, of which the separate plays constitute the rhapsodies. The principal features of the events are exhibited with such fidelity; their causes, and even their secret springs, are placed in such a clear light, that we may attain from them a knowledge of history in all its truth, while the living picture makes an impression on the imagination which can never be effaced. But this series of dramas is intended as the vehicle of a much higher and much more general instruction; it furnishes examples of the political course of the world, applicable to all times. This mirror of kings should be the manual of young princes; from it they may learn the intrinsic dignity of their hereditary vocation, but they will also learn from it the difficulties of their situation, the dangers of usurpation, the inevitable fall of tyranny, which buries itself under its attempts to obtain a firmer foundation; lastly, the ruinous consequences of the weaknesses, errors, and crimes of kings, for whole nations, and many subsequent generations. Eight of these plays, from *Richard the Second* to *Richard the Third*, are linked together in an uninterrupted succession, and embrace a most eventful period of nearly a century of English history. . . . The careless rule of the first of these monarchs, and his injudicious treatment of his own relations, drew upon him the rebellion of Bolingbroke; his dethronement, however, was, in point of form, altogether unjust, and in no case could Bolingbroke be considered the rightful heir to the crown. This shrewd founder of the House of Lancaster never as Henry IV. enjoyed in peace the fruits of his usurpation: his turbulent Barons, the same who aided him in ascending the throne, allowed him not a moment's repose upon it. On the other hand, he was jealous of the brilliant qualities of his son, and this distrust, more than any really low inclination, induced the Prince, that he might avoid every appearance of ambition, to give himself up to dissolute society. These two circumstances form the subject-matter of the two parts of *Henry the Fourth;* the enterprises of the discontented make up the serious, and the wild youthful frolics of the heir-apparent supply the comic scenes. (pp. 419-20)

The trilogies of the ancients have already given us an example of the possibility of forming a perfect dramatic whole, which shall yet contain allusions to something which goes before, and follows it. In like manner the most of these plays end with a very definite division in the history. . . . *The First Part of Henry the Fourth* . . . [is] rounded off in a less satisfactory manner. The revolt of the nobles was only half quelled by the overthrow of Percy, and it is therefore continued through the following part of the piece. . . . Shakspeare has fallen into this dramatic imperfection, if we may so call it, for the sake of advantages of much more importance. The picture of the civil war was too great and too rich in dreadful events for a single drama, and yet the uninterrupted series of events offered no more convenient resting-place. The government of Henry IV. might certainly have been comprehended in one piece, but it possesses too little tragical interest, and too little historical splendour, to be attractive, if handled in a serious manner throughout: hence Shakspeare has given to the comic characters belonging to the retinue of Prince Henry, the freest development, and the half of the space is occupied by this constant interlude between the political events. (pp. 421-22)

The first part of *Henry the Fourth* is particularly brilliant in the serious scenes, from the contrast between two young heroes, Prince Henry and Percy (with the characteristical name of Hotspur). All the amiability and attractiveness is certainly on the side of the prince: however familiar he makes himself with bad company, we can never mistake him for one of them: the ignoble does indeed touch, but it does not contaminate him; and his wildest freaks appear merely as witty tricks, by which his restless mind sought to burst through the inactivity to which he was constrained, for on the first occasion which wakes him out of his unruly levity he distinguishes himself without effort in the most chivalrous guise. Percy's boisterous valour is not without a mixture of rude manners, arrogance, and boyish obstinacy; but these errors, which prepare for him an early death, cannot disfigure the majestic image of his noble youth; we are carried away by his fiery spirit at the very moment we would most censure it. Shakspeare has admirably shown why so formidable a revolt against an unpopular and really an illegitimate prince was not attended with success: Glendower's superstitious fancies respecting himself, the effeminacy of the young Mortimer, the ungovernable disposition of Percy, who will listen to no prudent counsel, the irresolution of his older friends, the want of unity of plan and motive, are all characterized by delicate but unmistakable traits. After Percy has departed from the scene, the splendour of the enterprise is, it is true, at an end; there remain none but the subordinate participators in the revolts, who are reduced by Henry IV., more by policy than by warlike achievements. To overcome this dearth of matter, Shakspeare was in the second part obliged to employ great art, as he never allowed himself to adorn history with more arbitrary embellishments than the dramatic form rendered indispensable. The piece is opened by confused rumours from the field of battle; the powerful impression produced by Percy's fall, whose name and reputation were peculiarly adapted to be the watchword of a bold enterprise, make him in some degree an acting personage after his death. The last acts are occupied with the dying king's remorse of conscience, his uneasiness at the behaviour of the prince, and lastly, the clearing up of the misunderstanding between father and son, which make up several most affecting scenes. All this, however, would still be inadequate to fill the stage, if the

serious events were not interrupted by a comedy which runs through both parts of the play, which is enriched from time to time with new figures, and which first comes to its catastrophe at the conclusion of the whole, namely, when Henry V., immediately after ascending the throne, banishes to a proper distance the companions of his youthful excesses, who had promised to themselves a rich harvest from his kingly favour.

Falstaff is the crown of Shakspeare's comic invention. He has, without exhausting himself, continued this character throughout three plays, and exhibited him in every variety of situation; the figure is drawn so definitely and individually, that even to the mere reader it conveys the clear impression of personal acquaintance. Falstaff is the most agreeable and entertaining knave that ever was portrayed. His contemptible qualities are not disguised . . . ; and yet we are never disgusted with him. We see that his tender care of himself is without any mixture of malice towards others; he will only not be disturbed in the pleasant repose of his sensuality, and this he obtains through the activity of his understanding. Always on the alert, and good-humoured, ever ready to crack jokes on others, and to enter into those of which he is himself the subject, so that he justly boasts he is not only witty himself, but the cause of wit in others, he is an admirable companion for youthful idleness and levity. Under a helpless exterior, he conceals an extremely acute mind; he has always at command some dexterous turn whenever any of his free jokes begin to give displeasure; he is shrewd in his distinctions between those whose favour he has to win and those over whom he may assume a familiar authority. He is so convinced that the part which he plays can only pass under the cloak of wit, that even when alone he is never altogether serious, but gives the drollest colouring to his love-intrigues, his intercourse with others, and to his own sensual philosophy. Witness his inimitable soliloquies on honour, on the influence of wine on bravery, his descriptions of the beggarly vagabonds whom he enlisted, of Justice Shallow, &c. Falstaff has about him a whole court of amusing caricatures, who by turns make their appearance, without ever throwing him into the shade. The adventure in which the Prince, under the disguise of a robber, compels him to give up the spoil which he had just taken; the scene where the two act the part of the King and the Prince; Falstaff's behaviour in the field, his mode of raising recruits, his patronage of Justice Shallow, which afterwards takes such an unfortunate turn:—all this forms a series of characteristic scenes of the most original description, full of pleasantry, and replete with nice and ingenious observation, such as could only find a place in a historical play like the present. (pp. 424-27)

August Wilhelm Schlegel, "Criticisms on Shakespeare's Historical Dramas," in his Lectures on Dramatic Art and Literature, *edited by Rev. A.J.W. Morrison, translated by John Black, second edition, George Bell & Sons, 1892, pp. 414-445.*

SAMUEL TAYLOR COLERIDGE   (essay date 1808-18)

[Coleridge's lectures and writings on Shakespeare form a major chapter in the history of English Shakespearean criticism. As the channel for the critical ideas of the German Romantics and as an original interpreter of Shakespeare in the new spirit of Romanticism, Coleridge played a strategic role in overthrowing the last remains of the Neoclassical approach to Shakespeare and in establishing the modern view of Shakespeare as a conscious artist and masterful portrayer of human character. Coleridge's remarks on Shakespeare come down to posterity largely as fragmentary notes, marginalia, and reports by auditors on the lectures, rather

than in polished essays. Of Shakespeare's histories, Richard II *was the one most often and fully discussed by Coleridge; his remarks on the* Henry IV *plays are brief and scattered. The following excerpt was reproduced by the Coleridge editor T. A. Raysor from marginalia found in Coleridge's hand in an eight-volume edition of Shakespeare's works. The notes were apparently prepared for the series of lectures on Shakespeare which Coleridge delivered between 1808 and 1818. His brief comments on* Henry IV *reveal that Coleridge admired the plays but doubted they could be classified as pure histories.]*

[In] itself, and for the closet, I feel no hesitation in placing [*Richard II*] the first and most admirable of all Shakespeare's *purely* historical plays. For the two parts of *Henry IV.* form a species of themselves, which may be named the *mixt* drama. The distinction does not depend on the quanity of historical events compared with the fictions, for there is as much *history* in *Macbeth* as in *Richard,* but in the relation of the history to the plot. In the purely historical plays, the history *informs* the plot; in the mixt it *directs* it; in the rest, as *Macbeth, Hamlet, Cymbeline, Lear,* it subserves it. (pp. 142-43)

> *Samuel Taylor Coleridge, "Notes on the History Plays of Shakespeare: 'Richard II'," in his* Shakespearean Criticism, Vol. I, *edited by Thomas Middleton Raysor, Cambridge, Mass.: Harvard University Press, 1930, pp. 142-56.*

SAMUEL TAYLOR COLERIDGE [as reported by H. C. ROBINSON]   (essay date 1810)

[The following remarks by Coleridge on Falstaff were recorded in a memorandum by H. C. Robinson after his conversation with Coleridge on December 23, 1810. Coleridge's view that Falstaff is a character in whom the intellect predominates was developed by him on other occasions (see excerpts above, 1808-18, and below, 1813).]

Falstaff [Coleridge] also considered as an instance of the predominance of intellectual power. He is content to be thought both a liar and a coward in order to obtain influence over the minds of his associates. His aggravated lies about the robbery are conscious and purposed, not inadvertent untruths. On my observing that this account seemed to justify Cooke's representation [referring to a contemporary actor who had played Falstaff,] according to which a foreigner imperfectly understanding the character would fancy F[alstaff] to be the designing knave who actually does outwit the Prince, C[oleridge] answered that in his *own* estimation F[alstaff] is the superior who cannot easily be convinced that the prince has escaped him; but that as in other instances S[hakespeare] has shewn us the defeat of mere intellect by a noble feeling, the Prince being the superior moral character who rises above his insidious companion. (p. 210)

> *Samuel Taylor Coleridge [as reported by H. C. Robinson], in a detached memoranda of December 23, 1810, in his* Shakespearean Criticism, Vol. II, *edited by Thomas Middleton Raysor, Cambridge, Mass.: Harvard University Press, 1930, pp. 208-30.*

SAMUEL TAYLOR COLERIDGE [as reported by the *BRISTOL GAZETTE*]   (essay date 1813)

[The following excerpt is taken from an unsigned account of Coleridge's sixth Shakespeare lecture in Bristol, delivered November 16, 1813. It was first published as "Mr. Coleridge" in Bristol Gazette, *in 1813. In his notes to this lecture, editor T. M. Raysor states that Coleridge complained of inaccuracy in this newspaper*

account. The sentences that Raysor believes to have been most garbled have been omitted here. Coleridge's scattered remarks on Falstaff all appear, in some fashion, in the lecture.]

Shakespeare, possessed of wit, humour, fancy, and imagination, built up an outward world from the stores within his mind, as the bee builds a hive from a thousand sweets, gathered from a thousand flowers. He was not only a great poet but a great philosopher. The characters of Richard III., Iago, and Falstaff, were the characters of men . . . who place intellect at the head. . . . Richard, laughing at conscience, and sneering at religion, felt a confidence in his intellect, which urged him to commit the most horrid crimes, because he felt himself, although inferior in form and shape, superior to those around him; he felt he possessed a power that they had not. Iago, on the same principle, conscious of superior intellect, gave scope to his envy, and hesitated not to ruin a gallant, open, and generous friend in the moment of felicity, because he was not promoted as he expected. . . . Falstaff, not a degraded man of genius, like Burns, but a man of degraded genius, with the same consciousness of superiority to his companions, fastened himself on a young prince, to prove how much his influence on an heir apparent could exceed that of statesmen. With this view he hesitated not to practise the most [contemptible] of all characters—an open and professed liar: even his sensuality was subservient to his intellect, for he appeared to drink sack that he might have occasion to shew his wit. One thing, however, worthy of observation, was the contrast of labour in Falstaff to produce wit, with the ease [with] which Prince Henry parried his shaft, and the final contempt which such a character deserved and received from the young king, when Falstaff, calling his friends around him, Nym, Bardolph, Pistol, &c., expected the consummation of that influence which he flattered himself to have established. (pp. 286-87)

> *Samuel Taylor Coleridge [as reported by the* Bristol Gazette], "Lecture VI: Richard III, Falstaff, Iago, Shakespeare As a Poet," in his Shakespearean Criticism, Vol. II, *edited by Thomas Middleton Raysor (excerpted by permission of the President and fellows of Harvard College), Cambridge, Mass.: Harvard University Press, 1930, pp. 285-88.*

JOHANN WOLFGANG von GOETHE   (essay date 1815)

[Goethe is an outstanding figure of German literature and a distinguished poet, dramatist, and novelist. His reverance for Shakespeare was inspired early in his career by his friendship with the German Romantic writer Johann Gottfried Herder. Many of Goethe's works bear Shakespeare's influence, particularly his first published drama, Götz von Berlichingen mit der eisernen Hand *(1773), which is written in the manner of Shakespeare's history plays. In the excerpt below, written in 1815, he briefly discusses the effect of the conventional theater on Shakespeare's genius, which he considers more poetic than dramatic, and in many instances restricted by the limits of the stage.]*

A universally recognized talent may make of its capacities some use which is problematical. Not everything which the great do is done in the best fashion. So Shakespeare belongs by necessity in the annals of poetry; in the annals of the theater he appears only by accident. (p. 66)

Shakespeare's works are in [one] sense highly dramatic; by his treatment, his revelation of the inner life, he wins the reader; the theatrical demands appear to him unimportant, and so he takes it easy, and we, spiritually speaking, take it easy with him. We pass with him from place to place; our power of imagination provides all the episodes which he omits. We even feel grateful to him for arousing our imagination in so profitable a way. Since he exhibits everything in dramatic form, he renders easy the working of our imaginations; for with the "stage that signifies the world" we are more familiar than with the world itself, and we can read and hear the most fantastic things, and still imagine that they might pass before our eyes on the stage. This accounts for the frequently bungling dramatizations of favorite novels.

Strictly speaking, nothing is theatrical except what is immediately symbolical to the eye: an important action, that is, which signifies a still more important one. That Shakespeare knew how to attain this summit, that moment witnesses where the son and heir in *Henry IV* takes the crown from the side of the slumbering king, who lies sick unto death—takes the crown and marches proudly away with it. But these are only moments, scattered jewels, separated by much that is untheatrical. Shakespeare's whole method finds in the stage itself something unwieldly and hostile. His great talent is that of a universal interpreter, or "epitomizer" (*Epitomator*), and since the poet in essence appears as universal interpreter of Nature, so we must recognize Shakespeare's great genius as lying in this realm; it would be only falsehood—and in no sense is this to his dishonor—were we to say that the stage was a worthy field for his genius. These limitations of the stage, however, have forced upon him certain limitations of his own. (pp. 66-7)

In closing, let us proceed to the solution of the riddle. The primitiveness of the English stage has been brought to our attention by scholars. There is no trace in it of that striving after realism, which we have developed with the improvement of machinery and the art of perspective and costuming, and from which we should find it hard to turn back to that childlike beginning of the stage—a scaffolding, where one saw little, where everything was *signified,* where the audience was content to assume a royal chamber behind a green curtain; and the trumpeter, who always blew his trumpet at a certain place, and all the rest of it. Who would be content today to put up with such a stage? But amid such surroundings, Shakespeare's plays were highly interesting stories, only told by several persons, who, in order to make somewhat more of an impression, had put on masks, and, when it was necessary, moved back and forth, entered and left the stage; but left to the spectator nevertheless the task of imagining at his pleasure Paradise and palaces on the empty stage. (p. 68)

> Johann Wolfgang von Goethe, "Shakespeare ad Infinitum," translated by Randolph S. Bourne, in Shakespeare in Europe, edited by Oswald LeWinter, The World Publishing Company, 1963, pp. 57-70.

WILLIAM HAZLITT (essay date 1817)

[*Hazlitt is generally considered to be a leading Shakespearean critic of the English Romantic movement. A prolific essayist and critic on a wide range of subjects, Hazlitt remarked in the preface to his* Characters in Shakespeare's Plays, *first published in 1817, that he was inspired by the German critic August Wilhelm Schlegel and was determined to supplant what he considered the pernicious influence of Samuel Johnson's Shakespearean criticism. Hazlitt's criticism is typically Romantic in its emphasis on character studies. Unlike Samuel Taylor Coleridge, Hazlitt was a dramatic critic whose experience of Shakespeare in the theater influenced his interpretations. In the following excerpt, he continues in the tradition of Corbyn Morris (1744) and Maurice Morgann (1777) in his celebration of Falstaff as the central figure in* Henry IV. *But Hazlitt's deprecating remarks on Prince Hal mark a turning point*

in Henry IV *criticism: Hazlitt is the first critic to state openly "that Falstaff is the better man of the two." This interpretation has been supported by such later critics as Charles Cowden Clarke (1863), A. C. Bradley (1902), J. B. Priestley (1925), and Roy Battenhouse (1975). However, many other commentators—most notably Samuel Johnson (1765), G. G. Gervinus (1849-50), L. C. Knights (1934), J. Dover Wilson (1943), and Arthur Sewell (1951)—have all regarded Prince Hal as the center of the plays and Falstaff as a licentious figure unworthy of the attention he has received.*]

If Shakespear's fondness for the ludicrous sometimes led to faults in his tragedies (which was not often the case) he has made us amends by the character of Falstaff. . . . He would not be in character, if he were not so fat as he is; for there is the greatest keeping in the boundless luxury of his imagination and the pampered self-indulgence of his physical appetites. He manures and nourishes his mind with jests, as he does his body with sack and sugar. He carves out his jokes, as he would a capon or a haunch of venison, where there is *cut and come again;* and pours out upon them the oil of gladness. His tongue drops fatness, and in the chambers of his brain "it snows of meat and drink." He keeps up perpetual holiday and open house, and we live with him in a round of invitations to a rump and dozen.—Yet we are not to suppose that he was a mere sensualist. All this is as much in imagination as in reality. His sensuality does not engross and stupify his other faculties, but "ascends me into the brain, clears away all the dull, crude vapours that environ it, and makes it full of nimble, fiery, and delectable shapes." His imagination keeps up the ball after his senses have done with it. He seems to have even a greater enjoyment of the freedom from restraint, of good cheer, of his ease, of his vanity, in the ideal exaggerated description which he gives of them, than in fact. He never fails to enrich his discourse with allusions to eating and drinking, but we never see him at table. He carries his own larder about with him, and he is himself "a tun of man." His pulling out the bottle in the field of battle is a joke to shew his contempt for glory accompanied with danger, his systematic adherence to his Epicurean philosophy in the most trying circumstances. Again, such is his deliberate exaggeration of his own vices, that it does not seem quite certain whether the account of his hostess's bill, found in his pocket, with such an out-of-the-way charge for capons and sack with only one halfpenny-worth of bread, was not put there by himself as a trick to humour the jest upon his favourite propensities, and as a conscious caricature of himself. He is represented as a liar, a braggart, a coward, a glutton, &c., and yet we are not offended but delighted with him; for he is all these as much to amuse others as to gratify himself. He openly assumes all these characters to shew the humorous part of them. The unrestrained indulgence of his own ease, appetites, and convenience, has neither malice nor hypocrisy in it. In a word, he is an actor in himself almost as much as upon the stage, and we no more object to the character of Falstaff in a moral point of view than we should think of bringing an excellent comedian, who should represent him to the life, before one of the police offices. We only consider the number of pleasant lights in which he puts certain foibles (the more pleasant as they are opposed to the received rules and necessary restraints of society) and do not trouble ourselves about the consequences resulting from them, for no mischievous consequences do result. Sir John is old as well as fat, which gives a melancholy retrospective tinge to the character; and by the disparity between his inclinations and his capacity for enjoyment, makes it still more ludicrous and fantastical.

The secret of Falstaff's wit is for the most part a masterly presence of mind, an absolute self-possession, which nothing can disturb. His repartees are involuntary suggestions of his self-love; instinctive evasions of every thing that threatens to interrupt the career of his triumphant jollity and self-complacency. His very size floats him out of all his difficulties in a sea of rich conceits; and he turns round on the pivot of his convenience, with every occasion and at a moment's warning. His natural repugnance to every unpleasant thought or circumstance, of itself makes light of objections, and provokes the most extravagant and licentious answers in his own justification. His indifference to truth puts no check upon his invention, and the more improbable and unexpected his contrivances are, the more happily does he seem to be delivered of them, the anticipation of their effect acting as a stimulus to the gaiety of his fancy. The success of one adventurous sally gives him spirits to undertake another: he deals always in round numbers, and his exaggerations and excuses are "open, palpable, monstrous as the father that begets them." (pp. 117-19)

The true spirit of humanity, the thorough knowledge of the stuff we are made of, the practical wisdom with the seeming fooleries in the whole of the garden-scene at Shallow's country-seat, and just before in the exquisite dialogue between him and Silence on the death of old Double, have no parallel anywhere else. In one point of view, they are laughable in the extreme; in another they are equally affecting, if it is affecting to shew *what a little thing is human life*, what a poor forked creature man is!

The heroic and serious part of these two plays founded on the story of Henry IV. is not inferior to the comic and farcical. The characters of Hotspur and Prince Henry are two of the most beautiful and dramatic, both in themselves and from contrast, that ever were drawn. They are the essence of chivalry. We like Hotspur the best upon the whole, perhaps because he was unfortunate.—The characters of their fathers, Henry IV. and old Northumberland, are kept up equally well. Henry naturally succeeds by his prudence and caution in keeping what he has got; Northumberland fails in his enterprise from an excess of the same quality, and is caught in the web of his own cold, dilatory policy. Owen Glendower is a masterly character. It is as bold and original as it is intelligible and thoroughly natural. The disputes between him and Hotspur are managed with infinite address and insight into nature. (p. 124)

The peculiarity and the excellence of Shakespear's poetry is, that it seems as if he made his imagination the hand-maid of nature, and nature the plaything of his imagination. He appears to have been all the characters, and in all the situations he describes. It is as if either he had had all their feelings, or had lent them all his genius to express themselves. There cannot be stronger instances of this than Hotspur's rage when Henry IV. forbids him to speak of Mortimer, his insensibility to all that his father and uncle urge to calm him, and his fine abstracted apostrophe to honour, "By heaven methinks it were an easy leap to pluck bright honour from the moon," &c. After all, notwithstanding the gallantry, generosity, good temper, and idle freaks of the mad-cap Prince of Wales, we should not have been sorry, if Northumberland's force had come up in time to decide the fate of the battle of Shrewsbury; at least, we always heartily sympathise with Lady Percy's grief, when she exclaims,

Had my sweet Harry had but half their numbers,
To-day might I (hanging on Hotspur's neck)
Have talked of Monmouth's grave.
[*2 Henry IV*, II. iii. 43-5]

The truth is, that we never could forgive the Prince's treatment of Falstaff; though perhaps Shakespear knew what was best, according to the history, the nature of the times, and of the man. We speak only as dramatic critics. Whatever terror the French in those days might have of Henry V. yet, to the readers of poetry at present, Falstaff is the better man of the two. We think of him and quote him oftener. (pp. 124-25)

Henry V. is a very favourite monarch with the English nation, and he appears to have been also a favourite with Shakespear, who labours hard to apologise for the actions of the king, by shewing us the character of the man, as "the king of good fellows." He scarcely deserves this honour. He was fond of war and low company:—we know little else of him. He was careless, dissolute, and ambitious;—idle, or doing mischief. In private, he seemed to have no idea of the common decencies of life, which he subjected to a kind of regal licence; in public affairs, he seemed to have no idea of any rule of right or wrong, but brute force, glossed over with a little religious hypocrisy and archiepiscopal advice. His principles did not change with his situation and professions. His adventure on Gadshill was a prelude to the affair of Agincourt, only a bloodless one; Falstaff was a puny prompter of violence and outrage, compared with the pious and politic Archbishop of Canterbury, who gave the king *carte blanche,* in a genealogical tree of his family, to rob and murder in circles of latitude and longitude abroad—to save the possessions of the church at home. This appears in the speeches in Shakespear, where the hidden motives that actuate princes and their advisers in war and policy are better laid open than in speeches from the throne or woolsack. (pp. 125-26)

William Hazlitt, "'Henry IV', in Two Parts" and "'Henry V'," in Characters of Shakespeare's Plays & Lectures on the English Poets, *Macmillan and Co., Limited, 1903, pp. 117-25, 125-33.*

A. S. PUSHKIN   (essay date 1836)

[*Pushkin is considered the greatest poet and dramatist of nineteenth-century Russia. Shakespeare was a dominant influence on his work; he wrote several adaptations of the plays and used Shakespeare's work as the source for a number of his poems and dramas. Acknowledging his indebtedness to Shakespeare, he wrote of his drama Boris Gudonov: "Not disturbed by any other influence, I imitated Shakespeare in his broad and free depiction of characters, in the simple and careless combination of plots." The following excerpt, in which Pushkin calls Falstaff a "coward" and a "sissy," is closer in spirit and content to the eighteenth-century view of Sir John as a debauched character than the Romantic celebration of his wit and personality. This essay was first written in 1836 and first published in the* Sovremenik *in 1837.*]

But nowhere, perhaps, is reflected with such multiformity Shakspere's many-sided genius as in Falstaff, whose vices, entangled one with another, form an amusing and ugly chain resembling an ancient bacchanalia. Analyzing the character of Falstaff, we see that his principal trait is lust. From the time of his youth, probably, a coarse, cheap gallantry was his first preoccupation; but he is already in his fifties. He has grown fat, senile; gluttony and wine have subdued Venus. Besides, he is a coward; but, having spent his life with young rakes, he covers up his cowardice with an evasive and scoffing impertinence; he is a braggart by habit and by calculation. Falstaff is by no means stupid; on the contrary, he has the habits of a man who at times gives the impression of being good company. He has no principles whatsoever. He is a sissy. He needs strong

T H E
Second part of Henrie

the fourth, continuing to his death,
and coronation of Henrie
the fift.

With the humours of fir Iohn Fal-
ſtaffe, and ſwaggering
Piſtoll.

As it hath been ſundrie times publikely
acted by the right honourable, the Lord
Chamberlaine his feruants.

Written by William Shakeſpeare.

L O N D O N
Printed by V.S. for Andrew Wiſe, and
William Aſpley.
1600.

Title page of the Quarto of Henry IV, Part II *(1600). By permission of the Folger Shakespeare Library.*

Spanish wine (sack), huge dinners and money for his mistresses; to get these he is ready for anything provided it involves no visible danger. (pp. 120-21)

> A. S. Pushkin, "Notes on Shylock, Angelo and Falstaff," translated by Albert Siegel, in The Shakespeare Association Bulletin, *Vol. XVI, No. 1, January, 1941, pp. 120-21.**

HERMANN ULRICI   (essay date 1839)

[*A German scholar, Ulrici was a professor of philosophy and an author of works on Greek poetry and Shakespeare. The following excerpt is taken from an English translation of his* Über Shakespeares dramatische Kunst, und sein Verhältnis zu Calderon und Göthe, *first published in 1839. This work exemplifies the "philosophical criticism" developed in Germany during the nineteenth century. The immediate sources for Ulrici's critical approach appear to be August Wilhelm Schlegel's notion of the play as an organic, interconnected whole and Georg Wilhelm Friedrich Hegel's view of the drama as embodying the conflict of historical forces and ideas. Unlike his fellow German Shakespearean G. G. Gervinus, Ulrici saw himself as developing a specifically Christian aesthetics, but one which, as he carefully points out in the introduction to the work mentioned above, in no way intrudes on "that unity of idea, which preeminently constitutes a work of art a living creation in the world of beauty." Ulrici's interest in the problem of unity is well illustrated in the following remarks. He describes the plays as "the second act" of Shakespeare's "grand five-act historical drama," which begins with* Richard II *and closes with* Richard III. *A similar interpretation of Shakespeare's histories was also put forth by August Wilhelm Schlegel (1808), Beverley Warner (1894), and E.M.W. Tillyard (1944). Like most critics before him,*

Ulrici maintains that Prince Hal is the central figure of Henry IV, *"the living tie between the comic parts and the serious historical action." He thus relegates Falstaff to a subservient role, claiming that his comic interludes serve as an ironic parody of the historical plot. This idea is reiterated in the twentieth century by L. C. Knights (1933) and William Empson (1935). For more commentary on Prince Hal's function in the plays, see the excerpts by Jeremy Collier (1698), William Warburton (1733), Samuel Johnson (1765), G. G. Gervinus (1849-50), William Butler Yeats (1901), J. Dover Wilson (1943), and E. M. W. Tillyard (1944).*]

The character of Falstaff evidently borders close on caricature, without, however, overstepping the boundary line of reality. Both in his internal peculiarities and in his outward appearance he is evidently an *ideal* personality, and yet he possesses so much of living freshness and of portrait-like reality, that we feel almost sure of having somewhere or other met with his original; he keeps himself so nicely on the fine line of demarcation between the general and the individual, as to appear the true mean between both, where the two extremes are fused together into organic unity. This alone constitutes him a true artistic picture—a perfect work of art. No doubt all other dramatic figures are likewise ideal personages, in whom the general and individual are combined; but what distinguishes Falstaff from all others is, that whereas each one of them depends on the common action of, and a combination with, the other characters of the piece, for the development of its full personal peculiarities, Falstaff independently accomplishes this in and by himself. He appears the very personification of human weakness and infirmity, sensualism and lust; he is sunk in the lowest depths of moral perversity, and yet he is not absolutely *evil;* for the evil that he does is not for his own sake, but merely as a means of attaining what he calls life and pleasure, and which, in his belief, every one not only does but ought to pursue. Happiness, to which man certainly may and even *ought* to aspire, even because his *destination* is to union with God, is in his case . . . , through lying and self-delusion, corrupted into mere gratification of the flesh. He is so far a mere natural man, and we shall not fail to observe occasionally, if not often, the sparklings of a certain naïveté, harmless good-nature, and of a laughing light-hearted joyousness; but a child of nature, who not only is placed in the midst of a high state of civilization, but who, as the exquisite luxury and variety of his pleasure, and the artifices which he employs for their gratification prove, has imbibed much of this high-wrought and artificial refinement. And this constitutes the first inconsistency—the first comic ingredient in his character.

But Falstaff not only does not love what is properly base and wicked, but he has also within him a germ of good, a small and faint ray of that true nobility which invests all Shakspeare's characters, and Falstaff among them; for all proceed from the likeness of God. We see this in his superiority to other weaklings and fools comparatively more virtuous, and still more so when we compare him with his usual companions, Bardolph, Nym, Pistol, &c., but chiefly in the significant description of his last moments, in "Henry the Fifth." (Act II. Scene 3.) . . . It is even upon this better basis of his nature that Falstaff's clear *consciousness* of his own moral weakness and depravity is founded, which never leaves him entirely, and occasionally breaks out into the most amusing irony and persiflage of himself. It is the source of the best part of his wit. While his fleshly lusts are at continual war with his better spirit, which they are ever taxing for the means of their gratification, and spite of their momentary victory, are ever being broken by the power of objective goodness, they are reflected at the same time in his own better consciousness, which sees and derides their nakedness even when he is continually overcome by them. The double-tongued sophistic conversation which Falstaff is continually holding with himself, the dialectic with which he designedly brings his real character to light, the irony with which he dissects both himself and the whole world, as well as, on the other hand, the unceasing paralysis which moral weakness and perversity bring upon themselves both *subjectively* and *objectively,* not only afford a lively picture of the moral infirmity of man, but are also at the same time a lively exhibition of the idea of Comedy. Falstaff's individuality becomes, in short, the immediate expression of the comic view of life. (pp. 326-28)

From the 15th century downwards, the true spirit of chivalry . . . rapidly declined. To what humourous foppery and masquerade, empty splendour and display, had it for instance been degraded at the court of the Burgundian princes, and especially of Charles IV.! Mind and spirit had departed from it, and it had sunk into an empty spectacle, and a hollow fantastic form. In different lands it passed through as many different forms of corruption as there were many causes of the process of its final dissolution. While with the grandees of Spain, in the 16th century, it was carried to that pitch of absurdity which Cervantes so exquisitely ridicules in his Don Quixote, the sound sense of England, ever directed to the real and practical, without neglecting the poetical, turned chivalry into external luxury, sensual enjoyment, and extravangances of all kinds, seasoned with the most fantastic spirit of adventure. . . . In Falstaff's character we discern the exact portrait of such a chivalry, when corrupted into sensuality, and a love for gratification; he is, as it were, the satirical extract of it, in which all its faults and weaknesses have passed off and evaporated. . . . [In] "Henry IV." he appears in direct contrast to the noble chivalry of the prince, which, although in inmost core it is still sound and vigorous, has manifestly been smitten by the prevailing distemper. While the early heroism and valiant deeds of the future conqueror of France form one aspect of chivalry, Falstaff presents the other face of it, which took pleasure in a low but merry adventurous life, in which the prince with *good* example preceded the younger chevaliers of his kingdom. But the satirical design . . . in "Henry IV." falls into the back-ground behind the historical objectivity of the representation. . . . (pp. 331-32)

"Richard the Second" is the first part of the grand five-act historical drama which closes with "Richard the Third." It is evident that the guilt of Bolingbroke's rebellion was not lessened by the injustice of Richard, of which, however, it was the just punishment. This truth is strikingly set forth in the two following pieces, which bear the title of *"Henry the Fourth."* His usurped dignity reminds us in the first place of the stolen majesty of John. The circumstances of Henry the Fourth take, however, a different shape and hue. John was opposed by a pretender to the crown, supported by the church, by France, and the English nobles, and the chief interest was derived from the corruption, weakness, and abuse of the spiritual as well as of the temporal power, which, in their conflict with each other, shook in pieces the whole frame of society. Henry the Fourth, on the other hand, has only to contend with a few of his own barons, with whom are joined, it is true, some of the bishops and clergy, but rather as dignitaries of the kingdom than as representatives of the church. Consequently the whole action moves, as in "Richard the Second," within the limits of England, and in this respect the two parts of "Henry the Fourth"

form, on one hand, the continuation, and, on the other, a contrast, to the former drama.

For whereas in "Richard the Second" a mere outward title is insufficient, in the absence on *intrinsic* right and justice, to protect the state from devastation, dissension, and rebellion, the same disturbances and civil broils appear in "Henry the Fourth," because the inward qualifications for a crown, which Bolingbroke undoubtedly possessed in his moderation, prudence, and courage, are not associated with the *outward* right. The two ought never in fact to be disunited, but being blended organically together, to render to each other a mutual support. This is the unceasing requisition of moral order and of experience. Henry's inward *capacity* is in itself no inward *justification.* This he had irretrievably lost, when, instead of being content with the vindication of his own rights, he had presumed to usurp those of Richard; and when by robbing him of his crown, he became, whether intentionally or unintentionally, the cause of his sovereign's murder. This act had sapped the moral foundation of his private and public position. . . . It is not merely that though possessed of the inward right he is without the outward title—but the usurpation also of Henry is not contested, as the rightful throne of Richard the Second was, by violated *justice;* the *aggressions* upon it of his adversaries are equally unjustifiable. We have here wrong set against wrong, and usurpation struggling with usurpation, and the final decision rests with the *superiority* of mental and material power. Accordingly, Henry's high qualifications for governing gain the day; his own prudence and the bravery of his son are victorious over the weakness and incapacity of his adversaries. Henry dies in the undisturbed possession of his kingly dignity and power. But he dies without pleasure in life, and yet not rejoicing in death, distracted and disturbed by the discontent of his own conscience, and the worry of the ceaseless efforts he is called upon to make in order to defend a questionable and unrighteous acquisition. He leaves the crown to his son; but in the memory of the people, and beneath the very throne of his successors, the embers of unsatisfied wrongs are smouldering, and await only more favourable circumstances to fan them into flames.

Thus, in the second act of this grand drama, does Shakspeare lay open before us the course of history. In "Richard the Second" disturbed from within, it here clears a way for itself by repelling injustice by injustice, and gaining by the preponderance of talent and power a resting place, and a starting point for further progress. But at the same time we see how, mindful of this inward disturbance, history refuses peace to the authors of it, and intrinsically sick itself, restlessly advances, and cannot repose until the true harmony of moral order is restored.

This fundamental idea divides itself in the two parts as it were into principal branches. Both together form the proper whole, although each has its organic centre. Whereas the object of the "King John" pre-eminently was to set forth the true relation of the ecclesiastical power to the civil, and of "Richard the Second" to elucidate the real import of the sovereignty, the *first part* of "Henry the Fourth" places in a conspicuous light the power of the nobles, and the *essence of chivalry,* with its historical foundation of personal *prowess.* The very barons, to whose assistance principally Henry owed his throne, are now at war with and in rebellion against him. But their object is not, as it was in "King John" or "Richard the Second," to maintain their violated rights; the successful defence of their just dues has raised their pretensions, and they arrogate others which do not actually belong to them; they wish to dictate to the royal authority. Against such pretensions the right is with Henry. For his defective title is with them but a pretext for their own encroachments. What they really trust to is their own power and prowess; like many others in all ages and countries, whether consciously or unconsciously, they turn the possession of a good into a claim for greater. . . . The First Part also strikingly demonstrates Henry's fitness for command by the possession of undoubted bravery and great military experience. It is important to recognize Henry's superiority in this respect over his antagonists; we must feel that he owes his victory to himself, and not to the personal heroism of his son. And yet the character of the *Prince,* who plays so prominent a part in both pieces, was for other reasons absolutely indispensable. In the first place, it was requisite to illustrate the true nature of that personal valour which was the foundation of chivalry, and of its great influence. Of courage there are two kinds—two different qualities, bearing, however, the same names; one is, an inborn natural *daring*—the confidence of the physical man in his own personal prowess, which leads him to contend against all difficulties, and unreflectingly and ignorantly exposes itself to all dangers; in short, seeks them out, and finds a pleasure in them, either as indispensable for its own development, or for its emancipation from the restraints which unsubdued difficulties impose upon it. But the other species of bravery is altogether of an *intellectual* nature, and consists in the mind's conscious superiority over any danger that may threaten, by which it either overcomes it, or, in spite of outward discomfiture, is nevertheless the conqueror. . . . Both species are exhibited in this drama; the latter in the person of Prince Henry, the former in that of the Earl of Douglas, but still more so in that of the young Percy. . . . He displays towards every one the same restrained bluntness and forced vehemence, and the same defiance and haughtiness. On the other hand, it was no less necessary to bring out clearly and pregnantly the superior character of the Prince. Evidently it was not possible for his open and buoyant disposition to develope itself freely in the narrow circle of the court, and under the restraints which the King's humours and formality of nature would have placed upon it; in so sultry an atmosphere it could not live and flourish; it longed for a freer and more stirring air, and this it found in the society of Falstaff and his crew. The more he differed from these both inwardly and outwardly, the more necessary was it that his superior energies should shine forth brilliantly—as, for instance, in the fight with Percy—and eventually more fully realize themselves in the greatest achievements.

The *second part* exhibits Henry's *political capacity* for the throne. The civil war was in fact decided by the fight at Shrewsbury, and if the rebellious barons still kept the field, the attempt failed by its own impotence. From this day it was Henry's object to make the best use of his victory, and of his adversaries to make the best terms they could; all depended upon the superior political skill of the two parties. Of war there could be no question now—all chance of it had gradually died away, and the statesman's prudence appears from henceforward the true and sole lever of historical deeds and events. Secondly, Shakspeare has elucidated under this aspect also, the character, not only of the king, but of his opponents likewise, and at the same time assigned to the noble orders their true place and influence in the state. . . . They are like boys, therefore, caught by the smooth cunning of a beardless youth. The rest of the properly historical action is taken up with the description of the king's state of mind, and uneasy conscience, and with his cares for his crown and kingdom, as well as for his son and successor, which, agreeably to the respective characters of the Two Parts, find their place more appropriately in the second

than in the first. The whole is fittingly closed with the death of Henry. The Prince, in perfect consistency with his character as here drawn, takes no active or direct part in the historical action of the piece, in which the chief actors are the king and his immediate adherents, and the Prince John, in all things so unlike his noble brother. The *historical* importance of Prince Henry, in this portion of the play, is limited to his restoration to his father's favour and affection, and to some regulations rendered necessary by his accession.

While, therefore, the two parts of this dramatic poem stand apart in characteristic difference, they nevertheless readily coalesce into organic unity. But here arises the question—what is the meaning of the *comic view* which runs through the whole piece, and assumes so large a space relatively to the whole fable? . . . With his wit and humour Falstaff has sadly plagued the critics; no one seems to have known exactly what he had taken in hand in attempting to examine his character, or how to assign him his appropriate place in the mechanism of the fable; and yet all seem to have had an inexplicable feeling of his necessity; none would or could dispense with him. . . . The true explanation, although it lay near enough to the surface, has not yet been given. These comic scenes evidently contain a deep satire upon the represented history, their *parodical* bearing cannot be mistaken; they were designed to parody the hollow pathos of political history, and to tear from it its state robes and parade, in order to exhibit it in its true shape. To history herself—that is, to her mere semblance—the false tinsel splendour—the mere outward and arrogated importance with which she would pass for truly great and influential, and in purple mantle, and with crown and sceptre, step proudly forward to higgle about kingdoms, or to lay about her with the sharp lash of war, the poet has dared, in the mirror of satire and irony, to shew her her true features:—a bold stroke, which none but Shakspeare would have hazarded with success. Rebellions and wars, the setting up and overthrow of kingdoms, the intrigues of political cunning and high-sounding speeches about rights and wrongs, all these are alike mere outward shew, the mere mask of history. The rebellious barons had no care to dethrone the unrighteous usurper—this was but the pretext with which they veiled their own selfish objects. It is not from any want of an outward title that the king's position is inwardly and outwardly weak; he is deficient in true inward title of moral strength. It was not the constant factions and disturbances, nor the arts and practices of his opponents, that broke the peace of Henry's reign; it was easy enough for him to overcome these difficulties, but the weakness of the king, as well as of all the nobles and the popular leaders, was occasioned by grave moral faults: caprice, selfishness, and inability to controul both their intellectual and sensual nature. No reign ever was so poor in true historical influence, in moral force, in creative, formative, or organizing ideas; nay, even in true destructive energy, and the ferment which gives rise to new shapes and forms of things; and yet, on the other hand, it was indispensable in regard both to past and future. Without real worth or independence in itself, it nevertheless formed the oscillating point of transition for the further development of the great historical tragedy which had commenced with the dethronement of Richard the Second. Taken in itself it was without any principle of intrinsic vitality, and its interest centred solely and entirely in the *external* confirmation of the unjust acquisition of the royal dignity. Closely examined, accordingly, it resolves itself into the most empty and superficial formalism and untrue semblance; first by Richard, and afterwards by his own confession, Bolingbroke is proclaimed to be an excellent actor. The elucidation of the character of Henry the Fourth's reign, and its mere semblance and want of real depth, was the conscious or unconscious design of the poet in interweaving these circumstances with the proper historical action of the drama. (pp. 370-75)

The pursuit of external power, influence and authority, is essentially no less immoral and material than the carnal and sensual pleasures of Falstaff. His false and braggart swaggering forms a rare parody on the fiery character of young Hotspur; his comic circumspection and indecision, his effeminacy and love of ease, his rambling reflections on warfare and politics, and his musings on a super-terrestrial existence, travestie no less amusingly the chief traits in the characters of the Earl of Northumberland, Mortimer, the Archbishop of York, and Glendower, while his inexhaustible talent of misrepresentation, and the appearance of virtue which he so skilfully assumes, are a fine satire on the King, whose place he sustains in the first part so cleverly and so delightfully. His trencher fellows, too—the cowardly Peto and Gadshill—the sneaking bully Pistol, with his big words—the drunken Bardolph, ready for anything and fit for nothing—the shrewd, witty page, with his corrupted innocence—the ingenious, serviceable Poins—figures which are only necessary to give a living dramatic movement to the parody—appear merely as partial reflections of, and foils to Falstaff's character. To these, the hostess Doll Tear-Sheet, the two justices Shallow and Silence, Falstaff's recruits, and some other subordinate characters, are added in order to fill up the picture, to round off the whole, and to maintain the connection with the first part.

Thus furnished out, the comedy reflects the proper historic action in all its principal turnings and essential elements. In the first half, the expedition of Falstaff and his companions against the travellers at Gad's Hill, which is here the focus of all the wit and humour, forms the most thorough parody on the folly and worthlessness of the civil war, which, in so far as it was carried on for personal interests, is without historical significance or value. The scene at the Inn, which immediately follows, where Falstaff in the person of the King rebukes the Prince for the life he is leading, affords a witty and truthful description of the heads of the rebellion, as well as of Henry himself. The scenes at the close, where Falstaff appears at the council of war, and where he pretends to be the conqueror of Percy, are direct parodies on the war itself. In the second part, on the other hand, the tricks with which the Prince and Poins mystify the old sinner, and expose his lies and evasions, and the mode in which Falstaff deludes the two Justices, and makes use of them for his own purposes, and above all, with which he succeeds in gaining credit for courage, respectability, and influence; his escape from the rigid judge, and the final disappointment of all his hopes and plans by the Prince's stern decision upon his accession to the throne:—all this, again, is a happy parody upon the common cunning and the low intrigue of so-called political wisdom, which, as we have already remarked, forms the chief motive of the historical action in the second part; while Falstaff's recruiting services, and his very employment as a military officer, is a delightful satire on the fast sinking importance of the profession of war. Thus, then, do the comic parts completely and distinctly illustrate, in their own way, the general idea of the entire piece under both the aspects which it respectively assumes in the two parts. In the first, it is shewn of war, and in the second of politics—the two leading pursuits of the noble orders—that even when they are directed to the greatest objects, to interests externally the most important, they are without true historical value, which is of an ideal and moral nature, and that, consequently, whenever the moral basis, on which the various interests of history adjust

themselves, is overthrown, although there may be an outward calm, and although it may seem to be entering upon fresh directions, its course is nevertheless unsteady, and affords peace to none of its members until it resumes again its essential resting point.

It is manifest, therefore, that the complaint so frequently urged against this poem, that it is deficient in unity of action and interest, is no less groundless than many other objections. . . . But even the unreasonable demand, that the unity of interest should be found to centre itself in some one personage, appears in the present piece to be satisfied. Prince Henry may well pass for such a leading character. By disposition and conduct he is not only the organic opposite of his father, as well as of Percy and the other leaders of the revolt, but he is also the living tie between the comic parts and the serious historical action. His character well deserves the ample development which Shakspeare has bestowed upon it in three dramas, and if Hazlitt [1817] has wretchedly misunderstood it, his own political prejudices, and his blind hatred of a monarchy, are to blame. In Henry all the divergent interests of the *exhibited* story will be found to re-unite themselves. In the peril of the King's rights, his also are at stake; all his father's care and anxiety are for him; his victory over Percy decides the fortune of the war; he is the sun of all Falstaff's hopes, and a word from his mouth extinguishes them for ever. Hazlitt, and many others, have pronounced the Prince's conduct in this instance harsh and unfeeling, and no doubt the poor knight, with his dreams of bliss so suddenly cut short, is an object of compassion. And yet his lot could not well have been different, if we consider either his own character or that of the Prince. The latter was far from being a model of virtue; Shakspeare does not paint him is such a heroic light. On the contrary, we see at once that it was no venial aberration in his otherwise noble disposition to form such a connection as that with Falstaff and his followers. Such an acquaintance could only be broken off violently; the intrusive rabble must be roughly shaken off, and because of the rest of the crew, it was necessary to get rid of Falstaff himself. As usually happens, the first fault—and such his intimacy with Falstaff undoubtedly was—can only be repaired by a new one of ingratitude and injustice. That Falstaff, too, does but meet with his deserts, no one can doubt for a moment who is not accustomed to mistake his own momentary feelings for justice and right. It would have been the greatest mistake, both historically and poetically, to reward his worthless and unprofitable career with honours and distinction. (pp. 375-78)

Hermann Ulrici, "'Merry Wives of Windsor'—'Troilus and Cressida'" and "'Henry IV'," in his Shakspeare's Dramatic Art: And His Relation to Calderon and Goethe, *translated by A.J.W. Morrison, Chapman, Brothers, 1846, pp. 323-41, 368-78.*

G. G. GERVINUS (essay date 1849-50)

[*One of the most widely read Shakespearean critics of the latter half of the nineteenth century, Gervinus was praised by such eminent authors of his day as Edward Dowden, F. J. Furnivall, and James Russell Lowell; however, he is little known in the English-speaking world today. Like his predecessor, Hermann Ulrici, Gervinus wrote in the tradition of the "philosophical criticism" developed in Germany in the mid-nineteenth century. Under the influence of August Wilhelm Schlegel's literary theory and Georg Wilhelm Friedrich Hegel's philosophy, German critics like Gervinus tended to focus their analyses around a search for the literary work's organic unity and ethical import. Gervinus be-*

lieved Shakespeare's works contained a rational ethical system independent of any religion—in contrast to Ulrici, for whom Shakespeare's morality was basically Christian. In the following excerpt first published in 1849-50, Gervinus maintains that the unity of Henry IV *consists of a system of parallels and interconnections formed by the major characters, and he foreshadows such historical critics as J. Dover Wilson (1943) and E.M.W. Tillyard (1944) in placing Hal at the center of that dramatic system. His praise of Hal is perhaps the highest given that character in the history of* Henry IV *criticism. For earlier interpretations of Prince Hal's character, see the excerpts by Jeremy Collier (1698), William Warburton (1733), Charlotte Lennox (1754), Samuel Johnson (1765), and Hermann Ulrici (1839). Gervinus also considers Hal's rejection of Falstaff to be Shakespeare's final verdict on Sir John, whom he characterizes as "the personification of the inferior side of man." He is particularly critical of William Hazlitt's sympathetic view of Falstaff (see excerpt above, 1817), and because of this view he was later criticized by J. B. Priestly (1925) for failing to comprehend the humorous nature of Falstaff's character. For other sympathetic readings of Sir John's personality, see the excerpts by Corbyn Morris (1744), Charles Algernon Swinburne (1880), A. C. Bradley (1902), J.I.M. Stewart (1948), and Roy Battenhouse (1975).]*

In the series of historical plays, Shakespeare takes the same leap in [the two parts of *Henry IV.*] as in the series of love plays he does in *Romeo and Juliet.* But the effect must have been incomparably greater. For *Romeo* is a work the enjoyment of which was limited to those of Shakespeare's select public who possessed the greatest refinement of feeling; but in *Henry IV.* the richest entertainment was afforded for spectators of every class. Shakespeare has indeed scarcely written another play of such fulness and diversity in fascinating and sharply delineated characters, bearing at the same time such a native stamp, and interwoven with a subject so national, and so universally interesting—a play, in fact, of such manifold and powerful force of attraction. When *Henry IV.* first appeared, an immoderate delight must have seized the spectators of every nature and of every passion; a tumultuous joy must have been its effect; for the genius of a nation has never appeared on any stage in such bright cheerfulness, and, at the same time, in such quiet modesty, as in these plays. (pp. 299-300)

In the two parts of *Henry IV.*, the political theme which the poet had begun in *Richard II.* is continued. Richard's right, he has there shown us, could not exempt him from the fulfilment of his duty; when he neglected this he lost his title and his divine consecration. Legitimacy, as such, joined even to a fine natural character, could not protect the crown for the king. From Henry IV.'s rule we shall learn, on the other hand, that royal zeal for duty may indeed maintain the usurped position, but cannot atone for the injustice thus committed; and that a kingdom illegally gained is not secured from the greatest commotions by mere merit, combined even with the most able and crafty character. Shakespeare may have read the idea of this historical retribution even in Holinshed's *Chronicle;* it speaks of the cup of civil war as well deserved by the people who had assisted Henry IV. against Richard, and it shows the justice of that punishment against disorder which visited Henry IV. and his successors for the deposition of Richard II. The curse of the murdered king now reaches its fulfilment. Shakespeare does not mechanically represent this, as the *Chronicle* does, as an arbitrary punitive decree of God, but he exhibits it as the necessary fruit of a natural seed in the characters and actions of men. (pp. 301-02)

The character of the king is worked out by Shakespeare with that perfect penetration which is peculiar to him, as a prototype of diplomatic cunning and of complete mastery over fair ap-

pearance and all the arts of concealment. The difference between that which a man is and that which he appears occupies the poet in this character as it does in *Richard III.* But Henry IV. is rather a master in concealment than in dissimulation; he cannot, like the other, play any part required with dramatic skill; he can only exhibit the good side of his nature; he can steal kindness and condescension from Heaven; he is a Prometheus in diplomatic subtlety, and, as Percy calls him, 'a king of smiles.' That which separates him and his deep political hypocrisy from [*Richard III.*], as far as day from night, is that he possesses this good side, and has only to exhibit it and not to feign it. Far removed from authorising murder like the other, and delighting in the iron-hearted assassin, wading ever deeper from blood to blood and deadening conscience, he has rather wished than ordered Richard's death, and has cursed and exiled the murderer; conscience is roused in him immediately after the deed, and he wishes to expiate largely for the once suggested bloodshed. At the close of *Richard II.*, and at the beginning of this play, we find him occupied with the idea of making a crusade to the Holy Land in expiation of Richard's death. Strangely in this reserved mind, which fears to look into itself, does the domination of a worldly nature interweave itself with the stimulus of remorse; devout and serious thoughts of repentance are joined in this design with the most subtle political motives; earnestness of purpose and inclination to allow the purpose to be frustrated jar in a manner which the poet has made perfectly evident in the facts, though not more evident in the king's reflections than is natural to such a nature. We are in doubt whether the worldly man hesitates at the serious realisation of his religious design, or whether by the decree of Heaven the expiation of that murder was to be denied him as the natural consequence of his earlier deeds. He is in earnest about the crusade, but mostly when he is ill; then his fleet and army are in readiness. (pp. 302-03)

From this analysis of Bolingbroke's character we perceive the political relation and bearing of Henry IV. to Richard II.; but from the profound treatment of the principal characters these pieces are raised from the sphere of political historical plays into that of the true ethical dramas, the freer creations of Shakespeare; beyond the political theme of the pieces there appears also a moral centre of thought, as in *Richard III.* We arrive at this moral centre of the play by attentively considering the principal figures, Henry Percy and Prince Henry of Wales.

Shakespeare makes Henry Percy, in order that he may obtain a more complete contrast to the prince, of the same age as the latter, although historically he is far rather contemporary with King Henry, and twenty years older than the prince. He is the soul of the undertaking against the king, and the brilliant figure in the centre of the rebels, extorting love and admiration even from his enemies. Never was a more living character delineated in poetry; ballads designed to sing his glory might have borrowed their boldest traits and images from this drama. . . . Henry Percy is the ideal of all genuine and perfect manliness, and of that active nature which makes the man a man. In jesting exaggeration the prince well characterises him with the one touch, that he kills six or seven dozen of Scots at a breakfast, and says to his wife, 'Fye upon this quiet life! I want work!' As a model of genuine chivalry, Shakespeare has delineated the lion-hearted youth with characteristics as refined as they are great. He gives him the name of the war-god; report compares his victories to Caesar's: Achilles' motto is his: 'the time of life is too short to spend that shortness basely;' and when he has fallen, Henry says over his grave what so often has been said of Alexander:—

> When that this body did contain a spirit,
> A kingdom for it was too small a bound;
> But now, two paces of the vilest earth
> Is room enough.
>
> [*1 Henry IV*, V. iv. 89-92]
> (pp. 307-08)

It would be difficult to any poet to produce a hero superior to [Percy]. But least of all should it appear that Shakespeare wished or ventured to place his Prince Henry before him. Thus at any rate it could not have appeared to those interpreters who discovered a kind of injustice and an inconsistency in Percy's fall through Henry, after the early relations between the two. His own father indeed calls the prince in contrast to that king of honour, almost a king of ignomiy, and declares Percy more worthy of the throne than his own son! The prince, he asserts, in league with the low mob, is more dishonourably in war against the state than Percy! Ridiculing all knightly customs, he fights at tournaments with the glove of base prostitutes on his spear! He has even laid hands on the Lord Chief Justice, and has been for this placed in confinement and expelled from the Privy Council! Where in such a man could lie the right and the talents to be lord over a hero so splendidly endowed as Percy, unless some accident of history or some inconceivable caprice on the part of the poet dictated such a conclusion, which seems ill to accord with the just laws of a well organised world, such as that into which we wish poetry to transport us.

The prince indeed in his first soliloquy announces to us that he is perfectly aware of the wild actions of his youth, and that he intends some day to throw off this loose behaviour, and to redeem time lost. Frivolity seems accompanied with prudence and reflection, and behind the mask of folly we seem to hear a wise man speaking. Let us attentively follow out this double part, in order that we may discover the true nature of this chameleon. For how easily might that soliloquy be imagined less strong and solemn than it is intended! (pp. 313-14)

Richard II.'s intercourse was one with relatives and nobles, at least outwardly equal in birth. Prince Henry, on the contrary, roves about with men of the lowest class. It is not even the intellectual excellence of the wit which exclusively charms and attracts him. His game with the young drawer shows us his harmless delight even in the most innocent jokes; he roams about with vintners, with whom he assumes the greatest air of courtesy, so that Falstaff, compared to him, appears an insolent and proud fellow. This condescension is blamed by the king, whose art it was to 'show himself like a feast, seldom but sumptuous,' sparing of the courtesy which his son lavishes extravagantly. According to that soliloquy, however, the prince too seemed to act from a policy in no wise dissimilar. He wished to imitate the sun, which conceals itself behind the clouds that it may be more wanted and more wondered at; he indulges in his 'loose behaviour' upon the same principle of 'rare accidents,' only he seemed, if he did not presume too far, to wish to apply this principle as a great man. It was not his person, his robe of majesty, that was to form the 'rare accident,' the surprise, the sun-gleam, and the holiday, but his deeds. As long as he was not directly called to these, he shunned not to turn from the artificial nature round the throne to the original characters and the natural creations of the lower classes. He takes pleasure in human nature in its bare condition and unvarnished form; poverty of mind and of the necessaries of life is a study for him; his plain homely nature, contrasted with

Percy's knightly aristocratic bearing, is most at ease among the true-hearted fellows of Eastcheap, who call him a good boy, and tender him their service when he shall be King of England. Perhaps there is policy even in this, that he seeks to win the hearts of the people when so little reliance can be placed on the nobles, before whose assaults his father's throne is continually tottering.

With these propensities the prince wastes much time; idle and careless, whenever no positive business binds him, he is away from the court, like a son who is ill at ease in the narrow home circle. To his wild tricks, his madness, and his condescension, is added the idleness of this carousing life, on which account the king is ever holding before him the active life of Harry Percy. (pp. 315-16)

But if this may be called levity, it may also be indicative of calmness of mind. He trembles not in the least before the frightful alliance of Percy, Douglas, and Glendower. Does there not lie, at the bottom of his composure at this revolt, a firm consciousness and self-reliance? Does not a good conscience appear through all this carelessness, wantonness, and unrestraint; whilst his father, oppressed with suspicion and anguish, is suffering in his prosperity? In the silent manner in which he hears his father's suspicion, what humility and good childlike nature is exhibited! And when it is necessary, when the severe fight at Shrewsbury is threatened, does it not surprise us all, after this unrestrained life and conduct, as it surprises Percy, to read Vernon's splendid picture of the prince and his companions, like that of ostriches and eagles that wing the wind? Does it not appear as if necessity alone could call him to show himself as valiant and eager for war as Percy is always from a strong natural impulse? (p. 317)

On which shall we rely in this character—on the evil appearance, which we have exhibited, or on the sparks on honour and of a better nature which throughout we see glancing forth, and which might indicate a kernel of the rarest quality?

The idea which we have seen Shakespeare pursue throughout this whole period of his life . . . is exhibited in this character in its most perfect development. Appearance is against this wonderful man. Indifferently, indeed even wilfully, he fosters this show of evil, because in himself he is sure of the perfect essence of a genuine humanity. He sports with public opinion, because any hour he can give it the lie. On the accusation of sins worthy of death, he has in his proud self-reliance no answer but deeds. A many-sided, versatile being, he suffers life to influence him from all sides; he wishes to enjoy it as long as it offers him room for enjoyment, but in this leisure for recreation and jesting, he wishes, like the Macedonian Philip and like the Egyptian Amasis, only to steel and strengthen himself for the time of action and seriousness. . . . That which with Hamlet is a principle only of words is with him one carried into effect:—

> Rightly to be great,
> Is, not to stir *without great argument;*
> But greatly to find quarrel in a straw,
> *When honour's at the stake.*
>
> [*Hamlet*, IV. iv. 53-6]

And essentially in this principle is he a contrast to the fiery Percy, who in his passion certainly grows angry over 'the ninth part of a hair, even where no honour is at stake.'

Following out this principle, the thin, versatile, frivolous prince makes use of his time for jesting and mirth as long as it is given him. As soon as he has heard from his father that he is thought capable of watching for his father's death, and of treachery against his father's throne, he is struck with dismay, unsuspicious of having stood so low in the opinion of others. Hereafter he determines to be more himself, and he proves in his combat how truly and helpfully he stands by his father's side. . . . And thus urged by this smouldering fire of ambition, he encounters Percy's flaming passion for glory; the modest man meets his despiser, the idler in knightly deeds meets the master of chivalry, and he overcomes him, in no wise because the arbitrary fancy of the poet so willed it, but because the good cause thus required it, and the good powerful nature of the prince thus permitted it—a nature in which qualities were inherent which far outshone even the great gifts of Harry Percy.

For now, when the victory over Percy has given him a higher position, there appear qualities which make him greater than this great one. He stands over the conquered with admiration, with forgiveness, with emotion and pity. It had been his burning ambition to kill Percy; and now it is done the flame is at once extinguished, and gives place to the beautiful human emotions of the heart. And yet more; he gives to the foolish Falstaff the honour of having killed Percy, with the intention of re-establishing his old friend's sullied honour by yielding him this renown; he silently suppresses his self-confidence and renounces a fame only just obtained; with ready modesty he strips the glory from himself, the first time that it falls upon his misjudged life, with a feeling within of that highest honour and dignity, which is content with the self-consciousness and needs not the outward honour. (pp. 317-20)

We are struck at once with the relation in which Falstaff, the fourth principal figure in the first part of *Henry IV.*, stands to the rest. . . . By the side of these heroes of honour he seems utterly deprived of all sense of honour and of shame, and it is not possible to him to imitate dignity even in play. A respect for the opinion of others and a need of self-esteem are foreign to him; it is selfishness alone which places this machine in motion. In this contrast especially we will look at this remarkable character, who, like a living acquaintance, is on the lips and in the knowledge of all. To analyse it in all its fulness would be, moreover, as difficult as it would be unacceptable, because the critical analysis of a comic character cannot but destroy it, without yielding the compensation which in a noble character arises from the grand conception presented more distinctly to view through the analysis itself. (pp. 321-22)

The picture of a mass of indolence and incapability for action, [Falstaff] is the personification of the inferior side of man, of his animal and sensual nature. All the spiritual part of man, honour and morality, refinement and dignity, has been early spoiled and lost in him. The material part has smothered in him every passion, for good or for evil; he was perhaps naturally good-natured, and only from trouble and bad company became ill-natured, but even this ill-nature is as short as his breath, and is never sufficiently lasting to become real malice. His form and his mere bulk condemn him to repose and love of pleasure; laziness, epicurean comfort, cynicism, and idleness, which are only a recreation for his prince, are for him the essence, nature, and business of life itself; and whilst Percy loses appetite and sleep from the excitement of his aspiring spirit, Falstaff, on the contrary, is all care about his subsistence. In virtue, therefore, of this animal excess and demand, and the moral stupefaction which is its result, he holds to the natural right of animals: if the young dace be a bait for the old pike, he sees no reason in the law of nature why he may not snap

at the simple, the insipid, the dull, and the brisk among mankind. (p. 323)

Opposed to every political and judicial regulation, and to every moral precept, the preponderance of the material nature has made him obtuse, and thus opposed to all intellectual nourishment. His wit, the only mental gift which he possesses, must itself serve to his subsistence. . . . [Hazlitt] has utterly distorted this character, by maintaining that Falstaff is a liar, a coward, and a wit, only for the sake of amusing others and to show the humorous side of these qualities; an actor himself just as much as on the stage [see excerpt above, 1817]. Falstaff is indeed so far conscious of his jesting powers that he knows what makes the prince laugh; but in their exercise in every single instance the perfect instinct of habit and nature alone is expressed, and a calculated play of words is never manifested. His whole comic power lies in his unintentional wit and in his dry humour; natural mother-wit ever appears in this way; comic genius, like genius of every kind, moves in the undistinguishable line between consciousness and instinct. It is just this happy medium which Shakespeare assigned to his Falstaff; and *this* medium, and his position as bantering and bantered, as a mark for wit just as much as a dealer in it himself assigns to him the social place which he always occupied. The life and literature of that period distinguished between the popular and the court fool, between the unschooled mother-wit in the one, and the mask of wisdom in the other, between the clown and the fool, between the man who by nature and exterior provoked the love of laughter and raillery among the people and the man schooled to ridicule honest folly, between the man to whom a well-practised roguery was wit and the man who performed his pranks only with his tongue. Falstaff, not indeed holding any official function, unites both species of jesters in his person, with a natural though not easily distinguishable preponderance of the former. . . . (pp. 324-25)

How comes it, nevertheless, that we do not abhor the cowardly Jack as such; that, on the contrary, we find ourselves even feeling undisturbed delight in him? There are many complex causes which tend to moderate and even entirely to bribe over our moral judgment upon this character. Readily and involuntarily we mingle pleasure in the delineation of the poet with pleasure in the subject delineated. The liveliness of the picture; the abundance of the choicest wit; the unusually skilful touch in the choice of the ridiculous and the comic in the mere exterior of this phenomenon; and finally the blending of the ideal with the individual, which allows us to recognise in Falstaff now a typical character, and now an actual well-known personage; all this is done with such masterly power, that it is excusable if any transfer their admiration from the work of art to the subject of it. But even the subject itself has that within it which exercises a corrupting influence upon the estimate of its moral value. (p. 327)

Hazlitt, went so far as to say we could as little blame Falstaff's character as that of the actor who plays him; we should only consider the agreeable light in which he placed certain weaknesses, careless of the consequences, and from which, moreover, no pernicious consequences arose! He will not forgive the prince his treatment of Falstaff, for to the readers of poetry in the present day, he says that Falstaff appears as *the better man of the two*! This is indeed the acme of moral bluntness into which the aesthetic criticism of a man who has, however, made many striking remarks upon Shakespeare, has unwarily erred. . . . Our romanticists have pitied Falstaff's end, and have condemned the judgment which proffers the choice of a competence in life to the reformed, and disgrace to the incorrigible; they have indeed even supposed that Shakespeare might have written another conclusion. Even so severe a moralist as Johnson has considered Falstaff's vices contemptible rather than detestable [see excerpt above, 1765]; it seemed as if cowardice, lying, sensual gratification, baseness, robbery, ingratitude, and all the crimes in the world were to be made absolvable just because they are thus accumulated in Falstaff. The pernicious consequences which just before the act of disgrace led to murder in Hostess Quickly's house were wholly disregarded by the jealous interpreters. Falstaff's intercourse (and this was indeed a masterpiece of effect) appeared not only ensnaring and alluring to the prince, but also the the reader; the delight of seeing us well entertained prevented the blame of immorality from gaining ground. Thus far had the poet reached his object with ourselves, thus far did we all feel with the prince. But on his sentence of judgment we would no longer comprehend him. In this we fell far short of the prince in moral severity and nobility, and in the true dignity of man; far short of the prince and of the poet, who knew very well what he was doing, and what he made his Henry do. (pp. 328-29)

Upon the second part of *Henry IV.* we have but few words to say, since the political and ethical idea of the first part is here only continued, and is not replaced by a new one in a new group of characters and actions. The great characters in the first part—Glendower, Douglas, Percy—have disappeared, the king's physical constitution is broken, and a mental change appears to have begun in the prince; the space which Falstaff and his companions occupy is wider than formerly, but it loses in attraction. The threatening of the state in the little war of these freebooters stands out all the more glaringly as the great revolt of the Percys recedes. The exertion of the great powers in the first part is followed by a universal exhaustion in the second; and only secretly is a new energy preparing itself in Prince Henry, which is subsequently developed in the following play of *Henry V.* As soon as we consider the tetralogy in connection, the lower range of this third piece appears as necessary in an aesthetic as in an ethical sense. (p. 331)

> *G. G. Gervinus, "'Henry IV, Part I'" and "'Henry IV, Part II'," in his* Shakespeare Commentaries, *translated by F. E. Bunnèt, revised edition, Smith, Elder, & Co., 1877, pp. 298-330, 331-38.*

CHARLES COWDEN CLARKE (essay date 1863)

[*Clarke's praise of Shakespeare's powers of characterization is typical of nineteenth-century Shakespearean criticism. Although he praises Maurice Morgann (1777) for his sympathetic interpretation of Falstaff, he also argues that Morgann's essay reads in many respects like a "barrister's defense" of Falstaff's actions, rather than an objective "inquiry after truth." His essay was first published in 1863.*]

[The heroic plot of *Henry IV*] is conceived in the very highest spirit of chivalry and martial daring. The terrible valour of Percy, and the flaunting heroism of Prince Harry, are drawn with a fervour and dramatic fitness and art, and contrasted with wonderful brilliancy of effect. This power that Shakespeare possessed was in itself almost miraculous, carried, as he carried it, to such a point of perfection; but when we come to the *detail* in the characters, to the casual development of remote and subsidiary thoughts, feelings, and actions, it really seems as if he were indued with all the peculiarities of each individual character, or that he had imparted to them all *his* genius, that they might deliver themselves perfectly.

The two most important, if not the *chief* actors in the serious scenes of this drama, are Prince Harry and Harry Percy, of whom a remarkable list of references might be made confirmatory of the "individuality" sustained in the portraiture of the two men, from the outset to the close of their career. The former will hereafter come under examination; here, therefore, it were sufficient simply to remark, that as Hal the roysterer, as Prince Harry, and afterwards, in isolated royalty, as Henry V., he appears accurately and consistently, one and the same man. (p. 416)

The *manner* as well as the language of Percy are sustained with wonderful consistency of individuality. One of the most prominent features of his personal character is that of *perpetual restlessness,* to which may be added abundant determination, always combined with rashness and indiscretion. . . . [In Hotspur] we have constant allusion to some *peculiarity* or other, which makes us feel as though we had known him. First, there is the total lack of repose, already alluded to: he is like a wild beast newly confined. Then, his impetuosity of disposition naturally shows itself in perpetual interruptions during consultations. . . . (pp. 417-18)

Whether in council, whether in the field, even whether he is in the society of ladies, Percy is the same restless, untiring individual. Another striking personal characteristic in the man (and which is referred to several times) is his thick and inarticulate utterance,—a blemish which Lady Percy says of him was turned into a grace. (p. 420)

Among the second and third rate members of the drama may be instanced, first, that rancorous and uncompromising partisan, the Earl of Worcester, whose hatred of Henry, seated by himself and Northumberland on the throne of Richard, induces him even to betray his trust as messenger between the king and the rebel party on the eve of the Shrewsbury battle. (pp. 421-22)

[How] distinctly manifest, in these great historical dramas, is the fact, that from the era of John downwards, the monarchy in this country has almost always been, more or less, in abeyance to the aristocracy, and has indeed been sustained by the antagonism of parties in their own order; and these instinctively nourished and fostered by royalty itself, to preserve its own individuality, and even its "local habitation and name."

Vernon is by much the noblest of all the "subordinates" in the play. His constancy to the rebel party does not prevent his bearing honourable testimony to the merits of their opponents. His admiration of the gallant bearing of Prince Harry is in the purest spirit of chivalry, and *true* chivalry always carried honour—which is justice—to the verge of romance in generous dealing. It is Vernon who gives that superb description of the prince and his comrades, whom he had seen preparing for the campaign, in the 1st scene of the 4th Act, Part I. (pp. 422-23)

In direct contrast to the character of Vernon, may be cited that notable instance of treachery and meanness, Prince John of Lancaster, younger son of the king. Here is the phylactery of his vices—wily, wary, cold, calculating, indirect, faithless. In act, treacherous and cruel. No wonder Falstaff hates him; he hates him personally and socially, and *no* wonder, with his own quicksilver nature; because, as he says, "A man *cannot make him laugh.*" Beyond this playful reason, however, (containing a profound instinct beneath its apparent superficiality and lightness,) the acute perception and shrewd wit of Falstaff discerned the heartless nature of the young fellow, and he loathed him accordingly, with all the genuine disgust of a genial and cordial spirit. (p. 423)

In proceeding to notice the comic characters in the two parts of ''Henry IV.,'' can it be conceded that Falstaff was a ''subordinate''? A subordinate!—is he not almost the sole preoccupier of the mind whenever it recurs to these plays? Why, Sir John is principal and paramount in all places, and on all occasions. He makes his entry, and the scene is filled; he makes his exit, and our ''eyes are *idly* bent on him who enters next.'' He played second to no one. Prince Hal understood him as well as any of them; but the whole synod could never take the lead when Sir John was present. He was no subsidiary,—no attendant planet of any orb; he was himself a constellation,— a system! His path was eccentric, and comet-like; I will therefore (''by particular desire,''—of myself) depart from the general plan of the work, and devote a few words to this immortal and unequalled character. And first of all, truly speaking, Falstaff is a secondary person in these dramas,—he *is* a ''subordinate;'' the main plot of the play could proceed without him. (p. 430)

The character of Sir John Falstaff is, I should think, the most witty and humorous combined that ever was portrayed. So palpably is the person presented to the mind's eye, that not only do we give him a veritable location in history; but the others, the real characters in the period, compared with him, appear to be the idealised people, and invented to be his foils and contrasts. As there is no romance like the romance of real life, so no real-life character comes home to our apprehensions and credulities like the romance of Sir John Falstaff. He is one grand identity. His body is fitted for his mind,—bountiful, exuberant, and luxurious; and his mind was well appointed for his body,—being rich, ample, sensual, sensuous, and imaginative. The very fatness of his person is the most felicitous correspondent to the unlimited opulence of his imagination; and but for this conjunction, the character would have been out of keeping and incomplete. Fancy a human thread-paper with Sir John's amount of roguish accomplishment! . . . He keeps both body and mind in one perpetual gaudy-day; his is the saturnalia, the carnival of the intellect, and his body he rejoices with sack-posset, and his mind with jokes and roars of laughter; and with him each acts upon and with the other,— the true sign of a strong constitution. Falstaff's is not a ''clay that gets muddy with drink;'' his sensuality does not sodden and brutify his faculties, but it quickens their temper and edge. (p. 431)

Falstaff is equal to any exigence; he is never foiled, but usually comes off with flying colours by means of his astounding, and always laughable, effrontery. When this is recognised and resisted, he still saves himself with a flash of humour or a quirk. No one but Shakespeare could have brought such a character in competition with the Lord Chief Justice of England, and yet have maintained the supremacy of each party. (p. 434)

Gross as the knight is, and wonderfully as the poet has relieved that grossness by the most brilliant flashes of wit and drollery, no mortal, it is to be presumed, ever arose from reading the plays in which he shines with a less firm appreciation of the wealth of virtue in all its senses; still less could any one desire to mimic his propensities. (p. 436)

One eminent writer, several years ago, (Mr. Barnes, editor of the *Times*,) contributed some ingenious papers which appeared in the *Examiner*, their object being to prove that Falstaff was not a coward. What to say to this, decidedly, is questionable.

''Decidedly'' he ran away at Gadshill; he counterfeited death at the Shrewsbury fight when Douglas attacked him; and he stabbed the *dead* Percy in the thigh, which act, with the lie crowning it, villainous as it was, may rather come under the denomination of knavery than non-bravery, because he turned it to sordid advantage. And, lastly, when the sheriff's officers are proceeding to arrest him, he bids Bardolph ''cut off the villain's head;'' he offers no personal resistance himself. Nevertheless, and notwithstanding all these and more ''counts'' that might be adduced against him, the imputed cowardice of Falstaff does not arise so much from a principle of fear— downright, pallid horror—as from a constitutional love of ease, a sense of enjoyment, and repugnance—from inability—to disagreeable exertion. (pp. 437-38)

What can be a finer hoax than his pulling out his bottle of sack during the fight, when the prince desires him to lend him his sword? In short, I think with Mackenzie, in his essay upon the character [see excerpt above, 1786], that ''his cowardice may be placed to his *sagacity,* and that he has a lively sense of danger, but not the want of self-possession which arises from fear.'' But the finest dissertation upon the character of Falstaff is decidedly the essay by Mr. Morgann [see excerpt above, 1777]. As a specimen of neat and elegant writing, with ingenious special-pleading, it stands distinguished in our literature; at the same time it must be acknowledged that the author is so bent upon proving Shakespeare to have intended the fat knight to be considered a man of courage—absolute ''courage''—that the essay has more the air of a barrister's defence than a calm dispassionate inquiry after truth. (p. 439)

The last scene that we have with the fat old mountain of flesh and iniquity is a somewhat affecting one; and it should seem, by common consent, that the poet has visited his sins upon him with a degree of harshness. Moreover, it is not unusual with the critics to impute to cold-heartedness Henry V.'s peremptory and sudden dismissal of all his old co-rioters. It may be asked, however, what other course he could pursue, upon taking the reins of government? and, at all events, to Falstaff he promised ''competence of life, that lack of means enforce him not to evil;'' and he concludes with enjoining the Lord Chief-Justice *''to see performed the tenor of his word.''* (p. 441)

In the concourse and train of kings and princes, knights and highwaymen, it is pleasant to come upon that little scene in the inn-yard at Rochester, and listen to the natural talk of those carriers, puddering about with their lanterns, telling the hour of the night by the constellation ''Charles's wain over the new chimney,'' and grumbling at the new ostler's corn. ''The peas and beans are as dank as a dog,'' and they ''give the poor jades the bots.'' All things have gone wrong ''since Robin ostler died; he never joyed after the price of oats rose.'' The whole scene, with all its still-life accompaniments, is like a picture by Teniers, or a rival chiaro-scuro by Rembrandt. (p. 443)

After Falstaff, the most perfect characters in the play are Shallow and Silence; the Gloucestershire justices. Here again we have Shakespeare's astonishing power in individuality-portraiture. It is impossible to conceive a stronger contrast, a more direct antipodes in mental structure than he has achieved between Falstaff and Shallow; the one all intellect, all acuteness of perception and fancy, and the other, the justice, a mere compound of fatuity, a *caput mortuum* of understanding. Not only is Shallow distinguished by his eternal babble, talking ''infinite nothings,'' but with the flabby vivacity, the idiotic restlessness that not unfrequently accompany this class of mind; (if such a being may be said to possess mind at all;) he not only tattles on—''whirr, whirr, whirr,'' like a ventilator, but he fills up the chinks in his sentences with *repetitions,* as blacksmiths continue to tap the anvil in the intervals of turning the iron upon it. (pp. 443-44)

As if it were not sufficient triumph for the poet to have achieved such a contrast as the two intellects of Falstaff and Shallow,—in the consciousness and the opulence of unlimited genius, he stretches the line of his invention, and produces a foil even to Shallow—a climax to nothing—in the person of his cousin, Silence.

Silence is an embryo of a man,—a molecule,—a graduation from nonentity towards intellectual being,—a man dwelling in the suburbs of sense, groping about in the twilight of apprehension and understanding. He is the second stage in the ''Vestiges;'' he has just emerged from the tadpole state. Here again a distinction is preserved between these two characters. Shallow gabbles on from mere emptiness; while Silence, from the same incompetence, rarely gets beyond the shortest replies. The firmament of his wonder and adoration are the sayings and doings of his cousin and brother-justice at Clement's Inn, and which he has been in the constant habit of hearing, without satiety and nausea, for half-a-century. (pp. 445-46)

Not content with filling his scene with three such worthies as Falstaff, Shallow, and Silence, the poet stretches on the career of his imagination, and introduces that whiskered cat-a-mountain, Ancient Pistol; a character quite as grotesque and amusing in his walk as the half-witted justices. Pistol, however, is not an original invention of Shakespeare's; but he was intended to be a satire upon some euphuistic and bombastious characters that are to be found in other plays of his time; and Mackenzie says that he has even taken identical passages, in all their ''robustious periwig-pated'' absurdity, and putting them into Pistol's mouth, they become the natural effusions of a braggart and a poltroon.

If Shakespeare really intended to represent Falstaff as a coward, a white-livered fellow, although very questionable that such was his design, he has produced a complete distinction in the effects of the passion in the two men. In Falstaff it was policy; in Pistol it was negation, an incompetence of the principle of self-respect, as in Parolles. (p. 448)

> *Charles Cowden Clarke, '''Henry IV','' in his* Shakespeare-Characters. Chiefly Those Subordinate, *AMS Press, 1974, pp. 413-50.*

VICTOR HUGO   (essay date 1864)

[*Hugo was the leading poet and novelist of French Romanticism. In his study* William Shakespeare *(1865), he maintains that Shakespeare is a reincarnation of Aeschylus and regards the poet as a genius who explored the limits of human experience. Hugo was also interested in Shakespeare's use of the supernatural and claimed that the poet ''believed profoundly in the mystery of things.'' In the following remarks, he characterizes Falstaff as a ''miscarriage'' of the comic tradition exemplified by François Rabelais's Panurge and Miguel de Cervantes's Sancho Panza. Nearly twenty years later, Algernon Charles Swinburne (1880) challenged Hugo's appraisal of Falstaff as the moral inferior of Panurge and Sancho Panza, claiming instead that he is superior to both of these characters in moral integrity.*]

Deformity in the person of the tyrant [as in *Richard III*] is not enough for this philosopher [Shakespeare]; he must have it also in the shape of the valet, and he creates Falstaff. The dynasty of commonsense, inaugurated in Panurge, continued in Sancho

Panza, goes wrong and miscarries in Falstaff. The rock which this wisdom splits upon is, in reality, lowness. Sancho Panza, in combination with the ass, is embodied with ignorance. Falstaff—glutton, poltroon, savage, obscene, human face and stomach, with the lower parts of the brute—walks on the four feet of turpitude; Falstaff is the centaur man and pig. (p. 141)

Shakespeare is a human mind; he is also an English mind. He is very English,—too English. He is English so far as to weaken the horror surrounding the horrible kings whom he places on the stage, when they are kings of England; . . . so far as expressly to make a scapegoat, Falstaff, in order to load him with the princely [misdeeds] of the young Henry V.; so far as to partake in a certain measure of the hypocrisies of a pretended national history. . . . But at the same time, let us insist upon this,—for it is by it that he is great,—yes, this English poet is a human genius. Art, like religion, has its *Ecce Homo.* Shakespeare is one of those of whom we may utter this grand saying: He is Man. (p. 253)

> *Victor Hugo, ''Shakespeare—His Genius'' and ''After Death—Shakespeare—England,'' in his* The Works of Victor Hugo: Shakespeare, *Vol. X,* The Jefferson Press, *1864, pp. 134-55, 247-68.*

REV. H. N. HUDSON   (essay date 1872)

[*On the basis of the following two commentaries, J. Dover Wilson credited the Shakespearean editor Hudson with anticipating several key points of his own interpretation of* Henry IV, *particularly his conclusion that Prince Hal and Falstaff are opposing passions in an elaborate morality drama (see excerpts below, 1943 and 1944). Hudson's first excerpt consists of a digression on* Henry IV *from his criticism of* The Merry Wives of Windsor. *The second begins with a footnote that explores the character of Hal and examines the connection between Hal and Falstaff as the struggle between virtue and vice. Hudson's commentary concludes with a criticism of* Henry V *which explains Hal's rejection of Sir John.*]

[All] through the period of *King Henry the Fourth,* [Falstaff] keeps growing worse and worse, while the Prince is daily growing better. Out of their sport-seeking intercourse he picks whatever is bad, whereas the other gathers nothing but the good. As represented in the Comedy he seems to be in the swiftest part of this worsening process. At the close of the First Part of the History, the Prince freely yields up to him the honour of Hotspur's fall; thus carrying home to him such an example of self-renouncing generosity as it would seem impossible for the most hardened sinner to resist. And the Prince appears to have done this partly in the hope that it might prove a seed of truth and grace in Falstaff, and start him in a better course of life. But the effect upon him is quite the reverse. Honour is nothing to him but as it may help him in the matter of sensual and heart-steeling self-indulgence. And the surreptitious fame thus acquired, instead of working in him for good, merely serves to procure him larger means and larger license for pampering his gross animal selfishness. His thoughts dwell not at all on the Prince's act of magnanimity, which would shame his egotism and soften his heart, but only on his own ingenuity and success in the stratagem that led to that act. So that the effect is just to puff him up more than ever with vanity and conceit of wit, and thus to give a looser rein and a sharper stimulus to his greed and lust; for there is probably nothing that will send a man faster to the Devil than that sort of conceit. The result is, that Falstaff soon proceeds to throw off whatever of restraint may have hitherto held his vices in check, and to wanton in the arrogance of utter impunity. (pp. 305-06)

Rev. H. N. Hudson, "Shakespeare's Characters," in his Shakespeare: His Life, Art, and Characters, Vol. I, *revised edition, Ginn & Company, 1872, pp. 259-474.*

REV. H. N. HUDSON   (essay date 1872)

[In a footnote, Hudson states:] Our sympathies [in *Henry IV*] would be almost wholly with Hotspur and his friends, had not the Poet raised up a new interest in the chivalrous bearing of Henry of Monmouth, to balance the noble character of the young Percy. Rash, proud, ambitious, prodigal of blood, as Hotspur is, we feel that there is not an atom of meanness in his composition. He would carry us away with him, were it not for the milder courage of young Harry,—the courage of principle and of mercy. Frank, liberal, prudent, gentle, but yet brave as Hotspur himself, the Prince shows us that, even in his wildest excesses, he has drunk deeply of the fountains of truth and wisdom. The wisdom of the King is that of a cold and subtle politician; Hotspur seems to stand out from his followers as a haughty feudal lord, too proud to have listened to any teacher but his own will; but the Prince, in casting away the dignity of his station to commune freely with his fellowmen, has attained that strength which is above all conventional power: his virtues as well as his frailties belong to our common humanity; the virtues capable, therefore, of the highest elevation; the frailties not pampered into crimes by the artificial incentives of social position. His challenge to Hotspur exhibits all the attributes of the gentleman as well as the hero,—mercy, sincerity, modesty, courage. Could the Prince have reached this height amidst the cold formalities of his father's Court? We think that Shakespeare meant distinctly to show that Henry of Monmouth, when he ''sounded the very basestring of humility,'' gathered out of his dangerous experience that spirit of sympathy with human actions and motives from which a sovereign is almost necessarily excluded.

(pp. 79-80)

[King Henry IV's] great force of character would needs give shape and tone to Court and Council-board, while his subtlety and intricacy might well render the place any thing but inviting to a young man of free and generous aptitudes. That the Prince, as Shakespeare conceived him, should breathe somewhat hard in such an atmosphere, is not difficult to understand. However he may respect such a father, and though in thought he may even approve the public counsels, still he relucts to share in them, as going against his grain; and so is naturally drawn away either to such occupations where his high-strung energies can act without crossing his honourable feelings, or else to some tumultuous merry-makings where, laying off all distinct purpose, and untying his mind into perfect dishabille, he can let his bounding spirits run out in transports of frolic and fun. The question then is, to what sort of attractions will he betake himself? It must be no ordinary companionship that yields entertainment to such a spirit even in his loosest moments. Whatever bad or questionable elements may mingle in his mirth,

it must have some fresh and rich ingredients, some sparkling and generous flavour, to make him relish it. Any thing like vulgar rowdyism cannot fail of disgusting him. His ears were never organized to that sort of music.

Here then we have a sort of dramatic necessity for the character of Falstaff. To answer the purpose, it was imperative that he should be just such a marvellous congregation of charms and vices as he is. None but an old man could be at once so dissolute and so discerning, or appear to think so much like a wise man even when talking most unwisely; and he must have a world of wit and sense, to reconcile a mind of such native rectitude and penetration to his profligate courses. In the qualities of Sir John we can easily see how the Prince might be the madcap reveller that history gives him out, and yet be all the while laying in choice preparations of wisdom and virtue, so as to need no other conversion than the calls of duty and the opportunities of noble enterprise. (pp. 83-4)

If I were to fix upon any one thing as specially characteristic of Falstaff, I should say it is an amazing fund of good sense. His stock of this, to be sure, is pretty much all enlisted in the service of sensuality, yet nowise so but that the servant still overpeers and outshines the master. Then too his thinking has such agility, and is at the same time so pertinent, as to do the work of the most prompt and popping wit; yet in such sort as to give the impression of something much larger and stronger than wit. (p. 84)

And Falstaff is well aware of his power in this respect. He is vastly proud of it too; yet his pride never shows itself in an offensive shape, his good sense having a certain instinctive delicacy that keeps him from every thing like that. In this proud consciousness of his resources he is always at ease; hence in part the ineffable charm of his conversation. Never at a loss, and never apprehensive that he shall be at a loss, he therefore never exerts himself, nor takes any concern for the result; so that nothing is strained or far-fetched: relying calmly on his strength, he invites the toughest trials, as knowing that his powers will bring him off without any using of the whip or the spur, and by merely giving the rein to their natural briskness and celerity. Hence it is also that he so often lets go all regard to prudence of speech, and thrusts himself into tight places and predicaments: he thus makes or seeks occasions to exercise his fertility and alertness of thought, being well assured that he shall still come off uncornered, and that the greater his seeming perplexity, the greater will be his triumph. Which explains the purpose of his incomprehensible lies: he tells them, surely, not expecting them to be believed, but partly for the pleasure he takes in the excited play of his faculties, partly for the surprise he causes by his still more incomprehensible feats of dodging. Such is his story about the men in buckram who grew so soon from two to eleven; and how ''three misbegotten knaves in Kendall green came at my back, and let drive at me;—for it was so dark, Hal, that thou couldst not see thy hand'';—lies which, as himself knows well enough, are ''gross as a mountain, open, palpable.'' These, I take it, are studied self-exposures, to invite an attack. Else why should he thus affirm in the same breath the colour of the men's clothes and the darkness of the night? The whole thing is clearly a scheme, to provoke his hearers to come down upon him, and then witch them with his facility and felicity in extricating himself. (pp. 85-6)

In all that happens to Falstaff, the being cast off at last by the Prince is the only thing that really hurts his feelings. And as this is the only thing that hurts him, so it is the only one that does him any good: for he is strangely inaccessible to inward suffering; and yet nothing but this can make him better. His character keeps on developing, and growing rather worse, to the end of the play; and there are some positive indications of a hard bad heart in him. His abuse of Shallow's hospitality is exceedingly detestable, and argues that hardening of all within which tells far more against a man than almost any amount of mere sensuality. . . . In the matter about Justice Shallow we are let into those worse traits of Falstaff, such as his unscrupulous and unrelenting selfishness, which had else escaped our dull perceptions, but which, through all the disguises of art, have betrayed themselves to the apprehensive discernment of Prince Henry. . . . The bad usage which Falstaff puts upon Shallow has the effect of justifying to us the usage which he at last receives from the Prince. And something of the kind was needful in order to bring the Prince's character off from such an act altogether bright and sweet in our regard. For, after sharing so long in the man's prodigality of mental exhilaration, to shut down upon him so, was pretty hard. (pp. 98-9)

[But the] practical working of [the Prince's] choice composure is well shown in what happened at the killing of Hotspur. No sooner had Prince Henry slain the valiant Percy than he fell at once to doing him the offices of pious and tender reverence; and the rather, forasmuch as no human eye witnessed the act. He knew that the killing of Hotspur would be enough of itself to wipe out all his shames, and "restore him into the good thoughts of the world again"; nevertheless he cheerfully resigned the credit of the deed to Falstaff. He knew that such a surreptitious honour would help his old companion in the way wherein he was most capable and needy of help; while, for himself, he could forego the fame of it in the secret pledge it gave him of other and greater achievements: the inward conscience thereof sufficed him; and the sense of having done a generous thing was dearer to him than the beguiling sensation of "riding in triumph on men's tongues." This noble superiority to the breath of present applause is what most clearly evinces the solidity and inwardness of his virtue.

Yet in one of his kingliest moments he tells us, "If it be a sin to covet honour, I am the most offending soul alive." But honour is with him in the highest sense a social conscience, and the rightful basis of self-respect: he deems it a good chiefly as it makes a man clean and strong within, and not as it dwells in the fickle breath of others. As for that conventional figment which small souls make so much ado about, he cares little for it, as knowing that it is often got without merit, and lost without deserving. Thus the honour he covets is really to deserve the good thoughts of men: the inward sense of such desert is enough: if what is fairly his due in that kind be withheld by them, the loss is theirs, not his. (p. 123)

Rev. H. N. Hudson, "Shakespeare's Characters: Historical Plays," in his Shakespeare: His Life, Art, and Characters, Vol. II, revised edition, Ginn & Company, 1872, pp. 5-202.

ALGERNON CHARLES SWINBURNE   (essay date 1880)

[Swinburne was an English poet, dramatist, and critic who devoted much of his literary career to the study of Shakespeare and other Elizabethan writers. His three books on Shakespeare—A Study of Shakespeare (1880), Shakespeare (1909), and Three Plays of Shakespeare (1909)—all demonstrate his keen interest in Shakespeare's poetic talents and, especially, his major tragedies. In the following excerpt, he challenges Victor Hugo's unfavorable comparison of Falstaff with Sancho Panza and Panurge

(see excerpt above, 1864), offering instead his own theory that Falstaff is not a "downward" gradation from these two characters but a moral improvement. Swinburne also praises Maurice Morgann (1777) for his sympathetic study of Sir John.]

The great national trilogy [King Henry IV, Parts 1 and 2, King Henry V], which is at once the flower of Shakespeare's second period and the crown of his achievements in historic drama—unless indeed we so far depart from the established order and arrangement of his works as to include his three Roman plays in the same class with these English histories—offers perhaps the most singular example known to us of the variety in fortune which befell his works on their first appearance in print. None of these had better luck in that line at starting than King Henry IV.; none had worse than King Henry V. (p. 103)

[It should] be noted that the finest touch in the comic scenes, if not the finest in the whole portrait of Falstaff, is apparently an afterthought, a touch added on revision of the original design [of King Henry IV]. . . . It is as grievous as it is inexplicable that the Shakespeare of France [Victor Hugo]—the most infinite in compassion, in "conscience and tender heart," of all great poets in all ages and all nations of the world—should have missed the deep tenderness of this supreme and subtlest touch in the work of the greatest among his fellows [see excerpt above, 1864]. . . . Even Pistol and Nym can see that what now ails their old master is no such ailment as in his prosperous days was but too liable to "play the rogue with his great toe." "The king hatt run bad humours on the knight:" "his heart is fracted, and corroborate." And it is not thus merely through the eclipse of that brief mirage, that fair prospect "of Africa, and golden joys," in view of which he was ready to "take any man's horses." This it is that distinguishes Falstaff from Panurge; that lifts him at least to the moral level of Sancho Panza. I cannot but be reluctant to set the verdict of my own judgment against that of Victor Hugo's; I need none to remind me what and who he is whose judgment I for once oppose, and what and who am I that I should oppose it; that he is he, and I am but myself; yet against his classification of Falstaff, against his definition of Shakespeare's unapproached and unapproachable masterpiece in the school of comic art and humoristic nature, I must and do with all my soul and strength protest. The admirable phrase of "swine-centaur" (centaure du porc) is as inapplicable to Falstaff as it is appropriate to Panurge. Not the third person but the first in date of that divine and human trinity of humourists whose names make radiant for ever the century of their new-born glory—not Shakespeare but Rabelais is responsible for the creation or the discovery of such a type as this. "Suum cuique is our Roman justice"; the gradation from Panurge to Falstaff is not downward but upward; though it be Victor Hugo's very self who asserts the contrary. Singular as may seem the collocation of the epithet "moral" with the name "Falstaff," I venture to maintain my thesis; that in point of feeling, and therefore of possible moral elevation, Falstaff is as undeniably the superior of Sancho as Sancho is unquestionably the superior of Panurge. (pp. 105-08)

The actual lust and gluttony, the imaginary cowardice of Falstaff, have been gravely and sharply rebuked by critical morality; we have just noted a too recent and too eminent example of this; but what mortal ever dreamed of casting these qualities in the teeth of his supposed counterpart [Panurge]? The difference is as vast between Falstaff on the field of battle and Panurge on the storm-tossed deck as between Falstaff and Hotspur, Panurge and Friar John. No man could show cooler and steadier nerve than is displayed in either case—by the lay as well as the clerical namesake of the fourth evangelist. If ever fruitless but endless care was shown to prevent misunderstanding, it was shown in the pains taken by Shakespeare to obviate the misconstruction which would impute to Falstaff the quality of a Parolles or a Bobadil, a Bessus or a Moron. (p. 110)

It is needless to do over again the work which was done, and well done, a hundred years since, by the writer whose able essay in vindication and exposition of the genuine character of Falstaff elicited from Dr. Johnson as good a jest and as bad a criticism as might have been expected [see excerpt above by Maurice Morgann, 1777]. His argument is too thoroughly carried out at all points and fortified on all hands to require or even to admit of corroboration; and the attempt to appropriate any share of the lasting credit which is his due would be nothing less than a disingenuous impertinence. I may here however notice that in the very first scene of this trilogy which introduces us to the ever dear and honoured presence of Sir John, his creator has put into the mouth of a witness no friendlier or more candid than Ned Poins the distinction between two as true-bred cowards as ever turned back and one who will fight no longer than he sees reason. In this nutshell lies the whole kernel of the matter; the sweet, sound, ripe, toothsome, wholesome kernel of Falstaff's character and humour. He will fight as well as his princely patron, and, like the prince, as long as he sees reason; but neither Hal nor Jack has ever felt any touch of desire to pluck that "mere scutcheon" honour "from the pale-faced moon." Harry Percy is as it were the true Sir Bedivere, the last of all Arthurian knights; Henry V. is the first as certainly as he is the noblest of those equally daring and calculating statesmen-warriors whose two most terrible, most perfect, and most famous types are Louis XI. and Caesar Borgia. Gain, "commodity," the principle of self-interest, which never but in word and in jest could become the principle of action with Faulconbridge—himself already far more "a man of this world" than a Launcelot or a Hotspur,—is as evidently the mainspring of Henry's enterprise and life as of the contract between King Philip and King John. (pp. 111-12)

> *Algernon Charles Swinburne, "Second Period: Comic and Historic," in his* A Study of Shakespeare, *R. Worthington, 1880, pp. 66-169.*

EDWARD DOWDEN　(essay date 1881)

[*Dowden was an Irish critic and biographer whose* Shakespeare: A Critical Study of His Mind and Art *was the leading example of the biographical criticism popular in the English-speaking world near the end of the nineteenth century. Biographical critics sought in the plays and poems a record of Shakespeare's personal development. As that approach gave way in the twentieth century to aesthetic theories with greater emphasis on the constructed, artificial nature of literary works, Dowden and other biographical critics came to be considered limited. His remarks on* Henry IV, *like those of Jeremy Collier (1698), Samuel Johnson (1765), Hermann Ulrici (1839), G. G. Gervinus (1849-50), E. E. Stoll (1914), J. Dover Wilson (1943), and E.M.W. Tillyard (1944), place Hal at the center of the plays and justify the rejection of Falstaff. Dowden, however, contends that Hal is Shakespeare's ideal "in the sphere of practical achievement" rather than a representative of a general ideal of humanity.*]

Shakspere has judged Henry IV., and pronounced that his life was not a failure; still, it was at best a partial success. Shakspere saw, and he proceeded to show to others, that all which Bolingbroke had attained, and almost incalculably greater possession of good things, could be attained more joyously by nobler means. The unmistakable enthusiasm of the poet about his

Henry V. has induced critics to believe that in him we find Shakspere's ideal of manhood. He must certainly be regarded as Shakspere's ideal of manhood in the sphere of practical achievement—the hero and central figure, therefore, of the historical plays.

The fact has been noticed that with respect to Henry's youthful follies, Shakspere deviated from all authorities known to have been accessible to him. "An extraordinary conversion was generally thought to have fallen upon the Prince on coming to the crown—insomuch that the old chroniclers could only account for the change by some miracle of grace or touch of supernatural benediction." Shakspere, it would seem, engaged now upon historical matter, and not the fantastic substance of a comedy, found something incredible in the sudden transformation of a reckless libertine (the Henry described by Caxton, by Fabyan, and others) into a character of majestic force and large practical wisdom. Rather than reproduce this incredible popular tradition concerning Henry, Shakspere preferred to attempt the difficult task of exhibiting the Prince as a sharer in the wild frolic of youth, while at the same time he was holding himself prepared for the splendid entrance upon his manhood, and stood really aloof in his inmost being from the unworthy life of his associates.

The change which effected itself in the Prince, as represented by Shakspere, was no miraculous conversion, but merely the transition from boyhood to adult years, and from unchartered freedom to the solemn responsibilities of a great ruler. We must not suppose that Henry formed a deliberate plan for concealing the strength and splendor of his character, in order, afterwards, to flash forth upon men's sight, and overwhelm and dazzle them. When he soliloquizes (*1 Henry IV.*, act i., sc. 2), having bidden farewell to Poins and Falstaff,

> I know you all, and will awhile uphold
> The unyoked humor of your idleness:
> Yet herein will I imitate the sun,
> Who doth permit the base contagious clouds
> To smother up his beauty from the world,
> That, when he please again to be himself,
> Being wanted, he may be more wondered at,
> By breaking through the foul and ugly mists
> Of vapors, that did seem to strangle him.
> 　　　　　　　　　　　　[*1 Henry IV*, I. ii. 195-203]

—when Henry soliloquizes thus, we are not to suppose that he was quite as wise and diplomatical as he pleased to represent himself, for the time being, to his own heart and conscience. The Prince entered heartily, and without reserve, into the fun and frolic of his Eastcheap life; the vigor and the folly of it were delightful; to be clapped on the back, and shouted for as "Hal," was far better than the doffing of caps and crooking of knees, and delicate, unreal phraseology of the court. But Henry, at the same time, kept himself from subjugation to what was really base. He could truthfully stand before his father (*1 Henry IV.*, act iii., sc. 2) and maintain that his nature was substantially sound and untainted, capable of redeeming itself from all past, superficial dishonor.

Has Shakspere erred? Or is it not possible to take energetic part in a provisional life which is known to be provisional, while, at the same time, a man holds his truest self in reserve for the life that is best and highest and most real? May not the very consciousness, indeed, that such a life is provisional enable one to give one's self away to it, satisfying its demands with scrupulous care, or with full and free enjoyment, as a man could not if it were a life which had any chance of engaging his whole personality, and that finally? Is it possible to adjust two states of being, one temporary and provisional, the other absolute and final, and to pass freely out of one into the other? Precisely because the one is perfect and indestructible, it does not fear the counterlife. May there not have been passages in Shakspere's own experience which authorized him in his attempt to exhibit the successful adjustment of two apparently incoherent lives?

The central element in the character of Henry is his noble realization of fact. To Richard II., life was a graceful and shadowy ceremony, containing beautiful and pathetic situations. Henry IV. saw in the world a substantial reality, and he resolved to obtain mastery over it by courage and by craft. But while Bolingbroke, with his caution and his policy, his address and his ambition, penetrated only a little way among the facts of life, his son, with a true genius for the discovery of the noblest facts, and of all facts, came into relation with the central and vital forces of the universe, so that, instead of constructing a strong but careful life for himself, life breathed through him, and blossomed into a glorious enthusiasm of existence. And, therefore, from all that was unreal, and from all exaggerated egoism, Henry was absolutely delivered. A man who firmly holds, or, rather, is held by, the beneficent forces of the world, whose feet are upon a rock, and whose goings are established, may with confidence abandon much of the prudence and many of the artificial proprieties of the world. For every unreality Henry exhibits a sovereign disregard—for unreal manners, unreal glory, unreal heroism, unreal piety, unreal warfare, unreal love. The plain fact is so precious it needs no ornament.

From the coldness, the caution, the convention, of his father's court (an atmosphere which suited well the temperament of John of Lancaster), Henry escapes to the teeming vitality of the London streets, and the tavern where Falstaff is monarch. There, among hostlers, and carriers, and drawers, and merchants, and pilgrims, and loud robustious women, he at least has freedom and frolic. "If it be a sin to covet honor," Henry declares, "I am the most offending soul alive." But the honor that Henry covets is not that which Hotspur is ambitious after:

> By heaven, methinks it were an easy leap
> To pluck bright honor from the pale-faced moon.
> [*1 Henry IV*, I. iii. 201-02]

The honor that Henry covets is the achievement of great deeds, not the words of men which vibrate around such deeds. Falstaff, the despiser of honor, labors across the field, bearing the body of the fallen Hotspur, the impassioned pursuer of glory, and, in his fashion of splendid imposture or stupendous joke, the fat Knight claims credit for the achievement of the day's victory. Henry is not concerned, on this occasion, to put the old sinner to shame. To have added to the deeds of the world a glorious deed is itself the only honor that Henry seeks. Nor is his heroic greatness inconsistent with the admission of very humble incidents of humanity:

> *Prince*. Doth it not show vilely in me to desire small beer?
> *Poins*. Why, a prince should not be so loosely studied as to remember so weak a composition.
> *Prince*. Belike, then, my appetite was not princely got; for, by my troth, I do now remember the poor creature, small beer. But indeed these humble considerations make me out of love with my greatness.

[*2 Henry IV*, II. ii. 5-12]

Henry, with his lank frame and vigorous muscle (the opposite of the Danish Prince, who is "fat, and scant of breath"), is actually wearied to excess, and thirsty—and he is by no means afraid to confess the fact; his appetite, at least, has not been pampered. (pp. 186-91)

The same noble and disinterested loyalty to the truth of things renders it easy, natural, and indeed inevitable that Henry should confirm in his office the Chief-justice who had formerly executed the law against himself; and equally inevitable that he should disengage himself absolutely from Falstaff and the associates of his provisional life of careless frolic. To such a life an end must come; and, as no terms of half-acquaintance are possible with the fat knight, exorbitant in good-fellowship as he is, and inexhaustible in resources, Henry must become to Falstaff an absolute stranger:

> I know thee not, old man: fall to thy prayers:
> How ill white hairs become a fool and jester!
> [*2 Henry IV*, V. v. 47-8]

Henry has been stern to his former self, and turned him away forever; therefore he can be stern to Falstaff. There is no faltering. But at an enforced distance of ten miles from his person (for the fascination of Falstaff can hardly weave a bridge across that interval) Falstaff shall be sufficiently provided for. . . . (pp. 192-93)

> *Edward Dowden, "The English Historical Plays,"*
> *in his* Shakspere: A Critical Study of His Mind and
> Art, *third edition, Harper & Brothers Publishers,*
> *1881, pp. 144-97.*

RICHARD GRANT WHITE (essay date 1885)

In ["King Henry IV." in its two parts], which, like "King John," are true "histories" as far as the treatment of their main incidents is concerned, and in the poetical parts of which an increased weight of thought and momentum of utterance is observable, with a freedom of versification required, and to a certain degree caused, by the former qualities, Shakespeare introduced for the first time a representation of English social life. It was the social life of his own day; for never was there less the spirit of a literary antiquarian than in William Shakespeare. (p. 29)

In "Henry IV." we have the highest manifestation of Shakespeare's humor; but not in Falstaff only, whose vast unctuosity of mind as well as body has, to the general eye, unjustly cast his companions into eclipse. Prince Hal himself is no less humorous than Falstaff, while his wit has a dignity and a sarcastic edge not observable in the fat knight's random and reckless sallies. Falstaff, however, is peerless in a great measure because he is reckless, and because Shakespeare, fully knowing the moral vileness of his creature, had yet, as a dramatist, a perfect intellectual indifference to the character of the personage by whom he effected his dramatic purpose. But besides these principals, the attendants upon their persons and the satellites of their blazing intellects, Pointz, Bardolph, Nym, Pistol, Mrs. Quickly, Justice Shallow, Silence, and the rest, form a group which for its presentation of the humorous side of life has never been equalled in literature. It surpasses even the best of "Don Quixote," as intellectual surpasses practical joking. This history, take it all in all, is the completest, although far from being the highest, exhibition of Shakespeare's varied powers as poet and dramatist. No other play shows his various faculties at the same time in such number and at such a height. The greatest Falstaff is that of the Second Part. He is in every trait the same as he of Part First; but his wit becomes brighter, his humor more delicate, richer in allusion, and more highly charged with fun; his impudence attains proportions truly heroic. (pp. 29-30)

> Richard Grant White, "On Reading Shakespeare," in his Studies in Shakespeare, *second edition, Houghton Mifflin and Company, 1886, pp. 1-57.*

BERNARD SHAW (essay date 1891)

[*Shaw, an Irish dramatist and critic, was the major English playwright of his generation. In his Shakespearean criticism, he consistently attacked what he considered to be Shakespeare's inflated reputation as a dramatist. Shaw did not hesitate to judge the characters in the plays by the standards of his own values and prejudices, and much of his commentary is presented—as the prominent Shaw critic Edwin Wilson once remarked—"with an impudence that had not been seen before, nor is likely to be seen again." Shaw's hostility towards Shakespeare's work was due in large measure to his belief that it was interfering with the acceptance of Henrik Ibsen and the new social theater he so strongly advocated. In the following excerpt, first published in his* The Quintessence of Ibsenism *in 1891, he questions the comedy of Shakespeare's debauched characters in* Henry IV, *and suggests in what ways the poet might have developed if he had written under different circumstances.*]

Falstaff is introduced as a subordinate stage figure with no other function than to be robbed by the Prince and Poins, who was originally meant to be the *raisonneur* of the piece, and the chief figure among the prince's dissolute associates. But Poins soon fades into nothing, like several characters in Dickens's early works; whilst Falstaff develops into an enormous joke and an exquisitely mimicked human type. Only in the end the joke withers. The question comes to Shakespear: *Is* this really a laughing matter? Of course there can be only one answer; and Shakespear gives it as best he can by the mouth of the prince become king, who might, one thinks, have the decency to wait until he has redeemed his own character before assuming the right to lecture his boon companion. Falstaff, rebuked and humiliated, dies miserably. His followers are hanged [in *Henry V*], except Pistol, whose exclamation "Old do I wax; and from my weary limbs honor is cudgelled" is a melancholy exordium to an old age of beggary and imposture.

But suppose Shakespear had begun where he left off! Suppose he had been born at a time when, as the result of a long propaganda of health and temperance, sack had come to be called alcohol, alcohol had come to be called poison, corpulence had come to be regarded as either a disease or a breach of good manners, and a conviction had spread throughout society that the practice of consuming "a half-pennyworth of bread to an intolerable deal of sack" was the cause of so much misery, crime, and racial degeneration that whole States prohibited the sale of potable spirits altogether, and even moderate drinking was more and more regarded as a regrettable weakness! Suppose (to drive the change well home) the women in the great theatrical centres had completely lost that amused indulgence for the drunken man which still exists in some out-of-the-way places, and felt nothing but disgust and anger at the conduct and habits of Falstaff and Sir Toby Belch! Instead of *Henry IV* and *The Merry Wives of Windsor*, we should have had something like Zola's *L'Assommoir*. Indeed, we actually have Cassio, the last of Shakespear's gentleman-drunkards, talking like a temperance reformer, a fact which suggests that

Shakespear had been roundly lectured for the offensive vulgarity of Sir Toby by some woman of refinement who refused to see the smallest fun in giving a knight such a name as Belch, with characteristics to correspond to it. Suppose, again, that the first performance of *The Taming of the Shrew* had led to a modern Feminist demonstration in the theatre, and forced upon Shakespear's consideration a whole century of agitatresses, from Mary Wollstonecraft to Mrs. Fawcett and Mrs. Pankhurst, is it not likely that the jest of Katharine and Petruchio would have become the earnest of Nora and Torvald Helmer? (pp. 106-07)

> Bernard Shaw, "'Henry IV, Part I'," in his Shaw on Shakespeare: An Anthology of Bernard Shaw's Writings on the Plays and Production of Shakespeare, *edited by Edwin Wilson, E. P. Dutton, Inc., 1961, pp. 101-07.*

BEVERLEY E. WARNER (essay date 1894)

[*Warner's* English History in Shakespeare's Plays *was an early attempt to demonstrate that a coherent historical vision could be discerned in Shakespeare's history plays. His contention that* Henry IV *depicts the overthrow of feudalism prefigures the twentieth-century commentaries of Sigurd Burckhardt (1966) and Alvin Kernan (1969), while his interpretation of Falstaff as a satire of decaying chivalry anticipates T. A. Jackson's argument that he represents a "grotesque parody" of the feudal state (see excerpt below, 1936). Warner also regards the English histories from* Richard II *to* Richard III *as a "great national epic," a claim which was also made by August Wilhelm Schlegel (1808), Hermann Ulrici (1839), and E.M.W. Tillyard (1944).*]

[In *Henry IV*,] Shakespeare paints the death throes of feudalism with a master hand. The shadow of its passing enshrouded the whole reign of the first Lancastrian. (p. 95)

Shakespeare invariably links together the five dramatic epochs of his great national epic, from *Richard II.* to *Richard III.*, by causing the titular hero to share our interest with his successor. In this way the figure of Bolingbroke casts a shadow forward from *Richard II.*, Prince Hal from *Henry IV.*, and Richard Gloster from *Henry VI.* It is as if to remind kings that in the evolution of affairs they must pass, while their kingdoms remain. This is one of the great and noble lessons which the poet-historian sought to teach. England was greater than any personage who might for the time rule or misrule from her throne. The royal policy of this or that sovereign might seem at any stage of national progress to be the one policy. But underneath the ripples of change, the surface commotions of man's passions and greed, the calm tide of nationalism rose and fell, obeying higher laws than the edicts of kings or parliaments.

From Canute downward, this tide has been controlled for men and not by men.

The delineation of the young Prince Hal in the first part of this play is thus not only a following out of the poetic and dramatic habit of Shakespeare, but is a logical necessity of the historical situation. (pp. 109-10)

Whatever his faults of personal ambition, [Henry IV] saw the evil that lay curled about the root of England's noblest development—the feudal system—and struck it such a deadly blow as finally destroyed it. The people first in his reign grew to look upon their king as their natural leader, rather than upon their feudal lords. It was a great step in advance, as transforming England from an aggregation of small camps each clustered about the pennon of some noted baron, into a powerful host under a common commander, to whom was owed supreme homage. (p. 123)

From a contemplation of the decline of feudalism under Henry, we turn to consider one important element in these two plays concerning which, in an historical study, we might seem to have little to say.

I have abstained from touching upon the comedy of the drama for two reasons: First, save in one particular, it has nothing to do with English history; second, it deserves a chapter entirely devoted to it, as the richest vein of Shakespeare's humour. In one particular, however, Falstaff and his ragged crew have a very vital connection with the phase of English history marked by the passing of feudalism. What Shakespeare always intended to accomplish by the introduction of specific characters, and the grouping of them, we may not be sure. What he did accomplish he that runs may read. (pp. 123-24)

Falstaff, Pistol, Bardolph, and all their horde of petty followers with loud braggadocio and easily pricked cowardice, are set forth as a travesty upon the highborn but pseudo-chivalry, then on its last legs, and destined soon to pass away entirely. Chivalry had lived its noblest long before. The thing that masqueraded under its name is roughly typified in Falstaff with his shrewd knavery, his animal appetite, his gross trading on the name and title of gentleman; above all, his self-admitted knowledge that he was in certain important ways a humbug. Hear him, for example, soliloquize on honor. But he is not the arrant coward and time server he would have us believe. He speaks here very much in the spirit of Falconbridge . . . , when he determines to make the "vile commodity" his god. In these words we may read a commentary on the boasted chivalry of the fourteenth century. It was a painted simulacrum of the fair original.

Observe too the attitude of Prince Hal toward these "lewd fellows of the baser sort," with whom he found his lot cast for a while. The careful reader of these plays will readily note that while the wild Prince was often in Eastcheap Tavern, he was never of it. He is banished by his own restlessness from the solemn ceremonies of his father's court. He has no part nor lot with his eminently proper and respectable brothers. He seeks in dissipation, which it will be noted is never more than reckless and indifferent, never vile, the change such natures amidst such surroundings have ever sought; more's the pity. But he looks on the antics of his pot-room companions with a heavy heart and forced smile, valuing them, and through them the shams they represent in higher quarters, at their true worth. (pp. 124-25)

[The casting off of Falstaff by Hal] is cruel as we read it, but it was the poetic way of marking a point in the evolution of Hal's character, which the careful reader perceives is taking place all along.

Falstaff is not a real character, but a personification of the reckless youth of the Prince, under which lay ripening the splendid potency of his manhood. No one of all Shakespeare's heroes grows under our eye as this one of Henry V. One stage marking the changing of the old order, is the banishment of Falstaff and his fellows from court. And yet there is a side to Falstaff which inevitably draws us to him. We see that the Prince must have cast him off, and that he considered his old age enough to provide a comfortable resting-place for the gray head. We hear of him but once again. It is this scene, probably, which causes sentiment to enter so deeply into our reading of the pseudo-knight's character. It is among roughs, and the message is borne by an outcast, but it is the death of Jack Falstaff, who "fumbled wi' the sheets, and played with flowers, and smiled upon his fingers' ends, and babbled o' green fields," and they said the "king has killed his heart."

So died the shadow of that once proud knighthood which was dying all about him; with now and then a flickering gleam of its old splendid spirit, and now and then a flaming up in the socket of its former glorious power, but passing because its time was past. New figures were on the stage. New scenes occupied them. England was rousing herself from the old lair of feudal tyranny, and shaking the mighty spears of her serried yeomanry, led as of old by the barons, loyal as not of old, first to the nation, and not to men whose quarrel might any time turn them against their king. And so came Henry of that name the Fifth to rule the sceptred isle of England, and to extend her sway again across the seas, bringing back from France a new kingdom at his girdle and a noble wife at his side. (pp. 129-30)

Beverley E. Warner, "'Henry IV'—The Passing of Feudalism," in his English History in Shakespeare's Plays, Longmans, Green, and Co., 1894, pp. 93-130.

GEORGE BRANDES   (essay date 1895-96)

[Brandes was a scholar and the most influential literary critic of late nineteenth-century Denmark. His William Shakespeare, first published in 1895-96, was translated and widely read in his day. A writer with a broad knowledge of literature, Brandes placed Shakespeare in a European context, comparing him with other important dramatists. While Brandes praises 1 Henry IV as "one of the great masterpieces of the world's literature," he considers Part Two a lesser work, and its Falstaff not the "glorious" creation of Part One. This conclusion was also reached by Richard Cumberland (1786) and Caroline F. E. Spurgeon (1935).]

[The First Part of Henry IV is] the play in which Shakespeare first attains his great and overwhelming individuality. At the age of thirty-three, he stands for the first time at the summit of his artistic greatness. In wealth of character, of wit, of genius, this play has never been surpassed. Its dramatic structure is somewhat loose, though closer knit and technically stronger than that of the Second Part. But, as a poetical creation, it is one of the great masterpieces of the world's literature, at once heroic and burlesque, thrilling and side-splitting. And these contrasted elements are not, as in Victor Hugo's dramas, brought into hard-and-fast rhetorical antithesis, but move and mingle with all the freedom of life.

When it was written, the sixteenth century, that great period in the history of the human spirit, was drawing to its close; but no one had then conceived the cowardly idea of making the end of a century a sort of symbol of decadence in energy and vitality. Never had the waves of healthy self-confidence and productive power run higher in the English people or in Shakespeare's own mind. Henry IV., and its sequel Henry V., are written throughout in a major key which we have not hitherto heard in Shakespeare, and which we shall not hear again.

Shakespeare finds the matter for these plays in Holinshed's Chronicle, and in an old, quite puerile play, The Famous Victories of Henry the fifth, conteining the Honorable Battell of Agin-court, in which the young Prince is represented as frequenting the company of roisterers and highway robbers. It was this, no doubt, that suggested to him the novel and daring

Part I. Act II. Scene iii. Prince Henry, Poins, Falstaff. Frontispiece to Rowe edition (1709). By permission of the Folger Shakespeare Library.

idea of transferring direct to the stage, in historical guise, a series of scenes from the everyday life of the streets and taverns around him, and blending them with the dramatised chronicle of the Prince whom he regarded as the national hero of England. To this blending we owe the matchless freshness of the whole picture. (pp. 175-76)

[G. Walter Thornbury, in his *Shakespeare's England,*] has aptly remarked that the characteristic of the Elizabethan age was its sociability. People were always meeting at St. Paul's, the theatre, or the tavern. Family intercourse, on the other hand, was almost unknown; women, as in ancient Greece, played no prominent part in society. The men gathered at the tavern club to drink, talk, and enjoy themselves. (p. 177)

At the taverns, writers and poets met in good fellowship, and carried on wordy wars, battles of wit, sparkling with mirth and fantasy. They were like tennis-rallies of words, in which the great thing was to tire out your adversary; they were skirmishes in which the combatants poured into each other whole volleys of conceits. (p. 178)

Among the members of the circle which Shakespeare in his youth frequented, there must, of course, have been types of every kind, from the genius down to the grotesque; and there were some, no doubt, in whom the genius and the grotesque,

the wit and the butt, must have quaintly intermingled. As every great household had at that time its *jester,* so every convivial circle had its clown or buffoon. The jester was the terror of the kitchen—for he would steal a pudding the moment the cook's back was turned—and the delight of the dinner-table, where he would mimic voices, crack jokes, play pranks, and dissipate the spleen of the noble company. The comic man of the tavern circle was both witty himself and the cause of wit in others. He was always the butt of the others' merriment, yet he always held his own in the contest, and ended by getting the best of his tormentors. (pp. 178-79)

In his close-woven and unflagging mirthfulness, in the inexhaustible wealth of drollery concentrated in his person, Falstaff surpasses all that antiquity and the Middle Ages have produced in the way of comic character, and all that the stage of later times can show. (p. 179)

In the century after he came into existence, Spain and France each developed its own theatre. In France there is only one quaint and amusing person, Moron in Molière's *La Princesse d'Élide,* who bears some faint resemblance to Falstaff. In Spain, where the great and delightful character of Sancho Panza affords the starting-point for the whole series of comic figures in the works of Calderon, the *Gracioso* stands in perpetual contrast to the hero, and here and there reminds us for a moment of Falstaff, but always only as an abstraction of one side or another of his nature, or because of some external similarity of situation. (pp. 179-80)

Nevertheless there is among Shakespeare's predecessors a great writer, one of the greatest, with whom we cannot but compare him; to wit, Rabelais, the master spirit of the early Renaissance in France. He is, moreover, one of the few great writers with whom Shakespeare is known to have been acquainted. . . .

If we compare Falstaff with Panurge, we see that Rabelais stands to Shakespeare in the relation of a Titan to an Olympian god. Rabelais is gigantic, disproportioned, potent, but formless. Shakespeare is smaller and less excessive, poorer in ideas, though richer in fancies, and moulded with the utmost firmness of outline. (p. 180)

[Falstaff] was, as it were, the wine-god of merry England at the meeting of the centuries. Never before or since has England enjoyed so many sorts of beverages. There was ale, and all other kinds of strong and small beer, and apple-drink, and honey-drink, and strawberry-drink, and three sorts of mead (meath, metheglin, hydromel), and every drink was fragrant of flowers and spiced with herbs. (pp. 182-83)

There were fifty-six varieties of French wine in use, and thirty-six of Spanish and Italian, to say nothing of the many home-made kinds. But among the foreign wines none was so famous as Falstaff's favourite sherris-sack. It took its name from Xeres in Spain, but differed from the modern sherry in being a sweet wine. It was the best of its kind, possessing a much finer bouquet than sack from Malaga or the Canary Islands (Jeppe paa Bjergets, "Canari-Saek"), although these were stronger and sweeter. Sweet as it was too, people were in the habit of putting sugar into it. The English taste has never been very delicate. Falstaff always put sugar into his wine. Hence his words when he is playing the Prince while the Prince impersonates the king (Pt. First, ii.4):—"If sack and sugar be a fault, God help the wicked." He puts not only sugar but toast in his wine: "Go fetch me a quart of sack, put a toast in it" (*Merry Wives,* iii. 5). On the other hand, he does not like (as others did) to have it mulled with eggs: "Brew me a pottle of sack . . . simple of itself; I'll no pullet-sperm in my brewage'' (*Merry Wives,* iii. 5). And no less did he resent its sophistication with lime, an ingredient which the vintners used to increase its strength and make it keep: "You rogue, here's lime in this sack, too. . . . A coward is worse than a cup of sack with lime in it" (I. *Henry IV.,* ii.4). Falstaff is as great a wine-knower and wine-lover as Silenus himself. But he is infinitely more than that.

He is one of the brightest and wittiest spirits England has ever produced. He is one of the most glorious creations that ever sprang from a poet's brain. There is much rascality and much genius in him, but there is no trace of mediocrity. He is always superior to his surroundings, always resourceful, always witty, always at his ease, often put to shame, but, thanks to his inventive effrontery, never put out of countenance. He has fallen below his social position; he lives in the worst (though also in the best) society; he has neither soul, nor honour, nor moral sense; but he sins, robs, lies, and boasts, with such splendid exuberance, and is so far above any serious attempt at hypocrisy, that he seems unfailingly amiable whatever he may choose to do. Therefore he charms every one, although he is a butt for the wit of all. He perpetually surprises us by the wealth of his nature. He is old and youthful, corrupt and harmless, cowardly and daring, "a knave without malice, a liar without deceit; and a knight, a gentleman, and a soldier, without either dignity, decency, or honour." [See excerpt above by Maurice Morgann, 1777.] The young Prince shows good taste in always and in spite of everything seeking out his company. (pp. 183-84)

But if he has not been led astray, neither is he the "abominable misleader of youth" whom Prince Henry, impersonating the King, makes him out to be. For to this character there belongs malicious intent, of which Falstaff is innocent enough. It is unmistakable, however, that while in the First Part of *Henry IV.* Shakespeare keeps Falstaff a purely comic figure, and dissipates in the ether of laughter whatever is base and unclean in his nature, the longer he works upon the character, and the more he feels the necessity of contrasting the moral strength of the Prince's nature with the worthlessness of his early surroundings, the more is he tempted to let Falstaff deteriorate. In the Second Part his wit becomes coarser, his conduct more indefensible, his cynicism less genial; while his relation to the hostess, whom he cozens and plunders, is wholly base. In the First Part of the play he takes a whole-hearted delight in himself, in his jollifications, his drolleries, his exploits on the highway, and his almost purposeless mendacity; in the Second Part he falls more and more under the suspicion of making capital out of the Prince, while he is found in ever worse and worse company. The scheme of the whole, indeed, demands that there shall come a moment when the Prince, who has succeeded to the throne and its attendant responsibilities, shall put on a serious countenance and brandish the thunderbolts of retribution.

But here, in the First Part, Falstaff is still a demi-god, supreme alike in intellect and in wit. With this figure the popular drama which Shakespeare represented won its first decisive battle over the literary drama which followed in the footsteps of Seneca. We can actually hear the laughter of the ''yard'' and the gallery surging around his speeches like waves around a boat at sea. It was the old sketch of Parolles in *Love's Labour's Won* . . . , which had here taken on a new amplitude of flesh and blood. There was much to delight the groundlings—Falstaff is so fat and yet so mercurial, so old and yet so youthful in all his tastes

and vices. But there was far more to delight the spectators of higher culture, in his marvellous quickness of fence, which can parry every thrust, and in the readiness which never leaves him tongue-tied, or allows him to confess himself beaten. Yes, there was something for every class of spectators in this mountain of flesh, exuding wit at every pore, in this hero without shame or conscience, in this robber, poltroon, and liar, whose mendacity is quite poetic, Münchausenesque, in this cynic with the brazen forehead and a tongue as supple as a Toledo blade. (pp. 184-85)

Clothed in renown, and ever more insatiate of military honour, [Hotspur] is proud from independence of spirit and truthful out of pride. He is a marvellous figure as Shakespeare has projected him, stammering, absent, turbulent, witty, now simple, now magniloquent. His hauberk clatters on his breast, his spurs jingle at his heel, wit flashes from his lips, while he moves and has his being in a golden nimbus of renown.

Individual as he is, Shakespeare has embodied in him the national type. From the crown of his head to the sole of his foot, Hotspur is an Englishman. He unites the national impetuosity and bravery with sound understanding; he is English in his ungallant but cordial relation to his wife; in the form of his chivalry, which is Northern, not Romanesque; in his Viking-like love of battle for battle's and honour's sake, apart from any sentimental desire for a fair lady's applause.

But Shakespeare's especial design was to present in him a master-type of manliness. He is so profoundly, so thoroughly a man that he forms the one counterpart in modern poetry to the Achilles of the Greeks. Achilles is the hero of antiquity, Henry Percy of the Middle Ages. The ambition of both is entirely personal and regardless of the common weal. For the rest, they are equally noble and high-spirited. The one point on which Hotspur is inferior to the Greek demigod is that of free naturalness. His soul has been cramped and hardened by being strapped into the harness of the feudal ages. Hero as he is, he is at the same time a soldier, obliged and accustomed to be over-bold, forced to restrict his whole activity to feuds and fights. He cannot weep like Achilles, and he would be ashamed of himself if he could. He cannot play the lyre like Achilles, and he would think himself bewitched if he could be brought to admit that music sounded sweeter in his ears than the baying of a dog or the mewing of a cat. He compensates for these deficiencies by the unyielding, restless, untiring energy of his character, by the spirit of enterprise in his manly soul, and by his healthy and amply justified pride. It is in virtue of these qualities that he can, without shrinking, sustain comparison with a demigod.

So deep are the roots of Hotspur's character. Eccentric in externals, he is at bottom typical. The untamed and violent spirit of feudal nobility, the reckless and adventurous activity of the English race, the masculine nature itself in its uncompromising genuineness, all those vast and infinite forces which lie deep under the surface and determine the life of a whole period, a whole people, and one half of humanity, are at work in this character. Elaborated to infinitesimal detail, it yet includes the immensities into which thought must plunge if it would seek for the conditions and ideals of a historic epoch.

But in spite of all this, Henry Percy is by no means the hero of the play. He is only the foil to the hero, throwing into relief the young Prince's unpretentious nature, his careless sporting with rank and dignity, his light-hearted contempt for all conventional honour, all show and appearance. Every garland with which Hotspur wreathes his helm is destined in the end to deck the brows of Henry of Wales. (pp. 192-93)

[The Second Part of *Henry IV.* and *Henry V.*] are not to be compared with this First Part of *Henry IV.*, which in its day made so great and well-deserved a success. It presented life itself in all its fulness and variety, great typical creations and figures of racy reality, which, without standing in symmetrical antithesis or parallelism to each other, moved freely over the boards where a never-to-be-forgotten history was enacted. Here no fundamental idea held tyrannical sway, forcing every word that was spoken into formal relation to the whole; here nothing was abstract. No sooner has the rebellion been hatched in the royal palace than the second act opens with a scene in an inn-yard on the Dover road. It is just daybreak; some carriers cross the yard with their lanterns, going to the stable to saddle their horses; they hail each other, gossip, and tell each other how they have passed the night. Not a word do they say about Prince Henry or Falstaff; they talk of the price of oats, and of how "this house is turned upside down since Robin ostler died." Their speeches have nothing to do with the action; they merely sketch its locality and put the audience in tune for it; but seldom in poetry has so much been effected in so few words. The night sky, with Charles's Wain "over the new chimney," the flickering gleam of the lanterns in the dirty yard, the fresh air of the early dawn, the misty atmosphere, the mingled odour of damp peas and beans, of bacon and ginger, all comes straight home to our senses. The situation takes hold of us with all the irresistible force of reality. (p. 198)

> *George Brandes, in his* William Shakespeare, *translated by William Archer, Mary Morison, and Diana White, Heinemann, 1920, 721 p.*

BERNARD SHAW   (essay date 1896)

[*This essay was first published in* The Saturday Review, *London, in 1896.*]

Everything that charm of style, rich humor, and vivid natural characterization can do for a play are badly wanted by *Henry IV,* which has neither the romantic beauty of Shakespear's earlier plays nor the tragic greatness of the later ones. One can hardly forgive Shakespear quite for the worldly phase in which he tried to thrust such a Jingo hero as his Harry V down our throats. The combination of conventional propriety and brute masterfulness in his public capacity with a low-lived black-guardism in his private tastes is not a pleasant one. No doubt he is true to nature as a picture of what is by no means uncommon in English society, an able young Philistine inheriting high position and authority, which he holds on to and goes through with by keeping a tight grip on his conventional and legal advantages, but who would have been quite in his place if he had been born a gamekeeper or a farmer. We do not in the first part of *Henry IV* see Harry sending Mrs. Quickly and Doll Tearsheet to the whipping-post, or handing over Falstaff to the Lord Chief Justice with a sanctimonious lecture; but he repeatedly makes it clear that he will turn on them later on, and that his self-indulgent good-fellowship with them is consciously and deliberately treacherous. His popularity, therefore, is like that of a prizefighter: nobody feels for him as for Romeo or Hamlet. Hotspur, too, though he is stimulating as ginger cordial is stimulating, is hardly better than his horse; and King Bolingbroke, preoccupied with his crown exactly as a miser is preoccupied with his money, is equally useless as a refuge for our affections, which are thus thrown back un-

divided on Falstaff, the most human person in the play, but none the less a besotted and disgusting old wretch. And there is neither any subtlety nor (for Shakespear) much poetry in the presentation of all these characters. They are labelled and described and insisted upon with the roughest directness; and their reality and their humor can alone save them from the unpopularity of their unlovableness and the tedium of their obviousness. Fortunately, they offer capital opportunities for interesting acting. Bolingbroke's long discourse to his son on the means by which he struck the imagination and enlisted the snobbery of the English people gives the actor a chance comparable to the crafty early scenes in Richelieu. Prince Hal's humor is seasoned with sportsmanlike cruelty and the insolence of conscious mastery and contempt to the point of occasionally making one shudder. Hotspur is full of energy; and Falstaff is, of course, an unrivalled part for the right sort of comedian. Well acted, then, the play is a good one in spite of there not being a single tear in it. Ill acted—O heavens! (pp. 101-03)

> *Bernard Shaw, "'Henry IV, Part I'," in his* Shaw on Shakespeare: An Anthology of Bernard Shaw's Writings on the Plays and Production of Shakespeare, *edited by Edwin Wilson, E. P. Dutton & Co., Inc., 1961, pp. 101-07.*

W. B. YEATS   (essay date 1901)

[*Yeats, an Irish poet, dramatist, and essayist, is considered one of the greatest poets of the modern era. He was prompted to write the following essay in 1901 after reviewing the collection in the library of the Shakespeare Institute at Stratford-upon-Avon. He discusses the way in which Shakespearean criticism has "become a vulgar worshipper of success" by making heroes out of figures like Hal, whom Yeats finds to be "gross" and "coarse." In particular, he refers to Edward Dowden (1881) as one of the most prominent critics who have transformed the prince into an "ideal" of humanity. Yeats contrasts Hal unfavorably with Richard II, characterizing the successful monarch and soldier as a "vessel of clay" and the deposed Richard as a "vessel of porcelain." For other critical appraisals of Hal's character, see the excerpts by William Hazlitt (1817), A. C. Bradley (1902), H. B. Charlton (1935), and Harold C. Goddard (1951).*]

[William] Blake has said that 'the roaring of lions, the howling of wolves, the raging of the stormy sea, and the destructive sword are portions of Eternity, too great for the eye of man,' but Blake belonged by right to the ages of Faith, and thought the State of less moment than the Divine Hierarchies. Because reason can only discover completely the use of those obvious actions which everybody admires, and because every character was to be judged by efficiency in action, Shakespearian criticism became a vulgar worshipper of success. I have turned over many books in the library at Stratford-on-Avon, and I have found in nearly all an antithesis, which grew in clearness and violence as the century grew older, between two types, whose representatives were Richard II., 'sentimental,' 'weak,' 'selfish,' 'insincere,' and Henry V., 'Shakespeare's only hero.' These books took the same delight in abasing Richard II. that school-boys do in persecuting some boy of fine temperament, who has weak muscles and a distaste for school games. And they had the admiration for Henry V. that school-boys have for the sailor or soldier hero of a romance in some boys' paper. I cannot claim any minute knowledge of these books, but I think that these emotions began among the German critics, who perhaps saw something French and Latin in Richard II., and I know that Professor Dowden, whose book I once read carefully, first made these emotions eloquent and plausible.

He lived in Ireland, where everything has failed, and he meditated frequently upon the perfection of character which had, he thought, made England successful, for, as we say, 'cows beyond the water have long horns.' He forgot that England, as Gordon has said, was made by her adventurers, by her people of wildness and imagination and eccentricity; and thought that Henry V., who only seemed to be these things because he had some commonplace vices, was not only the typical Anglo-Saxon, but the model Shakespeare held up before England; and he even thought it worth while pointing out that Shakespeare himself was making a large fortune while he was writing about Henry's victories. In Professor Dowden's successors this apotheosis went further; and it reached its height at a moment of imperialistic enthusiasm, of ever-deepening conviction that the commonplace shall inherit the earth, when somebody of reputation, whose name I cannot remember, wrote that Shakespeare admired this one character alone out of all his characters. (pp. 107-09)

To pose character against character was an element in Shakespeare's art, and scarcely a play is lacking in characters that are the complement of one another, and so, having made the vessel of porcelain Richard II., he had to make the vessel of clay Henry V. He makes him the reverse of all that Richard was. He has the gross vices, the coarse nerves, of one who is to rule among violent people, and he is so little 'too friendly' to his friends that he bundles them out of doors when their time is over. He is as remorseless and undistinguished as some natural force, and the finest thing in his play is the way his old companions fall out of it broken-hearted or on their way to the gallows; and instead of that lyricism which rose out of Richard's mind like the jet of a fountain to fall again where it had risen, instead of that phantasy too enfolded in its own sincerity to make any thought the hour had need of, Shakespeare has given him a resounding rhetoric that moves men, as a leading article does to-day. His purposes are so intelligible to everybody that everybody talks of him as if he succeeded, although he fails in the end, as all men great and little fail in Shakespeare. . . . (p. 113)

> W. B. Yeats, "At Stratford-on-Avon," in his Ideas of Good and Evil, A. H. Bullen, 1903, pp. 99-116.

A. C. BRADLEY   (essay date 1902)

[*Bradley is a major Shakespearean critic whose work culminated the method of character analysis initiated in the Romantic era. He is best known for his* Shakespearean Tragedy, *a close analysis of* Hamlet, Othello, King Lear, *and* Macbeth. *Bradley concentrated on Shakespeare as a dramatist, and particularly on his characters, excluding not only the biographical questions so prominent in the works of his immediate predecessors but also the questions of poetic structure, symbolism, and thematics which became prominent in later criticism. He thus may be seen as a pivotal figure in the transition in Shakespearean studies from the nineteenth to the twentieth century. He has been a major target for critics reacting against Romantic criticism, but he has continued to be widely read to the present day. Bradley's "The Rejection of Falstaff," first published in 1902 in* The Fortnightly Review, *is an important work in the history of* Henry IV *criticism, epitomizing the concept that Falstaff is a major character who transcends the plays in which he appears and that Hal's rejection of him was heartless. Bradley acknowledges that Maurice Morgann (1777) influenced his interpretation of Falstaff, a gesture which greatly enhanced Morgann's reputation in the twentieth century. For other so-called pro-Morgann assessments of Falstaff's character, see the excerpts by William Hazlitt (1817), Charles Cowden Clark (1863), J. B. Priestley (1925), Louis Cazamian*

(1934), H. B. Charlton (1935), J.I.M. Stewart (1948), and Roy Battenhouse (1975). Bradley's ideas have been explicitly attacked or questioned by E. E. Stoll (1914), John Webster Spargo (1922), J. Dover Wilson (1943), John F. Danby (1949), and Samuel Hemingway (1952).]

What are our feelings during [the scene of Falstaff's rejection]? They will depend on our feelings about Falstaff. If we have not keenly enjoyed the Falstaff scenes of the two plays, if we regard Sir John chiefly as an old reprobate, not only a sensualist, a liar, and a coward, but a cruel and dangerous ruffian, I suppose we enjoy his discomfiture and consider that the King has behaved magnificently. But if we *have* keenly enjoyed the Falstaff scenes, if we have enjoyed them as Shakespeare surely meant them to be enjoyed, and if, accordingly, Falstaff is not to us solely or even chiefly a reprobate and ruffian, we feel, I think, during the King's speech, a good deal of pain and some resentment; and when, without any further offence on Sir John's part, the Chief Justice returns and sends him to prison, we stare in astonishment. These, I believe, are, in greater or less degree, the feelings of most of those who really enjoy the Falstaff scenes (as many readers do not). Nor are these feelings diminished when we remember the end of the whole story, as we find it in *Henry V.*, where we learn that Falstaff quickly died, and, according to the testimony of persons not very sentimental, died of a broken heart. (p. 251)

[What] troubles us is not only the disappointment of Falstaff, it is the conduct of Henry. It was inevitable that on his accession he should separate himself from Sir John, and we wish nothing else. It is satisfactory that Sir John should have a competence, with the hope of promotion in the highly improbable case of his reforming himself. And if Henry could not trust himself within ten miles of so fascinating a companion, by all means let him be banished that distance: we do not complain. These arrangements would not have prevented a satisfactory ending: the King could have communicated his decision, and Falstaff could have accepted it, in a private interview rich in humour and merely touched with pathos. But Shakespeare has so contrived matters that Henry could not send a private warning to Falstaff even if he wished to, and in their public meeting Falstaff is made to behave in so infatuated and outrageous a manner that great sternness on the King's part was unavoidable. And the curious thing is that Shakespeare did not stop here. If this had been all we should have felt pain for Falstaff, but not, perhaps, resentment against Henry. But two things we do resent. Why, when this painful incident seems to be over, should the Chief Justice return and send Falstaff to prison? Can this possibly be meant for an act of private vengeance on the part of the Chief Justice, unknown to the King? No; for in that case Shakespeare would have shown at once that the King disapproved and cancelled it. It must have been the King's own act. This is one thing we resent; the other is the King's sermon. He had a right to turn away his former self, and his old companions with it, but he had no right to talk all of a sudden like a clergyman; and surely it was both ungenerous and insincere to speak of them as his 'misleaders,' as though in the days of Eastcheap and Gadshill he had been a weak and silly lad. We have seen his former self, and we know that it was nothing of the kind. He had shown himself, for all his follies, a very strong and independent young man, deliberately amusing himself among men over whom he had just as much ascendency as he chose to exert. Nay, he amused himself not only among them, but at their expense. In his first soliloquy—and first soliloquies are usually significant—he declares that he associates with them in order that, when at some future time he shows his true character, he may be the more wondered at for his previous aberrations. You may think he deceives himself here; you may believe that he frequented Sir John's company out of delight in it and not merely with this cold-blooded design; but at any rate he *thought* the design was his one motive. And, that being so, two results follow. He ought in honour long ago to have given Sir John clearly to understand that they must say good-bye on the day of his accession. And, having neglected to do this, he ought not to have lectured him as his misleader. It was not only ungenerous, it was dishonest. It looks disagreeably like an attempt to buy the praise of the respectable at the cost of honour and truth. And it succeeded. Henry *always* succeeded.

You will see what I am suggesting, for the moment, as a solution of our problem. I am suggesting that our fault lies not in our resentment at Henry's conduct, but in our surprise at it; that if we had read his character truly in the light that Shakespeare gave us, we should have been prepared for a display both of hardness and of policy at this point in his career. And although this suggestion does not suffice to solve the problem before us, I am convinced that in itself it is true. Nor is it rendered at all improbable by the fact that Shakespeare has made Henry, on the whole, a fine and very attractive character, and that here he makes no one express any disapprobation of the treatment of Falstaff. For in similar cases Shakespeare is constantly misunderstood. His readers expect him to mark in some distinct way his approval or disapproval of that which he represents; and hence where *they* disapprove and *he* says nothing, they fancy that he does *not* disapprove, and they blame his indifference, like Dr. Johnson [see excerpt above, 1765], or at the least are puzzled. But the truth is that he shows the fact and leaves the judgment to them. (pp. 253-55)

Both as prince and as king [Henry] is deservedly a favourite, and particularly so with English readers, being, as he is, perhaps the most distinctively English of all Shakespeare's men. . . . [He] has been described as Shakespeare's ideal man of action; nay, it has even been declared that here for once Shakespeare plainly disclosed his own ethical creed, and showed us his ideal, not simply of a man of action, but of a man.

But Henry is neither of these. The poet who drew Hamlet and Othello can never have thought that even the ideal man of action would lack that light upon the brow which at once transfigures them and marks their doom. . . . Nor is it merely that his nature is limited: if we follow Shakespeare and look closely at Henry, we shall discover with the many fine traits a few less pleasing. Henry IV. describes him as the noble image of his own youth; and, for all his superiority to his father, he is still his father's son, the son of the man whom Hotspur called a 'vile politician.' Henry's religion, for example, is genuine, it is rooted in his modesty; but it is also superstitious—an attempt to buy off supernatural vengeance for Richard's blood; and it is also in part political, like his father's projected crusade. Just as he went to war [in *Henry V.*] chiefly because, as his father told him, it was the way to keep factious nobles quiet and unite the nation, so when he adjures the Archbishop to satisfy him as to his right to the French throne, he knows very well that the Archbishop *wants* the war, because it will defer and perhaps prevent what he considers the spoliation of the Church. This same strain of policy is what Shakespeare marks in the first soliloquy in *Henry IV.*, where the prince describes his riotous life as a mere scheme to win him glory later. It implies that readiness to use other people as means to his own ends which is a conspicuous feature in his father; and it reminds

us of his father's plan of keeping himself out of the people's sight while Richard was making himself cheap by his incessant public appearances. (pp. 256-58)

Thus I would suggest that Henry's conduct in his rejection of Falstaff is in perfect keeping with his character on its unpleasant side as well as on its finer; and that, so far as Henry is concerned, we ought not to feel surprise at it. And on this view we may even explain the strange incident of the Chief Justice being sent back to order Falstaff to prison (for there is no sign of any such uncertainty in the text as might suggest an interpolation by the players). Remembering his father's words about Henry, 'Being incensed, he's flint,' and remembering in *Henry V.* his ruthlessness about killing the prisoners when he is incensed, we may imagine that, after he had left Falstaff and was no longer influenced by the face of his old companion, he gave way to anger at the indecent familiarity which had provoked a compromising scene on the most ceremonial of occasions and in the presence alike of court and crowd, and that he sent the Chief Justice back to take vengeance. And this is consistent with the fact that in the next play we find Falstaff shortly afterwards not only freed from prison, but unmolested in his old haunt in Eastcheap, well within ten miles of Henry's person. His anger had soon passed, and he knew that the requisite effect had been produced both on Falstaff and on the world.

But all this, however true, will not solve our problem. It seems, on the contrary, to increase its difficulty. For the natural conclusion is that Shakespeare *intended* us to feel resentment against Henry. And yet that cannot be, for it implies that he meant the play to end disagreeably; and no one who understands Shakespeare at all will consider that supposition for a moment credible. No; he must have meant the play to end pleasantly, although he made Henry's action consistent. And hence it follows that he must have intended our sympathy with Falstaff to be so far weakened when the rejection-scene arrives that his discomfiture should be satisfactory to us; that we should enjoy this sudden reverse of enormous hopes (a thing always ludicrous if sympathy is absent); that we should approve the moral judgment that falls on him; and so should pass lightly over that disclosure of unpleasant traits in the King's character which Shakespeare was too true an artist to suppress. Thus our pain and resentment, if we feel them, are wrong, in the sense that they do not answer to the dramatist's intention. But it does not follow that they are wrong in a further sense. They may be right, because the dramatist has missed what he aimed at. And this, though the dramatist was Shakespeare, is what I would suggest. In the Falstaff scenes he overshot his mark. He created so extraordinary a being, and fixed him so firmly on his intellectual throne, that when he sought to dethrone him he could not. The moment comes when we are to look at Falstaff in a serious light, and the comic hero is to figure as a baffled schemer; but we cannot make the required change, either in our attitude or in our sympathies. We wish Henry a glorious reign and much joy of his crew of hypocritical politicians, lay and clerical; but our hearts go with Falstaff to the Fleet, or, if necessary, to Arthur's bosom or wheresomever he is. (pp. 258-60)

Falstaff's ease and enjoyment are not simply those of the happy man of appetite [see excerpt above by William Hazlitt, 1817]; they are those of the humorist, and the humorist of genius. Instead of being comic to you and serious to himself, he is more ludicrous to himself than to you; and he makes himself out more ludicrous than he is, in order that he and others may laugh. Prince Hal never made such sport of Falstaff's person as he himself did. It is *he* who says that his skin hangs about him like an old lady's loose gown, and that he walks before his page like a sow that hath o'erwhelmed all her litter but one. And he jests at himself when he is alone just as much as when others are by. It is the same with his appetites. The direct enjoyment they bring him is scarcely so great as the enjoyment of laughing at this enjoyment; and for all his addiction to sack you never see him for an instant with a brain dulled by it, or a temper turned solemn, silly, quarrelsome, or pious. The virtue it instils into him, of filling his brain with nimble, fiery, and delectable shapes—this, and his humorous attitude towards it, free him, in a manner, from slavery to it; and it is this freedom, and no secret longing for better things (those who attribute such a longing to him are far astray), that makes his enjoyment contagious and prevents our sympathy with it from being disturbed.

The bliss of freedom gained in humour is the essence of Falstaff. His humour is not directed only or chiefly against obvious absurdities; he is the enemy of everything that would interfere with his ease, and therefore of anything serious, and especially of everything respectable and moral. For these things impose limits and obligations, and make us the subjects of old father antic the law, and the categorical imperative, and our station and its duties, and conscience, and reputation, and other people's opinions, and all sorts of nuisances. I say he is therefore their enemy; but I do him wrong; to say that he is their enemy implies that he regards them as serious and recognises their power, when in truth he refuses to recognise them at all. They are to him absurd; and to reduce a thing *ad absurdum* is to reduce it to nothing and to walk about free and rejoicing. This is what Falstaff does with all the would-be serious things of life, sometimes only by his words, sometimes by his actions too. (pp. 261-63)

No one in the play understands Falstaff fully, any more than Hamlet was understood by the persons round him. They are both men of genius. Mrs. Quickly and Bardolph are his slaves, but they know not why. 'Well, fare thee well,' says the hostess whom he has pillaged and forgiven; 'I have known thee these twenty-nine years, come peas-cod time, but an honester and truer-hearted man—well, fare thee well.' Poins and the Prince delight in him; they get him into corners for the pleasure of seeing him escape in ways they cannot imagine; but they often take him much too seriously. Poins, for instance, rarely sees, the Prince does not always see, and moralising critics never see, that when Falstaff speaks ill of a companion behind his back, or writes to the Prince that Poins spreads it abroad that the Prince is to marry his sister, he knows quite well that what he says will be repeated, or rather, perhaps, is absolutely indifferent whether it be repeated or not, being certain that it can only give him an opportunity for humour. (pp. 263-64)

The main source, then, of our sympathetic delight in Falstaff is his humorous superiority to everything serious, and the freedom of soul enjoyed in it. But, of course, this is not the whole of his character. Shakespeare knew well enough that perfect freedom is not to be gained in this manner; we are ourselves aware of it even while we are sympathising with Falstaff; and as soon as we regard him seriously it becomes obvious. His freedom is limited in two main ways. For one thing he cannot rid himself entirely of respect for all that he professes to ridicule. He shows a certain pride in his rank: unlike the Prince, he is haughty to the drawers, who call him a proud Jack. He is not really quite indifferent to reputation. . . . [And] he has

affection in him—affection, I think, for Poins and Bardolph, and certainly for the Prince; and that is a thing which he cannot jest out of existence. Hence, as the effect of his rejection shows, he is not really invulnerable. And then, in the second place, since he is in the flesh, his godlike freedom has consequences and conditions; consequences, for there is something painfully wrong with his great toe; conditions, for he cannot eat and drink for ever without money, and his purse suffers from consumption, a disease for which he can find no remedy. . . . And so he is driven to evil deeds; not only to cheating his tailor like a gentleman, but to fleecing Justice Shallow, and to highway robbery, and to cruel depredations on the poor woman whose affection he has secured. All this is perfectly consistent with the other side of his character, but by itself it makes an ugly picture.

Yes, it makes an ugly picture when you look at it seriously. But then, surely, so long as the humorous atmosphere is preserved and the humorous attitude maintained, you do not look at it so. You no more regard Falstaff's misdeeds morally than you do the much more atrocious misdeeds of Punch or Reynard the Fox. You do not exactly ignore them, but you attend only to their comic aspect. This is the very spirit of comedy, and certainly of Shakespeare's comic world, which is one of make-believe, not merely as his tragic world is, but in a further sense—a world in which gross improbabilities are accepted with a smile, and many things are welcomed as merely laughable which, regarded gravely, would excite anger and disgust. The intervention of a serious spirit breaks up such a world, and would destroy our pleasure in Falstaff's company. Accordingly through the greater part of these dramas Shakespeare carefully confines this spirit to the scenes of war and policy, and dismisses it entirely in the humorous parts. Hence, if *Henry IV.* had been a comedy like *Twelfth Night,* I am sure that he would no more have ended it with the painful disgrace of Falstaff than he ended *Twelfth Night* by disgracing Sir Toby Belch.

But *Henry IV.* was to be in the main a historical play, and its chief hero Prince Henry. In the course of it his greater and finer qualities were to be gradually revealed, and it was to end with beautiful scenes of reconciliation and affection between his father and him, and a final emergence of the wild Prince as a just, wise, stern, and glorious King. Hence, no doubt, it seemed to Shakespeare that Falstaff at last must be disgraced, and must therefore appear no longer as the invincible humorist, but as an object of ridicule and even of aversion. And probably also his poet's insight showed him that Henry, as he conceived him, *would* behave harshly to Falstaff in order to impress the world, especially when his mind had been wrought to a high pitch by the scene with his dying father and the impression of his own solemn consecration to great duties.

This conception was a natural and a fine one; and if the execution was not an entire success, it is yet full of interest. Shakespeare's purpose being to work a gradual change in our feelings towards Falstaff, and to tinge the humorous atmosphere more and more deeply with seriousness, we see him carrying out this purpose in the Second Part of *Henry IV.* Here he separates the Prince from Falstaff as much as he can, thus withdrawing him from Falstaff's influence, and weakening in our minds the connection between the two. In the First Part we constantly see them together; in the Second (it is a remarkable fact) only once before the rejection. Further, in the scenes where Henry appears apart from Falstaff, we watch him growing more and more grave, and awakening more and more poetic interest; while Falstaff, though his humour scarcely flags to the end, exhibits more and more of his seamy side. (pp. 269-72)

Yet all these excellent devices fail. They cause us momentary embarrassment at times when repellent traits in Falstaff's character are disclosed; but they fail to change our attitude of humour into one of seriousness, and our sympathy into repulsion. And they were bound to fail, because Shakespeare shrank from adding to them the one device which would have ensured success. If, as the Second Part of *Henry IV.* advanced, he had clouded over Falstaff's humour so heavily that the man of genius turned into the Falstaff of the *Merry Wives*, we should have witnessed his rejection without a pang. This Shakespeare was too much of an artist to do—though even in this way he did something—and without this device he could not succeed. As I said, in the creation of Falstaff he overreached himself. He was caught up on the wind of his own genius, and carried so far that he could not descend to earth at the selected spot. It is not a misfortune that happens to many authors, nor is it one we can regret, for it costs us but a trifling inconvenience in one scene, while we owe to it perhaps the greatest comic character in literature. For it is in this character, and not in the judgment he brings upon Falstaff's head, that Shakespeare asserts his supremacy. To show that Falstaff's freedom of soul was in part illusory, and that the realities of life refused to be conjured away by his humour—this was what we might expect from Shakespeare's unfailing sanity, but it was surely no achievement beyond the power of lesser men. The achievement was Falstaff himself, and the conception of that freedom of soul, a freedom illusory only in part, and attainable only by a mind which had received from Shakespeare's own the inexplicable touch of infinity which he bestowed on Hamlet and Macbeth and Cleopatra, but denied to Henry the Fifth. (pp. 272-73)

> *A. C. Bradley, "The Rejection of Falstaff," in his* Oxford Lectures on Poetry, *Macmillan & Co Ltd, 1959, pp. 247-78.*

E. K. CHAMBERS (essay date 1906)

[Chambers occupies a transitional position in Shakespearean criticism, one which connects the biographical sketches and character analyses of the nineteenth century with the historical, technical, and textual criticism of the twentieth century. While a member of the education department of Oxford University, Chambers earned his reputation as a scholar with his multivolume works, The Medieval Stage *and* The Elizabethan Stage, *while he also edited* The Red Letter Shakespeare. *Chambers both investigated the purpose and limitations of each dramatic genre as Shakespeare presented it, and speculated on how the dramatist's work was influenced by contemporary historical issues and his frame of mind. In 1930, he completed his series on the Elizabethan stage with* William Shakespeare: A Study of Facts and Problems. *In it, Chambers collated biographical and historical data and interpreted the results in relation to Shakespeare's canon. In the following excerpt, written in 1906, he praises Shakespeare's characterization in* Henry IV, *particularly the portrait of Falstaff, whom Chambers regards as "a coward" and "a cheat." For a similar interpretation of Falstaff's character, see the excerpts by John Dryden (1668 and 1679), Samuel Johnson (1765), A. S. Pushkin (1836), Victor Hugo (1864), Leo Tolstoy (1906), E. E. Stoll (1914), L. C. Knights (1934), and Arthur Sewell (1951).]*

In *Henry the Fourth* chronicle history becomes little more than a tapestried hanging, dimly wrought with horsemen and footmen, in their alarums and their excursions, which serves as a background to groups of living personages, conceived in quite another spirit and belonging to a very different order of reality. Shakespeare set out in the beginning to tell of 'old, unhappy, far-off things, and battles long ago'; but he turned, with a growing mastery of realistic delineation and an unabated interest in all that lay before his eyes, to interpolate his narrative with scenes that bore no tincture of antiquity, and to show the very age and body of the time his form and pressure in vivid transcripts of contemporary life as it was lived from day to day in a Midland country-side or in the crowded streets of London town. Not since Chaucer painted, one by one, his pilgrims as they issued beneath the low archway of the Tabard in Southwark, had literature deigned to put upon record so ample a breadth of the varied web of English society. Here a group of carriers grumble to each other as they pack their horses by the light of a lanthorn in order to reach Charing-cross before nightfall. Here a leisurely country gentleman talks with his bailiff of the sowing of the headland with red wheat and the merits of a local dispute, or regales his friends with a last year's pippin and a dish of caraways in the quiet of his scented orchard. And in the narrow passages of an Eastcheap tavern drawers bustle to and fro scoring pints of bastard in the Half-Moon; Hostess Quickly gossips with Mistress Keech the butcher's wife, who has come in to borrow a mess of vinegar for a dish of prawns; and a gang of riotous youths, with a disreputable old knight in their midst, drink limed sack and profit by the attentions of Mistress Dorothy Tearsheet and her fellow-pagans, to the enlivening accompaniment of Sneak's noise.

In its turn all this revel of local colour and rapidly-shifting detail becomes the setting of a single great comic figure, and thereby the plays attain the unity, which their intermediate position in the dramatic cycle that begins with *Richard the Second* and ends with *Henry the Fifth* makes it difficult for them to accomplish in any other way. Instead of the dynamic unity of an emotional issue set and resolved in the course of the action, they have the static unity of a pervading humorous personality. Sir John Falstaff represents the top of Shakespeare's achievement in the creation of an immortal comic type. Individual in the fullest sense, since general characteristics meet and mingle in him as in a veritable creature of flesh and blood, he is none the less typical and symbolical in that these general characteristics reach in him their most complete and monumental expression. In such a figure literature provides a standard to which ever after we refer half-insensibly our judgments not only of art but of humanity. We none of us know a Falstaff; but we all of us know persons some at least of whose traits find in Falstaff their archetype and quintessence. Shakespeare never produced anything else quite so great as Falstaff and in the same vein. (pp. 118-20)

He is a sot, a lecher, a coward, a cheat, a braggart, and a hypocrite. And since it is by means of the visible and physical infirmities of frail humanity that farce most easily calls up the unquenchable guffaw, Falstaff is not only eternally thirsty, but also incredibly and ridiculously fat. (p. 121)

Comedy is differentiated from farce, not merely by the more temperate gusts of laughter which it awakes, but also by the fact that it calls the brain to its assistance, and finds material for its diversion, less in the visible infirmities of the body and soul of man than in the underlying inadequacies and inconsistencies of motive and ideal which a subtle psychological analysis lays bare. In the portrayal of Falstaff the moods of comedy and of farce are curiously interwoven. The comic spirit is busiest with him when he is aroused to an uneasy consciousness that his earthy mode of life requires some sort of justification. This justification generally takes the form of depreciation of other persons on whom he chooses to lay the responsibility for his degradation. . . . With characteristic impudence he upbraids Prince Henry himself. 'Thou hast done much harm upon me, Hal. God forgive thee for it! Before I knew thee, Hal, I knew nothing; and now am I, if a man should speak truly, little better than one of the wicked.' Or it is the 'costermonger times' that are out of joint, and simple virtue can hardly hold its own. 'In the state of innocency Adam fell; and what should poor Jack Falstaff do in the days of villainy?' An extra cup of sack readily works him up to the heights of self-pity. 'Go thy ways, old Jack; die when thou wilt! If manhood, good manhood, be not forgot upon the face of the earth, then am I a shotten herring. There live not three good men unhanged in England, and one of them is fat and grows old. God help the while! A bad world, I say!' All this is not wholly insincere. (pp. 123-24)

E. K. Chambers, "Henry the Fourth," in his Shakespeare: A Survey, Sidgewick & Jackson, Ltd., 1925, pp. 118-26.

LEO TOLSTOY   (essay date 1906)

[Tolstoy is regarded as one of the greatest novelists of world literature and an outstanding exponent of the realist style of fiction. His essay excerpted below is perhaps the most famous vituperative attack on Shakespeare ever written. The commentary concentrates on King Lear, but Falstaff is criticized as well. The eighteenth-century Russian writer A. S. Pushkin (1836) expressed a similar dislike of Shakespeare's character.]

"But Falstaff, the wonderful Falstaff," Shakespeare's eulogists will say, "of him, at all events, one can not say that he is not a living character, or that, having been taken from the comedy of an unknown author, it has been weakened."

Falstaff, like all Shakespeare's characters, was taken from a drama or comedy by an unknown author, written on a really living person, Sir John Oldcastle, who had been the friend of some duke. This Oldcastle had once been convicted of heresy, but had been saved by his friend the duke. But afterward he was condemned and burned at the stake for his religious beliefs, which did not conform with Catholicism. It was on this same Oldcastle that an anonymous author, in order to please the Catholic public, wrote a comedy or drama, ridiculing this martyr for his faith and representing him as a good-for-nothing man, the boon companion of the duke, and it is from this comedy that Shakespeare borrowed, not only the character of Falstaff, but also his own ironical attitude toward it. In Shakespeare's first works, when this character appeared, it was frankly called "Oldcastle," but later, in Elizabeth's time, when Protestantism again triumphed, it was awkward to bring out with mockery a martyr in the strife with Catholicism, and, besides, Oldcastle's relatives had protested, and Shakespeare accordingly altered the name of Oldcastle to that of Falstaff, also a historical figure, known for having fled from the field of battle at Agincourt.

Falstaff is, indeed, quite a natural and typical character; but then it is perhaps the only natural and typical character depicted by Shakespeare. And this character is natural and typical because, of all Shakespeare's characters, it alone speaks a language proper to itself. And it speaks thus because it speaks in that same Shakespearian language, full of mirthless jokes and unamusing puns which, being unnatural to all Shakespeare's

other characters, is quite in harmony with the boastful, distorted, and depraved character of the drunken Falstaff. For this reason alone does this figure truly represent a definite character. Unfortunately, the artistic effect of this character is spoilt by the fact that it is so repulsive by its gluttony, drunkenness, debauchery, rascality, deceit, and cowardice, that it is difficult to share the feeling of gay humor with which the author treats it. Thus it is with Falstaff. (pp. 68-70)

Leo Tolstoy, "Tolstoy on Shakespeare," in his Tolstoy on Shakespeare: A Critical Essay on Shakespeare, translated by V. Tchertkoff and I.F.M., Funk & Wagnalls, 1906, pp. 1-126.

C. F. TUCKER BROOKE   (essay date 1911)

[In this essay, Brooke, general editor of the Yale Shakespeare, discusses Henry IV in terms of Shakespeare's conception of responsible leadership. Brooke presents Hal as an ideal prince, whom Shakespeare created to contrast with Richard II and Henry IV. He thus follows in a tradition begun by August Wilhelm Schlegel (1808) and continued by G. G. Gervinus (1849-50), Edward Dowden (1881), E.M.W. Tillyard (1944), and John F. Danby (1949). For a dissenting view of Hal, see the excerpt by W. B. Yeats (1901).]

[Shakespeare's] "Henry IV" and "Henry V" plays form a closely connected series presenting a well-matured theory of royal responsibility and governmental ethics by means of their picture of the character evolution of a great national leader. It is the figure of the prince, as heir apparent, and as king, that gives unity and purpose to the trilogy—less, indeed, as the conventional dramatic hero who shapes the action, than as the ideal hypothetical type by which Shakespeare illustrates his philosophy of statecraft and kingship.

It can scarcely be doubted that the play of "Henry V," regularly announced in the Epilogue to "Henry IV, Part II," was definitely under contemplation when the first part of "Henry IV" was conceived. Indeed, an unnecessary allusion in the last act of "Richard II" (V,iii,1-22) to the young prince's "dissolute and desperate" character, through which Bolingbroke discerns "some sparks of better hope, which elder years May happily bring forth," makes it probable that the poet was already considering the dramatic portrayal of this figure. It may very reasonably be questioned, however, whether, when Shakespeare undertook, about 1596 or 1597, to follow up his study, in Richard II and Bolingbroke, of two imperfect and antagonistic monarchic types by a delineation of his ideal prince, he had any idea of devoting more than a single play to that prince's preparation for sovereignty and another to his triumphant reign. The second part of "Henry IV," like the second part of "Tamburlaine," seems to be an originally unpremeditated addition, occasioned by the enormous effectiveness of the by-figure of Falstaff. This genial character must have expanded in its development far beyond the limits at first intended for it, and thus necessitated the splitting of the political matter of Henry IV's reign, in itself hardly sufficient for a single drama, into two plays. The result is that the serious historical theme, which certainly represents the poet's primary conception, is continually being threatened with eclipse by the anachronistic comic scenes of sixteenth-century merriment and topical allusion. It is even true that the portrayal of the prince's preparation for government, besides being thus thrust into the background, is actually obscured by the division. The first play ends abruptly in order to leave scope for the second; yet much of the second part is notwithstanding a mere variation of material already used in the first; and the effect of the two parts when taken together is less that of steady dramatic progress than of march and counter-march. The great scenes, for example, which depict Falstaff's arrest at the suit of Dame Quickly and his impressment of soldiers in Gloucestershire (Part II, II, i; III, ii) are brilliant amplifications of suggestions more hastily and prodigally thrown out in the first part [III,iii,54-174; IV,ii]. Naturally, the tendency to repetition is yet more striking in the historical scenes, where actual scantiness of material could less readily be eked out by imagination. Virtually everything necessary to fit the Henry IV plays for their original purpose as preliminary to a drama on the reign of Henry V is accomplished in the first part. The triumph of the prince's nobler aspirations over the attractions of dissolute company, his reconciliation with his father, and the supreme vindication of his heroic valor in the overthrow of Hotspur are here complete. The play needs only scenes indicating the King's death and the final dismissal of Falstaff to stand forth as we may suspect it was first designed, perfect in itself and a full induction to the treatment of the hero's triumphant reign. As it is, however, the demand for more Falstaff scenes brings the prince back among his old irresistible but unedifying companions with a sudden revulsion which, after the exalted strain on which the first part ends, makes his character appear a little weak. Again he loses his father's confidence, and has this time to regain it by means of declamation rather than action. Meantime, the memory of the laurels won from Hotspur at Shrewsbury—an episode intended surely as the prelude which should usher in the wars of France and introduce the conqueror of Agincourt—grows dim through long unmartial acts where the prince appears but seldom, and the reader's attention follows the chicaneries of Northumberland and Prince John or the equally irrelevant knaveries of Falstaff.

There will hardly be found a critic to wish for one play of "Henry IV" instead of two. Falstaff is assuredly as great a favorite with the universal modern public as he seems to have been with Shakespeare and Queen Elizabeth. But it is necessary to consider the degree in which this most tremendous of comic figures probably affected Shakespeare's treatment of history, in order to gauge the intention of the political scenes in "Henry IV" and to understand the reason in part also for his abrupt cutting off in the pure history play of "Henry V." Had Falstaff been dealt with as summarily as Mercutio in "Romeo and Juliet," the trilogy we are considering would have lost immeasurably in human interest, but surely it would have gained in homogeneity. As matters stand, the student of the individual plays is almost certain, in reading either of the first two, to be diverted from the state of Plantagenet England to Shakespeare's Gloucestershire and the streets of contemporary London. Yet when the entire series is viewed comprehensively, as it should be, it is not difficult to see the lesson which the poet read behind the progress of events, and which he has here intended to enforce. The moral of the three Henry V plays is that which Shakespeare has strongly expressed elsewhere: the responsibility of the ruler both to his subjects and to higher power. This feeling inspires everywhere Shakespeare's repugnance to anything amateurish in government, whether expressed in the mob-rule of Jack Cade and the Roman rabble or in the anointed incapacity of Richard II. But though he shows clearly that Richard II deserved to fall, he emphasizes no less strongly, in the prophecies of the Bishop of Carlisle and Richard himself, and in the continual misery of the crowned Bolingbroke, that an equal scourge afflicts him who by any indirection seizes the royal burden with him who seeks to escape it. "Henry IV" paints the gradual development in the young prince of the ideals

of kingly service, capacity, justice, and patriotic fervor which Shakespeare demanded of the monarch; and "Henry V" is a triumphant finale, to be considered, not separately, but in closest connection with the study in character building which it immediately followed and completed. As "Richard II" and "Henry IV" both demonstrate the punishment of those who trifle with royalty, so this play pictures the enormous possibilities of personal glory and national service within the reach of that ruler who performs unshrinkingly and thoroughly the full duties of justly assumed dominion. (pp. 333-36)

> C. F. Tucker Brooke, "The History Play," in his *The Tudor Drama: A History of English National Drama to the Retirement of Shakespeare,* Houghton Mifflin Company, 1911, pp. 297-351.*

ELMER EDGAR STOLL   (essay date 1914)

[*Stoll was one of the earliest critics to attack the method of character analysis that had dominated nineteenth-century Shakespearean criticism. Instead, he maintained that Shakespeare was primarily a man of the professional theater and that his works had to be interpreted in the light of Elizabethan stage conventions and understood for their theatrical effects, rather than their psychological insight. Stoll has in turn been criticized for seeing only one dimension of Shakespeare's art. The following essay on Falstaff exemplifies Stoll's approach. He attacks Maurice Morgann (1777) and A. C. Bradley (1902) as romantics who in their views of Falstaff mistook a stage illusion for an actual human being. Stoll claims that Falstaff is instead an example of a traditional stage type, the* miles gloriosus, *or "braggart soldier," from classical Latin comedy. For additional comment on Stoll's essay, see the excerpts by J.I.M. Stewart (1949) and Samuel Hemingway (1952), both of whom consider Stoll's approach to Shakespeare's characters as mechanical and overly simplified.*]

In Shakespeare criticism, as in most things Anglo-Saxon but sport, there has been little professionalism. The best as well as the worst of our scientists and artists have done their work without learning how to do it, and our critics, like our soldiers, have won their Waterloos on cricket fields. For two hundred and fifty years Englishmen and Americans have been writing about the character of Falstaff, and hardly three or four of these have been students of the stage. Since 1777 they have followed in the steps of Maurice Morgann, a country gentleman of philosophic bent and literary taste who seems to have known little of the acted drama and to have loved it less. . . . Time establishes institutions, not truth. . . . What might be called the external history of the drama has been explored, but technique has been neglected, and still anybody ventures to write on Shakespeare who has a style and taste. Few among these would appreciate the remark of Stevenson that to read a play is as difficult as to read musical score. And to read an old play is as difficult as to read old score.

Morgann reads like a true Romantic, and discovers in the effect of Falstaff upon us in the two Parts of *Henry IV* an opposition between feeling and the understanding. . . . At times the critic goes farther, and, in the faith that Shakespeare's characters are "essentially different from those of other writers," considers Falstaff as if he were an "historic rather than dramatic being," inquiring adventurously into his hopeful youth, his family, and his station, and inferring from these that he must have had the constitutional instincts of courage although he had lost the principles which ordinarily accompany them. (pp. 65-7)

Not only is Morgann strangely confused and contradictory in that, finding the circumstances creditable to Falstaff thrown into the background, and the "follies and the buffoonery" thrown into the foreground, he calls us, who attach greater importance to the latter, the dupes of our wisdom and systematic reasoning, but thus and otherwise he betrays a total misapprehension of dramatic method, whether of his own or of an earlier time. It is all too plain that he cannot read score. To him, as to many another philosopher and literateur, Shakespeare is not score to be played, but a book to be read; and a really great dramatist is one who dupes us, deliberately misplaces the emphasis, transcendentally baffles men's wits. Yet of all dramatists down to Dumas and Ibsen—and even of them—the contrary is the case. What is in the foreground is important; what is in the background is less important, and, in Shakespeare and the Elizabethans, often epically, rather than dramatically and psychologically, in keeping. And what stands first in the play, as the cowardly flight from Gadshill, is most important of all and dominates the whole. Besides these simple principles of dramatic emphasis and perspective, which in our discussion will constantly be illustrated, Morgann and his followers ignore the various hints of the poet as embodied in the established conventions of the time—the confessions in soliloquy, the comments and predictions of important undiscredited characters like the Prince and Poins, and various devices and bits of "business," like Falstaff's roaring as he runs and his falling flat in battle. All these are as much means of expression as the Elizabethan vocabulary of the text, and yet they are treated as if they had no fixed and definite meaning—as if, as someone has said, the book had dropped from the skies; and the playwright and his time vanish from his play. So far has this gone that, as we have seen, inquiry presses coolly by him to the character's lineage, financial and social experiences, and his past as a whole. It was but yesterday that an Elizabethan scholar contended that we had a right to do this, and that characters in plays, particularly in Shakespeare's were not unreal like statues and paintings. They can think, talk, and walk—they are bits of real life, not art!

On the principle that what is most prominent is most important surely there is no need to dwell: of art it is the beginning and end. . . . Falstaff is as much of a coward sprawling on Shrewsbury Field as running down Gadshill. What, then, do these facts mean? as Mr. Bradley asks after having detailed the "secret impressions". "Does Shakespeare put them all in with no purpose at all, or in defiance of his own intention?" He never defies his own intention, I suppose, save in the hands of us critics. The incongruities, as I hope presently to show, are either necessarily or traditionally involved in the type of the *miles gloriosus* which he is here undertaking to exhibit; or they are incidental to the current convention of the professional comic person on the stage; or else they are such contradictions and irrelevancies as Shakespeare, writing for the stage and not for the study, slips into continually, examples of which in one play have, with admirable discernment, been collected by Mr. Bradley himself [in his *Shakesperean Tragedy*].

Meantime we take it that, standing first, "this unfortunate affair" of Gadshill is *meant* to prejudice us. In itself it is an example of the old device of a practical joke on the stage, not disdained by Molière and Goldoni, Goldsmith and Sheridan, any more than by the Elizabethans, and in farce not extinct today. According to Elizabethan usage a foolish character—a braggart, or a coward, or a conceited ass like Malvolio, or even a merry misogynist like Benedick—is, by conspiracy, fooled to the top of his bent, and in the end made aware of it and jeered at. Of this there are many instances in the comedies of Shakespeare, as in those of Marston, Chapman, Dekker,

and the rest of the craft. Always the expectations of the practical jokers—as here in Falstaff's cowardly conduct and "incomprehensible lies"—are fulfilled, and the victim's ridiculous sayings and doings cast in his teeth. Sometimes he loses temper, like Malvolio and Benedick; sometimes he takes to his wits to cover his retreat, like Falstaff. But at the outset he steps into the trap laid for him, unawares. There is no instance of a character making a fool of himself on purpose—playing the coward on purpose and then playing the ludicrous braggart afterward. (pp. 68-71)

Falstaff's cowardice appears still more clearly when the Gadshill incident is viewed in detail. There is the testimony of the Prince, Poins, and Falstaff himself. Four times the Prince flatly calls him coward to his face. The only time Falstaff attempts to deny it—on Gadshill—the Prince replies, "Well, we leave that to the proof"; and it comes speedily. Poins's estimate of his character has been subjected to the most undramatic and hair-splitting comment imaginable. "Well, for two of them, I know them to be as true-bred cowards as ever turned back; and for the third, if he fight longer than he sees reason, I'll forswear arms" [Part I, I,ii,183-86]. Certainly the latter half of the sentence contains no praise, however faint; it is followed by the remark about "the incomprehensible lies that this same fat rogue will tell us." Here or anywhere Poins, or Shakespeare himself, is not the man to distinguish between conduct and character, principles and constitution, a coward and a courageously consistent Epicurean; and this can only be a case of understatement and irony. Falstaff himself admits that he was a coward on instinct [Part I, II,iv,272-73], and at Shrewsbury says to himself, "I fear the shot here," "I am afraid of this Percy," and makes his words good by stabbing the corpse. Against such an interpretation Morgann and his followers murmur, bidding us remember his age and his peculiar philosophy, the corrupting example of his associates, the odds against him, and the suddenness of the assault; but on the Elizabethan comic stage, or any popular stage, where of course there are no relentings toward cowardice (there being none even toward things beyond control, as cuckoldom, poverty, physical ugliness, or meanness of birth), nobody confesses to fear but a coward, a child, or a woman. All of Shakespeare's cowards, like his villains, bear their names written in their foreheads, and his true men, like Don Quixote in the eyes of Sancho, neither know nor understand what fear or dismay is. (pp. 72-3)

In the Second Part the "satyr, lecher, and parasite" in Falstaff are uppermost, and the captain rests on his laurels. But we all know how they were won, and cannot take to heart his reputation for valor with certain ladies of Eastcheap, Justice Shallow, or even the enemy at Shrewsbury and at Gaultree Forest. The effect of Dame Quickly's and Doll Tearsheet's praise of his prowess in stabbing and foining would be inconsiderable even if, with most of the English critics, including Professor Bradley himself, we failed to detect the palpable double entendre. (p. 77)

The famous soliloquy . . . on sack as the cause of all wit and valor, is the epilogue to the old reveller's military career and an epitome of his character. It is an old saw and familiar fact that wine makes cowards brave, and Falstaff speaks out (though behind his hand) when he says that men are but fools and cowards without it. (p. 78)

I have suggested that many of the "secret impressions of courage" are contradictions inherent in the type of the braggart captain. For to this type Falstaff unquestionably belongs. He has the increasing belly and decreasing leg, the diminutive page for a foil, the weapon (his pistol) that is no weapon, but a fraud, as well as most of the inner qualities of this ancient stage-figure—cowardice and outlandish bragging, gluttony and lechery, sycophancy and pride. Also he is a recruiting officer and (though in the *Merry Wives of Windsor*) a suitor gulled. All these traits are manifest, except his sycophancy, which appears in his dependence on the Prince and his cajoling ways with him; and except his pride, which appears in his insistence on his title on every occasion [Part II, II,ii,109-16], and in his reputation for a proud jack among the drawers. (pp. 79-80)

In the first scene in which he appears Falstaff falters in his jollity and vows that he will give over this life, being now little better than one of the wicked. "Where shall we take a purse tomorrow, Jack?" "Zounds!" he shouts, "where thou wilt, lad!" On a blue Monday at the Boar's Head he is for repenting once more as he moodily contemplates his wasting figure. Bardolph complains of his fretfulness. "Why, *there* is it. Come sing me a bawdy song; make me merry!" If in this he be self-conscious, how annoying and unnatural! Those numerous critics who to keep for Falstaff his reputation as a humorist have him here play a part, seem to do so at the expense of their own. It is not to be wondered at in Hegel and some few German critics that, with philosophy in their every thought, they should shake their heads at the unenlightenment of Aristophanes, and turning their backs on Shakespeare, Cervantes, and Molière should proclaim the highest species of humor to be intentional and conscious; but it is to be wondered at in Englishmen. What joke could be made of this equal to the unconscious comical effect of the old sensualist plunged in penitence, and spontaneously buoyed up again, as by a specific levity? "Peace, good Doll"—and here, too, he is not jesting but saying it with a shudder—"do not speak like a death's head; do not bid me remember mine end." The pith of the humor lies in the huge appetite for purses, or mirth, bursting in an instant the bonds of his penitence; just as it lies in his thirst swallowing up the memory that his lips are not yet dry. "Give me a cup of sack! I am a rogue if I drunk to-day!" He is as unconscious as inconsistency has been on the comic stage ever since—as Molière's philosopher who declaims against wrath and presently gives way to it, or the duennas of Steele and Sheridan, who deprecate love and marriage for their nieces at the moment when they seek it for themselves.

Naïve, then, as well as witty, and quite as much the cause of mirth in other men when he is least aware, Falstaff is less "incomprehensible" both in his lies and, as we shall presently see, in his conduct generally. His wit is expended, not in making himself ridiculous for the sake of a joke unshared and unuttered, but, by hook or by crook, in avoiding that. (pp. 88-9)

A coward, then, if ever there was one, has Falstaff a philosophy? Military freethinking has been attributed to him to lift the stigma on his name. Believing not in honor, he is not bound by it. And by the Germans [such as Ulrici and Gervinus, see excerpts above, 1839 and 1849-50] and Mr. Bradley, as we have remarked, the scope of his philosophy has been widened, and he has been turned into a practical Pyrrhonist and moral nihilist, to whom virtue is "a fig," truth absurd, and all the obligations of society stumbling-blocks and nuisances. In various ways, by the English and the Germans alike, he has been thought to deny and destroy all moral values and ideals of life, not only for his own but for our behoof. So in a certain sense he is inspired by principle—of an anarchistic sort—not void of it.

Only at one ideal—honor—does Falstaff seem to me to cavil, and that he is only shirking and dodging. How does he, as Mr. Bradley thinks, make truth absurd by lying; or law, by evading the attacks of its highest representative; or patriotism, by abusing the King's press and filling his pockets with bribes? Or matrimony (logic would not forbear to add) by consorting with Mistresses Ursula, Quickly, and Tearsheet, thus lifting us into an atmosphere of freedom indeed? It fairly makes your head turn to see a simple picaresque narrative like that of Panurge or Sir Toby Belch brought to such an upshot as that.

As it seems to me, his catechism on the battlefield and his deliverances on honor are to be taken not as coming from his heart of hearts but from his wits and to cover his shame. Like disreputable characters in mediaeval and Renaissance drama and fiction without number, he unconsciously gives himself away. His "philosophy" is but a shift and evasion, and in his catechism he eludes the calm of honor when put by his conscience just as he does when put by the Prince and Poins. When he declares discretion to be the better part of valor there is no more philosophy in him than in Panurge and the Franc Archier de Baignollet when they avow that they fear nothing but danger, or than in himself when he swears that instinct is a great matter, and purse-taking no sin but his vocation. When he cries "Give me life" and "I like not the grinning honor that Sir Walter hath," there is no more Pyrrhonism or Epicureanism in him than there is idealism when, in defending his choice of the unlikeliest men for his company, he cries, "Give me the spirit, Master Shallow," meaning, "give me the crowns and shillings, Mouldy and Bullcalf." Here as there, he only dodges and shuffles. As in his fits of remorse we have seen, he is not "dead to morality" or free from its claims; neither does he frankly oppose them, or succeed in "covering them with immortal ridicule"; but in sophistry he takes refuge from them and the ridicule rebounds on his own head. (pp. 96-7)

One reason why in [Falstaff's speech on honor], we fail to penetrate this mask of unrealistic and malicious portrayal and take his words to heart, is that they are in soliloquy. A man does not banter himself. But on the stage in those times and before them a man did, and all soliloquy is phrased more as if the character were addressing himself or the audience than as if he were thinking aloud. Hence in comic soliloquy allowances are to be made, just as later, when Falstaff holds forth on sack as the cause of valor, which is another underhand confession of cowardice, and when Benedick declares that the world must be peopled, which is a confession of a tenderer sort. It is an irony which touches the speaker, not the thing spoken of, and dissolves away not all the seriousness of life but the speaker's pretenses; it is the exposure, not the expression, of his "inmost self." When Falstaff seems to be talking principle, he is, as we now say, only "putting it mildly": in his own time he gave himself away; in ours he takes the learned in.

But the main reason for our failure to penetrate the mask is that in or out of soliloquy this particular method of dramatic expression is a thing outworn, outgrown. Characters are no longer driven to banter or expose themselves, or the better audiences resent it if they are. Psychology—born of sympathy—will have none of it, as a method too external, ill-fitting, double-tongued. If the person be taken to be consciously jesting—the widow about wedding while mourning, Falstaff about the vanity of honor . . .—he seems then and there to be out of character; yet it is hard to see how he can have been unconscious, either, and it is manifest that the author is more intent on the jest, or, in the case of Quickly above, on the double entendre, than on the main or philosophic drift;—and yet (once again) this self-consciousness and mirth surely do not imply, as in the writing of today they must needs imply, "freedom" or detachment, any measure of indifference or superiority to the pleasure of incontinently taking one's valet, keeping one's arms and legs whole, or sponging in bibulous sloth. The pith of the matter, then, is that the lines of the character are, for us, confused, the author seems to peer through and wink at the audience, and our modern sympathy and craving for reality are vexed and thwarted, somewhat as they are by the self-consciousness of the villains or by the butt-and-wit-in-one. Indeed, unless the character be taken to be unconscious, we seem here to have a case of butt-and-wit-in-one at one and the same moment. For these reasons this method of comic portrayal, which goes back at least to the Middle Ages, and occurs not only in Elizabethan comic drama but in the greatest comic drama since—in Congreve, Sheridan, not to mention Molière—has, like butt-and-wit-in-one or self-conscious villainy, been dropped by the modern spirit as a strange, ill-fitting garment, and, since Robertson and Gilbert, has been relegated to frank satire and farce.

How petty and personal Falstaff's philosophy is on the face of it! . . . It is the "grin" that he "likes not," and since the beginning of things no philosophy has been needed for that.

For Falstaff is simple as the dramatist and his times. By him the chivalric ideal is never questioned; Hotspur is comical only for his testiness, not for the extravagance and fanaticism of his derring-do. To some critics Falstaff seems a parody or burlesque of knighthood, and they are reminded of the contemporary Quixote and his Squire. But the only parallel or contrast between knight and clown suggested is on the battlefield, and there as in Calderon's comedies the ridicule is directed at the clown alone. In the story of Cervantes himself it is so; the chivalric ideal stands unchallenged, though the romantic and sentimental extravagances are scattered like the rear of darkness thin. Even by these Shakespeare is untroubled, and true to the spirit of the Renaissance all his heroes cherish their fame and worship glory. To him as to Molière and Cervantes himself Moron's confession that he had rather live two days in the world than a thousand years in history, would, even in less compromising circumstances, have seemed but clownish and craven, though to us it would seem neither, in our mystical adoration of life and indifference to fame. "Give me life!"—we sadly mistake the ascetic, stoical, chivalric principles, coming down from the earliest times through the Renaissance even to our own, if we fancy that in England or in Italy there were many who could keep a good conscience and say it. Romeo, Hamlet, Brutus, Othello and Desdemona, Antony and his queen, are, like the ancients, far from saying it, though only happiness, not honor, is at stake. The men of the Renaissance loved life because they had found it sweet, but—especially the Elizabethans—they had not learned to think much better of it than the world had thought before. They loved it as well as we, but not, like us, from principle and as a tenet of their faith.

As incapable as is Shakespeare (in the person of his heroes) of swerving from the conventional standard of honor himself, so incapable is he of comprehending those who swerve. For his clowns the standard is set as for his villains. Sometimes, indeed, though only as rebels, the villains set up a standard of their own, as when Iago asserts the supremacy of his will, calls virtue a fig and reputation an idle and most false imposition. But Falstaff is neither rebel nor critic. As clown he is supposed

to have neither philosophy nor anti-philosophy, being a comic contrast and appendate to the heroes and the heroic point of view. (pp. 101-03)

Mr. Bradley does not mind saying that he for one is glad that Falstaff ran away on Gadshill; . . . and Hazlitt, lost in sympathy with Falstaff in the blighting of his hopes at the succession, resentfully asserts that he was a better man than the Prince [see excerpt above, 1817]. That is, the character is lifted bodily out of the dramatist's reach. Falstaff is a rogue, and people cannot like him: twice Morgann protests that in order to be comical at all he must be "void of evil motive." Lying for profit and jesting for profit, the cheating and swindling of your unsophisticated admirers, gluttony, lechery, extortion, highway robbery, and cowardice—pray, what is funny about all these? Hence the profit has been turned to jest, the misdemeanors to make-believe. (p. 105)

For those who have not learned to think historically cannot stomach the picaresque. It matters not to them that nearly all the professional comic characters of Elizabethan drama, as of all drama before it, have a vein of roguery in them—Sir Toby as well as Autolycus, the Clown as well as the Vice; or that in those days high and low were rejoicing in the roguery romances, English, French, or Spanish. Yet these people delighted in Falstaff as unreservedly as does the Prince in the play. That they did not take him for an innocuous mimic and merrymaker numerous allusions in the seventeenth century . . . attest. And Hal loved him . . . not for his humor only but for his lies and deviltry. They had their notions of "a character" as we have ours. (pp. 105-06)

Morals and sentiments alike, in the lapse of time, obliterate humor. Laughter is essentially a *geste social,* as Meredith and Professor Bergson have truly told us; and the immediate and necessary inference, which no doubt they themselves would have drawn, is that it languishes when the tickled *mores* change. Much that was funny to the Elizabethans or to the court of the Grand Monarch has since become pathetic. . . . On the stage and in the study much of the comedy in Shakespeare and Molière has been smothered out of them from the Romantic Revival unto this day, and yet we smile at the Middle Ages Christianizing the classics. (pp. 107-08)

Elmer Edgar Stoll, "Falstaff," in Modern Philology,
Vol. XII, No. 4, October, 1914, pp. 65-108.

[C. F.] TUCKER BROOKE (essay date 1918)

[*Brooke's comparison of Iago with Falstaff is perhaps the most fully developed of several attempts to define a similarity between these two characters. For other comparative essays on the character of Falstaff, see the excerpts by Henry Mackenzie (1786), Samuel Taylor Coleridge (1810), and Wyndham Lewis (1927). Brooke's essay originally appeared in* The Yale Review *in 1918.*]

The coupling of Falstaff and Iago may seem bizarre, and their relation is indeed a kind of Jekyll-Hyde affair; but that Shakespeare saw a likeness seems capable of proof, and each throws welcome light upon the character of the other. We need not dwell long upon their more social aspects, since exigencies of plot, which multiplied scenes of jovial merrymaking almost to the point of fatty degeneration in the Falstaff plays, reduced to the minimum the treatment of the corresponding side of Iago. Yet it is clear that Iago, like Sir John, has heard the chimes at midnight and been merry twice and once. Only a seasoned habitué of the taverns could talk as he talks in the scene of the arrival at Cyprus and in the brawl scene, or sing as he sings:

> And let me the canakin clink, clink;
> And let me the canakin clink:
> A soldier's a man;
> Oh, man's life's but a span;
> Why, then, let a soldier drink.
>
> [*Othello*, II. iii. 69-73]

In Iago's intellectual attitude we find reminiscences of Falstaff's way of thinking, just as we find reminiscences of Brutus in Hamlet. Falstaff's famous words on honor are virtually paraphrased in Iago's definition of reputation. "O, I have lost my reputation!" cries the disgraced Cassio. "I have lost the immortal part of myself!" "As I am an honest man," answers Iago, "I thought you had received some bodily wound; there is more sense in that than in reputation. Reputation is an idle and most false imposition, oft got without merit and lost without deserving: you have lost no reputation at all, unless you repute yourself such a loser." (pp. 49-50)

Falstaff and Iago are indeed Shakespeare's two great studies in materialism. Mentally and morally, they are counterparts. That they affect us so differently is due to the difference between the comic and the tragic environment. Still more it is due to difference in age. Falstaff, with his load of years and flesh, is a static force. Taking his ease at his inn, he uses his caustic materialistic creed and his mastery of moral paradox but as a shield to turn aside the attacks of a more spiritual society. Iago has looked upon the world for only four times seven years. His philosophy is dynamic. It drives him to assume the offensive, to take up arms against what he thinks the stupidity of a too little self-loving world. The flame, which in Falstaff only warms and brightens, sears in Iago; but it is much the same kind of flame and it attracts the same kind of moths. One may even imagine with a mischievous glee the warping and charring of green wit which would have resulted if Prince Hal and Poins had fluttered about Falstaff when he too was twenty-eight and "not an eagle's talon in the waist."

Iago is no more a born devil than Falstaff. He too might have gone merrily on drinking and singing, consuming the substance of two generations of Roderigos, till he too waxed fat and inert and unequivocally comic. His diabolism is an accident, thrust upon him early in the play, when in seeking to convince Roderigo of his hate for Othello he convinces himself likewise, and suddenly finds himself over head and ears in the depths of his own egoism, vaguely conscious that he is being used for the devil's purposes but incapable either of shaping the direction or checking the progress of his drift. (p. 52)

Iago's ruin results from two by-products of his Falstaffian materialism. In the first place, the materialistic theory of life corrodes the imagination. In Iago's case, as in Falstaff's, it cuts its victim off from his future and ultimately severs his bond of sympathy with his fellows. It leaves him only the sorry garden patch of present personal sensation. (p. 53)

A natural corollary is that the materialist makes large and ever larger demands upon the present. Like the clown in Marlowe's *Faustus*, when he buys his shoulder of mutton so dear, he "had need have it well roasted and good sauce to it." Ennui grows constantly more unendurable and more unavoidable. Falstaff's life is a series of desperate escapes from boredom; it is for this that he joins the Gadshill party, that he volunteers for the wars. It is for this that he so carefully husbands Shallow: "I will devise matter enough out of this Shallow to keep Prince Harry

in continual laughter the wearing out of six fashions." And Falstaff thinks with rueful envy of the capacity of romantic youth for sensation: "O, it is much that a lie with a slight oath and a jest with a sad brow will do with a fellow that never had the ache in his shoulders!" (pp. 53-4)

> . . . What is a man,
> If his chief good and market of his time
> Be but to sleep and feed? A beast, no more.
>
> [*Hamlet*, IV. iv. 33-5]

Iago illustrates Hamlet's words. So, less luridly, does Falstaff, and the parallel may explain the poet's alleged harshness in the rejection of Falstaff by his king. But Falstaff's creator, as he brought Iago to a realization of Cassio's "daily beauty," gave sir John also at his death a glimpse of the ideal: "A' babbled of green fields." (p. 56)

> [C. F.] *Tucker Brooke, "The Romantic Iago," in his* Essays on Shakespeare and Other Elizabethans, *Archon Books, 1969, pp. 46-56.*

JOHN WEBSTER SPARGO   (essay date 1922)

[*In the following essay, Spargo takes issue with the anti-Hal, pro-Falstaff positions of William Hazlitt (1817) and A. C. Bradley (1902), whose emphasis on Falstaff as the central figure in* Henry IV *indicates what he considers to be a misreading of the plays. Instead, Spargo suggests that Falstaff represents the character of "Vice" from the traditional morality play, and Prince Hal acts the role of Everyman. Spargo's interpretation anticipates the findings of J. Dover Wilson (1943) and E.M.W. Tillyard (1944), both of whom claim that* Henry IV *embodies a "divine-right-of-kings" theory—with Hal representing the ideal king—and that the dramatic structure of the plays is based on the Everyman medieval morality drama, with Sir John manifesting elements of the vice figure.*]

An examination of the critical history of the two *Parts* of *King Henry the Fourth* reveals the fact that this play presents problems of interpretation only less interesting to Shakespearean criticism than those afforded by *Hamlet*.

These problems center about two situations in the play. The first occurs at the close of Scene ii, Act I, *Part One*, when Hal delivers the soliloquy accounting for his presence in an Eastcheap tavern. The other occurs a few lines before the end of *Part Two*, when the Chief Justice banishes Falstaff to the Fleet, with the consent of Falstaff's erstwhile boon-companion and fellow-roysterer, the newly-crowned King Henry V. (p. 119)

The modern reader, from Hazlitt on is more than likely to loathe Hal at once, at the very inception, almost, of the play, and this loathing has its effect later when one revolts at Hal's repudiation of the round knight. Up to the time of this soliloquy we enjoy Hal profoundly: he is a jolly, witty youth sowing his wild oats in a relatively harmless way, assisted by the most delightful and merry of companions. But in this soliloquy he exposes himself as the coldest, most calculating wretch at large. Our sympathy for Hal is gone; and as we lose it, our partisanship for Falstaff grows. (p. 120)

Professor Bradley, in his article on Falstaff agrees to a large extent with Hazlitt. . . . We are to imagine Shakespeare as busying himself devising some sort of a lame conclusion for a play in which he had so far lost sight of dramatic effectiveness, of character values, of the entire art of stagecraft, as to stress a subsidiary character to such an extent that he overshadows the protagonist. I am not one of those to whom it appears sacrilegious to accuse Shakespeare of committing errors. But to assume such blindness to fundamental dramatic principles on his part appears a trifle steep.

I know of but one other theory designed to account for this apparently paradoxical situation. *Henry IV* was written shortly after the Armada scare, during a period when English patriotism was at white heat. Shakespeare's audience came knowing the story of the play. They knew that Prince Hal would overcome his youthful habits and mature into England's hero-king. Therefore, no matter by what means this process was achieved, it would be satisfactory; they were obsessed by the divine-right-of-kings theory, and hence whatever Hal did must be right. In any case, the future of England depended upon Hal, so that any act of policy, anything on his part, would be countenanced because the audience felt it was all "for the good of England." Such an explanation has its plausible points, but I believe it is assuming too much to assert that an Elizabethan audience would be likely to allow historical propriety to supersede dramatic effectiveness; or, even if it were allowed, Shakespeare's skill as a dramatic artist would be gravely questioned. The contemporaneous popularity of the play would argue against this. It is certainly true that Shakespeare was very sensitive to popular taste. Would not the Elizabethans demand that their nation-hero Hal be depicted as favorably as possible? (pp. 123-24)

Having rejected the existing theories, I suggest that Falstaff be regarded as an emanation from the Vice of the Morality Plays. If we examine him from this point of view remarkable similarities may be observed. Considering him as the prototype of the Vice, we have the Chief Justice functioning as the Virtue, with Hal functioning as Mankind, or Humanum Genus, or Everyman; that is to say, as the Morality type for the human race. That this parallel is formal and allegorical, and was interpreted as such by the Elizabethans, I do not believe at all. But that there is a strong possibility that the Elizabethans perceived in Falstaff an emanation from the Vice I hope to show in the following pages.

The Morality Play was one of the chief forms of dramatic entertainment in England during the fifteenth and the first half of the sixteenth centuries. Although this is generally recognized, it is not so generally recognized that moralities continued to be published and performed until the end of Elizabeth's reign, if not later. (pp. 125-26)

The general plan of the purely allegorical Morality is briefly this: the type representing humanity in general is subject to two sets of influences, the good being represented by the Virtues, the bad by the Vices. At first the bad influences triumph; the Vices and Virtues have verbal clashes, in which the Vices' witty remarks generally gain the upper hand, while the Virtues retire discomfited, the type representing humanity going off stage in the company of the Vices to enjoy their pleasures. Later Man returns, this time more than willing to accept the advice of the Virtues. The Vices are in this second argument brought to submission; sometimes they are beaten, sometimes they retire to their subterranean residence with Tityvillus, sometimes, as remarked, some Virtue acts as a judge and executes sentence upon them for their crimes. (pp. 126-27)

If we examine the Chief Justice's speeches in the play, we find them all characterized by the same stilled tone of conscious virtue as that used by the types in the allegories; Falstaff's replies are of the disrespectful, profane variety usually indulged in by the Vice. (p. 129)

In *Part I* of *Henry IV* we see Falstaff having the better of the Chief Justice in every encounter. As the play progresses, Falstaff's superiority gradually diminishes until at the end the Chief Justice sends him to the Fleet.

In the earlier Moralities, the type representing humanity often became very impatient at the Virtue's exhortations, sometimes going so far as to beat him. Compare the incident when Hal strikes the Chief Justice.

As has been noticed, the Morality frequently ends with Man's complete reconciliation with the Virtue. At the conclusion of *Henry IV* the new king has announced his intention of retaining the Chief Justice in that capacity; and, paralleling the ancient Morality even more closely, he causes the Chief Justice to pass sentence on Falstaff.

How does this theory affect the interpretation of the play? Take the opening lines of Act I scene ii, *Part 1* where Hal and Falstaff first appear.

> *Fal.* Now, Hal, what time of the day is it, lad?
> *Prince.* Thou art so fat-witted, with drinking
> of old sack and unbuttoning thee after supper
> and sleeping upon benches after noon, that thou
> hast forgotten to demand that truly which thou
> wouldest truly know. What a devil hast thou to
> do with the time of day? Unless hours were
> cups of sacks, and minutes capons, and clocks
> the tongues of bawds, and dials the signs of
> leaping-houses, and the blessed sun himself a
> fair hot wench in flame-coloured taffeta, I see
> no reason why thou shouldest be so superfluous
> as to demand the time of the day.
>
> [*1 Henry IV*, I. ii. 1-12]

Imagine the effect of this opening speech upon an audience steeped in the tradition of the Morality, as sketched above. That it is vastly funny, we agree. But it is funny in the typical Vice way, with, of course, rich additions. It is low comedy, decidedly. That in itself would tend to recall the Vice to an audience so familiar with that type. But consider the words themselves. Look at them from the point of view which the audience almost certainly had: "Thou art so fat-witted, with drinking of old sack and unbuttoning thee after supper and sleeping upon benches after noon,—."

Whom would this call to the mind of a person thoroughly orientated in Morality usage, in church homiletics where the Seven Deadly Sins were as familiar as our common Enemy, but Gluttony? And, similarly, the reference in the last section would just as unfailingly cause an Elizabethan to think of Lechery. We can imagine the audience as leaning back with a sigh of satisfaction at the prospect of a few hours' entertainment afforded by a fat jovial knight who has two qualities capable of affording vast merriment. Yet, all the while, due to the strength of a tradition as strong as any of the Greek drama, they were subconsciously aware of the fact that this hilarious wretch was doomed to eventual banishment, simply because he was what he was—gluttony and lechery, in the flesh. Hal, on the other hand, the future governor of the realm, would be recognized at once as the parallel of Humanum Genus, in the toils of sin; and naturally their intellectual sympathy went out to him, while for the moment they devoted themselves completely to the enjoyment of the round knight's merriment.

There are further instances in the play which may be considered as more conclusive evidence:

Prince [speaking of Falstaff] . . . . that reverend vice, that grey iniquity, that father ruffian, that vanity in years?

Prince. That / villainous abominable misleader of youth, Falstaff, that old white-bearded Satan.

[*1 Henry IV,* II. iv. 453-54, 462-63]

"Vice," "Iniquity," "Satan," all would almost unquestionably have called to mind what I believe Falstaff was intended to be. (pp. 130-31)

With this theory in mind, the play takes its action in the most easily explicable manner in the world. Falstaff goes on, exercising his genial wiles upon the prince, and the prince continues to enjoy them, but all the while the audience reads between the lines to discern the widening gap between the two men, all the while Falstaff is becoming more and more of the flesh. (p. 132)

[At the rejection scene the] time had come for dramatic retribution. What else could Shakespeare have done other than show the complete humiliation of Falstaff? His audience would have rebelled at introducing "that horson round man" into the splendid King Henry V's court. The King's temptation has been triumphantly survived, the dramatic need for Falstaff is gone. Shakespeare did not kill Falstaff because he was "the better man of the two." He killed him because he was Vice, because death was the only fate compatible with poetic justice; Falstaff had sinned, sinned grievously, in that he had made the attempt

To smother up his beauty from the world.

(p. 133)

John Webster Spargo, "An Interpretation of Falstaff," in The Washington University Studies, *Vol. IX, No. 2, April, 1922, pp. 119-33.*

J. B. PRIESTLEY (essay date 1925)

[*Priestley concentrates on the minor comic characters in* Henry IV *and comments briefly in praise of Samuel Johnson (1765), Maurice Morgann (1777), and A. C. Bradley (1902) for their seminal essays on the character of Falstaff. He also criticizes G. G. Gervinus (1849-50) for his inability to perceive the essentially comic nature of Sir John.*]

With the exception of Hamlet, no character in literature has been more discussed than . . . Falstaff, who is, like Hamlet, a genius, fastening immediately upon the reader's imagination, living richly in his memory, and inviting comment and interpretation that varies with the personality and point of view of every new reader. So splendid is the progress of this great figure in the earlier part of the drama, when he bestrides all Cockaigne like a colossus, so strange and puzzling is his rejection by the new king, so melancholy his end, with a heart "fracted and corroborate," that he engages all our attention and interest, dwarfing everybody with whom he comes into contact. For this reason, the comic grotesques who form his circle and are his foils, Pistol, Bardolph, Hostess Quickly, Doll Tearsheet, Justice Shallow and his cousin, Silence, have hardly been noticed, although most of the comedy in the second part of *Henry IV.* is of their making. But though we would rather bask in the warmth and light of this great sun of humour, the fantastic little planets that revolve about it deserve some attention. We will leave Sir John in peace for a while, nodding over his tankard, and creep away to the anteroom where his friends and followers are assembled.

Bardolph, attendant to Sir John and corporal in his service, is not witty in himself, but he is certainly the cause that wit is in other men. His face is his fortune, for at sight of it the comic fancy takes wing. His famous nose, that everlasting bonfire which Falstaff says has saved him a thousand marks in links and torches, is for ever igniting gunpowder trails of comic metaphor. Such a nose is not cheaply burnished, and Falstaff contends that the sack Bardolph has drunk would have bought lights as cheap at the dearest chandler's in Europe; but Bardolph's nose, that salamander consuming the fire of sack, has not been an unprofitable investment. This is proved by the fact that Bardolph has been with his master two and thirty years, after first being hired or "bought" in St. Paul's churchyard, where masterless servants, usually bad ones, were to be had at that time. That he has served his master very faithfully there can be no doubt: it is he who supplies us with one of the most striking tributes to Falstaff's ascendancy over his companions and to his power of winning affection, for after his master's death it is he who cries: "Would I were with him, wheresome'er he is, either in Heaven or in Hell!"—a genuine cry this, for ever thrown in the blank face of the universe by bereaved humanity. (pp. 69-71)

But if Bardolph is good, his superior officer, Ancient Pistol, is even better. His character is that of the common tavern bully of the period, a fellow who tries to make up for his want of courage and ability by his boldness of address, a mad moustachio'd, loud-voiced craven, whose scars are the marks of pots hurled in tavern brawls and of public beatings. This is a character that brags and swaggers his way throughout Elizabethan comedy. . . . But Pistol differs from the other fellows of his class in the fact that he has a mode of speech all his own. Indeed, he is actually one of those comic characters that hardly pretend to real existence at all and are obviously nothing but grotesque shadows, figures from a comic day-dream. Pistol's type was common enough, but the Ancient himself is not of this world. He is a walking parody of dramatic high-falutin. . . . The comic *idea* in Pistol is very slight and is amply covered by what has been said above; it is his actual speeches themselves, which we could not possibly invent for him, that make him so funny; and for this reason there are many admirable persons, lacking the ability to taste, as it were, the absurdity of a phrase, who cannot enjoy Pistol. . . . When he tells Falstaff that he is now one of the greatest men in the realm, and Silence, emboldened by his wine, calls attention to goodman Puff of Barson, some dim rural idol of his, what could be more ludicrous than Pistol's tremendous "Puff! Puff in thy teeth, most recreant coward base!" or his retort upon a further interruption, this time in song, by Silence?—

Shall dunghill curs confront the Helicons?
And shall good news be baffled?
Then, Pistol, lay thy head in Furies' lap.

[*2 Henry IV,* V. iii. 104-06]

Nothing less than blank verse, and blank verse at its wildest, will satisfy Pistol in a moment of excitement. How he raves of "golden times, and happy news of price," of "Africa and golden joys"; and as he stands there under the apple trees raving, a whole school of drama is being parodied by this ragged grotesque. There is one common type of romantic literature that is summed up to perfection in the single question he addresses to Shallow: "Under which king, Besonian? speak or die." After the great collapse, Pistol marries Hostess Quickly (and we would give much to hear the phrases he used to assault that battered heart), goes to the French wars, there to steal and run away, and, like Bardolph, comes at last to a bad end. He is not a caricature of something in life, but of something in literature; his flesh is paper, and his blood ink. (pp. 72-6)

[Hostess Quickly] is the mother of a great line of comic Cockney landladies, charwomen, and the like, in her wandering but vehement speech, her absurd mispronunciations, her oscillation between a native delight in mirth and easy living and an equally innate desire for respectability and a good name in the parish. The type changes very little. Both she and Doll, and particularly Doll, who has forfeited all title to it, are lovers of respectability. Nothing could be truer to nature than Doll's shrill abuse of Pistol, the mere ensign, when his captain is present and willing. The whole scene, with the gross raillery of Falstaff and Doll (and Hostess Quickly's sentimental delight in it—"By my troth, this is the old fashion; you two never meet but you fall to some discord''); the pretended delicacy of the easy dames, with their mutual encouragement, two women among men; Doll's delight in Falstaff as a man of war; his lordly "What stuff wilt have a kirtle of''—the secretly delighted male; the whole scene of broad comedy through which there flickers, as a glance of firelight, a touch of natural unforced sentiment (Doll's "Come, I'll be friends with thee, Jack: thou art going to the wars; and whether I shall ever see thee again or no, there is nobody cares'' is masterly), is a creation of sheer genius, and lifts Shakespeare as high above his fellows as does any of his great tragic scenes, for they tried in play after play to make such scenes come to life and yet did nothing like this, seemingly thrown out carelessly. (pp. 77-8)

All these figures about Falstaff, comic as they are in themselves, chiefly serve as foils to him; they are the grotesque landscape lit up by the summer lightning of his wit and humour. Not one is a better foil than Justice Shallow. Except in years, he is everything that Falstaff is not. When they made Sir John, the gods dipped their hands deep in the stuff of creation, so that he overflows with everything that a man could have, short of virtue. . . . Shallow, his contemporary, is the shadow of a lenten breakfast, who, even in his youth, was "like a man made after supper of a cheese-paring,'' a forked radish, with a head fantastically carved upon it with a knife, and now that his wisp of a carcase and his wisp of a mind have entered into their winter, there is hardly anything left of him but a few bones, a mouthful of silly phrases, and an idea or two, kept together only by his notion of his own importance. He has little to say, being as feeble in mind as in body, but being the greatest man in the district, and feeling that he ought to be saying something all the time, he repeats himself over and over again, without paying much attention to the person to whom he is talking, in a manner peculiar to half-witted self-important old men. This fussy empty mode of speech has never been caught so well as it is in Shallow: "Come on, come on, come on, sir; give me your hand, sir; give me your hand, sir; an early stirrer, by the Rood.'' These accents may be overheard any day in the smoking room of almost any club. After hearing Shallow talk, Falstaff, the clear-sighted old rascal, exclaims: "Lord, Lord, how subject we old men are to this vice of lying.'' That wild youth of his, to which Shallow so often refers, to the admiration of Silence, is entirely imaginary. . . . (pp. 80-2)

Silence is one of those characters (Slender and Sir Andrew Aguecheek are two others) that only Shakespeare could bring on the stage and leave us convinced of their reality. As Hazlitt has remarked: "In point of understanding and attainments, Shallow sinks low enough; and yet his cousin Silence is a foil to him; he is the shadow of a shade, glimmers on the very edge of downright imbecility, and totters on the brink of nothing'' [see excerpt above, 1817]. Revolving round the great roaring sun of Falstaff, we discover, in the far outer spaces, this dim fantastic planet of a Shallow, and yet this poor cinder in the darkness has its satellite, Silence, its faint little moon. So slight is Silence's demand upon life that he can bask even in the meagre bleak sunshine of his cousin, the Justice, and hear things even in this orchard that add colour to his dreams. Nay, when there has been an unusually liberal allowance of sack at supper, in honour of the great Sir John's presence, he can not only sit in the garden with the rest but can break into song without encouragement, lifting his faint voice like some roistering sparrow, some care-free sprawling field-mouse. Should Falstaff, with ironic appraisement, declare that he had not thought Master Silence had been a man of such mettle, he can reply "Who, I? I have been merry twice and once ere now,'' and thus flash a light upon his Sahara of an existence through which has trickled a tiny wasted brook of sack and song. Poor Silence!—we leave him, drowned by the last bumper, stunned by the fiery rhetoric of Pistol, asleep under the apple trees. (pp. 83-4)

Into these grotesques, these dim rural shades, Shakespeare has breathed the life that he could spare for all his creatures. No one but he could have written that dialogue between Shallow and Silence when we first meet them, that dialogue which Hazlitt and others have so rightly singled out for praise, a passage of talk so ludicrous and yet so commonplace, so characteristic of the speakers and yet so touched with universality. The fussy, vain, trivial, prattling Justice, determined to talk and yet not able to keep to one point for two sentences together, never forgetting, whatever he is saying, his own importance, the figure he cuts in the eyes of his companion; and Silence, so proud of being where he is and of talking so familiarly to his great relative, so foolish and simple; and both of them, in their vanity and simplicity, so very human that their silly talk lights up, for a moment, the whole strange business of this life:

> SHALLOW. Certain, 'tis certain; very sure, very sure: death, as the Psalmist saith, is certain to all; all shall die. How a good yoke of bullocks at Stamford fair?
> SILENCE. Truly, cousin, I was not there.
> SHALLOW. Death is certain. Is old Double of your town living yet?
> SILENCE. Dead, sir.
> SHALLOW. Jesu, Jesu, dead!—'a drew a good bow; and dead!—'a shot a fine shoot: John o' Gaunt loved him well, and betted much money on his head. Dead!—'a would have clapped i' the clout at twelve score; and carried you a forehand shaft a fourteen and fourteen and a half, that it would have done a man's heart good to see. How a score of ewes now?
> SILENCE. Thereafter as they be: a score of good ewes may be worth ten pounds.
> SHALLOW. And is old Double dead?
>
> [2 Henry IV, III. ii. 36-52]

Let us leave the two old men, nodding and talking, creasing their wintry faces in the sunshine. They have said everything, foolish as they are. Even old Double, who shot a fine shoot and was loved by John o' Gaunt, is dead, and a score of good ewes may be worth ten pounds, and death is certain. This is the world's news, and this is the world's history, and all the philosophers have told us little more.

As a purely literary figure that has seized hold upon men's imagination, aroused their curiosity and won their affection, Falstaff has only two rivals or superiors, namely, Hamlet, the great figure of tragedy, and Don Quixote, the great figure of ironic tragi-comedy or romance; and in his own sphere of the comic, he has no rival. So much has been written about him that any new study cannot be simply an essay in interpretation, a lightning sketch portrait, as the other chapters of this volume are, but must inevitably be a criticism of previous interpretations. The best of these are Maurice Morgann's *Essay on the Dramatic Character of Sir John Falstaff* and *The Rejection of Falstaff* in Mr. A. C. Bradley's Oxford Lectures on Poetry. The worst are everywhere. Among commentators of any importance, the account of Falstaff by Gervinus, who does not appear to have had a glimmer of humour and should have kept out of the fat knight's company, must take one of the highest places as a monument of obtuseness and critical density. It is Gervinus who tells us, while shaking his head over Falstaff's incorrigible coarseness and lewdness, that the little page was given to him in order that the tenderly nurtured lad might have a refining influence, instead of which—alas!—he is himself corrupted. Gervinus, too, is one of those simple souls who imagine that Falstaff's moments of "sighing and grief" are moments of real repentance, that the knight would be good if he could but is somewhat weak-willed and easily led astray. Why persons who are willing to admit Falstaff is a great humorist should insist upon taking every remark he makes as a serious literal statement is a mystery. (pp. 84-7)

It has been said, more than once, that Shakespeare, realising that his Falstaff of the First Part is too engaging and that we must be ready to approve his final rejection, deliberately blackens him in the Second Part. This is a mistake. Absurd as it is to act the magistrate with this great comic figure, drawing up a list of his misdemeanours in the order of their importance, we have only to think of the action of the two parts to realise that there is nothing in the theory. Falstaff's gravest offence is probably the one which first shows him in action, the highway robbery. What Shakespeare did do, towards the end of the Second Part, was to emphasise the fact that Falstaff as a companion and confidant of a serious ruler was impossible, a fact that was obvious throughout but perhaps needed to be emphasised in order that the issue should be clear. When Pistol rushes in with the great news and Falstaff talks as if the realm were already in his pocket, it is plain that disaster is imminent. Henry has to choose between kingship and Falstaff, and being, at heart, a very ambitious young man, he naturally chooses the former. It is inevitable, and, as we know, something like it actually happened. His conduct at the conclusion of the play is perfectly natural. Being a converted rake, very conscious of his improvement, it is natural that he should talk like a prig. He never was at any time a gentleman. (pp. 90-1)

Like most really great figures and great works of art, Falstaff has an equally successful appeal on many different levels. That is why there are so many Falstaffs, all heartily praised as great comic characters. As our sense of humour and character mellows and grows more subtle, so too the Falstaff to whom we inevitably return changes with us; we begin with a bloated old buffoon, whose gluttony, cowardice, lying are on such a colossal scale that we cannot help being amused by them; we end with the comic genius, busy dramatising himself, as it were, that may be discovered in the pages of Morgann and

Mr. A. C. Bradley. Don Quixote has had a similar history, for he too can be enjoyed at all levels and changes with the reader. That is why discussions of such things as Falstaff's apparent cowardice and love of boasting, though both interesting and amusing, are not really important. If we think that real cowardice and boasting are much funnier than pretended cowardice and boasting, if, in short, we prefer a real butt to an apparent one, then we shall continue to say that Falstaff is simply a coward and a boaster. His character is, as it were, a test of our sense of humour. (pp. 92-3)

There is no mystery, as some critics would have us suppose, about the appeal of such comic characters as Falstaff. Their crimes and vices, such as they are (and they are never very grave), have little or no effect upon us; they are so distant from us that we can regard them without moral indignation; it is not *our* sack they drink nor *our* money they borrow or steal or "convey"; it is no more possible to work ourselves up into a state of moral indignation over them than it is for us to grow angry at the thought of all the bandits existing in the remoter provinces of China, or tearful over the sexual laxity of the aborigines. On the other hand, though such fellows do not borrow *our* money and get drunk in *our* houses, so that their little weaknesses do not trouble us, it is for us, in the last resort, that these amusing rascals go through their various antics; their depredations are distant in time and space, but their jokes are here and now. Thus we can afford to be indulgent and to encourage them. It is often forgotten that Falstaff, after all, stands for something that is good in itself. He is the embodiment of masculine comradeship, ease, and merriment. He turns the whole world into the smoking-room of a club. He is the supreme example of the clubbable man. That word brings Dr. Johnson to our minds, and Dr. Johnson was a moralist by nature, and a somewhat severe moralist, but he loved company and ease and mirth, loved them all the more because there was in him a decided streak of melancholy and despondency. He does not understand Falstaff, but how he enjoys him, in spite of himself—"But *Falstaff* unimitated, unimitable *Falstaff,* how shall I describe thee?" he begins, throwing his judicial manner, the wig and robes of his office as a critic, to the winds. It is the clubbable man in him that is responding to the immortal master of the revels, the patron saint of all who love to assemble a few choice spirits, golden lads, shut the doors upon gravity and decorum, duty, and responsibility, and fleet the time in unbuttoned ease. (pp. 97-8)

We see the scenes that Falstaff dominates and makes his own against an ideal background for them, a world of statecraft and war, policy and cabals, of men whose armour seems to have grown upon them like a skin, so angular and stiff, so lacking in spontaneity are most of these barons. After spending some time in the company of these personages, we return to Falstaff with a glorious sense of freedom and spontaneity; the natural man is loose again; it is as if we ourselves had suddenly doffed our armour. And that indeed is what we have done, for we have doffed the armour of duties and obligations and rights and responsibilities. All the secret fears, the reservations, the conflicts are suddenly dropped from our minds and we can step out as free as the wind. (p. 99)

Henry went forward to Agincourt and became a popular hero, a figure for patriots in a noisy mood. Falstaff, who had the larger heart and the better mind, went forward into immortality and has since gained undreamed-of honours, presiding in spirit wherever there have been boon companions, ease and laughter. He was rejected once, but he has never been rejected again.

Whenever the choice spirits of this world have put the day's work out of their minds and have seated themselves at the table of goodfellowship and humour, there has been an honoured place at the board for Sir John Falstaff, in whose gigantic shadow we can laugh at this life and laugh at ourselves, and so, divinely careless, sit like gods for an hour. (pp. 104-05)

> *J. B. Priestley, "Falstaff and His Circle," in his* The English Comic Characters, *John Lane/The Bodley Head, 1925, pp. 69-105.*

HARRY T. BAKER   (essay date 1926)

[*Baker's essay is a continuation of the commentary begun by John Upton (1748), in its assessment of* 1 Henry IV *and* 2 Henry IV *as two distinct plays. Baker takes the position that* 2 Henry IV *was an unplanned sequel to* 1 Henry IV *and was written in response to public demand for more of Falstaff. Other critics who have reached a similar conclusion to Baker's include E. E. Stoll (1914), Robert Adger Law (1927), M. A. Shaaber (1948), and Muriel C. Bradbrook (1965).*]

When Shakespeare began his first play on Henry IV, he probably did not intend to write a sequel. The dramatic possibilities of Henry's reign would be largely exhausted after the Battle of Shrewsbury. Prince Hal would already have reformed, and Hotspur, his rival, would be dead. But dramatists and novelists never know just how popular a child of their brain is to be.

Act V. Scene iv. Falstaff. By Robert Smirke (1794). From the Art Collection of the Folger Shakespeare Library.

Shakespeare apparently found that his public was clamorous for a sequel to Falstaff's adventures. Accordingly he "came in and satisfied them." (p. 289)

About 55 per cent of *I Henry IV* is history; in the sequel, about the same percentage is devoted to comedy. But this does not sufficiently represent the difference. In Part I the crisis occurs, as is usual with Shakespeare, in the third act, when the Prince promises to turn over a new leaf. In the sequel, he "backslides" from this resolution and does not reaffirm his reform until the fifth scene of the fourth act. . . . This is certainly very casual structure, if we regard the serious scenes as the dominant ones. That Shakespeare's audience did not so regard them there is excellent evidence in the play itself. Falstaff dominates [Part II] even more than in Part I. He becomes king for four acts, even if he is deposed at the end by dramatic necessity. As various critics are agreed, he is a better man than his princely rival. His wit has a richer, more unctuous flavor and is not marred by thought of succession to the throne. What Shakespeare wrote in *II Henry IV* is comedy with history, not history with comedy. (pp. 289-90)

That Shakespeare had no didactic purpose in separating Falstaff from the Prince in Part II is suggested by the novelty and richness added to the comic action not only by Pistol and Doll but by Shallow and Silence. In plenitude of invention this sequel differs from any other that the present writer can recall. It would have been fatal to have Falstaff and Hal indulge in as many wit combats as in Part I. Shakespeare could not have exceeded himself, and the repetition would inevitably have become a little tiresome, even to the enthusiastic groundlings who applauded the repartee, blissfully ignorant that they were often listening to high comedy rather than to farce. With Pistol and Doll, the humor broadens—a fairly sure sign that Shakespeare was not neglecting "the understanding gentlemen of the ground." He allows the Archbishop to say

> An habitation giddy and unsure
> Hath he that buildeth on the vulgar heart.
>   [2 *Henry IV*, I. iii. 89-90]

But he himself goes right on building upon that foundation, probably remembering that even in the Elizabethan Age the supply of gentlemen in the audience was limited. Any gentleman, however, ought to be able to enjoy Pistol. . . . Pistol's scraps of old plays, generally misquoted, but improved, reveal him as the phoenix of bombastic humor. He speaks "of Africa and golden joys." Like Falstaff himself, he bids us forget the present. (pp. 290-91)

As for Doll Tearsheet, her replies to Falstaff are quite as good as the Prince's were in Part I. And does not the Prince himself call her an "honest, virtuous, civil gentlewoman"? Her sharp tongue is too much for Pistol, who is reduced to almost speechless rage before he is driven downstairs by Falstaff in what John Masefield has called the finest tavern scene ever written— and Mr. Masefield is an authority, having worked in a New York tavern himself in his pre-poetic days. If, then, this scene (II, 4), which corresponds in position to the similar one in *I Henry IV*, is superior, Shakespeare outdid himself in the longest comic scene of the sequel. He went back to the Boar's Head, not to repeat but to rise to "the brightest heaven of invention." Nor, I think, can it successfully be maintained that the wonderful countryside scenes with Shallow and Silence show any inferiority to the comedy of *I Henry IV*. Professor C. H. Herford testifies that the opening dialogue between the two old men in the second scene of the third act is "admirable literature completely denuded of literary phrase.'' There is nothing even remotely like it in Part I. Never did Shakespeare use common conversation more magically. Later in the scene, Shallow says: "O, Sir John, do you remember since we lay all night in the windmill in Saint George's field?'' There is something embarrassing in the reminiscence, for the knight replies, ''No more of that, good Master Shallow, no more of that.'' And Silence, a moment later, murmurs: "That's fifty-five year ago."

What a gusto Shakespeare imparts to this talk of old times! But for *II Henry IV,* we should never have known this side of Falstaff's life. The combination of the poetic-reminiscent with the comic is almost unique. These Gloucestershire scenes alone would be enough to justify Shakespeare in writing his sequel. (pp. 291-92)

Shakespeare, then, was not merely repeating in his sequel the kind of comic success he had scored in the first play. He gave us virtually a new comedy, with Falstaff and the Prince installed in the new group of fun-makers. He even reserved for this new play Falstaff's greatest speech, his encomium on sack, which "ascends me into the brain; dries me there all the foolish and dull and crudy vapors which environ it; makes it apprehensive, quick, forgetive [from forge, not from forget], full of nimble, fiery and delectable shapes.'' It is a comic monologue which reminds us that Falstaff's atmosphere is that of vaudeville plus brilliantly intellectual phrasing. Stevenson has described him, unintentionally, in his *Apology for Idlers:* "A happy man or woman is a better thing to find than a five-pound note. . . . Their entrance into a room is as though another candle had been lighted.'' And Professor A. C. Bradley, in his essay *The Rejection of Falstaff* [see excerpt above, 1902], adds that the true mission of the fat knight is to show us that life is not real and earnest. This contrast between Falstaff and Longfellow is priceless.

Yet Falstaff must be rejected to make a Coronation holiday. The Prince must become the priggish king. No doubt the Elizabethan audience accepted the dramatic necessity. It is a tribute to Shakespeare's remarkable character drawing that we do not. Falstaff got away from his creator. He established his popularity over the Prince, in perpetuity, so far as modern readers are concerned. Whether Shakespeare originally intended to have him rejected at the end of a sequel to *I Henry IV* and to refer to his death in *Henry V* is at least doubtful. (pp. 292-93)

Many things, then, seem to point to one play alone as Shakespeare's original plan for the treatment of the reign of Henry IV. The extraordinary success of the comedy material probably surprised him. It was a new treatment of history and, like all experiments, was somewhat hazardous. There had been no comedy figure comparable to Falstaff in Shakespeare's previous historical plays. And Shakespeare was in 1597 too mature a dramatist to plan in advance a second part of *Henry IV* which would be deficient in historical interest and in orderly progress of serious plot. His dramatic material was weak in history but strong in comedy. Unless he foresaw the triumph of Falstaff, he can hardly have envisaged a *II Henry IV* as a dramatic opportunity. There seems to the present writer no evidence that this sequel was written hastily, however. The comic scenes have a finish that is not exceeded by those of the first play. As for the serious scenes, although they contain many fine poetic speeches such as Northumberland's lament over the death of his son Hotspur, they are not and could not be—from lack of dramatic material—rivals of those in which Falstaff and his new cronies, Pistol, Doll, Shallow, and Silence, reign and revel. As Mistress Quickly says of Falstaff at his death, they

are all "in Arthur's bosom." They dwell perpetually in a Celtic paradise presided over by an angel with a flaming sword who admits to their company no reader without a sense of humor! The deathless critic who goes on record with the assertion that Shakespeare deliberately blackened the character of Falstaff by showing him in company with Doll Tearsheet will, I feel sure, arrive at another destination. As well say that the Prince is forever blackened by participating in the robbery at Gadshill! Hal, by the way, was a more attractive young man *before* he turned over a new leaf. (pp. 293-94)

Harry T. Baker, "The Problem of 'II Henry IV',"
in English Journal, *Vol. XV, No. 4, April, 1926, pp. 289-98.*

ROBERT ADGER LAW (essay date 1927)

[*Like such earlier critics as John Upton (1748), E. E. Stoll (1914), and Harry T. Baker (1926), Law claims that the two* Henry IV *plays are independent of each other. However, unlike these commentators, and most others before him, Law considers Part Two a well-structured and satisfying play. This opinion was also voiced by Clifford Leech (1951) and L. C. Knights (1959).*]

That each of the two parts of *Henry the Fourth,* particularly the *Second Part,* utterly lacks unity of plot-structure has been asserted or tacitly assumed by many Shakespeare critics of the past half-century, wherein so much stress has been laid on dramatic technique. It is the object of this paper to show that each of the two plays is carefully planned as an organic unit, and that the lack of sequence noted by Brooke [see excerpt above, 1908], when the two parts are taken together as the first two members of a trilogy, is the natural result of the entirely new framework that is employed for an "unpremeditated addition" to *Part I.*

The First Part of Henry the Fourth is built up around a conflict between protagonist and antagonist, Prince Hal and Percy, better known as Hotspur, which culminates in the Battle of Shrewsbury when Hal slays Hotspur. To this battle, which marks the one meeting between the two Harries, the first scene of the play definitely looks forward and we are frequently reminded of the conflict in every act. (pp. 223-24)

The fact that the author keeps so definitely before us the figures of Hal and Hotspur and the name of Shrewsbury, that he stresses so the contrast between the two Harries in the mouth of the King and those of the rivals themselves, that in defiance of history he makes Hotspur and Hal of the same age and stresses this point also, and that the catastrophe of the play is the long-anticipated duel to the death between them on the field of Shrewsbury—all this signifies what Shakespeare conceived to be the central theme of the *First Part.*

An oft-quoted paragraph from Holinshed's *Chronicle,* in description of the Battle of Shrewsbury, deserves careful analysis. The paragraph reads:

> The prince that daie holpe his father like a lustie
> yoong gentleman: for although he was hurt in
> the face with an arrow, so that diuerse noble
> men that were about him, would haue conueied
> him foorth of the field, yet he would not suffer
> them so to doo, least his departure from amongst
> his men might happilie haue striken some feare
> into their harts: and so without regard of his
> hurt, he continued with his men, and neuer
> ceassed, either to fight where the battell was

most hot, or to incourage his men where it seemed most need. This battell lasted three long houres, with indifferent fortune on both parts, till at length, the king crieng saint George victorie, brake the arraie of his enimies, and aduentured so farre, that (as some write) the earle Dowglas strake him downe, and at that instant slue sir Walter Blunt, and three other apparelled in the kings sute and clothing, saieng: I maruell to see so many kings thus suddenlie arise one in the necke of an other. The king in deed was raised, and did manie a noble feat of armes, for as it is writen, he slue that daie with his owne hands six and thirtie persons of his enimies. *The other on his part* incouraged by his doings, fought valiantlie, and slue the lord Persie, called sir Henrie Hotspurre. To conclude, the kings enimies were vanquished, and put to flight, in which flight, the earle of Dowglas, for hast, falling from the crag of an hie mountaine, brake one of his cullions, and was taken, and for his valiantnesse, of the king frankelie and freelie deliuered.

In copying this passage I have italicized five words, but otherwise have attempted to make a literal transcription. (p. 227)

Shakespeare's most important change in this account, generally speaking, was to diminish the part played by the King, while magnifying the Prince's part. More specific changes were (1) to bring Prince John into the fight, his valor serving as a foil to set off the greater valor of Prince Henry; (2) to bring Falstaff in for the comic effect; (3) to make Hal rescue his father; (4) to make Hal set Douglas free; (5) to make Hal slay Hotspur.

But are we certain that in making Hal slay Hotspur, the culminating incident of the entire plot, Shakespeare was changing Holinshed? To be sure, this is the unquestioned view of the critics. As one of them puts it: "Here once more Shakespeare deviated from his sources; Hotspur fell by an unknown hand." Yet let us examine again the five words that I have italicized in Holinshed's account. Now I believe that the first interpretation that an intelligent reader would put upon the sentence so beginning would be that *other* refers to the Prince, whose valor is so praised at the first of the paragraph, and that *on his part* is a connective phrase, contrasting the King with his son. We may compare a somewhat similar phrase used by Holinshed in a sentence a page or two later: "Serlo knowing there was no waie with him but death, would not utter any other, but confessed *for his owne part,* he was worthie for that wicked deed to die ten thousand deaths."

In other words, I believe one's first impression would be that Holinshed is telling us that the Prince, emulating his father's brave example, slew Hotspur. But this first impression is incorrect. Closer examination convinces one that *other* is plural, and *on his part* means *of the King's side.* But as Shakespeare actually makes Hal slay Hotspur, is it reasonable to suppose that on first reading Holinshed he was misled into thinking that Hotspur was slain by Prince Hal? If so, we have in this error the germ of the whole plot. In passing we may remark that each one of Shakespeare's changes in this account, with a single exception, tends to exalt the character of Prince Hal, and so is consistent with his purpose in the entire play. (pp. 228-29)

The *Second Part* . . . does not stress any conflict between King or Prince and any of the rebels, but does magnify the unhis-

torical, comic character of Falstaff. What is the theme of the incidents related in the play?

In reality there seem to be three themes, or at least, three lines along which the action develops. Two of these three are historical, having to do (1) with the Northumberland-York rebellion, and (2) with the death of King Henry IV and the accession of Hal as Henry V; one is entirely imaginative, recounting (3) Falstaff's relations with his friends and his enemies. As will be brought out later, there is definite effort to link together these three themes, but they remain distinct and to that extent interfere with the structural unity of the play.

The Northumberland-York rebellion, one of three armed disturbances that King Henry has simultaneously to quell, but the only one that Shakespeare is interested in, is anticipated in the Prologue, where Rumour tells of the false reports emanating from the Battle of Shrewsbury, a conscious effort on the dramatist's part to join more closely the two plays. (p. 230)

[Nine] scenes, or nearly half of the play, are devoted primarily to actual history, covering the rebellion of York and Northumberland, and the death of King Henry IV, with the accession of his son. The remaining ten scenes have to do chiefly with Falstaff, who, though always a comic figure, is pictured consistently in these scenes as a man of war. . . . [The tavern scene in the second part] shows Poins and Prince Hal plotting to be present in the disguise of waiters at a supper given by Falstaff in honor of two of his female friends. They carry out this plan to surprise Falstaff in II. iv, but meanwhile Falstaff has to drive out of doors the "swaggering Pistol" for his drunken brawling. The Prince, after a very brief conversation, is summoned to his father's bedside at Westminster, while Falstaff is called to colors. Hal bids Falstaff good night for the last time. This point seems to be the climax of the plot, where all three lines of action meet. It certainly marks a turning-point in Falstaff's fortunes. . . . The final scene, as already mentioned, combines serious and comic elements in the coronation of Henry V, with his pitiless condemnation and punishment of Falstaff and his crew. Here from Falstaff's standpoint the comedy becomes tragedy.

Thus the play turns chiefly on the fortunes of Falstaff, but he is consistently portrayed against a background of history. The first half of the drama presents the rebellion which Falstaff helps to quell. The second half looks forward to, and then shows the accession of the new King, who is to break Falstaff's heart in the moment of his triumph. (pp. 231-32)

Again, we are constantly reminded in the first three Acts of the play that King Henry is having to send three armies in as many directions to fight his enemies. Of these three, Shakespeare focuses our attention on that led by John of Lancaster against York and Northumberland, the army to which Falstaff is attached, rather than that directed by the King himself and Prince Hal. (p. 233)

Sir John Falstaff is pictured to us in the *First Part* chiefly as a tavern lounger who is caught up in the maelstrom of war; in the *Second Part* he is by vocation a soldier, who sometimes dallies with other business or pleasure. . . . Thus even the comic scenes keep reminding us of the war and the forces led by John of Lancaster.

About the middle of the play, it has been noted, the theme of the serious scenes shifts from the wars to the dying King. But this note, dominant henceforth, has been sounding as an undertone for some time. . . . The more and more serious development of this illness in several scenes of Act IV has already been discussed.

It will be seen that while Shakespeare stresses in this play mainly incidents connected with Falstaff, he emphasizes only to a less degree the two serious themes of the York-Northumberland rebellion and the death of King Henry as historical background for Falstaff, who serves in the army of Lancaster and who is tremendously affected by the death of the King. Indeed, the chief topic of conversation in the new King's household immediately before and after the older King's death is whether Hal will "cast off his followers" [IV.iv.75], or "assemble . . . the apes of idleness" [IV.v.121-22], by whom "all will be overturn'd" [V.ii.19]. Even the new King's brothers fear the worst, and advise the Chief Justice to "speak Sir John Falstaff fair" [V.ii.23].

All these links serve to unify the genuine history of the *Second Part* around the comic adventures of Falstaff, and perhaps justify applying the title, "The Second Part of Henry the Fourth, Containing His Death and the Coronation of Henry the Fifth," to what is really an historical comedy. But one other device for connecting the serious with the lighter scenes should not be overlooked. Act III, scene i, is given up to King Henry IV's reminiscences over his past life, particularly the reign of Richard II. This is immediately followed by the comic scene relating Justice Shallow's reminiscences over the same period, when Mowbray and John of Gaunt, Richard's uncle, were in power. One is reminded of the similar trick of having Henry V in the play of that name make his famous eloquent speech beginning, "Once more unto the breach, dear friends, once more" [III.i.1], only to be echoed by Bardolph in the very next scene, "On, on, on, on, on! to the breach, to the breach!" [III.ii.1]. Again, where, in V. i, Davy asks Justice Shallow to "countenance" a knave "at his friend's request," he is similarly parodying the offence of Prince Hal against the Chief Justice, an offence which finally sent Hal to prison, and which is so often mentioned in the play. Shall we not believe that these represent efforts on Shakespeare's part to unify material that of itself appears heterogeneous?

The one scene that tends more strongly than any other in the drama to give unity to all this heterogeneous material, particularly to unite the serious and the comic lines of action, is, of course, the final scene. . . . Although this episode of the rejection of Falstaff has caused more dissension among the critics than has any other part of the play, it has been carefully prepared for throughout the *Second Part.* (pp. 234-36)

We have already alluded to the fact that the struggle that chiefly concerns us in this story is not between the King, or the Prince, and any or all of the rebels, as in the *First Part.* It is between the Chief Justice and the royal household on one side, and Sir John Falstaff on the other. And the theme of dispute is the person of the future King.

This struggle comes to the fore in the second scene of Act I where the Chief Justice gloats over the King's separation of Hal from Falstaff, by assigning them to different armies, and Falstaff quickly rejoins, "I thank your pretty sweet wit for it." . . . The Chief Justice again meets Sir John in II. i, denounces him for mistreating the Hostess and for dawdling about his military duties, receives a sharp reply, and exchanges with him the dangerous appellation of "fool." At their next meeting, in the closing scene, the Chief Justice condemns his enemy to the Fleet. (pp. 237-38)

If the plot of the *Second Part,* then, centres about Falstaff, and its main theme is the struggle between Falstaff and his enemies

for the favor, or the very soul, of Prince Hal, a struggle that begins in the second scene of the play and ends with the Chief Justice's notable victory in the last scene, on what type of framework is the plot built? This question has already been answered, I believe, by Sir Arthur Quiller-Couch, in discussing "The Story of Falstaff." Concluding his study of the two Parts, and noting particularly the Prayer for the Queen at the end of the *Second Part,* a device he attributes to the interlude, inherited from the morality, Sir Arthur adds:

> The whole of the business is built on the old Morality structure, imported through the Interlude. Why, it might be labelled after the style of a Morality title *Contentio inter Virtutem et Vitium de anima Principis.*

To a similar conclusion, at least, so far as Falstaff is concerned, comes a young American scholar, Mr. J. W. Spargo [see excerpt above, 1922]. (p. 240)

My own position is somewhat different from that of either critic just quoted. I am not contending that Falstaff was considered by the Elizabethan audience as a definite incarnation of Sin, deadly or otherwise, though I believe certain elements inherited from the Morality figures went into the creation of his uncommonly real character. Nor do I see clear traces of the Morality influence in the *First Part* save in Hal's characterization of Falstaff as "that reverend Vice, that grey Iniquity, that father Ruffian, that Vanity in years." But throughout that play Prince Hal is entirely too active to be Man's Soul, or a mere "bone of contention." Moreover, the delightfully romantic Hotspur belongs not at all to the Morality atmosphere. Again, it must be remembered that the entire plot turns on Hal and Hotspur.

But the *Second Part* tells another story. Hal is remarkably passive until the very last Act. Falstaff, though still real, seems the lineal descendant of Gluttony and Lechery, intensified more than ever; of Sloth, in his tardiness to fight; of Avarice, in his financial dealings with the Hostess, the drafted soldiers, and Master Shallow; of Pride, in his talk immediately before his fall. Although no one could so misjudge the old knight as to find in him personified Envy or Wrath, he may well enfigure just five of the Seven Deadly Sins. The cold John of Lancaster joins with the Chief Justice in his zealous pursuit of Virtue, and in the end they together snatch Hal as a brand from the burning and piously provide a limbo for Vice. Our sympathy or hostility toward the forces of Light depends on our own attitude towards the spirit of Puritanism.

In general, then, I believe that Shakespeare knew what he was about in the composition of both of these plays. In them we have, not a single ten-act play, though the titles would give that impression, but two plays written with different purposes in view. The *First Part,* based probably on a misinterpretation of a passage in Holinshed, sets forth the conflict between Hal and Hotspur, culminating at Shrewsbury. The *Second Part,* "originally unpremeditated," but written in response to a public demand for more of Falstaff, depicts the conflict between Sir John and the Chief Justice, after the manner of the Moralities, for the soul of Prince Hal. In its essence this resembles the contest in *Twelfth Night* between Sir Toby and Malvolio, with a different conclusion. But here we have not the typical structure of comedy; we have rather the framework of the Moral Play, such as Marlowe used in *Dr. Faustus,* yet with far more care for the unity of structure. (pp. 241-42)

Robert Adger Law, "Structural Unity in the Two Parts of 'Henry the Fourth'," in Studies in Philology, Vol. XXIV, No. 2, April, 1927, pp. 223-42.

WYNDHAM LEWIS (essay date 1927)

[*Lewis wrote in a deliberately provocative style and outside the mainstream of Shakespearean criticism. The excerpt below is taken from his unusual study* The Lion and the Fox, *a title which refers to the struggle between world views which Lewis believes dominated Shakespeare's age. The lion stands for the mystical and feudalistic vision of the age of chivalry; the fox for the rationalism of the coming age of science and industry. Shakespeare himself, according to Lewis, did not take sides in any simple way, but his plays reflect the conflict of both world views. His lions range from the heroic Othello to the problematic Coriolanus, his foxes from the archvillain Iago to—as he argues in the following excerpt—"the humorous figure* par excellence," *Falstaff. For Lewis, Falstaff's instrument of transformation, his humor, is, like Iago's scheming, a manipulative tool. Lewis agrees with such earlier critics as Maurice Morgann (1777) and Hermann Ulrici (1839), in the first case that Falstaff is not a coward, and in the second that he is something like a "child" or "naif." Yet, he also questions Morgann's "affected defense" as obscuring a true psychological understanding of the man. Lewis's method of linking Falstaff and Iago may be compared with similar approaches by Samuel Taylor Coleridge (1810) and C. F. Tucker Brooke (1918).*]

Sancho Panza's *catechism* under the tree outside Toboso [in Cervantes's *Don Quixote*], "Let us know now, brother Sancho, where you are going," has often been compared with Falstaff's famous *catechism* on the field of Shrewsbury. But it has never suggested, I believe, the natural conclusion of where we should look, in english literature, for our knight.

This is all the more so as *Henry IV.* is, as the german critic Gervinus says, that play where more than elsewhere the full power of the english "national poet" is associated with a theme inalienably english ("The genius of a nation has never appeared on any stage in such bright cheerfulness," etc.) [see excerpt above, 1849-50]. To match Cervantes (if it were a question of comparing the two artists) I should choose myself some play of Shakespeare's where this "national cheerfulness" played a less important rôle. And *Don Quixote* is too wide and too personal to be "spanish" first and foremost. But all allowances made, and conceding that *Henry IV.* is not *Shakespeare's* most significant work, though it may be *the national poet's,* and that you could get as *spanish* a production as *Don Quixote* without the great personal genius of Cervantes; nevertheless these works can be confronted as peculiarly representative of their respective countries.

It may be as well to recall by reproducing it the well-known soliloquy of Falstaff:

> Can honour set to a leg? no: or an arm? or take away the grief of a wound? No. Honour hath no skill in surgery, then? no. What is honour? a word. What is in that word, honour? air. A trim reckoning!—Who hath it? he that died o' Wednesday. Doth he feel it? no. Doth he hear it? no. 'Tis insensible, then? yea, to the dead. But will it not live with the living? no. Why detraction will not suffer it:—therefore, I'll none of it.

> [*1 Henry IV*, V. i. 131-40]

There is the characteristic reasoning, but with a rapider and more informed cunning, of Sancho Panza. Only the english Sancho Panza, if Falstaff is he, is ten times the size of the spanish one. He is also a *knight;* so in a sense the rôles are reversed. He is a man of the world—a compendium of rosy vices, very pleasant and amusing: fallen on rather evil times, he displays himself as in reality a cutpurse, drunkard and sneak. And, without very much fancifulness, we could pursue the parallel, and show him surrounded (in Shakespeare's *Henry IV.*) with rather dull and boorish specimens of *real* chivalry, against which background he shows off to good advantage. (pp. 207-08)

"The wound that phantom gave me!" is an exclamation [by Don Quixote] illustrating the quixotic attitude to the environing world, which, if it lends qualities to things they do not possess, restores in a sense the balance by not bestowing on any existence quite the harshness of the analytic eye of common sense. Don Quixote is of course one of the many demented characters inhabiting the region of great fiction. Hamlet, Lear, Othello, Timon are all demented or hallucinated, as so many of the celebrated figures in nineteenth-century russian fiction were. It is the supreme liberty that it is possible to take with your material. (p. 215)

"The defeat of the hero" to see "the splendid triumph of his heroism" is in accord with the definitely tragic nature of the jest, and the movement of thought beneath the symbolization. That Don Quixote has not a ceremonious *pathos,* and that he only fights with *phantoms* which we know under homely shapes, does not make him any less a hero. . . . Don Quixote is, in literature, a lonely hero, and even in that responds to one of the chief requirements of tragedy, approximating at the same time to one of the conditions of madness. (pp. 215-16)

Whether Falstaff (Shakespeare's "knight," as Don Quixote was Cervantes') was only a whimsical invention to amuse; or how far certain more fundamental things—and what things—were involved, has, like most of the matters connected with this very rich and complex work [*Henry IV*]—overcrowded with startlingly real figures—been much discussed. (p. 217)

Where Ulrici says that Falstaff is the "impersonification of the whole of this refined and artificial civilization"—and more closely still that he is a *child,* a *naif*—he has, I think, established one of the important things about him. (p. 218)

If you imagine Shakespeare taking Falstaff all through his plays—or through as many more as possible—then we should have, still more, a central and great figure (which would also be an *idea*) to place beside Cervantes' knight.

"These scenes [the comic falstaffian ones in *Henry IV.*] fill almost one half of the whole play. In no other historical drama of Shakespeare's do we find such a total disregard of the subject. Here . . . the comic and unhistorical portions are so surprisingly elaborate, that the question as to their justification becomes a vital point. . . ." [Ulrici] (pp. 218-19)

Ulrici's solution is that the comic is set to dog the historic in *Henry IV.* on purpose to show up its influence. . . . (p. 219)

Ulrici thinks that the contrast was necessary only because of the emptiness of this *particular* history, in short. It is very easy, in view of the so-called enigmatical play of *Troilus and Cressida,* and in the view upheld here of a great many other points in all the plays, to *extend* this estimate of Ulrici to the whole of Shakespeare's works. (p. 220)

I will now show how all these various questions we have passed in review during the last few chapters can be combined, and how they each contribute to the fixing a psychical centre of control which is responsible for all of them. First of all, what I named *shamanization* must be reverted to: its effects will be found a necessary ingredient of one of the most celebrated attributes of Shakespeare—namely, his humour. . . .

For those who are not familiar with the phenomenon of *shamanization,* still universally prevalent among the subarctic tribes, I will briefly describe it.

A *shaman* is a person following the calling of a magician or priest: and the word *shamanization* that I have employed would refer to a shaman (the most typical of them) who had in addition transformed himself. (p. 221)

Generally speaking, the process of shamanizing himself confers on a man the feminine advantages. It signifies either a desire to experience the sensual delights peculiar to the female organization; or else an ambition to identify himself with occult powers. But it is further a withdrawal from masculine responsibilities in every sense, and an adoption of the spectator's rôle of the woman (freed further, in his case, from the cares of motherhood). That this is a very radical and even inversely heroic, or heroically inverse, proceeding is evident. If we now turn to . . . the "man of the world" (a figure with whom by implication Shakespeare is compromised, but from identification with whom this analysis should, in effect, rescue him)— we shall find that there is nothing that exactly corresponds to the transformed shaman. Like the latter, as it is his strategy to include among his numerous advantages those possessed by the woman, he has a tincture of the *shaman* in him. Hotspur (one of Shakespeare's lesser heroes) tells in a famous speech how he meets on the battlefield a shamanizing sprig of nobility, whom he describes as chiding soldiers carrying dead bodies near him "for bringing a slovenly unhandsome corpse between the wind and his nobility." This exquisite was not necessarily a wholly shamanized man, but possibly only a macaroni of the time. He would in that case be a "man of the world" of a very extravagant type, very extravagantly *shamanized.* He would have on the field of battle all the privileges of a woman, only frowned at—and perhaps hustled—by the blustering Percy.

It is at this point that, fully prepared, we can address ourselves to the subject that can be regarded as the centre one in Shakespeare—that of his *humour.*

The *humour* of Falstaff achieves the same magical result as Don Quixote's chivalrous delusion—namely, it makes him immune from its accidents. The battles he finds himself engaged in are jokes; his opponents, the Douglas, Colevile of the dale, are "phantoms" (of a different sort, it is true), just as Don Quixote's are. The contrast of these two knights is a contrast in two unrealities—two specifics to turn the world by enchantment into something else. One is the sense of humour, the other is the mysticism of chivalry; the first a negation, the latter a positive inspiration. The one, the magic of being *wide awake* (very wide awake—beyond normal common sense): the other of having your eyes naturally sealed up, and of *dreaming.*

The "sense of humour," again, provides us with an exceptionally english or american attribute of worldliness.

In Falstaff, Shakespeare has given us a very interesting specimen indeed of consummate worldliness, with a very powerfully developed humorous proclivity, which served him better than any suit of armour could in the various vicissitudes of his

life. An excellent substitute even for a *shamanizing* faculty, and enabling its possessor to escape the inconveniences and conventional disgrace of being feminine—at the same time it provides him with most of the social advantages of the woman. The sense of humour is from that point of view the masterpiece of worldly duplicity and strategy. On the field of battle at Tewkesbury, Falstaff avails himself of it in a famous scene, and gives us a classical exhibition of its many advantages, and the graceful operation of its deceit. It does not cut off its practitioner from "men" of the rough "hero type," but on the contrary endears him to them. So it becomes even a substitute for courage. There is no lack that it does not cover. With it Falstaff is as safe on the battlefield as the shamanized noble noticed by Percy Hotspur.

So if Falstaff is the embodiment of a mass of worldly expedient, this is of course all directed to defeating the reality as much as Don Quixote's. He is a walking disease, but his disease is used to evade the results of that absence of a sense of humour which is so conspicuous a characteristic of nature and natural phenomena. The sense of humour is woven into a magic carpet; with it he progresses through his turbulent career, bearing a charmed life. This "sense" performs for Falstaff the office of a psychological liberator; it is of magic potency, turning the field of Tewkesbury into a field of play, and cheating death wherever they meet.

The man would indeed be a coward who, possessed of this magic, was seriously timid. Falstaff was evidently not that: yet Morgann thought it necessary to write a book defending his "honour" in this respect. "He had from nature," he said, "as I presume to say, a spirit of boldness and enterprise". . . .

Being a humorous figure *par excellence,* it was not possible for him to be brave in the hero's way, any more than it would be proper for the circus clown to be an obviously accomplished athlete. Gaucherie and laughable failure is, in both cases, of the essence of their rôle. But boldness and enterprise—as far as that was compatible with the necessity of advertising a lack of courage—he possessed to a great degree. (pp. 222-25)

Morgann's affected defence (of Falstaff's physical courage) is successfully achieved—but at the expense of every psychologic requirement of the case.

Morgann makes a point of Falstaff's freedom from malice:

"He [Falstaff] seems by nature to have had a mind free of malice or any evil principle; but he never took the trouble of acquiring any good one. He found himself (from the start) esteemed and loved with all his faults, nay *for* his faults, which were all connected with humour, and for the most part grew out of it." So "laughter and approbation attend his greatest excesses."

This is of course the "man of the world" in Falstaff—the *anti-Machiavel* of the type of Frederick the Great. But the "good fellow" in Falstaff, as it is in anybody almost, was no more innocent than, actually not as innocent as, Machiavelli's "bad fellow" or *male persona.* There is, in short, much method in such sanity. (pp. 225-26)

Falstaff is a "man of wit and pleasure," and could generally be described as a very good specimen of a "man of the world." But the same thing applies to him as to Iago: the "man of the world" is never so dramatically and openly cynical as Falstaff, any more than he is so candid as Machiavelli. He is not dramatic at all. To come to one of the necessary conclusions in this connexion, if the *Machiavel* were an Englishman he would be

like Falstaff. This laziness, rascality and "good fellow" quality, crafty in the brainless animal way, is the english way of
being a "deep-brained Machiavel."

But Falstaff is a "child," too, a "naïf," as Ulrici says. A
worldly mixture of any strength is never without that ingredient. The vast compendium of worldly bluff that is Falstaff
would have to contain that. It was like "any christom child"
that he "went away," Mistress Quickly says.

He is armed from head to foot with sly feminine inferiorities,
lovable weaknesses and instinctively cultivated charm. He is
a big helpless bag of guts, exposing himself boldly to every
risk on the child's, or the woman's, terms. When he runs away
or lies down he is more adorable than any hero "facing fearful
odds."

His immense girth and stature lends the greatest point, even,
to his character. He is a hero run hugely to seed: he is actually
heavier and bigger than the heaviest and biggest true colossus
or hero. He is in that respect, physically, a mock-hero. Then
this childishness is enhanced by his great physical scale, so
much the opposite of the child's perquisite of smallness. And
because of this meaninglessness, unmasculine immensity he
always occupies the centre of the stage, he is the great landmark
in any scene where he is. It all means nothing, and is a physical
sham and trick put on the eye. And so he becomes the embodiment of bluff and worldly practice, the colossus of the
little. (pp. 226-27)

> *Wyndham Lewis, "The Two Knights," in his* The
> Lion and The Fox: The Role of the Hero in the Plays
> of Shakespeare *(© 1927 Wyndham Lewis and the
> Estate of Mrs. G. A. Wyndham Lewis; by permission
> of The Wyndham Lewis Memorial Trust, a registered
> charity), G. Richards, 1927, pp. 201-27.*

S. ASA SMALL (essay date 1932)

In the evolution of the English stage-fool from a crude type
like the country simpleton to a complex super-clown like Falstaff, we find every sort of stage device. Falstaff is, in a sense,
an epitome of this evolution. The range of his mental outlook
extends all the way from a rough material attitude, symbolized
in his large body, to successful wit combats with the Prince
of Wales. There are three strata of humor which Shakespeare
uses in the characterization of Falstaff: the material, the rhetorical, and the imaginative. Each of these levels of humor will
be illustrated in turn. (p. 114)

Falstaff's materialism, which is apparent everywhere in the
play, needs only a little illustration. It is alluded to time and
again by himself and by others in the play. For example, he
always speaks sympathetically about his physical troubles. He
shows momentary anger at the Prince and Poins when they
make his body the butt of their jokes. When they see the fat
knight trying to keep up with the life of youth around him,
they, as do those in the audience, feel a keen sense of humor. . . . But even in the handling of these crude matters which
belong to the clown proper, Shakespeare at times gives Falstaff
a mental attitude that shapes these materials with artistic thought.
This brings us to the rhetorical side of Falstaff's mind.

To illustrate this mental coloring, a number of cases will be
cited in which Falstaff skilfully makes use of a sudden change
of tone or key to cast ridicule on himself. When the Prince
tells him of the need of haste to stop Percy, he calls out to the
hostess:

> Rare words! brave world! Hostess, my breakfast, come!
> O, I could wish this tavern were my drum!
>   [*1 Henry IV*, III.iii.205-06]

Again, at the beginning of the battle, Falstaff thinks of a feast:

> Well,
> To the latter end of a fray and the beginning of a feast
> Fits a dull fighter and a keen guest. . . .
>   [*1 Henry IV*, IV.ii.79-80]

The Prince asks Falstaff how long it has been since he has seen
his knee. His reason for his fatness is, of course, a deliberate
shift in thought:

> My own knee? When I was about thy years,
> Hal, I was not an eagle's talon in the waist; I
> could have crept into an alderman's thumb-
> ring. A plague of sighing and grief! it blows a
> man up like a bladder.   [*1 Henry IV*, II.iv.329-33]
>   (pp. 114-16)

Let us now turn to a higher type of humor, which Falstaff uses
to baffle others. These intellectual turns are all invested with
a kind of reasoning that is so obviously illogical that no one
can take them seriously. . . .

Falstaff, all through the play, has little solid evidence behind
his reasoning, but he is prodigal of argument. He is like many
people in real life who show great earnestness in the line of
logic they hit upon, yet they are little concerned about the main
premises of their reasoning. Falstaff says to the Prince that
purse-taking is justifiable, for "'Tis no sin for a man to labour
in his vocation." The same touch of false reasoning is obvious
when he upbraids the Prince thus: "There's neither honesty,
manhood, nor good fellowship in thee, nor thou cam'st not of
the blood royal, if thou dar'st not stand for ten shillings."
(p. 117)

The fascination of Falstaff's personality consists in the large
range of his mental life. This range begins, as I have shown,
with a childish sensitiveness about his infirmities and rises to
a height that is colorful whenever he attempts to persuade others
through false reasoning. In two places his mind revels in the
region of pure fancy: first, when he plays the part of the king
to defend his name, and, later, at the end of the play, when
he pretends to have slain Percy and carries him away on his
back. (p. 118)

It is clear that the dramatic continuity of the play, so far as
Prince Hal and Falstaff are concerned, is worked out on the
principle of contrast. The morose humor of the Prince, displayed in his love of goading the fat knight to the highest
reaches of the imagination, is just as important to the humorous
tissue of the play as the direct wit of Falstaff. The talkative
temperament of Falstaff is woven around the sly reserve [of]
Prince Hal. The play is divided into two equal parts, each part
containing a crescendo of humor, beginning with a predominating amount of realism and ending in a glow of romantic
humor. The flight of Falstaff at the robbery scene [at II,ii,103]
is an act of real cowardice which the sensitive knight at first
vigorously denies until his mind colors the act with an exaggerated lie and gradually becomes romantic in the last speech
[II,iv,398-481] of the pretended scene where the Prince and
Falstaff each take turns in speaking from the mouth of the king.
The romantic humor is carried over in Falstaff's speech about
Bardolph's nose [III,iii,29-48]. In the second part of the play,
made up predominantly of historical matter, the Prince is interested only in the serious business of state. The second cres-

cendo of humor begins in the realistic scene in the tavern in
Eastcheap [III,iii,52ff], and ends in romantic humor when Fal-
staff counterfeits death and claims the credit of slaying Hotspur.
Thus we see that the dramatic continuity of the *The First Part
of Henry the Fourth* is effected by two crescendos of humor,
which are made possible by the reserved temperament of the
Prince, on the one hand, and the contrastingly large range of
Falstaff's mind, on the other. (pp. 121-22)

> S. Asa Small, ''The Structure of Falstaff's Humor,''
> in The Shakespeare Association Bulletin, *Vol. VII,
> No. 1, January, 1932, pp. 114-22.*

L. C. KNIGHTS   (essay date 1933)

[*A renown English Shakespearean scholar, Knights is perhaps
best known for his* How Many Children Had Lady Macbeth?
*(1933)—a milestone study in the twentieth-century reaction to the
Shakespearean criticism of the previous century. In this work,
Knights criticizes the traditional emphasis on ''character'' as an
approach which inhibits the reader's total response to Shakespeare's plays. In the following essay, originally published in*
Scrutiny *in 1933, Knights argues that the emphasis on Falstaff's
character epitomized by Maurice Morgann (1777) and other so-
called post-Morgannites has obscured critical understanding of
the plays' dramatic structure and unity. His idea that the Falstaff
plot acts as satirical commentary on the main plot is similar to
the theories of Hermann Ulrici (1839) and William Empson (1935).*]

Henry IV does not fit easily into any of the critical schemata,
though 'incongruity' has served the critics in good stead. But
at any rate since the time of Morgann [see excerpt above, 1777],
Falstaff has received a degree of sympathetic attention (how
we love the fat rascal!) that distorts Shakespeare's intention in
writing the two plays. We regard them as a sandwich—so much
dry bread to be bitten through before we come to the meaty
Falstaff, although we try to believe that 'the heroic and serious
part is not inferior to the comic and farcical'. Actually each
play is a unity, sub-plot and main plot co-operating to express
the vision which is projected into the form of the play. And
this vision, like that of all the great writers of comedy, is pre-
eminently serious. (p. 121)

Throughout we are never allowed to forget that Henry is a
usurper. (p. 122)

The rebels of course are no better. . . . The satire is general,
directed against statecraft and warfare. Hotspur is the chief
representative of chivalry, and we have only to read his speeches
to understand Shakespeare's attitude towards 'honour'; there
is no need to turn to Falstaff's famous soliloquy. The description of the Mortimer-Glendower fight has just that degree of
exaggeration that is necessary for not too obvious burlesque,
though oddly enough it has been used to show that Hotspur
'has the imagination of a poet'. But if the image of the Severn—

> Who then, affrighted with their bloody looks,
> Ran fearfully among the trembling reeds,
> And his his crisp head in the hollow bank—
> > [*1 Henry IV*, I. iii. 104-06]

is not sufficient indication the rhyme announces the burlesque
intention:

> He did confound the best part of an hour
> In changing hardiment with great Glendower.
> > [*1 Henry IV*, I. iii. 100-01]

There is the same exaggeration in later speeches of Worcester
and Hotspur; Hotspur's 'huffing part'—'By Heaven methinks

it were an easy leap'—did not need Beaumont's satire. In the
battle scene the heroics of 'Now, Esperance! Percy! and set
on', the chivalric embrace and flourish of trumpets are immediately followed by the exposure of a military dodge for the
preservation of the King's life. 'The King hath many marching
in his coats.'—'Another King! they grow like Hydra's heads.'

The reverberations of the sub-plot also help to determine our
attitude towards the main action. The conspiracy of the Percys
is sandwiched between the preparation for the Gadshill plot
and counter-plot and its execution. Poins has 'lost much honour' that he did not see the 'action' of the Prince with the
drawers. When we see the Court we remember Falstaff's joints-
tool throne and his account of Henry's hanging lip. . . . The
nobles, like the roarers, prey on the commonwealth, 'for they
ride up and down on her and make her their boots'.

The Falstaff attitude is therefore in solution, as it were, throughout the play, even when he is not on the stage; but it takes
explicit form in the person and speeches of Sir John. We see
an heroic legend in process of growth in the account of his
fight with the men in buckram. The satire in the description
of his ragged regiment is pointed by a special emphasis on
military terms—'soldiers', 'captain', 'lieutenant', 'ancients,
corporals . . . gentlemen of companies'. His realism easily
reduces Honour to 'a mere scutcheon'. Prince Henry's duel
with Hotspur is accompanied by the mockery of the Douglas-
Falstaff fight, which ends with the dead and the counterfeit
dead lying side by side. If we can rid ourselves of our realistic
illusions and their accompanying moral qualms we realize how
appropriate it is that Falstaff should rise to stab Hotspur's body
and carry him off as his luggage on his back.

The satire on warfare, the Falstaff attitude, implies an axis of
reference, which is of course found in the gross and vigorous
life of the body. We find throughout the play a peculiar insistence on imagery deriving from the body, on descriptions of
death in its more gruesome forms, on stabbing, cutting, bruis-
ing and the like. We expect to find references to blood and
death in a play dealing with civil war, but such references in
Henry IV are of a kind not found in a war play such as *Henry
V*. In the first scene we hear of the earth 'daubing her lips with
her own children's blood'. War is 'trenching', it 'channels'
the fields and 'bruises' the flowers. 'The edge of war' is 'like
an ill-sheathed knife' which 'cuts his master'. Civil war is an
'intestinal shock', and battles are 'butchery'. We learn that the
defeated Scots lay 'balk'd in their own blood', and that 'beastly
shameless transformation' was done by the Welsh upon the
corpses of Mortimer's soldiers. Later Hotspur mentions the
smell of 'a slovenly unhandsome corpse', and we hear of Mortimer's 'mouthed wounds'. So throughout the play. The dead
Blunt lies 'grinning', Hotspur's face is 'mangled', and Falstaff
lies by him 'in blood'. Falstaff's 'honour' soliloquy insists on
surgery, on broken legs and arms.

To all this Falstaff, a walking symbol, is of course opposed.
'To shed my dear blood drop by drop i' the dust' for the sake
of honour appears an imbecile ambition. Falstaff will 'fight no
longer than he sees reason'. His philosophy is summed up
when he has escaped Douglas by counterfeiting death. (pp.
123-28)

Once the play is read as a whole the satire on war and policy
is apparent. It is useful to compare the first part of *Henry IV*
with *King John* in estimating the development of Shakespeare's
dramatic power. *King John* turns on a single pivotal point—
the Bastard's speech on Commodity, but the whole of the latter

play is impregnated with satire which crystallizes in Falstaff. Now satire implies a standard, and in *Henry IV* the validity of the standard itself is questioned; hence the peculiar coherence and universality of the play. 'Honour' and 'state-craft' are set in opposition to the natural life of the body, but the chief body of the play is, explicitly, 'a bolting-hutch of beastliness'.—'A pox on this gout! or a gout on this pox, I should say.' Other speeches reinforce the age and disease theme which, it has not been observed, is a significant part of the Falstaff theme. (pp. 128-29)

The stability of our attitude after a successful reading of the first part of *Henry IV* is due to the fact that the breaking-down process referred to above is not simple but complex; one set of impulses is released for the expression of the Falstaff-out-look; but a set of opposite complementary impulses is also brought into play, producing an effect analogous to that caused by the presence of comedy in *King Lear* (compare the use of irony in *Madame Bovary*). *Lear* is secure against ironical assault because of the irony it contains; *Henry IV* will bear the most serious ethical scrutiny because in it the serious is a fundamental part of the comic effect of the play. (pp. 130-31)

No theory of comedy can explain the play; no theory of comedy will help us to read it more adequately. Only a morbid pedantry would be blind to the function of laughter in comedy, but concentration upon laughter leads to a double error: the dilettante critic falls before the hallucination of the Comic Spirit, the more scientifically minded persuade themselves that the jokes collected by Bergson and Freud have something to do with the practice of literary criticism. (p. 131)

> *L. C. Knights, "Notes on Comedy," in* Determinations: Critical Essays, *edited by F. R. Leavis, Chatto & Windus, 1934, pp. 109-31.**

LOUIS CAZAMIAN   (essay date 1934)

[*Cazamian and Samuel B. Hemingway (1952) are among a group of critics who have attempted to reconcile the apparently antagonistic interpretations of* Henry IV *by Maurice Morgann (1777), A. C. Bradley (1902), E. E. Stoll (1914), and J. Dover Wilson (1943). Cazamian makes it clear, however, that he considers himself a disciple of Bradley and Morgann in their sympathetic interpretations of Falstaff's character. Cazamian's essay is taken from a speech originally delivered in 1934.*]

I, for one, regard it as a fact that if the question is raised, of what was Shakespeare's conscious, dramatic purpose when he assigned a part to Falstaff in *Henry IV*, there can be only one answer: he was bent on turning to use the rich possibilities of a type that had always been a godsend to comic playwrights, the bragging and cowardly soldier. Scholarship has conclusively shown the long chain of historical development, from the "miles gloriosus" to Sir John, and after.

> [Cazamian adds in a footnote:] The outstanding name in that controversy is of course that of Professor Stoll. . . . That even his weight of comparative erudition fails to destroy the "romantic" view of Falstaff, while effectively checking its excesses, would be the conclusion of the present writer. Bradley's intuition can be profoundly true, although Stoll's argument is in a way irrefutable. The two do not really clash, because they do not meet on the same plane.

(p. 2)

But all that leaves us *our* Falstaff—a perfectly legitimate growth; the character that our modern mind has fashioned out of the Elizabethan figure, and which is in no wise arbitrary, since it develops and actualizes suggestions which Shakespeare's genius did create, and of which he cannot have been himself entirely unaware; though they are to be found, no doubt, at a level in his imaginative life where his clearer self-consciousness did not probably reach. In that sense, our Falstaff is the real Falstaff—to us; and in every sense that matters, he has not ceased to be Shakespeare's Falstaff.

The discovery of the modern Sir John, everybody knows, began as early as the eighteenth century. Then it was (in 1777) that Maurice Morgann, in a brilliant essay since reprinted and much discussed, aired the view that the fat knight has really no vile qualities, but only indulges his whim in playing the part of vileness [see excerpt above].

As an historical interpretation—and it gave itself out for such—that is not tenable. Morgann was wrong in affirming that Falstaff is not intended to make us laugh by the absurdity of his brag and the shamelessness of his cowardice. But he was right when he intuitively perceived in Falstaff elements of a very different nature, which set him in an altogether different light to our sense of moral and artistic values.

Among the followers of Morgann I must then, in all due modesty, take my stand; and more precisely, with the little knot of would-be psychological analysts, led by Professor A. C. Bradley, of Oxford. The stimulus under which the present study was undertaken, is the fond hope that a closer examination of Falstaff as a humorist may help us to draw the line more clearly between his purely Elizabethan self and his eternal being. . . . The duality, properly so called, is not in Shakespeare's hero; it is in Shakespeare himself. The character that he had selected and animated to play a given part in his drama, assumed in the making not only an importance, but a significance that went far beyond; and Shakespeare's less conscious creative purpose—his subconscious purpose, if we needs must use the phrase—made his bragging coward grow into something much more rare, interesting, and original.

Of that originality, the very essence is humor. (pp. 3-4)

When we speak of Falstaff's humor, we should take the word in as precise a meaning as possible. . . .

To all practical purposes, "humor" at the present day—in America more definitely than in England—has become a general name for the amusing. It simply means whatever tickles us to laughter. (p. 4)

To me—and, I have pleasure in adding, not to me alone—humor is indeed a special manner of pleasantry. The humorist calls up in us the perception of the comic discreetly, in a gingerly way, without seeming to perceive it himself; he is apparently impervious to the value of his own jokes, and the contrast between what he says and the fashion in which he says it, adds not a little zest to the flavor of the fun. That contrast between matter and manner in the presentment of the comic is essential; there is no humor, in the stricter sense, unless we are given a rich comedy, in which two kinds of fun are added one to the other, setting each other off: the fun of the absurdities of things, and that of a seeming, a paradoxical unawareness of those very absurdities.

The significance of such a contrast is that it betokens a subtle mental approach in the humorist; he is the man who sees a joke, and at the same time sees through his joke; he has detachment, since he can live at once on two different planes of thought; and being alive to the seriousness of the comic, and to the comedy of the serious, he is steeped, as it were, in the sense of the relativity of things. All humorists, worthy of the name, have been in that way, and to that degree, philosophers. Humor implies not only a reflective mood, since it checks the immediate laughter of the body, and replaces it by the smile of the intellect; but a freedom to move as one chooses among the virtual comedy which life presses upon us, letting some elements just pass through us, and express themselves directly, normally; subjecting the others, on the contrary, to such a queer twist, that they are translated into words which fit them but oddly; that oddness revealing, as it were, a victory of the human mind upon life; since the mind adds to the simple fun of things another and a sophisticated comedy, the source of which is in itself. (pp. 5-6)

The Falstaff of tradition, the bragging and lying soldier, is mostly a farcical figure, that will raise in us broad laughter, and will himself, being jocular, make jokes of the same quality. Good fun that, and which it would be silly to despise, since Shakespeare and Molière did not at all look down upon it. But if Shakespeare's Falstaff were nothing else, we could hardly speak of Falstaff's humor, in the proper sense. The super-Falstaff, the glorious creature that somehow grows upon the first—a growth that takes place, we must not forget, in the creative mind of Shakespeare—is, on the contrary, the greatest example of humor in English literature, from the earliest days to the end of the eighteenth century. (p. 6)

[The] richer expansion of Falstaff's character has a tendency to occur, neither at the beginning nor at the end, but in the middle sections of the two *Henry IV,* and especially of the first part. The reason is obvious: the setting of a plot under way, and its winding up, being the occasions on which the freedom of the playwright's mind is most restricted by technical cares, the moments of greatest ease, those in which Shakespeare would let himself go, are those in which Falstaff is allowed to assume his fullest originality. (pp. 6-7)

In the first scene where he appears at all (I, ii), so free, spontaneous and above board is his gaiety, that it is Prince Henry, not he, whose cool self-command and detachment in pleasantry would better fit in with our notion of humor.

And yet, we feel all along in that scene, and in the next where Falstaff appears (II, ii), that his jollity is not simply what it looks on the surface; it rings with an undertone, which, from the moment we are aware of it, becomes more and more audible. The impression is borne in upon us, that the fat knight is perfectly conscious of himself, and plays with his whole personality, physical and moral, as he plays upon words. Such a triumphant exhibition of his own foibles is a comedy that the rogue is giving himself, and so to say a part which he performs, as for a wager. He knows that the part sits well upon him—being, indeed, in a way, the projection, the glorification of his own nature—and into the playing of that part, the essence of which seems to be pure irresponsibility, he throws a cool-headed feeling of artistry. There is archness, for instance, and a subtle understanding of stage effect, in his putting up a pretence that he wishes to reform: "Before I knew thee, Hal, I knew nothing; and now am I, if a man should speak truly, little better than one of the wicked. I must give over this life, and I will give it over; by the Lord, an I do not, I am a villain!" (I, ii). He says that with his tongue in his cheek; and where the tongue perceptibly protrudes into the cheek, we have at least a flavor of the humorous; since one thing is said, and

another meant; the conditions are roughly realized, which Mr. J. B. Priestley summed up in his definition of humor: "Speaking in jest, and thinking in earnest."

How is it that we are actually sure of such a background in Falstaff's mind? We proceed, if I may say so, on a principle, unformulated and instinctive, of analogy and probability. The nimbleness of wit, the readiness of tongue, the mental agility of which Falstaff shows himself past master, do not possibly go, in our experience, along with the naïve unconsciousness, the dull sluggishness of inner sense, the blindness to one half, and that the better half, of mental life, which his acts and speech would imply, if he did not see any further than what he says. Now, his nature must be more or less of a piece; the moral incompatibilities that exist for us, must somehow exist for him; and so the bluntness of perception which Sir John parades again and again, can be but a mask which he puts on and enjoys putting on. At this stage, we are already far from the stock figure of the bragging cowardly soldier; out of the clown which he received, Shakespeare has made a complex being, with a wealth of individual peculiarities, a talent for farce, a gift of more subtle comedy, and gleams of genuine humor. But it is not long before his creation assumes the full stretch of its originality.

With the fourth scene of Act II, Falstaff rises to new heights of paradoxical extravagance, of poetical impudence, and of humor. (pp. 7-9)

The climax of dramatic irony, and the most suggestive humor, are reached soon after in the mock dialogue where Falstaff, impersonating first the King, then the Prince, puts in a plea for himself with roguish indirectness. This is not only the most brilliant demonstration of his mental resourcefulness; the fun has depth, because the clever handling of another person's point of view is a lesson in the relativity of our judgment; because, at the same time, the praise of Falstaff which Falstaff himself makes the King supposedly deliver is piquantly unexpected upon those lips; because that praise, meanwhile, takes on a very different coloring, when we realize that it comes from the very person who is being praised; because, the impudence of the fiction being seen through, the validity of the plea is crushingly, ridiculously impaired, no one being a disinterested judge of himself; because the rogue's audacity, finally, turns out successful after all, and his argument recovers the validity it had lost, when we reflect that under the cloak of comedy Falstaff is seriously pleading for himself, and that his earnestness is more than justified from the practical or the human angle: he is getting old, the Prince is moving away from him, and that is a friendship he cannot afford to lose. His call to pity under the disguise of farce and fun is plainer still at the end, when it is into the mouth of the Prince that Falstaff puts his exquisitely clever and soberly moving appeal to the indulgence of the young man, whose heart he feels is more and more hardening against him.

We have here a wonderfully subtle handling of the finer and implicit shades that enter into the composition of humor; what is said, and what is understood, are both involved in infinitely complex relations; the dialogue reverberates through our minds in long echoes of amusement, thought, and feeling. The essence of that playing with the hard and fast notions and judgments of normal life, through the effect of which they are brought into paradoxical suggestive connections with one another, is the veriest essence of philosophical humor. (pp. 12-13)

Louis Cazamian, "The Humor of Falstaff," in The Johns Hopkins Alumni Magazine, *Vol. XXIII, No. 1, November, 1934, pp. 2-24.*

H. B. CHARLTON (essay date 1935)

[*An English scholar, Charlton is best known for his* Shakespearian Tragedy *and* Shakespearian Comedy—*two important studies in which he argues that the proponents of New Criticism, particularly T. S. Eliot and I. A. Richards, were reducing Shakespeare's drama to its poetic elements and in the process losing sight of his characters. In his introduction to* Shakespearian Tragedy, *Charlton described himself as a "devout" follower of A. C. Bradley, and like his mentor he adopted a psychological, character-oriented approach to Shakespeare's work. Charlton follows Bradley (1902) in his remarks on* Henry IV, *describing Hal as priggish and Falstaff as a comic hero with an "unslakeable thirst for life." But he differs from Bradley in his claim that Falstaff was rejected not only by Hal, but also by Shakespeare. For further discussion of Hal's rejection of Falstaff, see the excerpts by Corbyn Morris (1744), Samuel Johnson (1765), William Hazlitt (1817), G. G. Gervinus (1849-50), Edward Dowden (1881), E. E. Stoll (1914), J. B. Priestley (1925), J. Dover Wilson (1943), E.M.W. Tillyard (1944), and J.I.M. Stewart (1948). The essay was first published in* Bulletin of the John Rylands Library *in 1935.*]

With hardly a dissentient voice, the later world has scorned Hal for his offense against humanity [in rejecting Falstaff]. Mr. Masefield lets it colour all Henry V's subsequent deeds, and writes him down for a heartless schemer. "Prince Henry is not a hero, he is not a thinker, he is not even a friend; he is a common man whose incapacity for feeling enables him to change his habits whenever interest bids him" [see excerpt above, 1911]. (pp. 165-66)

There is scarcely a reader who will not sympathise with Mr. Masefield's attitude, though perhaps few would press the case so far. It is indeed hardly thinkable that Shakespeare expected us to feel so bitterly against Prince Hal. Yet it is equally unthinkable that our feelings towards him can remain sympathetically genial. (p. 166)

Shakespeare's characters are incessantly striving to break into life. Dramatically this lends a larger dare to his great enterprise. But it has its greater hazards. Hal's conversion must be grounded in character. To make it credible and consonant with Henry V, it must follow a deliberate motive or an unconscious but convincing prompting from the stuff of his nature. Hence the cumulative priggishness of the young royster. His attempts to salve in words the long-grown wounds of his intemperance, his plea that he is only upholding the unyoked humour of his idle confederates for a while, his admission that he is deliberately experimenting, toying with a political practice to falsify men's hopes, and, by reformation, ultimately to show more goodly—all this is an offence against humanity, and an offence which dramatically never becomes a skill. (p. 169)

[What] is the humour, the ruling passion, the distinctive quiddity of Sir John Falstaff? Fundamentally, it is his infinite capacity for extricating himself from predicaments. Circumstance hems him in at the corner of a room, and, as his opponents stretch out their hands to lay hold of him, this huge mountain of flesh slips through the key-hole. So adept is he in this art of extrication that he revels in creating dilemmas for himself to enjoy the zest of coming triumphantly out of them. He is insatiably curious to provide situations which test or even strain his genius for overcoming them. Mastery of circumstance is his pride: it is also his supreme qualification to be a hero of comedy.

These are traits which supply the mainspring of the plot. Falstaff has an unslakeable thirst for life. "Give me life" [*I Henry IV*, 5.3.59]—he cries—and the cry is in soliloquy, no fetch therefore to delude listeners. Life is his *summum bonum*. "Young

men must live" [*Ibid.*, 2.2.90-91]—and he identifies himself with youth—"You that are old consider not the capacities of us that are young" [*II Henry IV*, 1.2.173-74]. Life is most intoxicating when a jest is forward and spirits are high. Life is indeed itself the greatest of frolics. (pp. 178-79)

One need not, of course, claim 'courage' for Falstaff. But one cannot indite him of cowardice. Neither are relevant terms. What he has is absolute self-possession and an aptitude to employ all the elements of his being for the furtherance of his own welfare. His counterfeiting of death is policy, just as was the King's scheme for avoiding death in battle by having many others disguised in his clothes. Falstaff's is as successful for his purpose as is the King's for his, and it does not, as does the King's, cost anybody his life. Indeed, in Falstaff's vocabulary, it is not counterfeiting at all. "Counterfeit? I lie, I am no counterfeit: to die is to be a counterfeit; for he is but the counterfeit of a man who hath not the life of a man: but to counterfeit dying, when a man thereby liveth, is to be no counterfeit, but the true and perfect image of life indeed" [*I Henry IV*, 5.4.114-19]. Almost always, since Falstaff's values are his own and not the conventional ones, he will find it necessary to twist words and things from their normal functions to apparently ludicrous ones. But their ludicrousness is caused by unexpected suddenness, not by inherent absurdity. Going into battle, Falstaff arms himself with a bottle of sack, not with a pistol. (pp. 183-84)

It might be, and has been, claimed that the original Falstaff overgrew his part, and had to be turned out of the cycle at the point when Hal became king. As has been seen, there is matter in the second *Henry IV* to suggest that Shakespeare was leading Falstaff to his dismissal: matter, also, hinting that he did it reluctantly. But if Sir John had necessarily to go, could he not have been allowed a death-bed—a more certain dismissal than a king's rejection—before Hal's coronation? An apoplexy, any affliction to which the body of man is liable might, without stretch of likelihood, have been called in to remove a Falstaff who, on a professional diagnosis, "might have more diseases than he knew for" [*II Henry IV*, 1.2.4-5]. Moreover, his removal by mere royal edict brought technical troubles with it, the dubieties surrounding the character of Hal. Why then did Shakespeare rest satisfied with Henry's rejection of Falstaff as the expedient by which to get rid of him? Is it indeed Henry, or is it Shakespeare who rejects Falstaff? (p. 196)

The figure which the dramatist's imagination had intuitively compounded, had seemed infinitely better provided than any of his predecessors with the gifts of the comic hero. With such a spirit, such a mind, such intuitions, and such an outlook on life, he appeared to bear within his own nature a complete guarantee of survival and of mastery of circumstance, the pledge of the perfect comic hero. But somehow or other, when the intoxication of creating him is momentarily quieter, hesitancies begin to obtrude and the processes of creation are different. The clogging becomes stronger. Falstaff must be cast off, as he is cast off at the end of the second *Henry IV*. But a pathetic hope persists, and is spoken in the Epilogue: it may still be possible to save Sir John: "our humble author will continue the story with Sir John in it, and make you merry with fair Katherine of France: where, for any thing I know, Falstaff shall die of a sweat, unless already a' be killed with your hard opinions" [*II Henry IV*, Epilogue]. But before the play with Katherine in it is written, the issue is settled. Falstaff is irrevocably discredited, fit for nothing more but Windsor forest [i.e., in *The Merry Wives of Windsor*]. (pp. 196-97)

In efficiency, indeed, efficiency to live the life to which one is called, there is only one person in the play to set beside Falstaff, namely, the King himself. A comparison of them at length would take us into a consideration of Shakespeare's view of kingship. . . . The King's immediate task is to maintain the welfare of the state of England; Falstaff's is to preserve the well-being of the corporation of Sir John. There is a striking similarity in the obligations imposed by each of these purposes, and in the means by which each of the actors secures his ends. The wit of Falstaff and the policy of the King are instruments which rest on similar assumptions. Morality enters into the schemes of neither of them: they remain free from the constraints of all conventions and of all generally accepted principles. Each in his own sphere is the perfect exponent of expediency. "Are these things then necessities? Then let us meet them like necessities." For both of them "nothing can seem foul to those that win." But the political necessities which are the King's sphere require him to purchase success by the complete subjugation of personal affection, human sentiment, and natural instinct. . . . [As] a social creature for whom life is not, unless it be with his fellows and nowise aloof from them, Falstaff can employ his wit without renouncing the instinctive promptings of his humanity or, at least, of his flesh. At the end, he emerges no less successful than the King, and insuperably superior to this cold-blooded politician in his claims on our regard. Falstaff, without doubt has demonstrated his right to be considered a matchless victor in the world which is the world of affairs and of comedy. But no less certainly, he has been cast out of it.

Why then did Shakespeare reject him? (pp. 203-04)

"Honour," "a good name," not only to Falstaff but also to Hotspur, may appear to be an article of commerce, a commodity to be bought. But in the certified records of human existence, it has been something more, something infinitely more. Honour, faith, love, truth, self-sacrifice—these are things in the light of which men have lived joyously,—the matter for comedy—and at the bidding of which they have happily died— the matter for tragedy, or, may be, for a divine comedy. But for Falstaff they have no existence. "Sirrah, there's no room for faith, truth, nor honesty in this bosom of thine; it is all filled up with guts and midriff" [*I Henry IV*, III.iii.153-55].

That is Falstaff's failure. It was in this realisation of Falstaff's incompleteness on the eve before Shrewsbury that Shakespeare felt the wine of life begin to taste like gall and wormwood on his tongue. But, though for a moment, and indeed for a more protracted stretch, the memory of Falstaff as he had seemed to be, excited a sense of disillusionment . . . yet with wider imaginative experience something of Falstaff was finally saved— his common sense, his intuitive apprehension of the facts of existence within the limits which life itself imposes, and his insatiable thirst for such a life amongst the rest of mortals.

But the world in which Falstaff's successors in comedy would have to prove their genius for mastery, would necessarily have to be a larger and a richer world than Falstaff's, one in which room would be found for the things unknown to Falstaff, things proved now to be no less necessary to life, things such as love and faith and truth and honour. Falstaff had indeed acquired a mastery of life. But it was by denying to his universe the very things which give life its supreme values. He had conquered a world, only to reveal that such a world was not worth conquest.

It is a devastating end to such a gigantic effort. It might well appear that Shakespeare had come to a dead end in his progress

towards the ideal of comedy. Falstaff had seemed so near it, and Falstaff had failed. To go farther Shakespeare would have to save himself from his own Falstaff. His imagination would have to cast about for a being bigger than Falstaff—*absit omen*— a being in whom the elements of human nature would be richer than in Falstaff, one who would by nature be endowed with a sense for those forces in human life which enrich it immeasurably, and which for Falstaff had been as if they were not. (pp. 206-07)

H. B. Charlton, "Falstaff," in his Shakespearian Comedy, *Methuen & Co. Ltd., 1938, pp. 161-207.*

M. NECHKINA   (essay date 1935)

[*The communist and socialist movements of the 1930s produced a large body of politically inspired literary criticism, including many attempts to interpret Shakespeare in the light of Marxist theory. In the following excerpt, the Russian critic M. Nechkina selects some of Marx's scattered remarks on Shakespeare to discuss Falstaff. Her contention that Sir John demonstrates Shakespeare's rejection of the growing "bourgeois world" was challenged vigorously by T. A. Jackson (1936).*]

Marx counted Shakespeare among his strongest literary attachments. He had a thorough knowledge of him and had several times read his works completely. . . . Marx's use of the character of Falstaff is extremely interesting. It is safe to say that the analysis of this character in Marxist literary research cannot but lose a great deal if the corresponding places in Marx's works are overlooked. Falstaff for Marx was a kind of "personified capital" of the epoch of the dawn of capitalism, which gave birth to the bourgeois of the epoch of primitive accumulation. An unpardonable liar, a narrow pleasure seeker, thinking only of his own material interests, a dissolute rake openly showing his contempt for all the religious mummery of feudalism, a highwayman and yet at the same time an arrant coward, a swindler and merry wine-bibber, ready to sell all his knightly virtues for a pound note—Falstaff is a clearcut type of the epoch of primitive accumulation. The fragments of feudal ideas are merely the building material for his new bourgeois morality. Saving his own skin by wile in the middle of the battle, (Falstaff, one will remember, threw his sword on the ground at the first advance of the enemy and pretended to be dead), he argues that to save one's own life is the first knightly virtue. Plundering, seizing, stealing, borrowing without repaying while swearing to the contrary, calling upon the Virgin Mary and all the mediaeval saints are amongst Falstaff's favorite tricks. Shakespeare, regretfully watching the downfall of the feudal world, showed his rejection of the coming bourgeois world in the comic character of Falstaff. (p. 75)

M. Nechkina, "Shakespeare in Karl Marx's 'Capital'," translated by N. Goold-Verschoyle, in International Literature, *No. 3, March, 1935, pp. 75-81.*

CAROLINE F.E. SPURGEON   (essay date 1935)

[*Spurgeon's* Shakespeare's Imagery *inaugurated the "image-pattern analysis" method of studying Shakespeare's plays, one of the most widely used methods of the mid-twentieth century. In this work, she interprets the thematic structure of the plays through an examination of patterns in the imagery. Spurgeon also sought to learn about Shakespeare's personality from a study of his images, a course which few of her disciples followed. Since publication of her book, earlier works on image patterns in Shakespeare have been discovered, but none was so important in the history of Shakespearean criticism as Spurgeon's. In the following re-marks on Falstaff, Spurgeon aligns herself with such earlier critics as Francis Gentleman (1774), Richard Cumberland (1786), and George Brandes (1895-96), all of whom detect a deterioration in Falstaff's character in Part Two.]*

In the first part of *Henry IV* one might argue, only from the images he uses, that Falstaff is a man of parts, of wit, sweet temper and charm, and of some reading and culture. One rarely finds facts from books or drama referred to by Shakespeare in his imagery, yet four of such images, out of a total of five in this play, are Falstaff's. He calls Mistress Quickly 'Dame Part-let the hen' (from either Reynard the Fox or Chaucer), com-pares himself to Turk Gregory (probably from Fox's *History*, or possibly from an old tragedy), and speaks in 'King Cam-byses' vein' (alluding to the old play of Preston's *Cambyses*, 1570). He has some knowledge too of the romances, for his name for Bardolph, 'the Knight of the Burning Lamp' is a skit (like the *Knight of the Burning Pestle* later) on the heroes of the old romances, he refers to the Knight of the Sun in a Spanish romance [I *H.IV*, I.ii.15-16] and in his jesting recommendation to the prince that when he is king, 'let not us that are squires of the night's body be called thieves of the day's beauty: let us be Diana's foresters, gentlemen of the shades, minions of the moon', he reveals, not only a feeling for and knowledge of chivalry and pageantry, but also a very charming gift of poetical expression. He has some acquaintance with the clas-sics, and declares that he is as 'valiant as Hercules'. Apart from his image drawn from Pharaoh's lean kine, it is certain from his language that he knows his Bible well [I *H.IV*, II.iv.473, etc.]. He clearly also knows his Lyly and enjoys the humour of the far-fetched comparisons, which he copies [I *H.IV*, II.iv.399-402]; he appreciates the 'drone of a Lincolnshire bag-pipe' [I *H.IV*, I.ii.76], he also notices pictures, a trait rare on the whole in Shakespeare, and refers, evidently with intimate knowledge, to Lazarus in the painted cloth, and to Dives, who lived in purple, burning in his robes. His, too, are the only images from heraldry in the play, honour is a 'mere scutcheon', and his soldier's half shirt is 'two napkins tacked together and thrown over the shoulders like a herald's coat without sleeves'. (pp. 377-78)

I do not think it is mere chance that Falstaff's images in the second part of the play show less trace of genuine feeling, cultivation and reading, and partake more of grotesqueness and ribaldry than in the first part. Witty they always are, for else Falstaff would no longer be Falstaff, but I believe that, in the course of the two plays, Shakespeare definitely pictured a cer-tain deterioration of spirit in the fat knight which is subtly reflected in his images.

One may compare, for instance, the charm of tone of his jesting reference to romance and the moon [I *H.IV*, I.ii.25] already quoted, with the roughness of his semi-satirical threat later to Prince John, that if his valour be not recognised he will have a ballad made to commemorate his deeds 'with mine own picture on the top on't, Coleville kissing my foot: to the which course if I be enforced, if you do not all show like gilt two-pences to men, and I in the clear sky of fame o'ershine you as much as the full moon doth the cinders of the element, which show like pins' heads to her, believe not the word of the noble' [2 *H.IV*, IV.iii.53].

As in the first part, the only two biblical images in the play are his (a comparison with Job and with the glutton in hell) and he alludes to Shallow as a 'Vice's dagger', but otherwise, with the exception of his calling his tailor 'a whoreson Achi-

tophel', we find in his images in 2 *H. IV* no references to books or drama, chivalry or painting.

On the other hand, there is quite a number of grotesque—and if not 'unsavoury' [I *H.IV*, I.ii.79] then of rough and somewhat coarse—similes, as in his anger with his tailor, who, instead of sending him satin, has the nerve to demand 'security', which calls forth Falstaff's curse "Let him be damned like the glutton, pray God his tongue be hotter!' and later his double-edged description of how he may 'sleep in security' [2 *H.IV*, I.ii.45]. His pungent pictures of Shallow's temperament and appearance and of Bardolph's face [2 *H.IV*, II.iv.333] are also of this nature.

The brilliant flashes of wit which light up a whole scene are in the second as well as the first part, as when he describes himself walking in front of his diminutive page 'like a sow that hath overwhelmed all her litter but one', or selects Shadow as the ideal soldier because 'the foeman may with as great aim level at the edge of a pen knife'; also his inimitable touches of vivid description, as of Prince Hal, who laughs 'till his face be like a wet cloak ill laid up'; but there is no sustained, good-humoured, sweet-flavoured wit of the quality of the immortal scene in the Boar's Head Tavern when in King Cambyses' vein he plays the part of the king reproving his erring son. (pp. 379-80)

Caroline F.E. Spurgeon, in her appendices to her Shakespeare's Imagery and What It Tells Us, Cambridge at the University Press, 1968, pp. 357-84.

WILLIAM EMPSON   (essay date 1935)

[Empson's Seven Types of Ambiguity *(1930), with its emphasis on interpreting a literary work as a complex combination of mul-tiple meanings, was a major influence in the development of New Criticism. In* Some Versions of Pastoral *(1935), excerpted below, Empson continued his exploration of the positive value of literary ambiguity, touching on* Henry IV *at two different points. He discusses the ambiguities generated through the juxtaposition of the heroic and comic plots which reaches its climax in Part One with the feigned death of Falstaff and the actual death of Hotspur. In the following comments, he turns to the Hal-Falstaff relation-ship, arguing that the contradictory emotions the playwright ex-presses regarding Hal are replicated in Shakespeare's Sonnet 94, which Empson interprets as a depiction of Shakespeare's bitter relationship with a patron. For more commentary on the relation of the Falstaff plot to the rest of the play, see the excerpts by Hermann Ulrici (1839) and L. C. Knights (1933).]*

The crucial first soliloquy of Prince Henry was put in to save his reputation with the audience; it is a wilful destruction of his claims to generosity, indeed to honesty, if only in Falstaff's sense; but this is not to say that it was a mere job with no feeling behind it. It was a concession to normal and decent opinion rather than to the groundlings; the man who was to write *Henry V* could feel the force of that as well as take care of his plot; on the other hand, it cannot have been written without bitterness against the prince. (p. 86)

We would probably find the prince less puzzling if Shakespeare had re-written *Henry VI* in his prime. The theme at the back of the series, after all, is that the Henries are usurpers; however great the virtues of Henry V may be, however rightly the nation may glory in his deeds, there is something fishy about him and the justice of Heaven will overtake his son. In having some sort of double attitude to the prince Shakespeare was merely doing his work as a history-writer. For the critic to drag in a personal situation from the Sonnets is neither an attack nor a justification; it claims only to show where the feelings the play needed were obtained.

Sir Walter Raleigh said that the play was written when Shakespeare was becoming successful and buying New Place, so that he became interested in the problems of successful people like Henries IV and V rather than in poetical failures like Richard II. On this view we are to see in Prince Henry the Swan himself; he has made low friends only to get local colour out of them, and now drops them with a bang because he has made money and grand friends. It is possible enough, though I don't know why it was thought pleasant; anyway such a personal association is far at the back of the mind and one would expect several to be at work together. Henry might carry a grim externalization of self-contempt as well as a still half-delighted reverberation of Southampton; Falstaff an attack on some rival playwright or on Florio as tutor of Southampton as well as a savage and joyous externalization of self-contempt. But I think only the second of these alternatives fits in with the language and echoes a serious personal situation. Henry's soliloquy demands from us just the sonnets' mood of bitter complaisance; the young man must still be praised and loved, however he betrays his intimates, because we see him all shining with the virtues of success. So I shall now fancy Falstaff as Shakespeare (he has obviously some great forces behind him) and Henry as the patron who has recently betrayed him.

> I know you all, and will a-while vphold
> The vnyoak'd humor of your idlenesse:
> Yet heerein will I imitate the Sunne,
> Who doth permit the base contagious cloudes
> To smother vp his Beauty from the world,
> That when he please again to be himselfe,
> Being wanted, he may be more wondred at,
> By breaking through the foule and vgly mists
> Of vapours, that did seeme to strangle him.
>
> [*1 Henry IV*, I. ii. 195-203]

This seems quite certainly drawn from the earliest and most pathetic of the attempts to justify W. H.

> Fvll many a glorious morning haue I seene, . . .
> Anon permit the *basest cloudes* to ride, . . .
> With *ougly* rack on his celestiall face, . . .
> *Suns* of the world may staine, when heauens sun
>   staineth
>
> [Sonnet 33]

But it is turned backwards: the sun is now to free itself from the clouds by the very act of betrayal. 'Oh that you were yourself' (13) and 'have eyes to wonder' (106) are given the same twist into humility; Shakespeare admits, with Falstaff in front of him, that the patron would be better off without friends in low life. The next four lines, developing the idea that you make the best impression on people by only treating them well at rare intervals, are a prosaic re-hash of 'Therefore are feasts so solemn and so rare', etc. (52); what was said of the policy of the friend is now used for the policy of the politician, though in both play and sonnet they are opposed. The connexion in the next lines is more doubtful.

> So when this loose behaviour I throw off
> And pay the debt I never promised
> By so much better than my word I am
> By so much shall I falsify men's hopes
>
> [*1 Henry IV*, I. ii. 208-11]

(He does indeed, by just so much.) This *debt* looks like an echo of the debt to nature there was so much doubt about W.

H.'s method of paying; it has turned into a debt to society. At any rate in the sonnet-like final couplet

> I'll so offend, to make offence a skill
>
> [*1 Henry IV*, I. ii. 216]

('The tongue that tells the story of thy days . . . Cannot dispraise but in a kind of praise') we have the central theme of all the sonnets of apology; the only difference, though it is a big one, is that this man says it about himself.

One element at least in this seems to reflect a further doubt on to the sonnet I have considered; the prince may be showing by this soliloquy that he can avoid infection, or may be an example of how sour a lord and owner can turn in his deeds on Coronation Day. The last irony and most contorted generosity one can extract from the sonnet is in the view that Shakespeare himself is the basest weed, that to meet him is to meet infection, that the result of being faithful to his friendship would be to be outbraved even by him, that the advice to be a cold person and avoid the fate of the lily is advice to abandon Shakespeare once for all.

This interpretation is more than once as firmly contradicted by Falstaff as it will be by my readers. He first comes on in a great fuss about his good name; he has been rated in the streets for leading astray Harry. At the end of the scene we find that this was unfair to him; the prince makes clear by the soliloquy that he is well able to look after himself. Meanwhile Falstaff amuses himself by turning the accusation the other way round.

> O, thou hast damnable iteration, and art indeede
> able to corrupt a Saint. Thou hast done much
> harme vnto me *Hal*, God forgiue thee for it.
> Before I knew thee *Hal*, I knew nothing: and
> now I am (if a man shold speake truly) little
> better than one of the wicked. I must giue ouer
> this life, and I will giue it over: and I do not,
> I am a Villaine. Ile be damn'd for never a Kings
> sonne in Christendome.
> PRIN. Where shall we take a purse tomorrow,
> lacke?
>
> [*1 Henry IV*, I. ii. 90-9]

The audience were not expected to believe this aspect of the matter, but there may well be some truth in it if applied to the situation Shakespeare had at the back of his mind. The other aspect is also preserved for us in the Sonnets.

> I may not euer-more acknowledge thee,
> Least my bewailed guilt should do thee shame,
> Nor thou with publike kindnesse honour me,
> Vnlesse thou take that honour from thy name:
>
> [Sonnet 36]

'I not only warn you against bad company; I admit I am part of it.' One could throw in here that letter about Southampton wasting his time at the playhouse and out of favour with the Queen.

There are two sums of a thousand pounds concerned, so that the phrase is kept echoing through both parts of the history; it seems to become a symbol of Falstaff's hopes and his betrayal. The first he got by the robbery at Gadshill, and the prince at once robbed him of it; supposedly to give back to its owner, if you take his reluctance to steal seriously (he does give it back later, but one is free to suspect only under threat of exposure). He says he will give it to Francis the drawer, and Falstaff pacifies the hostess by saying he will get it back. . . .

But Falstaff gets another thousand pounds from Shallow, and the phrase is all he clings to in the riddling sentence at his final discomfiture: 'Master Shallow, I owe you a thousand pound.' This is necessary, to seem calm and reassure Shallow; it is either a sweeping gesture of renunciation ('What use to me now is the money I need never have repaid to this fool?') or a comfort since it reminds him that he has got the money and certainly won't repay it; but it is meant also for the king to hear and remember ('I class you with Shallow and the rest of my friends'). (pp. 86-90)

It is as well to look at Falstaff in general for a moment, to show what this tender attitude to him has to fit in with. The plot treats him as a simple Punch, whom you laugh at with good humour, though he is wicked, because he is always knocked down and always bobs up again. (Our attitude to him as a Character entirely depends on the Plot, and yet he is a Character who very nearly destroyed the Plot as a whole.) People sometimes take advantage of this to view him as a lovable old dear; a notion which one can best refute by considering him as an officer.

        Part I. V. iii. 35-8

> I haue led my rag of Muffins where they are
> pepper'd: there's not three of my 150 left alive,
> and they for the Townes end, to beg during
> life.

We saw him levy a tax in bribes on the men he left; he now kills all the weaklings he conscripted, in order to keep their pay. A fair proportion of the groundlings consisted of disbanded soldiers who had suffered under such a system; the laughter was a roar of hatred here; he is 'comic' like a Miracle Play Herod. (Whereas Harry has no qualities that are obviously not W. H.'s.) And yet it is out of his defence against this, the least popularizable charge against him, that he makes his most unanswerable retort to the prince.

> PRINCE. Tell me, Jack, whose fellows are these
> that come after?
> FAL. Mine, Hal, mine.
> PRINCE. I never did see such pitiful rascals.
> FAL. Tut, tut; good enough to toss; food for
> powder, food for powder; they'll fill a pit as
> well as better; tush, man, mortal men, mortal
> men.
>
>   [*1 Henry IV*, IV. ii. 61-7]

Mortal conveys both 'all men are in the same boat, all equal before God' and 'all you want is slaughter'. No one in the audience was tempted to think Harry as wicked as his enemy Hotspur, who deserved death as much as Lear for wanting to divide England. But this remark needed to be an impudent cover for villainy if the strength of mind and heart in it were not to be too strong, to make the squabbles of ambitious and usurping persons too contemptible.

On the other hand, Falstaff's love for the prince is certainly meant as a gap in his armour; one statement (out of many) of this comes where the prince is putting his life in danger and robbing him of the (stolen) thousand pounds.

> I haue forsworne his company hourely any time
> this two and twenty yeares, and yet I am be-
> witcht with the Rogues company. If the Rascal
> haue not giuen me medecines to make me loue

him, Ile be hang'd; it could not be else; I haue drunke Medecines.

        [*1 Henry IV*, II. ii. 15-20]

He could continually be made to say such things without stopping the laugh at him, partly because one thinks he is pretending love to the prince for his own interest; 'never any man's thought keeps the roadway' as well as those of the groundlings who think him a hypocrite about it, but this phrase of mockery at them is used only to dignify the prince; the more serious Falstaff's expression of love becomes the more comic it is, whether as hopeless or as hypocrisy. But to stretch one's mind round the whole character (as is generally admitted) one must take him, though as the supreme expression of the cult of mockery as strength and the comic idealization of freedom, yet as both villainous and tragically ill-used. (pp. 90-1)

> *William Empson, "They That Have Power," in his*
> Some Versions of Pastoral: A Study of the Pastoral
> Form in Literature, *Penguin Books, 1966, pp. 75-
> 96.*

T. A. JACKSON (essay date 1936)

[*In response to Nechkina's remarks on Falstaff (see excerpt above, 1935), the British Marxist T. A. Jackson poses the theory that Falstaff represents not bourgeois society, but the values of a*

Part II. Act IV. Scene iv. Henry IV and Prince Henry. By Robert Smirke (1795). From the Art Collection of the Folger Shakespeare Library.

decaying feudal world. Jackson's article shares two features with J. Dover Wilson's well-known study The Fortunes of Falstaff *(see excerpt below, 1943): a condemnation of "sentimental" critics who see Falstaff as a hero wronged by Hal, and an emphasis on Falstaff's affinities with the Vice figure of medieval morality-plays. Other commentators who have interpreted* Henry IV *as a morality drama include John Webster Spargo (1922) and E.M.W. Tillyard (1944).]*

Netchkina says: "Falstaff is a clear-cut type of the epoch of primitive accumulation. The fragments of feudal ideas are merely the building materials for his *new bourgeois morality* . . . Shakespeare *regretfully* watching the downfall of the feudal world, *showed his rejection of the coming bourgeois world* in the comic character of Falstaff" [see excerpt above, 1935].

That Falstaff is a comic character is true, that Shakespeare showed by his handling of Falstaff that he "rejected" the "world" which Falstaff stood for, is true likewise. But we deny, categorically, that Falstaff's morality was "bourgeois" or that he typified in any sense of the word the "coming bourgeois world." Consequently, we draw from the character of Falstaff, and Shakespeare's handling thereof, deductions exactly opposite to those of Netchkina.

To make the issue—a crucial one—clear, we must consider the character of Falstaff in relation to the drama in which he appears, and then its significance as a social-historical phenomenon.

Considered as a piece of dramatic machinery Falstaff is first of all a "clown." He is, that is to say, a large, fat man, gluttonous and debauched,—so huge, and so gross, that "men of all sorts take pride to gird at me: the brain of this foolish-compounded clay, Man, is not able to invent anything that tends to laughter, more than I invent or is invented on me: I am not only witty in myself, but the cause that wit is in other men." This type of character, the "clown," whose every entrance raised an anticipatory guffaw—and whose function on the stage was to supply a comic relief for both actors and auditors between spells of tragedy, or farcical relief from the more tense episodes in a comedy drama—was a well-established convention in Shakespeare's day. It can in fact be traced back in the evolution of the drama to the *Devil* in the mediaeval "mystery" dramas and the *"Vice"* in their successors, the "morality" plays or "interludes."

In the "Mysteries" the "Devil" was brought in at appropriate moments—or was present all the time with his attendant imps on the lowest deck of the three-decker stage (which represented Hell, Earth and Heaven respectively). Grotesquely hideous in get-up he appeared on "Earth" (to the accompaniment of hoots, missiles and general merriment) either to fail ignominiously in an endeavour to corrupt the righteous or to carry off a convicted villain to his doom in "Hell."

The "Vice" evolved from the attendants upon the Devil in the religious "mystery" pageant dramas. These attendants were first specialised to represent one or other of the seven "deadly" sins, and were then elaborated into characters in which these "vices" were predominant. Along the latter line of development they finally broke away from their origin to become comedy or tragedy characters in the naturalistic drama, which the Elizabethan dramatists succeeded in evolving.

A specialised development from the "Vice" conventionalised to absurdity, is the "character" whose whole function is to be absurd. Originally there were Seven Vices. These, for economy's sake, became one generalised "Vice," which, in turn,

became both a substitute for the Devil (who by convention had always to be defeated and humiliated after a period of temporary triumph) as well as an embodiment of absurdity. (The ultimate outcome of this latter development survives in the "clown" of the circus or the pantomime.) Shakespeare, breaking away from the convention at an earlier stage, evolved out of the universal "butt" into which the Devil-Vice had degenerated, the whole series of his inimitable "clowns" of whom Falstaff is the chief.

It is important to remember this functional origin in estimating the significance of Falstaff as a *character*. In his role as a piece of dramatic machinery, Falstaff's descent from the mediaeval Devil is as apparent as is also, his descent from the devil's absurd duplicate, the "Vice." In the latter aspect Falstaff's huge girth and grotesque appearance (both, taken over by Shakespeare from the older dramatic work upon which his own was based—very few of "Shakespeare's" plays being *wholly* his own invention) are clear links with the past: In the former aspect the link is provided by the fact that alike in *Henry IV* and the *Merry Wives* of *Windsor* Falstaff is a *tempter* who is cheated, robbed of his ill-gotten gains, made a laughing-stock, and, finally, reduced to complete humiliation.

Sentimental bourgeois critics, Falstaff-"Fans", are all of them rather indignant with Shakespeare because in the *Merry Wives,* Falstaff is made a butt all through, and has not even a brief interval of triumph. They fail to realise that in *Henry IV* his ultimate humiliation is even more profound and follows closely the lines of the mediaeval flinging-down of the Devil into Hell. (pp. 81-2)

Connected closely with Falstaff's "Devil" function is the fact that he appears as the chief of a whole group of satellites (relics of the original vices attendant upon the Devil), Dame Quickly, Doll Tearsheet, Lieutenant Peto, Ancient (i.e. Ensign) Pistol, Corporals Bardolph and Nym, and the Page. But this fact that he is presented as the Knight-Commander of a company (of broken-down military men and their whole or part-time harlots, whose headquarters are at a quasi-tavern, quasi-bawdy house) also gives him his *representative* significance. This crew of satellites—into whose number are included, intermittently, Gadshill (a thieves' "bonnet"), Prince Hal and Poins (in their roystering, gentleman-highwayman stage) and Master Justice Shallow, with his satellite Silence, (burlesque memories of rowdy law students)—constitutes Falstaff's "tail." Their attendant relation to him gives him the standing of a petty king attended by his Court, a feudal lord surrounded by his household following, or (what was no uncommon sight in Shakespeare's London, and an unfailing source of mirth) a Scottish chief or an Irish "righ" followed by his tail of "ghillies" on "dhuine wassalls."

To grasp the full significance of the "rejection" implicit in Shakespeare's presentation of Falstaff he must be seen not only in his aspect of "Devil" but also in his aspect of a *grotesque parody of feudal state and status*.

It must, of course, be remembered, that, such is Shakespeare's artistry that these mechanical and symbolical functions of Falstaff and his "tail," become apparent only after analysis. In their actual stage appearance, each and every one of them is a complete and unique character. . . . Shakespeare's genius did not consist in making Falstaff out of *nothing;* it consisted in making him out of *less than nothing,* out of a mechanical abstraction,—the conventionalised "Devil"—"Vice" he was before Shakespeare gave him a human life and personality.

Originally, Falstaff's "Devil" function consisted in tempting the young Prince of Wales into wild and dissolute courses. For that purpose he had to be a glutton and a wine-bibber, a haunter of taverns and bawdy-houses, a gamester, a brawler and a pimp. It is notable that in Shakespeare's version, although the gross bulk of Falstaff—(that "huge hill of flesh'')—still remains as a vehicle for all the Seven deadly sins, they survive in Falstaff, except in respect of gluttony and sloth, only in their grotesquely degenerate forms. (pp. 82-3)

[Pride] has shrunk almost to vanishing point, his lust is now a thing to occasion jests on the marvel that "desire should so long outlive performance", his "anger''—(in the conventional sense of disposition towards murder)—is more than inhibited by his gluttony-begotten sloth, his "covetousness" is now the money-hunger of the chronically impecunious—that of the sponger and the highway-robber. This degeneration of the qualities necessary for his "Vice" function is, however, an enhancement of the qualities necessary for his representative function, that of presenting an aspect of feudal society in the last stages of degeneration. (p. 83)

Lest any reader not familiar with Shakespeare and the Elizabethan stage convention might be confused by this confounding of the chronology of *Henry IV* and that of Shakespeare's own day, it should be noted that *historical* realism was no part of Shakespeare's purpose. Falstaff and the members of his circle appear quite cheerfully in a *contemporary* Elizabethan comedy. . . . Whatever the scenes of one of Shakespeare's dramas, and whatever the nominal period, it is always the England of Shakespeare's own day which is presented. (pp. 83-4)

The Tudor monarchy he established was already *post*-feudal. It rested on the basis of an alliance between the town burghers—particularly the wealthy merchants of London—and the Crown. The absolutism of the Crown which was consolidated and extended all through the Tudor reigns until it became an intolerable grievance under the Stuarts, was in fact, the weapon with which,—to the complete satisfaction of the town burghers, and especially of the London merchants aforesaid—all the *local* sovereignties of the feudal baronage were destroyed. (p. 84)

When the bands of feudal retainers were dispersed, and again when the monasteries were blown-up, burned-down or converted into mansions for the new "kulak" aristocracy . . . what became of these retainers, these monks, and nuns? The statute-book, as Marx shows in his chapter, "Bloody Legislation Against the Expropriated" tells us part of the story. The rest can be pieced together from contemporary records. Briefly summarised, we may cite two great "canals" into which these masses of "unemployed" were drained off—except, of course, in so far as, in time, they found employment as proletarians in industry, which, however, was a prolonged and slow process. The feudal retainers went in the main "to the wars," that is to say, they became professional soldiers, and, between spells of service, cut-purses, highway-robbers, tavern-bullies, whores' "protectors" and general spongers. The unfrocked clerics partly went the same road; chiefly they supplied England with its first form of literary-intelligentsia. The whole amazing literary upsurge which has Shakespeare as its supreme height had its roots in this class and in the circumstances consequent upon its coming into being. Out of the de-classed strata of feudal retainers arose such types as Falstaff and his tail. Out of the strata of unfrocked clergy arose the class of scriveners, school-masters, lawyers, and also the new literary odd-job class, and their creations, the Elizabethan drama, and ultimately the work of William Shakespeare. Only in this sense is it correct to identify Falstaff (and his creator) with the epoch of primitive accumulation. (p. 85)

In form Falstaff's company is a quasi-feudal military company headed by a knight. In substance and in fact they are a crew of degenerate thieves, parasites, and spongers, foot-pads, tavern bullies, souteneurs and tricksters. Their lives and their ends follow closely the line followed in actual fact by Francois Villon in Paris, a century before Shakespeare's birth, while as more or less amusing scoundrels they form one of the earliest examples of the *picaresque*—the line of Sancho Panza, Gil Blas, Sganarelle and the rest, which is, as Maxim Gorki has pointed out, the nearest to an *heroic* line, persisting all though bourgeois literature from its beginnings in Boccaccio (1313-1375), Villon (1431- ? 1463), Rabelais (1483-1553) and Cervantes (1547-1616) to the crime literature of today. Falstaff in his combination of fleshly enjoyment with wit has affinities with Panurge. In general he is a species of inverted Quixote, with touches of the scoundrel-philosophy of Sancho-Panza. But taken over all, along with his comapny, his affinities are closest with Villon and the *lumpen-proletariat* produced by the decadence of feudalism. Since there is no reason at all to suppose that Shakespeare ever met with a line of Villon's work, the conclusion is obvious, that Shakespeare drew from life the late sixteenth century London equivalent of the low-life of fifteenth century Paris. (p. 86)

So thorough and devastating is Shakespeare's disposal of Falstaff and his crew—(its only parallel in English literature is Dickens' disposal of Fagin and his crew in *Oliver Twist,* where however the end has been clearly foreseen from the beginning)—that sentimentalists have made it a charge against Shakespeare that he cruelly sacrificed his puppets on the altar of conventional morality. The charge is baseless. At their most mirthprovoking, Falstaff's crew, contain within them the potentiality of no other end. Falstaff for all his wit was a self-indulgent parasite doomed to die as a parasite dies as soon as its source of nourishment is cut off. Sentimentalism was not for such an artist as William Shakespeare. He was artist enough to show in Falstaff, and in each one of his crew, traits of common humanity, such as would show that the gulf between them and the (presumably) normal respect-worthiness of the audience was not an absolute one. But he knew too, as an artist, that a drunken sponger to whom drunkenness and sponging had grown second-nature, could have no other end than that of a drunken-sponger worn out—however brisk his unfuddled wits, and however diverting he may have been in his cups. How else could Nell Quickly and Doll Tearsheet end but, sooner or later, penniless, of the disease special to their trade? How else could such as Nym and Bardolph end but on the gallows, convicted egregiously of some stupidly petty theft? What other end was possible to Pistol once he was cudgelled into facing actual reality but that of living (and dying) by the only job he was fit for—that of door-keeper and beer fetcher at a brothel, with a little pocket picking as a side line?

Sentimentalists are, after all, only bourgeois moralists looking through rose-coloured spectacles. Because poor, garrulous, ungrammatical, Nell Quickly is as good-hearted as she is high-spirited, and because Doll Tearsheet, when she is not fuddled with drink, or preoccupied with her profession, is a lively lass with no end of pluck, these sentimentalists think Shakespeare might have contrived some other end for them. Did they expect him to make them *reform*? Shakespeare being an artist as great as the sentimentalists are little, knew first of all that women of their profession usually are in fact plucky, generous, and good-hearted. At the same time, he was artist enough to know that (short of a reform which in their cases was artistically unthinkable) no other end for them could be envisaged realistically than the one he indicated.

In a word: Shakespeare in depicting Falstaff and his crew depicted from life, in vivid truth, the phenomena of *decadence*, the degeneration and decomposition of an absolute class—that of the dependants upon the feudal order. In showing their *rejection* by life, and by reality, Shakespeare showed his sense that the bourgeois order had come, and could not be *rejected* by any man except as pain of extinction.

Netchkina's assertion that "Falstaff for Marx was a kind of 'personified capital' of the epoch of the dawn of capitalism, which gave birth to the bourgeoisie of the epoch of primitive accumulation" is outrageously false at every point. It is, as we have seen, false as to the epoch indicated. It is grotesquely, and even cruelly false as to Falstaff as Shakespeare presents him. Does a "kind of 'personified capital'" speak his mind thus:—

> I can get no remedy against this consumption
> of the purse. Borrowing only lingers, and lin-
> gers it out, but the disease is incurable.
>
> [*2 Henry IV*, I. ii. 236-38]

There is not much "accumulation" there, whether primitive or otherwise; and it is a positive affront to Marx's intelligence to suggest that he could possibly have mistaken Falstaff for an "accumulation" of capital. (pp. 86-7)

The whole farce of the Falstaff scenes in *Henry IV* turns on [the] grotesque contrast between the feudal status as it was and that into which it has degenerated. The whole of the tragedy underlying the farce and giving it body and force, is the utter incompatibility between this status and relationship and the new bourgeois world which has come into being, throbbing with exuberant life, and finding fresh outlets for expansion every hour. If Shakespeare pities Falstaff and his crew—and his picture would not have been artistically complete if he had not done so—it is from this angle, from a sense of their hopelessly irredeemable helplessness; which turns from sheer excess into its opposite,—a recognition that to be *what* they are, they need no help. They are no more in need of sustenance than a ghost! For ghost of a departed order, lingering belated on the scene, is precisely what they are. In no other sense was it possible for Marx to envisage them; and in so far as he, too, pities them, it is in the same sense that at their worst they are, being as much victims as victimisers, not so different morally from their contemporaries as they seem to be. . . .

The whole comedy of Falstaff, as well as the whole tragedy which is its converse, lies in the fact that he personifies greatness and magnificence, utterly decadent and grotesquely out of place. And as these are just the qualities the bourgeoisie does not exhibit particularly in its epoch of primitive accumulation such a comparison could not possibly have been made by Marx. (p. 88)

Netchkina is, perhaps, most of all mistaken in supposing that Falstaff's morals are bourgeois (under a *quasi-feudal* disguise).

Very much to the contrary: Falstaff in his morals presents a phenomenon which recurs at every crisis of social transition, the phenomenon of the man who has lost the old morality and not yet found a new one—the phenomenon of *a-moralist egoism*.

As the highest point reached by the philosophy (and morality) of class-divided society is that of "the single individual in civil society" (Marx: *Theses on Feuerbach*) so its lowest point is that of the single individual who repudiates all social claims and obligations. This is, *par excellence,* the standpoint of the parasite who is weakly inefficient enough, even as a parasite, to feel the need of disguising his parasitism to himself under a guise of romantic pretence. In that sense Falstaff is startlingly "up-to-date" in a way Shakespeare could not have foreseen. For instance: Falstaff leads the plunder raid upon the merchants on Gads-Hill, with this slogan:—

> Strike! Down with them! Cut the villains' throats!
> Ah! whores on catterpillars! bacon-fed knaves!
> *they hate us youth!* Down with them! fleece
> them!
>
> [*1 Henry IV*, II. ii. 83-5]

That Falstaff is in fact "some fifty years of age, or may be three-score" only makes this use of the term "youth" all the more startlingly "modern." Do we not know this "youth"? And also its *a-moralism*—its affectation of a super-Nietzschean "transvaluation" of Good and Evil? (p. 89)

Falstaff's grossness of body, the product of a love of life with no moral scruple or sense of responsibility to keep it within bounds, or to harness it to a worthy cause, is, in fact, a tragedy of degeneration against which Falstaff, in melancholy moments, struggles fitfully, but in vain. His cowardice is not the mere cowardice of the flesh, of which in fact, when he is put to it, he is not really guilty. His is the cowardice of the innermost spirit—the canker consumption of a soul which has lost its bearings in a state of social transition, and has in consequence nothing but his own naked egoism to serve as his moral criterion and his object in life.

His is, in fact, the typical tragedy of a cynical degenerate egoism. He clings on to life: but has no use for his life when he has saved it at the cost of reputation, and everything else which would make it worth the saving. To cling on to life at any price is an even greater madness, a more irrational romanticism than to squander it at the demand of any and every conventional call of so-called "duty." And, thus, Falstaff's degenerate egoism comes to be prophetic of the new degeneracy of today.

If, now, the character of Falstaff and his circle has been made clear, whether taken in themselves or as a reflection, dramatically presented, of an objective social phenomenon, we can proceed to the consideration of Shakespeare's own political attitude—conscious or unconscious—to his time.

It was, as we have seen, fundamentally a time of transition, a period of unstable equilibrium between two great upheavals, the Reformation and the Puritan Revolution. The relative calm was, however, dramatically conditioned by a whole series of counter-tendencies. (p. 90)

The only foundation for a faith in the future lay in a healthy, well-poised, sceptical, melioristic *humanism*. After all, at bedrock bottom, the problem of problems was the problem of Man himself. Solve that—and all these "fribble-frabbles," these ready-made schemes of "reformation" in Church and State would be seen for the futilities they were.

It is this sceptical-humanist-meliorist attitude, the most profoundly far-sighted and philosophically penetrating attitude then possible which is the attitude of William Shakespeare. Before the coming of Marx and Marxism—and apart from Leninist-

Marxism—it was, as it remains, the highest standpoint attainable by the artist-philosopher. (p. 92)

To expect from Shakespeare (in between the years 1590-1612) the same appreciation of the revolutionary potentialities of the proletariat as was possible to the genius of Marx and Engels *in and after* 1844, would be to expect an anachronistic miracle. But it is both pertinent and proper to perceive in Shakespeare's never failing persistence in emphasizing in all his clowns—even the most degenerate, the Falstaff group—their universal humanity despite all their absurdity, an artistic intuition of the fact that however much these particular specimens might be doomed to fade away into futility and extinction, the pit from which they were dug was the one from which the future would extract its richest and rarest ore. (p. 97)

> *T. A. Jackson, "Letters and Documents: Marx and Shakespeare," in* International Literature, *No. 2, February, 1936, pp. 75-97.*

JOHN MIDDLETON MURRY   (essay date 1936)

As Bolingbroke in *Richard II* [Henry IV] was a clamorous nonentity, because Shakespeare was not interested in him; as a crowned king, he remains a non-entity, again because Shakespeare is not interested in him. But the causes of Shakespeare's indifference to him are different. He was not interested in Bolingbroke in *Richard II*, because he was interested for a moment not in the fact but in the problem of rebellion. The problem of the deposing of an anointed king interested him; therefore he was not interested in the mere instrument of his deposition. Now that Bolingbroke himself is an anointed king, Shakespeare is not interested in him, because he is not interested in history any more: it is become an excuse and framework for creating characters—characters with a national significance: Englishmen. This is good history: far better history indeed than would ever be written until the age of authentic history began, because it is not history at all. It is imaginative drama of contemporary England. (p. 171)

History itself killed Hotspur, Falstaff had to be killed by Shakespeare's fiat.

Falstaff, indeed, had to be killed twice over. He had to be dismissed by King Harry; and then he had to die. Those who complain of the King's treatment of Sir John show indeed that they have good hearts, which are most necessary to have, but they have not entered very deeply into the necessities imposed on the creative imagination. Falstaff had, somehow, to be brought back into the framework of 'history'; and Prince Hal's character had to be sacrificed in the process. The commiseration of the kind hearts goes to the wrong address. It is not Falstaff who needs to be pitied, but Prince Hal. From another congenial madcap, he had to be changed for the moment into an ingrate and a hypocrite—a painful and an arbitrary transformation, but no less drastic an operation was necessary if the fragments of exploded history were to be put together again.

There is evidence that Shakespeare was embarrassed by the necessity. That he was poetically embarrassed is plain from the words with which his Prince abandons Falstaff:

> FAL.   My King! my Jove! I speak to thee, my heart!
> KING. I know thee not, old man: fall to thy prayers;
>   How ill white hairs become a fool and jester!
>   I have long dream'd of such a kind of man,
>   So surfeit-swelled, so old and so profane;
>   But, being awak'd, I do despise my dream.
>   [*2 Henry IV*, V.v.46-51]

It was the best Shakespeare could do; but neither he, nor anyone else, could alter the fact that the dream was the reality, and the reality the dream. The words are, of course, preposterous on Prince Hal's lips: but their preposterousness reflects the hiatus that now yawned between the world of Shakespeare's spontaneity, or imaginative truth, and the world of theatrical necessity, or historical fact. To fill the hiatus, in appearance only, for the chasm is unbridgable, Falstaff is cast off, and the King made a dastard. Neither deserved it, and neither suffers from it: because it happens in a different world from that in which they have their being. Their ghosts merely are entangled in this summary process of rejoining earth.

It was a job of work that had to be done, in order to bring *Henry IV* to an end. (pp. 175-76)

> *John Middleton Murry, "Falstaff and Harry," in his* Shakespeare, *Jonathan Cape, 1936, pp. 170-87.*

MARK VAN DOREN   (essay date 1939)

No play of Shakespeare's is better than "Henry IV." Certain subsequent ones may show him more settled in the maturity which he here attains almost at a single bound, but nothing that he wrote is more crowded with life or happier in its imitation of human talk. The pen that moves across these pages is perfectly free of itself. The host of persons assembled for our pleasure can say anything for their author he wants to say. The poetry of Hotspur and the prose of Falstaff have never been surpassed in their respective categories; the History as a dramatic form ripens here to a point past which no further growth is possible; and in Falstaff alone there is sufficient evidence of Shakespeare's mastery in the art of understanding style, and through style of creating men.

The vast dimensions of the comic parts should not be permitted to obscure the merit of the rest. History is enlarged here to make room for taverns and trollops and potations of sack, and the heroic drama is modified by gigantic mockery, by the roared voice of truth; but the result is more rather than less reality, just as a cathedral, instead of being demolished by merriment among its aisles, stands more august. The King of the play is more remote from the audience than any of Shakespeare's kings have been; he is more formal, and speaks with a full organ tone which as Bolingbroke he never used; but that is as it should be in a work which has so much distance to fill between laughter and law, between the alehouse and the throne. Henry wears his robes regally, and his sighs because they weigh him down are dignified and sonorous. (pp. 116-17)

We shall not end by liking Hal better than the Hotspur whom he challenges and kills, or by preferring the new king of England to the sometime prince of London's stews. The life of "Henry IV," indeed, is not in the handsome boy who will be Henry V. But he is the foil to that life, the brocaded curtain against which we watch it moving; he is the mold it is trying to break, the form of which it is the foe. If he could be broken the life would spill itself meaninglessly; whereas nothing is meaningless in "Henry IV." . . . (pp. 119-20)

Not that Hotspur is less the gentleman than Harry, but that he is more the person, the created speaking man. (p. 120)

[Shakespeare] must have been fond of his creation: of this high-strung youth who was so far above liking the art he mastered, who could be a fine poet without knowing that he was, who indeed made his poetry out of a hot love for nothing except reality and hard sense. For the paradox of Hotspur is the paradox of Shakespeare; the best poet least pampers and preens his talent, and in public at any rate would rather abuse it than take off its edge by boasting of its power to cut. Shakespeare lets Hotspur be proud of his plainness—"By God, I cannot flatter" (I-IV,i,6), but never of his poetry. (p. 125)

[Northumberland's speech upon hearing of Hotspur's death in *2 Henry IV*, I, i] is an adequate tribute to the finest figure Shakespeare has been able to carve for the serious portion of his History. For Hotspur was very serious. He was almost, indeed, insanely serious. He did not know that he was amusing. He did not understand himself—could not have named his virtues, would never have admitted his limitations. As handsome as Hamlet, and apparently as intelligent, he was not in fact intelligent at all. He was pure illusion, pure act, pure tragedy, just as Falstaff at the opposite pole of "Henry IV" is pure light, pure contemplation, pure comedy.

Falstaff understands everything and so is never serious. If he is even more amusing to himself than he is to others, that is because the truth about himself is something very obvious which he has never taken the trouble to define. His intelligence can define anything, but his wisdom tells him that the effort is not worth while. We do not know him in our words. We know him in his—which are never to the point, for they glance off his center and lead us away along tangents of laughter. His enormous bulk spreads through "Henry IV" until it threatens to leave no room for other men and other deeds. But his mind is still larger. It is at home everywhere, and it is never darkened with self-thought. Falstaff thinks only of others, and of the pleasure he can take in imitating them. He is a universal mimic; his genius is of that sort which understands through parody, and which cannot be understood except at one or more removes. He is so much himself because he is never himself; he has so much power because he has more than that maximum which for ordinary men is the condition of their identity's becoming stated. His is not stated because there is no need of proving that he has force; we feel this force constantly, in parody after parody of men he pretends to be. The parodist, the artist, is more real than most men whom we know. But we cannot fix him in a phrase, or claim more for ourselves than that we have been undeniably in his living presence. (pp. 126-27)

The essence of Falstaff is that he is a comic actor, most of whose roles are assumed without announcement. (p. 130)

What now of his vices, and why is it that they have not the sound of vices? None of them is an end in itself—that is their secret, just as Falstaff's character is his mystery. He does not live to drink or steal or lie or foin o' nights. He even does not live in order that he may be the cause of wit in other men. We do not in fact know why he lives. This great boulder is balanced lightly on the earth, and can be tipped with the lightest touch. He cannot be overturned. He knows too much, and he understands too well the art of delivering with every lie he tells an honest weight of profound and personal revelation. (pp. 134-35)

Mark Van Doren, "'Henry IV'," in his Shakespeare, *Henry Holt and Company, 1939, pp. 116-35.*

THEODORE SPENCER   (essay date 1942)

[*Spencer is a well-known historical critic whose interpretation of* Henry IV *as two plays which demonstrate the disruption of social rebellion was later attacked by Leonard Dean (1944), who regarded the historical approach as "inadequate" to a proper understanding of Shakespeare's work.*]

In his second great trilogy, the two parts of *Henry IV* and *Henry V*, there is, as everyone knows, an enormous expansion both of Shakespeare's extraordinary capacity for creating character, and of his ability to weave different threads of plot into the texture of a single dramatic unity. And here again he owes much to dramatic convention and to the traditional views of kingship. Some scholars have even gone so far as to see, especially in the second part of *Henry IV*, a direct use of the technique of the morality play, with Falstaff "as the lineal descendant" of Gluttony, Lechery, Sloth, Avarice and Pride—five of the seven deadly sins rolled into . . . one "grey Iniquity" [see excerpts above by Robert Law, 1927, and J. W. Spargo, 1922]. (p. 77)

This is certainly a possible way of thinking about the matter, though I doubt if Shakespeare himself had quite so formal a scheme in mind. One imagines him as being more interested in character than in imitating directly a dramatic form which he must have known was out of date, and even if he did have the morality technique in mind as he wrote, he went beyond it in his actual performance. And yet the conventional scheme of the older serious drama is clearly present—the scheme which was a blending of the Biblical play and the morality into the serious chronicle play. A kingdom is in the chaos of civil war, and is only restored to order by the right kind of king. Henry V is, of course, a much more important figure in this trilogy than Richmond is in the earlier [plays, *Henry VI, Parts 1, 2, and 3*]; he is present from the first as a major character who, in typical royal fashion, the first time he speaks seriously, compares himself to the sun:

> I know you all, and will awhile uphold
> The unyok'd humour of your idleness:
> Yet herein will I imitate the sun,
> Who doth permit the base contagious clouds
> To smother up his beauty from the world,
> That when he please again to be himself,
> Being wanted, he may be more wonder'd at.
>
> [Part 1,I.ii.195]

In this speech Shakespeare wants to reassure his audience about Hal's true character; he is not the wastrel he seems to be, and it is perhaps not far-fetched to see, in his use of the familiar analogy, a means of re-inforcing that assurance: if Hal thinks along those lines, the audience will say, he must surely be a reliable prince. (pp. 77-8)

It is in *Henry V*, the third part of the trilogy, that we find the fullest description of what government and kingship should be. (p. 79)

Theodore Spencer, "The Dramatic Convention and Shakespeare's Early Use of It," in his Shakespeare and the Nature of Man, *Macmillan, 1942, pp. 51-92.*

J. DOVER WILSON   (essay date 1943)

[*Dover Wilson is a widely read and highly regarded Shakespearean scholar whose career has involved him in several aspects of Shakespearean studies. As an editor of the* New Cambridge Shakespeare, *Dover Wilson made numerous contributions to twentieth-century textual criticism, making use of the scientific bibliography developed by W. W. Greg and Charlton Hinman. As a critic, he combines several approaches and does not fit easily into any one critical "school." He is concerned with character analysis in the tradition of A. C. Bradley, he delves into Elizabethan culture like the historical critics, and his interest in visualizing possible dra-*]

matic performances of the plays links him with his contemporary Harley Granville-Barker. Dover Wilson divided his commentary on Henry IV *into two works: a discussion of Falstaff, from which the following excerpt is drawn, and a separate introduction to the plays as a whole (see excerpt below, 1944). His is the best-known argument that Falstaff is dramatically descended from the Vice or Devil figures of the medieval drama and that Hal's rejection of him should be regarded as a version of Everyman overcoming the sins of worldly existence. Dover Wilson credits Samuel Johnson (1765) and H. N. Hudson (1872) with influencing his views on* Henry IV; *other critics who have discussed the possible influence of the morality plays on* Henry IV *include John Webster Spargo (1922), T. A. Jackson (1936), and E.M.W. Tillyard (1944). Dover Wilson's controversial findings have been praised by Tillyard, but numerous later critics—most notably Cleanth Brooks and Robert B. Heilman (1945), M. A. Shaaber (1948), Harold C. Goddard (1951), Samuel Hemingway (1953), and Harold Jenkins (1955)—have all criticized his historical approach as ill-suited to a full understanding of Shakespeare's plays.]*

Falstaff may be the most conspicuous, he is certainly the most fascinating, character in *Henry IV,* but all critics are agreed, I believe, that the technical centre of the play is not the fat knight but the lean prince. Hal links the low life with the high life, the scenes at Eastcheap with those at Westminster, the tavern with the battlefield; his doings provide most of the material for both Parts, and with him too lies the future, since he is to become Henry V, the ideal king, in the play that bears his name; finally, the mainspring of the dramatic action is . . . the choice he is called upon to make between Vanity and Government, taking the latter in its accepted Tudor meaning, which includes Chivalry or prowess in the field, the theme of Part I, and Justice, which is the theme of Part II. Shakespeare, moreover, breathes life into these abstractions by embodying them, or aspects of them, in prominent characters, who stand, as it were, about the Prince, like attendant spirits: Falstaff typifying Vanity in every sense of the word, Hotspur Chivalry, of the old anarchic kind, and the Lord Chief Justice the Rule of Law or the new ideal of service to the state.

Thus considered, Shakespeare's *Henry IV* is a Tudor version of a time-honoured theme, already familiar for decades, if not centuries, upon the English stage. (p. 17)

[Medieval miracle and morality plays,] and much more of a like character, gave the pattern for Shakespeare's *Henry IV.* Hal associates Falstaff in turn with the Devil of the miracle play, the Vice of the morality, and the Riot of the interlude, when he calls him 'that villainous abominable misleader of Youth, that old white-bearded Satan' [Pt. I, II.iv.462-63], 'that reverend Vice, that grey Iniquity, that father Ruffian, that Vanity in years' [*Ibid.* II.iv.453-54], and 'the tutor and the feeder of my riots' [Pt. II, V.v.62]. 'Riot', again, is the word that comes most readily to King Henry's lips when speaking of his prodigal son's misconduct [Pt. I, I.i.85; Pt. II, IV.iv.62 and IV.v.135]. And, as heir to the Vice, Falstaff inherits by reversion the functions and attributes of the Lord of Misrule, the Fool, the Buffoon, and the Jester, antic figures the origins of which are lost in the dark backward and abysm of folk-custom. We shall find that Falstaff possesses a strain, and more than a strain, of the classical *miles gloriosus* as well. In short, the Falstaff-Hal plot embodies a composite myth which had been centuries amaking, and was for the Elizabethans full of meaning that has largely disappeared since then: which is one reason why we have come so seriously to misunderstand the play. (p. 20)

[Shakespeare] made the myth his own, much as musicians adopt and absorb a folk-tune as the theme for a symphony. He glorified it, elaborated it, translated it into what were for the Elizabethans modern terms, and exalted it into a heaven of delirious fun and frolic; yet never, for a moment, did he twist it from its original purpose, which was serious, moral, didactic. Shakespeare plays no tricks with his public. He did not, like Euripides, dramatize the stories of his race and religion in order to subvert the traditional ideals those stories were first framed to set forth. Prince Hal is the prodigal, and his repentance is not only to be taken seriously, it is to be admired and commended. Moreover, the story of the prodigal, secularized and modernized as it might be, ran the same course as ever and contained the same three principal characters: the tempter, the younker, and the father with property to bequeath and counsel to give. It followed also the fashion set by miracle, morality and the Christian Terence by devoting much attention to the doings of the first-named. Shakespeare's audience enjoyed the fascination of Prince Hal's 'white-bearded Satan' for two whole plays, as perhaps no character on the world's stage had ever been enjoyed before. But they knew, from the beginning, that the reign of this marvellous Lord of Misrule must have an end, that Falstaff must be rejected by the Prodigal Prince, when the time for reformation came. And they no more thought of questioning or disapproving of that finale, than their ancestors would have thought of protesting against the Vice being carried off to Hell at the end of the interlude. (pp. 21-2)

Prince Hal and Falstaff, for us merely characters in a play, were for the Elizabethans that and a great deal more. They embodied in dramatic form a miscellaneous congeries of popular notions and associations, almost all since gone out of mind, in origin quasi-historical or legendary, pagan and Christian, ethical and political, theatrical, topographical, and even gastronomic. (p. 36)

We begin with act I, scene 2, in which both principals make their first appearance, and which must be followed carefully as it gives us the earnest glimpse we have of the relationship between them. It should open, I believe, with an empty stage, but with the sound of stertorous snoring, as of a gigantic sow, issuing from behind the curtain at the back. Enter a youth of about twenty, evidently a prince of the realm, listens a moment, then lifts the curtain and discovers an enormously fat old man asleep upon a bench. He shakes him hard; whereupon, with a huge yawn, vast chaps opening like gates upon their hinges to reveal dim caverns of throat, the sleeper slowly awakens and begins the dialogue with a drowsy 'Now Hal, what time of day is it, lad?' This setting is, of course, editorial stage-direction; that is to say, its only basis is my fancy. What is certain is that the question gives the Prince an opening for a humorous but exceedingly candid statement both of Falstaff's way of life and of his own attitude towards it. Listen:

> Thou art so fat-witted with drinking of old sack
> and unbuttoning thee after supper and sleeping
> upon benches after noon, that thou hast for-
> gotten to demand that truly which thou would-
> est truly know. What a devil hast thou to do
> with the time of day? Unless hours were
> cups of sack, and minutes capons, and clocks
> the tongues of bawds, and dials the signs of
> leaping-houses, and the blessed sun himself a
> fair hot wench in flame-coloured taffeta, I see
> no reason why thou shouldst be so superfluous
> to demand the time of day.
>   [*1 Henry IV*, I. ii. 2-12]

The clock, that is to say, symbol of regularity, register of human duties, controller of the world's business, has no relevance whatever to the existence of so 'superfluous and lust-dieted' [*King Lear*, IV.i.67] a being as Falstaff. It is a devastating abstract and brief chronicle of his life, so devastating that he attempts no retort but shifts to the more entertaining ground of highway robbery, where he finds himself pressed scarcely less hard. In this first scene, at any rate, Falstaff comes off second best in his wit-combats with the Prince. (pp. 36-7)

Hal is easy, good-tempered, amused throughout; Falstaff, for all his familiarity and impudent sallies, is circumspect, even at times deferential. He throws out a hint about Hal's interest in a 'sweet wench', but does not venture to follow it up. He suggests that the 'heir apparent' has stretched his credit up to the limit of his expectations, and then breaks off short. And, though he condemns Hal's similes as 'unsavoury', he calls him a 'sweet young prince' immediately afterwards, while the complaint that his morals have been corrupted by Hal's company is as quickly contradicted by a second jest on his own vocation of purse-taking. Clearly everything he says is spoken with the object of entertaining his royal patron; and as clearly the entertainment is at once keenly enjoyed and taken as merely pastime. Falstaff's function, in short, as defined by this opening scene, is to act as 'the prince's jester' [cf. *Much Ado About Nothing*, II.i.137], and the Prince is not thereby in the least committed to countenance his way of living, still less to share in it. (p. 38)

One purpose, then, of the opening Falstaff scene is exposition. As he writes it Shakespeare is pointing his audience to the end of the play, hinting at the denouement, so that they may be at ease and surrender themselves with a free conscience to all the intervening fun and riot, in the assurance that at last the Prodigal will repent—is he not beginning to repent already?—and the Tempter be brought to book. This means that Falstaff must be clearly seen for what he is, viz. an impossible companion for a king and governor, however amusing as jester to the heir apparent; and Shakespeare, accordingly, insists upon his shadier aspects, aspects which will fade into partial obscurity in the blaze of merriment that illuminates scenes to follow, but will show up distinctly again in Part II. It means also that the weakness of the hold he has upon his patron must be emphasized. This is, indeed, exhibited as a preoccupation of his mind. 'When thou art king' runs like a refrain through what he has to say, and reveals the anxieties beneath the jesting. (p. 39)

As for what is to happen when Henry of Monmouth [Hal] succeeds Henry of Lancaster [Henry IV], the chief person concerned leaves us in no doubt on that score. For Hal also must be seen for what he is at the opening of the play. And so, when Falstaff has gone and Poins has gone, we are given in soliloquy a glimpse of his mind, the only direct view that Shakespeare vouchsafes in either part of the play.

The soliloquy seems callous and hypocritical to many modern critics. It was assuredly nothing of the kind to Shakespeare's original audience. Why not? The answer is, in the first place, that we have here a piece of dramatic convention, common in the Elizabethan theatre, but now over three hundred years out of date. The soliloquy, itself an outworn convention to us, is in this instance more than usually obsolete, since it belongs to what may be called the expository type, a type already becoming old-fashioned towards the end of the sixteenth century and seldom used again by Shakespeare after *Henry IV*. Its function was to convey information to the audience about the general drift of the play, much as a prologue did. . . . Prince Hal informs us that he is determined to prove a worthy king, despite all appearances to the contrary: 'I will be good' he promises,

as Victoria did on a later and different occasion. The sign-post is the more necessary in Hal's case, because two full-length performances are to intervene between promise and fulfilment. And when Part I was first staged, Part II not being yet in existence, the audience would not see the fulfilment at all. To charge him with meanness, therefore, for not communicating to Falstaff what Shakespeare makes him, for technical reasons, tell the theatre is absurd. (pp. 40-1)

It is a strange comment on the vagaries of criticism that [Hal's soliloquy], which seems to one living Shakespearian 'an offence against humanity, and an offence which dramatically never becomes a skill' [see excerpt above by H. B. Charlton, 1934], and to another [Arthur Quiller-Couch] 'the most damnable piece of workmanship to be found' in Shakespeare, should be praised by Johnson as a skilful expedient 'to keep the Prince from appearing vile'! [See excerpt above, 1765.] (p. 43)

In the battle scenes . . . , Shakespeare bends all his energy to enhance the honour of his hero [Prince Hal], even departing from the chroniclers to do so. The conspicuous part he plays is exhibited in marked contrast to that of the King. The King, for example, dresses many men in his coats so as to shield himself: the wounded Hal refuses to withdraw to his tent, yet is all the while glowing with pride at his younger brother's prowess. . . . Indeed, throughout the battle we are made to feel that the Prince is the real leader and inspirer of the royal army, a role which Holinshed ascribes to the King. There follows the encounter and fight with Hotspur, also taken from Daniel, which would be realistically played on the Elizabethan stage, and the tender, almost brotherly, speech which he utters over his slain foe. This last is Shakespeare's alone. (p. 66)

As he turns from the body of Hotspur, Hal sees a vaster corpse nearby, and is moved to utter another epitaph in a different key.

> What! old acquaintance! could not all this flesh
> Keep in a little life? poor Jack, farewell!
> I could have better spared a better man:
> O, I should have a heavy miss of thee,
> If I were much in love with vanity!
>   [*1 Henry IV*, V. iv. 102-06]

There is a genuine sorrow here; Falstaff had given him too much pleasure and amusement for him to face his death without a pang. But the tone, which may be compared with Hamlet's when confronted with Yorick's skull, is that of a prince speaking of his dead jester, not of friend taking leave of familiar friend; and what there is of affection is mainly retrospective. In the new world that opens up at Shrewsbury there is little place left for the follies of the past.

> O, I should have a heavy miss of thee,
> If I were much in love with vanity.
>   [*1 Henry IV*, V. iv. 105-06]

It is Hal's real farewell to the old life; and after Shrewsbury Falstaff is never again on the same terms with his patron.

The two epitaphs are deliberately placed side by side. Can there be any reasonable doubt which seemed to Shakespeare the more important? The overthrow of Hotspur is the turning point not only of the political plot of the two Parts but also in the development of the Prince's character. The son has fulfilled the promises made to his father; the heir has freed the monarchy of its deadliest foe; the youth has proved, to himself, that he need fear no rival in Britain as soldier and general. Yet these are not the considerations first in his mind; for himself and his own affairs are never uppermost in the consciousness of this character. The epitaph on Hotspur contains not a word of triumph; its theme is the greatness of the slain man's spirit, the tragedy of his fall, and what may be done to reverence him in death. With such solemn thoughts does Shakespeare's hero turn to Falstaff. Is it surprising that he should be out of love with Vanity at a moment like this? The point is of interest technically, since the moment balances and adumbrates a still more solemn moment at the end of Part II in which he also encounters Falstaff and has by then come to be even less in love with what he represents. (pp. 67-8)

[There is] nothing whatever in Part I to indicate that Falstaff possesses a military reputation of any kind. Certainly, Hal and Poins do not credit him with one; and if the former procures him his charge of foot, that is the least he could do to get him to Shrewsbury, where Shakespeare required his presence. It is from Part II that Morgann draws his evidence, such as it is [see excerpt above, 1777]. And the 'why' for this is plain as way to parish church, though, owing to the habit of knowing and judging by what is *going* to happen, all the critics seem to have missed it. Falstaff only becomes what Bradley calls 'a person of consideration in the army' after the battle of Shrewsbury, after, that is, he has slain, or helped to slay, the mighty Hotspur, chief of the rebels. In Part I he is Jack Falstaff with his familiars; in Part II he is Sir John with all Europe.

The words of the messenger, who gives old Northumberland tidings of the death of his son, show us that the true facts of the fight with Harry Monmouth had been observed by at least one man. But no other witness is quoted and, as we have seen, not even King Henry himself appears to realize what has taken place. The Prince is as good as his word; he gilds Falstaff's lie with the happiest terms at his command; and the Lord Chief Justice's grudging admission: 'Your day's service at Shrewsbury hath a little gilded over your night's exploits on Gad's Hill [Pt. II, I.ii.148-49] assures us that the gilding had passed current for true gold. Shakespeare leaves the particulars vague—the more a dramatist defines the less freedom he allows to himself—but makes it certain that, whether wholly or in part, the glory of Hotspur's overthrow belongs, not to Harry Monmouth, but to his 'brawn, the hulk Sir John' [*Ibid.* I.i.19].

Thus the 'established fame and reputation of military merit claimed for Falstaff [by Morgann] rests solely upon his 'day's service at Shrewsbury', which explains all the 'facts' alleged in support of it. (pp. 88-9)

[Falstaff's manipulation of Mistress Quickly in Part 1] is a palmary example of his dexterity in manipulation, and the dramatist is no less skilful in his presentation of the incident. Its sequel, too, the second great Boar's Head scene, one of the finest instances of Shakespeare's craftmanship in the canon, is as brilliant in its way as the first. Yet, how different is the atmosphere! We are no longer made to see Falstaff as 'splendid, and immortal, and desirable'; he is now the aged roué, taking his pleasures with the dregs of the population. The note is set, first, by the character of the jests that pass between him and his Doll, of which it is sufficient to remark with Johnson that an interpretation 'deserves not laborious research', and later by the Pistol episode, which develops into a drunken brawl between a braggart and a whore. (pp. 106-07)

As for

  I know thee not, old man. Fall to thy prayers,
         [*2 Henry IV,* V. v. 47]

and the rest of it, while such sentiments may be harsh, to call them 'ungenerous' is to misapprehend the relationship between the knight and his patron, and to call them 'dishonest' is even more absurd. The terms are again Bradley's [see excerpt above, 1902], who goes so far as to stigmatize the speech as 'an attempt to buy the praise of the respectable at the cost of honour and truth'. Charges of this kind would never, I think, have occurred to a critic before the end of the nineteenth century. Respectability, the word and the social quality, were of mid-eighteenth century origin, and did not even begin to fall into disfavour until at least a hundred years later; about which time the phenomenon of conversion, of which the change in Henry Monmouth is an instance, also ceased to be regarded as normal or desirable by average serious-minded persons. King Henry V is a new man; he had buried his 'wildness' in his father's grave; he speaks as the representative and embodiment of

  The majesty and power of law and justice.
         [*2 Henry IV,* V. ii. 78]

I cannot believe that members of an Elizabethan audience would have felt the 'sermon' anything but fine and appropriate. And if some, as Rowe suggests, may have 'in remembrance of the diversion' Falstaff 'had formerly afforded 'em, been sorry to see his friend Hal use him so scurvily', others would assuredly have retorted with Johnson:

> but if it be considered that the fat knight has never uttered one sentiment of generosity, and with all his power of exciting mirth, has nothing in him that can be esteemed, no great pain will be suffered from the reflection that he is compelled to live honestly, and maintained by the King, with a promise of advancement when he shall deserve it.

As for ourselves, how characteristically muddle-headed it is that a generation which has almost universally condemned a prince of its own for putting private inclinations before his public obligations, should condemn Hal as a cad and a prig for doing just the opposite.

But more important than all these questions of moral decorum, which are the plague of modern dramatic criticism, are those of dramatic decorum, in which critics of a former age took greater interest. And here, at any rate, there can be no question of the rightness of Shakespeare's finale. Preparing his audience for the rejection from the beginning, and making it appear ever more inevitable the nearer he approaches to it, in the end he springs it upon them in the most striking and unexpected fashion possible. Under the conditions of stage-performance, the only conditions which Shakespeare contemplated, both the encounter outside the Abbey and the speech of the King are extraordinarily effective. (pp. 122-23)

[What] the commiserators of Falstaff appear to overlook is that the delicious old sinner has no need of their pity. Shakespeare does not dismiss him in silence and with bowed head; he gives him his word, and a later word than the King's. It is a word too in which we see the dramatist holding, as ever, his balance even. We have applauded Majesty turning from Vanity in his hour of consecration towards the austere path of law and government; we have now to admire the demeanour of the Tempter thus suddenly cast down from the very gate of Heaven. The scene, indeed, affords not the slightest indication of that fat heart being 'fracted and corroborate' [as reported in *Henry V*]. On the contrary, never does it give clearer proof of stout intrepidity, not even when the sheriff in Part I interrupts the interlude at the Boar's Head. . . . [Instead] of replying to his royal Hal with reproachful reminders of past friendship, he counts his blessings and rejoices, like Milton's Satan, that 'all is not lost'. 'Master Shallow,' he remarks with a wicked smile to the chap-fallen justice at his side, when the procession has swept on, 'I owe you a thousand pound!' He had dreamed of that thousand ever since it was taken and retaken on Gad's Hill; he had made out that Hal was indebted to him for it; he had actually on one occasion tried to borrow it from the Lord Chief Justice himself. And now he has lifted it from the pocket of an old father antic in Gloucestershire and has it safe in his own, let Hal rave and storm as he will at his iniquities. Nor is this sheer effrontery. There is method in it. No sooner does he realize that his credit with the King is bankrupt than his eager intellect is busily at work trying to brazen it out with those in his party. 'I shall be sent for in private to him, look you,' he assures them; 'he must seem thus to the world: fear not your advancements—I will be the man yet that shall make you great.' And when his old enemies Fang and Snare, who turn up again in the train of the Chief Justice, close in upon him, his protesting shouts, 'My lord, my lord', tell us that a 'confident brow' is his to the very end and that 'the throng of words that come with such more than impudent sauciness' from him is only cut short because he is hustled out of earshot on his way to the Fleet.

Thus, though Shakespeare's Prince rejects Falstaff, and Shakespeare shows the rejection to be both right and necessary, Falstaff is never rejected by Shakespeare himself as some suppose. On the contrary, we are sent away with the assurance that full and ample provision has been made for his future. The King promises a 'competence of life', and this is enlarged upon by Prince John, who is presumably in the know and, what is dramatically more important, with those words we take our final leave of Falstaff in the play:

> I like this fair proceeding of the King's:
> He hath intent his wonted followers
> Shall all be *very well provided for*.
> [*2 Henry IV*, V. v. 107-09]

Let us not forget either that in addition to this allowance from the privy purse, there is Justice Shallow's £1000, not a penny of which will ever see Gloucestershire again. (pp. 125-27)

The feeling is something more than delightful: it is just. Shakespeare sends us home happy, but neither hoodwinked nor duped, as our theatrical entertainers too often dismiss us. We are not to imagine that, because kings should be virtuous and society needs a framework of decency, order, and justice to hold it together, there shall be no more cakes and ale, or that ginger will cease to be hot in the mouths of succeeding generations of men. Indeed, the progressive organization of the world during the last three centuries, which has caused the claims of social and political obligation to become ever more insistent and compelling, has also by reaction caused the invincibility of Falstaff to seem increasingly precious and significant. In a little book on Shakespeare published some years ago [*The Essential Shakespeare*], I suggested that Falstaff, for all his descent from a medieval devil, has become a kind of god in the mythology of modern man, a god who does for our imaginations very much what Bacchus or Silenus did for those of the ancients; and this because we find it extraordinarily exhilarating to contemplate a being free of all the conventions, codes and moral ties that control us as members of human society, a being without shame, without principles, without even a sense of decency, and yet one who manages to win our admiration by his superb wit, his moral effrontery, his intellectual agility, and his boundless physical vitality.

Yet the English spirit has ever needed two wings for its flight, Order as well as Liberty; and in none of Shakespeare's plays is the English spirit more explicit, or more completely expressed, than in *Henry IV*. The play celebrates a double coronation, that of our English Bacchus who, with the sprig of rue in his garland, reigns for ever from his state at the Boar's Head, and that of English Harry, in whose person Shakespeare crowns *noblesse oblige,* generosity and magnanimity, respect for law, and the selfless devotion to duty which comprise the traditional ideals of our public service. This balance which the play keeps between the bliss of freedom and the claims of the common weal has been disturbed by modern critics through a failure to preserve a similar balance in themselves. For . . . our liberty of interpreting Shakespeare must be constantly checked and reinspired by the discipline of Shakespearian scholarship. In the foregoing attempt to discover Shakespeare's intentions and to recapture glimpses of the vision which this widest of all his dramatic horizons opened up to the Elizabethan public, both in the popular playhouse and at court, I have endeavoured to do something to readjust the balance. In effect, it has meant trying to put Falstaff in his place, his place within the frame of the drama from which Morgann and his successors, to the confusion of criticism, had inadvisedly released him. I offer no apologies for constraining the old boar to feed in the old frank: for it is a spacious pinfold, with room and to spare for even the greatest of comic creations. (pp. 127-28)

> *J. Dover Wilson, in his* The Fortunes of Falstaff,
> *Cambridge at the University Press, 1943, 143 p.*

LEONARD F. DEAN   (essay date 1944)

[*Dean's essay on* Henry IV *is one of the earliest critiques of the historical school of Shakespearean criticism. In the excerpt below, he attacks, in particular, Theodore Spencer (1942) for his attempt to interpret* Henry IV *according to Elizabethan manners and ideas— an approach he considers "inadequate" to a proper understanding of Shakespeare's work.*]

The basic problems of Shakespearean criticism are continually revealed to be those of philosophy and criticism in general. Scholarly disclosure of the milieu in which Shakespeare worked has helped to correct and strengthen speculative nineteenth-century commentary. Scientific scholars have of course gone beyond this to suggest new and important aesthetic evaluations of their own. The difficulty arises from the fact that those evaluations are not purely the product of the historical method which is openly employed and championed. The result is to obscure what is actually happening in the critical process, to employ criteria that are insufficiently examined, and to produce a specious union of history and criticism rather than the real one which is sought. . . . [John W. Draper asserts in his *The "Hamlet" of Shakespeare's Audience*] that what is needed as the basis for interpretation is an account of Elizabethan manners and ideas. These "furnish the most fundamental, the most revelatory, background; for the plays of Shakespeare are the expression of very life." This enlargement of the historical basis for criticism has in fact been going on for some time; it is evident in this country in the writings of Professor Hardin Craig, Lily B. Campbell, O. J. Campbell, Theodore Spencer, and others. Professor Spencer declares that it is necessary to take in nothing less than the Elizabethan conception of man, of the social order, and of the whole universe.

The method in practice is familiar. Since Shakespeare was not in fact a learned man, it is argued with apparent reason that his moral and social ideas must have been those that were commonly held in his day and that found expression in the more popular manuals and compendiums. From these sources, rather than from the works of original thinkers, a fairly elaborate world picture is drawn. This is easily done, as Professor Spencer observes, because of "the remarkable unanimity with which all serious thinkers, at least on the popular level, express themselves about man's nature and his place in the world." The next step is to examine the plays for signs of this reconstructed world picture. A great many such signs are to be found. Shakespeare's knowledge of the prevailing ideas about the proper hierarchical order of society, of man's faculties, and so on, is thoroughly established. At this point there is a temptation to pass beyond historical annotation to a normative conclusion. It is this: Shakespeare always attempted to illustrate and confirm conventional ideas; he is most successful as a dramatist when he does this most completely.

This positive criterion is of course never adopted openly, but it does operate subterraneously in a negative form. The critic should not condemn Shakespeare for failing to espouse ideas that are popular today but that were not popular or were perhaps not even known in the Elizabethan period. Professor Spencer argues, for example, that the two plays dealing with Henry IV are meant to demonstrate the disaster that is caused by rebellion in the established social order. "A kingdom is in the chaos of civil war, and is only restored to order by the right kind of king." It is clear that Professor Spencer, like a good many others, privately doubts that Henry V is the right kind of king. Nevertheless, he proceeds to the rigorous conclusion that it "is in *Henry V* . . . that we find the fullest description of what government and kingship should be. Hal has reformed . . . , and though to modern readers his behavior as Henry V by no means makes him a perfect individual, there can be no doubt that Shakespeare intended him to embody all that a king should be . . .". (pp. 414-16)

The problem may be generalized to that of the function of literature with respect to tradition and change. When reality is conceived as static perfection, the literature produced is exemplary and allegorical. Since the flux of circumstance is mere appearance without real status, it is not binding on the artist; he manipulates its deceptively alluring details in order to illustrate the reality which is absolutely known. The golden world so pictured in allegory and *exempla* is familiar; it appears in the medieval saint's life and in the latest doctrinaire novel. The intention is to present a purified picture of experience as a guide and stimulus to action. Something like this is being implied about Shakespeare's plays when it is asserted that they can be no more than dramatic illustrations of conventional beliefs; but this of course is not the final explicit judgment of the historical critics in question. Professor Spencer states near the end of his study that the "second fact that emerges from our picture of Shakespeare's work as a whole—and this is something at which I have previously only hinted—is that though he drew very largely on what he inherited of the conventional concepts of man . . . , nevertheless Shakespeare's vision of human life transcends anything given him by his time . . . it is the individual human life, the thing itself underlying codification that Shakespeare gives us, and which makes him . . . 'not of an age but for all time.'"

This way of organizing a critical study seems to be very dangerous. During the lengthy historical annotation, the critic em-

phasizes Shakespeare's knowledge of conventional ideas by adopting an aesthetic that must ultimately be repudiated. A prefatory warning that the historical interpretations are deliberately incomplete does not explain how satisfactory interpretations of any length can be produced from inadequate assumptions. (pp. 416-17)

The social pattern which is dominant in the first part of *Henry IV* is certainly that of the tranquil and orderly state based on monarchy, degree, and vocation. It is announced in the King's opening speech, and then immediately broken by news of rebellion and by sight of Prince Hal failing to fulfill his vocation. At this point there are two possibilities: the rebels can succeed and Hal become wholly corrupt, or the King can put down the rebels and Hal can reform. Historical fact requires the second, but the details can be safely adjusted so that the defeat of the rebels and the reformation of the prince are parts of the same action. This is the orthodox Tudor use of history. The lesson from the past is neat and unmistakable. When nobles leave their place and when princes are irresponsible there is public trouble. Order can be restored only by the prince's return to his vocation. But to end analysis here is to ignore other important effects of the play, and that these effects were intended may be presumed from the fact that they are produced by elements that Shakespeare himself invented or developed. All readers agree that Hotspur is presented sympathetically. His gallantry and energy are of course a useful contrast to Hal's sloth, but they are also admirable in themselves. The result is to make us think critically about a social scheme that would automatically condemn all rebels. By the end of the play Hotspur is degraded and destroyed so that Hal can acquire his virtues, but he is never allowed to become easily detestable. The uncalculating quality of his ambition, his refusal to consider himself a skulking rebel, the healthy and high-spirited affection between him and his wife—these and other elements complicate the orthodox reaction to him as a rebel. The manner of his degradation is also significant. His gallant energy is made to appear excessive and sophomoric; his failing is a caricature of his virtue; but it is a fault as common to respectable people as to rebels. Hal perceives his opponent's weakness and thereby rises in our estimation. At the same time, Henry V at his noisy worst is not far away.

Another complication is introduced through the long invented speeches of warning addressed by the King to Hal. It was natural for Henry to compare his former situation with Richard II to that of Hal and Hotspur. The only lesson from history that he wishes to suggest is that social confusion results from unkingly behavior, that a king should keep his person fresh and new and thereby gain authority to maintain order. This intention and the device of the set speech itself are thoroughly conventional. But in the course of pretending the comparison Henry is made to show that history poses other and more basic questions about the nature of the royal vocation. He is so sincerely eager for Hal to reform that he exposes his own previous dissimulation as an example of proper conduct. The sanctity of kingship is thus damaged by the suggestion that it may often rest on little more than skilful play-acting. Even a rebel, as Henry himself was, may become a respectable king by means of expedient behavior. We recall Claudius, who failed; but who was opposed by a Hamlet.

Falstaff is of course the play's chief critic of respectable beliefs. Historical research shows his relation to characters on the stage and to persons in real life, and thus helps to explain his obvious theatrical function; but in the course of the play he is developed from these antecedents into an instrument for revealing that good people lead unexamined lives and that the aphorisms of the status quo may indeed be empty verbalisms. "'Tis no sin for a man to labour in his vocation." "Company, villanous company, hath been the spoil of me." "I was as virtuously given as a gentleman need to be." "Thou know'st in the state of innocency Adam fell; and what should poor Jack Falstaff do in the days of vallany." And so on to the show-piece catechism of honor. When Hal complains that Falstaff has enlisted pitiful rascals, Shakespeare gives the fat knight a famous cliché for answer. "Tut, tut; good enough to toss; food for powder, food for powder; they'll fit a pit as well as better. Tush, man, mortal men, mortal men." "Ay," agrees the respectable Westmoreland almost automatically, "but Sir John, methinks they are exceedingly poor and bare, too beggarly." I'm not responsible for that, returns Falstaff. The effect is unsettling. The efficient and approved officers are confounded by Falstaff's bland use of the conventional opinions to which they subscribe. His words are proper, but the occasion is not. He should have saved this speech for the battlefield where it would have been a comfortable thing to say over the bodies of dead commoners.

Falstaff's judgment on the war is a kind of summary of his position and function. "Well, God be thanked for these rebels, they offend none but the virtues. I laud them, I praise them." It is easy to be virtuous, that is, in a world of black and white; but Shakespeare has been careful not to present such a world. So it comes about that when the King draws the final moral, "Thus ever did rebellion find rebuke," the words mean something more than they did at the beginning of the play. The conventional social pattern has been so thoroughly examined that we reaccept it with the understanding that it is no more than a convention. We do not reject it, because we now better understand the need for it; but its claim to absoluteness has been exposed. Despite the big and proper words with which it is buttressed, it is revealed as only another make-shift account of reality, a necessary but temporary pattern of black and white that does not quite match the moving colors of full experience. The truth of the play, in short, is not to be found in any one element or set of elements but in the interaction of them all. It is neither radically modern nor conventionally Elizabethan, but a revelation of the deeper truth that organizations for action are essential yet finite.

To deny that something like this was Shakespeare's intention is to ignore the most effective elements in the play; and to deny that Elizabethan spectators could perceive such an intention is to refuse to grant them any power of attaining self-knowledge. Furthermore, it seems possible along this line to arrive at satisfactory aesthetic evaluations and at the same time to make full use of our historical information. Historians can tell us what the popular Elizabethan ideas actually were. It is better to have too much information of that sort rather than too little, for there is a constant need to correct the notion that today's assumptions have always been dominant. But on the other hand, Shakespeare's intentions and accomplishments can be inferred only from a full analysis of the plays. Without being unhistorical we may ask that he treat popular ideas in the philosophic manner that has been described. If investigation shows that *Henry V* is somewhat sentimental, nothing prevents us from saying so. Chauvinism is reprehensible at any time. It is clear that drama detached from its intellectual setting is meaningless; it should be equally clear that drama which merely confirms conventional beliefs is inconsequential. Great drama,

like all great art, examines and revitalizes traditional ideas. (pp. 419-23)

Leonard F. Dean, "Shakespeare's Treatment of Conventional Ideas," in The Sewanee Review, *Vol. LII, No. 3, Summer, 1944, pp. 414-23.*

BENJAMIN T. SPENCER   (essay date 1944)

[*Spencer's essay contains one of the earliest discussions of "time" as a major concept in* 2 Henry IV. *He relates the rejection of Falstaff to the atmosphere created by the motif of time. For further discussions of the element of time in* Henry IV, *see the excerpts by Clifford Leech (1951) and L. C. Knights (1959).*]

One of the oldest of Shakespearean cruxes is Hal's renunciation of Falstaff. . . . [The] crux is so genuine and the play is in its very essence so wholly the embodiment and expression of what is involved in the renunciation scene that no statement can entirely resolve it. The crux here, as in *Hamlet*, is evidence of the success of the play as a complete expression of experience, not of its failure. It implies neither Shakespeare's technical ineptness nor a Machiavellian heart and mind, but merely his "negative capability," to employ the useful Keatsian phrase. Therefore it cannot be resolved in any terms approaching poetic justice. It can be clarified, I believe, through exploration of what is implicit in the renunciation scene in terms of the play itself.

Indispensable to Shakespeare and omnipresent in his work is the concept of "time." Occurring in *2 Henry IV* in forty-three instances, only in *1 Henry IV, Cymbeline* and *Hamlet* is the word found as often, and in those plays it tends to be used in the first rather than the second sense in which Shakespeare employed it: in the first it concretely refers to specific occasions or eras; in the second it is regarded as an entity or force, abstractly or metaphysically conceived. (p. 394)

Omitting, therefore, such references to time in the play as Northumberland's "The times are wild" [I.i.9] or Falstaff's "these costermonger times" [I.ii.169], which refer to actual conditions of an historical period, one finds throughout the play among all the characters a special consciousness of the demands of time. Enraged and cynical old Northumberland regards it as an accomplice of spite, the two bringing in "the ragged'st hour," which one must be prepared to meet with courage [I.i.151]. Later, as a somewhat fearful opportunist, he again acknowledges the power of time to fix human destiny, and accordingly he delays conjunction with the other rebels on the grounds that he must wait "Till time and vantage crave my company" [II.iii.68]. King Henry IV more sombrely and religiously sees time as the inevitable flux of all things, a "book of fate" wherein one can perceive "the revolution of the times Make mountains level, and the continent . . . melt itself Into the sea" [III.i.45-49]. Warwick also sees a fatalistic pattern running through "the times deceas'd" and affecting man as well as nature, so that one may prophesy the future from "the hatch and brood of time" [III.i.81-86]. Hence it is natural for him to prophesy that "in the perfectness of time" [IV.iv.74] Hal will cast off his rowdy followers. To Morton the chief characteristic of time is its swiftness, which serves as a ceaseless goad and will give man no rest. . . . (p. 395)

It is the words of Hastings at the end of Act I, however, which most completely comprehend the sense in which time undergirds the structure of the play: "We are Time's subjects, and Time bids be gone" [I.iii.110]. Here is suggested most adequately that adjustment of human intention to the rigid necessity of time which constitutes the realism adopted by Hal at the end of the drama. What is more significant, Hal avows the same view of time as he confesses his weariness to Poins and sadly recognizes his obligation to forswear his old, carefree life and assume the duties of the world of affairs: "Well, thus we play the fools with the time, and the spirits of the wise sit in the clouds and mock us" [II.ii.142-43]. The same consciousness of time as the omnipresent gauge of his acts he soon voices again: "By heaven, Poins, I feel me much to blame, So idly to profane the precious time" [II.iv.361-62]. And having reached this conclusion, it is not strange that he abruptly cries, "Falstaff, good night." Indeed, here is the real renunciation scene in the play.

Falstaff's relation to time is more obliquely portrayed. Whereas the political figures of the play acknowledge and defer to the mighty potentialities of time, Falstaff rather regards it with an unmitigated dread. To him it is the ultimate horror of life which must be evaded. Its insatiable maw is the fearful consumer not of beauty, as in the sonnets, but of the animal vitality which is the essence of life. . . . "I am old, I am old," he reminds Doll [II.iv.271] and when she suggests that he patch up his old body for heaven, he pleads that she "not bid me remember mine end" [II.iv.234-35]. Similarly in the scenes with Justice Shallow, Falstaff cannot endure the Justice's reminiscences of the irrecoverable indulgences of their youth and abruptly commands that there be "No more of that" [III.ii.196]. Falstaff has brilliantly devoted himself to turning his back on time, to evading it rather than meeting it, through a life of sensual satisfaction and whimsical sophistry. Throughout the play there are increasing signs that his evasions have been in vain.

From all these instances the conclusion that time is central in the structure of the play and constitutes a version of the dramatic problem seems inescapable. Not only does nearly every major character by explicit statement evidence a constant concern with time, but also Shakespeare gives further emphasis to it by devoting the closing lines of three scenes (I. iii; II. iii; III. ii) to memorable statements of its power. Though shades and variations in its purport are present—it is sometimes the challenger of human desires, sometimes an intruder into the human scene from another realm, sometimes an inscrutable enemy thwarting human hopes, sometimes a maze through which blinded man stumbles to frustration—inclusively time is regarded as something against which man mut pit himself. It is a hovering, a relentless agent in human affairs. Therefore, Hal's rejection of Falstaff, as the crucial scene in the drama, cannot well be interpreted apart from so persistent a theme. In fact, it is the frame of reference in which the drama is set. In other words, the subject of 2 Henry IV is man against time.

Hal's two speeches to Poins on time are notably consistent and show not only that Shakespeare had integrally imagined his character but also that early in the play Hal is brooding over his relation to time and is earnestly moving toward a solution of it. He has come to view his existence as constituted of "precious time," a brief span not to be profaned by private inaction, as it is by his companions of the Boar's Head who "play the fools with the time" and in their attempt to find oblivion are mocked by "the spirits of the wise." It might be said that Hal has come to view time quantitatively and objectively and absolutely, whereas Falstaff persists (like Cleopatra: "Give me to drink mandragora . . . That I might sleep out this great gap of time My Antony is away") in a qualitative and subjective and relative view. Time has ceased to become a

function of the imagination for Hal, and has become a function of the will. Falstaff's pervasive scepticism as to the worth of social action could only issue in an idle profanation of "the precious time," for social action implies a constructive use of time and a belief in progress. What Hal renounces in renouncing Falstaff is a whole complex of attitudes (one cannot say values), a complex which can most readily be explored through the recurrent theme of time in the play. Falstaff conceives of time, like honour, as but a name, relatively conditioned by the mind of man. Hal, like the other public figures of the play, convinced of the reality of time, is impelled toward a life of action and public achievement as the most valid human effort to counteract the power of time. Hal's political realism is merely another name for his belief in the reality of time. (pp. 396-98)

The rejection is neither pathetic nor comic, but historical, and that not merely in the sense that, as Priestley has observed, it "shows us what happened" [see excerpt above, 1925]. In a larger sense it shows us what does happen, and in giving us this knowledge leaves the crux of actuality for the perennial reflection and delight of aftertimes. (p. 399)

Benjamin T. Spencer, " '2 Henry IV' and the Theme of Time," in University of Toronto Quarterly, *Vol. XIII, No. 4, July, 1944, pp. 394-99.*

JOHN DOVER WILSON (essay date 1944)

[*The following essay was first written in 1944.*]

It is commonly held that 2 Henry IV was an afterthought on Shakespeare's part, or, as one writer puts it, like 2 Tamburlaine 'an unpremeditated addition, occasioned by the enormous effectiveness of the by-figure of Falstaff' [see excerpt above by Tucker Brooke, 1908]. . . . [In partial agreement with such critics,] I admit at once that 1 Henry IV, which was probably being acted on Shakespeare's stage while 2 Henry IV was still in the process of composition and rehearsal, exhibits a certain unity that its sequel lacks. Neither, however, is in any true dramatic sense complete or self-contained, as are for instance Richard II and Henry V, the first and fourth of the same series; and the comparison with Marlowe's Tamburlaine only serves to bring out the fundamental distinction between the two cases. 1 Tamburlaine is a play, rounded off and clearly written without thought of a second part, which was only added in the hope of repeating the harvest reaped from Part I. 1 Henry IV, on the contrary, is as patently only part of a whole, inasmuch as at its close all the strands of the plot are left with loose ends. The rebels, Northumberland and Archbishop Scroop, are still at large after the battle of Shrewsbury; and the Archbishop is introduced and given a scene to himself in 4.4 in order to prepare the audience for the expedition of Prince John in Part 2. The relations of the Prince with his father, eased by the interview in 3.2 and his brilliant conduct in battle, still await that final clarification which, as Elizabethan auditors acquainted with the merest outline of the life of Henry of Monmouth would know, belonged to the death-bed scene in the Jerusalem chamber. Most striking of all perhaps is that stone of stumbling to modern interpreters, the soliloquy at the end of the second scene of Part I, which looks forward not only to the coronation of Henry V but also to the rejection of Falstaff, neither of which occurs until the very end of Part 2. If Part I be an integral drama, and Part 2 a mere afterthought, the soliloquy is inexplicable; indeed, the failure of critics to explain it is itself largely due to their absorption in the first part and their neglect of, or contempt for, the second. In short, the political and dynastic business of this history play, which is twofold, the defeat of the rebels and the repentance of the Prince including his reconciliation with his father, is only half through at the end of Part I. As for the comic underplot, by treating the drama as two plays critics have unwittingly severed and so overlooked all sorts of subtle threads of character and action belonging to it. (pp. ix-x)

On the other hand, think of the two parts as one, and the structure of the whole is revealed in its proper proportions. The normal dramatic curve, so to say, in Shakespeare is one that rises in intensity up to the middle of the play, e.g. in the trial scene of *The Merchant*, the play scene of *Hamlet*, the deposition scene of *Richard II;* relaxes during act 4, partly in order to gather up loose secondary threads of the plot, partly to give the principal actors a much-needed rest, and partly to relieve the strain upon the attention of the audience; and mounts again for the second and final climax of act 5, which we call catastrophe in tragedy and solution in comedy. Such and no other is the shape of *Henry IV,* in which the battle of Shrewsbury is the nodal point we expect in a third act, while the political scenes of minor interest, which in Part 2 round off the rebellion and dismiss the old king's troubles before the auspicious accession of his son, are just the kind of hang-over we get in a Shakespearian fourth act. And the curve, so plain to the eye in the rebellion plot, is to be traced as surely, if less obviously, in other plots also, which all, it may be noted, find their acme or turning-point in the battle of Shrewsbury. There Prince and King, as I said, come to a temporary understanding, to drift asunder again for most of Part 2, only to reach harmony in the moments before death separates them for ever. There Falstaff, as the accepted slayer of Hotspur, attains the height of his credit and his fortunes, which then fluctuate during the first half of Part 2, take an upward turn (which deludes him but not us), with his prospects of a loan from Justice Shallow and of becoming chief favourite at the court of the young King, and finally come crashing to the ground outside the Abbey. There, too, the Prince's friendship for him finds its tenderest expression in the epitaph over his vast corpse on the stricken field, is obscured for the next four acts (because Shakespeare deliberately keeps the two characters apart except for the brief and, from Falstaff's point of view, doubtful meeting in the presence of Doll Tearsheet), and once again reaches finality at their second meeting, after the coronation. Yet another indication of planning is the symbolic arrangement, which excludes the Lord Chief Justice from Part I, though there are indications that he appeared early in the pre-Shakespearian version, restricts that part to the theme of the truant prince's return to Chivalry, and leaves the atonement with Justice, or the Rule of Law, as a leading motive for its sequel. In short, when the Queen of the blue-stockings [Elizabeth Montagu] remarks, 'I cannot help thinking that there is more of contrivance and care in Shakespeare's execution of this play than in almost any he has written' [see excerpt above, 1769], one cannot help thinking she is right. . . . Taking the play as two and not one, [many critics] have never seen it as a whole, nor guessed that it might have been planned as a single structure, and probably intended when completed to be acted by the Lord Chamberlain's men on alternate afternoons. Until it be thus thought of, it will continue to languish in the undeserved neglect into which it has fallen since the eighteenth century. Once its unity is accepted by readers and producers, it will stand revealed as one of the greatest of dramatic masterpieces.

Henry IV is Shakespeare's vision of the 'happy breed of men' that was his England. Here he meets Chaucer on his own ground, and stretches a canvas even wider and more varied than that of *The Canterbury Tales.* True, he was to paint vaster worlds still in *King Lear* and *Antony and Cleopatra;* but those worlds, despite the animation of the titans which inhabit them, are of necessity remote and somewhat indistinct, whereas in the great expanse of *Henry IV* every incident and personage, whether tragic or comic, momentous or trivial, bears the hallmark, not merely of poetic genius, but of pure English gold, standard and current in the realm of Her Majesty Queen Elizabeth. (pp. xi-xiii)

> *John Dover Wilson, in his introduction to* The First
> Part of the History of Henry IV *by William Shakespeare, edited by John Dover Wilson, Cambridge at
> the University Press, 1946, pp. vii-xxviii.*

E.M.W. TILLYARD   (essay date 1944)

[*Tillyard's* Shakespeare's History Plays *(1944), one of the most influential twentieth-century works in Shakespearean studies, is considered a leading example of historical criticism. Tillyard's thesis, which is shared, with variations, by other historical critics, discerns a systematic world view in Shakespeare's plays—and one common to educated Elizabethans—in which reality is understood to be structured in a hierarchical Great Chain of Being. On a social level such a philosophy valued order, hierarchy, and civil peace as the chief political goals. Further, Tillyard notes a basic acceptance in Shakespeare's histories of "the Tudor myth," the critic's term for an interpretation of English history from Richard II to Henry VIII. This myth, which was established during the Elizabethan era, maintains that the chaos experienced by England between the reigns of Henry IV and Richard III, culminating in the War of the Roses, was a form of divine punishment exacted upon the kingdom for the usurpation of the throne by Henry IV and the continued illegitimate reign of his successors. It also claims that order and legitimate rule were not reestablished until the accession of Henry VII and his marriage to the Princess of York—a union which reunited the two rightful families to the throne, the House of Lancaster and the House of York. England under Queen Elizabeth, who was a Tudor and the granddaughter of Henry VII, experienced a growth in prosperity, a lessening of civil strife, and a new faith in a divine order throughout the universe, all of which were seen as the eventual result of the reestablishment of the legitimate king. In his remarks on* Henry IV, *Tillyard supports J. Dover Wilson's reading of the plays, although he does not accept Wilson's preoccupation with Falstaff's dramatic ancestry (see excerpt above, 1943). For Tillyard, Hal is an idealized Renaissance prince, while Falstaff represents the forces of disorder which Tillyard believed were unacceptable to the Elizabethan (and Shakespeare's) world view. Tillyard's influence has been great, but a reaction against his theses became widespread in the 1970s. For specific discussions of his work as it pertains to* Henry IV, *see the excerpts by M. A. Shaaber (1948), John F. Danby (1949), Clifford Leech (1951), G. K. Hunter (1954), Sigurd Burckhardt (1966), James Winny (1968), H. A. Kelly (1970), Robert Ornstein (1972), Edward Pechter (1980).*]

In an article on *Structural Unity in the two Parts of "Henry IV"* R. A. Law maintains that Part Two is a new structure, an unpremeditated addition [see excerpt above, 1927]. I think so decidedly the other way that I shall treat the two parts as a single play. . . . (p. 264)

The reason why Law wishes to separate the two parts is that he thinks their motives are different. According to him Part One shows the struggle of the Prince and Hotspur culminating in the Battle of Shrewsbury, while Part Two, in strong contrast, shows the Prince in the background not fighting but fought

*Part II. Act V. Scene v. Henry V, Chief Justice, Falstaff.
By Robert Smirke (1795). From the Art Collection of the
Folger Shakespeare Library.*

over, as in the Moralities, by the royal household and the Lord
Chief Justice on the one hand and by Falstaff, the epitome of
the Seven Deadly Sins, on the other. Law was right in seeing
the Morality pattern in Part Two, but wrong in not seeing it
in Part One likewise. The struggle between the Prince and
Hotspur is subordinate to a larger plan.

The structure of the two parts is indeed very similar. In the
first part the Prince (who, one knows, will soon be king) is
tested in the military or chivalric virtues. He has to choose,
Morality-fashion, between Sloth or Vanity, to which he is
drawn by his bad companions, and Chivalry, to which he is
drawn by his father and his brothers. And he chooses Chivalry.
The action is complicated by Hotspur and Falstaff, who stand
for the excess and the defect of the military spirit, for honour
exaggerated and dishonour. Thus the Prince, as well as being
Magnificence in a Morality Play, is Aristotle's middle quality
between two extremes. Such a combination would have been
entirely natural to the Elizabethans, especially since it occurred
in the second book of the *Fairy Queen*. (p. 265)

Now the Morality pattern of *Henry IV* will have mainly a formal
or historical interest, if its hero is an insignificant figure. Of
what use thrusting the Prince into the centre, if all the time we
look to left and right at Falstaff and Hotspur? The Prince as a
character has failed to please greatly, because he appeals less
to softer sentiment than Hotspur or Antony, while his imputed
Machiavellianism is quite without the glamour of the same
quality in an out-and-out villain like Richard III. Yet I believe

that current opinion is wrong and that he can hold his own
with any character in *Henry IV*. Dover Wilson in his *Fortunes
of Falstaff* deserves gratitude for having helped to redress the
balance between the Prince and Falstaff [see excerpt above,
1943]; but as I do not see the Prince altogether as he does, I
will give my version of him.

The Prince as depicted in *Henry IV* (and what follows has no
reference whatever to Henry V in the play which goes by that
name) is a man of large powers, Olympian loftiness, and high
sophistication, who has acquired a thorough knowledge of human nature both in himself and in others. He is Shakespeare's
studied picture of the kingly type: a picture to which his many
previous versions of the imperfect kingly type lead up: the
fulfilment of years of thought and of experiment. Shakespeare
sets forth his character with great elaboration, using both direct
description and self-revelation through act and word. Though
all the subtlety is confined to the second, there is no important
discrepancy between the two versions. (p. 269)

Those who cannot stomach the rejection of Falstaff assume
that in some ways the Prince acted dishonestly, that he made
a friend of Falstaff, thus deceiving him, that he got all he could
out of him and then repudiated the debt. They are wrong. The
Prince is aloof and Olympian from the start and never treats
Falstaff any better than his dog, with whom he condescends
once in a way to have a game. It is not the Prince who deceives,
it is Falstaff who deceives himself by wishful thinking. The
most the Prince does is not to take drastic measures to disabuse
Falstaff; doing no more than repeat the unkind truths he has
never spared telling. His first speech to Falstaff (''Thou art so
fat-witted . . .'') is, as well as much else, a cool statement of
what he thinks of him. And the epithet ''fat-witted,'' so plainly
the very opposite of the truth in most of its application, is
brutally true of Falstaff's capacity for self-deceit. The Prince
has a mind far too capacious not to see Falstaff's limitations.
In the same scene he plays with him (and with a coolness in
full accord with the rejection), when he refers to the gallows.
Falstaff dislikes the subject, but the Prince will not let him off.
And when later Falstaff tries to attach the Prince to him with
''I would to God thou and I knew where a commodity of good
names were to be bought,'' he gets not the slightest encouragement. The Prince just watches and tells the truth. And not
in this place alone: it is his habit. He also relishes the ironic
act of telling the truth in the assurance that he will thereby
deceive: indeed, to such an extent that he once takes big risks
and says things which if believed he would have been far too
proud to utter. I refer to the episode in the second part (II. 2,
at the beginning). (pp. 271-72)

[The prince] is at once contemptuous of Poin's perception—
Poins who had enjoyed his company and who had not the
excuse of the general public for knowing nothing of his mind—
fascinated at the display of human nature, and relieved at having opened his mind even to some one whom in so doing he
completely bewildered.

So much for the Prince's ironic detachment: the characteristic
and most attractive side of his deliberate way of acting. His
comprehensive nature comes out most brilliantly in an episode
that is usually taken as trivial if not positively offensive: the
foolery of the Prince and Poins with Francis and the other
drawers in the Eastcheap tavern, before Falstaff arrives from
the Gadshill robbery. . . . The Prince has been drinking and
making friends with the drawers of the tavern. He has won
their hearts and learnt their ways:

To conclude, I am so good a proficient in one quarter of an hour that I can drink with any tinker in his own language during my life. I tell thee, Ned, thou hast lost much honour that thou wert not with me in this action.

[*1 Henry IV*, II. iv. 17-21]

In other words the Prince has won a signal victory and great honour in having mastered this lesson so quickly. It was Johnson who perceived that the Prince's satire on Hotspur is logically connected with what goes before and not a mere unmotivated outburst [see excerpt above, 1765]. But later critics have not given due weight to that perception. Poins and the Prince have just had their game with Francis, Poins being as ignorant of the Prince's true meaning as he was in the scene from the second part just examined.

> *Poins*. But hark ye; what cunning match have you made with this jest of the drawer? Come, what's the issue?
> *Prince*. I am now of all humours that have showed themselves since the old days of goodman Adam to the pupil age of this present twelve o'clock at midnight.
>
> *Re-enter* Francis.
>
> What's o'clock, Francis?
> *Fran*. Anon, anon, sir. *Exit*.
> *Prince*. That ever this fellow should have fewer words than a parrot, and yet the son of a woman! His industry is upstairs and downstairs; his eloquence the parcel of a reckoning. I am not yet of Percy's mind, the Hotspur of the north. . . .

[*1 Henry IV*, II. iv. 89-102]

Johnson saw that the reference to Hotspur connects with the Prince's declaration that he is "now of all humours," the entry and exit of Francis with the Prince's comment being a mere interruption. The Prince's wealth of humours is contrasted with the single humour of Hotspur. Once again the Prince says just what he means but in words that will bear another meaning. On the face of it his words mean that he is greatly excited, being ruled simultaneously by every human motive that exists; but he also means that having learnt to understand the drawers he has mastered all the springs of human conduct, he has even then completed his education in the knowledge of men. We can now understand his earlier talk of honour: he has won a more difficult action than any of Hotspur's crudely repetitive slaughters of Scotsmen. Bearing this in mind, we may perceive things at the beginning of the episode which can easily be passed over. To Poins's question where he has been the Prince answers:

> With three or four loggerheads among three or four score hogsheads. I have sounded the very base string of humility. Sirrah, I am sworn brother to a leash of drawers and can call them all by their christen names, as Tom Dick and Francis. They take it already upon their salvation that though I be but Prince of Wales yet I am the king of courtesy.

[*1 Henry IV*, II. iv. 4-11]

When the Prince speaks of sounding the base string of humility he uses a musical metaphor. He means in one sense that he has touched the bottom limit of condescension. But he means something more: he is the bow that has got a response from the lowest string of the instrument, namely the drawers. We are to think that he has sounded all the other human strings already: he has now completed the range of the human gamut; he is of all humours since Adam. Now the idea of the world as a complicated musical harmony was a cosmic commonplace, which would evoke all the other such commonplaces. The drawers are not only the base or lowest string of the instrument; they are the lowest link in the human portion of the chain of being and as such nearest the beasts. And that is why the Prince directly after compares them to dogs by calling them "a leash of drawers." . . . It is not for nothing too that the Prince says the drawers think him the king of courtesy. As I shall point out later this is precisely what Shakespeare makes him, the *cortegiano*, the fully developed man, contrasted with Hotspur, the provincial, engaging in some ways, but with a one-track mind.

There remains a puzzle. Why should the Prince, after Francis has given him his heart, and, symbol of it, his pennyworth of sugar (which he wished he could make two) join with Poins to put him through a brutal piece of horseplay? Is not Masefield [see excerpt above, 1911] justified in his bitter attack on the Prince for such brutality? The answer is first that the Prince wanted to see just how little brain Francis had and puts him to the test, and secondly that in matters of humanity we must not judge Shakespeare by standards of twentieth century humanitarianism. In an age when men watched the antics of the mad and the sufferings of animals for sport we must not look for too much. Further we must remember the principle of degree. At the siege of La Rochelle costly dishes were carried into the town under a flag of truce to a Catholic hostage of noble birth, through a population dying of starvation; and such discrimination between classes was taken for granted. It may look strange when Shakespeare in one play represents the beautiful tact of Theseus in dealing with Bottom and his fellows, and in another allows his king of courtesy to be ungrateful and brutal to Francis. But Francis was a base string; Bottom a tenor string, a man in his way of intelligence and substance. Francis could not expect the same treatment. The subhuman element in the population must have been considerable in Shakespeare's day; that it should be treated almost like beasts was taken for granted.

From what I have said so far about the Prince it turns out that far from being a mere dissolute lout awaiting a miraculous transformation he is from the very first a commanding character, deliberate in act and in judgement, versed in every phase of human nature. But he is more than that. When the drawers think him the "king of courtesy" they know him better than his enemy Hotspur and even his own father do. And when Shakespeare put the phrase in their mouths he had in mind the abstract Renaissance conception of the perfect ruler. I will discuss how this conception enters and affects the play.

First, it is not for nothing that Elyot's *Governor* provided Shakespeare with the episode of the Prince being committed by the Lord Chief Justice. True, Shakespeare modified the episode to suit his special dramatic ends; but he must have known that Elyot held up Prince Hal, even during his father's lifetime, as one who was able to subordinate his violent passions to the sway of his reason. If Shakespeare got an episode from the *Governor* concerning his hero, it is likely that in shaping him he would have heeded the class of courtly manual to which the *Governor* belongs and of which Castiglione's *Cortegiano* was the most famous example. Then, there are passages in *Euphues* which are apt enough to the Prince's case.

I do not mean that Shakespeare used them directly, but that, occurring in a conventional didactic book on the education of a typical gentleman, they exemplify the assumptions Shakespeare would have been forced to go on if he meant to picture his perfect prince in accord with contemporary expectation. . . . Now the Prince in addition to skill in arms has a brilliant and well-trained intellect, which shows itself in his talk with Falstaff, of whose extraordinary character the recollection of a good education is an important part. But the Prince makes not the slightest parade of his intelligence, being apparently negligent of it. And this leads to another mark of the courtier. This is the quality of *sprezzatura* (which Hoby translates by *disgracing* or *recklessness* and to which *nonchalance* may be a modern approximation) considered by Castiglione to be the crown of courtliness, and the opposite of the vice of *affettazione* (translated by Hoby *curiousness*):

> I find one rule that is most general, which in this part, me think, taketh place in all things belonging to a man in word or deed, above all other. And that is to eschew as much as a man may, and as a sharp and dangerous rock, too much curiousness and (to speak a new word) to use in everything a certain disgracing to cover art withal and seem whatsoever he doth and saith to do it without pain and, as it were, not minding it.

Sprezzatura is a genuine ethical quality of the Aristotelian type: the mean between a heavy and affected carefulness and positive neglect. It is in the gift of this crowning courtly quality that the Prince so greatly excels Hotspur. He takes the Percies' rebellion with apparent lightness yet he is actually the hero in it. He gets news of it through Falstaff in the tavern scene after the Gadshill robbery. "There's villainous news abroad" says Falstaff, and goes on to name the different rebels. The Prince, quite unmoved apparently, makes a few idle remarks about Douglas and then goes on to the game of letting Falstaff act his father. Yet at the very end of the scene he lets out his true sentiments with the casual remark, "I'll to the court in the morning." Alone with his father at the court, he is forced by his father's reproaches out of his nonchalance into declaring the full seriousness of his intentions. But this does not stop him in the next scene from relapsing into his apparent frivolity:

> *Enter the* Prince *and* Peto *marching, and* Falstaff *meets them playing on his truncheon like a fife.*
>
> [S.D., *1 Henry IV*, III. iii. 87]

This may be too frivolous for the Italianate courtliness of Castiglione, but Vernon's description of the Prince vaulting with effortless ease onto his horse . . . is the perfect rendering of it. Finally there is the Prince's nonchalant surrender to Falstaff of his claim to have killed Hotspur and his good-humoured but sarcastic willingness to back up Falstaff's lie:

> For my part, if a lie may do thee grace,
> I'll gild it with the happiest terms I have.
>
> [*1 Henry IV*, V. iv. 157-58]

Hotspur both offends against the principle of *sprezzatura* in his blatant acclamation of honour, and is satirised by the Prince for the extreme clumsiness of his would-be nonchalance in the very scene where the Prince takes the news of the rebellion so coolly. . . . [The Prince] is the complete, sophisticated, internationally educated courtier ridiculing the provincial boorishness of Percy, the Hotspur of the north, much like a character in Restoration Comedy ridiculing the country bumpkin.

This is not to say that Hotspur is not a most engaging barbarian; adorable in the openness and simplicity of his excesses, infectious in his vitality, and well-flavoured by his country humour. The child in him goes straight to the female heart; and when his wife loves him to distraction for all his waywardness, we are completely convinced. (pp. 274-80)

I fancy there are still many people who regard Hotspur as the hero of the first part of the play. They are wrong, and their error may spring from two causes. First they may inherit a romantic approval for mere vehemence of passion, and secondly they may assume that Shakespeare must somehow be on the side of any character in whose mouth he puts his finest poetry. . . . But to interpret the poetry as a sign of Shakespeare's sympathy with Hotspur's excesses is as wrong as to imagine that Shakespeare approved of Cleopatra's influence on Antony's character because he puts such poetry into her mouth. What the poetry proves is that Shakespeare was much interested in these characters and that he had something important to say through them.

Why then did Shakespeare develop Hotspur's character so highly and put such poetry into his mouth, when a less elaborate figure would have done to symbolise, as was necessary for the play's structure, the principle of honour carried to an absurd excess? It is that he uses him as one of his principal means of creating his picture of England, of fulfilling in a new and subtle way the old motive of Respublica. For though, as said above, Hotspur is satirised as the northern provincial in contrast to that finished Renaissance gentleman, the Prince, he does express positive English qualities and in so doing has his part in the great composite picture Shakespeare was constructing. (pp. 282-84)

If Hotspur is in some way local, very much of an Englishman and contemporary in that he makes us think of Elizabethan and not medieval England, Falstaff enlarges the play, as none of Shakespeare's hitherto had been enlarged, into the ageless, the archetypal. Though richly and grossly circumstantiated, though quite at home in Elizabethan London from court to brothel, he reaches across the ages and over the earth. . . . Or one might say that Falstaff was in unseen attendance on Satan in the Garden of Eden to make the first frivolous remark and the first dirty joke, after the Fall. It is surprising that Miss Bodkin did not seize on him for one of her archetypal patterns.

Not that Falstaff is no more than the symbol of the ribald in man. He is a complicated figure combining several functions which it might tax the greatest author to embody in even separate persons. (p. 285)

As well as being the eternal child Falstaff is the fool. . . . Roaring in panic at Gadshill, falling down as if dead before Douglas at the Battle of Shrewsbury, he fulfils the fool's crude function of "mere safety-valve for the suppressed instincts of the bully," instincts common to every member of the audience. But far more often he fulfils the more complicated and more characteristic function of providing by his powers of recovery "a subtler balm for the fears and wounds" of the oppressed. He is kin to Brer Rabbit and Fool Schweik. (p. 286)

The Prince [tells] Falstaff that his concern is with disorder and misrule not with order and regularity. And Falstaff blandly admits it and seeks to attach the Prince to his own side when he answers:

> Indeed, you come near me now, Hal; for we
> that take purses go by the moon and the seven
> stars and not by Phoebus—
>
> [*1 Henry IV,* I. ii. 13-15]

With Falstaff here symbolising disorder, an Elizabethan audience would identify the Prince with Phoebus and know that Falstaff was trying to undermine his true kingly function of shining by day. And Falstaff later recalls this conversation when in the tavern he poses as Henry IV reproving his son and says:

> Shall the blessed sun of heaven prove a micher
> and eat blackberries? a question not to be asked.
> Shall the son of England prove a thief and take
> purses? a question to be asked.
>
> [*1 Henry IV,* II. iv. 407-10]

This is not the only place where Falstaff is academic as well as amusing. Indeed he utters as many cosmic or scientific commonplaces as the king himself. His disquisition on sherris-sack, for instance, is a perfectly correct parody of the physical organisation of the microcosm and of its correspondence with another sphere of existence, the body politic. . . . Of course this academic side of Falstaff has more than one job. It makes his antics far funnier. . . . But its immediate relevant job is that it helps to elevate Falstaff into the great symbolic figure of misrule or disorder that he is. To be effectively disorderly he must be learned in the opposite of disorder.

As such a symbol Falstaff is much more than a prolongation of the traditional lord of misrule; he stands for a perpetual and accepted human principle. (pp. 288-89)

[Falstaff,] though he stands for disorder, is after all a comic figure and is not solemn enough to represent the Elizabethan notion of chaos; chaos being what the Prince would have represented if he had made the wrong choice. When the Prince calls Falstaff "that villainous abominable misleader of youth, that old white-bearded Satan," he speaks truth only as far as might concern himself. Falstaff's exquisite mendacity about his own character gives us the general truth:

> If sack and sugar be a fault, God help the wicked!
> if to be old and merry be a sin, then many an
> old host that I know is damned; if to be fat be
> to be hated, then Pharaoh's lean kine are to be
> loved. No, my good lord; banish Peto, banish
> Bardolph, banish Poins: but for sweet Jack Fal-
> staff, kind Jack Falstaff, true Jack Falstaff, val-
> iant Jack Falstaff and therefore more valiant
> being, as he is, old Jack Falstaff, banish not
> him thy Harry's company, banish not him thy
> Harry's company. Banish plump Jack, and ban-
> ish all the world.
>
> [*1 Henry IV,* II. iv. 470-80]

With our virtuous selves we know he is lying; with our unofficial selves we back up the lie, agreeing to call the misleader of youth plump Jack. But only for the moment. We end by banishing the misleader of youth. But it is not the end, for once the misleader of youth has been disposed of, with a "Here we are again" plump Jack reappears; only to be banished again when he becomes too threatening. There is thus no need to be ashamed of having an affection for Falstaff, as long as we

acknowledge that we must also cast him out. The school of criticism that furnished him with a tender heart and condemned the Prince for brutality in turning him away was deluded. Its delusions will probably be accounted for, in later years, through the facts of history. The sense of security created in nineteenth century England by the predominance of the British navy induced men to rate that very security too cheaply and to exalt the instinct of rebellion above its legitimate station. They forgot the threat of disorder which was ever present with the Elizabethans. Schooled by recent events we should have no difficulty now in taking Falstaff as the Elizabethans took him.

The things I have treated of so far in this chapter have little to do with *Henry IV* as a pair of plays in a great historical sequence; they concern the plays' innovations. The exception was this: that in the Prince Shakespeare at last completes the many attempts he had made to define the perfect ruler. But there is far more political content than this. Shakespeare indeed carries on (and with sufficient emphasis to give it a place in the background when politics are not the theme) the total historical doctrine I have expounded in the course of this book, and the specific historical theme (the curse incurred through the murder of Woodstock, one of Edward III's seven sons, and not merely passed on but greatly intensified by the murder of Richard) that connects and animates the whole sequence of eight plays from the reign of Richard II to that of Henry VII. (pp. 290-91)

It remains to support my assertion that in *Henry IV* Shakespeare gives his version of contemporary England, a version allying him to the writers of epic.

Now as the stylistic mark of tragedy is intensity, that of the epic, though tragic intensity may occur, is breadth or variety. And in *Henry IV* there is a variety of style, fully mastered, which is new in Shakespeare and which can hardly be matched even in his later work. This variety contrasts, and I believe was meant deliberately to contrast, with the comparative monotony of *Richard II*. (p. 295)

As a kind of backbone, and corresponding to the high political theme of the plays, is the stately but no longer stiff blank verse used to describe the great happenings which are the main nominal theme. It is the stylistic norm that Shakespeare inherited from the whole series of History Plays he had already written and it is now his absolute servant. One may still call it Shakespeare's official style, but there is not the slightest sense of his using it because he should, and not because he would. It is the perfect correlative of his sincere and solemn heed of the awful and exemplary unfolding of history. Take, for instance, the induction to Part Two, where Rumour tells of the false reports he has spread. It is high-sounding rhetoric; strongly, even violently, metaphorical: and it moves with a gait that is at once ceremonial and consummately athletic. . . . But there are many passages which depart from the norm and in so doing borrow and repay a virtue which in isolation they would not possess. Hotspur's hearty homeliness gains enormously by being set against Shakespeare's official style. . . . (pp. 295-96)

But it is through his use of prose, and of a varied prose, that Shakespeare creates the fullest range of contrast with his blank verse norm. Indeed, some of the prose has a perfect polish that may go beyond any similar quality in the verse. This prose is the property of the Prince and of Falstaff; it is derived from the best things in Lyly's plays; and it looks forward to the elegancies of Congreve. Like its original and its offspring it is founded on the normal speech-cadence of the most intelligent and highly-educated of the aristocracy. It is simple, but measured and deliberate; and so highly wrought that not a syllable can be altered with impunity. . . . Falstaff commands not only the most exquisite conversational vein, but the Euphuism, of Lyly; and his exhibition of it when he poses as the king reproving the Prince is satirical much in the manner of Congreve exhibiting the affectation of contemporary fashions of speech. But the prose ranges through most ranks of society, through the country gossiping of the two Justices and the plainness of Davy to the Dickensian ramblings of Mrs. Quickly. It embraces a large portion of English life. Taken together, the verse and prose of the play are a stylistic exhibition of most phases of the commonwealth.

The theme of Respublica, now given a new turn and treating not merely the fortunes but the very nature of England, what I am calling the epic theme, is subtly contrived. And the contrivance depends on two conditions: first that the two parts of the play are a single organism, and secondly that we are assured from the start that the Prince will make a good king. By itself the first part does not fulfil the theme of England, which occurs only in hints or patches; by itself the second part with so much business in Gloucestershire would contain an overbalance of provincial England: but treat the two parts as a single play, and the theme of England grows naturally till its full compass is reached when Henry V, the perfect English king, comes to the throne. (pp. 297-99)

Henry IV shows a stable society and it is crowded, like no other play of Shakespeare, with pictures of life as it was lived in the age of Elizabeth. There is nothing archaistic about the Eastcheap tavern and its hostess, about the two carriers in the inn yard at Rochester, about the bill found in Falstaff's pocket, about the satin ordered from Master Dombleton for Falstaff's short cloak and slops, or about the life Shallow liked to think he had led at the Inns of Court: they are all pure Elizabethan. But opinions will differ on how they are to be interpreted. The hard-boiled critics will see no more in them than lively bits of local colour serving to make the heavy historical stuff more diverting to a mixed audience. Those who, like myself, believe that Shakespeare had a massively reflective as well as a brilliantly opportunist brain will expect these matters of Elizabethan life to serve more than one end and will not be surprised if through them he expresses his own feelings about his fatherland. It is also perfectly natural that Shakespeare should have chosen this particular point in the total stretch of history he covered, as suited to this expression. Henry V was traditionally not only the perfect king but a king after the Englishman's heart; one who added the quality of good mixer to the specifically regal virtues. The picture of England would fittingly be connected with the typical English monarch. The details of that picture bear out the notion that Shakespeare deliberately contrived such a connection.

First, it is difficult to deny a deliberate contrast between the play's first scene showing the remoteness of Henry IV from his own people, accentuated by his desire to leave his country for a crusade, and the second scene showing the Prince's easy mixing in the less reputable life of London. . . . And the Prince's soliloquy at the end of the scene, promising that he will exhibit all the proper regal virtues, reassures us that we have been justified, that we have been safe, in identifying the Prince with English life generally. And the process is repeated whenever the Prince condescends to take part in events, in Kent or London. Thus it is that when the Prince is crowned, and even though he is then in anything but a condescending mood, we

identify him with the picture of England, then complete.

And there are many things, in which the Prince has no share, that make up this picture. How Hotspur helps in this has been described above; and nowhere more effectively than in the scene in Wales with Glendower and Mortimer. Indeed one of this whole scene's main functions is to create a sense of England through a contrast with Wales. Here not only is the bluff anglicism of Hotspur contrasted with Glendower's Welsh romanticism, but Lady Percy's school-girlish simplicities—"Go, ye giddy goose," and "Lie still, ye thief, and hear the lady sing in Welsh"—are very English and contrast equally with Lady Mortimer's lyricism which Glendower interprets to her husband:

> She bids you on the wanton rushes lay you down
> And rest your gentle head upon her lap.
> [*1 Henry IV*, III. i. 211-12]
> (pp. 299-300)

It is in the scenes in Gloucestershire that the theme of England is completed. But here there is the question of interpretation. Dover Wilson considers these scenes "a studied burlesque of provincial life and manners for the hilarious contempt of London spectators," and if he is right they will be far from creating an epic picture of England. I think that he is wrong and that his opinion falsifies and impoverishes the scenes themselves and goes against the whole trend of Shakespeare's feelings about the country. Shallow and Silence may be ridiculous characters; some of the yokels gathered for recruiting may be pathetic: but these persons are no more a satire on country England than Nym and Bardolph are a satire on Elizabethan London. From first to last Shakespeare was loyal to the country life. He took it for granted as the norm, as the background before which the more formal or spectacular events were transacted. Shakespeare tells us this; when he slips in the spring and winter songs after the prolonged affectations in *Love's Labour's Lost*, or when he inserts the English realism of Petruchio's country house into the Italianate complexities of the *Taming of the Shrew*. And at the end of his career he made the wholesomeness of the pastoral life in the *Winter's Tale* redeem the barren and tortured jealousy of Leontes. Far from being a satire, the Gloucestershire scenes in *Henry IV* complete the picture of England and put the emphasis where Shakespeare meant it to be: on the life of the English countryside. And that emphasis is given precisely as the Prince becomes Henry V. (pp. 301-02)

E.M.W. Tillyard, "The Second Tetralogy," in his Shakespeare's History Plays, Chatto & Windus, 1944, pp. 234-314.

UNA ELLIS-FERMOR (essay date 1945)

[*Ellis-Fermor focuses on the four plays of the Henriad, but touches as well on the Roman plays and the tragedies as she attempts to chart a basic shift in Shakespeare's political thinking after* Henry V. *Although she only briefly examines* Henry IV, *Ellis-Fermor provides an evaluation of Prince Hal/Henry V which became increasingly prominent in subsequent attempts to understand the ambiguities of Hal's rejection of Falstaff: she found that he is an ideal king who in the very process of becoming an ideal figure loses a portion of his humanity. For a similar interpretation of Prince Hal's development, see the excerpts by Cleanth Brooks and Robert B. Heilman (1945) and D. A. Traversi (1948). Ellis-Fermor's essay was first published in 1945.*]

The central and continuous image in [*Richard II, 1 and 2 Henry IV, and Henry V*], more specific than a mood, more comprehensive than a character, is, I believe, a composite figure—that of the statesman-king, the leader and public man, which Shakespeare builds up gradually through the series of the political plays from *Henry VI* to *Henry V*. This figure recurs, in varying forms, through the greater part of Shakespeare's drama, for after the picture is completed in the political plays he appears to revise and reconsider it, studying it from a different angle in several of the tragedies and late plays. (p. 36)

The portrait of the statesman-king is the result of a series of explorations, now the study of a failure, now of a partial success; a vast, closely articulated body of thought imaged always in terms of actual character, yet completely incorporated in no one character. The figure that finally emerges is not Falconbridge or Theseus or Henry IV or Henry V, yet it would be incomplete if any one of them were taken away; nor is it the mere opposite of Henry VI or John or Richard III or Richard II, yet it would also be incomplete if one of these were destroyed. These separate images are but statements or qualifications contributing to that vaster image, no one of them in itself coextensive with the composite whole. It is this which gives coherence to the material of the history plays, which nevertheless remain individual works of art. (pp. 36-7)

The keystone of [the ordered hierarchical state] was the figure of the perfect public man, of Henry V. All the implications of the foregoing plays point to this ultimate emergence of the complete figure. In all the anticipations that lead up to him, and particularly in the later scenes of the second part of *Henry IV*, Shakespeare has, he would seem to imply, 'in this rough work, shaped out a man'; the great art of conduct, and of public conduct at that, is at last truly understood.

But has he? Or has he, as it were unawares, and led already on to some perception beyond his immediate purpose, shaped out instead something that is at once more and less than a man. Henry V has indeed transformed himself into a public figure; the most forbidding thing about him is the completeness with which this has been done. He is solid and flawless. There is no attribute in him that is not part of this figure, no desire, no interest, no habit even that is not harmonized with it. He is never off the platform; even when, alone in a moment of weariness and of intense anxiety, he sees with absolute clearness the futility of privilege and the burden of responsibility, he still argues his case in general terms, a king's life weighed against a peasant's, peasant against king. No expression of personal desire escapes him; though he makes almost the same comparison as Henry VI, he is detached alike from king and shepherd, commenting upon them, but wasting no more strength on imagining what cannot be than on deluding himself, like Richard, with the empty glories of his state. He has inured himself so steadfastly to the life of a king, lived so long in councils and committees, weighing, sifting, deciding, commanding, that his brain automatically delivers a public speech where another man utters a cry of despair, of weariness or of prayer. It is in vain that we look for the personality of Henry behind the king; there is nothing else there. (p. 45)

I think Shakespeare was profoundly interested in this particular study. Not, indeed, by the character, for there is no character, but by the singular circumstances of its disappearance. Neither we the readers nor Henry himself nor his God ever meets the individual that had once underlain the outer crust that covers a Tudor monarch, for there is nothing beneath the crust; all has been converted into it; all desires, all impulses, all selfhood, all spirit. (p. 46)

For the truth is that Shakespeare himself, now that he has built the figure with such care, out of the cumulative experience of eight plays, begins to recoil from it. It has been an experiment, an exploration, like, but for its larger scale, his brief but effective exploration of the system of Machiavelli, and, as he did with that system, so he does with this vast body of assembled evidence on public life: he rejects its findings as invalid before the deeper demands of the less explicit but immutable laws of man's spirit. (p. 47)

That citadel of absolute truth, the inner self hardly known to the man himself, may be corrupted by the effort to stage himself to the public eye, and to surrender to the demand of public life may well be fatal to that core of the spirit wherein is stored its potential immortality.

Shakespeare's final position is an uncompromising declaration of individual freedom and responsibility, that supreme virtue of which the Jacobeans knew so well the value. 'I have in this rough work shaped out a man.' He has, indeed, throughout the Jacobean period: Brutus, Hamlet, Macbeth, Lear, Timon, Antony, Cleopatra, Prospero. And the shaping has involved the rejection not of Falstaff, but of Henry V. (p. 54)

*Una Ellis-Fermor, "Shakespeare's Political Plays,"
in her* The Frontiers of Drama, *Methuen & Co Ltd,
1964, pp. 34-55 .*

CLEANTH BROOKS and ROBERT B. HEILMAN (essay date 1945)

[*The following excerpt is representative of New Criticism. The New Critics were heavily influenced by the English critic William Empson, and like Empson they tended to emphasize the ironies and ambiguities of a literary text. Brooks and Heilman criticize J. Dover Wilson's* Fortunes of Falstaff *(see excerpt above, 1943) as a one-sided defense of Hal's rejection of Sir John. They assert instead that through Hal's development into a successful king, a substantial portion of his natural humanity is lost. This interpretation, suggested earlier by Una Ellis-Fermor (1945), influenced subsequent criticism of* Henry IV, *and is evident in the essay by D. A. Traversi (1947-48). This essay was first published in 1945.*]

Falstaff has been charged with being a coward and has been vehemently defended against the charge, first by Maurice Morgann in the later eighteenth century [see excerpt above, 1777], and since that time by numerous critics on down to the present day. Actually the charge and the defense tend to miss the whole point.

If it is a little absurd to attempt to prove in the face of the Gadshill scene that Falstaff is a valiant man, it is only a little less absurd to use the scene to prove Falstaff's cowardice. Even a thief possessed of a good measure of personal valor will make good his escape if there is a good chance that standing his ground will increase the risk of his identification or capture. Even a rather brave thief, in Falstaff's position, might have run, for to be attacked themselves was the last thing that the successful thieves counted on.

Falstaff is no braver than he should be, doubtless, but he is certainly not a fool. He knows that a bag of gold filched without too much risk is one thing, but that the same bag, if it involves the risk of hanging, is quite another. He knows, on the other hand, as he recovers his breath after making good his escape, that it is a likely tale to turn up with—this story that he had made good the robbery and then by strange coincidence was at once robbed himself. . . . But Falstaff knows how much that story will bear—he sizes up the situation quickly and expertly—and he is able to shift his ground rapidly enough to remain in command of the situation at the end. For, when the prince in triumph asks, "What trick, what device, what starting-hole, canst thou now find out to hide thee from this open and apparent shame?" Falstaff is not even for a moment at a loss. His story about being brave by instinct is absurd, of course (he uses *instinct* as if it were a technical term, without moral significance, the use of which could remove his act from the realm of moral significance); but the "instinct" that prompts the story is not absurd at all. Falstaff is completely at home now. He never lacks a device. The gold is safe, after all, he now knows. First things first. The lads have the money; the joke has been a good joke; and Falstaff has capped the joke for them. "What, shall we be merry! shall we have a play extempore?" (pp. 345-46)

Falstaff and his companions . . . have most of [Act II of Part One]. The relatively short Scene iii seems intended, on the surface, to do little more than remind us of the political activities which are shortly to become more important in the play. We see a further contrast between Hal and Hotspur; and we see a further step taken in one "plot" while the other "plot" is almost completed.

Perhaps, however, Shakespeare is doing a little more than merely, as it were, reserving a future place for Hotspur. As Hotspur reads the letter, for instance, we see, in the relationship among the conspirators, certain parallels to the relationship among the hold-up men. The letter-writer says, for instance, that Hotspur's plot is "too light" to meet "so great an opposition"; when Peto had asked, "How many be there of them?" and Gadshill had answered "Some eight or ten," Falstaff had replied, "'Zounds, will they not rob us?" [II.ii.65]. That is, both great and small plots tend, ironically, to evoke the same thoughts and attitudes.

The comparison goes a step further: just after the passage quoted above, Hotspur calls the writer "cowardly hind" and "frosty-spirited rogue"; and just after Falstaff expresses his fear, Hal taunts him with being a coward. Then, with some shift of characters, the parallel becomes more complex. When he first enters after the robbery, Falstaff introduces a new refrain, "A plague on all cowards!" (he says it four times), addressing his words to the men he thought had *not* participated in the hold-up—Hal and Poins (here *they* are comparable to the writer of the letter to Hotspur). And a great deal more is said about cowardice. Does Shakespeare not appear, then, to be carrying on the theme of cowardice which runs through all the rest of the act and which . . . is a very complex one? Not only is cowardice not easy to define, but, ironically, the same charges are called forth by both comic and serious plots.

Hotspur's next sentence appears to provide a still more marked continuation of a theme that runs through the first two acts: his friends, he says, are "*true* and constant . . . good friends . . . very good friends," and the writer of the letter is "an *infidel*." It is difficult not to believe that Shakespeare is here picking up a concept which was first introduced in Act I, as we saw, when Falstaff said that the "*true* prince" might become a "*false* thief." . . . (pp. 347-48)

[May the repetitions in many contexts of the words "true" and "false"] not be a reminder, perhaps, of the complexities one runs into when one sets out to define *true* and *false* (like the difficulties presented by the word *coward*)? What *is* truth? If Falstaff's fellow-hold-up men do not observe their commitments to him, they are in one sense not *true;* if Hotspur's party do not stick to him, they are not *true*. But if the associates are

not *true* to Falstaff and Hotspur respectively, are they not, in another sense, the more *true* to the king? It may be just to suggest that here we have a *relativistic* view of what is true and false; if that is so, it immediately leads us to ask the question, "Is Shakespeare, in presenting the complexities of truth, going to be content to say that it is relative, or, in the political world about which he writes here, will he present, finally, an *absolute truth*?" The answer, of course, we must find in the rest of the play, and, it is clear, we must find it in the conduct of Hal. In what way will he be *true*? Or will he be *true* in several ways at once? (pp. 348-49)

If *Henry IV, Part I* does have a principle of unity, it is obviously one which allows for, and makes positive use of, an amazing amount of contrast. . . . There is the contrast between the king's hopes for his son and the life which Prince Hal has actually been leading; the contrast between the pomp and state of the councils at court which are called to debate the state of the realm and those other councils at the Boar's Head which take measures for the better lifting of travelers' purses. Moreover . . . Prince Hal and Percy Hotspur are obvious foils for each other; they are specifically contrasted again and again throughout the play. But one of the most important contrasts developed in the play is that between Falstaff and Percy Hotspur.

On one level, it ought to be pretty obvious, the play involves a study in the nature of kingship—not an unduly solemn study, to be sure—but a study, nevertheless, of what makes a good king. In this study, of course, Prince Hal is the central figure, and the play becomes, then, the study of his development.

On this level of consideration, Percy Hotspur not only is Hal's rival but also furnishes an ideal of conduct toward which Hal might aspire (and toward which his father, the king, actually wishes him to aspire). Falstaff represents another ideal of conduct—and here, consequently, finds his foil in Hotspur. (p. 377)

Consider the matter of honor. Hotspur represents one extreme, Falstaff, the other. . . .

Falstaff's common sense is devastating; but it is also crippling—or would be to a prince or ruler. If it does not cripple Falstaff, it is because Falstaff frankly refuses to accept the responsibilities of leadership. Perhaps he chooses wisely in so refusing. By refusing he achieves a vantage point from which he can perceive the folly and pretentiousness which, to a degree, always tend to associate themselves with authority of any kind.

But Hotspur's chivalry is crippling too. He wants to fight for honor's sake: he will not wait for reinforcements because it will beget more honor to fight without waiting for them; but, on the other hand, he will not fight at all (Worcester fears) if he hears of the king's mollifying offer, for then his pride will be saved, his honor preserved, and the political aspects of the rebellion can go hang; for Hotspur has little or no interest in them. (p. 378)

Yet Shakespeare does not give us an oversimplified picture of either extreme. Falstaff redeems himself for most of us by his humor, by his good nature, by his love of life, and perhaps, most of all, by a thoroughgoing intellectual honesty. Hotspur also has his attractive side. There is a kind of abandon, a kind of light-hearted gaiety—in his whole-souled commitment to the pursuit of honor, in his teasing of his wife, and in his laughing at the pompous mystery-mongering of Glendower—which puts him, like Falstaff, *above* the plots and counter-plots that fill up the play.

Yet—if we assume the necessity for leadership and authority—both Falstaff and Hotspur are *below* the serious concerns that fill the play. About both of them there is a childlike quality which relieves them of the responsibility of mature life, a frankness which is the opposite of the pretense and hypocrisy so apparent in the adult world.

This suggestion that there is something childlike and immature about Falstaff and Hotspur must, of course, be heavily qualified. There is a sense in which Hotspur is the epitome of manliness and aggressive masculinity, and certainly he thinks of himself as anything but childish. Moreover, Falstaff, in spite of the war cry with which he sets upon the travelers, "They hate us youth: down with them; fleece them," is old in the ways of vice, and indeed possesses a kind of wisdom which makes the solemn concerns of Henry IV's court appear callow and naïve beside it.

And yet, even so, the pair do not stand quite on the level of the adult world where there are jobs to be done and duties to be performed. They are either below it or else they transcend it; and Shakespeare is wise enough to let them—particularly Falstaff—do both. That is, they appear sometimes *childish* in their attitudes and sometimes *childlike*, for Shakespeare exploits both aspects of their characters in the play.

The childlike qualities, of course, are found predominantly in Falstaff—in his vitality and in his preservation of a kind of innocence. But Hotspur, too, has a kind of innocence which sets him apart from the more calculating of his fellow-conspirators. He is impulsive where they are Machiavellian; boyish, in his love of adventure, where they are playing coldly for high stakes. But the childlike innocence (or, if one prefers, the boyish impulsiveness) merges into childish foolhardiness when he insists on fighting the king at Shrewsbury before reinforcements can be brought up. (pp. 378-79)

Here we come to the crucial problem of unity: what attitude, finally, are we to adopt toward Falstaff and the prince? Which is right? With which of the two are our sympathies finally to rest? Those readers who have felt the charm of Falstaff and who have sensed the fact that Shakespeare is not disposed to defend the duplicities of the king are surely right in refusing to dismiss Falstaff as a coward or a buffoon. Furthermore, they may be right in feeling that Shakespeare has even revealed in Prince Hal himself a certain cold-blooded calculation.

The probability is that we shall miss the play if we assume that Shakespeare is forcing upon us a choice of the *either-or* variety. Is it not possible that Shakespeare is not asking us to choose at all, but rather to contemplate, with understanding and some irony, a world very much like the world that we know, a world in which compromises have to be made, a world in which the virtues of Falstaff become, under changed conditions, vices, and the vices of the Prince Hal become, under certain conditions, necessary, and thus, in a sense, accommodated to virtue? (One might well reverse the form of this statement. From the point of view of an Elizabethan audience, one would almost certainly have to reverse it thus: Falstaff's vices partake of virtue and the virtues of the prince—an easy camaraderie, a genial understanding, an unwillingness to stand on a haughty dignity—are revealed to him ultimately as vices which must be put away.)

Human beings live in a world of time, and a world in which—except at rare heroic moments—compromises have to be made. Falstaff lives, as we have already suggested, in a world of the eternal present, a timeless world which stands apart from the time-harried world of adult concerns. Yet Shakespeare keeps the balance with complete fairness. Each world has its claims. For the prince to be able to retire for awhile into Falstaff's world is worth something to him. It testifies to his humanity, since Falstaff's world is a part of the human world. It probably makes him a better king than he would be if he followed his more calculating and limited father's wishes. Bathed in the light of Falstaff's world, the coldness, the pomposity, the pretentiousness of the world of high concerns is properly exposed. Yet, after all, men must act; responsibilities must be assumed. To remain in Falstaff's world is to deny the reality of the whole world of adult concerns.

It is ironic, of course, that the human being is thus divided between the claims of two aspects of life. It is ironic, from one point of view, that men must grow up at all—must grow away from the innocence of the timeless and amoral world of childhood into the adult world, where except when crises evoke extraordinary devotion and resolution, compromises and scheming are a regular, and perhaps inevitable, part of human experience. Prince Hal, for example, in entering into the world of affairs, loses something as well as gains something—a matter which the play (particularly in its second part) rather clearly indicates. Falstaff may belong to a world unshadowed by time, but it is not for nothing that Prince Hal appears in a "history" play. He belongs to history—to the world of time—and in the Battle of Shrewsbury he enters into history.

The problem of Shakespeare's attitude toward Hal and Falstaff has been argued for a long time, and doubtless will continue to be argued. (pp. 383-85)

That the matter of our attitude toward the Falstaff-Hal relationship is important comes out clearly if we consult the most recent book on the subject, Dover Wilson's *Falstaff*. Wilson sees the plays as involving basically a study in kingship. Falstaff has to be rejected. Though, for Wilson, he remains brilliantly witty, even through the whole of *Henry IV, Part Two*, he becomes more boastful, with a correspondent weakening of our sympathy for him. And Wilson defends the terms of the rejection: Hal is not a "cad or a prig." Falstaff, after all, is not visited with a heavy punishment. The king sees to it that he, along with his other "wonted followers," is "very well provided for."

To repeat, the present analysis agrees on the need of having the matter both ways. Surely, Wilson is at his soundest when he argues that Shakespeare keeps the balance most impartially between Hal and Falstaff; but perhaps he might, on the whole, have made out a more convincing case had he pressed this argument further still instead of trying to mitigate the terms of Falstaff's rejection or to argue that the later Falstaff becomes less attractive than the earlier Falstaff. Is not the real point this: that in Hal's rejection of Falstaff something is lost as well as gained—that a good king, one grants, must reject Falstaff, but that in the process by which a man becomes a good king, something else—something spontaneous, something in itself good and attractive—must be sacrificed; that growing up is something which man must do and yet that even in growing up he loses, necessarily, something that is valuable?

Shakespeare does not sentimentalize the situation. The rejection is necessary if Hal is to become the king that he ought to be and that England doubtless needs; and yet Falstaff's dashed hopes are presented with due pathos. The sentimentalist will doubtless need to blacken Falstaff's character a little—suppress his sympathy for him—in order to be able to accept his being turned off; or, if he is unable to do this, he will, in order to justify Falstaff's rejection, doubtless have to blacken the prince's character, reading into it more of the "vile politician Bolingbroke'' than Shakespeare ever intended. The stern moralist (and he is nearer allied to the sentimentalist than is usually suspected) will do much the same: he will probably applaud the rejection of Falstaff whole-heartedly, or, just possibly and perversely, he will condemn the prince for his acceptance of pomp and power and for his cold heart.

Neither the sentimentalist nor the moralist, then, will be able to accept the play in its fullness. It is possible, of course, that even for the mature reader, the play finally lacks unity—that the balancing of attitudes which has been argued for in this analysis is something which perhaps Shakespeare should have attempted to accomplish but did not, for one reason or another, actually succeed in accomplishing. This, of course, each reader must decide for himself. For the reader who remains unconvinced of any totality of effect, the play will probably remain a collection of brilliant but ill-assorted fragments—the wonderful tavern scenes juxtaposed oddly with passages of dull and pawky history.

For the reader, however, for whom the play does achieve a significant unity it may well seem that here Shakespeare has given us one of the wisest and fullest commentaries on human action possible to the comic mode—a view which scants nothing, which covers up nothing, and which takes into account in making its affirmations the most searching criticism of that which is affirmed. For such a reader, Shakespeare has no easy moral to draw, no simple generalization to make.

Moreover, it will be evident that Shakespeare's final attitude toward his characters (and toward the human predicament. generally) is one of a very complex irony, though it is an irony which will be either missed altogether, or easily misinterpreted as an indifferent relativism—that is, a mere balancing of two realms of conduct and a refusal to make any judgment between them. The world which Shakespeare portrays here is a world of contradictions and of mixtures of good and evil. His vision of that world is ultimately a comic vision—if not gaily comic, and surely not bitterly comic, yet informed with the insights of mature comedy, nonetheless. For the comic writer does not attempt to transcend the world of compromises, even though the more thoughtful writer of comedy, as here, may be fully aware of the seriousness of the issues. (pp. 385-86)

If the prince must choose between two courses of action—and, of course, he must choose—we as readers are not forced to choose: indeed, perhaps the core of Shakespeare's ironic insight comes to this: that man must choose and yet that the choice can never be a wholly satisfactory one. If the play is a comedy in this sense, then the ''comic'' scenes of the play turn out to be only an aspect of, though an important aspect of, the larger comedy. (p. 387)

> *Cleanth Brooks and Robert B. Heilman, ''Shakespeare, 'Henry IV, Part I','' in their* Understanding Drama: Twelve Plays, *Holt, Rinehart and Winston, 1948, pp. 317-88.*

D[EREK] A. TRAVERSI (essay date 1947-48)

[*Focusing on the roles of Falstaff and Prince Hal and their relationship to each other, Traversi maintains that the central concern of* Henry IV *is the cleavage between ''unbridled impulse'' and ''the cold spirit of successful self-control which inevitably becomes inhuman.'' A similar conclusion was reached by Una Ellis-Fermor (1945) and Cleanth Brooks and Robert Heilman (1945), all of whom see in Hal's political development a subsequent deterioration in his humanity.*]

The Prince, as Shakespeare found him in the popular account on which he based his play, was an outstanding example of the familiar story of the dissolute young man who underwent a kind of moral conversion when faced by grave responsibilities and finally made good in the great sphere of political action to which he was called. The story, conceived in these terms, was too familiar and too popular to be ignored by a practical dramatist; on the other hand its conception of human character and motive was too naïvely optimistic to appeal to a Shakespeare moving at this stage towards the mood that was shortly to produce *Hamlet*. Faced with this dilemma Shakespeare chose to accept the very improbability of the story and to turn it to account. The Prince, from his very first appearance, looks forward to a reformation which, just because it is too good to be true, is seen to be moved by a political calculation which clearly reflects the character of his father. If his character is to change, as he announces in his very first soliloquy, it is because a transformation of this kind will attract popularity: for 'nothing pleaseth but rare accidents'. The whole process of 'reformation', as the Prince himself describes it, has a surface quality which Shakespeare is clearly concerned to emphasize. It is seen 'glittering' with metallic speciousness over previous faults, 'like bright metal on a sullen ground'; and its purpose, above all, is to '*show*' more goodly' and 'attract more eyes'. The conversion, thus transformed from an edifying example to an instrument of political success, enters fully into the permanent characteristics of the House of Lancaster. The future Henry V, already regarded as an example of the perfect political figure, begins by consciously abstaining from the finer aspects of human nature; for behind Shakespeare's acceptance of a traditional story lies the conviction that success in politics implies a spiritual loss, commonly involves the sacrifice of more attractive qualities which are distinctively personal.

The character of the Prince as it is developed through the play brings home this conception with a variety of detail. It is the character of a man whose keen if limited intelligence is placed consistently at the service of his political interests. . . . His intelligence is of the kind that judges all men by their value in relation to a coldly conceived political scheme; that is the reason both for his success and his inhumanity. (pp. 26-8)

It is as though the Prince, whose every action is based on calculation, felt for Falstaff, who represents in himself the vitality and the weakness of human flesh, the semi-conscious repulsion felt by the cold practical intellect for something which it can neither understand, ignore, nor, in the last resort, use. The Prince, echoing Falstaff's idiom, brings to it a cold, efficient intensity that points to an underlying aversion. The flesh, with which the finished politician needs to reckon, is nevertheless an object of repulsion to him. Beneath the burlesque and the rowdiness we may already look forward to the ultimate rejection of Falstaff. That rejection indeed is actually anticipated in the same scene. Falstaff, in a plea that is not less pathetic for being a parody based on monstrous presumption, concludes by begging the Prince not to banish him: 'banish plump Jack and banish all the world' (II, iv). Banish Falstaff, in other words, and banish everything that cannot be reduced to an instrument of policy in the quest for empty success. It is true to the Prince's character and to the tragedy of his family that he already replies without hesitation 'I do, I will'. (pp. 28-9)

Falstaff is given in the play a position of peculiar significance which enables him to transcend the political action in which he moves and to provide a sufficient comment on it. He serves, in a sense, as a connecting-link between two worlds, the tavern world of comic incident and broad humanity in which he is at home and the world of court rhetoric and political intrigue to which he also has access. So situated in two worlds and limited by neither, Shakespeare uses him as a commentator who passes judgment on the events represented in the play in the light of his own superabundant comic vitality. Working sometimes through open comment, sometimes even through open parody, his is a voice that lies outside the prevailing political spirit of the play, that draws its cogency from the author's own insight expressing itself in a flow of comic vitality. He represents, we might say, all the humanity which it seems that the politician bent on the attainment of success must necessarily exclude. That humanity, as it manifests itself in the tavern scenes, is full of obvious and gross imperfections; but the Falstaff of the play, whilst he shares these imperfections, is not altogether limited by them. His keen intelligence, his real human understanding, his refusal to be fobbed off by empty or hypocritical phrases—all these are characteristics that enable him to transcend his world and to become the individual expression of the conscience of a great and completely serious artist. In the elaboration of this point we approach the very heart of Shakespeare's conception in this play.

The true nature of Falstaff becomes most apparent when we realize that he comes to be in this series of plays a complete and significant contrast to the figure of the Prince. . . . It becomes fully clear for the first time in the scene of tavern parody when the two men caricature the relationship of Henry IV and his son (II, iv). . . . The description [Falstaff] gives of the Prince, using his father's supposed words, is in itself a criticism, realistic and sardonic, of the whole family: 'That thou art my son, I have partly thy mother's word, partly my own opinion, but chiefly a villanous trick of thine eye, and a foolish hanging of thy nether lip, that doth warrant me'. It is not thus that Henry does actually speak to his son, nor is it true to say that the relationship between them is of this kind. That relationship is on the contrary truly tragic, and becomes more so as the father grows older and more conscious of the weariness that besets him through life; but the disillusioned clarity, even the coarseness, of Falstaff's description corresponds to something really present, that makes itself felt time and again in the Prince's attitude towards his life in the taverns and is a symptom of the detached inhumanity which is one ingredient of his political sense. (pp. 32-3)

[Particularly revealing] because based on sentiments more deeply human beneath the comic vision, is [Falstaff's] attitude towards the pressed troops placed under his command to lead into battle. He has, as always, no particular illusion about the nature and the origins of this human material, 'the cankers of a calm world and a long peace' (IV, ii); but this very account of them in the same speech as 'discarded unjust serving-men, younger sons to younger brothers, revolted tapsters, and ostlers trade-fallen', together with many other references, implies an awareness of social issues possessed by no other character in the play. This awareness is based in its turn upon Falstaff's outstanding quality, the capacity for human sympathy which marks him out in a world of calculation and inspires the respect for human life implied in his magnificent ironic reply to the Prince when the latter sums up his contingent as so many 'pitiful rascals'— 'Tut, tut; good enough to toss; food for powder, food for powder; they'll fill a pit as well as better; tush, man, mortal men, mortal men' (IV, ii). For the Prince as for all his world, soldiers are mere pawns, the wretched instruments of political calculation to be considered from the point of view of their possible efficiency in the tasks imposed upon them by their leaders; for Falstaff alone they are human victims, individuals

exposed to the manipulations of discreditable interests, 'mortal men' and as such to be respected after detached and unsentimental scrutiny in the very sordidness of their tragedy. It is his sense of humanity in its weakness and its irreducibility that prompts Falstaff's behaviour in the battle. Precisely because he is so human himself in his very irony he has no desire to die, to pay the debt of death 'before his day' (V, i); and precisely because he can realize in others the human desire to survive which he feels so strongly in himself he is keenly aware that 'honour' in the mouths of politicians who have been brought to battle by a combination of past selfishness and present refusal to face their responsibilities is an empty word and a delusion. 'I like not such grinning honour as Sir Walter hath' (V, iii) is his final comment, at once human and dispassionate, on the waste implied in a battle based on causes so suspect; and inspired by its spirit he moves through the conflict without being subdued to its tone, viewing it and himself with characteristic frankness and dominating it, when all is said and done, by the very force of his vitality.

These observations bring us to a third characteristic of Falstaff, the one which is perhaps the ultimate source of his strength and the key to Shakespeare's deepest conception in this play. There is in Falstaff a true and rare combination of the warm, alert humanity we have already noted with a background, sometimes accepted and sometimes rebelled against, but continually present, of inherited Christian tradition. It is reasonable to suppose that the latter element makes itself felt in a spontaneous acceptance of the inheritance, still not so distant from Shakespeare, of the mediaeval religious theatre. . . . Falstaff's utterances, indeed, are steeped in tradition, at once religious and theatrical, of this kind. He shares with his audience a whole world of imagery, drawn upon in such phrases as that in which his troops are described as 'slaves as ragged as Lazarus in the painted cloth, where the glutton's dogs licked his sores' (IV, ii). Such were the advantages for Shakespeare of inheriting— I say inheriting because the question of personal belief need not arise—a set of spiritual conceptions at once simple enough to be popular and sufficiently profound to cover the wealth of human experience. We need not say—should not say—that Falstaff simply accepts the Christian tradition. Part of him, what we may call the flesh, clearly does not; but the tradition is there, alive in his utterances and giving him even in his refusal to conform a vitality that enables him to dominate the play. (pp. 33-5)

The emphasis, which had still lain in *Part I* on the clash of conflicting wills and interests, is [in *Part II*] rather upon common helplessness. The King himself, vastly changed from the politician and man of action represented by Bolingbroke in *Richard II*, has lost in this play most of his sense of political vocation and with it most of the practical attributes he still showed in *Part I*. The loss is, in the last analysis, a loss of interest. Old and sick now, the fundamental division noted in *Part I* between his distant aspiration for just and unsullied kingship and a present sense of his usurpation as a continual source of rebellion has now assumed a definitely tragic quality. The enterprises planned in the earlier part of his reign have all remained without fulfilment. Accepting this frustration as part of the nature of things, Henry's strongest emotion has now become a nostalgia for peace and sleep. (p. 120)

The English state is the universe of this play, and its disease is a disunion within that universe: a disunion which transcends mere political divisions and proceeds, in the last analysis, from elements still largely obscure in the author's own experience.

We may say, if we will, that in images of this kind the problem of political unity, or 'degree', and that of personal order are being brought into the closest relationship. Just as the state is regarded in its divisions as a diseased body ravaged by a consuming fever, so is the individual torn between the violence of his passions and the direction of reason; and just as the political remedy lies in an unquestioned allegiance to authority divinely constituted, so does personal coherence depend upon the submission to reason of our uncontrolled desires. In *Henry IV—Part II*, however, the disease, the sense of disunity, is far more evident than the possible remedy, the submission to rule; in fact the consequences of submission, with its accompanying problems, have yet to be seriously posed in a political organism whose infirmities, though clearly acute, are still far from defined in the utterances of those who compose it. (pp. 122-23)

The original presentation of monarchy as the necessary guarantee of order in a world where human experience can still aspire to value and significance continues to be valid for *Henry IV—Part II;* it might even be said that its validity has been strengthened by a growing association of the political with the personal order, by the presence of deepening individual needs seeking expression through the political symbol. What has changed is the presentation of the conception of kingship in relation to political realities. The responsibilities abdicated by Henry are taken over by Prince Hal and his more disagreeable echo, John of Lancaster, representatives of a new generation for which political success has become the sufficient end of existence. The attitude of father and sons, though founded upon a common idea of 'necessity', becomes increasingly different as time passes. What in Henry IV is predominantly tragic, a sense of profound weariness, is in his sons a practical sense of human limitations. Having played no part in the crime which had originally brought their father to the throne, the Prince and his brother are free from its consequences in tragedy and frustration, free therefore to achieve in the practical order all that he no longer hopes to attain. Yet the achievement itself is less satisfactory than it might have been earlier. The victory at Gaultree Forest is, morally speaking, a hollow victory. (p. 123)

Even Falstaff, in his own way, is affected by the prevailing spirit. No longer is he felt, as in *Part I*, to be outside the action in which he participates, transcending and criticizing it by his own vitality. He has become subdued to the life around him. Death, disease, and the flesh now dominate his thoughts, so much so that the critics have detected the realistic, moral influence of Ben Jonson. No doubt that influence exists in the great prose scenes, but Shakespeare's emphasis is profoundly individual and perfectly in tone with the rest of the play. It represents, in fact, a deepening into tragedy of the Christian tones we have already detected in some of the most important passages of the previous play. The prevailing note is not grotesque or farcical, even in the serious meaning with which the word can be applied—following Mr. Eliot's hint—to some Elizabethan writing; it insists rather on tragic pathos, and on the corruption of human values by a combination of time and ill-living. (p. 124)

Shakespeare not only accepted the artistic difficulty involved in [the rejection of Falstaff], imposed on him by the nature of the material he inherited, but wove it into the conception of his play; it is a most revealing example of the subjugation of plot to the growing necessities of dramatic expression. For the cleavage between Falstaff and Prince Hal is only a projection of one fundamental to the play, one between unbridled impulse, which degenerates into swollen disease, and the cold spirit of

successful self-control which inevitably becomes inhuman. . . . The precise meaning, in terms of the poet's sensibility, of this bitter contrast between aged dissolution, and the controlled coldness so unnaturally attributed to youth, needs to be defined in relation to the Sonnets, to *Troilus and Cressida*, and to *Measure for Measure*. The Second Part of *Henry IV* provides, in a word, through the presentation of a society in which all the normal attributes are subject to a peculiar and most disquieting inversion, a fruitful approach to the issues more completely handled by Shakespeare in the first plays of his maturity. (pp. 125-27)

> D[erek] A. Traversi, "'Henry IV—Part I'" and
> "'Henry IV—Part II'," in Scrutiny, Vol. XV, Nos.
> 1 and 2, Winter, 1947 and Spring, 1948, pp. 24-35;
> 117-27.

HERBERT MARSHALL McLUHAN   (essay date 1948)

[*Best known for his pioneering work in media theory, McLuhan follows in the tradition of the "anti-Romantic" critics in his discussion of* Henry IV. *He explicitly censures Maurice Morgann (1777), as well as Samuel Taylor Coleridge (1810 and 1813), William Hazlitt (1817), and A. C. Bradley (1902), for their emphasis on character, specifically the character of Falstaff, as a means of reconstructing the organic unity in the plays. For McLuhan, such a method isolates character from the dramatic context, and therefore deprives it of function.*]

One of the curiosities of the history of Shakespearean criticism concerns the application of the metaphor of organic completeness to the genius of Shakespeare. In the seventeenth century the estimate of Shakespeare as a child of nature rather than of art prepared the way for his acceptance in a new mode by the romantic enemies of art and convention both in literature and in society. As a child of nature, as one vibrating in sympathy with the laws of the universe, Shakespeare could do no wrong. As William Empson has said that

> Magnolias, for instance, when in bud,
> Are right in doing anything they can think of,

so the Shakespearean idolaters were ready to assign to all Shakespearean phenomena a sensitive fidelity to a logic distinct from that of the meddling intellect. The spirit of Morgann was upon Quiller-Couch when he wrote apropos of Falstaff: "No true artist develops or fashions a real character, once brought to birth, any more than a mother thenceforth develops or fashions a child." The force of metaphor in lulling the powers of perception can no further go.

In general, the idolaters dealt with his "imperfections" in the manner in which Pope managed the problem of evil. Shakespeare's Nature was but Art unknown to classicists, his haphazard direction which they could not see. So that his plays were made to seem the products of an almost superhuman provenance. And the method of exploring their internal relationships became, in the hands of Coleridge, not unlike the method which Freud was to use in exploring dream symbols.

One of the first results of viewing Shakespeare's creative activity in accordance with the metaphor of organic unity and coherence appears in Maurice Morgann's view of the character of Falstaff. Character became the point of focus for this organic perspective in Hazlitt, Lamb, and Coleridge. And so it remained for Bradley. The typical result was to isolate character from the dramatic context, and therefore to deprive character of function. But in the past twenty years the organic perspective has shifted focus from character to the plays themselves, as appears in the work of Wilson Knight, Granville-Barker, Caroline Spurgeon, D. A. Traversi, and many others. Along with this shift in focus has come a renewed, if qualified, respect for the pre-Romantic critics of Shakespeare.

Few are likely to quarrel with the view that contemporary erudition has achieved a much surer-footed procedure in the literature of the Renaissance than was possible in the nineteenth century. But we must also confess that much of the erudition has been a recovery of knowledge of Renaissance rhetoric, psychology, and cosmology which was still present to Dryden and Johnson. Professor Tillyard's astonishment at the scope and unity of the Elizabethan world picture, newly recovered, would have struck them as somewhat naïve. Going hand-in-hand with the advance of contemporary erudition has been an improvement in the methods of literary analysis. Granville-Barker's approach to Shakespeare is now typical. "He was liker to a musician, master of an instrument, who takes a theme and, by generally recognized rules, improvises on it; or even to an orator, so accomplished that he can carry a complex subject through a two-hour speech, split it up, run it by divers channels, digress, but never for too long, and at last bring the streams abreast again to blend them in his peroration."

The themes on which Shakespeare descants in the "Henriad" are associated with honour, the desire and the deserving of the praise of good men. Henry Bolingbroke is, however, both usurper and regicide. . . . No peace and no honour was possible under a usurper. And the death of Henry, like that of Claudius and Hamlet, changes the mode from discord to harmony, from corruption to honour, and from base to heroic. The mode of Henry is throughout that of Machiavellian "policy," always sharply contrasted with disinterested adherence to principle. He is treacherous, alternately whining with self-pity and sternly vindictive. He lectures Hal in all the hypocrisies of statecraft and then proposes the imprudent and choleric Hotspur as a model for him. Prince John of Lancaster is in the same mode of the court. He lectures Falstaff priggishly just after he himself has broken faith with the rebels who have accepted his amnesty. The eloquent contempt of Falstaff's ensuing panegyric on wine is not only Shakespeare's verdict on "this same sober-blooded boy" but is a key (if one were needed) to a principal theme of the play, that when the head of the state is corrupt then the belly and the members must find their law solely within their own appetites.

There are, then, three themes and three groups of characters in *Henry IV:* the court, the Boar's-Head group, and the rebels. The court is corrupt. Not principle but policy rules there in the service of ambition and illegitimate power. So Prince Hal's integrity requires that he assume an antic disposition, some protective colouring of dishonour. And since Shakespeare's ethics are traditional it appears in Hal that it is infinitely less dangerous and corrupting to permit disorder in the lower appetites than in the intellectual faculties. . . . So Hal's resort is the Boar's-Head. (We may ask was not Hamlet's mistake to attempt to meet policy with policy?) But the first lines he speaks alone on the stage (I, ii) are to reassure the audience:

> I know you all, and will awhile uphold
> The unyoked humour of your idleness.
> > [*1 Henry IV*, I. ii. 195-96]

Falstaff, Bardolph, and Poins are the types of the riot and disorder emanating from the corrupt court to the commons of England. When the head does not perform its functions the belly and the members are left to self-indulgent idleness. Yet no principle of order can proceed from the sway of the lower appetites. So Falstaff, the cynic about government, judiciary, and honour, can only discover positive motives of action in the gratification of his lusts. If the court lives for the hubristic appetite of power, then he will live for common appetite. His wit at once serves his appetites and is an aspect of them. His escapades as a recruiting officer like his exploits on the battlefield are consistent extensions and illustrations of this theme. In this light his relations with Justices Shallow and Silence, as well as with the Lord Chief Justice, acquire artistic coherence. Over Shallow he quickly gains an ascendancy which is born of smoking-room jocularity and reminiscence. Shakespeare is saying as flatly as he knows how that justice is shallow and silent when rooted in appetite, and that all justice tends to this state when the king is corrupt. But *vis-à-vis* the Lord Chief Justice, Falstaff appears as the moral absurdity he is. . . . In making these very simple intellectual distinctions in accordance with centuries of unbroken ethical conviction, Shakespeare could hardly have foreseen an audience hostile to reason itself and one which would take Falstaff to its muddle-crass bosom in the manner of Titania and Bottom.

The third group consists principally of Northumberland, Hotspur, Worcester, Glendower, and the Archbishop of York. It is significant that while King Henry is allowed no clerical support in the play, the rebels are. The rebels not only show, in part, the face of honour but of religion. (*Henry V*, by contrast, opens with the praise of Hal by the Archbishop of Canterbury.) But there is a simple key to these facts. Like Henry, Northumberland and his colleagues are guilty of upsetting monarchy. In Hotspur, however, the mode is changed to honour, as in Hal. Hotspur is guiltless of his father's connivings. And he is above them. But what can honour do among rebels? It is as useless as Hal's would be at court. Eccentric to the mode of the court, it can only flash fiery and comet-like. So the character of Hotspur is given an exaggeration, symbolically equivalent to Falstaff's. He is all air and fire as Falstaff is all earth and water. But his character is the unmistakable touchstone (as King Henry admits) for the defections of the court. This is brought out in a very forceful way in the first act of Part I. In Act I, Scene i, Hotspur's Scottish victory leads Henry to contrast this "son who is the theme of honour's tongue" with "my young Harry" in whom he sees only "riot and dishonour." And in Act I, Scene iii, Hotspur excuses his peremptory refusal of prisoners on the ground that the request for them came from a "popinjay" who was "perfumed like a milliner,"

> When I was dry with rage and extreme toil,
> Breathless and faint, leaning upon my sword.
> > [*1 Henry IV*, I. iii. 31-2]

The mode of the court is brought into the sharpest possible contrast with the mode of active honour and exploit in this long passage. (Precisely the same contrast occurs in *Hamlet* when Osric is entrusted to arrange the duel with Laertes. (pp. 152-55)

That Hotspur is honourable there is, then, no question. But that he is not fit for princely office is equally manifest. As Worcester says (V, ii) he is

> A hair-brain'd Hotspur, governed by a spleen.
> > [*1 Henry IV*, V. ii. 19]

And Hotspur's contempt for letters and mincing poetry ("'Tis like the forced gait of a shuffling nag") would have "placed" him very definitely for an Elizabethan audience [because of the emphasis on oratorical training for an ideal prince in educational writings of the period].

> Better consider what you have to do
> Than I, that have not well the gift of tongue,
> Can lift your blood up with persuasion.
>
> [1 Henry IV, V. ii. 76-8]
> (p. 158)

After [the] brief epiphany of his true character at Shrewsbury, Hal returns to the mode of his antic disposition. His time is not yet. But he is much less the *habitué* of the Boar's-Head in [Part II]. Of obvious significance in the second part is Henry's crowning breach of faith with the rebels at Gaultree Forest. When he receives word of this "success" in Act IV, Scene iv, he is typically engaged in bemoaning Hal's faults:

> Most subject is the fattest soil to weeds;
> And he, the noble image of my youth,
> Is overspread with them. . . .
>
> [2 Henry IV, IV. iv. 54-6]

Then he receives the good news:

> And wherefore should these good news make me sick?
>
> [2 Henry IV, IV. iv. 102]

Henry is sick to death. He, so long the source of sickness in the commonwealth, is finally poisoned by success. So Shakespeare prepares us for a "change of mode," but not until Henry's moral sickness has vented itself in several long speeches of whining self-pity. Just how we are to view him in this mood is not left in doubt. When he supposes that Hal has filched the crown from his pillow he breaks out (IV, v):

> How quickly nature falls into revolt
> When gold becomes her object!
> For this the foolish over-careful fathers
> Have broke their sleep with thoughts, their brains with care,
> Their bones with industry;
> For this they have engrossed and piled up
> The canker'd heaps of strange-achieved gold. . . .
>
> [2 Henry IV, IV. v. 65-71]

This is one of the great Elizabethan commonplaces, the miser who must bequeath his wealth to a prodigal. Henry assumes that his own greed for wealth and power necessarily has made Hal a prodigal. He knows he has no right to expect anything else.

> Henry the fifth is crown'd: up, vanity!
> Down royal state! all you sage counsellors, hence!
> And to the English court assemble now,
> From every region, apes of idleness!
>
> [2 Henry IV, IV. v. 119-22]

These are not idle words. Falstaff will soon be spurring joyfully to London. The politic Prince John expects the court to be changed from one of policy to revels. And his brother Clarence says to the Lord Chief Justice:

> Well, you must now speak Sir John Falstaff fair;
> Which swims against your stream of quality.
>
> [2 Henry IV, V. ii. 33-4]

To which the Chief Justice retorts, pointing up the central theme:

> Sweet princes, what I did, I did in honour.
>
> [2 Henry IV, V. ii. 35]

Seen in this light the concluding scenes concerning the discomfiture of Doll Tearsheet, Mistress Quickly, Silence, Shallow, and Falstaff have a perfect propriety. They are evident tokens of the fact that the death of Henry "changes the mode" from base to heroic. (p. 160)

> *Herbert Marshall McLuhan, "'Henry IV,' a Mirror for Magistrates," in* University of Toronto Quarterly, *Vol. XVII, No. 2, January, 1948, pp. 152-60.*

M. A. SHAABER (essay date 1948)

[*Shaaber disputes the claims of J. Dover Wilson (1944) and E.M.W. Tillyard (1944) that* 1 *and* 2 Henry IV *constitute a single, ten-act play. Other critics who have considered the plays as separate works include John Upton (1748), E. E. Stoll (1914), Harry T. Baker (1926), Robert Adger Law (1927), and Muriel C. Bradbrook (1965).*]

The fact that, in the last three or four years, two persuasive and influential critics [J. Dover Wilson and E.M.W. Tillyard] have offered us interpretations of Shakespeare's *Henry IV* plays which assume that these plays form a unified whole invites us once more to consider this assumption. There is nothing new about it (it is at least as old as Dr. Johnson [see excerpt above, 1765]), but it has rarely been assumed so confidently or worked into so elaborate an interpretation. . . .

Professor Dover Wilson proclaimed the unity of the two plays in *The Fortunes of Falstaff* (1943), but without making much attempt to prove it. . . . But in his edition of *1 Henry IV . . .* he offers some justification of his opinion. . . . (p. 217)

Dr. E.M.W. Tillyard, in *Shakespeare's History Plays* [1944], [also] argues for the unity of the two plays. . . . (p. 218)

The incompleteness [of *Part I*] assumed by both interpreters is not apparent to me. Of course, the reign of Henry IV is incomplete; as long as Shakespeare chose to make the Battle of Shrewsbury the climax of his play it could not be otherwise. The rebels, to be sure, are not completely quelled, but then they never are. The announcement that they have been thoroughly scotched a moment before Henry IV dies is an invention of Shakespeare's intended, I think, to add a poignant irony to the king's death. But the inheritors of their quarrel rise up against Henry V at the beginning of his reign, and indeed it is the argument of Dr. Tillyard's book that the rebel cause draws its motive from the wrong done Richard II, a wrong which plagues Henry IV and his successors all their lives and is not expiated till the end of the Wars of the Roses. So far as the play is incomplete, it is incomplete because history is an endless chain, and Shakespeare is dramatizing history. And if the theme of *1 Henry IV* is what Dr. Tillyard says it is, I do not understand how the play can be called incomplete.

> In the first part [he says] the Prince . . . is tested
> in the military or chivalric virtues. He has to
> choose, Morality-fashion, between Sloth or
> Vanity, to which he is drawn by his bad com-
> panions, and Chivalry, to which he is drawn
> by his father and his brothers. And he chooses
> Chivalry.

Indeed he does, unequivocally and completely. Fully reconciled with his father, he seems to have set the issue between them completely at rest. I cannot think what need have or could have been added to show that Hal was indeed the true prince. (pp. 218-19)

1 Henry IV, IV, iv is very commonly pointed out as a reason for taking the two plays as a unit. It has even been said that this appearance of the archbishop ''has no meaning unless his conspiracy was to follow.'' On the contrary, the scene has an obvious meaning in the dramatic scheme of *1 Henry IV* and is not ''almost irrelevant'' to it. Its business is to foreshadow the outcome of the Battle of Shrewsbury. There the rebels are to meet with a decisive check, and Shakespeare, after his usual fashion, anticipates what is to come. This scene signifies that the rebel cause is in a bad way indeed if one of its ringleaders has grave misgivings about it. The same thing might have been, and is, signified otherwise, but this is by no means the only place where Shakespeare, even near the end of a play, has brought forward a new character to serve some purpose of the moment and dismissed him as soon as his work was done. If *1 Henry IV* had never had a sequel, Shakespeare, judged by his practice elsewhere, might well have put this scene into his play. (pp. 219-20)

The idea that the relations of the prince and the king, ''eased by the interview in III.ii. and his brilliant conduct in battle,'' still await ''final clarification'' is adroitly stated [by Professor Wilson]. Much virtue in *eased*. Is there really the slightest hint in *1 Henry IV* that the king and the prince are not completely and triumphantly reconciled? Does ''Thou has redeem'd thy lost opinion'' [V. iv. 48] really mean ''I feel a bit easier about you than I did before, but the final showdown is still to come''? I cannot think that the impression left by *1 Henry IV* is anything but that of a complete vindication of the prince in his father's eyes. To be sure, in *2 Henry IV* we find him as much misunderstood as ever, but to interpret the first part by the second is what Professor Wilson himself objects to as ''the fallacy of omniscience, that is, of treating a play like a historical document and collecting evidence in support of a particular reading of character or situation from any point of the text without regard to its relation to the rest.'' If one does not fall into this fallacy, there is no reason whatever for supposing that the end of *1 Henry IV* is anything but an end. The prince has broken through the clouds ''that did seem to strangle him,'' has falsified men's hopes; the premises from which the play took its start have been carried to a conclusion. (p. 220)

Besides imputing weakness to the arguments in favor of a unified plan, I submit that there are other reasons for viewing the idea skeptically. The first is the similarity of the structure of the two plays. Structurally *2 Henry IV* is almost a carbon copy of the first play. According to the scene-division of modern editions, there is exactly the same number of scenes in both plays; according to that of the folio, there are three more in the first part. By either count the number of scenes is exactly the same in the first, second, and last acts. What is more impressive, the sequence of scenes developing the historical plot and that of the comic scenes is almost exactly the same. . . . In the first two acts the correspondences are remarkably close. I, iii represents a conference of the rebels in both plays; II, iii is a domestic scene among the Percies; II, iv is a tavern scene. The last is, I think, especially significant. In the third act the plan is, in a very general way, the same (historical matter followed by a Falstaff scene), but in *2 Henry IV* the comic material outweighs the historical. . . . In *1 Henry IV* the historical and the comic material are interwoven; in *2 Henry IV* they are separated until the last scene. The question is, then, would Shakespeare be more likely to plan the plays in this fashion if he were working out, in a single fit of creation, a play of ten acts or if, after *1 Henry IV* proved a resounding success, he aimed at repeating it? To me the latter view is the more probable.

Another reason for hesitating to see the two plays as one is, I think, the fact that in the second the clock is turned back most flagrantly. At the end of *1 Henry IV* the king and the prince are *en rapport* and united against the Welsh; in *2 Henry IV* we find them estranged all over again so that they must be reconciled a second time. No new cause of musunderstanding is shown; the situation simply reverts to what it was in the beginning. Shakespeare sets the clock back adroitly, but set it back he does. I know that Professor Wilson will have it otherwise: the king and the prince are only tentatively reconciled at the end of *1 Henry IV;* their relations are only ''eased.'' I can only repeat what I have said above, that I defy a candid reader to detect any flaws in the understanding between them as it is presented at the end of *1 Henry IV*. What becomes of the triumphant close of the play if the king and the prince are still somewhat at odds? How could this imperfect sympathy possibly be acted? Thus the question arises, if Shakespeare planned both plays as a whole, would he have planned to bring the king and the prince together, separate them covertly, and then bring them together once more? Would he have invented the reconciliation at the Battle of Shrewsbury, about which *The Famous Victories* and Holinshed are silent, knowing that there was a second reconciliation to come later? Or is it more likely that he would have done what he did because the immoderate popularity of *1 Henry IV* forced him to write an unpremeditated sequel for which he needed the death-bed scene as climax? It is hard for me to believe that an experienced playwright who from the first contemplated making the death-bed scene the climax of his picture of the relations of father and son would have anticipated their reconciliation in his version of the Battle of Shrewsbury and the events leading up to it.

Finally, the question of the unity of *Henry IV* raises larger questions about cyclical plays. Professor Wilson sees the implications of his argument clearly and faces them boldly. ''Part II,'' he says, ''was written to be played immediately, or at not more than twenty-four hours' interval, after Part I.'' And indeed his interpretation is highly esoteric unless the plays were so performed. What is the likelihood that they were?

So far as I know, there are no recorded performances of the two plays on the same day or on successive days before the twentieth century. (pp. 221-23)

Perhaps the practice of other playwrights will help us to estimate the likelihood of Shakespeare's having planned *Henry IV* as a unit. In the sixteenth and seventeenth centuries, I cannot find a real example of an integrated cycle of plays, of two or more plays which must be considered as one if their import is to be grasped. (p. 224)

It would seem then that, if *Henry IV* is a fully integrated unit, it is virtually unique. What Shakespeare did no other playwright of his time attempted. Obviously Shakespeare is by no means debarred from venturing upon untrodden ground and the singularity of such a scheme hardly disproves it. But one may still ask what Shakespeare would have gained by it, what advantage a highly integrated scheme gave him in attracting audiences to the theater. From a purely practical point of view, surely none at all; successive performances, separated by an interval of not more than twenty-four hours, require a degree of cooperation of the audience difficult to obtain. For obviously such a cycle of plays can achieve its full effect only so far as the same audience attends both performances. (pp. 224-25)

This is not to say that there are no links between the two parts of *Henry IV* or that the experience of seeing *2 Henry IV* is not the richer for having seen the first part. It is only to say that I cannot square what I think a knowledgeable playwright would do in writing two linked plays with Professor Wilson's description of *Henry IV*, and that therefore I am suspicious of his description. The unity which he attributes to the two plays seems to me to be a theatrical impossibility.

> [Shaaber adds in a footnote:] The structure which Professor Wilson attributes to the two plays is, I suspect, equally impossible. According to him . . . , the normal dramatic curve of a five-act Shakespearian play here encompasses ten acts. Now the structure of an effective play presses the spectator forward at an accelerating pace till his interest is carried to the climax and is satisfied by the dénouement. There are minor relaxations of the tension along the way, but there can be no real interruption of this continuous and progressive interest without disastrous results. How is it possible to send him home overnight midway in this continuous and progressive development without seriously impairing its effect? What experienced playwright would ever dream of doing such a thing?
>
> (p. 226)

One word more. I hope I do Professor Wilson and Dr. Tillyard no injustice by inferring that when they defend the unity of *Henry IV* they think they are vindicating Shakespeare's art, they think that a unified *Henry IV* is artistically superior to two plays linked by catch-as-catch-can methods. To that assumption I would demur. The logic of a play is no necessary cause of its greatness and at most but a minor cause. . . . For two hundred years captious critics have been trying to make sense of Falstaff's hyperbolical account of the action on Gadshill, trying to make it acceptable to our minds. They have not succeeded. But the scene remains ineffable comedy just the same; in other words, whether the mind can accept it has very little to do with the matter. Sense is only sense; it is not drama. Critics who put so heavy an emphasis on it are barking up the wrong tree. What happens in Shakespeare's plays (like what happens in human life) sometimes defies explanation, especially easy explanation, but if this fact is of any importance to the profound and lasting impressions that the plays make it is because our interest is quickened and our impressions heightened, as in life itself, by what is not transparently clear. Explain away the puzzles, the incongruities, the diversities and you take away some of the amazement, the awe, the sense of the complexity and the inscrutability of life which they excite. We do not need to impose an airtight logical scheme on Shakespeare's plays to justify them artistically; we come much closer to the radiant core of their interest by other avenues of approach. (pp. 226-27)

> *M. A. Shaaber, "The Unity of 'Henry IV'," in* Joseph Quincy Adams: Memorial Studies, *James G. McManaway, Giles E. Dawson, Edwin E. Willoughby, eds., Folger Shakespeare Library, 1948, pp. 217-27.*

J[OHN] I[NNES] M[ACKINTOSH] STEWART (essay date 1949)

[In contrast to Marshall McLuhan (1948), Stewart praises Maurice Morgann (1777) and considers his exclusive focus on character a viable approach to an understanding of the organic unity of Shakespeare's art. Stewart supplements this method with the insights of modern anthropological theory. He is the first critic to suggest the relevance of the scapegoat ritual to the rejection of Falstaff; for a similar interpretation, see the excerpt by C. L. Barber (1955). Stewart particularly disapproves of E. E. Stoll's essay on Falstaff, which he argues attributes too much to tradition, and not enough to Shakespeare's imagination, in the creation of Falstaff's character (see excerpt above, 1914).]

In Shakespeare's characters . . . we are aware, just as we are in actual people, of depths and facets not immediately rendered in behaviour. They seem to carry about with them a fuller and more complex humanity than is required by the exigencies of their rôle. It is this that makes them so lifelike, and our intuitive apprehension of the *whole* character is an important part of our experience of the play. At first the understanding pronounces Falstaff to be indeed a coward—the mere braggart soldier Stoll sees [see excerpt above, 1914]. But at the same time we are aware that Shakespeare "has contrived to make secret Impressions upon us of Courage." And if we respect these impressions, if we treat them as a trained historian might treat his underlying sense of some historical portrait's being as yet incomplete, if we work by inference from what is overt to what is concealed—if we do this we shall eventually vindicate our intuition before the bar of the understanding, and appreciate that the entire artistry in Shakespeare's creation of Falstaff consists in the disparity between real or whole character (which is courageous) and the partial or apparent character (which is cowardly). (p. 118)

Why does a man write plays or novels, after all; and how does he possess himself of the people who feel and act in them? On this Morgann himself has something to say—not much, but sufficient to set us on our road:

> But it was not enough for *Shakespeare* to have formed his characters with the most perfect truth and coherence; it was further necessary that he should possess a wonderful facility of compressing, as it were, his own spirit into these images, and of giving alternate animation to the forms. This was not to be done *from without;* he must have *felt* every varied situation, and have spoken thro' the organ he had formed. Such an intuitive comprehension of things and such a facility must unite to produce a *Shakespeare.* . . . The characters of *Shakespeare* are thus *whole,* and as it were original [see excerpt above, 1777].

"Compressing, as it were, his own spirit into these images." Coleridge, Morgann's immediate successor in the great line of Shakespeare critics—and another who believed that "Shakespeare's characters are like those in life, to be *inferred* by the reader"—takes us further when he notes

> Shakespeare's mode of conceiving characters out of his own intellectual and moral faculties, by conceiving any one intellectual or moral faculty in morbid excess and then placing himself, thus mutilated and diseased, under given circumstances.

Coleridge's words here take colouring from their being directed at an elucidation of the character of Hamlet, but the perception underlying them is clear. The artist does not get the essence of his characters from camera-work, as Mr. Draper would suppose; nor yet from a filing-cabinet of traditional literary types, which is the belief Professor Stoll constantly expresses with what softening word he can. He gets his characters from an interplay of these with something inside. And it is because he has a particular sort of inside, or psychic constitution, that he is obliged to get them. Falstaff and his peers are the product of an imagination working urgently from within. The sum of the characters is a sort of sum—nay, gives something like the portrait—of Shakespeare: a truth which Walter Bagehot realises in his essay, *Shakespeare—the Man*. ("If anybody could have any doubt about the liveliness of Shakespeare, let him consider the character of Falstaff.") (pp. 120-21)

And a man writes plays or novels, I conceive, partly at least because he is beset by unexpressed selves; by the subliminal falling now into one coherent pattern and now into another of the varied elements of his total man—elements many of which will never, except in his writing, find play in consciousness. It is this that gives the characters their "independence as well as relation"; their haunting suggestion of reality and of a larger, latent being unexhausted in the action immediately before us; their ability to beckon beyond the narrow limits of their hour. And here, too, we see how characters "come alive"—how Falstaff came alive. It was not that Shakespeare took a traditional figure and clothed it with the spurious animation of a dazzling dress. It was that he took that figure and infused into it as much—and only as much—of the Falstaff-being in himself as the exigencies of his design would admit. Of what more there was unused the bouquet, it may be, floats across the stage in those "secret impressions" which Morgann felt. And sherris and ambrosia mingle there.

We have discovered, I think, why Morgann's essay is so much nearer to Shakespeare than Stoll's. Morgann better understands being creative. Stoll sees Shakespeare making his book as Stoll would make a book: knowing just what he would do, assembling his material from all available sources, and then constructing according to the best professional specifications of his age. But Morgann knows that nothing was ever born alive this way, and that despite all the artist owes to tradition and convention his is an inner travail still. That he draws from tradition is assured, and he will be the better, perhaps, for having before him the idea of the literary kind to which he would contribute. But *what* he contributes will be his own, or nothing in art. It will be radically his own, and not an old thing resurfaced. For the essence of his task is in exploring an inward abundance. When he does this in drama his characters, sympathetically received, will inevitably suggest to us a life beyond the limits of their rôle. And Shakespeare, from the vast heaven of his mind, expresses whole constellations of emotion in personative form; it is nothing other than this that Morgann means when he asks:

> For what is *Falstaff*, what *Lear*, what *Hamlet*, or *Othello*, but different modifications of *Shakespeare's* thought?
>
> (pp. 121-22)

The "scurvy" treatment of Falstaff [in the rejection scene] is quite in keeping with certain insensibility in the Elizabethans which appears in many gulling scenes on the stage. But we are liable to feel it not consonant either with Shakespeare's humanity to a major creation, or with the sympathy and admiration which must surely be claimed from us for Hal, a character who is being "groomed" (as the studios say) for the

field of Agincourt. We may now consider more at large certain efforts as a solution of the problem.

Can we find some light in which the rejection of Falstaff commends itself to our sympathies while operating wholly within the sphere of psychological realism? I must say in advance that I think the answer to be "No." All through the trilogy there are penetrations enough into a deeper Harry Monmouth, and the rejection can be analysed in terms of these. But, by and large, I think something profounder is operating here than Shakespeare's understanding of the son of Henry Bolingbroke. There are times in all drama when immemorial forces come into play, and with the end of Falstaff we touch once more what Professor Schücking is fond of calling the limits of Shakespearian realism. (p. 127)

When Shakespeare makes Falstaff die "ev'n just betweene Twelve and One, ev'n at the turning o' th' Tyde" [in *Henry V*], he is touching a superstition, immemorial not only along the east coast of England from Northumberland to Kent but in many other parts of the world too—one shared by Dickens's Mr. Peggotty (who speaks of it expressly) and the Haidas on the Pacific coast of North America. But there is more of magic about Falstaff than this; and Dover Wilson, whom the editing of Shakespeare has schooled in a fine awareness of the reverberations of English words, is more than once well on the scent. "How doth the Martlemas, your Master?" Poins asks Bardolph. And Dover Wilson comments:

> Martlemas, or the feast of St. Martin, on 11 November, was in those days of scarce fodder the season at which most of the beasts had to be killed off and salted for the winter, and therefore the season for great banquets of fresh meat. Thus it had been for centuries, long before the coming of Christianity. In calling him a "Martlemas" Poins is at once likening Falstaff's enormous proportions to the prodigality of fresh-killed meat which the feast brought, and acclaiming his identity with Riot and Festivity in general.

Falstaff, in fact, is the "sweet beef," the roasted Manning-tree ox with the pudding in his belly," who reigns supreme on the board of the Boar's Head in Eastcheap—"a London tavern . . . almost certainly even better known for good food than for good drink." There is thus from the first a symbolical side to his vast and genuine individuality; and again and again the imagery in which he is described likens him to a whole larder of "fat meat."

> 'Call in Ribs, call in Tallow' is Hal's cue for Falstaff's entry in the first great Boar's Head scene; and what summons to the choicest feast in comedy could be more apt? For there is the noblest of English dishes straightaway: Sir John as roast Sir Loin-of-Beef, gravy and all.

Is it not—I find myself asking—as if the "brawn," Sir John, "the sow that hath overwhelmed all her litter but one," were some vast creature singled out from the herd and dedicated to a high festival indeed? But such festivals commemorate more than the need to reduce stock against a winter season. They commemorate a whole mythology of the cycle of the year, and of sacrifices offered to secure a new fertility in the earth.

Now, anthropologists are always telling us of countries gone waste and barren under the rule of an old, impotent and guilty king, who must be ritually slain and supplanted by his son or another before the saving rains can come bringing purification and regeneration to the land. Is not Henry IV in precisely the situation of this king? (pp. 137-38)

Perhaps, then, we glimpse here a further reason why the rejection of Falstaff is inevitable—not merely traditionally and moralistically inevitable but symbolically inevitable as well. And this may be why, when in the theatre, we do not really rebel against the rejection; why we find a fitness too in its being sudden and catastrophic. As long as we are in the grip of drama it is profoundly fit that Hal, turning king and clergyman at once, should run bad humours on the knight, should kill his heart. For the killing carries something of the ritual suggestion, the obscure *pathos,* of death in tragedy. (p. 138)

Falstaff's rejection and death are very sad, but Sir James Frazer would have classed them with the Periodic Expulsion of Evils in a Material Vehicle, and discerned beneath the skin of Shakespeare's audience true brothers of the people of Leti, Moa and Lakor.

If this addition of another buried significance to the composite myth of Hal and Falstaff should seem extravagant, or an injudicious striving after Morgann's "lightness of air," let it be remembered that drama, like religious ritual, plays upon atavic impulses of the mind. All true drama penetrates through representative fiction to the condition of myth. And Falstaff is in the end the dethroned and sacrificed king, the scapegoat as well as the sweet beef. For Falstaff, so Bacchic, so splendidly with the Maenads Doll and Mistress Quickly a creature of the wine-cart and the cymbal, so fit a sacrifice (as Hal early discerns) to lard the lean, the barren earth, is of that primitive and magical world upon which all art, even if with a profound unconsciousness, draws. (pp. 138-39)

> J[ohn] I[nnes] M[ackintosh] Stewart, "The Birth and Death of Falstaff," in his Character and Motive in Shakespeare: Some Recent Appraisals Examined, Longmans, Green and Co., 1949, pp. 111-39.

JOHN F. DANBY (essay date 1949)

[In the following essay, Danby attempts to reconcile the "Romantic" approaches of William Hazlitt (1817) and A. C. Bradley (1902), both of whom regarded Falstaff as the rejected hero of Henry IV, with the twentieth-century critics J. Dover Wilson (1943) and E.M.W. Tillyard (1944), who argued that Hal was the real hero of the plays, and that Falstaff was the "deservedly rejected" villain. Danby claims that it is impossible to choose between Hal and Falstaff, because they represent "false alternatives," the true synthesis of which Shakespeare provides in King Lear. Other critics who have attempted to mitigate the "Romantic" and "anti-Romantic" views of Henry IV include Harold C. Goddard (1951) and Samuel B. Hemingway (1952).]

Discussion of [Henry IV Parts 1 and 2] turns round the relations of Falstaff and Hal. As a . . . preliminary we might be allowed to describe at the outset the assumptions which govern the discussion following. It is admitted, with audiences from Shakespeare's day to ours and with critics from Hazlitt to Bradley, that Falstaff walks off with both parts of Henry IV. It is admitted, too, with critics up to and including Coleridge, and with Dr. Tillyard and Prof. Dover Wilson of recent commentators, that Shakespeare's intention was to make Hal the real hero of both parts, and Falstaff the deservedly rejected, utterly discredited, villain. It is suggested that both admissions are compatible: Hal is the end of the old period in Shakespeare's

development, Falstaff the portent of a new; Hal is Shakespeare's tired consciousness, Falstaff the sign of meanings growing unconsciously; Hal is part of a dying Shakespeare, Falstaff the promise of rebirth. (p. 82)

The world we see [in Henry IV] is one that has disintegrated into mutually exclusive spheres—the worlds of the Court (Prince John of Lancaster), of the tavern, of Shallow's Gloucestershire, of the rebellious lords: frigid opportunism, riotous irresponsibility, fatuous inconsequence, quarrelsome 'honour'—with no common term except the disease of each. 'England' is sometimes said to be the heroic composite thing that is portrayed. If this is so, it is an England seen in her most unflattering aspects—an England pervaded throughout court, tavern, and country retreat by pitiless fraud. Pity is the reconciling sweetness that the world of the plays most lacks. It is the absence of pity in Hal's dealings with Falstaff that explains the 'romantic' recoil from the Prince. (The age of the romantics rediscovered pity.) We can readily admit that the newly-crowned King must stop being the old prince; but only sophistry could see proper 'kindliness' in the manner of his dealings with Falstaff at the end of Henry IV, Part 2. We might admit, with Dr. Tillyard, that the Prince is Shakespeare's attempt to construct a good man on Aristotelian norms; but we should still insist that such a conception, with its absence of pity, represents a real loss in comparison with the unconscious Christian norms of Richard and Falconbridge [in King John]. It is Falstaff, of course, who makes the great appeal to the spectator's sense of pity. But Falstaff himself is the most pitiless creature in the play—Falstaff deceiving Shallow, recruiting his Gloucestershire yokels, ruining Mistress Quickly, despising Hal; predatory Falstaff about to swoop on the body politic and make it his new prey. The absence of pity makes for spiritual incoherence in the world of the play as a whole, and for lack of moral integrity in the individuals that compose it. Even inside the separate spheres there is no cohesion. Hotspur quarrels with Glendower, Northumberland's sickness leads to his son's defeat, Poins and the Prince have purposes between them at odds with those of their fellows, the devotion of Mistress Quickly and Bardolph to Falstaff gains them no euqivalent return from him, Hal and his father are estranged, John of Lancaster is distinct from both even after the family reconciliation. No character in the plays provides a satisfying point of rest—unless for rest we turn from the smaller confusions of Northumberland, Hotspur, Bolingbroke, Prince John, Mistress Quickly, Shallow, Doll Tearsheet, Poins and Hal, to lose ourselves in perplexity among the roomier contradictions of Falstaff. If anything unifies this congeries of unharmonized monads it is 'Commodity'—commodity unavowed by any, but duly observed by all, commodity acted upon unconsciously, the condition that ensures its greatest efficiency as a motive for conduct.

Richard III and King John both centre round a dominant figure who in his own consciousness experiences the polarity of 'commodity' and 'pity'. It goes without saying that the Prince Henry plays cannot include such a consciousness. Prince Arthur [in King John] is dead, and Shakespeare knows it. No one in Henry IV, however, can be permitted the same awareness. The world must now go on as if he had never existed. The problem is to find a makeshift ideal which can stand in the 'tempest' of 'the times' now that 'the life, the right, and truth' are departed. Such a makeshift Shakespeare invents in Prince Hal.

It is a critical commonplace that Hal is Shakespeare's ideal king in the Chronicle plays. He is not, however, ideal absolutely. (pp. 84-5)

It was idle of the Elizabethan censor to be afraid of the implications of *Henry IV*. It represents a view of history which makes sedition impossible. Whatever is, is right, provided it is strong: right in a makeshift way, to be tested by the secular standard of success, justified by its ability to hold what it has: the right, the life, the truth of all this realm is fled to heaven.

These then are the limits to the ideal. But within these limits Hal is still Shakespeare's hero. He carried on Shakespeare's conscious intent to come to terms with contemporary social reality. (p. 88)

Hotspur is Hal's proxy on the field of chivalry as Falstaff is on Gadshill. As befits a prince, Hal does none of the labouring in either case. He appears at the right time to rob both champions of their spoil. Hal is never involved directly either in the 'tug and scamble', the shady work of Eastcheap, or in the pot-hunting for 'honour'. These are implications—the indignities in which his dignity is rooted. Hal's inclusiveness as the perfect all-rounder must be asserted, but his princeliness must also be maintained. He is the distilled essence of the new humanity, not its crude original forms. . . . Just as the lack of coherence in the world of the play as a whole is compensated for by an amazing vividness and surface life in the individual components, Hal's lack of inner depth is balanced by a brilliant range and facility of gesture. But not even Shakespeare's virtuosity can dispel the impression of hollowness in the end. Hal remains a façade.

In Hal the figure of the machiavel undergoes a further and most surprising development. The full machiavel strategy is retained, but it is machiavellism turned inside out. Hal is the sheep in wolf's clothing, a machiavel of goodness:

> I know you all, and will a while uphold
> The unyoak'd humor of your idlenesse. . . .
>
> [*1 Henry IV*, I. ii. 195-96]

This is a bold attempt to enlist the machiavel in the ranks of virtue. But virtue itself wilts when it is made the object of a machiavellian strategy. It sinks to reputation, and that to the acclamation of one's dupes. The externals have again replaced the internals. To pseudo-goodfellowship in Hal must be added pseudo-morality. (pp. 89-90)

Hal, we have said, is Shakespeare's tired consciousness, Falstaff Shakespeare's unconscious. . . . There can be no doubt that [Hal] is intended for a new model King, a sixteenth-century paragon. The model itself, however, . . . falls short of the absolute ideal Shakespeare has educated us already to expect. In the preceding chronicle plays [*Henry VI, Parts 1, 2,* and *3*], the issues raised had been wider: Is the King right or wrong? Is the state just or unjust?—Even in the person of Jack Cade these questions are posed. In *Henry IV, Parts 1 and 2* the questions are reduced and vulgarized: Is the King strong or weak? Is the state secure or insecure? Shakespeare's first machiavel [Richard III] descried the actual mechanics of human motive in society. Richard appreciated the importance of self-interest, approved it, and decided on a ruthless employment of his intelligence to encompass the ends proposed by appetite. 'Pity, love, and fear' he dismissed as irrelevancies. But Richard was wicked. Shakespeare insists that his choice was wrongful. Then the machiavel, and the society he interprets, is submitted to a process of whitewashing. This process ends in the machiavel of goodness, Prince Hal. Hal is no longer aware that society might be wicked. He espouses the aims and the means of the society to hand, he equips himself to be good in accordance with the terms of the State he will ultimately govern:

> Ile so offend, to make offence a skill.
>
> [*1 Henry IV*, I. ii. 216]

This line gives the masterly essence of the new morality. Crude machiavellism says that the end justifies the means. Refined machiavellism merely says: Let what you can do indicate what you can do better: technique is the thing, let the ends look after themselves. It is the attitude underlying sixteenth-century capitalist development (in war, mining, and trade) and the attitude implied in the scientific programmes which grew out of that development.

This twofold attitude to Hal involves a twofold attitude to Falstaff. In so far as we see Hal as the model chronicle-hero, in accordance with Shakespeare's intention, Falstaff will then be the decided villain of the plays. If we tend to criticize Shakespeare's model as an inadequate ideal, compared with his early chronicle plays and with his later tragedies, then Falstaff will tend to acquire merit (deserved or undeserved) from his rejection. Critics have followed both paths. There has been a 'Hal party' and a 'Falstaff party'. The point missed in the debate has been, I think, the most important one: that Falstaff and Hal belong together, that they can be accepted together or rejected together. Shakespeare in *Henry IV* is a Shakespeare in transition. It is impossible to deny that he has already moved on in the Hal plays themselves. And he is still moving. As Hal turns away from Falstaff Shakespeare himself turns away from Hal. (pp. 90-2)

Coleridge groups Falstaff with Richard III and Iago [see excerpt above, 1811]. . . . It is not the popular view of Falstaff, though a similar view has been recently revived by Dr. Tillyard and Prof. Dover Wilson. It answers to something really sinister, however, in Falstaff's make-up, something not allowed to reveal itself as menacing until the old King is dead:

> Boote, boote, Master *Shallow*, I know the young
> King is sick for mee. Let us take any mans
> Horsses: the Lawes of England are at my command'ment. Happie are they which have been
> my Friendes: and woe unto my Lord Chiefe
> Justice.
>
> [*2 Henry IV*, V. iii. 134-38]

This is an unusual piece of self-revelation. Malice, vindictiveness, and overweening arrogance have not hitherto displayed themselves so openly in Falstaff. Nor, up to now, has he shown any sign of the fatal defect now apparent—the taking of himself seriously. This breach in his cynicism we are not prepared for, and not quite able to stomach. Falstaff sees the throne vacated for himself to occupy—a prospect not likely to lead to any more fun. Coleridge and Dr. Tillyard are right to take Falstaff seriously. (pp. 92-3)

Falstaff can be no more tolerated in court than Lear's rioting can be borne in the 'graced palace' of Goneril and Regan. From the point of view of responsible governors both old men are equally disgraceful ruffians: and both deserve banishment.

The parallel between the rejection of Falstaff and the banishment of Lear by his daughters is an exact one. If it is nonsense to plead that Lear's rejection was justified that is because of a development in Shakespeare's world-view beyond the impasse of *Henry IV*. *King Lear* provides a synthesis which resolves the unresolved oppositions of the Hal tetralogy. It gives the ground for a true solution of the false alternatives of Hal or Falstaff. (p. 94)

What we have called Authority (or Power) and Appetite Dr. Tillyard calls Order and Disorder (or Riot) and accounts for *Henry IV, Parts 1 and 2* in these terms. Dr. Tillyard makes an absolute distinction between the two. Order is a real absolute value, Riot a real immorality. Hal turns his back irrevocably on Riot and is converted to the party of My Lord Chief Justice—*Justitia*. The view proposed here as an alternative to Dr. Tillyard's makes no such absolute difference between Hal and Falstaff. The opposition into which they are thrown is an appearance rather than a reality. When Hal moves from Eastcheap to the Court, from Falstaff to My Lord Chief Justice, he is merely leaving the unofficial sphere of Elizabethan life for the official sphere. The two are different, and require different habits. But the difference is not essentially a moral difference. It is a difference of social function. On the view proposed here Authority (or Power) and Appetite occupy the same plane. Both are essential to the running of the Elizabethan state. Equally immoral, both collaborate to maintain an iniquitous world. The Elizabethan state was such a world, a corrupt society. (pp. 96-7)

Hal and Falstaff, then, go together. They are to be accepted together, or rejected together. Certainly Hal's rejection of Falstaff must not be regarded as more significant than his long association with the rogue. (p. 97)

John F. Danby, "Edmund's Ancestry," in his Shakespeare's Doctrine of Nature: A Study of "King Lear," *Faber and Faber Ltd, 1949, pp. 57-101.*

EDMUND WILSON   (essay date 1950)

The great salient patterns of Shakespeare that give us symbols for what is most personal and most profound are beginning to take shape in [the two parts of *Henry IV*]. The reader finds his sympathy weighted (as no doubt the Elizabethans did, since Falstaff became so tremendously popular) for Falstaff as against Hal, because Shakespeare, though he can give us both sides and holds the dramatic balance, is identifying himself with Falstaff in a way he cannot do with the Prince. He has already made us sympathize queerly with those of his characters who have been bent out of line by deformities or social pressures, whose morality is twisted, whose motives are mixed. Faulconbridge runs away with *King John*, and Shylock, the villain of *The Merchant of Venice*, becomes by a single speech a great deal more interesting than Antonio. Has not even Richard III in his horrid way a fascination—as of a Quilp or a Punch whose motives we have been made to understand—which the author could not possibly give Richmond? Falstaff is not deformed in quite the same obvious way as these others, but he is both physically and morally monstrous, and his nature is also mixed. And from Falstaff through Brutus to Hamlet is not such a great step. Hamlet is also complex and also out of tune, though what is wrong with him is less obvious still; like Falstaff, he is at once quick-witted and extremely inept at action, a brilliant and constant talker and a man always at odds with his social group. The opposition between Falstaff and Henry unmistakably reappears in the contrast between Hamlet and Fortinbras; and "Master Shallow, I owe you a thousand pound," with the deathbed scene that follows, is to flower into the tragic eloquence of that series of final scenes in which Shakespeare is to make us feel that Hamlet and Othello and Lear and Antony and Coriolanus, for all their confusion and failure, have been rarer and nobler souls than the opponents, unworthy or worthy, who have brought their destruction about. In *Hamlet*, the Falstaff figure, with changed mask but a similar voice, holds the un-

disputed center of the stage; Prince Henry has dwindled to Fortinbras, who is felt mainly as an offstage force, but still represents the straight man of action who is destined to take over in the end. But later we shall have Antony and Octavius, Coriolanus and Aufidius. Here, too, the balance will be evenly held, and we shall never get melodrama. We are not allowed to sentimentalize over Antony any more than we are over Falstaff. Octavius is perfectly right: he does his duty as Henry does; but we shall always like Antony better, just as we did poor old Falstaff. Falstaff and Richard II are the two most conspicuous prototypes of Shakespeare's tragic heroes. (pp. 166-67)

Edmund Wilson, "J. Dover Wilson on Falstaff," in his Classics and Commercials: A Literary Chronicle of the Forties, *Farrar, Straus and Giroux, 1950, pp. 161-67.*

CLIFFORD LEECH   (essay date 1951)

[*Like R. A. Law (1927) and L. C. Knights (1959), Leech considers* 2 Henry IV *an autonomous play with its own thematic unity. Also, like John F. Danby (1949), he finds a "darker" side to the play, similar in atmosphere to the problem comedies of Shakespeare's later career. Leech explicitly questions the position of E.M.W. Tillyard (1944) on the unity of Parts One and Two and his assumption that Shakespeare uncritically incorporated Elizabethan social prejudices into his work. For further critiques of Tillyard and other historical critics, see the excerpts by Leonard Dean (1944), Cleanth Brooks and Robert Heilman (1945), M. A. Shaaber (1948), Harold C. Goddard (1951), and Samuel B. Hemingway (1952). This essay is derived from a paper given in 1951.*]

In arguing that Part II [of *Henry IV*] was an "unpremeditated addition", which need not concern us here, R. A. Law has emphasized the morality characteristics of that Part, the placing of Prince Henry between the personified representations of order (in the Lord Chief Justice) and disorder (in Falstaff). This account of the play's structure has been elaborated by Tillyard, though of course he disagrees with Law on the play's origin. It does indeed now seem beyond question that the Prince, no longer on the field of battle, is exhibited as slowly abandoning his old associations with disorder and becoming ultimately at one with its opposite. Not that we have a 'conversion', as in the old moralities, but rather a manifestation of a hitherto concealed adherence. This part of the play's substance becomes most noticeable towards its end, when Falstaff is ready to steal any man's horses because his "dear boy" is on the throne, and Doll and the Hostess are taken to prison for being concerned in a man's death. To demonstrate this second phase in Hal's apprenticeship is the overt intention of this Part, as we may say that the overt intention of *Macbeth* is to demonstrate the ills that come upon a man and his country when he murders his King and steals the crown. But just as we may think that there is a secondary intention to *Macbeth*, to hint at a protest against the very frame of things, so in this Second Part of *Henry IV* we may feel that the dramatist, in giving us the preparation for Agincourt, hints also at a state of dubiety concerning basic assumptions in the great historical scheme. He shows us the new King adhering to political order, yet makes us half-doubt whether that order is worth its price, whether in fact it is of the deepest importance to men. And with this element of doubt, the poet's awareness of mutability grows more intense.

Whether Part II was a new play or a continuation of one already begun, the battle of Shrewsbury had marked the end of a phase.

Part II. Act I. Scene ii. Falstaff and the Chief Justice. By F. Barnard (n.d.). From the Art Collection of the Folger Shakespeare Library.

Shakespeare, returning to his subject, and to a more sober aspect of that subject (for law has not the manifest attractiveness of chivalrous encounter), was bound to approach his task with less light-heartedness, with a cooler and more objective view. Just as Marlowe in *Tamburlaine* appears to see his hero with less enthusiasm in Part II than in Part I, recognizing his excess as such and not keeping him immune from ridicule, so here Shakespeare weighs his characters more carefully and questions even the accuracy of his balance.

This note in the play is, I think, struck in the Induction itself. Clearly Shakespeare needed an introductory speech here, both to remind his auditors of what had happened at Shrewsbury and to make plain the irony of the false news brought to Northumberland in the first scene of the play. But he is not content with a simple Prologue. His speaker is a quasi-morality figure, and no pleasant one. Rumour expresses scorn for the credulity of men, and even—though irrelevantly—for their love of slander. The scorn is brought home when Rumour calls the audience he addresses "my household". In tone this Induction is similar to the Prologue to *Troilus and Cressida:* there too the speaker was in a costume appropriate to the mood of the play—"A Prologue arm'd . . . suited in like conditions as our argument"—and there too the tone was not gentle.

In the play we at once meet Northumberland, who has not gained much of our affection in either of the two earlier plays

in which he appeared. Here he is the first of a series of old and sick men that we are to encounter. Falstaff and Justice Shallow, King Henry IV and the Lord Chief Justice, are all burdened with their years, and the only one in full command of his wits and his body is the character given no personal name and conceived almost as a morality-presentment of the Justice which he executes. . . . The comedy [at the Boar's Head] and in Gloucestershire has a sharper savour because we are never allowed to forget the evidence of decay. Justice Shallow, wrapping his thin frame in a fanciful tapestry of wild youth, is comedy of the rarest sort, but "Jesu, the days that we have seen!" is a line with a barb in it for us all. And the King, in his different way, belongs with these men. When we first meet him in Act III, he is longing for the sleep denied him; he cannot rid himself of guilt, ever more and more pathetically he talks of the crusade he will never make; and when he is dying he asks to be carried to the chamber called Jerusalem, so that the prophecy may be fulfilled and he may derive consolation from submitting to what has been decreed. (pp. 17-18)

It is no surprise to us when Northumberland's defection is shown, and it seems appropriate that these rebels, so given to sober talk, should be vanquished by a verbal trick before a blow is exchanged. In Holinshed it is not Prince John of Lancaster but the Earl of Westmoreland who dupes the rebels: Shakespeare uses Westmoreland as an ambassador of Prince

John, but gives to the King's son all the doubtful credit of the action. The change can, I think, only be explained by the assumption that Shakespeare wanted to bring this line of conduct more closely home to the royal house. Because Prince John is the King's son and Hal's brother, the stain of the exploit falls partly on them. Perhaps some will claim that such conduct was justified in the cause of law and order, that an Elizabethan would simply admire the skill of it. Yet is it possible not to find irony in John's concluding speech in the scene of Gaultree Forest?

> I promised you redress of these same grievances
> Whereof you did complain; which, by mine honour,
> I will perform with a most Christian care.
>
> > *[2 Henry IV, IV. ii. 113-15]*

In the mouth of the astute Prince John the word "Christian" has an effect gross and palpable. When he proceeds to claim "God, and not we, hath safely fought to-day", we seem to recognize blasphemy. . . . Nor should we overlook Shakespeare's reminder that Prince John's adroit handling of the situation is but a momentary trick. Hastings has told him that, if this revolt is put down, others will rise against the House of Lancaster:

> And though we here fall down,
> We have supplies to second our attempt:
> If they miscarry, theirs shall second them;
> And so success of mischief shall be born,
> And heir from heir shall hold this quarrel up,
> Whiles England shall have generation.
>
> > *[2 Henry IV, IV. ii. 44-9]*

To that John replies:

> You are too shallow, Hastings, much too shallow,
> To sound the bottom of the after-times.

It is Hastings who is right: John is too vain to see the total situation. (p. 19)

In Shakespearian drama there is often a condition of tension between the play's overt meaning and its deeper implications. The gaiety of *Twelfth Night* is enriched by the thread of sadness that runs through it, but we cannot say that the baiting of Malvolio is in easy accord with the play's surface texture. In *Macbeth* the enfolding of the tragic idea within a morality pattern leaves us with a feeling of suspended judgement in which we resent Malcolm's concluding reference to "this dead butcher, and his fiend-like queen". So in this Second Part of *Henry IV* the deeper, more disturbing implications impinge directly on the main action of the drama, and then, as in *Macbeth*, the writer appears to strain for the re-establishment of the original framework. We get this feeling in the harshness of the words that Henry V uses to Falstaff, for we have come to wonder a little whether there is ultimately much to choose between Falstaff and Prince John, and indeed we greatly prefer Falstaff's company. And the same feeling emerges, I think, in the often praised scene where Hal is reconciled to his father. Justifying his taking of the crown when he believed his father dead, he says:

> I spake unto this crown as having sense
> And thus upbraided it: 'The care on thee depending,
> Hath fed upon the body of my father;
> Therefore, thou best of gold art worst of gold.
> Other, less fine in carat, is more precious,
> Preserving life in medicine potable:
> But thou, most fine, most honour'd, most renown'd,
> Hast eat thy bearer up.' Thus, my most royal liege,

> Accusing it, I put it on my head,
> To try with it, as with an enemy
> That had before my face murder'd my father,
> The quarrel of a true inheritor.
>
> > *[2 Henry IV, IV. v. 157-68]*

The elaborateness of the imagery is notable: the burden of the crown is a devouring monster, its gold is contrasted to *aurum potabile*, it is a murderer with whom the dead man's son must wage a blood-feud. In this scene and in the new King's rejection of Falstaff, the note of sternness and sobriety is heavily, almost clumsily, pressed down, in an attempt to silence the basic questions that so often in the play demand to be put. And perhaps, when he had done, Shakespeare realized that this close was altogether too ponderous for a play that had taken us to the Boar's Head and into Gloucestershire, and altogether too assured for a play persistently though not obtrusively concerned with change and ineradicable frailty. So he gave us the dancer's epilogue, in tripping prose, with its casual half-promise that Falstaff would come again in the next play: the banishment was to be merely from the King, and not from us. Later he was to change his mind again, perhaps because he realized that Sir John was no longer a figure of delight: around him had grown a small forest of disturbing thoughts, which might well choke the brief glory of Agincourt. (pp. 20-1)

In Law's paper on *Henry IV*, to which I have already acknowledged a debt, the darker side of Part II is in no way brought out. But Law does draw attention to the comic echoing of serious things in the play. . . . In Part I [Falstaff] has this exchange with the Prince when the battle of Shrewsbury is about to begin:

> *Fal.*   I would 'twere bed-time, Hal, and all well.
> *Prince* Why, thou owest God a death.
> *Fal.*   'Tis not due yet; I would be loath to pay him
>   before this day.
>
> > *[1 Henry IV, V. i. 125-28]*

Then there follows the 'catechism' on 'Honour'. In Part II the despised Feeble has a moment of splendour when, unlike Bullcalf and Mouldy, he does not attempt to escape from impressment:

> By my troth, I care not; a man can die but once:
> we owe God a death: I'll ne'er bear a base mind:
> an't be my destiny, so; an't be not, so: no man
> is too good to serve's prince: and let it go which
> way it will, he that dies this year is quit for the
> next.
>
> > *[2 Henry IV, III. ii. 234-38]*

There is of course an absurdity in these words of bravery poured from so weak a vessel, yet they demand respect. Bardolph's reply, "Well said; thou'rt a good fellow", cannot be wholly ironic, and the impressiveness of the effect is only mitigated, not destroyed, when Feeble comes out again with his "Faith, I'll bear no base mind". The interplay of feelings in this Second Part is so complex that our sympathy resides securely nowhere. Falstaff can be used to direct our feelings, as he does with Prince John, and often through the play we prefer his gross and witty animality to the politic management of the Lancastrians. But just as the dramatist makes no attempt to disguise his age and sickness or even a churlish arrogance in him, so here he is put down by Feeble's curious, inverted echo of his own words in the First Part. I am of course not suggesting that Shakespeare could expect an audience to note the echo: for us, however, it seems to indicate a trend of feeling in the writer's mind.

The remarkable degree of objectivity in the presentation of the characters reminds us of certain later plays of Shakespeare, those that we call the 'dark comedies'. . . . And *2 Henry IV* is close to these plays also in the peculiarly acrid flavour of certain generalized utterances. On his first appearance in the play, the King sees the process of time in geological change and in the pattern of a human life, and there is no comfort in the vision, only a desire to have done:

> O God! that one might read the book of fate,
> And see the revolution of the times
> Make mountains level, and the continent,
> Weary of solid firmness, melt itself
> Into the sea! and, other times, to see
> The beachy girdle of the ocean
> Too wide for Neptune's hips; how chances mock
> And changes fill the cup of alteration
> With divers liquors! O, if this were seen,
> The happiest youth, viewing his progress through,
> What perils past, what crosses to ensue,
> Would shut the book, and sit him down and die.
>   [*2 Henry IV*, III. i. 45-56]
>   (pp. 21-2)

It seems probable that *2 Henry IV* was written some three years before *Troilus*, some six before *Measure for Measure*, yet here Shakespeare anticipates that objectivity of manner, fused with a suggestion of deep and personal concern, which is characteristic of these two later plays. The sequence of the histories depends on the cardinal assumption that order in a commonwealth is a prime good: it is not altogether surprising that, as his task came towards its conclusion, and with the additional effort required in writing a second play on a young king's apprenticeship, Shakespeare should have reached a condition of dubiety, should have felt less secure in his assumptions. The 'dark comedies' come during the tragic period, and in their way give evidence of a similar slackening of grasp. The basic assumption made by the tragic writer is that a personal goodness, inexplicable and apparently futile, can nevertheless be realized. But, unless the writer has the sense of a direct revelation, this assumption can be maintained only by strong effort: in the 'dark comedies' the mind is not kept tragically taut. (p. 23)

When one is interpreting a Shakespeare play, one is always in danger of being reminded that Shakespeare was an Elizabethan, that his assumptions and standards of judgement were therefore different from ours. Tillyard has commented thus on Prince Hal's treatment of Francis in Part I:

> The subhuman element in the population must
> have been considerable in Shakespeare's day;
> that it should be treated almost like beasts was
> taken for granted.

But is not this to overlook the fact that Shakespeare can make us resent the ill-treatment of any human being, and respect the most insignificant of creatures, a Feeble or a servant of the Duke of Cornwall? In *Measure for Measure* he reminds us even that an insect shares with us the experience of death and corporal suffering. He was an Elizabethan certainly: he made assumptions about kingship and 'degree' and incest and adultery that perhaps we may not make. But he was also a human being with a remarkable degree of sensitivity: it is indeed for that reason that he can move us so much. If he merely had

skill in 'putting over' characteristic Tudor ideas, we could leave him to the social and political historians. Because his reaction to suffering, his esteem for good faith, his love of human society, his sense of mutability and loss, his obscure notion of human grandeur, his ultimate uncertainty of value, are not basically different from ours—though more deeply felt and incomparably expressed—he belongs supremely to literature. We do him, I think, scant justice if we assume that he could write complacently of Prince John of Lancaster, and could have no doubts about Prince Hal. (p. 24)

Clifford Leech, "The Unity of '2 Henry IV'," in Shakespeare Survey: An Annual Survey of Shakespearean Study and Production, Vol. 6, *edited by Allardyce Nicoll, Cambridge University Press, 1953, pp. 16-24.*

ARTHUR SEWELL (essay date 1951)

[*Sewell's study is a good example of the twentieth-century reaction to the character studies of the previous century. In the following excerpt, he criticizes Maurice Morgann (1777) for opening the debate over Falstaff's "cowardice," maintaining that such an approach to Shakespeare's characters is misleading in that it considers dramatic figures as real people with psychological motivations, rather than the characters of a play.*]

It was surely a mistake ever to ask the question: Is Falstaff a coward? Morgann, who first asked it, very rightly made the distinction between the Understanding, which deals in actions, and the Impression made upon us, often at variance with the Understanding. Morgann also affirmed of character-presentation that 'just so much is shewn as is requisite, just so much as is impressed': but he went on to say that this 'just so much' is able to imply a character which, though 'seen in part', may yet be 'capable of being unfolded and understood as a whole'. He therefore believed it possible to answer the question and proper to put it: Is Falstaff a coward? One might answer that the facts say that he is, but our impression of him, our attitude to him, says that he is not. Falstaff ran away, pretended to be dead; and to do these things was to put the safety of his skin above his human dignity, and this might be thought to be a sort of 'cowardice'. But not when we are dealing with Falstaff, for Falstaff was very doubtful about 'honour', and if we do not believe in 'honour' the word 'cowardice' has no meaning. Falstaff is not to be judged, as a real person might be judged, in terms of the ordinary moral categories. His running away, his pretending to be dead, his speech on 'honour' are all part of his attitude to his world, and it is this that calls from us the ambiguous, even face-saving, judgement of laughter. We do not ask, Was Falstaff a coward? just because we are ourselves infected with Falstaff's notion that perhaps, after all, the question is not so important as we thought it was.

Falstaff is a character, not a real person. What wholeness and consistency he has comes not from within but from the address of his personality *vis-à-vis* his world as it transforms itself into speech and behaviour. The world is his stooge, and so magnanimously does he present himself, he is his own stooge. He subdues and transforms the matter of the moment—even his own monstrous belly—to the purposes of his superlatively comic vision. Such a representation of personality is to be found in a work of art, and its consistency is not psychological but aesthetic. It is the notable distinction of Falstaff's being that he has been conceived quite independently of psychological motivation. His delights, like ours, are aesthetic, even though they have their play in the uncertain world of our moral scruples.

Falstaff is aware of his audience, on and off the stage, and the comic artistry is part of the comic character. His life within the play—the only life he has—is a sustained vaudeville turn. The audience is necessary to his being. Nor is he alone of Shakespeare's characters in this. . . . [The truth is] that in the creation of these persons Shakespeare's identification of himself is not with the character but with the actor. And this identification does not make him ask, What does it feel like to be Falstaff, Iago, Jaques, Richard III? but rather, What effect is Falstaff, Iago, Jaques, Richard III, to make on his audience? A very different matter. This effect is the product of an address to the world, here and now made concrete in the address to the audience. (pp. 13-15)

It is the experience of many of us, I fancy, that in the theatre or in the cinema—perhaps after a very good dinner—we have sat with a lump in our throats and tears welling just beneath our eyelids, devoutly hoping that the lights will not go up too soon. Cheap drama, like cheap music, can be curiously potent. And the reason for this seems to be that we are moved by the spectacle of what is happening to this man, this particular man—there, in front of us!—because there is nothing else for us to concern ourselves about. We are at the mercy of the simple stimulus. We are overwhelmed by the tearful situation, because the imagination and the intellect are not otherwise engaged. For the moment, we are debauched.

In Shakespeare's plays, however, what pity we feel, what terror, is of quite a different kind. The stimulus is by no means simple. We have a great deal else to concern ourselves about. And very often, when something like actuality, perhaps unbidden, breaks through, we are at a loss. We become, in fact, at the mercy of the simple stimulus.

I believe that this happens in Shakespeare's final dealings with Falstaff in *Henry IV, Part II*. In general the truly comic character, *qua* comic character, has no interior mode of existence, and what he feels has no relevance in our attitude towards him. Who asks what Falstaff is *feeling*, when he runs away at Gadshill, or counterfeits death at Shrewsbury? Who cares? Are his knees knocking? Do his limbs tremble? Does his heart miss a beat, except for the unusual exercise? Who asks these questions? But, in the end, when the king rejects him, questions of this sort must be asked. At that moment—all the attempts to excuse the king prove this point—we are compelled to ask: What is Falstaff feeling about all this? At last he is brought up to it—a situation which he cannot turn to his own comic purposes, intractable as it is to the subduing magic of personality, his address to the world. This address had never had to reckon with such a moment, and, for the moment, it is quite put down. We are a little ashamed of ourselves. The Falstaff we knew has never asked for our pity. We can do no more than fumble with our sympathies, tell ourselves that it had to be, bear in mind Henry V, justify (or condemn) the king that acts so. And all this because without the transforming power profanity, old age, and surfeit-swelling are no other than themselves, and we had thought them otherwise. We have to treat Falstaff—with what loss!—as a real person. We pity this fat old man; but we cannot say 'The pity of it!' And it is only when we pity and can also say, enlarging the moment in its significance, 'The pity of it!' that pity is more than self-indulgence. Unless what happens to the character is a mode of bringing together into more poignant relationship the character's way of meeting his world and the comprehensive vision

of the play, the character becomes no other than a 'real person', and we may be affected more, but moved less. The emotion, like the incident which arouses it, should be a catalyst by means of which vision is released and enriched, so that the particular case is apprehended in terms of the general case of Man. (pp. 34-6)

Arthur Sewell, "Character and Vision," in his *Character and Society in Shakespeare*, Oxford University Press, Oxford, 1951, pp. 1-37.

HAROLD C. GODDARD (essay date 1951)

[*Goddard combines the reactions of both the "Romantics" and "anti-Romantics" toward Falstaff and Prince Hal and presents the theory that Shakespeare intended to create two Henrys, as well as two Falstaffs, in the* Henry IV *plays. For Goddard, the dual personalities of these central characters explain the dissention among critics over what exactly each one comes to mean: Hal is both the reckless, good-natured son and the self-disciplined, cold-hearted king, while Falstaff is both the "Immoral and the Immortal Falstaff." Goddard's essay is in part a response to E. E. Stoll (1914) and J. Dover Wilson (1943), both of whom he sees as limiting the dimensions of Falstaff's character in their condemnations of his habits. For a similar interpretation of Falstaff and Prince Hal, see the excerpt by Leonard Unger (1956).*]

In *Richard II* Shakespeare interred the doctrine of the divine right of kings. In *Henry IV* he tries out what can be said for the opposing theory. (p. 161)

The hypocrite has always been a favorite subject of satire. Henry IV is one of the most subtly drawn and effective hypocrites in literature, in no small measure because the author keeps his portrayal free of any satirical note. But not of any ironical note. Richard II had done Henry an injustice in banishing him and confiscating his inheritance. Coming back, the exile discovers that the opportunity to right his personal wrongs coincides with the chance to rid his native land of a weak king. So he finds himself ascending the throne almost before he knows it. Or so at least he protests later. . . . From the moment Henry gave the hint that ended in Richard's death to the moment of his own death at the end of *II Henry IV*, his life became a continuous embodiment of the strange law whereby we come to resemble what we fear. The basis of that law is plain. What we are afraid of we keep in mind. What we keep in mind we grow like unto. (p. 162)

One cannot help loving Hotspur for his blunt honesty. It seems almost his central quality. And yet his very honesty is based on a lie, a degenerate form of the medieval conception of "honour." The fact that Hotspur talks so incessantly and extravagantly about "honour" shows that he distrusts his own faith in it. He is another who "doth protest too much." This fact is clinched by his uneasy sleep, which his wife reveals. He fights all night long in his dreams. We are reminded of Richard III's "timorous dreams," which *his* wife reveals. Far as the noble Hotspur is from the villainous Richard, the psychology is the same. It is fear begotten by falsehood. (p. 166)

With [a] glimpse of the heir to the throne added to what we have seen of the other three Henrys, the political pattern of these plays becomes clear. Henry IV, by deposing his legitimate sovereign, Richard, has committed himself to the best-man theory of kingship, which, in practice, is equivalent to the strong-man theory. Between himself and Richard, in his own opinion and in that of many others, there could be no question of relative merit. But here is Hotspur, the incarnation of valor (and brother-in-law incidentally of Mortimer, legal heir to the throne). And here is his own good-for-nothing son. What about the succession in this case, on the King's own theory?

Plainly Henry's revised version of the divine right of kings is in for trouble. He is caught in his own trap. And the nemesis is personal as well as political. "What the father hath hid cometh out in the son," says Nietzsche, "and often have I found the son a father's revealed secret." There was never a better illustration of this truth. In his concentration on power the elder Henry has suppressed both the playful and the passionate tendencies of his nature.

> My blood hath been too cold and temperate.
> [*1 Henry IV*, I. iii. 1]

What he has kept under comes out in Hal, who leads a life of abandon under the tutelage of Falstaff. (p. 168)

Though it comes later, it is Henry's great soliloquy on sleep that confirms all this. It is the nocturnal part of a man that receives what he puts behind his back or under his feet in the daytime. In the apostrophe to sleep this victim of insomnia reveals the unrealized half of his soul. The lines have been called out of character. They are Shakespeare the poet, we are told, running away with Shakespeare the dramatist; Henry was incapable of anything so imaginative. On the contrary, the soliloquy is a measure of the amount of imagination that must be repressed before nature will permit one of her own creatures to be tranformed into a worldling. It defines the distance Henry has travelled from innocence, and, in contrast with his diurnal aspect, the thickness of the mask that rank imposes. (p. 169)

On top of our first glimpse of the carefree Hal, [his soliloquy "I know you all . . ." comes] with a painful shock, casting both backward and forward, as they do, a shadow of insincerity. (p. 171)

The speech just doesn't cohere with the Hal we love, his admirers protest. It is out of character. It is Shakespeare speaking, not Henry. And in support of them, the historical critics point out that the poet was merely following a familiar Elizabethan convention of tipping off the audience that they might be in the secret. It is odd, however, if it is just Shakespeare, that he made the speech so long and detailed and chose to base it on a metaphor that was forever running through Henry's mind. The playwright could have given the necessary information in a quarter of the space.

It is true that the soliloquy is unlike Hal. Yet there is not a speech in the role more strictly in character. How can that be? It can be for the simple reason that it is not Hal, primarily, who makes the speech at all. The Prince makes it. There are two Henrys. This is no quibble; it is the inmost heart of the matter. . . . If we need authority for what page after page of the play drives home, we have it in Falstaff, who makes just this distinction:

> Prince: Darest thou be as good as thy word
> now?
> Falstaff: Why, Hal, thou knowest, as thou art
> but man, I dare; but as thou art Prince, I fear
> thee as I fear the roaring of the lion's whelp.
> [*1 Henry IV*, III. iii. 143-47]

Hal and the Prince: we shall never get anything straight about this story if we confuse them or fail to mark the differences, the connections, and the interplay of the two. Talk about the

Prodigal Son! There is indeed more than a touch of him in Hal; but in the deliberately and coldly ambitious Prince not a spark. In him the Prodigal was reformed before he ever came into existence.

The Henry who is the Prince is, appropriately, like the Henry who is the King, the son like the father. And Shakespeare takes the utmost pains to point this out. The theme of the famous soliloquy is the function of the foil. The Prince says he will imitate the sun and suddenly appear from behind clouds at the theatrical moment to dazzle all beholders. Well, turn to that heart-to-heart talk between the King and his heir that ends in the latter's promise to amend his ways, and straight from the father's mouth we have the son's philosophy. . . . But the father kept himself rare, it will be said, while the son made himself common, acting like Richard instead of following his father's example. That was indeed the ground of the King's complaint. But he got the truth there exactly upside down. He did not see that his son was acting far more like himself than he was like Richard. The Prince was doing precisely what his father had done, only in a wilier way. The King had kept himself literally hidden and then suddenly appeared. The Prince was keeping himself figuratively hidden by his wild ways in order to emerge all at once as a self-disciplined king. As between the two, who can question which was the more dramatic and effective? But we like neither father nor son for his tricks, no matter how well contrived or brilliantly executed. (pp. 171-73)

The moment we follow Falstaff's lead and cease thinking of Henry as Henry and conceive him as Hal-and-the-Prince we see how right Shakespeare was to build this play on an alternation of "tavern" scenes and political-military ones. Instead of being just chronicle play relieved by comedy (as historians of the drama are bound to see it), what we have is a genuine integration, both psychological and dramatic, the alternating character of the scenes corresponding to the two sides of a dual personality. (p. 175)

The disparagers of Falstaff generally make him out a mixture, in varying proportions, of [the Falstaff of *The Merry Wives of Windsor*], Sir Toby Belch, and Parolles, each of whom was an incalculably inferior person. But to assert that Falstaff is another man is not saying that he does not have many or even all of the vices of the "old wretch" for whom his defamers mistake him. Salt is not sodium, but that is not saying that sodium is not a component of salt. The truth is that there *are* two Falstaffs, just as there are two Henrys, the Immoral Falstaff and the Immortal Falstaff, and the dissension about the man comes from a failure to recognize that fact. That the two could inhabit one body would not be believed if Shakespeare had not proved that they could. That may be one reason why he made it so huge.

Curiously, there is no more convincing testimony to this double nature of the man than that offered by those who are most persistent in pointing out his depravity. In the very process of committing the old sinner to perdition they reveal that they have been unable to resist his seductiveness. Professor Stoll, for instance, dedicates twenty-six sections of a long and learned essay to the annihilation of the Falstaff that his congenital lovers love. And then he begins his twenty-seventh and last section with the words: "And yet people like Falstaff"! And before his first paragraph is done, all his previous labor is obliterated as we find him asserting that Falstaff is "supremely poetic" (even his most ardent admirers would hardly venture that "supremely") and that "his is in many ways the most marvellous prose ever penned.'' (It is, but how did the old sot, we wonder, ever acquire it?) Before his next paragraph is over, Stoll has called Falstaff ''the very spirit of comradeship,'' ''the king of companions,'' and ''the prince of good fellows.'' ''We, too, after all, like Prince Hal and Mrs. Quickly,'' he goes on, ''take to a man because of his charm, if it be big enough, not because of his virtue; and as for Falstaff, we are bewitched with the rogue's company.'' (A Falstaff idolater could scarcely ask for more than that.) ''Under the spell of his presence and speech,'' Stoll concludes, we should forget, as she does, the wrong he has done Mrs. Quickly, ''did we not stop to think.'' (pp. 175-76)

Those who think about Falstaff before they fall in love with him may say some just things about him but they will never enter into his secret. ''Would I were with him, wheresome'er he is, either in heaven or in hell!'' Those words of poor Bardolph on hearing the account of Falstaff's death remain the highest tribute he ever did or ever could receive. . . .

The scholars have attempted to explain Falstaff by tracing his origins. He has been found, variously, to have developed from the Devil of the miracle plays, the Vice of the morality plays, the boasting soldier of Plautine comedy, and so on. Now roots, up to a certain point, are interesting, but it takes the sun to make them grow and to illuminate the flower. (p. 177)

If I were seeking the embryo of Falstaff in Shakespeare's imagination, I should consider the claims of Bottom—of Bottom and another character in *A Midsummer-Night's Dream*. ''What!'' it will be said, ''the dull realistic Bottom and the lively witty Falstaff? They are nearer opposites.'' But embryos, it must be remembered, seldom resemble what they are destined to develop into. Bottom, like the physical Falstaff at least, is compact of the heaviness, the materiality, the reality of earth; and the ass's head that Puck bestows on him is abundantly deserved, not only in special reference to his brains but in its general implication of animality. But instead of letting himself be humiliated by it, Bottom sings, and Titania, Queen of the Fairies, her eyes anointed by the magic flower, awakening, mistakes him for an angel, and taking him in her arms, lulls him to sleep. The obvious meaning of the incident of course is that love is blind. . . . By a stroke of genius [Shakespeare] turns a purely farcical incident into nothing less than a parable of the Awakening of Imagination within Gross Matter. It is the poet's way of saying that even within the head of this foolish plebeian weaver a divine light can be kindled. . . . The dreamer may still be Bottom. But the dream itself is Puck. For one moment the two are one. Ass or angel? Perhaps Titania was not so deluded after all. (pp. 177-78)

I am not suggesting that Shakespeare ever consciously connected Puck and Bottom with Falstaff in his own mind. . . . That at any rate is what Falstaff is: Imagination conquering matter, spirit subduing flesh. (p. 178)

Is there any activity of man that involves the same factors that we find present in this Falstaff: complete freedom, an all-consuming zest for life, an utter subjugation of facts to imagination, and an entire absence of moral responsibility? Obviously there is. That activity is play.

Except for that little item of moral responsibility, ''play'' expresses as nearly as one word can the highest conception of life we are capable of forming: life for its own sake. . . . Play is the erection of an illusion into a reality. It is not an escape from life. It is the realization of life in something like its fulness. What it *is* an escape from is the boredom and friction

of existence. Like poetry, to which it is the prelude, it stands for a converting or winning-over of facts on a basis of friendship, the dissolving of them in a spirit of love, in contrast with science (at least the science of our day), which, somewhat illogically, stands first for a recognition of the absolute autonomy of facts and then for their impressment and subjection to human demands by a kind of military conquest.

Now Falstaff goes through life playing. He coins everything he encounters into play, often even into *a* play. He would rather have the joke on himself and make the imaginative most of it than to have it on the other fellow and let the fun stop there. Whenever he seems to be taken in because he does not realize the situation, it is safer to assume that he does realize it but keeps quiet because the imaginative possibilities are greater in that case.

Watching him, we who in dead earnest have been attending to business or doing what we are pleased to call our duty suddenly realize what we have been missing. (pp. 183-84)

Dover Wilson would have us take *Henry IV* as a morality play wherein a madcap prince grows up into an ideal king. Falstaff is the devil who tempts the Prince to Riot. Hotspur and especially the Lord Chief Justice are the good angels representing Chivalry and Justice or the Rule of Law. It is a struggle between Vanity and Government for the possession of the Royal Prodigal.

The scheme is superbly simple and as moral as a Sunday-school lesson. But it calmly leaves the Immortal Falstaff quite out of account! If Falstaff were indeed just the immoral creature that in part he admittedly is, Wilson's parable would be more plausible, though even then the words he picks to characterize Falstaff are singularly unfortunate. ''Vanity'' by derivation means emptiness or absence of substance, and ''riot'' quarrelsomeness. Imagine calling even the Immortal Falstaff empty or lacking in substance—or quarrelsome! He had his vices but they were not these. For either vanity or riot there is not a single good word to be said. To equate Falstaff with them is to assert that not a single good word can be said for him—a preposterous proposition. Wit, humor, laughter, good-fellowship, insatiable zest for life: are these vanity or does Falstaff *not* embody them? That is the dilemma in which Mr. Wilson puts himself. And as for the Lord Chief Justice, he is indeed an admirable man; a more incorruptible one in high position is not to be found in Shakespeare. But if the poet had intended to assign him any such crucial role as Mr. Wilson thinks, he certainly would have presented him more fully and would have hesitated to let Falstaff make him look so foolish. For the Chief Justice's sense of justice was better developed than his sense of humor. And even justice is not all.

Henry IV does have a certain resemblance to a morality play. The two, however, between whom the younger Henry stands and who are in a sense contending for the possession of his soul are not Falstaff and the Chief Justice, but Falstaff and the King. It is between Falstaff and the Father—to use that word in its generic sense—that Henry finds himself. (p. 185)

Concede the utmost—that is, take Falstaff at his worst. He was a drunkard, a glutton, a profligate, a thief, even a liar if you insist, but withal a fundamentally honest man. He had two sides like a coin, but he was not a counterfeit. And Henry? He was a king, a man of ''honour,'' of brains and ability, of good intentions, but withal a ''vile politician'' and respectable hypocrite. He *was* a counterfeit. Which, if it comes to the choice, is the better influence on a young man? Shakespeare, for one, gives no evidence of having an iota of doubt. (pp. 185-86)

"But how about Falstaff's honor?" it will be asked. "Thou owest God a death," says the Prince to him before the battle of Shrewsbury. "'Tis not due yet," Falstaff answers as Hal goes out. [Here Goddard quotes Falstaff's "catechism" on honour]. (p. 187)

["Honour"] in its decayed feudal sense of glory, fame, even reputation, as page after page of these Chronicle Plays records, had outlived its usefulness and the time had come to expose its hollowness. The soul, lifted up, declared Saint Teresa (who died in 1582), sees in the word "honor" "nothing more than an immense lie of which the world remains a victim. . . . She laughs when she sees grave persons, persons of orison, caring for points of honor for which she now feels profoundest contempt. . . . With what friendship we would all treat each other if our interest in honor and in money could but disappear from the earth! For my own part, I feel as if it would be a remedy for all our ills."

Saint Teresa and Sir John Falstaff! an odd pair to find in agreement—about honor if not about money. In the saint's case no ambiguity is attached to the doctrine that honor is a lie. In the sinner's, there remains something equivocal and double-edged. Here, if ever, the two Falstaffs meet. The grosser Falstaff is himself a parasite and a dishonorable man, and coming from him the speech is the creed of Commodity and the height of irony. But that does not prevent the man who loved Hal and babbled of green fields at his death from revealing in the same words, as clearly as Saint Teresa, that life was given for something greater than glory or than the gain that can be gotten out of it.

"Give me life," cries Falstaff on the field of Shrewsbury. "Die all, die merrily," cries Hotspur. That is the gist of it. The Prince killed Hotspur in the battle, and Falstaff, with one of his most inspired lies, claimed the deed as his own. But Falstaff's lies, scrutinized, often turn out to be truth in disguise. So here. Falstaff, not Prince Henry, did kill Hotspur. He ended the outworn conception of honor for which Hotspur stood. The Prince killed his body, but Falstaff killed his soul—or rather what passed for his soul. (pp.187-88)

[Of the scene of Falstaff's rejection, the] best we can say for Henry is that it is an outburst of that temper of which his father told us he was a victim ("being incens'd, he's flint"), sudden anger at Falstaff's highly untactful appearance at such a time and place. The worst we can say is that the King had deliberately planned to rebuke Falstaff publicly at the first opportunity for the sake of the moral contrast with his own past and in fulfilment of the promise of his first soliloquy. Unfortunately for Henry, however much anger he may have felt at the moment, Falstaff's explanation of the calamity to Shallow: "He must seem thus to the world," seems the most psychologically plausible account of what happened. . . .

This much at any rate is certain: we cannot imagine Shakespeare, no matter how high he might have risen in worldly place or esteem, rejecting a former friend by preaching him a sermon in public, no matter how low his friend might have fallen. So unthinkable is it that it seems almost silly to reduce the idea to words. (p. 204)

When Falstaff has been rebuffed, and he and his followers have been carried off to the Fleet, the play is a dozen lines from its end. Those lines (except for six significantly terse and reticent

words from the Chief Justice) are all spoken by John of Lancaster. Why does Shakespeare, who is so fond of remarking that "the end crowns the whole," give the crowning speeches of this play to a person whose sole distinction lies in the fact that he is the most dastardly character in it? Why does he permit him, and him alone, to pass judgment on his brother's act in rejecting Falstaff?

> I like this fair proceeding of the king's.
> [*2 Henry IV*, V. v. 97]

If you know the devil's opinion, you can infer the angels'. The safest way to vote is to find out how the most "intelligently" selfish man in the community is voting and then vote the other way. It was in recognition of this principle, I believe, that Shakespeare reserved the most emphatic place in his play for the judgment on the King's rejection of Falstaff by the man whom Falstaff, in just six words, caused *us* to cast forth into everlasting darkness: "a man cannot make him laugh." Dostoevsky declares that a man's character can be read by the way he laughs. By that token John of Lancaster had no character. He "doth not love me," said laughing John of sober John. And so when sober John welcomes the humiliation and degradation of laughing John by saying,

> I like this fair proceeding of the king's,

it sounds like a statement straight from Shakespeare that the proceeding was not fair and that he did not like it.

But there is more evidence than this (not counting that in the next play). In Shakespeare, as in life, things do not happen unprepared for. If we look back, we find a little scene in which the rejection of Falstaff was specifically forecast. More than forecast, rehearsed.

The place is the Boar's Head Tavern in Eastcheap, and the time just after the "discomfiture" of Falstaff in the matter of the robbery. (pp. 205-06)

This little play within a play, two plays within a play, each with its player-king, may well warn us that *Hamlet* itself is barely around the corner. Indeed, this mousetrap catches not only the conscience of a king but the conscience of a king-to-be. The play scene in Shakespeare's tragic masterpiece to come scarcely surpasses this one in the subtlety of its psychology or the intricacy of its interwoven meanings. Here, if anywhere, here, if ever, the truth is brought home that we are not single personalities, nor even double ones, but bundles rather of actual and potential, emerging and expiring selves, as many as there are people who love or hate us, or whom we love or hate. Each one out there evokes a different one in here. The relation between two individuals is itself an individual relation, and, when it is set up, something that never was before on sea or land is created. Within the confines of this brief scene, to the success of which Mrs. Quickly, as audience, makes a memorable if mainly silent contribution, half-a-dozen Falstaffs and Henrys jostle and elbow, come in and go out, split, disintegrate, and recombine, a veritable phantasmagoria of spiritual entities. Who would undertake even to enumerate, fet alone characterize them? When Falstaff plays Hal's father, for instance, he is partly King Henry rebuking the Prince for his wildness and partly the Falstaff who loves Hal as if he were his own son, and who longs to have Hal love him as if he were his father and consequently pictures himself as the sort of ideal father he would actually like to be to him. When, the parts exchanged, Falstaff plays Hal, he is first the subdued and respectful Prince in the presence of authority, and then the Hal whom Falstaff loved, and who, as Falstaff acts him, loved him as the real Falstaff longed to have the real Hal love him, and as, alas, he never did. When Hal acts himself, he is modest and reticent, not to say a bit scared, speaking scarcely a dozen words, but when he becomes his father he grows dominating and forbidding, and evokes in his description of his son's dissolute misleader the drunken debauched Falstaff who, it is especially worth noting, is otherwise totally and conspicuously absent from the scene. The Prince, *as his father*, says exactly what Sir John's bitterest enemies among critics and readers have been saying of him ever since:

> That bolting-hutch of beastliness. . . . Wherein is he good, but to taste sack and drink it? wherein neat and cleanly, but to carve a capon and eat it? wherein cunning, but in craft? wherein crafty, but in villainy? Wherein villanous, but in all things? wherein worthy, but in nothing?
>
> [*1 Henry IV*, II. iv. 449-59]

—while Hal, *impersonated by Falstaff*, describes the sweet, kind, true, valiant Jack that all the world loves, except the above-mentioned dissenters. It is all wonderful fun and we laugh. Yet underneath the mirth, how beautiful and tragic implications, how beyond comprehension the miracle by which so much is compressed into so little! And hovering over it all, over all these subordinate personalities that glide in and glide out like ghosts, is the evoker and master of them all (for it is only in his presence that Hal ever rises to such imaginative height), the Immortal Falstaff, the sweet Jack Falstaff whom Henry should never have rejected to the end of his days. (pp. 208-09)

> *Harold C. Goddard, "'Henry IV, Part I'; 'Henry IV, Part II' ('The Merry Wives of Windsor')," in his* The Meaning of Shakespeare, *University of Chicago Press, 1951, pp. 161-214.*

SAMUEL B. HEMINGWAY   (essay date 1952)

[*Hemingway proposes a "two-leveled" critical method for assessing Falstaff's character which utilizes both the traditional approaches of Maurice Morgann (1777) and A. C. Bradley (1902)— who regarded Falstaff as a real person given substance in Shakespeare's imagination—and E. E. Stoll (1914) and J. Dover Wilson (1943)—who considered him more of a stage convention. For other interpretive readings of Falstaff's character which combine both "pro-Morgann" and "anti-Morgann" sentiments, see the excerpts by John F. Danby (1949) and Harold C. Goddard (1951).*]

During the past twenty years some two hundred scholars have discussed, briefly or at length, the character of Sir John Falstaff. Much of what has been written is a dishing up of funeral baked meats, much is controversial; and in the controversies there is, not infrequently, a tendency to set up straw men for the sole purpose of knocking them down: attitudes of mind are attributed to the "romantics" which they would scarcely recognize, finality is attributed too to the dicta of "historical" critics which few of them would either claim or deserve.

Is a Harmony of the Gospels concerning Falstaff impossible— the Gospel according to Morgann and Bradley, the Gospel according to Stoll, and the newer (and less consistent) Gospel according to Dover Wilson? [See excerpts above 1777, 1902, 1914, and 1943.] To many who have lived with Falstaff, in class room or study, over a period of time, each Gospel seems valid as far as it goes, but no one of them seems complete. The Morgann and Bradley School sees, in Shakespeare's cre-

ations, the Shakespeare "of all time"; Stoll stresses the Shakespeare "of an age"; Dover Wilson wavers between the two without ever achieving a true synthesis; the modern student of Shakespeare should perhaps make a slight emendation in Ben Jonson's famous line and remember that Shakespeare was *both* of an age and of all time.

If this is true, should we not approach Shakespeare on two levels, and not regard the two as mutually exclusive? We can go every step (or almost every step) of the way with Professor Stoll, and we can feel great gratitude to him for the light that he has thrown on the Elizabethan Shakespeare and on the Falstaff of the stage of 1596: Shakespeare *was* (among other things) a commercial artist, a follower of stage traditions and conventions (and it is of the utmost importance that we should realize how far he was "conditioned" by them): he was writing for a theater audience, and not for readers, scholars, and posterity; he was giving his public what it wanted and would pay for. But is that all? Was he not also a great creative artist who transformed and transcended the conventions he inherited? The audience got what it wanted, but it got God's plenty in addition. And so, when we have finished Professor Stoll's brilliant analysis, we are likely to say: "Yes, this is true; 'only he comes too short.'" (p. 307)

A young novelist was once advised by a veteran in his craft to write a full biography of each of his principal characters before he started to construct his novel. Much that was in the biographies would never appear in the novel, but the parts that did appear would fit harmoniously into his concept of the whole character. It is the unwritten biography of Falstaff, the Life of Falstaff as it existed in his creator's mind, that is the chief concern of the Morgann-Bradley School. And who shall say them nay? Is not the mind of Shakespeare, the quality of his creative imagination, quite as worthy of our attention as the study of Elizabethan stage traditions and conventions? Shakespeare inherited plots and characters. His "originality" was not in "invention." But certain characters, functional puppets perhaps in his sources, took hold of his fancy and suffered a sea-change into something rich and strange. . . . In a sense then (*pace* Professor Stoll), Falstaff and Shylock, Hamlet and Cleopatra, Benedick and Beatrice, and others are "real people" and not puppets, real people who lived in Shakespeare's mind.

Let us apply the "two-level approach" to specific incidents. The Falstaff of Gadshill, to first-nighters and first readers, is obviously a coward. He runs away, roaring for mercy—there is no denying that fact. But when the whole Falstaff and the whole play are recollected in tranquillity this one display of abject cowardice seems out of character: in every other emergency Falstaff is at least cool-headed. Is it possible, we begin to wonder, that at Gadshill, Falstaff, recognizing the men in buckram, is playing a part? The hint as to the true nature of Falstaff's cowardice (or courage), given by Poins in I. ii—"if he fight longer than he sees reason," etc.—and the Q1 stage-direction in II. ii—"They all run away, and Falstaff, after a blow or two, runs away too"—would, we admit, pass unnoticed in the theater; they are not clues or hints provided by Shakespeare for spectators. But there they are. Why did he write them? To the reader of the play, or to the re-reader, who (to use Dover Wilson's phrase) "comes again" and again to the play, reading each part in the light of the whole, these two brief sentences may give a clue to Shakespeare's own answer to the eternally debated question of Falstaff's cowardice. (pp. 308-09)

Professor Stoll stresses the importance of the first impression an audience gets of a character. The first impression we get of Falstaff comes from Prince Hal's raillery in I. ii, and the first epithet applied to him is "fat-witted." To the first-night audience he is, and perhaps remains, "fat-witted" in the sense that he seems always to be the victim of the more clever Hal and Poins. But if we "come back" to this first Falstaff scene after reading the nine-and-a-half acts that follow, do we not radically modify this first impression? Indeed, do we not become more aware of the lack of perception on the part of the Prince than of any stupidity on the part of Falstaff? (p. 309)

Yes; great as [*Henry IV*] is as a stage play, its true greatness and its riches lie in the imagination of its maker which transcends the limits of the physical stage. We must, I maintain, follow Professor Stoll in his study of Shakespeare the Elizabethan dramatist; but if we stay permanently on this level we see in the Falstaff plot nothing but magnificent farce. Then we have to account for the eternal popularity of Falstaff himself with readers and interpreters of the play. Is it not significant that though much is written about Falstaff in the twentieth century, we are seldom given an opportunity to see him on the stage? *Henry IV* is no longer a popular stage-play, but except for *Hamlet*, it is the most discussed play of the Elizabethan age. The "book Falstaff," the Falstaff of Morgann and Bradley, has outlived the stage Falstaff. (pp. 309-10)

Dover Wilson's brilliant but exasperating *Fortunes of Falstaff* [see excerpt above] might so easily have been the Harmony of the Gospels concerning Falstaff. It fails, I believe, because Wilson's heart is always with Bradley (whom he calls "still the greatest of modern Shakespearean critics") and his head with Stoll (from whom "I have learnt something"). His first presentation of Falstaff, however, out-Stolls Stoll. His "editorial stage-directions" . . . tend to emphasize the repulsiveness of the physical Falstaff: "sterterous snoring as of a gigantic sow," "Vast chaps opening like gates upon their hinges to reveal dim caverns of throat"; Falstaff "one of a pack of scurvy rascals," Falstaff "Prince's Jester, Lord of Misrule," etc. This is Falstaff seen from one angle only, and the other side of Falstaff, even in I. ii, is not presented. . . . Professor Wilson rightly differentiates between "the impressions of a reader, indeed of an editor who must ponder his text much and deeply" and the impressions of a spectator with whom "such pondering is impossible . . . Nevertheless there the impressions are. Shakespeare is responsible for them, and the closer one examines them the stronger they grow." This is sound doctrine. Would that Professor Wilson had consistently applied it to the details of the play.

Dover Wilson, like Professor Stoll, stresses the importance of first impressions; but there seems to be a negation of this principle when he comes to the perennial question of Falstaff's cowardice. He imagines a young gentleman from the Inns of Court challenging Shakespeare at the tavern after the first performance of the play with the question: "But *was* Falstaff a coward?" and Shakespeare answering: "Come again tomorrow, and see." It is this coming again and again to the text of the play, as Wilson admits, that helps us to answer our question. One could wish that Professor Wilson had "come again" to I. ii before drawing his initial portrait of Falstaff. In *The Fortunes of Falstaff* we get, intermittently, the Falstaff of Morgann and Bradley and the Falstaff of Stoll; but we fail to get the complete Falstaff of Shakespeare's mind, who, it is my contention, is visible in every Falstaff episode. (pp. 310-11)

Samuel B. Hemingway, "On Behalf of That Falstaff," in Shakespeare Quarterly, *Vol. III, No. 4, October, 1952, pp. 307-11.*

G. K. HUNTER   (essay date 1954)

[*Hunter, along with M. A. Shaaber (1948) and H. Edward Cain (see Additional Bibliography), challenges the views of J. Dover Wilson (1944) and E.M.W. Tillyard (1944) on the continuity and unity of* 1 *and* 2 Henry IV. *But Hunter discerns in the two dramas another form of unity, common to several Elizabethan two-part plays, based on a parallelism of their respective incidents. For a slightly different interpretation of the unity of Parts 1 and 2 see the excerpt by Harold Jenkins (1955).*]

Mr. Shaaber and Mr. Cain have demonstrated that the 'unity and continuity' which Dr. Dover Wilson and Dr. Tillyard find in *Henry IV* is based on inadequate or illusory evidence. The points made by Mr. Shaaber and Mr. Cain bear, however, against 'continuity' rather than 'unity'; the sensitive reader who continues to detect 'unity' in *Henry IV* can be justified if 'unity' can be found to have a meaning (appropriate to Shakespeare) which is dissociated from the untenable 'continuity'. (p. 236)

I contend that the connexion between the two parts of *Henry IV* formalizes a unity [of theme]: the unity of the play is that of a diptych, in which repetition of shape and design focuses attention on what is common to the two parts.

The use of such features to unify a two-part play does not seem to have found any justification in critical theory, but appears to have been conscious to the extent that we can find a technique and a history attached to the form, and it is with these that I shall be concerned in the rest of this paper. . . . [There is] one small group of Elizabethan two-part plays which have a method of unification in common. If we examine these plays, we uncover an approach to the construction of *Henry IV* which, though it does not tell us anything about Shakespeare's original intentions, does give us information about his later view of the completed structure. (pp. 237-38)

[The two-part plays analysed are Chapman's *Byron*, Marlowe's *Tamburlaine I and II*, and Marston's *Antonio and Mellida*].

[Such] unity as we can find in Elizabethan two-part plays depends on a parallel setting-out of the incidents rather than on any picking-up of all the threads of Part One. The plays we have examined all use this method, with a greater or lesser degree of success, and it is the only method I have been able to find. Does Shakespeare use this method in *Henry IV*, or is that play unique among Elizabethan two-part plays in possessing a different or more complex organization of its parts?

It was pointed out as long ago as 1877 by Dr. König [in *Shakespeare-Jahrbuch*, 1877] and more recently by Mr. Shaaber [see excerpt above, 1948] that the two parts of *Henry IV* are built up on parallel lines, but neither author has noted the full extent of this parallelism, so I shall set out the two parts to illustrate this:

ACT I

Sc. i.	[1H4] The disruption of peace by rebellion is hinted at.
	[2H4] News of Shrewsbury is given, with news of a second rebellion—in the north.
Sc. ii.	[1H4] Poins details the plan of the Gadshill robbery; Poins and Hal plan a comic defeat for Falstaff.
	[2H4] Falstaff prepares to join the army; he is rebuked by the Chief Justice.
Sc. iii.	[1H4] Turned off by the king, Hotspur, Worcester, and Northumberland plan their revolt.
	[2H4] The Northern conspirators meet and plan their revolt.

ACT II

Sc. i. [1H4] Preparations are made for the Gadshill robbery.
[2H4] Falstaff is arrested at the instance of Mrs. Quickly, but manages to escape.

Sc. ii. [1H4] Falstaff robs the travellers; Hal and Poins prepare the fun of II. iv by their counter-robbery.
[2H4] Hal and Poins plan the fun of II. iv.

Sc. iii. [1H4] Harry Percy and his wife discuss the revolt; he sets out.
[2H4] Northumberland and his wife discuss the revolt; he flees to Scotland.

Sc. iv. [1H4] The big comic scene: in the Eastcheap tavern the prince mingles with the drawers. Falstaff is discovered in lies, but jests his way out of the discovery. At the end of the scene the outer world breaks in upon the fun.
[2H4] The big comic scene: in the Eastcheap tavern Falstaff swaggers and blusters till Hal and Poins (disguised as drawers) discover him; he jests his way out of the discovery. At the end of the scene the outer world breaks in upon the fun.

ACT III

Sc. i. [1H4] The conspirators seal their bonds and prepare to fight. [This scene has no parallel in Part II]

Sc. ii. [1H4] The king reproaches Hal, who promises to amend.
[Sc. i., 2H4] The king mourns his unquiet reign.

Sc. iii. [1H4] Falstaff quarrels with the hostess, prepares for the war.
[Sc. ii., 2H4] Falstaff recruits in Gloucestershire.

ACT IV

Sc. i. [1H4] Rebellion suffers setbacks: Northumberland will not join and Glendower cannot.
[2H4] Northumberland will not join the rebels, who are tricked and defeated.

Sc. ii. [1H4] Falstaff, on his way to the battlefield, expatiates on the tricks he has employed in recruiting.
[2H4] (Modern sc. iii—but I take modern scenes i and ii to be continuous.) Falstaff captures Coleville while on his way to the battlefield; he expatiates on the virtues of sack.

Thereafter the structure is not parallel.

(pp. 243-45)

[We] find, as in the plays already examined, a structure which shows the relationship between two incompatibles—Rebellion and Order, in the state and in the mind of the prince; the first is subordinated to the second at the end of Part One, but by showing us the preparations of the Archbishop of York and by resurrecting Falstaff from his sham death, Shakespeare keeps his conclusion from being irretrievably final. The incompatibles clash again in Part Two and a final conclusion is only produced when one is destroyed by the other. Both parts have the same design, but in the second we have a change of direction and a different atmosphere. (p. 245)

The struggle of Part Two is not the struggle of coming-of-age, nor indeed a personal struggle of this kind at all. Its interest is that it draws from the interaction of Rebellion and Order in court and country (the same framework as in Part One) a more abstract and meditative view of kingship. The first part may be said to deal with the question: 'What is the relationship between the princely mind and the common disorder of experience?'; the second part raises a rather different question: 'What is the cost of kingliness in a world of duties rather than achievements?' In most respects the kind of development from Part One to Part Two which Shakespeare devises for his hero is very different from that of Marlowe or Chapman, but the sense of difficulty in sustaining a role achieved at the end of Part One in a world more searching and more severe is the same in all these plays. (p. 246)

Falstaff's career also follows the two-part play's normal design of rise and fall; the zenith of his success is reached at the end of Part One, his claim to have killed Hotspur being allowed by the prince. Though his career in Part Two does not show anything like a steady decline, he is never again able to enjoy such prestige and security. He performs a similar feat in Part Two—the capture of Sir John Coleville—but John of Lancaster is a different kind of person from Hal, and the action does not yield similar results. . . . I do not think that an audience which sees the two parts played continuously ought to sense that Falstaff is a different kind of person in Part Two, but certainly it ought to notice that the temper of the world he lives in has become less amenable to his methods. (pp. 246-47)

Though there may not be any exact continuity in *Henry IV,* we see that the word 'unity' can be applied to it, in the limited sense of 'diptych-unity'; that is, the form of the play depends *primarily* on a parallel presentation of incidents (as in the other two-part plays examined here) and only secondarily on a preservation of traits of character or strands of the plot. An absence of continuity in such features cannot be used to prove a lack of unity, for the 'unity' of *Henry IV* does not depend primarily on these factors. There can be no doubt, of course, that the diptych-unity disciplines a greater complexity of material in *Henry IV* than in any of the other 'unified' two-part plays—a subplot which merges into the main plot, and a wide range of principal characters—but the methods employed are, in general, the same; it follows that the justification of the word 'unity' must be the same.

The evidence that we have been examining here does not tell us anything about the genesis of *Henry IV.* We see that Marlowe, in what was presumably a catchpenny sequel, and Chapman, designing a two-part play from the beginning, both used the methods of 'unity in duality' to link together the two parts of their plays. The fact that Shakespeare used the same methods does not tell us whether he should be associated with Chapman or with Marlowe. Some of the arguments used by Shaaber and Cain—'setting the clock back' at the beginning of Part Two, the unstable conditions of Elizabethan production, for example—apply to *Byron* [which clearly seems to have been planned as a two-part play] not less than to *Tamburlaine* [in which Part Two clearly seems to be an unplanned sequel]; therefore they cannot be used to weigh the evidence either for or against any idea that Shakespeare planned *Henry IV* from the beginning as a two-part play. This is not to say that all the evidence advanced by these scholars must be discounted; indeed I would allow that enough evidence remains to establish their view that Shakespeare composed *I Henry IV* without any intention of composing its sequel. Nevertheless, it seems to me that in propagating this truth they allow (and so propagate) a view at least as misleading—the view that the natural alternative to 'unity and continuity' is 'two plays linked by catch-as-catch-can methods'. It is as important to see Shakespeare here as an artist painstakingly concerned about the 'unity' which was possible and significant within the terms of his art as to avoid seeing him with intentions he is unlikely to have possessed. (pp. 247-48)

G. K. Hunter, "'Henry IV' and the Elizabethan Two-Part Play," in The Review of English Studies, *n.s. Vol. V, No. 19, July, 1954, pp. 236-48.*

HAROLD JENKINS (essay date 1955)

[*Jenkins takes issue with such earlier critics as Samuel Johnson (1765), J. Dover Wilson (1944), and E.M.W. Tillyard (1944) and posits his own theory on the question of the unity of* Henry IV, Part 1 *and* Part 2: *that the two dramas are both unified and separate; complementary, though at many points incompatible. He justifies his hypothesis by claiming that somewhere along the way Shakespeare changed his mind and decided that one play was insufficient for the action he wished to present; thus, a sequel was written which compliments the first, but which also, for reasons of dramatic integrity, reiterates much of what was presented in* Henry IV, Part 1. *Because of this repetition, Jenkins maintains, each play appears complete, though only in reading both do we realize their dependence on each other. This essay was originally given as a lecture in 1955.*]

[In *Henry IV* Part I, Hal and Hotspur are opposed] to one another throughout the play, constantly spoken of together, [but] are nevertheless kept apart till the fifth act, when their first and last encounter completes in the expected manner the pattern of their rivalry that began in the opening words. The two have exchanged places. Supremacy in honour has passed from Hotspur to the Prince, and the wayward hero of the opening ends by exhibiting his true princely nature.

What then is one to make of the view of Professor Dover Wilson that the Battle of Shrewsbury, in which the Prince kills Hotspur, is not an adequate conclusion but merely the "nodal point we expect in a third act" [see excerpt above, 1944]? (p. 8)

[Although] *Henry IV* Part I . . . from its first act directs our interest to the time when Hal will be king, it is not of course until the last act of Part 2 that Pistol comes to announce, "Sir John, thy tender lambkin now is king." It is not until the last act of Part 2 that the Prince is able to institute the new régime which makes mock of Falstaff's dream-world. And it is not of course till the final scene of all that the newly crowned king makes his ceremonial entrance and pronounces the words that have threatened since he and Falstaff first were shown together. "I banish thee." (p. 13)

The last act of Part 2 thus works out a design which is begun in the first act of Part I. How then can we agree with Kittredge that each part is a complete play? Such a pronouncement fits the text no better than the opposite view of Johnson [see excerpt above, 1765] and Dover Wilson that Part I, though it ends in Hotspur's death and the Prince's glory, is yet only the first half of a play. If it were a question of what Shakespeare intended in the matter, the evidence provided by what he wrote would not suggest either that the two parts were planned as a single drama or that Part 2 was an "unpremeditated sequel".

An escape from this dilemma has sometimes been sought in a theory, expounded especially by Professor Dover Wilson and Dr. Tillyard, that what *Henry IV* shows is one action with two phases [see excerpt above by Tillyard, 1944]. While the whole

drama shows the transformation of the madcap youth into the virtuous ruler, the first part, we are told, deals with the chivalric virtues, the second with the civil. In the first part the hero acquires honour, in the second he establishes justice. But I see no solution of the structural problem here. For though it is left to Part 2 to embody the idea of justice in the upright judge, the interest in justice and law is present from the start. On Falstaff's first appearance in Part I he jibes at the law as "old father antic". And he goes further. Included within his bubble is a vision of his future self not simply as a man freed from "the rusty curb" of the law but as a man who actually administers the law himself. "By the Lord, I'll be a brave judge", he says, making a mistake about his destined office which provokes Hal's retort, "Thou judgest false already." It is in the last act of Part 2 that we have the completion of this motif. Its climax comes when on Hal's accession Falstaff brags, "The laws of England are at my commandment", and its resolution when the true judge sends the false judge off to prison. But it begins, we see, in the first act of Part I. The Prince's achievement in justice cannot, then, be regarded simply as the second phase of his progress. Certainly he has two contests: in one he outstrips Hotspur, in the other he puts down Falstaff. But these contests are not distributed at the rate of one per part. The plain fact is that in *Henry IV* two actions, each with the Prince as hero, begin together in the first act of Part I, though one of them ends with the death of Hotspur at the end of Part I, the other with the banishment of Falstaff at the end of Part 2.

Now, since the Falstaff plot is to take twice as long to complete its course, it might well be expected to develop from the beginning more slowly than the other. Certainly if it is to keep symmetry, it must come later to its turning-point. But is this in fact what we find? Frankly it is not. On the contrary, through the first half of Part I the Hotspur plot and the Falstaff plot show every sign of moving towards their crisis together.

Both plots, for example, are presented, though I think both are not usually observed, in the Prince's soliloquy in the first act . . . foretelling the banishment of his tavern companions. It is unfortunate that this speech has usually been studied for its bearing on Falstaff's rejection; its emphasis is really elsewhere. It is only the first two lines, with the reference to the "unyoked humour" of the Prince's companions, that allude specifically to them, and what is primarily in question is not what is to happen to the companions but what is to happen to the Prince. In the splendid image which follows of the sun breaking through the clouds we recognize a royal emblem and behold the promise of a radiant king who is to come forth from the "ugly mists" which at present obscure the Prince's real self. Since Falstaff has just been rejoicing at the thought that they "go by the moon . . . and not by Phoebus", it is apparent that his fortunes will decline when the Prince emerges like Phoebus himself. It is equally apparent, or should be, that the brilliant Hotspur will be outshone. There is certainly no clue at this stage that the catastrophes of Hotspur and Falstaff will not be simultaneous.

Our expectations that they will be is indeed encouraged as the two actions now move forward. While Hotspur in pursuit of honour is preparing war, Falstaff displays his cowardice (I use the word advisedly) at Gadshill. While Hotspur rides forth from home on the journey that will take him to his downfall, the exposure of Falstaff's make-believe in the matter of the men in buckram is the foreshadowing of his. The news of Hotspur's rebellion brings the Falstaffian revels to a climax at the same time as it summons the Prince to that interview with his father which will prove, as we have seen, the crisis of his career and the "nodal point" of the drama. (pp. 14-17)

The various dooms of Hotspur and Falstaff are now in sight; and we reasonably expect both dooms to be arrived at in Act 5. What we are not at all prepared for is that one of the two will be deferred till five acts later than the other. The symmetry so beautifully preserved in the story of Hotspur is in Falstaff's case abandoned. Statistics are known to be misleading, and nowhere more so than in literary criticism; but it is not without significance that in *Henry IV* Part I Falstaff's speeches in the first two acts number ninety-six and in the last two acts only twenty-five. As for Falstaff's satellites, with the exception of a single perfunctory appearance on the part of Bardolph, the whole galaxy vanishes altogether in the last two acts, only to reappear with some changes in personnel in Part 2. Falstaff, admittedly, goes on without a break, if broken in wind; and his diminished role does show some trace of the expected pattern of development. His going to war on foot while Hal is on horseback marks a separation of these erstwhile companions and a decline in Falstaff's status which was anticipated in jest when his horse was taken from him at Gadshill. When he nevertheless appears at one council of war his sole attempt at a characteristic joke is cut short by the Prince with "Peace, chewet, peace!" A fine touch, this, which contributes to the picture of the Prince's transformation: the boon companion whose jests he has delighted in is now silenced in a word. There is even the shadow of a rejection of Falstaff; over his supposed corpse the Prince speaks words that, for all their affectionate regret, remind us that he has turned his back on "vanity". But these things, however significant, are details, no more than shorthand notes for the degradation of Falstaff that we have so confidently looked for. What it comes to is that after the middle of Part I *Henry IV* changes its shape. And that, it seems to me, is the root and cause of the structural problem.

Now that this change of shape has been, I hope I may say, demonstrated from within the play itself, it may at this stage be permissible to venture an opinion about the author's plan. I do not of course mean to imply that *Henry IV*, or indeed any other of Shakespeare's plays, ever had a plan precisely laid down for it in advance. But it has to be supposed that when Shakespeare began a play he had some idea of the general direction it would take, however ready he may have been to modify his idea as art or expediency might suggest. Though this is where I shall be told I pass the bounds of literary criticism into the province of biography or worse, I hold it reasonable to infer from the analysis I have given that in the course of writing *Henry IV* Shakespeare changed his mind. I am compelled to believe that the author himself foresaw, I will even say intended, that pattern which evolves through the early acts of Part I and which demands for its completion that the hero's rise to an eminence of valour shall be accompanied, or at least swiftly followed, by the banishment of the riotous friends who hope to profit from his reign. In other words, hard upon the Battle of Shrewsbury there was to come the coronation of the hero as king. This inference from the play is not without support from other evidence. The prince's penitence in the interview with his father in the middle of Part I corresponds to an episode which, both in Holinshed and in the play of *The Famous Victories of Henry the Fifth*, is placed only shortly before the old king's death. And still more remarkable is the sequence of events in a poem which has been shown to be one of Shakespeare's sources. At the historical Battle of Shrewsbury the Prince was only sixteen years old, whereas Hotspur was thirty-nine. But in Samuel Daniel's poem, *The Civil Wars*, Hotspur is made "young" and "rash" and encounters a prince of equal age who emerges like a "new-appearing glorious star". It is

Daniel, that is to say, who sets in opposition these two splendid youths and so provides the germ from which grows the rivalry of the Prince and Hotspur which is structural to Shakespeare's play. And in view of this resemblance between Daniel and Shakespeare, it is significant that Daniel ignores the ten years that in history elapsed between the death of Hotspur and the Prince's accession. Whereas in Holinshed the events of those ten years fill nearly twenty pages, Daniel goes straight from Shrewsbury to the old king's deathbed. This telescoping of events, which confronts the Prince with his kingly responsibilities directly after the slaying of Hotspur, adumbrates the pattern that Shakespeare, as I see it, must have had it in mind to follow out. The progress of a prince was to be presented not in two phases but in a single play of normal length which would show the hero wayward in its first half, pledging reform in the middle, and then in the second half climbing at Shrewsbury the ladder of honour by which, appropriately, he would ascend to the throne.

The exact point at which a new pattern supervenes I should not care to define. But I think the new pattern can be seen emerging during the fourth act. At a corresponding stage the history play of *Richard II* shows the deposition of its king, *Henry V* the victory at Agincourt, even *Henry IV* Part 2 the quelling of its rebellion in Gaultree Forest. By contrast *Henry IV* Part I, postponing any such decisive action, is content with preparation. While the rebels gather, the Prince is arming and Falstaff recruiting to meet them. Until well into the fifth act ambassadors are going back and forth between the rival camps, and we may even hear a message twice over, once when it is despatched and once when it is delivered. True, this is not undramatic: these scenes achieve a fine animation and suspense as well as the lowlier feat of verisimilitude. But the technique is obviously not one of compression. Any thought of crowding into the two-hour traffic of one play the death of the old king and the coronation of the new has by now been relinquished, and instead the Battle of Shrewsbury is being built up into a grand finale in its own right. In our eagerness to come to this battle and our gratification at the exciting climax it provides, we easily lose sight of our previous expectations. Most of us, I suspect, go from the theatre well satisfied with the improvised conclusion. (pp. 18-22)

Part 2 itself does not require extended treatment. For whenever it was "planned", it is a consequence of Part I. Its freedom is limited by the need to present what Part I so plainly prepared for and then left out. Falstaff cannot be allowed to escape a second time. His opposition to the law, being now the dominant interest, accordingly shapes the plot; and the law, now bodied forth in the half-legendary figure of the Lord Chief Justice, becomes a formidable person in the drama. The opening encounter between these two, in which Falstaff makes believe not to see or hear his reprover, is symbolic of Falstaff's whole attitude to law—he ignores its existence as long as he can. But the voice which he at first refuses to hear is the voice which will pronounce his final sentence. The theme of the individual versus the law proves so fertile that it readily gives rise to subplots. Justice Shallow, of course, claims his place in the play by virtue of the life that is in him, exuberant in the capers of senility itself. He functions all the same as the Lord Chief Justice's antithesis: he is the foolish justice with whom Falstaff has his way and from whom he wrings the thousand pounds that the wise justice has denied him. Even Shallow's servant Davy has his relation to the law; and his view of law is that though a man may be a knave, if he is my friend and I am the justice's servant, it is hard if the knave cannot win. In this humane sentiment Davy takes on full vitality as a person; but he simultaneously brings us back to confront at a different angle the main moral issue of the play. Is he to control the law or the law him? In fact, shall Falstaff flourish or shall a thief be hanged?

It has sometimes been objected that Falstaff runs away with Part 2. In truth he has to shoulder the burden of it because a dead man and a converted one can give him small assistance. Part 2 has less opportunity for the integrated double action of Part I. To be sure, it attempts a double action, and has often been observed to be in some respects a close replica of Part I—"almost a carbon copy", Professor Shaaber says [see excerpt above, 1948]. . . . [In Part 2, with] history and Holinshed obliging, rebellion can break out as before; yet the rebellion of Part 2, though it occupies our attention, has no significance, nor can have, for the principal characters of the play. The story of the Prince and Hotspur is over, and the King has only to die.

The one thing about history is that it does not repeat itself. Hotspur, unlike Sherlock Holmes, cannot come back to life. But there are degrees in all things; conversion has not quite the same finality as death. And besides, there is a type of hero whose adventures always can recur. Robin Hood has no sooner plundered one rich man than another comes along. It is the nature of Brer Fox, and indeed of Dr. Watson, to be incapable of learning from experience. In folk-lore, that is to say, though not in history, you can be at the same point twice. And it seems as if Prince Hal may be sufficient of a folk-lore hero to be permitted to go again through the cycle of riot and reform. In Part 2 as in Part I the King laments his son's unprincely life. Yet this folk-lore hero is also a historical, and what is more to the point, a dramatic personage, and it is not tolerable that the victor of Shrewsbury should do as critics sometimes say he does, relapse into his former wildness and then reform again. The Prince cannot come into Part 2 unreclaimed without destroying the dramatic effect of Part I. Yet if Part 2 is not to forgo its own dramatic effect, and especially its spendid last-act peripeteia, it requires a prince who is unreclaimed. This is Part 2's dilemma, and the way that it takes out of it is a bold one. When the King on his deathbed exclaims against the Prince's "headstrong riot", he has not forgotten that at Shrewsbury he congratulated the Prince on his redemption. He has not forgotten it for the simple reason that it has never taken place. The only man at court who believes in the Prince's reformation, the Earl of Warwick, believes that it will happen, not that it has happened already. Even as we watch the hero repeating his folk-lore cycle, we are positively instructed that he has not been here before:

> The tide of blood in me
> Hath proudly flow'd in vanity till now.
> [*2 Henry IV*, V. ii. 129-30]

In the two parts of *Henry IV* there are not two princely reformations but two versions of a single reformation. And they are mutually exclusive. Though Part 2 frequently recalls and sometimes depends on what has happened in Part I, it also denies that Part I exists. Accordingly the ideal spectator of either part must not cry with Shakespeare's Lucio, "I know what I know." He must sometimes remember what he knows and sometimes be content to forget it. This, however, is a requirement made in some degree by any work of fiction, or as they used to call it, feigning. And the feat is not a difficult one for those accustomed to grant the poet's demand for "that

willing suspension of disbelief . . . which constitutes poetic faith".

Henry IV, then, is both one play and two. Part I begins an action which it finds it has not scope for but which Part 2 rounds off. But with one half of the action already concluded in Part I, there is danger of a gap in Part 2. To stop the gap Part 2 expands the unfinished story of Falstaff and reduplicates what is already finished in the story of the Prince. The two parts are complementary, they are also independent and even incompatible. What they are, with their various formal anomalies, I suppose them to have become through what Johnson termed "the necessity of exhibition" [see excerpt above, 1765]. Though it would be dangerous to dispute Coleridge's view that a work of art must "contain in itself the reason why it is so", that its form must proceed from within, yet even works of art, like other of man's productions, must submit to the bondage of the finite. Even the unwieldy novels of the Victorians, as recent criticism has been showing, obey the demands of their allotted three volumes of space; and the dramatic masterpieces of any age, no less than inaugural lectures, must acknowledge the dimensions of time. (pp. 23-7)

> *Harold Jenkins, in his* The Structural Problem in Shakespeare's "Henry the Fourth," *Methuen & Co Ltd., 1956, 28 p.*

LEONARD UNGER   (essay date 1956)

[*Like Harold C. Goddard (1951), Unger considers "deception and self-deception" the theme of* Henry IV *and maintains that both Hal and Falstaff adopt an exterior disguise in order to conceal their true motivations.*]

[The] theme of deception and self-deception, of motive obscuring motive, of confusion and rationalization, is not only developed in the character of the King [Henry IV] but is given full orchestration throughout [the two parts of *Henry IV*]. At the opening of Part I we find the King and his helpers to the crown mutually suspicious. He suspects them of feeling that he is inordinately indebted to them for their help. They suspect him of having this suspicion. And thus each party is justified in its own extravagant and unyielding selfishness. (p. 7)

One could follow the theme of egotistical motivation, of suspicion, deception and self-deception in such characters as Northumberland, Worcester, and Glendower. But it is with the protagonists, Falstaff and Prince Hal, that Shakespeare gives the theme its central operation and its structural significance in the plays, thus emphasizing the essential unity of the two parts of *Henry IV*. In addition to being the central characters of the dramatic surface, these two are centrally placed in psychological perspective on the gallery of the other characters. They see through all the others, and as well, through each other. It is they who concentrate and intensify the vision of human motives that Shakespeare has otherwise elaborated in the plays. Hal encompasses the pattern of the manipulating of motives in his whole career as prince, and Falstaff embodies it in almost every moment, we may say in the very fact, of his existence. Their relationship with each other, their common and individual adventures, are a ritualistic parody of the larger plot in which they are involved, and a symbol of that aspect of humanity which Shakespeare has dramatized.

One of the most obvious characteristics of Falstaff is his ironical parallelism to, his debunking of, the noble characters. The "honor" which is their common code and which is epitomized in Hotspur, is for Falstaff "a mere scutcheon" and it belongs to "he that died o' Wednesday." That Prince Hal, to his father's grief, shares this critical detachment from the code is shown by his whole Falstaffian career, and particularly by his comment on Hotspur:

> I am not yet of Percy's mind, the Hotspur of
> the North, he that kills me some six or seven
> dozen Scots at a breakfast, washes his hands,
> and says to his wife, "Fie upon this quiet life!
> I want work." "O my sweet Harry," says she,
> "how many hast thou killed today?" "Give
> my roan horse a drench," says he, and answers
> "Some fourteen" an hour after—"a trifle, a
> trifle." . . .
>
> [*1 Henry IV*, II. iv. 101-08]

Hal's similar contempt for the solemnity of court and crown is shown in the same scene. Although he ends the speech above with the plan that he and Falstaff mockingly "play" at being Hotspur and his wife, he decides later that they "play" at being the King while he is scolding and advising the Prince. (pp. 7-8)

While Prince Hal shares in some measure Falstaff's critical perspective on the other characters, it is he who is drawn most fully in ironical parallelism with the fat knight. It is these two who carry the theme of deception and self-deception as a continuous strand throughout the plays. Prince Hal's great deception is, of course, announced in his first soliloquy:

> I know you all, and will a while uphold
> The unyoked humor of your idleness.
> Yet herein will I imitate the sun. . . .
>
> [*1 Henry IV*, I. ii. 195-97]
> (p. 10)

The dramatic significance of this passage, like the rejection of Falstaff at the end of Part II, has been much disputed. Our interpretation of the play is here in accord with Dr. Johnson's admirable comment: "The speech is very artfully introduced to keep the Prince from appearing vile in the opinion of the audience; it prepares them for his future reformation, and *what is yet more valuable, exhibits a natural picture of a great mind offering excuses to itself, and palliating those follies which it can neither justify nor forsake*" [see excerpt above, 1765]. The italics are mine, but the emphasis is Dr. Johnson's—"what is yet more valuable." Dr. Johnson recognized the complex purposes to which Shakespeare had adjusted his material and saw the self-deception that was being practiced behind the announced deception. . . . As a good prince [Hal] would still have been in the shadow of the King and the brightness of his princely virtues would have been mere appendages to the inherent glory of the King. So he chose to be with Falstaff and the tavern crowd, a prince among small beer, a big fish in a little pond until he could be the biggest fish in the ocean. But the little pond is of course only incidental, or instrumental, to the satisfaction he sought in being a bad prince and not just a prince. Until he could have the ultimate distinction of kingship, he chose the distinctness of being a bad prince: "I'll so offend, to make offense a skill." He could thus be a prince to the tavern and an offender to the court, something out of the ordinary in either case and hence something whole and independent to himself. (pp. 11-12)

The ironical parallelism between Hal and Falstaff appears most vividly in the scene where Hal is caught in a desperately awkward situation. Caught holding the crown of the still-living

King whom he took for dead, he can at first only weakly explain, "I never thought to hear you speak again." (p. 13)

Hal's mistaking his father's sleep for death and his taking the crown from the room show his keenness for the noble role he has at last assumed. The Falstaffian aspect of Hal's character and behavior is epitomized in his being discovered with the crown and in his weak and brief excuse, "I never thought to hear you speak again"—a situation bordering closely on the comic. He remains holding the embarrassing crown, while his father opens a bitter tirade against him with the accusation, "Thy wish was father, Harry, to that thought." That Hal has had time during his father's speech to collect his wits and prepare a more forceful justification is pointed up by the opening words of his own speech.

> Oh, pardon me, my liege! But for my tears,
> The moist impediments unto my speech,
> I had forestalled this dear and deep rebuke
> Ere you with grief had spoke and I had heard
> The course of it so far.
>
> [*2 Henry IV*, IV. iv. 138-42]

To make this observation is not to say that this statement, or the rest of Hal's humble and noble speech, is not sincere. The point is that Shakespeare is persuasively consistent in representing the complexity of what men call sincerity in such a way as to indicate its coexistence with unexpressed or unrealized motives. Hal had certainly not planned being caught with the crown, but he can, like Falstaff, turn a huge *faux pas* to his advantage, "Pleading so wisely in excuse of it!" as the quickly forgiving King exclaims. Hal can explain his action in such a way as to gain his father's blessing. Indeed, he can so reform as to make reform a skill. In his exoneration of himself from the appearance of overeagerness for the crown, one can see again the theme of motive concealing motive. If there is something Falstaffian about the awkwardness of Hal's situation, there is also about his successful escape from it. Even the King recognizes that the *faux pas* was a lucky occasion, leading to a fuller and more impressive reconciliation than might otherwise have occurred. (pp. 14-15)

It has been observed that Brutus is a precursor of Hamlet in the develoment of Shakespeare's pageant of characters. And Hal is a still earlier precursor. All are characters peculiarly isolated, struggling with confused motives, extremely self-preoccupied but showing attractive personal features. All show a capacity, seemingly without plan or effort, of reproducing in others the love they bear toward themselves. The "small beer" scene . . . is most Hamlet-like. Hal appears quite sympathetically here, letting his hair down ever so slightly and with dignity, at once melancholy, witty, and superior. Poins has chided him with the trifling life he leads while his father is sick. His reply is that his "heart bleeds inwardly" and that everyone would think him a hypocrite were he to weep openly. His sentiments here are convincing, but not his logic. He would rather be thought a waster and a heartless son than a hypocrite. He is more concerned with what men like Poins think than with what his father thinks. It would be hypocritical to weep now, it would be out of character. He will weep when he is ready to step out of that character into another, when he performs the somersault of reformation, when he and the time are ready for him to put his heart into the act and the crown on his head. The *he* will not think himself a hypocrite, and that is what matters.

The somersault of reformation has turned Hal's joke into a dream and his revels now are ended. But there is a sense in which the dream continues and in which the joke and the dream have existed side by side. The period of Hal's "loose behavior" was a joke to the extent that it was a conscious deception, but it was like a dream to the extent that it was a self-deception. And the self-deception continues, of course, in the transformation of the joke into the dream. Hal, like his father, is impelled to recreate reality according to his own egotistical needs. Indeed, once he has properly assumed the crown, he becomes visibly much like his father. We have earlier observed an implicit parallelism between father and son, but now, when Hal is also King Henry, this likeness comes to the foreground. (pp. 16-17)

> Leonard Unger, *"Deception and Self-deception in Shakespeare's 'Henry IV*,'" *in his* The Man in the Name: Essays on the Experience of Poetry, *University of Minnesota Press, Minneapolis, 1956, pp. 3-17.*

ROBERT LANGBAUM (essay date 1957)

[*Langbaum praises Maurice Morgann's interpretation of Falstaff as a precursor of the Romantic, or "existential," approach to literature developed in the nineteenth century (see excerpt above, 1777). At the same time, he criticizes E. E. Stoll (1914) for his contention that a character cannot be treated historically, beyond the dramatic or narrative plot, but only as a fictitious element in a creative work of art. For Langbaum, Falstaff's courage consists not in his moral integrity, in which he fails according to the Elizabethan codes of honor, justice, and chivalry, but in his "existential" integrity—his determination to realize his individuality and to impress his vision upon the world. It is this suggestion, Langbaum claims, that makes Morgann's essay one of the most significant in the history of Shakespearean criticism.*]

Sympathy would seem to have been responsible in the first place for the psychological interpretation of Shakespeare, and it is no coincidence that the new interpretation made its first appearance in the latter eighteenth century when we note the decline of the dogmatic and the beginning of the sympathetic or humanitarian attitude. (p. 168)

The modern interest—what we mean by *character* in fact—is in just that which is incongruent with the moral category. The modern reader can sympathize with any character, regardless of his moral position in the plot, provided only that he is sufficiently central to claim our attention, and has a sufficiently definite point of view and sufficient power of intellect and will to hold our interest. Thus, sympathy is likely to be more important than moral judgment in the modern interpretation not only of Iago but also of Shakespeare's Richard III, Macbeth, Shylock and Falstaff, and Marlowe's Tamburlaine, Faustus and Jew of Malta. (p. 169)

Since the comic effect depends specifically on the exclusion of sympathy, it is even more important in comedy than in tragedy that we keep the offended mores in mind—which is why fewer comedies than tragedies survive, and why the comedies that do survive do so through the pathetic or psychological interest that modern readers think they find there.

Falstaff's comic effect has not been impaired. But that is because his comic role has been made philosophical by the modern elevation of his character, an elevation which Stoll attributes to the decline of the chivalric code of honour [see excerpt above, 1914]. We laugh with Falstaff when he makes the common-sense attack upon honour ("Can honour set to a leg?"), because we see him as the witty philosopher of a rival world-

view. But according to Stoll, the Elizabethans laughed at him for his transparent attempt to justify his cowardice. They saw him as a self-describing coward turning the general perspective against himself by poking sarcastic fun at himself. Stoll even suggests that Falstaff might have winked at the audience as he "descanted on the duty of discretion." Such humorous self-betrayal would have been no more unpsychological than the startling self-betrayal of Shakespeare's villains in the tragedies.

But whether or not we are willing to go along with Stoll on this point (there is, after all, reason to believe that the laugh on chivalry had begun by Shakespeare's time), the issue between the psychological and anti-psychological interpretations of Falstaff is whether as coward, lecher and glutton he is the butt of the comedy and deservedly outwitted in the end; or whether he is the maker of the comedy, playing the butt for the sake of the humour which he turns upon himself as well as everyone else—whether he is, in other words, victorious in all the wit combats whatever his circumstantial defeat. It is essentially the issue of Hamlet and Macbeth criticism, whether they confront their difficulties or create them; and of Iago criticism, whether he is the villain or as maker of the plot merely playing the villain. In other words, are the characters agents of the plot with only as much consciousness as the plot requires; or have they a residue of intelligence and will beyond what the plot requires and not accounted for by it, so that they stand somehow above the plot, conscious of themselves inside it? The latter view assumes that we can apprehend more about the characters than the plot tells us, assumes our sympathetic apprehension of them.

The Falstaff question has been only less important than the Hamlet question in establishing the psychological interpretation of Shakespeare. Both Hamlet and Falstaff began to appear in their new complex and enigmatic character in the 1770's, the decade of Werther and of a European Wertherism that owed much to an already well-established sentimental tradition in England. Of such a propitious age for psychological criticism, Maurice Morgann, the projector of the new Falstaff, was one of the advanced spirits—liberal in politics, humanitarian in sentiment, and in literature endowed with the new sensibility.

Morgann's sensibility is abundantly illustrated in the *Essay on the Dramatic Character of Sir John Falstaff* [see excerpt above, 1777] . . . where the perceptions are far in advance of the dialectic. It is his fundamental sympathy for Falstaff that Morgann is trying to explain when he undertakes to prove that, in spite of cowardly actions, "Cowardice *is not* the *Impression,* which the *whole* character of *Falstaff* is calculated to make on the minds of an unprejudiced [i.e. sympathetic] audience." And it is on the ground of experience that he makes the novel distinction between our *"mental Impressions"* and our *"Understanding"* of character—whereby "we often condemn or applaud characters and actions on the credit of some logical process, while our hearts revolt, and would fain lead us to a very different conclusion." (pp. 169-71)

Unfortunately, Morgann is a bit frightened by the revolutionary nature of his case, and tries to prove it to his eighteenth-century readers on their own rationalistic and moral grounds. His essay is therefore valuable for its scattered insights rather than for the hair-splitting, text-citing argument destructive of the dramatic and comic context which he employs in order to uncover in the *actions* he says do not *matter* evidences of Falstaff's courage. It would have required the dialectical equipment of the next century for Morgann to have granted the moral case against Falstaff and accounted for his sympathetic *impression* of him by quite another order of value. Yet the other order of value is certainly implied by Morgann's distinction between the *first principles* of character which we apprehend sympathetically and its manifestations which we judge. (pp. 171-72)

It follows—though Morgann does not specifically articulate the conclusion—that our judgment of Falstaff's moral courage must be problematical because based on a shifting idea of honour; whereas our apprehension of his *constitutional* courage must be certain because based on what he is in himself. Only the double apprehension of character could have given rise to Morgann's perception that character may be incongruous with action, that "the *real* character of *Falstaff* may be different from his *apparent* one," and that an author may give wit, dignity and courage to a character made to seem ridiculous, ignoble and cowardly by all external appearances. The recognition that our *impressions* of a character and even of certain of the character's sentiments and actions may be contradictory of his moral category yet "we know not why, natural," leads to the essential method of all psychological criticism in that it compels us "to look farther, and examine if there be not something more in the character than is *shewn.*"

Now it is just the habit in Shakespeare criticism of looking for more than is shown that makes Stoll see red, since he contends that this is to treat the character as historical and that there can be no more in a fictitious character than *is* shown. It is true enough that psychological criticism treats the character as though he had a life of which the action presents only a portion; yet Stoll defines the issue, I think, inadequately. For if we conceive the play as larger than the plot, the part of character uncovered by psychological criticism falls not outside the play but outside the moral categories of the plot. The plot, which we understand through moral judgment, becomes a clearing in the forest; while the play shades off to include the penumbra of forest fringe out of which the plot has emerged, a penumbra which we apprehend through sympathy. Such a conception makes room for psychological criticism by dissolving the limits of character and of the play, by suggesting that the limits are always in advance of comprehension. That is how we come by the modern idea of a masterpiece as an enigma whose whole meaning can never be formulated. Comprehension becomes an unending process, historical and evolutionary; while the play itself moves inviolate down the ages, eluding final formulation yet growing, too, in beauty and complexity as it absorbs into its meaning everything that has been thought and felt about it. (pp. 172-73)

The fact that our *feelings* should have occasion to revolt against our *understanding* means that we judge this residue of consciousness by an order of value other than moral. Morgann's *courage* and *ability* are existential virtues, virtues which make for the sheer survival of the personality apart from any moral purpose toward which the personality is directed. He speaks at length of the indestructible nature of Falstaff, who, unlike Parolles and Bobadil, is never defeated and never even loses stature from his several disgraces. That is because the disgraces, like the "ill habits, and the accidents of age and corpulence, are no part of his essential constitution . . . they are second natures, not *first.*" (p. 174)

Falstaff's courage, remember, is not moral but *constitutional.* It is not Hotspur's kind of courage. It is too bad that Morgann did not undertake the contrast with Hotspur, for it holds good under his interpretation—not to be sure as between cowardice and heroism, but as between two kinds of heroism. If Hotspur is the chivalric hero, Falstaff is the natural hero, the Hero of

Existence. His is the courage to be himself, to realize his individuality. He is a hero because of his hard core of character, his fierce loyalty to himself, because he is more alive than other people. By this peculiarly modern reading, Falstaff and Hotspur would represent opposite kinds of heroism both of which go down to defeat; while the Prince, who temporizes between the two extremes, appropriating from each the virtues he can turn to his advantage, becomes prudence triumphant.

Although the eighteenth century could not supply the concepts and vocabulary by which Falstaff might be called a hero, Morgann is already dealing in the distinctive virtues of the new heroism when he attacks as mere prudence the moral virtues Falstaff lacks, and glorifies Falstaff on the ground of his imprudence. . . . The attack on prudence is the beginning of the romantic ethics. Hypocrisy (the denial of one's own nature) is its worst sin, sincerity (another name for existential courage) its prime virtue. Morgann's Falstaff has the virtues Blake was to recommend in *The Marriage of Heaven and Hell:* "Prudence is a rich, ugly old maid courted by Incapacity," "He who desires but acts not, breeds pestilence," "The road of excess leads to the palace of wisdom." *Excess* explains Falstaff's nature; his girth, his appetites, his laughter, even his style of wit and the rich redundancy of his language—all derive their character from excess; yet they are not for that reason vices, as they would be according to the Aristotelian ethics of the Golden Mean. According to the new ethics, Falstaff's excesses are at once the cause of his failure and of his distinction.

For he commits what Shelley was to call the "generous error," the error of those who try to live life by a vision of it, thus transforming the world about them and impressing upon it their character. This is the secret of Falstaff's appeal. His vision of life takes over whenever he is on the stage; and everyone on stage with him, most notably the Prince, is drawn into his characteristic atmosphere. The only characters who resist his influence are those who, like the King and Hotspur, never confront him. Yet Falstaff's genius for creating his own environment is dangerous, since the single vision of life cannot be identical with reality and must eventually collide with it. That is why the "generous error" distinguishes the Hero of Existence from what Shelley calls the "trembling throng," who "languish" and are "morally dead," who live eclectically because they have not the courage to live out the implications of their own natures, who are too prudent to venture all on what must turn out to have been a noble delusion.

Dr Johnson, who saw where Morgann's kind of criticism was leading, said of him: "Why, Sir, we shall have the man come forth again; and as he has proved Falstaff to be no coward, he may prove Iago to be a very good character." Johnson thought he was indulging in witty hyperbole, but the admiration for Falstaff was in fact to be accompanied in the next century by an admiration for Iago and for all characters alive enough to take over the scene, to assert their point of view as the one through which we understand the action. The new existential rather than moral judgment of character was to dissolve dramatic structure by denying the authority of the plot—making the psychologically read play, like the dramatic monologue, depend for its success upon a central character with a point of view definite enough to give meaning and unity to the events, and the strength of intellect, will and passion, the imaginative strength, to create the whole work before our eyes, to give it a thickness and an atmosphere, an inner momentum, a life.

It is, however, in the isolation of character from plot that we can best see the psychological interpretation of Shakespeare as dissolving dramatic structure and leading us toward the dramatic monologue. For in concentrating on the part of character in excess of plot requirements, and in claiming to apprehend more about character than the plot reveals, the psychological interpretation isolates character from the external motivation of plot (such as money, love, power). It makes of character an autonomous force, motivated solely by the need for self-expression. (pp. 175-77)

> *Robert Langbaum, "Character versus Action in Shakespeare," in his* The Poetry of Experience: The Dramatic Monologue in Modern Literary Tradition, *Random House, Inc., 1957, pp. 160-81.*

W. H. AUDEN   (essay date 1959)

[*Auden, an Anglo-American poet, essayist, and critic, is considered a major literary figure of the twentieth-century. His Shakespearean criticism takes many forms, including essays, introductions, and miscellaneous observations. Here he interprets Falstaff as a "comic symbol for the supernatural order of charity as contrasted with the temporal order of Justice symbolized by Henry of Monmouth." This position was later praised and amplified by Roy Battenhouse (1975). Auden's essay was originally published in* Encounter *in 1959.*]

The experience of reading a play and the experience of watching it performed are never identical, but in the case of *Henry IV* the difference between the two is particularly great.

At a performance, my immediate reaction is to wonder what Falstaff is doing in this play at all. At the end of *Richard II*, we were told that the Heir Apparent has taken up with a dissolute crew of "unrestrained loose companions." What sort of bad company would one expect to find Prince Hal keeping when the curtain rises on *Henry IV*? Surely, one would expect to see him surrounded by daring, rather sinister, juvenile delinquents and beautiful gold-digging whores. But whom do we meet in the Boar's Head? A fat, cowardly tosspot, old enough to be his father, two down-at-heel hangers-on, a slatternly Hostess and only one whore, who is not in her earliest youth either; all of them seedy, and, by any worldly standards, in-

Part II. Act II. Scene iv. Hostess Quickly, Falstaff, Doll Tearsheet, Bardolph, the Page, Pistol (n.d.). From the Art Collection of the Folger Shakespeare Library.

cluding those of the criminal classes, all of them *failures*. Surely, one thinks, an Heir Apparent, sowing his wild oats, could have picked himself a more exciting crew than that. As the play proceeds, our surprise is replaced by another kind of puzzle, for the better we come to know Falstaff, the clearer it becomes that the world of historical reality which a Chronicle Play claims to imitate is not a world which he can inhabit.

If it really was Queen Elizabeth who demanded to see Falstaff in a comedy, then she showed herself a very perceptive critic. But even in *The Merry Wives of Windsor*, Falstaff has not and could not have found his true home because Shakespeare was only a poet. For that he was to wait nearly two hundred years till Verdi wrote his last opera. Falstaff is not the only case of a character whose true home is the world of music; others are Tristan, Isolde, and Don Giovanni.

Though they each call for a different kind of music, Tristan, Don Giovanni, and Falstaff have certain traits in common. They do not belong to the temporal world of change. One cannot imagine any of them as babies, for a Tristan who is not in love, a Don Giovanni who has no name on his list, a Falstaff who is not old and fat, are inconceivable. (pp. 182-84)

For Falstaff time does not exist, since he belongs to the *opera buffa* world of play and mock-action governed not by will or desire, but by innocent wish, a world where no one can suffer because everything they say and do is only a pretence. (p. 184)

There are at least two places in the play where the incongruity of the *opera buffa* world with the historical world is too much, even for Shakespeare, and a patently false note is struck. The first occurs when, on the battlefield of Shrewsbury, Falstaff thrusts his sword into Hotspur's corpse. Within his own world, Falstaff could stab a corpse because, there, all battles are mock battles, all corpses straw dummies; but we, the audience, are too conscious that this battle has been a real battle and that this corpse is the real dead body of a brave and noble young man. Pistol could do it, because Pistol is a contemptible character, but Falstaff cannot; that is to say, there is no way in which an actor can play the scene convincingly. So, too, with the surrender of Colevile to Falstaff in the Second Part. In his conversation, first with Colevile and then with Prince John, Falstaff talks exactly as we expect—to him, the whole business is a huge joke. But then he is present during a scene when we are shown that it is no joke at all. How is any actor to behave and speak his lines during the following?

> LANCASTER—Is thy name Colevile?
> COLEVILE—It is, my lord.
> LANCASTER—A famous rebel art thou, Colevile?
> FALSTAFF—And a famous true subject took him.
> COLEVILE—I am, my lord, but as my betters are, that led me hither. Had they been ruled by me, You would have won them dearer than you have.
> FALSTAFF—I know not how they sold themselves but thou, kind fellow, givest thy self away gratis, and I thank thee, for thee.
> LANCASTER—Now have you left pursuit?
> WESTMORELAND—Retreat is made and execution stay'd.
> LANCASTER—Send Colevile, with his confederates, to York, to present execution.
>   [*2 Henry IV*, IV. iii. 61-74]

The Falstaffian frivolity and the headsman's axe cannot so directly confront each other. (pp. 184-85)

As the play proceeds, we become aware, behind all the fun, of something tragic. Falstaff loves Hal with an absolute devotion. "The lovely bully" is the son he has never had, the youth predestined to the success and worldly glory which he will never enjoy. He believes that his love is returned, that the Prince is indeed his other self, so he is happy, despite old age and poverty. We, however, can see that he is living in a fool's paradise, for the Prince cares no more for him as a person than he would care for the King's Jester. He finds Falstaff amusing but no more. If we could warn Falstaff of what he is too blind to see, we might well say: Beware, before it is too late, of becoming involved with one of those mortals

> That do not do the thing they most do show,
> Who, moving others, are themselves as stone. . . .
> [Sonnet 94]

Falstaff's story, in fact, is not unlike one of those folk tales in which a mermaid falls in love with a mortal prince: the price she pays for her infatuation is the loss of her immortality without the compensation of temporal happiness. (pp. 191-92)

Seeking for an explanation of why Falstaff affects us as he does, I find myself compelled to see *Henry IV* as possessing, in addition to its overt meaning, a parabolic significance. Overtly, Falstaff is a Lord of Misrule; parabolically, he is a comic symbol for the supernatural order of charity as contrasted with the temporal order of Justice symbolised by Henry of Monmouth. (p. 198)

Before the battle of Shrewsbury, he first conscripts those who have most money and least will to fight and then allows them to buy their way out, so that he is finally left with a sorry regiment of "discarded unjust serving men, younger sons to younger brothers, revolted tapsters and ostlers trade fallen. . . ." Before the battle of Gaultree Forest, the two most sturdy young men, Mouldy and Bullcalf, offer him money and are let off, and the weakest, Shadow, Feeble, and Wart, taken.

From the point of view of society this is unjust, but if the villagers who are subject to conscription were to be asked, private individuals, whether they would rather be treated justly or as Falstaff treats them, there is no doubt as to their answer. What their betters call just and unjust means nothing to them; all they know is that conscription will tear them away from their homes and livelihoods with a good chance of getting killed or returning maimed "to beg at the town's end." Those whom Falstaff selects are those with least to lose, derelicts without home or livelihood to whom soldiering at least offers a chance of loot. Bullcalf wants to stay with his friends, Mouldy has an old mother to look after, but Feeble is quite ready to go if his friend Wart can go with him.

Falstaff's neglect of the public interest in favour of private concerns is an image for the justice of charity which treats each person, not as a cypher, but as a unique person. The Prince may justly complain:

> I never did see such pitiful rascals.
> [*1 Henry IV*, IV. ii. 64]

but Falstaff's retort speaks for all the insulted and injured of this world:

> Tut tut—good enough to toss, food for powder, food for powder.
> They'll fill a pit as well as better. Tush, man, mortal men, mortal men. . . .
> [*1 Henry IV*, IV. ii. 65-7]

These are Falstaff's only acts: for the rest, he fritters away his time, swigging at the bottle and taking no thought for the morrow. As parable, both the idleness and the drinking, the surrender to immediacy and the refusal to accept reality, become signs for the Unworldly Man as contrasted with Prince Hal who represents worldliness at its best. (pp. 203-04)

Falstaff makes the same impression on us that the Sinner of Lublin made upon his rabbi.

> In Lublin lived a great sinner. Whenever he went to talk to the rabbi, the rabbi readily consented and conversed with him as if he were a man of integrity and one who was a close friend. Many of the hassidim were annoyed at this and one said to the other: "Is it possible that our rabbi who has only to look once into a man's face to know his life from first to last, to know the very origin of his soul, does not see that this fellow is a sinner? And if he does see it, that he considers him worthy to speak to and associate with." Finally they summoned up courage to go to the rabbi himself with their question. He answered them: "I know all about him as well as you. But you know how I love gaiety and hate dejection. And this man is so great a sinner. Others repent the moment they have sinned, are sorry for a moment, and then return to their folly. But he knows no regrets and no doldrums, and lives in his happiness as in a tower. And it is the radiance of his happiness that overwhelms my heart."

Falstaff's happiness is almost an impregnable tower, but not quite. "I am that I am" is not a complete self-description; he must also add—"The young prince hath misled me. I am the fellow with the great belly, and he is my dog."

The Christian God is not a self-sufficient being like Aristotle's First Cause, but a God who creates a world which he continues to love although it refuses to love him in return. He appears in this world, not as Apollo or Aphrodite might appear, disguised as a man so that no mortal should recognise his divinity, but as a real man who openly claims to be God. And the consequence is inevitable. The highest religious and temporal authorities condemn Him as a blasphemer and a Lord of Misrule, as a Bad Companion for mankind. Inevitable because, as Richelieu said, "the salvation of States is in this world," and history has not as yet provided us with any evidence that the Prince of this world has changed his character. (pp. 207-08)

W. H. Auden, "The Prince's Dog," in his The Dyer's Hand and Other Essays, *Random House, Inc., 1962, pp. 182-208.*

L. C. KNIGHTS (essay date 1959)

[*Knights enters into the long-standing argument over the question of unity in the* Henry IV *plays, claiming that* 1 Henry IV *and* 2 Henry IV *are indeed two distinct works. Knights rests his conclusion on the theory that Shakespeare shifted his interests significantly from the first to the second parts: from a study of political ethics in Part One, to an examination of "time and change" in Part Two. Unlike such earlier critics as Francis Gentleman (1774), Richard Cumberland (1786), George Brandes (1895-96), and Caroline F.E. Spurgeon (1935), Knights considers* Henry IV, Part 2 *superior to its predecessor, as well as one of the first plays "in which we recognize the great Shakespeare" and see the beginning of his "darkening" vision of life—a vision which culminated in* King Lear. *For further discussions of the element of time in* Henry IV, *see the excerpts by Benjamin T. Spencer (1944) and Clifford Leech (1951). Also, see the excerpts by Leech and John F. Danby (1949) for additional commentary on the "darkening" mood in Shakespeare's history. Knights's essay was first published in 1959.*]

In the First Part of *King Henry IV* the question that Shakespeare is asking is, What does it mean to use force for political ends, to seek and keep power? The facts of the situation—I mean the dramatic facts, not any that may be brought in from historical knowledge extraneous to the play—are clear. Henry Bolingbroke is a usurping king, who is now meeting the consequences of usurpation in precisely the way that was foretold in *Richard II.* . . . It is certain that the rebels, the Northumberland faction, do not enlist our sympathy. Indeed they are often presented satirically, as in the comedy of their first meeting, where Worcester and Hotspur take turns in deflating each other's rhetoric. . . . (pp. 38-9)

Yet the rebels' view of how the king came to his throne—and they revert to it often enough—is not far from what Henry himself admits. Hotspur speaks of 'murderous subornation' [I. iii. 163], of a hypocritical pretense of righting wrongs, whereas Henry speaks of 'necessity',

. . . necessity so bow'd the state,
That I and greatness were compell'd to kiss
[2 Henry IV, III. i. 73-4]

but even he admits to his son that he used considerable astuteness to 'pluck allegiance from men's hearts' [*1 Henry IV,* III. ii. 52ff.], and, as he says on his death-bed,

God knows, my son,
By what by-paths and indirect crook'd ways
I met this crown.
[2 Henry IV, IV. v. 183-85]

What we have in *Henry IV* therefore is a realistic portrayal of the ways of the world and an insistent questioning of the values by which its great men live—with a consequent ironic contrast between public profession and the actuality. (p. 40)

In *Henry V,* in *Julius Caesar* and, later, in *Coriolanus,* Shakespeare was to continue his exploration of the public world and its tragic contradictions, and of the rôle of the Governor. But between *Henry IV* and *Henry V* Shakespeare wrote *2 Henry IV;* and the Second Part of *King Henry IV* is a different kind of play from the first Part. There is certainly continuity, but there is also a new direction of interest and the action is contrived for new purposes: there is a greater involvement of the dramatist in his fable. . . . [A] shrewd understanding of men in their political and public aspects and relations (not 'disillusioned', because that implies an attitude to the self quite foreign to Shakespeare, but certainly without illusions) was an essential condition of Shakespeare's exploration of experiences that come to each man simply as individual man in his more directly personal life and relationships. It meant that the inwardness was to be something utterly different from the results of an engrossed introspection. (p. 44)

Great poetry demands a willingness to meet, experience and contemplate all that is most deeply disturbing in our common fate. The sense of life's tragic issues comes to different men in different ways. One of the ways in which it came to Shakespeare is not uncommon; it was simply a heightened awareness of what the mere passage of time does to man and all created things. There are many of the Sonnets that show the impact

of time and mutability on a nature endowed with an uncommon capacity for delight. And it is surely no accident that one of the first plays in which we recognize the great Shakespeare—the Second Part of *King Henry IV*—is a play of which the controlling theme is time and change. In that play, and in the sonnets on time, we see clearly the beginning of the progress that culminates in *King Lear* and the great tragedies. (p. 45)

2 Henry IV, a tragi-comedy of human frailty, is about the varied aspects of mutability—age, disappointment and decay. The theme of 'policy' is of course continued from Part I, and sometimes it is presented with similar methods of ironic deflation; but we cannot go far into the play without becoming aware of a change of emphasis and direction, already marked indeed by the words of the dying Hotspur at Shrewsbury,

But thought's the slave of life, and life time's fool:
And time, that takes survey of all the world,
Must have a stop.
[*1 Henry IV,* V. iv. 81-3]

Each of the three scenes of the first act gives a particular emphasis to elements present in Part I, though largely subdued there by the brisker tone, by the high-spirited satire. Now the proportions are altered. Act I, scene i is not comic satire: it is a harsh reminder of what is involved in the hard game of power politics—the desperate resolve ('each heart being set On bloody courses. . .') and the penalties for failure; and for some thirty lines, throughout Northumberland's elaborate rhetoric of protestation against ill news [I. i. 67-103], the word 'dead' (or 'death') tolls with monotonous insistence. Now just as the comedy of the first meeting of the conspirators in Part I was in keeping with the Falstaffian mode that so largely determined the tone of that play, so this scene is attuned to the appearance of a Falstaff who seems, at first perplexingly, to be both the same figure as before and yet another: it is as though we had given a further twist to the screw of our binoculars and a figure that we thought we knew had appeared more sharply defined against a background that he no longer dominated. When Falstaff enters with his page ('Sirrah, you giant, what says the doctor to my water?'), throughout his exchange with the Lord Chief Justice, and in his concluding soliloquy, it is impossible to turn the almost obsessive references to age and disease, as the references to Falstaff's corpulence are turned in Part I, in the direction of comedy. Later, Falstaff will try again his familiar tactics of evasion—'Peace, good Doll! do not speak like a death's-head; do not bid me remember mine end' [II. iv. 234-35] but from the scene of his first appearance the well-known *memento mori,* if not—as in *The Revenger's Tragedy*—actually present on the stage, has certainly been present to the minds of the audience. 'Is not . . . every part about you blasted with antiquity?'—to that question wit in its wantonness must make what reply it can. (pp. 52-3)

The world of *King Henry IV, Part II*—the world we are introduced to in the first Act—is a world where men are only too plainly time's subjects, yet persist in planning and contriving and attempting by hook or by crook to further their own interests. Most of them, drawing a model of a desirable future beyond their power to build, are, in the course of the play, disappointed. (p. 55)

The tone of the play is sombre; but it could not possibly be called pessimistic or depressed. Not only is there the vigour of mind with which the political theme is grasped and presented, there is, in the Falstaff scenes, a familiar comic verve together with an outgoing sympathy—even, at times, liking—

for what is so firmly judged. It is important, here, to say neither more nor less than one means, and humour is of all literary qualities the most difficult to handle. (p. 59)

And Shakespeare shows a further characteristic of great genius: he can feel for, can even invest with dignity, those representative human types who, in the complex play of attitudes that constitute his dramatic statement, are judged and found wanting. When Falstaff celebrates with Doll Tearsheet, at the Boar's Head Tavern, his departure for the wars (II. iv), there is nothing comic in the exhibition of senile lechery. Yet the tipsy Doll can move us with, 'Come, I'll be friends with thee, Jack: thou art going to the wars; and whether I shall ever see thee again or no, there is nobody cares'. And at the end of the scene Mrs Quickly too has her moment, when sentimentality itself is transformed simply by looking towards those human decencies and affections for which—the realities being absent—it must do duty:

> Well, fare thee well: I have known thee these twenty nine years, come peascod time; but an honester and truer-hearted man,—well, fare thee well.
>
> [2 Henry IV, II. iv. 382-84]

There is nothing facile in Shakespeare's charity; it is simply that Shakespeare, like Chaucer, is not afraid of his spontaneous feelings, and his feelings are not—so to speak—afraid of each other.

Here, then, is one way in which the insistent elegiac note is both qualified and deepened. There is yet another. We have already noticed the repeated references to Falstaff's age and diseases. But it is not only Falstaff who is diseased. Northumberland is sick, or 'crafty-sick'; the King is dying; and the imagery of disease links the individuals to the general action.

> Then you perceive the body of our kingdom
> How foul it is; what rank diseases grow,
> And with what danger, near the heart of it. . . .
>
> [2 Henry IV, III. i. 38-40]
> (pp. 60-1)

Shakespeare never explicitly points a moral; and it will be some years before he fully reveals in terms of the awakened imagination why those that follow their noses are led by their eyes, or what it really means to be the fool of time. For the moment we are only concerned with the direction that his developing insight is taking; and it seems to me that what is coming into consciousness is nothing less than an awareness of how men make the world that they inhabit, an understanding of the relation between what men are and the kind of perceptions they have about the nature of things. It is this growing awareness, linking the overt social criticism with the more deep-lying and pervasive concern with time's power, that explains our sense of fundamental issues coming to expression. It explains why the tone of 2 Henry IV is entirely different from the tone of detached observation of the earlier plays. (pp. 62-3)

Henry IV, Part II, is markedly a transitional play. It looks back to the Sonnets and the earlier history plays, and it looks forward to the great tragedies. In technique too we are beginning to find that more complete permeation of the material by the shaping imagination which distinguishes the plays that follow it from those that went before. The words do not yet strike to unsuspected depths (it is significant that some of the most vividly realized scenes are in prose); but in the manner of its working the play is nearer to *Macbeth* than to *Richard III;* the

imagery is organic to the whole, and the verse and prose alike are beginning to promote that associative activity that I have tried to define as the distinguishing mark of great poetic drama. It is this imaginative wholeness that allows us to say that Shakespeare is now wholly *within* his material. As a result the play has that doubleness which, as T. S. Eliot says, is a characteristic of the greatest poetry, and the more obvious qualities of action, satire, humour and pathos are informed and integrated by a serious vision of life subjected to time. (pp. 63-4)

> *L. C. Knights, "The Public World: First Observations" and "Time's Subjects: The Sonnets and 'King Henry IV',"* in his *Some Shakespearean Themes, Stanford University Press, 1960, pp. 26-44, 45-64.*

U. C. KNOEPFLMACHER (essay date 1963)

I should like to suggest that Shakespeare's subtle metaphoric use of the Elizabethan theory of humors provides the basis for a symbolic nucleus which binds [*1 Henry IV*'s] abundant references to blood, sickness and the four elements to those related to heavenly bodies and to time, and stresses the Christian import of Prince Hal's transcendence. These seemingly disjointed images have a common function: they serve to distinguish the identity of the prince from those characters who, like his father, Hotspur, or Falstaff, are hopelessly enmeshed in a protean world of changes and "counterfeit"; they punctuate the conversion of a companion of thieves into an ideal Christian monarch; and they help to resolve the basic paradox posed by Hal's uncertain claim to an usurped throne.

According to the theories fashionable in Shakespeare's time, the distemper of a patient was determined by the preponderance of one or more of the four humors. The melancholic humor, corresponding to the element of "Earth," was cold and dry; the phlegmatic humor, corresponding to "Water," was cold and moist; the choleric humor, "Fire," was hot and dry; and the sanguine humor, "Air," was hot and moist. In *1 Henry IV*, the opposition between a world of mutability and a world of static truths is depicted through the contrast between King Henry, Hotspur and Falstaff on one hand, and Prince Hal on the other. The humors of the King, of Hotspur, and of Falstaff are fragmented, causing their identities to merge and overlap. The Prince, on the other hand, is the man whose humors are well commingled. He shakes off his adopted "intemperance" in order to become "of all humors that showed themselves humors since the days of goodman Adam." The nature of the "base contagious clouds" above which he must rise is depicted in the first three scenes of the play through the unbalance of humors which exists in the characters of the King, Hotspur, and Falstaff, the "foils" to his "glitt'ring" reformation.

The opening speech of *1 Henry IV* is that of a melancholic man, a shaken King, "wan with care," who prescribes a crusade to the Holy Land as the sole remedy for "the intestine shock" suffered by his own, disease-ridden country. . . . The King's melancholic speech is an imposture, for the grave and sober ruler hides the crime of a young man who was once, like the Hotspur he admires but resents, "drunk with choler." The England described by the King is thirsty, hot and dry: "the land is burning." . . . By the third scene of Act I, the King has revealed his true humor: his "blood hath been too cold and temperate," and he clashes angrily with the man he would have liked to have had as a son. The fester implanted by this "ingrate and cankered Bolingbroke" promises to spread over his kingdom, mocking the hopes of his son and his own yearning to wash away his stains at the site of Christ's "bitter cross."

If King Henry changes from feigned melancholy to open choler, his rival, young Harry Percy, lapses from a choleric outburst of temper into the most sanguine of hopes. The King's elements are Earth and Fire; Hotspur's are Fire and Air. Eager to dethrone his King, ready to leap through the skies to pluck "bright honor from the pale-faced moon," willing to fly like a thunderbolt, "hot horse to horse," Hotspur is himself the "unruly wind" with which he taunts Glendower's allusions to heavenly fires. For Hotspur, like the King, is "altogether governed by humors." (pp. 497-98)

If the first scene of Act I opens on the humor of Melancholy only to give way to the Choler predominant in scene three, the scene wedged in between introduces the humor of Phlegm. Lethargic, drowsy, and "fat-witted with the drinking of old sack," a yawning Falstaff asks for the time of day. His element is Water, or, more properly, wine. He and his band of thieves belong to a world as inconstant as that of the King who deprived Richard of his throne and that of the "noble" rebels led by Hotspur who haggle over their "promises" like the coarse assembly at the Boar's Head Tavern. Falstaff and his men are "governed as the sea is, by our noble and chaste mistress the moon, under whose countenance we steal." (pp. 498-99)

The humor of Choler was associated by the Elizabethans with the symbols of the sun and of Mars; the sun itself was regarded as an emblem for earthly and divine kingship. It is significant that neither King Henry nor Hotspur is depicted as being sunlike. (p. 499)

Hal's sun-like rise and his concomitant detachment from the earthly vanities of all other characters is presented in two separate cycles. The first takes place in scenes one, two and four of Act II, and portrays Hal's gradual ascendancy over the "thieves of day's beauty," Falstaff's "minions of the moon." The second cycle takes place at Shrewsbury where, after Hal's displacement of Hotspur and his assumption of properties absent in his father, it becomes evident that the "true prince" will become a Christian monarch faithful to his promise to "redeem time." The first of these cycles begins at night and ends in the early dawn; the second begins at dawn and ends in "the closing of some glorious day." . . . After the robbery and the plunder by the "two rogues in buckram" has taken place, Hal still pretends to "drive away the time till Falstaff come." But he plays a cat-and-mouse game with Francis the drawer of ale, which clearly prefigures his later charade with Falstaff. As he kicks away the hesitant Francis, the Prince concludes that the time has come: "I am now of all humors that have showed themselves humors since the old days of goodman Adam to the pupil age of this present twelve o'clock." From that point on Hal begins his ascent. The "true prince" has taken over, as he mocks Falstaff's "instinct" and obliquely announces his separation from his former companion. When the Sheriff who looks for Falstaff takes his leave with a "good night, my noble lord," the Prince retorts, "I think it is good morrow, is it not?" The officer is puzzled: "Indeed, my lord, I think it be two o'clock." The scene ends with the exchange of "good morrow" between Hal and a respectful Peto. Falstaff is sound asleep, but the prince has divested himself of the nightly humor of idleness and is ready to become the rising sun that breaks "through the foul and ugly mists." He will face his father and then meet Hotspur at a fixed "dial's point," at the appointed "hour." (p. 500)

Hal's rise, in imitation of the sun and the Son, is parodied by Falstaff's "counterfeit" resurrection. But the Prince is now aloof. Not even Falstaff's false claim for a "reward" for his own "valor" in killing Hotspur can prompt him into anger. The "true prince" has detached himself from the "double man" who asks mockingly whether the truth is not the truth. . . .

1 Henry IV ends with the glimpse of a sun-like Prince who has already broken through "the foul and ugly mists / Of vapors that did seem to strangle him." The "vapors" still remain. The figure of Falstaff, clinging greedily to the mangled corpse of Hotspur, provides a grotesque contrast to the "fair rites of tenderness" uttered by the Prince for his antagonist's spirit. King Henry's vengeful execution of Worcester, whom he accuses of bearing himself unlike a "Christian," is the ugly counterpart of Hal's release of Douglas, "ransomless and free." Falstaff and the King are "still much in love with vanity." The civil butchery is not ended. But a new sun has arisen. It is the spilled blood of a new Hal, armed in the cross of St. George, and not the proposed pilgrimage to the far-away tomb of Christ, which has "salved" the "long-grown wounds" of his "intemperance" and of the England that is to be his own. (p. 501)

U. C. Knoepflmacher, "The Humors As Symbolic Nucleus in 'Henry IV, Part I'," in College English, Vol. 24, No. 7, April, 1963, pp. 497-501.

C. L. BARBER   (essay date 1963)

[*In his* Shakespeare's Festive Comedy, *Barber explores the festive element in several of Shakespeare's plays, which he asserts has its roots in Elizabethan holiday celebrations. In his essay on* Henry IV, *Barber traces Shakespeare's use of the Saturnalian tradition, particularly the scapegoat ritual and the figure of the Lord of Misrule, in connection with the character of Falstaff. For an earlier discussion of the Falstaff plot as a dramatization of the scapegoat ritual, see the excerpt by J.I.M. Stewart (1948). Barber also takes issue with Hermann Ulrici (1839), Victor Hugo (1864), L. C. Knights (1933), and William Empson (1935) for their interpretation of the Falstaff comedy as a satire of the historical action of the plays; instead, Barber claims that the relation between the comedy and the history is Saturnalian, not satiric, and that* Henry IV *is therefore a skillful dramatization of a ritualized behavior. It is in this light that Barber regards the rejection of Falstaff: not as a moral reaction, but as a dramatization of the traditional banishment of the Lord of Misrule enacted in numerous cultures during holiday festivities.*]

It is in the Henry IV plays that we can consider most fruitfully general questions concerning the relation of comedy to analogous forms of symbolic action in folk rituals; not only the likenesses of comedy to ritual, but the differences, the features of comic form which make it comedy and not ritual. Such analogies, I think, prove to be useful critical tools: they lead us to see structure in the drama. And they also raise fascinating historical and theoretical questions about the relation of drama to other products of culture. One way in which our time has been seeing the universal in literature has been to find in complex literary works patterns which are analogous to myths and rituals and which can be regarded as archetypes, in some sense primitive or fundamental. I have found this approach very exciting indeed. But at the same time, such analysis can be misleading if it results in equating the literary form with primitive analogues. (pp. 192-93)

Shakespeare was the opposite of primitivistic, for in his culture what we search out and call primitive was in blood and bone as a matter of course; the problem was to deal with it, to master it. The Renaissance, moreover, was a moment when educated men were modifying a ceremonial conception of human life to create a historical conception. The ceremonial view, which assumed that names and meanings are fixed and final, expressed experience as pageant and ritual—pageant where the right names could march in proper order, or ritual where names could be changed in the right, the proper way. The historical view expresses life as drama. People in drama are not identical with their names, for they gain and lose their names, their status and meaning—and not by settled ritual: the gaining and losing of names, of meaning, is beyond the control of any set ritual sequence. Shakespeare's plays are full of pagentry and of action patterned in a ritualistic way. But the pageants are regularly interrupted; the rituals are abortive or perverted; or if they succeed, they succeed against odds or in an unexpected fashion. The people in the plays try to organize their lives by pageant and ritual, but the plays are dramatic precisely because the effort fails. This failure drama presents as history and personality; in the largest perspective, as destiny.

At the heart of the plays there is, I think, a fascination with the individualistic use or abuse of ritual—with magic. There is an intoxication with the possibility of an omnipotence of mind by which words might become things, by which a man might "gain a deity," might achieve, by making his own ritual, an unlimited power to incarnate meaning. This fascination is expressed in the poetry by which Shakespeare's people envisage their ideal selves. But his drama also expresses an equal and complementary awareness that magic is delusory, that words can become things or lead to deeds only within a social group, by virtue of a historical, social situation beyond the mind and discourse of any one man. This awareness of limitations is expressed by the ironies, whether comic or tragic, which Shakespeare embodies in the dramatic situations of his speakers, the ironies which bring down the meaning which fly high in winged words. (pp. 193-94)

In creating the Falstaff comedy, [Shakespeare] fused two main saturnalian traditions, the clowning customary on the stage and the folly customary on holiday, and produced something unprecedented. He was working out attitudes towards chivalry, the state and crown in history, in response to the challenge posed by the fate he had dramatized in *Richard II*. The fact that we find analogies to the ritual interregnum relevant to what Shakespeare produced is not the consequence of a direct influence; his power of dramatic statement, in developing saturnalian comedy, reached to modes of organizing experience which primitive cultures have developed with a clarity of outline comparable to that of his drama. The large and profound relations he expressed were developed from the relatively simple dramatic method of composing with statement and counterstatement, elevated action and burlesque. The Henry IV plays are masterpieces of the popular theater whose plays were, in Sidney's words, "neither right tragedies nor right comedies, mingling kings and clowns." . . .

The relation of the Prince to Falstaff can be summarized fairly adequately in terms of the relation of holiday to everyday. As the non-historical material came to Shakespeare in *The Famous Victories of Henry the Fifth*, the prince was cast in the traditional role of the prodigal son, while his disreputable companions functioned as tempters in the same general fashion as the Vice of the morality plays. At one level Shakespeare keeps the pattern, but he shifts the emphasis away from simple moral terms. The issue, in his hands, is not whether Hal will be good

or bad but whether he will be noble or degenerate, whether his holiday will become his everyday. (p. 195)

In his early history play, *2 Henry VI* . . . Shakespeare used his clowns to present the Jack Cade rebellion as a saturnalia ignorantly undertaken in earnest, a highly-stylized piece of dramaturgy, which he brings off triumphantly. In this more complex play the underworld is presented as endemic disorder alongside the crisis of noble rebellion: the king's lines are apposite when he says that insurrection can always mobilize

> moody beggars, starving for a time
> Of pell-mell havoc and confusion.
>
> [*1 Henry IV*, V. i. 81-2]

Falstaff places himself in saying "Well, God be thanked for these rebels. They offend none but the virtuous. I laud them, I praise them."

The whole effect, in the opening acts, when there is little commentary on the spectacle as a whole, is of life overflowing its bounds by sheer vitality. Thieves and rebels and honest men—"one that hath abundance of charge too, God knows what" [II.ii.58-9]—ride up and down on the commonwealth, pray to her and prey on her. . . .

When [Hal] stands poised above the prostrate bodies of Hotspur and Falstaff, his position on the stage and his lines about the two heroes express a nature which includes within a larger order the now subordinated parts of life which are represented in those two: in Hotspur, honor, the social obligation to courage and self-sacrifice, a value which has been isolated in this magnificently anarchical feudal lord to become almost everything; and in Falstaff, the complementary *joie de vivre* which rejects all social obligations with "I like not such grinning honour as Sir Walter hath. Give me life" [V.iii.58-9]. (pp. 204-05)

But Falstaff does not stay dead. He jumps up in a triumph which, like Bottom coming alive after Pryramus is dead, reminds one of the comic resurrections in the St. George plays. He comes back to life because he is still relevant. His apology for counterfeiting cuts deeply indeed, because it does not apply merely to himself; we can relate it, as William Empson has shown, to the counterfeiting of the king [see excerpt above, 1935]. Bolingbroke too knows when it is time to counterfeit, both in this battle, where he survives because he has many marching in his coats, and throughout a political career where, as he acknowledges to Hal, he manipulates the symbols of majesty with a calculating concern for ulterior results. L. C. Knights, noticing this relation and the burlesque, elsewhere in Falstaff's part, of the attitudes of chivalry, concluded with nineteenth-century critics like Ulrici and Victor Hugo that the comedy should be taken as a devastating satire on war and government. But this is obviously an impossible, anachronistic view, based on the assumption of the age of individualism that politics and war are unnatural activities that can be done without. Mr. Knights would have it that the audience should feel a jeering response when Henry sonorously declares, after Shrewsbury: "Thus ever did rebellion find rebuke." This interpretation makes a shambles of the heroic moments of the play—makes them clearly impossible to act. My own view, as will be clear, is that the dynamic relation of comedy and serious action is saturnalian rather than satiric, that the misrule works, through the whole dramatic rhythm, to consolidate rule. But it is also true, as Mr. Empson remarks, that "the double plot is carrying a fearful strain here." Shakespeare is putting an enormous pressure on the comedy to resolve the challenge posed by the ironic preceptions presented in his historical action.

The process at work, here and earlier in the play, can be made clearer, I hope, by reference now to the carrying off of bad luck by the scapegoat of saturnalian ritual. We do not need to assume that Shakespeare had any such ritual patterns consciously in mind; whatever his conscious intention, it seems to me that these analogues illuminate patterns which his poetic drama presents concretely and dramatically. After such figures as the Mardi Gras or Carnival has presided over a revel, they are frequently turned on by their followers, tried in some sort of court, convicted of sins notorious in the village during the last year, and burned or buried in effigy to signify a new start. . . . One such scapegoat figure, as remote historically as could be from Shakespeare, is the Tibetan King of the Years, who enjoyed ten days' misrule during the annual holiday of Buddhist monks at Lhasa. At the climax of his ceremony, after doing what he liked while collecting bad luck by shaking a black yak's tail over the people, he mounted the temple steps and ridiculed the representative of the Grand Llama, proclaiming heresies like "What we perceive through the five senses is no illusion. All you teach is untrue." A few minutes later, discredited by a cast of loaded dice, he was chased off to exile and possible death in the mountains. One cannot help thinking of Falstaff's catechism on honor, spoken just before another valuation of honor is expressed in the elevated blank verse of a hero confronting death: "Can honour . . . take away the grief of a wound? No . . . What is honour? a word. What is that word, honour? Air." Hal's final expulsion of Falstaff appears in the light of these analogies to carry out an impersonal pattern, not merely political but ritual in character. After the guilty reign of Bolingbroke, the prince is making a fresh start as the new king. At a level beneath the moral notions of the personal reform, we can see a nonlogical process of purification by sacrifice—the sacrifice of Falstaff. (pp. 205-06)

But this process of carrying off bad luck, if it is to be made *dramatically* cogent, as a symbolic action accomplished in and by dramatic form, cannot take place magically in Shakespeare's play. When it happens magically in the play, we have, I think, a failure to transform ritual into comedy. In dealing with fully successful comedy, the magical analogy is only a useful way of organizing our awareness of a complex symbolic action. The expulsion of evil works as dramatic form only in so far as it is realized in a movement from participation to rejection which happens, moment by moment, in our response to Falstaff's clowning misrule. We watch Falstaff adopt one posture after another, in the effort to give himself meaning at no cost; and moment by moment we see that the meaning is specious. So our participation is repeatedly diverted to laughter. The laughter, disbursing energy originally mobilized to respond to a valid meaning, signalizes our mastery by understanding of the tendency which has been misapplied or carrried to an extreme. (p. 207)

Freud's account of bad luck, in *The Psychopathology of Everyday Life,* sees it as the expression of unconscious motives which resist the conscious goals of the personality. This view helps explain how the acting out of disruptive motives in saturnalia or in comedy can serve to master potential aberration by revaluing it in relation to the whole of experience. (pp. 208-09)

In *Part One,* Falstaff reigns, within his sphere, as Carnival; *Part Two* is very largely taken up with his trial. To put Carnival on trial, run him out of town, and burn or bury him is in folk

custom a way of limiting, by ritual, the attitudes and impulses set loose by ritual. Such a trial, though conducted with gay hoots and jeers, serves to swing the mind round to a new vantage, where it sees misrule no longer as a benign release for the individual, but as a source of destructive consequences for society. This sort of reckoning is what *Part Two* brings to Falstaff.

But Falstaff proves extremely difficult to bring to book—more difficult than an ordinary mummery king—because his burlesque and mockery are developed to a point where the mood of a moment crystallizes as a settled attitude of scepticism. As we have observed before, in a static, monolithic society, a Lord of Misrule can be put back in his place after the revel with relative ease. The festive burlesque of solemn sanctities does not seriously threaten social values in a monolithic culture, because the license depends utterly upon what it mocks: liberty is unable to envisage any alternative to the accepted order except the standing of it on its head. But Shakespeare's culture was not monolithic: though its moralists assumed a single order, scepticism was beginning to have ground to stand on and look about—especially in and around London. So a Lord of Misrule figure, brought up, so to speak, from the country to the city, or from the traditional past into the changing present, could become on the Bankside the mouthpiece not merely for the dependent holiday scepticism which is endemic in a traditional society, but also for a dangerously self-sufficient everyday scepticism. When such a figure is set in an environment of sober-blooded great men behaving as opportunistically as he, the effect is to raise radical questions about social sanctities. At the end of *Part Two,* the expulsion of Falstaff is presented by the dramatist as getting rid of this threat; Shakespeare has recourse to a primitive procedure to meet a modern challenge. We shall find reason to question whether this use of ritual entirely succeeds.

But the main body of *Part Two,* what I am seeing as the trial, as against the expulsion, is wonderfully effective drama. The first step in trying Carnival, the first step in ceasing to be his subjects, would be to stop calling him "My Lord" and call him instead by his right name, Misrule. Now this is just the step which Falstaff himself takes for us at the outset of *Part Two;* when we first see him, he is setting himself up as an institution, congratulating himself on his powers *as* buffoon and wit. . . . In the early portion of *Part One* he never spoke in asides, but now he constantly confides his schemes and his sense of himself to the audience. We do not have to see through him, but watch instead from inside his façades as he imposes them on others. Instead of warm amplifications centered on himself, his talk now consists chiefly of bland impudence or dry, denigrating comments on the way of the world. Much of the comedy is an almost Jonsonian spectacle where we relish a witty knave gulling fools. (pp. 213-15)

Many of the basic structures in this action no doubt were shaped by morality-play encounters between Virtues and Vices, encounters which from my vantage here can be seen as cognate to the festive and scapegoat pattern. The trial of Falstaff is so effective *as drama* because no one conducts it—it happens. Falstaff, being a dramatic character, not a mummery, does not know when he has had his day. (p. 216)

But I do not think that the dramatist is equally successful in justifying the rejection of Falstaff as a mode of awareness. The problem is not in justifying rejection morally but in making the process cogent *dramatically,* as in *Part One* we reject magical majesty or intransigent chivalry. The bad luck which in *Part Two* Falstaff goes about collecting, by shaking the black yak's tail of his wit over people's heads, is the impulse to assume that nothing is sacred. In a play concerned with ruthless political maneuver, much of it conducted by impersonal state functionaries, Falstaff turns up as a functionary too, with his own version of maneuver and impersonality: "If the young dace be a bait for the old pike, I see no reason in the law of nature but I may snap at him" [*2 Henry IV*, III.ii.330-32]. Now this attitude is a most appropriate response to the behaviour of the high factions beneath whose struggles Falstaff plies his retail trade. In the Gaultree parleys, Lord John rebukes the Archbishop for his use of the counterfeited zeal of God—and then himself uses a counterfeited zeal of gentlemanly friendship to trick the rebels into disbanding their forces. The differences between his behavior and Falstaff's is of course that Lancaster has reasons of state on his side, a sanction supported, if not by legitimacy, at least by the desperate need for social order. This is a real difference, but a bare and harsh one. After all, Falstaff's little commonwealth of man has its pragmatic needs too: as he explains blandly to the Justice, he needs great infamy, because "he that buckles him in my belt cannot live in less" [*2 Henry IV*, I.ii.138-39].

The trouble with trying to get rid of this attitude merely by getting rid of Falstaff is that the attitude is too pervasive in the whole society of the play, whether public or private. It is too obviously *not* just a saturnalian mood, the extravagance of a moment: it is presented instead as in grain, as the way of the world. Shakespeare might have let the play end with this attitude dominant, a harsh recognition that life is a nasty business where the big fishes eat the little fishes, with the single redeeming consideration that political order is better than anarchy, so that there is a pragmatic virtue in loyalty to the power of the state. But instead the dramatist undertakes, in the last part of the play, to expel this view of the world and to dramatize the creation of legitimacy and sanctified social power. Although the final scenes are fascinating, with all sorts of illuminations, it seems to me that at this level they partly fail.

We have seen that Shakespeare typically uses ritual patterns of behavior and thought precisely in the course of making clear, by tragic or comic irony, that rituals have no *magical* efficacy. The reason for his failure at the close of *Part Two* is that at this point he himself uses ritual, not ironically transformed into drama, but magically. To do this involves a restriction instead of an extension of awareness. An extension of control and awareness is consummated in the epiphany of Hal's majesty while he is standing over Hotspur and Falstaff at the end of *Part One*. But *Part Two* ends with drastic restriction of awareness which goes with the embracing of magical modes of thought, not humorously but sentimentally. (pp. 216-17)

The priggish tone [of Hal's rejection speech], to which so many have objected, can be explained at one level as appropriate to the solemn occasion of a coronation. But it goes with a drastic narrowing of awareness. There are of course occasions in life when people close off parts of their minds—a coronation is a case in point: Shakespeare, it can be argued, is simply putting such an occasion into his play. But even his genius could not get around the fact that to block off awareness of irony is contradictory to the very nature of drama, which has as one of its functions the extension of such awareness. Hal's lines, redefining his holiday with Falstaff as a dream, and then despising the dream, seek to invalidate that holiday pole of life, instead of including it, as his lines on his old acquaintance did at the end of *Part One*. (Elsewhere in Shakespeare, to dismiss

dreams categorically is foolhardy.) And those lines about the thrice-wide grave: are they a threat or a joke? We cannot tell, because the sort of consciousness that would confirm a joke is being damped out: "Reply not to me with a fool-born jest" [*2 Henry IV*, V.v.55]. If ironies about Hal were expressed by the context, we could take the scene as the representation of his becoming a prig. But there is simply a blur in the tone, a blur which results, I think, from a retreat into magic by the *dramatist*, as distinct from his characters. Magically, the line about burying the belly is exactly the appropriate threat. It goes with the other images of burying sin and wildness and conveys the idea that the grave can swallow what Falstaff's belly stands for. To assume that one can cope with a pervasive attitude of mind by dealing physically with its most prominent symbol— what is this but magic-mongering? It is the same sort of juggling which we get in Henry IV's sentimental lines taking literally the name of the Jerusalem chamber in the palace. . . An inhibition of irony goes here with Henry's making the symbol do for the thing, just as it does with Hal's expulsion of Falstaff. A return to an official view of the sanctity of state is achieved by sentimental use of magical relations.

We can now suggest a few tentative conclusions of a general sort about the relation of comedy to ritual. It appears that comedy uses ritual in the process of redefining ritual as the expression of particular personalities in particular circumstances. The heritage of ritual gives universality and depth. The persons of the drama make the customary gestures developed in ritual observance, and, in doing so, they project in a wholehearted way attitudes which are not normally articulated at large. At the same time, the dramatization of such gestures involves being aware of their relation to the whole of experience in a way which is not necessary for the celebrants of a ritual proper. In the actual observance of customary misrule, the control of the disruptive motives which the festivity expresses is achieved by the group's recognition of the place of the whole business within the larger rhythm of their continuing social life. No one need decide, therefore, whether the identifications involved in the ceremony are magically valid or merely expressive. But in the drama, perspective and control depend on presenting, along with the ritual gestures, an expression of a social situation out of which they grow. So the drama must control magic by reunderstanding it as imagination: dramatic irony must constantly dog the wish that the mock king be real, that the self be all the world or set all the world at naught. When, through a failure of irony, the dramatist presents ritual as magically valid, the result is sentimental, since drama lacks the kind of control which in ritual comes from the auditors' being participants. Sentimental "drama," that which succeeds in being neither comedy nor tragedy, can be regarded from this vantage as theater used as a substitute for ritual, without the commitment to participation and discipline proper to ritual nor the commitment to the fullest understanding proper to comedy or tragedy.

Historically, Shakespeare's drama can be seen as part of the process by which our culture has moved from absolutist modes of thought towards a historical and psychological view of man. But though the Renaissance moment made the tension between a magical and an empirical view of man particularly acute, this pull is of course always present: it is the tension between the heart and the world. By incarnating ritual as plot and character, the dramatist finds an embodiment for the heart's drastic gestures while recognizing how the world keeps comically and tragically giving them the lie. (pp. 219-21)

C. L. Barber, "Rule and Misrule in 'Henry IV'," in Shakespeare's Festive Comedy: A Study of Dramatic Form and Its Relation to Social Custom *by C. L. Barber, World Publishing Co., 1963, pp. 192-221.*

JAN KOTT   (essay date 1964)

[Kott is a Polish-born critic and professor of English and comparative literature now residing in the United States. In his well-known study Shakespeare, Our Contemporary *he interprets several of the plays as presenting a tragic vision of history in which one tyrant succeeds another in an endless and futile process. Kott calls this historical pattern the Grand Mechanism. He considers* Henry IV, *however, as a play quite different from the other histories, claiming that it is the only one that presents a true protagonist and that can be regarded as "cheerful." Kott's essay was first published in his* Szkice o Szekspirze *in 1964.]*

Of all the important works written by Shakespeare before 1600, i.e. in what nineteenth-century scholars called his optimistic period, only *Henry IV* can be called a cheerful play. In both the *Richard* plays, and in the other *Henrys*, history is the only *dramatis persona* of the tragedy. The protagonist of *Henry IV* is Falstaff.

The great feudal barons are still butchering one another. King Henry IV, who had recently deposed Richard II, and let him be murdered together with his followers, did not atone for his crimes by a journey to the Holy Land. The allies who have put him on the throne are rebelling. For them he is a new tyrant. Wales and Scotland rise. History will begin from the beginning. But in *Henry IV* history is only one of many actors in the drama. It is being played out not only in the royal palace and in courtyards of feudal castles; not only on battlefields, in dungeons of the Tower, and in the London street where frightened townsmen are hurrying by. Nearby the royal palace there is a tavern called "The Boar's Head". In it Falstaff is king. Somehow, between the chapters of an austere historical chronicle there has been interpolated a rich Renaissance comedy about a fat knight, unable for many years to see his own knees under his huge belly. (pp. 48-9)

Shakespeare never renounces his great confrontations. It is only that he poses them differently. Against the feudal barons butchering one another he sets the gargantuan figure of Falstaff. Sir John Falstaff not only personifies the Renaissance lust for life and thunderous laughter at heaven and hell, at the crown and all other laws of the realm. The fat knight possesses a plebeian wisdom and experience. He will not let history take him in. He scoffs at it.

There are two excellent scenes in *Henry IV*. The first one shows Falstaff as a newly created captain walking with his men to the place where the army has assembled. He has recruited only cripples and the poorest wretches in rags and tatters, because all those who had a little money could evade enlistment. The young prince looks aghast at this sorry army. But Falstaff, undisturbed, replies:

> Tut, tut! good enough to toss; food for powder,
> food for powder. They'll fill a pit as well as
> better. Tush, man, mortal men, mortal men.
>
> *[1 Henry IV, IV. ii. 65-8]*

This entire scene might have been put, as it stands, into a play by Brecht. And only on reading it does one realize how much Brecht has taken from Shakespeare.

The other scene shows Falstaff on the battlefield. He soliloquizes while looking for the best place to hide himself:

> What is honour? A word. What is that word
> honour? Air. A trim reckoning! Who hath it?
> He that died a Wednesday. Doth he feel it? No.
> Doth he hear it? No. 'Tis insensible then? Yea,
> to the dead. But will it not live with the living?
> No. Why? Detraction will not suffer it. Therefore I'll none of it. Honour is a mere scutcheon—and so ends my catechism.
>
> *[1 Henry IV, V. i. 133-41]*

In *Henry IV* two notions of England are continuously set in contrast to each other. The feudal barons slaughter one another. The young crown prince robs merchants on the highways and has a gay time in taverns with a band of rascals. *Henry IV* is one of the few apologetic dramas written by Shakespeare. The young prince grows up to become a wise and brave king. There is, however, a sting on the moral. It appears that the company of Falstaff and cutpurses is a far better school for royalty than the feudal slaughter. (pp. 49-50)

Jan Kott, "The Kings," in his Shakespeare, Our Contemporary, *translated by Boleslaw Taborski, Anchor Books, 1966, pp. 3-56.*

MURIEL C. BRADBROOK   (essay date 1965)

[The following essay was originally a paper delivered at the Shakespeare Seminar in 1965.]

There was once a summer school . . . where in two successive hours, a first speaker said that anyone who doubted the unity of the great continuous ten-act play [*Henry IV*, Parts 1 and 2] was disqualified to understand Shakespeare; while a second said that anyone who thought *Henry IV*, Part 2 more than a feeble 'encore' must be illiterate. The link that I would see is that of adaptability, the imaginative ability to create a part and to play it. In Part 1, this playful, heroic, or sometimes merely crafty capacity distinguishes each of the main characters. In the second part, the role-taking (to use familiar jargon) is subtle, Machiavellian and by no means subjected to plain ethical judgements of right and wrong. In dismissing Falstaff, Henry V appears both kingly *and* treacherous—because his two roles can no longer be played by the same man; the King cannot be true to the reveller of Eastcheap. In the play as a whole, the width of reference and ambiguity of response shows Shakespeare's full maturity. . . . 'We are much beholden to Machiavelli,' said Bacon, 'who openly and unfeignedly declares . . . what men do, and not what they ought to do.' A famous book on princely education, Elyot's *Book of the Governor*, had aimed in the early sixteenth century at producing a traditionally good, well-equipped and high-principled ruler. Machiavelli perceived the emergence of secular sovereignty; and the rest of the world was horrified at what he saw. . . . *Henry IV*, Part 2 came out shortly after the first edition of Bacon's essays; these men, however different their minds, were observing the same phenomenon. Shakespeare gave it imaginative form, Bacon gave it definition. (pp. 168-69)

Against Falstaff's instinctive mobility, Hal's role-taking looks deliberate. He early casts himself for the role of Percy, playing it in a mixture of admiration and irony; in his Revels, he plays the part of Prodigal Prince, with Falstaff as his father; and then, assuming the King, deposes and banishes Falstaff as later he will do in earnest. But he can play the potboy in a leather apron equally well. The fantasy life of Eastcheap (even the robbery is a jest), playing at capital crime, at exhortation, at soldiering, is sharply dismissed by the prince, even while he enjoys it. It is Idleness—according to Puritan opponents, the capital sin of all players. (p. 172)

Henry IV, as in the play of *Richard II*, stands for the life of judgement against that of the fantasy and imagination; it is his superior skill in deploying his forces that defeats the dash and fire of Hotspur.

Percy's scornful mimicry of the popinjay lord reveals that he, like Hal and Falstaff, lives in the life of the imagination. To think of a plot is enough for him; he can feed on his motto *Esperance*; mappery and closet-war are quite alien to him. Yet when he meets the more primitive imagination of Glendower with its cressets and fiery shapes, its prophecies out of the common lore, Hotspur baits Glendower mercilessly. Glendower is Hotspur's Falstaff. (p. 173)

Harry of Monmouth and Hal of Eastcheap are different roles for the same young man, who had learnt many-sidedness among the pots of ale where Hotspur contemptuously places him. The opening soliloquy shows the Prince as a passionless manipulator of events, whereas Hotspur is carried away by rage, ardour or mockery. In his presence, calculation fails; his uncle Worcester, the supreme Machiavellian gives up schooling him and at the last dupes him. (p. 175)

Interplay of character, exchange of roles, melting of mood into mood and free range combine to give Part 1 its 'divine fluidity'. All is lucent, untrammelled in the consequence. The consequences are presented in Part 2.

Here the characters are sharper, clearer, more definite; they do not blend but contrast. Instead of lambent interplay, division or fusion of roles is provided, with clear separation of man and Office. There is more oration and less action: the action belongs to the common people, while the King utters his great soliloquies and Falstaff talks directly to the audience on the virtues of sherris sack. (p. 177)

No one, least of all Bolingbroke, denies the guilt of usurpation or the conflicts it brings. Treachery in the political sphere replaces the mock robberies of Part 1; the presiding Genius is not Valour but Wit, not Chivalry but Statecraft. God send us His peace, but not the Duke of Lancaster's, the commons might exclaim. (p. 179)

It has been said that we always fundamentally talk about ourselves, or aspects of ourselves; so, if Falstaff represents something of Shakespeare's own assessment of himself, may not Pistol be a player's nightmare? A parody of Ned Alleyn's rant, perhaps, but also an embodiment of Shakespeare's deepest fear—a wild tatterdemalion spouter of crazy verses. Hopelessly mistaken in all he says and does, thrown off even by Falstaff. Pistol embodies the life of dream, of playmaking at its most distorted and absurd. It is fitting that he brings the deceptive good news of Hal's succession to Falstaff. (pp. 179-80)

The audience feels no compulsion to take the side of law and order; indeed the tragic themes predominate in reading, but on the stage this is Falstaff's play. The imaginative life of the action lies less in the sick fancies, the recollections and foreshadowing of Bolingbroke than in the day dreams and old wives' tales of Mistress Quickly and Justice Shallow. Neither Hal nor Falstaff daff the world aside with quite the carelessness they had shown before. (pp. 183-84)

The uncertainty of the public view of Truth has been demonstrated. 'Thou art a blessed fellow', says Truth's champion, Prince Hal, to Poins, 'to think as every many thinks; never a man's thought in the world keeps the roadway better than thine.' There is no need for an unconditional identification with Falstaff; indeed there is no possibility of it; for the virtue of Shakespeare is to present many incompatibles not reconciled, but harmonized. (pp. 184-85)

> *Muriel C. Bradbrook, "'King Henry IV'," in* Strat-ford Papers: 1965-67, *edited by B.A.W. Jackson, McMaster University Library Press, 1969, pp. 168-85.*

A. R. HUMPHREYS   (essay date 1966)

[*Humphreys, reviewing the long debate on the unity of* 1 *and* 2 Henry IV, *argues in favor of their being considered a single, unified work. This conclusion follows in the tradition of such earlier critics as Samuel Johnson (1765), Hermann Ulrici (1839), G. G. Gervinus (1849-50), and E.M.W. Tillyard (1944). Humphreys also concurs with Clifford Leech (1951) that Part Two is more "thoughtful" and "inquiring" than its predecessor. Other critics who have voiced this sentiment include Robert Adger Law (1927) and L. C. Knights (1959).*]

Discussions of how Part 2 [of *Henry IV*] relates to Part 1 go back over two centuries. In his *Critical Observations on Shakespeare* (1746) John Upton [see excerpt above] observed that

> these plays are independent each of the other. . . . To call [them], *first and second parts,* is as injurious to the author-character of Shakespeare as it would be to Sophocles, to call his two plays on Oedipus, *first and second parts of King Oedipus.*

To this, Johnson [see excerpt above, 1765] firmly rejoined in his edition:

> Mr *Upton* thinks these two plays improperly called the *first* and *second parts* of *Henry* the *fourth* . . . [yet they] will appear to every reader, who shall peruse them without ambition of critical discoveries, to be so connected that the second is merely a sequel to the first; to be two only because they are too long to be one.
>
> (pp. xxi-xxii)

But did Shakespeare, perhaps, mean to stop with Hotspur's defeat? This is most unlikely. In Part 1, five scenes point significantly towards events after Shrewsbury:

(*a*) In I. ii Falstaff repeatedly asks Hal what will happen 'when thou art king'. Hal answers cryptically, but clearly time will show. Hal's soliloquy in that scene promies that idleness will not always be upheld and that he will shine forth unclouded (this, though Shrewsbury is an earnest of it, must point to the coronation);

(*b*) In II. iv the theme of banishment is sounded. 'Banish plump Jack, and banish all the world', Falstaff says, as a pure hypothesis: 'I do, I will,' Hal replies, though no one pays any attention;

(*c*) in IV. iv the Archbishop, fearing Hotspur's defeat, perhaps further hostilities by writing to his friends, including Scroop and Mowbray (neither at Shrewsbury, but Mowbray to be a leading rebel in Part 2);

(*d*) in V. v the King is equally anticipating further action. He sends Westmoreland and Prince John 'To meet Northumberland and the prelate Scroop', while he and Hal go off against Glendower;

(*e*) and, not least, in V. iv, there are aspects of prince John and Falstaff which call for further treatment. Presumably Prince John figures at Shrewsbury (unhistorically—he was only thirteen) because, like the archbishop, he is to appear in a later action and so has already engaged Shakespeare's interest. John, not his elder brother Thomas of Clarence, must be chosen because of his later Gaultree eminence; Gaultree is already foreseen, and Shakespeare is unobtrusively preparing both leaders there, the Prince and the Archbishop. As for Falstaff, this is the scene where, after Hotspur's death, he follows 'for reward'. He is at the height of his prospects, favoured as never before, with Hal countenancing the most preposterous of his japes, and the looked-for retribution is still not in sight. Clearly, both serious and comic themes require further stages of the action.

Those critics who consider Part 2 as an 'unpremeditated addition', therefore, are going against the evidence. They have on their side the fact that Shrewsbury is a wonderful climax and Part 1 superbly handled, and acceptable in itself. But of course no play patently dependent on another would satisfy its customers; historical dramas must be dramatically complete, even though history itself is incomplete. Shrewsbury is an interim triumph, but the stress of the whole story requires an end beyond Shrewsbury. No matter where Shakespeare looked in the chronicles he would find that the expected counterpart to the overthrow of Richard II was the unquiet time of Henry IV—that was what the reign of Henry meant. And Falstaff must curve downwards to his doom. So the heroics and gaiety of Part 1 must yield to the darker history and more ominous comedy of Part 2. Part 2 is the necessary complement of Hal's evolution, and Henry's, and Falstaff's. (pp. xxiv-xxv)

Shakespeare shows every sign of strong interest, from the lines in which Rumour conjures up a nation in tumult, through the tragic urgency of Northumberland's and Morton's exchanges and the council of war, to the confrontation of the opponents. Henry appears late and infrequently, but there is a moving power in his utterance. Falstaff lacks Hal, but his exchanges with the Lord Chief Justice, Mistress Quickly, and Shallow are boldly impudent. Shakespeare is extending his range in the psychology of ambiguous motives and making that exploration of the national life of which Eastcheap, in its new Hogarthian character, and Gloucestershire are the remarkable discoveries. Professor Clifford Leech has indicated in Part 2 a unity of more thoughtful tone and inquiring implications than in Part 1. The morality-elements endemic in much of Part 1's idiom, as well as in Hal's poise between opposed incentives, are here more deeply realized; human life is, in general, more complicated and precarious than the confident enjoyable matter it had been in Part 1. More miscellaneous though it is, and less co-ordinated by a total creative impulse, Part 2 is hardly less powerful as an act of the imagination, with a vitality and indeed violence in its comedy, a passion and thoughtfulness in its history, without which the canon of the plays would be much the poorer. It is unified by the powerful treatment of a nexus of themes. (pp. xliii-xliv)

Playgoers have discussed Falstaff's dismissal for centuries. (p. lviii)

Shakespeare's problem was not wholly tractable. The Wild-Prince stories presented a licentious ribald miraculously con-

verted, which was material rather for a romance than a history. A Wild Prince, on the other hand, whom his fellow-nobles knew to be grooming himself for responsibility would contravene the chronicles and forfeit that dramatic emergence into virtue which was integral to the legend. Shakespeare effects a skilful compromise. Hal is reputedly dissolute but, as far as one sees him, harmless enough. He is aware of his destiny. While the crown is remote, and Falstaff's japes are innocuous, he enjoys the Boar's Head, though hinting that the revelry must end. As the accession grows nearer and Falstaff grosser, he avoids him. Three things make his course seem heartless in a way Shakespeare probably never intended: these are Hal's soliloquy . . . , Warwick's declaration that Hal frequents the Boar's Head simply to recognize and disclaim vice . . . , and the rejection speech. But these three need taking with care. Hal's soliloquy is a morality-manifesto rather than heartless policy, Warwick is providing a gloss to console the dying King, and the rejection speech is official rather than personal, a required public demonstration. The general tenor of Hal's evolution deserves respect. . . . The opposed evolutions of Falstaff and Hal, rightly observed, will dispel any notion that Falstaff is scurvily treated; only the most careless reading could take the rejection as a melodrama prepared by a calculating Prince against a hoodwinked crony. . . .

> 'Dickens', Sir Alfred Duff Cooper suggests [in his *Sergeant Shakespeare*], would have settled Falstaff down with a pension in a country cottage, with honeysuckle round the door, and a hospitable inn hard by, where the old gentleman, grown quite respectable, would have recounted tales of the riotous past, to the wondering yokels, and where the King would have paid him an occasional visit. But Shakespeare did not live in a sentimental age.

In fact, unsentimental though Falstaff's dismissal is, Shakespeare provided a future for him at the end of *2 Henry IV* not far different from that thus humorously described—though no Shakespearean Falstaff, one hopes, would grow 'quite respectable', whatever a Dickensian one might do. The rejection, in short, is necessary, well-prepared, and executed without undue severity.

'And yet', Mr. Dipak Nandy writes to me, 'might not something more be said? One asks why, despite all these considerations, one's feelings are nevertheless jarred. Why is there, in Morgann's terms [see excerpt above, 1777], such a gap between one's understanding and one's impressions?' He makes three suggestions. First, the rejection dislocates not only Falstaff's self-esteem but our very 'taking' of him as a splendid performer in his own role. However reprehensible in real terms, he has appreciatively acted out the great enlargement of comedy, and 'the success of a role depends in large part on the acceptance of the role-player *as a role-player*.' Falstaff not only has been enjoyable, he has shown himself a virtuoso in relishing his part. 'I know thee not, old man' strips him bare of the gorgeous assumptions he has donned for our pleasure, and turns him into an aged cast-off: 'in rejection, the multitude of roles we call Falstaff seems to become suddenly humanized into a person; and this', Mr. Nandy observes, 'I find pathetic'. Second, the terms of Henry's reproof—fool, jester, a dream he despises—though accurate in sense, destroy that balance of judgments so well held in Part I, by which Falstaff is a rascal and yet contributes wisdom to a world of harsh purpose. They invite us to assume the same tone, to accuse ourselves in the same terms, as Henry uses; and this we are wholly unwilling to do. To do so would in some sense be treachery to ourselves. So strict a rejection of what has pleased us may be the tribute duty owes to responsiblity; yet it impoverishes our sense of life. And third, though the rejection is inevitable, its very necessity marks a narrowing (not less regrettable because absolutely requisite) in Henry himself. 'Are we not', Mr. Nandy writes, 'witnessing the disjunction between the King and the man that the histories stress as, at moments of crisis, their kings have to confront in their own souls the realization that they are men no more? Is it not possible for the sentimentalists to argue that the sense of loss they feel at the rejection derives not only from the loss of Falstaff, not only from the decease of a human relationship, but also from the loss of something, some generosity perhaps (not in what he *does* to Falstaff, which is mild enough, but in what he *says*), in Henry himself, from the feeling that the transformation of Hal into Henry involves— and that ''necessarily''—some sacrifice?'

This is said well; it reflects something of what we feel; and we cannot but regret that stroke which eclipses the gaiety of nations and impoverishes the public stock of harmless pleasure. Yet taking all in all—the seamier streaks, the dangerously predatory impulses, revealed in Falstaff, Hal's disciplining through grief, the noble idea of justice that dominates the accession, the need for unmistakable severance, and the comfortable leniency of the sentence—it is still possible to hold that Shakespeare *has* here achieved a balanced complexity of wisdom not inferior to that in Part I, the acknowledgement of necessity with its double face of grief and consolation; that Hal as deepened, not narrowed; and that Falstaff (at a distance of ten miles) can fleet the time carelessly with his cronies, remedying the long consumption of his purse at the expense of the royal exchequer. His well-wishers need ask no more. (pp. lix-lxi)

A. R. Humphreys, in his introduction to The Second Part of King Henry IV *by William Shakespeare, edited by A. R. Humphreys, Methuen & Co Ltd, 1966, pp. xi-xci.*

SIGURD BURCKHARDT　(essay date 1966)

[*Burckhardt takes issue with E.M.W. Tillyard's theory that Shakespeare's histories embody a stable ''Elizabethan world picture'' influenced by a prevailing ''Tudor myth'' (see excerpt above, 1944). This ''myth,'' according to Tillyard, claimed that the chaos and tribulations experienced by England between the reigns of Henry IV and Richard III, culminating in civil war, were a form of divine punishment exacted upon the kingdom for the usurpation of the throne by Henry IV and the continued illegitimate reign of his successors. The ''myth'' maintains that order and legitimate rule were not reestablished until the accession of Henry VII and his marriage to the Princess of York—a union which reunited the two rightful families to the throne. In the excerpt below, Burckhardt argues that the ''Tudor myth'' regards the movement of history as ''restorative''—towards a reassertion of cosmic order following a period of chaos and civil strife—but that Shakespeare's tetralogy on Prince Hal does not satisfy this assumption, but instead ''moves toward the accession and 'victorious acts' of a king whose title is almost non-lineal, one short link removed from the breach.'' For a similar interpretation of Shakespeare's relation to the ''Tudor myth,'' see the excerpt by Edward Pechter (1980). Burckhardt's essay was written in 1966.*]

Symmetry is so satisfying an arrangement because it gives scope to our secret lust for combat and disorder even while reassuring us that we are ultimately safe. We may think as we wish of Hal's famous soliloquy in *I Henry IV*—''I know you

all, and will a while uphold''—we *are* reassured by it. Between rebellion and misrule, between hot pride and slippery wit, sword-edged honor and fat-bellied self-indulgence, we know there is an axis of symmetry and a *tertius ridens*. Order will emerge in the end, not necessarily because it has proved its superior title but because the two kinds of disorder will kill and çancel each other.

I Henry IV seems to reach this point of satisfying resolution when Hal stands between what he assumes to be the corpses of Hotspur and Falstaff and speaks over each the appropriate obsequies. If the stage were simply a mirror of reality, its order and disorders, here the ordering would seem achieved. But of course it is not; no sooner has Hal walked off than disorder arises in massive palpability:

> 'Sblood, 'twas time to counterfeit. . . . Counterfeit? I lie, I am no counterfeit. To die is to be a counterfeit, for he is but the counterfeit of a man who hath not the life of a man; but to counterfeit dying when a man thereby liveth, is to be no counterfeit, but the true and perfect image of life indeed. . . . I am afraid of this gunpowder Percy though he be dead. How, if he should counterfeit too and rise? By my faith, I am afraid he would prove the better counterfeit. Therefore I'll make him sure; yea, and I'll swear I killed him. Why may not he rise as well as I?
>
> [*1 Henry IV*, V. iv. 113-26]

Not only *may* Hotspur rise but he *will*—as soon as the scene is ended and his ''body''has been lugged off the stage. Like other leading actors in tragedies and histories, he makes a living by counterfeit dying, and to do so ''is to be no counterfeit, but the true and perfect image of life indeed.'' Falstaff's rising destroys all kinds of reassuring symmetries, the first being that of stage and world. *Sub specie realitatis*, his claim to being Hotspur's killer is exactly as good, or bad, as Hal's, just as his pretense of having died on the field of honor is exactly as good, or bad, as Hotspur's. Simply by refusing to submit to the agreeable fiction that there is an axis of symmetry between on-stage and off-stage and that reality and its representation correspond to each other in perfect balance, Falstaff throws us and the play back into dizzying confusion. (pp. 146-48)

Falstaff is ready to split the credit for Hotspur's killing: if Hal supports him in his ''lie,'' he will sustain Hal in Hal's ''lie.'' And this bargain does represent some sort of truth, or at least of justice. For no matter who has run his sword through Hotspur in the make-belief of the stage, dramatically and morally it is Falstaff's role to kill him and to be killed by him; in the dialectic of the play's structure, he is a hero, while Hal is the *tertius ridens*. Strangely, it is he, the creature of Shakespeare's imagination rather than of history, who in the end asserts himself as the reality principle incarnate, reminding us that disorder is not slain as neatly and inexpensively as the calculated symmetrics of dialectics would have us believe. (pp. 148-49)

I Henry IV is designed toward the release of combat. We watch the opponents quarrel; lay their plans, and gather their forces; march toward Shrewsbury, and fail in last-minute negotiations, until by Act v, scene iii, we are ready for that discharge of tension which of itself seems to create a sense of order.

2 Henry IV promises to repeat the design. Once again the rebels plot and march; once again the king takes countermeasures. But this time the encounter takes place in the first part of Act

IV—and in Gaultree Forest of infamous memory. We are denied the release of battle; the confrontation ends in the treachery of John of Lancaster. The rebels, promised redress of their grievances, are tricked into dismissing their army; as soon as they have done so, they are seized and executed, while their dispersing soldiers are pursued and slain.

In the innocent days of moral and psychological criticism, John's bloody equivocation used to be roundly condemned; critics made no secret of their distaste for a play which seemed, for its satisfactory outcome, to depend on so mean a stratagem. Of late we have become more sophisticated; we talk about the larger political design, the education of Hal, and the utter wickedness of rebellion in Tudor doctrine. We are warned not to take Gaultree Forest too seriously: for an Elizabethan audience, rebels deserved no better. What Prince John dispenses is, after all, a kind of "justice," though somewhat "rigorous": "Temperamentally [Hal] strikes the balance between . . . John and . . . Falstaff . . . The justice of John in his cold-blooded treatment of the rebels verges on rigour; Falstaff has no general standard of justice at all" [see excerpt above by E.M.W. Tillyard, 1944].

I suggest that if an interpreter finds himself driven, by the tenor of his argument, into such euphemizing, there is something badly wrong with the argument. We always misread Shakespeare if our reading compels us to make light of cruelty and treachery—especially where these are not condemned and in some manner disowned in the play itself. (pp. 149-50)

Two things about *2 Henry IV* are clear: it is designed to culminate in Hal's accession; and it disappoints our expectation (aroused by the play itself) of reaching that point through the "plain shock and even play of battle." To gauge our disappointment, we need only imagine the following: that Shakespeare had written *Henry IV* in one part, climaxing in the battle of Shrewsbury; that the king had died right after the battle, so that Hal's accession would have followed immediately upon his battlefield triumph; and that Hal had at that point exposed Falstaff's cowardice and lies, making them the occasion of rejecting him and signifying his own resolution to be a just and sober as well as valiant king. The distortion and telescoping of historical facts would have been no worse than what Shakespeare permits himself elsewhere; and I am by no means the first to suggest that such a way of managing the story would have been dramatically much more satisfying than the two-part arrangement Shakespeare chose. (pp. 156-57)

In fact, up to the point of his seizing the crown, it appears that Hal is quite deliberately being kept *out of* [Part II]. Of the only two scenes he is given prior to that point, the second (II, iv) is almost wholly dominated by Falstaff and his gentlewomen; the Prince's puny jest is just sufficient—and is *meant*—to remind us of the lost glories of the corresponding scene in Part I (II, iv). (pp. 158-59)

Clearly the theory that in Part II Hal proves himself just (as in Part I he proved himself valorous), while it has a certain *a priori* plausibility, is sadly lacking in dramatic substance. But just as clearly the play is *about* Hal and culminates in his accession. What, then, is Hal's role; what does he *do*, except remind us that he is doing nothing? The answer is simple: prior to his accession, Hal has one role only—that of heir, of *successor*. (p. 161)

Our seeing Hal as stripped of all roles except that of successor helps us account for several oddities. It accounts for the omission of the scene in which Hal strikes the Chief Justice; it

accounts for his non-appearance at court and his non-participation in the affairs of the realm. (p. 162)

It would seem that we need to think carefully about the problem of *succession*. What is it? What does it rest on? What does it entail? (p. 163)

It has been shown that the governing theme of the history plays, derived by Shakespeare from Hall's *Union of the Noble and Illustre Fameiles of Lancastre and Yorke,* is that of the disturbed succession. But I shall argue that for Shakespeare the disturbance was vastly more radical and encompassing than we have realized; that it involved not merely England but the entire moral universe; and, most importantly, that its consequences were *irreversible*. To put it somewhat provocatively: in the deposition of Richard II Shakespeare discovered the decomposition of a world picture; we are wrong in assuming that his world picture was still that of Hall and Tudor doctrine. (p. 164)

At first glance it seems obvious that Shakespeare's histories recognize only one mode of succession as truly legitimate: Primogeniture. Other modes—particularly succession by combat, as described in Frazer's *Golden Bough*—seem clearly illegitimate; indeed they are not alternate modes so much as lapses into chaos. (Succession by popular election can readily be interpreted as a variant of succession by combat.) All the same it would be very easy for an anthropological critic to read the history plays as recording a series of successions by combat, in which kings who are lacking in potency are supplanted (and usually killed) by others who prove their right to the title by their ability to seize it. Indeed, if this critic were rigorously descriptive and inferred the law of succession in the histories strictly from the actual events, he could not possibly arrive at the law of primogeniture. Richard II to Henry IV, Henry VI to Edward IV, Edward V to Richard III, Richard III to Henry VII—by the combat mode this succession is close to "unbroken," certainly much less broken than under the mode of primogeniture. Depending on the model we choose, the same sequence will appear as either reasonably orderly or disastrously chaotic.

Of course, if we chose the combat model we would completely pervert the meaning of Hall and other Tudor historians and do at least some violence to Shakespeare's. Still I cannot help asking: how much violence? Tudor political theorists and propagandists were always ready to quote St. Paul to the effect that all power is from God, whence it followed that the subject owed obedience, as a matter of religious duty, to the *de facto* ruler. It does not take much thought to discover that this argument implies a combat model of succession; a little more thought may even lead to the suspicion that there is a remarkably close, perhaps necessary, connection between this model and a divinely ruled universe. However that may be, the Tudors were not foolhardy enough to rest their title on the Pauline principle alone; a great deal of effort and ingenuity was expended in proving that the title was (primogenitively) legitimate. Tudor propaganda left little to chance; it worked both sides of the royal road. The title was legitimate beyond question; and even if it was not, it still was. Heads the king won, tails the doubting subject lost—his head most likely if he was rash enough to ask for the toss.

I do not mean that the deception was conscious; the apologists of the Tudor establishment were, I expect, all honorable men, and in any case there is hardly a limit to the inconsistencies men manage sincerely to believe where their needs and vital interests are at stake. . . . Under these circumstances it was natural that even thoughtful men should, as occasions demanded, feel quite untroubled about applying one or the other of these concepts of legitimacy, or even both simultaneously, without realizing that they entailed mutually inconsistent world pictures. But I believe that Shakespeare—who was a more than ordinarily thoughtful man—did see the inconsistency. (pp. 166-68)

I am aware that my ideas on the meaning of "succession" must seem wholly un-Shakespearean in spirit. Few things are as firmly established as that the history plays adopt and follow the great scheme of Tudor history. Far from being caused by the law of primogeniture, England's troubles from Richard II to Henry VII were both the result of and the punishment for the *breach* of that law. (We note in passing how in this account the two models—causal and juridical—are mixed.) Of all the lessons to be learned from history, that is the one most insistently pointed by Hall, as well as by many of Shakespeare's characters. Even Henry V recites it when he implores God's help in the night before Agincourt.

The argument, I grant, looks strong; all the same I find it less and less tenable. What does the orthodox scheme entail? Most importantly it entails the belief that in the long run, if not in the short, the movement of history is *restorative*. The cosmic order has been disturbed by man; after a while, and often at great cost to man, it reasserts itself. The scheme of Hall's *Union* satisfies this assumption perfectly; it traces English history from the fatal breach to the happy restoration. But Shakespeare's histories do *not* satisfy it; his second tetralogy ends in the middle of the story, with the usurper Henry V at the high tide of glory and good fortune. (pp. 172-73)

The structure of the second tetralogy . . . is *not* restorative. It moves toward the accession and "victorious acts" of a king whose title is almost non-lineal, one short link removed from the breach. This king is not sent by God as a redeemer; we observe him grooming himself for his role with the cool calculation of Richard III (though of course by wholly different means). I think we need to be cautious about calling Henry V Shakespeare's "ideal king"; but to a remarkable degree he is *self-made*. His title is legitimized largely by his self-nurtured qualities and by his achievements; when God "crowns" him with victory, that legitimation is *ex post facto*. (p. 174)

We misread the second tetralogy if we think of it as "really" the first. The chronology that counts is not that of English history but that of Shakespeare's plays—which is to say, of his development as a dramatist. There is no evidence for considering the second tetralogy a revision of some lost plays; but there are some very good reasons for considering it as a revision of the first tetralogy—as a revision dictated by the discovery that restoration is a false ideal. Time, like a line, moves in one direction only; and drama, especially historical drama, is action in time. (p. 176)

The burden of my argument—the point of this interpretation of the Hal trilogy—is this: Shakespeare, having discovered that the "most fine, most honoured, most renowned" golden unity of the Elizabethan world picture was in truth a lethal mixture of two mutually inconsistent and severally inadequate models of succession, but that to reject both meant imprisonment and sterility, first tried a dialectical solution (*I Henry IV*) and next a dis-solution (*2 Henry IV* and *Henry V*). The solution, he found, rested on a *petitio principii* [begging the question]; the several dis-solutions entailed severe sacrifices—most importantly, the sacrifice of true legitimacy. Each in its own way

was "swoll'n with some other grief"; but it was a grief that had to be borne and born, if bearing, generation, succession was to continue.

I realize that I have credited Shakespeare with what appears to be a very modern and still largely scientific concept: that of the *model*. I must now credit him with another, closely related one: *complementarity*. I am in fact saying that, some three centuries before Niels Bohr, Shakespeare discovered the need of complementarity—i.e., of operating with two mutually inconsistent and severally inadequate models because, and as long as, a single, consistent, and adequate model has not been found. Complementarity differs from and is superior to mixing because it remains aware of its "illegitimacy" and *pays the price* of choosing one model or the other. It does not pretend to be a solution, hence does not close the road of discovery but on the contrary compels us to take the risk of following it. Its passionate demand for order forces us to leave the safe prison of a static, once-for-all world picture, to suffer the grief of imperfection and disorder and the joy of genuine action and creativity. Complementarity, in short, asserts the value of *human action in time*—which is to say, of history, of drama.

I credit Shakespeare with discovering these concepts not because I want to "modernize" him but because I see no other way of accounting for the observable facts of the second tetralogy. How else are we to explain the sequence Shrewsbury-Gaultree Forest-Agincourt? How else are we to explain the strange frustration of our combativeness, which appears to be the "law" of *2 Henry IV*, and on the other hand the almost total indulgence of this same combativeness which governs most of *Henry V*? . . .

How—to mention one more item from what could easily be extended into a very long list—are we to explain the fact that the crown comes to Hal both by seizure and by lineal descent—that he takes, before the appointed time, what becomes his at the appointed time? Why this filial, lineal piety so oddly yoked with creative impatience? Wherever we look, we find complementarity.

Hal's seizure of the crown is the figure of Shakespeare's "seizure" of history. Of course, he found the episode in his sources, but that is precisely the point. He likewise found other episodes in his sources—most signally that of Hal's striking the Chief Justice. Many of these he reduced to dramatic insignificance, but this one he makes his own. Not wilfully, not for theatrical effect, but because in it he discovers the very metaphor of his effort and enterprise: to write "creative history," to find meaning and order both in the succession of historical events and in the succession of his dramatic explorations. Truly and reverently looked at, recorded history answers *to* his quest and question; but it does not *answer* it. Instead of providing him with the definitive model of succession and success, to be retraced by him in simple piety—or instead of meeting him with blank silence and leaving him free to impose on it whatever pattern happens to suit him—it supplies him with a metaphor. And the metaphor is one of *complementarity*, of either-or. It is neither a mixture nor a synthesis, but a metaphor: that strange entity which demands to be analytically dissolved because it *means* and creatively "made good" because it *is*. It is pregnant, hence promises birth; but the birth is never certain, while labor and pain *are* certain. Is even the father certain? Can we be sure of legitimacy? Will the offspring be the child of passion or of duty, of self-assertive lust or submissive routine? There are no guarantees, only the risk and the will—the need—to order.

To state my argument in terms of the "price paid," the following schema emerges. Richard II, refusing to pay any price whatever, in the end pays most heavily; he finds himself compelled to retreat into the sterile though poignant pathos of non-success and non-succession. Prince Hal of *1 Henry IV* tries to avoid paying the price by dialectical design: he exploits the combat model by pitting disorder against rebellion, but hopes to escape the consequences of this model by superior management. He is literally the "know-you-all," the omniscient and almost omnipotent dramatist, seemingly involved but actually secure. And he almost brings it off; *1 Henry IV* is not by accident the "best play" of the trilogy. If the problem of succession were solvable by dramaturgic skill, here it would be solved; if dialectical "wit" were the ultimate wisdom, Hal's obsequies over Hotspur and Falstaff might be the last word. But, as we saw, Hal's solution is half a lie; to sustain it, he must also sustain Falstaff's half-lie. Disorder is not vanquished; Falstaff survives by playing dead, and the rebellion survives, at least in part, by Northumberland's playing sick. If disorder has lost a good deal of its vitality, so has order (witness *2 Henry IV*), for the simple reason that order, under the dialectical scheme, depends on disorder as symmetry depends on contrast. Without two such splended foils as Hotspur and Falstaff to flash in mock-heroic combat, Hal finds himself sadly reduced.

In *2 Henry IV* he (and Shakespeare—the two are the same) accepts the necessity of paying the price; and the price is self-denial, withdrawal. Now there is no theatrical cashing in on the combat model: on exciting clashes and encounters, on tense confrontations; the "due process" of lineality prevails. A fetid domesticity, a weary rather than vigorous air of expectancy, blankets the whole. What vigor there is comes from Falstaff and even so is generated by contrast. . . . (pp. 183-86)

Sigurd Burckhardt, "'Swoll'n with Some Other Grief':
Shakespeare's Prince Hal Trilogy," in his Shakespearean Meanings, *Princeton University Press, 1968,
pp. 144-205.*

*Part I. Act V. Scene iv. Prince Henry and Henry Percy. By
H. Corbould (n.d.). From the Art Collection of the Folger
Shakespeare Library.*

JAMES WINNY (essay date 1968)

[Winny argues for the relative autonomy of 1 and 2 Henry IV.
*He also regards Shakespeare's English histories as unified only
in their common exploration of the theme of self-deception, specifically with respect to the kings. He thus contradicts August
Wilhelm Schlegel (1808), Hermann Ulrici (1839), Beverley Warner (1894), and E.M.W. Tillyard (1944), all of whom identify
Shakespeare's English histories as a unified "epic" of either eight
or ten plays. For a similar interpretation of the autonomy of* Henry
IV, *Parts 1 and 2, see the excerpts by John Upton (1748), E. E.
Stoll (1914), Harry T. Baker (1926), Robert Adger Law (1927),
and M. A. Shaaber (1948).]*

Belief that the history-plays act out the moral argument of the Homilies has encouraged an assumption that eight of the plays form tetralogies, to be read as a continuous work showing the evil consequences of deposing Richard II, which were to trouble England for the next eighty years. This view of the Histories is open to several objections. The most obvious is that their order of composition suggests no such purpose. Had Shakespeare intended from the outset to make the crime of deposing a lawful king responsible for all the disorder and havoc which the two tetralogies depict, he would hardly have chosen to begin his series with *Henry VI*, historically the midpoint of the whole timespan which his plays cover. . . . It is more reasonable to suppose that if the Histories contain some collective

meaning, it is compatible with their order of composition. (pp. 18-19)

[In all of the histories] the efforts of a king to impose his authority upon an unruly kingdom, or to resist the challenge of open rebellion, is a matter of first account. The persistence of this subject, from *Henry VI* onwards, hs been the main support of interpretations based upon the political morality of the Homilies, and of the argument that the two tetralogies show the consequnces of lifting hands against God's deputy. If, instead, we assume that Shakespeare used the matter of the English chronicles for an essentially imaginative purpose, the repeated—and generally unsuccessful—attempts of a king to assert his authority over rebellious subjects take on a very different appearance. It now becomes a point of imaginative significance that none of the six kings in these eight plays enjoys an undisputed title to the crown, and must fight to retain it. The first of Shakespeare's sovereigns, 'in infant bands crowned king', is the weakest and least effectual in resisting the challenge to his title and possession; the last the strongest and most assured of his legitimacy. This development running through the Histories, by which the king acquires an increasing force of authority, shows why it must be mistaken to treat the series as though it were intended to begin with the deposition of Richard and to end with the accession of Henry Tudor. The historical order of the six reigns is not relevant to Shakespeare's imaginative purpose: the chronological order of the plays is.

The historical matter is treated in a sequence which illustrates that purpose; beginning at the point of greatest political confusion and national weakness, with a king incapable of ruling his insubordinate subjects, and ending after a great victory by the only English monarch whom Shakespeare presents as a national hero. (pp. 38-9)

In each of the later Histories the king is forced to come to terms with the nature of the royal identity which he has tried to assume, and to recognise a disparity between his ideal of majesty and his personal ability to fill the role assigned to him. The costume is laid out and the part rehearsed, but the performance falls short in respects which both actor and audience acknowledge. The player is not the king. However alluring in prospect, and however confidently the part is accepted, the task of realising this major role proves destructively taxing. The unachieved magnificence of the king finally appears to lie beyond human reach; a part which the actor relinquishes in the disillusioned spirit expressed by the poet of the Sonnets:

> Thus have I had thee as a dream doth flatter;
> In sleep a king, but waking no such matter.
>   [Sonnet 97]
>   (p. 46)

The imaginative concerns of his plays relate to the world which the poet brings into existence, and not to the experiences of actual life. The task of self-identification, and the actor's struggle to become the part he plays, are issues which Shakespeare's creative consciousness never drops for long. In the later Histories they join to form a central theme of attention; using the image of king to embody the natural sovereignty which Renaissance man believed himself to possess, and the chronicler's records as a dramatic field where this exalted identity could be put to the test. (p. 47)

It is of course clear that Bolingbroke has the natural gifts of a politician and no inclination to suppress private interest when [in *Richard II*] the crown appears within his grasp; but the interpretation put upon his past behavior in *Henry IV* goes well beyond the limits of fair inference. Too much of the later Bolingbroke is incompatible with his namesake in *Richard II* for the two figures to be accepted as the same man. Like all Shakespeare's plays, *Henry IV* determines its own conditions without referring to other works with which it is nominally connected.

The shift of ground which comparison with *Richard II* reveals provides a helpful indication of Shakespeare's more complex purpose in *Henry IV*. The King is a practised hypocrite and dissembler, an oath-breaker and a confirmed bad debtor. . . . (p. 89)

His personal debts and his spiritual guilt are irksome facts which Bolingbroke evades as far as he can, adopting a façade of moral respectability which hardens into a character he himself accepts as authentic. The regal manner which he assumes does not suggest the impudence of a usurper, conscious that he is merely impersonating the king, but a monarch whose legal right is established beyond dispute. His imperviousness to the fact of being himself a successful rebel makes his high-toned dealing with the Percy faction particularly ironic, and invites the kind of satirical comment which Holinshed attributes to Hotspur after the King's 'fraudulent excuse' for not ransoming Mortimer:

> Behold, the heire of the relme is robbed of his
> right, and yet the robber with his owne will not
> redeeme him.

Henry IV does not lack characters who keep the plain facts of Bolingbroke's greed, fraudulence and double-dealing in clear view, against the figure of unruffled majesty which he tries to present to the world.

There is some apparent disagreement over the means by which Bolingbroke acquired the crown. It is clear to the rebels that the deposition had been methodically planned, that Bolingbroke's undertakings at his return from exile were cynically insincere, and that he had never had any intention of honouring the debts he contracted to them. He remains, especially in the early scenes of the play, deeply tainted by perjury and dissimulation as well as by the unabsolved crime of Richard's death. Yet despite his long record of deceit, Bolingbroke appears genuinely unaware of the course of deliberate subversion and treachery which brought him to the throne. He speaks of his accession as though the crown had come into his hands by accident, and with no connivance on his part. . . . There is a further surprise in his admission of bewilderment at the working of political forces which have plainly not been in his command. 'God knows, my son,' he says, expressing a perplexity that again seems unassumed,

> By what by-paths and indirect crook'd ways
> I met this crown.
>   [2 *Henry IV*, IV.v.183-85]

The crooked ways may have been the course of deceit and concealment which enabled him to outwit both Richard and his own supporters, but there is a sense of puzzled uncertainty in the speech which suggests that events have followed an enigmatic purpose of their own, using Bolingbroke to fulfil purposes which he still does not comprehend. This is probably the significance of his repeated claim to have had no designs on the crown. In his function as character, Bolingbroke embodies an ambition for power which exploited every means of attaining its end, however dishonourable. Only a memory as evasive as his political motives could misrepresent truth so badly as to tell Warwick that he was obliged to assume the crown in the interests of good government. But as a history-play, *Henry IV* is concerned to show the underlying irony of political events, which reverses reasonable hopes in the unforeseen consequences of actions simple enough in themselves. (pp. 93-5)

Falstaff and Bolingbroke are linked in a comic relationship whose nature is indicated during the play-acting scene in which Falstaff impersonates the King. At the most obvious level of appreciation, this is a farcical interlude justified by Hal's need to 'practise an answer' for the approaching audience with his father; but the scene rapidly develops beyond this practical purpose. As Falstaff snatches up impromptu regalia, taking a stool for his throne, a cushion as crown, and a dagger as makeshift sceptre, he presents more than a merely clownish figure of barnstorming majesty. The parody relates specifically to Bolingbroke, whose character Falstaff has assumed; and these comic properties have a satirical point as sharp as the dagger which this alehouse king clutches as his badge of authority. The usurper whose crimes have debased the dignity of his royal office enjoys as much right to crown and throne as Falstaff's makeshift properties suggest, and he too guards his stolen property with a ready knife. Yet despite this illicit possession of Richard's crown and the naked show of force, the King maintains an outward majesty which Falstaff parodies in his comic stateliness and aplomb. . . . (pp. 106-07)

The comic parallel begins to be drawn with the earliest low-life scenes, where preparations for the Gad's Hill robbery call in references to theft and fraud. The robbery is manifestly a comically scaled-down version of Bolingbroke's original crime, followed by a matching sequel in which a group of fellow-conspirators attempt to snatch the booty from their successful partners; incidentally revealing the cowardice of the original thief. (p. 109)

Falstaff is carrying out his satirical function by behaving in a fashion which encourages the Price to castigate him in terms appropriate to Bolingbroke. This is not the only occasion, in either part of the play, when Hal seems to be tacitly denouncing his father's viciousness by attacking the same faults in Falstaff. This means of registering moral disapproval of Bolingbroke's crimes indirectly allows the Prince to dissociate himself completely from a lawless régime without overt disloyalty to his father. When we realise that Falstaff is unwittingly standing-in for the man whose moral character he shares, we may feel less uneasy about the gratuitousness of Hal's sometimes scathing attacks upon Falstaff, whose company he is not obliged to tolerate. . . . At such moments Falstaff becomes the scapegoat for Bolingbroke, and the target of a satirical venom whose shafts are often ambiguously appropriate to both. This ambiguousness is particularly evident in Hal's speech from the throne denouncing

>   that reverend vice, that grey iniquity, that father ruffian.
>   [*1 Henry IV*, II. iv. 453-54]

His satirical terms fit Bolingbroke rather better than Falstaff. Sir John may deserve 'reverend vice' for his jocular pretence of respectability, but the King—a crowned robber, holding sacred office in defiance of right—has a stronger claim to the description. (pp. 113-14)

Like so many of Falstaff's actions and comments, the catechism of honour which seems to typify his own shameless outlook puts in plain terms the principles underlying Bolingbroke's behaviour:

>   What is honour? a word. What is in that word
>   honour? What is that honour? Air. A trim reck-
>   oning! Who hath it? He that died a-Wednesday.
>   [*1 Henry IV*, V. i. 133-36]

Of all the combatants at Shrewsbury, only the King and his grotesque counterpart try to save their own skins; both of them by means of the counterfeiting that is so deeply charactersitic of Bolingbroke. Hotspur, the Prince, and the other combatants throw themselves whole-heartedly into the battle, as though calling attention to the King's reluctance to expose himself in a fight to determine his own authority. The catechism of honour is not directed satirically against Hotspur's rapturous ideal of knighthood

>   O gentlemen, the time of life is short!
>   To spend that shortness basely were too long
>   [*1 Henry IV*, V. ii. 81-2]

or against Hal's more sober respect for noble reputation. Its target is Bolingbroke. Falstaff is himself of course involved in the satirical consequences of his defence of cowardice, but knowingly; making himself ridiculous by the deliberate sophistry of his argument in order to reveal the unspoken, un-admitted purpose which prompts Bolingbroke's ruse. (pp. 120-21)

The general parallel between Falstaff and Bolingbroke as diseased and ageing men, and between the King and his unhealthy realm, is too plain to be overlooked. The association goes well

beyond this general likeness. When the Lord Chief remarks that Falstaff and the King seem to be troubled with the same complaint, Falstaff makes the nice distinction that it is 'the disease of not listening, the malady of not marking', that he suffers from; which confirms their kinship. The moral 'sleeping in the blood' which Falstaff represents in broad physical terms by unbuttoning after supper and sleeping on benches after noon is the manifestation of a spiritual deafness. Similarly in Bolingbroke the 'lethargy' diagnosed by Falstaff is not only physical; and the 'kind of deafness' which afflicts him is a bodily counterpart of his stifling of conscience and disregard of moral law. By admitting his own malady of not marking, Falstaff draws their single identity more closely about himself and the King, making it difficult to separate the two characters into distinct beings. For this reason, every reference to Falstaff's increasing age and ill-health takes on an ambiguous significance, as though spreading beyond its explicit object and impelling attention towards a second figure, sensed rather than seen in the half-light behind him. (p. 125)

When the new King speaks of a father who has gone 'wild into his grave' he means, at the simplest level of interpretation, that his own riotousness is buried with Bolingbroke. Other meanings are involved, which suggest the King's agony of spirit as he dies with his guilt still unpurged. The arrest of Falstaff brings to an end a parallel career of infamy and misrule in a form which, behind its low comedy, hints ominously at the spiritual reckoning to which Bolingbroke has been summoned. The hour which both men struggled to put off has at last struck, and a long overdue account has been brought to settlement.

Unlike the truly profligate Falstaff, Prince Hal has few friends among critics of the play. His popularity is readily accountable. A lone wolf playing a double game to which not even his anxious father is admitted, he is seen waiting to acquire moral estimation by humiliating an old friend in the moment of triumph, and to hoodwink his subjects by a sham reformation prepared well in advance. His behavior has attracted understandably scornful criticism; and the acknowledgement that this cynical opportunist is to become the dauntless Harry of Harfleur and Agincourt has only added puzzlement to the distaste of readers who cannot forgive his callous deception of Falstaff. (pp. 131-32)

The difficulty of explaining Hal's actions in terms of human character has to be admitted. There are Shakespearian figures whose behavior is determined to an appreciable extent by the imaginative design of the play, without first regard to their human plausibility. The Prince is one of them. The incompleteness of his human motivation is at once evident in Shakespeare's vague and contradictory suggestions of what moves Hal to abandon Westminster for Eastcheap and to choose riotous companions, concealing his true character until the time is ripe to disclose himself. The Prince himself prefers to be obscure about his motives. . . . (p. 132)

Hal is wasting time fruitlessly, and the discovery that Eastcheap provided an important part of his education is not to be made in this play. . . . The empty existence which the Prince shares with Falstaff serves no constructive purpose. It involves forcing a tedious and wantonly trivial way of life upon a young man whose tastes are entirely serious and responsible, denying him the absorbing occupation which his temperament demands, and compelling him to dissipate his energies upon an endless, exasperating holiday from the crucial affairs about him. The indignity is self-imposed, but the obvious frustration of Hal's serious moral impulse in the frivolous life to which he is committed must rule out any later suggestion that Eastcheap provided valuable experience. (p. 134)

In many important respects Hal presents . . . an antithesis to Bolingbroke so pointed that his dramatic character seems largely determined by the terms of this inverted relationship. If Falstaff is comic shadow to Bolingbroke, the Prince is his reverse image, duplicating his father's habits in the opposite moral sense, by presenting virtue in the guise of vice. Where Hal's behaviour is not psychologically accountable we may look for its explanation in the imaginative design which obliges him to act as though in deliberate contrast to Bolingbroke, taking a path which tacitly dissociates him from all that his father represents. (p. 136)

Bolingbroke, Hotspur and the Prince have more in common than the name Harry, which helps to suggest an obscure relationship between all three. Each has adopted a moral disguise, the two impostors passing themselves off as authentic, and the true prince deliberately bringing his genuineness into doubt. Bolingbroke grudgingly acknowledges his heir, but envies Northumberland his Harry, and wishes their sons might be exchanged; not appreciating that the traitor Harry Hotspur might fittingly regard him as father of his lawless enterprise, and that Hal is indeed a stranger to him except in blood. Their likeness of moral character makes it appropriate that the King should wish to recognise Hotspur as heir, and that Hotspur should act the part of prodigal son to this father-figure; but Hal has imperative reasons for insisting upon his legitimacy, and for offering positive proof of the identity which Hotspur is trying to steal from him. 'I will redeem all this on Percy's head,' he promises Bolingbroke;

> And in the closing of some glorious day
> Be bold to tell you that I am your son,
> When I will wear a garment all of blood,
> And stain my favours in a bloody mask,
> Which, washed away, shall scour my shame with it.
> [*1 Henry IV*, III. ii. 133-37].
> (p. 143)

Hal's descent to the murky world of the taverns does not prepare him for kingship. It represents the adoption of a moral attitude exactly opposite to the position taken up by Bolingbroke and Hotspur in common, a mask of dishonour assumed as though in protest against the spurious nobility of both. The audience is invited to recognise the Prince as the moral antithesis of Bolingbroke, and to find assurance in Hal's behaviour that the next king will reverse all the practices by which Bolingbroke has corrupted law and truth. The killing of Hotspur, an image of the prince whom Bolingbroke wishes his son to be, is an earnest of Hal's ultimate intention. The purpose which he discloses at his accession admits more than his own past wildness. 'The tide of blood in me,' he tells the Lord Chief Justice,

> Hath proudly flowed in vanity till now;
> Now doth it turn and ebb back to the sea,
> Where it shall mingle with the state of floods,
> And flow henceforth in formal majesty.
> [*2 Henry IV*, V. ii. 129-33].

The tide withdrawing from inland creeks to the open sea represents the Prince who has abandoned Eastcheap for ever, but much more the final dissociation of the blood-royal from the dishonours which Bolingbroke rather than Hal has brought upon it. Although Hal's moral reformation involves some calculated pretence, it is not simply hypocritical. The change of

character which he appears to undergo is a true index of the transformation worked upon the king's office and person as Hal restores dignity to both. By concealing his nobility under the moment of his accession, he is able to show in himself how completely sovereignty is to renounce its long association with crime. A prince who had not disguised his respect for law would be incapable of making this deeply symbolic gesture, whose purpose is not to illuminate Hal's character but to round off the imaginative design of the play in a strong dramatic image. (pp. 145-46)

This reinstating of justice [Hal's reappointment of the Lord Chief Justice] after the confusions of Bolingbroke's imposture restores the positive standards which the old king's falseness has thrown into question. By presenting his actual nobility as dishonour, Hal has made himself a strange to the inverted moral values upheld by Bolingbroke, and shown his critical discrimination between the substance and form of truth; while the King, through habitual counterfeiting, has lost his power of distinguishing between the false and the authentic. The new king now brings his discrimination to bear upon the ambiguous appearances which have checked and harassed the process of law during the reign of a usurper, and chooses without hesitation between the real and the spurious figures of justice which claim the office. In making this disclosure of his true self, Hal also restores the image of sovereignty defaced by his father, whose dissimulating of royalty set an example of doubling and equivocation throughout his kingdom. With the passing of old Double and the public rejection of the father-figure in whom Bolingbroke's vices are impudently parodied, the moral inversions of the reign are brought to an end. The prodigal father is succeeded by a just son; and the royal estate is inherited by an heir whose personal truth, in its various senses, is made imaginatively equivalent with an unchallengeable right to the name of king. (pp. 150-51)

> *James Winny, "Introduction" and "The Royal Counterfeit," in his* The Player King: A Theme of Shakespeare's Histories, *Chatto & Windus, 1968, pp. 9-47, 86-167.*

ALVIN KERNAN   (essay date 1969)

[*Kernan presents a new version of the concept that* 1 *and* 2 Henry IV *are part of a larger Shakespearean epic, claiming that* Richard II, 1 Henry IV, 2 Henry IV, *and* Henry V *make up what he calls* The Henriad—*an epic dramatization of England's transition from the Middle Ages to the modern world. For a brief examination of such "epic" readings of Shakespeare's histories, see the excerpt by James Winny (1968).*]

Taken together, Shakespeare's four major history plays, *Richard II, 1 Henry IV, 2 Henry IV,* and *Henry V* constitute an epic, *The Henriad*. Obviously these four plays are not an epic in the usual sense—there is no evidence that Shakespeare even planned them as a unit—but they do have remarkable coherence and they possess that quality which in our time we take to be the chief characteristic of epic: a large-scale, heroic action involving many men and many activities, tracing the movement of a nation or people through violent change from one condition to another. . . .

In *The Henriad*, the action is the passage from the England of Richard II to the England of Henry V. This dynastic shift serves as the framework for a great many cultural and psychological transitions which run parallel to the main action, giving it body and meaning. In historical terms the movement from the world of Richard II to that of Henry V is the passage from the Middle Ages to the Renaissance and the modern world. In political and social terms it is a movement from feudalism and hierarchy to the national state and individualism. In psychological terms it is a passage from a situation in which man knows with certainty who he is to an existential condition in which any identity is only a temporary role. In spatial and temporal terms it is a movement from a closed world to an infinite universe. In mythical terms the passage is from a garden world to a fallen world. In the most summary terms it is a movement from ceremony and ritual to history and drama. [In *Richard II*, the "fall" from feudal certainties to the modern world takes place.] (p. 3)

Looking back on the lost past, the men of *The Henriad* see the "fall" occurring at that fatal moment when Richard threw down his warder, the symbol of his office and his duty, to stop for political reasons the ritual trial by combat between Bolingbroke and Mowbray. In *Richard II* the effects of that act are focused in the person of Richard and his passage into tragic existence. In the two parts of *Henry IV*, however, the effects are exploded into an entire dramatic world and the many various characters who inhabit it. Richard's disorders and conflicting values grow into the increasingly bitter political and social disorders of a world racked by rebellion, strife, ambition, self-seeking, squabbling, and desperate attempts to hold things together. (pp. 10-11)

Richard's discovery that man is a creature of infinite possibilities ranging all the way from dust to god, beggar to king, is projected in the Henry plays into the wide and varied cast of characters, each of whom seems to be not a whole man but a fragment, some singular component of human nature isolated and carried to its extreme. "Homo" may be, as Gadshill says, "a common name to all men" [*1 Henry IV*, II.i.95], but the adjective which should follow is constantly questioned. Does man realize his humanity properly in power? pleasure? learning? love? order? glory? Is the truly human setting the place of pleasure and fellowship, the Boar's Head Tavern in Eastcheap? the council table in the palace at Westminster? the desperate battlefields far to the north and west along the Scottish and the Welsh marches? Glendower's castle where old songs of love are played and the vast mysteries of the universe are discussed? These are the principal symbolic places in the Henry plays, the places in which man now works out, in a sudden surge of freedom and released energy, his destiny and his nature. Each of these symbolic places has a resident deity, a genius of the place, whose speeches and actions embody its attitudes and values.

The Glendower world, which focuses the values of magic, science, poetry, and love, remains strangely peripheral, as if, despite the high value Shakespeare elsewhere places on these powers, they were not of fundamental importance in *The Henriad*. There is perhaps a disqualifying sensitivity here, a tendency to withdraw from the power struggle, for when Hotspur—who finds love trivial—offends Glendower by laughing at his magic, the Welshman simply withdraws his support and is not heard of again.

Falstaff presides over the tavern world, and, when first seen, this latter-day Bacchus is waking from a nap on a bench. (p. 12)

The old knight is enormously fat, a walking version of the roast beef of Old England, given over entirely to epicurean pleasures. He never pays his debts; he is a liar, a thief, a drunkard, the very energy of disorder and lawlessness. For him

a true man follows the pleasures of the belly and the bed, avoiding pain and labor whenever possible. He takes what he wants without worrying about property rights or morality. . . . He is a master at staying alive and comfortable in an extremely difficult, dangerous, and potentially painful world.

Viewed from a sternly moral direction, Falstaff is a vice, a demi-devil, a tempter, a mere caterpillar of the commonwealth. When viewed from a more tolerant perspective, Falstaff is an amusing and cunning old rogue, but still an obvious, slow-witted glutton and braggart, a victim of his own appetites and a figure of fun. But Falstaff meets these challenges more than halfway by asking continually the eternal "cool" questions: "What is so important about a well-run state? Why all this strange passion for this 'grinning honor,' this order and honesty, which cost so much pain and suffering?" These questions are usually asked indirectly, by means of parody and wit, and the shrewdness of mind and the style of execution are exquisite.

Each of Falstaff's parodies presents both the pretense of virtue and the reality lying behind the pretense, and as the play progresses he stages ever more pointed demonstrations of the gap between appearance and reality. (pp. 13-14)

Henry Percy, Hotspur, is the exact opposite of Falstaff. . . . But the contrast between the two characters is best understood in terms of their distinct aims: where Falstaff always seeks pleasure, Hotspur always seeks fame, honor, *gloire*. (pp. 14-15)

Honor, as Hotspur understands it, is no longer the honor of the medieval knight, of Roland or Galahad, achieved by humbling one's self to the difficult tasks imposed by one's God, one's feudal lord, or one's lady. It is instead the Renaissance thirst for individual fame, for immortality of reputation in a world where all else dies and is forgotten, and it possesses Hotspur utterly. Even his sleep is a restless impatient dream of battle, which culminates in a breath-taking vision of Fame:

> And in thy face strange motions have appear'd,
> Such as we see when men restrain their breath
> On some great sudden hest.
>
> [*1 Henry IV*, II.iii.60-2]
> (p. 15)

Hotspur's life is a surging rush onward which endures no obstacles. . . . The thirst for fame is death-marked even before it dies on Shrewsbury Field. Its republican cry for liberty cries also for blood, "If we live, we live to tread on kings." It tastes the pleasure of the battle, feels the charge like a thunderbolt, is all on fire to hear that victims are coming to be offered to its god, "the fire-ey'd maid of smoky war." Honor contains a sensual delight in the nearness of death, death for the self and death for all others. "Doomsday is near; die all, die merrily.". . . (pp. 15-16)

A life and values which have so much death in them cannot endure for long, and Hotspur shortly dies at the hands of a more efficient and more durable force, embodied in the greatest of the Lancastrian kings, Prince Hal, later to be Henry V. As Hotspur dies, he glimpses, as Richard had earlier, the vast, infinite reaches of time in which men briefly live, die, and are forgotten, where life and fame are but the fools of time, and where in some distant future even time itself gives way to some unthinkable emptiness:

> But thoughts, the slaves of life, and life, time's fool,
> And time, that takes survey of all the world,
> Must have a stop. O, I could prophesy,

But that the earthy and cold hand of death
Lies on my tongue. No, Percy, thou art dust
And food for—
                [*Dies.*]
           [*1 Henry IV*, V.iv.81-6]

Hal's completion of Percy's thought, "for worms," suggests the extent to which he understands and shares this modern vision of time and space.

It is the work of the realistic politician to control and adjust such extremes as Hotspur's idealism and Falstaff's sensuality, which threaten civil order in the pursuit of what they take as the good. Superb politician though he may be, it is Henry IV's fate to spend his lifetime trying to order such contraries as these, and it is equally his fate never to succeed in doing so. (p.16)

Struggling with endless rebellions and increasing savagery, Henry IV comes at last to the place where Richard and Hotspur have already stood—where Adam stands in Books 11 and 12 of *Paradise Lost*—looking out on that vast span of time and change which swallows hope and obliterates the meaning of individual life:

O God! that one might read the book of fate,
And see the revolution of the times
Make mountains level, and the continent,
Weary of solid firmness, melt itself
Into the sea; and other times to see
The beachy girdle of the ocean
Too wide for Neptune's hips; how chances mock,
And changes fill the cup of alteration
With divers liquors! O, if this were seen,
The happiest youth, viewing his progress through,
What perils past, what crosses to ensue,
Would shut the book and sit him down and die.
           [*2 Henry IV*, III.i.45-56]
              (pp. 18-19)

At the same time that he breaks into the vastness of time and space, the endlessness of change, man also discovers the iron law of historical necessity, Having rejected the old social restrictions of obedience, submission to tradition and ritual, and maintenance of assigned station and rank, having chosen freedom, men now begin to discover that freedom leads, ironically, to another kind of necessity, the tragic necessity which forces you to endure the unsuspected consequences of what you are and what you have done. In the tragic world of *The Henriad* the past is never done with until you are dead, and even as Henry lies dying, the "polished perturbation" for which he has suffered so much lying beside him, Hal enters and, thinking his father dead, carries the crown away. The act is innocent, perhaps, but it reenacts another crime in which the wish was also father to the deed and the crown was also taken from its rightful possessor before he was dead. That crown which glittered so attractively has become for Henry "a rich armour worn in heat of day, that scald'st with safety," and so it will also be for the man who now carries it away.

The continuing turmoil and suffering of the new world are intensified by the will to power and the incompatibility of its individual energies. The sensualist, the idealist, and the politician—each seeks to be king, to become, as it were, the whole world. (pp. 19-20)

Out of these antagonisms rises the plot of the play. The politician seeks social order and stability but runs athwart honor's

headlong search for glory and sensuality's absolute rejection of any kind of restraint. Sensuality and idealism in turn find that the social need for order imposes upon them limits which they cannot endure. . . . Politics and sensuality mix better than either does with idealism and its death-directedness, and Falstaff, marches uneasily with the forces of order. Idealism, honor, and raw courage lack the sense and control needed for a world where only the fittest survive, and Hotspur's body, with the strange wound in his thigh, is borne off on the back of Falstaff. Falstaff's quick opportunism, raw common sense, and cat-footed sense of survival; and the politician's hard, clear objectivity, practicality, and ability to control passions are the virtues which do persist.

Despite all the disorders of *1 Henry IV*, the release of energy and the exhilarating effects of freedom—the positive side of the transition from the Middle Ages to the Renaissance—are so attractive that disorder seems almost a small price to pay for the wit and pleasure in life of Falstaff, the fiery idealism and high courage of the knight Harry Percy, the political skill and masterful strategy of statesmen like Henry IV and the Earl of Worcester. The possibilities of human nature and the mind of man come into view, and men begin to discover what they and their world are really like. As in *Paradise Lost*, the first experience of disobeying God, satisfying appetite, and eating of the tree of knowledge is hot and pleasurable. But as in Milton, so in *2 Henry IV* men soon learn that knowledge is knowledge of good *and* evil. The first joy of power and pleasure soon passes and the previously hidden side of freedom begins to turn into view. Justice Shallow and his cousin Silence sitting talking of the old days that are gone and agreeing that "Death is certain" set the tone of this darkening world. (pp. 20-1)

The banishment of Falstaff and the destruction of wit and pleasure do not teach a moral lesson but present a tragic necessity. Henry V is not here making a wrong choice but simply instrumenting the inevitable triumph of politics over pleasure. (p. 23)

> Alvin Kernan, "The Henriad: Shakespeare's Major History Plays," in The Yale Review, Vol. LIX, No. 1, October, 1969, pp. 3-32.

HENRY ANSGAR KELLY (essay date 1970)

[*Kelly concentrates on the theme of providence in the Hal tetralogy and claims that in none of these plays does Shakespeare depict the Lancastrian kings, of whom Henry IV was the first, as "being punished by God for their acquisition and continued possession of the throne." Although Kelly does not refer directly to the "Tudor myth," as originally put forth by E.M.W. Tillyard (1944), his argument definitely opposes its central assumption that all the English kings, from Henry IV to Richard III, experienced some degree of strife and tribulation as a divine punishment for their illegitimate possession of the throne. For further discussions of the "Tudor myth" and its relation to Shakespeare's histories, see the excerpts by Sigurd Burckhardt (1966) and Robert Ornstein (1972).*]

[Throughout *1 Henry IV*, King Henry] regards himself as the rightful king, supported by human and divine right against rebellion. And this is the viewpoint of the chroniclers in general, especially Walsingham, Vergil, and Hall, for the events covered in this play.

This characterization of Henry is made very evident in his dealings with his son. When he calls him in to give an account of himself, the king addresses him as follows:

I know not whether God will have it so,
For some displeasing service I have done,
That, in his secret doom, out of my blood
He'll breed revengement and a scourge for me;
But thou dost in thy passages of life
Make me believe that thou art only marked
For the hot vengeance and the rod of heaven
To punish my mistreadings. Tell me else,
Could such inordinate and low desires,
Such poor, such bare, such lewd, such mean attempts,
Such barren pleasures, rude society,
As thou art matched withal and grafted to,
Accompany the greatness of thy blood
And hold their level with thy princely heart?

[*1 Henry IV*, III. ii. 4-17]

In this remarkable speech we are told that Henry is not conscious of any sin that God could be punishing him for. Furthermore, the audience is well aware that he is completely mistaken in his analysis of God's dispositions toward him as far as the prince is concerned; he has not bred revenge for him in his son; if anything he has blessed him with the most glorious son and successor that a king ever had.

Of course, it could be held that Shakespeare introduced the providential theme here for its rhetorical effectiveness in its immediate context, in spite of the fact that it goes counter to a larger theme in the play. Shakespeare rather frequently employs this kind of rhetorical abstraction from the plot of his plays; for instance, he has Hamlet declare that no one ever returns to this world from the dead, just after he has received a rather convincing visitor from the other world in the person of his own father. But the evidence for a "greater theme" of the providential punishment of Henry IV is completely lacking in this play. And if we are to assume that the theme is wholly taken for granted on Shakespeare's part, we must protest that a speech like this one of Henry's would practically negate such an implied theme, unless one were to postulate an extraordinarily subtle kind of irony in the king's words. (pp. 215-17)

On the other hand, if irony were intended, the audience would be expected to believe that Henry is really suffering the pangs of a remorse he always feels but never acknowledges, even in soliloquy, and that he knows or suspects that God is punishing him for his crimes against Richard, in allowing or forcing his son to follow his disastrous course. Perhaps one could even make a case for saying that God is actually punishing Henry in allowing him to believe that his son is on the path to destruction; there is no doubt that the king does suffer much in this regard. But if so, we must also admit that God very shortly calls a halt to this punishment, for Henry realizes his mistake when the prince answers him. He now realizes what the audience already knows, that his son will turn out well, and that therefore God is not punishing him as he feared; the prince will have fulfilled his promise abundantly by the end of the play.

Furthermore, the theory that Henry is meant to be afflicted with remorse for his offenses against Richard throughout the play is decisively refuted in this very scene. The king is clearly thinking of the way he acquired the crown, but it is in terms precisely the opposite of remorse. He recalls his achievement with pride, and he chides his son for not imitating the deportment that enabled him to succeed as he did; he compares the prince's actions with Richard's and warns that a fall like Richard's may be his lot as well. (p. 217)

The heavy emphasis upon the Percys as rebels is strengthened . . . by Henry's prayer to God to befriend his side, because of the justice of his cause [*1H4*, V.i.120]. It is true that Hotspur also assures his men that their own cause is just [*1H4*, V.ii.87-8], but just before this his uncle Worcester characterized their action as treason [*1H4*, V.ii.1-11]. It is evident that Shakespeare has put the burden of blame for this rebellion and the losses suffered in the battle upon Worcester, and no doubt Henry's closing sentiments are to be taken as an honorable summation of the play's events, especially since they reflect Prince Henry's victory and vindication as well as his own. (p. 221)

The moral situation of the second play on Henry IV reverts to that of *Richard II* in some aspects that were altered in *I Henry IV*. For one thing, it seems evident that Henry feels remorse for his treatment of Richard and seeks God's pardon for it. Then again, Richard's prophecy to Northumberland is picked up, and the theme of an alternate claimant to the crown disappears. There is no suggestion that Henry is keeping the realm from a rightful heir, and Archbishop Scrope's rising is for the reform of Henry's rule, not for his overthrow.

The archbishop's motives appear somewhat less worthy in the characterization they receive in Northumberland's camp than they do in his own person. In Morton's speech to Percy on the matter (deleted from the quarto edition of the play), he says that the gentle Archbishop of York binds his followers with a double surety. Hotspur had only their bodies, for their souls were frozen up in the belief that rebellion was unlawful;

But now the bishop
Turns insurrection to religion. . . .

[*2 Henry IV*, I.i.200-01]
(p. 222)

In Scrope's own analysis of the situation, he blames the fickle people most of all for the present troubles: "The commonwealth is sick of their own choice." The sickness he likens to that of a dog whose ravenous greed has left it nauseated. (p. 223)

The sickness of the commonwealth is matched by Henry's own illness and unrest, which is described by Falstaff [*2H4*, I.ii.111-17]. The king's soliloquy at the beginning of the third act, his first appearance in the play [*2H4*, III.i.4-31], is simply a dissertation on the worries and trials of kings in general. . . . (pp. 223-24)

At the risk of excessive repitition, let us stress once more that the crown in *2 Henry IV* is definitely regarded as the rightful possession of the Henrys; and [the speeches on the crown by Hal and Henry] are the strongest expressions of this view we have yet seen. Admittedly, the crown was wrongfully acquired, but Henry prays (and, we presume, hopes) for pardon for this offense. And he prays further for God to grant that his son may possess it in true peace. He most certainly does not ask for forgiveness for cutting off his former allies. Their assistance was wrong ("fell") in the first place, as was his ascent to the throne. But their turning upon him was equally wrong, and he only did what was right in putting them down. (p. 230)

We have witnessed the pious death of a good king, who is at peace with God. There is no indication at this point, in his references to the troubles he experienced during his reign, that they were in any way a punishment from God for his sins in acquiring the throne; and he expresses no qualms about punishment after death. The final act of the play is taken up with King Henry V's appearance as the worthy successor of his father. He says that he survives his father to frustrate prophecies and to refute the ''rotten opinion'' that has judged him according to appearances; and, ''God consigning to my good intents,'' no one will have just cause to wish, ''God shorten Harry's happy life one day!'' [2H4, V.ii.125-45] And the play ends with Prince John's surmise of Henry's eagerness to undertake the conquest of France [2H4, V.v.105-08].

We must therefore conclude that in neither of the plays named after Henry IV are the Lancastrians dramatized as being punished by God for their acquisition and continued possession of the throne. Henry's uneasiness might be interpreted as a fear of God's punishment; but in the event this fear proves unfounded. And if his apprehension itself is to be considered a divine punishment (a rather forced interpretation), the punishment must be said to end whenever his fears are relieved—specifically, when he gains confidence in his son in I Henry IV, III.ii and II Henry IV, IV.v, and when his enemies are defeated in I Henry IV, V.v and II Henry IV, IV.iv. (p. 232)

> Henry Ansgar Kelly, ''Shakespeare's Double Tetralogy,'' in his Divine Providence in the England of Shakespeare's Histories, Cambridge, Mass.: Harvard University Press, 1970, pp. 203-95.

ROBERT ORNSTEIN   (essay date 1972)

[Ornstein's essay is a broad attack on the historical critics' approach to Shakespeare; thus he allies himself with such earlier critics as Leonard Dean (1944), Cleanth Brooks and Robert Heilman (1945), Harold C. Goddard (1951), Samuel B. Hemingway (1953), Harold Jenkins (1955), Sigurd Burckhardt (1966), James Winny (1968), and Alvin Kernan (1969). In particular, he centers his discussion on E.M.W. Tillyard (1944), whom he considers incorrect in his assumption that Shakespeare's English histories represent an orthodox Elizabethan view of life. Ornstein also criticizes Tillyard's contention that Shakespeare based his chronicles on the Tudor myth popular during his lifetime, maintaining that such a utilitarian view of Shakespeare's art is overly simplistic and contradicted by the text of the plays themselves. Other critics, most notably Burckhardt and Henry Ansgar Kelly (1970), question the presence of the Tudor myth in Shakespeare's histories. Edward Pechter (1980) later praised Ornstein as the most systematic of a number of recent critics writing in reaction to Tillyard and historical criticism.]

The scholarly insistence on the orthodoxy of the History Plays would be more tolerable if it were tinged with some regret that the Soul of the Age lent his great art to doctrinaire purposes. But instead of regret, there seems to be pleasure in the scholarly discovery of the orthodoxy of this character's thought and the ''correctness'' of that character's acts. If there is a left and right wing in the criticism of Shakespeare, one libertarian (or Falstaffian) in sympathies, the other conservative and mindful of the need for authority and discipline, then the party of the right (and of Prince Hal) seems entrenched in the scholarship on the History Plays. Rather than complain of the bias of particular scholars, however, I would point out the inherent bias of the historical method toward what is conventional and orthodox in Elizabethan culture, because any search for the ''norms'' of Elizabethan thought must lead to a consensus of truisms and pieties. In sketching the main contours of Elizabethan thought, scholarship often smooths out the jagged edges and wrinkles of individual opinion. It does not maintain that all Elizabethans were typical, but it often creates the impression that there were only two categories of Renaissance thought and art—the orthodox and the deviant—and it seems to insist that

we place Shakespeare on one side of the angels or another. (pp. 3-4)

Insisting on the primacy of Shakespeare's didactic intention, scholarship would have us believe that the interpretation of the History Plays does not depend on sensitivity to nuances of language and characterization or awareness of Shakespeare's poetic and dramatic methods; it depends instead on the appropriate annotation of the doctrine of the plays. Where the interpreter of Bach hopes through historical research to transcend history, the literary scholar insists that historicity is the goal of interpretation. Convinced that the ''Elizabethan response'' which he postulates is the authentic one, he assures us that if we were Elizabethan enough in our attitudes, we would have no difficulty in interpreting Shakespeare correctly. If, for instance, we recognized that York's stance in Richard II is impeccably orthodox, we would not think his eagerness to have his only son executed unconscionable or, as it seems in the play, somewhat comic. (p. 8)

A case in point is the scene in Henry IV Part I (II.iv), where Hal, aided by Poins, plays a joke on Francis, the drawer. Perhaps it is wrong to be slightly pained by the callousness of Hal's treatment of Francis, but if we are pained, at least we are responding immediately and honestly to the lines which Shakespeare wrote and to a human situation which we can understand because we have experienced or witnessed its analogue in our own lives. We recognize Hal's boredom in the tavern, and his condescension to those who are his inferiors. We recognize, too, the pleasure which he takes in playing cat-and-mouse games with other people—with Poins, Falstaff, and the Lord Chief Justice in Henry IV Part II, and with the English traitors and the French Princess Katherine in Henry V. Arguing that ''we must not judge Shakespeare by standards of twentieth-century humanitarianism,'' Tillyard would have us believe that Elizabethan audiences (in which apprentices far outnumbered princes) would not have been troubled at all by Hal's conduct because they thought the Francises of the world hardly human. If we accept this dubious generalization about Shakespeare's contemporaries, however, we do not respond ''properly'' to Shakespeare's representation of life; what we respond to is a learned admonition against modern sentimentality which saves Hal's ideality by degrading Shakespeare's humanity and cheapening his art. If Tillyard is correct, the Francis episode is not a fascinating revelation of Hal's personality; it is an irrelevant and purposeless bit of low humor, which exposes Shakespeare's ''Elizabethan'' snobbery and coarseness. (p. 9)

It is worth noting that Poins, Hal's assistant in the game, who is as coarse and common in his outlook as any Elizabethan one would ever want to meet, seems to lack the proper Elizabethan outlook, because he does not get the joke of baiting Francis and asks Hal the point of it.

The appeal to Elizabethan attitudes is frequent enough in the literature on the History Plays for us to wonder why it should be easier to predict the responses of Shakespeare's audience than to interpret his artistic intentions from the thousands of lines which embody them. If we grant that there was in Shakespeare's England a community of shared values and beliefs which scholarship can cautiously describe, we must grant too that a wide range of individual and group attitudes must have existed in his society, which knew more than its share of religious and political turmoil and social and economic change. When we consider how reluctant we would be to generalize about the attitudes of our contemporaries—or to define the beliefs of our next-door neighbors, for that matter—we must be astonished at the confidence with which scholars characterize Elizabethan convictions. Perhaps the Elizabethans seem simpler and more transparent than do our contemporaries, because we know less about the diversity, contradictions, shadings, and facets of their beliefs—or because these nuances are not apparent in the documents and treatises which we consider the repositories of Elizabethan "thought." In any event, Shakespeare's contemporaries sometimes appear in scholarly portraits as a fundamentally naive and credulous folk, who managed to create a highly sophisticated civilization and great monuments of art while retaining simple emotional enthusiasms and stock responses.

More unfortunate still is the curiously Philistine blueprint for Elizabethan culture sometimes implicit in the scholarship that looks always outside the realm of literature to explain and annotate literary ideas. Such an approach creates the impression that Elizabethan poets and dramatists made no significant contribution to the thought of their age, that they found their moral values in sermons and took their psychology from treatises on the humors, their political ideas from the Tudor and Elizabethan Homilies. What an approach to the era of Shakespeare, Marlowe, Spenser, Jonson, and Donne! (p. 10)

Tillyard's claim that the picture of English history in the tetralogies is based on the Tudor myth which Hall promulgated in his Chronicle and which supposedly moralizes the calamity of the War of the Roses in the following way:

> Over against Richard [II]'s inability is set Henry IV's crime, first in usurping the throne and secondly in allowing Richard to be killed against his oath. God punished Henry by making his reign unquiet but postponed full vengeance till a later generation, for Henry (like Ahab) humbled himself. But Henry was none the less a usurper and this was a fact universally accepted by the Elizabethans. Hall notes the immediate jealousy of the house of York when Richard was deposed. Henry V by his politic wisdom and his piety postpones the day of reckoning. He learns from the example of past history and chooses good counsellors; he banishes his evil companions; he does his best to expiate his father's sin by having Richard reburied in Westminster. But his wisdom does not stretch to detecting the danger from the House of York. With Henry VI the curse is realised and in the dreaded form of a child being king—"woe to the nation whose king is a child."

Because Tillyard's exposition of the Tudor myth seems to explain the form and comprehend the substance of Shakespeare's tetralogies, it has had an enormous influence on the criticism of the History Plays. To be sure, skeptics have pointed out that the pattern of the Tudor myth is eccentrically set forth in the tetralogies, which begin with the funeral of Henry V and end with the famous victory of Agincourt. Others have noted that the political lesson which is supposedly at the heart of Hall's Chronicle and Shakespeare's History Plays is remarkably obscure in the tetralogies. The three brief references to the deposition of Richard II in the first tetralogy scarcely convince us that it was the cause of Henry VI's calamities. And though Shakespeare has the opportunity to drive his lesson home in the Epilogue to *Henry V*, which comments on the tragedy of the War of the Roses, he makes no mention of the

original sin committed against Richard II for which later generations supposedly paid with their blood.

There is very good reason to doubt that Shakespeare wrote his tetralogies to set forth what Tillyard calls the Tudor myth of history. There is reason also to question whether the view of history which Tillyard sets forth as the Tudor myth was in fact the Tudor myth and can be attributed as such to Hall. (pp. 15-16)

Like most Henrician writers, Hall dwells on the horrors of civil war, and on the unnaturalness of dissension, strife, and factionalism in England. He does not, however, propagandize for the Tudor doctrine of obedience; he never postulates the sacredness of royal authority, nor does he exclaim against the sin of rebellion. (p. 17)

What Tillyard and other Shakespeareans call the Tudor myth of history might more correctly be called the Yorkist myth of history, because it corresponds in essential details to the argument set forth by the Duke of York to the English Parliament after the battle of Northampton, when he claimed the throne as its rightful heir. It is Holinshed in 1577, not Hall in 1548, who accepts this Yorkist view of the past, who condemns Bolingbroke as a usurper, and who dwells on the fits of remorse and guilty fears that supposedly plagued Bolingbroke's later years as king. (pp. 18-19)

Can we believe . . . that Shakespeare was so shallow in his assessment of the temper of his countrymen, and so fearful of the threat of incipient anarchy, that he wrote play after play to persuade his audiences of the need for order and obedience? If we may judge from his characterizations of common men in the History Plays, he knew that his fellow Englishmen were neither giddy nor eager for change. He may even have suspected that as a people the English were far more conservative than were their Tudor monarchs, who came to power by armed rebellion, who changed the established religion, radically altered the Church, dissolved the monastic orders, and centralized political power under the throne—all the while proclaiming that whatever is is right. When, as in sixteenth-century England, the government becomes revolutionary, it is likely that those who rebel are conservatives who resort to arms in attempts to restore traditional ways of life. (p. 25)

A master of theatrical spectacle, Shakespeare could appreciate the need for spectacle in politics, for the ceremonies which make all the world a stage for the mystery of power. He could also appreciate the mythopeic genius of the Tudors, who traced their descent to legendary kings and who consciously imitated the splendor of Plantagenet rule in their courtly pomp and stately progresses. Where Henry VII had ascended the throne as a savior-bridegroom whose marriage to the Yorkist princess Elizabeth reunited the royal houses of England, Elizabeth presented herself to the nation as the bride of England—as the Virgin Queen who loved her people so well that she would accept no other husband. Aware that all successful leaders create their personal mythologies, Shakespeare does not hesitate to grant the Lancastrian kings the political instincts of the Tudors. Where the Chronicles tell of a Prince Hal whose youth was misspent but who put on a new man when crowned, Shakespeare depicts a prince who deliberately fashions the legend of his prodigality and miraculous reformation, even as his father had artfully made himself seem a man of destiny who obeyed heaven's will in becoming King. (p. 30)

Robert Ornstein, "The Artist As Historian," in his
A Kingdom for a Stage: The Achievement of Shake-

speare's History Plays, *Cambridge, Mass.: Harvard University Press, 1972, pp. 1-32.*

HERBERT B. ROTHSCHILD, JR.   (essay date 1973)

[*In the following excerpt, Rothschild suggests that in addition to the traditional interpretations of Falstaff as the braggart soldier of classical New Comedy, the Vice figure of medieval morality plays, and the "King of Misrule" originating in the popular holiday festivals of archaic cultures, he may also be regarded as a descendent of the picaro, or rogue, of Renaissance fiction. Rothschild bases this reading on the numerous similarities between Falstaff and the picaro, particularly the inability of each to "respond to value beyond the material." For leading examples of the traditional interpretations of Falstaff's character, see the excerpts by E. E. Stoll (1914), J. Dover Wilson (1943), and C. L. Barber (1963).*]

The complexity of Falstaff, witnessed not merely by disparate critical and scholarly interpretations but at times by rather heated differences in emotional response to the character, is by now beyond dispute. Shakespeare has taken a number of traditional figures and shaped them into a unique creation encompassing and yet transcending them all. Each source so far explored has shed its own particular light on the character, and beyond him to the play as a whole. The braggart soldier of classical New Comedy and Udall's *Ralph Roister Doister*; the vice of native morality plays, who tended to get amalgamated with the witty and pandering slaves of Plautus and Terence; the King of Misrule releasing in popular festivals the aberrant impulses of society until his holiday reign expires; these sources have been isolated and their implications discussed. In this paper I should like to do the same for another figure not yet so treated, that of the *picaro*, or rogue, of Renaissance fiction; and at its close briefly suggest how Shakespeare continued to make use of the figure as his dramatic vision matured.

The picaresque genre can be said to have been created in 1533 with the publication of *Lazarillo de Tormes*, an episodic tale narrated in the first person. The anonymous author established the form and the type of irony which characterized the work of his successors in the sixteenth and seventeenth centuries. *Lazarillo* was translated into English in 1586, and from its great popularity and an allusion in *Much Ado About Nothing* we can conclude that Shakespeare very probably knew the book. (p. 14)

The *picaro* usually originates in the lower classes—Lazarillo's father is a miller, Pablo's a barber (and both are dishonest)—though this is not invariably the case. More importantly, he tends to lose his social ties very quickly either through the destruction of his family, his running away, or an unstable apprenticeship. From that point on until the end of his career, the *picaro* is never integrated into society's structures. Whatever his situation as beggar, camp follower, strolling player, servant, card sharp, or high-society poseur, he develops no personal relationships or vested interests binding him in the social matrix. The peripatetic inclinations of the *picaro* have all too frequently been taken as the main characteristic of the genre, and any plot featuring a wandering protagonist, such as those found in Smollett's work, has been dubbed picaresque. To do so is to miss the point. The *picaro*'s movements are incident to his nature and situation—an outsider with no ties, he follows the pickings. (p. 15)

The *picaro*'s roguery is quite unambitious. With a bagful of petty tricks and ruses he manages to eke out a poor living. Cheating at dice, shoplifting food, purloining from the master's larder, conning free meals, begging under false pretences, in short, the unorganized, day-to-day, shifts of survival are his stock-in-trade. In no picaresque fiction is the accent on villainy as a means of accumulating wealth and power. What is gained is quickly and entirely consumed; nothing is left to show for it. The *picaro* has no ambition to impose his will on the world, because he sees neither it nor his relation to it coherently enough to give birth to sustained initiative. Perhaps the upper limit of his ambition is best expressed by a passage [in Quevedo's *Pablo the Sharper*] in which a fellow rogue sings to Pablo the praises of Madrid: 'In that city I never want for five or six crowns in my pocket; nor a bed, meat and drink; nor, on occasion, the married man's pastime: for the possession of wit in Madrid is like the philosopher's stone, which converts all it touches into gold.' 'This discourse', says Pablo, 'opened a great vista before me'. . . .

If, because of the modesty of his ambition, the *picaro* seems to pose a far less serious threat to the social and moral order than does someone like Epicure Mammon [in Jonson's *The Alchemist*], whose imaginative vista, opened by promise of the philosopher's stone, is much grander in its self-seeking, then the implications of the picaresque attitude are misunderstood. For just as the pressure for material survival is itself the most subversive of all forces working against human value, so too the man geared only toward survival is the least responsive to those values. Unintegrated into the social fabric of humankind, the *picaro* is also, and relatedly, unintegrated into its symbolic structure. For him the test of truth and goodness is as unpretentious as his goal: what is real is what assists survival; what is good is what provides. Life is tested by the belly and the gonads, and the results are simple, strange, and disconcerting.

Other people exist for the *picaro* only as means to his ever-pressing end—satisfaction of the primal appetites. Thus they tend to get reduced in his vision to what they are for him. (p. 16)

Under such circumstances all human contact is superficial, predatory, and shortlived. If any lasting arrangements are formed, it is economic convenience which cements them. (p. 17)

The essence of the picaresque vision, then, is an incapacity to respond to value beyond the material. Filtered through the rogue's sensibility, symbols become denuded of their value and reduced to the material reality which is his ever present concern. The most instructive example of this desymbolization—and an episode which completely epitomizes the picaresque genre—is found in *Lazarillo*. The priest keeps his bread locked in a trunk, to which the starving boy has been able to get a duplicate key. After one theft, however, the priest counts his loaves and Lazarillo is afraid to remove any more for fear of exposure: 'He went out, and in order to console myself, I opened the chest, and when I saw the bread I began to adore it, not daring to receive it'. . . . The language here is an obvious allusion to the Holy Eucharist. For Lazarillo, the priest's loaf is literally, not symbolically, the bread of life. Under pressure of material necessity, the symbol is emptied of its content and is collapsed back into the physical. Unlike satire, in which symbolic values are introduced to remind the reader of the ways in which they are being violated, picaresque fiction introduces them only to indicate how they are being negated.

In the light of the foregoing discussion, it is not difficult to see how Falstaff conforms to the picaresque life and attitude. Whatever station in life his birth originally gave him, the fat knight frequents no court but the tavern where he reigns over

433

a pack of common scamps. His title, and particularly his friendship with the prince, barely enable him to stay on the edge of social tolerance, and there are hints from the first that his margin of safety is precarious. 'I would to God thou and I knew where a commodity of good names were to be bought', he tells Hal in their first scene [I.2.82-3]. The wars come none too soon for Falstaff, because the social upheaval leaves the authorities with little leisure to cope with everyday parasites. In the disarray men generally are too concerned with their own survival to scrutinize the means by which others are keeping their heads above water.

Falstaff's life on this social fringe is marked by a chronic impecuniosity, which he relieves mainly with his wit. The hostess of the tavern seems to have been his chief mark. From her he cadges bed and board, clothing, and, in the words of Pablo's fellow rogue, 'on occasion, the married man's pastime'. 'You owe me money, Sir John', she tells him. 'I bought you a dozen of shirts to your back. . . . You owe money here besides, Sir John, for your diet, and by-drinkings, and money lent you, four and twenty pound' [III.3.66-74]. It is in the Prince himself, however, that Falstaff finds his gold mine. Whether Hal is paying his debts, countenancing his thefts, or procuring him a commission in the wars, it is he on whom Falstaff relies to keep afloat. How one is to evaluate Falstaff's attachment to the Prince is a matter of individual response to the character. Whether one believes his several protestations of affection, which tend to cluster in the first half of Part I, or whether one leans more heavily on the second half of that play and on Part II and concludes that he cultivates Hal for his obvious self-interest, makes the difference between a sympathetic and a cynical reading. I myself feel that Shakespeare allows Falstaff to expose himself increasingly as cynical and self-serving in his relationships. His final speech in Part I, delivered as Hal leaves the stage, suggests nothing of affection: 'I'll follow, as they say, for reward. He that rewards me, God reward him!' [V.iv.162]. While this evolution of the character does not suffice to dismiss totally the earlier impression of a more genial companion, at least it casts back a long shadow of suspicion. Minimally one must say that by the end of Part I and and throughout Part II, Falstaff's personal relationships are marked by arrangements of economic convenience and motivated by predatory instincts. (pp. 17-18)

This attitude toward other people, one which by implication denies to them any value above the material and finds its expression in a diction which equates people with stuff, is, as we saw earlier, a hallmark of the *picaro*'s sensibility and language. Falstaff's criteria of value are precisely those of the *picaro*—does it provide, does it contribute to survival?—and he applies them with the same results. The famous battlefield catechism assumes its fullest implications in the context of our investigation. He questions what honour is worth: 'Can honour set to a leg? No. Or an arm? No. Or take away the grief of a wound? No.' What then is honour? In the course of Falstaff's answer we see that process of desymbolization which was termed earlier the very essence of the picaresque vision. 'What is honour? A word. What is in that word honour? What is that honour? Air' [*1 Henry IV*, V.i.133-35]. In the rogue's mind the urgency of life's physical dimension is such that no reality is conceded to exist beyond it. The dead man is the counterfeit, 'for he is but the counterfeit of a man, who hath not the life of a man: but to counterfeit dying, when a man thereby liveth, is to be no counterfeit, but the true and perfect image of life indeed' [*1 Henry IV*, V.iv.116-19]. (pp. 18-19)

Yet in the context of the play as a whole, Falstaff's attitude, while not shared by other characters, threatens to become a pervasive one. Though we do not see the world only as it is filtered through his sensibility, still his presence is powerfully felt and tends to cast doubt, first on the political behavior of the high characters, and then beyond them on the very possibility of investing political behaviour with legitimate value. (p. 19)

Shakespeare . . . does not confront with full awareness and honesty the questions raised in *Henry IV* by Falstaff. It is noteworthy that when he does come to confront them, to pose those questions he uses figures bearing some resemblance to his *picaro*. I have Iago and Edmund in mind. If they remind us at times of Falstaff, it is not only because the Vice, the witty mischief-maker, is a shared ancestor; also it is because their view of what is real, or rather (since they are essentially mockers), their view of what is not real, corresponds to that of the *picaro*. Of course Iago and Edmund are active agents of evil, so that to yoke their names closely with Falstaff's may produce uneasiness. Yet just as in the mature tragedies, Shakespeare is far more purposive than in the histories about exploring and universalizing attitudes toward order and value, so Iago and Edmund are far more purposive than Falstaff (and any *picaro*) about establishing the validity of their own attitudes, of their denials. One may say that Iago, and to a lesser degree Edmund, are actively evil because they feel threatened by the possibility of their being wrong about what reality encompasses, and therefore they feel compelled to justify themselves by subverting and destroying the exponents of competing values. (p. 21)

Herbert B. Rothschild, Jr., "Falstaff and the Picaresque Tradition," in The Modern Language Review, *Vol. 68, No. 1, January, 1973, pp. 14-21.*

ROY BATTENHOUSE   (essay date 1975)

[*Battenhouse is well known for his studies on religion and literature and for his theory that Shakespeare's works embody a specifically Christian world view. In the following excerpt, he combines the centuries-old discussion of Falstaff's morality with the idea that Falstaff's outer behavior is a mask for inner charity and holiness. Battenhouse cites W. H. Auden (1959) as a precursor of his views, but his argument parallels in some ways Maurice Morgann's contention that there is an inner, courageous Falstaff belying the outward appearance of cowardice (see excerpt above, 1777). Battenhouse's thesis is disputed by Roger Cox (1975).*]

It was suggested by Lord Fitz Roy Raglan, in 1936 [in his *The Hero*] that "Shakespeare had in the back of his mind the idea that Falstaff was a holy man." And W. H. Auden, more recently, has argued in cryptic fashion that Falstaff, while overtly a Lord of Misrule, is nevertheless at heart "a comic symbol for the supernatural order of charity" [see excerpt above, 1959]. By other scholars there has been an understandable reluctance to pick up or probe this possibility. For it fits not at all with Prince Hal's view when banishing Falstaff as a profane fool and abominable misleader. And no doubt few of today's playgoers think of imputing charity to a Falstaff whose prankish chicanery and braggadocio seem to make him the very image of traditional vice, garnished at one time or other with all the Seven Deadlies. Yet may not the fulsome display of reprobation be more mask than inner man? One of Auden's most tantalizing points is to remind us that the Sermon on the Mount enjoins Christians to show charity through a secret almsgiving unto men to fast. Could this be a clue to the enigma of Falstaff's

Part I. Act III. Scene i. Hotspur, Worcester, Mortimer, Glendower. By R. Westall (1803).

character? Perhaps so, I think, provided we put beside it Lord Raglan's intuition that Falstaff's vocation, in the public world, is that of court fool and soothsayer. Such a double hypothesis, in any case, seems to me to warrant a trying out and testing. For it could mean that while as "allowed fool" Falstaff is shamming vices and enacting parodies, his inner intent is a charitable almsgiving of brotherly self-humiliation and fatherly truth-telling.

It could mean, further, that the relation of Falstaff to the Lollard martyr Oldcastle, a matter that scholars have puzzled over ever since Shakespeare juggled their names, is a relation of paradoxical affinity. For on the one hand, as the play's Epilogue tells us, Falstaff is not the man Oldcastle (a solemn martyr for views unconventional in his times); yet is not Falstaff, though comic, also a nobleman whose seeming affronts to officialdom make him a martyr? The mode of witnessing is of course different. A clown, if and while Christian at heart, must mask his piety under absurd posturings and perhaps facial leers. His office is to offer spectacle of himself in the lineaments of folly, as a mirror to the great of their own imperfections. But such a vocation runs the risk of banishment at the hands of princes whose morals are those of worldly self-advantage and political expediency. By such princes the Fool's mirror is rejected as disreputably profane, even when marginally it reflects Christian premises. (p. 32)

Let it be said at the start that my thesis, novel though it largely is, and perhaps at first glance preposterous, is not without

wayside support from the observations of other scholars. For while some have emphasized the vice characteristics of Falstaff, Alfred Harbage has remarked acutely:

> Falstaff is the least effective wrongdoer that ever lived. He is a thief whose booty is taken from him, a liar who is never believed, a drunkard who is never befuddled, a bully who is not feared. . . . Even his lechery is a doubtful item. . . .

The real Falstaff is in full control of his wits at all times, despite his praise of sack and despite those wine bills which he has, as clown, no doubt planted in his pocket for the sake of the comedy they will produce when his pockets are picked. And as for a lechery which Harbage terms doubtful, how can we believe it at all of the fat sixty-year-old whom we see in Mistress Quickly's tavern? The pose of fornicator, says W. H. Auden, is jolly pretense, while all that we actually see Falstaff doing in this scene is defending Nell from a bully, Pistol, then setting Doll on his knee and making her cry out of affection and pity for him. . . .

Falstaff differs in one very important respect from a vice character such as Ambidexter in Thomas Preston's *Cambises:* Ambidexter goes about planting suspicion, tempting Cambises to hatred and fratricide, and constantly glorying in his skill as a beguiler. By contrast there is in Falstaff, as various scholars have noted, none of this vicious guile. Time is the only thing Falstaff beguiles; through his role as fall guy and buffoon he is a comic butt of laughter and by his wit a cause of wit in others. (p. 33)

Critics who have seen in Falstaff a Lord of Misrule may be correct, except for their own inadequate understanding of the role's implications. It developed historically, we need to be reminded, as a Christian holiday exercise. Its licensed mimicking of inverted moral order served two concurrent purposes: (1) that of releasing mimetically, and thus confessing, the disorders of Old Adam behavior which Everyman has in him; and (2) that of clarifying thereby the mystery of the New Adam to which Everyman is properly called and obligated. . . . It is paralleled also in medieval graphic art: in cloister decorations which portray monkey figures amid the foliage adjacent to saints; in cathedrals whose gargoyles spout healthful rainwater; and on manuscript borders, where ass-eared humans can be found presided over, for instance, by Moses and David and trumpeting angels. The medieval Feast of Fools was underpinned by this large sense of the landscape of history. It was devoted to celebrating, as Harvey Cox has pointed out in a recent book, the mystery of Christ the harlequin, a spirit of play amid a world of utilitarianism, and a concept (as Cox phrases it) of "prayer as joke or the joke as prayer." It sanctioned as overdoing and "living it up," precisely in order to recognize the delinquencies with which man is vexed, viewing these not cynically but with a confidence in the ultimate goodness of life. Cox urges us to revive this sense of festivity, reminding us that one of the catacomb etchings of Christ depicts a crucified figure with the head of an ass. . . .

Do we doubt that Falstaff belongs within this tradition? Let us recall that Poins terms him "the martlemas," that is, a St. Martin's Day summer [*2H4* II.ii]. Or let us recall that Doll affectionately calls him a Bartholomew boar-pig [*2H4* II.iv]. Bartholomew was the disciple, elsewhere in the Gospels named Nathaniel, whom Jesus described as a man "in whom there is no guile" (John I.47); and from the twelfth century on into the nineteenth his Saint's Day was the occasion of a great public Fair including sideshows and rowdy entertainment. This Fair owes its origin, moreover, to a monk who had been a court jester under King Henry I. Having decided to become a monk, he built first a monastery near the shrine of St. Bartholomew and soon afterward an annual fair in the saint's honor. (p. 35)

Throughout Falstaff's whole pose of deafness [in his interview with the Chief Justice], it should be evident that he is slyly commenting on a deafness in his superiors, a disease in *them*. He has heard, he says, that the king has fallen into a discomfort—an apoplexy, a lethargy, a whoreson sleepiness, a kind of deafness. And Falstaff implies that it is *this* he is troubled about, whereas the Chief Justice lacks the *patience* to *digest* its significance. . . .

The times, Falstaff goes on to say, are coster-monger times—that is, times when everything is measured by its cash value. Because of "the malice of this age," the gifts most "appertinent to man" are disvalued, and valor is reduced to a taming of bears—which implies, I would say, that the function of bearherd has replaced that of Shepherd. And the times are also those of no true repentance, even on Prince Hal's part. Rather, merely a comic substitute, a repenting "not in ashes and sackcloth, but in new silk and old sack." In other words, old wine in new bottles—the reverse of New Testament injunction. Or, a secondary meaning of Falstaff's phrase could be: "old ransacking in new silken rhetoric," the old destructiveness clothed now in sleek diplomacy. These facts of his times, it seems to me, Falstaff knows and is teasingly making jest of while insisting, with equal truth, that *he* is no ill angel, nor in any way a misleader of the Prince. Rather, the Prince is misleading *him*: "God send the companion a better Prince." . . .

The mock-trial situation has given Falstaff an opportunity for putting on record (as if making a legal "deposition") his answer to the charge that he is a white-bearded Satan. Not so, he replies, unless you regard it a sin to be old and merry. To banish Falstaff would be as perverse a mistake, he warns, as to hate Pharaoh's fat kine while cherishing lean kine. There are fascinating implications in this biblical allusion. Through it Falstaff is intimating, I would say, that England under King Henry is comparable to an Egypt of spiritual darkness under a troubled Pharaoh, and that Falstaff embodies within his English-Egypt a God-given plenty that could save England from the famine figured in lean Prince Hal. (p. 36)

The implications hidden under Shakespeare's biblical echoes have been sadly neglected by commentators. . . . [Such] study can vastly repay our attention, especially when allusions to Scripture appear in the talk of so canny a fellow as Falstaff. They can be, in fact, something like the tip of an iceberg, signalizing a subsurface context of Bible story which is relevant by analogy to the events taking place in Shakespeare's story. (p. 37)

Falstaff when comically impersonating King Henry includes some pompous sermonizing as follows:

> There is a thing, Harry, which thou hast often
> heard of, and it is known to many in our land
> by the name of pitch. This pitch, as ancient
> writers do report, doth defile; so doth the com-
> pany thou keepest.
>
> [*1 Henry IV*, II. iv. 410-14]

As editors note, the allusion is to Ecclesiasticus xiii.1. But why does Falstaff's Henry ascribe it vaguely to "ancient au-

thors"? Very likely because Henry, here being impersonated as a Euphuist, is being credited with a pretentiously shallow knowledge like that of John Lyly's Euphues. The neo-Greek Euphues was a showy moralist who pirated scraps of authority from sources he knew only superficially, using their adages in utilitarian fashion to give himself a reputation as wiseman, while himself living a wanton life and betraying friends by slippery preachments. Perhaps, therefore, Falstaff is analogizing Euphues to King Henry: England's king of politics is about as trustworthy as Lyly's king of rhetoricians in Shakespeare's own day, each being (if rightly assessed) an absurd morality. . . . In Henry's case, readers who remember his practices during his rise to power ought to realize how little right he has to lecture against thievery. And, indeed, Henry's chief concern, as portrayed by Falstaff, is not so much to upbraid Hal's thievery as to mend Hal's reputation for respectability: what offends is that Hal is "pointed at" for keeping disreputable company. In the interview scene which follows in the drama's next act, we will hear Henry object ot Hal's associating with "rude society," with "shallow jesters and rash bavin wits," and recommend instead a courtesy "stolen" from heaven and dressed in robes pontifical. Falstaff's prior parody of this attitude contains a very accurate characterization and forecast of the ethics of King Henry's courtliness or courtesy.

But to return to our biblical allusion: Was "rude society" what the author of Ecclesiasticus had in mind when warning against pitch? Only in a very different sense from King Henry's. Henry understands pitch as referring to social inferiors, "vulgar company" [III.ii.41], rude in their rash deportment. But what the Bible writer Ben Sira means by pitch is high and mighty persons who are morally rude in offering a friendship that is false and beguiling. . . . It is evident that what *pitch* signifies for Ben Sira is the high-stationed manipulator who uses a hollow courtesy to hoodwink the unwary, offering an unmerciful companionship which turns out to be false friendship. . . . King Henry, if compared with Ben Sira, is a counterfeit moralist. Hence he warrants Falstaff's impersonation of him as comic in his preaching, in that when invoking an ancient author's text whose true meaning he does not know he distorts it and overlooks its application to himself. (This is much like the Wife of Bath's sermonizing as portrayed by Chaucer: she alludes to texts from St. Paul which, did she but know it, condemn her out of her own mouth.) (pp. 37-8)

If only Prince Hal were less shallow he would perceive that here, in moral fact, is the truth about his father Henry; and he would guess at Falstaff's hidden warning to expect in Henry's love a conscience eager to entangle Hal in its own pitch. Falstaff is implying that if Hal, like Cambises' queen, risks a liaison with this King, he can expect a bedfellow who will cherish him only so long as he condones the King's bloody policy and supports it. But alas, throughout this scene, what Hal appreciates is solely the absurdity of Falstaff's supposedly madcap language and foolery, not the insight into England's cultural situation and its headmaster which Falstaff's swiftly moving vignettes have capsulized as babble and oracle rolled into one. (p. 39)

My own commentary, I fear, must seem pedantically tedious, since to expound jokes is to appear flatfooted. Ideally, perhaps, one ought to dance out the meaning like a striptease artist, tossing off veils of enigma one by one until at last the bare secret is flickeringly revealed. But to do so would seem disreputable scholarship, to which my audience would no doubt respond with catcalls for more proof. So I must be content with the humdrum rules of my vocation as armchair professor and systematically spell out the hidden. (p. 40)

The farce at Gad's Hill enacts a political parody. Its moral is stated in Falstaff's comic cry, "A plague upon it when thieves cannot be true one to another." . . . In effect, King Henry is thieving from the Percies, while all they can do is fulminate and concoct a retaliation which turns out to be politically about as farcical as Falstaff's concocted story of how he peppered and paid home two men in buckram suits. . . . We can easily infer that Falstaff has been deliberately playing a mock-Hotspur role in the whole jest, even to the point of magnifying valiancy as Hotspur is later satirized for doing—taking on "some fourteen" in an hour. The difference between main plot and subplot is merely that whereas Hotspur undertook a real rebellion and a genuine thievery when prompted by the devious King Henry, Falstaff undertook only a mock thievery and a storybook retaliation against his treacherous setter-on, Prince Hal. That is the difference between history and art. Yet art has its own truth, a figurative truth, which refutes Prince Hal's notion that Falstaff's story is a mere pack of lies. "Art thou mad?" replies Falstaff. "Is not the truth the truth?" It is not here Falstaff who is clay-brained or stupid. "By the Lord," he concludes, "I knew ye as well as he that made ye." When Falstaff swears by the Lord, we had better believe him. (p. 41)

The Dives allusion is one Falstaff cannot let alone. He turns to it again in Part II of the play, when talking about the refusal of a certain "Master Dumbledon" to provide him clothes:

> Let him be damned, like the glutton! Pray God
> his tongue be hotter! A whoreson Achitophel!
> [*2 Henry IV*, I. ii. 34-5]

Here the Dives of hot tongue is being compared to Achitophel, the traitor who for a hoped-for worldly advantage deserted the good King David to serve instead a vain and self-righteous Absalom. Whom could Falstaff be glancing at? If we recall that Achitophel was a vile politician who helped bring in Absalom on a "reform" platform, we can scarcely miss the object of Falstaff's comment since either Henry IV or later his son fits this pattern. (p. 43)

The basic reason why Falstaff prompts dialogue about disease and tailoring on his first entrance into Part II of the play is that these two motifs now characterize the drift of England's history and will do so throughout the play's subsequent action. Since the commonwealth is sick, as various other characters in this play tell us, Falstaff's talk is about the nature of this sickness. But as we have already noted, he finds the land's Chief Justice deaf to any true understanding. The Justice, like his superiors, is interested only in tailoring a new military expedition for his own security. To Falstaff, such a prescription for the land's disease is mere waste (or waist); it ignores the *heart* of the matter. "I can get no remedy," he laments, "against this consumption of the purse." His chief meaning is that bankruptcy is the ironic result of the public seeking for "security." Exhaustion of the spiritual exchequer is the looming fate of Bolingbroke and his opponents alike, after a lifetime of extended credit and unpaid debts. (p. 44)

It is Falstaff who has been practicing the true sense of Ephesians V: redeeming time through making manifest "unfruteful workes of darkenes" in "dayes [that] are evil," while secretly "speaking *unto your selves* in psalmes and hymnes, and spiritual songs, singing and making melodie to the Lord *in your hearts*" (Geneva; italics mine). Prince Hal's purpose has been but a counterfeit redeeming, reductively political, which Falstaff re-*deems* in the sense of re-estimates, re-evaluates. This has been the ironic base of the playfulness between Falstaff and his world. (p. 47)

My survey of Falstaff's entire role has shown how wise he is about the ways of Caesar, Cambises, Euphues, gay Corinthians, and Ephesians of the *old* church (i.e., worshipers of Diana, servitors of illusion, in a comedy-of-errors world of enticingly silver but actually coppersmith values). And his insight for understanding this world of fog and moonshine, I have argued, derived from St. Paul, the Gospels, Psalms and Proverbs, the Apocalypse, and the piety of an urbane Ben Sira, that ancient contender against the Hellenists who outdid them with his Ecclesiasticus. Out of a perspective grounded in this heritage, Falstaff was able to devise his double-sided mirrors of comic nonsense and authentic truth, while combining in his own person a heavenly vocation with the earthly one of Fool.

By repeated references to the parable of Dives and Lazarus, Falstaff has figured his times as those of the rich fool Dives, and himself as the age's Lazarus, fated to enjoy only crumbs from the table of its rulers, but with an inner faith in the table of Psalm xxiii. The Lazarus parable, in my reading of the play, is more central than that of the Prodigal Son, at least for interpreting Falstaff. For although Falstaff may have been a once-upon-a-time prodigal, he is at heart now a Lazarus, mirroring in his merrily accepted "sores" the wounded relationships of the Dives world, "the injuries of a wanton time" [*1H4*, V.i.50]. As jester he can offer, for the taking away of grief, a delightful mockery of the "honor" catechism of present Diveses, and simultaneously can covertly witness his own inner Holy Land pilgrimage, while glancing at the aborted one of King Henry and Prince Hal. Their plight is indeed humorous—and as old as that of Goodman Adam fallen among thieves (through traveling, as Augustine would say, to Jericho's city-of-the-moon and leaving man's mystical Jerusalem). For what is history if not the existential manifestations of some latent paradigm; and what is art if not the simultaneous hiding and disclosing of the present's radical significance through *figura*?

Since Dover Wilson turned to parable for his well-know interpretation to the *Henry IV* plays [see excerpt above, 1943] may not I be pardoned for doing so, too? The structure of the dramatic action, Wilson believes, rests on the Prodigal Son story, since Shakespeare's hero is a prodigal young Hal, who repents by returning to his father's house; he returns to Chivalry in Part I, and to Good Government in Part II. The analogy here tendered is a tantalizing one. Yet as a parallel to the biblical hero something is askew, especially when Wilson himself explains that Hal's sin was "not against God," but a sin of Vanity in violation of Chivalry and Justice. Critics of Wilson's analogy have objected that Hal is a much more businesslike traveler into a far country than his anonymous predecessor; he assures us he is going to enjoy *just enough* riotous living to make his father glad to see him home again, and this purpose makes his action chiefly political. But the basic difference . . . is total: the father to whom Prince Hal returns is no heaven-virtued father, but instead a counterfeit of the Bible's father. While King Henry may *seem* like the biblical father in proposing for his son a royal "robe," that robe (ironically) is Hal's own blood which, as calf, he is being asked to risk; and the "ring" (or crown), which Hal is given in Part II, establishes on him nothing but the "giddy" justice of a tennis-game war. The whole transaction, thus, is secularized man's ironic substitute for true chivalry and true good government. What Hal has come home to, spiritually, is the swine owner's Dives table in a far country: that is what makes him a true prodigal, unreformed of heart, but now newly "busy" instead of idle. Sloth in a physical sense he has put behind; but sloth in its medieval spiritual sense of a dried-up heart is his now more than ever.

This carefully ambiguous "placing" of Hal's success—a return to Respectability achieved, but by a forfeiting of Humaneness—is the measure of Shakespeare's sense of history in his drama *Henry IV*. The new Harry will be a "mirror of all Christian Kings," but alas in a rather Turkish way (if we consider substance more than surface) which merely counterfeits Christian values. His reign will be as colorful as his justice is shallow, and with barren consequences. Falstaff rightly divined and forecast "a good shallow" bread-chipper. The very quality of Falstaff's diction, throughout the drama, has reflected an intelligence superior to Hal's. The fat knight's prose can pirouette and vault, where thin Hal's is pedestrian and repetitious. (pp. 47-8)

Falstaff is inevitably downgraded as compared to Hal by critics insensitive to tonalities of rhythm and allusion. Some, seeking to schematize the drama within a formula of Aristotelian ethics, credit to Hal a golden mean between the extremes of moral excess they see in Falstaff and Hotspur. Others prefer a Hegelian formula, by which they can see Hal as outwitting Falstaff and outfighting Hotspur, thus transcending them both. And still others, trying for a "balanced" views, read both Falstaff and Hotspur as irresponsible and childlike, while Hal is said to mature into the responsible king England needs, though sacrificing inevitably a child's attractive spontaneity. But none of these interpretations can explain the drama's sandwich-style placing of main plot and comic-plot scenes. And in supposing that maturity and childlikeness must be qualities exclusive of each other, a medieval *topos* is being ignored, that of the *puer senex* (the old young man, more charming than in youth), inspired by Bible texts which value a spiritualized childlikeness. According to Ernst R. Curtius [in his *European Literature and the Latin Middle Ages*], one extrabiblical instance of this topos is the *Passio SS. Perpetuae et Felicitatis*, where the martyrs are vouchsafed a vision of God "as a hoary old man with snow-white hair and a youthful countenance."

We need to have this topos in mind when we read Falstaff's dialogue with the Lord Chief Justice. Falstaff poses a riddle by saying: "You that are old consider not the capacities of us that are young" [*2H4*, I.ii. 173-74]. The Justice then expresses incredulity that Falstaff should call himself young, in view of his white beard, among other things. To which Falstaff replies:

> My Lord, I was born about three of the clock
> in the afternoon, with a white beard and some-
> thing a round belly. . . . The truth is, I am only
> old in judgment and understanding.
>
> [*2 Henry IV*, I. ii. 187-92]

Here, wittily stated, in the *puer senex* or *senex iuvenis* paradox. (p. 48)

If readers object that my interpretations require an unbelievably close reading, I can only say that medieval and Renaissance artists valued obscurity, following in this respect the view of St. Augustine in his *De Doctrina Christiana*. And besides, in the Bible itself, parables were a form of art for hiding the meaning from some and revealing it to others. . . .

A groundling who after attending a performance of *Henry IV* goes away with the haunting feeling that he has seen a jolly old St. Nick or a Robin Hood cannot be altogether wrong. For the play not only shows Falstaff outwitting "St. Nicholas' clerks," but, much later, in backwoods Gloucestershire, offering "a health" to Justice Silence and thus loosing the tongue of this dumb man to sing—of Shrovetide, and of "Robin Hood, Scarlet, and John." That is miracle enough. Let skeptics try to evaporate it if they can. But if they suppose preferable the counterfeit miracle of Hal's "conversion," or the sanctimony with which Hal's brother John hails Falstaff's banishment as a "fair proceeding," generations of Falstaff lovers must and will demur. Unless, of course, one means by *fair* a Vanity Fair's ironic comedy. (p. 49)

Roy Battenhouse, "Falstaff As Parodist and Perhaps Holy Fool," in *PMLA*, Vol. 90, No. 1, January, 1975, pp. 32-52.

ROGER L. COX (essay date 1975)

[*In the following excerpt, Cox responds to Roy Battenhouse's interpretation of Falstaff as a "holy fool" (see excerpt above, 1975), arguing that this "romantic view" of Sir John essentially inverts the play's meaning and destroys the irony which permeates the plays.*]

In his article "Falstaff as Parodist and Perhaps Holy Fool" Roy Battenhouse employs a method of literary interpretation that needs to be carefully analyzed. It is at one and the same time incredibly complicated and remarkably simplistic. Battenhouse self-consciously observes that his own commentary "must seem pedantically tedious" . . . ; and a little further on . . . he clearly identifies Falstaff with Shakespeare in a way that reflects his consistent determination to regard this one character as the author's privileged spokesman—"It is a stroke of genius on Falstaff's part (alias Shakespeare's). . . ." A direct consequence of such identification is that the irony that thus envelops Falstaff apparently does not even touch the other characters. Thus, when Falstaff hails the newly crowned Henry V, who is supposedly no more than a ruthless opportunist, as "My King! My Jove!" his words are to be understood as "an impeccably Christian prayer or plea" . . . ; but when Hal assures his father of his own reformation, "the father to whom Prince Hal returns is no heaven-virtued father, but instead a counterfeit of the Bible's father." . . .

Such interpretation, by the critic's own admission, is necessarily based upon "wayside evidence tucked here and there" . . . ; and it finds only "wayside support from the observations of other scholars." . . . This wayside evidence, inconclusive as it is, can be used as the basis for general interpretation only if the interpretive statement begins with a formula that disarms the reader with its apparent modesty and at the same time allows almost any conclusion the critic cares to draw. . . .

But why resort to wayside evidence when the obvious signposts are so clear? . . . The answer seems inescapable, and it is this: because such a method enables the critic to impose an interpretation upon the text that the text itself stubbornly resists. In this case the interpretation is a highly romantic view of Falstaff which holds that the marvelous old reprobate is in fact a "holy fool," subject to humiliation and ridicule by those with whom he associates though he is clearly superior to them in both wisdom and righteousness. By a feat of rationalization worthy of Falstaff himself, he is represented not as the "old man," whom the relevant passage in Ephesians enjoins us to "cast off," but as the "new man, which after God is created in righteousness, and true holiness." . . . Thus the meaning of the work is effectively stood on its head; and the irony that permeates the Henry plays is not enriched but destroyed. When Falstaff complains that "company, villainous company, hath been the spoil of me," he refers quite straightforwardly to the corrupting influence of Prince Hal, whose own "conversion" is no more than a "counterfeit miracle." Ignore the fact that a result of the Reformation, from which perspective Shakespeare wrote, was to identify the interests of religion with those of the state; ignore (or gloss over) Shakespeare's explicit reference to Henry V as "the mirror of all Christian kings"; ignore everything but wayside evidence concerning "plump Jack Falstaff," whose wisdom shines forth from behind empty bottles of sack and baseless pretensions to lechery, both of which are merely a mask for a spirit rich in Christian virtues. (p. 919)

Roger L. Cox, "Interpreting Falstaff," in PMLA, Vol. 90, No. 5, October, 1975, pp. 919-20.

JOSEPH A. PORTER   (essay date 1979)

[*In the following excerpt, Porter turns to the "speech-act" theory of British philosopher J. L. Austin in an attempt to resolve the problem of interpreting Hal's first soliloquy. Porter concludes that the "illocutionary force" and "direction of address" of Hal's famous soliloquy—two terms he uses for denoting the kind of "act" any speech performs in relation of its audience—support its assessment as a promise "directed to himself or to an unnamed hearer such as God." For Porter, this evidence repudiates the theory that Hal is a "scheming hypocrite."*]

In many interchanges it is possible to establish that one of the parties is controlling the conversation. There may or may not be apparent reasons for his control, and the reasons may be of various kinds (the speaker's office, his "strength of character," etc.). But within the speech action itself there are fairly definite and constant manifestations of control. In Henry's "private conference" with Hal (III.ii. . .), the king's imperatives are his most obvious bids for control. Any imperative may be a bid for control, of course; but Henry's have particularly to do with control *within speech action* because they are in fact commands to speak, which Hal finally obeys satisfactorily. Furthermore, Henry's control and Hal's obedience are manifested by the fact that it is always Henry, and never Hal, who introduces a topic of conversation. (pp. 59-60)

In the first brief scene with Henry, Lancaster, Westmoreland, Blunt, and others, we have a decorously ordered court in which there is genuine interaction controlled entirely by the king. Henry speaks at times to everone present (the first vocative is his "friends, l. 18) but only Westmoreland replies, so that the scene amounts to a kind of dialogue in which the control is most obviously manifest in the transitions from one speaker to the other.

Henry initiates the action, first addressing all present and then concluding his speech with an address to Westmoreland:

Then let me hear
Of you, my gentle cousin Westmoreland,
What yesternight our Council did decree
In forwarding this dear expedience.
[*1 Henry IV*, I.i.30-3]

The change of address in mid-speech is an assertion of authority—Henry will address whom he pleases—and the concluding command or request to Westmoreland is a bid for control of the interaction. Westmoreland accepts the bid, replying as requested about the appointed subject. (pp. 60-1)

All this is to say that the direction of control of the interaction is constant and unchallenged throughout the scene. (p. 61)

In interaction like that between Henry and Westmoreland where from speech to speech there is no change in the configuration of the variables that constitute control, we can give a simple description of the action as a whole in terms of control—for example, the first scene is controlled by Henry. But in the scene with Hal and Falstaff we find, moving from speech to speech, virtually every possible configuration of these variables so that, while at any point we can give a local description in terms of control, such a description of the entire action cannot be simple. Still, in the interchange taken as a whole, the play of control does not have a design whose significance we apprehend much as we apprehend the significance of musical patterns. In this interaction, for instance, the state of complete and unchallenged control by Hal is like the tonic key with reference to which we order the movement, and to which we know it must return. This is not because most of the action transpires in that state—it does not—but rather because of the context in which it occurs. For example, in the interchanges discussed it is significant that the configuration of control variables shifts, never being quite the same from speech to speech, until Falstaff refuses to obey Hal's "demand." He makes a "demand" of his own, thus moving farther than before from the "tonic," at which point the action modulates immediately into the "tonic," with the control variables remaining constant now through several speeches. So it is that the first scene with Hal and Falstaff establishes a kind of key for the entirety of their interaction. (p. 66)

[One] pronounced characteristic of Hal's language deserves particular note. While his linguistic flexibility is manifest in his perfoming and mentioning a considerable variety of kinds of speech act, there is one which he mentions and performs frequently, distinctively, and emphatically enough for it to be considered typical of him. This is the group of *promising* and other similar speech acts such as vowing, swearing, and giving one's word. (p. 74)

Regarding Hal thus as a central promiser involves taking into account, as far as possible, all his promising and certainly his explicit references to the act of promising. In particular it involves attending to his

So when this loose behaviour I throw off,
And pay the debt I never promised,
By how much better than my word I am,
By so much shall I falsify men's hopes.
[*1 Henry IV*, I.ii.208-11]

This occurs in his famous, or notorious, soliloquy at the end of his first scene, a speech which has often figured in the critical controversy about his character. It is favorite evidence of hypocrisy and mean conniving for those who find these qualities in Hal, and has been something of a thorn in the flesh of those who do not. Although my concerns and approach differ from the traditional ones in that controversy, I think that the troublesome aspect of the speech can be brought into sharper focus by the notion of speech act.

Samuel Johnson's comment [see excerpt above, 1765] is representative of a certain critical fuzziness which has persisted:

This speech is very artfully introduced to keep the prince from appearing vile in the opinion of the audience: it prepares them for his future reformation, and, what is yet more valuable, exhibits a natural picture of a great mind offering excuses to itself, and palliating those follies which it can neither justify nor forsake.

It seems odd, in the first place, that Johnson is telling us *what the speech does*, rather than what *Hal* is doing—the latter is more directly relevant to a moral judgement of the character.

What Hal is doing is, in fact, strange and difficult to define. In the four lines quoted above, the characteristic seriousness and scrupulousness about promising and keeping one's word pose no problem; but there is a problem in that the disclaimer of promising is part of an apparent promise—indeed the whole soliloquy looks like a kind of promise.

But if the speech is a promise, it is fundamentally different from what Johnson's representative comment seems to imply. To Johnson it seems that the speech is a report, with excuses and palliations, of a state of mind, so that the parts of the speech referring to future actions are not promises but statements of intention.

This ambiguity can arise because, since the act is not explicit (i.e., Hal says neither "I hereby promise" nor "I hereby state my intentions"), we must infer the illocutionary force. That the question is important for a moral assessment of Hal can be seen, I think, if we consider rough translations which are unambiguously

> (A) *statement of intent:* "My intention is to throw off this loose behavior, falsify men's hopes, etc."

and

> (B) *promise:* "I promise to throw off this loose behavior, falsify men's hopes, etc."

With (A) Hal is autonomous—he has a plan which he deigns to state; and this fits with the picture of him as a sort of hypocritical schemer. With (B), however, Hal is placing himself under an obligation to act in a certain way—he is being morally responsible. Thus it is important to decide of what sort Hal's illocutionary act is.

The decision is made easier by considering direction of address. The speech begins—

> I know you all, and will a while uphold
> The unyok'd humour of your idleness
> [*1 Henry IV*, I.ii.195-96]

—so that the first possibility to be considered is that it is entirely an apostrophe, explicitly directed to "you all"; Poins, Falstaff, and company. This is incorrect, however, because (1) Shakespeare is usually careful about marking the extent of apostrophe by repeatedly making the direction of address explicit throughout, while here, after the first sentence, there are no more markers for an apostrophe to "you all"; and (2) Falstaff, Poins, and company must be included in the "men" whose hopes Hal is going to falsify by redeeming time when they least expect it, implying that he is no longer addressing them—otherwise he would be using a second, not a third person.

It seems therefore that the direction of address must change after the first sentence, and that we must take the remainder of the speech as being addressed to himself, to the play's audience, or to an unnamed, vague, and general third hearer such as God. This, in the first place, removes the apparent contradiction of his promising to pay a debt he never undertook: he can be promising to the present addressee what he never

vowed to "men." With that difficulty removed, Hal's references to keeping one's word and promising could support our regarding the speech itself as a promise. As the only references to illocutionary action in the speech these direct our attention toward promising, give us that mental set, and show the one specific kind of speech act that occupies Hal's mind.

If we further consider direction of address, the speech taken as (A), a declaration of state of mind including intent and addressed to a general unnamed hearer such as God, seems rather pointless, this sort of hearer presumably being omniscient; but as (B), a promise, the speech makes sense so addressed—God is just the sort of hearer to whom people (including Hal later in his career) make promises. If we take the speech as addressed to himself, (B) continues to be more probable. Although a declaration to oneself of the state of one's mind is conceivable, it would seem normally to occur only at the moment of discovering or understanding that state of mind—as with Richard's final soliloquy. And in fact, Hal's speech does not give the impression that he is discovering or understanding a state of mind as he enunciates it to himself. On the other hand, there is nothing strange about making a vow or promise (a "resolution") to oneself.

If we take the speech as being directed to the play's audience, the balance might seem to rest either way, but such an address seems far less likely than the other two. The matter is complicated by the dramatic irony of the audience's knowledge that Hall *will* reform. There would be some justification for his stating his intention to reform inasmuch as the audience does not know that at this point in his career he already has that intention. There would also be justification of his promising the play's audience to reform, since their foreknowledge does in a sense constitute an obligation for him. However, this direction of address still seems less likely than the other two because Hal does not elsewhere seem to take the play's audience into account.

Thus a consideration of the illocutionary force and direction of address of Hal's famous soliloquy supports its being understood as a promise directed to himself or to an unnamed hearer such as God, and thus it provides evidence for a moral assessment of him, evidence that apparently makes it impossible to regard him as a scheming hypocrite. (pp. 75-9)

With regard to quotation, . . . Hal sets himself apart from most of the other characters. In IV.v.[of Part Two] he surprisingly and interestingly misquotes something he has said a few lines earlier. Indeed "misquote" with its suggestion of an attempt to quote accurately, is hardly the word, for the words Hal ascribes to himself,

> I spake unto this crown as having sense,
> And thus upbraided it: "The care on thee depending
> Hath fed upon the body of my father;
> Therefore thou best of gold art worst of gold. . .
> [*2 Henry IV*, IV.v.157-60]

are quite different from those we have just heard him utter. Sigurd Burckhardt is, I think, right in his belief that "this is one of the many instances where Shakespeare does something odd because he wants to startle us into paying close attention" [see excerpt above, 1966]. Burckhardt finds that the difference in the content of Hal's two speeches elucidates Shakespeare's conception of kingship. But what I find interesting is that the mere fact of the discrepancy shows Hal radically high-handed where others are most timid—in his attitude toward the word. I say "high-handed" rather than "double-dealing" because I agree with Burckhardt that we cannot take Hal for a hypocrite and liar. Considering his other behavior in the tetralogy, I think we must assume that what he says to his father is true. That is, we must assume that for him the original utterance and the quoted one are in some sense the same. And this is to say that Hal looks very deeply beneath the surface of speech action.

It is also to distinguish him from the play's other notably inaccurate reporter of speech acts. Falstaff lies in *1H4,* but in *2H4* there seems to be a certain specificity in his lying. His false reports here tend to be about other people's speech acts, to their discredit. Inasmuch as he is especially concerned with what people say, he manifests the play's general tendency to retreat from general problems of speech action—not to mention general problems of action or of language—and to focus on the mere locutionary act, the act of saying such-and-such a thing. And inasmuch as his reports are of the acts of others, to their discredit and false, he is the play's most prominent practitioner of the act named by Rumour, slander. (pp. 98-9)

> *Joseph A. Porter, "'1 Henry IV'" and "'2 Henry IV'," in his* The Drama of Speech Acts: Shakespeare's Lancastrian Tetralogy, *University of California Press, 1979, pp. 52-88, 89-115.*

EDWARD PECHTER　(essay date 1980)

[*Pechter argues that* 1 Henry IV *is an "open" play resistant to conceptualization as a whole. He places his own essay in the context of the modern reaction against E.M.W. Tillyard's historical approach to Shakespeare's histories (see excerpt above, 1944). Other contemporary critics who oppose Tillyard's assumptions, particularly his conception of Elizabethan society, include Sigurd Burckhardt (1966), Henry Ansgar Kelly (1970), and Robert Ornstein (1972).*]

I wish to argue here that a central strategy of *1 Henry IV* is to involve the spectator from the beginning in a sequence or problematic expectations about the ways in which the play can or should end, making us increasingly conscious of the nature of our desires for order and for disorder, and of the different needs these desires seek to satisfy in both dramatic and actual experience.

It is highly unlikely that I could argue this way if it were not for the dramatic shift in contemporary critical attitudes toward Shakespeare's history plays. Until quite recently, the thematic approach as typified by E.M.W. Tillyard's *Elizabethan World Picture* and *Shakespeare's History Plays* was a generally accepted orthodoxy. This sort of approach has been challenged in a wide variety of ways in recent years, perhaps most systematically by Robert Ornstein, who argues, among other things, that the authors of that body of doctrine that has been called the Tudor Myth were signficantly more flexible than has been allowed in that they emphasized the decisive human agency in the shaping of history, rather than—or at least in addition to—the hand of Providence. In the light of Ornstein's work, E.A.J. Honingmann wittily declares that "the Elizabethan World Picture has now been shown up as a copy from an unidentifiable original, if not a complete fake," and in general it appears that contemporary critical opinion has turned against Tillyard with something approaching unanimity.

In terms of my own interests in this essay, in resolution and dramatic closure, it is Tillyard's holism that is particularly problematical. In effect, Tillyard transformed Shakespeare's two "tetralogies" (the use of this term is itself the problem) into a single, unified work, with a beginning in Richard's

deposition and murder, a middle describing the providential punishment visited upon England in civil wars, and a conclusive ending in *Richard III* with the final purgation of the guilty generations and the restoration of divine favor in the form of the accession of the Tudor dynasty that is and was and—so an audience is presumably meant to feel—shall be evermore. Tillyard's Great Idea subsumed within it, or frankly ignored, some rather striking matters of an apparently contradictory nature. The order of composition is one, but the most important for my purposes is production practice, the lack of any evidence to suggest that the plays were presented to Elizabethan audiences as a group, as part of a single sustained dramatic experience, like Greek tragedy or the medieval cycles or Wagner at Bayreuth. Without such evidence, it seems to me questionable to interpret the multiple references in Shakespeare's histories to each other as articulating the grand design of an overriding unity. On the contrary, as I think, they serve rather to make us sense in each individual play a stubborn resistance to achieving wholeness and closure in itself. (pp. 212-14)

At the end of *Shakespeare's History Plays,* Tillyard writes that "it is not likely that anyone will question my conclusion that Shakespeare's Histories with their constant pictures of disorder cannot be understood without assuming a larger principle or order in the background." We can hardly fail to smile now at the opening words, but the irony I wish to emphasize is directed no longer at Tillyard but at the Tillyard-bashing, my own and others', that is so much a part of contemporary criticism. In fact Tillyard's confidence was justified: for an entire generation of scholars without effective exception, Tillyard's conclusions were indeed accepted. How were we all so fooled? Why did this view so generally satisfy us? Tillyard himself provides an answer in his assumption that art is understood through (and by implication valued for) its manifestation of order. Tillyard wrote in the 1940s and for the 1950s, and we have moved in these last two decades to a diametrically opposed position. For the time being, literary theory and Shakespearean commentary have waffled toward Dionysius, toward theatrical experience rather than thematic neatness, and have asserted man's rage for chaos, as Morse Peckham puts it [in his *Man's Rage for Chaos*], the value of literary openness, as Robert M. Adams puts it [in his *Strains of Discord*]. But the counterneeds—the rage for order and for closure—will surely reassert themselves, for the need satisifed by Tillyard to perceive unity, harmony, and resolution is a basic human need. Like the playful and the serious in Richard Lanham's brilliant recent book, *The Motives of Eloquence* (to which I am deeply indebted for the approach in this essay), these are the extremes between which we oscillate in an attempt to find a balanced response to the whole range of human need. And this oscillation is what the recent history of critical response to the history plays, and the history plays themselves, are all about. (p. 215)

To put it baldly, what I wish to suggest is that *1 Henry IV* is not only about civil war, but furnishes an experience of civil war for its audience. Our initiation into the world of the play provides its primary datum: a king and no king, a player-king, not wholly secure and not wholly trustworthy. In other words, it is a world lacking a clear center of authority, and the major dramatic business of the rebellion describes a competition to attain to the seat of authority or to consolidate one's position upon it. The competing characters represent not only particular claims to the throne, but conflicting points of view as to the relative value of, say, freedom (or is it anarchy, riotous misrule?) and the law (or is it resolution-fubbing suppression?), a thematic debate that is often developed in terms of honor, a

Part I. Engraving from Verplanck edition (1847). By permission of the Folger Shakespeare Library.

term and concept as much up for grabs, so to speak, as the throne itself. We in the audience of the play, like the figures within it, lack a center of authority; not a king in our case, but a dramatic hero. Or perhaps there are too many heroes—namely, especially, Hal and Falstaff (though Hotspur must figure there too), one the structural and technical hero, the other the affective center of the play. The *pas de deux* that these two figures dance through the play, especially the first half, acts to reproduce within us the kind of self-division that the play is about. As we are pulled alternately toward and away from these two figures, we are made to experience a kind of psychomachia or internal civil war. This effect is not limited to the Hal-Falstaff material; it is produced by the presentation of many other odd couples in the play, as we find ourselves confronting a range of figures, each of whom is in some way admirable or attractive, but each of whom is also in some way deficient or repellent. The effect is comparable to Hal's joke on Francis: like the little drawer, we are pulled in different directions, recognizing voices on either side to which we are bound, but lacking a single figure that contains all these qualities in himself, a hero in whom we can fully place our confidence.

The analogy with Francis cannot be pushed too far, however, for what is an anxious experience for him is for us a deeply pleasurable one. Unlike Francis, who has to choose sides, we are left free to enjoy all sides in their differences, free to

acknowledge the needs of our nature represented in the full range of the play's experience—in short, the pleasures of variety. (pp. 216-17)

This variety is presented primarily in terms of style, accent, tone of voice. Our attention is insistently drawn to the stylistic interplay—neutrally mimetic, playfully parodic, openly antagonistic—among a range of assumed roles, conscious presentations of self. (p. 217)

It is almost as if the civil war were predicated upon a divergence of styles, a variety of address, and this brings us back to the incongruity I remarked earlier in connection with Francis. There is a difference between living amidst civil war and watching a dramatic representation of civil war; what we would register as intolerable disorder in an actual situation (or in experiencing the play as a "mimesis of life") is sensed as a pleasurable diversity in a dramatic situation (or in experiencing the play as a "literary-theatrical artifice"). . . . The explosive vitality and rich variety we enjoy in the play have civil war as their necessary basis or precondition. There is simply too much energy to be contained within the confines of peaceful rule, too much variety to march all one way. What Hal says to Percy near the end has a meaning beyond his own intentions:

> Two stars keep not their motion in one sphere,
> Nor can one England brook a double reign
> Of Harry Percy and the Prince of Wales. . . .
> [*1 Henry IV*, V.iv. 65-7]

Hal asserts a kind of happy ending, the restoration of a homogeneous political order, but what we sense in his assertion here, as in his similar assertions throughout, is not just the virtue but the defect of a conventionally happy ending, the ruthless delimitation of various possibilitites, the rounding out but also the closing down of experience: in short, the falsification of our hopes.

The words are from Hal's soliloquy at the end of the second scene:

> So when this loose behaviour I throw off,
> And pay the debt I never promised,
> By how much better than my word I am,
> By so much shall I falsify men's hopes. . . .
> [*1 Henry IV*, I. ii. 208-11]

In this context, falsifying men's hopes strikes a discordant note, since what he is talking about is falsifying men's fears, fears that he will continue to be what even now he really is only in show—vain, idle, dissolute. Some editors try to explain away this problem by appealing to a secondary significance of "hopes," but even if such an explanation were convincing, the problem would not go away, for it is the problem of the soliloquy as a whole. John Dover Wilson [see excerpt above, 1943] and the others are right, surely, to tell us that the soliloquy has a reassuring effect in terms of what it tells us both about the prince and about the play's structure. Hal knows what he is doing, and we can trust him to choose the appropriate moment for redeeming time, restoring England to political harmony, and giving us a rounded ending. Yet William Empson and the others are also right, surely, in their insistence that the soliloquy has a very unreassuring effect as well. The unease centers on the figure of Hal himself. We probably wonder about his motives, and we certainly worry about his intentions for Falstaff. (pp. 218-20)

This same ambivalence is at the heart of our experience of the great tavern scene (II.iv). The scene is Hal's at the beginning, with three bits all focusing upon the prince as a player of roles. In the first of these, Hal describes his self-consciously assuming the style of a humble man-of-the-people: "I have sounded the very base-string of humility" [*1H4*, II.iv.5-6]. A cool audience will see a calculated exercise in flesh-pressing in order to guarantee popular support; a warmer one might emphasize that, by learning their language, Hal learns the way the common people think and feel and thus equips himself uniquely, indeed literally, to be their spokesman. In either event (in both, I am inclined to hope), we see Hal methodically preparing himself to be king, and in that context we come to the second bit of role-playing, the Francis joke. (p. 220)

The Hotspur business that follows seems surprising because of the apparent non sequitur, but, as many have perceived, the subject does not really change. Hotspur is another role for Hal to perform, another exercise in mimesis. Though Hal has to give up his plan to "play Percy" [*1H4*, II.iv.109] when Falstaff enters, and never revives it, he already has played him. It is a parody performance, but only in part; the key predicative words, "I am not yet of Percy's mind" [*1H4*, II.iv.101-02], make it clear that he will be of Percy's mind eventually, soon, anon. Or rather, that what is good in Percy will be assimilated into Hal's great sponge of a consciousness, another voice, another style, another role in the ever-expanding repertory with some traces of honor in it, another one from among the totality of human types ("all humours") that will collectively authorize Hal's final role as king. (p. 221)

Falstaff, too, is a role-player, but his mode contrasts completely with Hal's. . . . Falstaff's performances have essentially no motive beyond (in the words of Thomas F. Van Laan) "the high degree of pleasure he obviously derives from shaping and executing the . . . different parts he gets a chance to play." (And from entertaining his audience as well, one ought to add.) They certainly are not intended to be believed, or to be judged by their reflection of any truth outside their own realization. Maurice Morgann was right in his observation that the sheer extravagance of Falstaff's monstrous inventions precludes our sense that he is trying to convince anybody [see excerpt above, 1777]. Even the confirming details that we hear about later—the hacked swords, the blood-beslubbered garments—take their place as stage props, contributing more to heighten his performance as a performance than to persuade us of its validity as reportage. (pp. 221-22)

Inconsistency and contradiction are at the heart of Falstaff's role-playing. For Hal, with his relentlessly single-minded pursuit of kingship, this is unnatural lying, but for Falstaff, whose mode of action denies the validity of a unitary selfhood, this is the source of delightful variety. (p. 222)

What the balance of the play does, however, is to bring us round to an acceptance of the inevitable end, employing a number of strategies that make Falstaff seem a much less and Hal a more endearing figure. . . . As a consequence when Hal, drawing out Falstaff's pistol from the holster and finding it to be a bottle of sack, asks, "What, is it a time to jest and dally now? [*1H4*, V. iii. 55], an audience is inclined—or so it seems to me—to agree with its intention as a rhetorical question. No, it is not, we feel, not *now*. And when in the next scene Hal stands over the corpses of Hotspur and Falstaff in a moment rich in dramatic closure, we are inclined—though again the point is debatable—not only to acknowledge but to approve the climactic inevitability.

What cannot be debated is the closural effect here, primarily in terms simply of the stage image. Hal's standing between

the two corpses suggests a resolution that is at once thematic (the mean, absorbing the virtues of the extremes) and structural (the completion of the two actions which we have been encouraged from the beginning of the play to expect). And the style confirms the effect still further. Obsequy strikes a conventionally closural note, and Hal's last six lines on Falstaff even break into rhyme. Of course, the play cannot quite end here: guts will have to be lugged, and we expect Henry to reenter with some ennobling rhetoric. But nonetheless, the pause (yet another pregnant pause) that follows Hal's exit is one we naturally tend to fill with a sense of the lay in its totality as an integrated and purposeful structure that has moved inevitably to this point of termination.

When Falstaff rises, we feel the same delighted surprise that we experienced in his great triumph earlier in the tavern scene:

> Embowelled? If thou embowel me today, I'll give you leave to powder me and eat me too tomorrow. 'Sblood. 'twas time to counterfeit, or that hot termagant Scot had paid me, scot and lot too. Counterfeit? I lie, I am no counterfeit: to die is to be a counterfeit, for he is but the counterfeit of a man, who had not the life of a man: but to counterfeit dying, when a man thereby liveth, is to be no counterfeit, but the true and perfect image of life indeed.
> [*1 Henry IV*, V. iv. 111-19]
> (pp. 226-27)

And then, in the balance of Falstaff's speech, there follows an astounding second *volte-face*:

> The better part of valour is discretion, in the which better part I have saved my life. 'Zounds, I am afraid of this gunpowder Percy, though he be dead; how if he should counterfeit too and rise? By my faith, I am afraid he would prove the better counterfeit: therefore I'll make him sure, yea, and I'll swear I killed him. Why may not he rise as well as I? Nothing confutes me but eyes, and nobody sees me: therefore, sirrah [*stabbing him*], with a new wound in your thigh, come you along with me.
> [*1 Henry IV*, V. iv. 121-29]

[Our] instinctive revulsion from Falstaff, as he mutilates Hotspur's corpse, constitutes a total repudiation of the character and a repudiation, further, of precisely the kind of dramatic experience we had shared with him in the earlier part of the speech. For us, Hotspur is not just an actor who, as Sigurd Burckhardt points out, not only may but surely will rise as well as Falstaff himself [see excerpt above, 1966]. In Hotspur's lifeless form we sense qualities of nobility that really existed and that really exist as historical and actual possibilities. The play is now experienced once again as a mimetic work, a reflection of reality, within whose condition actions have real consequences and thus must be rendered consistent with a coherent moral purpose. From this perspective, the absolute freedom we have enjoyed in Falstaff comes to seem not only undesirable, but intolerable.

With their ingenious metadramatic analyses, both Burckhardt and Calderwood [see excerpt above, 1973] get very close to the heart of the experience we feel watching this scene, but both of them seem to me fundamentally misleading in the way they interpret the scene as shattering a desirable coherence. For Burckhardt, "Falstaff's rising destroys all kinds of reassuring symmetries'' that seem to guarantee the existence of a coherent structure of political authority. . . . But this is a half-truth; it ignores the delight we feel in Falstaff's rising, and the need, which that delight proves upon our pulses to be real, to escape from such a coherent structure. . . . Calderwood manages, by a conceptual analysis whose finesse is extraordinary even for him, to rescue the play from its own incoherence, and in the process to develop the same sort of poetic theory he had projected onto *A Midsummer Night's Dream* in an earlier work. But the split is there, in the play as a whole and in this scene in particular, for the modes of dramatic experience whose value we are made to recognize, and the two kinds of human need that they make us acknowledge, are indeed irrevocably antagonistic.

In its ending as throughout, the play resists all endeavors to make it conform to a normative, coherent structure. The ending is neither comic nor tragic; indeed, it is and is not an ending. On the one hand, there is ample material to give a sense of closure. Hal's last speech, redeeming Douglas, goes back to Henry-Hotspur in I.iii, where the rebellion began. Unlike his father, the ''vile politican'' [*1H4*, I.iii.241] who would not redeem Mortimer, but unlike Hotspur too in his monomaniacal egotism (''So he that doth redeem [honor] thence might wear / Without corrival all her dignities'' [*1H4*, I.iii.206-07], Hal both redeems the prisoner and generously transfers the honor to another, thereby confirming his promise in the soliloquy to achieve a true nobility of authority under which England may now unite. On the other hand, however, Falstaff survives, unrepentant as ever (since surely the very terms by which he imagines repentance deny its spiritual reality). Yet no one should want it any other way. Falstaff dead or banished might cohere better with the upbeat of Hal's last speech (which we also want), but what price coherence? And as for Falstaff truly repentant, that would be a fate worse than death.

It is all in the play's last words. After Hal's great speech, Henry rises to tell us that England is not yet united, that more battles are to come. ''If we are to consider this 'first part' as an entire play,'' Hartley Coleridge says, ''King Harry's closing speech offends sadly against Aristotle. . . . It is a conclusion in which nothing is concluded.'' But this irresolution is a resolution. (pp. 228-30)

> *Edward Pechter, ''Falsifying Men's Hopes: The Ending of '1 Henry IV','' in* Modern Language Quarterly, *Vol. 41, No. 3, September, 1980, pp. 211-30.*

ADDITIONAL BIBLIOGRAPHY

Ainger, Alfred. ''Sir John Falstaff.'' In his *Lectures and Essays, Vol. I*, pp. 119-55. London: Macmillan & Co., Limited, 1905.
    Interprets Falstaff as having evolved from oral traditions that portrayed the historical John Oldcastle as a corrupt Lollard, through the convention of the comic Vice figure of medieval morality drama.

Aldus, Paul J. ''Analogical Probability in Shakespeare's Plays.'' *Shakespeare Quarterly* VI, No. 4 (Autumn 1955): 397-414.
    Asserts that Shakespeare's plays generally achieve unity through the use of analogues—complex interrelations between scenes, characters, and language—so that what may appear as casual dialogue or extraneous matter is often part of a larger pattern. The casual references to time and the interactions of the comic and serious throughout *Henry IV* are cited as major examples of this procedure. Aldus also discusses *Antony and Cleopatra* and *Julius Caesar* in this connection.

Alexander, Franz. ''A Note on Falstaff.'' *Psychoanalytic Quarterly* II (1933): 592-606.
    A Freudian analysis of Falstaff. For Alexander, Falstaff represents the id, or the ''non-social portions of the personality,'' and his banishment illustrates a dramatic enactment of repression.

Baines, Barbara J. ''Kingship of the Silent King: A Study of Shakespeare's Bolingbroke.'' *English Studies* 61, No. 1 (February 1980): 24-36.
    Focuses on *Richard II* and parts of *Henry IV* and argues that Bolingbroke/Henry IV displays a ''tough-minded pragmatism'' shared by Hal and largely approved by Shakespeare. The Shakespearean concept of kingship that emerges has nothing to do with the theory of divine right, but instead blends Christian ethics and Machiavellian statecraft.

Baker, George Pierce. ''The Chronicle Plays.'' In his *The Development of Shakespeare As A Dramatist*, pp. 142-80. New York, London: Macmillan, 1907.
    Proposes that in *1* and *2 Henry IV* Shakespeare carried the chronicle play to its limit, and suggests that this form evolved eventually into comedy of manners, romance, and, to some extent, tragedy. Baker asserts that Part Two is indeed more memorable for its comedy of manners than for its historicalness, and that in both Part One and Part Two, episode and characterization are more important than plot.

Baker, Harry T. ''The Two Falstaffs.'' *Modern Language Notes* XXXV, No. 8 (December 1919): 470-74.
    Argues that the Falstaff of *The Merry Wives of Windsor* is a faithful continuation of the Falstaff of *Henry IV*. Baker goes against accepted critical opinion with this theory.

Baker, Herschel. Introduction to *Henry IV, Parts 1 and 2*. In *The Riverside Shakespeare*, by William Shakespeare, edited by G. Blakemore Evans, pp. 842-46. Boston: Houghton Mifflin, 1974.
    An overview of *1* and *2 Henry IV* that emphasizes the plays' ambiguities and intricate systems of character parallels. Hal's rejection of Falstaff is seen as ''necessary and painful.''

Bass, Eben. ''Falstaff and the Succession.'' *College English* 24, No. 7 (April 1963): 502-06.
    Interprets Falstaff as a complex Vanity figure who parallels the flattering counselors of *Richard II*, but retains traces of his historical source, Sir John Oldcastle. Bass posits that by rejecting Falstaff Hal avoids repeating Richard II's errors, and proves himself worthy of succession.

Beauchamp. Gorman. ''Falstaff and Civilization's Discontents.'' *College Literature* III, No. 2 (Spring 1976): 94-101.
    Employs the theories of Sigmund Freud and Herbert Marcuse in an attempt to explain the ''pronounced . . . ambiguity in our response to Falstaff and his fate at the hands of Henry V.'' Beauchamp considers *Henry IV* a ''dramatic objectification'' of the conflict between the pleasure principle, embodied by Falstaff, and the reality principle, embodied by Hal. This argument basically supplements the views of A. C. Bradley.

Berkeley, David, and Eidson, Donald. ''The Theme of *Henry IV, Part 1*.'' *Shakespeare Quarterly* XIX, No. 1 (Winter 1968): 25-31.
    Contends that Hal does not change during the play, but follows the cautious policy of dissimulation recommended by Renaissance conduct books. The play does not deal with the education of a prince, and the theme of honor is secondary; the main theme is ''the politic concealment and exhibition of seminally transmitted virtue.''

Berlin, Normand. ''William Shakespeare.'' In his *The Base String: The Underworld in Elizabethan Drama*, pp. 172-229. Rutherford, N.J.: Fairleigh Dickinson University Press, 1967.
    A discussion of the Elizabethan underworld as social phenomenon and literary theme, in which the underworld of *Henry IV* is seen as a metaphor for usurpation and rebellion at society's highest

level. Berlin interprets Falstaff's ambiguous nature as a reflection of Elizabethan literature's portrayal of the underworld as both colorful and socially dangerous.

Berman, Ronald. "The Nature of Guilt in the 'Henry IV' Plays." *Shakespeare Studies* I (1965): 18-28.
Analyzes the motifs of disease and counterfeiting in *2 Henry IV*. Berman asserts that these motifs reveal a corrupt world that is cured by Hal's final act of counterfeiting: his adoption of the "royal image" role.

Berry, Edward I. "The Rejection Scene in *2 Henry IV*." *Studies in English Literature 1500-1900* XVII, No. 2 (Spring 1977): 201-18.
Attempts to synthesize the conflicting interpretations of Hal's rejection of Falstaff, which are epitomized by the opposing views of A. C. Bradley and J. Dover Wilson. Berry finds both approaches partially correct, and argues that Hal indeed plays roles, but not hypocritically, since his roles are "extensions of the self, not masks to disguise it."

Boas, Frederick S. "The Chief Group of Chronicle-History Plays." In his *Shakespeare and His Predecessors*, pp. 235-81. New York: Charles Scribner's Sons, 1896.
Focuses on King Henry, Hal, Hotspur, and Falstaff, and finds Hal and Falstaff preferable to the king and Hotspur.

Boughner, Daniel C. "Traditional Elements in Falstaff." *Journal of English and Germanic Philology* XLIII, No. 4 (October 1944): 417-28.
Theorizes that Falstaff's main dramatic ancestor from continental drama is the "braggart soldier," derived from the Italian theater.

Bowers, Fredson. "Theme and Structure in *King Henry IV, Part 1*." In *The Drama of the Renaissance: Essays for Leicester Bradner*, edited by Elmer M. Blistein, pp. 42-68. Providence: Brown University Press, 1970.
Examines the dramatic structure of *1 Henry IV*, defining Henry and Worcester as the play's formal antagonists. According to Bowers, Hal and Hotspur are their agents, embodying the thematic conflict between the modern state and feudalism. Falstaff is a structural necessity invented to occupy Hal until the denouement.

Bradbrook, M. C. "Comical-Historical." In her *Shakespeare and Elizabethan Poetry*, pp. 189-211. London: Chatto & Windus, 1951.
Places *1* and *2 Henry IV* in the tradition of "comical history," a minor genre characterized by freedom of invention and a jovial atmosphere of good fellowship.

Bryant, J. A., Jr. "Prince Hal and the Ephesians." *The Sewanee Review* LXVII, No. 2 (Spring 1959): 204-19.
Compares Hal's rejection of Falstaff to St. Paul's exhortation to the Ephesians on the need to recognize and cast off the "old" penchant for sin.

Cain, H. Edward. "Further Light on the Relation of *1* and *2 Henry IV*." *Shakespeare Quarterly* III, No. 1 (January 1952): 21-38.
An influential essay which claims that *2 Henry IV* was the unplanned sequel to *1 Henry IV* and should be read accordingly. Cain bases his case on entries in the Stationers' Register regarding Shakespeare's use of sources, and on alleged inconsistencies in the treatment of Hal's reformation in the two plays.

Campbell, Lily B. "The Unquiet Time of Henry IV." In her *Shakespeare's 'Histories': Mirrors of Elizabethan Policy*, pp. 213-54. San Marino, Calif.: The Huntington Library, 1947.
Discusses the relation of the Falstaff plot to the historical action of *Henry IV*. Campbell maintains that the Falstaff story obscures the historical movement of the plays.

Champion, Larry S. "History into Drama: The Perspective of *Henry IV*." *Journal of General Education* XXX, No. 3 (Fall 1978): 185-202.
Finds *1 Henry IV* holding a middle ground between two extremes of Shakespeare's early dramatic technique: the use of an "internalized protagonist" as in *Julius Caesar* and *Richard II*, and the "fragmented perspective and the static characterizations" of *1, 2*, and *3 Henry VI*.

Claeyssens, Astere E. "*Henry IV, Part 1*." In *Lectures on Four of Shakespeare's History Plays*, pp. 19-34. Carnegie Series in English, No. 1. Pittsburgh: Carnegie Institute of Technology, 1953.
Discusses Hal, Hotspur, Falstaff, and, briefly, Henry IV, asserting that at the end of Part 1, Hal achieves a precarious synthesis between the child-worlds of Hotspur and Falstaff and the brute realities of politics.

Council, Norman. "Prince Hal: Mirror of Success." *Shakespeare Studies* VII (1974): 125-46.
Places *1 Henry IV* in the context of Renaissance writings about honor and Aristotle's ethics. Hotspur is seen as the embodiment of the Renaissance ideal of honor, Falstaff as his opposite, and Hal as a pragmatic figure who uses honor only as a means to his own end.

Courtenay, Thomas Peregrine. *Commentaries on the Historical Plays of Shakspeare*, 2 Vols. London: Henry Colburn, Publisher, 1840.
The first systematic attempt to determine the accuracy of the events depicted in Shakespeare's histories. Courtenay surveys several of Shakespeare's sources and examines nineteenth-century historical accounts.

Crane, Milton. "Shakespeare: The Comedies." In his *Shakespeare's Prose*, pp. 66-127. Chicago: University of Chicago Press, 1951.
Contains a section which analyzes the use of prose and verse in *Henry IV*, concluding that they delineate the worlds of comedy and history in the plays.

Croce, Benedetto. "Motives and Development of Shakespeare's Poetry." In his *Ariosto, Shakespeare, and Corneille*, translated by Douglas Ainslie, pp. 163-273. 1920. Reprint. New York: Russell & Russell, 1966.
Views Shakespeare's histories as "without passion for any sort of particular ideals, but . . . animated with sympathy for the varying lots of striving humanity."

Davis, Jo Ann. "Henry IV: From Satirist to Satiric Butt." In *Aeolian Harps: Essays in Honor of Maurice Browning Cramer*, edited by Donna G. Fricke and Donald C. Fricke, pp. 81-93. Bowling Green, Ohio: Bowling Green University Press, 1976.
Argues that in *Richard II* Bolingbroke/Henry IV satirizes Richard's empty ritual, while in *1* and *2 Henry IV* he unsuccessfully attempts to reinstate the order and ritual he had overthrown, becoming the butt of Falstaff's satire and a version of the *senex iratus* of Greek and Latin comedy.

Doran, Madeleine. "Imagery in *Richard II* and in *Henry IV*." *Modern Language Review* XXXVII, No. 2 (April 1942): 113-22.
Asserts that "the images in *Richard II* tend to be direct or explicit, complete, correspondent, point to point, to the idea symbolized and separate from one another; whereas the images in *1 Henry IV* tend to be richer in implicit suggestion and in ambiguity, not fully developed, fluid in outline and fused with one another."

Draper, John W. "Sir John Falstaff." *Review of English Studies* VIII, No. 32 (October 1932): 414-24.
Critiques A. C. Bradley and E. E. Stoll, and interprets Falstaff as an Elizabethan social type: the professional military man.

Draper, John W. "Falstaff and the Plautine Parasite." *The Classical Journal* XXXIII, No. 7 (April 1938): 390-401.
Posits that an important ancestor in Falstaff's complex dramatic lineage was the figure of the "parasite" in the classical Latin comedies of Plautus. This figure lived by his wits in single-minded pursuit of food and drink by flattering and entertaining wealthy patrons. But Draper concludes that a realistic portrayal of Elizabethan mores was a more important influence on Falstaff's character.

Eastmen, Richard M. "Political Views in *Henry IV, Part One*: A Demonstration of Liberal Humanism." *College English* 33, No. 8 (May 1972): 901-07.
The "liberal" half of a debate on *Henry IV* meant to illustrate the differences between Marxist and liberal approaches to literature. While Eastman considers the emphasis on hierarchy and

divine will in *1 Henry IV* outdated, he believes that the play's demonstration of the corrosive effects of rebellion and the important symbolic functions played by the Renaissance monarchy is relevant to the twentieth century.

Emmett, V. J., Jr. "*1 Henry IV*: Structure, Platonic Psychology, and Politics." *Midwest Quarterly* XIX, No. 4 (Summer 1978): 355-69.
>   Interprets *1 Henry IV* through the categories of Plato's analysis of the soul: Falstaff represents appetite, Hotspur the "spirited element," and Hal characterizes reason. The plot depicts Hal's struggle to subordinate Falstaff and his world while assimilating Hotspur's values, achieving a synthesis with reason in control.

Evans, Gareth Lloyd. "The Comical-Tragical-Historical Method: *Henry IV*." In *Early Shakespeare*, edited by John Russell Brown and Bernard Harris, pp. 145-63. Stratford-upon-Avon Studies 3. London: Edward Arnold, 1961.
>   A reading of *1* and *2 Henry IV* as a unified complex of thematic opposites: the "natural" and "political," the comic and the serious, the public and the private. Evans suggests that Shakespeare presents a multi-dimensional reality that paves the way for *Hamlet* and the other great tragedies.

Farnham, Willard, "The Mediaeval Comic Spirit in the English Renaissance." In *Joseph Quincy Adams: Memorial Studies*, edited by James G. McManaway, Giles E. Dawson, and Edwin E. Willoughby, pp. 429-37. Washington: The Folger Shakespeare Library, 1948.*
>   Considers Falstaff a descendent of the grotesque figure in Medieval literature. Farnham maintains that Shakespeare, in his portrait of Falstaff, returned to the acceptance of an imperfect world as understood during the Middle Ages and presented his grotesque fool without moral condemnation.

Fehrenbach, Robert J. "The Characterization of the King in *1 Henry IV*." *Shakespeare Quarterly* 30, No. 1 (Winter 1979): 42-50.
>   Asserts that the methods of characterization used to portray King Henry—irony, contrasts with other characters, descriptions by other characters, and the unsaid—mirror the secretive Machiavellian traits of his personality.

Freeman, Leslie. "Shakespeare's Kings and Machiavelli's Prince." In *Shakespeare Encomium*, edited by Anne Paolucci, pp. 25-43. The City College Papers I. New York: The City College, 1964.*
>   A detailed study of the influence of Machiavelli's *The Prince* on the politics of Richard II, Henry IV, and Henry V. Freeman claims that Richard II ignored Machiavellian policy to his peril, while the two Henrys followed *The Prince*'s essential ideas and demonstrated their effectiveness.

Frye, Northrop. "The Argument of Comedy." *English Institute Essays*, 1948, pp. 58-73.
>   Notes that Shakespearean comedy features an idealized "green world" as the main locus of comic life, and that the characters move back and forth between it and the historical world. According to Frye, Falstaff's tavern society constitutes such a world, but *1* and *2 Henry IV* lack true comic resolution.

Gillett, Peter J. "Vernon and the Metamorphosis of Hal." *Shakespeare Quarterly* 28, No. 3 (Summer 1977): 351-53.
>   A close reading of the speech in which Vernon praises the newly armed Hal. Gillett argues that the opining seven lines are purposely ambiguous and can be interpreted as mockery or as praise. The main purpose of the speech, Gillett believes, is to prepare the audience for Hal's transformation.

Goldman, Michael. "Falstaff Asleep." In his *Shakespeare and the Energies of Drama*, pp. 45-57. Princeton, N.J.: Princeton University Press, 1972.
>   Focuses on Hal's rejection of Falstaff. Goldman agrees with most twentieth-century critics that Falstaff's banishment was necessary to the health of the English nation, but he attempts to reconcile this necessity with an equally strong conviction that Falstaff is important as a sympathetic figure who balances the thematics of the plays.

Gottschalk, Paul A. "Hal and the 'Play Extempore' in *1 Henry IV*." *Texas Studies in Literature and Language* XV, No. 4 (Winter 1974): 605-14.
>   Appraises *1 Henry IV* as a play without a climax. The critic states that Shakespeare compensates for this flaw by arranging three incidents which expose Hal's ultimate characterization to the audience while hiding it from his comtemporaries: Hal's first soliloquy, the 'play extempore,' and the confrontation with Henry IV after the tavern scenes.

Harbage, Alfred. "Paradoxes." In his *As They Liked It: An Essay on Shakespeare and Morality*. pp. 73-82. New York: Macmillan, 1947.
>   Finds Falstaff an ineffective wrongdoer whose sins become sources of delight through Shakespeare's paradoxical art. Harbage notes that "delight in [Falstaff] is a test of our normality."

Hardy, Barbara. *Dramatic Quicklyisms: Malaproic Word Technique in Shakespeare's 'Henriad,'* 2 Vols. Salzburg Studies in English Literature. Salzburg: Institut für Englische Sprache und Literatur, Universität Salzburg, 1979.
>   An attentive examination of Mistress Quickly's language in the three plays in which she appears. This work contains detailed surveys of literature on a number of topics related to the main subject and a lengthy bibliography.

Hawking, Sherman H. "Virtue and Kingship in Shakespeare's *Henry IV*." *English Literary Renaissance* 5, No. 3 (Autumn 1975): 313-43.
>   Discusses *Henry IV* in the light of Elizabethan and classical writings on kingship and the education of the prince. In Part One, according to Hawkins, Hal learns fortitude and temperance; in Part Two, he learns justice and wisdom.

Hibbard, G. R. "*Henry IV* and *Hamlet*." *Shakespeare Survey* 30 (1977): 1-12.
>   Sees *Hamlet* and *Henry IV* as "break-through" or "growth point" plays in which Shakespeare made major advances in his art. Hibbard asserts that *Henry IV* and *Hamlet* share a variety of material: ironically paralleled characters, deft counterpointing between prose and verse, and major characters (Hamlet and Falstaff) who transcend the plays in which they appear.

Holland, Norman N. Introduction to *Henry IV, Part Two*. In *The Complete Signet Classic Shakespeare*, by William Shakespeare, edited by Sylvan Barnet, pp. 678-85. New York: Harcourt Brace Jovanovich, 1972.
>   Finds that *2 Henry IV* is built around betrayals and mocked expectations, and is closer in mood to the tragedies and problem plays than Part One.

Hunter, G. K. "Shakespeare's Politics and the Rejection of Falstaff." *The Critical Quarterly* I, No. 3 (1959): 229-36.
>   Briefly surveys *Henry IV* criticism from Dryden to L. C. Knights, dividing commentators into two major camps: "those who see Shakespeare as protected by a layer of irony from any identificaiton with the ethics of political success", and those who "see Shakespeare as primarily the spokesman of his own age." The crux of their differences is the rejection of Falstaff.

Hunter, G. K. Introduction to *Shakespeare: 'Henry IV, Parts I and II's: A Casebook*, By William Shakespeare, edited by G. K. Hunter, pp. 9-20. London: Macmillan, 1970.
>   Surveys three centuries of major criticism of *Henry IV*, focusing on the following topics: the history plays as genre, the politics of the plays, their unity, Falstaff, and Hal's relation to Falstaff.

Hunter, Robert G. "Shakespeare's Comic Sense As It Strikes Us Today: Falstaff and the Protestant Ethic." In *Shakespeare: Pattern of Excelling Nature*, edited by David Bevington and Jay L. Halio, pp. 125-32. Newark: University of Delaware Press, 1978.
>   Maintains that *The Henriad* dramatizes, through the rejection of Falstaff, the victory of the Protestant ethic over the decadence of sensual gratification.

Hunter, William B., Jr. "Falstaff." *South Atlantic Quarterly* L, No. 1 (January 1951): 86-95.

Contends that Hal represents the Aristotelian golden mean between the vicious excesses of Falstaff and Hotspur.

Jember, Gregory K. "Glory, Jest, and Riddle: The Three Deaths of Falstsff." *Toth* 12, No. 3 (Spring/Summer 1972): 30-8.

Discovers three separate but related Falstaffs in the Henriad. In Part One, he is the embodiment of the comic spirit; in Part Two, a mortal jester; and with the report of his death in *Henry V*, he becomes a mystery with hitherto unsuspected qualities.

Jorgensen, Paul A. "Valor's Better Parts: Backgrounds and Meanings of Shakespeare's Most Difficult Proverb." *Shakespeare Studies* IX (1976): 141-58.

A wide-ranging inquiry into the precise meaning of Falstaff's famous dictum. Jorgensen claims that the statement is Shakespeare's gnomic rendering of sentiments expressed in a large body of classical and Renaissance writings on the relation of courage and wisdom. Jorgensen finds no single meaning for the statement, but a number of serious and humorous implications, including sexual ones.

Kaiser, Walter. *Praisers of Folly: Erasmus, Rabelais, Shakespeare.* Cambridge: Harvard University Press, 1963. 318 p.*

A comparative study of three great Renaissance "Fools": Erasmus's Stultitia in *The Praise of Folly;* Rabelais's Panurge in *The Third Book of Pantagruel;* and Shakespeare's Falstaff. Falstaff is interpreted as the most secular of the fools, the only one who does not approach the status of "fool of Christ." But his relationship with Hal shares the complex ironic interplay found between Don Quixote and Sancho Panza.

Kingsford, C. L. "Fifteenth-Century History in Shakespeare's Plays." In his *Prejudice and Promise in Fifteenth-Century England;* pp. 1-21. 1925. Reprint. London: Frank Cass & Co., 1962.

Analyzes the historical accuracy of Shakespeare's history plays through survey of Holinshed, Hall, and Stow. Kingsford credits Hall, with his "Tudor and Protestant sympathies," as the ultimate source of Shakespeare's interpretation of the Lancastrian period.

Kittredge, George Lyman. Introduction to *The First Part of King Henry the Fourth*, by William Shakespeare, edited by George Lyman Kittredge, pp. vii-xiv. New York: Ginn and Company, 1940.

Brief, general essay on *1 Henry IV*, including discussions of the historical drama, and the major characters.

Knight, Charles. Supplementary Notice to *King Henry IV, Parts I and II.* In *The Comedies, Histories, Tragedies, and Poems of William Shakespeare, Vol. 5,* by William Shakespeare, edited by Charles Knight, pp. 254-77. 1842. Reprint. New York: AMS Press, 1968.

A reading of *1* and *2 Henry IV* based on the scattered remarks of Coleridge. Knight states that the plays' central thematic purpose is to display the evils of civil war, and that the dramatic center is Hal's change of character.

Knight, G. Wilson. "This Sceptred Isle: A Study of Shakespeare's Kings." In his *The Sovereign Flower,* pp. 11-92. London: Methuen, 1958.

Briefly points out that the theme of kingship is basic to the plays. Hal is described as a characteristically English hero-to-be, and Falstaff as an essential tutor to him.

Knights, L. C. "Shakespeare's Politics: With Some Reflections on the Nature of Tradition." In *Proceedings of the British Academy,* pp. 115-32. London: The Oxford University Press, 1957.

Groups *1* and *2 Henry IV* with *Julius Caesar* and *Henry V* as plays that pose the problem of humane political action, a problem explored on a deeper level in *King Lear, Macbeth,* and *Coriolanus.* Knights sees a political legacy to the twentieth century in Shakespeare's awareness of the need to "know the soul" to preserve a sense of humanity in politics.

Knowles, Richard. "Unquiet and the Double Plot of '2 Henry IV'." *Shakespeare Studies* II (1966): 133-40.

Examines the motif of sound in *Henry IV, Part 2* and demonstrates how it informs both the historical and comic plots, particularly with respect to the play's central theme of disorder and turbulence.

Knowlton, E. C. "Falstaff Redux." *Journal of English and Germanic Philology* XXV (1926): 193-215.

Reacts largely to E. E. Stoll's view of Falstaff, claiming that Falstaff is neither a coward nor a *miles gloriosus,* but a type of old veteran soldier found more in life than in literature.

Kris, Ernst. "Prince Hal's Conflict." *The Psychoanalytic Quarterly* XVII, No. 4 (1948): 487-506.

Psychoanalytic interpretation of the father-son conflicts of *Henry IV* in terms of Sigmund Freud's theory of the Oedipal complex.

La Branche, Anthony. "'If Thou Wert Sensible of Courtesy': Private and Public Virtue in *Henry IV, Part One.*" *Shakespeare Quarterly* XVII, No. 4 (Autumn 1966): 371-82.

Posits, contrary to E.M.W. Tillyard, that Hotspur is not subordinate to Hal in the hierarchy of values in the play. La Branche decides that Shakespeare strikes a moral balance between the two, and treats them with a complex interplay of irony and contrast.

La Guardia, Eric. "Ceremony and History: The Problem of Symbol from *Richard II* to *Henry V.*" In *Pacific Coast Studies in Shakespeare,* edited by Waldo F. McNeir and Thelma Greenfield, pp. 68-88. Eugene: University of Oregon Books, 1966.

Studies the naturalistic/symbolic dichotomy in the Henriad, arguing that Shakespeare sought to define an "uneasy equilibrium" between the demands of imagination and experience in the plays. Henry V's final achievement is seen as possessing a definite "Pyrrhic quality."

Lawry, Jon S. "Born to Set It Right: Hal, Hamlet, and Prospero." *Ball State Teachers College Forum* V, No. 3 (Autumn 1964): 16-24.

Notes that the themes of usurpation and corruption, a play-within-the-play, and a purging hero are common elements in *1 Henry IV, Hamlet,* and *The Tempest.*

Levin, Harry. "Falstaff Uncolted." *Modern Language Notes* XLI, No. 4 (April 1946): 305-10.

Claims that, although Elizabethan stage conventions forbade the use of horses on stage, Shakespeare's language compensates for the lack, particularly in *1 Henry IV,* which contains more equine references than any other Shakespeare play. Despite the limitations of the stage, the play achieves "all the range and mobility of the picaresque."

Levin, Lawrence L. "Hotspur, Falstaff, and the Emblem of Wrath in *1 Henry IV.*" *Shakespeare Studies* X (1977): 43-65.

Links Hotspur and Falstaff with Renaissance emblems depicting the capital sin of wrath. This is achieved with Falstaff through parody and Hotspur by tragedy.

Macisaac, Warren J. "A Commodity of Good Names in the *Henry IV* Plays." *Shakespeare Quarterly* 29, No. 3 (Summer 1978): 417-19.

Analyzes the distribution of the prince's three names—Henry, Hal, and Harry—through *1* and *2 Henry IV.* "Hal" is, with a single exception, a name only Falstaff uses, while "Harry" distinguishes him from his father and links the prince with Hotspur. The name "Henry" occurs only three times.

Manheim, Michael. "New Thoughts to Deck Our Kings." In his *The Weak King Dilemma in the Shakespearean History Play,* pp. 161-82. Syracuse: Syracuse University Press, 1973.

Interprets *Henry IV* as the "triumph of the Machiavellian spirit over the human" as Shakespeare realizes that government is "life-destroying even as it performs its imperative function of preserving life." *Henry IV* is subordinate to *Henry V* for purposes of this thematic study.

Mathews, Brander. "The Falstaff Plays." In his *Shakespere As a Playwright,* pp. 117-41, New York: Charles Scribner's Sons, 1913.

Claims that Part One is superior to Part Two and that Falstaff deteriorates in Part Two. The critic posits that the plays represent a regression in dramatic construction (compared with *Romeo and Juliet),* but an advance in characterization.

Matthews, Honor. "The Character of the Usurper." In his *Character and Symbol in Shakespeare's Plays,* pp. 44-67. Cambridge: At the University Press, 1962.

Argues that the Hal of both *Henry IV* and *Henry V* is a character of a deeply divided mind, sumultaneously humane and Machiavellian.

McGuire, Richard L. "The Play-within-the-Play in *1 Henry IV*." *Shakespeare Quarterly* XVIII, No. 1 (Winter 1967): 47-52.

Cites the "play extempore" as the occasion for a struggle between the world views of Hal and Falstaff, and identifies it as a major turning point in the play.

McNamara, Anne Marie. "*Henry IV*: The King as Protagonist." *Shakespeare Quarterly* X, No. 3 (Summer 1959): 423-31.

Asserts that, because of their status as Tudor history plays, *1* and *2 Henry IV* should be considered separate plays in which the title character is also the protagonist of each play.

McNier, Waldo R. "Structure and Theme in the First Tavern Scene of *1 Henry IV*." In *Pacific Coast Studies in Shakespeare*, edited by Waldo F. McNeir and Thelma N. Greenfield, pp. 89-105. Eugene: University of Oregon Books, 1966.

Treats the first tavern scene as a miniature five-act drama in its own right. According to McNeir, it foreshadows Hal's reformation and the rejection of Falstaff.

Meyers, Walter E. "Hal: The Mirror of All Christian Kings." In *A Fair Day in the Affections: Literary Essays in Honor of Robert B. White, Jr.*, edited by Jack D. Durant and M. Thomas Hester, pp. 67-77. Raleigh, N. C.: Winston Press, 1980.

A character analysis of Hal in *Henry IV* that finds him cruel, calculating, and addicted to role-playing.

Moorman, F. W. "Shakespeare's History-Plays and Daniel's *Civil Wars*." *Jahrbuch der Deutschen Shakespeare—Gesellschaft, 1904*, pp. 69-83.*

A detailed comparison of *1* and *2 Henry IV* and Samuel Daniel's epic poem *The Civil Wars*. Moorman finds significant similarities to the latter in the details of Hal's heroics at Shrewsbury and Henry's deathbed scenes.

Morgan, A. E. *Some Problems of Shakespeare's "Henry the Fourth"*. London: Shakespeare Association, 1924, 43 p.

Posits the existence of a lost play as the common source of the anonymous *The Famous Victories of Henry V* and a supposed early Shakespeare version of *1 Henry IV*. Evidence adduced to support this view includes identification of "verse fossils" in Falstaff's prose speeches and an otherwise unexplained fragment in the hand of playwright John Day: a dramatic blank-verse speech that alludes to the dead body of Percy, but has no analogue in any extant play.

Morris, Harry. "Prince Hal: Apostle to the Gentiles." *Clio* 7, No. 2 (Winter 1978): 227-45.

Claims that Hal embodies the roles of priest and apostle which are assigned to Christ in Paul's Epistle to the Hebrews. The plays do not describe the education of a prince, states Morris, but rather the prince's efforts to purge himself and to "redeem the time" and the other characters.

Murry, John Middleton. "The Creation of Falstaff." In his *John Clare and Other Studies*, pp. 181-207. London: Peter Nevill, 1950.

Maintains that only in *1 Henry IV* is Falstaff the greatest of all comic characters, because the Falstaff of *2 Henry IV* and *The Merry Wives of Windsor* is marred by the time constraints under which Shakespeare composed those plays.

Palmer, D. J. "Casting Off the Old Man: History and St. Paul in *Henry IV*." *Critical Quarterly* 12, No. 3 (Autumn 1970): 265-83.

Asserts that allusions to Paul's Epistle to the Ephesians are central to the meaning of *Henry IV*.

Pettigrew, John. "The Mood of *Henry IV, Part 2*." In *Stratford Papers, 1965-67*, edited by B.A.W. Jackson, pp. 145-67. Shannon: Irish University Press, 1969.

Defends *2 Henry IV* from charges that it is inferior to *1 Henry IV*. Pettigrew feels that Part Two is thematically unified, but in a darker tone than the relatively sunny Part One, and he sees Part Two as "more profound, mature, and searching."

Pierce, Robert B. "The *Henry IV* Plays." In his *Shakespeare's History Plays: The Family and the State*, pp. 171-217. Columbus: Ohio State University Press, 1973.

Examines *Henry IV* in terms of the interplay between the public and the private as it is manifested in the dual relations of Henry IV and Hal: father and son, king and prince. Pierce regards Hal as the hero, and Falstaff as an impediment to Hal's personal and political maturity.

Pinciss, G. M. "The Old Honor and the New Courtesy: *1 Henry IV*." *Shakespeare Survey* 31 (1978): 85-91.

Analyzes Hal and Hotspur by the standards of two influential Renaissance handbooks of aristocratic behavior: Baldassar Castiglione's *The Courtier* and Thomas Elyot's *The Governour*. Pinciss concludes that Hotspur exemplifies medieval chivalry, while Hal excels in Renaissance courtly skills.

Planchon, Roger. "Advancing with Shakespeare: No Falstaffs in Formosa?" *The Times Literary Supplement*, No. 3262 (September 3, 1964): 817-18.

Discussion of *Henry IV* as a viable commentary on the abuses of power in the modern world.

Raleigh, Walter. "Story and Character." In his *English Men of Letters: Shakespeare*, pp. 128-208. London: Macmillan, 1907.

Regards Falstaff as the hero of the plays, a kind of "comic Hamlet" who had to be eliminated if the heroics of *Henry V* were to be effective.

Reese, M. M. *The Cease of Majesty: A Study of Shakespeare's History Plays*. London: Edward Arnold, 1961, 350 p.

Argues that *Henry IV* depicts the education of a prince who overcomes three different temptations which are represented by his father, Hotspur, and Falstaff.

Reik, Theodor. "Rosenkavalier Waltzes." In his *The Haunting Melody: Psychoanalytic Experiences in Life and Music*, pp. 121-46. New York: Farrar, Straus, and Young, 1953.*

Contains an aside which identifies Falstaff with the "obese cycloid personality type" and suggests latent homosexuality in his feelings for the prince.

Reno, Raymond H. "Hotspur: The Integration of Character and Theme." In *Renaissance Papers*, edited by George Walton Williams and Peter G. Phialas, pp. 17-25. Durham, N.C.: The Southeastern Renaissance Conference, 1963.

Modern reaction against the character studies of the nineteenth century. Reno maintains that no critic should view character merely as a representation of theme, but should regard it as embodying theme "so as to articulate it through the unique psychological pattern of the character himself." Reno demonstrates this idea with respect to the character of Hotspur, whom he sees as psychologically embodying, as well as projecting onto the play's structure, the theme of disorder.

Ribner, Irving. "Bolingbroke, A True Machiavellian." *Modern Language Quarterly* 9, No. 2 (June 1948): 177-84.

Primarily discusses *Richard II*, maintaining that Bolingbroke's actions are Machiavellian, not in the tradition of the stage villain Machiavelli of Elizabethan drama, but in the vein of the political philosophy in Machiavelli's *The Prince*.

Ribner, Irving. "Shakespeare's Second Tetralogy." In his *The English History Play in the Age of Shakespeare*, rev. ed., pp. 151-93. London: Methuen, 1965.

Sees *1* and *2 Henry IV* concerned primarily with the education of the prince, with Falstaff representing the antithesis of the values embodied in an ideal king.

Rossiter, A. P. "Ambivalence: The Dialectic of the Histories." In his *Angel with Horns and Other Shakespeare Lectures*, edited by Graham Storey, pp. 40-64. London: Longmans, Green and Co., 1961.

States that *Henry IV* should be read as ironically structured and dramatically ambivalent. The plays, according to Rossiter, contain both an assertion of Tudor orthodoxy and a critique of it.

Saccio, Peter. *Shakespeare's English Kings: History, Chronicle, and Drama.* New York: Oxford University Press, 1977, 268 p.

Recounts current knowledge of the events which Shakespeare depicted in his history plays. Saccio compares and contrasts actual history with the action of plays.

Sanders, Norman. "The True Prince and the False Thief: Prince Hal and the Shift of Identity." *Shakespeare Survey* 30 (1977): 29-34.

Describes a number of parallels between Hal and the other characters of *Henry IV*, and discerns a "pattern of dislocation of self and society" that is thematically central to the plays. Hal's apparent criminality is interpreted as his radical attempt to break away from a diseased social order. Sanders believes that, unlike Hamlet, Hal discovers a morally viable public role.

Schell, Edgar T. "Prince Hal's Second 'Reformation'." *Shakespeare Quarterly* XXI, No. 1 (Winter 1970): 11-16.

Characterizes Hal's apparent reformation in Part Two as a change in his father's perceptions, unlike the true reform that was presented in Part One. Schell asserts that Hal's "second reformation" is Shakespeare's skillful response to the structural problem created by his decision to write a continuation of Part One.

Schuchter, J. D. "Prince Hal and Francis: The Initation of an Action." *Shakespeare Studies* III (1967): 129-37.

Suggests that a main trait of Hal is his propensity to think his way through situations by "theatricalizing" through play-action and impersonations. The "play extempore," Francis the drawer, and Hal's discussion of Hotspur exemplify this trait.

Schucking, Levin L. "Motives for Action." In his *Character Problems in Shakespeare's Plays*, pp. 203-36. 1922. Reprint. Gloucester, Mass.: Peter Smith, 1959.

Treats Hal's first soliloquy as an example of a "primitive" monologue used as a choral device to aid the exposition of the play. Unlike Hamlet's soliloquies, Schucking asserts, Hal's first speech is not to be regarded as a clue to personality.

Seltzer, Daniel. "Prince Hal and Tragic Style." *Shakespeare Survey* 30 (1977): 31-40.

Discusses Hal's characterization as the point in Shakespeare's dramatic career in which he became capable of representing the interior life of characters in the process of change.

Sen Gupta, S. C. "Sir John Falstaff." In his *Shakespearian Comedy*, pp. 250-75. Delhi: Oxford University Press, 1950.

Praises Bradley's reading of *Henry IV* and rejects that of Gervinus. Sen Gupta describes Falstaff as a kind of artist who lives "an amoral philosophy of joy" which is "anterior to moral evaluation."

Sen Gupta, S. C. "The Second Tetralogy." In his *Shakespeare's Historical Plays*, pp. 113-50. London: Oxford University Press, 1964.

Maintains that the eight English history plays share a common "amoral vision of history" and that, in *Henry IV*, Hal is not privileged over Falstaff, who is the real center of Part Two.

Sicherman, Carol Marks. "'King Hal': The Integrity of Shakespeare's Portrait." *Texas Studies in Literature and Language* 21, No. 4 (Winter 1979): 503-21.

Analyzes the language used by Hal in *Henry IV* and *Henry V*. Sicherman finds continuity rather than disjunction between Hal as prince and as king, though only when the masks that young Hal adopts as prince are correctly understood.

Siegel, Paul N. "Shakespeare and the Neo-Chivalric Cult of Honor." In his *Shakespeare in His Time and Ours*, pp. 122-62. Notre Dame: University of Notre Dame Press, 1964.

States that Hotspur represents an individualistic cult of honor found in Tudor duelling manuals, which are based on sixteenth-century Italian attitudes, while Hal represents Christian humanism.

Sims, Ruth E. "The Green Old Age of Falstaff." *Bulletin of the History of Medicine* XIII, No. 2 (February 1943): 144-57.

A detailed study of Falstaff's age, health, and humors in the light of Elizabethan medical treatises. Sims concludes that Falstaff is at least 62, and that, while showing signs of the other humors, he is predominantly a "choleric type."

Smith, Gordon Ross. "A Rabble of Princes: Considerations of Touching Shakespeare's Political Orthodoxy in the Second Tetralogy." *Journal of the History of Ideas* (1980): 29-48.

Discusses Shakespeare's acceptance of the Tudor myth and its presence in *Henry IV*. Smith disputes Tillyard's claim that *Henry IV* dramatizes elements of the Tudor myth popular during Shakespeare's lifetime, and even maintains that the text itself contradicts this type of interpretation.

Snider, Denton J. "King Henry IV." In his *The Shakespearian Drama: A Commentary: The Histories*, pp. 345-406. 1889. Reprint. Danville, Ind.: Indiana Publishing Co., 1894.

Claims that Hal is the hero of *Henry IV*, a "colossal figure" who synthesizes traits of Hotspur and Falstaff and personifies the rise of the national spirit. Snider finds Falstaff a self-conscious personification of the comic spirit who lacks moral instinct and is rightly rejected by Hal.

Spencer, Benjamin T. "The Stasis of *Henry IV, Part II*." *Tennessee Studies in Literature* VI (1961): 61-9.

Contends that 2 *Henry IV* dramatizes the stasis or "still-stand" which often precedes periods of national greatness, and that the dramatic form of the play mirrors this theme.

Spivack, Bernard. "Falstaff and the Psychomachia." *Shakespeare Quarterly* VIII, No. 4 (Autumn 1957): 449-59.

A contribution to the critical discussion of Falstaff's dramatic ancestry. Like several critics before him, Spivack considers Falstaff to be descended from medieval morality plays; he also cites the fourth-century Latin poem *Psychomachia* as a source for the character. In addition, Spivack attempts to define how the allegorical tradition interacts with realism to form the synthesis of *Henry IV*.

Sprague, Arthur Colby. "Gadshill Revisited." *Shakespeare Quarterly* IV, No. 2 (April 1953): 125-37.

Surveys the major contributors to the long debate about Falstaff's alleged cowardice, including Samuel Johnson, Maurice Morgann, A. C. Bradley, E. E. Stoll, and J. Dover Wilson. Sprague himself favors the view that Falstaff is indeed cowardly.

Stoll, E[lmer] E[dgar]. "Henry V." In his *Poets and Playwrights: Shakespeare, Jonson, Spencer, Milton*, pp. 31-54. Minneapolis: University of Minnesota Press, 1930.

A discussion of *Henry V* containing asides which cite *1 Henry IV* as Shakespeare's greatest history play. Stoll praises the play's realism, characterization, and unity of comic and serious plots.

Stoll, Elmer Edgar. "A Falstaff for the 'Bright'." *Modern Philology* LI, No. 3 (February 1954): 145-59.

Criticizes J. Dover Wilson's *Fortunes of Falstaff*, arguing that, like Maurice Morgann and A. C. Bradley, Wilson sentimentalizes Falstaff while ignoring Johnson's firm insistence that Falstaff is a coward.

Stone, William B. "Literature and Class Ideology: *Henry IV, Part One*." *College English* 33, No. 8 (May 1972): 891-900.

The Marxist half of a debate that illustrates the differences between Marxist and liberal approaches to literature. To Stone, *1 Henry IV* reveals an Elizabethan nationalistic ideology which he believes aided in the destruction of feudalism and the development of the modern state. According to Stone, Hotspur represents feudalism, Falstaff the commoners, and Hal the emerging state. Richard M. Eastman presents the liberal argument (see annotation above).

Vickers, Brian. "The World of Falstaff." In his *The Artistry of Shakespeare's Prose*, rev. ed., pp. 89-170. London: Methuen, 1968.

Closely analyzes the prose portions of the four plays concerning Falstaff. Vickers claims that Falstaff's verbal facility allows him to reinterpret his deeds in a self-serving way, particularly through equivocations. Hal's role is to find instances of Falstaff's speciousness.

Waldock, A.J.A. "The Men in Buckram." *Review of English Studies* XXIII, No. 89 (January 1947): 16-23.

Replies to Dover Wilson's contention that Falstaff knew all along that Hal and Poins were disguised in buckram at Gadshill. Waldock maintains that Falstaff was not aware of the disguise, and that his blatant lying was simply vaudevillian humor.

Walker, Saxon. "Mime and Heraldry in *Henry IV, Part I*." *English* XI, No. 63 (Autumn 1956): 91-6.

Examines the speeches of Hotspur, Hal, Falstaff, and the King for instances of the mimicry of other characters. Walker demonstrates how this mimicry helps to define the numerous parallels and ironic contrasts in the play. He also discusses examples of imagery derived from heraldry.

Webber, Joan. "The King's Symbolic Role: From *Richard II* to *Henry V*." *Texas Studies in Literature and Language* IV, No. 4 (Winter 1963): 530-38.

A study of the themes of rhetoric and kingship, language and reality in the Henriad. Webber notes that Hal recognizes the symbolic and imaginative role a king must play to be an effective leader.

Welsford, Enid. *The Fool: His Social and Literary History*. New York: Farrar & Rinehart, 1935, 374 p.

Contains only brief remarks on Falstaff as a buffoon. However, the critic's account of the history of fools, parasites, buffoons, lords of misrule, and clowns "in reality and in imagination" is of great relevance to the study of Falstaff's literary and social ancestry.

Wendell, Barrett. "The Plays of Shakespere, from *A Midsummer Night's Dream* to *Twelfth Night*." In his *William Shakspere: A Study in Elizabethan Literature*, pp. 103-220. New York: Charles Scribner's Sons, 1895.

A reading of *Henry IV* as closet drama and as an anticipation of Walter Scott. Wendell interprets Falstaff as a character originally intended as a satirical attack against Puritans.

Whittier, Gayle. "Falstaff as a Welshwoman: Uncomic Androgyny." *Ball State University Forum* XX, No. 3 (Summer 1979): 23-35.

Suggests that understanding Falstaff as a "submerged androgyn— a false woman" accounts for the ambiguities surrounding Falstaff in the history of criticism.

Wilson, J. Dover. "The Political Background of Shakespeare's *Richard II* and *Henry IV*." *Shakespeare-Jahrbuch* LXXV (1939): 36-51.

A lecture delivered before the German Shakespeare Society. Dover Wilson asserts that Shakespeare fused Lancastrian and Yorkist accounts of the historical events in *Richard II* and *Henry IV* in a viewpoint that stresses the evils of civil war and the value of Tudor stability.

Wilson, J. Dover. "The Origins and Development of Shakespeare's *Henry IV*." *The Library* XXVI, Fourth Series, No. 1 (June 1945): 2-16.

Speculates on the genesis of the two parts of *Henry IV*. Dover Wilson traces the development of the Wild Hal legends, contending that Samuel Daniel and John Stow were important sources for the plays. He believes that the two extant *Henry IV* plays are revisions of a single, largely verse drama which Oldcastle's descendants forced Shakespeare to withdraw, and which he later revised to its present two-play form.

Young, David P. Introduction to *Twentieth Century Interpretations of "Henry IV, Part Two": A Collection of Critical Essays*, edited by David P. Young, pp. 1-12. Englewood Cliffs, N. J.: Prentice-Hall, 1968.

Treats *2 Henry IV* as an autonomous play organized around the themes of change, decay, disease, and misapprehension.

Zeeveld, W. Gordon. "'Food for Powder'—'Food for Worms'." *Shakespeare Quarterly* III, No. 3 (July 1952): 249-53.

An image-pattern analysis in which the critic argues that Falstaff's catechism on honor and Hotspur's death interact to create a sense of the limitations of both views of life.

Timon of Athens

DATE: The consensus of recent criticism dates *Timon*'s composition between 1604 and 1609, with the year 1607 a favorite hypothesis. There is no external evidence to help date the play: no record exists of a performance in Shakespeare's lifetime, and its earliest appearance in print was in the First Folio (1623). In the absence of external evidence, scholars have attempted to date the play by comparing its style, theme, and metrics to more authenticated plays in the canon. But metrical and stylistic tests are uncertain because of the "rough" state of the text of the First Folio. The strong possibility that the text is unfinished, corrupted in the printing, or written in collaboration with another playwright argues caution in applying such measures—which, however, have been relied on by many scholars in arriving at the 1607 conjecture.

TEXT: *Timon* is one of eighteen Shakespearean plays printed for the first time in the First Folio, but the circumstances of its placement in the Folio make it unique. It occupies the gap between *Romeo and Juliet* and *Julius Caesar* that had been created by the withdrawal of *Troilus and Cressida* from that position, perhaps because of copyright difficulties. Critics are able to trace the change because *Timon* required fewer pages than *Troilus*, and the substitution led to misnumberings of the pages, a blank, and other technical anomalies. In addition, a few copies of the Folio retain the cancelled leaf on which *Romeo and Juliet* ends and *Troilus* begins on the facing page.

Editors since Samuel Johnson have agreed that the text of *Timon* seems unusually corrupt and problematic. Some speeches contain a mixture of prose, blank verse, and rhymed couplets; in others prose seems to have been printed as verse or the verse is unusually loose in metric structure. There are numerous inconsistencies in the naming and spelling of the names of the characters and some stage directions seem misplaced or unclear. Many scholars have suspected that sections that would have clarified these points are lost. This would help explain other more substantial questions like the relation of Alcibiades's scene with the Senate to the main plot or the exact manner of Timon's death.

SOURCES: The name Timon was proverbial in the Renaissance for misanthropy; among numerous examples are an allusion by Shakespeare himself to "critic Timon" in *Love's Labor's Lost*. The story of Timon was treated in a number of works, all deriving ultimately from two classical treatments of the Timon story by Plutarch and Lucian.

It is almost certain that Shakespeare made use of Sir Thomas North's English translation of Plutarch's *Lives of the Noble Grecians and Romans*, the source also for *Julius Caesar, Antony and Cleopatra, Coriolanus*, and parts of other plays. The two apparently contradictory epitaphs used by Shakespeare in *Timon*'s last scene are taken almost word for word from North's Plutarch. But the story told by Plutarch is so brief and undetailed that it seems certain Shakespeare made use of additional sources; however, there has been no consensus among scholars on which ones he may have used. Among those suggested are Lucian's second century A.D. dialogue in Greek, *Timon, or the Misanthrope;* Matteo Boiardo's Italian drama *Timone* (c. 1487), based on Lucian; Pedro Mexía's version of the story in Spanish, contained in *La Silva de varia lección* (1545); a ver-

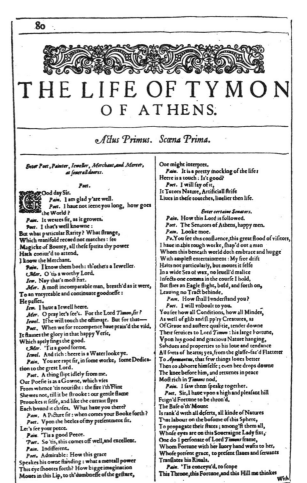

sion of the story in English indebted to Mexía, in William Painter's *Palace of Pleasure;* and additional material in Plutarch's *Lives*, particularly on Alcibiades.

Of special interest is the English academic comedy *Timon*, which has survived in manuscript and which was published by Alexander Dyce for the Shakespeare Society in 1842. While the play comes from Shakespeare's era, it has been impossible to date it exactly, and critics have argued variously that it is a source for Shakespeare's play, that it came later and was influenced by Shakespeare's play, and that the two share a common lost source. The comedy seems clearly designed for a school audience, with numerous parodic allusions to school classics, but it contains two features in common with Shakespeare not found in other sources: a mock banquet and a faithful servant similar to Shakespeare's steward, Flavius.

CRITICAL HISTORY: Opinion on the play's importance has ranged from G. Wilson Knight's imaginative but little-supported argument that *Timon* is a great tragedy in ways that make *Lear* and *Hamlet* seem childish, to the influential argument of Una Ellis-Fermor that *Timon* fails as a work of art because it was left unfinished and artistically unrealized.

Timon first received critical attention in the eighteenth century. At that time there was already the disparity of interpretation and evaluation that has become the hallmark of *Timon* criticism. Even the earliest commentators were unable to bring about unanimity of opinion on *Timon*. An anonymous defender of Shakespeare in 1698 saw Timon's misanthropy as "Manly and Generous" and Timon himself as an admirable tragic hero. But near the end of the Neoclassical era George Steevens argued that the character of Timon failed to meet the criteria for a tragic hero set by Aristotle in his *Poetics*, that he was fit only for ridicule, and that the play's morality was a hoax. However, Steevens's outright rejection of the play was exceptional for his epoch. Nicholas Rowe and John Potter gave high praise to the character of Apemantus for his powers of satirical commentary, and Robert Gould praised *Timon* as an "image" of Shakespeare's "unbounded mind." Potter pointed to its "beauties"—individual passages and touches—while criticizing its irregularities of diction and plot. Samuel Johnson combined several of these themes into a judicious pronouncement of the play as an artfully written "domestick tragedy," an opinion which was to be repeated years later by Coleridge.

William Richardson's study of Timon established a critical controversy over Shakespeare's protagonist that has continued to the present day. Specifically, this controversy consists of whether Shakespeare intended Timon to be a "flawed" personality, as argued by Richardson, or whether he was meant to be a noble and generous figure destroyed by a corrupt society, as maintained by such later critics as G. G. Gervinus and G. Wilson Knight.

The comments of the Romantic critics on *Timon* were just as varied as those of their Neoclassical predecessors. August Wilhelm Schlegel noted that *Timon* is neither a comedy, tragedy, nor history, but contains elements of all these, as well as of satire. Coleridge compared *Timon* unfavorably to *Lear* ("a *Lear* of the satirical drama . . . without [*Lear*'s] soul-scorching flashes, its ear-cleaving thunderclaps, its meteoric splendors"), sounding a theme to be echoed by dozens of later commentators. William Hazlitt praised *Timon* for its intensity and sincerity. For Leigh Hunt, *Timon* was a play for the closet and not the stage, a masterful character sketch of much poetry but little drama. The brevity of the Romantics' comments seems to indicate that the play lacked sufficient appeal to sustain their interests.

Post-Romantic nineteenth-century editors and scholars found in *Timon* a fascinating puzzle, for the play's textual irregularities and late inclusion in the Folio provided tantalizing clues for the deductive powers of literary historians. Johnson and Coleridge had made brief allusions to the possibility of some textual corruptions in *Timon*, but in his 1838 edition of the complete plays, Charles Knight theorized that the text's irregularities had come about because two playwrights, and not Shakespeare alone, had written *Timon*. To Knight, it seemed likely that Shakespeare had partially revised an older play, adding scenes on Timon and the story of Alcibiades which were not present in the original version. But another editor, Gulian C. Verplanck, theorized in his 1846 edition of Shakespeare's works that, on the contrary, Shakespeare's unfinished first draft was revised by some second playwright, possibly Thomas Heywood. Theories proliferated particularly as to the identity of the supposed second author. George Chapman, Thomas Middleton, Cyril Tourneur, John Day, and Thomas Heywood were all championed as candidates. A minority, however, notably the German critic Hermann Ulrici, held that Shakespeare was the sole author of *Timon*, and this theory eventually became the accepted view of the twentieth century.

Later nineteenth-century criticism of *Timon* was dominated by German critics and those influenced by German thought. The commentaries on *Timon* by Gervinus and Ulrici constitute the fullest analyses of the play until well into the twentieth century. Gervinus studied the play as a dramatic system and showed how Apemantus and Alcibiades are foils to the central character and contribute to the play's thematic unity. He was also one of the few critics of the nineteenth century who regarded Timon as an essentially noble figure, thereby opposing Richardson's view of him as a deceitful, self-serving individual. Ulrici's study combines praise and blame of Timon in a subtle analysis emphasizing both Timon's nobility and the roots of his downfall in false idealizations, a tendency which led him from one-sided philanthropy to one-sided misanthropy. Ulrici was also one of the earliest critics to suggest a correspondence between the pessimistic vision of *Timon* and Shakespeare's own "dark" moods towards the end of his life—an opinion which further led him to consider it as one of Shakespeare's last plays. Karl Marx utilized Timon's invective against gold to help formulate his own ideas on money and alienation in remarks which became influential in the twentieth century. Denton J. Snider's reading of *Timon* as a study of a personality type who fails through his own excesses differs from other German-influenced studies and anticipates some twentieth-century critics. Also influential to this period was George Brandes, who was the first critic to point out the parable-like quality of the play and to link it with *Coriolanus*.

In the late nineteenth century, Edward Dowden attempted to determine the correspondences between events in Shakespeare's life and the pessimistic vision evident in *Timon*. Influenced by Gervinus, Dowden regarded *Timon* as a study of various responses to the world's injustice and argued that Timon's "fruitless and suicidal rage" was rejected by Shakespeare. Frank Harris's deliberately outrageous biography forms an interesting pendent to Dowden's more measured work, but Harris's comments also reveal a strong response to *Timon*.

E. K. Chambers's and Walter Raleigh's commentaries mark the change in tide dividing nineteenth- and twentieth-century *Timon* scholarship. Both critics rejected the divided authorship theory, not because of any new evidence, but because of their impatience with the highly speculative nature of that hypothesis. They argued that it is simpler to assume that the play had been left unfinished by Shakespeare. Each of them, however, ends his essay with a brief flight of speculative biography—Chambers suggesting that *Timon* was the last play of Shakespeare's "tragic phase" and Raleigh arguing that it was a piece of "journey-work" which Shakespeare later expanded at the demand of the theater for more of his work.

In the twentieth century, G. Wilson Knight's praise of *Timon* as a masterpiece was a tribute that brought about some rethinking of the play's qualities as a work of art, but few if any critics have ranked *Timon* as high as Knight. In his study *The Wheel of Fire*, he called *Timon* among the best of Shakespeare's tragedies and interpreted it as a cosmic allegory which traces the gradual emancipation of a "Titanic" soul from the finite symbols of the universe into the infinite realm of nonexistence. More representative of the general twentieth-century response is J. C. Maxwell's view that in *Timon* one sees "Shakespeare at the height of his powers struggling with material which even for him proves recalcitrant." However, no single formula can be considered really typical of the diversity of critical interpretations and estimates that characterize *Timon* criticism during the last half-century.

Knight's challenging reading was answered by Una Ellis-Fermor, who argued that *Timon* was not only unfinished in a technical sense, but was also unfinished in a conceptual sense, which she attributed to the inconspicuousness of Timon's character. Andor Gomme also assailed Knight's interpretation, maintaining that his attempt to demonstrate a transcendent vision at the play's end amounts to nothing more than a gross "sentimentalization of the central figure." Continuing the debate, L. C. Knights criticized Knight indirectly but firmly in an essay that quoted approvingly from William Richardson's eighteenth-century critique of Timon's self-indulgent liberality. But G. Wilson Knight has returned repeatedly to *Timon* throughout his career with the same enthusiasm and high praise.

Besides their focus on textual and linguistic preoccupations, twentieth-century Shakespearean critics have also emphasized an historical approach to *Timon*. John W. Draper initiated a discussion of the relation of social forces in Tudor England to the events depicted in *Timon*, arguing that Shakespeare's reason for writing the play was to portray the collapse of traditional aristocratic and Christian values at the hands of the growing middle class. Among other historical approaches to the play is W. M. Merchant's discussion of the controversies in art theory lying behind the Painter and Poet's dialogue.

Among the most controversial issues in twentieth-century criticism of *Timon* is the debate over the play's genre. A. S. Collins has called *Timon* a "morality play," while Anne Lancashire modified this assessment and interpreted the play as a work similar to Marlowe's *Dr. Faustus*, labeling it a "secularized anti-traditional drama." Northrop Frye provided a fresh perspective by noting *Timon*'s partially comic structure, a point also emphasized by Andor Gomme. Still other critics, most notably William W. E. Slights and Lesley W. Brill, have attempted to synthesize several of these generic approaches, suggesting that Shakespeare adapted a number of literary conventions in the construction of his work.

Winifred M. T. Nowottny inaugurated a new wave of readings of *Timon* by claiming that the play is based essentially on an ironic inversion of traditional Christian values. This interpretation, and those which followed it in a similar manner, all considered the play's anomalies as part of its overall theme, as well as those elements which convey a vision of reality as fragmented and morally ambiguous. Other essays on this matter have been written by Brill, Richard D. Fly, Cyrus Hoy, and Susan Handelman, the last of whom undertakes a reading of the play through Freudian, Marxian, and feminist categories.

Timon of Athens, then, may be considered as one of the most widely disputed and variously interpreted plays in Shakespeare's canon. Perhaps the only certainty in the prismatic world of *Timon* criticism is that the play is no longer one of Shakespeare's most neglected dramas, but a work which continues to fascinate and confound contemporary critics of all persuasions.

ROBERT GOULD (essay date 1685)

[*In the following excerpt from a satirical poem on the contemporary English theater, Gould places* Timon *in the company of* The Tempest *and* King Lear. *Gould's poem, from which the following lines are taken, was originally published in 1685 in* The Works of Robert Gould.]

　　But if with *Profit* you wou'd reap *Delight*,
Lay *Shakespeare*, *Ben*, and *Fletcher* in Your sight:
Where Human Actions are with Life express'd,
Vertue advanc'd, and *Vice* as much depress'd.

There the kind Lovers with such Zeal complain,
You in their Eyes behold their inmost Pain,
And pray such Truth may not be Plac'd in vain. . . .
　　　　　　　　　　　　　　　　　　　　　(p. 414)

In *Timon*, *Lear*, the *Tempest*, we may find
Vast Images of thy Unbounded Mind:
These have been alter'd by our *Poets* now,
And with Success, too, that we must allow:
Third Days they get when *Part of THEE* is shown,
Which they but Seldom do when *All*'s their own.
　　　　　　　　　　　　　　　　　　　　　(p. 415)

> *Robert Gould, in his extract from "The Play-House: A Satyr," in* Shakespeare: The Critical Heritage, 1623-1692, Vol. 1, *edited by Brian Vickers, Routledge & Kegan Paul, 1974, pp. 414-16.*

A DEFENCE OF DRAMATICK POETRY AND *A FARTHER DEFENCE OF DRAMATICK POETRY* (essay date 1698)

[*The anonymous author of the following excerpt is defending Shakespeare, and drama in general, from the moralistic attacks of Jeremy Collier's* A Short View of the Immorality, and Profaneness of the English State *(1698). The critic chooses* Timon *to refute Collier's condemnation of drama for exciting the passions, arguing that tragedy indeed raises the passions, but that these passions are not necessarily ignoble. The essay from which the following excerpt is drawn was originally published as* A Defence of Dramatick Poetry *and* A Farther Defence of Dramatick Poetry *in 1698.*]

Tragedy indeed does raise the Passions; and its chief work is to raise *Compassion*. For the great Entertainment of Tragedy is the moving that tenderest and noblest Humane Passion, *Pity*. And what is it we pity there but the Distresses, Calamities and Ruins of *Honour*, *Loyalty*, *Fidelity* or *Love*, &c. represented in some True or Fictitious, Historick or Romantick Subject of the Play? (p. 89)

'Tis true a Character that has not all the perfections of true Honour or Innocence, nay a Vicious one sometimes, may move Compassion. But then 'tis not the Vice or Blemishes in the Character that moves that Pity. . . .

Thus we pity *Timon of Athens*, not as the Libertine nor Prodigal, but the *Misanthropos*: when his Manly and Generous Indignation against the Universal *Ingratitude* of Mankind makes him leave the World and fly the Society of Man; when his open'd Eyes and recollected Virtue can stand the Temptation of a Treasure he found in the Woods enough to purchase his own Estate again; when all this glittering Mine of Gold has not Charm to bribe him back into a hated World, to the Society of *Villains*, *Hypocrites* and *Flatterers*. (p. 90)

> *Extracts from* Shakespeare, the Critical Heritage: 1693-1733, Vol. 2, *edited by Brian Vickers, Routledge & Kegan Paul, 1974, pp. 89-92.*

NICHOLAS ROWE (essay date 1709)

[*Rowe was the editor of the first critical edition of Shakespeare's plays (1709) and the author of the first authoritative Shakespeare biography. In the following excerpt, which first appeared in Rowe's 1709 edition of* The Works of Mr. William Shakespeare, *he calls* Timon *a masterpiece of "ill Nature and satyrical Snarling."*]

[Shakespeare's] Clowns, without which Character there was hardly any Play writ in that Time, are all very entertaining; and, I believe, *Thersites* in *Troilus and Cressida,* and *Apemantus* in *Timon* will be allow'd to be Master-Pieces of ill Nature and satyrical Snarling. (p. 196)

> *Nicholas Rowe, in his extract from "Some Account of the Life, &c. of Mr. William Shakespeare," in* Shakespeare, the Critical Heritage: 1693-1733, Vol. 2, *edited by Brian Vickers, Routledge & Kegan Paul, 1974, pp. 190-202.*

CHARLES GILDON   (essay date 1710)

[*Gildon was the first critic to write an extended commentary on Shakespeare's plays. Like many other Neoclassicists, Gildon regarded Shakespeare as an imaginative playwright who nevertheless lacked knowledge of the dramatic "rules" necessary for correct writing. In the following excerpt, taken from Gildon's remarks first published in the 1710 edition of* The Works of Mr. William Shakespeare, *he argues that Shakespeare made direct use of Lucian's* Timon *as a source for his play, an assessment which modern critics are less certain to admit.*]

[*Timon of Athens*] is plainly taken from *Lucian's Timon,* and I wonder that *Shakespeare* rather chose to give *Roman* Names to his Persons as *Lucius, Lucullus,* &c. than *Gnathonides, Philiades, Demeas* a flattering Orator, from whence our Author seems to have taken his Poet; *Thrasycles* a Philosopher but not of *Apemantus*'s kind, but a Lover of Money or rather a Hypocrite; *Blapsius, Laches, Gniphon. Apemantus* is indeed *Shakespeare*'s own, and much better for the End he introduces him than *Thrasycles* cou'd have been, tho' the later is better in *Lucian. Shakespeare* has thrown the Infamy on the Poet which *Lucian* threw on the Orator, not considering that Poets made another sort of Figure in *Athens* (where the Scene lies) than they do in *England,* the State thinking them so useful to the Public that on the Death of *Eupolis* in a Sea Fight all Poets were for the future forbid to go to the War. Yet a Poet methinks shou'd have more regard to his Art and himself than to bring in a Character of one mean or ridiculous. But Mr. *Shadwell,* who has pretended to alter this Play, has made him a very Scoundrel, and the Players always take Care in Dress and Action to make him more so. (pp. 254-55)

The Play is full of Moral Reflections and useful Satire. The Characters are well mark'd and observ'd, and the Diction generally speaking expressive. . . .

The trying and Refusal of the Friends is very touching, and too natural and obvious to need a Comment; a Hint of this is in the latter End of *Lucian*'s Dialogue of *Timon.* . . .

The false Supper *Timon* invites his false Friends to is all *Shakespeare*'s Contrivance. *Timon*'s Curses on Athens in the Beginning of the fourth Act is worthy his Rage and Passion. (p. 255)

The Scene betwixt him, *Alcibiades,* Timandra, &c. is full of wholesome Satire against Whoring &c. . . . (p. 256)

> *Charles Gildon, in his extract from "Remarks on the Plays of Shakespeare," in* Shakespeare, the Critical Heritage: 1693-1733, Vol. 2, *edited by Brian Vickers, Routledge & Kegan Paul, 1974, pp. 226-62.*

LEWIS THEOBALD   (essay date 1719)

[*During the first half of the eighteenth century, Theobald was considered one of the greatest and most competent of Shakespearean critics. However, after his death in 1744 his reputation suffered a severe decline, probably due to his misguided attempts to revise many of Shakespeare's plays according to Neoclassical ideas of unity of action and dignity of character. In the brief remarks below, he considers* Timon *proof that Shakespeare knew the classics and used them as models for his work—a practice seen by the Neoclassicists as absolutely necessary for producing the best verse drama. This excerpt is taken from Theobald's preface, dated 1719, to Shakespeare's* The Tragedy of King Richard II.]

As to particular Passages in [Shakespeare's] Works, to prove he was no inconsiderable Master of the *Greek* Story there are but Two Plays, his *Timon of Athens* and *Troilus and Cressida,* that can furnish me with Instances, but they are so numerous in These as to leave it without Dispute or Exception. But to prove that he owed several of his Thoughts and Sentiments to the Antients, whoever will take the Pains to dip into his Works with that View, I dare engage, will find evident Traces of Imitation where he could expect them neither from the Characters nor Fable. (p. 356)

> *Lewis Theobald, in an extract from his preface to "The Tragedy of King Richard II" in* Shakespeare, the Critical Heritage: 1693-1733, Vol. 2, *edited by Brian Vickers, Routledge & Kegan Paul, 1974, pp. 352-56.*

SAMUEL JOHNSON   (essay date 1765)

[*Johnson has long held an important place in the history of Shakespearean criticism. He is considered the foremost representative of moderate English Neoclassicism and is credited by some literary historians with freeing Shakespeare from the strictures of the three unities valued by strict Neoclassicists: that dramas should have a single setting, take place in less than twenty-four hours, and have a causally connected plot. More recent commentators portray him as a critic who was able to synthesize existing critical theory rather than as an innovative theoretician. Johnson was a master of Augustan prose style and a personality who dominated the literary world of his day. The following excerpts are taken from his editorial notes to his text of* Timon *included in his 1765 edition of Shakespeare's plays. In accordance with the practice of Arthur Sherbo, editor of* Johnson on Shakespeare, *the act, scene, and line references given in the excerpt below refer to W. Aldis Wright's Cambridge edition of Shakespeare, but the Shakespearean text to which Johnson's notes refer comes from his own first edition. Perhaps the most significant aspect of Johnson's remarks on* Timon *is his interpretation of the play as a "domestick tragedy." Although the question of the exact genre of Shakespeare's play has existed since the eighteenth century, many critics—most notably Samuel Taylor Coleridge (1808-18), Hermann Ulrici (1839), Bernard Paulin (1964), and Rolf Soellner (1979)—agree with Johnson that* Timon *is essentially a tragedy.*]

I.i.23   POET.   Our poesy is as a gum, which oozes
From whence 'tis nourished. The fire i'th' flint
Shews not, 'till it be struck: our gentle flame
Provokes itself, and like the current flies
Each bound it chafes.

This speech of the poet is very obscure. He seems to boast the copiousness and facility of his vein, by declaring that verses drop from a poet as gums from odoriferous trees, and that his flame kindles itself without the violence necessary to elicite sparkles from the flint. What follows next? that it, "like a current, flies each bound it chafes.'' This may mean, that it expands itself notwithstanding all obstructions: but the images in the comparison are so ill sorted, and the effect so obscurely expressed, that I cannot but think something omitted that connected the last sentence with the former. It is well known that the players often shorten speeches to quicken the representation; and it may be suspected, that they sometimes performed their amputations with more haste then judgment. (p. 707)

II.ii.51 [Stage direction] Enter Apemantus, and Fool.

I suspect some scene to be lost, in which the entrance of the fool, and the page that follows him, was prepared by some introductory dialogue, and the audience was informed that they were the fool and page of Phrynia, Temandra, or some other courtisan, upon the knowledge of which depends the greater part of the ensuing jocularity. (p. 718)

IV.ii.1 [Stage direction] Enter Flavius, with two or three servants.

Nothing contributes more to the exaltation of Timon's character than the zeal and fidelity of his servants. Nothing but real virtue can be honoured by domesticks; nothing but impartial kindness can gain affection from dependants. (p. 728)

IV.iii.251 TIMON. Hadst thou, like us from our first swath, proceeded

Through sweet degrees that this brief world affords

There is in this speech a sullen haughtiness, and malignant dignity, suitable at once to the lord and the manhater. The impatience with which he bears to have his luxury reproached by one that never had luxury within his reach, is natural and graceful. (p. 736)

IV.iii.274 TIMON. If thou hadst not been born the worst of men,

Thou hadst been knave and flatterer.

Dryden has quoted two verses of Virgil to shew how well he could have written satires. Shakespeare has here given a specimen of the same power by a line bitter beyond all bitterness, in which Timon tells Apemantus, that he had not virtue enough for the vices which he condemns.

Dr. Warburton explains ''worst'' by ''lowest,'' which somewhat weakens the sense, and yet leaves it sufficiently vigorous.

I have heard Mr. Burke commend the subtilty of discrimination with which Shakespeare distinguishes the present character of Timon from that of Apemantus, whom to vulgar eyes he would now resemble. (p. 737)

V.i.1 [Stage direction] Enter Poet and Painter.

The Poet and the Painter were within view when Apemantus parted from Timon, and might then have seen Timon, since Apemantus, standing by him, could see them: but the scenes of the ''thieves'' and the ''steward'' have pass'd before their arrival, and yet passed, as the drama is now conducted, within their view. It might be suspected that some scenes are transposed, for all these difficulties would be removed by introducing the Poet and Painter first, and the thieves in this place. Yet I am afraid the scenes must keep their present order; for the Painter alludes to the thieves, when he says, ''he likewise enriched poor straggling soldiers with great quantity.'' This impropriety is now heighten'd by placing the thieves in one act, and the Poet and Painter in another: but it must be remembered, that in the original edition this play is not divided into separate acts, so that the present distribution is arbitrary, and may be changed if any convenience can be gained, or impropriety obviated by alteration. (pp. 741-42)

V.iii.4 SOLDIER. Some beast read this; here does not live a man. . . .

There is something elaborately unskilful in the contrivance of sending a soldier, who cannot read, to take the epitaph in wax, only that it may close the play by being read with more solemnity in the last scene. (p. 744)

The play of *Timon* is a domestick tragedy, and therefore strongly fastens on the attention of the reader. In the plan there is not much art, but the incidents are natural, and the characters various and exact. The catastrophe affords a very powerful warning against that ostentatious liberality, which scatters bounty, but confers no benefits, and buys flattery, but not friendship.

In this tragedy are many passages perplexed, obscure, and probably corrupt, which I have endeavoured to rectify or explain with due diligence; but having only one copy, cannot promise myself that my endeavours will be much applauded. (p. 745)

Samuel Johnson, ''Notes on Shakespeare's Plays,'' in his The Yale Edition of the Works of Samuel Johnson: Johnson on Shakespeare, Vol. VIII, *edited by Arthur Sherbo, Yale University Press, 1968, pp. 706-45.*

JOHN POTTER (essay date 1771)

[*Potter was an eminent English classical scholar whose studies of Plutarch and St. Basil were considered the standard works until the middle of the nineteenth century. In the excerpt below, he refers to a 1771 stage adaptation of* Timon *by the playwright Richard Cumberland, criticizing the author's additions and revisions as ''very inadequate to the Sterling of* Shakespeare.''*]

[*Timon of Athens*], as we have it from *Shakespeare*, is extremely faulty in point of Regularity, many of the Passages being very perplexed, while others appear to have been corrupted through the ignorance or inattention of Transcribers. It contains many beautiful Passages; but, upon the whole, it is not one of those Plays in which either the extent of *Shakespeare*'s views or elevation of his fancy is fully displayed, for he has not exerted much invention in the Conduct of his Plot. Tho' it must be confessed that he has diversified his Characters so as to make a very pleasing and interesting variety, and preserved most of them with great exactness.—The most remarkable Character in the Piece is that of *Apemantus*, which is probably as highly finished as any thing to be met with in the whole of *Shakespeare*'s Works. . . . Some of his Strokes discover great knowledge of Men and Things, and afford many useful hints to the vain, the extravagant, and the profligate. (p. 437)

And as we think Mr. *Cumberland*'s Additions very inadequate to the Sterling of *Shakespeare* we cannot help wishing that some Writer of sufficient ability would think it worth his while once more to revise this Tragedy; and, by treating it with a more sparing hand than Mr. *Cumberland* has done, and improving it upon *Shakespeare*'s original plan, render it sufficiently interesting; which would entitle it to an equal immortality with the best of this celebrated Author's Pieces. This would be paying a pleasing and a grateful tribute to the memory of the greatest Dramatic Writer, the world ever produced. (p. 438)

John Potter, " 'Timon of Athens'," in Shakespeare: The Critical Heritage, 1765-1774, Vol. 5, edited by Brian Vickers, Routledge & Kegan Paul, 1979, pp. 432-43.

JEREMY COLLIER [pseudonym of George Steevens] (essay date 1772)

[Brian Vickers, in his Shakespeare: The Critical Heritage, has attributed the following essay to George Steevens, an English scholar who collaborated with Samuel Johnson on a ten-volume edition of Shakespeare's works in 1773. The subsequent revisions of this collection, along with Steevens's own edition of 1793, formed the textual basis for the first two Variorum editions of Shakespeare's plays. Many modern scholars also contend that Steevens was the sole theater critic for the General Evening Post, in which the essay below was originally published on February 8-11, 1772. Steevens's use of Jeremy Collier's name was probably meant to be satirical and, therefore, the following excerpt should not be confused with Collier's influential book A Short View of the Immortality, and Profaneness of the English Stage. Unlike Samuel Johnson (1765), Steevens considers Timon hardly a true tragedy because it fails to excite pity and arouse terror.]

[Timon of Athens is] so radically wrong as to affirm that it must speedily return to the oblivion from whence it was lately called forth by the industry of the Drury-lane managers.

When I speak of this play it is not my intention to examine whether the alterations made by Mr. Cumberland are, or are not, judicious: I will suppose them, for argument sake, to be as masterly as the hand of human nature could form them; yet still I must contend that a dramatic edifice reared on a tottering foundation can never stand the smallest storm of criticism, but on the contrary at the first shock must instantly crumble into dust.

The two grand passions to be excited in tragedy are pity and terror; pity for the miseries of the worthy, and terror at the punishments inflicted upon guilt: neither of these passions however is excited in Timon of Athens. The hero, held out as an object of compassion, is an object only of ridicule; when he talks of his misfortunes we actually smile at his follies, and see him so undistinguishing a prodigal that we no way detest the ingratitude of his parasites; Timon's sole merit consists in giving away his money profusely, and in entertaining every man at his table with magnificence who stoops to be his flatterer. This is not generosity but weakness; it is not benevolence, but dishonesty; for he lets many of his lawful creditors go unpaid while he is squandering mines of wealth upon a gang of contemptible rascals. When, therefore, Timon, in the hour of adversity, lays claim to our sympathy in the character of a liberal man ruined by his virtues, our hearts indignantly refuse to participate in his distress. We consider him as a blockhead very properly undone by his extravagance, and even rejoice in his sufferings as in the natural execution of poetical justice.

The man who is to interest us most strongly in his misfortunes being thus palpably no object of pity, it necessarily follows that every thing said to raise our emotion is a false attack upon the passions, and, like the woman's absurd wish for the ladle, turns what should be great into absolute farce. Decorate the play, therefore, as we may; act it as we will; and subscribe as we chuse to the beauty of the language; still the main principle on which the whole rests, the great axis upon which all is to turn, Timon's distress, not being of a nature either to affect or terrify, the representation at the best must freeze upon the mind,

and move us little more than the fate of Macheath in the *Beggar's Opera*.

To encrease the absurdity of this play besides, Timon himself runs into the very crime for which he not only execrates his sycophants but at last forsakes the society of mankind. The people that most oblige him he insults with the grossest brutality, and even arraigns the equity of Providence because he has acted the part of an ungrateful spendthrift in prostituting the bounties which Heaven graciously poured upon his head. Thus in prosperity he is an idiot, in calamity he is a blasphemer; he behaves foolishly when surrounded with flatterers, and wickedly when abandoned. Yet in the midst of all his lunacy on the one hand, and all his impiety on the other, we are to commiserate his sufferings and to think that both men and Gods have treated him very dirtily.

The poet who would interest us for his hero should always take care that his distresses are of a natural kind, and such as may properly operate upon the feelings. A man madly throwing his treasures into the sea, and afterwards desiring the world to pity him because he wants a guinea is too ridiculous a character to wake the sensibility even of the most compassionate heart. But if to folly so egregious he adds ingratitude, nay, irreligion; if he detests all the worthy, merely for having been the voluntary dupe of the profligate, and questions the justice of Omnipotence because he has himself shamefully abused its bounty;—the author who desires us to weep for such a fellow strikes no less at the morality than the reason of the stage, and will in the end commit a dramatic suicide if in the beginning he is not sacrificed to the honest indignation of the public. (pp. 490-92)

Jeremy Collier [pseudonym of George Steevens], "Theatrical Review: 'Timon of Athens'," in Shakespeare, the Critical Heritage: 1765-1774, Vol. 5, edited by Brian Vickers, Routledge & Kegan Paul, 1974, pp. 490-92.

WILLIAM RICHARDSON (essay date 1784)

[Richardson was a Scottish author and educator whose philosophical leanings led him to focus on the psychological and moral aspects of Shakespeare's major characters, drawing from each a philosophical lesson, or what he termed a "ruling principle." For Richardson, such guiding principles served to establish the psychological aspects of Shakespeare's characters—their motives, fears, delusions—and in the process defined the action of each play. In the following excerpt, Richardson considers Timon's "ruling principle" his "love of distinction." Although Richardson suggests that Timon's philanthropy has its basis in good intentions, the motive behind these intentions is essentially destructive, consisting as it does in vanity and self-deceit. The question of whether Timon was meant to be a truly idealistic hero tragically destroyed by a corrupt society, or a flawed personality deceived by his need for recognition and adulation—as suggested by Richardson—is a central controversy in both nineteenth- and twentieth-century interpretations of the play. For more on this topic, see the excerpts by August Wilhelm Schlegel (1808), Hermann Ulrici (1839), G. G. Gervinus (1849-50), G. Wilson Knight (1930), and L. C. Knights (1969). The study from which the following excerpt is taken was first published in 1784.]

Shakespeare, in his *Timon of Athens*, illustrates the consequences of that inconsiderate profusion which has the appearance of liberality, and is supposed even by the inconsiderate person himself to proceed from a generous principle; but which, in reality, has its chief origin in the love of distinction. Though this is not the view usually entertained of this singular dramatic character, I persuade myself, if we attend to the design of the poet in all its parts, we shall find, that the opinion now advanced is not without foundation.

The love of distinction is asserted to be the ruling principle in the conduct of Timon; yet it is not affirmed, nor is it necessary to affirm, that Timon has no goodness of heart. He has much goodness, gentleness, and love of society.—These are not inconsistent with the love of distinction: they often reside together; and in particular, that love of distinction which reigned in the conduct of Timon, may easily be shewn to have received its particular bias and direction from original goodness. For, without this, what could have determined him to chuse one method of making himself conspicuous rather than another? Why did he not seek the distinction conferred by the display of a military or of a political character? Or why did he not aspire after pageantry and parade, the pomp of public buildings, and the ostentation of wealth, unconnected with any kind of beneficence? (pp. 85-7)

Guided by early or inherent predilection, men actuated by the love of distinction, seek the idol of their desires in various situations; in the bustle of active life, or in the shade of retirement. (p. 87)

[Early] or inherent goodness may be subverted by the love of distinction. A person of good dispositions, inclined by his temper and constitution to perform acts of beneficence, receives pleasure in the performance. He also receives applauses. He has done good, and is told of it. Thus he receives pleasure, not only from having gratified a native impulse, but from the praise of mankind, and the gratitude of those whom he may have served. (p. 92)

Perhaps it may now seem probable, that a man of constitutional goodness may perform beneficent actions, not from principles of humanity, though these may actually reside in his breast; but from the desire of being distinguished as a generous person; and that in the mean while, not discerning his real motives, he shall imagine himself actuated by pure generosity. That such characters may exist, is all that is hitherto asserted. That Shakespeare has exhibited an illustration, accurately defined and exquisitely featured, in his *Timon of Athens*, we will now endeavour to shew. We will endeavour to ascertain and trace, in the conduct of Timon, the marks of that beneficence which proceeds from the love of distinction. We will, at the same time, endeavour to trace the causes of the strange alteration that took place in his temper; and delineate the operations of those circumstances that changed him from being apparently social, and full of affection, into an absolute misanthrope.

Real goodness is not ostentatious. Not so is the goodness of Timon. Observe him in the first scene of the tragedy: trumpets sound; Timon enters; he is surrounded with senators, poets, painters, and attendants; chuses that moment to display his beneficence; and accompanies his benefits with a comment on his own noble nature.

> I am not of that feather, to shake off
> My friend when he most needs me.
>   [I. i. 100-01]

He is impatient of admonition. Knowing that he was formerly influenced by sentiments of humanity, he supposes that their power is abiding; and that, as he continues to do good, his principles of action are still the same. He is exposed to this self-imposition, not only by the tendency which all men have to deceive themselves, but by the flatteries and praises he is fond of receiving.—Of consequence, he would suffer pain by

being undeceived; he would lose the pleasure of that distinction which he so earnestly pursues; the prevailing passion would be counteracted: thus, there is a disposition in his soul, which leads him to be displeased with the truth; and who that is offended with the truth, can endure admonition? (pp. 94-6)

The same self-deceit which renders him deaf to counsel, renders him solicitous and patient of excessive applause. He endures even the grossest adulation. Notwithstanding the covering which hides him from himself, he cannot be quite confident that his principles are just what he wishes and imagines them to be. The applauses he receives tend to obviate his uncertainty, and reconcile him to himself. Yet, it is not affirmed, that the man of conscious merit is either insensible of fame, or careless of reputation. He feels and enjoys them both; but having less need of external evidence to strengthen him in the belief of his own integrity, he is less voracious of praise, and more acute in the discernment of flattery.

The favours bestowed by Timon, are not often of such a kind as to do real service to the persons who receive them. Wishing to be celebrated for his bounty, he is liberal in such a manner as shall be most likely to draw attention, and particularly to provoke the ostentation of those, on account of his munificence, whom he is inclined to benefit. (pp. 97-8)

He acts in the same manner, in the choice he makes of those whom he serves, and on whom he confers his favours. He is not so solicitous of alleviating the distress of obscure affliction, as of gratifying those who enjoy some degree of distinction, or have it in their power to proclaim his praises. He is not represented as visiting the cottage of the fatherless and widow; but is wonderfully generous to men of high rank and character. He is desirous of encouraging merit; but the merit must be already known and acknowledged. Instead of drawing bashful worth from obscurity, he bestows costly baubles on those eminent or reputable persons who shall be attended to, if they publish his praises. These are such displays of beneficence, as a man of genuine goodness would be apt to avoid. Yet, the persons whom Timon honours and obliges, are loquacious poets, flattering painters, great generals, and mighty elders. (pp. 98-9)

Yet, this seeming want of discernment in Timon, is not to be considered as a proof of weak understanding. Our poet, who has omitted nothing to render the features of this character, though perhaps not obvious, yet so distinct, consistent, and perfectly united, that there is scarcely a lineament too little or too much, has guarded him from this objection, and represents him as a man of ability. When the state, and rulers of Athens, in the hour of extreme urgency and distress, are threatened with an assault by Alcibiades, whom they had treated with disrespect, they have recourse for advice and assistance to no other than Timon. (p. 100)

Timon is not more ostentatious, impatient of admonition, desirous of applause, injudicious in his gifts, and undistinguishing in the choice of his friends, than he is profuse. Desirous of superlative praises, he endeavours, by lavish beneficence, to have unbounded returns. (p. 101)

The poet, with judicious invention, deduces the chief incident in the play, namely the reverse of Timon's fortune, from this circumstance in his conduct. The vanity of Timon renders him profuse; and profusion renders him indigent.

The character we are describing, sets a greater value on the favours he confers than they really deserve. Of a mind undisciplined by reason, and moved by a strong desire, he conceives the state of things to be exactly such as his present mood and desire represent them. Wishing to excite a high sense of favour, he believes he has done so, and that the gratifications he bestows are much greater than what they are. He is the more liable to this self-imposition, that many of those he is inclined to gratify, are no less lavish of their adulation than he is of his fortune. He does not perceive that the raptures they express are not for the benefit they have received, but for what they expect; and imagines, that while his chambers

> Blaze with lights, and bray with minstrelsy;
> [II. ii. 161]

while his cellars weep "with drunken spilth of wine"; while he is giving away horses, and precious stones; entertaining the rulers and chief men of Athens, he fondly fancies that he is kindling in their breasts a sense of friendship and obligation. He fondly fancies, that in his utmost need, he will receive from them every sort of assistance; and without reserve or reluctance, lays immediate claim to their bounty. (pp. 101-03)

Need we be surprised that Timon, and men of his character, should meet with disappointment? Howsoever they may impose upon themselves, and believe they are moved by real friendship, and believe that they are conferring real benefits, the rest of mankind discern, and disapprove of their conduct. Even those very persons, who, by adulation, and a mean acceptance of favours, have contributed to their delusion, feel, or conceive themselves, under no obligation. The benefits they received were unsolicited, or unimportant; and the friendship of their benefactor was not so genuine as he believed. Thus, then, Timon demands a requital of his good deeds: he meets with refusal; when he solicits the affections of his professing friends, he is answered with coldness. (pp. 103-04)

There is no one passage in the whole tragedy more happily conceived and expressed than the conduct of Timon's flatterers. Their various contrivances to avoid giving him assistance, shew diversity of character; and their behaviour is well contrasted, by the sincere sorrow and indignation of Timon's servants. They are held out to deserved scorn, by their easy belief that the decay of their benefactor's fortunes was only pretended, and by their consequent renewal of mean assiduities.

It remains to be mentioned, that such disappointment, in tempers like that of Timon, begets not only resentment at individuals, but aversion at all mankind.

Timon imposes on himself; and while he is really actuated by a selfish passion, fancies himself entirely disinterested. Yet he has no select friends; and no particular attachments. He receives equally the deserving and undeserving; the stranger and the familiar acquaintance. Of consequence, those persons with whom he seems intimate, have no concern in his welfare; yet, vainly believing that he merits their affections, he solicits their assistance, and sustains disappointment. His resentment is roused; and he suffers as much pain, though perhaps of a different kind, as, in a similar situation, a person of true affection would suffer. But its object is materially different. For against whom is his anger excited? Not against one individual, for he had no individual attachment; but against all those who occasioned his disappointment: that is, against all those who were, or whom he desired should be, the objects of his beneficence; in other words, against all mankind. In such circumstances, the violence of resentment will be proportioned to original sensibility; and Shakespeare, accordingly, has represented the wrath of Timon

as indulging itself in furious invective, till it grows into lasting aversion. (pp. 105-07)

Apemantus, a character well invented and well supported, has no other business in the play, than to explain the principles of Timon's conduct. His cynic surliness, indeed, forms a striking contrast to the smoothness of Timon's flatterers; but he is chiefly considered as unveiling the principal character. His manners are fierce; but his intentions are friendly: his invectives are bitter; but his remarks are true. He tells the flattering poet who had written a panegyric on Timon, that he was worthy of him; and adds, even in Timon's presence, "He that loves to be flattered, is worthy of the flatterer." He tells Timon, inviting him to his banquet—"I scorn thy meat; 'twould choke me, for I should ne'er flatter thee." Elsewhere he gives him admonitions to the very same purpose; and finding his advice undervalued, he subjoins—"I will lock thy heaven from thee"; meaning, as a commentator has well explained it, the pleasure of being flattered. (pp. 108-09)

There are few instances of a dramatic character executed with such strict regard to unity of design, as that of Timon. This is not all. It is not enough to say, that all the parts of his conduct are consistent, or connected with one general principle. They have an union of a more intimate nature. All the qualities in his character, and all the circumstances in his conduct, lead to one final event. They all co-operate, directly or indirectly, in the accomplishment of one general purpose. It is as if the poet had proposed to demonstrate, how persons of good temper, and social dispositions, may become misanthropical. He assumes the social dispositions to be constitutional, and not confirmed by reason or by reflection. He then employs the love of distinction to bring about the conclusion. He shews its effects, in superseding the influence of better principles, in assuming their appearance, and so, in establishing self-deceit. He shews its effects, in producing ostentation, injudicious profusion, and disappointment. And lastly, he shews, how its effects contributed to excite and exasperate those bitter feelings which estranged Timon from all mankind. Timon, at the beginning of the drama, seems altogether humane and affectionate; at the end he is an absolute misanthrope. Such opposition indicates inconsistency of character; unless the change can be traced through its causes and progress. If it can be traced, and if the appearance shall seem natural, this aspect of the human mind affords a curious and very interesting spectacle. Observe, in an instance or two, the fine lineaments and delicate shadings of this singular character. The poet refuses admission even to those circumstances which may be suitable, and consistent enough with the general principle; but which would rather *coincide* with the main design, than *contribute* to its consummation. Timon is lavish; but he is neither dissolute nor intemperate. He is convivial; but he enjoys the banquet not in his own, but in the pleasure of his guests. Though he displays the pomp of a masquerade, Phrynia and Timandria are in the train not of Timon, but of Alcibiades. He tells us, alluding to the correctness of his deportment,

> No villainous bounty yet hath pass'd my heart;
> Unwisely, not ignobly, have I given.
> [II. ii. 173-74]

We may observe, too, that he is not so desirous of being distinguished for mere external magnificence, as of being distinguished for courteous and beneficent actions. He does some good, but it is to procure distinction; he solicits distinction, but it is by doing good. (pp. 109-12)

William Richardson, "On the Dramatic Character of Timon of Athens," in his Essays on Shakespeare's Dramatic Characters of "Richard the Third," "King Lear," *and* "Timon of Athens", *AMS Press, 1974, pp. 85-112.*

AUGUST WILHELM SCHLEGEL   (essay date 1808)

[*A prominent German Romantic critic, Schlegel holds a key place in the history of Shakespeare's reputation in European criticism. His translations of thirteen of the plays are still considered the best German translations of Shakespeare. Schlegel was also a leading spokesman for the Romantic movement which permanently overthrew the Neoclassical contention that Shakespeare was a child of nature whose plays lacked artistic form. In the following excerpt, taken from an essay first written in 1808 and originally published as* Über dramatische Kunst und Literatur *in 1811, Schlegel considers* Timon *more of a satire than either a tragedy or comedy. He also concurs with the conclusion reached by William Richardson (1784) that* Timon *is essentially a "flawed" protagonist whose major fault resides in his vanity and his desire to be extraordinary. For further discussion of Timon's character, see the essays by Hermann Ulrici (1839), G. G. Gervinus (1849-50), Denton J. Snider (1887), G. Wilson Knight (1930), and L. C. Knights (1969).*]

Timon of Athens, and *Troilus and Cressida,* are not historical plays; but we cannot properly call them either tragedies or comedies. . . . (p. 417)

Timon of Athens, of all the works of Shakspeare, possesses most the character of satire:—a laughing satire in the picture of the parasites and flatterers, and Juvenalian in the bitterness of Timon's imprecations on the ingratitude of a false world. The story is very simply treated, and is definitely divided into large masses:—in the first act the joyous life of Timon, his noble and hospitable extravagance, and around him the throng of suitors of every description; in the second and third acts his embarrassment, and the trial which he is thereby reduced to make of his supposed friends, who all desert him in the hour of need;—in the fourth and fifth acts, Timon's flight to the woods, his misanthropical melancholy, and his death. The only thing which may be called an episode is the banishment of Alcibiades, and his return by force of arms. However, they are both examples of ingratitude,—the one of a state towards its defender, and the other of private friends to their benefactor. As the merits of the General towards his fellow-citizens suppose more strength of character than those of the generous prodigal, their respective behaviours are not less different; Timon frets himself to death, Alcibiades regains his lost dignity by force. If the poet very properly sides with Timon against the common practice of the world, he is, on the other hand, by no means disposed to spare Timon. Timon was a fool in his generosity; in his discontent he is a madman: he is every where wanting in the wisdom which enables a man in all things to observe the due measure. Although the truth of his extravagant feelings is proved by his death, and though when he digs up a treasure he spurns the wealth which seems to tempt him, we yet see distinctly enough that the vanity of wishing to be singular, in both the parts that he plays, had some share in his liberal self-forgetfulness, as well as in his anchoritical seclusion. This is particularly evident in the incomparable scene where the cynic Apemantus visits Timon in the wilderness. They have a sort of competition with each other in their trade of misanthropy: the Cynic reproaches the impoverished Timon with having been merely driven by necessity to take to the way of living which he himself had long been following of his free

choice, and Timon cannot bear the thought of being merely an imitator of the Cynic. In such a subject as this the due effect could only be produced by an accumulation of similar features, still, in the variety of the shades, an amazing degree of understanding has been displayed by Shakspeare. What a powerfully diversified concert of flatteries and of empty testimonies of devotedness! It is highly amusing to see the suitors, whom the ruined circumstances of their patron had dispersed, immediately flock to him again when they learn that he has been revisited by fortune. On the other hand, in the speeches of Timon, after he is undeceived, all hostile figures of speech are exhausted,—it is a dictionary of eloquent imprecations. (pp. 417-18)

> *August Wilhelm Schlegel, "Criticisms on Shakspeare's Historical Dramas," in his* Lectures on Dramatic Art and Literature, *edited by A.J.W. Morrison, translated by John Black, George Bell & Sons, 1892, pp. 414-46.*

SAMUEL TAYLOR COLERIDGE   (essay date 1808-18)

[*Coleridge's lectures and writings on Shakespeare form a major chapter in the history of English Shakespearean criticism. As the channel for the critical ideas of the German Romantics and as an original interpreter of Shakespeare in the new spirit of Romanticism, Coleridge played a strategic role in overthrowing the last remains of the Neoclassical approach to Shakespeare and in establishing the modern view of Shakespeare as a conscious artist and masterful portrayer of human character. Coleridge's remarks on Shakespeare come down to posterity largely as fragmentary notes, marginalia, and reports by auditors on the lectures, rather than as polished essays. The following remarks on* Timon of Athens *were taken from marginalia in Coleridge's personal copy of a two-volume edition of Shakespeare's plays. Their date is uncertain: they obviously could not have been written before 1807, since that is the publication date of the two-volume edition mentioned above, and presumably they date from the years of Coleridge's public lectures on Shakespeare (1808-18). His comment that* Timon *is "a Lear of domestic or ordinary life" is close to Samuel Johnson's interpretation of the play as a "domestick tragedy" (see excerpt above, 1765).*]

[*Timon of Athens*] is a *Lear* of the satirical drama, a *Lear* of domestic or ordinary life—a local eddy of passion on the high road of society, while all around are the week-day goings on of wind and weather—a *Lear,* therefore, without its soul-scorching flashes, its ear-cleaving thunder-claps, its meteoric splendors, without the contagion and fearful sympathies of nature, the Fates, the Furies, the frenzied elements dancing in and out, now breaking thro' and scattering, now hand in hand with, the fierce or fantastic group of human passions, crimes, and anguishes, reeling on the unsteady ground in a wild harmony to the swell and sink of the earthquake. (pp. 108-09)

> *Samuel Taylor Coleridge, "Notes on the Comedies of Shakespeare: 'Troilus and Cressida'," in his* Coleridge's Shakespearean Criticism, Vol. 1, *edited by Thomas Middleton Raysor, Cambridge, Mass.: Harvard University Press, 1930, pp. 108-11.*

CHARLES LAMB   (essay date 1811)

[*Lamb is considered one of the leading figures of the Romantic movement and an authority on Elizabethan drama. Although he was, like William Hazlitt, a theatrical critic, Lamb argued that the stage was an improper medium for Shakespeare's plays, mainly because visual dramatizations marred their artistic and lyrical effects. Like Samuel Taylor Coleridge, Lamb reverenced Shake-*

speare as a poet rather than a playwright. Although many scholars consider his views sentimental and subjective, and his interpretations of Shakespeare's characters as often extreme, Lamb remains an important contributor to the nineteenth-century's re-evaluation of Shakespeare's genius. In the excerpt below, he compares Timon with William Hogarth's Rake's Progress, both of which Lamb considers as portraits of men driven through extravagance to solitude. The essay from which this excerpt is drawn was originally published in The Reflector, April-September, 1811.]

I was pleased with the reply of a gentleman, who being asked which book he esteemed most in his library, answered,— 'Shakspeare': being asked which he esteemed next best, replied,—'Hogarth.' His graphic representations are indeed books: they have the teeming, fruitful, suggestive meaning of *words*. Other pictures we look at,—his prints we read.

In pursuance of this parallel, I have sometimes entertained myself with comparing the *Timon of Athens* of Shakspeare . . . and Hogarth's *Rake's Progress* together. The story, the moral, in both is nearly the same. The wild course of riot and extravagance, ending in the one with driving the Prodigal from the society of men into the solitude of the deserts, and in the other with conducting the Rake through his several stages of dissipation into the still more complete desolations of the madhouse, in the play and in the picture are described with almost equal force and nature. The levee of the Rake, which forms the subject of the second plate in the series, is almost a transcript of Timon's levee in the opening scene of that play. We find a dedicating poet, and other similar characters, in both.

The concluding scene in the *Rake's Progress* is perhaps superior to the last scenes of *Timon*. If we seek for something of kindred excellence in poetry, it must be in the scenes of Lear's beginning madness. . . . (pp. 92-3)

> *Charles Lamb, "On the Genius and Character of Hogarth," in* The Works in Prose and Verse of Charles and Mary Lamb: Miscellaneous Prose, Elia, Last Essays of Elia, Vol. I *by Charles Lamb and Mary Lamb, edited by Thomas Hutchinson, Oxford University Press, London, 1908, pp. 91-111.*

LEIGH HUNT (essay date 1816)

[*Hunt, like William Hazlitt and Charles Lamb, was a theatrical critic, and as such his criticism usually focuses on the technical or representational aspects of Shakespeare's plays, such as advice to actors on the interpretation of their roles. Also like Lamb, Hunt felt that the stage could rarely do justice to Shakespeare's work. In general, he typifies the growing Romantic worship of Shakespeare as a poet and as a skillful analyst of human types. The excerpt below is taken from a review of an 1816 stage version of Timon which starred the famous Shakespearean actor Edmund Kean. Hunt's comments on the new adaptor of the play refer to George Lamb, a writer who restored most of Shakespeare's original text and repressed most but not all of the additions of earlier adaptors. Unlike Samuel Johnson (1765) and William Richardson (1784), Hunt concludes that the moral of Timon is neither "that he conferred bounties only and no benefits, nor that he mistook the love of distinction for generosity, but that human nature will allow no excess."*]

[The parts of *Timon of Athens*] which contain the dramatic interest are comparatively few; the moral, though strong, is obvious, and in fact too easily anticipated; and when *Timon* has once fallen from his fortunes, there is little to excite further attention in the spectator. The *reader* is still delighted, but he would be still more so in his closet, where he could weigh every precious sentence at leisure, and lose none of the text either by the freaks of adapters or the failure of actors' voices.

Timon's story is short. He is a magnificent liver, who wastes a princely fortune in gifts and entertainments, and finding he can get no assistance from those who devoured it, turns misanthrope, and dies in the woods. Dr. Johnson says that the play affords "a very powerful warning against that ostentatious liberality, which scatters bounty, but confers no benefits, and buys flattery, but not friendship" [see excerpt above, 1765]. Professor Richardson too sees nothing but "inconsiderate profusion" in *Timon*, "a profusion," says he, "which is supposed even by the inconsiderate person himself to proceed from a generous principle, but which in reality has its chief origin in the love of distinction" [see excerpt above, 1784]. . . . The fact is, that *Timon* is really a generous man, spoiled by habitual good fortune and the enjoyment of his animal spirits. The moral of his tragedy is, not that he conferred bounties only and no benefits, nor that he mistook the love of distinction for generosity, but that human nature will allow of no excess; and that, if we set out in this world with animal spirits which lead us to think too highly of it, we shall be disappointed. Shakspeare never wrote commonplace morals. He flattered virtuous men no more than he did vicious. In the very play we are now talking of, he seems to have been before-hand with the complacency of the dogmatic; and will not allow the cynic philosopher *Apemantus*, who had been bred up in different circumstances and never been flattered, to rail at *Timon*, without a bitter rebuke for the mistakes of his own egotism.

The whole play indeed abounds in masterly delineations of character, and in passages equally poetical and profound; though the latter unfortunately reduced the adapter of the piece [George Lamb] to an awkward dilemma; for they constitute its main beauty, and yet he seems to have felt himself obliged to cut them short, either for fear of making it drag with the spectators, or in compliance with a sophisticated decorum. Thus many of the most striking pieces of satire are left out; and we see nothing of the two females who come in upon *Timon*'s retreat with *Alcibiades*. Yet a character of *Alcibiades* himself survives and furnishes a singular sort of cooler to the two burning, theoretical spirits of *Timon* and *Apemantus*. Shakspeare seems to have well appreciated this celebrated pupil of Socrates, at least the better part of him, and perhaps to have liked him. He makes him utterly careless of pretension of any sort, brave, open, generous, pleasurable, making allowances for other people, and revenging himself of his enemies rather out of contempt for their not being generous, also, than from any graver self-love of his own, though still he does not affect to be exempt from it. (pp. 134-36)

If *Timon* had been only ostentatious, he would hardly have been so willing to borrow, and to think all his friends as generous as himself: he would have run mad for pride; whereas his misanthropy is really owing, as in almost all instances, to an unexpected and extreme conviction of the hollowness of the human heart. (p. 137)

> *Leigh Hunt, " 'Timon of Athens'," in his* Dramatic Criticism: 1808-1831, *edited by Lawrence Huston Houtchens and Carolyn Washburn Houtchens, Columbia University Press, 1949, pp. 134-39.*

WILLIAM HAZLITT (essay date 1817)

[*Hazlitt is generally considered to be a leading Shakespearean critic of the English Romantic movement. A prolific essayist and critic on a wide range of subjects, Hazlitt remarked in the preface to his* Characters in Shakespeare's Plays *that he was inspired by the German critic August Wilhelm Schlegel and was determined to supplant what he considered the pernicious influence of Samuel Johnson's Shakespearean criticism. Hazlitt's criticism is typically Romantic in its emphasis on character studies. Unlike his fellow Romantic critic Samuel Taylor Coleridge, Hazlitt was a dramatic critic whose experience of Shakespeare in the theater influenced his interpretations. In the excerpt below, first published in the 1817 edition of his* Characters in Shakespeare's Plays, *he considers* Timon *the most "intense" of all Shakespeare's plays and the one work in which he never relaxes his efforts, nor loses sight of "the unity of his design." Like Schlegel (1808) and Coleridge (1808-18), Hazlitt contends that* Timon *is as much a "satire as a play."*]

Timon of Athens always appeared to us to be written with as intense feeling of his subject as any one play of Shakespear. It is one of the few in which he seems to be in earnest throughout, never to trifle nor go out of his way. He does not relax in his efforts, nor lose sight of the unity of his design. It is the only play of our author in which spleen is the predominant feeling of the mind. It is as much a satire as a play: and contains some of the finest pieces of invective possible to be conceived, both in the snarling, captious answers of the cynic Apemantus, and in the impassioned and most terrible imprecations of Timon. The latter remind the classical reader of the force and swelling impetuosity of the moral declamations in *Juvenal,* while the former have all the keenness and caustic severity of the old Stoic philosophers. The soul of Diogenes appears to have been seated on the lips of Apemantus. The churlish profession of misanthropy in the cynic is contrasted with the profound feeling of it in Timon, and also with the soldier-like and determined resentment of Alcibiades against his countrymen, who have banished him, though this forms only an incidental episode in the tragedy. (p. 38)

The fable consists of a single event;—of the transition from the highest pomp and profusion of artificial refinement to the most abject state of savage life, and privation of all social intercourse. The change is as rapid as it is complete; nor is the description of the rich and generous Timon, banqueting in gilded palaces, pampered by every luxury, prodigal of his hospitality, courted by crowds of flatterers, poets, painters, lords, ladies, who—

> Follow his strides, his lobbies fill with tendance,
> Rain sacrificial whisperings in his ear;
> And through him drink the free air—   [I. i. 80-3]

more striking than that of the sudden falling off of his friends and fortune, and his naked exposure in a wild forest digging roots from the earth for his sustenance, with a lofty spirit of self-denial, and bitter scorn of the world, which raise him higher in our esteem than the dazzling gloss of prosperity could do. He grudges himself the means of life, and is only busy in preparing his grave. How forcibly is the difference between what he was, and what he is, described in Apemantus's taunting questions, when he comes to reproach him with the change in his way of life!

> ————What, think'st thou,
> That the bleak air, thy boisterous chamberlain,
> Will put thy shirt on warm? will these moist trees
> That have out-lived the eagle, page thy heels,
> And skip when thou point'st out? will the cold brook,
> Candied with ice, caudle thy morning taste
> To cure thy o'er-night's surfeit? Call the creatures,
> Whose naked natures live in all the spight

> Of wreakful heav'n, whose bare unhoused trunks,
> To the conflicting elements expos'd,
> Answer mere nature, bid them flatter thee.
>   [IV. iii. 221-31]

The manners are every where preserved with distinct truth. The poet and painter are very skilfully played off against one another, both affecting great attention to the other, and each taken up with his own vanity, and the superiority of his own art. Shakespear has put into the mouth of the former a very lively description of the genius of poetry and of his own in particular. (p. 39)

> ————A thing slipt idly from me.
> Our poesy is as a gum, which issues
> From whence 'tis nourish'd. The fire i' th' flint
> Shews not till it be struck: our gentle flame
> Provokes itself—and like the current flies
> Each bound it chafes.   [I. i. 20-5]

The hollow friendship and shuffling evasions of the Athenian lords, their smooth professions and pitiful ingratitude, are very satisfactorily exposed, as well as the different disguises to which the meanness of self-love resorts in such cases to hide a want of generosity and good faith. The lurking selfishness of Apemantus does not pass undetected amidst the grossness of his sarcasms and his contempt for the pretensions of others. Even the two courtezans who accompany Alcibiades to the cave of Timon are very characteristically sketched; and the thieves who come to visit him are also "true men" in their way.—An exception to this general picture of selfish depravity is found in the old and honest steward Flavius, to whom Timon pays a full tribute of tenderness. Shakespear was unwilling to draw a picture *"ugly all over with hypocrisy."* He owed this character to the good-natured solicitations of his Muse. His mind might well have been said to be the "sphere of humanity."

The moral sententiousness of this play equals that of Lord Bacon's Treatise on the Wisdom of the Ancients, and is indeed seasoned with greater variety. Every topic of contempt or indignation is here exhausted; but while the sordid licentiousness of Apemantus, which turns every thing to gall and bitterness, shews only the natural virulence of his temper and antipathy to good or evil alike, Timon does not utter an imprecation without betraying the extravagant workings of disappointed passion, of love altered to hate. Apemantus sees nothing good in any object, and exaggerates whatever is disgusting: Timon is tormented with the perpetual contrast between things and appearances, between the fresh, tempting outside and the rottenness within, and invokes mischiefs on the heads of mankind proportioned to the sense of his wrongs and of their treacheries. (p. 40)

One of the most decisive intimations of Timon's morbid jealousy of appearances is in his answer to Apemantus, who asks him,

> What things in the world can'st thou nearest compare
>   with thy flatterers?
> *Timon.* Women nearest: but men, men are the things
>   themselves.
>   [IV. iii. 318-21]

Apemantus, it is said, "loved few things better than to abhor himself." This is not the case with Timon, who neither loves to abhor himself nor others. All his vehement misanthropy is forced, up-hill work. From the slippery turns of fortune, from the turmoils of passion and adversity, he wishes to sink into the quiet of the grave. On that subject his thoughts are intent, on that he finds time and place to grow romantic. He digs his own grave by the sea-shore; contrives his funeral ceremonies amidst the pomp of desolation, and builds his mausoleum of the elements. . . .

[Thus, Timon makes] the winds his funeral dirge, his mourner the murmuring ocean; and seeking in the everlasting solemnities of nature oblivion of the transitory splendour of his lifetime. (p. 42)

William Hazlitt, "'Timon of Athens'," in his Characters of Shakespear's Plays & Lectures on the English Poets, *Macmillan and Co. Limited, 1903, pp. 38-42.*

HERMANN ULRICI (essay date 1839)

[*A German scholar, Ulrici was a professor of philosophy and an author of works on Greek poetry and Shakespeare. The following excerpt is taken from an English translation of his* Über Shakspeares dramatische Kunst, und sein Verhältnis zu Calderon und Göthe. *The German edition was originally published in 1839. This work exemplifies the "philosophical criticism" developed in Germany during the nineteenth century. The immediate sources for Ulrici's critical approach appear to be August Wilhelm Schlegel's conception of the play as an organic, interconnected whole and Georg Wilhelm Friedrich Hegel's view of the drama as an embodiment of the conflict of historical forces and ideas. Unlike his fellow German Shakespearean critic G. G. Gervinus, Ulrici sought to develop a specifically Christian aesthetics, but one which, as he carefully points out in the introduction to the work mentioned above, in no way intrudes on "that unity of idea, which preeminently constitutes a work of art a living creation in the world of beauty." In the following excerpt, he agrees with such earlier commentators as William Richardson (1784) and August Wilhelm Schlegel (1808) in judging Timon as an individual deceived by his own actions. Ulrici characterizes Timon's major fault—that element upon which the play evolves—as his tendency to idealize both his own nature and the nature of the world. The debate over whether Timon was meant to be a "flawed" personality or a "noble" and generous idealist destroyed by an essentially corrupt society has dominated the nineteenth- and twentieth-century criticism of Shakespeare's play. For further commentary on this topic, see the excerpts by G. G. Gervinus (1849-50), Denton J. Snider (1887), G. Wilson Knight (1930), J. C. Maxwell (1948), and L. C. Knights (1969). Like Samuel Johnson (1765) and Samuel Taylor Coleridge (1808-18), Ulrici regards* Timon *as a true tragedy, and one comparable to Shakespeare's other great tragedies. The controversy over the exact genre of* Timon *has been discussed by numerous critics in the nineteenth and twentieth centuries, but most thoroughly by Schlegel, G. Wilson Knight (1930), John W. Draper (1934), A. S. Collins (1946), G. B. Harrison (1951), Andor Gomme (1959), Northrop Frye (1963), and Rolf Soellner (1979). Ulrici was also one of the earliest critics to comment on the gloom and darkness surrounding* Timon, *an interpretation which led him to consider it one of Shakespeare's last, if not his final play. Other critics who have attempted to draw a correlation between Shakespeare's mental state and the pessimism of his final plays include G. G. Gervinus (1849-50), Edward Dowden (1881), Wilhelm Wendlandt (1888), George Brandes (1895-96), E. K. Chambers (1908), and Frank Harris (1909).*]

A right understanding of Timon's character is essential to obtain an insight into the profound meaning of this wonderful drama. . . . Born and brought up in the lap of luxury, in a well-regulated home, and undoubtedly beneath the eye of noble parents, faithful teachers, and servants; great and blessed, not more by external advantages than by high and noble qualities,

and, therefore, universally caressed and admired, he had been accustomed to look upon all men as no less equally noble and virtuous with himself; wholly devoid of vanity and pride, he regarded them all as brothers, and members of one great family, who had received from the friendly gods their several shares of a common inheritance and stewardship. Accordingly his own property was in his eyes but for the common benefit of all; he resolves to repay twofold and threefold for the use of it, and outward splendour is nothing to him, but the love of men everything. He is ignorant, it is true, of human nature; not so much from any fault of his own, as because he has only studied its bright side. His ardent philanthropy, his undoubting belief in human virtue, is no doubt a great error, but one infinitely more lovely and noble than the mournful truth. Who will blame him, if, in the elevation of his pure fancy and his own noble feeling, he took men for what they *ought* to be, and such as he himself believed them? That common-sense which laughs in pity at such idealists, is in truth the poorest and most prosaic worldly wisdom, whose treasure of experience, on which it prides itself, makes its possessor the poorer and more needy by every increase.

What, then, is the true reason of the fall of this nobel and princely character? Feeling and fancy are evidently the predominant qualities of his disposition; in these lies all its energy, and to them he resigns himself entirely, as he sails along the quiet and prosperous current of life. He appears to possess intellect, shrewdness, and wit, only on occasions and upon compulsion; they sleep as long as there is no external stimulus to set them in action. Such men have, perhaps, a rare exuberance of thought and intellectual riches, but it is only within a partial and limited sphere that they exert themselves. The mental activity of such characters usually revolves around a single leading and fundamental idea. Accordingly, Timon is not more boundless in discovering occasions for the display of his disinterested philanthropy, than he is ingenious, consistent, and inexhaustible in the exercise of his hatred. To idealise is the vital principle of his mental activity. Thus has he idealised himself first of all, not subjectively only, but likewise objectively; his *acts* are in perfect conformity with his thoughts. However eccentric, therefore, his love and esteem for others may at first appear, it is equalled in extravagence by his subsequent hatred and contempt both of himself and whatever bears the name of man. This is a consequence of his highly sanguine, and at the same time highly choleric temperament. This idealising humour, this exuberance of fancy and feeling, bring him eventually to a complete knowledge *of himself*. He had sedulously suppressed the consciousness of his *own* sinfulness, although the very fact that he shrunk from indulging a thought of its possibility, as troublesome and uneasy, was in itself sufficient proof of its existence. In the intoxication of virtue, he had drowned the still voice of conscience, which would have told him that even this ardour of love—and desire of self-sacrifice—this gush of affection and regard for others as well as himself, was sinful, even because it made himself and his fellow men the sole centre of all his thoughts and actions. This is the heavy immorality which weighs upon and ultimately crushed him: man alone, and not God, was in all his thoughts; he made man alone the business of his whole life, and, accordingly, all his plans came to nought. As soon, therefore, as this his only prop was broken, his whole life and being was crushed and annihilated. He inevitably rushed from one extreme into the opposite, because the connecting mean between the two, that inward organic centre of human existence, the knowledge and the love of God, was wanting. But as this ideal love of man was alone the element of his life, a no less ideal misanthropy was an atmosphere of poison to him; and he was therefore of necessity the victim of his annihilating rage against himself and all mankind. This is the ground-idea of this thoughtful work, and renders it the worthy companion of "Romeo," "Othello," "Lear," "Macbeth," and "Hamlet." As in these five master-pieces of art, the fundamental principles of human life—love, marriage, domestic life,—the state with the power of will as its foundation and preservative, and, lastly, the power of thought, as the basis of science, art, and philosophy, are severally exhibited in the weakness and sinfulness which attach to them as soon as man, however great and noble, gives himself up entirely to them, and builds on them alone his whole scheme of life; so in the present piece, the whole of humanity, and its greatest earthly good—universal philanthropy—proves a tottering column, which falls and buries beneath its ruins all that lean upon it.

Wonderful is the skill with which the poet has moulded so unmanageable a subject into a living and deeply interesting fable. This he has accomplished, as in his other pieces, partly by establishing an active relation between the conduct and fortune of individuals, and a whole people and state, but principally by furnishing in the other chief personages of the drama a triple contrast to the character of Timon. In the first place, how strong a light is thrown upon his sterling sincerity by the worthless flattery of the parasites who prey upon him, and affect the same friendship, liberality, and love of mankind! They are all equally rotten, and as like as one pea to another; and yet, with delicate irony, the poet has succeeded in giving each his peculiar shade, which shews itself in the different manner they severally receive and resist Timon's petition for assistance. Opposed to this motley crew of false friends is the warm-hearted affection of Timon's household, and especially of his steward, whom Timon proclaims the only honest man. In an over civilized and morally corrupt state, in which the nobles are usurers, and the people, generally abandoned to luxury and gluttony, either banish the more virtuous from among them, or suffer them to perish by neglect; where the army cannot take the field without its concubines, and turns its arms against its country; the little of virtue that is left often takes refuge among the lowest classes. The Cynic, Apemantus, forms the second contrast to Timon. A deeper shade is cast upon his genuine hatred of mankind by the spurious misanthropy of the philosopher. To the latter, we might justly address the question: what hast thou done for men that thou presumest so profoundly to hate and despise them? Apemantus himself is but half a man, he is but half human, and so his treatment both of himself and his fellow men is naturally currish. Because fortune has denied to him her best gifts, because he cannot arrive at consideration and respect by any other way, he misemploys his talents, his rich wit and more than common strength of purpose, in order to make himself felt by the liberty of a cynic's life, and by the unblushing impudence of his censures and the abuse with which he falls foul of every body. The contempt into which he has brought himself is his impunity. Injuries from him are not injuries; in his mouth even the justest reproach loses its truth and force. So he goes about like a ridiculous phantom—useless, a burthen both to himself and to others, a warning example against a corrupt view of life similar to Timon's, but still its perfect opposite. At last he is outdone by Timon in his own art, and we may assume that he fell sick of vexation and grew better. Lastly, the character of Alcibiades, while it exhibits the connection between the private fortunes of the great hero, and the great public of his state and people, stands also in direct opposition to Timon. He, like all the other characters of the piece, is absolutely indispensable as a component part of the whole, and necessary both for the working out of the ground idea, and for the particular march of the action which inevitably follows from that idea. He exhibits, for instance, in his person, the way in which *such* a state and *such* a people must be treated. He repels injustice by injustice, force by force, and preaches reason and morality sword in hand. But thus his *right* way of regulating life is only suited for this particular *immoral* state of mankind, and is therefore itself *unjust* and immoral.

Now it is this very-fact, that Alcibiades is made ultimately to appear in the right, that constitutes the great defect of the piece. The immediate impression which "Timon of Athens" leaves on the mind, is without the *atoning* and *soothing* element of true tragedy; and it is in the absence of this, that its affinity with "Titus Andronicus" consists. If Alcibiades be in the right, then life is not worth its pains; then is there no truth in the doctrine of an overruling Providence; and we must exclaim in tears with Flavius:—

Strange, unusual brood,
When man's worst sin is he does too much good!
Who then dares to be half so kind again,
For bounty, that makes gods, does still mar men.
[IV. ii. 38-41]

Act IV. Scene iii. Alcibiades, Soldiers, Phrynia, Timandra, Timon of Athens. Frontispiece to Rowe edition (1709). By permission of the Folger Shakespeare Library.

Then would sin and injustice reign supreme, with no other check and corrective but their own conflicts. In such a case the tragic view of things becomes merged into the comic, without however allowing to the latter its full force. Accordingly, in spite of the lavish expenditure of art with which the several subordinate motives are made to co-operate with the fundamental idea of the whole, and to reflect it in varying light and shade, so as to furnish another striking proof, to those who question it, of our poet's truly dramatic skill, with which he invariably combines the several parts of his plot into an organic whole; and in spite of all the particular beauties, and the profound view of things, which forms the ground-work of the whole, we yet rise from the perusal of this drama with the mournful impression of an irremediable discord pervading human life. Indeed, who will deny that such does really exist and works in it? But still human life is not *simply* a dissonance; it also bears within it a principle of harmony. However, it is not *shown* to us at all in the present piece, and in order to discover it by the aid of *reflection on* the story, we must bring to the task a firm faith in its existence.

"Timon of Athens" forms the beautiful close of Shakspeare's poetical career. It reflects more clearly than any other piece, the poet's consciousness of the nothingness of human life and nature in themselves, and a christian reliance on God, as the source of all that is abiding and permanent. We distinctly see him abandoning the trifling pursuits and contentions of this life, for calm heavenly meditation; but at the same time we see, that before he could arrive at this repose, his path had been crossed by many and heavy conflicts. Indeed, when we compare this tragedy with others which belong probably to his latest labours, the confession is forced from us that his view of the world and things, even in its *artistic* side, must have been somewhat troubled in the latter years of his career. Even in "Macbeth" and "Othello," the expiatory moment of the tragic idea, that mild splendour of the setting sun, does not shine forth in the same vigour and brilliancy, as in the deaths of Romeo, Lear, and Hamlet. Over the "Winter's Tale," "Cymbeline," the "Tempest," and in some parts of "Measure for Measure," a profound and grave earnestness is spread, which is almost too heavy indeed for the motley sportiveness of the comic view of things. The shadows have been continually thickening, until at last, in 'Timon,'' the perfect night overtakes us, and it is only on the other side of the fable, as on the other side of human life, that a brighter day glimmers. No one could have painted misanthropy with such truth and force without having at some time or other experienced its bitter agony. Shakspeare's tone of mind must momentarily, at least, have been in unison with that of Timon; otherwise his choice of such a subject is wholly inexplicable, especially as it possesses no dramatic fitness to recommend it. Moreover, there were outward causes and reasons enough, not only in the last years of our poet's career, to embitter it, but the memory also of his whole life. . . . He was doomed to look on, while that on which he had spent all his mental energy was profaned and blackened by rude hands; he was doomed to see genuine poetry, and with it the deep seriousness of the christian view of life, banished from the age. It was, therefore, but natural that he should have had misgivings, lest his name and all his labours would be soon forgotten, perhaps, for ever; as indeed in truth, for a whole century, his countrymen were unconscious that the greatest poet of all ages had issued from among themselves. (pp. 239-44)

> Hermann Ulrici, '' 'Titus Andronicus', and 'Timon
> of Athens','' in his Shakspeare's Dramatic Art: And

His Relation to Calderon and Goethe, *translated by A.J.W. Morrison, Chapman, Brothers, 1846, pp. 233-45.*

CHARLES KNIGHT   (essay date 1843)

[*Knight, an English author and publisher, dedicated his career to providing education and knowledge to the Victorian middle class. In the essay from which this excerpt is taken, first published in 1843, Knight criticizes the practice of eighteenth-century Shakespearean editors known as "regulation," a process by which lines that had been originally printed as prose were transposed into verse, and those that had been rendered in the original as verse were changed into prose. Knight argues that this practice altered the text of* Timon, *"disguising" certain features of it—particularly, in his view, stylistic evidence that suggests two separate authors had written the play, and not Shakespeare alone. Knight was one of the earliest critics to contend that* Timon *was essentially an early play which Shakespeare partially rewrote, specifically those scenes confined to the character of Timon. The question of the authorship of* Timon *has persisted to the present day and has been discussed by such other critics as Gulian C. Verplanck (1847), F. G. Fleay (1874), George Brandes (1895-96), Walter Raleigh (1907), E. K. Chambers (1908), Una Ellis-Fermor (1942), G. B. Harrison (1951), and Charlton Hinman (1969).*]

The disguises of the ancient text, which have been so long accepted without hesitation, have given to the 'Timon of Athens' something of the semblance of uniformity in the structure of the verse; although in reality the successive scenes, even in the modern text, present the most startling contrarieties to the ear which is accustomed to the versification of Shakspere. The ordinary explanation of this very striking characteristic is, that the ancient text is corrupt. This is the belief of the English editors. Another theory, which has been received in Germany, is, that the 'Timon' being one of the latest of Shakspere's performances, has come down to us unfinished. The conviction to which we have ourselves arrived neither rests upon the probable corruption of the text, nor the possibility that the poet has left us only an unfinished draft of his performance; but upon the belief that the differences of style, as well as the more important differences in the cast of thought, which prevail in the successive scenes of this drama, are só remarkable as to justify the conclusion that it is not wholly the work of Shakspere. We think it will not be very difficult so to exhibit these differences in detail, as to warrant us in requesting the reader's acquiescence in the principle which we seek to establish, namely, that the 'Timon of Athens' was a play originally produced by an artist very inferior to Shakspere, and which probably retained possession of the stage for some time in its first form; that it has come down to us not wholly re-written, but so far remodelled that entire scenes of Shakspere have been substituted for entire scenes of the elder play; and lastly that this substitution has been almost wholly confined to the character of Timon. . . . (pp. 170-71)

The contrast of style which is to be traced throughout this drama is sufficiently striking in the two opening scenes which now constitute the first act. Nothing can be more free and flowing than the dialogue between Poet and the Painter. It has all the equable graces of Shakspere's facility, with occasional examples of that condensation of poetical images which so distinguishes him from all other writers. For instance:—

> All those which were his fellows but of late,
> (Some better than his value,) on the moment
> Follow his strides, his lobbies fill with tendance,

Rain sacrificial whisperings in his ear,
Make sacred even his stirrup, and through him,
Drink the free air.   [I. i. 78-83]

The foreshadowing of the fate of Timon in the conclusion of this dialogue is part of the almost invariable system by which Shakspere very early infuses into his audience a dim notion of the catastrophe,—most frequently indeed in the shape of some presentiment. When Timon enters we feel certain that he is the Timon of Shakspere's own conception. He is as graceful as he is generous; his prodigality is without the slightest particle of arrogance; he builds his munificence upon the necessity of gratifying without restraint the deep sympathies which he cherishes to all of the human family. He is the very model too of patrons, appearing to receive instead of to confer a favour in his reward of art,—a complete gentleman even in the act of purchasing a jewel of a tradesman. That the Apemantus of this scene belongs wholly to Shakspere is not to our minds quite so certain. There is little of wit in any part of this dialogue; and the pelting volley of abuse between the Cynic, the Poet, and the Painter, might have been produced by any writer who was not afraid of exhibiting the *tu quoque* style of repartee which distinguishes the angry rhetoric of fish-wives and school-boys. (pp. 171-72)

If, in the first scene, it would be very difficult to say with certainty what is not Shakspere's, so in the second scene it appears to us equally difficult to point out what is Shakspere's. We believe that scarcely any part of this scene was written by him; we find ourselves at once amidst a different structure of verse from the foregoing. We encounter this difference remarkably in the first speech of Timon:—

I gave it freely ever; and there's none
Can truly say he gives, if he receives:
If our betters play at that game, we must not dare
To imitate them; faults that are rich are fair.
                                    [I. ii. 10-13]

In the first scene we do not find a single rhyming couplet;—in the second scene their recurrence is more frequent than in any of Shakspere's plays, even the earliest. (pp. 172-73)

The whole of the senate scene in 'Timon' is singularly unmetrical; but wherever the verse becomes regular, it is certainly not the metre of Shakspere. Mark the pause, for example, that occurs at the end of every line of the first speech of Alcibiades. ''The linked sweetness long drawn out'' is utterly wanting. The last scene of the fifth act has the same peculiarity. But in addition to the structure of the verse, the character of the thought is essentially different from that of the true Shaksperian drama. Where is our poet's imagery? From the first line of this scene to the last, the speeches, though cast into the form of verse, are in reality nothing but measured prose. The action of this scene admitted either of passion or reflection; and we know how Shakspere puts forth either power whenever the occasion demands it. The passion of Alcibiades is of the most vapid character:—

Now the gods keep you old enough; that you may live
Only in bone that none may look on you!
                                    [III. v. 103-04]
                                    (p. 177)

It is scarcely necessary for us very minutely to follow the successive passages of the fourth and fifth acts, in our endeavours to trace the hand of Shakspere. We may, however, briefly point out the passages which we believe *not* to be his. The second scene of the fourth act, between the Steward and the servants, has some touches undoubtedly of the master's hand; the Steward's speech, after the servants have left, again presents us the rhyming couplets, and the unmetrical blank-verse. The scene between the Poet and the Painter, at the commencement of the fifth act, is so unmetrical, that it has been printed as prose by all modern editors, and we scarcely know how to avoid following the example. (p. 180)

It is not by looking apart at the scenes and passages which we have endeavoured to separate from the undoubted scenes and passages of Shakspere in this play, that we can rightly judge of their inferiority. They must be contrasted with the great scenes of the fourth act, and with Timon's portion of the fifth,—the essentially tragic portions of this extraordinary drama. In power those scenes are almost unequalled. They are not pleasing—they are sometimes positively repulsive in the images which they present to us; but in the tremendous strength of passionate invective we know not what can be compared to them. In 'Lear,' the deep pity for the father is an ever-present feeling, mingling with the terror which he produces by his denunciations of his daughters; but in 'Timon,' the poet has not once sought to move our pity: by throwing him into an attitude of undiscriminating hostility to the human race, he scarcely claims any human sympathy. (p. 181)

The all-absorbing defect of Timon—the root of those generous vices which wear the garb of virtue—is the entire want of discrimination, by which he is also characterized in Lucian's dialogue. Shakspere has seized upon this point, and held firmly to it. He releases Ventidius from prison,—he bestows an estate upon his servant,—he lavishes jewels upon all the dependants who crowd his board;—

Methinks I could deal kingdoms to my friends,
And ne'er be weary.   [I. ii. 220-21]

That universal philanthropy, of which the most selfish men sometimes talk, is in Timon an active principle; but let it be observed that he has no preferences. It appears to us a most remarkable example of the profound sagacity of Shakspere, to exhibit Timon without any especial affections. It is thus that his philanthropy passes without any violence into the extreme of universal hatred to mankind. Had he loved a single human being with that intensity which constitutes affection in the relation of the sexes, and friendship in the relation of man to man, he would have been exempt from that unjudging lavishness which was necessary to satisfy his morbid craving for human sympathy. Shakspere, we think, has kept this most steadily in view. His surprise at the fidelity of his steward is exhibited, as if the love for any human being in preference to another came upon him like a new sensation. (p. 186)

In lavishing his wealth as if it were a common property, he had believed that the same common property would flow back to him in his hour of adversity. "O, you gods, think I, what need we have any friends, if we should never have need of them? they were the most needless creatures living, should we ne'er have use for them: and would most resemble sweet instruments hung up in cases, that keep their sounds to themselves." His false confidence is at once, and irreparably, destroyed. If Timon had possessed one friend with whom he could have interchanged confidence upon equal terms, he would have been saved from his fall, and certainly from his misanthropy. If he had even fallen by false confidence, he would have confined his hatred to his

> Most smiling, smooth, detested parasites,
> Courteous destroyers, affable wolves, meek bears.
>
> [III. vi. 94-5]

But his nature has sustained a complete revulsion, because his sympathies were forced, exaggerated, artificial. It is then that all social life becomes to him an object of abomination:—

> Piety and fear,
> Religion to the gods, peace, justice, truth,
> Domestic awe, night-rest, and neighbourhood,
> Instruction, manners, mysteries, and trades,
> Degrees, observances, customs, and laws,
> Decline to your confounding contraries
> And yet confusion live!—Plagues incident to men,
> Your potent and infectious fevers heap
> On Athens, ripe for stroke! thou cold sciatica,
> Cripple our senators, that their limbs may halt
> As lamely as their manners! lust and liberty
> Creep in the minds and marrows of our youth;
> That 'gainst the stream of virtue they may strive,
> And drown themselves in riot! itches, blains,
> Sow all the Athenian bosoms; and their crop
> Be general leprosy! breath infect breath;
> That their society, as their friendship, may
> Be merely poison! [IV. i. 15-32]

Nothing can be more tremendous than this imprecation,—nothing, under the circumstances, more true and natural. (p. 187)

> *Charles Knight, in his introduction to "Timon of Athens," in* The Comedies, Histories, Tragedies, and Poems of William Shakespere, *edited by Charles Knight, second edition, AMS Press, 1968, pp. 167-90.*

KARL MARX (essay date 1844)

[*Marx is often considered one of the most important and influential figures of the modern age. Although he began his career as a student of literature and continued throughout his life to be interested in aesthetics and literary theory, Marx wrote no serious theoretical pronouncements until after his association with Friedrich Engels. In general, Marx believed that literature should be, above all things, realistic; characters should be drawn as concrete universals, individual yet representative, and that modern tragedy should be based on a conflict between equal historical forces. Informing Marx's view of literature is not a system of rigid economic determinism, which many so-called "Marxists" later developed as the cornerstone of their aesthetics, but a general philosophy of history as a force which shapes individual consciousness. Like other Germans of his generation, Marx greatly admired Shakespeare, and read his complete plays every year. The excerpt below, first written in 1844 and later published in* Das Kapital, *praises Shakespeare for his shrewd understanding of the "real nature of* money."]

By possessing the *property* of buying everything, by possessing the property of appropriating all objects, *money* is thus the *object* of eminent possession. The universality of its *property* is the omnipotence of its being. It therefore functions as almighty being. Money is the *pimp* between man's need and the object, between his life and his means of life. But *that which* mediates *my* life for me, also *mediates* the existence of other people *for me.* For me it is the *other* person. . . .

Shakespeare in *Timon of Athens:*

> Gold? Yellow, glittering, precious gold? No, Gods,
> I am no idle votarist! . . . Thus much of this will make
>   black white, foul fair,
> Wrong right, base noble, old young, coward valiant.
> . . . Why, this
> Will lug your priests and servants from your sides,
> Pluck stout men's pillows from below their heads:
> This yellow slave
> Will knit and break religions, bless the accursed;
> Make the hoar leprosy adored, place thieves
> And give them title, knee and approbation
> With senators on the bench: This is it
> That makes the wappen'd widow wed again;
> She, whom the spital-house and ulcerous sores
> Would cast the gorge at, this embalms and spices
> To the April day again. Come, damned earth,
> Thou common whore of mankind, that putt'st odds
> Among the rout of nations.
>
> [IV. iii. 26-43]

And also later:

> O thou sweet king-killer, and dear divorce
> Twixt natural son and sire! thou bright defiler
> Of Hymen's purest bed! thou valiant Mars!
> Thou ever young, fresh, loved and delicate wooer,
> Whose blush doth thaw the consecrated snow
> That lies on Dian's lap! Thou *visible God!*
> That solder'st *close impossibilities,*
> And makest them kiss! That speak'st with every tongue,
> To every purpose! O thou touch of hearts!
> Think, thy slave man rebels, and by thy virtue
> Set them into confounding odds, that beasts
> May have the world in empire!
>
> [IV. iii. 381-92]

Shakespeare excellently depicts the real nature of *money.* (pp. 165-67)

Shakespeare stresses especially two properties of Money: (1) It is the visible divinity—the transformation of all human and natural properties into their contraries, the universal confounding and overturning of things: it makes brothers of impossibilities. (2) It is the common whore, the common pimp of people and nations.

The overturning and confounding of all human and natural qualities, the fraternization of impossibilities—the *divine* power of money—lies in its *character* as men's estranged, alienating and self-disposing *species* nature. Money is the alienated *ability* of mankind. (pp. 167-68)

> *Karl Marx, "The Power of Money in Bourgeois Society," in his* Economic and Philosophic Manuscripts of 1844, *edited by Dirk J. Struik, translated by Martin Milligan, International Publishers Co., Inc., 1964, pp. 165-69.*

GULIAN C. VERPLANCK (essay date 1847)

[*Verplanck was a nineteenth-century American journalist, politician, lawyer, scholar, and editor, and one of the earliest American Shakespearean scholars. His major contribution to American letters was a three-volume biographical edition of Shakespeare's plays in 1847. In the following excerpt, taken from that work, he takes issue with both the hypotheses of Hermann Ulrici (1839) and Charles Knight (1843) on the authorship of* Timon *and its chronological place in Shakespeare's canon. Verplanck asserts that* Timon *was originally written by Shakespeare, but was left unfinished and taken up years later by another playwright, possibly Thomas Heywood. Verplanck refutes the idea that Timon was Shakespeare's last play on the grounds that it does not "resemble the unfinished work of a great master." For more commentary on the question of Timon's place in Shakespeare's canon, see the excerpts by F. G. Fleay (1874), George Brandes (1895-96), Walter Raleigh (1907), E. K. Chambers (1908), Una Ellis-Fermor (1942), G. B. Harrison (1951), and Charlton Hinman (1969).]*

[Charles Knight's] theory has much to give it probability, and may possibly give the true solution of the question. Yet there are some weighty reasons that may be opposed to it.

We have lately been made acquainted, through Mr. Dyce's edition of 1842, with the original drama of *Timon*, referred to by Stevens, and other editors, who had seen or heard of it in manuscript. This is certainly anterior to Shakespeare's *Timon*, and the manuscript transcript is believed to have been made before 1600. It is the work of a scholar, and it appears to have been acted. But to this *Timon*, it is apparent that Shakespeare was under no obligation of the kind required by Mr. Knight's theory, although it may possibly have been the medium through which he derived one or two incidents from Lucian. We must then presume the existence of another and more popular drama, on the same subject, of which all other trace is lost, and of a piece which, if it even existed, could not have been from any despicable hand; for the portions of the Shakespearian drama ascribed to it, however inferior to the glow and vigour of the rest, are yet otherwise, as compared with the writings of preceding dramatists, written with no little dramatic spirit and satiric humour. This is surely a somewhat unlikely presumption.

But what weighs most with me is this: that, great as the discrepancy of style and execution may be, yet in the characters, and the whole plot, incidents, and adjuncts required to develope them, there is an entire unison of thought, as if proceeding from a single mind; much more so, for instance, than in the *Taming of the Shrew*, where the materials may be distinctly assigned to different workmen, as well as the taste and fashion of the decoration.

Another theory is patronized by Ulrici [see excerpt above, 1839], and is said to be the opinion commonly received in Germany, where Shakespeare has of late years found so many ardent admirers and acute critics. It is that *Timon* is one of Shakespeare's very latest works, and has come down to us unfinished.

To the theory as thus stated I must object, that so far as we can apply to a great author any thing resembling those rules whereby the criticism of art is enabled so unerringly to divide the works of great painters into their several successive "manners," and to appropriate particular works of Raphael or Titian to their youth, or their improved taste and talent in their several changes until maturity; we must assign *Timon*, not to the latest era of Shakespeare's style and fancy, as shown in the *Tempest* and the *Winter's Tale*, but to the period where it is placed by Hallam and Coleridge, as of the epoch of *Measure for Measure*, the revised *Hamlet*, and *Lear*.

But the conclusive argument against this opinion is, that the play does not, except in a very few insulated passages, resemble the unfinished work of a great master, where parts are finished, and the rest marked out only by the outline, or still more imperfect hints. On the contrary, it is like such a work left incomplete and finished by another hand, inferior, though not

without skill, and working on the conceptions of the greater master.

This is precisely the hypothesis to which the examination of the other theories has brought my own mind. The hypothesis which I should offer—certainly with no triumphant confidence of its being the truth, but as more probable than any other—is this: Shakespeare, at some time during that period when his temper, state of health, or inclination of mind, from whatever external cause, strongly prompted him to a severe judgment of human nature, and acrimonious moral censure, adopted the canvass of *Timon*'s story as a fit vehicle for poetic satire, in the highest sense of the term, as distinguished alike from personal lampoons and from the playful exhibition of transient follies. In this he poured forth his soul in those scenes and soliloquies, the idea of which had invited him to the subject; while, as to the rest, he contented himself with a rapid and careless composition of some scenes, and probably on others, (such as that of Alcibiades with the Senate,) contenting himself with simply sketching out the substance of an intended dialogue to be afterwards elaborated. In this there is no improbability, for literary history has preserved the evidence of such a mode of composition in Milton and others. The absence of all trace of the piece from this time till it was printed in 1623, induces the supposition that in this state the author threw aside his unfinished work, perhaps deterred by its want of promise of stage effect and interest, perhaps invited by some more congenial theme. When, therefore, it was wanted by his friends and "fellows," Heminge & Condell, after his death, for the press and the stage, some literary artist like Heywood was invited to fill up the accessory and subordinate parts of the play upon the author's own outline; and this was done, or attempted to be done, in the manner of the great original, as far as possible, but with little distinction of his varieties of style.

Upon this hypothesis, I suppose the play to be mainly and substantially Shakespeare's, filled up indeed by an inferior hand, but not interpolated in the manner of Tate, Davenant, or Dryden, with the rejection and adulteration of parts of the original; so that its history would be nearly that of many of the admired paintings of Rubens and Murillo, and other prolific artists, who often left the details and accessories of their work to be completed by pupils or dependents.

The reader must decide for himself among these contending conjectures, where nothing is certain but the fact of a singular discrepancy of taste, style, and power of execution in the same piece, combined with a perfect unity of plot, purpose, and intent. (pp. 6-7)

> *Gulian C. Verplanck, "Introductory Remarks," in* Shakespeare's Plays: With His Life, Tragedies, Vol. III *by William Shakespeare, edited by Gulian C. Verplanck, Harper & Brothers, 1847, pp. 3-9.*

G. G. GERVINUS (essay date 1849-50)

[One of the most widely read Shakespearean critics of the latter half of the nineteenth century, the German critic Gervinus was praised by such eminent authors of his day as Edward Dowden, F. J. Furnivall, and James Russell Lowell; however, he is little known in the English-speaking world today. Like his predecessor Hermann Ulrici, Gervinus wrote in the tradition of the "philosophical criticism" developed in Germany in the mid-nineteenth century. Under the influence of August Wilhelm Schlegel's literary theory and Georg Wilhelm Friedrich Hegel's philosophy, German critics like Gervinus tended to focus their analyses around a search

*for the literary work's organic unity and ethical import. Gervinus
believed Shakespeare's works contained a rational ethical system
independent of any religion—in contrast to Ulrici, for whom
Shakespeare's morality was basically Christian. In the following
excerpt, Gervinus briefly addresses the issue of* Timon's *authorship, concluding that the inconsistencies and contradictions in the
play can be attributed to two causes: the "unfathomable" state
of Shakespeare's mind at the time he wrote the play and his idea
that* Timon *is a play with "scarcely any real story." Unlike most
earlier commentators, particularly William Richardson (1784)
and Hermann Ulrici (1839), who viewed* Timon *as the "flawed"
personality of the play—and even as an individual corrupt in his
self-deception, his philanthropy, and his eventual misanthropy—
Gervinus regards Timon as a human being whose only true fault
is his over-abundant affection for humanity. He regards Apemantus as the evil figure in the drama, and views him as a character whose cynicism and total disregard for humanity far out-
weigh Timon's misguided love. Other critics who have debated
this issue include August Wilhelm Schlegel (1808), Denton J.
Snider (1887), G. Wilson Knight (1930), and L. C. Knights (1969).
The essay from which the following excerpt is taken was originally
published in German as* Shakespeare, 1849-50.]

The impression made on most readers by *Timon* is that of great
inequality. The versification is loose, and either unusually irregular or corrupted. Some portions of the piece are worked
out with love, others appear to have been most carelessly treated.
The many indifferent personages with no distinctly marked
characters make the scenes here and there disconnected. The
intensity and depth of feeling with which the subject, as a
whole, is carried out cannot be denied; but, compared with
this earnestness, the burlesque scenes, where the borrowing
servants of Timon are turned off, are too sharply contrasted.
The composition is arranged with the old attention to unity of
idea, but in some points it is loose and, as it were, unfinished. . . . In Act V. sc. 3 it is intimated that Alcibiades has
undertaken the war against Athens partly on Timon's account,
but nothing further is said of this in the play. The reason of
his rebellion is given in Act III. sc. 5. He there pleads in vain
for a friend who has been condemned to death for killing a
man in a duel. . . . But the discussion concerns some one
entirely unknown; we learn nothing whatever of the man's
person or home. Singularly enough, all commentators pass over
this circumstance without remark, although no similar disconnected scene is to be found in the whole of Shakespeare. How
these irregularities are to be accounted for is a matter of dispute.
Coleridge thought that the original text of Shakespeare had
been spoiled by actors. Knight considered the piece to be a
revision of an older play, of which portions only were retained
[see excerpt above, 1843], so that *Timon* was to be looked
upon as a companion piece to *Pericles*. Delius regards the play
as an unfinished work, the outlines of which were left incomplete for representation. We, on our side, however, content
ourselves with the opinion we expressed in our remarks upon
Antony, where we attributed the carelessness in a number of
plays of this date to one common, though unfathomable, cause—
the state of the poet's mind. We must, however, add that some
of the peculiarities in this or other works of the same date may
arise also from the subject itself. Timon is a play with scarcely
any real story. (pp. 769-71)

With a mind unfortified and of little strength [Timon] cannot
overcome the injuries of fate; his spirit is drowned and lost in
misfortune, which he has never been inured to bear; the mere
man of the world whose mind has hitherto been only seen with
a smooth surface, is now roused by the storm of passion, which
reverses all things. We have before us the most lively image
of the transition from one extreme to another; the want of

moderation peculiar to him in one instance is evident here in
the other. In this point of view Coleridge styled *Timon* the
Lear of domestic and ordinary life [see excerpt above, 1808-
18]. He who but now was surrounded and worshipped by all
is forsaken and despised. . . . (p. 779)

In the extremity of his obdurate and immoderate hatred, the
humane poet has not forgotten the original nature of the man,
nor neglected to make the traces of his former goodness dis-
cernible through all his fury and curses. This, too, contributes
not a little to keep in view in this play a better human nature.
When Alcibiades first disturbs his repose, he pours out his fury
upon him in all its strength. Immediately afterwards there flows
from his lips, which he desired only to open for cursing, an
involuntary prayer for blessing. He wishes that bounteous 'nature out of her fertile and conceptious womb' may rather engender unheard-of monsters than bring forth 'ingrateful man';
he bids her 'dry up her unctuous morsels, vines, and marrows,'
and refuse to nourish the ingrates she had borne. Apemantus
torments him, and against him Timon rises with all the self-
consciousness of his nobler nature; but even in discourse with
him a kinder expression insinuates itself, proving that he thought
better of women than men, not having had such evil experiences
of them. The thieves come; he is kinder towards them, because,
at least, they do not seem different to what they are. Even with
them, as we said above, his curse works a blessing. His steward's fidelity staggers him completely. He is forced to recognise
one upright man, who demands exemption from his systematic
hatred; he acknowledges for once that he has gone to an immoderate excess; he confesses his 'exceptless rashness,' and
prays the 'perpetual sober' gods to forgive him. But the weak
man is unable to remain in this wholesome state of mind, which
might have saved him; an obstinate consistency has taken hold
of him, and at the same moment that he sees and confesses
the fault of 'exceptless' condemnation of humanity, he
strengthens his resolution to avoid all exception but this one.
He returns to his obdurate hatred, in which, however, such a
nature as his could not long abide. 'Philanthropy,' says Ulrici,
'was his element; misanthropy suffocated him; he could not
breathe in it long' [see excerpt above, 1839]. It is usually
understood that he dies of a broken heart; to us the intention
of suicide seems evident in his last words. (pp. 780-81)

[Shakespeare] contrasts in Timon and Apemantus the cyrenaic
and cynic systems, which divided antiquity between them; and
he allows it evidently and strongly to be felt that both, by
representing happiness as the aim of human endeavours, set
up a false standard, and that the being intent upon extreme
principles will not, after all, lead to this false aim. The open
and refined nature of Timon, who seeks happiness in nourishing
and fostering, and in accumulating and satisfying the wants of
men, who considers culture and improvement, which are the
distinguishing privilege of our race, to be inseparably connected with this, who sees in sociability the best means for
this refinement of all external and internal gifts and enjoyments,
is contrasted with this proletary of antiquity, this cynic philosopher at the opposite extreme of Rousseau's 'Theory of
Nature.' Confused by the caprice of his principles, he is extreme in frugality; born poor and needy, he makes the abnegation of all things his system; the renunciation of everything
that makes man human, the degradation of human nature to
brutish, the most entire self-denial, the avoidance of society
and social meetings, these are the principles of his wisdom.
In his one-sidedness, that poorest of all humours, he is opposed
to all humanity; wine and the marrow of the earth have not
made his spirit indolent, but water has drowned it from his

youth. He despises art and artists; all enjoyment, dancing, and pomp are madness in his eyes. Compared with the sensitiveness of Timon's soft heart, his is quite stiff and frozen. Born in poverty, he was destined to labour, to activity, and business more than Timon, who made his money work for him; but if it were a fault in the latter that he imitated the gods in his enjoyment and bestowal of good things, the indolence and inactivity of Apemantus are much more culpable and contemptible. Timon would have helped him daily out of his beggary, if this, according to the uncorrupted opinion of our forefathers, had been considered as a disgrace by him; but he was proud of it, gloried in not being a prodigal like Timon, though abstinence was not meritorious in his case; in the literal sense of the words he made a virtue of necessity. If the beggarly pride of this man contrasts with Timon's modesty to the immeasurable advantage of the latter, much more does Timon's disinterestedness shine by comparison with the selfishness of Apemantus, whose prayer is only for himself, notwithstanding his pretence of self-abhorrence. For all this self-degrading, this intentional impoverishment and isolation, is only, according to that suggestion of Lucian's, an affectation of originality and a real vanity to attract the eyes of mankind. Compared with this innate vanity how pardonable is that of the prodigal, generated and nourished by the thanks, the admiration, and the love of hundreds of hypocritical flatterers! If Apemantus were no flatterer except to misery, if he spoke truths and cutting truths to everyone, why should his straightforwardness be judged better than Timon's genial and considerate love of society, since the cynic's candour had its origin in nothing but his beggarly pride and vanity? He stood on the lowest step, where there was none beneath for a flatterer to stand upon, from whence he therefore refused to flatter those above him; his plain speaking flowed from the malice of a venomous, envious, and violent nature; by an instinctive acuteness it spied out every bad quality and experience, and refused to see the good; unlike Timon's endeavour to show love and kindness to all, he indulged in a habit of blame and slander; his abuse had no other aim than to enrage men, 'the office of a knave or a fool.' Contrary to the proverb, anger was in him lasting and stinging; misanthropy, which in Timon arose out of the shattering of his faith in human nature, was in him a profession, the effect of innate inhumanity and of his vain and malicious disposition. If Timon carried his love and trust to excess, so did this man his hatred and mistrust. How clearly shines the uncorrupted nature of that most spoilt of mortals, still holding his belief in human virtue; how bright the splendour of his friendship mania, compared with the suspicious disposition of this egotist, who believes in no integrity, who wonders that men dare trust themselves with men, who implores the gods to preserve him from the folly of trusting anyone! He who possesses nothing has attained to the hard-heartedness of the miser, who pretends to possess nothing. (pp. 782-83)

Between these two eccentric beings Alcibiades is placed as the man of practical life, which generally blunts extremes. He is by no means shown in a very favourable light, lest he should prejudice the chief character. Shakespeare represents him without any ideality, as a man of coarse texture, who is in no way enthusiastic about the extreme ends of things; a complete soldier, who carries about with him the pleasures of peaceful life; who knows how to be poor and to be rich; not the worst of Timon's friends, who, needy himself, yet willingly offers him money for his support, and, though reviled by him, espouses his cause as his own. . . . Where Timon nourishes universal hatred Alcibiades punishes with severity, but with discrimination. On hearing that the walls which he is about to overthrow

were not built by those who have injured him he desists from the attempt. 'All have not offended,' they tell him. They offer him decimation 'if his revenges hunger for that food which nature loaths.' The warrior throws down his glove to certify that he will only punish his enemies; reconciliation quickly follows his substantial revenge and active hatred, whilst Timon, in his enmity against humanity, does not think decimation satisfaction enough. This limitless fury necessarily recoils fatally on the impotent hater. Fate had restored to him in a wonderful manner the means of taking the sweetest revenge on his false friends. He despised in obstinate bitterness what prodigal chance had freely given into his prodigal hands, and died desolate, a subject of malicious joy perhaps to his pretended friends, while the poor Alcibiades, with unpaid soldiers, preserving moderation in his aims and in his passions, punishes ingratitude, spares the penitent, and triumphs over all. (pp. 785-86)

G. G. Gervinus, "Third Period of Shakespeare's Dramatic Poetry: 'Timon of Athens',' in his Shakespeare Commentaries, translated by F. E. Bunnètt revised edition, Smith, Elder, & Co., 1877, pp. 769-86.

F. G. FLEAY (essay date 1874)

[*Fleay was an English clergyman, scholar, and critic who, as a member of the New Shakspere Society, joined F. J. Furnivall as a pioneer in the area of standardized verse analysis tests, a method which "scientifically" investigated the metrical variations in Shakespeare's verse. Fleay constructed a statistical table that evaluated each of Shakespeare's plays with a numerical breakdown of blank verse, prose, rhyme, short and long lines, and redundant syllables. The results of his tests indicated that a number of passages that had been accepted as the work of Shakespeare were the work of another author. Fleay and Furnivall laid the foundation for succeeding disintergration theorists. Despite its initial appeal, most twentieth-century scholars have come to reject Fleay's verse analysis method and the conclusions both Fleay and Furnivall drew from their experiments. In the following excerpt, Fleay agrees with Gulian C. Verplanck (1847) that Shakespeare was the original author of* Timon, *and that its inconsistencies are due to the revisions or completions of a later writer, whom Fleay speculates was Cyril Tourneur. Other critics, most notably Charles Knight (1843), have argued that* Timon *was originally the work of an unknown author, and that Shakespeare revised and added scenes of his own. Still others, such as Walter Raleigh (1907), E. K. Chambers (1908), Una Ellis-Fermor (1942), G. B. Harrison (1951), and Charlton Hinman (1969) contend that the play is totally Shakespeare's work, although they also disagree as to whether it is finished or unfinished.*]

The object of the present paper is to shew that the nucleus, the original and only valuable part of [*Timon of Athens*], is Shakspere's; and that it was completed for the stage by a second and inferior hand. . . .

In Act I. Sc. 1, I find nothing that we can reject except the prose parts. . . . (p. 130)

Act I. Sc. 2, on the other hand, has not a trace of Shakspere in it. . . . As to the poor humour, poorer metre, and wretched general style of this scene, I need say nothing: it is manifest on a mere cursory reading, but I give a specimen of the *poetry*, the best I can find.

He commands us to prowide, and give great guifts,
     and all out of an empty Coffer:

Nor will he know his Purse, or yeeld me this,
To shew him what a Begger his heart is,
Being of no power to make his wishes good.
His promises flye so beyond his state,
That what he speaks is all in debt: he owis for every
   word;
He is so kind that he now pays interest for't,
His Land's put to their Bookes.

                     [I. ii. 192-200]

However fine this may be, it is certainly not in the style of
Shakspere, or of the preceding scene.

But in Act II. Sc. 1 we come on the genuine play again.

                      For I do feare,
When every Feather stickes in his own wing,
Lord Timon will be left a naked gull,
Which flashes now a Phoenix.

                      [II. i. 29-32]

There is the true ring in this. (pp. 131-32)

But I have only done one part of my work. I have next to show
how this curious treatment of a play of Shakspere's came to
be adopted. His share of the play was written undoubtedly
about 1606. Delius places it with *Pericles* rightly. The rhyme
test places it there also. But I believe that *Timon* differs from
the others in not being finished in Shakspere's lifetime at all,
though I do not advance this as *certain*, but as *probable* only.
[Here Fleay explains the anomalies of the pagination of *Timon*
in the First Folio]. . . .

This space, then, of pp. 80-108, which would have just held
the *Troylus and Cressida*, being left unfilled, it became necessary to fill it. But if, as I conjecture, all the following plays
from *Julius Caesar* to *Cymbeline* were already in type, and
had been printed off, there was nothing to fall back on but
Pericles and the unfinished *Timon*. I have given reasons in my
paper on *Pericles* for believing that the Editors would not have
considered it respectful to Shakspere's memory to publish the
Pericles; they therefore took the incomplete *Timon*, put it into
a playwright's hands, and told him to make it up to 30 pages.
Hence the enormous amount of padding and bombast in his
part of the work: hence the printing of prose in cut-up into
short lines as if it were verse, which is a very common characteristic of spurious or otherwise irregular editions:—hence
the Dumas style of dialogue so frequent in the Apemantus parts:
hence the hurry that left uncorrected so many contradictions,
and unfilled so many omissions. The hypothesis is bold even
to impudence; but it accounts for the phenomena, and no other
can I find that will. (pp. 136-37)

I have only to add that the *essential* part of this Paper is the
proof that the Shakspere part of this play was written *before*
the other part: the theory how this came to be done is accessory
and unimportant. If any one likes to believe as I did in 1869
that the unfinished play of Shakspere was given to another
theatre-poet to finish in 1608-9, he is welcome to his belief:
he avoids some difficulties and incurs others. But that Knight's
theory as held by Delius, &c., is untenable, I hold to be proven:
the un-Shaksperian parts were certainly the latest written. (p. 139)

      F. G. Fleay, ''On the Authorship of 'Timon of Ath-
      ens','' in Transactions of the New Shakespeare So-
      ciety, *first series, N. Trubner & Co., 1874, pp. 130-*
      51.

EDWARD DOWDEN (essay date 1881)

[*Dowden was an Irish critic and biographer whose* Shakespeare:
A Critical Study of His Mind and Art *was the leading example
of the biographical criticism popular in the English-speaking world
near the end of the nineteenth century. Biographical critics sought
in the plays and poems a record of Shakespeare's personal development. As this approach gave way in the twentieth century
to aesthetic theories with greater emphasis on the constructed,
artificial nature of literary works, Dowden and other biographical
critics came to be considered limited. In the following excerpt,
he views the story of* Timon *as more than a dramatic study, or
a portrait for the sake of ''moral edification''; for him, it is an
intimate chronicle, a tale of an individual close to the poet himself.
Dowden considers such tragic, though fascinating, characters as
Hamlet, Lear, and Timon as creative embodiments of the dark
side of Shakespeare's own personality. This biographical approach to Shakespeare's work, and* Timon *in particular, can also
be seen in the excerpts by Hermann Ulrici (1839), G. G. Gervinus
(1849-50), Wilhelm Wendlandt (1888), George Brandes (1895-
96), E. K. Chambers (1908), and Frank Harris (1909).*]

[*Timon of Athens*] may actually lie, in point of time, at a
considerable distance from those discoveries of evil in man's
heart which inspired the soliloquies of Hamlet and the frenzied
utterances of Lear; but in Timon indignation has attained its
ideal expression; it is the decuman wave which sets shoreward
from that infinite and stormy sea of human passion.

Timon of Athens, although deservedly one of the least popular
of Shakspere's plays, belongs to his best period, and was written by the poet with no half-hearted regard for his subject. (pp.
338-39)

It would seem that about this period Shakspere's mind was
much occupied with the questions, In what temper are we to
receive the injuries inflicted upon us by our fellow-men? How
are we to bear ourselves towards those that wrong us? How
shall we secure our inward being from chaos amid the evils of
the world? How shall we attain to the most just and noble
attitude of soul in which life and the injuries of life may be
confronted? Now, here in Timon we see one way in which a
man may make his response to the injuries of life; he may turn
upon the world with a fruitless and suicidal rage. Shakspere
was interested in the history of Timon, not merely as a dramatic
study, and not merely for the sake of moral edification, but
because he recognized in the Athenian misanthrope one whom
he had known, an intimate acquaintance, the Timon of Shakspere's own breast. Shall we hesitate to admit that there was
such a Timon in the breast of Shakspere? We are accustomed
to speak of Shakspere's gentleness and Shakspere's tolerance
so foolishly that we find it easier to conceive of Shakspere as
indulgent towards baseness and wickedness than as feeling
measureless rage and indignation against them—rage and indignation which would sometimes flash beyond their bounds
and strike at the whole wicked race of man. And it is certain
that Shakspere's delight in human character, his quick and
penetrating sympathy with almost every variety of man, saved
him from any persistent injustice towards the world. But it can
hardly be doubted that the creator of Hamlet, of Lear, of Timon,
saw clearly, and felt deeply, that there is a darker side to the
world and to the soul of man. (pp. 340-41)

In the character of Timon, Shakspere gained dramatic remoteness from his own personality. It would have been contrary to
the whole habit of the dramatist's genius to have used one of
his characters merely as a mask to conceal his visage, while
he relieved himself with lyrical vehemence of the feelings that
oppressed him. No; Shakspere, when *Timon* was written, had

attained self-possession, and could transfer himself with real disinterestedness into the person of the young Athenian favorite of fortune. This, in more than one instance, was Shakspere's method—having discovered some single central point of sympathy between his chief character and his past or present self, to secure freedom from all mere lyrical intensity by studying that one common element under conditions remote from those which had ever been proper or peculiar to himself. (p. 342)

Having never made discovery of human virtue, the first incursion of veritable fact upon Timon, the first in his whole life, is that of the selfishness, ingratitude, and baseness of man. The entire dream-structure of his life topples, totters, and crashes down. The mirage of universal brotherhood among men vanishes, and he is left in the barren wastes of the world. And because Timon has lived carelessly, with relaxed moral fibre, now, when calamity overtakes him, he is wanting in all capacity for patient endurance of the heart. He is "passion's slave:"

> A pipe for Fortune's finger
> To sound what stop she please.
>
> [*Hamlet,* III. ii. 70-1]

Shakspere in an earlier play—that from which these words are borrowed—had pictured a man who had taken "Fortune's buffets and rewards with equal thanks." But the character of Horatio was not lax and self-indulgent; he was "more an antique Roman than a Dane." Timon is unable to accept his sorrow, and hold his nature strenuously under command until it can adjust itself to the altered state of things. He flings himself from an airy, unreal philanthropy into passionate hatred of men. He is a revolter from humanity. He foams at the mouth with imprecation. He shakes off the dust of Athens from his feet, and strives to maintain himself in isolation, the one protester in the world against the cruelty and selfishness and baseness of the race. (p. 343)

Gervinus has rightly noticed that Shakspere, in several of his dramas, reflects his main plot in a secondary plot, making the latter serve to illustrate and illuminate the former. Thus the story of Gloucester and his unnatural Edmund is a secondary plot reflecting the story of Lear and his daughters; the thunder of that moral tempest rolls away with reverberations, which prolong and intensify its menace. In *Hamlet,* the position of Laertes, who had lost a father by foul means, and who hastens to revenge his death, repeats the position of the Danish prince himself. In *The Tempest,* the treasonable attempt of Caliban, Stephano, and Trinculo upon the life of Prospero is by its wickedness and its folly a kind of parody upon the treason of Antonio and Sebastian against the King of Naples. Here, in *Timon of Athens,* the story of Alcibiades, so ill connected by external points of contact with that of the principal character, fulfils the same ethical and aesthetic purpose that the secondary plots fulfil in *Lear,* in *Hamlet,* and in *The Tempest.* (p. 344)

Alcibiades comes before the Athenian senate to plead on behalf of the life of a friend who had slain one who wronged his honor:

> With a noble fury and fair spirit,
> Seeing his reputation touch'd to death,
> He did oppose his foe.   [III. v. 18-20]

It was precisely such plain loyalty of friendship as this shown by Alcibiades which Timon had not found, and, not finding which, he had abandoned himself to desperation. The senators—whose words are excellent words, but wholly unreal—

utter wise maxims about the patient bearing of injuries and the unworthiness of revenge.

> He's truly valiant that can wisely suffer
> The worst that man can breathe, and make his wrongs
> His outsides, to wear them like his raiment, carelessly,
> And ne'er prefer his injuries to his heart
> To bring it into danger.   [III. v. 31-5]

But Alcibiades, who is of an active, practical, unideal character, is not able to discover wisdom in the suffering of evils, which, by opposing, a man may end.

> Why do fond men expose themselves to battle,
> And not endure all threats? Sleep upon 't,
> And let the foes quietly cut their throats
> Without repugnancy?   [III. v. 42-5]

Alcibiades, for daring the anger of the Senate, is sent into perpetual banishment. He, like Timon, is compelled to experience the ingratitude of his fellows. But Alcibiades has been living in the real world, and is able immediately to assign its place to this ingratitude and baseness in a world in which evil and good are mingled.

Although possessed of none of the potential nobleness of Timon, Alcibiades possesses one virtue—that of perceiving such facts as lie within the range of his limited observation. He does not see the whole world, but he sees the positive limited half of it rightly in the main. He is less than Timon, and yet greater; for Timon miserably fails through want of the one gift which Alcibiades possessed. In like manner, Hamlet had failed for want of the gift which Fortinbras possessed; and yet Hamlet's was beyond all measure a larger and rarer soul than that of the Prince of Norway. Alcibiades has, at least, not been living in a dream; he lays hold of the positive and coarser pleasures of life, and endures its positive, limited pains, definite misfortunes which lie within appreciable bounds. No absolute, ideal anguish like that of Timon can overwhelm him. Accordingly, instead of wasting himself in futile rage against mankind, Alcibiades resolves to set himself in active opposition to those who have wronged him. While Timon is lifting weak hands of indignation to the gods, Alcibiades advances against Athens with swords and drums. To him the Senate will bow with humble entreaties for grace. Timon had fiercely thrust away their advances, because he could not accept benefits or render service in a base world which was remote from the ideal he had dreamed. Alcibiades, who deals with the world as it is, will punish and will pardon. The rage of Timon had been barren; it is hushed at last under the sands and the wash of waves. (pp. 345-48)

Yet the idealist Timon was infinitely interesting to the imagination of Shakspere. The practical and limited character of Alcibiades was esteemed highly by him, but did not really interest him. In like manner, Hamlet, who failed, interested Shakspere; Fortinbras, who succeeded, seemed admirable to him, but in his presence Shakspere's sympathies and imagination were not deeply moved. Can we miss the significance of such a fact as this? Can we doubt that the Hamlets and Timons of Shakspere's plays represent the side of the dramatist's own character in which lay his peculiar strength, and also his special danger and weakness? An Alcibiades or a Fortinbras represents that side of his character into which he threw himself for protection against the weakness of excess of passion or excess of thought. It was the portion of his being which was more elaborated than the rest, and less spontaneous; and therefore he highly esteemed it, and loved it little. (p. 349)

Edward Dowden, ''Shakspere's Last Plays,'' in his Shakspere: A Critical Study of His Mind and Art, *third edition, Harper & Brothers Publishers, 1881, pp. 336-82.*

DENTON J. SNIDER (essay date 1887)

[*Snider suggests an interpretation of Timon similar to that of William Richardson (1784) and Hermann Ulrici (1839), both of whom considered Timon as an individual whose tragic flaw resides in his inability to control a certain element of his personality. This assessment is perhaps most vehemently opposed by G. G. Gervinus (1849-50) and G. Wilson Knight (1930), both of whom characterize Timon as a noble and overly generous soul in a corrupt society.*]

The character [of Timon] is common to all times and places; it shows a man who through his own excess falls into adversity from prosperity, experiences ingratitude, lays the blame on civilization, and flees to the woods. But in the present case there is afterwards no return to society, such as Shakespeare portrays in some of his comedies; the character of Timon is such that he draws no blessing from his trial; he seems the more hardened in hate by his discipline; the flight into Nature brings to him no healing mediation, but becomes the last flight into the realm beyond.

The character runs on a line with the poet's great tragic characters, showing a deed, a disposition or a passion, which being pushed beyond its true limit, lands in the opposite of itself. Timon is liberal without bounds, and so passes to being illiberal without bounds; generosity becomes its own tragedy, the unbalanced passion hastes to be antipathetic to itself. When the citizens show their ingratitude, it throws him into ingratitude; he was unable to remain generous in spirit, when his property was gone. As he finds no rational principle in property, so he finds none in himself; as he loses his wealth, so he loses his humanity. His open-handedness we find to be a selfish indulgence of a passion, which, when the means of gratification is gone, turns to the bitterest hate; his generosity is not centered at the heart; even philanthropy, if self-seeking, gets to be self-contradictory, and becomes its own opposite, namely, misanthropy. This transition in a human soul is what the poet has sought to portray in the character of Timon.

The play is, however, one of the less celebrated and less attractive among Shakespeare's works. The theme itself is not the most enticing, and its treatment must be pronounced to be in many respects unsatisfactory. The inequality of the execution will be acknowledged by every careful reader. Some parts are wrought out with great skill and completeness; others are hastily and rudely sketched, while certain necessary links seem to be omitted altogether. The versification is often a mystery, and the prose frequently appears to be written with exceeding carelessness. But the main characteristic of the play is the dark coloring in which it portrays social life. (pp. 12-14)

The relation of the individual and of society to property and the conflicts which arise therefrom constitute the fundamental theme of the play. For property is also an ethical principle—not the highest by any means, perhaps the lowest, still an ethical principle—to violate which within its sphere is guilt, and not to subordinate which outside of its sphere is also guilt. A person, therefore, who disregards it utterly, and a person who esteems it as the highest end, may, both of them, become involved in a tragic destiny. These two forms occur in the present drama, whose general movement shows the course of

the property-despising man, through prodigality to misanthropy and death; and of the property-loving society, through avarice to the loss of national independence. (pp. 14-15)

Let us now consider, in a brief statement, the structure of the work. There are two Movements in the play, as we usually find in Shakespeare's tragedies—two grand sweeps of the Ethical World of the poet into and out of a corrupted condition. The First Movement extends to the time when both Timon and Alcibiades, who have not their end in gain, take their departure from Athens on account of the above-mentioned conflict; a money-getting society drives them away. The Second Movement depicts the conduct of these two persons in exile. Timon becomes a misanthrope, turns not only against his own city, but curses all mankind as a property-acquiring race, and is involved in his own curse, finally perishing, it would seem, by suicide. Alcibiades, the soldier and man of action, returns with an army, humiliates and punishes his country for its wrongs. Thereby is indicated that the nation, having banished its best general, can no longer defend itself, but is sapped within by its exclusive devotion to property. In this subjection would naturally begin its discipline and purification, but the poet in the present instance does not show his disordered Ethical World restored, as he has done in some other tragedies—in which fact we may mark an imperfection, comparing this drama with his better procedure. The First Movement embraces the first three Acts, the Second Movement the last two Acts; wherein we observe another rule of structure, to which the poet, for the most part adheres.

The Threads around which the action centers are two, that of Timon and that of Alcibiades. Both these persons are in a conflict with the society in which they live, as respects property; that society is devoted primarily to the acquisition of wealth, yet with a decided relish for the gratification of the senses. These two men are alike in not seeking gain, though otherwise different enough. (pp. 16-17)

But this society, so selfish and sensual, has naturally produced its opposite. Here is the example, Apemantus, the cynic. This character really belongs to history—to the days of the ancient Greek and Roman world, in its decline and corruption. We now behold an individual who, instead of gratifying the senses, abuses them, and thrusts from him all the reasonable comforts of life. To the flatterer succeeds the scoffer; to abject servility succeeds intentional discourtesy. The love of property has no place in his breast; on the contrary, he has become the hater of men, from their pursuit of gain. He is just the person to expose the rotten condition of society, because he contemns it so deeply. His main function in the play is, therefore, to reflect the age in its negative phases. He holds up to Timon, for whom alone he seems to have some affection, the consequences of prodigality; he speaks openly and bitterly, exposing the flattery and treachery of the whole crowd of followers. But not alone to Timon, but also to all persons with whom he comes in contact, he tells with stinging satire what they are; he is the mirror which reflects the inner character of each individual of the company. Thus, amid all this hollow formality, the real spirit is shown; a man may utter his polite phrases, but Apemantus is there in his presence to cast his true image. Moreover, Apemantus is now the picture of that which Timon is destined to become, namely, the misanthrope. Still another trait must be added, which, however, appears with distinctness only in the latter part of the drama. It is the vein of affectation which lies deep in the character of Apemantus. His cynicism is largely the result of vanity, and not of conviction. Insincerity must thus attach to him in a certain degree, and he is a true member of this false and dissembling Athenian world. (pp. 19-20)

Timon excites our admiration by his lofty enthusiasm, and by his noble striving after an ideal life in which all things are common and all men are brothers. But such a principle is an absurdity, an impossibility, for it rests upon a one-sided view of human nature. Man must be individual to be man; he cannot be absorbed into a universal humanity. Society also is based on the fact that each member of it seeks to own—that is, to acquire and to retain. One contributes his labor in order to get in return, and to keep as much as is reasonable. The consciousness of Timon is contrary to the organization of society, which cannot rest on spending alone, but also on obtaining. As everybody else is seeking to acquire and retain, Timon must soon be deprived of his property. It is at this point that we can see the ethical guilt of Timon; his principle and his conduct are logically destructive to society.

But there is one class which remains honest and faithful in this corrupt community—the servants of Timon. His own household shares in his true nature. Flavius, his steward, has also warned him of the consequences of his conduct, has done everything to stem the tide of extravagance, and is, in fact, the most rational character in the drama. It is a contrast between the high and the low; integrity and honor have taken refuge in the humblest class of people. Thus there still remains a sound part of society, though the top is rotten; there is still a source from which a new life is possible. But it is only one bright and small ray in a very dark picture. (pp. 21-2)

[The] play, as a whole, leaves the impression of a sketch completely filled out in some portions, in other portions possessing the barest outlines of the characters and action. Motives are inserted which are not afterwards used, some are omitted which ought to have been mentioned; both redundancy and deficiency are easy to be pointed out. Several unexpected differences between the First and Second Movements occur in the characterization. . . . The work, therefore, seems to lack the final revision which gives to every element its proper relief, and organizes the whole into a consistent unity. The reason of this incompleteness has often been conjectured, but never can be known. Still, the conception of the play is eminently worthy of the great Dramatist, but it remains a grand fragment of his genius, which, had it been completed, might have taken an equal rank alongside of *Lear*, whose coloring and treatment it often resembles. But, in its present condition, there is much passion in it but no patience, much vengeance but no endurance. Timon never says, as Lear does, "I can be patient"; even in his prayer he grows satirical toward the Gods. (p. 33)

> Denton J. Snider, "'Timon of Athens'," in his The
> Shakespearian Drama, a Commentary: The Trage-
> dies, *Sigma Publishing Co., 1887, pp. 11-35.*

WILHELM WENDLANDT　(essay date 1888)

[*In his study of* Timon, *Wendlandt focuses on a number of issues discussed by a host of critics since the eighteenth century. Perhaps most significant is his contention that Shakespeare's play clearly demonstrates "certain conditions in Shakespeare's own life and times," particularly the bitterness and melancholy he felt towards the end of his life. This point is also made by Hermann Ulrici (1839), G. G. Gervinus (1849-50), Edward Dowden (1881), George Brandes (1895-96), E. K. Chambers (1908), and Frank Harris (1909). Wendlandt's view of Timon as a noble and kind individual whose benevolence ceases only after his bounty ends and his*

friends desert him has been affirmed by Gervinus and, most vehemently, G. Wilson Knight (1930).]

Timon was written in Shakespeare's last period when he knew so much about the world that it had become almost a sickness. Shakespeare's protagonists from that period reflect these traits, notably the tragic fate of being ahead of one's time and thus isolated and cut off from 'real' life. Seen in this light, *Timon* proves to be the exact counterpart to Prospero. . . .

While Prospero embodies love, life and wellness of spirit, Timon embodies hate, death and sickness of spirit. This sickness of spirit and the nature of Timon's decline follow the same pattern as in three other late plays: *Troilus and Cressida, Antony and Cleopatra*, and *Coriolanus*.

Timon of Athens is, of course, not a run-of-the-mill tragedy. Goethe spoke of it as being actually a subject for comedy. We concur . . . and find . . . the characteristic ambivalence between comic and tragic subject typically Shakespearean. Only Shakespeare could have successfully given tragic treatment to a comic subject. Only Shakespeare could have thought of writing a play about a man-hater as tragedy—material which would be better suited for comedy. . . .

We believe . . . that *Richardson* and *Schlegel* misunderstood Timon as tragic figure [see excerpts above, 1784 and 1808]. Richardson says that his tendency to boast of his generosity prevents him from being a tragic figure; Schlegel says he couldn't tolerate the thought of merely being an imitator of Apemantus. We see the tragic truth about Timon in his noble blindness about the nature of his fellowmen whose benevolence stops as soon as his bounty stops. And thus Timon's kindness and benevolence eventually die at the root and turn into poison.

In Timon's material decline Shakespeare portrays his own spiritual fate. He had thrown his pearls before swine when he offered up his great, rich heart to a forgetful nation; he had sacrificed himself to a hungry public. *Timon*, like the late sonnets, reflected certain conditions in Shakespeare's own life and times: the retirement in Stratford; the time for reflection and contemplation of contemporary social and political conditions; his psychological condition after leaving London. The theater people forgot quickly what gifts he had bestowed on them; the theater crowd now being made up mostly of powerful protectors and unprincipled flatterers. Shakespeare foresaw that all this would soon lead to the disintegration of the theater as he had known it.

Timon . . . reflects this mood: inexhaustible generosity, the wasting of incredible wealth, sudden poverty, disloyalty, ingratitude, bitterness and finally escape from the world. *Timon* and Shakespeare's last *sonnets* (whose writing Shakespeare resumed after his retirement to Stratford) are two essentially inseparable counterpieces which provide a mutual commentary on each other. Most likely Shakespeare wrote *Timon* in Stratford after settling his affairs: expending his last energies, he created a gravestone both for himself and his century, whose inscription is just as disillusioned as that on his own gravestone in the church of his native town:

> Good friend, for Jesus' sake, forbear
> To dig the dust enclosed here.
> Blessed be he that spares these stones,
> And cursed be he that moves my bones.

The same words could have been written on Timon's gravestone, for they bear witness to a passionate longing for peace and deliverance.

The objective source for *Timon of Athens* is Plutarch's Life of Antonius, the Dialogue of Lucian, and existing comedies. The subjective source is Shakespeare's own dark emotions. . . . Timon, in his kinship with Shakespeare as well as his completeness, greatness and believability, could only have been a product of Shakespeare's own hand. The same . . . can be said of the other main characters in the play; those parallel figures always present in Shakespeare's plays. Here: Alcibiades, Apemantus and Flavius. These three together comprise the idea which Timon, the tragic hero, is to embody. Across from them is the group of flatterers and false friends, gluttonous lords, artists and merchants, senators and usurers with their servants; and finally the group of faithful, loyal servants led by Flavius.

Timon represents the idea of a completely guileless, benevolent man of undisputed social and spiritual superiority who, through unexpected disappointments, is propelled so far into hatred that no return to earth is possible.

Alcibiades represents the idea of a proud, self-confident soldier/ warrior who punishes disappointments with the sword. Alcibiades and Timon are friends by congeniality.

Apemantus is a poor soul who, from birth on, is alienated from the world.

Flavius is the very essence of loyalty, kindred in spirit to Kent in *Lear*. He takes on the role of the apologia for Timon.

The composition itself consists of 2 acts, closely interwoven and unified through theme (although different in mood and concept). Their function and impact as counterparts of each other, as contrasting, an-tithetical images, is uniquely Shakespearean. The architecture of the play is flawless, particularly its parallelism; . . . the parallelism of the characters whose gradation of minor and major figures can be compared to the technique used in *Hamlet, Richard III* and *Lear*. The skillful structuring of the material . . . isn't lacking in the characteristic decorative figures: the fool and a deteriorating, depraved nation. We consider . . . the play superior to all Shakespeare plays in its artistic structure. . . .

> Wilhelm Wendlandt, *''Shakespeare's 'Timon oon Athen','' in* Jahrbuch der Deutschen Shakespeare Gesellschaft, *1888, pp. 1-11 [translated for this publication].*

GEORGE BRANDES (essay date 1895-96)

[*Brandes was a scholar and the most influential literary critic of late nineteenth-century Denmark. His work on Shakespeare was translated and widely read in his day. A writer with a broad knowledge of literature, Brandes placed Shakespeare in a European context, comparing him with other important dramatists. In the excerpt below, Brandes focuses on the inconsistencies and contradictions in* Timon *and suggests that the play is the work of more than one author. Unlike some earlier commentators who have attempted to determine whether* Timon *was the work of another playwright, which Shakespeare revised (see excerpt above by Charles Knight, 1843), or whether Shakespeare wrote the original version, which some later writer adapted or revised (see excerpt above by F. G. Fleay, 1874), Brandes merely states that the play clearly demonstrates that more than one author contributed to its creation. Brandes also presents a biographical reading of the play and concludes that in the character of Timon Shakespeare gave release to all the suffering he had endured during the last years of his life. For other biographical analyses of Timon, see the excerpts by Hermann Ulrici (1839), G. G. Gervinus (1849-50), Edward Dowden (1881), Wilhelm Wendlandt (1888), E. K. Chambers (1908), and Frank Harris (1909). This excerpt*

Act IV. Scene iii. Alcibiades, Soldiers, Phrynia, Timandra, Timon of Athens. Frontispiece to Hanmer edition by F. Hayman (1744). By permission of the Folger Shakespeare Library.

is taken from an essay which was first published in Danish as William Shakespeare *in 1895-96.*]

Timon of Athens has come down to us in a pitiable condition. The text is in a terrible state, and there are, not only between one scene and another, but between one page and another, such radical differences in the style and general spirit of the play as to preclude the possibility of its having been the work of one man. The threads of the story are often entirely disconnected, and circumstances occur (or are referred to) for which we were in no way prepared. The best part of the versification is distinctly Shakespearian, and contains all that wealth of thought which was characteristic of this period of his life; but the other parts are careless, discordant, and desperately monotonous. The prose dialogue especially jars, thrust as it is, with its long-winded straining after effect, into scenes which are otherwise compact and vigorous.

All Shakespeare students of the present day concur in the opinion that *Timon of Athens*, like *Pericles*, is but a great fragment from the master-hand. (p. 254)

The non-Shakespearian elements of the play do not prevent his genius and master-hand from pervading the whole, and it is easy to see how this work grew out of the one immediately preceding it [*Coriolanus*], to trace the connecting links between the two plays.

When Coriolanus is exasperated by the ingratitude of the plebeians, he joins the enemies of his country and people, and becomes the assailant of his native city. When Timon falls a victim to the thanklessness of those he has loaded with benefits, his hatred embraces the whole human race. The contrast is very suggestive. The despair of Coriolanus is of an active kind, driving him to deeds and placing him at the head of an army. Timon's is of the passive sort: he merely curses and shuns mankind. It is not until the discovery of the treasure determines him to use his wealth in spreading corruption and misery that his hatred takes a semi-practical form. This contrast was not an element of the drama until Shakespeare made it so. (p. 259)

Like *Coriolanus*, this play was undoubtedly written in a frame of mind which prompted Shakespeare less to abandon himself to the waves of imagination than to dwell upon the worthlessness of mankind, and the scornful branding of the contemptible. There is even less inventiveness here than in *Coriolanus:* the plot is not only simple, it is scanty—more appropriate to a parable or didactic poem than a drama. Most of the characters are merely abstractly representative of their class or profession, *e.g.* the Poet, the Painter, the servants, the false friends, the flatterers, the creditors and mistresses. They are simply employed to give prominence to the principal figure, or rather, to a great lyrical outburst of bitterness, scorn, and execration. (p. 260)

We must now, with a view to defining the non-Shakespearian elements of the play, devote some attention to its dual authorship. In the first act it is particularly the prose dialogues between Apemantus and others which seem unworthy of Shakespeare. The repartee is laconic but laboured—not always witty, though invariably bitter and disdainful. The style somewhat resembles that of the colloquies between Diogenes and Alexander in Lyly's *Alexander and Campaspe*. The first of Apemantus's conversations might have been written by Shakespeare—it seems to have some sort of continuity with the utterances of Thersites in *Troilus and Cressida*—but the second has every appearance of being either an interpolation by a strange hand, or a scene which Shakespeare had forgotten to score out. Flavius's monologue (Act I. sc. 2) never came from Shakespeare's pen in this form. Its marked contrast to the rest shows that it might be the outcome of notes taken by some blundering shorthand writer among the audience.

The long conversation, in the second act, between Apemantus, the Fool, Caphis, and various servants, was, in all probability, written by an alien hand. It contains nothing but idle chatter devised to amuse the gallery, and it introduces characters who seem about to take some standing in the play, but who vanish immediately, leaving no trace. A Page comes with messages and letters from the mistress of a brothel, to which the Fool appears to belong, but we are told nothing of the contents of these letters, whose addresses the bearer is unable to read.

In the third act there is much that is feeble and irrelevant, together with an aimless unrest which incessantly pervades the stage. It is not until the banqueting scene towards the end of the act that Shakespeare makes his presence felt in the storm which bursts from Timon's lips. The powerful fourth act displays Shakespeare at his best and strongest; there is very little here which could be attributed to alien sources. I cannot understand the decision with which English critics (including a poet like Tennyson) have condemned as spurious Flavius's monologue at the close of the second scene. Its drift is that of the speech in the following scene, in which he expresses the whole spirit of the play in one line: "What viler things upon

the earth than friends!" Although there is evidently some confusion in the third scene (for example, the intimation of the Poet's and Painter's appearance long before they really arrive), I cannot agree with Fleay that Shakespeare had no share in the passage contained between the lines, "Where liest o' nights, Timon?" and "Thou art the cap of all the fools alive."

One speech in particular betrays the master-hand. It is that in which Timon expresses the wish that Apemantus's desire to become a beast among beasts may be fulfilled:

> If thou wert the lion, the fox would beguile
> thee: if thou wert the lamb, the fox would eat
> thee: if thou wert the fox, the lion would suspect
> thee when, peradventure, thou wert accused by
> the ass: if thou wert the ass, thy dulness would
> torment thee: and still thou livedst but as a
> breakfast to the wolf: if thou wert the wolf, thy
> greediness would afflict thee, and oft thou
> shouldst hazard thy life for thy dinner.
>
> [IV. iii. 328-35]

There is as much knowledge of life here as in a concentrated essence of all Lafontaine's fables.

The last scenes of the fifth act were evidently never revised by Shakespeare. It is a comical incongruity that makes the soldier who, we are expressly told, is unable to read, capable of distinguishing Timon's tomb, and even of having the forethought to take a wax impression of the words. There is also an amalgamation of the two contradictory inscriptions, of which the first tells us that the dead man wishes to remain nameless and unknown, while the last two lines begin with the declaration, "Here lie I, Timon." Notwithstanding the shocking condition of the text, the repeatedly occurring confusion of the action, and the evident marks of an alien hand, Shakespeare's leading idea and dominant purpose is never for a moment obscured. Much in *Timon* reminds us of *King Lear*, the injudiciously distributed benefits and the ingratitude of their recipients are the same, but in the former the bitterness and virulence are tenfold greater, and the genius incontestably less. Lear is supported in his misfortunes by the brave and manly Kent, the faithful Fool, that truest of all true hearts, Cordelia, her husband, the valiant King of France. There is but one who remains faithful to Timon, a servant, which in those days meant a slave, whose self-sacrificing devotion forces his master, sorely against his will, to except one man from his universal vituperation. In his own class he does not meet with a single honestly devoted heart, either man's or woman's; he has no daughter, as Lear; no mother, as Coriolanus; no friend, not one.

How far more fortunate was Antony! It is a corrupt world in the process of dissolution that we find in *Antony and Cleopatra*. Most of it is rotten or false, but the passion binding the two principal characters together by its magic is entirely genuine. (pp. 263-65)

Shakespeare has intentionally veiled the defects of nature and judgment which deprive Timon to some extent of our sympathy, both in his prosperity and his misfortunes. He had never in his bright days attached himself so warmly to any heart that he felt it beat in unison with his own. Had he ever been powerfully drawn to a single friend, he would not have squandered his possessions so lightly on all the world. Because he only loved mankind in the mass, he now hates them in the mass. He never, now as then, shows any powers of discrimination. (p. 266)

When Alcibiades, who appears in company with two hetaerae, addresses Timon in friendly fashion, the latter turns to abuse one of the women, declaring that she carries more destruction with her than the soldier does in his sword. (p. 267)

The women, seeing his wealth, immediately beg him for gold, and he answers, "Hold up, you sluts, your aprons mountant." They are not to swear, for their oaths are worthless, but they are to go on deceiving, and being "whores still," they are to seduce him to attempts to convert them, and to deck their own thin hair with the hair of corpses, that of hanged women preferably; they are to paint and rouge until they themselves lie dead: "Paint till a horse may mire upon your face."

They shout to him for more gold; they will "do anything for gold." Timon answers them in words which Shakespeare, for all the pathos of his youth, has never surpassed, words whose frenzied scathing has never been equalled:

> Consumptions sow
> In hollow bones of men: strike their sharp shins,
> And mar men's spurring; crack the lawyer's voice,
> That he may never more false title plead,
> Nor sound his quillets shrilly: hoar the flamen,
> That scolds against the quality of flesh,
> And not believes himself: down with the nose,
> Down with it flat: take the bridge quite away
> Of him that, his particular to foresee,
> Smells from the general weal: make curled-pate ruffians
>   bald,
> And let the unscarred ruffians of the war
> Derive some pain from you: plague all:
> That your activity may defeat and quell
> The source of all erection. There's more gold:
> Do you damn others, and let this damn you,
> And ditches grave you all.
> *Phrynia and Timandra.* More counsel with more gold,
> bounteous Timon.
>
>   [IV. iii. 151-67]

The passion in this is overpowering. One need only compare it with Lucian to realise the fire that Shakespeare has put into the old Greek, whose reflections are only savage in substance, being absolutely tame in expression—"The name of misanthrope shall sound sweetest in my ears, and my characteristics shall be peevishness, harshness, rudeness, hostility towards men," &c. (pp. 268-70)

These are his last words. May pestilence rage amongst men! May it infect and destroy so long as there is a man left to dig a grave! May the world be annihilated as Timon is about to annihilate himself. The light of the sun will presently be extinguished for him; let it be extinguished for all!

This is not Othello's sorrow over the power of evil to wreck the happiness of noble hearts, nor King Lear's wail over the ever-threatening possibilities and the heaped-up miseries of life: it is an angry bitterness, caused by ingratitude, which has grown so great that it darkens the sky of life and causes the thunder to roll with such threatening peals as we have never heard even in Shakespeare. All that he has lived through in these last years, and all that he has suffered from the baseness of other men, is concentrated in this colossal figure of the desperate man-hater, whose wild rhetoric is like a dark essence of blood and gall drawn off to relieve suffering. (p. 270)

> *George Brandes, "'Timon of Athens'—Hatred of Mankind," translated by Diana White with Mary Morison, in his* William Shakespeare: A Critical Study,

Vol. II, *Frederick Ungar Publishing Co., 1963, pp. 254-70.*

FREDERICK S. BOAS   (essay date 1896)

[*Boas considers* Timon *flawed in two respects: it is more like lyrical poetry than dramatic verse, and its subplot, which recounts the tribulations of Alcibiades, is not artistically woven into the texture of the main action.*]

Timon of Athens, as it stands, cannot represent a complete, genuine Shaksperean work. The contrast between the noble verse and imagery in the finer scenes, and the halting metre and insipid dialogue of other parts, is too striking to be entirely attributed to the dramatist in the maturity of his powers. Yet these inequalities have been exaggerated, and all attempts to rigidly separate the genuine from the spurious parts of the work must be viewed with suspicion.

The play, as it has come down to us, has, apart from faults of detail, two cardinal defects. Its main plot lacks sufficient action, and dwindles in its latter stages into mere passionate declamation. As *King Lear* by introducing a plethora of incidents becomes epic rather than dramatic in structure, so *Timon* through an insufficiency of incidents verges towards the close on lyrical method and temper. Secondly, its underplot with Alcibiades as hero, though its subtle variation on the main theme is essentially Shaksperean, is not closely enough interwoven into the texture of the piece. Yet, in spite of these weaknesses, *Timon* is a notable and highly characteristic product of the tragic period, of which it is the fiercest as *Lear* is the most stupendous expression. (p. 495)

Though the scene is laid in Athens, Shakspere shows as little power of creating a Greek environment for his story as he had done years ago in *A Midsummer Night's Dream.* Except for a brief allusion to the 'great towers, trophies, and schools,' which Alcibiades is begged to spare, there is not a hint to show that the dramatist had any conception of the artistic and intellectual glories of Athens in its prime. He was evidently as unfamiliar with the conditions of Periclean Greece as of Homeric. We are introduced, it is true, into a cultured and wealthy society, but its features are in no way distinctive, and it might belong to any age or nation which had advanced to a certain stage of material refinement. The representative of its art are not sculptors or dramatists, but a painter, and a poet who has allegorized for Timon's benefit the commonplace moral of the fickleness of fortune. The philosopher Apemantus is not a product of the Hellenic schools, but is a specimen of the ubiquitous curmudgeon type that from native perversity delights to snarl at the heels of humanity. The young lords who are Timon's associates, with their presents of four milk-white horses and two brace of greyhounds, remind us, like Theseus in *A Midsummer Night's Dream,* of Tudor nobles rather than genuine Athenian aristocrats. But though Shakspere does not transport us back into the atmosphere of the fifth century B.C., he achieves his purpose of placing before our view an idle, luxurious society, of which Timon is the leading figure. The rich lord, a spoiled child of fortune from his cradle, holds a court among parasites and fair-weather friends. He keeps open house for all and sundry, and scatters his gifts with reckless prodigality. . . . As he declares himself, he could deal kingdoms to his friends and ne'er be weary. And this lavishness does not spring from ostentation, but from genuine goodwill towards all mankind. He is as ready to bestow upon his servant the wherewithal to contract an advantageous marriage as to shower jewels or plate upon his equals. But this munificence has its seamy side in a criminal indifference to the elementary duty of balancing income and expenditure. It is in vain that the faithful steward, Flavius (who like Adam in *As You Like It* is a Teutonic, and not a classical type), warns his master, account-book in hand, that bankruptcy stares him in the face, and that when his wealth is flown, his friends will take flight too. . . . (pp. 496-97)

But Timon's fatal error at this crisis is that he does not stop to consider how far he is himself accountable for what has happened, and whether there is any surer way into men's hearts than prodigal hospitality. His idealism of nature proves his ruin, for, wrenched out of its original shape, it recoils in the form of savage hatred of humanity. With bitter curses he turns his back upon the whole race:

> Be abhorr'd
> All feasts, societies, and throngs of men!
> His semblable, yea, himself, Timon disdains:
> Destruction fang mankind!
>
> [IV. iii. 20-3]

He plunges into forest solitudes, and lives upon roots, but Shakspere, as appears from *As You Like It,* had no illusions about the healing properties of Nature on a radically diseased mind. Indeed, Timon himself, with a curious anticipation of modern scientific doctrines, realizes that Nature is 'one with rapine,' that the struggle for existence produces war and treachery in the animal world, and that one primordial matter breeds humanity and the lower forms of life. The 'self-same mettle, whereof'

> Arrogant man is puff'd,
> Engenders the black toad, and adder blue,
> The gilded newt, and eyeless venom'd worm,
> With all the abhorred births below crisp heaven.
>
> [IV. iii. 180-83]

Even the inanimate world is one wide area of mutual pillage:

> The sun's a thief, and with his great attraction
> Robs the vast sea; the moon's an arrant thief,
> And her pale fire she snatches from the sun;
> The sea's a thief, whose liquid surge resolves
> The moon into salt tears; the earth's a thief,
> That feeds and breeds by a composture stolen
> From general excrement; each thing's a thief.
>
> [IV. iii. 436-42]

Thus Timon's rage, though it has man for its prime object, includes in its comprehensive sweep the whole universe. This Titanic passion, the agonized outburst of a noble nature shattered to its base, is thrown into splendid relief by being contrasted with the mean, venomous ill-humour of the professional cynic. Apemantus, doomed from his birth to a dog's life, tries to avenge himself by mocking at all the gifts which fortune showers upon her favourites, and from which he is for ever shut out. The grapes are hung well beyond his reach, and it gives him a sinister satisfaction to make them out as sour as possible. When Timon turns his back upon the world, Apemantus hurries to the forest to claim him as a disciple, and to pour fresh poison into his wounds. But the man who has been driven to hatred of his fellows by a convulsion of his moral being, turns with scorn from this petty-minded railer at society, whose cynicism is as truly the veneer of selfish hardness of heart as the jovial good-fellowship of Timon's former boon-

companions. He exposes his sham philosophy in all its nakedness, as he overwhelms him with bitterly truthful words:

> I, to bear this,
> That never knew but better, is some burden:
> Thy nature did commence in sufferance, time
> Hath made thee hard in 't. Why should'st thou hate men!
> They never flatter'd thee: what hast thou given! . . .
> Poor rogue hereditary. Hence! begone!—
> If thou hadst not been born the worst of men,
> Thou hadst been a knave and flatterer.
>
> [IV. iii. 266-76]
> (pp. 499-500)

Frederick S. Boas, "The Plutarch Series of Plays," in his Shakspere and His Predecessors, *Charles Scribner's Sons, 1896, pp. 454-503.*

WALTER RALEIGH   (essay date 1907)

[*In the excerpt below, first published in his study* Shakespeare *in 1907, Raleigh derides those scholars who contend that another writer adapted and revised* Timon, *suggesting instead that Shakespeare wrote it himself as a piece of journey work, or as a "slight" drama, before the Elizabethan theaters demanded more developed plays, and also that he only revived it years later because of the demand for more of his work. For additional commentary on the question of Shakespeare's authorship of* Timon, *see the essays by Charles Knight (1843), Gulian C. Verplanck (1847), F. G. Fleay (1874), George Brandes (1895-96), E. K. Chambers (1908), Una Ellis-Fermor (1942), G. B. Harrison (1951), and Charlton Hinman (1969).*]

Timon of Athens is the exhibition of a single character in contrasted situations. Timon is rich and generous, which is matter for the First Act; his riches and his friends fail him in the Second and Third Acts; he retires to a desert place outside the city, curses mankind, and dies, which climax is the theme of the Fourth and Fifth Acts. There is nothing in all Shakespeare's work more stupendous than the colossal figure of Timon, raining his terrible imprecations on the littleness and falsehood of mankind. Yet the play as a whole is unsatisfying, because the cause is inadequate to produce the effect. No one can read the play and believe that Shakespeare intended a satire on misanthropy: Timon's passion is heart-rending and awe-inspiring; desolation and despair never spoke with more convincing accents. Yet when we examine the events that lead up to the crisis, and the characters who are grouped around Timon, they seem like excuses and shadows, hastily sketched as a kind of conventional framework for the great central figure. The machinery is carelessly put together, and the writing, in these outlying parts of the play, is often flat. The critics have been busy with this case, and have called in the inevitable collaborator. . . . [Shakespeare] was a purveyor to the public stage, and surely must have been pressed, as the modern journalist is pressed, to supply needed matter. Many authors who have suffered this pressure have settled their account with their conscience by dividing their work into two kinds. Some of it they do frankly as journey-work, making it as good as time and circumstances permit. The rest they keep by them, revising and polishing it to satisfy their own more exacting ideals. Shakespeare did both kinds of work, and the bulk of his writing has come down to us without distinction made between the better and the worse. (pp. 112-13)

There is good reason to think that many of his comedies are recasts of his own earlier versions, now lost to us. . . . When the theatre came to its maturity, complete five-act plays, with two plots and everything handsome about them, were required to fill the afternoon. The earlier and slighter plays and interludes were then enlarged and adapted to the new demands. It was not easy, even for Shakespeare, to supply his best work, freshly wrought from fresh material, at the rate of two plays a year. For certain marvellous years he almost did it; and, as likely as not, the effort killed him. The Vicar of Stratford says that he died of a drinking-bout, but a drinking-bout seldom gives more than the *coup de grâce*. No man, not even one who was only a little lower than the angels, could live through the work that Shakespeare did, from *Hamlet* to *Antony and Cleopatra*, without paying for it in health. He must have bowed under the strain, ''unless his nerves were brass or hammered steel.'' But the theatre, having devoured the products of his intense labour, was as hungry as ever, and unremitting in its demands. In *Timon of Athens* we see how these demands were met. The close likeness between Timon and King Lear has often been noticed, so that it is not unfair to say that in *King Lear* Shakespeare treated the very theme of *Timon*, and treated it better, with all added circumstances of likelihood. The passion of the lonely old king on the heath passes by degrees into the fiercest misanthropy, but it carries our sympathy with it, for we have watched it from its beginning, and have been made to feel the cruelty of the causes that provoked it. After *King Lear*, nothing new could be made of the same figure in a weaker setting. But if, as seems likely, *Timon* is a first sketch of *King Lear*, set aside unfinished because the story proved intractable and no full measure of sympathy could be demanded for its hero, the position is explained. Shakespeare, the artist, had no further use for Timon; Shakespeare, the popular playwright, laid his hand on the discarded fragment of a play, and either expanded it himself, or, more probably, permitted another to expand it, to the statutory bulk of five acts. (pp. 114-15)

Walter Raleigh, ''The Theatre,'' in his Shakespeare, *Macmillan and Co., Limited, 1909, pp. 94-127.*

E. K. CHAMBERS   (essay date 1908)

[*Chambers occupies a transitional position in Shakespearean criticism, one which connects the biographical sketches and character analyses of the nineteenth century with the historical, technical, and textual criticism of the twentieth century. While a member of the education department at Oxford University, Chambers earned his reputation as a scholar with his multivolume works,* The Medieval Stage *and* The Elizabethan Stage, *while he also edited* The Red Letter Shakespeare. *Chambers both investigated the purpose and limitations of each dramatic genre as Shakespeare presented it, and speculated on how the dramatist's work was influenced by contemporary historical issues and his own frame of mind. In the excerpt below, first published in The Red Letter Edition of* The Works of William Shakespeare *in 1908, he enters into the authorship controversy over* Timon *and offers his own explanation for the play's inconsistencies and contradictions. Chambers speculates that* Timon *was the last drama of Shakespeare's final tragic phase, an "ultimate summing up" of his "long and remorseless analysis of human nature." However, during his writing of the play Shakespeare experienced a new turn of mind, a new mood— as evidenced in his later romances—which made the prospect of completing his initial task unbearable. Other critics who have examined the authorship question include Charles Knight (1843), Gulian C. Verplanck (1847), F. G. Fleay (1874), George Brandes (1895-96), Walter Raleigh (1907), Una Ellis-Fermor (1942), G. B. Harrison (1951), and Charlton Hinman (1969). For a discussion of the relation between the mood of* Timon *and Shakespeare's state of mind, see the essays by Hermann Ulrici (1839), G. G. Gervinus (1849-50), Edward Dowden (1881), Wilhelm Wendlandt (1888), and Frank Harris (1909).*]

Critics are agreed that there is something enigmatic about *Timon of Athens,* that its genesis and composition present a literary problem which cannot as yet be thought to have quite reached its solution. . . . Its general conception is continuous with the development of pessimistic thought which is traceable along the whole line of the tragedies. The ruin and eclipse of Timon's soul in the discovery of human baseness is a vision which was assuredly not revealed to another than the delineator of Lear and of Othello. And from beginning to end of the play, especially where Timon himself is to the front, there are passages whose magnificent phrasing bears the indubitable craftmark of the Shakespearean workshop. The opening scene takes up the tradition, with its—

A most incomparable man, breathed, as it were,
To an untirable and continuate goodness,

[I. i. 9-10]

and hands it down to the last noble utterance which winds up all the whirling words—

Come not to me again, but say to Athens,
Timon hath made his everlasting mansion
Upon the beached verge of the salt flood,
Who once a day with his embossed froth
The turbulent surge shall cover; thither come,
And let my grave-stone be your oracle.

[V. i. 214-19]

Nevertheless, the instinct is a right one which refuses to accept *Timon of Athens* as a complete and jointed Shakespearean whole. There are impossibilities in it. The moment the eye passes from the dominant figure of Timon himself, it falls upon scenes which appear to be in different planes from that of the main composition. What, for example, is the spiritual relation between Alcibiades and Timon? Is some effect of contrast intended, or is Alcibiades merely Timon over again, in a weaker and less clearly motived version of the disillusioned child of fortune? And what is the precise dramatic purpose served by the good steward Flavius and his sentimentalities, which seem to give the lie to Timon's wholesale condemnation of humanity, without any appreciable effect upon its direction or its force? These are structural incoherencies which it would have been more Shakespearean to have cleared away, or at least to have glossed over, so as to prevent their jarring, as they undeniably do jar, against the ready acceptance of the play. Alcibiades ought to mean something, and is introduced as though he were going to mean something; and the reader very naturally resents the discovery of how very little, if anything, he does in the end mean. Nor is it only a question of structure. There are certain scenes or parts of scenes, in which the expression is so halting, so lacking in the golden mastery of speech, as to raise a doubt whether they can be Shakespeare's. These passages are fairly well marked off from the rest. They include a conversation between Timon, Apemantus, and the Steward in the banquet scene of the First Act; the three scenes in which Timon's servants endeavour to borrow money, the scene between the Steward and the creditors, and the scene between Alcibiades and the Senate, in the Third Act; the Steward's resolve to follow Timon, and his subsequent dialogue with Timon, in the Fourth Act; and Timon's interview with the Poet and the Painter in the Fifth Act. They are all subordinate passages; the great scenes of Timon's agonies and denunciations, although the flow of their verse is sometimes broken, give no such impression of uncouthness and want of finish. And, as will be observed, they are largely scenes in which Alcibiades and the Steward, the two personages who have already been noted as imperfectly fused into the plot, make their appearance. Certain other scenes, mainly prose passages in which the cynical philosopher Apemantus takes a principal part, have also been questioned, but on less satisfactory grounds. They are by no means of an un-Shakespearean type; and although they are certainly not inspired, there is no reason why they should not have been written by Shakespeare in the somewhat jaded mood of which at least one other play, *Coriolanus,* closely contemporary with *Timon of Athens,* shows decided signs. The nature of the passages that remain under suspicion may be well illustrated by the following lines, which are spoken by the Steward—

> O, the fierce wretchedness that glory brings us!
> Who would not wish to be from wealth exempt,
> Since riches point to misery and contempt?
> Who would be so mocked with glory, or to live
> But in a dream of friendship?
> To have his pomp and all what state compounds,
> But only painted, like his varnished friends?
> Poor honest lord, brought low by his own heart,
> Undone by goodness! Strange, unusual blood,
> When man's worst sin is, he does too much good!
> Who, then, dares to be half so kind again?
> For bounty, that makes gods, does still mar men.
> My dearest lord, blessed, to be most accurst,
> Rich, only to be wretched, thy great fortunes
> Are made thy chief afflictions. Alas, kind lord!
> He's flung in rage from this ingrateful seat
> Of monstrous friends; nor has he with him to
> Supply his life, or that which can command it.
> I'll follow and enquire him out.
> I'll ever serve his mind with my best will;
> Whilst I have gold, I'll be his steward still.
>
> [IV. ii. 30-50]

The peculiarities of rhythm which are to be noted here, and in especial the alternation of jolting rhymed couplets with lines in which the metre seems suddenly to come to an abrupt stop, are repeated in the other suspected passages, and differentiate them clearly enough from the undoubted Shakespearean matter.

The explanations of scholars, in other respects sufficiently divergent, generally assume the presence of a second hand in the play. There can hardly be any question of direct collaboration, such as we find somewhat later in *Henry the Eighth* and *The Two Noble Kinsmen,* for the share to be assigned on this hypothesis to a collaborator would not have been worth dividing off. Nor is it a very plausible suggestion that Shakespeare was working on the text of an older play, and that the passages to be accounted for represent surviving fragments of that text. There is no evidence of the existence of any such older play, and nothing to show that, wherever Shakespeare may have gone for the plots of his plays, he ever, after the days of his apprenticeship, found any advantage in using the dialogue of a predecessor. Moreover, the theory does not really remove the difficulty which it professes to remove, since, even if there were an older play, it would still be necessary to ask why the process of adaptation was so incomplete, and why Shakespeare was willing to accept the sketchy characters and the halting lines bequeathed to him. One is thrown back on the alternative of a play unfinished by Shakespeare; and in fact most editors explain the origin of *Timon of Athens* as we now have it, by supposing that such a play was handed over to an inferior playwright and eked out by him with additional scenes, either for performance on the stage, or, according to a less

plausible version of the hypothesis, to fill up blank pages in the First Folio. Some bold spirits have even gone further, and have attempted to find stylistic analogies to the suspected passages in the work of one or another contemporary writer, Tourneur, or Heywood, or Wilkins, or Chapman, whom they have then saddled with the responsibility of the patchwork.

I should be sorry to dismiss the second hand as altogether out of the question, but it does not seem to me that its presence is rigidly necessitated by the conditions of the problem. May not *Timon of Athens* have been left unfinished by Shakespeare, and be unfinished still? The soliloquy of the Steward quoted above gives me the impression of being not so much un-Shakespearean as incompletely Shakespearean. The themes, even the phrases—the 'dream of friendship' and the 'varnished friends'— might have found their place readily enough in a rhythmic and developed period from the master's hand. So it is with the other suspected passages. They might be rough notes, first drafts of scenes, jotted down in half prose or gnomic couplets, just as they came to the surface in the early stages of composition, to be taken up and worked over again during the process of revision. This is a very natural way of writing, and there is no reason why Shakespeare should not have practised it. The famous statement of the editors of the First Folio, that 'what he thought, he uttered with that easiness, that we have scarce received from him a blot in his papers,' is hardly convincing evidence that he never made a rough copy before he prepared his final manuscript for the actors. So far as the substance of the doubtful scenes is concerned, it is on the whole more likely that they were originally shaped by Shakespeare than that they were interpolated in his work by someone commissioned to complete a task which he had laid aside. (pp. 268-74)

As to the reason why *Timon of Athens* should have remained unfinished at all, conjecture alone is possible. The metrical evidence forbids that it should be regarded as the last of Shakespeare's plays. But it might very well be the last of his tragedies, and it is in some sort the ultimate summing-up of that long and remorseless analysis of human nature and divine ordering of which the tragedies must be taken as the expression. Its immediate predecessors were most probably *Antony and Cleopatra* and *Coriolanus.* In the one of these the love of woman, in the other the honour of man, is put through the crucible, and reduced to ash and nothingness. And then Shakespeare seems to have gathered himself together for a last and bitterest effort, in which no longer one sex only, but the whole of humanity, was to receive its meed of utter and comprehensive scorn. . . . Tragedy, in *Timon of Athens,* is not yet robbed of awe; but the finer ear may perhaps detect in the play a want of balance and of measure, a touch almost of hysteria in the vituperation, which suggests that the stress of pessimistic thought is becoming a little more than the imagination can endure, and that in the brain of Timon's creator some strange crisis is at hand. That the crisis took place is indisputable. With *Timon of Athens* pessimism ends abruptly. Between its temper and that of any of the work that followed it there is a spiritual gulf fixed. It is tempting to suppose that the deep waters closed over Shakespeare's head while he was still elaborating the play, and that when he faced the world once more in his new mood the inclination to finish the task had left him. (pp. 275-76)

E. K. Chambers, "'Timon of Athens'," in his Shakespeare: A Survey, *Sidgewick & Jackson, Ltd., 1925, pp. 268-76.*

FRANK HARRIS   (essay date 1909)

[*Harris attempted to find a pattern in Shakespeare's work that would shed light on the nature of Shakespeare's life. His theories have been either ignored or ridiculed by most Shakespearean scholars. In the following two excerpts, he argues that* Timon *is the "ultimate" of Shakespeare's tragedies because it deals with the two greatest weaknesses of the dramatist's personality: "trust and generosity." Harris considers* Timon *a good indication of Shakespeare's mental and physical breakdown because the play consists mainly of "futile, feeble cursings" carelessly directed against all humanity. In the second excerpt, he asserts that the undramatic quality of the play can be attributed to the "exceeding bitterness" of Shakespeare's soul. For other biographical readings of* Timon, *see the excerpts by Hermann Ulrici (1839), G. G. Gervinus (1849-50), Edward Dowden (1881), Wilhelm Wendlandt (1888), George Brandes (1895-96), and E. K. Chambers (1908).*]

"Timon" marks the extremity of Shakespeare's suffering. It is not to be called a work of art, it is hardly even a tragedy; it is the causeless ruin of a soul, a ruin insufficiently motived by complete trust in men and spendthrift generosity. If there was ever a man who gave so lavishly as Timon, if there was ever one so senseless blind in trusting, then he deserved his fate. There is no gradation in his giving, and none in his fall; no artistic crescendo. The whole drama is . . . a scream of suffering, or rather, a long curse upon all the ordinary conditions of life. The highest qualities of Shakespeare are not to be found in the play. There are none of the magnificent phrases which bejewel "Lear"; little of high wisdom, even in the pages which are indubitably Shakespeare's, and no characterization worth mentioning. The honest steward, Flavius, is the honest Kent again of "Lear," honest and loyal beyond nature; Apemantus is another Thersites. Words which throw a high light on Shakespeare's character are given to this or that personage of the play without discrimination. One phrase of Apemantus is as true of Shakespeare as of Timon and is worth noting:

> The middle of humanity thou never knewest,
> but the extremity of both ends.
>
> [IV. iii. 300-01]
> (pp. 337-38)

In so far as Timon is a character at all he is manifestly Shakespeare, Shakespeare who raves against the world, because he finds no honesty in men, no virtue in women, evil everywhere—"boundless thefts in limited professions." This Shakespeare Timon swings round characteristically as soon as he finds that Flavius is honest:

> Had I a steward
> So true, so just, and now so comfortable?
> It almost turns my dangerous nature mild.
> Let me behold thy face. Surely this man
> Was born of woman.
> *Forgive my general and exceptless rashness,*
> *You perpetual-sober Gods!* I do proclaim
> One honest man—mistake me not—but one. . . .
>
> [IV. iii. 490-97]

I cannot help putting the great and self-revealing line in italics; a line Tolstoi would, no doubt, think stupid-pompous. Timon ought to have known his steward, one might say in Tolstoi's spirit, as Lear should have known his daughters; but this is still the tragedy, which Shakespeare wishes to emphasize that his hero was blind in trusting. (p. 338)

"Timon" is the true sequel to "The Merchant of Venice." Antonio gives lavishly, but is saved at the crisis by his friends.

Timon gives with both hands, but when he appeals to his friends, is treated as a bore. Shakespeare had travelled far in the dozen years which separate the two plays.

All Shakespeare's tragedies are phases of his own various weaknesses, and each one brings the hero to defeat and ruin. Hamlet cannot carry revenge to murder and fails through his own irresolution. Othello comes to grief through mad jealousy. Antony fails and falls through excess of lust; Lear through trust in men, and Timon through heedless generosity. All these are separate studies of Shakespeare's own weaknesses; but the ruin is irretrievable, and reaches its ultimate in Timon. Trust and generosity, Shakespeare would like to tell us, were his supremest faults. In this he deceived himself. Neither "Lear" nor "Timon" is his greatest tragedy; but "Antony and Cleopatra," for lust was his chief weakness, and the tragedy of lust his greatest play.

Much of "Timon" is not Shakespeare's, the critics tell us, and some of it is manifestly not his, though many of the passages rejected with the best reason have, I think, been touched up by him. The second scene of the first act is as bad as bad can be; but I hear his voice in the line:

> Methinks, I could deal kingdoms to my friends,
> And ne'er be weary.
>
> [I. ii. 220-21]

At any rate, this is the keynote of the tragedy, which is struck again and again. Shakespeare probably exaggerated his generosity out of aristocratic pose; but that he was careless of money and freehanded to a fault, is, I think, certain from his writings, and can be proved from the facts known to us of his life. (pp. 339-40)

The wheel has swung full circle: Timon is almost as weak as "Titus Andronicus"; the pen falls from the nerveless hand. Shakespeare wrote nothing for some time. Even the critics make a break after "Timon," which closes what they are pleased to call his third period; but they do not seem to see that the break was really a breakdown in health. In "Lear" he had brooded and raged to madness; in "Timon" he had spent himself in futile, feeble cursings. His nerves had gone to pieces. He was now forty-five years of age, the forces of youth and growth had left him. He was prematurely old and feeble. (p. 341)

Frank Harris, "The Drama of Despair: 'Timon of Athens'" and "The Latest Works: All Copies, 'Winter's Tale'; 'Cymbeline'; 'The Tempest'," in his *The Man Shakespeare and His Tragic Life Story, Frank Palmer, 1909, pp. 337-40, 341-55.*

FRANK HARRIS   (essay date 1911)

Timon breeds new thoughts in me; it is a poor play, and yet it increases my admiration of Shakespeare's wisdom, and in proportion diminishes my already chastened opinion of his commentators. (p. 169)

The more I read *Timon* the more convinced I am that it is all Shakespeare's, and Shakespeare's alone, from beginning to end.

My readers, I think, will trust me now without proof; but as I go through the play selecting the most characteristic passages, I must just notice the fact that the very finest work is ascribed to the "unknown writer" by all the commentators. The amusing thing is that the critics are unanimous in rejecting, not Shakespeare's vulgarities and inanities, but the gems of his thought, the rays of purest insight in him. *Timon* is all his, I say again deliberately. The weakest work in the play, the word disputes with Apemantus and others, are in his manner; the undramatic monotony of it is due to his exceeding bitterness of soul. For instance, Timon's gentlemen go to borrow for their lord: when they're refused, instead of smiling at their own wisdom in finding expectancy fulfilled, they curse the ungrateful friends in Timon's own vein. Life has so bruised Shakespeare that he is one ache; his very soul is sore. Love and friendship, which he held most sacred, have betrayed him; his friend has proved a vulgar cad, his love a wanton. The gold which he has always tried to despise, he now sees is the master-key of every lock in the world. . . . (pp. 169-70)

Frank Harris, "'Lear' and 'Timon': Erotic Mania," *in his* The Women of Shakespeare, *Methuen & Co Ltd, 1911, pp. 164-78.*

THOMAS MARC PARROTT   (essay date 1923)

[*In the following excerpt, Parrott posits that* Timon's *interest resides purely in its textual and authorial problems, and states that the play itself is a dramatic failure.*]

For the critical student of Shakespeare *Timon of Athens* has an attraction peculiarly its own. It is perhaps the most interesting work that has come down to us from his later years at once fascinating, perplexing, and disappointing. Gleams of Shakespeare's unmistakeable gift of dramatic expression, fitful flashes of his genial characterization, noble strains of his inimitable music are all here, but surrounded, encumbered, buried, one might almost say, by masses of incoherent, prosaic and often manifestly mutilated matter. The theme, the ruin of a frank and generous soul by ingratitude, public and private, is no unfit subject for tragedy, the treatment of this theme in *Timon* presents some very effective scenes, yet as it stands it is a simply impossible play. (p. 3)

The explanation of the dramatic impossibility of *Timon* is after all, quite simple. There is not enough of the creative power of Shakespeare in the play to quicken the whole into dramatic life. *Timon* must always remain a play for a study rather than for the stage, and the problem that confronts the student is to determine first how much of Shakespeare can be found in the work; and, secondly, how it comes to be there. (pp. 3-4)

Thomas Marc Parrott, in his The Problem of "Timon of Athens", *Oxford University Press, London, 1923, 34 p.*

WYNDHAM LEWIS   (essay date 1927)

[*Lewis wrote in a deliberately provocative style and outside the mainstream of Shakespearean criticism. The excerpt below is taken from his unusual study* The Lion and the Fox, *a title which refers to the struggle between world views which Lewis believes dominated Shakespeare's age. The lion stands for the mystical and feudalistic vision of the age of chivalry; the fox for the rationalism of the coming age of science and industry. Shakespeare himself, according to Lewis, did not take sides in any simple way, but his plays reflect the conflict of both world views. Ultimately for Lewis, Shakespeare's vision is nihilistic, a point of view which he often portrayed as madness in his plays. In the excerpt below, Lewis considers* Timon *one of Shakespeare's great tragedies, as well as an imaginative investigation of two of the great heroes of nihilism, Timon and Apemantus. For more commentary on the nihilistic outlook in Shakespeare's play, see the excerpt by Jarold W. Ramsey (1966).*]

Shakespeare, like Cervantes, was occupied always with cases of insanity . . . : that could be said to be a great characteristic of his. . . . And madness accounts for the nihilism that surges up in every tragedy of Shakespeare, once the characters have become "mad" enough with suffering. . . . It is as outcasts, as men already in a sense out of life, and divested of the functional machinery of their rôles (which would necessitate their being *objects* only—things *looked at* and not *looking*), that speak objectively—an objective, and not a functional, truth. Lear, Hamlet, Timon, Thersites [in *Troilus and Cressida*] and so forth, are in the position of disincarnate spirits, but still involved with and buffeted by life. Their "truth" is an angry one usually, but they have the advantage of having no "axe to grind."

Thersites is always in that unfortunate position: Lear and Hamlet only become so when they grow demented: or rather (as we usually meet them first when they are already in this prophetic condition), we assume that if undisturbed by calamity they would be respectable members of society, and not have, much less express, all these horrible thoughts. It is this *assumption* of conditions that do not exist at all in the plays (for, as just remarked, in a tragedy the figures from the start are usually very excited) that is usually the basis of english shakespearian criticism. The remarks made by a whole sequence of characters in shakespearian tragedy are the ravings of madmen, it would imply. They have no relation to the settled mind of their great author, but are unfortunate aberrations in which he is compelled to deal. . . . (pp. 248-49)

A man is either (1) a philosopher, or (2) not a philosopher: or he is (1) mad, or (2) not mad. Where (in shakespearian tragedy) a man becomes *mad,* he shows a strange tendency to become what we usually call a *philosopher.* That is to say, of course, he is transformed, and becomes somebody else. Should any character in a play of Shakespeare's *before he went mad,* express himself as, let us say, Schopenhauer constantly was in the habit of doing, a scandal would at once ensue—or if not a scandal, a disturbing *problem* would have been posed for the english shakespearian critic. Under the stress of some great emotion, or belaboured by some particularly evil circumstances—like Job—even the best of men is apt to make remarks that he will subsequently regret. But in cold blood, and in his sober senses, no man—or no gentleman, which is the same thing—ever says, or thinks even, things of that description.

This situation is justly parodied by Shakespeare in the squabble of Apemantus and Timon. Apemantus (who, contrary to what it is usual to affirm, has the best of the argument) comes to Timon to put him out of conceit with himself. Timon gets angrier and angrier: and at length they part in a storm of mutual abuse. Apemantus (described as "a churlish philosopher") argues with Timon that he is only imitating him, Apemantus, and other cynics, because he has been *forced* to this by circumstances, and has not elected to live "the philosophic life" of his own free choice; and is indeed very "churlish" and disagreeable about it. What the churlish philosopher says is, of course, quite true: and the contempt of Apemantus for the spiteful worldling, stealing the thunders of Diogenes to bombard his old associates, who are neither better nor worse than himself, is justified. Or rather it would be justified if we were not assured that there was a streak of generosity and *naïveté* in Timon that saved him from fulfilling the rôle suggested to us for him by Apemantus.

It is usually said that Apemantus is introduced by Shakespeare, with his invariable resourcefulness and tact, to contrast Timon with this cynic philosopher, to the disadvantage of the latter, and to enable us to see how superior Timon was to such people, and to relieve our minds on a point on which they might have been uneasy. For otherwise we might have said to ourselves that after all Timon is only a cynic philosopher!—and "cynic" is an unpopular word.

This explanation is on a par with many others of a similar order. In reality it seems much more that Apemantus is introduced, and is intended, to occupy the position of the nihilistic chorus or the *fool*. . . . [His] rôle is a revelatory and truth-bearing one. The reason for it could be that without such a voice giving *the other side of the case,* and showing where Timon's advocacy is apt to break down, the spoilt-child bellowings of Timon would arouse answers in the audience, perhaps: for the answer to this very one-sided heroism is too palpable to be missed; and for the success of this figure a vent must be provided for criticism. Apemantus could be regarded, from this point of view, as the chorus, or the critical *vent* of the audience, baiting with dangerous arguments the dying god, and accusing him of plagiarism:

> men report
> Thou dost affect my manners. . . .
>
>   [IV. iii. 199-99]

And he describes this affectation of Timon's as:

> A poor unmanly melancholy sprung
> From change of fortune.
>
>   [IV. iii. 203-04]

The melancholy outburst of nearly every shakespearian hero could be described from this standpoint as "unmanly," or at least highly unreasonable, and as the wild bellowing of the spoilt-child of fortune, fallen on evil times from the height of tragical *hubris*. (pp. 249-51)

Timon arguing with Apemantus is a typical shakespearian hero arguing about his rôle. All shakespearian heroes being the result of the conventional tragic drop from *hubris* and happiness to misery and disaster, it is always mechanically assumed that it is this rapid and unexpected fall that shakes out of them the marvellous music of the shakespearian blank verse, and the dark fury of their gibing. It is further assumed that humanity in general—unless taken up aloft a certain way by the devil, and allowed to have a godlike peep around it, and then cast down again from this dangerous height—is incapable of such things. But the situation in reality, where Shakespeare's plays are concerned, lacks the simple definition of this accepted formula. For the "great line" invented by Marlowe, the music of verse, and the soul of Shakespeare, complicate it to such an extent that confusion is inevitable. But disentangled as best it can be, this is how it must be read.

First, there is Timon's reply to Apemantus. It is the logical reply of the protagonist of a tragic performance. What he answers quite directly and with truth is somewhat as follows: "*You,* Apemantus, are not the hero of a tragedy, nor ever will be. But I, Timon, am. Therefore, in order to produce the effect, as you know, it was necessary that I should be very rich or eminent in some way, and then suddenly lose all my money or my social position." He argues that his *cynicism,* unlike that of Apemantus (which is natural, inborn cussedness), is the result of this unexpected and undesired obvention. For:

>   I, to bear this,
> That never knew but better, is some burden.
>
>   [IV. iii. 266-67]

This very reasonable complaint could hardly be met otherwise than with sympathy. But he proceeds then to deny to Apemantus the right to be a cynic, because Apemantus has never been rich, like him, and so has nothing to complain about:

> Thy nature did commence in sufferance, time
> Hath made thee hard in't. Why shouldst thou hate men?
> They never flatter'd thee: what hast thou given?
> If thou wilt curse, thy father . . .
> Must be thy subject; who, in spite, put stuff
> To some she beggar and compounded thee.
>
>   [IV. iii. 268-73]
>   (pp. 251-52)

Apart from the abuse with which Timon accompanies these remarks, Apemantus could hardly be expected to agree to the latter part of this statement of his. Timon asks him: "Why should you hate men? They never flattered you!" To which probably Apemantus would reply: "That is why I hate them!" (p. 253)

Apemantus does not think much of tragedy, or the poetry of its spoilt children in adversity; and has a strong professional objection to their stealing the thunders of the cynic philosopher: and is prepared even to pursue them into their adversity and rebuke them for it. Timon, on the other hand, does not believe in cynic philosophy, or any other philosophy, without *tragedy:* he does not believe that philosophy can exist without tragedy; and he thinks that to have the right to gibe and bellow you must have been either a king, a field-marshal or a millionaire first: *dropped* from that height (in which you will have displayed *hubris*): and then, as the day succeeds the night, or as you put a penny in the slot and the figure works, you will utter the organ-notes of shakespearian despair, and almost certainly give an exhibition of the *altofronto* Hamlet technique. For Timon is very conventional: that is because he is a puppet, mechanically worked, and seeing nothing beyond his mechanism—which is the traditional mechanism of the european formula for tragedy.

But *we* must be aware of several things undreamt of in Timon's philosophy. We agree more with Apemantus than we do with Timon. We know, for instance, that ninety-nine per cent. of human beings—however *high up* you may transport them, however much insolence they may deploy when they discover themselves so *high up,* and however far you drop them *down,* and however much despair they may feel as they strike the bottom—will never show the least tincture of philosophy. They will never, we know, make even a tenth-rate tragic hero; and will neither produce, automatically, an organ-music like Bach, nor a mournful and gigantic rhetoric like that of Timon. (pp. 253-54)

We know therefore (however much we are told that it is the *drop* of a normal man or woman that causes the great afflatus in a shakespearian tragedy) that that is not so. Emotional beauty of diction, depth and strangeness of philosophical understanding, are not produced by this means; any more than Shelley's verse or Kant's philosophy is produced by dropping a person over the edge of a cliff. But the scientific *sans gêne* which characterizes our attitude of mind to-day will enable us to get a closer view of this perplexing phenomenon, even, than our reasoning so far has given us. For we can say: "Was the man who wrote these plays himself a tragic hero? What was the nature of his experience?" etc. And we should find that Shakespeare himself was neither a prince nor a wealthy man, but on the contrary a very poor and humbly placed one: who, like

Apemantus, had never any chance to *drop* from anywhere, and consequently, according to Timon's reasoning, had no occasion to hate his fellow-men. In spite of this handicap, he seems to have understood very well the nature of grief, to have possessed a mind of a philosophic cast; and—being a matchless artist— he was able, as we know, to perform these tragical operations far better than they ever happen in life.

Shakespeare's knowledge of the ins and outs of human character was so wide, and he displayed such a varied power and self-restraint in portraying different sorts of men in a lifelike way, that people are inclined to forget, perhaps, that the art of the drama, and all its purgational greek rules of jealous gods (and envious audiences), of revenge for grandeur, and of well-turned and melodious death, is a game: and that what is enacted in a heroic play bears very little resemblance to *life*. In none of its details is it the least *likely*. Timon would probably, after a life of overeating, have caught a cold immediately in his damp cave, or been at once prostrated with rheumatism. (p. 255)

> *Wyndham Lewis, "Apemantus and Timon," in his* The Lion and the Fox: The Role of the Hero in the Plays of Shakespeare, *G. Richards, 1927, pp. 247-56.*

G. WILSON KNIGHT (essay date 1930)

[*One of the most influential of modern Shakespearean critics, Knight helped shape the twentieth-century reaction against the biographical and character studies of the nineteenth-century Shakespeareans. Knight's analytic practice stresses what he calls, in his study* The Wheel of Fire, *the "spatial" aspects of imagery, atmosphere, theme, and symbol in the plays. He thus parallels the New Critics with his emphasis on verbal texture; his discussions of symbolism are similar to Samuel Taylor Coleridge's notion of the symbolic as indefinite with multiple meanings. The excerpt below on* Timon *is taken from Knight's much-discussed and controversial chapter in his* The Wheel of Fire, *first published in 1930. The aim of the essay is primarily interpretive: to communicate to the reader what Knight believes to be a Shakespearean vision reformulated in the language of the modern era. On the basis of this interpretation, Knight moves to evaluation, and judges* Timon *to be one of Shakespeare's greatest plays. Along with the nineteenth-century German critic G. G. Gervinus (1849-50), Knight remains one of the leading proponents of the idea that* Timon *is a noble figure whose generosity is abused by a vicious and ignoble world. Knight sees Timon's only shortcoming as his failure to realize that his society cannot maintain his boundless love, a failure which eventually results in his renunciation of the world and life itself. Knight interprets Timon's story as an allegory or parable relating the unfaltering course of a "Titanic" soul which gradually realizes its fulfillment in death. For other, more negative assessments of Timon's character, see the excerpts by William Richardson (1784), August Wilhelm Schlegel (1808), Hermann Ulrici (1839), Denton J. Snider (1887), J. C. Maxwell (1948), and L. C. Knights (1969).*]

In this essay I outline the nature of a tragic movement more precipitous and unimpeded than any other in Shakespeare; one which is conceived on a scale even more tremendous than that of *Macbeth* and *Lear;* and whose universal tragic significance is of all most clearly apparent. My purpose will be to concentrate on whatever is of positive power and significance, regarding the imaginative impact as all-important however it may appear to contradict the logic of human life. My analysis will first characterize the imaginative atmosphere of the early acts and indicate its significance as a setting for the personality of Timon; next, it will show how the subsidiary persons and choric speeches are so presented that our sympathy is directed into

certain definite channels; and, finally, I shall point the nature of the second half of the play, contrasting it strongly with the earlier acts and indicating the reversal of symbolic suggestion. Such an analysis will inevitably reveal important facts as to the implicit philosophy, exposing its peculiar universality, and the stark contrast of the partial and imperfect nature of humanity and the world of the senses with the strong aspiration toward infinity and perfection and the ultimate darkness of the unknown embodied in the two parts of the play.

The first acts convey the impression of riches, ease, sensuous appeal, and brilliant display. The curtain rises on a blaze of magnificence and the first persons are the Poet, Painter, Jeweller, and Merchant. In no play of Shakespeare is the opening more significant. Art, wealth, trade are represented, things which stand for human intercourse, progress, civilization, worldly success and happiness. Here poet and painter enjoy leisure to hold forth on their art, and jeweller and merchant await high payment for their wares. In the early acts we are continually reminded of wealth. . . . These acts scintillate with the flash of gold coins and rich metals and stones. They delight the imagination's eye and touch, as the glittering proper names delight the ear. These, however, are but elements in a single effect of wealth, ease, refined luxury, and, in the earliest scenes especially, sensuous joy. . . . We are lost in a riot of display, a gold-mist of romance and pleasures of the senses. The setting is brilliant, the wealth apparently inexhaustible, the pleasures free. We can imagine the rich food and wine, the blare and clash of music, embraces, laughter, and passages of glancing love; the coursing of blood, the flushed cheek, the mask of fair dancers and Cupid.

Timon's world is sensuous and erotic, yet not vicious or ignoble. . . . The early atmosphere of *Timon of Athens* is thus as the poetic atmosphere of *Antony and Cleopatra.* In both there is the same kind of atmospheric technique that focuses our vision to the unique differing worlds of gloom of *Macbeth* and *King Lear;* and in both this sensuous blaze is conceived as a setting for a transcendent love. Only by subduing our more independent faculties in abeyance to the imaginative quality of these early scenes shall we receive the play as poetry and know its meaning. A true interpretative faculty in the reader must be the bride of the poet's imagination, since only so can it give birth to understanding. So, by dwelling inwardly on the points I have adduced to indicate the imaginative quality of Timon's setting, our consciousness will be, as it were, tuned to respond to and appreciate the true erotic richness of Timon's soul.

The world of Timon and the soul of Timon are thus interdependent, and our consideration of the total imaginative impact illuminates his personality. Though at first sight there may seem something barbaric and oriental in Timon's generosity and sense of display, yet we are confronted in reality not with barbarism, but humanism. . . . His love, too, is the love not of the saint, but the lover; a rich erotic perception welling up from his soul, warm-blooded, instinctive, romantic and passionate. It is the love of Othello for Desdemona, of Antony for Cleopatra, of Shakespeare for the fair boy of the Sonnets. These we understand; so, too, we form some contact with the self-renouncing, ascetic, all-embracing love of the saint. But Timon's is the passionate, somewhat selfish, love of one lover for another, physical and spiritual, of the senses as of the soul; yet directed not toward one creature or one purpose but expanding its emotion among all men.

Timon is a Universal Lover, not by principle but by nature. His charity is never cold, self-conscious, or dutiful. He with-

Act IV. Scene iii. Soldiers, Phrynia, Timandra, Timon of Athens. By J. Opie (1803).

holds nothing of himself. His praise to the painter . . . is sincere appreciation; his jests with the jeweller . . . kind and not condescending; his chance of doing good to his servant whose lack of wealth forbids his desired marriage is one of those god-sent adventures in kindness that make the life of Timon a perpetual romance. . . . If, as Shakespeare's imagery sometimes suggests, the lover sees his own soul symbolized in his love, then we can say that Timon projects himself into the world around him; mankind is his own soul; a resplendent and infinite love builds an earthly paradise where it may find complete satisfaction in the inter-communion of heart with heart, and gift with gift. (pp. 207-12)

The most striking subsidiary figure is Apemantus. Contrasted with Timon's faith and love, we have a churlish cynicism and disgust. Timon is a universal lover, Apemantus a universal cynic. His mind functions in terms of the foul, bestial, and stupid attributes of man. . . . He makes lascivious jests. He loaths the shape of man powerfully as Timon loves it:

> The strain of man's bred out
> Into baboon and monkey.   [I. i. 250-51]

and,

> What a coil's here!
> Serving of becks and jutting out of bums!
>   [I. ii. 230-31]

His cynicism is a compound of ridicule, foul suggestion, and ascetic philosophy. Timon shows him a picture:

> *Timon.* Wrought he not well that painted it?
> *Apemantus.* He wrought better that made the painter;
>   and yet he's but a filthy piece of work.
>   [I. i. 197-98]

Thus swiftly is condemned God, man, and man's aspiration and endeavour. The pregnancy of this answer is amazing in its compactness and the poignance of its sting. As he watches the observances of respect, the greetings and smiles attendant on Alcibiades' entry, he comments:

>   So, so, there!
> Aches contract and starve your supple joints!
> That there should be small love 'mongst these sweet knaves,
> And all this courtesy!   [I. i. 247-50]

Entertainment is a mockery to him, for his thoughts are centred on the transience of shows, the brittleness of the armour of manners with which civilized man protects the foulness within from the poisoned dart of truth. Therefore he sits apart during the feast, refusing the food of Timon, gnawing roots, drinking water. . . . His respect for Timon is, however, clearly noted:

>   Even he drops down
> The knee before him and returns in peace
> Most rich in Timon's nod.   [I. i. 60-2]

Therefore the presence of Apemantus serves many purposes. It points us to the insincerity of Timon's friends and the probable course of events; it shows us that even the cynic cannot help but honour and respect Timon; and it makes us feel how repellent is this very cynicism, which is the opposite of Timon's faith and love. Apemantus thus enlists our respect for Timon, and even at their final meeting, when Timon has left Athens, we are again shown that Timon's hate is not as Apemantus'.

But we are repelled not alone by the churlish philosopher: we are even more repelled by the false friends of Timon. The incident of Lucullus' refusal is exquisitely comic, yet bitterly satiric. Nothing more meanly unpleasant could well be imagined, and yet its truth to human nature cannot be denied. His greed, flattery, hypocrisy, and finally open confession of baseness, are drawn in swift, masterly strokes, culminating in:

> 'Here's three solidares for thee; good boy, wink
> at me, and say thou saw'st me not,' and 'Ha!
> now I see thou art a fool and fit for thy master.'
> [III. i. 43-5, 49-50]

The poet and painter—whatever they may be as artists—are also depicted as time-servers: towards the end of the play, when they come to Timon to gain his favour, their dialogue with each other exposes their clear hypocrisy. . . . The theme of Alcibiades is close-woven with that of Timon, and both endure ingratitude from the Senate, symbol of the state of Athens. We feel, in fact, that Timon's personality alone is responsible for any pleasure we have received in this Athens. It is a state of greed and ingratitude. The fine flower of civilization to which I have referred is evidently not in itself existent here, but purely a projection of Timon's mind. There are, however, certain persons who appear both good and rational: all these emphasize Timon's nobility. (pp. 212-15)

The faithfulness of Timon's servants is indeed a major theme in the drama. After the final failure, and Timon's retirement to the woods, they meet, not as servants to the same lord, but rather as disciples to a loved and world-crucified master. . . . It is as though the spirit of Timon's former love and generosity has settled among them as an everlasting bond of love. We begin to know that we have been watching something more than the downfall of a noble gentleman:

> *Third Servant.* Yet do our hearts wear Timon's livery;
>   That see I by our faces; we are fellows still,
>   Serving alike in sorrow: leak'd is our bark,
>   And we, poor mates, stand on the dying deck,
>   Hearing the surges threat: we must all part
>   Into this sea of air.
> *Flavius.*   Good fellows all,
>   The latest of my wealth I'll share amongst you.
>   Wherever we shall meet, for Timon's sake,
>   Let's yet be fellows; let's shake our heads, and say,
>   As 'twere a knell unto our master's fortunes,
>   'We have seen better days'. Let each take some;
>   Nay, put out all your hands. Not one word more:
>   Thus part we rich in sorrow, parting poor.
> [IV. ii. 17-29]

'Nay, put out all your hands'. . . . The still poetry of deepest emotion, the grandest simplicity of the human soul, indeed do not sound their noblest notes in this play till the pages thereof are become 'rich in sorrow': and then they touch a music, as in this speech, of a more wondrous simplicity and a more mighty and heart-quelling beauty than anything in *King Lear*

or *Othello*. This, however, is to forestall—this scene occurs after the shadow of eternity has overcast the drama.

Enough has been said to indicate the nature of the technique that loads and all but overcharges the first part of this play with a clear honour and love of Timon's generosity and freehearted soul; that indicts an overplus of humanity with the uttermost degree of despisal; that leaves us in the naked knowledge of the inevitable ignition and the dynamite of passion that thunders, reverberates, and dies into silence through the latter acts. The poet unfalteringly directs our vision: to ignore the effect of these massed speeches condemning Timon's friends and all but deifying Timon is to blur our understanding, to refuse the positive and single statement of this the most masterfully deliberate of Shakespeare's sombre tragedies. Then shall we fail before the deep music of the two final acts. But if yet more definite indication be needed, it is to be found in the poet's early speech, a unique Shakespearian introduction to his own play:

> I have, in this rough work shaped out a man,
> Whom this beneath world doth embrace and hug
> With amplest entertainment.   [I. i. 43-5]

It is all there, a clear description of the play's theme. Even the peculiar universality is clearly noted, especially in the next lines:

>   . . . my free drift
> Halts not particularly, but moves itself
> In a wide sea of wax: no levell'd malice
> Infects one comma in the course I hold;
> But flies an eagle flight, bold and forth on,
> Leaving no tract behind.   [I. i. 45-50]

This is manifestly not true of Shakespeare's Poet, who has composed his poem for Timon alone, but profoundly true of Shakespeare himself. Again:

> Sir, I have upon a high and pleasant hill
> Feign'd Fortune to be throned: the base o' the mount
> Is rank'd with all deserts, all kind of natures,
> That labour on the bosom of this sphere
> To propagate their states: amongst them all,
> Whose eyes are on this sovereign lady fix'd,
> One do I personate of Lord Timon's frame,
> Whom Fortune with her ivory hand wafts to her;
> Whose present grace to present slaves and servants
> Translates his rivals.   [I. i. 63-72]

The sequel is as the action of *Timon of Athens.* Thus *Timon of Athens* is a parable, or allegory; its rush of power, its clean-limned and massive simplicity, its crystal and purposive technique—all these are blurred and distorted if we search for exact verisimilitude with the appearances of human life. It is sublimely unrealistic. But if we recognize its universal philosophic meaning, it is then apparent in all its profundity and masterly construction. We are here judging the chances of the spirit of perfected man to embrace Fortune and find love truly interfused in this 'beneath world': to build his soul's paradise on 'the bosom of this sphere'. Thus Timon is the archetype and norm of all tragedy. (pp. 218-20)

[When] next Timon appears the iron of enduring hate has entered his soul. True, he has one more banquet; invites his friends to it; withholds his rage till he has made one speech of withering scorn—then volleys the titanic fury of his kingly nature in hate sovereign as tremendous as his sovereign love. There is no tragic movement so swift, so clean-cut, so daring and so terrible in all Shakespeare as this of Timon. We pity Lear, we dread for Macbeth: but the awfulness of Timon, dwarfing pity and out-topping sympathy, is as the grandeur and menace of the naked rock of a sky-lifted mountain, whither we look and tremble. Deserting Athens, he steps from time into eternity. The world of humanity tilts over, and is reversed. We see now, not with the vision of man, but henceforth with that of the aspiring spirit of love that has scorned mankind for ever. Timon will tolerate no disorder, within and without his mind, like Lear, torn betwixt love and loathing, division which is madness. The chaos which his imprecations are to call on man will be as a concord within the soul of him whose love is reversed, and who is no longer of this world. Thus Timon preserves the grander harmony of loneliness and universal loathing, and fronts his destiny, emperor still in mind and soul, wearing the imperial nakedness of hate. This unswerving majesty is a grander thing than the barbaric fury of Othello, or the faltering ire of Lear. The heart's-gold in Timon has seen the ingrateful and miserly greed that would coin for use the infinity of a great soul's love. So Timon leaves Athens.

His long curses are epics of hatred, unrestrained, limitless, wild. The whole race of man is his theme. His love was ever universal, now his hate is universal, its theme embraces every grade, age, sex, and profession. . . . The poet has shown us a supreme love, dissociated from other qualities, and this love, trusting finite symbols of itself, has failed disastrously. It now appears as a naked force, undirected towards any outward manifestations, diffused and bodiless, no longer fitted to the finite, a thing inhuman, unnatural, and infinite. Timon, naked and fierce-eyed, is no longer personal, no longer one of mankind. He is pure passion, a naked rhythmic force, a rush and whirl of torrential energy loosed from any contact or harmony with temporal and confining things, a passion which

> . . . like the current flies
> Each bound it chafes.   [I. i. 24-5]

There is thus less imaginative unity in *Timon of Athens:* rather a strongly marked duality. The latter part of the play is contrasted with and related logically to the beginning. In *Hamlet* we see the tragic superman incongruously set in a normal social unit and working chaos therein; in *Macbeth* and *King Lear,* he is given a world of the same nature as himself, a single visionary universe woven in the pattern of imagination's truth. Here there is a curious time-sequence. The hero is first a resplendent man among men, superhuman, perhaps, but not inhuman: now he becomes inhuman. We need not question Timon's Athens: save for Timon himself, prince-hearted and lord of love, it is the world we know, first sensuous, and attractive, then trivial, poor-spirited, dishonest. Timon alone, with his shadow Apemantus, is in his latter hate of the anti-social and wayward nature of Hamlet and Lear. Thus in *Timon* we have a logical exposition of the significance of earlier plays. The hero's passion is clearly juxtaposed and related logically to a normal human society. The play is in two firmly contrasted parts. During the second our universe changes with the change in Timon, and after the brilliance of Athens the shadow of an infinite gloom broods over the desert solitudes where Timon communes with his hate. Mankind are then dim spectres only, and Timon's passion alone reality. (pp. 221-23)

Timon's original force of soul is ultimate. First infused into love of man, thence driven, it expresses itself, first in a positive and passionate aversion from all finite forms—that is, he must love or hate. Second, we have clear signs of the reality toward which this primary energy is directing him: the infinite and

ineffable to which he is bound. There is a swift movement toward infinity. From the gold-haze of the mystic dream of a universal love on earth have emerged stark contours of base ingratitude: then the outward world of man and its shapes swiftly vanishes, and the inward world of infinite spirit takes its place, first expressing its nature by aversion from the other mode of life, then turning towards all that is vast, inhuman, illimitable, void.

The course is direct. There is no tragic conflict, and therefore no dramatic tempest-symbolism occurs to heighten our imagination of storm and stress: Timon's curses will not ring weak. Nor is there any divagation from his inhuman quest. Thus in the latter scenes we are aware of two modes in the utterance of Timon: passionate hate, and a solitary contemplation of the infinite, the two interfused or alternate; and of three orders of dramatic persons—(i) pale ghosts of mankind, linking us to the world we have left; (ii) Timon; and (iii) a wild ocean, a breadth of nature, the great earth and its sun and moon, agents interacting in a cosmic drama mightier than man's puppet-play, yet finally dwarfed too by the grander soul of Timon, unsatiated in thought by the farthest limits of the material universe. . . . In these scenes the Shakespearian poetry takes on a mighty and compulsive rhythm, a throb and pulse unknown in other plays. As Timon severs all contact with the finite world and, like some majestic liner, cleaves the dark seas of infinity, we voyage too, put off from land on the big loom of that leviathan, to leave safe coasts and plough forthward into the unknown, bosomed on the swell and heave of ocean, by the lode-star of a titanic love.

Apemantus comes to Timon, the philosopher of hate to the prophet of hate. The incident points the difference between them, and is important. Apemantus first advises Timon to return to mankind, to turn flatterer himself. He points out that this life of hardship serves no purpose of revenge, and that nature will be no less cruel than men. Will the bleak air, the trees, the creatures hardened in nature's battle with a cruel heaven, come to Timon's bidding, and flatter? Timon, however, angrily bids him depart. . . . Apemantus and Timon hate with a difference: one, because he is less than mankind—the other because he is greater. Hence Timon is particularly disgusted with Apemantus, who apes, and enjoys, the bitter passion of his own enduring soul.

This dialogue is most important for our understanding of the essential meaning of the play. The two hates are juxtaposed. Apemantus upholds the worth of his as a thing of judgement, systematized into a way of life. To Timon that is abhorrent, and witnesses a gross nature. Now Apemantus is right when he tells Timon that death is the only hope left for him. Apemantus has scorned humanity, but lives on with them, feeding his scorn; he continues 'vexing' men, which is, says Timon, 'a villain's office or a fool's' . . . ; and he enjoys doing it, which proves him a 'knave.' . . . Apemantus has hated life, yet loves to live. But for Timon, who has uncompromisingly broken from mankind, and whose sweeping condemnation includes not alone humanity and the beasts of nature . . . but even sun and moon . . . : for Timon there is, as Apemantus points out, only death. (pp. 224-27)

Timon knows the end to which he aspires. It is so clear—so implicit in the whole allegorical movement—that no cause of death is given or needed:

> Then, Timon, presently prepare thy grave;
> Lie where the light foam of the sea may beat
> Thy grave-stone daily.   [IV. iii. 377-79]

And:

> Come not to me again: but say to Athens,
> Timon hath made his everlasting mansion
> Upon the beached verge of the salt flood;
> Who once a day with his embossed froth
> The turbulent surge shall cover: thither come,
> And let my grave-stone be your oracle.
>
> [V. i. 214-19]

The void of death, darkness; the Shakespearian 'nothing' which brings Timon 'all things.' . . . The dark sea which is infinite formlessness, infinite depth, the surge and swell within the soul of man, the deeps beyond intellect, or sight, or sound. It is this surge that has throbbed within the poetry of tremendous symbols, this tide of emotion that breaks and sobs in Timon's passion when, his active hate subdued, he speaks the language of a soul beyond the world of manifestation and tuned to its own solitary music; the psalmody of earth and sun and the wide sea of eternal darkness beating on the rocks of creation.

We are given no chance to sentimentalize Timon's hate. Its nobility derives solely from its utter reversal of love. It is thus not a spiritual atrophy, a negation, a cold vacuum of the soul, like the pain of Hamlet, but a dynamic and positive thing, possessing purpose and direction. Therefore, though impelled to its inevitable death-climax, the tragic movement of this play leaves us with no sense of the termination of the essential Timon: its impact on the imagination is rather that of a continuation, circling within and beyond the mysterious nothing of dissolution, in a new dimension congruous with the power and the passion which have forced him toward death. The especial reality of Timon is this of powerful, torrential movement to freedom: which freedom from all that we call 'life' is so necessary and excellent a consummation to the power and the direction of Timon's passion, that it can in no sense be imaged as a barrier or stoppage. It is rather as though the rushing torrent, so long chafed by the limits of its channel, breaks out into the wide smoothness of the living sea. The death-theme in *Timon of Athens* is thus of the greatest importance, the crowning majesty of the play's movement. (pp. 230-31)

We have watched a swift unwrapping of fold on fold of life's significances—civilized man, beasts, the earth, the objective universe itself, till we reach the core of pure and naked significance, undistorted by any symbol, in the nothingness of death. Yet at every step in Timon's history we have been aware, not of a lessening, but of an increase of his grandeur; that is, at every stripping of the soul of Timon we have known that what was taken is but another rag, what remains, the essence, the reality. For Timon, at the end, is pure essence of significance, beyond the temporal, in touch with a conquering knowledge of his furthest destiny. Nothing will be proved the largesse of all things. So he cries:

> Graves only be men's works and death their gain!
> Sun, hide thy beams! Timon hath done his reign.
>
> [V. i. 222-23]

Again is emphasized the completeness with which Timon's love is reversed. It is not alone a turning away from mankind: rather a passionate turning inward from all forms and shapes of actuality, all manifestation, from the cosmic scheme. He would wish the race die out, the sun blackened, the glass of time exhausted. Only the rhythm of the tireless beat of waves, the crash and the whispering retraction, these alone signify some fore-echoing of the thing which is to receive Timon. This

is only the last step, into the cold night of death, of the movement we have been watching all along. It is truly spoken that

> Timon is dead, who hath outstretch'd his span.
>
> [V. iii. 3]

His hate of man was ever but one aspect, or expression, of the turning inward of his soul toward death, and since he flung back titanic curse on Athens, his being has been centred not in time but throughout the otherness of eternity. (pp. 232-33)

[The poetry is] loaded with a massive, compulsive emotion, in comparison with which the words of Hamlet, Troilus, Othello, and even Lear, are as the plaintive accents of children. A mighty rhythm of a race's longing, of human destiny unalterable and uncomplained, sounds through the whole play, and wakes an unearthly majesty of words in the symphonic harmonies of the final acts. There is no turning aside, no regret in all the passion of Timon, but it

> flies an eagle's flight, bold and forth on,
> Leaving no tract behind—   [I. i. 49-50]

until, in the poetry of the latter half of the play, the mind is a-voyage on unfathomed and uncharted seas, whose solid deeps of passion but wanly and waveringly reflect the vastest images that man can dream. In this recurrent solemnity of utterance more grand for its massive and fathomless simplicity, we joy in that we listen not to the accents of mortality but to those of the spirit of a race. Therefore, though Flavius saves mankind from utter condemnation by one act of faith, we know that the organ notes of implacable hatred cannot so be stilled, since by them alone the soul of Timon pursues its course. He is no 'idle votarist' . . . :

> Hate all, curse all, show charity to none.
>
> [IV. iii. 527]

The profoundest problems of racial destiny are here symbolized and fought out. In no other play is a more forceful, a more irresistible, mastery of technique—almost crude in its massive, architectural effects—employed. But then no play is so massive, so rough-hewn into Atlantean shapes from the mountain rock of the poet's mind or soul, as this of Timon. 'I have in this rough work shap'd out a man . . .' It is true. No technical scaffolding in Shakespeare has to stand so weighty and shattering a stress. For this play is *Hamlet, Troilus and Cressida, Othello, King Lear,* become self-conscious and universal; it includes and transcends them all; it is the recurrent and tormenting hate-theme of Shakespeare, developed, raised to an infinite power, presented in all its tyrannic strength and profundity, and—killed. Three acts form the prologue. Our vision thus with infinite care and every possible device focused, we await the onrush of a passion which sums in its torrential energy all the lesser passions of those protagonists foregone. Timon is the totality of all, his love more rich and oceanic than all of theirs, all lift their lonely voices in his universal curse. Christlike, he suffers that their pain may cease, and leaves the Shakespearian universe redeemed that Cleopatra may win her Antony in death, and Thaisa be restored to Pericles. (pp. 235-36)

G. Wilson Knight, "The Pilgrimage of Hate: An Essay on 'Timon of Athens'," in his The Wheel of Fire: Interpretations of Shakespearian Tragedy, revised edition, Methuen & Co Ltd, 1949, pp. 207-39.*

JOHN W. DRAPER (essay date 1934)

[*Draper applies a socio-economic approach to* Timon *and interprets the play as Shakespeare's negative portrait of the collapse of traditional aristocratic and Christian values and the rise of the merchant class in England. For other discussions of the role of money and social class in* Timon, *see the excerpts by Karl Marx (1844) and Kenneth Muir (1947).*]

In the Elizabethan age, the old feudal nobility had reached an economic *impasse* that might well arouse one's sympathy and that produced overwhelming social changes. Religious, military, political and economic causes were bringing about a peaceful revolution that was very generally deplored. Many of the old county families were still Roman Catholic, and so fell under special taxation and other disabilities. The final abandonment of the feudal military system during the 1590's, moreover, and the substitution of professional soldiers ended the military power of the aristocracy; and the romantic independence of knight-errantry degenerated into Falstaffian escapades necessarily embarked upon to pay, or to avoid paying, the 'shot' of tavern bills. The lucrative Court positions went to the upstarts of Tudor creation, and it was they who directed the corrupt machinery of the law which was displacing feudal custom. Cheap money, moreover, from the mines of Mexico and Peru caused a constant rise in prices which enriched the merchants at the expense of the other classes; for persons with fixed incomes such as feudal rents suffered from the fallen purchasing power of money. Dekker is bitter against this flow of gold from America; and Timon's several tirades against gold, the 'common whore of mankind,' seem to refer to this condition. (pp. 23-4)

The merchants meanwhile, after the commercial decay of the early Tudor period, were more and more enriched, and competed with the noblemen in equipage and magnificence. . . . So the old aristocracy was threatened with 'loss of all distinction'; and their places were taken by merchants who looked to their tenants for income rather than for feudal services, who dismissed superfluous retainers, enclosed the common land, increased the rents, and spent a large part of their time away in London. No wonder a general outcry arose against the change. Usury seemed the cause that enriched the new families and destroyed the old. Land was the one conservative investment of the age; and land was, therefore, the immediate prize of rich merchants who hoped to found great families; and thus the landed aristocracy was the especial object of their attack. (pp. 25-6)

If usury then was responsible for this social disintegration and the misery it entailed, one can easily see why Antonio and even Timon were so sympathetic to an Elizabethan audience, which saw itself, like them, in the clutches of griping creditors. . . . [In] *Timon of Athens*, Alcibiades' attacks on 'usury That makes the senate ugly' and on 'the usuring senate' supply obvious motivation for his rebellion, and to the Elizabethans would clearly link his cause to Timon's. Thus Shakespeare, though he flew in the face of tradition in interpreting a popular story, did so in order to express the popular resentment against usurers; and tumult and proscription seemed a fitting outcome in a state that permitted usury to subvert the feudal and the Christian virtues. . . . The play, indeed, is Shakespeare's *Gulliver,* a fierce and sweeping indictment of the ideals and social ethics of the age, an indictment largely consonant with popular opinion of the time. In *Lear,* Shakespeare depicts the social chaos consequent upon the abdication of royal authority; in *Timon of Athens,* upon the economic ruin of the nobility. (pp. 27-8)

That Shakespeare had in mind the very conditions of his day and was not merely moralising in the abstract is evident not only in the intense bitterness of the lines but in numerous immediate and contemporary details. He supports the very virtues, liberality and valour, that rising capitalism was obliging society to abandon, and points directly towards the legal decisions against duels. Timon himself is a characteristic noble: his wealth is in 'land'; he is a soldier of no mean repute; he even refers to his 'reign'; as if he were a semi-independent prince, very different from the Timone of Boiardo whose father made the family fortune through usury. Indeed, Shakespeare's Timon comes of a great 'house.' Like so many of the Elizabethan aristocracy, he is ruined with incredible speed by forfeitures and rapidly compounding interest. The usurers and Timon's devouring friends are described as 'knaves' or 'slaves and peasants.' . . .

The Elizabethan attitude towards usury is the key to *Timon of Athens:* it gives the purpose to the play, which former scholars could not find; it explains the change in Timon, links to the former acts the final episode of Alcibiades' revenge, and so gives unity to character and to plot; it gives a reason for Shakespeare's change in attitude toward the Timon of tradition; and, by showing that he meant the play to be a commentary on current life, it explains his utter disregard of classical authenticity. (p. 29)

*John W. Draper, "The Theme of 'Timon of Athens',"
in* The Modern Language Review, *Vol. XXIX, No. 1, January, 1934, pp. 20-31.*

CAROLINE F.E. SPURGEON   (essay date 1935)

[*Spurgeon's* Shakespeare's Imagery, *originally published in 1935, inaugurated the "image-pattern analysis" method of studying Shakespeare's plays, one of the most widely used methods of the mid-twentieth century. In this work, she interprets the thematic structure of the plays through an examination of patterns in the imagery. Spurgeon also sought to learn about Shakespeare's personality from a study of his images, a course which few of her disciples followed. Since publication of her book, earlier works on image patterns in Shakespeare have been discovered, but none was so important in the history of Shakespearean criticism as Spurgeon's. In the following excerpt, she claims that though most critics have considered "gold" the ruling image in* Timon, *the true unifying picture, that which "runs as an undertone throughout the whole play," is the image of dogs "fawning and eating." Kenneth Muir (1947) challenges Spurgeon's conclusion.*]

A recent critic, in a most profound and suggestive essay on *Timon of Athens,* has said that 'gold-symbolism' is persistent, and, he suggests, dominant, throughout the play [see excerpt above by G. Wilson Knight, 1930]. This is a good example of how misleading it may be in a study of this sort to trust to the impression rather than to the fact. Undoubtedly gold is constantly spoken of and kept before our minds; in one scene alone . . . the word is repeated twenty times, considerably more than in the whole of any other one play, there is a number of images (ten to be exact) of which gold is the subject, such as 'delicate wooer', 'visible god', 'touch of hearts', 'yellow slave', 'strong thief', and so on; the metal symbols, 'base metal', 'iron heart', 'flinty mankind', all hard and valueless, are clearly used in contrast to the idea of the precious quality of pure gold; *but there is only one image from gold throughout the play.* This is at the end of the first scene, when the richness and brilliance of Timon's surroundings are pictured to us with the flash of jewels and the beauty of art, culminating in the description of his bounty:

> He pours it out; Plutus, the god of gold,
> Is but his steward;

[I. i. 276-77]

which leaves us with a vision of an endless stream of gold issuing from his hands in unmeasured abundance.

But gold, however much it may be emphasised, was not the *picture* which was constantly before Shakespeare's eyes as he threw himself into this story of man's greed and ingratitude. It was a quite different picture, but an extraordinarily characteristic one. . . . It is the imaginative picture always linked in Shakespeare's mind with the theme of false friends and flatterers, which is the subject of this play: dogs, fawning and eating and lapping, with 'gluttonous maws' devouring their 'lord's meat', eating remnants, licking sweets and melting the sugar. This is the picture which runs as an undertone throughout the whole play. (pp. 344-45)

> Caroline F.E. Spurgeon, "Leading Motives in the Tragedies," in her Shakespeare's Imagery and What It Tells Us, Cambridge at the University Press, 1968, pp. 309-56.

MARK VAN DOREN (essay date 1939)

[In the excerpt below, Van Doren voices a complaint which many commentators on Timon have suggested, namely that the play reads better as poetry than as drama.]

If Aristotle was right when he called plot the soul of tragedy, "Timon of Athens" has no soul. There are those who claim to know that Shakespeare's soul is in it, exposed at a crisis which experts on the inner lives of authors can read at a glance; but that is an additional way of saying that the play does without complications. Its action is the simplest that can be imagined. Upon the refusal of four friends to lend him money when he needs it Timon passes from the extreme of prodigality to the extreme of misanthropy. "The middle of humanity," whence tragedy no less than comedy derives its strength, he never knows; he knows "but the extremity of both ends." The words are those of Apemantus, who as the churl of the piece is privileged also to say that Timon's transformation is from a madman to a fool, from a flashing phoenix to a naked gull. Apemantus is a harsh critic, but he is a critic. The author's interest is entirely confined to the absolutes of Timon's illusion and disillusion. Not only has he taken no pains to motivate his hero's change of mind, for the episode of the friends' ingratitude is perfunctory; he has taken no pains whatever to put more than lyric force into Timon's utterances before and after. The play is two plays, casually joined at the middle; or rather two poems, two pictures, in swan white and raven black. The contrast is all. This is where the spiritual biographers of Shakespeare come in. The poetry of either half being radical in its intensity and impossible to ignore, they argue that the feeling behind it must be Shakespeare's instead of Timon's, and that the play was never anything but an excuse to rid the poet's bosom of its perilous stuff—granted, to be sure, that he is responsible for all of it as it stands. Assuming that he is, we can agree that the play as written leaves him open to the charge of having expressed himself rather than his theme. But the field of conjecture is so wide that any step taken across it may be in the right direction, and we may wish to escape into an alternative theory which starts from the supposition that "Timon of Athens" is Shakespeare's last tragedy and that it was never finished. (pp. 288-89)

No play of Shakespeare's confesses its limits more frankly. It is content to be abstract, to leave unclothed the symbols of which its poetry is made. . . .

    This yellow slave
    Will knit and break religions, bless the accurs'd,

    Make the hoar leprosy ador'd, place thieves
    And give them title, knee, and approbation
    With senators on the bench. This is it
    That makes the wappen'd widow wed again;
    She, whom the spital-house and ulcerous sores
    Would cast the gorge at, this embalms and spices
    To the April day again. Come, damn'd earth,
    Thou common whore of mankind, that puts odds
    Among the rout of nations, I will make thee
    Do thy right nature.

                                    [IV. iii. 34-44]

Such a speech has its terrors, and with many another speech in the play it belongs somewhere near the top of Shakespeare's poetry. But it is not terrible that Timon should be saying such things as it was terrible that Lear should say the things he said. Gold has been a symbol wherewith Timon could express his love. Now it is a symbol wherewith he can express his hate. That is all. It is as naked a piece of poetic property as the hole he stands in, as the root he throws up, as the cave he enters and leaves, and as the sea by which he is to die. (pp. 289-90)

He himself is pure symbol, a misanthrope and not a man.

The play confesses as much in the conduct of such action as it has. Schematism is everywhere apparent. There are three malcontents: Timon, Apemantus, and Alcibiades. Three servants enter Timon's hall bearing gifts [I. ii]. Three friends refuse money to Timon in three consecutive scenes [III. i, ii, iii] and three strangers comment upon the triple outrage [III. ii]. In his solitude Timon is visited by three significant individuals: Alcibiades, Apemantus, Flavius. And the banditti who come are three in number. This is obviously the work of a playwright who does not care how much his machinery shows, just as the poetry is the work of a man who does not mind announcing his themes—in the first half they are friendship, music, love, praise, and summer tears, in the second half they are hate, rage, roots, gold, bleak earth and sky, unvesseled sea, and winters too hard for weeping. (pp. 291-92)

> Mark Van Doren, "'Timon of Athens'," in his Shakespeare, Henry Holt and Company, 1939, pp. 288-92.

JOHN W. DRAPER (essay date 1940)

Elizabethan psychological theory was based on the concept of the four 'humours', or fluids, that were thought to govern the bodily and mental functions. The predominance of blood made a man 'sanguine'; and such persons were thought to be particularly fortunate, for they were under the astral influence of the planet Jupiter, 'the greatest fortune', and blood was considered the best of all the humours: the Timon of Act I, with his host of friends and his 'large fortune', certainly seems a lucky man. The sanguine temper, moreover, was appropriate to 'Noblemen'; and 'the Lord Timon', with his wide stretch of landed estates, is clearly and Athenian noble. The bodily attributes of the sanguine type were a 'persuasive' voice and a 'comely' stature; and Timon would seem to have been a personable man. Such people were 'mery' and witty to their fellows; and Timon was certainly a jovial companion. In character, they were reckoned 'just, true, benevolent, liberall, faithfull, milde, godly, shamefast, magnanimous . . . and happie'; and the earlier Timon is all these things. Both Timon's own acts at the outset of the play and the comment of the other characters bring out these sanguine traits. . . . (p. 522)

In sharp contrast to this sanguine Timon are the sub-major characters of the play. The Senators, despite their position and wealth, lack the liberality of the sanguine humour, and indeed descend to usury. . . . This 'cold' disposition, together with their 'dotage', suggests that they are supposed to be melancholy. This humour was chill and dry, unlucky and associated with death, in diametric opposition to the warm and damp and vital attributes of the sanguine type. Timon's steward Flavius seems to be actuated by the phlegmatic humour, which was dull but well-intentioned: Flavius deplores somewhat helplessly his master's prodigality, but does not even get to warn him until it is too late. The churlish Apemantus illustrates the fourth humour, and is certainly choleric: he constantly rails, and is described as 'ever angry'. This same choleric disposition, which was supposed to be appropriate to military men, appears also in Timon's friend, the soldier Alcibiades: the sack of Athens that he threatens in revenge for the wrongs that the Senate has committed is closely parallel to the Emperor's despoiling of Milan, likewise in revenge; and this latter event was attributed to choler. Thus the early and middle scenes of the drama, like *Romeo and Juliet*, present in sharp dramatic contrast the types of all four humours. (pp. 522-23)

Shakespeare has depicted a psychological evolution in Timon appropriate to his actions in the original story and also to the change in point of view that the dramatist intended: his sanguine nature, through bitter adversity, gives place to the choleric, and this in turn burns out to a bitter melancholy, which possibly runs its course to madness, or at all events concludes with suicide. Thus character and plot are perfectly integrated; and the Elizabethan theory of humours supplies the hero with an inevitable psychological evolution. Just so in a contemporary play, Shakespeare makes Coriolanus begin with military pride, pass on to choler and so to revenge and ruin. In the comedies, in the figures of Petruchio, Corporal Nym and Falstaff, he had depicted men pretending to humours that they did not by right possess; in *Romeo and Juliet*, he had combined the theory of humours with astrology to give motive to the plot; in *Twelfth Night*, the Duke's love-melancholy is used to explain his sudden marriage to Viola at the end; in *Hamlet*, melancholy is the hero's natural reaction at the frustration of his purposes; and in *Lear* it appears as incident to the King's old age; but, in his latest tragedies, Shakespeare uses the humours, not incidentally, but as the very warp and woof of plot and character and as the main support to his political or social theme. Coriolanus and Timon, as characters, could not have been what they were, nor could the plays have reasonably followed the course of action that the theme required and that tradition had established, but for the motivating psychology of the humours. (p. 525)

John W. Draper, "The Psychology of Shakespeare's Timon," in The Modern Language Review, *Vol. XXXV, No. 4, October, 1940, pp. 521-25.*

UNA ELLIS-FERMOR (essay date 1942)

[*The following essay has been seen as something of a definitive statement on the authorship question of* Timon *and on the status of the drama in Shakespeare's canon. Ellis-Fermor concludes that* Timon *is more than likely the sole work of Shakespeare, but a work which he, for unknown reasons, failed to finish. What sets Ellis-Fermor apart from a host of other critics on this point is her contention that the play is not only unfinished in a technical sense, but also in a conceptual sense, because its main character remains the most troublesome of all its shortcomings. E.A.J. Honigmann opposes this interpretation, arguing that Ellis-Fermor misinterprets Shakespeare's intentions in the play (see excerpt*

below, 1961). For more commentary on the authorship question of Timon, *see the essays by Charles Knight (1843), Gulian C. Verplanck (1847), F. G. Fleay (1874), George Brandes (1895-96), Walter Raleigh (1907), E. K. Chambers (1908), G. B. Harrison (1951), and Charlton Hinman (1969).*]

The play of *Timon* has disturbed Shakespeare's critics from an early period and continues to do so. In nearly every respect, from details of style to major characteristics of structure, it is now like, now unlike Shakespeare. Many conjectural explanations of this condition have been offered, but it seems more than usually difficult to reach agreement. Either Shakespeare worked upon an older play of which he retained parts, or he left an unfinished play which was completed by someone else, or the Folio (our only text) is full of cuts and corruptions difficult to explain, or we have merely an unfinished play in which the other 'hand' is negligible or non-existent. These four interpretations are, clearly, not easy to reconcile. (p. 270)

It is as an unfinished play . . . that I should like to consider it, a play such as a great artist might leave behind him, roughed out, worked over in part and then abandoned; full of inconsistencies in form and presentation, with fragments (some of them considerable) bearing the unmistakable stamp of his workmanship scattered throughout. Such a text makes it difficult to believe 'another hand' has been at work upon it, for the confusion, whether it affects details of style or the relations of characters and scenes, is precisely what that hand would have been paid to reduce to order. But if we believe that we have here a unique case in the Shakespeare canon, a play abandoned when only half-worked, and read it through scene by scene in the light of this assumption, we find little which does not seem to be explained thereby. (p. 271)

The imagery and the prosody of the opening passages mark them as mature Shakespearean poetry; scenes in which such imagery and such prosody are found must be taken seriously; they will contain presumably, something that Shakespeare intended to present. The immediate opening up to the entrance of Timon is, it is true, unlike the induction of any other play of his; but we may notice that that is also true of nearly all the plays he wrote after he reached full stature; the theme, in all these, makes its own form. The Jacobean drama offers us a series of notable inductions, and Shakespeare is here, as usual, profoundly original in an age of virtuosos. This passage gives us, moreover, in the poet's allegory, the ironic forewarning of Timon's fall, a warning which precedes the detailed presentation of his wealth and extravagance that occupies the first two acts, and is picked up at intervals like a melody, subordinate in the early movements of a symphony and becoming dominant at the climax. (pp. 271-72)

The latter part of this scene (from the entrance of Apemantus) offers some difficulties, but they are not insuperable. It is certainly a thin patch of writing. There are very few touches of live imagery or music, and these . . . occur in the later part. Even Apemantus, afterwards an integral part of the play's content and structure affecting both the outer and the inner action, lacks sinew here and is no more than a kind of conventional Diogenes crossed with a little diluted Thersites. I can see no artistic reason for this flatness, but we must admit that there is some, though not so much, of the same kind in other plays that are psychologically related to *Timon*—in *All's Well*, in *Measure for Measure* and even in *Troilus and Cressida*. One might venture the suggestion that this part was roughed out and not finished: it compares badly with the first half of the scene, which was either worked over after roughing out or written more eagerly in the first instance. For one reason or for the other, the earlier seems more fully imagined and so more finished.

There is nothing in the second scene to make us withdraw. In fact, the design of the outward action seems sound and broadly based up to the end of the act. As a first act, that is, this one does its work. If the next four had been lost we should have no reason to suspect artistic confusion or collapse in what was to follow. (pp. 272-73)

Moreover, two of the chief characters that appear here are built strongly into the play and do, in fact, maintain their shape and position later when much else goes to wreck. Apemantus' mood seems at first to run counter to that of the play, in churlish opposition. But when the crisis has turned the tide, it is found to be the dominant stream that carries all with it; as the play goes on, there is a slowly deepening power and increasing relevance in his speech which indicates design. Flavius, again, is planted firmly in the action both of events and of ideas. He has, moreover, the special function of uttering in more precise definition the vague warnings and threats of the poet's allegory at the beginning. This theme, which we are never allowed to escape for long, has clearly been foreseen from the beginning.

But beside these indications of deliberate planning of the functional relations of the characters to the main theme, we notice signs of unfinished work in the details of this act. The broken and irregular lines, the patch-work effect of many even of the finest speeches, have long troubled Shakespeare's critics here. They are indeed extremely difficult to explain in terms of any kind of corruption known to bibliographical critics; with the best will in the world, I cannot see how playhouse additions or excisions or the most illegible palimpsest that was ever handed to a compositor in the form of a prompt-copy could have produced just this condition. But I can see without any difficulty at all how a man who was roughing out a scene might leave a speech in this form: it is to my mind as strong evidence as we can find that whoever wrote these passages did not finish them. And the presence of many such in the play, and in speeches of undeniable majesty and power, is likewise the best evidence I could ask that Shakespeare wrote the rest of the play also, and, similarly, left it unfinished. (pp. 273-74)

I incline to think that what we have here is Shakespeare's work in varying degrees of completion and at varying levels of imaginative intensity but still substantially the first act that he planned, with some of the later action and the main theme already in his mind, and that parts of the design here conceived were strongly enough formed to emerge firm and powerful throughout the play. I think also that he was experimenting with structure. . . . What was the experiment in this case and what the consequent form it may be hard to discover. (pp. 274-75)

Where the first act had been extended and in parts almost leisurely, as fits the induction to an inner action of vast scope, [the] second act is correspondingly rapid; the audience may be presumed to have grasped what is involved and the action can go forward. Its relation to the preceding act seems sound enough, too, in actual plotting; the change in the direction of Timon's fortunes, for which we have been consciously or unconsciously prepared, is now presented. There are flat passages again, it is true, but the mixture of tediousness with vigorous commentary . . . has the same function as similar passages in *Measure for Measure*, it reveals a background that we must take into account if we are to perceive justly the relations of values in the play. And the later part of the second scene . . . we can

by no means dismiss, for some of the verbal music and its imagery is as powerful as in any play of this period; here at least we have finished or relatively finished work.

But one thing disturbs us in this act, our first meeting with a conspicuous and inexplicable loose end in the character of the Fool. Although the passage in which he appears is well enough written, he is not built into the play. We do not know who he is or where he comes from. We hardly know to whom he belongs. And he disappears never to appear again. We are forced to one of two assumptions: either that he ceased to be part of Shakespeare's design by a change of intention after this scene, or that the scenes or passages in which his function and relation to the play would have appeared were never written or were lost. He is the first, but not the last disturbing element of this kind that we shall find in the play. (p. 275)

[The third act gives] an impression of being planned; but there is no consistent carrying through of the plan as in the first and to some degree in the second. Apart from the fact that the first three scenes are much more closely grouped than those that follow and that the climax in the sixth scene seems only a sketch, falling far short of the expectation that has been raised in us, there is the strange and startling incursion made by the fifth scene. This scene has given the commentators more trouble than any other in the play. Professor Boas long ago declared strongly in favour of Shakespeare's authorship of this scene and there does not seem any reason, in the light of what has been said since, to reject it. It is a fine Shakespearean scene: the difficulty lies not in its quality but in its function. . . . Questions beset us as we read. What is this trial that is in progress? For whom is Alcibiades pleading? What has happened? And when? What has it to do with what goes before? Or, as we are presently in a position to ask, with what follows? It tumbles suddenly into the action with the bewildering inconsequence of an episode in a dream and its power and its vividness only strengthen this impression. Worse still, perhaps, they convince us that Shakespeare wrote this scene with considerable enthusiasm; he either cared enough about it to work over it until it was coherent and vigorous, or he came to it with a measure of artistic delight great enough to carry it through, clear and shapely, at the first writing. (pp. 277-78)

Either, it is clear, the scene belongs to some alternative action or sub-plot which was finally discarded, in which case it has presumably strayed into the text . . . , or it is an essential part of the action of the play as it was planned and its supporting scenes are lost or were never written. It may be noticed that, though it has as it stands no connection with the preceding action of the play, it has some kinship with the theme, for the changes are rung here, as all through the play, on the contrast between generous friendship and ingratitude. If it was a part of Shakespeare's design, nothing remains to confirm this or to show how it was to be related to the foregoing scenes except one or two hints in Alcibiades' speech [IV. iii. 94-5] and in the senators' embassy to Timon [V. i. 149-66] which suggest that it was Timon himself who had committed the murder and was the subject of the trial. This of course presupposes that a supporting scene or passage earlier in the act has been lost (or never written) as well as the necessary references that must have followed. But it does at least, if we can agree to it, clear away several difficulties. This scene, characteristically Shakespearean as it is in style, might, in that case, have been functional, taking up its place in the action of the play; the relationship of Alcibiades to the rest of the play could thereupon become firm and coherent instead of disturbing us as it does by its inconclusiveness; the action of the final scenes of the play would take on a substance and a coherence that it badly lacks, and, in fact, the whole of Act V could be related to the main action. It becomes increasingly difficult to resist the idea that a series of passages is missing containing such essential parts of the story as would have made the structure of the last three acts solid by relating Timon clearly to Alcibiades and both to Athenian politics. (pp. 278-79)

The fourth act presents no such interruptions to the scheme of the play. . . . The full working-out of the thought, fuller than in any other part, and the potency of the imagery, which is not only cogent and impressive, but significant of the main lines of thought throughout, convince me that here again we have something which is substantially Shakespeare's intention. It relates itself closely to *Troilus and Cressida* on the one hand and to *Lear* on the other, the two plays which seem to stand nearest to *Timon* in their mood and interpretation.

The fifth act is again uneven. So erratic is the relating of its parts that we sometimes feel as if we are reading a mixture of two different plays. Yet all through it are the signs of mature writing which make us hesitate to say that it has not been touched by Shakespeare. . . . [We cannot help] the suspicion that the condition of the play is more than a matter of scenes that have not been worked over and a minor character, like the fool, who has not been clearly related. For from the middle of the third act there are major inconsistencies, most noticeable in the unexplained appearance of III. v, always involving Alcibiades and the Athenians and ending in the structural disjunction of the fifth act. As we have reason to believe that the plot was firmly designed, we can only assume that the design is not fairly represented by what remains. (pp. 279-80)

But we have avoided mention so far of the greatest weakness in the play, that which gives us more ground for uneasiness than all of these—the character of Timon. This goes deep into the fabric of the play and we cannot explain it away by saying that something has been lost or not written or not worked-over. This is a matter of conception, not of working-out. For our complaint concerning Timon is not that we do not see enough of him, but that, in spite of the length of time during which he occupies the stage, he fails to leave a deep, coherent impression of his personality. And this is at its worst in the first two acts which we found no reason for supposing unfinished or unrepresentative of Shakespeare's intention regarding the central theme. Timon here is negative. There *is* no individuality. There is, it is true, a picture of great wealth and extravagant squandering, but this is not fit to support either so mighty a theme as is foreshadowed at the beginning, or a conversion such as the mood of the fourth and fifth acts presuppose. (pp. 280-81)

And this impression of negation and isolation is deepened, not dissipated, as we look closer. We do not know him and we do not know about him. Indeed, we begin to wonder whether he is not, himself, the greatest of the unrelated elements in the play. For he is only real by reason of his continual presence. Apart from that, he is hardly better built into his society on the grand scale than the fool is on a small scale. What, after all, do we know of his circumstances and relations, past and present, compared with all that we know or can divine of Hamlet, Lear or Coriolanus? If we begin to ask ourselves some of the questions to which Shakespeare generally provides unobtrusive answers, how many of them can we in fact answer? What is the source of his wealth; is it inherited or acquired? If inherited, how long has he had complete control of it? If

acquired, by what means did he acquire it? Who were his parents and when did they die—if indeed they are dead? How long has he been an orphan—if he indeed is? Has he no blood relations? How and where was he brought up? If it was out of touch with courts, why are we not told so? If in the court, why is he so little aware of its pitfalls? How old is he? If he is very young, why has he not some of the characteristics of youth? Why, above all, is he not in love? If he is of mature age, why is he such a fool? And why again, in that case, does he bear no signs of the experience he must have met, above all, the acute knowledge of man that palace intrigue would have given to a strong intelligence? (pp. 281-82)

Timon is an unfinished play in a far deeper sense than that which is implied by saying Shakespeare left off writing before he had set down all that was in his mind. It *is* unfinished in this way also, it is true. But, what matters more, it is unfinished in conception. We can explain the broken verse and the loose ends easily; we can explain nearly as easily the imperfections of the plot; we can even isolate the main theme and show how unworthy of it is the working-out in the later acts. What we cannot explain is our impression that this play is indeed 'Hamlet without the Prince of Denmark', the character of Timon being often a blank. Here is that rarest of all weaknesses in Shakespeare's work, an element which is not wholly functional; a character which does not convince us, upon inspection, that, given its nature and these events, the resultant action presented to us is inevitable. Dare we suggest that, for some reason at which we can only dimly guess, Shakespeare chose the wrong character to support his theme, and, consequently, the wrong outer action as the image of the inner action? This obviously leaves us as far as ever from real knowledge of the cause of the play's collapse, but it may suggest one reason why it came to a standstill, was 'unfinished' in the more limited and technical sense also. How Shakespeare, with his unsurpassed artistic and psychological sureness, came to make so colossal a blunder is a matter on which we dare not conjecture. Were there other plays which also miscarried, which have not survived? Did this survive against his intention? All that we can say with any certainty is that here is a design not wholly comprehended and subdued by the shaping spirit of imagination. (p. 283)

Una Ellis-Fermor, " 'Timon of Athens': An Unfinished Play," in The Review of English Studies, *Vol. 18, No. 71, July, 1942, pp. 270-83.*

A. S. COLLINS (essay date 1946)

[*Collins argues that the lack of characterization in* Timon *and the play's unusual design can be understood if we interpret it as Shakespeare intended it to be read, as a "medieval morality play." This assessment has also been reached by such commentators as Peter Ure (1964) and Anne Lancashire (1970), but has been vehemently denounced by J. C. Maxwell (1948), L. C. Knights (1969), and Rolf Soellner (1979).*]

The continued neglect and misunderstanding of *Timon of Athens* is a puzzle. Not all critics have wanted appreciation of its qualities and merits. Hazlitt said that '*Timon of Athens* always appeared to us to be written with as intense a feeling of his subject as any one play of Shakespear' [see excerpt above, 1817]. Saintsbury called it 'the most Shakespearean of all plays not the greatest'. But those who have approved it have been few. Extremes of judgment are by no means uncommon even from the best critics, and not least so in recent years, as when Sir Edmund Chambers suggested that the play must have been

Act III. Scene vi. Timon of Athens and Lords. Frontispiece to Verplanck edition (1847). By permission of the Folger Shakespeare Library.

written 'under conditions of mental and perhaps physical stress, which led to a breakdown'. Yet *Timon of Athens* is a play which one might have expected our day, particularly the recent decades, to see very clearly and appreciatively. It is such a satire upon a cold-hearted commercial community, fearfully reinforcing its security by a heartless legalism, as Mr. W. H. Auden might well have envied. Its teaching, that although the head must rule the heart, yet in the heart lies the essential truth of personal relationships and thereby the health of the state, is the teaching Mr. E. M. Forster has had so much in mind to reawaken us to. Nevertheless, the general run of criticism has been against it. . . . Critics continue to find the lack of individual characterisation, especially in Timon himself, a marked defect. Perhaps it is the disappointment aroused by expecting the usual Shakespearean characterisation that has made it less easy for critics to discover a unity in the play, and hence the various speculations of earlier critics as to an earlier play, partly revised by Shakespeare, and perhaps supplemented by some contemporary dramatist. Particularly, critics seem to have been driven to the conclusion that it is, to an exceptional extent, unfinished. (pp. 96-7)

Certainly it is an unusual experiment of Shakespeare's, even if, with Saintsbury, we admit it to be 'the most Shakespearean of all plays not the greatest'. But 'even if' is illogical. It is very Shakespearean partly because it is so unusual an experiment, for it is of the very essence of Shakespeare to experiment. . . . In fact, the unending variety of his dramatic experiments is so obvious that it should be easy to see that, if *Timon* is the most striking of his experiments, it is by that all the more surely Shakespeare's, a bold departure typical of him and not of any other. Could any play more clearly declare its deliberate intention to be different? There is really no characterisation in the usual sense, except in Alcibiades. Amazingly in a Shakespearean play there are no women, for the Mask of Ladies as Amazons is only a Mask, and Phrynia and Timandra are mere stage properties. There is very little spectacle, and a

minimum of action. It is not a play therefore popular in appeal, or ever likely to be so. But against these negatives, what of the positive? The characters are subtilized Virtues and Vices, the staple of the play is satire and argument, and it is a play that could well appeal to a select thinking audience, for it covers much of the ground of Baconian essays on Friendship, Traffic, True and False Misanthropy, Law and Mercy, but, of course, with a most un-Baconian feeling. . . . Professor Dover Wilson writes of *Henry IV* that it 'is Shakespeare's great morality play'. Indeed it is, but *Timon* is his true morality play in the straight sense. It is the medieval morality play, only so much altered as to bring it very near to perfection.

There are two master keys to the play—the Three Strangers in III. ii, and the great scene (III. v) of Alcibiades before the senate. The first lets us into the secret of the nature of the play, its Morality nature: the second is the key to the play's very heart, the nature of its feeling; and until that is fully apprehended, the argument of the play remains cold, intellectual, and obviously, from the many dissatisfied critics, a bad argument. (pp. 97-8)

Scene ii of the Third Act is only a short scene, but what a power it carries. The crash of Timon is in the air: 'common rumours' tell how his 'happy hours are done and past, and his estate shrinks from him'. The servants of the usurers have been bidden to 'put on a most importunate aspect, a visage of demand', the senators have denied the pleas of Flavius, and the first 'friend', Lucullus, has denied Timon's servant. Now, in the hearing of the Three Strangers, Lucius too denies him help, pleading with an assumed bitterness of remorse, 'I have no power to be kind'. Almost abruptly the First Stranger assumes the role of a judge, or messenger of God, detached from all the action, to declare the truth about the world of Athens. 'Why, this is the world's soul', he declares:

> Men must learn now with pity to dispense;
> For policy sits above conscience.
>
> [III. ii. 86-7]

The ingratitude of Lucius is not individual ingratitude; he and all his like in Athens share it, and in the only words of the Third Stranger, breaking in with a quiet and damning solemnity, 'Religion groans at it.' And there is nothing personal in the First Stranger's feeling: 'I never tasted Timon in my life.' Detached, he sees clearly, but he also feels: he knows Timon's quality—'right noble mind, illustrious virtue, and honourable carriage' above all, 'so much I love his heart'. And we too must love Timon's heart so much if we are to understand Shakespeare's intentions. But why, then, does not the First Stranger help Timon? It is not that kind of play; the First Stranger and his colleagues have no individual dramatic function, for this is not a play of individuals. Look at the list of *dramatic personae* understandingly and the personal names almost vanish—it is only three flattering lords, one false friend, a selfish father, some senators, money lenders and their servants, a faithful steward and some honest servants, a painter, a poet, a jeweller, a merchant, two mistresses, a page, a fool, two banditti; there are left only Timon, Alcibiades, and Apemantus. Look a little longer, and these three, too, to a large extent lose their individual qualities. Apemantus is a fairly simple 'humour' of Railing Envy, Timon is Ideal Bounty and Friendship, Alcibiades alone is a man, a soldier, practical, sensual, yet a true friend, but still barely individualized. But, if we had not realized already the morality nature of this play, we should not for a moment doubt it after the incursion of the Three Strangers: they are symbolical, they sum it up beyond a doubt, as they lift the whole matter to a universal moral level. (pp. 98-9)

For Timon is not only no mere bountiful man, or mere Bounty, but Ideal Bounty, whose twin soul is Ideal Friendship, and you cannot bind such a figure to property and talents. No man could be such a fool as Timon in respect of his money (and yet have been such a great general and pillar of the state), if you once begin to consider Timon as a normal man in a normal non-morality play. In brief, what matters is why Timon is so completely insulated from reality.

'So much I love his heart', says the First Stranger. That is the key to the whole matter. When the Poet, forecasting Timon's tragedy, speaks of 'his good and gracious nature', he is speaking only plain truth. That nature is consumed with an ideal of friendship. Timon's first words in the play are: 'Imprison'd is he, say you?' And at once there follows:

> I am not of that feather to shake off
> My friend when he must need me.
> [I. i. 100-01]

and

> 'Tis not enough to help the feeble up,
> But to support him after.   [I. i. 107-08]
> (p. 100)

The signs of an unfinished play are there, as notably in the incursion of the Fool, but they do not affect the steady development: it builds steadily up to the great scene of Alcibiades before the senate. Now we know what kind of a city this Athens is. Before Timon throws his last 'feast', and is off, mad, to the desert, Shakespeare will teach his lesson beyond mistaking. Or does the scene 'tumble suddenly into the action with the bewildering inconsequence of an episode in a dream'? [See excerpt above by Ellis-Fermor, 1942.]

At a first reading, perhaps, Alcibiades comes to his great stature abruptly. But is it so when the play is seen whole and steadily? After the rather tedious interchange between Timon and Apemantus, Alcibiades is announced with 'some twenty horse'. Arrived, he cries to Timon: 'I feed hungerly on your sight'; and at once they leave the stage. But we must remember the staging: surely Alcibiades has a presence, and his arrival has caused a stir, and the audience has expectations. In the banqueting room his words are few, but he stands apart, drawing one's eyes, for he alone is sincere: he would rather 'be at a breakfast of enemies' 'so they were bleeding new'. In the hall, as they return from hunting, he is Timon's special friend, 'my Alcibiades'; he says nothing; the two of them are off the stage again quickly, and we see him no more until he is before the senate. But on the stage, we have noted him, and so we can, if we will, in the study, a noble figure, isolated in his sincerity, apart from all these flatterers, not involved in the tale of Timon's ruin, for he is a soldier, and feasts and flattery are not his world.

Now this brief, packed, cogent dramatic argument opens, and with its first words we learn what issues from this usuring senate of cold hearts—pitiless fear that strikes ruthlessly at any offender against its security.

> *First Sen.* My lord, you have my voice to it; the fault's
> Bloody; 'tis necessary he should die:
> Nothing emboldens sin so much as mercy.
> *Sec. Sen.* Most true; the law shall bruise him.
> [III. v. 1-4]

From this moment every word tells: it is as telling as the short, packed sentences that speak the verdicts of the jurymen at the trial of Faithful in *Pilgrim's Progress.* . . . Ideal Friendship has been driven to fury and verges upon madness, because, losing its power to be bountiful, it has lost all. Now Alcibiades picks up the theme, his simple, soldierly words quick with irony:

> It pleases time and fortune to lie heavy
> Upon a friend of mine.   [III. v. 10-11]

When he pleads that his soldier saw 'his reputation touch'd to death', he is told he is too paradoxical, 'striving to make an ugly deed look fair'. The argument of the First Senator is all of a kind with the reply of the senators to the pleas of Flavius: this was no true courage of a man to defend his honour—no, 'he's truly valiant that can wisely suffer', and indeed to risk life for honour is 'folly'. Alcibiades can hardly interject a word, as the Second Senator follows the First. But he breaks in, to 'speak like a captain', to argue that such a man as they would have, a man able to endure insult, is no soldier to defend them. Urgently he tries to get at their hearts: 'Who cannot condemn rashness in cold blood?' But from thin, tight lips comes the response: 'You breathe in vain.' Surely the soldier's services to the state at Lacedaemon and Byzantium 'were a sufficient briber for his life'? But the First Senator is either too stupid or too contemptuous to understand. 'What's that?' he asks. (And what had it availed Timon in his pleas that he had 'deserved this hearing' 'even to the state's best health'?) To the Second Senator it is enough that it is said 'his days are foul and his drink dangerous'. Not even the pledge of Alcibiades, knowing how their 'reverend ages love security', to pawn his victories and all his honours in their service will suffice. This soldier's violence has been like a dagger at their cold hearts, and the vehemence of Alcibiades only gives an edge to their grinding fears. 'We are for law: he dies: urge it no more.' When Alcibiades cries, 'My wounds ache at you', they are beyond themselves with rage. Unaccustomed human feeling battering at their hearts' doors begets their furious anger. The soldier shall die, and Alcibiades shall be banished. Nothing must break into the cold security of their money-getting: they are for law, for money is more than men, and law than mercy. Alcibiades, alone, may curse them, and resolve upon revenge, but his banishment makes little stir in this society—a matter of tattle among the jostling crowd pressing into Timon's last feast, a day's wonder that can keep: 'I'll tell you more anon. Here's a noble feast toward.'

So the play has come to its climax and turning point. First, Ideal Friendship, displaying Noble Bounty, has stated its case; gradually, with increasing scope and detail, the baseness of Athenian society has appeared; then, where all have talked of Friendship, and none but Timon has meant it, when the abstract Virtue is almost ready to be transformed to a similarly abstract Vice, a real man has pleaded for his friend, a fellow soldier. This is the true transformation of the old morality play: we start with the general, and come to the particular, remembering with Blake that 'General Forms have their vitality in Particulars; and every Particular is a Man'. And it is most proper that the scene before the senate should come before Timon's last feast. After that, Timon's madness will be monstrous. In his compromise Shakespeare has inevitably had to allow some humanity to Timon, and Timon will appear an incredible monster of a man. But already we have seen how the realization of the true nature of this society affects an ordinary man: every word of Alcibiades before the senate has come from his very human heart, and upon him as a man, not a part-man, part-Virtue, like Timon, what is the effect? A cold, consuming hatred and spirit of revenge. Alcibiades declares himself 'worse than mad' to have been the dupe and tool of men like these. (pp. 102-05)

Shakespeare has given us an unusual play, perhaps a unique play, but surely not so unique that it cannot be seen, especially now, as Hazlitt said it, a piece of peculiarly cogent thinking. When we think of how Shakespeare has exalted his Ideal Friendship and Bounty, let us not see mere stupid extravagance in Timon, but rather feel with Yeats that 'only the wasteful virtues earn the sun'. Let us remember with Wordsworth the lesson:

> Give all thou canst; high Heaven rejects the lore
> Of nicely calculated less and more.

This is one of the plays of Shakespeare that Francis Bacon could not have even begun to write. (pp. 107-08)

A. S. Collins, "'Timon of Athens': A Reconsideration," in The Review of English Studies, *Vol. 22, No. 88, October, 1946, pp. 96-108.*

KENNETH MUIR (essay date 1947)

[*In his refutation of Caroline F.E. Spurgeon's argument that "gold" is not the unifying symbol in* Timon *(see excerpt above, 1935), Muir puts forth an interpretation of the play which recalls that of John W. Draper (1934): that* Timon *represents Shakespeare's commentary on the collapse of the traditional order of his age and the growth of capitalism as the sole means of human interaction. The essay from which the following excerpt is taken was originally published in* Modern Quarterly Miscellany *in 1947.*]

Miss Spurgeon, in a footnote, unjustly disposed of Wilson Knight's essay on *Timon of Athens* [see excerpts above, 1935 and 1930]; for though she was perfectly right to say that there is no gold imagery in the play, she was wrong to brush aside the two hundred references to gold. As the essential nature of an image is that it should throw light on an idea or object by means of a comparison, it was impossible for Shakespeare to use gold as the basis of his imagery. But gold-symbolism is used throughout the play. Wilson Knight claims that it is used as a symbol of Timon's golden heart; but its significance is surely not this. He is nearer the truth when he suggests that there is 'a contrast between gold and the heart's blood of passionate love of which it is a sacrament: the association of the metaphorical value of gold and the value of love'. Gold is also a symbol of man's greed and of the economic basis of society. It is a symbol of the way in which the means of generosity corrupt the recipient, and of the way in which gross inequality in society destroys disinterestedness in love. It is not only Timon's friends who are corrupted by the wealth he dispenses. Timon himself is prevented from being fully human by the weight of his own riches, as Lear was by the weight of Authority. Timon tried to buy love with gold and was himself guilty, to a lesser extent, of the fault for which he blamed his friends. (p. 66)

In Athens, it is clear, love is a commodity like everything else. The only women we see are masquers and harlots. The sex nausea of Timon is an appropriate criticism of a society which is dominated by the acquisitive principle, a society which is bound together by what Marx calls the cash-nexus. (p. 67)

Some of the most impressive speeches in [*Timon*] describe the overthrowing of order by the power of gold. Shakespeare chooses as his hero, not a king, a statesman, or a great warrior, but a man whose eminence depends entirely on his wealth, and whose power vanishes with his wealth. It is as though he realized, at the beginning of the capitalist era, that power was shifting from one class to another and that authority was decreasingly invested in the nominal rulers. It is for this reason that the play may be said to continue the debate on order and authority. Money, the new basis of authority, is the destroyer of order. The intricate and all-embracing idea of order, inherited from the medieval world, may have been undermined by Luther, Copernicus, and Machiavelli; but Hooker's conception of order differs very little from that of pre-Reformation thinkers, the new astronomy substitued a new order for that which it disproved, and Machiavelli, though his influence on political morality was disintegrating, was primarily concerned with the maintenance of order in the State. Shakespeare, even though he may have accepted Copernican theories with his mind, continued to assume the Ptolemaic system in his poetry. He could reject Machiavellianism as a temporary aberration. But the new domination of money was clearly a threat to the conception of order Shakespeare shared with his contemporaries: it substituted for it an order divorced from morality, an authority without responsibility, a power animated entirely by self-interest.

When Timon, digging for roots, discovers gold, he exclaims:

> Gold? Yellow, glittering, precious gold? No, gods,
> I am no idle votarist. Roots, you clear heavens!
> Thus much of this will make black white, foul fair,
> Wrong right, base noble, old young, coward valiant.
>
> [IV. iii. 26-30]

There follow the scenes with Alcibiades and Apemantus. Just before the latter goes out, Timon again addresses the newly found gold:

> O thou sweet king-killer, and dear divorce
> 'Twixt natural son and sire! thou bright defiler
> Of Hymen's purest bed! thou valiant Mars!
>
> [IV. iii. 381-83]

In the work from which I have already quoted . . . Marx quotes both the above passages. . . . Marx then provides the following analysis and commentary [see excerpt above, 1844]. . . . (pp. 69-71)

Marx uses the quotations from *Timon of Athens* to support his criticisms of an acquisitive society. One might go further and say that some of these criticisms were suggested by Shakespeare, and that Shakespeare was one of the spiritual godparents of the *Communist Manifesto*. Marx would doubtless have become a Communist even if he had never read *Timon of Athens*, but his reading of that play helped him to crystallize his ideas. (p. 75)

Kenneth Muir, "'Timon of Athens' and the Cash-Nexus," in his The Singularity of Shakespeare and Other Essays, *Barnes & Noble, 1977, pp. 56-75.*

J. C. MAXWELL (essay date 1948)

[*Maxwell contends that in portraying Timon as he did, Shakespeare was not attempting an edifying portrait of "Noble Bounty"—as argued by A. S. Collins (1946)—but instead a critical dramatization of an individual's excessive luxury in both virtue and vice. In this respect, Maxwell's assessment comes closest to the conclusions of William Richardson (1784), August Wilhelm Schlegel (1808), Hermann Ulrici (1839), and Denton J. Snider (1887), all of whom see in Timon's generosity a misunderstanding of the real world and a tendency towards self-gratification.*]

There is perhaps no other play of Shakespeare in which attention is so much concentrated on the central figure [as in *Timon*], and even a slight misinterpretation of the way in which he is presented will gravely impair the understanding of the whole play. In this it differs somewhat from most of the other plays, in which there are a number of firmly placed characters to give us our bearings, so that if we make a mistake about one, we can pull ourselves up by seeing that our reading does not fit into the general pattern. *Timon* is not devoid of pointers of this kind, but they are less obtrusive, and so error can propagate itself more easily.

The majority of critics have seen that the presentation of Timon is intensely critical throughout. His character has no balance or coherence; as Apemantus says: 'The middle of humanity thou never knewest, but the extremity of both ends'—and this in behaviour as well as in fortune. On this score at least, there can be no objection to the sharp duality in the structure of the play—it is a clear schematic presentation of an unintegrated personality. And we are prepared for what happens right from the start: the Jacobean audience can have had no difficulty in making the right response to prodigality and susceptibility to flattery. (p. 196)

The play is perhaps the one which, of all Shakespeare's, falls most easily within the framework of an Aristotelian moral scheme, and Timon, both before and after his fall, is clearly an example of excess. Prodigality is a vice, but the natural disposition on which it depends is intrinsically good, and, if properly directed by reason, manifests itself in the virtue of generosity. Potentially, then, Timon does possess all the noble qualities with which he is credited. If anything more is required to account for the force with which the Stranger in particular expresses himself [III. i], it can be found in the fact that, whatever Timon's faults, he has certainly been wronged by those whom he has benefited—even unreasoning prodigality creates some claim to requital. Moreover Timon's prodigality is shown as a particular manifestation of the pursuit of false values by Athens as a community—he has been corrupted by the corruption of the state. To take only one instance in which this motif is employed, when the senators propose to Timon that he should return to Athens they offer him—significant juxtaposition—'heaps and sums of love and wealth'. . . . (p. 197)

[The] crucial opening scene holds the balance delicately between the two extremes to be avoided in our attitude towards Timon. It is the one scene in which there is clear indication of genuine personal feeling in his generosity, and it is shown in contrast with a typical representative of the spirit of Athens, the 'old Athenian'. . . . Timon cannot really overcome it; he can only outbid it in its own currency of gold—and it is a further irony that he cannot, by now, even do that: the audience is already conscious that his 'to build his fortune I will strain a little' is a grim understatement of his financial embarrassments. This theme of the impossibility of genuinely defeating the ethos of Athens is perhaps best expressed in a passage of detached comment at the end of the scene, where one of the Lords remarks: 'no gift to him But breeds the giver a return exceeding All use of quittance' [I. i. 278-80]. We are soon to learn that Timon has been having recourse to usurers in the literal sense, but the implications of these lines are more profound: by his habit of lavish recompense Timon is turning even those who ostensibly give him free gifts into usurers, more

successful usurers than the real ones: the word 'breeds' evokes all the traditional doctrines about 'barren metal'. In this sense of the guilt shared both by lender and borrower, and infecting all transactions in a usurious society, lies the advance in complexity in Shakespeare's treatment of usury since *The Merchant of Venice*. For this reason, I am unable to go very far with J. W. Draper [see excerpt above, 1934], who uses the fact that the theme occurs in both plays as evidence for an idealizing picture of Timon as 'a sort of liberal young Bassanio, who, without the moneyed backing of Antonio and Portia, experienced to his sorrow the hard economic facts of the Jacobean age'. In the fairytale atmosphere of *The Merchant of Venice* we have a clear naïve contrast between good and bad; there is no consciousness that Antonio and Bassanio are contributing to the debasement of moral standards by having recourse to Shylock, who can be lightheartedly treated as a scapegoat. No doubt Draper is right in suggesting that the Jacobean audience would still have been willing to accept a presentation in these terms, but Shakespeare was no longer prepared to give it to them. In *The Merchant of Venice* there is no criticism implied of Antonio, whose losses were 'enow to press a royal merchant down' [IV. i. 29], in the more politically conscious milieu of *Timon*, as I hope to show, words like 'royal' have a different connotation.

This first scene has foreshadowed the approaching fall, and has shown us in some measure how even the more genuinely fine sides of Timon's nature are corrupted by the spirit of his society, but on the whole we have so far seen him at his best. It is in the second scene that his failings become more apparent. It is here that the conceptions of 'bounty' and 'goodness' begin to receive penetrating criticism. Already in I, ii, the merchant's obviously interested reference to Timon's 'untirable and continuate goodness' has caught our attention. Perhaps we are already meant to have a sense of its being too much 'on tap'— 'automatic' in Campbell's phrase . . .—and when Lucilius says 'never may That state or fortune fall into my keeping Which is not owed to you!' it is clear that Timon is in danger of complacently accepting superhuman honours. But in the second scene this aspect of the treatment is greatly elaborated, and there is much more stress on Timon's attitude towards his own behaviour. He has no true sense of reciprocity in friendship: 'there's none Can truly say he gives if he receives', and if he seems to recant that later in the scene—'what need we have any friends, if we should ne'er have need of them?'—the contradiction merely emphasizes his irresponsible attitude, and throughout this speech his ideal of 'brothers commanding one another's fortunes' does not get beyond the stage of daydreaming. By this time it has already been clearly indicated that Timon is not merely emotionally self-indulgent but also presumptuous. Apemantus has struck the warning note with his gnomic: 'Feasts are too proud to give thanks to the gods', and once the true situation of Timon's fortunes has been revealed by Flavius, the references come faster. Timon, says one of the Lords, is 'the very soul of bounty'. He himself says: 'Methinks, I could deal kingdoms to my friends, And ne'er be weary', and he regrets that Apemantus baulks him in the indulgence of his temperament: 'if thou wert not sullen, I would be good to thee'. It is not merely that he lives in an unreal world: he is soaring, like Icarus . . . , into a sphere that is not his as a man and a private individual. The honours he aspires to are now royal, now even divine. Right to the end he clings to these presumptions, and when he finally takes leave of the world, it is as a king manqué, and with an exhortation to his macrocosmic counterpart to join him in oblivion: 'Sun, hide thy beams! Timon hath done his reign' [V. i. 223]. (pp. 198-200)

The critical attitude towards this sort of 'goodness' is firmly established by the time we come, after the fall, to Flavius's paradoxical summing-up of Timon's fate:

> Undone by goodness. Strange, unusual blood,
> When man's worst sin is, he does too much good!
> Who then dares to be half so kind again?
> For bounty, that makes gods, does still mar men.
> [IV. ii. 38-41]

I think Shakespeare is here using his gnomic technique with a good deal of subtlety. We are meant to accept what Flavius says, but not to regard him as having adequate insight into Timon's nature, and the special connotations that the play has given to 'goodness' and 'bounty' enable us to achieve both these ends at once. For Flavius, his old master is in a straight-forward sense 'too good for this world', but the audience is meant to take his comments, which for the speaker are really a confession of inability to understand the ways of the universe, as literal truth. The audience can see, if Flavius—his heart stronger than his head—cannot, that an attempt on the part of man to ape divine bounty, ever spontaneously giving without receiving anything in return, is presumptuous and must inevitably be frustrated. It is characteristic of Timon that he cannot grasp the notion of the necessary reciprocity of creation. This is the point of the curious lines, IV, iii, 436-42, beginning: 'the sun's a thief'. Since for Timon giving must be only giving, receiving only receiving, even if he has in his adversity expected a reversal of the roles, the normal processes of give-and-take in nature appear as thievery, on the analogy of the corrupted society of Athens, which has also lost the notion of reciprocity; which has, indeed, destroyed it in Timon's mind. Flavius's own goodness, in contrast, is the genuine, human thing, his determination to seek out Timon and serve him is immediately and ironically followed by Timon's soliloquy: 'O blessed breeding sun'. And human, *costing* generosity has already been presented in III, v, a scene introducing a motif which I suspect Shakespeare would have exploited more fully if he had completed the play. Alcibiades, who pleads for his friend's life, and has kept back the state's foes is 'rich only in large hurts'. . . . (p. 201)

The following of these themes through the play has, I hope, shown the coherence of Shakespeare's attitude towards Timon's 'bounty'. It is now time to look more closely at certain peculiarities of the play's structure. It is only a very superficial study that can give rise to the judgment sometimes made that it is really two plays 'casually joined at the middle' [see excerpt above by Mark Van Doren, 1939]. But some of the defences of Shakespeare against charges that need never have been brought are unsatisfactory. Several critics have commented on the 'bare nature of the drama' (Campbell), and the 'queer formal schematism' . . . , and both Van Doren and A. S. Collins [see excerpt above, 1946] stress the abstract, morality treatment. This is clearly an element in the play's technique, but neither of these critics has escaped the danger of treating forms and conventions as if they had more explanatory force than they have. When, for instance, Van Doren writes: 'Timon is not so much a man as a figure representing Munificence, an abstraction in whom madness may not matter' . . . , one asks why should it not matter. If the Morality convention had this sort of irrelevance to real problems, it would be a curiously frivolous thing. And in fact there is no need for any such subterfuges. Timon is, if you like, a simplified, schematized figure; but Shakespeare makes it quite clear that his madness does 'matter', that his prodigality is to be judged by ordinary moral

standards. Equally inacceptable is Collins's version in which 'the abstract Virtue' of Bounty is transformed 'to a similarly abstract Vice'. . . . Collins does not really, as the better parts of his valuable essay show, read the play as any such unearthly ballet of bloodless categories, but he is betrayed into this account through taking as the moral of the early acts that 'such Ideal Bounty should have infinity of riches to draw on, for it is Noble Bounty'. . . . That, complete to the capital letters, is no doubt how Timon sees himself in the distorting mirror provided by his flatterers, but it is not how the audience sees him, and it does not make sense of the play. The two halves of it are contrasting studies in excess, and both excesses quite intelligibly belong to the same character. This element of the play is summed up in Timon's reply to Apemantus's statement that he is proud 'that I was No prodigal'—'I, that I am one now' [IV. iii. 278-79]. It is the same nature that, according to circumstances and the twist they have given him, can turn to love or hate, but to each with prodigality, and the gold that embodies the corrupted and corrupting spirit of Athens affords an equally fit instrument for the expression of each.

Timon's invective has often been compared with that of Lear. . . . The difference between him and Lear after their falls is that Lear learns by his misfortune as Timon does not. That does not mean that there is no substance in his tirades—much of them consists of the stock-in-trade of the traditional moral satirist—but there is no hint of insight or wisdom behind them. One might express the difference between Lear and Timon by saying that Lear in affliction comes to *see* as he never did before; the utmost Timon attains to is to *see through* particular shams and injustices. Unlike Lear who finally welcomes and values love, he grudges it when the disinterested affection of Flavius forces him to modify his wholesale condemnation of mankind [IV. iii. 495ff.]. When, a few lines earlier, he has said: 'I never had honest man about me; ay all I kept were knaves, to serve in meat to villains' [IV. iii. 477-78], he has not merely exaggerated, he has been utterly wrong, since at the risk of undue simplification Shakespeare has insisted that all Timon's servants, in contrast to his flatterers, are faithful to him and have a genuine affection for him [IV. ii]. The picture is perhaps modified by the curious incomplete suggestions of a wisdom by withdrawal to be achieved only in death, but there is no direct connection between that and his sufferings—it is *'nothing'* that brings him 'all things' [V. i. 188].

If Collins invokes the morality form in order to escape seeing some of the very un-ideal elements in the presentation of Timon's 'bounty', Campbell's classification of the play as through and through satiric errs in the opposite direction. The comparison with Jonson's *Sejanus* and *Volpone* illuminates much, but it involves cavalier treatment of several portions of the play, and leads Campbell into at least one manifest misreading of what actually happens. It is part of his thesis that an attitude of scorn and mockery persists right to the end, and in order to help him to believe this he has persuaded himself to follow those critics who have held that Timon's death is suicide, a view for which the text affords no warrant. Reaction against what he regards as the sentimentality of Wilson Knight and Van Doren has induced in him such a hardboiled attitude that he can write: 'even his choice of a grave is food for scorn' . . . , and quote in the same paragraph:

> Come not to me again; but say to Athens,
> Timon hath made his everlasting mansion
> Upon the beached verge of the salt flood,

> Who once a day with his embossed froth
> The turbulent surge shall cover: thither come,
> And let my grave-stone be your oracle.
>
>   [V. i. 214-19]

One may distrust such biographical conjectures as that 'in Timon's tomb Shakespeare buried his own bitterness', but to deny that something has happened to Timon here that does not happen to Sejanus or Volpone is to refuse to read the text. So with:

> my long sickness
> Of health and living now begins to mend,
> And nothing brings me all things.
>
>   [V. i. 186-88]

It is perhaps a fair comment that this is fragmentary, that Shakespeare has not really developed it organically out of the theme, even that failure to do so may have been his reason for abandoning the play unfinished, but it is no good pretending that it is not there: and it disrupts Campbell's neat scheme.

Having followed Timon's progress to this intangible and mysterious consummation (which is itself qualified by the admittedly 'satiric' final couplet uttered by Timon: V. i. 222-23), I must turn to a brief consideration of some of the subordinate themes of the play, which bear, more than the central one, the marks of incompleteness. The political theme of the corruption and materialism of Athenian society I have referred to at several points. . . . It is not, I think, notably incomplete except where it interlocks with the Alcibiades theme. Most critics have seen the importance of the contrast between Timon and Alcibiades in their responses to Athenian baseness. Collins has given perhaps the best account of what Alcibiades means for the play, in stressing how in III, v, 'a real man has pleaded for his friend' . . . , and how, at the end of the play with Alcibiades' return to Athens 'sanity, with common decency, is restored: there shall be human-heartedness again' . . . ; but he destroys some of the effect of his criticism by exaggerating the contrast in technique between the handling of Timon and that of Alcibiades—the criticism of Timon that is implied in the figure of Alcibiades is much more telling than it would be if Timon were, as Collins writes, an 'abstract Virtue almost ready to be transformed to a similarly abstract Vice'. . . . In fact it is hard to see how a play could successfully work simultaneously on those two levels. The contrast is not . . . between Idealism and Realism but between an inhuman excess and a balanced humanity. Alcibiades can see what is wrong with Athens: 'Banish usury' [III. v. 98], and he is not provoked to indiscriminate hatred: 'I will use the olive with my sword' [V. iv. 82]. Only the outlines of the theme are indicated, but the intention is clear. The other exemplar of human-heartedness in the play, the steward Flavius, is treated in more detail, in several of Shakespeare's most tenderly beautiful scenes. (I find it significant that Campbell, in making out the treatment to be satirical throughout, is led to ignore the roles of both Flavius and Alcibiades in the play). In him, and in Timon's other servants, we see genuine personal affection, contrasting strongly with Timon's automatism.

In the absence of a full development of the Alcibiades theme, the other main contrast of the play, that between Timon and Apemantus, perhaps assumes undue prominence. Here there is no doubt that especially in Act IV this part of the play is relatively near completion. There is less of Apemantus in the first three Acts, but perhaps about as much as Shakespeare meant there to be. In the earlier scenes, Apemantus falls easily

enough under the type of 'scurrilous and profane jester' first introduced by Jonson in *Every Man out of his Humour* in the person of Carlo Buffone. No radical criticism of a specific kind is conveyed by his railing. In Act IV he is able to argue with Timon on equal terms, and is given some of the most impressive poetry of the play. In spite of this and in spite of the superficially keen play of dialectic, he seems even more ineffective than before. In the earlier scene his effectiveness had been neutralized in advance by the information that

> even he drops down
> The knee before him, and returns in peace,
> Most rich in Timon's love.   [I. i. 60-2]

And in Act IV the audience knows that he is arguing on false premises, since Timon has discovered his new store of gold, and does not act the misanthrope 'enforcedly' [IV. iii. 241]. But even if this were not so, we can see that Timon would still be right in saying 'thou flatter'st misery' [IV. iii. 234]. Apemantus's speech beginning 'thou has cast away thyself' [IV. iii. 219] is such a characteristic piece of Shakespeare's mature verse that we tend to overlook how unnecessary it is for Timon to have all this pointed out to him. It is not only unnecessary, it becomes clear as the scene proceeds that from Timon's point of view it is a falsely romantic picture. Apemantus for all his cynicism has a picture of a finely incorruptible 'nature' refusing to flatter man—a picture made in his own image, and one to which, in turn, he strives to approximate even more closely. The core of Timon's criticism of cynicism is in the long speech beginning at IV, iii, 327: 'a beastly ambition'. The real animal world, in contrast to Apemantus's idealized picture, is just as full of conflict and inequality as the human—'what beast couldst thou be, that were not subject to a beast'. If Timon himself later wishes 'that beasts may have the world in empire', it is from pure hatred of mankind, not from any idealization of beasts. All this does not mean that we are asked to share Timon's total vision—I have already commented on the failure of insight shown in the speech, 'the sun's a thief'—but it does dispose of Apemantus's essentially sentimental and self-indulgent cynicism. One could have prophesied Shakespeare's attitude towards a philosophy of life that took the dog as its ideal.

It would be natural to hope to follow up a piece-meal treatment of themes by an attempt to see them together in a coherent picture, and it is the radical criticism of the play that, unless I have badly failed to read it aright, this is not possible. At a highly abstract level, it is easier to summarize without serious distortion than any other of the plays. To say that it is a study of a potentially noble but unbalanced and prodigal nature, corrupted by a usurious and materialistic society with its flattery, and thrown off his balance and plunged into an equally extreme and indiscriminate misanthropy when the loss of his wealth discovers the falsehood of his friends—to say this is probably a less hopelessly inadequate account of 'what the play is about' than could be given for any other important play of Shakespeare. But once we descend from such generalities, and attempt an analysis in terms of individual themes, there seems to be less over and above, or rather encompassing, those themes than in the greatest works. Each is worked out with passion and brilliance, though to different degrees of completeness; yet whole-hearted encomiums of the play as a whole always give the impression of special pleading, and all attempts to make it out to be all of a piece are unduly schematic and incomplete. Nor does this mean simply that the play is too rich and varied to be brought under a systematic description. On the contrary one feels that it is a play that ought to have been neat and shapely—it aims more at the qualities of *Coriolanus* than of *Antony and Cleopatra* or *Lear,* and it has the promise of a more interesting and profound play than *Coriolanus.* It is easy to be wise after the event, and to say that Shakespeare chose a theme that was too exaggerated or too monotonous or what you will. There is no harm in such conjecture. All we can say for certain—a few critics would deny even this—is that Shakespeare did not bring his work on the play to a satisfying state of completion. That he could not have done so, who would venture to say? (pp. 203-08)

> *J. C. Maxwell, "'Timon of Athens',"* in Scrutiny, *Vol. XV, No. 3, Summer, 1948, pp. 195-208.*

G. WILSON KNIGHT   (essay date 1948)

[*In the following excerpt, Knight continues his interpretation of* Timon *which he first began in his influential study* The Wheel of Fire *(see excerpt above, 1930).*]

Timon of Athens is the most revealing of Shakespeare's tragedies. Horror at ingratitude, a primary theme throughout the plays, is here raised to titanic, almost grotesque, proportion and extended to a condemnation of man and all his works of oppression, dishonesty, and greed, with imprecations of war. Shakespeare writes at a period when a time-honoured feudal order was rapidly disintegrating before a rising commercialism. He feels something of great worth and aristocratic value slipping away, while the acquisitive instincts, freed from traditional checks, wait to push mankind towards chaos. . . . [Timon] is, indeed, Shakespeare's 'superman', and therefore inclusive. He contains the courtier-grace of Hamlet, the soldiership of Othello and Antony, the pride of Coriolanus, the disillusioned agony of Lear, together with the inherent princeliness of the not dissimilar Richard II and the noble magnanimity of Theseus; but the criminal types, Richard III and Macbeth, are not reflected. In Timon's rejection of Athens and imprecation of disasters on a people grown decadent with greed and ease the poetic genius of Shakespeare, from a Nietzschean standpoint, summons to account—as did Goethe's *Faust*—the future civilisation of the western world.

Money, to-day, percolates everywhere, and is in peacetime all but the main currency of human intercourse; and, as property and private power, relates most intimately to that individual personality with which all poetry is primarily concerned; so that, in studying, normally, everything but economics, great poetry necessarily studies, though indirectly, economics too. Now *Timon of Athens,* perhaps alone in the history of highest drama, directly witnesses this identity, imposing on the crude facts of human greed and selfishness the mighty periods of great poetry. Timon in his self-chosen banishment from man addresses the gold he has dug from earth as the 'common whore of mankind' that sets 'odds among the rout of nations' [IV. iii. 43-4]. Yet his almost loving, if ironic, respect is also significant:

> O thou sweet king-killer, and dear divorce
> 'Twixt natural son and sire; thou bright defiler
> Of Hymen's purest bed, thou valiant Mars,
> Thou every young, fresh, lov'd and delicate wooer,
> Whose blush doth thaw the consecrated snow
> That lies on Dian's lap! thou visible god,
> That solder'st close impossibilities,
> And mak'st them kiss; that speak'st with every tongue,

> To every purpose: O thou touch of hearts!
> Think thy slave man rebels, and by thy virtue
> Set them into confounding odds, that beasts
> May have the world in empire!
>
> [IV. iii. 381-92]

The gold is felt as power, as 'virtue', itself an essence, a divinity almost; and in this central 'virtue' Timon, unlike Apemantus, never quite loses trust. The fault lies not in man's deepest instincts, but in his use of them; in the grasping partiality, but not the inspiration, of his craving. (pp. 223-24)

Each curse of Timon is barbed by a truth and winged by fierce love, while the gold he discovers in his wild retreat, which he hands, with imprecations, to those who visit him, symbolises still his compulsion to give, to expend himself, though with bitterest denunciations. The new-found gold remains symptomatic of that soul-worth Athens—or London—has rejected. His continued obsession with it signifies a respect, which Apemantus could never have understood, for the gold-essence, the dynamic within the straining upward of man's virtues and vices alike, for that royal heritage and destiny being desecrated. Timon personifies that princely essence. Oedipus was banished from Thebes as unclean that his city might survive; but Athens suicidally rejects its own potential saviour and golden wisdom. Timon is the inmost genius of man throughout the centuries unwanted and thence embittered by man's own degraded social consciousness. He is all but poetry incarnate and his story, like that of Hamlet or Prospero, the story of genius in any age. . . . (pp. 225-26)

We must, indeed, respond not merely to the language but also to the drama, which involves visualisation. Timon's deliberately assumed nakedness during the latter scenes is deeply significant, confronting human vice with the physical impact of an essential humanity. . . . [And] just as the crucified Christ challenges through the centuries man's self-seeking head-culture not by argument, nor even alone by poetic speech, but pre-eminently by his body, so Timon, through a dramatic conception of staggering simplicity recalling the contrast of coin and human life in *The Merchant of Venice,* hurls at man not only metallic gold but also the other golden powers of the human form.

The long falling movement of *Timon of Athens* is indeed less a human narrative than a cosmic exploration, like Shelley's *Prometheus* or the *Book of Job.* The individual soul has proved unable to realise its own perfection in social intercourse and the world of sense-enjoyment; and beyond Swiftian rejections looms the yet darker record of a complete mental and emotional severance from all temporal commitments whatsoever, calling down through a succession of mighty speeches that sense of the numinous, of other-worldly powers and presences—what Nietzsche called the Dionysian as opposed to the Apollonian—usually attending only the final impact of great tragedy. Timon's hate is nearer prophecy than neurosis and his denunciations are Hebraic. At the last he is, like Wordsworth's Newton [in *The Prelude*], felt as 'voyaging through strange seas of thought, alone' . . . , more truly at home with a wild nature, a surging ocean, and imagery of sun and moon, than human purposes. Into such infinities his story fades. (pp. 227-28)

> *G. Wilson Knight, "King and Superman,"* in his Christ and Nietzsche: An Essay in Poetic Wisdom, *Staples Press, 1948, pp. 219-38.*

G. B. HARRISON   (essay date 1951)

[*Harrison agrees with E. K. Chambers (1908) that Shakespeare probably left* Timon *unfinished; but whereas Chambers believed its incompletion was a result of the poet's mental breakdown, Harrison suggests that Shakespeare abandoned the project out of sheer boredom. He calls the play neither a tragedy nor a tragicomedy, but a "misanthropy," based solely around the railings of one or more characters. For more on the authorship of* Timon *and its place in Shakespeare's canon, see the essays by Charles Knight (1843), Gulian C. Verplanck (1847), F. G. Fleay (1874), George Brandes (1895-96), Walter Raleigh (1907), Una Ellis-Fermor (1942), and Charlton Hinman (1969).]*

Timon of Athens was included with the Tragedies by the editors of the First Folio but apparently as an afterthought. . . . It could hardly be called Comedy, if that word was to be associated with laughter, even with derisive laughter, or to denote a play without an unhappy ending. Neither was it a tragedy, however loosely the word might be defined, nor even a mongrel tragi-comedy. It belongs rather to a kind of drama for which enough specimens remain to justify a new category—Misanthropy. Misanthropies are plays designed mainly to display the rottenness of human nature. They always include scenes of sordid meanness and one or more persons who rail on humanity at considerable length and with great satisfaction to themselves. Plays of this kind were particularly fashionable in the decade 1598 to 1608 when Ben Jonson's *Every Man in his Humour* and its successors popularized the mode.

Nevertheless, even as a Misanthropy, *Timon* is an unsuccessful play seldom acted or read except by students and, to add to the difficulties, the text is distressingly uneven. At times the play runs smoothly, with speeches well written and the action consistent, and then for whole scenes the diction breaks down completely and is neither blank verse, rhymed verse, free verse or prose, but a medley of all four. (p. 253)

[The] first scenes reveal the essential weakness of the play, which is more of a morality than a drama. All the characters are personifications and none at any time becomes an individual. Timon is simply Reckless Prodigality; he has no human relations, no wife, child, parent, friend or even mistress. He remains therefore a type for whom we may feel neither intimacy nor common interest; nor is his nobility or his friendship impressive, for his good deeds are merely acts of the purse which in no way discommode him. Of the other characters, Apemantus is a wearisome convention who does nothing but rail, while the steward, like dear old Adam in *As You Like It*, is no more than Faithful Service. Even Alcibiades is but vaguely sketched as a typical gay young soldier. (pp. 258-59)

Timon is in every way an unsatisfactory play. Apart from the curiously chaotic verse and a last Act which is little more than disjointed fragments, there are two noticeable weaknesses. The first is that, though some of the best speeches and incidents would be effective on the stage, the play is full of imitations and echoes; it is second-hand work, Shakespeare repeating or paraphrasing himself, or borrowing ideas from others because his own inspiration is flat. There is more than a suggestion of Jonson's *Volpone*, which the King's Men had acted in 1606. The theme in both plays is that all men are vendible and will do anything for gold. In Jonson's play Volpone amuses himself by exploiting this venality of his fellows, who will commit any sin for the sake of riches. Volpone is a rogue, but he has a shrewd, though depraved, sense of values. Timon, however, is a simple-minded lord and learns of the depravity of man by the hard way of experience.

The conception of Timon's character is another weakness in the play, for the moral values are confused and perverted; and a moral sense, it was suggested, is an essential ingredient of

true tragedy. . . . Timon is another specimen of the prodigal, but with this difference, that the Prodigal Son of the parable realized that he had made a fool of himself, repented, and went home to ask forgiveness and to start afresh. It never occurs to Timon to blame himself for an elementary lack of common prudence. Instead, he heaps curses on mankind, which may be justified, but not in Timon's mouth. From the beginning to the end he is essentially stupid, and the moralizings of fools are not to be taken too seriously. There might indeed have been a fine tragedy, even in this conception of the character, for stupidity is one of the major ingredients in the tragedy of Lear, Othello and Macbeth; but in truth Shakespeare seems not to have regarded Timon as a tragic figure.

How then can this failure be explained? (pp. 267-68)

Shakespeare was a working playwright, and he did not forget his public or his fellows. When *Richard II* was selling well in print, he followed it up with a sequel in the *First Part of Henry IV*. When Falstaff was surprisingly popular in the first part of the play, he hastily extended the successful features into the second part. When Queen Elizabeth demanded Falstaff in love, he obliged with the *Merry Wives*. When some piece of Scottish history was needed to please King James, he wrote *Macbeth*. So here, it is not too much to guess that someone—his fellows, maybe, or one of his patrons—suggested that Shakespeare should write a Misanthropy, a play about Timon.

He knew the general outline of the story, and he went back to his Plutarch and re-read the brief anecdote of Timon. Then he sketched out a plot and started to write; but the theme was elusive. He had already emptied himself of his own misanthropy in Thersites, in Lear, in Coriolanus. The vein was exhausted and the best he could do was to repeat himself or to imitate others. Inventiveness ran dry and speeches refused to come alive. He laid the papers away. Besides, the public had had a surfeit of these railing fellows, and now that Beaumont and Fletcher were beginning to write for the King's Men, the new tragi-comedies were all the fashion. Chambers was right in supposing that *Timon of Athens* was never finished, but the reason was not mental breakdown but sheer boredom. (pp. 269-70)

> G. B. Harrison, "'Timon of Athens'," in his Shakespeare's Tragedies, *Routledge and Kegan Paul Ltd, 1951, pp. 253-70.*

W. M. MERCHANT (essay date 1955)

[Focusing on the opening scene between the painter and the poet, Merchant defines the two major themes in Timon: *the conflict between "deceitful appearance" and reality and the betrayal of trust and friendship. Merchant demonstrates how Shakespeare dramatically fuses these two themes in the character of Timon.]*

In the opening scene [of *Timon of Athens*] the poet and painter are given a long passage of close and technical discussion which is manifestly disproportionate if the sole function of the introductory scenes is to show Timon's uncritical bounty to his friends. Their argument concerns the mystery of their crafts. The painter has brought to Timon a portrait which the poet praises in terms both of contemporary rhetorical gesture and of the "expressionism" of Italian renaissance figure-painting

> How this grace
> Speakes his owne standing; what a mentall power

This eye shootes forth. How bigge imagination
Moves in this Lip, to th'dumbnesse of the gesture
One might interpret.

[I. i. 30-4]

From this praise it is but a short step to another contemporary commonplace, to considering art as imitation, counterfeiting life:

It is a pretty mocking of the life:
Heere is a touch: Is't good?

[I. i. 35-6]

to which the poet responds:

I will say of it,
It Tutors Nature, Artificiall strife
Lives in these toutches, livelier then life.

[I. i. 36-8]

This theme, with ironic undertones, is to be resumed later in the play . . . , but meanwhile the two artists have still a lengthy dialogue before their introduction of the play is complete. It becomes the poet's turn to demonstrate his craft. He does so by summarizing an allegorical poem reflecting on Timon's state, the subject of which is Fortune, enthroned and on a high hill. This exaltation of Timon in the poem corresponds to the "bigge imagination" of the painter's portrait. But the poetic allegory goes further than the painter's analysis of "magnificence"; its description of Timon's sycophantic adherents, loyal so long as his fortune holds, but with hurried withdrawal at his decline in fortune, serves as a prologue to the play and an epitome of it; it directs attention not so much to the pernicious nature of wealth as to the dual theme of the false appearance of friendship and the uncertainty of fortune.

But this does not exhaust the function and argument of the prologue. The painter comes back with a counterclaim; he declares that the poem employs a characteristic theme of the painter's art:

This Throne, this Fortune, and this Hill me thinkes
. . . Would be well exprest
In our Condition.

[I. i. 73-6]

The poet brushes the interruption aside with a description of the life and movement of the poem, implying a contrast with the static quality of the painter's art. But he has an adequate technical riposte:

A thousand morall Paintings I can shew,
That shall demonstrate these quicke blowes of Fortunes
More pregnantly then words.

[I. i. 90-2]

And the claim is just; allowing for the pardonable exaggeration in "a thousand morall Paintings", he refers quite rightly to the mediaeval allegory of Fortune set, and sometimes enthroned, on a high hill, and he claims very properly that in this allegorizing the painter's art is not static. The mediaeval device of multiple action in one setting was admirably suited to render mutability; it is found not infrequently in tapestry and painted cloth in Shakespeare's own day, and has an immediate relevance to stage practice. (pp. 249-50)

But there is a further interest in the dialogue, in the deeper rivalry implied between poet and painter—"more pregnantly than words". Professor Anthony Blunt has drawn attention here to a probable echo of the *Paragone* controversy in which

Leonardo da Vinci was a principal protagonist. This controversy concerned the status of the painter in society and his refusal to accept a position lower in the scale than the poet's. (pp. 250-51)

This controversy had two main aspects. The one which mainly concerned Leonardo was his struggle to obtain recognition for painting as a liberal art. . . . The other aspect is more fundamental: it claims for the visual arts, which constantly lay under judgment as panders to the lust of the eyes, an insight into reality which had until the high renaissance been reserved for the operation of "the word", philosophy and poetry. By Shakespeare's day the controversy, still active, had clarified itself. The artist's status in society was scarcely now in question. (p. 251)

If then, as seems likely, Shakespeare was commenting in the opening scenes of *Timon of Athens* on the material of the *Paragone* argument which had become a commonplace of intellectual society, he explores there not its more obvious social elements, but its profounder implications, the competence with which painting and poetry render "appearance" as a revelation of "reality".

At this point the function of the dialogue between the poet and the painter as a prologue to the play is complete. They have established one aspect of the theme, man's subordination to Fortune; they have stated the case for the status of their respective arts in the intellectual economy of society; now the two artists are brought into the current of the plot itself. With the entrance of Timon they are given the opportunity to present their gifts. Timon pays the most generous compliment to the painter:

Painting is welcome.
The Painting is almost the Naturall man:
For since Dishonor Traffickes with man's Nature,
He is but out-side; These Pensil'd Figures are
Even such as they give out. I like your worke,
And you shall finde I like it.

[I. i. 156-61]

This speech has an unexpected tone at this moment in the play. Timon in the first act is genial, all unsuspecting generosity and cordial friendship. Yet his commendation of painting has this dark reference to dishonor which isolates the speech from his prevailing cordiality and stresses its significance. And the momentary, shadowed mood is expressed in terms of appearance and deception which anticipate the still darker tones at the end of the play. Painting, in this view of its function, exhibits the natural man, and so far from showing merely the "out-side", which is the conventional view of its purpose, it alone reveals true nature in its inward reality. This is indeed Leonardo's claim raised to moral stature. (p. 252)

[Before] the final catastrophe, two related themes have been established in the plot: deceitful appearance, introduced by the technical consideration of painting and poetry in their arts of imitation; and betrayal of trust and friendship, related to the scriptural theme of an ideal of charity and its denial. Now, by the deepest use of irony, the two themes become dramatically one. The former, of deceitful appearance, is attached to the character of Timon himself; in his generosity he is not what he seems, and criticism, when it is directed for the first time against him, is made not in the comparatively neutral terms of art, which Timon had used in the opening scene, but with the theological overtones of sin and judgment. Moreover we shall see that Timon is involved in the second theme, in the same condemnation as his treacherous friends; that, even though it be in a lesser degree, he too is but "out-side", appearance not fulfilling the ideal which he professes.

The criticism begins with Apemantus. Among the signs of Timon's generosity have been the masques and shows with which he entertained his friends. But these are given a new aspect by Apemantus:

> If I should be brib'd too, there would be none
> left to raile upon thee, and thou wouldst sinne
> the faster. Thou giv'st so long *Timon* (I feare
> me) thou wilt give away thy selfe in paper
> shortly. What needs these Feasts, pompes, and
> Vaine-glories.
>
> [I. ii. 238-43]

In this speech all apparent values in the play are reversed. Apemantus is no longer a mere railer; but for him Timon would "sinne the faster", the first indication that Timon's generosity is regarded as wicked prodigality, though founded on the admirable precepts of charity. In the fourth act he explicitly declares his pride that, unlike Timon, he was no prodigal. The highly commended masques and pageants are to him no more than "Vaine-glories". When once this criticism is begun by Apemantus, others pursue it. A Senator in the same scene (II. i) describes Timon's lavishness:

> Still in motion.
> Of raging waste? It cannot hold, it will not.
>
> [II. i. 3-4]

Timon's just steward, Flavius, makes the same open declaration:

> No care, no stop, so senseless of expence,
> That he will neither know how to maintain it,
> Nor cease his flow of Riot.
>
> [II. ii. 1-3]

With these criticisms, Timon's dark commendation of painting, that in its rendering of reality, searching below superficial appearance, it exceeds nature, has had an early, ironic fulfilment. Men are certainly not what they seem; they are treacherous, self-seeking flatterers. But neither is Timon what he seems; his generosity has in its excess become corrupted into prodigality and "Riot".

This union of the two main themes raises an apparent ambiguity in Shakespeare's treatment of character. Timon's dignity and moral worth at the opening of the play make it appropriate that he should pass judgment on artists and on art as a moral revelation. Later, however, the scriptural source of his ideal conduct and the reiteration of the Judas reference invite the supposition that Timon is a Christlike figure betrayed in a like manner. If this be so, the condemnation of his generosity and charity as riotous excess involves a moral ambiguity in the texture of the character. But the terms of the problem as they are implied here involve a misconception of Shakespeare's method (paralleled by some current misunderstanding of the quasi-divine acts of the Duke in *Measure for Measure*). In each case, the clearest analogy in method is with the limited, univocal nature of character in the New Testament parables; that of the Importunate Widow and the Unjust Judge provides a convenient instance. The parable involves teaching on the necessity of reiterated and sincere prayer to God; but God is not thereby to be identified with an Unjust Judge whose caprice is overruled by repeated pleading. The betrayal of Timon in his highest ideal of charity properly invites the Judas reference

to betrayal in the course of hospitality, but Timon is no more to be identified with Christ than the Duke of Vienna—or the Unjust Judge—with God.

This is not to deny that there is an uncomfortable shifting of values in the character of Timon, quite unlike the development and revelation of character in the great tragedies. The ultimate moral judgment on Timon remains in doubt through the greater part of the play and the ambiguity is increased by the conduct of his character, of Apemantus and of Alcibiades in the latter part of the play. We have seen that Apemantus is made the means of a transformation of values in the middle of the plot. The last ironic reversal of judgment we shall find at the final appearance of the poet and the painter, but meanwhile Timon himself becomes the vehicle for the theme of deceitful appearance and in a manner and with terms different from those of art or of theology, which have hitherto been examined. It begins with Timon's farewell to Athens, in which he prays for the overthrow of all established values and truths:

> Piety, and Feare,
> Religion to the Gods, Peace, Justice, Truth,
> Domesticke awe, Night-rest, and Neighbour-hood,
> Instruction, Manners, Mysteries, and Trades,
> Degrees, Observances, Customes, and Lawes,
> Decline to your confounding contraries. . . .
>
> [IV. i. 15-20]

But in fact Timon's prayer is but an extension of his own condition which is also in a state of "confounding contraries". The actual discovery of gold enables him to make still more explicit the reversal of values of which he is so tragically aware. . . . Having rejected all the values of society, Timon proceeds to conjure Nature to reverse her properties and functions, even though in the midst of his sickness of soul she is still in his judgment a "bounteous housewife". Twice in the course of this address to Nature Timon makes "ingrateful Man", Lear's sick phrase, the occasion of his prayer:

> Common Mother, thou
> Whose wombe unmeasureable, and infinite brest
> Teems and feeds all . . .
> Enseare thy Fertile and Conceptious wombe,
> Let it no more bring out ingratefull man.
> Goe great with Tygers, Dragons, Wolves, and Beares,
> Teeme with new Monsters.
>
> [IV. iii. 177-90]

This is the point in the play at which the original theme is resumed, and art is again made the occasion for comment on appearance, illusion and reality. After Timon's departure from Athens, Flavius, his steward, describes the falsity of reputation:

> Who would be so mock'd with Glory, or to live
> But in a Dreame of Friendship.
> To have his pompe, and all what state compounds,
> But onely painted like his varnish't Friends.
>
> [IV. ii. 33-6]

A mockery, a dream and a varnished portrait—or complexion—are here equally an illusion and the illusion involves "Glory" and "Friendship". Timon has now reached the utter rejection of the values by which he had lived, and with the entry of the poet and the painter the cycle is complete. The commendation of the painter's art in the first scene is recalled, the artist's revelation of the true man beneath the exterior corrupted by the trafficking of dishonor. Now, in the fourth act, both painting and poetry are rejected; they too are illusion, a deceitful appearance, like the false behavior of his friends and his own apparent generosity. (pp. 253-56)

[Two] attitudes, the acceptance and rejection of art as a means of revelation, are present in Timon; they are functions of his predominant moods in the play: a generous ''magnificence'', the attribute of the art-loving courtier; and the sickened rejection of all grace, charity and beauty. The more seriously, therefore, we take the opening scene, in establishing the status, authority and power of revelation in the visual arts, the more deeply Shakespeare involves the character of the painter in the problem of ''appearance'' as it is examined in the play. Timon's initial acceptance of his art commends it at its highest renaissance value: it is the revelation of truth in appearance. His subsequent rejection of the painter and the poet corresponds to his profound disgust with all appearance, his conviction that all human action is hypocritical, all humanity bestial, and all law corrupt.

This completion of the fourth act by a return to the subject of the opening scene and its ironic rejection is structurally important. . . . [When] the painter and the poet have been dismissed and the intellectual tensions completed, if not resolved, the fifth act enters upon profounder intuitions, which, in the form in which the play was left, are not wholly realized in dramatic terms. The human problems explored up to that point were dramatically expressible in terms of ostentatious generosity, covetousness, law and its rejection, a reduction of man to brutality, and the judgment over all that human action and life are corrupt or illusory, a cheat of the senses. But the fifth act has a different tone; it begins that exploration of dereliction and despair which anticipates the more penetrating intuitions of *King Lear.* (pp. 256-57)

> W. M. Merchant, '''Timon' and the Conceit of Art,''
> in Shakespeare Quarterly, *Vol. VI, No. 3, Summer,*
> *1955, pp. 249-57.*

ANDOR GOMME   (essay date 1959)

[*Gomme takes issue directly with G. Wilson Knight's interpretation of* Timon *as Shakespeare's major tragedy (see excerpt above, 1930)—a claim which Gomme regards as a ''sentimentalisation of the central figure, producing a grotesque black and white analysis of the action of the play.'' Unlike Knight, Gomme finds in Timon's ''virtue of generosity'' a reflection of the intellectual and moral shortcomings of his society; Timon's eventual disenchantment with humanity Gomme describes as something ''ignoble, just because it is as gross and unjustified as his self-confident luxury was earlier.'' In many respects, Gomme's understanding of Timon's character further substantiates the findings of William Richardson (1784), August Wilhelm Schlegel (1808), Hermann Ulrici (1839), Denton J. Snider (1887), and L. C. Knights (1969).*]

[Ever] since Professor Wilson Knight's essay, 'The Pilgrimage of Hate', appeared in 1930 [see excerpt above], it has been clear that the play needs more careful consideration than it has normally been given. And however much one may feel that the claims he makes for *Timon of Athens* are grotesquely extravagant, his position, stated as it is in a book of considerable authority and distinction, is one that has to be answered. Two recent productions and two new editions suggest enough interest in the play to prompt an attempt at an answer. The sentimentalisation of Shakespeare's 'noble heroes' is a process to which people seem to be continually attracted. It stems presumably from a perhaps unconscious feeling that we are, in a tragedy, being invited always to feel with the 'hero', even

Frontispiece to Verplanck edition (1847). By permission of the Folger Shakespeare Library.

to identify ourselves with him, and the consequent desire to think as well of him as possible. (pp. 107-08)

If the practice has been less frequent with *Timon,* it is only because the play has excited less interest. And Professor Knight's essay, the only considerable recent attempt that I know to establish the play as a complete and major work of art, seems to me to amount finally to just this, a sentimentalisation of the central figure, producing a grotesque black and white analysis of the action of the play. This romanticising goes to such lengths as to find in *Timon* 'the flower of human aspiration'. . . . Professor Knight is unable to see 'his world' except through a haze of brilliant lights:

> We are lost in a riot of display, a gold-mist of
> romance and pleasures of the senses. The set-
> ting is brilliant, the wealth apparently inex-
> haustible, the pleasures free. We can imagine
> the rich food and wine, the blare and clash of
> music, embraces, laughter, and passages of
> glancing love; the coursing of blood, the flushed
> cheek, the mask of fair dancers and Cupid. . . .

There is, unfortunately, no evidence that Professor Knight's use of such words as 'riot' and 'blare' is any indication of his being aware of a possible alternative attitude to the scene which he 'imagines'. Thus Timon's world is 'sensuous and erotic, yet not vicious or ignoble' . . . , his pleasures 'are in themselves excellent, the consummation of natural desire and harmony with the very spirit of man's upward endeavour towards the reality of art, the joys of civilisation, and love universal.

Timon's world is poetry made real, lived rather than imagined'. . . .

It is indeed true that Timon appears in the early acts boundlessly rich: there is a sense of luscious extravagance welling round him, so that he is unable to think in any other terms. But we are left in little doubt about the character of the 'world' with which Timon has surrounded himself: the five who meet at the start of the play are openly mercenary. And nowhere is there any real doubt that Timon will accept what they have to offer; there is no hint of criticism or discrimination in him. . . . Correspondingly, those who hang on Timon's purse have a cringing lack of vitality which stamps the whole scene of luxury as oversoft and decaying. The poet allows things to 'slip idlely' from him [I. i. 20], his is a 'gentle flame' [I. i. 23], poet and painter discuss their arts with an air of superior detachment amounting to dilettantism, full of conceits with no substantial purpose underneath. Everything depends on fortune, in default of which there will be no more friendship. (pp. 108-10)

Against this background Timon's generosity strikes a fresh note, but there is already a hint of self-satisfaction, at least of complacency:

> 'Tis not enough to help the feeble up,
> But to support him after.   [I. i. 107-08]

And immediately afterwards we find it confirmed that his generosity, real and extensive though it is, is realised in terms of wealth alone. J. C. Maxwell [see excerpt above, 1948] points out that the Lucilius episode breaks the similarity of Timon's response to each one of his adulators in turn: 'but at the same time it does show the subtle corruption exercised by the materialistic spirit of Athens. Timon cannot overcome it; he can only outbid it in its own currency of gold—and it is a further irony that he cannot, by now, even do that.' But has Timon any idea that the materialistic spirit of Athens is something he ought to overcome? The pointers to what constitute Timon's riches are the continual references to gold and money and gifts, and the perpetual feasting. These are what make up Timon's world. And its character is defined by Flavius, the only one in it who can maintain a fairly balanced viewpoint:

> No care, no stop, so senseless of expense,
> That he will neither know how to maintain it
> Nor cease his flow of riot. Takes no account
> How things go from him, nor resume no care
> Of what is to continue: never mind,
> Was to be so unwise, to be so kind.
>   [II. ii. 1-6]

The 'kind' is contradicted by 'senseless' and 'riot'; and the impression left is of distaste slightly flavoured with bewildered admiration for Timon's generosity. The crucial passage occurs a little later when Flavius has at last made Timon listen to him:

> So the Gods bless me,
> When all our offices have been oppress'd
> With riotous feeders, when our vaults have wept
> With drunken spilth of wine; when every room
> Hath blaz'd with Lights, and bray'd with minstrelsy,
> I have retired me to a wasteful cock,
> And set mine eyes at flow.   [II. ii. 157-62]

[For Professor Knight], there is here 'a grand profusion, an aristocratic brilliance and richness of entertainment [which] yet pleasures us'. . . . But the lack of depth beneath the rich surface is plain to see. The offices are 'oppress'd', the feasters are in a drunken spilth of wine: the striking effect of the rich

word 'spilth', with its scornful sound reminiscent of 'filth' ('filthy' is a word which Apemantus does not allow us to forget), is carried on by the broad associations of 'brayed'— the music has become coarse and asinine; and the tone of the speech is clinched by the 'wasteful cock' associated with Flavius's weeping. All Timon's show is finally a display of waste. (pp. 110-11)

We return, then, to the essential fact of the superficiality of 'Timon's world': the world whose concern is for surface glitter, which is directed by a blatant appeal to the senses, which are not at the fingertips of the intellect, but merely used to the end of their own gratification. And again it must be said that Timon, for all that he stands for the best side of it, is part of this world, a world of which Timon, Apemantus and the Lords represent three simultaneous aspects. The function of the Lords is clear: they demonstrate the final decay of a civilisation which defines itself in terms of wealth and luxury. From this point of view there is no real distinction between the three whom we see at fairly close hand; each represents a slightly different side of the same selfish meanness bred inevitably by the society on which Timon depends, on which he tells Apemantus not to rail, because he cannot accept its failure. Apemantus, too, as Professor Knight has convincingly shown, cannot live without this society: if it were gone he would have nothing on which to pour his scorn. He is the inverted parasite, but as much conditioned and supported by the decaying world as any of the fawning courtiers. And in this world Timon stands out only by virtue of a generosity which depends for its existence on a narrowness of outlook, a failure of intellectual awareness, which finally appears as moral weakness. . . . (pp. 113-14)

Timon has failed to achieve a proper response to his situation: his failure is at once an intellectual and a moral one. And the result, when the crisis comes, is the catastrophic slide from one end of the (same) scale to the other. As far as Timon is concerned the transformation is astonishingly abrupt (though not, I think, unconvincingly so): in one short scene the whole direction of his general attitude is reversed. From him we get nothing more in preparation for the desperation of the final acts. But immediately after his departure from Athens comes the important scene between his servants, which contains some of the best verse in the play.

> As we do turn our backs
> From our companion, thrown into his grave,
> So his familiars to his buried fortunes
> Slink all away, leave their false vows with him
> Like empty purses pick'd; and his poor self
> A dedicated beggar to the air,
> With his disease, of all shunn'd poverty,
> Walks like contempt alone.   [IV. ii. 8-15]

One senses here the mature Shakespeare: the use of the vivid verb 'slink' at an emphatic position at the beginning of a line, with its strong emotive tone; the contemptuously exact placing given by the alliterated p's in the fifth line; the slight strangeness of the vow/purse simile (picked purses are not first offered like vows, though the reference to the characteristic action of the false friends is fully realised); all these immediately call up a sharpened attention to prepare us for the superb image in the last three lines. One says 'image', but the word is inexact: any picture which one may have thought up will certainly be inaccurate (the verse of course does not—any more than, say, 'The morn in russet mantle clad'—if read as it deserves to be read, encourage the formation of pictures). But the abrupt halt on the strong word 'contempt' stops the progress of thought which has been developing in the last half-dozen lines. There is in it something of the oddity of Macbeth's

> pity, like a naked new-born babe
> Striding the blast.   [*Macbeth*, I. vii. 21-2]

There isn't, of course, the profound subtlety and firmness of thought that we find in the *Macbeth* passage, but a similar emphatic direction of meaning is given by an apparent reversal of sense: contempt has become personified, but it is not Timon who, in the previous lines, has been the despiser. Now *he* walks like contempt alone: it is the prefiguring of the position of Timon in the final acts. (pp. 115-16)

[From] here on the play is dominated by Timon's unbridled hatred, which calls down curses on all men because he has been deceived: it is the logical culmination of the moral weakness which the earlier acts have exposed. For Professor Knight this hatred is essentially 'noble'. . . . (p. 117)

[Rather] is one impelled to call it something fundamentally ignoble, just because it is as gross and unjustified as his self-confident luxury was earlier. In this respect Timon produces a perverse sentimentalisation of himself, which is then transferred to the attitude to the position of mankind displayed in the extravagant metaphor on thievery:

> The Sun's a thief, and with his great attraction
> Robs the vast Sea. The Moon's an arrant thief,
> And her pale fire, she snatches from the Sun,
> The Sea's a thief, whose liquid surge, resolves
> The Moon into salt tears. The Earth's a thief,
> That feeds and breeds by a composure stolen
> From gen'ral excrement: each thing's a thief.
> The Laws, your curb and whip, in their rough power
> Has uncheck'd theft . . .
> All that you meet are thieves.
>
>   [IV. iii. 436ff]

The grounds for Timon's consuming passion simply do not exist; and the quality of it is characterised by the continual references to disease which are now so evident. (p. 118)

Timon of Athens, then, has considerable merits, though not, it seems to me, those that Professor Knight finds, nor to such a degree. The verse has, fitfully, many qualities which stamp it as coming from Shakespeare's maturity. There is, for example, the brilliant conciseness of Apemantus's 'He wrought better that made the Painter, and yet he's but a filthy piece of work' [I. i. 198-99], in which, as Professor Knight says, the whole of Apemantus's rejection of God, of man and of man's work is made clear. . . . (pp. 122-23)

These are occasional achievements, in themselves minor but significant; they ensure that the play cannot be lightly dismissed. And yet for all the local successes attained, *Timon* is certainly a failure; and on the whole it is not difficult to see why. There is little of the richness of meaning, given by the tactual and visual immediacy apparent in the language of the other plays of this time: the imagery is not properly controlled and has no coherent development; the rhythm is sluggish, both in individual speeches and as a whole. Again, the position of Alcibiades is hard to account for fully. His triumph at the end suggests an attempt to give an answer to the problem set by Timon's reaction to his world and to Athens. But though he himself has been a part of that world and has reacted against it, he hardly represents a distinct and reputable standard of his own: he is in fact nowhere given enough body, enough moral

substance, to take that part in the development of the action and theme of the play which he has to bear at the end.

It is true, too, that the framework adopted by Shakespeare does not make possible the kind of social analysis which appears to be being attempted. Timon is shown, I have suggested, a product of the society in which he lives, and his failure of moral and intellectual awareness is the failure of the society. But the crude outlines in which the situation is drawn give no proper scope for the irony which was one of the greatest achievements of this phase of Shakespeare's work. In fact at times the play reads like a grotesque. The three scenes in which Timon's servants are repulsed by his false friends have a monstrous comedy in which the Lords are caricatured. They suggest that here is the material less for tragedy than for satiric comedy. And the choice of subject-matter prompts this too: as in the other play in which money appears as the dominant interest—*The Merchant of Venice*—Shakespeare seems not to know exactly how to treat it. It was something that Jonson could manage perfectly, but it produced, of course, an analysis of society far less profound than Shakespeare at his greatest was able to achieve. (pp. 123-24)

The play which it is obviously tempting to compare *Timon* with is *Coriolanus*. There is an apparent similarity of plot (Coriolanus looking rather like a fusion of Timon and Alcibiades), which prompts the view that *Timon* might have been in some sense a study for the later play. That is, assuming it is the later; but the tremendous success in *Coriolanus* of the kind of social analysis which I suppose Shakespeare to have been trying for in *Timon* makes the assumption reasonable: it might explain why, if E. K. Chambers is right [see excerpt above, 1908], *Timon* was never finished—Shakespeare had realised his mistake and started again on the right track. The comparison, however, when examined closely, shows little essential similarity between the plays, though it does give some suggestion for the basic reason for the failure of *Timon*. In *Coriolanus* the tragedy . . . [derives] from the conflict between natural humanity and an unnatural discipline of 'honour'. It is clearly a great opportunity for the kind of analytic penetration of which only Shakespeare was capable. But in Timon, as Professor Knight has observed, there is no conflict: on the contrary, there is an identification of life and pleasure. There is in Timon no natural humanity struggling against the unnatural pressure of luxurious extravagance; and when pleasure is denied Timon, there is no life to take its place. In the end, the society, and Timon with it, appears too decadent, too unnatural for Shakespeare's purpose; and the only action which could develop out of the original situation proved a moral and artistic impasse. (pp. 124-25)

Andor Gomme, "'Timon of Athens'," in Essays in Criticism, *Vol. IX, No. 2, April, 1959, pp. 107-25.*

WINIFRED M.T. NOWOTTNY (essay date 1959)

[*Nowottny argues that* Timon *represents Shakespeare's inversion of the Christian myths of Order and Natural Law. Through a succession of revelatory scenes, Nowottny asserts, Shakespeare replaces these divine myths with secular substitutes, such as the myth of Prostitution and the myth of Natural Thievery. By the end of the play, Timon is an Antichrist figure preaching his new doctrine of salvation. This final assessment echoes a conclusion reached by Cyrus Hoy (1973), who views Timon as a "monstrous parody of Christ." For additional commentary on the religious elements in* Timon, *see the excerpt by Jarold W. Ramsey (1966).*]

In his article in *Shakespeare Quarterly* . . . , W. M. Merchant draws attention to some scriptural references in Acts I-III of *Timon of Athens* and argues that they establish in the play a theme of "betrayal of trust and friendship, related to the scriptural theme of an ideal of charity and its denial" and goes on to deal with the difficulties encountered in trying to relate this theme to what he sees as the other main theme of the play, that of "deceitful appearance, introduced by the technical consideration of poetry and painting in their arts of imitation" [see excerpt above, 1955]. . . . My comment will be limited to the proffering of these observations: (a) that the significant echoing of scriptural phrases is not confined to Acts I-III; (b) that in Timon's "overthrow of all established values and truths" there is a clearly articulated sequence, and that in this sequence the climactic inversion is of values specifically Christian; (c) that this climactic inversion is more intimately related to the processes of Timon's imagination, as represented in Acts IV and V, than is the theme of art's counterfeiting.

It will be best to consider first to what extent one may rightly say that the Timon of Acts IV and V is more than a speech-prefix to a number of indifferently-placed diatribes. The first diatribe [IV. i. 1-41] calls for the subversion of the degrees and duties of ordered society and its conclusion decisively rejects the "accommodations" of civilization in the words "Nothing Ile beare from thee / But nakednesse, thou detestable Towne". The second diatribe [IV. iii. 1-23] is an exposure of the falsity of the myth of Order and a restatement of the structure of society as a function of Fortune operating upon the basic villainy of man's nature; it reaches its climax, just before the discovery of the gold, in a call for the destruction of mankind. The gold provokes a third diatribe [IV. iii. 26-44], in which gold as a symbol of Fortune is seen as confounding abstract categories of value and as transforming or transferring human attributes. This progression from a repudiation couched in the terms of society's own current myth, to the construction of a new myth of Fortune and man's villainy, and thence to the discernment that the physical substance of gold ("This yellow Slaue" and "damn'd Earth") has the powers, usually attributed only to the divine, of conferring blessing and the attraction of adoration and veneration, of making whole again and indeed, after a fashion, resurrecting ("This Embalmes and Spices / To' th' April day againe"), is not only a progression in acuity of discernment, as may be seen simply by considering the content of the successive speeches; it is also a progression from poetry that declaims and states, to poetry that discovers a symbol capable of subsequent co-ordinating use and lays down the lines of its coming development. Timon's discovery of the properties of gold is closely comparable to Lear's discovery of the properties of the flesh. . . . In *Lear* the symbol of the suffering, begetting, guilty, knowing flesh is more successful than the symbol of Timon's gold, because it can itself be the symbol for all Lear's major concerns, whereas Timon's gold is not so much a prime and perfected symbol as a maker of collateral symbols, but none the less the symbolic nature of the subsequent processes of Timon's imagination is clear. Gold in this third diatribe is discovered to be the paradoxical embodiment, in the form of damned and slavish earth, of a power having effects comparable to those of divine power, and this prepares the way for the great speech of Act IV [IV. iii. 381-92] in which a brilliant array of paradox and oxymoron attains its most compelling luminosity when it draws on religious formulations more and more closely associated with Christianity ("Thou visable God" . . . "that speak'st with euerie Tongue" . . . "thou touch of hearts") and also prepares for the great incantatory speeches of Act V in which Timon (with

an apparent simplicity of diction, recalling the apparent simplicity of Lear's speeches after the reunion with Cordelia) preaches a doctrine of despair in words that almost openly invert the message of Christ: Timon, having already preached thievery to the thieves, now speaks of his tree, inviting each man who desires to "stop Affliction" to "take his haste; / Come hither ere my Tree hath felt the Axe, / And hang him-selfe", and finally cries out, in words that have many reverberations against the Gospel story,

> *Come not to me* againe, but say to Athens
> Timon hath made his *euerlasting Mansion*
> Vpon the Beached Verge of the Salt Flood,
>   . . . thither come,
> And let my grave-stone be your Oracle:
> . . . .
> Graues onely be *mens workes, and Death their gaine;*
> *Sunne, hide thy Beames,* Timon *hath done his Raigne.*
>   [V. i. 214-23]
>   (pp. 493-94)

A development more immediate than this, however, is the transition, in IV. iii, from gold as the symbol of the confusion of moral, physical and social distinctions [IV. iii. 28-42] to a further symbolization of gold as the "common whore" [IV. iii. 43], leading to the diatribe [IV. iii. 151-66] that presents prostitution as being, in fact, a leveller of society to a featureless and rotten lump and, in symbol, a means of revealing that a featureless and rotten lump is what society in reality is. This latter I take to be the true *aculeus* of the identification of gold and prostitution. The identification begins, at IV. iii. 42-4, with an explanatory analogy (nations will quarrel over gold as men do over their whores), but its reference is very swiftly extended and particularized when it is stressed that each member of the metaphorical connection (the gold itself and the whore herself) is in actuality and not merely in metaphor as destructive as Alcibiades' sword. That Timon's imagination moves symbolically . . . is I think clearly shown in the fourth diatribe, Timon's speech to Alcibaides [IV. iii. 107-28], in which Timon sees Alcibiades as the scourge of sexuality: as the "plague" of some "high-Vic'd City", of usury (earlier described as a bawd), of the counterfeit matron who is really a bawd, of "Milke pappes that . . . bore at mens eyes", and of the babe who is to be thought of as a bastard, all these instances having as common factor some association with base sexuality hidden under the appearance of being a traditionally fit object of piety; this common factor indicates that the movement of Timon's imagination is towards a vision of society as presenting a varied *superficies* covering the one reality of base and undiscriminating human appetite; and it is for that reason that Timon adjures Alcibiades to "Sweare against Objects", for "Objects" has here its usual Shakespearian sense of that-which-is-looked-upon. The "theme of deceitful appearance" (to which my remarks would now seem to be approximating) has, in this part of the play, a vital, complex and in some respects implicit connection with its instance, prostitution—not, as in the poet and painter scene of Act V, an explicit and relatively simple instance in the counterfeiting of art. These speeches on prostitution in Act IV (the fifth and sixth diatribes) present baseness and utter absence of discrimination ("Thatch / Your poore thin Roofes with burthens of the dead, / (Some that were hang'd) no matter;") as being the hidden reality and social distinctions as being only superficial and false; thus in Timon's imagination the prostitute is at once the symbol of the real baseness underlying the pretence of ordered society, an actual agent of its actual destruction, and an agent such that her activities will have effects at once concrete and symbolical of the real truth: "Downe with the Nose, / Downe with it flat, take the Bridge quite away" . . . "defeate and quell / The sourse of all Erection". These curses, venereally particularized, have their impetus and form from the identification of the prostitute with the social leveller, who reduces Order, the appearance, to shapeless rottenness, the reality. Thus Timon's view of the real nature of man in society is expressed by his substituting the myth of Prostitution for the myth of Order.

The preoccupation with society as a structure has reached an imaginative climax, and the interest of the dialogue now turns to Nature. Timon in his seventh diatribe [IV. iii. 176-96], discovering that though he is sick of man's unkindness, he is still prompted by Nature to eat, turns to scrutinize her and addresses her as the "Common Mother", the main drift of the speech being that Nature is indifferent, neutral, showing no principle of discrimination, whether between her "proud Childe (arrogant man)" and the "venom'd Worme", or between the normal and what is "abhorred"; she merely "Teemes and feeds all". . . . Timon is moving towards an inversion of the argument from "the book of the creatures" and indeed towards inversion of the whole argument from "correspondences". When, therefore, in the next diatribe [IV. iii. 374-92] he speaks of his sickness with "this false world", the phrase sums up not only his experiences of so-called friendship but also his vision of a world devoid of any true source or embodiment of values (whether in society, man or nature) and he immediately goes on, as indeed the inner logic of his repudiation demands, to address that power which he now discerns to be greater than anything in the world, namely, his gold—seen, now, as cancelling every bond between man and what is godlike (kingship, the relation between father and son, marriage, heroism, love, chastity, consecration) and finally as being itself, impossibly, a god ("Thou visible God / That souldrest close Impossibilities"), at whose pentecost appear the tongues in which money talks, the one touchstone and toucher of hearts, the "yellow slave" now revealed as master of its slave, man.

This neo-God, gold, now becomes the prime mover in a new cosmology, which is announced in Timon's encounter with the thieves, to whom he preaches a new interpretation of the exemplifying in natural phenomena of the divine plan for the world. The speech on universal thievery [IV. iii. 425-49], like the speeches on prostitution, has more to it than an indiscriminate misanthropy taking temporary color from whatever confronts it in encounters dictated in the first place by a plot. As in *Lear*, the function of the plot itself, in this part of the play, is to provide encounters with people who will appear to have suggested to the hero precisely those symbols upon which the dramatist's imagination is at work. Timon's cosmology of Thievery is connected only dramaturgically with the actual entry of actual thieves; the basic connection of the Thievery-symbol with what has gone before lies in its dialectic with the concept of the expression of the divine in the natural order, just as the Prostitution-symbol had its dialectical relation to the concept of Order in society. God's law in Nature . . . fixes demarcations; in so far as the phenomena of the natural order provide examples to society, they do so by exemplifying (as in Shakespeare's fable of the bees in *Henry V* and in that of the belly and the members in *Coriolanus*) hierarchical functions operating for mutual benefit, or "common weal"; Timon on the contrary sees the physical universe in terms of usurpation and flux, exemplifying social relations of mutual robbery. Thus the myth of Natural Law is challenged by the myth of Natural

Thievery, just as the myth of Order in society was challenged by the myth of Prostitution.

Thus far in Acts IV and V, it seems to me clear that one continuous imaginative process shapes the sequence of Timon's encounters and speeches. It is not clear to me what relation obtains between this process and the ensuing encounters with the steward and with the poet and the painter. I should perhaps mention, in order to clarify for the reader the point of view from which I write this article, that I think *Timon* to be the work of two hands and, whilst I am convinced that there is no compelling case for supposing Shakespeare to have written any more of Acts I to III than the dialogue of Timon and Flavius in Act II, scene 2, the area of my bafflement on the authorship question is, precisely, from [IV. iii. 458] (the entry of Flavius, after the thieves' exit) to the end of the play. Within this stretch of the play all that I feel sure of is that Shakespeare did write Timon's speeches to the senators and Alcibiades' comment on the epitaph. For here, surely, is the last efflux of that imaginative process by which there has been substituted for the whole Elizabethan world-picture the twin myths of prostitution and thievery associated with the god gold, a last efflux in which Timon, when society resorts to him to save it, repudiates that society at its very foundation and preaches as Anti-Christ his ironic message of salvation. The high incantatory style has a slow long-swinging calm that would be hard to match from anywhere in Shakespeare's work. . . . (pp. 495-97)

Timon's witness is of course ironic, and the play is not to end without Alcibiades' reinterpretation of Timon's life and death. I do not fully understand this closing speech, but I think that if I did, I should find that I understood the relation between Shakespeare's tragedies and his last plays, for, in a sense surely important for our understanding of the last phase of Shakespeare's art, Timon's words, "Lippes, let soure words go by, and Language end", must precede discovery of the richness of that conceit whereby, over his submerged tomb, vast Neptune is to "weep for aye . . . on faults forgiuen". (p. 497)

Winifred M.T. Nowottny, "Acts IV and V of 'Timon of Athens'," in Shakespeare Quarterly, Vol. X, No. 4, Autumn, 1959, pp. 493-97.

E.A.J. HONIGMANN (essay date 1961)

[*Honigmann maintains that* Timon *was written completely by Shakespeare, and that its structural faults—plot inconsistencies, indefinite structure, and unsatisfying conclusion—have either been invented by critics or blown out of proportion. Honigmann takes particular issue with Una Ellis-Fermor (1942), and rejects her assertion that the characterization of Timon is the greatest weakness of the play. According to Honigmann, Timon is incompletely characterized in order to demonstrate his lack of self-knowledge. He argues that it is the chief irony of the play that we should "remain perplexed about the borders between Timon's nobility and his stupidity."*]

Despite the gap of six or so years between them, *Timon* is now often placed beside *Troilus*, and this common intuition of kinship prompts some further conjectures. . . . The question arises whether the stage-histories of the two plays, and not only their contents, have anything in common? If the now very widely accepted opinion that *Troilus* was designed for an Inn of Court holds for one play it will hold for two. After all, in his special study of Elizabethan audiences, Harbage earmarked two Shakespearian plays as "not out of place" in the coterie-theatre category: *Troilus* and *Timon*. If *Timon* too was produced at an

Inn of Court this would be just the sort of company in which one would expect to find the pedantic author of the MS. *Timon*.

Such an hypothesis disposes economically of various loose ends in the tangled history of *Timon*. . . . Stylistic and textual peculiarities have been overstressed while the vital fact that *Timon* appears to be an almost finished play has escaped the attention it deserved. (p. 14)

The high degree of foresight and planning evident in the works of [Shakespeare's] maturity reduces to absurdity the customary assumption that he blundered blindly through *Timon*, drew up in dismay at the end and flung his abortion aside. Once we dismiss Shakespeare's "mythical sorrows" and breakdown, as C. J. Sisson's admirable lecture compels us, once the passionate poetry of *Timon* is seen in the context of the eminently sane and critical presentation of the hero, we must face up to the difficulty that a great dramatist in his prime would hardly bring a play to near-completion and then wonder that it was not what he meant it to be. I think it more likely that *Timon*, like the other plays of Shakespeare of this time, carries out his intentions. In short, the view that *Timon* would never have been performed because the only text that happens to survive looks like a rough draft ignores all the decisive factors—the printers' dilemma, the craftsmanship of Shakespeare, the possibility of a special design for a special audience, and the state of the play as we have it.

Though short compared with Shakespeare's other tragedies (which, it should be remembered, would have to be cut, since most of them were too long), *Timon* would be just the right length for an Elizabethan play, just the same length as *King John, Much Ado,* and *The Tempest*. Equally indicative I find the finish of the beginnings and endings of scenes: though some adjustments were probably intended (with the clown, with the entrance of poet and painter in V. i. 1, etc.), Shakespeare had obviously advanced beyond the stage of fragmentary jottings, he knew precisely where he was going. Plotlessness may be one of the faults of the play, but it is possible that the author foresaw and resigned himself to this, in which case it is our duty to try and explain his motives.

Quietly passing over the high standard of completion of individual scenes, some nevertheless place great emphasis on structural deficiencies. Were once-planned scenes never written? The need for some preliminary puff for Alcibiades and his friend [III. v. 7ff], a favorite instance of postulated "missing scenes", was denied by A. S. Collins, who rightly insisted that the sudden prominence of Alcibiades in the middle of Act III should come as no surprise: his stage-presence earlier would prepare for his role, his stature would be suggested—"a noble figure, isolated in his sincerity, apart from all these flatterers" [see excerpt above, 1946]. Many other "structural weaknesses" are, I think, equally figmentary. Oddities, even if pronounced and unfamiliar in a "typical Shakespearian play" (whatever that may be), should not be allowed to obscure the issue—for *Timon* should rather be judged with its like and its contemporaries.

(1) The "isolation of the hero" occurs also with the Duke in *Measure for Measure,* with Pericles, with Henry VIII, differently each time, but one may legitimately regard this as deliberate, not as a fault which Shakespeare would have swept away in a miraculous last-minute reworking.

A far larger structural peculiarity affects the secondary characters, Alcibiades, Flavius, Apemantus: they speak and clash with Timon, with the play's nonentities, but do not stand in any sort of relationship to each other. This sacrifice of one major source of conflict again seems no accident. As often elsewhere, Shakespeare mirrors the predicament of his hero in these subordinate figures: Laertes, Fortinbras and Pyrrhus must avenge a father's death like Hamlet. Similarly Timon's loneliness reappears in Apemantus, the professional outsider, in Flavius, whose apartness shines through most unmistakably in the one scene where the fellowship of Timon's servants is stressed (IV.ii), and in Alcibiades, whose long silences in Act I together with the restrained courtesy of his replies when addressed mark him out as singularly as his unquestioned captainship in Acts IV and V. To see *Timon* as a study of different forms of loneliness (among other things), a theme that occupied Shakespeare more and more after the creation of Prince Hal and Jaques, helps to place it in his "development", and also to appreciate the hazards in such an essentially undramatic subject.

Miss Ellis-Fermor, in her brilliant and damaging critique of the play, has insisted that Timon, the hero, is its greatest weakness. "We do not know him and we do not know about him"; he "fails to leave a deep, coherent impression of his personality," and lacks "a wide variety of enthusiasms and richness of personality." This is to judge one hero against an invariable, rigid general standard and to forget the special requirements of what is after all a very special play. I think, too, that a recognition of Timon's extraordinary emotionalism will explain why he seems to differ so radically from the other tragic heroes. Much more than Othello and Antony, Timon reduces all his experiences (and thus himself) to overwrought posturing and rhetoric, he forever loses himself in an *O altitudo*—literally loses himself, depersonalizing himself in the process. Though the audience will not misapprehend this for the grand manner and will understand him more completely than he can understand himself, it is one of the concerted ironies of the play that we remain perplexed about the borders between Timon's nobility and his stupidity—perhaps, then, the vagueness of his characterization serves a purpose in the analysis of unwise magnanimity.

A "master passion" always narrows the personality, and Timon's extravagance thus ranges him with the characters of comedy, satire, melodrama (Sir Epicure Mammon, Malvolio, Barabas), yet few will concede that he fails to leave a deep impression of personality. When Miss Ellis-Fermor concluded that "Shakespeare may, it is true, have intended to throw the character into isolation", I feel she was on a more rewarding tack: when she rejected the possibility, because Shakespeare did not underline his intention "with a fulness and clarity that left no room for mistake", one can only reflect that the reiterated warnings of Apemantus and Flavius were indeed in vain.

(2) The episodic nature of the action, again, may be not so much Shakespeare's slack planning as an intended effect. Many scenes are placed side by side rather than closely integrated with one another, a feature which goes hand in hand with the diminished individualization of the minor characters. *Pericles* resembles *Timon* in this looseness of the plot, but after *Othello*, perhaps his masterpiece in "cause and effect" writing, parallelism and analysis begin to challenge suspense in the arrangement of Shakespeare's dramatic forms: one thinks of the elaborate juxtapositionings of *Lear*, the second half of *Macbeth*, and of the controlled slowness of the romances. From 1604/5 onwards, too, increasing numbers of type-characters (lords, physicians, etc.), psychologically unsubtilized, confirm the new trend.

(3) A comparison with *Troilus* and the private theatre play resolves many other "problems" which have vexed the critics.

(a) Is the end of the play incoherent, "disturbing us as it does by its inconclusiveness"? [See excerpt above by Ellis-Fermor, 1942.] The same sort of "conclusion in which nothing is concluded" was devised for *Troilus*, against the chronology of the sources, against the familiar facts of "history", for the sake of intellectual outrageousness: it may be that Shakespeare thought that his special audience (if any) would prefer disturbing questions in place of the usual heavy-handed resolutions of tragedy. Thus Timon's suicide is hinted at but not definitely asserted, the reformation of Athens proposed but not demonstrated. I do not say that this is aesthetically more satisfying than the crashing chords at the end of grand tragedy: yet the "dark comedies" corroborate that in his probing plays Shakespeare found it rewarding to ask frightening questions and close them with perfunctory answers, fading out without the high moral seriousness and conviction of his greatest purging catastrophes.

(b) The same causes probably induced Shakespeare to attempt the intellectualism which saps the vitality of the two plays. Not only in the characterization of subsidiaries, but in Timon's long denunciations, in the essentially detached "putting of the case" by Alcibiades in III.v, in the chit-chat of poet and painter, even in the contrived contrast of Timon's earlier and later speeches, Shakespeare seems to assume his audience's *penchant* for abstraction and generalization. The comparison of the reactions of the parasites to the request for money (Act III), and of the reactions of Timon and the rest to the discovered gold (Acts IV, V), affords the clearest proof that Shakespeare's structural principles here must not be confused with those of the tragedies. His leisurely schematism runs counter to his usual tragic concentration: to propound that the play is "unfinished in conception" is to assume too lightly that it was cast in the same mould as its great predecessors.

(c) Timon's sex-disgust, commencing in IV.i, once regarded as simply an intrusion of Shakespeare's personal feelings, therefore a sign of artistic irresponsibility, may lose some of its unexpectedness if placed beside *Troilus*. (pp. 14-17)

The dresses and demeanor of extras could easily convey in Acts I-III the sex-atmosphere which is so vividly described thereafter. Plutarch's indignation against sexual debaucheries in the "Alcibiades" and the "Marcus Antonius" surely prepared this theme for Shakespeare, as perhaps did the French translator of Lucian who transformed the Greek's (male) Plutus into a (female) whore, Richesse . . .—but quite as important for our purposes is the fact that Inn of Court literature dwells with enormous relish upon every sort of unchastity. . . . The shock-tactics in the employment of the sex-theme in *Timon* seem to me not so much a personal obsession as a necessary ingredient, much like Pandar and Thersites.

(4) Fourthly, it cannot be sufficiently emphasized that though *Timon* is riddled with inconsistencies and loose ends, this does not set it apart from Shakespeare's other works but rather confirms its authenticity. The notes at the end of Bradley's *Shakespearean Tragedy*, as also Laqueur's further discoveries in *Shakespeares Dramatische Konzeption* (1955), suggest that loose ends were the unavoidable secondary manifestations of his genius, and there would be more cause for disquiet if they were absent. (pp. 17-18)

We have been told over and over again that *Timon* is a failure: because Shakespeare reworked another man's play, because he did not complete his own play; it is "a first sketch of *King Lear*, set aside unfinished because the story proved intractable and no full measure of sympathy could be demanded for its hero" [see excerpt above by Walter Raleigh, 1907], or it is the left-overs of *King Lear*, an "after vibration". The same misconceptions fuddled the interpretation of the dark comedies and the romances. Compared with the tragedies these do indeed seem to be a falling-off: nevertheless, eloquent advocates persuade us that they exist successfully in their own right. I fear that the traditional bracketing of *Timon* and *King Lear* has done far more harm. Despite many and striking likenesses, which, to be sure, are frequent in plays written in close proximity even if belonging to different genres (e.g. *Hamlet* and *Troilus*), the *forms* of *Timon* and *King Lear* are so utterly unlike that their collocation can only be misleading.

The recognition that *Timon* may have been meant as something other than the regular tragedy has come slowly. I do not think that we should call it a "tragical satire," yet we cannot hope to be fair to this unique and embarrassing drama by lazily lumping it together with the grand tragedies. If a point of reference is required, the most useful would be *Troilus*, with which it has much more affinity than I have been able to demonstrate. A coterie audience, especially one made up of termers, would resolve many of its difficulties, both of value and technique. The absence of a satisfactory source explains others, Plutarch's Timon anecdote being too short, so that the "Marcus Antonius" and the "Coriolanus" were drawn upon, and Lucian's dialogue being a few loosely connected episodes rather than a narrative. As regards the text, the agents of transmission must be given some credit for its irregularities, and the very nearly finished version that survives in no sense obviates the possibility of a cleaner and final fair copy blessed with the author's approval. At the same time, of course, *Timon* belongs to the end of the "tragic period", when Shakespeare began casting about for a new manner, so that his touch was not always happy. All these accidents may help us to understand why the play is so "unusual", but they do not justify the too prevalent refusal to take it seriously—"because Shakespeare did not put his heart into it", or "because he put too much of himself into it." (p. 20)

E.A.J. Honigmann, "'Timon of Athens'," in Shakespeare Quarterly, Vol. XII, No. 1, Winter, 1961, pp. 3-20.

BERNARD PAULIN (essay date 1964)

[*In the following excerpt, Paulin focuses on the debate over the specific genre of* Timon, *criticizing those commentators who have either interpreted the play as a comedy, a moraltiy drama, a satire, or even a tragic-satire. Instead, Paulin believes that* Timon *was written as a tragedy, since Timon's suicide at the end of the play is understandable only within the tragic mode. For a discussion of the generic classification of* Timon, *see the excerpts by August Wilhelm Schlegel (1808), G. Wilson Knight (1930), John W. Draper (1934), A. S. Collins (1946), Kenneth Muir (1947), Andor Gomme (1959), Peter Ure (1964), Northrop Frye (1965), L. C. Knights (1969), and Anne Lancashire (1970).*]

Shakespeare's *Timon*, a difficult and indubitably incomplete play, leaves in obscurity any number of issues, frequently important ones. The death of the protagonist is certainly not the least significant of these shadowy zones. Although the play is entitled *The Life of Timon of Athens*, it is Timon's death which constitutes, in fact, an essential moment of the drama.

One can certainly opine that the mystery adds to the beauty of the work. One can appreciate the charm of the unfinished quality. One can, like G. Wilson Knight, deem that the precise details are unnecessary [see excerpt above, 1930]. Still, nothing dispenses us from seeking to know and to understand.

How does Timon die? The critics are divided on this question. For some, it is a matter of suicide: A. C. Bradley, O. J. Campbell, and Lawrence Babb are of this opinion. For others, such as J. C. Maxwell [see excerpt above, 1948], the suicide is not a proven fact. A third group takes refuge in abstention; included here are G. Wilson Knight, E.A.J. Honingmann [see excerpt above, 1961] and W.I.D. Scott. Can we settle among these critics, whose differences are, moreover, often very subtle? We will study in succession the facts as they present themselves, then the presumptions, and finally the options which seem necessary.

Three witnesses seem to have been the last people to converse with Timon: two senators and Flavius [V. i.]. All that these witnesses can say is that Timon let it be understood that his death was imminent before retiring into his cave [V. i. 214-23]. The stage direction does not help us, for it is vague and, in any case, it does not apper in the folio.

One witness, on the other hand, claims to have found Timon's tomb: Alcibiades' soldier who, having been sent by his general, arrives too late to find him alive [V. iii]. He is able to provide us with three documents: the three versions of the epitaph [V. iii. 3-4, V. iv. 70-73]. He is of no help to us concerning the manner in which Timon died.

Dr. Scott declares that Timon is ill from the beginning of the play and that his improvident behavior is due to syphilis. That the kind of blind optimism which he evidences might be a symptom of this disease in general does not oblige us to arrive at this diagnosis here, unless the rest of the play leaves no doubt whatsoever on the subject. But when arguments lean simply one on the other, they amount to nothing more than a house of cards. However that may be, if Timon is diseased from the first act, why does he become a misanthrope (and a misogynist) only after his ruin and the flight of his supposed friends?

The only possibilities that seem to us worth keeping in mind are suicide and a death of chagrin or exhaustion.

Suicide is rarely accidental; it festers initially, sometimes for a long while, in a person's heart. Without a doubt, Timon's personality shows potential for self-destruction, to use an expression dear to psychologists. It is certainly not his material ruin which pushes him to suicide. Nor is it syphilis, as we have seen. Nor is it madness: although he suffers from a certain dose of melancholy—an agent of suicide according to Burton—he is not mad in the clinical sense of the term. Nevertheless his excessive nature in prosperity just as in adversity, his lack of moderation and proportion could contribute to his arming against himself. Disappointment and despair eat away at him. He is hateful, violent. A suicide of refusal would be in keeping with his temperament. It would stand as an indication, as well, of the tragic grandeur of his solitude. *Timon* is "a study of different forms of solitudes". The protagonist is, actually, alone from the beginning until the end of the play. And isolation is frequently a cause of suicide. The hatred that Timon professes to have for all men is a hatred for all human life, including his own:

"His semblable, yea himself, Timon disdains."

[IV. iii. 22]

These are only suppositions here however. . . . [The critic] has to choose among several interpretations of the play. Depending on these options suicide will be impossible, desirable, or necessary.

Rather curiously, some critics have claimed to see in *Timon* a sort of comedy in the classical tradition: Timon is the misanthrope. F. L. Losey says that the play is "a somewhat pleasant satire". If one accepts this hypothesis—a fairly implausible one, since Shakespeare is not presenting simply a failing or a vice, but a man—the death of the main character, no matter what its nature, threatens to lend to the comedy a quite "rough hilarity".

The notion of a morality play has also been brought up, a sort of survival from medieval theatre, in which the characters would be rather more allegorical than real. This is A. S. Collins' opinion [see excerpt above, 1946]. In this perspective, suicide is inconceiveable. . . . [In] the Middle Ages, Judas is the only character to hang himself on stage and suicide is still seen as reprehensible. . . .

If one makes of *Timon* a satiric tragedy—or a tragic satire—in the manner of Ben Jonson's *Sejanus*, as Campbell proposes, one meets up again with the detestable *Timon* of recurring tradition. He is odious.

How to reconcile the hideous traits of such a character with Timon's nobleness, attested by different people who, themselves, inspire confidence?

It is certain that Timon has faults and problems, if not he would not interest us. But witnesses worthy of our trust prevent us from seeing in him only a simple scoundrel. Paradoxically, we feel sympathy for this enemy of sympathy. A dishonourable suicide is then out of the question.

There remains the option of tragedy, be it a successful one or not. The tragic interpretation imposes the solution of suicide. It is not simply coincidence that the most prominent of the partisans of the suicide theory is Bradley, author of the classic work on Shakespearean tragedy. If Timon is a tragic figure, he will not die of distress, like a child. Othello cannot die at the executioner's hands; nor can he survive his crime. Antony and Cleopatra cannot surrender to Octavius; leaving behind a world too small for them, they go, as immortal lovers, to join Dido and Aeneas. Brutus, related to the great Cato, cannot accept defeat. In the plays inspired from antiquity, the hero's suicide is viewed as the supreme expression of freedom. . . . If Timon is of the same calibre as the other characters mentioned above, he does not submit to his destiny, he rises to it. He is not simply a malcontent, satisfied to condemn verbally and to show his fig tree to the Athenians: he matches his acts to his words in destroying his own life. A heroic gesture, arousing admiration as much as pity—but certainly not horror—his suicide reveals this same noble nature attested by the good characters in the play, but not so apparent in the action. Logical with himself, courageous, proud, Timon dies like a Roman.

As the supreme protest, Timon's suicide sets up the framework for the last phase of the tragic process: the revival. Timon has paid, and not with gold.

Suicide attentuates a little the weaknesses of this play by giving to Timon a tragic stature, by clarifying the conclusion and by lending movement to a character otherwise frozen in a perpetually sterile and sterilizing invective.

Bernard Paulin, ''La mort de 'Timon d'Athens','' in
Etudes Anglaises, *Vol. XVII, No. 1, January-March,
1964, pp. 1-8 [translated for this publication]*.

PETER URE (essay date 1964)

[*The view that* Timon *is a lesser, artistically flawed version of*
King Lear *goes back at least to Samuel Taylor Coleridge (1808-
18), but in the following excerpt Ure develops the comparison
with greater detail than had previously been attempted. Also significant is Ure's contention that though most critics refuse to see*
Timon *as a ''medieval morality Shakespearianized,'' many commentators have recognized the play's similarity to traditional morality drama. This point is further developed by A. S. Collins
(1946) and Anne Lancashire (1970).*]

[In Act III of *Timon of Athens*] Timon stage-manages the revelation of how his own nature has itself been transformed from
sweetness and dreamy abundance into bitterness and withdrawal as though he were the *régisseur* of some desperate anti-
masque, fitly opposite to the masque of Cupid performed at
[an] earlier feast. He still gives and gives out, but what he
gives are stones, projected from him in hurling movements of
fury.

Up to this point the play has been marked by that controlled
forward movement of event and character which is so characteristic of Shakespeare's and of most successful dramatic art.
It is easy to believe that Timon's trust in his friends, built as
it is on complete unawareness about them, should, when washed
by so icy a wave of reality, corrode into violent repugnance.
The very obviousness of the moral paradigm helps us to believe
that so, indeed, it did happen. It is not suggested in this part
of the play that the pattern of experience which has befallen
Timon is uniquely strange and never before traced out. . . .
The sense that Timon's experience illustrates a general truth,
while it need not detract from the sharpness of his own les-
soning, is precisely that quality which gives the play its character of a moral apologue. All the commentators have recognized that character, even though they may not all wish to see
it simply as a medieval morality Shakespearianized.

But in the last two Acts of the play both the enlightening
generalization of the theme and the forward-looking behaviour
of the protagonist are almost completely checked. For the whole
point about Timon is that he now becomes unique, strange,
the archetype of his kind, the famous Misanthrope: 'I am Misanthropos, and hate mankind.' The only change that does occur
is the enlargement of his hatred to include the whole cosmic
process. The extraordinary inclusiveness of his condemnation
of all human and animal life and of all Nature is a thing for
wonder and dismay. We contemplate him with amazement
because he goes so far; but after a while the amazement palls,
just as the magnified creatures of Dryden's heroic plays—'as
far above the ordinary proportion of the stage, as that is beyond
the words and actions of common life'—at first may make us
gasp and stretch our eyes, but later begin to languish before
our desire that they should do more than just parade their
excess. For the complement to Timon's uniqueness is his un-
changeability. Movement within him ceases, and he becomes
fixed for much of the rest of the play in an eternal gesture of
repugnance as though his last banquet had been like that mythological one at which the guests were turned to stone.

Timon's speeches in the last two Acts contain some very great
poetry (though much of it is only doubtfully *dramatic* poetry)
which reminds all their readers of the terrible curses and in-

vocations of Lear. His situation, driven out into the wilderness
by ingratitude, is very like Lear's. But Lear's vision of the
great world wearing itself out to naught is one which, in Keats's
words, he 'burns through'. As he opens his mind at length to
the truth about himself, pain alters to insight, and he is able
to overcome the poisons of ingratitude and the desire to punish.
This never happens to Timon. The poisons blacken all his
vision, even though his enemies are commoner and smaller
than Lear's. The faithful love of his steward is treated by him
(IV.iii) only as a grudgingly received exception to his obses-
sional rule that all men are contemptible. (pp. 48-51)

In the end Timon's tone grows tedious. His voice seeks again
and again the same pitch of bitter fury. The long speeches,
which as isolated curses or poems of hatred are charged with
some of Shakespeare's most effective and resonant images,
oppress the imagination. We soon realize that the face Timon
presents to his visitors, who come to watch him prowling up
and down in the cage of his hatred, will always be the same;
he seems to have passed beyond that ability to be modified by
his experience which is the continuing life of a dramatic character. It is a blessed relief when, with the approach of death,
invective gives way to elegy, in lines of grave and bitter beauty
unsurpassed in Shakespeare:

> I have a tree, which grows here in my close,
> That mine own use invites me to cut down,
> And shortly must I fell it. Tell my friends,
> Tell Athens, in the sequence of degree
> From high to low throughout, that whoso please
> To stop affliction, let him take his haste,
> Come hither ere my tree hath felt the axe,
> And hang himself. I pray you do my greeting . . .
>
> Come not to me again; but say to Athens,
> Timon hath made his everlasting mansion
> Upon the beached verge of the salt flood,
> Who once a day with his embossed froth
> The turbulent surge shall cover. Thither come,
> And let my grave-stone be your oracle.
> Lips, let four words go by and language end:
> What is amiss, plague and infection mend!
> Graves only be men's works, and death their gain!
> Sun, hide thy beams; Timon hath done his reign.
> [V. i. 205-23]

When, later, in the Senate of a yielding and contrite city Alcibiades reads Timon's bitter epitaph on himself, what Alcibiades says and does makes it clear enough that Timon's misanthropy is no statement of the poet's own judgement on the
world. The state can still be purged of breathless wrong and
pursy insolence; there is still the faithful steward; and even if
men forbid themselves tenderness, then Nature herself will
supply the recompense:

> Though thou abhorr'dst in us our human griefs,
> Scorn'st our brain's flow, and those our droplets which
> From niggard nature fall, yet rich conceit
> Taught thee to make vast Neptune weep for aye
> On thy low grave, on faults forgiven.   [V. iv. 75-9]
>   (pp. 51-2)

If we want to say that *Timon of Athens* is unsatisfying primarily
because [Shakespeare's] instinct for choosing the 'right' source
and subject seems for once to have failed him, the reasons for
failure, if it is admitted, in *All's Well* are different: he missed
opportunities which his story seemed to provide. As Shakespeare's experiments they are of course more instructive than

the successes of lesser men, especially since he was at the height of his poetic powers when he wrote them. The powers and the experimentation are both seen in the other two plays. *Measure for Measure* is the beneficiary of the lessons learnt in the making of *All's Well* (as *Lear* may well be of *Timon*). . . . (p. 53)

> Peter Ure, "'Timon of Athens'," in his William Shakespeare, the Problem Plays: "Troilus and Cressida," "All's Well That Ends Well," "Measure for Measure," "Timon of Athens", *revised edition, Longmans, Green & Co., 1964, pp. 44-51.*

NORTHROP FRYE (essay date 1965)

[*One of the most widely acclaimed critics of contemporary letters, Frye is best known for the theory and practice of "myth criticism" as elaborated especially in his* Anatomy of Criticism. *In the following excerpt, he characteristically analyzes* Timon *in terms of universal comic forms and character types that are for him aspects of a universal myth-making capacity in all human beings. Frye considers* Timon *much more akin to comedy than to tragedy. Although most critics still regard* Timon *as a tragedy, numerous others have described it variously as a satire, a morality play, and a social commentary. For readings in these different classifications, see the excerpts by August Wilhelm Schlegel (1808), G. Wilson Knight (1930), John W. Draper (1934), A. S. Collins (1946), Kenneth Muir (1947), Andor Gomme (1959), Peter Ure (1964), L. C. Knights (1969), and Anne Lancashire (1970).*]

[Comedy] is a structure embodying a variety of moods, the majority of which are comic in the sense of festive or funny, but a minority of which, in any well-constructed comedy, are not. Similarly, comedy presents a group of characters, the majority of which advance toward the new society of the final scene and join it. But, again, in any well-constructed comedy there ought to be a character or two who remain isolated from the action, spectators of it, and identifiable with the spectator aspect of ourselves.

Of these spectator roles two are of particular importance. One of them is the fool or clown, who, contrary to what we might expect, often preserves a curious aloofness from the comic action. The fool, when technically so, is frequently (Lavache, Touchstone, Feste) said to belong to the older generation, his jokes in a different idiom from what the society of the comedy wants and expects. He is often (Lavache, Costard, Gobbo, and Feste if that is the implication of Olivia's "dishonest") said to be lustful, more inclined to get girls into trouble than to take any responsibility for them afterward. References are made (Costard, Touchstone, Lavache) to his being whipped or imprisoned. The clown is significantly linked—usually by antagonism, for isolated characters do not form a society—with another role in which a character personifies a withdrawal from the comic society in a more concentrated way. There is, as usual, no word for this role, and I am somewhat perplexed what name to give it. Names which I have used elsewhere, such as *pharmakos* and churl, belong rather to the different character types that may or may not have this role. I select *idiotes*, more or less at random. The *idiotes* is usually isolated from the action by being the focus of the anticomic mood, and so may be the technical villain, like Don Juan, or the butt, like Malvolio and Flastaff, or simply opposed by temperament to festivity, like Jaques. Although the villainous, the ridiculous, and the misanthropic are closely associated in comedy, there is enough variety of motivation here to indicate that the *idiotes* is not a character type, like the clown, though typical features recur, but a structural device that may use a variety of characters. (pp. 92-3)

In tragedy, of course, the hero is always something of an *idiotes*, isolated from the society in which he has his being. Perhaps the most concentrated study of social isolation in the tragedies is *Coriolanus*, where the hero is a man whose "heart's his mouth," who, like Moliere's Alceste in a comic setting, carries sincerity to the extreme of a social vice. In Plutarch the Greek counterpart, or rather contrast, to Coriolanus is Alcibiades, who also returns in revenge to the city that has exiled him, and it would be a logical development for Shakespeare to go from the isolation of Coriolanus to the isolation of Alcibiades's friend Timon. It may seem an irresponsible paradox to speak of *Timon of Athens* as a comedy. Yet if we think of it simply as a tragedy, we are almost bound to see it as a failed tragedy, comparing it to its disadvantage with *King Lear*. But we can hardly suppose that Shakespeare was foolish enough to attempt the same kind of thing that he attempted in *King Lear* with so middle-class and un-titanic a hero. It seems to me that this extraordinary play, half morality and half folk tale, the fourth and last of the Plutarchan plays, is the logical transition from *Coriolanus* to the romances, and that it has many features making for an *idiotes* comedy rather than a tragedy. If we were to see the action of *Twelfth Night* through the eyes of the madly used Malvolio, or the action of *The Merchant of Venice* through the eyes of the bankrupt and beggared Shylock, the tone would not be greatly different from that of the second half of *Timon of Athens*. (p. 98)

In the first half of this play Timon is surrounded by the rare triumphs of love and fortune, for a masque of Cupid in his honor takes place at his banquet and his painter depicts him as under the favor of fortune. It gradually dawns on us that what seems to be generosity is rather, or is also, a humor of prodigality. Timon is never released from his humor; the humor merely goes into reverse, and in his exile he keeps flinging gold at his visitors from opposite motives. His story is, in the words of Launce, a parable of the prodigious son who has spent his proportion, but he is as prodigal with curses as blessings, and his misanthropy represents as much of a social half-truth as his benevolence did before. The fact that there is no heroine in this play, nor in fact any females at all except a brace of whores attached to Alcibiades, reinforces the sense of the play as a comedy of humor with no focus for a comic development.

In the festive society of Timon's prosperous days the *idiotes* is Apemantus. Apemantus is something of a clown too, but the *idiotes* is normally higher in social rank than the clown, and Apemantus carries a fool around with him partly to make this point. Apemantus is, like Jaques, a philosopher, of the Cynic school, though his ideal is the Stoic one of invulnerability, as his name, which means "suffering no pain," signifies. After Timon becomes a misanthrope, he takes over the *idiotes* role, and Apemantus comes to visit him and point out that his motivation is suspect. From the point of view of comic structure, what he is really protesting about is being himself degraded to the rank of clown as Timon becomes the *idiotes*. In the quarrel that ensues between them, each is trying to assert that the other is really a fool and not a genuine misanthrope. (pp. 99-100)

What fascinates us about the *idiotes* and clown is that they are not purely isolated individuals: we get fitful glimpses of a hidden world which they guard or symbolize. They may be able to speak for their world, like Jaques, or it may remain locked up in their minds, breaking through suddenly and involuntarily. The world we glimpse may be evil, like Don John's cave of spleen, or ridiculous, like the world of Malvolio's fantasies which are, in Olivia's parody of the Song of Songs, sick of self-love. But it is never a wholly simple world, and it exerts on the main action a force which is either counter-dramatic or antidramatic. Some of the most haunting speeches in Shakespeare are connected with these shifts of perspective provided by alienated characters. (p. 101)

> *Northrop Frye, "The Triumph of Time," in his* A Natural Perspective: The Development of Shakespearean Comedy and Romance, *Columbia University Press, 1965, pp. 72-117.*

JAROLD W. RAMSEY   (essay date 1966)

[*Whereas Winifred M. T. Nowottny (1959) regarded the transformation of the world in Timon's imagination as one that overthrows traditional Christian values and replaces them with corrupt secular ones, Ramsey argues that Timon's transformation into the "hater of man" suggests not a new system of beliefs but a vision of "utter desolation" and total nihilism. The nihilistic vision in Shakespeare's play has also been examined by Wyndham Lewis (1927).*]

Timon of Athens is Shakespeare's starkest dramatization of his perception of the painful disjunctive logic in which Either/Or

THERE'S·MORE GOLD ACT·IV·SCENE·III

Act IV. Scene iii. Timon of Athens, Phrynia, Timandra. By Byam Shaw (1902). From the Art Collection of the Folger Shakespeare Library.

as moral alternatives become Neither/Nor. The play's major events all involve, in some way, a violation of consequentiality and normal expectation; its major sympathetic characters are all caught in what Timon calls "confounding contraries"—the contradictions that are *inherent* in human institutions and values. . . . My experience with the play is that, within the rather narrow limits of its artistic validity, it is disturbingly pessimistic, a kind of *elenchus* to certain received moral ideals of the Christian faith. It is as if Shakespeare were following out to their bitter ends the implications of [one of] Greville's paradoxes, his famous apology: "I know the world, and believe in God."

In confronting us with the unresolved conflict of two sets of values, those demanded by God and those enforced by "the world," *Timon of Athens* makes a bold and immediate challenge to the teachings the New Testament urges men to live by. The idealism of Christian ethics is seen as potentially cruel, destructive, perhaps impossible to live by. I think Timon's career is calculated to ask us, "Well now, what are the basic assumptions of our morality? List them, please; now observe that this man Timon seems to agree with us. Very well, let us extend these assmptions as far as we humanly can—because, if they are truly and fundamentally good in themselves, as we are taught, we cannot enact them to excess, can we? What sense is there in obeying Christ in moderation? His Gospels contain no grounds for it. Timon will perform the noble experiment for us . . . but alas, poor Timon? Has his ruin nullified our Christian assumptions, *reductio ad absurdum*?"

Consider the governing themes of *Timon of Athens*—which are specified so insistently in this insistent play that there is no question about what topics Shakespeare had on his mind. They are: Bounty, Friendship, Fortune, and Nature; they can be abstractly defined and schematized roughly as follows. For Timon in Acts One and Two, the Good Life is the life of bountiful magnificence, of noble and generous commerce between friends. His categorical imperative is thus based upon a principle of reciprocal bounty or largesse: "We are born to do benefits" for each other. Gratitude is the unspoken but cardinal emotion in such a system; it is the guarantee that the reciprocal (but not necessarily proportional) exchange of charity and love will be continued. At the heart of Timon's pre-misanthropic philosophy is an essentially Christian vision of universal harmony: God (here, "the gods") displays His benevolence through a benevolent natural order; Man, Nature's favored creature, is obliged to establish his society, by analogy to natural law, on the ideals of social harmony and unstinting bounty. And as an integral part of the natural order, man's own nature allows him to keep this obligation. A "lord" should be *Lordly* in his performance of charity; on such a life, Fortune can only smile.

The thematic oppositions of the drama can be defined in terms of a series of puns on these abstractions. Timon's "trencher-friends" talk a great deal about Fortune, too; but for them, she is only a punning metaphor for the portable fortune that Timon gives away so liberally. The only god recognized by the aristocrats of Athens is the visible god Pecunia; but they are glad to assist Timon in the rites of Friendship and Bounty, so long as Fortune continues to smile on him, and his fortunes continue to rain on them. The Poet and Painter, Ventidius and Sempronius and the rest of Timon's circle represent, then, the exact denial of his ideal system. Art, ideally the representation of Nature, instead falsifies it; Generous Friendship becomes Greedy Hypocrisy; Bounty, the reward of Fortune, becomes the means to it; Magnificence becomes mean Ingratitude; the Natural Order becomes what men make of it, for their own selfish purposes. In Athens, usury constitutes a radical denial of the Timonian ideal of free and loving exchange: usurers like Isidore and Varro demand interest on what is given. Timon's "Masque of Cupid" (I.ii) is perverted by his friends into a masque of cupidity. In short, the drama poises Timon's concept of a coherent and benevolent nature, of which human nature is a consistent part, against the wholly artificial outlook of the Athenian aristocracy, artificial in the sense that it recognizes no natural imperative higher than those of man himself. Athens is a walled city. (pp. 162-63)

At the center of the contradictions in *Timon of Athens*, there is a pattern of allusions, verbal echoes, and events that has never been adequately dealt with by critics of the play, for one reason or another. It is simply this: in trying to obey the higher "law" to which he feels bound, Timon becomes a figure of Christ, a painfully human caricature of the Son of God. (p. 166)

[Timon] is portrayed as a pre-Christian and unconscious Christ-figure; he only plays the role he thinks "the gods" have assigned him, and he plays it without stint. So, in his second appearance in the drama, he declines the offer of Ventidius to repay as a loan what Timon meant as a free-will gift:

> there's none
> Can truly say he gives, if he receives.
> If our betters play at that game, we must not dare
> To imitate them; faults that are rich are fair.
>
> [I. ii. 10-13]

That is, though the gods expect reverential "payment" for *their* generosity, men should not imitate them in this expectation; if it is a fault not to accept repayment nor to offer it on the human level, it is a "rich" fault. The general idea is, of course, fundamental to Christ's teachings; Timon's phrasing of it is most closely matched by one of His corollaries from the Golden Rule, in the Sermon on the Mount:

> And if ye lend to them of whom ye hope to receive, what hope have ye? For sinners also do even the same.

and by the quotation of Christ in *Acts*, xx.35: "It is more blessed to give, than to receive"—a "rich fault," in other words. Timon's general concept of the divine precedent for human charity is best glossed by one of Christ's first instructions to the apostles. In *Matt.*, x.8: "freely ye have received, freely give."

But, though suggestive, these are allusions, not identifications. Shakespeare begins to color Timon's identity in earnest a little later, during his first banquet. . . . What is the banquet, in other words, but a monstrous parody of the Communion of the Last Supper, with every guest playing Judas Iscariot to Timon's Christ? "It has been proved." Let a mere man devote himself to a life of "freely giving," and his brethren will turn cannibal and eat him up—before they betray him. Out of this hideous vision flow the images of anthropophagy which lie just behind Timon's later curses, becoming explicit more than once. (pp. 166-67)

The climax of denial comes when Timon himself is accosted by a pack of stewards, who "attack" him with their masters' claims. Timon's maddened response is to offer his flesh and

blood for the remission, not of his debtors sins of ingratitude, but of his debts!

> Knock me down . . . cleave me to the girdle. . . .
> Cut my heart in sums. . . .
> Tell out my blood. . . .
> Take me, tear me, and the gods fall upon you.
>
> [III. iv. 90, 92, 94, 99]

"Take, eat, this is my body. . . . Drink ye all of it, for this is my blood of the new testament, which is shed for the remission of sins." (*Matt.*, xxvi.26-28)

This ritual butchery seems to suggest to Timon the idea of another banquet for his man-eating friends, a fierce mockery of the first. (p. 168)

In this final phase of Timon's parody of Christ, after his rejection by men, he dwells for a time in a suggestive cave, emerging to condemn all humanity. And the parodic pattern is completed when, instead of rising from the cave to be transfigured, he descends from it to be merely obliterated in the sands of the seashore. (p. 169)

This image of Timon's end is powerfully suggestive, and a majority of commentators have understood Alcibiades' rather obscurely-worded interpretation of it as Shakespeare's own. To Alcibiades, it conveys a sense of affirmation:

> Though thou abhor'dst in us our human griefs,
> Scorn'dst our brains' flow, and those our droplets which
> From niggard nature fall; yet rich conceit
> Taught thee to make vast Neptune weep for aye
> On thy low grave, on faults forgiven. Dead
> is noble Timon, of whose memory
> Hereafter more.　　　　　　　　　　[V. iv. 75-81]

But isn't this essentially a final rather glib sentimentalization of Timon, acceptable neither as a prophecy of moral regeneration nor as a confirmation of the unity of man and Nature? . . . *Rich conceit*: the motive of Timon's choice of a grave-site is just that. Like his great Christian vision of a life of unchecked bounty and friendship between men ("We are born to do benefits"), his final concept of a sympathetic inanimate Nature is shown to be, alas, an ideal, a figment, a truly pathetic fallacy. One sees at once the ideal nobility of each "conceit," and the real form it takes in the play: Timon the figure of Christ—in reality, prodigal, impercipient, something of a fool; Timon the enshrined martyr—in point of fact, simply nullified under an indifferent tide. Alcibiades, the generous friend and military opportunist, leads his whores back to Athens, to a politic compromise with the city that is hard to stomach; the faithful Flavius and the Apostles of Timon have vanished; and the "soul of bounty" himself—"of whose memory / Hereafter more"—is simply dead, although the memory of Timon Misanthropus, the ferocious Hater of Man, will certainly live on. It is an image, almost unparalleled in the plays, of utter desolation, of nihilism, of *nada*. Shakespeare has given us the Either and the Or of Timon's experience as impossibilities, either the unqualified Imitation of Christ or the life and death of misanthropy; he has given us no viable middle term. (pp. 170-71)

Jarold W. Ramsey, "Timon's Imitation of Christ," in Shakespeare Studies: An Annual Gathering of Research, Criticism, and Reviews, *Vol. II, 1966, pp. 162-73.*

L. C. KNIGHTS (essay date 1969)

[*A renowned English Shakespearean scholar, Knights followed the precepts of I. A. Richards and F. R. Leavis and sought for a total evaluation of a work of literature. His* How Many Children Had Lady Macbeth? *(1933)—a milestone study in the twentieth-century reaction to the Shakespearean criticism of the previous century— criticizes the traditional emphasis on "character" as an approach which inhibits the reader's total response to Shakespeare's plays. In the excerpt below, Knights follows in the tradition of such earlier critics as William Richardson (1784), Hermann Ulrici (1839), and Denton J. Snider (1887), all of whom consider Timon more of a self-serving, deceitful individual than a generous and noble person destroyed by a corrupt world. This latter interpretation of Timon's character was perhaps most forcefully argued by G. Wilson Knight (1930), whom Knights criticizes in the essay below. Although Knights cannot accept the interpretation of Timon as a tragedy of an honorable, altruistic idealist overcome by an evil society, he also cannot accept the drama as simply a morality play, an assessment put forth most thoroughly by A. S Collins (1946). Instead, he claims that Timon is Shakespeare's dramatic portrait of an individual whose false vision of himself and his world is totally destroyed when his external "supports"— in Timon's case his wealth and public recognition—are removed. Knights characterizes Timon's eventual misanthropy, not as an appropriate response to reality, but as a "primitive rage at the destruction of an ego-ideal."*]

One of the most interesting problems in Shakespeare criticism—as indeed in the criticism of all great literature—is the problem of divergent interpretations. I do not refer to shifts of emphasis and approach inevitable as times change, or to the mysterious power of works of art to reveal *more* meaning in the course of centuries, but to radically incompatible accounts of 'the meaning' of a work among readers who respect each other's standards and general powers of judgment. A glance at the history of opinion about Shakespeare's *Timon of Athens* suggests that the critic who chooses to write on this most puzzling of Shakespeare's plays must take especial care to expose the grounds of his judgment. An attempt to do this is my tribute to the author of *The Wheel of Fire* and *The Imperial Theme* [see excerpt above by G. Wilson Knight, 1930], works which, more than any others available at the time, helped my generation in the arduous and endlessly rewarding task of reading Shakespeare for themselves.

There seems no doubt that *Timon of Athens* is an unfinished play: not in the sense that it lacks a formal conclusion, but in the sense that it has not been finally worked over for presentation on the stage. It is, however, very much more than a mere draft; it is a play moving towards completion; and although the great variety of critical opinion warns us that it is not easy to get at the meaning, there is no reason why we should not trust our impression that Shakespeare is saying something important, and use our wits to determine what that something may be. Our best course, as usual, is to trust our immediate sense of dramatic power, to begin by concentrating on those parts where our minds and imaginations are most fully engaged, and to ask ourselves how these are related to each other and to the remainder of the play—to those parts of lesser intensity that serve to reinforce, to modify or to cast a fresh light on what is more prominent. I am not advocating simple concentration on dramatic highlights: all I am saying is that understanding has to start somewhere, and we run less risk of going astray if we start with whatever it may be that most engages us.

Timon is no exception to the rule that Shakespeare's plays are always superbly well planned. When we look back on *Timon,* after directly experiencing it, we recall three episodes or phases of great dramatic effectiveness. The first is the presentation of Timon in his prosperity, surrounded by suitors, friends and parasites. This begins about a third of the way through the first scene and continues throughout the second (that is to say, to the end of the first Act). The second is the scene of the mock banquet (III.vi), where Timon serves covered dishes of warm water to the friends whose utter falseness has been exposed, denounces them for the fawning parasites they are ('Uncover, dogs, and lap'), beats them, and drives them out. The third is the exhibition of Timon's misanthropy: this consists of the tirade of IV.i, and the tirades and curses of IV.iii, when Timon is confronted, in turn, with Alcibiades, Apemantus, the bandits, and other intruders on his solitude. There is in addition a kind of prologue, when Poet, Painter, Jeweller and Merchant congregate at Timon's house, and the Poet describes the common changes and chances of Fortune's Hill; and a kind of epilogue, where the cowed Senators of Athens submit to Alcibiades, Timon's death is reported, and Alcibiades speaks a formal valediction.

All these major scenes, and all but one of the intervening scenes, concentrate on Timon with an unremitting attention. The question that any producer, like any reader, must ask himself is, how is Timon presented? how are we to take him? Now it is obviously possible to take him as a truly noble man, ruined by his own generosity—'Undone by goodness', as the Steward says—someone, quite simply too good for the society that surrounds him. Roy Walker, in an interesting review of the Old Vic 1956 production, says, 'it was presumably the poet's intention to show how selfish society drives out true generosity'. (pp. 1-3)

Of remarks such as these I can only say that they seem to me completely to miss the point of the opening scenes. Timon is surrounded by the corrupt and the self-seeking: this is made very plain, and he must have been rather stupid or else possessed by a very strong emotional bias to have had no glimmer of it. Of course it is good to use one's money to redeem a friend from a debtor's prison or to enable a poor serving-gentleman to marry the girl of his choice. But it is not good to engage in a perpetual potlatch. (p. 3)

Gifts, to be meaningful and not part of a ritual of exchange or display, must be person to person. Timon, who does not pause to look at the Painter's picture or to glance at the Poet's book, hardly *attends* to anyone. . . . When, therefore, he voices the incontrovertible sentiments we have had quoted as an expression of his magnanimity—'We are born to do benefits. . . . O what a precious comfort 'tis to have so many like brothers commanding one another's fortunes'—it is not moral truth that we recognize but self-indulgence in easy emotion. . . . Compared with those who have idealized the early Timon for his generosity, the eighteenth-century critic, William Richardson, surely came nearer to the truth when he wrote:

> Shakespeare, in his *Timon of Athens,* illustrates
> the consequences of that inconsiderate profu-
> sion which has the appearance of liberality, and
> is supposed even by the inconsiderate person
> himself to proceed from a generous principle;
> but which, in reality, has its chief origin in the
> love of distinction [see excerpt above, 1784].

Tragedy of course takes us beyond bare moral judgment. But moral judgment necessarily enters into our experience of tragedy: and it is worth remarking how sharply, in this play, Shakespeare seems to insist on the moral issue, even to the extent of using techniques reminiscent of the morality plays. In the first part of the opening scene (in what I have called the Prologue) Timon's situation is presented with a formal simplification that suggests a moral *exemplum* rather than any kind of naturalistic portrayal. (pp. 3-4)

Now it is of course true that the tradition of didactic simplification was still active in Shakespeare's lifetime. A rather dull little morality called *Liberality and Prodigality* was revived and acted before the Queen in 1601. As in our play Money is shown as in the gift of Fortune; Prodigality gets rid of Money with something of Timon's unthinking ease—

> Who lacks money, ho! who lacks money?
> But ask and have: money, money, money!

—and when Virtue hands over Money to 'my steward Liberality'—Prodigality having proved unworthy—her servant Equity preaches the golden mean ('Where reason rules, there is the golden mean') in the manner of Apemantus moralizing to Timon about 'the middle of humanity'. But we have only to put *Timon of Athens* beside *Liberality and Prodigality,* or beside a more sophisticated play in the same tradition such as Ben Jonson's *The Staple of News,* to see how inappropriate, here, any kind of Morality label would be. For myself I think we get closer to Shakespeare's play by recognizing the didactic elements than by a too ready responsiveness to Timon as the disillusioned idealist. But to see the play as straight didactic moralizing directed *at* Timon as Prodigality—as though he were merely an illustration of a moral thesis—that too feels inadequate. The verse is often too powerful to allow us that kind and degree of detachment as we judge. (pp. 5-6)

Timon of Athens, in so far as it is a direct satire on the power of money, can be seen as Shakespeare's response to certain prominent features in the economic and social life of his own day. And the satire, as we have just seen, has the kind of bite that makes it relevant to *any* acquisitive society, our own as much as Shakespeare's. (It was almost inevitable that Karl Marx should quote Timon's denunciation of 'gold . . . this yellow slave' in an early chapter of *Capital* [see excerpt above, 1844].)

But—and here comes the difficulty—when Timon first gives expression to his outraged feelings and curses Athens, in forty lines of invective the only reference to money is short, incidental and indirect [IV. i. 8-12]. He does, on the other hand, have a lot to say about sexual corruption; just as in encouraging Alcibiades to destroy Athens his catalogue of the city's vices, after a brief mention of usury, plunges into a lengthy diatribe against an anarchic sexuality. Nothing in the play has prepared us for this (apart from the dance of the Amazons in I.ii, Timon seems to have lived in an exclusively masculine society). And although Timon does of course denounce money, and although he subsequently gives some of his new-found gold to Alcibiades to pay troops levied against Athens, and some to the harlots to encourage them to spread diseases, it is not money-satire, or satire on ingratitude, that forms the substance of the long dialogue in the woods with Apemantus. In short, given the obvious data of the play, and given the obvious grounds for Timon's rejection of a society shown as corrupt and usurous, there is nevertheless something excessive in the *terms* of his rejection, just as there is something strange (and, if you see the play solely in terms of a *saeva indignatio* directed against society, even tedious) in the slanging match with Apemantus in the woods. What, then, is Shakespeare up to?

I suggest that as in all the greater plays Shakespeare is using the outward action to project and define something deeply inward. I do not mean simply that in *Lear* or *Macbeth* or *Othello* Shakespeare observes character with a rare psychological penetration, though he does of course do this. I mean that in a variety of ways he uses the forms of dramatic action, external conflict and event, to reveal inner conflicts and distortions, basic potentialities for good and evil, at a level where individual characteristics take second place to human nature itself. In short he demonstrates precisely what T. S. Eliot meant when he wrote:

> A verse play is not a play done into verse, but a different kind of play: in a way more realistic than 'naturalistic drama', because, instead of clothing nature in poetry, it should remove the surface of things, expose the underneath, or the inside, of the natural surface appearance.

In *Timon,* as in *Lear* and *Othello,* Shakespeare is revealing what is 'underneath . . . the natural surface appearance'— sometimes in a naive Morality way (as when the mock feast of steam and stones instead of nourishment shows us what the earlier feast really was—not a feast at all), sometimes with the force and subtlety of the great tragedies.

In *Timon* the surface appearance is lightly sketched in the suggestions of a corrupt society, where the business of individuals is very much to feather their own nests: more firmly, though in a rather schematized way, in the presentation of Timon's friends and parasites. But the surface appearance on which, in the first Act, attention is most sharply concentrated is Man in Prosperity, the ego sustained in a fixed posture by an endless series of reflections which show it just as it thinks itself to be. . . . That this picture—of what the Steward, allowing himself a touch of satire, calls 'Great Timon, noble, worthy, royal Timon'—has to be drawn again and again betrays a compulsive need. What supports Timon in his self-idolatry, what buys him reassurance ('You see, my lord, how amply y'are belov'd'), is of course his wealth. But the wealth is secondary in dramatic importance to what it serves: means to the same end could have been extorted professions of filial affection, as in *Lear,* or any of the familiar tricks that we use to cut a fine figure in our own eyes. Towards the end of Act II the Steward points the action:

> Heavens, have I said, the bounty of this lord!
> How many prodigal bits have slaves and peasants
> This night englutted! Who is not Timon's?
> What heart, head, sword, force, means, but is Lord
>   Timon's.
> Great Timon, noble, worthy, royal Timon?
> Ah, when the means are gone that buy this praise,
> The breath is gone whereof this praise is made,
> Feast-won, fast-lost.   [II. ii. 164-71]

At virtually one stroke the props to Timon's self-esteem are removed, and he is reduced to 'unaccommodated man'. He is stripped, so to speak, of his protective covering, and, as in *Lear,* his physical appearance reflects an inner state. 'Nothing I'll bear from thee But nakedness, thou detestable town!' [IV. i. 32-3.] (pp. 7-10)

There, I think, you have the central interest of the play. In a world such as the men of great tragic vision have always known it to be, a world where you clearly cannot remove all the threats—the inner and the outer threats—to your security, how, quite simply, do you keep going? Life only allows a limited number of choices. Either you live by some kind of integrating principle through which even potentially destructive energies can be harnessed, stability and movement combined; or, plumping for security—for 'a solid without fluctuation', like Blake's Urizen—you seek artificial supports for a fixed posture. Unfortunately the concomitant of a fixed posture is unremitting anxiety to maintain itself; and it is in the nature of artificial supports, sooner or later, to break down. This is what happens to Timon. When his supports are removed, 'when the means are gone that buy this praise', he is left, like Lear, with 'nothing'—nothing, that is, but a vision of a completely evil world that partly, of course, reflects a social reality, but is also an expression of his own self-hatred and self-contempt. . . . (p. 10)

It is this, surely, that explains the nature of Timon's first great speech of invective, where there is very little about money and nothing about ingratitude, but much about sexual incontinence and general anarchy. . . . It is a little like what Conrad's Marlow glimpsed on his voyage up the river to the heart of darkness, though perhaps more specifically realized. Timon's horror is of anarchic impulses that he knows within himself when the picture of noble Timon is destroyed. It is true of course that Timon presently denounces the inequalities bred by fortune, the corruption caused by money; and throughout the scenes in the woods, when he is visited by Alcibiades and the harlots, the bandits, and various former hangers-on who have heard of his newly discovered wealth, the satire on money-lust continues. All this is clearly very near the dramatic centre of the play. But to treat it as *the* controlling centre, *the* dominant theme, is to see things entirely from Timon's point of view, from the point of view of a man who feels unjustly treated by others,—as of course he is. But the play only makes sense as a whole when we see him as self-betrayed, his revulsion against the city as equally a revulsion against himself. (pp. 10-11)

If Shakespeare's intention was in fact, as I suppose, to portray self-revulsion, the shattering of an unreal picture and the flight from hitherto concealed aspects of the self that are found insupportable, this would also explain the drawn-out exchanges with Apemantus in the woods. In the opening of the play Apemantus, as professional cynic, is not an attractive figure. But he is no Thersites. It is from him, almost as much as from the Steward, that we get a true picture of Timon's 'bounty' and its effects. . . . But if Apemantus is not Thersites, neither is he Lear's Fool, the disinterested teller of unwelcome truths: the emotional bias, like the ostentatious poverty, is too marked. It is this that explains his dual and ambiguous role in the later scene. On the one hand he is the objective commentator, a mentor that Timon ignores at his peril; and since this is so clearly intended it is a mistake to play him simply as the abject and railing cynic. (p. 12)

Some of this, perhaps, is matter for dispute. What is abundantly clear is that Timon's misanthropy is in no essential way an approach to reality; it is primitive rage at the destruction of an ego-ideal, horror and hated at what is revealed when support for that ideal picture is withdrawn. Denied the absolute and one-sided endorsement that he had claimed, the self-esteem that his wealth had enabled him to buy, he refuses to see his claims for what they were. Instead he projects onto the world at large his own desire to get what he wanted by means that were essentially dishonest. He has been, in effect, a thief. (p. 13)

I am of course aware that this unfavourable view of Timon has against it not only the opinions of many critics but, more

important, certain pronouncements within the play itself—pronouncements that, unlike the eulogies of the parasites, are disinterested, and must therefore be given due weight. There is the unwavering loyalty of the Steward, for whom Timon is

> Poor honest lord, brought low by his own heart,
> Undone by goodness . . .   [IV. ii. 37-8]

and there is the eulogy by Alcibiades that virtually concludes the play. . . . But I do not think that either substantially modifies the account that I have given. The Steward, playing Kent to Timon's Lear, reminds us in his devotion that love and loyalty see further than the eye of the mere spectator; there is no need to doubt the potentiality of goodness that is in Timon. But in the play it remains unrealized. The most that this old servant's undemanding devotion can wring from Timon is the recognition that his undiscriminating condemnation of mankind must allow of one exception:

> You perpetual-sober gods! I do proclaim
> One honest man. Mistake me not, but one,
> No more, I pray. . . .   [IV. iii. 496-98]
>   (pp. 14-15)

Some of our perplexities [brought about by the final scene] may be due to the play's unfinished state. But if we take the scene in conjunction with III.v—the previous confrontation of Alcibiades with apparently representative Athenians—it suggests a world of hazy verbiage. (What right has Alcibiades to reproach Athens with being 'lascivious'? When last seen he was trailing about with a couple of mistresses. As for the Senators, anything goes, so long as they can save their skins and plaster the situation with appropriate platitude.) And this does not only contrast with Timon's blazing hatred, it offers a parallel. Men set themselves up for judges, when the underlying attituds, from which their judgments spring, are distorted by evasions, self-exculpations, and lack of self-knowledge. All that is said in this final scene is, for Alcibiades and the Senators, an easy way out—the world's way when confronted with any kind of absolute, of negation or affirmation. In this context, 'Dead is noble Timon' suggests a bitter irony. Timon's self-composed epitaph was not noble; and his wholesale condemnation of the world, though not an easy way, was easier than the pain of self-recognition.

Presumably we shall never know when *Timon of Athens* was written, nor why it was not finally completed. . . . My own guess, for what it is worth, is that *Timon* was drafted when *Lear* was already taking shape in Shakespeare's mind. Both plays are about a man 'who hath ever but slenderly known himself', who tries to buy love and respect, who has genuine reason to feel wronged, and whose sense of betrayal releases an indictment of the world that can't be shrugged off as 'madness' or 'misanthropy', but a man also whose sense of betrayal by others masks a deep inward flaw; in both the stripping away of all protective covering reveals with fierce clarity a world of evil. But there the major resemblances cease. *Timon of Athens* contains a loyal and decent Steward; it does not contain a Cordelia. Timon goes almost as far in hatred and revulsion as Lear; there is nothing in his mind that corresponds to Lear's gropings towards self-knowledge. And it is the active presence in *King Lear* of positive and affirmative elements that, paradoxically, makes its presentation of pain and evil so much more deeply disturbing. You can disengage from *Timon of Athens,* for all its power: you have to live with *King Lear.* And when the greater theme took possession of Shakespeare's mind, the more partial one could be abandoned: Timon had 'done his reign'. (pp. 16-17)

L. C. Knights, "'Timon of Athens'" (reprinted by permission of the author), in The Morality of Art: Essays Presented to G. Wilson Knight by His Colleagues and Friends, edited by D. W. Jefferson, Routledge & Kegan Paul Ltd, 1969, pp. 1-17.

CHARLTON HINMAN   (essay date 1969)

[Unlike most earlier critics who have dealt with the authorship question in Timon, Hinman argues that the play is indeed a complete work and was not left unfinished by Shakespeare. Hinman concludes that Timon stands as "a whole play," its scenes and acts coherently interrelated, its progress systematic, and its conclusion definite and complete. For more commentary on the authorship question, see the excerpts by Charles Knight (1843), Gulian C. Verplanck (1847), F. G. Fleay (1874), George Brandes (1895-96), Walter Raleigh (1907), E. K. Chambers (1908), Una Ellis-Fermor (1942), and G. B. Harrison (1951).]

[The opening scene of Timon of Athens] is lively, colorful, full of both movement and matter. It has abundant variety, yet its numerous components are coherently interrelated and form a unified whole. The economy with which so much is so quickly imparted is striking: in less than three hundred lines the atmosphere in which the action of the first part of the play is to take place is well established; the theme of this action is both announced and in due course vigorously restated; all the most important characters save one—Timon's steward, Flavius, who is to appear in the next scene—are introduced; the essential qualities of Timon, or at any rate of Timon in his prosperity, are already fairly clear; and the likelihood of future disaster is made plain. Even in King Lear (to which Timon is so similar as regards the general structure of its opening scene) the exposition, the initial presentation of situation and character, is hardly managed more adroitly.

To point out these virtues is of course not to affirm that there are no defects whatever. On the contrary, the most serious faults with which the play as a whole can be charged . . . are to some extent shared by its initial scene. Alcibiades' part here seems slighted, for example, and the relationship between him and Timon is not made clear; nor is Timon's nobility of soul, though frequently mentioned, made convincing. Notwithstanding these weaknesses, however, the many-faceted excellence of this scene is hardly to be denied; and one may add at once that dramaturgical skill of a high order is evident throughout Timon. Still, there are some notable lapses. The passage of approximately seventy lines devoted to the fool and the page (see II, ii, 47-119) is dramatically unnecessary, has small intrinsic merit, and seems at best an infelicitous interruption of the serious business in hand. But this particular kind of artlessness, of which there are instances enough in other Shakespearean plays, is rare, whereas examples of superior craftmanship abound. The various ingredients that make up the long second scene of Act I are as skillfully combined as those in the first; and what immediately follows, the very short contrasting scene in which the imminence of Timon's fall is made plain (II, i), is equally effective in its very different way. Especially illuminating are the three consecutive scenes at the beginning of Act III which, collectively, provide the play's crucial demonstration of its central figure's betrayal by his fair-weather friends. Here, each of the lords most deeply in Timon's debt is in turn appealed to for help, which he declines to give. The scenes in question are all short, and precisely the same story is told in each. Yet monotony is skillfully avoided. In less than two hundred lines Lords Lucullus, Lucius, and Sempronius become distinct individuals, each loathsome in his own

special way; and even Timon's three servants are to some extent individualized. The second, who is much meeker than the other two (one notes that he is called Servilius), is appropriately denied a final speech of passionate denunciation like that given each of his fellows. The vileness of Lord Lucius receives its full share of castigation, however, from the "three strangers" whose presence effectively differentiates the second of these scenes from the first and the third. There is no doubt some artificiality in this, but there is art as well. And there is more art and less trickery later on. It must be acknowledged that the misanthropic tirades of Timon in his latter days (Acts IV and V) are long-drawn-out; but while in aim and mood they are all alike, the virtuosity they nonetheless show as a succession of variations on a single theme is remarkable indeed.

More remarkable still, to be sure, is the poetry in this part of the play. What above all else makes Timon of Athens an extraordinary work of art is the magnificence of the language in which its hero, to whom life at its best has become no more than a long disease, pours out his bitterness of soul, his anguished contempt for all humanity, and his longing for the nothingness of death. But the poetic excellence of Acts IV and V has long been recognized, whereas the lesser merits of the play, though both pervasive and real, have tended to be overlooked. Critical interest has usually been directed instead to the reasons for Timon's failure to produce at last, despite the eloquence of its concluding scenes, the kind of effect we regard as essential to all really great tragedy. And much attention has also been given to certain peculiarities in the only authoritative text that has come down to us, peculiarities that are without parallel elsewhere. These are especially interesting, and are not without relevance to questions about the play's literary qualities, as indications that Shakespeare left Timon of Athens unfinished.

"Unfinished," however, is a misleading term. Timon is a whole play. That there is a marked difference between Acts I-III and IV-V does not imply incoherence or betray any lack of plan. What may be called the two movements of the play are evidently intended to produce the very striking before-and-after contrast that we find: the first three acts are a necessary preparation for the last two; progress is systematic throughout; and when the last speech of Alcibiades comes to a close ("Let our drums strike") there can be no more doubt that a conclusion has been reached than when Fortinbras issues a similar command ("Go, bid the soldiers shoot") and Hamlet ends.

Emphatically, then, Timon is not a mere fragment. It is complete, or at least very nearly so. (pp. 1136-37)

Charlton Hinman, in his introduction to "The Life of Timon of Athens," in William Shakespeare: The Complete Works, Alfred Harbage, General Editor, revised edition, Penguin Books Inc., 1969, pp. 1136-68.

ANNE LANCASHIRE   (essay date 1970)

[In a conclusion comparable to that of A. S. Collins (1946), Lancashire regards Timon not as a tragedy but as a "secularized, anti-traditional morality play," similar in many respects to the medieval morality Everyman play. Where Shakespeare departs from the traditional morality formula, Lancashire claims, is in choosing not to redeem his hero, but to make him refuse the secular knowledge of himself and humanity offered by Apemantus.]

In Dr. Faustus, as has often been demonstrated, Marlowe makes use, in structure and theme, of the morality tradition of plays such as *Mankind,* with its alternating serious and comic scenes and its theme of the psychomachia—the conflict within a man between virtue and vice, with virtue eventually triumphant. Marlowe works against tradition in that Faustus, his mankind hero, is not saved but damned at the end of the play; and to the extent that Marlowe presents Faustus as an historical individual, and his self-inflicted fall as tragedy, he personalizes and somewhat secularizes the morality tradition. But, although secularized and personalized, *Dr. Faustus* is definitely a morality play, with an anti-traditional ending; Marlowe is consciously working both *in* and *against* the morality tradition, and the force of the play comes above all from his use of the morality scheme combined with his deliberate departures from it.

I suggest that in *Timon of Athens* Shakespeare, like Marlowe in *Faustus,* is writing his own secularized, anti-traditional morality play. Like Marlowe, Shakespeare chooses as subject matter a well-known story in which the hero is finally destroyed rather than saved—and through his own willful choice. Like Marlowe, Shakespeare draws upon the theme and structure of morality drama, working at once within, against, and beyond its framework. Where Marlowe uses the form and theme of the psychomachia drama, as exemplified in *Mankind,* Shakespeare uses the tradition of plays such as *Everyman,* in which the mankind hero is brought, by the experience of some material disaster, to a realization of the transitory nature of worldly goods, and accordingly turns to spiritual values. Where Marlowe employs morality devices such as the Good and Evil Angels, Shakespeare gives us, among other traditional features, *Everyman*'s traditional appeal to and rejection by false friends. Where Marlowe reverses the stock morality-play ending of spiritual salvation, Shakespeare too rejects the redemption of *Everyman,* and essentially shows Timon going to death "unredeemed", a self-made exile from human society. Like *Faustus,* Timon is most powerful and meaningful when seen in this way, as secularized, anti-traditional everyman drama; and many in Shakespeare's audience may be expected to have been fully conscious that Shakespeare was using the morality tradition to create an anti-*Everyman.* (p. 35)

A careful comparison of *Timon* and *Everyman* reveals that Shakespeare is definitely working within the *Everyman* tradition. The morality opens with its protagonist at the height of material prosperity; but the speech of the Messenger, which begins the play, forecasts the ruin to come—because life inevitably ends in death and judgment. Similarly, *Timon of Athens* opens with a hero at the peak of material and social prosperity. Material wealth is emphasized throughout the play, from the jewels and rewards of the first scene to the gold that Timon finds in the forest; and the vocabulary of the play is strongly commercial, with words such as "bonds", "accounts", and "dues" continually recurring. And, as in *Everyman,* there is a note of foreboding present from the opening speeches of the play. . . . Everyman has had no thought for anything but material and social pleasures; and so he is threatened with eternal damnation when God calls him to a "reckoning". . . . Similarly, the Timon of the opening of Shakespeare's play is a materialistic, sociable man, a patron of the five senses [I. ii. 123-24]: indeed, the traditional prodigal Timon, a heedless man, unaware of the real nature of his world, his friends, and even himself. And for him, as for Everyman, a time of "reck'ning" [II. ii. 150] will come, though for Timon, since the world of the play is secular, it will be a secular, not a spiritual,

reckoning and will thus be expressed in terms of material payment: bonds, dues, bills.

In *Everyman,* the hero's fall occurs almost immediately. As soon as Everyman enters, . . . disaster strikes. Death summons him; and Everyman learns the transitory nature of worldly goods and of life itself. He turns for help to those who were his friends in his prosperity—Fellowship, Kindred and Cousin, Goods; he appeals to them one by one, and one by one, on material grounds, with contrived excuses, they reject him. Good Deeds, Everyman's last hope, he finds to be too weak to aid him, and Everyman despairs. In *Timon,* the fall of the protagonist from material prosperity is a process extending through three acts; but it takes place, otherwise, almost exactly on the *Everyman* pattern—and this pattern exists in none of Shakespeare's known probable sources, nor in the old *Timon,* in which the protagonist does ask friends for help, but not in the patterned series of requests and refusals that we have in Shakespeare's play. (pp. 36-7)

At this point *Everyman* begins the second half of its circle, swinging upward from despair towards the spiritual victory with which the play closes. Knowledge (a mercy figure) appears, gives Everyman hope, and leads him to repentance and absolution, which ultimately bring him to salvation. Everyman is thus saved through acquiring *knowledge* of himself and of the material and spiritual worlds in which, as a mortal man, he participates. Parallel to the Knowledge of *Everyman* is a "mercy figure" in *Timon* who offers "redemption" of a kind, through true knowledge of the world, to the protagonist. This mercy figure is Apemantus, the cynical philosopher, who believes in "plain-dealing" [I. i. 211] and attempts to give Timon a clear-sighted view of the nature of men and of the society they create. Through this secular knowledge, or worldly wisdom, Timon can become like Apemantus: a man with no illusions about men and their world, but not, because of this, cutting himself off from society, but rather, remaining in the world and, through railing at it, attempting to "redeem" it. Apemantus is concerned with reform—with destroying ignorance, pretence, deceit—though he is cynical about his chances of success. He sees clearly the evil in man; but he also sees the potential for goodness, and he condemns Timon for his extremes of, first, complete love of the world, and, second, entire hatred of it. "The middle of humanity thou never knewest, but the extremity of both ends" [IV. iii. 300-01]. Apemantus, then, parallels in *Timon* the Knowledge of *Everyman,* rational philosophy (knowledge of self and of human nature and society in general) being the classical, pagan equivalent to the truths about man (secular and spiritual) presented by Christianity and to which Knowledge leads Everyman; and this Apemantus is seemingly a deliberate change by Shakespeare from the Timon-like, misanthropic Apemantus of two of Shakespeare's probable sources, Plutarch's *Lives* and Painter's *Palace of Pleasure.* (There is no Apemantus in Lucian's *Timon* or in the old *Timon.*) Apemantus preaches, in his own way, simply full knowledge of the world as it is, good and bad, and thus offers Timon a kind of pagan salvation: a way to live successfully in a world without God, a way in which Timon may set himself within the framework of society while rejecting its false values and pretences and accepting only the true values of self-knowledge and knowledge of general human nature and fortune. Similarly, Everyman learns from Knowledge the real value of material goods and the true nature of a life of social and physical pleasure; but Everyman, as a Christian, can go beyond this world, as Timon cannot, to give his life direction and meaning. Apemantus, as Knowledge, makes possible for

Timon only a partial recovery from despair, because we are, in *Timon*, in a secular world, and full recovery from the evils of life is possible only to spiritual man. Everyman is offered spiritual as well as secular knowledge; Timon can be given only the latter.

At this point Shakespeare, like Marlowe in *Dr. Faustus*, deliberately leaves the morality tradition, turning it against itself. Faustus, who has followed the pattern of the hero of *Mankind*, departs from morality tradition in maintaining to the end of the play his choice of evil over good, devil over God; and Timon, offered the classical equivalent of spiritual knowledge, rational philosophy, rejects it, unlike Everyman, for a meaningless life outside society, cut off from his fellowmen, just as Faustus cuts himself off from God. Like Faustus, again, Timon holds to his choice to the end of the play. Thus, like Faustus, Timon denies himself the only "salvation" possible for him. That knowledge can be salvation is made explicit in *Timon* as early as I.ii.

> Tim.   Nay, and you begin to rail on society
>   once, I am sworn not to give regard to
>   you. Farewell, and come with better
>   music.
> Apem. So. Thou wilt not hear me now; thou
>   shalt not then. I'll lock thy heaven from
>   thee.
>
> [I. ii. 244-48]

Unlike Everyman, Timon rejects knowledge: knowledge, first (to be found in Apemantus' railings), of man's potential for evil; then, after his disillusionment, knowledge (the "better music") of man's potential for good. He also explicitly rejects both order [e.g. IV. i. 3-32] and "good deeds". Even in his state of misery in the forest, it is possible for him to do good for his fellowmen; but he uses his newly-acquired gold only to bring ruin to mankind. . . . Unlike Everyman, he is made so bitter by his experience with false friends and fickle fortune that he cannot accept redemption; and, like Lear, he rails against his fellowmen, seeing himself as "more sinn'd against than sinning", without ever coming to Lear's (or Everyman's) realization of his own faults. He moves from one extreme position to another, and each extreme gives him only a partial view of life. Thus, through extremism, Timon rejects true knowledge of the world. Shakespeare is here working with the well-known tradition of Timon the misanthrope; the Timon story, as found in common legend and in sources such as Plutarch and Painter, was ideal for Shakespeare's purpose of depicting willful, secular self-destruction.

As Timon, however, goes down to self-inflicted damnation, Shakespeare presents to us a second everyman, Alcibiades, who is also mistreated by a selfish and materialistic Athens but whose subsequent conduct is eventually in sharp contrast to that of Timon. . . . The proper mode of conduct for everyman is not Timon's but that made explicit in the suggestion of the First Senator to Alcibiades in V.iv:

> . . . like a shepherd,
> Approach the fold and cull th'infected forth,
> But kill not all together.   [V. iv. 42-4]

Alcibiades himself practises this behavior, not only in sparing Athens but also in his final eulogy of "noble Timon" [V. iv. 80], a final gesture of mercy, of forgiveness, extended even to the "misanthropos" [IV. iii. 54] the "noble Timon" had become. The play thus ends almost as positively as *Everyman*, with the establishment of mercy; but because, in *Timon*, we

are confined to this physical world, there can be no spiritual soaring beyond it into complete harmony and goodness, but, rather, only a complex and difficult reconciliation of contraries. (pp. 37-41)

Timon has been called a bare play; but a clean, stark plot line is essential to morality drama, as is the technique of formal structuring through contrasting a number of different though parallel episodes. The play has been condemned for not being a *King Lear*; . . . but Shakespeare clearly was not trying in *Timon* to write another *Lear*. He was aiming, not at tragedy, but at a kind of morality drama, and at richness and complexity of quite a different sort from that found in *Lear*: that found in *Faustus*, which comes from working within, around, and against a longstanding tradition, built upon theological complexity and enriched and compressed through centuries of dramatic presentation and clerical and lay debate. (p. 44)

> Anne Lancashire, "'Timon of Athens': Shake-
> speare's 'Dr. Faustus'," in Shakespeare Quarterly,
> Vol. XXI, No. 1, Winter, 1970, pp. 35-44.

HARRY LEVIN   (essay date 1972)

[*Levin contends that* Timon *is essentially two plays: one about a philanthropist, the other about a misanthropist, and that the transition from the first part to the second is undramatic, and therefore ineffective, because Shakespeare failed to present the necessary psychological insight into Timon's personality. In conclusion, Levin asserts that Shakespeare, "so adept and far-ranging in his sympathy," was artistically unable to convincingly portray the misanthropy of his hero. The essay from which the following excerpt is taken was originally delivered as a lecture at the 15th International Conference of the Shakespeare Institute from August 26 to September 1, 1972.*]

We do not need Herman Melville to warn us that *Timon of Athens* is an ambush for critics. Yet, in his nondescript edition of Shakespeare now at Harvard University, it is one of the plays most heavily marked. Marginal annotations are rare but pithy. Thus, when Timon urges the Bandits to plunder the shops of Athens, two of them are almost dissuaded from banditry. The third, an opportunist, tells his colleagues that it would be better to reform when less plunder is available: 'There is no time so miserable but a man may be true' [IV. iii. 456-57]. This has been didactically paraphrased by the anonymous editor: 'There is no hour in a man's life so wretched, but he always has it in his power to become *true*, i.e. honest.' And Melville, in the margin, has glossed the comment, after crossing it out: 'Peace, peace! Thou ass of a commentator!' His own feelings come to the surface when Timon drives his false friends out of the banquet hall, and Melville comments with Yankee succinctness: 'Served 'em right.' In his other reading he would frequently return to his misanthropic touchstone. Where La Bruyère wrote skeptically about friendship, Melville commented: 'True, Shakespeare goes further: None die but somebody spurns them into the grave.' Melville's misquotation is even more absolute than the words of Shakespeare's Apemantus: 'Who dies that bears not one spurn to the grave / Of their friends' gift?' [I. ii. 141-42.]

Timon of Athens provided a moral backdrop for Melville's *Confidence-Man*, as *Hamlet* had for *Pierre* and *King Lear* for *Moby Dick*. His literary career bogged down at the stage that his biographers would call Timonism, and *The Confidence-Man*—with its masquerade of Emersonian ideals and Hawthornesque doubts, its dialectic between a self-deluding optimism and an ever-deepening mistrust—was the last work of fiction he published. But from first to last he worshipped at the Shakespearian pantheon, and ranked Timon with Lear and Hamlet as a spokesman for those bitter truths to which he felt the American public was deaf. (p. 89)

In 'Some Thoughts on Playwriting' Thornton Wilder remarked: 'The exposition of the nature of misanthropy . . . in Shakespeare's *Timon of Athens* has never been a success.' Solitude, after all, is antisocial by definition, and anchorites can express their distaste for society by undramatically avoiding it. Molière's *Misanthrope,* on the other hand, takes place in a highly social setting. To be sure, its hero is constantly contemplating a retirement to some desert island. . . . Yet it takes the mundanity of the court to bring out the misanthropy of Alceste; his intransigent sincerity has its foil in the worldly hypocrisy of the courtiers; and we end by wondering which has been the more sharply satirized. *Timon of Athens,* by contrast, moves in the direction of a monodrama which is unresolved. The isolated protagonist is subject to successive interrogations. If he is being tested like Job, he does not survive the ordeal. If he is being punished like Prometheus, he retaliates by verbal castigations and assumes the final responsibility for his own victimization.

He can be brought nearer to his Jacobean context if we view him as a malcontent. But malcontents, while cursing their lot, undertake to set things right: to retrieve a princely heritage or avenge a sister's rape. Hamlet wears his antic disposition as a cloak to mask his vengeance. The ingrained malignity of Iago, or of Webster's disgruntled adventurers, seeks to vent itself in action. A closer prototype would be the melancholy Jaques, who cultivates melancholia for its own sake. . . . In comparison, we must remember that Timon did not begin as a Timonist. He was, as one Senator puts it, a phoenix before he became a gull [II. i. 31-2]. Legend has preserved him in the posture of a reclusive curmudgeon; in his prime he had personified the image of a gregarious prodigal. The problem of recreating that earlier personality, and registering the stages of alienation and decline, was one to overtax the flexibility and resourcefulness of Shakespeare himself. His philanthropist is one man, his misanthropist another, and the transition between them is a sudden recoil rather than a gradual disillusionment.

All this, in bald outline, corresponds well enough with the basic patterns of medieval or Renaissance tragedy. Seldom indeed has a downfall been so precipitate from such lavish prosperity to such crouching adversity. But, whereas the traditional sacrifice was a throne, a high office, or a beloved partner, here the loss is reckoned in financial terms. Fortune still is the presiding goddess, although her precipitating symbol is not a wheel but a hill, which the competitive crowd is climbing up or sliding down. The venal allegory of the Poet, which serves as an expository device, is rounded out by his reappearance with a moralistic satire. The barometric references to Timon's *fortune* indicate both his destiny and his affluence. Romeo is 'fortune's fool' because he is crossed by fate; Timon's 'trencher-friends' are 'fools of fortune' because they would do anything for wealth [III. vi. 93-7]. The key-words of the play, employed more often than anywhere else in Shakespeare, *friend* and *gold,* almost seem to cancel each other out. Timon learns, from his painful experience with his selfish following, to equate them. (pp. 90-1)

His relations with his fellow men have been predicated upon 'a dream of friendship', from which—his steward Flavius perceives—he was bound to be rudely awakened [IV. ii. 33-6]. Much of what we hear about his nobility is attested by those who have something to gain from their flattery. . . . The test of magnanimity on both sides, the process of debasement and undeception, comprises a three-act drama in itself. (p. 91)

The last scene of the third act, where the fair-weather flatterers are invited to a mock-banquet and told off, is a kind of dénouement. We may well then feel, as Melville apparently did, that the curtain of poetic justice has fallen at last. 'Served 'em right.'

The first three acts attempt to trace, so to speak, the etiology of Timon's malaise. The treatment is somewhat diagrammatic, as in a morality play. Instead of the psychological insight that revealed, step by step, how a Macbeth could become steeped in blood or an Othello corrupted by unworthy suspicions, we are confronted with the overt theatricalism of a Leontes overcome by jealousy in a single instantaneous seizure. As in *The Winter's Tale* likewise, there is a sharp disjunction between the first three acts and acts IV and V. Yet, insofar as the characterization of Timon is concerned, the real break occurs in act III. During his absence from the stage, bills have been accumulating and loans put off. One of the servants alerts the others to the fact that an identity crisis is brewing: 'my lord leans wondrously to discontent' [III. iv. 70]. When Timon reappears soon afterward, he is—as the stage direction specifies—'*in a rage*'. No longer the easy-going host of act I or the bewildered patron of act II, he is abruptly ready to denounce his duns, summon his ever-greedy *clientèle* to an anti-feast, and emerge as a full-fledged misanthrope: 'Henceforth hated be / Of Timon, man and all humanity!' [III. vi. 104-05.] (pp. 91-2)

Timon, the man-hater of the last two acts, has hardened into his monolithic attitude. If his prior self seems in retrospect shallow, it is attributable to his thoroughly extroverted disposition. But how much deeper does his embitterment go? In the 'better days' of lordly innocence, he held no mental reservations [IV. ii. 27]; hence he needed no asides or soliloquies. In his 'latter spirits' he continues to speak out directly [V. iv. 74]. But he cannot be said to have moved from the one extreme to the other through the medium of introspection; nor does he, as an ascetic hermit, engage his thoughts in spiritual meditation. The first scene of act IV constitutes a soliloquy merely because, for the first time it would seem, he stands alone. This has its counterpart in the climactic episode of *Coriolanus,* where at the gates of Rome the exiled general pronounces his personal decree of banishment against his fellow citizens. Henceforth the speeches of Timon extend and intensify the acrid rhetoric of Coriolanus: the invective vein, the serried style, the pregnant imagery. Timon's farewell to Athens is a baneful prayer that the laws of nature reverse themselves, a litany of curses, 'multiplying bans' [IV. i. 34]. Since obligations to him have not been met, let all sanctions be broken: 'Degrees, observances, customs and laws, / Decline to your confounding contraries' [IV. i. 18-19]. Timon prays for everything that Ulysses warned the Greek generals against. No wonder Karl Marx relished Shakespeare's imprecation against gold [see excerpt above, 1844]. (p. 92)

The redeeming virtue of Flavius modifies the scope, if not the intensity, of Timon's hatred. Diogenes the Cynic might have been happy to have encountered a single honest man—might have become, in Melville's phrase, 'a genial misanthrope'. And Melville, who on occasion could out-Timon Shakespeare, sharpens a nice distinction in *The Confidence-Man:* 'tell me, was not that humor, of Diogenes, which led him to live, a merry-andrew, in the flowermarket, better than that of the less wise Athenian, which made him a skulking scarecrow in pine-barrens? An injudicious gentleman, Lord Timon.' It remains an open question whether Timon's experience should be viewed as one man's hard-luck story or as an indictment of the human race. Other tragic heroes have undergone worse tribulations than bankruptcy, and have not arrived at so wholesale a condemnation of their fellow men. Since Timon is the victim of callousness rather than cruelty, his sufferings are not to be compared with those of King Lear. Grief, which has a humanizing effect on Lear, dehumanizes Timon. Should the limitation be ascribed to the character or to the playwright? Could it be that Shakespeare, so adept and far-ranging in his sympathy, was balked at the portrayal of antipathy? It seems clear that he, who empathized with such numerous and varied themes, found this an uncongenial one. It would be signficant if his uncertainties over Timon of Athens marked his transition from tragedy to romance.

Not that there is much romance about Timon. Its subject-matter would, by neo-classical standards, relegate it to the bourgeois sphere of comedy, where parasites and moneylenders flourish and rich men like Trimalchio entertain. Actually it has few comic moments, if any, and its Fool is Shakespeare's dimmest and dullest. Molière's misanthrope has his laughable aspects, which were sorely resented by Rousseau. Timon himself had been a laughing-stock of the Old Comedy; he would be mocked again in an eighteenth-century harlequinade. Shakespeare, taking him seriously, focused attention on the object of his grim mockery: not on money itself, but on the colluding attributes of greed and guile. These, of course, are the mainsprings of Jonson's comedies and of many others—though not, on the whole, of Shakespeare's. Living in the same society at its hour of capitalistic emergence, he cannot have been less aware than they were of acquisition and dispossession as a timely theme. They embodied it in the coney-catching [swindling] of the London underworld. He conceived it as a cosmic projection, when Timon assures the thieves that sun and moon and sea and earth are bent on pilfering and pillaging. This is darker than those occasional glimpses of anarchy which rift the chain of being from play to play. Possibly it is intended to estrange us, like the sardonic harshness of Bertolt Brecht, and unlike the brigher and warmer vistas that we think of as more characteristically Shakespearian. Shakespeare himself was so far from being Misanthropos, so very far from hating all mankind, that for once his negative capability got in the way of his dramaturgy. (p. 94)

Harry Levin, "Shakespeare's Misanthrope," in Shakespeare Survey: An Annual Survey of Shakespearean Study and Production, Vol. 26, Cambridge University Press, 1973, pp. 89-94.

RICHARD D. FLY (essay date 1973)

[Fly maintains that we must interpret Timon from two different points of view: Timon's and his society's. In doing this, Fly contends, we come to a fuller understanding of the play, for it is only through a juxtaposition of these two viewpoints that we can assess the significance of Timon's suicide, as well as the effect of society on the individual.]

In its stark refusal to fuse its disparate parts into an organic whole Timon of Athens achieves, at best, a magnificence of a disturbingly uneven and disjunctive nature. Perhaps the most serious and damaging disjunction, in what M. C. Bradbrook calls "this drama of the gaps," appears in the apparent lack of coherent synchronization between the Alcibiades subplot and the Timon main action. The discontinuity between the two story lines is sporadically bothersome throughout Timon—especially in III, v—but causes the fifth act in particular to appear extremely unsatisfactory. Because of this structural bifurcation the conclusion of Timon, rather like the troublesome ending of Troilus, seems to conclude nothing, to leave the play distressingly open and unresolved. G. B. Harrison's charge that the fifth act of Timon "is little more than disjointed fragments" [see excerpt above, 1951], for example, would probably be accepted by most commentators as equally applicable to the last act of Troilus. . . . In what follows I propose to reexamine the problem of Timon's last act in order to see if a more satisfactory understanding of its disjunctive structure can be achieved. (pp. 242-43)

Univocal "either/or" critical responses to Shakespeare's plays are usually distorting and reductive, and this may be true also of the Alcibiades/Timon controversy. Critical debate on this level can quickly descend to appeal to moral biases and reliance on rhetorical flourishes. Perhaps a more rewarding approach is one which recognizes the presence of a double perspective that permits the audience to respond to the play's conclusion from two different and even contrasted viewpoints simultaneously: that is, from the tragic protagonist's angle of vision and from his society's angle of vision. When understood in this manner Timon of Athens becomes an apt title for a tragedy that splits the audience's attention almost equally between the technical hero and his carefully defined society—between Timon and Athens. Hamlet's Denmark, Lear's pre-Christian England, and Macbeth's Scotland have undeniable dramatic significance; but the only other Shakespearean play outside the English history plays to create the kind of accentuated social perspective equal to Timon's is Coriolanus, and again the protagonist is required to share the title of the play with the name of a city.

But we must not think that Shakespeare was drawn to this dual perspective because of an increasing interest in the "ethos" of a particularly circumscribed pagan culture—his historical and ethnological sense was surely not this disciplined. What seems to have drawn Shakespeare back to Plutarch, rather, was that Plutarch's accounts of the besieged societies within the walled city-states of Rome and Athens made possible the kind of dramatic "scene" that was most admirably suited for an exploration of the relations between the heroic individual and the demands of his society. By acknowledging that Timon's interest is just as much a parable as history should permit us a less reductive response to the action of the play's bifurcated conclusion.

Both Timon and Coriolanus have unique fifth act structures that contrast a scene of joyful social regeneration and salvation with a scene dealing with the isolated death of the banished tragic protagonist. The audience, therefore, seems to be required simultaneously to condemn the society to some extent for causing through its baseness the death of the hero, and to praise the society for its constructive efforts to purge its evil elements and to come to better terms with its past failings. Its attitude towards the hero is also ambivalent. Because of the marked interplay between hero and society one senses that the partial regeneration of the society is somehow related magically to the sacrificial death of the hero. From one possible viewpoint, then, the hero becomes a scapegoat carrying off with his death the crimes of the community and making civic improvement possible. The emotion elicited in this regard is associated primarily with communion. But from another equally valid viewpoint one tends to suppress his social concern and to focus his attention on the suffering and eventual death of the hero. The emotions elicited in this case are pity and terror and the result should be tragic *catharsis*. (pp. 244-45)

Timon commands a centrifugal movement away from society towards total isolation and death—a movement suggesting tragedy and eliciting emotions associated with *catharsis*. Alcibiades is less fully portrayed as the leader of a centripetal movement back into reunion with society—an action suggesting primarily history and eliciting communal emotions. But should the triumphant re-entry of Alcibiades into Athens be viewed as the dramatic resolution to the problems presented in *Timon*, or should Timon's abandoned death be—or is this the wrong way to state the question? . . . Because of the increased dramatic significance of Athens in *Timon* one is . . . equally concerned with the nature of Alcibiades' reconciliation with Athens as well as with Timon's death. Finally, the suggestion is also present that Timon's action makes a more timeless, ahistorical, even allegorical, comment on the human condition, while Alcibiades' action is more firmly bound by the temporal realm of history. The suggestion is that Athenian society can come to terms with Alcibiades but man cannot by himself come to terms with the imperfections of his nature. By keeping these distinctions in mind we may now be better able to account for the contrasting reactions of Timon and Alcibiades to the ingratitude of the Athenians. (p. 246)

A recurrent idea in Shakespeare's tragedies—one difficult for modern readers to understand—is that an individual's real existence is manifested primarily through his social relatedness. And the terror usually associated with banishment in these plays, therefore, results from this ontological context. Withdrawal from society, whether forced or willingly undertaken, is seen as a frighteningly absolute gesture: an annihilating confrontation with chaos and nothingness. The "nothing" motif which rings disturbingly through *Lear* and *Timon*, when properly understood, gives focus to this complex of social and ontological meanings. Because of this interpenetration of meaning, Timon's self-banishment can suggest the disintegration of both his society and himself to "nothing." At the climatic moment of Timon's second banquet, as his wrath explodes in words of absolute social repudiation, he punctuates his abdication with the term "nothing": "For these may present friends, as they are to me nothing, so in nothing bless them, and to nothing are they welcome" [III. vi. 82-4]. "Nothing" here means not so much loss of existence as a more horrible loss of authentic "being." The term recurs frequently in the scenes immediately following this pivotal moment: "Nothing I'll bear from thee / But nakedness, thou detestable town," Timon cries; [IV. i. 32-3] and Timon's servants moan, "Are we undone? cast off? nothing remaining?" [IV. ii. 2]. And at the moment of Timon's own annihilation, this nihilistic motif emphatically sounded again:

> My long sickness
> Of health and living now begins to mend,
> And nothing brings me all things.
>
> [V. i. 186-88]

By this subtle cross-reference of the term "nothing" one becomes aware that Timon's suicide is the ontological analogue to his former repudiation of society—on both levels a demand for the bliss of nothingness. Timon's suicide leaves the universe totally devoid of meaning, and informed by a vision of absurdity and futility. (pp. 250-51)

Alcibiades' actions, of course, do not penetrate to this visionary level, and so we need to readjust our former understanding of the complementary nature of Timon's conclusion. Alcibiades' actions at the end of the play are all designed to get his stunned and frightened society functioning again in its usual ordinary manner. . . . Timon may lie in his lonely sea-side grave, but the tides of history will continue to ebb and flow. Alcibiades is, thus, a figure we meet often at the close of Shakespeare's plays: he is an order-figure somewhat like Lucius or Richmond, Antony or Octavius, Malcolm, Fortinbras, or Albany who, with widely varying degrees of emotional effect and thematic validation, brings a fractured society back to its natural rhythms.

But, more so than in any of these other plays, *Timon*, finally, throws this resolving orderfigure and his restorative actions into a bitterly ironic perspective. Athens and Alcibiades can come to terms, life in the city can resume its normal course, and disruptive bestiality can ostensibly be contained within the reestablished "bounds" of "public laws." But Timon's "gravestone" remains in their midst as an everpresent "oracle" constantly reminding them of the futility of their efforts. "Thither come," Timon says, "And let my gravestone be your oracle" [V. i. 218-19]. "Make thine epitaph," Timon tells himself, "That death in me at others' lives may laugh" [IV. iii. 379-80]. From the perspective which terminates Timon's experience with society, life itself appears as only a joke, and this circumambient diabolic laughter echoes faintly through the reconciliation between Alcibiades and Athens as the play closes. This vision of existential absurdity, as Northrop Frye perceives, "contains and enfolds the vision of the turning wheel of fortune," and one can, therefore, take little comfort in the ostensibly optimistic conclusion of the play. (pp. 251-52)

> *Richard D. Fly, "The Ending of 'Timon of Athens':*
> *A Reconsideration," in* Criticism, *Vol. XV, No. 3*
> *(Summer, 1973), pp. 242-52.*

CYRUS HOY (essay date 1973)

[*Hoy contends that* Timon *deals specifically with the theme of human alienation, symbolized in the recurring imagery of money and commodities. It also depicts an individual's inability to discern appearance from reality, as well as that individual's failure to break out of the "narcissism" of his misanthropy once he has come to recognize the true motives of his society. Hoy sees Timon as a "monstrous parody of Christ," broken by suffering but uninstructed by it, overwhelmed by sorrows that only his mind, and not his heart, can respond to. Other critics, most notably Winifred M.T. Nowottny (1959), have regarded Timon as something of an Antichrist figure.*]

The imaginative vision that produced Shakespeare's Jacobean tragedies was conditioned by that crisis of the Renaissance—that counter-Renaissance, as it is sometimes termed—brought on by those innovations in science and religion, political and moral philosophy that are associated with the names of Copernicus and Luther, Machiavelli and Montaigne. The effects of these have been often described. They issue in the recognition that truth is not absolute and completely objective but relative, that morality has a double standard (one for rulers, the other for the ruled), that the intellect is of no avail in scrutinizing the wisdom of God, that the earth is not the centre of the universe. It would be odd if so thorough-going a revolution in man's conception of himself, his world, and his relation to deity—all accomplished within the limits of a single century—had not left its impact on the art of the sixteenth and early seventeenth centuries and of course it has done so, both

"Timon," by Wyndham Lewis (1913). From the Art Collection of the Folger Shakespeare Library.

on the art of literature, and on the arts of painting, architecture and sculpture. (p. 49)

In no major body of tragic drama have deceptions, disguises, the manipulation of appearances loomed so large as in that of Shakespeare and his Jacobean contemporaries. Their concern with masks is directly related to the fact that long before the end of the sixteenth century the question of what is real and what is not had become a problem; reality had become, in a word, problematic, which is what the crisis of the Renaissance is about. . . . Tragic personages such as Hamlet, Othello, Lear and Timon must pick their way through a maze of conflicting appearances that have been wilfully erected by the unscrupulous to confound the image of truth, and the contradictions that encompass them are their undoing. . . .

Timon's betrayal by his flattering friends follows the familiar example of Othello betrayed by Iago, and Lear by his false daughters, but the play continues (in its last two acts), as it examines what betrayal has done to Timon, into regions of the soul that the dramatist had not explored before, but which— in the figures of Macbeth and Coriolanus—he would shortly be exploring again. Lear, even in his outcast state, is never without attendant and beneficent spirits: Kent, the Fool, later Cordelia. Timon in his exile is alone with his hate for mankind, and his periodic shouting matches with Apemantus or Alci-

biades but confirm the finality of his alienation, of which he is indeed an archetypal figure. Hauser has termed alienation 'the key to mannerism', and has gone on to declare that the psychology of alienation is narcissism; and there is something distinctly narcissistic about Timon's misanthropy. (p. 58)

[Hoy adds in a footnote:]

> Alienation, Hauser affirms, appeared for the first time in conscious form as the crisis of the Renaissance; concerning its process, he writes: 'Man created objects, forms, and values, and became their slave and servant instead of their master. The works of his hand and mind assumed an autonomy of their own, and became independent of him while he became dependent on them. . . . In the classical meaning of the term . . . alienation means divestiture of the self, the loss of subjectivity; a turning inside out of the personality, exteriorising and driving out what ought to remain within, with the result that what is ejected in this way assumes a nature completely different from the self, becomes alien and hostile to it, and threatens to diminish and destroy it. Meanwhile the self loses itself in its objectifications, faces an alienated form of itself in them'. . . . Hauser stresses the importance of economic factors in the process of alienation in the sixteenth century, where 'the concept of commodities became the fundamental category of social life and reshaped and refashioned every field of human endeavour'. . . . The effect of this is to turn the worker and his work alike into a saleable object. The middle of the sixteenth century, Hauser notes, 'saw the real birth of the art trade' . . . , and the sense of artists as dealers in commodities is clearly evident in the figures of the poet and the painter in *Timon of Athens*. 'Nothing,' says Hauser . . . 'illustrates the process of alienation in economic and social life more strikingly and significantly than the part played by money in modern capitalism'; *Timon of Athens*, where everything turns on the power of money, is Shakespeare's demonstration of this.
>
> (n.pp. 58-9)

[The narcissim of Timon's misanthropy] accounts for the complete stasis of the figure of Timon himself throughout the last half of the play where he is frozen into an immobility that permits him only to go on staring relentlessly into the image of his hate as this turns into a passion for universal ruin on a scale sufficient to satisfy his outrage at the fact of human ingratitude.

Shakespeare had dealt with narcissistic types before, notably in the person of Hamlet. What is new about the psychological condition that is being explored in the last two acts of *Timon of Athens* is its depiction of a figure bent on making his actions square with his words, and both actions and words square with his inner desire, regardless of how destructive this may be: in effect, the unfulfilled ideal so basic to the tragedy of *Hamlet*. Early in the play Timon has commended the Painter for his art whose 'pencilled figures are / Even such as they give out' [I. i. 159-60], which is more than can be said for the figures of human nature which, stained with dishonor, are too often 'but outside'. And much later in the play he commends the bandits for frankly professing to be what in truth they are: 'Yet thanks I must you con / That you are thieves professed, that you work not / In holier shapes' [IV. iii. 425-27]. Timon, with his huge invective against mankind, is acting on the injunction of Edgar at the close of *Lear*, speaking what he feels, not what he ought to say, and achieving thereby a rare coherence of intention and word whose only precedent hitherto in Shakespearian tragedy has been Cordelia, with her refusal to speak other than as she feels. But the achievement is totally self-destructive, and Timon ends as some monstrous parody of Christ: one who dies for hate of mankind. He is in every way a paradoxical creation: broken by suffering but uninstructed by it, a sorrowing figure whose sorrows only the mind—and not the heart—responds to. With its tragic sense of the contradictory nature of things, of the appalling chasm that separates appearance from truth, the play is in fact one of Shakespeare's most mannerist performances, and its mannerist features extend to the different degrees of reality which it exhibits: Timon's rage is far more fully rendered than Timon in prosperity, and the periphery of the play is populated by wraith-like figures who are hardly more than sketched in. The play is a mannerist work in the way that Michelangelo's *Pietà Rondanini* is mannerist: the mode of representation is irrational, anti-natural, but informed with a profound spiritual vision which both Michelangelo and Shakespeare seem ultimately to have despaired of translating adequately into material form. The *Pietà Rondanini* is unfinished, and so, I suspect, is *Timon of Athens*. (pp. 59-60)

> *Cyrus Hoy, "Jacobean Tragedy and the Mannerist Style," in* Shakespeare Survey: An Annual Survey of Shakespearean Study and Production, *Vol. 26, Cambridge University Press, 1973, pp. 49-67.*

WILLIAM W.E. SLIGHTS   (essay date 1977)

[*Slights attempts to demonstrate that Shakespeare combined elements from a number of literary genres to produce "a satiric analysis of the decay of authority in Timon's Athens." For other points of view regarding the genre of Shakespeare's play, see the essays by Samuel Johnson (1765), August Wilhelm Schlegel (1808), Samuel Taylor Coleridge (1808-18), Hermann Ulrici (1839), G. Wilson Knight (1930), John W. Draper (1934), A. S. Collins (1946), Kenneth Muir (1947), Andor Gomme (1959), Peter Ure (1964), Northrop Frye (1965), Anne Lancashire (1970), and Rolf Soellner (1979).*]

We seek in vain for the stamp of generic purity in the variegated *Life of Timon of Athens*. It is neither tragedy nor comedy, morality nor history. Shakespeare has not ignored genre as a means of shaping his material, but he has used that tool of his craft in a far more flexible way than has generally been understood. His subject, an examination of the proper uses of authority in an established social order, was ideally suited to satire. His problem was to find or construct a dramatic form that would create multiple perspectives capable of challenging illegitimate claims to authority and strengthening what he saw as valid ones. In this he was not wholly successful, to judge from most readers' reactions; yet it is instructive to watch him blending and modifying the resources of dramatic genre in order to piece together a balanced, satiric analysis of the decay of authority in Timon's Athens. The process is particularly evident in this play where the connections are not always smooth and the satiric vision of the play as a whole so clearly exceeds that of its central figure. (pp. 40-1)

The point of the satire is, I think, not to condemn Timon's folly but to present to our understanding the series of con-

founding dilemmas that makes an essentially good man decide to withdraw from the human community.

The special kind of attention Shakespeare pays to the problems of community in *Timon* can be seen in his use of the masque form in Act I. Timon, an apparently wealthy and highly regarded citizen in Athens, reaches the height of his fortunes with the mounting of a lavish spectacle, an Ovidian banquet of sense, culminating in a masque of Amazons. The masque marks the turning point in Timon's fortunes and hence in the action of the entire play. It has a different position and function from any other embedded masque in Shakespeare. Unlike those in the romantic comedies and the romances, which occur late and celebrate the action of reunion, this masque is prominently placed at the end of Act I to establish the precarious norm of civilized behavior which is soon lost in Athens. Cupid, whose handiwork is elsewhere conspicuously absent from the play, acts as presenter of the masque. He speaks in praise of Timon, Athens' foremost patron of the five senses. (p. 42)

Timon's purpose in mounting the masque is to delight his friends and to reassure them that the disruptive forces in his society, symbolized by the conquered Amazons, are being held in check by art and manners. These friends in turn join in a ritual re-enactment of their grateful respect for Timon's authority, in particular his power to authorize a sumptuous pageant whose theme is the extension and continuation of their own social order. If carried out with proper decorum, the masque will fix Timon at the head of the established order. But the mythic, political, and ritualistic resonances set off by the masque find a poor sounding-board in the commentary of Apemantus, the cynic, to whom "the glory of this life," particularly the present entertainment, exemplifies vanity, madness, folly, flattery, spite, envy, and depravity [I. ii. 132-40]. Apemantus can comment prophetically, "I should fear those that dance before me now / Would one day stamp upon me," without altering Timon's sense that the masquers "have added worth . . . and lustre" to his evening's entertainment [I. ii. 143-44, 149-50]. These two opposed views, of man as depraved brute and man as the source of generosity and civilization, are held in temporary stasis by the masquing situation. From Timon's perspective in the center of the experience the masque celebrates the permanent value of communal harmony. To Apemantus, the brevity of the spectacle serves as a reminder of the impermanence of Timon's good fortune. (pp. 43-4)

Shakespeare, then, has used the masque form to establish the subject of his play, and the need for a satiric corrective. His substantial achievement in *Timon* is to show not only that in any age the ideals of shared communal life may be despised by the disruptive forces of greed, violence, and cynical opportunism, but that when the order instituted by right-minded men to preserve these ideals becomes corrupt, it must, however painfully, be revised. This assault on the ground of authority itself, which reaches its crisis shortly after the masquing sequence, has been carefully prepared for since the opening lines of the play. (p. 45)

If Timon glimpses the cloud-capped towers of the pageant world in Act I, the action which immediately follows is antimasque and satiric commentary on Timon's lost authority. The characteristic progression of action in the masque is reversed in this play. Instead of proceeding from fast-moving comic action to the stately main masque to revels and finally to the tranquil parting of the masquers, Shakespeare accelerates the tempo and madness of Timon's career, moving from the opening processions and ceremonial courtliness to the burlesque banquet, Timon's retreat from the city, his discovery of buried gold, his rejection of the Athenian suppliants, and desperate renunciation of life. As the action speeds up with the series of brief encounters in the middle acts, the noise-level rises proportionately: Act III concludes with the clatter of hurled serving dishes, Act IV with the noisy flyting between Apemantus and Timon. Timon himself is master of these antic revels, which remind us more of the disruptive Humours and Affections of the anti-masque in Jonson's *Hymenaei* or the swashbuckling fencer in *Pan's Anniversarie* than the actions of Shakespeare's tragedies.

The transition from masque to comic anti-masque is evident not only in the action but also in Shakespeare's presentation of character. Timon's antagonists, a group of usurers and fair-weather friends, are stock characters from morality plays and citizen comedy that were frequently pressed into service in Jacobean satiric plays. One of these is the money-lending Athenian senator who coaches his servant in the techniques of dunning in the brief opening scene of Act II. . . . Timon will be offered no chance to rise victorious from his phoenix-like self-destruction. The greedy senator changes the phoenix image, so appropriate to celebrations of heroic virtue, into the predatory image of the satiric gull. He speaks for a ruthless form of economic authority that has expanded to fill the vacuum left by Timon's shrunk fortunes and loss of moral authority. With the references to the naked gull Shakespeare has evoked the moral perspective of Jacobean city comedy to make a specific point: value in the community is henceforth to be determined solely in monetary terms. (pp. 48-9)

Timon himself participates in the movement away from the moral perspective of masque to that of satiric comedy. We see him as a satiric manipulator in the splendidly contrived mock-banquet scene [III. vi]. Timon greets his skeptical guests, designated now simply by numbers; then he calls for the regal music of trumpets, and the banquet dishes arrive, all of them covered, thus promising only the finest fare. After Timon's bitterly ironic prayer for ingratitude, reminiscent of Apemantus' Grace in the earlier banquet scene, Timon uncovers the dishes and hurls their watery contents in the faces of the guests; he also curses them with the paradoxical epithets "Courteous destroyers, affable wolves, meek bears" [III. vi. 95]. Each of Timon's oxymorons wittily captures the true horror of a civilized world in a state of collapse. The flood of water and words, the clatter of dishes, and the guests' mad scramble for hats and cloaks all fit the decorum of comic disaster. Still, in the midst of this scene we are forced to recognize that chaos is come again and that Timon, by mocking the ceremonies of civilization, is the author of his own isolation. His comedic outburst ends with a misanthropic curse.

> Burn house! sink Athens! henceforth hated be
> Of Timon man and all humanity!
>
>   [III. vi. 104-05]

When the spectacle of the banquet is violently overturned, so too are the ideals of generosity and order which it originally celebrated. It is not surprising, then, that the next time we see Timon he is in the guise of Misanthropos. Behind this mask he is unapproachable as a human being; the civilizing influence of masquerading has been destroyed. (pp. 50-1)

[In Act IV] Timon has become totally transformed; rather than the naive masque-maker of the early acts we see something akin to the cunning malcontent in the plays of Marston, Webster, and Ford. . . . Although it has occurred to Timon that

his fall may have been a fortunate one and that he is well rid of corrupting civilization [IV. iii. 4-23], still his suffering is feelingly conveyed. Whereas Apemantus wishes to be transformed, along with the rest of mankind, into a beast, Timon seeks to retain his identification with humanity. He realizes, however, that there is no way to return to civilized life once ceremony has been utterly rejected. Unlike Lear, Timon has no loving child to lead him back to the ordered world he has renounced. Nor is he comfortable in the role of satirist. He is not finally a profiteering manipulator like Volpone, who creates an imaginary golden world in which he can feel invulnerable. Such characters are legion in Jacobean satire; they lose sight of the real world and are tripped up by it at the moment of exposure. Though the numerous allusions to the genre of satiric comedy have prepared us for this moment, it never comes. It is impossible to expose Timon because mask and self have become one and the same. His dilemma is a composite of Lear's and Volpone's; he makes their mistakes, yet he is denied both the glee of the comic villain and the noble stature of the tragic hero. When he refuses for the last time to defend his native Athens against the disaffected Alcibiades, we may well share the second senator's feeling that "Our hope in him is dead" [V. i. 226]. Timon is left to do explicitly what he has been doing implicitly all along; he digs his own grave. (pp. 54-5)

While it is true that Shakespeare's Timon . . . lacks judgment, his folly eventually becomes his tragedy. Though in comedy deceitful characters always run the risk of being found out, they do not ordinarily face the graver danger of finding out anything about themselves. Timon has been a fool, deceived both by himself and by others, and he responds to this revelation, as we have seen, with a kind of antic disposition that suits his newly acquired sense of identity. He chooses to live in isolation; he suffers the knowledge that men who once seemed worthy of his gifts are unfeeling mercenaries; and he dies with no more faith in justice than Lear has. The idea of community has not only proved unattainable for him, but remains for him a mockery. The tragic dimension of the play thus is subordinated to the controlling satiric idea that no man is left undiminished by an imperfect world. (p. 56)

I have tried thus far to demonstrate that Shakespeare has considerably broadened the range of effects available to the Jacobean stage satirist first by contrasting the masque and satiric anti-masque movements in his play, then by adding a tragic dimension to his satirized-satirist figure, Timon. And these are only the most prominent generic elements in Shakespeare's experiment with *genera mixta*. Not far off in the constellation of dramatic kinds to which Shakespeare alludes with the short-hand of tag-names, adages, and epigrams are the *Respublica* histories, prodigal son plays, and *Mankind*-moralities. Each kind carries with it a disposition toward certain values—community, restraint, fortitude—values by which Shakespeare's characters are measured under the unforgiving light of satire. No single generic frame would quite serve Shakespeare's purpose. (pp. 57-8)

William W.E. Slights, "'Genera mixta' and 'Timon of Athens'," in Studies in Philology, *Vol. LXXIV, No. 1, January, 1977, pp. 36-62.*

LESLEY W. BRILL (essay date 1979)

[*Because* Timon's *main action deals with self-analysis and the presentation of the diverse nature of truth, Brill argues that Shakespeare intended his play to elicit a variety of responses, for it is only through considering all contradictory views of reality that the individual comes closest to the truth. For Brill, then, the majority of disagreements over the play arise only when critics accept the words or actions of one character as containing the meaning of the play.*]

The meaning of Shakespeare's *Timon of Athens*, the integrity of its text, the moral status of its important characters, and its genre have all been the subject of extensive debate. What qualities in the play encourage such a multiplicity of responses? Unlike *Hamlet*, Shakespeare's most famous conundrum, *Timon* lacks complexity of plot and character. Nor is its poetry, even at its most powerful, unusually rich in imagery or ideas. It may be that part of the ambiguity of *Timon* originates in this very simplicity, for scarcity of data invites variance in interpretation. What *Timon* lacks in complexity of plot, character, and language, however, it more than makes up in abundance of internal commentary. Its main action, in fact, is self-analysis. But like the analyses of its critics, its interior explanations remain equivocal, their abundance as confusing as the spareness of plot and character. I propose to argue that the diversity of critical response to *Timon* leads us, paradoxically, to an understanding of its unity; that the play itself demands a variety of responses; and that its cosmology implicitly explains why multiple and contradictory views of reality bring men as close as they can approach to the truth. In works of art, the most formal and obviously false of men's redactions of life, we come closest to true commentary, even when those works suggest, as *Timon* does, that no such truth is possible. (p. 17)

Looking at *Timon* and the scholarship surrounding it from outside any particular critical position, what are we to suppose? Surely it is unlikely that only one of [the many] analyses has any substantial accuracy. Less likely still is the idea that nobody has yet discovered "the truth about *Timon*." It seems more plausible that many truths have been expounded about this puzzling play. When we actually examine various interpretations, moreover, we find most of them well buttressed by textual evidence. The diversity of responses to *Timon*, then, must derive from its polysemous construction rather than from the whimsey of contentious teachers of literature.

The development of the plot of *Timon* proceeds as smoothly as anything Shakespeare ever wrote. . . . *Timon* contains few incidents and fewer surprises—with one crucial exception: after renouncing Athens and mankind and departing into the woods, Timon accidentally uncovers an immense treasure. It is, apparently, enough to buy anything except peace of mind. A single bump in a Shakespearean main plot is several fewer than usual, however, and it remains accurate to characterize the plotting of *Timon* as clean and simple. This simplicity, coupled with the meager development of the subplot, makes commentary problematical, for the incidents are sufficient to evoke many possible responses but insufficient to rule many out. The plot of *Timon* appears to be a verbal seed from which almost any moral organism may be bred.

Like the plot, characterization in *Timon* is markedly spare. Indeed, the bald characterization of virtually all its figures is frequently cited as evidence of its status as a morality. Timon appears as innocent and loving generosity in the first movement of the play, as bitterly disillusioned misanthropy in the second. Apemantus is a cynic throughout. The lords are flatterers, Timon's servants loyal retainers, the senators hypocrites; the usurers are mercilessly avaricious, the whores shamelessly venal; and the Poet, Painter, Merchant, and Jeweller are essentially functions of the crafts their names indicate. Only Alcibiades threatens to flesh out as a character of some complexity, but we see

so little of him that he remains no more than a passably honest and energetic soldier and politician. As the spareness of the plot of *Timon* leaves us free to put on it what interpretation we will, so does the coarseness of its characterization. (pp. 20-1)

The main role played by every figure in *Timon* is that of commentator. Nowhere else in Shakespeare's work do so many characters comment so copiously upon such scanty action. *Timon* may be imagined as a colossal dramatization of the story of the blind men and the elephant; it is a collection of commentaries on data as enigmatic as they are spectacular. In *Timon* the audience too is blind, and its idea of the elephant remains as uncertain as the ideas of its blind guides.

The opening scene of Act I sets forth a paradigm for the entire play. The Poet and the Painter have just greeted one another when the Poet asks, "How goes the world?" The Painter replies, "It wears, sir, as it grows." Deeming the answer banal, if true, the Poet responds: "Ay, that's well known" [I.i.2-3]. This evidently unremarkable opening exchange . . . establishes in small a discursive shape that will dominate the play at every order of magnitude: we are presented with a "fact" (here, the world), a comment on it, then a reformulation of the comment. The play immediately proceeds to a similar sequence. The Merchant exclaims to the Jeweller, "O, 'tis a worthy lord." The Jeweller answers, much as the Poet did the Painter, "Nay, that's most fix'd" [I.i.9]. Again the sequence presents us with a "fact" (implicitly, Timon), a commentary, and, in this case, an evaluation of the comment. It is typical of *Timon* that in both these opening interchanges most of the emphasis falls on the commentaries, very little on the subjects to which they apply. Neither the world nor Timon appears as more than an excuse for small talk. (p. 22)

Timon begins with a prologue which in effect instructs its audience about what it is watching—a commentary upon, presumably, the facts of life—and how it is to respond—by working its own criticisms or reformulations of that commentary. As the play proceeds, every action and circumstance becomes an occasion for comment and countercomment. The audience is never allowed to forget that the world is what one makes of it, and that what one makes of it is always subject to dispute and redefinition.

After the prologue, Timon enters and displays his generosity by paying the debts of an imprisoned friend and by making a gift of money which enables one of his servants to marry. Besides Timon's openhandedness, we may notice his tendency to moralize his own actions, a tendency that continues the penchant for self-commentary of the drama. An aphoristic style surfaces here, as it did earlier, and as it will throughout the play: "'Tis not enough to help the feeble up, / But to support him after" [I.i.107-08]. Spilling pronouncements upon everything that catches his attention, Timon moves judiciously through the action of Act I. . . . Like everyone else in the play, Apemantus is ever ready to serve as a commentator. He judges not only the jewel and the painting, but the company of Timon's flatterers, Athenians generally, the art of poetry, the venality of the Merchant, the quality of the feast and the masque, and Timon himself. Nor are Timon and Apemantus the only commentators in Act I. Virtually everyone at the feast offers an opinion, frequently with considerable pomp, on some facet of his surroundings. As in the opening exchanges, the comments are themselves immediately subjected to scrutiny and criticism, especially but not exclusively from Apemantus. The self-analytic mode of *Timon* is firmly established in its opening lines and is intensified as the play continues. One would be obliged to quote practically all the rest of the drama in order to trace fully this tendency of the characters to serve as commentators upon the action of their play and as reformulators of each other's commentaries. (pp. 23-4)

The works of the Poet and the Painter are examples of art within art. They emphasize formal expression of feelings and ideas within the larger aesthetic unit of the play as a whole. Such conventional expression persists throughout *Timon* in gift-giving and feasts, in speechifying, in the masque of the Amazons, in the frequent introduction of music, and in tirades with elegantly ordered topoi. (p. 24)

In the woods as in his palace, Timon's actions inspire radically diverse responses among those who witness them. All utterances and all gestures in *Timon* are rendered equivocal by the variety of responses they evoke.

Timon ends, as it began and as it proceeded, with an efflorescence of internal commentary. As usual, this commentary is elevated at the expense of the actions upon which it comments. Timon dies off stage, and we learn of his death only from the report of the soldier who finds his tomb. The other action at the end of the play, Alcibiades' attack upon Athens, is diminished and deemphasized when Alcibiades enters the city peacefully. Thus there is little activity to distract us from the play's final remarks upon itself. Timon's polemical impulse transcends his very death, and his moralizing reaches us across his grave in a series of angry epitaphs. . . . The inconsistencies among Timon's epitaphs have been regarded as evidence of the incomplete state of the drama as we have it, the assumption being that Shakespeare would have canceled one or two of them when he gave a final polishing to the play. But their contradiction of each other has a broad consistency both with Timon's career and with the multiplicity of contradictory commentaries that accompany it. Through his epitaphs, Timon offers his final commentary and so concludes a life that consisted of a series of formal gestures of uncertain import. He writes the poem of his death as he wrote the poem of his life. (pp. 25-6)

Though nothing be good or bad but thinking makes it so, in *Timon* there is so much and such contradictory thinking that moral truth practically disappears into a whirlwind of contending opinions. The simplicity of plot leaves enormous room for speculation, and the prolixity of internal analysis does little to circumscribe this interpretative space. This pervasive self-commentary accounts for much of the diversity of critical response which the play has evoked: all reasonable interpretations are set forth in a plenty that is finally as undiscriminating as paucity. The simplicity of characterization in *Timon*, surprisingly, does not clarify this confusion, for although sympathetic and unsympathetic characters are strongly differentiated, they are not distinguished in terms of reliability.

Virtually all the characters comment on the action of the play from narrow and self-serving viewpoints. (p. 27)

Timon is unlikely, obviously, to be a less interested or more reliable interpreter of his own story than the figures who surround him. Thus every character's interpretation of the action of *Timon* comes from a point of view which is limited and colored by self-interest or "humor." This assertion implies, not that everyone in the play is entirely untrustworthy, but that no one is wholly reliable. The majority of disagreements about *Timon* arise when critics adopt as normative or choral the words and actions of particular characters. Timon's critical defenders

find in his intemperance truth and goodness, and dismiss the caveats of characters in the play as caviling. His detractors cull the play for criticisms of Timon's most attractive qualities, which they then use to debunk any ideas of Timon's nobility. Those who find *Timon* a lofty tragedy fix upon the stature of the hero and the extremity of his sufferings; those who argue that the drama is essentially a satire cite the absurdity of Timon's behavior when considered from a prudential perspective. The play provides evidence for both viewpoints. If we adopt the standards of Apemantus, the world view in *Timon* becomes one of unadulterated cynicism; if we adopt those of Alcibiades, the play figures forth a rational and even mildly optimistic model of the functioning of men and nations. Again, both viewpoints are partly validated by the drama. (p. 30)

The corruption of man and of his world produces a disorder in which moral categories, like other phenomena, are hopelessly tangled and mixed. At the beginning of the play, Timon behaves as if he were still living in a Golden Age. When he discovers that he is not, he continues to roar his curses at the fallen world from the perspective of a prelapsarian one. For all their simple truth, these judgments are as extreme and naïve as were his prodigal love and bounty before his bankruptcy. The "justice" Timon calls down on Athens and mankind is like the inflexible law of the Senators or the undiscriminating iron flail of Spenser's Talus; it lacks "equity," that understanding mercy which takes into account the complex circumstances of an imperfect world. Equally simple in love and in hate, Timon is quite out of place in a world where black and white have run to gray. (pp. 33-4)

In such a dark and muddled world, it is questionable whether man can apprehend even fragmentary truth. If he can, however, the play suggests that he is likeliest to do so in works of art. *Timon* is exceptionally rich in representations of art and artful formality, an emphasis of crucial importance to its meaning. One of the central paradoxes of this protean work is its suggestion that the lying of such self-seeking artists as the Poet and the Painter may be as near as man can approach to the truth. (p. 34)

In a world where "all's obliquy; / There's nothing level in our cursed natures / But direct villainy" [IV.iii.18-20], an admitted pretender like the Poet or the Painter must be the most honest of men. The feigning that is his profession represents a profound acknowledgment of the deception inherent in all man's acts. Timon speaks accurately when he tells the Poet in a wonderfully resonant line that "thou art even natural in thine art" [V.i.85]. In addition to possessing talents appropriate to his lying profession, the Poet (and the Painter also) is "natural" in the sense of ingenuous or simple-minded. His allegories are not well calculated to coin the gold he seeks from Timon. One must therefore conclude either that the Poet does not understand what he writes or that he cannot control it, which may be saying the same thing. . . . When Timon asks Apemantus how he likes the Painter's picture, Apemantus replies, "The best, for the innocence" [I.i.196]. He means, of course, crudity. But the Painter's innocence has to do with his relative lack of guilt as well, for he, like the Poet, is an admitted illusionist and therefore an honest man. The "innocence" of his art resides also in its moral superiority to its maker. "Excellent workman," says Timon, "thou canst not paint a man so bad as is thyself" [V.i.31-2]. (pp. 35-6)

The world of *Timon* is one of infinite moral complexity. It is a world in which truth and falsehood are as hard to separate as the making and the lying in a poet's feigning. Timon is at once Ideal Bounty and Reckless Prodigality; the play will not allow us to claim one without acknowledging the other. He is heroic and ridiculous, "bless'd to be most accurs'd, / Rich only to be made wretched—[his] great fortunes / Are made [his] chief afflictions" [IV.ii.42-4]. By presenting all interpretations of its action, *Timon* prevents us from wholly advocating any one. It excludes only exclusivity and fixes the ambiguity of life unambiguously. It claims for the lies of art and for feigning artists a special honesty. It traps its readers, like its characters, into thinking that they have discovered the truth about a false world. It is an ocean; it is very like a camel, a weasel, a whale; it fairly strives to appear foul, rots to grow ripe. It is nothing, and it is all things. (p. 36)

Lesley W. Brill, "Truth and 'Timon of Athens'," in Modern Language Quarterly, *Vol. 40, No. 1, March, 1979, pp. 17-36.*

SUSAN HANDELMAN   (essay date 1979)

[*Handelman describes* Timon *as the depiction of a world in which the correspondences and interrelationships between opposites—men and women, love and hate, self and other, ideal and real—break down, leaving a world of negation, misanthropy, and rage. Handelman claims that the absence of women in Timon's society represents that society's, as well as Timon's, refusal to accept the balancing order which the love of women sustains. It also suggests the narcissistic attitude in Timon's society based on the society's attempts to construct a community exclusively of men. When Timon discovers that his idealized brotherly communion is only a "mutual devouring" of human lives, Handelman continues, his response is not guilt or shame but "rage and primitive hatred."*]

For Shakespeare, the dreams and diseases of the narcissistic ego were of particular fascination. His stage is peopled with characters who represent in both comic and tragic modes the manifold forms which these dreams and disorders may assume. Malvolio and Lear, for example, are so different and yet so similar, for the cornerstone of their characters is an infantile narcissism which abruptly conflicts with a reality which negates their dreams of omnipotence, confines the boundaries of their egos, and denies them the objects of their desires. And Shakespeare gives them both very harsh therapy. (p. 45)

Shakespeare's characters frequently express an obsession with the problems of creation, illusion, boundaries, dreams. The anxiety that the symbolic world will break down, vanish and leave not a rack behind, is present in all the plays, and perhaps accounts for their obsessive self-reflexiveness—their constant reflection on their own origins, their own natures as plays. The anxiety of the artist's ego is another variant of the primal shock to our universal narcissism. But with those characters who insist on retaining and trying obstinately to recapture that original state, Shakespeare is often not kind.

The inability to accept loss may express itself in the creation of higher narcissistic illusions or heightened rage. In Lear, both reactions exist simultaneously—holding dead Cordelia in his arms, he cries "Never, never, never," etc. etc., and yet looks for signs of breath on her lips—"The feather stirs; she lives! If it be so, / It is a chance which does redeem all sorrows / that ever I have felt" [*King Lear*, V. iii. 262-67]. *Timon of Athens* follows *Lear* and is a play so close and yet so far from *Lear* because it asks the question: How do we go on living *after* Cordelia is dead? In *Timon of Athens* disillusion is absolute, no substitute is acceptable, there are no rituals of atonement, no provisions for mourning. The play is less about the experience of loss itself than a demonstration of the rage which

refuses to accept loss. Perhaps this is why it is generally considered to be a bad play—it does not do what we expect of art in general: help us to accept loss.

All the questions about its authorship, which stem from the many confusions and disjunctions in the text, indicate an unfinished play which somewhere broke down, would not allow itself to be composed. But that indeed, I think, is itself what the play is about—a breakdown of all those ways in which rage, pain, and loss can somehow be accepted, made sense of, transformed into life-affirming energies. That transformation indeed requires a magic power, and the magic of art which is always engaged in denying loss by making something from nothing, making dead matter live, conjuring presences, thieving immortality from time, does not work in this play—both structurally and symbolically.

In *Timon*, Shakespeare does not believe in his own art, and that is why the play is unfinished. *Timon* tells us something that the artist himself cannot dwell on too long: that mourning is never finished, that we can't and don't really know how to accept or redeem loss, that we are always pained and enraged. Says Alcibiades, "To be in anger is impiety; / But who is man that is not angry?" [III. v. 56-7]. (pp. 46-8)

In the world of *Timon* nothing can redeem sorrow. Nothing can come of nothing. There are no acceptable substitutes; loss is irrevocable. Therefore, Timon does not mourn, he rages. In a world without Cordelia, without an embodied ideal of love, art, nature, man himself is not man, but a beast. What Apemantus says also applies to the modern city: "The commonwealth of Athens is become a forest of beasts." What Timon asks him is also the question of contemporary history: "What beast couldst thou be, that were not subject to a beast? And what a beast art thou already, that sees not thy loss in transformation!" [IV. iii. 343-45]. (pp. 48-9)

That the embodied principle of good is often an idealized woman in Shakespeare is significant. In *Timon*, there is neither good art nor good women. The play itself is in part about the cultural and individual disaster of execution of the female. A world without women is a world not only without art, but without order. In *Lear*, the good woman, the ideal of pure love was exiled, but not murdered until the end of the play. In *Timon*, she never existed; there is no feminine representative of goodness and constancy. When woman as nourisher is perceived as devourer, and relation with her as feared dependency; when the wish for a gratifying union with her is seen as threatening destruction only; when she is not only banished, but hated and murdered, then there can be neither manhood nor brotherhood, neither human being, nor society. That is the condition of the world in *Timon of Athens*.

Accepting woman, however, means accepting loss, accepting not only the gap between self and other, but also the gap between self and self—recognizing the illusion of narcissistic omnipotence, knowing that one is limited, imperfect, dependent and not projecting that part of one's nature onto a conveniently hated and abhorred weak, false female. The world cannot be split, as Timon originally splits it, into a male brotherly good and a female fatal bad. Woman herself cannot be split, as the cultural myth splits her, into the Sacred Virginal Good and Profane Prostitute Bad. Accepting woman means accepting art itself. The world which excludes woman splits itself apart; the man who denies the female divides his own self and like Timon becomes his opposite, Misanthropos, monster, and beast. In *Timon of Athens*, there is no way back to humanity.

Thus, the world of *Timon* is a world of negations, mutually destructive oppositions—male-female, good-bad, love-hate, man-beast, friend-enemy, forgiveness-revenge. Contraries do not mutually exist, differences and separations are not tolerated; the gap between self and other, presence and absence, ideal and real, loss and recovery is unbridgeable. The adjoining "bonds" are broken. The structure of the play itself operates on the principle of splitting, of incorporation and expulsion, orally ambivalent perception. The first half of the play centers around Timon's communal feasts, the second half around his solitary exile; the imagery turns from the intake of nourishing food to the vomiting of poison and disease. In place of an internal principle of integration which Timon lacks and cannot find, he had depended on a false, external, reified, material means of mutuality: money.

Seen in terms of the relation of loss and return, money, art, and love are all intimately connected. All are attempts to bridge the gap between self and other, wish and need. All are ways to deny loss, to find recompense. (pp. 49-50)

The problem of loss is the problem of need and want, the problem of wholeness, an integrated and not split identity. Art, money, law, love, all bonds and means of exchange between men, civilization itself, are means to recover loss. Timon's primitive communism is a dream of restored communion, an attempt to defend against primal loss, to become both Self and Other, to be fed by his friends' flattery and feed them from the overflow of his bounty—to be simultaneously the passive nursing one, and the beneficent nourishing Mother. Yet he can only replace the flow of female milk with the rigid exchange of male money. Timon's attempted identification with the role of the Mother is a way to deny the loss of that primal one who gratified the infant's every wish, and to thereby be autonomous, not dependent on any female, not in need or vulnerable to any woman. But his primitive communism is, in fact, a feudal lordship, a narcissistic dream of adoration from his retainers under the guise of a Holy Brotherhood, one which admits no women. (p. 53)

Loss can be denied by identification with the lost object and by attempted appropriation of female magic. For Shakespeare, Timon's magic, however, is impotent because it is narcissistic, substitutive, cannibalistic, and not transformative. Coins, jewels, food, are nonhuman, inert matter that cannot gratify the wish to be at one. The failure of all narcissistic substitutions leads to expulsion, spitting, and vomiting out all with which Timon had identified—women, friends, food, money, art:

> Therefore, be abhorred
> All feasts, societies, and throngs of men!
> His semblable, yea, himself, Timon disdains.
> Destruction fang mankind!   [IV. iii. 20-4]

> *Alcibiades:* Why, fare thee well:
> Here is some gold for thee.
> *Timon:*   Keep it, I cannot eat it. [IV. iii. 100-01]
>   (p. 54)

The first scene of the play contains in miniature the critique of the impossible feast of civilization in its art, love, money and law. The poet in line 6 exclaims, "See, / Magic of bounty / All these spirits thy power / Hath conjured to attend." The poet, too, though, is in attendance not because of free love, nor is his art a free gift, but rather a counter to be exchanged for monetary recompense. The painter's art is described as a "pretty mocking of the life" [I. i. 35]. The mentality of art as imitation is the same mentality as literal, externalized sub-stitution—as the mentality of money and the merchant. Art mocks nature by holding up the mirror, by copying and aping. In Renaissance thought, over against this kind of art, is the idealized power of Nature—the divinely created order of things, the procreative power which art might tutor or tame, but which art does not possess itself. To transfer the belief in that kind of natural transformative and freely creative power to Art, as we have done since the Romantics, and as Shakespeare plays with doing especially in the later works, signifies the loss of the divinely ordered scheme (and not incidentally the rise of bourgeois capitalism).

The Shakespearean moment is one in which the theological hierarchy gives way to the chaos of history (and regulated value to the chaotic fluctuation of the capitalistic market). In the Great Chain of Being, differences are dissolving, and all things are dangerously confusing their places (especially if money can transform identities), "place thieves / And give them title, knee, and approbation / With senators on the bench" [IV. iii. 36-8]. Men and beasts are transformed into each other. Art itself cannot mirror life, correspond in a one-to-one relationship to a nature no longer based on a hierarchical set of correspondences. (pp. 54-5)

The inability to accept change as the inability to accept difference is also the Shakespearean theme of loss as ingratitude—of betrayal as lack of faith and constancy. Woman is the first betrayer of constancy, not only because she is different, but because she forces separation from her body, through birth and weaning, and because she cannot be possessed by the child as the father possesses her. Thus it is that the changes and petulance of "Fortune" are personified, especially in the Renaissance, as female. Fortune is a fickle and false lady; the poet in the first scene of *Timon* likewise portrays Timon's ascent and fall from Fortune as a climbing of a female body. . . . (pp. 56-7)

When Timon discovers that his idealized brotherly communion is a cannibalistic mutual devouring, his response is not guilt or shame as it would be in the case of Freud's totemistic brotherhood, but rage and primitive hatred (what in Freud would precede the murder of the father). This rage is directed against and placed in terms of women, not men; the breeding and feeding generosity of the mother must be accepted as beneficent bounty or it becomes detested as parasitic dependence. Before he can give his gift, Timon needs to learn how to accept and receive the gift of nature, love, grace; he must accept the power of women. Instead, he tries to omnipotently become the woman and nourisher himself. He refuses to accept generation from the female, and thus *all* generation, all creation of something from nothing is detestable debt and abhorred birth. . . . including the breeding of capital. . . . (p. 61)

Outside of the two whores who appear briefly with Alcibiades in Act IV, the only women in the play are, significantly, Amazons in a masque—threatening, warlike women placed under formalized and ritual control through art (the same defensive strategy used in *The Tempest*). . . . After he loses his money, devoured by his debts, woman becomes also for Timon a ravenous destroyer:

> This fell whore of thine
> Hath in her more destruction than thy sword,
> For all her cherubin look.   [IV. iii. 62-4]

> Strike me the counterfeit matron;
> It is her habit only that is honest, herself's a bawd.

Let not the virgin's cheek
Make soft thy trenchant sword; for those milk paps
That through the window [bars] bore at men's eyes,
Are not within the leaf of pity writ.
But set them down horrible traitors.   [IV. iii. 113-19]
                                                    (p. 62)

The taking in of nourishing milk reverses to the vomiting of poison; communion with the mother and the other is now a source of corruption and syphillitic disintegration. But Timon's hatred, while it is a schizophrenic reversal is itself still a refusal to accept loss, a refusal to reconstruct, and recover new objects, to transform or metamorphose. He cannot find a substitute ideal. His rage remains primitively narcissistic. His hatred is as orgasmic, diffuse, and undifferentiated as his love. It contains both the desire to control and enclose the whole world, and the desire passively to see oneself as a victim of universal corruption. On the one hand, it represents an all-or-nothing split between ideas of good and evil, pure and impure, and the outward projection of the primitive hatred at the recognition of the discrepancy between self and other into the outside world. The original unity of love and hate in oral ambivalence becomes undone and in place of incorporation is expulsion. Yet Timon's curses all center around the confusion of opposites and boundaries, the collapse of splitting divisions:

    To general filth
    Convert 'i the 'instant green virginity. . . .
    Instruction, manners, mysteries, and trades,
    Degrees, observances, customs, and laws,
    Decline to your confounding contraries,
    And let confusion live!   [IV. i. 6, 7, 18-21]

To convert everything into its opposite means to negate and destroy one term of the existing contraries; such was the original aim of Timon's love and his use of money. His hate has the same purpose of destroying difference, of denying mourning and recovery. His split ego, even in its construction of a nightmare world is seeking still a way back to primal undifferentiated unity. To hate is a way to retain his relation to his objects; only when he becomes indifferent does he die. (pp. 62-3)

Both cultural and individual identity demand the establishment of differences, the toleration of mutually co-existing opposites of self and other. The precariousness of these differences and of this toleration is the threat of inner violence which suddenly wells up to cause a breakdown of differentiation, a collapse of things into their opposite, of Timon into Misanthropos, noble warrior into revengeful rebel. (p. 66)

Where Antony and Cleopatra's dream is of a marriage between male and female, an interpenetration of opposites, Timon's dream is of a male fantasy of exclusive brotherhood, based on an identity which needs to destroy the other. The difference between the two dreams is the difference between the art of recovering loss by metamorphosis (identity-in-difference) and the recovery of loss by substitution (identity as sameness, incorporation, internalization). One is transformative, the other sacrificial. One allows for surplus value as free gift; the other demands exact recompense. One represents mercy, love, art; the other money, law, capitalism, artifice.

Timon of Athens is a dead end. Such transformative magic does not exist in its world. Antony and Cleopatra must necessarily follow upon Timon's heels if the rest is not to be silence. Once recognized and accepted, one can render to Caesar that which is Caesar's. The transformative power of art means another world than this one. Art can no longer imitate nature, but just transform it into "something rich and strange." Yet the world remains Caesar's. The world which is the province of art, the part of nature which can become a part of paradise exists in the realm of the idealizing imagination. But Shakespeare was not a Romantic; Prospero needs to abjure his art so that we can return to Naples, to face death. Yet in facing death, we need the imaginative dream of Cleopatra, a dream that is permitted to us only for a few moments. (pp. 67-8)

    *Susan Handelman, "'Timon of Athens': The Rage
    of Disillusion," in* American Imago, *Vol. 36, No. 1,
    Spring, 1979, pp. 45-68.*

ROLF SOELLNER (essay date 1979)

[*Soellner argues that the pessimistic vision in* Timon *inhibits many critics from accepting the play as a tragedy. Although* Timon *does not conform to the classical rules for tragedy, Soellner maintains, it nonetheless produces in us the response of pity and awe, similar to that engendered by classical tragedy. In defining* Timon *as a "pessimistic tragedy," Soellner refutes those interpretations of the drama as either a morality play or a satire (see excerpts above by August Wilhelm Schlegel, 1808; A. S. Collins, 1946; Andor Gomme, 1959; Peter Ure, 1964; and Anne Lancashire, 1970). He considers the categorization of a morality play too limiting because none of the characters, particularly Timon himself, can be reduced to such allegorical figures as Noble Bounty, Prodigality, Commercialism, or Greed. He also regards the classification of the play as a satire to be inappropriate since it fails to account for Timon's extreme pessimism and misanthropy.*]

That a number of critics have found *Timon* lacking in tragic qualities is symptomatic of the general feeling that it is in some manner different from Shakespeare's other tragedies, that it lies, to use Willard Farnham's phrase, at the frontiers of tragedy. But, to my mind, it is still clearly within these. This is not, I think, an academic argument, because a critic's attitude toward all aspects of a work is influenced by what he judges the whole to be. (p. 15)

Well into the nineteenth century, most critics, whose judgments were formed by the standards of Greek tragedy, or rather some select Greek tragedies, were averse to using the term for Shakespeare's. And when Shakespeare was accepted into the canon, it was at first for a small number of plays. Bradley's singling out of *Hamlet, Othello, Lear,* and *Macbeth* made it fashionable to think only of these as true tragedies, and some were even excluded one or the other of them. There are few now who would deny that *Romeo and Juliet* and the Roman plays are also tragedies. But *Timon* is still in most critics' limbo if not somewhere in an upper circle of hell; and this, I think, is unfortunate. This is not to say that it is in the same league as *Hamlet, Othello, Lear,* and *Macbeth;* but I think that it belongs to the next group, being in kind no less powerful than *Antony and Cleopatra* and *Coriolanus,* Shakespeare's other late tragedies. If it has not been so ranked, by and large, this has been due to an overemphasis on the defectiveness of the text and to preconceptions on the need for tragedy to uplift and edify, preconceptions, I believe, that are restrictive and really quite arbitrary. (pp. 15-16)

Of the claims that *Timon* belongs to a genre different from tragedy, the one easiest to refute is that it is a "morality." True, its outcome is in a sense predictable; but then, in what Shakespearean tragedy is it not? For that matter, all tragedies make us anticipate their general endings since these must rest on some inevitability. The dramatic strategy of *Timon* is not as simple as some would have it; the outcome is not altogether anticipated by the poet's allegory of Fortune, and certainly the moral is not contained in it or the play would be both cynical and banal. Although the allegory anticipates the major turn of the action (leaving out, however, the Alcibiades movement), it makes of Timon a mere favorite and victim of Fortune, and, for better or worse, he is something more. . . . Granted that the "vices" that oppose Timon, taken *en bloc,* represent something like "Commercialism" or "Exploitation," not a single one represents a clearly defined particular vice, such as Pecunia or Luxuria or Dissimulatio. And there is certainly no character that embodies a definite pattern of virtue: Timon the philanthropist is also prodigal; Apemantus the philosopher is also vain and envious; Flavius is loyal but also interested in gold. We do not have the feeling of a clear moral orientation to which Timon could and should adjust himself. (p. 17)

Timon is a pessimist, a nihilist, a prophet of annihilation; above all, he is a misanthrope. Among Shakespeare's heroes, who are all extremists, he is the most extreme; to call him a satirist is to put him into a frame from which he breaks.

That Timon is killed by the nature of satire sounds better in the study or the classroom than when seeing the play or reading it as theater of the mind. What is self-destructive is Timon's misanthropy, which is an extreme reaction to the villainy and ingratitude of his friends, and this misanthropy is fed by his recognition of the general venality of Athens, which he generalizes into that of man. Timon's death derives with tragic logic from his character and circumstances; it does not matter that it occurs offstage if one attends to classical models, as Shakespeare appears to have done. Timon's death certainly dominates the catastrophe in tragic manner. (p. 19)

Certainly satire is one of its defining elements, but there are other components that equally claim attention.

One of these is the particular domestic quality of the play—in fact, "domestic tragedy" was Dr. Johnson's label for it [see excerpt above, 1765]. The action turns on the misfortune of a citizen of Athens, and the fall of his great house provides some of its pathos. (p. 20)

In one respect *Timon* does move closer to Shakespeare's romances: in the large role given to spectacle—to the banquets, the masque, music, and dancing. The very settings are spectacular: Timon's splendid house, the walls that symbolize the large city, the wild, wooded land that contains Timon's cave, and beyond them the universe evoked in Timon's apocalyptic imagination. (p. 21)

We have so far characterized *Timon* as tragical-satirical-domestical-spectacular, a hyphenization that views with Polonius's "tragical-comical-historical-pastoral." In effect, all of Shakespeare's plays are hyphenated things; *Hamlet,* for instance, could be called "tragical-historical-satirical-psychological." *Timon* follows an even more complex recipe. We must yet add that other adjective that keeps recurring to the hyphenization that characterizes the play: pessimistic. Pessimism, of course, is as much a matter of reaction to what is presented as it is inherent in the play: what may strike one reader or viewer as a deeply discouraging statement about mankind may register only mildly on another; but experience has proved that the play manipulates its audience toward pessimism, a manipulation some have resented.

In this pessimism lies the major problem for the play's appreciation as a tragedy. . . . Tragedy, we are urged, reconciles

us in some manner to the universe or teaches us something about the working of retributive justice or edifies us about the dignity of man. . . . If such affirmation of a transcendent order via the assertion of human dignity is *de rigeur* for tragedy, *Timon* does not qualify; its hero does his best to prove human indignity, and rather succeeds in it. But then, how many Jacobean tragedies would qualify? The pervasive corruption of society, the quirkiness of fate, and the impotence of the good in Webster's tragedies are not recommended reading for those who want their faith in mankind restored. To derive an even moderately optimistic lesson from *Lear* requires a particularly benign reaction in view of the cataclysmic ending. (pp. 22-3)

A pessimistic moral for tragedy was suggested to the Renaissance by the ubiquitous commonplace of life as a play, the *theatrum mundi,* which always has a melancholy message: life is a lamentable or ridiculous performance under the aegis of Fortune, who assigns the roles and directs the action. It is generally a tragedy the catastrophe of which is death. The frequent use of this commonplace by writers of tragedy shows that it was very much in their minds. It could be used with an explicitly Christian script that recalled that the danger in the game of fortune was to sell one's soul to the world. It could also be without theological implications and with classical-pagan exemplification. (pp. 23-4)

Shakespeare's play is a tragedy of fortune in a wider sense than that of presenting the fall of a great man—the classical Renaissance formula. The hero's change of fortune is associated with a fundamental change of attitude toward the world and with an equally radical change in the attitudes of his friends toward him. Fortune dominates this world in a crude and materialistic way to which we are not accustomed in Shakespeare but which is not so unlike that of Chapman's tragedies (and, for that matter, in this respect at least, of Jonson's *Sejanus*). As in Chapman, virtue is doomed here. (p. 24)

Like Shakespeare's other tragic heroes (Brutus is an exception), Timon is highly passionate; Shakespeare's tragedies still bear a faint imprint of the humanistic genre with its warning against excessive passion. The passion of Timon, like that of other tragic heroes, is articulated and given significance by being set in a relationship to similar but not identical passions of characters who function at least partially as foils. What Laertes and Fortinbras do for our understanding of the ways in which the grief of Hamlet and his desire for revenge express themselves is accomplished by Apemantus and Alcibiades for the wrath and misanthropy of Timon. The low-burning anger of Apemantus and the quickly aroused but also quickly controlled temper of Alcibiades show up the self-harming fury of Timon. The more vulnerable personality, he is also, not the least because of the magnitude of his passion, a man of larger sympathies and capacities. In tragic terms, Timon's wild misanthropy is his claim to greatness.

This greatness is one that isolates the tragic hero, and Timon, more than any of Shakespeare's tragic heroes with the possible exception of Coriolanus, is a lonely figure. . . . Shakespeare certainly shows that Timon's isolation is not merely self-created. Misanthropy, of course, is by definition an isolating passion, but philanthropy should be a fusing and a synthesizing one; if it fails in that, the meanness around Timon is at least as much to blame as his own foolishness.

The isolation of the philanthropic Timon is the one we moderns know best: the loneliness in the midst of the crowd. Timon, the giver, is a loner even when among his admiring friends.

His most ironic, tragically ironic, sentiment is that of the first banquet: "I have often wish'd myself poorer that I might come nearer to you" [I.ii.100-01]—at the very moment when he glories in opulent togetherness, he feels most alone. When in the same speech he compares his friends to instruments hung up in cases, instruments that "keep their sound to themselves," he unwittingly characterizes himself and his longings as much as his friends. They mask their true selves deliberately, and in the process they stifle the free development of his own self even though outwardly they encourage it. His wish to be poorer and thus to come closer to them expresses a hidden desire to put everything at stake in order to break out of his dimly felt isolation and become free. But Timon's remains an "unsounded self" to the very end. Only death brings him health and freedom. (pp. 26-7)

But can a pessimistic tragedy, we are asked, produce a *catharsis*? Let us leave aside here the question of what Aristotle really meant by this term—purgation, purification, or clarification—and whether he wanted it to be that of the hero, the dramatic characters in general, or the audience. Let us adopt the common conception that the hero's tragic predicament and fall must produce a feeling of pity and fear (or awe) in us that we can relate to our own lives. Does then Timon have this effect on us? Actually, every reader must answer this question for himself, but I shall keep the editorial "we" here for persuasion's sake. Timon, it must be said, alienates more than attracts us. He never seems much like us, and even if we are rather pessimistic about man and the world, misanthropy in such force bothers us. Yet we are not without some pity for him. This pity, I think, is of a special kind, different from that which we accord to Hamlet, Othello, or Lear but resembling what we feel for Macbeth in some respects and for Coriolanus in others. Macbeth is really not much like us either. Do we really think ourselves capable of murder except in self-defense? Macbeth, of course, overcomes our antipathy by his sensitive moral imagination that makes us aware of man's potential greatness. Although Timon lacks Macbeth's poetic apprehensiveness, he has qualities that we admire in other contexts, and he achieves a rhetorical triumph in his protest against man. He has a total commitment to the two causes to which he dedicates his life, and he shows an uncompromising courage in throwing off the fetters of the society that is bent on his ruin. We feel some pity for him, if for no other reason than that he is born into the exploitive society of Athens. This is a pity similar to that which we feel for Coriolanus for having been born a Roman, a patrician, and the son of Volumnia; Timon, like Coriolanus, is cut off from life-nourishing springs. We feel pity for Timon also because he has something in him that would be admirable if it found a different outlet, a tremendous human power that bestows on him a paradoxical glamor even when he is at his worst. The alienation and pity Timon engenders in us are mixed with awe. His misanthropy is an awesome phenomenon to watch. Much like the fear of Macbeth, it is heightened beyond the human scale and enlarges our comprehension of what man is capable of feeling. He pursues his pessimism with a total consistency to the very end to which we dare not or, shall we say, must not go. (pp. 27-8)

Many of our modern ills resemble the Athenian or, better, Jacobean ones Timon attacks. Pessimistic and apocalyptic strains have risen in volume and insistence in contemporary fiction and poetry. What is presented on our stages as tragic (although we have become shy of the word) is not the dignity of man and the consoling cosmos but the insecurity, fragility, and smallness of man and the menacing inscrutability of the universe. As we have become greater pessimists because we are plagued with much of what *Timon* depicts as hateful, we find the tragic misanthropy of Timon less repelling than have preceding ages. If we are to experience a feeling analogous to the play's catharsis for Jacobean England, we must imagine a modern Timon standing in our lands, denouncing the towns and cities for the evil they harbor, and we must feel this evil in us and around us, but also in some measure in him. And if this Timon despairs of a mankind that has created and suffered such conditions, we must feel his predicament—and ours—as tragic. I do not think that this is too difficult an imaginative exercise. (pp. 28-9)

> *Rolf Soellner, in his* Timon of Athens: Shakespeare's Pessimistic Tragedy, *Ohio State University Press, 1979, 245 p.*

ADDITIONAL BIBLIOGRAPHY

Adams, Joseph Quincy, Jr. "The Timon Plays." *Journal of English and Germanic Philology* IX, No. 4 (October 1910): 506-24.
> Useful discussion of the three known Elizabethan plays founded on the Timon story: Shakespeare's *Timon of Athens*, an anonymous *Timon* comedy which survived in manuscript, and an interlude in Francis Beaumont and John Fletcher's *The Triumph of Time*. Adams also discusses the possible sources for these plays.

Alexander, Peter. "The Third Period." In his *Shakespeare's Life and Art*, pp. 139-97. London: James Nisbet and Co., 1939.
> Considers the argument between Alcibiades and the Senate as central to the meaning of *Timon*, which revolves around Timon's humanity and the world's injustice.

Anderson, Ruth L. "Excessive Goodness a Tragic Fault." *Shakespeare Association Bulletin* XIX, No. 2 (April 1944): 85-96.
> Argues that Michel de Montaigne and other Renaissance and classical authors established the idea that excessive goodness may leave a person defenseless against guile, and that this idea forms the basic theme to *Timon of Athens* and other Shakespeare plays.

Bailey, John. "The Later Plays." In his *Shakespeare*, pp. 139-208. London: Longmans, Green and Co., 1929.
> Characterizes *Timon* as "a dull failure which contains some speeches of passionate genius."

Bergeron, David M. "*Timon of Athens* and Morality Drama." *CLA Journal* X, No. 3 (March 1967): 181-88.
> Compares *Timon* with the medieval play *Everyman*. Bergeron agrees with A. S. Collins that *Timon* is in many ways a morality drama.

Bevington, David. Introduction to *Timon of Athens* in *The Complete Works of William Shakespeare*, by William Shakespeare, rev. ed., edited by Hardin Craig and David Bevington, pp. 1017-42. Glenview, Ill.: Scott, Foresman and Co., 1972.
> Regards *Timon* as a satire against greed and finds it similar to *King Lear*, although it lacks the compassion of the latter work.

Bizley, W. H. "Language and Currency in *Timon of Athens*." *Theoria* XLIV, No. 44 (May 1975): 21-42.
> Focuses on *Timon*'s numerous references to money. Bizley attempts to define the evolution of an epoch's "sensibility" when its older feudal modes of thought give way to a new commercial spirit.

Bond, R. Warwick. "Lucian and Boiardo in *Timon of Athens*." *Modern Language Review* XXVI, No. 1 (January 1931): 52-68.
> Argues that Boiardo's Italian comedy *Timone* (1487?), which was itself based on Lucian's dialogue *Timon, or the Misanthrope*, was an important source for Shakespeare's play.

Bradbrook, M. C. *The Tragic Pageant of ''Timon of Athens.''* Cambridge: Cambridge University Press, 1966, 38 p.
Isolates the elements of spectacle in *Timon* and maintains that the play is best understood as an ''anti-shew'' or tragical pageant structured emblematically rather than dramatically. Bradbrook's lecture links *Timon*'s peculiarities as a drama to a supposed search by Shakespeare for more spectacular theater, a search initiated in order to accomodate the new Blackfriars theater.

Bradley, A. C. ''Lecture VII: *King Lear.*'' In his *Shakespearean Tragedy: Lectures on ''Hamlet,'' ''Othello,'' ''King Lear,'' ''Macbeth,''* pp. 243-79. 2nd ed. London: Macmillan and Co., 1905.
Reference to *Timon* in which the play is linked, both in theme and in date of composition, to *King Lear.* Bradley regards *Timon* as ''weak, ill-constructed and confused.''

Brownlow, F. W. ''Conclusion: *Timon of Athens*'' and ''Epilogue.'' In his *Two Shakespearean Sequences: ''Henry VI'' to ''Richard II'' and ''Pericles'' to ''Timon of Athens,''* pp. 216-32, 233-34. Pittsburgh: University of Pittsburgh Press, 1977.
Detailed thematic argument which contends that *Timon* was a neoclassically influenced ''metaphysical tragedy'' left unfinished at Shakespeare's death.

Bulman, James C., Jr. ''Shakespeare's Use of the *Timon* Comedy.'' *Shakespeare Survey* 29 (1976): 103-16.
Considers the *Timon* comedy the main source for Shakespeare's play.

Burke, Kenneth. ''*Timon of Athens* and Misanthropic Gold.'' In his *Language As Symbolic Action: Essays on Life, Literature, and Method,* pp. 115-24. Berkeley: University of California Press, 1966.
Characterizes *Timon* as a cohesive dramatic structure. In an analysis informed by Freud, Marx, and image pattern studies, Burke argues that Shakespeare's play possesses a thematic consistency that threatens to become ''monotonic.'' This theme he regards as the idea of human ''scurrility.''

Butler, Francelia. *The Strange Critical Fortunes of Shakespeare's ''Timon of Athens.''* Ames: Iowa State University Press, 1966, 188 p.
Survey of the history of *Timon* criticism.

Campbell, Oscar James. ''Timon of Athens.'' In his *Shakespeare's Satire,* pp. 168-97. New York: Oxford University Press, 1943, 227 p.
Disputes G. Wilson Knight's interpretation of *Timon* as an allegory and characterizes the play instead as a ''tragic-satire.''

Chambers, E. K. ''Plays of the First Folio: *Timon of Athens.*'' In his *William Shakespeare: A Study of Facts and Problems,* Vol. 1, pp. 480-84. Oxford: Oxford University Press, 1930.
Briefly surveys the controversies surrounding the authorship, textual anomalies, sources, and date of *Timon.* For Chambers the play is structurally incoherent, and he believes it is a draft Shakespeare left unfinished.

Champion, Larry S. ''The Social Dimensions of Tragedy: *Timon of Athens, Coriolanus, Antony and Cleopatra.*'' In his *Shakespeare's Tragic Perspective,* pp. 201-65. Athens: University of Georgia Press, 1976.
Sees *Timon* as a failure, though one which established the techniques Shakespeare would use later in *Coriolanus* and *Antony and Cleopatra.*

Charney, Maurice. Introduction to *Timon of Athens.* In *The Complete Signet Classic Shakespeare* by William Shakespeare, edited by Sylvan Barnet, pp. 1367-1406. New York: Harcourt, Brace, Jovanovich, 1972.
Reading of *Timon* as a ''dramatic fable.'' Charney's interpretation is similar to those earlier readings of the work as a morality play or allegory.

Clemen, Wolfgang H. ''*Timon of Athens.*'' In his *The Development of Shakespeare's Imagery,* pp. 168-76. London: Methuen & Co., 1951.
Finds the play's imagery similar in function to that of *King Lear,* but less integrated into the dramatic structure.

Cook, David. ''*Timon of Athens.*'' *Shakespeare Survey* 16 (1963): 83-94.

Determines that *Timon*'s major theme is ''the need to accept and love man as he is, and to acknowledge our human condition.''

Davidson, Clifford. ''*Timon of Athens:* The Iconography of False Friendship.'' *The Huntington Library Quarterly* XLIII, No. 3 (Summer 1980): 181-200.
Focuses on the visual aspects of *Timon* as a stage drama. Davidson argues that a series of ''visual tableaux'' in the play reproduces images from Renaissance iconography and illuminates the play's meaning. He also contends that Timon is a foolish figure whose misanthropy is irrational, but considers his friends even worse.

Draper, R. P. ''*Timon of Athens.*'' *Shakespeare Quarterly* VIII, No. 2 (Spring 1957): 195-200.
Argues that Timon's problem stems from the conflict between his ''idealistic communism'' and the corruption of his age.

Eagleton, Terence. ''A Note on *Timon of Athens.*'' In his *Shakespeare and Society: Critical Studies in Shakespearean Drama,* pp. 172-76. London: Chatto & Windus, 1967.
Regards Timon's major problem as his ability to give but not receive.

Elliott, Robert C. ''The Satirist Satirized; Studies of the Great Misanthropes: *Timon of Athens.*'' In his *The Power of Satire: Magic, Ritual, Art,* pp. 141-67. Princeton: Princeton University Press, 1960.
Places *Timon* within the historical development of satirical literature. Elliott relates both Timon and Apemantus to character types borrowed from primitive satire; but he also contends that these two characters are further defined by Shakespeare's own irony—an effect which serves to undercut Timon's invective and present his misanthropy as a kind of folly.

Empson, William. ''Timon's Dog.'' In his *The Structure of Complex Words,* pp. 175-84. 1951. 3d ed. London: Chatto & Windus, 1979.
Examines Shakespeare's use of the word ''dog'' in *Timon.* Empson concludes that Shakespeare's word usage constitutes a radically complex verbal structure in which he transfers a simple metaphor into a ''symbol,'' but at the same time refuses to accept its symbolism.

Farnham, Willard. ''Timon of Athens.'' In his *Shakespeare's Tragic Frontier: The World of His Final Tragedies,* pp. 39-78. Berkeley and Los Angeles: University of California Press, 1950.
Considers *Timon* in relation to *Macbeth, Antony and Cleopatra,* and *Coriolanus.* Farnham groups all these plays together as Shakespeare's final tragedies and concludes that each one is similar in its portrayal of a ''deeply flawed hero.''

Fergusson, Francis. ''Timon of Athens.'' In his *Shakespeare: The Pattern in the Carpet,* pp. 258-63. New York: Delacorte Press, 1970.
Maintains that *Timon* is more like ''classical comedy'' than tragedy. Fergusson characterizes the play as something of a farce, punctuated only by Timon's eventual misanthropy.

Fly, Richard. ''Confounding Contraries: The Unmediated World of *Timon of Athens.*'' In his *Shakespeare's Mediated World,* pp. 117-42. Amherst: University of Massachusetts Press, 1976.
Considers *Timon* the most extreme of Shakespeare's last three tragedies, all of which renounce various kinds of mediating characters—particularly ''middleman'' characters like Iago or the Duke in *Measure for Measure*—and instead abandon their respective worlds to ''self-destructive . . . unarbitrated extremes.''

French, Marilyn. ''Chaos Come Again; Ideals Banished: *Timon of Athens.*'' In her *Shakespeare's Division of Experience,* pp. 276-82. New York: Summit Books, 1981.
Interprets *Timon* as a portrait of the worst and best that the ''masculine principle'' can achieve without the aid of the ''complementary principle.''

Goldstein, Leonard. ''Alcibiades's Revolt in *Timon of Athens.*'' *Zeitschrift für Anglistik und Amerikanistik,* XV, No. 3 (1967): 256-78.
Recent example of the 1930s-style Marxist approach to Shakespeare. Goldstein argues that Alcibiades, though a ''quasi-feudal'' militarist, leads a genuinely populist army whose alliance is based on a mutual distrust of capitalism.

Griffith, Elizabeth. "Timon." In her *The Morality of Shakespeare's Drama Illustrated*, pp. 379-99. 1775. Reprint. London: Frank Cass & Co., 1971.

Example of the seventeenth- and eighteenth-century practice of reading Shakespeare for his treatment of certain "topics" or "commonplaces," i.e. isolating passages from their dramatic context and enjoying them as general observations on a given subject. In the present essay, Griffith confronts the moral questions in Shakespeare's play and concludes by interpreting *Timon* as a warning against "ostentatious liberality."

Holloway, John. "*Coriolanus, Timon of Athens.*" In his *The Story of the Night: Studies in Shakespeare's Major Tragedies*, pp. 121-34. Lincoln: University of Nebraska Press, 1961.

Regards *Timon* and *Coriolanus* as two plays which present, "almost barely and baldly," the essential pattern of Shakespearean tragedy.

Hulme, Hilda M. "Proverb and Proverb-Idiom." In her *Explorations in Shakespeare's Language: Some Problems of Lexical Meaning in the Dramatic Text*, pp. 39-88. New York: Barnes & Noble, 1962.

Interprets problematical passages in *Timon* according to Elizabethan proverb idioms.

Hunter, G. K. "The Last Tragic Heroes." In *Later Shakespeare*, edited by John Russell Brown and Bernard Harris, pp. 11-28. Stratford-upon-Avon Studies 8. London: Edward Arnold Publishers, 1966.

Groups *Timon* with *Macbeth, Coriolanus*, and *Antony and Cleopatra* and contrasts these late tragedies with *King Lear*. Hunter views the late tragedies, and *King Lear*, as plays about exile, but contends that the tragedies differ from *Lear* fundamentally in that their respective heroes fail to create an internal alternative source of value against the revealed corruption of the world.

Kermode, Frank. Introduction to *Timon of Athens*. In *The Riverside Shakespeare*, by William Shakespeare, edited by G. Blakemore Evans, pp. 1141-43. Boston: Houghton Mifflin Co., 1973.

Sees the play as consisting of two halves, each illustrating Timon's contrasting and excessive modes of existence. Kermode considers Alcibiades as the dramatically unsuccessful mediator between Timon's two extremes.

Kernan, Alvin. "Tragical Satire." In his *The Cankered Muse: Satire of the English Renaissance*, pp. 192-246. New Haven: Yale University Press, 1959.

Claims that satire is a specific Renaissance genre and that in *Timon* Shakespeare dissected "the satiric sense of life." Kernan finds that both Shakespeare's and Timon's "sense of life" is diseased and distorted, since, carried to the ultimate conclusion, it refuses to accept any evidence of human goodness.

Knight, G. Wilson. "*Timon of Athens* and Buddhism." *Essays in Criticism* XXX, No. 2 (April 1980): 105-23.

Most recent of Knight's series of writings on *Timon*. Knight argues that although *Timon* has strong Greek and Hebraic elements, Timon's views on death at the play's end evoke the paradoxical and ambiguous concept of Nirvana in the Buddhist tradition.

Lake, David J. Appendix V, "Middleton in Shakespeare: *Timon of Athens*." In his *The Canon of Thomas Middleton's Plays: Internal Evidence for the Major Problems of Authorship*, pp. 279-86. Cambridge: Cambridge University Press, 1975.

Argues on the basis of selected traditional linguistic tests that a strong case exists to justify the possibility of Middleton's presence as coauthor of Shakespeare's *Timon*. Lake also takes issue with aspects of Una Ellis-Fermor's widely accepted explanation for the rough verse of parts of *Timon*.

Leech, Clifford. "*Timon* and After." In his *Shakespeare's Tragedies and Other Studies in Seventeenth-Century Drama*, pp. 113-36. London: Chatto & Windus, 1950.

Sees *Timon* as a transition between the tragedies and romances. Leech claims that *Timon* approaches tragedy, but lacks tragedy's sense that "something admirable in mankind is possible"; and, like the romances, it shifts from public to private concerns.

Leech, Clifford. "Shakespeare's Greeks." In *Stratford Papers on Shakespeare*, edited by B. W. Jackson, pp. 1-20. Toronto: W. J. Gage, 1964.

Argues that *Timon, Troilus and Cressida, Pericles, The Winter's Tale, Midsummer Night's Dream* and *Comedy of Errors* form a group of "Greek plays" which, despite their great diversity, share in common a freedom of dramatic form and a liberty of alteration of the sources. Leech's discussion centers primarily on *Troilus and Cressida*, secondarily on *Timon*.

Maxwell, J. C. Introduction to *Timon of Athens*, by William Shakespeare, edited by J. C. Maxwell, pp. ix-xlii. Cambridge: Cambridge University Press, 1957.

Follows the lines of his 1948 article in *Scrutiny*. Maxwell critiques the theories of Una Ellis-Fermor, A. S. Collins, and J. W. Draper and concludes that the play is an interesting failure.

Miola, Robert S. "Timon in Shakespeare's Athens." *Shakespeare Quarterly* 31, No. 1 (Spring 1980): 21-30.

Surveys Renaissance attitudes critical of democracy, particularly the democracy of classical Athens, and argues that Shakespeare presupposed such attitudes in constructing *Timon*'s negative image of that city.

Morley, Henry. Introduction to *Timon of Athens*, by William Shakespeare, edited by Henry Morley, pp. 5-11. London: Cassell & Co., 1888.

Discusses Shakespeare's possible sources, giving close attention to Lucian's dialogue, and concludes that Shakespeare, like Lucian, meant to present Timon as foolish. Morley's edition of the play also reprints the anonymous *Timon* comedy as an appendix.

Neiditz, Minerva. "Primary Process Mentation and the Structure of *Timon of Athens*." *University of Hartford Studies in Literature* 11, No. 1 (1979): 24-35.

Claims that the play follows the logic of "primary process mentation," the logic of dreams and intoxication, rather than of waking life. Timon is seen as suffering from separation anxiety and seeks a psychic return to the mother.

Oliver, H. J. Introduction to *Timon of Athens*, by William Shakespeare, edited by H. J. Oliver, pp. xiii-lii. The Arden Edition of the Works of William Shakespeare. London: Methuen & Co., 1959.

Argues that *Timon* lacks dramatic conflict and that the central character lacks depth, but agrees with William Hazlitt's praise of the play's intensity and unity.

Paolucci, Anne. "Marx, Money, and Shakespeare: The Hegelian Core in Marxist Shakespeare-Criticism." *Mosaic* V, No. 3 (Spring 1977): 134-56.

Discusses the writings on Shakespeare, especially on *Timon of Athens*, by Karl Marx, Georg Lukacs, Georg Friedrich Hegel, Jan Kott, and others. Although Paolucci demonstrates a continuity in the work of these writers, she does not always properly distinguish the views of Marx from his Russian and Russian-influenced followers.

Pettet, E. C. "*Timon of Athens*: The Disruption of Feudal Morality." *Review of English Studies* 23, No. 92 (October 1947): 321-36.

Considers Timon an idealized feudal lord who becomes a misanthrope only after he discovers that the world no longer shares his medieval values. Pettet concludes that stripped "of its flimsy Athenian trappings, *Timon* is a straightforward tract for the times."

Phillips, James Emerson, Jr. "Social Corruption in *Troilus and Cressida* and *Timon of Athens*." In his *The State in Shakespeare's Greek and Roman Plays*, pp. 112-46. New York: Columbia University Press, 1940.

States that in *Timon* Shakespeare depicted a degenerate political society that had "placed material welfare before virtue as its activating purpose."

Pogson, Beryl. "*Timon of Athens*." In his *In the East My Pleasure Lies: An Esoteric Interpretation of Some Plays of Shakespeare*, pp. 78-84. London: Stuart & Richards, 1950.

Regards the play as a demonstration of the idea that the senses perceive only an illusory world.

Robertson, J. M. *Shakespeare and Chapman.* 1917. Reprint. St. Clair Shores, Mich.: Scholarly Press, 1971, 303 p.
> Through stylistic, metrical, and vocabulary comparisons, argues that *Timon* is Shakespeare's poorly revised draft of an earlier play by George Chapman.

Rockas, Leo. "Notes Toward a More Finished *Timon.*" *Essays in Arts and Sciences* VII (May 1978): 21-36.
> Speculative essay in which Rockas suggests plot developments that might make *Timon* a more finished drama.

Ruszkiewicz, John J. "Liberality, Friendship, and *Timon of Athens.*" *Thoth* 16, No. 1 (1975-76): 3-17.
> Surveys Renaissance ideas on friendship as background material to *Timon.* Ruszkiewicz views Timon as a foolish character because of his inability to distinguish true friends from false.

Scott, W.I.D. "Timon—The General Paralytic." In his *Shakespeare's Melancholics,* pp. 108-30. London: Mills & Boon, 1962.
> Medical diagnosis of Timon as suffering from "the tertiary stage of syphilis." Scott also links Timon's personality to Jung's introverted, sensation-dominated type of individual.

Somerville, H. "Timon's Megalomania." In his *Madness in Shakespearean Tragedy,* pp. 187-96. London: Richards Press, 1929.
> Diagnosis by a member of the Royal Medico-Psychological Association of Timon's mental illness, said to be caused by syphilis.

Spencer, T.J.B. "'Greeks' and 'Merrygreeks': A Background to *Timon of Athens* and *Troilus and Cressida.*" In *Essays on Shakespeare and Elizabethan Drama in Honor of Hardin Craig,* edited by Richard Hosley, pp. 223-33. Columbia: University of Missouri Press, 1962.
> Discussion of the Elizabethan attitude towards Greek culture and how that attitude influenced Shakespeare's writing of *Timon.*

Spencer, Terence. "Shakespeare Learns the Value of Money: The Dramatist at Work on *Timon of Athens.*" *Shakespeare Survey* 6 (1953): 75-8.
> Claims that Shakespeare changed his mind in the course of writing *Timon* about the value of the talent, a unit of currency in the play. Because Shakespeare never went back and made his usage consistent, Spencer believes the play was undoubtedly left unfinished. J. M. Robertson used the same evidence in his argument for dual authorship of *Timon* (see entry above).

Spencer, Theodore. "Shakespeare's Last Plays." In his *Shakespeare and the Nature of Man,* pp. 177-202. New York: Macmillan, 1942.
> Argues that *Timon* lacks true tragic dimension and inner dramatic coherence.

Stauffer, Donald A. "Roads to Freedom: *Timon of Athens, Antony and Cleopatra, Coriolanus.*" In his *Shakespeare's World of Images: The Development of His Moral Ideas,* pp. 221-66. New York: Norton, 1949.
> Characterizes *Timon* as a tragedy *manqué,* or abortive tragedy, lacking an effective dramatic structure.

Swigg, R. "*Timon of Athens* and the Growth of Discrimination." *Modern Language Review* 62, No. 3 (July 1967): 385-94.
> Considers *Timon* a play constructed to offer its readers a series of moral distinctions. Swigg argues that it is the reader who must determine who is right and who is wrong through the course of the drama.

Thomson, Patricia. "The Literature of Patronage, 1580-1630." *Essays in Criticism* II, No. 3 (July 1952): 267-84.

Interprets the discussion between Poet and Painter in *Timon's* first scene as reflecting the dynamics of the poet-patron relation during the Elizabethan age.

Traversi, D. A. "The Mature Tragedies: *Timon of Athens.*" In his *An Approach to Shakespeare,* 3d ed., pp. 474-90. Garden City, N.Y.: Doubleday & Co., 1968.
> Interprets *Timon* as a kind of morality drama in which the hero exemplifies two forms of vicious excess, bounty and misanthropy. Traversi sees the conclusion as producing "a gesture of reconciliation in favor of the processes of life renewed."

Waggoner, G. R. "*Timon of Athens* and the Jacobean Duel." *Shakespeare Quarterly* XVI, No. 2 (Spring 1965): 303-11.
> Believes that Alcibiades's reference to duelling in his scene with the Senate reflects Shakespeare's unsympathetic response to James I's attempts to abolish the custom.

Walker, Lewis. "Fortune and Friendship in *Timon of Athens.*" *Texas Studies in Literature and Language* XVIII, No. 4 (Winter 1977): 577-600.
> Discusses medieval and Renaissance concepts of fortune, and the Roman goddess Fortuna, and argues that *Timon* reflects tensions between Christian and classical views of fortune.

Walker, Lewis. "Money in *Timon of Athens.*" *Philological Quarterly* 57, No. 2 (Spring 1978): 269-71.
> Response to J. M. Robertson's and Terence Spencer's arguments that there are contradictory values for the talent, a unit of currency in *Timon.* For Walker the various sums mentioned are fully congruent with the dramatic situations in which they are mentioned, and their disparities don't support the claims that *Timon* is an unfinished draft or the work of two authors.

Wecter, Dixon. "Shakespeare's Purpose in *Timon of Athens.*" *PMLA* XLIII (1928): 701-21.
> One of the latest arguments for dual authorship. Wecter thinks Shakespeare was the author of a lost version of the play, which was subsequently rewritten by an inferior playwright, probably Thomas Middleton, resulting in the Folio text of *Timon.* In addition, Wecter suggests that the play recalls elements of the downfall of Shakespeare's patron, the Earl of Essex, in particular Bacon's alleged perfidy towards him.

White, Howard B. "The Decay of the Polity: Timon." In his *Copp'd Hills towards Heaven: Shakespeare and the Classical Polity,* pp. 25-42. International Archives of the History of Ideas, No. 32. The Hague: Martinus Nijhoff, 1970.
> Examines the image of the city of Athens in *Timon* and finds it representative of the corruption of the post-Classical era. White fails to distinguish between Athens as Shakespeare conceived it and the historical Athens he has studied from classical sources.

Wilson, Harold S. "Antithesis: *Troilus and Cressida* and *Timon of Athens.*" In his *On the Design of Shakespearean Tragedy,* pp. 115-56. University of Toronto Department of English Studies and Texts, No. 5. Toronto: University of Toronto Press, 1966.
> Regards *Timon* as the dramatization of one man's total renunciation of human value, and artistically as the extreme limit of Shakespeare's tragic vision.

Woods, Andrew H. "Syphilis in Shakespeare's Tragedy of *Timon of Athens.*" *American Journal of Psychiatry* 91 (July 1934): 95-107.
> Argues that Timon's unusual behavior in the play can be explained as the symptoms of "paretic dementia," a particular form of syphilitic brain desease.

Wright, Ernest Hunter. *The Authorship of Timon of Athens.* New York: Columbia University Press, 1910, 104 p.
> Monograph which argues on structural and stylistic grounds that there must have been two authors of *Timon.*

Twelfth Night

DATE: It is generally accepted that Shakespeare composed *Twelfth Night, or What You Will* between 1600 and 1602. This date links the play with the other "happy comedies" thought to be composed at this time, *As You Like It* and *Much Ado About Nothing,* and places it before the "problem comedies," such as *Troilus and Cressida* and *Measure for Measure.* The earliest record of a performance also helps in dating the play; it was provided by John Manningham, who reported in his diary that he saw *Twelfth Night* at the Middle Temple on February 2, 1602. Leslie Hotson presented evidence in his *The First Night of "Twelfth Night"* that the play was composed specifically for a Twelfth Night performance on January 6, 1601, in honor of a visiting dignitary, Virgino Orsino, Duke of Bracciano.

TEXT: No quarto edition of *Twelfth Night* exists, and the text of the play in the First Folio is considered authoritative. Probably taken from a prompt-copy, the text is remarkably clean. Certain references in the play would suggest that some of the songs in *Twelfth Night,* all assigned to Feste in the Folio, were originally performed by Viola. This has led some critics to speculate that the original copy might have been altered to accommodate changes in the personnel of Shakespeare's company. It is a minor point of contention, however, regarding a text that is generally conceded to be free of problems.

SOURCES: Critics consider Shakespeare's chief source for *Twelfth Night* to be the story of "Apolonius and Silla" by Barnabe Riche, taken from his *Riche, His Farewell to the Military Profession,* published in 1581. Riche's story is derived from the Italian comedy *Gl' Ingannati,* written around 1531. Another version of the story was given by Matteo Bandello in his *Novelle* of 1554, which was translated into French in 1579 by François de Belleforest as part of his *Histoires tragiques.* Scholars believe that Shakespeare had read either Bandello or Belleforest at the time he was writing *Much Ado About Nothing,* so it would seem that the story of *Twelfth Night* was available to him from a variety of sources.

Within Shakespeare's canon, *Twelfth Night* has been linked to *The Comedy of Errors* because they share the similar plot-device of twinning, first developed by Shakespeare in *Comedy* and derived from the *Menaechmi* of Plautus. And *Twelfth Night* shares with *The Two Gentlemen of Verona* the theme of a girl disguised as a page, who must woo another woman for the man she loves.

CRITICAL HISTORY: *Twelfth Night* is often praised as the most elegant, charming, and perfectly constructed of Shakespeare's comedies. Because of this, critics have discussed the importance of *Twelfth Night* in terms of Shakespeare's achievement in the comedic form, focusing on the central themes, characterization, and artistic unity of the play. Eighteenth-century observers were divided over the play's success as a unified entity: Charles Gildon and George Steevens praised the construction of the play, while others, such as Charlotte Lennox and Samuel Johnson, faulted the work for its want of credibility.

In the nineteenth century, commentators focused on several critical issues which were developed in twentieth-century crit-

Title page of Twelfth Night taken from the First Folio (1623). By permission of the Folger Shakespeare Library.

icism. The German Romantic critic August Wilhelm Schlegel stressed the organic unity of the play, noting Shakespeare's ability to fuse the graver and lighter aspects of the comedy. William Hazlitt, another Romantic critic, praised the play for its well-rounded, nonsatirical characters. Later in the nineteenth century, the French critic E. Montégut interpreted the play as a carnival farce, and identified the themes of madness and self-deception, points which were developed in twentieth-century interpretations of the play. Also in the late nineteenth century, Frederick Furnivall identified a theme which was to reverberate throughout the history of comment on *Twelfth Night.* He noted the "shadow of death and distress across the sunshine" in the play, and thus prefigured a century of criticism on the darker aspects of the work. The late nineteenth century also produced the first interpretation of *Twelfth Night* as a play with a specific focus on the social conventions of Shakespeare's time, particularly in the character of Malvolio.

Early in the twentieth century, E. K. Chambers pointed out the theme of self-deception, which harkened back to Montégut's interpretation and anticipated a similar strain in later debate. Joseph H. Summers developed this theme in an essay which focuses on the motif of masks and masking in the play. Further expanding on this idea, Bertrand Evans theorized that

Shakespeare's dramatic method is predicated on a system of "discrepant awareness," a method that gives an audience the advantage of seeing and knowing elements of the plot not known by the characters.

Focusing on the Saturnalian aspects first noted by Montégut, a variety of commentators in the twentieth century have found a thematic unity in the play. Enid Welsford found the play's unity in the character of Feste, as Lord of Misrule of the Twelfth Night festivities. L. G. Salingar, too, noted that the elements of the feast of Misrule pervade the play. For C. L. Barber, the Saturnalian qualities which inform *Twelfth Night* are based on specific Elizabethan customs. Barbara Lewalski offered an interpretation of the play's holiday theme based on the Christian concept of Epiphany. Several critics discuss the theme of indulgence versus moderation. Morris P. Tilley found that the play is unified by this theme, which for him imparts a philosophical and moral seriousness to the play. John Hollander developed the theme in two essays; in one, he concentrated on the theme of order through an analysis of the play's music, and in the other he discussed the concepts of appetite and satiety as they evolve to express a specifically moral attitude.

Many twentieth-century critics concentrate on the idea of *Twelfth Night* as Shakespeare's "farewell to comedy," seeing in the play both his highest achievement in the genre and elements which prefigure his later tragedies and bitter comedies. Arthur Quiller-Couch found Illyria nearer to Elysium than to the world of the previous comedies, and John Middleton Murry noted the "silvery undertone of sadness" in the play. For Mark Van Doren, this darkness casts a melancholy tone on *Twelfth Night,* and E. C. Pettet speculated that at this point in his dramatic career Shakespeare was perhaps tiring of the love romance. W. H. Auden felt that the darkness verges on thoughts of death and described Shakespeare's mood in *Twelfth Night* as distinctly uncomic. For G. K. Hunter, the ending of the play borders on tragedy, a comment that was echoed by Albert Gérard, who saw the play as near tragedy, but lacking a tragic vision. Clifford Leech observed elements in *Twelfth Night* which make us ill at ease and which distort the harmony of the play. Jan Kott maintained that the atmosphere is bitter and unharmonious, and that the air is filled with "erotic madness." Philip Edwards, through his explication of the songs, found the play far darker in tone than its predecessor, *As You Like It.*

Although William Archer claimed in the late nineteenth century that Shakespeare did not intend to recreate a historically accurate Elizabethan world, many twentieth-century critics place *Twelfth Night* in the context of specific Elizabethan social and literary customs, and some find that this impedes modern appreciation of the play. For John Draper, *Twelfth Night* is based on Elizabethan societal conventions and is not a love comedy at all, but a comedy of "social security," an aspect that he feels is lost on modern audiences. Harley Granville-Barker claimed that the comedy of the play is least accessible to modern audiences because the humor is topical. For Karl F. Thompson, an understanding of *Twelfth Night* is predicated on a comprehension of the courtly love tradition which the play imitates and satirizes. The common Elizabethan device of sex-role reversal in the character of Viola/Cesario is problematical for both Leech and Kott, who noted the complicated sexual overtones this role reversal implies.

Many critics discuss Shakespeare's handling of the theme of love. To H. B. Charlton, *Twelfth Night, Much Ado About Nothing,* and *As You Like It* show Shakespeare's concept of characters who are emotionally complex and who enlarge the scope of comedy through their exploration of the meaning of love. John Russell Brown examined the characters of *Twelfth Night* in terms of their attitudes toward love's truth, wealth, and order. For Harold Jenkins, the theme of the play is the manifestation of one of the primary principles of comedy: the education of a man or woman in the correct attitude toward love. Alexander Leggatt focused on the theme of solitude and unrequited love in the play.

Shakespeare's characterization in *Twelfth Night* has become the focus for many critical studies. Some commentators discuss the way in which one character provides the tone or focal point of the play; Viola, Malvolio, and Feste have often been cited in this role. Viola has been studied as a character whose traits and viewpoint mark her as the central figure. For Hazlitt, she is the "great and secret charm" of *Twelfth Night.* Hudson and Fleming both identified her as the unifying character of the play. In his discussion of masking, Summers asserted that because Viola is able to see through the masks of all the other characters, she is the center of the play. In a similar vein, Evans regarded Viola as the most important masquerader of the comedies; she purposely continues her masque as Cesario until the last moment of the play, thus heightening the effect of the denouement. Hollander also focused on Viola in his explication of the themes of music and appetite in *Twelfth Night.* He described her as "the affective, instrumental, prematurely Baroque music" of the play, and as the figure who destroys the gourmandizing of Olivia and Orsino while redirecting their appetites in love. In his discussion of love in *Twelfth Night,* Brown singled out Viola as the character who will "generously give and hazard love," and one who knows "love's true wealth." A rather untraditional view of Viola is offered by Draper, who found the romantic nature of her character to be in vivid contrast to the dominant realism of the play and he faulted the Romantic critics for giving her character unwarranted prominence. A number of critics characterize Viola as Shakespeare's ideal of love in her patience and attitude of self-sacrifice. In her discussion of the religious aspects of the play, Lewalski noted that this selfless love distinguishes her from her fellow characters and found that Viola and her twin Sebastian represent "the word made flesh," and thus reflect the spirit of Epiphany and Christmas.

Malvolio, more than any other character, has captured the imagination of critics. Manningham, the play's first known commentator, praised the gulling of the steward, and the fascination with Malvolio's treatment at the hands of his tormentors, Sir Toby and Maria, has remained strong throughout the centuries. Charles I crossed out the original title of the play in his copy of the Second Folio (1632) and renamed it "Malvolio," which indicates the continued interest that the role held for seventeenth-century audiences. Nineteenth-century commentators raised the question of whether or not Malvolio was a Puritan, and they speculated that he should be considered a prototype of the emerging bourgeois class. Joseph Hunter was the first critic to interpret the characterization of Malvolio as a "grand attack on Puritanism," and F. Kreyssig believed the characterization pointed to Shakespeare's dislike of Puritans. Kreyssig's argument was developed in a historical context by H. N. Hudson, who saw in Malvolio a satirical attack on the Puritans and on the censorship of the Privy Council of the early seventeenth century. William Archer rejected this notion, stating that Malvolio is less a Puritan than a Philistine. In the twentieth century, Tilley asserted that Malvolio is punished as a Puritan and condemned as a hypocrite. Both Van Doren and O. J. Campbell noted that Malvolio represents the "new order,'' which poses a menacing threat to the society depicted in *Twelfth Night*.

Critics have also debated the severity of Malvolio's punishment, and whether Shakespeare intended him to be an object of our derision or our pity. Hazlitt was the first to express uneasiness about the punishment of Malvolio, but the strongest defender of the steward was Charles Lamb, who claimed that the character possesses ''dignity,'' and that neither his manners nor his morals fit the world of *Twelfth Night*. Lamb's interpretation elicited comment in subsequent criticism and is examined in depth by Sylvan Barnet in the twentieth century. Reacting to the variety of response which he felt mistakenly elevates the character, Harold Jenkins stated that Malvolio is not of great importance to the play. Yet, Melvin Seiden saw Malvolio as a scapegoat sacrificed to the gods of comedy. T. Kenny and others found Malvolio's punishment ''coarse and excessive,'' while Milton Crane asserted that we share in Toby's ''sadistic pleasure'' in the gulling of the steward. The variety of opinion on the character attests to his continuing appeal.

Another character of great interest to critics is Feste. L. G. Salingar pronounced him ''the most finished portrait of the fool,'' in Shakespeare's work and he is considered by many to be the finest of Shakespeare's clowns. Many commentators mark his as a pivotal role, and for many he personifies the essence of *Twelfth Night* and the source of its unity. Ulrici thought that the meaning of the play was concentrated in the fool, and Gervinus wrote that Feste is ''conscious of his superiority.'' For Hudson, comedy and romance meet in Feste. Noting that music is all important to the play and that the music is centered in Feste, Bradley concluded that Feste supplies Shakespeare's own comment on the play, especially in his songs. Welsford, focusing on the Saturnalian aspects of the play, found Feste to be a Lord of Misrule, and marked his role as the play's focal point. For G. K. Hunter, the casting of Feste as the objective, central observer in the play indicates a change in the overall design of Shakespeare's work. G. Wilson Knight found in Feste's final song a macrocosm of the play, and stated that Feste embodies the essence of the comedy.

Twelfth Night begins with an invocation to music and ends with one of the most discussed of Shakespeare's songs, Feste's ''When that I Was.'' The history of discussion on the song begins with George Steevens, who struck an iconoclastic note by insisting that it is ''utterly unconnected to the play'' and, further, claiming that Shakespeare did not write the song. His only support came from E. K. Chambers, who suggested that none of Feste's songs have relevance to the play's theme. Charles Knight, representing the majority opinion, took issue with Steevens and praised it as the ''most philosophical'' of any fool's song. Several twentieth-century critics have discussed the song; Tilley concluded that it evokes the play's fundamental idea. Noting again the darker, more melancholy aspects of the play, such critics as Murry commented on the passing of innocence which is chronicled in the song, and Barber found Feste contemplating here the ''limitations of revelry.'' Thus, many critics concur with Salingar, who finds in the enigmatic fool's song ''the epilogue to the whole group of Shakespeare's romantic comedies.''

JOHN MANNINGHAM (essay date 1602)

[*The following excerpt from the* Diary of John Manningham, *published in 1868, contributed to the accepted dating of* Twelfth Night *as 1600 to 1602. Manningham, in a typical Elizabethan response, particularly praises the gulling of Malvolio. His comment about the* ''Italian called *Inganni'' is considered by most scholars to be a reference to the Italian comedy* Gl' Ingannati.]

At our feast wee had a play called *Twelve Night, or what you will,* much like the commedy of erro*r*es, or Menechmi in Plau*t*us, but most like and neere to that in Italian called *Inganni.* A good practise in it to make the steward beleeve his lady widdowe was in love with him, by counterfayting a letter as from his lady, in generall termes, telling him what shee liked best in him, and prescribing his gesture in smiling, his apparaile, &c., and then when he came to practise making him beleeve they tooke him to be mad. (p. 98)

> *John Manningham, in an extract from his diary entry on February 2, 1602, in* The Shakspere Allusion-Book: A Collection of Allusions to Shakspere from 1591 to 1700, *Vol. I, edited by John Munro, revised edition, Oxford University Press, London, 1932, pp. 98-9.*

LEONARD DIGGES (essay date 1640)

[*Digges was a poet and translator who contributed a poem in Shakespeare's memory to the First Folio. The following poem, first published in Shakespeare's* Poems *in 1640, is noted for its interpretation of Shakespeare's comic characters and attests to the early popularity of Malvolio.*]

　　　　　　let but *Beatrice*
And *Benedick* be seene, loe in atrice
The Cockpit Galleries, Boxes, all are full
To heare *Malvolio* that crosse garter'd Gull.
Briefe, there is nothing in his wit fraught Booke,
Whose sound we would not heare, on whose worth looke
Like old coynd gold, whose lines in every page,
Shall passe true currant to succeeding age.
　　　　　　　　　　　　　　　　　　　(p. 28)

> *Leonard Digges, ''Upon Master William Shakespeare, the Deceased Authour, and His Poems,'' in* Shakespeare, the Critical Heritage: 1623-1692, *Vol. 1, edited by Brian Vickers, Routledge & Kegan Paul, 1974, pp. 27-9.*

CHARLES GILDON (essay date 1710)

[*Gildon was the first critic to write an extended commentary on Shakespeare's plays. Like many other Neoclassicists, Gildon regarded Shakespeare as an imaginative playwright who nevertheless lacked knowledge of the dramatic ''rules'' necessary for correct writing. Gildon here praises Shakespeare for his achievement in interweaving the plot and subplot of* Twelfth Night. *The excerpt is taken from Gildon's remarks first published in* The Works of Mr. William Shakespeare *in 1710.*]

[In *Twelfth Night* there] is a sort of under-Plot of Sir *Toby*'s bubbling Sir *Andrew* in hopes of his having *Olivia,* of their imposing on *Olivia*'s Steward *Malvolio* as if his Lady was in Love with him, and the Quarrel promoted betwixt *Caesario* and Sir *Andrew,* which yet are so interwove that there is nothing that is not necessary to the main Plot but that Episode of the Steward. . . .

The Captain's Description of *Sebastian*'s coming ashoar is fine, and if compar'd with that before of *Ferdinand*'s Escape (describ'd in the *Tempest*) wou'd show the Fertility of the Author in his Variety on the same Subject. . . .

Olivia's Declaration of Love to *Viola* is very fine and pathetick. . . . (p. 244)

> *Charles Gildon, in an extract from his "Remarks on the Plays of Shakespeare," in* Shakespeare, the Critical Heritage: 1693-1733, Vol. 2, *edited by Brian Vickers, Routledge & Kegan Paul, 1974, pp. 226-62.*

RICHARD STEELE (essay date 1711)

[*The essay from which the following excerpt is taken was first published in* The Spectator *on December 3, 1711.*]

It sometimes happens that even Enemies and envious Persons bestow the sincerest Marks of Esteem when they least design it. Such afford a greater Pleasure as extorted by Merit and freed from all Suspicion of Favour or Flattery. Thus it is with *Malvolio*. He has Wit, Learning, and Discernment, but temper'd with an Allay of Envy, Self-Love, and Detraction. *Malvolio* turns pale at the Mirth and good Humour of the Company if it center not in his Person; he grows jealous and displeased when he ceases to be the only Person admired, and looks upon the Commendations paid to another as a Detraction from his Merit and an Attempt to lessen the Superiority he affects; but by this very method he bestows such Praise as can never be suspected of Flattery. His Uneasiness and Distastes are so many sure and certain Signs of another's Title to that Glory he desires and has the Mortification to find himself not possessed of. (p. 271)

> *Richard Steele, in an extract in* Shakespeare, the Critical Heritage: 1693-1733, Vol. 2, *edited by Brian Vickers, Routledge & Kegan Paul, 1974, pp. 270-71.*

LEWIS THEOBALD (essay date 1733)

[*During the first half of the eighteenth century, Theobald was considered one of the greatest and most competent of Shakespearean critics. However, after his death in 1744 his reputation suffered a severe decline, probably due to his misguided attempts to revise many of Shakespeare's plays according to Neoclassical ideas of unity of action and dignity of character. In the following excerpt, first published in Theobald's edition of* The Works of Shakespeare *in 1733, he speculates that Viola's famous "smiling at grief" speech had its source in a poem by Chaucer, and praises Shakespeare for his improvement upon his supposed model.*]

I cannot pass over the remarkable Conundrum betwixt Sir *Andrew* wishing he had follow'd the *Arts* and Sir *Toby*'s Application of This to the using *Art* in improving his *Hair*, because I would observe what Variety and what a Contrast of Character the Poet has preserv'd in this Pair of ridiculous Knights. Sir *Toby* has moderate natural Parts, and a smattering of Education, which makes him always to be running his Wit, and gives him a Predominance over the other. Sir *Andrew* is a Blockhead by Nature, and unimprov'd by any Acquirements from Art, and so is made the very Anvil to Imposition and Ridicule. . . .

> She pined in Thought;
> And, with a green and yellow Melancholy,
> She sate like *Patience* on a Monument,
> Smiling at *Grief*.
>
> [II.iv.112-15]

This very fine Image [from *Twelfth Night*, II, IV], which has been so universally applauded, it is not impossible but our Author might originally have borrow'd from CHAUCER in his *Assembly of Foules*.

> And her besidis wonder discretlie,
> Dame *Pacience ysittinge* there I fonde
> With *Face pale*, upon an *hill* of *sonde*.

If he was indebted, however, for the first rude Draught, how amply has he repaid that Debt in heightning the Picture! How much does the *green* and *yellow Melancholy* transcend the Old Bard's *Face pale;* the *Monument,* his *Hill* of *Sand;* and what an additional Beauty is *smiling at Grief,* for which there are no Ground nor Traces in the Original! (p. 499)

> *Lewis Theobald, in an extract from his essay in* Shakespeare, the Critical Heritage; 1693-1733, Vol. 2, *edited by Brian Vickers, Routledge & Kegan Paul, 1974, pp. 475-528.*

[CHARLOTTE LENNOX] (essay date 1753)

[*Lennox was an American-born novelist and Shakespearean scholar who compiled a three-volume edition of translated texts of the sources used by Shakespeare in twenty-two of his plays, including some analyses of the ways in which he used these sources. Here she faults* Twelfth Night *for lacking the Neoclassical precepts of credibility and decorum, a position taken later by Samuel Johnson (1765). Her view that both Viola's disguise and Olivia's passion for a lowly page are evidence of the sensual "impropriety of manners" in all the characters is disputed by John Potter in 1772 and by Anna Jameson in 1833. Lennox compares the play with one of its possible sources, the* Novelle *of Bandello, and stresses that Shakespeare's version is inferior to Bandello's in action and characterization.*]

It is really surprising to see the Admirers of *Shakespear* so solicitous to prove he was very conversant with the Antients; they take all Opportunities to find in his Writings Illusions to them; Imitations of their Thoughts and Expressions; and will not scruple to allow their Favourite to have been guilty of some little Thefts from their Works, provided it will make out his Claim to an Acquaintance with them.

It is very much to be doubted whether or not he understood the *Italian* and *French* Languages, since we find he made Use of Translations from both when he borrowed of their Authors; and still less probable is it that he understood and studied the *Greek* and *Latin* Poets, when he, who was so close a Copyer has never imitated them in their chief Beauties, and seems wholly a Stranger to the Laws of dramatic Poetry, well does the Poet [Milton] say of him,

> *Shakespear*, Fancy's sweetest Child,
> Warbles his native Wood-Notes wild.

His true Praise seems to be summ'd up in those two Lines; for wild, though harmonious, his Strains certainly are; and his modern Admirers injure him greatly, by supposing any of those Wood-Notes copied from the Antients; *Milton*, by calling them *native*, allows them to have been untaught, and all his own; and in that does Justice to his vast imagination, which is robbed of great Part of its Merit by supposing it to have received any Assistance from the Antients, whom if he understood, it must be confessed he has profited very little by, since we see not the least Shadow of their Exactness and Regularity in his Works.

Though it should be granted that *Shakespear* took the Hint of *Sebastian* and *Viola*'s Resemblance from the *Maenechmi* and *Amphitrio* of *Plautus*, yet he might have done that without understanding *Latin*, since there were Translations of both those

Plays in his Time; and to his own Invention, had that been the Case, might be attributed almost all the perplexing Adventures which the Resemblance of the Brother and Sister gave rise to in the *Twelfth-Night,* and which are very different from those in the *Latin* Author.

But *Shakespear* had a much more ample Supply for the Fable of this Comedy in [Bandello's *Novel*], from whence he undoubtedly drew it, and which not only furnished him with the Hint of the Resemblance between *Sebastian* and *Viola,* but also with the greatest Part of the Intrigue of the Play. (pp. 240-42)

Though *Shakspear* has copied the Novelist in [several] Particulars, yet he differs from him in others, which very much lessens the Probability of the Story.

Sebastian and *Viola* in the Play are parted by a Shipwreck, and *Viola* is cast upon the Coast of *Illyria;* but we are not told with what Intention this Brother and Sister embarked, or whither their Voyage was bound.

The Poet had Occasion for them in *Illyria,* and there they are at the Service of the Audience; no Matter if introduced with Propriety or not; we must be contented to take them as we find them: Well; *Viola,* after giving some Tears to the Memory of her Brother, whom she fears is drowned, is desirous of being recommended as an Attendant to a Lady with whom the Sovereign of the Country is in love; but being told it would be difficult to procure Admission to her, she all of a sudden takes up an unaccountable Resolution to serve the young Batchelor-Duke in the Habit of a Man. . . . (p. 243)

A very natural Scheme this for a beautiful and virtuous young Lady to throw off all at once the Modesty and Reservedness of her Sex, mix among Men, herself disguised like one; and, prest by no Necessity, influenced by no Passion, expose herself to all the dangerous Consequences of so unworthy and shameful a Situation.

We find this Incident managed with much more Decency in the *Novel.*

Nicuola is violently in love with and beloved by *Lattantio;* and finding that, during. a short Absence from him, he became enamoured of *Catella,* upon hearing he had lost his Page and wanted another, she disguises herself like a Boy, and offers her Service to wait upon him with a View of recalling his Affections by this extraordinary Instance of her Tenderness and Fidelity, and of seizing every Opportunity of traversing his new Passion for *Catella.*

This Project, though not altogether prudent and wise, was far from being inconsistent with the Temper and Circumstances of *Nicuola,* stimulated as she was by Love, Jealousy and Despair, to attempt something extraordinary for the Recovery of her Lover.

But what are *Viola's* Motives for so rash an Enterprize? She is neither in love with or abandoned by the Duke, and cannot reasonably propose to herself any Advantage by thus hazarding her Virtue and Fame: His Person she had never seen; his Affections she was informed were engaged; what then were her Views and Designs by submitting to be his Attendant?

Bandello does not even make *Nicuola* resolve upon such an Expedient till the Design was suggested to her by over-hearing *Lattantio* lament the Loss of his Page and wish for another.

But the Novellist is much more careful to preserve Probability in his Narration than the Poet in his Action: The Wonder is

that *Shakespear* should borrow so many Incidents from him, and yet task his Invention to make those Incidents unnatural and absurd.

The Passion of *Olivia,* the Duke's Mistress, for the disguised Lady, is attended with Circumstances that make it appear highly improbable and ridiculous: She is represented as a noble and virtuous Lady, overwhelmed with Grief for the Death of a beloved Brother; her Grief indeed is of a very extraordinary Nature. . . . (pp. 244-45)

This sorrowful Lady, however, makes her first Appearance in the Company of a Jester, with whom she is extremely diverted; and notwithstanding her Vow which we are told of in another Place, not to admit the Sight or Company of Men, she permits the Duke's Page to approach her, shews him her Face, and bandies Jests and smart Sentences with all the lively Wit of an airy Coquet.

Then follows her sudden Passion for the supposed Youth, which is as suddenly declared, without any of those Emotions that Bashfulness, Delicacy, and a Desire of preserving the Decorum her Sex and Birth oblige her to observe, must raise in the Mind of a Woman of Honour.

Had *Shakespear,* by mixing so much Levity in the Character of *Olivia,* designed a Satire on the Sex, he would have certainly led us by some Reflexions on the Inconsistency of her Behaviour to have made that Inference; but this is not the Case; for *Olivia* is every where highly extolled for her Virtues.

It is his injudicious Conduct of the Fable that gives so much Impropriety to the Manners of his Persons, at least in this Instance, which is the more surprizing, as the Novel furnished him with one much better contrived, and Characters more suitable to the Action.

Catella acts the same Part in the Novel that *Olivia* does in the Play; but *Catella* is a young gay libertine Girl, whose Birth was but mean, and Education neglected; it was not therefore surprizing that she should so easily fall in Love with a Page, indecently court him, and resolve to marry him, such an inconsiderate Conduct was agreeable to her Character; but in the noble and virtuous *Olivia,* 'tis unnatural and absurd, and what makes it still more so is, that as *Shakespear* has ordered the Matter, *Olivia* is disgracefully repulsed by this Youth, and yet continues her Suit, whereas *Catella* meets with a ready Compliance from the supposed *Romulo,* who sees his Designs on *Lattantio* likely to succeed by his Mistress's fortunate Passion for him.

Olivia's taking *Sebastian,* the Brother of the disguised *Viola,* for the beautiful Page, and marrying him, is with very little Variation borrowed from *Bandello;* but *Paolo* in the Novel is much more naturally introduced than *Sebastian* in the Play.

Paolo comes to *Efi* to seek for his Father and Sister, but we are not acquainted with *Sebastian's* Motives for going to *Illyria;* the Poet indeed had Business for him there, and there he lugs him without the least Shadow of a Reason for it, which is left to the Imagination of the Reader to supply.

The Behaviour of *Lattantio* in the Novel is more natural and consistent, than the Duke's in the Play: They both marry the Women that had attended on them disguised, but the Difference of their Stations, Circumstances, and Characters, makes the same Action natural in one, which in the other is absurd and ridiculous.

Lattantio had been in Love with *Nicuola,* but her Absence, joined to the natural Inconstancy of Youth, so wild and inconsiderate as his, transferred his Affections from her to *Catella;* she slights him, and he being informed that his abandoned *Nicuola,* impelled by the Violence of her Passion for him, had disguised herself in Boy's Cloaths, and waited on him as his Page; he repents of his Falsehood, and charmed with her Tenderness and Fidelity makes her his Wife.

This Conduct in *Lattantio* is very natural, but why should the Duke, a sovereign Prince who so passionately adored *Olivia,* all at once take a Resolution to marry *Viola,* a Stranger whom he had never seen in her proper Garb, because she had served him in Disguise; 'tis absurd to suppose he could in a Moment pass from the most extravagant Passion imaginable for *Olivia,* to one no less extravagant, for a Person, whom till then he had always believed to be a Boy; and 'tis also highly improbable that a great Prince would so suddenly resolve to marry a Girl, who had no other Title to his Favour than an imprudent Passion, which had carried her greatly beyond the Bounds of Decency.

The Duke's Reasons for this extraordinary Action are far from being convincing. (pp. 246-49)

And as *Viola* at first had not even Love to plead as an Excuse for her indecent Disguise, she is still less worthy of the Fortune she was raised to.

There is a great deal of true Comic Humour in the inferior Characters of this Play, which are entirely of the Poet's Invention; the Mistakes *Antonio* is led into by the Resemblance of *Sabastian* and *Viola,* are no doubt Hints borrowed from the *Amphitrio* and the *Maenechmi* of *Plautus,* for which it is probable he consulted the *French,* or rather the *English* Translations of those Comedies extant in his Time; but these Mistakes, however diverting, take their Rise from a very improbable Circumstance.

Antonio, a Sea Captain, delivers *Sebastian* from the Fury of the Waves; the Youth being obstinately determined to go to the Court, *Antonio,* who in a Sea-fight had done great Mischief to the Duke's Galleys, resolves, out of the Violence of his Friendship, to follow him thither, notwithstanding he knew his Life would be in manifest Danger if he was seen in *Illyria.*

How unaccountably extravagant is this Kindness in a Stranger? what more could a long continued Friendship, confirmed by mutual Obligations have produced? But this Play is full of such Absurdities, which might have been avoided, had the Characters as well as the Action been the same with the Novel. (pp. 249-50)

> [*Charlotte Lennox*], "*Observations on the Use Shakespear Has Made of the Foregoing Novel, in His Comedy Called 'Twelfth Night', or 'What You Will',*" in her Shakespear Illustrated: Or the Novels and Histories on Which the Plays of Shakespear Are Founded, *Vol. I, A. Millar, 1753, pp. 237-50.*

SAMUEL JOHNSON (essay date 1765)

[*Johnson has long held an important place in the history of Shakespearean criticism. He is considered the foremost representative of moderate English Neoclassicism and is credited by some literary historians with freeing Shakespeare from the strictures of the three unities valued by strict Neoclassicists: that dramas should have a single setting, take place in less than twenty-four hours, and have a causally connected plot. More recent scholars portray him as a critic who was able to synthesize existing critical theory*

rather than as an innovative theoretician. Johnson was a master of Augustan prose style and a personality who dominated the literary world of his epoch. Like Charlotte Lennox (1753), Johnson states that Twelfth Night *lacks credibility and verisimilitude, and, further, fails to instruct the audience. This latter position is countered by John Potter (1772). The excerpt below is taken from a note in Johnson's edition of* The Plays of Mr. William Shakespeare *published in 1765.*]

[*Twelfth Night*] is in the graver part elegant and easy, and in some of the lighter scenes exquisitely humorous. *Ague-cheek* is drawn with great propriety, but his character is in a great measure that of natural fatuity, and is therefore not the proper prey of a satirist. The soliloquy of *Malvolio* is truly comick; he is betrayed to ridicule merely by his pride. The marriage of *Olivia* and the succeeding perplexity, though well enough contrived to divert on the stage, wants credibility, and fails to produce the proper instruction required in the drama, as it exhibits no just picture of life.

> *Samuel Johnson, in his end-note to "Twelfth Night,"* in Shakespeare, the Critical Heritage: 1765-1774, *Vol. 5, edited by Brian Vickers, Routledge & Kegan Paul, 1979, p. 109.*

HIC et UBIQUE [pseudonym of GEORGE STEEVENS] (essay date 1772)

[*Steevens was an English scholar who collaborated with Samuel Johnson on a ten-volume edition of Shakespeare's works in 1773. The subsequent revisions of this collection, along with Steevens's own edition of 1793, formed the textual basis for the first two Variorum editions of Shakespeare's plays. The following excerpt, first published in* St. James's Chronicle, *January 23-25, 1772, is attributed to Steevens by Brian Vickers, editor of* Shakespeare: The Critical Heritage. *Here Steevens praises the construction of* Twelfth Night *and Shakespeare's handling of the comedic form.*]

One of the most entertaining Plays in any Language, or upon any Stage is now to be considered; and let me remark, by the Bye, that it is become almost a Term of Reproach that a Comedy should have any Resemblance of a Novel. . . . Without justifying or condemning the Practice at present, I shall only remark that Shakespeare, in the Play under our Consideration, as well as in *As you like it, All's well,* &c. *Much ado, Measure for Measure, Merchant of Venice,* &c. has chosen Novels for the Foundations on which to erect the most extraordinary and exquisite Edifices of Art and Nature! The late Dr. Akenside, whose Genius and Taste are well known by various Performances, pronounced this Comedy of *Twelfth Night* the Perfection of the Comic Drama. The Doctor, perhaps, was too warm in his Admiration; but surely when we consider the Variety and proper Contrast of Characters, the many uncommon Situations to unfold and bring forth the several Humours, Passions, and Peculiarities of the *Dramatis Personae,* there is no Performance of five short Acts which contains such Matter for Mirth, arising from the happy Disposition of the Scenes and from the natural, though unexpected, Mistakes of the Characters. All the Parts being thus well and easily connected with the whole commands that Attention, mixed with Pleasure, which real Criticks acknowledge to be the best Proof of the Genius of a Comic Writer.

Twelfth Night is an admirable Comedy; and first let us pay our Respects to that most consummate Coxcomb, that ridiculous Composition of stiff Impertinence and uncommon Conceit—*Malvolio.* . . . (p. 446)

Sir *Toby Belch,* never sober but always delightfully mischievous, is the true Picture of an old shameless Debauchee, reduced by his Intemperance to be a Hanger-on, and distressing his Niece by his Love of Drink, Noise, and Quarrelling. . . .

Sir Andrew Ague-cheek, who admires Sir Toby, and without any one Requisite to keep him Company adds much to the *Vis-comica* of the Piece. He quarrels without Courage, drinks himself sick, and becomes the Maudlin Echo of Sir Toby, without Wit, Humour, Spirit, Fancy, or Force; and yet Shakespeare has shewn all of 'em in the Production of this most inimitable Nothing! (pp. 446-47)

> *Hic et Ubique [pseudonym of George Steevens],*
> *"Dramatic Strictures: Upon the Comedy of 'Twelfth*
> *Night',"* in Shakespeare, the Critical Heritage: 1765-
> 1774, Vol. 5, *edited by Brian Vickers, Routledge &*
> *Kegan Paul, 1979, pp. 243-50.*

[JOHN POTTER]   (essay date 1772)

[*Potter was an eminent English classical scholar whose studies of Plutarch and St. Basil were considered standard until the middle of the nineteenth century. Addressing Samuel Johnson (1765), who complained that* Twelfth Night *lacks credibility and fails to instruct, Potter pleads for an understanding of the play as "exquisite entertainment," a work which, although not instructive, is innocent and free from obscenity. He also challenges the contention of Charlotte Lennox (1753) that Olivia's passion for Viola is indecorous, stating that the situation is both true to life and based on honorable principles. The excerpt below is taken from Potter's review of* Twelfth Night *first published in his* The Theatrical Review *in 1772.*]

We acknowledge ourselves of the Doctor's opinion, but we think he has been somewhat sparing of praise in his general Character of this pleasing Comedy. It is true, it does not exhibit a just picture of life, and on this account fails to produce instruction, which should be the grand aim of the Drama; but as all amusements do not professedly unite themselves with instruction, tho' it is best when they do, surely a Piece full of exquisite entertainment, founded on innocent circumstances, displaying Characters inoffensive in themselves, and Dialogue untainted either with licentiousness or obscenity is entitled to a considerable degree of approbation.—The Plot of this Piece is well contrived, and the Incidents in general are sufficiently probable to be pleasing. The Characters are numerous, and marked with great variety; and tho' some of them are not exact portraits of nature they are not so much on the extreme as either to disgust or be unpleasing. A more innocent set of beings were probably never grouped together. If any one of them can be said to be reprehensible it is *Olivia,* whose sudden love for *Viola* in man's attire, and precipitate marriage with *Sebastian* thro' the mistake of dress, is not altogether consistent with a woman in her exalted situation; and yet we frequently meet with instances of this sort in real life, which derive their origin from chaste love and have their foundation in the principles of honour and virtue. . . . With respect to the Character of *Sir Toby Belch,* it may be objected that he is a drunkard. This we acknowledge, but in other respects he is inoffensive. What is observed above [by Johnson] of *Sir Andrew Ague-cheek* is undoubtedly just; and *Malvolio* is drawn rather in the extreme. Yet surely, tho' there is something singularly ridiculous in this fantastical Character it is rather deserving of applause than censure, and the trick played him by *Sir Toby,* and *Maria* exhibits such contrivance and contains so much true humour as cannot fail of affording exquisite entertainment to the Spec-

tators.—*Clowns* were Characters in which *Shakespeare* delighted; and tho' there was hardly a Play wrote in that time without one, he has varied the *Clown* in this Play with considerable distinction from those in his other Pieces.—*Viola* is a very pleasing Character, yet her conduct is very singular and unaccountable. She forms a deep design with very little premeditation. She is thrown by shipwreck on an unknown Coast, hears that the Prince is a Batchelor, and resolves to supplant the Lady whom he courts. This is not a little extraordinary, and the only excuse to be made is that her resolution was necessary to *Shakespeare's* Plan. (pp. 439-40)

> [*John Potter*], *in an extract from his review of "Twelfth Night," in* Shakespeare, the Critical Heritage: 1765-
> 1774, Vol. 5, *edited by Brian Vickers, Routledge &*
> *Kegan Paul, 1979, pp. 432-43.*

GEORGE STEEVENS   (essay date 1780)

[*Steevens is the first of many critics to comment on the music in* Twelfth Night. *Presenting a position that will be argued throughout the criticism, Steevens objects to Feste's final song, finding it "utterly unconnected" to the play, and proposing that Shakespeare did not write it. For further commentary on the importance of Feste's song, see the essays by Charles Knight (1842), E. K. Chambers (1907), Morris P. Tilley (1914), A. C. Bradley (1916), G. Wilson Knight (1932), John Middleton Murry (1936), L. G. Salingar (1958), and C. L. Barber (1959). Steevens's comments first appeared in 1780 as a supplement to* The Plays of William Shakespeare.]

Though we are well convinced that Shakspeare has written slight ballads for the sake of discriminating characters more strongly, or for other necessary purposes, in the course of his mixed dramas, it is scarce credible, that after he had cleared his stage, he should exhibit his Clown afresh, and with so poor a recommendation as this song ["When that I was a little tiny boy"], which is utterly unconnected with the subject of the preceding comedy. I do not therefore hestitate to call the nonsensical ditty before us, some buffoon actor's composition, which was accidentally tacked to the prompter's copy of *Twelfth-Night,* having been casually subjoined to it for the diversion, or at the call, of the lowest order of spectators. (p. 501)

> *George Steevens, in his footnote to "Twelfth Night, or, What You Will,"* in The Plays and Poems of William Shakspeare, with the Corrections and Illustrations of Various Commentators: Comprehending a Life of the Poet, and an Enlarged History of the Stage, Vol. XI, *edited by J. Boswell, AMS Press, Inc., 1966, pp. 500-01.*

AUGUST WILHELM SCHLEGEL   (essay date 1808)

[*A leading German Romantic critic, Schlegel holds a key place in the history of Shakespeare's reputation in European criticism. His translations of thirteen of the plays are still considered the best German translations of Shakespeare. Schlegel was also a leading spokesman for the Romantic movement which permanently overthrew the Neoclassical contention that Shakespeare was a child of nature whose plays lacked artistic form. Schlegel stresses the unity of* Twelfth Night, *noting that the "ideal follies" of the main plot are fused with the "naked absurdities" of the subplot to provide comment on the central theme of love. Schlegel also discusses Shakespeare's concept of "fancy," which, according to Schlegel, was meant to imply both love and imagination. This theory is further developed in the comments of Hermann Ulrici (1839). Schlegel also implies that* Twelfth Night *was Shakespeare's last play, a point that was challenged by Charles Knight*

(1842). The essay from which the following excerpt is drawn was originally delivered as a lecture in 1808.]

The Twelfth Night, or What you Will, unites the entertainment of an intrigue, contrived with great ingenuity, to a rich fund of comic characters and situations, and the beauteous colours of an ethereal poetry. In most of his plays, Shakespeare treats love more as an affair of the imagination than the heart; but here he has taken particular care to remind us that, in his language, the same word, *fancy,* signified both fancy and love. The love of the music-enraptured Duke for Olivia is not merely a fancy, but an imagination; Viola appears at first to fall arbitrarily in love with the Duke, whom she serves as a page, although she afterwards touches the tenderest strings of feeling; the proud Olivia is captivated by the modest and insinuating messenger of the Duke, in whom she is far from suspecting a disguised rival, and at last, by a second deception, takes the brother for the sister. To these, which I might call ideal follies, a contrast is formed by the naked absurdities to which the entertaining tricks of the ludicrous persons of the piece give rise, under the pretext also of love: the silly and profligate Knight's awkward courtship of Olivia, and her delcaration of love to Viola; the imagination of the pedantic steward Malvolio, that his mistress is secretly in love with him, which carries him so far that he is at last shut up as a lunatic, and visited by the clown in the dress of a priest. These scenes are admirably conceived, and as significant as they are laughable. If this were really, as is asserted, Shakspeare's latest work, he must have enjoyed to the last the same youthful elasticity of mind, and have carried with him to the grave the undiminished fulness of his talents. (p. 392)

> *August Wilhelm Schlegel, "Criticisms on Shakspeare's Comedies," in his* Lectures on Dramatic Art and Literature, *edited by Rev. A.J.W. Morrison, translated by John Black, second edition, George Bell & Sons, 1892, pp. 379-99.*

WILLIAM HAZLITT (essay date 1817)

[Hazlitt is generally considered to be a leading Shakespearean critic of the English Romantic movement. A prolific essayist and critic on a wide range of subjects, Hazlitt remarked in the preface to his Characters of Shakespeare's Plays, *first published in 1817, that he was inspired by the German critic August Wilhelm Schlegel, and was determined to supplant what he considered the pernicious influence of Samuel Johnson's Shakespearean criticism. Hazlitt's criticism is typically Romantic in its emphasis on character studies. Unlike his fellow Romantic critic Samuel Taylor Coleridge, Hazlitt was a dramatic critic whose experience of Shakespeare in the theater influenced his interpretations. While professing a greater fondness for the tragedies than for the comedies, Hazlitt acknowledged Shakespeare's breadth and scope in comedic characterization. He believed that Shakespeare's personae are drawn with a fullness and naturalness which distinguish them from the characters of Restoration drama, for they elicit our laughter, but not our derision. In this they resemble the characters of Cervantes and Molière. Hazlitt here initiates the long tradition of sympathetic response to the gulling of Malvolio. For other sympathetic interpretations of the character of Malvolio, see the excerpts by Charles Lamb (1822), Charles Knight (1842), T. Kenny (1864), and William Archer (1884).]*

[Twelfth Night] is justly considered as one of the most delightful of Shakespeare's comedies. It is full of sweetness and pleasantry. It is perhaps too good-natured for comedy. It has little satire, and no spleen. It aims at the ludicrous rather than the ridiculous. It makes us laugh at the follies of mankind, not despise them, and still less bear any ill-will towards them. Shakespeare's comic genius resembles the bee rather in its power of extracting sweets from weeds or poisons, than in leaving a sting behind it. He gives the most amusing exaggeration of the prevailing foibles of his characters, but in a way that they themselves, instead of being offended at, would almost join in to humour; he rather contrives opportunities for them to show themselves off in the happiest lights, than renders them contemptible in the perverse construction of the wit or malice of others. (p. 201)

[The] spirit of his comedies is evidently quite distinct from that of [Congreve, Wycherly, Vanbrugh, &c.], as it is in its essence the same with that of Cervantes, and also very frequently of Molière, though he was more systematic in his extravagance than Shakespeare. Shakespeare's comedy is of a pastoral and poetical cast. Folly is indigenous to the soil, and shoots out with native, happy, unchecked luxuriance. Absurdity has every encouragement afforded it; and nonsense has room to flourish in. Nothing is stunted by the churlish, icy hand of indifference or severity. The poet runs riot in a conceit, and idolizes a quibble. His whole object is to turn the meanest or rudest objects to a pleasurable account. The relish which he has of a pun, or of the quaint humour of a low character, does not interfere with the delight with which he describes a beautiful image, or the most refined love. The clown's forced jests do not spoil the sweetness of the character of Viola; the same house is big enough to hold Malvolio, the Countess, Maria, Sir Toby, and Sir Andrew Aguecheek. . . . How Sir Toby, Sir Andrew, and the Clown . . . *chirp over their cups,* how they 'rouse the night-owl in a catch, able to draw three souls out of one weaver'!—What can be better than Sir Toby's unanswerable answer to Malvolio, 'Dost thou think, because thou art virtuous, there shall be no more cakes and ale?' In a word, the best turn is given to everything, instead of the worst. There is a constant infusion of the romantic and enthusiastic, in proportion as the characters are natural and sincere: whereas, in the more artificial style of comedy, everything gives way to ridicule and indifference, there being nothing left but affectation on one side, and incredulity on the other.—Much as we like Shakespeare's comedies, we cannot agree with Dr. Johnson that they are better than his tragedies; nor do we like them half so well. If his inclination to comedy sometimes led him to trifle with the seriousness of tragedy, the poetical and impassioned passages are the best parts of his comedies. The great and secret charm of *Twelfth Night* is the character of Viola. Much as we like catches and cakes and ale, there is something that we like better. We have a friendship for Sir Toby; we patronize Sir Andrew; we have an understanding with the Clown, a sneaking kindness for Maria and her rogueries; we feel a regard for Malvolio, and sympathize with his gravity, his smiles, his cross-garters, his yellow stockings, and imprisonment in the stocks. But there is something that excites in us a stronger feeling than all this—it is Viola's confession of her love. . . . Shakespeare alone could describe the effect of his own poetry

> Oh, it came o'er the ear like the sweet south
> That breathes upon a bank of violets,
> Stealing and giving odour.
>
> [I. i. 5-7]

What we so much admire here is not the image of Patience on a monument, which has been generally quoted, but the lines before and after it. 'They give a very echo to the seat where love is throned.' How long ago it is since we first learnt to repeat them; and still, still they vibrate on the heart, like the sounds which the passing wind draws from the trembling strings of a harp left on some desert shore! (pp. 202-05)

Yet after reading other parts of this play, and particularly the garden-scene where Malvolio picks up the letter, if we were to say that his genius for comedy was less than his genius for tragedy, it would perhaps only prove that our own taste in such matters is more saturnine than mercurial. . . . If poor Malvolio's treatment afterwards is a little hard, poetical justice is done in the uneasiness which Olivia suffers on account of her mistaken attachment to Cesario, as her insensibility to the violence of the Duke's passion is toned for by the discovery of Viola's concealed love of him. (pp. 206-08)

> *William Hazlitt, " 'Twelfth Night; or, What You Will',"*
> *in his* Characters of Shakespeare's Plays, *Oxford*
> *University Press, London, 1959, pp. 201-08.*

CHARLES LAMB (essay date 1822)

[*Lamb is considered one of the leading figures of the Romantic movement and an authority on Elizabethan drama. Although he was, like William Hazlitt, a theatrical critic, Lamb argued that the stage was an improper medium for Shakespeare's plays, mainly because visual dramatizations marred their artistic and lyrical effects. Like Samuel Taylor Coleridge, Lamb reverenced Shakespeare as a poet rather than a playwright. Although many scholars consider his views sentimental and subjective and his interpretations of Shakespeare's characters as often extreme, Lamb remains an important contributor to the nineteenth century's re-evaluation of Shakespeare's genius. His defense of Malvolio is well known. Lamb perceived Malvolio as an estimable character, not as a comic butt for the abuse he receives from Sir Toby and Maria. Lamb asserts that neither Malvolio's morality nor his manners fit the revels of Illyria. According to Lamb, Malvolio is curiously out of place, and his fate borders on the tragic. For additional commentary on the role of Malvolio, see the excerpts by Joseph Hunter (1845), F. Kreyssig (1862), H. N. Hudson (1872), Morris P. Tilley (1914), Mark Van Doren (1939), and O. J. Campbell (1943). In a section of the essay not excerpted here, Lamb discusses the interpretation of Malvolio by the actor Robert Bensley. The effect of Lamb's interpretation of Bensley is discussed by Sylvan Barnett (1954). Lamb's essay originally appeared in* The London Magazine *in February, 1822.*]

Malvolio is not essentially ludicrous. He becomes comic but by accident. He is cold, austere, repelling; but dignified, consistent, and, for what appears, rather of an over-stretched morality. Maria describes him as a sort of Puritan; and he might have worn his gold chain with honour in one of our old round-head families, in the service of a Lambert, or a Lady Fairfax. But his morality and his manners are misplaced in Illyria. He is opposed to the proper *levities* of the piece, and falls in the unequal contest. Still his pride, or his gravity, (call it which you will) is inherent, and native to the man, not mock or affected, which later only are the fit objects to excite laughter. His quality is at the best unlovely, but neither buffoon nor contemptible. His bearing is lofty, a little above his station, but probably not much above his deserts. We see no reason why he should not have been brave, honourable, accomplished. His careless committal of the ring to the ground (which he was commissioned to restore to Cesario), bespeaks a generosity of birth and feeling. His dialect on all occasions is that of a gentleman, and a man of education. We must not confound him with the eternal old, low steward of comedy. He is master of the household to a great Princess; a dignity probably conferred upon him for other respects than age or length of service.

Olivia, at the first indication of his supposed madness, declares that she 'would not have him miscarry for half of her dowry.' Does this look as if the character was meant to appear little or insignificant? Once, indeed, she accuses him to his face—of what?—of being 'sick of self-love,'—but with the gentleness and considerateness which could not have been, if she had not thought that this particular infirmity shaded some virtues. His rebuke to the knight, and his sottish revellers, is sensible and spirited; and when we take into consideration the unprotected condition of his mistress, and the strict regard with which her state of real or dissembled mourning would draw the eyes of the world upon her house-affairs, Malvolio might feel the honour of the family in some sort of his keeping; as it appears not that Olivia had any more brothers, or kinsmen, to look to it—for Sir Toby had dropped all such nice respects at the buttery hatch. That Malvolio was meant to be represented as possessing estimable qualities, the expression of the Duke in his anxiety to have him reconciled, almost infers. 'Pursue him, and entreat him to a peace.' Even in his abused state of chains and darkness, a sort of greatness seems never to desert him. He argues highly and well with the supposed Sir Topas, and philosophises gallantly upon his straw. There must have been some shadow of worth about the man; he must have been something more than a mere vapour—a thing of straw, or Jack in office—before Fabian and Maria could have ventured sending him upon a courting-errand to Oliva. There was some consonancy (as he would say) in the undertaking, or the jest would have been too bold even for that house of misrule. (pp. 53-55)

Who would not wish to live but for a day in the conceit of such a lady's love as Olivia? Why, the Duke would have given his principality but for a quarter of a minute, sleeping or waking, to have been so deluded. The man seemed to tread upon air, to taste manna, to walk with his head in the clouds, to mate Hyperion. O! shake not the castles of his pride—endure yet for a season bright moments of confidence—'stand still ye watches of the element,' that Malvolio may be still in fancy fair Olivia's lord—but fate and retribution say no—I hear the mischievous titter of Maria—the witty taunts of Sir Toby—the still more insupportable triumph of the foolish knight—the counterfeit Sir Topas is unmasked—and 'thus the whirligig of time,' as the true clown hath it, 'brings in his revenges.' (p. 56)

> *Charles Lamb, "The Comedies: 'The Old Actors',"*
> *in his* Charles Lamb on Shakespeare, *edited by Joan*
> *Coldwell, Barnes & Noble, 1978, pp. 50-62.*

MRS. [ANNA] JAMESON (essay date 1833)

[*In the following excerpt, first published in her* Characteristics of Women *in 1833, Jameson opposes the Neoclassical view that Olivia's passion for a lowly page is indecorous (see excerpt above by Charlotte Lennox, 1753), finding the situation amusing and not reproachful.*]

As the innate dignity of Perdita in *The Winter's Tale* pierces through her rustic disguise, so the exquisite refinement of Viola triumphs over her masculine attire. Viola is, perhaps, in a degree less elevated and refined than Perdita, but with a touch of sentiment more profound and heart-stirring; she is 'deep-learned in the lore of love,'—at least theoretically,—and speaks as masterly on the subject as Perdita does of flowers. . . .

What beautiful propriety in the distinction drawn between Rosalind and Viola! The wild sweetness, the frolic humour which sports free and unblamed amid the shades of Ardennes, would ill become Viola, whose playfulness is assumed as part of her disguise as a court-page, and is guarded by the strictest delicacy. She has not, like Rosalind, a saucy enjoyment in her own incognito; her disguise does not sit so easily upon her; her heart does not beat freely under it. (p. 392)

Contrasted with the deep, silent, patient love of Viola for the Duke, we have the lady-like wilfulness of Olivia; and her sudden passion, or rather fancy, for the disguised page takes so beautiful a colouring of poetry and sentiment that we do not think her forward. Olivia is like a princess of romance, and has all the privileges of one; she is, like Portia, high-born and high-bred, mistress over her servants—but not, like Portia, 'queen o'er herself.' She has never in her life been opposed; the first contradiction, therefore, rouses all the woman in her, and turns a caprice into a headlong passion. . . .

The distance of rank which separates the Countess from the youthful page—the real sex of Viola—the dignified elegance of Olivia's deportment, except where passion gets the better of her pride—her consistent coldness towards the Duke—the description of that 'smooth, discreet, and stable bearing' with which she rules her household—her generous care for her steward Malvolio, in the midst of her own distress,—all these circumstances raise Olivia in our fancy, and render her caprice for the page a source of amusement and interest, not a subject of reproach. *Twelfth Night* is a genuine comedy—a perpetual spring of the gayest and the sweetest fancies. In artificial society men and women are divided into castes and classes, and it is rarely that extremes in character or manners can approximate. To blend into one harmonious picture the utmost grace and refinement of sentiment and the broadest effects of humour, the most poignant wit and the most indulgent benignity, in short, to bring before us in the same scene Viola and Olivia, with Malvolio and Sir Toby, belonged only to Nature and to Shakespeare. (pp. 392-93)

> *Mrs. [Anna] Jameson, in her extract in* A New Variorum Edition of Shakespeare: Twelfe Night, or, What You Will, Vol. XIII, *edited by Horace Howard Furness, J. B. Lippincott Company, 1901, pp. 392-93.*

HERMANN ULRICI (essay date 1839)

[A German scholar, Ulrici was a professor of philosophy and an author of works on Greek poetry and Shakespeare. The following excerpt is from an English translation of his Uber Shakspeare's dramatische Kunst, und sein Verhaltniss zu Calderon und Göthe. *This work exemplifies the ''philosophical criticism'' developed in Germany during the nineteenth century. The immediate sources for Ulrici's critical approach appear to be August Wilhelm Schlegel's conception of the play as an organic, interconnected whole and Georg Wilhelm Friedrich Hegel's view of the drama as an embodiment of the conflict of historical forces and ideas. Unlike his fellow German Shakespearean critic G. G. Gervinus, Ulrici sought to develop a specifically Christian aesthetics, but one which, as he carefully points out in the introduction to the work mentioned above, in no way intrudes on ''that unity of idea, which preeminently constitutes a work of art a living creation in the world of beauty.'' Continuing the discussion initiated by August Wilhelm Schlegel (1808) regarding love as ''fancy'' in* Twelfth Night, *Ulrici observes that Shakespeare creates a world in which love is a ''mere humour of fancy,'' a world in which contradiction, fantastic elements, and ''the chaotic medley of accident and caprice'' are ordered through the dialectic of Shakespeare's irony. For Ulrici, the comedy of fancy reconciles the external nature of experience and the fantastic quality of the inner world. He finds the meaning of* Twelfth Night *centered in Feste, claiming that this character alone, with full consciousness, observes and comments on the others. For additional commentary on Feste's central*

role in the play, see the excerpts by A. C. Bradley (1916), G. Wilson Knight (1932), Enid Welsford (1935), E. J. West (1949), and G. K. Hunter (1962). Ulrici's Uber Shakspeare's dramatische Kunst, und sein Verhaltniss zu Calderon und Gothe *was first published in 1839.]*

The Comedies of Shakespeare may . . . be arranged in two grand divisions; which, however, are by no means absolutely distinct from each other. Among all his pieces we do not meet with *one* pure comedy of fancy, nor one of *pure* intrigue. These two characteristics—the fantastic or capricious, and the intriguing or intentional—are but the leading elements of the self-same idea of comedy; not two essentially different *forms of art,* but merely two aspects of *one and the same.* Accordingly, it is possible that comedies may exist in which the two elements are combined together in such equal proportions, that neither decidedly predominates. This epicene species will properly form, therefore, at once the mean and the transition between the two ordinary species. (p. 246)

It is necessary, in the first place, to remind our readers, that . . . the essence of the Comedy of Fancy does not merely consist in giving a wonderful shape to *external* nature, repugnant to the ordinary reality, but also in an *intrinsic* fancifulness, which consists essentially in the dominion of a pure contingency, subjective and objective, and therefore in an ideal humourousness, an intrinsic causelessness and aimlessness, whether resting ultimately in the play of chance, or in the caprices, mistakes, the folly, or perversity of men. Keeping this in mind we shall readily discern the fantastic colouring of [''Twelfth Night, or What You Will'']. There is nothing in the outward circumstances of the fable inconsistent with ordinary experience; for even the great resemblance of the twins, Viola and Sebastian, is nothing singular; the inner world, on the contrary, with its influence on the outer world, exhibits the most wonderful combination of rare freaks and complicated incidents. Here we at once recognize the fanciful element in the *whimsical* resolve of Viola to play the man, in the Duke's absurd passion for Olivia, and the no less capricious and sudden liking of the latter for the disguised Viola, and in the sudden change in the humour of both which leads to the marriage of Viola with the Duke, and of her brother Sebastian with Olivia; not less of caprice is there in the foolish freak of Sir Andrew Ague-cheek to become a suitor to Olivia: on the other hand, the complications brought about by mere chance, and the accidental delivery of Sebastian, and his finding Viola in Illyria, and meetings with Olivia, Sir Toby, and the rest. On the other hand, the *intriguing portion* of this play is easily recognized in the deliberateness with which Viola acts throughout, and with which she assumes her disguise and attempts to woo Olivia, and to cure her of her aversion for the Duke; but, above all, in the merry tricks which Maria, with the aid of Sir Toby and Fabian, play upon Sir Andrew and Malvolio.

The slightest consideration of the structure of this piece suffices to discover all the usual springs and motives of comedy in full action. Subjective caprice, folly, error, and perversity, are associated ith objective contingency and chance; the oddest freaks and humours, as well as the most deliberate intrigue, cross and re-cross each other, so as to form altogether a lively and diversified web. All the principal elements of the comic view are here combined; subjective caprice paralyses and is paralysed by objective chance; the well-laid intrigue is frustrated by chance, as in the duel between Viola and Sir Andrew, while in the relation of Viola and her brother to Olivia the results of accident are obviated by intrigue. Thus wonderfully does the dialectic of Shakspeare's irony maintain itself, dissolving perversity and folly, wilfulness and accident, as well as the mutual conflict of intrigues, into their proper worthlessness, so as to produce in the end universal harmony, and to give the victory to that which is just and rational.

But the more pregnantly, as it thus appears, the general comic view of things is expressed in the "Twelfth Night," the more difficult is it to ascertain the *special modification* which forms the ground-work of this particular comedy. In vain does the attentive reader search amid this combined mass of all the separate elements of the comic view of things for the slightest indication to guide him to discover where the preponderance lies. At the first glance it might almost be thought that the end in view was a comic exhibition of love, which, indeed, may well be the subject of Comedy, in so far as it forms an essential principle of human existence, and as life, when considered from it, assumes a peculiar aspect. But it is not the real, and in this sense so influential passion of love, that we have to do with in this piece. Love here is rather a mere humour of fancy—a chameleon-like play of the feelings, a motley garb which the soul puts on and off with the changing fashion of the hour. The Duke's passion for Olivia bursts out into flame for Viola as suddenly as love for him was kindled in her heart; Olivia's liking for Viola is easily satisfied with the substitution of her brother, who, on his part, has no scruple to be put in his sister's place, and Malvolio's and Sir Andrew's tenderness for Viola is, after all, but a bubble. And even Antonio's friendship for Sebastian possesses the same characters of caprice and groundlessness. Thus does the motley capriciousness of love appear the chief impulse in the merry game of life, which is here laid open to our sight, and we cannot for a moment recognize any more serious view of it in the ground-work of this piece. (pp. 246-48)

[Shakespeare] has allowed all the principal elements of the comic view of things to play their part in unison, and he has with wonderful ability placed them all in such balance that no one can claim the preponderance over the rest. With the same view, he has carefully avoided all allusion to any special modification of the general view, which could only have led the reader astray. It was his design to exhibit life exactly in the light that it appears to the comic apprehension of things, as a curiously inwrought but suggestive arabesque, as a realm of contradictions and semblance, and a fantastic, chaotic medley of accident and caprice, of error and perversity, which nothing but the dialectic of irony which rules in comedy can ever reduce to order.

With great propriety, it is only in the title that the author gives the slightest hint or information how the whole is to be taken. . . . ["Twelfth Night"] corresponds entirely to the spirit and essence of the piece, which sets forth life itself, like the Feast of the Three Kings, as a merry and fantastic lottery. The second title, "What You Will," is still more clear and significant. It refers, no doubt, to the relation between the public and the piece, but not in the inadmissible sense in which some have undertsood it, as if poesy could take any meaning and signification that the spectator might choose to assign to it. For such is never the case; for poesy has no other law of its creations than its own will, and whatever it presents, is, by an intrinsic necessity, even such as she offers it. But because the groundwork of the piece is the general comic view itself, and because it does not here assume any modification, but all its motives and elements are put forth at once, it is left to the spectator to select at pleasure from them all, and to give to the whole the special signification and reference that may suit him, and to

apply it according to his own personal humour and circumstances.

A closer consideration of the *leading characters* of the piece would, if it were necessary, still more clearly establish the interpretation we have just given of the groundwork of the piece. (pp. 248-49)

[All these] characters are thrown off in such easy flowing outline, and in such transparent colours, and harmonize so well together, that the slightest alteration would tear the varied, light, and airy, but ingenious web that is spun around them. In drawing the characters, Shakspeare has as it were but brushed off the light pollen of the flower—a ruder and a bolder hand would have torn the fine threads off its anthers. The clever contrast between the fool by profession, and the involuntary simpletons, Malvolio, Sir Andrew, and Sir Toby, is perhaps the most carefully worked out of the whole piece. While their own folly and absurdity, notwithstanding all their struggles, does but force the cap-and-bells over their ears, the clown in his adopted gown of motley moves with inimitable ease, and pins the pied lappets of his wit to the backs of all the rest. In his person the meaning of the entire poem is as it were concentrated. He alone with full consciousness looks upon life as a merry Twelfth-Night, on which every one must play his allotted part, so as to afford the greatest possible amusement and diversion, both to himself and others. What he wishes is nothing more nor less than to be a fool in the great fool's house, the world; hence he has an unconquerable aversion for all starched wisdom and reserve, and for all hollow unmeaning gravity, which can neither understand nor bear a joke, and on this account is he on such ill terms with Malvolio. He alone feels respect for his cap-and-bells; for he knows that fun and laughter, joke and jest, belong in short to life, and that there is more depth and meaning in witty folly like his own, than in the sour looks of so-called wise folk. And this is the profound seriousness which serves as a foil to this merry drama. (p. 250)

The chief moments of the *action* spontaneously evolve themselves out of the fundamental idea, and the characters which so aptly correspond to it. The characters fall into two principal groups; which again divide into subordinate ones, and occasionally mingling and approaching, act and react upon each other. On one side stands the Duke, with Olivia, Viola, and Sebastian; on the other, Sir Toby, Sir Andrew, and the household of Olivia. Chance, caprice, and intrigue—Viola's preservation and disguise—furnish the groundwork and plan of the fable. First of all, love and chance lead a merry game with the first group. Viola, who means only to toy with the love of others, falls herself into a heavy love sickness: the Duke, the slave of the scornful Olivia, is happily emancipated in order to work the cure of Viola; and Olivia, in punishment of her cruelty, falls desperately in love with one of her own sex;—all, however, is happily set right by chance, which introduces Sebastian on the scene. In the second of the principal groups, Sir Toby and Sir Andrew are in the most amusing manner lashed by their folly and perversity, while the silly and conceited Malvolio is made the laughing-stock of the Clown, Maria, and Fabian, and in order to heighten the complication, chance and mistake entangle Antonio and Sebastian in the capricious net wherein reason, prudence, and all the prosaic virtues of every-day life, are caught. But chance and caprice again disentangle the intricate web, and by a happy fate every one obtains his wish. The common-place prosaic Malvolio alone reaps his due in mockery and derision; for the unenthusiastic prose, which indeed is always immoral, meets with no mercy at the comic tribunal.

The *language* of the piece flows on full of grace and wit; and thus in this piece, again, we discover an intrinsic harmony between the characterization, action (invention), and diction. All springs up out of the view of life which is made the basis of the piece (ground-idea), with such organic necessity, that the composition appears not less masterly here than in Shakspeare's best tragedies.

As this admirable comedy stands between the two classes of Shakspeare's comedies, so also in date it belongs to the middle of our poet's career. It admits of no doubt that it was already written in 1599. In support of this view we may appeal to the language and versification, the tone and keeping of the whole, and especially to this view of life which is not usually met with in the young or old, but to the fresh and vigorous season at which the gifted mind hs gained the summit of life, and has not yet taken a step in descent. (pp. 251-52)

> Hermann Ulrici, *"Criticisms of Shakspeare's Dramas: 'Twelfth Night',"* in his Shakespeare's Dramatic Art: And His Relation to Calderon and Goethe, *translated by A.J.W. Morrison, Chapman Brothers, 1846, pp. 246-53.*

CHARLES KNIGHT (essay date 1842)

[*Knight, an English author and publisher, dedicated his career to providing education and knowledge to the Victorian middle class. In his discussion of* Twelfth Night, *first published in his 1842 edition of Shakespeare's works, he disputes several earlier commentators on a variety of points. He disproves August Wilhelm Schlegel (1808), who speculated that the play was Shakespeare's last, by citing John Manningham (1602) and by presenting internal evidence which links* Twelfth Night *to Shakespeare's happy comedies. Knight continues the discussion of the importance of Malvolio by declaring that the steward is neither central to the play nor to the comic subplot; he is a comical rather than a serious character, as "poetical as Don Quixote," to be both laughed at and pitied. Finally, Knight contests George Steevens (1772), who commented that Feste's final song is "utterly unconnected" with the play, terming it "the most philosophical clown's song upon record."*]

There is something to our minds very precious in that memorial of Shakspere which is preserved in the little Table-book of the Student of the Middle Temple: "Feb. 2, 1601 [2]. At our feast we had a play called *'Twelve night or what you will'*." And the actual roof under which the happy company of benchers, and barristers, and students first listened to that joyous and exhilarating play, full of the truest and most beautiful humanities, especially fitted for a season of cordial mirthfulness, is still standing; and we may walk into that stately hall and think,— Here Shakspere's 'Twelfth Night' was acted in the Christmas of 1601; and here its exquisite poetry first fell upon the ear of some secluded scholar, and was to him as a fragrant flower blooming amidst the arid sands of his Bracton and his Fleta; and here its gentle satire upon the vain and the foolish penetrated into the natural heart of some grave and formal dispenser of justice, and made him look with tolerance, if not with sympathy, upon the mistakes of less grave and formal fellow-men; and here its ever-gushing spirit of enjoyment,—of fun without malice, of wit without grossness, of humour without extravagance,—taught the swaggering, roaring, overgrown boy, miscalled student, that there were higher sources of mirth than affrays in Fleet Street, or drunkenness in Whitefriars. (pp. 238-39)

Accepting, though somewhat doubtingly, the statement of the commentators that 'Twelfth Night' was produced as late as 1614, Schlegel says, "If this was really the *last work* of Shakspere, as is affirmed, he must have enjoyed to the last the same *youthfulness of mind,* and carried with him to the grave the whole fulness of his talents." There is something very agreeable in this theory; but we can hardly lament that the foundation upon which it rests has been utterly destroyed. Shakspere did, indeed, carry "with him to the grave the whole fulness of his talents," but they were talents, perhaps not of a higher order, but certainly employed upon loftier subjects, than those which were called out by the delicious comedies of the Shakspere of forty. His "youthfulness of mind" too, even at this middle period of his life, is something very different from the honeyed luxuriance of his spring-time—more subjected to his intellectual penetration into the hidden springs of human action—more regulated by the artistical skill of blending the poetical with the comic, so that in fact they are not presented as opposite principles constrained to appear in a patchwork union, but are essentially one and the same creation of the highest imaginative power. We are told that of 'Twelfth Night' the scenes in which Malvolio, and Sir Toby, and Sir Andrew appear are Shakspere's *own.* The Duke, and Olivia, and Viola, and Sebastian, belong to some one else, it is said, because they existed, before he evoked them from their hiding-places, in the rude outlines of story-books without poetry, and comedies without wit. . . . Now it is [the] penetration of his own imaginative power in and through all his materials which renders it of little more account than as a matter of antiquarian curiosity where Shakspere picked up hints for the plots of his plays. He might have found the germ of Viola in Barnaby Rich; and he might have altogether invented Malvolio: but Viola and Malvolio are for ever indissolubly united, in the exact proportions in which the poetic and the comic work together for the production of a harmonious effect. The *neutral* title of 'Twelfth Night'—conveying as it does a notion of genial mirth—might warrant us in thinking that there was a preponderance of the comic spirit. Charles I. appears to have thought so, when, in his copy of the second edition of Shakspere, he altered the title with his own pen to that of '*Malvolio.*' But Malvolio is not the predominant idea of the comedy; nor is he of that exclusive interest that the whole action, even of the merely comic portions, should turn upon him. When Shakspere means one character to be the centre of the dramatic idea, he for the most part tells us so in his title:—Hamlet, Othello, Lear, Macbeth, Timon. Not one of the comedies has such a personal title, for the evident reason that the effect in them must mainly depend upon the harmony of all the parts, rather than upon the absorbing passion of the principal character. The 'Twelfth Night' is especially of this description. It presents us with the golden and the silver sides of human life,—the romantic and the humorous. But the two precious metals are moulded into one statue. (pp. 239-41)

It is impossible, we think, for one of ordinary sensibility to read through the first act without yielding himself up to the genial temper in which the entire play is written. "The sunshine of the breast" spreads its rich purple light over the whole champain, and penetrates into every thicket and every dingle. From the first line to the last—from the Duke's

> That strain again;—it had a dying fall,
>
> [I.i.4]

to the Clown's

> With hey, ho, the wind and the rain,
>
> [V.i.406]

there is not a thought, nor a situation, that is not calculated to call forth pleasurable feelings. The love-melancholy of the Duke is a luxurious abandonment to one pervading impression—not a fierce and hopeless contest with one o'ermastering passion. It delights to lie "canopied with bowers,"—to listen to "old and antique" songs, which dally with its "innocence,"—to be "full of shapes," and "high fantastical." The love of Viola is the sweetest and tenderest emotion that ever informed the heart of the purest and most graceful of beings with a spirit almost divine. Perhaps in the whole range of Shakspere's poetry there is nothing which comes more unbidden into the mind, and always in connexion with some image of the ethereal beauty of the utterer, than Viola's "She never told her love." The love of Olivia, wilful as it is, is not in the slightest degree repulsive. With the old stories before him, nothing but the refined delicacy of Shakspere's conception of the female character could have redeemed Olivia from approaching to the anti-feminine. But as it is we pity her, and we rejoice with her. These are what may be called the serious characters, because they are the vehicles for what we emphatically call the poetry of the play. But the comic characters are to us equally poetical—that is, they appear to us not mere copies of the representatives of temporary or individual follies, but embodyings of the universal comic, as true and as fresh to-day as they were two centuries and a half ago. Malvolio is to our minds as poetical as Don Quixote; and we are by no means sure that Shakspere meant the poor cross-gartered steward *only* to be laughed at, any more than Cervantes did the knight of the rueful countenance. He meant us to pity him, as Olivia and the Duke pitied him; for, in truth, the delusion by which Malvolio was wrecked, only passed out of the romantic into the comic through the manifestation of the vanity of the character in reference to his situation. But if we laugh at Malvolio we are not to laugh ill-naturedly, for the poet has conducted all the mischief against him in a spirit in which there is no real malice at the bottom of the fun. Sir Toby is a most genuine character,—one given to strong potations and boisterous merriment; but with a humour about him perfectly irresistible. His *abandon* to the instant opportunity of laughing at and with others is something so thoroughly English, that we are not surprised the poet gave him an English name. And like all genuine humorists Sir Toby must have his butt. What a trio is presented in that glorious scene of the second act, where the two Knights and the Clown "make the welkin dance;"—the humorist, the fool, and the philosopher!—for Sir Andrew is the fool, and the Clown is the philosopher. We hold the Clown's epilogue song to be the most philosophical Clown's song upon record; and a treatise might be written upon its wisdom. It is the history of a life, from the condition of "a little tiny boy," through "man's estate," to decaying age—"when I came unto my bed;" and the conclusion is, that what is true of the individual is true of the species, and what was of yesterday was of generations long past away—for

A great while ago the world begun.

[V.i.405]

Steevens says this "nonsensical ditty" is utterly unconnected with the subject of the comedy. We think he is mistaken. (pp. 241-43)

Charles Knight, "Supplementary Notice: 'Twelfth Night'," in The Comedies, Histories, Tragedies, and Poems of William Shakspere, Vol. III, *edited by Charles Knight, second edition, AMS Press, 1968, pp. 238-43.*

JOSEPH HUNTER (essay date 1845)

[*Although not the first to mention Malvolio's Puritanism, Hunter is the first to perceive the character, and the play as a whole, as a "grand attack" on Puritanism. According to Hunter, the gulling of Malvolio is designed to mark him and his fellow Puritans as objects of ridicule. Additional commentary on Malvolio as a Puritan is found in the excerpts by G. G. Gervinus (1849), William Archer (1884), Edward Dowden (1903), and Morris P. Tilley (1914). The essay from which the following excerpt is taken first appeared in Hunter's* New Illustrations of the Life, Studies and Writings of Shakespeare *in 1845.*]

Though in other plays of Shakespeare we have indirect and sarcastical remarks on the opinions or practices by which the Puritan party in the Reformed Church of England were distinguished, casually introduced, it is in [*Twelfth Night*] that we have his grand attack upon them; here in fact there is a systematic design of holding them up to ridicule, and of exposing to public odium what appeared to him the dark features of the Puritan character. Not only does this appear in particular expressions and passages in the play, but to those who are acquainted with the representations which their enemies made of the Puritan character, it will appear sufficiently evident that Shakespeare intended to make Malvolio an abstract of that character, to exhibit in him all the worst features, and to combine them with others which were simply ridiculous. The character which his mistress gives him is that he is 'sad and civil,' and that he 'suits as a servant with her fortune,' in her state of affliction. This shows that, previously to the introduction into his mind of the fantastic notions which afterwards possessed him, it was intended that he should be of a formal, grave, and solemn demeanour, and, as to his attire, dressed with a Quaker-like plainness, which would heighten the comic effect when afterwards he decked himself with all manner of finery when he sought to please, as he supposed, his mistress. As we proceed we find that he is a person not moved to cheerfulness by any innocent jest; he casts a malign look on every person and everything around him; he seeks to depreciate everything and everybody; even Feste, the poor innocent domestic fool, who plays his part admirably, is not too far removed below the line of a rational jealousy to be free from the effects of his malign disposition: 'I saw him put down the other day by an ordinary fool.' At the same time he has a most inordinate conceit of himself, 'sick of self-love;' and, without possessing any of the qualities by which a generous ambition may and does effect its designs, he aims at objects which he ought to have regarded as without the range of his desires, even so far as to seek to possess himself of the hand and fortune of his mistress. Under a show of humility he hides a proud and tyrannical heart; in what he says of Sir Toby he shows the petty tyranny which he will exercise when the golden opportunity shall arrive. He begrudges any little service to any one, even that belonging to the office which he holds; and when there is anything in which he is employed, where he has the chance of smoothening or roughening asperities, or when he has to form a judgement on what he witnesses, he invariably takes the unkinder part, and shows at the same time that he has pleasure in taking it. His first introduction to the audience is with the remark which he makes, 'Yes, and shall do till the pangs of death shake him;' and he makes his final exit exclaiming, 'I'll be revenged on the whole pack of you.' Such is Malvolio, who thus answers to his name, and who is perhaps one of the most finished characters drawn by Shakespeare, or any other dramatist. As the representative of a class, however, it is overcharged with what is unamiable. It was no part of the object of Shakespeare to soften or to mix those redeeming features which were to be found in the Puritan character. His object was to hold up the Puritan to aversion; and the moment he entered, the spectators would perceive by his attire the kind of person brought before them, or, if that were not sufficient, there was no mistaking the words of Maria: 'Sometimes he is a kind of Puritan.'

In Malvolio's general character the intention was to make the Puritan odious; in the strategem of which he is the victim to make him ridiculous. It seems as if it were originally the poet's intention to deliver him up into the hands of Falstaff. Sir Toby is corpulent and witty, needy, dishonest, shifting, drunken, and 'much a liar,' with all Falstaff's address in extricating himself from a difficulty. Several of his expressions are quite in the Falstaff vein. Strip Falstaff, in short, of his military character and court brocade, and send him from the taverns of London to a well-replenished hall in the country, and we have the character of Sir Toby. In his companion Sir Andrew we have Slender again under a new name, even to the trick of *quoting,* the main characteristic of Slender. A stroke or two may be perceived, just sufficient to discriminate them, but such strokes, if such exist, are few; so few that there can be hardly a doubt that the poet's original intention, or perhaps a suggestion made to him, was that the Puritan should be delivered up into the hands of Falstaff. Falstaff's aera was, however, too decidedly fixed, and this rendered it expedient to invent a new name, and perhaps to introduce certain new features into the character. (pp. 397-98)

> *Joseph Hunter, in an extract from* A New Variorum Edition of Shakespeare: Twelfe Night, or, What You Will, *Vol. XIII,* edited by Horace Howard Furness, *J. B. Lippincott Company, 1901, pp. 397-98.*

GULIAN C. VERPLANCK (essay date 1847)

[*Verplanck was a nineteenth-century American lawyer, journalist, politician, scholar, and editor, and one of the earliest American Shakespearean scholars. His major contribution to American letters was a three-volume biographical edition of Shakespeare's plays in 1847. Here he praises the characterization of Malvolio and, like Joseph Hunter (1845), compares Toby with Falstaff.*]

[*Twelfth Night,*] with all its admirable points, and its delightful variety of poetic feeling and humorous invention, yet certainly has not those indications of the fulness of its author's talent which may be traced in his later works, even in those not of the highest comparative rank. After the succession of his great tragedies, *Othello, Macbeth, Lear,* including the deeper sentiment and sadder philosophy at that time infused into his before merely dramatic *Hamlet,* he seems to have written nothing which does not retain some trace, in thought and expression, of that storm-like inspiration which had thus swept over his mind. The poetry of the *Twelfth Night* is exquisite in fancy and feeling, but has none of that intense idiosyncrasy of thought and expression—that unparalleled fusion of the intellectual with the passionate—which discriminates the poetry of *Lear* from that of the *Merchant of Venice,* not only in the general spirit, but in more transient images and phrases, and even single epithets. All this does not detract from the exquisite delicacy and grace of the poetic scenes of this comedy, but still it marks that the very highest and most peculiar powers of the author's mind had not yet been so developed and made familiar by use, and his genius had become (as it did afterwards) wholly "indued unto that element." (pp. 5-6)

The *Twelfth Night* is wholly pleasurable in its intent and in its feeling, the gay and the ludicrous predominating over and yet assimilating with its higher dramatic poetry; because the passion of that is not of strong emotion, but of fancy and sentiment. Thus its characters claim immediate brotherhood with that throng of comic inventions which seem to have been spontaneously developed in the Poet's mind between his thirtieth and fortieth year, amid the excitement and variety of a great city, when he probably mixed widely in various society, and enjoyed the passing scenes of "many-coloured life" with the joyous buoyancy of youth and health, and successful genius; at the same time that he scanned the foibles and caprices of his companions with an artist's eye.

I do not maintain that all these indications of the period of the author's life at which he wrote this agreeable and beautiful drama are so conclusive as alone to settle that question definitively; for the highest probabilities of this nature are often refuted by stubborn facts; but I am glad to find that this view of the subject, which appears to throw some light on the intellectual as well as the personal history of the great dramatist, is confirmed by the recently discovered evidence of facts. Mr. Collier first ascertained "that it was acted on the celebration of the Readers' Feast, at the Middle Temple, on Feb. 2, 1602. The fact of its performance we have on the evidence of an eye-witness, who seems to have been a barrister, and whose 'Diary,' in his own hand-writing, is preserved in the British Museum [see excerpt above by Manningham, 1602]. (p. 6)

Thus we may safely fix the date of this comedy about the year 1600 or 1601, and class it among the later productions of that period of Shakespeare's life when his mind most habitually revelled in humorous delineation, while his luxuriant fancy, turning aside from the sterner and painful passions, shed its gayest tints over innumerable forms of grace and beauty. He seems, by his title of the *Twelfth Night,* to apprise his audience of the general character of this agreeable and varied comedy—a notice intelligible enough at that time, and still not without its significance in a great part of Europe, though quite otherwise among our un-holiday-keeping people cn this side of the Atlantic. The *Twelfth Night* (twelfth after Christmas) was, in the olden times, the season of universal festivity—of masques, pageants, feasts, and traditional sports. This comedy then would not disappoint public expectation, when it was found to contain a delightful combination of the delicate fancy and romantic sentiment of the poetic masque, with a crowd of revelling, laughing, or laugh-creating personages, whose truth all would recognize, and whose spirit and fun no gravity could resist. He gave to these the revelling spirit, and the exaggeration of character necessary for the broadest comic effect, but still kept them from becoming mere buffoon masquers by a truth of portraiture which shows them all to be drawn from real life. Malvolio—the matchless Malvolio—was not only new in his day, to comic delineation of any sort, but I believe has never since had his fellow or his copy, in any succeeding play, poem, essay, or novel. The gravity, the acquirement, the real talent and accomplishment of the man, all made ludicrous, fantastical and absurd, by his intense vanity, is as true a conception as it is original and droll, and its truth may still be frequently attested by actual comparison with real Malvolios, to be found everywhere, from humble domestic life up to the high places of learning, of the state, and even of the church. Sir Toby certainly comes out of the same associations where the Poet saw Falstaff hold his revels. He is not Sir John, nor a fainter sketch of him, yet with an odd sort of family likeness to him. Dryden and other dramatists have felicitated themselves upon success in grouping together their comic underplots with their more heroic personages. But here, all, grave and gay, the lovers, the laughers, and the laughed-at, are made to harmonize in one scene and one common purpose. I cannot help adding—though perhaps it may be a capricious over-refinement—that to my mind this comedy resembles *Macbeth,* in one of the marked characteristics of that great drama; appearing, like it, to have been struck out at a heat, as if the whole plot, its characters and dialogue, had presented themselves at once, in one harmonious group, before the ''mind's eye'' of the Poet, previously to his actually commencing the formal business of writing, and bearing no indication either of an original groundwork of incident, afterwards enriched by the additions of a fuller mind, or of thoughts, situations, and characters accidentally suggested, or growing unexpectedly out of the story, as the author proceeded. (pp. 6-7)

> *Gulian C. Verplanck, in his introductory remarks to "Twelfth Night," in* Shakespeare's Plays, with His Life: Comedies, Vol. II, *edited by Gulian C. Verplanck, Harper & Brothers, Publishers, 1847, pp. 5-7.*

G. G. GERVINUS   (essay date 1849-50)

[*One of the most widely read Shakespearean critics of the latter half of the nineteenth century, the German critic Gervinus was praised by such eminent authors of his day as Edward Dowden, F. J. Furnivall, and James Russell Lowell; however, he is little known in the English-speaking world today. Like his predecessor Hermann Ulrici, Gervinus wrote in the tradition of the "philosophical criticism" developed in Germany in the mid-nineteenth century. Under the influence of August Wilhelm Schlegel's literary theory and Georg Wilhelm Friedrich Hegel's philosophy, German critics like Gervinus tended to focus their analyses around a search for the literary work's organic unity and ethical import. Gervinus contended that Shakespeare's works contained a rational ethical system independent of any religion, in contrast to Ulrici, who believed that Shakespeare's morality was basically Christian. Gervinus's comment that Orsino is "more in love with his love than with his mistress" is perhaps the most often-repeated comment on the character. He praises the unified structure of the play and stresses Shakespeare's achievement in the delineation of human nature. Of Feste's role, he notes that the clown is not part of the play's action, but is a commentator on the action of the other characters and is conscious of his superiority unlike any other of Shakespeare's fools. In this Gervinus echoes the interpretation of Ulrici (1839). The essay from which the following excerpt is drawn first appeared in German as* Shakespeare *in 1849-50.*]

[Manningham] was struck with the similarity of ['Twelfth-Night'] to Plautus' 'Menaechmi' and the Italian play *Gl' Inganni* [see excerpt above, 1602]. . . . It is hard to say to which of these sources Shakespeare is most indebted, as he in truth stands equally remote from all; so remote indeed, that we may leave the connection of his comedy with them wholly unexamined. The comic elements are entirely Shakespeare's own; the love-affairs are treated in those tales and comedies so superficially, so coarsely and so dissimilarly in every way, that the bare externals of the plot can alone have afforded the poet a mere suggestion; namely the series of confusions between the duke who loves the countess, and the countess who loves the page, and the page who loves the duke, until the brother of the page steps between, and the difficulties vanish. Even in this circumstance, the errors which arise from the similarity of the twins Sebastian and Viola, and which call to mind the 'Menaechmi,' are Shakespeare's addition. By this addition the

scene acquires greater extent; it connects the main action with the occurrences between Sir Toby and Sir Andrew, the intricacy and liveliness is increased, and the wholly unexpected conclusion, the surprising and exciting catastrophe is gained by it, and this contrasts peculiarly with the quiet issue of 'As you Like It.'

However successfully the plot is woven out of these complexitites, no importance is laid upon it, as is the case in all Shakespeare's more finished works. The progress of the poet compared to the time when he executed the 'Comedy of Errors,' may be proved here by a tangible instance. That was truly a comedy of intrigue; in [a previous] discussion of the play we . . . indicated how much unnaturalness was comprehended in this mere definition, and to how many improbabilities the writer was exposed. Shakespeare has here avoided this. The similarity of the twins pre-supposed, the possibility of the mistake is accounted for by the fact that Viola has intentionally put on the same dress as her brother; the probability of the meeting is a matter of course, as both, after they have suffered shipwreck, would from their station and acquaintance seek safety at the court of the inhospitable Illyria. The unnaturalness of the seeking brother not being reminded at the first mistake of the one sought, is here wholly avoided. . . . The matter in question in this play, as in all others, is not the plot, the outward web of the action, but the actors themselves and their nature and motives; it is not the effect, but the cause and the agencies. If we examine these, the resemblance of the story with that of the 'Comedy of Errors' is at once wholly lost sight of, and we discover rather an affinity between this piece and 'Love's Labour's Lost,' where the importance of the plot was so small, and so remarkable a stress was laid upon the motives for action. (pp. 423-24)

As in 'Love's Labour's Lost,' so in 'What you Will,' two different strata of society are represented—characters of a more refined organization, and caricatures in which the vices of human nature grow as luxuriantly as weeds. Just as in 'Love's Labour's Lost,' taking our start from glaring sketches of this sort, we more readily found the key to the less obvious characters of the nobler personages, so is it also here; these characters are Shakespeare's addition, and precisely in them must he all the more distinctly indicate the reason for which he added them, and brought them to bear on the original part of the story. In the centre of this lower group stands Malvolio. He is an austere puritan; his crossed garters point him out as such; to him therefore the demand, required of him from the clown in his character of parson, is doubly wicked, namely that he should hold the opinions of Pythagoras on the transmigration of souls. Pedantic, more than economical, conscientious and true, grave and sober, he is a servant suitable to Olivia's melancholy bias, to her moral severity, and to her maidenly reserve; she prefers him, and he ingratiates himself into her favour, he watches an opportunity for punishing the rough youngsters, who make an alehouse of his lady's palace; he acts the talebearer and informer; his eye is everywhere; he brings Fabian out of favour about a bear-baiting; the captain, who saved Viola, is scarcely landed, when Malvolio has him apprehended on account of a quarrel. He regards himself as far superior to the society in his mistress' house; he considers the wise men, who can be pleased with fools and their jests no better than fools themselves; he looks down contemptuously on the 'shallow things,' Toby, Fabian, and Maria, who persecute him with the bitterest malevolence on account of his time-serving, his affectation, and his assumed importance. . . . He regards the happiness, into the haven of which he thinks to steer in perfect security, as the direct work of the care of Jove for his highly important person, when in fact only the 'shallow things,' whom he considered so far beneath him, are making him run aground on the shoals of his own self-conceit. Self-love is, therefore, in this comical character also the distinguishing feature of his nature; it has degenerated into that degree of self-conceit which fancies itself able to master all, because it sees itself not only at the aim of perfection, but also of the happiness which belongs to this perfection. In Malvolio, therefore, this self-conceit imagines a 'desert,' without a shadow of reality having given cause for it, and even without an emotion of his own love being called into play. Like the false love of glory in those caricatures of Holofernes and Armado, his self-conceit had instinctively grown up to such a degree that it is unconscious of itself, that nothing brings it to self-knowledge or improvement; the follies and caprices which spring up in him grow into gigantic size, whether trampled down or nurtured.

The reverse to this caricature is the squire Sir Andrew. He is a melancholy picture of what man would be without any self-love, the source indeed of so many weaknesses. To this straight-haired country squire, life consists only in eating and drinking; eating beef, he himself fears, has done harm to his wit; in fact he is stupid even to silliness, totally deprived of all passion, and thus of all self-love or self-conceit. . . . He repeats indeed after Sir Toby that he too was adored by any; but we see, while he says it, by the stupid face, that on *this* point beyond any other he is totally without experience. He has never been so conceited as to believe himself seriously regarded by any: his mistrust of himself is as great as his mistrust of others is small. . . . Sir Andrew is at best to be compared with his cousin Slender, whose love of bear-baiting he also shares. His apathy and cowardice are all the more plainly brought to life from his quarrelsome disposition, and from the disputes into which he is led. . . . Between [Sir Andrew and Malvolio], in a skilfully sketched, though rather remote contrast, the poet has placed Sir Toby, who cheats his friend of his horses and ducats, whilst he decoys him with the prospect of his niece's hand. A drunkard, a coarse realist of the lowest sort, he yet possesses a slyness in seeing through the weaknesses of men who do not lie beyond his range of vision; rough and awkward in his manners, he yet so far knows how to assume the fashions of the town as to impose on Sir Andrew; impudent enough to make an alehouse of Olivia's palace, and to take no heed when she orders him to leave, he yet knows how to keep on good footing with the servants of the house. He has nothing of the high soaring vanity of Malvolio, but yet he looks down with blunt pride not merely upon Sir Andrew and Malvolio, but upon the clown and Olivia; and he believes himself adored by Maria, the only one whose volubility gives him the impression of superiority. However, his egotism manifests itself in that dangerous manner in which Falstaff considered inferior minds as his natural prey; he avails himself of the weaknesses of others, that he may play them deceitful or teasing tricks. (pp. 425-28)

As in 'Love's Labour's Lost,' the caricatures of the burlesque part of the comedy are placed by the side of a series of characters in whom the same fault lies concealed, which in those caricatures shot forth like a wild growth of nature into extravagant forms; a fault, indiscernible outwardly from the veil of refined cultivation, but in its nature not dissimilar from that manifested in them; so it is in this play. This same Olivia, to whom Malvolio's thoughts soar in laughable fashion, attracts also the eyes and the heart of the duke Orsino, a man who is so endowed with personal pretensions and excellencies, that

he seems separated from Malvolio by a still greater distance than the King of Navarre in the other play is from Armado. . . . A tender poetic soul, the Duke with delicate feeling has made his favourite poetry the popular song of the spinning-room, which is more exquisite and simple in its touching power than aught that lyric art has created in the erotic style; he revels even to satiety in the enjoyment of these soft heart-felt tunes, which are like an echo to the heart. This proneness to go to extremes in his love, in his melancholy, and in all inclinations which are congenial to and in accordance with his ruling passion, is expressed in all that the Duke says and does. . . . But this very inclination to exaggeration induces us to look more closely into the genuineness of this most genuine love. It almost seems as if the Duke were more in love with his love, than with his mistress; as if like Romeo with Rosalind he rather speculated in thought over his fruitless passion, than felt it actually in his heart; as if his love were rather a production of his fancy than a genuine feeling. It startles us, that just that which in a paroxysm of self-loving commendation he said of his own love compared to the love of woman, he himself contradicts in a calm thoughtful moment, when he says to Viola that the fancies of men are more giddy than women's are, more longing, but yet more wavering, sooner lost and worn. Thus is it with his own. To give an air of importance to their love, to pride themselves and to presume upon it, is in truth the habit or rather the bad habit of men. Viola tells him, what is just his case, that men make more words about their love, that they say more, swear more, but their shows are more than will, for they prove much in their vows, but little in their love. Olivia must feel this throughout the urgent suit of the Duke; she calls his love heresy, and turns coldly away from his seeming fervour. (pp. 429-30)

The fool, no less than Olivia, has seen through the Duke's disease, and he tells him of an excellent remedy. 'I would have men of such constancy,' he says, 'put to sea, that their business might be everything, and their intent everywhere; for that's it, that always makes a good voyage of nothing.' Thus, those natures which, forgetful of all else, become absorbed in one constant affection, he would drive into the very element of adventure, that they might forget their ponderings upon one intent, that in a natural course of life they might be delivered from the hard service of one idol, that that freshness might be restored to them which permits a man even in matters of love to reach his aim more quickly and easily, while the weak votaries of love forfeit their end. Shakespeare has illustrated this in the young Sebastian. For he is just such a youth, free-hearted, un-injured, and virgin-like, who, seeking adventures with his sister, apparently without any definite object, undertook a voyage, suffered shipwreck, and proved himself in the shipwreck a man of courage and hope, a man provident in peril; being cast ashore, he laments for his sister with the utmost tenderness; but, like his sister, he quickly and practically embraces a plan for his immediate future, appearing throughout quick in resolve, vigorous, never weary, and free in mind and action. Inoffensive, trusting to fortune and his good nature, he receives a purse from his captain, without knowing how he is to repay it; he gives a liberal present out of it to be free from a troublesome companion; unexpectedly involved in an adventure of the most strange, most magic nature, he enters into it with deliberate circumspection; drawn into the quarrel of the squires, he at one stroke gives back the blows due, and proves to Olivia that he would know how to free her from her dissolute guests. The charm exercised by a nature at once so fresh and so victorious, Olivia is not alone to experience. The poet has taken care that the instinctive feeling of the Countess should not be construed into womanly weakness, for men of strong nature entirely share it with her. The rough captain Antonio is attracted to this youth by an equally blind impulse of pleasure and love. . . . (p. 431)

There yet remains to us to say a word upon the fool Feste, to whom the poet has in this play assigned a very peculiar position. He appears quite out of all the action, out of the reach both of chance and of the passions which are at work throughout the play. We could almost fancy that he was brought into the different scenes only to act the witty entertainer, or, as he calls himself, the corrupter of words, or indeed that his part was designed for a favourite singer. It is striking that in all the comedies which we have been now examining—indeed in all Shakespeare's plays of this period, in 'Henry VIII.,' in 'Measure for Measure,' in 'Hamlet,' 'Othello,' and 'Caesar'—the musical element appears. . . . [The] fool appears as a singer by profession, singing with equal skill love-songs of a merry and tragic nature, comic jigs and heart-rending canons. With all this he is a careless cheerful fellow, troubling himself about nothing, placed in the midst of the busy company, a wise fool among the foolish wise. No other of Shakespeare's fools is so conscious of his superiority as this one. He says it indeed too often, and he shows still oftener that his foolish wisdom is in fact no folly, that it is a mistake to call him a fool, that the cowl does not make the monk, that his brain is not so motley as his dress. The poet has not in this play brought the words and actions of the fool into relation with the one main idea of the piece, but he has opposed him rather to the separate characters in separate expressions. It is in this play that that instructive passage occurs, which designates the fool's difficult office as demanding that he should 'observe their mood on whom he jests, the quality of persons, and the time, and check at every feather that comes before his eye;' this is exactly the part which Shakespeare has made the fool here play. He is fit for anything; he lives with each after his own fashion, knowing their weaknesses, considering their nature, carefully adapting himself to the mood of the moment. (pp. 437-38)

In common with the 'Merry Wives of Windsor' and the 'Taming of the Shrew,' 'What You Will' is the purest and merriest comedy which Shakespeare has written. In the 'Comedy of Errors,' in 'Love's Labour's Lost,' in 'As You Like It,' in 'Much Ado About Nothing,' tragic incidents interrupt the course of comedy. Here there is nothing of the kind; even the sentimental and at first somewhat elegiac connection between the lovers takes a cheerful turn from the mistakes between Sebastian and Viola. In this manner the burlesque part of the comedy becomes conspicuous, reaching such an extent of excess and wantonness, that even Fabian declared that the self-conceit of Malvolio, represented on the theatre, would appear an improbable invention, and he calls the absurdity of Sir Andrew suitable to a Carnival frolic. . . . [The] piece in truth is constituted throughout to make a strong impression of the maddest mirth. Rightly conceived and acted by players who even in caricature do not miss the line of beauty, it has an incredible effect. (p. 439)

> G. G. Gervinus, "Comedies: 'Twelfth Night: Or,
> What You Will'," in his Shakespeare Commentaries,
> translated by F. E. Bunnètt, revised edition, smith,
> Elder, & Co., 1877, pp. 423-40.

F. KREYSSIG (essay date 1862)

[*Like Hermann Ulrici (1839) and G. G. Gervinus (1849-50), Kreyssig praises the unity and structure of* Twelfth Night. *He also concurs with Joseph Hunter (1845) in proposing that* Twelfth Night *is an indication of Shakespeare's aversion to the Puritan movement. Feste's masquerade as Sir Topas, is, according to Kreyssig, a satire of the Puritan clergy. The following excerpt is taken from an essay which was originally published in German in Kreyssig's* Vorlesungen über Shakespeare, seine Zeit und seine Werke *in 1862.*]

[In *Twelfth Night*] Shakespeare erected the exquisite, graceful structure of the most perfect of his comedies, and at the same time, by the most complete scheme and by a rarely full range of characters, he drew the attention from external circumstances and concentrated it on the inner life of the action, and by giving an absolute unity of interest he breathed into it all the true dramatic soul. That saying of Goethe: 'That in every finished work of Shakespeare there could be found a central idea,' here finds its justification in fullest measure. Let it be supposed that Shakespeare had set himself the task to show, within the limit of one treatment, like a recapitulation, every combination of comedies in one single comedy, and it would not be difficult to prove that in *Twelfth Night* the task had been successfully accomplished. Just consider, for a moment, the three wooers who aspire to the fair Olivia's hand, observe Olivia's relation to Viola, and enlarge this series of enamoured situations by glancing at Maria's victorious campaign against the bibulous Knight, and we shall have a shaded series, tolerably complete, of amourous folly or foolish amourousness in an ascending scale from the wooing of a charming woman by a feeble-minded, senseless ninnyhammer, on through the self-seeking of inane puffed-up stupidity and of downright shrewd intriguing, up to the fantastic youthful follies of natures, noble and gifted, to be sure, but untried and still ignorant of their own quality. And inasmuch as it is not Shakespeare's wont to base the action of his comedies on the requirements of frivolous wit or even of malicious slander, thus in this play we do not fail to hear the lovely ground-tone, which at first softly sounding, at last rises triumphantly above the chaos of clashing tones, and in the most delightful way harmonises all discords; I mean the portrayal of deep and true love in sound healthy natures. Then at the close this victory puts an end to all mistakes within and without, and leaves us in a mood of serene and joyous peace, an emotion which it is the aim of true comedy to produce, just as the subsidence of passion into a manly resignation is that of tragedy. (p. 381)

In Feste, who is far more deeply involved in the plot than Touchstone, or any others of his class (except, perhaps, the Fool in *Lear*), we have the accomplished Fool, the allowed Merryman, in the full exercise of his skill; but, in accordance with the innocent and joyous character of the comedy, without the stinging satire which we feel so keenly in *As You Like It*. On the contrary, it is his aim by ingenious jokes and harmless teasings to add spice to the flagging entertainment, and, at the same time, he is at full liberty accurately to gauge the characters about him, and as opportunity gives benefit to proffer jestingly to them his opinion of them; even this, however, he does with the greatest prudence; and (which is noteworthy) he speaks ill of no one behind the back. Thus it is that he is become perfect in his difficult position, and well deserves Viola's praise: 'This fellow is wise enough to play the fool,' etc. [III.i.60]. In this sense he may well say to Olivia: '*Cucullus non facit monachum*, I wear not motley in my brain.' Of course he is placed in the sharpest contrast to Malvolio, the personification of insipid arrogance. It would, indeed, be a radical defect in that insufferable pedant if he could take a joke; if he did not invariably regard bird-bolts as cannon-bullets as soon as ever they hit his worthy person. . . . It is against this principle, therefore, of which Malvolio is the representative, and against this principle alone that Feste makes an earnest front. His remarks about the changeable taffeta of the Duke's doublet, and about Olivia's weak mourning for her brother, are purely good humoured; he never elsewhere indulges his satire against classes or ranks, unless it be where he compares husbands and fools to pilchards and herrings. But when it comes to flouting the arrogant pietistic steward, who would banish cakes and ale and witty foolery, then he marshalls all his talents, and, when donning the gown of [Sir Topas], permits himself to utter the first and only sharp thrust at earnest and dangerous people: 'I would I were the first that ever dissembled in such a gown.' The passage is all the more striking, inasmuch as the whole disguise, as Maria afterwards remarks, is needless. It may be incidentally remarked, that throughout the conjuration scene the Fool imitates the unctuous tone of the Puritanic divines, whereas the priest, to whom Olivia entrusts her fate, is to be regarded clearly as a Catholic monk; a further indication of Shakespeare's almost instinctive repugnance to the whole canting and pietistic Puritanical movement which, shortly after his death, proscribed his masterpieces, together with all other sports of merry England, and to whose folly it is to be ascribed that only by wading through the slough of the demoralised comedy of the Restoration, could England find the way to return to her Shakespeare. (p. 404)

> *F. Kreyssig, in extracts, translated by Horace Howard Furness, in* A New Variorum Edition of Shakespeare: Twelfe Night, or, What You Will, Vol. XIII, *edited by Horace Howard Furness, J. B. Lippincott Company, 1901, pp. 381, 404.*

THOMAS KENNY (essay date 1864)

[*Kenny's guarded praise of* Twelfth Night *is reminiscent of several Neoclassical commentaries in its disapproval of the extravagant and improbable elements of the play. He also finds Malvolio's punishment "coarse and excessive" and in this he echoes the comments of Charles Lamb (1822). Kenny differs from the majority of critics in his low opinion of the characterization in the play. The following excerpt was first published in Kenny's* The Life and Genius of Shakespeare *in 1864.*]

The grace and vigour of Shakespeare's genius are frequently observable throughout the whole of the incidents of [*Twelfth Night*]; but we cannot class this work among his highest achievements, and the admiration with which we regard it is by no means free from any qualification. There is much of extravagance and improbability in the development of its more romantic incidents, and it thus frequently becomes less purely creative and less absolutely truthful than less striking productions of the poet's genius. The treatment of the story is sometimes manifestly melodramatic, as, for instance, in the appearance of Antonio, and his arrest by the officers; and, we think we may add, in the hurried and strange marriage contract between Olivia and Sebastian. The disguise of Viola is one of those artifices which are only possible in the large domain of poetry; and the freedom of poetry itself seems somewhat abused in the representation of the supposed complete likeness between her and her brother. The merely comic business of the play is more naturally executed. Many people will probably regard the misadventures of the befooled and infatuated Malvolio as its most vigorous and amusing episode. But we cannot help thinking that the punishment to which the vanity of Malvolio is exposed, is somewhat coarse and excessive. In spite of the bad character which he bears in his very name, there is nothing

in his conduct, as far as we can see, to justify the unscrupulous persecution of his tormentors. . . . We confess that, as exemplifications of Shakespeare's wonderful comic power, we prefer to this humiliation and discomfiture of Malvolio the scenes in which Sir Toby and Sir Andrew make the welkin ring to the echo of their uproarious merriment. It is often in lighter sketches of this description that the hand of Shakespeare is most distinguishable and most inimitable; and this triumphant protest against the pretensions of a narrow and jealous austerity will no doubt last as long as social humour forms one of the elements of human life:—'Dost thou think, because thou art virtuous, there shall be no more cakes and ale?' We find in *Twelfth Night* no striking indication of Shakespeare's power in the delineation of character. Such a display was, perhaps, hardly compatible with the general predominance of the lighter romantic element throughout the whole work. The passion of the Duke for Olivia is neither very deep nor very dramatic. It is merely dreamy, restless, longing, and enthralling desire. It is the offspring of a mood which, we cannot help thinking, was specially familiar to the poet himself; and it seems directly akin to the state of feeling which he has revealed in his Sonnets. . . . Neither Viola nor Olivia can be ranked among his finest female characters. The former has a difficult and a somewhat unnatural part to sustain; and although she fills it with considerable brilliancy and spirit, she scarcely enlists our strongest sympathies in her favour. The allusion, however, to her untold love is one of the bright passages in Shakespeare's drama, and will for ever form for tender hearts a cherished remembrance. The character of Olivia suffers much more from the perplexities or temptations to which she becomes exposed, and she certainly fails to display, amidst those trials, the highest maidenly purity and refinement. *Twelfth Night* is, we think, on the whole, one of the bright, fanciful, and varied productions of Shakespeare's less earnest dramatic mood; but it possesses neither complete imagination nor complete natural truthfulness; and it seems to us to be more or less deficient throughout in consistency, in harmony, in the depth and firmness of touch, which distinguish the finer creations of his genius. (pp. 381-82)

> *Thomas Kenny, in an extract from* A New Variorum Edition of Shakespeare: Twelfe Night, or, What You Will, Vol. XIII, *edited by Horace Howard Furness, J. B. Lippincott Company, 1901, pp. 381-82.*

E. MONTÉGUT (essay date 1867)

[*Montégut is the first critic to present the theory that* Twelfth Night *is a masquerade and carnival farce. In a comment that will be repeated in twentieth-century criticism, Montégut asserts the importance of the ambiguity in the play and discusses how the characters are "slaves" of their individual defects and perspectives. For additional discussions on the theme of self-deception in the play, see the excerpts by E. K. Chambers (1907), Joseph H. Summers (1955), and Bertrand Evans (1960). The following excerpt was originally published in French in Montégut's* Oeuvres complètes de Shakspeare *in 1867.*]

Twelfth Night is a masquerade, slightly grotesque, as befits a play whereof the title recalls one of those festivals which were most dear to the jocund humour of our forbears. This festival was the day whereon in every family a king for the nonce was crowned after he had been chosen by lot, sometimes it fell to a child to be the ruler over the whole family, again a servant was crowned by his master, for the moment it was the world turned upside down, a rational hierarchy topsy-turvy, authority created by chance, and the more grotesque the surprise, the merrier the festival. . . . The whole episode of the wild orgy of Toby and of the crotchety Malvolio is drawn incomparably to the life; Shakespeare has there, so to speak, surpassed himself, for he has there shown himself a consummate master of a species of composition which has been many a time denied to him, namely, comedy. That Shakespeare, in the comedy of fancy, of caprice, of adventure, is without a peer is acknowledged by every one; but he has been gravely reproached with not being able to stand a comparison with those masters who draw their resources exclusively from those faculties whence alone true comedy springs; in a word, with not being sufficiently in his comedies exclusively comic. The episodes of Sir Toby and Malvolio correct this judgement of error; Rabelais is not more of a buffoon, and Molière not more exclusively comic than Shakespeare in these two episodes.

The sentimental and romantic portions of the play are stamped with that inimitable grace which especially characterises Shakespeare; but even here this comedy remains faithful to its title of *Twelfth Night;* for ambiguity still reigns sovereign mistress there, and treats the real world under its double form, the reality of nature and that of society, like a carnival farce. The characters instigated by their whims or the spitefulness of chance are deceived as to condition and sex and become involved in an imbroglio of charming and dangerous complications. Beneath the real piece, another can be read at the will of the reader, just as by certain artifices one image may be seen beneath another image, and herein lies the delicate point of this charming work for which that famous saying appears to have been expressly written: 'Glide, mortals, bear not heavily.' A surly reader or a stern critic might say that this poetic Viola is merely an amiable adventuress. And her brother, Sebastian, her living mirror, so charming that the friendships which he inspires cling to him like lichens on a rock—is he not too womanish? in sooth, he needed but the whim of donning woman's clothes to become *una feminuccia*, as the Italians say in their expressive diminutives. Of the Countess Olivia, with her singular mistakes, may we not also have some doubts? We might suspect that Toby, with his unmannerly perverted wit, who knew his world and fathomed his niece, was not far wrong when he said she was a 'Cataian,' herein alluding to that land of Cathay whence came, with the Italian renaissance, and that princess Angelique through whom Medor was made happy and Roland desperate, all the magicians, sorceresses, enchantresses, and sirens who ruled all hearts in the chivalric literature of the sixteenth century. But, hush! youth, grace, beauty, with all their dreams, their illusions and their charms, enwrap these adventures. We are here in fairyland; why should we try to discover the real nature of these personages? They are the children of the imagination, of caprice, graceful fairies, sylphs and imps, *piccolini stregoni*.

In Shakespeare's plays philosophy is rarely lacking; is there then a philosophy in this poetic masquerade? Ay, there is one here, and to its fullest depth. In two words it is: we are all, in varying degrees, insane; for we are all the slaves of our defects, which are genuine chronic follies, or else we are the victims of dreams which attack us like follies at an acute stage. Man is held in leash by his imagination, which deceives him even to the extent of reversing the normal conditions of nature and the laws of reality. An image, ordinary but true, of man in every station is this silly Malvolio, whose folly unavowed and secretly cherished, bursts forth on a frivolous pretext. Malvolio is, no question, a fool, but this sly waiting woman who ensnares him by an all-revealing strategem, is she herself exempt from the folly of which she accuses Malvolio? and if the steward believes himself beloved by his mistress, does she not pursue the same ambitious dream of making a match with Sir Toby, who, however degraded and drunken, is at least a gentleman and the uncle of Olivia? It is the same dream under very different conditions which Viola pursues,—a dream which would never have come true, if luck had not extricated her from the *cul de sac* whither her temerity had led her. What is to be said of Olivia but that her imagination, suddenly smitten, could go so far astray as to stifle in her the instinct which should have revealed to her that Viola was of her own sex? The friendship of Antonio for Sebastian,—a friendship which involves him in perils so easily foreseen,—is a sentiment exactly twin with the love of Olivia for Cesario-Viola. All dream, all are mad, and differ from another only in the kind of their madness,—some have a graceful and poetic madness, others a madness grotesque and trivial. And after all, some of these dreams come true. Must we ascribe the honour of success to the good sense of the happy ones who see their secret desires crowned? Ah no, we must ascribe it to nature. We all dream,—it is a condition of humanity; but in this multitude of dreams, Nature accepts only certain ones which are in harmony with grace, with poesy, and with beauty; for Nature is essentially platonic, and thrusts aside as a revolt and a sin, every dream wherein ugliness intrudes. Hence it is that Viola's secret dream comes true, while Malvolio's is condemned to remain for ever a grotesque chimera. Very humble indeed should all of us be, for we are only a little less mad than our neighbours; it is Nature alone who is our arbiter and decides which of us she wishes to pose as sages, and which of us she intends to retain in the rank of fools. (pp. 382-84)

> *E. Montégut, in an extract, translated by Horace Howard Furness, in* A New Variorum Edition of Shakespeare: 'Twelfe Night or, What You Will', Vol. XIII, *edited by Horace Howard Furness, J. B. Lippincott Company, 1901, pp. 382-84.*

H. N. HUDSON (essay date 1872)

[*Suggesting that* Twelfth Night *reveals Shakespeare "at peace with himself and all the world," Hudson praises the graceful style and humor of the play. He continues the discussion of Shakespeare's supposed aversion to the Puritans of his time. The critic maintains that Shakespeare, reacting to the restrictive orders of the Privy Council which governed stage performances in 1600, created Malvolio as a satire on the Puritans. Hudson believes that Shakespeare wanted us to pity Malvolio, and that is why his punishment is so excessive.*]

In Act iii., scene 1 [of *Twelfth Night*], the Clown says to Viola, "But, indeed, words are very rascals, since bonds disgraced them." This may be fairly understood as referring to an order issued by the Privy Council in June, 1600, and laying very severe restrictions upon stage performances. (p. 352)

Therewithal it is to be noted that the Puritans were specially forward and zealous in urging the complaints which put the Privy Council upon issuing this stringent process; and it will hardly be questioned that the character of Malvolio was partly meant as a satire on that remarkable people. That the Poet should be somewhat provoked at their action in bringing about such tight restraints upon the freedom of his art, was certainly natural enough. Nor is it a small addition to their many claims on our gratitude, that their aptness to "think, because they were virtuous, there should be no more cakes and ale," had the effect of calling forth so rich and withal so good-natured a piece of retaliation. (p. 353)

I am quite at a loss to conceive why *Twelfth Night* should ever have been referred to the Poet's latest period of authorship. The play naturally falls, by the internal notes of style, temper, and poetic grain, into the middle period of his productive years. It has no such marks of vast but immature powers as are often met with in his earlier plays; nor, on the other hand, any of "that intense idiosyncrasy of thought and expression,—that unparalleled fusion of the intellectual with the passionate,"— which distinguishes his later ones. Every thing is calm and quiet, with an air of unruffled serenity and composure about it, as if the Poet had purposely taken to such matter as he could easily mould into graceful and entertaining forms; thus exhibiting none of that crushing muscularity of mind to which the hardest materials afterwards or elsewhere became as limber and pliant as clay in the hands of a potter. Yet the play has a marked severity of taste; the style, though by no means so great as in some others, is singularly faultless; the graces of wit and poetry are distilled into it with indescribable delicacy, as if they came from a hand at once the most plentiful and the most sparing: in short, the work is everywhere replete with "the modest charm of not too much"; its beauty, like that of the heroine, being of the still, deep, retiring sort, which it takes one long to find, forever to exhaust, and which can be fully caught only by the reflective imagination in "the quiet and still air of delightful studies." Thus all things are disposed in most happy keeping with each other, and tempered in the blandest proportion of Art. . . . (pp. 356-57)

Malvolio, the self-love-sick Steward, has hardly had justice done him, his bad qualities being indeed of just the kind to defeat the recognition of his good ones. He represents a perpetual class of people, whose leading characteristic is moral demonstrativeness, and who are never satisfied with a law that leaves them free to do right, unless it also give them the power to keep others from doing wrong. (p. 359)

Maria, the little structure packed so close with mental spicery, has read Malvolio through and through; she knows him without and within; and she never speaks of him, but that her speech touches the very pith of the theme; as when she describes him to be one "that cons State without book, and utters it by great swaths; the best-persuaded of himself, so crammed, as he thinks, with excellences, that it is his ground of faith that all who look on him love him." Her quaint stratagem of the letter has and is meant to have the effect of disclosing to others what her keener insight has long since discovered; and its working lifts her into a model of arch, roguish mischievousness, with wit to plan and art to execute whatsoever falls within the scope of such a character. (pp. 360-61)

The scenes where the waggish troop, headed by this "noble gull-catcher" and "most excellent devil of wit," bewitch Malvolio into "a contemplative idiot," practising upon his vanity and conceit till he seems ready to burst with an ecstasy of self-consequence, and they "laugh themselves into stitches" over him, are almost painfully diverting. It is indeed sport to see him "jet under his advanced plumes"; and during this part of the operation our hearts freely keep time with theirs who are tickling out his buds into full-blown thoughts: at length, however, when he is under treatment as a madman, our delight in his exposure passes over into commiseration of his distress, and we feel a degree of resentment towards his ingenious persecutors. The Poet, no doubt, meant to push the joke upon him so far as to throw our sympathies over on his side, and make us take his part. For his character is such that perhaps nothing but excessive reprisals on his vanity and conceit could make us do justice to his real worth. (p. 361)

It strikes me, withal, as a rather note-worthy circumstance that both the comedy and the romance of the play meet together in [Feste], as in their natural home. He is indeed a right jolly fellow; no note of mirth springs up but he has answering susceptibilities for it to light upon; but he also has at the same time a delicate vein of tender pathos in him; as appears by the touchingly-plaintive song he sings. . . . (p. 362)

All this array of comicalities, exhilarating as it is in itself, is rendered doubly so by the frequent changes and playings-in of poetry breathed from the sweetest spots of romance, and which "gives a very echo to the seat where Love is thron'd"; ideas and images of beauty creeping and stealing over the mind with footsteps so soft and delicate that we scarce know what touches us. (p. 363)

In Shakespeare's delineations as in nature, we may commonly note that love, in proportion as it is deep and genuine, is also inward and reserved. To be voluble, to be fond of spreading itself in discourse, or of airing itself in the fineries of speech, seems indeed quite against the instinct of that passion; and its best eloquence is when it ties up the tongue, and *steals* out in other modes of expression, the flushing of the cheeks and the mute devotion of the eyes. In its purest forms, it is apt to be a secret even unto itself, the subjects of it knowing indeed that something ails them, but not knowing exactly what. So that the most effective love-making is involuntary and unconscious. And I suspect that, as a general thing, if the true lover's passion be not returned before it is spoken, it stands little chance of being returned at all.

Now, in Orsino's case, the passion, or whatever else it may be, is too much without to be thoroughly sound within. Like Malvolio's virtue, it is too glass-glazing, too much enamoured of its own image, and renders him too apprehensive that it will be the death of him, if disappointed of its object. Accordingly he talks too much about it, and his talking about it is too ingenious withal; it makes his tongue run glib and fine with the most charming divisions of poetic imagery and sentiment; all which shrewdly infers that he lacks the genuine thing, and has mistaken something else for it. (pp. 366-67)

In Viola, divers things that were else not a little scattered are thoroughly composed; her character being the unifying power that draws all the parts into true dramatic consistency. Love-taught herself, it was for her to teach both Orsino and Olivia how to love: indeed she plays into all the other parts, causing them to embrace and cohere within the compass of her circulation. And yet, like some subtle agency, working most where we perceive it least, she does all this without rendering herself a special prominence in the play. (p. 367)

Sundry critics have censured, some of them pretty sharply, the improbability involved in the circumstance of Viola and Sebastian resembling each other so closely as to be mistaken the one for the other. Even so just and liberal a critic as Hallam has stumbled at this circumstance, so much so as quite to disconcert his judgment of the play [see excerpt above, 1839]. The improbability is indeed palpable enough; yet I have to confess that it has never troubled me, any more than certain things not less improbable in *As You Like It*. But even if it had, still I should not hold it any just ground for faulting the Poet, inasmuch as the circumstance was an accepted article in the literary faith of his time. (p. 369)

[Sebastian and Viola] are really as much alike in the inward texture of their souls as in their visible persons; at least their mutual resemblance in the former respect is as close as were compatible with proper manliness in the one, and proper womanliness in the other. Personal bravery, for example, is as characteristic of him as modesty is of her. In simplicity, in gentleness, in rectitude, in delicacy of mind, and in all the particulars of what may be termed complexional harmony and healthiness of nature,—in these they are as much twins as in birth and feature. . . .

The conditions of the plot did not require nor even permit Sebastian to be often or much in sight. We have indeed but little from him, but that little is intensely charged with significance; in fact, I hardly know of another instance in Shakespeare where so much of character is accomplished in so few words. (p. 370)

The society delineated in this play is singularly varied and composite; the names of the persons being a mixture of Spanish, Italian, and English. Though the scene is laid in Illyria, the period of the action is undefined, and the manners and costumes are left in the freedom of whatever time we may choose antecedent to that of the composition, provided we do not exceed the proper limits of imaginative reason.

This variety in the grouping of the persons, whether so intended or not, very well accords with the spirit in which, or the occasion for which, the title indicates the play to have been written. Twelfth Day, anciently so called as being the twelfth after Christmas, is the day whereon the Church has always kept the feast of "The Epiphany, or the Manifestation of Christ to the Gentiles." So that, in preparing a Twelfth-Night entertainment, the idea of fitness might aptly suggest, that national lines and distinctions should be lost in the paramount ties of a common Religion; and that people the most diverse in kindred and tongue should draw together in the sentiment of "one Lord, one Faith, one Baptism"; their social mirth thus relishing of universal Brotherhood.

The general scope and plan of *Twelfth Night, as a work of art,* is hinted in its second title; all the comic elements being, as it were, thrown out simultaneously, and held in a sort of equipoise; so that the readers are left to fix the preponderance where it best suits their several bent or state of mind, and each, within certain limits and conditions, may take the work in *what sense he will.* For, where no special prominence is given to any one thing, there is the wider scope for individual aptitude or preference, and the greater freedom for each to select for virtual prominence such parts as will best knit in with what is uppermost in his thoughts.

The significance of the title is further traceable in a peculiar spontaneousness running through the play. Replete as it is with humours and oddities, they all seem to spring up of their own accord; the comic characters being free alike from disguises and pretensions, and seeking merely to let off their inward redundancy; caring nothing at all whether everybody or nobody sees them, so they may have their whim out, and giving utterance to folly and nonsense simply because they cannot help it. Thus their very deformities have a certain grace, since they are genuine and of Nature's planting: absurdity and whimsicality are indigenous to the soil, and shoot up in free, happy luxuriance, from the life that is in them. And by thus setting the characters out in their happiest aspects, the Poet contrives to make them simply ludicrous and diverting, instead of putting upon them the constructions of wit or spleen, and thereby making them ridiculous or contemptible. . . . Moreover the high and the low are here seen moving in free and familiar intercourse, without any apparent consciousness of their re-

spective ranks: the humours and comicalities of the play keep running and frisking in among the serious parts, to their mutual advantage; the connection between them being of a kind to be felt, not described. (pp. 371-72)

In no one of his dramas, to my sense, does the Poet appear to have been in a healthier or happier frame of mind, more free from the fascination of the darker problems of humanity, more at peace with himself and all the world, or with Nature playing more kindly and genially at his heart, and from thence diffusing her benedictions through his whole establishment. (p. 373)

Rev. H. N. Hudson, "Shakespeare's Characters: 'Twelfth Night'," in his Shakespeare: His Life, Art, and Characters, Vol. I, *revised edition, Ginn & Company, 1872, pp. 351-73.*

F. J. FURNIVALL   (essay date 1877)

[*One of the leading philologists of the nineteenth century, Furnivall founded the New Shakspere Society and was among the first scholars to apply the principles of scientific investigation to the study of Shakespeare's work. The New Shakspere Society set out to measure Shakespeare's poetic and dramatic growth by means of "verse tests"—detailed examinations of variations in the metrical features of Shakespeare's dramatic verse. Furnivall's work is indicative of the influence which nineteenth-century scientism exerted in the field of literary scholarship. While noting that* Twelfth Night *reflects the happy spirit of Shakespeare's "bright, sweet time," Furnivall observes that there is a "shadow of death and distress" in the play. The perception of* Twelfth Night *as a farewell to mirth is echoed by such twentieth-century commentators as Arthur Quiller-Couch (1930), Mark Van Doren (1939), E. C. Pettet (1949), and G. K. Hunter (1962). The excerpt below is taken from Furnivall's introduction to* The Leopold Shakspere, *first published in 1877.*]

[*Twelfth Night* is still] one of the comedies of Shakspere's bright, sweet time. True, that we have to change Rosalind's rippling laugh for the drunken catches and bibulous drollery of Sir Toby and his comrade, and Touchstone for the Clown; but the leading note of the play is fun, as if Shakspere had been able to throw off all thought of melancholy, and had devised Malvolio to help his friends 'fleet the time carelessly,' as they did in the golden world. Still though, as ever in the comedies, except *The Merry Wives,* there's the shadow of death and distress across the sunshine, Olivia's father and brother just dead, Viola and Sebastian just rescued from one death, Viola threatened with another, and Antonio held a pirate and liable to death. And still the lesson is, as in *As You Like It,* 'Sweet are the uses of adversity'; out of their trouble all the lovers come into happiness, into wedlock. The play at first sight is far less striking and interesting than *Much Ado* and *As You Like It.* No brilliant Beatrice or Benedick catches the eye, no sad Rosalind leaping into life and joyousness at the touch of assured love. The self-conceited Malvolio is brought to the front, the drunkards and Clown come next; none of these touches any heart; and it's not till we look past them, that we feel the beauty of the characters who stand in half-light behind. Then we become conscious of a quiet harmony of colour and form that makes a picture full of charm, that grows on you as you study it, and becomes one of the possessions of your life.

F. J. Furnivall, in an extract from A New Variorum Edition of Shakespeare: Twelfe Night, or, What You Will, Vol. XIII, *edited by Horace Howard Furness, J. B. Lippincott Company, 1901, p. 385.*

WILLIAM ARCHER (essay date 1884)

[*Scottish theater critic and playwright, Archer is noted primarily for his English translations of Henrik Ibsen and his efforts to promote the so-called "new drama" of the 1890s. Archer argued, as did Bernard Shaw, that the drama of his own age was as good or even superior to the work of the ancients and Elizabethans, both of whom he considered overvalued in many respects. This attitude is often apparent in his criticism of Shakespeare's drama. To Archer, Shakespeare was concerned only with the externals of Elizabethan life, and had "no eye for the social, political, or religious tendencies of his day." His opinion is challenged in the twentieth century by critics who study* Twelfth Night *and all of Shakespeare's works in light of their historical context (see excerpts below by John W. Draper (1950), Karl F. Thompson (1952), and C. L. Barber (1959).) In opposition to Joseph Hunter (1845), F. Kreyssig (1862), and H. N. Hudson (1872), Archer states that Malvolio is not a Puritan, but a Philistine, and his punishment is "excessive to the point of barbarity." But, unlike Charles Lamb (1822), Archer maintains that this does not interfere with an audience's pleasure in the play. Unlike the majority of commentators, Archer asserts that Feste is "one of the shallowest of Shakespeare's jesters."*]

It is the fashion to speculate on Shakespeare's astonishment could he see the luxury and completeness of illusion with which his plays are now put on the stage. I sometimes wonder whether he would not be even more suprised at the bare fact of his plays holding the stage at all.

Let us examine Shakespeare's own definition of the function of the drama—"to show the very age and body of the time his form and pressure." A definition this which every one accepts without demur. But it is one thing to accept a maxim, and another thing to act and think up to it. We do not in our drama show the age and body of the time his form and pressure, any more than we turn the left cheek to him who smites us on the right. And did Shakespeare himself obey his own precept any better than we? Assuredly not. He imagined the mere externals of Elizabethan life, because the limited historic sense of his time cared nothing for painstaking reconstructions of the manners of distant ages and nations; but he had no eye for the social, political, or religious tendencies of his day; America scarcely existed for him, the Reformation was not, no one had less foreboding than he of the coming baptism in blood of our infant democracy. What he did was to show the age and body of *all* time his form and pressure; in other words, to see and interpret the spirit of man, unconditioned by time and space, as the great art of the Italian Renaissance had seen and interpreted his body. This he did through the medium of fables gathered from many sources—classical and national history, northern legend and southern romance. (pp. 271-72)

Our Asmodeus-Shakespeare would, on reflection, cease to wonder at finding the passing fantasy of 1601 regenerated and glorified in 1884. He would see in it an aesthetic plaything as good as any other and better than most—a thing of mere beauty, and therefore a joy for ever. Utility passes away, but beauty remains. Just because Shakespeare did not show the age and body of his time its form and pressure, his plays, in so far as they have the perennial gift of pure beauty, are acceptable to a generation which does not care, or dare, to see its own form and pressure on the stage. (p. 272)

Beauty and humour . . . are the two imperishable elements for which we have to look in estimating the claim of a Shakespearean comedy to hold the stage. In both qualitites *Twelfth Night* ranks high, if not highest, among its fellows. It has practically only one competitor, *As You Like It*, in which I, for my part, find the beauty fresher, robuster, less evanescent on the stage, and the humour at once less obsolete and more intimately blended with the beauty; but this is a mere individual impression, a question of "as you like it," and nothing more. Two other fantastic comedies, *A Midsummer Night's Dream* and *The Tempest*, are put out of court by the inherent impossibility of adequate stage presentation. . . . Who shall lay down the boundary between the land of faery and the land of fantasy? It is merely the line on one side of which the spirits are visible, while on the other they play their pranks unseen. Puck is as active in Illyria as in Attica, though we see him only in his works; Ariel is as much at home in Ardennes as in the Enchanted Island. Who does not feel that the air of our *Twelfth Night* Illyria is full of influences quite absent from the atmosphere of *Much Ado* or of *The Merchant of Venice?* This distinction cannot be too strongly insisted on, for it involves the question of what critical standard we are to apply. Our moral judgments are as inapplicable to *Twelfth Night* as to an Arabian Night; *Much Ado*, on the other hand, should stand the ethical test as well as [George Eliot's] *Middlemarch*—if it does not, so much the worse.

The elements of beauty and of humour are kept very much apart in *Twelfth Night*. It contains two actions in one frame—a romantic intrigue borrowed from Italy, and a pair of practical jokes, or "good practices," as Mr. Manningham hath it [see excerpt above, 1602], invented by Shakespeare. These two actions can be said really to touch at only one point, and then, as it were, unwillingly; for it is where Viola's blade crosses Sir Andrew's. . . . The play has just as much unity as two spheres in contact.

The history of the romantic intrigue is curious, and affords one example of Charles Kingsley's somewhat rash generalisation as to Shakespeare's "truly divine instinct for finding honey where others found poison." The sister disguised in male attire and mistaken for her twin-brother appears in Cinthio's *Hecatommithi*, but it is in Bandello that the tale first takes the shape we know. . . . Bandello's tale is rambling and very licentious, burdened with heavy fathers, confidants, and the other stock figures of the Italian bourgeois life it depicts, the separation of the brother and sister being supposed to take place at the sack of Rome. . . . That Shakespeare borrowed mainly from Rich [sic] cannot be doubted. . . . It was Rich who changed the characters of the tale from Italian bourgeois into romantic dukes and dames; it was Rich who placed the scene by the sea and introduced a shipwreck, though not as the means of the separation between Silla and Silvio. Strangely enough Rich had greatly improved upon Bandello's tale, introducing a novel comic motive towards the close, and bringing about the revelation of his heroine's sex better than any of his predecessors. This modification, however, involved two scenes of such immodesty as Beaumont and Fletcher would have revelled in. Not so Shakespeare, who rejected them even at the sacrifice of a certain amount of constructive finish. The change is due to a refined sense of tone and keeping which he did not always evince so clearly. He felt that the love which breathes through the play must be "high-fantastical," and that its grosser phenomena must for the nonce be ignored. In a fairy tale everything must be sensuous, nothing sensual; and *Twelfth Night* is a fairy tale.

This well understood, all the crudities and absurdities of the romance become so many inseparable characteristics of the form. The exact likeness between Viola and Sebastian, extending even to the fashion and colour of their clothes; Olivia's sudden love for Viola; the complaisant philosophy with which Sebastian consents to marry a woman he has never seen before; the Duke's barbarous whim of sacrificing "the lamb that he doth love, to spite a raven's heart within a dove;" the failure of Viola and Sebastian instantly to recognise one another—all these details are bad drama but good fairy tale. And how fresh and exquisite, how gracious and stately, are the figures which move through these fantastic mazes! Viola is a shade more ethereal and fragile than Rosalind; to take an illustration suggested by their two names, she is as a violet to a moss-rose. "Ganymede" would probably have done more credit to his "swashing, martial outside" in the duel with Sir Andrew than did the shrinkingly sensitive "Cesario." For the rest they are equally modest, yet equally frank, equally self-reliant, yet equally womanly. Olivia is a model of the gracious chatelaine, even while she is a victim to the mischievous love-philtres of the unseen Puck of the play. . . . What a princely carriage has the languid egoist Orsino, in whose mouth the poet has placed some of his loveliest snatches of verbal melody! What a fine fresh buoyancy of youth do we find in Sebastian! How pleasant is the bluff tenderness of the old seaman Antonio! The play begins with a symphony, and ends with a song, and should, on the stage, be steeped in music. It is a fugue of graceful fantasies.

So much for the fairy tale: now for the farce. Its construction is entirely Shakespeare's, and affords a good specimen of his manner. Given the pompously fatuous character of Malvolio, the "practise" put upon him is a very simple invention. Much more ingenuity is shown in the second practical joke of the duel, with its recoil upon the head of its perpetrator through the intervention of Sebastian. All these scenes—the scene of the letter, of the cross-garters, of the duel and its consequences—are theatrically effective by reason of their skilful dialogue, which a little judicious pruning renders fairly comprehensible to modern ears. On the other hand there are many passages which can at no time have been reasonably good dialogue—such as the first meeting between Maria and Sir Andrew, and several of the scenes in which the Clown is concerned. Such inane word-strainings may have been true to nature, since the professional fools of the day, bound to be funny at all hazards, must often have resorted to them; but they are none the less puerile, and should drop away on the modern stage to the great advantage of all concerned. Feste is, on the whole, one of the shallowest of Shakespeare's jesters. When he says of himself that he is not Olivia's fool, but her corrupter of words, there is more than a spice of truth in the remark. Compared with Touchstone, he sinks into absolute insignificance. The parts can scarcely have been written for the same actor; Touchstone was probably designed for a comedian of authoritative genius, Feste for a mere singing clown.

As to the other characters in this portion of the play, only one of them, Malvolio, presents any difficulties. Of Sir Toby Belch and Sir Andrew Ague-cheek, it is an old remark, but none the less a true one, that the former is a vulgarised Falstaff, the latter a caricatured Slender. It is to be noted that in the chronological sequence *Twelfth Night* follows almost immediately the two parts of *Henry IV*, and *The Merry Wives of Windsor*. Shakespeare doubtless found the popularity of these types unexhausted, and, moreover, he had probably the actors of Sir John and Slender ready to hand. He accordingly deprived the knight of his consummate intellectual supremacy of scoundreldom, giving him a somewhat weaker head for liquor, and a somewhat stronger heart for fighting; he added to Slender a dash of Ben Jonson's Master Stephen; and he placed the two figures in his

Act IV. Scene ii. Malvolio, Feste, Sir Toby Belch, Maria. Frontispiece to Rowe edition (1709). By permission of the Folger Shakespeare Library.

fairy Illyria as he had formerly placed Bottom, Snout, and Starveling in his fairy Attica.

And lastly, of Malvolio. I confess that he has always been to me one of the most puzzling of Shakespeare's creations. The theory, so popular with German, and with some English, commentators, which makes of him a satirical type of the Puritan as Shakespeare conceived him, will not hold ground for a moment. It is founded on one or two detached speeches wrested from their context. Maria says of him that "he is sometimes a kind of a Puritan," only to say in the next breath that "the devil a Puritan" is he; and when Sir Andrew expresses a desire to beat him, Sir Toby derisively asks, "What, for being a Puritan? Thy exquisite reason, dear knight?" Is it likely that Shakespeare was himself guilty of the stupidity which even Sir Toby ridicules in his gull? Yet Kreyssig, as a rule one of the most common-sense commentators, does not hesitate to speak as if the poet, in this character, took revenge for the Puritan attacks upon his craft, as Molière, in *Tartuffe*, lashed his enemies the bigots. If this was Shakespeare's intention, he must have been a blundering satirist, for there is nothing of the typical Puritan in Malvolio. He carries out his lady's orders in remonstrating with her kinsman for making her house a noisy tavern, and by so doing he draws down upon himself the vengeance of the leagued spirits of misrule. If it be Puritanism to do his duty as a man of sense and a faithful steward in attempting to put a stop to drunken ribaldry, then the poet seems rather to eulogise than to satirise Puritanism. On the other hand, his misfortunes, so far as he is himself responsible for them, spring from defects by no means characteristically Puritan. Spiritual pride is the besetting sin of the "unco 'guid"; it is physical vanity which leads Malvolio so readily to swallow his tormentors' bait. A scorn, real or affected, for the things of this life is the mark of the Puritan; Malvolio, however little taste he may have for the gross "cakes and ale" of the boon companions, has not the slightest desire to conceal his worldliness beneath a mask of other-worldliness. But such argument is futile. No one who reads the play without a preconceived theory can find in Malvolio the smallest trace of the zealot. All that can by any stretch of language be called Puritanism in his conduct rebounds entirely to his honour.

To me it seems that Shakespeare, in drawing him, had not so clear an idea as usual of the precise phase of character he wished to represent. He was more concerned to obtain comic effects than to create a consistent, closely-observed type. We do not *know* Malvolio as we know Polonius, Jacques, Mercutio, Dogberry. This may be a mere personal impression, but I seem to trace in the commentators something of the uncertainty which has always troubled me with reference to his character. The very fact that he has been so grievously misinterpreted proves that there is a certain vagueness in his characterisation. Lamb has drawn with his usual delicacy of insight the externals, so to speak, of the part. . . . If I may hazard a theory, I should say that he is not a Puritan but a Philistine. The radical defect of his nature is a lack of that sense of humour which is the safety-valve of all our little insanities, preventing even the most expansive egoism from altogether over-inflating us. He takes himself and the world too seriously. He has no intuition for the incongruous and grotesque, to put the drag upon his egoistic fantasy, "sick of self-love." His face, not only smileless itself but contemptuous of mirth in others, has acted as a damper upon the humour of the sprightly Maria and the jovial Sir Toby; he has taken a set pleasure in putting the poor Clown out of countenance by receiving his quips with a stolid gravity. Hence the rancour of the humorists against a fundamentally antagonistic nature; hence, perhaps, their whim of making him crown his absurdities by wearing a forced smile, a grimace more incongruous with his pompous personality than even cross-garters or yellow stockings. He is a being, in short, to whom the world, with all its shows and forms, is intensely real and profoundly respectable. He has no sense of its littleness, its evanescence, without which he can have no true sense of its greatness and its mystery. In common life this absorption in the shows of things manifests itself in a deficient feeling for proportion and contrast. He has no sense of humour—that is the head and front of his offending.

That his punishment, strictly considered, is excessive to the point of barbarity, cannot, I think, be doubted; but the air of the fairy tale inter-penetrates the farce, and we do not demand a strict apportionment of justice either poetical or practical. It is certain that no sense of painful injustice has generally been found to interfere with the pleasure to be derived from the play. . . . Nor can we doubt that its attractiveness on the stage has hitherto been due to the farce rather than to the fairy-tale, whose iridescent beauties are apt to be lost in the harsh light of the theatre. Whether he clearly defined his character or not, Shakespeare evidently succeeded in making of Malvolio an effective comic figure. (pp. 272-77)

William Archer, "'Twelfth Night' at the Lyceum," in Macmillan's Magazine, *Vol. L, No. 298, August, 1884, pp. 271-79.*

BARRETT WENDELL (essay date 1894)

[*Wendell points out that each element of* Twelfth Night *is slightly reworked from other of Shakespeare's plays; thus, he concludes, it is a "masterpiece not of invention but of recapitulation." He also states that* Twelfth Night *exhibits no philosophical seriousness and is a source rather of "unthinking pleasure." This position is countered by such twentieth-century critics as Morris P. Tilley (1914) and John Hollander (1956), both of whom focus on the philosophic depth of the play.*]

To dwell on *Twelfth Night* in detail . . . would be unusually pleasant. For our purposes, however, which are merely to fix its place, if we can, in the artistic development of Shakspere, we need only glance at it. (p. 206)

The one fact for us to observe, and to keep in mind, is the surprising contrast between the free, rollicking graceful, poetic *Twelfth Night* which any theatre-goer and any reader of Shakspere knows almost by heart, and the *Twelfth Night* which reveals itself to whoever pursues such a course of study as ours. Taken by itself, the play seems not only admirably complete but distinctly fresh and new,—spontaneous, vivid, full of fun, of romantic sentiment, and of human nature, and above all individually different from anything else. This Illyria, for example, is a world by itself, whither one might sail from the Messina of Benedick and Beatrice, or perhaps travel from the Verona of Romeo and Juliet, to find it different from these, much as regions in real life differ one from another. For all the romance and the fun of *Twelfth Night,* its plausibility is excellent; and so its individuality seems complete.

As everybody can feel, all this is lastingly true. What is also lastingly true, yet can be appreciated only by those of us who have begun to study Shakspere chronologically, is that, to a degree hitherto unapproached, what is distinct and new in *Twelfth Night* is only the way in which the play is put together. From beginning to end, as we scrutinize it, we find it a tissue of incidents, of characters, of situations which have been proved effective by previous stage experience. . . . [The] more one looks for familiar things in new guise, the more one finds. What conceals them at first is only that *Twelfth Night* resembles *As You Like It* in being full of a romantic sentiment peculiarly its own, with a less palpable but still sufficient undercurrent of delicate melancholy. Throughout, too, the infusion of this new spirit into these old bodies is made with the quiet ease which we have begun to recognize as the mark of Shakspere's handiwork.

Together with *As You Like It,* then, we may call *Twelfth Night* light, joyous, fantastic, fleeting, a thing to be enjoyed, to be loved, to be dreamed about; but never, if one would understand, to be taken with philosophic seriousness. Plays in purpose, poems in fact, these two comedies alike are best appreciated by those who find in them only lasting expressions and sources of unthinking pleasure.

While *As You Like It,* however, differs from Shakspere's other work by translating into permanent dramatic form a dull novel of a kind not before found among the sources of his plays, *Twelfth Night,* far from being essentially different from his former plays, is perhaps the most completely characteristic we have yet considered. Again and again we have . . . remarked in Shakspere a trait which will appear throughout. For what reason we cannot say—indolence we might guess in one mood, prudence in another—he was exceptionally economical of invention, except in mere language. Scenes, characters, situations, devices which had once proved themselves effective he would constantly prefer to any bold experiment. This very economy of invention, perhaps, contained an element of strength; it left his full energy free for the masterly phrasing, and the spontaneous creation of character, which has made his work lasting. Strong or weak, however, the trait is clearly becoming almost as characteristic as the constant concreteness of his style; and nowhere does it appear more distinctly or to more advantage than when we recognize in *Twelfth Night*—with all its perennial delights—a masterpiece not of invention but of recapitulation. (pp. 206-09)

> Barrett Wendell, "The Plays of Shakspere, from 'A Midsummer Night's Dream' to 'Twelfth Night'," in his William Shakspere: A Study in Elizabethan Literature, *Charles Scribner's Sons, 1894, pp. 103-220.*

EDWARD DOWDEN   (essay date 1903)

[*Dowden was an Irish critic and biographer whose* Shakespeare: A Critical Study of His Mind and Art *was the leading example of the biographical criticism popular in the English-speaking world near the end of the nineteenth century. Biographical critics sought in the plays and poems a record of Shakespeare's personal development. As that approach gave way in the twentieth century to aesthetic theories with greater emphasis on the constructed, artificial nature of literary works, Dowden and other biographical critics came to be considered limited. In his brief remarks on* Twelfth Night, *Dowden speculates that Shakespeare had perhaps encountered a "starched Puritan" who served as the model for Malvolio. For additional commentary on Malvolio as a Puritan, see the excerpts by Joseph Hunter (1845), F. Kreyssig (1862), H. N. Hudson (1872), William Archer (1884), and Morris P. Tilley (1914). The following essay was first published in 1903.*]

The midsummer of Shakespeare's comedy is reached in *Twelfth Night*. Was it his effort to resist the invasion of sadder thought which raised its mirth to the reeling heights of Sir Toby's Illyrian bacchanals? We dare not venture such a surmise, for the light and warmth are at flood-tide. The voluptuous love-languors of the Duke and Olivia's luxury of grief fatten the idle soil for the blossoming of the rose. The disease of overmuch prosperity in the palaces of Illyria seems set over against the sanity of adversity in the forest of Arden. Viola, in her disguises as Cesario, has a harder task than the banished Rosalind; for instead of assisting at her own wooing, she is required to plead as an envoy of love against herself. In place of the dilettante egotist Jaques, who would range through all experiences, we have here the solemn self-lover, Malvolio, pinnacled in his own sense of importance and his code of formal propriety, yet toppling from his heights to so grotesque a fall. Had Shakespeare encountered some starched Elizabethan Puritan, who looked sourly on the theatre, and thought that because he was virtuous there should be no more cakes and ale, and did the dramatist read a humorous lesson to his time on an error more deep-seated in the human heart than the excesses of a joyous temper? Was the comic spirit here a swordsman armed with the blade of reason and good sense? If such was the case, Shakespeare was assuredly no partisan, and Sir Toby Belch is hardly his ideal representative of a liberal humanism. (pp. 655-56)

> Edward Dowden, "Shakespeare As a Comic Dramatist," in Representative English Comedies: From the Beginnings to Shakespeare, Vol. I, *edited by*

Charles Mills Gayley, *Macmillan Publishing Company, 1912, pp. 635-61.*

E. K. CHAMBERS   (essay date 1907)

[*Chambers occupies a transitional position in Shakespearean criticism, one which connects the biographical sketches and character analyses of the nineteenth century with the historical, technical, and textual criticism of the twentieth century. While a member of the education department of Oxford University, Chambers earned his reputation as a scholar with his multivolume works,* The Medieval Stage *and* The Elizabethan Stage, *while he also edited* The Red Letter Shakespeare. *Chambers both investigated the purpose and limitations of each dramatic genre as Shakespeare presented it, and speculated on how the dramatist's work was influenced by contemporary historical issues and his own frame of mind. Chambers discusses the subject of deception and self-deception in* Twelfth Night, *which was first noted by E. Montégut (1867) and later developed by Joseph H. Summers (1955) and Bertrand Evans (1960). He also echoes the position of George Steevens (1780) in regard to the relevance of Feste's songs to* Twelfth Night *and asserts that they have no relation to the play's theme. The essay from which the following excerpt is taken was first published in Chambers's* The Red Letter Shakespeare *in 1907.*]

[*Twelfth Night*] is the comedy of the sentimentalists, of the tendency of minds pent in the artificial atmosphere of cities to a spiritual self-deception, whereby they indulge in the expression of emotions not because they really have them, but because they have come to be regarded by themselves or others as modish or delightful emotions to have.

Thus Orsino, like the young Romeo before the crisis of his fate, is a thistle-down amorist. He is in love, not with Olivia, but with being in love with Olivia. (pp. 174-75)

Orsino and Olivia are self-deceivers, the dupes of their own sentimentalisms. And the play touches them with such delicate irony of criticism that its sting might fail to reach the bosoms of an audience not exceptionally tickle o' the sere. But Shakespeare's dramaturgy is ready with a device to meet the contingency. He will illustrate and interpret the subtler situation by the juxtaposition of others like in kind, but grosser and more obvious of purport. Beside his principal characters, who befool themselves, he places subordinate personages, who are befooled by others; and thus he succeeds in evoking an atmosphere of malicious chicanery and deception, which attunes the spectator to his main intention. The play, indeed, is full of gulls; and one at least, who spends the best part of his sober hours in laying schemes to abuse others, is himself most notoriously abused. This is the arch-plotter, Sir Toby Belch. . . . [It] is through sheer devilry that he tricks Sir Andrew and the supposed Cesario into the duel which each, at any loss to dignity, would avoid; while revenge is the motive which leads him to conspire with Maria for the undoing of Malvolio. And in the end his rogueries recoil upon him. Not only does he take Sebastian for Cesario, and get his head broken accordingly, but he is so fascinated with the incomparable capacity for intrigue displayed by 'the youngest wren of nine' that when things are cleared up he finds his head in the ultimate noose of marriage with a waiting-maid. If Sir Toby is the arch-plotter of the piece, Malvolio may claim to be its arch-victim. . . . Yet, hard as is his fate, it cannot be denied that it serves admirably to vindicate comic justice. Like Orsino and like Olivia he is a notable self-deceiver. . . . He has the austerity of a puritan and the insolence of a jack-in-office; and how should a free-thinking, free-living Elizabethan playhouse not split its sides in exultant hilarity at his downfall?

Like all Shakespeare's comedies, *Twelfth Night* is desultory in texture, and contains various threads of interest besides the central comic idea on which its dramatic unity depends. This comic idea must not be pressed too far as regards details. There is much excellent and irresponsible fooling for its own sake, and the charming songs assigned to Feste the jester have no particular relation to the principal theme. After all, a comedy must entertain. The sort of criticism which endeavours to trace and interpret topical allusions in Shakespeare's plays can easily be overdone, and has, as a matter of fact, in recent years been overdone. An Elizabethan dramatist was not likely to take the love-affairs of the queen, or the fortunes of the house of Stuart or the house of Devereux, as the deliberate groundwork of his plot. It is not to be supposed that the censorship is so modern an institution as that kind of theory implies. But in all ages the drama has been ready to glance, as occasion allowed, at events of public interest and at personages much in the public eye; nor is it probable that the Elizabethan age, which was by no means averse to gossip, afforded any exception to the rule. A touch of courtly compliment or a discreet allusion to the latest jest or scandal of the backstairs would be a palatable spice to the comedy destined to furnish forth the Christmas merriment of Hampton Court or Whitehall. (pp. 175-78)

The weakness of comedy generally lies in the difficulty of finding any device whereby to keep the wheels of the plot moving onwards. This is met in *Twelfth Night* by the introduction of the romantic story of Sebastian and Viola, their lamentable separation and joyous reunion. This motive . . . is neatly woven into the fortunes of Olivia and Orsino; but it is kept in proper subordination, since it is no part of the dramatist's intention to turn the play into a melodrama. An interesting contribution to the total dramatic effect is made by the character of Viola, which in its naturalness and transparent honesty seems designed to heighten and set off by deliberate contrast the insincerities which it is the purpose of the comic muse to correct. Into the perfumed chamber of Olivia's sentimentality Viola comes like a breath of spring air, with her grave and contemptuous rebukes of the fine lady's poses. . . . And when love, a love that must be hidden, grows like a flower in her own soul, she bears herself with a gallant and sensitive pathos that informs the scenes in which she appears with touches of exquisite poetry. Surely it is Viola, not Olivia, of whom it should have been written—

> Methought she purged the air of pestilence.
> 　　　　　　　　　　　　　　　　　[I.i.18]

With the specific of simple truth she purges the pestilence of artifice and rhetoric. (pp. 179-80)

> E. K. Chambers, " 'Twelfth Night'," in his *Shakespeare: A Survey*, 1925 (and reprinted by Oxford University Press, New York, 1926), pp. 172-80.

HARLEY GRANVILLE-BARKER (essay date 1912)

[*Granville-Barker was a noted actor, playwright, director, and critic. His work as a Shakespearean critic is at all times informed by his experience as a director, for he treats Shakespeare's plays not as works of literature better understood divorced from the theater, as did many Romantic critics, but as pieces meant for the stage. As a director, he emphasized simplicity in staging, set design, and costuming. He believed that elaborate scenery obscured the poetry which was of central importance to Shakespeare's plays. Granville-Barker also eschews the approach of directors who scrupulously reconstructed a production based upon Elizabethan stage techniques; he felt that this, too, detracted from*

the play's meaning. In the following excerpt, first published in his preface to Twelfth Night: An Acting Edition *in 1912, he recommends a bare platform stage as the most meaningful setting for* Twelfth Night, *because this setting best reflects the clarity and simplicity of the writing. Granville-Barker discusses two points of difficulty in* Twelfth Night *for modern audiences. He maintains that in order for the Viola/Cesario device to work, the play must be viewed "with Elizabethan eyes." Accustomed to seeing young boys cast in the roles of female characters, Elizabethan audiences saw Cesario as a boy, just as Orsino and Olivia see him. The "strain of make-believe" to modern audiences results from seeing Cesario played by an actress, which confounds our understanding of the love scenes. This point touches on the theme of sexual ambiguity in the play developed by Jan Kott (1964) and Clifford Leech (1965). The second problem concerns the humor of the play, which, according to Granville-Barker, draws much of its vigor from topical references, and therefore has lost its "salt" for modern audiences.*]

[*Twelfth Night*] is classed, as to the period of its writing, with *Much Ado About Nothing, As You Like It,* and *Henry V.* But however close in date, in spirit I am very sure it is far from them. I confess to liking those other three as little as any plays [Shakespeare] ever wrote. I find them so stodgily good, even a little (dare one say it?) vulgar, the work of a successful man who is caring most for success. . . . It was a turning point and he might have remained a popular dramatist. But from some rebirth in him that mediocre satisfaction was foregone, and, to our profit at least, came *Hamlet, Macbeth, Lear,* and the rest. (p. 26)

Twelfth Night is, to me, the last play of Shakespeare's golden age. I feel happy ease in the writing, and find much happy carelessness in the putting together. It is akin to the *Two Gentlemen of Verona* (compare Viola and Julia), it echoes a little to the same tune as the sweeter parts of the *Merchant of Venice,* and its comic spirit is the spirit of the Falstaff scenes of *Henry IV,* that are to my taste the truest comedy he wrote.

There is much to show that the play was designed for performance upon a bare platform stage without traverses or inner rooms or the like. It has the virtues of this method, swiftness and cleanness of writing and simple directness of arrangement even where the plot is least simple. It takes full advantage of the method's convenience. The scene changes constantly from anywhere suitable to anywhere that is equally so. The time of the play's action is any time that suits the author as he goes along. Scenery is an inconvenience. I am pretty sure that Shakespeare's performance went through without a break. Certainly its conventional arrangement into five acts for the printing of the Folio is neither by Shakespeare's nor any other sensitive hand; it is shockingly bad. If one must have intervals (as the discomforts of most theatres demand), I think the play falls as easily into the three divisions I have marked as any. [Intervals after II. iii and IV. i.]

I believe the play was written with a special cast in mind. Who was Shakespeare's clown, a sweet-voiced singer and something much more than a comic actor? He wrote Feste for him, and later the Fool in *Lear.* At least, I can conceive no dramatist risking the writing of such parts unless he knew he had a man to play them. And why a diminutive Maria—Penthesilea, the youngest wren of nine—unless it was only that the actor of the part was to be such a very small boy? I have cudgelled my brains to discover why Maria, as Maria, should be tiny, and finding no reason have ignored the point.

I believe too (this is a commonplace of criticism) that the plan of the play was altered in the writing of it. Shakespeare sets out upon a passionate love romance, perseveres in this until (one detects the moment, it is that jolly midnight revel) Malvolio, Sir Toby and Sir Andrew completely capture him. Even then, perhaps, Maria's notable revenge on the affectioned ass is still to to be kept within bounds. But two scenes later he begins to elaborate the new idea. The character of Fabian is added to take Feste's share of the rough practical joke and set him free for subtler wit. Then Shakespeare lets fling and works out the humorous business to his heart's content. That done, little enough space is left him if the play is to be over at the proper hour, and, it may be (if the play was being prepared for an occasion, the famous festivity in the Middle Temple Hall or another), there was little enough time to finish writing it in either. From any cause, we certainly have a scandalously ill-arranged and ill-written last scene, the despair of any stage manager. But one can discover, I believe, amid the chaos scraps of the play he first meant to write. Olivia suffers not so much by the midway change of plan, for it is about her house that the later action of the play proceeds, and she is on her author's hands. It is on Orsino, that interesting romantic, that the blow falls.

> Why should I not, had I the heart to do it,
> Like to the Egyptian thief at point of death,
> Kill what I love?—a savage jealousy
> That sometime savours nobly.
>   [V.i.117-20]

On that fine fury of his—shamefully reduced to those few lines—I believe the last part of the play was to have hung. It is too good a theme to have been meant to be so wasted. And the revelation of Olivia's marriage to his page (as he supposes), his reconciliation with her, and the more vital discovery that his comradely love for Viola is worth more to him after all than any high-sounding passion, is now all muddled up with the final rounding off of the comic relief. The character suffers severely. Orsino remains a finely interesting figure; he might have been a magnificent one. But there, it was Shakespeare's way to come out on the other side of his romance.

The most important aspect of the play must be viewed, to view it rightly, with Elizabethan eyes. Viola was played, and was meant to be played, by a boy. See what this involves. To that original audience the strain of make-believe in the matter ended just where for us it most begins, at Viola's entrance as a page. Shakespeare's audience saw Cesario without effort as Orsino sees him; more importantly they saw him as Olivia sees him; indeed it was over Olivia they had most to make believe. One feels at once how this affects the sympathy and balance of the love scenes of the play. One sees how dramatically right is the delicate still grace of the dialogue between Orsino and Cesario, and how possible it makes the more outspoken passion of the scenes with Olivia. Give to Olivia, as we must do now, all the value of her sex, and to the supposed Cesario none of the value of his, we are naturally quite unmoved by the business. Olivia looks a fool. . . . Now Shakespeare has devised one most carefully placed soliloquy where we are to be forcibly reminded that Cesario is Viola; in it he has as carefully divided the comic from the serious side of the matter. That scene played, the Viola, who does not do her best, as far as the passages with Olivia are concerned, to make us believe, as Olivia believes, that she is a man, shows, to my mind, a lack of imagination and is guilty of dramatic bad manners, knocking, for the sake of a little laughter, the whole of the play's romantic plot on the head. (pp. 26-9)

I do not think that Sir Toby is meant for nothing but a bestial sot. He is a gentleman by birth, or he would not be Olivia's

uncle (or cousin, if that is the relationship). He has been, it would seem, a soldier. He is a drinker, and while idleness leads him to excess, the boredom of Olivia's drawing-room, where she sits solitary in her mourning, drives him to such jolly companions as he can find: Maria and Fabian and the Fool. . . . [To] found an interpretation of Sir Toby only upon a study of his unfortunate surname is, I think, for the actor to give us both less and more than Shakespeare meant.

I do not believe that Sir Andrew is meant for a cretinous idiot. His accomplishments may not quite stand to Sir Toby's boast of them. . . . But Sir Andrew, as he would be if he could—the scholar to no purpose, the fine fellow to no end, in short the perfect gentleman—is still the ideal of better men than he who yet can find nothing better to do. (pp. 29-30)

Fabian, I think, is not a young man, for he hardly treats Sir Toby as his senior, he is the cautious one of the practical jokers, and he has the courage to speak out to Olivia at the end. . . .

Feste, I feel, is not a young man either. There runs through all he says and does that vein of irony by which we may so often mark one of life's self-acknowledged failures. We gather that in those days, for a man of parts without character and with more wit than sense, there was a kindly refuge from the world's struggle as an allowed fool. Nowadays we no longer put them in livery.

I believe Antonio to be an exact picture of an Elizabethan seaman-adventurer, and Orsino's view of him to be just such as a Spanish grandee would have taken of Drake. 'Notable pirate' and 'salt-water thief,' he calls him. (p. 30)

The keynotes of the poetry of the play are that it is passionate and it is exquisite. It is life, I believe, as Shakespeare glimpsed it with the eye of his genius in that half-Italianised court of Elizabeth. Orsino, Olivia, Antonio, Sebastian, Viola are passionate all, and conscious of the worth of their passion in terms of beauty. To have one's full laugh at the play's comedy is no longer possible, even for an audience of Elizabethan experts. Though the humour that is set in character is humour still, so much of the salt of it, its play upon the time and place, can have no savour for us. Instead we have learned editors disputing over the existence and meaning of jokes at which the simplest soul was meant to laugh unthinkingly. I would cut out nothing else, but I think I am justified in cutting those pathetic survivals.

Finally, as to the speaking of the verse and prose. The prose is mostly simple and straightforward. True, he could no more resist a fine-sounding word than, as has been said, he could resist a pun. They abound, but if we have any taste for the flavour of a language he makes us delight in them equally. There is none of that difficult involuted decoration for its own sake in which he revelled in the later plays. The verse is still regular, still lyrical in its inspiration, and it should I think be spoken swiftly. . . . (p. 31)

> *Harley Granville-Barker, "Preface to 'Twelfth Night'," in* More Prefaces to Shakespeare *by Harley Granville-Barker, edited by Edward M. Moore, Princeton University Press, 1974, pp. 26-32.*

MORRIS P. TILLEY (essay date 1914)

[*Tilley judges* Twelfth Night *to be philosophically and morally serious, a unified work centered around a "philosophical defence of a moderate indulgence in pleasure." For Tilley,* Twelfth Night *presents the historical struggle between the warring ideologies of the Renaissance and the Reformation, between the Puritanical restraint embodied in Malvolio and the wise moderation represented by Viola and Feste. In considering the conflict in its historical context, Tilley supports the criticism of Joseph Hunter (1845), F. Kreyssig (1862), and H. N. Hudson (1872). Because Malvolio is shown to be a religious hypocrite, his punishment is, for Tilley, neither excessive nor undeserved. Unlike George Steevens (1772) or E. K. Chambers (1907), Tilley claims that Feste's final song evokes the central meaning of the play, and gives voice to the theme of moderation. John Hollander (1959) also focuses on the theme of indulgence in* Twelfth Night.]

There is no agreement among Shakespearian critics with regard to the organic unity of *Twelfth Night*. Dr. Furnivall in one place believes that "the leading note of the play is fun." In another place he says less aptly that "the lesson is, sweet are the uses of adversity" [see excerpt above, 1877]. . . . Schlegel is representative of a group of critics who believe that "love regarded as an affair of the imagination rather than of the heart, is the fundamental theme running through all the variations of the play" [see excerpt above, 1808]. Most commentators, however, have agreed that the leading thought of this play may be discovered in its title; that the words *Twelfth Night, or What You Will*, are themselves the key-note of the play; that Shakespeare's first thought was to provide a comedy suitable for the festival. No one of these critics has thought that an organic idea has been more than incidental in this creation of pure mirth. So purely comic are its scenes, and so entirely sufficient are all of its incidents, that critics have not gone behind its gay life to look for an underlying moral law.

But such a moral law does exist as the fundamental idea of the play. *Twelfth Night* is a philosophical defence of a moderate indulgence in pleasure, in opposition on the one hand to an extreme hostility to pleasure and on the other hand to an extreme self-indulgence. Of the two extremes, the course of life that would banish all indulgence is emphasized as the more objectionable. In contrast to both, wise moderation is held up as the course to follow.

In opposing the extreme of excessive austerity Shakespeare is taking up cudgels for the stage in its struggle against the puritans; for the dramatists and the puritans fell out about the question of pleasure and pastime. (pp. 550-51)

The puritan's aversion to pleasure did not cease with his withdrawing of himself from pastimes and plays. He strove to make it impossible for others to enjoy what he thought a sin. It was not enough that, being virtuous, he did not care for cakes and ale, and ginger hot in the mouth; he was determined that others enjoying these things of the flesh should join him in giving them up, if not of their own free will, then by force of legislation or of arms. As a result the puritans stood out prominently and disagreeably in the mind of the average man of the street in Shakespeare's day, for their hostile attitude towards pleasure, and their zeal in trying to force their opinion upon others.

To the dramatist the name of puritan was, therefore, anathema; and he savagely attacked him in his most effective way. On every stage he held him up to scorn as a man who merely affected holiness. This he gave out to be the real puritan. In these attacks he presented the puritan condemning all pastimes, not that the puritan might grow strong by righteous living, but that he might enjoy the good opinion of others for a piety which in reality he did not possess. In short the dramatist made the puritan out to be a religious hypocrite: to the world a strict observer of religious forms, but at heart a self-seeker. (p. 552)

Shakespeare's method of attacking the puritans, however, is far less obvious than that of his fellow dramatists. By some he has even been thought to pass over with indifference the dispute of the theatre with the puritans. His infrequent mention of puritans lends appearance to this view, as does the fact that in his dramas we find only infrequent, and then only obscured, satire of puritan costume, speech, and manner. However, he does take part in the dispute, but in his distinctive way. (p. 553)

The theme of *Twelfth Night*, closely related as I believe that it is to the actual thought of the day, required less explanation at that time than it requires now. Malvolio's dress, his starched gait, his close cut hair, his nasal intonation of voice, told the Elizabethan audience what has frequently been doubted by critics since that time, that Malvolio was none other than a puritan.

The organic idea quickening and giving life to *Twelfth Night* was born of the strife of Shakespeare's day. Written at a time when the renaissance and the reformation had come in England to the parting of the ways, *Twelfth Night* bears testimony of the influence of these contending currents of freedom and of restraint. (p. 554)

Shakespeare, one of the sanest men that ever lived, viewed the struggles about him with a calmness that refused to allow him to become a partisan on either side. When the reformers were sweeping aside all pastime, and their opponents in reaction were sinking to new follies in their opposition, Shakspeare composed *Twelfth Night* in praise of the much-needed, well-balanced nature, to extoll that happy union of judgment and of feeling which is the basis of a higher sanity. He does this so deftly, with so little intrusion of his purpose in other than the most perfect dramatic form, that we of another time, removed from the strife of the puritan age, enjoy the result without realizing the purpose behind the finished production. Only the figure of Malvolio stands out in his hostility to all forms of amusement, to remind us that he is Shakespeare's contribution to the portraits of those enemies of art and of life in its fullest development, which aroused the Elizabethan dramatists to energetic and continued opposition.

The problem of life as Shakespeare saw it, and reveals it to us in this play, is basic; far greater than that of any group or sect of persons. It is the conflict in human nature between the reason and the emotions; and he suggests to us in the perfect sanity of Viola and of Feste that the solution lies not in the exclusion of the one or the other, but in the union of the two. In two groups of characters in the play he presents to us the evil results of following, to the exclusion of the other, either reason or emotion. In the self-conceited Malvolio and the strict Olivia he gives us representatives of those reformers of his day who, ignoring the moderate, gravitate to an extreme course of life in which reason is exalted to the exclusion of the emotions. Similarly, in Sir Andrew and Sir Toby, the other extreme from a well-ordered life is represented, one in which pleasure and folly make up the whole existence of man. (pp. 556-57)

There is general agreement among critics with regard to the excellence and the sanity of the characters of Viola and Feste. To them Shakespeare has given self-control and a penetration that guide them in their course of life, without exposing them to the extreme either of folly or of austerity. They represent the golden mean of temperance, in whom reason and emotion are at poise. (p. 558)

[This] ability to see and to think clearly, and to control her affections when necessary, was Viola's part in Shakespeare's plan of the play. As a further result of her well-balanced character, the plan of the play rewards her with the husband of her choice, while Orsino and Olivia are defeated in the aims of their affections. Similarly Feste in the sub-plot does not meet disappointment as do Andrew and Malvolio, but remains the happy son of mirth, to whom Shakespeare has given in goodly measure his own penetration into the motives of others.

In the persons of Orsino and Sir Andrew we have characters that are accepted as examples, in different degrees, of ungoverned natures. Orsino has surrendered himself entirely to his passion for Olivia, that will "bide no denay." No check of reason holds him back from his extravagance of love; and when count is taken at the end, his suit for the hand of Olivia is no more successful than that of the witless Sir Andrew, who has wasted his time in "fencing, dancing, and bear-baiting." So far as they are shown to us they have acted without reference to the guidance of reason; and are the products of their surrender to their unchecked inclinations.

With Sir Andrew may be included Sir Toby, Maria, and Fabian, as representatives of the extreme of mirth and frivolity. (p. 559)

The character of Olivia is open to no misunderstanding. She is the most impulsive of the whole impulsive group; nor do we feel the smallest surprise when her exaggerated grief gives sudden place to exaggerated passion. With regard to grouping her with Malvolio, however, it is important to dwell upon her determination to spend seven years in mourning. Her actions and words ally her with "her sad and civil steward," who suits so well with her fortunes. Her nature and his agree in looking upon life with severity. Her austere attitude is natural to her, so that it is not solely because of the recent death of her brother that she hath abjured the company and the sight of men. Until her distracting frenzy for Cesario seizes upon her, she not only rules pleasure out of her own life but regulates the life of her household with severity. The reproofs that she administers to Feste and to Cesario, upon her first visit, reveal her a stern governess of her household. (p. 560)

It is to this model of virtue that comes the distracting frenzy of falling in love with Viola disguised as a messenger from Orsino. Her self-discipline does not save her from the folly of loving Viola madly in spite of her resolution not to admit the suit of man. She is conscious of her revolt from her standard of reason and refers to it several times:

> There is something in me that reproves my fault
> But such a headstrong potent fault it is,
> That it but mocks reproof.
>
> [III.iv.203-05]

> I love thee so, that maugre all thy pride,
> Nor wit nor reason can my passion hide.
>
> [III.i.151-52]

Olivia is only one of a number of examples that Shakespare gives us in his plays, to show the futility of the aims of those who would be wiser than nature; and seek, in ruling out of life the emotions, to exalt the single standard of reason to supreme importance.

Malvolio shares with Olivia the distinction of representing the extreme of austerity, and is similarly brought to see his error. The placing of Olivia and Malvolio in the center of the plot interest, points to Shakespeare's intention in this play of emphasizing the inability of the puritans to rule out of life pleasure and pastime.

Those critics who have found Malvolio's punishment both coarse and excessive have failed to conceive Malvolio as the hypocrite that Shakespeare intended him to be [see excerpts above by Kenny (1864) and Archer (1884)]. This was the Elizabethan dramatist's usual denunciation of the puritans who ordered their life after Malvolio's principles. He is not as he seems, a genuinely pious man. It is only sometimes that he is a kind of a puritan. His puritanism is a pose that he adopts to advance himself at this time when with his mistress puritanical mannerisms are in favor. (pp. 560-61)

The inconsistencies in Malvolio's character that Mr. Archer and other critics have noted and have attributed to Shakespeare's incomplete mastery in the delineation of Olivia's steward, are not defects, but the natural inconsistencies that would arise in such a conflict between the real Malvolio and the part that he is acting.

It is probable that to the audience of his day, Malvolio appeared as a designing steward, who hoped to win his lady's favor by playing the puritan in her household. Feste had a shrewd suspicion of his motive when he wished him a "speedy infirmity for the better increasing his folly." Maria also saw through him. She based her plot of the letter on this weakness. Finally we hear Malvolio confessing in secret that his thoughts are upon the days when he shall be Count Malvolio by reason of marriage to his lady. If we keep this motive of his in mind, and measure his desire to please Olivia accordingly, there will arise no doubt in our mind as to whether his punishment is excessive. (pp. 562-63)

At the end of *Twelfth Night* is a song sung by Feste that is thought by some to be full of wisdom and by others to be hardly intelligible. . . .

> When that I was and a little tiny boy,
> A foolish thing was but a toy.
>
> But when I came to man's estate,
> Gainst Knaves and Thieves men shut their gate.
>
> But when I came alas to wive,
> By swaggering could I never thrive.
>
> But when I came unto my beds,
> With tosspots still had drunken heads.
>
> A great while ago the world begun,
> But that's all one, our play is done,
> And we'll strive to please you every day.
>
> [V.i.389-408]

In these words we have Feste touching lightly upon the fundamental idea of the play. Experience, coming to him with man's estate, has taught him the difference between men who are knaves and men who are not. The third and fourth stanzas of his song give his division of knaves into two classes, representatives of each of which he finds in his fellows of the sub-plot. Malvolio, who by swaggering tries to thrive in his suit for Olivia's hand, is his reference to the one class; and Sir Toby, Olivia's drunken cousin, and his foolish dupe Sir Andrew Aguecheek, whom canary has put down, are the point of his allusion to the tosspots, who go to bed with drunken heads. This division of knaves by Feste is his reference to the followers of the two extremes in the play. Experience has taught him that against both "men shut their gates." (pp. 564-65)

Thus it is that Feste, the wise discerner of motives throughout the play, gives us in this his song, and the last words of the comedy, assistance in penetrating to its fundamental idea; and in so doing adds his word to the support of the theory that Shakespeare in *Twelfth Night* scorns the folly of extremes, and holds up to high praise the mean that we term golden. (pp. 565-66)

Morris P. Tilley, "The Organic Unity of 'Twelfth Night'," in PMLA, 29, *Vol. XXIX, No. 4, December, 1914, pp. 550-66.*

A. C. BRADLEY (essay date 1916)

[*Bradley is a major Shakespearean critic whose work culminated the method of character analysis initiated in the Romantic era. He is best known for his* Shakespearean Tragedy, *a close analysis of* Hamlet, Othello, King Lear, *and* Macbeth. *Bradley concentrated on Shakespeare as a dramatist, and particularly on his characters, excluding not only the biographical questions so prominent in the works of his immediate predecessors, but also the questions of poetic structure, symbolism, and thematics which became prominent in later criticism. He thus may be seen as a pivotal figure in the transition in Shakespearean studies from the nineteenth to the twentieth century. He has been a major target for critics reacting against Romantic criticism, but he has continued to be widely read to the present day. In his essay on* Twelfth Night, *first published in* A Book of Homage to Shakespeare *in 1916, Bradley focuses on Feste, who, according to him, supplies Shakespeare's comment on the play. Noting the importance of music to the comedy, Bradley observes that "almost all the music and the praise of music comes from Feste or has to do with Feste." He opposes George Steevens (1772) regarding the relevance and authorship of Feste's final song: he claims that Shakespeare wrote the song, and, further, that it provides insight into the relationship between the clown and the playwright, because Shakespeare and Feste share the roles of servant and jester for their audience. For additional commentary on Feste's role in the play see the excerpts by Hermann Ulrici (1839), G. Wilson Knight (1930), Enid Welsford (1935), E. J. West (1949), and G. K. Hunter (1962).*]

Lear's Fool stands in a place apart—a sacred place; but, of Shakespeare's other Fools, Feste, the so-called Clown in *Twelfth Night,* has always lain nearest to my heart. He is not, perhaps, more amusing than Touchstone, to whom I bow profoundly in passing; but I love him more.

Whether Lear's Fool was not slightly touched in his wits is disputable. Though Touchstone is both sane and wise, we sometimes wonder what would happen if he had to shift for himself. Here and there he is ridiculous as well as humorous; we laugh *at* him, and not only *with* him. We never laugh at Feste. He would not dream of marrying Audrey. Nobody would hint that he was a "natural" or propose to "steal" him. . . He is as sane as his mistress; his position considered, he cannot be called even eccentric, scarcely even flighty; and he possesses not only the ready wit required by his profession, and an intellectual agility greater than it requires, but also an insight into character and into practical situations so swift and sure that he seems to supply, in fuller measure than any of Shakespeare's other Fools, the poet's own comment on the story. (pp. 207-08)

All the agility of wit and fancy, all the penetration and wisdom, which Feste shows in his calling, would not by themselves explain our feeling for him. But his mind to him a kingdom is, and one full of such present joys that he finds contentment there. Outwardly he may be little better than a slave; but Epictetus was a slave outright and yet absolutely free: and so is Feste. That world of quibbles which are pointless to his audience, of incongruities which nobody else can see, of flitting fancies which he only cares to pursue, is his sunny realm. . . .

But for this inward gaiety he could never have joined with all his heart in the roaring revelry of Sir Toby; but he does not need this revelry, and, unlike Sir Toby and Sir Toby's surgeon, he remains master of his senses. Having thus a world of his own, and being lord of himself, he cares little for Fortune. His mistress may turn him away; but, "to be turned away, let summer bear it out." This "sunshine of the breast" is always with him and spreads its radiance over the whole scene in which he moves. And so we love him.

We have another reason. The Fool's voice is as melodious as the "sweet content" of his soul. To think of him is to remember "Come away, come away, Death," and "O Mistress mine," and "When that I was," and fragments of folk-song and ballad, and a catch that "makes the welkin dance indeed." To think of *Twelfth Night* is to think of music. It opens with instrumental music, and ends with a song. All Shakespeare's best praise of music, except the famous passage in *The Merchant of Venice,* occurs in it. And almost all the music and the praise of music comes from Feste or has to do with Feste. In this he stands alone among Shakespeare's Fools; and that this, with the influence it has on our feeling for him, was intended by the poet should be plain. It is no accident that, when the Duke pays him for his "pains" in singing, he answers, "No pains, sir; I take pleasure in singing, sir"; that the revelry for which he risks punishment is a revelry of song; that, when he is left alone, he still sings. And, all being so, I venture to construe in the light of it what has seemed strange to me in the passage that follows the singing of "Come away." Usually, when Feste receives his "gratillity," he promptly tries to get it doubled; but here he not only abstains from any such effort but is short, if not disagreeably sharp, with the Duke. The fact is, he is offended, not as Fool, but as music-lover and artist. We others know what the Duke said beforehand of the song, but Feste does not know it. Now he sings, and his soul is in the song. Yet, as the last note dies away, the comment he hears from this noble aesthete is, "There's for thy pains"!

I have a last grace to notice in our wise, happy, melodious Fool. He was little injured by his calling. He speaks as he likes; but from first to last, whether he is revelling or chopping logic or playing with words, and to whomsoever he speaks or sings, he keeps his tongue free from obscenity. The fact is in accord with the spirit of this ever-blessed play, which could not have endured the "foul-mouthed" Fool of *All's Well.* . . . (pp. 210-12)

It remains to look at another side of the whole matter. One is scarcely sorry for Touchstone, but one is very sorry for Feste; and pity, though not a painful pity, heightens our admiration and deepens our sympathy. The position of the professional jester we must needs feel to be more or less hard, if not of necessity degrading. In Feste's case it is peculiarly hard. He is perfectly sane, and there is nothing to show that he is unfit for independence. In important respects he is, more than Shakespeare's other fools, superior in mind to his superiors in rank. And he has no Celia, no Countess, no Lear, to protect or love him. He had been Fool to Olivia's father, who "took much delight in him"; but Olivia, though not unkind, cannot be said to love him. We find him, on his first appearance, in disgrace and (if Maria is right) in danger of being punished or even turned away. His mistress, entering, tells him that he is a dry fool, that she'll no more of him, and (later) that his fooling grows old and people dislike it. Her displeasure, doubtless, has a cause, and it is transient, but her words are none the less significant. Feste is a relic of the past. The steward, a person highly valued by his lady, is Feste's enemy. Though Maria likes him, and, within limits, would stand his friend, there is no tone of affection in her words to him, and certainly none in those of any other person. We cannot but feel very sorry for him.

This peculiar position explains certain traits in Feste himself which might otherwise diminish our sympathy. One is that he himself, though he shows no serious malevolence even to his enemy, shows no affection for any one. . . . The fact is, he recognizes very clearly that, as this world goes, a man whom nobody loves must look out for himself. Hence (this is the second trait) he is a shameless beggar, much the most so of Shakespeare's Fool's. He is fully justified, and he begs so amusingly that we welcome his begging; but shameless it is. But he is laying up treasures on earth against the day when some freak of his own, or some whim in his mistress, will bring his dismissal, and the short summer of his freedom will be followed by the wind and the rain. And so, finally, he is as careful as his love of fun will allow to keep clear of any really dangerous enterprise. He must join in the revel of the knights and the defiance of the steward; but from the moment when Malvolio retires with a threat to Maria, and Maria begins to expound her plot against him, Feste keeps silence; and, though she expressly assigns him a part in the conspiracy, he takes none. The plot succeeds magnificently, and Malvolio is shut up, chained as a lunatic, in a dark room; and that comic genius Maria has a new scheme, which requires the active help of the Fool. But her words, ''Nay, I prithee, put on this gown and this beard,'' show that he objects; and if his hesitation is momentary, it is not merely because the temptation is strong. For, after all, he runs but little risk, since Malvolio cannot see him, and he is a master in the management of his voice. And so, agreeing with Sir Toby's view that their sport cannot with safety be pursued to the upshot, after a while, when he is left alone with the steward, he takes steps to end it and consents, in his own voice, to provide the lunatic with light, pen, ink, and paper for his letter to Olivia.

We are not offended by Feste's eagerness for six-pences and his avoidance of risks. By helping us to realize the hardness of his lot, they add to our sympathy and make us admire the more the serenity and gaiety of his spirit. And at the close of the play these feelings reach their height. He is left alone; for Lady Belch, no doubt, is by her husband's bedside, and the thin-faced gull Sir Andrew has vanished, and the rich and noble lovers with all their attendants have streamed away to dream of the golden time to come, without a thought of the poor jester. There is no one to hear him sing; but what does that matter? He takes pleasure in singing. And a song comes into his head; an old rude song about the stages of man's life, in each of which the rain rains every day; a song at once cheerful and rueful, stoical and humorous; and this suits his mood and he sings it. But, since he is even more of a philosopher than the author of the song, and since, after all, he is not merely a Fool but the actor who is playing that part in a theatre, he adds at the end a stanza of his own:

> A great while ago the world begun,
>   With hey, ho, the wind and the rain;
> But that's all one, our play is done,
>   And we'll strive to please you every day.
> > [V. i. 405-08]

Shakespeare himself, I feel sure, added that stanza to the old song; and when he came to write *King Lear* he, I think, wrote

yet another, which Feste might well have sung. To the immortal words,

> Poor Fool and knave, I have one part in my
> heart That's sorry yet for thee,

the Fool replies,

> He that has and a little tiny wit,
>   With hey, ho, the wind and the rain,
> Must make content with his fortunes fit,
>   Though the rain it raineth every day.
> > [*King Lear*, III. ii. 72-7]

So Shakespeare brings the two Fools together; and, whether or no he did this wittingly, I am equally grateful to him. But I cannot be grateful to those critics who see in Feste's song only an illustration of the bad custom by which sometimes, when a play was finished, the clown remained, or appeared, on the stage to talk nonsense or to sing some old ''trash''; nor yet to those who tell us that it was ''the players'' who tacked this particular ''trash'' to the end of *Twelfth Night*. They may conceivably be right in perceiving no difference between the first four stanzas and the last, but they cannot possibly be right in failing to perceive how appropriate the song is to the singer, and how in the line

> But that's all one, our play is done,
> > [V. i. 407]

he repeats an expression used a minute before in his last speech [''I was one, sir, in his interlude; one Sir Topas, sir; *but that's all one*'']. We owe these things, not to the players, but to that player in Shakespeare's company who was also a poet, to Shakespeare himself—the same Shakespeare who perhaps had hummed the old song, half-ruefully and half-cheerfully, to its accordant air, as he walked home alone to his lodging from the theatre or even from some noble's mansion; he who, looking down from an immeasurable height on the mind of the public and the noble, had yet to be their servant and jester, and to depend upon their favour; not wholly uncorrupted by this dependence, but yet superior to it and, also, determined, like Feste, to lay by the sixpences it brought him, until at last he could say [in *The Tempest*], ''Our revels now are ended,'' and could break—was it a magician's staff or a Fool's bauble? (pp. 212-17)

A. C. Bradley, ''Feste the Jester,'' in his A Miscellany, *Macmillan and Co., Limited, 1929, pp. 207-17.*

J. B. PRIESTLEY (essay date 1925)

[*Priestley observes that Malvolio is outside the comic tradition and is not treated by Shakespeare as a purely comic character. Instead, he represents an intolerant, self-seeking type whom Shakespeare ''clearly detested.'' Additional commentary on Shakespeare's intent in the characterization of Malvolio is provided in the excerpts by Joseph Hunter (1845), F. Kreyssig (1862), H. N. Hudson (1872), Morris P. Tilley (1914), Mark Van Doren (1939), and O. J. Campbell (1943).*]

Our present inquiry takes us into the society of the low, the drunken and disreputable company, the comic Illyrians. (It is difficult even to sound the name and remain sober.) Whether Malvolio, who was himself neither drunken nor disreputable but essentially a ''grave liver,'' should have place in the company, is a very debatable question. Most of the comic scenes in the play revolve around him, and it is his antics, his sudden rise and his awful collapse, that form the basis of most of the broader comedy of the piece; his self-love and swelling vanity, which make him an easy butt for Maria and her grinning troupe, his gravity and pompous airs, are all served up, without mercy, for our entertainment. Yet Malvolio, strictly speaking, is not a comic character. He stands outside the real comic tradition. Although Shakespeare gives some of his speeches a most delicious flavour of absurdity, he does not treat Malvolio as he treats his purely comic figures, whom he regards not merely with a humorous tolerance but with positive delight and relish, encouraging them, as it were, to indulge their every whim. The difference between, let us say, Malvolio and Sir Andrew Aguecheek is that Shakespeare handles the one and dandles the other. Sir Andrew is really a much more contemptible figure than the serious and capable steward, but then he is so manifestly ridiculous that he evades criticism altogether, escapes into a world of his own, where every fresh piece of absurdity he commits only brings him another round of laughter and applause. Times change, and we are more likely to regard Malvolio with some measure of sympathy than was Shakespeare; indeed, in spite of his vanity, to us he is a figure not untouched by pathos, for the possibility of Olivia falling in love with him (and she admits his value as an employee) appears to us not entirely preposterous, nor do his portentous gravity and puritanical airs seem to us so offensive, now that our Sir Tobies have been steadily rebuked in the manner of Malvolio for at least two generations. . . . Malvolio, we may say, has been steadily coming into his own for a long time, so that it is difficult for us to regard him as an unpleasant oddity as Shakespeare did. And perhaps it says something for our charity that, sitting as we are among ever-diminishing supplies of cakes and ale, we can still see something pathetic in this figure.

Shakespeare's sympathies were so wide and his dramatic genius so universal that it is always dangerous to give him a point of view and dower him with various likes and dislikes. Nevertheless it is true to say that certain types of character very clearly aroused his dislike; and it is also true to say that these are the very types of character that appear to have some fascination for our world. In short, his villains are rapidly becoming our heroes. Thus, Shakespeare clearly detested all hard, unsympathetic, intolerant persons, the over-ambigious and overweening, the climbers and careerists, the "get on or get outs" of this world. When the will and the intellect in all their pride were divorced from tolerance, charity, a love of the good things of this world, they formed the stuff out of which the Shakespearean villains were made. But the Bastard and Iago and Richard the Third are the very characters that some of our modern dramatists would select to adorn three acts of hero-worship. So too, to come down the scale, our friend Malvolio, the pushing puritan, is, under various disguises, the hero of almost one-half of all the American novels that were ever written. . . . While this conceited and over-ambitious steward struts cross-gartered on the lawn for our entertainment, there flutters across his path, for one fleeting moment, the terrible shadow of that other ambitious underling, Iago. So Malvolio is deceived, abused, locked up and treated as a madman for a short space, and this is his purgation, for Shakespeare saw that his soul was in danger and so appointed for him two angels of deliverance, namely, Maria and Sir Toby Belch.

In the very first speech that Sir Toby makes, when we discover him talking with Maria, he remarks that "care's an enemy to life," and this we may take to be his philosophy. His time is spent in putting a multitude of things, oceans of burnt sack,

mountains of pickled herrings, between himself and the enemy, Care; and he may be shortly described as a Falstaff without genius, who would have made the fat knight a very able lieutenant. (pp. 44-7)

[Sir Toby] is by no means a simpleton. Nor is he, on the other hand, a comic genius like Falstaff, whose world has been transformed into an ideally comic world, whose whole life, whose every speech and action, are devised to further ease, enjoyment, and laughter. Sir Toby, in his own coarse, swashbuckling manner, is witty, but he is not the cause of wit in other men. He does not transform himself into an object of mirth, content so long as men are laughing and the comic spirit is abroad, but, like any bullying wag of the tap-room, looks for a butt in the company. (pp. 49-50)

Of one of Sir Toby's boon companions, Feste the Clown, there is little to be said. Viola, after a bout of wit with him, sums up the matter admirably:

This fellow's wise enough to play the Fool;
And to do that well craves a kind of wit:
He must observe their mood on whom he jests,
The quality of persons, and the time;
Not, like the haggard, check at every feather
That comes before his eyes. This is a practice
As full of labour as a wise man's art:
For folly, that he wisely shows, is fit;
But wise men's folly, shown, quite taints their wit.

[III.i.60-8]

This is an accurate description of Feste's own practice, for as he lounges in and out of the scene, it will be noticed that always he plays up to his company. He is a professional entertainer and gives his audiences what he knows will please them. . . . With Sir Toby and Maria, Feste appears at his ease and, as it were, with his wit unbuttoned, bandying broad jests with them; while for the delectation of Sir Andrew, a great admirer of his, he utters the first nonsense that comes into his head. Indeed, in this company of boon companions and midnight caterwaulers, his humour is all for wild nonsense of a Rabelaisian cast. Such ridiculous speeches as "I did impeticos thy gratillity; for Malvolio's nose is no whipstock; my lady has a white hand, and the Myrmidons are not bottle-ale houses" cast a spell over the rural wits of Sir Andrew, who pronounces it to be "the best fooling, when all is done." (pp. 57-9)

Sir Andrew Aguecheek is one of Shakespeare's family of simpletons: he is first cousin to Slender and Silence. Life pulses to faintly in this lank-haired, timid, rustic squire that he is within a stride of utter imbecility. . . . At first sight, it seems astonishing that a comic character of any dimensions could possibly be created out of such material, and, indeed, only a great genius could have taken these few straws and made of them a creature whose every odd remark and quaint caper is a delight. But it is Sir Andrew's amazing simplicity, his almost pathetic naïvety, his absolute lack of guile, that make him so richly absurd. And with these there goes a certain very characteristic quality, the unanalysable factor, that is present in every remark he makes; every speech has a certain Aguecheek flavour or smack that is unmistakable; even as we read we can hear the bleating of his plaintive little voice. (pp. 60-1)

Our last glimpse of him is somewhat moving, for he has a broken head, received in the company of Sir Toby, who has himself been given "a bloody coxcomb," but nevertheless his admiration and faith are undiminished. . . . But his idol turns and rends him, calling him an ass-head and a coxcomb and a knave, a thin-faced knave, a gull. These are hard sayings but not too hard for Sir Andrew to swallow, and perhaps they made their peace together afterwards. If not, we can only hope that our simpleton went on his travels and somehow in the end contrived to find his way into Gloucester and into the orchard of Justice Shallow, for there he would find company after his own heart, the great Shallow himself and Silence and Slender, and take his place among such boon companions, seat himself at the pippins and cheese and try to disengage from his tangled mind such confused memories as remained there of Illyria and the roystering Illyrians, his foolish face aglow beneath the unfading apple blossom. (pp. 67-8)

> *J. B. Priestley, "The Illyrians," in his* The English Comic Characters, *John Lane, 1925, pp. 43-68.*

ARTHUR QUILLER-COUCH (essay date 1930)

[*Quiller-Couch was editor with J. Dover Wilson of the New Cambridge edition of Shakespeare's works. In his study* Shakespeare's Workmanship, *and in his Cambridge lectures on Shakespeare, Quiller-Couch based his interpretations on the assumption that Shakespeare was mainly a craftsman attempting, with the tools and materials at hand, to solve particular problems central to his plays. He interprets Illyria and its inhabitants as so ethereal and unearthly that their world more closely resembles Elysium than the life-like settings of the previous comedies. This comment supports Frederick Furnivall (1877) and prefigures the comments of Mark Van Doren (1939), E. C. Pettet (1949), W. H. Auden (1957), G. K. Hunter (1962), Jan Kott (1964), Albert Gérard (1964), Clifford Leech (1965), and Philip Edwards (1968) who see in* Twelfth Night *the seeds of a darker mood which Shakespeare developed in the problem comedies.*]

Structurally *Twelfth Night* is a piece of fun as primitive as a harlequinade. Misrule rules all the while in Olivia's household; songs and catches turn night into day: and the culprits work their final jest upon the Steward who would suppress it. His downfall, again, is just of the sort to tickle a child's humour—the sort of risibility that does not reach beyond the sheer fun, for instance, of seeing a solemn personage slip up heels-aloft on a slide of butter.

Let us remind ourselves, too, that *Twelfth Night* contains no bawdry: that Feste, while one of the most philosophical of Shakespeare's clowns, is also the cleanest mouthed; that the jolly back-chat of Sir Toby, Sir Andrew, Maria, Fabian runs innocent throughout as battledore and shuttlecock: that the plentiful disorder of Olivia's household, in short, is never that of a disorderly house. Even the love-making never passes beyond such simple romantic play as children have learnt from their fairy-books and take as much for granted as the glass slipper fitted by the Prince on Cinderella. No hearts break; passion never obtrudes upon sentiment, save by a hint. . . . Everything ends happily and, as it began, to the pretty illusion of music. (pp. xviii-xix)

Orsino, but for the grace of God and the clemency of circumstance, might have come to as evil an end as King Richard II. He has the same gift of saying things beautifully when they do not help the immediate situation. . . . He toys with [love] as with a lap-dog, stroking its ears: he feeds it on music—'Give me excess of it'. . . . As for the music, Shakespeare knew a great deal about it: knew about it from the music of the spheres down to triple time, plain-song, tonic intervals and the proper handling of lute and viol. . . . But as in the last Act of *The Merchant,* as in the 'moated grange song' in *Measure for Measure,* so in this play, it is Shakespeare who brings in the music exactly to the mood *he* commands: and here he commands better than Orsino—the wayward, wistful singing of Feste. Orsino, commanding much music and a page with the impressive name of Cesario, finds himself in the end fortunately possessed of a—Viola. (pp. xxi-xxiii)

[Malvolio] is not a 'Puritan' in any historical sense, but a Puritan only as an incarnation of the abstract Puritan's besetting foible—that of self-righteousness, of making himself a judge of others. Through this, and through the complacent arrogance bred by that habit of mind, he comes to grief. As the Comic Spirit might put it, he tries to lift himself up by his own cross-garters: and he is incorrigible as a nagging woman—as all such kill-joys are. . . . We all know that type of man and have a sort of pitying respect for him because he will never learn. But we should not allow his figure to dominate this play any more than we should allow his kind to dominate our daily life. (p. xxiv)

[By] contrast with Rosalind Viola appears less a creature of flesh and blood; diaphanous somewhat; a princess out of fairy-tale; yet indubitably a princess, born to arrive after pretty adversities at her heart's desire and live happy ever after. To put it in one way, she is just the sort of maiden that a sound middle-aged man, with a heart not unresponsive to youth and romance, would choose for a ward: to put it in another, she is one of those Shakespearian women—such as Perdita and Miranda—concerning whom one feels that on a perfect stage they could only be impersonated by one gifted by the gods to combine fresh transient beauty with inherited breeding. (p. xxv)

[With] all respect to Malvolio, to his hold upon 'star' actors, to all his claim, not disputed, upon Shakespeare's sole begetting, we must hold and insist on holding Feste, Master of the Revels, to be the master-mind and controller of *Twelfth Night,* its comic spirit and president, even as Puck is comic spirit and president of *A Midsummer-Night's Dream.* Unscathed by the slaps and side-blows of the plot, in the end he gets dismissed out into the cold: and that is Shakespeare's last word of irony—as it is with his last word on the poor loyal Fool in *Lear.* But while the play lasts, and his business, Feste has it in charge. (p. xxvi)

[*Twelfth Night*] has been called Shakespeare's farewell to mirth: and for this leave-taking . . . Shakespeare summons up a troop of characters recognisable by us as our old favourites—with a difference. Delightful to read—and so delightful to witness that no one who has missed seeing it staged can guess the full of its charm or the thrill of that truly Aristotelian [recognition scene] upon which it concludes—a play of one piece compact, compelling and holding you to its mood—this *Twelfth Night,* analysed in the study, becomes a texture or tissue of shadows, of afterthoughts, the ghostlier the more poetical. Arden, with its greenwood sunshine, has faded into Illyria, perilously near fading into Elysium. The mirth abides; but it reaches us from a distance, its *dramatis personae* move in the beams of a lunar rainbow. They move to music, but to music with a dying fall as a fountain in a garden at night, and it has changed from the robust note of 'Love is crownéd with the prime' to 'Youth's a stuff will not endure'—a very slight change, but subtle, delicate, if we listen. The reader, aware of this change, becomes aware also that the play, for all its gaiety, is agonising a spell upon him. . . . A most subtle play, belonging (in the Malvolio business especially) to the highest, most ancient traditions of Comedy. . . . (pp. xxvii-xxviii)

> *Arthur Quiller-Couch, in his introduction to* Twelfth Night or What You Will *by William Shakespeare,*

Cambridge at the University Press, 1930, pp. vii-
xxviii.

G. WILSON KNIGHT (essay date 1932)

[*One of the most influential of modern Shakespearean critics,
Knight helped shape the twentieth-century reaction against the
biographical and character studies of the nineteenth-century
Shakespeareans. Knight's analytic practice stresses what he calls,
in his study* The Wheel of Fire, *the "spatial" aspects of imagery,
atmosphere, theme, and symbol in the plays. He thus parallels
the New Critics with his emphasis on verbal texture; his discussions of symbolism are similar to Samuel Taylor Coleridge's notion of the symbolic as indefinite with multiple meanings. The
essay below is excerpted from Knight's* The Shakespearean Tempest, *in which he focuses on the unity of* Twelfth Night *through
a discussion of the imagery of the sea, music, love, and precious
stones. For additional commentary on the unity of the play, see
the excerpts by August Wilhelm Schlegel (1808), Hermann Ulrici
(1839), G. G. Gervinus (1849-50), Morris P. Tilley (1914), Enid
Welsford (1935), and John Russell Brown (1957).*]

Twelfth Night is an exquisite blending of *The Comedy of Errors*
and *The Merchant of Venice:* the plot of the one charged with
the imaginative richness and deep emotions of the other. Again
the tempest-music opposition is exquisitely developed. Wrecked
and divided, the twins, Viola and Sebastian, find themselves
in Illyria, land of music and romance. Music is here stronger
than in any other of these romantic comedies, and the pattern
of romantic love more exquisitely therewith entwined. The
tempest which prologues the action is described for us:

> *Viola.* And what should I do in Illyria?
> 　My brother he is in Elysium.
> 　Perchance he is not drown'd: what think you, sailors?
> *Captain.* It is perchance that you yourself were saved.
> *Viola.* O my poor brother! and so perchance may he be.
> *Captain.* True, madam: and, to comfort you with chance,
> 　Assure yourself, after our ship did split,
> —When you and those poor number saved with you
> 　Hung on our driving boat, I saw your brother,
> 　Most provident in peril, bind himself,
> 　Courage and hope both teaching him the practice,
> 　To a strong mast that lived upon the sea;
> 　Where, like Arion on the dolphin's back,
> 　I saw him hold acquaintance with the waves
> 　So long as I could see.　　　　　　　[I.ii.3-17]

The association of the sea and 'chance' is important. The thought
is ever embedded in this tempest imagery: waves are fickle as
fortune, the sea suggests all the chances of mortality. This
description of Sebastian in the waters is close to a similar
passage on Ferdinand in *The Tempest.* Now Sebastian, too,
recalls the wreck. He is with Antonio, bereft of his loved sister,
derelict and purposeless: 'my determinate voyage is mere extravagancy' [II.i.11]: here all human adventure is a 'voyage'
and nearly every one employs the metaphor. Sebastian tells
Antonio of his father, and twin sister; then,

> . . . some hour before you took me from the
> breach of the sea was my sister drowned.
> 　　　　　　　　　　　　　　　[II.i.21-23]

There follows a characteristic image:

> . . . She is drowned already, sir, with salt wa-
> ter, though I seem to drown her remembrance
> again with more.
> 　　　　　　　　　　　　　　　[II.i.30-31]

Antonio later recalls how he rescued Sebastian

> From the rude sea's enraged and foamy mouth.
> 　　　　　　　　　　　　　　　[V.i.78]

'Enraged' again. 'A wreck past hope he was', says Antonio.
So a tempest here disperses and divides, setting the stage for
reunion and joy.

Twelfth Night takes us to a world of music:

> If music be the food of love, play on;
> Give me excess of it, that, surfeiting,
> The appetite may sicken and so die.
> That strain again! it had a dying fall:
> O, it came o'er my ear like the sweet sound,
> That breathes upon a bank of violets,
> Stealing and giving odour.　　　　[I.i.1-7]

'Violets'. The name Viola suggests both flowers and music,
music of the 'viol', mentioned in *Pericles.* Music and soft
zephyrs: we shall find them again in the person of Imogen.
Viola can speak 'in many sorts of music' [I.ii.58]. This is a
natural phrase. Personal qualities tend to reflect poetic associations. Thus love heroines are continually gifted with love
associations: Portia has riches, Viola, Desdemona, Marina and
many others are musical, Perdita and Ophelia carry flowers,
Imogen is 'a piece of tender air'. But in this play music is
more important than any other love suggestion:

> *Duke.* Give me some music. Now, good morrow, friends.
> 　Now, good Cesario, but that piece of song,
> 　That old and antique song we heard last night;
> 　Methought it did relieve my passion much,
> 　More than light airs and recollected terms
> 　Of these most brisk and giddy-paced times:
> 　Come, but one verse.　　　　　　[II.iv.2-7]

Orsino reminds us of Cleopatra: 'music, moody food of us that
trade in love' (where, by the way, we may observe the typical
merchandise metaphor 'trade'). Music plays.

> *Orsino.*　　　　　. . . How dost thou like this tune?
> *Viola.* It gives a very echo to the seat
> 　Where Love is throned.　　　　[II.iv.20-22]

Here is another fine love-music comparison:

> *Olivia.* But, would you undertake another suit,
> 　I had rather hear you to solicit that
> 　Than music from the spheres.　　[III.i.108-10]

Feste sings a song which 'dallies with the innocence of love'.
[II.iv.47] Feste embodies the play's essence. Humour and music are blent in his person. And in his earlier song, too, singing
and love are close-twined:

> O mistress mine, where are you roaming?
> O stay and hear; your true love's coming,
> 　That can sing both high and low.　[II.iii.39-41]

And there are some fine phrases spoken in Viola's embassy of
love to Olivia. First she tells how her master loves

> With adorations, fertile tears,
> With groans that thunder love, with sighs of fire. . . .

A curious passage where love, to suit Viola's purpose, itself
becomes imaginatively a thing of terrible, god-like power to

which mortality must submit. Next, she tells how she, in her master's place, would sing her love:

> *Olivia.*   Why, what would you?
> *Viola.* Make me a willow cabin at your gate,
>   And call upon my soul within the house;
>   Write loyal cantons of contemned love
>   And sing them loud, even in the dead of night;
>   Holla your name to the reverberate hills,
>   And make the babbling gossip of the air
>   Cry out 'Olivia!' O you should not rest
>   Between the elements of air and earth
>   But you should pity me!   [I.v.267-276]

Throughout, however, sea thought and voyages are inwoven in our world of music. Sebastian's sudden lovejoy at the end is a 'flood of fortune'. [IV.iii.11]. Orsino's love, 'receiveth as the sea' and is 'all as hungry as the sea', infinite as the ocean itself [I.i.11; II.iv.100]. And, like the ocean, he is changeable, uncertain. . . . 'I am for all waters', he says later [IV.ii.63]. Sir Toby is 'drowned' in drink [I.v.136], just as the mind is often imaged as 'drowned' by any mastering emotion. Malvolio says of Cesario: ''tis with him in standing water, between boy and man' [I.v.158-59], a queer image such as we find in *Antony and Cleopatra*. Viola is love's ambassador and therefore, as happens elsewhere in *The Merry Wives of Windsor*, and *Troilus*, imaged as a ship:

> *Maria.* Will you hoist sail, sir? here lies your way.
> *Viola.* No, good swabber; I am to hull here a little longer. . . .
>   [I.v.202-04]

There is rich jewel imagery, too. Rings and pearls are associated with love, and Orsino makes a fine 'jewel' comparison:

> But 'tis that miracle and queen of gems
> That nature pranks her in, attracts my soul.
>   [II.iv.85-86]

Maria, whom Sir Toby eventually marries, is his 'metal of India' [II.v.14]. Such Eastern imagery variously accompanies Shakespearian love. So Orsino compares himself to an angry lover of legend: 'the Egyptian thief' [V.i.118], and a lover's smile is compared to a map of the 'Indies' [III.ii.80]. But tragic sea-adventures are in our background. Antonio is throughout a tragic figure, associated with sea-fights and stern events:

> Once, in a sea-fight, 'gainst the count his galleys
> I did some service.   [III.iii.26-27]

Orsino describes the action:

> That face of his I do remember well;
> Yet, when I saw it last, it was besmear'd
> As black as Vulcan in the smoke of war:
> A bawbling vessel was he captain of,
> For shallow draught and bulk unprizable,
> With which such scathful grapple did he make
> With the most noble bottom of our fleet,
> That very envy and the tongue of loss
> Cried fame and honour on him.   [V.i.51-59]

He is a 'notable pirate' and 'salt-water thief' [V.i.69], according to Orsino. His passionate love of Sebastian causes him to make a metaphorical 'voyage' in following him [III.iii.7]. His love is tragically passionate, a more dangerous reality than our other love themes: he is a forecast of Othello. But tragedy

is not given much freedom here. Terror is often humorous, as in the duel scene. There a 'bear' is mentioned as an image of terror [III.iv.323]. Malvolio was originally annoyed about a bear, too [II.v.9]. All, however, if we except Malvolio, is blended in a final joy. At the moment of reunion the amazed Sebastian cries:

>   I had a sister,
> Whom the blind waves and surges have devour'd. . . .
>   [V.i.228-29]

Sebastian, too, has risen from 'his watery tomb' [V.i.234]. Both find that 'tempests are kind and salt waves fresh in love' [III.iv.384].

Here, then, we find a pattern of music, love, and precious stones, threaded by the sombre strands of a sea tempest and a sea fight. Finally there is love, reunion, and joy. Even Orsino has a share 'in this most happy wreck' [V.i.266]. 'Journeys end in lovers meeting', sings Feste [II.iii.43]: they are sea journeys, the storm-tossed life of man voyaging to love's Illyrian coasts. Like Christopher Sly's strange experience, this golden romance is all like a sweet dream come true, or a bad dream gone. . . . Continually the Shakespearian imagination plays on this thought of dream; and his romances are dreamland actualized. But never was the whole world of sweet dream so perfectly and harmoniously bodied into a purely human plot as here. And even Malvolio only falls by aspiring to the fine and rich delight of an impossible love. All tragic and tempestuous things are finally blended in the music of Feste's final song, with its refrain,

>   With hey, ho, the wind and the rain. . . .

and

>   The rain it raineth every day.
>   [V.i.390-92]

Which song presents a microcosm of the play: tempests dissolved in music. Perhaps this is the most harmonious of Shakespeare's human romances. (pp. 121-26)

> *G. Wilson Knight, "The Romantic Comedies," in his* The Shakespearian Tempest, *Oxford University Press, London, 1932, pp. 75-168.*

ENID WELSFORD   (essay date 1935)

[*Welsford discusses the Saturnalian aspects of* Twelfth Night. *She describes Feste as less a critic of the play's action than a Lord of Misrule who unifies the play and preserves its comic proportion. For additional commentary on the Saturnalian elements of the play, see the excerpts by E. Montégut (1867), C. L. Barber (1958), L. G. Salingar (1959), and Barbara K. Lewalski (1965). The following excerpt is taken from Welsford's* The Fool: His Social and Literary History, *first published in 1935.*]

Like *As You Like It*, *Twelfth Night* is a poem of escape, where our sympathies go out to those who evade reality or rather realize a dream; so that it is but natural that the fool should be a prominent and attractive figure and make an important contribution to the action. Nevertheless, Shakespeare does not in this case repeat himself, and, in spite of obvious resemblances, Feste and Touchstone play very different parts in very different plays. *As You Like It* deals with the flight from civilization into an imaginary golden world, and Touchstone is the merry critic of various would-be practitioners of the simple life. In *Twelfth Night*, which, as its name suggests, is a play intended for the Christmas season, Shakespeare transmutes into poetry the quintessence of the Saturnalia. The revellers at that festive holiday were too busily engaged in celebrating a temporary freedom from the restraints of law and order to have inclination or leisure for Arcadian day-dreaming. Illyria is a country permeated with the spirit of the Feast of Fools, where identities are confused, 'uncivil rule' applauded, cakes and ale successfully defended against virtuous onslaughts, and no harm is done. In Illyria therefore the fool is not so much a critic of his environment as a ringleader, a merry-companion, a Lord of Misrule. Being equally welcome above and below stairs, his musical mirth gives unity to a play which, like the Duke's mind, 'is a very opal'. His only enemy is Malvolio, the killjoy who takes himself too seriously and whose very virtues as a steward are vices in a world where nothing is of value save romantic love and lusty revelling. Malvolio, like Jaques, excludes himself from the final comic harmony; while Feste, who has triumphed over him completely, is given the last word and is left in possession of the stage.

This reversal of dignity and impudence is not only in accordance with the Saturnalian tradition, it has something of the more subtle spirit of the sottie. Feste is no mere mischief-making Vice, but a fool who sees the truth and is wiser than his betters. In proving Olivia to be the true fool, he acts in accordance with the traditions of the fool-societies; and in poking fun at the sentimentality of Olivia and the Duke he is, like Touchstone, claiming his jester's privilege of licensed criticism. (pp. 251-52)

Feste, then, is, in his humble way, a sage-fool, who sees the truth; but what is this truth that he sees? Well, he has no particularly profound remarks to make, but is a living embodiment of the comic truth that it is a pity to be too portentous. Even if Malvolio 'thinks nobly of the soul', he, like Sir Toby Belch, should remember that 'care's an enemy to life' and that revellers and romantic lovers have more to say for themselves than the worldly wise are willing to admit. But even about this there is no need to be over-serious. In these plays Shakespeare does indeed support the cause of youth and gaiety, but he does so not as a moralist but as an entertainer. The deliberate unreality of the romantic comedies is part of their charm, and the jester's main function is to preserve proportion, while helping on the game of make-believe. It is but fitting that a fool should be called Touchstone in a play called *As You Like It;* and that the jester, Feste, should sum up *Twelfth Night, or What you Will* by dissolving the Illyrian comedy of errors into a nonsense song.

Yet it cannot be denied that this final trifling is a little sad. Meaningless, illogical as it is, the old folk-rhyme, with its recurrent refrain and plaintive melody, conveys a suggestion of regret for youth, for the fading of romance into a hard reality, where fools no longer lead the revels. . . . (pp. 252-53)

But is this sense or nonsense? Is life so much less transient than youth; is the world so much more solid than romantic comedy?

> 'A great while ago the world begun,
> With hey, ho, the wind and the rain;
> But that's all one, our play is done,
> And we'll strive to please you every day.'
> [V.i.405-08]

The next time we hear this refrain it will still be sung by a fool, but by a fool in bitter earnest, by a fool who stands with his master, a vagabond caught in a storm, outside gates which men have most effectually shut against him. (p. 253)

Enid Welsford, "The Court-Fool in Elizabethan Drama," in her The Fool: His Social and Literary History, *Farrar & Rinehart, Incorporated, 1936, pp. 243-72.*

JOHN MIDDLETON MURRY (essay date 1936)

[*Middleton Murry echoes Frederick Furnivall (1877) and Arthur Quiller-Couch (1930) in noting the "silvery undertone of sadness" which permeates* Twelfth Night. *For additional commentary on the darker aspects of the play, see the excerpts by Mark Van Doren (1939), E. C. Pettet (1949), W. H. Auden (1957), G. K. Hunter (1962), Jan Kott (1964), Albert Gérard (1964), Clifford Leech (1965), and Philip Edwards (1968).*]

[In *Twelfth Night* there is] a silvery undertone of sadness, which makes it perhaps the loveliest of all Shakespeare's high comedies. Maybe, in this, my ear is super-subtle, and self-deceived; but the impression is unfailing. In *Twelfth Night* even 'fooling grows old': Feste is an older, sadder, wiser man than Touchstone; and he has outworn his favour. Though Malvolio alone bears him any ill-will, nobody cares for him. Since Malvolio grudges Feste his place, we accommodate ourselves to Malvolio's baffling: but, as such things are in life, it is a little excessive and leaves a wry taste in the mouth. Malvolio should have been more malevolent to deserve all his punishment. The songs are tinged with sadness. (p. 225)

Viola is but a girl; Sebastian but a boy: but ages are deceptive in *Twelfth Night.* This girl is older, if not in years, then in experience, than Beatrice or Rosalind or Portia. She has neither their high-spirited gaiety, nor the new-born innocence of Perdita or Miranda. A mood which seems to hover in the background of *The Merchant of Venice,* and is there thrust under by the bravery of youth and the ecstasy of love, now suffuses the whole of a comedy. The Duke in *Twelfth Night* is the counterpart of Antonio in the *Merchant;* but whereas in the tragicomedy he fades into the background, in the comedy he subtly dominates the whole.

His is not the perfunctory and conventional lover's melancholy, of which Shakespeare had so often and so happily made fun. It is the Melancholy of Keats' ode, the sovereign goddess who

> Dwells with beauty, beauty that must die
> And joy whose hand is ever at his lips
> Bidding adieu.

It looks back on gaiety and confidence as belonging to the past. And *Twelfth Night* is, to my sense, the most perfect example of the way in which Shakespeare could make his mood override his fable. Than the actual story of *Twelfth Night,* what could be happier? There are no disturbing villainies as there are in *Much Ado* and even in *As You Like It.* The plot is as innocent as that of the *Dream.* Yet the thing is sad: sad, partly with the weight of its own beauty, but sad also with a wistfulness to which Shakespeare could not help giving direct expression. The song the Duke loves—'Come away, come away, death'—contains it in part; there is something of it in the ambiguous twist of Malvolio's taking down: but most of all it is contained in Feste, and in his singing. There is a strange aloofness in Feste: he is attached, as Dr. Bradley has remarked, to nobody [see excerpt above, 1916]. He is woven in and out the play like a careless wraith. Nothing matters to him. If he is turned away, 'let summer bear it out'. His fooling has a different flavour from the fooling of any other fool. It is almost metaphysical in its aloofness. And—once more as Dr. Bradley has remarked—it seems natural that he should be, as he is, more unblushing in his demands for money than any other of Shakespeare's fools. He has no illusion about his own precariousness. It sorts with this that at one moment he appears to be abrupt and careless of his reward—after singing 'Come away, death'. 'There's for thy pains', says the Duke. 'No pains, sir, I take pleasure in singing', says Feste. At all events, it is clear that he does take pleasure in singing—more truly than any other character in a play which begins and ends in music, and is saturated with it. For the others, music is the food of love, or languor, or mirth: for Feste it is an art—aloof, abstract, akin to himself. At the last, he is left on the stage alone—not unlike Firs at the end of *The Cherry Orchard*—as it were in anticipation of his end:

> And unregarded age in corners thrown.

There he stands and sings. Perhaps it was an old song, not of Shakespeare's making. But whether he made it, or merely put it there, just as magically as the final song in *Love's Labour* gathers up the hidden potentiality of that gay and clumsy and youthful play, so is the bitter-sweet of *Twelfth Night* caught into the first verse of Feste's song:

> When that I was and a little tiny boy,
> 　With hey, ho, the wind and the rain,
> A foolish thing was but a toy,
> 　For the rain it raineth every day.
>
> 　　　　　　　　　　　　　[V.i.389-92]

It is almost nonsense, yet it seems like a perfect lament over the passing of innocence, the passing of all things. *Surgit amari aliquid medio de fonte leporum.* (pp. 226-28)

> *John Middleton Murry, ''The Shakespeare Man,'' in*
> *his* Shakespeare, *Jonathan Cape, 1936, pp. 212-34.**

H. B. CHARLTON (essay date 1937)

[*An English scholar, Charlton is best known for his* Shakespearian Tragedy *and* Shakespearian Comedy—*two important studies in which he argues that the proponents of New Criticism, particularly T. S. Eliot and I. A. Richards, were reducing Shakespeare's drama to its poetic elements and in the process losing sight of his characters. In his introduction to* Shakespearian Tragedy, *Charlton described himself as a ''devout'' follower of A. C. Bradley, and like his mentor he adopted a psychological, character-oriented approach to Shakespeare's work. Charlton discusses* Twelfth Night, Much Ado About Nothing, *and* As You Like It *as Shakespeare's finest achievements in comedy. Stressing the romantic aspects which distinguish Elizabethan comedy, he explores Shakespeare's conception of men and women who are emotionally complex and who enlarge and vitalize the world of comedy. Charlton stresses particularly that the heroines of the best comedies embody the generosity, guiltlessness, and freshness of disposition necessary to practice the ''art of life'' that Shakespeare promotes in these plays. Shakespeare's handling of the theme of love is also discussed by E. C. Pettet (1949), John Russell Brown (1957), Harold Jenkins (1959), and Alexander Leggatt (1974). The excerpt below is drawn from Charlton's essay which first appeared in the* Bulletin of the John Rylands Library *in October, 1937.*]

[With *Much Ado About Nothing, Twelfth Night,* and *As You Like It,*] Shakespearian comedy realises its most perfect form, and therefore in them Shakespeare's comic idea, his vision of the reach of human happiness in this world of men and women, is richer, deeper, more sustained, and more satisfying than in any other of his plays. They embody his surest clue to the secret of man's common and abiding welfare. Being that, they are also, technically speaking, his happiest examples of the characteristically Elizabethan kind of romantic comedy, the

plays in which he most fully satisfies the curiously Elizabethan aesthetic demand for a drama which would gratify both the romantic and the comic instincts of its audience. (p. 266)

[Shakespeare's so-called romances, *The Tempest, Cymbeline,* and *The Winter's Tale,*] have, of course, their own virtue. But there could be no clearer evidence of the weakening of Shakespeare's dramatic genius. For our own particular argument, its most manifest symptom is seen by comparing the heroines of the romances with those of the mature comedies. To set a Perdita or a Miranda by the side of a Rosalind or a Viola is to put a slip of girlhood by the side of women who have grown into the world, become a part of its fabric and enriched their personality by traffic with affairs and with other men and women. For the purposes of comedy, which by its nature seeks to envisage the way to happiness in a material world, the experience of a Viola or of a Rosalind is worth infinitely more than the charming innocence and ignorance of the world which are the peculiar virtue of a Perdita and a Miranda. Let there be no mistake. Shakespeare's last plays, the romances, are rich in such pleasure as none but Shakespeare could provide. But, as comedies, they are of little account. . . . For our enquiry, the peak is reached by *Much Ado, Twelfth Night,* and *As You Like It.* (p. 269)

On a purely and superficially formal consideration, it is remarkable that [Shakespeare's] mature plays seem to exhibit little progress in such external things as plotcraft and dramatic illusiveness when set beside [his] earlier experiments in comedy. . . . *Twelfth Night* builds itself formally on circumstances like those of *A Comedy of Errors,* and even increases the theatrical improbability of all plays of mistaken identity by adding sex-disguise to make stage-illusion still more difficult. . . . But the appearance of casualness in plotcraft is delusory. These plays are held together, not by the nexus of external circumstance, but by the coherence of their spiritual substance. Their apparent diversity is moulded into unity by what Coleridge would have called an esemplastic power. They are the unified shape of an embodied idea, the representation of a created world which has become an organic universe because its every operation manifests the universality of its own proper laws.

To see these plays as a form of comedy, it is perhaps easiest to begin by realising that in kind they are essentially and obviously different from traditional classical comedy. Their main characters arouse admiration; they excite neither scorn nor contempt. They inspire us to be happy with them; they do not merely cajole us into laughing at them. Therein lies the fundamental difference between classical and Shakespearian comedy. Classical comedy is conservative. It implies a world which has reached stability sufficient for itself. Its members are assumed to be fully aware of the habits and the morals which preserve an already attained state of general well-being. The main interest is the exposure of offenders against common practice and against unquestioned propriety in the established fitness of things. Hence, its manner is satire, and its standpoint is public common sense. But Shakespearian comedy is a more venturesome and a more imaginative undertaking. It does not assume that the conditions and the requisites of man's welfare have been certainly established, and are therefore a sanctity only to be safeguarded. It speculates imaginatively on modes, not of preserving a good already reached, but of enlarging and extending the possibilities of this and other kinds of good. Its heroes (or heroines, to give them the dues of their sex) are voyagers in pursuit of a happiness not yet attained, a brave new world wherein man's life may be fuller, his sensations more exquisite and his joys more widespread, more lasting, and so more humane. But as the discoverer reaches this higher bliss, he (or rather she) is making his conquests in these realms of the spirit accessible not only to himself but to all others in whom he has inspired the same way of apprehending existence. He has not merely preserved the good which was; he has refined, varied, and widely extended it. Hence Shakespearian comedy is not finally satiric; it is poetic. It is not conservative; it is creative. The way of it is that of the imagination rather than that of pure reason. It is an artist's vision, not a critic's exposition. (pp. 276-78)

"This is the air, this is the glorious sun." But it is not only in its geographical atmosphere that the world of these comedies is so vastly larger than that of classical comedy, so much more radiant than that of Shakespeare's earlier romantic comedies, and so much more rich than that of Falstaff's Eastcheap. In its own turn, the world of the spirit has been equally extended. As one obvious sign of it, man has become more exquisitely conscious of music. Of course, there has always been a human impulse for caterwauling; and, in their cups, men have commonly felt themselves to be such dogs at a catch that they could rouse the night-owl and make the welkin dance. But it is in these great plays that men are suddenly brought up against the stupendous and apparently incredibly foolish circumstance that sheep's guts are potent to hale the souls out of their bodies. (pp. 279-80)

It is not only that song and music irradiate these plays—the very clown of one of them has almost lost his clownage to qualify as a singer—the important point is that the men and women of the play, and Shakespeare and his audience, are becoming conscious of what the spell of music implies. 'That strain again'; these old and antique songs were apt to arouse amorousness in Orsino and yet "to relieve him of his passion much". To recognise the palpable effect of music was the first step: to become aware of its implications was another. In men's secular lives, music ministered most powerfully to their passion of love. "If music be the food of love, play on." And so they found themselves at the very heart of the mystery, the recognition that, however strange, sheep's guts did in fact hale their souls out of their bodies. They were feelingly aware that the soul is susceptible to strange and unaccountable impulses, and that, responding to them, it enters a rich and novel spiritual kingdom.

What this means for the purposes of Shakespearian comedy is this. Man had discovered that he was a much less rational and a much more complex creature than he had taken himself to be. His instincts and his intuitions, his emotions and his moods were as real and as distinctive a part of him as his reason and his plain common sense. (pp. 280-81)

So, amongst the themes of Elizabethan comedy, love had now justified its primacy. . . . It is noteworthy, however, that though these three great comedies are even more exclusively the plays of lovers and their wooing than are the earlier ones, seldom does Shakespeare allow their wooing to express itself through the full gamut of its lyric modulations. Its utterance is adapted to a dramatic, and, indeed, to a comic scene: depth of affection is displayed rather by hints and by deeds than by the conventional phrase of the love poet. (p. 281)

Rosalind, Viola, and, to a less extent, Beatrice, are Shakespeare's images of the best way of love. They, and the men in whom they inspire love, are Shakespeare's representation

of the office of love to lift mankind to a richer life. So, by the entry into it of love, not only has the world of these comedies become a bigger world: the men and women who inhabit it have become finer and richer representatives of human nature. . . . They have left Theseus far behind; they have also outgrown Falstaff.

But if the new world of these mature comedies is one of which Falstaff could never have attained the mastery, there is yet room in it for much even of the corporeal and for all of the immortal parts of him. He is relegated, however, to his proper place therein. Perhaps Sir Toby is as much of him as will survive a final approbation. To both Toby and Falstaff, care is the chief enemy of life; its main sustenance is capons and canary. Their values are much the same: Falstaff's deepest contempt is for a brewer's horse; Sir Toby's symbol of a world without life is an unfilled can. Both live by their wits, deluding the gullible into disbursing. "Let's to bed, knight; thou hadst need send for money." But if Toby never attains the plenitude of Falstaff's dominion, at least he escapes rejection, and achieves ultimately a more settled survival. (pp. 283-84)

[The] acceptance of Toby as an integral part of the ideal world of romantic comedy does not fully indicate how much of the essential virtue of Falstaff Shakespeare, after the antipathy of his dark comedies, endeavoured to find permanently serviceable to humanity. For Toby has not the full measure of Falstaff's wit. Perhaps Beatrice of *Much Ado* is Shakespeare's completest picture of the way in which sheer wit may serve the cause of human sanity in human society and thereby extend the scope of its possible happiness. (p. 284)

Shakespeare's enthronement of woman as queen of comedy is no mere accident, and no mere gesture of conventional gallantry. Because they are women, these heroines have attributes of personality fitting them more certainly than men to shape the world towards happiness. . . . [His] heroes, in effect, are out of harmony with themselves, and so are fraught with the certainty of tragic doom. Their personality is a mass of mighty forces out of equipoise: they lack the balance of a durable spiritual organism. It was in women that Shakespeare found this equipoise, this balance which makes personality in action a sort of ordered interplay of the major components of human nature. In his women, hand and heart and brain are fused in a vital and practicable union, each contributing to the other, no one of them permanently pressing demands to the detriment of the other, yet each asserting itself periodically to exercise its vitality, even if the immediate effect be a temporary disturbance of equilibrium, for not otherwise will they be potent to exercise their proper function when the whole of their owner's spiritual nature is struck into activity. (pp. 285-86)

It is unnecessary here to attempt to describe these heroines one by one, or even to name in detail all their generic traits. It will be enough to indicate one or two of their characteristic virtues. They have all the gift of inspiring and of returning affection. They have the good will of all who know them. They are simply human and patently natural in their response to emotional crises like that of falling in love. . . . Once they are conscious of their own desire they are master-hands in reaching it. . . . Viola resolves at once to remedy her lot by taking service with the Duke; and immediately becomes his confidant and his private minister. She overcomes all the ceremonial obstacles which bar access to Olivia, using, when need be, the bluster and the rudeness which she learns from her opponents. She seizes a situation on the instant; and even when the outcome is not clearly to be foreseen, she acts in a manner which will save unnecessary suffering to others: "she took the ring of me," is her lie to Malvolio, guessing at once how the distraught Olivia had tried to hide her device from her steward and messenger. In crises, all of them, Rosalind, Viola, and Beatrice, are guided by intuitive insight. Beatrice acclaims Hero's innocence in the face of damning evidence. Viola judges her ship's captain by the same inner vision, and she confides in him implicitly. Yet the instinct and the intuition are always open-eyed and cautiously safeguarded against mere casual vagary or whimsical sentimentality. When Viola judges the captain's worth by his fair and outward character, she remembers that nature with a beauteous wall doth oft close in pollution. . . . Yet, with all the efficiency and savoir faire of which these heroines prove themselves to be possessed, they are amazingly modest. It is this modesty which prevents them from endeavouring to compass what is beyond mortal reach. Fortune, they know, is but a blind worker; and she doth most mistake in her gifts to woman. Viola undoubtedly is confident, but not overconfident: she will do what she can, but

> O time! thou must untangle this, not I;
> It is too hard a knot for me to untie.
>
> [II.ii.40-1]

And Rosalind never forgets how full of briers is this work-a-day world. But in the end, they triumph; and they triumph because they are just what they are, the peculiar embodiment in personality of those traits of human nature which render human beings most loveable, most loving, and most serviceable to the general good.

But these ladies are not only doers and inspirers of action. Merely by their presence in the play, they serve as standards whereby degrees of worth and worthlessness in other characters are made manifest. Hence the rich variety of theme, of episode, and of person in these plays is knit together and holds as a coherent structure. The beneficence of emotion and of intuition is no wise belittled by the revelation of the follies which spring from feeling in less stable creatures than are the heroines. So, *Twelfth Night* is largely occupied with the disclosure of unbalanced sentiment. There is the enervating sentimentality of Orsino, there is the unrestrained emotionalism of Olivia. . . . Indeed, once the positive construction of their larger world has been effected by the heroines, there is now place, not only for their own safeguards for it, such as this perpetual alertness to expose the dangers of unbalanced sentiment, there is also place for the sort of direct satire and the forthright comicality which were the manner of the older classical tradition. Just as Sir Toby finds his station in *Twelfth Night*, so do Andrew and even Malvolio; there, in Andrew's case, simply to display his own foolish inanity as do the witless in all sorts of comedy; and in Malvolio's, to enter almost as Jonson gave his characters entry, for a more subtle but still classical kind of discomfiture. As Malvolio in *Twelfth Night*, so Jaques in *As You Like It*, another of the few attempts of Shakespeare to project malcontentism for comic purposes. Besides these, traditional clowns may now also play their part, whether the English Shakespearian ones of the tribe of Bottom, such as Dogberry and Verges, or the more technical ones, Feste and Touchstone, grown now by contact with natural Costards into something more substantial and more homely than the mere traditional corrupters of words, and therefore playing not the part of an added funny interlude, but an essential rôle in the orientation of the idea of comedy. . . . [The] motley of romantic comedies is subtler than the slapdash skittle-knocking of the satire in classical comedy. Their reformatory way, too, is fundamentally differ-

ent from the simple exposure of ludicrous abnormality which had been the approved manner of older comedy. They entice to a richer wisdom by alluring the imagination into desire for larger delights. They are not mainly concerned to whip offenders into conventional propriety by scorn and by mockery. They persuade one to the better state by presenting it in all its attractiveness: they depict a land of heart's desire, and, doing that, reveal the way of human and natural magic by which it is to be attained.

Hence, in the last resort, the greatness of these greatest of Shakespeare's comedies will be measured by the profundity and the persuasiveness of the apprehension of life which they embody, by the worth, that is, of their underlying worldly wisdom. What then is this comic idea of which these plays are the dramatic revelation?

Something of the answer has already been given in estimating the characteristics of the heroines. But the conclusions may be made more general: in the first place, however, it must be noted that though these romantic comedies break through the traditional scope of classical comedy, their sphere is still rigorously confined within the proper orbit of comedy. They limit themselves to acquaintance with life here and now; the world, and not eternity, is their stage. It is, of course, a world presenting many more woeful pageants than comedy is capable of transmuting to happiness: and comedy must confine itself to those threats of fate and those rubs of circumstance which can be reconciled with man's reach for assured joy in living. In these ripest of Shakespeare's comedies, comedy is seeking in its own artistic way to elucidate the moral art of securing happiness by translating the stubbornness of fortune into a quiet and a sweet existence.

It finds that this art comes most easily to those who by nature are generous, guiltless, and of a free disposition, just, indeed, as are Shakespeare's heroines. It finds the art crippled, if not destroyed, in those who lack the genial sense of fellowship with mankind. A Malvolio, sick of self-love, thanking God that he is not of the element of his associates, sees the rest of men merely as specimens of the genus 'homo,'—"why, of mankind". The springs of sympathy are dried up within him. He becomes merely a time-server, planning only for his own selfish gain. The aptitude to do this successfully had been a positive asset to the earlier, even to the Falstaffian, kind of comic hero. But now, in the radiance of these maturer plays, it is seen in truer light. Malvolio has lost the art of life; his very genius is infected. (pp. 286-90)

> *H. B. Charlton, "The Consummation," in his* Shakespearian Comedy, *Methuen & Co. Ltd., 1938, pp. 266-97.*

MARK VAN DOREN (essay date 1939)

[*Indicative of the tendency of critics to note the melancholy, elegaic tone of* Twelfth Night, *Van Doren finds a menacing Malvolio at the center of the play. In his discussion of Malvolio as representative of a "rewarder" class which threatens the static social world of the play, Van Doren presages the approaches of O. J. Campbell (1943) and John Draper (1950). For additional commentary on the dark aspects of the play, see the excerpts by F. J. Furnivall (1877), Arthur Quiller-Couch (1930), John Middleton Murry (1936), E. C. Pettet (1949), W. H. Auden (1957), G. K. Hunter (1962), Jan Kott (1964), Albert Gérard (1964), Clifford Leech (1965), and Philip Edwards (1968).*]

If so absorbing a masterpiece as ''Twelfth Night'' permits the reader to keep any other play in his mind while he reads, that play is ''The Merchant of Venice.'' Once again Shakespeare has built a world out of music and melancholy, and once again this world is threatened by an alien voice. The opposition of Malvolio to Orsino and his class parallels the opposition of Shylock to Antonio and his friends. The parallel is not precise, and the contrast is more subtly contrived; Shakespeare holds the balance in a more delicate hand, so that the ejection of Malvolio is perhaps less painful to our sense of justice than the punishments heaped upon Shylock until he is crushed under their weight. But the parallel exists, and nothing provides a nicer opportunity for studying the way in which Shakespeare, returning to a congenial theme, could ripen and enrich it.

Orsino's opening speech is not merely accompanied by music; it discusses music, and it is music in itself. Furthermore, a suggestion of surfeit or satiety occurs as early as the second line: this suggestion, so consonant with Orsino's melancholy tone, to be developed throughout a speech of considerable complexity. For at more than one point ''Twelfth Night'' foreshadows the concentration and even the difficulty which will be found in the poetry of the later plays.

> If music be the food of love, play on!
> Give me excess of it, that, surfeiting,
> The appetite may sicken, and so die.
> That strain again! It had a dying fall.
> O, it came o'er my ear like the sweet sound
> That breathes upon a bank of violets
> Stealing and giving odour. Enough! no more!
> 'T is not so sweet now as it was before.
> O spirit of love, how quick and fresh art thou,
> That, notwithstanding thy capacity
> Receiveth as the sea, nought enters there,
> Of what validity and pitch soe'er,
> But falls into abatement and low price
> Even in a minute! So full of shapes is fancy
> That it alone is high fantastical.
>
> [I.i.1-15]

The music of, ''The Merchant of Venice'' is freer than this, more youthful and less tangled with ideas of sickness; and the bank of violets has aged beyond the simple sweetness of Lorenzo's bank whereon the moonlight slept. Orsino's love for Olivia turns in upon him and torments him. He is as mannerly in his sadness as Antonio was, but he knows, or thinks he knows, the origin of his state. He may not wholly know; his melancholy is in part a fine convention of his class, like the preference he feels for olden days and the gentle idiom of an outmoded music. . . . Orsino is indeed an exquisitely finished portrait of his type. His is the luxury of a ''secret soul'' [I.iv.14], and it is natural that he should so easily understand the young gentleman who is Viola in disguise, and who lets concealment, like a worm i' the bud, feed on her damask cheek [II.iv.111-12]. Viola's variety of melancholy is green and yellow. Olivia's is ''sad and civil'' [III.iv.5]. But all of them are graced with sadness. It is the mark of their citizenship in a world which knows a little less than the world of ''The Merchant of Venice'' did what to do with its treasure of wealth and beauty, and whose spoken language has deepened its tone, complicated its syntax, learned how to listen to itself. (pp. 161-63)

Sir Toby Belch is a gentleman too, or at any rate he belongs. He is an old relation and retainer in the somewhat cluttered household of Olivia. ''The Merchant of Venice'' never took us so deep into domestic details. The household of Olivia is old-world, it is Merry England. . . . [Sir Toby] is as old-fashioned as Falstaff, and as functionless in the modern world. ''Am not I consanguineous? Am I not of her blood?'' [II.iii.77-78]. He even talks like Falstaff, puffingly and explosively, as he reminds Maria that he is Olivia's uncle. And for another thing he belongs. Old households harbor such old men. They are nuisances to be endured because they are symbols of enduringness, signs of the family's great age. . . . It is a crowded household, swarming with gross life behind high walls of custom. (pp. 163-64)

It is to Sir Toby that Malvolio is most alien. ''Dost thou think, because thou art virtuous, there shall be no more cakes and ale?'' This most famous sentence in the play is more than Sir Toby disposing of his niece's steward; it is the old world resisting the new; it is the life of hiccups and melancholy trying to ignore latter-day puritanism and efficiency. . . . [Malvolio's] existence somehow challenges their right to be freely what they are. He is of a new order—ambitious, self-contained, cold and intelligent, and dreadfully likely to prevail. That is why Sir Toby and his retinue hate him. . . . Puritan or not, Malvolio has offended them as a class. They could have forgiven his being a climber, his having affection for himself, if he had been any other kind of man than the cool kind he is.

The earliest protest against his disposition is made in fact by Olivia herself, on the occasion when Feste has been amusing her with samples of his wit and Malvolio, asked for his opinion of the stuff, cuts in with this commentary:

> I marvel your ladyship takes delight in such a barren rascal. I saw him put down the other day with an ordinary fool that has no more brain than a stone. Look you now, he's out of his guard already. Unless you laugh and minister occasion to him, he is gagg'd. I protest, I take these wise men, that crow so at these set kind of fools, no better than the fools' zanies.
>
> [I.v.83-89]

He has appeared to be judging the kind of fool Feste is, and his success within that kind; but Olivia sees through to the root of the matter, which is that he does not like jesting at all.

> O, you are sick of self-love, Malvolio, and taste with a distemper'd appetite. To be generous, guiltless, and of free disposition, is to take those things for bird-bolts that you deem cannon-bullets. There is no slander in an allow'd fool, though he do nothing but rail; nor no railing in a known discreet man, though he do nothing but reprove.
>
> [I.v.90-6]

She gives him, in brief, a lesson in the manners of her breed. If he supposes Feste's jibes at her to have been slanderous, that is because he does not understand how little time her people spend in thinking of themselves; if they are free and generous, and know the code, they will laugh at things which to an outsider must sound outrageous. Malvolio may have a sense of humor, but it is not the kind that goes with her code.

Olivia does not bother with him again until he comes, cross-gartered and smiling, to make her think him mad. Meanwhile the roysterers within her gates carry the criticism on. And Malvolio is given a voice which perfectly explains the criticism. The fatal difference between his nature and that of the drunken singers in Olivia's cellar rings out as clearly as if notes had been struck on a warning bell. To begin with there is the fact that Malvolio hates music; as Shylock had declared the harmonies of a carnival to be wrynecked and squealing, so he denounces the strains of "O mistress mine, where are you romaing?" as "the gabble of tinkers" [II.iii.87]. And then there is the icy, tight-lipped fashion of his speech, a fashion that contrasts with the thoughtless, bawling, open-throated style of Sir Toby as frost contrasts with foam, and with the grave, rich style of Orsino or Olivia as steel contrasts with gold. In his niggard's nature he has developed a mannerism which he forces to do all the work of his thought. It is economical and efficient, and it attests his trained intelligence, but it cuts offensively into the hearing of his foes.

> Do ye make an alehouse of my lady's house,
> that ye squeak out your coziers' catches *without*
> *any mitigation or remorse of voice?* . . .
>   [II.iii.88-91]

> And then *to have the humour of state;* and *after*
> *a demure travel of regard,* . . . to ask for my
> kinsman Toby. . . . Seven of my people, *with*
> *an obedient start,* make out for him. . . . I
> extend my hand to him thus, *quenching my*
> *familiar smile with an austere regard of con-*
> *trol.* . . .
>   [II.v.52-66]

> I am no more mad than you are. Make the trial
> of it *in any constant question.*
>   [IV.ii.48-49]

> And tell me, *in the modesty of honour.* . . . .
>   [V.i.335]

> And, acting this *in an obedient hope.* . . . .
>   [V.i.340]

The syntax is brilliantly condensed, but the tone is condescending; a man speaks who thinks of himself as master and frowns the while, tapping the floor till it tinkles like iron and winding up his watch as if it kept time for a universe of "lighter people" [V.i.339]. No wonder his enemies loathe him. "O, for a stone-bow, to hit him in the eye!" [II.v.46]. And no wonder, since their ears are clever, that they mimic his precious manner when they compose the note he is to read as a love-letter from Olivia:

> Let thy tongue tang *arguments of state;* put
> thyself into the trick of singularity.
>   [II.v.150-52]

They have not failed to notice his lordly way with the little word "of," or the practice of his hand as he plucks the string of any other preposition, or the miracle by which he can give an effect of terseness to polysyllables. And they have studied his vocabulary as though it were an index of terms never to be used again. (pp. 165-68)

"He hath been most notoriously abus'd" [V.i.379]. Olivia's line rights Malvolio's wrong, but her household will never grant him the last justice of love. Where there is such difference there cannot be love. That is what "Twelfth Night" is most interested in saying, and saying with an impartiality which precludes sentiment. The balance between Malvolio and his enemies is delicate; they are attractive, as all loose livers are, yet there is an integrity in his tightness, a loftiness other than the misguided one, which we cannot but respect. Modern audiences have bestowed more sympathy upon Malvolio than

Shakespeare perhaps intended, so that the balance is now not what it was. It can scarcely be overthrown, however, whatever changes the whirligig of time brings in. The foundation for comedy here is too firm for that, the counterpoint of effects is too sanely arranged. This world of music and mannerly sadness is not sentimentally conceived. Even within its gates the violin voice of Orsino is corrected by the bawling bass of Sir Toby, and the elegant neuroses of the nobility are parodied on servants' tongues. . . . A balance of tones is maintained, indeed, everywhere in "Twelfth Night." Nature and artifice, sanity and sentiment, are so equally at home here that they can with the greatest difficulty be distinguished from one another; nor in our delight are we disposed to try.

All the while, of course, a story of twins is being told, and three cases of love at first sight (Viola and Orsino, Olivia and Viola, Sebastian and Olivia) are being dove-tailed into a pattern of romance. Shakespeare's interest in Viola cannot be doubted.

> My father had a daughter lov'd a man,
> As it might be, perhaps, were I a woman,
> I should your lordship.   [II.iv.107-09]

Nor can that of the audience, for she is Julia grown to greatness. But other portions of the pattern deserve and are given only such attention as is necessary. The confusion of the twins and the farce of the fencing-match are not what the comedy is essentially about, any more than the marriage of Olivia and Sebastian is—and the perfunctoriness of Shakespeare's feeling with respect to that marriage is clearly confessed in the kind of verse he gives the priest to speak [V.i.156-63]. Even Viola, much as we like her, stands a little to one side of the center. The center is Malvolio. The drama is between his mind and the music of old manners. (pp. 168-69)

> *Mark Van Doren, " 'Twelfth Night'," in his* Shake-
> speare, *Henry Holt and Company, 1939, pp. 161-
> 69.*

OSCAR JAMES CAMPBELL   (essay date 1943)

[*In a discussion that contrasts Ben Jonson's 'humor' characters with those of* Twelfth Night, *Campbell contributes to the continuing commentary on Malvolio. With Mark Van Doren (1939), he claims that Malvolio is typical of a class of upstarts or "coystrils" who sought to gain recognition during a time of social change. Malvolio's punishment is a cruel farce, asserts Campbell, but for the Elizabethan audience, his is a "deserved purgation." For additional commentary on Malvolio's punishment, see the excerpts by William Hazlitt (1817), Charles Knight (1842), T. Kenny (1864), H. N. Hudson (1872), William Archer (1884), Milton Crane (1955), and Melvin Seiden (1961).*]

Acute critics have long recognized the similarities between *Twelfth Night* and Jonson's first humor comedy [*Every Man in His Humour*]. Herford calls it 'the most Jonsonian comedy of Shakespeare.'C. R. Baskervill is also aware of the general relation of both this comedy and *The Merry Wives* to what he calls 'the humor trend that was associated with satire.' And two American scholars have worked out many of the details of Jonson's influence upon the construction of *Twelfth Night.* The characters in the comedy who are most obviously Jonsonian are Sir Andrew Aguecheek and Malvolio.

The former is a gull, who imitates Sir Toby Belch as mechanically as Labesha aped Dowsecer, or as Matthew did Bobadill. Sir Andrew also possesses some of the characteristics of Stephen, Jonson's country gull. The two are alike in being

Engraving from Hanmer edition (1744). By permission of the Folger Shakespeare Library.

unadulterated fools and in their countrified imitation of what they believe to be the manners of a gentleman. (pp. 80-1)

[Most] of the time Sir Andrew needs no urging to exhibit his fatuity. Like Stephen in *Every Man in His Humour* he requires only an ear into which to pour his fat-witted talk. He echoes every remark of his hero. To the Clown's exclamation that Sir Toby is 'in admirable fooling,' Sir Andrew proudly replies, 'Ay, he does well enough if he be disposed and so do I too. He does it with a better grace, but I do it more natural' [II.iii.82-83]. Yet when he hears the graceful compliments which Viola pays Olivia, he is greatly impressed and determines to learn by heart all her most glowing words:

> VIOLA. Most excellent accomplished lady, the
>   heavens rain odors on you.
> ANDREW [*aside*]. That youth's a rare courtier.
>   'Rain odors'—well!
> VIOLA. My matter hath no voice, lady, but to
>   your own most pregnant and vouchsafed ear.
> ANDREW [*aside*]. 'Odors,' 'pregnant' and
>   'vouchsafed'—I'll get 'em all three ready.
>   [III.i.83-91]

This perfectly simple dramatic method serves admirably for the display of Sir Andrew's fatuity. But Shakespeare clearly felt that the unmasking of his cowardice demanded more artifice. Accordingly he falls back upon a booby trap which he

has Sir Toby and Fabian set. They urge the gull to send an eloquent and insulting challenge to Cesario, his apparent rival for the hand of Olivia. (p. 82)

Toby sees to it that the duel takes place. So the two draw their swords and approach each other with farcical attitudes of fright, only to be interrupted by Antonio, who is searching for Sebastian, Viola-Cesario's twin brother. The next time that Andrew thinks he has overtaken Viola, he encounters Sebastian, who soundly thrashes both Sir Andrew and Sir Toby.

The last view that we gain of the precious pair is when they later appear before Olivia and the Duke with their heads broken. Toby is drunk and Andrew completely crestfallen. As they go off to have their wounds dressed, Sir Andrew offers to help Sir Toby out. Then Toby turning on him fires a parting shot, a final characterization of the gull: 'Will you help—an ass-head and a cox-comb and a knave—a thin-faced knave—a gull?' [V.i.206-07].

Sir Andrew then is a gull—Shakespeare's composite of Matthew and Stephen, Jonson's city and country gulls. He is derided, exposed, and ejected from the company of the wise and the sane, as are all ridiculed figures in satire of any sort. But Shakespeare's lampooning of Sir Andrew is utterly devoid of malice. The gull entertains every audience in the same hilarious fashion in which he entertains Sir Toby. His folly is inoffensive. No one expects or desires his reform. We cannot share Sir Toby's final disgust with his dear manikin. We hope that he has run away only to return to amuse us on another day. At no point is the difference between the comic art of Jonson and that of Shakespeare more obvious than in their conception of their gulls. Jonson's Matthew and Stephen are personifications of an eccentricity—frank caricatures. Sir Andrew is just as farcically drawn, but always a human being, even when he is most idiotic. His follies may be wild exaggerations of human foibles, but they never completely obliterate the silly man.

In his characterization of Malvolio, Shakespeare approaches much closer to Jonson's satiric methods. Malvolio is a humor figure in being, as Olivia tells us, 'sick of self-love,' or as Maria puts it, 'The best persuaded of himself, so crammed, as he thinks, with excellencies, that it is his ground of faith that all that look on him love him' [II.iii.150-52]. His self-conceit so puffs him up with false dignity that he thinks simple fun of every sort utterly, exasperatingly trivial. This lofty scorn leads Maria to say, 'Marry sir, sometimes he is a kind of Puritan'—a remark that has misled many critics to imagine that in Malvolio Shakespeare satirizes the Puritans. (pp. 83-4)

Malvolio's self-love has filled him with an ambition presumptuous in one of his lowly social position. 'Art thou any more than a steward?' asks Sir Toby contemptuously, when Malvolio rebukes him and Sir Andrew for their riotous noise in the hall. Maurice Evans in his recent production of *Twelfth Night* made Malvolio's social inferiority immediately obvious to his audiences by the anachronistic device of giving the steward a cockney accent. This established him at once as a rank social outsider. His aspiring to be Olivia's husband is therefore colossal presumption, gross and palpable self-conceit.

The plot which Maria devises to drive his humor into exaggerated display is quite properly based on his faith that Olivia has but to look on him to love him. Maria explains in detail the nature of the trap in which she is to catch the booby, and even describes the grotesque struggles in which he will indulge when securely caught in the toils. She will drop in his path some obscure epistles of love which he will imagine come from Olivia. She knows he will then act most like the 'affectioned ass' he is. In no humor play is the conventional device for exhibiting the fool made more obvious or its mechanism more carefully described.

In *Twelfth Night* the rogues have a valid motive for wishing to humiliate Malvolio. Unlike Lemot in Chapman's comedy, they are not professional entertainers who plan to show off the fools merely to amuse their mistress. They have a good reason for resenting Malvolio's officious pretensions. They see in him an enemy to everything in life which they enjoy. (pp. 84-5)

[The] rogues, with the help of Feste, torture Malvolio in a way which seems cruel to modern spectators, but to an Elizabethan audience was merely a hilarious form of deserved purgation. For Malvolio is purged; at least for the moment he seems to be washed clean of his ambition to marry Olivia and of the crudest of his social affectations.

Twelfth Night, however, does not close, as did *Every Man in His Humour*, with a merry ceremony in which the humor figures take joy in their reformation and are welcomed back into the company of the psychologically balanced and socially competent, by a Dionysiac celebration. Malvolio appears in the final scene to learn all about the plot of which he has been the victim. He is neither amused nor purged. Instead he rushes off the stage in a passion of anger and wounded pride, shouting, 'I'll be revenged on the whole pack of you!' And he is followed by the scornful laughter of satire.

Malvolio is Shakespeare's representative of the upstart, who was the butt of all the satirists, formal and dramatic, of the 1590's. Like the rest of the writers of the age, Shakespeare takes the conservative side in the struggle of the new classes for social recognition. Malvolio is a 'coystril.' Having no right to bear arms, he is regarded by the gentlemen as a menial and therefore an impossible husband for the lady Olivia. Shakespeare clearly agrees with them that the steward's hope to marry his mistress is consummate impudence.

In another respect Shakespeare seems to take sides against Malvolio. He is the major-domo of the Tudor country house, and, as the official responsible for the economy of Olivia's establishment, he is dead against the extravagances which are relics of life in the medieval castle. He quite properly regards Sir Toby as an anachronism, as a debased representative of the armed retainers who once defended the castle from its foes and in return were given their board and keep. Though when off duty they brawled indoors and out, they were tolerated because of their help in time of trouble. Sir Toby contributes as much uproar to Olivia's household as his forebears used to do, but he performs no other service. Yet he demands all the cakes and ale that he can swallow and the right to introduce his boon companions into the hall to roister when and how they please. To this conduct Malvolio objects. He is an enemy to the time-honored English hospitality and liberality because of the strain it puts upon his lady's purse. He detests Toby's revelry, not because it is wicked, but because it is both indecorous and expensive. Shakespeare is obviously against this upstart of the new social dispensation.

Other satirists of his day, and indeed most Elizabethan writers, bewail the passing of the days of the free table, of the lavish dispensing of hospitality. To them such entertainment was the cornerstone of Merry England. To Shakespeare, also, this change in social custom was something to lament. He believed that the security of gentle folk was endangered by the transition

going on in noble households like that of Olivia. Consequently he makes the merchant-minded enemy of the good old days a kill-joy, a conceited ass, an inept social parvenu.

Malvolio is thus elevated above the artificial simplicity of the typical humor figure. In the process he has become an almost pathetically ridiculous human being. In spite of this transformation Shakespeare puts him through the conventional satiric routine of a man caught in the toils of his humor and forced to struggle and grimace there for our amusement. It is Malvolio's routine that forms the center of the robust comic subplot of *Twelfth Night*. It provides merry interludes to the sentimental story of Viola, Orsino, and Olivia. It also enables Shakespeare to employ satiric conventions established by Chapman and Jonson in a way to create the most vivid and human of all the humor figures in Elizabethan comedy. (pp. 86-8)

> *Oscar James Campbell, "'Humor' Characters," in his* Shakespeare's Satire, *Oxford University Press, New York, 1943, pp. 65-88.*

E. J. WEST (essay date 1949)

[*West, like A. C. Bradley (1916), is fascinated by the character of Feste. He challenges the opinion of Harley Granville-Barker (1912), who regarded the clown as a "self-acknowledged failure," and he supports G. G. Gervinus (1849-50) in recognizing Feste's "intellectual superiority." For additional commentary on Feste's role in the play, see the excerpts by Hermann Ulrici (1839), G. Wilson Knight (1932), Enid Welsford (1935), and G. K. Hunter (1962).*]

[Like] many of my elders and betters, I have fallen inescapable prey to the peculiar fascination of the character of the Fool in *Twelfth Night*. . . . [With] A. C. Bradley I must confess that of all Shakespeare's fools Feste "has always lain nearest to my heart," and that "I love him more" than any of his professional fellows. I am aware that the general critical view of the play, willing or no, has assigned to Malvolio the chief masculine interest of the play. Indeed, in a relatively recent and well-received book, innocent from cover to cover of any apparent recognition that Shakespeare designed his plays for the stage rather than for the study, Mark Van Doren goes further: "Even Viola, much as we like her, stands a little to one side of the center. The center is Malvolio. The drama is between his mind and the music of old manners" [see excerpt above, 1939]. One wishes that Van Doren had perceived that part of Feste's power is that he is the personified music of old manners. (p. 265)

[Granville-Barker] in an acting edition of the play emphasized Feste's maturity, but strangely found in him "that vein of irony by which we may so often mark one of life's self-acknowledged failures," "a man of parts without character and with more wit than sense," who sought "a kindly refuge from the world's struggles as an allowed fool."

This, from so acute a critic, somewhat surprises me. All criticism savors necessarily of the impressionism which is the impact of the age, and Feste is frequently ironic; but I submit that his irony is that of his own realization of his intellectual superiority and not that of James Thurber's indubitably and profoundly revealing contemporary Middle Aged Man. And surely Feste lacks neither character nor sense. . . . Feste could justly say, "I wear not motley in my brain," and to the various examples cited by Bradley to demonstrate his ready wit, his mental agility and his real perception of character and situation, we might add the glancing irony of his question to Toby and Andrew: "Would you have a love song, or a song of good life?"; his refusal to explain to Viola the rascality of words: "words are grown so false I am loath to prove reason with them"; his reflection, as "an honest man and a good house-keeper," while donning the robe of Sir Topas: "I would I were the first that ever dissembled in such a gown"; his pithy retort to Malvolio, "I say there is no darkness but ignorance"; and the dignity of his wish that even the flighty Orsino should not "think that my desire is the sin of covetousness." I find much justice in Bradley's contention that in his own words (and we must remember that these include the words of his songs), we may in truth find "the poet's own comment on the story." And in the words of the other characters concerning him, surely the most impersonal, those which most sound like "the poet's own comment" on Feste, are those of Viola, who alone perceived "This fellow is wise enough to play the fool," who appreciates Feste's nice calculation of the "mood" and "quality of persons, and the time," and who realizes that the "folly that he wisely shows, is fit." (pp. 266-67)

In opposition to the "kindly refuge" theory of Granville-Barker, I would claim that part of the fascination and appeal of Feste lies really in our sympathetic sense of sorrow and pity for him. Viola, as I have noted, alone of his fellows in the play seems to see him clearly, and that dear innocent, despite Tilley [see excerpt above, 1914], is much too preoccupied with her own troubles really to *feel* for or with Feste. . . . [We] who read the play sensitively and appreciatively, I trust, do more than "take much delight in him;" we love him—we love him for his insight and philosophy, for his ability to build up for himself a world of fancy born of his acute observation of the world as it is, for his genuine and deep love of music, for his freedom from obscenity (Bradley's contrast here is the "foul-mouthed" Fool of *All's Well*, but Feste in this respect is eminently more endearing than even the much-loved Beatrice of *Much Ado*) and from bad taste generally. Surely it is intentional that Fabian is introduced late in the play to take the part originally assigned to Feste by Maria in the gulling of Malvolio, and that when the necessity for a conspirator of his professional talents does finally draw him into the plot against the steward, "he takes steps to end it and consents, in his own voice, to provide the lunatic with light, pen, ink, and paper for his letter to Olivia." Feste is incapable of harboring a grudge, even against his professed enemy.

One point, already implied in the insistence upon Feste's possession of sense, I should like to remark on further. The play, it has been noted, is full of gulls. Only that bright and lovely creature Viola and Feste himself seem not to be deceived in one way or another, self-deceived or deceived by their fellows. If the play were produced as I suspect possibly Shakespeare meant it to be produced, that is, with Orsino and Olivia definitely comic characters, as humorous in their self-deception as Malvolio himself, I rather suspect we should more than ever see clearly how brightly shine forth the purity of mind and spirit of both Viola and Feste. Occasional difficulties arise in production today from an apparent conflict between the romance of the Orsino-Olivia-Viola-Sebastian-Antonio motif and the farce of the Malvolio-Maria-Toby-Andrew-Fabian motif; the usual remedy is to attempt to soften the farce to bring it into harmony with the romance. I personally would like to see the experiment of bringing more of the romantic characters into the comedy. Probably it wouldn't work; certainly Feste could not be forced into farce. An innate dignity of character keeps him aloof from the antics and schemes of Toby and Andrew.

This dignity is part of his maturity, and emphasizes that he must be played by a man, not a boy. (pp. 267-68)

[Today] it is commonly granted that ["The Wind and the Rain"] fits the play, and that it exquisitely fits the character, which Bradley rightly noted as distinguished for the "serenity and gaiety of his spirit," reflected in this "old rude song about the stages of man's life, in each of which the rain rains every day; a song at once cheerful and rueful, stoical and humorous." (p. 270)

When some years before his death I first suggested to the late Tucker Brooke some of the ideas here expressed, he replied: "There is a peculiar quality about *Twelfth Night,* I think, that you have illustrated impressively. More than in the other high comedies, each of the greater characters, if you begin studying him, becomes a kind of peephole into infinity." . . . Herein I have merely recorded something of my own attachment to that "peephole into infinity" whose name, hauntingly and ironically, is Feste the Fool. (p. 271)

> E. J. West, "Bradleyan Reprise: On the Fool in *'Twelfth Night'*," in The Shakespeare Association Bulletin, Vol. 24, No. 4, October, 1949, pp. 264-74.

E. C. PETTET (essay date 1949)

[*Pettet conjectures that in* Twelfth Night, Much Ado About Nothing, *and* As You Like It *Shakespeare was growing tired of the love romance. In* Twelfth Night, *"love is a subsidiary factor completely lacking the romantic spirit." He notes that there are no courtship dialogues in this play like those in the earlier comedies, and he finds its comic spirit to be satirical and close in mood to the comedy of Ben Jonson. For additional commentary on Shakespeare's handling of the theme of love in the play, see the excerpts by H. B. Charlton (1937), John Russell Brown (1957), Harold Jenkins (1959), and Alexander Leggatt (1974).*]

Much Ado About Nothing, As You Like It and *Twelfth Night* may conveniently be taken together not only on account of their dates of composition (1598-1601) and level of excellence as the peaks of Shakespeare's comedy, but also because of certain broad similarities in their attitudes towards the romantic tradition.

Up to the time of this trilogy, the 'romantic' comedies had followed a fairly consistent formula: the core of each one had been a love romance, serious in the main, though often treated comically and frequently lightened with wit. Woven in and around this romantic centre there had been comic diversions and incidents, sometimes serving as a burlesque or anti-masque to the main love romance.

Now one of the chief points to be noticed about these three great comedies that Shakespeare composed at the turn of the century—probably in the order *Much Ado, As You Like It* and *Twelfth Night*—is the shift of dramatic gravity away from the love romance. It would obviously be incorrect to say that Shakespeare rejected the romantic narrative, since *As You Like It* is an almost perfect specimen of a dramatised romance. But *Much Ado* and *Twelfth Night* do afford the first clear signs that he was growing—temporarily at least—tired or dissatisfied with this type of story. (p. 122)

In *Twelfth Night* the romantic part of the plot is admittedly rather more to the foreground [than in *Much Ado*]. But at least as prominent as this, and certainly more entertaining, is again Shakespeare's own invention—the gulling of Malvolio, Sir

Toby's confidence tricks on Sir Andrew, and Sir Andrew's duel with Viola. Once more this original creation has little to do with romance. The action in these episodes is farcical intrigue; love is a subsidiary factor completely lacking the romantic spirit; the main characters are middle-aged men and women; and the comedy is to a large extent satirical, a mocking exposure of human foibles and weaknesses. With Sir Andrew the satire is light-hearted and kindly enough. But when we contemplate the great satiric portrait of Malvolio and the harsh indignities to which he is subjected, we feel ourselves transported from the genial atmosphere of the earlier comedies to a region not very far removed from the raw, vigorous and unromantic comic world that Jonson was about to create.

Nor is it merely that the dramatic centre of gravity in these three comedies is shifting away from the romantic story. Love-making, so essential a part of romance, is dwindling too—even in the romantic parts of the comedies. . . . In *Twelfth Night* the love-making is by proxy and constantly interrupted by the raillery of Olivia, while there is no courtship between Viola and the Duke or between Olivia and Sebastian, who are all united in a somewhat perfunctory manner. (pp. 123-24)

[It] is certainly a remarkable feature of the three main comedies that the high romantic liturgy of love almost disappears from them. (p. 125)

There are some few passages of the old romantic love parlance in *Twelfth Night*, but these are spoken either by the Duke, who is momentarily in love with love's mood rather than with any woman, or by Viola, who recites them to Olivia, only to be mocked at for her pains. Not that Viola can have been greatly grieved by Olivia's response, for all her fine love speeches have usually a casual note, sometimes even a suggestion of parody. Moreover, there is a good deal of contradiction in the Duke's attitude. If we can believe his opening words, there is a part of him that would really prefer not to be in love, while he seems to share Duke Theseus' conviction that love is 'high fantastical'. Certainly, for all his indulgence, he does not believe in the romantic doctrine of the elevating powers of love, which is, he states, like the sea:

> Nought enters there,
> Of what validity and pitch soe'er,
> But falls into abatement and low price.
> 　　　　　　　　　　　　　　　　[I.i.11-13]

Later, in conversation with Viola, he utters two further heresies: he has no faith in the lover's fidelity—

> Our fancies are more giddy and unfirm,
> More longing, wavering, sooner lost and worn
> Than women's are—　　　　　　　　[II.iv.33-35]

and, in spite of this, he has a low, unchivalric opinion of a woman's love that none of the earlier romantic lovers would have shared:

> Alas, their love may be call'd appetite,
> No motion of the liver, but the palate,
> That suffer surfeit, cloyment and revolt.
> 　　　　　　　　　　　　　　　　[II.iv.97-99]
> 　　　　　　　　　　　　　　　　(p. 127)

E. C. Pettet, ''Shakespeare's Detachment from Romance,'' in his Shakespeare and the Romance Tradition, *Staples Press, 1949, pp. 101-35.*

JOHN W. DRAPER (essay date 1950)

[*In his detailed exploration of the social world of Shakespeare's era, Draper stresses that modern audiences are too far removed from the conventions of Elizabethan society to grasp the true meaning of* Twelfth Night. *While he echoes, in part, the earlier response of Harley Granville-Barker (1912) and the comments of J. B. Priestley (1925) and Mark Van Doren (1939), Draper goes farther. He concludes that* Twelfth Night *is not a love comedy, but a comedy of the social struggles of the time; it is Shakespeare's play of ''social security.'' Norman A. Brittin (1956) challenges Draper's interpretation.*]

The interpretation of *Twelfth Night* might well begin, as do Chaucer's *Canterbury Tales*, with the characterization of a knight. Sir Toby Belch and his crony and gull, Sir Andrew Aguecheek, form one of those comic pairs, incongruous foils to each other, whose physiques and minds and characters parody the extreme vagaries of human nature. Sir Toby appears in ten of the eighteen scenes, and speaks some four hundred complete or partial lines—more than any other character. He is linked with all the currents of the action. . . . Shakespeare would seem to have taken him, as he doubtless did Falstaff, not so much from theatrical tradition as from actual Elizabethan life. Indeed, most of these traits and actions derive as much from contemporary reality as from the shadow world of the stage: the roistering soldier who bilked callow, gilded youths was a common tavern type; Elizabethan gentlemen could, and did, commonly sing part songs; and every age has known eavesdropping and the gulling of fools. Sir Toby is truly of the earth, earthy, a very Teniers study in the genre. (pp. 19-20)

He is woven more skillfully and fully into the major plot than is Falstaff in *Henry IV*, and so, not only furnishes amusement in both dialogue and intrigue, but also welds the parts of the play together. He and Sir Andrew, moreover, give variety to the types of comedy: Orsino and Olivia supply high comedy, Feste an effervescent mockery, and, in the two knights, wit verges on slapstick farce. Thus the economy of Shakespeare's art makes one figure serve many ends. (p. 39)

Shakespeare's final disposition of his characters generally accords with the social judgments of his time, and the reason why Sir Toby in the end fares so much better than does Falstaff is that the audience despised the latter as a coward, whereas Sir Toby has done nothing that the age would not condone. (p. 40)

Though Sir Andrew has a speaking part of only some hundred and eighty lines and appears in less than half the scenes, his role is probably the most obviously comic in this play of comic characters. (p. 41)

If the essence of comedy be incongruity, Sir Andrew represents the very *summa* of the comic both in body and mind and in his social status: physically he is incongruously tall and incongruously complacent of his broomstick legs; mentally, his phlegmatic stupidity is incongruous, especially after Sir Toby's panegyric, for he does not know wit from nonsense and, in his challenge to Viola, cannot put two sentences coherently together; spiritually, his knightly title and his clownish courtesy and sense of humor, his bragging and his craven cowardice cry out at one another. . . . Gull, prodigal, and coward, he is the *reductio ad absurdum* of a man. In chivalry, he is the perfect foil to His Grace, the Duke Orsino; in arms, to the brave Sebastian; in wealth, to the impecunious Sir Toby. He is cousin germane only to the despised Malvolio, for both are social upstarts—and both have their reward.

Sir Toby and Sir Andrew are a far cry from Chaucer's "worthy knight," and for good historic reason: in the Renaissance, among the old families, chivalry had so declined that it could support its lackland followers only as ragtag hangers-on of their landed relatives, living in time of peace at home on charity or by theft and chicanery in London, and in time of war by theft abroad. The Falstaff plays depict this vividly. Of such stripe also was Sir Toby. Or, among the bourgeois newly rich, knighthood was merely an outer gilding, a title and a few empty prerogatives hastily donned to flaunt before the vulgar and give a spurious show of gentle birth: of such was Sir Andrew. . . . [Both] reflect the decay of chivalry, the gilded upstart and his mentor, the tosspot knight. With all these differences, however, both are actuated by the same human motive, the urge for security in a mutable world and a transition age: Sir Toby wants the economic security of future years of "Cakes and Ale"; Sir Andrew, the social security of a titled wife and a son and heir. Sir Toby seems to achieve his lofty purpose, but Fate in the person of Shakespeare has drawn a kindly curtain over Sir Andrew's future: the world punishes fools more harshly than it does shrewd knaves, and Sir Andrew's wealth and knighthood and pre-eminent folly made him a shining mark. So, in the end, he follows Sir Toby out to have his head bound up, and such slight impression had he made on friend and foe and chosen fiancée, that no one troubles to make inquiry or remark. Sir Andrew is just one of those persons that simply do not matter. (pp. 68-9)

[Maria] rides out the teapot tempest of household transition and intrigue, and finally takes the precious prizes of a husband and a title of respect. Her Shakespearean ancestor is not the outrageous Quickly, but the sprightly Nerissa, who is likewise a lady and likewise gains a proper husband, though with less ado; but beside Maria, Nerissa is a pale figure, with little clarity of motive or device. Shakespeare, indeed, when he conceived *Twelfth Night*, knew much more about the ordering of noble households, and about the men and women who composed them, than when he wrote *The Merchant of Venice;* and this greater knowledge shows in the lifelike realism and sharp individuality of Maria. Her inner psychology and her outward social status deviously or directly permeate her every motive, speech, and action. (p. 84)

[Malvolio] has not lacked the *obiter dicta* of critics. His yellow stockings and the question of his Puritanism have caused some debate; but the main subject of discussion has been whether or not he deserves the practical jokes that he endures. The older and more usual view seems to be that Malvolio merits his fate. Manningham, who saw the play in 1602 (N.S.), thought the Malvolio plot a "good practise" [see excerpt above, 1602]. Dr. Johnson (1765) declared the Steward's soliloquy "truly comick," and felt that pride justified his fall [see excerpt above]. Hunter (1845), likewise blamed his "proud and tyrannical heart" [see excerpt above]. Montégut called him "crotchety" [see excerpt above, 1807]. Giles imputed his folly to love and "masculine vanity" [see excerpt above, 1868]; but is Malvolio really in love? Ruggles blames his "inordinate vanity''; Furnivall calls him the "self-conceited" [see excerpt above, 1877]; Conrad, the "narrow and prosaic Malvolio''; and Winter says that he is "the image of overweening self-love, of opinionated self-conceit, of narrow-minded, strutting, consequential complacency." The Tudor editors, like Dr. Johnson, consider him "essentially ridiculous." This group of critics does not find in him any violation of poetic justice.

The Romantic point of view, in literary criticism as in life, tended to emphasize all human beings as particularly good or

bad: thus it made Iago an inhuman monster and Falstaff, because of his seductive wit, a man of principle, sincere in purpose and truly good at heart. Its democratic bias ruined King Claudius, but turned a sympathetic ear to the vaulting ambitions of Malvolio. Thus, his character became stuff of serious drama rather than of satiric comedy of manners. Charles Lamb and the actor Bensley seem to have set this style [see excerpt above, 1822]. Of course, it throws the part quite out of focus, spoils our enjoyment of Maria's stratagem, precludes poetic justice in the play; and, while it leaves in comic vein the plots of Olivia's marriage and Maria's, it makes the gulling of Malvolio an unresolved tragedy. (pp. 86-7)

Some scholars would call Malvolio a Puritan and so explain Shakespeare's unsympathetic attitude; but the charge of Puritanism is only the casual fling of a detractor, and calling bad names is rarely done with nicety, and a moment later the term is half-recalled. Malvolio's reiterated belief in his "Fortunes" and his "starres" and like astrological phenomena belies his Puritanism; moreover, he indulges in mild oaths, and he quotes a despised ballad, "Please one, please all." Sir Toby, to be sure, sneers at him as "vertuous," but his fundamental motive is not godly zeal but a longing for the gauds and vanities of this world. . . . But the wrath of Sir Toby and the "lighter people" is chiefly aroused, not against his imputed religion or even his sedate demeanor, but against his outrageous ambition to become the husband of a Countess, a most un-Puritanical ambition. (p. 89)

Elizabethans of the serving class, being employed more and more for work rather than for prowess, were losing their hereditary status. Shakespeare would seem to have transferred to Illyria an English household in this transition, with a licensed jester, gently born retainers, dependent relatives, and uninvited guests as in the Middle Ages, and also a Renaissance staff of actual servants headed by the competent and all-too-hopeful Malvolio.

The two knights, Maria, and Fabyan, were gentles all; but, within this charmed circle, Malvolio did not belong. Feste, to be sure, once ironically calls him "M[aster] Malvolio"; and once Olivia pityingly terms him a "poore Gentleman," though she elsewhere calls him a "servant"; and he is quite willing to allude to himself as a "Gentleman," and to reprimand Viola as an equal. On the other hand, he is "a steward . . . the fellow of servants." (p. 92)

Malvolio's humble place, in comic contrast to his exalted aspirations, appears best symbolized by the references to costume in the play. . . . About 1600, Malvolio's yellow stockings and cross-garters seem to have had a plebeian connotation; and thus he aspires to court the Countess in clothes that imply his humble origins. . . . Malvolio then, in the very act of his social apotheosis, is gulled into donning the habiliments, partly of the humble yeomanry whence he seems to have sprung, and partly of the household servitor, the very class from which he is trying to escape. This is an irony even finer than Ben Jonson's treatment of the incongruous coat of arms with which Sogliardo, like Malvolio, attempts to gain gentility. (pp. 93-4)

Most Elizabethans regarded the structure of society as divinely ordained and so immutable; and men were therefore supposed to be content with the station in life to which God had appointed them. (p. 94)

[Not] only was change per se unwelcome, but Malvolio, as the symbol of a change that was generally deplored and was associated with obvious social evils and painful maladjustments—Malvolio, flaunting his impudent designs before his social betters and glorying in the dominion that he hopes shortly to assume—would naturally present to the Elizabethans a most odious figure and thus become a Saint Sebastian for every shaft of satire. (p. 96)

Intelligent people who knew and accepted the science of the age, i.e., astrology and alchemy and the theory of the humors, must have noted scores of human anomalies about them: rulers, like Lear, who were not choleric; merchants, like Antonio, who were not mercurial; courtiers, like Don John, who were not sanguine; and a playwright, with his eye upon theatrical effect, must have seen in these misfits and psychosocial incongruities striking opportunity for comic and tragic effects. Just such a misfit is Malvolio, the choleric steward, whose choler makes him aspire, and aspire especially through marriage. His disparity of humor is the perfect complement to Sir Toby's and Sir Andrew's: as knights, they should be choleric, but by the fact of birth are actually phlegmatic; Malvolio, as a servant, should be phlegmatic, but by birth is choleric. Indeed, this minor plot is a sort of every man out of his humor; and, as the piece followed shortly after Jonson's, it might be taken (had not Shakespeare used humors so amply in earlier plays) as an example of Jonsonian influence. In any case, this disparity of personality with social station produces the incongruity that is the essence of the comic, and makes that unstable equilibrium that sets plot in motion, the plot of high comedy based in character. (pp. 105-06)

Malvolio is indeed a master portrait; but the world has moved so far away from him that generations of accumulated change have begrimed the colors, erased detail, and obliterated the background. The modern reader, with his modern democracy and his modern liking for efficient management at any cost, finds Malvolio a rather commonplace, perhaps even a pathetic, type. The Industrial Revolution has made us used to social change and its hardships and its social interlopers: we do not condemn ambition that reaches out beyond its class, nor see in Malvolio's the symbol of social misery and disorganization. We neither suffer from, nor see, the hardships that these household changes shown in the play effected in the Elizabethan world; and so, as in the case of Shylock, the bitterness of the dramatist and of the other characters finds no answering chord in us. This is the tragedy of great art, that a thing of beauty cannot be a joy forever, unless one can recapture the essential background of the age that brought it forth. Not only do we fail to see Malvolio's social implications, but we also miss his choleric nature and the implications of this choler; for, not merely social structure but intellectual beliefs and scientific theories are passing, temporal things. Thus we have either spoiled the comedy of the play by making Malvolio a sympathetic character, or tried to explain his disagreeable qualities on the mere basis of his being disagreeable, without realizing that his actions arise from a psychology that clashed with his lowly station and from a social change that made both his social class and his ambitions pernicious and odious. (pp. 111-12)

The Countess, by all the proprieties, should have married the Duke and so made him the Orlando-Romeo of the comedy. Until Act V, he cannot believe that she really means to refuse him, and thus his action in the play is a prolonged and bootless importunity, until he finally cures his passion by a second choice. (p. 113)

Despite this reduction in Orsino's part, he remains a major character. His ducal rank alone would give him importance in Elizabethan eyes. . . . The love-melancholy, moreover, from

which he suffers, would also have made him a sympathetic figure. Unfortunately, however, the twentieth century does not care for dukes, takes no stock in love-melancholy, and prefers success to failure even in love affairs; *ergo*, Orsino has passed under a cloud, and is usually presented on the modern stage, like the King in *Hamlet*, as a rather wooden type. (pp. 113-14)

Orsino is genuinely ill with a mild case of a serious disease, and his cure in the end is essential to the comic conclusion of the play. He is not a ''thistle-down amorist,'' as Sir E. K. Chambers would suppose [see excerpt above, 1904], but, like the Prince in Ford's *Lover's Melancholy,* he is sincerely and seriously in love; and Viola doubtless makes him a better wife than the self-willed Olivia would have.

The narrative form in which Riche cast his *Apolonius* allowed time for the hero to recover at leisure; but Shakespeare was forced by the confines of drama to greater speed and compression. Orsino's illness becomes a sort of frame to the play, and helps to give it the predominant tone of high-life elegance that belongs to comedy of manners. (p. 131)

Shakespeare's Viola appears in the second scene, a young lady without a past, without visible means of support (though she has ''gold'' to give the worthy Captain), and indeed without most of those trappings of current realism so apparent in Sir Toby and Maria. Like a fairy princess, she appears from nowhere in particular, her ship, of unrecorded port and destination, has been wrecked; and no one ever tells the purpose of this voyage that she so readily abandons. The truculent waves merely toss her on the Illyrian shore, and the comedy begins. (p. 133)

Viola's eccentric orbit can be explained only in part by Shakespeare's source and only in part by contemporary realism. How far she is the creature of Elizabethan stage convention remains to be explored. Her entire role, except for the beginning and the end, is played in the disguise of a man, a common device fostered by boy actors' taking women's parts. . . . The trouble with mistaken identity on the stage is that it hardly carries conviction; and, though Viola says that she is imitating her twin brother in ''fashion, colour, ornament,'' and though the Duke testifies to the perfect likeness of the two, yet this convention, which so dominates her role, is sufficiently unconvincing, no matter what the dramatist might do, to tune her whole part to romance rather than to reality. . . . Truly, it must have seemed impossible to give Viola's inexplicable past, improbable disguise, and phenomenal success any sort of workaday Elizabethan realism; and so Shakespeare perforce gave her the allurement of romance, and let our delight in her charms persuade us to accept that mixture of a lie that doth ever add pleasure. Her role is, indeed, a tissue of common stage devices. . . . In fact, stage convention contributes more to the situations—and so to the character—of Viola than to any other figure in the play. The conventions in which Sir Toby is involved belong not only to the stage but to Elizabethan life, and so reinforce his realism; but Viola's have no tang of the earth earthy or the workaday world. Thus she is more stagy and less true to life; but, since she was not Elizabethan in the first place, she has had less to lose by the passing of the Elizabethan age, and this may account for her popularity with actresses in recent times. (pp. 136-38)

The early critics indeed accept Viola with little or no comment. The ''appreciative'' Romantics of the nineteenth century have luxuriated over the wide expanses of her role that Shakespeare left to random conjecture; and so, both as a star part on the stage and also in the critical heavens, she has climbed to the very zenith, and is generally accounted one of Shakespeare's loveliest creations and the heroine of the play. . . . Thus Viola, though Shakespeare so reduced her part that she has fewer lines than Sir Toby and is much less central to the plot than Olivia, has risen, because she charmed the Romantic nineteenth century, to a supremacy where all unite to praise her virtues and excuse her faults and flaws. Of course, the very fact that she is less true to Elizabethan life has made her lose less vividness in the whirligig of time. She is not so much a portrait as a decorative piece, and time cannot wither nor custom stale the grace of purely decorative forms. (pp. 138-39)

The Romantic critics are perhaps right in celebrating Viola as the nonpareil of virtue and loveliness; but are they right in making her the central figure of the play, or even its heroine? . . . In fact, [Viola] seems, like Maria in her plainness, to be rather a mere foil to the others who are intended to stick fiery off. The last scene, moreover, disposes of her future in a few rapid lines, and Malvolio's release and anger get its final climax. Indeed, Viola seems to be a romantic contrast to the dominant realism of the play—low-life realism in the case of Sir Toby's schemes and Maria's aspirations, and high-life realism in the case of the self-willed and astute Olivia; but Viola is a silver strand of romance, glinting here and there to set off this kersey web of everyday buffs and browns and mourning black, a necessary part of Shakespeare's complex pattern, but hardly a part predominant.

Viola in the beginning sets foot on the firm shores of Illyria and proceeds to treat it like fairyland; and Illyria, for all its Sir Andrew and Sir Toby and their "Cakes and Ale," responds in kind, and, as if it were a fairy godmother, grants her the three wishes of her brother's life, her own security, and the husband of her choice. How different from Maria's shrewd maneuvering that finally gains her the bare recompense of Sir Toby! But Maria is only common clay. Viola does not need to toil or spin; the world is her oyster; and, for all her quick wit, her matter-of-fact talk, and her fear of melancholy, she is really a fairy princess for whom it opens at a word. She may have no past, but her roseate future is as assured as fairyland itself. . . . Orsino is a bit too realistic for a fairy prince; but at least they both are sanguine, and so, according to high medical authority, should enjoy together the serenest marital felicity. Thus unquestionably, Orsino's wedded bliss, like Sir Toby's, is assured; and Viola has security and a fortune and a husband; and both he and she, as in all good fairy tales, doubtless live happily forever after. (pp. 150-51)

If Viola is a fairy princess, then her twin brother Sebastian should be a fairy prince, with no more past and no more realism of action and dialogue than she. All this, however, is not obvious, for he is sketched in pastel shades, and thus, on his own account, is hardly noticeable. Like Fortinbras in *Hamlet*, who is likewise essential only to the conclusion of the piece, he is early spoken of by others, and here and there appears *personâ propriâ* so that his part in the ending will not seem too unconvincing a surprise. He is among those present in only five scenes; and his hundred and twenty-odd lines contain no purple patches. Indeed, Shakespeare does not even present on the stage either his formal betrothal or his marriage. (p. 152)

[The] convention of mistaken identity overwhelms his part; and, although the events are hardly more convincing, their point in the plot is at least clear and unquestionable, for they lead

him to Olivia and to the altar, where all good comedies should end. (p. 155)

Twelfth Night, like most Elizabethan plays, depicts a wide range of social types, though not as wide as *Hamlet*, for the former does not show the great mass of English peasantry represented in the gravediggers. Nevertheless, the gamut of classes between the duke and the steward was a wide one; and, within this field, Shakespeare gives many types: soldiers and servingmen, shading downward into menials and upward into public servants and courtiers; and he illustrates the clergy and knighthood and the nobility. Thus the upper strata of social Illyria are put before our eyes as a going concern, with their several ambitions and fears and very human struggle for existence. Viola, Sebastian, and Antonio, to be sure, have one foot in the land of make-believe; but, for the most part, even the minor characters (in the words of the Preface to Shakespeare's *Troilus*) "are so fram'd to the life that they serve for the most common commentaries of all the actions of our lives." (pp. 166-67)

The Lady Olivia is a realist in a romantic situation: her youth and charm and wealth make her the cynosure of neighboring sheep's eyes, and everyone has plans to marry her off or to be married to her. Thus, while the castaway Viola desperately seeks a husband and protector, the much-bereaved but hard-headed Olivia seeks to avoid wooers, and so gives time for more and more to cluster, buzzing and droning about the honey-pot of her attractions until at last she finds a suitable candidate; and then she swiftly follows the ancient maxim of *fortiter in re.* . . .

Although Olivia appears in only six scenes and speaks fewer lines than Viola or Sir Toby, she is truly the crux of *Twelfth Night*. Her role of melancholy mourning—seclusion, veil, and fertile tears—keeps her behind the scenes. Indeed, she appears but once in the first act and not at all in the second; but repeated reference to her makes her a pervading presence, and she is the center of the plots, which, as in contemporary Italian comedy, chiefly concern her lovers. (p. 168)

According to Elizabethan stage convention, the introduction of a character generally gave a clue as to his personality, his place, and his importance in the play; and there is probably no one in Shakespeare who has a more lengthy and elaborate introduction than Olivia. Her appearance is a sort of climax to Act I, most amply and ingeniously prepared for. . . . Indeed, though the Countess takes up but part of a single scene, she dominates the act; and her meeting with Viola not only gives it a brilliant climax of color and grouping upon the stage but also starts the major complication, which in the end defeats the well-laid plans of steward and knights and duke. Surely, the playwright Shakespeare, having given Olivia such an introduction, must have considered her crucially important. (pp. 169-70)

Olivia's speech, though not fast for the Elizabethan stage, presents a clear contrast to Viola's slow utterance. . . . Her tempo seems to express the balanced restraint in which her precarious situation obliges her to hold herself—a sanguine temper tinged with enough choler to make her independent, and with the melancholy that begins to arise from her unrequited love for Viola. In short, the very rhythms of her speech seem to express the impact of the plot on her humor and character, and so imply her fundamental realism. (pp. 184-85)

If a comedy is to be convincing and significant, the final wedding bells should seem to lead to a happy married life. Sir

Toby and Maria, both phlegmatic, would not be sufficiently dynamic personalities to run great risk of marital discord; the fairy princess, Viola, like all fairy princesses, of course becomes the perfect wife; and Orsino's virtues, set forth even by Olivia, give ample warrant of his success as a husband. But what of the brave Sebastian and his strong-minded Countess? Here surely was the tinder for a marital conflagration. Sebastian, however, being his sister's twin, had enough in him of the fairy prince to guarantee success at anything; and Olivia, likewise, if she could negotiate the dangers of an unprotected maidenhood and an unassisted spousal, could surely rise to the demands of simple matrimony. The Elizabethans, moreover, would see ampler reasons than all this to look forward to her happy marriage: Sebastian seems to represent the fortunate balance of humors that gave the harmony of perfect physical and mental health; and Olivia is innately sanguine. This humor was "the paragon of complexions," made one "liberall, faithfull and mild," and was especially adapted to wedded bliss. (p. 187)

[Olivia] rules the plot as Shakespeare revised it; and any effort to dethrone her throws the whole comedy out of joint. How can Viola be the heroine, and Sir Toby or Malvolio the comic hero, as most critics would suggest, when this hero and this heroine have little or no relation with each other in the plot? The identity of the hero is possibly open to question; but undoubtedly the heroine, as the early actresses who chose the role well knew, is clearly the Countess Olivia. Whereas Shakespeare reduced the role of Viola from his source, his chief additions—Toby, Andrew, Maria, Feste, Malvolio—all center around Olivia; whereas he filled out Viola's not-too-convincing part with the facile stuff of stage convention, he made Olivia a realistic portrayal of a current type; and, to accent her part further, he gave her as fully and carefully prepared a grand entry as he gave any character in all his plays. Olivia is far from a wooden convention, as some critics seem to think; she is a vital and realistic force in a comedy of manners—a woman whose decisions (as a countess' decisions should) rule the fortunes and lives of those about her and so determine the plot. She can quietly make up her mind and bide her time and have her way, and doubtless she proved an able administrator of her domain. Indeed, she is perhaps the most psychologically true-to-Elizabethan-life of Shakespeare's long list of great ladies; and yet, especially in her grand passion, she is very human—in short, a counterpart of Queen Elizabeth herself, but luckier in loving a Sebastian rather than a Leicester or an Essex. (pp. 189-90)

Feste is a fool; but, if he ever committed any folly, he has apparently long since married and repented at leisure. Indeed, when he settled down and commenced fooling in earnest, he seems, according to some critics, to have turned philosopher beneath the guise of his motley; and, for all his workaday gaiety, moreover, he is a shrewd appraiser of persons and something of a manager of affairs, even of the affair between Olivia and Sebastian. His profession and outward character are like his name, festive; and this festival guise helps to give the comedy that illusion of romantic unreality that blinds the uninitiated not only to its essential realism but also to Feste's own essential truth to life. He is a gleeful stage manager to the *comédie humaine* of Shakespeare's Illyria; and critics have been too busy enjoying the performance he puts on to look much behind the scenes or to inquire deeply into his life and character, even though he takes curtain calls before the audience in seven scenes and speaks over three hundred lines. They

enjoy the effect, but miss the means—so subtle is Shakespeare's art. (p. 191)

[Feste,] as one might expect in Shakespeare, stems less from the theater than from life. Far from being a country boor, he is sophisticated, worldly-wise, and even learned in a fashion; far from being an innocent, or a "natural," he appears to the consensus of opinion as sage, if not serious, and even philosophic. One should therefore seek his prototype among the fools, not of the stage but of the courts, an ancient and time-honored, if not honorable, profession. . . . [Robert Armin] was doubtless the greatest living authority on court-foolery; and, in creating for him the part of Feste, the dramatist surely intended to capitalize his professional fame and bring to the common public some of the quips and cranks with which he regaled the great. The present study makes no claim that the part of Feste is a biography of Armin; but it does suggest that this role, perhaps the first portrayal of a court fool in Elizabethan drama, evolved, not from mere stage convention, but from life as Armin knew it and as Shakespeare himself saw it in contemporary fooldom.

What references we have to Feste's early life come from the Epilogue—if Shakespeare wrote it and if we may take it at face value. . . . [The] fact that the story it tells is phrased in the first person singular suggests that . . . it is a sketch of Feste's own biography. If this be true . . . then a brief review of its statements is in order. In paraphrase it says: when I was a child, my follies were trifles in the common course of nature; but, when I grew to be a man, I found that men shut their gates against knaves and thieves; and, when I married, I found that playing the bravo and the swaggerer brought in no money, and that drunkards got merely addled brains. Apparently, this realization led Feste to seek respectable steady employment as court jester. (pp. 194-95)

Feste has the sagacity of the finished and perfect fool, a virtuoso in the art of courtly entertainment, who can select from his repertory of effects what style or technique he will to fit the person or occasion. He can use music or speech or action; he entertains the Duke and Sir Toby with songs; he fends off Maria with impudence; he woos Sir Andrew with innocuous nonsense, and outwits his mistress with syllogistic paradox; he knows that he cannot entertain Malvolio at all, and so he entertains himself at Malvolio's expense. (p. 204)

[Feste's] more significant raillery, like that of Swift, is aimed at the foibles and shams of mankind; his very name, suggestive of the Italian *festa* or *festare,* is the perfect expression of the holiday mood in which kings clothed the serious business of their courts. (p. 205)

Feste, except perhaps for Olivia, is the shrewdest person in the play. When he has once made up his mind which way his wind blows he sets his sail accordingly, seeks and obtains Cesario's good opinion of his fooling (as he had the Duke's) and, when the two knights set upon the youngster to do him injury, Feste runs off to "tell my Lady straight," for he knows that she will be furious if they harm her lover. (p. 208)

He joins in the practical jokes on Malvolio; he woos the Duke for reasons of obvious policy; and, for like reasons, he helps Olivia woo Cesario, and even on occasion becomes her trusted messenger. Over all this plays the lambent sparkle of his badinage. Like so many clever people, he lives on two planes of being, an outward façade of professional raillery, and a serious inner urge for the good things of the great world to which he was not born. He is truly chameleon-like, and eats the air promise-crammed—chameleon-like in his varied wit to half a dozen sorts of people, and planning and plotting that the promise of his future livelihood may be fulfilled, as in the end under Olivia and Sebastian, it seems to be fulfilled to the merriment of all.

Shakespeare thought of character in terms of bodily humors and planets, which dominated contemporary science. The covetous, like Feste, were thought to be melancholy, and melancholy might produce a bitter wit, but the frolicsome Feste, as he himself avers, is no cold "dry" fool. . . . Our Feste . . . seems outwardly at least to be a mercurial fellow, in vivid contrast to the ardent melancholy of Viola and the Duke, to the fine balance of Sebastian, to the phlegmatic humors of the two knights and Maria.

The fool tradition that came down from the Middle Ages saw the world as topsy-turvy, and all society as fools, except the fool, and *Twelfth Night,* seen from one angle, is a comedy of all-too-human fools whom Shakespeare depicts as fooled to the top of their several bents, Feste perhaps the least of all. Olivia fools Orsino by refusing him; and Viola fools him and marries him; Sebastian unwillingly makes a fool of himself and of Olivia by letting her lead him to the altar; Olivia fools Sir Toby and Sir Andrew; and they fool Malvolio; and Feste, in this world of chance and caprice and change, though fooled as to Olivia's marrying the Duke, is perhaps less of a fool than any of the rest. There are two noble fools, Orsino, who thinks he can win Olivia, and Olivia, who thinks she can win Viola; two knightly fools, Sir Toby who thinks he can marry off his niece, and Sir Andrew who thinks he can espouse her; a commoner fool, Malvolio, who thinks he can wed a Countess; and a fool-by-vocation, Feste, who knows the others for what they are: such is this gay Illyrian world of realistic foolery, quite in the tradition of *The XXV Orders of Fooles* and Tarlton's *Jests* and Armin's *Nest of Ninnies. Twelfth Night* is also a play of foils and vivid contrasts: Viola and Maria and Orsino who seek marriage, over against Olivia and Sir Toby who seek to avoid it; the contrasting humors of the several figures; and above all the two arch-fools of the comedy, Feste and Sir Andrew, the court fool and the fool-courtier whose difference may be phrased in Feste's own remarks, "Better a witty fool than a foolish wit." (pp. 210-12)

Love is, of course, the subject of most comedies, and . . . Professor Craig, and others have so interpreted *Twelfth Night* [see excerpt above, 1948]. Certainly Olivia has manifold wooers, and there are also the courtships of Maria and Viola; but, if love were the theme, would not at least one of these courtships, as in *Much Ado,* follow normal Elizabethan convention? But in each case, the girl, unaided and unadvised, chooses the man, an unusual procedure in actual Elizabethan life. In *Twelfth Night,* neither father nor brother nor next of kin bestows the hand of Viola, Maria, or Olivia. Moreover, is it really love in any strict sense between Maria and Sir Toby, or between Olivia and most of her wooers? Immediate practical considerations seem rather to be the mainspring of their courtship; Olivia herself in her final choice is governed by such motives and by accident as well as by her passion. Viola is perhaps a Juliet in the play; but it certainly lacks a Romeo. Indeed, the whole comedy has a worldly-wise and humorous tone far removed from *Love's Labour's Lost* and *Romeo and Juliet,* and comparable rather to *The Shrew.* (pp. 247-48)

Twelfth Night is rather the comedy of the social struggles of the time: Orsino wishes to fulfill his duty as head of the house and prolong his family line by a suitable marriage; Maria wants

the security and dignity of marriage to a gentleman—a difficult accomplishment in view of her lack of dowry. Feste and Sir Toby want the security of future food and lodging; Viola and Sebastian hope to reassume their doffed coronets; and Sir Andrew and Malvolio are arrant social climbers, who long to acquire a gentility that neither can possess. In short, this is Shakespeare's play of social security; and, in time of peace, marriage was the chief means by which this prize was gained or lost—one's own marriage, or the marriage of one's friend, overlord, or master. The universal urge of all humanity is said to be survival; and this in turn resolves itself into food, lodging, and a mate. Every important character in the play is scheming for one or all of these: even Feste is looking to his future when he runs away to court the Duke who seems about to wed his mistress; and Fabyan in making Malvolio ridiculous is paying the steward back for denouncing his bearbaiting to Olivia. Every major action in the plot is governed by this urge; and the conclusion shows all the characters with whom the audience would sympathize rewarded with as much certainty of future as one can hope for in this world.

The changes that Shakespeare made from his source in Riche's story give definite support to the theory that he intended social security to be the theme of the comedy. In Riche, Silla (Viola) has the protection of a royal father at whose court Apolonius (Orsino) has been visiting, and she deliberately follows her lover to Constantinople; nothing of this appears in Shakespeare. In Riche, Julina (Olivia) is a widow, and as such does not occupy the uncertain social status of an unmarried young heiress without protection of a father or a brother; in Shakespeare, Olivia has only Sir Toby, who is more of a danger than a protection. In Riche, Silvio (Sebastian) is not shipwrecked, and leaves home merely to seek his errant sister. Riche's story, therefore, is merely a love romance: Julina's marriage to Silvio had no apparent motive of social security on either side, nor did Silla's marriage to Apolonius. Thus Shakespeare's interest in the theme of social security seems to account for his major changes from his source. This reconstituted plot requires a group of characters who will show the dangers of Olivia's position, a persistent noble suitor who will not be gainsaid, a presumptuous menial who aspires to be Count, and a self-seeking uncle who (as was common in that age) insists on a suitor calculated to his own advantage. Thus the main plot concerning Olivia's lovers (suggested in part by the conventional action of Italian comedy) was necessary to illustrate this social theme. Likewise, the shipwreck of Viola and Sebastian, and the seeming fact that they are orphans bring into their lives an insecurity that was not in Riche's story. (pp. 249-51)

The present interpretation of *Twelfth Night* finds the action of the play a complex but well-integrated unity with the minor plots dependent on the major in both commencement and conclusion, and with the episodes developing on the whole naturally and reasonably from the initial situation, from the characters, and from one another. The personalities are highly diversified both in humor and in social types; the part each plays would have seemed to an Elizabethan audience either realistically motivated or so glamourously romantic as to be imaginatively acceptable. The methods of characterization are as diverse as the characters themselves: the personalities express their traits in talk, gesture, and action, in physique, age, and humor, and also appear in the attitude of others toward them. The setting is "Illyria," not a Land of Nowhere (indeed an actual region on contemporary maps), but so little known to the Elizabethans that it could be used to reflect the generalized conditions of the Renaissance, its elegance and brilliance, and its problems of social and economic change. The style of the play is expository, or lyrical, or witty, as the particular scene required—some characters pithy in speech, some elaborate or prolix, as they would be in life. The theme is social security, generally attained through marriage; for security in that age, as today, was generally an economic matter, and the wealth that gave economic safety was usually gained (or was supposed to be, at least) by inheritance or family alliance. Thus, three pairs of heroes and heroines achieve their desires, and the action at last slows down to a static equilibrium in which all who deserve it live happily ever after. The play is all of a piece; the threads are perfectly interwoven; each character does what such a person might be expected to do, and this is also what he should do to further the plot; and all their careers illustrate the comic solution of a single significant theme—significant in all ages but especially in the changes and chances of Shakespeare's time. Above all, the laughter of the piece, supplied partly by the action, partly by the style, arises without strain from the plot and the characters, and is expressed in a swift and brilliant dialogue replete with epigram, allusion, and fine ironies, somewhat elusive to the modern ear. Such is the comedy of *Twelfth Night*. (pp. 253-54)

> *John W. Draper, in his* The "Twelfth Night" *of Shakespeare's Audience, Stanford University Press, 1950, 280 p.*

KARL F. THOMPSON (essay date 1952)

[*Like John W. Draper (1950), Thompson concludes that Shakespeare's romantic comedies are difficult for modern audiences to enjoy. He asserts that we must consider them within the correct literary and historical context which is, according to Thompson, the English courtly love tradition.*]

[Shakespeare's romantic comedies] confuse us, and for the modern audience or reader they are the hardest of his plays to enjoy. . . . Perhaps, we say in our moments of candor with ourselves, perhaps the only reason these comedies survive and pass as sound literary coin is that they have the mint stamp of Shakespeare's name. They seem, though, so old-fashioned; somewhat naive, or contrived to suit popular tastes that have long since vanished; so preposterous with their sudden conversions of villains, disguised maidens, transvestitism carried to an extreme, ridiculous outlaws, foolish heroes, and wise heroines—all these, we think, tax too much our capacity willingly to suspend our disbelief. These objections are valid if we insist on listening to these comedies with ears attuned to catching the subtleties of Noel Coward, the metaphysical wit bandied about at Cocktail Parties, or the brusqueries of Kaufmann and Hart. Yet a case can be made for these antiquated romantic comedies. The enjoyment of them requires, however, an altered point of view, an adjusted receptivity, or at least a more informed one. We are not, perhaps, sophisticated enough to enjoy romance.

The greatest hindrance to our enjoyment of these comedies is that they abound in echoes of a literary tradition that has, in large measure, passed away. They depend for their effect upon the audience's ability to hear these echoes and to perceive how the playwright is using the elements of that tradition.

This tradition, made up of themes, tags, characters, references, and situations, is the courtly love tradition, which from eleventh-century Provence spread throughout western Europe and influenced literature for some five centuries. In Shakespeare's time it was still vital, although modified by Italian and English

writers of the Renaissance. The problem here, then, is to see how these comedies depend upon their observance of, departure from, and ironical use of the conventions of the courtly tradition and to consider if Shakespeare had a genuine respect for or faith in a tradition that seems so old, tired, nonsensical to us. We must try to decide if Shakespeare accepted the tradition, or whether he changed it to suit his personal views and finally gave it up as ridiculous and unsuitable for drama.

The origin and growth of the courtly love tradition is too well known and its history too complicated to be treated more than cursorily here. In summation one can say that from its beginnings in Provence, through its dissemination throughout France and Italy, the tradition contained these elements:

1) The feudal metaphor places the lady in the same relationship to her lover that the lord is to his vassal. Conversely, the lover owes unquestioning and unfaltering obedience to his lady.

2) The religion of love metaphor creates a god or goddess of love whose devotees do quasi-liturgical observances. Lovers often refer to their ladies as saints, objects of semi-religious veneration. Implicit in the metaphor is the idea that as God is everything that is good in eternity, so is *amor* everything *in soeculo bonum*.

3) The lord of love (a feudal lord) commands his subjects to do his will in several ways. Noble youths must perform deeds of heroism; ladies must at last grant their favor when the petitions of their suffering lovers, who journey to love's court, are granted. The lord of love commands armies, too, and his servants are loyal soldiers.

4) The commandments of love are a code of conduct to be followed by the true lover.

5) Scoffers at love are punished and converted, and their repentance, confession, and penance connects this converted scoffer convention with the religion of love metaphor.

6) The school of love is the lessons which the converted scoffer learns. Here the religion of love metaphor and the court of love blend. The commandments of love or code of the lover are announced to the repentant lover, who subscribes to them and forthwith takes up his feudal service of his lady. (pp. 1079-81)

Shakespeare turned . . . for his manner of handling plots, actions, and incidents . . . to what I shall call the English tradition of courtly love, stemming from Chaucer, elaborated by the fifteenth-century Chaucerians and changed by their sixteenth-century successors. This English tradition added to the medieval tradition these two elements: the romance of marriage, which replaced the romance of adultery, and humorous mockery of the conventions. The romance of marriage resolved the conflict between *amor in soeculo* and sempiternal love which had compelled the older romancers to add palinodes, but no palinode is necessary when romance ends in the sacrament of marriage. Mockery of the conventions was brought into the open and made an integral part of romance, whereas in continental romances it had been rather covert, an addition or a coda. English clowns are permitted, indeed required, to ape their betters and to court and woo. (p. 1081)

Twelfth Night, or What You Will (ca. 1600), is the half-way mark of Shakespeare's dramatic career. But in this play Shakespeare's dependence upon the tradition is still strong. He does not show impatience with the conventions or a desire to be rid of them. The Petrarchistic conceits of the Duke, it is true, are extremely farfetched, but that is the kind of person the Duke Orsino is. He likes to refer to love as the "rich, golden shaft"; and such conceited phraseology and a few languid gestures are the extent of his courtship of the lady Olivia. Yet he boasts that "such as I am all true lovers are":

> Unstaid and skittish in all motions else
> Save in the constant image of the creature
> That is belov'd.   [II.iv.18-20]

This kind of deportment is not dramatically promising if exhibited by more than the one person whom it characterizes as a tired aesthete and egotist. But the playwright has the Duke, after saying that he pines for love, turn to questioning Cesario, Viola in disguise, about the lady Olivia. This is a dramatically effective exchange because Viola's disguise, which permits her to be the aggressor and to direct considerable attention to herself, and the Duke's languid mannerisms are ironically contrasted.

The ironical use of the feudal metaphor is one of the sources of the comedy. Viola merely pretends to be a servant, whereas she is really the lady to whom the Duke should be servant. On the other hand, Malvolio is an actual servant, who, when he attempts to be the love-servant, becomes ridiculous. Malvolio may be, of course, other things, but he is principally the ridiculous love-servant.

The other characters of the sub-plot also conform to the conventions. The courtly code demanded deeds of valor. Therefore, Sir Toby and Fabian make their appeal to Sir Andrew to show himself worthy of his lady. What better way than to overcome a rival in a passage of arms which, fortunately for the outcome of the play, serves to reveal the identities of Sebastian and Viola? (pp. 1090-91)

In *Twelfth Night* as in *Love's Labor's Lost* Shakespeare put the conventions to dramatic use. Of course he has had sport with them, for they lend themselves to jest as well as to seriousness. . . . The tradition itself allows for jesting, for it sees the ridiculousness that is inherent in man's habits of courtship—as indeed it is in most of human activity. Carry our seriousness too far in our adherence to social codes and the ludicrous takes over. The muse of comedy is always in the wings ready to steal the scene from the tragic muse should she overact.

This is what Shakespeare does with the tradition: somewhere in most of the comedies he presents the tradition reversed. Then he turns it right again. Or he adds a flourish, an extra character or scene that exaggerates the traditional situation. Or he parodies the tradition with a set of purely comic characters acting out their own homely romances. And he often uses the standard reversal of the converted scoffer at love, provided by the tradition itself. He toys with the tradition, it is true, teases the audience's expectations by addition here, reversal there, new situations, parody and jest. For Shakespeare knew as well as we that *variatio delectat*. But it must be a variation of the familiar to result in pleasure. Shakespeare therefore always maintains a balance for his audience by offering them recognition of the familiar and exploration of, the new and diverting. His use of the tradition thus creates tension in his comedies and gives them a unity of action.

Shakespeare had an aesthetic faith in the tradition sufficiently strong to allow him to employ it as the unifying theme of his romantic comedies. Now, reasonably well-constructed comedies result in what can be called the comic catharsis, that is,

the purgation of such socially involved emotions as spite, malice, hatred, lust, and envy. Of these, romantic comedy concentrates upon lust and envy. It does this, in Shakespeare's comic vein, by directing the attention of the audience to such socially harmful actions as treachery to friends and betrayal of trust. But in the world of comedy such actions fail and are defeated by love, loyalty, and honor.

After this consideration of Shakespeare's aesthetic faith in the conventions and his reliance upon them, the question arises: did Shakespeare accept the morality that is inherent in the Anglicized courtly tradition? . . . The practising dramatist does not often violate the morality of his age. On the other hand, he reflects that morality through his perceptive intelligence. He gives the audience what it wants—if that is what he wants too. Quite often the two desires coincide. Shakespeare, like his audience, probably accepted the morality of the old conventions.

Shakespeare has been credited by some with having amended romantic comedy by introducing the respectable bourgeois notion of marriage. . . . Love is loyalty—this is the proper answer to the question of the relation of sex to society. *Amor* is sexual; loyalty is a social as well as a personal emotion. But Shakespeare refused to employ the fascinating comic situations promised by deviation from that equation. His jests about cuckoldry are wordplay merely. One view has it that Shakespeare's patrons wouldn't have tolerated the condoning of illicit love. Another says that it was to Shakespeare's credit that he refused to portray illicit love. Actually it is both. Shakespeare adopted the idea that love is loyalty because it suited his moral sense and because it had been introduced into romance long before his time. Audiences had already become accustomed to the reformed medieval romance. That reformation of the romance of adultery had been accomplished by Shakespeare's English predecessors: by Hawes, Nevill, Gavin Douglas, and by John Heywood. What Shakespeare did was to work in the English tradition of romance, reinforce it, dramatize it.

We return to the ancient tradition every time and find in it aid in seeing Shakespeare's romantic comedies as in themselves they really are. At the very least, we can say that knowledge of the conventions gives savor to the plays. But we can also claim that these comedies which depend so greatly upon the courtly tradition do perform the whole function of comedy, the purgation from human nature of painful desires by transforming them in art. Paradoxically, what the modern audience must do, and can do, is to take these comedies more seriously. They are more than pretty fancies. The courtly tradition upon which they are based should not, therefore, be neglected. For the altars of the god and goddess of love in the old dispensation have been too long barren. (pp. 1091-93)

> *Karl F. Thompson, "Shakespeare's Romantic Comedies," in PMLA, 67, Vol. LXVII, No. 2, March, 1952, pp. 1079-93.*

SYLVAN BARNET   (essay date 1954)

[*The following response to Charles Lamb's defense of Malvolio (see excerpt above, 1822) concerns the interpretation of the character by the nineteenth-century actor, Robert Bensley. Barnet quotes sources who witnessed Bensley's performances to prove that Lamb was unique in seeing Malvolio as a tragic character. Barnet concludes that Lamb's interpretation of Malvolio is "not Bensley's, not the age's, but his own."*]

[Charles Lamb's essay] "On Some of the Old Actors," is largely devoted to a recollection of the Malvolio of Robert Bensley, a role which Lamb regarded as having tragic affinities. "I confess," he wrote, "that I never saw the catastrophe of this character, while Bensley played it, without a kind of tragic interest." (p. 178)

Closest to Lamb in his view of *Twelfth Night* is Hazlitt; who was a bit upset at the fun made of Malvolio [see excerpt above, 1817]. "If poor Malvolio's treatment afterwards is a little hard, poetical justice is done in the uneasiness which Olivia suffers on account of her mistaken attachment to Cesario." Aware that in comedy poetic justice must reign, Hazlitt has sought by his interpretation of Olivia to redress the balance which he overset when he took Malvolio too seriously. But besides Lamb, no Romantic went, in his sympathy for Malvolio, even as far as Hazlitt. And Hazlitt himself concentrated attention not on the Steward, but upon the romantic aspects of the play. . . . (p. 179)

Shakespeare's play is, of course, a romantic comedy, with even less of a threat to a happy outcome than there is in his other plays in this genre. No Shylock whets his knife, no Don John lurks malignantly in the shadows; indeed, there is not even a Charles who threatens to crack an Orlando's ribs. . . . [Earlier spectators] did find that Malvolio was a major figure (though not a tragic one) in the play. When John Manningham of the Middle Temple confided to his diary his comments on the play, which he saw following the feast on February 2, 1602, he did not remark on the love of Viola for Orsino, but on the good trick of making a steward think his mistress was in love with him, and then making the poor gull believe that others in the household thought him mad [see excerpt above, 1602]. And several decades later Charles I crossed out the title of the play in the royal copy of the Second Folio (1632), and replaced it with "Malvolio." In short, the earliest evidence we have, scanty though it is, indicates that the Steward was the center of interest, while later evidence (even more scanty) suggests that during the Restoration he was not. Certainly he was never conceived tragically before the late eighteenth century, and I shall endeavor to show that in the early nineteenth century Lamb was unique in his conception of the part, and thus is largely responsible for the tragic Malvolio. (p. 180)

Malvolio is potentially tragic, for he finds that past modes of behavior are no longer suitable, no longer meaningful in his present relationship with the world. His self-love is no longer adequate. In tragedy, the protagonist comes to some such realization, and by a heroic, and exhausting, endeavor, readjusts the balance. But in *Twelfth Night* Malvolio rejects the challenge to alter himself, and grotesquely continues to defy his antagonists, who are not villains of great power, but jovial tipplers. The struggle is unworthy as well as unheroic. Our sympathies are all with Malvolio's foes, who represent a way of life which gains, at least within the playhouse, our approval. The world of Goneril and Regan, of King Claudius, of Iago, we reject, and our sympathy goes out to the man partly entrapped in it. But Illyria is another thing, and he who would war against it forfeits our approval, since he has forfeited his love of humanity. (pp. 181-82)

[Lamb] found great dignity and merit in Malvolio, and though he granted that the Steward was flawed with pride, he held that "if an unseasonable reflection of morality obtruded itself, it was a deep sense of the pitiable infirmity of man's nature, that can lay him open to such frenzies—but in truth you rather admired than pitied the lunacy while it lasted—you felt that an hour of such mistake was worth an age with the eyes open."

The pattern which Lamb establishes is clearly a tragic one. A man of considerable worth falls from weal to woe, through an infirmity in his nature, and even in his infirmity there is a kind of greatness. Furthermore, his fall inspires us to think of the weakness and yet the majesty of human nature. Lamb asserts that Bensley's playing, more than earlier or later performances, paralleled this interpretation. . . . As Lamb was only twenty-one when Bensley retired from the stage on May 6, 1796, he was by no means a mature critic during Bensley's acting career. His account of *Twelfth Night*, written more than a quarter of a century after Bensley had retired, is the work of a sophisticated critic (however wrongheaded we feel the essay may be), and is based more on nostalgic reminiscence than on fresh observation. (p. 183)

Most of Bensley's contemporaries who wrote about him at all praised his Malvolio. For example, the author of *Memoirs of Mrs. Crouch* observed that "Mr. Bensley, in the vain fantastical Malvolio, was excellent," and John Adolphus, in his biography of John Bannister, alluded to "Bensley's solemn deportment and ludicrous gullibility in Malvolio." If we are accustomed to seeing Bensley only through Lamb's eyes, these words have a strange sound. (p. 184)

The dignity which Lamb felt invested Bensley, Bensley's contemporaries often felt was comic. The testimonies from which I have quoted indicate over and over that his Malvolio was a grotesque figure, not a serious or tragic one. His gravity was a symbol of his conceit, of his self-love. . . . (p. 185)

Lamb's interpretation of Bensley as Malvolio not only fails to correspond with contemporary opinions, but is strangely inconsistent with his own theory of comedy. As he realized (even in "On the Artificial Comedy of the Last Century"), comedy is frequently a lighthearted protest against some of its characters. Prudish parents, jealous husbands, misers, and all such troublemakers, are held up to derision, and the ideal comic world agrees with Sir Toby Belch that "care's an enemy to life." Those who intrude, however, into the world of comedy must not be taken too seriously, and must ultimately be dismissed with a laugh and a shrug. The subjects of mirth in art are, in real life, not necessarily amusing, but they are deviations from a norm. Lamb knew that some of these deviations, the miser, for example, depicted realistically on the stage would not afford laughter, and he wisely suggested that the actor must not be too natural, but, indeed, must make his role engaging by presenting a cartoon of his subject. The real miser, the real jealous husband, however, though not always amusing, is, by his deviation, out of place even in the real world, for his excessive attention to a particular matter sets him apart from other men. He does not quite "fit" in real life, and comedy capitalizes on his incompatibility. But Lamb suggests that Malvolios are necessary and at home in the real world, and that Shakespeare's Steward is comic only because he has been taken out of the realm of reality and thrust into the fairyland of Illyria. Such an interpretation eliminates or at best minimizes both Malvolio's self-love and his consequent attempt to foist his own ideas upon others. It sees in him only a diligent man thrust into a world free from worry, and it overlooks the fact that his diligence is chiefly exerted in self-advancement. In short, I suggest that Malvolio is intrinsically comic, a deviation from the norm of life, and in Illyria, of course, he is doubly so. Malvolio seeking to rise in the social scale, Malvolio fondling his chain and imagining it to be some rich jewel—these are comic, and not only in Illyria. Lamb merely grants that Malvolio is out of place in Illyria, and hence he gives him a great measure of sympathy. In fact, so great is his sympathy that he shifts the object of value from Illyria to Malvolio, and thus brings us into the tragic realm, where the hero often is superior to his environment.

Lamb's discussion of Bensley, I think, is Lamb writing of his own Malvolio, rather than of Bensley's. The evidence of Bensley's contemporaries clearly suggests that the actor's Malvolio was not that which Lamb depicted twenty-six years after Bensley had retired. Perhaps Lamb's memory was partly at fault, but the distortion also arises, I think, from his creative faculty. His interpretation of the play is wrong, but it is an interpretation which could only be produced by a sensitive mind in contact with a great work of art. (pp. 186-87)

Sylvan Barnet, "Charles Lamb and the Tragic Malvolio," in Philological Quarterly, Vol. XXXIII, No. 2, April, 1954, pp. 177-88.

MILTON CRANE (essay date 1955)

[*Crane interprets* Twelfth Night *as representative of Shakespeare at the height of his comic powers. He challenges the sympathetic response of nineteenth- and twentieth-century commentators to the gulling of Malvolio. Crane believes that the audience is intended to share Sir Toby's "sadistic pleasure" in the deception of the steward. Although he is central to the structure of* Twelfth Night, *Malvolio does not engage Shakespeare's attention. For additional commentary on the punishment of Malvolio, see the excerpts by William Hazlitt (1817), Charles Lamb (1822), Charles Knight (1842), T. Kenny (1864), H. N. Hudson (1872), William Archer (1884), O. J. Campbell (1943), and Melvin Seiden (1961).*]

A work productive of mirth, frequently employing a love-story as its basic matter, agreeably resolving a disturbing or even dangerous situation or group of incidents, and exposing vice or correcting folly: such is Elizabethan comedy. *Twelfth Night* is an admirable example of this synthesis of the romantic and the didactic; but we may do well to recall that Shakespeare came to such a synthesis by way of an orderly development.

The plays generally classed together as Shakespeare's comedies, if we omit the chronicle histories with substantial comic subplots, fall into four major groups: (1) the early comedies and farces, including such plays as *The Comedy of Errors* and *The Taming of the Shrew;* (2) the great comedies: *Twelfth Night* and *As You Like It;* (3) the so-called dark comedies; and (4) the romantic comedies or tragi-comedies of Shakespeare's last years. Now the earliest plays are simple, even classical, in their comic structure; and they make capital of every device known to the writer of farce. (pp. 3-4)

About the early plays, then, we may assume that no great difficulty exists. The main action of each play is normally paralleled by a subplot of clowns: the Antipholuses have their Dromios; King Ferdinand and the Princess have their Berowne and Rosaline and even their Armado and Jacquenetta; the loves of Lysander and Hermia are answered by the marvelous triangle of Oberon, Titania, and Bottom.

As we approach the great comedies of Shakespeare's middle period, we are faced by serious questions concerning the structure of dramatic action and the nature of dramatic effect. What has the tragic—or at least melodramatic—story of Hero and Claudio to do with the comedy of Beatrice and Benedick? How does the sentimental romance of Orsino and Viola come to be played to the raucous accompaniment of Sir Toby Belch? *Twelfth*

Night deserves special consideration because it has the greatest complexity of plot structure, and because the net effect of the play, in spite of Malvolio, is not comic. *Twelfth Night* is, moreover, a crucial case in the study of Shakespearian comedy, as it exhibits the chief problems that are to be raised and resolved less successfully in the problem comedies and the last plays. If it is possible to demonstrate the pattern that Shakespeare employed in *Twelfth Night*—a combination of consistent and ingenious variations on a favorite theme of classical comedy—then Shakespeare's technique of comic inversion becomes clearly recognizable; it is this technique which, when pressed too far and insufficiently controlled by comic decorum, produces such baffling and irritating works as *Measure for Measure*.

Twelfth Night is compounded of three plots. Central to the play, as Mark Van Doren has well said [see excerpt above, 1939], is Malvolio, the gull, critical and waspish, an efficiency expert, a busybody. To pay him back for his insults, Sir Toby, Sir Andrew, and Maria contrive to lead him by the nose until he has disgraced himself with Olivia, been confined as a madman, and put out of his humor publicly in the presence of his mistress and his tormentors. He is a comic protagonist *par excellence;* his ambition and his vanity are precisely the comic vices by means of which he is plagued. The counterfeited letter is exquisitely designed so that he will put just such a construction on it as will gratify his self-love and lead him to his own destruction. (pp. 4-5)

This is such a plot as would have delighted Ben Jonson or any writer of classical satirical comedy. . . . Its mainspring is the unmasking of a gull by his own witless conceit; it is enhanced by the parallel action in which Sir Andrew is persuaded to court Olivia, only to have his head broken by way of reward. The baiting of Malvolio is unrelieved in its comic heartlessness, and is not even superficially moral in its purpose. Others may prate about reforming the gull by putting him out of his humor; there can be no doubt, as we watch the undoing of Malvolio, that we are intended to share Sir Toby's sadistic pleasure in the process, and that no one takes the slightest interest in whether all this will make a better man of Malvolio. (p. 5)

At the risk of laboring the obvious, I should like to recall the essential elements of Malvolio's story: the progress toward self-recognition of a man who is partly self-deceived and partly deceived by others; who assumes a form of disguise in order (as he thinks) to achieve his end, but who must ultimately divest himself of it; who loves, but—as he comes to realize—in vain. He is at length brought to utter confusion, but his downfall produces pain only in himself, a ridiculous figure (in spite of nineteenth- and twentieth-century romanticizing) and therefore worthy of suffering the typical fate of a comic protagonist.

The second of the three plots of *Twelfth Night* deals with the frustrated love of Olivia for Viola-Cesario and its happy resolution in the marriage of Olivia and Sebastian. The first interview of Olivia and the disguised Viola is a brilliantly contrived comic exchange, the end of which is tempered by Olivia's confession of love for the supposed youth. Here are all the elements of a romantic plot of frustrated love in the manner of Beaumont and Fletcher. Shakespeare, however, is content to develop the emotional possibilities of this situation for only one additional scene; then, using precisely such a casual, perfunctory, and mechanical device as he had unblushingly exploited in the farcical *Comedy of Errors*, he substitutes Sebastian for Viola and packs the lovers off to a priest. Let no one tell us of the profound psychology that Shakespeare here displays in making Viola and Sebastian identical twins in wit and intellect as well as in form and feature. Shakespeare is merely hustling his minor characters off the stage with the least possible trouble, whatever the cost in plausibility. In this respect, at least, *Twelfth Night* is no less a romance than *The Winter's Tale*.

Note, however, that the story of Viola, Olivia, and Sebastian, like that of Malvolio, turns on Olivia's awakening from a deception—actually a double deception, produced partly by a disguise and partly by lack of self-knowledge. She first is made to realize, when she becomes infatuated with Viola, that her determination to mourn her brother seven years can be overcome in a twinkling:

> Even so quickly may one catch the plague?
> Methinks I feel this youth's perfections
> With an invisible and subtle stealth
> To creep in at mine eyes.   [I.v.295-98]

Similarly, she must presently abase herself before the young page, beg his hand in marriage, and hale him before a priest, offering no seemlier excuse for her unladylike haste than

> Plight me the full assurance of your faith
> That my most jealous and too doubtful soul
> May live at peace.   [IV.iii.26-8]

The most radiant, exquisite, and unmatchable beauty has indeed learned to humble herself. From this point forward, she has little to do in the play but to help complete the confusion of Malvolio.

The third plot is, of course, the story of Viola and Orsino. Just as Malvolio is deceived by Maria and Sir Toby, and Olivia by Viola, so Orsino is baffled partly by his infatuation for Olivia (which steeps him in a fashionable melancholy) and by his inability to penetrate the disguise of the unfortunate Viola. This is a comedy of errors in which the only character who is fully aware of the situation is powerless to remedy it, and can only apostrophize her page's garments. . . . Now, whereas we take satisfaction in the untrussing of Malvolio, and we never really fear that the awakening of Olivia will pass beyond the boundaries of comedy (as is made altogether plain by the simple and mechanical contrivance that extricates her from her predicament), the story of Viola and Orsino is something else again. Although unmistakably comic in outline, in its development this action seizes every opportunity to develop sentimental suggestions and implications. It may be argued that comic decorum does not exclude sentiment. On this point authorities disagree; nevertheless, when Rosalind permits her mind to run on Orlando and her wished-for joys, she almost at once mocks herself for so doing. Viola cannot; not only is her situation beyond her control, but she is temperamentally one with Hero and Celia, not with Rosalind or Beatrice. In other words, she is the kind of heroine whom one does not expect to find playing a leading role in comedy, but rather serving as a Julia to a Kate Hardcastle. . . .

Now the curious thing about *Twelfth Night* is not only that Viola plays the leading feminine part, but that the patently comic action of Malvolio, central though it be to the structure of the play, is clearly the action that least engages Shakespeare's attention. In short, here is a play that inverts what we may regard as the normal order of elements in a comedy, with respect to the importance it assigns to each. The sentimental story of Viola and Orsino is in first place; closely connected

with it but clearly subordinate to it is the more overtly comic story of Olivia, Viola, and Sebastian; and in last place is the comic gulling of Malvolio. All three plots have fundamentally the same structure: a comic protagonist is gulled by another person, and is at length forced to recognize and take account of the imposition that has been practiced upon him. But it makes a very great difference whether, on the one hand, the gull is Orsino, unwillingly deceived by Viola, or whether, on the other hand, Maria and Sir Toby are joyfully hoodwinking Malvolio. Shakespeare has so harmonized the three actions that they answer one another on different levels and with different effects; but there can be no doubt as to which of these actions seemed to him of paramount interest and importance. He invented the story of Malvolio, and used it with rare skill as the foundation of his play; but he was concerned first of all with Viola and secondarily with Olivia. (pp. 5-7)

Shakespeare, beginning with a theme of classical comedy, proceeded to devise a series of variations on this fundamental action, variations that departed more and more from comedy in their effects though not in their methods. If the total effect of *Twelfth Night*, owing to the predominance of Viola's story, suggests *la comédie larmoyante* more than a Goldsmith could approve, we should not seek to explain this fact by postulating special theories of Shakespearian comedy or by atomizing Shakespeare's plays into individual scenes. Above all, we should not neglect the importance in the play's structure of the grossly anti-romantic plot of Malvolio and his tormentors.

Twelfth Night, together with Shakespeare's other great comedies, leads one to conclude that Dr. Johnson's praise of Shakespeare's comic genius was hardly exaggerated, although one hesitates to affirm with him that the comedies surpass the tragedies in excellence. One cannot agree with Dr. Johnson, however, that Shakespeare's plays were neither comedies nor tragedies. The early comedies, such as *A Midsummer-Night's Dream*, are surely true comedies; and in them Shakespeare employed a comic structure and method that he, like his colleagues, had inherited from the ancients and turned to his own uses. The dark comedies depart from Shakespeare's normal practice in comedy because in them he fails to reconcile conflicting elements of romance and satire. The great comedies such as *Twelfth Night* show, on the contrary, Shakespeare working effectively within the tradition of classical comedy and enlarging it to encompass a rich and harmonious development of fundamentally comic matter. (pp. 7-8)

> *Milton Crane, "'Twelfth Night' and Shakespearian Comedy," in* Shakespeare Quarterly, *Vol. VI, No. 1, Winter, 1955, pp. 1-8.*

JOSEPH H. SUMMERS   (essay date 1955)

[*Continuing the discussion of the theme of self-deception in* Twelfth Night, *Summers interprets the play as a "dance of Maskers" in which each character wears a mask and plays a role. In this he sounds again a chord first struck by E. Montégut (1867) and E. K. Chambers (1907) and anticipates the essay by Bertrand Evans (1960).*]

Love and its fulfillment are primary in Shakespeare's comedies. Its conflicts are often presented in terms of the battle of the generations. At the beginning of the plays the bliss of the young lovers is usually barred by an older generation of parents and rulers, a group which has supposedly experienced its own fulfillment in the past and which is now concerned with preserving old forms or fulfilling new ambitions. The comedies usually end with the triumph of young love, a triumph in which the lovers make peace with their elders and themselves assume adulthood and often power. The revolutionary force of love becomes an added element of vitality in a re-established society.

Twelfth Night does not follow the customary pattern. In this play the responsible older generation has been abolished, and there are no parents at all. In the first act we are rapidly introduced into a world in which the ruler is a love-sick Duke—in which young ladies, fatherless and motherless, embark on disguised actions, or rule, after a fashion, their own households, and in which the only individuals possibly over thirty are drunkards, jokesters, and gulls, totally without authority. All the external barriers to fulfillment have been eliminated in what becomes almost a parody of the state desired by the ordinary young lovers, the Hermias and Lysanders—or even the Rosalinds and Orlandos. According to the strictly romantic formula, the happy ending should be already achieved at the beginning of the play: we should abandon the theater for the rites of love. But the slightly stunned inhabitants of Illyria discover that they are anything but free. Their own actions provide the barriers, for most of them know neither themselves, nor others, nor their social world.

For his festival entertainment, Shakespeare freshly organized all the usual material of the romances—the twins, the exile, the impersonations—to provide significant movement for a dance of maskers. Every character has his mask, for the assumption of the play is that no one is without a mask in the serio-comic business of the pursuit of happiness. The character without disguises who is not ridiculous is outside the realm of comedy. Within comedy, the character who thinks it is possible to live without assuming a mask is merely too naive to recognize the mask he has already assumed. He is the chief object of laughter. As a general rule, we laugh with the characters who know the role they are playing and we laugh at those who do not; we can crudely divide the cast of *Twelfth Night* into those two categories.

But matters are more complicated than this, and roles have a way of shifting. All the butts except perhaps Sir Andrew Aguecheek have moments in which they are the masters of our laughter; yet all the masters have moments in which they appear as fools. In our proper confusion, we must remember the alternative title of the play, "What You Will." It may indicate that everyone is free to invent his own title for the proceedings. It also tells the author's intention to fulfill our desires: we wish to share in the triumphs of love and we wish to laugh; we wish our fools occasionally to be wise, and we are insistent that our wisest dramatic figures experience our common fallibility. Most significantly, the title may hint that what "we" collectively "will" creates all the comic masks—that society determines the forms of comedy more directly than it determines those of any other literary genre.

At the opening of the play Orsino and Olivia accept the aristocratic (and literary) ideas of the romantic lover and the grief-stricken lady as realities rather than as ideas. They are comic characters exactly because of that confusion. Orsino glories in the proper moodiness and fickleness of the literary lover; only our own romanticism can blind us to the absurdities in his opening speech. Orsino first wishes the music to continue so that the appetite of love may "surfeit"; immediately, however, he demands that the musicians stop the music they are playing to repeat an isolated phrase—an awkward procedure and a comic bit of stage business which is rarely utilized in produc-

tions. Four lines later the music must stop entirely because the repeated "strain" no longer *is* sweet, and the appetite is truly about to "surfeit." (pp. 25-6)

In the same scene, before we ever see the lady, Olivia's state is as nicely defined. Valentine, Orsino's messenger, has acquired something of his master's extraordinary language, and his report on his love mission manages both to please the Duke and to convey his own incredulity at the excess of Olivia's vow for her brother. In his speech the fresh and the salt are again confused. It is impossible to keep fresh something so ephemeral as grief; Olivia can make it last and "season" it, however, by the process of pickling—the natural effect of "eye-offending brine." (p. 26)

Both Orsino and Olivia have adopted currently fashionable literary postures; yet neither of them is a fool. We are glad to be reassured by the Captain that Orsino is "A noble duke, in nature as in name," and that his present infatuation is only a month old. Sir Toby's later remark "What a plague means my niece, to take the death of her brother thus?" indicates that Olivia too had seemed an unlikely candidate for affectation. She is also an unconvincing practitioner. . . . Outraged nature has its full and comic revenge when Olivia falls passionately in love with a male exterior and acts with an aggressiveness which makes Orsino seem almost feminine. Still properly an actor in comedy, Olivia quickly changes from the character who has confused herself with a socially attractive mask to one who fails to perceive the mask which society has imposed on another.

Viola's situation allows time for neither love- nor grief-in-idleness. A virgin, shipwrecked in a strange land, possessing only wit and intelligence and the Captain's friendship, she must act immediately if she is to preserve herself. She, like Olivia, has "lost" a brother, but the luxury of conventional mourning is quickly exchanged for a *willed* hope that, as she was saved, "so perchance may he be." With Viola's wish for time to know what her "estate is," before she is "delivered to the world," we are reminded that society often requires a mask, neither for the relief of boredom nor the enjoyment of acting, but merely for self-preservation. . . . Viola suffers from no failure of discretion or imagination. She must assume a disguise as a boy and she must have help in preparing it. (pp. 26-7)

We have in this second scene not only the beginning of one strand of the complicated intrigue, but also the creation of the one character active in the intrigue who provides a measure for the comic excesses of all the others. (Feste's role as observer is analogous to Viola's role as "actor.") Although Viola chooses to impersonate Cesario from necessity, she later plays her part with undisguised enjoyment. She misses none of the opportunities for parody, for confession, and for *double entendre* which the mask affords, and she never forgets or lets us forget the biological distance between Viola and Cesario. Except in the fencing match with Sir Andrew Aguecheek, she anticipates and directs our perception of the ludicrous in her own role as well as in the roles of Orsino and Olivia.

Sebastian is the reality of which Cesario is the artful imitation. Viola's twin assumes no disguises; Viola and the inhabitants of Illyria have assumed it for him. He is, to the eye, identical with Viola, and his early scenes with Antonio serve to remind us firmly of his existence as well as to introduce an initial exhilarating confusion at the entrance of either of the twins. When he truly enters the action of the play in Act IV he is certainly the object of our laughter, not because he has confused himself with an ideal or improper mask, but because he so righteously and ineffectually insists on his own identity in the face of unanimous public opposition. (pp. 27-8)

[Sir Andrew] would hardly exist without Sir Toby Belch: the gull must have his guller. Sir Toby may fulfill Sir Andrew's idea of what a gentleman should be, but Sir Toby himself has no such odd idea of gentility. (Sir Andrew may be "a dear manikin to you, Sir Toby," but Sir Toby has a superlatively good reason for allowing him to be: "I have been dear to him, lad, some two thousand strong, or so.") Even at his most drunken, we are delightfully unsure whether we laugh at or with Sir Toby, whether he is or is not fully conscious of the effects as well as the causes of his "mistakes," his verbal confusions, and even his belches. Like another drunken knight, and like Viola, Toby possesses a range of dramatic talents and he enjoys using them. . . . But like other knowing players, Sir Toby is vulnerable to deception. He is object rather than master of our laughter from the time when he mistakes Sebastian for Cesario and attempts to assert his masculine ability as a swordsman.

In the business of masking, Feste is the one professional among a crowd of amateurs; he does it for a living. He never makes the amateur's mistake of confusing his personality with his mask—he wears not motley in his brain. Viola recognizes his wisdom and some kinship in the fact that each "must observe their mood on whom he jests." But though Feste may have deliberately chosen his role, society determines its conditions. Now that he is growing old, the conditions become difficult: "Go to, you're a dry fool, I'll no more of you. Besides, you grow dishonest." While all the other characters are concerned with gaining something they do not have, Feste's struggle is to retain his mask and to make it again ingratiating. He is able to penetrate all the masks of the others, and he succeeds in retaining his own.

However fanciful its dreams of desire, the play moves within a context of an almost real world, from one disguise and half-understood intrigue to another, until all its elements are whirled into a complexly related and moving figure. With the constant contrasts and parallels and reversals in character, situation, and intrigue, we find ourselves at last, along with Malvolio and Olivia and Viola and the rest, in a state of real delirium. Until the concluding scene, however, we can largely agree with Sebastian: if we dream, we do not wish to wake; if this is madness, it is still comic madness, and we do not envy the sane. The attempts at false and inflexible authority are being defeated, the pretentious are being deflated, and the very sentimentality of the likeable sentimentalists has led them close to biological reality. We are particularly delighted with Viola. Young, intelligent, zestful, she is a realist. She cuts through the subterfuges and disguises of the others with absolute clarity, and she provides us with a center for the movement, a standard of normality which is never dull. In her rejection of the artificial myths of love, moreover, Viola never becomes the advocate of a far more terrifying myth, the myth of absolute rationality. In a completely rational world, Shakespeare never tires of pointing out, what we know as love could not exist. We have never desired such a world.

From the time of her first aside to the audience after she has seen Orsino ("Yet a barful strife! / Whoe'er I woo, myself would be his wife"), Viola directly admits her irrational love. She differs, then, from Orsino and Olivia not in any invulnerability to blindness and passion, but in the clarity and simplicity with which she recognizes and accepts her state. . . .

Viola needs a miracle. Although she may imagine herself as "Patience on a monument, smiling at grief," she remains as close as possible to her loved one and waits for the miracle to happen. Since we have seen Sebastian, we know that the miracle will occur; yet through our identification with Viola we come to know the comic burden, the masker's increasing weariness of the mask which implies that love is still pursued rather than possessed.

The burden becomes comically unbearable only in the final scene, when it is cast off. Here Shakespeare underscores all those possibilities of violence and death which are usually submerged in comedy. Antonio is arrested and in danger of his life. Orsino, finally recognizing the hopelessness of his suit to Olivia, shows the vicious side of sentimentality. After considering the possibility of killing Olivia "like to the Egyptian thief," he determines to do violence to "Cesario." . . . Olivia is hysterical at what seems to be the baseness of Cesario. Sir Toby has a broken pate to show for his one major failure to penetrate a mask. The dance must stop. The miracle must occur.

The entrance of Sebastian is "what we will." It is the most dramatic moment of the play. The confrontation of Sebastian and Cesario-Viola, those identical images, concludes the formal plot and provides the means for the discarding of all the lovers' masks. The moment must be savored and fully realized. As Viola and Sebastian chant their traditional formulas of proof, both the audience and the other characters on the stage undistractedly view the physical image of the duality which has made the confusion and the play. The masks and the play are to be abandoned for a vision of delight beyond delight, in which lovers have neither to wear nor to penetrate disguises since they are at last invulnerable to error and laughter.

Yet the play does not resolve into a magic blessing of the world's fertility as does A Midsummer Night's Dream. We have been promised a happy ending, and we receive it. We are grateful that the proper Jacks and Jills have found each other, but the miracle is a limited miracle, available only to the young and the lucky. Not every Jack has his Jill even in Illyria, and after the general unmasking, those without love may seem even lonelier. Malvolio, of course, is justly punished. He has earned his mad scene, and with the aid of Feste he has made it comic. As a result of his humiliation he has also earned some sort of redress. Yet he is ridiculous in his arrogance to the end, and his threatened revenge, now that he is powerless to effect it, sustains the comedy and the characterization and prevents the obtrusion of destructive pathos.

It is Feste rather than Malvolio who finally reminds us of the limitations and the costs of the romantic vision of happiness with which we have been seduced. However burdensome, masking is his career, and romantic love provides no end for it. Alone on the stage at the end of the play, he sings a song of unfulfilled love which shows the other side of the coin. For Feste, as for his audience, the mask can never be finally discarded: the rain it raineth every day. His song has those overtones, I believe, but they are only overtones. The music, here and elsewhere in the play, provides an element in which oppositions may be resolved. And the song itself, like the movement which must accompany it, is crude and witty as well as graceful and nostalgic. However far it may have missed the conventionally happy ending, Feste's saga of misfortunes in love is comic, even from his own point of view. The exaggeration so often operative in the refrains of Elizabethan lyrics emphasizes that the watery as well as the sunny vision can become funny: it doesn't rain every day by a long shot.

The song, which begins as the wittiest observer's comment on the denouement of the play, ends as a dissolution of the dramatic fiction:

> A great while ago the world begun,
>   With hey, ho, the wind and the rain,
> But that's all one, our play is done,
>   And we'll strive to please you every day.
>
> [V. i. 405-08]

The audience has been a participant in the festivity. As the fictional lovers have unmasked to reveal or realize their "true" identities, it is only proper that the clown, the only character who might move freely in the environs of Bankside, as well as in the realm of Illyria, should unmask the whole proceeding for the imitation of a desired world which it has been. The audience must be returned from "What You Will" to its own less patterned world where the sea rarely disgorges siblings given up for lost, where mistaken marriages rarely turn out well, where Violas rarely catch Dukes, and where Malvolios too often rule households with disturbing propriety. The lovers have met, and Feste announces that present laughter has come to an end. But the actors, those true and untiring maskers, will continue to "strive to please" us. They will find few occasions in the future in which their efforts will be more sure of success.

Twelfth Night is the climax of Shakespeare's early achievement in comedy. The effects and values of the earlier comedies are here subtly embodied in the most complex structure which Shakespeare had yet created. But the play also looks forward: the pressure to dissolve the comedy, to realize and finally abandon the burden of laughter, is an intrinsic part of its "perfection." Viola's clear-eyed and affirmative vision of her own and the world's irrationality is a triumph and we desire it; yet we realize its vulnerability, and we come to realize that virtue in disguise is only totally triumphant when evil is not in disguise —is not truly present at all. Having solved magnificently the problems of this particular form of comedy, Shakespeare was evidently not tempted to repeat his triumph. After *Twelfth Night* the so-called comedies require for their happy resolutions more radical characters and devices—omniscient and omnipresent Dukes, magic, and resurrection. More obvious miracles are needed for comedy to exist in a world in which evil also exists, not merely incipiently but with power. (pp. 28-32)

Joseph H. Summers, "The Masks of 'Twelfth Night'," in The University of Kansas City Review, *Vol. XXII, No. 1, Autumn, 1955, pp. 25-32.*

NORMAN A. BRITTIN (essay date 1956)

[*In his reply to John W. Draper's* The "Twelfth Night" *of Shakespeare's Audience (see excerpt above, 1950), Brittin faults what he feels to be Draper's straining after realism in his interpretation of* Twelfth Night.]

Professor Draper rightly stresses the realistic elements of the comedy: the persuasively realistic setting of the Countess Olivia's household, and the recognizable Elizabethan characters who live there. . . . And yet I do not feel satisfied that Draper has rightly judged the high-comedy characters, that he has seen the plot in just perspective, or that he has correctly identified the theme of the comedy when he calls it "Shakespeare's play of social security".

Draper regards Olivia as the most important character in the play, an efficient, self-willed, independent, clear-sighted, and calculating woman realistically portrayed; whereas Viola is merely a bundle of stage conventions, an unrealistic fairy princess, whose role has been greatly over-emphasized. Both Orsino and Olivia, he thinks, are realistically drawn, the former in the real and sympathetically presented pangs of love-melancholy, the latter in the midst of her cleverly utilized mourning which provides her a shield against unwelcome wooers. If we look at them through Elizabethan eyes, we should take them seriously: they are not sentimental; Orsino is seeking a mate so that there will be an heir to carry on his name; Olivia is arranging matters so that she can preserve her independence by marrying—in her own good time—a man whom she can dominate. This is the way in which many Elizabethans proceeded, and it would be sensible to suppose that Orsino and Olivia are also proceeding thus. And yet—though this may be a matter of subtle emphases—I doubt that even the Elizabethan audience could look on the noble duke and countess with entire sympathy for their pangs of love and for their basic practicality.

I have always felt that Orsino is somewhat ostentatious about his love-pangs, somewhat sentimental in his indulgence in sighs, music, flowers, and bombast about "the beating of so strong a passion". . . . In spite of his nobility Orsino belongs among those comic figures that achieve their comic quality by falling in love and taking it too hard; he is akin to Sylvius in *As You Like It*—"sure I think did never man love so"—who breaks "from company Abruptly", crying "O Phebe, Phebe, Phebe!" [*As You Like It*, II.iv.29,40ff].

Though we may for the most part agree with Draper's analysis of Olivia . . . [he] attributes to her more decisiveness and more activity than are due her. (pp. 211-12)

I believe that Olivia also becomes a figure of sport—Draper acknowledges . . . that "we have no great compassion for her". Her grief for her brother may seem pitiable; but when we learn that she has vowed to keep veiled for seven years during which she will weep daily for her brother's death, we feel that here is an excess of grief, or grief made ostentatious, which is similar to Orsino's ostentation in love. Draper believes . . . that Olivia made this vow "in the shock of her first grief . . . ; but, as time wore on and her youth reasserted itself, this rigid mourning became more and more a matter of convenience. He calls her "artful" and "astute". Yet he says too that

> for months Olivia has been living as a cloistress
> and weeping daily; and then Feste comes back
> from his sojourn at the Duke's and . . . she is
> tricked into laughter, and so recoils to her nat-
> ural, sanguine self. . . .

The critic cannot have it both ways. If she is artful and her mourning has become a matter of convenience, then we can hardly think her sincere about it at the opening of the play; nor can we believe that she begins to laugh at Feste's jokes "before she knows it". . . . It seems more reasonable to think that she has made a hasty vow, given excessive hostages to grief, but that by the time the play opens, some ten months at least since her brother's death, she has resumed normal living, though she has not advertised this fact to the world. At any rate, she has to send Maria to bring her veil; she is not wearing it when Viola seeks admission. Furthermore, she shows herself delightfully vulnerable by the alacrity with which she breaks the vow that we have been hearing about; obviously she cannot bear for this handsome young stranger not to see her face; she is eager enough to show it and, what is more, to ask for his comment on its beauty. For all her efficiency as a chatelaine, on which Draper rightly insists, she is still a woman who, blinded by self-confidence perhaps, does not know herself very well. This beauty and cynosure of neighboring eyes who handles her suitors so deftly nevertheless sprawls most undeftly into love.

The plot requires her to do so. As I see it, the key speech of the play is Viola's:

> Love make his heart of flint that you shall love;
> And let your fervour, like my master's, be
> Placed in contempt.　　　　　　　　[I.v.286-88]

This speech foreshadows the whole situation of Olivia from then on. Six lines later she is asking: "Even so quickly may one catch the plague?" And thus the tables are turned on the independent (if not haughty) countess. "The strong-willed but shrewd Olivia is a dominating figure", Draper declares. . . . Therefore the fun lies in placing her in the situation of the mistress mastered, the scorner scorned, the independent become dependent. . . . Her situation might seem pitiful, wondrous pitiful, but the audience knows that she is outrageously deceived, and since she is in love—helplessly, futilely—with a *woman,* she becomes a figure of fun. . . . (pp. 213-14)

Thus Olivia is fair game; and so is Orsino, poor fool, importuning a countess who will not listen, while ignorant of the love that is at hand, blooming day-long about him.

Draper says that *Twelfth Night* is not a story of love

> but of the very realistic struggles and intrigues
> over the betrothal of a rich Countess, whose
> selection of a mate determines the future of all
> the major and most of the minor charac-
> ters. . . . This is not a play of passion, but of
> marriage in its most prudential aspects. . . .

Now it seems to me that "struggles" and "intrigues" are terms far too strong to describe properly the actual situation in the play; it is essentially a play of comic mistakes, not a play of intrigue. Sir Andrew, though he has Sir Toby's support, is no serious threat; his courtship constitutes neither a struggle nor an intrigue. Olivia is not even aware, until the very end of the comedy, that Malvolio has considered himself a suitor; and he could hardly have done so with any assurance unless he had been "most notoriously abused" . . . by the sportful malice of his enemies. Orsino's courtship does involve an opposition of wills, but not intrigue. I believe, further, that Draper reads into the play as actualities far too many elements that are only possibilities because they occurred in Elizabethan life—possibilities nevertheless that never occurred to Shakespeare or that he discarded. Draper says that *Twelfth Night* is "the comedy of the social struggles of the time: Orsino wishes to fulfill his duty as head of the house and prolong his family line by a suitable marriage" . . . but there is not a line, not a word, about this in the play. Similarly, "Sir Toby might . . . try to betroth [Olivia] as he pleased, or he might even connive at an abduction". . . . The play contains no hint of such actions.

To call *Twelfth Night* a play of social security seems to me to make it over into something like a Middleton comedy of London life—*A Trick to Catch the Old One,* perhaps. That is really a play of social security. But it is not much like *Twelfth Night.* I feel that Professor Draper, in his eagerness to show the importance of the realistic elements of the comedy and to establish

Olivia as its most important figure, has somewhat distorted the picture Shakespeare meant us to see. For the romantic elements (granting that Viola *is* a sort of fairy princess) are not merely excrescences upon, or adornments of, or foils to, the realistic elements. The coming of the romantic twins determines, after all, the outcome of the plot. The main dramatic question is not: Which of these suitors will Olivia choose, but rather, how will Olivia be got out of the way so that Viola can have the man she loves? Actually, in what Draper says about the excellent qualities of Viola, he has the key to the theme of the play. Viola is a fairy princess; she is perfect; she is ideal. Her love is deep, true love—true unto death. And of course Sebastian, her identical twin, must be just like her.

Viola is not merely a contrast but a determiner. She and Sebastian bring the ideal into the midst of the realism, which, lacking the ideal, is insufficient. "With this play," wrote the late Professor Stauffer, "Shakespeare touches the pinnacles of romantic love. . . . Harmony achieved through unselfish love—how all the Golden Comedies point to that as the moral ideal!" The theme of the comedy is not social security. For without the ideal, which Viola represents, the realism of the "good catch" angled after by various undesirable suitors is inadequate to Shakespeare's purposes. The theme of the comedy is, rather, the power of true love, romantic, self-sacrificing love with a minimum of prudential consideration, to give happiness; and the superiority of this love to earthier matches of prudence and convenience.

Draper says . . . that he has prepared a short biography of each character "so far as the play states or implies the facts". But Draper tries to read too much between the lines, and thus he arrives at some ludicrous ideas. For example:

> Viola's late unhappy voyage has apparently given
> her an occasional nautical turn of phrase, and
> she knows that sailors swab decks and that the
> London watermen cried "Westward hoe" to
> tell the direction they were going.

But this is to consider too curiously. Perhaps Draper's basic assumption is at fault. He declares . . . that the allusions each character makes, "if a play is truly drama",

> should . . . illustrate, when collected and sys-
> tematically arranged, the character who is
> speaking—his education and interests and men-
> tal bent—and so furnish a clue to his motives
> and psychology and also to his former life. . . .

Thus he asserts . . . , to demonstrate that Olivia is "a very Portia", that "she knows something of law, understands the office of 'Crowner', . . . the technical terms of heraldry . . . , and itemized inventories. . . ." Her references to text and homily, the devil tempting souls to hell, and insane persons being possessed of devils, prove to Draper that "she has been duly instructed in religion". He is surprised to find that the few lines of the captain who saved Viola "strangely enough, draw their allusions, not from the sea but from the court and classics. Therefore the captain is "not only traveled but also educated—in fact, a cut above his class . . .". Thus Draper makes Shakespeare look like a naturalistic novelist, a Zola or a Sinclair Lewis, who prepares a *dossier* for each character before ever touching pen to paper. One may be permitted to doubt that Shakespeare curbed himself thus (to put it one way) or (to put it another way) was so exquisitely meticulous in adjusting language to character.

Draper complains . . . that most critics of Shakespeare are irresponsible, wandering "fancy-free over the field, strewing obiter dicta up and down. . . ." But Draper's approach leads inevitably to considering literary characters as real people, who have an independent life outside Shakespeare's lines. Every time we encounter a "perhaps" in Draper's pages, we may expect some snatch of his fancy. In this respect Draper is as irresponsible as the critics whom he condemns. (pp. 214-16)

> *Norman A. Brittin, "The 'Twelfth Night' of Shakespeare and of Professor Draper," in* Shakespeare Quarterly, *Vol. VII, No. 2, Spring, 1956, pp. 211-16.*

JOHN HOLLANDER (essay date 1956)

[*Hollander's essay on* Twelfth Night, *which was originally presented as a paper before the English Institute on Music and Poetry in 1956, begins with a summary of the musical theories of the Neoplatonist philosopher Boethius, who divided music into three types:* musica mundana, musica humana, *and* musica instrumentalis. *Hollander suggests that* musica humana, *which emphasizes abstract order and harmony, dominates* Twelfth Night, *as evidenced in the theme of feasting and appetite. Hollander further examines the themes of appetite and satiety in his 1959 essay on* Twelfth Night *(see excerpt below). His emphasis on the theme of order in* Twelfth Night *supports the earlier comments of Morris P. Tilley (1914).*]

[The] authority of Boethius on many general musical questions remained unshaken up through the Renaissance, and his famous tripartite division between *musica mundana, musica humana,* and *musica instrumentalis* helped to blur many distinctions between speculative and practical music in later writers. By *musica mundana* Boethius meant the harmony of the universe, including the cosmological order of elements, astral bodies, and seasons. By human music he meant "that which unites the incorporeal activity of the reason with the body . . . a certain mutual adaptation and as it were a tempering of high and low sounds into a single consonance." This paralleled the cosmic music in causing "the blending of the body's elements." The third category is simply practical music. The first two designate what is in fact not music at all, but figurative ascriptions of a regularity to nature. The harmony of the universe and the tempering of warring elements in the human character are both metaphors from Greek thought, in which the extended sense of the term "harmony" did not preserve the same implications that it holds for us. By and large, we must understand the word *harmonia* as ordered melody, and, when extended, as the rationalized proportions of whole numbers that were seen to generate the intervals between musical tones. (p. 58)

The concept of the music of the spheres was a popular one, passed down from antiquity through Plato, Cicero, and Macrobius' commentary on Cicero's *Somnium Scipionis*. It is of interest not only because of its embodiment of universal harmony, but because of its implications of both human and actual music, Boethius' second and third categories, as well. (p. 60)

[Microcosmic] man, imitating in his *musica instrumentalis* or practical music the ideal order of the *harmonia mundi,* can regain in some small way the *musica humana*, the ordering of his being, that characterizes the music of the spheres. (p. 62)

The order of the heavens, political concord, and the organic unity of individual men, each a "little world, made cunningly," were all thus embraced under the extended metaphor

of harmony. It was the singular accomplishment of the sixteenth century, however, to incorporate into its *musica speculativa* so much of its practical music. This had for centuries been generating its own forms and conventions independently of the almost hermetically-sealed body of literary discourse that comprised musical speculation. (p. 64)

In sixteenth-century England, then, the word "music" could suggest a wealth of speculation to an informed mind. Both a variety of actual practice, and an even more complex intellectual institution were embraced in a dialectic that unified inherited Medieval traditions, more recently acquired information about Antiquity, and the bare facts of how and what people played and sang. Traditional divisions of music into practical and theoretical, or into Boethius' cosmological, psychological, and instrumental were all retained in one way or another. And any answer to the question "What is music?" would involve a confusion between an abstract institution and a concrete practice that a modern philosopher might deplore, but one that we need only consider as an intricate yet unified series of metaphors.

When seen in the light of the richness of sixteenth-century musical thought, the modern academic question of "Shakespeare and Music" tends to be more blinding than the glittering of its generality would warrant. With the aid of the musicological studies of the past thirty years, we are better able than ever before to reconstruct the actual music performed, and referred to, in Shakespeare's plays. The growth of study in the History of Ideas has given us models for understanding how words and customs that have misleadingly retained their forms to this day reverberated differently in various historical contexts. The forays of sixteenth- and seventeenth-century poets into *musica speculativa*, consequently, can now be understood as more than either the fanciful conceits or the transmission of quaint lore that many nineteenth-century readers took them to be. But the recent critical traditions that read all of Shakespeare with the kind of attention previously devoted to other kinds of poetry has tended to create a third, queer category of symbolic music. G. Wilson Knight in particular has employed the images of tempest and music in his criticism to suggest the universal themes of disorder and resolving, reconciling order [see excerpt above, 1932]. These concepts stem largely from his invaluable early work on the last plays, in which, trivially speaking, storm and music do appear to alternate in profound and general ways. But more recently, Professor Knight has elevated his rather *symboliste* construction of the word "music" to the heights proclaimed in Verlaine's manifesto: *"De la musique avant toute chose."* One result of this has been, I feel, to credit Shakespeare's imagination with the creation of what, for hundreds of years, had been fairly widely received ideas. Worse than this, however, has been the failure to see exactly to what degree Shakespeare's poetic intelligence utilized these received ideas about music, both speculative and practical, analyzing and reinterpreting them in dramatic contexts. Finally, and perhaps worst of all, some of Shakespeare's amazingly original contributions to *musica speculativa* have been lost sight of.

Twelfth Night represents, I feel, an excellent case in point. Probably written late in 1600, its treatment of the theme of music is considerably more complex than that of the plays preceding it. By and large, the bulk of the references in all the plays is to practical music, which is cited, satirized, and praised in various contexts like any other human activity. Of particular interest to Shakespeare always was the richness of various technical vocabularies, and much of the wit in all but the later

plays consists of puns and twisted tropes on technical terminology, often that of instrumental music. (pp. 66-8)

[In *Twelfth Night*] the role of music is so obviously fundamental
to the spirit of the play that it is momentarily surprising to find
so little speculative music brought up for discussion. But I
think that, on consideration of the nature of the play itself, the
place of both active and intellectual music, and the relations
between them, emerge as something far more complex than
Shakespeare had hitherto cause to employ. *Twelfth Night* is,
in very serious ways, a play about parties and what they do to
people. Full of games, revels, tricks, and disguises, it is an
Epiphany play, a ritualized Twelfth Night festivity in itself,
but it is much more than this: the play gives us an analysis,
as well as a representation, of feasting. It develops an ethic of
indulgence based on the notion that the personality of any
individual is a function not of the static proportions of the
humors within him, but of the dynamic appetites that may more
purposefully, as well as more pragmatically, be said to govern
his behavior. Superficially close to the comedy of humors in
the characterological extremes of its *dramatis personae,* the
play nevertheless seems almost intent on destroying the whole
theory of comedy and of morality entailed by the comedy of
humors.

The nature of a revel is disclosed in the first scene. The materials are to be music, food and drink, and love. The basic
action of both festivity in general, and of the play itself, is
declared to be that of so surfeiting the appetite that it will
sicken and die, leaving fulfilled the tempered, harmonious self.
The movement of the whole play is that of a party, from
appetite, through the direction of that appetite outward toward
something, to satiation, and eventually to the condition when,
as the Duke hopes for Olivia, "liver, brain and heart / These
sovereign thrones, are all supplied, and filled / Her sweet perfections with one self king." The "one self king" is the final
harmonious state to be achieved by each reveller, but it is also,
in both the Duke's and Olivia's case, Cesario, who kills "the
flock of all affections else" that live in them, and who is shown
forth in a literal epiphany in the last act.

The Duke's opening speech describes both the action of feasting, and his own abundant, ursine, romantic temperament. But
it also contains within it an emblematic representation of the
action of surfeiting:

> If music be the food of love, play on.
> Give me excess of it, that, surfeiting,
> The appetite may sicken, and so die.
> That strain again! It had a dying fall.
> Oh, it came o'er my ear like the sweet sound
> That breathes upon a bank of violets,
> Stealing and giving odor! Enough, no more.
> 'Tis not so sweet now as it was before.   [I.i.1-8]

The one personage in the play who remains in a melancholy
humor is the one person who is outside the revels and cannot
be affected by them. Olivia's rebuke cuts to the heart of his
nature: "Thou art sick of self love, Malvolio, and taste with
a distempered appetite." Suffering from a kind of moral indigestion, Malvolio's true character is revealed in his involuted,
Puritanic sensibility that allows of no appetites directed outward. His rhetoric is full of the Devil; it is full of humors and
elements as well. No other character tends to mention these
save in jest, for it is only Malvolio who believes in them. Yet
real, exterior fluids of all kinds, wine, tears, sea-water, urine,
and finally the rain of inevitability bathe the whole world of
Illyria, in constant reference throughout the play.

The general concern of *Twelfth Night,* then, is *musica humana,*
the Boethian application of abstract order and proportion to
human behavior. The literalization of the universal harmony
that is accomplished in comedy of humors, however, is unequivocally rejected. "Does not our life consist of the four
elements?" catechizes Sir Toby. "Faith, so they say," replies
Sir Andrew, "but I think it rather consists of eating and drinking." "Thou'rt a scholar," acknowledges Sir Toby. "Let us
therefore eat and drink." "Who you are and what you would
are out of my welkin—I might say 'element,' but the word is
overworn," says Feste, who, taking offense at Malvolio's characterization of him as a "dry fool" touches off the whole
proceedings against the unfortunate steward. The plot to ridicule Malvolio is more than the frolicsome revenge of an "allowed fool"; it serves both to put down the "party-pooper"
and to affirm the psychology of appetite and fulfillment that
governs the play. To the degree that the *musica humana* of
Twelfth Night involves the substitution of an alternative view
to the fairly standard sixteenth-century descriptions of the order
of the passions, an application of the musical metaphor would
be trivial, and perhaps misleading. But the operation of practical music in the plot, the amazingly naturalistic treatment of
its various forms, and the conclusions implied as to the nature
and effects of music in both the context of celebration and in
the world at large, all result in some musical speculation that
remains one of the play's unnoticed accomplishments.

The actual music in *Twelfth Night* starts and finishes the play,
occurring throughout on different occasions and in different
styles. The presumably instrumental piece in which the Duke
wallows at the opening dampens his desire for it very quickly,
but that desire returns before long. Orsino's appetite at the start
of the play is purportedly for Olivia, who hungers for, and
indulges herself in, her own grief. The Duke's actual love,
too, is for his own act of longing, and for his own exclamations
of sentiment. Both of these desires are directed outward before
the play is over. But until a peculiar musical mechanism, which
will be mentioned later on, as has been set to work, the Duke
will hunt his own heart, and his desires, "like fell and cruel
hounds," will continue to pursue him. The music in Act II,
scene iv, is of just such a nature to appease the Duke's extreme
sentimentality. Orsino makes it plain what sort of song he wants
to hear:

> Now, good Cesario, but that piece of song,
> That old and antique song we heard last night.
> Methought it did relieve my passion much,
> More than light airs and recollected terms
> Of these most brisk and giddy-pacèd times.
>   [II.iv.2-6]

Orsino's favorite song, he says,

>   is old and plain.
> The spinsters and the knitters in the sun
> And the free maids that weave their thread with bones
> Do use to chant it. It is silly sooth,
> And dallies with the innocence of love,
> Like the old age.   [II.iv.43-48]

Actually the song that Feste sings him is a highly extravagant,
almost parodic version of the theme of death from unrequited
love. Its rather stilted diction and uneasy prosody are no doubt
intended to suggest a song from an old miscellany. "Come
away" is a banal beginning, appearing at the start of four song
texts in Canon Fellowes' collection. (pp. 73-7)

It is just one of these "light airs and recollected terms," however, with which Sir Toby and Feste plague Malvolio in their

big scene of carousal (II.iii). A setting of "Farewell, dear heart" appears in Robert Jones' first book of airs, published in 1600. Of the other songs in the same scene, one is a round, a more trivial form of song, certainly with respect to its text, than the sophisticated and intricate lewdness of the post-Restoration catch. The other is a "love song" sung by Feste, and preferred by Sir Toby and Sir Andrew to "a song of good life," perhaps with a pious text. It is of the finest type of Shakesperian song that catches up the spirit of overall themes and individual characters, ironically and prophetically pointing to the end of a plot or bit of action. All of "Oh mistress mine" is in one sense an invocation to Olivia to put off her self-indulgent grief, her courting of her dead brother's memory. In particular, the first stanza refers to Viola, the boy-girl true love, "that can sing both high and low."

Feste's songs to Malvolio in his madman's prison are both of an archaic cast. The first is a snatch of a song of Wyatt's, "A robyn, joly robyn" that was set to music by William Cornish during the reign of Henry VIII. The other one, a parting jibe at Malvolio's cant about the Devil, suggests the doggerel of an old Morality, invoking Malvolio as the Devil himself, and continuing the game of mocking him by appealing to his own rhetoric.

All of these occurrences of practical music function in the plot as well as with respect to the general theme of feasting and revels. The one reference to *musica speculativa* is a very interesting one, however, and leads to the most important aspect of the operation of music in *Twelfth Night*. Olivia is exhorting Viola to refrain from mentioning the Duke to her, and implying that she would rather be courted by his messenger:

> I bade you never speak of him again.
> But would you undertake another suit,
> I had rather hear you to solicit that
> Than music from the spheres.   [III.i.107-10]

The citation of the music of the spheres here has the tone of most such references during the later seventeenth century in England. With the exception of poets like Milton and Marvell, who used metaphors from the old cosmology for intricate poetic purposes of their own, the music of the spheres became, in Cavalier and Augustan poetry, a formal compliment, empty of even the metaphorical import that the world view of the centuries preceding had given to it. Just as the word "heavenly," used in exclamations of praise, long ago became completely divorced from its substantive root, the music of the spheres gradually came to designate the acme of effective charm in a performer. (pp. 78-9)

As in the case of Dryden's music that would "untune the sky," references to the heavenly harmony had nothing to do with received ideas of music's importance during the later seventeenth century, which were more and more becoming confined to a rhetorical ability to elicit passion, on the one hand, and to provide ornament to the cognitive import of a text, on the other. . . . Most important of all, traditional *musicà speculativa* gradually ceased being a model of universal order, and was replaced by a notion of music as a model of rhetoric, whose importance lay in its ability to move the passions, rather than in its older role of the microcosmic copy of universal harmony. The Apollonian lute-harp-lyre constellation, once an emblem of reason and order, became an instrument of passion in the hands of Caravaggio's leering boys, and in the hands of Crashaw's musician who slew the nightingale by musically ravishing her, as even her avatar Philomela was never so ravished, to death.

Act IV. Scene iii. The Priest, Olivia, Sebastian. By W. Hamilton (1794). From the Art Collection of the Folger Shakespeare Library.

With these considerations in mind, the crucial role of Viola as an instrument of such a rhetorical music becomes quite clear. It is unfortunate that we have no precise indication of an earlier version of the play, presumably rewritten when the superior singer Robert Armin entered Shakespeare's company, in which some of the songs may have been assigned to Viola. She declares herself at the outset:

> I'll serve this Duke.
> Thou shalt present me as a eunuch to him.
> It may be worth thy pains, for I can sing,
> And speak to him in many sorts of music,
> That will allow me very worth his service.
>   [I.ii.55-59]

She will be the Duke's instrument, although she turns out to be an instrument that turns in his hand, charming both Olivia and himself in unexpected fashion. Orsino is given an excess of music in Viola. As Cesario, she wins Olivia for her alter ego Sebastian who is himself, in his few scenes, rhetorically effective almost to the point of preciosity, and who is likened to the musician Arion who charmed his way to safety. Viola is the affective, instrumental, prematurely Baroque music in *Twelfth Night,* and it is she whose charm kills off the gourmandizing sentimentality in both Orsino and Olivia, directing their appetites of love outward, in fact, towards herself. Among the characters to whom Malvolio refers as "the lighter people," it is Feste, the singer and prankster, whose pipe and tabor serve as a travesty of Viola's vocal chords. The operation of Viola's "music" involves charming by the use of appearances; the effects of the trickery instigated by Feste are to make Malvolio appear, until he is undeceived, to be Olivia's ridiculously amorous swain. (It is, of course, the phrase "To be Count Malvolio" that appears on his lips after reading the forged letter.) Through the mechanism of fooling, the travesty of music below stairs, Sir Andrew is chastened, Sir Toby is soberly married to Maria, Malvolio is made to act out the madness of which he falsely accused Feste, and "the whirligig of time brings in his revenges."

The music that brings about the conclusion of the revels is thus a figurative music. It pervades the symbolic enactment of indulgence and surfeit in the plot as the actual music, relegated to its several uses and forms with considerable eye to details of practice in Shakespeare's own day, pervades the spectacle of *Twelfth Night*. The play is about revelry, and, in itself, a revels; so too, there is music in it, and a working out of a theme in speculative music that strangely coincides with later views on the subject. The *Ursprung* of Viola's music is certainly in the action of the play; it is not to be implied that *Twelfth Night* is anything of a formal treatise, and the music in Illyria all serves its immediately dramatic purposes. Within the context of the play's anti-Puritan, anti-Jonsonian treatment of moral physiology, the role of music seems to have become inexorably defined for Shakespeare. Set in a framework of what, at this point, might be almost coy to call a study in *musica humana*, practical music becomes justified in itself. Free of even the scraps of traditional musical ideology that had been put to use in the plays preceding it, *Twelfth Night* represents a high point in one phase of Shakespeare's musical dramaturgy. It is not until *Antony and Cleopatra* and the last romances that the use of an almost supernatural music, perhaps imported to some degree from the musical *données* of the masque, comes to be associated with the late, great themes of reconciliation and transformation. (pp. 79-82)

> John Hollander, "*Musica Mundana and Twelfth Night*," in *Sound and Poetry, edited by Northrop Frye, Columbia University Press, 1957, pp. 55-82.*

W. H. AUDEN (essay date 1957)

[*Auden, an Anglo-American poet, essayist, and critic, is considered a major literary figure of the twentieth century. His Shakespearean criticism takes many forms, including essays, introductions, and miscellaneous observations. Like many critics, Auden notes dark elements pervading* Twelfth Night. *Unlike others, however, notably Arthur Quiller-Couch (1930) and John Middleton Murry (1936), who maintain that the melancholy tone enhances the play, Auden asserts that the darker elements express Shakespeare's mood of "puritanical aversion" which "keeps disturbing, even spoiling, the comic feeling." Auden also claims that while, read separately, the songs in* Twelfth Night *are beautiful, within the context of the play "these lines are the voice of elderly lust, afraid of its own death." For additional commentary on the dark aspects of the play, see the excerpts by F. J. Furnivall (1877), Mark Van Doren (1939), E. C. Pettet (1949), G. K. Hunter (1962), Albert Gérard (1964), Jan Kott (1964), Clifford Leech (1965), and Philip Edwards (1968). The essay from which the following excerpt is drawn was originally published in* Encounter *in 1957.*]

I have always found the atmosphere of *Twelfth Night* a bit whiffy. I get the impression that Shakespeare wrote the play at a time when he was in no mood for comedy, but in a mood of puritanical aversion to all those pleasing illusions which men cherish and by which they lead their lives. The comic convention in which the play is set prevents him from giving direct expression to this mood, but the mood keeps disturbing, even spoiling, the comic feeling. One has a sense, and nowhere more strongly than in the songs, of there being inverted commas around the "fun."

There is a kind of comedy, *A Midsummer Night's Dream* and *The Importance of Being Earnest* are good examples, which take place in Eden, the place of pure play where suffering is unknown. In Eden, Love means the "Fancy engendered in the eye." The heart has no place there, for it is a world ruled by wish not by will. (p. 520)

To introduce will and real feeling into Eden turns it into an ugly place, for its native inhabitants cannot tell the difference between play and earnest and in the presence of the earnest they appear frivolous in the bad sense. The trouble, to my mind, about *Twelfth Night* is that Viola and Antonio are strangers to the world which all the other characters inhabit. Viola's love for the Duke and Antonio's love for Sebastian are much too strong and real.

Against their reality, the Duke, who up till the moment of recognition has thought himself in love with Olivia, drops her like a hot potato and falls in love with Viola on the spot, and Sebastian, who accepts Olivia's proposal of marriage within two minutes of meeting her for the first time, appear contemptible, and it is impossible to believe that either will make a good husband. They give the impression of simply having abandoned one dream for another.

Taken by themselves, the songs in this play are among the most beautiful Shakespeare wrote and, read in an anthology, we hear them as the voice of Eden, as "pure" poetry. But in the contexts in which Shakespeare places them, they sound shocking.

Act II, Scene 3.

SONG: O mistress mine, where are you roaming?
AUDIENCE: Sir Toby Belch, Sir Andrew Aguecheek.
[II.iii.39]

Taken playfully, such lines as

> What's to come is still unsure:
> In delay there lies no plenty;
> Then come kiss me, sweet-and-twenty.
> Youth's a stuff will not endure

[II.iii.49-52]

are charming enough, but suppose one asks, "For what kind of person would these lines be an expression of their true feelings?" True love certainly does not plead its cause by telling the beloved that love is transitory; and no young man, trying to seduce a girl, would mention her age. He takes her youth and his own for granted. Taken seriously, these lines are the voice of elderly lust, afraid of its own death. Shakespeare forces this awareness on our consciousness by making the audience to the song a couple of seedy old drunks.

Act II, Scene 4.

SONG: Come away, come away, death.
AUDIENCE: The Duke, Viola, courtiers.
[II.iv.51]

Outside the pastures of Eden, no true lover talks of being slain by a fair, cruel maid, or weeps over his own grave. In real life, such reflections are the daydreams of self-love which is never faithful to others.

Again, Shakespeare has so placed the song as to make it seem an expression of the Duke's real character. Beside him sits the disguised Viola, for whom the Duke is not a playful fancy but a serious passion. It would be painful enough for her if the man she loved really loved another, but it is much worse to be made to see that he only loves himself, and it is this insight which at this point Viola has to endure. In the dialogue about the difference between man's love and woman's which follows on the song, Viola is, I think, being anything but playful when she says:

> We men say more, swear more; but, indeed,
> Our vows are more than will; for still we prove
> Much in our vows, but little in our love.
>
> [II.iv.116-18]
> (pp. 521-22)

W. H. Auden, "Music in Shakespeare," in his The Dyer's Hand and Other Essays, *Random House, 1962, pp. 500-27.*

JOHN RUSSELL BROWN (essay date 1957)

[*Brown discerns three predominant qualities of love presented in Shakespeare's comedies: love's wealth, love's truth, and love's order; he analyzes the characters of* Twelfth Night *in terms of their attitudes toward these qualities of love. For additional commentary on Shakespeare's handling of the theme of love, see the excerpts by H. B. Charlton (1937), E. C. Pettet (1949), Harold Jenkins (1959), and Alexander Leggatt (1974).*]

It has often been remarked that *Twelfth Night* repeats characters, situations, and dramatic devices from earlier comedies; it also repeats their implicit judgements, and modifies and enlarges them by new associations. This play cannot be fitly considered in the light of any one of the three basic ideas [of love's wealth, love's truth, and love's order]; the three threads must be held in the hand all the time.

Twelfth Night begins with music, but it does not express an ordered harmony; Orsino, the lord of Illyria, longs for an 'excess' of it, hearkens after one particular strain, and then abruptly sends the musicians away. . . . His love knows no 'order', and it knows no 'wealth'; he is far from Valentine who can feed upon 'the very naked name of love', from Portia who would be 'trebled twenty times' herself only to 'stand high' in Bassanio's account, or from Juliet who likens her love to the sea as Orsino does, but in a far different sense:

> My *bounty* is as *boundless* as the sea,
> My love as deep; the more I *give* to thee
> The more I have, for both are *infinite*.
> [*Romeo and Juliet*, II.ii.133-35]

Orsino's love is not 'boundless as the sea', but

> . . . all as *hungry* as the sea,
> And can digest as much. . . .
> [II.iv.100-01]

Instead of finding love's wealth, he finds 'abatement and low price'. . . . He mars no trees with his verses, attempts no tasks of 'faith and service'; he does not find a new and comprehensive

'order' in love, but in solitariness indulges his fancy, leaving the stage with:

> Away before me to sweet beds of flowers:
> Love-thoughts lie rich when canopied with bowers.
> [I.i.39-40]

Instead of seeking opportunities to 'give and hazard', he passively takes what seeming pleasures can be his.

The first scene also contains a picture of Olivia, Orsino's beloved. She has been left sorrowful and unprotected by the death of her brother, and, not returning Orsino's love, she has resolved to shut the gate upon the world. . . . Olivia is like the young men of *Love's Labour's Lost,* or like Romeo's Rosaline, all of whom swear to live alone and 'in that sparing' make 'huge waste'; in the words of the sonnets, Olivia has determined to be a 'profitless usurer', to 'abuse The bounteous largess' given her to give; she has determined to hazard nothing of her potential 'wealth' in love.

This first scene is a mere forty lines and it is followed by one only slightly longer, but with an immediate contrast in tone; the dialogue is now brisk, the characters active. Viola, like Olivia, has lost her twin brother and only guardian, and is even more unprotected, being shipwrecked and friendless on the strange shore of Illyria. . . . Viola's entry upon the scene, rising mysteriously from the sea, is strange, and her sudden 'intent' to serve Orsino is strange also; but her activity, her willingness to trust the outcome to 'time' [I.i.60], and her brisk exit—'I thank thee: lead me on.'—are all in clear contrast to the earlier scene. On her next appearance as Cesario, Orsino's page, the contrast is clearer still, for she is one who will generously give and hazard for love—she will do her best to woo Orsino's lady though she herself 'would be his wife' [I.iv.42]. On her third appearance she is one who knows love's true wealth; to her way of thinking, Olivia 'usurps' herself, for what is hers to 'bestow' is not hers 'to reserve' [I.v.187-89]. When Olivia asks what Cesario would do in Orsino's predicament, Viola's ardent description of a lover's restless and possibly absurd activity is in direct contrast to her master's indulgence, and in Olivia it awakens admiration, generosity, and the willingness to hazard.

Shakespeare has not presented Orsino and Olivia in a directly satirical manner. . . . But the judgement which Shakespeare's ideal of love's wealth leads us to expect, is implicit in the dialogue, and is made dramatically apparent by the contrast of Viola; the first two scenes leave the audience delighted and charmed, and also uncertain; youth, beauty, and the wealth of love are already in question.

Sir Toby Belch begins the next scene with

> What a plague means my niece, to take the
> death of her brother thus? I am sure care's an
> enemy to life.
>
> [I.iii.1-3]

and, at once, there is another contrast. Sir Toby is a hanger-on in Olivia's household, indulging in wine and good fellowship at the buttery-bar. The cares of either mourner or lover are not for him. He does, however, profess friendship, and his 'love' for the foolish knight, Sir Andrew Aguecheek, contrasts him directly with the more courtly characters. The ideals of love's wealth are doubly outraged in this friendship, for he encourages Sir Andrew to recoup his fortune by paying court to Olivia and uses this as a pretext to fleece his 'friend' on his own account. (pp. 162-66)

This travesty of love's wealth in friendship is immediately contrasted in a scene between Sebastian and Antonio, the friend by whose help he has survived the shipwreck. . . . These true friends delight to give before they are asked, and demand no surety or promises.

The characters of this play seem to take up formal relationships to each other in the light of their attitudes to love's wealth. Malvolio, Olivia's steward, is another instance; he affects to love Olivia, but truly he loves only himself. . . . Malvolio shows his lover's disposition in soliloquy; he indulges the fancy—somewhat like Orsino—that his dreams have come true, and we hear his wildest hopes. In these he thinks only of the wealth and importance which love will bring to himself; Olivia doesn't even come into the picture, nor the service that he can do for her. . . . If in courting Olivia, Sir Andrew strives for 'that which many men desire', Malvolio is fool enough to 'assume desert' and to choose 'as much as he deserves'; loving only himself, thinking only of what will accrue to him, failing to be *'generous'* and 'of *free* disposition, he is unable to realize the true 'wealth' of love.

Having presented these characters in terms of love's wealth, Shakespeare developed the action by many of the devices associated with the ideal of love's truth. Most obvious is Viola's disguise as Cesario. When Olivia falls in love with the seeming boy, Viola at once suspects that she has been charmed merely by her 'outside' [II.ii.18]. Viola is constantly aware of the difference between appearance and reality. . . . (pp. 166-68)

Viola's disguise shows love's truth in another way, for it means that she must act a part. Viola is not that she 'plays' [I.v.183-85], and so in praising Olivia she must use her art, remembering a well-penned speech. Eventually she has to improvise and becomes Olivia's 'fool' [III.i.144], 'dallying nicely with words' [III.i.14-15]. Yet when she is asked how she herself would love, she can speak clearly and freely although such a speech is 'out of her part' [I.v.179]; her lover's imagination takes over and she acts with complete 'truth'. (p. 168)

As one good actor on a stage will make bad ones more conspicuous, so Viola's 'acting' shows up that of others. Olivia has to appear disinterested, but she cannot maintain the part and at last declares her passion for Cesario. Even Orsino, who believes that he loves Olivia completely and ardently, is liable to seem a poor actor when he speaks of her, and a 'truthful' one when he speaks of Cesario. (p. 169)

Malvolio is one to whom life has never given a part answerable to his imagination; as we witness, he can only rehearse in soliloquy his favourite role of 'Count Malvolio' [II.v.35]; lacking an audience he must always be 'practising behaviour to his own shadow' [II.v.17]. But when Maria, Olivia's waiting-gentlewoman, writes a letter in her mistress' handwriting addressed 'To the unknown beloved' and leaves it where he must find it, Malvolio is encouraged to bring his performance before the world. So powerful is his imagination that he can see no trick; he believes that Olivia loves him because he had always imagined that she must. . . . Success goes to his head and he is unaware that he is being ridiculous in the eyes of others, that the 'truth' of his imagination, though strong, is also absurd. . . . When all's done he is a 'poor fool', 'baffled' by others [V.i.369]; the lack of 'generosity', the failure to recognize his own faults, a disposition not 'free' in his dealing with an allowed fool, have made him, in his turn, a laughing-stock for others; to get 'what he deserves', to act to the height of his imagination, is to choose a fool's head. He gives the

performance of his career, and, at the last, is forced to see that his audience does not admire; if it were 'played upon a stage', it would be condemned 'as an improbable fiction' [III.iv.127-28]. (pp. 170-71)

Malvolio's is not the only absurd performance. Following the subjective truth of their imaginations, each of the lovers may appear foolish or mad in the eyes of those who have not the imagination to 'amend' their performances. Antonio, exclaiming against the seeming perjury of Sebastian, seems 'mad' to disinterested observers [III.iv.371]; Olivia acknowledging her love for Cesario thinks she is as 'mad' as Malvolio could ever be [III.iv.15]; Sebastian surprised by Olivia's welcome and beauty thinks likewise that he himself is 'mad' [IV.i.61]. The essential difference between these follies and Malvolio's is in the imagination that prompts them. True lovers are willing to hazard their reputation to affirm the truth they see. . . . Malvolio cannot do this; to call him madman when he is affirming his own greatness is to defeat his very object. (p. 171)

In *Twelfth Night,* as in Shakespeare's other comedies, 'barbarous' disorder may always threaten the ordered peace of society. So Sir Toby's indulgent roistering is liable to disturb the 'peace' of Olivia's household. Yet we can scarcely judge him harshly, for in contrast Olivia's cloistered good order seems zestless. . . . (p. 173)

Shakespeare's ideal of order is implicit in the affairs of love as in those of society; Sir Toby's thirst is not the only appetite to threaten good order. Olivia has no sooner rebuked him than she herself becomes 'much out of quiet' [II.iii.133]; the enchantment of Cesario's beauty and eloquence has released a new disordering element within her and she finds her honour

> . . . at the stake
> And *baited* . . . with all the *unmuzzled* thoughts
> That *tyrannous* heart can think.
>
> [III.i.118-20]

Orsino suffers the same disorder; when he first saw Olivia her beauty seemed to 'purge the air of pestilence', but within him disorder ensued:

> That instant was I turn'd into a hart;
> And my desires, like fell and cruel *hounds,*
> E'er since pursue me.
>
> [I.i.20-3]

As Cesario the page, Viola understands her master's disordered state, for she, 'poor *monster,* fond[s] as much on him' [II.ii.34]. By these turbulent, animal images, Shakespeare has shown at what risk of disorder love's order is finally established; he has shown the force behind the lovers' desire to 'live at peace' [IV.iii.28].

He is also at pains to show that, as love's truth may be 'madness' in the eyes of society, so love's order may cut across society's notions of decorum. This comedy is called *Twelfth Night* to good purpose, for during the festivities of that night, the lowliest persons may become as lords, acting for general merriment the role of the Lord of Misrule. Its title is a figure of Olivia's lovemaking; she who manages her household with 'smooth, discreet and stable bearing' [IV.iii.19], for the sake of her notion of love's truth must acknowledge the lordship of the 'man' and not the 'master' [I.v.294], must sue to her 'servant's servant' [III.i.102]. It is a figure too of Orsino's love and Viola's; she who called him 'master' for so long, becomes her 'master's mistress' and his 'fancy's queen' [V.i. 24-6, 388]. The order of love is 'what you will', the assumption of the roles of master and servant according to the individual, subjective truth of love's imagination.

Not every one who claims love's truth is able to establish such an order. Malvolio knows that there is 'example' [II.v.39] for 'Twelfth Night' reversals in the name of love, but, seeking the greatness and not the service, seeking to honour himself and not his mistress, he attempts to assert love's order only to give further proof that he lacks the warrantry of a lover's imagination. He is not only absurd in the unquestioning way in which he follows the directions detailed by Maria, or in his overweening self-confidence; he is also absurd as indecorum is absurd. For courtly address he can only summon 'Sweet lady, ho, ho'; for conversation he can only remark on his own discomfort; and for a love sonnet he can only quote a common ballad. His interview with his lady ends in a delighted recitation of his own greatness. The antithesis to this performance is Antonio's willing offers of service when he discovers that his friend is one whom the world would call his master. Malvolio is put in a dark house for a madness and indecorum that has no authority beyond his own love of himself; since he only wishes to 'lime' his lady [III.iv.74], the mutual order of love can never justify his folly.

With the interplay of generosity and possessiveness, of subjective truth and order and subjective folly, and of good-humoured disorders and natural fooling, Shakespeare has mingled the artful wisdom of Feste the fool; here is another contrast:

> For folly that he wisely shows is fit;
> But wise men, folly-fall'n, quite taint their wit.
>
> [III.i.67-8]

He *seems* to be a 'merry fellow' who cares 'for nothing', but in fact he makes it clear that he does 'care for something' [III.i.28-30]. It is not at all obvious what that 'something' is; it might be the money he so often begs for his fooling, or it might be his skill, 'As full of labour as a wise man's art' [III.i.66]; but it is most likely to be his attempt to find that 'foolish thing' [V.i.391] which would content himself rather than his audience. In the meantime he fulfils his calling; he 'walk[s] about the orb like the sun' [III.i.38-9] and by the light of his folly discovers kinship with other mortals.

But as well as showing the follies of others, Feste is used by Shakespeare to introduce a new theme to this comedy, or rather to give greater prominence to a subsidiary theme which he had hinted at in earlier comedies. In *Love's Labour's Lost,* the lovers are attentive to the cuckoo and the owl, and are willing to test their 'world-without-end' bargains by submitting the 'gaudy blossoms' of their love to the 'frosts and fasts' of time's reckoning. In *As You Like It,* Jaques, the detached critic, brings to the enjoyment of simple pleasures the remembrance of the seven ages of man, the 'strange eventful history' all must fulfil. So Feste, the professional, detached jester, is also time's remembrancer. As Ariel, the airy spirit, alone can sing of summer as Prospero draws men together for forgiveness and resignation, so Feste, the professional fool, sings in the youthful Illyria of death and the passage of time; the shadow of the cypress falls across the Twelfth Night merriments when he sings that

> Youth's a stuff will not endure.
>
> [II.iii.52]
> (pp. 174-77)

This note is echoed several times in the course of the play. Sir Andrew, so unsuccessful in his present endeavours, remembers that he 'was adored once, too' [II.iii.181], and, at the outset,

Olivia reminds us of time by her contempt or ignorance of it. Olivia believes that she can keep her brother's love 'fresh And lasting in her sad remembrance', and that her own beauty will 'endure wind and weather'; she does not heed Feste's warning that 'As there is no true cuckold but calamity, so beauty's a flower', but defies time in cutting seven years from her life in the world. (p. 177)

A poignant echo of Feste's songs is heard when Viola and Orsino speak of the tune for 'Come away, come away, death'. Viola, who is serving Orsino as Cesario the page, has to hear her master say:

> . . . women are as roses, whose fair flower
> Being once display'd, doth fall that very hour.
>
> [II.iv.38-9]

In her generous love for Orsino she does what he desires and forwards his suit to Olivia; 'giving' is her only resource and the rest she commits 'to time' [I.ii.60]. She must 'sit like patience on a monument' while concealed love, 'like a worm i' the bud', feeds on her own beauty [II.iv.111-15]. Knowing all this and thinking of the passage of time, she can only answer Orsino with:

> And so they are: alas, that they are so;
> To die, even when they to perfection grow!
>
> [II.iv.40-1]
> (pp. 177-78)

Twelfth Night is also distinguished for its ardent poetry. Benedick and Beatrice, Rosalind and Orlando had wooed chiefly in prose, and one must go back to *A Midsummer Night's Dream* or *The Merchant of Venice* to find heroes and heroines who speak so consistently in poetry—and their poetry, except for set pieces like the casket scene or trial scene in *The Merchant,* is much lighter and quicker than that which springs from 'unpremeditated' dialogue in *Twelfth Night.* As Viola acknowledges that beauty is a flower, a deeper and more sustained lyrical note is heard than in any of the previous comedies.

These two characteristics, combined with the judgements inherent in any expression of Shakespeare's ideals, give a strange intensity and beauty to the end of *Twelfth Night.* Although its dialogue is almost wholly in verse, the rapidity of this last scene allows no opportunity for the full expression of thought and feeling; nevertheless our interest and feelings have already been engaged and, as the characters take up their final relationships, the merest word can be charged with meaning. In the light of Shakespeare's threefold ideal of love, the contrasts and conflicts of this comedy are resolved like the last inevitable moves in a game of chess; implicit in each swift alteration there is a tally of earlier successes and failures. But this simile will not fully hold, for the object is not to defeat pieces of a certain colour; it is rather to range all in due order; the only 'defeat' is an inability to find a place in that order.

Lightheartedly, save for a disguised purposefulness in Orsino, the characters begin to take up their places; but as Antonio enters under arrest, bloodshed, envy, and disorder are remembered from his half-hidden past; the violent words—'Vulcan', 'smoke of war', 'scathful grapple', '. . . That took the Phoenix', '. . . that did the Tiger board'—seem to tear apart the fabric of the dialogue. But Antonio's concern is with the more immediate past, with the 'rude sea's enraged and foamy mouth' from which he had redeemed Sebastian, and with the 'witchcraft' which has drawn him into new danger. Explanations are prevented by Olivia's entry and Orsino's subsequent discovery of disorder and danger within his own heart. Because Olivia is concerned for Cesario and not for him, Orsino asks why he should not 'kill' the one he loves. . . . Orsino's heart is as disordered as seafight or tempest, and Viola can only continue to 'give and hazard'; she merely reiterates her love and her willingness to die a thousand deaths to give him 'rest' [V.i.133]. And Olivia must acknowledge her new order which will seem but a 'Twelfth Night' folly to others; so she calls Cesario 'husband' before the contemptuous glance of Orsino. She brings the friar to witness, and he acknowledges the 'contract of eternal bond of love' in formal words and measured sentences.

Quickly the action moves forward with Sir Andrew and Sir Toby entering to protest their own folly and hence their own place in the order of things. Then Sebastian enters and full recognitions ensue. Olivia finds that she was contracted to a man who had dared to trust the dream-like truth he had found; however much her eye had proved a 'flatterer for her mind', she had not formally given and hazarded until she found one who could answer fully to her 'soul' [IV.iii.27]. And Orsino's perturbation is quieted; instead of desiring 'the dove' whom he had loved for that which 'nature pranks her in' [II.iv.86], he learns to value 'the lamb' whom he had loved even in 'masculine usurp'd attire'—Viola's generous and patient love is thus attractive. Orsino's jealous savagery towards Cesario in this last scene had betrayed his true bias, even as, earlier, his close attention to Cesario's tale had shown where his imagination truly lay. (pp. 178-80)

As these characters join hands in mutual accord, others take up their due places. We hear that Sir Toby has married Maria in recompense for the trick she had played on Malvolio. He would claim this as a generous impulse for he asks 'no other dowry . . . but such another jest' [II.v.184-85], but he could scarcely hope for a greater; the best of his bargain is that he has become a 'bond-slave' [II.v.191] to one who he believes 'adores' him [II.iii.180] and one who tries to confine his habits 'within the modest limits of order'. Then Malvolio enters having been released from the dark room in which Sir Toby has bound him; his kind of love has proved the most foolish, the most a prey to the mockery of others, and now it appears to be incurable. Still believing that Olivia wrote the letter, he seeks redress for the 'madly-used Malvolio', yet when he is disabused he is silent, unable to accept his own absurdity. When injuries on both sides are considered, the 'sportful malice' of his persecutors 'May rather pluck on laughter than revenge' [V.i.366]; but Malvolio's self-love will not allow this. When Feste reminds him that he had previously mocked a fool as a 'barren rascal' and that 'the whirligig of time brings in his revenges', Malvolio still cannot accept the judgement; he must, in his own right, be 'revenged on the whole pack' of those who had mocked and tormented him. He cannot be taught to have a generous, guiltless, and free disposition.

In earlier comedies, the characters who rejected the ordered conclusions have left the stage without the lovers sparing much thought for them; so, in the eyes of others, Shylock has 'but justice' and no one but the Duke asks Jaques to stay; and so Don John is thought on only so that the morrow may devise brave punishments for him. But in *Twelfth Night*, Malvolio is considered; Olivia remembers a 'most extracting frenzy' of her own [V.i.281] and Orsino's violent disorder is still in his mind. There is no move in the last scene which is so inevitable as Malvolio's exit thinking of revenge, but nevertheless Olivia, echoing his own words, acknowledges that he has been most 'notoriously' abused [V.i.379], and Orsino commands that he

should be sent after and entreated 'to a peace' [V.i.380]. There is no communal feast, music, or dance to close this play—that must wait until 'golden time convents' [V.i.382]; but as the lovers leave the stage together we know that their generosity and desire for harmony can, after the realization of their own follies and disorders, reach to one who has 'had but justice', and that but a kind of wild justice.

We must do more than delight in this conclusion of the lovers' wooing. Feste is left alone on the stage to sing of man's folly and disorder, of the passing of time, and of 'the wind and the rain'. The theme of the comedy moves beyond that of particular love-making and its key is transposed from a major to minor; Feste's professional, disinterested view brings us to a contemplation of the whole course of man, and of the need for a generous, guiltless, and free acceptance of all things. And his song ended, Feste is a lonely figure requiring our applause. (pp. 180-82)

> *John Russell Brown, "'Twelfth Night or What You Will'," in his* Shakespeare and His Comedies, *Methuen & Co Ltd, 1957, pp. 160-82.*

L. G. SALINGAR (essay date 1958)

[*Salingar proposes that Shakespeare's purpose in* Twelfth Night *is to reveal the varying responses to the power of love. For Salingar, the Saturnalian spirit pervades the play, and the reversals that this spirit induces spring from the nature of love. He explores Shakespeare's use of dramatic contrivances as a means of understanding* Twelfth Night *and discusses how, in altering his sources, Shakespeare made the situations more romantically improbable, more melancholy, and more fantastic. In focusing on the Saturnalian aspects of* Twelfth Night, *Salingar echoes the comments of E. Montégut (1867) and Enid Welsford (1935) and anticipates the interpretations of C. L. Barber (1959) and Barbara Lewalski (1965).*]

Most readers of *Twelfth Night* would probably agree that this is the most delightful, harmonious and accomplished of Shakespeare's romantic comedies, in many ways his crowning achievement in one branch of his art. They would probably agree, too, that it has a prevailing atmosphere of happiness, or at least of "tempests dissolved in music" [see excerpt above by G. Wilson Knight, 1932]. Yet there are striking differences of opinion over the design of *Twelfth Night*. Is it, for example, a vindication of romance, or a depreciation of romance? [See excerpt above by Karl F. Thompson, 1952.] Is it mainly a love-story or a comedy of humours; a "poem of escape" or a realistic comment on economic security and prudential marriage? [See excerpt above by John W. Draper, 1950.] And there are further variations. The principal character, according to choice, is Viola, Olivia, Malvolio, or Feste.

To some extent, the play itself seems to invite such varying reactions: *Twelfth Night; or, What You Will*. Shakespeare here is both polishing his craftsmanship and exploring new facets of his experience, so that the play has the buoyancy of a mind exhilarated by discovery, testing one human impulse against another, and satisfied with a momentary state of balance which seems all the more trustworthy because its limits have been felt and recognized. But in consequence, Shakespeare's attitude towards his people comes near to humorous detachment, to a kind of Socratic irony. He refrains from emphasizing any one of his themes at the expense of the rest. He carefully plays down and transforms the crisis of sentiment in his main plot, while giving unusual prominence to his comic sub-plot. He distributes the interest more evenly among his characters than in *As You Like It* or the other comedies, providing more numerous (and more unexpected) points of contact between them, not only in the action but on the plane of psychology. And the whole manner of *Twelfth Night* is light and mercurial. The prose is full of ideas, but playful, not discursive. The poetry, for all its lyrical glow, gives a sense of restraint and ease, of keenly perceptive and yet relaxed enjoyment, rather than of any compelling pressure of emotion.

Perhaps this attitude on Shakespeare's part is responsible for the inconsistency of his interpreters. Those who dwell on the romantic side of the play seem uncertain about its connection with the comic realism; while those who concentrate on the elements of realism have to meet the kind of objection gravely stated by Dr. Johnson—that "the marriage of Olivia, and the succeeding perplexity, though well enough contrived to divert on the stage, wants credibility, and fails to produce the proper instruction required in the drama, as it exhibits no just picture of life" [see excerpt above, 1765]. The question to be interpreted, then, is how Shakespeare is using the instrument of theatrical contrivance, which is present, of course, in all his comedies, but which he uses here with exceptional delicacy and freedom.

Briefly, Shakespeare has taken a familiar kind of love-story and transformed it so as to extend the interest from the heroine to a group of characters who reveal varying responses to the power of love. He has modified the main situation further, and brought home his comments on it, by using methods of construction he had mastered previously in his *Comedy of Errors*. And he has added a sub-plot based on the customary jokes and revels of a feast of misrule, when normal restraints and relationships were overthrown. As the main title implies, the idea of a time of misrule gives the underlying constructive principle of the whole play.

In *Twelfth Night,* as Miss Welsford puts it, Shakespeare "transmutes into poetry the quintessence of the Saturnalia" [see excerpt above, 1935]. The sub-plot shows a prolonged season of misrule, or "uncivil rule", in Olivia's household, with Sir Toby turning night into day; there are drinking, dancing, and singing, scenes of mock wooing, a mock sword fight, and the gulling of an unpopular member of the household, with Feste mumming it as a priest and attempting a mock exorcism in the manner of the Feast of Fools. Sir Andrew and Malvolio resemble Ben Jonson's social pretenders; but Shakespeare goes beyond Jonson in ringing the changes on the theme of Folly and in making his speakers turn logic and courtesy on their heads. A girl and a coward are given out to be ferocious duellists; a steward imagines that he can marry his lady; and finally a fool pretends to assure a wise man that darkness is light. In Feste, Shakespeare creates his most finished portrait of a professional fool; he is superfluous to the plot, but affects the mood of the play more than any other of Shakespeare's clowns.

Moreover, this saturnalian spirit invades the whole play. In the main plot, sister is mistaken for brother, and brother for sister. Viola tells Olivia "That you do think you are not what you are"—and admits that the same holds true of herself. The women take the initiative in wooing, both in appearance and in fact; the heroine performs love-service for the lover. The Duke makes his servant "your master's mistress" and the lady who has withdrawn from the sight of men embraces a stranger. The four main actors all reverse their desires or break their vows before the comedy is over; while Antonio, the one single-minded representative of romantic devotion, is also the only character in the main plot who tries to establish a false identity

and fails [III.iv.329-30]; and he is left unrewarded and almost disregarded. Such reversals are, as Johnson says, devices peculiar to the stage, but Shakespeare makes them spring, or seem to spring, from the very nature of love. (pp. 117-19)

The analysis of love as a kind of folly was a common theme of Renaissance moralists, who delighted in contrasting it with the wisdom of the stoic or the man of affairs. Shakespeare's treatment of the theme in *Twelfth Night* is a natural development from his own previous work, but he could have found strong hints of it in the possible sources of his Viola-Orsino story. Bandello remarks, for instance, that it arouses wonder to hear of a gentleman disguising himself as a servant, and still more in the case of a girl: but when you realize that love is the cause, "the wonder ceases at once, because this passion of love is much too potent and causes actions much more amazing and excessive than that"; a person in love has "lost his liberty, and . . . no miracle if he commits a thousand errors". And Barnabe Riche tells his readers that in his story of *Apolonius and Silla,* "you shall see Dame Error so play her part with a leash of lovers, a male and two females, as shall work a wonder to your wise judgement". In effect, then, what Shakespeare could take for granted in his audience was not simply a readiness to be interested in romance, but a sense of the opposition between romance and reason.

On this basis, Shakespeare can unite his main action with his sub-plot, bending a romantic story in the direction of farce. By the same contrivances, he can disclose the follies surrounding love and celebrate its life-giving power. And he can do this, without sacrificing emotional reality—which is not exactly the same as Dr. Johnson's "just picture of life"—because he takes his stage machinery from the traditions of a feast of misrule, where social custom has already begun to transform normal behavior into the material of comic art. The whole play is a festivity, where reality and play-acting meet. By presenting his main story on these lines, Shakespeare can develop his insight into the protean, contradictory nature of love with more economy and force than by keeping to the lines of an ordinary stage narrative. At the same time he can extend this theme through his realistic images of "uncivil rule" in the sub-plot, disclosing the conflicting impulses of an aristocratic community in a period of social change, and touching on the potentially tragic problems of the place of time and order in human affairs. (pp. 119-20)

Shakespeare's situations were part of the common stock of classical and medieval romance, as Manningham saw at one of the first performances of *Twelfth Night,* when he noted in his diary that it was "much like the Comedy of Errores, or Menechmi in Plautus, but most like and neere to that in Italian called *Inganni*" [see excerpt above, 1602]. . . . (pp. 120-21)

There are four essential characters common to *Gl'Ingannati,* Bandello, Riche, and Shakespeare; namely, a lover, a heroine in his service disguised as a page, her twin brother (who at first has disappeared), and a second heroine. The basic elements common to all four plots are: the heroine's secret love for her master; her employment as go-between, leading to the complication of a cross-wooing; and a final solution by means of the unforeseen arrival of the missing twin.

If Shakespeare knew Bandello or *Gl'Ingannati,* he altered their material radically. The Italians both take the romance motif of a heroine's constancy and love-service, set it in a realistic bourgeois environment, and rationalize it with respectful irony. In Bandello, the irony is severely rational—because it is a tale of love, "the wonder ceases at once". In *Gl'Ingannati*, the tone is whimsical. "Two lessons above all you will extract from this play", says the Prologue: "how much chance and good fortune can do in matters of love; and how much long patience is worth in such cases, accompanied by good advice". Both Italian authors give the heroine a strong motive for assuming her disguise, in that the lover has previously returned her affection, but has now forgotten her and turned elsewhere. Both provide her with a formidable father in the background and a foster-mother like Juliet's Nurse, who admonishes and helps her; and both credit her with the intention of bilking her rival if she can. On the other side, they both respect the code of courtly love to the extent of stressing the lover's penitence at the end, and his recognition that he must repay the heroine for her devotion. "I believe", he says in the play, "that this is certainly the will of God, who must have taken pity on this virtuous maiden and on my soul, that it should not go to perdition. . . ."

Riche keeps this framework of sentiment, vulgarizes the narrative, and changes some of the material circumstances, generally in the direction of an Arcadian romance.

Shakespeare, for his part, changes the story fundamentally, broadening the interest and at the same time making the whole situation more romantically improbable, more melancholy at some points, more fantastic at others. He stiffens the heroine's loyalty, but deprives her of her original motive, her initiative, and her family. In place of these, he gives her the background of a vague "Messaline" and a romantic shipwreck, for which he may have taken a hint, but no more, from the episode of the shipwreck in Riche. Shakespeare's Viola, then, is a more romantic heroine than the rest, and the only one to fall in love *after* assuming her disguise. At the same time, however, Shakespeare enlarges the role of her twin brother and gives unprecedented weight to coincidence in the dénouement, which in both Italian stories is brought about more rationally, by the deliberate action of the heroine and her nurse; so that Shakespeare's Viola is also unique in that her happiness is due to "good fortune" more than "long patience", and to "good advice" not at all.

In his exposition, therefore, Shakespeare sketches a situation from romance in place of a logical intrigue. But the purpose, or at any rate, the effect, of his plan is to shift attention at the outset from the circumstances of the love story to the sentiments as such, especially in their more mysterious and irrational aspects. . . . [The comedy] consists in the triumph of natural love over affectation and melancholy. And, taken together, the leading characters in *Twelfth Night* form the most subtle portrayal of the psychology of love that Shakespeare had yet drawn.

Viola's love is fresh and direct, and gathers strength as the play advances. When she first appears, Viola mourns her brother, like Olivia, and by choice would join Olivia in her seclusion:

> O, that I serv'd that lady,
> And might not be deliver'd to the world,
> Till I had made mine own occasion mellow,
> What my estate is.   [I.ii.41-4]

Shakespeare makes the most here of the vagueness surrounding Viola; she seems the child of the sea, and of time. But even when her feelings and her problem have become distinct she still commits herself to "time" with a gentle air of detachment:

> What will become of this? As I am a man,
> My state is desperate for my master's love;
> As I am a woman,—now alas the day!—
> What thriftless sighs shall poor Olivia breathe!

> O time, thou must untangle this, not I,
> It is too hard a knot for me t'untie.
>
>   [II.ii.36-41]

She has none of the vehement determination of the Italian heroines, and, though nimble-witted, she is less resourceful and high-spirited than Rosalind. She foreshadows Perdita and Miranda in the romantically adolescent quality of her part. (pp. 121-22)

Shakespeare begins the play with Orsino. He follows Riche in making the lover in his comedy a duke (not, as with the Italians, a citizen), who has been a warrior but has now "become a scholar in love's school". Orsino suffers from the melancholy proper to courtly and "heroical" love; and Shakespeare fixes attention on his passion, which is more violent and "fantastical" than in the other versions of the story, by keeping Orsino inactive in his court to dramatize his own feelings like Richard II. . . . Orsino's love for Olivia is self-destructive, subject to time and change. Although, or rather, because, it is "all as hungry as the sea", it is impossible to satisfy. And it seems almost without an object, or incommensurate with an object, or incommensurate with any object, a "monstrosity" in the same sense as Troilus' love for Cressida, in its grasping after the infinite.

Moreover, Orsino's "spirit of love" seems something outside the rest of his personality, a tyrant from whom he longs to escape. His desires pursue him "like fell and cruel hounds". He wants music to diminish his passion, to relieve it with the thought of death. And when at last he confronts Olivia, something like hatred bursts through his conventional phrases of love-homage: "yond same sovereign cruelty" (II.iv) is now (V.i) a "perverse", "uncivil lady", "ingrate and unauspicious", "the marble-breasted tyrant". . . . In all this, however, there is as much injured vanity as anything else. His "fancy" is at the point of dying, not his heart; and it is fully consistent with his character that he can swerve almost at once to Viola, gratified and relieved by the surprise of her identity and the full dislosure of her devotion to himself. His emotions, then, give a powerful upsurge to the play, but they are kept within the bounds of comedy. His real "error", in Shakespeare, is that he only imagines himself to be pursuing love. Olivia's, correspondingly, is that she only imagines herself to be flying from it.

With Olivia, even more than with Orsino, Shakespeare diverges from his possible sources, making her a much more prominent and interesting character than her prototypes. In the Italian stories, the second heroine is heiress to a wealthy old dotard, is kept out of sight most of the time, and is treated with ribald irony for her amorous forwardness. In *Apolonius and Silla*, she is a wealthy widow. In all three, she is considered only as rival and pendant to the Viola-heroine. Shakespeare, however, makes her a virgin, psychologically an elder sister to Viola, and better able to sustain the comedy of awakening desire. At the same time, she is the mistress of a noble household, and hence the focus of the sub-plot as well as the main plot. (pp. 123-25)

The comic reversal of Olivia's attitude culminates in her declaration of love to Viola, the most delicate and yet impressive speech in the play. . . . It is now Olivia's turn to plead against "scorn", to "unclasp the book of her secret soul" to Viola [I.iv.13-14]—and, equally, to herself. After two lines, she turns to the same verse form of impersonal, or extra-personal, "sentences" in rhyme that Shakespeare gives to other heroines at their moment of truth:

> O, what a deal of scorn looks beautiful
> In the contempt and anger of his lip!
> A murd'rous guilt shows not itself more soon
> Than love that would seem hid: love's night is noon.
> Cesario, by the roses of the spring,
> By maidhood, honour, truth, and every thing,
> I love thee so, that, maugre all thy pride,
> Nor wit nor reason can my passion hide.
> Do not extort thy reasons from this clause,
> For that I woo, thou therefore hast no cause;
> But rather reason thus with reason fetter,
> Love sought is good, but given unsought is better.
>
> [III.i.144-56]

Having already thrown off her original veil, Olivia now breaks through the concealments of her pride, her modesty, and her feminine "wit". Her speech is mainly a vehement persuasion to love, urged "by the roses of the spring". Yet she keeps her dignity, and keeps it all the more in view of the secondary meaning latent in her words, her timid fear that Cesario's scorn is not the disdain of rejection at all but the scorn of conquest. Logically, indeed, her first rhyming couplet implies just this, implies that his cruel looks are the signs of a guilty lust rising to the surface; and this implication is carried on as she speaks of his "pride" (with its hint of sexual desire), and into her last lines, with their covert pleading not to "extort" a callous advantage from her confession. But in either case—whatever Cesario's intentions—love now appears to Olivia as a startling paradox: guilty, even murderous, an irruption of misrule; and at the same time irrepressible, fettering reason, and creating its own light out of darkness. And, in either case, the conclusion to her perplexities is a plain one—"Love sought is good, but given unsought is better". This is Shakespeare's departure from the moral argument of his predecessors, and it marks the turning-point of *Twelfth Night*. (pp. 126-27)

[From] the point of her declaration to Viola, the way is clear for the resolution of the whole comedy on the plane of sentiment. In terms of sentiment, she has justified her gift of love to a stranger. She is soon completely sure of herself, and in the later scenes she handles Sir Toby, Orsino, and Cesario-Sebastian with brusque decision; while her demon of austerity is cast out through Malvolio. The main action of *Twelfth Night*, then, is planned with a suggestive likeness to a revel, in which Olivia is masked, Orsino's part is "giddy" and "fantastical", Viola-Sebastian is the mysterious stranger—less of a character and more of a poetic symbol than the others—and in the end, as Feste says of his own "interlude" with Malvolio, "the whirligig of time brings in his revenges".

Although Olivia's declaration forms the crisis of the main action, the resolution of the plot has still to be worked out. And here Shakespeare departs in a new way from his predecessors. Shakespeare's Sebastian, by character and adventures, has little in common with the brother in *Gl'Ingannati*, and still less with Silla's brother in Riche; but nearly everything in common—as Manningham presumably noticed—with the visiting brother in Plautus, Menaechmus of Syracuse. And Antonio's part in the plot (though not his character) is largely that of Menaechmus' slave in Plautus, while his emotional role stems from the Aegeon story that Shakespeare himself had already added to *Menaechmi* in *The Comedy of Errors*. These Plautine elements in the brother's story have been altered in *Gl'Ingannati* and dropped from, or camouflaged in, *Apoloniu and Silla*. Which-

ever of the latter Shakespeare used for Viola, therefore, he deliberately reverted to Plautus for Sebastian, sometimes drawing on his own elaborations in *The Comedy of Errors*, but mainly going back directly to the original.

Hence the second half of *Twelfth Night* is largely more farcical than its predecessors, whereas the first half had been, in a sense, more romantic. Shakespeare thus provides a telling finale, proper, as Dr. Johnson observes, to the stage. But he does much more than this. His farcical dénouement gives tangible shape to the notion of misrule inherent in his romantic exposition. Faults of judgment in the first part of *Twelfth Night* are answered with mistakes of identity in the second, while the action swirls to a joyful ending through a crescendo of errors. And by the same manoeuvre, Shakespeare charges his romance with a new emotional significance, bringing it nearer to tragedy. (pp. 127-28)

In the Italian stories, the heroine reaches an understanding with her master by her own devices and the aid of her nurse, without any kind of help from the arrival of her brother; and this is a logical solution, since the heroine's love-service is the clear center of interest. But Shakespeare has been more broadly concerned with love as a force in life as a whole. He has shifted the emphasis to the two older lovers, keeping Viola's share of passion in reserve. And even after the crisis, he continues to withhold the initiative the Italians had given her. Shakespeare is alone in making the heroine reveal herself *after* her brother's marriage with the second heroine, as a consequence of it. And the whole Plautine sequence in *Twelfth Night* is designed to lead to this conclusion. Hence, while the first half of Shakespeare's comedy dwells on self-deception in love, the second half stresses the benevolent irony of fate.

In the early scenes, fate appears to the speakers as an overriding power which is nevertheless obscurely rooted in their own desires (the obverse, that is, to Orsino's "spirit of love", which springs from himself, yet seems to dominate him from without). Thus, Viola trusts herself to "time"; Olivia, falling in love, cries, "Fate, show thy force: ourselves we do not owe"; and the letter forged in her name yields an echo to her words: "Thy Fates open their hands; let thy blood and spirit embrace them". Antonio and Sebastian strengthen this motif and clarify it.

Antonio stands for an absolute devotion that is ultimately grounded on fate; he is the embodiment of Olivia's discovery, and his speeches on this theme are interwoven with hers. Shortly after her first lines about fate—and chiming with them—comes his declaration to Sebastian . . . :

> But, come what may, I do adore thee so,
> That danger shall seem sport, and I will go. . . .
>
> [II.i.47-8]

In the last scene, again, he proclaims to Orsino—

> A witchcraft drew me hither:
> That most ingrateful boy there by your side,
> From the rude sea's enrag'd and foamy mouth
> Did I redeem.
>
> [V.i.76-9]

The resonant sea-image of destiny here dominates the bewildered tone still appropriate, at this point, to a comedy of errors.

Sebastian's part runs parallel with this. When he first appears (II.i), he feels the same melancholy as his sister, and shows a similar vague self-abandonment in his aims: ''My determinate voyage is mere extravagancy''. [II.i.11-2] The Captain has told Viola to ''comfort [herself] with chance''; Sebastian is ''provident in peril'', on friendly terms with destiny. When he bobs up resurrected at the end, accordingly, he does precisely what Malvolio had been advised to do, grasps the hands of the Fates and lets himself float with ''the stream'', with ''this accident and flood of fortune'' [IV.i.60, IV.iii.11]. By the same turn of mind, moreover, he imparts to the dénouement a tone as of clarity following illusion, of an awakening like the end of *A Midsummer Night's Dream:*

> Or I am mad, or else this is a dream. . . . . . .
> [IV.i.61]

> This is the air; that is the glorious sun;
> This pearl she gave me, I do feel't and see't;
> And though 'tis wonder that enwraps me thus,
> Yet 'tis not madness. . . . . . .   [IV.iii.1-4]

''Mad'' the lady may appear; but Sebastian—like Olivia before him, except that he does it in all coolness—is ready to ''wrangle with his reason'' and welcome the gift of love. The comedy of errors in which he figures is thus both counterpart and solution to the initial comedy of sentiment. Riche had called his lovestory the work of ''Dame Error''; Shakespeare, in effect, takes the hint, and goes back to Plautus.

Having planned his dénouement on these lines, moreover, Shakespeare goes further, adding a superb variation on his Plautine theme in the farcical scene leading up to Viola's meeting with Antonio (III.iv). This scene as a whole, with its rapid changes of mood and action, from Olivia to the sub-plot and back towards Sebastian, braces together the whole comic design. It brings to a climax the misrule, farcical humours, and simulated emotions of the play—with Olivia confessing ''madness'', Sir Toby triumphant, Malvolio *in excelsis* (''Jove, not I, is the doer of this . . .''), Sir Andrew allegedly ''bloody as the hunter'', and Viola, after her unavoidable coldness to Olivia, submitted for the first time to the laughable consequences of her change of sex. And the duel with its sequel perfect this comic catharsis. This duel, or what Sir Toby and Fabian make of it, bears a strong affinity to the sword dances and Mummers' play combats of a season of misrule; it becomes another encounter between St. George and Captain Slasher, the Turkish Knight. . . . [This] episode of misrule contains the principal conflict between the serious and the ludicrous forces in the play; it prepares emotionally for the resurrection of Sebastian; and, by a further swerve of constructive irony, the additional, gratuitous comedy of errors involving Antonio gives new force to the main theme of the romance.

As it concerns Viola, the dialogue here restores the balance in favor of her character, in that her generosity and her lines against ''ingratitude'' prepare the audience for her culminating gesture of self-sacrifice in the last act. But, more than this, Antonio's speeches stress the paradox of love that has been gathering force through the play:

> *Antonio:* Let me speak a little. This youth that you see here
>   I snatch'd one half out of the jaws of death,
>   Reliev'd him with such sanctity of love,
>   And to his image, which methought did promise
>   Most venerable worth, did I devotion.
> *Officer:* What's that to us? The time goes by: away!

> *Antonio:* But, O, how vile an idol proves this god.
>   Thou hast, Sebastian, done good feature shame.
>   In nature there's no blemish but the mind;
>   None can be call'd deform'd but the unkind:
>   Virtue is beauty, but the beauteous evil
>   Are empty trunks o'erflourished by the devil.
> *Officer:* The man grows mad: away with him! . . .
> [III.iv.359-71]

It is in keeping with the comedy of errors that Antonio here has mistaken his man, to the point of seeming ''mad'', that Viola, happy to hear of her brother again, promptly forgets him—as Sir Toby notices [III.iv.385-88]—and that Antonio, as it turns out, should help Sebastian most effectively by so being forgotten. But this same quirk of fate brings the mood of the play dangerously near the confines of tragedy. The comedy has no answer to his problem of sincere devotion given to a false idol.

Antonio stands outside the main sphere of the comedy. He belongs to the world of merchants, law, and sea-battles, not the world of courtly love. His love for Sebastian is irrational, or beyond reason, and his danger in Orsino's domains is due, similarly, to irrational persistence in an old dispute [III.iii.24-8]. But he gives himself completely to his principles, more seriously than anyone else in the play, and tries to live them out as rationally as he can. In contrast to the lovers (except possibly Viola), he is not satisfied with truth of feeling, but demands some more objective standard of values; in his world, law and ''time'' mean something external, and harder than the unfolding of natural instinct. His problems are appropriate to *Troilus* or *Hamlet.* In one way, therefore, he marks a limit to festivity. Nevertheless, precisely because he takes himself so seriously, he helps to keep the comic balance of the play.

The comedy of errors in the main plot, the element of mummery and misrule, implies a comment on the serious follies of love, and bring a corrective to them. In the sub-plot (or -plots)—his addition to the Viola story—Shakespeare makes this corrective explicit and prepares for the festive atmosphere at the end. ''What a plague means my niece, to take the death of her brother thus? I am sure care's an enemy to life. . . .'' ''Does not our lives consist of the four elements?—Faith, so they say; but I think it rather consists of eating and drinking.'' Sir Toby, Maria, Feste, Fabian stand for conviviality and the enjoyment of life, as opposed to the melancholy of romance.

At the same time, however, the sub-plot action reproduces the main action like a comic mirror-image, and the two of them are joined to form a single symmetrical pattern of errors in criss-cross. Shakespeare had attempted a similar pattern before, in *The Comedy of Errors, A Midsummer Night's Dream,* and *Much Ado,* for example, but nowhere else does he bring it off so lightly and ingeniously. (pp. 128-32)

The interest of the sub-plot is more varied, moreover, and its links with the main plot are more complex, than a bare summary of the action can indicate. In relation to the main plot, the comic figures are somewhat like scapegoats; they reflect the humours of Orsino and Olivia in caricature and through them these humours are purged away. Secondly, the sub-plot is a Feast of Fools, containing its own satire of humours in Malvolio and Sir Andrew. And, from another point of view, Sir Toby's ''uncivil rule'' is complementary to the problem of ''time'' in the main plot.

Besides Malvolio, Sir Toby and Sir Andrew are to some extent parodies of Orsino. One will drink Olivia's health till he is "drowned" or "his brains turn o' the toe like a parish-top"; the other is a model of gentlemanly indecision, hopes to woo Olivia without speaking to her, and attacks Viola from jealousy. The strains of unconscious parody in the sub-plot help to amplify the general theme of delusion and error.

On Olivia's side, moreover, the disorder in her household is a direct reaction to her attitude at the beginning of the play. Malvolio affects a grave austerity to please her, but the instincts are in revolt. Sir Toby redoubles the clamor of love for her and personifies her neglect of time and the reproach of the clock [III.i.130]. Sir Andrew, a fool, helps to find her a husband. In Malvolio's "madness" she comes to see a reflection of her own [III.iv.14-15], and at the end he takes her place in cloistered darkness.

In addition, the comic dialogue echoes the thought of the serious characters and twists it into fantastic shapes. To the serious actors, life is a sea-voyage: the comic actors deal with journeys more specific, bizarre, and adventurous than theirs, ranging in time from when "Noah was a sailor" to the publishing of "the new map with the augmentation of the Indies", and from the Barents Sea to the gates of Tartar or the equinoctial of Queubus. The serious actors scrutinize a fate which might be pagan in its religious coloring: the comic speakers, for their part, are orthodox Christians, and their dialogue is peppered with biblical and ecclesiastical references. . . . In part, these ecclesiastical jokes reinforce the suggestion of Twelfth Night foolery and of mock sermons like Erasmus' sermon of Folly; from this aspect, they lead up to Feste's interlude of Sir Topas. But in part, too, their tone of moral security to the degree of smugness gives a counterweight to the emotions of the serious actors.

Moreover, Sir Andrew and Sir Toby are both alike in feeling very sure of their ideal place in the scheme of things. They are contrasted as shrewd and fatuous, parasite and gull, Carnival and Lent; but they are both, in their differing ways, "sots", and both gentlemen. (pp. 133-34)

Malvolio is a more complex and formidable character. Evidently Maria's "good practise" on this overweening steward was the distinctive attraction of *Twelfth Night* to Stuart audiences; but that does not mean (as some critics would have it, reacting against Lamb [see excerpt above, 1822]) that Malvolio is presented as a contemptible butt. An audience is more likely to enjoy and remember the humiliation of someone who in real life would be feared than the humiliation of a mere impostor like Parolles. Malvolio is neither a puritan nor an upstart, though he has qualities in common with both. . . . With his unconscious hypocrisy in the exercise of power and his rankling sense of injustice, he comes midway between Shylock and the Angelo of *Measure for Measure*.

Sir Toby, Sir Andrew and Malvolio—all three—are striving to be something false, whether novel or antiquated, which is out of place in a healthy community; they are a would-be retainer, a would-be gallant, a would-be "politician". But the conflict over revelry between Malvolio and Sir Toby is a conflict of two opposed reactions towards changing social and economic conditions. In Malvolio's eyes, Sir Toby "wastes the treasure of his time". So he does; and so, in their ways, do Olivia and Orsino. A natural way of living, Shakespeare seems to imply, must observe impersonal factors such as time as well as the healthy gratification of instinct—and in the last resort, the two may be incompatible with each other. Hence Malvolio in the end is neither crushed nor pacified. He belongs,

like Antonio, to the world of law and business, outside the festive circle of the play. Both are imprisoned for a while by the others. They stand for two extremes of self-sacrifice and self-love, but they share a rigid belief in principle. And neither can be fully assimilated into the comedy.

There are discordant strains, then, in the harmony of *Twelfth Night*—strains of melancholy and of something harsher. As far as any one actor can resolve them, this task falls to Feste.

Feste is not only the most fully portrayed of Shakespeare's clowns, he is also the most agile-minded of them. He has fewer set pieces than Touchstone and fewer proverbs than the Fool in *Lear*. He is proud of his professional skill—"better a witty fool than a foolish wit"—but he wields it lightly, in darting paradoxes; he is a "corrupter of words". Yet, besides being exceptionally imaginative and sophisticated, he is exceptionally given to scrounging for tips. This trait is consistent with the traditional aspect of his role, especially as the fool in a feast of misrule, but it helps to make him more like a real character and less like a stage type.

This money-sense of Feste and his awareness of his social status bring him within the conflict of ideas affecting the other actors. Although he depends for his living on other people's pleasure, and can sing to any tune—"a love-song or a song of good life"—Feste is neither a servile entertainer nor an advocate of go-as-you-please. On the contrary, he is a moralist with a strong bent towards scepticism. "As there is no true cuckold but calamity, so beauty's a flower. . . . Truly, sir, and pleasure will be paid, one time or another. . . . The whirligig of time brings in his revenges": one factor will always cancel another. As against Malvolio, he belittles the soul; but he shows hardly any more confidence in the survival-value of folly, and marriage is the only form of it he recommends. For Feste himself could very easily belong to the ship of fools he designates for Orsino, having his business and intent everywhere and making "a good voyage of nothing". (The same thought is present when he tells Viola that foolery "does walk about the orb like the sun; it shines every where".) There is a persistent hint, then, that his enigmas glance at himself as well as others, and that he feels his own position to be insecure. And it is consistent with this that he should be the only character in Shakespeare to take pleasure, or refuge, in fantasies of pure nonsense: "as the old hermit of Prague, that never saw pen and ink, very wittily said to a niece of King Gorboduc, 'That that is is'." It is impossible to go further than a non-existent hermit of Prague.

Feste is not the ringleader in *Twelfth Night,* nor is he exactly the play's philosopher. He is cut off from an independent life of his own by his traditional role in reality and on the stage, and what he sees at the bottom of the well is "nothing". He knows that without festivity he is nothing; and he knows, in his epilogue, that misrule does not last, and that men shut their gates against tosspots, lechers, knaves, and fools. A play is only a play, and no more. Yet it is precisely on this finely-poised balance of his that the whole play comes to rest. Orsino, Olivia, Viola, Sebastian, Sir Toby, Maria, Malvolio, Feste himself—nearly everyone in *Twelfth Night* acts a part in some sense, but Feste is the only one who takes this aspect of life for granted. The others commit errors and have divided emotions; but Feste can have no real emotions of his own, and may only live in his quibbles. Yet by virtue of this very disability, he sees the element of misrule in life more clearly than the rest, appreciating its value because he knows its limitations.

A play to Feste may be only a play, but it is also the breath of life.

Feste is the principal link between the other characters in *Twelfth Night*. Unless Puck is counted, he is the only clown for whom Shakespeare provides an epilogue. And as it happens, his is the epilogue to the whole group of Shakespeare's romantic comedies. (pp. 134-37)

> *L. G. Salingar, "The Design of 'Twelfth Night',"*
> in Shakespeare Quarterly, *Vol. IX, No. 2, Spring,*
> *1958, pp. 117-39.*

S. NAGARAJAN (essay date 1959)

[*Nagarajan explores the themes of appetite and will in* Twelfth Night, *basing his interpretation of the play on Aquinian concepts. The theme of appetite in the play is also studied by Morris P. Tilley (1914) and John Hollander (1956 and 1959).*]

"What You Will", the alternate title of *Twelfth Night*, is generally interpreted as Shakespeare's liberal invitation to his readers and spectators to choose the title of the play themselves, and such invitation is read as an appropriate sign of the light-hearted gaiety that informs Shakespearian comedy. Light-hearted gaiety, of course, there is in the comedy Shakespearian—that explains its perennial attraction—but to treat the alternate title of the play as a sign of it is to misread the serious artistic intent that causes the play's unity of structure. . . .

The theme of *Twelfth Night* is unrequital in love; this is a theme which exists in *All's Well, Troilus and Cressida,* and *Measure for Measure.* The unrequital is linked with a prior act of self-deception in the lover; in Bertram, in Troilus, and in Angelo. In *Twelfth Night,* the act of self-deception consists in imposing on oneself a vision that does not really belong to oneself. Orsino, Olivia, and Malvolio are all creatures of self-deception. (p. 61)

The words "appetite" and "will" often occur in the play and merit some explanation in terms of the thought that generally prevailed in Shakespeare's day. Without doing any violence to the intellectual diversity of the Elizabethan age or to the authority of the defining process that goes on in the play itself, we may be permitted to draw on external explication of the language of the play to strengthen our growing appreciation of the medieval affinities of Shakespeare's work. I have drawn on Aquinas here, who, though not of the Middle Ages, does belong . . . to the Middle Ages. I am not suggesting that Shakespeare pored over the *Summa;* well-deliberated opinion, however, is becoming charier of minimizing the dramatist's scholarship. I am not claiming Aquinas as a "source"; I am merely suggesting that a knowledge of Aquinas will be a legitimate help in giving precision to the medieval aspect of Shakespeare's work. (pp. 61-2)

According to Aquinas, in everything there is an inclination or propensity to a particular form of behavior. The word "inclination" suggests a conscious tending towards an object; but Aquinas uses it in a very general sense, which would cover, to use his example, the natural upward movement of fire. "Propensity follows form. In the case of things without knowledge, each possesses one form limiting it to one existence or condition of natural being. The resulting propensity is called natural appetite." "Material things are, as it were, bound and stiffened with matter and so they are not self-directing; their tendencies follow a physical determinism and are shaped by the outside principle of their nature." In things which are

capable of knowledge, however, we find an appetite which follows apprehension of an object as good or desirable. As present on the level of sensitive life, this appetite is called the animal or sensitive appetite. "Within each power, there is its own natural appetite for a suitable object; but, over and above, there is a special type of appetite, termed the animal appetite, resulting from perception and going for an object, not merely because it is congruous to this or that power, as seeing for the sight or hearing for the ear, but also because it is wanted by the whole organism." Aquinas also calls the sensitive appetite "sensuality." . . . The sensitive appetite is in no way disordered. On the contrary it is natural and tends to the objective good of the thing which possesses it. This sensitive appetite is, of course, found in man. But in man there is also a rational or intellectual appetite by which he desires a good consciously apprehended by the reason. "The sensitive appetite is at the stage between natural appetite and the higher rational appetite which is termed will. . . . Objects of sense and of intelligence are at different levels; in consequence, the intellectual appetite or will is a power distinct from the sensitive appetite."

When we are dealing with the particular and the contingent and not the universal good, after cogitation, we decide on a course of action; our "election" of one means out of many to achieve the contingent end proposed, includes both the deliberation of reason and the decision of the will. Reason and understanding are required for deliberation and for judgment as to which means seem preferable. The will is required for assent to these means and for election; that is, for preferred choice for one of them. "Only acts controlled by man through his reason and will are properly termed human: they proceed from deliberation. Others may be called acts of the man but they are not human in the specific sense of the term." The "sensuality" is called reasonable only in so far it obeys the reason. But when intelligence is obsequious to sensuality, derangement results.

The action of the play must be seen against this background, and the interpretation of "What You Will" suggested here will not seem, I hope, fantastic.

When Orsino murmurs:

> If music be the food of love, play on;
> Give me excess of it, that, surfeiting,
> The appetite may sicken and so die.
>
> [I.i.1-3]

pretty as the conceit may be, it is apparent that instead of achieving a reasonable sensuality, he has incited appetite by withdrawing the control of a rational will. "Irrelevant daydreamings which flourish when a man ceases to exercise intellectual habits, will distract him to contraries so much so that unless the imagination be refined by frequent use of intellectual habits, a man will get out of practice in making right judgments, indeed sometimes will become quite impotent." Orsino grows weary because "fatigue is incidental to the enjoyment of sensible activities; it comes from strain on their organs."

> That strain again! it had a dying fall:
> O! it came o'er my ear like the sweet sound
> That breathes upon a bank of violets,
> Stealing and giving odour. Enough! no more:
> 'Tis not so sweet now as it was before.
>
> [I.i.4-8]

Throughout the play, we find it difficult to take him seriously; he is so obviously not grown up. (In spite of Dr. Hotson! [See

Additional Bibliography, *The First Night of "Twelfth Night"*])
He is suffering from superfluous concupiscence—intemperance, as Aquinas would say. . . . Perfect enjoyment demands intelligence, says Aquinas.

When we hear again how Olivia is deliberately plunged into grief and seeks to nurse and augment it, her malady also is the enthronement of appetite in her personality. Her grief is not wrong but she has abandoned all prudence. . . . The point of Feste's exchanges in I.v with Olivia is to show up the unnaturalness, the "imprudence" of her life, of trying to wed calamity, ignoring that beauty is a flower that fades, of mourning excessively for her dead brother, the excess consisting in the supersedure of reason. Hence he sings later: "What is love? 'Tis not hereafter"; and Sir Toby with the song running in his befuddled brain says roundly, "My lady is a Cataian", trying to cheat herself, her youth and her beauty. This is the abnormality in Olivia that provides the staple of the comedy. . . . When we find Olivia tumbling into love much against her resolve, our response to the situation is a laughter that is truly in the comic spirit since it arises from our intellectual perception of how in Olivia will and appetite have ceased to be distinct powers. The tenor of her love with Viola is controlled by the loss of this distinction.

It is because this source of the comic in the play is overlooked that Orsino's marriage is often criticized as much too sudden. Precisely in the suddenness consists the comedy as it relates to Orsino. Just as Olivia before she knows what is happening falls head over heels in love with Cesario, bringing to surface the difference between idea and instinct, even so Orsino discovers that his love for Olivia was purely self-conjured. In Orsino, we have Shakespeare's still imperfect realization of what M. Hubert Benoit has called an "adoring" lover; Orsino leads the way to Troilus. (pp. 62-5)

Again, it was the insufficient appreciation of the animating principle of the comedy, the difference between what we will and what we are, that induced Charles Lamb to speak of Malvolio as comic by accident only and still causes the play to be divided into plot and underplot [see excerpt above, 1822]. After all, the gulling of Malvolio, which is regarded as the underplot of the play, reveals his self-deception, the irrationality of his will. It has its parallel in Orsino's fanciful reading of Feste's pretty party song and in Olivia's pursuit of Viola. With this difference: the self-deception of Malvolio, springing from haughty self-conceit, involves others in discomfort. The innocent jesting of Feste is rebuked by him and this creates the impression that Malvolio is a kill-joy. . . . This impression controls our interpretation of Malvolio's attempt to curb Sir Toby and his associates. It is love of love with Orsino; it is the *sickness* of self-love with Malvolio. While well-ordered self-love is right and natural, pride in the sense of an inordinate desire of one's own private excellence is a special sin. . . . Just as in Molière, the theatrical convention of the actor's mask ceases to be a jejune convention and becomes a symbol of Molière's conception of the comic, even so the nature of the punishment awarded to Malvolio is a scenic representation of what has taken place in Malvolio's nature. Besides, we think of Malvolio's imprisonment as an unbearable weight on the character because we have uncritically abstracted the character from the comic setting of Sir Thopas' colloquy. Malvolio is no more tragic than Harpagon or Tartuffe. Any embarrassment that we may feel when he is discomfited arises from a change not in the character's mode of existence but in the kind of responses that the character once evoked and does so no longer;

the kind of society for which the comedy was written—and comedy is a particularly social art—no longer exists. The enormous self-love of Malvolio, his overweening self-conceit, his wilfulness, his lack of balance, involving wickedness toward others, inevitably demanded the treatment he receives, and hence it is difficult to agree with the contention that Malvolio is faced by or brought to a situation for which his previous address to the world had never covenanted. . . . He should be compared with Molière's deliberately single-trait characters who end as they begin in accordance with the principles of dramatic construction adopted by the dramatist. (pp. 65-6)

Among *Hamlet, Troilus and Cressida, All's Well* and *Measure for Measure,* there is a thematic kinship strengthened by chronological neighborhood. The theme of unrequital in love which occurs in these plays in a wide range of characterization, extending from Olivia to Helena and Mariana, has great tragic potentialities which require an utterly new type of comedy if a comic form is sought for the theme. The trick of confused identity, derived from the romances, gives *Twelfth Night* a comic conclusion, no doubt, but leaves us emotionally unsatisfied; the style is felt to be somewhat inadequate to the intrinsic demands and scope of the "idea" of the play. Hence we have that odd feeling, glimpsed sometimes in the midst of our admiration, that in this play [according to J. C. Maxwell in his essay "Shakespeare: The Middle Plays,"] "there is a certain lack of warmth, a sense that the poet is not creating from the deepest springs of his experience." It is significant that this feeling does not arise with Malvolio's characterization. (pp. 66-7)

S. Nagarajan, "'What You Will': A Suggestion," in Shakespeare Quarterly, *Vol. X, No. 1, Winter, 1959, pp. 61-7.*

HAROLD JENKINS (essay date 1959)

[*Jenkins proposes that* Twelfth Night *manifests one of the primary principles of comedy: the education of a man or woman. He challenges the position of Charles Lamb (1822), Milton Crane (1955), and others on the importance of Malvolio. Jenkins decides that Malvolio is relegated to the subplot and that his purpose is to provide a contrast with Olivia, who learns to love, whereas Malvolio is confined to the prison of his self-love. For additional commentary on Shakespeare's handling of the theme of love, see the excerpts by H. B. Charlton (1937), E. C. Pettet (1949), John Russell Brown (1957), and Alexander Leggatt (1974). Jenkins's essay, from which the following excerpt is taken, was originally published in* The Rice Institute Pamphlet *in January, 1959.*]

It was several years before the Twelfth Night entertainment of 1601—certainly not later than 1594—that Shakespeare first wrote a play about identical twins who were separated from one another in a shipwreck and afterwards mistaken for one another even by the wife of one of them; and it was at a similarly early stage in his career that Shakespeare wrote another play about a woman who served her lover as a page, and who in her page's disguise carried messages of love from her lover to another woman. When Shakespeare makes these things happen in *Twelfth Night* he is, in fact, combining the plots of *The Comedy of Errors* and *The Two Gentlemen of Verona.* He does not, however, combine them in equal degree. The heartsick heroine who in page's disguise takes messages of love to another woman provided little more than an episode in the complicated relations of the two gentlemen of Verona; but in *Twelfth Night* this episode has grown into the central situation from which the play draws its life. On the other hand, the confusion of twins which entertained us for five acts of *The Comedy of Errors* appears now as little more than an adroit device to bring about a happy ending. These shifts of emphasis show clearly enough the direction that Shakespeare's art of comedy has taken. When Sebastian appears in *Twelfth Night* we see that Shakespeare can still delight in the jolly mix-up of mistaken identities, not to mention their consequence of broken pates, but his plot now gives chief attention to the delineation of romantic love. This is more than just a preference for one situation rather than another: it means that a plot which turns on external appearances—a resemblance between men's faces—gives way to an action which involves their feelings. In *The Comedy of Errors*, though the physical resemblance between twins is no doubt a fact of nature, the confusion is really the result of accidental circumstances and is as accidentally cleared up. But in *Twelfth Night* the confusion is in the emotions and no *dénouement* is possible until the characters have grown in insight to the point where they can acknowledge the feelings that nature has planted in them. Thus *Twelfth Night* exhibits in its action one of the fundamental motifs of comedy: the education of a man or woman. For a comedy, as everyone knows, is a play in which the situation holds some threat of disaster but issues in the achievement of happiness; and those comedies may satisfy us most deeply in which danger is averted and happiness achieved through something that takes place within the characters. Orsino and Olivia come to their happy ending when they have learnt a new attitude to others and to themselves. (pp. 72-3)

[Unlike *The Two Gentlemen of Verona*,] *Twelfth Night* has no unfaithful lover. But it cannot escape notice that Orsino's love is repeatedly compared to the sea—vast, hungry, but unstable, while his mind appears to Feste like an opal, a jewel of magical but ever-changing colors. The changeable man is there, but he has undergone a subtle transformation, and to notice this is, I think, of far more importance than to object, as Charlotte Lennox did in the eighteenth century, that Shakespeare in *Twelfth Night* has ruined the story of Bandello which she regarded as "undoubtedly" Shakespeare's source [see excerpt above, 1753]. Shakespeare, she objects, deprives the story of probability because he neglects to provide his characters with acceptable motives. Viola, she says, "all of a sudden takes up an unaccountable resolution to serve the young bachelor-duke in the habit of a man." And since Viola has not even the excuse of being in love with the duke to start with, this goes "greatly beyond the bounds of decency." But if Shakespeare had wanted to make Viola assume her man's disguise because she was already in love with Orsino, he did not need Bandello to teach him; he had already tried that situation with Julia and Proteus, and it had necessarily involved Proteus in that heartless infidelity from which Orsino is to be spared. The emotional situation of *Twelfth Night* is of a much less obvious kind.

The most important source for *Twelfth Night*, one might therefore say, is *The Two Gentlemen of Verona*. For it is only by a paradox of scholarship that the word *source* is usually restricted to material that an author draws on from someone else's work. But that there were other sources for *Twelfth Night* I readily admit. (p. 74)

But that Shakespeare read up these plays and novels for the express purpose of writing his own play is perhaps another matter. The similarities between Shakespeare and these others are certainly interesting; yet to point out similarities will usually end in drawing attention to their difference. For instance, *Twelfth Night* seems to echo Riche's tale when Olivia, declaring her unrequited love for Cesario, says she has "laid" her "honor too unchary out." But in Riche the lady said that she had "charity preserved" her "honor." The phrasing is reminiscent; but Riche's lady boasts of her honor after she has sacrificed her chastity, while Shakespeare's Olivia reproaches herself for being careless of her honor when her chastity of course is not in question. Riche's lady is anxious lest she has lost her reputation in the eyes of the world, Olivia lest she has fallen from her own high ideal of conduct. Without accepting Furness's view that any reference to the act of sex is coarse and repulsive, we may easily find it significant that Shakespeare leaves it out. His delineation of Olivia's love for the page, in contrast to most of the earlier versions, omits all the physical demonstrations. The usual way when the lady falls in love with the page is for her to astonish him by falling on his neck and kissing him. In Secchi's play of *Gl'Inganni* the relations between them reach the point where the woman page is expected to play the man's part in an actual assignation and she gets out of it by the cunning substitution of her brother. In the play of *Gl'Ingannati*, which comes closer to Shakespeare, the lady takes the brother by mistake, but he goes to bed with her just the same. In Riche's story this incident has consequences, which force the lady so chary of her honor to demand marriage of the page, who can only establish innocence by the disclosure of *her* sex. Shakespeare appropriates this convenient brother as a husband for Olivia, but since he could easily have invented Viola's twin, and in *The Comedy of Errors* had, one might say, already tried him out, this debt is not a profound one. What is more remarkable, the similarity as usual embracing a contrast, is that when Olivia mistakes Sebastian for Cesario she takes him not to bed but to a priest. Olivia no less than Orsino is kept free of moral taint. And this is no mere matter of prudishness. The reckless abandonment of scruple shown by all these earlier lovers —both by the gentlemen who desert their mistresses and the ladies who fling themselves upon the page-boys—cannot coexist with the more delicate sentiment which gives *Twelfth Night* its character. In Shakespeare, even the twin brother, prop to the plot as he may be, shares in this refinement. When Olivia takes charge of Sebastian's person, what he gives her is less his body than his imagination. He is enwrapped, he says in "wonder." And it is his capacity to experience this wonder that lifts him to the level of the other lovers in the play, so that he becomes a worthy partner for Orsino's adored one and Viola's adorer.

Now if *Twelfth Night* is the greatest of Shakespeare's romantic comedies, it is partly because of its success in embodying these feelings of wonder in the principal persons of the play. Stories of romantic love owe something of their perennial appeal, we need not be ashamed to admit, to the taste for tales of pursuit and mysterious adventure, as well as to what psychologists no doubt explain as the sublimation of the natural impulses of sex. But the devotion which the romantic lover bestows upon a woman as pure as she is unattainable may also symbolize the mind's aspiration towards some ever alluring but ever elusive ideal. . . . Orsino, with whom *Twelfth Night* begins and who draws us from the start into the aura of his imagination, is in some ways the most perfect of Shakespeare's romantic lovers simply because he is so much more. This is easily appreciated if we compare him with his earlier prototypes in *The Two Gentlemen of Verona*. He is, as I have suggested, the inconstant

Proteus transformed. But he is also the other gentleman, the constant Valentine. He is

> Unstaid and skittish in all motions else
> Save in the constant image of the creature
> That is beloved.   [II.iv.18-20]

So, simultaneously volatile and steadfast, he combines in a single figure those aspects of man's nature which in the earlier comedy had been systematically contrasted and opposed.

In Valentine, of course, we recognize the typical victim of the passion of courtly love. He tells us himself how he suffers

> With bitter fasts, with penitential groans,
> With nightly tears and daily heartsore sighs.
>   [*The Two Gentlemen of Verona*, II.iv.131-32]

That these groans and sighs survive in Orsino is clear when Olivia asks "How does he love me?" and the messenger replies,

> With adorations, with fertile tears,
> With groans that thunder love, with sighs of fire.
>   [I.v.255-56]

The danger of such a hero is, as Professor Charlton has remarked, that, in fulfilling his conventional role, he may to the quizzical eye seem a fool. Shakespeare guards against this danger by anticipating our ridicule; but his mockery of Valentine and Orsino is quite different in kind. The romantic Valentine is given an unromantic servant who pokes broad fun at his conduct: "to sigh like a schoolboy that has lost his A.B.C.; to weep like a young wench that had buried her grandam; to fast like one that takes diet," and so forth. But Orsino, instead of a servant who laughs at him for loving, has a page who can show him how to do it. "If I did love you in my master's flame," says Cesario, I would

> Make me a willow-cabin at your gate
> And call upon my soul within the house
>   [I.v.268-69]

till all the hills reverberated with the name of the beloved. This famous willow-cabin speech, often praised for its lyricism, is of course no less a parody of romantic love than are Speed's gibes at Valentine. The willow is the emblem of forsaken love and those songs that issue from it in the dead of night apostrophizing the mistress as her lover's "soul"—they are easily recognizable as the traditional love-laments. But the parody, though it has its hint of laughter, is of the kind that does not belittle but transfigures its original. So it comes as no surprise when Olivia, hitherto heedless of sighs and groans, suddenly starts to listen. To the page she says, "*You* might do much," and these words are her first acknowledgement of love's power. Orsino, content to woo by proxy a woman who immures herself in a seven-year mourning for a dead brother, may have the glamor of a knight of romance but he is *not* quite free from the risk of absurdity. He seems, they tell us with some justice, in love not so much with a woman as with his own idea of love. But what they do not so often tell us is how splendid an idea this is. His very groans go beyond Valentine's; they were said, it will have been noticed, to *thunder*, and his sighs were *fire*. If he indulges his own emotions, this is in no mere dilettantism but with the avidity of hunger.

> If music be the *food* of love, play on,
> Give me *excess* of it, that *surfeiting*,
> *The appetite* may sicken and so die.
>   [I.i.1-3]

This wonderful opening speech suggests no doubt the changeableness of human emotion. "Play on . . . that strain again! It had a dying fall. . . . Enough, no more! 'Tis not so sweet now as it was before." But if the spirit of love is as transitory as music and as unstable as the sea, it is also as living and capacious. New waves form as often as waves break; the shapes of fancy, insubstantial as they are, make a splendor in the mind, and renew themselves as quickly as they fade. So Orsino's repeated rejections by his mistress do not throw him into despair. Instead he recognizes, in her equally fantastic devotion, a nature of surpassingly "fine frame" and he reflects on how she *will* love when the throne of her heart shall find its "king." How too will *he* love, we are entitled to infer, when his inexhaustible but as yet deluded fancy shall also find the true sovereign it seeks. This of course it does at the end of the play when he exchanges all his dreams of passion for the love of someone he has come to know. In the play's last line before the final song he is able to greet Viola as "Orsino's mistress and his fancy's queen."

Before this consummation Orsino and Viola have only one big scene together, and in view of all that depends on it it will need to be a powerful one. Again it finds a model in *The Two Gentlemen of Verona*, where already there is a scene in which a man declares his love for one woman in the hearing of another woman who loves *him*. The technique is in each case that of a scene that centers upon a song, which makes a varying impact upon the different characters who hear it. In *The Two Gentlemen of Verona* a song of adoration to a mistress is presented by a faithless lover and is overheard by the woman he has deserted, while her heartbreak goes undetected by her escort, who calmly falls asleep. This is admirably dramatic, but its irony may seem a trifle obvious when set beside the comparable scene in *Twelfth Night*. The song here is one of forsaken love and it is sung to two constant lovers. Most artfully introduced, it is called for by Orsino, whose request for music sustains the role in which he began the play; and the way in which he calls for the song characterizes both him and it before its opening notes are heard. It is to be an old and antique song, belonging to some primitive age, the kind of song chanted by women at their weaving or their knitting in the sun. It will appeal to Orsino in its simple innocence, or, we may say if we wish, by its ideal immunity from fact. So the rational mind can disengage itself from the sentiment in advance, and as soon as the song is ended its effect is counteracted by the jests of the clown who has sung it and the practical necessity of paying him. Yet the sentiment of the song remains to float back and forth over the dialogue which surrounds it as Orsino and Viola tell us of their love. The contrast here is not, as in *The Two Gentlemen of Verona*, between the faithful and the faithless, the heartbroken and the heartwhole. It is between one who is eloquent about an imaginary passion and one who suffers a real grief in concealment. Orsino appropriates the song to himself, yet it is Viola who hears it

> a very echo to the seat
> Where Love is throned.
>
>   [II.iv.21-2]

Orsino is still sending messages to one he calls his "sovereign," but *his* throne, we may say, is still unoccupied. For his splendid fantasies are as yet self-regarding. When Viola objects, "But if she cannot love you, sir?" he dismisses this with "I cannot be so answered." Yet when she simply retorts, "Sooth, but you must," he receives his first instruction in the necessity of accommodating his fantasies to practical realities.

And soon he begins, however unwittingly, to learn. As Viola tells the history of her father's daughter, though he does not see that she is speaking of herself, he finds himself for the first time giving attention to a sorrow not his own. "But died thy sister of her love, my boy?" he asks. To this Viola can only reply, "I know not"; for at this stage in the drama the issue is still in the balance, though Orsino's new absorption in another's plight will provide us with a clue to the outcome. (pp. 75-9)

In the emotional pattern of the play Viola represents a genuineness of feeling against which the illusory can be measured. As the go-between she is of course also at the center of the plot. It is her role to draw Orsino and Olivia from their insubstantial passions and win them to reality. But her impact upon each of them is inevitably different. Orsino, whom she loves but cannot tell her love, responds to her womanly constancy and sentiment; Olivia, whom she cannot love but has to woo, is to be fascinated by her page-boy effrontery and wit.

Now in all the stories of the woman-page who woos for her master and supplants him, the transference of the mistress's affections must be the pivot of the action. In *The Two Gentlemen of Verona*, of course, the lady fails to fall in love with the page at all, which is really a little surprising of her, since she had done so in Shakespeare's source. It is almost as though Shakespeare were reserving this crowning situation, in which the mistress loves the woman-page, for treatment in some later play. At any rate, in *Twelfth Night* he takes care to throw the emphasis upon it from the first. Viola is got into her page-boy clothes before we are halfway through the first act. The plausibility of this, notwithstanding Mrs. Lennox and Dr. Johnson [see excerpts above, 1753 and 1765], is not the question. What matters is that the encounter of the lady and the page, upon which the plot is to turn, shall be momentous. And there is no encounter in Shakespeare, not even that of Hamlet with the ghost, which is more elaborately prepared for. Olivia's situation is referred to in each of the first four scenes before she herself appears in the fifth. . . . All these varied views are insinuated naturally into the dialogue, but their cumulative effect is to give Olivia's situation in the round and to make us curious to see her for ourselves. When after all this she appears, curiosity is not satisfied but intensified; she is not, I think, what we expected. Instead of the veiled lady sprinkling her chamber with tears there enters a mistress commanding her household, and her first words are, "Take the fool away." Equally unexpected is the fool's retort, "Do you not hear, fellows? Take away the lady." This great dame is called a fool by one of her own attendants, who then goes on to prove it:

> *Clown.* Good madonna, why mourn'st thou?
> *Olivia.* Good fool, for my brother's death.
> *Clown.* I think his soul is in hell, madonna.
> *Olivia.* I know his soul is in heaven, fool.
> *Clown.* The more fool, madonna, to mourn for
>   your brother's soul being in heaven.
>   Take away the fool, gentlemen.
>   [I.v.65-72]

Now this is excellent fooling, but Shakespeare's incidental gaieties have a way of illuminating important matters and our conception of Olivia is one of them. It is only a fool who calls her a fool, but, as the fool himself has suggested, a fool "may pass for a wise man," while those who think they have wit "do very oft prove fools." The question of Olivia's folly remains open. It is kept alive below the surface of the quipping dialogue which entertains us while Olivia defends the fool and

is thanked by the fool in characteristically equivocal terms. "Thou hast spoke for us, madonna, as if thy eldest son should be a fool." One could hardly say more than that. Yet the suggestion that her eldest son might be a fool is at best a left-handed compliment. The fool is quick to right it with a prayer that Jove may cram his skull with brains, but it seems that Jove's intervention may be necessary, for—as Sir Toby enters—"one of thy kin has a most weak pia mater." The chances of brains or folly in the skull of any son of Olivia seem then to be about equal. But what is surely most remarkable is the notion of Olivia's ever having a son at all. We have been made to associate her not with birth but death. The weeping cloistress, as Orsino's gentleman put it, was seasoning a "dead love," and what plagued Sir Toby about this was that care was "an enemy to life." Yet the fool seems to see her as available for motherhood. The remarks of a fool—again—strike as deep as you choose to let them—that is the dramatic use of fools—but Olivia interests us more and more.

By now the page is at the gate. Indeed three different messengers announce him. Sir Toby of the weak pia mater is too drunk to do more than keep us in suspense, but Malvolio precisely catalogues the young man's strange behavior, till we are as curious to see him as is Olivia herself. "Tell him he shall not speak with me," she has insisted; but when this changes to "Let him approach," the first of her defences is down. Our interest in each of them is now at such a height that the moment of their meeting cannot fail to be electric.

How different all this is from what happened in *The Two Gentlemen of Verona*, where only a single soliloquy prepared us before the page and Sylvia just came together pat. But it is interesting to see how the seeds strewn in the earlier play now germinate in Shakespeare's mature inventiveness. When the page came upon Sylvia, he did not know who she was and actually asked her to direct him to herself. This confusion gave a momentary amusement and the dramatic importance of the encounter was faintly underlined. But as Sylvia at once disclosed her identity, this little gambit came to nothing. In *Twelfth Night*, however, Cesario only pretends not to recognize Olivia so as to confound her with his raillery. "Most radiant, exquisite and unmatchable beauty," he begins and then breaks off to enquire whether the lady before him is the radiant unmatchable or not. As he has never seen her, how can he possibly tell? This opens up a brilliant series of exchanges in the course of which the familiar moves of the conventional courtship are all similarly transformed. In *The Two Gentlemen of Verona* Proteus was simply following the usual pattern of suitors when he instructed the page,

> Give her that ring and therewithal
> This letter . . . Tell my lady
> I claim the promise for her heavenly picture.
>   [*The Two Gentlemen of Verona*, IV.iv.85-7]

To be fair, even in this early play the conventional properties, the ring, the letter, and the picture, each made a dramatic point: for Sylvia recognized the ring as that of her rival and so refused to accept it, while she tore the letter up; and if she compliantly handed over her portrait, she was careful to add the comment that a picture was only a shadow and might appropriately be given for a fickle lover to worship. But in *Twelfth Night* the letter, the picture, and the ring are changed almost out of recognition. Shakespeare's superbly original invention allows Orsino to dispense with them; yet they are all vestigially present. Instead of bearing missives, the page is given the task of acting out his master's woes, and so instead of the lover's own letter we are to have the page's speech. This cunningly diverts attention from the message to the messenger, and the effect is still further enhanced when even the speech never gets delivered apart from its opening words. Instead there is talk about the speech—how "excellently well penn'd," how "poetical" it is—and are you really the right lady so that I may not waste the praise I have taken such pains to compose? Olivia in turn delights us by matching Cesario's mockery, but as we watch them finesse about how and even whether the speech shall be delivered, their mocking dialogue says more than any formal speech could say. In fact the very circumventing of the speech brings them to the heart of its forbidden theme. And so we come to the picture. There is of course no picture, any more than there was a letter; but the convention whereby the lover asks for a picture of his mistress is made to provide a metaphor through which the witty duel may proceed. Olivia draws back the curtain and reveals a picture, they talk of the colors that the artist's "cunning hand laid on," and Cesario asks for a copy. But the curtain Olivia draws back is her own veil, the artist is Nature, and the copy of Nature's handiwork will come as the fruit of marriage. Again the suggestion that Olivia could have a child. The cloistress who dedicates herself to the dead is reminded of the claims of life. She waves them aside for the moment by deftly changing the application of the metaphor. Certainly there shall be a copy of her beauty; why not an inventory of its items? As she catalogues them—"two lips, indifferent red . . . two grey eyes, with lids to them"—she ridicules the wooer's praises; but at the same time, it may not be too much to suggest, she robs her womanhood of its incipient animation. Yet the cloistress has removed her veil and presently there is the ring. Orsino again sent no ring, but that need not prevent Olivia from returning it. And with this ruse the ring no less than the picture takes on a new significance. By means of it Olivia rejects Orsino's love but at the same time declares her own. And as Malvolio flings the ring upon the stage it makes its little dramatic *éclat*.

Shakespeare's portrait of Olivia has usually, I think, been underrated. The critics who used to talk about Shakespeare's heroines fell in love with Viola, and actresses have naturally preferred the bravura of her essentially easier role. Besides there is the risk of the ridiculous about a woman who mistakenly loves one of her own sex. But the delicacy of Shakespeare's handling, once more in contrast with that of his predecessors, steers the situation right away from farce and contrives to show, through her potentially absurd and undisguisedly pathetic plight, the gradual awakening of that noble nature which Orsino detected from the first. . . . [Is] there not the suggestion that when Olivia ceases to mourn the dead and gives herself to the pursuit of the living, she has advanced some small way towards wisdom?

There is one character in the play who, unlike Olivia and Orsino, is unable to make this journey. And that brings me to the subplot. For it will already be apparent that I do not agree with a recent paper in the *Shakespeare Quarterly* which makes Malvolio the central figure of the play [see excerpt above by Milton Crane, 1955]. The mistake is not a new one. The record of a court performance in the year of the First Folio actually calls the play *Malvolio* and there are other seventeenth-century references, beginning with Manningham in 1602 [see excerpt above], which go to show that the sublime swagger with which Malvolio walks into the box-hedge trap to emerge in yellow stockings was largely responsible, then as now, for the play's theatrical popularity. The distortion of emphasis this implies is a tribute to Shakespeare's invention of the most novel sit-

uation in the play, but if I venture to suggest that it does no great credit to his audience, no doubt some one will rise up like Sir Toby and ask me, "Dost thou think because thou art virtuous there shall be no more cakes and ale?" All I think is that the cake-and-ale jollifications are very jolly indeed so long as they stay, whether in criticism or performance, within the bounds of a subplot, which the whole technique of the dramatic exposition marks them out to be. These more hilarious goings-on make an admirable counterweight to the more fragile wit and sentiment of which the main plot is woven; but attention is firmly directed to the love story of Orsino, Olivia, and Viola before Sir Toby and Malvolio are heard of, and the courtships are well in progress by the time we come to the midnight caterwaulings. So the love-delusions of Malvolio, brilliant as they are, fall into perspective as a parody of the more delicate aberrations of his mistress and her suitor. Like them Malvolio aspires towards an illusory ideal of love, but his mistake is a grosser one than theirs, his posturings more extravagant and grotesque. So *his* illusion enlarges the suggestions of the main plot about the mind's capacity for self-deception and if, as Lamb maintained, it gives Malvolio a glory such as no mere reason can attain to [see excerpt above, 1822], still "lunacy" was one of Lamb's words for it and it is to the madman's dungeon that it leads.

Malvolio's fate, like Falstaff's, has been much resented by the critics. But drama, as Aristotle indicated and Shakespeare evidently perceived, is not quite the same as life, and punishments that in life would seem excessive have their place in the more ideal world of art. In the ethical scheme of comedy, it may be the doom of those who cannot correct themselves to be imprisoned or suppressed. Olivia and Prince Hal, within their vastly different realms, have shown themselves capable of learning, as Malvolio and Falstaff have not.

The comparison between Olivia and Malvolio is one that the play specifically invites. He is the trusted steward of her household, and he suits her, she says, by being "sad and civil." This reminds us that it was with her authority that he descended on the midnight revels to quell that "uncivil rule." Have you no manners, he demands of Sir Toby and his crew; and his rebuke is one that Olivia herself will echo later when she calls Sir Toby a barbarian fit to dwell in "caves Where manners ne'er were preached." But if Olivia and Malvolio are united in seeking to impose an ordered regimen on these unruly elements, that does not mean, though I have found it said, that they share a doctrine of austerity [see excerpt above by M. P. Tilley, 1914]. Indeed the resemblance between them serves to bring out a distinction that is fundamental to the play. It is clearly marked for us on their first appearance. Significantly enough, they are brought on the stage together and placed in the same situation, as if to attract our attention to their contrasting reactions. The first remark of each of them is one of dissatisfaction with the fool, and the fool's retaliation is first to prove Olivia a fool and then to call Malvolio one. But Olivia is amused and Malvolio is not. "I marvel your ladyship takes delight in such a barren rascal." What Olivia delights in, Malvolio finds barren. "Doth he not mend?" she says, suggesting that the fool is getting wittier. But Malvolio rejoins, Yes, he is mending by becoming a more perfect fool—"and shall do till the pangs of death shake him." Olivia too has given her thoughts to death, but whereas she mourns the dead, prettily if absurdly, Malvolio threatens the living in words which betray a cruel relish. This is his first speech in the play and it carries a corresponding emphasis. There are already signs that Olivia may be won from death to life, but the spirit of Malvolio can only be destructive. (pp. 79-84)

As the action proceeds, Olivia opens her heart to the new love that is being born within her, but Malvolio is only confirmed in that sickness of self-love of which she has accused him. At the height of his love-dream, his imaginings are all of his own advancement—"sitting in my state," "in my branched velvet gown," "calling my officers about me" as I "wind up my watch or play with my—some rich jewel." When he showed resentment at the fool, Olivia reproached Malvolio for his lack of generosity and now his very words freeze every generous impulse—"I frown the while," "quenching my familiar smile with an austere regard of control." This is not the language of Olivia. She speaks of the impossibility of quenching those natural feelings which rise up within her, and which we are made to recognize even in the comicality of her predicament:

Cesario, by the roses of the spring,
By maidhood, honour, truth and everything,
I love thee so that maugre all thy pride,
No wit nor reason can my passion hide.
[III.i.149-52]

So Olivia, notwithstanding her mistakes, is allowed to find a husband while Malvolio is shut up in the dark.

The ironic fitness of Malvolio's downfall is dramatically underscored in every detail of his situation. When he dreamed of his own greatness he pictured Sir Toby coming to him with a curtsey and he told Sir Toby to amend his drunkenness: it is now his bitterest complaint that this drunken cousin has been given rule over him. When he rebuked the tipsy revellers, he began, "My masters, are you mad?" and their revenge upon him is to make it seem that he is mad himself. Particularly instructive is the leading part taken in his torment by the fool he began the play by spurning. The fool taunts him in the darkness of the dungeon and he begs the fool to help him to some light. It is to the fool that the man contemptuous of fools is now made to plead his own sanity. But his insistence on his sanity—"I am as well in my wits, fool, as thou art"—leaves the matter in some ambiguity, as the fool very promptly retorts: "Then you are mad indeed, if you be no better in your wits than a fool." And Malvolio ends the play as he began by being called a fool. And if at first it was only the fool who called him so, now it is his mistress herself. Even as she pities him for the trick that has been played on him, "Alas, poor fool" are the words that Shakespeare puts into her mouth.

What then is folly and what wisdom, the comedy seems to ask. The question first appeared in that early cross-talk with the fool which brought Olivia into contrast with Malvolio even while we were awaiting her reception of Cesario. So that the manner in which Malvolio's story is begun clearly puts it into relation with the main plot of the wooing. And of course it is only appropriate that scenes of romantic love should be surrounded by a comic dialogue which gaily tosses off its hints about whether these characters are fools. For the pursuit of the ideal life is not quite compatible with reason. And, as another of Shakespeare's comedies puts it, those who in imagination see more than "reason ever comprehends" are the lover, the poet, and the lunatic. So where does the noble vision end and the madman's dream begin? The greatness and the folly that lie in the mind of man are inextricably entangled and the characters in *Twelfth Night* have each their share of both. Malvolio's moment of lunacy may be, as Lamb suggests, the moment of his glory. Yet Malvolio, so scornful of the follies of others,

would persuade us that his own are sane. His sanity is indeed established, but only to leave us wondering whether sanity may not sometimes be the greater folly. What the comedy *may* suggest is that he who in his egotism seeks to fit the world to the procrustean bed of his own reason deserves his own discomfiture. But Olivia, who self-confessedly abandons reason, and Orsino, who avidly gives his mind to all the shapes of fancy, are permitted to pass through whatever folly there may be in this to a greater illumination. Although what they sought has inevitably eluded them, it has nevertheless been vouchsafed to them in another form.

Yet is is the art of Shakespeare's comedy, and perhaps also its wisdom, to make no final judgments. The spirit of the piece, after all, is that of Twelfth Night and it is in the ideal world of Twelfth Night that Malvolio may be justly punished. Perhaps we should also remember, as even the Twelfth Night lovers do, to pause, if only for a moment, to recognize his precisian virtues. Olivia agrees with him that he has been "notoriously abused" and the poet-lover Orsino sends after him to "entreat him to a peace," before they finally enter into the happiness to which "golden time" will summon them. "Golden time"— the epithet is characteristically Orsino's. It is only the wise fool who stays to sing to us about the rain that raineth every day. (pp. 85-7)

> Harold Jenkins, "Shakespeare's 'Twelfth Night'," in Shakespeare, the Comedies: A Collection of Critical Essays, *edited by Kenneth Muir, Prentice-Hall, Inc., 1965, pp. 72-87.*

JOHN HOLLANDER (essay date 1959)

[*Hollander here develops his theory on the concepts of appetite and satiety in* Twelfth Night, *which he had briefly outlined in his earlier essay on music in the play (see excerpt above, 1956). He concludes that* Twelfth Night *is a moral comedy distinct from a Jonsonian humour comedy in its fully dramatized metaphors of feasting and satiety. According to Hollander, the moral nature of* Twelfth Night *can be approached through Malvolio, and he further asserts that Charles Lamb (1822) missed the point: Malvolio is presented not as part of a group of bourgeois usurpers, but rather as "a case of indigestion due to self-love, the result of a perverted, rather than an excessive appetite." The theme of appetite in* Twelfth Night *is also discussed by Morris P. Tilley (1914) and S. Nagarajan (1959).*]

To say that a play is "moral" would seem to imply that it represents an action which concretizes certain ethical elements of human experience, without actually moralizing at any point, and without having any of the characters in it state univocally a dogma, precept, or value that would coincide completely with the play's own moral intention. It was just this univocal didacticism, however, which characterized what was becoming in 1600 a prevailing comic tradition. The moral intent of the Jonsonian "comedy of humours" was direct and didactic; its purpose was to show

the times deformitie
Anatomiz'd in euery nerue and sinnew
With constant courage, and contempt of feare.

For moral purposes, a humour is an identifying emblem of a man's moral nature, graven ineradicably onto his physiological one. In the world of a play, a humour could be caricatured to

Act III. Scene iv. Sir Andrew Aguecheek, Sir Toby Belch, Viola. By H. Hoffman (n.d.). From the Art Collection of the Folger Shakespeare Library.

such a degree that it would practically predestine a character's behavior. It was made to

> . . . so possess a man, that it doth draw
> All his affects, his spirits and his powers,
> In their confluctions, all to runne one way,
> This may be truly said to be a Humour.
>
> (p. 220)

Now *Every Man In His Humour* was first acted in 1598, and it is known that Shakespeare appeared in it. He seems in *Twelfth Night* (for which I accept the traditional date of 1600-1601) to have attempted to write a kind of moral comedy diametrically opposed to that of Jonson, in which "the times deformitie" was not to be "anatomiz'd," but represented in the core of an action. For a static and deterministic Humour, Shakespeare substituted a kinetic, governing Appetite in the action, rather than in the bowels, of his major characters. In his plot and language, he insists continually on the fact and importance of the substitution. Characters in a comedy of humours tend to become caricatures, and caricatures tend to become beasts, inhuman personifications of moral distortions that are identified with physiological ones. I believe that it was Shakespeare's intention in *Twelfth Night* to obviate the necessity of this dehumanization by substituting what one might call a moral process for a moral system. While it is true that the play contains quite a bit of interesting discussion of humours as such, and

that there is some correspondence between appetites and humours, it is equally true that the only person in the play who believes in the validity of humourous classifications, who, indeed, lives by them, is himself a moral invalid. . . . [The] primary effective difference between Shakespeare's and Jonson's techniques in making moral comedy is the difference between what is merely a display of anatomy, and a dramatization of a metaphor, the difference between a Pageant and an Action.

The Action of *Twelfth Night* is indeed that of a Revels, a suspension of mundane affairs during a brief epoch in a temporary world of indulgence, a land full of food, drink, love, play, disguise and music. But parties end, and the reveller eventually becomes satiated and drops heavily into his worldly self again. The fact that plays were categorized as "revells" for institutional purposes may have appealed to Shakespeare; he seems at any rate to have analyzed the dramatic and moral nature of feasting, and to have made it the subject of his play. His analysis is schematized in Orsino's opening speech.

The essential action of a revels is: To so surfeit the Appetite upon excess that it "may sicken and so die". It is the Appetite, not the whole Self, however, which is surfeited: the Self will emerge at the conclusion of the action from where it has been hidden. The movement of the play is toward this emergence of humanity from behind a mask of comic type.

Act I, Scene 1, is very important as a statement of the nature of this movement. Orsino's opening line contains the play's three dominant images:

> If music be the food of love, play on.
> Give me excess of it, that, surfeiting,
> The appetite may sicken, and so die. . . .
>
> [I.i.1-3]

Love, eating, and music are the components of the revelry, then. And in order that there be no mistake about the meaning of the action, we get a miniature rehearsal of it following immediately:

> That strain again! It had a dying fall.
> Oh, it came o'er my ear like the sweet sound
> That breathes upon a bank of violets
> Stealing and giving odor! Enough, no more.
> 'Tis not so sweet now as it was before.
> O spirit of love, how quick and fresh art thou!
> That, notwithstanding thy capacity
> Receiveth as the sea, naught enters there,
> Of what validity and pitch soe'er,
> But falls into abatement and low price,
> Even in a minute! So full of shapes is fancy
> That it alone is high fantastical. . . .
>
> [I.i.4-15]

A bit of surfeiting is actually accomplished here; what we are getting is a proem to the whole play, and a brief treatment of love as an appetite. The substance of a feast will always fall into "abatement and low price" at the conclusion of the feasting, for no appetite remains to demand it. We also think of Viola in connection with the "violets / Stealing and giving odor," for her actual position as go-between-turned-lover is one of both inadvertent thief and giver. The Duke's rhetoric is all-embracing, however, and he immediately comments significantly upon his own condition.

> Oh, when mine eyes did see Olivia first,
> Methought she purged the air of pestilence!
> That instant was I turned into a hart,
> And my desires, like fell and cruel hounds,
> E'er since pursue me. . . .
>
> [I.i.18-22]

Like Actaeon, he is the hunter hunted; the active desirer pursued by his own desires. As embodying this overpowering appetite for romantic love, he serves as a host of the revels.

The other host is Olivia, the subject of his desire. We see almost at once that her self-indulgence is almost too big to be encompassed by Orsino's. . . . "To season a brother's dead love": she is gorging herself on this fragrant herb, and though she has denied herself the world, she is no true anchorite, but, despite herself, a private glutton. The Duke looks forward to the end of her feast of grief,

> . . . when liver, brain, and heart,
> These sovereign thrones, are all supplied, and filled
> Her sweet perfections with one self king! . . .
>
> [I.i.36-8]

The trinitarian overtone is no blasphemy, but a statement of the play's teleology. When everyone is supplied with "one self king", the action will have been completed.

The first three scenes of the play stand together as a general prologue, in which the major characters are introduced and their active natures noted. Viola is juxtaposed to Olivia here;

she is not one to drown her own life in a travesty of mourning. It is true that she is tempted to "serve that lady" (as indeed she does, in a different way). But her end in so doing would be the whole play's action in microcosm; the immersion in committed self-indulgence would result in the revelation of herself:

> And might not be delivered to the world
> Till I had made mine own occasion mellow,
> What my estate is.   [I.ii.42-4]

She will serve the Duke instead, and use her persuasive talents to accomplish the ends to which his own self-celebrating rhetoric can provide no access. "I can sing," she says, "and speak to him in many sorts of music." Her sense of his character has been verified; the Captain tells her that his name is as his nature. And "what is his name?" she asks. "Orsino," answers the Captain. Orsino—the bear, the ravenous and clumsy devourer. Her own name suggests active, affective music; and the mention of Arion, the Orpheus-like enchanter of waves and dolphins with his music, points up the connotation. Orsino's "music," on the other hand, is a static well of emotion in which he allows his own rhetoric to submerge; Viola's is more essentially instrumental, effective, and convincing.

The third scene of Act I completes the prologue by further equating the moral and the physiological. Here we first encounter the world of what Malvolio calls "Sir Toby and the lighter people" (it is indeed true that there is none of Malvolio's element of "earth" in them). The continued joking about *dryness* that pervades the wit here in Olivia's house, both above and below stairs, is introduced here, in contrast to Olivia's floods of welling and self-indulgent tears. The idea behind the joking in this and the following scenes is that drinking and merriment will moisten and fulfill a dry nature. As Feste says later on, "Give the dry fool drink, then the fool is not dry." Toby's sanguine temperament and Aguecheek's somewhat phlegmatic one are here unveiled. They are never identified as such, however; and none of the wit that is turned on the associations of "humours," "elements" and "waters," though it runs throughout the play, ever refers to a motivating order in the universe, except insofar as Malvolio believes in it.

What is most important is that neither Feste, the feaster embodying not the spirit but the action of revelry, nor Malvolio, the ill-wisher (and the *bad appetite* as well), his polar opposite, appears in these introductory scenes. It is only upstairs in Olivia's house (I.v) that the action as such commences. The revels opens with Feste's exchange with Maria in which she attempts three times to insist on innocent interpretations of "well-hanged" and "points." But Feste is resolute in his ribaldry. Thus Olivia, momentarily voicing Malvolio's invariable position, calls Feste a "dry fool," and "dishonest"; Malvolio himself refers to him as a "barren rascal." From here on in it will be Feste who dances attendance on the revelry, singing, matching wit with Viola, and being paid by almost everyone for his presence. To a certain degree he remains outside the action, not participating in it because he represents its very nature; occasionally serving as a comic angel or messenger, he is nevertheless unmotivated by any appetite, and is never sated of his fooling. His insights into the action are continuous, and his every remark is telling. "*Cucullus non facit monachum.* That's as much as to say I wear not motley in my brain." Indeed, he does not, but more important is the fact that his robe and beard are not to make him a *real* priest later on. And neither he as Sir Thopas, nor Olivia as a "cloistress," nor Malvolio in his black suit of travestied virtue, nor the transvestite Viola is what he appears to be. No one will be revealed in his true dress until he has doffed his mask of feasting. (pp. 221-26)

Every character in the play, however, is granted some degree of insight into the nature of the others. It is almost as if everyone were masked with the black side of his vizard turned inwards; he sees more clearly past the *persona* of another than he can past his own. (p. 227)

Olivia's retort to Malvolio in [I.v.]: "O you are sick of self-love, Malvolio, and taste with a distempered appetite" . . . provides the key to his physiological-moral nature. "Sick of self-love" means "sick with a moral infection called self-love," but it can also mean "already surfeited, or fed up with your own ego as an object of appetite." Malvolio's "distempered appetite" results from the fact that he alone is not possessed of a craving directed outward, towards some object on which it can surfeit and die; he alone cannot morally benefit from a period of self-indulgence. Actually this distemper manifests itself in terms of transitory desires on his part for status and for virtue, but these desires consume him in their fruitlessness; he is aware of the nature of neither of them. This is a brilliant analysis of the character of a melancholic, and Shakespeare's association of the melancholy, puritanic and status-seeking characters in Malvolio throws considerable light on all of them. The moral nature of the plot of *Twelfth Night* can be easily approached through the character of Malvolio, and this, I think, is what Lamb and his followers missed completely in their egalitarian sympathy for his being no "more than steward" [see excerpt above, 1822]. For Malvolio's attachment to self-advancement is not being either aristocratically ridiculed or praised as an example of righteous bourgeois opposition to medieval hierarchies. In the context of the play's moral physiology, his disease is shown forth as a case of indigestion due to his self-love, the result of a perverted, rather than an excessive appetite. In the world of feasting, the values of the commercial society outside the walls of the party go topsy-turvy: Feste is given money for making verbal fools of the donors thereof; everyone's desire is fulfilled in an unexpected way; and revellers are shown to rise through realms of unreality, disguise and luxurious self-deception. We are seduced, by the revelling, away from seeing the malice in the plot to undo Malvolio. But whatever malice there is remains peculiarly just. It is only Malvolio who bears any ill-will, and only he upon whom ill-will can appear to be directed. He makes for himself a hell of the worldly heaven of festivity, and when Toby and Maria put him into darkness, into a counterfeit-hell, they are merely representing in play a condition that he has already achieved.

The plot against Malvolio, then, is no more than an attempt to let him surfeit on himself, to present him with those self-centered, "time-pleasing" objects upon which his appetite is fixed. In essence, he is led to a feast in which his own vision of himself is spread before him, and commanded to eat it. The puritan concern with witchcraft and the satanic, and its associations of them with madness are carried to a logical extreme; and once Malvolio has been permitted to indulge in his self-interest by means of the letter episode, he is only treated as he would himself treat anyone whom he believed to be mad. (pp. 227-29)

It is interesting to notice how carefully Shakespeare analyzed another characteristic of the melancholic in his treatment of Malvolio. L. C. Knights has suggested [in his *Drama and Society in the Age of Jonson*] that the vogue of melancholy at the turn of the 17th century was occasioned to some degree by

the actual presence in England of a large number of *"intellectuels en chômage"* (in Denis de Rougement's words), unemployed, university-trained men whose humanistic education had not fitted them for any suitable role in society. Malvolio is no patent and transparent university intellectual (like Holofernes, for example). He contrives, however, to over-rationalize his point (where the Duke will over-sentimentalize it) on almost every occasion. Even his first introduction of Viola, as has been seen before, is archly over-reasoned. His venture into exegesis of a text is almost telling.

It is not merely self-interest, I think, that colors the scrutiny of Maria's letter. His reading is indeed a close one: he observes that, after the first snatch of doggerel, "The numbers altered." But Malvolio is incapable of playing the party-game and guessing the riddle. Of "M, O, A, I doth sway my life," he can only say "And yet, to crush this a little it would bow to me, for every one of these letters are in my name." He even avoids the reading that should, by all rights, appeal to him: Leslie Hotson [in his *The First Night of "Twelfth Night"* (see Additional Bibliography)] has suggested that "M, O, A, I" probably stands for *Mare, Orbis, Aer* and *Ignis,* the four elements to which Malvolio so often refers. Malvolio himself fails as a critic, following a "cold scent" that, as Fabian indicates, is "as rank as a fox" for him in that it tantalizes his ambition. (p. 229)

The prank played on Malvolio is not merely an "interwoven" second story, but a fully-developed double-plot. Like the Belmont episodes in *The Merchant of Venice,* it is a condensed representation of the action of the entire play. In *Twelfth Night,* however, it operates in reverse, to show the other side of the coin, as it were. For Malvolio there can be no fulfillment in "one self king". His story effectively and ironically underlines the progress toward this fulfillment in everybody else, and helps to delineate the limitations of the moral domain of the whole play. In contrast to Feste, who appears in the action at times as an abstracted spirit of revelry, Malvolio is a model of the sinner.

The whole play abounds in such contrasts and parallels of character, and the players form and regroup continually with respect to these, much in the manner of changing of figurations in a suite of brambles. Viola herself indulges in the festivities in a most delicate and (literally) charming way. She is almost too good a musician, too effective an Orpheus: "Heaven forbid my outside have not charmed her," she complains after her first encounter with Olivia. But as soon as she realizes that she is part of the game, she commits herself to it with redoubled force. If her "outside" is directed towards Olivia, her real identity and her own will are concentrated even more strongly on Orsino. In the most ironic of the love-scenes, she all but supplants Olivia in the Duke's affections. Orsino, glutting himself on his own version of romantic love, allows himself to make the most extravagant and self-deceptive statements about it:

> Come hither, boy. If ever thou shalt love,
> In the sweet pangs of it remember me;
> For such as I am all true lovers are,
> Unstaid and skittish in all motions else
> Save in the constant image of the creature
> That is beloved. . . .   [II.iv.15-20]

This skittishness, beneath the mask of the ravenous and constant bear, is obvious to Feste, at least: "Now, the melancholy god protect thee, and the tailor make thy doublet of changeable taffeta, for thy mind is a very opal. I would have men of such constancy put to sea, that their business might be everything and their intent everywhere; for that's it that always makes a good voyage of nothing." (pp. 230-31)

Orsino also gives us a curious version of the physiology of the passions on which the plot is based; it is only relatively accurate, of course, for he will be the last of the revellers to feel stuffed, to push away from him his heaping dish.

> There is no woman's sides
> Can bide the beating of so strong a passion
> As love doth give my heart, no woman's heart
> So big to hold so much. They lack retention.
> Alas, their love may be called appetite—
> No motion of the liver, but the palate—
> They suffer surfeit, cloyment and revolt.
> But mine is all as hungry as the sea
> And can digest as much.   [II.iv.93-101]
>   (pp. 231-32)

Viola has been giving him her "inside" throughout the scene, and were he not still ravenous for Olivia's love he could see her for what she is: a woman with a constancy in love (for himself and her brother) that he can only imagine himself to possess. She is indeed an Allegory of Patience on some baroque tomb at this point. She is ironically distinguished from Olivia in that her "smiling at grief" is a disguising "outside" for her real sorrow, whereas Olivia's is a real self-indulgent pleasure taken at a grief outworn. It is as if Olivia had misread Scripture and taken the letter of "Blessed are they that mourn" for the spirit of it. Her grief is purely ceremonial.

The "lighter people," too, are engaged in carrying out the action in their own way, and they have more business in the play than merely to make a gull of Malvolio. Toby's huge stomach for food and drink parallels the Duke's ravenous capacity for sentiment. The drinking scene is in one sense the heart of the play. It starts out by declaring itself in no uncertain terms. "Does not our life consist of the four elements?" catechizes Sir Toby. "Faith, so they say," replies Andrew, "but I think it rather consists of eating and drinking." No one but Feste, perhaps, really knows the extent to which this is true, for Andrew is actually saying "We are not merely comic types, mind you, being manipulated by a dramatist of the humours. The essence of our lives lies in a movement from hunger to satiety that we share with all of nature."

When Toby and Andrew cry out for a love song, Feste obliges them, not with the raucous and bawdy thing that one would expect, but instead, with a direct appeal to their actual hostess, Olivia. This is all the more remarkable in that it is made on behalf of everyone in the play. "O Mistress Mine" undercuts the Duke's overwhelming but ineffectual mouthings, Viola's effective but necessarily misdirected charming, and, of course, Aguecheek's absolute incompetence as a suitor. The argument is couched in purely naturalistic terms: "This feast will have to end, and so will all of our lives. You are not getting younger ('sweet and twenty' is the contemporaneous equivalent of 'sweet and thirty,' at least). Give up this inconstant roaming; your little game had better end in your marriage, anyway." The true love "That can sing both high and low" is Viola-Sebastian, the master-mistress of Orsino's and Olivia's passion. (Sebastian has just been introduced in the previous scene, and there are overtones here of his being invoked as Olivia's husband.) Sebastian has, aside from a certain decorative but benign courtly manner, no real identity apart from Viola. He is the

fulfillment of her longing (for she has thought him dead) and the transformation into reality of the part she is playing in the *ludus amoris*. The prognostication is borne out by Sebastian's own remark: "You are betrothed both to a man and maid." He is himself characterized by an elegance hardly virile; and, finally, we must keep in mind the fact that Viola was played by a boy actor to begin with, and that Shakespeare's audience seemed to be always ready for an intricate irony of this kind.

But if Viola and Sebastian are really the same, "One face, one voice, one habit, and two persons, A natural perspective that is and is not," there is an interesting parallel between Viola and Aguecheek as well. Both are suitors for Olivia's hand: Andrew, ineffectively, for himself; Viola for Orsino, and (effectively) for Sebastian. Their confrontation in the arranged duel is all the more ironic in that Andrew is an effective pawn in Toby's game (Toby is swindling him), whereas Viola is an ineffective one in the Duke's (she is swindling him of Olivia's love).

Feste's other songs differ radically from "O Mistress Mine." He sings for the Duke a kind of languorous ayre, similar to so many that one finds in the songbooks. It is aimed at Orsino in the very extravagance of its complaint. It is his own song, really, if we imagine him suddenly dying of love, being just as ceremoniously elaborate in his funeral instructions as he has been in his suit of Olivia. (pp. 232-34)

If Feste's purpose is to serve as a symbol of the revels, however, he must also take a clear and necessary part in the all-important conclusion. *Twelfth Night* itself, the feast of the Epiphany, celebrates the discovery of the "True King" in the manger by the Wise Men. "Those wits," says Feste in Act I, Scene 5 "that think they have thee [wit] do very oft prove fools, and I that am sure I lack thee may pass for a wise man." And so it is that under his influence the true Caesario, the "one self king," is revealed. The whole of Act V might be taken, in connection with "the plot" in a trivial sense, to be the other *epiphany,* the perception that follows the *anagnorisis* or discovery of classic dramaturgy. But we have been dealing with the Action of *Twelfth Night* as representing the killing off of excessive appetite through indulgence of it, leading to the rebirth of the unencumbered self. The long final scene, then, serves to show forth the Caesario-King, and to unmask, discover and reveal the fulfilled selves in the major characters.

The appearance of the priest (a real one, this time) serves more than the simple purpose of proving the existence of a marriage between Olivia and "Caesario." It is a simple but firm intrusion into the world of the play of a way of life that has remained outside of it so far. The straightforward solemnity of the priest's rhetoric is also something new; suggestions of its undivided purpose have appeared before only in Antonio's speeches. The priest declares that Olivia and her husband have been properly married:

> And all the ceremony of this compact
> Sealed in my function, by my testimony.
> Since when, my watch hath told me, toward my grave
> I have travelled but two hours. . . .
>   [V.i.160-63]

It is possible that the original performances had actually taken about two hours to reach this point. At any rate, the sombre acknowledgment of the passage of time in a real world is there. Antonio has prepared the way earlier in the scene; his straightforward confusion is that of the unwitting intruder in a masquerade who has been accused of mistaking the identities of two of the masquers.

That the surfeiting has gradually begun to occur, however, has become evident earlier. In the prison scene, Sir Toby has already begun to tire: "I would we were well rid of this knavery." He gives as his excuse for this the fact that he is already in enough trouble with Olivia, but such as this has not deterred him in the past. And, in the last scene, very drunk as he must be, he replies to Orsino's inquiry as to his condition that he hates the surgeon, "a drunken rogue." Self-knowledge has touched Sir Toby. He could not have said this earlier.

As the scene plays itself out, Malvolio alone is left unaccounted for. There is no accounting for him here, though; he remains a bad taste in the mouth. "Alas poor fool," says Olivia, "How have they baffled thee!" And thus, in Feste's words, "the whirligig of time brings in his revenges." Malvolio has become the fool, the "barren rascal." . . . His business has never been with the feasting to begin with, and now that it is over, and the revellers normalized, he is revealed as the true madman. He is "The Madly-Used Malvolio" to the additional degree that his own uses have been madness.

For Orsino and Viola the end has also arrived. She will be "Orsino's mistress and his fancy's queen." He has been surfeited of his misdirected voracity; the rich golden shaft, in his own words, "hath killed the flock of all affections else" that live in him. "Liver, brain and heart" are indeed all supplied; for both Olivia and himself, there has been fulfillment in "one self king." And, lest there be no mistake, each is to be married to a Caesario or king. Again, "Liver, brain and heart" seems to encompass everybody: Toby and Maria are married, Aguecheek chastened, etc.

At the end of the scene, all exit. Only Feste, the pure fact of feasting, remains. His final song is a summation of the play in many ways at once. Its formal structure seems to be a kind of quick rehearsal of the Ages of Man. In youth, "A foolish thing was but a toy": the fool's bauble, emblematic of both his *membrum virile* and his trickery, is a trivial fancy. But in "man's estate," the bauble represents a threat of knavery and thievery to respectable society, who shuts its owner out of doors. The "swaggering" and incessant drunkenness of the following strophes bring Man into prime and dotage, respectively. Lechery, trickery, dissembling and drunkenness, inevitable and desperate in mundane existence, however, are just those activities which, mingled together in a world of feasting, serve to purge Man of the desire for them. The wind and the rain accompany him throughout his life, keeping him indoors with "dreams and imaginations" as a boy, pounding and drenching him unmercifully, when he is locked out of doors, remaining eternal and inevitable throughout his pride in desiring to perpetuate himself. The wind and the rain are the most desperate of elements, that pound the walls and batter the roof of the warm house that shuts them out, while, inside it, the revels are in progress. Only after the party is ended can Man face them without desperation.

It is the metaphor of the rain that lasts longest, though, and it recapitulates the images of water, elements and humours that have pervaded the entire play. Feste himself, who tires of nothing, addresses Viola: "Who you are and what you would are out of my welkin—I might say 'element' but the word is overworn." He adroitly comments on Malvolio's line "Go to; I am not of your element" by substituting a Saxon word for a Latin one. The additional association of the four elements

with the humours cannot be overlooked. It is only Malvolio, of course, who uses the word "humour" with any seriousness: "And then to have the humour of State," he muses, as he imagines himself "Count Malvolio." Humours are also waters, however. And *waters,* or fluids of all kinds, are continually being forced on our attention. Wine, tears, sea-water, even urine, are in evidence from the first scene on, and they are always being metaphorically identified with one another. They are all fluids, bathing the world of the play in possibilities for change as the humours do the body. Feste's answer to Maria in the prison scene has puzzled many editors; if we realize, however, that Feste is probably hysterically laughing at what he has just been up to, "Nay, I'm for all waters" may have the additional meaning that he is on the verge of losing control of himself. He is "for all waters" primarily in that he represents the fluidity of revelling celebration. And finally, when all is done, "The rain it raineth every day," and Feste reverts to gnomic utterance in a full and final seriousness. Water is rain that falls to us from Heaven. The world goes on. Our revels now are ended, but the actors solidify into humanity, in this case. "But that's all one, our play is done / And we'll strive to please you every day."

In this interpretation of *Twelfth Night,* I have in no sense meant to infer that Malvolio is to be identified as Ben Jonson, or that the play functioned in any systematic way in the war of the theatres. There are, of course, a number of propitious coincidences: Marston's *What You Will,* coming some six or seven years after *Twelfth Night,* devotes much effort to lampooning Jonson. What could have been meant by the title, however, as well as Shakespeare's real intention in his sub-title, remains obscure. Perhaps they both remain as the first part of some forgotten proverb to the effect that what you will (want) may come to you in an unexpected form. Perhaps they are both merely throw-away comments to the effect that the play is really "whatyoumaycallit". (It has been frequently suggested that it is a translation of Rabelais' *"Fay ce que vouldras."*) Then there is the dig, in *Every Man Out of His Humour,* at a comedy with a romantic (Italianate) plot more than vaguely resembling that of *Twelfth Night. Every Man Out* has been dated in 1599, but the idea that Shakespeare may have chosen just such a "romantic" story with which to oppose Jonson's comic theories is not inconceivable.

My point, however, is that *Twelfth Night* is opposed by its very nature to the kind of comedy that Jonson was not only writing, but advocating at the time; that it is a moral comedy, representing human experience in terms of a fully dramatized metaphor rather than a static emblematic correspondence; and, finally, that it operates to refute the moral validity of comedy of humours in its insistence on the active metaphor of surfeiting the appetite, upon which the whole plot is constructed. It is only romantic in that it shares, with *As You Like It* (and with *Love's Labours Lost,* too, for that matter) a hint of the world of transformation of the last plays. Its moral vision is as intense as that of the problem comedies. (pp. 234-38)

John Hollander, "'Twelfth Night' and the Morality of Indulgence," in The Sewanee Review, *Vol. LXVII, No. 2, Spring, 1959, pp. 220-38.*

C. L. BARBER   (essay date 1959)

[*In the tradition of Enid Welsford (1935) and L. G. Salingar (1958), Barber focuses on the Saturnalian pattern of* Twelfth Night. *He explores the festive element in the play, which he feels is based on Elizabethan holiday celebrations. Each of Shake-*

speare's festive comedies concentrates on a particular kind of folly, ''a basic movement which can be summarized in the formula, through release to clarification.'' For Barber, the temporary sex-role reversals in Twelfth Night *reinforce the normal pattern of male-female relationships; this idea is challenged by Jan Kott (1964) and Clifford Leech (1965), both of whom stress the theme of sexual ambiguity in the play. In an interesting comment on the dating of* Twelfth Night, *Barber theorizes that the accepted chronology, in which* Twelfth Night *comes before* Hamlet *and the dark comedies, is perhaps too much based on the perceived unity of a happy mood in the early comedies. He speculates that, for Shakespeare's audience, the mood of* Twelfth Night *was not necessarily so different from that of* Measure for Measure *and* All's Well That Ends Well. *Barber's essay, from which the following excerpt is drawn, was originally published in his* Shakespeare's Festive Comedy *in 1959.*]

[In *Twelfth Night*] Shakespeare can be inclusive in his use of traditions because his powers of selection and composition can arrange each element so that only those facets of it show which will serve his expressive purpose. He leaves out the dungeon in which Rich's jealous Orsino shuts up Viola, as well as Sebastian's departure leaving Olivia with child; but he does not hesitate to keep such events as the shipwreck, or Sebastian's amazing marriage to a stranger, or Orsino's threat to kill Viola. It is not the credibility of the event that is decisive, but what can be expressed through it. Thus the shipwreck is made the occasion for Viola to exhibit an undaunted, aristocratic mastery of adversity—she settles what she shall do next almost as though picking out a costume for a masquerade:

> I'll serve this duke,
> Thou shalt present me as an eunuch to him;
> It may be worth thy pains. For I can sing,
> And speak to him in several sorts of music . . .
>   [I.ii.55-8]

What matters is not the event, but what the language says as gesture, the aristocratic, free-and-easy way she settles what she will do and what the captain will do to help her. The pathetical complications which are often dwelt on in the romance are not allowed to develop far in the play; instead Viola's spritely language conveys the fun she is having in playing a man's part, with a hidden womanly perspective about it. One cannot quite say that she is playing in a masquerade, because disguising *just* for the fun of it is a different thing. But the same sort of festive pleasure in transvestism is expressed.

It is amazing how little happens in *Twelfth Night,* how much of the time people are merely talking, especially in the first half, before the farcical complications are sprung. Shakespeare is so skillful by now in rendering attitudes by the gestures of easy conversation that when it suits him he can almost do without events. In the first two acts of *Twelfth Night* he holds our interest with a bare minimum of tension while unfolding a pattern of contrasting attitudes and tones in his several persons. Yet Shakespeare's whole handling of romantic story, farce, and practical joke makes a composition which moves in the manner of his earlier festive comedies, through release to clarification.

Olivia's phrase in the last act, when she remembers Malvolio and his ''madness,'' can summarize the way the play moves:

> A most extracting frenzy of mine own
> From my remembrance clearly banish'd his.
>   [V.i.281-82]

People are caught up by delusions or misapprehensions which take them out of themselves, bringing out what they would

keep hidden or did not know was there. *Madness* is a key word. The outright gull Malvolio is already ''a rare turkey-cock'' from ''contemplation'' [II.v.30-1] before Maria goes to work on him with her forged letter. (pp. 241-42)

What they bring about as a ''pastime'' [III.iv.138], to ''gull him to a nayword, and make him a common recreation'' [II.iii.134-35], happens unplanned to others by disguise and mistaken identity. (p. 243)

The farcical challenge and ''fight'' between Viola and Sir Andrew are another species of frantic action caused by delusion. ''More matter for a May morning'' [III.iv.142] Fabian calls it as they move from pretending to exorcise Malvolio's devil to pretending to act as solicitous seconds for Sir Andrew. When Antonio enters the fray in manly earnest, there is still another sort of comic error, based not on a psychological distortion but simply on mistaken identity. This Plautine sort of confusion leads Sebastian to exclaim, ''Are all the people mad?'' [IV.i.27] Just after we have seen ''Malvolio the lunatic'' [IV.ii.22] baffled in the dark room (''But tell me true, are you not mad indeed? or do you but counterfeit?'' [IV.ii.113-14], we see Sebastian struggling to understand his wonderful encounter with Olivia:

> This is the air; that is the glorious sun;
> This pearl she gave me, I do feel't and see't;
> And though 'tis wonder that enwraps me thus,
> Yet 'tis not madness.   [IV.iii.1-4]

The open-air clarity of this little scene anticipates the approaching moment when delusions and misapprehensions are resolved by the finding of objects appropriate to passions. Shakespeare, with fine stagecraft, spins the misapprehensions out to the last moment. He puts Orsino, in his turn, through an extracting frenzy, the Duke's frustration converting at last to violent impulses toward Olivia and Cesario, before he discovers in the page the woman's love he could not win from the countess.

That it should all depend on there being an indistinguishable twin brother always troubles me when I think about it, though never when I watch the play. Can it be that we enjoy the play so much simply because it is a wish-fulfillment presented so skillfully that we do not notice that our hearts are duping our heads? Certainly part of our pleasure comes from pleasing make-believe. But I think that what chance determines about particular destinies is justified, as was the case with *The Merchant of Venice,* by the play's realizing dynamically general distinctions and tendencies in life.

The most fundamental distinction the play brings home to us is the difference between men and women. To say this may seem to labor the obvious; for what love story does not emphasize this difference? But the disguising of a girl as a boy in *Twelfth Night* is exploited so as to renew in a special way our sense of the difference. Just as a saturnalian reversal of social roles need not threaten the social structure, but can serve instead to consolidate it, so a temporary, playful reversal of sexual roles can renew the meaning of the normal relation. One can add that with sexual as with other relations, it is when the normal is secure that playful aberration is benign. This basic security explains why there is so little that is queazy in all Shakespeare's handling of boy actors playing women, and playing women pretending to be men. This is particularly remarkable in *Twelfth Night,* for Olivia's infatuation with Cesario-Viola is another, more fully developed case of the sort of crush Phebe had on Rosalind. . . . When on her embassy

Viola asks to see Olivia's face and exclaims about it, she shows a woman's way of relishing another woman's beauty—and sensing another's vanity: "'Tis beauty truly blent. . . ." "I see you what you are—you are too proud" [I.v.239,250]. Olivia's infatuation with feminine qualities in a youth takes her, doing "I know not what," from one stage of life out into another, from shutting out suitors in mourning for her brother's memory, to ardor for a man, Sebastian, and the clear certainty that calls out to "husband" in the confusion of the last scene. (pp. 244-45)

The particular implausibility that there should be an identical man to take Viola's place with Olivia is submerged in the general, beneficent realization that there is such a thing as a man. Sebastian's comment when the confusion of identities is resolved points to the general force which has shaped particular developments:

> So comes it, lady, you have been mistook.
> But nature to her bias drew in that.
>
> [V.i.259-60]
> (p. 246)

Over against the Olivia-Cesario relation, there are Orsino-Cesario and Antonio-Sebastian. Antonio's impassioned friendship for Sebastian is one of those ardent attachments between young people of the same sex which Shakespeare frequently presents, with his positive emphasis, as exhibiting the loving and lovable qualities later expressed in love for the other sex. Orsino's fascination with Cesario is more complex. In the opening scene, his restless sensibility can find no object: "naught enters there, . . . / But falls into abatement . . . / Even in a minute" [I.i.11-14]. Olivia might be an adequate object; she at least is the Diana the sight of whom has, he thinks, turned him to an Acteon torn by the hounds of desires. When we next see him, and Cesario has been only three days in his court, his entering question is "Who saw Cesario, ho?" [I.iv.10] and already he has unclasped to the youth "the book even of [his] secret soul" [I.iv.14]. He has found an object. The delight he takes in Cesario's fresh youth and graceful responsiveness in conversation and in service, is one part of the spectrum of love for a woman, or better, it is a range of feeling that is common to love for a youth and love for a woman. For the audience, the woman who is present there, behind Cesario's disguise, is brought to mind repeatedly by the talk of love and of the differences of men and women in love. . . . This supremely feminine damsel, who "sat like patience on a monument," is not Viola. She is a sort of polarity within Viola, realized all the more fully because the other, active side of Viola does not pine in thought at all, but instead changes the subject: ". . . and yet I know not. / Sir, shall we to this lady?—Ay, that's the theme" [I.iv.121-22]. The effect of moving back and forth from woman to sprightly page is to convey how much the sexes differ yet how much they have in common, how everyone who is fully alive has qualities of both. Some such general recognition is obliquely suggested in Sebastian's amused summary of what happened to Olivia:

> You would have been contracted to a maid;
> Nor are you therein, by my life, deceiv'd:
> You are betroth'd both to a maid and man.
>
> [V.i.261-63]
> (pp. 246-47)

[Each] of the festive comedies tends to focus on a particular kind of folly that is released along with love—witty masquerade in *Love's Labour's Lost*, delusive fantasy in *A Midsummer Night's Dream*, romance in *As You Like It*, and, in *The Merchant of Venice*, prodigality balanced against usury. *Twelfth Night* deals with the sort of folly which the title points to, the folly of misrule. But the holiday reference limits its subject too narrowly: the play exhibits the liberties which gentlemen take with decorum in the pursuit of pleasure and love, including the liberty of holiday, but not only that. Such liberty is balanced against time-serving. As Bassanio's folly of prodigality leads in the end to gracious fulfillment, so does Viola's folly of disguise. There is just a suggestion of the risks when she exclaims, not very solemnly,

> Disguise, I see thou art a wickedness
> Wherein the pregnant enemy does much.
>
> [II.ii.27-8]

As in *The Merchant of Venice* the story of a prodigal is the occasion for an exploration of the use and abuse of wealth, so here we get an exhibition of the use and abuse of social liberty.

What enables Viola to bring off her role in disguise is her perfect courtesy, in the large, humanistic meaning of that term as the Renaissance used it, the *corteziania* of Castiglione. Her mastery of courtesy goes with her being the daughter of "that Sebastian of Messalina whom I know you have heard of": gentility shows through her disguise as does the fact that she is a woman. . . . We think of manners as a mere prerequisite of living decently, like cleanliness. For the Renaissance, they could be almost the end of life as the literature of courtesy testifies. *Twelfth Night* carries further an interest in the fashioning of a courtier which, as Miss Bradbrook points out [in *Shakespeare and Elizabethan Poetry* (see *Additional Bibliography*)], appears in several of the early comedies, especially *The Two Gentlemen of Verona*, and which in different plays Shakespeare was pursuing, about the same time as he wrote *Twelfth Night,* in *Hamlet* and *Measure for Measure*. People in *Twelfth Night* talk of courtesy and manners constantly. But the most important expression of courtesy of course is in object lessons. It is their lack of breeding and manners which makes the comic butts ridiculous, along with their lack of the basic, free humanity which, be it virile or feminine, is at the center of courtesy and flowers through it.

Mr. Van Doren, in a fine essay, observes that *Twelfth Night* has a structure like *The Merchant of Venice*. "Once again Shakespeare has built a world out of music and melancholy, and once again this world is threatened by an alien voice. The opposition of Malvolio to Orsino and his class parallels the opposition of Shylock to Antonio and his friends. The parallel is not precise, and the contrast is more subtly contrived; Shakespeare holds the balance in a more delicate hand. . . ." [See excerpt above, 1939.] One way in which this more delicate balance appears is that the contest of revellers with intruder does not lead to neglecting ironies about those who are on the side of pleasure. We are all against Malvolio, certainly, in the great moment when the whole opposition comes into focus with Toby's "Dost thou think, because thou art virtuous, there shall be no more cakes and ale?" [II.iii.115-16]. The festive spirit shows up the killjoy vanity of Malvolio's decorum. The steward shows his limits when he calls misrule "this uncivil rule." But one of the revellers is Sir Andrew, who reminds us that there is no necessary salvation in being a fellow who delights "in masques and revels sometimes altogether" [I.iii.114]. There was no such ninny pleasure-seeker in *The Merchant of Venice;* his role continues Shallow's, the would-be-reveller who is comically inadequate. To put such a leg as his into "a flame-coloured stock" only shows how meager it is. This thin creature's motive is self-improvement: he is a version of the stock type of prodigal who is gulled in trying to learn how to be gallant. (pp. 248-50)

Sir Toby is gentlemanly liberty incarnate, a specialist in it. He lives at his ease, enjoying heritage, the something-for-nothing which this play celebrates, as *The Merchant of Venice* celebrates wealth—what he has without having to deserve it is his kinsman's place in Olivia's household. . . . He is like Falstaff in maintaining saturnalian paradox and in playing impromptu the role of lord of misrule. But in his whole relation to the world he is fundamentally different from Prince Hal's great buffoon. Falstaff makes a career of misrule; Sir Toby uses misrule to show up a careerist.

There is little direct invocation by poetry of the values of heritage and housekeeping, such as we get of the beneficence of wealth in *The Merchant of Venice*. But the graciousness of community is conveyed indirectly by the value put on music and song, as Mr. Van Doren observes. . . . [The] significance of music in relation to community is suggested in the Duke's lines about the "old and antique song":

Mark it, Cesario; it is old and plain.
The spinsters and the knitters in the sun,
And the free maids that weave their thread with bones,
Do use to chant it. It is silly sooth,
And dallies with the innocence of love
Like the old age.   [II.iv.43-8]

The wonderful line about the free maids, which throws such firm stress on "free" by the delayed accent, and then slows up in strong, regular monosyllables, crystallizes the play's central feeling for freedom in heritage and community. It is consciously nostalgic; the old age is seen from the vantage of "these most brisk and giddy-paced times" [II.iv.6].

Throughout the play a contrast is maintained between the taut, restless, elegant court, where people speak a nervous verse, and the free-wheeling household of Olivia, where, except for the intense moments in Olivia's amorous interviews with Cesario, people live in an easy-going prose. The contrast is another version of pastoral. The household is more than any one person in it. People keep interrupting each other, changing their minds, letting their talk run out into foolishness—and through it all Shakespeare expresses the day-by-day going on of a shared life. . . . Maria's character is a function of the life of "the house"; she moves within it with perfectly selfless tact. "She's a beagle true-bred," says Sir Toby: her part in the housekeeping and its pleasures is a homely but valued kind of "courtiership."

All of the merrymakers show a fine sense of the relations of people, including robust Fabian, and Sir Toby, when he has need. The fool, especially, has this courtly awareness. We see in the first scene that he has to have it to live: he goes far enough in the direction of plain speaking to engage Olivia's unwilling attention, then brings off his thesis that *she* is the fool so neatly that he is forgiven. What Viola praises in the fool's function is just what we should expect in a play about courtesy and liberty:

This fellow is wise enough to play the fool,
And to do that well craves a kind of wit.
He must observe their mood on whom he jests.
The quality of persons and the time . . .
      [III.i.60-3]

It is remarkable how little Feste says that is counterstatement in Touchstone's manner: there is no need for ironic counterstatement, because here the ironies are embodied in the comic butts. Instead what Feste chiefly does is sing and beg—courtly occupations—and radiate in his songs and banter a feeling of liberty based on accepting disillusion. "What's to come is still unsure. . . . Youth's a stuff will not endure" [II.iii.49,52]. In *The Merchant of Venice*, it was the gentlefolk who commented "How every fool can play upon the word!" but now it is the fool himself who says, with mock solemnity: "To see this age! A sentence is but a chev'ril glove to a good wit!" [III.i.11-12]. He rarely makes the expected move, but conveys by his style how well he knows what moves are expected:

so that, conclusions to be as kisses, if your four
negatives make your two affirmatives, why then,
the worse for my friends and the better for my
foes.
Duke. Why, this is excellent.
Feste. By my troth, sir, no; though it pleases
you to be one of my friends.
      [V.i.20-5]
      (pp. 250-53)

Viola, who as "nuntio" moves from tense court to relaxed household, has much in common with Feste in the way she talks, or better, uses talk; but she also commands effortlessly, when there is occasion, Shakespeare's mature poetic power:

It gives a very echo to the seat
Where love is throned.
      [II.iv.21-2]

"Thou dost speak masterly," the Duke exclaims—as we must too. Part of her mastery is that she lets herself go only rarely, choosing occasions that are worthy. Most of the time she keeps her language reined in, often mocking it as she uses it, in Feste's fashion. (pp. 253-54)

Olivia says that "it was never merry world / Since lowly feigning was called compliment" [III.i.98-9]. As Sir Toby is the spokesman and guardian of that merry world, Malvolio is its antagonist. . . . [The] "stubborn and uncourteous parts" in Malvolio's character, to which Fabian refers in justifying the "device," are precisely those qualities which liberty shows up. Malvolio wants "to confine himself finer than he is," to paraphrase Toby in reverse: he practices behavior to his own shadow. His language is full of pompous polysyllables, of elaborate syntax deploying synonyms:

Do ye make an alehouse of my lady's house,
that ye squeak out your coziers' catches without
any mitigation or remorse of voice? Is there no
respect of place, persons, nor time in you?
      [II.iii.88-92]

In "loving" his mistress, as Cesario her master, he is a kind of foil, bringing out her genuine, free impulse by the contrast he furnishes. He does not desire Olivia's person; *that* desire, even in a steward, would be sympathetically regarded, though not of course encouraged, by a Twelfth-Night mood. What he wants is "to be Count Malvolio," with "a demure travel of regard—telling them I know my place, as I would they should do theirs" [II.v.35,53-4]. His secret wish is to violate decorum himself, then relish to the full its power over others. No wonder he has not a free disposition when he has such imaginations to keep under! (pp. 254-55)

In his "impossible passages of grossness," he is the profane intruder trying to steal part of the initiates' feast by disguising himself as one of them—only to be caught and tormented for his profanation. As with Shylock, there is potential pathos in his bafflement, especially when Shakespeare uses to the limit the conjuring of devils out of a sane man, a device which he had employed hilariously in *The Comedy of Errors*. There is no way to settle just how much of Malvolio's pathos should be allowed to come through when he is down and out in the dark hole. Most people now agree that Charles Lamb's sympathy for the steward's enterprise and commiseration for his sorrows is a romantic and bourgeois distortion [see excerpt above, 1822]. But he is certainly pathetic, if one thinks about it, because he is so utterly cut off from everyone else by his anxious self-love. He lacks the freedom which makes Viola so perceptive, and is correspondingly oblivious. . . . The dark house is, without any straining, a symbol: when Malvolio protests about Pythagoras, "I think nobly of the soul and no way approve his opinion," the clown's response is "Remain thou still in darkness." The pack of them are wanton and unreasonable in tormenting him; but his reasonableness will never let him out into "the air; . . . the glorious sun" [IV.iii.1] which they enjoy together. To play the dark-house scene for pathos, instead of making fun out of the pathos, or at any rate out of most of the pathos, is to ignore the dry comic light which shows up Malvolio's virtuousness as a self-limiting automatism.

Malvolio has been called a satirical portrait of the Puritan spirit, and there is some truth in the notion. But he is not hostile to holiday because he is a Puritan; he is like a Puritan because he is hostile to holiday. Shakespeare even mocks, in passing, the thoughtless, fashionable antipathy to Puritans current among gallants. Sir Andrew responds to Maria's "sometimes he is a kind of Puritan," with "if I thought that, I'd beat him like a dog" [II.iii.141-42]. "The devil a Puritan he is, or anything constantly," Maria observes candidly, "but a time-pleaser" [II.iii.147-48]. Shakespeare's two greatest comic butts, Malvolio and Shylock, express basic human attitudes which were at work in the commercial revolution, the new values whose development R. H. Tawney described in *Religion and the Rise of Capitalism*. But both figures are conceived at a level of esthetic abstraction which makes it inappropriate to identify them with specific social groups in the mingled actualities of history: Shylock, embodying ruthless money power, is no more to be equated with actual bankers than Malvolio, who has something of the Puritan ethic, is to be thought of as a portrait of actual Puritans. Yet, seen in the perspective of literary and social history, there is a curious appropriateness in Malvolio's presence, as a kind of foreign body to be expelled by laughter, in Shakespeare's last free-and-easy festive comedy. He is a man of business, and, it is passingly suggested, a hard one; he is or would like to be a rising man, and to rise he *uses* sobriety and morality. One could moralize the spectacle by observing that, in the long run, in the 1640's, Malvolio *was* revenged on the whole pack of them.

But Shakespeare's comedy remains, long after 1640, to move audiences through release to clarification, making distinctions between false care and true freedom and realizing anew, for successive generations, powers in human nature and society which make good the risks of courtesy and liberty. And this without blinking the fact that "the rain it raineth every day."

Twelfth Night is usually placed just before *Hamlet* and the problem plays to make neat groupings according to mood, but it may well have been written after some of these works. In thinking about its relation to the other work of the period from 1600 to 1602 or 1603, it is important to recognize the independent artistic logic by which each play has its own unity. There are features of *Twelfth Night* that connect it with all the productions of this period. There is the side of Orsino's sensibility, for example, which suggests Troilus' hypersensitivity:

> Enough, no more!
> 'Tis not so sweet now as it was before.
>
> [I.i.7-8]

> How will she love when the rich golden shaft
> Hath kill'd the flock of all affections else
> That live in her; when liver, brain, and heart,
> Those sovereign thrones, are all supplied and fill'd,
> Her sweet perfections, with one self king!
> Away before me to sweet beds of flow'rs!
>
> [I.i.34-9]

Troilus carries this sort of verse and feeling farther:

> What will it be
> When that the wat'ry palates taste indeed
> Love's thrice-repured nectar? Death, I fear me;
> Sounding destruction; or some joy too fine,
> Too subtile-potent, tun'd too sharp in sweetness
> For the capacity of my ruder powers.
>
> [*Troilus*, III.ii.20-5]

Troilus' lines are a much more physical and more anxious development of the exquisite, uncentered sort of amorousness expressed by Orsino. But in *Twelfth Night* there is no occasion to explore the harsh anti-climax to which such intensity is vulnerable, for instead of meeting a trivial Cressida in the midst of war and lechery, Orsino meets poised Viola in a world of revelry. The comparison with *Troilus and Cressida* makes one notice how little direct sexual reference there is in *Twelfth Night*—much less than in most of the festive comedies. It may be that free-hearted mirth, at this stage of Shakespeare's development, required more shamefastness than it had earlier, because to dwell on the physical was to encounter the "monstruosity in love" which troubled Troilus: "that the desire is boundless and the act a slave to limit" [*Troilus*, III.ii.81-3]. (pp. 255-58)

It is quite possible that *Measure for Measure* and *All's Well That Ends Well* did not seem to Shakespeare and his audiences so different from *Twelfth Night* as they seem to us. Both of them use comic butts not unlike Andrew and Malvolio: Lucio and Parolles are, each his way, pretenders to community who are shown up ludicrously by their own compulsions, and so expelled. Our difficulty with these plays, what makes them problem plays, is that they do not feel festive; they are not merry in a deep enough way. (p. 258)

[The] fool in *Twelfth Night* has been over the garden wall into some such world as the Vienna of *Measure for Measure*. He never tells where he has been, gives no details. But he has an air of knowing more of life than anyone else—too much, in fact; and he makes general observations like

> Anything that's mended is but patch'd; virtue
> that transgresses is but patch'd with sin, and
> sin that amends is but patch'd with virtue. If
> that this simple syllogism will serve, so; if it
> will not, what remedy?
>
> [I.v.47-51]

His part does not darken the bright colors of the play; but it gives them a dark outline, suggesting that the whole bright revel emerges from shadow. In the wonderful final song which he is left alone on stage to sing, the mind turns to contemplate the limitations of revelry: "By swaggering could I never thrive. . . ." The morning after, the weather when the sky changes, come into the song:

> With tosspots still had drunken heads
> For the rain it raineth every day.
>
> [V.i.403-04]

It goes outside the garden gate:

> But when I come to man's estate,
> With hey, ho, the wind and the rain,
> 'Gainst knaves and thieves men shut their gate,
> For the rain it raineth every day.
>
> [V.i.389-92]

Yet the poise of mirth, achieved by accepting disillusion, although it is now precarious, is not lost:

> A great while ago the world begun,
> With hey, ho, the wind and the rain;
> But that's all one, our play is done,
> And we'll strive to please you everyday.
>
> [V.i.405-08]

There is a certain calculated let-down in coming back to the play in this fashion; but it is the play which is keeping out the wind and the rain.

The festive comic form which Shakespeare had worked out was a way of selecting and organizing experience which had its own logic, its own autonomy: there is no necessary reason to think that he did not play on that instrument in *Twelfth Night* after making even such different music as *Hamlet*. Indeed, across the difference in forms, the comedy has much in common with the tragedy: interest in courtesy and free-hearted manners; consciousness of language and play with it as though a sentence were but a chev'ril glove; the use of nonsequitur and nonsense. Malvolio absurdly dreams of such a usurpation of heritage, "having come from a day bed, where I have left Olivia sleeping," as Claudius actually accomplishes. The tragedy moves into regions where the distinction between madness and sanity begins to break down, to be recovered only through violence; the fooling with madness in the comedy is an enjoyment of the control which knows what is mad and what is not. (pp. 259-61)

For sheer power of wit and reach of comic vision, there are moments in *Hamlet* beyond anything in the comedies we have considered. But to control the expression of the motives he is presenting, Shakespeare requires a different movement, within which comic release is only one phase. After *Twelfth Night*, comedy is always used in this subordinate way: saturnalian moments, comic counterstatements, continue to be important resources of his art, but their meaning is determined by their place in a larger movement. So it is with the heroic revels in *Antony and Cleopatra*, or with the renewal of life, after tragedy, at the festival in *The Winter's Tale*. (p. 261)

C. L. Barber, "Testing Courtesy and Humanity in 'Twelfth Night'," in his Shakespeare's Festive Comedy: A Study of Dramatic Form and Its Relation to Social Custom, *The World Publishing Company, 1963, pp. 240-61.*

BERTRAND EVANS   (essay date 1960)

[*Evans states that "Shakespeare's dramatic method relied heavily on arrangements of discrepant awarenesses," a method which gives an audience the advantage of seeing and knowing elements of the plot not known by the characters. In* Twelfth Night, *the vantage point of the individual character is arranged so that each looks over the shoulder of the other, aware of some, but not all of the discrepancies. Evans here contributes to a long history of criticism that focuses on the theme of self-deception and masking in the play; additional commentary on this theme is found in the excerpts by E. Montégut (1867), E. K. Chambers (1907), and Joseph H. Summers (1955).*]

In the world of *Twelfth Night,* as in the worlds of the comedies just preceding, the spirit of the practiser prevails. Seven of the principal persons are active practisers, and they operate six devices. All action turns on these, and the effects of the play arise from exploitation of the gaps they open. During all but the first two of eighteen scenes we have the advantage of some participant; in seven—an unusually high proportion—we hold advantage over all who take part. In the course of the action, every named person takes a turn below our vantage-point, and below the vantage-point of some other person or persons: in this play neither heroine nor clown is wholly spared. Although Viola shares the great secret with us alone, Shakespeare early establishes our vantage-point above hers, and once even makes her the unwitting victim of another's practice. Although Feste is either 'in' on most practices or unaffected by them, he, with all Illyria, is ignorant of the main secret of the play, the identity of 'Cesario'. Here, then, even heroine and clown stand below us, and below them the others range down to the bottom, where sit Aguecheek and Malvolio in chronic oblivion. Though also victims of others' practices, neither needs deceiving to be deceived—Nature having practised on them once for all.

But if all are exposed at some time in ignorance of their situations, yet all but Orsino and Malvolio have compensatory moments when they overpeer others: even Aguecheek, though a fool the while, briefly enjoys advantage over Malvolio. The awarenesses in *Twelfth Night* are so structured that an overpeerer gloating in his advantage is usually himself overpeered by another participant or by us: thus Sir Toby exults in his advantage over 'Cesario', knowing that Sir Andrew is not the 'devil in a private brawl' he would have 'Cesario' believe—but at the same time 'Cesario' holds advantage over him in knowing that 'Cesario' is a fiction; and the last laugh is ours, on Sir Toby, for even he would hardly have made his jest of a duel had he known 'Cesario' truly. From much use of such arrangements, in which a participant's understanding is inferior with respect to some elements of a situation and superior with respect to others, emerge the richest effects of *Twelfth Night* and some of the finest in Shakespeare.

Of the six practices, the central one is of course the heroine's masquerade. It is the longest, and, in its relations with the play as a whole, the most important such masquerade in the comedies. . . . [The] force of Viola's masquerade in *Twelfth Night* prevails in all but the opening scenes and relates to every incident and person. Though it most affects two victims, Viola's is truly a practice on the whole world of Illyria, as Duke Vincentio's is on the world of *Measure for Measure,* and as, in tragedy, Iago's is on his world and as Hamlet's antic disposition is on the whole world of Denmark. Viola rightly belongs in this company of most notable masqueraders in all the plays.

Viola takes up her masquerade with somewhat less urgency and altruism than moved Portia, but with somewhat more of both than moved Rosalind to perpetrate her fraud in the Forest of Arden. Washed up on the shore of Illyria, she goes to work at once. Quickly ascertaining the name of the place, the name of its ruler, and the fact that he is still a bachelor, she makes up her mind.

> I'll serve this duke.
> Thou shalt present me as an eunuch to him.
> It may be worth thy pains, for I can sing
> And speak to him in many sorts of music
> That will allow me very worth his service.
> What else may hap, to time I will commit,
> Only shape thou thy silence to my wit.
>
> [I. ii. 55-61]

This speech creates at one stroke the discrepancy in awarenesses which will endure until the closing moments of the play, giving advantage to us and disadvantage to all Illyria. And as swiftly as he creates the gap, Shakespeare begins its exploitation. When next we see Viola, in man's attire, after three days at Orsino's court and already his favourite, Valentine's remarks give first expression to the general Illyrian error:

> If the Duke continue these favours towards you,
> Cesario, you are like to be much advanc'd. He
> hath known you but three days, and already
> you are no stranger.
>
> [I. iv. 1-4]

But a stranger, of course, this 'Cesario' is to the Duke, and to all others. The Duke's unawareness is next exploited: 'Cesario,' he says, 'thou know'st no less but all'—and so she does, more than he dreams. When Orsino directs her to bear his lovesuit to Olivia, his remarks come near enough to strike sparks from the truth, and these flashes of irony are the first to result from the great discrepancy:

> . . . they shall yet belie thy happy years,
> That say thou art a man. Diana's lip
> Is not more smooth and rubious; they small pipe
> Is as the maiden's organ, shrill and sound;
> And all is semblative a woman's part.
>
> [I. iv. 30-4]

As the scene ends, the basic exploitable gap is opened wider; says Viola,

> I'll do my best
> To woo your lady,—(*aside*) yet, a barful strife!
> Whoe'er I woo, myself would be his wife.
>
> [I. iv. 40-2]

As suddenly as her adoption of disguise created the first discrepancy, this confession creates a second. Henceforth her advantage, and ours, over the Duke is double: the secret of her right identity and the secret of her love.

The first major clash of the discrepant awarenesses of Viola and Illyria occurs, however, not in the Duke's court but in Olivia's house. . . . [The] principal exploitation occurs in the interview with Olivia, whose attitude changes in the course of 100 lines from haughty scorn to flirtatious interest and finally to love. The effect of exploitation of the difference between our understanding and Olivia's is here not merely comic, although that is certainly part of the total. Though the play is not yet a full act old, the dramatist has already packed our minds with so much that simple laughter is an inadequate response. (pp. 118-21)

Until the end of this scene, when Olivia, moved by a passion she thinks futile to resist—not knowing how futile it is to succumb—dispatches Malvolio to run after 'that same peevish messenger' and give him a ring—'He left this ring behind him / Would I or not'—Shakespeare has established only two levels of awareness. . . . The instant effect of Sebastian's appearance, safe and sound on the very coast where Viola had inquired 'What country, friends, is this?' and been advised 'This is Illyria, lady' is the creation of a third level, a vantage-point above Viola's, to be held by ourselves alone until the end of Act III—and possibly but not probably until the last moments of Act V.

The placement of the scene informing us of Sebastian's survival and immediate destination—'I am bound to the Count Orsino's court'—is a notable example of Shakespeare's way of handling the awarenesses. It is the more significant for being conspicuously early in the action, and the more conspicuous for its rather awkward interruption of the expected sequence of incident. Our notification of his rescue and arrival in Illyria might readily have been postponed until Act IV, when, in front of Olivia's house, the Clown mistakes Sebastian for 'Cesario'. Or he might have been introduced inconspicuously between almost any two scenes in either Act II or Act III. Instead, he is thrust between Viola's departure from Olivia's house and her meeting with Malvolio on the street. Ordinarily, no scene would intervene in this space, as is demonstrable many times over in the plays. . . . [The] introduction of Sebastian splits the sequence with a scene of some fifty lines that entails also a shift from the vicinity of Olivia's house to the sea-coast. From the first history play onward, Shakespeare's method avoided violence to the normal order of action unless there was something special to be gained. By the time of *Twelfth Night*, certainly, the only disruptions of sequence are calculated ones. In the present case the dramatist evidently wished us to learn as early as possible that Sebastian is alive, and, more precisely, to learn it *just before Viola discovers that Olivia has fallen in love with her*.

In short, Sebastian's introduction is our assurance that all is well and will end well, an assurance which contradicts Viola's distress on recognizing what seems a hopeless entanglement:

> She loves me, sure. . . . If it be so, as 'tis,
> Poor lady, she were better love a dream.
> Disguise, I see thou art a wickedness
> Wherein the pregnant enemy does much.
>
> [II. ii. 22, 25-8]

When we saw her leave Olivia's house, her vantage-point was ours. Now, overtaken by Malvolio—who is himself wrapped in fourfold ignorance—she has slipped below, for we have seen Sebastian. She is nevermore quite the match of Rosalind, who overpeered all and was never overpeered. Yet her mind is packed with almost as much understanding as ours: she realizes, by the ring that Olivia, ignorant of 'Cesario's' sex, has fallen in love; she recognizes that Malvolio, besides being a fool, is ignorant also of her sex and of his mistress's meaning in sending the ring; and certainly she observes irony's bright flashes about his head when, with intolerable condescension, he announces that Olivia had commanded 'Cesario' to come no more 'unless it be to report your lord's taking of this'—thereupon tossing Olivia's, not Orsino's, ring on the ground. But her mind is chiefly on Orsino and his oblivion, which includes ignorance of her identity, of her love for him, and of the fact that just now his beloved has given her heart to 'Cesario':

> My master loves her dearly;
> And I, poor monster, fond as much on him;
> And she, mistaken, seems to dote on me.
> What will become of this?
>
> [II. ii. 33-6]

By making Viola voice dismay for the several matters that burden her awareness, Shakespeare bids our own be alert; he comes as near as a dramatist can to saying: 'Bear this in mind, and this, and yet this.' (pp. 121-23)

Sebastian's introduction is thus a strategic move, giving us assurance that all is and will be well. But it is also a tactical move, multiplying the possibilities of exploitation. Sebastian's unawareness—exploitable the instant he appears on the seacoast, weeping for a 'drowned' sister who is in fact doing quite well for herself in Illyria—provides one such possibility. All Illyria's unawareness that Sebastian is not 'Cesario'—who, of course, is not 'Cesario' either—provides another. Add to these the possibilities already in existence, including the main secret of Viola-'Cesario' and the subordinate ones born of Aguecheek's and Malvolio's chronic oblivions, and it is evident that by the start of Act II the exploitable potentiality is enormous.

Although Sebastian's appearance gives us advantage over Viola, her demotion is hardly damaging to her prestige as heroine and prime practiser. Her ignorance that her brother is at hand does not expose her to ridicule or pity, for the truth that she cannot see is better than the appearance. (pp. 123-24)

During Act II, however, except that she does not know about Sebastian, Viola escapes unawareness and enjoys an advantage over Orsino that matches Rosalind's over poor Orlando and Portia's over Bassanio. Indeed, her advantage grows during this period. When she left for her first interview with Olivia, Orsino was ignorant only of her identity. When she returns, he is still ignorant of that, of the fact that she loves him, that she is loved by Olivia, and that therefore his suit to Olivia is truly hopeless. His fourfold ignorance is the exploitable substance of the second Viola-Orsino interview. Shakespeare capitalizes the opportunity fully but tenderly, and the result is an artistic triumph. Lacking the complexity of some later scenes, in which stair-stepped levels of awareness provide the structure for dazzling cross-play, the scene nevertheless makes a powerful demand for simultaneous conflicting responses. Luxuriating in melancholy, loving love, affecting the agony of the disdained lover, feasting on music and song that aggravate his craving, Orsino stands naked to laughter—a foolish plight for a hero, like that into which Shakespeare previously thrust Orlando, rehearsing with 'Ganymede' his love for Rosalind.

Like Orlando's, then, a brutally ludicrous representation of romantic masculinity, Orsino's exposure should inspire roaring laughter. Yet as the scene moves on laughter becomes inappropriate and is perhaps finally made impossible by the force of a contradictory impulse. The latter force is enhanced by the music, song, and poetry of the scene—but its original stimulation is the presence of Viola, whose quality is as right for this moment as are the qualities of Rosalind and Orlando for their wooing scene. Whereas Orsino sees nothing, Viola sees too much; her mind is burdened with understanding. . . . Everything that she does know, beyond Orsino's knowledge, hurts her; and what she does not know—that the dramatist has taken care to have *us* know—hurts her also. Deliberately, with a

psychologically shrewd manoeuvre, Shakespeare has balanced our own awarenesses between laughter and pain.

These contradictory impulses, equal in power, stimulated by complex awarenesses, do not cancel each other out, leaving indifference; they battle for supremacy, and the intensity of their struggle determines the degree of our involvement. Shakespeare's way in the great scenes is to involve us deeply, by packing our minds with private awarenesses that confer a sense of personal responsibility toward the action. (pp. 124-25)

In the second Viola-Olivia interview, Shakespeare deals gently with Olivia's unawareness. Here, if he chose, he might cause a lady to look as ridiculous as Orlando rehearsing for 'Ganymede'. It is not so: we are required to pity Olivia, for she has caught the plague. (p. 126)

Viola did not take up the masquerade for the love of mockery. Hers is not a mocking nature. The thing she starts threatens to get out of hand almost at once. Hopelessly wooing Olivia for Orsino, hopelessly loving Orsino, hopelessly loved by Olivia, ignorant that Sebastian is alive to make all right at last, she is caught in what is to her a frightening dilemma such as Rosalind would never be caught in—for Rosalind is superior to dilemmas. It is in accord with her nature that Viola bears her advantage mercifully in the second interview, and the gap between the pair is exploited tenderly: 'A cypress, not a bosom, / Hides my heart', Olivia begins, and Viola replies, 'I pity you'. . . . Yet the frame of the situation is comic, even grotesque: the reversal of roles, the woman wooing the man, an incongruity in society if not in nature, is a perennial subject of jest; and the fact that this 'man' is not even a man adds a joke to what is already a joke. But within this laughable frame the presentation of human qualities stifles laughter. Olivia's nature conflicts with her plight; her genuineness disarms laughter. And the 'man' is not only a woman, but a woman of rare sensitivity, who carries her masquerade with uncertainty, in a sprightly manner but with rising alarm and forced bravado. Earlier heroines—Julia, Portia, Rosalind—had no such difficulty with this role. Besides the fact that their capabilities were greater, they had female companions to confide in: before donning men's clothes Julia jests with Lucetta, Portia with Nerissa, Rosalind with Celia. They carry their roles with a certain elation. But in her disguise Viola is as much alone in the great world as when she floundered in the sea. Acutely feminine, she finds the role hard, is distressed by it, comes soon to wish she had not undertaken it: 'Disguise, I see thou art a wickedness / Wherein the pregnant enemy does much.'

The emotional conflict which rises from this unlaughable treatment of a laughable situation, complex already, is further complicated by the force of the crowning fact in our superior awareness: our knowledge that Sebastian lives and must now be close at hand. If Olivia can love 'Cesario', she can love Sebastian. . . . Thus while the laughter implicit in the situation is drowned in the sympathy demanded by the gentleness of both women, the struggle is also flooded with comforting assurance; all is well and will end well.

And there is more: the total effect of this scene is lightened by the character of the action which surrounds it. The scene which immediately precedes it has ended on a high note of promised hilarity as Maria speaks of Malvolio to her accomplices:

> If you will then see the fruits of the sport, mark
> his first approach before my lady. He will come
> to her in yellow stockings, and 'tis a colour she

abhors, and cross-garter'd, a fashion she detests; and he will smile upon her, which will now be so unsuitable to her disposition, being addicted to a melancholy as she is, that it cannot but turn him into a notable contempt. If you will see it, follow me.

[II. v. 197-204]

This invitation is followed by the entrance of Viola, who matches wits with Feste, then proceeds to the interview with Olivia. *Maria's promise of the ludicrous spectacle that is to be the highest point of hilarity in all the action thus hangs over the tender scene.* (pp. 127-29)

Shakespeare's preparation of our minds for the climactic scene of the yellow stockings and cross-gartering has been long and elaborate. It has included introduction to the back stairs of that household in which Olivia—exhibited in a predicament as deliciously ironical as any in Shakespeare—has vainly vowed to walk for seven years in mourning veil 'And water once a day her chamber round / With eye-offending brine: all this to season / A brother's dead love'. It is not only Orsino's suit that threatens her solemn purpose; the stamp of futility is set on her vow by the lunatic character of her household: vain dream, to pass seven years in weeping under the same roof with Malvolio, Maria, Belch, and Aguecheek! Before it is visited by Viola, practising as 'Cesario', and before Maria devises her practice on Malvolio, Olivia's house harbours another practice: Sir Toby is revelling at Sir Andrew's cost, the bait being Olivia. This practice was begun before the action of the play commences, and it continues until the final scene. . . . Though inconspicuous, this long-standing practice is central to much action, for it precipitates both Maria's practice on Malvolio and Toby's practice on Sir Andrew and Viola-'Cesario' which brings them near to duelling and very nearly ends Viola's masquerade; indeed, it underlies the entire secondary action, which itself provides the comic environment for the main 'Cesario-Orsino-Olivia-Sebastian plot. (p. 129)

Before we see him, then, we hold advantage over Sir Andrew in knowing that he is being gulled. At first sight, in I. iii, we gain another: we perceive at once that his ignorance of Toby's practice is only an acute manifestation of a native condition. Of the race of Bottom, Sir Andrew would be at a disadvantage if he were not being gulled; being gulled, he is doubly 'out'.

The practice on Sir Andrew goes forward in back-room caterwauling; and it is this caterwauling that precipitates the practice on Malvolio, whose high-handed manner of relaying Olivia's command that the bacchanal cease provokes the wrath of the revellers and inspires Maria's genius: 'If I do not gull him into a nayword, and make him a common recreation, do not think I have wit enough to lie straight in my bed.' Her device is adapted precisely to that singular lack of self-perspective which is Malvolio's whole vice and whole virtue. . . . Besides other attributes, Maria has a gift for forgery: 'I can write very like my lady your neice.' Says Toby,

He shall think, by the letters that thou wilt drop, that they come from my niece, and that she's in love with him.

[II. iii. 164-66]

Such is the practice which places Maria and her accomplices, with ourselves, on a level above Malvolio and Olivia. Our advantage over Malvolio, however, like that over Sir Andrew, is double. Possibly Malvolio's pit is the darker, since Sir Andrew has moments when he apprehends the possibility that he

lacks wit: 'I am a great eater of beef and I believe that does harm to my wit.' Though foolish enough to dream of Olivia's hand, he is scarcely hopeful. . . . Sir Andrew, then, is deceived, and foolish, but not self-deceived. (p. 130)

Malvolio, on the other hand, is self-deceived before he is deceived. Sir Hugh Evans and Justice Shallow together cannot arouse real hope in Slender's breast; Sir Toby's assurances do not allay Sir Andrew's grave doubts. But Malvolio's fire is the product of spontaneous combustion, and his sense of worthiness is unalloyed by misgivings. Shakespeare makes this fact clear by exhibiting the man's vainglory just before he finds the forged letter: 'To be Count Malvolio!' and, again:

> Having been three months married to her, sitting in my state. . . . Calling my officers about me, in my branch'd velvet gown, having come from a day-bed, where I have left Olivia sleeping. . . .

[II. v. 44-9]

This exhibition of self-deception continues until Malvolio picks up the letter, when deception is welded to self-deception by a gaudy flash of irony: 'What employment have we here?' The 100 lines that follow, during which Malvolio manages to find his own name in the letters M, O, A, I, and arrives at confirmation—'I do not now fool myself, to let imagination jade me; for every reason excites to this, that my lady loves me'—make simultaneous exploitation of deception and self-deception:

> M, O, A, I; this simulation is not as the former. And yet, to crush this a little, it would bow to me, for every one of these letters are in my name.

[II. v. 139-41]

Exhibiting the seduction of a mind eager to be seduced, the scene surpasses everything resembling it in Shakespeare. (p. 131)

'Observe him, for the love of mockery', said Maria to her accomplices. Hidden in the box-tree, they hold a triple advantage over Malvolio, in that they watch him when he does not suspect, recognize his self-kindled folly, and, of course, know that the letter which sets him ablaze is forged. Yet the master practiser here is Shakespeare, whose way it is to set participants where they overpeer others while they are also overpeered. The practice on Malvolio is contained by frames which the practisers do not suspect, as we are privately reminded when Maria describes Olivia as 'addicted to a melancholy', a disposition which will render Malvolio's smiles intolerable to her. The fact is that Olivia is not now addicted to a melancholy, but is in love with 'Cesario'—and her world has changed. Hence even Maria, knowing nothing of the change, drops below our level. (pp. 131-32)

The climactic scene does not follow immediately: Maria's promise, suspended, conditions the environment of three scenes before it is fulfilled. The first of these, the pathetic interview of 'Cesario' with Olivia, totally encircled by past, continuing, and promised hilarity, has already been examined. Sentimentally conceived, permeated with emotion, Olivia's declaration of love demands sympathy: yet, placed where it is, it gathers an echo from Malvolio's affair: Olivia's passion for 'Cesario' is as preposterous as Malvolio's for Olivia. The second scene (III. ii) is affected also, but differently: Sir Toby, assisted by Fabian, puffs up Sir Andrew's collapsing hopes of winning Olivia, and Sir Andrew, foolish and practice-ridden, fails to see in Malvolio's delusion the very portrait of his own. (p. 132)

The third scene set between Maria's promise and its fulfilment shows Sebastian on a street in Illyria and confirms our long-held, comforting assumption that the solution to Viola's 'insoluble' problem is at hand. Placed between the announcement of Sir Toby's practice (the challenge) which will surely terrify 'Cesario', and the exploitation of multiple practices in the climactic scene, Sebastian's declaration that he will walk abroad to view the town is our reassurance that all is well. It comes just as the climactic scene of the yellow stockings begins and is the dramatist's last bid to make certain that all useful information is in our minds.

And it is truly an enormous bundle of awarenesses that we must carry into this scene, during the action of which all nine of the persons present are blind to some part of the situation. Though not the first of Shakespeare's scenes in which everyone stands below our vantage-point, it is the most complex of such scenes until the climactic portion of *Cymbeline*. Four principal situations comprise the scene: first, that in which Malvolio's delusion is central; second, that in which Olivia's unawareness of 'Cesario's' identity is central; third, that in which Viola and Sir Andrew's unawareness of Toby's practice is central; fourth, that in which Antonio's mistaking of 'Cesario' for Sebastian is central. Yet these are only the basic situations. The total context which has been established in our minds and from which the action draws its full meaning is beyond explicit description; yet it is in the totality that the cream of the jest—or of four jests—lies.

First up for exploitation is Malvolio's unawareness—but Shakespeare delays Malvolio yet again, until we have been reminded of the state of Olivia's mind. Her remarks stand like the topic sentence for what follows:

> *(Aside.)* I have sent after him; he says he'll
> come. How shall I feast him? What bestow of
> him? For youth is bought more oft than begg'd
> or borrow'd.
>
> [III. iv. 1-3]

Not Malvolio, as he thinks, or her dead brother, as Maria and her accomplices suppose, but 'Cesario' fills her mind: *we are not to be allowed to forget, even at the very edge of it, that Malvolio's outrageous performance before his lady is set within the frame of Viola's masquerade.* Remembrance of Olivia's vain love thus is made to hang darkly over the hilarious spectacle very much as, earlier, Maria's promise of this hilarity hung brightly above the tender and embarrassed interview of Viola and Olivia. The second fold of Olivia's ignorance is next exposed:

> Where is Malvolio? He is sad and civil,
> And suits well for a servant with my fortunes.
> Where is Malvolio?
>
> [III. iv. 5-7]

Malvolio's gulling is also Olivia's; says Maria:

> Your ladyship were best to have some guard
> about you, if he come; for, sure, the man is
> tainted in's wits.
>
> [III. iv. 12-3]

Unaware of Maria's forgery, both servant and lady are victims of the practice. But Olivia stands on the higher level: mystification is up the scale from oblivion. Maniacally smiling, cross-gartered, yellow-stockinged, a veritable bodying-forth of ignorance, Malvolio is the central figure amid circles of error. His smile, his garters, his stockings are unawareness rendered

visible; his words, unawareness rendered audible. Orlando's unawareness of 'Ganymede' and Orsino's of 'Cesario' are exploited mainly by words whose flares illuminate the space between their depths and our height. But Malvolio's is ignorance not so much of another person as of himself, hence is aptly exhibited not only by words but by physical signs—like Bottom's superadded head and Falstaff's horns. 'His very genius', says Sir Toby, when the incident is past, 'hath taken the infection of the device.' The smile, the garters, the stockings—the immediate effects of Maria's practice on him—are ultimately the signs of Malvolio's practice on himself.

Here and in Feste's later practice (IV. ii) Malvolio's exposure to derision is well deserved. Not only is his aspiration self-kindled, lacking the excuse that it was set going by an external practice, but it is contemptible in its nature. Sir Andrew, with Toby's prompting, aspires to Olivia's hand because, in his booby fashion, he loves her. But Malvolio sees Olivia as means to Great Place. Shakespeare exhibits four such deceived, futile aspirants: Sir Andrew and Malvolio of *Twelfth Night*, Slender of *The Merry Wives of Windsor*, and, in the tragic case, Roderigo of *Othello*. Sir Andrew's aspiration is nearest Slender's in its innocence; Malvolio's, tainted with self-love and social ambition, nearest Roderigo's, which is lust. (pp. 133-34)

Amid preparations for Toby's newest practice, Shakespeare sets the third interview of 'Cesario' and Olivia, which reminds us—should the several interludes have obscured the fact—that Olivia's passion is real enough. Though brief, the interview is indispensable: it looks before and after, and its twenty lines bind together the four episodes of this very long climactic scene.

The third of these episodes, which primarily exploits Sir Andrew's ignorance, is at once the result of Sir Toby's old practice on him and of 'Cesario's' practice on all Illyria. The episode parallels that of the yellow stockings: his aspiration fed by Maria's practice, Malvolio makes a spectacle of himself before Olivia; his aspiration fed by Sir Toby's practice, Sir Andrew makes a spectacle of himself by challenging 'Cesario'. 'Marry', says Toby, when the opponents are brought front to front, 'I'll ride your horse as well as I ride you.' Even Malvolio is not so practice-ridden as is Sir Andrew at this moment. Victim, first of all, of nature's practice, he has next been deceived by Sir Toby into supposing that Toby's dry gullet is the way to Olivia's heart; next, he is deceived by Viola's practice into supposing that 'the Count's serving-man' is a serious rival; next, egged on to challenge 'Cesario', he is abused when his foolish letter is replaced by Toby's description of his ferocity: 'this letter, being so excellently ignorant, will breed no terror in the youth; he will find it comes from a clodpole'; and, finally, he is abused by Toby's exaggerated report of his adversary: 'Why, man, he's a very devil; I have not seen such a firago. . . . They say he has been fencer to the Sophy.' The densest concentration of the Illyrian fog which rolled in from the sea with Viola here settles about the head of Sir Andrew. . . . When the time comes, Sir Andrew's resolution is shattered by the terrifying images looming through his wall of fog: 'Let him let the matter slip, and I'll give him my horse, grey Capilet.'

If it concerned him alone, the effect of the episode would be purely comic. But Sir Toby's device makes sport of 'Cesario' also: 'This will so fright them both that they will kill one another by the look, like cockatrices.' For the very first time, yoked with a booby as the butt of a joke, Viola is in danger of looking ridiculous. Hitherto our only advantage over her has been our knowledge of Sebastian's survival—an advantage that has provided comforting assurance but given no cause for laughter. Yet again, as in the case of Olivia stricken with passion for 'Cesario', though the plight is laughable the victim is not. It bears repeating that Viola is one of the most feminine of Shakespeare's heroines. No other heroine is less suited to brave it in man's role—unless it were Hero, who would not dare. . . . From the outset the trials in which Viola's disguise involves her have been hard; this one frightens her nearly to surrendering her secret: 'A little thing would make me tell them how much I lack of a man.'

The line prods our awareness at a crucial moment: the grotesque basis of the duel, the blubbering terror of Sir Andrew, and the swaggering, gross humour of Sir Toby would assuredly tip the scales to the side of hilarity if we should momentarily forget what 'Cesario' is. Further, this particular line of Viola's, being set just after Sir Toby's loudest exhortation to the reluctant duellists, subtly reminds us that Sir Andrew and Viola are not the only butts of this joke: they are the butts in Sir Toby's perspective, but Sir Toby is the butt in ours. . . . This is the cream of the cream: that the boisterous manipulator, perpetrator of multiple practices on Sir Andrew, overpeerer also of 'Cesario' by virtue of his better acquaintance with the silly knight's valour, absolute master, in his own perspective, of all elements in the situation, as self-assured as Malvolio in his utterances—should be all the while ignorant of the most important fact in the entire action. 'Marry', he tells us confidentially of Aguecheek, 'I'll ride your horse as well as I ride you.' But Shakespeare has enabled us to ride Sir Toby.

Perhaps, then, Viola gets off free here, when her unawareness invites laughter at her expense. But in the final episode of the scene, though she escapes laughter, she is exposed under an unflattering light. The fault, of course, is not hers, but Antonio's, in mistaking her for Sebastian. In a sense, Antonio's level is lower than Illyria's, for Orsino, Olivia, and others have only supposed Viola to be 'Cesario', while Antonio, ignorant alike of 'Cesario' and Viola, takes her to be Sebastian. Yet in another sense Illyria's error is deeper, for 'Cesario' is a fiction, whereas Sebastian is a fact.

For this episode the dramatist has so arranged the awarenesses that they set contradictory responses fighting for supremacy. Here again, also, the initial preparation lies far back, in the scene which first shows us Sebastian. Antonio has saved him from the sea, weeps with him for his drowned sister, is solicitous for his welfare, begs to serve him, and, finally, braving old enemies in Orsino's court, insists on accompanying him: 'I do adore thee so / That danger shall seem sport, and I will go.' When next we see the pair, the expression of Antonio's regard for his young friend is emphatic to the point of being conspicuous; what is more, it is backed up by action: 'Hold, sir, here's my purse.' (pp. 135-37)

Sebastian's magnanimous Antonio is like Bassanio's; hence, when he mistakes 'Cesario' for Sebastian, is arrested, asks return of his purse—'It grieves me / Much more for what I cannot do for you / Than what befalls me'—is stared at and refused, our knowledge of his kindness compels sympathy for him—and resentment towards the cause of this sudden shock given to his nature:

> Will you deny me now?
> Is't possible that my deserts to you
> Can lack persuasion?
>
> [III. iv. 347-49]

It is a moment shrewdly wrought, which brings into conflict two urgent awarenesses—of Antonio's selflessness and of Viola's femininity and perfect innocence. Though we know Antonio to be in error and Viola blameless, yet in the eyes of this kind man she is terribly guilty. Shakespeare's devotion to such moments of extreme tension sometimes leads him to the edge of psychological calamity; perhaps there he goes too near, and his heroine, despite our awareness that she is innocent and despite her eagerness to do what she can for Antonio—'My having is not much. / I'll make division of my present with you'—is singed by an involuntary flash of our resentment.

The incident closes the scene. Presenting four interlocked episodes all the relationships of which are constantly exposed to our Olympian view; parading forth nearly all the persons of the play in their relative states of ignorance, none understanding all, and some—Malvolio, Aguecheek, Olivia, Antonio—understanding nothing that is going on; moving from the hilarious exhibition of Malvolio's delusion to the painful representation of Antonio's sudden disillusionment with humankind, it is, from the point of view of the creation, maintenance, and exploitation of multiple discrepant awarenesses, the most remarkable achievement in Shakespearian comedy before *Cymbeline*.

The brief scene which follows is the very cap atop the action of the play, the tip of the summit. In short space are exploited the gaps between the several levels—all inferior to ours—of the six persons who enter. In Shakespeare's comedies, almost infallibly, two contrasting moments make the great peaks: first, the moment in which, errors having been compounded and various lines of action brought to a central point, confusion is nearest universal, visibility nearest zero; second, that in which confusion is dispelled. In the present scene, the first moment is marked by Feste's doubly ironical expostulation with Sebastian:

> No, I do not know you; nor I am not sent to
> you by my lady, to bid you come speak with
> her; nor your name is not Master Cesario; nor
> this is not my nose neither. Nothing that is so
> is so.
>
> [IV. i. 5-9]

So speaks the Clown, wise enough to *play* the fool, yet lost like the others in the Illyrian fog. He is the first of five who in quick succession mistake Sebastian for 'Cesario'. The formula is the same on which the entire action of *The Comedy of Errors* is based, but it is here used with a difference. In the early play, when Adriana mistakes Antipholus of Syracuse for her husband, she is only once removed from the truth apparent to us—for there is indeed an Antiphilus of Ephesus. But the 'Cesario' for whom Sebastian is mistaken is himself a fiction. All five persons, thus, being twice removed from truth, hold a level even lower than Sebastian's. For Sebastian, though he has come from outside into a situation of which he is totally ignorant—knowing neither that Viola lives nor that she poses as 'Cesario', that Olivia loves this 'Cesario', or that Sir Andrew is jealous of him—is nevertheless well enough aware that he is himself Sebastian and no other; not seeing the illusion that blinds the others, he is nearer reality than they. Oblivion is a lower level than mystification; they are oblivious, and he is mystified:

> What relish is in this? How runs the stream?
> Or I am mad, or else this is a dream.
>
> [IV. i. 60-1]

His mystification continues through his next scene, when it contrasts with Olivia's blissful error as she draws him home in the company of a priest. In all Shakespeare's comedies, only the twin brothers of *The Comedy of Errors*, masters and servants, remain longer in this precise degree of awareness. . . . [Sebastian's] relation to the illusion-ridden city of Illyria differs in one particular from that of Antipholus of Syracuse to Ephesus. Until Antipholus and his Dromio arrived, no illusion existed in Ephesus; what follows is all of their own making. But when Sebastian came out of the sea to Illyria, Viola had preceded him, bringing in the fog that now engulfs everyone. 'Madman, thou errest', the Clown tells Malvolio in the continuing practice on this most extreme case of the Illyrian affliction. 'I say, there is no darkness but ignorance, in which thou art more puzzl'd than the Egyptians in their fog.' Malvolio best represents also the Illyrians' inability to perceive their illusion: 'I tell thee, I am as well in my wits as any man in Illyria.' In contrast, coming from outside into all this, Sebastian knows enough to be mystified; though he cannot see through the fog, he can see that it is there: 'There's something in't / That is deceivable.'

At the opening of Act V the burden of the context which preceding acts have established in our minds is staggering. *During Acts II, III, and IV no fully aware person except Viola has appeared before us*—and during part of this time she too has lacked full vision. At precisely what moment she rejoins us in our omniscience is the final question to be considered; indeed, the question of the state of Viola's awareness during the last two acts is the great question of the play.

At the close of Act IV we saw Olivia and Sebastian go to be married. We therefore hold advantage over Viola and Orsino upon their entrance in Act V. Over Orsino, of course, we hold other advantages also—the same that we have held for three acts. But are we to suppose that we hold any additional advantage over Viola? She is ignorant that her brother—in a state like that of shock—is now repeating the marriage oath before Olivia's priest. But is she still ignorant that he escaped drowning and has arrived in Illyria?

At the end of Act III, when Antonio interrupted her match with Sir Andrew, the cause of his error was as open to her as to us. That she then perceived the truth there can be little doubt:

> Methinks his words do from such passion fly
> That he believes himself; so do not I.
> Prove true, imagination, O, prove true,
> That I, dear brother, be now ta'en for you!
> [III. iv. 373-76]

And again:

> He nam'd Sebastian. I my brother know
> Yet living in my glass; even such and so
> In favour was my brother, and he went
> Still in this fashion, colour, ornament,
> For him I imitate.
> [III. iv. 379-83]

But now, at the opening of Act V, with Orsino, again meeting Antonio, she speaks with wide-eyed amazement:

> He did me kindness, sir, drew on my side,
> But in conclusion put strange speech upon me.
> I know not what 'twas but distraction.
> [V. i. 66-8]

'That most ingrateful boy there by your side, / From the rude sea's enrag'd and foamy mouth / Did I redeem', asserts An-

tonio. . . . From the first she had entertained hope; then Antonio had mistaken her and named Sebastian, whom she imitated in her masquerade; and, finally, Antonio describes a sea-rescue that accords with other evidence of Sebastian's survival. When Antonio has finished his account of the rescue and his three-months' life with Sebastian, Viola could, with few words, disabuse the tormented fellow, whose experience with ingratitude is maddening him. Instead, wide-eyed as before, she inquires, 'How can this be?'

That is to say, she holds to her masquerade in spite of all at this crucial moment—and even, in feigning ignorance, grafts a new practice on the old. Why does she do so? A damning answer is that Shakespeare is willing to sacrifice plausibility in order to preserve to the last moment the richly exploitable gap between Illyria's oblivion and Viola's awareness, so that when all lines have converged upon that moment, he can achieve a spectacular denouement, with Illyria's awareness shooting up like a rocket when Sebastian and 'Cesario' come face to face. That Shakespeare always set a high rate on exploitable gaps and that he here forces the situation to yield its utmost effect before he explodes it is unquestionable. But that he sacrifices plausibility in doing so is not so sure.

At the opening of Act V Viola is yet ignorant of one fact: that Olivia and Sebastian are married. *If she knew that,* she would know that time, on which she early set her hope—'O time! thou must untangle this, not I'—has already solved her problem. Not knowing it, and being Viola, feminine as no other, she maintains her old fiction and compounds a new one of silence and innocence. Like Portia and Rosalind, Vincentio and Prospero in that she plays the role of chief practiser and controlling force, she is unlike these in her attitude toward it. She has found no joy in the role; she has been tempted to abandon it: 'A little thing would make me tell them how much I lack of a man.' More significantly, whereas the other controlling forces manipulate persons and contrive practices to bring their ends about, she has contrived nothing beyond her initial disguise. . . . When at last Antonio's error advised her of her brother's survival, her hope took ecstatic new life: the end was in sight. Being Viola, she could not then break faith with time, even to save the good Antonio from misanthropy. Feminine in her patient waiting, she is no less so in her persistence: it is not enough that the end is in sight; it must actually be reached. When the Duke berates her, even threatening death, she opposes her patience to his fury:

> And I, most jocund, apt, and willingly,
> To do you rest, a thousand deaths would die.
> [V. i. 132-33]

The final silent moments of her masquerade are the hardest.

So great is her subtlety at the last that it is difficult to identify the instant at which she perceives that time has performed its final chore in her behalf. But she must be fully aware by the time of Olivia's exclamation: 'Cesario, husband, stay!' Nevertheless, to the Duke's enraged 'Her husband, sirrah!' she replies with a wide-eyed denial that we should perhaps take instead as a victory whoop: 'No, my lord, not I.' The priest confirms Olivia's word that 'Cesario' is her husband. Sir Andrew and Sir Toby berate 'Cesario' for hurting them. Still Viola keeps silent, except to deny the charges. Then follow fifty lines of dialogue in the course of which Sebastian enters and astonishes all Illyria except herself. And still she speaks never a word. The arrival of Sebastian cannot be a surprise to her; his tender greeting of Olivia can be none. The long, superb silence, more wonderful than the Illyrians' ejaculations of amazement, is almost but not quite the extremest demonstration of her femininity. That demonstration comes only after Sebastian has subjected her to direct questioning, when she replies with wide-eyed and incredible incredulity:

> Such a Sebastian was my brother too;
> So went he suited to his watery tomb.
> If spirits can assume both form and suit,
> You come to fright us.
>
> [V. i. 233-36]

In this last instant before giving over her long masquerade, she thus devises a final fiction: neither husband, brother, nor sister-in-law will ever learn from her lips anything other than that she had been ignorant, *until this instant,* of her brother's survival, his arrival in Illyria, and his marriage. This shred of a great secret she will never give up, that she had ridden her masquerade to the very end, biding time—'O time! thou must untangle this, not I'—until it took Olivia off her hands and gave her Orsino. (pp. 137-43)

> Bertrand Evans, "The Fruits of the Sport: 'Twelfth Night'," in his Shakespeare's Comedies, Oxford at the Clarendon Press, Oxford, 1960, pp. 118-43.

MELVIN SEIDEN (essay date 1961)

[*Seiden claims that the comic strategy of* Twelfth Night *is devious. In his view of Malvolio as a character of low self-esteem, Seiden departs from the great majority of nineteenth- and twentieth-century critics, who treat Malvolio as a victim of self-love. He finds that Shakespeare manipulates Malvolio as his comic instrument, and uses him not to reveal and describe the evils of Puritanism, as critics such as Joseph Hunter (1845) and F. Kreyssig (1862) claim, but to serve as a scapegoat to the "amoral, bacchanalian gods of comedy." For additional commentary on the punishment of Malvolio, see the excerpts by William Hazlitt (1817), Charles Lamb (1822), Charles Knight (1842), T. Kenny (1864), H. N. Hudson (1872), William Archer (1884), O. J. Campbell (1943), and Milton Crane (1955).*]

Twelfth Night is a triumphant hoax. Outwardly a conventional Elizabethan comedy, it is witty, complicated, ingenious, and devious to the end that we may be gratified by its high spirits. But unlike the other comedies of Shakespeare there is in this equivocal work a subterranean deviousness and ingenuity that aims to deceive us in a special way. To the extent to which the play is successful as a comedy, it can be said that the trickery which operates at our expense is also successful.

No one can have failed to recognize the violent incongruity between the tone and texture of the Viola-Olivia-Orsino action (which is gentle, lyrical, and musically amorous) and the harsh punishment inflicted upon Malvolio. And so we have puzzled over the moral question, Is the punishment deserved? whereas the more pertinent question is, Why, matters of justice aside, did Shakespeare feel compelled to provide us with this singularly uncharacteristic spectacle of a Juvenalian (or Jonsonian) scourging of a comic villain? To answer this we must follow the crooked stream of Shakespeare's comic art to its subterranean sources. (p. 105)

Shakespeare treats his star-crossed lovers with the utmost gentleness and tact. Modern critics tell us that Shakespeare is satirizing Orsino's mooney-eyed love-*schmerz* and slyly spoofing Olivia's extravagant sorrow for the death of her brother; and these critics cite the excesses of language—self-indulgent, artificial, and hyperbolic—that Shakespeare has them mouth.

But the proof of the pudding in drama is not and can never successfully be in the language or the subtleties of imagery and symbolism, but in the action. As in so many different ways E. E. Stoll has never tired of pointing out, in drama the character *is* what he *does;* and what is remarkable here is the total omission of any action that might function comically at the expense of these three lovers. They are never caught up in the ludicrous predicaments that their situation and the impingement of the other comic developments insistently suggest should be their fate. (p. 106)

Shakespeare's grand strategy is to divert the current of our expectations into another channel, to provide us with another object for our promiscuous and destructive laughter in the figure of Malvolio. . . . It is not Sir Andrew Aguecheek and Sir Toby Belch, patricians manqué, who are the true surrogates for the comic-"tragedies" that are never permitted to embroil the lovers, but the puritan Malvolio. He is the scapegoat; he is the man who undergoes a sacrificial comic death so that they may live unscathed; he is the man who, because of offensive seriousness (made to appear an antithetical ridiculousness) allows what is also ludicrous in the lovers to maintain its sober-faced pretense of impregnable seriousness.

Malvolio stands condemned of a mean, life-denying, but nevertheless principled utilitarianism. Shakespeare wants to excite our antipathy to Malvolio's anti-comic sobriety, his sour bourgeois version of Aristotle's ethical golden mean, and he provides us with many appropriate occasions for venting our antipathies. What Shakespeare does not want us to recognize, and what becomes clear once we are no longer involved emotionally in the play, is the fact that just as Malvolio is a creature of utility for his mistress Olivia, winning for his assiduous services only scorn and abuse, so for his creator Malvolio becomes an infinitely serviceable comic instrument. We recognize that without Malvolio the comedy of *Twelfth Night* would be impoverished; I would go farther and argue that without him the comedy, the play as a whole, would not *work,* and it is precisely this indebtedness to Malvolio's multifarious utilitarianism that Shakespeare cannot acknowledge, since we are not meant to see what the old magician has up his sleeve or in his hat.

The social issues involved in the struggle between Malvolio's code of calculating utility and the comic values suggested by the title of the play (the bacchanalia, before the holiday ends) are not as clear as some critics have made them out to be. Tallying Malvolio's traits, we have no trouble seeing what these stand for. He is efficient, music-hating, fun-denying, power-seeking, austere, pompous, officious, and melancholy—in short, he is a Puritan and, in the first decade of the seventeenth century, an ur-version of the man of the future, the petty bourgeois. Curiously, however, these values are not pitted against the lovers' aristocratic ones; the conflict is *not* between Malvolio's excessively rigid and stifling code of responsibility and that of love, leisure, music, sensibility, elegance, and the higher irresponsibility. Shakespeare is particularly careful to avoid representing a direct clash between Malvolio and his aristocratic betters. He is gulled, baited, and scourged by Maria and Feste, socially his inferiors, who are aided by Sir Toby and Sir Andrew, and the latter are grossly perverted specimens of nobility. We need not look any farther than Falstaff to see that for Shakespeare the fallen aristocrat can be morally worse than the erect man of lower degree. (pp. 106-07)

The conflict in *Twelfth Night* is then between aristocracy at its worst (Toby and Aguecheek, aided by the roisterers)—perverted, and thus the antithesis of what is implied in the ideal of *noblesse oblige*—and a representative of the new bourgeoisie presented in its most perfect archetypal form, since Malvolio, whatever else he is not, is true to the principles he represents. He has a radical existential authenticity; he is the quintessential bourgeois.

Shakespeare's overt—but I think questionable—point is that in its purest manifestation such dour puritanism is worse even than the corrupt patrician irresponsibility of the Belches and Aguecheeks. The point that he is at some pains to conceal— or rather, what he wishes to avoid making a point of—is that he must avoid challenging the values of the patrician lovers with those of Malvolio.

Why? For one thing, the antithesis between Malvolio's grubby puritanism and the lovers' exquisite manners is not the unequivocal conflict between beauty and the beast that so many of our critics have made it out to be. We all recognize that Malvolio stands for work, order, duty, sobriety—everything, in short, that permits a society to function. Olivia clearly recognizes this. She understands that Malvolio's stewardship is necessary to the functioning of her household. As steward, then, Malvolio represents the police force: law and order. The love-making, the sweet melancholy of long leisure hours spent in contemplation, the delight in music, the poeticizing of life— all this is possible because of the mean prose of Malvolio's labors as a steward. (p. 108)

His arrogance is not the swollen amour-propre it seems to be. Clearly this is a man who believes in work and in particular in his own work. He is fanatically conscientious in trying to enforce law and order, not as the play so slyly makes us believe merely because he is temperamentally opposed to fun and play, but because he is also by principle antagonistic to whatever threatens to subvert the orderly social machinery of his mistress's household.

We in America have made a cult of that ambiguous virtue we call "a sense of humor." And so one hears it said, "If only Malvolio had a sense of humor, it would be possible to like him a little." What is being asked for here is that Malvolio be critical and detached, able to view his policeman's job skeptically and perhaps with the saving grace of an irony that would puncture the hypocrisies inherent in the job itself and his own seriousness. But this is impossible. Such a Malvolio would be a deeply divided man. Having the insight to see that in being Olivia's lackey he demeans himself and makes himself an object of contempt, Malvolio would indeed become what he comes perilously close to being in that extraordinary scene in which he suffers Feste's catechistic torments—a tragic figure. The so-called romantic critics assert that in this bitter, punitive scene, ending with the victim's impotent oath, "I'll be reveng'd on the whole pack of you!" Malvolio is in fact something like a tragic figure. But romantic critics and those who dismiss this view of Malvolio as sentimentality agree that it cannot have been Shakespeare's intention (or, seeking to avoid the dread intentional fallacy: that of the play) to endow Malvolio with tragic stature. Granting Malvolio the complex attitudes of a man with a sense of humor could all too easily engender tragic consequences. (pp. 108-09)

Olivia, it can be assumed, would be the first to be displeased by a Malvolio who, winking broadly at Toby, had said, "Dost thou think because I must feign a steward's virtue I desire not the joys of cakes and ale?" Malvolio's frigid personality reflects his stern policies, and these are his mistress's. He is her surrogate, her cop; he is all super-ego in a libidinous society; and as we all come round to saying when we must justify whatever it is we do, Malvolio might have said, "That is what I'm paid to do." Malvolio, like the petty Nazi hireling defending himself at the Nuremberg trials, would have had to be a revolutionary to be different from what he was—not just a better man, but a radical critic of the society that created him, gave him employment, and provided sustenance.

Early in the play, in answer to Malvolio's contempt for the verbal tomfoolery with which Feste amuses his mistress, Olivia sums up Malvolio's chief vice neatly (and famously) in the line: "O, you are sick of self-love, Malvolio, and taste with a distemper'd appetite." The tag has stuck. Self-love seems to explain almost everything. But does it? Is Malvolio's behavior that of a man who, thinking well of himself, thinks poorly of others? One ought not answer Yes too quickly.

A common schematic analysis of the theme of love in *Twelfth Night* is the following: all of the major characters, with the exception of Viola, are seen to be motivated by some heretical or distorted version of love. Orsino is in love with love itself, Olivia is in love with grief, Malvolio is smitten with self-love, and only Viola expresses true—that is, a properly directed and controlled—love. In this account, Malvolio's narcissistic love disables him from loving others.

Now it is certainly true that more than anything else it is the passionless, calculating, mercenary fashion in which Malvolio responds to the imaginary love of his mistress that makes him so repugnant. Despite the social impropriety, we might forgive him were he to court his mistress with passion. If he were a man by love possessed, unable to control an imperious passion, he would be the type of the romantic sinner we have no difficulty forgiving. And, so far as the proprieties are concerned, it is no accident that the witty Maria, blessed because she is a wit, is fortunate enough to marry above her station. Only a twentieth century reader of the play, his mind corrupted by democratic and psychological principles alien to the world of *Twelfth Night*, will question Maria's good luck. For the Elizabethan, it cannot have much mattered that Toby is an ass; even an ass, if affiliated with nobility, may be a good catch for one of the downstairs folk. The point then is that Shakespeare's social hierarchy can, for comic purposes, be flexible enough to permit one of those who has ingratiated herself to us by ingeniously performing her role as maker of comedy the good fortune of succeeding as a social climber.

Malvolio's social climbing is therefore not evil per se. In comedy, success is conferred only upon those who please us by aiding and abetting the flow of the comedy. Malvolio is the very embodiment of the anti-comic spirit and the failure of his social climbing is due not simply or primarily to the immorality and impiety of the aim itself, but to his not having as it were bribed us by affording us comic pleasure. If Malvolio had been an agent of joy and comic abandon, Shakespeare would have had little difficulty in winning the sympathy of his audience for a man who at play's end inherits rather than becomes, as he does become, dispossessed.

The critics agree that Malvolio is a loveless Snopes, and the orthodox view, based on Olivia's judgment, is that inflated self-love incapacitates him for loving others. I want to suggest that what seems to Olivia to be self-love in Malvolio is more likely to be a deficiency of self-esteem. Like all those whose work is primarily that of imposing discipline, coercing obedience, enforcing respect and orderly behavior, checking "the natural man'' in whatever guise he may assume with the ''civilizing'' force of control, constraint, and censorship, Malvolio is well suited to this job precisely because he does not possess a well developed, assertive ego. . . . Those whose social roles require, as does Malvolio's, that they be constantly saying no to others must first learn to be deaf to the alluring siren songs within themselves. (pp. 109-11)

If Malvolio loved himself more one can imagine him loving his policeman's work less. If this seeming self-love were genuine, Malvolio might have allowed himself to be caught up in the fun, the irresponsible high jinks, the holiday mood of the revelers. True self-love, witnessing the privileged hedonism of irresponsibility says, ''Why should I be excluded? Why must I be the servant of fasting while others feast?'' . . . Malvolio acts and talks like one whose show of strength is only a fantasy, the purpose of which is to abrogate a reality that is all weakness and self-contempt. It is no accident that in the first great scene of Malvolio's comic humiliation, where he is ensnared into ludicrous courtship of his mistress, it is precisely the fantasist in Malvolio that is played upon so outrageously and brilliantly by Maria and the other wits. And, if it be objected that the motives we impute to Malvolio are too serious, too sympathetic, the reply must be that we do not necessarily sympathize more with a self-deceived puritan than a simple moral bully, and, comedy or no comedy, Malvolio is a serious character; it is precisely his seriousness that we are asked to see as comic in the context of the others' horseplay. (p. 111)

I have described the comic strategies of *Twelfth Night* as devious. It can also be said that they are curiously un-Shakespearean. In particular, I refer to the emotional and moral implications of the mechanism for resolving a comic action that is analogous to catharsis in tragedy.

It is a commonplace of the critical tradition to find in Shakespeare's Falstaff the embodiment of the comic spirit. Modern scholarship has tended to reinforce this tradition by showing that Falstaff derives from the character of Vice or Riot in the medieval morality plays. Because he is Riot, Falstaff represents the principle of the transvaluation of all normal values. The comedy of the *Henry IV* plays inheres precisely in the subverting of the normal, sane, responsible, ordered, workaday world. (pp. 111-12)

Because more than being an impresario of comedy Falstaff *is* comedy, it is inevitable that Falstaff be banished, purged, symbolically sacrificed after he has outlived his comic usefulness. The pattern of the *Henry IV* plays seems to be an archetypal one: the sane, sober, unmagical world of work and duty is turned topsy-turvy by comic anarchy; comic anarchy flourishes, evoking in us pleasure and wonder; the forces representing what most of us unphilosophically think of as ''reality'' reassert themselves, thus re-establishing a world that, whatever else it may be, is always a non-comic one.

This re-establishing of a non-comic world is, of course, equivalent to the return to a non-tragic world in tragic works. Indeed, the whole pattern is more than similar in comedy and tragedy: in both there is a radical overturning of that gray reality we all know best, followed by a return to equilibrium at every level at which the disharmony and disequilibrium had previously existed. What comedy and tragedy have in common is that in both a kind of insanity (one terrible, the other delightful) has been allowed to reign and is then purged.

Everything that has given us pleasure in *Henry IV* took place under the aegis of Falstaff. No wonder we are saddened and perhaps even indignant when we are forced to witness the humiliation of the fantastic creature that made all of this possible. The tensions of tragedy become increasingly intolerable and we demand that they be resolved. But we want the holidaying of comedy to go on and on—in our dreams, even forever. In both cases, however, we understand that life always provides a Fortinbras to insure that man and society will survive and that, for a similar but antithetical reason, King Henrys, judges, wives, babies, and empty cupboards contrive to bring the raptures of a comic holiday to an end.

There is no Falstaff in *Twelfth Night;* there are only those grossly inferior comedians, Feste, Maria, Toby, and Aguecheek and—quintessential antagonist to everything that Falstaff is and represents, that harsh and melancholy voice of the anticomic spirit: Malvolio.

How clever of Shakespeare to get us to believe that puritanism is bad or ugly—so at least hundreds of college students of Shakespeare have unanimously believed—when in fact Malvolio's fundamental sin (I am tempted to say his only sin) is that in his very being he threatens the comic, holiday world that Maria, Feste and company are so gaily creating. It is irrelevant that Shakespeare the man may have loathed puritanism and everything it stood for. In this play, Malvolio's puritanism is a pretext, a convenient catch-all for traits and attitudes inimical to the lovely anarchy of comedy. He must be humiliated, gulled, baited, scourged, made to suffer the melancholy consequences of his melancholy personality, and, above all, rendered impotent so that the fever of comedy can range with full potency. If Malvolio is not the perfect mythic scapegoat, where in our literature does one find a figure who can be called a scapegoat? No, it simply will not do to say that one is sentimentalizing in describing Malvolio as a scapegoat sacrificed to the amoral, bacchanalian gods of comedy. To insist upon Malvolio's sacrificial status is not to excuse or justify his clearly repugnant personality. Least of all is it a covert plea for sympathy. Malvolio's function is to ''die'' a kind of comic death so that comedy may live. And so, throughout the play we see him ''dying'' in various ways. However, the immense—and in my opinion, unsatisfactorily resolved—problem arises when the comedy itself, as is always the case, must ''die.'' What does—what can—the dramatist do with Malvolio at that point?

The logic that ought to impose itself upon Shakespeare would seem to be as follows: since the re-instituting of the non-comic world in *Henry IV* requires the literal and symbolic sacrificing of the patron of riot and comedy who is Falstaff, the same strategic necessities in *Twelfth Night* ought to allow Malvolio, by virtue of his antithetical role, to come into his own with the ''dying'' of the comedy. He is the patron of the non-comic and it would seem natural that he should preside over the re-establishment of the hegemony of the non-comic that ends the play. But Shakespeare has provided himself with no machinery and aroused in us no expectations that would permit Malvolio to receive the blessing of a magic (and thus appropriately comic) and symbolic rebirth. Lodged uncomfortably at the center of this genial, loving, musical comedy is the harsh, unpurged punitive fate of Malvolio. Olivia says, ''He hath been most notoriously abus'd''; and that is the only soft chord in the dissonant Malvolio music.

Let us be perfectly clear about this point. If Shakespeare is ''unfair'' in his treatment of Malvolio it is not in the severity of the punishments meted out to him during the course of the play; it is in Shakespeare's trying to have it both ways. Denier of comedy and its claims that Malvolio is, by comedy's standards he "deserves" his fate, but, when the resolution of the action itself denies, negates, "kills" the comedy, one expects that with the return to the world that Malvolio has been immolated for upholding, Malvolio himself will have his day. But Malvolio has been totally discredited in serving this world. He is like the politician who lives to see his name become anathema while the principles that soiled his good name, having once been defeated, return triumphantly. But these principles, miraculously, are no longer associated with the man who gave them their name.

Malvolio is Shakespeare's comic Coriolanus, a man beset by the wolves who are his enemies and the jackals who are or ought to be his friends. In America no one loves a cop—even when he's called a policeman. In Illyria the natives are apparently no different, and even light-hearted Illyrian comedy turns out to be a cannibalistic affair, at bottom. (pp. 112-14)

Melvin Seiden, "Malvolio Reconsidered," in The University of Kansas City Review *(copyright University of Kansas City, 1961), Vol. XXVIII, No. 2, December, 1961, pp. 105-14.*

G. K. HUNTER (essay date 1962)

[*Writing within the critical tradition which identifies* Twelfth Night *as Shakespeare's farewell to comedy, Hunter discerns a darkness in the play which prefigures the tragedies. In the casting of Feste as the objective, central observer in* Twelfth Night, *Hunter detects a change in the overall design of Shakespeare's work. He also notes how affectation and self-indulgence plague major and minor characters alike, and the way in which their paths toward self-awareness include self-sacrifice. For Hunter, the happiness at the end of* Twelfth Night *is tentative, sounding tragic chords which prepare the way for* Hamlet, Troilus and Cressida, *and the end of Shakespeare's comedy. For additional commentary on the dark aspects of the play, see the excerpts by F. J. Furnivall (1877), Arthur Quiller-Couch (1930), John Middleton Murry (1936), Mark Van Doren (1939), E. C. Pettet (1949), W. H. Auden (1957), Albert Gérard (1964), Jan Kott (1964), Clifford Leech (1965), and Philip Edwards (1968).*]

A reading of *As You Like It* together with *Twelfth Night* will soon reveal that the two plays are by the same hand. Both centre on the vision of happiness through love, as it is seen by a highly-born heroine who is condemned to serve out her love in a strange country, disguised as a boy. Both plays set the loving self-awareness of this heroine against a gallery of poseurs, lamed by self-love (and the consequent lack of self-awareness), and show her depth of sanity in her capacity to play the strange role that the harsh world sets her, with efficiency but without losing faith in the true identity to which fate and her own efforts will eventually return her. Both plays contain important 'wise-fool' roles, in which the fool (Touchstone or Feste) is largely detached from the loving and self-loving world, knowing better than most the inevitability of self-deception, but less than at least one (the heroine) the value of implication in the Human Dilemma.

The likeness of the two plays is considerable, but it appears in the mechanics rather than the effects. The two professional fools may indeed serve to focus the differences as well as the similarities. A. C. Bradley remarked of Feste that 'he would never have dreamed of marrying Audrey' [see excerpt above, 1916]. Critics today are properly chary about the kind of criticism which tries to fit characters out of one play into another ('we can imagine the difference at Elsinore if only Hamlet

could have been married to Lady Macbeth') but in this case the remark seems to compress conveniently an important difference between the two plays. Feste (unlike Touchstone) has no history, and this affects his function in the play. . . . Feste has no personal life to use as a 'stalking horse'; there is no self-parody in his statements; his gaze is fixed relentlessly on the temperaments and actions of others, with a clear eye for their foibles and weaknesses. . . . It is typical of Feste's role as the detached onlooker that we are uncertain if he was ever fully involved in the plot against Malvolio. Certainly he was willing to appear as the 'wise' Sir Topas ministering to the 'fool' Malvolio, for that demonstrated neatly how 'the whirligig of time brings in his revenges', but the involvement seems limited to this intellectual kind of pleasure in consequences. Feste is not to be circumscribed by the subplot grouping of Sir Toby, Maria, Sir Andrew, nor can he be supposed to share their 'eat, drink and be merry' philosophy, except as it suits his purpose. He is the onlooker who judges but is never judged; in this way he is bound to be much nearer to the centre of the play than is Touchstone.

The changed and more central role of the fool in this play is symptomatic of a change of focus in the whole design. No longer is affectation or self-indulgence a weakness which can be put aside blandly, as it is by Rosalind. In *As You Like It* Phebe and Jaques can be put in their places, in a dance of living and loving, by self-control and self-awareness, but without self-sacrifice. In *Twelfth Night*, affectation is everywhere—among the heroic as among the foolish, among the central characters as among the marginal—and self-sacrifice is necessarily involved if it is to be defeated. Rosalind is able to use her disguise as a genuine and joyous extension of her personality; Viola suffers constriction and discomfiture in *her* role. It is properly representative that the most famous speeches by the disguised Rosalind are her teasing comments on Orlando. . . :

> The poor world is almost six thousand years old, and in all this time there was not any man died in his own person, videlicet, in a love-cause . . . men have died from time to time, and worms have eaten them, but not for love.
> [*As You Like It*, IV. i. 94ff.]

while the most famous speech of the disguised Viola is the melancholy description of her own imagined fate:

> She never told her love,
> But let concealment, like a worm i' th' bud,
> Feed on her damask cheek. She pin'd in thought;
> And with a green and yellow melancholy
> She sat like Patience on a monument
> Smiling at grief. Was not this love indeed?
> [II. iv. 110-15]

—further constricted, as the speech is, in the context of Orsino's assumption that women cannot love.

The vision of happiness is thus for Viola a smiling through tears, a vision all the more poignant for its unlikeliness to be fulfilled. To say this is to make Viola sound like the archetype for much modern 'brave little woman' sentimentality. And she is not: the play is too busy to let her even seem so. The sentiment is placed in a current of cross-intrigues which keeps it from the stagnation of sentimentality. Happiness is a perpetual possibility which has to be shelved away as soon as it is exposed (for matters, not hostile, but more immediately pressing, always intervene); it is a single thread in a broadloom that is largely made up of threats and deceptions. It is one of the functions of the large-scale and fully developed subplot of this play to complicate each of the visits that Viola makes to the house of Olivia, and to cross-hatch the final comedy of errors between Sebastian and Viola.

But the complications introduced by the sub-plot are not to be limited to the intrigues it contains; what we have here is not a simple world of below-stairs bumbling and aping (as in *Much Ado*) but a real, even if easily deflected, threat to the security of princely natures and developed sensibilities. On the self-indulgence of Olivia and Orsino must be laid at least some of the blame for the presumptuousness of Malvolio and the idle mischief of Sir Toby. Malvolio's aspiration to join the aristocracy is not absurd; his disguise in smiles and yellow stockings can be seen as a nastier variant of the 'mental disguise' of Orsino and Olivia—their willingness to act on temporary obsessions, and to forget the continuity of their lives. All are presented as victims of a need to hide from the isolated truth (and here Viola, though her disguise is forced on her and not chosen, must be joined with the others): Olivia cannot bear to be known for what she is—a healthy and nubile woman; Viola cannot permit herself to be known for what she is—a girl; Orsino cannot bear to be known for what he is—a lover in love with the idea of love; Sir Toby cannot bear to be known for a parasite, Sir Andrew for a fool, Malvolio for a steward. The process of the play is one which allows these truths to be bearable (or socially organized) at the end of the action, not by developing characters to a greater understanding, but simply by moving the plot around till the major characters each find themselves opposite a desirable partner and an escape hatch from absurdity. . . . It is true that there is a degree of 'Jonsonian' social realism in the play's image of an effete aristocracy threatened by a determined upstart; the economic basis of the relationship between Sir Toby and Sir Andrew is clearly stated [II. iii. 181ff.], and the marriage of Sir Toby and Maria is more a piece of social justice than a contribution to any final dance of reconciliation. But this dance itself is not to be explained in social terms; the principal emotion involved in the denouement is the sense of release from the complexity and isolation of outer disguise or inner obsession; and this is a personal and individual matter, to which society is merely accessory:

> When . . . golden time convents,
> A solemn combination shall be made
> Of our dear souls. Meantime, sweet sister,
> We will not part from hence, Cesario, come;
> For so you shall be, while you are a man;
> But when in other habits you are seen,
> Orsino's mistress, and his fancy's queen.
>
> [V. i. 382-89]

But we may well feel that the play has related the dream world of 'golden time' too securely to the class struggle around it to allow this to be more than a partial reconciliation. The amount of space that the denouement gives to Malvolio (about one hundred lines out of a total of one hundred and seventy-five) may seem to be indicative of Shakespeare's waning interest in these glamorous aristocrats. . . . The happiness of the lovers would seem to have been bought at a price which excludes Malvolio, and we may feel that this circumscribes and diminishes the final effect of their happiness.

It is another function of the subplot in *Twelfth Night* to complement the lyric world of the high-born characters with a robust and self-sufficient grossness so that a more complete image of society emerges. . . . *Twelfth Night* is not . . . a comedy of wit. It is, on the other hand, the most poetical (and musical) of the comedies; this is not to say that a higher proportion of the lines are poetry, but that it is more shot through and through by the lyric abandon of poetic utterance. . . . Poetic abandon of this kind is required in *Twelfth Night*, because there is so little that the characters, disguised, obsessed and frustrated as they are, can do; they are obliged to live out their potentialities rather than deeds—potentialities . . . dramatically enlarged in the mirror of a nostalgia for the impossible. This powerfully affects the image of the lover that the play gives us. In *As You Like It* we met the absurdity of the lover in Orlando's verses; but the verse is only a by-product of the loving personality. In Orsino, on the other hand, as in Olivia, the poetic abandon of love is given its bent and allowed a full range of languorous evocation. . . . (pp. 43-50)

Orsino and Olivia are too powerful to be scored against and pushed aside. Both indeed are, as has been remarked, 'unlikely candidates for affectation'; Orsino is categorically stated, in the exposition, to be

> A noble duke, in nature as in name.
>
> [I. ii. 25]

and Olivia, in her rule of her household and her distinction between Feste and Malvolio, shows a rare poise, even in the midst of her excess:

> O, you are sick of self-love, Malvolio, and taste
> with a distemper'd appetite. To be generous,
> guiltless, and of free disposition, is to take those
> things for bird-bolts that you deem cannon bul-
> lets. There is no slander in an allow'd fool,
> though he do nothing but rail; nor no railing in
> a known discreet man, though he do nothing
> but reprove.
>
> [I. v. 90-6]

If such people are deluded, then their poetical delusions must be *self*-cured; it is for this reason, I suppose, that the play offers, beside *their* worlds, other worlds of experience which they can react to and discover, and discovering, evaluate properly (because of their fundamental nobility); with this evidence we judge them on their potential insight, seen against the others' incurable blindness. That love is both absurd and ennobling is a point that all these comedies have made; here in a world where all are disguised or deluded we need the grosser loves (and delusions) of Andrew, Toby and Malvolio, whose sensuality is an important element in his character, to give a scale to the high poetical delusions of Orsino and Olivia. A glance at a long and complex scene, like Act III, scene iv, may indicate how this is achieved. The scene opens with the comic incoherence of an Olivia plagued by love—very similar to the comedy of Rosalind . . .—but it moves immediately to the related love-madness of Malvolio, the relevance of this being stated categorically:

> *Olivia.* Go call him hither. I am mad as he,
> If sad and merry madness equal be.
>
> [III. iv. 14-15]

Malvolio's lunatic power to find encouragement in insults reflects directly on Olivia's refusal to accept Viola's words, but it also highlights the self-knowledge she shows in the face of her own madness; for he flies straight into a state where he is the very puppet of his own obsession, incapable of human conversation. . . . (pp. 50-1)

The next episode contrasts the cowardice of Viola with that of Sir Andrew, and again the contrast is handled as one between laughing at the person and laughing at the situation. Andrew is sublimely ignorant of the difference between noble and ig-noble behaviour:

> Plague on't; an I thought he had been valiant,
> and so cunning in fence, I'd have seen him
> damn'd ere I'd have challeng'd him. Let him
> let the matter slip, and I'll give him my horse,
> grey Capilet.
>
> 　　　　　　　　　　　　　　　　[III. iv. 282-87]

To Fabian and Sir Toby the comedy of the cowardly Cesario is no different from that of the cowardly Sir Andrew:

> *Sir Toby.* I have his horse to take up the quarrel:
> I have persuaded him the youth's a devil.
> *Fabian.* He is as horribly conceited of him; and
> pants and looks pale, as if a bear were at his
> heels,
>
> 　　　　　　　　　　　　　　　　[III. iv. 292-95]

but we react differently. Viola directs our attention to her inner dilemma:

> Pray God defend me! A little thing would make
> me tell them how much I lack of a man.
> 　　　　　　　　　　　　　　　　[III. iv. 302-03]

and so (while we laugh) we share her view of the situation; the gross level of the practical joke that Fabian and Sir Toby are conducting is being judged by Viola's reaction to it no less than she is being judged by their contrived situation.

In among these pranks Shakespeare places two passages of high-bred sensibility. Olivia and Viola meet briefly (for seventeen lines) and reveal their natures:

> *Olivia.* I have said too much unto a heart of stone,
> And laid mine honour too unchary out:
> There's something in me that reproves my fault;
> But such a headstrong potent fault it is,
> That it but mocks reproof.
> *Viola.* With the same 'haviour that your passion bears
> Goes on my master's griefs. 　　[III. iv. 201-07]

In the context of the fake conflict of Sir Andrew's challenge, this real conflict of sensibilities and self-awarenesses make an immediate effect of noble honesty; it is not the self-indulgence that we note so much as the effort to deal with emotion. A second and more extended expression of the emotional world of noble persons comes at the end of the scene. Sir Toby's plan to trap Viola in her cowardice is turned back on his own head (quite literally) by the intervention of Antonio; but the farce turns towards tragedy in the arrest and apparent betrayal of Antonio.

Shakespeare's handling of this is extremely complex: the natural release by a just revenge on the bullies is suspended; they are left plotting new torments for Viola, while Antonio is hauled away to prison; but the centre of the episode is in none of these, but in the sudden and rapturous vision that the refined sensibility will not always have to endure the context of disguise and discomfiture:

> *Viola.* He nam'd Sebastian: I my brother know
> Yet living in my glass; even such and so
> In favour was my brother; and he went
> Still in this fashion, colour, ornament,

> For him I imitate: O, if it prove,
> Tempests are kind, and salt waves fresh in love!
> 　　　　　　　　　　　　　　　　[III. iv. 379-84]

Beside this vision of escape and reconciliation, the difficulties of denouement fall away, and the threat from the bullies, still crouching in the corner, suddenly seems absurd and unimportant. . . . (pp. 50-3)

But the reconciliation is an *escape* here, not a conquest, as in *As You Like It*. The final dance of reconciliation is bound to seem circumscribed, for the role of Chance (which brings Sebastian to Illyria) is (unlike that of Hymen) that of the master and not servant to the heroine:

> What will become of this? As I am man,
> My state is desperate for my master's love;
> As I am woman—now alas the day!—
> What thriftless sighs shall poor Olivia breathe!
> O time! thou must untangle this, not I;
> It is too hard a knot for me t'untie.
> 　　　　　　　　　　　　　　　　[IV. ii. 36-41]
> 　　　　　　　　　　　　　　　　(p. 53)

The play ends with a nonsense-song which earlier critics thought was plain nonsense and therefore spurious, but which modern critics usually see as an extended comment on the central ideas of the play:

> When that I was and a little tiny boy,
> 　　　With hey, ho, the wind and the rain,
> A foolish thing was but a toy,
> 　　　For the rain it raineth every day.
>
> But when I came to man's estate, etc.
> 'Gainst knaves and thieves men shut their gate, etc.
>
> But when I came, alas! to wive, etc.
> By swaggering could I never thrive, etc.
>
> But when I came unto my beds, etc.
> With toss-pots still had drunken heads, etc.
>
> A great while ago the world began, etc.
> But that's all one, our play is done,
> 　　　And we'll strive to please you every day.
> 　　　　　　　　　　　　　　　　[V. i. 389-408]

Very little is clear in this; maturing seems to be looked at as a process in which folly loses its status, though most things stay the same ('the rain it raineth every day'), and have stayed the same since the world began. The song ends with a deliberate refusal to philosophize even this far, however: 'don't look for causal connections; a play is a play and not a treatise.' In its illogicality and its bittersweet sense of the need to submit to illogicality, the song is a fitting conclusion to the play in which happiness itself is seen as illogical and chancy. The very name of the play should suggest the same mood to us. 'Twelfth night' is often taken as meaning simply 'revelry', but though it is still in the season of Misrule, twelfth night is at the very limit of the season. . . . (p. 54)

Seen in the context of Shakespeare's *oeuvre*, this melancholy mood of comedy in *Twelfth Night* cannot well be kept apart from the tragic vision of the plays like *Troilus and Cressida* and *Hamlet* which are its contemporaries. The comedy ends with happiness for some, but the happiness has no inevitability, and the final song sounds perilously like a tune whistled through the surrounding darkness. The fate of Malvolio is proper enough in the context of revelry, but the context is hardly strong enough to drown completely the overtones of *Hamlet;* the malcontented outsider is not *always* despicable. In *Twelfth Night* the impetus towards reconciliation is sufficiently tentative to allow such thoughts, and in such thoughts lies the death of Comedy. (p. 55)

> G. K. Hunter, "'Twelfth Night'," in his William Shakespeare, the Later Comedies: "A Midsummer-Night's Dream," "Much Ado About Nothing," "As You Like It," "Twelfth Night," *Longmans, Green & Co., 1962, pp. 43-55.*

ALBERT GÉRARD (essay date 1964)

[*Like many critics before him, Gérard examines* Twelfth Night *for "premonitory signs and ominous portents" of the darkening tone that Shakespeare was to adopt in his later works. He finds the play near to tragedy, but lacking a tragic vision. Gérard writes that in* Twelfth Night *Shakespeare had reached the limits of his comic vision and that his insight into human nature had led him to conclude that humankind is controlled by blindness and self-love. After that, according to Gérard, only satire and tragedy remained as dramatic vehicles for Shakespeare's concept of the human condition. F. J. Furnivall (1877), Arthur Quiller-Couch (1930), John Middleton Murry (1936), Mark Van Doren (1939), E. C. Pettet (1949), W. H. Auden (1957), G. K. Hunter (1962), Jan Kott (1964), Clifford Leech (1965), and Philip Edwards (1968) also discuss the play's dark aspects.*]

[Although] we are not likely ever to know with any degree of certainty what it was, in Shakespeare's experience and awareness of life, that caused him to turn away from the pleasant world of his comedies to the disquieting topsy-turvy universe of *Hamlet* and *Troilus and Cressida,* we can at least attempt to discover whether there is any factor of continuity underlying this frightful and apparently sudden and unpredictable development. At first sight *Twelfth Night* seems hardly the place to look for such premonitory signs and ominous portents. No one in his senses would dream of denying that the last of Shakespeare's comedies is also the purest gem of Shakespearian comedy, romantic and gay, ironic and farcical. But it was too . . . Shakespeare's farewell to comedy, and as such, it might carry some secret intimation that Shakespeare was beginning to outgrow the pure mirth of the comic vision.

As it happens, the *Concordance* informs us with statistical peremptoriness that there is no other Shakespearian play in which the words 'fool', 'folly', 'mad', 'madman', 'madness' recur with such high frequency. And however distrustful we may legitimately feel towards the procrustean science of statistics, it is a matter of ascertainable fact that the characters of *Twelfth Night* have a most undistinguished habit of calling each other fool—so much so that to quote all the relevant passages would very nearly involve reprinting the whole play. This, of course, should not be assumed to be automatically significant. But Shakespeare has a knack of making the anecdotal meaningful by throwing in here and there some general observation which causes a number of apparently scattered and casual remarks to fall into proper perspective. In ancient drama this task of suggesting an ideological and ethical frame of reference was performed by the chorus. In *Twelfth Night,* as in many Shakespearian plays, the function of the chorus is thrust upon the shoulders of the Clown, whose outspokenness is sheltered by his motley, although he does not wear motley in his brain [I. v. 57]. And the essential sanity of Feste, his wisdom, the shrewdness of his psychological insight, are emphasized time and again, both in words and through action. When, therefore, the clown says to Viola-Cesario: 'Foolery, sir, does walk about the orb like the sun, it shines everywhere', [III. i. 38-9] it is

perhaps not entirely unwarranted to consider this utterance not as a mere piece of jesting, or as the expression of a fleeting mood of cynicism, but as the proper way in which comedy can convey a view of man which is, to put it mildly, rather sarcastic. (pp. 109-10)

By the time the curtain falls, it has become clear that Viola and Sebastian had the same appointed mission of Fortinbras in *Hamlet* and the English army in *Macbeth:* they are there to throw into relief the anomalies, ludicrous or otherwise, of the microcosmic world and, ultimately, to restore order where everything was upside down. The folly that characterizes Illyria in *Twelfth Night* is the comic correlative and the comic anticipation of the rottenness of Denmark and the chaos of Scotland in the two later plays. If this is so, it becomes worthwhile to inquire into the nature of Illyrian folly, for Illyria is Shakespeare's *Narrenschiff* [Ship of Fools], and Orsino is its captain. (p. 110)

As a man, Orsino is what in a flash of partial self-awareness he claims to be: 'unstaid and skittish' [II. iv. 18]. His sudden dismissal of the music he had just longed to hear is a *figura* that sets the pattern of his behaviour in the other sphere of his ducal activity: love. That Orsino is not distinguished for coherent thinking, emerges from his *ex tempore* disquisitions on love and woman. By the side of his enthusiastic praise of Olivia's constancy [I. i. 32-40], must be placed his unconsciously contemptuous opinion of woman: 'women are as roses, whose fair flower / Being once displayed doth fall that very hour' [II. iv. 38-39]. (p. 111)

Obviously, there is nothing constant about the image of the beloved which Orsino is fond of entertaining in his mind: Viola will take the place of Olivia without undue friction. Moreover, the fact that Orsino's image of Olivia herself is distorted reveals another aspect of his oceanic capacity for delusion.

There is nothing inherently funny in Olivia's predicament and this is certainly the reason why Shakespeare found it suitable to bias the mind of the audience in a comic direction by introducing Olivia through Valentine long before she actually appears on the stage. In that way we are compelled to overlook the intrinsic pathos of her situation because we have already accepted Valentine's view of her behaviour as highly ridiculous, a view which is conveyed through his choice of similes and metaphors [I. i. 33-40].

The consequence is that when we first see Olivia, we are struck by the contradiction between her ostentatious show of irrational sentimentality as reported by Valentine and by the captain, and her essentially sane and natural being as it is unveiled when she falls in love with Viola-Cesario. She does not even attempt to maintain her mask of grief. Implicitly, she admits that her romantic ideal of constant sorrow (which, of course, reflects Orsino's ideal of constant passion) was just a passing whim, a sentimental piece of foolishness, as the Clown, with crazy but irrefutable logic, had proved it to be.

But the point is that the Duke is never aware of the true nature of Olivia. Being a fool, he cannot find in himself the objective criteria that might make him conscious of her type of insanity. His mistaken faith in his own constancy (in love) prevents him from realizing the implausibility of her constancy (in grief), in spite of Valentine's innuendoes. (p. 112)

[The] reason why he rejoices in his erroneous appraisal of Olivia's nature and behaviour is his unshakable conviction that, ultimately, he will be the one to enjoy her constancy. And so, having peeled off layer after layer of Orsino's folly, we reach its central core, which is self-love. . . . It is this curious strain of obtuseness which drives him to use Viola-Cesario as a love messenger on the ground that the latter's 'constellation is right apt / For this affair' [I. iv. 35-36]. With felicitous dramatic irony, Shakespeare shows in the next scene how apt, indeed, Viola-Cesario's constellation is, and how efficient. And the audience is made to understand, in a sense that Orsino himself could never have thought of, the meaning of the Duke's prophecy:

> And thou shalt live as freely as thy lord,
> To call his fortunes thine.   [I. iv. 39-40]

Orsino is blissfully unaware of this danger, confident as he is that Olivia must inevitably fall in love with him, although she has been rejecting him for a long time. And of this aspect of his character, Malvolio is the caricature. Indeed on his first appearance we are informed by Olivia herself that he is 'sick of self-love' [I. v. 90]. Orsino feels secure in his satisfaction of knowing, as does everybody, including Olivia, that he is

> noble,
> Of great estate, of fresh and stainless youth;
> In voices well divulged, free, learned and valiant,
> And in dimensions and the shape of nature
> A gracious person.   [I. v. 258-62]

Malvolio likewise finds encouragement in what he supposes to be Olivia's appreciation of his fine countenance and behaviour. . . . And just as it is Orsino's self-confidence which drives him to use the services of a messenger that soon becomes a rival, so it is Malvolio's self-esteem which ensures the success of Maria's fake message.

While the theme of appearance vs. reality is central to *Twelfth Night*, it is clear that the action of the play exploits its more playful potentialities, as is suitable in comedy. But there are three passages where the non-Illyrian characters refer to it in language which is not entirely consonant with the usual tone of light comedy, and which implies serious moral valuation.

When Viola lands ashore, she addresses the sea-captain as follows:

> There is a fair behaviour in thee, captain,
> And though that nature with a beauteous wall
> Doth oft close in pollution, yet of thee
> I will believe thou hast a mind that suits
> With this thy fair and outward character.
>
>   [I. ii. 47-51]

Viola, of course, is the most conspicuous illustration of the theme of appearance and reality. But her disguise is merely physical and has been forced upon her by circumstances: she cannot enter the service of Olivia, who 'will admit no kind of suit' [I. ii. 45]; nor can she serve the bachelor Duke if she presents herself as a woman. But she is soon made aware of the danger of her stratagem, and when she notices that Olivia is falling in love with her, she exclaims:

> Disguise, I see thou art a wickedness,
> Wherein the pregnant enemy does much.
>
>   [II. ii. 27-28]

And in the third Act, Viola herself becomes the victim of her own disguise and is harshly blamed by Antonio when she cannot return the purse which he had given to Sebastian:

> how vile an idol proves this god!
> Thou hast, Sebastian, done good feature shame.
> In nature there's no blemish but the mind;

> None can be called deformed but the unkind;
> Virtue is beauty, but the beauteous evil
> Are empty trunks o'erflourished by the devil.
>
>   [III. iv. 365-70]

'Pollution', 'wickedness', 'evil', 'devil' are very strong words indeed. After all, there is little evidence of actual corruption or devilish actions in Illyria. For the folly of Illyria is high fantastical, and the sun of folly ends its course in no murkier night than the night of ignorance: 'There is no darkness but ignorance', Feste says [IV. ii. 42-3]. But this is only true in the comic cosmos, where the logic of ignorance leads the worse characters to mild punishments and the better ones to redeeming impulses. The fundamental generosity of Orsino and Olivia, however ill-informed, makes it possible for their non-Illyrian guardian angels to steer them to their own non-Illyrian shores, where appearance and reality coincide, where identities are established. In Illyria, as the Clown says, 'Nothing that is so is so' [IV. i. 8-9], but Viola knows how to lift the painted veil, and the world of Sebastian is a place where things are what they are. . . . (pp. 112-14)

Nevertheless, in that very folly of self-love and self-deception, the possibility of evil and tragedy is lurking, and critics have become sensitive, of late, to the fact that the slightest twist could have turned *Twelfth Night* into a dark comedy or a tragedy. L. C. Salingar noticed, a few years ago, that 'Orsino's love . . . seems almost without an object, or incommensurate with any object, a "monstrosity" in the same sense as Troilus' love for Cressida, in its grasping after the infinite' [see excerpt above, 1958]; and he went on to say that Antonio's reproaches in the third act 'bring the mood of the play dangerously near the confines of tragedy'; of Malvolio, he observed that 'with his unconscious hypocrisy in the exercise of power and his rankling sense of injustice, he comes midway between Shylock and the Angelo of *Measure for Measure*'. . . . Sir Toby would be a perfect Pandarus if only his niece were a Cressida, while his parasitic relationship to Sir Andrew is only equalled by Iago's cynical zest in sponging on another halfwit. And how the mild dusk of foolish ignorance points the way to the darkest depths of gloom is exemplified in *King Lear*. So that with *Twelfth Night*, Shakespeare's insight into the world of man appears to have reached a point of no return. It is indeed a sheer marvel of dramatic genius that the play never topples into tragedy, for it contains everything that is necessary for tragedy—except the tragic vision. But also, it both stretches the comic sense of life to the uttermost and reaches the outer limits of comedy, thus maintaining a precarious and wholly admirable balance. The primrose path of comic perception had led Shakespeare to the pathetic core of human nature: man's helplessness as he finds himself controlled by his own blindness and self-love. From this point, there were only two courses left, each of which Shakespeare was to follow to the bitter end: the savagery of satire and the cathartic awe of tragedy. (p. 115)

Albert Gérard, "Shipload of Fools: A Note on 'Twelfth Night'," in English Studies, Vol. XLV, No. 2, 1964, pp. 109-15.

JAN KOTT (essay date 1964)

[*Kott is a Polish-born critic and scholar now residing in the United States. He characterizes Shakespeare's Illyria as "bitter," especially in the sex-role reversals. That Cesario should be a eunuch is "shocking," and, according to Kott, Shakespeare intended that reaction. Like Clifford Leech (1965), who also considers the sex-role reversals problematical, Kott finds the play unharmonious, and like E. Montégut (1867), he stresses the ambiguity of the piece. For additional commentary on the dark aspects of the play, see the excerpts by F. J. Furnivall (1877), Arthur Quiller-Couch (1930), John Middleton Murry (1936), Mark Van Doren (1939), E. C. Pettet (1949), W. H. Auden (1957), G. K. Hunter (1962), Albert Gérard (1964), Clifford Leech (1965), and Philip Edwards (1968). The study from which the following excerpt is taken was originally published in Polish as* Szkice o Szekspirze *in 1964.]*

Twelfth Night opens with a lyrical fugue accompanied by an orchestra:

> If music be the food of love, play on,
> Give me excess of it, that, surfeiting,
> The appetite may sicken, and so die.
> That strain again! It had a dying fall.

> [I. i. 1-4]

The exposition gives one the impression of a broken string; broken by itself, or by someone. It is like an overture in which the instruments got mixed up. From the first scene, music and lyrical elements sound in disharmony. The orchestra has stopped, then begins again. In vain:

> . . . Enough, no more!
> 'Tis not so sweet now as it was before.

> [I. i. 7-8]

The passions are hungry, but choke with their own appetite. The Duke's monologue is spoken in the style and poetic diction we know from the Sonnets. The style is refined, the diction authentic. There is tension and anxiety in it. Love is an entry into the sphere of risk and uncertainty; everything in it is possible.

> O spirit of love, how quick and fresh art thou! . . .
> . . . So full of shapes is fancy
> That it alone is high fantastical.

> [I. i. 9, 14-15]

This hurrying of images we also know from the Sonnets. The lyrical fugue breaks just as suddenly as the music. The dialogue becomes brutal and quick:

> CURIO
> Will you go hunt, my lord?
> DUKE
>   What, Curio?
> CURIO
> The hart.

> [I. i. 16]

From the very first lines everything in *Twelfth Night* is ambiguous. The hunt is for Olivia. But the hunter has been hunted down himself. The Duke himself is both Actaeon and stag. (pp. 255-56)

Viola with the Captain will presently be shipwrecked ashore the very same country of Illyria. Shakespeare deals with the plot of a sister losing her twin brother in a sea storm, in just

Act III. Scene iv. Malvolio, Olivia, and Maria. By D. Maclise (n.d.). From the Art Collection of the Folger Shakespeare Library.

a couple of lines. The plot is a pretext. The theme of the play is disguise. (p. 257)

Disguise was not anything out of the ordinary. But in this first scene between Viola and the Captain we observe the striking brutality of the dialogue. In the first version of the comedy, say the experts, Viola was to sing the songs later given to the Clown, and that is why the Captain introduces her to the Duke as an Italian *castrato*. But even with this correction there is something shocking in the proposition. A young girl is to turn into a eunuch. It is as if a chill went down our spines. As with everything in Shakespeare, this is intended. (pp. 257-58)

Disguise was nothing out of the ordinary, but in *Twelfth Night* there is something disturbing in it. A girl disguised herself as a boy, but first a boy had disguised himself as girl. On the Elizabethan stage female parts were acted by boy actors. That was a limitation, as theatre historians well know. Female parts in Shakespeare are decidedly shorter than male parts. Shakespeare was well aware of the limitations of boy actors. They could play girls; with some difficulty they could play old women. But how could a boy act a mature woman? In all Shakespeare's plays, in the whole of Elizabethan drama even, there are very few such parts. . . . But on at least two occasions Shakespeare used this limitation as the theme and theatrical instrument of comedy. *Twelfth Night* and *As You Like It* were written for a stage on which boys played the parts of girls. The disguise is a double one; played on two levels as it were: a boy dresses up as girl who disguises herself as boy.

> 'Tis beauty truly blent, whose red and white
> Nature's own sweet and cunning hand laid on.
> Lady, you are the cruell'st she alive
> If you will lead these graces to the grave,
> And leave the world no copy.
>
> [I. v. 239-43]

This passage has been compared with the Sonnets. Even the actual words are similar:

> She carv'd thee for her seal, and meant thereby
> Thou shouldst print more, not let that copy die.
>
> [Sonnet XI]

That appeal was addressed by a man to a youth who was his lover and patron at the same time. In *Twelfth Night* the lines are spoken by the Duke's page to Countess Olivia; by a girl disguised as boy, to a boy disguised as girl. But the girl disguised as boy is a boy disguised as girl.

> What country, friends, is this?
> This is Illyria, lady.
>
> [I. ii. 1-2]

We are still in Illyria. In that country ambiguity is the principle of love as well as of comedy. For, in fact, Viola is neither a boy nor a girl. Viola-Cesario is the "master mistress" of the Sonnets. The music of *Twelfth Night* has been written for that particular instrument. Viola is an ephebe and an androgyny. (pp. 258-59)

Duke Orsino, Viola, Olivia are not fully drawn characters. They are blank, and the only element that fills them is love. They cannot be dissociated from one another. They have no independent being. They exist only in and through mutual relationships. They are infected, and they infect, with love. Orsino is in love with Olivia, Olivia is in love with Cesario, Cesario is in love with Orsino. That is how things look on the surface of the dialogue, on the upper level of Shakesperean

disguise. A man, a youth, a woman: love has three faces, as in the Sonnets. . . .

Everyone in Illyria speaks about love in verse. It is a refined, occasionally too contrived verse. Authentic drama takes place under the surface of that court rhetoric. (p. 260)

Every character here has something of the fair youth and the Dark Lady. Every character has been endowed with a bitter knowledge about love. Love in Illyria is violent and impatient; it cannot be gratified or reciprocated. . . .

As in the Sonnets, the three characters exhaust all forms of love. Olivia loves Cesario, Cesario loves Orsino, Orsino loves Olivia. But Cesario is Viola. On the middle level of Shakespearean disguise Olivia loves Viola, Viola loves Orsino, Orsino loves Olivia. Shakespeare's triangle has been modified: there are now two women and one man, or rather a man, a girl, and a woman. . . .

Viola seems to Olivia a girlish youth and to Orsino a boyish girl. A Shakespearean androgyne acts a youth for Olivia and a girl for Orsino. This triangle is now commuted for the third time. Olivia and Orsino are now simultaneously in love with Cesario-Viola, with the youth-girl. Illyria is a country of erotic madness. Shakespearean names and places often have hidden associations. The circle has been closed, but it is a *circulus vitiosus*. In all metamorphoses, on all levels of Shakespearean disguise, these three—Olivia, Viola, and Orsino—chase one another, unable to join. (p. 261)

The appearance of Sebastian does not really make any difference. Sebastian is a character in the plot of the play, but does not participate in the real love drama. He was taken over by Shakespeare lock, stock, and barrel from the Italian story to provide the solution proper for a comedy. But even in the adventures of this conventional character Shakespeare does not abandon ambiguity. In Illyria the aura of inversion embraces everybody:

> I could not stay behind you. My desire,
> More sharp than filed steel, did spur me forth.
>
> [III. iii. 4-5]

Antonio, the other captain of the ship, is in love with Sebastian. He has saved him from shipwreck and now accompanies him on his adventures, following him round Illyria. He is faithful and brave, but also ridiculous and common. He should be big and fat, very ugly, should have an uncouth beard and look amazingly like the first Captain who accompanied Viola. Shakespeare frequently repeats in the *buffo* tone a theme previously dealt with seriously or lyrically. Sebastian is Viola's twin and double. If Viola is boyish, Sebastian must be girlish. A bearded giant now chases a girlish youth round Illyria. This is the last but one of *Twelfth Night*'s metamorphoses.

The appearance of Sebastian does not dispel the basic ambiguity of erotic situations in Illyria, but, on the contrary, seems to aggravate it even more. Who has been deceived? Olivia or Orsino? Who has been deluded by appearance? Is desire part of the order of nature, or of love? Love is mad. But what about nature? Can nature be mad and irrational? Olivia fell in love with Cesario; Cesario turned out to be Viola. But Viola changed again into Sebastian. . . . (p. 262)

A youth fell in love with the Duke; the youth was a disguised girl. Nothing stands in the way of another marriage to be concluded. . . .

The comedy is over. *Twelfth Night; or, What You Will.* What will you have: a boy, or a girl? The actors take off their costumes: first the Duke, then Viola and Olivia. The last metamorphosis of the amorous triangle has been accomplished. What remains is a man and two youths. "But nature to her bias drew in that." A boy acted girl who acted boy; then the boy changed again into a girl who again turned into a boy. Viola transformed herself into Cesario, then Cesario became Viola, who turned into Sebastian. Ultimately then, in this comedy of errors, what was just an appearance? There is only one answer: sex. Love and desire pass from a youth to a girl and from a girl to a youth. Cesario is Viola, Viola is Sebastian. The court model of ideal love has been ironically analysed to the end. Or rather, presented more realistically. (p. 263)

Passion is one; it only has different faces: of man and woman; of revulsion and adoration; of hate and desire.

There have been productions of *Twelfth Night* in which Sebastian and Viola were acted by one and the same person. This seems the only solution, even if its consistent treatment requires the epilogue to be dealt with in a thoroughly conventional manner. But it is not enough for Cesario-Viola-Sebastian to be acted by one person. That person must be a man. Only then will the real theme of Illyria, erotic delirium or the metamorphoses of sex, be shown in the theatre. (p. 264)

Jan Kott, "Shakespeare's Bitter Arcadia," in his Shakespeare, Our Contemporary, *translated by Boleslaw Taborski, Anchor Books, 1966, pp. 57-74.*

BARBARA K. LEWALSKI (essay date 1965)

[*Developing the critical view that* Twelfth Night's *theme is informed by the feast of misrule associated with the pagan celebration of Twelfth Night, Lewalski examines the Christian concept of Epiphany she discerns in the play. Lewalski finds Feste's song to be integrally related to the Christian themes and proposes that "When that I Was" alludes to verses in the New Testament. For additional commentary on the Saturnalian elements in the play, see the excerpts by E. Montégut (1867), L. G. Salingar (1958), and C. L. Barber (1959).*]

[Though] the point has received little attention, I believe it can be shown that the central themes and motifs of [*Twelfth Night*] contain something of the religious significance associated with Epiphany and with the spirit of Christmastide. By this statement I do not imply that the play is an allegory in which characters and incidents are designed to stand for or mean abstract qualities or religious personages. Nor is Shakespeare's method here much like Plato's mode of allegory, in which a particular sensible object (here the dramatic fiction) has its own kind of reality but yet reflects or images forth something in the realm of Forms or Archetypes which is more real. Rather, Shakespeare's method resembles, and was probably formed by, that other tradition of allegorical interpretation which was still influential in the Renaissance, namely the tradition of Christian typology, whereby certain real historical events and personages from the Old Testament and (more significantly for the present purposes) from certain classical fictions such as the *Metamorphoses* or the *Aeneid* were seen to point to aspects of Christ and of the Gospel story without losing their own historical or fictional reality. . . . In *Twelfth Night* Shakespeare's incorporation of certain religious significances into his dramatic fiction rather resembles the typological treatment of some classical stories and completely reverses the Platonic emphasis, being incarnational rather than transcendent in focus. In Shake-

speare's play the particular story, the created fiction, draws into itself and embodies larger meanings and significances but the focus remains always on the dramatic microcosm: the word is made flesh and continues to dwell among us. However limited or widespread such a mode of vision may be in Shakespeare's total work, it is obviously wholly appropriate in a play celebrating the Christmas festival.

Illyria is one of several idealized locales in Shakespeare's romantic comedies and romances, a "second world" markedly different from and in most respects better than the real world by reason of its pervasive atmosphere of song and poetry, its dominant concern with love and the "good life" (that is, the life of revelry), and its freedom from any malicious villany. Other idealized locales such as the Forest of Arden, the forest of *A Midsummer Night's Dream,* Prospero's island, and Perdita's pastoral refuge, present what Northrop Frye terms "green worlds" or John Vyvyan labels "retreats in the wilderness" into which characters move from the world outside, within which they establish new comic relationships and clarifications, and from which they then return to the real world. But the case with Illyria is different: the characters who enter it from outside, Viola and Sebastian, do not leave it again; moreover they are not formed or altered by it, or in it, or under its influence, but they are themselves the chief agents in reordering and perfecting Illyrian life.

Something of the special quality of Illyria is indicated by the first use of the name in the dialogue, as Viola specifically contrasts Illyria with Elysium:

> *Viola:* What country, friends, is this?
> *Captain:* This is Illyria, lady.
> *Viola:* And what should I do in Illyria?
> My brother he is in Elysium.

[I. ii. 1-4]

At the same time, however, Illyria is related to Elysium through the melodic, romantic sound of the two words and their identical syntactical positions. Indeed the dominant Illyrian concern with song, music, poetry, good cheer, and love gives the place an idyllic, Elysium-like atmosphere. This idyllic aspect may be more precisely defined when one considers that the avowed antagonist of Illyria's accustomed life and activities is Malvolio—Bad Will—whose name is justified and interpreted by Olivia's comment, "O, you are sick of self-love, Malvolio, and taste with a distempered appetite. To be generous, guiltless, and of free disposition, is to take those things for birdbolts that you deem cannon bullets" [I. v. 90-3]. If Malvolio's "Bad Will" (self-love) constitutes the antagonistic force to the life of Illyria we may be directed by this fact to the recognition that the Elysium-like quality of this place emanates from a festival atmosphere of *Good Will* which has banished active malice and radical selfishness and has created a genuine community. These terms invite recall of the Christmas message proclaimed by the angels, rendered in the Geneva bible as "peace on earth, and towards men good will," and in the Rheims New Testament as "on earth peace to men of good will." Illyria would seem to be a realm ready for, open to, and perhaps already experiencing in some measure the restoration and "peace" promised in the angelic message: the charity of the play's spirit is such that Malvolio himself is invited at the conclusion to share in this special condition. This context gives significance to the full title of the play, "Twelfth Night: Or, What you Will." Instead of being merely an invitation to whimsical response and interpretation the subtitle would seem to point to the thematic opposition of Good and Bad Will in the play, and to the fact that the promises of the Christmas season attend upon or include the spirit of Good Will.

But if Illyria is in some respects related to Elysium as a place of Good Will exhibiting the spirit of the season, it is also a place much in need of the restoration and peace of the Christmastide promises. The name Illyria may be intended to suggest *illusion* in the sense of distortion, disorder, and faulty perception of self and others; at any rate, as J. R. Brown has pointed out, these are all dominant features of Illyrian life [see excerpt above, 1957]. Barber notes that "madness" is a key word in this play [see excerpt above, 1959]; almost every character exclaims about the madness and disorder afflicting other people and sometimes himself as well. . . . This pervasive "madness," while it is not malicious or vicious and may even be in some respects restorative, nevertheless leads each person whom it afflicts towards a culpable self-centeredness and a potentially dangerous indulgence of emotional excess. Illyria is badly in need of restoration to order and peace, but such a restoration as will also preserve the merriment, spontaneity, and sense of human community displayed in the "mad" state.

Malvolio, by repudiating any share in the Illyrian "madness" shows himself more lunatic than any, for he repudiates thereby the greatest goods of human life and the common bonds of human kind, love and merrymaking. . . . One whose self-regard, self-delusion, and absurd ambition cause him to exclude himself deliberately from human merriment and human love is obviously a greater madman than the most abandoned reveller or the most fantastic lover in Illyria, and Maria's trick, which causes Malvolio to be taken for a lunatic, points symbolically to the real lunacy of his values. Since he so richly deserves his exposure, and so actively cooperates in bringing it upon himself, there seems little warrant for the critical tears sometimes shed over his harsh treatment and none at all for a semi-tragic dramatic rendering of his plight in the "dark house." (pp. 169-71)

Opposition to the forces of self-love and disorder in Illyria is offered by certain characters who embrace wholeheartedly the human activities of love and merrymaking but who are preserved from "madness" by positive ordering principles within themselves and who project these principles as forces to restore and reorder the community.

Maria embodies one such restorative force within Illyria: sheer wit. Early in the play Feste points to her special quality, terming her "as witty a piece of Eve's flesh as any in Illyria" [I. v. 27-8]. Maria employs her wit as contriver and executor of the masterful plot against Malvolio: her faked letter is cleverly framed so as to confirm Malvolio's self-delusions about Olivia's regard for him, and the letter's recommendations that Malvolio affect yellow stockings, cross-garters, constant smiles, and surly behavior are brilliantly calculated to insure his self-exposure. The power of Maria's wit is thus addressed to the revelation and punishment of the "madness" involved in self-delusion, self-love, and hypocritic affectation of virtue. Maria's wit becomes an instrument for further reformation when Sir Toby Belch out of sheer delight in her witty plot offers to marry her: there can be little doubt from her success in managing Sir Toby and his associates throughout the play that she will succeed henceforward through wit in controlling Toby's excesses without in the least repressing his gaiety.

The clown Feste is the second force working from within to reorder and perfect Illyria. In many respects he is Malvolio's opposite, incarnating the spirit of festival Good Will. . . . His foolery is a consciously adopted and controlled foolery which is a far cry from the madness and disorder rampant in Illyria; it is compacted of wit and song and is firmly aligned with the forces of love and merrymaking, but is conscious also of other perspectives and harsh realities. (p. 173)

Feste in the guise of Sir Topas the curate (the topaz stone was traditionally thought to cure madness) endeavors to cure Malvolio's "lunacy" by witty mockery designed to point out the true madness of his attitudes. Responding to Malvolio's constant protestations of his sanity, Feste replies, "Madman, thou errest. I say there is no darkness but ignorance, in which thou are more puzzled than the Egyptians in their fog" [IV. ii. 42-4]. The exchange about Pythagoras' opinion concerning the transmigration of souls is not merely comic dialogue since it deals with the sources of Malvolio's lunacy: lack of sensitivity to others, lack of concern for any life beyond his own. Feste accordingly declares that Malvolio should be left alone in darkness until he embraces Pythagoras' opinion, "and fear to kill a woodcock, lest thou dispossess the soul of thy grandam" [IV. ii. 59-60]. Sir Topas also mocks Malvolio as one possessed of the devil or as himself a kind of comic Satan cast into a dungeon dark "as hell" [IV. ii. 34-5]. Assuming the tones of an exorcist he calls, "Out, hyperbolical fiend!" [IV. ii. 25], and again, "Fie, thou dishonest Satan. . . . I am one of those gentle ones that will use the devil himself with courtesy" [IV. ii. 31-3]. These exchanges are brilliant comedy, but they also point to the fact that Malvolio's ill will derives ultimately from the Satanic principle: self-love directed toward self-advancement. Finally, resuming his own form, Feste achieves Malvolio's release by carrying a letter from him to Olivia—identifying himself in this action as the "old Vice" of the morality-play tradition serving the "goodman devil" [IV. ii. 124, 131].

The forces of wit and festival—of Good Will—can do much to reorder and restore Illyria but they cannot do everything. They can in large part reclaim Olivia from melancholic surrender to excessive grief, they can control and care for Sir Toby, they can expose the real "lunacy" of Malvolio and cast him forth as comic Satan into the bondage and darkness which was supposedly the fate of Satan himself at the nativity of Christ. But they cannot reform Malvolio, they cannot deal effectively with the love disorders of Orsino and Olivia, and they cannot restore the community as a whole to the "peace" that is the special promise of the season. For this a force must come from outside, presenting a pattern of perfect love and perfect order, and having power to produce these qualities in the community. Such a force enters the Illyrian world in the persons of the twins, Viola and Sebastian.

Though the two are dramatically separate, Viola and Sebastian represent thematically two aspects of the same restorative process. This fact is suggested partly by an identity in their physical appearances so absolute that they themselves recognize no differences. . . . More important, there is a remarkable identity in the events of their lives: both endure a sea tempest, both are saved and aided by good sea captains, both are wooed by and in a manner of speaking woo Olivia, Both are forced to duel with Andrew Aguecheek, both give money to Feste, both are in the end betrothed to their proper lovers. By these parallels the twin motif is made to do much more than to provide occasion for comic misapprehension and misunderstanding, though it does that also in good measure.

Viola, disguised throughout the play as the page Cesario, is the embodiment of selfless love (as Maria is the embodiment of wit and Feste of festival foolery); as such she provides a direct contrast to the self-centered passions of Orsino and Olivia and at length inspires both to a purified love. . . . This pattern of selfless love acts finally to inspire right love in Olivia and Orsino: Olivia's attraction to the 'outside' but also to the inner worth of Viola-Cesario brings her to discard completely her self-indulgent grief and readies her for the final transfer of her affection to Sebastian, Viola's alter ego and the right recipient of her love. Orsino is inspired almost at once to love of his "boy" Cesario (Valentine comments on the suddenness and depth of the affection in I. iv. 1-3) and is so moved by the story of Viola's constant love and hard service undertaken for him that he loves her at last in her own person.

Because her love is selfless. Viola is able to embrace love fully, freely, and at once, to share in the common human turbulence of feeling attending upon love without ever giving way to the madness and disorder that accompany the selfish passions of Orsino and Olivia; she is thus a pattern of the ordered self as well as of selfless love. (pp. 174-75)

Also, because she is ruled by selfless love Viola can wait patiently upon time for the manifestation, the epiphany which must resolve the difficulties. This waiting observes the finest balance between inaction and precipitancy. . . . [Despite] the steadily mounting pressure upon her resulting from the mistaken identities—Antonio's rage, Olivia's chiding, Orsino's offer to kill her—she gives no hint that she has a twin brother who may hold the key to the confusions. The epiphany must be allowed to come when it will, and she endures in patience until the revelation is given.

Sebastian's role is to bring to determination the issues which Viola begins, and to resolve the difficult situations which she must endure until his manifestation. Whereas Viola must constantly give selfless love and service to others, Sebastian is able at once to inspire selfless, devoted love for himself: his friend Antonio risks danger and imprisonment to minister to Sebastian's needs in the strange town, and later risks life itself for him in undertaking a duel in his supposed defence. The pattern is repeated when Olivia (thinking him Cesario) proclaims her love for him at first sight and proposes a betrothal. His immediate decision to accept that betrothal despite his perception that it is grounded in some error, and his forthright response to the attack of Andrew and Toby in which he gives each a "bloody coxcomb" show a power of firm determination which make possible the restoration of order to the land.

The complementary roles of Viola and Sebastian in Illyria may on the basis of what has been said be seen to reflect the dual nature and role of the incarnate Divine Love, Christ, in accordance with the Christmastide theme implied in the play's title. Recognition of such a dimension does not, it should be reëmphasized, make the Viola-Sebastian story an allegory of Christ's action in the world, but rather presents this dramatic fiction as a type of that ultimate manifestation of Divine Love— a reflection, an analogue, another incarnation of it. (p. 176)

An Elizabethan "Postill" or exposition of the Gospel for Epiphany . . . points to the paradoxical duality of Christ's manifestation to the Magi: "For as the Maunger in which he lay, argueth that his kingdome is not of this world: so the starre appearing from Heaven declareth him to bee a heavenly king. And like as the Maunger sheweth him to be base in the sight of the worlde: even so the starre setteth out the maiestie of his kingdome for us to behold." . . . Accordingly, an audience would be prepared through the significances commonly associated with the Epiphany message to find in a play entitled

Twelfth Night and presenting twins who embody complementary aspects of the role and power of love, a reflection of the dual manifestation of Christ's action in the world as Divine Love incarnate.

In *Twelfth Night* Viola's role alludes to the human dimension. Christ's role as patient servant, willing sufferer, model of selfless love. Her offer to Orsino, "And I, most jocund, apt, and willingly, / To do you rest a thousand deaths would die" [V. i. 132-33] is perhaps the most direct verbal reference to this role. Sebastian reflects the divine dimension, pointed up especially in Antonio's language to and about Sebastian: "I do *adore* thee so / That danger shall seem sport" [II. i. 47-8] and again, "to his image, which methought did promise / Most venerable worth, did I *devotion*" [III. iv. 362-63], and then in disillusionment, "But, O, how vile an *idol* proves this *god*" [III. iv. 365]. The bloody pates dealt out to Toby and Andrew present Sebastian in the role of judge and punisher, and the final betrothal to Olivia suggests Christ's role as destined "husband" of the perfected soul and of the reordered society, the Church.

In the "epiphany" in the final scene when Sebastian is at length manifested and the double identity is revealed, some of the language points directly to the theological dimension here noted, but at the same time resists simplistic allegorical equations. When the twins are first seen together by the company the Duke's comment suggests and reverses the usual formula for defining Christ as incorporating two natures in one person, observing that here is "One face, one voice, one habit, and two persons" [V. i. 216]. Antonio makes a similar observation, "How have you made division of yourself? / An apple cleft in two is not more twin / Than these two creatures" [V. i. 222-24]. But the other formulation, a mysterious duality in unity, is suggested throughout the play in Viola's dual masculine-feminine nature, and is restated in the last scene in Sebastian's words to Olivia. "You are betrothed both to a maid and man" [V. i. 263]. Elsewhere in the final scene Sebastian denies any claim to "divinity" in terms that at the same time relate him to such a role: "I never had a brother; / Nor can there be that deity in my nature / Of here and everywhere" [V. i. 226-28]. And again, "A spirit I am indeed, / But am in that dimension grossly clad / Which from the womb I did participate" [V. i. 236-38].

Sebastian and Viola do indeed bring the "peace" of the season to Illyria through a reordering of its life and its loves. The seven years' peace throughout the Roman world before the traditional date of Christ's birth was commonly seen as a sign of that peace. . . . In the conclusion of the play Fabian virtually echoes the Isaiah prophecy in pointing to the wondrous peace established in Illyria: "let no quarrel, nor no brawl to come, / Taint the condition of this present hour, / Which I have wond'red at" [V. i. 356-58]. The right betrothals are made though Viola may not yet put off her disguise: that must wait upon finding the sea-captain who has her "maids garments" and who "upon some action / Is now in durance, at Malvolio's suit" [V. i. 275-76]. When we remember that Malvolio has been identified as comic devil the line seems to point to the condition of mankind held in durance by the devil's "suit" as a result of the Fall, and reminds us that only after the atonement for that Fall has been made may Christ's passive, suffering servant's role be put aside. Sir Toby and Sir Andrew have endured the token punishment for their disorders meted out by Sebastian, Toby will wed Maria and reform, and even Malvolio is freed and invited to participate in the general "peace" if he will,

"Pursue him and entreat him to a peace" [V. i. 380]. The Duke's concluding statement shows him taking firm hold of affairs in his kingdom for the first time since the play began, auguring well for the preservation of the land in order and peace. And the Duke's declaration that the weddings will take place when "golden time convents" suggests that the reordering made possible by this fictional embodiment of the significance and themes of Christmastide looks forward to the reëstablishment of the golden age, or in Christian terms, to the millennium.

Feste's final song, contrary to much critical opinion, is integrally related to the themes of the play, as developed above. Its opening lines,

> When that I was and a little tiny boy,
> With hey, ho, the wind and the rain,
> A foolish thing was but a toy,
> For the rain it raineth every day.
> But when I came to man's estate,
> With hey, ho, the wind and the rain,
> 'Gainst knaves and thieves men shut their gate,
> For the rain it raineth every day　　　[V. i. 389-96]

seem to allude to I Cor., xiii. 11, "When I was a childe, I spake as a childe: I understoode as a childe, I thought as a childe: but when I became a man, I put away childish things." This echo also recalls Paul's classic definition of Christian love which immediately precedes the verse cited and which needs only to be quoted in part for its relevance to the play to be apparent:

> Love suffereth long: it is bountifull: love envieth not:
> 　Love doth not boast it selfe: it is not puffed up:
> It doth no uncomely thing: it seeketh not her owne
> 　things: it is not provoked to anger: it thinketh no
> 　evill:
> It suffereth all things: it beleeveth all things: it hopeth
> 　all things: it endureth all things.　　(I Cor. xiii, 4-7)

And the verse just following the echo mentioned, "For nowe we see thorow a glasse darkely: but then shall wee see face to face. Nowe I know in part: but then shall I knowe even as I am knowen" (I Cor. xiii. 12), with its graphic symbol for the imperfections of the present life in relation to the ideal fulfillment of love in the future state relates to the tone and burden of Feste's song. His sad and haunting references to the wind and the rain, the thieves and the tosspots, the swaggering and the drunken heads which have been part of life from birth to death since the world began set the play suddenly in a new perspective, that of the real world. Bringing the Twelfth Night celebration to a close, Feste reminds us that the world we live in is a very great distance from the land of good will that is Illyria, that the restorative forces which had a comparatively easy time there have much more resistant materials to work upon in the real world, and that the golden age foreseen as imminent at the end of the play is in the real world only a far-off apocalyptic vision. (pp. 177-79)

> *Barbara K. Lewalski, "Thematic Patterns in 'Twelfth Night'," in* Shakespeare Studies: An Annual Gathering of Research, Criticism, and Reviews, *Vol. 1, 1965, pp. 168-81.*

CLIFFORD LEECH　(essay date 1965)

[*Leech, like other recent critics, perceives a darkness in the tone of* Twelfth Night. *He argues that there are elements in the play that make us feel ill at ease, and that these elements distort the harmony of the work. In contrast with Charles Lamb (1822) and his followers, Leech does not find Malvolio a character of tragic proportions; rather, he believes that like Parolles in* All's Well That Ends Well, *Malvolio is subjected to a humiliation that sparks our sympathy. Leech also finds the sex-role reversals problematical in* Twelfth Night, *an opinion that counters that of C. L. Barber (1959), but seconds the interpretation of Jan Kott (1964). For additional commentary on the dark aspects of the play, see the excerpts by F. J. Furnivall (1877), Arthur Quiller-Couch (1930), John Middleton Murry (1936), Mark Van Doren (1939), E. C. Pettet (1949), W. H. Auden (1957). G. K. Hunter (1962), Jan Kott (1964), and Albert Gerard (1964).*]

[*Twelfth Night*] is gay and a little sad and certainly high-fantastical. Its material is human nature, but the angle of vision is unusual, the range of vision highly selective. And for the fun and ingenuity of it we are invited, and are willing, to take a little of the impossible as a seasoning to genuine observation. Illyria is not everyday Elizabethan London or even the court at Whitehall. It is a land with some of its own laws, where things ripen fast, and sometimes with grace, where men are almost always at leisure for love or wine or practical jesting. Its humour . . . is less sharp than is often found in comedy: if at the end Malvolio is at odds with his fellows, they at least feel a warm desire that rancour should not be nourished. Were the play all this and nothing more, it would give us much to take pleasure in. But there remains that sense of uneasy affection that the play does, I think, generally induce. To see *Twelfth Night* is to be reminded of occasions when we are making merry with those who are closest to us in sympathy and affection, and yet, though the pleasure is keen and genuine, we are fractionally conscious that the formula is not quite right, so that we cannot quite keep it from ourselves that an effort is needed for the contrivance of harmony. On such occasions the moment comes when we look coldly on the merry-making and the good relationship and see the precariousness of our tolerance for one another, the degree of pretence in all sociability. But that moment of disillusioned insight does not invalidate the experience of brief rejoicing that is possible in human encounters. There is an important sense in which any goodness in life is an artifact. Illyria, with the events it frames, is Shakespeare's image for this contrived thing: it impresses us the more deeply because from time to time Shakespeare seems deliberately to make us aware of the contrivance. (pp. 42-3)

[First] of course, there is the problem of Malvolio. Lamb says: "I confess that I never saw the catastrophe of this character, while Bensley played it, without a kind of tragic interest." . . . But in saying that, Lamb has rather bedevilled the issue. We are not concerned with tragedy in *Twelfth Night*. "Tragedy" implies a whole view of the universe, in which man's sureness of defeat is seen at odds with his magnitude of spirit. The dominant attitude of *Twelfth Night* is far from that: the play is concerned, rather, with man's subjection to a relatively kindly puppet-master, and Malvolio, however he may suffer, is not a symbol of human greatness. If we are to look for a resemblance between him and other Shakespearian characters, we shall find his kin not among the tragic heroes but rather in the Parolles of *All's Well that Ends Well*. Parolles is a braggart and a coward, who is finally exposed when he shows himself willing to buy his life with treachery. The world of *All's Well* is much darker than that of *Twelfth Night*, and fittingly, therefore, Parolles' failings are deeper than Malvolio's. But their resemblance lies in our response to their humiliation. Both of them become aware of solitude. When that happens to Parolles, he shows an interesting resilience: "Even the thing I am shall make me live," he says, and he is willing to accept the scorn of men who are safe in their noble station, if they will, nevertheless, find a place in their charity for him. Malvolio shows not resilience but a sense of outrage. "Madam, you have done me wrong, notorious wrong" is his cry to Olivia when he is brought from the darkness of his cell to the bright end of the comedy, and his final words, "I'll be revenged on the whole pack of you," leave us uneasy at the gull's intransigence and wincing at the word "pack." Thus he becomes a stronger, more independent figure than Parolles, but they are alike in our sense of discomfort in their baiting. Illyria, like the France and Italy of *All's Well*, cannot exist without a strain of cruelty, of persecution. We cannot have our Illyria, in fact, without an echo of the common world. . . . Olivia and the Duke, the persons of authority in this play's world, are anxious that all shall be put right. Yet it is apparent that it cannot be put right. The humiliation of Malvolio is the price that one pays for practical jesting: one cannot strip the self-important and the puritanical without sharing their embarrassment at nakedness. To put Malvolio on a tragic level is to disregard the general effect of his appearance on the stage: rather, he is one of those comic figures at whom it is too easy to laugh, so easy that, before we know it, we have done harm and are ashamed. At the end of *All's Well* we may feel more in sympathy with Parolles than with any other character. That is not the case with Malvolio and *Twelfth Night*, for the dominant mood of this comedy is gentler and we are here more closely in tune with the dénouement.

Yet even in this relaxed comedy, with its conclusion in Viola's victory over Orsino's heart and Olivia's winning at least the appearance of the man she had fallen in love with, we are not long allowed to forget the harshness of things. Malvolio is suddenly brought to Olivia's mind in the last scene because Viola mentions the imprisonment "at Malvolio's suit" of the captain who had helped her when she arrived in Illyria. It is evident that the ambitious steward has exercised authority with a long arm: our realization of that moderates our pity for him. Then, when "the madly us'd Malvolio" is brought onstage, and the whole story is told, Feste runs through the matter of the gulling, with a special sourness in recalling how Malvolio had spoken contemptuously of him at the beginning of the play. . . .

> Why, "Some are born great, some achieve greatness, and some have greatness thrown upon them." I was one, sir, in this interlude—one Sir Topas, sir; but that's all one. "By the Lord, fool, I am not mad!" But do you remember— "Madam, why laugh you at such a barren rascal? An you smile not, he's gagg'd"? And thus the whirligig of time brings in his revenges.
>
> [V. i. 370-77]

It is hard to be reminded of one's own words, especially at the moment of humiliation, and Feste's remorselessness here, while not putting us on Malvolio's side, makes us realize what it is like to be in his situation. The "whirligig of time" only for a moment appears to be a light-hearted and irreverent way of referring to Fortune's wheel: the fun evaporates with the word "revenges." This is a vindictive Fortune, a Fortune who not only turns her wheel but punishes. Her spokesman is the clever and engaging Fool.

Against Fortune, against the general laughter of Orsino's and Olivia's people, there stands the mock-madman madly used,

the petty tyrant who now in his turn talks of revenge. We are made conscious that this despised man, the man outside the orbit of harmony, makes, almost like Gregers Werle in Ibsen's *The Wild Duck*, his "demand of the ideal." We feel, like Olivia and the Duke, the pity of life's refusal even in this comedy to sort itself out with a uniformity of happiness. The play is the stronger for its sense of this impossibility.

There are other traces of human suffering in this play. Antonio's relation with Sebastian has its poignancy. On his first appearance he tells Sebastian of the danger he runs in coming near Orsino's court, but he is willing to risk that to be near his friend. His language here is curiously emphatic:

> I have many enemies in Orsino's court,
> Else would I very shortly see thee there.
> But come what may, I do adore thee so
> That danger shall seem sport, and I will go.
>
> [II. i. 45-8]

"Adore" is a strong word in Shakespeare. It prepares us for Antonio's violence of language when he believes that Sebastian has betrayed him in his time of necessity. . . . And in the last scene of the comedy he speaks at length of his "love" and of the ingratitude it has met with. . . . Immediately afterwards Orsino is reproaching the disguised Viola in similar terms, thinking that the boy he has befriended has shown a perfidy like that which Antonio has believed himself to find in Sebastian: the parallelism is comic and prevents us from taking Antonio's plight over-seriously for more than a moment. Yet for that moment he brings to us a strong sense of disillusioned friendship. If we compare it with Valentine's disappointment with Proteus in *The Two Gentlemen of Verona*, we see that here Shakespeare has much more fully imagined the situation. And while Antonio remains on the stage, we have before us a reminder that humanity is vulnerable through its attachments, that affection puts a man in another's power.

Now we have a more difficult matter to turn to. On the Elizabethan stage the women's parts were of course played by boys, and some time before Shakespeare began to write the dramatists saw the piquancy of a situation in which a boy-player, acting the part of a young woman, had to wear the dramatic disguise of a boy. This could produce sexual overtones of a complicated kind, and the effect was increased rather than diminished by the general reticence in Elizabethan times concerning homosexual feeling. (pp. 43-8)

More than usually in Shakespeare we are made conscious of the sex of the players, the sex of the characters they are playing, and the double disguise of the boy playing Viola. The thing is a jest, but we cannot take it quite light-heartedly because of the extent to which Shakespeare has suggested a disturbance of mind in both Olivia and Viola. We are not in the world of the Christmas pantomime of the English theatre, with its principal-girl and principal-boy, both played by actresses, where the affections are only conventionally suggested: Olivia, conscious of her love for a mere page, as she thinks, has a touch of Angelo's shame in *Measure for Measure*, when he finds the saintly Isabella arousing his lust; and Viola, more aware of the situation, can exclaim in soliloquy:

> Disguise, I see thou art a wickedness
> Wherein the pregnant enemy does much.
>
> [II. ii. 27-8]

The tone of her speech as a whole remains comparatively light, but the vocabulary is weighted in these two lines. (pp. 49-50)

It is difficult to speak of this element in *Twelfth Night* without appearing to exaggerate its significance in the whole pattern, and we must remember that in a modern production the use of actresses for the women's parts materially lessens the disturbing quality. Because on our stage the transvestism is single and not double, the effect has not the specially troubling character that emerges when a boy playing a girl becomes emotionally involved with a boy playing a girl disguised as a boy: with that complexity we reach a point where sexual distinctions begin to dissolve. If we can imagine the play as acted at Shakespeare's Globe Theatre, we may feel that Illyrian love is presented with a touch of wryness, that a jovial absurdity is not its only hazard.

Moreover, the ending of the play suggests a refusal to take a love-attachment with a full measure of sympathy. Orsino turns quickly from Olivia to Viola, as years before Proteus in *The Two Gentlemen of Verona* had turned from Silvia to Julia. And Olivia is content with Viola's brother, having married him in place of the boy-girl-boy that had banished her own brother's memory. So much, it seems implied, for rhapsody of all sorts.

As comic error may arouse a sense of danger, so the lyric fluency of *Twelfth Night*'s verse may sometimes disguise a quality of harshness in what is said and may, on the other hand, sometimes provoke a resistance in the hearer through an over-cultivation of the dying fall. In the play's opening Orsino is languorous at love's and music's joint command:

> If music be the food of love, play on,
> Give me excess of it, that, surfeiting,
> The appetite may sicken and so die.
> That strain again! It had a dying fall;
> O, it came o'er my ear like the sweet sound
> That breathes upon a bank of violets,
> Stealing and giving odour!
>
> [I. i. 1-7]

Two lines later the Duke turns his thought to love's power to destroy: nothing, he says, will keep its worth in the love-charged mind, which has room for but one value:

> O spirit of love, how quick and fresh art thou!
> That, notwithstanding thy capacity
> Receiveth as the sea, nought enters there,
> Of what validity and pitch soe'er,
> But falls into abatement and low price
> Even in a minute.
>
> [I. i. 9-14]

We may think of the lovesick Troilus and Paris in *Troilus and Cressida*, for whom the laws of Nature and of nations, the continuance of their city's life, were not things of moment, and we may remember that *Troilus and Cressida* was probably written within a year or two of *Twelfth Night*. (pp. 50-1)

The most famous love-passages in the play, those where devotion is most freely and picturesquely embodied, have a cloyingness that comes near to dulling our appetite and to making us question the impulse behind them. That the effect was operative for Shakespeare as it is for us is, I think, evident from the frankness of Orsino's words (whatever their tone). And when Olivia's beauty is unveiled in I. v, there is a startling bluntness in Viola's comment: "Excellently done, if God did all." . . . The line has a sharpness in its general reference, in its scepticism and note of challenge, in its envy and impatience of the power of beauty. . . . Sidney saw comedy as depending on the spectator's "delight," on his acceptance of the con-

trolled and often absurd motions of the characters for the sake of the graceful pattern that is made. But the kind of comedy that holds us most conveys a hint of resentment too. Madame Ranevsky in [Anton Chekhov's] *The Cherry Orchard*, Alceste in [Molière's] *Le Misanthrope*, Volpone in Jonson's play, the lovers in [William Congreve's] *The Way of the World*—all these must utter the words and perform the actions that their characters and situations decree, and there is a pleasing appropriateness in their varying discomfitures; yet along with our pleasure goes a greater or less, a never wholly subdued, never dominant, regret that things are as they are. *Twelfth Night* has hardly the inclusiveness of the comedies that I have just mentioned. Yet it shares their sense of recoil; from it, too, from what it implies but cannot of its nature put over-plainly, we infer the limitations of the comic form.

At the very end of the play, the dramatist gives over the comic idea. Feste sings his epilogue, bringing us back from Illyria to the wind and the rain that every day beat on human heads. It is not uncommon to suggest that at the end of a comedy we emerge from a dream to a waking condition. . . . [This] epilogue to *Twelfth Night* has an epilogue of its own in the heart of *King Lear*. There we find an additional stanza for the song:

> He that has and a little tiny wit
> With heigh-ho, the wind and the rain—
> Must make content with his fortunes fit,
> Though the rain it raineth every day.
>
> [*King Lear*, III. ii. 74-7]

It is again a Fool singing, and the "tiny wit" is an implied antithesis to the great bauble and the other thing that he carries. Now the stress is on human vulnerability and the human desire to come to terms. In *Twelfth Night* there was something of truculence in Feste's ending. Men's gates have been shut against him, his swaggering has not availed him, his cups have brought headache and ignoble company, and this has been making a continuous pattern since "A great while ago the world begun"; yet he confesses it all with a shrug and a defiance, and ends by reminding us that he is an entertainer. He has amused us, and enriched our transient Illyria, but will not let us go without claiming a common humanity with us. (pp. 52-4)

The shifting of viewpoint that comes with the *Twelfth Night* epilogue is remarkable. Orsino has, in the last lines of the play itself, referred to Viola as "Orsino's mistress and his fancy's queen," and for the moment we seem securely in the world of make-believe, the world where the clue to love's labyrinth is successfully followed, where fancy is free and yet has its queen. And then at once we are among toss-pots and their drunken heads. Yet the transition is bridged by music. Feste has been a singer, of love and of "good life," within the play, and it is therefore in character that his epilogue should be sung. In the 1800 Preface to the *Lyrical Ballads* Wordsworth pointed out that the use of metrical form could soften the effect of a painful narrative. Even more powerful in this respect is the singing voice. Shakespeare here dismisses his comedy and our acceptance of it, but the total effect is not harsh. We leave the theatre with a tune in our ears, and the harmony of *Twelfth Night* is after a fashion maintained. Later we may recall what Feste's words have been, as we recall Malvolio's treatment and the other disturbing reverberations of the comedy, but none of them will, during the time of performance or the time it takes to leave the theatre, obtrude much on our consciousness. There has, after all, been song at Illyria's departure from us. (pp. 54-5)

Clifford Leech, "'Twelfth Night', or What Delights You," in his "Twelfth Night" and Shakespearian Comedy, *University of Toronto Press*, 1965, pp. 29-55.

D. J. PALMER (essay date 1967)

[*Palmer examines the way in which the Ovidian concept of metamorphosis informs the theme of mutability in* Twelfth Night.]

The improbable fictions which are the material of Shakespearian comedy have often embarrassed those who find Shakespeare's genius in his truth to nature, but delighted those who admire the plays above all for their formal qualities, for their creation of a self-contained world that obeys only the laws of imagination. Since delight is a surer guide than embarrassment to an understanding of the comedies, criticism that first accepts the unreality of the comic world is usually more successful. The difficulty is to show why such unnatural and preposterous dramatic fictions should possess any meaning or significance other than sheer fantasy. Yet, despite their far-fetched plots, few of us would dismiss the comedies as absurd. (p. 201)

The story of *Twelfth Night* contains many conventional elements: a shipwreck on a strange coast to initiate the action, a pair of identical twins each believing the other dead, the consequent confusions of mistaken identity and the ironic situations arising from these, and from the additional complications of disguise, the cross-purposes of amorous intrigue, and the remarkable series of coincidences which eventually and conveniently bring about a happy ending. A plot of this kind, in *Twelfth Night* and the other comedies, certainly provides fullness and variety. It also produces a paradoxical effect of both artifice and artlessness. Highly artificial in its extravagant improbabilities, it is for the same reasons curiously naïve. The impression of a loosely-knit, apparently random sequence of events, following no natural laws of causality or necessity, is a basic feature of romance and of Shakespearian comedy. . . . [The] imaginative experience of such a plot is not one of pressing forward to a conclusion, but rather the sense of a meandering and illogical succession of episodes which seem to take us further and further away from any feeling of inevitability. This is surely an important effect of dramatic composition, since it contributes significantly to what we feel as the liberating experience of Shakespearian comedy, the sense of life as a pastime. It also suggests that behind the apparently naïve artlessness of romance convention there lies a deliberate and sophisticated art. (pp. 201-02)

In *Twelfth Night* the multiplicity of incident and the wayward progress of the plot not only serve to create the scope and freedom of the comic world: what seem from one point of view to be merely looseness of design and arbitrariness of event, characteristic of romance narrative, here of themselves dramatise the play's concern with the instability and impermanence of life. The dramatic form corresponds to the flux and changefulness represented in each situation. Orsino's moody restlessness is matched by the perversity of Olivia, who first withdraws from life to mourn a dead brother, and then suddenly finds herself wooing her suitor's servant. Malvolio's influence over his young mistress at the beginning of the play is a kind of usurpation, an upsetting of the natural order, to say nothing of the more outrageous ambitions he nourishes in her direction. The clamorous revelry of Malvolio's enemies, Sir Toby and company, constitutes a parallel source of unrest, for they refuse to confine themselves "within the modest limits of order".

Feste, the ubiquitous fool, adds further to this unsettled state of affairs in his restless wandering through the play.

Nothing is fixed or still in Illyria: an impression of capricious and elaborate artifice in the plot is directly related to a major theme of the play, the theme of mutability. The confusions and accidents of romance convention, the circuitous movement of events, are features of the structure that move us to an immediate experience of what the play also states more philosophically, that "all is Fortune". The unity of *Twelfth Night* is therefore formulated in terms of its apparent lack of unity as a romance, and an attempt to resolve its complex harmonies into a single theme must be qualified by the reminder that what we are aware of as we see or read the play is not a neat, logical scheme being worked out, but an apparently casual and random power controlling the fortunes of the characters it has brought together. (pp. 202-03)

Chance and fortune govern this world, where "as giddily as Fortune" is a byword, and nature is subject to what Feste calls "the whirligig of Time".

We hear the word "time" often enough in the course of the play. The muddle in which Viola finds herself between Orsino and Olivia is a knot which she says Time must untangle, and in time it does; for the waywardness of fortune is perfectly capable of producing Sebastian and so precipitating the happy ending. Sir Toby's drunken merry-making belies his claim that he keeps time in his catches; his anti-social hours send time topsy-turvy, and logic along with it: "To be up after midnight, and to go to bed then, is early; so that to go to bed after midnight is to go to bed betimes."

The confusions and disorders brought about by fortune and time are exploited both for comedy and for the melancholy lyricism which pervades the play. The general condition of mutability produces situations of farcical absurdity, but it also manifests itself in the more wistful sadness of Viola's reflections on her situation, cast ashore believing her brother drowned, and then impossibly in love with Orsino. Moreover, the giddiness of fortune, it seems, can turn men's wits, and there is much talk of madness in the play, from the innocent "natural" folly of Sir Andrew to the darker, crueller torments suffered by Malvolio. (p. 203)

The play has a remarkable fluidity of mood, reflected in the ease with which shifts of feeling and tension are made, even within a single scene. Music is of great importance in creating and dissipating these dramatic moods, and the lyrical texture of much of the verse similarly gives an ethereal and dreamlike insubstantiality to these modulations and changes of tempo. Indeed, language itself seems at times to be swayed by the extravagant and mutable conditions that govern in the play: Sir Toby appropriately displays an inebriated state of speech in his fondness for pedantic and exotic phrases, while Sir Andrew exposes his lack of wit and of bravery in his verbal pretensions to them. Feste's quibbling and punning show that words possess no more stability or fixity than anything else in Illyria. . . .

Like Shakespeare's other comedies, *Twelfth Night* is a love story. But love in this play participates in the waywardness and impermanence that affects all things in Illyria. The lover's mind is a microcosm, for, as Orsino says,

> For such as I am all true lovers are,
> Unstaid and skittish in all motions else
> Save in the constant image of the creature
> That is belov'd.   [II. iv. 17-20]
>   (p. 204)

If the references to ''appetite'' and ''surfeit'' ironically recall Orsino's description of his own feelings in the opening speech of the play, the imagery of the sea . . . relates the lover's changeful moods to the vicissitudes of fortune. The sea as a mirror of nature's mutability, a metaphor of destruction and renewal, eternally ebbing and flowing and therefore associated with the influence of time and fortune, is familiar enough in Shakespeare's work from beginning to end of his career; the associations he draws upon, both in poetic imagery and in the action of his plots, were part of the common property of the age. (p. 205)

Shakespeare seems to have developed a particular interest at this time in the aberrations of the fantasy, for within a year of 1600 he gave us Brutus, Orsino, and Hamlet, in each of whom, despite their very different situations, melancholy and an agitated fancy are mutually sustaining. Nobody in *Twelfth Night*, however, judges Orsino as severely as many critics have done, and while his egocentric lovesickness, projected upon Oliva, is akin to other types of madness in the play, he is more than the languid fop that he has often been made to seem. The ironic contrast between his unstable self-absorbed passion, and the selfless fidelity of Viola, certainly doesn't work in his favour; but at least, like Romeo's languishing for Rosaline, the very shallowness and unreality of this love prepares the ground for transferring the affections to a more genuine object: ''Love is not love which alters when it alteration finds.'' Moreover, Orsino is clearly invested with a certain aristocratic magnificence, and the lyrical voluptuousness of his melancholy contributes to the play a splendour and beauty that is not altogether disqualified by his comic extravagance. . . .

Such is the changeableness and confusion in Illyria, and in the passion-tossed minds of the lovers, that delusions and the mistaking of false for true easily prevail in the love affairs of the play. Orsino is kept apart from Olivia until the end of the play, so that his love is inspired and fed by music and poetry, by art rather than nature. (p. 207)

If Orsino's passion is nourished by art, not nature, then Olivia's plight is no better, for she falls in love with a fiction, mistaking art for nature. ''Poor lady, she were better love a dream'', says Viola, pitying the confusion her disguise has caused. But the dream proves true, for Cesario is an artificial copy of reality, and Olivia's marriage to Sebastian involves no change of her affections. (p. 208)

While the confusions and caprices of the lovers are exploited for comedy, the theme of mutability also assumes a more nostalgic, elegiac form in the play's awareness of the transience of youth and beauty. Such shifts of dramatic mood themselves create a sense of changefulness, and like the imagery of the sea, relate the lovers to a world whose very nature is impermanence and vicissitude. (p. 209)

Shakespeare converts into dramatic feeling the great Elizabethan commonplaces associated with the theme of mutability. For commonplaces though they are, these ideas had a profound imaginative appeal to the Elizabethan sensibility, whether they found expression in the epic majesty of the fragments concluding Spenser's *Faerie Queene*, or in the lyric simplicity of songs like Peele's ''His golden locks time hath to silver turned.''

Behind the Elizabethan awareness of mutability there lies a long and complex tradition of medieval and classical thought, but there is one figure whose influence upon Shakespeare it would be difficult to exaggerate. This is Ovid, whose *Metamorphoses* seemed to the Elizabethans not only a delightful collection of mythological stories on the theme of transformation, but also a philosophical work dealing with the mutability of nature. According to his sixteenth-century translator, Arthur Golding, Ovid's meaning in these tales of mortals changed into beasts and birds and trees was

> That nothing under heaven doth ay in stedfast state
>   remain,
> And next that nothing perisheth: but that each substance
>   takes
> Another shape than that it had.

(pp. 209-10)

Ovid's relevance to our understanding of *Twelfth Night* extends beyond this conception of nature's flux and impermanence. The Ovidian metamorphosis is a magical rather than a natural change, a transformation to a more enduring plane of existence, removed from the vicissitudes of time and fortune. As the Elizabethans interpreted it, metamorphosis was a symbolic change which altered the form in order to express its true nature. For example, they understood the transformation of Ulysses' sailors into swine to signify the domination of animal appetites that yielded to Circe's temptation.

In *Twelfth Night*, the conception of metamorphosis informs Shakespeare's use of disguise, and its function as a particular kind of change in a world subject to changefulness is similar in spirit to that of Ovid's stories. Viola, who is the constant and unchanging heart at the centre of several shifting and unstable attachments, first suffered an accident of fortune in the shipwreck, but survives in a changed shape as Cesario. Her disguise adds to the delusions of those around her, but it seems to translate her to an order of existence beyond the flux of nature. Cesario is not of nature, but of art: a fiction in himself, he nevertheless mirrors nature by expressing others' truth. Thus to Orsino, Cesario embodies his suit to Olivia; to Olivia, though she doesn't understand how until the end of the play, Cesario embodies the man she loves and will marry; to Viola herself, Cesario is a vehicle for the expression and revelation of her love for Orsino. Cesario has no fixed identity of his own, but changes his role chameleon-like in this world of ceaseless change. He is a figure of change by renewal, the complement to the theme of love's transitoriness and loss. Just as Viola survives in him, and as Orsino renews his courtship through him, so Olivia is restored to the living from mourning the dead, when she falls in love with him, and Sebastian also survives in him. When the disguise is dropped, the termination of Cesario's existence allows a new set of relationships to come into being, based on truth and harmony.

Viola's is not the only metamorphosis in the play. Malvolio is encouraged to ''cast off thy humble slough, and appear fresh'', and he dresses up in yellow garters, and puts on ridiculous airs, to win his mistress Olivia. He is the antithesis of Viola, who dresses as a boy to be Orsino's servant; moreover, while adversity causes Viola to assume disguise, Malvolio thinks it is his good fortune that tempts him to change his appearance. But in his disguise, like Viola in hers, he is manifesting the true nature of his secret desires and ambitions. Feste also disguises himself at one point in the play, to act Sir Topas for the benefit of the imprisoned Malvolio. In pretending to cast out the devil possessing Malvolio, he speaks truth as jest, and jest as truth, for in reality the fool is saner than Malvolio, whose madness and delusion come from pride. The whole of this pantomime really is arranged to exorcise the devil from Malvolio, to purge him of his humour. Feste, however, *in propria persona,* is like Cesario: he reveals no personal emotions, and lives only in his art, his quibbles and his songs.

The poetry which most beautifully captures this pervading sense of transient nature transformed into art comes in Cesario's fiction of his dead sister, who is Viola herself:

> She never told her love,
> But let concealment, like a worm i' th' bud,
> Feed on her damask cheek. She pin'd in thought;
> And with a green and yellow melancholy
> She sat like Patience on a monument,
> Smiling at grief.   [II. iv. 110-15]

The figure of Patience, the cherub above the grave, is a metamorphosis of love translated into a sphere beyond change and death, "smiling at grief".

Twelfth Night is a play in which art and nature are constantly changing places. It shows us nature becoming art, and at the end of the play we and the characters finally attain that harmony, wholeness and completeness, that poise and balance which transcend mutability. These are the qualities of perfection felt too in the songs:

> What is love? 'Tis not hereafter;
> Present mirth hath present laughter;
>   What's to come is still unsure.
> In delay there lies no plenty,
> Then come kiss me, sweet, and twenty;
> Youth's a stuff will not endure.
>   [II. iii. 47-52]

Both in its theme and in its form, this song holds in suspension all the fleeting transience and fragile beauty of the play. Insubstantial though it is, an interlude in a scene which is itself an interlude, the song fixes and holds by its highly-wrought art the fluidity and unconfined movement of feeling that "leaps all civil bounds". Thus, while the play includes the song, the song also contains the play; just as the play, art itself, contains and orders the capricious mutability and confusion of nature. (pp. 210-12)

> D. J. Palmer, "Art and Nature in 'Twelfth Night'," in Critical Quarterly, *Vol. 9, No. 3, Autumn, 1967, pp. 201-12.*

BRIAN VICKERS (essay date 1968)

[*In his discussion of the use of language in* Twelfth Night, *Vickers explores Shakespeare's use of verbal humor, the relationship of prose to poetry in the play, and the imagery.*]

The value of taking *Twelfth Night* [after *As You Like It* and *Much Ado About Nothing*], and not after *Julius Caesar* and *Hamlet,* where it probably belongs, is not only that we associate it with the two comedies whose mood it clearly shares but that by juxtaposition within these comedies we can see how Shakespeare, having had a holiday with Wit in *As You Like It,* returns to the application of prose to plot which he had so strongly achieved in *Much Ado.* One of the first things that we notice about *Twelfth Night* is the absence of any of the long, witty, solo speeches which dominate *As You Like It:* any prose soliloquies, such as those by Malvolio, are not performances at some point midway between the play and the audience, . . . but are the consistent expressions of such a character in such a situation. Developing this observation, we notice how Feste's wit, although being partly the normal expression of a clown, is quite integral to the situations which develop within the play.

And as we follow through the parallel characters in the lower plots—Sir Toby Belch, Aguecheek, Maria, Malvolio—we realize that we have left behind the separate, Lyly-like development of *As You Like It* (where Phebe was the only link between two plot-levels, and a tenuous one at that) to return to Shakespeare's own personal dramatic structure, where the various levels of the action cross and interact, providing significant oppositions as well as fruitful parallels. However, we must not take these observations too far, for the lower worlds of this play do not come into such meaningful contact with those above them as in *Much Ado,* and although the proportion of prose to verse is actually greater here than in *As You Like It* the prose-scenes contain much less of the central experience of the play: of all the witty comedies, *Twelfth Night* has the finest, and the most important poetry, together with the more delicate and responsive moods proper to verse.

Some of the differences between *Twelfth Night* and the preceding plays are simply accidental results of the major decisions which shaped the plot. Thus as there are no prose characters whose wit is changed by the experience of falling in love, then one type of stylistic change is absent. Indeed there is little stylistic development or 're-application' in the play (Malvolio does not change—that is his tragedy) and little extended verbal wit or rhetorical structure. This time the clown is restricted to logic, and elsewhere the syntactical norm is that of prose conversation, enlivened only by the individualizing details for certain characters. Perhaps the greatest determinant cause of this decline in verbal humour here is the increased use of the comedy of situation, as befits a play which turns on disguise, deception, and the mistakes of confused identity. The major comic scenes in the play show this move away from verbal wit towards a humour which depends on our knowledge of certain incongruities hidden from the characters involved, as with the first over-hearing of Malvolio, and still more with his appearance to Olivia cross-gartered. . . . (pp. 220-21)

Although it plays a smaller part than usual, Shakespeare feels bound to include some verbal humour in the play, and having constructed a full noble household complete with Fool, Steward, and hangers-on, he makes Feste the major repository of wit. Throughout the play Feste gradually comes into contact with each of the main characters for a bout of wit, and although these are usually the real-life exchanges between the witty clown meeting a new arrival at the house and jesting with him for sixpences, (incidentally, by such and other means Olivia's house is given a substantial dramatic presence), these combats have the added significance, as usual in Shakespeare, of showing the superior wit of whoever wins the bout. . . . [Olivia] appears, and with an invocation for dexterity (like Hal before the entry of Falstaff after Gadshill) Feste attacks her complaint that he is 'dry' and 'dishonest' with a piece of logic which is so dazzling that it sends any editor into contortions:

> Two faults, madonna, that drink and good
> counsel will amend. For give the dry fool drink,
> then is the fool not dry. Bid the dishonest man
> mend himself; if he mend, he is no longer dis-
> honest; if he cannot, let the botcher mend him.
> Any thing that's mended is but patched; virtue
> that transgresses is but patched with sin; and
> sin that amends is but patched with virtue. If
> that this simple syllogism will serve, so; if it
> will not, what remedy? As there is no true cuck-
> old but calamity, so beauty's a flower.
>   [I. v. 45-52]

That is as witty a piece of logic as anything by Touchstone, and far less peremptory. Feste is now brought closer to the play, for his 'catechism' of Olivia shows to her and to us that her mourning is superfluous: 'The more fool, madonna, to mourn for your brother's soul being in heaven.' His wit is then used to make a still more important dramatic point, for it is contrasted with the sour 'self-love' of Malvolio, whose arrogant dismissal—'Infirmity, that decays the wise, doth ever make the better fool'—inevitably reminds us of Feste's earlier words, and an idea which Shakespeare harps on throughout the play: 'Better a witty fool than a foolish wit', a sentence which could be taken as a motto for Malvolio, Belch, Aguecheek—to go no further.

Feste's other appearances have less relationship with the plot, although in addition to their significance in terms of their outcome it is noticeable that Feste is always used to begin a scene, as a humorous 'warming-up'. Thus when Viola encounters him alone (III, i) he takes the absolute equivocating manner of the obstreperous clown:

> VIOLA. Save thee friend, and thy music. Dost
> thou live by thy tabor?
> FESTE. No, sir, I live by the church.
> VIOLA. Art thou a churchman?
> FESTE No such matter sir, I do live by the church;
> for I do live at my house, and my house doth
> stand by the church.
>
> [III. i. 1-7]

The quickness of Viola's wit is now shown in the way she immediately spots the device (*antanaclasis*, taking the second meaning) and returns it with an *antimetabole:*

> So thou mayst say the king lies by a beggar, if
> a beggar dwell near him; or the church stands
> by the tabor, if thy tabor stand by the church. . . .
>
> [III. i. 8-10]

Shakespeare's clowns are never far from the 'conclusions' of syllogistic reasoning, and although a taste for verbal wit—and particularly the abuse of logic—is perhaps the last thing that the modern reader of Shakespeare develops, it is a necessary faculty if we are to appreciate his many subtleties, and when we have it we are guaranteed much quiet amusement—and increasingly a deeper understanding of the mental processes of his characters.

The prose of *Twelfth Night* is largely given to the lower orders of society and to the upper representatives when they come into contact with their servants and dependants. With Viola it is sometimes associated with her disguise, and when she is left alone at the end of a prose-scene she sometimes naturally ascends to the higher dignity of verse for a soliloquy (as at the end of II, ii; III, iv, and left alone III, i, 67-75). The only scene in which upper characters speak prose to each other is—again quite naturally within Shakespeare's conventions—also the most mocking and ironic scene between any of them, Viola's first embassy to Olivia (I, v). Here we find almost the only piece of that direct mockery of Romance (there is, I take it, much indirect mockery in the character and verse of Orsino) which had been so important for Shakespeare in his younger comedies, but one which does fulfil here its normal function in being ironic comment accompanying a love-interest which is ultimately to be taken seriously. However this deflation of the Romance code is put to a new and piquant dramatic situation, for the romantic pretensions of Orsino are not deflated directly but in the form of his ambassador, in a way which

while preserving Orsino's dignity inevitably reflects back on him. (pp. 222-25)

The detail of the mockery is built up of several of the most familiar prose devices, especially imagery: while Olivia's attendants are still present, Viola refrains from launching into her full declaration (although there is some amusing play with the 'speech' and her 'part'), and is given (or uses, as it seems to us in the theatre) images which are suitably extravagant for a young gallant: 'by the very fangs of malice I swear, I am not that I play' . . . 'What I am, and what I would, are as secret as maidenhead; to your ears, divinity; to any other's, profanation.' This is the romantic verging on the blasphemous again, as with Rosalind, and as they are left alone Olivia takes up the image in a witty piece of repartee:

> OLIVIA. Now sir, what is your text?
> VIOLA. Most sweet lady—
> OLIVIA. A comfortable doctrine, and much may
> be said of it. Where lies your text?
> VIOLA. In Orsino's bosom.
> OLIVIA. In his bosom? In what chapter of his
> bosom?
> VIOLA. To answer by the method, in the first
> of his heart.
> OLIVIA. O, I have read it; it is heresy.
>
> [I. v. 219-28]

This is the only time in the play (apart from the duel, and there for other reasons) that Viola is not dominant by her wit, and it is only right that Olivia should be allowed to win, being after all joint heroine. . . . Viola now launches into verse, into her prepared speech, and into the conventional arguments for marriage which are found in the early *Sonnets,* only for Olivia to seize on the conventional image 'And leave the world no *copy*' and deflate it by taking it quite literally and then arranging it in 'inventorial' form:

> O sir, I will not be so hard-hearted. I will give
> out divers schedules of my beauty. It shall be
> inventoried, and every particle and utensil la-
> belled to my will—
>   as, item two lips, indifferent red;
>   item two gray eyes, with lids to them;
>   item one neck
>   one chin
>   and so forth.
>
> [I. v. 244-49]

But although Olivia mocks the vocabulary of romance here, Viola's persistency impresses her, and she is magnetically drawn up to the level of verse and so to the medium and the mood in which Cupid can strike.

As that final exchange showed, Shakespeare's sensitivity to the way in which a character will react to the images used by another character is considerable: we have seen several examples of the significance of the failure to understand an image, and in Olivia's play with 'text' and 'copy' we see the function of the acceptance or refusal of an image (I suppose this is an instance of the 'forensic' category of imagery, with a character perceiving what effect the image is meant to have and then rejecting it). . . . [Throughout] *Twelfth Night* almost everyone is deflated at some time or another, either by the situation, or by imagery ranging from the lighthearted to the more corrective poles (Orsino and Olivia are the only ones to be spared direct irony, unless it be in the confusion of sexes which deceives them for so long—but they are the less important for being spared) and the normal equality of wit and status in Shakespearian comedy is perfectly demonstrated here, as a current of mockery of varying strengths leaves no idols standing, bringing everyone down to the same human level.

The biggest comic object of mockery, and indeed a comic butt *par excellence* in that' our sympathies are never likely to be aroused for him, is Andrew Aguecheek. (pp. 225-27)

Aguecheek is all of a piece feeble throughout, but the most original sign of his limited comprehension is his reaction to abuse. Like most of the significant stylistic effects in Shakespeare's prose, this is twice repeated: first he does not see the Clown's joke against him in the catch 'Hold thy peace, thou knave':

> FESTE. I shall be constrained in't to call thee knave, knight.
> ANDREW. 'Tis not the first time I have constrained one to call me knave.
>
> [II. iii. 63-6]

His passivity is ludicrous because he has wit enough to record the abuse, but not enough to see or resent the implication. The second time is when they overhear Malvolio's fantasy speech to Toby:

> MALVOLIO. Besides, you waste the treasure of your time with a foolish knight—
> ANDREW. That's me I warrant you.
> MALVOLIO. One Sir Andrew—
> ANDREW. I knew 'twas I, for many do call me fool.
>
> [II. v. 77-81]

This is still more amusing as he is actually pleased at having identified himself. (pp. 229-30)

Sir Toby Belch's images are universally abusive, a detail which shows his bluff egotism and irreverence for all—in this as in other things he is a pocket-sized Falstaff. But for his intended, Maria, his images are naturally more affectionate and also serve to characterize him by the two main sources from which he draws them: first, his sporting life: 'She's a beagle, true-bred' [II. iii]; 'Shall I play my freedom at tray-trip' (a game with dice); 'the youngest wren of nine'; secondly his pretentions to learning: 'my metal of India' [II. v], 'To the gates of Tartar' [II. v], 'Good night, Penthesilea' [II. iii]—an allusion to the Queen of the Amazons, killed at Troy by Achilles (Belch?). Toby's irreverence (which provides the force for the much needed correction of Malvolio—'Sneck up! . . . Art any more than a steward? Dost thou think because thou art virtuous, there shall be no more cakes and ale?') is also seen in his scornful wit, especially in his use of equivocation to evade the issue;

> MARIA. Your cousin, my lady, takes great exceptions to your ill hours.
> TOBY. Why let her except before excepted.
> MARIA. Ay, but you must confine yourself within the modest limits of order.
> TOBY. Confine? I'll confine myself no finer than I am. These clothes are good enough to drink in, and so be these boots too. . . .
>
> [I. iii. 5-12]

Sir Toby is an example of the economy of Shakespeare's stylistic characterization, for his words are only a small guide to his personality—it is more what he says and does, than how he says it.

But for the major prose-character of the play, Malvolio, the details of language are again significant. His arrogance is es-

tablished mainly by his attitude, actions, and by external comment, but is also seen in his imagery: Viola's epicene appearance is 'As a squash is before 'tis a peascod, or a codling when 'tis almost an apple. 'Tis with him in standing water, between boy and man'; the nocturnal trio 'gabble like tinkers' and 'squeak out' their 'coziers' catches' [II. iii]. Toby finds an appropriate image for this arrogance: 'the niggardly rascally sheep-biter'. (pp. 230-32)

But the great deflation of Malvolio is of course the overhearing-scene, the most amusing deception in all the comedies. Malvolio is heralded by Maria: 'he has been yonder i' the sun practising behaviour to his own shadow this half-hour'—like Ford in the *Merry Wives*, the prior existence of an obsession is greater argument for deflating it. He is discovered daydreaming—'To be Count Malvolio'—on that favourite Renaissance topic, the relative power of Virtue and Fortune in shaping a man's career: unlike Machiavelli, he has little confidence in *virtu* (or excuses his own lack of it): ''Tis but fortune, all is fortune.' As he develops this fantasy world with Malvolio as Prince a fine stylistic detail is the way that the intensity of his wish expresses itself in the verb tenses he uses: not 'then I could' or 'then I might', but the present *definite* (with a brief use of the infinitive and the present perfect), especially the present participle, which is used to suggest the action, situation, and circumstantial detail that have just preceded this moment—the verb tenses dramatize his savouring of the experience of *having* power:

> *Having been* three months married to her, *sitting* in my state—*Calling* my officers about me, in my branched velvet gown; *having come* from a daybed, where *I have left* Olivia *sleeping*— And then *to have* the humour of state; and after a demure travel of regard—*telling* them I *know* my place, as I would they should do theirs— *to ask* for my kinsman Toby—Seven of my people with an obedient start, *make* out for him, I *frown* the while, and . . .
>
> [II. v. 44-59]

and so on: the immediacy of Malvolio's vision, as revealed in the verb-tenses, is so strong that we can almost see him in action (it is like Mistress Quickly's reminiscence of Falstaff's broken promise, for here too through the details of style we see the man himself). But of course, although Malvolio does not realize it, his pretensions are being undermined both by the revelation of his dissembling and the conscious surface which he can vary ('after a *demure* travel of regard'—'quenching my familiar smile with an *austere* regard of control'), and also by the fact that his hypothetical present tense is being accompanied by the real present happening, the comments of the plotters: 'O, for a stone-bow to hit him in the eye!'. Here for almost the first time the prose aside has the function of also releasing our feelings towards the person being mocked by it, as Toby's long-suppressed abuse expresses what we would like to do—'And does not Toby take you a blow o' the lips then?'

The plot has been laid, and Malvolio walks into it. The image that naturally presents itself is of an animal being caught in a trap, and as in the twin deception scenes of *Much Ado* Shakespeare is at pains to punctuate the gulling of Malvolio with trap metaphors which will focus the action verbally, and remind us of the situation being exploited. This situational use of imagery here does not seem to have been noticed, although it is perfectly consistent. Maria announces his arrival: 'for here comes the trout that must be caught with tickling' [II. v. 22], and Fabian comments on his as yet uncorrected arrogance with an image similar to that used for Pistol immediately before his hubris was punctured by Fluellen: 'Contemplation makes a rare turkey-cock of him; how he jets under his advanced plumes.' As he steps further into the trap the images express the situation with remarkable detail and variety:

> FABIAN. Now is the woodcock near the dish.
> [II. v. 83]

> TOBY. Marry hang thee brock!
> [II. v. 103]

> FABIAN. What dish o'poison has she dressed him!
> TOBY. And with what wing the staniel checks at it!
> [II. v. 112-14]

> MALVOLIO. Softly—M, O, A, I—
> TOBY. O ay, make up that, he is now at a cold scent.
> FABIAN. Sowter will cry upon't for all this, though it be as rank as a fox.
> MALVOLIO. M—Malvolio—M—why that begins my name.
> FABIAN. Did not I say he would work it out; the cur is excellent at faults.
> [II. v. 120-28]
> (pp. 232-34)

Malvolio is a 'time-server', a politician, with all the unpleasant connotations which that word had for an Elizabethan, as reflected elsewhere in the play, in Aguecheek's naïve distrust of 'policy': 'An't be any way, it must be with valour, for policy I hate, I had as lief be a Brownist as a politician' [III. ii], and still more sharply in Falstaff's saturnalian inversion: 'we are politicians, Malvolio's a Peg-a-Ramsey' [II. iii]. This being so, it was an ingenious idea of Shakespeare's to cast the letter laid to deceive him into the style of the very authors which an ambitious politician would study, the style nourished on the pregnant aphorisms of Machiavelli and Guicciardini and boiled down to precepts at their barest: the English versions might be the aculeate memoranda of Gabriel Harvey's *Marginalia*, or Bacon's *Essays* in their first form (1597) or indeed in many cruder examples of the 'Advice' literature. The precept in the form of a bare imperative, such as we find it in this letter— 'let thy tongue tang arguments of state'—is more characteristic of Harvey and the cruder works (or Polonius), but the balancing of observation in parallel clauses beginning with 'some' is more like Bacon, as in the opening of 'Studies': 'Some bookes are to be tasted, others to be swallowed, and some few to be chewed and digested.' I do not want to suggest any definite source for this style, but rather to refer briefly to a whole convention of terse advice for self-betterment.

Shakespeare catches perfectly the mnemonic balances of this tradition, and also its direct, pithy imperatives:

> Some are born great,
> some achieve greatness, and
> some have greatness thrust upon them.
> Thy Fates open their hands,
> let thy blood and spirit embrace them; . . .
> cast thy humble slough, and appear fresh.

> Be opposite with a kinsman,
> surly with servants.
> Let thy tongue tang arguments of state;
> put thyself into the trick of singularity.
> [II. v. 145-52]

These are the bare bones of advice for getting on (of course, perfectly adapted to this dramatic situation), and the final reference to touching 'Fortune's fingers' brings us back both to Malvolio's own reflections and recalls the central place of ambition in the literature of the *Faber Fortunae* (as in Gabriel Harvey's anguished recognition of lost opportunities). Malvolio's reaction to the letter is ideal, couched in the same bare style and correctly answering the imperative 'do' with the future 'I will,' but even more precisely (as, too, with his translation of the vagueness of 'a kinsman'—as in a horoscope— into the specific: 'Sir Toby'):

> I will be proud,
> I will read politic authors,
> I will baffle Sir Toby,
> I will wash off gross acquaintance,
> I will be point-devise, the very man.
> [II. v. 161-63]

These might almost be sub-titled 'Malvolio's Resolves', but the ruthless dignity here revealed is shattered for us as he answers the final imperative, 'Remember who commended thy yellow stockings', with an undignified rush of resolves, his haste now dropping the repeated 'I will': 'I will be strange, stout, in yellow stockings, and cross-gartered, even with the swiftness of putting on.' But we are reminded of the inevitable outcome by the cool symmetries with which Maria balances 'resolve' and reaction:

> He will come to her
> in yellow stockings, and 'tis a colour she abhors,
> and cross-gartered, a fashion she detests.
> [II. v. 198-200]

The outcome of the plot is one of Shakespeare's most brilliant visual and situational comic scenes, especially as Olivia is given an ironic reminder of Malvolio's previous character:

> Where is Malvolio? He is sad and civil,
> And suits well for a servant with my fortunes.
> [III. iv. 5-6]
> (pp. 235-36)

The final exploitation of style and character comes in the last scene, as after his dignified and bitter letter Feste explains the whole device (doubtless with appropriate mimicry), recalling Fortune's precepts but with a crude version of the third term: 'some have greatness thrown upon them'. And the recollection of Malvolio's initial mock now completes the sense of the philosophical *antimetabole*, 'Better a witty fool than a foolish wit' with an image appropriate to the clown and his toys: 'But do you remember—"madam, why laugh you at such a barren rascal, an you smile not, he's gagged."' And thus the whirlgig of time brings in his revenges.' It is worth noting that of all Shakespeare's comic butts so far, Malvolio has received the sharpest, least humane, most humiliating correction. But it has not been the statutory mock of a semi-stereotyped comic figure unimportant to the action, rather a perfectly realistic attack on the faults of a fully-defined personality. Indeed everything in *Twelfth Night* is organized in coherent terms of situation and character: there is no superfluous wit (to adopt for the moment a modern attitude to wit in comedy), for Feste is a jester, and even the gaffes of Aguecheek, the last of the simpletons, are fully in character; nor are there any superfluous rhetorical symmetries, for the norm of naturalistic conversation is only substantially broken for Malvolio's letter and his reactions to it, and this piece of stylistic invention captures not just the man but the milieu. In this last matter *Twelfth Night* is a turning-point in Shakespearian Comedy, for in future the prose of wit—with unimportant exceptions—is subordinated to character and situation more naturalistically conceived. (pp. 238-39)

> Brian Vickers, "Gay Comedy," in his The Artistry of Shakespeare's Prose, *Metheun & Co Ltd, 1968, pp. 171-239.*

PHILIP EDWARDS   (essay date 1968)

[*Edwards, comparing the songs and the sentiment of* Twelfth Night *with those of* As You Like It, *concludes that* Twelfth Night *is the darker play. In the reunion of Viola and Sebastian, Edwards detects a theme which harkens back to* The Comedy of Errors *and prefigures* Pericles. *He suggests that perhaps Shakespeare, wearied by the "celebration of achieved love," had found in the happy reunion of families a focus for his literary efforts. For additional commentary on the dark aspects of the play, see the excerpts by F. J. Furnivall (1877), Arthur Quiller-Couch (1930), John Middleton Murry (1936), Mark Van Doren (1939), E. C. Pettet (1949), W. H. Auden (1957), G. K. Hunter (1962), Albert Gérard (1964), Jan Kott (1964), and Clifford Leech (1965).*]

For all its vitality and humour, *Twelfth Night* is not only darker than *As You Like It*; it is in many respects an uncomfortable play. Both comedies are plays of liberation. But in *As You Like It* the liberation is by means of escape, whereas in *Twelfth Night* the liberation is by inversion and misrule. *As You Like It* is a parable of healing: from the habitations where there is

Engraving from Verplanck edition (1847). By permission of the Folger Shakespeare Library.

hatred in families, the characters escape into a magic place which cures malice and provides for lovers their proper partners. In *Twelfth Night*, we remain in the city. Liberation means the temporary lordship of Sir Toby Belch, the subjugation of Malvolio and the deception of almost every character in the play. 'Healing' is an inappropriate word. A brother and sister are re-united by chance, and the initial unhappiness of Olivia and Orsino is resolved in a way that may seem a satire of the 'Jack shall have Jill' theme. Shakespeare, re-peopling an abandoned cave is perhaps a little weary of his duty, and exposes his comedy to questioning at every point.

Morley's settings of the central songs in *As You Like It* and *Twelfth Night* beautifully convey the differences between the plays. *It was a lover and his lass* is the happiest account of love finding its fulfilment in the spring time. What do the lovers themselves sing? Cutting out the refrain, the song goes,

> This carol they began that hour,
> How that love was but a flower,
> And therefore take the present time,
> For love is crowned with the prime.
> [*As You Like It*, V. iii. 26-32]

There is really not much noise of Time's winged chariot hurrying near. Love may be a flower, but it is robustly in bloom at the moment. It is the joy of taking the present time that is dominant, not the fear of growing old. But in the second stanza of *O mistress mine*, the dominance is elsewhere.

Feste sings *O mistress mine* at the height of the saturnalia in II, iii, the after-hours revelry which is Sir Toby's victory over care. Sir Toby has of course demanded 'a love song' rather than a 'song of good life'.

> What is love? 'Tis not hereafter;
> Present mirth hath present laughter;
>   What's to come is still unsure.
> In delay there lies no plenty,
> Then come kiss me, sweet and twenty;
>   Youth's a stuff will not endure.
> [II. iii. 47-52]

Love is encompassed by darkness here. Love is something seized to lighten the darkness rather than a free giving and fulfilment. What's to come is still unsure. In spite of the light ironical tone, this is jet-black melancholy besides which everyone else's is a pretty silvered grey. The two songs fall either side of *carpe diem*. In the first there is no real sense of the menace of time; in the second, there is no real delight in love. The darkness is visible: in the first stanza, isn't the lover looking for his mistress in the dark?

> O mistress mine, where are you roaming?
> O stay and hear, your true love's coming.
> [II. iii. 39-40]

As we go on, we hear the voice of Puck ('Jack shall have Jill')

> Journeys end in lovers' meeting
> Every wise man's son doth know.
> [II. iii. 43-4]

This is how plays end. When this play is rounded off, with the meetings of lovers who have (one might say) bumped into each other in the dark, Feste the clown is left alone on the stage and he sings his weird plaint as epilogue to the play. The 'folly' which serves him in a world of play in which Malvolio is the measure of sanity only antagonizes the world outside:

> But when I came to man's estate
>   With hey, ho, the wind and the rain,
> 'Gainst knaves and thieves men shut their gate,
>   For the rain it raineth every day.
>
> [V. i. 393-96]

Love is different:

> But when I came, alas! to wive,
>   With hey, ho, the wind and the rain,
> By swaggering could I never thrive,
>   For the rain it raineth every day.
>
> [V. i. 397-400]

The obscure fourth stanza seems to reflect, like the first three, on the 'reality' of the spheres which were transmuted in the comedy world. Clowning, hostility, love are now followed by drink: 'But when I came unto my beds . . . With tosspots still had drunken heads.'

> A great while ago the world begun,
>   With hey, ho, the wind and the rain,
> But that's all one, our play is done,
>   And we'll strive to please you every day.
>
> [V. i. 405-08]

Has simplicity and casualness ever been made to convey so much? As Barber says, 'It is the play which is keeping out the wind and the rain' [see excerpt above, 1959]. Or, it is the play which makes the light in the darkness. Not love, but comedy's presentation of love. Experience has made Feste sad, as it made Jaques sad, but he is too urbane, has too strong a sense of humour to go around protesting against self-deception, or to bore the audience with a parade of his knowledge. (pp. 63-5)

As Feste's 'minority voice' is more delicate and more subtle, and more far-reaching, than that of Jaques, so the play he is to 'see through' is more vulnerable than *As You Like It*. There is much play, in the Malvolio scenes, about which is the world of sanity and which the world of madness. (The word 'mad' is used more often in *Twelfth Night* than in any other play of Shakespeare's.) The man responsible for decency and order in the household, who has called his opponents mad, is imprisoned as a madman by those opponents. 'You have put me into darkness and given your drunken cousin rule over me.' He protests his sanity to a priest who is a clown in disguise. This comedy world is a very bad dream indeed for the representative of discipline and sobriety. The fantasy of liberation demands that the upholder of authority be simply an object of derision and it is as ridiculous to be sentimental about Malvolio as it is to be priggish about Sir Toby's financial exploitation of Sir Andrew. But it is difficult to respond wholeheartedly to the inversion of the standards of sanity and order, and probably Shakespeare meant it to be difficult. (pp. 65-6)

Orsino, with his voluptuous delight in the 'sweet pangs' of his own love-melancholy, calls in Feste to sing an 'old and antique song' that 'dallies with the innocence of love' and 'did relieve my passion much'. He wants the kind of music which relieves his passion, not by curing it with surfeit of food, as he extravagantly demanded in the very first lines of the play, but by feeding it and sentimentalizing it until his passion becomes a detached object to commune with and worship.

Feste has no objection to living off the patrons whom he knows better than they know themselves and he provides for the Duke the saccharine he will pay for. The melancholy of his song,

so thickly laid on, is poles apart from the real depression underlying the light irony of *O mistress mine*. (p. 67)

I have spoken before of the follies of infatuation, which certainly include the enjoyment of sighs and suffering, as being cheerfully included by Shakespeare in the necessary procession towards Thalamos. 'As all is mortal in nature, so is all nature in love mortal in folly.' But there seems to me a world of difference between amusing absurdity and the kind of mood which Orsino and his pupil are in: a strange sinking mood of abandonment into thinking about passion. The falsity of Feste's song colours the whole 'lovers' meeting' between Orsino and Viola. (I am ignoring the argument that it was not originally intended that Feste should sing this song: we must take the play as we have it.)

What is the truest thing in *Twelfth Night*, if there is a falseness in the lovers and their meetings? Surely it is the greeting of brother and sister, Viola and Sebastian, who had been parted by shipwreck.

> —I had a sister
> Whom the blind waves and surges have devour'd.
> Of charity, what kin are you to me?
> What countryman, what name, what parentage?
>
> —Of Messaline; Sebastian was my father.
> Such a Sebastian was my brother too.
> So went he suited to his watery tomb;
> If spirits can assume both form and suit,
> You come to fright us.
>
> —A spirit I am indeed,
> But am in that dimension grossly clad
> Which from the womb I did participate.
> Were you a woman, as the rest goes even,
> I should my tears let fall upon your cheek,
> And say, 'Thrice welcome, drowned Viola!'
>
> [V. i. 228-41]

This has been foreshadowed in *Comedy of Errors* and itself foreshadows the reunions in families broken by shipwreck in *Pericles* and *The Tempest*. It is so much greater, in this play, than the ritual of converging lovers, which seems sardonically treated in comparison. There was something here to hold on to, when the celebration of achieved love may have wearied Shakespeare. (pp. 68-9)

> *Philip Edwards, "The Abandon'd Cave," in his* Shakespeare and the Confines of Art, *Methuen & Co Ltd, 1968, pp. 49-70.*

M. C. BRADBROOK (essay date 1968)

[*The part of Feste and other of Shakespeare's clowns is thought to have been written for the actor Robert Armin. Bradbrook discusses how Armin might have influenced the characters of Feste, Lear's Fool, and Touchstone in* As You Like It. *Bradbrook's essay, from which the following excerpt is taken, was originally delivered as a lecture at Trinity College in 1968.*]

[What] Armin seems to have provoked in Shakespeare (and membership of the company in Armin) was the integrated comic vision of an Erasmus or a More of the world of fools; the idea of what Erasmus had first termed the 'foolosopher' (a word picked up by Armin). 'He uses folly as a stalking horse and under cover of that he shoots his wit' defines Touchstone, in words close to Armin's own definition: 'Fools natural, are prone to self-conceit / Fools artificial with their wits lay wait.'

Feste is Malvolio's first and principal antagonist, parish clerk to Lady Folly.

He never uses such gross terms of familiarity as earlier clowns, but he can conjure money from old friends like the Duke or strangers like the twins; he invents wonderful mock authorities to edify Sir Andrew; he can parody the church service as readily as Erasmus himself.

Very early, he foresees the fate which overtakes Malvolio; 'God send *you*, Sir, a speedy infirmity for the better increasing of your folly' [I. v. 78-9].

At the end Feste recognizes the rounded and absurd perfection of the comedy—'Thus the Whirligig of time bringeth in his revenges'. There was a feeling that the clown ought to be able to deal with anything—perhaps from his taking on all comers. . . . The new kind of wit depended on being able to adjust to a varied audience, to play a multiplicity of rôles. The clown was losing his independence as an entertainer; he was no longer a challenger but a servant. As Viola recognizes, this asks sensitive responses to mood and company:

> This fellow's wise enough to play the fool;
> And to do that well craves a kind of wit:
> He must observe their mood on whom he jests,
> The qualities of persons and the times,
> And like the haggard check at every feather
> That comes before his eye.
> This is a practice
> As full of labour as a wise man's art.   [III. i. 60-6]

No confident jig for such a character—he ends with a melancholy song. And in his next appearance a household jester Yorick has long been dead, and Armin the clown is digging a grave. The association of the Fool and Death in the famous pictures of Hans Holbein had haunted Shakespeare's imagination since he wrote of the antic Death crouching within the hollow crown circling a king's brow (*Richard II*, III. ii. 160-70).

Although his writings are broken and confused, and his history with the players too seems a broken and uncertain one, Armin's sympathetic *rapport* can be sensed in the full, gratified unity of conception that makes *As You Like It*, *Twelfth Night*, and *King Lear* each in so different a way macrocosmic, a complete world whose inhabitants live in a special glow, or light that suffuses them:

> Folly, sir, doth walk about the orb like the sun,
>   it shines everywhere.   [III. i. 38-9]
>   (pp. 57-9)

To King Charles the play was known as *Malvolio*, and from an early admirer we learn that it was Malvolio the crowds went to see [see excerpt above by Digges, 1640]. Van Doren says of Toby's attack on Malvolio, 'It is the old world resisting the new; it is the life of hiccups and melancholy, trying to ignore latter day puritanism and efficiency' and between his mood and the music of old manners it may be felt that Malvolio is 'dreadfully likely to prevail' [see excerpt above, 1939]. Certainly Olivia would not have this important and necessary officer miscarry for half of her dowry; but when he resents the quips of Feste, she diagnoses him acutely: 'O you are sick of Self-Love, Malvolio, and taste with a distempered appetite'.

Self-Love, as many authorities from Erasmus to Ben Jonson bear witness, is the chief attendant on Folly; and Folly, as again Erasmus and other authors had made clear, held her rule in the world of fools by delegation from Fortune, or Lady

Luck. The unity of this play comes from the Rule of Fortune over the lives of Orsino, Olivia and the twins, and the Rule of Folly over life below stairs. As a victim of Self-Love, Malvolio tries to climb the wheel of Folly's Mistress, Fortune. 'All is Fortune' he remarks as he picks up the deceptive love letter from 'the fortunate-unhappy' [II. v. 23]. But it is Folly that guides him—the penalty of his aspiration to be Count Malvolio is to be taken for a madman; when all is revealed, Olivia tacitly withdraws her offer to let him judge his own case—'Alas, poor Fool, how have they baffled thee!' (pp. 59-60)

So Malvolio is drawn into the kingdom of folly. Ecclesiastes has said the number of fools is infinite, and the idea of a kingdom of fools was familiar in carnival and sottie. Malvolio in fact performs a kind of little play to his appreciative stage audience, and when he is bound in the dark room, Feste performs one of the regular clowning acts by holding a dialogue in which he sustains both parts, demanding that Malvolio subscribe to the heretical doctrine of transmigration and in his own person challenging the devil, now inhabiting Malvolio, to combat. (p. 61)

Within the fantasy there is a very clear sense—an actor's sense, or a jester's—of precise social distinctions. The most poignant comes at the end of Feste's last song when he suddenly turns into Armin himself, as the wind and rain of January fall, the world returns to work again, ending foolish things and childish toys. For the Players' offerings, unlike those of the old households, *will* go on, as part of a workaday world.

> A great while since the world began
> With hey ho, the wind and the rain,
> But that's all one, our play is done,
> And we'll strive to please you *every day*.
>   [V. i. 405-08]

Here, the moment of comic truth is the moment when the old world of the revels turns into the new world of the theatre, and when the craft of the player is laid aside for a final bow as he turns to 'woo the twopenny room for a plaudite'. The new fool is a fool *deferring to an audience*. (pp. 61-2)

The comic vision was more elusive than the tragic, but in *Twelfth Night*, it is fully embodied. To attribute this to the presence of a gifted clown rather than the presence of an Italian Duke (as Leslie Hotson would have it in *The First Night of Twelfth Night*) implies that Shakespeare had left behind that ceremonious kind of drama which he perfected in *A Midsummer Night's Dream*, and that he was as deeply influenced by his fellow-actor as by his audience. A momentary compliment, a skilful improvisation might be part of the play; but the play itself had become a craft mystery.

Twelfth Night, because it was made for one company at one time by a master of craft carries the self-adjustive elasticity of all great drama; being so complete and beautifully balanced in itself between the world of revels and the January cold, it absorbs the imbalance of those who would present or accept it. (pp. 66-7)

M. C. Bradbrook, "The New Clown: 'Twelfth Night'," in her Shakespeare, the Craftsman: The Clark Lectures, 1968, *Chatto & Windus, 1969, pp. 49-74.*

ANNE BARTON (essay date 1972)

[*For Barton, the tone of* Twelfth Night *becomes harsh in the final act, where images of death threaten the heightened world of the comedy. Like E. Montégut (1867) and Jan Kott (1964), Barton explores the madness which prevails in the play.*]

All of *Twelfth Night*, up to the final scene, takes place in a heightened world. There is no contrasting environment, no Athens or Duke Frederick's court, to set against Illyria. Messaline, the place from which Viola and Sebastian have come, is even more shadowy than Syracuse in *The Comedy of Errors*, or those wars from which Don Pedro, Claudio and Benedick find release in Messina. Messaline has no character whatever, and certainly no claim to be regarded as that normal world to which characters have so often returned at the end of a Shakespearian comedy. Illyria itself, on the other hand, has a very distinct character and declares it from the opening moments of the play. The sea-captain, appealed to by Viola for information about the country in which she has so unexpectedly arrived, might just as well have said to her what the Cheshire Cat says to Alice: 'They're all mad here.' Even before the unsettling appearance of twin Cesarios, both the ruler of Illyria and his reluctant mistress have manoeuvred themselves into unbalanced states of mind. They are surrounded, moreover, by characters even madder than they: Sir Toby Belch, Sir Andrew Aguecheek, or Feste, the man whose profession is folly. Malvolio in his dark room may seem to present the play's most extreme image of insanity, yet Olivia can confess that 'I am as mad as he, / If sad and merry madness equal be' [III. iv. 14-5]. Sebastian, bewildered by Olivia's passionate claims upon him, will earnestly debate the question of his own sanity. Antonio, already bewitched as he sees it by Sebastian, is accused of madness by Orsino's officer when he tries to explain his situation.

The eruption onto the stage of identical twins is calculated to make people distrust the evidence of their own senses. *The Comedy of Errors*, which plays the same game of mistaken identity in a doubled form, had also made use of images of madness. Yet the lunacy of *Twelfth Night* is both more widespread and more various. It is part of the whole atmosphere of the Feast of Fools suggested by the play's title, not simply a product of the failure to understand that there are two Cesarios and not just one. For Elizabethans this title would have stirred immemorial and continuing associations with a period of time in which normal rules were suspended, in which the world turned ritually upside down, allowing the plain man to become king and pleasure to transform itself into a species of obligation. Certainly the spirit of holiday reigns in Illyria, particularly in the household of the mourning Olivia. The countess herself may disapprove from a distance of the nightly chaos presided over by Sir Toby: only Malvolio tries in earnest to repress it. As soon as he does so, he places himself in danger. He becomes the churl at the banquet, the sobersides at the carnival. The revellers, forgetting their own private dissensions, recognize him at once for the common enemy and hunt him from their midst. As feasters, men living in a celebratory world that, temporarily at least, is larger than life, they instinctively protect themselves against the niggard who refuses to yield himself to the extraordinary.

As members of the *Twelfth Night* audience, we too are sharers in the extraordinary, a fact which perhaps explains why Malvolio has found tender-hearted apologists in the study but very few sympathizers in the playhouse. His humiliation at the hands of Feste, Maria, Fabian and Sir Toby removes a threat to our own equilibrium, to the holiday mood induced by the comedy in its early stages. . . . By means of laughter, we too cast Malvolio out. As soon as the steward has pieced together the meaning of the mock letter to his own satisfaction, as soon as

he has swallowed the bait, he ceases to be a threat. Yellow-stockinged and cross-gartered, trying to produce some rusty approximation to a smile, Malvolio has become part of precisely that heightened world of play-acting, revelry and lack of control which he so despised. Festivity has made him its unwilling prey. Thereafter, it will do with him what it likes, until the moment of awakening.

This moment of awakening is in some ways the most distinctive feature of *Twelfth Night*. Sir Toby is the first to scent the morning air. At the end of Act IV, he is wishing that 'we were well rid of this knavery', and that some means of releasing Malvolio 'conveniently' might be devised before the mood of holiday inconsequence breaks [IV. ii. 65-8]. Act V displays a marked harshening of tone. It begins by massing together images of death in a fashion that harks back to Shakespeare's preferred comic practice in the plays written before *As You Like It*. In this respect, as in its renewed emphasis on plot, *Twelfth Night* breaks away from the classicism of its predecessor. (pp. 171-73)

[As Sir Toby and Sir Andrew] are being helped away in a state of debility and antagonism, Shakespeare exchanges prose for verse and radically alters the mood of the scene. He allows Sebastian, that comedy resolution personified, at last to confront his twin sister, to assure Olivia of his faith, to renew his friendship with Antonio and to enlighten Orsino. There will be a happy ending. It is, however, a happy ending of an extraordinarily schematized and 'playlike' kind. Viola has already had virtual proof, in Act III. that her brother has survived the wreck. They have been separated for only three months. Yet the two of them put each other through a formal, intensely conventional question and answer test that comes straight out of Greek New comedy:

> *Viola:*   My father had a mole upon his brow.
> *Sebastian:* And so had mine.
> *Viola:*   And died that day when Viola from her birth
>   Had numb'red thirteen years.
> *Sebastian:* O, that record is lively in any soul!
>   He finished indeed his mortal act
>   That day that made my sister thirteen years.
> [V. i. 242-48]

This recognition scene is intensely moving. Its emotional force and purity derive, however, from consonances that are recognizably fictional. In the theatre, the fact that an audience will always be more struck by the *dissimilarity* in appearance of the actors playing Viola and Sebastian than by that marvellous identity hailed so ecstatically by the other characters, also serves to drive a wedge between fact and literary invention. We are dealing here, Shakespeare seems to announce, with a heightened, an essentially implausible world.

For Olivia and Sebastian, Viola and Orsino, this heightened world perpetuates itself. For them, there will be no return from holiday, no need to leave Illyria. Yet the little society which they form at the end of the play is far more fragmentary and insubstantial than the one that had been consolidated in Arden. The final pairings-off are perfunctory. Olivia accepts Sebastian for himself. Orsino, rather more surprisingly, accepts a Viola he has never seen as a woman. Rosalind had returned in her own guise as a girl at the end of *As You Like It*, uniting Ganymede with the lady Orlando loved first at Duke Frederick's court. Considering the abruptness of Orsino's resolve to substitute Viola for Olivia in his affections, an unknown Viola only guessed at beneath her 'masculine usurp'd attire' [V. i. 250], Shakespeare might well have done something similar here. Instead, he treats this joining of hands summarily, and turns away at once to the very different issue of Malvolio.

In the final act of *Twelfth Night,* a world of revelry, of comic festivity, fights a kind of desperate rearguard action against the cold light of day. It survives only in part, and then by insisting upon an exclusiveness that is poles apart from the various and crowded dance at the end of *As You Like It.* Viola and Orsino, Olivia and Sebastian may no longer be deluded, yet it is still Illyria in which they live: an improbable world of hair's-breadth rescues at sea, romantic disguises, idealistic friendships and sudden, irrational loves. This is not quite the country behind the North Wind, but it approaches those latitudes. The two romantic couples stand on the far side of a line dividing fiction from something we recognize as our own reality, and the society they epitomize is too small to initiate a dance. Of the other main characters, no fewer than four are conspicuous by their absence. Maria, Sir Toby and Sir Andrew are not present to witness the revelations and accords of the closing moments. Malvolio intrudes upon them briefly, but entirely uncomprehendingly. Like Sir Toby and Sir Andrew, he comes as a figure of violence and leaves unreconciled, meditating a futile revenge. For him too, the dream is over and the moment of awakening bitter. Jacques had walked with dignity out of the new society; Malvolio in effect is flung.

There is only one character who can restore some sense of unity to *Twelfth Night* at its ending, mediating between the world of the romantic lovers and our own world, which is (or is about to be) that of the chastened Sir Andrew, the sobered Belch and the unbending Malvolio. In a sense, he has been doing just this all along in preparation for some such ultimate necessity. Throughout *Twelfth Night,* Feste has served as commentator and Chorus, mocking the extravagance of Orsino, the wasteful idealism of Olivia's grief, Viola's poor showing as a man. He has joined in the revels of Sir Toby and Sir Andrew while remaining essentially apart from them, aware of their limitations. Most important of all, he has kept us continually aware of the realities of death and time: that 'pleasure will be paid one time or another' [II. iv. 70-1], that 'beauty's a flower' [I. v. 52] and youth 'a stuff will not endure' [II. iii. 52]. Two contradictory kinds of time have run parallel through the comedy, diverging only at its end. One is the time of holiday and of fiction, measureless and essentially beneficent, to which Viola trusts when she remains passive and permits the happy ending to work itself out with no positive assistance from her [II. ii. 40-1]. The other time is remorseless and strictly counted. Although even Viola and Orsino catch glimpses of it, its chief spokesman has been Feste.

At the very end of *Twelfth Night* these two attitudes towards time distinguish two groups of characters, dividing a world of fiction from one of fact. The audience leaving the theatre faces its own jolt into reality, into the stern time of a world beyond holiday, but at least it is given Feste and not Malvolio as its guide. Left alone on the stage, Feste sings his song about the ages of man, a song which draws its material from the same source as Jaques' pessimistic catalogue. This time, there will be no attempt at qualification or correction. Yet the song itself is curiously consoling. It leads us gently and in a way that is aesthetically satisfying from the golden world to the age of iron which is our own. A triumph of art, it builds a bridge over the rift which has opened in the comedy at its conclusion.

Feste is tolerant as Jaques, on the whole, was not. He does not attempt to judge, or even to reason. He simply states fact. The child is allowed his fancies: a foolish thing is but a toy.

When he grows up he pays for them, or else discovers that the self-deceptions in which he is tempted to take refuge are easily penetrated by the world. Marriage ultimately becomes tedious, and so do the infidelities to which it drives a man. The reality of wind and rain wins out, the monotony of the everyday. The passing of time is painful, may even seem unendurable, but there is nothing for it but resignation, the wise acceptance of the Fool. All holidays come to an end; all revels wind down at last. Only by the special dispensation of art can some people, Viola and Orsino, Olivia and Sebastian, be left in Illyria. For the rest of us, the play is done; fiction yields to fact, and we return to normality along with Sir Toby and Maria, Sir Andrew and Malvolio. (pp. 175-78)

> *Anne Barton, "'As You Like It' and 'Twelfth Night': Shakespeare's Sense of an Ending," in* Shakespearian Comedy, *Stratford-Upon-Avon Studies, No. 14, John Russell Brown and Bernard Harris, General Editors, Edward Arnold (Publishers) Ltd, 1972, pp. 160-180.*

JOAN HARTWIG (essay date 1973)

[*Hartwig characterizes the conflicts of* Twelfth Night *as contests "between human will and suprahuman control." She proposes that the characters of the play, particularly Feste, are subservient to the benevolent, larger design, symbolized by Feste's "whirligig of time."*]

Shakespeare's plays frequently counterpose the powers of human and of suprahuman will, and the antithesis usually generates a definition of natures, both human and suprahuman. (p. 501)

Many of the conflicts of *Twelfth Night* seem to be concerned with the contest between human will and suprahuman control; yet, the latter manifests itself in various ways and is called different names by the characters themselves. As each contest between the human will and another designer works itself out, the involved characters recognize that their will is fulfilled, but not according to their planning. The individual's will is finally secondary to a design that benevolently, but unpredictably, accords with what he truly desires. For example, when Olivia, at the end of Act I, implores Fate to accord with her will in allowing her love for Cesario to flourish, she has no idea that her will must be circumvented for her own happiness. Yet the substitution of Sebastian for Cesario in her love fulfills her wishes more appropriately than her own design could have done. Inversely, when Duke Orsino says in the opening scene that he expects to replace Olivia's brother in her "debt of love," he doesn't realize that literally he will become her "brother" [I. i. 33-40]. . . . When the play's action accords with Duke Orsino's "will," the discrepancy between intention and fulfillment is a delightful irony which points again to the fact that "what you will" may be realized, but under conditions which the human will cannot manipulate. Orsino's desire to love and be loved, on the other hand, is fulfilled by his fancy's true queen, Viola, more appropriately than his design for Olivia would have allowed.

The one character whose true desires are not fulfilled in the play is Malvolio. His hope to gain Olivia in marriage results in public humiliation at the hands of Feste, who takes obvious satisfaction in being able to throw Malvolio's former haughty words back at him under their new context of Malvolio's demonstrated foolishness. . . . Feste's assertion that the "whirligig of time" has brought this revenge upon Malvolio neglects the fact that Maria has been the instigator and Feste the enforcer of the plot to harass Malvolio. Time's design, insofar as Malvolio is concerned, depends upon Maria's and Feste's will, which differs significantly from a central point that the main plot makes—that human will is not the controller of events. The characters in the main plot learn from the play's confusing action that human designs are frequently inadequate for securing "what you will," and that a design outside their control brings fulfillment in unexpected ways. Feste's fallacy, of course, makes the results of the subplot *seem* to be the same as the results of the main plot, but Time's revenges on Malvolio are primarily human revenges, and this particular measure for measure is thoroughly within human control. Feste's justice allows no mitigation for missing the mark in human action; and the incipient cruelty that his precise justice manifests is felt, apparently, by other characters in the play. (pp. 501-03)

Feste's "whirligig of time brings in his revenges," and Malvolio quits the stage with, "I'll be revenged on the whole pack of you!" [V. i. 378]. The forgiveness that should conclude the comic pattern is "notoriously" missing from the subplot and cannot be absorbed successfully by the Duke's line, "Pursue him and entreat him to a peace." Malvolio seems unlikely to return. The major differences between the subplot and the main plot is clearest at this dramatic moment: revenge is a human action that destroys; love, graced by the sanction of a higher providence, creates a "golden time."

Feste's "whirligig" seems to be a parody of Fortune's wheel in its inevitable turning, particularly with its suggestions of giddy swiftness and change. It provides a perfect image for the wild but symmetrical comic conclusion of the play's action. Feste's speech which includes it gives the appearance of completion to a mad cycle of events over which no human had much control. Only in Malvolio's case was human control of events evident. In her forged letter, Maria caters to Malvolio's "will" and, by encouraging him to accept his own interpretation of circumstances as his desire dictates, she leads him not only into foolishness, but also into a defense of his sanity. (pp. 504-05)

In the darkness of his prison, Malvolio literally is unable to see, and Feste makes the most of the symbolic implications of Malvolio's blindness. The audience perceives with Feste that the house is not dark (that hypothetical Globe audience would have been able to see the literal daylight in the playhouse), yet the audience also knows that Malvolio is being "abused" because he cannot see the light. The audience is therefore led to a double awareness of values in this scene: we are able to absorb the emblematic significance of Malvolio's separation from good-humored sanity and to know at the same time that Malvolio is not mad in the literal way that Feste, Maria, and Sir Toby insist. Although the literal action engenders the emblematic awareness, the literal action does not necessarily support the emblematic meaning. This pull in two opposite directions occurs simultaneously and places the audience in a slightly uncomfortable position. We prefer to move in one direction or in the other. Yet it seems that here Shakespeare asks us to forgo the either-or alternatives and to hold contradictory impressions together. Malvolio cannot be dismissed as a simple comic butt when his trial in the dark has such severe implications.

The ambiguities of his situation are clear to everyone except Malvolio, but he rigidly maintains his single point of view. Because he refuses to allow more than his own narrowed focus, he is *emblematically* an appropriate butt for the harsh comic action that blots out his power to see as well as to act. He must

ultimately depend upon the fool to bring him "ink, paper, and light" so that he may extricate himself from his prison, a situation which would have seemed to Malvolio earlier in the play "mad" indeed. Feste thus does force Malvolio to act against his will in submitting to the fool, but Malvolio fails to change his attitudes. (pp. 508-09)

In the very next scene, Sebastian presents a contrast which delineates even more clearly the narrowness of Malvolio's response to an uncontrollable situation. Sebastian, too, confronts the possibility that he is mad: his situation in Illyria is anything but under his control.

> This is the air; that is the glorious sun;
> This pearl she gave me, I do feel't and see't;
> And *though* 'tis wonder that enwraps me thus,
> *Yet* 'tis not madness. . . .
> For *though* my soul disputes well with my sense
> That this may be some error, *but* no madness,
> *Yet* doth this accident and flood of fortune
> So far exceed all instance, all discourse,
> That I am ready to distrust mine eyes
> And wrangle with my reason that persuades me
> To any other trust *but* that I am mad,
> *Or else* the lady's mad.   [IV. iii. 1-16: my italics]

Sebastian's pile of contrasting conjunctions ("though," "yet," "but") underlines his hesitance to form a final judgment, unlike Malvolio, whose point of view never changes despite the onslaught of unmanageable circumstances. The contradictions of his sensory perceptions lead Sebastian to a state of "wonder" in which he is able to suspend reason and delay judgment, and this signifies a flexibility of perception which Malvolio cannot attain. . . . Sebastian's ability to sense the "wonder" in a world where cause and effect have been severed gives him a stature that Malvolio cannot achieve. Yet the difference between them is due to the source of their manipulation as well as to their response. Sebastian is manipulated by Fate or by Fortune; Malvolio, by Maria and Feste. Human manipulators parody suprahuman control and because they do, Maria and Feste define both levels of action. (pp. 509-10)

Feste's attribution of revenge to this "whirligig of Time" points up the difference between the two controls. The whirligig becomes a parodic substitute for the larger providence that other characters talk about under other titles: Time, Jove, Fate, Fortune, or Chance. Significantly, Malvolio's humiliation is the only humanly designed action that fulfills itself as planned. The subplot performs its parody in many other ways, but in Feste's summary "whirligig" it displays the double vision that Shakespearean parody typically provides. The foibles of the romantics in Illyria are seen in their reduced terms through Sir Toby, Maria, and Sir Andrew, but the limitations of the parodic characters also heighten by contrast the expansive and expanding world of the play. Love, not revenge, is celebrated.

But even Feste's whirligig takes another spin and does not stop at revenge: in the play's final song the playwright extends an embrace to his audience. Feste's song creates an ambiguity of perspective which fuses the actual world with an ideal one: "the rain it raineth every day" is hardly the world described by the play. Romantic Illyria seems to have little to do with such realistic intrusions. Yet, the recognition of continuous rain is in itself an excess—it does not rain every day in the actual world, at least not in the same place. Thus, the pessimistic excess of the song balances the optimistic excesses of the romance world of Illyria; neither excess accurately reflects the actual world. Despite the apparent progress the song describes of a man's growing from infancy to maturity and to old age, it remains something of an enigma. The ambiguities of the first four stanzas build to a contrast of direct statements in the final stanza.

> A great while ago the world begun,
> > With hey, ho, the wind and the rain;
> But that's all one, our play is done,
> > And we'll strive to please you every day.
>
> > > > > [V. i. 405-08]

The first line of this stanza seems to imply that the world has its own, independent design; and it also suggests that man's actions must take their place and find meaning within this larger and older pattern. The specific meaning of that larger design, however, remains concealed within the previous ambiguities of Feste's song. His philosophic pretensions to explain that design are comically vague and he knows it. (pp. 510-11)

Turning to the audience and shattering the dramatic illusion is typical in epilogues, but Feste's inclusion of the audience into his consciousness of the play as a metaphor for actual experience has a special significance here. Throughout *Twelfth Night*, Feste has engaged various characters in dialogues of self-determination. . . . In each situation, Feste provides the other person with a different perspective for seeing himself. Thus, it is more than merely appropriate that at the end of the play Feste engages the audience in its own definition of self. By asking them to look at their participation in the dramatic illusion, Feste is requesting them to recognize their own desire for humanly willed happiness.

The playwright, like the comic providence in the play, has understood "what we will" and has led us to a pleasurable fulfillment of our desires, but in ways which we could not have foreseen or controlled. The substitution of the final line, "And we'll strive to please you every day," for the refrain, "For the rain it raineth every day," is a crucial change. Like the incremental repetition in the folk ballad, this pessimistic refrain has built a dynamic tension which is released in the recognition that the play is an actual experience in the lives of the audience, even though it is enacted in an imagined world. The players, and the playwright who arranges them, are engaged in an ongoing effort to please the audience. The providential design remains incomplete within the play's action and only promises a "golden time"; similarly, the playwright promises further delightful experiences for his audience. The subplot's action, on the other hand, is limited within the framework of revenge: the revenge of the subplot characters elicits Malvolio's cry for revenge.

Malvolio is the only one who refuses to see himself in a subservient position to a larger design. And possibly because that design is too small, we cannot feel that his abuse and final exclusion from the happy community of lovers and friends allows the golden time to be fulfilled within the play. Feste's manipulation of Malvolio resembles the playwright's manipulation of his audience's will, but in such a reduced way that we cannot avoid seeing the difference between merely human revenge and the larger benevolence that controls the play's design. (pp. 512-13)

> Joan Hartwig, "Feste's 'Whirligig' and the Comic
> Providence of 'Twelfth Night'," in ELH, Vol. 40,
> No. 4, Winter, 1973, pp. 501-13.

ALEXANDER LEGGATT   (essay date 1974)

[*In his study of Shakespeare's love comedies, Leggatt stresses the variety rather than the unity of these works. In the following*

excerpt, he points out the differences in Shakespeare's handling of theme, plot development, and characterization in Twelfth Night *and* As You Like It, *and explores the concept of unrequited love. For additional commentary on Shakespeare's handling of the theme of love in the play, see the excerpts by H. B. Charlton (1937), E. C. Pettet (1949), John Russell Brown (1957), and Harold Jenkins (1959).*]

As You Like It and *Twelfth Night* are often seen as the twin peaks of Shakespeare's achievement in romantic comedy, yet within the conventions of the genre they could hardly be more different. It is as though the later play was created by taking the major impulses behind its predecessor and throwing them into reverse. While *As You Like It* was almost without conventional comic intrigue, *Twelfth Night* bristles with plot complications. Instead of enjoying the freedom of the forest, with the organic cycles of nature in the background, the characters are enclosed in houses and formal gardens, and in the background is not the familiar countryside but the implacable, mysterious sea. Instead of the swift, decisive matings and friendly courtship games of the earlier play, we have unrequited love (a minor motif in *As You Like It*) expressing itself through unreliable messengers. Not since *The Two Gentlemen of Verona* has there been such emphasis on the pains rather than the pleasures of love; not since *Love's Labour's Lost* have we been so aware that love's means of expression are unreliable. It is as though the ground won in the intervening plays—and most notably in *As You Like It*—has been deliberately surrendered.

A civilized liberty was the keynote of the earlier play. *Twelfth Night* is, by comparison, strictly divided into compartments. In the earlier play, prose and verse mingled freely, and both could be used for moments of casual naturalism, or moments of formality. Here there is a stricter division, and a tighter logic—prose for comic or naturalistic effects, verse for formal and romantic ones. This reflects a firmer separation of romantic and comic figures: the plotlessness of *As You Like It* allowed a casual mingling; in *Twelfth Night* each set of characters has a plot to tend to, and is largely kept within the confines of that plot. When a character from one plot becomes involved in the other, the effect is not so much to unify the play as to create a comic shock. Viola among the clowns, and Malvolio trying to be a lover, are both laughably out of their depth. There is also a sharp division between the two households that dominate the play. Orsino's is dramatically simple—a single figure surrounded by attendants, who except for Viola are functional and characterless—and even Viola is utterly dedicated to her master. Olivia's household is dramatically more open and complex: there is a fully developed life below stairs, largely unconcerned with Olivia's problems, and even the attendants who appear with their mistress, Malvolio and Maria, spend most of the action engaged in their own affairs.

The 'dykes that separate man from man', upon which, according to W. B. Yeats, 'comedy keeps house', are nowhere more apparent in Shakespeare's comedies than they are in *Twelfth Night*. In plays like *A Midsummer Night's Dream* and *As You Like It* the confrontation of different minds was mostly stimulating and entertaining—a celebration of human variety. In *Twelfth Night*, however, we see the other side of this vision: each individual is locked in his own private understanding, and his ability to escape from himself and share experiences with others is limited. . . . [We] are aware of each character as an individual, out on his own, the lovers trying to make contact but with limited success, and the comic figures either openly hostile or forming relationships based on temporary expediency. If the frequent comparisons between *Twelfth Night* and

Jonsonian comedy have any basis, it may be in this sense of sharply distinguished individuals adrift in a fragmented world, each with his own obsession. Certainly individual characters come more clearly into focus than in any previous comedy of Shakespeare's, and the sense that they can be bound together in a common experience is weaker. The play ends not with a dance or a procession of couples trooping off to bed, but with the solitary figure of Feste, singing of the wind and the rain. And this image of solitude echoes and reverberates throughout the play.

The solitude of the lovers results from their experience of unrequited love, an experience that leaves them frustrated and restless. (pp. 221-23)

The lovers are confined by circumstance as much as by their own natures: so long as their love is misdirected, they find no relief or satisfaction. The figures of the comic plot are trapped in another way—by limited, clearly defined comic personalities. In Sir Toby Belch's opening pun, 'Confine? I'll confine myself no finer than I am' [I. iii. 10-1], there may be an extra significance of which he is not aware. To be occasionally drunk may be the sign of a free spirit; to be consistently drunk is not. Sir Toby may challenge the restrictions of Olivia's household, but he is too bound by his addiction to the bottle to put genuine liberty in their place. . . . Sir Andrew yearns for better things: he imagines for himself the full life of the courtier, soldier and scholar: dancing, duelling, masques and revels. He envies the fool's singing voice, and Cesario's gift with words; and he will, if goaded, try almost anything once. But the aspirations of Sir Philip Sidney are wedded to the capacities of Sir Andrew Aguecheek. However earnestly he may try to improve himself, he suffers a comic paralysis of will; his weakness ties him to the more decisive character of Sir Toby, and he is confined in Sir Toby's narrow world of eating and drinking. . . . Sir Toby has the capacities of a gentleman—he is shrewd, witty and not afraid of swordplay; but his talents have no outlet. He has come to terms with life, but in a way that belittles and restricts him. Sir Andrew has the ambition but not the capacity; both are trapped by their own natures—comically, but, the more we look at them, pathetically too.

It is more difficult to see pathos in Malvolio—in his early scenes, at least. He too is in the prison of his ego, but for him it is a gorgeous palace. His egotism kills his capacity for ordinary pleasure. . . . He takes no pleasure, that is, if it is provided by anyone else—by Feste, for example. But he is an endless source of pleasure to himself. Like Orsino, he leads a fantasy life, 'practising behaviour to his own shadow' [II. v. 17]. In the long soliloquy of the letter scene the stiff constraint of his ordinary manner disappears, and he becomes urbane and expansive, revelling in the details of his dream. In fact Malvolio is fully happy only when he is alone; his prickly manner at other times is his reaction to the presence of other people, whose very existence is an irritating intrusion: 'Go off; I discard you. Let me enjoy my private' [III. iv. 89-90]. Malvolio is the most obviously solitary figure in Illyria, but his solitude is also a striking comic variant on the confinement suffered by Orsino and Olivia, indulging fantasies of love that cannot be gratified, and the restriction of personality that lies behind the gregariousness of the drunken knights. (pp. 226-28)

[Both Viola and Feste] show, in their different ways, a sensitivity to the people they deal with. Feste in his role as commentator and entertainer has to understand the minds of his audience, and tune his speech to their moods. . . . From this point of view, Malvolio is the sort of audience every comedian

dreads, for he knows just how much depends on him, and he refuses to co-operate: 'Look you now, he's out of his guard already; unless you laugh and minister occasion to him, he is gagg'd' [I. v. 86-8]. But the others, at one time or another, fall under Feste's spell, and in this respect he goes some way towards drawing together the broken world of Illyria. He can unite Sir Toby and Sir Andrew into a silent, appreciative audience by singing to them of love; he can rouse Olivia and Orsino to laughter. On the rare occasions when he takes a direct part in the action, it is to bring people together: he fetches Olivia to her first meeting with Sebastian, and he delivers the letter that clears up the confusion surrounding Malvolio. But these direct interventions are rare. If his role as entertainer gives him freedom of movement, it also gives him a certain detachment. . . . An important condition of his professional freedom is that he does not become too closely involved with any member of his audience. His role, in the end, is both liberating and confining.

In Viola we see an intuitive, outgoing sympathy, an ability to share in the predicaments of others: her involvement is greater than Feste's, for she lacks his professional detachment. Like Olivia, she begins by mourning for a brother, and when she hears of the Countess's grief, she exclaims 'O that I serv'd that lady' [I. ii. 41]. But her sympathy for both Olivia and Orsino finally depends on a shared experience of unrequited love. When Orsino tells her 'It shall become thee well to act my woes' [I. iv. 26], he is speaking more truly then he knows, for she feels for him what he feels for Olivia—and what, ironically, Olivia feels for her. E. K. Chambers writes of Viola, 'With the specific of simple truth she purges the pestilence of artifice and rhetoric'' [see excerpt above, 1907]. On the contrary, she uses the rhetoric of love for all it is worth. (pp. 230-31)

When Viola comes to Olivia's house as the messenger of Orsino's love, barrier after barrier falls. Sir Toby is ordered away from the gate, and replaced by the more formidable Malvolio; but when Malvolio reports his attempt to keep Viola out, the messenger sounds so interesting that she is admitted after all. In the interview itself the process continues: Viola is left alone with Olivia; and then Olivia unveils. Step by step, but rapidly, Viola is allowed to take liberties that would have seemed unthinkable at the beginning of the scene. This progressive removal of inhibition is reflected in the way language is used. At first we may wonder how seriously Viola is taking her own mission:

> Most radiant, exquisite, and unmatchable
> beauty—I pray you tell me if this be the lady
> of the house, for I never saw her. I would be
> loath to cast away my speech; for, besides that
> it is excellently well penn'd, I have taken great
> pains to con it.
>
> [I. v. 170-74]

She emphasizes that she is putting on an act, and thus calls into question the sincerity of her words; she denies the reality of Orsino's love, for reasons we can guess—'Whoe'er I woo, myself would be his wife' [I. iv. 42]. Olivia responds in the same spirit, asking 'Are you a comedian?' [I. v. 182]. Like the ladies of Love's Labour's Lost, she mistrusts the conventional words of love, and Viola's emphasis on the theatrical nature of her mission makes this mistrust greater—as it is presumably intended to. . . . (p. 232)

When Viola creates an image of yearning, unrequited love ('Make me a willow cabin at your gate . . .') she fuses her understanding of Orsino's love with her own experience of passion, and the conventional posture of adoration expresses the truth of her own situation. As it was in *As You Like It*—but this time more swiftly and directly—the satiric view is swept aside, and we see that through convention love can find its truest expression. Moreover, the sheer ambiguity of the speech—does it refer to Orsino, or Viola, or both?—cuts it loose from any specific love affair, and makes it a general image of unrequited love, conventional, recognizable, and therefore available to anyone. (pp. 233-34)

[Viola's] disguise is also a barrier: it prevents Olivia from seeing how misdirected her love is, and it prevents Orsino from knowing how far his affection for Cesario may really go. Viola herself continually strains against the disguise, dropping broad hints: 'I am not that I play' [I. v. 184]; 'I am not what I am' [III. i. 141]. Orsino unwittingly looks behind the disguise to the reality:

> For they shall yet belie thy happy years
> That say thou art a man: Diana's lip
> Is not more smooth and rubious; thy small pipe
> Is as the maiden's organ, shrill and sound,
> And all is semblative a woman's part.
>
> [I. v. 30-4]

Normally, when another character describes one of these disguised heroines, the emphasis is on the pert boyishness one imagines as a quality of the boy actor himself. This emphasis on the femininity of Cesario is unusual; it is as though Orsino is trying to wish the disguise away. (p. 235)

[In Act II, Scene iv.] Orsino depicts his love as an active, selfish, insatiable appetite; Viola portrays hers as passive, selfless, but at bottom sterile and self-enclosed, like his own. The two are complementary and therefore drawn to each other; but neither suggests any capacity for sharing or for mutual sympathy. The irony is that Orsino and Viola, in exchanging experiences as they do, demonstrate a sympathy they cannot express: the images they have found for love belittle and even betray it, concentrating on its privateness, but the interplay of minds that surrounds these images suggests a deeper capacity for love than either of them can make articulate. The scene ends, like the scene with Olivia, on a note of frustration.

Both scenes are lively and moving in their depiction of the efforts people make to reach each other across the barriers of situation and personality. As in *The Merchant of Venice*, characters react to a fantastic situation with behaviour that is convincingly, frustratingly human. As in *Much Ado*, more is expressed in the subtext than appears on the surface of the dialogue. And one of the basic problems of Shakespearian comedy is here explored eloquently: we see the conventions of speech, the literary images, that characters use in an attempt to make contact with each other; and we see that these conventions both help and betray them, just as Viola's disguise frees and imprisons her at the same time. There is nothing didactic in this: it is not an abstract exploration of the nature of language. Rather, it is a theatrical demonstration of language in action, of the complex dilemmas involved in the characters' efforts, spurred on by love, to break out of the privateness of the individual mind.

The comic figures operate in quite a different way, and their scenes are dramatically simpler. There is no subtext, for there are no hidden depths of feeling: the self-indulgence, the pretensions, and the mutual hostility are out in the open. And while the lovers struggle with misunderstandings they have not

created and cannot solve themselves, the misunderstandings of the comic plot, centred on Malvolio, are deliberately manufactured by Maria and her cohorts. Here, the barriers that separate people are actually fortified. The hostility between Malvolio and the rest of the household has a sharpness unusual among Shakespeare's comic figures. (pp. 237-38)

Malvolio's letter scene shows how radically different are the dramatic methods Shakespeare employs in the two plots. Instead of the subtle mingling of sympathy and concealment in the scenes with the lovers, we are shown two quite separate trains of thought, operating independently. Malvolio figuratively enclosed in his private fantasy, and the listeners literally enclosed in their boxtree, engage in competition rather than dialogue:

MALVOLIO:	To be Count Malvolio!
SIR TOBY:	Ah, rogue!
SIR ANDREW:	Pistol him, pistol him.
SIR TOBY:	Peace, peace!
MALVOLIO:	There is example for't: the Lady of the Strachy married the yeoman of the wardrobe.
SIR ANDREW:	Fie on him, Jezebel!
FABIAN:	O, peace! Now he's deeply in; look how imagination blows him.
MALVOLIO:	Having been three months married to her, sitting in my state—
SIR TOBY:	O, for a stone-bow to hit him in the eye!

[II. v. 35-46]

This is the Jonsonian device of putting a character on display, while others make sardonic remarks about him (a device Shakespeare uses again in Parolles's drum scene in *All's Well That Ends Well*). The effect is not so much to provide a comic dislocation of Malvolio—that is hardly necessary, for he is sufficiently ridiculous on his own—as to let each party strike sparks off the other. (p. 239)

The scene is splendidly funny in performance, and we do not ask awkward questions about the characters' behaviour. But like so many great comic scenes it is based on a view of humanity—in this case, of competing egotists—that is anything but sanguine. The lovers' awkward but earnest attempts at contact are thus thrown into relief. The difference between the two plots is finally not just a matter of dramatic idiom or technique, but a basic difference of vision. (p. 241)

[The] final, crucial difference between the two plots lies in the manner of their respective endings. The deceptions of the love plot are partly the result of chance, and chance can take a hand in resolving them. But the deceptions of the comic plot are man-made, the result of fixed, antagonistic, personalities. And there is no easy or satisfying solution for this plot. After our initial amusement, we become aware of the inherent cruelty of the jokes against Malvolio. We have seen in earlier plays, notably *The Merchant of Venice* and *Much Ado*, that wit is not always in season, and in *Twelfth Night* the same realization grows towards the end. We are not bothered by the letter scene, whose pace and *brio* prevent any awkward emotional involvement; but when Malvolio is shut in a dark room, begging for light, we see the victim's sufferings a little too clearly, and our laughter acquires an edge of distaste. (p. 243)

The comic plot is conventionally full of false images—Maria's letter, Feste's disguise, Sir Toby's description of Sir Andrew as a dangerous swordsman. And when Malvolio adopts the external shows of love, in yellow stockings, cross-gartered and relentlessly smiling, the result is simply absurd. In this plot, images and appearances have no validity except as signs of comic confusion. But the romantic plot operates by a different set of rules. . . . Throughout the romantic plot, a trust in appearances, though it may lead to temporary confusion, is justified in the long run. To Orsino, Cesario looks like a woman; he is a woman. To Olivia, he looks like a man; he is a man. (pp. 245-46)

This trust in images is made possible by the special handling of the figure of Cesario, in which the extension of personality implied in disguise is taken further, and exploited in a more daring way, than in any previous comedy of Shakespeare's. When Viola and Sebastian meet at the end of the play, the reactions of the others suggest something more than the simple discovery that there are two characters who look alike. Orsino exclaims 'One face, one voice, one habit, and two persons! / A natural perspective, that is and is not' [V. i. 216-17]. Antonio asks 'How have you made division of yourself?' [V. i. 222], and even Sebastian holds back for a moment the natural explanation of the seeming miracle:

> Do I stand there? I never had a brother;
> Nor can there be that deity in my nature
> Of here and everywhere.
>
> [V. i. 226-28]

The reunion of the twins is a moment of still, poised formality: action freezes in the contemplation of a miracle, and natural explanations emerge only slowly. Theatrically this moment counts for more than the pairing of the lovers, and so it should. The joining of the twins is the crucial action; after it has been accomplished the lovers can slip easily into couples, for the problem is already solved. But the plot significance of this moment is a clue to something deeper. The single being in a double body is an image of love to set against the opposing image of the solitary ego—Malvolio in his dark room. . . . In other comedies a single personality is extended by disguise, but the extension is temporary and finally withdrawn; this is the only case in which the new figure created by disguise has also an objective reality, a life of its own. Viola's creation of Cesario is confirmed, as no ordinary comic pretence could be, by the existence of Sebastian. It is as though mind has actually created matter, and the distinction between spirit and body, like other distinctions, is blurred. (pp. 246-48)

The resolution of the love plot does not depend on the will, or the knowledge, of individuals. It is an impersonal, organic process: confusion gathers to a head, and breaks. Sebastian has no Prospero-like authority: he solves the lover's problems not by what he knows, but by what he is. He provides a true version of the false, comic images of the subplot—a real lover for Olivia, a real fighter who can put the two knights in their place. (p. 248)

The pairing of the lovers in the final scene is likewise beyond considerations of individual temperament. It is, like the meeting of the twins, a generalized image of love. Within that image, the pairing of Orsino and Viola carries some psychological conviction: their interest in each other is already established, and even when Olivia appears, Orsino's greeting, 'Here comes the Countess; now heaven walks on earth' [V. i. 97], is rendered perfunctory by the speed with which he goes back to what really interests him—a conversation about Cesario. His joking with Feste, and the references to the sea fight, suggest that Orsino's personality may be more balanced and complete, and his capacities wider, than mere indulgence in love melancholy. There is enough material here to make us see his match with Viola as satisfying, if we are inclined to ask for

satisfaction in psychological terms. Even so, Orsino's actual transfer of affection is too swift and simple to bear much literal-minded inspection. And Olivia's marriage to Sebastian, seen literally, would be a clear case for immediate annulment. We are not, however, encouraged to take it this way. . . . There are no apologies or statements of forgiveness as the lovers join hands; indeed their minds are hardly examined at all. The ending takes little account of the reasons for particular attachments; it is, on the contrary, a generalized image of love.

As such, its significance is limited. We can easily think of Rosalind and Orlando married and producing children, for they think of themselves that way; but the union of lovers in *Twelfth Night* is more a freezing of the moment of romantic contemplation, before the practical business of marriage. . . . It is also both miraculous and exclusive: it cannot touch the ordinary world. While Touchstone and Audrey can join the procession of couples in *As You Like It*, the comic figures of *Twelfth Night* pass through the final scene untouched by its harmony. (pp. 250-51)

In *As You Like It* time was primarily the medium of fulfilment; it was also admitted to be the medium of decay, but that view was firmly placed as secondary. In *Twelfth Night* the two views are more closely balanced. Time brings the lovers to each other, untangling the knot as Viola said it would; but we are constantly reminded that times does other work as well. . . . At the end, [the] sense that time finally destroys our illusions and brings us to decay is centred on the broken figures of the clowns. Time as the medium of fulfilment belongs to the lovers. And the special moment of the play's title shares this double significance: Twelfth Night celebrates the Epiphany, the showing forth of a miraculous birth; but it is also the last night of a revel, before the cold of winter closes in.

The last scene is neither a still point of harmony nor a simple dying fall: it is the busiest, most complex scene in the play, as the private, magic happiness of the lovers vies for attention with the larger, uncontrollable world of time inhabited by the clowns. . . . This kind of tension is basic to Shakespearian comedy: it is at bottom a tension between stylized and realistic art. The lovers, having engaged our feelings as human beings, are now fixed in a harmony we can believe in only by trusting the power of fantasy; the clowns, stylized in their own way at first, have lost some of the immunity of comedy and now present an image of defeat that is uncomfortably real.

The tension is resolved, unexpectedly, in Feste's last song. It seems at first to belong to the vision of the comic plot. Feste sings of our decay through time, from the folly of childhood to the knavery of manhood to a drunken collapse in old age. The lovers have disappeared, and there is a solitary figure on stage. His experience, as often in the comedies, is linked to ours through the medium of nature—this time the wind and the rain. Yet before we sink too easily into melancholy, the song concludes: 'But that's all one, our play is done, / And we'll strive to please you every day' [V, i. 407-08]. In *As You Like It* the play was put aside as an illusion, but its vision of humanity walking to the Ark in pairs was confirmed by the audience itself. In *Twelfth Night* the triumph of love is put at a distance, as a strange and special miracle that cannot touch everyone. But the vision of decay that opposes it is also, in the last analysis, one more illusion, part of a play. The one thing that is permanent is the work of art itself: tomorrow it will be there to entertain us again, even if we are all a day older. As in Shakespeare's sonnets, art is a means, perhaps the only means, of cheating time, of holding human experience in permanent form. . . . We have seen in the play as a whole the power of conventional images to touch their hearers. The same may be true of the stylized image of the lovers in the final scene: the fact that it is obviously a matter of literary artifice does not make it invalid; on the contrary, its bold stylization strikes through to the heart of experience. When Feste is left alone on stage the vision of an uncontrollable world of time and decay may seem for a moment to overwhelm the happiness of the lovers. But just as, in *As You Like It,* satire fights a sudden rearguard action at the end, so in *Twelfth Night* there is, against all odds, a final rescue for artifice. (pp. 251-54)

Alexander Leggatt, " 'Twelfth Night'," in his Shake-speare's Comedy of Love, *Methuen & Co Ltd, 1974, pp. 221-54.*

ELIZABETH M. YEARLING (essay date 1982)

[*Yearling's essay deals specifically with the language of* Twelfth Night. *She discusses the way in which Shakespeare exposes the falsity of language and concludes that the play presents the "conflict of truth and illusion."*]

Half-way through [*Twelfth Night*] Viola and Feste meet and jest about words and meaning [III. i. 1-59]. The significance of their exchange is uncertain. . . . Yet this is the only meeting between Shakespeare's heroine and his fool. Their quibbling shows the two-facedness of words. . . .

[Often in *Twelfth Night* Shakespeare] shows words to be frivolous, conventional, or false. Apart from Feste's comments there is Olivia's remark about the poetical being 'the more like to be feigned' [I. v. 196]. (p. 80)

[Tired] or inflated vocabulary brings us to one of the play's complexities. A rich source of cliché was the language of compliment, the store of polite but often insincere courtesies which came naturally to the well-bred but had to be taught to the uncourtly in manuals which suggested the right phrases for wooing and suing. And it is the heroine who is the play's main speaker in this fossilized, conventional style. . . . Much of Viola's language, especially to Olivia, is affected, courtly, artificial, not the style we expect of a Shakespearian heroine. But Shakespeare exploits this conventional speech brilliantly. . . . [Act I, scene v] turns on Viola's semi-serious use of conventional vocabulary and images, her knowledge of what she is doing, and our share in that knowledge. Yet there is more. The stereotyped language conveys a considerable depth of feeling. ''Tis beauty truly blent' is a genuine appreciation of Olivia's beauty and of Viola's task as a rival. 'Make me a willow cabin . . . 'is a powerful love speech. The strength and truth of feeling make it wrong to concentrate on the clichés and stock motifs, or on the speech's deception. Viola uses words devalued by overexposure; she speaks them as Cesario, whose existence is illusory, but their emotion convinces. (pp. 80-1)

[Viola's] style expresses her nature. She is a linguistic chameleon who adapts her style to her companion. Her vocabulary ranges from courtly compliment to rude jargon [I. v. 203-05]. But her variousness is not just verbal: her nature is to deal confidently with sudden changes. And the assumed registers, coupled often with sincere feelings, capture the blend of truth and illusion which Viola represents. It is difficult not to see a convincing personality breaking through the polite fiction which is Cesario. (p. 81)

Although *Twelfth Night* includes Feste's scepticism and many instances of verbal folly and deception, Shakespeare's practice encourages a positive belief in the power of words. Character and theme emerge from the nature of the words and the way they are combined. Here we are a little closer to the Platonic theory of names. Several characters in *Twelfth Night* have an individual vocabulary and syntax. . . . New words are common in Orsino's vocabulary, especially words of several syllables ending in suffixes. His syntax is appropriate. . . .

Sir Toby is an interesting contrast. He also invents long words—'substractors' [I. iii. 34-5], 'consanguineous' [II. iii. 77], 'intercepter' [III. iv. 222]. And his syntax is mannered. . . . But Sir Toby's long words and patterned syntax are not enough to elevate his speech. His long words occur in prose, not verse, and their use undercuts their impressiveness: 'substractor' is a nonce-word meaning 'detractor' and it *sounds* like a drunken fumbling for words. (p. 82)

Malvolio's language indicates constraint. He introduces fewer new words than either Orsino or Sir Toby, but his mouth is full of pompous phrases and long words without the poetry of Orsino or the colloquialism of Sir Toby. He is at his worst in contemplation, in the letter scene [II. v. 23-179]. Inflated vocabulary is not simply a public front but is his very nature. . . .

When we read or hear *Twelfth Night* we learn about the characters by attending to their vocabulary and syntax. Besides expressing character, the words and sentence structure can also clarify themes. One of the play's contrasts is between holiday and the work-a-day world. Although the title suggests festivity, recent criticism has qualified C. L. Barber's treatment of *Twelfth Night* as a festive comedy [see excerpt above, 1959]. Many modern critics dwell on the play's melancholy mood, but in more positive opposition to festivity are the characters' working lives. (p. 83)

The contrast between holiday and work results in an interesting structural device. There are repeated movements from musing or conversation back to some necessary task. These shifts are embodied in the dialogue, and centre on Viola. It is easy to note the difference between the first scene's languor and the second scene's sense of purpose, but even within scene 2 there is a distinct change of mood. Viola and the Captain discuss her brother's fate and she is encouraged to hope for his safety:

> Mine own escape unfoldeth to my hope,
> Whereto thy speech serves for authority,
> The like of him.   [I. ii. 19-21]

The lines are in verse, the first has a formal old-fashioned -*eth* verb ending, and the object is delayed by a subordinate clause. Viola then switches to practical questions about her present situation: 'Know'st thou this country?'; 'Who governs here?' The crisper -*s* ending for the third-person verb belongs with the simple questions and short prose lines which contrast with the Captain's verse replies. Viola's interest in what has or may have happened to her brother is superseded by a need to sort out her own affairs, and her style changes correspondingly. . . . In act I scene 5, she is Orsino's messenger to Olivia. At first she fences with Olivia but she suddenly returns to duty:

> *Olivia.* Are you a comedian?
> *Viola.* No, my profound heart: and yet, by the
> very fangs of malice I swear, I am not that I
> play. Are you the lady of the house?

Her ambiguity about herself is accompanied by an obscure oath. With her question, the conversation becomes more straightforward only to dissolve in wordplay again. (p. 84)

Other characters move similarly into action. Olivia's style in act I, scene 5 also involves syntactical contrasts although her questions are misleadingly direct. She lingers over jokes such as the inventory of her beauty, but follows with a pertinent question: 'Were you sent hither to praise me?' [I. v. 249]. She continues with what seem to be the same sort of inquiries: 'How does he love me?'; 'Why, what would you?'; 'What is your parentage?' [I. v. 254, 268, 277]. She is pursuing what has become important to her, but she has moved from the interview's business—Orsino—to Cesario-Viola, and she stops herself with crisp commands and statements which are more to the purpose.

> Get you to your lord:
> I cannot love him: let him send no more,
> Unless, perchance, you come to me again,
> To tell me how he takes it. Fare you well:
> I thank you for your pains: spend this for me.
>
>   [I. v. 279-83]

The short clauses emphasize her business-like manner. (pp. 84-5)

[We] might note a recurring syntactic pattern which embodies the deceptions of *Twelfth Night*. Earlier I quoted 'I am not that I play' from Viola's first encounter with Olivia. This takes up her request to the Captain, 'Conceal me what I am' [I. ii. 53] and prefigures a cryptic exchange with Olivia in act 3, scene 1:

> *Olivia.*
>   I prithee tell me what thou think'st of me.
> *Viola.*
>   That you do think you are not what you are.
> *Olivia.*
>   If I think so, I think the same of you
> *Viola.*
>   Then think you right; I am not what I am.
>
>   [III. i. 138-43]

The setting of negative against positive in conjunction with the verb 'to be' is repeated at the end of the play when Orsino finds Sebastian and Viola forming 'A natural perspective, that is, and is not!' [V. i. 217]. And it is mocked in Feste's joking: '"That that is, is": so I, being Master Parson, am Master Parson; for what is "that" but "that"? and "is" but "is"?' [IV. ii. 14-16]. In fact here, that that is, is not. Feste is more accurate, but without knowing it, when he tells Sebastian, whom he mistakes for Cesario, 'Nothing that is so, is so' [IV. i. 8-9]. The repeated formula captures the confusion of actuality and fiction which these characters experience. Again the syntax tells us a truth while agreeing that words and events themselves can lie.

We cannot be certain about reality and falsehood when the genuine emotion of 'My father had a daughter loved a man' can move us so. Shakespeare's achievement with language in *Twelfth Night* is to encapsulate the conflict of truth and illusion, and to remind us that facts and truth are not necessarily the same, that the truest poetry often *is* the most feigning. (p. 86)

Elizabeth M. Yearling, "Language, Theme, and Character in 'Twelfth Night'," in Shakespeare Survey: An Annual Survey of Shakespearian Study and Production, Vol. 35, edited by Stanley Wells, Cambridge University Press, 1982, pp. 79-86.

ADDITIONAL BIBLIOGRAPHY

Baker, Herschel. "Introduction." In *William Shakespeare: 'Twelfth Night; or, What You Will'*, edited by Herschel Baker, pp. xxiii-xxxi. New York: The New American Library, Inc., 1965.
> Proposes that *Twelfth Night* offers both the verisimilitude and universality necessary to make it relevant to contemporary audiences.

Bevington, David. Introduction to *Twelfth Night; or, What You Will*. In *The Complete Works of Shakespeare*, by William Shakespeare, edited by Hardin Craig and David Bevington, pp. 615-18. Rev. ed. Glenview, Ill.: Scott, Foresman and Company, 1973.
> Summarizes available criticism on the date, sources, and plot of *Twelfth Night*. Bevington accentuates the themes in the play of enjoying life while "one is still young" and the brevity of the "release from responsibility." He also maintains that Malvolio deserves his "come-uppance."

Bradbrook, M. C. "Comical-Fantastical: 'Love's Labour's Lost', 'As You Like It', 'Twelfth Night'." In her *Shakespeare and Elizabethan Poetry: A Study of His Earlier Work in Relation to the Poetry of the Time*, pp. 212-33. 1951. Reprint. Cambridge: Cambridge University Press, 1979.
> Compares *Love's Labour's Lost, As You Like It*, and *Twelfth Night*, finding that "the combination of delicacy and penetration in *Twelfth Night*" offers a more rarefied atmosphere than the other comedies. Bradbrook terms the play Shakespeare's farewell to comedy.

Brown, John Russell. *"Twelfth Night."* In his *Shakespeare's Dramatic Style*, pp. 132-39. New York: Barnes & Noble, Inc., 1971.
> A close exploration of syntax and diction in three extracts from *Twelfth Night*. Brown directs his comments to both the student and the actor, and cites his experience as both teacher and director in handling a play which he feels "needs the lightest touch and quietest perception."

Bullough, Geoffrey. Introduction to *Twelfth Night*. In *Narrative and Dramatic Sources of Shakespeare, Vol. II*, edited by Geoffrey Bullough, pp. 269-85. London: Routledge and Kegan Paul, 1958.
> A discussion of Shakespeare's sources and his use of them in *Twelfth Night*. The introduction is followed by the texts of the sources.

Burton, Philip. "Malvolio." In his *The Sole Voice: Character Portraits from Shakespeare*, pp. 188-200. New York: The Dial Press, 1970.
> Describes Malvolio as a man of dignity, "soured and embittered by the impossibility of his ambition, an impossibility determined by his birth in a society where one's social limits were fixed by one's ancestry, where everything is decided by fortune, the luck of the cradle."

Cecil, David. "Shakespearean Comedy." In his *The Fine Art of Reading and Other Literary Studies*, pp. 37-106. Indianapolis and New York: The Bobbs-Merrill Company, Inc., 1957.
> Praises *Twelfth Night* for its dramatic structure and the perfection of its comic form. Cecil characterizes Malvolio as a figure of both fun and pathos for Shakespeare, and he proposes that Feste's final song reveals the fragility of Illyria.

Champion, Larry S. "The Comedies of Identity." In his *The Evolution of Shakespeare's Comedy*, pp. 60-95. Cambridge: Harvard University Press, 1970.
> Explores the theme of identity in *Twelfth Night* and the other comedies.

Coleridge, Samuel Taylor. "Notes on the Comedies of Shakespeare." In his *Shakespearean Criticism, Vol. I*, edited by Thomas Middleton Raysor, pp. 83-126. New York: E. P. Dutton, Inc., 1960.
> Faults the Shakespearean editor, William Warburton, for his humorless alteration of Feste's speech in V.i.

Collier, John Payne. "The Eighth Conversation." In his *The Poetical Decameron; or, Ten Conversations on English Poets and Poetry, Par-*

ticularly of the Reigns of Elizabeth and James I, Vol. II, pp. 133-96. Edinburgh: Archibald Constable and Co., 1820.

A discussion of Shakespeare's sources for *Twelfth Night* and his handling of the characters. The discussion also examines Samuel Johnson's objections to Viola's quickness to pursue the Duke and concludes that her actions would not have affected Elizabethan audiences as it does modern ones.

Conrad, Hermann. An extract from his article in *Preussische Jahrbuch* (July 1887), translated by Horace Howard Furness. In *A New Variorum Edition of Shakespeare: Twelfe Night, or, What You Will, Vol. XIII*, edited by Horace Howard Furness, pp. 387-88. New York: J. B. Lippincott Company, 1901.

Commends the organic combination of the "material" and "personal" plots in *Twelfth Night* and states that Olivia, like Bassanio in *The Merchant of Venice*, unites the two plots in the play.

Craig, Hardin. "The End of the Century." In his *An Interpretation of Shakespeare*, pp. 154-77. New York: The Citadel Press, 1948.

Extols the structure and workmanship of *Twelfth Night* and observes that Malvolio's "exaggerated superior bearing offers opportunity for caricature."

Downer, Alan S. "Feste's Night." *College English* 13, No. 5 (February 1952): 258-65.

Finds that Feste provides the unity of *Twelfth Night* as the figure who exposes the follies of the other characters.

Draper, John W. "Olivia's Household." *PMLA* XLIV, No. 3 (September 1934): 797-806.

An interpretation of Malvolio which is developed and expanded to include the entire world of *Twelfth Night*.

Eagleton, Terrence. "Language and Reality in *Twelfth Night*." *Critical Quarterly* 9, No. 3 (Autumn 1967): 217-28.

Discusses the destructive power of language in *Twelfth Night*.

Farjeon, Herbert. "*Twelfth Night*: Random Notes." In his *The Shakespearean Scene: Dramatic Criticisms*, pp. 68-76. London: Hutchinson & Co (Publishers) Ltd, 1949.

Contains a brief discussion of the songs in *Twelfth Night*.

Fleming, William H. "*Twelfth Night*." In his *Shakespeare's Plots: A Study in Dramatic Construction*, pp. 319-82. New York: G. P. Putnam's Sons, 1901.

Praises the lyrical element of *Twelfth Night* as the "perfect technique" for expressing the theme of love. Fleming also discusses humor, farce, and satire in the play.

Forbes, Lydia. "What You Will." *Shakespeare Quarterly* XIII, No. 4 (Autumn 1962): 475-85.

Identifies the themes of deception and self-knowledge in *Twelfth Night*.

Giles, Henry. An extract from his *Human Life in Shakespeare*. 1868. In *A New Variorum Edition of Shakespeare: 'Twelfe Night; or, What You Will', Vol. XIII*, edited by Horace Howard Furness, pp. 398-99. New York: J. B. Lippincott Company, 1901.

Examines Malvolio as "an excellent specimen of the sentimental fool," at whom we "*must* laugh" even though we pity him.

Griffith, Elizabeth. "*Twelfth Night; or, What You Will*." In her *The Morality of Shakespeare's Drama Illustrated: Eighteenth Century Shakespeare*, edited by Arthur Freeman, pp. 119-23. 1775. Reprint. London: Frank Cass & Co. Ltd., 1971.

Commends Shakespeare's description of love in *Twelfth Night*.

Hall, Peter. Introduction to *Twelfth Night* by William Shakespeare, pp. 3-9. London: The Folio Society, 1966.

Identifies Feste as the central figure of the play. Hall describes Feste as bitter, insecure, and cynical.

Hart, John A. "Foolery Shines Everywhere: The Fool's Function in the Romantic Comedies." In *'Starre of Poets': Discussions of Shakespeare*, pp. 31-48. Carnegie Series in English, No. 10. Pittsburgh: Carnegie Institute of Technology, 1966.

Claims that Shakespeare's clowns become of focal importance in the romantic comedies, a trend which culminates in Feste's final

song, which, according to Hart, sounds the "death knell of comedy."

Hotson, Leslie. *The First Night of "Twelfth Night."* London: Rupert Hart-Davis, 1954, 256 p.

Proposes that *Twelfth Night* was commissioned by Queen Elizabeth for a Twelfth Night performance given in 1600-01, in honor of Virginio Orsino, Duke of Bracciano. Hotson's theories have been disputed, but his book is regarded as a full and entertaining account of Elizabeth and her court.

Hunt, Hugh. "*Twelfth Night*." In his *Old Vic Prefaces: Shakespeare and the Producer*, pp. 53-81. London: Routledge & Kegan Paul Ltd., 1954.

From a collection of prefaces used by Hunt to familiarize actors with Shakespeare's plays and with Hunt's approach as a producer. In his production of *Twelfth Night*, Hunt emphasized the "poetic and fantastic" aspects of the play.

Kermode, Frank. "The Mature Comedies." In *Early Shakespeare*, edited by John Russell Brown and Bernard Harris, pp. 211-27. Stratford-upon-Avon Studies, No. 3. London: Edward Arnold, 1961.

Discusses *Twelfth Night* as a comedy dealing with the problem of identity which is "set in the borders of wonder and madness."

King, Walter N. "Shakespeare and Parmenides: The Metaphysics of *Twelfth Night*." *Studies in English Literature* VIII, No. 2 (Spring 1968): 283-306.*

Suggests that Shakespeare's treatment of the theme of appearance and reality is more sophisticated than critics generally allow.

Langbaine, Gerard. "William Shakespeare." In his *An Account of the English Dramatick Poets; or, Some Observations and Remarks*, pp. 453-69. 1691. Reprint. New York: Burt Franklin, 1969.

Esteems Shakespeare's plays more than "any that have ever been published in our language" and briefly comments on each one. Langbaine states that he does not know Shakespeare's source for *Twelfth Night*, but that he recognizes plot similarities with the plays of Plautus.

Legouis, Emile. *The Bacchic Element in Shakespeare's Plays*. London: Oxford University Press, 1926, 20 p.

Describes Sir Toby as a "thoroughly real" successor to Falstaff and "a very convincing tippler" whose "fearless love of fun" and "innate jollity" make him wholly sympathetic.

Levin, Richard A. "Viola: Dr. Johnson's 'Excellent Schemer'." *The Durham University Journal* LXXI, No. 2 (June 1979): 213-22.

A close examination of Samuel Johnson's interpretation of Viola. Levin discovers "an important element of calculation in her personality."

Markels, Julian. "Shakespeare's Confluence of Tragedy and Comedy." In *Shakespeare 400: Essays by American Scholars on the Anniversary of the Poet's Birth*, edited by James G. McManaway, pp. 75-88. New York: Holt, Rinehart, and Winston, 1964.

Compares *Twelfth Night* and *King Lear* on many points with the object of showing how Shakespeare drew from similar sources and character types, specifically Lear and Malvolio, to create his finest comedy and tragedy.

Manheim, Leonard F. "The Mythical Joys of Shakespeare; or, What You Will." In *Shakespeare Encomium*, edited by Anne Paolucci, pp. 100-12. The City College Papers, Vol. I. New York: The City College, 1964.

A psychoanalytical study of *Twelfth Night*. Manheim sees in the play the wish-fulfilling fantasies of Shakespeare.

Mueschke, Paul, and Fleisher, Jeannette. "Jonsonian Elements in the Comic Underplot of *Twelfth Night*." *PMLA* XLVIII, No. 3 (September 1933): 722-40.

Compares and contrasts *Twelfth Night* with Ben Jonson's early comedies *Every Man in His Humour* and *Every Man out of His Humour*. Because Shakespeare probably acted in the former Jonson play, Jonsonian influences are, according to Mueschke and Fleisher, abundant in *Twelfth Night*.

Noble, Richmond. *"Twelfth Night."* In his *Shakespeare's Use of Song: With the Text of the Principle Songs,* pp. 78-87. 1923. Reprint. London: Oxford University Press, 1966.

　　Discusses the songs of *Twelfth Night* and concludes that Feste's final song "serves as a commentary on the events of the play."

Parrott, Thomas Marc. "The Master Craftsman." In his *Shakespearean Comedy,* pp. 134-90. New York: Oxford University Press, 1949.

　　Discusses the play's sources, the integration of plot and subplot, the percentage of prose to verse, and Charles Lamb's interpretation of Malvolio.

Phialas, Peter G. *"Twelfth Night."* In his *Shakespeare's Romantic Comedies: The Development of Their Form and Meaning,* pp. 256-80. Durham, N.C.: The University of North Carolina Press, 1966.

　　Discerns in *Twelfth Night* an ideal of love which emerges through the juxtaposition of Viola's selfless love and the self-indulgent love of Orsino and Olivia.

Preston, Dennis R. "The Minor Characters of *Twelfth Night*." *Shakespeare Quarterly* XXI, No. 2 (Spring 1970): 167-76.

　　Finds that the minor characters have a greater importance in *Twelfth Night* than in the other comedies and discusses how they enhance the play.

Prouty, Charles Tyler. *"Twelfth Night."* In *Stratford Papers: 1965-67,* edited by B.A.W. Jackson, pp. 110-28. Hamilton, Ontario: McMaster University Library Press, 1969.

　　Theorizes that the happy comedies are based on complex Elizabethan social customs and are therefore difficult for modern readers to understand.

Pyle, Fitzroy. *"Twelfth Night, King Lear* and *Arcadia."* *The Modern Language Review* XLIII, No. 4 (October 1948): 449-55.*

　　Claims that Sir Philip Sidney's *Arcadia* was one of Shakespeare's sources for *Twelfth Night,* and notes that it particularly influenced the subplot.

Schwartz, Elias. *"Twelfth Night* and the Meaning of Shakespearean Comedy." *College English-*28, No. 7 (April 1967): 508-19.

　　Interprets Shakespeare's comedies as non-Aristotelian in concept and tone. Whereas Aristotle proposed a formula in which characters imitate people who are worse than we are, Shakespeare created characters who are equal to, or better than we are. Their actions elicit our indulgence rather than satiric laughter.

Scott, W.I.D. "Orsino—The Immature." In his *Shakespeare's Melancholics,* pp. 50-60. London: Mills & Boon Limited, 1962.

　　A psychological approach to Orsino. Scott speculates that Shakespeare found it painful to probe Orsino's true personality, because there was a good deal of Shakespeare himself in the Duke.

Sen Gupta, S. C. "Middle Comedies." In his *Shakespearian Comedy,* pp. 129-73. London: Oxford University Press, 1950.

　　Considers William Hazlitt's classification of three types of comedy in *Twelfth Night:* the comedy of artificial life, the comedy of refined sentiment, and the comedy of nature.

Shanker, Sidney. "Ambition, the Murderous Appetite." In his *Shakespeare and the Uses of Ideology,* pp. 25-43. The Hague: Mouton & Co. N.V., Publishers, 1975.

　　Proposes that Malvolio's ambition parallels the political and social events of Shakespeare's time.

Sisson, C. J. "Tudor Intelligence Tests: Malvolio and Real Life." In *Essays on Shakespeare and Elizabethan Drama: In Honor of Hardin Craig,* edited by Richard Hosley, pp. 183-200. Columbia, Mo.: University of Missouri Press, 1962.

　　Parallels Malvolio's "insanity trial" in IV. ii of *Twelfth Night* with the idiocy trial of Henry Windsor in England in 1550. Sisson concludes that Malvolio's trial has no basis in the public process of English law at the time of the play's composition.

Stauffer, Donald A. "The Garden of Eden." In his *Shakespeare's World of Images: The Development of His Moral Ideas,* pp. 67-109. New York: W. W. Norton & Company, 1949.

　　Examines the way in which Shakespeare presents the themes of liberty, liberality of spirit, and the idealization of love. Stauffer describes Viola as "the quintessence of love."

Strong, L.A.G. "Shakespeare and the Psychologists." In *Talking of Shakespeare,* edited by John Garrett, pp. 187-208. Toronto: Max Reinhardt, 1954.

　　Identifies Orsino, Olivia, and Malvolio as victims of fantasy.

Symons, Arthur. *"Twelfth Night."* In his *Studies in the Elizabethan Drama,* pp. 35-43. 1889. Reprint. London: William Heinemann, 1920.

　　Describes *Twelfth Night* as Shakespeare's "farewell to mirth."

Weiss, John. An extract from his *Wit, Humor, and Shakespeare: Twelve Essays* (1876). In *A New Variorum Edition of Shakespeare: Twelfe Night; or, What You Will, Vol. XIII,* edited by Horace Howard Furness, pp. 405-06. New York: J. B. Lippincott, 1901.

　　Declares that Feste is "the only cool and consistent character in *Twelfth Night.*"

Willbern, David. "Malvolio's Fall." *Shakespeare Quarterly* XXIX, No. 1 (Winter 1978): 85-90.

　　Discerns erotic overtones in the language of *Twelfth Night.* Willbern focuses particular attention on Malvolio's diction and discovers evidence of the steward's repressed sexual desires.

Wilson, John Dover. *"Twelfth Night."* In his *Shakespeare's Happy Comedies,* pp. 163-83. London: Faber and Faber Limited, 1962.

　　Describes *Twelfth Night* as the most exquisite of Shakespeare's comedies and concludes that the play is Shakespeare's farewell to comedy.

Winter, W. An extract from his *Shadows of the Stage* (1895). In *A New Variorum Edition of Shakespeare: Twelfe Night; or, What You Will, Vol. XIII,* edited by Horace Howard Furness, pp. 394-95, 401. New York: J. B. Lippincott Company, 1901.

　　Notes that Viola is Shakespeare's "ideal of the patient idolatry and devoted, silent self-sacrifice of perfect love." Winter also states that we miss the meaning of Malvolio's character if we only laugh at him, instead of contemplating the human frailties Shakespeare reveals in his character.

Woolf, Virginia. *"Twelfth Night* at the Old Vic." In her *The Death of the Moth and Other Essays,* pp. 34-7. 1933. Reprint. London: The Hogarth Press, 1942.

　　Proposes that Shakespeare wrote *Twelfth Night* in such a way that "from the echo of one word is born another word, for which reason, perhaps, the play seems as we read it to tremble perpetually on the brink of music."

Appendix

The following is a listing of all sources used in Volume 1 of *Shakespearean Criticism*. Included in this list are all copyright and reprint rights and acknowledgments for those essays for which permission was obtained. Every effort has been made to trace copyright, but if omissions have been made, please let us know.

THE EXCERPTS IN SC, VOLUME 1, WERE REPRINTED FROM THE FOLLOWING PERIODICALS:

American Imago, v. 36, Spring, 1979. Copyright 1979 by The Association for Applied Psychoanalysis, Inc. Reprinted by permission of the Wayne State University Press.

Blackwood's Edinburgh Magazine, v. II, February, 1818.

Bulletin of the John Rylands Library, v. 15, January, 1931; v. 19, January, 1935; v. 21, October, 1937; v. 26, April-May, 1942. © The John Rylands Library, 1931, 1935, 1937, 1942. All reprinted by permission.

College English, v. 24, April, 1963. Copyright © 1963 by the National Council of Teachers of English. Reprinted by permission of the publisher.

Critical Quarterly, v. 9, Autumn, 1967. Reprinted by permission of Manchester University Press.

Critical Review, v. I, April, 1756.

Criticism, v. XV, Summer, 1973. Copyright 1973, Wayne State University Press. Reprinted by permission of the Wayne State University Press.

Current Literature, v. XLII, March, 1907.

ELH, v. 40, Winter, 1973. Reprinted by permission.

English Journal, v. XV, April, 1926 for "The Problem of 'II Henry IV'" by Harry T. Baker. Copyright © 1926 by the National Council of Teachers of English. Reprinted by permission of the publisher.

English Studies, v. XLV, 1964.

Etudes Anglaises, v. XVII, January-March, 1964 for "La mort de 'Timon d'Athens'" by Bernard Paulin. © Didier-Erudition, Paris, 1964. Translated for this publication and copyright © 1983 by Gale Research Company.

Essays in Criticism, v. IX, April, 1959.

Fortnightly Review, v. 77, May, 1902. Reprinted by permission of Contemporary Review Company Limited.

General Evening Post, January 1-2, 1772; February 6-8, 1772; February 8-11, 1772.

International Literature, March, 1935; February, 1936.

Jahrbuch der Deutschen Shakespeare Gesellschaft, 1888, for "Shakespeares 'Timon von Athen'," by Wilhelm Wendlandt. Translated for this publication and copyright © 1983 by Gale Research Company.

The Johns Hopkins Alumni Magazine, v. XXIII, November, 1934.

London Chronicle; or, Universal Evening Post, January 25, 1757.

Lounger, May 20 and 27, 1786.

Macmillan's Magazine, v. L, August, 1884.

Mirror, April 17 and 22, 1780.

Modern Language Quarterly, v. 40, March, 1979; v. 41, September, 1980. © 1979, 1980 University of Washington. Both reprinted by permission.

Modern Language Review, v. XII, October, 1917; v. XIII, April, 1918; v. XXIX, January, 1934; v. XXV, October, 1940./ v. 68, January, 1973. © Modern Humanities Research Association 1973. Reprinted by permission.

Modern Philology, v. XII, October, 1914. © 1914 by The University of Chicago. Reprinted by permission of The University of Chicago Press.

The Observer: Being a Collection of Moral, Literary and Familiar Essays, v. III, 1786.

Philological Quarterly, v. XXXIII, April, 1954. Copyright 1954 by The University of Iowa. Reprinted by permission.

PMLA, v. XLI, September, 1926; v. LXVII, March, 1952./ v. XXIX, December, 1914; v. LXX, September, 1955; v. 90, January, 1975; v. 90, October, 1975. Copyright © 1914, 1955, 1975 by the Modern Language Association of America. All reprinted by permission of the Modern Language Association of America.

The Prompter, October 24, 1735.

The Reflector, April-September, 1811.

A Review of English Literature, v. 5, October, 1964. © Longmans, Green & Co. Ltd. 1964. Reprinted by permission.

The Review of English Studies, v. 18, July, 1942; v. 22, October, 1946; n.s. v. V, July, 1954. All reprinted by permission of Oxford University Press, Oxford.

The Rice Institute Pamphlet, v. XLV, January, 1959. Reprinted by permission of Rice University.

St. James's Chronicle, January 23-25, 1772; February 18-20, 1772.

Scrutiny, v. XV, Winter, 1947; v. XV, Spring, 1948; v. XV, Summer, 1948. All reprinted by permission of Cambridge University Press.

The Sewanee Review, v. LII, Summer, 1944. Published 1944 by The University of the South; v. LXI, Winter and Spring, 1953. © 1953, copyright renewed © 1981, by The University of the South; v. LXII, Winter, 1954. © 1954, copyright renewed © 1982, by The University of the South; v. LXVII, Spring, 1959. © 1959 by The University of the South. All reprinted by permission of the editor.

The Shakespeare Association Bulletin, v. VII, January, 1932./ v. XVI, January, 1941; v. 24, October, 1949. Copyright, 1941, 1949, by The Shakespeare Association of America, Inc. Both reprinted by permission.

Shakespeare Quarterly, v. III, October, 1952./ v. IV, October, 1953; v. VI, Winter, 1955; v. VI, Summer, 1955; v. VII, Spring, 1956; v. IX, Spring, 1958; v. X, Winter, 1959; v. X, Autumn, 1959; v. XII, Winter, 1961; v. XXI, Winter, 1970; v. XXII, Winter, 1971. © The Folger Shakespeare Library 1953, 1955, 1956, 1958, 1959, 1961, 1970, 1971. All reprinted by permission.

Shakespeare Studies, v. I, 1965. © Shakespeare Studies 1965; v. II, 1966. © The Center for Shakespeare Studies, 1967; v. V, 1970. © The Center for Shakespeare Studies, 1970. All reprinted by permission.

THE EXCERPTS IN SC, VOLUME 1, WERE REPRINTED FROM THE FOLLOWING BOOKS:

Abel, Lionel. From *Metatheatre: A New View of Dramatic Form*. Hill and Wang, 1963. Copyright © 1960, 1962, 1963 by Lionel Abel. Reprinted by permission of Hill and Wang, a division of Farrar, Straus and Giroux, Inc.

Addison, Joseph. From "Ride si sapis," in *The Spectator*, Vol. I. Edited by Donald F. Bond. Oxford at the Clarendon Press, Oxford, 1965.

Anthony, Earl of Shaftesbury. From *Characteristics of Men, Manners, Opinions, Times, Vol. I*. Fifth edition. John Darby, 1732.

Auden, W. H. From "Music in Shakespeare," in *The Dyer's Hand and Other Essays*. Random House, 1962. Copyright © 1957 by W. H. Auden. Reprinted by permission of Random House, Inc.

Auden, W. H. From "The Prince's Dog," in *The Dyer's Hand and Other Essays*. Random House, 1962. Copyright © 1958 by W. H. Auden. Reprinted by permission of Random House, Inc.

Baldwin, Thomas Whitfield. From his introduction to *The Comedy of Errors*. By William Shakespeare, edited by Thomas Whitfield Baldwin. D. C. Heath, 1928.

Barber, C. L. From "From Ritual to Comedy: An Examination of 'Henry IV'," in *English Stage Comedy: English Institute Essays, 1954*. Edited by W. K. Wimsatt, Jr. Columbia University Press, 1955. Copyright 1955 by Columbia University Press. Reprinted by permission of the publisher and the author.

Barber, C. L. From *Shakespeare's Festive Comedy: A Study of Dramatic Form and Its Relation to Social Custom*. Princeton University Press, 1959. Copyright © 1959 by Princeton University Press. Reprinted by permission of Princeton University Press.

Barton, Anne. From "'As You Like It' and 'Twelfth Night': Shakespeare's Sense of Editing," in *Shakespearian Comedy*, Stratford-Upon-Avon Studies, No. 14. Edited by John Russell Brown and Bernard Harris. Arnold, 1972. © Edward Arnold (Publishers) Ltd, 1972. Reprinted by permission.

Barton, Anne. From her introduction to "The Comedy of Errors," in *The Riverside Shakespeare*. By William Shakespeare, edited by G. Blakemore Evans. Houghton Mifflin, 1974. Copyright © 1974 by Houghton Mifflin Company. Reprinted by permission of Houghton Mifflin Company.

Boas, Frederick S. From *Shakespere and His Predecessors*. Charles Scribner's Sons, 1896. Reprinted with permission of Charles Scribner's Sons.

Bonazza, Blaze Odell. From *Shakespeare's Early Comedies: A Structural Analysis*. Mouton, 1966. © copyright 1966 Mouton & Co., Publishers. Reprinted by permission of Mouton Publishers, a division of Walter de Gruyter & Co.

Bradbrook, M. C. From *Shakespeare, the Craftsman: The Clark Lectures, 1968*. Chatto & Windus, 1969. © M. C. Bradbrook 1969. Reprinted by permission of the author and Chatto & Windus.

Bradbrook, Muriel C. From "King Henry IV'," in *Stratford Papers: 1965-67*. Edited by B. A. W. Jackson. McMaster University Library Press, 1969. Reprinted by permission.

Bradley, A. C. From *Shakespearian Tragedy: Lectures on "Hamlet", "Othello", "King Lear", "Macbeth"*. Second edition. Macmillan, 1905. Reprinted by permission of Macmillan, London and Basingstoke.

Bradley, A. C. From "Feste the Jester," in *A Book of Homage to Shakespeare*. Edited by Israel Gollancz. Oxford University Press, Oxford, 1916. Reprinted by permission of Oxford University Press.

Brandes, George. From *William Shakespeare: A Critical Study, Vols. I & II*. Translated by William Archer, Mary Morison, and Diana White. Heinemann, 1898. Copyright 1898 by William Heinemann. Reprinted by permission.

Brooke, C. F. Tucker. From *The Tudor Drama: A History of English National Drama to the Retirement of Shakespeare*. Houghton Mifflin, 1911. Copyright, 1911, copyright renewed © 1939, by C. F. Tucker Brooke. Reprinted by permission of Houghton Mifflin Company.

Brooks, Cleanth, and Heilman, Robert B. From *Understanding Drama: Twelve Plays*. Holt, 1945. Copyright © 1945, 1948. Copyright renewed © 1972, by Henry Holt and Company, Inc. Reprinted by permission of the authors.

Brooks, Harold. From "Themes and Structure in 'The Comedy of Errors'," in *Early Shakespeare*, Stratford-Upon-Avon Studies, No. 3. John Russell Brown and Bernard Harris, General Editors. Arnold, 1961. © Edward Arnold (Publishers) Ltd 1961.

Brower, Reuben A. From *Hero & Saint: Shakespeare and the Graeco-Roman Heroic Tradition*. Oxford University Press, New York, 1971. Copyright © 1971 by Oxford University Press. Reprinted by permission.

Brown, John Russell. From *Shakespeare and His Comedies*. Methuen, 1957. Reprinted by permission of Methuen & Co Ltd.

Brown, John Russell. From "Love's Wealth and the Judgement of 'The Merchant of Venice'," in *Shakespeare and His Comedies*. Second edition. Methuen, 1962. Reprinted by permission of Methuen & Co Ltd.

Burckhardt, Sigurd. From *Shakespearean Meanings*. Princeton University Press, 1968. Copyright © 1968 by Princeton University Press. Excerpts reprinted by permission of Princeton University Press.

Campbell, Oscar James. From *Shakespeare's Satire*. Oxford University Press, New York, 1943. Copyright 1943 by Oxford University Press, Inc. Renewed 1971 by Mrs. Robert L. Goodale, Mrs. George W. Meyer, and Robert F. Campbell. Reprinted by permission of Oxford University Press, Inc.

Chambers, E. K. From *Shakespeare: A Survey*. Sidgwick & Jackson, 1925. Reprinted by permission of Oxford University Press, Inc.

Champion, Larry S. From *The Evolution of Shakespeare's Comedy: A Study in Dramatic Perspective*. Cambridge, Mass.: Harvard University Press, 1970. Copyright © 1970 by the President and Fellows of Harvard College. Excerpted by permission.

Clarke, Charles Cowden. From *Shakespeare-Characters. Chiefly Those Subordinate*. Smith Elder & Co., 1863.

Clemen, Wolfgang H. From *The Development of Shakespeare's Imagery*. Methuen, 1951. Reprinted by permission of Methuen & Co Ltd.

Coleridge, Samuel Taylor. From *The Literary Remains of Samuel Taylor Coleridge, Vol. 2*. Edited by Henry Nelson Coleridge. W. Pickering, 1837.

Coleridge, Samuel Taylor. From *Seven Lectures on Shakespeare and Milton*. Chapman & Hall, 1856.

Coleridge, Samuel Taylor. From *Shakespearean Criticism, Vols. I & II*. Edited by Thomas Middleton Raysor. Cambridge, Mass.: Harvard University Press, 1930. Excerpted by permission of the President and Fellows of Harvard College.

Collier, Jeremy. From *A Short View of the Immorality and Profaneness of the English Stage*. S. Keble, 1698.

Craig, Hardin. From *An Interpretation of Shakespeare*. The Citadel Press, 1948.

Cruttwell, Patrick. From "The Morality of Hamlet—'Sweet Prince' or 'Arrant Knave'?" in *Hamlet,* Stratford-Upon-Avon Studies, No. 5. John Russell Brown and Bernard Harris, General Editors. Arnold, 1963. © Edward Arnold (Publishers) Ltd., 1963. Reprinted by permission.

Danby, John F. From *Shakespeare's Doctrine of Nature: A Study of "King Lear."* Faber and Faber, 1949. Reprinted by permission of Faber and Faber Ltd.

A Defence of Dramatick Poetry and *A Farther Defence of Dramatick Poetry*. Eliz. Whitlock, 1698.

Digges, Leonard. From "Upon Master William Shakespeare, the Deceased Authour, and His Poems," in *Poems*. By William Shakespeare. Thomas Cotes, 1640.

Dowden, Edward. From *Shakespeare: A Critical Study of His Mind and Art*. Third edition. Harper & Brothers Publishers, 1881.

Dowden, Edward. From "Shakespeare As a Comic Dramatist," in *Representative English Comedies: From the Beginnings to Shakespeare, Vol. I*. Edited by Charles Mills Gayley. Macmillan Publishing Company, 1903.

Drake, James. From *The Antient and Modern Stages Survey'd; or, Mr. Collier's View of Immorality and Profaneness of the English Stage Set in a True Light*. 1699.

Draper, John W. From *The "Twelfth Night" of Shakespeare's Audience*. Stanford University Press, 1950.

Dryden, John. From *Of Dramatick Poesie: An Essay*. Henry Herringman, 1668.

Dryden, John. From *Troilus and Cressida; or, Truth Found Too Late*. 1679.

Edwards, Philip. From *Shakespeare and the Confines of Art*. Methuen, 1968. © 1968 Philip Edwards. Reprinted by permission of Methuen & Co Ltd.

Eliot, T. S. From *Selected Essays*. Harcourt Brace Jovanovich, 1950. Copyright 1950 by Harcourt Brace Jovanovich, Inc.; 1978 by Esme Valerie Eliot. Reprinted by permission of the publisher and Faber and Faber Ltd.

Ellis-Fermor, Una. From *The Frontiers of Drama*. Methuen, 1945. Reprinted by permission of Methuen & Co Ltd.

Empson, William. From *Some Versions of Pastoral: A Study of the Pastoral Form in Literature*. Chatto & Windus, 1935. Copyright © William Empson, 1935. Reprinted by permission of the author and Chatto & Windus.

Evans, Bertrand. From *Shakespeare's Comedies*. Oxford at the Clarendon Press, Oxford, 1960. © Oxford University Press, 1960. Reprinted by permission of Oxford University Press.

Fergusson, Francis. From *The Idea of a Theatre: A Study of Ten Plays; The Art of Drama in Changing Perspective*. Princeton University Press, 1949. Copyright 1949 © renewed 1977 by Princeton University Press. Reprinted by permission of Princeton University Press.

Fleay, F. G. From "On the Authorship of 'Timon of Athens'," in *Transactions of the New Shakespeare Society*. First Series. N. Trubner & Co., 1874.

Freud, Sigmund. From *The Interpretation of Dreams*. Edited and translated by James Strachey. Basic Books, 1955. © 1956 by Basic Books, Inc., Publishers. Reprinted by permission of the publishers. In Canada by George Allen & Unwin (Publishers) Ltd.

Frye, Northrup. From "The Argument of Comedy," in *English Institute Essays*. Edited by Rudolf Kirk & others. Columbia University Press, 1949. Copyright 1949, copyright renewed © 1977, by Columbia University Press. Reprinted by permission of the publisher.

Frye, Northrup. From *A Natural Perspective: The Development of Shakespearean Comedy and Romance*. Columbia University Press, 1965. Copyright © 1965 Columbia University Press. Reprinted by permission of the publisher.

Fuller, Thomas. From *The History of the Worthies of England*. Edited by Thomas Fuller. J.G.W.L. & W. G., 1662.

Furnivall, F. J. From his introduction to *The Leopold Shakespeare*. By William Shakespeare. Cassell, Petter & Galpin, 1877.

Gardner, Helen. From *The Business of Criticism*. Oxford at the Clarendon Press, Oxford, 1959. © Oxford University Press, 1959. Reprinted by permission of Oxford University Press.

Gentleman, Francis. From his notes to "1 Henry IV" and "2 Henry IV," in *Bell's Edition of Shakespeare's Plays: Shakespeare's Poems, Vol. IX*. By William Shakespeare. J. Bell, 1774.

Gervinus, G. G. From *Shakespeare Commentaries*. Translated by F. E. Bunnett. Revised edition. Smith, Elder, & Co., 1877.

Gildon, Charles. From his "Remarks on the Plays of Shakespeare," in *The Works of Mr. William Shakespeare, Vol. 7*. By William Shakespeare. E. Curll and E. Sanger, 1710.

Gildon, Charles. From *The Laws of Poetry Explain'd and Illustrated*. 1721.

Goddard, Harold C. From *The Meaning of Shakespeare*. University of Chicago Press, 1951. Copyright 1951 by The University of Chicago. Copyright renewed © 1979 by Margaret G. Holt and Eleanor G. Worthen. Reprinted by permission of The University of Chicago Press.

Goethe, Johann Wolfgang von. From *Wilhelm Meister's Apprenticeship*. Translated by R. Dillon Boylan. Bell & Daldy, 1873.

Goethe, Johann Wolfgang von. From *Goethe's Literary Essays*. Edited by J. E. Springarn, translated by Randolph S. Bourne. Harcourt Brace Jovanovich, Inc. Copyright 1921 by Harcourt Brace Jovanovich, Inc. Reprinted by permission of the publisher.

Gould, Robert. From *The Works of Robert Gould*. W. Lewis, 1709.

Granville-Barker, Harley. From his preface to *Twelfth Night: An Acting Edition*. By William Shakespeare. William Heinemann, 1912. Reprinted by permission of the Society of Authors as the Literary Representatives of the Harley Granville-Barker Estate.

Granville-Barker, Harley. From *Prefaces to Shakespeare, Vol. I*. Princeton University Press, 1946. Copyright © 1946 by Princeton University Press, © renewed 1974 by Princeton University Press. Excerpts reprinted by permission of Princeton University Press.

Griffith, Elizabeth. From *The Morality of Shakespeare's Drama Illustrated*. T.Cadell, 1775.

Guthrie, William. From *An Essay Upon English Tragedy*. 1747.

Hallam, Henry. From *Introduction to the Literature of Europe in the 15th, 16th, and 17th Centuries*. A. and W. Galignani, 1837.

Halliday, F. E. From an anonymous critic in "Gray's Inn Records," in *Shakespeare and His Critics*. Gerald Duckworth & Co. Ltd., 1949.

Harris, Frank. From *The Man Shakespeare and His Tragic Life Story*. Frank Palmer, 1909. Reprinted by permission of the Literary Estate of Frank Harris.

Harris, Frank. From *The Women of Shakespeare*. Methuen & Co. Ltd., 1911.

Harrison, G. B. *From Shakespeare's Tragedies*. Routledge & Kegan Paul Ltd, 1951.

Hazlitt, William. From *Characters of Shakespear's Plays*. C. H. Reynell, 1817, Taylor and Hessey, 1817.

Hinman, Charlton. From his introduction to "The Life of Timon of Athens," in *William Shakespeare: The Complete Works*. By William Shakespeare, edited by Alfred Harbage. Revised Edition. Penguin Books Inc., 1969. Copyright © 1969 by Penguin Books Inc. Reprinted by permission of Viking Penguin Inc.

Hollander, John. From "Musica Mundana and 'Twelfth Night'," in *Sound and Poetry*. Edited by Northrup Frye. Columbia University Press, 1957. Copyright © 1957 Columbia University Press. Reprinted by permission of the publisher.

Holt, John. From his preface to *An Attempte to Rescue the Aunciente, English Poet, and Play-wrighte, Maister Williaume Shakespere, from the Maney Errours, Fausley Charged on Him*. Manby and Cox, 1749.

Hudson, Rev. H. N. From *Shakespeare: His Life, Art, and Characters, Vols. I & II*. Revised edition. Ginn & Company, 1872.

Hugo, Victor. From *The Works of Victor Hugo: Shakespeare, Vol. X*. The Jefferson Press, 1864.

Humphreys, A. R. From his introduction to *The Second Part of King Henry IV*. By William Shakespeare, edited by A. R. Humphreys. Methuen, 1966. © 1966 Methuen & Co Ltd. Reprinted by permission of Methuen & Co Ltd.

Hunt, Leigh. From *Dramatic Criticism: 1808-1931*. Edited by Lawrence Huston Houtchens and Carolyn Washburn Houtchens. Columbia University Press, 1949. Copyright 1949 Columbia University Press, New York. Copyright renewed © 1977 by Lawrence H. Houtchens and Carolyn W. Houtchens. Reprinted by permission of the publisher.

Hunter, G. K. From *William Shakespeare, the Later Comedies: "A Midsummer-Night's Dream," "Much Ado About Nothing," "As You Like It."* Longmans, Green & Co., 1962. © G. K. Hunter, 1962. Reprinted by permission of Profile Books Limited.

Hunter, Joseph. From *New Illustrations of the Life, Studies and Writings of Shakespeare, Vol. I*. J. B. Nichols and Son, 1845.

Inchbald, Elizabeth. From "Remarks: 'King Henry IV, First Part'" and "Remarks: 'King Henry IV, Second Part'," in *The British Theatre; or, A Collection of Plays, Vol. II*. 1808.

James, D. G. From *The Dream of Learning*. Oxford at the Clarendon Press, Oxford, 1951. Reprinted by permission of Oxford University Press.

Jameson, Anna. From *Characteristics of Women: Moral, Poetical, and Historical, Vol. I*. Second edition. 1833.

Jenkins, Harold. From *The Structural Problem in Shakespeare's "Henry the Fourth"*. Methuen, 1956. Reprinted by permission of Methuen & Co Ltd.

Johnson, Samuel. From his notes on "Hamlet," "Henry IV," and "Twelfth Night," in *The Plays of William Shakespeare*. By William Shakespeare, edited by Samuel Johnson. J. & R. Tonson, 1765.

Johnson, Samuel. From *The Yale Edition of the Works of Samuel Johnson: Johnson on Shakespeare, Vol. VIII*. Edited by Arthur Sherbo. Yale University Press, 1968. © 1968 by Yale University. Reprinted by permission.

Jones, Ernest. From *Hamlet and Oedipus*. Norton, 1949, Victor Gollancz, Ltd, 1949. Copyright 1949 by Ernest Jones. Copyright renewed 1982 by Merwyn Jones. Reprinted by permission of W. W. Norton & Company, Inc. In Canada by Victor Gollancz Ltd.

Jorgensen, Paul A. From his introduction to "The Comedy of Errors," in *William Shakespeare: The Complete Works*. By William Shakespeare, Alfred Harbage, General Editor. Revised edition. Penguin Books, Inc., 1969. Copyright © 1969 by Penguin Books Inc. Reprinted by permission of Viking Penguin Inc.

Kelly, Henry Ansgar. From *Divine Providence in the England of Shakespeare's Histories*. Cambridge, Mass.; Harvard University Press, 1970. Copyright © 1970 by the President and Fellows of Harvard College. Excerpted by permission.

Kenny, Thomas. From *The Life and Genius of Shakespeare*. Longman, Green, Longman, Roberts, and Green, 1864.

Kierkegaard, Søren. From *Stages on Life's Way*. Translated by Walter Lowrie. Princeton University Press, 1940. Copyright 1940, © renewed 1968 by Howard Johnson. Excerpts reprinted by permission of Princeton University Press.

Kitto, H.D.F. From *Form and Meaning in Drama: A Study of Six Greek Plays and of "Hamlet."* Methuen, 1956. Reprinted by permission of Methuen & Co. Ltd.

Knight, Charles. From his "Supplementary Notice: 'Twelfth Night'," in *The Comedies, Histories, Tragedies, and Poems of William Shakespeare, Vol. III*. By William Shakespeare, edited by Charles Knight. Second edition. Charles Knight and Co., 1842.

Knight, Charles. From his introduction to "Timon of Athens," in *The Comedies, Histories, Tragedies, and Poems of William Shakespeare, Vol. X*. By William Shakespeare, edited by Charles Knight. Second edition. Charles Knight and Co., 1843.

Knight, G. Wilson. From *The Shakespearian Tempest*. Oxford University Press, London, 1932. Reprinted by permission of the author.

Knight, G. Wilson. From *Christ and Nietzsche: An Essay in Poetic Wisdom*. Staples Press, 1948. Reprinted by permission of Granada Publishing Limited.

Knight, G. Wilson. From *The Wheel of Fire: Interpretations of Shakespearian Tragedy*. Revised edition. Methuen, 1949. Reprinted by permission of Methuen & Co Ltd.

Knights, L. C. From "Notes on Comedy," in *Determinations: Critical Essays*. Edited by F. R. Leavis. Chatto & Windus, 1934.

Knights, L. C. From *Shakespearean Themes*. Stanford University Press, 1960. © 1959 by L. C. Knights. Reprinted with the permission of the publishers, Stanford University Press.

Knights, L. C. From *An Approach to "Hamlet."* Stanford University Press, 1961. © 1960 by L. C. Knights. Reprinted with the permission of the publishers, Stanford University Press.

Knights, L. C. From "'Timon of Athens'," in *The Morality of Art: Essays Presented to G. Wilson Knight by His Colleagues and Friends*. Edited by D. W. Jefferson. Routledge & Kegan Paul Ltd, 1969. Reprinted by permission of the author.

Kott, Jan. From *Shakespeare, Our Contemporary*. Translated by Boleslaw Taborski. Doubleday, 1964. Copyright © 1964, 1965, 1966 by Doubleday & Company, Inc. In Canada by Jan Kott. Reprinted by permission. Originally published as *Szkice o Szekspirze*. Państwowe Wydawnicto Naukowe, 1964. Copyright © 1964 Państwowe Wydawnictwo Naukowe. Reprinted by permission.

Kott, Jan. From "Shakespeare's Bitter Arcadia," in *Shakespeare, Our Contemporary*. Translated by Boleslaw Taborski. Anchor Books, 1966. Copyright © 1964, 1965, 1966 by Doubleday & Company, Inc. Reprinted by permission of Doubleday & Company, Inc. In Canada by Jan Kott.

Kreysig, F. From his extracts in *A New Variorum Edition of Shakespeare: "Twelfe Night; or, What You Will," Vol. XIII*. By William Shakespeare, edited by Horace Howard Furness. J. B. Lippincott, Company, 1901.

Lamb, Charles. From his "On the Tragedies of Shakespeare: Considered with Reference to Their Fitness for Stage Representation," in *The Works in Prose and Verse of Charles and Mary Lamb, Vol. I*. By Charles Lamb and Mary Lamb, edited by Thomas Hutchinson. Oxford University Press, Oxford, 1908.

Lamb, Charles. From *Charles Lamb on Shakespeare*. Edited by Joan Coldwell. Barnes & Noble, 1978.

Langbaum, Robert. From *The Poetry of Experience: The Dramatic Monologue in Modern Literary Tradition*. Random House, 1957. Copyright © 1957 by Robert Langbaum. Reprinted by permission of Random House, Inc.

Leech, Clifford. From *"Twelfth Night" and Shakespearean Comedy*. University of Toronto Press, 1965. © University of Toronto Press 1965. Reprinted by permission.

Leggatt, Alexander. From *Shakespeare's Comedy of Love*. Methuen, 1974. © 1973 Alexander Leggatt. Reprinted by permission of Methuen & Co Ltd.

Lennox, Charlotte. From her notes on "Twelfth Night," "Hamlet," and "Henry IV," in *Shakespear Illustrated; or, The Novels and Histories, on Which the Plays of Shakespear Are Founded, Vols. I, II, & III*. A. Millar, 1753.

Lessing, Gotthold Ephraim. From *Hamburgische Dramaturgie*. Verlag Philipp Reclam jun., 1972. Translated for this publication and copyright © 1983 Gale Research Company.

Levin, Harry. From *The Question of "Hamlet."* Oxford University Press, New York, 1959. Copyright © 1959 by Oxford University Press, Inc. Reprinted by permission of Oxford University Press, Inc.

Lewis, Charlton M. From *The Genesis of "Hamlet."* Henry Holt and Company, 1907.

Lewis, Wyndham. From *The Lion and the Fox: The Role of the Hero in the Plays of Shakespeare*. G. Richards, 1927. © 1927 Wyndham Lewis and the Estate of Mrs. G. A. Wyndham Lewis. Reprinted by permission of The Wyndham Lewis Memorial Trust, a registered charity.

Mack, Maynard, Jr. From *Killing the King: Three Studies in Shakespeare's Tragic Structure*. Yale University Press, 1973. Copyright © 1973 by Yale University. Reprinted by permission.

Madariaga, Salvador de. From *On Hamlet*. Hollis & Carter, 1948. Reprinted by permission of the Literary Estate of Salvador de Madariaga.

Manningham, John. From his diary entry in *The Shakspere Allusion-Book: A Collection of Allusions to Shakspere from 1591 to 1700, Vol. I*. Edited by John Munro. Revised edition. Oxford University Press, London, 1932. Reprinted by permission of Oxford University Press.

Marx, Karl. From *Economic and Philosophic Manuscripts of 1844*. Edited by Dirk J. Struik, translated by Martin Milligan. International, 1964. Translation © 1964 by International Publishers Co., Inc. Reprinted by permission.

Montagu, Elizabeth. From *An Essay on the Writings and Genius of Shakespeare*. J. Dodsley, 1769.

Montégut, E. From his extract in *A New Variorum Edition of Shakespeare: "Twelfe Night; or, What You Will," Vol. XIII*. Edited by Horace Howard Furness. J. B. Lippincott, 1901.

Morgann, Maurice. From *An Essay on the Dramatic Character of Sir John Falstaff*. T. Davies, 1777.

Morris, Corbyn. From *An Essay Towards Fixing the True Standards of Wit, Humour, Raillery, Satire, and Ridicule*. 1744.

Muir, Kenneth. From *The Singularity of Shakespeare and Other Essays*. Barnes & Noble, 1977. Copyright © 1977 by Kenneth Muir. By permission of Barnes & Noble Books, a Division of Littlefield, Adams & Co., Inc.

Murphy, Arthur. From *The Works of Arthur Murphy: "Gray's Inn Journal," Vol. V*. T. Cadell, 1786.

Murray, Gilbert. From "Hamlet and Orestes," in *The Classical Tradition in Poetry: The Charles Eliot Norton Lectures*. Cambridge, Mass.: Harvard University Press, 1927. Copyright 1927 by the President and Fellows of Harvard College. © renewed 1955 by Gilbert Murray. Excerpted by permission.

Murry, John Middleton. From *Shakespeare*. Jonathan Cape, 1936. Reprinted by permission of The Society of Authors as the Literary Representative of the Estate of John Middleton Murry.

Nietzsche, Friedrich. From *The Birth of Tragedy and The Case of Wagner*. Translated by Walter Kaufmann. Vintage Books, 1967. Copyright © 1967 by Random House, Inc. Reprinted by permission of the publisher.

Ornstein, Robert. From *The Moral Vision of Jacobean Tragedy*. University of Wisconsin Press, 1960. Copyright © 1960, by the Regents of the University of Wisconsin. Reprinted by permission.

Ornstein, Robert. From *A Kingdom for a Stage: The Achievement of Shakespeare's History Plays*. Cambridge, Mass.: Harvard University Press, 1972. Copyright © 1972 by the President and Fellows of Harvard College. Excerpted by permission.

Parrott, Thomas Marc. From *The Problem of "Timon of Athens."* Oxford University Press, London, 1923. Reprinted by permission of Oxford University Press.

Pettet, E. C. From *Shakespeare and the Romance Tradition*. Staples Press, 1949. Reprinted by permission of Granada Publishing Limited.

Phialas, Peter G. From *Shakespeare's Romantic Comedies: The Development of Their Form and Meaning*. University of North Carolina Press, 1966. Copyright © 1966 by The University of North Carolina Press. Reprinted by permission.

Porter, Joseph A. From *The Drama of Speech Acts: Shakespeare's Lancastrian Tetralogy*. University of California Press, 1979. Copyright © 1979 by The Regents of the University of California. Reprinted by permission of the University of California Press.

Potter, John. From "Timon of Athens" and "Twelfth Night," in *The Theatrical Review; or, New Companion to the Playhouse*. Edited by John Potter. S. Crowder, 1772.

Priestley, J. B. From *The English Comic Characters*. John Lane/The Bodley Head, 1925. Reprinted by permission of The Bodley Head.

Prosser, Eleanor. From *Hamlet & Revenge*. Second edition. Stanford University Press, 1971. Copyright, 1967, 1971 by the Board of Trustees of the Leland Stanford Junior University. Reprinted with the permission of the publishers, Stanford University Press.

Appendix

Steevens, George. From his end-note to ''The Comedy of Errors,'' in *The Plays of William Shakespeare, Vol. II.* By William Shakespeare, edited by George Steevens and Samuel Johnson. 1773.

Steevens, George. From his footnote to ''Twelfth Night; or, What You Will,'' in *The Poems of William Shakespeare, Vol. XI.* By William Shakespeare, edited by J. Boswell. F. C. & J. Rivington, 1821.

Stewart, John Innes Mackintosh. From *Character and Motive in Shakespeare: Some Recent Appraisals Examined.* Longmans, Green and Co., 1949. Reprinted by permission of Penguin Books Ltd.

Stoll, Elmer Edgar. From *Art and Artifice in Shakespeare: A Study in Dramatic Contrast and Illusion.* Cambridge at the University Press, 1933.

Strachey, Edward. From *Shakespeare's Hamlet: An Attempt to Find the Key to a Great Moral Problem, by Methodical Analysis of the Play.* J. W. Parker, 1848.

Stubbes, George/Hanmer, Thomas. From *Some Remarks on the Tragedy of Hamlet.* 1736.

Swinburne, Algernon Charles. From *A Study of Shakespeare.* R. Worthington, 1880.

Talbert, Ernest William. From *Elizabethan Drama and Shakespeare's Early Plays: An Essay in Historical Criticism.* University of North Carolina Press, 1963. Copyright © 1963 by The University of North Carolina Press. Reprinted by permission.

Theobald, Lewis. From his preface to *The Tragedy of King Richard II.* By William Shakespeare, edited by Lewis Theobald. G. Strahan, W. Mears, 1720.

Theobald, Lewis. From his essay in *The Works of Shakespeare, Vol. II.* By William Shakespeare, edited by Lewis Theobald. A. Bettesworth & C. Hitch, 1733.

Tillyard, E.M.W. From *Shakespeare's History Plays.* Chatto & Windus, 1944. © 1944 by Macmillan Publishing Company. Copyright renewed © 1971 by Stephen Tillyard, Mrs. V. Sankaran and Mrs. A. Ahlers. Reprinted by permission of the author's literary estate and Chatto & Windus.

Tillyard, E.M.W. From *Shakespeare's Problem Plays.* University of Toronto Press, 1949. Copyright, Canada, 1949, by University of Toronto Press. Reprinted by permission.

Tillyard, E.M.W. From *Shakespeare's Early Comedies.* Chatto & Windus, 1965. © Stephen Tillyard 1965. Reprinted by permission of Stephen Tillyard and Chatto & Windus.

Tolstoy, Leo. From *Tolstoy on Shakespeare: A Critical Essay on Shakespeare.* Translated by V. Tchertkoff and I.F.M. Funk & Wagnalls, 1906. Reprinted by permission of William Heinemann Limited.

Traversi, Derek. From *William Shakespeare: The Early Comedies.* British Council, 1960. © Profile Books Ltd., 1960.

Ulrici, Hermann. From *Shakespeare's Dramatic Art: And His Relation to Calderon and Goethe.* Translated by Rev. A.J.W. Morrison. Chapman, Brothers, 1846.

Unger, Leonard. From *The Man in the Name: Essays on the Experience of Poetry.* University of Minnesota Press, Minneapolis, 1956. © 1956 by Leonard Unger. Reprinted by permission of the author.

Upton, John. From *Critical Observations on Shakespeare.* Second edition. G. Hawkins, 1748.

Ure, Peter. From *William Shakespeare, the Problem Plays: "Troilus and Cressida," "All's Well That Ends Well," "Measure for Measure," "Timon of Athens."* Revised edition. Longmans, Green & Co., 1964. © Peter Ure, 1961, 1964. Reprinted by permission of Profile Books Limited.

Van Doren, Mark. From *Shakespeare.* Henry Holt and Company, 1939.

Verplanck, Gulian C. From ''Introductory Remarks,'' in *Shakespeare's Plays: With His Life, Vols. II & III.* By William Shakespeare, edited by Gulian C. Verplanck. Harper & Brothers, 1847.

Vickers, Brian. From *The Artistry of Shakespeare's Prose.* Methuen, 1968. © 1968 Brian Vickers. Reprinted by permission of Methuen & Co Ltd.

Vickers, Brian, ed. *Shakespeare: The Critical Heritage, Vols. 1-6.* Routledge & Kegan Paul, 1974-81.

Voltaire, F. M. From his essay in *Readings on the Character of Hamlet: 1661-1947*. Edited by Claude C. H. Williamson. Allen & Unwin, 1950. Reprinted by permission of Gordian Press, Inc. In Canada by George Allen & Unwin (Publishers) Ltd.

Waldock, A.J.A. From *"Hamlet": A Study in Critical Method*. Cambridge at the University Press, 1931.

Warburton, William. From his preface to *The Works of Shakespeare*. By William Shakespeare, edited by Lewis Theobald. A. Bettesworth, and C. Hitch, 1733.

Warner, Beverly E. From *English History in Shakespeare's Plays*. Longmans, Green and Co., 1894.

Weiss, Theodore. From *The Breath of Clowns and Kings: Shakespeare's Early Comedies and Histories*. Atheneum, 1971. Copyright © 1971 by Theodore Weiss. Reprinted with the permission of Atheneum Publishers, New York.

Welsford, Enid. From *The Fool: His Social and Literary History*. Faber and Faber, 1935. Reprinted by permission of Faber and Faber Ltd.

Wendell, Barrett. From *William Shakespeare: A Study in Elizabethan Literature*. Charles Scribner's Sons, 1894.

Werder, Karl. From *The Heart of Hamlet's Mystery*. Translated by Elizabeth Wilder. G. P. Putnam's Sons, 1907.

West, Rebecca. From *The Court and the Castle: Some Treatments of a Recurrent Theme*. Yale University Press, 1957. © 1957 by Yale University Press, Inc. Reprinted by permission.

White, Richard Grant. From *Studies in Shakespeare*. Second Edition. Houghton Mifflin and Company, 1886. Copyright, 1885, by Alexina B. White. Reprinted by permission.

Wilson, Edmund. From *Classics and Commercials: A Literary Chronicle of the Forties*. Farrar, Straus and Giroux, 1950. Copyright 1950 by Edmund Wilson. Copyright renewed © 1978 by Elena Wilson. Reprinted by permission of Farrar, Straus and Giroux, Inc.

Wilson, J. Dover. From *What Happens in "Hamlet."* Cambridge at the University Press, 1935.

Wilson, J. Dover. From *The Fortunes of Falstaff*. Cambridge at the University Press, 1943.

Wilson, John Dover. From his introduction to *The First Part of the History of Henry IV*. By William Shakespeare, edited by John Dover Wilson. Cambridge at the University Press, 1946.

Winny, James. From *The Player King: A Theme of Shakespeare's Histories*. Chatto & Windus, 1968. © James Winny 1968. Reprinted by permission of the author.

Yeats, W. B. From *Ideas of Good and Evil*. A. H. Bullen, 1903. Reprinted by permission of Michael and Anne Yeats.

Cumulative Index to Critics

Abel, Lionel
Hamlet 1:237

Addison, Joseph
Hamlet 1:75
Henry IV, 1 and 2 1:287

Anthony, Earl of Shaftesbury
Hamlet 1:75

Archer, William
Twelfth Night 1:558

Auden, W. H.
Henry IV, 1 and 2 1:410
Twelfth Night 1:599

Baker, Harry T.
Henry IV, 1 and 2 1:347

Baldwin, Thomas Whitfield
The Comedy of Errors 1:21

Barber, C. L.
Henry IV, 1 and 2 1:414
Twelfth Night 1:620

Barnet, Sylvan
Twelfth Night 1:588

Barton, Anne
The Comedy of Errors 1:61
Twelfth Night 1:656

Battenhouse, Roy
Henry IV, 1 and 2 1:434

Boas, Frederick S.
Timon of Athens 1:476

Bonazza, Blaze Odell
The Comedy of Errors 1:50

Bowers, Fredson
Hamlet 1:209

Bradbrook, Muriel C.
Henry IV, 1 and 2 1:418
Twelfth Night 1:655

Bradley, A. C.
Hamlet 1:120
Henry IV, 1 and 2 1:333
Twelfth Night 1:566

Brandes, George
Hamlet 1:116
Henry IV, 1 and 2 1:329
Timon of Athens 1:474

Brill, Lesley W.
Timon of Athens 1:526

Brittin, Norman A.
Twelfth Night 1:594

Brooke, C. F. Tucker
Henry IV, 1 and 2 1:337, 341

Brooks, Cleanth
Henry IV, 1 and 2 1:375

Brooks, Harold
The Comedy of Errors 1:40

Brower, Reuben A.
Hamlet 1:259

Brown, John Russell
The Comedy of Errors 1:36
Twelfth Night 1:600

Burckhardt, Sigurd
Henry IV, 1 and 2 1:421

Campbell, Oscar James
Twelfth Night 1:577

Campbell, Thomas
Hamlet 1:97

Cazamian, Louis
Henry IV, 1 and 2 1:355

Chambers, E. K.
The Comedy of Errors 1:16
Henry IV, 1 and 2 1:336
Timon of Athens 1:478
Twelfth Night 1:561

Champion, Larry S.
The Comedy of Errors 1:56

Charlton, H. B.
The Comedy of Errors 1:23
Hamlet 1:166
Henry IV, 1 and 2 1:357
Twelfth Night 1:573

Clarke, Charles Cowden
Henry IV, 1 and 2 1:321

Clemen, Wolfgang H.
Hamlet 1:188

Coleridge, Samuel Taylor
The Comedy of Errors 1:14
Hamlet 1:94, 95
Henry IV, 1 and 2 1:310, 311
Timon of Athens 1:459

Collier, Jeremy
See also **Steevens, George**
Hamlet 1:73
Henry IV, 1 and 2 1:286
Timon of Athens 1:456

Collins, A. S.
Timon of Athens 1:492

Cox, Roger L.
Henry IV, 1 and 2 1:438

Craig, Hardin
The Comedy of Errors 1:31

Crane, Milton
Twelfth Night 1:590

Cruttwell, Patrick
Hamlet 1:234

Cumberland, Richard
Henry IV, 1 and 2 1:305

Danby, John F.
Henry IV, 1 and 2 1:391

Dean, Leonard F.
Henry IV, 1 and 2 1:370

Digges, Leonard
Twelfth Night 1:539

Dowden, Edward
The Comedy of Errors 1:16
Hamlet 1:115
Henry IV, 1 and 2 1:326
Timon of Athens 1:470
Twelfth Night 1:561

Drake, James
Hamlet 1:73

Draper, John W.
Timon of Athens 1:487, 489
Twelfth Night 1:581

Dryden, John
Henry IV, 1 and 2 1:285

Edwards, Philip
Twelfth Night 1:654

Eliot, T. S.
Hamlet 1:142

Elliott, G. R.
The Comedy of Errors 1:27

Ellis-Fermor, Una
Henry IV, 1 and 2 1:374
Timon of Athens 1:490

Empson, William
Hamlet 1:202
Henry IV, 1 and 2 1:359

Evans, Bertrand
The Comedy of Errors 1:37
Twelfth Night 1:625

Everett, Barbara
Hamlet 1:268

Ewbank, Inga-Stina
Hamlet 1:270